D1418583

University Casebook Series

March, 1989

ACCOUNTING AND THE LAW, Fourth Edition (1978), with Problems Pamphlet (Successor to Dohr, Phillips, Thompson & Warren)

George C. Thompson, Professor, Columbia University Graduate School of Business.

Robert Whitman, Professor of Law, University of Connecticut.

Ellis L. Phillips, Jr., Member of the New York Bar.

William C. Warren, Professor of Law Emeritus, Columbia University.

ACCOUNTING FOR LAWYERS, MATERIALS ON (1980)

David R. Herwitz, Professor of Law, Harvard University.

ADMINISTRATIVE LAW, Eighth Edition (1987), with 1983 Problems Supplement (Supplement edited in association with Paul R. Verkuil, Dean and Professor of Law, Tulane University)

Walter Gellhorn, University Professor Emeritus, Columbia University.

Clark Byse, Professor of Law, Harvard University.

Peter L. Strauss, Professor of Law, Columbia University.

Todd D. Rakoff, Professor of Law, Harvard University.

Roy A. Schotland, Professor of Law, Georgetown University.

ADMIRALTY, Third Edition (1987), with Statute and Rule Supplement

Jo Desha Lucas, Professor of Law, University of Chicago.

ADVOCACY, see also Lawyering Process

AGENCY, see also Enterprise Organization

AGENCY—PARTNERSHIPS, Fourth Edition (1987)

Abridgement from Conard, Knauss & Siegel's Enterprise Organization, Fourth Edition.

AGENCY AND PARTNERSHIPS (1987)

Melvin A. Eisenberg, Professor of Law, University of California, Berkeley.

ANTITRUST: FREE ENTERPRISE AND ECONOMIC ORGANIZATION, Sixth Edition (1983), with 1983 Problems in Antitrust Supplement and 1988 Case Supplement

Louis B. Schwartz, Professor of Law, University of Pennsylvania.

John J. Flynn, Professor of Law, University of Utah.

Harry First, Professor of Law, New York University.

BANKRUPTCY (1985)

Robert L. Jordan, Professor of Law, University of California, Los Angeles.

William D. Warren, Professor of Law, University of California, Los Angeles.

BANKRUPTCY AND DEBTOR–CREDITOR LAW, Second Edition (1988)

Theodore Eisenberg, Professor of Law, Cornell University.

BUSINESS ORGANIZATION, see also Enterprise Organization

BUSINESS PLANNING, Temporary Second Edition (1984)

David R. Herwitz, Professor of Law, Harvard University.

BUSINESS TORTS (1972)

Milton Handler, Professor of Law Emeritus, Columbia University.

CHILDREN IN THE LEGAL SYSTEM (1983) with 1988 Supplement

Walter Wadlington, Professor of Law, University of Virginia.
Charles H. Whitebread, Professor of Law, University of Southern California.
Samuel Davis, Professor of Law, University of Georgia.

CIVIL PROCEDURE, see Procedure

CIVIL RIGHTS ACTIONS (1988), with 1988 Supplement

Peter W. Low, Professor of Law, University of Virginia.
John C. Jeffries, Jr., Professor of Law, University of Virginia.

CLINIC, see also Lawyering Process

COMMERCIAL AND DEBTOR–CREDITOR LAW: SELECTED STATUTES, 1988 EDITION

COMMERCIAL LAW, Second Edition (1987)

Robert L. Jordan, Professor of Law, University of California, Los Angeles.
William D. Warren, Professor of Law, University of California, Los Angeles.

COMMERCIAL LAW, Fourth Edition (1985)

E. Allan Farnsworth, Professor of Law, Columbia University.
John Honnold, Professor of Law, University of Pennsylvania.

COMMERCIAL PAPER, Third Edition (1984)

E. Allan Farnsworth, Professor of Law, Columbia University.

COMMERCIAL PAPER, Second Edition (1987) (Reprinted from COMMERCIAL LAW, Second Edition (1987))

Robert L. Jordan, Professor of Law, University of California, Los Angeles.
William D. Warren, Professor of Law, University of California, Los Angeles.

COMMERCIAL PAPER AND BANK DEPOSITS AND COLLECTIONS (1967), with Statutory Supplement

William D. Hawkland, Professor of Law, University of Illinois.

COMMERCIAL TRANSACTIONS—Principles and Policies (1982)

Alan Schwartz, Professor of Law, University of Southern California.
Robert E. Scott, Professor of Law, University of Virginia.

COMPARATIVE LAW, Fifth Edition (1988)

Rudolf B. Schlesinger, Professor of Law, Hastings College of Law.
Hans W. Baade, Professor of Law, University of Texas.
Mirjan P. Damaska, Professor of Law, Yale Law School.
Peter E. Herzog, Professor of Law, Syracuse University.

COMPETITIVE PROCESS, LEGAL REGULATION OF THE, Third Edition (1986), with 1987 Selected Statutes Supplement

Edmund W. Kitch, Professor of Law, University of Virginia.
Harvey S. Perlman, Dean of the Law School, University of Nebraska.

CONFLICT OF LAWS, Eighth Edition (1984), with 1987 Case Supplement

Willis L. M. Reese, Professor of Law, Columbia University.
Maurice Rosenberg, Professor of Law, Columbia University.

CONSTITUTIONAL LAW, Eighth Edition (1989)

Edward L. Barrett, Jr., Professor of Law, University of California, Davis.
William Cohen, Professor of Law, Stanford University.
Jonathan D. Varat, Professor of Law, University of California, Los Angeles.

CONSTITUTIONAL LAW, CIVIL LIBERTY AND INDIVIDUAL RIGHTS, Second Edition (1982), with 1987 Supplement

William Cohen, Professor of Law, Stanford University.
John Kaplan, Professor of Law, Stanford University.

CONSTITUTIONAL LAW, Eleventh Edition (1985), with 1988 Supplement (Supplement edited in association with Frederick F. Schauer, Professor of Law, University of Michigan)

Gerald Gunther, Professor of Law, Stanford University.

CONSTITUTIONAL LAW, INDIVIDUAL RIGHTS IN, Fourth Edition (1986), (Reprinted from CONSTITUTIONAL LAW, Eleventh Edition), with 1988 Supplement (Supplement edited in association with Frederick F. Schauer, Professor of Law, University of Michigan)

Gerald Gunther, Professor of Law, Stanford University.

CONSUMER TRANSACTIONS (1983), with Selected Statutes and Regulations Supplement and 1987 Case Supplement

Michael M. Greenfield, Professor of Law, Washington University.

CONTRACT LAW AND ITS APPLICATION, Fourth Edition (1988)

Arthur Rosett, Professor of Law, University of California, Los Angeles.

CONTRACT LAW, STUDIES IN, Third Edition (1984)

Edward J. Murphy, Professor of Law, University of Notre Dame.
Richard E. Speidel, Professor of Law, Northwestern University.

CONTRACTS, Fifth Edition (1987)

John P. Dawson, Professor of Law Emeritus, Harvard University.
William Burnett Harvey, Professor of Law and Political Science, Boston University.
Stanley D. Henderson, Professor of Law, University of Virginia.

CONTRACTS, Fourth Edition (1988)

E. Allan Farnsworth, Professor of Law, Columbia University.
William F. Young, Professor of Law, Columbia University.

CONTRACTS, Selections on (statutory materials) (1988)

CONTRACTS, Second Edition (1978), with Statutory and Administrative Law Supplement (1978)

Ian R. Macneil, Professor of Law, Cornell University.

COPYRIGHT, PATENTS AND TRADEMARKS, see also Competitive Process; see also Selected Statutes and International Agreements

COPYRIGHT, PATENT, TRADEMARK AND RELATED STATE DOCTRINES, Second Edition (1981), with 1988 Case Supplement, 1987 Selected Statutes Supplement and 1981 Problem Supplement

Paul Goldstein, Professor of Law, Stanford University.

UNIVERSITY CASEBOOK SERIES—Continued

COPYRIGHT, Unfair Competition, and Other Topics Bearing on the Protection of Literary, Musical, and Artistic Works, Fourth Edition (1985), with 1985 Statutory Supplement

Ralph S. Brown, Jr., Professor of Law, Yale University.
Robert C. Denicola, Professor of Law, University of Nebraska.

CORPORATE ACQUISITIONS, The Law and Finance of (1986), with 1988 Supplement

Ronald J. Gilson, Professor of Law, Stanford University.

CORPORATE FINANCE, Third Edition (1987)

Victor Brudney, Professor of Law, Harvard University.
Marvin A. Chirelstein, Professor of Law, Columbia University.

CORPORATE READJUSTMENTS AND REORGANIZATIONS (1976)

Walter J. Blum, Professor of Law, University of Chicago.
Stanley A. Kaplan, Professor of Law, University of Chicago.

CORPORATION LAW, BASIC, Third Edition (1989), with Documentary Supplement

Detlev F. Vagts, Professor of Law, Harvard University.

CORPORATIONS, see also Enterprise Organization

CORPORATIONS, Sixth Edition—Concise (1988), with Statutory Supplement (1988)

William L. Cary, late Professor of Law, Columbia University.
Melvin Aron Eisenberg, Professor of Law, University of California, Berkeley.

CORPORATIONS, Sixth Edition—Unabridged (1988), with Statutory Supplement (1988)

William L. Cary, late Professor of Law, Columbia University.
Melvin Aron Eisenberg, Professor of Law, University of California, Berkeley.

CORPORATIONS AND BUSINESS ASSOCIATIONS—STATUTES, RULES AND FORMS (1988)

CORPORATIONS COURSE GAME PLAN (1975)

David R. Herwitz, Professor of Law, Harvard University.

CORRECTIONS, SEE SENTENCING

CREDITORS' RIGHTS, see also Debtor-Creditor Law

CRIMINAL JUSTICE ADMINISTRATION, Third Edition (1986), with 1988 Case Supplement

Frank W. Miller, Professor of Law, Washington University.
Robert O. Dawson, Professor of Law, University of Texas.
George E. Dix, Professor of Law, University of Texas.
Raymond I. Parnas, Professor of Law, University of California, Davis.

CRIMINAL LAW, Fourth Edition (1987)

Fred E. Inbau, Professor of Law Emeritus, Northwestern University.
Andre A. Moenssens, Professor of Law, University of Richmond.
James R. Thompson, Professor of Law Emeritus, Northwestern University.

CRIMINAL LAW AND APPROACHES TO THE STUDY OF LAW (1986)

John M. Brumbaugh, Professor of Law, University of Maryland.

CRIMINAL LAW, Second Edition (1986)

Peter W. Low, Professor of Law, University of Virginia.
John C. Jeffries, Jr., Professor of Law, University of Virginia.
Richard C. Bonnie, Professor of Law, University of Virginia.

CRIMINAL LAW, Fourth Edition (1986)

Lloyd L. Weinreb, Professor of Law, Harvard University.

CRIMINAL LAW AND PROCEDURE, Seventh Edition (1989)

Ronald N. Boyce, Professor of Law, University of Utah.
Rollin M. Perkins, Professor of Law Emeritus, University of California, Hastings College of the Law.

CRIMINAL PROCEDURE, Third Edition (1987), with 1988 Supplement

James B. Haddad, Professor of Law, Northwestern University.
James B. Zagel, Chief, Criminal Justice Division, Office of Attorney General of Illinois.
Gary L. Starkman, Assistant U. S. Attorney, Northern District of Illinois.
William J. Bauer, Chief Judge of the U.S. Court of Appeals, Seventh Circuit.

CRIMINAL PROCESS, Fourth Edition (1987), with 1988 Supplement

Lloyd L. Weinreb, Professor of Law, Harvard University.

DAMAGES, Second Edition (1952)

Charles T. McCormick, late Professor of Law, University of Texas.
William F. Fritz, late Professor of Law, University of Texas.

DECEDENTS' ESTATES AND TRUSTS, Seventh Edition (1988)

John Ritchie, Late Professor of Law, University of Virginia.
Neill H. Alford, Jr., Professor of Law, University of Virginia.
Richard W. Effland, Professor of Law, Arizona State University.

DISPUTE RESOLUTION, Processes of (1989)

John S. Murray, President and Executive Director of The Conflict Clinic, Inc., George Mason University.
Alan Scott Rau, Professor of Law, University of Texas.
Edward F. Sherman, Professor of Law, University of Texas.

DOMESTIC RELATIONS, see also Family Law

DOMESTIC RELATIONS, Successor Edition (1984) with 1988 Supplement

Walter Wadlington, Professor of Law, University of Virginia.

EMPLOYMENT DISCRIMINATION, Second Edition (1987), with 1988 Supplement

Joel W. Friedman, Professor of Law, Tulane University.
George M. Strickler, Professor of Law, Tulane University.

EMPLOYMENT LAW (1987), with 1987 Statutory Supplement and 1988 Case Supplement

Mark A. Rothstein, Professor of Law, University of Houston.
Andria S. Knapp, Adjunct Professor of Law, University of California, Hastings College of Law.
Lance Liebman, Professor of Law, Harvard University.

ENERGY LAW (1983) with 1986 Case Supplement

Donald N. Zillman, Professor of Law, University of Utah.
Laurence Lattman, Dean of Mines and Engineering, University of Utah.

ENTERPRISE ORGANIZATION, Fourth Edition (1987), with 1987 Corporation and Partnership Statutes, Rules and Forms Supplement

Alfred F. Conard, Professor of Law, University of Michigan.
Robert L. Knauss, Dean of the Law School, University of Houston.
Stanley Siegel, Professor of Law, University of California, Los Angeles.

ENVIRONMENTAL POLICY LAW 1985 Edition, with 1985 Problems Supplement (Supplement in association with Ronald H. Rosenberg, Professor of Law, College of William and Mary)

Thomas J. Schoenbaum, Professor of Law, University of Georgia.

EQUITY, see also Remedies

EQUITY, RESTITUTION AND DAMAGES, Second Edition (1974)

Robert Childres, late Professor of Law, Northwestern University.
William F. Johnson, Jr., Professor of Law, New York University.

ESTATE PLANNING, Second Edition (1982), with 1985 Case, Text and Documentary Supplement

David Westfall, Professor of Law, Harvard University.

ETHICS, see Legal Profession, Professional Responsibility, and Social Responsibilities

ETHICS AND PROFESSIONAL RESPONSIBILITY (1981) (Reprinted from THE LAWYERING PROCESS)

Gary Bellow, Professor of Law, Harvard University.
Bea Moulton, Legal Services Corporation.

EVIDENCE, Sixth Edition (1988 Reprint)

John Kaplan, Professor of Law, Stanford University.
Jon R. Waltz, Professor of Law, Northwestern University.

EVIDENCE, Eighth Edition (1988), with Rules, Statute and Case Supplement (1988)

Jack B. Weinstein, Chief Judge, United States District Court.
John H. Mansfield, Professor of Law, Harvard University.
Norman Abrams, Professor of Law, University of California, Los Angeles.
Margaret Berger, Professor of Law, Brooklyn Law School.

FAMILY LAW, see also Domestic Relations

FAMILY LAW Second Edition (1985), with 1988 Supplement

Judith C. Areen, Professor of Law, Georgetown University.

FAMILY LAW AND CHILDREN IN THE LEGAL SYSTEM, STATUTORY MATERIALS (1981)

Walter Wadlington, Professor of Law, University of Virginia.

FEDERAL COURTS, Eighth Edition (1988)

Charles T. McCormick, late Professor of Law, University of Texas.
James H. Chadbourn, late Professor of Law, Harvard University.
Charles Alan Wright, Professor of Law, University of Texas, Austin.

FEDERAL COURTS AND THE FEDERAL SYSTEM, Hart and Wechsler's Third Edition (1988), with the Judicial Code and Rules of Procedure in the Federal Courts (1988)

Paul M. Bator, Professor of Law, University of Chicago.
Daniel J. Meltzer, Professor of Law, Harvard University.
Paul J. Mishkin, Professor of Law, University of California, Berkeley.
David L. Shapiro, Professor of Law, Harvard University.

FEDERAL COURTS AND THE LAW OF FEDERAL–STATE RELATIONS, Second Edition (1989)

Peter W. Low, Professor of Law, University of Virginia.
John C. Jeffries, Jr., Professor of Law, University of Virginia.

FEDERAL PUBLIC LAND AND RESOURCES LAW, Second Edition (1987), with 1984 Statutory Supplement

George C. Coggins, Professor of Law, University of Kansas.
Charles F. Wilkinson, Professor of Law, University of Oregon.

FEDERAL RULES OF CIVIL PROCEDURE and Selected Other Procedural Provisions, 1988 Edition

FEDERAL TAXATION, see Taxation

FOOD AND DRUG LAW (1980), with Statutory Supplement

Richard A. Merrill, Dean of the School of Law, University of Virginia.
Peter Barton Hutt, Esq.

FUTURE INTERESTS (1958)

Philip Mechem, late Professor of Law Emeritus, University of Pennsylvania.

FUTURE INTERESTS (1970)

Howard R. Williams, Professor of Law, Stanford University.

FUTURE INTERESTS AND ESTATE PLANNING (1961), with 1962 Supplement

W. Barton Leach, late Professor of Law, Harvard University.
James K. Logan, formerly Dean of the Law School, University of Kansas.

GOVERNMENT CONTRACTS, FEDERAL, Successor Edition (1985)

John W. Whelan, Professor of Law, Hastings College of the Law.

GOVERNMENT REGULATION: FREE ENTERPRISE AND ECONOMIC ORGANIZATION, Sixth Edition (1985)

Louis B. Schwartz, Professor of Law, Hastings College of the Law.
John J. Flynn, Professor of Law, University of Utah.
Harry First, Professor of Law, New York University.

HEALTH CARE LAW AND POLICY (1988)

Clark C. Havighurst, Professor of Law, Duke University.

HINCKLEY, JOHN W., JR., TRIAL OF: A Case Study of the Insanity Defense (1986)

Peter W. Low, Professor of Law, University of Virginia.
John C. Jeffries, Jr., Professor of Law, University of Virginia.
Richard C. Bonnie, Professor of Law, University of Virginia.

INJUNCTIONS, Second Edition (1984)

Owen M. Fiss, Professor of Law, Yale University.
Doug Rendleman, Professor of Law, College of William and Mary.

UNIVERSITY CASEBOOK SERIES—Continued

INSTITUTIONAL INVESTORS, (1978)

David L. Ratner, Professor of Law, Cornell University.

INSURANCE, Second Edition (1985)

William F. Young, Professor of Law, Columbia University.
Eric M. Holmes, Professor of Law, University of Georgia.

INTERNATIONAL LAW, see also Transnational Legal Problems, Transnational Business Problems, and United Nations Law

INTERNATIONAL LAW IN CONTEMPORARY PERSPECTIVE (1981), with Essay Supplement

Myres S. McDougal, Professor of Law, Yale University.
W. Michael Reisman, Professor of Law, Yale University.

INTERNATIONAL LEGAL SYSTEM, Third Edition (1988), with Documentary Supplement

Joseph Modeste Sweeney, Professor of Law, University of California, Hastings.
Covey T. Oliver, Professor of Law, University of Pennsylvania.
Noyes E. Leech, Professor of Law Emeritus, University of Pennsylvania.

INTRODUCTION TO LAW, see also Legal Method, On Law in Courts, and Dynamics of American Law

INTRODUCTION TO THE STUDY OF LAW (1970)

E. Wayne Thode, late Professor of Law, University of Utah.
Leon Lebowitz, Professor of Law, University of Texas.
Lester J. Mazor, Professor of Law, University of Utah.

JUDICIAL CODE and Rules of Procedure in the Federal Courts, Students' Edition, 1988 Revision

Daniel J. Meltzer, Professor of Law, Harvard University.
David L. Shapiro, Professor of Law, Harvard University.

JURISPRUDENCE (Temporary Edition Hardbound) (1949)

Lon L. Fuller, late Professor of Law, Harvard University.

JUVENILE, see also Children

JUVENILE JUSTICE PROCESS, Third Edition (1985)

Frank W. Miller, Professor of Law, Washington University.
Robert O. Dawson, Professor of Law, University of Texas.
George E. Dix, Professor of Law, University of Texas.
Raymond I. Parnas, Professor of Law, University of California, Davis.

LABOR LAW, Tenth Edition (1986), with 1986 Statutory Supplement

Archibald Cox, Professor of Law, Harvard University.
Derek C. Bok, President, Harvard University.
Robert A. Gorman, Professor of Law, University of Pennsylvania.

LABOR LAW, Second Edition (1982), with Statutory Supplement

Clyde W. Summers, Professor of Law, University of Pennsylvania.
Harry H. Wellington, Dean of the Law School, Yale University.
Alan Hyde, Professor of Law, Rutgers University.

LAND FINANCING, Third Edition (1985)

The late Norman Penney, Professor of Law, Cornell University.
Richard F. Broude, Member of the California Bar.
Roger Cunningham, Professor of Law, University of Michigan.

LAW AND MEDICINE (1980)

Walter Wadlington, Professor of Law and Professor of Legal Medicine, University of Virginia.
Jon R. Waltz, Professor of Law, Northwestern University.
Roger B. Dworkin, Professor of Law, Indiana University, and Professor of Biomedical History, University of Washington.

LAW, LANGUAGE AND ETHICS (1972)

William R. Bishin, Professor of Law, University of Southern California.
Christopher D. Stone, Professor of Law, University of Southern California.

LAW, SCIENCE AND MEDICINE (1984), with 1989 Supplement

Judith C. Areen, Professor of Law, Georgetown University.
Patricia A. King, Professor of Law, Georgetown University.
Steven P. Goldberg, Professor of Law, Georgetown University.
Alexander M. Capron, Professor of Law, University of Southern California.

LAWYERING PROCESS (1978), with Civil Problem Supplement and Criminal Problem Supplement

Gary Bellow, Professor of Law, Harvard University.
Bea Moulton, Professor of Law, Arizona State University.

LEGAL METHOD (1980)

Harry W. Jones, Professor of Law Emeritus, Columbia University.
John M. Kernochan, Professor of Law, Columbia University.
Arthur W. Murphy, Professor of Law, Columbia University.

LEGAL METHODS (1969)

Robert N. Covington, Professor of Law, Vanderbilt University.
E. Blythe Stason, late Professor of Law, Vanderbilt University.
John W. Wade, Professor of Law, Vanderbilt University.
Elliott E. Cheatham, late Professor of Law, Vanderbilt University.
Theodore A. Smedley, Professor of Law, Vanderbilt University.

LEGAL PROFESSION, THE, Responsibility and Regulation, Second Edition (1988)

Geoffrey C. Hazard, Jr., Professor of Law, Yale University.
Deborah L. Rhode, Professor of Law, Stanford University.

LEGISLATION, Fourth Edition (1982) (by Fordham)

Horace E. Read, late Vice President, Dalhousie University.
John W. MacDonald, Professor of Law Emeritus, Cornell Law School.
Jefferson B. Fordham, Professor of Law, University of Utah.
William J. Pierce, Professor of Law, University of Michigan.

LEGISLATIVE AND ADMINISTRATIVE PROCESSES, Second Edition (1981)

Hans A. Linde, Judge, Supreme Court of Oregon.
George Bunn, Professor of Law, University of Wisconsin.
Fredericka Paff, Professor of Law, University of Wisconsin.
W. Lawrence Church, Professor of Law, University of Wisconsin.

LOCAL GOVERNMENT LAW, Second Revised Edition (1986)

Jefferson B. Fordham, Professor of Law, University of Utah.

MASS MEDIA LAW, Third Edition (1987)

Marc A. Franklin, Professor of Law, Stanford University.

MENTAL HEALTH PROCESS, Second Edition (1976), with 1981 Supplement

Frank W. Miller, Professor of Law, Washington University.
Robert O. Dawson, Professor of Law, University of Texas.
George E. Dix, Professor of Law, University of Texas.
Raymond I. Parnas, Professor of Law, University of California, Davis.

MUNICIPAL CORPORATIONS, see Local Government Law

NEGOTIABLE INSTRUMENTS, see Commercial Paper

NEGOTIATION (1981) (Reprinted from THE LAWYERING PROCESS)

Gary Bellow, Professor of Law, Harvard Law School.
Bea Moulton, Legal Services Corporation.

NEW YORK PRACTICE, Fourth Edition (1978)

Herbert Peterfreund, Professor of Law, New York University.
Joseph M. McLaughlin, Dean of the Law School, Fordham University.

OIL AND GAS, Fifth Edition (1987)

Howard R. Williams, Professor of Law, Stanford University.
Richard C. Maxwell, Professor of Law, University of California, Los Angeles.
Charles J. Meyers, Dean of the Law School, Stanford University.
Stephen F. Williams, Judge of the United States Court of Appeals.

ON LAW IN COURTS (1965)

Paul J. Mishkin, Professor of Law, University of California, Berkeley.
Clarence Morris, Professor of Law Emeritus, University of Pennsylvania.

PATENTS AND ANTITRUST (Pamphlet) (1983)

Milton Handler, Professor of Law Emeritus, Columbia University.
Harlan M. Blake, Professor of Law, Columbia University.
Robert Pitofsky, Professor of Law, Georgetown University.
Harvey J. Goldschmid, Professor of Law, Columbia University.

PLEADING AND PROCEDURE, see Procedure, Civil

POLICE FUNCTION, Fourth Edition (1986), with 1988 Case Supplement

Reprint of Chapters 1–10 of Miller, Dawson, Dix and Parnas's CRIMINAL
JUSTICE ADMINISTRATION, Third Edition.

**PREPARING AND PRESENTING THE CASE (1981) (Reprinted from THE LAW-
YERING PROCESS)**

Gary Bellow, Professor of Law, Harvard Law School.
Bea Moulton, Legal Services Corporation.

PROCEDURE (1988), with Procedure Supplement (1988)

Robert M. Cover, late Professor of Law, Yale Law School.
Owen M. Fiss, Professor of Law, Yale Law School.
Judith Resnik, Professor of Law, University of Southern California Law Center.

**PROCEDURE—CIVIL PROCEDURE, Second Edition (1974), with 1979 Supple-
ment**

The late James H. Chadbourn, Professor of Law, Harvard University.
A. Leo Levin, Professor of Law, University of Pennsylvania.
Philip Shuchman, Professor of Law, Cornell University.

PROCEDURE—CIVIL PROCEDURE, Fifth Edition (1984), with 1988 Supplement

Richard H. Field, late Professor of Law, Harvard University.
Benjamin Kaplan, Professor of Law Emeritus, Harvard University.
Kevin M. Clermont, Professor of Law, Cornell University.

PROCEDURE—CIVIL PROCEDURE, Fourth Edition (1985), with 1988 Supplement

Maurice Rosenberg, Professor of Law, Columbia University.
Hans Smit, Professor of Law, Columbia University.
Harold L. Korn, Professor of Law, Columbia University.

PROCEDURE—PLEADING AND PROCEDURE: State and Federal, Fifth Edition (1983), with 1988 Supplement

David W. Louisell, late Professor of Law, University of California, Berkeley.
Geoffrey C. Hazard, Jr., Professor of Law, Yale University.
Colin C. Tait, Professor of Law, University of Connecticut.

PROCEDURE—FEDERAL RULES OF CIVIL PROCEDURE, 1988 Edition

PRODUCTS LIABILITY (1980)

Marshall S. Shapo, Professor of Law, Northwestern University.

PRODUCTS LIABILITY AND SAFETY (1980), with 1985 Case and Documentary Supplement

W. Page Keeton, Professor of Law, University of Texas.
David G. Owen, Professor of Law, University of South Carolina.
John E. Montgomery, Professor of Law, University of South Carolina.

PROFESSIONAL RESPONSIBILITY, Fourth Edition (1987), with 1989 Selected National Standards Supplement

Thomas D. Morgan, Dean of the Law School, Emory University.
Ronald D. Rotunda, Professor of Law, University of Illinois.

PROPERTY, Fifth Edition (1984)

John E. Cribbet, Professor of Law, University of Illinois.
Corwin W. Johnson, Professor of Law, University of Texas.

PROPERTY—PERSONAL (1953)

S. Kenneth Skolfield, late Professor of Law Emeritus, Boston University.

PROPERTY—PERSONAL, Third Edition (1954)

Everett Fraser, late Dean of the Law School Emeritus, University of Minnesota.
Third Edition by Charles W. Taintor, late Professor of Law, University of Pittsburgh.

PROPERTY—INTRODUCTION, TO REAL PROPERTY, Third Edition (1954)

Everett Fraser, late Dean of the Law School Emeritus, University of Minnesota.

PROPERTY—REAL AND PERSONAL, Combined Edition (1954)

Everett Fraser, late Dean of the Law School Emeritus, University of Minnesota.
Third Edition of Personal Property by Charles W. Taintor, late Professor of Law, University of Pittsburgh.

PROPERTY—FUNDAMENTALS OF MODERN REAL PROPERTY, Second Edition (1982), with 1985 Supplement

Edward H. Rabin, Professor of Law, University of California, Davis.

PROPERTY—PROBLEMS IN REAL PROPERTY (Pamphlet) (1969)

Edward H. Rabin, Professor of Law, University of California, Davis.

SECURITY INTERESTS IN PERSONAL PROPERTY, Second Edition (1987)

Douglas G. Baird, Professor of Law, University of Chicago.
Thomas H. Jackson, Professor of Law, Stanford University.

SECURITY INTERESTS IN PERSONAL PROPERTY (1985) (Reprinted from Sales and Sales Financing, Fifth Edition)

John Honnold, Professor of Law, University of Pennsylvania.

SENTENCING AND THE CORRECTIONAL PROCESS, Second Edition (1976)

Frank W. Miller, Professor of Law, Washington University.
Robert O. Dawson, Professor of Law, University of Texas.
George E. Dix, Professor of Law, University of Texas.
Raymond I. Parnas, Professor of Law, University of California, Davis.

SOCIAL RESPONSIBILITIES OF LAWYERS, Case Studies (1988)

Philip B. Heymann, Professor of Law, Harvard University.
Lance Liebman, Professor of Law, Harvard University.

SOCIAL SCIENCE IN LAW, Cases and Materials (1985)

John Monahan, Professor of Law, University of Virginia.
Laurens Walker, Professor of Law, University of Virginia.

TAX, POLICY ANALYSIS OF THE FEDERAL INCOME (1976)

William A. Klein, Professor of Law, University of California, Los Angeles.

TAXATION, FEDERAL INCOME (1989)

Stephen B. Cohen, Professor of Law, Georgetown University

TAXATION, FEDERAL INCOME, Second Edition (1988)

Michael J. Graetz, Professor of Law, Yale University.

TAXATION, FEDERAL INCOME, Sixth Edition (1987)

James J. Freeland, Professor of Law, University of Florida.
Stephen A. Lind, Professor of Law, University of Florida and University of California, Hastings.
Richard B. Stephens, Professor of Law Emeritus, University of Florida.

TAXATION, FEDERAL INCOME, Successor Edition (1986), with 1988 Legislative Supplement

Stanley S. Surrey, late Professor of Law, Harvard University.
Paul R. McDaniel, Professor of Law, Boston College.
Hugh J. Ault, Professor of Law, Boston College.
Stanley A. Koppelman, Professor of Law, Boston University.

TAXATION, FEDERAL INCOME, VOLUME II, Taxation of Partnerships and Corporations, Second Edition (1980), with 1988 Legislative Supplement

Stanley S. Surrey, late Professor of Law, Harvard University.
William C. Warren, Professor of Law Emeritus, Columbia University.
Paul R. McDaniel, Professor of Law, Boston College.
Hugh J. Ault, Professor of Law, Boston College.

TAXATION, FEDERAL WEALTH TRANSFER, Successor Edition (1987)

Stanley S. Surrey, late Professor of Law, Harvard University.
Paul R. McDaniel, Professor of Law, Boston College.
Harry L. Gutman, Professor of Law, University of Pennsylvania.

UNIVERSITY CASEBOOK SERIES—Continued

TAXATION, FUNDAMENTALS OF CORPORATE, Second Edition (1987)

Stephen A. Lind, Professor of Law, University of Florida and University of California, Hastings.
Stephen Schwarz, Professor of Law, University of California, Hastings.
Daniel J. Lathrope, Professor of Law, University of California, Hastings.
Joshua Rosenberg, Professor of Law, University of San Francisco.

TAXATION, FUNDAMENTALS OF PARTNERSHIP, Second Edition (1988)

Stephen A. Lind, Professor of Law, University of Florida and University of California, Hastings.
Stephen Schwarz, Professor of Law, University of California, Hastings.
Daniel J. Lathrope, Professor of Law, University of California, Hastings.
Joshua Rosenberg, Professor of Law, University of San Francisco.

TAXATION, PROBLEMS IN THE FEDERAL INCOME TAXATION OF PARTNER-SHIPS AND CORPORATIONS, Second Edition (1986)

Norton L. Steuben, Professor of Law, University of Colorado.
William J. Turnier, Professor of Law, University of North Carolina.

TAXATION, PROBLEMS IN THE FUNDAMENTALS OF FEDERAL INCOME, Second Edition (1985)

Norton L. Steuben, Professor of Law, University of Colorado.
William J. Turnier, Professor of Law, University of North Carolina.

TAXES AND FINANCE—STATE AND LOCAL (1974)

Oliver Oldman, Professor of Law, Harvard University.
Ferdinand P. Schoettle, Professor of Law, University of Minnesota.

TORT LAW AND ALTERNATIVES, Fourth Edition (1987)

Marc A. Franklin, Professor of Law, Stanford University.
Robert L. Rabin, Professor of Law, Stanford University.

TORTS, Eighth Edition (1988)

William L. Prosser, late Professor of Law, University of California, Hastings.
John W. Wade, Professor of Law, Vanderbilt University.
Victor E. Schwartz, Adjunct Professor of Law, Georgetown University.

TORTS, Third Edition (1976)

Harry Shulman, late Dean of the Law School, Yale University.
Fleming James, Jr., Professor of Law Emeritus, Yale University.
Oscar S. Gray, Professor of Law, University of Maryland.

TRADE REGULATION, Second Edition (1983), with 1987 Supplement

Milton Handler, Professor of Law Emeritus, Columbia University.
Harlan M. Blake, Professor of Law, Columbia University.
Robert Pitofsky, Professor of Law, Georgetown University.
Harvey J. Goldschmid, Professor of Law, Columbia University.

TRADE REGULATION, see Antitrust

TRANSNATIONAL BUSINESS PROBLEMS (1986)

Detlev F. Vagts, Professor of Law, Harvard University.

TRANSNATIONAL LEGAL PROBLEMS, Third Edition (1986) with Documentary Supplement

Henry J. Steiner, Professor of Law, Harvard University.
Detlev F. Vagts, Professor of Law, Harvard University.

TRIAL, see also Evidence, Making the Record, Lawyering Process and Preparing and Presenting the Case

TRUSTS, Fifth Edition (1978)

George G. Bogert, late Professor of Law Emeritus, University of Chicago.
Dallin H. Oaks, President, Brigham Young University.

TRUSTS AND SUCCESSION (Palmer's), Fourth Edition (1983)

Richard V. Wellman, Professor of Law, University of Georgia.
Lawrence W. Waggoner, Professor of Law, University of Michigan.
Olin L. Browder, Jr., Professor of Law, University of Michigan.

UNFAIR COMPETITION, see Competitive Process and Business Torts

UNITED NATIONS LAW, Second Edition (1967), with Documentary Supplement (1968)

Louis B. Sohn, Professor of Law, Harvard University.

WATER RESOURCE MANAGEMENT, Third Edition (1988)

Charles J. Meyers, Esq., Denver, Colorado, formerly Dean, Stanford University Law School.
A. Dan Tarlock, Professor of Law, II Chicago-Kent College of Law.
James N. Corbridge, Jr., Chancellor, University of Colorado at Boulder, and Professor of Law, University of Colorado School of Law.
David H. Getches, Professor of Law, University of Colorado School of Law.

WILLS AND ADMINISTRATION, Fifth Edition (1961)

Philip Mechem, late Professor of Law, University of Pennsylvania.
Thomas E. Atkinson, late Professor of Law, New York University.

WORLD LAW, see United Nations Law

WRITING AND ANALYSIS IN THE LAW (1989)

Helene S. Shapo, Professor of Law, Northwestern University
Marilyn R. Walter, Professor of Law, Brooklyn Law School
Elizabeth Fajans, Writing Specialist, Brooklyn Law School

University Casebook Series

EDITORIAL BOARD

DAVID L. SHAPIRO
DIRECTING EDITOR
Professor of Law, Harvard University

EDWARD L. BARRETT, Jr.
Professor of Law, University of California, Davis

ROBERT C. CLARK
Professor of Law, Harvard University

OWEN M. FISS
Professor of Law, Yale Law School

JEFFERSON B. FORDHAM
Professor of Law, University of Utah

GERALD GUNTHER
Professor of Law, Stanford University

THOMAS H. JACKSON
Dean of the School of Law, University of Virginia

HARRY W. JONES
Professor of Law, Columbia University

HERMA HILL KAY
Professor of Law, University of California, Berkeley

PAGE KEETON
Professor of Law, University of Texas

ROBERT L. RABIN
Professor of Law, Stanford University

CAROL M. ROSE
Professor of Law, Northwestern University

SAMUEL D. THURMAN
Professor of Law, Hastings College of the Law

HART AND WECHSLER'S

THE FEDERAL COURTS

AND

THE FEDERAL SYSTEM

THIRD EDITION

By

PAUL M. BATOR
John P. Wilson Professor of Law,
University of Chicago Law School

DANIEL J. MELTZER
Professor of Law, Harvard Law School

PAUL J. MISHKIN
Emmanuel S. Heller Professor of Law,
University of California, Berkeley School of Law

DAVID L. SHAPIRO
William Nelson Cromwell Professor of Law,
Harvard Law School

Westbury, New York
THE FOUNDATION PRESS, INC.
1988

COPYRIGHT © 1953, 1973 THE FOUNDATION PRESS, INC.
COPYRIGHT © 1988 By THE FOUNDATION PRESS, INC.
615 Merrick Ave.
Westbury, N.Y. 11590

Library of Congress Cataloging-in-Publication Data

Hart, Henry Melvin.

  Hart and Wechsler's the federal courts and the federal system.—
3rd ed. / by Paul M. Bator ... [et al.]
    p.   cm.—(University casebook series)
  Includes index.

  ISBN 0-88277-647-9

  1. Courts—United States—Cases. 2. Jurisdiction—United States—
Cases. I. Wechsler, Herbert, 1909–   . II. Bator, Paul.
III. Title. IV. Title: Federal courts and the federal system.
V. Series.
KF8718.H32 1988
347.73'2—dc19
[347.3071]
                                                                88-16486
                                                                CIP

Hart & Wechsler—Fed. Courts & System 3d Ed. UCB
1st Reprint—1989

The first edition of this book was dedicated
TO FELIX FRANKFURTER
who first opened our minds
to these problems

The second edition was dedicated to the memory of
HENRY M. HART, JR.
profound and passionate
student and teacher

The editors of the third edition add a dedication
to the memory of
HENRY J. FRIENDLY
man for all seasons in the law;
master of this subject

*

PREFACE
TO THE
THIRD EDITION

Authors of new editions tend to brag about how much there is that is new. In contrast, we are particularly pleased that so much of the classic First Edition remains alive in this, the Third. We have sought to retain the historical and analytical richness of the first two editions, as well as their editorial method, which connects the relatively few leading cases with a series of detailed monographs that discuss the background of the case and further developments in the field. We continue to believe, with the editors of the First Edition, that "over-simplification is no service to advanced students," and therefore have continued to raise in the notes more questions than can be answered. (The quotation is from the Preface to the First Edition, which is reprinted hereafter.) And we have persisted in the aim of treating the subject with the sophistication that will make the book useful to practitioners, judges, and scholars as well as law students. We have preserved the "great" historical cases, believing that students should read (rather than merely hear about) Marbury v. Madison, Martin v. Hunter's Lessee and Murdock v. Memphis, McCardle and Osborn v. Bank, Swift v. Tyson and Erie. Indeed, we have added, as leading cases, some of the "classics" (Ex parte Young; United States v. Lee; Brown v. Allen; Monroe v. Pape; Rooker v. Fidelity Trust) that were not printed as leading cases in the first two editions.

Alas, the First Edition's general (though not invariable) practice of printing leading cases in their entirety, without editing, has been made increasingly impracticable by the loquaciousness of the modern Supreme Court; we have thus, increasingly, resorted to the common modern habit of presenting the cases in reduced form.

In this edition, as in the Second, we have attempted to retain the special flavor brought to the book by the styles and personalities of the two remarkable original editors, Herbert Wechsler and the late Henry Hart. In particular, as in the Second Edition, we have kept intact the entire text of Hart's celebrated "Dialogue" on congressional power to restrict the jurisdiction of the federal courts (using footnotes and additional text notes to bring the material up to date).

II.

The organization of the book has much that is old and some that is new.

The first five chapters follow the organization of the First and Second Editions. Chapter I provides a brief introductory overview of the history of Article III and of the federal judicial system and its workings. The second chapter is devoted to the "case or controversy" problem and related problems of justiciability. The third is a study of the Supreme Court's original jurisdiction. The fourth deals with congressional power to control federal and state court jurisdiction. And the fifth studies Supreme Court review of state court judgments.

Old Chapter VI, on the law applied in the federal district courts, has been divided into two, with a new separate Chapter VII covering federal common law. Innovations here include an attempt, in Section 4 of Chapter VI, to collect the scattered parts of the old editions that dealt with the varied effects of state law on exercise of federal court jurisdiction. The new Chapter VII reflects the huge growth of the federal common law, already shown by voluminous additions made to the Second Edition by the 1977 and 1981 Supplements. The subject of implied rights of action, in particular, has been greatly expanded. Chapter VII now also includes the materials on federal common law crimes and on the implication of rights of action by the United States (formerly found in old Chapter IX on federal government litigation).

Chapter VIII (covering the first half of "old" Chapter VII) deals with the rules governing the "arising under" jurisdiction of the federal district courts. To this has been added a new separate section on federal question removal (which includes the materials on civil rights removal and federal official removal). The last section of Chapter VIII, on "related heads of jurisdiction," contains brief notes on the admiralty jurisdiction and on criminal and civil cases initiated by the federal government.

Chapters IX and X represent a substantial innovation in the organization of the book. Chapter IX covers suits against federal and state governments and their officials, collecting in one chapter (and greatly expanding) materials that formed parts of Chapters VII and IX of the previous editions. The new form of organization allows a more integrated treatment of subjects such as sovereign immunity and official immunity. The chapter reflects, too, the enormous growth in this subject since 1973; it thus includes large bodies of new material—for instance, on the various forms of immunity to suit, and on § 1983 cases against state officials.

Chapter X covers statutory rules and judicial doctrines based on notions of federalism and comity that limit the exercise of district court jurisdiction, primarily (but not exclusively) in cases against state and local governments and officials. Treatment of all the various forms of abstention are now collected in this chapter.

Chapter XI is devoted to federal habeas corpus. Chapter XII is entirely new: called "Advanced Problems in Judicial Federalism," it deals with res judicata problems and with special "borderline" problems that have developed at the intersections of doctrines such as res judicata, comity, and exhaustion. Chapter XIII presents the diversity materials that used to form part of Chapter VII. Chapter XIV is devoted to "Additional Problems of District Court Jurisdiction": challenges to jurisdiction, process and venue, jurisdictional amount, removal, and conflicts among federal courts. Chapter XV, finally, covers the federal appellate system and the certiorari jurisdiction.

III.

We realize, of course, that no course (in any except a fantasized law school) could cover this entire work. Teachers may be interested in some suggestions as to selecting materials. We view Chapter I as important background reading for any course. The materials in Chapter II are dealt with in many basic constitutional law courses; and most of Chapter VI (Erie; Guaranty Trust, Hanna; etc.) is usually covered in the basic course in Civil Procedure. A teacher of a three semester-hour course who is using this book might, therefore, try to cover Sections 1A and 2 of Chapter IV; Sections 1, 2A, and 2B of Chapter V (together with the relevant pages of Chapter XI that are incorporated by reference at p. 628); a few selections from VI; VII; VIII (Sections 1–4); IX (Section 2); and X (Sections 1 and 2A–2C). Some or all of Chapter XII could be added. A teacher of a four semester-hour course could add some or all of the rest of Chapters IV, V, VIII, IX, X, and XII, and also cover some of Chapters II, XI, and XIII.

IV.

The active work in preparing this edition was done by Professors Bator, Meltzer and Shapiro, with Professors Mishkin and Wechsler providing important advice and commentary. The allocation of responsibilities was as follows:

Bator: Chapters III; IV (Section 1B); V; VIII; XI; and XII.

Meltzer: Chapters II (Section 3); IX; X.

Shapiro: Chapters I; II (Sections 1–2, 4–6); IV (except Section 1B); VI; VII; XIII; XIV; and XV.

V.

A few notes on questions of form are in order. Although we recognize that the denial of certiorari by the Supreme Court may have some significance to persons besides the litigants themselves, we have economized on space by omitting this reference in the citation of state and lower federal court cases, except in the few instances where it has special relevance. With respect to principal cases and quotations in text, no indication of footnotes or of citations omitted is given; those footnotes that have been retained carry their original numbers. All other omissions, whether of a few words, a paragraph, or several pages, are indicated by * * *.

One work that is frequently cited in these materials is the American Law Institute Study of the Division of Jurisdiction Between State and Federal Courts—a study that was published in 1969 and that has been the subject of extensive legislative, judicial, and scholarly consideration. It is cited throughout simply as the ALI Study.

VI.

The important work of Professor Stanley Katz as consultant on the historical materials in Chapter I, done in connection with the Second Edition, has been carried forward into this edition. The perceptive comments of Professor Vicki Jackson of Georgetown University greatly improved Chapter IX. Timothy Bishop, Esquire, of Mayer, Brown & Platt in Chicago, was of immense help in the revision of Chapter XI.

The following graduate and undergraduate students also helped at various times with research, the preparation and checking of the manuscript, and the preparation of the index: Gregory Baer, Amy Chua, Owen Clements, Douglas Masters, Barbara Fried, Robert Gilbert, Michael Levy, William Levy, Peter Mulhern, Miriam Nemetz, Seth Tucker, and Scott Winkelman. Their valuable assistance is gratefully acknowledged.

Our thanks also to Beth Drufva, Brenda Huffman, Maura Kelley, and Fabienne Lentz for their able secretarial assistance and unfailing patience and good cheer.

The research on Chapters V, VIII, XI and XII was aided by the Russell J. Parsons Faculty Research Fund of the University of Chicago Law School. The firm of Mayer, Brown & Platt, in Chicago, led by Robert A. Helman and Leo Herzel, made its resources generously available to Professor Bator for his part of the work; we are most grateful.

VII.

Various authors participated in various ways as counsel in some of the cases discussed in this book. After some discussion among us, we came to the conclusion that it would constitute an excess of scruple and pedantry to advert in each case, by footnote, to such participation. We are confident that our editorial process has fairly guarded us against partisan treatment (or undue leaning-over-backwards) with respect to the cases in question.

VIII.

Permission to quote from the following is gratefully acknowledged:

Hon. Henry Friendly, *In Praise of Erie—And of the New Federal Common Law*, 39 N.Y.U. Law Review 383 (1964), © 1964 by New York University.

Hon. Henry Friendly, *Is Innocence Irrelevant? Collateral Attack on Criminal Judgments*, 38 U. Chicago Law Review 142 (1970), © 1970 by the University of Chicago.

Professor Peter Linzer, *The Meaning of Certiorari Denials*, 79 Columbia Law Review 1227 (1979), © 1979 by the Directors of the Columbia Law Review Association, Inc.

P.M.B.
D.J.M.
D.L.S.

May 1988

*

PREFACE
TO THE
FIRST EDITION

I.

One of the consequences of our federalism is a legal system that derives from both the Nation and the states as separate sources of authority and is administered by state and federal judiciaries, functioning in far more subtle combination than is readily perceived. The resulting legal problems are the subject of this book. They are examined here mainly from the point of view of the federal courts and of Congress when it legislates respecting the judicial system. The frequently neglected problems posed in the administration of federal law by state courts have not, however, been ignored.

The jurisdiction of courts in a federal system is an aspect of the distribution of power between the states and the federal government. Federal jurisdiction, as our subject is usually called, would surely be a sterile topic were it not explored in this perspective. Questions of jurisdiction, however, bear commonly a subordinate or derivative relation to the distinct problem of determining the respective spheres of operation of federal and state law. It is in the effort to identify and to delineate these areas of federal and state authority that the nature of federalism and its crucial problems are, in our view, most significantly revealed. The book is concerned, therefore, with the relationship of federal and state law, both as guides to judicial decision and in everyday affairs, no less than with the jurisdiction of the federal courts and the relation of those courts to the tribunals of the states.

Problems of federal and state legislative competence are, of course, the main subject of elementary courses in constitutional law. Such courses tend, however, to deal with issues of this kind as they arise in clear-cut instances of conflict between federal and state assertions, calling for the adjudication of competing claims of power. These dramatic conflicts touch only the beginnings of the problems, as the materials in this volume should make clear. For every case in which a court is asked to invalidate a square assertion of state or federal legislative authority, there are many more in which the allocation of control does not involve questions of ultimate power; Congress has been silent with respect to the displacement of the normal state-created norms, leaving courts to face the problem as an issue of the choice of law. The book tries to suggest something of the variety of these questions and of their significance; it points to the importance of the postulates of federalism in the common run of litigation; it asks the question whether Congress cannot profitably give increased attention to these issues and attempts to show respects in which such conscious management of our federalism, on this mundane, working level, might produce important gains. Without depreciating the importance of the problems facing courts, we are concerned throughout with the issues of legislative policy that the nature of our system puts to Congress. The legislative possibilities have received less attention than they merit, though they arise throughout the field.

The book deals mainly with these problems of federal-state relationships but it also has two secondary themes. In varying contexts we pose the issue of what courts are good for—and are not good for—seeking thus to open up the whole range of questions as to the appropriate relationship between the federal courts and other organs of federal and state government. We also pose throughout problems of the organization and management of the federal courts, wishing to promote understanding of the task of federal judicial administration and of the means available for its improvement.

The study of federal jurisdiction has commonly been coupled with that of federal procedure. What has been said will make clear why it is uncoupled here. Procedural problems remain in plenty, to be sure, as they must in any study of law administration, but they are raised and dealt with only as incidents of other problems posited by the main themes. In the editors' own schools, systematic instruction in federal practice takes place in procedure courses built around the Federal Rules of Civil Procedure or in which those Rules play a central part. Independently of this, however, we are convinced that studying procedure for its own sake, as of course it should be studied, is alien to the main inquiries projected by this book. The effort to combine them in law teaching serves, in our view, to produce a misalliance that accords to neither subject the attention it deserves.

II.

Though this book was planned and executed in the hope that it might be of use in practice as well as in the schools, it is primarily a teaching book, designed to lay the basis for an advanced course in public law. The course that we envisage would be offered to students who are grounded both in constitutional law and in conflicts of laws or, at the least, are studying those subjects simultaneously. In present curricula, courses suited for this purpose vary in length from two to four semester hours, and the book has been designed for accommodation to this fact, as a brief summary of its contents will disclose.

The opening chapter is intended primarily for introductory reading rather than classroom discussion. Looked at either historically or contemporaneously, the federal judicial system is an organic unity; and this chapter seeks to meet the difficulty that effective study of any part of the system necessarily presupposes some familiarity with the whole. It has also the purpose of enabling instructors in shorter courses to confine intensive work to selected aspects of the subject without undue impairment of general understanding.

Most teachers of two or three semester hour courses will probably decide to omit both the second chapter on the nature of the federal judicial function and the third chapter on the Supreme Court's original jurisdiction. The elements of the concept of a case or controversy are ordinarily considered in basic courses in constitutional law. In an advanced course, accordingly, choice lies between thorough study and either complete omission or review of only the basic principles dealt with in the introductory section of the chapter. The practical importance of the original jurisdiction obviously does not match its theoretical interest. But if this jurisdiction is to be studied at all, the editors believe it should be studied at an early stage. It exemplifies the simplest and most basic form of federal judicial organization, and affords both an illuminating introduction to central problems of federal law and an understanding of the practical considerations which, in the United States, have compelled reliance, for the vindication of federal interests, upon the more complex devices of federal review of state court decisions and the establishment of a full-fledged hierarchy of federal trial and appellate courts. The jurisdiction is rich, too, in suggestions of the problems and possibilities of supra-national judicial organization.

The next five chapters (Chapters IV to VIII, inclusive) are the core of the book and have been conceived as providing the main substance of a two or three semester hour course.

Apart from the Supreme Court's original jurisdiction, the jurisdiction of the federal courts and of the state courts in federal matters are both subject to broad powers of congressional regulation. The fourth chapter examines the main alternatives which are open to Congress under the Constitution in the exercise of these powers. The severe compression of a two semester hour course may force an instructor to deal lightly with the relatively specialized and complex problems of partial or total denial of jurisdiction in any court, although these are among the most challenging in the whole subject. An understanding of the constitutional powers of Congress simply to distribute jurisdiction between state and federal courts, however, is an essential foundation for consideration, throughout the remainder of the course, of the issues of legislative and interpretive policy which the existence of these powers must continually pose.

The scheme of the next three chapters, broadly speaking, is to examine first of all problems of the delimitation of *issues* of federal cognizance before proceeding to the more complex problems of delimitation of *cases* of federal cognizance.

The fifth chapter accordingly begins with the study of Supreme Court review of state court decisions. The Supreme Court, of course, asserts power on occasion to reexamine the decisions of state courts on questions of state law. But these assertions are few and carefully justified in terms of the need of safeguarding federal rights against frustration or evasion. Generally, questions of jurisdiction and of identification of the applicable law are coextensive, with the qualification only that an admittedly federal issue will not be decided unless the decision will control the Court's judgment. Regarded only in terms of abstract jurisdictional doctrine, the cases on the Supreme Court's authority to review state court decisions can be reduced to a few relatively simple propositions. Regarded from the point of view of the considerations which have prompted the identification of particular issues as state or federal, however, they become a rich storehouse for the study of federalism.

Against this background, the sixth chapter turns to questions of identification of the applicable law in the district courts. Some of these questions, it will be observed, are of the same type as those encountered in the preceding chapter. Others, however, are of different types, reflecting crucial differences between an appellate and an original jurisdiction. Some of the new questions result from the peculiar difficulties of a federal jurisdiction based simply upon diversity of citizenship. Others, more significantly, reveal afresh the essentially interstitial nature of federal law and its characteristic inadequacy as a complete guide to the disposition in the first instance even of actions founded upon claims of federal right.

The next chapter (Chapter VII) explores the fundamentals of federal question and diversity jurisdiction. The important section on federal question jurisdiction builds upon the previous study of identification of federal issues, bringing in only the added complexity of distinguishing between those federal issues which serve as a basis of original federal jurisdiction and those which do not. The third section in the chapter singles out for special consideration the distinctive problems presented by actions claiming federal constitutional protection against state officials.

The eighth chapter on general aspects of district court jurisdiction is the last in the central group of basic chapters. It begins with examination of more technical, workaday questions of venue, process, and litigating capacity, jurisdictional amount, and removal jurisdiction. In the concluding sections, however, issues of federalism move again to the forefront in the consideration of special limitations upon the use of the federal courts as tribunals for the administration of state law and of problems of the conflicts of jurisdiction between federal and state courts.

The ninth and tenth chapters reflect a decision to deal in some detail with two of the federal specialities and no others. The book touches upon federal jurisdiction in admiralty and bankruptcy and in patent, trade-mark, and copyright cases only to the extent that doctrines in those fields illuminate general principles. Specialized problems in these fields had better be left to specialized courses. With respect to federal habeas corpus and federal government litigation, however, a different judgment was reached. These matters are not commonly the subject of separate law school courses. They are of high importance and, as even the severely condensed treatment in this volume shows, they have suffered too long from both scholarly and professional neglect. Instructors who are unable to reach these chapters may find it possible and profitable to supplement Chapters VII and VIII by reference to part of this material.

The concluding chapter (Chapter XI) deals with appellate review of federal decisions and with the certiorari policy. The main outlines of federal appellate jurisdiction are implicit, and often explicit, in the cases considered in the main body of the book. The function of the first two sections of this final chapter, accordingly, is one largely of summary and clarification of important technical points. The last section focuses attention on the far-reaching problems of governmental and judicial administration raised by the Supreme Court's vast power, in the review of both federal and state decisions, not only to decide cases but also to decide what cases it is willing to decide.

III.

A word should be said about editorial method. The principal cases, less than a hundred and fifty in number, have been chosen with a view to their usefulness as the chief centers of classroom discussion. Related cases are abstracted, and related problems discussed, in the accompanying text notes. The text notes, it will be evident, raise many more questions than class discussion can hope to explore. We have proceeded here on the conviction that over-simplification is no service to advanced students and have tried to put before the reader something of the breadth of background and knowledge that an experienced teacher brings to a subject—or a teacher's manual seeks to give an inexperienced one. The general, if not invariable, rule, moreover, has been that references to variant decisions or important secondary discussions ought not to be blind. An effort has accordingly been made to tell enough about the decision or comment referred to so that the reader will not need to get the book from the shelf before he can begin to think about the problem. This relative fullness of discussion, it is hoped, will enhance the usefulness of the book to practitioners as well as to students.

Successive classes of students, using a series of temporary editions of these materials at both the Columbia and Harvard Law Schools, have made suggestions contributing inestimably to the final product. Professor Paul Mishkin of the University of Pennsylvania Law School has made helpful comments from an instructor's point of view. For assistance in preparing drafts of various notes we are particularly indebted to Sterling F. Black of the class of 1949, Columbia; Roger S. Kuhn of the class of 1951, Columbia; Stanton S. Oswald of the class of 1952, Harvard; M. Bernard Aidinoff, Jack A. Hamer and Aram Jack Kevorkian, all of the class of 1953, Harvard. We gratefully acknowledge also the labors of Mrs. Jerome Edward Feinberg of New York City and Mrs. Byron D. Coney of Seattle, Washington, in preparing the manuscript for the printer; of Aram Jack Kevorkian, in making up the index; and of George E. Shertzer of the class of 1953, Columbia; and Alan N. Cohen of the class of 1954, Columbia, in working on the proofs.

H. M. H., Jr.
H. W.

August, 1953

*

SUMMARY OF CONTENTS

SUMMARY OF CONTENTS

SUMMARY OF CONTENTS

*

Page

TABLE OF CONTENTS

TABLE OF CONTENTS

Page

xlv

TABLE OF CASES

Principal cases are in italic type. Cases cited or discussed are in roman type. References are to Pages.

li

THE CONSTITUTION OF THE UNITED STATES OF AMERICA

We the People of the United States, in Order to form a more perfect Union, establish Justice, insure domestic Tranquility, provide for the common defence, promote the general Welfare, and secure the Blessings of Liberty to ourselves and our Posterity, do ordain and establish this Constitution for the United States of America.

ARTICLE I

Section 1. All legislative Powers herein granted shall be vested in a Congress of the United States, which shall consist of a Senate and House of Representatives.

Section 2. The House of Representatives shall be composed of Members chosen every second Year by the People of the several States, and the Electors in each State shall have the Qualifications requisite for Electors of the most numerous Branch of the State Legislature.

No Person shall be a Representative who shall not have attained to the Age of twenty five Years, and been seven Years a Citizen of the United States, and who shall not, when elected, be an Inhabitant of that State in which he shall be chosen.

Representatives and direct Taxes shall be apportioned among the several States which may be included within this Union, according to their respective Numbers, which shall be determined by adding to the whole Number of free Persons, including those bound to Service for a Term of Years, and excluding Indians not taxed, three fifths of all other Persons. The actual Enumeration shall be made within three Years after the first Meeting of the Congress of the United States, and within every subsequent Term of ten Years, in such Manner as they shall by Law direct. The Number of Representatives shall not exceed one for every thirty Thousand, but each State shall have at Least one Representative; and until such enumeration shall be made, the State of New Hampshire shall be entitled to chuse three, Massachusetts eight, Rhode Island and Providence Plantations one, Connecticut five, New York six, New Jersey four, Pennsylvania eight, Delaware one, Maryland six, Virginia ten, North Carolina five, South Carolina five, and Georgia three.

When vacancies happen in the Representation from any State, the Executive Authority thereof shall issue Writs of Election to fill such Vacancies.

The House of Representatives shall chuse their Speaker and other Officers; and shall have the sole Power of Impeachment.

Section 3. The Senate of the United States shall be composed of two Senators from each State, chosen by the Legislature thereof, for six Years; and each Senator shall have one Vote.

Immediately after they shall be assembled in Consequence of the first Election, they shall be divided as equally as may be into three Classes. The Seats of the Senators of the first Class shall be vacated at the Expiration of the second Year, of the second Class at the Expiration of the fourth Year, and of the third Class at the Expiration of the sixth Year, so that one third may be chosen every second Year; and if Vacancies happen by Resignation, or otherwise, during the Recess of the Legislature of any State, the Executive thereof may make temporary Appointments until the next Meeting of the Legislature, which shall then fill such Vacancies.

No Person shall be a Senator who shall not have attained to the Age of thirty Years, and been nine Years a Citizen of the United States, and who shall not, when elected, be an Inhabitant of that State for which he shall be chosen.

The Vice President of the United States shall be President of the Senate, but shall have no Vote, unless they be equally divided.

The Senate shall chuse their other Officers, and also a President pro tempore, in the Absence of the Vice President, or when he shall exercise the Office of President of the United States.

The Senate shall have the sole Power to try all Impeachments. When sitting for that Purpose, they shall be on Oath or Affirmation. When the President of the United States is tried, the Chief Justice shall preside: And no Person shall be convicted without the Concurrence of two thirds of the Members present.

Judgment in Cases of Impeachment shall not extend further than to removal from Office, and disqualification to hold and enjoy any Office of honor, Trust, or Profit under the United States: but the Party convicted shall nevertheless be liable and subject to Indictment, Trial, Judgment, and Punishment, according to Law.

Section 4. The Times, Places and Manner of holding Elections for Senators and Representatives, shall be prescribed in each State by the Legislature thereof; but the Congress may at any time by Law make or alter such Regulations, except as to the Places of chusing Senators.

The Congress shall assemble at least once in every Year, and such Meeting shall be on the first Monday in December, unless they shall by Law appoint a different Day.

Section 5. Each House shall be the Judge of the Elections, Returns, and Qualifications of its own Members, and a Majority of each shall constitute a Quorum to do Business; but a smaller Number may adjourn from day to day, and may be authorized to compel the Attendance of absent Members, in such Manner, and under such Penalties as each House may provide.

Each House may determine the Rules of its Proceedings, punish its Members for disorderly Behaviour, and, with the Concurrence of two thirds, expel a Member.

Each House shall keep a Journal of its Proceedings, and from time to time publish the same, excepting such Parts as may in their Judgment require Secrecy; and the Yeas and Nays of the Members of either House on any question shall, at the Desire of one fifth of those Present, be entered on the Journal.

Neither House, during the Session of Congress, shall, without the Consent of the other, adjourn for more than three days, nor to any other Place than that in which the two Houses shall be sitting.

Section 6. The Senators and Representatives shall receive a Compensation for their Services, to be ascertained by Law, and paid out of the Treasury of the United States. They shall in all Cases, except Treason, Felony and Breach of the Peace, be privileged from Arrest during their Attendance at the Session of their respective Houses, and in going to and returning from the same; and for any Speech or Debate in either House, they shall not be questioned in any other Place.

No Senator or Representative shall, during the Time for which he was elected, be appointed to any civil Office under the Authority of the United States, which shall have been created, or the Emoluments whereof shall have been encreased during such time; and no Person holding any Office under the United States, shall be a Member of either House during his Continuance in Office.

Section 7. All Bills for raising Revenue shall originate in the House of Representatives; but the Senate may propose or concur with Amendments as on other Bills.

Every Bill which shall have passed the House of Representatives and the Senate, shall, before it become a Law, be presented to the President of the United States; If he approves he shall sign it, but if not he shall return it, with his Objections to that House in which it shall have originated, who shall enter the Objections at large on their Journal, and proceed to reconsider it. If after such Reconsideration two thirds of that House shall agree to pass the Bill, it shall be sent together with the Objections, to the other House, by which it shall likewise be reconsidered, and if approved by two thirds of that House, it shall become a Law. But in all such Cases the Votes of both Houses shall be determined by Yeas and Nays, and the Names of the Persons voting for and against the Bill shall be entered on the Journal of each House respectively. If any Bill shall not be returned by the President within ten Days (Sundays excepted) after it shall have been presented to him, the Same shall be a Law, in like Manner as if he had signed it, unless the Congress by their Adjournment prevent its Return in which Case it shall not be a Law.

Every Order, Resolution, or Vote, to Which the Concurrence of the Senate and House of Representatives may be necessary (except on a question of Adjournment) shall be presented to the President of the United States; and before the Same shall take Effect, shall be approved by him, or being disapproved by him, shall be repassed by two thirds of the Senate and House of Representatives, according to the Rules and Limitations prescribed in the Case of a Bill.

Section 8. The Congress shall have Power To lay and collect Taxes, Duties, Imposts and Excises, to pay the Debts and provide for the common Defence and general Welfare of the United States; but all Duties, Imposts and Excises shall be uniform throughout the United States;

To borrow Money on the credit of the United States;

To regulate Commerce with foreign Nations, and among the several States, and with the Indian Tribes;

To establish an uniform Rule of Naturalization, and uniform Laws on the subject of Bankruptcies throughout the United States;

To coin Money, regulate the Value thereof, and of foreign Coin, and fix the Standard of Weights and Measures;

To provide for the Punishment of counterfeiting the Securities and current Coin of the United States;

To Establish Post Offices and Post Roads;

To promote the Progress of Science and useful Arts, by securing for limited Times to Authors and Inventors the exclusive Right to their respective Writings and Discoveries;

To constitute Tribunals inferior to the supreme Court;

To define and punish Piracies and Felonies committed on the high Seas, and Offences against the Law of Nations;

To declare War, grant Letters of Marque and Reprisal, and make Rules concerning Captures on Land and Water;

To raise and support Armies, but no Appropriation of Money to that Use shall be for a longer Term than two Years;

To provide and maintain a Navy;

To make Rules for the Government and Regulation of the land and naval Forces;

To provide for calling forth the Militia to execute the Laws of the Union, suppress Insurrections and repel Invasions;

To provide for organizing, arming, and disciplining, the Militia, and for governing such Part of them as may be employed in the Service of the United States, reserving to the States respectively, the Appointment of the Officers, and the Authority of training the Militia according to the discipline prescribed by Congress;

To exercise exclusive Legislation in all Cases whatsoever, over such District (not exceeding ten Miles square) as may, by Cession of particular States, and the Acceptance of Congress, become the Seat of the Government of the United States, and to exercise like Authority over all Places purchased by the Consent of the Legislature of the State in which the Same shall be, for the Erection of Forts, Magazines, Arsenals, dock-Yards, and other needful Buildings;—And

To make all Laws which shall be necessary and proper for carrying into Execution the foregoing Powers, and all other Powers vested by this

Constitution in the Government of the United States, or in any Department or Officer thereof.

Section 9. The Migration or Importation of Such Persons as any of the States now existing shall think proper to admit, shall not be prohibited by the Congress prior to the Year one thousand eight hundred and eight, but a Tax or duty may be imposed on such Importation, not exceeding ten dollars for each Person.

The Privilege of the Writ of Habeas Corpus shall not be suspended, unless when in Cases of Rebellion or Invasion the public Safety may require it.

No Bill of Attainder or ex post facto Law shall be passed.

No Capitation, or other direct, Tax shall be laid, unless in Proportion to the Census or Enumeration herein before directed to be taken.

No Tax or Duty shall be laid on Articles exported from any State.

No Preference shall be given by any Regulation of Commerce or Revenue to the Ports of one State over those of another: nor shall Vessels bound to, or from, one State be obliged to enter, clear, or pay Duties in another.

No Money shall be drawn from the Treasury, but in Consequence of Appropriations made by Law; and a regular Statement and Account of the Receipts and Expenditures of all public Money shall be published from time to time.

No Title of Nobility shall be granted by the United States: And no Person holding any Office of Profit or Trust under them, shall, without the Consent of the Congress, accept of any present, Emolument, Office, or Title, of any kind whatever, from any King, Prince, or foreign State.

Section 10. No State shall enter into any Treaty, Alliance, or Confederation; grant Letters of Marque and Reprisal; coin Money; emit Bills of Credit; make any Thing but gold and silver Coin a Tender in Payment of Debts; pass any Bill of Attainder, ex post facto Law, or Law impairing the Obligation of Contracts, or grant any Title of Nobility.

No State shall, without the Consent of the Congress, lay any Imposts or Duties on Imports or Exports, except what may be absolutely necessary for executing its inspection Laws: and the net Produce of all Duties and Imposts, laid by any State on Imports or Exports, shall be for the Use of the Treasury of the United States; and all such Laws shall be subject to the Revision and Controul of the Congress.

No State shall, without the Consent of Congress, lay any Duty of Tonnage, keep Troops, or Ships of War in time of Peace, enter into any Agreement or Compact with another State, or with a foreign Power, or engage in War, unless actually invaded, or in such imminent Danger as will not admit of delay.

ARTICLE II

Section 1. The executive Power shall be vested in a President of the United States of America. He shall hold his Office during the Term of four Years, and, together with the Vice President, chosen for the same Term, be elected, as follows:

Each State shall appoint, in such Manner as the Legislature thereof may direct, a Number of Electors, equal to the whole Number of Senators and Representatives to which the State may be entitled in the Congress; but no Senator or Representative, or Person holding an Office of Trust or Profit under the United States, shall be appointed an Elector.

The Electors shall meet in their respective States, and vote by Ballot for two Persons, of whom one at least shall not be an Inhabitant of the same State with themselves. And they shall make a List of all the Persons voted for, and of the Number of Votes for each; which List they shall sign and certify, and transmit sealed to the Seat of the Government of the United States, directed to the President of the Senate. The President of the Senate shall, in the Presence of the Senate and House of Representatives, open all the Certificates, and the Votes shall then be counted. The Person having the greatest Number of Votes shall be the President, if such Number be a Majority of the whole Number of Electors appointed; and if there be more than one who have such Majority, and have an equal Number of Votes, then the House of Representatives shall immediately chuse by Ballot one of them for President; and if no Person have a Majority, then from the five highest on the List the said House shall in like Manner chuse the President. But in chusing the President, the Votes shall be taken by States, the Representation from each State having one Vote; A quorum for this Purpose shall consist of a Member or Members from two thirds of the States, and a Majority of all the States shall be necessary to a Choice. In every Case, after the Choice of the President, the Person having the greater Number of Votes of the Electors shall be the Vice President. But if there should remain two or more who have equal Votes, the Senate shall chuse from them by Ballot the Vice President.

The Congress may determine the Time of chusing the Electors, and the Day on which they shall give their Votes; which Day shall be the same throughout the United States.

No person except a natural born Citizen, or a Citizen of the United States, at the time of the Adoption of this Constitution, shall be eligible to the Office of President; neither shall any Person be eligible to that Office who shall not have attained to the Age of thirty five Years, and been fourteen Years a Resident within the United States.

In case of the removal of the President from Office, or of his Death, Resignation or Inability to discharge the Powers and Duties of the said Office, the Same shall devolve on the Vice President, and the Congress may by Law provide for the Case of Removal, Death, Resignation or Inability, both of the President and Vice President, declaring what Officer shall then act as President, and such Officer shall act accordingly, until the Disability be removed, or a President shall be elected.

The President shall, at stated Times, receive for his Services, a Compensation, which shall neither be encreased nor diminished during the Period for which he shall have been elected, and he shall not receive within that Period any other Emolument from the United States, or any of them.

Before he enter on the Execution of his Office, he shall take the following Oath or Affirmation: "I do solemnly swear (or affirm) that I will faithfully execute the Office of President of the United States, and will to the best of my Ability, preserve, protect and defend the Constitution of the United States."

Section 2. The President shall be Commander in Chief of the Army and Navy of the United States, and of the militia of the several States, when called into the actual Service of the United States; he may require the Opinion, in writing, of the principal Officer in each of the executive Departments, upon any Subject relating to the Duties of their respective Offices, and he shall have Power to grant Reprieves and Pardons for Offenses against the United States, except in Cases of Impeachment.

He shall have Power, by and with the Advice and Consent of the Senate, to make Treaties, provided two thirds of the Senators present concur; and he shall nominate, and by and with the Advice and Consent of the Senate, shall appoint Ambassadors, other public Ministers and Consuls, Judges of the supreme Court, and all other Officers of the United States, whose Appointments are not herein otherwise provided for, and which shall be established by Law; but the Congress may by Law vest the Appointment of such inferior Officers, as they think proper, in the President alone, in the Courts of Law, or in the Heads of Departments.

The President shall have power to fill up all Vacancies that may happen during the Recess of the Senate, by granting Commissions which shall expire at the End of their next Session.

Section 3. He shall from time to time give to the Congress Information of the State of the Union, and recommend to their Consideration such Measures as he shall judge necessary and expedient; he may, on extraordinary Occasions, convene both Houses, or either of them, and in Case of Disagreement between them, with Respect to the Time of Adjournment, he may adjourn them to such Time as he shall think proper; he shall receive Ambassadors and other public Ministers; he shall take Care that the Laws be faithfully executed, and shall Commission all the Officers of the United States.

Section 4. The President, Vice President and all civil Officers of the United States, shall be removed from Office on Impeachment for, and Conviction of, Treason, Bribery, or other high Crimes and Misdemeanors.

ARTICLE III

Section 1. The judicial Power of the United States, shall be vested in one supreme Court, and in such inferior Courts as the Congress may from time to time ordain and establish. The Judges, both of the supreme and inferior Courts, shall hold their Offices during good Behaviour, and shall, at stated Times, receive for their Services a Compensation, which shall not be diminished during their Continuance in Office.

Section 2. The judicial Power shall extend to all Cases, in Law and Equity, arising under this Constitution, the Laws of the United States, and Treaties made, or which shall be made, under their Authority;—to all Cases affecting Ambassadors, other public Ministers and Consuls;—to all Cases of admiralty and maritime Jurisdiction;—to Controversies to which the United States shall be a Party;—to Controversies between two or more States;—between a State and Citizens of another State;—between Citizens of different States;—between Citizens of the same State claiming Lands under the Grants of different States, and between a State, or the Citizens thereof, and foreign States, Citizens or Subjects.

where? All ?

In all Cases affecting Ambassadors, other public Ministers and Consuls, and those in which a State shall be a Party, the supreme Court shall have original Jurisdiction. In all the other Cases before mentioned, the supreme Court shall have appellate Jurisdiction, both as to Law and Fact, with such Exceptions, and under such Regulations as the Congress shall make.

The trial of all Crimes, except in Cases of Impeachment, shall be by Jury; and such Trial shall be held in the State where the said Crimes shall have been committed; but when not committed within any State, the Trial shall be at such Place or Places as the Congress may by Law have directed.

Section 3. Treason against the United States, shall consist only in levying War against them, or, in adhering to their Enemies, giving them Aid and Comfort. No Person shall be convicted of Treason unless on the Testimony of two Witnesses to the same overt Act, or on Confession in open Court.

The Congress shall have Power to declare the Punishment of Treason, but no Attainder of Treason shall work Corruption of Blood, or Forfeiture except during the Life of the Person attained.

ARTICLE IV

Section 1. Full Faith and Credit shall be given in each State to the public Acts, Records, and judicial Proceedings of every other State. And the Congress may by general Laws prescribe the Manner in which such Acts, Records and Proceedings shall be proved, and the Effect thereof.

Section 2. The Citizens of each State shall be entitled to all Privileges and Immunities of Citizens in the several States.

A Person charged in any State with Treason, Felony, or other Crime, who shall flee from Justice, and be found in another State, shall on demand of the executive Authority of the State from which he fled, be delivered up, to be removed to the State having Jurisdiction of the Crime.

No Person held to Service or Labour in one State, under the Laws thereof, escaping into another, shall, in Consequence of any Law or Regulation therein, be discharged from such Service or Labour, but shall be delivered up on Claim of the Party to whom such Service or Labour may be due.

Section 3. New States may be admitted by the Congress into this Union; but no new State shall be formed or erected within the Jurisdiction of any other State; nor any State be formed by the Junction of two or more States, or Parts of States, without the Consent of the Legislatures of the States concerned as well as of the Congress.

The Congress shall have Power to dispose of and make all needful Rules and Regulations respecting the Territory or other Property belonging to the United States; and nothing in this Constitution shall be so construed as to Prejudice any Claims of the United States, or of any particular State.

Section 4. The United States shall guarantee to every State in this Union a Republican Form of Government, and shall protect each of them against Invasion; and on Application of the Legislature, or of the Executive (when the Legislature cannot be convened) against domestic Violence.

ARTICLE V

The Congress, whenever two thirds of both Houses shall deem it necessary, shall propose Amendments to this Constitution, or, on the Application of the Legislatures of two thirds of the several States, shall call a Convention for proposing Amendments, which, in either Case, shall be valid to all Intents and Purposes, as part of this Constitution, when ratified by the Legislatures of three fourths of the several States, or by Conventions in three fourths thereof, as the one or the other Mode of Ratification may be proposed by the Congress; Provided that no Amendment which may be made prior to the Year One thousand eight hundred and eight shall in any Manner affect the first and fourth Clauses in the Ninth Section of the first Article; and that no State, without its Consent, shall be deprived of its equal Suffrage in the Senate.

ARTICLE VI

All Debts contracted and Engagements entered into, before the Adoption of this Constitution, shall be as valid against the United States under this Constitution, as under the Confederation.

This Constitution, and the Laws of the United States which shall be made in Pursuance thereof; and all Treaties made, or which shall be made, under the Authority of the United States, shall be the supreme Law of the Land; and the Judges in every State shall be bound thereby, any Thing in the Constitution or Laws of any State to the Contrary notwithstanding.

The Senators and Representatives before mentioned, and the Members of the several State Legislatures, and all executive and judicial Officers, both of the United States and of the several States, shall be bound by Oath or Affirmation, to support this Constitution; but no religious Test shall ever be required as a Qualification to any Office or public Trust under the United States.

ARTICLE VII

The Ratification of the Conventions of nine States shall be sufficient for the Establishment of this Constitution between the States so ratifying the Same.

ARTICLES IN ADDITION TO, AND AMENDMENT OF, THE CONSTITUTION OF THE UNITED STATES OF AMERICA, PROPOSED BY CONGRESS, AND RATIFIED BY THE LEGISLATURES OF THE SEVERAL STATES PURSUANT TO THE FIFTH ARTICLE OF THE ORIGINAL CONSTITUTION.

AMENDMENT I [1791]

Congress shall make no law respecting an establishment of religion, or prohibiting the free exercise thereof; or abridging the freedom of speech, or of the press; or the right of the people peaceably to assemble, and to petition the Government for a redress of grievances.

AMENDMENT II [1791]

A well regulated Militia, being necessary to the security of a free State, the right of the people to keep and bear Arms, shall not be infringed.

AMENDMENT III [1791]

No Soldier shall, in time of peace be quartered in any house, without the consent of the Owner, nor in time of war, but in a manner to be prescribed by law.

AMENDMENT IV [1791]

The right of the people to be secure in their persons, houses, papers, and effects, against unreasonable searches and seizures, shall not be violated, and no Warrants shall issue, but upon probable cause, supported by Oath or affirmation, and particularly describing the place to be searched, and the persons or things to be seized.

AMENDMENT V [1791]

No person shall be held to answer for a capital, or otherwise infamous crime, unless on a presentment or indictment of a Grand Jury, except in cases arising in the land or naval forces, or in the Militia, when in actual service in time of War or public danger; nor shall any person be subject for the same offence to be twice put in jeopardy of life or limb; nor shall be compelled in any criminal case to be a witness against himself, nor be deprived of life, liberty, or property, without due process of law; nor shall private property be taken for public use, without just compensation.

Amendment VI [1791]

In all criminal prosecutions, the accused shall enjoy the right to a speedy and public trial, by an impartial jury of the State and district wherein the crime shall have been committed, which district shall have been previously ascertained by law, and to be informed of the nature and cause of the accusation; to be confronted with the witnesses against him; to have compulsory process for obtaining witnesses in his favor, and to have the Assistance of Counsel for his defence.

Amendment VII [1791]

In Suits at common law, where the value in controversy shall exceed twenty dollars, the right of trial by jury shall be preserved, and no fact tried by jury, shall be otherwise re-examined in any Court of the United States, than according to the rules of the common law.

Amendment VIII [1791]

Excessive bail shall not be required, nor excessive fines imposed, nor cruel and unusual punishments inflicted.

Amendment IX [1791]

The enumeration in the Constitution, of certain rights, shall not be construed to deny or disparage others retained by the people.

Amendment X [1791]

The powers not delegated to the United States by the Constitution, nor prohibited by it to the States, are reserved to the States respectively, or to the people.

Amendment XI [1798]

The Judicial power of the United States shall not be construed to extend to any suit in law or equity, commenced or prosecuted against one of the United States by Citizens of another State, or by Citizens or Subjects of any Foreign State.

Amendment XII [1804]

The Electors shall meet in their respective states and vote by ballot for President and Vice-President, one of whom, at least, shall not be an inhabitant of the same state with themselves; they shall name in their ballots the person voted for as President, and in distinct ballots the person voted for as Vice-President, and they shall make distinct lists of all persons voted for as President, and of all persons voted for as Vice-President, and of the number of votes for each, which lists they shall sign and certify, and transmit sealed to the seat of the government of the United States, directed to the President of the Senate;—The President of the Senate shall, in the presence of the Senate and House of

Representatives, open all the certificates and the votes shall then be counted;—The person having the greatest number of votes for President, shall be the President, if such number be a majority of the whole number of Electors appointed; and if no person have such majority, then from the persons having the highest numbers not exceeding three on the list of those voted for as President, the House of Representatives shall choose immediately, by ballot, the President. But in choosing the President, the votes shall be taken by states, the representation from each state having one vote; a quorum for this purpose shall consist of a member or members from two-thirds of the states, and a majority of all the states shall be necessary to a choice. And if the House of Representatives shall not choose a President whenever the right of choice shall devolve upon them before the fourth day of March next following, then the Vice-President shall act as President, as in the case of the death or other constitutional disability of the President.—The person having the greatest number of votes as Vice-President, shall be the Vice-President, if such number be a majority of the whole number of Electors appointed, and if no person have a majority, then from the two highest numbers on the list, the Senate shall choose the Vice-President; a quorum for the purpose shall consist of two-thirds of the whole number of Senators, and a majority of the whole number shall be necessary to a choice. But no person constitutionally ineligible to the office of President shall be eligible to that of Vice-President of the United States.

AMENDMENT XIII [1865]

Section 1. Neither slavery nor involuntary servitude, except as a punishment for crime whereof the party shall have been duly convicted, shall exist within the United States, or any place subject to their jurisdiction.

Section 2. Congress shall have power to enforce this article by appropriate legislation.

AMENDMENT XIV [1868]

Section 1. All persons born or naturalized in the United States, and subject to the jurisdiction thereof, are citizens of the United States and of the State wherein they reside. No State shall make or enforce any law which shall abridge the privileges or immunities of citizens of the United States; nor shall any State deprive any person of life, liberty, or property, without due process of law; nor deny to any person within its jurisdiction the equal protection of the laws.

Section 2. Representatives shall be apportioned among the several States according to their respective numbers, counting the whole number of persons in each State, excluding Indians not taxed. But when the right to vote at any election for the choice of electors for President and Vice President of the United States, Representatives in Congress, the Executive and Judicial officers of a State, or the members of the Legislature thereof, is denied to any of the male inhabitants of such State, being twenty-one years of age, and citizens of the United States, or in any way abridged, except for participation in rebellion, or other crime, the basis of representation therein shall be reduced in the proportion which the number of such male citizens shall bear to the whole number of male citizens twenty-one years of age in such State.

Section 3. No person shall be a Senator or Representative in Congress, or elector of President and Vice President, or hold any office, civil or military, under the United States, or under any State, who having previously taken an oath, as a member of Congress, or as an officer of the United States, or as a member of any State legislature, or as an executive or judicial officer of any State, to support the Constitution of the United States, shall have engaged in insurrection or rebellion against the same, or given aid or comfort to the enemies thereof. But Congress may by a vote of two-thirds of each House, remove such disability.

Section 4. The validity of the public debt of the United States, authorized by law, including debts incurred for payment of pensions and bounties for services in suppressing insurrection or rebellion, shall not be questioned. But neither the United States nor any State shall assume or pay any debt or obligation incurred in aid of insurrection or rebellion against the United States, or any claim for the loss or emancipation of any slave; but all such debts, obligations and claims shall be held illegal and void.

Section 5. The Congress shall have power to enforce, by appropriate legislation, the provisions of this article.

AMENDMENT XV [1870]

Section 1. The right of citizens of the United States to vote shall not be denied or abridged by the United States or by any State on account of race, color, or previous condition of servitude.

Section 2. The Congress shall have power to enforce this article by appropriate legislation.

AMENDMENT XVI [1913]

The Congress shall have power to lay and collect taxes on incomes, from whatever source derived, without apportionment among the several States, and without regard to any census or enumeration.

AMENDMENT XVII [1913]

[1] The Senate of the United States shall be composed of two Senators from each State, elected by the people thereof, for six years; and each Senator shall have one vote. The electors in each State shall have the qualifications requisite for electors of the most numerous branch of the State legislatures.

[2] When vacancies happen in the representation of any State in the Senate, the executive authority of such State shall issue writs of election to fill such vacancies: *Provided,* That the legislature of any State may

empower the executive thereof to make temporary appointments until the people fill the vacancies by election as the legislature may direct.

[3] This amendment shall not be so construed as to affect the election or term of any Senator chosen before it becomes valid as part of the Constitution.

AMENDMENT XVIII [1919]

Section 1. After one year from the ratification of this article the manufacture, sale, or transportation of intoxicating liquors within, the importation thereof into, or the exportation thereof from the United States and all territory subject to the jurisdiction thereof for beverage purposes is hereby prohibited.

Section 2. The Congress and the several States shall have concurrent power to enforce this article by appropriate legislation.

Section 3. This article shall be inoperative unless it shall have been ratified as an amendment to the Constitution by the legislatures of the several States, as provided in the Constitution, within seven years from the date of the submission hereof to the States by the Congress.

AMENDMENT XIX [1920]

[1] The right of citizens of the United States to vote shall not be denied or abridged by the United States or by any State on account of sex.

[2] Congress shall have power to enforce this article by appropriate legislation.

AMENDMENT XX [1933]

Section 1. The terms of the President and Vice President shall end at noon on the 20th day of January, and the terms of Senators and Representatives at noon on the 3d day of January, of the years in which such terms would have ended if this article had not been ratified; and the terms of their successors shall then begin.

Section 2. The Congress shall assemble at least once in every year, and such meeting shall begin at noon on the 3d day of January, unless they shall by law appoint a different day.

Section 3. If, at the time fixed for the beginning of the term of the President, the President elect shall have died, the Vice President elect shall become President. If the President shall not have been chosen before the time fixed for the beginning of his term, or if the President elect shall have failed to qualify, then the Vice President elect shall act as President until a President shall have qualified; and the Congress may by law provide for the case wherein neither a President elect nor a Vice President elect shall have qualified, declaring who shall then act as President, or the manner in which one who is to act shall be selected, and such person shall act accordingly until a President or Vice President shall have qualified.

Section 4. The Congress may by law provide for the case of the death of any of the persons from whom the House of Representatives may choose a President whenever the right of choice shall have devolved upon them, and for the case of the death of any of the persons from whom the Senate may choose a Vice President whenever the right of choice shall have devolved upon them.

Section 5. Sections 1 and 2 shall take effect on the 15th day of October following the ratification of this article.

Section 6. This article shall be inoperative unless it shall have been ratified as an amendment to the Constitution by the legislatures of three-fourths of the several States within seven years from the date of its submission.

Amendment XXI [1933]

Section 1. The eighteenth article of amendment to the Constitution of the United States is hereby repealed.

Section 2. The transportation or importation into any State, Territory, or possession of the United States for delivery or use therein of intoxicating liquors, in violation of the laws thereof, is hereby prohibited.

Section 3. This article shall be inoperative unless it shall have been ratified as an amendment to the Constitution by conventions in the several States, as provided in the Constitution, within seven years from the date of the submission hereof to the States by the Congress.

Amendment XXII [1951]

Section 1. No person shall be elected to the office of the President more than twice, and no person who has held the office of President, or acted as President, for more than two years of a term to which some other person was elected President shall be elected to the office of President more than once. But this Article shall not apply to any person holding the office of President when this Article was proposed by the Congress, and shall not prevent any person who may be holding the office of President, or acting as President, during the term within which this Article becomes operative from holding the office of President or acting as President during the remainder of such term.

Section 2. This article shall be inoperative unless it shall have been ratified as an amendment to the Constitution by the legislatures of three-fourths of the several States within seven years from the date of its submission to the States by the Congress.

Amendment XXIII [1961]

Section 1. The District constituting the seat of Government of the United States shall appoint in such manner as the Congress may direct:

A number of electors of President and Vice President equal to the whole number of Senators and Representatives in Congress to which the District would be entitled if it were a State, but in no event more than the least populous state; they shall be in addition to those appointed by the states, but they shall be considered, for the purposes of the election of President and Vice President, to be electors appointed by a state; and they shall meet in the District and perform such duties as provided by the twelfth article of amendment.

Section 2. The Congress shall have power to enforce this article by appropriate legislation.

AMENDMENT XXIV [1964]

Section 1. The right of citizens of the United States to vote in any primary or other election for President or Vice President, for electors for President or Vice President, or for Senator or Representative in Congress, shall not be denied or abridged by the United States or any State by reason of failure to pay any poll tax or other tax.

Section 2. The Congress shall have power to enforce this article by appropriate legislation.

AMENDMENT XXV [1967]

Section 1. In case of the removal of the President from office or of his death or resignation, the Vice President shall become President.

Section 2. Whenever there is a vacancy in the office of the Vice President, the President shall nominate a Vice President who shall take office upon confirmation by a majority vote of both Houses of Congress.

Section 3. Whenever the President transmits to the President pro tempore of the Senate and the Speaker of the House of Representatives his written declaration that he is unable to discharge the powers and duties of his office, and until he transmits to them a written declaration to the contrary, such powers and duties shall be discharged by the Vice President as Acting President.

Section 4. Whenever the Vice President and a majority of either the principal officers of the executive departments or of such other body as Congress may by law provide, transmit to the President pro tempore of the Senate and the Speaker of the House of Representatives their written declaration that the President is unable to discharge the powers and duties of his office, the Vice President shall immediately assume the powers and duties of the office as Acting President.

Thereafter, when the President transmits to the President pro tempore of the Senate and the Speaker of the House of Representatives his written declaration that no inability exists, he shall resume the powers and duties of his office unless the Vice President and a majority of either the principal officers of the executive department or of such other body as Congress may by law provide, transmit within four days to the President pro tempore of the Senate and the Speaker of the House of Representatives their written declaration that the President is unable to discharge the powers and duties of his office. Thereupon Congress shall decide the issue, assembling within forty-eight hours for that purpose if not in session. If the Congress, within twenty-one days after receipt of the latter written declaration, or, if Congress is not in session, within twenty-one days after Congress is required to assemble, determines by two-thirds vote of both Houses that the President is unable to discharge the powers and duties of his office, the Vice President shall continue to discharge the same as Acting President; otherwise, the President shall resume the powers and duties of his office.

AMENDMENT XXVI [1971]

Section 1. The right of citizens of the United States, who are eighteen years of age or older, to vote shall not be denied or abridged by the United States or by any State on account of age.

Section 2. The Congress shall have power to enforce this article by appropriate legislation.

THE FEDERAL COURTS

AND

THE FEDERAL SYSTEM

Chapter I

THE DEVELOPMENT AND STRUCTURE OF THE FEDERAL JUDICIAL SYSTEM

INTRODUCTORY NOTE: THE JUDICIARY ARTICLES IN THE CONSTITUTIONAL CONVENTION AND THE RATIFICATION DEBATES

The great and crucial decision of the Convention that met in Philadelphia in May, 1787, was the decision that a federal government should be established with powers to act directly upon individuals and not simply upon the member states.[1] And this was buttressed by the corollary decision that the "Constitution, and the Laws of the United States which shall be made in Pursuance thereof; and all Treaties made, or which shall be made, under the Authority of the United States, shall be the supreme Law of the Land".

The principal decisions which more particularly concerned the federal courts may be grouped under five headings:

First, That there should be a federal judicial power operating, like the legislative and executive powers, upon both states and individuals;

Second, That the courts and the judges exercising the power should be "as independent as the lot of humanity will admit"; and that the power exercised should be judicial only but should include, as a necessary incident, the power to pass upon the constitutionality of both state and federal legislation;

---

1. Charles Warren, The Making of the Constitution 3–54 (1937 ed.) (hereafter cited as Warren) gives one account of the background of this determination. For an opposing view of the era of the Confederation, see Jensen, The Articles of Confederation: An Interpretation of the Social-Constitutional History of the American Revolution 1774–1781 (1940), and The New Nation: A History of the United States During the Confederation, 1781–1789 (1950). Writing in the tradition of Charles Beard, Jensen sees the movement for the Constitution as a conservative response to the democratic excesses of the early 1780s. Jensen demythologizes the Framers and argues that the Constitution was not a necessary product of the instability of the Confederation. See also Lynd, Class Conflict, Slavery, and the United States Constitution: Ten Essays (1967). For a contemporaneous anti-Federalist account, see Lynd, *Abraham Yates's History of the Movement for the United States Constitution,* 20 Wm. & Mary Q. 223 (1963). See also Wood, The Creation of the American Republic (1969); McDonald, E. Pluribus Unum: The Formation of the American Republic, 1776–1790 (1965); McDonald, Novus Ordo Seclorum: The Intellectual Origins of the Constitution (1985); Ferguson, The Power of the Purse: A History of American Public Finance, 1776–1790 (1961); Ferguson, *The Nationalists of 1781–1783 and the Economic Interpretation of the Constitution,* in The Confederation and the Constitution—The Critical Issues 1 (Wood ed. 1973).

The nationalist position is extended beyond reasonable limits of history in Crosskey, Politics and the Constitution in the History of the United States (1953). Professor Crosskey asserts that the Framers intended a completely national, rather than a federal system of government. For highly critical reactions see the reviews by Professors Brown and Hart, 67 Harv.L.Rev. 1439, 1456 (1954), and Goebel, *Ex Parte Clio,* 54 Colum.L.Rev. 450 (1954). Crosskey should still be consulted for the wide range of sources he utilizes.

Third, That the power should be vested in a Supreme Court to be established at all events, and in such inferior federal courts as Congress might choose to establish;

Fourth, That the power should extend to nine specified classes of cases; and

Fifth, That in certain of these cases the Supreme Court should have original jurisdiction and in the remainder "appellate Jurisdiction, both as to Law and Fact, with such Exceptions, and under such Regulations as the Congress shall make."

To understand these decisions it is helpful to have a general picture of the way in which the Convention worked. Its deliberations can be divided into three main phases.

The settlement of general principles (May 30 to July 26).[2] In this first phase the four main plans before the Convention were presented and most of the principal decisions made. On May 29 Governor Randolph of Virginia proposed a series of resolutions.[3] These became the order of business the next day when the Convention resolved itself into a Committee of the Whole to begin serious deliberation. On the same day Charles Pinckney of South Carolina proposed a draft of a constitution[4] which was also referred to the committee. Randolph's resolutions, however, were the focus of discussion and became, as amended, the substance of the first report of the Committee of the Whole to the Convention on June 13.

The nationalism of Randolph's plan precipitated a counter-proposal by William Paterson of New Jersey,[5] which was in turn referred to the

2. For the events of this phase, see Farrand, The Framing of the Constitution 68–123 (1913); Warren 134–367. More recent accounts of the proceedings of the Convention are: Rossiter, 1787: The Grand Convention (1966); Murphy, The Triumph of Nationalism: State Sovereignty, The Founding Fathers, and the Making of the Constitution (1967); Goebel, History of the Supreme Court of the United States: Antecedents and Beginnings to 1801, at 196–250 (1971) (hereafter cited as Goebel; this is Volume I of the Oliver Wendell Holmes Devise History of the Supreme Court of the United States); Collier & Collier, Decision in Philadelphia (1986).

For studies of the Convention as the outcome of forces at work over a long period, see Greene, Peripheries and Center: Constitutional Development in the Extended Politics of the British Empire and the United States, 1607–1788 (1986); Morris, The Forging of the Union, 1781–1789 (1987). For informative monographs, see Rogow, *The Federal Convention: Madison and Yates,* 60 Am.Hist.Rev. 323 (1955); Roche, *The Founding Fathers: A Reform Caucus in Action,* 55 Am.Pol.Sci.Rev. 799 (1961); Mason, *The Constitutional Convention,* in The Confederation and the Constitution—Critical Issues 37 (Wood ed. 1973).

Biographical studies of the Framers include: Brant, James Madison: Father of the Constitution, 1787–1800 (1950); Smith, James Wilson, Founding Father, 1742–1798 (1956); Rossiter, Alexander Hamilton and the Constitution (1964); Zahniser, Charles Cotesworth Pinckney: Founding Father (1967); Morris, Present at the Creation: Hamilton, Madison, Jay, and the Constitution (1985).

3. 1 Farrand, The Records of the Federal Convention 20–23 (1911) (hereafter cited as Farrand). This is the basic document for the study of the Convention. Three volumes were published in 1911; a fourth volume, published in 1937, has recently been revised and expanded. Hutson, Supplement to Max Farrand's Records of the Federal Convention of 1787 (1987).

Professors Kurland and Lerner have assembled a five volume anthology, The Founders' Constitution (1987), which presents views expressed on constitutional problems before, during, and after the Convention, through the year 1835. The volumes are keyed to the provisions of the Constitution and the first twelve amendments.

4. 3 Farrand 595–609 (Appendix D).

5. 1 *Id.* 242–45; 3 *id.* 611–16 (Appendix E).

Committee of the Whole. In the course of the crucial four-day debate that followed, Alexander Hamilton of New York presented the fourth and last of the complete plans [6] before the Convention. (In addition, the Convention probably had before it a draft, of a judiciary article only, in the handwriting of John Blair of Virginia, which was later found in the papers of George Mason.[7]) This debate ended on June 19 when the Committee voted, seven states to three with Maryland divided, to adhere to its original report of the Randolph resolutions.

There followed the second major round of debate, in the Convention proper, on the report of the Committee of the Whole, in the course of which most of the major issues outstanding were compromised and settled.

The elaboration of detail (July 27 to September 10).[8] The Convention adjourned from July 27 to August 6 while a Committee of Detail, with John Rutledge as chairman, prepared the first definite draft of the Constitution.[9] The Committee built upon the votes of the Convention adopting or modifying Randolph's Virginia Plan, but it drew heavily also on the other plans that had been submitted, as well as on a 1781 report of a committee of the old Congress to revise the Articles of Confederation, consisting of Randolph, Oliver Ellsworth, and James M. Varnum, and on the provisions of various state constitutions. The report of the Committee of Detail introduced the third major round of debate, in which the Convention disposed not only of this report but of various special reports on the remaining problems of general principle.

Final settlement and polishing (September 10 to 15).[10] A Committee on Style, which made more than stylistic changes, reported to the Convention on September 12.[11] There ensued a final review, in which minor amendments were made, culminating in the engrossed Constitution signed on Monday, September 17.

Every commentator has agreed with Farrand that to "one who is especially interested in the judiciary, there is surprisingly little on the subject to be found in the records of the convention".[12] But silence may speak as eloquently as debate. It is illuminating to observe what matters aroused controversy and what did not.

A. A Federal Judicial Power

"That there should be a national judiciary," says Farrand, "was readily accepted by all." [13]

In the first day of debate in the Committee of the Whole (May 30) Randolph moved a substitute resolution "that a national government ought to be established consisting of a supreme Legislative, Judiciary, and Executive." This was carried with New York divided and Connecticut alone opposing.[14] On June 4 Madison records in his notes: "It was then moved and seconded to proceed to the consideration of the Ninth Resolution

6. 1 *Id.* 291–93; 3 *id.* 617–30 (Appendix F).

7. 2 *Id.* 432–33. See also Warren 538n.

8. This phase is described in Farrand, The Framing of the Constitution 124–75, and Warren 368–685.

9. 2 Farrand 177–89.

10. For this final phase, see Farrand, The Framing of the Constitution 176–95, and Warren 686–721.

11. 2 Farrand 590–603.

12. Farrand, The Framing of the Constitution 154.

13. *Id.* 79.

14. 1 Farrand 30–31.

submitted by Mr. Randolph; when on motion to agree to the first clause, namely, 'Resolved that a national Judiciary be established', it passed in the affirmative, *nem. con.* [no one opposed]" [15]

What was thus agreed to, without discussion or further question, was a substantial innovation in American experience. The idea of a national tribunal had, of course, the partial precedent from colonial times of the Committee for Hearing Appeals of the Privy Council. Besides exercising the function of disallowance of colonial legislation, the Privy Council had had jurisdiction both of ordinary appeals and of border disputes between colonies.[16] The new states, too, had themselves tried to settle border disputes, by the device of *ad hoc* tribunals.[17] And in one instance a regular national court had been established to deal with cases of captures.[18] But

15. Madison's Journal 108 (Scott ed. 1895). (Madison's Notes of Debates in the Federal Convention of 1787 are also available in a paperback edition (Koch ed., Norton, 1969).) See also 1 Farrand 104.

16. See Joseph Henry Smith, Appeals to the Privy Council from the American Plantations (1950). For a brief summary, see Frank, *Historical Bases of the Federal Judicial System,* 13 Law & Contemp.Prob. 3, 5–6 (1948).

17. In 1775 Congress was presented with the spectacle of actual fighting between Pennsylvania and Connecticut over territory on the banks of the Susquehanna river known as Wyoming. A special committee of Congress was appointed, which recommended the terms of an armistice that should govern until the dispute could be settled. Carson, The Supreme Court of the United States 67–68 (1891).

In 1777 it was provided in the Articles of Confederation that "The United States in Congress assembled, shall also be the last resort on appeal in all disputes and differences now subsisting or that hereafter may arise between two or more States concerning boundary, jurisdiction, or any other cause whatever. * * *" The Articles then went on to provide a cumbersome machinery whereby the two States selected seven judges by joint consent, any five of whom could constitute a quorum. If judges could not be agreed upon, Congress was to select three men from each State and the court would be arrived at by alternate striking of these names. The judgment of the court so selected was to be final. Articles of Confederation, Art. IX.

In March, 1781, the Articles were ratified by the last State, and in November Pennsylvania petitioned Congress for a hearing. On the appointed day agents for the two states appeared. Connecticut made various motions, one of which was to postpone the proceedings "until after the termination of the present war". Connecticut's objections were overruled and the two States were directed to appoint a court

in the manner specified in the Articles of Confederation.

A court was appointed by joint consent and it sat in Trenton, New Jersey for forty-two days. It rendered a unanimous judgment against Connecticut. Years later it was discovered that the judges had considered the business of rendering a judgment in a dispute between sovereign states so delicate that they agreed on the following course before determining the controversy: the reasons for the determination should never be given, and the minority should permit the determination to be rendered as unanimous. Individual Connecticut settlers were unwilling to cede their lands, even though Connecticut herself acquiesced in the judgment. The excitement did not really die down until a few years later when Pennsylvania passed a series of Acts whereby the lands of actual Connecticut settlers were confirmed to them. Carson, *supra,* at 67–74.

No other cases were ever settled by the judgment of such a court. The temporary nature of the court was not calculated to inspire confidence in the states. Resort to this machinery was further discouraged by the fact that Congress lacked power to enforce the judgment either against the state or individuals. "Accordingly, while the mere fact of the existence of the Court induced a few States to settle their disputes by compact, and without litigation, most of the boundary conflicts remained unsettled. And it was realized that some stronger means must be found of dealing with such State controversies." Warren, The Supreme Court and Sovereign States 13 (1924).

18. In 1775, Washington, harassed by disputes over captures by Continental vessels, and finding the Massachusetts condemnation law limited to captures by vessels operating under authority of the Massachusetts Assembly, recommended to Congress the establishment of a court to hear cases involving prizes captured by Continental ships. Shortly thereafter Con-what was now proposed was much more than a specialized tribunal. It was a national judicial power joined with executive and legislative powers as part of a national government.

The Convention's unhesitant agreement upon such a power, of course, cloaked lively disagreements about the kinds of tribunals that should exercise it and the exact scope of the jurisdiction they should have. But the unanimity bespoke impressively the general understanding that a government is not a government without courts.[19]

gress suggested that the several states set up courts to determine all cases of capture in the first instance, or confer such jurisdiction on their then existing courts. In all such cases an appeal was to lie to Congress, or such person or persons as they should appoint. All the states but New York complied. The first appeal came up in August of 1776, and Congress appointed a special committee to hear it. The practice of appointing special committees continued until January, 1777, when a five-member Standing Committee was appointed.

The Articles of Confederation were approved by Congress in November, 1777. Article IX, relating to powers of Congress, among other things conferred the power of "appointing courts for the trial of piracies and felonies committed on the high seas and establishing courts for receiving and determining appeals in all cases of captures, providing that no member of Congress shall be appointed a Judge of said courts." No independent federal courts were ever established under the provision relating to piracies and felonies, but in 1781 Congress provided for trial of such offenses by certain designated state judges. However, in January, 1780, Congress resolved "that a Court be established for trial of all appeals from the Courts of Admiralty in these United States, in cases of capture, to consist of 3 Judges appointed and commissioned by Congress ∗ ∗ ∗." The court was called "The Court of Appeals in Cases of Capture". See Carson, note 17, *supra*, at 41–64.

This was the first national court. Its creation represented Congress' recognition of a grave need. But the time was not ripe for the granting of powers to a federal court commensurate with the need. Several important provisions had been stricken from the original draft. Among them were provisions that the Judges have the powers of a court of record in fining and imprisoning for contempt and disobedience, that the state admiralty courts should execute its decrees, and that a marshal be appointed. Tenure of the Judges was uncertain. The Court was never really independent of its creator. In the case of the brig "Susannah", involving a delicate question of national power arising out of conflict between a New Hampshire statute and the act of Congress creating the Court of Appeals, Congress ordered that all proceedings upon the sentence of the Court be stayed, and attempted to determine the dispute itself. Congress never took any final action in the case, but during the debate it was moved that it was improper for Congress in any manner to reverse or control the decisions, judgments or decrees of the Court of Appeals, and the motion was defeated. In December, 1784, business had dwindled; the Court had cleared its docket; and after a few more occasional sessions, the Court ceased to function on May 16, 1787. But "some 118 cases were disposed of by the congressional committees and the Court of Appeals, and the idea became well fixed that admiralty and maritime cases pertained to federal jurisdiction". Hockett, The Constitutional History of the United States 157 (1939).

See also Jameson, *The Predecessor of the Supreme Court,* in Essays in the Constitutional History of the United States 1–45 (1889).

19. Courts were thought of in part, of course, as instruments for the protection of individuals. Thus Madison wrote in October, 1787: "The mutability of the laws of the States is found to be a serious evil. The injustice of them has been so frequent and so flagrant as to alarm the most steadfast friends of Republicanism. I am persuaded I do not err in saying that the evils issuing from these sources contributed more to that uneasiness which produced the Convention, and prepared the public mind for a general reform, than those which accrued to our national character and interest from the inadequacy of the Confederation to its immediate objects. A reform, therefore, which does not make some provision for private right must be materially defective." 5 Writings of James Madison 27 (Hunt ed. 1904).

But the sheer weakness of the Confederation was the most urgent reason for change and the one most frequently assigned. "[T]he United States afford the extraordinary spectacle of a government destitute even of the shadow of constitutional power to enforce the execution of its own laws." The Federalist, No. 21. In

B. Separation and Independence of the Judicial Power

1. Appointment of Judges

The method of appointment of the judges became a nearly major issue. On June 13 the Committee of the Whole, rejecting Randolph's proposal for appointment by the legislature, agreed upon appointment by the Senate. There was sharp debate whether this should be replaced by appointment by the executive, with or without the approval of the Senate; but the Convention adhered to its decision on July 21.[20] Not until the closing days, on September 7, was the issue resolved, as part of a general settlement on appointments, in favor of appointment by the executive with the advice and consent of the Senate.[21]

2. Tenure and Salary

The provisions protecting the tenure and salary of judges received almost complete assent. All four of the principal plans provided that the judges should hold office during good behavior, and the Randolph, Pinckney and Paterson plans forbade either a decrease or an increase in salary during continuance in office.

What chiefly stirred debate was the proposal to prevent the temptation of increases. After first being accepted in the Committee of the Whole,[22] it was rejected in the general debate in the Convention and again in the debate on the report of the Committee of Detail.[23] But the rejection was largely on the practical ground that the cost of living might rise, and it prevailed only over the strong opposition of Madison and the votes of Virginia and North Carolina.

The lone assault on the principle of tenure was made in the debate on the report of the Committee of Detail, when Dickinson of Delaware, seconded by Gerry and Sherman, moved that the judges "may be removed by the Executive on the application by the Senate and House of Representatives"; but the motion was strongly opposed and only Connecticut supported it.[24]

---

this aspect courts were thought of as indispensable instruments for the vindication of national authority.

20. The first proposal for appointment by the President with the concurrence of the Senate was made by Hamilton on June 5. Motions for executive appointment alone, or executive appointment subject to Senate approval, were defeated on several occasions thereafter. See 1 Farrand 128, 224, 232–33; 2 Farrand 80–83; Warren 327–29.

21. Appointment by the Senate was retained in the draft reported by the Committee of Detail. 2 Farrand 132, 155, 169, 183. The final compromise was worked out between August 25 and September 7. See id. 498, 538–40; Warren 639–42. For Hamilton's comments on the matter, see

The Federalist, Nos. 76, 77. See generally Harris, The Advice and Consent of the Senate ch. II (1953).

22. 1 Farrand 121.

23. 2 Id. 44–45, 429–30; Warren 532–34. See also Rosenn, The Constitutional Guaranty Against Diminution of Judicial Compensation, 24 U.C.L.A. L.Rev. 308, 311–18 (1976).

24. 2 Farrand 428–29; Warren 532. For the conflict over judicial tenure in the colonial period, see Klein, Prelude to Revolution in New York: Jury Trials and Judicial Tenure, 17 Wm. & Mary Q. 439 (1960). For an extensive analysis of the problems of tenure and removal in the Constitution, see Berger, Impeachment: The Constitutional Problems (1973).

3. Extra–Judicial Functions

In an impressive series of votes the Convention defeated a variety of proposals to give non-judicial functions to the courts or judges.

Randolph's eighth resolution proposed to create a council of revision composed of "the Executive and a convenient number of the National Judiciary" with authority, first, "to examine every act of the National Legislature before it shall operate", and, second, to review every negative exercised by the National Legislature upon an act of a state legislature, pursuant to a power proposed in the sixth resolution, before it "shall be final". The dissent of the council was to "amount to a rejection, unless the Act of the National Legislature be again passed, or that of a particular Legislature be again negatived by [blank] of the members of each branch".[25]

This plan to associate the judges with the processes of enacting laws the Convention rejected eight votes to two, when it was first discussed in Committee of the Whole, and substituted a purely executive veto of national legislation.[26] Two days later it adhered to the rejection, eight votes to three, on Wilson's and Madison's motion for reconsideration.[27] Wilson and Madison renewed the proposal in the later debate on the report of the Committee of the Whole; and again it was rejected, four votes to three with two states divided.[28] They renewed it a third time in the debate on the report of the Committee of Detail, and for a fourth time it was defeated.[29]

The proposal was debated at length and strongly supported as a necessary check upon legislative aggrandizement and as an assurance of wiser laws. The arguments that prevailed against it were concisely stated by Gerry and King at the outset:

"Mr. Gerry doubts whether the Judiciary ought to form a part of it [the council of revision], as they will have a sufficient check agst. encroachments on their own department by their exposition of the laws, which involved a power of deciding on their Constitutionality. In some States the Judges had actually set aside laws as being agst. the Constitution. This was done too with general approbation. It was quite foreign from the nature of ye. office to make them judges of the policy of public measures."

To which King added "that the Judges ought to be able to expound the law as it should come before them, free from the bias of having participated in its formation".[30]

Influenced apparently by similar considerations, the Convention permitted two other plans for using judges non-judicially to die. The first was a suggestion advanced by Ellsworth and put in more elaborate form by Gouverneur Morris to make the Chief Justice a member of the projected Privy Council of the President.[31] The second was a proposal by Charles

---

25. 1 Farrand 21.

26. *Id.* 97–104, 108–110 (June 4). As to the proposal for a negative of state laws, see note 36, *infra*.

27. *Id.* 138–140 (June 6).

28. 2 *Id.* 73–80 (July 21).

29. *Id.* 298 (August 15). The form of the proposal this time was somewhat different.

30. 1 Farrand 97–98, 109 (June 4).

31. See generally Warren 643–50.

Ellsworth revived previous discussion of an executive or privy council with a definite proposal, on August 18, of a council to consist of the President of the Senate, the Chief Justice, and the heads of certain departments. Gerry at once objected to allowing the heads of departments to "have any thing to do in business connected with legislation", and "mentioned the

Pinckney that "Each branch of the Legislature, as well as the Supreme Executive shall have authority to require the opinions of the supreme Judicial Court upon important questions of law, and upon solemn occasions".[32]

The last important reference to extra-judicial functions occurred near the close of the Convention when Dr. Johnson moved to extend the judicial power to cases arising under the Constitution of the United States, as well as under its laws and treaties. Then:

"Mr. Madison doubted whether it was not going too far to extend the jurisdiction of the Court generally to cases arising under the Constitution, & whether it ought not to be limited to cases of a Judiciary Nature. The right of expounding the Constitution in cases not of this nature ought not to be given to that Department."

However: "The motion of Docr. Johnson was agreed to *nem. con.*: it being generally supposed that the jurisdiction given was constructively limited to cases of a Judiciary nature." [33]

4. The Power to Declare Statutes Unconstitutional

The grant of judicial power was to include the power, where necessary in the decision of cases, to disregard state or federal statutes found to be unconstitutional. Despite the curiously persisting myth of usurpation, the Convention's understanding on this point emerges from its records with singular clarity.[34]

Chief Justice also as particularly exceptionable". 2 Farrand 328–29.

Morris's more elaborate plan, supported by Pinckney, called for a Council of State with the Chief Justice as a member and as president of the body in the absence of the President. It provided further that the Chief Justice should "from time to time recommend such alterations of and additions to the laws of the U.S. as may in his opinion be necessary to the due administration of Justice, and such as may promote useful learning and inculcate sound morality throughout the Union". *Id.* 342–44 (August 20). The Committee of Detail, to which the proposal was referred, eliminated this last provision but approved the scheme of a council with the Chief Justice as a member. *Id.* 367. The Convention, however, never voted on the scheme, apparently regarding the eventual provision empowering the President to require written opinions from the heads of departments as a substitute.

32. *Id.* 340–41 (August 20). Pinckney's proposal went to the Committee of Detail, but was never reported out.

33. *Id.* 430 (August 27).

34. The classical work on the matter is Beard, The Supreme Court and the Constitution (1912). Berger, Congress v. The Supreme Court (1969), makes the strongest historical case that can be made for the intention of the Framers and the first Congress to confer the power of judicial review upon the Supreme Court. See also Hart, Book Review, 67 Harv.L.Rev. 1456 (1954), rejecting Crosskey's argument (2 Politics and the Constitution 1007) that "judicial review was not meant to be provided generally in the Constitution, as to acts of Congress, though it was meant to be provided generally as to the acts of the states, and a limited right likewise was intended to be given to the Court, even as against Congress, to preserve its own judiciary prerogatives intact." Boudin, Government by Judiciary (1932) remains the most sober case against the constitutionality of judicial review. In spite of doubts expressed by Judge Learned Hand, The Bill of Rights (1958), the Beard-Hart-Berger position now commands almost universal scholarly respect.

Wood, The Creation of the American Republic 453–63 (1969), argues that developments in political theory in the 1780s, especially the substitution of popular sovereignty for the traditional Blackstonian notion of legislative sovereignty, made possible the institution of judicial review. He also contends that the idea of judicial review was associated with the revival of morality as a necessary ingredient of law, with courts as protectors of the public against legislative error or excess. It now seems clear that judicial review was also related to the resurgence of separation of powers theory in the Revolutionary era.

In the debate on the judiciary article itself, the power of judicial review was taken for granted, as Madison's comment on Dr. Johnson's motion indicates. It was in the debate on additional safeguards against excesses of state and federal legislation that the understanding was made explicit.

The crux of the long controversy over the proposed congressional negative of state laws was whether the check of judicial invalidation of unconstitutional state laws was a sufficient safeguard or whether an additional one was needed.[35] The existence of this power in the federal courts was common ground, unquestioned throughout the debate. And the issue in the end was settled by acceptance of Luther Martin's proposal of the supremacy clause, strengthening the judicial check by express statement of the parallel power and responsibility of state judges.[36]

The existence of a judicial safeguard against unconstitutional federal laws was similarly recognized on both sides in the debates over the proposal

See Vile, Constitutionalism and the Separation of Powers (1967); Bailyn, The Ideological Origins of the American Revolution (1967).

Recent decades have seen an important revision of attitudes toward the intellectual climate in which the Constitution was conceived. Historians now place less emphasis on the natural law—natural rights philosophy of the Revolution; instead they stress the English origins of revolutionary political ideas and the importance of ideal notions of English government in assessing American political experience. The general direction of this work is best summed up in Wood, *supra*. See also Colbourn, The Lamp of Experience: Whig History and the Intellectual Origins of the American Revolution (1965); The Works of James Wilson (McCloskey ed. 1967); Bailyn, The Origins of American Politics (1968); Stourzh, Alexander Hamilton and the Idea of Republican Government (1970); Adair, *The Tenth Federalist Revisited*, 8 Wm. & Mary Q. 48 (1951); Diamond, *Democracy and The Federalist: A Reconsideration of the Framers' Intent*, 53 Am.Pol.Sci.Rev. 52 (1959); Katz, *The Origins of American Constitutional Thought*, in 3 Perspectives in American History 474 (Bailyn & Fleming, eds. 1969). But see Lynd, Intellectual Origins of American Radicalism (1982).

Nelson, *Changing Conceptions of Judicial Review: The Evolution of Constitutional Theory in the States, 1790–1860*, 120 U.Pa.L.Rev. 1166 (1972), gives an interesting account of the evolution of judicial review into "an unchallenged dogma" in the period between Marbury v. Madison and the Civil War.

35. Wilson thus summarized the proponents' case: "The power of self-defence has been urged as necessary for the State Governments—It was equally necessary for the General Government. The firmness of Judges is not of itself sufficient. Something further is requisite—It will be better to prevent the passage of an improper law, than to declare it void when passed." 2 Farrand 391 (August 23).

36. For the history of the proposal for a Congressional negative on state laws, see generally Warren 164–71, 316–24. On the Supremacy Clause, see further note 39, *infra*.

The proposal of a legislative negative, first advanced and vigorously supported throughout by Madison, was embodied in Randolph's sixth resolution, which authorized a negative only of state laws "contravening in the opinion of the National Legislature the articles of Union". 1 Farrand 21. In this form it was initially approved by the Committee of the Whole on May 31 without debate or dissent. *Id.* 54. The plan was first discussed on June 8 when the Committee rejected Charles Pinckney's motion to extend the negative to "all laws which they shd. judge to be improper". Rumblings of opposition then appeared and culminated in a debate in the Convention of July 17, when the plan was rejected.

Madison, in support, urged that states "can pass laws which will accomplish their injurious objects before they can be repealed by the Genl Legislre, or be set aside by the National Tribunals". Sherman and Gouverneur Morris, in opposition, relied upon the courts to set aside unconstitutional laws. Sherman saying that the proposal "involves a wrong principle, to wit, that a law of a State contrary to the articles of the Union, would if not negatived, be valid and operative". None doubted the judicial power. When the negative was defeated, Luther Martin at once proposed the first version of the Supremacy Clause, "which was agreed to *nem. con.*" 2 Farrand 27–29. See also *id.* 390–91.

for a council of revision of acts of the national legislature. Gerry's statement of the power, already quoted, was repeated at least eight times.[37]

The only note of challenge was struck in the fourth and last debate on the proposal when Mercer, a recently arrived delegate, speaking in support of the alternative plan of judicial participation in the veto, said that he "disapproved of the Doctrine that the Judges as expositors of the Constitution should have authority to declare a law void". Dickinson then observed that he was impressed with Mr. Mercer's remark and "thought no such power ought to exist" but "he was at the same time at a loss what expedient to substitute". Gouverneur Morris at once said that he could not agree that the judiciary "should be bound to say that a direct violation of the Constitution was law", and there the discussion ended.[38]

Meanwhile, the first version of the Supremacy Clause had been approved. At no time was there a suggestion that the responsibility of the judges under this clause was any less with respect to federal than state laws. On the contrary the changes in the clause in the closing days of the Convention seem designed to make clear that it was the same.[39] And it was made doubly clear by the Convention's matter-of-course approval of the express grant of jurisdiction in cases arising under the Constitution.[40]

C. The Tribunals Exercising the Power

Agreement upon a federal judicial power carried with it agreement upon at least one tribunal to exercise it. All the plans submitted provided for a Supreme Court.[41]

The proposal for inferior federal courts, however, aroused opposition in the Convention and major controversy in the ratification debates.

The Randolph and Pinckney plans provided for mandatory establishment of inferior federal courts. The Paterson plan did not provide for any such courts. Hamilton's plan empowered Congress to create them for the determination of all matters of general concern. John Blair's plan provided only for lower courts of admiralty.

The Committee of the Whole approved the Randolph proposal without discussion on June 4 and 5,[42] but Rutledge brought it up for reconsideration later in the second day. He urged that "the State tribunals might and ought to be left in all cases to decide in the first instance, the right of appeal to the supreme national tribunal being sufficient to secure the national rights & uniformity of Judgmts: that it was making an unnecessary encroachment on the jurisdiction of the States, and creating unnecessary

37. See Rufus King, 1 Farrand 109 (June 4); Wilson, 2 id. 73 (July 21); Madison, id. 74 (July 21), and 92–93 (July 23); Martin, id. 76 (July 21); Mason, id. 78 (July 21); Pinckney, id. 298 (August 15); G. Morris, id. 299 (August 15). See also Williamson, id. 376 (August 22).

38. 2 Farrand 298–99 (August 15).

39. In its original form the clause referred only to "Legislative acts of the United States made by virtue and in pursuance of the Articles of Union" and to treaties, and it declared them to be the supreme law only "of the respective States". 2 Farrand 28 (July 17). On August 23 the Conven-

tion amended the clause without debate to declare expressly the supremacy of "This Constitution and the laws of the United States made in pursuance thereof". Id. 389. The final draft of the Committee on Style declared the Constitution, laws and treaties to be "the supreme law of the land" and not merely "of the respective States". Id. 603. See generally Warren 318–22.

40. See text at note 33, supra.

41. 1 Farrand 21, 244, 292; 2 id. 432; 3 id. 600.

42. 1 Id. 104–05 (June 4), 119 (June 5).

obstacles to their adoption of the new system". Sherman supported him, dwelling on the expense of an additional set of courts.

Madison strongly opposed. He said that "unless inferior federal tribunals were dispersed throughout the Republic with *final* jurisdiction in *many* cases, appeals would be multiplied to a most oppressive degree". Besides, "an appeal would not in many cases be a remedy." "What was to be done after improper Verdicts in State tribunals obtained under the biassed directions of a dependent Judge, or the local prejudices of an undirected jury?" A new trial at the supreme bar would not be practicable. "An effective Judiciary establishment commensurate to the legislative authority, was essential. A Government without a proper Executive & Judiciary would be the mere trunk of a body without arms or legs to act or move." Wilson and Sherman spoke in the same vein, the former emphasizing the special need for an admiralty jurisdiction.

However, Rutledge's motion to strike out "inferior tribunals" carried, five states to four with two divided. Then, picking up a suggestion by Dickinson, Wilson and Madison moved "that the National Legislature be empowered to institute inferior tribunals", saying that "there was a distinction between establishing such tribunals absolutely, and giving a discretion to the Legislature to establish or not establish them". The compromise was agreed to, eight states to two with one divided.[43]

Opposition to a system of inferior federal courts was renewed when the report of the Committee of the Whole came before the Convention on July 18. But it was milder, Sherman saying that he "was willing to give the power to the Legislature but wished them to make use of the State Tribunals whenever it could be done with safety to the general interest". This time the vote accepting the compromise was unanimous,[44] and the decision stood without further question.[45]

The grounds of the Convention's action throw light on two questions that were later to become the subject of bitter political contention.

They show unmistakably, as the Judiciary Act of 1789 confirms, that the Framers contemplated the review by the Supreme Court of state court decisions on matters of federal concern. It was the states' righters themselves, indeed, who most strongly insisted upon the appropriateness of this method of protecting federal interests.

And it seems to be a necessary inference from the express decision that the creation of inferior federal courts was to rest in the discretion of Congress that the scope of their jurisdiction, once created, was also to be discretionary. This is supported not only by such statements as Sherman's but by numerous indications of an expectation that Congress in the beginning would go no further than to vest an admiralty jurisdiction in inferior federal courts.[46]

43. *Id.* 124–25 (June 5). The word "institute" in the text of the Wilson-Madison motion is used in Madison's notes; in the Convention Journal the word "appoint" is used. See Goebel, note 2, *supra*, at 211 & n. 76.

44. 2 Farrand 45–46 (July 18).

45. In the debate on the report of the Committee of Detail, a motion, recorded only in the Journal, was made and seconded to give the inferior federal courts only an appellate jurisdiction over decisions of state courts; but the motion was withdrawn. *Id.* 424 (August 27). Warren 537–38 states erroneously that this was voted, and the vote reconsidered.

46. See Warren 531.

Mention should be made, however, of two votes of the Convention on August 27, after the report of the Committee of Detail.

D. The Scope of Jurisdiction

All five of the plans respecting the judiciary which were put before the Convention specified various definite heads of federal jurisdiction. When the Committee of the Whole first discussed this subject on June 12 and 13, Randolph quickly concluded that it was "the business of a subcommittee to detail" the jurisdiction. He "therefore moved to obliterate such parts of the resolve so as only to establish the principle, to wit, that the jurisdiction of the national judiciary shall extend to all cases of national revenue, impeachment of national officers, and questions which involve the national peace or harmony", which was agreed to unanimously.[47]

In considering the report of the Committee of the Whole on July 18, the Convention again confined itself to general principle. But "several criticisms having been made on the definition [of jurisdiction]; it was proposed by Mr. Madison so to alter as to read thus—'that the jurisdiction shall extend to all cases arising under the Natl. laws: And to such other questions as may involve the Natl. peace & harmony.' which was agreed to nem. con." [48]

Thus it was that Section 2 of Article III began to take shape only after the reference to the Committee of Detail. Because of this, and because the discussion of the Committee's proposals was short and incompletely reported, the records of the Convention cast very little light on the special purposes of particular clauses. What is perhaps most illuminating is the

First, the Convention rejected (6–2) a proposal to insert in Article III the sentence "In all the other cases before mentioned the Judicial power shall be exercised in such manner as the Legislature shall direct." 2 Farrand 431 (August 27). (A similar provision had been proposed in the Committee of Detail, and had not been adopted. See 2 Farrand 146–47.) Second, the Convention voted (8–0) to strike from the report of the Committee of Detail the express provision that the "Legislature may assign any part of the jurisdiction above mentioned [which included the original and appellate jurisdiction of the Supreme Court] (except the trial of the President of the United States) in the manner, and under the limitations which it shall think proper, to such Inferior Courts as it shall constitute from time to time." 2 Farrand 186–87 (report), 431 (August 27).

The votes have no recorded explanation, Madison's notes for that important day being highly abbreviated. As for the first, it is not clear where the sentence was to be inserted, whether its purpose related to the scope of federal jurisdiction or its allocation between the Supreme Court and inferior courts, what its relation was to the provision governing the Supreme Court's appellate jurisdiction, or why it was rejected. And as to the second vote, it appears to have been part of a largely rhetorical change. The Committee's draft enumerated the various heads of federal jurisdiction as cases to which the "jurisdiction of the Supreme Court" shall extend. The later assignment clause was thus needed to provide for the jurisdiction of the inferior courts. Madison and Morris moved to substitute for the quoted words "judicial power", "which was agreed to nem. con." The assignment clause was then stricken, apparently as unnecessary, by a unanimous vote. 2 Farrand 431 (August 27).

Professor Clinton has argued that the first of these votes, coupled with the rejection of a similar proposal in the Committee of Detail, "would seem to refute any intention on the part of the Convention to create anything other than a mandatory, constitutionally established jurisdiction for the federal courts." Clinton, A Mandatory View of Federal Court Jurisdiction: A Guided Quest for the Original Understanding of Article III, 132 U.Pa.L.Rev. 741, 796 (1984). But this seems a slender reed on which to hang such a weighty conclusion.

For further discussion of this issue, and of other suggested limits on the power of Congress with respect to federal jurisdiction, see Chap. IV, Sec. I(A), infra.

47. 1 Farrand 238 (June 13, Yates' notes). See also id. 220 (June 12), 223–24, 232 (June 13).

48. 2 Farrand 46 (July 18).

knowledge that the Convention intended all these clauses to be, and treated them as, specifications of the general principle settled on July 18.[49]

The nine heads of federal jurisdiction that eventually emerged can usefully be regrouped around five major themes.

1. Vindication of Federal Authority

(a) *Cases Arising Under the Laws of the United States*

Faithful to the vote of July 18, the Committee of Detail placed at the head of its list of subjects of jurisdiction "all cases arising under laws passed by the Legislature of the United States".[50] The clause had antecedents, partial or complete, in all five of the judiciary plans.[51] Save only for the change in wording by the Committee of Style, it was accepted and incorporated into the Constitution without further question or discussion.[52]

(b) *Cases Arising Under the Constitution*

The matter of fact way in which this clause was inserted has already been described.[53] Only the Blair plan had included such a provision.[54]

(c) *United States a Party*

Under the Articles of Confederation the United States had to go into state courts for enforcement of its laws and collection of its claims.[55]

Of the five plans before the Convention, however, only Blair's included a general grant of jurisdiction in cases to which the United States was a

---

49. "By questions involving the National peace and harmony, no one can suppose more was meant than might be *specified* by the Convention, as proper to be referred to the Judiciary either by the Constitution or the Constitutional authority of the Legislature ∗ ∗ ∗. That the Convention understood the entire Resolutions of Mr. Randolph to be a mere sketch in which omitted details were to be supplied and the general terms and phrases to be reduced to their proper details is demonstrated by the use made of them in the Convention ∗ ∗ ∗. Candour discovers no ground for the charge that the Resolutions contemplated a Government materially different from, or more National than, that in which they terminated. ∗ ∗ ∗ The plan expressly aimed at a specification, and, of course, a limitation of the powers." Letter of Madison to John Tyler, 1833, as quoted in Warren 331.

50. 2 Farrand 186 (August 6).

51. Randolph: cases "which respect the collection of the National revenue", 1 *id.* 22; Pinckney: "all cases arising under the laws of the United States", 3 *id.* 600; Paterson: all cases "which may arise on any of the Acts for regulation of trade, or the collection of the federal Revenue", 1 *id.* 244; Hamilton: "all causes in which the revenues of the general Government ∗ ∗ ∗ are concerned", with power in the

legislature "to institute Courts in each State for the determination of all matters of general concern", *id.* 292; Blair: "all cases in law and equity arising under ∗ ∗ ∗ the laws of the United States", 2 *id.* 432.

52. 2 Farrand 600 (committee report), 628 (September 15, entire Article approved).

53. See note 33, *supra*, and accompanying text.

54. 2 Farrand 432.

55. Thus, even treason against the United States had to be left to trial in state courts by state law. In 1781 Congress recommended to the state legislatures that they pass laws punishing infractions of the law of nations, and erect courts or clothe existing courts with authority to decide what constituted such an offense. Where an official of the United States Post Office was guilty of misdemeanor in office, Congress could only prescribe penalties and let the Postmaster General bring an action in debt in a state court to recover them. In settling accounts of the military and in recovering debts from individuals, Congress recommended that the state legislatures pass laws empowering Congress' agents to bring such actions in state courts. Carson 83–86.

party.[56] Perhaps the clause was omitted in the others because the problem was thought to be taken care of through jurisdiction in cases arising under various federal laws. Perhaps for the same reason there was no such clause in the initial report of the Committee of Detail. But responding to a motion by Charles Pinckney, the committee later made a special recommendation, on August 22, that jurisdiction be given in controversies "between the United States and an individual State or the United States and an individual person".[57] The provision as it stands was inserted on the floor on August 27, on a motion by Madison and G. Morris apparently intended to reflect this recommendation. Soon after, on the same day, it was moved that "in cases in which the United States shall be a party the jurisdiction shall be original or appellate as the Legislature may direct", but the motion failed,[58] with the result that the jurisdiction of the Supreme Court was made appellate only.

2. Admiralty and Maritime Cases

Hamilton said in The Federalist, "The most bigoted idolizers of state authority, have not thus far shown a disposition to deny the National Judiciary the cognizance of maritime causes".[59] Although only Pinckney's and Blair's plans provided for admiralty jurisdiction,[60] the need for it had been widely recognized and its inclusion in the report of the Committee of Detail went unchallenged.[61]

The principal commerce of the period was, of course, maritime; and, as Wilson pointed out on the floor, it was in the admiralty jurisdiction that disputes with foreigners were most likely to arise.[62] But the roots of the prepossession toward federal authority lie deeper in history. Maritime law was a separate (although very narrow) corpus, which before the war had been administered by British vice-admiralty rather than colonial courts. General admiralty jurisdiction was thus not one that state courts had been accustomed to exercise; and state legislatures proved hesitant in conferring it upon them. And, as already seen,[63] in the one special field of maritime law in which jurisdiction was widely conferred upon state courts, that of prize cases, experience had shown the existence of federal concern and the need of a federal tribunal with adequate authority.

3. Foreign Relations

In October 1786, Jefferson wrote to Madison: "The politics of Europe rendered it indispensably necessary that with respect to everything external we be one nation firmly hooped together; interior government is what each State should keep to itself." [64] That the national government should have exclusive power to deal with foreign nations was common ground at

---

56. 2 Farrand 432. One version of the Paterson plan included a resolution that "provision ought to be made for hearing and deciding upon all disputes arising between the United States and an individual State respecting territory". 3 *Id.* 611.

57. 2 *Id.* 367 (August 22). This report was distributed to the members, *id.* 376, but seems not to have been acted upon. For Pinckney's earlier motion, see *id.* 342 (August 20).

58. *Id.* 424–25, 430.

59. No. 80.

60. 3 Farrand 600; 2 *id.* 432. However, both Randolph and Paterson gave jurisdiction of "piracies & felonies on the high seas" and "captures from an enemy"—Paterson's, of course, being appellate only. *Cf.* Warren 535n.

61. 2 Farrand 186.

62. 1 *Id.* 124 (June 5).

63. See note 18, *supra.*

64. Warren 46.

the Convention. Even the Articles of Confederation had attempted to lodge all such powers in the national Congress.[65]

From this premise several corollaries were drawn.

(a) *Arising Under Treaties Made or to be Made*

The Treaty with Great Britain had guaranteed the integrity of certain private debts owed to British subjects, provided for post-war return of certain British property interests acquired before the war, and limited private causes of action against British subjects arising out of legitimate war activities. Since then nearly all the states had passed statutes which in various ways violated these and other provisions of the treaty.

The experience of the national government in attempting to redeem its good faith had taught two lessons: first, that appeals to state legislatures to repeal the offending laws were ineffectual—such correction as took place had come from state courts which voided the statutes or gave them a forced construction; and second, that uniform interpretations of the treaty could not be expected from thirteen separate judiciaries.[66]

In his early proposal to settle the scope of jurisdiction in terms of general principle, Randolph made clear that "questions which involve the national peace and harmony" was intended to include questions of "the security of foreigners where treaties are in their favor".[67] All the other plans except Pinckney's contemplated a similar jurisdiction.[68] In addition, the Convention at one time had extended the proposed negative on state laws, upon motion by Benjamin Franklin, to include laws contravening "any treaties subsisting under the authority of the Union."[69] Nevertheless, the Committee of Detail omitted any express reference to treaties, perhaps because of the provisions giving jurisdiction when foreigners were parties. The present clause was inserted on the floor on motion of Rutledge *nem. con.*[70]

(b) *Affecting Ambassadors, Other Public Ministers or Consuls*

Under the Articles of Confederation, the United States could give no assurance of legal protection to the representatives of foreign countries living in the United States. Where legal proceedings involving such representatives were conducted in state courts, the foreign relations of all the states were in the hands of that particular judge or jury. "The Convention was convinced that if foreign officials were either to seek justice at law or be subjected to its penalties, it should be at the hand of the national government."[71]

All the plans contemplated such a jurisdiction.[72] The present clause was reported out of the Committee of Detail and passed without dispute,

65. 1 Farrand 133 (Sherman, June 6); Articles of Confederation, Art. IX.

66. Meigs, The Judiciary and the Constitution 80–100 (1919).

67. 1 Farrand 238 (June 13).

68. Paterson: appellate jurisdiction where construction of a treaty involved, 1 Farrand 244; Hamilton: where "citizens of foreign nations are concerned", *id.* 292;

Blair: cases arising under a treaty, 2 *id.* 432.

69. 1 *Id.* 54 (May 31).

70. 2 *Id.* 431 (August 27).

71. Frank, *Historical Bases of the Federal Judicial System,* 13 Law & Contemp. Prob. 3, 14 (1948).

72. The Paterson plan gave the Supreme Court appellate jurisdiction in cases

and also without dispute, was included in the Supreme Court's original jurisdiction.[73]

(c) States, or Citizens Thereof, and Foreign States, Citizens or Subjects

In April, 1787, Madison said in a letter to Randolph: "It seems, at least essential * * * that an appeal should lie to some national tribunal in all cases which concern foreigners, or inhabitants of other states." [74] And in the Virginia convention Madison said, "We well know, sir, that foreigners cannot get justice done them in these courts, and this has prevented many wealthy gentlemen from trading or residing among us." [75] All the plans except Pinckney's provided for jurisdiction where foreigners were interested; [76] and the need for a grant going beyond cases involving treaties and foreign representatives seems to have been undisputed. The clause came out of the Committee of Detail in its present form.[77]

4. Inter-State Umpiring

(a) Controversies Between Two or More States

Border disputes had plagued the new states.[78] In a speech introducing his resolutions, Governor Randolph said: "Are we not on the eve of war, which is only prevented by the hopes from the convention?" [79] And when the Convention was close to complete impasse, Gerry appealed to the members to keep trying. Without a Union, "We should be without an Umpire to decide controversies and must be at the mercy of events".[80] Sherman listed a national power to prevent internal disputes and resorts to force as one of the four basic objects of a Union.[81]

However, only the Blair plan proposed a specific jurisdiction in controversies between states, although this was perhaps intended to be included in Randolph's "national peace and harmony" provision and in a similar provision of Hamilton's.[82] Moreover, when the Committee of Detail reported, it qualified its proposed grant of jurisdiction to the Supreme Court in "controversies between two or more States" with an exception for "such as shall regard Territory or Jurisdiction". For these disputes it almost duplicated the cumbersome machinery of the Articles of Confederation, using the Senate to implement it.[83]

On the floor, in the debate on the legislative articles, Rutledge moved to strike these provisions, saying that they were "necessary under the

"touching the rights of ambassadors", as well as in cases "in which foreigners may be interested". 1 Farrand 244. The Pinckney plan gave the Court original jurisdiction in cases "affecting Ambassadors & other public Ministers". 3 Id. 600. The Blair plan added consuls, in substantially the language of the present grant. 2 Id. 432. The Randolph and Hamilton plans provided generally for jurisdiction where foreigners were concerned. 1 Id. 22, 292.

73. 2 Id. 186, 431.

74. 2 Papers of James Madison 633 (1840).

75. 3 Elliot's Debates 583 (1888).

76. See text at notes 67–70, supra.

77. 2 Farrand 186.

78. See note 17, supra.

79. 1 Farrand 26 (May 29).

80. Id. 515 (July 2).

81. Id. 133 (June 6).

82. Blair, 2 Farrand 432; Randolph, 1 id. 22; Hamilton, id. 292.

83. See the proposed Art. IX, Sec. 3, 2 Farrand 183–84. The provision seems to have originated in Randolph's draft in the Committee of Detail. Id. 144.

Confederation, but will be rendered unnecessary by the National Judiciary now to be established". Doubts were expressed whether the judiciary was appropriate, since "the Judges might be connected with the States being parties". But the motion to strike carried eight states to two, North Carolina and Georgia dissenting.[84]

(b) *State and Citizens of Another State*

The grant of jurisdiction in controversies between a state and citizens of another state had no specific forerunner in any of the five plans.[85] The clause first appears in a marginal note in Rutledge's handwriting on Randolph's draft for the Committee of Detail,[86] and was reported out by that committee in its present form.[87] There was no discussion of it. Without doubt the underlying considerations were akin to those that prompted the diversity clause—indeed, this clause is *a fortiori;* and the diversity jurisdiction, too, stirred no comment.[88]

(c) *Citizens of the Same State, Land Grants Under Different States*

The Blair plan alone touched the problem of this clause,[89] save as it may have been thought involved in "national peace and harmony". The Committee of Detail proposed the same mode of settling these controversies as for controversies over territory or jurisdiction between the states themselves; and both proposals were stricken by the same vote.[90] Sherman moved the insertion of the present provision in the later debate on the judiciary article, and the motion was agreed to *nem. con.*[91]

5. Controversies Between Citizens of Different States

The grant of diversity jurisdiction aroused bitter controversy in the ratification debates, and the controversy has continued intermittently ever since.[92] Strangely, the clause passed without question in the Convention, and thus without clarification of its purposes. Madison early said that he wished to add to Sherman's statement of the four principal objects of union "the necessity, of providing more effectually for the security of private rights, and the steady dispensation of Justice. Interferences with these were evils which had more perhaps than anything else, produced this convention".[93] Perhaps the diversity clause was responsive to these and

84. 2 *Id.* 400–01 (August 24).

85. Randolph's original resolution would have given jurisdiction to inferior federal courts in "cases in which foreigners or citizens of other States applying to such jurisdictions may be interested". 1 Farrand 22. But this would not have guarded against the possibility of antagonism when a state was suing in the courts of another state. And if Hamilton was right in *The Federalist,* No. 81, that the Convention did not contemplate that a state could be sued by a citizen of another state without its consent, it would have been of no assistance to an out-of-state citizen as plaintiff.

86. 2 Farrand 147.

87. *Id.* 186.

88. See heading 5, *infra.*

89. 2 Farrand 432.

90. See note 84, *supra.*

91. 2 Farrand 431–32 (August 27).

92. The problem is more fully treated in the *Note on the Historical Background of the Diversity Jurisdiction,* Chap. XIII, p. 1658, *infra.*

93. 1 Farrand 134 (June 6). He was addressing himself to the need for having one branch of the legislature elected by the people, so that it might be representative of all groups and thus a safeguard against domination by anyone.

similar expressions of concern, and not simply to the obvious intention to protect out-of-state litigants, rich or poor, from the bias of local tribunals. But this rationale was never articulated, and proposals more directly related to the security of commercial and property interests either were never made or not taken up.[94]

Randolph's initial plan provided for jurisdiction in "cases in which foreigners or citizens of other States applying to such jurisdictions may be interested",[95] in contrast with Paterson's, Hamilton's, and Blair's, which protected only foreigners, and Pinckney's, which had no provision against bias. When the Committee of the Whole first considered Randolph's proposal on June 12, it voted to give jurisdiction in "cases in which foreigners or citizens of two distinct States of the Union" may be interested.[96] This specification was submerged in the more general votes of principle on June 13 and July 18.[97] But in the report of the Committee of Detail it reappeared in its present form, and was accepted without challenge on August 27.[98]

E.   Jurisdiction of the Supreme Court

1.   Original Jurisdiction

The Randolph plan, which required the establishment of lower federal courts, made no provision for an original jurisdiction of the Supreme Court. But all the other plans did.   Paterson's, contemplating primarily an appellate jurisdiction from state courts, provided for original jurisdiction in cases of impeachment.[99]   Pinckney's gave original jurisdiction in impeachment and in cases affecting ambassadors and other public ministers; [100]   Hamilton's, in cases of captures; [101]   and Blair's, "in all cases affecting ambassadors, other public ministers and consuls, and those in which a State shall be a party, and suits between persons claiming lands under grants of different states".[102]

After it had been decided that the creation of inferior courts should be at the discretion of Congress, the Supreme Court's original jurisdiction took on new importance as the only available means of assuring access to a federal tribunal.[103]   In the Committee of Detail, one draft of the Constitution in Randolph's handwriting gave the Supreme Court original jurisdiction in cases of impeachment and such other cases as the legislature might prescribe.[104]   In a later draft in Wilson's handwriting, and in the draft submitted to the Convention, original jurisdiction was given in cases of

---

94. A striking proposal, in the light of the later development under Swift v. Tyson, Chap. VI, Sec. 2, *infra*, was that of jurisdiction in "any case which may arise • • • on the Law of Nations, or general commercial or marine Laws". This is contained in a draft in Wilson's handwriting among the records of the Committee of Detail, taken chiefly from the Paterson plan and hence providing only for appellate jurisdiction. 2 Farrand 157.

95. See note 85, *supra*.

96. 2 Farrand 431–32.

97. See notes 47 and 48, *supra*, and accompanying text.

98. 1 Farrand 22.

99. *Id.* 244.

100. 3 *Id.* 600.

101. 1 *Id.* 292.

102. 2 *Id.* 432.

103. The assurance was only at the option of the plaintiff, in view of the Court's ultimate ruling that lower federal courts and state courts could be given concurrent jurisdiction of cases within the original jurisdiction. See Chap. III, Sec. 1, *infra.* Compare the holding in Marbury v. Madison, Chap. II, Sec. 1, *infra,* that Congress is without power to enlarge the original jurisdiction.

104. 2 Farrand 147.

impeachment, in cases affecting ambassadors and other public ministers and consuls, and in cases in which a state was a party. This, however, was subject to a general power in the legislature to assign this jurisdiction, except for a trial of the President, to inferior federal courts.[105] The provision for impeachments and the legislative power of assignment were stricken on the floor.[106]

2. Appellate Jurisdiction

The decisions as to the scope of the Supreme Court's original jurisdiction settled that the balance of the jurisdiction should be appellate.[107] The important provision that the appellate jurisdiction should be subject to exceptions and regulations by Congress was contained in none of the plans.[108] It is foreshadowed in Randolph's draft for the Committee of Detail and then appears in a later draft in Wilson's handwriting in substantially the form in which the committee reported it.[109] There was no discussion in the Convention.

The provision that the jurisdiction should extend to both law and fact was added on the floor of the Convention. Together with the provision for inferior courts, it was to become a main target of attack in the ratification debates, but the Convention accepted it without question. A similar provision had been in the Paterson plan.[110] Blair's plan gave jurisdiction as to law only, except in cases of equity and admiralty.[111] But the point was not touched on in the report of the Committee of Detail. On the floor G. Morris asked if the appellate jurisdiction extended to matters of fact as well as law, and Wilson said he thought that was the Committee's intention. Dickinson then moved to add the words "both as to law and fact", and it was agreed to *nem. con.*[112]

The phrase "and fact" opened the Constitution to the charge that the Supreme Court was authorized to re-examine the verdicts of juries. The charge was made even as to criminal cases, where the right of trial by jury was guaranteed, but more especially as to civil cases, where it was not.[113]

---

105. *Id.* 173, 186–87.

106. See notes 46 and 47, *supra;* 2 Farrand 423–24, 430–31 (August 27).

107. For the expectation that this should include jurisdiction to review the decisions of state courts, see text following note 45, *supra.* Only Paterson's and Blair's plans provided in terms for such a jurisdiction. 1 Farrand 243–44; 2 *id.* 433.

108. All the plans would seem to have made the appellate jurisdiction a constitutional requirement and Blair's even went to the point of prescribing a constitutional jurisdictional amount.

109. 2 Farrand 147, 173, 186.

110. 1 *Id.* 243.

111. 2 *Id.* 433.

112. *Id.* 431 (August 27).

113. None of the five plans referred to trial by jury except Blair's. His plan, while contemplating the trial of crimes in state courts, required that the trial should be by jury. It said nothing of civil cases. *Id.* 433.

The provision in Article III for trial of crimes by jury first appears in a draft for the Committee of Detail in Wilson's handwriting, *id.* 173, and was included in the Committee's report. *Id.* 187. It was amended in the Convention to provide for the venue of trial for crimes not committed in any state and approved *nem. con.*, on August 28. *Id.* 438.

On September 12, while the report of the Committee of Style was being printed, Mr. Williamson "observed to the House that no provision was yet made for juries in Civil cases and suggested the necessity of it". Gorham said it was impossible "to discriminate equity cases from those in which juries are proper", and added that the "Representatives of the people may be safely trusted in this matter". Gerry supported Williamson. Mason said he saw the difficulty of specifying jury cases, but, broadening the discussion, said that a bill

It bore fruit, of course, in the Seventh Amendment, which not only established the right of trial by jury in civil cases but provided that "no fact tried by a jury, shall be otherwise re-examined in any Court of the United States, than according to the rules of the common law".

F. The Ratification Debates and Proposals for Amendment

The judiciary article, which had aroused only relatively minor disagreement in the Convention, became a storm center of controversy in the ratification debates. The conventions of six of the initially ratifying states suggested amendments, and all of these but South Carolina wanted changes in Article III.[114] No less than 19 of the 103 amendments proposed by these six states related to the judiciary or judicial proceedings.[115] As Charles Warren says:

"The principal Amendments which were regarded as necessary, relative to the Judiciary, were (a) an express provision guaranteeing jury trials in civil as well as criminal cases; (b) the confinement of appellate power to questions of law, and not of fact; (c) the elimination of any Federal Courts of first instance, or, at all events, the restriction of such original Federal jurisdiction to a Supreme Court with very limited original jurisdiction; (d) the elimination of all jurisdiction based on diverse citizenship and status as a foreigner." [116]

The scope and force of the objections to the judiciary provisions are perhaps best measured by the proposals for amendments which survived to be pressed, and formally acted upon, in the first Congress. Twelve amendments were approved for submission to the states of which, of course, only ten were eventually ratified.[117] Action on these amendments was concurrent with, and became enmeshed in, the process of framing the First Judiciary Act.[118]

Ames lists 173 amendments proposed in the first session of the first Congress, although the figure includes many repetitions of the same proposal as well as variants of essentially similar ones. Of these, 48 can be

of rights "would give great quiet to the people"; and Gerry and Mason moved that a committee be appointed to prepare such a bill. Sherman thought the state bills of rights sufficient, and repeated Gorham's points about juries. The Convention, plainly fatigued at this point, voted down the motion unanimously. *Id.* 587–88.

114. Rhode Island's belated convention in 1790 also proposed amendments to Article III. Ames, Proposed Amendments to the Constitution, 1789–1889, at 310 (1897) (hereafter cited as Ames).

On the process of ratification generally, and on the character of anti-federalist opinion, see Main, The Anti-Federalists: Critics of the Constitution, 1781–1788 (1961); Mason, The States Rights Debate: Antifederalism and the Constitution (1964); Kenyon, The Anti-Federalists (1966); Rutland, The Ordeal of the Constitution: The Anti-Federalists and the Ratification Struggle of 1787–1788 (1966); Goebel, *supra* note 2, at 251–91; Storing, The Com-

plete Anti-Federalist (1981). On the debate over the judiciary during the ratification process, see Clinton, note 46, *supra*, at 797–829.

In addition, publication is well underway of a projected 16 or 17 volume work entitled The Documentary History of the Ratification of the Constitution. The project is sponsored by The State Historical Society of Wisconsin.

115. Ames 307–10.

116. Warren, *New Light on the History of the Federal Judiciary Act of 1789*, 37 Harv.L.Rev. 49, 56 (1923).

117. The amendments which failed related to the compensation of members of Congress and the apportionment of representatives. Ames 317 (No. 243), 320 (No. 295).

118. A detailed and classic account both of the act and the amendments is contained in Warren, note 116, *supra*.

counted as primarily concerned with courts and court proceedings. Much the greater number, 36 in all, had to do with trial by jury and various rights of defendants in criminal proceedings.[119] The Fourth, Fifth, Sixth, Seventh, and Eighth Amendments reflect the substance of most of them.

Of the remaining proposals none brought into question the basic principle of a federal judiciary. The most drastic was an amendment, originating in the Virginia convention and offered only in the Senate, which would have substantially redrafted Article III, altering not only the structure of the courts but the scope and conception of the judicial power.[120] The rest of the fire, however, was with rifle rather than shotgun.

Virginia revived the proposal to forbid increases as well as decreases in judicial salary during incumbency, but coupled it this time with a provision for revision by general regulation at stated periods of not less than seven years.[121]

The sharpest and most persistent attack was directed at the power of Congress to establish inferior federal courts. In the House, Representative Tucker of South Carolina moved three times to limit this power to the establishment of courts of admiralty, and was three times defeated.[122] The same proposal was included in Virginia's shotgun measure in the Senate.

The only proposal in the House to change the scope of federal jurisdiction was a motion for an amendment, again by Mr. Tucker, to abolish the diversity jurisdiction.[123] In the Senate this likewise was included in Virgin-

119. Ames 310–21 (Nos. 135–38, 140, 142–43, 169–76, 183–86, 188–89, 213–14, 221–24, 226–27, 254–55, 258, 292–94, 297).

On the origins of the Bill of Rights, see generally Rutland, The Birth of the Bill of Rights, 1776–1791 (1955); Levy, Legacy of Suppression: Freedom of Speech and Press in Early American History (1960); Brant, The Bill of Rights: Its Origin and Meaning (1965); Goebel, note 2, *supra*, at 413–56; Schwartz, The Bill of Rights: A Documentary History (1971).

120. Ames 320 (No. 284), Senate Journal, 1st Cong., 1st Sess., p. 126. The amendment (capitals and punctuation modernized) provided as follows:

"That the judicial power of the United States shall be vested in one supreme court, and in such courts of admiralty as Congress may, from time to time, ordain and establish in any of the different states; the judicial powers shall extend to all cases in law and equity, arising under treaties made, or which shall be made, under the authority of the United States; to all cases affecting ambassadors, other foreign ministers, and consuls; to all cases of admiralty and maritime jurisdiction; to controversies to which the United States shall be a party; to controversies between two or more states; and between parties claiming lands under the grants of different states. In all cases affecting ambassadors, other foreign ministers, and consuls, and those in which a state shall be a party, the supreme court shall have original jurisdiction; in all oth-

er cases beforementioned the supreme court shall have appellate jurisdiction as to matters of law only, except in cases of equity, and of admiralty and maritime jurisdiction, in which the supreme court shall have appellate jurisdiction, both as to law and fact, with such exceptions, and under such regulations, as the Congress shall make. But the judicial power of the United States shall extend to no case where the cause of action shall have originated before the ratification of this constitution; except in disputes between states about their territory, disputes between persons claiming lands under the grants of different states, and suits for debts due to the United States."

See also 3 Elliot's Debates on the Federal Constitution 660–61 (2d ed. 1836).

This amendment withdrew any general jurisdiction in cases arising either under Acts of Congress or under the Constitution. Consider whether this would have served to negate power to find state or federal statutes unconstitutional, or only to reduce the types of cases in which it might be exercised.

121. Ames 320 (No. 287); Senate Journal, p. 127; 3 Elliot's Debates 661.

122. Ames 314 (No. 201), 315 (No. 208), 317 (No. 237); 1 Annals of Congress 791 (August 18, 1789), 807 (August 22, 1789).

123. Ames 315 (No. 209); 1 Annals of Congress 791 (August 18, 1789).

ia's plan. A more realistic effort, springing evidently from awareness that more drastic moves would fail, sought only to attach to the diversity jurisdiction a requirement of a minimum jurisdictional amount, but this failed also.[124]

Apart from the Seventh Amendment and the Virginia plan, only one proposal was made affecting the Supreme Court's appellate jurisdiction. This would have excluded appeals "where the value in controversy shall not amount to one thousand dollars". It had the powerful support of Madison, who urged that "great inconvenience has been apprehended to suitors from the distance they would be dragged to obtain justice in the Supreme Court of the United States". The amendment was reported out by the Select Committee of the House and approved in that branch but rejected in the Senate.[125]

———

EXCERPTS FROM THE FEDERALIST PAPERS

Of the eighty-five Federalist papers only five (Nos. 78 to 82) deal directly with the judiciary. But references to the courts and the judicial power are woven into the argument throughout. Of chief importance in showing the place of the courts in the frame of the analysis are the eight papers, five by Hamilton and three by Hamilton and Madison, concerning the defects of the confederacy (Nos. 15 to 22). These follow fourteen introductory papers about the need and utility of an effective union, and introduce the consideration of what is requisite to accomplish such a union.

In No. 15 Hamilton launches the argument with the proposition that:

"The great, and radical vice, in the construction of the existing confederation, is in the principle of *legislation* for *states* or *governments,* in their *corporate* or *collective capacities,* and as contradistinguished from the *individuals* of whom they consist."

The papers then develop, with many historic examples, the thesis that the absence of any effective peaceful process dooms a mere confederacy, having power only to act upon the member states, to disintegrating resort to violence. Hamilton says:

"Government implies the power of making laws. It is essential to the idea of a law, that it be attended with a sanction; or, in other words, a penalty or punishment for disobedience. If there be no penalty annexed to disobedience, the resolutions or commands which pretend to be laws, will in fact amount to nothing more than advice or recommendation. This penalty, whatever it may be, can only be inflicted in two ways; by the agency of the courts and ministers of justice, or by military force; by the COERCION of the magistracy, or by the COERCION of arms. The first kind can evidently apply only to men; the last kind must of necessity be employed against bodies politic, or communities or states. It is evident, that there is no process of a court by which their observance of the laws can, in the last resort, be enforced. Sentences may be denounced against them for violations of their duty; but these sentences can only be carried into execution by the sword. In an association, where the general authority is confined to

---

124. Ames 318 (No. 256); Senate Journal p. 119. The amount was $3,000 in the Supreme Court and $1,500 in lower courts.

125. Ames 316 (No. 225, drawn from Nos. 141, 181, 182); Senate Journal, p. 130.

the collective bodies of the communities that compose it, every breach of the laws must involve a state of war, and military execution must become the only instrument of civil obedience. Such a state of things can certainly not deserve the name of government, nor would any prudent man choose to commit his happiness to it."

And in the final paper of the series (No. 22) he concludes:

"A circumstance, which crowns the defects of the confederation, remains yet to be mentioned—the want of a judiciary power. Laws are a dead letter, without courts to expound and define their true meaning and operation."

The next group of papers (Nos. 23 to 51) deal with a series of general problems concerning the new plan of government, the last five papers on the separation of powers being of special interest. Then come three series devoted more particularly to the three branches of government, of which the series on the judiciary, all by Hamilton, is the last.

The first of the judiciary papers (No. 78), which is addressed immediately to the question of tenure and independence of the judges, contains Hamilton's famous argument on judicial review. While the paper, of course, is no more than suggestive of the conclusions of the Convention, it demonstrates beyond controversy that a formulated and matured theory of judicial review was in the forefront of the thinking of the times.

The next paper treats, more briefly, the protection of judicial independence by security of salary.

The first part of No. 80, excerpts from No. 81, and No. 82 are reproduced below. The final judiciary paper, which is not reproduced, discusses trial by jury.

No. 80, Hamilton

To judge with accuracy of the due extent of the federal judicature, it will be necessary to consider, in the first place, what are its proper objects.

It seems scarcely to admit of controversy, that the judiciary authority of the union ought to extend to these several descriptions of cases. 1st. To all those which arise out of the laws of the United States, passed in pursuance of their just and constitutional powers of legislation; 2nd. To all those which concern the execution of the provisions expressly contained in the articles of union; 3rd. To all those in which the United States are a party; 4th. To all those which involve the PEACE of the CONFEDERACY, whether they relate to the intercourse between the United States and foreign nations, or to that between the States themselves; 5th. To all those which originate on the high seas, and are of admiralty or maritime jurisdiction; and lastly, to all those in which the state tribunals cannot be supposed to be impartial and unbiassed.

The first point depends upon this obvious consideration, that there ought always to be a constitutional method of giving efficacy to constitutional provisions. What, for instance, would avail restrictions on the authority of the state legislatures, without some constitutional mode of enforcing the observance of them? The states, by the plan of the convention, are prohibited from doing a variety of things; some of which are incompatible with the interests of the union, others, with the principles of good government. The imposition of duties on imported articles, and the emission of paper money, are specimens of each kind. No man of sense will believe that such prohibitions would be scrupulously regarded, without some effectual power in the government to restrain or correct the infractions of them. This power must either be a direct negative on the state laws, or an authority in the federal courts, to over-rule such as might be in manifest contravention of the articles of union. There is no third course that I can imagine. The latter appears to have been thought by the convention preferable to the former, and I presume will be most agreeable to the states.

As to the second point, it is impossible, by any argument or comment, to make it clearer than it is in itself. If there are such things as political axioms, the propriety of the judicial power of a government being co-extensive with its legislative, may be ranked among the number. The mere necessity of uniformity in the interpretation of the national laws, decides the question. Thirteen independent courts of final jurisdiction over the same causes, arising upon the same laws, is a hydra in government, from which nothing but contradiction and confusion can proceed.

Still less need be said in regard to the third point. Controversies between the nation and its members or citizens, can only be properly referred to the national tribunals. Any other plan would be contrary to reason, to precedent, and to decorum.

The fourth point rests on this plain proposition, that the peace of the WHOLE ought not to be left at the disposal of a PART. The union will undoubtedly be answerable to foreign powers for the conduct of its members. And the responsibility for an injury ought ever to be accompanied with the faculty of preventing it. As the denial or perversion of justice by the sentences of courts is with reason classed among the just causes of war, it will follow that the federal judiciary ought to have cognizance of all causes in which the citizens of other countries are concerned. This is not less essential to the preservation of the public faith, than to the security of the public tranquillity. A distinction may perhaps be imagined, between cases arising upon treaties and the laws of nations, and those which may stand merely on the footing of the municipal law. The former kind may be supposed proper for the federal jurisdiction, the latter for that of the states. But it is at least problematical, whether an unjust sentence against a foreigner, where the subject of controversy was wholly relative to the *lex loci,* would not, if unredressed, be an aggression upon his sovereign, as well as one which violated the stipulations of a treaty, or the general law of nations. And a still greater objection to the distinction would result from the immense difficulty, if not impossibility, of a practical discrimination between the cases of one complexion and those of the other. So great a proportion of the controversies in which foreigners are parties, involve national questions, that it is by far most safe, and most expedient, to refer all those in which they are concerned to the national tribunals.

The power of determining causes between two states, between one state and the citizens of another, and between the citizens of different states, is perhaps not less essential to the peace of the union, than that which has been just examined. History gives us a horrid picture of the dissentions and private wars which distracted and desolated Germany, prior to the institution of the IMPERIAL CHAMBER by Maximilian, towards the close of the fifteenth century; and informs us, at the same time, of the vast influence of that institution, in appeasing the disorders, and establishing the tranquillity of the empire. This was a court invested with authority to decide finally all differences among the members of the Germanic body.

A method of terminating territorial disputes between the states, under the authority of the federal head, was not unattended to, even in the imperfect system by which they have been hitherto held together. But there are other sources, besides interfering claims of boundary, from which bickerings and animosities may spring up among the members of the union. To some of these we have been witnesses in the course of our past experience. It will readily be conjectured that I allude to the fraudulent laws which have been passed in too many of the states. And though the proposed constitution establishes particular guards against the repetition of those instances, which have heretofore made their appearance, yet it is warrantable to apprehend, that the spirit which produced them will assume new shapes that could not be foreseen, nor specifically provided against. Whatever practices may have a tendency to disturb the harmony of the states, are proper objects of federal superintendence and control.

It may be esteemed the basis of the union, that "the citizens of each state shall be entitled to all the privileges and immunities of citizens of the several states." And if it be a just principle, that every government *ought to possess the means of executing its own provisions, by its own authority,* it will follow, that in order to the inviolable maintenance of that equality of privileges and immunities to which the citizens of the union will be entitled, the national judiciary ought to preside in all cases, in which one state or its citizens are opposed to another state or its citizens. To secure the full effect of so fundamental a provision against all evasion and subterfuge, it is necessary that its construction should be committed to that tribunal, which, having no local attachments, will be likely to be impartial, between the different states and their citizens, and which, owing its official existence to the union, will never be likely to feel any bias inauspicious to the principles on which it is founded.

The fifth point will demand little animadversion. The most bigoted idolizers of state authority, have not thus far shown a disposition to deny the national judiciary the cognizance of maritime causes. These so generally depend on the laws of nations, and so commonly affect the rights of foreigners, that they fall within the considerations which are relative to the public peace. The most important part of them are, by the present confederation, submitted to federal jurisdiction.

The reasonableness of the agency of the national courts, in cases in which the state tribunals cannot be supposed to be impartial, speaks for itself. No man ought certainly to be a judge in his own cause, or in any cause, in respect to which he has the least interest or bias. This principle has no inconsiderable weight in designating the federal courts, as the proper tribunals for the determination of controversies between different states and their citizens. And it ought to have the same operation, in regard to some cases, between the citizens of the same state. Claims to land under grants of different states, founded upon adverse pretensions of boundary, are of this description. The courts of neither of the granting states could be expected to be unbiassed. The laws may have even prejudged the question, and tied the courts down to decisions in favour of the grants of the state to which they belonged. And where this had not been done, it would be natural that the judges, as men, should feel a strong predilection to the claims of their own government. * * *

PUBLIUS.

No. 81, Hamilton

Let us now return to the partition of the judiciary authority between different courts, and their relations to each other.

"The judicial power of the United States is to be vested in one supreme court, and in such inferior courts as the congress may from time to time ordain and establish." That there ought to be one court of supreme and final jurisdiction, is a proposition which is not likely to be contested. * * *[Hamilton here discusses the need for an independent judiciary and undertakes to refute claims that there is danger of encroachment by the judiciary department upon the legislative.]

Having now examined, and I trust removed, the objections to the distinct and independent organization of the supreme court; I proceed to consider the propriety of the power of constituting inferior courts,[1] and the relations which will subsist between these and the former.

The power of constituting inferior courts is evidently calculated to obviate the necessity of having recourse to the supreme court in every case of federal cognizance. It is intended to enable the national government to institute or *authorize* in each state or district of the United States, a tribunal competent to the determination of matters of national jurisdiction within its limits.

But why, it is asked, might not the same purpose have been accomplished by the instrumentality of the state courts? This admits of different answers. Though the fitness and competency of these courts should be allowed in the utmost latitude: yet the substance of the power in question may still be regarded as a necessary part of the plan, if it were only to authorize the national legislature to commit to them the cognizance of causes arising out of the national constitution. To confer upon the existing courts of the several states the power of determining such causes, would perhaps be as much "to constitute tribunals," as to create new courts with the like power. But ought not a more direct and explicit provision to have been made in favour of the state courts? There are, in my opinion, substantial reasons against such a provision: The most discerning cannot foresee how far the prevalency of a local spirit may be found to disqualify the local tribunals for the jurisdiction of national causes; whilst every man may discover that courts constituted like those of some of the states would be improper channels of the judicial authority of the union. State judges, holding their offices during pleasure, or from year to year, will be too little independent to be relied upon for an inflexible execution of the national laws. And if there was a necessity for confiding to them the original cognizance of causes arising under those laws, there would be a correspondent necessity for leaving the door of appeal as wide as possible. In

---

1. This power has been absurdly represented as intended to abolish all the county courts in the several states, which are commonly called inferior courts. But the expressions of the constitution are to constitute "tribunals INFERIOR TO THE SUPREME COURT," and the evident design of the provision is, to enable the institution of local courts, subordinate to the supreme, either in states or larger districts. It is ridiculous to imagine, that county courts were in contemplation.— Publius.

proportion to the grounds of confidence in, or distrust of the subordinate tribunals, ought to be the facility or difficulty of appeals. And well satisfied as I am of the propriety of the appellate jurisdiction, in the several classes of causes to which it is extended by the plan of the convention, I should consider everything calculated to give, in practice, an unrestrained course to appeals, as a source of public and private inconvenience.

I am not sure but that it will be found highly expedient and useful to divide the United States into four or five, or half a dozen districts; and to institute a federal court in each district, in lieu of one in every state. The judges of these courts may hold circuits for the trial of causes in the several parts of the respective districts. Justice through them may be administered with ease and dispatch; and appeals may be safely circumscribed within a narrow compass. This plan appears to me at present the most eligible of any that could be adopted, and in order to it, it is necessary that the power of constituting inferior courts should exist in the full extent in which it is seen in the proposed constitution.

These reasons seem sufficient to satisfy a candid mind, that the want of such a power would have been a great defect in the plan. Let us now examine in what manner the judicial authority is to be distributed between the supreme and the inferior courts of the union.

The supreme court is to be invested with original jurisdiction only "in cases affecting ambassadors, other public ministers and consuls, and those in which A STATE shall be a party." Public ministers of every class are the immediate representatives of their sovereigns. All questions in which they are concerned are so directly connected with the public peace, that as well for the preservation of this, as out of respect to the sovereignties they represent, it is both expedient and proper that such questions should be submitted in the first instance to the highest judiciary of the nation. Though consuls have not in strictness a diplomatic character, yet as they are the public agents of the nations to which they belong, the same observation is in a great measure applicable to them. In cases in which a state might happen to be a party, it would ill suit its dignity to be turned over to an inferior tribunal. * * *

[Hamilton here digresses to refute the objection that a state would be open to suit, without its consent, by a citizen of another state. See Monaco v. Mississippi, p. 306, *infra.*]

Let us resume the train of our observations; we have seen that the original jurisdiction of the supreme court would be confined to two classes of causes, and those of a nature rarely to occur. In all other cases of federal cognizance, the original jurisdiction would appertain to the inferior tribunals, and the supreme court would have nothing more than an appellate jurisdiction, "with such *exceptions,* and under such *regulations,* as the congress shall make."

The propriety of this appellate jurisdiction has been scarcely called in question in regard to matters of law; but the clamours have been loud against it as applied to matters of fact. * * *

The amount of the observations hitherto made on the authority of the judicial department is this: That it has been carefully restricted to those causes which are manifestly proper for the cognizance of the national judicature; that, in the partition of this authority, a very small portion of original jurisdiction had been reserved to the supreme court, and the rest consigned to the subordinate tribunals; that the supreme court will possess an appellate jurisdiction, both as to law and fact, in all the cases referred to them, but subject to any *exceptions* and *regulations* which may be thought advisable; that this appellate jurisdiction does, in no case, *abolish* the trial by jury; and that an ordinary degree of prudence and integrity in the national councils, will insure us solid advantages from the establishment of the proposed judiciary, without exposing us to any of the inconveniences which have been predicted from that source.

PUBLIUS.

No. 82, Hamilton

The erection of a new government, whatever care or wisdom may distinguish the work, cannot fail to originate questions of intricacy and nicety; and these may, in a particular manner, be expected to flow from the establishment of a constitution founded upon the total or partial incorporation of a number of distinct sovereignties. Time only can mature and perfect so compound a system, liquidate the meaning of all the parts, and adjust them to each other in a harmonious and consistent WHOLE.

Such questions accordingly have arisen upon the plan proposed by the convention, and particularly concerning the judiciary department. The principal of these respect the situation of the state courts, in regard to those causes which are to be submitted to federal jurisdiction. Is this to be exclusive, or are those courts to possess a concurrent jurisdiction? If the latter, in what relation will they stand to the national tribunals? These are inquiries which we meet with in the mouths of men of sense, and which are certainly entitled to attention.

The principles established in a former paper [1] teach us that the states will retain all *pre-existing* authorities, which may not be exclusively delegated to the federal head; and that this exclusive delegation can only exist in one of three cases; where an exclusive authority is, in express terms, granted to the union; or where a particular authority is granted to the union, and the exercise of a like authority is prohibited to the states; or, where an authority is granted to the union, with which a similar authority in the states would be utterly incompatible. Though these principles may not apply with the same force to the judiciary, as to the legislative power; yet I am inclined to think that they are in the main, just with respect to the former, as well as the latter. And under this impression I shall lay it down as a rule that the state courts will *retain* the jurisdiction they now have, unless it appears to be taken away in one of the enumerated modes.

The only thing in the proposed constitution, which wears the appearance of confining the causes of federal cognizance, to the federal courts, is contained in this passage: "The JUDICIAL POWER of the United States *shall be vested* in one supreme court, and in *such* inferior courts as the congress shall from time to time ordain and establish." This might either be construed to signify that the supreme and subordinate courts of the union should alone have the power of deciding those causes, to which their authority is to extend; or simply to denote that the organs of the national judiciary should be one supreme court, and as many subordinate courts, as congress should think proper to appoint; in other words, that the United States should exercise the judicial power with which they are to be

1. No. XXXII.—Publius.

invested, through one supreme tribunal, and a certain number of inferior ones, to be instituted by them. The first excludes, the last admits, the concurrent jurisdiction of the state tribunals: And as the first would amount to an alienation of state power by implication, the last appears to me the most defensible construction.

But this doctrine of concurrent jurisdiction is only clearly applicable to those descriptions of causes, of which the state courts have previous cognizance. It is not equally evident in relation to cases which may grow out of, and be *peculiar* to, the constitution to be established: For not to allow the state courts a right of jurisdiction in such cases can hardly be considered as the abridgement of a pre-existing authority. I mean not therefore to contend that the United States, in the course of legislation upon the objects entrusted to their direction, may not commit the decision of causes arising upon a particular regulation, to the federal courts solely, if such a measure should be deemed expedient; but I hold that the state courts will be divested of no part of their primitive jurisdiction, further than may relate to an appeal; and I am even of opinion, that in every case in which they were not expressly excluded by the future acts of the national legislature, they will, of course, take cognizance of the causes to which those acts may give birth. This I infer from the nature of judiciary power, and from the general genius of the system. The judiciary power of every government looks beyond its own local or municipal laws, and in civil cases, lays hold of all subjects of litigation between parties within its jurisdiction, though the causes of dispute are relative to the laws of the most distant part of the globe. Those of Japan, not less than of New York, may furnish the objects of legal discussion to our courts. When in addition to this we consider the state governments and the national governments, as they truly are, in the light of kindred systems, and as parts of ONE WHOLE, the inference seems to be conclusive, that the state courts would have a concurrent jurisdiction in all cases arising under the laws of the union, where it was not expressly prohibited.

Here another question occurs; what relation would subsist between the national and state courts in these instances of concurrent jurisdiction? I answer, that an appeal would certainly lie from the latter, to the supreme court of the United States. The constitution in direct terms, gives an appellate jurisdiction to the supreme court in all the enumerated cases of federal cognizance, in which it is not to have an original one; without a single expression to confine its operation to the inferior federal courts. The objects of appeal, not the tribunals from which it is to be made, are alone contemplated. From this circumstance, and from the reason of the thing, it ought to be construed to extend to the state tribunals. Either this must be the case, or the local courts must be excluded from a concurrent jurisdiction in matters of national concern, else the judiciary authority of the union may be eluded at the pleasure of every plaintiff or prosecutor. Neither of these consequences ought, without evident necessity, to be involved; the latter would be entirely inadmissible, as it would defeat some of the most important and avowed purposes of the proposed government, and would essentially embarrass its measures. Nor do I perceive any foundation for such a supposition. Agreeably to the remark already made, the national and state systems are to be regarded as ONE WHOLE. The courts of the latter will, of course, be natural auxiliaries to the execution of the laws of the union, and an appeal from them will as naturally lie to that tribunal, which is destined to unite and assimilate the principles of national justice and the rules of national decision. The evident aim of the plan of the convention is, that all the causes of the specified classes shall, for weighty public reasons, receive their original or final determination in the courts of the union. To confine, therefore, the general expressions which give appellate jurisdiction to the supreme court, to appeals from the subordinate federal courts, instead of allowing their extension to the state courts, would be to abridge the latitude of the terms, in subversion of the intent, contrary to every sound rule of interpretation.

But could an appeal be made to lie from the state courts, to the subordinate federal judicatories? This is another of the questions which have been raised, and of greater difficulty than the former. The following considerations countenance the affirmative. The plan of the convention, in the first place, authorizes the national legislature "to constitute tribunals inferior to the supreme court." [2] It declares in the next place, that "the JUDICIAL POWER of the United States *shall be vested in* one supreme court, and in such inferior courts as congress shall ordain and establish;" and it then proceeds to enumerate the cases, to which this judicial power shall extend. It afterwards divides the jurisdiction of the supreme court into original and appellate, but gives no definition of that of the subordinate courts. The only outlines described for them are, that they shall be "inferior to the supreme court," and that they shall not exceed the specified limits of the federal judiciary. Whether their authority shall be original or appellate, or both, is not declared. All this seems to be left to the discretion of the legislature. And this being the case, I perceive at present no impediment to the establishment of an appeal from the state courts, to the subordinate national tribunals; and many advantages attending the power of doing it may be imagined. It would diminish the motives to the multiplication of federal courts, and would admit of arrangements calculated to contract the appellate jurisdiction of the supreme court. The state tribunals may then be left with a more entire charge of federal causes; and appeals in most cases in which they may be deemed proper, instead of being carried to the supreme court, may be made to lie from the state courts, to district courts of the union.

PUBLIUS.

NOTE ON THE ORGANIZATION AND GROWTH OF THE FEDERAL JUDICIAL SYSTEM

A. The First Judiciary Act

The judiciary article of the Constitution was not self-executing, and the first Congress in its twentieth enactment accordingly passed "An Act to establish the Judicial Courts of the United States", approved September 24, 1789.[1] The Act was the beginning of an organic evolution. Special attention to the foundation that it laid is helpful in understanding the structure since built upon it.[2]

---

2. Section 8th, Article 1st.—Publius.

1. 1 Stat. 73.

2. The classic and indispensable account of the history of the federal judiciary acts is Frankfurter & Landis, The Business

1. Court Organization

The Supreme Court. The first section of the Act provided that "the supreme court of the United States shall consist of a chief justice and five associate justices". It called for two sessions annually at the seat of government, one commencing the first Monday of February and the other the first Monday of August.

The circuit and district courts. The "transcendent achievement"[3] of the First Judiciary Act was the decision to take up the constitutional option to establish a system of federal trial courts.[4]

The system seems a curious one today. The Act provided for two tiers of trial courts. The first tier consisted of district courts, each manned by its own district judge. The second consisted of circuit courts without judges of their own. The circuit courts, holding two sessions a year in each district within the circuit were to have a bench of three judges each, one of them a district judge and the other two Supreme Court justices sitting on circuit.

The Act divided the eleven states then in the union into thirteen districts with boundaries corresponding to state lines, except that the parts of Massachusetts and Virginia which later became Maine and Kentucky were made into separate districts. Thus, a precedent was established, which is still unbroken, against the crossing of state lines in setting the boundaries of federal judicial districts.

Eleven of the thirteen districts were in turn divided into three circuits, special provision being made for the remote Maine and Kentucky districts.[5]

2. Jurisdiction of the District and Circuit Courts

The jurisdiction of the district courts was entirely original. Part of the jurisdiction was exclusive of the state courts, as it still is today, and part was concurrent with them.

The circuit courts also had an important original jurisdiction. In addition, they had authority to review on writ of error final decisions of the district courts in civil cases in which the matter in controversy exceeded $50, and on appeal final decrees in admiralty and maritime cases in which the matter in controversy exceeded $300.

The original jurisdiction of both sets of courts can usefully be considered together, under the headings which the Administrative Office of the United States Courts currently uses in reporting statistics of the federal courts.

of the Supreme Court (1928). An elaborate account, bringing forward source material hitherto unnoticed, is Goebel, p. 2, note 2, *supra,* at 507–08. For a useful summary, see Bator, *Judiciary Act of 1789,* 3 Encyclopedia of The American Constitution 1075 (1986); Bator, *Judicial System, Federal, id.* at 1068–70. See also authorities cited, Chap. IV, Sec. 1(A), pp. 385–86, *infra.*

For a brief but valuable description of the historical development of the jurisdiction of the lower federal courts, see Frank-furter, *Distribution of Judicial Power Between United States and State Courts,* 13 Corn.L.Q. 499, 507–15 (1928).

3. Frankfurter & Landis 4.

4. See Frank, *Historical Bases of the Federal Judicial System,* 13 Law & Contemp.Prob. 3, 9–11 (1948).

5. The district courts here were authorized to sit also as circuit courts, a device afterward repeatedly used in outlying areas.

(a) *Private Civil Litigation*

Diversity jurisdiction. The Act made prompt use of the constitutional grant of judicial power in cases of diverse citizenship. But the initial grant was carefully and significantly limited to controversies "between a citizen of the State where the suit is brought, and a citizen of another State." To prevent defendants from being summoned long distances to defend small claims, the jurisdiction was restricted to cases in which the matter in dispute exceeded five hundred dollars. The jurisdiction was concurrent with state courts.[6]

The circuit courts were given a further jurisdiction dependent upon the character of the parties, also concurrent with the state courts, in all suits of a civil nature at common law or equity where an alien was a party, again when more than five hundred dollars was in dispute.

The district courts were given jurisdiction, exclusive of the state courts, of all suits against consuls and vice-consuls (except criminal cases triable in the circuit courts).[7] And they were given concurrent jurisdiction "of all causes where an alien sues for a tort only in violation of the law of nations or a treaty of the United States." (The successor provision is 28 U.S.C. § 1350.)

These various grants of jurisdiction dependent upon the character of the party were qualified by the famous "assignee clause," which with various changes survived until 1948. To avoid collusive assignments to create jurisdiction, no district or circuit court was to "have cognizance of any suit to recover the contents of any promissory note or other chose in action in favor of any assignee, unless a suit might have been prosecuted in such court * * * if no assignment had been made, except in cases of foreign bills of exchange." [8]

Federal question jurisdiction. In the sphere of private civil litigation, curiously, the Act made no use of the grant of judicial power over cases arising under the Constitution or laws of the United States.[9]

Admiralty jurisdiction. The district courts were given, in terms which in substance survive today, "exclusive original cognizance of all civil causes of admiralty and maritime jurisdiction, * * * saving to suitors, in all cases, the right of a common law remedy, where the common law is competent to give it".[10] This grant included jurisdiction of "all seizures under laws of impost, navigation or trade of the United States, where the seizures are made, on waters which are navigable from the sea by vessels of ten or more tons burthen, within their respective districts as well as upon the high seas."

(b) *United States Civil Litigation* [11]

The Act did not in terms contemplate the possibility of suits against the United States.

---

6. For the development of the diversity jurisdiction, see Chap. XIII, *infra.*

7. See Chap. III, Sec. 2, *infra.*

8. The successor provision is 28 U.S.C. § 1359. See Chap. XIII, Sec. 4, *infra.*

9. The development of later statutory grants of this jurisdiction is traced in Chap. VIII, pp. 960–66, *infra.*

10. For the current provision, see 28 U.S.C. § 1333; see also pp. 1071–79, *infra.*

11. For the later development, see Chap. VII, Sec. 2(A), Chap. IX, Sec. 1, *infra.*

The circuit courts were given concurrent jurisdiction with the state courts of all civil suits at common law or in equity in which "the United States are plaintiffs, or petitioners" and the matter in dispute exceeded five hundred dollars. The district courts were given jurisdiction, similarly concurrent, "of all suits at common law where the United States sue, and the matter in dispute amounts * * * to the sum or value of one hundred dollars."

In addition, the district courts were given "exclusive original cognizance of all seizures on land, or other waters than as aforesaid, made, and of all suits for penalties and forfeitures incurred, under the laws of the United States."

(c) *Criminal Cases*

The circuit courts were given "exclusive cognizance of all crimes and offences cognizable under the authority of the United States," subject to a concurrent jurisdiction of the district courts to try certain minor criminal offenses.[12]

(d) *Removal Jurisdiction* [13]

The First Judiciary Act originated the device, since continuously in use, of authorizing the removal to a federal court, before trial, of certain types of proceedings begun in the state courts. The device was restricted, initially, to the field of private civil litigation, in which its chief importance still lies. The removal was to a circuit court, and was subject to the jurisdictional amount requirement of five hundred dollars. The privilege of removing was given to three classes of parties:

(a) To a defendant who was an alien;

(b) To a defendant who was a citizen of another state, when sued by a plaintiff who was a citizen of the state where suit was brought; and

(c) To either party, where title to land was in dispute, if one party claimed under a grant from another state and the other party claimed under a grant of the state in which the suit was brought.

3. Jurisdiction of the Supreme Court

(a) *Original Jurisdiction* [14]

Either not foreseeing the later-established doctrine that the original jurisdiction of the Supreme Court is derived directly from the Constitution, or not content to rely on forecast, the framers of the First Judiciary Act specified just what that jurisdiction should be.

They made it nearly but not exactly coextensive with the constitutional grant. It included:

(1) "all controversies of a civil nature, where a state is a party, except between a state and its citizens;" and

(2)(a) "all such jurisdiction * * * as a court of law can have or exercise consistently with the law of nations" of suits "against ambassa-

12. The successor provision is 18 U.S.C. § 3231.

13. For the later history of the removal provisions, see Chap. VIII, Sec. 5, Chap. XIV, Sec. 4, *infra.*

14. See generally Chap. III, *infra.*

dors, or other public ministers, or their domestics, or domestic servants;" and

(b) "all suits brought by ambassadors, or other public ministers, or in which a consul, or vice consul, shall be a party."

The Act distinguished, as all later acts have done, between those instances in which this original jurisdiction was exclusive of other courts and those in which it was not. The jurisdiction was exclusive in the cases in clause (1), above, except suits "between a state and citizens of other states, or aliens", and in all the cases in clause 2(a).

(b) *Review of Circuit Court Decisions* [15]

The new Act did not provide for review of all decisions of the lower federal courts. Final judgments or decrees of the circuit courts in civil cases were made reviewable on writ of error if but only if "the matter in dispute exceeds the sum or value of two thousand dollars, exclusive of costs". There was no provision for review of criminal cases.

(c) *Review of State Court Decisions*

In its famous Section 25, the Act provided for Supreme Court review of final judgments or decrees "in the highest court of law or equity of a State in which a decision in the suit could be had," in three classes of cases:

(a) " * * * where is drawn in question the validity of a treaty or statute of, or an authority exercised under the United States, and the decision is against their validity;" or

(b) " * * * where is drawn in question the validity of a statute of, or an authority exercised under any State, on the ground of their being repugnant to the constitution, treaties or laws of the United States, and the decision is in favor of such their validity;" or

(c) " * * * where is drawn in question the construction of any clause of the constitution, or of a treaty, or statute of, or commission held under the United States, and the decision is against the title, right, privilege or exemption specially set up or claimed" thereunder. [16]

B. The First 100 Years

The structure of courts established by the First Judiciary Act remained stable both at the apex and at the base. [17] The jurisdiction of the courts, of course, has undergone a steady development, important details of which are recounted in succeeding chapters dealing with particular phases of existing jurisdiction. But the institutional changes have been less numerous. The Supreme Court has had a continuous existence since 1789, with changes only in its terms and in the number of associate justices. So also

15. See Chap. XV, Sec. 2, *infra.*

16. For the later development, see Chap. V, Sec. 1, *infra.*

17. For a detailed and fascinating account of the administration and business of the district and circuit courts under the First Judiciary Act from 1789 to 1801, see Henderson, Courts for a New Nation (1971); see also Goebel, p. 2 note 2, *supra,* at 552–661; Tachau, Federal Courts in the Early Republic: Kentucky 1789–1816 (1978).

Minutes of the sessions of the Supreme Court from 1789 to 1806 have been published in the American Journal of Legal History (Surrency ed.). See 5 Am.J. Legal Hist. 67, 166, 369 (1961); 6 *id.* 71 (1962); 7 *id.* 63, 165, 246, 340 (1963); 8 *id.* 72, 326 (1964).

have the district courts, although their numbers have greatly increased and their functions eventually were altered materially by absorption of the original jurisdiction of the circuit courts.

The circuit courts were the weak spot in the original system. The first weakness, disclosed almost at once, was the lack of any judges of their own, and the inordinate burden of circuit riding cast upon the Supreme Court justices. The burden was reduced in 1793 by requiring only one justice on the circuit court; [18] but this was at the cost of establishing a precedent of a two-judge court—creating a problem of split decisions.

In the closing days of the Federalist administration Congress came to grips with these problems in the famous Law of the Midnight Judges. The Act of February 13, 1801,[19] "combined thoughtful concern for the federal judiciary with selfish concern for the Federalist party".[20]

The new Act gave the district and circuit courts, taken together, a jurisdiction almost coextensive with the constitutional authorization. It created ten new judicial districts, each with a district judge; divided the total of 23 districts into six circuits; abolished circuit riding by Supreme Court justices; and manned five of the circuit courts with a bench of three circuit judges each and the sixth (the western circuit) with a single circuit judge. District court judgments were made reviewable directly by writ of error from the Supreme Court.

But the new circuit judges were all Federalists. The incoming Jeffersonians, their anger heightened by the behavior of some of the new judges, repealed the act and abolished the judgeships.[21] Soon afterward they passed their own "act to amend the judicial system".

The new Act of April 29, 1802,[22] with minor exceptions, maintained the *status quo ante*. It continued the system of circuit riding, to which Congress remained persistently attached as a means of keeping the justices in touch with the people. Six circuit courts were established, composed as before of one Supreme Court justice and one district judge. They were each to hold two sessions a year in each district within the circuit. There were seventeen districts, and the number grew steadily. To meet the burden of holding circuit court sessions in more and more districts, the Act reduced the number of Supreme Court sessions to one a year and authorized the holding of the circuit court by a single district judge. Circuit riding thus became a duty of imperfect obligation. This did not eliminate the burden; but as the country grew the privilege of non-attendance came increasingly to be used. Correspondingly, circuit court review of district court decisions became more and more frequently futile.

The Act did contain a few new jurisdictional provisions. In cases where the judges of the circuit court were divided in opinion they were authorized and in criminal cases required to certify the question at issue to

---

18. Act of March 2, 1793, 1 Stat. 333. See Frankfurter & Landis 14–30, and 1 Warren, The Supreme Court in United States History 85–90 (1926) for discussions of contemporary criticisms of the circuit riding obligation.

19. 2 Stat. 89. See generally Surrency, *The Judiciary Act of 1801,* 2 Am.J. Legal Hist. 53 (1958); Turner, *The Midnight Judges,* 109 U.Pa.L.Rev. 494 (1961); Turner, *Federalist Policy and the Judiciary Act of 1801,* 22 Wm. & Mary Q. 3 (1965).

20. Frankfurter & Landis 25.

21. Act of March 8, 1802, 2 Stat. 132. See Frankfurter & Landis 24–30; 1 Warren 184–230; 3 Beveridge cc. 1–4.

22. 2 Stat. 156, as amended by the Act of March 3, 1803, 2 Stat. 244.

the Supreme Court.[23] And in addition to its old jurisdiction in error the Supreme Court was empowered to hear appeals from the circuit courts in equity, admiralty, and prize cases where the amount in dispute exceeded $2,000.

Not until 1891 did Congress again take action with a view to the needs of the federal judicial system as a whole. The story of the intervening years is a story of near-unanimous recognition of the inadequacy of the judicial system, of interminable debate about remedies, and of long-delayed and meager action.

In 1807 a seventh circuit was created to meet the needs of Kentucky, Tennessee, and Ohio.[24] This automatically resulted in the appointment of a sixth associate justice for the new circuit. With the size of the Supreme Court thus tied to the circuit system, Congress found itself for twenty years unable to agree upon similar action for later-entering states, so that these remained outside the circuit system. At length, in 1837, the country was redivided into nine circuits, and the membership of the Supreme Court increased to nine.[25]

California (joined soon after by Oregon) became a tenth circuit in 1855;[26] and in 1863 a tenth justice was added to the Supreme Court.[27] But in 1866 the districts were again reorganized into nine circuits.[28] The 1866 Act also reduced the size of the Supreme Court to seven,[29] to keep President Johnson from filling vacancies; but three years later the number was restored to nine,[30] where it has ever since remained.

The Act of 1869, in addition, took a substantial, albeit inadequate, step toward relieving the intolerable burden upon the understaffed circuit system. In this act Congress at length yielded to the old Federalist plan for the appointment of circuit judges, and authorized one circuit judge for each of the nine circuits. At the same time it reduced the circuit-riding duty of the Supreme Court justices to attendance at one term every two years in each district of the circuit to which the justice was assigned.

Meanwhile, the growth of the country, and patchwork extensions of federal jurisdiction, had been placing increasing strain upon the Supreme Court's docket. The Court's term, as well as its membership, was several times enlarged.[31] And Congress kept adding to the Court's jurisdiction. The Court was authorized to review judgments rendered in the highest courts of the territories.[32] It was empowered to revise judgments in civil

---

23. On the review of criminal cases, see note 39, *infra.*

24. Act of Feb. 24, 1807, 2 Stat. 420, amended by the Act of March 22, 1808, 2 Stat. 477, and the Act of Feb. 4, 1809, 2 Stat. 516.

25. Act of March 3, 1837, 5 Stat. 176.

26. Act of March 2, 1855, 10 Stat. 631.

27. Act of March 3, 1863, 12 Stat. 794, amended by the Act of Feb. 19, 1864, 13 Stat. 4.

28. Act of July 23, 1866, § 2, 14 Stat. 209.

29. *Id.,* § 1.

30. Act of April 10, 1869, 16 Stat. 44.

31. A month was added by the Act of March 4, 1826, 4 Stat. 160, and another month by the Act of June 17, 1844, 5 Stat. 676. The anti-Johnson Act of 1866, *supra* note 28, authorized one term a year without specifying when it should begin. The Act of Jan. 24, 1873, 17 Stat. 419, fixed the second Monday of October as the beginning date, with freedom as to the end. At the Court's request this was changed to the first Monday of October by the Act of Sept. 6, 1916, § 1, 39 Stat. 726, where it has since stayed. 28 U.S.C. § 2.

32. *E.g.,* Act of Feb. 5, 1825, § 5, 4 Stat. 80, 81 (Michigan Territory); Act of April 17, 1828, § 7, 4 Stat. 261, 262 (Arkansas Territory); Act of Aug. 14, 1848, § 9, 9

rights,[33] habeas corpus,[34] and patent and copyright [35] cases without regard to jurisdictional amount.[36] In 1872 the system of certifying questions—a system that had existed since 1803—was abolished. At the same time, Congress provided that when the judges of a circuit court disagreed, judgment should be entered in accordance with the views of the presiding judge and the question which formerly could have been certified should then be reviewable on appeal or writ of error.[37] When at length a restriction on appellate jurisdiction was enacted, in 1875, it took the unhappy form of an increase in the jurisdictional amount to $5,000.[38] Even this restriction was partially offset by further enlargements in the years immediately following.[39]

The period from 1870 to 1891 represents the nadir of federal judicial administration. At the opening of the period lower courts and the Supreme Court alike were already swamped with more than they could do. Then suddenly, in the Judiciary Act of March 3, 1875,[40] Congress followed the Federalists of 1801 in expanding the statutory grant of jurisdiction almost to the full extent of the constitutional authorization. Both diversity and federal question jurisdiction were conferred in the language of the Constitution, limited only by a requirement of jurisdictional amount.[41] Whatever the wisdom of these and other extensions of federal trial jurisdiction, they unloosed a flood of litigation utterly beyond the existing capacity of the courts to handle.

The Supreme Court "began its 1870 Term with six hundred and thirty-six cases on its docket. This number nearly doubled within ten years. The October Term of 1880 begins with twelve hundred and twelve cases; the number steadily mounts in the years following, reaching a total of eighteen hundred and sixteen cases at the beginning of October Term, 1890." [42]

In the lower federal courts, which were the principal feeders of the stream, the condition was the same. "In 1873 the number of cases pending in the circuit and district courts was twenty-nine thousand and thirteen, of which five thousand one hundred and eight were bankruptcy cases. In

Stat. 323, 327 (Oregon Territory); Rev.Stat. § 702; Judicial Code of 1911, §§ 244–49, 36 Stat. 1087, 1157–59.

33. Act of April 9, 1866, § 10, 14 Stat. 27, 29; Act of April 20, 1871, 17 Stat. 13.

34. Act of Feb. 5, 1867, § 1, 14 Stat. 385, 386. An intermediate appeal to the circuit court was also provided for. Congress abolished appeals to the Supreme Court under this law by the Act of March 27, 1868, § 2, 15 Stat. 44, see p. 364, *infra*, but restored them by the Act of March 3, 1885, 23 Stat. 437.

35. Act of Feb. 18, 1861, 12 Stat. 130.

36. The Act of March 3, 1863, § 7, 12 Stat. 759, 760, and the Act of June 30, 1864, § 13, 13 Stat. 306, 310, provided for direct appeals from the district courts in prize cases.

37. Act of June 1, 1872, § 1, 17 Stat. 196.

38. Act of Feb. 16, 1875, § 3, 18 Stat. 315.

39. To the matters reviewable without regard to the amount in controversy were added more civil rights cases by the Act of March 1, 1875, § 5, 18 Stat. 335, 337, and jurisdictional questions by the Act of Feb. 25, 1889, 25 Stat. 693. In 1889, writs of error were for the first time permitted in cases of capital crime. Act of Feb. 6, 1889, § 6, 25 Stat. 655, 656. On the further development of appeals in federal criminal cases, see Chap. XV, *infra.*

40. 18 Stat. 470.

41. "In the Act of March 3, 1875, Congress gave the federal courts the vast range of power which had lain dormant in the Constitution since 1789. These courts ceased to be restricted tribunals of fair dealing between citizens of different states and became the primary and powerful reliances for vindicating every right given by the Constitution, the laws, and treaties of the United States." Frankfurter & Landis 65.

42. *Id.* 60.

1880, despite the fact that the repeal of the Bankruptcy Act had dried up that source of business, the number had increased to thirty-eight thousand and forty-five. The year 1890 brings the total to fifty-four thousand one hundred and ninety-four." [43]

C. The Evarts Act and the Judges' Bill of 1925

The chronically-deepening crisis reached the point of universal acknowledgement. But action was paralyzed by seemingly irreconcilable differences about remedies. One school of thought, with its voting strength in the Senate and its support in the East, sought the answer by adding to the capacity of the courts to dispose of business. The other, with its voting strength in the House and support in the South and West, sought the answer in restrictions upon jurisdiction.

Both remedies in truth had to be adopted, and both eventually were. The Judiciary Acts of 1887–1888 put a series of curbs on access to the lower federal courts. [44] But this was not enough. The problem called for structural change—the establishment of intermediate courts of appeal and the sharp restriction of double review as of right. In the Evarts Act (the Circuit Court of Appeals Act of 1891 [45]) Congress at length came to this solution.

Circuit courts of appeals, consisting of three judges each, were established in each of the nine existing circuits. An additional circuit judgeship was created in each circuit, thus providing two circuit judges in all the circuits except the second which, having received an additional judge in 1887, [46] now had three. The third place was ordinarily to be filled by a district judge, but Supreme Court justices were also eligible to sit. The Act specifically provided (as had the 1789 Act) that a district judge could not sit on review of his own judgments.

In deference to the traditionalists, the Act did not abolish the old circuit courts, although it took away their appellate jurisdiction over the district courts. For another twenty years there remained two sets of federal trial courts. [47]

43. Id.

44. Act of March 3, 1887, 24 Stat. 552, corrected by Act of Aug. 13, 1888, 25 Stat. 433. The specific restrictions of jurisdiction that the Act introduced were each relatively minor although considerable in the aggregate:

(1) The jurisdictional amount was raised to $2,000. (In 1911, in the first Judicial Code, it was raised again to $3,000. In 1958 the present figure of $10,000 was enacted.)

(2) The privilege of removal was withdrawn from plaintiffs and confined to defendants; in diversity cases it was confined to nonresident defendants.

(3) It was made clear that the general removal jurisdiction did not extend to any cases except those that might have been brought originally in a federal court.

(4) No longer was venue proper in any district in which the defendant "shall be found" but only in the district of which he was an "inhabitant," with an option in diverse citizenship cases of the district of either the plaintiff's or the defendant's residence.

(5) No longer were national banking associations to be allowed to sue in federal courts merely on the ground that they were incorporated under the laws of the United States.

(6) The assignee clause limiting diversity jurisdiction was broadened.

These restrictions of the 1887 act, however, were partly offset by the Tucker Act, 24 Stat. 505, which was signed on the same day. See Chap. IX, Sec. 1(C), infra.

45. Act of March 3, 1891, 26 Stat. 826.

46. Act of March 3, 1887, 24 Stat. 492.

47. See text at note 49, infra.

Under the Evarts Act, certain decisions of the trial courts were reviewable directly by the Supreme Court. These included questions—not whole cases—of the trial court's jurisdiction, and many other classes of cases.

The Act continued to allow double review as of right in important classes of cases, subject in general to a jurisdictional amount requirement of $1,000.

The most important innovation of the Act was the introduction of the now familiar principle of discretionary review by certiorari. Circuit court of appeals decisions were declared to be "final" in diversity litigation, in suits under the revenue and patent laws, in criminal prosecutions, and in admiralty suits; but in all such cases the Supreme Court, "by certiorari or otherwise," was authorized, regardless of the amount in controversy, to order the judgment brought before it for review. In addition, as remains true today, a circuit court of appeals was authorized to "certify to the Supreme Court * * * any questions or propositions of law concerning which it desires the instruction of that court for its proper decision." [48]

Between the Evarts Act and the Judges' Bill of 1925 came the Judicial Code of 1911, which finally abolished the old circuit courts.[49]

The next major reform of the Supreme Court's jurisdiction was the Act of February 13, 1925,[50] which was drafted by a committee of Supreme Court Justices (led by Justice Van Devanter). This Act did not make structural changes in the court system; its purpose was to reduce sharply the Supreme Court's burden by narrowing the scope of review as of right of decisions of state courts and of the circuit courts of appeals and replacing it with discretionary review by writ of certiorari. In addition, direct appeals from the district courts were sharply curtailed. Ever since, the principle of review at the Court's discretion has come to dominate its administration.[51]

D. The Court Packing Plan

Questions regarding the administration of the Supreme Court's business became entangled with broad political issues in connection with President Roosevelt's celebrated court-packing plan of 1937. The decisions of the Court in 1934–36 invalidating important portions of the New Deal program,[52] and fear for the remainder of that program,[53] persuaded President Roosevelt in 1936–37 that drastic action was necessary. A large number of possible measures were canvassed by the Administration, including restrictions on the courts' jurisdiction and substantive constitutional

48. See Chap. XV p. 1794, *infra.*

49. Act of March 3, 1911, 36 Stat. 1087.

50. 43 Stat. 936. See generally Frankfurter & Landis 255–94; Mason, William Howard Taft: Chief Justice 88–120 (1964).

51. On review of state court decisions, see further Chap. V, *infra;* on review of federal decisions, Chap. XV, *infra.* On the certiorari policy, see Chap. XV, Sec. 3, *infra.* The device of certiorari had also been used when the Congress extended the Supreme Court's jurisdiction to include the review of state court decisions favorable to

a claim of federal right. Act of Dec. 23, 1914, 38 Stat. 790.

52. See, *e.g.,* Panama Refining Co. v. Ryan, 293 U.S. 388 (1935); Railroad Retirement Board v. Alton R. Co., 295 U.S. 330 (1935); Schechter Poultry Corp. v. United States, 295 U.S. 495 (1935); United States v. Butler, 297 U.S. 1 (1936); Carter v. Carter Coal Co., 298 U.S. 238 (1936).

53. Two of the major measures considered to be jeopardized by the earlier rulings were the National Labor Relations Act and the Social Security Law.

amendments.[54] The proposal that was finally sent to Congress [55] had as its aim the reconstitution of the Court by the appointment of additional judges: if any federal judge (who had served 10 years) became seventy, and did not retire or resign, an additional judge would be appointed for that court. Not more than 50 additional judges were to be so appointed, and the membership of the Supreme Court was to be limited in any event to 15. The proposal would have had the effect of allowing the President to add six Justices to the Supreme Court, assuming that none of the sitting members over 70 stepped down.[56]

The plan was justified by the President on the basis, appearing highly disingenuous to many, that it was needed to keep the Supreme Court abreast of its work; in passing the President criticized the certiorari system.[57] The plan aroused wide-spread opposition as an attack on the

54. An admirable and detailed account of the origins and formulation of the plan is given in Leuchtenburg, *The Origins of Franklin D. Roosevelt's "Court–Packing" Plan*, 1966 Sup.Ct.Rev. 347. See also Burns, The Lion and the Fox ch. 15 (1956) (with critical bibliography at pp. 521–23).

55. S. 1392, 75th Cong., 1st Sess. (1937), printed in Sen.Rep. No. 711, 75th Cong., 1st Sess. (1937) (Reorganization of the Federal Judiciary).

56. The six over 70 were Justices Butler (71), Hughes (75), Sutherland (75), McReynolds (75), Van Devanter (78), and Brandeis (81).

57. See the President's Message to Congress of February 5, 1937, printed in Sen. Rep. No. 711, note 55, *supra*, at 25–27:

" * * *

"The judiciary has often found itself handicapped by insufficient personnel with which to meet a growing and more complex business. * * *

"The simple fact is that today a new need for legislative action arises because the personnel of the Federal judiciary is insufficient to meet the business before them. A growing body of our citizens complain of the complexities, the delays, and the expense of litigation in the United States courts. * * *

"The attainment of speedier justice in the courts below will enlarge the task of the Supreme Court itself, and still more work would be added by the recommendation which I make later in this message for the quicker determination of constitutional questions by the highest court.

"Even at the present time the Supreme Court is laboring under a heavy burden. Its difficulties in this respect were superficially lightened some years ago by authorizing the Court, in its discretion, to refuse to hear appeals in many classes of cases. This discretion was so freely exercised that in the last fiscal year, although 867 petitions for review were presented to the Su-

preme Court, it declined to hear 717 cases. If petitions in behalf of the Government are excluded, it appears that the Court permitted private litigants to prosecute appeals in only 108 cases out of 803 applications. Many of the refusals were doubtless warranted. But can it be said that full justice is achieved when a court is forced by the sheer necessity of keeping up with its business to decline, without even an explanation to hear 87 percent of the cases presented to it by private litigants?

"It seems clear, therefore, that the necessity of relieving present congestion extends to the enlargement of the capacity of all the Federal courts. * * *

"Modern complexities call also for a constant infusion of new blood in the courts, just as it is needed in executive functions of the Government and in private business. * * *

"I, therefore, earnestly recommend that the necessity of an increase in the number of judges be supplied by legislation providing for the appointment of additional judges in all Federal courts, without exception, where there are incumbent judges of retirement age who do not choose to retire or to resign. If an elder judge is not in fact incapacitated, only good can come from the presence of an additional judge in the crowded state of the dockets; if the capacity of an elder judge is in fact impaired, the appointment of an additional judge is indispensable. This seems to be a truth which cannot be contradicted. * * * "

Subsequently the President became much more forthright in justifying his plan on the ground that the Court's decisions were an intolerable obstacle to his program. See generally Burns, *supra* note 54. See also 6 The Public Papers and Addresses of Franklin D. Roosevelt lxv (1941): "I made one major mistake when I first presented the plan. I did not place enough emphasis upon the real mischief—the kind of decisions which, as a studied and continued policy, had been coming down from the

independence of the federal judiciary and on the principle of judicial review. The suggestion that the plan was justified by the needs of judicial administration was strongly rebutted by Chief Justice Hughes, speaking also for Justices Brandeis and Van Devanter, in a celebrated letter to Senator Wheeler,[58] which stated that the Court was abreast of its work and

Supreme Court. I soon corrected that mistake—in the speeches which I later made about the plan."

58. See Sen.Rep. No. 711, note 55, *supra,* at 38–40:

"MY DEAR SENATOR WHEELER: In response to your inquiries, I have the honor to present the following statement with respect to the work of the Supreme Court:

"1. The Supreme Court is fully abreast of its work. When we rose on March 15 (for the present recess) we had heard argument in cases in which certiorari had been granted only 4 weeks before—February 15.

"During the current term, which began last October and which we call 'October term, 1936', we have heard argument on the merits in 150 cases (180 numbers) and we have 28 cases (30 numbers) awaiting argument. We shall be able to hear all these cases, and such others as may come up for argument, before our adjournment for the term. There is no congestion of cases upon our calendar.

"This gratifying condition has obtained for several years. We have been able for several years to adjourn after disposing of all cases which are ready to be heard. * * *

"4. The act of 1925, limiting appeals as a matter of right and enlarging the provisions for review only through certiorari was most carefully considered by Congress. * * * That legislation was deemed to be essential to enable the Supreme Court to perform its proper function. No single court of last resort, whatever the number of judges, could dispose of all the cases which arise in this vast country and which litigants would seek to bring up if the right of appeal were unrestricted. * * *

"Under our Federal system, when litigants have had their cases heard in the courts of first instance, and the trier of the facts, jury or judge, as the case may require, has spoken and the case on the facts and law has been decided, and when the dissatisfied party has been accorded an appeal to the circuit court of appeals, the litigants, so far as mere private interests are concerned, have had their day in court. If further review is to be had by the Supreme Court it must be because of the public interest in the questions involved. * * *

"It is obvious that if appeal as a matter of right is restricted to certain described

cases, the question whether review should be allowed in other cases must necessarily be confided to some tribunal for determination, and, of course, with respect to review by the Supreme Court, that Court should decide.

"5. Granting certiorari is not a matter of favor but of sound judicial discretion. It is not the importance of the parties or the amount of money involved that is in any sense controlling. The action of the Court is governed by its rules. * * *

"These rules are impartially applied, as it is most important that they should be. * * *

"6. The work of passing upon these applications for certiorari is laborious but the Court is able to perform it adequately. * * *

"I think that it is safe to say that about 60 percent of the applications for certiorari are wholly without merit and ought never to have been made. There are probably about 20 percent or so in addition which have a fair degree of plausibility but which fail to survive critical examination. The remainder, falling short, I believe, of 20 percent, show substantial grounds and are granted. I think that it is the view of the members of the Court that if any error is made in dealing with these applications it is on the side of liberality.

"7. An increase in the number of Justices of the Supreme Court, apart from any question of policy, which I do not discuss, would not promote the efficiency of the Court. It is believed that it would impair that efficiency so long as the Court acts as a unit. There would be more judges to hear, more judges to confer, more judges to discuss, more judges to be convinced and to decide. The present number of Justices is thought to be large enough so far as the prompt, adequate, and efficient conduct of the work of the Court is concerned. As I have said, I do not speak of any other considerations in view of the appropriate attitude of the Court in relation to questions of policy.

"I understand that it has been suggested that with more Justices the Court could hear cases in divisions. It is believed that such a plan would be impracticable. A large proportion of the cases we hear are important and a decision by a part of the Court would be unsatisfactory.

that the appointment of additional Justices would impair the effectiveness of the Court.[59]

The court packing plan was adversely reported by the Senate Judiciary Committee in June, 1937.[60] In the meantime the Court had sustained the constitutionality of a number of regulatory statutes,[61] and Justice Van Devanter had retired. In late July the Senate allowed the core of the plan to die.[62]

E. The Federal Judicial System Today; Proposals for Change

The defeat of the Court-packing plan left the basic organization of the federal court system in the form given it by the Evarts Act and the Judges' Bill of 1925.[63] The Judicial Code of 1948 (which is the present codification of the organization and business of the federal courts) retained that structure while making many important changes in the statutory formulation governing the courts' jurisdiction. In 1958 came enactments restricting access to the federal courts by increasing the jurisdictional amount in federal question and diversity cases from $3,000 to $10,000 and by redefining corporate citizenship, and permitting certain interlocutory appeals to the courts of appeals from the district courts.

Since 1958, the major legislative changes in the federal judicial system have included:

1. The virtual elimination of the requirement that certain cases be heard before a district court of three judges, with a right of direct appeal to the Supreme Court.[64] The story of the rise and fall of this requirement is told in Chap. X, Sec. 1(B), *infra*.

2. Elimination of several other provisions for direct appeal to the Supreme Court of federal district court decisions.[65]

"I may also call attention to the provisions of article III, section 1, of the Constitution that the judicial power of the United States shall be vested 'in one Supreme Court' and in such inferior courts as the Congress may from time to time ordain and establish. The Constitution does not appear to authorize two or more Supreme Courts or two or more parts of a Supreme Court functioning in effect as separate courts.

"On account of the shortness of time I have not been able to consult with the members of the Court generally with respect to the foregoing statement, but I am confident that it is in accord with the views of the Justices. I should say, however, that I have been able to consult with Mr. Justice Van Devanter and Mr. Justice Brandeis, and I am at liberty to say that the statement is approved by them. * * * *"

59. On the circumstances of the writing of this letter, and on its impact, see 2 Pusey, Charles Evans Hughes 754–56, 766

(1951); Freund, *Charles Evans Hughes as Chief Justice*, 81 Harv.L.Rev. 4, 21–34 (1967). On reactions within the Court, see Mason, Harlan Fiske Stone ch. 28 (1956).

60. Sen.Rep. No. 711, note 55, *supra*.

61. See, in particular, West Coast Hotel Co. v. Parish, 300 U.S. 379 (1937); NLRB v. Jones & Laughlin Steel Corp., 301 U.S. 1 (1937). For the role of Justice Roberts in the Parish case see Frankfurter, *Mr. Justice Roberts*, 104 U.Pa.L.Rev. 311 (1955); Freund, note 59, *supra* at 29–30.

62. See Burns, note 54, *supra*, at 306–09.

63. The present Tenth Circuit had been created in 1929. Act of Feb. 28, 1929, 45 Stat. 1346.

64. Act of Aug. 12, 1976, 90 Stat. 1119.

65. See, *e.g.*, Omnibus Crime Control Act of 1970, 18 U.S.C. § 3731, as amended by Act of Jan. 2, 1971, § 14(a), 84 Stat. 1890; Act of Dec. 21, 1974, 88 Stat. 1708–09 (amending the Expediting Act).

3. Elimination of the amount-in-controversy requirement in federal question cases brought under 28 U.S.C. § 1331.[66]

4. Division of the Fifth Circuit into a new Fifth Circuit (Louisiana, Mississippi, and Texas), and a new Eleventh Circuit (Alabama, Florida, and Georgia).[67]

5. Numerous changes in the character and scope of the specialized federal courts, including the creation of a new Court of Appeals for the Federal Circuit. These changes are described in Part F of this Note.

Since the 1960s, there has been a renewed interest in fundamental changes in the jurisdiction of the federal courts and in the structure of the federal court system. A comprehensive American Law Institute Study, completed in 1969, made a number of proposals with respect to the jurisdiction of the district courts.[68] Included among these proposals was one substantially curtailing the diversity jurisdiction; since then, bills curtailing or virtually abolishing the diversity jurisdiction have frequently been introduced, and one such bill narrowly failed of congressional enactment.[69]

At the appellate and Supreme Court levels, there has been, for the first time in a century, serious interest in structural change—an interest actuated by a sense that the increase in the workload of these courts was approaching crisis proportions and that the Supreme Court was unable to fulfill its role in clarifying and developing federal law.[70] Thus in 1972, a

66. Act of Dec. 1, 1980, 94 Stat. 2369.

67. Act of Oct. 14, 1980, 94 Stat. 1994.

68. American Law Institute, Study of the Division of Jurisdiction Between State and Federal Courts (1969). For appraisals, see Wright, *Restructuring Federal Jurisdiction: The American Law Institute Proposals*, 26 Wash. & Lee L.Rev. 185 (1969); Currie, *The Federal Courts and The American Law Institute*, 36 U.Chi.L.Rev. I, 268 (1968–69). See also Hearings on S. 1876 Before the Subcomm. on Improvements in Judicial Machinery of the Senate Comm. on the Judiciary, 92d Cong., 1st & 2d Sess. (1971, 1972).

69. See Chap. XIII, Sec. 4, *infra.* The proposals to curtail or abolish diversity jurisdiction have been motivated in part by concern over crowded dockets in the district courts. For data bearing on this problem, see *Note on the Business of the District Courts*, p. 50, *infra.* For valuable overviews and critiques of federal court jurisdiction, and discussion of proposals for change, see Friendly, Federal Jurisdiction—A General View (1973); Posner, The Federal Courts: Crisis and Reform (1985). For a skeptical appraisal of the claims of a caseload crisis in American courts generally, and the federal courts in particular, see Galanter, *The Day After The Litigation Explosion*, 46 Md.L.Rev. 1 (1986).

70. For data on the burgeoning caseloads of the appellate courts and on the workload of the Supreme Court, see the Notes at pp. 55, 57, *infra.*

In addition to the reports described in the text, leading discussions of proposals for change include:

Symposium, *The Federal Courts: The Next 100 Years* (articles by A.E. Dick Howard, Charles Wright, Erwin Griswold, Paul Carrington, Edward Cooper, and James Underwood), 38 S.Car.L.Rev. 363 (1987); *Rx for an Overburdened Supreme Court: Is Relief in Sight?*, 66 Judicature 394 (1983) (report of panel discussion at Feb. 1983 mid-year meeting of American Judicature Society); Symposium, *Federal Appellate Justice* (articles by Roger Cramton, Maurice Rosenberg, Clement Haynsworth, Philip Kurland and Henry Friendly), 59 Cornell L.Rev. 571 (1974); Baker, *A Compendium of Proposals to Reform the Courts of Appeals*, 37 U.Fla.L.Rev. 225 (1985); Carrington, *Crowded Dockets and the Courts of Appeals: The Threat to the Function of Review and the National Law*, 82 Harv.L.Rev. 542 (1969); Edwards, *The Rising Workload and Perceived "Bureaucracy" of the Federal Courts: A Causation-Based Approach to the Search for Appropriate Remedies*, 68 Iowa L.Rev. 871 (1983); Hufstedler, *Courtship and Other Legal Arts*, 60 A.B.A.J. 545 (1974); Leventhal, *A Modest Proposal for a Multi–Circuit Court of Appeals*, 24 Am.U.L.Rev. 881 (1975); Levin, *Adding Appellate Capacity to the Federal System: A National Court of Appeals or an Inter-circuit Tribunal?*, 39 Wash. & L.Rev. 1 (1982); Meador, *The Federal Judiciary—Inflation, Malfunction and*

committee under the chairmanship of Professor Paul Freund, after concluding that the "conditions essential for the performance of the [Supreme] Court's mission do not exist," proposed elimination of the Court's obligatory review jurisdiction and creation of a new National Court of Appeals.[71] Under this proposal, the new court would have "screened" all petitions for certiorari from state and federal courts, and would have had final authority (a) to resolve certain inter-circuit conflicts on the merits and (b) to deny certiorari and preclude further review in all other cases. Cases thought potentially worthy of Supreme Court review (estimated at some 400–500 annually) would have been certified to that Court, which would have selected among them for full review on the merits.

The Freund Committee's proposal was greeted by a predominantly critical response, with the criticism centering primarily on the point that the Supreme Court's control over its own docket would be drastically reduced.[72] This defect was avoided in the next major proposal, which was issued by the National Commission on Revision of the Federal Appellate System (the Hruska Commission) in 1975.[73] The Commission proposed a new national court of appeals—to consist of seven judges—which was to be a "decisional" rather than a "screening" court, designed primarily to increase the capacity of the federal judicial system for definitive adjudication of issues of national law. The new court was to have (a) jurisdiction to decide cases referred to it by the Supreme Court[74] and (b) "transfer" jurisdiction to decide cases submitted to it (before decision) by any of the regional courts of appeals.[75] All of its decisions were to be subject to review by the Supreme Court on certiorari.

The Hruska Commission proposal for transfer jurisdiction ran into strong opposition from the outset; broader reservations to the plan as a whole focused on the point that more modest, or "traditional," reforms

a Proposed Course of Action, 1981 B.Y.U.L. Rev. 617.

For a general overview of the appellate process, see P. Carrington, D. Meador & M. Rosenberg, Justice on Appeal (1976). For further discussion of the work of the Supreme Court, see Casper & Posner, The Workload of the Supreme Court (1976).

71. Report of the Study Group on the Caseload of the Supreme Court (Federal Judicial Center 1972).

72. See, *e.g.,* Warren, *Let's Not Weaken The Supreme Court,* 60 A.B.A.J. 677 (1974); Brennan, *The National Court of Appeals: Another Dissent,* 40 U.Chi.L.Rev. 473 (1973); Black, *The National Court of Appeals: An Unwise Proposal,* 83 Yale L.J. 883 (1974); authorities cited in 13 Wright, Miller & Cooper, Federal Practice and Procedure § 3510 n. 10 (1975). For defense of the Committee's proposals by two of its members, see Bickel, The Caseload of the Supreme Court (1973): Freund, *Why We Need the National Court of Appeals,* 59 A.B.A.J. 247 (1973).

73. Commission on Revision of the Federal Court Appellate System, Structure and Internal Procedures: Recommenda-

tions for Change (1975) (reprinted in 67 F.R.D. 195 (1975)). The Act of Congress establishing the Commission, 86 Stat. 807 (1972), authorized it to study the structure and procedures of the courts of appeals; the study was not to embrace the jurisdiction of the district courts.

In addition to the proposal discussed in text, the Commission made a number of thoughtful suggestions for changes in the internal procedures of the courts of appeals and also recommended splitting the Fifth and Ninth Circuits. Congress did subsequently divide the Fifth Circuit. See note 67, *supra.*

74. Any case within the appellate jurisdiction of the Supreme Court in which Supreme Court review was sought was to be subject to such a reference. The Court could direct the National Court to decide the case on the merits or could leave it to that Court to determine whether to review.

75. The suggested criterion for transfer was the existence of a question that would benefit from prompt national resolution. The National Court could reject any transfer from a court of appeals.

should first be instituted and their effects studied.[76] Several such reforms were subsequently adopted: in 1976 Congress virtually eliminated three-judge courts; in 1976 and 1979 it expanded the role of magistrates (see p. 54, *infra*); in 1978 and again in 1984 it created a substantial number of new appellate and district court judgeships.[77]

The idea of a new national court of appeals surfaced again in 1983, stimulated by a proposal made by Chief Justice Burger at a meeting of the American Bar Association. Burger, *Annual Report on the State of the Judiciary,* 69 A.B.A.J. 442, 447 (1983). He advocated, as an interim step "which would provide relief and also provide a concrete experience and information," the creation of a special appellate panel. The panel was to consist of judges designated from each circuit, was to have a limited five-year existence, and was to "hear and decide all intercircuit conflicts and possibly, in addition, a defined category of statutory interpretation cases" (*id.*).

Following this proposal, bills were introduced in each House to establish an Intercircuit Tribunal consisting of 26 judges, two from each circuit, which was to sit in panels of five to hear cases referred to it by the Supreme Court on vote of five justices. The Tribunal's judgments were to be reviewable on certiorari by the Supreme Court but until modified or overruled were to be binding on all federal courts and, with respect to federal questions, on state courts. S.645, 98th Cong., 1st Sess. §§ 601–607 (1983); H.R. 1970, 98th Cong., 1st Sess. (1983).

A similar bill was introduced in the 99th Congress (S. 704); after hearings, it was reported out with amendments by the Judiciary Committee but never came to the floor. Strong support for the bill (with some suggested changes) was expressed by a number of practitioners, judges, and members of the academic community,[78] but support was far from universal. Opponents argued, inter alia, that the Supreme Court's caseload was not in a state of crisis; that much could be accomplished by more modest steps (like eliminating the Court's obligatory jurisdiction) and by more discriminating selection of cases for review; and that the creation of a new court might unduly narrow the scope of the Supreme Court's own work and create new and contentious issues of docket management.[79]

76. The proposals were ably presented and defended in 61 A.B.A.J. 819 (1975); Hruska, *The National Court of Appeals: An Analysis of Viewpoints,* 9 Creighton L.Rev. 286 (1975); Rosenberg, *Enlarging the Federal Courts, Capacity to Settle the National Law,* 10 Gonz.L.Rev. 709 (1975). Criticisms were voiced in, *e.g.,* Casper & Posner, The Workload of the Supreme Court (1976); The Needs of the Federal Courts (Report of the Dep't of Justice Comm. on Revision of the Fed'l Judicial System 1977); Feinberg, *A National Court of Appeals?,* 42 Brooklyn L.Rev. 611 (1976); Owens, *The Hruska Commission's Proposed National Court of Appeals,* 23 U.C.L.A.Rev. 580 (1976), and by a number of witnesses at Senate Hearings in May and November 1976, (*Proposed National Court of Appeals Act: Hearings on S. 2762 and S. 3423 Before the Subcomm. on Improvements in Judicial Machinery of the Senate Comm. on*

the Judiciary, 94th Cong., 2d Sess. (1976)). The Subcommittee did not report a bill.

77. Act of Oct. 20, 1978, 92 Stat. 1629; Act of July 10, 1984, 98 Stat. 333, 346.

78. See, *e.g., Intercircuit Panel of the United States Act: Hearings on S. 704 Before the Subcomm. on Courts of the Senate Comm. on the Judiciary,* 99th Cong., 1st Sess. (1985), at 151 (testimony of Prof. Daniel J. Meador), 229 (statement of Erwin N. Griswold), 256 (statement of Robert L. Stern). See also Baker & McFarland, *The Need for a New National Court,* 100 Harv. L.Rev. 1400 (1987); McCree, *To Preserve an Endangered Species,* 52 U.Cin.L.Rev. 248 (1983); Rehnquist, *The Changing Role of the Supreme Court,* 14 Fla.St.U.L.Rev. 1 (1986).

79. See, *e.g., Hearings* note 78, *supra,* at 94–121 (statements of Judges Patricia Wald, Harry Edwards, and Ruth Gins-

F. The Specialized Courts

1. Courts of the District of Columbia

The organization of the District of Columbia compelled the establishment of tribunals to perform the functions of local courts as well as of ordinary federal courts. From the beginning the District has had inferior courts with distinctively local jurisdiction. From 1863 to 1893 this judicial system was headed by a Supreme Court of the District of Columbia, which was comparable both to a circuit court and to a state supreme court. In the latter year the Court of Appeals of the District of Columbia was established as a superior tribunal corresponding to the new circuit courts of appeals.[80] Both these courts had a local as well as a federal jurisdiction. But by successive steps the former District supreme court was given the title and status of a district court of the United States, and the former court of appeals became a United States Court of Appeals.[81]

In 1970 the District of Columbia Court Reorganization Act [82] ended the system of combining federal and local jurisdictions in the courts of the District. Under this Act, the United States Court of Appeals for the District of Columbia Circuit and the United States District Court for the District of Columbia exercise only federal jurisdiction. The remaining local jurisdiction of those courts was transferred to two local courts. The highest local court continues to be the District of Columbia Court of Appeals,[83] an appellate court whose judgments are in turn reviewable by the Supreme Court under 28 U.S.C. § 1257 as if they were rendered by a state court.[84] The Superior Court of the District of Columbia is now the trial court of general jurisdiction,[85] and is divided into Civil, Criminal, Family, Probate, and Tax Divisions.[86] The judges of both these local courts serve for fifteen-

burg). See also Hellman, *The Proposed Intercircuit Tribunal: Do We Need It? Will It Work?*, 11 Hastings Const.L.Q. 375 (1984); Ginsburg & Huber, *The Intercircuit Committee,* 100 Harv.L.Rev. 1417, 1432 (1987) (proposing, instead of a new national court, a "new standing committee" of Congress, whose function would be "to examine court decisions construing federal statutes and to draft bills to resolve actual or potential conflicts"); Estreicher & Sexton, Redefining the Supreme Court's Role 111–15 (1986).

The book by Professors Estreicher & Sexton was based on an in-depth study of the Supreme Court's work during the 1982 Term. The study itself, entitled the New York University Supreme Court Project, is reported in three issues of the New York University Law Review beginning at 59 N.Y.U.L.Rev. 677 (1984). Its conclusions were summarized at the 1985 Hearings in a statement submitted by Professors Estreicher & Sexton in opposition to the proposed legislation. See *Hearings, supra,* at 163. (For further discussion of the Study, see p. 1874, *infra.*)

80. Act of Feb. 9, 1893, 27 Stat. 434. For the history of this court and of the old District supreme court, see O'Donoghue v. United States, 289 U.S. 516, 548 (1933).

81. For the present provisions, see 28 U.S.C. §§ 41, 43 (court of appeals), and §§ 88, 132 (district court).

82. Act of July 29, 1970, 84 Stat. 473. See generally Kern, *The District of Columbia Court Reorganization Act of 1970: A Dose of the Conventional Wisdom and a Dash of Innovation,* 20 Am.U.L.Rev. 237 (1971).

83. 11 D.C.Code §§ 11–701 *et seq.*

84. 11 D.C.Code § 11–102. On the question whether Supreme Court review is on appeal or certiorari, see Palmore v. United States, 411 U.S. 389 (1973); Key v. Doyle, 434 U.S. 59 (1977). These decisions establish that D.C.Code provisions are neither state statutes for purposes of 28 U.S.C. § 1257(2) nor statutes of the United States for purposes of § 1257(1).

85. 11 D.C.Code §§ 11–901 *et seq.*

86. 11 D.C.Code §§ 11–902, 11–1301.

year terms.[87] (For further discussion of the courts of the District of
Columbia, and especially of their status under the Constitution, see Palmore v. United States, 411 U.S. 389 (1973).)

2. The Territorial and Related Courts

The statutes organizing each of the territories have likewise had to
make provision for courts of local as well as federal jurisdiction. Today the
Commonwealth of Puerto Rico has a United States District Court for the
District of Puerto Rico,[88] exercising federal jurisdiction. In addition the
Commonwealth has a system of local courts, headed by the Supreme Court
of Puerto Rico; [89] decisions of the latter are reviewed by the United States
Supreme Court much as state court judgments are.[90]

Guam, the Virgin Islands, and the Northern Mariana Islands also have
district courts; these, however, exercise both local and federal jurisdiction.[91]

3. The Tax Court

Until 1969 the Tax Court of the United States, which hears taxpayer
petitions contesting deficiency determinations, was an independent agency
in the Executive Branch. It was then declared to be a "court." [92] Its
judgments are reviewed by the courts of appeals.

4. The Claims Court

The story of the establishment of the Court of Claims by statutes of
1855, 1863, 1866, and its replacement in 1982 by the United States Claims
Court, is summarized in Chap. II, Sec. 2.[93] Chapter 7 of the Judicial Code
contains the provisions governing the organization of the Claims Court and
Chapter 91 the provisions governing its jurisdiction.

87. 11 D.C.Code § 11–1502.

88. This district court is constituted
among the regular district courts by Chapter 5 of the Judicial Code, 28 U.S.C. §§ 119,
132. Its judges have life tenure by virtue
of the Act of September 12, 1966, 80 Stat.
764, amending 28 U.S.C. § 134(a). It is
attached to the First Circuit, 28 U.S.C.
§ 41, and its judgments are reviewable in
the normal manner under 28 U.S.C.
§§ 1291 and 1292.

89. See Puerto Rico Constitution Art.
V, superseding 48 U.S.C. § 861.

90. 28 U.S.C. § 1258.

91. These district courts are not included among the district courts constituted by
Chapter 5 of the Judicial Code; they are
separately created, and their judges are
appointed for a term of years. See 48
U.S.C. §§ 1405x, 1406 (Virgin Islands),
1424 (Guam), 1694 (Northern Mariana Islands). But many of the provisions of the
Judicial Code are expressly made applicable to these courts. See, e.g., 28 U.S.C.
§§ 1291, 1294(2), 1294(3) and 1294(4) (review by the Courts of Appeals of the Third
and Ninth Circuits of judgments of the

district courts of the Virgin Islands and
Guam). These territories also have local
inferior courts.

On the status of the courts of Guam, see
Territory of Guam v. Olsen, 431 U.S. 195
(1977).

92. Act of Dec. 30, 1969, 83 Stat. 730,
amending 26 U.S.C. § 7441. The Tax
Court is not an Article III court, and its
judges are appointed for 15–year terms.
26 U.S.C. § 7443(e).

For an exhaustive historical study of the
Tax Court, see the series of articles appearing in the Albany Law Review from 1975
to 1978 by Dubroff, Cook & Grossman.
The articles appear in Volume 40 at pp. 7,
53, and 253; Volume 41 at pp. 1 and 639,
and Volume 42 at pp. 161, 191, and 353.

93. See also Glidden Co. v. Zdanok, 370
U.S. 530 (1962); Chap. IX, Sec. 1(C), infra.
Under the 1982 statute, present Claims
Court judges are appointed for 15–year
terms. 28 U.S.C. § 172. For the concurrent jurisdiction of the district courts under the successor to the Tucker Act, note
44, supra, see 28 U.S.C. § 1346(a).

5. The Court of International Trade

In 1926 the old Board of General Appraisers, which had been established to hear in the first instance appeals from decisions of customs collectors, was given formal status as a specialized court with the name of the United States Customs Court.[94] The court was declared to be an Article III court in 1956,[95] and in 1980 was redesignated the United States Court of International Trade.[96] The provisions governing its organization are collected in Chapter 11 of the Judicial Code and the jurisdictional provisions in Chapter 95.[97]

6. The Court of Appeals for the Federal Circuit

In 1982, Congress created a new United States Court of Appeals for the Federal Circuit.[98] This court's exclusive appellate jurisdiction includes (1) appeals from the Claims Court,[99] (2) appeals from the Federal Merit System Protection Board, (3) appeals from agency boards of contract appeals under the Contract Disputes Act of 1978, (4) appeals from the Court of International Trade, (5) appeals from the Patent Office in patent and trademark cases,[100] (6) appeals from the district courts in certain actions in which district court jurisdiction was based in whole or in part on the "Little Tucker Act" (28 U.S.C. § 1346(a)(2)), and (7) appeals from the district courts in all patent cases in which district court jurisdiction was based in whole or in part on 28 U.S.C. § 1338.

Commenting on the significance of this new court, and especially of the seventh head of jurisdiction in the list just given, Judge Posner wrote:

"* * * [The new court] is a portent, though a slightly ambiguous one, of growing specialization in the federal judicial system. A merger of existing specialized courts, the new court will actually be less specialized than either of its predecessors. But it will be much more specialized than any of the regular federal courts of appeals, and its jurisdiction is being enlarged at their expense. Patent infringement will become the most

---

94. Act of May 28, 1926, § 1, 44 Stat. 669, 1948. See also Act of June 17, 1930, § 518, 46 Stat. 590, 737: Act of Oct. 10, 1940, 54 Stat. 1101; Act of June 2, 1970, 84 Stat. 278.

95. Act of July 14, 1956, 70 Stat. 532.

96. Act of Oct. 10, 1980, 94 Stat. 1727.

97. See generally Johnson, *The United States Customs Court—Its History, Jurisdiction, and Procedure,* 7 Okla.L.Rev. 393 (1954); Note, *Customs Court Reform,* 7 Int'l Trade L.J. 119 (1981–82).

98. The Federal Courts Improvement Act of 1982, 96 Stat. 25, 37–38. The relevant provision appears in the Judicial Code at 28 U.S.C. § 1295.

99. The relation between the new court of appeals and the Claims Court is similar in important respects to the relation between the judges of the former Court of Claims and the commissioners of that court. Indeed the present provision for sixteen Judges of the Claims Court, 28

U.S.C. § 171, parallels the former authorization, in 28 U.S.C. § 792 (now repealed) for the appointment of sixteen commissioners.

100. Items (4) and (5) embrace the jurisdiction of the former Court of Customs and Patent Appeals. That court was established in 1909 as the second of the specialized federal courts with nationwide jurisdiction, to hear appeals from the Board of General Appraisers—appeals that were then swamping some of the regular courts. Act of Aug. 5, 1909, 36 Stat. 11, 105. The court continued to hear these appeals after the board became the Customs Court in 1926, and in 1929 Congress gave the court the jurisdiction over appeals from the Patent Office that had been vested in the Court of Appeals of the District of Columbia. Act of March 2, 1929, 45 Stat. 1475. See also Act of June 17, 1930, § 646, 46 Stat. 590, 762; Act of Dec. 24, 1970, 84 Stat. 1558.

important area of specialized federal appellate jurisdiction we have ever had." [101]

7. Bankruptcy Courts

Until enactment of the Bankruptcy Act of 1978, the district courts acted as bankruptcy courts. Proceedings were generally conducted before court-appointed referees; the district court could at any time withdraw the case from the referee; and the referee's final order was appealable to the district court. In the 1978 Act, however, Congress created, as "an adjunct to the district court" for each district a "court of record known as the United States Bankruptcy Court." The judges of the new courts were to serve 14–year terms; they were removable by the judicial councils of the circuits; and their salaries were not protected against diminution.

The system of bankruptcy courts created by this statute failed to survive constitutional challenge. See Northern Pipeline Construction Co. v. Marathon Pipe Line Co., 458 U.S. 50 (1982), pp. 425–453, *infra*. After considerable delay and controversy, Congress in 1984 changed the system once again. Under the law as revised, bankruptcy judges are appointed as officers of the district courts for a term of fourteen years; appointments are made by the courts of appeals for the districts within their respective circuits, and the judges in each district "constitute a unit of the district court to be known as the bankruptcy court for that district." 28 U.S.C. §§ 151, 152.[102]

---

101. Posner, *Will the Federal Courts of Appeals Survive Until 1984? An Essay on Delegation and Specialization of the Judicial Function.* 56 S.Cal.L.Rev. 761, 776–77 (1983). Judge Posner later in the same article expressed his concern about this specialization (p. 782):

"I * * * question whether the usual arguments for the division of labor have much force applied to subject-matter specialization by courts, except in a handful of areas where the legal experts are generally accepted to be objective. * * * I doubt that patent law, where there is a deep cleavage * * * between those who believe that patent protection should be construed generously to create essential incentives to technological progress and those who believe that patent protection should be narrowly construed to accommodate the procompetitive policies of the antitrust laws, is such an area * * *."

For other perspectives, see, *e.g.*, Bator, *The Judicial Universe of Judge Posner* (Book Review), 52 U.Chi.L.Rev. 1146, 1154–56 (1985) (advocating "increased specialization at the court of appeals level" and arguing that specialization would "attract more real lawyers and fewer pseudo-politicians to the bench" and would subject them to the "kind of intellectual discipline that comes from having to demonstrate detailed substantive mastery over a field"); Griswold, *Cutting the Cloak to Fit the Cloth* (address at Catholic University Law

School, March 23, 1983, advocating, inter alia, expansion of the number of courts of appeals with "topical" jurisdiction).

For one court's expression of concern over the jurisdictional "quagmire" created by some of the provisions of the 1982 Act, see Van Drasek v. Lehman, 762 F.2d 1065, 1072 (D.C.Cir.1985). See also United States v. Hohri, 107 S.Ct. 2246 (1987) (ambiguity in 1982 Act is resolved by holding that Federal Circuit has exclusive jurisdiction over "mixed cases" involving claims under both the Little Tucker Act and the Tort Claims Act). See generally Comment, 36 Am.Univ.L.Rev. 943 (1987).

102. Mention should also be made of several other courts:

(a) *The Temporary Emergency Court of Appeals* was originally created by the 1971 amendments to the Economic Stabilization Act of 1970 (Act of Dec. 22, 1971, 85 Stat. 743) to hear all appeals from district court decisions arising under the Act or regulations. The duties of this court, staffed by appointment of regular federal judges from other courts, were later expanded to include appeals from the district courts in cases arising under the Emergency Petroleum Allocation Act of 1973, the Energy Policy and Conservation Act of 1975, and the Emergency Natural Gas Act of 1977.

(b) *The Judicial Panel on Multidistrict Litigation* is also staffed by appointment of regular federal judges from other courts.

NOTE ON THE BUSINESS OF THE DISTRICT COURTS

Chapter 5 of the Judicial Code of 1948 (Title 28, U.S. Code) codified the statutes establishing the district courts. It now provides for 91 district courts: 89 for the fifty states, and one each for the District of Columbia and Puerto Rico.[1]

Each state has at least one district court. The more populous states are divided into two, three, or four districts. Many districts are in turn divided into divisions. On June 30, 1986, there were 575 authorized district judgeships (117 of these were added in 1978 and 60 in 1984.) In addition, there were 156 senior district judges.[2]

Chapter 85 of the Code (§§ 1331–62) collects the principal grants to the district courts of original jurisdiction in civil cases. Chapter 90 deals with bankruptcy cases. The principal removal provisions are collected in Chapter 89. The criminal jurisdiction of the district courts rests upon 18 U.S.C. § 3231, which gives them in sweeping terms "original jurisdiction, exclusive of the courts of the States, of all offenses against the laws of the United States."

In the preparation of these codes, as of earlier codes, an effort was made to bring together all the statutory provisions affecting the jurisdiction of the federal courts. But the effort was not completely successful. Drafters of substantive statutes have persisted in inserting jurisdictional provisions as sections of those statutes rather than as amendments of the Judicial Code; and the codifiers have never been able wholly to unravel their work. In determining the jurisdiction of a district court over a particular proceeding, therefore, it remains necessary to examine not only the applicable code but also the relevant substantive statutes.

The current business of the district courts (as well as of other federal courts) is described in extensive detail in the Annual Reports of the Director of the Administrative Office of the United States Courts.[3] Although nothing ages more quickly than such statistics, this and the following Notes attempt to give a summary picture of the work of these courts.

This court is authorized by 28 U.S.C. § 1407 to transfer certain actions pending in different districts to a single district "for coordinated or consolidated pretrial proceedings."

(c) *The Rail Reorganization Court* was established by the Regional Rail Reorganization Act of 1973, primarily to determine the value of properties transferred pursuant to the Act by seven bankrupt railroads. The court is staffed by three federal judges designated by the Panel on Multi-district Litigation. The constitutionality of the statute creating the court was upheld in Regional Rail Reorganization Act Cases, 419 U.S. 102 (1974).

1. In addition, district courts are established for the Virgin Islands, Guam, and the Northern Mariana Islands. See p. 47, note 91, *supra*.

2. These figures are drawn from the 1986 Annual Report of the Director of the Administrative Office of the United States Courts, Table 3.

3. These will be cited hereafter in this chapter as Ad.Off.Rep. with the appropriate date. Except where otherwise stated, the statistics of current litigation which follow are taken from these reports. Various tables, however, have been derived from materials scattered through the reports.

For writings by political scientists about the work of the federal courts, see Richardson & Vines, The Politics of Federal Courts (1970); The Federal Judicial System: Readings in Process and Behavior (Goldman & Jahnige eds. 1968); for an analysis of one aspect of this work, see Dolbeare, *The Federal District Courts and Urban Public Policy*, in Frontiers of Judicial Research 373 (Grossman & Tanenhaus eds. 1969).

A detailed account of the history of the various district courts is Surrency, *Federal*

In fiscal 1986, 296,318 civil and criminal cases were commenced in the district courts—down from an all-time high of 313,170 the previous year. (By contrast, the Second Edition of this book noted that 127,280 civil and criminal cases were commenced in 1970 and 89,091 in 1960.) In addition a total of 477,856 bankruptcy petitions were filed (194,399 bankruptcy petitions were filed in 1970, and 110,034 in 1960.)

Civil and criminal suits commenced in fiscal 1986 broke down as follows (comparative figures noted in the Second Edition for 1970 are also given:) [4]

	1970	1986
Private civil cases:		
Federal Question (including admiralty)	34,846	98,747
Diversity	22,854	63,672
United States civil cases:		
U.S. plaintiff	13,310	60,779
U.S. defendant	11,655	31,051
Criminal cases:	39,959	41,490
TOTAL	122,624	295,739

Private Civil Cases. The table in the footnote lists some of the significant categories of private litigation commenced in 1986.[5]

The statistics may lead to exaggeration of the absolute burden of such litigation. Thus in 1986, 155,147 private civil cases were terminated in the district courts. Of these, 56,874 were ended without court action by

District Court Judges and the History of Their Courts, 40 F.R.D. 139 (1966). See also Clark, *Adjudication to Administration: A Statistical Analysis of Federal District Courts in the Twentieth Century*, 55 S.Calif.L.Rev. 65 (1981).

4. 4,656 cases in 1970, and 579 cases in 1986 involving local jurisdiction are not included in this table. Here and in the remainder of this Note, unless otherwise indicated figures for these and other years are derived from Table C–2 (for civil cases) and from Table D–1 (for criminal cases) in the annual Ad.Off.Reps.

5. Federal Question:

Antitrust	877
Civil rights (other than prisoner cases)	20,128
Commerce (ICC rates, etc.)	922
Copyright	2,198
Fair Labor Standards Act	405
Labor Mgmt Relations Act	3,681
Marine contracts	5,041
Marine torts	3,590
Patent	1,105
Prisoners' (state) petitions	
—Habeas corpus	9,040
—Mandamus, etc.	215
—Civil rights	20,071
Securities laws	3,059
Trademark	2,378

Diversity of Citizenship:

Contract actions	
—Insurance	6,776
—Other	25,095
Tort actions	
—Motor vehicle	6,634
—Asbestos	4,492
—Other	17,573

withdrawal or settlement; 61,962 were disposed of by court action before pretrial; and 26,048 by court action during or after pretrial. Only 10,263 such cases reached trial (of which 5,481 were before a jury). The proportion of cases reaching trial was 5.8% for federal question cases, 8.0% for diversity cases.[6]

In federal question litigation, growth has occurred in almost all categories, though with considerable variation. Illustrations (1986 and 1970 figures) are: securities laws (3,059/1,211); civil rights actions, other than prisoner petitions (20,128/3,586);[7] suits under the Labor Management Relations Act (3,681/1,228). With respect to prisoner petitions, after an explosive increase in habeas corpus petitions filed by state prisoners in the 1960s (872 in 1960; 8,963 in 1970), the number of these filings leveled off, and in 1986 stood at 9,040.[8] Other state prisoner petitions—complaining primarily of conditions of confinement—rose dramatically, however, from 2,653 in 1970 to 20,071 in 1986.[9]

Though the number of diversity cases filed has also increased substantially, the ratio of diversity filings to total civil filings has declined in recent decades—from 33.4% (17,048 diversity cases) in 1960 to 26.2% (22,854 diversity cases) in 1970, to 25.0% (63,672 diversity cases) in 1986.

United States Civil Cases. The table in the footnote lists some of the significant categories of litigation commenced in fiscal 1986 by and against the United States and its agencies and officers.[10] Cases involving the United States as defendant have increased from 5,854 in 1960, to 11,655 in 1970, to 31,051 in 1986; cases under the social security laws alone increased from 1,735 in 1970 to 14,376 in 1986. Federal prisoner petitions, which increased from 1,308 in 1960 to 4,185 in 1970 (or 220%) have risen more slowly since 1970, and stood at 4,432 in 1986.

Civil filings by the United States were relatively stable for many years, and actually declined from 1970 (13,310) to 1975 (12,742). But they rose

---

6. The figures in this paragraph are derived from 1986 Ad.Off.Rep. Table C–4.

7. The largest single category of civil rights cases in 1986 was 9,174 under the heading "Employment"—primarily cases under Title VII of the 1964 Civil Rights Act. For discussion of another category of cases that has substantially increased—actions under 42 U.S.C. § 1983—see Chap. IX, Sec. 2(C), *infra*.

8. These figures exclude a small number of local jurisdiction cases—100 in 1970 and 5 in 1986. The corresponding number of local jurisdiction cases for 1960 is not stated in the 1960 Ad.Off.Rep.

9. These figures also exclude local jurisdiction cases.

10. **United States plaintiff:**

Antitrust	25
Civil rights	570
Forfeiture and penalty	3,318
Labor laws	1,019
Securities laws	188
Tax suits	829
Recovery of overpayments and enforcement of judgments	40,544
Other contract actions	6,791
Real property actions	5,750

United States defendant:

Civil rights (excluding prisoner cases)	1,656
Prisoner petitions	
—Motions to vacate sentence	1,556
—Habeas corpus	1,679
—Mandamus and other	427
—Civil rights	770
Social security laws	14,376
Contract actions	922
Real property actions	951
Tort actions	3,177

sharply from 1975 to 1985, when they reached 79,371, and then declined to 60,779 in 1986. Of these filings, 57,888 in 1985 and 40,824 in 1986 were to recover overpayments and to enforce judgments, most of which were in connection with defaulted student loans and overpayment of veterans' benefits.[11]

Of 110,624 United States cases terminated in 1986, only 1,445 went to trial, and only 164 of those were tried to a jury. Thus the percentage of United States cases reaching trial (1.3%) was far less than the percentage for all civil filings (4.4%).[12]

Criminal Cases. The story on the criminal side is one of relative stability. Before World War I, filings ranged from 12,000 to 20,000 cases a year. During the Prohibition era, the number of annual filings climbed as high as 90,000, but well over half of these were prohibition cases. From 1934 to 1975, the number of filings ranged from about 30,000 to 50,000 with fluctuation due to such matters as price control and rationing cases during World War II, strenuous efforts to enforce the immigration laws in the fifties, and selective service cases in the early seventies. In the mid-seventies, the number of criminal prosecutions declined—partly as a result of efforts by the Justice Department to focus on organized and white collar crime and to transfer or divert other matters (*e.g.,* bank robberies, car thefts, cases involving juveniles) to the states. In the eighties, the number began to rise again because of increases in prosecutions involving drugs, weapons, and fraud. In 1986 total filings stood at 41,490.

In 1986, criminal cases terminated involved 50,040 defendants.[13] Cases involving 7,882 defendants were dismissed, and 1,418 defendants were acquitted (461 by the court and 957 by a jury). Of the 40,740 convicted, 35,448 pleaded guilty or nolo, 1,139 were convicted by the court, and 4,153 were convicted by a jury.

Bankruptcy Cases. The volume of bankruptcy cases is, of course, a function of both the size and the condition of the economy. Annual filings reached 70,000 in 1932, declined during World War II to a low of 10,000 in 1946, and with a few exceptions, have been climbing ever since. After some decline from 254,484 cases in the recession year of 1975,[14] the figure began to increase once again, jumping 31% in 1986 alone, and in that year filings reached an all-time high of 477,856.[15]

Of the 1986 total, 16% were business filings [16]—involving persons and companies who were farmers, professionals, merchants, manufacturers, and others in business. The vast majority of non-business bankruptcies involved wage earners.

The bulk of the work in bankruptcy cases is performed by the judges of the bankruptcy courts.[17]

11. See Galanter, *The Day After the Litigation Explosion,* 46 Md.L.Rev. 3, 17 (1986) (noting that approximately one-half of the increase in district court filings from 1975 to 1984 was accounted for by "recovery cases and social security cases").

12. The figures in this paragraph are derived from 1986 Ad.Off.Rep. Table C–4.

13. Figures in this paragraph are derived from 1986 Ad.Off.Rep. Table D–4.

14. 1975 Ad.Off.Rep. 151.

15. The figures for 1986 appear in 1986 Ad.Off.Rep. 33.

16. *Id.*

17. See pp. 49, *supra,* 753, *infra.*

Other Business.

(a) *The probation system.* Various classes of offenders against federal laws who are not in confinement are supervised by probation officers, appointed by the district court and responsible to it. At the close of fiscal 1986, the Federal Probation System had under supervision a total of 69,656 persons. This figure was the highest ever reported, and represented an increase of 5.5% over the prior year.[18]

(b) *Naturalization.* Since the first naturalization law was enacted in 1790, the granting of American citizenship to aliens has been a function of the federal as well as of designated state courts.[19] For 116 years the courts performed this function unaided. Since 1906, however, all the steps in the process of naturalization prior to final hearing have been handled administratively, by what is now the Immigration and Naturalization Service; and a representative of the Service also participates in the final hearing, as an aid to the court with authority to oppose the application if in the judgment of the agency the public interest so requires. The volume of naturalizations during the Second World War was very great, reaching a peak of 441,979 in fiscal 1944. In fiscal 1986, 252,679 persons were naturalized in the federal courts.[20]

Federal Magistrates. The position of "federal magistrate" was created by the Federal Magistrates Act of 1968, 82 Stat. 1108, as amended, 28 U.S.C. §§ 631 *et seq.* Magistrates are appointed by the federal district judges, in such numbers as the Judicial Conference may determine. They may be appointed on a full-time basis for an eight-year term, or on a part-time basis for a four-year term. They were initially given (a) the powers previously exercised by United States commissioners (*e.g.,* issuing warrants, conducting probable cause and other preliminary hearings in criminal cases), (b) jurisdiction to try "minor offenses," and (c) "such additional duties as are not inconsistent with the Constitution and laws" as might be established at the district court level, including service as special masters in civil cases, assistance in discovery or other pretrial proceedings, and preliminary review of applications for post-conviction relief.

The past fifteen years have witnessed considerable controversy over the proper role of magistrates, as well as a substantial increase in the authority conferred by Congress. In Wingo v. Wedding, 418 U.S. 461 (1974), the Supreme Court held that the 1968 Act did not alter the rule requiring evidentiary hearings in habeas corpus cases to be conducted by the judge personally. Congress responded with the Federal Magistrates Act of 1976,[21] which provides explicitly that district judges may designate a magistrate to conduct evidentiary hearings on certain "dispositive" motions (such as motions to suppress, motions for summary judgment, and motions to dismiss civil and criminal cases), and on prisoner petitions. Under this statute, the parties may file objections to any of the proposed findings and recommendations of the magistrate, and the district judge "shall make a de novo determination" with respect to matters to which such objection has been made. "The judge may also receive further evidence * * *."

---

18. 1986 Ad.Off.Rep. 41.

19. See 8 U.S.C. § 1421.

20. 1986 Ad.Off.Rep. 226. The district courts also processed 1,996 passport appli-

cations, a function now handled primarily by the U.S. Postal Service.

21. 90 Stat. 2729, amending 28 U.S.C. § 636(b).

Congress further expanded the role of magistrates in the Federal Magistrates Act of 1979,[22] which authorized magistrates to hear, determine, and enter final judgment in both jury and nonjury civil cases if all of the parties consent. Magistrates may also try criminal misdemeanor cases if the defendant consents. Appeal is, of course, provided for in all such cases (in some cases to the district court, in others to the court of appeals).[23]

The following table shows the growth in matters handled by magistrates from 1972, soon after the new system began, to 1986:[24]

	1972	1986
Trial Jurisdiction cases	72,082	91,570
—Petty offenses	62,915	79,272
—Misdemeanors	9,167	12,298
Preliminary Proceedings in Criminal Cases (warrants, arraignments, etc.)	131,522	129,526
Additional Duties	33,918	219,548
—Criminal (motions, pretrial conferences, etc.)	11,537	37,293
—Civil (motions, pretrial conferences, etc.)	15,595	158,451
—Prisoner litigation (habeas corpus, civil rights)	6,786	23,804
—Civil consent cases	—	4,931

NOTE ON THE BUSINESS OF THE COURTS OF APPEALS

Chapter 3 of the Judicial Code of 1948 changed the name of the former circuit courts of appeals to the United States Courts of Appeals, and codified the provisions establishing them. It now provides for thirteen judicial circuits: eleven in the various states, one for the District of Columbia, and one for the Federal Circuit, located in the District of Columbia and other places as the court may by rule direct. The number of judges on each circuit ranges from six (First) to 28 (Ninth). 28 U.S.C. § 44. As of the end of fiscal 1986, 168 judgeships were authorized and there were in addition 41 senior judges.[1]

The development of the statutory provisions governing the jurisdiction of the courts of appeals is described in Chap. XV. The courts' business can usefully be grouped in three categories: (1) review of decisions of district courts, including the district courts in the territories; (2) issuance of prerogative writs; and (3) review of decisions of certain administrative agencies and commissions.[2]

22. 93 Stat. 643, amending 28 U.S.C. §§ 604, 631, 633–36, 1915(b), 18 U.S.C. § 3401.

23. On the question of the consistency of the 1976 Act with Article III, see United States v. Raddatz, 447 U.S. 667 (1980), discussed at pp. 436–39, *infra.* For discussion of constitutional issues raised by the 1979 Act, see p. 472, *infra.*

For a comprehensive description of the magistrate system in operation, see Seron, The Roles of Magistrates in Federal District Courts (1985).

24. The table is derived from 1986 Ad. Off.Rep. 40 (Table 13).

1. 1986 Ad.Off.Rep. 7. The Federal Court Improvement Act of 1982 authorized 12 judgeships for the new Court of Appeals for the Federal Circuit; in the other circuits, 35 new judgeships were authorized in 1978 and 24 in 1984.

2. In addition, the Court of Appeals for the Federal Circuit reviews decisions of the Claims Court and of the Court of International Trade.

The statutory provisions conferring jurisdiction in the first category are codified in Chapter 83 of the Judicial Code. The jurisdiction of the courts of appeals to issue the prerogative writs rests on 28 U.S.C. § 1651.

The provisions for direct review by the courts of appeals of administrative decisions are dispersed among the various statutes establishing the agencies involved. This mode of review of administrative action was first adopted in 1914 in the Federal Trade Commission Act. The same pattern of review has since been followed for some or all of the decisions of many other agencies: *e.g.,* the Securities and Exchange Commission, the National Labor Relations Board, and The Federal Communications Commission.

Cases in the courts of appeals are normally heard and determined by panels of three judges, but each court may, by vote of a majority of the judges in regular active service, order a hearing or rehearing by the court in banc. 28 U.S.C. § 46(c).[3] Rehearings in banc are rare; original hearings in banc are even rarer.[4] A number of circuits, however, have specified that their decisions may be overruled only by the full bench sitting in banc. See, *e.g.,* Bonner v. City of Prichard, 661 F.2d 1206, 1209–11 (11th Cir.1981); United States v. Fatico, 603 F.2d 1053, 1058 (2d Cir.1979).[5]

The number of appeals filed in the courts of appeals rose from 3,899 in 1960, to 11,662 in 1970, and to 34,292 in 1986.[6] Of the 33,774 cases terminated in 1986, 2,848 were disposed of by consolidation, and an additional 12,727 were disposed of without hearing or submission to the court.

3. A court in banc consists of all circuit judges in regular active service, except that (a) a senior circuit judge who sat on the decision being reviewed is also eligible to participate and (b) circuits with more than fifteen active judges—currently the fifth and ninth—may prescribe by rule the number of members required to perform in banc functions.

4. See United States v. American-Foreign S.S. Corp., 363 U.S. 685, 689 (1960), (in banc courts "are the exception, not the rule.")

5. For examples of some of the difficulties that have arisen in the in banc process, see 16 Wright, Miller, Cooper & Gressman, Federal Practice and Procedure § 3981 (1977 and 1986 Supp.). For discussion of recent efforts to reduce the costs and delays of in banc proceedings, see Note, 34 Cleve.St.L.Rev. 531 (1986).

6. 1960, 1986 Ad.Off.Reps. Table B–1. (Unless otherwise indicated, all figures in this Note for this and other fiscal years are derived from Table B–1 in the annual Ad.Off. Reps.)

The number of appeals filed increased 5.9% from 1984 to 1985, and 2.8% from 1985 to 1986. See 1985 Ad.Off.Rep. Table 2; 1986 Ad.Off.Rep. Table 1.

The distribution of appeals filed in 1986 was as follows:

Criminal	5,134
U.S. prisoner petitions	1,569
Other U.S. civil	4,846
State prisoner petitions	5,423
Other private civil	12,453
Bankruptcy	977
Administrative appeals	3,187
Original proceedings	703

The burden of the sharply increased caseload has led to dramatic changes in the procedures of the courts of appeals. Opportunity for oral argument has been sharply reduced in most circuits,[7] and the proportion of cases decided without any opinion, or by per curiam opinion, has increased.[8] In addition, at the urging of the Judicial Conference, most circuits have adopted rules with respect to their "unpublished" opinions and orders—rules that in various ways restrict the citation and use of these opinions and orders as precedent.[9] Serious questions have been raised about the meaning, validity, desirability, and enforceability of these rules.[10] See, *e.g.*, Carrington, Meador & Rosenberg, Justice on Appeal 37–41 (1976); Walther, *The Noncitation Rule and the Concept of Stare Decisis*, 61 Marq.L. Rev. 581 (1978). See also Posner, note 7, *supra*, at 120–27; Reynolds & Richman, *An Evaluation of Limited Publication in the United States Courts of Appeals: The Price of Reform*, 48 U.Chi.L.Rev. 573 (1981).[11]

The problems of congestion in the courts of appeals has also led to increased reliance on "central" legal staffs,[12] and to proposals for such reforms as increased use of specialized courts, diversion of cases to alternative means of dispute resolution, an increase in the discretion of the appellate courts to deny review, statutory changes in the scope of review, and increased use of attorneys' fees awards to the prevailing party.[13]

NOTE ON THE BUSINESS OF THE SUPREME COURT

The statutory provisions establishing the Supreme Court are now codified in Chapter 1 of the Judicial Code, and the major provisions

7. "Once virtually all appeals were argued orally; now fewer than a third are. The length of the average oral argument has declined precipitously; today it is under 20 minutes per side. (In 1960 it was 45 minutes to an hour per side.)" Posner, The Federal Courts: Crisis and Reform 119 (1985).

8. Judge Posner reported that of all "contested terminations"—terminations after hearing or submission—the percentage disposed of by signed opinion declined from 74% in 1960 to 42% in 1983. Posner, note 7, *supra*, at 69–70.

9. One of the most elaborate of these rules is Rule 35 of the Rules of the Seventh Circuit, which after defining "publication" and providing for limited distribution of unpublished orders, provides that an unpublished order may not be cited or used as precedent "in any federal court within the circuit in any written document or in oral argument or ∗ ∗ ∗ by any such court for any purpose" except to support a claim of "res judicata, collateral estoppel or law of the case."

10. Does the rule quoted in note 9, for example, mean that an appellate court decision may be cited as binding authority in the district courts even though it is flatly inconsistent with a later unpublished order? That conflicting district court decisions within the circuit are of equal precedential value even though one has been affirmed (or reversed) in an unpublished order? That the appellate court itself may not be reminded that the identical question was dismissed as frivolous in an unpublished order in another case?

11. For contrasting views of the values and problems inherent in the sorting out of cases for some form of summary treatment, compare Carrington, *Ceremony and Realism: Demise of Appellate Procedure*, 66 A.B.A.J. 860 (1980), with Godbold, *Improvements in Appellate Procedure: Better Use of Available Facilities*, 66 A.B.A.J. 863 (1980).

12. For a comprehensive account of this and related developments in one circuit, see Hellman, *Central Staff in Appellate Courts: The Experience of the Ninth Circuit*, 68 Cal.L.Rev. 937 (1980).

13. These and other proposals are discussed in many of the authorities referred to in Part E of the *Note on the Organization and Growth of the Federal Judicial System*, pp. 42–45, *supra*, especially those cited at notes 70, 73, 101. See also 13 Wright, Miller & Cooper, Federal Practice and Procedure § 3510 (1984).

governing its jurisdiction in Chapter 81. The development of the provisions for review of state and federal court decisions is described in Chap. V, Sec. 1, *infra* (state decisions), and Chap. XV, Secs. 1, 2, *infra* (federal decisions).

The business of the Court is summarized in statistical tables appearing every year in the Annual Report of the Administrative Office (though these tables are less detailed than they once were), in United States Law Week, and in the "Supreme Court Note"—a survey, both statistical and substantive, of the Court's work that is published annually in the November issue of the Harvard Law Review.[1]

At its 1986 Term, which ended in July 1987, the Supreme Court disposed of 4,350 cases (compared to 3,318 in 1970, 1,911 in 1960, and 1,202 in 1950).[2] An appreciation of the significance of this number and its relation to the Court's capacity to decide cases depends on an understanding of the various categories of its business and of the ways in which it handles them.[3]

Original cases. The Court disposed of one case on its original docket in the 1986 Term. Original cases are few, but characteristically they are laborious and prolonged. Cases that are fully heard are usually referred to a master, and while they are pending call periodically for special consideration and interim orders.[4]

Appellate cases. The remaining 4,349 cases disposed of in the 1986 Term fell within the Court's appellate jurisdiction, with the vast majority coming from the courts of appeals and the state courts.[5] Of these, 4,062 were cases in which a petition for certiorari was denied or dismissed, an appeal was dismissed,[6] a petition for issuance of an extraordinary writ was denied or dismissed,[7] or the appeal or petition was withdrawn. The large

---

1. Statistics for the pre–World War II Terms following the Judiciary Act of 1925 were reviewed in a series of articles in the Harvard Law Review by Professor Frankfurter and a number of collaborators. See 42 Harv.L.Rev. 1 (1928) (with Landis); 43 *id.* 33 (1929); 44 *id.* 1 (1930); 45 *id.* 271 (1931); 46 *id.* 726 (1932); 47 *id.* 245 (1933) (with Hart); 48 *id.* 238 (1934); 49 *id.* 68 (1935); 51 *id.* 577 (1938) (with Fisher); 53 *id.* 579 (1940) (with Hart).

2. Figures for the 1986 Term here and in the following discussion are derived from 56 U.S.L.W. 3102 (1987) unless otherwise indicated. Figures for 1970 are from 85 Harv.L.Rev. 346 (1971), for 1960 from 75 Harv.L.Rev. 85 (1961), and for 1950 from 65 Harv.L.Rev. 179 (1951).

3. See also Chap. XV, Sec. 3, *infra.* For a lively comparison, see *The Supreme Court in 1848 and 1948: A Review of Two Terms,* 23 S.Cal.L.Rev. 460 (1950).

4. See generally Chap. III, *infra.*

5. A few cases come from the district courts, either on application for an extraordinary writ or pursuant to one of the remaining provisions for direct appeal, *e.g.,* 28 U.S.C. §§ 1252, 1253. (See Chap. XV, Sec. 2, *infra.*) With the establishment of

the Court of Appeals for the Federal Circuit, cases no longer go directly to the Supreme Court from the specialized courts that the new court has superseded.

6. Beginning in the 1971 Term of the Supreme Court, the statistics reported by the Clerk of the Supreme Court no longer distinguished between denials or dismissals of certiorari petitions on the one hand and dismissals of appeals on the other. See 86 Harv.L.Rev. 303 n.c (1972). A dismissal of an appeal from a state court decision, when based on the lack of a substantial federal question, is a disposition on the merits and does have precedential value. But these dismissals, usually without opinion, are typically given far less consideration by the Supreme Court than cases on plenary review. See Chap. V, Sec. 4, *infra.*

7. Like the other federal courts, the Supreme Court has authority under 28 U.S.C. § 1651 to issue extraordinary (or prerogative) writs—such as habeas corpus, mandamus, or prohibition—in aid of its jurisdiction. See Chap. III, § 3, *infra.* Separate statistics on applications received are no longer reported, but the number of such applications has always been relatively small. In the 1969 Term, for example,

majority of these dispositions were denials of petitions for certiorari. Such a denial is a decision only that the case will not be reviewed, and imports no adjudication on the merits.[8]

Of the summary denials and dismissals, 2,186, or more than one-half, were cases in which the appellant or petitioner was proceeding *in forma pauperis.* Under 28 U.S.C. § 1915, any court of the United States may permit an action to be begun or an appeal taken without prepayment of fees and costs, or security for them, if the litigant submits a proper affidavit of inability to bear these expenses.[9] In such cases also, an appellate court may dispense with printing of the record and other papers, or direct that these expenses be borne by the United States.

In the Supreme Court, a party who seeks the benefit of § 1915 is permitted to file a single copy of a motion and of the certiorari or other papers (typewritten if possible), along with a copy of the record below. See Sup.Ct. Rule 46. The Court then, in a proper case, grants the motion and at the same time acts on the underlying petition or appeal.

Most of the *in forma pauperis* cases are filed by criminal defendants seeking relief from conviction or imprisonment. The percentage of such cases granted review, *i.e.,* not summarily denied or dismissed, is far lower than the percentage of paid cases granted review.[10]

Of the relatively small number of cases surviving these various dispositions in the 1986 Term, 109 were affirmed, reversed, or vacated per curiam on the appeal or petition papers without full briefing or oral argument. Of the cases briefed, argued, and submitted, 164 were disposed of by signed opinion and 10 by per curiam opinion. (In addition, one case was set for reargument in the 1987 Term.)

Trends in the volume of business. Comparisons over time are complicated by changes in the methods of keeping and reporting statistics. But one useful comparison is the number of cases reported by the Harvard Law Review as disposed of by written opinion, including per curiam opinions containing substantial discussion: [11]

Term of Court:	1960	1970	1980	1984	1985	1986
Disposed of by Written opinion:	132	141	159	175	172	175

124 motions for leave to file an application for an extraordinary writ were received; of these, 121 were summarily denied or dismissed. 1970 Ad.Off.Rep. 208 (Table A–4).

8. See Chap. XV, Sec. 3, *infra.*

9. Prepaid cases are assigned docket numbers beginning with 1. *In forma pauperis* cases are assigned docket numbers beginning with 5001. (In both categories, numbers are preceded by a designation of the Term in which the case was filed.)

10. In the 1985 Term, for example, the Harvard Law Review reports that review was granted in 11.2% of the paid cases and only 1.3% of the *in forma pauperis* cases. See 100 Harv.L.Rev. 308 (1983).

11. The sources of the figures in this table are: for 1960, 75 Harv.L.Rev. 85 (1961); for 1970, 85 Harv.L.Rev. 346 (1971); for 1980, 95 Harv.L.Rev. 342 (1981); for 1984, 99 Harv.L.Rev. 326 (1985); for 1985, 100 Harv.L.Rev. 308 (1986); and for 1986, 101 Harv.L.Rev. 366 (1987).

Most of these opinions, but not all, were rendered after submission of briefs on the merits and oral argument. Some were disposed of on the certiorari petition or jurisdictional statement, though the number of such dispositions has declined in recent years. The total here given for 1985 differs from the total of 161 reported earlier in text because of the inclusion in this table of per curiam opinions containing "substantial legal reasoning."

The increase in the number of cases docketed since 1960 has, of course, been more dramatic (although that number has itself leveled off in recent years): [12]

Term of Court:	1960	1970	1980	1984	1985	1986
Cases docketed:	1,957	3,419	4,174	4,263	4,278	4,240

This table is slightly misleading, since the number of cases docketed during the 1970s did rise to approximately 4,200 before falling below 4,000 for several years and then rising again.[13] But the two tables taken together indicate that while the Court has only limited control over the number of cases brought to it for review, it does have the capacity to keep within bounds the number of cases selected for intensive consideration. Thus in the period 1960–70, when the number of cases docketed rose 76.2%, the number of cases disposed of by written opinion rose only 6.4%.

Questions remain, however, whether the increase in the Court's workload has led to inadequate attention to the screening process, to inability to grant full review to all those cases deserving such attention, or to insufficient consideration of the larger number of cases that are accepted for briefing and oral argument. All these questions are the subject of continuing dispute, as are the merits of the various proposals that have been made to alleviate the burden on the Court. See pp. 42–45, *supra*.[14]

NOTE ON THE ADMINISTRATION OF THE FEDERAL COURTS

From 1789 substantially to 1922 the federal courts were an aggregation of independent tribunals, tied together only by the authority of the superior courts to revise the judicial judgments of the inferior. Of administrative direction or coordination there was little or none.

" * * * The root conceptions of our federal judicial system were independence and localism. Life tenure for United States judges grew out of the doctrine of the separation of powers. An independent judiciary was part of the scheme of counterpoises in government. But not only were the judges rendered independent of the President and Congress; they were rendered independent of each other. * * *

"The system was without direction and without responsibility. Each judge was left to himself, guided in the administration of his business by his conscience and his temperament. The bases for informed public judgment and self-criticism were wanting, since adequate judicial statistics

12. These figures are derived from the tables published each year in United States Law Week.

13. For an analysis of why the number of applications to the Court could stabilize or even drop in the face of an expanding population and economy, see Casper & Posner, The Workload of the Supreme Court (1976), updated in Casper & Posner, *The Caseload of the Supreme Court: 1975 and 1976 Terms* 1977 Sup.Ct.Rev. 87.

14. In addition to the authorities cited at pp. 43–45, *supra*, see Wechsler, *The Ap-* *pellate Jurisdiction of the Supreme Court: Reflections on the Law and Logistics of Direct Review*, 34 Wash. & Lee L.Rev. 1043 (1977) (expressing concern whether the Supreme Court can exercise sufficient control over the adjudication of federal claims in the state courts) and the valuable research on the work of the Court in a series of articles by Professor Hellman, most recently, *Case Selection in the Burger Court: A Preliminary Inquiry*, 60 Notre Dame L.Rev. 947 (1985). A listing of these articles appears at *id.* n. 13.

were unknown. The types and volume of litigation, the character of the issues, the duration of trials, the speed of disposition, the delay of appeals,—these and kindred data must be known in order to determine competence or laxity in judicial administration. Such information is particularly indispensable for any fruitful scrutiny of the workings of a single system of courts extending over so vast an area as that of the United States. Without it, the demands of different districts for more judges have to be decided in the dark. Nor will statistics gotten up for the occasion serve the purpose. There must be recognized standards of interpretation and continuity of observation. Thus only can the system be subjected to scientific accountability." [1]

The defects of an uninformed and uncoordinated administration of justice appeared most acutely when questions of the need for new judges had to be decided. The play of political pressures was unchecked by any real knowledge. Congress had no way of finding out how many more judges were needed, where they were needed, or indeed if any were needed. In some areas the courts were seriously understaffed but in others they were overstaffed. Yet at first each judge, regardless of the state of his docket, was tied to his own court.[2] Before the first world war Congress took only a few cautious steps in authorizing the temporary transfer of judges with light workloads to districts with heavy loads.[3]

Increasing public and professional impatience with delays of justice after the first world war produced the necessary climate for reform. In the Act of September 14, 1922,[4] following the leadership of Chief Justice Taft, Congress laid the foundation for a comprehensive attack upon the whole problem of judicial administration.

The Act greatly liberalized the provisions for assignment of judges, substantially achieving the ideal of a mobile judicial force. More important, it established an administrative means for securing information about the needs of the federal judiciary, for promoting better administration within the framework of existing laws, and for formulating recommendations to Congress for changes in the laws.

The means adopted was a conference of the senior circuit judges of each circuit to be summoned annually by the Chief Justice of the United States. On the basis of reports from the judges and the Attorney General, the conference was directed to "make a comprehensive survey of the condition of business in the courts of the United States and prepare plans for assignment and transfer of judges to or from circuits or districts where the state of the docket or condition of business indicates the need therefor," and to "submit such suggestions to the various courts as may seem in the interest of uniformity and expedition of business."

On this foundation the Act of August 7, 1939,[5] built the present organization for the administration of the United States courts. That Act

1. Frankfurter & Landis 218, 220–21.

2. If a district judge could not act, the court had to be adjourned. Act of Sept. 24, 1789, § 6, 1 Stat. 73, 76.

3. See Frankfurter & Landis 219n. See also Act of Oct. 3, 1913, 38 Stat. 203 (authorizing assignment of district judges from elsewhere in the country to sit in the Second Circuit). Also in 1913, the Commerce Court was abolished, 38 Stat. 219, and its judges, who became circuit judges at large, were vastly useful in helping to reduce backlogs in overburdened courts.

4. 42 Stat. 837.

5. 53 Stat. 1223. For a history of the Act, see Fish, *Crises, Politics, and Federal Judicial Reform: The Administrative Office Act of 1939*, 32 J. Politics 599 (1970).

extended and strengthened the idea of the judicial conference as an instrument of coordination and direction of the judicial system. And it established the Administrative Office of the United States Courts, enabling the conferences to function more effectively by providing them with continuous, expert staff assistance.

The 1939 Act was modified and altered in minor respects by the Judicial Code of 1948. The provisions with regard to Judicial Conferences and Councils are collected in Chapter 15; those with regard to the Administrative Office constitute Chapter 41. The Code also codified (and collected in Chapter 13, §§ 291–96) the provisions regarding temporary assignments of judges.

The former conference of senior circuit judges is now named the Judicial Conference of the United States, and the Chief Justice is expressly directed to "submit to Congress an annual report of the proceedings of the Judicial Conference and its recommendations for legislation." [6]

The Judicial Conference operates in part through a large number of committees. Its reports are printed annually and bound with the reports of the Director of the Administrative Office.

By virtue of a provision added in 1958,[7] the Judicial Conference is charged with carrying on "a continuous study" of the rules of procedure prescribed by the Supreme Court and with making recommendations for changes and additions to the rules. Another 1958 amendment authorized the Judicial Conference to organize judicial "institutes and joint councils on sentencing" in order to achieve uniformity in sentencing procedures.[8] And an amendment in 1980 authorized the Conference, acting as such or through a standing committee, to exercise certain powers of investigation and judicial discipline provided in newly enacted subsection (c) of 28 U.S.C. § 372.[9]

The Code also provides (1) for annual judicial conferences of the district judges in each circuit to be summoned by the chief judge "for the purpose of considering the business of the courts and advising means of improving the administration of justice within such circuit," [10] and (2) for the calling of a semi-annual Judicial Council in each circuit, composed of the chief judge of the circuit and a number of circuit and district judges. Each Judicial Council has been given authority with respect to judicial discipline under 28 U.S.C. § 372, as well as broad authority to "make all necessary and appropriate orders for the expeditious administration of justice within its circuit." [11]

See also Chandler, *Some Major Advances in the Federal Judicial System 1922–1947*, 31 F.R.D. 307 (1963).

6. 28 U.S.C. § 331.

7. Act of July 11, 1958, 72 Stat. 356, added to 28 U.S.C. § 331. See further Chap. VI, Sec. 1, *infra*.

8. Act of Aug. 25, 1958, 72 Stat. 845, 28 U.S.C. § 334.

9. Act of Oct. 15, 1980, § 4, 94 Stat. 2040. See generally Remington, *Circuit Council Reform: A Boat Hook for Judge and Court Administrators*, 1981 B.Y.U.L. Rev. 695.

10. 28 U.S.C. § 333.

11. *Id.* § 332. See generally 16 Wright, Miller, Cooper & Gressman, Federal Practice and Procedure § 3939 (1977 and 1986 Supp.).

At the head of the Administrative Office of the United States Courts is a Director, who is appointed and subject to removal by the Supreme Court,[12] but who discharges his duties "under the supervision and direction of the Judicial Conference of the United States." [13]

The Administrative Office assists the Judicial Conference in a number of ways, most notably in preparation of the annual budget for the judicial system, in the collection and reporting of judicial statistics, and in the conduct of a wide variety of housekeeping tasks.

The tremendous growth in federal judicial business in recent decades has been accompanied by a corresponding expansion of administrative requirements. In 1960, the Administrative Office had a staff of 157 and a budget of $1.2 million. In 1986, the staff numbered 543 and the budget was $28.4 million. (The total budget for the federal judicial branch went from $48.3 million in 1960 to $1.044 billion in 1986. Total personnel went from 5,561 in 1960 to 18,277 in 1986. These figures exclude the budget and personnel of the Supreme Court.) [14]

In 1967 the judicial branch acquired a research arm by the creation of the Federal Judicial Center.[15] The Center, which is run by a Board (whose chairman is the Chief Justice) [16] and a Director [17] has four purposes: to conduct and stimulate "research and study of the operation of the [federal] courts"; to present to the Judicial Conference recommendations for improvements in the administration and management of the federal courts; to develop and conduct programs of continuing education for judges and other court personnel; and to provide research, staff, and planning assistance to the Judicial Conference and its committees.[18]

The proposal of a Judicial Conference in 1933 aroused the objection that it would give legislative and political functions to the courts. "It was the function of judges, so ran the sterile logic, to judge—not to watch the workings of the judicial system, to explore its defects and devise remedies." [19] The federal judges are now doing much more than judging. They have express responsibility for recommending judiciary legislation to Congress. In formulating procedural rules they exercise powers of subordinate legislation by delegation from Congress. And they have executive responsibility in supervising the manifold day-to-day tasks of operation of

12. 28 U.S.C. § 601.

13. *Id.* § 604. For useful accounts by a former Director of the Administrative Office, see Chandler, *The Administration of the Federal Courts,* 13 Law & Contemp.Prob. 182 (1948); Chandler, *Some Major Advances in the Federal Judicial System,* 31 F.R.D. 307, 396–420 (1963).

14. Figures for 1960 are taken from Meador, *The Federal Judiciary and its Future Administration,* 65 Va.L.Rev. 1031, 1038–39 (1979). Figures for 1986

are derived from 1986 Ad.Off.Rep. 50, 78.

15. Act of Dec. 20, 1967, 81 Stat. 664, adding Chapter 42 (§§ 620–29) to the Judicial Code. See Clark, *The New Federal Judicial Center,* 54 A.B.A.J. 743 (1968).

16. 28 U.S.C. §§ 621–24.

17. *Id.* § 625.

18. *Id.* § 620.

19. Frankfurter & Landis 240.

the judicial establishment. Wisely or unwisely, the principle has been accepted that "judging is also administration." [20]

20. Justice Burton, *"Judging Is Also Administration": An Appreciation of Constructive Leadership,* 33 A.B.A.J. 1099 (1947). See also Chief Justice Vinson, *The Business of Judicial Administration: Suggestions to the Conference of Chief Justices,* 35 A.B.A.J. 893 (1949); Chief Justice Warren, *Administrative Problems of the Federal Judiciary,* 23 Bus.Lawyer 7 (1967).

For a comprehensive, authoritative account of the history of the administration of the federal court system over the fifty year period following the creation of the Judicial Conference in 1922, see Fish, the Politics of Federal Judicial Administration (1973). See also Fish, *William Howard Taft and Charles Evans Hughes: Conservative Politicians as Chief Judicial Reformers,* 1975 Sup.Ct.Rev. 123.

For a discussion of recent administrative problems and suggestions for change, see Meador, *The Federal Judiciary and Its Future Administration,* 65 Va.L.Rev. 1031 (1979).

For articles warning of the hazards of increasing the administrative and managerial tasks that judges are required to perform, see Hoffman, *The Bureaucratic Spectre: Newest Challenge to the Courts,* 66 Judicature 66 (1982); Resnik, *Managerial Judges,* 96 Harv.L.Rev. 374 (1982); Rubin, *The Bureaucratization of the Federal Courts: The Tension Between Justice and Efficiency,* 55 Notre Dame L.Rev. 648 (1980).

Chapter II

THE NATURE OF THE FEDERAL JUDICIAL FUNCTION: CASES AND CONTROVERSIES

SECTION 1. GENERAL CONSIDERATIONS

CORRESPONDENCE OF THE JUSTICES (1793)[1]

Letter from Thomas Jefferson, Secretary of State, to Chief Justice Jay and Associate Justices:

Philadelphia, July 18, 1793.

Gentlemen:

The war which has taken place among the powers of Europe produces frequent transactions within our ports and limits, on which questions arise of considerable difficulty, and of greater importance to the peace of the United States. These questions depend for their solution on the construction of our treaties, on the laws of nature and nations, and on the laws of the land, and are often presented under circumstances *which do not give a cognizance of them to the tribunals of the country.* Yet their decision is so little analogous to the ordinary functions of the executive, as to occasion much embarrassment and difficulty to them. The President therefore would be much relieved if he found himself free to refer questions of this description to the opinions of the judges of the Supreme Court of the United States, whose knowledge of the subject would secure us against errors dangerous to the peace of the United States, and their authority insure the respect of all parties. He has therefore asked the attendance of such of the judges as could be collected in time for the occasion, to know, in the first place, their opinion, whether the public may, with propriety, be availed of their *advice on these questions?* And if they may, to present, for their advice, the abstract questions which have already occurred, or may soon occur, from which they will themselves strike out such as any circumstances might, in their opinion, forbid them to pronounce on. I have the honour to be with sentiments of the most perfect respect, gentlemen,

Your most obedient and humble servant,
Thos. Jefferson.

The following are some of the questions submitted by the President to the Justices:

1. Do the treaties between the United States and France give to France or her citizens a *right,* when at war with a power with whom the

---

1. The letters are taken from 3 Correspondence and Public Papers of John Jay 486–89 (Johnston ed. 1891), and the questions from 10 Sparks, Writings of Washington 542–45 (1836).

65

United States are at peace, to fit out originally in and from the ports of the United States vessels armed for war, with or without commission?

2. If they give such a *right*, does it extend to all manner of armed vessels, or to particular kinds only? If the latter, to what kinds does it extend?

3. Do they give to France or her citizens, in the case supposed, a right to refit or arm anew vessels, which, before their coming within any port of the United States, were armed for war, with or without commission?

4. If they give such a right, does it extend to all manner of armed vessels, or to particular kinds only? If the latter, to what kinds does it extend? Does it include an *augmentation* of force, or does it only extend to replacing the vessel *in statu quo*?

17. Do the laws of neutrality, considered as aforesaid, authorize the United States to permit France, her subjects, or citizens, the sale within their ports of prizes made of the subjects or property of a power at war with France, before they have been carried into some port of France and there condemned, refusing the like privilege to her enemy?

18. Do those laws authorize the United States to permit to France the erection of courts within their territory and jurisdiction for the trial and condemnation of prizes, refusing that privilege to a power at war with France?

20. To what distance, by the laws and usages of nations, may the United States exercise the right of prohibiting the hostilities of foreign powers at war with each other within rivers, bays, and arms of the sea, and upon the sea along the coasts of the United States?

22. What are the articles, by name, to be prohibited to both or either party?

25. May we, within our own ports, sell ships to both parties, prepared merely for merchandise? May they be pierced for guns?

29. May an armed vessel belonging to any of the belligerent powers follow *immediately* merchant vessels, enemies, departing from our ports, for the purpose of making prizes of them? If not, how long ought the former to remain, after the latter have sailed? And what shall be considered as the place of departure from which the time is to be counted? And how are the facts to be ascertained?

On July 20, 1793, Chief Justice Jay and the Associate Justices wrote to President Washington expressing their wish to postpone the answer to Jefferson's letter until the sitting of the Court. On August 8, 1793, they wrote to the President as follows:

Sir:

We have considered the previous question stated in a letter written by your direction to us by the Secretary of State on the 18th of last month, [regarding] the lines of separation drawn by the Constitution between the three departments of the government. These being in certain respects checks upon each other, and our being judges of a court in the last resort, are considerations which afford strong arguments against the propriety of our extrajudicially deciding the questions alluded to, especially as the power given by the Constitution to the President, of calling on the heads of departments for opinions, seems to have been *purposely* as well as expressly united to the *executive* departments.

We exceedingly regret every event that may cause embarrassment to your administration, but we derive consolation from the reflection that your judgment will discern what is right, and that your usual prudence, decision, and firmness will surmount every obstacle to the preservation of the rights, peace, and dignity of the United States.

NOTE ON ADVISORY OPINIONS

(1) To what extent was the Justices' decision controlled by the language and history of the Constitution?

Did the Justices have power to answer the questions authoritatively? If not, why not? Was the difficulty one of constitutional or statutory power, or simply of wisdom and appropriateness? Would the subject matter of the questions have been within the competence of the Court if they had been presented in the ordinary course of litigation? If so, was there any reason of substance why the Constitution should be read as requiring the Court to wait for a lawsuit, or a whole series of lawsuits, instead of deciding the questions then and there when the President needed the decisions? What light do the proceedings in the constitutional convention throw on the problem? The prior practice in the English and colonial courts? Analysis of the difference between "judicial" power and other kinds of official power? [1]

(2) Legal propositions consist of general directions or arrangements about what is to be done in future situations. Since the situations that may arise are of infinite, or near infinite, variety, and hence can be foreseen only imperfectly, the integrity and continued workability of the arrangements depend upon having some means of settling uncertain or controverted questions about their application to particular situations as and when the situations arise. The process of settlement of such questions is different from the process of making new arrangements in general terms for the future. The difference consists in the necessity of relating the conclusion about the particular application in question, in some intelligible and acceptable way, to previous understanding about the arrangement and its other applications.

Judicial decisions, of course, have consequences for persons other than the parties before the court. The doctrine of stare decisis and the related principle that like cases should be decided alike guarantee that. But the essential aspect of the judicial function (indeed, an inescapable one in any regime of law) is that of authoritative application, in such particular situations as may be presented for decision, of general propositions drawn from preexisting sources. This function includes, as a necessary incident, the task of determining the facts of the situation and of resolving uncertainties about the content of the applicable general propositions.

---

1. For an illuminating discussion of this incident, see Wheeler, *Extrajudicial Activities of the Early Supreme Court*, 1973 Sup. Ct.Rev. 123, 144–58. Wheeler concludes that "the 1793 incident was more than a refusal to give advice. It was part of a broader attempt by the early Supreme Court to deemphasize the obligatory extrajudicial service concept, so widely held in the early period" (p. 158).

In what respects, if any, would the Court have performed a significantly different function had it undertaken to reply to the questions of the President?

In considering this question, take into account:

(a) The sheer multiplication of matters to which attention must be directed, and the resulting dispersion of thought, when a legal proposition is formulated in the abstract;

(b) The importance, in the judicial development of law, of a concrete set of facts as an aid to the accurate formulation of the legal issue to be decided;

(c) The importance of an adversary presentation of evidence as an aid to the accurate determination of the facts out of which the legal issue arises;

(d) The importance of an adversary presentation of argument in the formulation and decision of the legal issue;

(e) The importance of a concrete set of facts in limiting the scope and broad policy implications of the legal determination, and as an aid to its accurate interpretation;

(f) The value of having courts function as organs of the sober second thought of the community appraising action already taken, rather than as advisers at the front line of governmental action at the stage of initial decision;

(g) The importance of all the factors enumerated in maximizing the acceptability of decisions.

The weight of these factors varies according to the type of legal proposition involved.[2] Compare, for example, the questions asked by Jefferson with the question whether a cause of action for defamation survives the death of the person defamed. Which type do you think is more representative of the hard questions of contemporary law, and especially of public law, that are likely to cause the greatest concern? See Note, 69 Harv.L.Rev. 1302 (1956); Note, 72 Harv.L.Rev. 723 (1959). See also Flast v. Cohen, 392 U.S. 83, 95–97 (1968).

Even when it is possible to formulate and answer legal questions in terms that do not significantly implicate the raw facts of particular situations, how complete is the guidance that the answers can afford in actual affairs or in later litigation?

To what extent would the objections to advisory opinions be lessened if the Court restricted itself to giving advisory rulings on definite states of fact, real or assumed? Consider the practices of administrative agencies in meeting the insistent demand for advance information of the agencies' policies and legal position. See generally Schwartz, Administrative Law 132–41 (2d ed. 1984).

(3) The value of a careful and discriminating adherence to the "case or controversy" limitation of Article III—and of the avoidance of advisory opinions not moored to the facts of an immediate dispute—is further supported from a somewhat different perspective in a thoughtful article by

---

2. Indeed, some would question their significance on more fundamental grounds relating to the appropriate role of the judiciary in constitutional adjudication. See *Note on Marbury v. Madison and the Function of Adjudication,* Paragraph (2)(a), p. 79, *infra.*

Brilmayer, *The Jurisprudence of Article III: Perspectives on the "Case or Controversy" Requirement*, 93 Harv.L.Rev. 297 (1979). Her theory rests on "three interrelated policies of Article III: the smooth allocation of power among courts over time; the unfairness of holding later litigants to an adverse judgment in which they may not have been properly represented; and the importance of placing control over political processes in the hands of the people most closely involved" (p. 302).

See also M. Eisenberg, *Participation, Responsiveness, and the Consultative Process: An Essay for Lon Fuller*, 92 Harv.L.Rev. 410, 430 (1978): "The underlying message of *Forms and Limits* [an article by Prof. Fuller] cannot be lightly disregarded: adjudication has a moral force, and this force is in major part a function of those elements that distinguish adjudication from all other forms of ordering. In the long run, the cost of departing from those elements may be a forfeiture of the moral force of the judicial role." [3]

(4) Note that Jefferson's questions to the Justices all sought clarification of existing law. Compare the proposal of Senator Schwellenbach in 1937 that the Supreme Court be requested to amend its rules so as to enable the Congress, on majority vote of both houses, to request and receive "advisory opinions as to the constitutionality of legislation pending before, and being considered by, the Congress of the United States." S.Res. 103, 75th Cong., 1st Sess., 81 Cong.Rec. 2804 (1937).

(5) Instances of extrajudicial expression of legal opinion by Justices of the Supreme Court have not been wanting. Three years before the *Correspondence,* President Washington wrote to the Justices, as they were about to set out on their first circuit riding, inviting them to feel free to communicate with him from time to time. Chief Justice Jay and "a minority of the Members of that Court" responded in a letter stating their belief that the act requiring Supreme Court justices to sit on circuit courts was unconstitutional. See 4 Am.Jur. & Law Mag. 293 (1830). (The letter may never have been sent. See Wheeler, note 1, *supra,* at 148.) The substantive point involved was later raised in Stuart v. Laird, 1 Cranch 299, 309 (U.S.1803), but the Court, without reference to the letter of 1790, disposed of the question summarily on the ground that the practice was too well established to be questioned at that late date.[4]

For later examples, see: Opinion given by Justice Johnson, with the approval of other members of the Court, to President Monroe, in 1 Warren, The Supreme Court in United States History 596–97 (1937 ed.); Letter of Chief Justice Hughes to Senator Wheeler, Chairman of the Senate Judiciary Committee, concerning President Roosevelt's proposals for reorganizing the Supreme Court, excerpted at p. 41, *supra;* Letter of Chief Justice Taney to Secretary of the Treasury Chase concerning the 1862 tax levied upon the salaries of federal judges, in Tyler, Memoir of Roger B. Taney 432–34 (1872).[5]

3. For further discussion of these and conflicting views of the nature of the judicial process, and their relation to questions of justiciability, see *Note on Marbury v. Madison and the Function of Adjudication,* Paragraph (2), p. 79, *infra.*

4. Compare a personal letter of November 13, 1790, by Chief Justice Jay to President Washington in 3 Correspondence and Public Papers of John Jay 405–08 (Johnston ed. 1891).

5. Taney protested that the tax was invalid, giving as his reason for the form of the protest that all the judges would be disqualified if the question arose in litigation. When the same question arose under the Revenue Act of 1918, the Supreme Court held the tax invalid, referring to

For a comprehensive review and compilation, see Westin, *Out-of-Court Commentary by United States Supreme Court Justices, 1790–1962: Of Free Speech and Judicial Lockjaw,* 62 Colum.L.Rev. 633 (1962). For instances of public statements by sitting Justices since 1962, see, *e.g.,* Stevens, *Life Span of a Judge–Made Rule,* 58 N.Y.U.L.Rev. 1 (1983); Brennan, *State Constitutions and the Protection of Individual Rights,* 90 Harv.L.Rev. 489 (1977); Rehnquist, *The First Amendment: Freedom, Philosophy, and the Law,* 12 Gonzaga L.Rev. 1 (1976); Stewart, *"Or of the Press,"* 26 Hastings L.J. 631 (1975); Black, A Constitutional Faith (1969); Fortas, Concerning Dissent and Civil Disobedience (1968); Douglas, The Bible and the Schools (1966); Clark, *Religion and the Law,* 15 S.C.L.Rev. 855 (1963).

(6) Part 2, ch. 3, art. 2 of the constitution of Massachusetts (1780) provides: "Each branch of the legislature, as well as the governor or the council, shall have authority to require the opinions of the justices of the supreme judicial court, upon important questions of law, and upon solemn occasions." There are variants of this provision in the constitutions of New Hampshire, Maine, Rhode Island, Florida, Colorado, and South Dakota. In at least two states, Alabama and Delaware, advisory opinions are authorized, in certain circumstances, by statute. The North Carolina Supreme Court renders advisory opinions without constitutional or statutory authority. See Edsall, *The Advisory Opinion in North Carolina,* 27 N.C.L.Rev. 297 (1949). Other states have had such a procedure in the past, but have abandoned it through judicial decision, statutory repeal, or constitutional amendment.[6]

If a state court renders an advisory opinion on a question of federal law, and if that opinion significantly affects the operations of state government, doesn't that raise all the difficulties noted in Paragraphs (2) and (3), *supra?* How may federal interests be protected in such a case? *Cf.* Tileston v. Ullman, p. 137, *infra;* Fidelity Nat'l Bank v. Swope, p. 235, *infra.*

(7) The advisory opinion has been used in other legal systems. See Davison, *The Constitutionality and Utility of Advisory Opinions,* 2 U. of Toronto L.J. 254 (1938) (Canadian practice); Wade, *Consultation of the Judiciary by the Executive,* 46 L.Q.Rev. 169 (1939) (English practice).

The Permanent Court of International Justice rendered 27 advisory opinions from 1922 to 1935.[7] Those opinions, however, were for the most part analogous to our declaratory judgments, since there were actual disputes, and adverse parties argued the points involved.[8] Its successor, the International Court of Justice, is authorized to answer interrogatories by the General Assembly, the Security Council, and other organs and

Taney's opinion. Evans v. Gore, 253 U.S. 245 (1920), substantially overruled in O'Malley v. Woodrough, 307 U.S. 277 (1939).

6. For critical commentary, favorable and adverse, on the advisory opinion practice, see Note, 29 Me.L.Rev. 305 (1978); Comment, 44 Fordham L.Rev. 81 (1975); Borchard, Declaratory Judgments 71–80 (2d ed. 1941); Frankfurter, *Advisory Opinions,* 1 Enc.Soc.Sci. 475 (1930); Hudson,

Advisory Opinions of National and International Courts, 37 Harv.L.Rev. 970 (1924).

7. Hudson, The Permanent Court of International Justice, 1920–1942 at 513–22 (1943).

8. See L.M. Goodrich, *The Nature of the Advisory Opinions of the Permanent Court of International Justice,* 32 Am.J.Int.L. 738 (1938); Hudson, *The Effect of Advisory Opinions of the World Court,* 42 Am.J.Int. L. 630 (1948).

agencies of the United Nations.[9] The present World Court has been significantly less active than the old, rendering only 17 advisory opinions from its creation in 1945 to 1984.[10]

(8) Since Jefferson's efforts to obtain advice from the Supreme Court failed, the Attorney General has been the principal legal adviser to the President and the executive departments. See 28 U.S.C. §§ 511, 512, derived from § 35 of the First Judiciary Act; Cummings & McFarland, Federal Justice 40, 78–92, 511–20 (1937); Nealon, *The Opinion Function of the Federal Attorney General,* 25 N.Y.U.L.Rev. 825 (1950); Rhodes, *"Opinions of the Attorney General" Revived,* 64 A.B.A.J. 1374 (1978).

Formal opinions of the Attorney General have been published since 1841. But their number has declined considerably in recent years. (Indeed, published opinions are so rare that the latest, still unbound volume (Vol. 43) contains fewer than 40 opinions from September 1975 to the present.) Beginning in 1977, however, the government began annual publication of the much more frequent opinions of the Office of Legal Counsel in the Department of Justice—the office that also prepares the opinions of the Attorney General.[11]

William Wirt, who took office in 1817, was the first Attorney General to maintain records and largely shaped the future practices of the office in the discharge of the opinion function. Among these practices are: limitation of the function to questions propounded by the President and heads of departments;[12] refusal to render formal opinions deciding questions of fact or arbitrating disputes between departments; and refusal to render formal opinions for the purpose of giving legal advice to Congress, either of its Houses, or their committees.[13]

In advising the President whether to sign an enrolled bill, the Attorney General may have to express an opinion about its constitutionality. But opinions on the constitutionality of enacted bills are rare, and an opinion of unconstitutionality might seriously prejudice the government's later position in litigation.

The flavor of politics hangs about the opinions of the Attorney General and may lighten their weight. But despite the inescapable context of politics, sometimes of the highest politics, most Attorneys General have adhered to the conception of the opinion function voiced by Wirt: "I do not consider myself as the advocate of the government, but as a judge, called to decide a question of law with the impartiality and integrity which characterizes the judician." (Quoted in Cummings & McFarland, *supra* at 90.)

9. U.N.Charter Art. 96.

10. International Court of Justice, Yearbook 1983–84, at 5–6.

11. Authority for the preparation of opinions of the Attorney General, originally delegated to the Solicitor General in 1925, is now delegated to this office pursuant to 28 U.S.C. § 510.

12. This limitation applies to the opinions of the Attorney General, but not to opinions of the Office of Legal Counsel.

13. One former head of the Office of Legal Counsel writes: "[I]t seems to me

that the practice was to draw a line (however unrealistic) between opinion-giving on the one hand and comment regarding pending legislation on the other. Both in writing and orally, the Attorney General and various Assistant Attorneys General frequently express views to congressional committees concerning the constitutionality of particular legislative proposals. * * * They are not, however, cast in the form of formal opinions." Letter from Antonin Scalia to David Shapiro, 10/14/83.

The opinions are seldom challenged within the government, and play a vital role in securing uniformity and reasonableness of governmental action. They can be and have been rejected by the courts,[14] but they have much more often been accepted, with due regard not only for the dignity of the Attorney General's office but also for the importance of stability in those administrative practices that the opinions have shaped.[15]

MARBURY v. MADISON

1 Cranch 137, 2 L.Ed. 60 (U.S.1803).
On Petition for Mandamus.

* * * the following opinion of the Court was delivered by the CHIEF JUSTICE:

Opinion of the Court. At the last term on the affidavits then read and filed with the clerk, a rule was granted in this case, requiring the secretary of state to show cause why a *mandamus* should not issue, directing him to deliver to William Marbury his commission as a justice of the peace for the county of Washington, in the district of Columbia.

No cause has been shown, and the present motion is for a *mandamus*. The peculiar delicacy of this case, the novelty of some of its circumstances, and the real difficulty attending the points which occur in it, require a complete exposition of the principles on which the opinion to be given by the court is founded.

These principles have been, on the side of the applicant, very ably argued at the bar. In rendering the opinion of the court, there will be some departure in form, though not in substance, from the points stated in that argument.

In the order in which the court has viewed this subject, the following questions have been considered and decided.

1st. Has the applicant a right to the commission he demands?

2d. If he has a right, and that right has been violated, do the laws of his country afford him a remedy?

3d. If they do afford him a remedy, is it a *mandamus* issuing from this court?

* * * [The Court here addressed the first question and concluded that the withholding of the commission was "violative of a vested legal right." It then considered the second question, and began by quoting Blackstone to the effect that "where there is a legal right, there is also a legal remedy by suit or action at law, whenever that right is invaded." (3 Blackstone, Commentaries *23.) This was followed by an extensive discussion designed to show that Marbury was entitled to a remedy, that his case was not within "the class of cases which come under the description of *damnum absque injuria.*"]

---

14. See, *e.g.*, Perkins v. Elg, 307 U.S. 325, 348–49 (1939). Sometimes, Supreme Court Justices even reject their own opinions as Attorney General. See McGrath v. Kristensen, 340 U.S. 162, 176–78 (1950) (Jackson, J., concurring).

15. See, *e.g.*, Foley Bros., Inc. v. Filardo, 336 U.S. 281, 286, 291–92 (1949), and cases cited in Cummings & McFarland 517.

It is, then, the opinion of the Court,

1st. That by signing the commission of Mr. Marbury, the President of the United States appointed him a justice of peace for the county of Washington, in the district of Columbia; and that the seal of the United States, affixed thereto by the secretary of state, is conclusive testimony of the verity of the signature, and of the completion of the appointment; and that the appointment conferred on him a legal right to the office for the space of five years.

2d. That, having this legal title to the office, he has a consequent right to the commission; a refusal to deliver which is a plain violation of that right, for which the laws of his country afford him a remedy.

It remains to be inquired whether,

3d. He is entitled to the remedy for which he applies. This depends on,

1st. The nature of the writ applied for; and,

2d. The power of this court.

1st. The nature of the writ.

Blackstone, in the 3d volume of his Commentaries, page 110, defines a *mandamus* to be "a command issuing in the king's name, from the court of king's bench, and directed to any person, corporation, or inferior court of judicature within the king's dominions requiring them to do some particular thing therein specified, which appertains to their office and duty, and which the court of king's bench has previously determined, or at least supposes, to be consonant to right and justice." * * *

Still, to render the *mandamus* a proper remedy, the officer to whom it is to be directed, must be one to whom, on legal principles, such writ may be directed; and the person applying for it must be without any other specific and legal remedy.

1st. With respect to the officer to whom it would be directed. The intimate political relation subsisting between the president of the United States and the heads of departments, necessarily renders any legal investigation of the acts of one of those high officers peculiarly irksome, as well as delicate; and excites some hesitation with respect to the propriety of entering into such investigation. Impressions are often received without much reflection or examination and it is not wonderful that in such a case as this the assertion, by an individual, of his legal claims in a court of justice, to which claims it is the duty of that court to attend, should at first view be considered by some, as an attempt to intrude into the cabinet, and to intermeddle with the prerogatives of the executive.

It is scarcely necessary for the court to disclaim all pretensions to such a jurisdiction. An extravagance, so absurd and excessive, could not have been entertained for a moment. The province of the court is, solely, to decide on the rights of individuals, not to inquire how the executive, or executive officers, perform duties in which they have a discretion. Questions in their nature political, or which are, by the constitution and laws, submitted to the executive, can never be made in this court.

But, if this be not such a question; if, so far from being an intrusion into the secrets of the cabinet, it respects a paper which, according to law, is upon record, and to a copy of which the law gives a right, on the payment of ten cents; if it be no intermeddling with a subject over which the executive can be considered as having exercised any control; what is there in the exalted station of the officer, which shall bar a citizen from asserting, in a court of justice, his legal rights, or shall forbid a court to listen to the claim, or to issue a *mandamus,* directing the performance of a duty, not depending on executive discretion, but on particular acts of congress, and the general principles of law?

If one of the heads of departments commits any illegal act, under colour of his office, by which an individual sustains an injury, it cannot be pretended that his office alone exempts him from being sued in the ordinary mode of proceeding, and being compelled to obey the judgment of the law. How, then, can his office exempt him from this particular mode of deciding on the legality of his conduct, if the case be such a case as would, were any other individual the party complained of, authorize the process?

It is not by the office of the person to whom the writ is directed, but the nature of the thing to be done, that the propriety or impropriety of issuing a *mandamus* is to be determined. Where the head of a department acts in a case, in which executive discretion is to be exercised; in which he is the mere organ of executive will; it is again repeated, that any application to a court to control, in any respect, his conduct would be rejected without hesitation.

But where he is directed by law to do a certain act affecting the absolute rights of individuals, in the performance of which he is not placed under the particular direction of the president, and the performance of which the president cannot lawfully forbid, and therefore is never presumed to have forbidden; as for example, to record a commission, or a patent for land, which has received all the legal solemnities; or to give a copy of such record; in such cases, it is not perceived on what ground the courts of the country are further excused from the duty of giving judgment that right be done to an injured individual, than if the same services were to be performed by a person not the head of a department. * * *

This, then, is a plain case for a *mandamus,* either to deliver the commission, or a copy of it from the record; and it only remains to be inquired,

Whether it can issue from this court.

The act to establish the judicial courts of the United States authorizes the supreme court, "to issue writs of *mandamus,* in cases warranted by the principles and usages of law, to any courts appointed or persons holding office, under the authority of the United States."

The secretary of state being a person holding an office under the authority of the United States, is precisely within the letter of the description; and if this court is not authorized to issue a writ of *mandamus* to such an officer, it must be because the law is unconstitutional, and therefore, absolutely incapable of conferring the authority, and assigning the duties which its words purport to confer and assign.

The constitution vests the whole judicial power of the United States in one supreme court, and such inferior courts as congress shall, from time to time, ordain and establish. This power is expressly extended to all cases arising under the laws of the United States; and, consequently, in some form, may be exercised over the present case; because the right claimed is given by a law of the United States.

In the distribution of this power it is declared, that "the supreme court shall have original jurisdiction in all cases affecting ambassadors, other public ministers and consuls, and those in which a state shall be a party. In all other cases, the supreme court shall have appellate jurisdiction."

It has been insisted, at the bar, that as the original grant of jurisdiction, to the supreme and inferior courts, is general, and the clause, assigning original jurisdiction to the supreme court, contains no negative or restrictive words, the power remains to the legislature, to assign original jurisdiction to that court in other cases than those specified in the article which has been recited; provided those cases belong to the judicial power of the United States.

If it had been intended to leave it in the discretion of the legislature to apportion the judicial power between the supreme and inferior courts according to the will of that body, it would certainly have been useless to have proceeded further than to have defined the judicial power, and the tribunals in which it should be vested. The subsequent part of the section is mere surplusage, is entirely without meaning, if such is to be the construction. If congress remains at liberty to give this court appellate jurisdiction where the constitution has declared their jurisdiction shall be original; and original jurisdiction where the constitution has declared it shall be appellate; the distribution of jurisdiction, made in the constitution, is form without substance.

Affirmative words are often, in their operation, negative of other objects than those affirmed; and in this case, a negative or exclusive sense must be given to them, or they have no operation at all.

It cannot be presumed that any clause in the constitution is intended to be without effect; and therefore, such a construction is inadmissible, unless the words require it.

If the solicitude of the convention, respecting our peace with foreign powers, induced a provision that the supreme court should take original jurisdiction in cases which might be supposed to affect them; yet the clause would have proceeded no further than to provide for such cases, if no further restriction on the powers of congress had been intended. That they should have appellate jurisdiction in all other cases, with such exceptions as congress might make, is no restriction; unless the words be deemed exclusive of original jurisdiction.

When an instrument organizing fundamentally a judicial system, divides it into one supreme, and so many inferior courts as the legislature may ordain and establish; then enumerates its powers, and proceeds so far to distribute them, as to define the jurisdiction of the supreme court, by declaring the cases in which it shall take original jurisdiction, and that in others it shall take appellate jurisdiction; the plain import of the words seems to be, that in one class of cases its jurisdiction is original, and not appellate; in the other it is appellate, and not original. If any other construction would render the clause inoperative, that is an additional reason for rejecting such other construction, and for adhering to their obvious meaning.

To enable this court, then, to issue a *mandamus*, it must be shown to be an exercise of appellate jurisdiction, or to be necessary to enable them to exercise appellate jurisdiction.

It has been stated at the bar that the appellate jurisdiction may be exercised in a variety of forms, and that if it be the will of the legislature that a *mandamus* should be used for that purpose, that will must be obeyed. This is true, yet the jurisdiction must be appellate, not original.

It is the essential criterion of appellate jurisdiction, that it revises and corrects the proceedings in a cause already instituted, and does not create that cause. Although, therefore, a *mandamus* may be directed to courts, yet to issue such a writ to an officer for the delivery of a paper, is in effect the same as to sustain an original action for that paper, and, therefore, seems not to belong to appellate, but to original jurisdiction. Neither is it necessary in such a case as this, to enable the court to exercise its appellate jurisdiction.

The authority, therefore, given to the supreme court by the act establishing the judicial courts of the United States, to issue writs of *mandamus* to public officers, appears not to be warranted by the constitution; and it becomes necessary to inquire whether a jurisdiction so conferred can be exercised.

The question, whether an act, repugnant to the constitution, can become the law of the land, is a question deeply interesting to the United States; but, happily, not of an intricacy proportioned to its interest. It seems only necessary to recognize certain principles, supposed to have been long and well established, to decide it.

That the people have an original right to establish, for their future government, such principles, as in their opinion, shall most conduce to their own happiness is the basis on which the whole American fabric has been erected. The exercise of this original right is a very great exertion; nor can it, nor ought it, to be frequently repeated. The principles, therefore, so established, are deemed fundamental. And as the authority from which they proceed is supreme, and can seldom act, they are designed to be permanent.

This original and supreme will organizes the government, and assigns to different departments their respective powers. It may either stop here, or establish certain limits not to be transcended by those departments.

The government of the United States is of the latter description. The powers of the legislature are defined and limited; and that those limits may not be mistaken, or forgotten, the constitution is written. To what purpose are powers limited, and to what purpose is that limitation committed to writing, if these limits may, at any time, be passed by those intended to be restrained? The distinction between a government with limited and unlimited powers is abolished, if those limits do not confine the persons on whom they are imposed, and if acts prohibited and acts allowed, are of equal obligation. It is a proposition too plain to be contested, that the constitution controls any legislative act repugnant to it; or, that the legislature may alter the constitution by an ordinary act.

Between these alternatives, there is no middle ground. The constitution is either a superior paramount law, unchangeable by ordinary means, or it is on a level with ordinary legislative acts, and, like other acts, is alterable when the legislature shall please to alter it.

If the former part of the alternative be true, then a legislative act, contrary to the constitution, is not law: if the latter part be true, then written constitutions are absurd attempts, on the part of the people, to limit a power in its own nature, illimitable.

Certainly all those who have framed written constitutions contemplate them as forming the fundamental and paramount law of the nation, and, consequently, the theory of every such government must be, that an act of the legislature, repugnant to the constitution, is void.

This theory is essentially attached to a written constitution, and is consequently, to be considered, by this court, as one of the fundamental principles of our society. It is not therefore to be lost sight of, in the further consideration of this subject.

If an act of the legislature, repugnant to the constitution, is void, does it, notwithstanding its invalidity, bind the courts, and oblige them to give it effect? Or, in other words, though it be not law, does it constitute a rule as operative as if it was a law? This would be to overthrow in fact what was established in theory; and would seem, at first view, an absurdity too gross to be insisted on. It shall, however, receive a more attentive consideration.

It is emphatically the province and duty of the judicial department to say what the law is. Those who apply the rule to particular cases, must of necessity expound and interpret that rule. If two laws conflict with each other, the courts must decide on the operation of each.

So, if a law be in opposition to the constitution; if both the law and the constitution apply to a particular case, so that the court must either decide that case conformably to the law, disregarding the constitution; or conformably to the constitution, disregarding the law; the court must determine which of these conflicting rules governs the case. This is of the very essence of judicial duty.

If then, the courts are to regard the constitution, and the constitution is superior to any ordinary act of the legislature, the constitution, and not such ordinary act, must govern the case to which they both apply.

Those, then, who controvert the principle that the constitution is to be considered, in court, as a paramount law, are reduced to the necessity of maintaining that courts must close their eyes on the constitution, and see only the law. This doctrine would subvert the very foundation of all written constitutions. It would declare that an act which, according to the principles and theory of our government, is entirely void, is yet, in practice, completely obligatory. It would declare that if the legislature shall do what is expressly forbidden, such act, notwithstanding the express prohibition, is in reality effectual. It would be giving to the legislature a practical and real omnipotence, with the same breath which professes to restrict their powers within narrow limits. It is prescribing limits, and declaring that those limits may be passed at pleasure.

That it thus reduces to nothing, what we have deemed the greatest improvement on political institutions, a written constitution, would of itself be sufficient, in America, where written constitutions have been viewed with so much reverence, for rejecting the construction. But the peculiar expressions of the constitution of the United States furnish additional arguments in favour of its rejection.

The judicial power of the United States is extended to all cases arising under the constitution.

Could it be the intention of those who gave this power, to say that in using it the constitution should not be looked into? That a case arising under the constitution should be decided, without examining the instrument under which it arises?

This is too extravagant to be maintained.

In some cases, then, the constitution must be looked into by the judges. And if they can open it at all, what part of it are they forbidden to read or to obey?

There are many other parts of the constitution which serve to illustrate this subject.

It is declared, that "no tax or duty shall be laid on articles exported from any state." Suppose, a duty on the export of cotton, of tobacco, or of flour; and a suit instituted to recover it. Ought judgment to be rendered in such a case? ought the judges to close their eyes on the constitution, and only see the law?

The constitution declares "that no bill of attainder or *ex post facto* law shall be passed."

If, however, such a bill should be passed, and a person should be prosecuted under it; must the court condemn to death those victims whom the constitution endeavors to preserve?

"No person," says the constitution, "shall be convicted of treason unless on the testimony of two witnesses to the same overt act, or on confession in open court."

Here the language of the constitution is addressed especially to the courts. It prescribes, directly for them, a rule of evidence not to be departed from. If the legislature should change that rule, and declare *one* witness, or a confession *out* of court, sufficient for conviction, must the constitutional principle yield to the legislative act?

From these, and many other selections which might be made, it is apparent, that the framers of the constitution contemplated that instrument as a rule for the government of courts, as well as of the legislature.

Why otherwise does it direct the judges to take an oath to support it? This oath certainly applies in an especial manner, to their conduct in their official character. How immoral to impose it on them, if they were to be used as the instruments, and the knowing instruments, for violating what they swear to support!

The oath of office, too, imposed by the legislature, is completely demonstrative of the legislative opinion on this subject. It is in these words: "I do solemnly swear that I will administer justice without respect to persons, and do equal right to the poor and to the rich; and that I will faithfully and impartially discharge all the duties incumbent on me as _____, according to the best of my abilities and understanding, agreeably to the *constitution* and laws of the United States."

Why does a judge swear to discharge his duties agreeably to the constitution of the United States, if that constitution forms no rule for his government? if it is closed upon him, and cannot be inspected by him?

If such be the real state of things, this is worse than solemn mockery. To prescribe, or to take this oath, becomes equally a crime.

It is also not entirely unworthy of observation, that in declaring what shall be the *supreme* law of the land, the *constitution* itself is first mentioned; and not the laws of the United States, generally, but those only which shall be made in *pursuance* of the constitution, have that rank.

Thus, the particular phraseology of the constitution of the United States confirms and strengthens the principle, supposed to be essential to all written constitutions, that a law repugnant to the constitution is void; and that *courts,* as well as other departments, are bound by that instrument.

The rule must be discharged.

NOTE ON MARBURY v. MADISON AND THE FUNCTION OF ADJUDICATION

(1) Would it be right to describe the parts of Marshall's opinion dealing with Marbury's title to the commission and the propriety of the remedy of mandamus as advisory? [1]

Was Marshall's interpretation of the section of the Judiciary Act of 1789 authorizing the Supreme Court to issue writs of mandamus a necessary one? His interpretation of the second paragraph of Article III, Section 2? [2]

(2) Marshall derives the Court's power to declare acts of Congress unconstitutional, and hence its power to make authoritative determinations of constitutional law, solely from its power to decide cases. Is there any other basis for attributing a law-declaring function of any kind to courts?

(a) Until recent years, most observers would have answered this question with a firm negative. But increasingly, a more diffused conception of the function of courts in public law matters has appeared (sometimes explicitly, sometimes assumed)—a conception that puts forward a judicial role other than as an incident of the power to resolve particular, ongoing disputes between identified litigants. This approach has at least three aspects. The first questions the importance of requiring that the plaintiff have a personal stake in the outcome of a lawsuit; in its purest form, it would permit any citizen to bring a "public action" to challenge allegedly unlawful government conduct. The second argues that the judiciary should not be viewed as a mere settler of disputes, but rather as an institution with a distinctive capacity to declare and explicate public values—norms that transcend individual controversies and that are con-

1. For the later history of this aspect of Marbury v. Madison, see *Note on Nonstatutory Review of Federal Official Action,* Chap. IX, Sec. 1(A), *infra.*

2. For further discussion of these questions, see Currie, *The Constitution in the*

Supreme Court: The Powers of the Federal Courts, 1801–1835, 49 U.Chi.L.Rev. 646, 651–55 (1982). For further material on the last question, see Chap. III, Sec. 3, pp. 353–55, *infra.*

cerned with the conditions of social and political life. The third defends the exercise by courts of broad remedial powers in cases challenging the operation of such public institutions as schools, prisons, and mental hospitals, arguing that relief cannot and should not be limited to undoing particular violations, but should involve judges (and their nominees) in the management and reshaping of those institutions.[3]

(b) The distinction between what may simplistically be called the "dispute resolution" and "public action" models does not involve watertight compartments.[4] School desegregation cases, for example—which many would regard as the epitome of the latter model—have their origin in individual grievances that plainly require the reshaping of institutions if the rights infringed are to be remedied. At the same time, the issues presented in such cases involve questions of social structure and of social life that often cannot be fully dealt with in the context of any one individual's complaint or within the educational career of any one student. To a significant degree, the devices of the class action, as well as other techniques of broadening the scope of litigation, constitute an effort to embrace these larger questions, and many of the tensions inherent in determining the proper role of the courts have been felt in the utilization of those devices.[5] See pp. 212–30, *infra.*

3. For a range of commentary elaborating this approach in one or more of these three aspects, see, *e.g.,* Chayes, *The Role of the Judge in Public Law Litigation,* 89 Harv.L.Rev. 1281 (1976); Chayes, *Foreword: Public Law Litigation and the Burger Court,* 96 Harv.L.Rev. 4 (1982); Dworkin, Taking Rights Seriously 131–49 (1977); Fiss, *Foreword: The Forms of Justice,* 93 Harv.L.Rev. 1 (1979); Jaffe, *The Citizen as Litigant in Public Actions: The Non-Hohfeldian or Ideological Plaintiff,* 116 U.Pa.L.Rev. 1033 (1968); Monaghan, *Constitutional Adjudication: The Who and When,* 82 Yale L.J. 1363 (1973); Tushnet, *The New Law of Standing: A Plea for Abandonment,* 62 Cornell L.Rev. 633 (1977); Vining, Legal Identity: The Coming of Age of Public Administrative Law (1978).

These three aspects often coincide in particular litigation. But the coincidence is hardly inevitable; for example, an effort to bring a public action seeking narrow declaratory or injunctive relief with respect to a specific government practice would clearly not implicate a broad remedial role for courts in restructuring public institutions. See Fallon, *Of Justiciability, Remedies, and Public Law Litigation: Notes on the Jurisprudence of Lyons,* 59 N.Y.U.L. Rev. 1, 3–9 (1984).

Support for this approach, particularly in constitutional adjudication, is found by some of these commentators in Marbury itself. Thus Monaghan, *supra,* in criticizing " 'the old notion that the power to decide constitutional questions is simply incident to the power to dispose of a concrete case,' " says that "Marbury itself provides the basis for a different model of judicial competence. In its repeated emphasis that a written constitution imposes limits on every organ of the state, Marbury welded judicial review to the political axiom of limited government" (82 Yale L.J. at 1370).

4. For valuable discussion of similar models from a comparative perspective see Damaska, The Faces of Justice and State Authority (1986). Professor Damaska develops the relationship between what he calls the "conflict solving" and "policy implementing" approaches to adjudication and visions of the state as "reactive" and "activist."

5. In his well-known essay, *The Forms and Limits of Adjudication,* 92 Harv.L. Rev. 353 (1978), Professor Fuller stresses the inappropriateness of adjudication for the resolution of "polycentric" disputes. He argues that such many-faceted disputes have too many ramifications, too many interdependent aspects, to yield to rational solution; they are far more suited to disposition by processes of negotiation and managerial intuition.

In a more recent essay on institutional reform litigation, Professor Horowitz notes the difficulties of casting the issues in such cases in terms of legal rights; the dangers of attempting to treat class plaintiffs and governmental defendants as if each side were always homogeneous and adverse to the other; the hazards of delegating authority to masters and of compromising judicial neutrality; and the inevitability of unintended consequences when judges necessarily "act on a piece, and neglect the

But the public action model also contemplates judicial action in situations in which the dispute resolution model plainly would not consider any action appropriate—when, for example, questions of constitutional validity are raised but no immediate interests of the parties before the court are at stake. It is unclear, however, whether the public action model would sanction the rendering of advisory opinions on the validity of proposed legislation, even if advocates could be found to present competing arguments with sufficient vigor, or whether the model would consider it appropriate for the court itself to generate the question for resolution and to appoint advocates to present it with the relevant issues and arguments. See generally *Note on Advisory Opinions*, p. 67, *supra*.

(c) To take a case that comes closer to the dispute resolution model, suppose that a state employee, claiming that she is threatened with discharge in violation of her constitutional rights, brings a federal court action to enjoin her discharge and to require her state employer to institute certain procedures for dealing with cases like hers in the future. Two days after the complaint is filed, the plaintiff dies of unrelated causes, and her lawyer resists a motion to dismiss on the ground that the case raises important constitutional questions about the procedures and structure of the state employer. He seeks to substitute his client's husband, who is not a state employee, as plaintiff.

Of the factors listed at p. 68, *supra*, some do not seem to be affected by the death of the original plaintiff, while others plainly are, but since only prospective relief was sought, her death surely eliminates any ongoing dispute that the court's judgment and decree might resolve. Nor is there any indication in the character of the lawsuit that other employees of this agency confront similar problems, or, if they do, that they wish to press any claim they might have. Would a decision of the Court passing on the constitutional question under these circumstances, and issuing an injunction requiring the agency to change its operations, be a legitimate exercise of judicial power? If you think so, would it matter if no evidence could be adduced that the original plaintiff had been threatened with discharge? If she had never been a public employee but had simply been seeking to determine whether the agency could discharge someone under certain conditions?

What are the functions and limitations that distinguish the judiciary from the other branches of government? If courts are to adjudicate such matters, is there a danger that they will become preoccupied with issues that are not of present concern to those who might be immediately affected? That they will be diverted from the task of authoritatively resolving disputes that *are* immediate and pressing? That they will act on the basis of inadequate information or without adequate sensitivity to the particular situation? That they will become too readily and too deeply immersed in the operation of other branches and in the allocation of limited resources? That their exercise of discretion in the formulation of remedies will not be subject to adequate controls? That they will jeopardize their position as the final arbiters of conformity to law?

rest." Horowitz, *Decreeing Organizational Change: Judicial Supervision of Public Institutions*, 1983 Duke L.J. 1265.

See also Fletcher, *The Discretionary Constitution: Institutional Remedies and Judicial Legitimacy*, 91 Yale L.J. 635 (1982); Stewart, *The Reformation of American Administrative Law*, 88 Harv.L.Rev. 1667, 1802–05 (1975); Stewart, *Reconstitutive Law*, 46 Md.L.Rev. 86, 103 (1986).

The contours of the dispute resolution model are sufficiently imprecise that even one who adheres to its tenets must confront many difficult questions. Thus one who is convinced that in the hypothetical case just put, the court should not proceed, would still have to grapple in similar cases with such questions as: How immediate must the threat of discharge be to warrant declaratory or prospective relief? May an action be pursued by an organization representing a class of employees or by an individual representative of that class? May such an individual continue to represent the class even after she has left her job? These are some of the issues explored in the remaining sections of this chapter. There, as here, one's perspective will be acutely affected by one's conception of the proper limits of judicial power.

(d) The Supreme Court has never embraced the public action model of the judicial role or abandoned the dispute resolution model. Indeed, its pronouncements have been consistently to the contrary. Thus, for example, the Court has held that a federal district court exceeded its Article III jurisdiction when it considered a constitutional issue not raised by the parties—even though it did so at the express direction of the court of appeals. Williams v. Zbaraz, 448 U.S. 358, 367 (1980). See also, *e.g.,* Princeton University v. Schmid, 455 U.S. 100, 102 (1982) ("if the State were the sole appellant and its jurisdictional statement simply asked for review and declined to take a position on the merits, we would have dismissed the appeal for want of a case or controversy"); Kirchberg v. Feenstra, 450 U.S. 455, 462 (1981) ("We decline to address appellant's concerns about the potential impact of the Court of Appeals decision on other mortgages * * *. The only question before us is whether the decision of the Court of Appeals applies to the mortgage in this case * * *.").[6]

Moreover, as will appear in the remainder of this Chapter, the Court has recurrently rejected litigation avowedly aimed at generally policing official conduct rather than seeking relief for the complaining party; see, *e.g.,* Sierra Club v. Morton, p. 123, *infra;* O'Shea v. Littleton, p. 256, *infra* ; City of Los Angeles v. Lyons, p. 266, *infra;* Rizzo v. Goode, p. 265, *infra;* United States v. Richardson, p. 125, *infra.* There are, however, some holdings that may be seen as reflecting—though not in terms—a shift in conception of the judicial role; see, *e.g.,* the developments discussed in the *Note on Mootness and Class Actions,* p. 225, *infra,* and in the *Note on the Scope of the Issue in First Amendment Cases,* p. 184, *infra.* Consider, as you work through these materials, whether a significant change in overall conception is occurring and, if so, whether such a change is warranted.

(3) If Marshall was right that the function of courts is to decide cases, was he also right that this function must include the power to inquire into the constitutionality of acts of Congress?

---

6. There are traditionally certain threshold issues, like subject-matter jurisdiction, that a court will consider whether the parties ask it to or not. See Chap. XIV, Sec. 1, *infra.* Thus in United States v. Will, 449 U.S. 200, 212 (1980), the Court considered the question whether all the justices were disqualified from passing on the validity of certain statutes affecting judicial salaries. Both parties agreed that they were not disqualified, but the Court said: "Notwithstanding this concurrence of views resulting from the Government's concession, the sensitivity of the issues leads us to address the applicability of § 455 [the disqualification statute] with the same degree of care and attention we would employ if the Government asserted that the District Court lacked jurisdiction or that § 455 mandates disqualification of all judges and Justices without exception."

In certain matters courts are content to accept as a basis of decision, without further inquiry, a formally correct determination of the legislative or executive branches, *e.g.,* a statement that a certain statute has in fact been enacted in accordance with the prescribed procedure, or that a certain government is the established government of a country. See, further, Sec. 6, *infra.* Why should they not, in all cases, similarly accept the determination of Congress and the President (or in the case of a veto, of a special majority of Congress) that a statute is duly authorized by the Constitution?

Does Congress in voting to enact a bill or the President in approving it actually make or purport to make such a determination? So far at least as concerns questions of the validity of the statute as applied in particular situations, how can they?

Both Congress and the President can obviously contribute to the sound interpretation of the Constitution. But clearly neither branch is so organized or staffed as to be able, without aid from the courts, to build up a body of coherent and intelligible constitutional principle, and to carry public conviction that these principles are being observed. Consider, for example, the differences among the branches in respect of experience and temperament of personnel, of procedure for decision, of means of recording decision, and of opportunity for close examination of particular questions.

How important is it that such a body of constitutional principle should be developed? That people believe that the principles guide decision? Is this equally important with respect to all constitutional provisions? Compare for example the Contract Clause and the Bill of Rights, on the one hand, with the provisions about how statutes shall be enacted and the guarantee to the states of a republican form of government, on the other. Is it equally important with respect to all kinds of official decisions? Or specially important with respect to decisions authoritatively applying the law to specific individuals?

(4) Does it follow from Marshall's reasoning that the executive and legislative departments have a similar responsibility to interpret and apply the Constitution when that is relevant to the proper discharge of executive or legislative functions? Does this view involve the potentiality of serious conflicts among the departments? What, if any, guides does the Constitution give for the resolution of such conflicts?

Consider the position taken by President Franklin D. Roosevelt in his much-quoted letter of July 6, 1935, to Congressman Samuel B. Hill concerning the questions of constitutionality that had arisen with respect to a bill to regulate the bituminous coal mining industry, 4 Public Papers and Addresses of Franklin D. Roosevelt 297–98 (1938). The letter opens with a brief argument in favor of the constitutionality of the measure. The last paragraph, of which only the last sentence is usually quoted, is as follows:

"Manifestly, no one is in a position to give assurance that the proposed act will withstand constitutional tests, for the simple fact that you can get not ten but a thousand differing legal opinions on the subject. But the situation is so urgent and the benefits of the legislation so evident that all doubts should be resolved in favor of the bill, leaving to the courts, in an orderly fashion, the ultimate question of constitutionality. A decision by the Supreme Court relative to this measure would be helpful as indicating, with increasing clarity, the constitutional limits within which this Government must operate. The proposed bill has been carefully drafted by employers and employees working cooperatively. An opportunity should be given to the industry to attempt to work out some of its major problems. I hope your committee will not permit doubts as to constitutionality, however reasonable, to block the suggested legislation."

Contrast Jackson's message of July 10, 1832, justifying his veto of the bill to continue the Bank of the United States in spite of Supreme Court decisions favorable to its constitutionality. 2 Richardson, Messages and Papers of the Presidents 576, 582 (1896). Jackson said:

"If the opinion of the Supreme Court covered the whole ground of this act, it ought not to control the coordinate authorities of this Government. The Congress, the Executive, and the Court must each for itself be guided by its own opinion of the Constitution. Each public officer who takes an oath to support the Constitution swears that he will support it as he understands it, and not as it is understood by others. It is as much the duty of the House of Representatives, of the Senate, and of the President to decide upon the constitutionality of any bill or resolution which may be presented to them for passage or approval as it is of the supreme judges when it may be brought before them for judicial decision. The opinion of the judges has no more authority over Congress than the opinion of Congress has over the judges, and on that point the President is independent of both. The authority of the Supreme Court must not, therefore, be permitted to control the Congress or the Executive when acting in their legislative capacities, but to have only such influence as the force of their reasoning may deserve."

Compare Lincoln's position in his first inaugural that in constitutional controversies with respect to which the Constitution is not explicit the minority must in the end acquiesce with the majority (6 *id.* 5, 9):

"I do not forget the position assumed by some that constitutional questions are to be decided by the Supreme Court, nor do I deny that such decisions must be binding in any case upon the parties to a suit as to the object of that suit, while they are also entitled to very high respect and consideration in all parallel cases by all other departments of the Government. And while it is obviously possible that such decision may be erroneous in any given case, still the evil effect following it, being limited to that particular case, with the chance that it may be overruled and never become a precedent for other cases, can better be borne than could the evils of a different practice. At the same time, the candid citizen must confess that if the policy of the Government upon vital questions affecting the whole people is to be irrevocably fixed by decisions of the Supreme Court, the instant they are made in ordinary litigation between parties in personal actions the people will have ceased to be their own rulers, having to that extent practically resigned their Government into the hands of that eminent tribunal. Nor is there in this view any assault upon the court or the judges. It is a duty from which they may not shrink to decide cases properly brought before them, and it is no fault of theirs if others seek to turn their decision to political purposes."

(5) Compare with the Presidential views the Supreme Court's statement of the binding nature of its decisions in Cooper v. Aaron, 358 U.S. 1 (1958): The Court was asked to postpone the implementation of a court-approved desegregation program for Little Rock, Arkansas, because of extreme public hostility. Previously, the Governor had called out the

National Guard to prevent black students from entering Little Rock Central High School and, though these troops were later withdrawn in response to a federal injunction against the Governor, black students were thereafter able to attend only under federal military protection. Though the School Board had been actively seeking to implement desegregation, it sought a two and one-half year postponement of the court-approved program. The District Court granted relief. The Court of Appeals reversed. The Supreme Court affirmed, denying delay, on the ground that "the constitutional rights of respondents are not to be sacrificed or yielded to the violence and disorder which have followed upon the actions of the Governor and Legislature" (p. 16).

The opinion of the Court, captioned in an extraordinary fashion with the names of all nine justices individually, continued (pp. 17–19):

"What has been said, in the light of the facts developed, is enough to dispose of the case. However, we should answer the premise of the actions of the Governor and Legislature that they are not bound by our holding in the Brown case. It is necessary only to recall some basic constitutional propositions which are settled doctrine.

"Article VI of the Constitution makes the Constitution the 'supreme Law of the Land.' In 1803, Chief Justice Marshall, speaking for a unanimous Court, referring to the Constitution as 'the fundamental and paramount law of the nation,' declared in the notable case of Marbury v. Madison, 1 Cranch 137, 177, that 'It is emphatically the province and duty of the judicial department to say what the law is.' This decision declared the basic principle that the federal judiciary is supreme in the exposition of the law of the Constitution, and that principle has ever since been respected by this Court and the Country as a permanent and indispensable feature of our constitutional system. It follows that the interpretation of the Fourteenth Amendment enunciated by this Court in the Brown case is the supreme law of the land, and Art. VI of the Constitution makes it of binding effect on the States 'any Thing in the Constitution or Laws of any State to the Contrary notwithstanding.' Every state legislator and executive and judicial officer is solemnly committed by oath taken pursuant to Art. VI, cl. 3, 'to support this Constitution.' * * *

"No state legislator or executive or judicial officer can war against the Constitution without violating his undertaking to support it. Chief Justice Marshall spoke for a unanimous Court in saying that: 'If the legislatures of the several states may, at will, annul the judgments of the courts of the United States, and destroy the rights acquired under those judgments, the constitution itself becomes a solemn mockery * * *.' United States v. Peters, 5 Cranch 115, 136. A Governor who asserts a power to nullify a federal court order is similarly restrained. If he had such power, said Chief Justice Hughes, in 1932, also for a unanimous Court, 'it is manifest that the fiat of a state Governor, and not the Constitution of the United States, would be the supreme law of the land; that the restrictions of the Federal Constitution upon the exercise of state power would be but impotent phrases * * *.' Sterling v. Constantin, 287 U.S. 378, 397–398."

Note that Cooper v. Aaron itself involved the integrity of a court order, and thus the Court's language and result is consistent with Lincoln's position, Paragraph (4), *supra*. Are any further assertions or implications concerning the pre-eminence of the Court's power of constitutional exposition warranted? Does Marbury support any broader position?

If one takes the view that "[u]nder Marbury, the Court decides a case; it does not pass a statute calling for obedience by all within the purview of the rule that is declared," does it follow that constitutional doctrine must remain unsettled? See Wechsler, *The Court and the Constitution*, 65 Colum.L.Rev. 1001, 1008 (1965), building on the excerpt from Lincoln's First Inaugural quoted above: "[N]ote the purpose of the limitation [there] stated: to allow for the 'chance' that the decision 'may be overruled and never become a precedent for other cases.' When that chance has been exploited and has run its course, with reaffirmation rather than reversal of decision, has not the time arrived when its acceptance is demanded, without insisting on repeated litigation? The answer here, it seems to me, must be affirmative, both as the necessary implication of our constitutional tradition and to avoid the greater evils that will otherwise ensue."

Cf. Jaffe, *Impromptu Remarks*, 76 Harv.L.Rev. 1111 (1963). See also Bickel, The Least Dangerous Branch 254–72, especially at 261 (1962).

(6) The travails of President Nixon's administration gave rise to several occasions for revisiting Marbury.

In United States v. Nixon, 418 U.S. 683 (1974) (the "Watergate" tapes case, in which a subpoena directed to the President was upheld) the Court dealt with the contention that the President's claim of privilege was not subject to judicial review by saying (p. 703): "In the performance of assigned constitutional duties each branch of the Government must initially interpret the Constitution, and the interpretation of its powers by any branch is due great respect from the others. The President's counsel * * * reads the Constitution as providing an absolute privilege of confidentiality for all Presidential communications. Many decisions of this Court, however, have unequivocally reaffirmed the holding of Marbury v. Madison * * * that '[i]t is emphatically the province and duty of the judicial department to say what the law is.' " The opinion then referred to a number of cases—admittedly none directly on point [7]—in which the power of judicial review had been exercised, and concluded this part of its discussion (p. 705): "We therefore reaffirm that it is the province and duty of this Court 'to say what the law is' with respect to the claim of privilege presented in this case. Marbury v. Madison * * *."

Was Marbury a sufficient response to the contention? Would it have been inconsistent with Marbury for the Court to hold that a President's determination that certain material was privileged had to be accepted as conclusive by the courts? Recall the instances noted previously (in Paragraph (3) of this Note) involving judicial acceptance of determinations by other branches as to compliance with procedures for the enactment of a statute or as to the identity of the "established" government of a foreign country.[8]

---

7. The references included the steel seizure case, Youngstown Sheet & Tube Co. v. Sawyer, 343 U.S. 579 (1952), p. 1129, *infra;* Powell v. McCormack, 395 U.S. 486 (1969); and a series of cases interpreting congressional members' immunity under the Speech or Debate Clause of Art. I, § 6 of the Constitution.

8. See Gunther, *Judicial Hegemony and Legislative Autonomy: The Nixon Case and the Impeachment Process*, 22 U.C.L.A.L. Rev. 30, 33–35 (1974); Karst & Horowitz, *Presidential Prerogative and Judicial Review*, 22 U.C.L.A.L.Rev. 47, 55–61 (1974). See also Section 6 of this Chapter.

Both United States v. Nixon and Marbury v. Madison were invoked in Nixon v. Fitzgerald, 457 U.S. 731 (1982), holding the President absolutely immune from civil damages liability for acts "within the 'outer perimeter' of his official responsibilities." Justice White, for four dissenters, urged that across-the-board, absolute immunity, based on what the majority described as the President's "unique position in the constitutional scheme," was inconsistent with the holding of United States v. Nixon that the President was subject to lawful process and with the Court's insistence in Marbury that "the very essence of civil liberty certainly consists in the right of every individual to claim the protection of the laws, whenever he receives an injury" (1 Cranch at 163). He argued that a "functional approach" to immunity questions—one that evaluated the effect of liability on governmental decisionmaking within a particular function—represented "an appropriate reconciliation of the conflicting interests at stake" (457 U.S. at 782–83 & n. 26).

Is it the case that a "right * * * to claim the protection of the laws" necessarily includes the right to sue a government official for *damages*? The rhetoric of Marbury surely cannot resolve the question of executive immunity from damage actions any more than it can determine the scope of executive privilege with respect to conversations and documents. Whether the result of Nixon v. Fitzgerald was right or wrong, Justice White's reliance on Marbury was severely undercut by his own willingness to recognize absolute or qualified immunity in other contexts.

(7) Does the power of judicial review upheld in Marbury carry with it a correlative duty to decide any claims of unconstitutionality in a properly presented case, or is there some measure of discretion to abstain from such decisions? In an important and controversial work, Professor Bickel argued that at the Supreme Court level (as distinguished from that of the lower federal courts), there must be flexibility to determine when it is appropriate to decide. This flexibility, he argued, is afforded not only by the discretion vested in the Court to grant or deny a writ of certiorari, but in the various doctrines of justiciability developed under such rubrics as standing, mootness, ripeness, and political question. Indeed, he suggests that these doctrines are best understood as techniques for avoiding the necessity of decision, not as principled bodies of law to be rigorously applied in particular cases. See Bickel, The Least Dangerous Branch—The Supreme Court at the Bar of Politics 111–98 (1962).

Bickel's thesis has been vigorously challenged on the grounds that it tolerates, and even encourages, unprincipled judicial action[9] and that it violates the basic tenets of Marbury itself. See, *e.g.*, Gunther, *The Subtle Vices of the "Passive Virtues"—A Comment on Principle and Expediency in Judicial Review*, 64 Colum.L.Rev. 1 (1964); Wechsler, *Book Review*, 75 Yale L.J. 672 (1966). See also Wechsler, *Toward Neutral Principles of Constitutional Law*, 73 Harv.L.Rev. 1, 6 (1959). The debate is one that arises not

Although President Nixon's attorney, as well as the President himself, indicated in advance that he might defy an order to produce, the attorney stated soon after the unanimous decision that the President would comply "fully." Van Alstyne, *A Political and Constitutional Review of United States v. Nixon*, 22 U.C.L.A.L.Rev. 116, 123 (1974).

9. Note especially that while Bickel prescribes his approach only for the Supreme Court, the justiciability doctrines he invokes are doctrines that purport to govern the propriety of judicial intervention by all federal courts.

only in the context of justiciability but in other instances of refusal to reach the merits of a constitutional claim. See, *e.g.,* pp. 342, 744, 1852, *infra.*

(8) Other questions of the separation of powers have also been considered in terms of the functions of adjudication articulated in Marbury and implicit in Article III. Prominent among these is the question of prospective overruling. In its landmark decision in <u>Linkletter v. Walker</u>, 381 U.S. 618 (1965), the Supreme Court held that the rule of Mapp v. Ohio, 367 U.S. 643 (1961), would not be applied retroactively to a state criminal conviction that had become final before Mapp was decided; one year later, in Johnson v. New Jersey, 384 U.S. 719 (1966), it determined that the criteria for deciding whether a new constitutional rule of criminal procedure would be retroactive were also applicable to convictions pending on direct review.

After several decades of debate over the propriety of the Johnson approach, and uncertainty over its application, the Court changed direction. In Griffith v. Kentucky, 107 S.Ct. 708 (1987), it decided that "failure to apply a newly declared constitutional rule to criminal cases pending on direct review violates basic norms of constitutional adjudication. * * * [A]fter we have decided a new rule in the case selected, the integrity of judicial review requires that we apply that rule to all similar cases pending on direct review" (p. 713). But the Court made clear that it would continue to adhere to a more flexible approach in civil cases (citing Chevron Oil Co. v. Huson, 404 U.S. 97, 106–07 (1971)). And it left open the question whether it would move toward the position, urged by Justice Harlan, that (with certain limited exceptions) a newly declared rule should not apply in collateral challenges to criminal convictions that had become final before the rule was announced. See Mackey v. United States, 401 U.S. 667, 675 (1971) (opinion of Harlan, J.).[10]

(9) For a comprehensive analysis of Marshall's opinion and a bibliography of major writings on the principles of the case, see Van Alstyne, *A Critical Guide to Marbury v. Madison,* 1969 Duke L.J. 1 (1969).

For a recent survey of the voluminous literature on the legitimacy of judicial review, see Gunther, Constitutional Law 13–21 (11th ed. 1985). See also Currie, note 2, *supra,* at 655–61; p. 8, *supra.*

---

10. For general discussion of the issues presented in these cases, compare Mishkin, *Foreword: The High Court, The Great Writ, and the Due Process of Time and Law,* 79 Harv.L.Rev. 56 (1965), with Schwartz, *Retroactivity, Reliability, and* *Due Process: A Response to Professor Mishkin,* 33 U.Chi.L.Rev. 719 (1966). See also Beytagh, *Ten Years of Non-retroactivity: A Critique and a Proposal,* 61 Va.L.Rev. 1557 (1975). Note, 71 Yale L.J. 907 (1962).

SECTION 2. PARTIES AND THE REQUIREMENT OF FINALITY

HAYBURN'S CASE

2 Dall. 409, 1 L.Ed. 436 (U.S.1792).
On Petition for Mandamus.

This was a motion for a *mandamus* to be directed to the *Circuit Court* for the district of *Pennsylvania*, commanding the said court to proceed in a certain petition of *Wm. Hayburn*, who had applied to be put on the pension list of the *United States*, as an invalid pensioner.

The principal case arose upon the act of Congress passed the 23d of *March*, 1792.

[The relevant sections of that Act, 1 Stat. 243, provided as follows:

[SEC. 2. *And be it further enacted,* That any commissioned officer, not having received the commutation of half pay, and any non-commissioned officer, soldier or seaman, disabled in the actual service of the United States, during the late war, by wounds or other known cause, who did not desert from the said service, shall be entitled to be placed on the pension list of the United States, during life or the continuance of such disability, and shall also be allowed such farther sum for the arrears of pension, from the time of such disability, not exceeding the rate of the annual allowance, in consequence of his disability, as the circuit court of the district, in which they respectively reside, may think just. *Provided,* That in every such case, the rules and regulations following shall be complied with; that is to say:—First. Every applicant shall attend the court in person, except where it shall be certified by two magistrates that he is unable to do so, and shall produce to the circuit court, the following proofs, to wit:—A certificate from the commanding officer of the ship, regiment, corps or company, in which he served, setting forth his disability, and that he was thus disabled while in the service of the United States; or the affidavits of two credible witnesses to the same effect.—The affidavits of three reputable freeholders of the city, town, or county, in which he resides, ascertaining of their own knowledge, the mode of life, employment, labour, or means of support of such applicant, for the last twelve months.—Secondly. The circuit court, upon receipt of the proofs aforesaid, shall forthwith proceed to examine into the nature of the wound, or other cause of disability of such applicant, and having ascertained the degree thereof, shall certify the same, and transmit the result of their inquiry, in case, in their opinion, the applicant should be put on the pension list, to the Secretary at War, together with their opinion in writing, what proportion of the monthly pay of such applicant will be equivalent to the degree of disability ascertained in manner aforesaid.

[SEC. 3. *And be it further enacted,* That the clerk of the district court, in each district, shall publish this act in such manner as the judge of the district court shall think effectual to give general information thereof to the people of the district, and shall give like information of the times and places of holding the circuit courts in such district. * * * And it shall be the duty of the judges of the circuit courts respectively, during the term of two years from the passing of this act, to remain at the places where the said courts shall be holden, five days at the least from the time of opening the sessions thereof, that persons disabled as aforesaid, may have full opportunity to make their application for the relief proposed by this act.

[SEC. 4. *And be it further enacted,* That the Secretary at War, upon receipt of the proofs, certificate and opinion aforesaid, shall cause the same to be duly filed in his office, and place the name of such applicant on the pension list of the United States, in conformity thereto: *Provided always,* That in any case, where the said Secretary shall have cause to suspect imposition or mistake, he shall have power to withhold the name of such applicant from the pension list, and make report of the same to Congress, at their next session.

[The temper in which this measure was passed is suggested by the following editorial in the National Gazette, April 12, 1792, quoted in 1 Warren, the Supreme Court in United States History 70n. (1926):

["Our poor, starving invalids have at length some provision made for them by Congress; and as the distresses of many of them are urgent in the extreme, it is to be hoped that not a moment's delay will be made by the public officers who are directed to settle their accounts * * * If through unavoidable delay any of those unfortunate men should starve before their pittance is paid, then it is to be hoped their widows and orphans will on the very first application receive it, that they may at least have something to purchase coffins for the deceased."]

The Attorney General (Randolph) who made the motion for the *mandamus,* having premised that it was done *ex officio,* without an application from any particular person, but with a view to procure the execution of an act of Congress, particularly interesting to a meritorious and unfortunate class of citizens, THE COURT declared that they entertained great doubt upon his right, under such circumstances, and in a case of this kind, to proceed *ex officio;* and directed him to state the principles on which he attempted to support the right. The Attorney General, accordingly, entered into an elaborate description of the powers and duties of his office:—

But the COURT being divided in opinion on that question, the motion, made *ex officio,* was not allowed.

The Attorney General then changed the ground of his interposition, declaring it to be at the instance, and on behalf of Hayburn, a party interested; and he entered into the merits of the case, upon the act of Congress, and the refusal of the Judges to carry it into effect.

The COURT observed, that they would hold the motion under advisement, until the next term; but no decision was ever pronounced, as the Legislature, at an intermediate session, provided, in another way, for the relief of the pensioners.

[The following was added by the reporter as a footnote to the above report:]

As the reasons assigned by the Judges, for declining to execute the first act of Congress, involve a great Constitutional question, it will not be thought improper to subjoin them, in illustration of Hayburn's case.

The Circuit Court for the district of New York (consisting of JAY, CHIEF JUSTICE, CUSHING, JUSTICE, and DUANE, DISTRICT JUDGE) * * * were * * * unanimously, of opinion and agreed.

"That by the Constitution of the United States, the government thereof is divided into *three* distinct and independent branches, and that it is the duty of each to abstain from, and to oppose, encroachments on either.

"That neither the *Legislative* nor the *Executive* branches, can constitutionally assign to the *Judicial* any duties, but such as are properly judicial, and to be performed in a judicial manner.

"That the duties assigned to the Circuit courts, by this act, are not of that description, and that the act itself does not appear to contemplate them as such; in as much as it subjects the decisions of these courts, made pursuant to those duties, first to the consideration and suspension of the Secretary at War, and then to the revision of the Legislature; whereas by the Constitution, neither the Secretary at War, nor any other Executive officer, nor even the Legislature, are authorized to sit as a court of errors on the judicial acts or opinions of this court.

"As, therefore, the business assigned to this court, by the act, is not judicial, nor directed to be performed judicially, the act can only be considered as appointing commissioners for the purposes mentioned in it, by *official* instead of *personal* descriptions.

"That the Judges of this court regard themselves as being the commissioners designated by the act, and therefore as being at liberty to accept or decline that office.

"That as the objects of this act are exceedingly benevolent, and do real honor to the humanity and justice of Congress; and as the Judges desire to manifest, on all proper occasions, and in every proper manner, their high respect for the National Legislature, they will execute this act in the capacity of commissioners. * * *" [1]

The Circuit court for the district of Pennsylvania, (consisting of WILSON, and BLAIR, JUSTICES, and PETERS, DISTRICT JUDGE) made the following representation, in a letter jointly addressed to the President of the United States, on the 18th of April, 1792.

"* * * It is a principle important to freedom, that in government, the *judicial* should be distinct from, and independent of, the legislative department. To this important principle the people of the United States, in forming their Constitution, have manifested the highest regard. * * *

"Upon due consideration, we have been unanimously of opinion, that, under this act, the Circuit court held for the Pennsylvania district could not proceed;

"1st. Because the business directed by this act is not of a judicial nature. It forms no part of the power vested by the Constitution in the courts of the United States; the Circuit court must, consequently, have proceeded *without* constitutional authority.

"2d. Because, if, upon that business, the court had proceeded, its *judgments* (for its *opinions* are its judgments) might, under the same act, have been revised and controuled by the legislature, and by an officer in

1. [Ed.] On the use of federal judges in other governmental roles, see generally *Note on Extra–Curricular Activities of Federal Judges* in the first edition of this book, at p. 102. See also the Code of Judicial Conduct approved by the American Bar Association, August 17, 1972; Canon 5(G) of the Code bars judges from accepting appointments to governmental commissions other than those concerned with the improvement of the law, the legal system, or the administration of justice.

the executive department. Such revision and controul we deemed radically inconsistent with the independence of that judicial power which is vested in the courts; and, consequently, with that important principle which is so strictly observed by the Constitution of the United States. * * *"

The Circuit court for the district of North Carolina, (consisting of IREDELL, JUSTICE, and SITGREAVES, DISTRICT JUDGE) made the following representation in a letter jointly addressed to the President of the United States, on the 8th of June, 1792. * * *

"1. That the Legislative, Executive, and Judicial departments, are each formed in a separate and independent manner; and that the ultimate basis of each is the Constitution only, within the limits of which each department can alone justify any act of authority.

"2. That the Legislature, among other important powers, unquestionably possess that of establishing courts in such a manner as to their wisdom shall appear best, limited by the terms of the constitution only; and to whatever extent that power may be exercised, or however severe the duty they may think proper to require, the Judges, when appointed in virtue of any such establishment, owe implicit and unreserved obedience to it.

"3. That at the same time such courts cannot be warranted, as we conceive, by virtue of that part of the Constitution delegating *Judicial power,* for the exercise of which any act of the legislature is provided, in exercising (even under the authority of another act) any power not in its nature *judicial,* or, if *judicial,* not provided for upon the terms the Constitution requires.

"4. That whatever doubt may be suggested, whether the power in question is properly of a judicial nature, yet inasmuch as the decision of the court is not made final, but may be at least suspended in its operation by the Secretary at War, if he shall have cause to suspect imposition or mistake; this subjects the decision of the court to a mode of revision which we consider to be unwarranted by the Constitution; for, though Congress may certainly establish, in instances not yet provided for, courts of appellate jurisdiction, yet such courts must consist of judges appointed in the manner the Constitution requires, and holding their offices by no other tenure than that of their good behaviour, by which tenure the office of Secretary at War is not held. And we beg leave to add, with all due deference, that no decision of any court of the United States can, under any circumstances, in our opinion, agreeable to the Constitution, be liable to a reversion [sic], or even suspension, by the Legislature itself, in whom no judicial power of any kind appears to be vested, but the important one relative to impeachments.

"These, sir, are our reasons for being of opinion, as we are at present, that this Circuit court cannot be justified in the execution of that part of the act, which requires it to examine and report an opinion on the unfortunate cases of officers and soldiers disabled in the service of the United States. The part of the act requiring the court to sit five days, for the purpose of receiving applications from such persons, we shall deem it our duty to comply with; for, whether in our opinion such purpose can or cannot be answered, it is, as we conceive, our indispensable duty to keep open any court of which we have the honor to be judges, as long as Congress shall direct."

[The judges then indicated that they were of the opinion that they could not regard the Act as appointing them commissioners for the purpose of its execution, since the Act appeared to confer power on the circuit courts and not on the judges personally. Acknowledging their doubts as to the propriety of giving an advisory opinion (no application under the Act had as yet been made to them), they concluded that the present situation called for an exception, "upon every principle of humanity and justice", but stated that they would "most attentively hear" argument on the points on which an opinion had been expressed in the event that an actual application were made.]

NOTE ON HAYBURN'S CASE AND THE PROBLEM OF PARTIES

(1) Jurisdiction in Hayburn's Case—that is, in the mandamus proceeding in the Supreme Court—was no doubt premised on the statute held unconstitutional in Marbury v. Madison. Did the Court overlook the problem of the constitutionality of that statute? Or is this case distinguishable? See Ex parte Peru and materials in Chap. III, Sec. 3.

(2) When the Attorney General reached in his pocket and pulled out Mr. Hayburn as a client, there were two perfectly good adverse parties in the Supreme Court. Who did the Attorney General think were the parties before then? Must a "case" or "controversy" always have at least two parties who are adverse to each other?

(3) Whom did the 1792 pension statute contemplate as parties to proceedings in the circuit courts? Was the lack of provision for any party defendant one of the reasons why the judges thought that the statute did not call for the exercise of "judicial power"? Is there any intrinsic difficulty in making a "case" out of an application by a private person for a grant by the government of money or other tangible property or of an intangible permission? See Tutun v. United States, below.

(4) If a party plaintiff was necessary, what was wrong with the United States? Is there any difficulty in the conception of the government as the party litigant? Generally? As a litigant whose interest is only in the enforcement of its own laws?

Why could not the Attorney General, proceeding *ex officio*, have been regarded as in substance representing the United States? Compare the traditional functions of the English Attorney General and many state attorneys general in relation to charities and in the enforcement of corporation laws. Was the difficulty here one simply of the Attorney General's authority? On what did that authority depend? [1]

---

1. In Marcus & Teir, *Hayburn's Case: A Misinterpretation of Precedent*, 1988 Wis.L.Rev. 4, the authors argue persuasively, on the basis of Justice Iredell's notes, that the three justices who were unwilling to let the Attorney General proceed were simply insisting on presidential authorization, while the other three were willing to let him proceed "completely on his own."

Cf. Massachusetts v. Feeney, 429 U.S. 66 (1976) (certifying to state supreme court the question of the authority of the state's Attorney General to maintain an appeal); Karcher v. May, 108 S.Ct. 388 (1987) (appellants, who intervened in lawsuit only in their official capacities as presiding officers of state legislature, may not pursue an appeal after they have left those offices).

In Pasadena City Bd. of Educ. v. Spangler, 427 U.S. 424 (1976), high school students and their parents brought an action seeking injunctive relief from allegedly unconstitutional racial segregation in the Pasadena school system. The United States intervened as a party plaintiff pursuant to 42 U.S.C. § 2000h–2, which provides that upon such intervention, "the United States shall be entitled to the same relief as if it had instituted the action." By the time the case (involving issues as to remedy) reached the Supreme Court, all the student plaintiffs had graduated. The Court held that the continued presence of the United States was authorized by the statute, and that the case was therefore not moot.

Did the United States necessarily have to take the same position as the original parties? Should that have made any difference? See pp. 197–99, *infra.* Should it have made any difference that the basis for relief was constitutional rather than statutory?

(5) Note that in Hayburn's case the original parties in the Supreme Court were the Attorney General and the Circuit Court for the District of Pennsylvania. Does the idea of a "case" entirely between the government and its own officials smack too much of the government litigating with itself? What if the adverse parties are both part of the same branch?

In United States v. Nixon, 418 U.S. 683 (1974), enforcement of a subpoena against the President was sought by the Watergate Special Prosecutor, appointed by the Attorney General and removable by him (under specified conditions). The Court said (pp. 692–97):

"In the District Court, the President's counsel argued that the court lacked jurisdiction to issue the subpoena because the matter was an intra-branch dispute between a subordinate and superior officer of the Executive Branch and hence not subject to judicial resolution. That argument has been renewed in this Court with emphasis on the contention that the dispute does not present a 'case' or 'controversy' which can be adjudicated in the federal courts. * * *

"The mere assertion of a claim of an 'intra-branch dispute,' without more, has never operated to defeat federal jurisdiction; justiciability does not depend on such a surface inquiry.[2] * * * Our starting point is the nature of the proceeding for which the evidence is sought—here pending criminal prosecution [against John Mitchell, the former Attorney General, and others for a number of offenses]. * * * Under the authority of Art. II, § 2, Congress has vested in the Attorney General the power to conduct the criminal litigation of the United States Government. 28 U.S.C. § 516. It has also vested in him the power to appoint subordinate officers to assist him in the discharge of his duties. 28 U.S.C. §§ 509, 510, 515, 533. Acting pursuant to those statutes, the Attorney General has delegated the authority to represent the United States in these particular matters to a Special Prosecutor with unique authority and tenure. * * * [The opinion here referred to the regulation promulgated by the Attorney General giving the Special Prosecutor independent powers and preventing his removal except for "extraordinary improprieties."]

2. The Court here cited, *inter alia,* United States v. ICC, 337 U.S. 426 (1949) (action by the U.S., as shipper, to set aside reparations order of ICC), and United States ex rel. Chapman v. FPC, 345 U.S. 153 (1953) (action by Secretary of Interior challenging authority of FPC to grant license). Both the FPC and the ICC are "independent agencies". Does this matter?

"So long as this regulation is extant it has the force of law. * * * [I]t is theoretically possible for the Attorney General to amend or revoke the regulation defining the Special Prosecutor's authority. But he has not done so. So long as this regulation remains in force the Executive Branch is bound by it, and indeed the United States as the sovereign composed of the three branches is bound to respect and to enforce it. * * *

"In light of the uniqueness of the setting in which the conflict arises, the fact that both parties are officers of the Executive Branch cannot be viewed as a barrier to justiciability. It would be inconsistent with the applicable law and regulation, and the unique facts of this case to conclude other than that the Special Prosecutor has standing to bring this action and that a justiciable controversy is presented for decision."

Whether or not the Court's stated ground was sufficient, wasn't the result correct on the issue of justiciability? So long as the Constitution permits the government to be structured so that some parts are not directly subordinate to others, can't a justiciable dispute exist between two factually independent units of government? [3]

NOTE ON HAYBURN'S CASE AND THE PROBLEM OF EXECUTIVE REVISION

(1) Why did the judges in the circuit courts think that the existence of an executive power of revision was fatal to the exercise of "judicial power"? Was it a matter simply of dignity and keeping face? Or would the recognition of the propriety of such a power have threatened in some fundamental way the integrity of the judicial process?

Note that the provision made perfectly good short-run practical sense. The judges were in a better position than the "Secretary at War" to appraise the personal good faith of claimants and the extent of their disability, which was the job they were given to do. But the Secretary was in a better position than the judges to check the official military records.

(2) Pursuant to the treaty of 1819 between the United States and Spain, Congress directed the judge of the territorial court, and later of the district court, in Florida to "receive, examine and adjudge" claims for losses suffered by certain Spanish citizens through operations of the American army in Florida. The judge was to report his decisions, if in favor of the claimants, together with the evidence upon which they were founded, to the Secretary of the Treasury, who, on being satisfied that the same were just and equitable, within the provisions of the treaty, was to pay the amount thereof. 3 Stat. 768, 6 *id.* 569, 9 *id.* 788. An appeal by the United States from an award by the district judge, acting under these provisions, was dismissed by the Supreme Court "for want of jurisdiction". The Court

---

3. For varying responses to these and other questions relating to the Nixon decision, see Freund, *Foreword: On Presidential Privilege,* 88 Harv.L.Rev. 13, 14–17 (1974); Kurland, *United States v. Nixon: Who Killed Cock Robin?,* 22 U.C.L.A.L.Rev. 68, 71–72 (1974); Mishkin, *Great Cases and Soft Law: A Comment on United States v. Nixon,* 22 U.C.L.A.L.Rev. 76, 81–83 (1974); Van Alstyne, *A Political and Constitution-* al *Review of United States v. Nixon,* 22 U.C.L.A.L.Rev. 116, 130–140 (1974); Bickel, *On Mr. Jaworski's Quarrel with Mr. Nixon,* N.Y. Times, May 23, 1974, at 41, col. 1; Bator, *Disputing Mr. St. Clair on the Jurisdictional Issue,* N.Y. Times, May 30, 1974, at 37, col. 1; Letter from A.M. Bickel to the Editor, N.Y. Times, June 3, 1974, at 30, col. 3.

said that the judge was not acting judicially, but as a commissioner. It noted but did not decide a question whether he could be appointed in that capacity by statute rather than by the President with the advice and consent of the Senate. United States v. Ferreira, 13 How. 40 (U.S.1852).

(3) In Chicago & Southern Air Lines v. Waterman S.S. Corp., 333 U.S. 103 (1948), the question for decision was whether an order of the Civil Aeronautics Board denying to one *citizen* air carrier and granting to another a certificate of convenience and necessity for an *overseas* and *foreign* air route was subject to judicial review. Section 801 of the Act provided that two kinds of orders concerning air routes must be submitted to the President before publication and were unconditionally subject to his approval. These were, first, orders granting or denying a certificate for any kind of route to a *foreign* air carrier, and, second, orders granting or denying a certificate for an overseas or foreign air route to a citizen carrier. The judicial review section of the Act provided that "any order, affirmative or negative, issued by the Board under this Act, except any order in respect of any *foreign* air carrier subject to the approval of the President as provided in section 801 of this Act, shall be subject to review by the circuit courts of appeals ＊ ＊ ＊."

The Court held that final orders approved by the President could not be reviewed because such orders "embody Presidential discretion as to political matters beyond the competence of the courts to adjudicate" (p. 114). The circuit court of appeals had avoided this difficulty by holding that after it had reviewed the final order the case should be resubmitted to the President so "that his power to disapprove would apply after as well as before the court acts". In rejecting this view, the Court said (pp. 113–14):

"＊ ＊ ＊ But if the President may completely disregard the judgment of the court, it would be only because it is one the courts were not authorized to render. Judgments within the powers vested in courts by the Judiciary Article of the Constitution may not lawfully be revised, overturned or refused faith and credit by another Department of Government.

"To revise or review an administrative decision which has only the force of a recommendation to the President would be to render an advisory opinion in its most obnoxious form—advice that the President has not asked, tendered at the demand of a private litigant, on a subject concededly within the President's exclusive, ultimate control. This Court early and wisely determined that it would not give advisory opinions even when asked by the Chief Executive. It has also been the firm and unvarying practice of Constitutional Courts to render no judgments not binding and conclusive on the parties and none that are subject to later review or alteration by administrative action."

Four justices, dissenting, thought that the order should be reviewed only after final action by the President, and that at that stage it would be feasible to separate those aspects of the order attributable to an exercise of Presidential discretion and review only those aspects relating to the validity of the Board's action.

Lower courts have held Waterman inapplicable "where the action of the Board ＊ ＊ ＊ is beyond the Board's power," on the theory that then, legally, the Board could have placed nothing before the President for action. American Airlines, Inc. v. CAB, 348 F.2d 349, 352 (D.C.Cir.1965); Pan American World Airways, Inc. v. CAB, 380 F.2d 770 (2d Cir.1967), aff'd by an equally divided Court, 391 U.S. 461 (1968). See also Pan American World Airways, Inc. v. CAB, 392 F.2d 483, 492–93 (D.C.Cir.1968).

Cf. McGrath v. Kristensen, 340 U.S. 162, 167–68 (1950).

(4) Was the power of Congress under the pension act to revise the decision of the judges open to the same objections as the power of the Secretary? Because the Act contemplated legislative review of the merits of cases? Suppose the Secretary had been directed to put all names certified by the courts on the pension roll, and Congress had simply retained power to refuse to pay any particular pension by virtue of its constitutional power over appropriations? See *Note on the Claims Against the United States and the Problem of Legislative Revision*, p. 102, *infra.*

(5) After the argument in Hayburn's Case, Congress repealed the second, third, and fourth sections of the 1792 act, declaring that they had been "found by experience inadequate to prevent the admission of improper claims to invalid pensions, and not to contain a sufficient facility for the allowance of such as may be well founded." Act of Feb. 28, 1793, 1 Stat. 324. The new act provided for the taking of certain described evidence, "upon oath or affirmation, before the judge of the district, in which such invalids reside, or before any three persons specially authorized by commission from the said judge." The district judge was then directed "to transmit a list of such claims, accompanied by the evidence herein directed, to the Secretary for the department of War, in order that the same may be compared with the muster-rolls, and other documents in his office; and the said Secretary shall make a statement of the cases of the said claimants to Congress, with such circumstances and remarks, as may be necessary, in order to enable them to take such order thereon, as they may judge proper."

Did the new act cure the constitutional infirmities of the old? [1]

---

1. The 1793 Act was evidently not a response to the view expressed by the judges in Hayburn's Case; rather, it was an effort to cut back on the judges' responsibilities because they had been too "sympathetic" in approving questionable applications. See Wheeler, *Extrajudicial Activities of the Early Supreme Court,* 1973 Sup.Ct.Rev. 123, 131–39.

A note by Chief Justice Taney, appended by direction of the Court to the report of United States v. Ferreira, 13 How. 40 (U.S.1851), describes the unreported case of United States v. Yale Todd, decided by the Supreme Court, Feb. 17, 1794. This was an "amicable action" by the United States to recover the amount of a pension paid under the 1792 act involved in Hayburn's Case. It was brought pursuant to a direction to the Attorney General in the repealing act of 1793 to take such measures as might be necessary to secure an adjudication from the Supreme Court "on the validity of such rights, claimed under the act aforesaid, by the determination of certain persons styling themselves commissioners"—a provision, said Taney, "manifestly occasioned by the difference of opinion upon that question which existed among the justices." Todd's pension had been paid on the certificate of Chief Justice Jay, Justice Cushing, and Judge Law. The Supreme Court, with Jay, Cushing, Wilson, Blair, and Patterson sitting, entered judgment for the United States, without opinion or notation of dissent.

TUTUN v. UNITED STATES

270 U.S. 568, 46 S.Ct. 425, 70 L.Ed. 738 (1926).
Certificate from the Circuit Court of Appeals for the First Circuit.

MR. JUSTICE BRANDEIS delivered the opinion of the Court.

These cases present, by certificate, the question whether the Circuit Courts of Appeals have jurisdiction to review a decree or order of a federal District Court denying the petition of an alien to be admitted to citizenship in the United States. * * *

The "jurisdiction to naturalize aliens as citizens of the United States" is conferred by Act of June 29, 1906, c. 3592, § 3, 34 Stat. 596 (Comp.St. § 4351) upon the District Courts, among others. Jurisdiction to review the "final decision in the District Courts * * * in all cases," except as otherwise provided, was conferred by Act of March 3, 1891, c. 517, § 6, 26 Stat. 826, 828, upon Circuit Courts of Appeals. * * * The substantial question is whether a petition for naturalization is a case within the meaning of the Circuit Court of Appeals Act.

The function of admitting to citizenship has been conferred exclusively upon courts continuously since the foundation of our government. See Act of March 26, 1790, c. 3, 1 Stat. 103. The federal District Courts, among others, have performed that function since the Act of January 29, 1795, c. 20, 1 Stat. 414. The constitutionality of this exercise of jurisdiction has never been questioned. If the proceeding were not a case or controversy within the meaning of article 3, § 2, this delegation of power upon the courts would have been invalid. Hayburn's Case, 2 Dall. 409; United States v. Ferreira, 13 How. 40; Muskrat v. United States, 219 U.S. 346. Whether a proceeding which results in a grant is a judicial one does not depend upon the nature of the thing granted, but upon the nature of the proceeding which Congress has provided for securing the grant. The United States may create rights in individuals against itself and provide only an administrative remedy. United States v. Babcock, 250 U.S. 328, 331. It may provide a legal remedy, but make resort to the courts available only after all administrative remedies have been exhausted. It may give to the individual the option of either an administrative or a legal remedy. Or it may provide only a legal remedy. Whenever the law provides a remedy enforceable in the courts according to the regular course of legal procedure, and that remedy is pursued, there arises a case within the meaning of the Constitution, whether the subject of the litigation be property or status. A petition for naturalization is clearly a proceeding of that character.

The petitioner's claim is one arising under the Constitution and laws of the United States. The claim is presented to the court in such a form that the judicial power is capable of acting upon it. The proceeding is instituted and is conducted throughout according to the regular course of judicial procedure. The United States is always a possible adverse party. * * * Section 9 (Comp.St. § 4368) provides that every final hearing must be held in open court, that upon such hearing the applicant and witnesses shall be examined under oath before the court and in its presence, and that every final order must be made under the hand of the court and shall be entered in full upon the record. The judgment entered, like other judgments of a court of record, is accepted as complete evidence of its own validity unless set aside. It may not be collaterally attacked. If a certificate is procured when the prescribed qualifications have no existence in fact, it may be canceled by suit. "It is in this respect," as stated in Johannessen v. United States, 225 U.S. 227, 238 "closely analogous to a public grant of land (Rev. Stat. § 2289 et seq. [Comp.St. § 4530]), or of the exclusive right to make, use and vend a new and useful invention (Rev.Stat. § 4883, et seq. [Comp. St. § 9427])."

The opportunity to become a citizen of the United States is said to be merely a privilege, and not a right. It is true that the Constitution does not confer upon aliens the right to naturalization. But it authorizes Congress to establish a uniform rule therefor. Article 1, § 8, cl. 4. The opportunity having been conferred by the Naturalization Act, there is a statutory right in the alien to submit his petition and evidence to a court, to have that tribunal pass upon them, and, if the requisite facts are established, to receive the certificate. See United States v. Shanahan (D.C.) 232 F. 169, 171. There is, of course, no "right to naturalization unless all statutory requirements are complied with." United States v. Ginsberg, 243 U.S. 472, 475; Luria v. United States, 231 U.S. 9, 22. The applicant for citizenship, like other suitors who institute proceedings in a court of justice to secure the determination of an asserted right, must allege in his petition the fulfillment of all conditions upon the existence of which the alleged right is made dependent, and he must establish these allegations by competent evidence to the satisfaction of the court. In re Bodek (C.C.) 63 F. 813, 814, 815; In re _____, 7 Hill (N.Y.) 137. In passing upon the application the court exercises judicial judgment. It does not confer or withhold a favor. * * *

Questions answered in the affirmative.

NOTE ON THE TUTUN CASE AND THE PROBLEM OF JUDICIAL REVISION

(1) Note the Court's statement that the district court's certificate could be cancelled on a subsequent judicial finding that "the prescribed qualifications have no existence in fact". Does the limited res judicata effect implied by the possibility of such re-examination raise any question concerning the consistency of the original naturalization proceeding with the judicial function?

(2) For many years the Court of Appeals of the District of Columbia had jurisdiction of appeals from certain decisions of the Patent Office denying patent applications and disposing of claims of interference, and also from similar decisions of the Commissioner of Patents in trade-mark proceedings.[1] The statute provided that the decision on appeal "shall govern the further proceedings in the case. But no opinion or decision of the court in any such case shall preclude any person interested from the right to contest the validity of such patent in any court wherein the same may be called in question." Rev.Stat. § 4914, 35 U.S.C. § 62 (1946).

---

1. From 1929 to 1982, this jurisdiction was vested in the Court of Customs and Patent Appeals. Act of March 2, 1929, 45 Stat. 1476. In 1982, that court was abol- ished and its jurisdiction transferred to the new Court of Appeals for the Federal Circuit. See p. 48, *supra*.

In Postum Cereal Co. v. California Fig Nut Co., 272 U.S. 693 (1927), the Court held that it was without jurisdiction under the Constitution to review a decision of the Court of Appeals of the District of Columbia in a trademark *inter partes* proceeding in which § 62 was applicable. (In the view that that court was not limited in its jurisdiction by Article III, no question was raised as to its power under the Constitution to hear such appeals.) Chief Justice Taft said (pp. 698–99):

" * * * The decision of the Court of Appeals * * * is not a judicial judgment. It is a mere administrative decision. It is merely an instruction to the Commissioner of Patents by a court which is made part of the machinery of the Patent Office for administrative purposes. In the exercise of such function, it does not enter a judgment binding parties in a case as the term case is used in the third article of the Constitution * * *. Neither the opinion nor decision of the Court of Appeals * * * precludes any person interested from having the right to contest the validity of such patent or trade-mark in any court where it may be called in question. This result prevents an appeal to this Court, which can only review judicial judgments."

The unsuccessful party in the Patent Office, after an unsuccessful appeal, could resort to a bill in equity in a federal district court, under 35 U.S.C. § 63 (1946), to compel the granting of his application.[2] The provisions of § 63 did not contain a provision like that of § 62 limiting the effect of the judgment. In Hoover Co. v. Coe, 325 U.S. 79 (1945), the Court entertained an appeal by an applicant for a patent whose claims had been finally dismissed by the Patent Office, and who had been unsuccessful in a suit to review this decision brought under § 63 in the district court for the District of Columbia. The court of appeals had held that the district court lacked jurisdiction. Without adverting to the Postum case, the Supreme Court reversed, holding that the final denial of claims for a patent was a reviewable decision.

In 1952 Title 35 of the United States Code was revised, and § 62 was essentially carried over into new § 144.[3] The provision of § 62 limiting the effect of the judgment was, however, omitted as "superfluous," the Reviser's Note pointing to the fact that, though § 63 had contained no equivalent provision, proceedings under that section had not precluded parties from subsequently raising questions of the patent's validity.

In Glidden Co. v. Zdanok, 370 U.S. 530, 576 (1962), Justice Harlan pointed to that earlier provision of § 62 as "evidently instrumental in prompting" the Postum decision and concluded that the decision did not apply to the authority of the Court of Customs and Patent Appeals under the statutory scheme in effect in 1962. (See note 1, *supra*.) He said:

"It may still be true that Congress has given to the equity proceeding a greater preclusive effect than that accorded to decisions of the Court of Customs and Patent Appeals. Even so, that circumstance alone is insufficient to make those decisions nonjudicial. Tutun v. United States, 270 U.S. 568, decided by the same Court as Postum and not there questioned, is controlling authority. * * *

2. By the Act of March 2, 1927, 44 Stat. 1335, the applicant was required to elect between the appeal to the court of appeals and the bill in equity, but the Supreme Court nonetheless adhered to the rule of the Postum case. See, *e.g.*, McBride v. Teeple, 311 U.S. 649 (1940).

3. Section 63 was incorporated in new § 145.

"Mr. Justice Brandeis, the author of the Tutun opinion, had also prepared the Court's opinion in United States v. Ness, 245 U.S. 319, which upheld the Government's right to seek denaturalization even upon grounds known to and asserted unsuccessfully by it in the naturalization court. Proceedings in that court, the opinion explained, were relatively summary, with no right of appeal, whereas the denaturalization suit was plenary enough to permit full presentation of all objections and was accompanied with appeal as of right. 245 U.S., at 326. These differences made it reasonable for Congress to allow the Government another chance to contest the applicant's eligibility.

"The decision in Tutun, coming after Ness, draws the patent and trademark jurisdiction now exercised by the Court of Customs and Patent Appeals fully within the category of cases or controversies. * * * Like naturalization proceedings in a District Court, appeals from Patent Office decisions under 35 U.S.C. § 144 are relatively summary—since the record is limited to the evidence allowed by that office—and are not themselves subject to direct review by appeal as of right. * * *

"We conclude that the Postum decision must be taken to be limited to the statutory scheme in existence before the transfer of patent and trademark litigation to that court" (pp. 577–79).

In Brenner v. Manson, 383 U.S. 519 (1966), the Court held that it could constitutionally review patent cases from the Court of Customs and Patent Appeals.

(3) In the Ness case (cited by Justice Harlan, *supra*), Justice Brandeis pointed out that some, relatively minor, issues resolved in the naturalization proceeding might be foreclosed from subsequent re-examination. The Court has since made clear that while the burden of proof in the original naturalization proceeding is on the applicant, *e.g.,* Berenyi v. District Director, 385 U.S. 630 (1967), in seeking denaturalization the government must establish its case by "clear, unequivocal, and convincing evidence", *e.g.,* Chaunt v. United States, 364 U.S. 350 (1960). The present statute also provides for denaturalization only on the grounds that the naturalization was "illegally procured" or "procured by concealment of a material fact or by willful misrepresentation." 8 U.S.C. § 1451(a).

Does the validity of the Tutun holding depend on these or similar restrictions on the scope of re-examination? On the "relatively summary" nature of the original proceedings? What is the problem in having a judgment subject to later judicial revision?

UNITED STATES v. JONES

119 U.S. 477, 7 S.Ct. 283, 30 L.Ed. 440 (1886).
Appeal from the Court of Claims.

Mr. Chief Justice Waite delivered the opinion of the Court.

The grounds of this motion [to dismiss the appeal] are:

1. That under the law as it now stands no appeal lies from a judgment of the Court of Claims to this court; * * *

The case of Gordon v. United States, 2 Wall. 561, holding that no appeal would lie from a judgment of the Court of Claims to this court, was announced March 10, 1865. The cause was originally submitted on the 18th of December, 1863, and on the 10th of April, 1864, it was ordered for argument on the second day of the next term. Chief Justice Taney died October 12, 1864, and the case was not reargued under the special order of the previous term until January 3, 1865. Consequently, the opinion published as an appendix to 117 U.S. 697 must have been prepared by him before the decision was actually made. The records of the court show that in announcing the judgment Chief Justice Chase said: "We think that the authority given to the head of an Executive Department by necessary implication in the 14th section of the amended Court of Claims Act, to revise all the decisions of that court requiring payment of money, denies to it the judicial power, from the exercise of which alone appeals can be taken to this court. The reasons which necessitate this conclusion may be more fully announced hereafter. At present, we restrict ourselves to this general statement, and to the direction that the cause be dismissed for want of jurisdiction." This differs somewhat from the case as reported by Mr. Wallace, and shows precisely the ground of the opinion, to wit, the special provisions of § 14. That section was as follows:

"Sec. 14. That no money shall be paid out of the Treasury for any claim passed on by the Court of Claims till after an appropriation therefor shall have been estimated for by the Secretary of the Treasury."

At the next session of Congress after this decision the objectionable section was repealed by the Act of March 17, 1866, c. 19, 14 Stat. 9, and the Court of Claims was directed to transmit, at the end of every term, a copy of its decisions to the heads of departments and certain other officers specially mentioned. From that time until the presentation of this motion it has never been doubted that appeals would lie. Indeed, immediately after the repealing act went into effect, and before the adjournment of the term then being held, a set of rules regulating such appeals was promulgated by this court, and it is safe to say that there has never been a term since in which many cases of the kind have not been heard and decided without objection from any one. * * *

Reference is also made to an Act of March 3, 1875, c. 149, 18 Stat. 481, which provides for "deducting any debt due the United States from any judgment recovered against the United States by such debtor;" but this gives the accounting officers of the government no authority to reexamine the judgment. It only provides a way of payment and satisfaction if the creditor shall, at the time of the presentation of his judgment, be a debtor of the United States for anything except what is included in the judgment, which is conclusive as to everything it embraces.

It is unnecessary to pursue this branch of the case further. We are entirely satisfied that, as the law now stands, appeals do lie to this court from the judgments of the Court of Claims in the exercise of its general jurisdiction. * * *

NOTE ON CLAIMS AGAINST THE UNITED STATES AND THE PROBLEM OF LEGISLATIVE REVISION

(1) Before 1855 no general statute gave the consent of the United States to suit on claims for money, and the only recourse of a claimant was

to petition Congress to redress his grievance by a private act. The burden on Congress of private bills, the delays and inequities of the private bill procedure, and the resulting impairment of government credit prompted the enactment of the Act of February 24, 1855, 10 Stat. 612, establishing the Court of Claims. But while the 1855 act authorized the court to "hear and determine" most types of money claims other than tort claims, and while the court made findings of fact and conclusions of law, its decision was to be embodied not in a judgment but in a report to Congress if the decision were adverse, or in a draft of a private bill if it were favorable. Since the Congressional committees were willing to re-examine claims *de novo* and to receive fresh evidence on either side, this procedure succeeded only in erecting an additional hurdle for proper claims to surmount.

The pressure of Civil War contracts led to the enactment of the Act of March 3, 1863, involved in the Gordon case, enlarging the court and authorizing it to render judgment.[1]

For the present jurisdiction of the United States Claims Court, which (along with the Court of Appeals for the Federal Circuit) has succeeded to the jurisdiction of the Court of Claims, see 28 U.S.C. §§ 1491–1507; pp. 1144–53, *infra*. The Claims Court is an Article I court, the new court of appeals an Article III court.

(2) Chief Justice Taney's draft opinion in the Gordon case, referred to in United States v. Jones, took a much wider ground than the actual decision as described in the Jones case. The opinion said that Congress, of course, could create the Court of Claims to help it pass upon claims against the United States, just as it could invoke the assistance of any executive or administrative officer. But, it said (117 U.S. at 702–03):

" * * * Congress cannot extend the appellate power of this Court beyond the limits prescribed by the Constitution, * * * nor can Congress authorize or require this Court to express an opinion on a case where its judicial power could not be exercised, and where its judgment would not be final and conclusive upon the rights of the parties, and process of execution awarded to carry it into effect.

"The award of execution is a part, and an essential part of every judgment passed by a court exercising judicial power. It is no judgment, in the legal sense of the term, without it. Without such an award the judgment would be inoperative and nugatory, leaving the aggrieved party without a remedy. * * *

"It is true the act speaks of the judgment or decree of this Court. But all that the Court is authorized to do is to certify its opinion to the Secretary of the Treasury, and if he inserts it in his estimates, and Congress sanctions it by an appropriation, it is then to be paid, but not otherwise. And when the Secretary asks for this appropriation, the propriety of the estimate for this claim, like all other estimates of the Secretary, will be opened to debate, and whether the appropriation will be made or not will depend upon the majority of each House. The real and ultimate judicial power will, therefore, be exercised by the Legislative Department, and not by that department to which the Constitution has confided it."

1. See generally Richardson, History, Jurisdiction and Practice of the Court of Claims (2d ed. 1885).

(3) The 1855, 1863, and 1866 acts all gave the Court of Claims certain advisory functions on reference from either house of Congress or from the head of an executive department. In Sanborn v. United States, 27 Ct.Cl. 485 (1892), Chief Justice Richardson, assuming his court to be one created under Article III, explained these functions as extra-judicial tasks voluntarily undertaken by the judges in the capacity of commissioners. The Supreme Court seems more often to have regarded these functions, as Chief Justice Taney did in the Gordon case, as those of a "legislative court" created under Article I and hence not subject to the restrictions of Article III. Action of the Court of Claims in the exercise of its advisory functions, of course, was not subject to review by the Supreme Court. In re Sanborn, 148 U.S. 222 (1893).

Note the assumption in United States v. Jones that review of a "judicial" decision by a "legislative court" (as the Court of Claims was then regarded) is an exercise of "appellate jurisdiction" within the meaning of Article III. The problem of legislative courts is dealt with further in Chap. IV, Sec. 1(b), *infra*.

In 1953, the Court of Claims was congressionally "declared to be a court established under article III," 28 U.S.C. § 171, and the departmental reference responsibility (28 U.S.C. § 1493) repealed. 67 Stat. 226. Following the Supreme Court's upholding of the general Article III characterization in Glidden Co. v. Zdanok, 370 U.S. 530 (1962), and its expression of doubt about the validity of the congressional reference advisory role, those functions were transferred from the Court of Claims itself to its chief commissioner. They are now vested in the chief judge of the United States Claims Court (which, as noted above, is an Article I court). See 28 U.S.C. § 1492.

(4) From 1956 to 1977, Congress provided that judgments of $100,000 or less were to be paid by the General Accounting Office; judgments in excess of that amount were to be certified by the Secretary of the Treasury to Congress for consideration. See Act of July 27, 1956, 70 Stat. 694.

The effect of that provision on the justiciability of money claims against the United States was considered by the Supreme Court on two occasions. In Glidden Co. v. Zdanok, 370 U.S. 530 (1962), the plurality opinion of Justice Harlan found such claims justiciable even when they exceeded $100,000. He referred to a study (46 Harv.L.Rev. 677, 685–86 n. 63 (1933)) that discovered only 15 instances in 70 years when Congress had refused to pay a judgment. "This historical record," he said, "surely more favorable to prevailing parties than that obtaining in private litigation, may well make us doubt whether the capacity to enforce a judgment is always indispensable for the exercise of judicial power" (p. 570). After discussing such earlier cases as La Abra Silver Mining Co. v. United States, 175 U.S. 423, 461–62 (1899), and South Dakota v. North Carolina, 192 U.S. 286, 318–21 (1904), he concluded: "If this Court may rely on the good faith of state governments or other public bodies to respond to its judgments, there seems to be no sound reason why the Court of Claims may not rely on the good faith of the United States" (p. 571).

The second occasion—the Regional Rail Reorganization cases (Blanchette v. Connecticut General Ins. Corp., 419 U.S. 102 (1974))—involved a challenge to the constitutionality of amendments to § 77 of the Bankruptcy Act enacted after eight northeastern railroads had filed for reorganization under that section. The amendments required creditors and shareholders of the railroad to exchange their interests for stock and debt in Conrail (a government-created but private, for-profit corporation) and also required the railroads to continue operating until the exchange occurred. The Court held that the Tucker Act remedy in the Court of Claims remained available to compensate for any deficiency in the value of the Conrail securities and for losses incurred by reason of the mandatory continued operation. Justice Brennan, for the Court, relied on the above-quoted language in Glidden to answer the contention that this remedy was inadequate. Justice Douglas's dissent, joined on this issue by Justice Stewart, argued that while Congress ordinarily pays judgments over $100,000 as a matter of routine, "this is an exceptional case, involving the possibility of judgments in the billions of dollars" (p. 180).

In 1977, Congress eliminated the dollar amount limitation in the statute and provided generally for payment by the Comptroller General of final judgments, awards, and compromise settlements against the United States. See 31 U.S.C. § 1304.

(5) So long as Congress makes lump sum appropriations, whether for judgments already entered or to be entered, particular judgments can be questioned only by means of an additional, separate legislative act. In the instances mentioned in the Harvard Note cited by Justice Harlan in Glidden, Paragraph (4), *supra*, such a special act was the means actually used. Could Congress, consistently with its constitutional assignment of responsibility for appropriations, properly surrender the power to enact such legislation?

Assuming that a particular judgment against the United States may be defeated by the adoption of later legislation forbidding its payment, what conclusion follows? May not other judgments similarly be deprived of practical effect by subsequent legislation? Consider, for example, the effect upon an injunction of a statute validating the prohibited conduct.[2]

Many cases have upheld statutes waiving the benefit of judgments in favor of a public right. *E.g.*, Pennsylvania v. Wheeling & Belmont Bridge Co., 18 How. 421 (U.S.1855) (statute declaring bridge not to be an obstruction to navigation, after Supreme Court had enjoined its maintenance); Hodges v. Snyder, 261 U.S. 600 (1923) (statute validating district bonds after a judgment of invalidity); Cherokee Nation v. United States, 270 U.S. 476 (1926) (statute waiving the benefit of a judgment in favor of the United States); Pope v. United States, 323 U.S. 1 (1944) (upholding a statute, which the Court of Claims had declared unconstitutional, directing that court to rehear a claim and give judgment according to a different principle of proof under which the calculation of the amount due would be largely mechanical); United States v. Sioux Nation of Indians, 448 U.S. 371 (1980) (upholding a statute providing for de novo review, by the Court of Claims, of Indian Claims against United States without regard to defenses of res judicata or

---

2. Compare Watson v. Mercer, 8 Pet. 88 (U.S.1834) (upholding power of state legislature to cure formal defects in deeds, thereby causing title to revest in one previously ousted in a state court action of ejectment); Paramino Lumber Co. v. Marshall, 309 U.S. 370 (1940) (upholding act of Congress directing review of a final adminis- trative award of disability and the issuance of a new award taking account of subsequently discovered complications; 149 Madison Ave. Corp. v. Asselta, 331 U.S. 795 (1947) (modifying earlier judgment to give district court authority "to consider any matters presented to it under the Portal-to-Portal Act of 1947").

collateral estoppel based on a prior Court of Claims proceeding; Justice Rehnquist, dissenting, argued that "Congress may not constitutionally require the Court of Claims to reopen this proceeding" (p. 424)).[3]

(6) The validity of congressional action questioning judgments of the Court of Claims against the United States has come into issue in only a few cases.

District of Columbia v. Eslin, 183 U.S. 62 (1901). Pending an appeal from the Court of Claims to the Supreme Court, Congress repealed the act under which the proceeding had been brought and directed that "no judgment heretofore rendered in pursuance of said act shall be paid". The Supreme Court dismissed the appeal, relying upon Chief Justice Taney's language in the Gordon case. The formal disposition of the case was as follows:

"As no judgment now rendered by this court would have the sanction that attends the exercise of judicial power, in its legal or constitutional sense, the present appeal must be dismissed for want of jurisdiction and without any determination of the rights of the parties."

Pocono Pines Assembly Hotels Co. v. United States, 73 Ct.Cl. 447 (1932), petition for writ of mandamus or prohibition denied, 285 U.S. 526 (1932). The Court of Claims having rendered judgment against the United States for $227,239.53, Congress, on a suggestion from the Comptroller General that the government had failed to present certain substantive defenses, passed a special act which "remanded" the case to the Court of Claims "with complete authority, the statute of limitations or rule of procedure to the contrary notwithstanding, to hear testimony as to the actual facts involved in the litigation and with instructions to report its finding of facts to Congress at the earliest practicable moment." The Court of Claims rejected an argument that the statute was unconstitutional. It construed the act as leaving the prior judgment unimpaired and as constituting simply a reference to the court in its advisory capacity to secure information to guide Congress in determining whether the judgment should be paid. The Supreme Court denied without opinion a petition for a writ to prevent the Court of Claims from proceeding under the statute. See the discussion of the case in Note, 46 Harv.L.Rev. 677 (1933).

See also United States v. Klein, 13 Wall. 128 (U.S.1872), pp. 368–69, *infra.*

----

3. The Court in the Sioux Nation case also held that the statute did not constitute an impermissible attempt to prescribe the outcome of a judicial decision, distinguishing United States v. Klein, 13 Wall. 128 (U.S.1871). See p. 369, *infra.*

SECTION 3. SOME PROBLEMS OF STANDING TO SUE

SUBSECTION A: PLAINTIFFS' STANDING

ALLEN v. WRIGHT

468 U.S. 737, 104 S.Ct. 3315, 82 L.Ed.2d 556 (1984).
Certiorari to the United States Court of Appeals for the
District of Columbia Circuit.

JUSTICE O'CONNOR delivered the opinion of the Court.

Parents of black public school children allege in this nation-wide class action that the Internal Revenue Service (IRS) has not adopted sufficient standards and procedures to fulfill its obligation to deny tax-exempt status to racially discriminatory private schools. They assert that the IRS thereby harms them directly and interferes with the ability of their children to receive an education in desegregated public schools. The issue before us is whether plaintiffs have standing to bring this suit. We hold that they do not.

I

The IRS denies tax-exempt status under §§ 501(a) and (c)(3) of the Internal Revenue Code, 26 U.S.C. §§ 501(a) and (c)(3)—and hence eligibility to receive charitable contributions deductible from income taxes under §§ 170(a)(1) and (c)(2) of the Code, 26 U.S.C. §§ 170(a)(1) and (c)(2)—to racially discriminatory private schools.[1] The IRS policy requires that a school applying for tax-exempt status show that it "admits the students of any race to all the rights, privileges, programs, and activities generally accorded or made available to students at that school and that the school does not discriminate on the basis of race in administration of its educational policies, admissions policies, scholarship and loan programs, and athletic and other school-administered programs." To carry out this policy, the IRS has established guidelines and procedures for determining whether a particular school is in fact racially nondiscriminatory. Failure to comply with the guidelines "will ordinarily result in the proposed revocation of" tax-exempt status.

The guidelines provide that "[a] school must show affirmatively both that it has adopted a racially nondiscriminatory policy as to students that is made known to the general public and that since the adoption of that policy it has operated in a bona fide manner in accordance therewith." The school must state its nondiscrimination policy in its organizational charter, and in all of its brochures, catalogs, and other advertisements to

---

1. As the Court explained last Term in Bob Jones University v. United States, 461 U.S. 574, 579 (1983), the IRS announced this policy in 1970 and formally adopted it in 1971. This change in prior policy was prompted by litigation over tax exemptions for racially discriminatory private schools in the State of Mississippi, litigation that resulted in the entry of an injunction against the IRS largely if not entirely coextensive with the position the IRS had voluntarily adopted. * * *

prospective students. The school must make its nondiscrimination policy known to the entire community served by the school and must publicly disavow any contrary representations made on its behalf once it becomes aware of them. * * * [T]he school must annually certify, under penalty of perjury, compliance with these requirements. * * *

* * *

In 1976 respondents challenged these guidelines and procedures in a suit filed in Federal District Court against the Secretary of the Treasury and the Commissioner of Internal Revenue. The plaintiffs named in the complaint are parents of black children who, at the time the complaint was filed, were attending public schools in seven States in school districts undergoing desegregation. They brought this nation-wide class action "on behalf of themselves and their children, and * * * on behalf of all other parents of black children attending public school systems undergoing, or which may in the future undergo, desegregation pursuant to court order [or] HEW regulations and guidelines, under state law, or voluntarily." They estimated that the class they seek to represent includes several million persons.

Respondents allege in their complaint that many racially segregated private schools were created or expanded in their communities at the time the public schools were undergoing desegregation. According to the complaint, many such private schools, including 17 schools or school systems identified by name in the complaint (perhaps some 30 schools in all), receive tax exemptions either directly or through the tax-exempt status of "umbrella" organizations that operate or support the schools. Respondents allege that, despite the IRS policy of denying tax-exempt status to racially discriminatory private schools and despite the IRS guidelines and procedures for implementing that policy, some of the tax-exempt racially segregated private schools created or expanded in desegregating districts in fact have racially discriminatory policies. [App.] 17–18 (IRS permits "schools to receive tax exemptions merely on the basis of adopting and certifying—but not implementing—a policy of nondiscrimination"); *id.,* at 25 (same).[11] Respondents allege that the IRS grant of tax exemptions to such racially discriminatory schools is unlawful.[12]

Respondents allege that the challenged Government conduct harms them in two ways. The challenged conduct

"(a) constitutes tangible federal financial aid and other support for racially segregated educational institutions, and

"(b) fosters and encourages the organization, operation and expansion of institutions providing racially segregated educational opportunities for white children avoiding attendance in desegregating public school districts and thereby interferes with the efforts of federal courts,

---

11. * * *

Contrary to Justice Brennan's statement, the complaint does not allege that each desegregating district in which they reside contains one or more racially discriminatory private schools unlawfully receiving a tax exemption.

12. The complaint alleges that the challenged IRS conduct violates several laws: § 501(c)(3) of the Internal Revenue Code, 26 U.S.C. § 501(c)(3); Title VI of the Civil Rights Act of 1964, 78 Stat. 252, as amended, 42 U.S.C. § 2000d *et seq.;* Rev. Stat. § 1977, 42 U.S.C. § 1981; and the Fifth and Fourteenth Amendments to the United States Constitution.

Last Term, in Bob Jones University v. United States, 461 U.S. 574 (1983), the Court concluded that racially discriminatory private schools do not qualify for a tax exemption under § 501(c)(3) of the Internal Revenue Code.

HEW and local school authorities to desegregate public school districts which have been operating racially dual school systems." *Id.,* at 38–39.

Thus, respondents do not allege that their children have been the victims of discriminatory exclusion from the schools whose tax exemptions they challenge as unlawful. Indeed, they have not alleged at any stage of this litigation that their children have ever applied or would ever apply to any private school. Rather, respondents claim a direct injury from the mere fact of the challenged Government conduct and, as indicated by the restriction of the plaintiff class to parents of children in desegregating school districts, injury to their children's opportunity to receive a desegregated education. The latter injury is traceable to the IRS grant of tax exemptions to racially discriminatory schools, respondents allege, chiefly because contributions to such schools are deductible from income taxes * * * and the "deductions facilitate the raising of funds to organize new schools and expand existing schools in order to accommodate white students avoiding attendance in desegregating public school districts."

Respondents * * * ask for a declaratory judgment that the challenged IRS tax-exemption practices are unlawful. They also ask for an injunction requiring the IRS to deny tax exemptions to a considerably broader class of private schools than the class of racially discriminatory private schools. * * * Finally, respondents ask for an order directing the IRS to replace its 1975 guidelines with standards consistent with the requested injunction.

* * * [P]rogress in the lawsuit was stalled for several years. During this period, the IRS reviewed its challenged policies and proposed new Revenue Procedures to tighten requirements for eligibility for tax-exempt status for private schools. In 1979, however, Congress blocked any strengthening of the IRS guidelines at least until October 1980.[16] The District Court thereupon considered and granted the defendants' motion to dismiss the complaint, concluding that respondents lack standing, that the judicial task proposed by respondents is inappropriately intrusive for a federal court, and that awarding the requested relief would be contrary to the will of Congress expressed in the 1979 ban on strengthening IRS guidelines. Wright v. Miller, 480 F.Supp. 790 (DC 1979).

The United States Court of Appeals for the District of Columbia Circuit reversed, concluding that respondents have standing to maintain this lawsuit. 656 F.2d 820 (D.C.Cir.1981). * * * The Court of Appeals also held that the 1979 congressional actions were not intended to preclude judicial remedies and that the relief requested by respondents could be fashioned "without large scale judicial intervention in the administrative process." The court accordingly remanded the case to the District Court

16. [Provisions in appropriations acts] specifically forbade the use of funds to carry out the IRS's proposed Revenue Procedures * * * [and] more generally forbade the use of funds to make the requirements for tax-exempt status of private schools more stringent than those in effect prior to the IRS's proposal of its new Revenue Procedures.

These provisions expired on October 1, 1980, but * * * were reinstated for the period December 16, 1980, through September 30, 1981. For fiscal year 1982, Congress specifically denied funding for carrying out not only administrative actions but also court orders entered after the date of the IRS's proposal of its first revised Revenue Procedure. No such spending restrictions are currently in force.

for further proceedings, enjoining the defendants meanwhile from granting tax-exempt status to any racially discriminatory school.

* * *

We granted certiorari, and now reverse.

II

A

Article III of the Constitution confines the federal courts to adjudicating actual "cases" and "controversies." As the Court explained in Valley Forge Christian College v. Americans United for Separation of Church and State, Inc., 454 U.S. 464, 471–476 (1982), the "case or controversy" requirement defines with respect to the Judicial Branch the idea of separation of powers on which the Federal Government is founded. The several doctrines that have grown up to elaborate that requirement are "founded in concern about the proper—and properly limited—role of the courts in a democratic society." Warth v. Seldin, 422 U.S. 490, 498 (1975).

> "All of the doctrines that cluster about Article III—not only standing but mootness, ripeness, political question, and the like—relate in part, and in different though overlapping ways, to an idea, which is more than an intuition but less than a rigorous and explicit theory, about the constitutional and prudential limits to the powers of an unelected, unrepresentative judiciary in our kind of government." Vander Jagt v. O'Neill, 699 F.2d 1166, 1178–1179 (1983) (Bork, J., concurring).

The case-or-controversy doctrines state fundamental limits on federal judicial power in our system of government.

The Art. III doctrine that requires a litigant to have "standing" to invoke the power of a federal court is perhaps the most important of these doctrines. "In essence the question of standing is whether the litigant is entitled to have the court decide the merits of the dispute or of particular issues." Warth v. Seldin, supra, at 498. Standing doctrine embraces several judicially self-imposed limits on the exercise of federal jurisdiction, such as the general prohibition on a litigant's raising another person's legal rights, the rule barring adjudication of generalized grievances more appropriately addressed in the representative branches, and the requirement that a plaintiff's complaint fall within the zone of interests protected by the law invoked. The requirement of standing, however, has a core component derived directly from the Constitution. A plaintiff must allege personal injury fairly traceable to the defendant's allegedly unlawful conduct and likely to be redressed by the requested relief.

Like the prudential component, the constitutional component of standing doctrine incorporates concepts concededly not susceptible of precise definition. The injury alleged must be, for example, " 'distinct and palpable,' " Gladstone, Realtors v. Village of Bellwood, 441 U.S. 91, 100 (1979) (quoting Warth v. Seldin, supra, at 501), and not "abstract" or "conjectural" or "hypothetical," Los Angeles v. Lyons, 461 U.S. 95, 101–102 (1983); O'Shea v. Littleton, 414 U.S. 488, 494 (1974). The injury must be "fairly" traceable to the challenged action, and relief from the injury must be "likely" to follow from a favorable decision. See Simon v. Eastern Kentucky Welfare Rights Org., 426 U.S. [26,] 38, 41 [(1976)]. These terms cannot be defined so as to make application of the constitutional standing requirement a mechanical exercise.

The absence of precise definitions, however, * * * hardly leaves courts at sea in applying the law of standing. Like most legal notions, the standing concepts have gained considerable definition from developing case law. * * * More important, the law of Art. III standing is built on a single basic idea—the idea of separation of powers. It is this fact which makes possible the gradual clarification of the law through judicial application. * * *

Determining standing in a particular case may be facilitated by clarifying principles or even clear rules developed in prior cases. Typically, however, the standing inquiry requires careful judicial examination of a complaint's allegations to ascertain whether the particular plaintiff is entitled to an adjudication of the particular claims asserted. Is the injury too abstract, or otherwise not appropriate, to be considered judicially cognizable? Is the line of causation between the illegal conduct and injury too attenuated? Is the prospect of obtaining relief from the injury as a result of a favorable ruling too speculative? These questions and any others relevant to the standing inquiry must be answered by reference to the Art. III notion that federal courts may exercise power only "in the last resort, and as a necessity," Chicago & Grand Trunk R. Co. v. Wellman, 143 U.S. 339, 345 (1892), and only when adjudication is "consistent with a system of separated powers and [the dispute is one] traditionally thought to be capable of resolution through the judicial process," Flast v. Cohen, 392 U.S. 83, 97 (1968).

B

Respondents allege two injuries in their complaint to support their standing to bring this lawsuit. First, they say that they are harmed directly by the mere fact of Government financial aid to discriminatory private schools. Second, they say that the federal tax exemptions to racially discriminatory private schools in their communities impair their ability to have their public schools desegregated.

* * *

* * * We conclude that neither suffices to support respondents' standing. The first fails under clear precedents of this Court because it does not constitute judicially cognizable injury. The second fails because the alleged injury is not fairly traceable to the assertedly unlawful conduct of the IRS.[19]

19. The "fairly traceable" and "redressability" components of the constitutional standing inquiry were initially articulated by this Court as "two facets of a single causation requirement." C. Wright, Law of Federal Courts § 13, p. 68, n. 43 (4th ed. 1983). To the extent there is a difference, it is that the former examines the causal connection between the assertedly unlawful conduct and the alleged injury, whereas the latter examines the causal connection between the alleged injury and the judicial relief requested. Cases such as this, in which the relief requested goes well beyond the violation of law alleged, illustrate why it is important to keep the inquiries separate if the "redressability" component is to focus on the requested relief. Even if the relief respondents request might have a substantial effect on the desegregation of public schools, whatever deficiencies exist in the opportunities for desegregated education for respondents' children might not be traceable to IRS violations of law—grants of tax exemptions to racially discriminatory schools in respondents' communities.

1

Respondents' first claim of injury can be interpreted in two ways. It might be a claim simply to have the Government avoid the violation of law alleged in respondents' complaint. Alternatively, it might be a claim of stigmatic injury, or denigration, suffered by all members of a racial group when the Government discriminates on the basis of race. Under neither interpretation is this claim of injury judicially cognizable.

This Court has repeatedly held that an asserted right to have the Government act in accordance with law is not sufficient, standing alone, to confer jurisdiction on a federal court. In Schlesinger v. Reservists Committee to Stop the War, 418 U.S. 208 (1974), for example, the Court rejected a claim of citizen standing to challenge Armed Forces Reserve commissions held by Members of Congress as violating the Incompatibility Clause of Art. I, § 6, of the Constitution. As citizens, the Court held, plaintiffs alleged nothing but "the abstract injury in nonobservance of the Constitution. . . ." More recently, in Valley Forge, *supra,* we rejected a claim of standing to challenge a Government conveyance of property to a religious institution. Insofar as the plaintiffs relied simply on " 'their shared individuated right' " to a Government that made no law respecting an establishment of religion, we held that plaintiffs had not alleged a judicially cognizable injury. * * *

Neither do they have standing to litigate their claims based on the stigmatizing injury often caused by racial discrimination. There can be no doubt that this sort of noneconomic injury is one of the most serious consequences of discriminatory government action and is sufficient in some circumstances to support standing. Our cases make clear, however, that such injury accords a basis for standing only to "those persons who are personally denied equal treatment" by the challenged discriminatory conduct.

* * *

If [an] abstract stigmatic injury were cognizable, standing would extend nationwide to all members of the particular racial groups against which the Government was alleged to be discriminating by its grant of a tax exemption to a racially discriminatory school, regardless of the location of that school. * * * A black person in Hawaii could challenge the grant of a tax exemption to a racially discriminatory school in Maine. Recognition of standing in such circumstances would transform the federal courts into "no more than a vehicle for the vindication of the value interests of concerned bystanders." United States v. SCRAP, 412 U.S. 669, 687 (1973). Constitutional limits on the role of the federal courts preclude such a transformation.

2

It is in their complaint's second claim of injury that respondents allege harm to a concrete, personal interest that can support standing in some circumstances. The injury they identify—their children's diminished ability to receive an education in a racially integrated school—is, beyond any doubt, not only judicially cognizable but, as shown by cases from Brown v.

Board of Education, 347 U.S. 483 (1954), to Bob Jones University v. United States, 461 U.S. 574 (1983), one of the most serious injuries recognized in our legal system. Despite the constitutional importance of curing the injury alleged by respondents, however, the federal judiciary may not redress it unless standing requirements are met. In this case, respondents' second claim of injury cannot support standing because the injury alleged is not fairly traceable to the Government conduct respondents challenge as unlawful.[22]

The illegal conduct challenged by respondents is the IRS's grant of tax exemptions to some racially discriminatory schools. The line of causation between that conduct and desegregation of respondents' schools is attenuated at best. From the perspective of the IRS, the injury to respondents is highly indirect and "results from the independent action of some third party not before the court." Simon v. Eastern Kentucky Welfare Rights Org., 426 U.S., at 42. * * *

The diminished ability of respondents' children to receive a desegregated education would be fairly traceable to unlawful IRS grants of tax exemptions only if there were enough racially discriminatory private schools receiving tax exemptions in respondents' communities for withdrawal of those exemptions to make an appreciable difference in public school integration. Respondents have made no such allegation. It is, first, uncertain how many racially discriminatory private schools are in fact receiving tax exemptions. Moreover, it is entirely speculative, as respondents themselves conceded in the Court of Appeals, whether withdrawal of a tax exemption from any particular school would lead the school to change its policies. It is just as speculative whether any given parent of a child attending such a private school would decide to transfer the child to public school as a result of any changes in educational or financial policy made by the private school once it was threatened with loss of tax-exempt status. It is also pure speculation whether, in a particular community, a large enough number of the numerous relevant school officials and parents would reach decisions that collectively would have a significant impact on the racial composition of the public schools.

---

22. Respondents' stigmatic injury, though not sufficient for standing in the abstract form in which their complaint asserts it, is judicially cognizable to the extent that respondents are personally subject to discriminatory treatment. See Heckler v. Mathews, 465 U.S. 728, 739–740 (1984). The stigmatic injury thus requires identification of some concrete interest with respect to which respondents are personally subject to discriminatory treatment. That interest must independently satisfy the causation requirement of standing doctrine.

In Heckler v. Mathews, for example, the named plaintiff (appellee) was being denied monetary benefits allegedly on a discriminatory basis. We specifically pointed out that the causation component of standing doctrine was satisfied with respect to the claimed benefits. In distinguishing the case from Simon v. Eastern Kentucky Welfare Rights Org., 426 U.S. 26 (1976), we said: "there can be no doubt about the direct causal relationship between the Government's alleged deprivation of appellee's right to equal protection and the personal injury appellee has suffered—denial of Social Security benefits solely on the basis of his gender." 465 U.S., at 741, n. 9.

In this litigation, respondents identify only one interest that they allege is being discriminatorily impaired—their interest in desegregated public school education. Respondents' asserted stigmatic injury, therefore, is sufficient to support their standing in this litigation only if their school-desegregation injury independently meets the causation requirement of standing doctrine.

The links in the chain of causation between the challenged Government conduct and the asserted injury are far too weak for the chain as a whole to sustain respondents' standing. In Simon v. Eastern Kentucky Welfare Rights Org., *supra*, the Court held that standing to challenge a Government grant of a tax exemption to hospitals could not be founded on the asserted connection between the grant of tax-exempt status and the hospitals' policy concerning the provision of medical services to indigents. The causal connection depended on the decisions hospitals would make in response to withdrawal of tax-exempt status, and those decisions were sufficiently uncertain to break the chain of causation between the plaintiffs' injury and the challenged Government action. The chain of causation is even weaker in this case. It involves numerous third parties (officials of racially discriminatory schools receiving tax exemptions and the parents of children attending such schools) who may not even exist in respondents' communities and whose independent decisions may not collectively have a significant effect on the ability of public school students to receive a desegregated education.

The idea of separation of powers that underlies standing doctrine explains why our cases preclude the conclusion that respondents' alleged injury "fairly can be traced to the challenged action" of the IRS. That conclusion would pave the way generally for suits challenging, not specifically identifiable Government violations of law, but the particular programs agencies establish to carry out their legal obligations. Such suits, even when premised on allegations of several instances of violations of law, are rarely if ever appropriate for federal-court adjudication. * * *

The same concern for the proper role of the federal courts is reflected in cases like O'Shea v. Littleton, 414 U.S. 488 (1974), Rizzo v. Goode, 423 U.S. 362 (1976), and Los Angeles v. Lyons, 461 U.S. 95 (1983). In all three cases plaintiffs sought injunctive relief directed at certain systemwide law enforcement practices. The Court held in each case that, absent an allegation of a specific threat of being subject to the challenged practices, plaintiffs had no standing to ask for an injunction. Animating this Court's holdings was the principle that "[a] federal court * * * is not the proper forum to press" general complaints about the way in which government goes about its business.

Case-or-controversy considerations, the Court observed in O'Shea v. Littleton, *supra*, at 499, "obviously shade into those determining whether the complaint states a sound basis for equitable relief." The latter set of considerations should therefore inform our judgment about whether respondents have standing. Most relevant to this case is the principle articulated in Rizzo v. Goode, *supra*, at 378–379:

> "When a plaintiff seeks to enjoin the activity of a government agency, even within a unitary court system, his case must contend with 'the well-established rule that the Government has traditionally been granted the widest latitude in the "dispatch of its own internal affairs." '"

When transported into the Art. III context, that principle, grounded as it is in the idea of separation of powers, counsels against recognizing standing in a case brought, not to enforce specific legal obligations whose violation works a direct harm, but to seek a restructuring of the apparatus established by the Executive Branch to fulfill its legal duties. The Constitution, after all, assigns to the Executive Branch, and not to the Judicial Branch, the duty to "take Care that the Laws be faithfully executed." U. S. Const., Art. II, § 3. We could not recognize respondents' standing in this case without running afoul of that structural principle.[26]

C

The Court of Appeals relied for its contrary conclusion on Gilmore v. City of Montgomery, 417 U.S. 556 (1974), [and] Norwood v. Harrison, 413 U.S. 455 (1973) * * *. * * * [No case], however, requires that we find standing in this lawsuit.

In Gilmore v. City of Montgomery, *supra*, the plaintiffs * * * alleged that the city was violating [their] equal protection right by permitting racially discriminatory private schools and other groups to use the public parks. The Court recognized plaintiffs' standing to challenge this city policy insofar as the policy permitted the exclusive use of the parks by racially discriminatory private schools * * *.

Standing in Gilmore thus rested on an allegation of direct deprivation of a right to equal use of the parks. * * *

In Norwood v. Harrison, *supra*, parents of public school children in Tunica County, Miss., filed a statewide class action challenging the State's provision of textbooks to students attending racially discriminatory private schools in the State. The Court held the State's practice unconstitutional because it breached "the State's acknowledged duty to establish a unitary school system." The Court did not expressly address the basis for the plaintiffs' standing.

In Gilmore, however, the Court identified the basis for standing in Norwood: "The plaintiffs in Norwood were parties to a school desegregation order and the relief they sought was directly related to the concrete injury they suffered." 417 U.S., at 571, n.10. Through the school-desegregation decree, the plaintiffs had acquired a right to have the State "steer clear" of any perpetuation of the racially dual school system that it had once sponsored. 413 U.S., at 467. The interest acquired was judicially cognizable because it was a personal interest, created by law, in having the State refrain from taking specific actions. * * *

* * *

III

"The necessity that the plaintiff who seeks to invoke judicial power stand to profit in some personal interest remains an Art. III requirement." Simon v. Eastern Kentucky Welfare Rights Org., 426 U.S., at 39. Respondents have not met this fundamental requirement. The judgment of the Court of Appeals is accordingly reversed, and the injunction issued by that court is vacated.

26. We disagree with Justice Stevens' suggestions that separation of powers principles merely underlie standing requirements, have no role to play in giving meaning to those requirements, and should be considered only under a distinct justiciability analysis. Moreover, our analysis of this case does not rest on the more general proposition that no consequence of the allocation of administrative enforcement resources is judicially cognizable. Rather, we rely on separation of powers principles to interpret the "fairly traceable" component of the standing requirement.

It is so ordered.

JUSTICE MARSHALL took no part in the decision of these cases.

JUSTICE BRENNAN, dissenting.

* * *

II

* * *

A

In these cases, the respondents have alleged at least one type of injury that satisfies the constitutional requirement of "distinct and palpable injury." [3] In particular, they claim that the IRS's grant of tax-exempt status to racially discriminatory private schools directly injures their children's opportunity and ability to receive a desegregated education.

* * *

The Court acknowledges that this alleged injury is sufficient to satisfy constitutional standards. It does so only grudgingly, however, without emphasizing the significance of the harm alleged. Nonetheless, we have consistently recognized throughout the last 30 years that the deprivation of a child's right to receive an education in a desegregated school is a harm of special significance; surely, it satisfies any constitutional requirement of injury in fact. * * *

* * *

B

* * *

Viewed in light of the injuries they claim, the respondents have alleged a direct causal relationship between the Government action they challenge and the injury they suffer: their inability to receive an education in a racially integrated school is directly and adversely affected by the tax-exempt status granted by the IRS to racially discriminatory schools in their respective school districts. Common sense alone would recognize that the elimination of tax-exempt status for racially discriminatory private schools would serve to lessen the impact that those institutions have in defeating efforts to desegregate the public schools.

The Court admits that "[t]he diminished ability of respondents' children to receive a desegregated education would be fairly traceable to unlawful IRS grants of tax exemptions . . . if there were enough racially discriminatory private schools receiving tax exemptions in respondents'

---

3. Because I conclude that the second injury alleged by the respondents is sufficient to satisfy constitutional requirements, I do not need to reach what the Court labels the "stigmatic injury." I note, however, that the Court has mischaracterized this claim of injury * * *. In particular, the respondents have not simply alleged that, as blacks, they have suffered the denigration injury "suffered by all members of a racial group when the Government discriminates on the basis of race." Rather, the complaint, fairly read, limits the claim of stigmatic injury from illegal governmental action to black children attending public schools in districts that are currently desegregating yet contain discriminatory private schools benefiting from illegal tax exemptions. Thus, the Court's "parade of horribles" concerning black plaintiffs from Hawaii challenging tax exemptions granted to schools in Maine is completely irrelevant for purposes of Art. III standing in this action. Indeed, even if relevant, that criticism would go to the scope of the class certified or the relief granted in the lawsuit, issues that were not reached by the District Court or the Court of Appeals and are not now before this Court.

communities for withdrawal of those exemptions to make an appreciable difference in public school integration," but concludes that "[r]espondents have made no such allegation." With all due respect, the Court has either misread the complaint or is improperly requiring the respondents to prove their case on the merits in order to defeat a motion to dismiss. For example, the respondents specifically refer by name to at least 32 private schools that discriminate on the basis of race and yet continue to benefit illegally from tax-exempt status. Eighteen of those schools—including at least 14 elementary schools, 2 junior high schools, and 1 high school—are located in the city of Memphis, Tenn., which has been the subject of several court orders to desegregate. * * * [T]here can be little doubt that the respondents have identified communities containing "enough racially discriminatory private schools receiving tax exemptions * * * to make an appreciable difference in public school integration." [6]

Moreover, the Court has previously recognized the existence, and constitutional significance, of such direct relationships between unlawfully segregated school districts and government support for racially discriminatory private schools in those districts. In Norwood v. Harrison, 413 U.S. 455 (1973), for example, we considered a Mississippi program that provided textbooks to students attending both public and private schools, without regard to whether any participating school had racially discriminatory policies. In declaring that program constitutionally invalid, we * * * [observed]:

> "The District Court laid great stress on the absence of a showing by appellants that 'any child enrolled in private school, if deprived of free textbooks, would withdraw from private school and subsequently enroll in the public schools.' * * * *We do not agree with the District Court in its analysis of the legal consequences of this uncertainty, for the Constitution does not permit the State to aid discrimination even when there is no precise causal relationship between state financial aid to a private school and the continued well-being of that school. A State may not grant the type of tangible financial aid here involved if that aid has a significant tendency to facilitate, reinforce, and support private discrimination.*" Id., at 465–466 (citations omitted) (emphasis added).

The Court purports to distinguish Norwood from the present litigation because " '[t]he plaintiffs in Norwood were parties to a school desegregation order' " and therefore "had acquired a right to have the State 'steer clear' of any perpetuation of the racially dual school system that it had once sponsored," whereas the "[r]espondents in this lawsuit * * * have no injunctive rights against the IRS that are allegedly being harmed." * * * Given that many of the school districts identified in the respondents' complaint have also been the subject of court-ordered integration, the standing inquiry in these cases should not differ. And, although the respondents do not specifically allege that they are named parties to any outstanding desegregation orders, that is undoubtedly due to the passage of time since the orders were issued, and not to any difference in the harm they suffer.

6. Even if the Court were correct in its conclusion that there is an insufficient factual basis alleged in the complaint, the proper disposition would be to remand in order to afford the respondents an opportunity to amend their complaint.

Even accepting the relevance of the Court's distinction, moreover, that distinction goes to the injury suffered by the respective plaintiffs, and not to the causal connection between the harm alleged and the governmental action challenged. The causal relationship existing in Norwood between the alleged harm (i.e., interference with the plaintiffs' injunctive rights to a desegregated school system) and the challenged governmental action (i.e., free textbooks provided to racially discriminatory schools) is indistinguishable from the causal relationship existing in the present cases, unless the Court intends to distinguish the lending of textbooks from the granting of tax-exempt status. * * *

Given these precedents, the Court is forced to place primary reliance on our decision in Simon v. Eastern Kentucky Welfare Rights Org., supra. In that case, the Court denied standing to plaintiffs who challenged an IRS Revenue Ruling that granted charitable status to hospitals even though they failed to operate to the extent of their financial ability when refusing medical services for indigent patients. The Court found that the injury alleged was not one "that fairly can be traced to the challenged action of the defendant." In particular, it was "purely speculative" whether the denial of access to hospital services alleged by the plaintiffs fairly could be traced to the Government's grant of tax-exempt status to the relevant hospitals, primarily because the hospitals were likely making their service decisions without regard to the tax implications.

Even accepting the correctness of the causation analysis included in that decision, however, it is plainly distinguishable from the cases at hand. The respondents in these cases do not challenge the denial of any service by a tax-exempt institution; admittedly, they do not seek access to racially discriminatory private schools. Rather, the injury they allege, and the injury that clearly satisfies constitutional requirements, is the deprivation of their children's opportunity and ability to receive an education in a racially integrated school district. This injury, as the Court admits, and as we have previously held in Norwood v. Harrison, is of a kind that is directly traceable to the governmental action being challenged. The relationship between the harm alleged and the governmental action cannot simply be deemed "purely speculative," as was the causal connection at issue in Simon v. Eastern Kentucky Welfare Rights Org. * * *

III

More than one commentator has noted that the causation component of the Court's standing inquiry is no more than a poor disguise for the Court's view of the merits of the underlying claims. The Court today does nothing to avoid that criticism. * * *

JUSTICE STEVENS, with whom JUSTICE BLACKMUN joins, dissenting.

Three propositions are clear to me: (1) respondents have adequately alleged "injury in fact"; (2) their injury is fairly traceable to the conduct that they claim to be unlawful; and (3) the "separation of powers" principle does not create a jurisdictional obstacle to the consideration of the merits of their claim.

I

Respondents, the parents of black schoolchildren, have alleged that their children are unable to attend fully desegregated schools because large numbers of white children in the areas in which respondents reside attend private schools which do not admit minority children. The Court, JUSTICE BRENNAN and I all agree that this is an adequate allegation of "injury in fact." * * *

II

In final analysis, the wrong respondents allege that the Government has committed is to subsidize the exodus of white children from schools that would otherwise be racially integrated. The critical question in these cases, therefore, is whether respondents have alleged that the Government has created that kind of subsidy.

* * *

* * * Only last Term we explained the effect of * * * preferential [tax] treatment:

"Both tax exemptions and tax deductibility are a form of subsidy that is administered through the tax system. A tax exemption has much the same effect as a cash grant to the organization of the amount of tax it would have to pay on its income. Deductible contributions are similar to cash grants of the amount of a portion of the individual's contributions." Regan v. Taxation With Representation of Washington, 461 U.S. 540, 544 (1983).

* * * If the granting of preferential tax treatment would "encourage" private segregated schools to conduct their "charitable" activities, it must follow that the withdrawal of the treatment would "discourage" them, and hence promote the process of desegregation.

* * *

This causation analysis is nothing more than a restatement of elementary economics: when something becomes more expensive, less of it will be purchased. * * * [W]ithout tax-exempt status, private schools will either not be competitive in terms of cost, or have to change their admissions policies, hence reducing their competitiveness for parents seeking "a racially segregated alternative" to public schools, which is what respondents have alleged many white parents in desegregating school districts seek. In either event the process of desegregation will be advanced in the same way that it was advanced in Gilmore and Norwood—the withdrawal of the subsidy for segregated schools means the incentive structure facing white parents who seek such schools for their children will be altered. * * *

III

Considerations of tax policy, economics, and pure logic all confirm the conclusion that respondents' injury in fact is fairly traceable to the Government's allegedly wrongful conduct. The Court therefore is forced to introduce the concept of "separation of powers" into its analysis. The Court writes that the separation of powers "explains why our cases preclude the conclusion" that respondents' injury is fairly traceable to the conduct they challenge.

The Court could mean one of three things by its invocation of the separation of powers. First, it could simply be expressing the idea that if the plaintiff lacks Art. III standing to bring a lawsuit, then there is no "case or controversy" within the meaning of Art. III and hence the matter is not within the area of responsibility assigned to the Judiciary by the Constitution. * * * While there can be no quarrel with this proposition, in itself it provides no guidance for determining if the injury respondents have alleged is fairly traceable to the conduct they have challenged.

Second, the Court could be saying that it will require a more direct causal connection when it is troubled by the separation of powers implications of the case before it. That approach confuses the standing doctrine with the justiciability of the issues that respondents seek to raise. The purpose of the standing inquiry is to measure the plaintiff's stake in the outcome, not whether a court has the authority to provide it with the outcome it seeks * * *.

Thus, the " 'fundamental aspect of standing' is that it focuses primarily on the *party* seeking to get his complaint before the federal court rather than 'on the issues he wishes to have adjudicated,' " United States v. Richardson, 418 U.S. 166, 174 (1974) (emphasis in original) (quoting Flast, 392 U.S., at 99). * * * If a plaintiff presents a nonjusticiable issue, or seeks relief that a court may not award, then its complaint should be dismissed for those reasons, and not because the plaintiff lacks a stake in obtaining that relief and hence has no standing. Imposing an undefined but clearly more rigorous standard for redressability for reasons unrelated to the causal nexus between the injury and the challenged conduct can only encourage undisciplined, ad hoc litigation * * *.

Third, the Court could be saying that it will not treat as legally cognizable injuries that stem from an administrative decision concerning how enforcement resources will be allocated. This surely is an important point. Respondents do seek to restructure the IRS's mechanisms for enforcing the legal requirement that discriminatory institutions not receive tax-exempt status. Such restructuring would dramatically affect the way in which the IRS exercises its prosecutorial discretion. The Executive requires latitude to decide how best to enforce the law, and in general the Court may well be correct that the exercise of that discretion, especially in the tax context, is unchallengeable.

However, as the Court also recognizes, this principle does not apply when suit is brought "to enforce specific legal obligations whose violation works a direct harm." For example, despite the fact that they were challenging the methods used by the Executive to enforce the law, citizens were accorded standing to challenge a pattern of police misconduct that violated the constitutional constraints on law enforcement activities in Allee v. Medrano, 416 U.S. 802 (1974). Here, respondents contend that the IRS is violating a specific constitutional limitation on its enforcement discretion. There is a solid basis for that contention. In Norwood, we wrote:

> "A State's constitutional obligation requires it to steer clear, not only of operating the old dual system of racially segregated schools, but also of giving significant aid to institutions that practice racial or other invidious discrimination." * * *

Respondents contend that these cases limit the enforcement discretion enjoyed by the IRS. They establish, respondents argue, that the IRS cannot provide "cash grants" to discriminatory schools through preferential tax treatment without running afoul of a constitutional duty to refrain from "giving significant aid" to these institutions. Similarly, respondents claim that the Internal Revenue Code itself, as construed in Bob Jones, constrains enforcement discretion. It has been clear since Marbury v. Madison, 1 Cranch 137 (1803), that "[i]t is emphatically the province and duty of the judicial department to say what the law is." Deciding whether the Treasury has violated a specific legal limitation on its enforcement discretion does not intrude upon the prerogatives of the Executive, for in so deciding we are merely saying "what the law is." * * *

In short, I would deal with the question of the legal limitations on the IRS's enforcement discretion on its merits, rather than by making the untenable assumption that the granting of preferential tax treatment to segregated schools does not make those schools more attractive to white students and hence does not inhibit the process of desegregation. I respectfully dissent.

_____

NOTE ON STANDING TO SUE

(1) *The Origins of Standing Doctrine.* The Supremacy Clause, and the decision in Marbury v. Madison, rather plainly imply that a litigant always has standing to challenge judicial action (including the use of a rule of decision) claimed to violate his constitutional rights. Thus, in cases involving coercive action against a defendant, there is little question that he may challenge the judicial coercion as violating his rights; the only difficult question, discussed in Subsection B, is in what circumstances he may invoke the rights of others. In the cases discussed in this Subsection, in which a plaintiff seeks a remedy other than relief from an adverse judicial action, the question of standing is more problematic.

"The word '*standing*' * * * does not appear to have been commonly used until the middle of our own century." Vining, Legal Identity: The Coming of Age of Public Law 55 (1978). Before then, most litigants asserted legal interests plainly recognized at common law. Even suits raising constitutional questions at first followed the private law model: the complaint would allege that official action invaded a legal interest protected at common law; to the defense of official authority, the plaintiff would respond that the authorization was unconstitutional, thereby leaving the official liable, like a private tortfeasor, for invasion of the protected interest. See *id.* at 20–27; Stewart, *The Reformation of American Administrative Law,* 88 Harv.L.Rev. 1667, 1717–18, 1723–24 (1975).[1]

The breakdown of the common-law model is attributable primarily to two causes. The first, the rise of the administrative state, created diffuse

1. Even in federal court actions, the common law was not viewed as a body of federal law, but either as state law or as a general body of jurisprudence not emanating from a particular jurisdiction. Federal equity practice, by contrast, was viewed as a distinctive body of federal law. See generally Chap. VI, Secs. 1(A), 3–4.

At times, the prerogative writs or other forms of action permitted suit by litigants not asserting traditional common law interests. See Paragraph (5), *infra.* And particular forms of relief were sometimes authorized by state or federal legislation. See generally Chap. IX, Sec. 1(A), *infra.*

rights shared by large groups, and new legal relationships, hard to capture in common law terms; it also gave rise to a need for judicial control of the exercise of power by administrative agencies. See generally Jaffe, *Standing to Secure Judicial Review: Public Actions,* 74 Harv.L.Rev. 1265, 1282–84 (1961); Stewart, *supra,* at 1674–81. The evolution of competitors' standing highlights this development. The traditional rule was that a businessman lacks standing to object to the government's support of competing activities, because the common law does not recognize an interest in freedom from competition. See Tennessee Elec. Power Co. v. Tennessee Valley Auth., 306 U.S. 118, 137–38 (1939) (power companies that sell electricity lack standing to enjoin the TVA's competing operations, which are alleged to be unconstitutional). See also Alabama Power Co. v. Ickes, 302 U.S. 464 (1938). A major shift occurred in FCC v. Sanders Bros. Radio Station, 309 U.S. 470 (1940), where a radio station sought judicial review of the FCC's award of a broadcast license to a competitor. Section 402(b) of the Communications Act allowed an appeal "by any * * * person aggrieved or whose interests are adversely affected by a decision of the Commission granting or refusing any such application." The complainant argued that the Act created a legal interest in freedom from competition, which required consideration by the FCC of the economic impact of the award on existing licensees. The Court rejected this argument, but upheld the complainant's standing (p. 477): "Congress * * * may have been of opinion that one likely to be financially injured by the issue of a license would be the only person having a sufficient interest to bring to the attention of the appellate court errors of law in the action of the Commission in granting the license. It is within the power of Congress to confer such standing to prosecute an appeal." See also Scripps–Howard Radio, Inc. v. FCC, 316 U.S. 4, 14 (1942) (under Sanders, "these private litigants have standing only as representatives of the public interest").

The emergence of a new conception of constitutional rights—as authorizing the award of affirmative relief to redress injury to distinctive constitutionally protected interests—also led standing doctrine away from common law benchmarks. (That development is traced in connection with the landmark decisions in Ex parte Young, 209 U.S. 123 (1908), p. 1173, *infra* (recognizing a judicially-created equitable cause of action for violation of the Fourteenth Amendment's Due Process Clause), and Bivens v. Six Unknown Named Agents of Federal Bureau of Narcotics, 403 U.S. 388 (1971), p. 917, *infra* (recognizing a judicially-created cause of action for damages for violation of the Fourth Amendment).) The constitutionally protected interests given recognition—for example, the interest of a voter in challenging a malapportioned legislative district, see Baker v. Carr, 369 U.S. 186 (1962), p. 270, *infra,* or of a public school pupil in challenging school prayer, see School Dist. v. Schempp, 374 U.S. 203 (1963)—differ markedly from those recognized at common law.

(2) *What Is Standing?* The Supreme Court has frequently stated that standing questions relate to parties—to the nature and sufficiency of the litigant's concern with the subject matter of the litigation—rather than to the fitness for adjudication of the legal issues tendered for decision. See, *e.g.,* Flast v. Cohen, 392 U.S. 83, 95 (1968), which follows this Note. Consider whether Allen v. Wright, and the decisions discussed in this Note, are consistent with that statement.

In Warth v. Seldin, 422 U.S. 490 (1975), the Court said that the question of standing "is whether the constitutional or statutory provision on which the claim rests properly can be understood as granting persons in the plaintiff's position a right to judicial relief" (p. 500). Is that the same question as whether the plaintiff has stated a valid claim for relief? See Albert, *Standing to Challenge Administrative Action: An Inadequate Surrogate for Claim for Relief,* 83 Yale L.J. 425 (1974); Currie, *Misunderstanding Standing,* 1981 Sup.Ct.Rev. 41 (1981). On the view stated in Warth, if one is to determine whether the plaintiffs in Wright stated a valid claim for relief, doesn't one need a substantive theory of the scope of the equal protection component of the Fifth Amendment and of the appropriate remedy for any violation found?

Or is the purpose of standing doctrine not only to limit relief to those litigants entitled to it, but also (i) to ensure that controversies will be concrete and genuine; (ii) to ensure that litigants will be energetic adversaries; (iii) to ration a scarce and expensive resource—access to the courts; (iv) to ensure that those most affected by a challenged practice are adequately represented; or (v) to facilitate discretionary, prudential judgments whether the time is right for resolution of a particular controversy? Did any of these concerns argue against deciding the claims asserted in Wright?

(3) *The Requirement of Injury in Fact.* The cases have long accepted the principle that Article III itself requires the plaintiff to show that he was injured by the conduct under challenge.

(a) In Sierra Club v. Morton, 405 U.S. 727 (1972), the Sierra Club sued the United States Forest Service, claiming that its approval of the development of a ski resort in the Sequoia National Forest violated federal statutes and regulations. Alleging that it had "a special interest in the conservation and sound maintenance of the national parks, game refuges, and forests of the country" and that the project would adversely affect the aesthetics and ecology of the area (p. 731), the Club claimed to be "adversely affected or aggrieved" under § 10 of the Administrative Procedure Act (APA), 5 U.S.C. § 702.[2]

The Court ruled that the plaintiff lacked standing because it had not alleged that it would suffer "injury in fact" from the challenged action. (The case was decided under the APA—which the Court had previously interpreted to require that the plaintiff have suffered injury in fact, see pp. 162–63, *infra*—but the decision that the Club suffered no injury had implications beyond cases brought under that statute). Though non-economic harm of the kind alleged could satisfy that requirement, "the 'injury in fact' test requires more than an injury to a cognizable interest. It requires that the party seeking review be himself among the injured. * * * Nowhere * * * did the Club state that its members use [the area in question] for any purpose, much less that they use it in any way that would be significantly affected by the proposed actions of the [defendants]. * * * [I]f any group with a bona fide 'special interest' could initiate such litigation, it is difficult to perceive why any individual citizen with the same bona fide special interest would not also be entitled to do so." The requirement of injury is a "rough attempt to put the decision as to whether

2. That section provides: "A person suffering legal wrong because of agency action, or adversely affected or aggrieved by agency action within the meaning of a relevant statute, is entitled to judicial review thereof."

review will be sought in the hands of those who have a direct stake in the outcome," a goal that would be "undermined" if organizations were permitted to sue under the APA merely to "vindicate their own value preferences through the judicial process" (pp. 734–35, 739–40).[3]

(b) In United States v. Students Challenging Regulatory Agency Procedures (SCRAP), 412 U.S. 669 (1973), a loose association of law students brought suit alleging that the ICC had failed to prepare an environmental impact statement, as required by federal law, before deciding not to suspend a temporary surcharge on railroad freight rates. The complaint averred that the surcharge, by raising the cost of recycled products, would increase consumption of natural resources, some of which might be taken from the Washington, D.C. area, which the association's members used for recreational purposes. The Supreme Court upheld the plaintiffs' standing. Unlike Sierra Club, the Court said, here the complaint alleged injury to the *members*—that they "used the forests, streams, mountains, and other resources in the Washington metropolitan area * * * and that this use was disturbed by the adverse environmental impact caused by the nonuse of recyclable goods brought about by a rate increase on those commodities" (p. 685).

(c) Was the dispute in SCRAP more genuine than the one in Sierra Club? Wasn't the Sierra Club likely to be at least as competent a litigant as the plaintiffs in SCRAP? Would it be proper for the Court to make ad hoc judgments about the litigating capacity of particular parties? Compare Scott, *Standing in the Supreme Court: A Functional Analysis,* 86 Harv.L. Rev. 645, 674 (1973) ("If plaintiff did not have the minimal personal involvement and adverseness which Article III requires, he would not be engaging in the costly pursuit of litigation.").

On one view, the critical defect in Sierra Club was one of pleading—the Club had not alleged that its members used the area in question. (On remand, standing was established after additional allegations and parties were added to the complaint. 348 F.Supp. 219 (N.D.Cal.1972).) This view requires, however, acceptance of the Court's premise that harm to an ideological interest does not constitute cognizable injury. By what standards does a court decide whether a particular claim of injury is cognizable? See Nichol, *Injury and the Disintegration of Article III,* 74 Calif.L. Rev. 1915 (1986).

In Allen v. Wright, could the Court, consistently with Sierra Club, have found the plaintiffs' claim that they were racially stigmatized by the IRS's conduct to be an adequate injury?

(d) In SCRAP, the Court said that if the allegations of standing were untrue, the defendant should have moved for summary judgment on the standing issue. But if the defendant could not prove on such a motion that the allegations were a sham, the case would proceed to trial, "where the plaintiff must prove the allegations in order to prevail" (p. 689). Accord,

---

3. Justice Blackmun (joined by Justice Brennan) dissented, calling for "an imaginative expansion of our traditional concepts of standing in order to enable an organization such as the Sierra Club, possessed, as it is, of pertinent, bona fide and well-recognized attributes and purposes in the area of the environment, to litigate environmental issues" (p. 757). Justice Douglas also dissented; he would have upheld standing "in the name of the inanimate object about to be despoiled, defaced, or invaded by roads and bulldozers and where injury is the subject of public outrage" (p. 741).

Gwaltney of Smithfield v. Chesapeake Bay Foundation, Inc., 108 S.Ct. 376, 386 (1987). However, following the Supreme Court's decision in SCRAP, the three-judge district court awarded partial relief to the plaintiffs, 371 F.Supp. 1291 (D.D.C.1974), an award that the Supreme Court reversed on the merits, Aberdeen & Rockfish R. Co. v. S.C.R.A.P., 422 U.S. 289 (1975). Neither court discussed whether the allegations found sufficient to confer standing had been proven.

(4) *Injury and Generalized Grievances.* Closely related to cases about the adequacy of injury are those involving widely-diffused harms, in which no single plaintiff suffers harm distinct from that suffered by many or all other citizens.

(a) Schlesinger v. Reservists Comm. to Stop the War, 418 U.S. 208 (1974), was a class action challenging the military reserve membership of certain Congressmen as inconsistent with the "Incompatibility Clause" of Article I, § 6, cl. 2 ("no Person holding any Office under the United States, shall be a Member of either House during his Continuance in Office"). The plaintiffs—present and former members of the military reserves, and an association of members opposed to the Vietnam War—alleged as their injury that Congressmen who belonged to the reserves would be subject to undue influence by the Executive, and that they had potentially conflicting obligations that would foster violations of their duties in each capacity to all citizens.

The Court, per Burger, C.J., held that the plaintiffs had failed to assert sufficiently concrete, individualized injury, and merely sought to air " 'generalized grievances' about the conduct of Government" (p. 217). The Court continued (pp. 220–22): "Concrete injury ＊ ＊ ＊ is that indispensable element of a dispute which serves in part to cast it in a form traditionally capable of judicial resolution. ＊ ＊ ＊

"Moreover, ＊ ＊ ＊ concrete injury removes from the realm of speculation whether there is a real need to exercise the power of judicial review in order to protect the interests of the complaining party," and "insures the framing of relief no broader than required by the precise facts to which the court's ruling would be applied. This is especially important when the relief sought produces a confrontation with one of the coordinate branches of the Government; here the relief sought would, in practical effect, bring about conflict between two coordinate branches." [4]

(b) In United States v. Richardson, 418 U.S. 166 (1974), decided the same day as Reservists, the Court ruled that the plaintiff lacked standing to litigate the question whether the CIA was violating Article I, § 9, cl. 7 (requiring "a regular Statement and Account of the Receipts and Expenditures of all public Money") by accounting for its expenditures, in accordance with a federal statute, "solely on the certificate of the Director." Chief Justice Burger's opinion actually addressed only the question whether the plaintiff had standing as a federal taxpayer (on that question, see the materials immediately following this Note); but it left no doubt that a complaint on behalf of a citizen-plaintiff would have fared no better (p. 179):

4. Dissenting, Justices Douglas and Marshall would have upheld plaintiffs' standing as citizens, while Justice Brennan would have upheld their standing as taxpayers, see pp. 138–54, *infra*.

"It can be argued that if respondent is not permitted to litigate this issue, no one can do so. In a very real sense, the absence of any particular individual or class to litigate these claims gives support to the argument that the subject matter is committed to the surveillance of Congress, and ultimately to the political process. Any other conclusion would mean that the Founding Fathers intended to set up something in the nature of an Athenian democracy or a New England town meeting to oversee the conduct of the National Government by means of lawsuits in federal courts. The Constitution created a *representative* Government with the representatives directly responsible to their constituents at stated periods * * *. Lack of standing within the narrow confines of Art. III jurisdiction does not impair [a citizen's] right to assert his views in the political forum or at the polls. Slow, cumbersome, and unresponsive though the traditional electoral process may be thought at times, our system provides for changing members of the political branches when dissatisfied citizens convince a sufficient number of their fellow electors that elected representatives are delinquent in performing duties committed to them." [5]

Justice Powell elaborated on this theme in his concurring opinion (pp. 188–91):

* * * [R]epeated and essentially head-on confrontations between the life-tenured branch and the representative branches of government will not, in the long run, be beneficial to either. The public confidence essential to the former and the vitality critical to the latter may well erode if we do not exercise self-restraint in the utilization of our power to negative the actions of the other branches. * * * Indeed, taxpayer or citizen advocacy, given its potentially broad base, is precisely the type of leverage that in a democracy ought to be employed against the branches that were intended to be responsive to public attitudes about the appropriate operation of government. * * *

* * *

"The power recognized in Marbury v. Madison, 1 Cranch 137 (1803), is a potent one. Its prudent use seems to me incompatible with unlimited notions of taxpayer and citizen standing. * * *

" * * * The irreplaceable value of the power articulated by Chief Justice Marshall lies in the protection it has afforded the constitutional rights and liberties of individual citizens and minority groups against oppressive or discriminatory government action. It is this role, not some amorphous general supervision of the operations of government, that has maintained public esteem for the federal courts and has permitted the peaceful coexistence of the countermajoritarian implications of judicial review and the democratic principles upon which our Federal Government in the final analysis rests."

5. The Court relied heavily on Ex parte Lévitt, 302 U.S. 633 (1937), a challenge by a citizen and member of the bar of the Supreme Court to the appointment of Justice Black. The suit alleged a violation of Art. I, § 6, cl. 2, which prohibits the appointment of any Senator or Representative to any federal office whose emoluments were increased during the time in which he served in Congress. The Court ruled that Lévitt lacked standing because he had suffered no "direct injury" and any interest he had was shared with "all members of the public" (p. 634). See also Fairchild v. Hughes, 258 U.S. 126 (1922) (plaintiff asserting rights of citizens, taxpayers, and members of the American Constitutional League denied standing to challenge the validity of the adoption of the Nineteenth Amendment).

Reviewing the "revolution in standing doctrine" of recent years, he concluded (pp. 194–95): "[D]espite the diminution of standing requirements in the last decade, the Court has not broken with the traditional requirement that, in the absence of a specific statutory grant of the right of review, a plaintiff must allege some particularized injury that sets him apart from the man on the street.

"I recognize that the Court's allegiance to a requirement of particularized injury has on occasion required a reading of the concept that threatens to transform it beyond recognition. *E.g.*, Baker v. Carr, [p. 270, *infra*]; Flast v. Cohen, p. 138, *infra*. But despite such occasional digressions, the requirement remains, and I think it does so for the reasons outlined above. In recognition of those considerations, we should refuse to go the last mile towards abolition of standing requirements that is implicit in * * * allowing a citizen *qua* citizen to invoke the power of the federal courts to negative unconstitutional acts of the Federal Government."

(c) Is there a difference between the kind of general judicial oversight feared by Chief Justice Burger, and judicial interpretation of a constitutional provision as granting enforceable rights in all citizens? Does the fact that a grievance is widely shared ensure that the political branches will respond to it—or that, if they do not, the grievance must not be very serious? Compare SCRAP, Paragraph (3)(b), *supra*, at 687–88 ("standing is not to be denied simply because many people suffer the same injury"; otherwise, "the most injurious and widespread Government actions could be questioned by nobody"). Does the purpose of the Incompatibility Clause make it a provision especially appropriate for judicial enforcement—enforcement that can be secured only by recognizing standing in a citizen as such?

Why isn't the lack of any other or better plaintiff an argument in favor of upholding a litigant's standing? See, *e.g.*, Mathews v. Heckler and Orr v. Orr, Paragraph (6)(e), *infra*. See also Meltzer, *Deterring Constitutional Violations by Law Enforcement Officials: Plaintiffs and Defendants as Private Attorneys General*, 88 Colum.L.Rev. 247, 297–306 (1988). If there is reason to fear that adjudication of sensitive issues of governmental relations would result, isn't the political question doctrine the appropriate rubric under which to deal with that fear? See Sec. 6, *infra*.

Allen v. Wright formulates the rule barring adjudication of generalized grievances as an independent reason, apart from the injury requirement, for denying standing. Accord, *e.g.*, Valley Forge Christian College v. Americans United for Separation of Church and State, Inc., 454 U.S. 464, 474–76 (1982); Warth v. Seldin, 422 U.S. 490, 499–502 (1975). Wright adds that the rule is a judicially self-imposed, rather than a constitutionally mandated, requirement. Is the Court justified in creating restrictions on standing not demanded by Article III? Reservists, by contrast, appears to argue that a mere generalized grievance does not constitute injury under Article III.

(5) *The Public Action.* The premise that a mere citizen lacks standing to challenge government illegality has been challenged by some commentators. Professor Berger argues that when the Constitution was adopted, "the English practice in prohibition, certiorari, quo warranto, and informers' and relators' actions encouraged strangers to attack *unauthorized action*." Berger, *Standing to Sue in Public Actions: Is It a Constitutional*

Requirement?, 78 Yale L.J. 816, 827 (1969). See also Jaffe, Judicial Control of Administrative Action 329–36, 459–75 (1965) (describing the history, in England and in the state and federal courts, of the prerogative writs and of citizen and taxpayer standing). Professor Jaffe has forcefully argued that effective advocacy does not require personalized injury; he adds that a so-called "public" action, rather than being inconsistent with democratic theory, can serve the important purposes of permitting citizen participation and fulfilling a widespread desire for a judicial pronouncement. Thus, he would allow courts, in their discretion, to entertain a public action brought by a wholly ideological citizen/plaintiff when the challenged conduct is clearly illegal and there is a strong public interest in ending the illegality. See Jaffe, *The Citizen as Litigant in Public Actions: The Non–Hohfeldian or Ideological Plaintiff*, 116 U.Pa.L.Rev. 1033 (1968).

Is there a sufficient interest in adjudicating a public action to justify the inherent risk of conflict with the other branches of government? Should it matter whether Congress has expressly authorized the federal courts to entertain a citizen suit? See Paragraph (9), *infra*.

(6) *Standing Requirements in Addition to Injury.* Allen v. Wright holds that Article III requires not merely a cognizable injury, but also one that is "fairly traceable" to the challenged action and that will be redressed by a favorable decision. These requirements—often called "causation" and "redressability"—evolved in a series of important and controversial decisions.[6]

(a) Linda R.S. v. Richard D., 410 U.S. 614 (1973), was a class action, brought by the mother of an illegitimate child, against state officials whose policy was to bring non-support prosecutions against only the fathers of legitimate children. Asserting that the policy violated the Equal Protection Clause, the complaint sought an injunction requiring prosecution of the fathers of illegitimate children. Justice Marshall's opinion for the Court found no standing (pp. 617–18): "in the unique context of a challenge to a criminal statute, appellant has failed to allege a sufficient nexus between her injury and the government action which she attacks to justify judicial intervention. * * * [T]he requested relief * * * would result only in the jailing of the child's father. The prospect that prosecution will, at least in the future, result in payment of support can, at best, be termed only speculative." The opinion also rested on the proposition that "in American jurisprudence at least, a private citizen lacks a judicially cognizable interest in the prosecution or nonprosecution of another" (p. 619).[7]

Since the suit was brought as a class action, is the result of prosecuting non-supporting fathers any more speculative than the general theory that the criminal law deters? Consider Professor Chambers' study, Making

6. For critical commentary, see Chayes, *Foreword: Public Law Litigation and the Burger Court*, 96 Harv.L.Rev. 4, 17–19 (1982); Nichol, *Causation as a Standing Requirement: The Unprincipled Use of Judicial Restraint*, 69 Ky.L.Rev. 185 (1981); Tushnet, *The New Law of Standing: A Plea for Abandonment*, 62 Cornell L.Rev. 663, 680–88 (1977).

7. Justices White and Douglas dissented, while Justices Blackmun and Brennan disposed of the case on other grounds.

See also Leeke v. Timmerman, 454 U.S. 83 (1981) (per curiam) (relying on Linda R.S. in reversing a lower court damage award in a suit against officials who allegedly had conspired in bad faith to block a magistrate's issuance of arrest warrants, and noting that even had the warrants been issued, the prosecutor in his discretion might have chosen not to press charges).

Fathers Pay: The Enforcement of Child Support (1979), which provides empirical evidence that aggressive prosecution of non-supporting fathers induces greater compliance. Should the decision in Linda R.S. be viewed instead as expressing doubts about the appropriateness of a judicial order requiring the prosecution of others?

(b) Warth v. Seldin, 422 U.S. 490 (1975), was an action alleging that the town zoning ordinance in Penfield, New York (located next to Rochester) violated the Constitution and federal civil rights statutes, by preventing persons of low and moderate means (many of them minorities) from living in the town. The Court, per Powell, J., affirmed the dismissal of the complaint.[8] In its opinion, the Court considered and rejected a number of theories of standing, of which two were central.

The first was asserted by several low-income individuals who did not reside in Penfield, but wished to, and who contended that enforcement of the ordinance against developers had prevented construction of low-income housing in which these individuals could live. The Court found that even if the zoning law had increased housing costs, the complaint fell short unless it "allege[d] facts from which it reasonably could be inferred that, absent the [defendants'] restrictive zoning practices, there is a substantial probability that [plaintiffs] would have been able to purchase or lease in Penfield and that, if the court affords the relief requested, the asserted inability of [plaintiffs] will be removed." That "the harm to [these plaintiffs] may have resulted indirectly does not in itself preclude standing[,] * * * [b]ut it may make it substantially more difficult to meet the minimum requirement of Art. III: to establish that, in fact, the asserted injury was the consequence of the defendants' actions, or that prospective relief will remove the harm" (pp. 504–05). The record referred to only two efforts to develop low income housing, and the Court found no "indication that these projects, or other like projects, would have satisfied [the plaintiffs'] needs at prices they could afford, or that, were the court to remove the obstructions attributable to [defendants], such relief would benefit [the plaintiffs]. Indeed, [plaintiffs'] descriptions of their individual financial situations and housing needs suggests precisely the contrary—that their inability to reside in Penfield is the consequence of the economics of the area housing market, rather than of [defendants'] assertedly illegal acts" (p. 506).[9]

The Court considered separately the standing of Metro–Act, a non-profit corporation interested in the housing needs of the poor. Metro–Act was permitted to serve as the representative of its members (see, on this point, pp. 159–60, *infra*), which led to consideration whether the members them-

---

8. Justice Brennan (joined by Justices White and Marshall) and Justice Douglas dissented.

9. Compare Village of Arlington Heights v. Metropolitan Housing Development Corp., 429 U.S. 252 (1977), in which a corporate housing developer, and a black would-be resident of the multiple-unit housing the developer planned to build, were each accorded standing to challenge the validity of an exclusionary single-family zoning ordinance. The developer had contracted to purchase the land for the project, engaged an architect, and begun design and other steps. The black plaintiff testified that he would qualify for the projected housing and would move there if it were built. The Court recognized (p. 261) that "[a]n injunction would not, of course, guarantee that [the development] will be built. [Developer] would still have to secure financing, qualify for federal subsidies, and carry through with construction. But all housing developments are subject to some extent to similar uncertainties. When a project is as detailed and specific as [this one], a court is not required to engage in undue speculation."

selves had standing. The Court ruled that the allegation that some members, who lived in Penfield, were deprived by the zoning ordinance of the benefits of living in a racially and ethnically integrated community did not state a judicially cognizable injury. In doing so, the Court had to deal with Trafficante v. Metropolitan Life Ins. Co., 409 U.S. 205 (1972), Paragraph (9), *infra,* which had upheld, in a suit specifically authorized by Congress for violations of the Civil Rights Act of 1968, the standing of tenants to sue their landlord for discrimination that deprived the tenants of the benefits of an integrated community. Trafficante was different, the Court argued in Warth, because it involved a statutory right of action, and "Congress may create a statutory right or entitlement the alleged deprivation of which can confer standing to sue even where the plaintiff would have suffered no judicially cognizable injury in the absence of statute" (p. 514).

Consider this second holding in Warth. Can the diminished ability of residents of Penfield to live in an integrated community, found wanting in Warth, be distinguished from the diminished ability of the plaintiffs in Wright to obtain an education in a racially integrated school, which the Court held was judicially cognizable?

Consider, next, Warth's holding that the ordinance did not cause (and relief from it would not redress) the absence of "affordable" housing in Penfield. Did the Court require "intricacies of pleading that would have gladdened the heart of Baron Parke"? See Chayes, *The Role of the Judge in Public Law Litigation,* 89 Harv.L.Rev. 1281, 1305 (1976), so arguing.[10] Isn't the question whether the zoning law restricted plaintiffs' ability to obtain housing in Penfield highly complicated? Is that question better answered at the threshold of the litigation, or after a full record has been developed? Do you agree with Professor Fallon that the Court is mistaken to view the question of "redressability" as part of the standing inquiry, rather than as an aspect of the appropriateness of a particular form of relief? See Fallon, *Of Justiciability, Remedies, and Public Law Litigation: Notes on the Jurisprudence of Lyons,* 59 N.Y.U.L.Rev. 1, 7, 43–47 (1984).

Could the plaintiffs have met the causation and redressability requirements by defining their injury differently—as the denial of the opportunity to participate in a housing market untainted by illegal conduct? Compare Regents of the University of California v. Bakke, 438 U.S. 265 (1978), involving a white plaintiff's challenge to the defendant's operation of a special admissions program for minority applicants to medical school. Some amici argued that Bakke lacked standing because he had not shown that his injury—exclusion from medical school—would be redressed by a favorable decision, as he might not have been admitted even absent any preference for minorities. In a portion of his opinion endorsed by four other Justices, Justice Powell affirmed Bakke's standing, arguing that relief would redress the injury Bakke had suffered by having been deprived, simply because of his race, of the chance to compete for every place in the entering class. The four Justices dissenting on the merits did not address the standing question.[11]

10. Compare Havens Realty Corp. v. Coleman, 455 U.S. 363, 377–78 (1982), Paragraph (9), *infra,* holding that the allegations of injury were inadequate, but remanding to permit amendment of the complaint; "[u]nder the liberal federal pleading standards, • • • dismissal on the pleadings is inappropriate at this stage of the litigation."

11. For other decisions that, like Bakke, interpret the causation and redressability requirements far less strictly than Warth, see, *e.g.,* Bryant v. Yellen, 447 U.S.

(c) Simon v. Eastern Kentucky Welfare Rights Org. [EKWRO], 426 U.S. 26 (1976), was a class action, on behalf of all persons unable to afford hospital services, against officials of the Treasury Department. The suit challenged a Revenue Ruling that eliminated a requirement that non-profit hospitals provide some care for indigents in order to qualify for favorable tax treatment. The plaintiffs, alleging injury in that the Ruling "encouraged" hospitals to deny services to indigents, argued that the Ruling violated the Internal Revenue Code and had been issued in violation of the Administrative Procedure Act.

The Court, per Powell, J., held that the plaintiffs lacked standing (pp. 42–44): "The complaint here alleged only that petitioners * * * had 'encouraged' hospitals to deny services to indigents. * * * But it does not follow * * * that the denial of access to hospital services in fact results from the petitioners' new Ruling, or that a court-ordered return by petitioners to their previous policy would result in these respondents' receiving the hospital services they desire. It is purely speculative whether the denials of service specified in the complaint fairly can be traced to petitioners' 'encouragement' or instead result from decisions made by the hospitals without regard to the tax implications.

" * * * So far as the complaint sheds light, it is just as plausible that the hospitals to which respondents may apply for service would elect to forgo favorable tax treatment to avoid the undetermined financial drain of an increase in the level of uncompensated services. * * * Thus, respondents' allegation that certain hospitals receive substantial charitable contributions, without more, does not establish the further proposition that those hospitals are dependent upon such contributions."

Justice Brennan, joined by Justice Marshall, concurred in the result on the ground that the plaintiffs had failed to establish either that the contested ruling altered the operation of all non-profit hospitals or that the tax-exempt status of the hospitals whose conduct affected the plaintiffs was in any way related to the ruling. He took sharp issue, however, with the Court's rationale.[12] Justice Stewart concurred with the majority, but noted specially (p. 46): "I add only that I cannot now imagine a case, at least outside the First Amendment area, where a person whose own tax liability was not affected ever could have standing to litigate the federal tax liability of someone else."

(d) In Duke Power Co. v. Carolina Environmental Study Group, 438 U.S. 59 (1978), an environmental organization, a labor union, and forty individuals sued the Nuclear Regulatory Commission and a utility company that was constructing two nuclear power plants. The suit sought a declaration that the Price–Anderson Act, 42 U.S.C. § 2210, which limits liability in the event of a nuclear accident, was an unconstitutional deprivation of property of potential accident victims. The Court, per Chief Justice Burger, affirmed standing and upheld the constitutionality of the Act.

352, 366–68 (1980); Larson v. Valente, 456 U.S. 228, 239–43 (1982).

12. " * * * Respondents' claim is not * * * that they have been and will be illegally denied the provision of indigent medical services by the hospitals. Rather, * * * it is that the Internal Revenue Code requires the government to offer economic inducements to the relevant hospitals only under conditions which are likely to benefit respondents. The relevant injury in light of this claim is, then, injury to this beneficial interest—as respondents alleged, injury to their 'opportunity and ability' to receive medical services * * *." (p. 56).

The Court said that Article III requires, first, a " 'distinct and palpable injury' to the plaintiff," and, second, a " 'fairly traceable' causal connection between the claimed injury and the challenged conduct" (p. 72). Sufficient injury was found in the potential thermal pollution of several lakes in the vicinity of the plants under construction, and in the likelihood of low-level radiation from the plants. The Court did not rely on the "possibility of a nuclear accident and the present apprehension generated by this future uncertainty" (pp. 73–74).

The Court found the second aspect of Article III standing satisfied by the District Court's finding that absent the Price–Anderson Act, there was a "substantial likelihood" that the utility would be unable to complete the two nuclear plants. The Court explicitly rejected any requirement, for Article III purposes, that the claimed injuries and the constitutional rights asserted have any connection. Restricting the "nexus" requirement of Flast v. Cohen (which follows this Note) to taxpayer suits, the Court refused to hold, in other kinds of lawsuits, that "a litigant must demonstrate anything more than injury in fact and a substantial likelihood that the judicial relief requested will prevent or redress the claimed injury" (p. 79).

Justice Stewart, dissented on the standing issue, arguing that "[s]urely a plaintiff does not have standing simply because his challenge, if successful, will remove the injury relied on for standing purposes *only* because it will put the defendant out of existence. Surely there must be *some* direct relationship between the plaintiff's federal claim and the injury relied on for standing" (p. 95). Justice Stevens objected on similar grounds, and added (pp. 102–03):

"The string of contingencies that supposedly holds this litigation together is too delicate for me. We are told that but for the Price–Anderson Act there would be no financing of nuclear power plants, no development of those plants by private parties, and hence no present injury to persons such as appellees; we are then asked to remedy an alleged due process violation that may possibly occur at some uncertain time in the future, and may possibly injure the appellees in a way that has no significant connection with any present injury. It is remarkable that such a series of speculations is considered sufficient * * * to establish appellees' standing."

Can the Duke Power decision on standing be reconciled with prior authority? If not, should it be viewed as overruling earlier cases, or should it be regarded as a "sport", responsive to particular ad hoc considerations— especially the desire to reverse on the merits the district court's ruling that the Act was unconstitutional? See Stewart, *Review, Standing for Solidarity*, 88 Yale L.J. 1559, 1574 n. 62 (1979). See also Varat, *Variable Justiciability and the Duke Power Case*, 58 Tex.L.Rev. 273 (1980).

(e) A recurring question of standing has arisen in equal protection actions brought by persons who claim a right to the more favorable treatment enjoyed by others. If a violation can be established, the inequality might be eliminated either by treating the plaintiff more favorably, or by denying the favorable treatment to others; in the latter case, the plaintiff would obtain no material benefit. The Supreme Court has nonetheless consistently upheld plaintiffs' standing in these cases. See, *e.g.*, Heckler v. Mathews, 465 U.S. 728 (1984); Orr v. Orr, 440 U.S. 268, 272 (1979); Stanton v. Stanton, 421 U.S. 7, 17–18 (1975); Iowa–Des Moines Nat.

Bank v. Bennett, 284 U.S. 239, 247 (1931), p. 585, *infra.* See generally Kovacic, *Remedying Underinclusive Statutes,* 33 Wayne L.Rev. 39 (1986).

In the Mathews case, Congress had provided larger benefit awards under the Social Security Act to certain women than to similarly situated men. A severability clause accompanying this legislation made clear that if the special provision were found to deny equal protection, men and women alike should receive the smaller rather than the larger amount. The Court upheld the standing of a male beneficiary to challenge the unequal treatment. Because he asserted "the right to receive 'benefits * * * distributed according to classifications which do not without sufficient justification differentiate * * * solely on the basis of sex,' and not a substantive right to any particular amount of benefits, [plaintiff's] standing does not depend on his ability to obtain increased Social Security payments. * * * Although the severability clause would prevent a court from redressing this inequality by increasing the benefits payable to [plaintiff], we have never suggested that the injuries caused by a constitutionally underinclusive scheme can be remedied only by extending the program's benefits to the excluded class. * * * [D]iscrimination itself, by perpetuating 'archaic and stereotypic notions' or by stigmatizing members of the disfavored group as 'innately inferior,' * * * can cause serious noneconomic injuries" (pp. 737–39).

Though, at least in a challenge to a *federal* statute, ordinarily "extension [of benefits] rather than nullification is the proper course, [Califano v. Westcott, 443 U.S. 76, 89 (1979)]," the Court explained that the question is one of legislative intent, and here Congress's clear expression of its preference for nullification should be honored (p. 739 n. 5). On the merits, the Court upheld the provision under attack.

Mathews is surely sound; to have denied standing would have effectively immunized the statute from judicial review. See Orr v. Orr, *supra,* 440 U.S. at 272. Can Mathews be squared, however, with the refusal in Allen v. Wright to find that the stigma suffered by plaintiffs was cognizable injury?

(7) *Standing and the Separation of Powers.* Article III's case or controversy requirement has often been said to implement the separation of powers. See, *e.g.,* Valley Forge Christian College v. Americans United for Separation of Church and State, Inc., 454 U.S. 464, 473–74 (1982); Flast v. Cohen, 392 U.S. 83, 95 (1968). But Allen v. Wright is distinctive in suggesting (see footnote 26) that the application of standing doctrine in a particular case should be guided by separation of powers considerations.[13] The Court was presumably concerned about the appropriate limits of relief against the Executive Branch. But if the Court was right that case-or-controversy considerations "shade into" the question of the appropriateness of equitable relief, wasn't it wrong that "[t]he latter set of considerations should therefore inform our judgment about whether [plaintiffs] have standing"? Can the need for a particular kind of relief—and its impact on the Executive Branch—be adequately judged on the pleadings? See Fallon,

---

13. Compare the discussion in Part III of the opinion in Flast v. Cohen, which follows, stressing that the question of standing "does not, by its own force, raise separation of powers problems related to improper judicial interference in areas committed to other branches of the Federal Government. Such problems arise, if at all, only from the substantive issues the individual seeks to have adjudicated" (pp. 100–01).

Paragraph (6)(b), *supra*, at 72. And aren't these equitable considerations, in any event, quite distinct from the question to which Wright deemed them relevant—namely, whether the IRS' conduct caused the harm in question? Compare Nichol, *Abusing Standing: A Comment on Allen v. Wright*, 133 U.Pa.L.Rev. 635 (1985), with Logan, *Standing to Sue: A Proposed Separation of Powers Analysis*, 1984 Wis.L.Rev. 37.

(8) *Asserting the Rights of Others.* Allen v. Wright notes that one of the Court's subconstitutional, "self-imposed limits on the exercise of federal jurisdiction * * * is a general prohibition on a litigant's raising another person's legal rights." A number of cases have, however, forged exceptions to this rule. In Pierce v. Society of Sisters, 268 U.S. 510 (1925), owners of a private school—whose enrollment had declined after enactment of a state law requiring parents to send their children to public schools—were permitted to enjoin enforcement of the statute on the ground that it violated the parents' rights to determine how their children should be educated. The Court relied on the "many * * * cases where injunctions have issued to protect business enterprises against interference with the freedom of patrons or customers" (p. 536).[14]

In Singleton v. Wulff, 428 U.S. 106 (1976), two physicians challenged the constitutionality of a Missouri statute denying Medicaid benefits to patients who underwent abortions that were not "medically indicated." All nine Justices found sufficient injury in the physicians' performance of abortions made non-reimbursable by the statute. Four members of the Court, in an opinion by Justice Blackmun, argued that in attacking the statute, the physicians could assert the rights of their patients, because of the physicians' relationship to their patients and the patients' asserted inability to press their own rights. Justice Stevens cast the fifth vote for that outcome: he was uncertain, however, whether a physician who had not suffered injury would have standing to assert his patients' rights, and refused to endorse the plurality's view that "it is generally appropriate to allow a physician to assert the rights of women patients as against government interference with the abortion decision" (pp. 117–18). Justice Powell, joined by the Chief Justice and Justices Stewart and Rehnquist, dissented on this point.

In City of Revere v. Massachusetts Gen. Hosp., 463 U.S. 239 (1983), municipal police officers wounded a suspect and then summoned an ambulance, which took the suspect to a private hospital for treatment. When the city refused to pay the bill, the hospital sued the city in state court. The state courts ruled for the hospital, concluding that the Cruel and Unusual Punishment Clause required that the city be held liable in order to ensure that persons in police custody receive adequate medical care. On review, the Supreme Court held that the hospital clearly had "standing in the Article III sense" because it sought directly to redress its economic loss for services rendered (p. 243). It would be a mistake, the Court continued, to refuse for "prudential reasons" to permit the hospital to assert the rights of persons in police custody: that assertion was not contested in the state

14. See also Buchanan v. Warley, 245 U.S. 60 (1917) (white vendor of land sued black vendee for specific performance; vendor, in responding to defense of breach of a contractual condition, was permitted to challenge the constitutionality of a city ordinance purporting to forbid blacks from residing on the property in question); Truax v. Raich, 239 U.S. 33 (1915) (permitting an alien to enjoin enforcement of a statute prohibiting an employer from hiring more than a specified percentage of alien employees).

courts, and a refusal would "leav[e] intact the state court's judgment in favor of [the hospital], the purportedly improper representative of the third party's constitutional rights." In a footnote, the Court argued that standing and the merits were here "inextricably intertwined"; both questions depended in part on "whether injured suspects will be deprived of their constitutional right to necessary medical care unless the government entity is required to pay hospitals for their services" (p. 243 n. 5). On the merits, the Court reversed.

Can any of these cases be explained as involving the assertion of the plaintiff's own right to engage in a constitutionally protected relationship? See Warth v. Seldin, Paragraph (6)(b), *supra,* 422 U.S. at 501, citing Pierce as an example of the Court's having "found, in effect, that the constitutional or statutory provision in question implies a right of action in the plaintiff." For fuller discussion of assertion of the rights of others, see *Note on Asserting the Rights of Others,* Subsection (B), pp. 166–75, *infra,* which discusses the more common situation of an actual or potential *defendant* who seeks to resist enforcement of a legal duty by asserting the rights of third persons.

(9) *The Pertinence of Congressional Legislation Conferring Standing.* May Congress confer standing in a case where it would not exist absent the legislation? Presumably Congress may do so if the barrier to suit is a "prudential" one, like the rule against asserting the rights of others. See, *e.g.,* Warth v. Seldin, Paragraph (6)(b), *supra,* 422 U.S. at 500–01; Gladstone, Realtors v. Village of Bellwood, 441 U.S. 91, 103 n. 9 (1979).

The problem is thornier if Congress purports to confer standing in a case in which, absent such legislation, the Court would find no injury under Article III. The Court's discussion of this question has not been a model of clarity.

In Trafficante v. Metropolitan Life Ins. Co., 409 U.S. 205 (1972), a white and a black tenant were held to have standing under § 810 of the Civil Rights Act of 1968, 42 U.S.C. § 3610, to seek injunctive relief and damages from their landlord for discriminating against non-white rental applicants. Section 810(d) of the Act provides that a "person aggrieved" may bring suit in federal court "to enforce rights granted or protected" by the Act. Section 810(a) defines "person aggrieved" to mean one "who claims to have been injured by a discriminatory housing practice ∗ ∗ ∗." The plaintiffs here claimed damages for (1) lost social benefits of living in an integrated community, (2) lost business and professional advantages, and (3) embarrassment and economic injury from being "stigmatized" as residents of a "white ghetto."

Justice Douglas, for a unanimous Court, held that the statute "showed 'a congressional intention to define standing as broadly as is permitted by Article III ∗ ∗ ∗' insofar as tenants of the same housing unit are concerned" (p. 209). Legislative history, consistent administrative construction, and the determination by HUD in this case that the plaintiffs were aggrieved were cited to support this conclusion. Further, the opinion inferred from the Act's structure that, in achieving compliance, "the main generating force must be private suits in which ∗ ∗ ∗ the complainants act not only on their own behalf but also 'as private attorneys general in vindicating a policy that Congress considered to be of the highest priority' " (pp. 210–11).[15]

Justice White, joined by Justices Blackmun and Powell, concurred in the opinion of the Court but wrote specially to note (p. 212): "Absent the Civil Rights Act of 1968, I would have great difficulty in concluding that petitioners' complaint in this case presented a case or controversy within the jurisdiction of the District Court under Article III of the Constitution. But with that statute purporting to give all those who are authorized to complain to the agency the right also to sue in court, I would sustain the statute insofar as it extends standing to those in the position of the petitioners in this case. * * *"

Justice White's approach was endorsed in Linda R.S. v. Richard D., Paragraph (6)(a), *supra*, 410 U.S. at 617 n. 3 (dictum) ("Congress may enact statutes creating legal rights, the invasion of which creates standing, even though no injury would exist without the statute"), and in Warth v. Seldin, Paragraph (6)(b), *supra*, 422 U.S. at 500–01 (dictum) (emphasis added) ("[t]he actual or threatened injury required by Art. III may exist *solely* by virtue of 'statutes creating legal rights, the invasion of which creates standing' ").

In Havens Realty Corp. v. Coleman, 455 U.S. 363, 372–74 (1982), the Court held that a black "tester"—who posed as a renter or purchaser of housing to collect evidence of racial steering practices—had standing to seek equitable and monetary relief against private parties under § 804 of the Fair Housing Act of 1968, 42 U.S.C. § 3604. The Court reasoned that the Act conferred on the tester an enforceable legal right not to be denied, because of racial steering, truthful information about the availability of housing. (A white tester, to whom the defendant had given truthful information, was held to lack standing under this theory). But the Court also insisted that "the sole requirement for standing to sue under [the Act] is the Art. III minima of injury in fact: that the plaintiff allege that as a result of the defendant's actions he has suffered 'a distinct and palpable injury' "; accord, *e.g.*, Gladstone, note 15, *supra*, at 100. Is it significant that the plaintiff in Havens sought damages as well as equitable relief?

The federal Clean Air Act provides that "any person may commence a civil action on his own behalf" against a polluter who violates the Act, or against the Administrator of EPA for failing to perform a nondiscretionary duty. 42 U.S.C. § 7604(a). In Metropolitan Washington Coalition for Clean Air v. District of Columbia, 511 F.2d 809, 814 n. 26 (D.C.Cir.1975) (per curiam), the D.C. Circuit ruled that a plaintiff suing under this provision did not need to allege injury in order to establish standing. Other courts have disagreed. See, *e.g.*, NRDC, Inc. v. U.S. EPA, 507 F.2d 905, 908–11 (9th Cir.1974). See generally Currie, *Judicial Review Under Federal Pollution Laws*, 62 Iowa L.Rev. 1221, 1271–80 (1977).

---

15. In Gladstone, *supra*, § 812 of the 1968 Civil Rights Act, which provides simply that specified rights granted by the Act "may be enforced by civil actions in appropriate United States district courts * * *," was given the same broad construction as § 810 had been in Trafficante. The Court held that a village and four white residents could sue realtors who allegedly were "steering" non-white homebuyers into, and white buyers away from, a particular neighborhood. The residents were held to have standing under Trafficante. The village's Article III standing was upheld on the basis of the profound adverse consequences to it that could result from manipulation of the racial composition of its neighborhoods.

Can the D.C. Circuit's view of congressional power be squared with the notion of "injury" as a constitutional limitation? Would its view endanger proper exercise of the judicial function? Does authorization of suit by Congress mitigate the separation of powers concerns that underlie Article III—even though Congress is authorizing the Judiciary to entertain suit against the Executive Branch? See Part III of Justice Harlan's dissenting opinion in Flast v. Cohen, 392 U.S. 83, 107 (1968), which follows this Note; Monaghan, *Constitutional Adjudication: The Who and When,* 82 Yale L.J. 1363, 1375–79 (1973). But *cf.* McClure v. Carter, 513 F.Supp. 265 (D. Idaho 1981) (dismissing, for lack of standing, a congressionally-authorized suit by a Senator who challenged the constitutional validity of a judicial appointment), *affirmed sub nom.* McClure v. Reagan, 454 U.S. 1025 (1981), pp. 156–57, *infra.*[16]

(10) *The Bearing of State Law on Standing.* Article III's definition of judicial power applies only to the federal courts. The state courts are thus free to adjudicate federal questions even when there is no "case or controversy" within the meaning of Article III; some state courts, for example, issue advisory opinions. See p. 70, *supra.*[17]

In Tileston v. Ullman, 318 U.S. 44 (1943) (per curiam), the Connecticut Supreme Court had rejected, on the merits, a physician's constitutional challenge to a state statute prohibiting the use or distribution of contraceptives. The Supreme Court dismissed his appeal on the ground that the only constitutional attack on the statute—that it worked a deprivation of life without due process—was based on the rights not of the physician but of his patients, which he had no standing to assert. See also Doremus v. Board of Educ., 342 U.S. 429, 434 (1952), p. 154, *infra* (dismissing, for want of standing, an appeal from a state judgment denying relief on the merits in a state taxpayer's challenge to a state statute).

Should the Connecticut Supreme Court's opinion be viewed as recognizing, under state law, a legal interest that protects physicians from official interference with proper professional treatment of their patients? Does Article III place any limits on the power of the states to create such legal interests, provided they are genuine? See Diamond v. Charles, 476 U.S. 54, 65 n. 17 (1986) (dictum) ("The Illinois Legislature, of course, has the power to create new interests, the invasion of which may confer standing. In such a case, the requirements of Art. III may be met.") See also Justice Frankfurter's separate opinion in Coleman v. Miller, 307 U.S. 433, 465–66

---

16. Congress has often given the Attorney General or other federal officials power to bring suit for the purpose of enforcing laws that do not benefit the agency or officials empowered to sue. See, *e.g.,* § 301 of the Voting Rights Act Amendments of 1975, 42 U.S.C. § 1973bb; Title VII of the Civil Rights Act of 1964, §§ 706–07, as amended, 42 U.S.C. §§ 2000e–5 to 2000e–6. In a regulatory scheme like the Clean Air Act, should Congress have equal power to use the device of suits by *private* attorneys general? See Fallon, Paragraph (6)(b), *supra,* at 30–35, 54–56.

17. For an argument that standing to raise a federal question in state court

should itself be a matter of federal law, see the comments of Professor Freund, in Supreme Court and Supreme Law 35 (E. Cahn ed. 1954); Varat, Paragraph (6)(d), *supra,* at 311–13.

May a state court refuse, on standing grounds, to hear a federal cause of action in which a federal court would uphold standing? See generally Chap. IV, Sec. 2, *infra;* Chap. V, Sec. 2A, pp. 581–90, *infra;* Gordon & Gross, *Justiciability of Federal Claims in State Court,* 59 Notre Dame L.Rev. 1145 (1984).

(1939), p. 156, *infra*. Compare the question of Congress's power to create new legal interests, Paragraph (9), *supra*.

Suppose Dr. Ullman proceeded to distribute contraceptives and was prosecuted under the statute. Could the state supreme court's prior judgment preclude litigation of any constitutional challenge in the state courts? In the Supreme Court, on review of a judgment affirming his conviction? See Fidelity Nat. Bank & Trust Co. v. Swope, 274 U.S. 123 (1927), p. 235, *infra*.

Assuming the correctness of the Supreme Court's holding in Tileston (a dubious assumption in light of later decisions), does it follow that the Court would have lacked power to review a state court judgment holding the statute unconstitutional on the merits and enjoining its enforcement? If so, unless a state prosecutor were willing to risk contempt, wouldn't the state court's decision of a matter of federal constitutional law be unreviewable? Compare City of Revere v. Massachusetts Gen. Hosp., Paragraph (8), *supra*.

FLAST v. COHEN
392 U.S. 83, 88 S.Ct. 1942, 20 L.Ed.2d 947 (1968).
Appeal from the United States District Court for the Southern
District of New York.

MR. CHIEF JUSTICE WARREN delivered the opinion of the Court.

In Frothingham v. Mellon, 262 U.S. 447 (1923), this Court ruled that a federal taxpayer is without standing to challenge the constitutionality of a federal statute. That ruling has stood for 45 years as an impenetrable barrier to suits against Acts of Congress brought by individuals who can assert only the interest of federal taxpayers. In this case, we must decide whether the Frothingham barrier should be lowered when a taxpayer attacks a federal statute on the ground that it violates the Establishment and Free Exercise Clauses of the First Amendment.

Appellants filed suit in the United States District Court for the Southern District of New York to enjoin the allegedly unconstitutional expenditure of federal funds under Titles I and II of the Elementary and Secondary Education Act of 1965, 20 U.S.C. §§ 241a et seq., 821 et seq. The complaint alleged that the seven appellants had as a common attribute that "each pay[s] income taxes of the United States," and it is clear from the complaint that the appellants were resting their standing to maintain the action solely on their status as federal taxpayers. The appellees, who are charged by Congress with administering the Elementary and Secondary Education Act of 1965, were sued in their official capacities.

The gravamen of the appellants' complaint was that federal funds appropriated under the Act were being used to finance instruction in reading, arithmetic, and other subjects in religious schools, and to purchase textbooks and other instructional materials for use in such schools. * * * Such expenditures of federal tax funds, appellants alleged, violate the First Amendment because "they constitute a law respecting an establishment of religion" and because "they prohibit the free exercise of religion on the part of the [appellants] * * * by reason of the fact that they constitute compulsory taxation for religious purposes." The complaint asked for a declaration that appellees' actions in approving the expenditure of federal funds for the alleged purposes were not authorized by the Act or, in the alternative, that if appellees' actions are deemed within the authority and intent of the Act, "the Act is to that extent unconstitutional and void." The complaint also prayed for an injunction to enjoin appellees from approving any expenditure of federal funds for the allegedly unconstitutional purposes. The complaint further requested that a three-judge court be convened as provided in 28 U.S.C. §§ 2282, 2284.

* * * The three-judge court * * * ruled on the authority of Frothingham that appellants lacked standing. * * * From the dismissal of their complaint on that ground, appellants appealed directly to this Court, 28 U.S.C. § 1253, and we noted probable jurisdiction. * * *

* * *

II.

This Court first faced squarely the question whether a litigant asserting only his status as a taxpayer has standing to maintain a suit in a federal court in Frothingham v. Mellon, *supra,* and that decision must be the starting point for analysis in this case. The taxpayer in Frothingham attacked as unconstitutional the Maternity Act of 1921, 42 Stat. 224, which established a federal program of grants to those States which would undertake programs to reduce maternal and infant mortality. The taxpayer alleged that Congress, in enacting the challenged statute, had exceeded the powers delegated to it under Article I of the Constitution and had invaded the legislative province reserved to the several States by the Tenth Amendment. The taxpayer complained that the result of the allegedly unconstitutional enactment would be to increase her future federal tax liability and "thereby take her property without due process of law." The Court noted that a federal taxpayer's "interest in the moneys of the treasury * * * is comparatively minute and indeterminable" and that "the effect upon future taxation, of any payment out of the [Treasury's] funds, * * * [is] remote, fluctuating and uncertain." As a result, the Court ruled that the taxpayer had failed to allege the type of "direct injury" necessary to confer standing.

Although the barrier Frothingham erected against federal taxpayer suits has never been breached, the decision has been the source of some confusion and the object of considerable criticism. The confusion has developed as commentators have tried to determine whether Frothingham establishes a constitutional bar to taxpayer suits or whether the Court was simply imposing a rule of self-restraint which was not constitutionally compelled.[6] * * * The opinion delivered in Frothingham can be read to support either position. The concluding sentence of the opinion states that, to take jurisdiction of the taxpayer's suit, "would be not to decide a judicial controversy, but to assume a position of authority over the governmental acts of another and co-equal department, an authority which plainly we do not possess." Yet the concrete reasons given for denying standing to a federal taxpayer suggest that the Court's holding rests on something less than a constitutional foundation. For example, the Court conceded that

---

6. The prevailing view of the commentators is that Frothingham announced only a nonconstitutional rule of self-restraint. See, *e.g.,* Jaffe, *Standing to Secure Judicial Review: Private Actions,* 75 Harv.L.Rev. 255, 302–303 (1961); Davis, *Standing to Challenge Governmental Action,* 39 Minn. L.Rev. 353, 386–391 (1955). * * *

standing had previously been conferred on municipal taxpayers to sue in that capacity. However, the Court viewed the interest of a federal taxpayer in total federal tax revenues as "comparatively minute and indeterminable" when measured against a municipal taxpayer's interest in a smaller city treasury. This suggests that the petitioner in Frothingham was denied standing not because she was a taxpayer but because her tax bill was not large enough. In addition, the Court spoke of the "attendant inconveniences" of entertaining that taxpayer's suit because it might open the door of federal courts to countless such suits "in respect of every other appropriation act and statute whose administration requires the outlay of public money, and whose validity may be questioned." Such a statement suggests pure policy considerations.

* * * Whatever the merits of the current debate over Frothingham, its very existence suggests that we should undertake a fresh examination of the limitations upon standing to sue in a federal court and the application of those limitations to taxpayer suits.

III.

* * * [T]he judicial power of federal courts is constitutionally restricted to "cases" and "controversies." * * * Embodied in the words "cases" and "controversies" are two complementary but somewhat different limitations. In part those words limit the business of federal courts to questions presented in an adversary context and in a form historically viewed as capable of resolution through the judicial process. And in part those words define the role assigned to the judiciary in a tripartite allocation of power to assure that the federal courts will not intrude into areas committed to the other branches of government. Justiciability is the term of art employed to give expression to this dual limitation placed upon federal courts by the case-and-controversy doctrine.

Justiciability is itself a concept of uncertain meaning and scope. * * *

Part of the difficulty in giving precise meaning and form to the concept of justiciability stems from the uncertain historical antecedents of the case-and-controversy doctrine. For example, Mr. Justice Frankfurter twice suggested that historical meaning could be imparted to the concepts of justiciability and case and controversy by reference to the practices of the courts of Westminster when the Constitution was adopted. Joint Anti-Fascist Refugee Committee v. McGrath, 341 U.S. 123, 150 (1951) (concurring opinion); Coleman v. Miller, 307 U.S. 433, 460 (1939) (separate opinion). However, the power of English judges to deliver advisory opinions was well established at the time the Constitution was drafted. 3 K. Davis, Administrative Law Treatise 127–128 (1958). And it is quite clear that "the oldest and most consistent thread in the federal law of justiciability is that the federal courts will not give advisory opinions." C. Wright, Federal Courts 34 (1963). Thus, the implicit policies embodied in Article III, and not history alone, impose the rule against advisory opinions on federal courts. * * *

Additional uncertainty exists in the doctrine of justiciability because that doctrine has become a blend of constitutional requirements and policy considerations. And a policy limitation is "not always clearly distinguished from the constitutional limitation." Barrows v. Jackson, 346 U.S. 249, 255 (1953). * * *

It is in this context that the standing question presented by this case must be viewed and that the Government's argument on that question must be evaluated. As we understand it, the Government's position is that the constitutional scheme of separation of powers, and the deference owed by the federal judiciary to the other two branches of government within that scheme, present an absolute bar to taxpayer suits challenging the validity of federal spending programs. * * * According to the Government, the resolution of such disagreements is committed to other branches of the Federal Government and not to the judiciary. Consequently, the Government contends that, under no circumstances, should standing be conferred on federal taxpayers to challenge a federal taxing or spending program.[17] An analysis of the function served by standing limitations compels a rejection of the Government's position.

* * *

Despite the complexities and uncertainties, some meaningful form can be given to the jurisdictional limitations placed on federal court power by the concept of standing. The fundamental aspect of standing is that it focuses on the party seeking to get his complaint before a federal court and not on the issues he wishes to have adjudicated. * * * In other words, when standing is placed in issue in a case, the question is whether the person whose standing is challenged is a proper party to request an adjudication of a particular issue and not whether the issue itself is justiciable. Thus, a party may have standing in a particular case, but the federal court may nevertheless decline to pass on the merits of the case because, for example, it presents a political question. * * *

When the emphasis in the standing problem is placed on whether the person invoking a federal court's jurisdiction is a proper party to maintain the action, the weakness of the Government's argument in this case becomes apparent. The question whether a particular person is a proper party to maintain the action does not, by its own force, raise separation of powers problems related to improper judicial interference in areas committed to other branches of the Federal Government. Such problems arise, if at all, only from the substantive issues the individual seeks to have adjudicated. Thus, in terms of Article III limitations on federal court jurisdiction, the question of standing is related only to whether the dispute sought to be adjudicated will be presented in an adversary context and in a form historically viewed as capable of judicial resolution. It is for that reason that the emphasis in standing problems is on whether the party

17. The logic of the Government's argument would compel it to concede that a taxpayer would lack standing even if Congress engaged in such palpably unconstitutional conduct as providing funds for the construction of churches for particular sects. The Government professes not to be bothered by such a result because it contends there might be individuals in society other than taxpayers who could invoke federal judicial power to challenge such unconstitutional appropriations. However, if as we conclude there are circumstances under which a taxpayer will be a proper and appropriate party to seek judicial review of federal statutes, the taxpayer's access to federal courts should not be barred because there might be at large in society a hypothetical plaintiff who might possibly bring such a suit.

invoking federal court jurisdiction has "a personal stake in the outcome of the controversy," Baker v. Carr, [369 U.S. 186, 204 (1962)], and whether the dispute touches upon "the legal relations of parties having adverse legal interests." Aetna Life Insurance Co. v. Haworth, [300 U.S. 227, 240–41 (1937)]. A taxpayer may or may not have the requisite personal stake in the outcome, depending upon the circumstances of the particular case. Therefore, we find no absolute bar in Article III to suits by federal taxpayers challenging allegedly unconstitutional federal taxing and spending programs. There remains, however, the problem of determining the circumstances under which a federal taxpayer will be deemed to have the personal stake and interest that impart the necessary concrete adverseness to such litigation so that standing can be conferred on the taxpayer *qua* taxpayer consistent with the constitutional limitations of Article III.

IV.

The various rules of standing applied by federal courts have not been developed in the abstract. Rather, they have been fashioned with specific reference to the status asserted by the party whose standing is challenged and to the type of question he wishes to have adjudicated. We have noted that, in deciding the question of standing, it is not relevant that the substantive issues in the litigation might be nonjusticiable. However, our decisions establish that, in ruling on standing, it is both appropriate and necessary to look to the substantive issues for another purpose, namely, to determine whether there is a logical nexus between the status asserted and the claim sought to be adjudicated. For example, standing requirements will vary in First Amendment religion cases depending upon whether the party raises an Establishment Clause claim or a claim under the Free Exercise Clause. Such inquiries into the nexus between the status asserted by the litigant and the claim he presents are essential to assure that he is a proper and appropriate party to invoke federal judicial power. Thus, our point of reference in this case is the standing of individuals who assert only the status of federal taxpayers and who challenge the constitutionality of a federal spending program. Whether such individuals have standing to maintain that form of action turns on whether they can demonstrate the necessary stake as taxpayers in the outcome of the litigation to satisfy Article III requirements.

The nexus demanded of federal taxpayers has two aspects to it. First, the taxpayer must establish a logical link between that status and the type of legislative enactment attacked. Thus, a taxpayer will be a proper party to allege the unconstitutionality only of exercises of congressional power under the taxing and spending clause of Art. I, § 8, of the Constitution. It will not be sufficient to allege an incidental expenditure of tax funds in the administration of an essentially regulatory statute. This requirement is consistent with the limitation imposed upon state-taxpayer standing in federal courts in Doremus v. Board of Education, 342 U.S. 429 (1952). Secondly, the taxpayer must establish a nexus between that status and the precise nature of the constitutional infringement alleged. Under this requirement, the taxpayer must show that the challenged enactment exceeds specific constitutional limitations imposed upon the exercise of the congressional taxing and spending power and not simply that the enactment is generally beyond the powers delegated to Congress by Art. I, § 8. When both nexuses are established, the litigant will have shown a taxpayer's stake in the outcome of the controversy and will be a proper and appropriate party to invoke a federal court's jurisdiction.

The taxpayer-appellants in this case have satisfied both nexuses to support their claim of standing under the test we announce today. Their constitutional challenge is made to an exercise by Congress of its power under Art. I, § 8, to spend for the general welfare, and the challenged program involves a substantial expenditure of federal tax funds. In addition, appellants have alleged that the challenged expenditures violate the Establishment and Free Exercise Clauses of the First Amendment. Our history vividly illustrates that one of the specific evils feared by those who drafted the Establishment Clause and fought for its adoption was that the taxing and spending power would be used to favor one religion over another or to support religion in general. James Madison, who is generally recognized as the leading architect of the religion clauses of the First Amendment, observed in his famous Memorial and Remonstrance Against Religious Assessments that "the same authority which can force a citizen to contribute three pence only of his property for the support of any one establishment, may force him to conform to any other establishment in all cases whatsoever." 2 Writings of James Madison 183, 186 (Hun ed. 1901). The concern of Madison and his supporters was quite clearly that religious liberty ultimately would be the victim if government could employ its taxing and spending powers to aid one religion over another or to aid religion in general. The Establishment Clause was designed as a specific bulwark against such potential abuses of governmental power, and that clause of the First Amendment [25] operates as a specific constitutional limitation upon the exercise by Congress of the taxing and spending power conferred by Art. I, § 8.

The allegations of the taxpayer in Frothingham v. Mellon, *supra*, were quite different from those made in this case, and the result in Frothingham is consistent with the test of taxpayer standing announced today. The taxpayer in Frothingham attacked a federal spending program and she, therefore, established the first nexus required. However, she lacked standing because her constitutional attack was not based on an allegation that Congress, in enacting the Maternity Act of 1921, had breached a specific limitation upon its taxing and spending power. The taxpayer in Frothingham alleged essentially that Congress, by enacting the challenged statute, had exceeded the general powers delegated to it by Art. I, § 8, and that Congress had thereby invaded the legislative province reserved to the States by the Tenth Amendment. To be sure, Mrs. Frothingham made the additional allegation that her tax liability would be increased as a result of the allegedly unconstitutional enactment, and she framed that allegation in terms of a deprivation of property without due process of law. However,

25. Appellants have also alleged that the Elementary and Secondary Education Act of 1965 violates the Free Exercise Clause of the First Amendment. This Court has recognized that the taxing power can be used to infringe the free exercise of religion. Murdock v. Commonwealth of Pennsylvania, 319 U.S. 105 (1943). Since we hold that appellants' Establishment Clause claim is sufficient to establish the nexus between their status and the precise nature of the constitutional infringement alleged, we need not decide whether the Free Exercise claim, standing alone, would be adequate to confer standing in this case. We do note, however, that the challenged tax in Murdock operated upon a particular class of taxpayers. When such exercises of the taxing power are challenged, the proper party emphasis in the federal standing doctrine would require that standing be limited to the taxpayers within the affected class.

the Due Process Clause of the Fifth Amendment does not protect taxpayers against increases in tax liability, and the taxpayer in Frothingham failed to make any additional claim that the harm she alleged resulted from a breach by Congress of the specific constitutional limitations imposed upon an exercise of the taxing and spending power. In essence, Mrs. Frothingham was attempting to assert the States' interest in their legislative prerogatives and not a federal taxpayer's interest in being free of taxing and spending in contravention of specific constitutional limitations imposed upon Congress' taxing and spending power.

We have noted that the Establishment Clause of the First Amendment does specifically limit the taxing and spending power conferred by Art. I, § 8. Whether the Constitution contains other specific limitations can be determined only in the context of future cases. However, whenever such specific limitations are found, we believe a taxpayer will have a clear stake as a taxpayer in assuring that they are not breached by Congress. Consequently, we hold that a taxpayer will have standing consistent with Article III to invoke federal judicial power when he alleges that congressional action under the taxing and spending clause is in derogation of those constitutional provisions which operate to restrict the exercise of the taxing and spending power. The taxpayer's allegation in such cases would be that his tax money is being extracted and spent in violation of specific constitutional protections against such abuses of legislative power. Such an injury is appropriate for judicial redress, and the taxpayer has established the necessary nexus between his status and the nature of the allegedly unconstitutional action to support his claim of standing to secure judicial review. Under such circumstances, we feel confident that the questions will be framed with the necessary specificity, that the issues will be contested with the necessary adverseness and that the litigation will be pursued with the necessary vigor to assure that the constitutional challenge will be made in a form traditionally thought to be capable of judicial resolution. We lack that confidence in cases such as Frothingham where a taxpayer seeks to employ a federal court as a forum in which to air his generalized grievances about the conduct of government or the allocation of power in the Federal System.

While we express no view at all on the merits of appellants' claims in this case, their complaint contains sufficient allegations under the criteria we have outlined to give them standing to invoke a federal court's jurisdiction for an adjudication on the merits.

Reversed.

MR. JUSTICE DOUGLAS, concurring.

While I have joined the opinion of the Court, I do not think that the test it lays down is a durable one for the reasons stated by my Brother Harlan. I think, therefore, that it will suffer erosion and in time result in the demise of Frothingham v. Mellon, 262 U.S. 447. It would therefore be the part of wisdom, as I see the problem, to be rid of Frothingham here and now.

I do not view with alarm, as does my Brother Harlan, the consequences of that course. Frothingham, decided in 1923, was in the heyday of substantive due process, when courts were sitting in judgment on the wisdom or reasonableness of legislation. * * *

When the Court used substantive due process to determine the wisdom or reasonableness of legislation, it was indeed transforming itself into the Council of Revision which was rejected by the Constitutional Convention. It was that judicial attitude, not the theory of standing to sue rejected in Frothingham, that involved "important hazards for the continued effectiveness of the federal judiciary," to borrow a phrase from my Brother Harlan. A contrary result in Frothingham in that setting might well have accentuated an ominous trend to judicial supremacy.

But we no longer undertake to exercise that kind of power. Today's problem is in a different setting.

* * *

The States have experimented with taxpayers' suits and with only two exceptions now allow them. A few state decisions are frankly based on the theory that a taxpayer is a private attorney general seeking to vindicate the public interest. Some of them require that the taxpayer have more than an infinitesimal financial stake in the problem. At the federal level, Congress can of course define broad categories of "aggrieved" persons who have standing to litigate cases or controversies. But, contrary to what my Brother Harlan suggests, the failure of Congress to act has not barred this Court from allowing standing to sue and from providing remedies. * * *

Taxpayers can be vigilant private attorneys general. Their stake in the outcome of litigation may be *de minimis* by financial standards, yet very great when measured by a particular constitutional mandate. * * *

The judiciary is an indispensable part of the operation of our federal system. With the growing complexities of government it is often the one and only place where effective relief can be obtained. If the judiciary were to become a super-legislative group sitting in judgment on the affairs of people, the situation would be intolerable. But where wrongs to individuals are done by violation of specific guarantees, it is abdication for courts to close their doors.

* * *

There need be no inundation of the federal courts if taxpayers' suits are allowed. There is a wise judicial discretion that usually can distinguish between the frivolous question and the substantial question, between cases ripe for decision and cases that need prior administrative processing, and the like. * * *

* * *

Mr. Justice Stewart, concurring.

I join the judgment and opinion of the Court, which I understand to hold only that a federal taxpayer has standing to assert that a specific expenditure of federal funds violates the Establishment Clause of the First Amendment. Because that clause plainly prohibits taxing and spending in aid of religion, every taxpayer can claim a personal constitutional right not to be taxed for the support of a religious institution. The present case is thus readily distinguishable from Frothingham v. Mellon, 262 U.S. 447, where the taxpayer did not rely on an explicit constitutional prohibition but instead questioned the scope of the powers delegated to the national legislature by Article I of the Constitution. * * *

Mr. Justice Fortas, concurring.

I would confine the ruling in this case to the proposition that a taxpayer may maintain a suit to challenge the validity of a federal expenditure on the ground that the expenditure violates the Establishment Clause. * * *

Perhaps the vital interest of a citizen in the establishment issue, without reference to his taxpayer's status, would be acceptable as a basis for this challenge. We need not decide this. But certainly, I believe, we must recognize that our principle of judicial scrutiny of legislative acts which raise important constitutional questions requires that the issue here presented—the separation of state and church—which the Founding Fathers regarded as fundamental to our constitutional system—should be subjected to judicial testing. This is not a question which we, if we are to be faithful to our trust, should consign to limbo, unacknowledged, unresolved, and undecided.

On the other hand, the urgent necessities of this case and the precarious opening through which we find our way to confront it, do not demand that we open the door to a general assault upon exercises of the spending power. The status of taxpayer should not be accepted as a launching pad for an attack upon any target other than legislation affecting the Establishment Clause. See concurring opinion of STEWART, J., ante.

MR. JUSTICE HARLAN, dissenting. * * *

I.

It is desirable first to restate the basic issues in this case. The question here is not, as it was not in Frothingham, whether "a federal taxpayer is without standing to challenge the constitutionality of a federal statute." It could hardly be disputed that federal taxpayers may, as taxpayers, contest the constitutionality of tax obligations imposed severally upon them by federal statute. * * *

The lawsuits here and in Frothingham are fundamentally different. They present the question whether federal taxpayers qua taxpayers may, in suits in which they do not contest the validity of their previous or existing tax obligations, challenge the constitutionality of the uses for which Congress has authorized the expenditure of public funds. These differences in the purposes of the cases are reflected in differences in the litigants' interests. An action brought to contest the validity of tax liabilities assessed to the plaintiff is designed to vindicate interests that are personal and proprietary. The wrongs alleged and the relief sought by such a plaintiff are unmistakably private; only secondarily are his interests representative of those of the general population. * * *

The complaint in this case, unlike that in Frothingham, contains no allegation that the contested expenditures will in any fashion affect the amount of these taxpayers' own existing or foreseeable tax obligations. Even in cases in which such an allegation is made, the suit cannot result in an adjudication either of the plaintiff's tax liabilities or of the propriety of any particular level of taxation. The relief available to such a plaintiff consists entirely of the vindication of rights held in common by all citizens. * * *

Nor are taxpayers' interests in the expenditure of public funds differentiated from those of the general public by any special rights retained by them in their tax payments. The simple fact is that no such rights can sensibly be said to exist. Taxes are ordinarily levied by the United States without limitations of purpose; absent such a limitation, payments received by the Treasury in satisfaction of tax obligations lawfully created become part of the Government's general funds. * * *

[T]he United States holds its general funds, not as stakeholder or trustee for those who have paid its imposts, but as surrogate for the population at large. * * *

Surely it is plain that the rights and interests of taxpayers who contest the constitutionality of public expenditures are markedly different from those of "Hohfeldian" plaintiffs,[5] including those taxpayer-plaintiffs who challenge the validity of their own tax liabilities. We must recognize that these non-Hohfeldian plaintiffs complain, just as the petitioner in Frothingham sought to complain, not as taxpayers, but as "private attorneys-general." The interests they represent, and the rights they espouse, are bereft of any personal or proprietary coloration. They are, as litigants, indistinguishable from any group selected at random from among the general population, taxpayers and nontaxpayers alike. These are and must be, to adopt Professor Jaffe's useful phrase, "public actions" brought to vindicate public rights.

It does not, however, follow that suits brought by non-Hohfeldian plaintiffs are excluded by the "case or controversy" clause of Article III of the Constitution from the jurisdiction of the federal courts. This and other federal courts have repeatedly held that individual litigants, acting as private attorneys-general, may have standing as "representatives of the public interest." Scripps–Howard Radio v. Federal Communications Comm., 316 U.S. 4, 14. See also [, *e.g.*,] Federal Communications Commission v. Sanders Bros. Radio Station, 309 U.S. 470, 477. And see, on actions *qui tam,* Marvin v. Trout, 199 U.S. 212, 225; United States ex rel. Marcus v. Hess, 317 U.S. 537, 546. The various lines of authority are by no means free of difficulty, and certain of the cases may be explicable as involving a personal, if remote, economic interest, but I think that it is, nonetheless, clear that non-Hohfeldian plaintiffs as such are not *constitutionally* excluded from the federal courts. The problem ultimately presented by this case is, in my view, therefore to determine in what circumstances, consonant with the character and proper functioning of the federal courts, such suits should be permitted.[8] * * *

II.

As I understand it, the Court's position is that it is unnecessary to decide in what circumstances public actions should be permitted, for it is possible to identify situations in which taxpayers who contest the constitu-

---

5. The phrase is Professor Jaffe's, adopted, of course, from W. Hohfeld, Fundamental Legal Conceptions (1923). I have here employed the phrases "Hohfeldian" and "non-Hohfeldian" plaintiffs to mark the distinction between the personal and proprietary interests of the traditional plaintiff, and the representative and public interests of the plaintiff in a public action. I am aware that we are confronted here by a spectrum of interests of varying intensities, but the distinction is sufficiently accurate, and convenient, to warrant its use at least for purposes of discussion.

8. I agree that implicit in this question is the belief that the federal courts may decline to accept for adjudication cases or questions that, although otherwise within the perimeter of their constitutional jurisdiction, are appropriately thought to be unsuitable at least for immediate judicial resolution. Compare Ashwander v. Tennessee Valley Authority, 297 U.S. 288, 345–348 (concurring opinion); H. Wechsler, Principles, Politics, and Fundamental Law 9–15 (1961); and Bickel, *Foreword: The Passive Virtues, The Supreme Court, 1960 Term,* 75 Harv.L.Rev. 40, 45–47 (1961).

tionality of federal expenditures assert "personal" rights and interests, identical in principle to those asserted by Hohfeldian plaintiffs. This position, if supportable, would of course avoid many of the difficulties of this case * * *. But, for reasons that follow, I believe that the Court's position is untenable.

The Court's analysis consists principally of the observation that the requirements of standing are met if a taxpayer has the "requisite personal stake in the outcome" of this suit. This does not, of course, resolve the standing problem; it merely restates it. The Court implements this standard with the declaration that taxpayers will be "deemed" to have the necessary personal interest if their suits satisfy two criteria: *first,* the challenged expenditure must form part of a federal spending program, and not merely be "incidental" to a regulatory program; and *second,* the constitutional provision under which the plaintiff claims must be a "specific limitation" upon Congress' spending powers. The difficulties with these criteria are many and severe, but it is enough for the moment to emphasize that they are not in any sense a measurement of any plaintiff's interest in the outcome of any suit. As even a cursory examination of the criteria will show, the Court's standard for the determination of standing and its criteria for the satisfaction of that standard are entirely unrelated.

It is surely clear that a plaintiff's interest in the outcome of a suit in which he challenges the constitutionality of a federal expenditure is not made greater or smaller by the unconnected fact that the expenditure is, or is not, "incidental" to an "essentially regulatory" program.[9] * * *

Presumably the Court does not believe that regulatory programs are necessarily less destructive of First Amendment rights, or that regulatory programs are necessarily less prodigal of public funds than are grants-in-aid, for both these general propositions are demonstrably false. The Court's disregard of regulatory expenditures is not even a logical consequence of its apparent assumption that taxpayer-plaintiffs assert essentially monetary interests, for it surely cannot matter to a taxpayer *qua* taxpayer whether an unconstitutional expenditure is used to hire the services of regulatory personnel or is distributed among private and local governmental agencies as grants-in-aid. His interest as taxpayer arises, if at all, from the fact of an unlawful expenditure, and not as a consequence of the expenditure's form. Apparently the Court has repudiated the emphasis in Frothingham upon the amount of the plaintiff's tax bill, only to substitute an equally irrelevant emphasis upon the form of the challenged expenditure.

The Court's second criterion is similarly unrelated to its standard for the determination of standing. The intensity of a plaintiff's interest in a suit is not measured, even obliquely, by the fact that the constitutional provision under which he claims is, or is not, a "specific limitation" upon Congress' spending powers. Thus, among the claims in Frothingham was

9. I must note at the outset that I cannot determine with any certainty the Court's intentions with regard to this first criterion. Its use of Doremus v. Board of Education, 342 U.S. 429, as an analogue perhaps suggests that it intends to exclude only those cases in which there are virtually no public expenditures. * * * On the other hand, the Court also emphasizes that the contested programs may not be "essentially regulatory" programs, and that the statute challenged here "involves a *substantial* expenditure of federal tax funds." Presumably this means that the Court's standing doctrine also excludes any program in which the expenditures are "insubstantial" or which cannot be characterized as a "spending" program.

the assertion that the Maternity Act, 42 Stat. 224, deprived the petitioner of property without due process of law. The Court has evidently concluded that this claim did not confer standing because the Due Process Clause of the Fifth Amendment is not a specific limitation upon the spending powers.[11] Disregarding for the moment the formidable obscurity of the Court's categories, how can it be said that Mrs. Frothingham's interests in her suit were, as a consequence of her choice of a constitutional claim, necessarily less intense than those, for example, of the present appellants? I am quite unable to understand how, if a taxpayer believes that a given public expenditure is unconstitutional, and if he seeks to vindicate that belief in a federal court, his interest in the suit can be said necessarily to vary according to the constitutional provision under which he states his claim.

The absence of any connection between the Court's standard for the determination of standing and its criteria for the satisfaction of that standard is not merely a logical ellipsis. Instead, it follows quite relentlessly from the fact that, despite the Court's apparent belief, the plaintiffs in this and similar suits are non-Hohfeldian, and it is very nearly impossible to measure sensibly any differences in the intensity of their personal interests in their suits. The Court has thus been compelled simply to postulate situations in which such taxpayer-plaintiffs will be "deemed" to have the requisite "personal stake and interest." The logical inadequacies of the Court's criteria are thus a reflection of the deficiencies of its entire position. These deficiencies will, however, appear more plainly from an examination of the Court's treatment of the Establishment Clause.

Although the Court does not altogether explain its position, the essence of its reasoning is evidently that a taxpayer's claim under the Establishment Clause is "not merely one of ultra vires," but one which instead asserts "an abridgment of individual religious liberty" and a "governmental infringement of individual rights protected by the Constitution." Choper, *The Establishment Clause and Aid to Parochial Schools*, 56 Calif.L. Rev. 260, 276. It must first be emphasized that this is apparently not founded upon any "preferred" position for the First Amendment, or upon any asserted unavailability of other plaintiffs.[12] The Court's position is instead that, because of the Establishment Clause's historical purposes, taxpayers retain rights under it quite different from those held by them under other constitutional provisions.

      *   *   *   [G]iven the ultimate obscurity of the Establishment Clause's historical purposes, it is inappropriate for this Court to draw fundamental distinctions among the several constitutional commands upon the supposed

---

11. It should be emphasized that the Court finds it unnecessary to examine the history of the Due Process Clause to determine whether it was intended as a "specific limitation" upon Congress' spending and taxing powers. Nor does the Court pause to examine the purposes of the Tenth Amendment, another of the premises of the constitutional claims in Frothingham.

12. The Court does make one reference to the availability *vel non* of other plaintiffs. It indicates that where a federal statute is directed at a specified class, "the proper party emphasis in the federal stand-

ing doctrine would require that standing be limited to the taxpayers within the affected class." Assuming *arguendo* the existence of such a federal "best-plaintiff" rule, it is difficult to see why this rule would not altogether exclude taxpayers as plaintiffs under the Establishment Clause, since there plainly may be litigants under the Clause with the personal rights and interests of Hohfeldian plaintiffs. See, *e.g.*, Board of Education of Central School District No. 1 v. Allen, 392 U.S. 236 [p. 158, *infra*], decided today.

authority of isolated dicta extracted from the clause's complex history. In particular, I have not found, and the opinion of the Court has not adduced, historical evidence that properly permits the Court to distinguish, as it has here, among the Establishment Clause, the Tenth Amendment, and the Due Process Clause of the Fifth Amendment as limitations upon Congress' taxing and spending powers.

The Court's position is equally precarious if it is assumed that its premise is that the Establishment Clause is in some uncertain fashion a more "specific" limitation upon Congress' powers than are the various other constitutional commands. It is obvious, first, that only in some Pickwickian sense are any of the provisions with which the Court is concerned "specific[ally]" limitations upon spending, for they contain nothing that is expressly directed at the expenditure of public funds. The specificity to which the Court repeatedly refers must therefore arise, not from the provisions' language, but from something implicit in their purposes. But this Court has often emphasized that Congress' powers to spend are coterminous with the purposes for which, and methods by which, it may act, and that the various constitutional commands applicable to the central government, including those implicit both in the Tenth Amendment and in the General Welfare Clause, thus operate as limitations upon spending. * * *

* * *

Even if it is assumed that such distinctions may properly be drawn, it does not follow that federal taxpayers hold any "personal constitutional right" such that they may each contest the validity under the Establishment Clause of all federal expenditures. The difficulty, with which the Court never comes to grips, is that taxpayers' suits under the Establishment Clause are not in these circumstances meaningfully different from other public actions. * * * To describe those rights and interests as personal, and to intimate that they are in some unspecified fashion to be differentiated from those of the general public, reduces constitutional standing to a word game played by secret rules.[18] * * *

III.

It seems to me clear that public actions, whatever the constitutional provisions on which they are premised, may involve important hazards for

---

18. I have equal difficulty with the argument that the religious clauses of the First Amendment create a "personal constitutional right," held by all *citizens,* such that any *citizen* may, under those clauses, contest the constitutionality of federal expenditures. The essence of the argument would presumably be that freedom from establishment is a right that inheres in every citizen, thus any citizen should be permitted to challenge any measure that conceivably involves establishment. Certain provisions of the Constitution, so the argument would run, create the basic structure of our society and of its government, and accordingly should be enforceable at the demand of every individual. Unlike the position taken today by the Court, such a doctrine of standing would at least be internally consistent, but it would also threaten the proper functioning both of the federal courts and of the principle of separation of powers. The Establishment Clause is, after all, only one of many provisions of the Constitution that might be characterized in this fashion. * * * [A]ny doctrine of standing premised upon the generality or relative importance of a constitutional command would, I think, very substantially increase the number of situations in which individual citizens could present for adjudication "generalized grievances about the conduct of government." I take it that the Court, apart from my Brother Douglas, and I are agreed that any such consequence would be exceedingly undesirable.

the continued effectiveness of the federal judiciary. Although I believe such actions to be within the jurisdiction conferred upon the federal courts by Article III of the Constitution, there surely can be little doubt that they strain the judicial function and press to the limit judicial authority. There is every reason to fear that unrestricted public actions might well alter the allocation of authority among the three branches of the Federal Government. It is not, I submit, enough to say that the present members of the Court would not seize these opportunities for abuse, for such actions would, even without conscious abuse, go far toward the final transformation of this Court into the Council of Revision which, despite Madison's support, was rejected by the Constitutional Convention. I do not doubt that there must be "some effectual power in the government to restrain or correct the infractions" of the Constitution's several commands, but neither can I suppose that such power resides only in the federal courts. * * * The powers of the federal judiciary will be adequate for the great burdens placed upon them only if they are employed prudently, with recognition of the strengths as well as the hazards that go with our kind of representative government.

Presumably the Court recognizes at least certain of these hazards, else it would not have troubled to impose limitations upon the situations in which, and purposes for which, such suits may be brought. Nonetheless, the limitations adopted by the Court are, as I have endeavored to indicate, wholly untenable. This is the more unfortunate because there is available a resolution of this problem that entirely satisfies the demands of the principle of separation of powers. This Court has previously held that individual litigants have standing to represent the public interest, despite their lack of economic or other personal interests, if Congress has appropriately authorized such suits. See especially Oklahoma v. United States Civil Service Comm., 330 U.S. 127, 137–139. Compare Perkins v. Lukens Steel Co., 310 U.S. 113, 125–127. I would adhere to that principle.[21] Any hazards to the proper allocation of authority among the three branches of the Government would be substantially diminished if public actions had been pertinently authorized by Congress and the President. I appreciate that this Court does not ordinarily await the mandate of other branches of the Government, but it seems to me that the extraordinary character of public actions, and of the mischievous, if not dangerous, consequences they involve for the proper functioning of our constitutional system, and in particular of the federal courts, makes such judicial forbearance the part of wisdom.[22] It must be emphasized that the implications of these questions

21. My premise is, as I have suggested, that non-Hohfeldian plaintiffs as such are not excluded by Article III from the jurisdiction of the federal courts. The problem is therefore to determine in what situations their suits should be permitted, and not whether a "statute constitutionally could authorize a person who shows no case or controversy to call on the courts * * *." Scripps–Howard Radio v. Comm., 316 U.S. 4, at 21 (dissenting opinion). I do not, of course, suggest that Congress' power to authorize suits by specified classes of litigants is without constitutional limitation. This Court has recognized a panoply of restrictions upon the actions that may properly be brought in federal courts, or reviewed by this Court after decision in state courts. It is enough now to emphasize that I would not abrogate these restrictions in situations in which Congress has authorized a suit. The difficult case of Muskrat v. United States, 219 U.S. 346, does not require more. Whatever the other implications of that case, it is enough to note that there the United States, as statutory defendant, evidently had "no interest adverse to the claimants." Id., at 361.

22. I am aware that there is a second category of cases in which the Court has entertained claims by non-Hohfeldian

of judicial policy are of fundamental significance for the other branches of the Federal Government.

Such a rule could readily be applied to this case. Although various efforts have been made in Congress to authorize public actions to contest the validity of federal expenditures in aid of religiously affiliated schools and other institutions, no such authorization has yet been given.

This does not mean that we would, under such a rule, be enabled to avoid our constitutional responsibilities, or that we would confine to limbo the First Amendment or any other constitutional command. The question here is not, despite the Court's unarticulated premise, whether the religious clauses of the First Amendment are hereafter to be enforced by the federal courts; the issue is simply whether plaintiffs of an *additional* category, heretofore excluded from those courts, are to be permitted to maintain suits. The recent history of this Court is replete with illustrations, including even one announced today (*supra*, at n. 12), that questions involving the religious clauses will not, if federal taxpayers are prevented from contesting federal expenditures, be left "unacknowledged, unresolved, and undecided." * * *

FURTHER NOTE ON STANDING: TAXPAYERS, GOVERNMENTS AND THEIR OFFICIALS, ORGANIZATIONS, AND INTERVENORS

(1) *Standing in Actions by Federal Taxpayers.* Three important decisions since Flast have addressed the issue of taxpayer standing.

(a) The first two, United States v. Richardson, 418 U.S. 166 (1974), and Schlesinger v. Reservists Comm. to Stop the War, 418 U.S. 208 (1974), were decided the same day, and in both the Court ruled against standing. (The facts of both cases are described at p. 125, *supra*.)

In Richardson, the Court stressed the narrowness of Flast and the vitality of "the Frothingham holding left undisturbed" by Flast. "[Plaintiff] makes no claim that appropriated funds are being spent in violation of a 'specific constitutional limitation upon the * * * taxing and spending power * * *.' [Flast], 392 U.S., at 104," but only that the CIA's expenditures had not been reported in the manner required by the Constitution's Statement and Account Clause. "[T]here is no 'logical nexus' between the asserted status of taxpayer and the claimed failure of the Congress to require the Executive to supply a more detailed report of the expenditures of that agency" (pp. 173–75).

In Reservists, the Court found the complaint deficient under Flast because it "did not challenge an enactment under Art. I, § 8, but rather the

plaintiffs: suits brought by state or local taxpayers in state courts to vindicate federal constitutional claims. A certain anomaly may be thought to have resulted from the Court's consideration of such cases while it has refused similar suits brought by federal taxpayers in the federal courts. This anomaly, if such it is, will presumably continue even under the standing doctrine announced today, since we are not told that the standing rules will hereafter be identical for the two classes of taxpayers. Although these questions are not now before the Court, I think it appropriate to note that one possible solution would be to hold that standing to raise federal questions is itself a federal question. See Freund, in E. Cahn, Supreme Court and Supreme Law 35 (1954). This would demand partial reconsideration of, for example, Doremus v. Board of Education, 342 U.S. 429. * * *

action of the Executive Branch in permitting Members of Congress to maintain their Reserve status" (p. 228).[1]

(b) Eight years later the Court decided Valley Forge Christian College v. Americans United for Separation of Church and State, Inc., 454 U.S. 464 (1982). A federal statute authorizes the lease or sale of surplus property to tax-exempt educational institutions, for a consideration that takes into account any benefit to the United States from the transferee's use of the property. Federal Property and Administrative Services Act of 1949 (FPASA), 40 U.S.C. § 471 et seq. Acting pursuant to this statute, federal officials transferred a closed army hospital and 77 acres of land to a nonprofit Christian college, which, after a 100% public benefit allowance, received property valued at $577,500 for free.

Americans United for Separation of Church and State, an organization with 90,000 taxpayer members, challenged the transfer under the Establishment Clause. The Supreme Court ruled that the members lacked standing, and therefore so did the organization as their representative. (On an organization's standing as the representative of its members, see Paragraph (8), infra). The taxpayers failed the first prong of Flast's test—permitting challenges only to "exercises of congressional power under the taxing and spending clause"—for two reasons: first, "the source of their complaint is not a congressional action, but a decision by HEW to transfer a parcel of federal property"; and second, the FPASA was "an * * * exercise of Congress' power under the Property Clause, Art. IV, § 3, cl. 2," rather than under the Taxing and Spending Clause (pp. 479–80).[2]

The Court also ruled (pp. 482–83) that standing could not be based on the claim of a "shared individuated right to a government that 'shall make no law respecting the establishment of religion.'" Reservists and Richardson rejected similar assertions of individuated rights under constitutional provisions, and "assertion of a right to a particular kind of Government conduct, which the Government has violated by acting differently, cannot alone satisfy the requirements of Art. III without draining those requirements of meaning."

Justice Brennan dissented, joined by Justices Blackmun and Marshall.[3] After reviewing the Establishment Clause's history, he concluded (p. 504) that "one of [its] primary purposes * * * was to prevent the use of tax

1. Justice Stewart concurred in Reservists, but (joined by Justice Marshall) dissented in Richardson. In his Richardson dissent, he argued (pp. 203–05) that the plaintiff was "in the position of a traditional Hohfeldian plaintiff. He contends that the Statement and Account Clause gives him a right to receive the information and burdens the Government with a correlative duty to supply it. Courts of law exist for the resolution of such right-duty disputes." Justice Stewart drew an analogy to the standing of citizens under the Freedom of Information Act to bring suit contesting the government's failure to disclose information, and added (p. 204) that "it does not matter that those to whom the duty is owed may be many." In his concurrence in Reservists, he said (pp. 228–29) "Here, unlike [Richardson], the [plaintiffs] do not allege that the [defendants] have refused to perform an affirmative duty imposed upon them by the Constitution." For criticism of this distinction between constitutional duties and prohibitions, see Justice Powell's concurrence in Richardson, 418 U.S. at 185–88.

Justices Brennan, Douglas and Marshall dissented in both cases.

2. In a footnote, the Court added the point—which it said was not necessary to its decision—that voiding the transfer would probably not increase government receipts, since the property would in all likelihood be transferred to "another nonprofit institution rather than a purchaser for cash" (pp. 480–81 n. 17).

3. Justice Stevens dissented separately.

moneys for religious purposes. *The taxpayer was the direct and intended beneficiary of the prohibition on financial aid to religion."* This history explained, he suggested, why Flast treated a taxpayer challenge under the Establishment Clause differently from other taxpayer suits.

Justice Brennan rejected the Court's effort to distinguish Flast. The Court's first distinction—between challenges to congressional and to executive action—was in his view doubly flawed: Flast challenged federal executive action in disbursing funds under a federal statute, just as in this case the plaintiffs challenged executive action under the FPASA; and in any event, "the First Amendment binds the Government as a whole, regardless of which branch is at work in a particular instance" (p. 511). The Court's second distinction—between statutes enacted under the spending power and under Article IV—was equally unavailing, for the Establishment Clause forbids the government from subsidizing religion, whether by the transfer of cash or of real property.

Is the majority's statement—that "assertion of a right to a particular kind of Government conduct, which the Government has violated by acting differently, cannot alone satisfy the requirements of Art. III without draining those requirements of meaning"—consistent with Mathews v. Heckler, pp. 132–33, *supra*? (Recall that Mathews upheld the standing of a male beneficiary under the Social Security Act to contest the Act's alleged denial of equal protection, even though no more tangible benefit would accrue to the plaintiff if he prevailed).[4]

(2) *State and Municipal Taxpayers' Actions.* Doremus v. Board of Educ., 342 U.S. 429 (1952), was a state court action to declare invalid under the federal Constitution a New Jersey statute requiring five verses of the Old Testament to be read without comment at the opening of every public school day. Each of the two plaintiffs stated that he was both a state and a municipal taxpayer, but neither asserted or showed any dollars-and-cents relation between his taxes and the statute complained of. The state court expressed misgivings about the plaintiffs' standing but entertained the action and ruled against them on the merits.

The Supreme Court dismissed the appeal for want of a justiciable controversy. Justice Jackson, speaking for the Court, said (pp. 434–35):

"We do not undertake to say that a state court may not render an opinion on a federal constitutional question even under such circumstances that it can be regarded only as advisory. But, because our own jurisdiction is cast in terms of 'case or controversy,' we cannot accept as the basis for review, nor as the basis for conclusive disposition of an issue of federal law without review, any procedure which does not constitute such.

"The taxpayer's action can meet this test, but only when it is a good-faith pocketbook action. It is apparent that the grievance which it is sought to litigate here is not a direct dollars-and-cents injury but is a religious difference. If appellants established the requisite special injury necessary to a taxpayer's case or controversy, it would not matter that their dominant inducement to action was more religious than mercenary.

---

4. On Valley Forge, see Nichol, *Standing on the Constitution: The Supreme Court and Valley Forge,* 61 N.C.L.Rev. 798 (1983). For earlier commentary on taxpayer standing, see Bittker, *The Case of the Fictitious Taxpayer: The Federal Taxpay-*er's Suit Twenty Years After Flast v. Cohen, 36 U.Chi.L.Rev. 364 (1969); Davis, *The Case of the Real Taxpayer: A Reply to Professor Bittker,* 36 U.Chi.L.Rev. 375 (1969).

It is not a question of motivation but of possession of the requisite financial interest that is, or is threatened to be, injured by the unconstitutional conduct."

Justice Douglas, joined by Justices Reed and Burton, dissented.

Are Doremus and Flast consistent, as the Flast opinion says?

In Frothingham v. Mellon, the Court said (p. 486): "The interest of a taxpayer of a municipality in the application of its moneys is direct and immediate and the remedy by injunction to prevent their misuse is not inappropriate. It is upheld by a large number of state cases and is the rule of this court." What do Doremus and Flast do to that "rule" of the Court? It seems to go without saying that a state or municipal taxpayer's action will be entertained where a federal taxpayer would have standing. See, e.g., Grand Rapids School Dist. v. Ball, 473 U.S. 373, 380 n. 5 (1985) (upholding state taxpayer standing to challenge, under the Establishment Clause, aid to nonpublic schools, and citing nine similar decisions). Should the converse also be true? Is there any reason why, if a state confers on its taxpayers a broad power to police expenditures, that should not be sufficient to establish standing for Supreme Court review of such actions? See Wieman v. Updegraff, 344 U.S. 183 (1952) (entertaining, without discussion by any justice, an appeal from a state court decision in a taxpayer's action to enjoin state officials from further payment of compensation to state employees who had failed to take a statutory loyalty oath). See generally pp. 137–38, *supra*.

(3) *Actions by States.* Consult at this point the *Note on the Standing of a State as Parens Patriae to Sue the Federal Government*, p. 331, *infra*.

See also the *Note on a State's Standing to Sue and Related Problems of Justiciability*, p. 324, *infra*, particularly at pp. 326–31.

(4) *Actions by Municipalities.* Municipal corporations have regularly been denied standing in the federal courts to attack state legislation as violative of the federal Constitution, on the ground that they have no rights against the state of which they are a creature. *E.g.,* Pawhuska v. Pawhuska Oil Co., 250 U.S. 394 (1919); Trenton v. New Jersey, 262 U.S. 182 (1923); Williams v. Mayor, 289 U.S. 36 (1933).[5]

(5) *Actions by Voters.* Many cases have recognized the standing of an individual voter to bring suit to protect the integrity of his vote. See, e.g., Smiley v. Holm, 285 U.S. 355 (1932); Leser v. Garnett, 258 U.S. 130 (1922).

In Baker v. Carr, 369 U.S. 186 (1962), p. 270, *infra*, registered state voters were held to have standing to challenge alleged malapportionment of the state legislature resulting in the dilution of their vote. The Court concluded that a sufficient "personal stake in the outcome of the adjudication" was alleged "to insure that concrete adverseness which sharpens the presentation of issues upon which the court so largely depends for illumination of difficult constitutional questions" (pp. 203–04). Justice Frankfurter,

5. In Rogers v. Brockette, 588 F.2d 1057 (5th Cir.1979), *noted*, 93 Harv.L.Rev. 586 (1980), however, the court upheld the standing of a local school district (which was treated as indistinguishable from a municipality for this purpose) to challenge state rules requiring the district to participate in the federal school lunch program. The rule against municipal standing was interpreted as a substantive holding that "the Constitution does not interfere in states' internal political organization"; this suit alleged, however, that the state rules violated federal statutes and regulations, and Congress "may interfere with a state's internal political organization in a way that the Constitution itself does not" (pp. 1069–70).

joined by Justice Harlan, dissented, resting in part on the inaptness of judicial remedies for such malapportionment. See also Wesberry v. Sanders, 376 U.S. 1 (1964); Gray v. Sanders, 372 U.S. 368 (1963).

Why weren't these voters asserting a mere "generalized grievance"?

(6) *Actions by Legislators.* In Coleman v. Miller, 307 U.S. 433 (1939), a bare majority of the Court held that Kansas state legislators who had voted against ratification of the Child Labor Amendment had standing to seek review of a state court's refusal to enjoin state officials from certifying that Kansas had ratified the amendment. One of the grounds of suit was that the amendment had been approved in the state Senate only by virtue of the vote of the Lieutenant-Governor, as presiding officer, to break a tie, and that under the Federal Constitution such a vote was ineffectual. The Court, however, recognized not only the standing of state senators to raise this issue, in protection of their official vote, but the standing of both state senators and representatives to urge also that the ratification was invalid because a previous rejection by Kansas was final, and because the proposed amendment, having been outstanding for what was claimed to be more than a reasonable time, was no longer susceptible of ratification.

To what extent was the decision dependent on the fact that the Kansas court had accorded standing to the legislators, while denying them on the merits the relief they sought? See also Karcher v. May, note 7, *infra.*

In recent years, Members of the House and Senate have often brought suit challenging official action alleged to impair their rights as legislators. The leading case upholding standing is Kennedy v. Sampson, 511 F.2d 430 (D.C.Cir.1974), in which Senator Kennedy sought a declaratory judgment that a bill passed by the House and Senate, but which the President had neither signed into law nor vetoed, had been enacted into law. The President took the position that because Congress had in the meantime adjourned, the bill had been subjected to a "pocket veto" and hence was invalid; the Senator contended that a pocket veto is unconstitutional. The court of appeals recognized his standing, on the ground that a pocket veto, if unconstitutional, improperly deprived him of an effective vote to enact legislation or to override a veto.[6] But standing has been denied when a Congressman seeks to challenge executive action as not in compliance with legislation for which he voted. See, *e.g.*, Harrington v. Bush, 553 F.2d 190 (D.C.Cir.1977).

With these cases, compare McClure v. Carter, 513 F.Supp. 265 (D.Idaho 1981), a challenge to the appointment of former Congressman Mikva to the United States Court of Appeals for the D.C. Circuit, on the ground that it

---

6. In Barnes v. Kline, 759 F.2d 21 (D.C. Cir.1984), *vacated as moot,* 107 S.Ct. 734 (1987), the court of appeals again held that plaintiffs—Members of Congress and the Senate itself (which filed suit pursuant to a Senate resolution)—could challenge a pocket veto, and on the merits found the veto unconstitutional. Judge Bork wrote a long dissent, arguing that recognition of Congressmen as plaintiffs was "a major shift in basic constitutional arrangements," was "inconsistent with the judicial function," and would "subvert[] the constitutional roles of our political institutions" (pp. 41–42). Recognition of standing here could

not be squared, he said, with the general requirements of standing set forth in recent decisions like Allen v. Wright, and with the decisions barring adjudication of "generalized grievances."

See also Goldwater v. Carter, 617 F.2d 697 (D.C.Cir.) (en banc) (per curiam) (upholding the standing of Senators and Congressmen to challenge President Carter's unilateral termination of a treaty with Taiwan), *vacated,* 444 U.S. 996 (1979) (per curiam), p. 290, *infra* (dispute held not justiciable; standing issue not reached).

violated Art. I, § 6, cl. 2, which prohibits the appointment of any Senator or Representative to any federal office whose emoluments were increased during the time for which he was elected. A special statute passed by Congress several weeks after Mikva's confirmation authorized any Senator or Member of the House to bring suit before a three-judge district court to challenge under the Emoluments Clause any judicial appointment to the D.C. Circuit made during the 96th Congress. When Senator McClure, who had opposed the appointment, brought suit under this statute, the district court ruled that he had no standing. Ex parte Lévitt, p. 126 note 5, *supra,* held that an ordinary citizen lacked standing to bring suit in just these circumstances. And unlike the legislators in Coleman v. Miller or Kennedy v. Sampson, Senator McClure could not assert that his vote had been impaired; he was simply on the losing side of the confirmation battle. Nor did the statutory authorization of suit change the outcome; "[i]t is difficult to see how this statute may, consistent with Article III, confer upon a senator or member of the House of Representatives a 'right' to seek a decision from a federal court that such a senator or member of the House would otherwise be powerless to procure" (p. 271). The Supreme Court summarily affirmed. McClure v. Reagan, 454 U.S. 1025 (1981).

Do the federal courts have a special role in settling questions of conformity to constitutional procedures defining the legitimacy of asserted governmental authority? Compare the decisions in Richardson and Reservists, Paragraph (1)(a), *supra.* Should it matter whether suit is brought by an individual legislator, by one House of Congress pursuant to a resolution thereof, or by Congress itself under a joint resolution?[7] If an individual legislator has standing to challenge a pocket veto because he has been denied an effective vote, why doesn't any constituent have standing on the theory that he has been denied effective representation?

7. In Barnes v. Kline, note 6, *supra,* the Senate was a plaintiff in a suit challenging the pocket veto. Compare, *e.g.,* United States v. American Tel. & Tel. Co., 551 F.2d 384 (D.C.Cir.1976) (subcommittee chairman allowed to intervene in suit by Executive to enjoin telephone company from complying with subcommittee's subpoena, where House retroactively passed resolution authorizing suit); Senate Select Committee on Presidential Campaign Activities v. Nixon, 498 F.2d 725 (D.C.Cir. 1974) (en banc) (congressional committee allowed to sue President to compel production of tape recordings of conversations between President and his former aide).

Cf. Karcher v. May, 108 S.Ct. 388 (1987), where, after New Jersey executive officials refused to defend the constitutionality of a "moment of silence" law challenged in federal court, the presiding officers of the New Jersey Senate and General Assembly intervened as defendants on behalf of the legislature. After the court of appeals affirmed the district court's judgment declaring the law unconstitutional, the two intervenor-defendants lost their leadership positions in the legislature. Though they appealed to the Supreme Court, their successors "withdrew" the appeal on behalf of the legislature. The intervenors nonetheless sought Supreme Court review as individual legislators and as representatives of the former legislature that had enacted the law, but the Court dismissed the appeal for want of jurisdiction. The Court stressed that whether or not the appellants could have intervened in either of those capacities, they had not done so, and hence could not appeal on that basis; they had intervened only as representatives of the incumbent legislature, and no longer had authority to pursue an appeal on that basis. The intervenors argued, alternatively, that if the case could not be heard, the judgment must be vacated for want of a proper party-defendant below. The Court rejected this contention, finding that under state law the New Jersey legislature has authority to represent the state's interests in the courts. Concurring in the judgment, Justice White stressed the Court's acknowledgement that a state legislature (and its representative) may defend the constitutionality of a state statute challenged in federal court.

Are there functional or prudential reasons to decline adjudication in cases like those just discussed? If so, should dismissal be based on lack of standing, lack of ripeness, the political question doctrine, or general equitable discretion? [8]

(7) *Actions Involving Executive Officials and Administrative Agencies.* Innumerable cases recognize the standing of an administrative or executive official to defend the constitutionality of the legislation that he is charged with administering or enforcing. *E.g.,* Boynton v. Hutchinson Gas Co., 291 U.S. 656 (1934), as explained in Coleman v. Miller, *supra,* 307 U.S. at 444.

On the other hand, the general rule at least until 1968 was that a state official lacks standing to attack the validity under the federal Constitution of the state statute that he is charged with enforcing. Smith v. Indiana, 191 U.S. 138 (1903); Braxton County Court v. West Virginia, 208 U.S. 192 (1908); Columbus & Greenville Ry. v. Miller, 283 U.S. 96 (1931).

In Board of Educ. v. Allen, 392 U.S. 236 (1968), however, members of a school board were allowed to maintain an action against the Commissioner of Education of New York to challenge the constitutionality of a state statute (N.Y.Educ.Law § 701) requiring them to lend textbooks free of charge to students in parochial schools. The Court disposed of the standing question in a footnote (p. 241 n. 5): "Appellees do not challenge the standing of appellants to press their claim in this Court. Appellants have taken an oath to support the United States Constitution. Believing § 701 to be unconstitutional, they are in the position of having to choose between violating their oath and taking a step—refusal to comply with § 701—that would be likely to bring their expulsion from office and also a reduction in state funds for their school districts. There can be no doubt that appellants thus have a 'personal stake in the outcome' of this litigation."

Are officials "better" litigants than taxpayers? Would routine litigation by officials to test the constitutionality of statutes they are charged with enforcing be desirable? If an official truly believes a statute to be invalid, should he be required to refuse to enforce it, and to raise the question as a defense to whatever sanction—*e.g.,* dismissal—he suffers for his refusal? [9]

---

8. In Riegle v. Federal Open Market Comm., 656 F.2d 873 (D.C.Cir.1981), the D.C.Circuit, following a suggestion offered by one of its members (see McGowan, *Congressmen in Court: The New Plaintiffs,* 15 Ga.L.Rev. 241 (1981)), ruled that as a matter of equitable discretion a federal court should dismiss a suit brought by a Congressman who had standing, but who "could obtain substantial relief from his fellow legislators through the enactment, repeal, or amendment of a statute" (p. 881). The complaint in the Riegle case— that a statute providing for appointment of members of the Federal Open Market Committee without Senate approval was unconstitutional—was dismissed, since the plaintiff could seek to have the statute amended. Under the approach of the Riegle case, should the suit in Kennedy v. Sampson have been dismissed, on the theory that Congress can hold up controversial bills passed just before a recess and send

them to the White House after Congress reassembles? (Senator Mansfield, the former majority leader, was reported to have followed this practice. See N.Y. Times, Nov. 10, 1974, § 1, at 44, col. 1.) But see Barnes v. Kline, note 6, *supra,* following Kennedy v. Sampson several years after the Riegle decision.

For additional commentary, see Dessem, *Congressional Standing to Sue: Whose Vote Is This, Anyway?,* 62 Notre Dame L.Rev. 1 (1986); Note, 90 Harv.L.Rev. 1632 (1977) (urging reliance on the political question rubric); Note, 82 Colum.L.Rev. 526 (1982).

9. To have standing under Allen, must an official face some realistic threat of a sanction for his failure to enforce the law? See City of South Lake Tahoe v. California Tahoe Regional Planning Agency, 625 F.2d 231 (9th Cir.1980), in which the court— reasoning that Allen had been undercut by subsequent Supreme Court decisions that

Bender v. Williamsport Area School Dist., 475 U.S. 534 (1986), also raised a question of a local official's standing. There, high school students sued their school district, school officials, and nine school board members, challenging the refusal to permit a student religious club to meet on school premises. The district court granted summary judgment to the plaintiffs; no injunction was entered, however, and no relief was granted against any defendant individually. A majority of the school board decided to comply with the ruling, but a dissenting board member (Youngman) filed an appeal. When the case reached the Supreme Court, it ruled that Youngman lacked standing to appeal. He had been sued only in his official capacity, and therefore had no financial stake in the outcome of the litigation. And "[g]enerally speaking, members of collegial bodies do not have standing to perfect an appeal the body itself has declined to take" (p. 544). Allen was distinguished on the ground that "[u]nlike the members of the school board *majority* in Allen who were put 'in the position of having to choose between violating their oath and taking a step * * * that would be likely to bring their expulsion from office * * *,' Mr. Youngman has voted his conscience and, as a member of the Board, must abide by its decision not to appeal * * *" (p. 544 n. 7).[10]

If the responsibility for carrying out the board's decision was vested exclusively in the school superintendent and his subordinates, wouldn't Youngman be in the same situation as a Congressman, who lacks standing to contest the constitutionality of a law passed by the legislature? See, *e.g.,* Harrington v. Bush, Paragraph (6), *supra.* If, instead, Youngman had some responsibility for complying with the district court's ruling, wouldn't he be in the same bind, when deciding whether to comply with the order, as the officials in Allen? Can the sentiment of a majority eliminate the injury to an individual's conscience that was of concern in Allen?

(8) *The Standing of Organizations.* Sierra Club v. Morton, p. 123, *supra,* held that organizations do not have standing to represent their particular conception of the public interest. The Court's position did not, however, restrict an organization's right to sue for injuries that it has itself suffered. For an expansive view of organizational injury, see Havens Realty Corp. v. Coleman, 455 U.S. 363, 378–79 (1982), p. 136, *supra* (nonprofit organization devoted to equal housing opportunity permitted to sue a landlord whose racial steering practices were alleged to impair the plaintiff's ability to provide services to low-income homeseekers, with a consequent drain on the organization's resources).

Nor did Sierra Club cast doubt on the common practice, frequently upheld, of permitting associations to litigate as representatives of their members, so long as the members themselves would have standing to sue. The Court summed up prevailing doctrine in Hunt v. Washington State Apple Advertising Comm'n, 432 U.S. 333, 343 (1977): "Thus we have recognized that an association has standing to bring suit on behalf of its members when: (a) its members would otherwise have standing to sue in

tighten standing requirements and clearly reject citizen standing—refused to accord standing to plaintiff officials where the risk of civil liability for failing to enforce a law they believed to be unconstitutional was slight. The Supreme Court denied certiorari, over three dissents. 449 U.S. 1039 (1980).

10. The Court also ruled that the record did not support Youngman's standing as a parent of a pupil; Chief Justice Burger, and Justices White and Rehnquist, dissented on this point.

their own right; (b) the interests it seeks to protect are germane to the organization's purpose; and (c) neither the claim asserted nor the relief requested requires the participation of individual members in the lawsuit."

The Washington State Commission in that case was not a membership organization but a statutory agency, consisting of 13 apple growers and dealers elected by growers and dealers. It was suing for declaratory and injunctive relief, on Commerce Clause grounds, against special grading and identifications requirements imposed by North Carolina on apples sold in that state. The Court found that the Commission performed the functions of a traditional trade association; that while there were no official "members" the relationship to the growers and dealers in fact carried all the indicia of membership; and, indeed, that the Commission itself could be affected by the outcome of the litigation, because its annual assessments were tied to the volume of sales of Washington apples. The Court noted but did not specifically respond to the defendants' argument that the growers could easily have sued on their own, and upheld the Commission's standing without dissent.[11]

In International Union, UAW v. Brock, 477 U.S. 274 (1986), the UAW, suing on behalf of its members, challenged rules, issued by the Secretary of Labor, limiting eligibility for a federal program providing benefits to workers laid off because of foreign competition. The government urged the Court to reject the principles of associational standing recognized in Hunt. It argued that, " 'at least absent a showing of particularized need,' " members of an organization should be permitted to litigate common questions of law or fact against the same defendant only by filing a class action in accordance with Rule 23—which, unlike organizational standing doctrine, requires the plaintiff to be an adequate representative so as to protect the interests of class members (p. 2532, quoting the government's brief). The Court disagreed, concluding that this argument overlooked the distinctive value of organizational plaintiffs, whose ability to "draw upon a pre-existing reservoir of expertise and capital * * * can assist both courts and plaintiffs" (pp. 2532–33). In addition, the Court observed that the primary reason that people join an organization—"to create an effective vehicle for vindicating interests that they share with others"—provides "some guarantee that the association will work to promote their interests" (p. 2533).

The Court noted, however, that if an organization were in fact an ineffective representative, due process principles might prevent a judgment against it from precluding claims by its members. The Court added (p. 2533): "And were we presented with evidence that such a problem existed * * * we would have to consider how it might be alleviated." But the Court found no reason to doubt the UAW's ability in the case at bar.[12]

---

11. Compare Harris v. McRae, 448 U.S. 297, 320–21 (1980) (denying the Women's Division of a Methodist Church standing to challenge, under the Free Exercise Clause, federal restrictions on Medicaid funding for abortions; the participation of individuals in the lawsuit was required because the claim required a showing of coercive effect on an individual's religious practice, and because there was a division of opinion within the plaintiff group on the abortion question); Warth v. Seldin, 422 U.S. 490, 515–16 (1975), p. 129, *supra* (association of developers lacks standing to challenge municipal zoning restrictions that are alleged to have harmed member firms; "the damages claims are not common to the entire membership, nor shared by all in equal degree," and thus "to obtain relief in damages, each member * * * who claims injury as a result of [the town's] practices must be a party to the suit").

12. Justice Powell dissented from the standing decision. He did not endorse the government's frontal attack on Hunt, fo-

Is it fair to say that the Court and the government differ on (i) whether the organization itself (rather than an affected member) can be the nominal plaintiff, and (ii) assuming the organization can be named as plaintiff, whether its adequacy as a representative should be presumed or must be proven? Are these important differences? See generally Note, 61 B.U.L. Rev. 174 (1981); Note, 1974 U.Ill.L.F. 663.

Should the UAW be required to identify particular members injured by the regulations, or does it suffice that the regulations will surely injure some members, even if it cannot now be shown which ones? Compare *Note on "Ripeness" in Public Actions Challenging Patterns or Practices in the Administration of the Law,* pp. 264–70, *infra,* especially LaDuke v. Nelson, p. 269, *infra* (holding justiciable a class action challenging an official practice likely to harm some members of the class but unlikely to affect any particular member).

(9) *Standing to Intervene and to Appeal.* In Director, Office of Workers' Compensation Programs v. Perini North River Associates, 459 U.S. 297 (1983), an administrative tribunal decided that an employee (Churchill) was not covered by the Longshoremen's and Harbor Workers' Compensation Act. Churchill sought review in the court of appeals, and the Director of the Office of Workers' Compensation Programs participated as a respondent, filing a brief supporting the employee. After the court of appeals affirmed the decision, the Director alone sought review in the Supreme Court, which upheld his standing to appeal. Though the Director, as a party respondent below, clearly had statutory authority under 28 U.S.C. § 1254(1) to seek certiorari, the Court observed that "he *may* not have Art. III standing to argue the merits of Churchill's claim ＊ ＊ ＊. However, the Director's petition makes Churchill an automatic respondent under our Rule 19.6, and in that capacity, Churchill 'may seek reversal of the judgment of the Court of Appeals on any ground urged in that court'" (p. 304).

A similar question arose in Diamond v. Charles, 476 U.S. 54 (1986). Diamond, a pediatrician opposed to abortion, was allowed to intervene as a defendant in a challenge to state legislation regulating abortions. After the court of appeals approved a permanent injunction against four sections of the statute, only Diamond appealed to the Supreme Court; the state merely filed a "letter of interest" noting that under the Court's rules it was an automatic appellee, and that its interest and Diamond's were identical. The Supreme Court dismissed the appeal on the ground that Diamond lacked standing. It first held that he could not ride "piggyback" on the state's undoubted ability to appeal; though the state was made a "party" by the Supreme Court's rules, it was not an appellant. The Court then rejected several theories under which Diamond claimed to have standing in his own right, one of which was based on his status as an intervenor. That status gave him a statutory right to seek review, but the Court ruled that he could continue the suit without the state's participation only "upon a showing ＊ ＊ ＊ that he fulfills the requirements of Art. III" (p. 68). The Court added (pp. 68–69): "We need not decide today whether a party

cusing instead on the Court's traditional reluctance to permit parties to assert the rights of third persons "for fear of inadequate representation" (p. 2536). Absent a showing that more than a small number of UAW members had a stake in the lawsuit, he argued, the union's interest might be insufficient to assure the "concrete adverseness" that previous decisions had demanded (p. 2537).

seeking to intervene before a District Court must satisfy not only the requirements of Rule 24(a)(2), but also the requirements of Art. III." [13]

Justice O'Connor, joined by Chief Justice Burger and Justice Rehnquist, concurred in part and concurred in the judgment. She agreed that Diamond in his own right had not alleged any injury cognizable under Article III, but thought the first part of the Court's opinion—holding that Diamond could not ride piggyback on the state's presence as a designated appellee—was inconsistent with the Perini decision. In Justice O'Connor's view, if Diamond was a proper party in the court of appeals, his statutorily-authorized appeal brought a justiciable controversy (to which the state was a party) before the Supreme Court. However, she argued that, at least in the court of appeals, Diamond was not a proper intervenor, and therefore she agreed that his appeal should be dismissed. [14]

NOTE ON STANDING TO CHALLENGE FEDERAL ADMINISTRATIVE ACTION

(1) Until 1970, the law of standing to challenge federal administrative action "was divided into three parts. In the absence of specific statutory provisions entitling designated persons or parties to judicial review, standing could be based upon present or threatened official infringement of an interest protected at common law; upon an interest substantively protected by a relevant organic statute (the statutorily protected-interest test); or upon an adverse economic impact when a relevant statute afforded standing to persons 'adversely affected' or 'aggrieved.'" Stewart, *Standing for Solidarity (Book Review)*, 88 Yale L.J. 1559, 1569 (1979). See also *Note on Standing to Sue*, p. 121, *supra*, Paragraph (1).

(2) A major doctrinal shift was announced in Association of Data Processing Service Orgs., Inc. v. Camp, 397 U.S. 150 (1970). Sellers of data processing services to businesses sought review under the Administrative Procedure Act (APA), 5 U.S.C. § 702, of a ruling by the Comptroller of the Currency permitting national banks to provide data processing services to other banks and to bank customers. (Section 702 provides: "A person suffering legal wrong because of agency action, or adversely affected or aggrieved by agency action within the meaning of a relevant statute, is entitled to judicial review thereof.") The district court dismissed for lack of standing, and the court of appeals affirmed, finding that the plaintiff must show either a "legal interest" or an explicit provision in the relevant

---

13. See generally Shapiro, *Some Thoughts on Intervention Before Courts, Agencies, and Arbitrators*, 81 Harv.L.Rev. 721, 726–28 (1968). Professor Shapiro argues that "there is a difference between the question whether one is a proper plaintiff or defendant in an initial action and the question whether one is entitled to intervene. * * * A may not have a dispute with C that could qualify as a case or controversy [under Article III], but he may have a sufficient interest in B's dispute with C to warrant his participation in the case once it has begun, and the case or controversy limitation should impose no barrier to his admission" (p. 726).

14. Compare Maine v. Taylor, 477 U.S. 131 (1986), a federal prosecution for transporting fish in interstate commerce in violation of state law. When the defendant contended that the state law unconstitutionally burdened interstate commerce, Maine intervened to defend the law. After the federal court of appeals reversed the defendant's conviction on the ground that the state law was indeed invalid, Maine (but not the United States) sought review. The Court ruled that Maine had standing to appeal in view of its interest in the continued enforceability of its statute and in the reinstatement of the defendant's conviction.

statute permitting suit by any party "adversely affected or aggrieved." The Supreme Court reversed, with Justice Douglas writing for the Court. After finding that the plaintiffs had suffered the requisite injury in fact, the Court rejected any requirement formulated in terms such as a "legally protected interest." He referred to Tennessee Elec. Power Co. v. TVA, 306 U.S. 118 (1939), p. 122, *supra*, which denied a competitor standing on the basis (which Justice Douglas quoted) that standing was unavailable "unless the right invaded is a legal right,—one of property, one arising out of contract, one protected against tortious invasion, or one founded on a statute which confers a privilege," and then continued:

"The 'legal interest' test goes to the merits. The question of standing is different. It concerns, apart from the 'case' or 'controversy' test, the question whether the interest sought to be protected by the complainant is arguably within the zone of interests to be protected or regulated by the statute or constitutional guarantee in question" (p. 153).

The opinion then referred to a statute that was not the principal ground of the plaintiffs' attack on the legality of the Comptroller's action, § 4 of the Bank Service Corporation Act of 1962, 12 U.S.C. § 1864: "No bank service corporation may engage in any activity other than the performance of bank services for banks." Although the Act itself had no provision authorizing review, the Court held that it established plaintiffs' standing because it "arguably brings a competitor within the zone of interests protected by it" (pp. 155–56).

In Barlow v. Collins, 397 U.S. 159 (1970), decided the same day as Data Processing, tenant farmers challenged a regulation of the Secretary of Agriculture as unauthorized by statute. The statute permitted farmers to assign certain government payments only "as security for cash or advances to finance making a crop." 16 U.S.C. § 590h(g). The challenged regulation defined this language to allow assignments to secure rent for a farm. Though this new definition increased the tenant farmers' freedom from governmental restraint, they objected because it allegedly permitted landlords to compel them to finance all their farm needs through the landlords at inflated cost. The court of appeals had denied the farmers standing on the ground that they had alleged no legally protected interest and also that they "have not shown us, nor have we found, any provision of the Food and Agriculture Act of 1965 which either expressly or impliedly gives [them] standing." Again speaking through Justice Douglas, the Court reversed. Relying on the legislative history of the specific substantive provision involved, which it viewed as indicating "a congressional intent to benefit the tenants," the Court held that "tenant farmers are clearly within the zone of interests protected by the Act." [1]

In Data Processing and Barlow, Justice Brennan, joined by Justice White, concurred in the judgment but disagreed with the Court's reasoning. In his view, the issue of standing presented a question only of injury in fact: "The Constitution requires for standing only that the plaintiff allege that actual harm resulted to him from the agency action" (p. 178). To be sure, "[b]efore the plaintiff is allowed to argue the merits, it is true that a canvass of relevant statutory materials must be made in cases challenging

1. Davis, *The Liberalized Law of Standing,* 37 U.Chi.L.Rev. 450, 455–56 (1970), argues that the focus on the interests of tenant farmers in general, rather than on the *particular interest* asserted in the litigation, was inconsistent with Data Processing, may have been due to inadvertence, and was in any event wrong.

agency action. But the canvass is made, not to determine *standing,* but to determine an aspect of *reviewability,* that is, whether Congress meant to deny or to allow judicial review of the agency action at the instance of the plaintiff." At this point, a footnote was appended: "Reviewability has often been treated as if it involved a single issue; whether agency action is conclusive and beyond judicial challenge by anyone. In reality, however, reviewability is equally concerned with a second issue: whether the *partic- ular* plaintiff then requesting review may have it" (p. 169 & n. 2).[2]

See also Arnold Tours, Inc. v. Camp, 400 U.S. 45 (1970) (travel agents accorded standing to challenge, on the basis of the same statute involved in Data Processing, a ruling by the Comptroller of the Currency that allowed national banks to provide travel services for their customers); Investment Company Inst. v. Camp, 401 U.S. 617 (1971) (investment companies and securities dealers accorded standing to challenge, on the basis of the Glass-Steagall Act, regulations allowing banks to operate mutual funds).

(3) Among the difficult questions raised by Data Processing and its immediate progeny were these: (i) Does the "zone of interests" test impli- cate the merits any less than the "legally protected interests" standard? (ii) May a plaintiff with standing nonetheless be defeated on the merits on the ground that the statute does not confer on him a legally protected interest?[3] (iii) Is the "zone of interests" test limited to cases under the APA? (iv) Do the grounds on which a litigant has been granted standing serve to limit the considerations he can raise on the merits?

For discussion of these and other questions, see Albert, *Standing to Challenge Administrative Action: An Inadequate Surrogate for Claim for Relief,* 83 Yale L.J. 425 (1974); Davis, note 1, *supra;* Jaffe, *Standing Again,* 84 Harv.L.Rev. 633 (1971); Scott, *Standing in the Supreme Court—A Functional Analysis,* 86 Harv.L.Rev. 645 (1973); Stewart, *The Reformation of American Administrative Law,* 88 Harv.L.Rev. 1667, 1723–47 (1975); Vining, Legal Identity: The Coming of Age of Public Law 34–35 (1978).

(4) In Control Data Corp. v. Baldridge, 655 F.2d 283, 291 (D.C.Cir.1981), the court of appeals observed that the Supreme Court had rarely invoked the test in recent years, and that at least one commentator believed the test had been abandoned.[4] The court also noted that some lower federal courts had expressed disagreement with the test, others had misapplied it, and still others had virtually ignored it. Believing that the test was still controlling, the court of appeals interpreted it as requiring some indicia, however slight, that Congress intended to protect, regulate, or benefit the plaintiff.

(5) In Clarke v. Securities Industry Ass'n, 107 S.Ct. 750 (1987), the Supreme Court once again invoked the zone of interests test in a case

---

2. Justice Brennan quoted as the "gov- erning principle" of reviewability the lan- guage of Abbott Laboratories v. Gardner, 387 U.S. 136, 140 (1967), that "judicial re- view of a final agency action by an ag- grieved person will not be cut off unless there is persuasive reason to believe that such was the purpose of Congress."

3. Data Processing warned that an ac- tion might be dismissed if the plaintiff's interest was not legally protected. 397

U.S. at 158. But see Sierra Club v. Mor- ton, 405 U.S. 727, 737 (1972), p. 123, *supra,* stating that a plaintiff with standing may argue "the public interest" in challenging agency action.

4. The commentator was Professor Da- vis, who later said that the Court "failed to mention the test in 27 opinions on standing since 1970, even when the test was rele- vant." 4 Davis, Administrative Law Trea- tise § 24:17, at 277 (2d ed. 1983).

involving review of agency action,[5] but rejected as too restrictive the interpretation offered in the Control Data case. The suit was brought by a securities industry trade association, which challenged a decision of the Comptroller of the Currency permitting national banks to provide discount brokerage services in branch offices from which, under the federal banking laws, they would be forbidden to provide banking services. The plaintiff contended that the brokerage operations themselves constituted "branch banks" in violation of the federal law. In upholding the association's standing, the Court, per Justice White, stressed two implications of Data Processing (p. 756): "*First.* The Court interpreted the phrase 'a relevant statute' in § 702 broadly; the data processors were alleging violations of [one statute], yet the Court relied on the legislative history of a much later statute * * * in holding that the data processors satisfied the zone of interest test. *Second.* The Court approved the 'trend * * * toward [the] enlargement of the class of people who may protest administrative action.'" He continued (p. 757): "The test is not meant to be especially demanding; in particular, there need be no indication of congressional purpose to benefit the would-be plaintiff."

In a footnote (p. 758 n. 16), the Court stressed that "[t]he principal cases in which the zone of interest test has been applied are those involving claims under the APA, and the test is most usefully understood as a gloss on the meaning of § 702. * * * Data Processing speaks of claims 'arguably within the zone of interests to be protected or regulated by the statute *or constitutional guarantee* in question.' We doubt, however, that it is possible to formulate a single inquiry that governs all statutory or constitutional claims. * * * We have occasionally listed the zone of interest inquiry among general prudential considerations bearing on standing, see, *e.g.,* Valley Forge Christian College v. Americans United for Separation of Church and State, Inc., 454 U.S. 464, 475 (1982), and have on one occasion conducted a zone of interest inquiry in a case brought under the Commerce Clause, see Boston Stock Exch. v. State Tax Comm'n, 429 U.S. 318, 320–21 n. 3 (1977)." But the latter case "should not be taken to mean that the standing inquiry under whatever constitutional or statutory provision a plaintiff asserts is the same as it would be if the 'generous review provisions' of the APA apply."

The Court then held that the trade association had standing under the APA. The Court found in the federal banking laws a concern not only with limiting branch banking by national banks in states where state banks were barred from operating branches, but also with "keep[ing] national banks from gaining a monopoly control over credit and money through unlimited branching" (p. 759). The interest asserted by plaintiff has a "plausible relationship to [these] policies": the plaintiff's members compete with banks in providing discount brokerage services, and those services "give banks access to more money, in the form of credit balances, and enhanced opportunities to lend money." On the merits, the Court upheld the Comptroller's decision.[6]

---

5. The test had also been invoked, and found satisfied, in Japan Whaling Ass'n v. Cetacean Soc'y, 106 S.Ct. 2860, 2866 n. 4 (1986).

6. Justice Stevens, joined by Chief Justice Rehnquist and Justice O'Connor, concurred in part and concurred in the judg-ment, but did not join the Court's standing discussion. Finding that "this case falls squarely within our decisions in [Data Processing, Arnold Tours, and Investment Company Institute]," he "decline[d] to join the Court's sweeping discussion of the zone

(6) Why didn't the Data Processing test govern many of the subsequent decisions involving challenges to federal administrative action—*e.g.*, Allen v. Wright; EKWRO, p. 131, *supra*; Richardson, p. 125, *supra*; Valley Forge, p. 153, *supra*? When the Data Processing test does apply, does its "injury in fact" requirement include the questions of "causation" and "redressability" emphasized in cases like Allen and EKWRO?

SUBSECTION B: DEFENDANTS' STANDING

NOTE ON ASSERTING THE RIGHTS OF OTHERS

(1) When a defendant in an enforcement proceeding resists the imposition of state force upon him, he clearly faces injury. The standing question in such a suit revolves around what issues he may raise in his defense: he may, of course, assert any claimed violation of his own rights, but he may or may not be entitled to defend on the ground that the law being enforced against him violates the rights of others.

(2) In Tileston v. Ullman, 318 U.S. 44 (1943) (per curiam), the Connecticut Supreme Court had rejected, on the merits, a physician's constitutional challenge to the application to him of a state statute prohibiting the use or distribution of contraceptives. The Supreme Court dismissed his appeal on the ground that the only constitutional attack on the statute—that it worked a deprivation of life without due process—was based on the rights not of the physician but of his patients, which he had no standing to assert. "No question is raised in the record with respect to the deprivation of appellant's liberty or property in contravention of the Fourteenth Amendment * * *. * * * Since the appeal must be dismissed on the ground that appellant has no standing to litigate the constitutional question which the record presents, it is unnecessary to consider whether the record shows the existence of a genuine case or controversy * * *" (p. 46).

Tileston is often cited as holding that a litigant may not assert the rights of third persons. Some have read the case more narrowly, as resting on the absence of any injury to the doctor himself: he failed to allege that the statute injured him economically, and the risk of a criminal prosecution was insufficiently ripe to constitute redressable injury. See Bickel, The Least Dangerous Branch 143–45 (1962); Scott, *Standing in the Supreme Court—A Functional Analysis,* 86 Harv.L.Rev. 645, 649 n. 14 (1973). On this view, the case stands merely for the proposition that a party not himself injured may not start a lawsuit solely to alleviate harm to others.

Dr. Tileston was formally a plaintiff, but he was also a prospective defendant, bringing an anticipatory action (seeking a declaratory judgment or injunction) against a criminal statute directed at his own conduct. Ordinarily, the plaintiff in such an action can allege cognizable injury—namely, the threat of enforcement of the statute against him. Is there any reason to bar a prospective defendant who brings an anticipatory action from making any legal arguments (including those based on the rights of others) that he would be entitled to raise in an enforcement proceeding

of interest test" (p. 766). Justice Scalia did
not participate.

against him? See note 5, *infra*. How great is the risk, in either an anticipatory attack or an enforcement action, that adjudication of the constitutional rights of third parties will be ill-defined?

(3) McGowan v. Maryland, 366 U.S. 420 (1961), was a prosecution of department store employees for Sunday sales in violation of the state's "Blue Laws". The Court denied the defendants' standing to assert their customers' First Amendment right to free exercise of religion (pp. 429–30):

"[A]ppellants ＊ ＊ ＊ allege only economic injury to themselves; they do not allege any infringement of their own religious freedoms due to Sunday closing. In fact, the record is silent as to what appellants' religious beliefs are. Since the general rule is that 'a litigant may only assert his own constitutional rights or immunities,' United States v. Raines, 362 U.S. 17, 22, we hold that appellants have no standing to raise this contention. Tileston v. Ullman, 318 U.S. 44, 46. ＊ ＊ ＊ Those persons whose religious rights are allegedly impaired by the statutes are not without effective ways to assert these rights. Cf. N. A. A. C. P. v. Alabama, 357 U.S. 449, 459–460; Barrows v. Jackson, 346 U.S. 249, 257. Appellants present no weighty countervailing policies here to cause an exception to our general principles. See United States v. Raines, *supra*." [1]

(4) In Barrows v. Jackson, 346 U.S. 249 (1953), a state court damage action against a white vendor of land for selling the land in breach of a racially restrictive covenant, the defendant was permitted to resist enforcement of the covenant on the ground that enforcement would amount to unconstitutional discrimination, even though she was not a member of the class discriminated against. Justice Minton wrote for the Court (pp. 255–57, 259):

"Ordinarily, one may not claim standing in this Court to vindicate the constitutional rights of some third party. ＊ ＊ ＊ The requirement of standing is often used to describe the constitutional limitation on the jurisdiction of this Court to 'cases' and 'controversies.' ＊ ＊ ＊ Apart from the jurisdictional requirement, this Court has developed a complementary rule of self-restraint for its own governance (not always clearly distinguished from the constitutional limitation) which ordinarily precludes a person from challenging the constitutionality of state action by invoking the rights of others. The common thread underlying both requirements is that a person cannot challenge the constitutionality of a statute unless he shows that he himself is injured by its operation. This principle has no application to the instant case in which respondent has been sued for damages totaling $11,600, and in which a judgment against respondent would constitute a direct, pocketbook injury to her.

"There are still other cases in which the Court has held that even though a party will suffer a direct substantial injury from application of a statute, he cannot challenge its constitutionality unless he can show that he is within the class whose constitutional rights are allegedly infringed. ＊ ＊ ＊ One reason for this ruling is that the state court, when actually faced with the question, might narrowly construe the statute to obliterate the objectionable feature, or it might declare the unconstitutional provisions separable. ＊ ＊ ＊ It would indeed be undesirable for this Court to

1. Note that in a companion case to McGowan involving Orthodox Jewish merchants, the Court rejected the free exercise challenge on the merits. See Braunfeld v. Brown, 366 U.S. 599 (1961).

consider every conceivable situation which might possibly arise in the application of complex and comprehensive legislation. Nor are we so ready to frustrate the expressed will of Congress or that of the state legislatures.

*   *   *

"This is a salutary rule, the validity of which we reaffirm. But in the instant case, we are faced with a unique situation in which it is the action of the state *court* which might result in a denial of constitutional rights and in which it would be difficult if not impossible for the persons whose rights are asserted to present their grievance before any court. Under the peculiar circumstances of this case, we believe the reasons which underlie our rule denying standing to raise another's rights, which is only a rule of practice, are outweighed by the need to protect the fundamental rights which would be denied by permitting the damages action to be maintained.

*   *   *

" *   *   * The relation between the coercion exerted on respondent and her possible pecuniary loss thereby is so close to the purpose of the restrictive covenant, to violate the constitutional rights of those discriminated against, that respondent is the only effective adversary of the unworthy covenant in its last stand. She will be permitted to protect herself and, by so doing, close the gap to the use of this covenant, so universally condemned by the courts."

(5) In NAACP v. Alabama, 357 U.S. 449 (1958), Alabama had brought suit to enjoin the NAACP from doing further business in the State because it had not registered. In response to an order to produce certain records, the NAACP refused to produce membership lists, for which it was held in contempt of court. Questioning the constitutionality of the order, the NAACP secured review in the Supreme Court, which reversed. On the standing issue, the Court said (pp. 458–60):

"The Association both urges that it is constitutionally entitled to resist official inquiry into its membership lists, and that it may assert, on behalf of its members, a right personal to them to be protected from compelled disclosure by the State of their affiliation with the Association as revealed by the membership lists. We think that petitioner argues more appropriately the rights of its members, and that its nexus with them is sufficient to permit that it act as their representative before this Court. *   *   *

"To limit the breadth of issues which must be dealt with in particular litigation, this Court has generally insisted that parties rely only on constitutional rights which are personal to themselves. Tileston v. Ullman, 318 U.S. 44 *   *   *. The principle is not disrespected where constitutional rights of persons who are not immediately before the Court could not be effectively vindicated except through an appropriate representative before the Court. See Barrows v. Jackson, 346 U.S. 249, 255–259; Joint Anti–Fascist Refugee Committee v. McGrath, 341 U.S. 123, 183–187 (concurring opinion).

"If petitioner's rank-and-file members are constitutionally entitled to withhold their connection with the Association despite the production order, it is manifest that this right is properly assertable by the Association. To require that it be claimed by the members themselves would result in nullification of the right at the very moment of its assertion. Petitioner is the appropriate party to assert these rights, because it and its members are in every practical sense identical. *   *   * The reasonable likelihood that the Association itself through diminished financial support and membership may be adversely affected if production is compelled is a further factor pointing towards our holding that petitioner has standing to complain of the production order on behalf of its members. *Cf.* Pierce v. Society of Sisters, 268 U.S. 510, 534–536."

Could the members have intervened, as "John Does", to oppose the order? If so, couldn't they have asserted their right to anonymity without losing it?

(6) In Griswold v. Connecticut, 381 U.S. 479 (1965), a doctor and the Executive Director of the Planned Parenthood League were convicted as accessories to violation of the Connecticut birth control statute involved in Tileston v. Ullman, Paragraph (2), *supra*. The Court had in the interim rejected another anticipatory attack, by doctor and patients, on the validity of that law, see Poe v. Ullman, 367 U.S. 497 (1961), p. 740 *infra*. But in Griswold, the Court went to the merits and held the underlying anti-"use" statute invalid as an invasion of "marital privacy". Justice Douglas wrote for the Court (p. 481):

"We think that appellants have standing to raise the constitutional rights of the married people with whom they had a professional relationship. Tileston v. Ullman, 318 U.S. 44, is different, for there the plaintiff seeking to represent others asked for a declaratory judgment. In that situation we thought that the requirements of standing should be strict, lest the standards of 'case or controversy' in Article III of the Constitution become blurred. Here those doubts are removed by reason of a criminal conviction for serving married couples in violation of an aiding-and-abetting statute. Certainly the accessory should have standing to assert that the offense which he is charged with assisting is not, or cannot constitutionally be, a crime.

"This case is more akin to Truax v. Raich, 239 U.S. 33, where an employee was permitted to assert the rights of his employer; to Pierce v. Society of Sisters, 268 U.S. 510, where the owners of private schools were entitled to assert the rights of potential pupils and their parents; and to Barrows v. Jackson, 346 U.S. 249, where a white defendant, party to a racially restrictive covenant, who was being sued for damages by the covenantors because she had conveyed her property to Negroes, was allowed to raise the issue that enforcement of the covenant violated the rights of prospective Negro purchasers to equal protection, although no Negro was a party to the suit. The rights of husband and wife, pressed here, are likely to be diluted or adversely affected unless those rights are considered in a suit involving those who have this kind of confidential relation to them."

Was the second quoted paragraph necessary? Was not defendants' standing to challenge the validity of the birth control statute clearly established by the state law which made the accessory convictions dependent upon the substantive criminal prohibition?

(7) Be sure to notice a distinction not always clearly made in the cases—between (i) third party standing (or *jus tertii*), the subject of the cases in this Note; and (ii) overbreadth challenges, discussed at pp. 181–96, *infra*. "The overbreadth claimant seeks to assert the rights of hypothetical third persons to whom the challenged law conceivably might apply in a manner that would violate their constitutional rights. The most common

example of such an attack arises under the first amendment, when a litigant whose speech may not itself be constitutionally protected claims that the relevant statute must be struck down because it could be applied to restrict speech that cannot constitutionally be burdened. Thus, overbreadth attacks involve both the application of the challenged law to the claimant and a different, hypothetical application of the law to third parties. Quite different from this sort of third party claim is an assertion of jus tertii—a litigant's claim that a single application of a law both injures him and impinges upon the constitutional rights of third persons." Note, *Standing to Assert Constitutional Jus Tertii*, 88 Harv.L.Rev. 423, 423–24 (1974).

(8) Eisenstadt v. Baird, 405 U.S. 438 (1972), involved the validity of a Massachusetts conviction for giving away a contraceptive.[2] The challenged law prohibited the dispensing, by anyone other than a registered physician or pharmacist administering to a married person, of any article for the prevention of conception. Mass.Gen.Laws c. 272, §§ 21, 21A. Baird, who was not a registered physician or pharmacist, challenged the statute on the ground that denial to unmarried persons of the same access to contraceptives as married persons violated the former's right to equal protection. His claim was upheld.

On the question of Baird's standing to assert the rights of unmarried distributees, the Court first noted (p. 443) that he unquestionably "ha[d] sufficient interest in challenging the statute's validity to satisfy the 'case or controversy' requirement of Article III of the Constitution."[3] The Court continued (pp. 444–46):

"[A]ppellant contends that Baird's conviction rests on the restriction in § 21A on permissible distributors and that that restriction serves a valid health interest independent of the limitation on authorized distributees. Appellant urges, therefore, that Baird's action in giving away the [contraceptive] foam fell squarely within the conduct that the legislature meant and had power to prohibit and that Baird should not be allowed to attack the statute in its application to potential recipients. In any event, appellant concludes, since Baird was not himself a single person denied access to contraceptives, he should not be heard to assert their rights. We cannot agree.

"The Court of Appeals held that the statute under which Baird was convicted is not a health measure. If that view is correct, we do not see how Baird may be prevented, because he was neither a doctor nor a druggist, from attacking the statute in its alleged discriminatory application to potential distributees. We think, too, that our self-imposed rule against the assertion of third-party rights must be relaxed in this case just as in Griswold v. Connecticut * * *. Appellant here argues that the absence of a professional or aiding-and-abetting relationship distinguishes this case from Griswold. Yet, as the Court's discussion of prior authority

2. The case came to the Supreme Court on review of a federal habeas corpus proceeding. Is there any significant difference with regard to standing between the defendant in the criminal case and the petitioner in habeas?

3. A footnote appended at this point said (p. 443 n. 4): "This factor decisively distinguishes Tileston v. Ullman, 318 U.S. 44 (1943), where the Court held that a physician lacked standing to bring an action for declaratory relief to challenge, on behalf of his patients, the Connecticut law prohibiting the use of contraceptives. The patients were fully able to bring their own action * * *."

in Griswold indicates, the doctor-patient and accessory-principal relationships are not the only circumstances in which one person has been found to have standing to assert the rights of another. Indeed, in Barrows v. Jackson, * * * [t]he relationship * * * between the defendant and those whose rights he sought to assert was not simply the fortuitous connection between a vendor and potential vendees, but the relationship between one who acted to protect the rights of a minority and the minority itself. * * * And so here the relationship between Baird and those whose rights he seeks to assert is not simply that between a distributor and potential distributees, but that between an advocate of the rights of persons to obtain contraceptives and those desirous of doing so. The very point of Baird's giving away the vaginal foam was to challenge the Massachusetts statute that limited access to contraceptives.

"In any event, more important than the nature of the relationship between the litigant and those whose rights he seeks to assert is the impact of the litigation on the third-party interests. In Griswold, the Court stated: 'The rights of husband and wife, pressed here, are likely to be diluted or adversely affected unless those rights are considered in a suit involving those who have this kind of confidential relation to them.' A similar situation obtains here. Enforcement of the Massachusetts statute will materially impair the ability of single persons to obtain contraceptives. In fact, the case for according standing to assert third-party rights is stronger in this regard here than in Griswold because unmarried persons denied access to contraceptives in Massachusetts, unlike the users of contraceptives in Connecticut, are not themselves subject to prosecution and, to that extent, are denied a forum in which to assert their own rights. *Cf.* NAACP v. Alabama, 357 U.S. 449 (1958); Barrows v. Jackson, *supra*. The Massachusetts statute, unlike the Connecticut law considered in Griswold, prohibits not use, but distribution.

"For the foregoing reasons we hold that Baird, who is now in a position, and plainly has an adequate incentive, to assert the rights of unmarried persons denied access to contraceptives, has standing to do so."

Justice White, joined by Justice Blackmun, pointed out that Baird had been convicted of giving away the contraceptive when he was not a physician or pharmacist, and not of giving it to an unmarried person; the state had not even offered proof as to the marital status of the recipient. He concurred in overturning the conviction on the limited ground that, since there was no indication that the foam involved danger to health, restriction of its distribution to medical channels was precluded by Griswold insofar as the recipients were married persons.

Chief Justice Burger dissented. On the standing question, he said that since Baird was not a physician or pharmacist and was on that basis prohibited by the statute from dispensing contraceptives to anyone, regardless of marital status, "the validity of this restriction on dispensing medicinal substances is the only issue before the Court, and appellee has no standing to challenge that part of the statute restricting the persons to whom contraceptives are available" (pp. 465–66). Substantively he found the limitation to professional distribution valid, and voted to uphold the conviction.[4]

4. Justices Powell and Rehnquist did not participate.

(9) Wasn't Justice White correct that, if the restriction of distribution by nonprofessionals were invalid, Baird's conviction should have been reversed on that limited ground, whatever the marital status of the distributee?

Suppose, however, that the record indicated that Baird's distributee was unmarried, and the state argued that whether or not the ban on nonprofessional distribution was valid, the ban on *any* distribution to unmarried persons certainly was. At that point, the question of Baird's right to challenge the validity of the distinction between married and unmarried persons becomes central.

Suppose, instead, that the Court believed it to be constitutional to prohibit a nonprofessional from distributing contraceptives. Should Baird be permitted to argue that his conviction should be overturned because the statute also makes an unconstitutional distinction between married and unmarried persons? This question raises a conventional severability problem: is the ban on distribution by nonprofessionals severable from the ban on distribution (by anyone) to unmarried persons? On severability, see, generally, the materials immediately following this Note.

(10) In Doe v. Bolton, 410 U.S. 179 (1973), a companion case to Roe v. Wade, 410 U.S. 113 (1973), the Court held that doctors who are consulted by pregnant women had standing, in an anticipatory attack, to challenge the constitutionality of a criminal statute prohibiting those doctors from performing abortions. That they could raise their patients' rights in the lawsuit was implicit but not clearly stated. The point was not important in that case, however, because joining the complaint was a woman plaintiff, who could assert her own rights. Since then, the Court has frequently permitted doctors to assert their patients' rights in actions challenging abortion restrictions. See, *e.g.*, Planned Parenthood Ass'n v. Ashcroft, 462 U.S. 476 (1983) (permitting, without discussion, Planned Parenthood, two physicians, and an abortion clinic to challenge the constitutionality of state abortion restrictions).

(11) Craig v. Boren, 429 U.S. 190 (1976), involved Oklahoma laws that made it unlawful to sell 3.2% beer to males under 21, but permitted sale to females over 18. A licensed beer vendor who brought an anticipatory attack against the laws was permitted to assert the equal protection rights of 18–20 year-old men. The Court noted that the rule against the assertion of *jus tertii* was not constitutionally mandated. This self-imposed rule of restraint should not be followed in this case, the Court argued, because the vendor's standing had not been challenged below and because the constitutional questions had been effectively presented.

The Court proceeded to hold (p. 194) that "[i]n any event," the vendor had independently established her standing to assert the young men's equal protection rights. The legal duties addressed to her clearly established her injury in fact, and she was "entitled to assert those concomitant rights of third parties that would be 'diluted or adversely affected' should her constitutional challenge fail and the statutes remain in force. Griswold v. Connecticut * * *. Otherwise, the threatened imposition of governmental sanctions might deter [the plaintiff] and other similarly situated vendors from selling 3.2% beer to young males, thereby ensuring that 'enforcement of the challenged restriction against the [vendor] would result indirectly in the violation of third parties' rights,' Warth v. Seldin,

422 U.S. 490, 510 (1975). Accordingly, vendors and those in like positions have been uniformly permitted to resist efforts at restricting their operations by acting as advocates of the rights of third parties who seek access to their market or function" (p. 194). The Court found particular support for its result in Eisenstadt v. Baird, Paragraph (8), *supra,* and concluded that since here, as there, the law prohibited distribution rather than use, the "obvious claimant" was the vendor, who, like Baird, was directly subject to the prohibition (p. 197).[5] (On the merits, the Court held the statute unconstitutional.)

Chief Justice Burger alone dissented on the standing issue. He stressed (p. 216) that there was "no barrier whatever to Oklahoma males 18–20 years of age asserting, in an appropriate forum, any constitutional rights they may claim to purchase 3.2% beer." Nor did Griswold control: "It borders on the ludicrous to draw a parallel between a vendor of beer and the intimate professional physician-patient relationship which undergirded relaxation of standing rules in that case." Even Eisenstadt was distinguishable, involving as it did "the relationship between one who acted to protect the rights of a minority and the minority itself'" (p. 216, quoting Eisenstadt).

After Craig, what is left of McGowan v. Maryland, Paragraph (3), *supra?* See also Secretary of State of Maryland v. Joseph H. Munson Co., Inc., 467 U.S. 947, 954–58 (1984) (seller of fundraising services to charities has standing, in challenging statute making some of its fundraising activities unlawful, to assert the rights of charities); Carey v. Population Services, Intern., 431 U.S. 678 (1977) (mail-order vendor of contraceptives has standing, in challenge to state law forbidding it to advertise or distribute contraceptives, to assert the rights of its potential customers); Village of Belle Terre v. Boraas, 416 U.S. 1 (1974) (landlord subject to criminal liability for violation of zoning ordinance permitted, without discussion, to raise tenants' rights of association and travel in anticipatory attack on the ordinance's restriction on occupancy).

(12) Should standing to assert the rights of others be permitted, as Chief Justice Burger suggested in his dissent in Craig, only when there is some barrier to the rightholders' asserting their own rights? In how many of the cases in this Note did such a barrier exist?

What of the Chief Justice's point that the vendor-vendee relationship is less important than the doctor-patient relationship? Can the importance of a relationship be analyzed in the abstract, without regard to the right at issue? Isn't the vendor-vendee relationship every bit as important, in connection with the right of young men to purchase beer on equal terms with young women, as the doctor-patient relationship is in the context of abortion or distribution of contraceptives?

What of the majority's point that in Craig (as in Barrows, Griswold, and Eisenstadt) a refusal to permit assertion of the rights of others will dilute those rights? Doesn't that risk exist whenever third persons can fully exercise their constitutional rights only through relationships with the class of persons to which the litigant belongs? Shouldn't a litigant

---

5. The Court refused to distinguish Eisenstadt v. Baird because it involved an actual defendant prosecuted for a violation, while the vendor in Craig was only a prospective defendant; "[t]he existence of Art. III 'injury in fact' and the structure of the claimant's relationship to the third parties are not altered by the litigative posture of the suit" (p. 196 n. 5).

always be free to challenge the imposition on him of a legal duty that prohibits him from acting in ways necessary for third parties to enjoy their constitutional rights—leaving to the merits the question whether, in fact, the third parties have such a right? See Note, Paragraph (7), *supra*, at 431–33. Doesn't Craig endorse that view?

(13) Are the cases in this Note that permit assertion of the rights of others better viewed as assertions by the litigant of his own rights? Professor Sedler has argued that a litigant asserts his own rights when (1) he and third persons have some relationship; (2) the relationship is the source of the deprivation of the third persons' rights by an invalid law; and (3) for the same reason that the law violates the rights of third persons, it violates the rights of the litigant. Sedler, *The Assertion of Constitutional Jus Tertii: A Substantive Approach*, 70 Calif.L.Rev. 1308, 1329 (1982). Professor Monaghan similarly asserts that a litigant "asserts his own rights (not those of a third person) when he seeks to void restrictions that directly impair his freedom to interact with a third person who himself could not be legally prevented from engaging in the interaction." Monaghan, *Third Party Standing*, 84 Colum.L.Rev. 277, 299 (1984).[6] Professor Monaghan suggests that this "first party" view is preferable because it eliminates "unanalyzed and ungrounded notions of judicial 'discretion.'" *Id.* at 278– 79. Note, moreover, that under the "rights of others" view, Congress could presumably pass legislation barring the Court from exercising its discretion to hear *jus tertii* claims; by contrast, under the "first party" view, Congress would lack power to enact a law barring courts (at least in enforcement proceedings) from adjudicating the rights at issue.[7]

(14) The Supreme Court has concluded that the Fourth Amendment's exclusionary rule does not prevent or redress any harm to the criminal defendant who invokes it, but instead simply helps to protect the citizenry at large by generally deterring constitutional violations. See, *e.g.*, United States v. Calandra, 414 U.S. 338, 353–54 (1974); United States v. Leon, 468 U.S. 897, 906 (1984). On this view, isn't the criminal defendant, in moving to suppress evidence, asserting the rights of others? The defendant surely has no relationship with citizens in general through which they exercise their Fourth Amendment rights. What then justifies this remedy? See generally Meltzer, *Deterring Constitutional Violations by Law Enforcement Officials: Plaintiffs and Defendants as Private Attorneys General*, 88 Colum.L.Rev. 247 (1988); Monaghan, Paragraph (13), *supra*, at 279–82, 310– 15.

6. For earlier suggestions along similar lines, see Albert, *Standing to Challenge Administrative Action: An Inadequate Surrogate for Claim for Relief*, 83 Yale L.J. 425, 464–68 (1974); Jaffe, *Standing to Secure Judicial Review: Private Actions*, 75 Harv.L.Rev. 255, 270 (1961); Lewis, *Constitutional Rights and the Misuse of "Standing,"* 14 Stan.L.Rev. 433, 446–47 (1962). For other commentary using the third person rubric, see Rohr, *Fighting for the Rights of Others: The Troubled Law of Third–Party Standing and Mootness in the Federal Courts*, 35 U.Miami L.Rev. 393 (1981).

7. The "first party" view can also apply to suits by plaintiffs seeking to assert the rights of others. Recall Singleton v. Wulff, 428 U.S. 106 (1976), p. 134, *supra*, in which physicians, who brought suit challenging the constitutionality of a Missouri statute that prohibited payment of Medicaid benefits for abortions that were not "medically indicated," were permitted to assert their patients' rights. Sedler, *supra*, at 1332, argues that the physicians should have been permitted to assert their own equal protection right to obtain payment for abortions as well as for other medical procedures; Monaghan, *supra*, at 306–07, disagrees, finding the interference with the doctor-patient relationship not sufficiently "direct" to violate the physicians' rights.

(15) Private litigants are often permitted to raise questions of federalism or separation of powers in challenging a law or a government action that, if valid, affects their interests. See, *e.g.*, San Diego Bldg. Trades Council v. Garmon, 359 U.S. 236 (1959) (private litigant permitted to assert that state law under which he was sued is preempted by the National Labor Relations Act); INS v. Chadha, 462 U.S. 919 (1983) (permitting an alien to challenge a legislative veto of a decision suspending a deportation order against him, on the ground that the veto violated the separation of powers). Should these litigants be viewed as invoking the rights of a government or one of its branches? (Chadha rejected the argument that the alien lacked standing because he was advancing the interests of the Executive Branch in a dispute with Congress). See Choper, Judicial Review and the National Political Process: A Functional Reconsideration of the Role of the Supreme Court 209–10 (1980). Or do these litigants assert their own right to be regulated in accordance with a valid rule?

YAZOO & MISSISSIPPI VALLEY R. R. v. JACKSON VINEGAR CO.

226 U.S. 217, 33 S.Ct. 40, 57 L.Ed. 193 (1912).
Appeal from the Circuit Court of Hinds County, Mississippi.

Mr. Justice Van Devanter delivered the opinion of the Court.

This was an action to recover damages from a railway company for the partial loss of a shipment of vinegar carried over the company's line from one point to another in the state of Mississippi. This case originated in a justice's court and was taken on appeal to the circuit court of Hinds county, where the plaintiff recovered a judgment for actual damages and $25 as a statutory penalty. That being the highest court in the state to which the case could be carried, it was then brought here. The position of the railway company, unsuccessfully taken in the state court and now renewed, is that the Mississippi statute providing for the penalty is repugnant to the due process of law and equal protection clauses of the 14th Amendment to the Constitution of the United States. The statute reads:

"Railroads, corporations, and individuals engaged as common carriers in this state are required to settle all claims for lost or damaged freight which has been lost or damaged between two given points on the same line or system, within sixty days from the filing of written notice of the loss or damage with the agent at the point of destination; and where freight is handled by two or more roads or systems of roads, and is lost or damaged, claims therefor shall be settled within ninety days from the filing of written notice thereof, with the agent by consignee at the point of destination. A common carrier failing to settle such claims as herein required shall be liable to the consignee for $25 damages in each case, in addition to actual damages, all of which may be recovered in the same suit: Provided that this section shall only apply when the amount claimed is $200 or less."

The facts showing the application made of the statute are these: The plaintiff gave notice of its claim in the manner prescribed, placing its damages at $4.76, and, upon the railway company's failure to settle within sixty days, sued to recover that sum and the statutory penalty. Upon the trial the damages were assessed at the sum stated in the notice, and judgment was given therefor, with the penalty. Thus, the claim presented in advance of the suit, and which the railway company failed to settle within the time allotted, was fully sustained.

As applied to such a case, we think the statute is not repugnant to either the due process of law or the equal protection clause of the Constitution, but, on the contrary, merely provides a reasonable incentive for the prompt settlement, without suit, of just demands of a class admitting of special legislative treatment. See Seaboard Air Line R. Co. v. Seegers, 207 U.S. 73; St. Louis, I. M. & S. R. Co. v. Wynne, 224 U.S. 354.

Although seemingly conceding this much, counsel for the railway company urge that the statute is not confined to cases like the present, but equally penalizes the failure to accede to an excessive or extravagant claim; in other words, that it contemplates the assessment of the penalty in every case where the claim presented is not settled within the time allotted, regardless of whether, or how much, the recovery falls short of the amount claimed. But it is not open to the railway company to complain on that score. It has not been penalized for failing to accede to an excessive or extravagant claim, but for failing to make reasonably prompt settlement of a claim which, upon due inquiry, has been pronounced just in every respect. Of course, the argument to sustain the contention is that, if the statute embraces cases such as are supposed, it is void as to them, and, if so void, is void *in toto*. But this court must deal with the case in hand, and not with imaginary ones. It suffices, therefore, to hold that, as applied to cases like the present, the statute is valid. How the state court may apply it to other cases, whether its general words may be treated as more or less restrained, and how far parts of it may be sustained if others fail, are matters upon which we need not speculate now. New York ex rel. Hatch v. Reardon, 204 U.S. 152, 160; Lee v. New Jersey, 207 U.S. 67, 70; Southern R. Co. v. King, 217 U.S. 524, 534; Collins v. Texas, 223 U.S. 288, 295; Standard Stock Food Co. v. Wright, 225 U.S. 540, 550.

The judgment is accordingly affirmed.

UNITED STATES v. RAINES

362 U.S. 17, 80 S.Ct. 519, 4 L.Ed.2d 524 (1960).
Appeal from the United States District Court for the Middle
District of Georgia.

MR. JUSTICE BRENNAN delivered the opinion of the Court.

[The United States sued local officials in Georgia, seeking preventive relief because of defendants' alleged discrimination against black voters, in violation of the Civil Rights Act of 1957. The federal district court ruled that the provision under which the suit was brought was unconstitutional because it would permit the Attorney General to sue to enjoin purely private action designed to deprive black citizens of the right to vote. Concluding that the Act was capable of application beyond the scope thought to be permissible under the Fifteenth Amendment, the district court treated it as unconstitutional in all its applications, and dismissed the complaint. 172 F.Supp. 552. The government brought a direct appeal under 28 U.S.C. § 1252.]

The very foundation of the power of the federal courts to declare Acts of Congress unconstitutional lies in the power and duty of those courts to decide cases and controversies properly before them. * * * This Court, as is the case with all federal courts, "has no jurisdiction to pronounce any statute, either of a state or of the United States, void, because irreconcilable with the constitution, except as it is called upon to adjudge the legal rights of litigants in actual controversies. In the exercise of that jurisdiction, it is bound by two rules, to which it has rigidly adhered: one, never to anticipate a question of constitutional law in advance of the necessity of deciding it; the other, never to formulate a rule of constitutional law broader than is required by the precise facts to which it is to be applied." Liverpool, New York & Philadelphia S. S. Co. v. Commissioners of Emigration, 113 U.S. 33, 39. Kindred to these rules is the rule that one to whom application of a statute is constitutional will not be heard to attack the statute on the ground that impliedly it might also be taken as applying to other persons or other situations in which its application might be unconstitutional. [Citing many cases, including Yazoo, and concluding with] Ashwander v. Tennessee Valley Authority, 297 U.S. 288, 347–348 (concurring opinion). In Barrows v. Jackson, 346 U.S. 249, this Court developed various reasons for this rule. Very significant is the incontrovertible proposition that it "would indeed be undesirable for this Court to consider every conceivable situation which might possibly arise in the application of complex and comprehensive legislation." * * * The Court further pointed to the fact that a limiting construction could be given to the statute by the court responsible for its construction if an application of doubtful constitutionality were in fact concretely presented. We might add that application of this rule frees the Court not only from unnecessary pronouncement on constitutional issues, but also from premature interpretations of statutes in areas where their constitutional application might be cloudy.

The District Court relied on, and appellees urge here, certain cases which are said to be inconsistent with this rule and with its closely related corollary that a litigant may only assert his own constitutional rights or immunities. * * * For example, where, as a result of the very litigation in question, the constitutional rights of one not a party would be impaired, and where he has no effective way to preserve them himself, the Court may consider those rights as before it. N. A. A. C. P. v. State of Alabama, 357 U.S. 449, 459–460; Barrows v. Jackson, *supra*. This Court has indicated that where the application of these rules would itself have an inhibitory effect on freedom of speech, they may not be applied. See Smith v. People of State of California, 361 U.S. 147, 151; Thornhill v. State of Alabama, 310 U.S. 88, 97–98. Perhaps cases can be put where their application to a criminal statute would necessitate such a revision of its text as to create a situation in which the statute no longer gave an intelligible warning of the conduct it prohibited. See United States v. Reese, 92 U.S. 214, 219–220; cf. Winters v. People of State of New York, 333 U.S. 507, 518–520. And the rules' rationale may disappear where the statute in question has already been declared unconstitutional in the vast majority of its intended applications, and it can fairly be said that it was not intended to stand as valid, on the basis of fortuitous circumstances, only in a fraction of the cases it was originally designed to cover. See Butts v. Merchants & Miners Transportation Co., 230 U.S. 126. The same situation is presented when a state statute comes conclusively pronounced by a state court as having an otherwise valid provision or application inextricably tied up with an invalid one, see Dorchy v. State of Kansas, 264 U.S. 286, 290; or possibly in that rarest of cases where this Court can justifiably think itself able confidently to discern that Congress would not have desired its legislation to stand at all unless it could validly stand in its every application. Cf. The Trade–Mark Cases, 100 U.S. 82, 97–98; The Employers' Liability Cases, 207 U.S. 463, 501. But we see none of the countervailing considerations suggested by these examples, or any other countervailing consideration, as warranting the District Court's action here in considering the constitutionality of the Act in applications not before it. This case is rather the most typical one for application of the rules we have discussed.

There are, to be sure, cases where this Court has not applied with perfect consistency these rules for avoiding unnecessary constitutional determinations * * *. The District Court relied primarily on United States v. Reese, *supra*. As we have indicated, that decision may have drawn support from the assumption that if the Court had not passed on the statute's validity *in toto* it would have left standing a criminal statute incapable of giving fair warning of its prohibitions. But to the extent Reese did depend on an approach inconsistent with what we think the better one and the one established by the weightiest of the subsequent cases, we cannot follow it here.

* * *

The District Court seems to us to have recognized that the complaint clearly charged a violation of the Fifteenth Amendment and of the statute, and that the statute, if applicable only to this class of cases, would unquestionably be valid legislation under that Amendment. We think that under the rules we have stated, that court should then have gone no further and should have upheld the Act as applied in the present action, and that its dismissal of the complaint was error. * * *

* * *

Reversed.

MR. JUSTICE FRANKFURTER, with whom MR. JUSTICE HARLAN concurs, joining in the judgment. * * *

NOTE ON THE SCOPE OF THE ISSUE AND THE PROBLEM OF SEPARABILITY

(1) Would it be open to the Mississippi courts to hold after Yazoo (a) that the statute involved in that case applied also to failure to settle groundless or excessive claims; (b) that as so applied the statute violated the federal Constitution; and (c) that the statute was inseparable, so that it could no longer be applied even to failure to settle claims which were sustained in full? If so, would this furnish a reason for permitting the railroad to anticipate these questions in the Yazoo litigation? If the state court had anticipated them, should the Supreme Court then have treated question (b) as open to review?

(2) In Dorchy v. Kansas, 264 U.S. 286 (1924), Dorchy sought review of his conviction under § 19 of the Court of Industrial Relations Act of Kansas, which he claimed was an unconstitutional restriction of the right

to strike. Pending the decision of this case, the Supreme Court held in another case that other provisions of the statute (providing for compulsory arbitration of labor disputes) violated the federal Constitution as there applied. The Court pointed out that it would be unnecessary to consider Dorchy's objections to § 19 if that section were inseparable from the arbitration provisions. It vacated the state court's judgment and remanded the case for a determination of that question. The Court said (pp. 289–91):

" * * * Provisions within the legislative power may stand if separable from the bad. * * * But a provision, inherently unobjectionable, cannot be deemed separable unless it appears both that, standing alone, legal effect can be given to it and that the legislature intended the provision to stand, in case others included in the act and held bad should fall. * * * Whether § 19 is so interwoven with the system held invalid that the section cannot stand alone, is a question of interpretation and legislative intent. * * *

"The task of determining the intention of the state legislature in this respect, like the usual function of interpreting a state statute, rests primarily upon the state court. Its decision as to the severability of a provision is conclusive upon this Court. * * * In cases coming from the lower federal courts, such questions of severability, if there is no controlling state decision, must be determined by this Court. * * * In cases coming from the state courts, this Court, in the absence of a controlling state decision, may, in passing upon the claim under the federal law, decide, also, the question of severability. But it is not obliged to do so. The situation may be such as to make it appropriate to leave the determination of the question to the state court. We think that course should be followed in this case."

(3) Where the highest court of a state has refused to deal with applications of a state statute not involved in the case before it, the Supreme Court has regularly followed the holding of the Yazoo case. See, in particular, Smiley v. Kansas, 196 U.S. 447, 454–55 (1905), where the Court said: "The Supreme Court of the State held that the acts charged and proved against the defendant were clearly within the terms of the statute, * * * and that the statute could be sustained as a prohibition of those acts irrespective of the question whether its language was broad enough to include acts and conduct which the legislature could not rightfully restrain. * * * We accept the construction given to a state statute by that court. * * * Nor is it material that the state court ascertains the meaning and scope of the statute as well as its validity by pursuing a different rule of construction from what we recognize."

The cases are collected in 13 Wright, Miller, & Cooper, Federal Practice and Procedure § 3531.9, at 589–90 & n. 87 (1984); Sedler, *Standing to Assert Constitutional Jus Tertii in the Supreme Court*, 71 Yale L.J. 599, 601–12 (1962); and Stern, *Separability and Separability Clauses in The Supreme Court*, 51 Harv.L.Rev. 76 (1937).

(4) Separability of a federal statute is, of course, an issue for the Supreme Court. Did the Court in Raines necessarily decide that the statute is separable and could be applied to state officials even if invalid as to private persons?

(5) In Electric Bond & Share Co. v. SEC, 303 U.S. 419 (1938), the Court held that a utility company could not escape the registration provisions of

the Public Utility Holding Company Act of 1935 by arguing that the "control" provisions of the same Act (which applied only after a company was registered) were unconstitutional. The Act contained a separability clause, which, the Court said (p. 434), "reverses the presumption of inseparability—that the legislature intended the Act to be effective as an entirety or not at all."

Does Electric Bond imply that a statute without a separability clause is presumed to be inseparable? In United States v. Jackson, 390 U.S. 570 (1968), the district court had dismissed a federal kidnapping indictment after holding unconstitutional the statute's death penalty provision. The Supreme Court agreed that the death penalty could not be imposed, but ruled that the kidnapping charge was nonetheless valid. Quoting Champlin Rfg. Co. v. Corporation Comm'n, 286 U.S. 210, 234 (1932), the Court said (p. 585): " 'Unless it is evident that the legislature would not have enacted those provisions which are within its power, independently of that which is not, the invalid part may be dropped if what is left is fully operative as a law.' " Though the statute at issue in Jackson (unlike that in Champlin) had no separability clause, the Court remarked that "the ultimate determination of severability will rarely turn on the presence or absence of such a clause" (p. 585 n. 27). Accord, Buckley v. Valeo, 424 U.S. 1, 108 (1976) (also quoting Champlin); Regan v. Time, Inc., 468 U.S. 641, 653 (1984) (plurality opinion) (severability "is largely a question of legislative intent, but the presumption is in favor of severability").

(6) Exactly what is the question of legislative intent that the Court asks in severability cases? In Alaska Airlines, Inc. v. Brock, 107 S.Ct. 1476 (1987), the Court considered federal statutory provisions requiring airlines, when filling a vacancy, to give preference to certain former airline employees who lost their jobs after airline deregulation. The statute authorized the Secretary of Labor to issue regulations, subject to a legislative veto. Several airlines brought suit, contending that the first-hire provisions were void because inseparable from the legislative veto, which under INS v. Chadha, 462 U.S. 919 (1983), was unconstitutional. The court of appeals, in rejecting that argument, stated that the veto was severable unless "Congress would have preferred no airline employee protection provision at all to the existing provision *sans* the veto provision." 766 F.2d 1550, 1561. The Supreme Court offered a somewhat different formulation: "the unconstitutional provision must be severed unless the statute created in its absence is legislation that Congress would not have enacted" (p. 1481). Was the Court right when it claimed (p. 1481 n. 7) that its standard and that of the court of appeals are "completely consistent"? [1]

1. In Alaska Airlines, the Supreme Court held that the veto provision was severable, stressing that the statute did not require the Secretary to issue regulations and "did not link specifically the operation of the first-hire provisions to the issuance of regulations" (p. 1482). The Court also reviewed the provisions' legislative history, which, it said, paid far more attention to employee protection than to legislative oversight.

Chadha itself involved a provision of the Immigration and Nationality Act that authorized the Attorney General to suspend a deportation, subject to a legislative veto. The Court refused to invalidate the provision in its entirety: "we need not embark on [the] elusive inquiry" demanded by the Champlin case, since the Act included a severability clause, which "gives rise to a presumption" that the provision should not be declared invalid *in toto* (p. 932). The Court did examine the legislative history of the provision, finding that its purpose—to free Congress of the burdens of private immigration bills—would be undercut if the veto were found not to be severable.

(7) United States v. National Dairy Prod. Corp., 372 U.S. 29 (1963), was a prosecution for violation of the Robinson–Patman Act, 15 U.S.C. § 13a, making it a crime to sell goods "at unreasonably low prices for the purpose of destroying competition * * *." Defendants, who were charged with having sold below cost for the proscribed purpose, challenged the statute as unconstitutionally vague. Relying in part on Raines, the Court held that "[i]n determining the sufficiency of the notice a statute must of necessity be examined in light of the conduct with which a defendant is charged" (p. 33). Proceeding to determine "whether the statute sufficiently warned that selling 'below cost' with predatory intent" was prohibited, the Court upheld the statute (p. 33). It noted, however, as is indicated in the materials that follow, that First Amendment cases apply a different approach—one focusing on the vagueness of the statute "on its face."

COATES v. CITY OF CINCINNATI

402 U.S. 611, 91 S.Ct. 1686, 29 L.Ed.2d 214 (1971).
Appeal from the Supreme Court of Ohio.

MR. JUSTICE STEWART delivered the opinion of the Court.

A Cincinnati, Ohio, ordinance makes it a criminal offense for "three or more persons to assemble * * * on any of the sidewalks * * * and there conduct themselves in a manner annoying to persons passing by * * *." The issue before us is whether this ordinance is unconstitutional on its face.

The appellants were convicted of violating the ordinance, and the convictions were ultimately affirmed by a closely divided vote in the Supreme Court of Ohio, upholding the constitutional validity of the ordinance. 21 Ohio St.2d 66, 255 N.E.2d 247. An appeal from that judgment was brought here under 28 U.S.C. § 1257(2), and we noted probable jurisdiction, 398 U.S. 902. The record brought before the reviewing courts tells us no more than that the appellant Coates was a student involved in a demonstration and the other appellants were pickets involved in a labor dispute. For throughout this litigation it has been the appellants' position that the ordinance on its face violates the First and Fourteenth Amendments of the Constitution.

In rejecting this claim and affirming the convictions the Ohio Supreme Court did not give the ordinance any construction at variance with the apparent plain import of its language. The court simply stated:

"The ordinance prohibits, *inter alia*, 'conduct * * * annoying to persons passing by.' The word 'annoying' is a widely used and well understood word; it is not necessary to guess its meaning. 'Annoying' is the present participle of the transitive verb 'annoy' which means to trouble, to vex, to impede, to incommode, to provoke, to harass or to irritate.

"We conclude, as did the Supreme Court of the United States in Cameron v. Johnson, 390 U.S. 611, 616, in which the issue of the vagueness of a statute was presented, that the ordinance 'clearly and precisely delineates its reach in words of common understanding. It is a "precise and narrowly drawn regulatory statute [ordinance] evincing a legislative

See generally Smith, *From Unnecessary Surgery to Plastic Surgery: A New Approach to the Legislative Veto Severability Cases,* 24 Harv.J.Legis. 397 (1987).

judgment that certain specific conduct be * * * proscribed." ' " 21 Ohio
St.2d, at 69, 255 N.E.2d, at 249.

Beyond this, the only construction put upon the ordinance by the state
court was its unexplained conclusion that "the standard of conduct which it
specifies is not dependent upon each complainant's sensitivity." Ibid. But
the court did not indicate upon whose sensitivity a violation does depend—
the sensitivity of the judge or jury, the sensitivity of the arresting officer, or
the sensitivity of a hypothetical reasonable man.

We are thus relegated, at best, to the words of the ordinance itself. If
three or more people meet together on a sidewalk or street corner, they
must conduct themselves so as not to annoy any police officer or other
person who should happen to pass by. In our opinion this ordinance is
unconstitutionally vague because it subjects the exercise of the right of
assembly to an unascertainable standard, and unconstitutionally broad
because it authorizes the punishment of constitutionally protected conduct.

Conduct that annoys some people does not annoy others. Thus, the
ordinance is vague not in the sense that it requires a person to conform his
conduct to an imprecise but comprehensible normative standard, but rather
in the sense that no standard of conduct is specified at all. As a result,
"men of common intelligence must necessarily guess at its meaning."
Connally v. General Construction Co., 269 U.S. 385, 391.

It is said that the ordinance is broad enough to encompass many types
of conduct clearly within the city's constitutional power to prohibit. And
so, indeed, it is. The city is free to prevent people from blocking sidewalks,
obstructing traffic, littering streets, committing assaults, or engaging in
countless other forms of antisocial conduct. It can do so through the
enactment and enforcement of ordinances directed with reasonable specificity toward the conduct to be prohibited. It cannot constitutionally do so
through the enactment and enforcement of an ordinance whose violation
may entirely depend upon whether or not a policeman is annoyed.

But the vice of the ordinance lies not alone in its violation of the due
process standard of vagueness. The ordinance also violates the constitutional right of free assembly and association. Our decisions establish that
mere public intolerance or animosity cannot be the basis for abridgment of
these constitutional freedoms. * * * The First and Fourteenth Amendments do not permit a State to make criminal the exercise of the right of
assembly simply because its exercise may be "annoying" to some people. If
this were not the rule, the right of the people to gather in public places for
social or political purposes would be continually subject to summary
suspension through the good-faith enforcement of a prohibition against
annoying conduct. And such a prohibition, in addition, contains an obvious
invitation to discriminatory enforcement against those whose association
together is "annoying" because their ideas, their lifestyle or their physical
appearance is resented by the majority of their fellow citizens.

The ordinance before us makes a crime out of what under the Constitution cannot be a crime. It is aimed directly at activity protected by the
Constitution. We need not lament that we do not have before us the
details of the conduct found to be annoying. It is the ordinance on its face
that sets the standard of conduct and warns against transgression. The
details of the offense could no more serve to validate this ordinance than

could the details of an offense charged under an ordinance suspending unconditionally the right of assembly and free speech.

The judgment is reversed.

MR. JUSTICE BLACK.

* * * As my Brother White states in his opinion (with which I substantially agree), this is one of those numerous cases where the law could be held unconstitutional because it prohibits both conduct which the Constitution safeguards and conduct which the State may constitutionally punish. Thus, the First Amendment which forbids the State to abridge freedom of speech, would invalidate this city ordinance if it were used to punish the making of a political speech, even if that speech were to annoy other persons. In contrast, however, the ordinance could properly be applied to prohibit the gathering of persons in the mouths of alleys to annoy passersby by throwing rocks or by some other conduct not at all connected with speech. It is a matter of no little difficulty to determine when a law can be held void on its face and when such summary action is inappropriate. This difficulty has been aggravated in this case, because the record fails to show in what conduct these defendants had engaged to annoy other people. In my view, a record showing the facts surrounding the conviction is essential to adjudicate the important constitutional issues in this case. I would therefore vacate the judgment and remand the case to the court below to give both parties an opportunity to supplement the record so that we may determine whether the conduct actually punished is the kind of conduct which it is within the power of the State to punish.

MR. JUSTICE WHITE, with whom THE CHIEF JUSTICE [BURGER] and MR. JUSTICE BLACKMUN join, dissenting.

* * * Any man of average comprehension should know that some kinds of conduct, such as assault or blocking passage on the street, will annoy others and are clearly covered by the "annoying conduct" standard of the ordinance. It would be frivolous to say that these and many other kinds of conduct are not within the foreseeable reach of the law.

It is possible that a whole range of other acts, defined with unconstitutional imprecision, is forbidden by the ordinance. But as a general rule, when a criminal charge is based on conduct constitutionally subject to proscription and clearly forbidden by a statute, it is no defense that the law would be unconstitutionally vague if applied to other behavior. Such a statute is not vague on its face. It may be vague as applied in some circumstances, but ruling on such a challenge obviously requires knowledge of the conduct with which a defendant is charged.

[Justice White then discussed several decisions—including United States v. National Dairy Prod. Corp., p. 181, *supra*]—rejecting vagueness challenges brought by litigants to whose conduct the statutes clearly applied.] This approach is consistent with the host of cases holding that "one to whom application of a statute is constitutional will not be heard to attack the statute on the ground that impliedly it might also be taken as applying to other persons or other situations in which its application might be unconstitutional." United States v. Raines, 362 U.S. 17, 21 (1960), and cases there cited.

Our cases, however, including *National Dairy*, recognize a different approach where the statute at issue purports to regulate or proscribe rights of speech or press protected by the First Amendment. Although a statute may be neither vague, overbroad, nor otherwise invalid as applied to the conduct charged against a particular defendant, he is permitted to raise its vagueness or unconstitutional overbreadth as applied to others. And if the law is found deficient in one of these respects, it may not be applied to him either, until and unless a satisfactory limiting construction is placed on the statute. The statute, in effect, is stricken down on its face. This result is deemed justified since the otherwise continued existence of the statute in unnarrowed form would tend to suppress constitutionally protected rights.

Even accepting the overbreadth doctrine with respect to statutes clearly reaching speech, the Cincinnati ordinance does not purport to bar or regulate speech as such. It prohibits persons from assembling and "conduct[ing]" themselves in a manner annoying to other persons. Even if the assembled defendants in this case were demonstrating and picketing, we have long recognized that picketing is not solely a communicative endeavor and has aspects which the State is entitled to regulate even though there is incidental impact on speech. In Cox v. Louisiana, 379 U.S. 559 (1965), the Court held valid on its face a statute forbidding picketing and parading near a courthouse. This was deemed a valid regulation of conduct rather than pure speech. The conduct reached by the statute was "subject to regulation even though [it was] intertwined with expression and association." *Id.*, at 563. The Court then went on to consider the statute as applied to the facts of record.

In the case before us, I would deal with the Cincinnati ordinance as we would with the ordinary criminal statute. The ordinance clearly reaches certain conduct but may be illegally vague with respect to other conduct. The statute is not infirm on its face and since we have no information from this record as to what conduct was charged against these defendants, we are in no position to judge the statute as applied. That the ordinance may confer wide discretion in a wide range of circumstances is irrelevant when we may be dealing with conduct at its core.

I would therefore affirm the judgment of the Ohio court.

NOTE ON THE SCOPE OF THE ISSUE IN FIRST
AMENDMENT CASES

(1) The first case to permit a defendant to attack a statute on its face for overbreadth was Thornhill v. Alabama, 310 U.S. 88 (1940). An Alabama statute made it a crime for anyone "without a just cause" to "go near to or loiter about" any business for the purpose of influencing others not to deal with or be employed by that business, or to "picket the works or place of business" for the purpose of "hindering, delaying, or interfering with or injuring" the business. Thornhill was convicted on a charge phrased substantially in the words of the statute. In reversing the conviction as unconstitutional under the First Amendment, the Court said (pp. 96–98):

"* * * The section in question must be judged upon its face.

"The finding against petitioner was a general one. It did not specify the testimony upon which it rested. The charges were framed in the words of the statute and so must be given a like construction. The courts below expressed no intention of narrowing the construction put upon the statute by prior State decisions. In these circumstances, there is no occasion to go behind the face of the statute or of the complaint for the purpose of determining whether the evidence, together with the permissible inferences to be drawn from it, could ever support a conviction founded upon different and more precise charges. 'Conviction upon a charge not made would be sheer denial of due process.' De Jonge v. Oregon, 299 U.S. 353, 362; Stromberg v. California, 283 U.S. 359, 367, 368. * * *

"There is a further reason for testing the section on its face. Proof of an abuse of power in the particular case has never been deemed a requisite for attack on the constitutionality of a statute purporting to license the dissemination of ideas. * * * The power of the licensor * * * is pernicious not merely by reason of the censure of particular comments but by reason of the threat to censure comments on matters of public concern. * * * One who might have had a license for the asking may therefore call into question the whole scheme of licensing when he is prosecuted for failure to procure it. Lovell v. Griffin, 303 U.S. 444; Hague v. C.I.O., 307 U.S. 496. A like threat is inherent in a penal statute, like that in question here, which does not aim specifically at evils within the allowable area of State control but, on the contrary, sweeps within its ambit other activities that in ordinary circumstances constitute an exercise of freedom of speech or of the press. The existence of such a statute, which readily lends itself to harsh and discriminatory enforcement by local prosecuting officials, against particular groups deemed to merit their displeasure, results in a continuous and pervasive restraint on all freedom of discussion that might reasonably be regarded as within its purview. * * * An accused, after arrest and conviction under such a statute, does not have to sustain the burden of demonstrating that the State could not constitutionally have written a different and specific statute covering his activities as disclosed by the charge and the evidence introduced against him. Schneider v. State, 308 U.S. 147, 155, 162, 163. Where regulations of the liberty of free discussion are concerned, there are special reasons for observing the rule that it is the statute, and not the accusation or the evidence under it, which prescribes the limits of permissible conduct and warns against transgression."

(2) In Cox v. New Hampshire, 312 U.S. 569 (1941), a New Hampshire statute prohibited holding a "parade or procession upon any public street or way * * * unless a special license therefor shall first be obtained." Defendants, Jehovah's Witnesses, were convicted for having marched on the streets of Manchester single file, in groups of 15–20, each marcher carrying a sign with "informational" inscriptions. The state supreme court, in upholding the convictions, ruled that the authority to license parades was not unfettered but called for a "systematic, consistent and just order of treatment, with reference to the convenience of public use of the highways," and that the statute sought only to control "organized formations of persons using the highways" and did not otherwise restrict the distribution of literature or the communication of facts and opinions. The Supreme Court unanimously affirmed (p. 576): "We find it impossible to say that the limited authority conferred by the licensing provisions of the statute in question as thus construed by the state court contravened any constitutional right."

In Shuttlesworth v. Birmingham, 394 U.S. 147 (1969), defendant was convicted of violating an ordinance that prohibited participation in any "parade or procession or other public demonstration" without a permit, but required the City Commission to issue a permit "unless in its judgment the public welfare, peace, safety, health, decency, good order, morals or convenience required that it be refused." Birmingham Gen.Code § 1159. The Supreme Court of Alabama upheld the conviction by construing the ordinance to authorize denial of a permit only in accordance with a "systematic, consistent and just order of treatment with reference to the convenience of the public use of the streets and sidewalks." The Supreme Court reversed (pp. 155–58):

" * * * We may assume that * * * the ordinance as now authoritatively construed would pass constitutional muster. It does not follow, however, that the severely narrowing construction put upon the ordinance by the Alabama Supreme Court in November of 1967 necessarily serves to restore constitutional validity to a conviction that occurred in 1963 under the ordinance as it was written. * * *[1]

"In Cox * * * [t]his Court accepted the state court's characterization of the statute, and its assurance that the appellants ' "had a right, under the Act, to a license to march when, where and as they did, if after a required investigation it was found that the convenience of the public in the use of the streets would not thereby be unduly disturbed, upon such conditions or changes in time, place and manner as would avoid disturbance." ' * * *

"In the present case we are confronted with quite a different situation. In April of 1963 * * * [i]t would have taken extraordinary clairvoyance for anyone to perceive that [the ordinance] meant what the Supreme Court of Alabama was destined to find that it meant more than four years later; and, with First Amendment rights hanging in the balance, we would hesitate long before assuming that either the members of the Commission or the petitioner possessed any such clairvoyance at the time of the Good Friday march.

"But we need not deal in assumptions. * * * [The Court reviewed the events preceding the march, including two attempts to secure a permit, and concluded:]

"These 'surrounding relevant circumstances' make it indisputably clear, we think, that in April of 1963—at least with respect to this petitioner and his organization—the city authorities thought the ordinance meant exactly what it said. The petitioner was clearly given to understand that under no circumstances would he and his group be permitted to demonstrate in Birmingham, not that a demonstration would be approved if a time and place were selected that would minimize traffic problems. * * *"

(3) In Gooding v. Wilson, 405 U.S. 518 (1972), Wilson was convicted of violating Georgia Code § 26–6303, making it a misdemeanor for any person "without provocation, [to] use to or of another, and in his presence * * * opprobrious words or abusive language, tending to cause a breach of the peace." He challenged the validity of the statute under the First Amendment on grounds of vagueness and overbreadth. Although the facts of the case involved "fighting words" clearly punishable under existing precedents, the only issue before the Supreme Court was the validity of the

---

1. But *cf.* Dombrowski v. Pfister, 380 U.S. 479, 491 n. 7 (1965), p. 1428, *infra.*

statute on its face. The Court held the statute invalid on the ground that the construction given it by the Georgia courts was overbroad (pp. 520–21):

"Section 26–6303 punishes only spoken words. It can therefore withstand appellee's attack upon its facial constitutionality only if, as authoritatively construed by the Georgia courts, it is not susceptible of application to speech, although vulgar or offensive, that is protected by the First and Fourteenth Amendments. Only the Georgia courts can supply the requisite construction, since of course 'we lack jurisdiction authoritatively to construe state legislation.' United States v. Thirty–Seven Photographs, 402 U.S. 363, 369 (1971). It matters not that the words appellee used might have been constitutionally prohibited under a narrowly and precisely drawn statute. At least when statutes regulate or proscribe speech and when 'no readily apparent construction suggests itself as a vehicle for rehabilitating the statutes in a single prosecution,' Dombrowski v. Pfister, 380 U.S. 479, 491 (1965), the transcendent value to all society of constitutionally protected expression is deemed to justify allowing 'attacks on overly broad statutes with no requirement that the person making the attack demonstrate that his own conduct could not be regulated by a statute drawn with the requisite narrow specificity,' *id.*, at 486. This is deemed necessary because persons whose expression is constitutionally protected may well refrain from exercising their rights for fear of criminal sanctions provided by a statute susceptible of application to protected expression."

Justice Blackmun, joined by Chief Justice Burger, dissented (pp. 534– 37):

"It seems strange indeed that in this day a man may say to a police officer, who is attempting to restore access to a public building, 'White son of a bitch, I'll kill you' and 'You son of a bitch, I'll choke you to death,' * * * and yet constitutionally cannot be prosecuted and convicted under a state statute which makes it a misdemeanor to 'use to or of another, and in his presence, opprobrious words or abusive language, tending to cause a breach of the peace. * * * ' This, however, is precisely what the Court pronounces as the law today.

"* * * Except perhaps for the 'big' word 'opprobrious'—and no point is made of its bigness—any Georgia schoolboy would expect that this defendant's fighting and provocative words to the officers were covered by § 26–6303. * * *

"The Court reaches its result by saying that the Georgia statute has been interpreted by the State's courts so as to be applicable in practice to otherwise constitutionally protected speech. It follows, says the Court, that the statute is overbroad and therefore is facially unconstitutional and to be struck down in its entirety. Thus Georgia apparently is to be left with no valid statute on its books to meet Wilson's bullying tactic. * * * If this is what the overbreadth doctrine means, and if this is what it produces, it urgently needs reexamination * * *."

(4) How persuasive is the premise of Gooding, Paragraph (3), *supra,* that an overbroad statute chills the conduct of constitutionally protected actors? Compare Note, *The First Amendment Overbreadth Doctrine,* 83 Harv.L.Rev. 844 (1970), and Note, *The Chilling Effect in Constitutional Law,* 69 Colum.L.Rev. 808 (1969), both supporting the premise, with Redish, *The Warren Court, The Burger Court, and the First Amendment Over-*

breadth Doctrine, 78 Nw.U.L.Rev. 1031 (1983), questioning it. If unprotected actors, like the defendant in Gooding, are willing to violate an overbroad statute, why is it that protected actors will be less willing to do so? Isn't "chilling" less likely in a case like Coates or Gooding—in which protected actors may neither know nor care about the scope of a statute or judicial decisions construing it—than in a case involving planned activity?

Experience certainly shows that many protected actors will violate an overbroad statute, though others may desist from fear of prosecution. Those who are in fact concerned about possible prosecution may be able to test the statute's constitutionality in a declaratory judgment action, though that course may be too burdensome or time-consuming to eliminate the chilling effect in every case.

Whatever the force of the chilling effect rationale, is it any less forceful when applied to statutes whose overbreadth violates constitutional provisions other than the First Amendment? In H.L. v. Matheson, 450 U.S. 398 (1981), the plaintiff (an unmarried 15–year old girl living with and dependent on her parents) challenged a law requiring a physician, before performing an abortion on any minor, to "[n]otify, if possible" her parents or guardian. The Court refused to entertain the plaintiff's facial attack, and upheld the law as applied to the plaintiff. Suppose, however, that other minors regulated by the statute—those who are mature and emancipated— do have a constitutional right to an abortion without parental notification. Couldn't the Court's approach chill their exercise of that right? [2]

Compare Aptheker v. Secretary of State, 378 U.S. 500 (1964), involving a challenge to § 6 of the Subversive Activities Control Act of 1950. This section prohibited the use of a passport by any person who belonged to an organization which, to his knowledge, was required to register under the Act. Two leaders of the Communist Party brought suit to enjoin the State Department's efforts to revoke their passports. The Supreme Court held the statute "unconstitutional on its face" because it "too broadly and indiscriminately restricts the right to travel and thereby abridges the liberty guaranteed by the Fifth Amendment" (p. 505). Though it did not deny that a statutory ban on passport use by leaders of the Party might be valid, the Court refused to uphold the statute as applied to the plaintiffs. It suggested that an effort to supply a limiting construction would constitute "judicial[ ] rewriting" of the statute and would "inject an element of vagueness into the statute's scope and application. * * * [S]ince freedom of travel is a constitutional liberty closely related to rights of free speech and association, we believe that appellants in this case should not be required to assume the burden of demonstrating that Congress could not have written a statute constitutionally prohibiting their travel" (pp. 515–17).

Were the difficulties of limiting the statute, or the risks of chilling protected conduct, any greater in Aptheker (or in Coates and Gooding) than in H.L. v. Matheson? Should Aptheker be regarded as a First Amendment case?

2. See also Bowers v. Hardwick, 106 S.Ct. 2841 (1986). There, a practicing homosexual attacked a state statute that prohibited sodomy. The Court upheld the statute as applied to consensual homosexual sodomy, but refused to consider its constitutionality as applied, for example, to the conduct of a married couple.

(5) Which of the following issues is a defendant in a state criminal proceeding entitled to raise in mounting a First Amendment attack on the statute he is charged with violating?

(a) The constitutionality of the statute as written?

(b) The constitutionality of the statute as construed by the state court?

(c) The constitutionality of the statute as applied to the conduct in which he is found to have engaged? [3]

Consider the argument in Monaghan, *Overbreadth,* 1981 Sup.Ct.Rev. 1., that there is no need or justification for a special standing doctrine in First Amendment overbreadth cases. Professor Monaghan argues that a litigant is always permitted to attack as constitutionally invalid the rule of law under which he is being sanctioned, whether or not the First Amendment is implicated, and whether or not his conduct is itself constitutionally protected. Under ordinary severability analysis, such an attack will succeed if the law's application to him, though itself constitutional, cannot be severed from other unconstitutional applications. For a narrowing construction to cure any possible invalidity, it must not only eliminate the statute's application to protected conduct; it must also leave the statute clear enough to withstand a challenge under the void-for-vagueness doctrine, which demands "a greater degree of specificity" in statutes regulating free expression than in other areas.[4] And for Professor Monaghan, in First Amendment cases as in any other case raising a severability question, there is no justification for striking down a statute on its face when a valid limiting construction is available.[5]

Note that this view would still call for overturning the conviction in a case like Shuttlesworth, Paragraph (2), *supra,* on the theory that an individual who has been denied a permit by local officials on an unconstitutional basis has the right to demonstrate without one, even if the denial violated state law. It could also call for overturning the convictions in Gooding, Paragraph (4), *supra,* and in Coates: the state court's construction of the laws there involved still reached protected conduct, so that the litigant could properly complain of conviction under an unconstitutional rule of law.[6]

3. These questions recur in Chap. V, Sec. 2(C), *infra.*

4. See, *e.g.,* Smith v. Goguen, 415 U.S. 566, 573 (1974); accord, *e.g.,* Hynes v. Mayor of Oradell, 425 U.S. 610 (1976).

But see the surprising ruling in Arnett v. Kennedy, 416 U.S. 134 (1974), where a majority of the Court, in rejecting a claim of facial overbreadth by a discharged federal civil service employee, construed in the following terms the statutory standard governing grounds for discharge (p. 162): "We hold that the language 'such cause as will promote the efficiency of the service' * * * excludes constitutionally protected speech, and that the statute is therefore not overbroad."

5. The Supreme Court has refused to strike down laws that were overbroad as written but that had already been given narrowing constructions by the state

courts. See, *e.g.,* Ward v. Illinois, 431 U.S. 767, 773–76 (1977) (obscenity statute narrowed to meet requirements of Miller v. California, 413 U.S. 15 (1973)); Colten v. Kentucky, 407 U.S. 104, 110–11 (1972) (disorderly conduct statute narrowed to extend only to cases involving no bona fide intention to exercise constitutional rights or to those in which the state's interest in public order clearly outweighs any interest in free expression).

6. See also Erznoznik v. City of Jacksonville, 422 U.S. 205 (1975), where plaintiff sought a declaratory judgment in state court against enforcement of an ordinance prohibiting display on screens visible from any public place of films containing nudity. The record did not clearly indicate whether the film whose exhibition was at issue was protected. Noting that the ordinance was not easily susceptible to a limiting

(6) In Gooding, would it have been appropriate for the Supreme Court to have (a) explained the contours of First Amendment protection in the context of regulation of breach of the peace; (b) indicated that the ordinance, as construed by the state court, still extended to protected conduct; (c) ruled that Gooding's conduct was unprotected; and (d) remanded to permit the state to redetermine, in light of a proper understanding of the First Amendment, whether to uphold the conviction under an interpretation of the ordinance that could pass constitutional muster? See generally Chap. V, Sec. 2(A), *infra,* discussing generally the appropriateness of the Supreme Court's remanding a case to permit the state courts to modify a prior interpretation of state law that was based on an erroneous understanding of federal law.[7]

Could the Court in Gooding have gone further still—and instead of vacating and remanding, as just suggested, upheld the conviction on the presumption (see the Yazoo case) that the state would sever the unconstitutional applications? *Cf.* Brockett v. Spokane Arcades, Inc., Paragraph (11), *infra.* At a minimum, doesn't the answer depend on whether the Court could have fairly viewed the ordinance as susceptible to a limiting construction that would not be void for vagueness?

(7) In United States v. Thirty–Seven (37) Photographs, 402 U.S. 363 (1971), the Court considered the validity of a *federal* law prohibiting the importation of obscene material and providing for its seizure by customs officials. In a federal civil enforcement proceeding to forfeit allegedly obscene photographs, the owner counterclaimed for injunctive relief, alleging that the law was unconstitutional on its face and as applied. It was stipulated that some or all of the photographs were intended for use in a commercially distributed book. A three-judge district court held the statute unconstitutional, in part on the ground that it was overbroad as applied to the importation of materials for private use. A majority of the Court rejected this approach. Justice White's plurality opinion, joined by Chief Justice Burger and Justices Brennan and Blackmun, took the position that the statute was valid even as applied to private use, but specifically stated that had the district court's contrary view been correct, the proper approach would have been to "construe [the law] narrowly and hold it valid in its application to [the owner]" (p. 375 n. 3). Justice Harlan, concurring separately, stated (p. 378) that the commercial importer "lacked standing to raise the overbreadth claim." Justice Stewart concurred in the judgment, concluding that the statute was valid as applied to the owner, while implying that it could not validly extend to importation for private use. Justices Black, Douglas, and Marshall dissented.[8]

construction, and that the state courts had made no effort to limit it, the Supreme Court struck it down as overbroad.

7. Compare Metromedia, Inc. v. City of San Diego, 453 U.S. 490 (1981), a state court declaratory judgment action challenging the constitutionality of a local ordinance that barred all outdoor display advertising, noncommercial as well as commercial. The state supreme court upheld the ordinance. In the Supreme Court, the plurality concluded that the ordinance was constitutional insofar as it regulated only commercial speech, but "[b]ecause [it]

reaches too far into the realm of protected speech [by regulating noncommercial speech], we conclude that it is unconstitutional on its face" (p. 521). In a footnote, the plurality added that, on remand, the state courts "may sustain the ordinance by limiting its reach to commercial speech, assuming the ordinance is susceptible to this treatment" (p. 522 n. 26).

8. In United States v. 12 200–Foot Reels, 413 U.S. 123 (1973), the Court later upheld that statute's constitutionality as applied to the importation of obscene material exclusively for private use.

The three-judge district court had also held that the statutory procedures for seizing obscene material were deficient because they did not contain time limits within which judicial review of any seizure must occur, as required by such cases as Freedman v. Maryland, 380 U.S. 51 (1965) and Teitel Film Corp. v. Cusack, 390 U.S. 139, 141 (1968). However, the Court found that "it is possible to construe the [law] to bring it in harmony with constitutional requirements," and distinguished its refusal to do so in Freedman and Teitel because the statutes there "were enacted pursuant to state rather than federal authority," and "we lack jurisdiction authoritatively to construe state legislation" (pp. 368–69). The Court held that its limiting construction applied in the present case.[9]

Freedman and Teitel each arose on review of a state conviction, where the state court had already had the chance to provide a limiting construction, and could be given another chance to do so on remand. In federal court actions seeking equitable relief from the enforcement of state laws alleged to be overbroad under the First Amendment, should the federal court abstain, or certify the question of state law to a state court, in order to obtain that court's authoritative construction of the statute? See Virginia v. American Booksellers Ass'n, Inc., 108 S.Ct. 636 (1988) (certifying state law questions in such an action). See generally Chap. X, Sec. 2(B), *infra*.

(8) In Broadrick v. Oklahoma, 413 U.S. 601 (1973), state employees whose conduct was concededly prohibited under Oklahoma's "Little Hatch Act" challenged the statute in federal court on First Amendment grounds, alleging vagueness and overbreadth. On appeal, the Court entertained the facial attack, rejecting it on the merits. Justice White's opinion for the Court said (pp. 612–16):

"[C]laims of facial overbreadth have been entertained in cases involving statutes which, by their terms, seek to regulate 'only spoken words.' Gooding v. Wilson, 405 U.S. 518, 520 (1972). * * * Overbreadth attacks have also been allowed where the Court thought rights of association were ensnared in statutes which, by their broad sweep, might result in burdening innocent associations. * * * Facial overbreadth claims have also been entertained where statutes, by their terms, purport to regulate the time, place, and manner of expressive or communicative conduct, * * * and where such conduct has required official approval under laws that delegated standardless discretionary power to local functionaries, resulting in virtually unreviewable prior restraints on First Amendment rights.
* * *

"The consequence of our departure from traditional rules of standing in the First Amendment area is that any enforcement of a statute thus placed at issue is totally forbidden until and unless a limiting construction or partial invalidation so narrows it as to remove the seeming threat or deterrence to constitutionally protected expression. Application of the overbreadth doctrine in this manner is, manifestly, strong medicine. It has been employed by the Court sparingly and only as a last resort. Facial overbreadth has not been invoked when a limiting construction has been or could be placed on the challenged statute. * * * Equally important, overbreadth claims, if entertained at all, have been curtailed when invoked

9. For other decisions upholding federal statutes after narrowing constructions, see, *e.g.*, Hamling v. United States, 418 U.S. 87, 114–15 (1974); Buckley v. Valeo, 424 U.S. 1, 44, 76–80 (1976).

against ordinary criminal laws that are sought to be applied to protected conduct. [Citing and discussing cases involving "breach of peace" charges.] Additionally, overbreadth scrutiny has generally been somewhat less rigid in the context of statutes regulating conduct in the shadow of the First Amendment, but doing so in a neutral, noncensorial manner. * * *

"It remains a 'matter of no little difficulty' to determine when a law may properly be held void on its face and when 'such summary action' is inappropriate. Coates v. City of Cincinnati, 402 U.S. 611, 617 (1971) (opinion of Black, J.). But the plain import of our cases is, at the very least, that facial overbreadth adjudication is an exception to our traditional rules of practice and that its function, a limited one at the outset, attenuates as the otherwise unprotected behavior that it forbids the State to sanction moves from 'pure speech' toward conduct and that conduct—even if expressive—falls within the scope of otherwise valid criminal laws that reflect legitimate state interests in maintaining comprehensive controls over harmful, constitutionally unprotected conduct. Although such laws, if too broadly worded, may deter protected speech to some unknown extent, there comes a point where that effect—at best a prediction—cannot, with confidence, justify invalidating a statute on its face and so prohibiting a State from enforcing the statute against conduct that is admittedly within its power to proscribe. To put the matter another way, particularly where conduct and not merely speech is involved, we believe that the overbreadth of a statute must not only be real, but substantial as well, judged in relation to the statute's plainly legitimate sweep. It is our view that [the Oklahoma statute] is not substantially overbroad and that whatever overbreadth may exist should be cured through case-by-case analysis of the fact situations to which its sanctions, assertedly, may not be applied."

Justice Brennan, in a dissent joined by Justices Stewart and Marshall, objected to the majority's result and to its criterion of "substantial overbreadth" (pp. 629–32): "We have never held that a statute should be held invalid on its face merely because it is possible to conceive of a single impermissible application, and in that sense a requirement of substantial overbreadth is already implicit in the doctrine. * * * Whether the Court means to require some different or greater showing of substantiality is left obscure * * * because the Court makes no effort to explain why the overbreadth of the Oklahoma Act, while real, is somehow not quite substantial. * * *

"More fundamentally, the Court offers no rationale to explain its conclusion that, for purposes of overbreadth analysis, deterrence of conduct should be viewed differently from deterrence of speech, even where both are equally protected by the First Amendment. * * * In any case, the conclusion that a distinction should be drawn was the premise of Mr. Justice White's dissenting opinion in Coates v. City of Cincinnati, * * * and that conclusion—although squarely rejected in Coates—has now been adopted by the Court.

"* * * Coates stood, until today, for the proposition that where a statute is 'unconstitutionally broad because it authorizes the punishment of constitutionally protected conduct', 402 U.S., at 614, it must be held invalid on its face whether or not the person raising the challenge could have been prosecuted under a properly narrowed statute. The Court makes no attempt to distinguish Coates, implicitly conceding that the decision has been overruled."

The requirement that overbreadth be substantial has had a confusing history, but the Court now appears prepared to apply the requirement not only to cases involving "conduct" but also to those involving "pure speech." [10]

(9) Overbreadth methodology necessarily involves consideration of hypothetical statutory applications not raised by the conduct of litigants before the court. But the "substantial overbreadth" requirement makes the adjudication more speculative still. No longer can the court merely identify some potential applications of the statute that would be unconstitutional; instead, the court must try to imagine all possible valid and invalid applications, and then somehow compare their number or importance. See Broadrick, 413 U.S. at 615–18; New York v. Ferber, note 10, *supra*, at 773. How manageable is that inquiry?

On the other hand, that inquiry will provide considerable guidance to the parties, and to other interested persons, about the scope of First Amendment protection in the context under review. Compare Gunther, *Reflections on Robel*, 20 Stan.L.Rev. 1140, 1147–48 (1968), criticizing overbreadth decisions for suggesting, when striking down overbroad laws, that less sweeping enactments would be valid without providing any guidance about how to draft them.

Suppose that a state statute is overbroad but not substantially so, and the state court has authoritatively ruled that the unconstitutional applications cannot be severed from the constitutional ones. Under ordinary separability principles, a litigant would be entitled to challenge the statute as unlawful, whether or not his conduct is protected. Should the require-

---

10. In Lewis v. City of New Orleans, 415 U.S. 130 (1974), the Court reversed a conviction under an ordinance making it unlawful "wantonly to curse or revile or to use obscene or opprobrious language" to a police officer. The Louisiana Supreme Court had interpreted that language as limited to "fighting words" uttered to specific persons at a specific time, but the Supreme Court found that even as narrowed the ordinance had "a broader sweep than the constitutional definition of 'fighting words' announced in Chaplinsky v. New Hampshire, 315 U.S. 568, 572 (1942)" (p. 132). Noting that the ordinance "punishes only spoken words," the Court struck it down as overbroad; neither the majority opinion nor Justice Blackmun's dissent mentioned Broadrick. See also Bigelow v. Virginia, 421 U.S. 809, 817 (1975), stating in dictum that the substantial overbreadth doctrine does not apply where "pure speech" is involved.

In Village of Schaumburg v. Citizens for a Better Environment, 444 U.S. 620 (1980), the Court struck down as overbroad an ordinance that prohibited solicitation of contributions by charities that used less than 75% of the receipts for charitable

purposes. The Court made no finding that the overbreadth was substantial, and it could hardly have found that the ordinance regulated "pure speech."

In New York v. Ferber, 458 U.S. 747 (1982), the Court affirmed that the requirement of *substantial* overbreadth "is sound and should be applied in the present context involving the harmful employment of children to make sexually explicit materials for distribution" (p. 771). Accordingly, the Court rejected the overbreadth challenge of a defendant convicted under a statute barring the distribution of materials depicting sexual performances by children under 16, ruling that any overbreadth was not substantial. And in Brockett v. Spokane Arcades, Inc., 472 U.S. 491, 503 n. 12 (1985), the Court expressly stated, in dictum, that Ferber had rejected the proposition that "the Broadrick substantial overbreadth requirement is inapplicable where pure speech rather than conduct is at issue." See also City of Houston v. Hill, 107 S.Ct. 2502, 2508 (1987) (invalidating as substantially overbroad an ordinance making it unlawful to "assault, strike, or in any manner oppose, molest, abuse or interrupt a policeman in the execution of his duty").

ment of "substantial" overbreadth be understood as making such challenges *less* available in free speech cases?

(10) Since Broadrick, the Court has created other restrictions on the overbreadth doctrine.

In Parker v. Levy, 417 U.S. 733 (1974), the Court rejected an overbreadth attack on general articles of the Uniform Code of Military Justice. In the Court's view, the reasons "dictating a different application of First Amendment principles in the military context" make less forceful the policies that support overbreadth attacks (p. 760).

In Bates v. State Bar of Arizona, 433 U.S. 350 (1977), in ruling that a state could not ban all advertising by attorneys and that the particular advertisement at issue in the case was protected, the Court refused to entertain an overbreadth challenge. "Since advertising is linked to commercial well-being, it seems unlikely that such speech is particularly susceptible to being crushed by overbroad regulation. * * * Moreover, concerns for uncertainty * * * are reduced; the advertiser seeks to disseminate information about a product or service that he provides, and presumably he can determine more readily than others whether his speech is truthful and protected" (p. 381).[11]

(11) In Brockett v. Spokane Arcades, Inc., 472 U.S. 491 (1985), only four days after the effective date of a Washington statute regulating obscenity, various purveyors of sexually-oriented books and movies brought a federal court challenge to that statute. The court of appeals ruled that the statute extended to protected as well as unprotected speech, and, finding that it "did not lend itself to a saving construction," declared it to be unconstitutional *in toto*. (In the court of appeals' view, the statute's vice was that it defined "prurient" to include "that which incites * * * lust," and thereby reached material that merely stimulated normal sexual responses). The Supreme Court reversed. Though Justice O'Connor, joined by Chief Justice Burger and Justice Rehnquist, argued for abstention to permit the state courts to construe the new statute, the Court, per Justice White, rejected that course. Instead, the Court ruled that the court of appeals should have invalidated the statute only insofar as it reached protected expression. The precedents support total invalidation, the Court said, when an unprotected actor challenges a statute as overbroad, but where the litigant challenging the statute is a protected actor, "[t]here is then no want of a proper party to challenge the statute, no concern that an attack on the statute will be unduly delayed or protected speech discouraged. The statute may forthwith be declared invalid to the extent that it reaches too far, but otherwise left intact" (p. 504). Total invalidation would be proper only if the state legislature had passed an inseverable statute or would not have passed the statute had its partial invalidity been recognized; under Washington law, however, there was a presumption of severability, and the statute included a severability clause.

Should Brockett be taken to announce the surprising proposition that the less protected a litigant's conduct is, the more completely he can have an overbroad statute declared unconstitutional? Would that proposition

---

11. See also Village of Hoffman Estates v. Flipside, Hoffman Estates, Inc., 455 U.S. 489, 496–97 (1982) (rejecting an overbreadth attack on an ordinance regulating the sale of drug paraphernalia, and stating that "it is irrelevant whether the ordinance has an overbroad scope encompassing protected commercial speech of other persons, because the overbreadth doctrine does not apply to commercial speech").

require, in a case like Coates, that the Court determine whether the defendant's actual conduct was protected, so that it could in turn determine whether, in reversing his conviction, it should hold the ordinance unconstitutional on its face or only as applied? Is the difference between narrow and total invalidation more significant in a suit for equitable relief like Brockett than in a criminal prosecution like Coates? [12]

(12) What is the relationship between vagueness and overbreadth challenges? Consider the explanation of Justice Marshall in Village of Hoffman Estates v. Flipside, Hoffman Estates, Inc., 455 U.S. 489, 494–95 (1982): "In a facial challenge to the overbreadth and vagueness of a law, a court's first task is to determine whether the enactment reaches a substantial amount of constitutionally protected conduct. If it does not, then the overbreadth challenge must fail. The court should then examine the facial vagueness challenge, and assuming the enactment implicates no constitutionally protected conduct, should uphold the challenge only if the enactment is impermissibly vague in all of its applications. A plaintiff who engages in some conduct that is clearly proscribed cannot complain of the vagueness of the law as applied to the conduct of others." See also Parker v. Levy, Paragraph (10), *supra*, 417 U.S. at 756. Is Coates consistent with this approach?

In Kolender v. Lawson, 461 U.S. 352 (1983), the plaintiff brought a facial attack against a California statute prohibiting loitering. The lower federal courts enjoined the law on the grounds that it was vague and that it violated the Fourth Amendment, and the Supreme Court affirmed on vagueness grounds. In dissent, Justice White, joined by Justice Rehnquist, argued that the statute did not implicate First Amendment concerns, and that because the statute was not vague in all of its possible applications, the Court's facial invalidation was inconsistent with the reasoning of cases like Hoffman Estates.[13] The majority, per O'Connor, J., responded (p. 359 n. 8) that his description of the precedents was inaccurate because (i) the Court permits facial challenges to laws that reach " 'a substantial amount of constitutionally protected conduct,' " quoting Hoffman Estates, and (ii) the standard of certainty is higher for criminal statutes. To Justice White's charge that the Court had confused overbreadth and vagueness, the Court responded "we have traditionally viewed vagueness and overbreadth as logically related and similar doctrines." Finally, the Court asserted that

---

12. Compare Secretary of State of Maryland v. Joseph H. Munson Co., Inc., 467 U.S. 947 (1984), a state court action by a fundraiser challenging the constitutionality of a state law that, subject to waiver provisions, prohibited charitable organizations from paying more than 25% of the proceeds of fundraising activities as expenses therefor. The Court of Appeals of Maryland struck down the statute on its face as overbroad, and the Supreme Court affirmed, 5–4. The majority cited 10 cases that it described as permitting facial rather than partial invalidation at the behest of a litigant claiming that his own conduct is protected. Facial attacks were permitted in these cases because "it was apparent that any application of the legislation 'would create an unacceptable risk of the suppression of ideas' " (p. 965 n. 13, quot-

ing City Council of Los Angeles v. Taxpayers for Vincent, 466 U.S. 789, 797 (1984)).

Justice Rehnquist and three other dissenters doubted "as a matter of original inquiry * * * whether an overbreadth challenge should ever be allowed" given the availability of declaratory and preliminary injunctive relief (p. 977). He viewed the statute under attack as constitutional in its "core" application to regulate the fees charged charities by outside fundraisers, and therefore not substantially overbroad.

13. Justice White added that "if the statute on its face violates the Fourth or Fifth Amendment—and I express no views about that question—the Court would be justified in striking it down" (p. 374).

"[n]o authority cited by the dissent supports its argument about facial challenges in the arbitrary enforcement context."

On vagueness, see generally Note, *The Void-for-Vagueness Doctrine in the Supreme Court,* 109 U.Pa.L.Rev. 67 (1960).

SECTION 4. FEIGNED AND MOOT CASES

UNITED STATES v. JOHNSON

319 U.S. 302, 63 S.Ct. 1075, 87 L.Ed. 1413 (1943).
Appeal from the District Court of the United States for the
Northern District of Indiana.

PER CURIAM. One Roach, a tenant of residential property belonging to appellee, brought this suit in the district court alleging that the property was within a "defense rental area" established by the Price Administrator pursuant to §§ 2(b) and 302(d) of the Emergency Price Control Act of 1942, 56 Stat. 23; that the Administrator had promulgated Maximum Rent Regulation No. 8 for the area; and that the rent paid by Roach and collected by appellee was in excess of the maximum fixed by the regulation. The complaint demanded judgment for treble damages and reasonable attorney's fees, as prescribed by § 205(e) of the Act, 50 U.S.C.A.Appendix, § 925(e). The United States, intervening pursuant to 28 U.S.C. § 401, filed a brief in support of the constitutionality of the Act, which appellee had challenged by motion to dismiss. The district court dismissed the complaint on the ground—as appears from its opinion (48 F.Supp. 833) and judgment—that the Act and the promulgation of the regulation under it were unconstitutional because Congress by the Act had unconstitutionally delegated legislative power to the Administrator.

Before entry of the order dismissing the complaint, the Government moved to reopen the case on the ground that it was collusive and did not involve a real case or controversy. This motion was denied. The Government brings the case here on appeal under § 2 of the Act of August 24, 1937, 50 Stat. 752, 28 U.S.C. § 349a, and assigns as error both the ruling of the district court on the constitutionality of the Act, and its refusal to reopen and dismiss the case as collusive. * * *

The affidavit of the plaintiff, submitted by the Government on its motion to dismiss the suit as collusive, shows without contradiction that he brought the present proceeding in a fictitious name; that it was instituted as a "friendly suit" at appellee's request; that the plaintiff did not employ, pay, or even meet, the attorney who appeared of record in his behalf; that he had no knowledge who paid the $15 filing fee in the district court, but was assured by appellee that as plaintiff he would incur no expense in bringing the suit; that he did not read the complaint which was filed in his name as plaintiff; that in his conferences with the appellee and appellee's attorney of record, nothing was said concerning treble damages and he had no knowledge of the amount of the judgment prayed until he read of it in a local newspaper.

Appellee's counter-affidavit did not deny these allegations. It admitted that appellee's attorney had undertaken to procure an attorney to represent the plaintiff and had assured the plaintiff that his presence in court during the trial of the cause would not be necessary. It appears from the district court's opinion that no brief was filed on the plaintiff's behalf in that court.

The Government does not contend that, as a result of this cooperation of the two original parties to the litigation, any false or fictitious state of facts was submitted to the court. But it does insist that the affidavits disclose the absence of a genuine adversary issue between the parties, without which a court may not safely proceed to judgment, especially when it assumes the grave responsibility of passing upon the constitutional validity of legislative action. Even in a litigation where only private rights are involved, the judgment will not be allowed to stand where one of the parties has dominated the conduct of the suit by payment of the fees of both. Gardner v. Goodyear Dental Vulcanite Co., 131 U.S.Appendix ciii.

Here an important public interest is at stake—the validity of an Act of Congress having far-reaching effects on the public welfare in one of the most critical periods in the history of the country. That interest has been adjudicated in a proceeding in which the plaintiff has had no active participation, over which he has exercised no control, and the expense of which he has not borne. He has been only nominally represented by counsel who was selected by appellee's counsel and whom he has never seen. Such a suit is collusive because it is not in any real sense adversary. It does not assume the "honest and actual antagonistic assertion of rights" to be adjudicated—a safeguard essential to the integrity of the judicial process, and one which we have held to be indispensable to adjudication of constitutional questions by this Court. Chicago & G.T. Ry. Co. v. Wellman, 143 U.S. 339, 345; and see Lord v. Veazie, 8 How. 251; Cleveland v. Chamberlain, 1 Black 419; Bartemeyer v. Iowa, 18 Wall. 129, 134, 135; Atherton Mills v. Johnston, 259 U.S. 13, 15. Whenever in the course of litigation such a defect in the proceedings is brought to the court's attention, it may set aside any adjudication thus procured and dismiss the cause without entering judgment on the merits. It is the court's duty to do so where, as here, the public interest has been placed at hazard by the amenities of parties to a suit conducted under the domination of only one of them. The district court should have granted the Government's motion to dismiss the suit as collusive. We accordingly vacate the judgment below with instructions to the district court to dismiss the cause on that ground alone. * * *

Judgment vacated with directions.

NOTE ON FEIGNED CASES

(1) Why didn't the government's intervention in the Johnson case, pursuant to what is now 28 U.S.C. § 2403, cure the difficulty of lack of a party genuinely interested in supporting the constitutionality of the legislation?

(2) The government's immediate interests in the Johnson case might have been better served by an early Supreme Court determination of the

constitutional issues involved. If so, was the government wise in pressing the objection that the action was collusive? Was the Solicitor General under a duty to do so?

(3) If one party agrees with the position of the other, does that necessarily preclude the presence of a case or controversy? See Moore v. Charlotte–Mecklenburg Bd. of Educ., 402 U.S. 47 (1971), where, "confronted with the anomaly that both litigants desire precisely the same result, namely, a holding that the anti-busing statute is constitutional," the Court held, "There is, therefore, no case or controversy within the meaning of Art. III of the Constitution. Muskrat v. United States, 219 U.S. 346 (1911) [p. 231, *infra*]." But *cf.* GTE Sylvania, Inc. v. Consumers Union, 445 U.S. 375, 382–83 (1980) (parties do not desire "precisely the same result" when federal agency defendant would have been willing to disclose information sought by the plaintiff but could not do so because of outstanding injunction in another proceeding); Immigration and Naturalization Service v. Chadha, 462 U.S. 919, 939–40 (1983) (in a challenge to the constitutionality of the legislative veto in an immigration case, a case or controversy exists, even though the Attorney General, representing the INS, agrees with Chadha and the decision of the court below that the legislative veto is unconstitutional; the INS had concluded that, if not for that decision, it would be required to comply with the order of the House of Representatives that Chadha be deported).[1]

What should government counsel do if he believes that the case against the government is sound? When the government is seeking review, its counsel can presumably withdraw the appeal or other petition, leaving the decision below in effect. When the government has prevailed below, the problem is stickier; in a number of such instances the Solicitor General has confessed error in that judgment and asked to have it vacated or reversed. These confessions are generally accepted, but the Court not infrequently recites that it does so "upon an independent examination of the record." See, *e.g.*, Pope v. United States, 392 U.S. 651 (1968); Rosengart v. Laird, 405 U.S. 908 (1972).[2]

The Court's policy as applied to criminal cases was explained in Young v. United States, 315 U.S. 257, 259 (1942):

1. In Chadha, the Court thus concluded that there was "adequate Article III adverseness" even before the Senate and House of Representatives were allowed to intervene as parties to defend the validity of the legislative veto (p. 939). But the Court also noted that any "prudential" concerns were dispelled by the participation of both Houses of Congress in the proceeding.

See also Kentucky v. Indiana, 281 U.S. 163 (1930); Bob Jones University v. United States, 461 U.S. 574, 585 n. 9 (1983).

2. In Watts v. United States, 422 U.S. 1032 (1975), the Solicitor General agreed with the judgment below rejecting petitioner's claim of double jeopardy but sought permission to dismiss the prosecution because it did not conform to a Department of Justice policy applicable in the event of a prior state court conviction involving the same acts. The Court vacated and remanded to allow dismissal, with three dissenters arguing that it was "not a judicial function" to aid the Department in implementation of its internal policies (p. 1036). See also Thompson v. United States, 444 U.S. 248 (1980).

Would the dissenters have thought it similarly inappropriate for the trial court to dismiss on such a representation prior to trial? If not, why was it inappropriate now? The dissenters implicitly answered this question by expressing displeasure at having to "sacrifice the careful work of the District Court and the Court of Appeals—to say nothing of the public funds which that work required—to the vagaries of administrative interpretation" (*id.*).

"The public interest that a result be reached which promotes a well-ordered society is foremost in every criminal proceeding. That interest is entrusted to our consideration and protection as well as to that of the enforcing officers. Furthermore, our judgments are precedents, and the proper administration of the criminal law cannot be left merely to the stipulation of parties."

Moreover, in civil proceedings in which the government has found itself aligned with its adversary on one or more critical issues, the Court has on occasion appointed an *amicus curiae* to argue the other side. *E.g.,* Bob Jones University v. United States, 456 U.S. 922 (1982) (decided on the merits, 461 U.S. 574 (1983)); Cheng Fan Kwok v. Immigration Service, 392 U.S. 206 (1968).

How can these actions by the Court be reconciled with the view of the judicial function expressed in cases like Williams v. Zbaraz, 448 U.S. 358, 367 (1980), p. 82, *supra?* On occasion, the Court may suspect, or may be informed, that the Solicitor General's views are not shared by other agencies or branches of the government; in those instances the appointment of an *amicus* may be tantamount to allowing intervention by that other agency or branch.[3] But in the absence of any such indication, is it an adequate reason for independent consideration that acceptance of the confession of error will create a precedent? In Casey v. United States, 343 U.S. 808 (1952), the Court, without an independent examination, accepted a confession of error that there had been an unreasonable search and seizure, saying that to do so "in this case * * * would not involve the establishment of any precedent." Three justices dissented vigorously, arguing that "[w]hatever action we take is a precedent" and that "[o]nce we accept a confession of error at face value and make it the controlling and decisive factor in our decision, we no longer administer a system of justice under a government of laws" (pp. 811–12).[4]

(4) With the Johnson case, compare:

Lord v. Veazie, 8 How. 251 (U.S.1850). Veazie having executed a deed to Lord warranting that he had certain rights claimed by third persons, an action on the covenant by Lord against Veazie "was docketed by consent," and the circuit court "gave judgment for the defendant *pro forma,* at the request of the parties, in order that the judgment and question might be brought before" the Supreme Court. On the third person's motion the Court dismissed the case, saying that the judgment below was a nullity upon which no writ of error would lie, and that "the whole proceeding was in contempt of the court, and highly reprehensible."

3. See, *e.g.,* United States v. Lovett, 328 U.S. 303 (1946), where counsel for Congress appeared and argued as *amicus* by authority of a joint resolution and by special leave of Court; *Cf.* INS v. Chadha, note 1, *supra,* where formal intervention was allowed.

4. In Mariscal v. United States, 449 U.S. 405 (1981), the Court vacated and remanded per curiam "[i]n light of the Solicitor General's concession in this Court that the [petitioner's] mail fraud convictions were invalid." Justice Rehnquist, dissenting, suggested that the Court had been routinely vacating judgments on the basis of such concessions without independent examination. "[Congress] has not to my knowledge moved the Office of the Solicitor General from the Executive Branch of the Federal Government to the Judicial Branch. Until it does, I think we are bound by our oaths either to examine independently the merits of a question presented for review on certiorari, or in the exercise of our discretion to deny certiorari" (p. 407).

Chicago & Grand Trunk Ry. Co. v. Wellman, 143 U.S. 339 (1892). A Michigan statute established a fixed rate per mile for transportation of passengers by railroad, graduated according to the earnings of the railroad per mile of road. On the day the law took effect, the plaintiff tried to buy a ticket from Port Huron to Battle Creek at the reduced statutory rate and was refused. He brought an action for damages. The railroad answered promptly, and the case was quickly tried on an agreed statement of facts, together with testimony from two witnesses. The case came to the Supreme Court on writ of error from a decision of the state supreme court upholding the trial court's refusal to charge that the statute was unconstitutional. The Court affirmed the judgment, on the ground that unchallenged assertions about earnings and expenses afforded no adequate ground for declaring such a statute unconstitutional. Justice Brewer said (pp. 344–45):

" * * * The theory upon which, apparently, this suit was brought is that parties have an appeal from the legislature to the courts; and that the latter are given an immediate and general supervision of the constitutionality of the acts of the former. Such is not true. Whenever, in pursuance of an honest and actual antagonistic assertion of rights by one individual against another, there is presented a question involving the validity of any act of any legislature, State or Federal, and the decision necessarily rests on the competency of the legislature to so enact, the court must, in the exercise of its solemn duties, determine whether the act be constitutional or not; but such an exercise of power is the ultimate and supreme function of courts. It is legitimate only in the last resort, and as a necessity in the determination of real, earnest and vital controversy between individuals. It never was the thought that, by means of a friendly suit, a party beaten in the legislature could transfer to the courts an inquiry as to the constitutionality of the legislative act." [5]

(5) Does the rule against feigned cases defeat the planning of a test case by the parties to a real controversy? See Evers v. Dwyer, 358 U.S. 202 (1958), in which the plaintiff (who was black) boarded a bus once, refused to obey an order to sit in the rear, got off, and brought a class action for a declaratory judgment against the segregation. The Court held the action justiciable despite findings by the district court that the plaintiff had ridden a city bus on only that one occasion and then for the purpose of instituting the litigation. (Compare O'Shea v. Littleton, p. 256, *infra.*) See also Bankamerica Corp. v. United States, 462 U.S. 122, 124 (1983), in which the Court decided on the merits an issue of federal antitrust law after noting that the proceedings before it were "companion test cases" brought by the United States against ten corporations and five individuals. *Cf.*

---

5. See also Vermont v. New York, 417 U.S. 270 (1974), and New Hampshire v. Maine, 426 U.S. 363 (1976), p. 324, *infra,* Swift & Co. v. Hocking Valley Ry. Co., 243 U.S. 281 (1917) (disregarding a stipulation inconsistent with the record on the ground that to do otherwise would present "a moot or fictitious case" beyond the judicial power to decide); South Spring Hill Gold Mining Co. v. Amador Medean Gold Mining Co., 145 U.S. 300 (1892) (holding that once control of the two contesting corporations had come into the hands of the same per-

sons, the litigation had ceased to be between adverse parties and had to be dismissed).

In at least two cases prior to Lord v. Veazie, the Supreme Court reached the merits even though it appeared that the controversy was feigned or collusive. Hylton v. United States, 3 Dall. 171 (U.S.1796); Fletcher v. Peck, 6 Cranch 87 (U.S.1810). These cases are discussed in 1 Warren, The Supreme Court in United States History 147, 392–95 (Rev. ed. 1926).

Buchanan v. Warley, 245 U.S. 60 (1917), a challenge to a segregated housing law which had every appearance of a test case and in which the Court reached the merits without discussion of justiciability.

DeFUNIS v. ODEGAARD

416 U.S. 312, 94 S.Ct. 1704, 40 L.Ed.2d 164 (1974).
Certiorari to the Supreme Court of Washington.

PER CURIAM.

In 1971 the petitioner Marco DeFunis, Jr., applied for admission as a first-year student at the University of Washington Law School, a state-operated institution. The size of the incoming first-year class was to be limited to 150 persons, and the Law School received some 1,600 applications for these 150 places. DeFunis was eventually notified that he had been denied admission. He thereupon commenced this suit in a Washington trial court, contending that the procedures and criteria employed by the Law School Admissions Committee invidiously discriminated against him on account of his race in violation of the Equal Protection Clause of the Fourteenth Amendment to the United States Constitution.

DeFunis brought the suit on behalf of himself alone, and not as the representative of any class, against the various respondents, who are officers, faculty members, and members of the Board of Regents of the University of Washington. He asked the trial court to issue a mandatory injunction commanding the respondents to admit him as a member of the first-year class entering in September 1971, on the ground that the Law School admissions policy had resulted in the unconstitutional denial of his application for admission. The trial court agreed with his claim and granted the requested relief. DeFunis was, accordingly, admitted to the Law School and began his legal studies there in the fall of 1971. On appeal, the Washington Supreme Court reversed the judgment of the trial court and held that the Law School admissions policy did not violate the Constitution. By this time DeFunis was in his second year at the Law School.

He then petitioned this Court for a writ of certiorari, and Mr. Justice Douglas, as Circuit Justice, stayed the judgment of the Washington Supreme Court pending the "final disposition of the case by this Court." By virtue of this stay, DeFunis has remained in law school, and was in the first term of his third and final year when this Court first considered his certiorari petition in the fall of 1973. Because of our concern that DeFunis' third-year standing in the Law School might have rendered this case moot, we requested the parties to brief the question of mootness before we acted on the petition. In response, both sides contended that the case was not moot. The respondents indicated that, if the decision of the Washington Supreme Court were permitted to stand, the petitioner could complete the term for which he was then enrolled but would have to apply to the faculty for permission to continue in the school before he could register for another term.[2]

---

2. By contrast, in their response to the petition for certiorari, the respondents had stated that DeFunis "will complete his third year [of law school] and be awarded his J.D. degree at the end of the 1973–74 academic year regardless of the outcome of this appeal."

We granted the petition for certiorari on November 19, 1973. 414 U.S. 1038. The case was in due course orally argued on February 26, 1974.

In response to questions raised from the bench during the oral argument, counsel for the petitioner has informed the Court that DeFunis has now registered "for his final quarter in law school." Counsel for the respondents have made clear that the Law School will not in any way seek to abrogate this registration.[3] In light of DeFunis' recent registration for the last quarter of his final law school year, and the Law School's assurance that his registration is fully effective, the insistent question again arises whether this case is not moot, and to that question we now turn.

The starting point for analysis is the familiar proposition that "federal courts are without power to decide questions that cannot affect the rights of litigants in the case before them." North Carolina v. Rice, 404 U.S. 244, 246 (1971). The inability of the federal judiciary "to review moot cases derives from the requirement of Art. III of the Constitution under which the exercise of judicial power depends upon the existence of a case or controversy." Liner v. Jafco, Inc., 375 U.S. 301, 306 n. 3 (1964); see also Powell v. McCormack, 395 U.S. 486, 496 n. 7 (1969); Sibron v. New York, 392 U.S. 40, 50 n. 8 (1968). Although as a matter of Washington state law it appears that this case would be saved from mootness by "the great public interest in the continuing issues raised by this appeal," 82 Wash.2d 11, 23 n. 6, 507 P.2d 1169, 1177 n. 6 (1973), the fact remains that under Art. III "[e]ven in cases arising in the state courts, the question of mootness is a federal one which a federal court must resolve before it assumes jurisdiction." North Carolina v. Rice, *supra*, at 246.

The respondents have represented that, without regard to the ultimate resolution of the issues in this case, DeFunis will remain a student in the Law School for the duration of any term in which he has already enrolled. Since he has now registered for his final term, it is evident that he will be given an opportunity to complete all academic and other requirements for graduation, and, if he does so, will receive his diploma regardless of any decision this Court might reach on the merits of this case. In short, all parties agree that DeFunis is now entitled to complete his legal studies at the University of Washington and to receive his degree from that institution. A determination by this Court of the legal issues tendered by the parties is no longer necessary to compel that result, and could not serve to prevent it. DeFunis did not cast his suit as a class action, and the only remedy he requested was an injunction commanding his admission to the Law School. He was not only accorded that remedy, but he now has also been irrevocably admitted to the final term of the final year of the Law School course. The controversy between the parties has thus clearly ceased to be "definite and concrete" and no longer "touch[es] the legal relations of parties having adverse legal interests." Aetna Life Ins. Co. v. Haworth, 300 U.S. 227, 240–241 (1937).

It matters not that these circumstances partially stem from a policy decision on the part of the respondent Law School authorities. The respondents, through their counsel, the Attorney General of the State, have

3. In their memorandum on the question of mootness, counsel for the respondents unequivocally stated: "If Mr. DeFunis registers for the spring quarter under the existing order of this court during the registration period from February 20, 1974, to March 1, 1974, that registration would not be canceled unilaterally by the university regardless of the outcome of this litigation."

professionally represented that in no event will the status of DeFunis now be affected by any view this Court might express on the merits of this controversy. And it has been the settled practice of the Court, in contexts no less significant, fully to accept representations such as these as parameters for decision. See Gerende v. Election Board, 341 U.S. 56 (1951) * * *.

There is a line of decisions in this Court standing for the proposition that the "voluntary cessation of allegedly illegal conduct does not deprive the tribunal of power to hear and determine the case, *i.e.*, does not make the case moot." United States v. W.T. Grant Co., 345 U.S. 629, 632 (1953); United States v. Trans-Missouri Freight Assn., 166 U.S. 290, 308–310 (1897) * * *. These decisions and the doctrine they reflect would be quite relevant if the question of mootness here had arisen by reason of a unilateral change in the *admissions procedures* of the Law School. For it was the admissions procedures that were the target of this litigation, and a voluntary cessation of the admissions practices complained of could make this case moot only if it could be said with assurance "that 'there is no reasonable expectation that the wrong will be repeated.'" United States v. W.T. Grant Co., *supra*, at 633. Otherwise, "[t]he defendant is free to return to his old ways," *id.*, at 632, and this fact would be enough to prevent mootness because of the "public interest in having the legality of the practices settled." *Ibid.* But mootness in the present case depends not at all upon a "voluntary cessation" of the admissions practices that were the subject of this litigation. It depends, instead, upon the simple fact that DeFunis is now in the final quarter of the final year of his course of study, and the settled and unchallenged policy of the Law School to permit him to complete the term for which he is now enrolled.

It might also be suggested that this case presents a question that is "capable of repetition, yet evading review," Southern Pacific Terminal Co. v. ICC, 219 U.S. 498, 515 (1911); Roe v. Wade, 410 U.S. 113, 125 (1973), and is thus amenable to federal adjudication even though it might otherwise be considered moot. But DeFunis will never again be required to run the gantlet of the Law School's admission process, and so the question is certainly not "capable of repetition" so far as he is concerned. Moreover, just because this particular case did not reach the Court until the eve of the petitioner's graduation from law school, it hardly follows that the issue he raises will in the future evade review. If the admissions procedures of the Law School remain unchanged,[4] there is no reason to suppose that a subsequent case attacking those procedures will not come with relative speed to this Court, now that the Supreme Court of Washington has spoken. This case, therefore, in no way presents the exceptional situation in which the Southern Pacific Terminal doctrine might permit a departure from "[t]he usual rule in federal cases * * * that an actual controversy must exist at stages of appellate or certiorari review, and not simply at the date the action is initiated." Roe v. Wade, *supra*, at 125; United States v. Munsingwear, Inc., 340 U.S. 36 (1950).

4. In response to an inquiry from the Court, counsel for the respondents has advised that some changes have been made in the admissions procedures "for the applicants seeking admission to the University of Washington law school for the academic year commencing September, 1974." The respondents' counsel states, however, that "[these] changes do not affect the policy challenged by the petitioners * * * in that * * * special consideration still is given to applicants from 'certain ethnic groups.'"

Because the petitioner will complete his law school studies at the end of the term for which he has now registered regardless of any decision this Court might reach on the merits of this litigation, we conclude that the Court cannot, consistently with the limitations of Art. III of the Constitution, consider the substantive constitutional issues tendered by the parties.[5] Accordingly, the judgment of the Supreme Court of Washington is vacated, and the cause is remanded for such proceedings as by that court may be deemed appropriate.

It is so ordered.

MR. JUSTICE DOUGLAS, dissenting.

I agree with MR. JUSTICE BRENNAN that this case is not moot, and because of the significance of the issues raised I think it is important to reach the merits.

* * *

MR. JUSTICE BRENNAN, with whom MR. JUSTICE DOUGLAS, MR. JUSTICE WHITE, and MR. JUSTICE MARSHALL concur, dissenting.

I respectfully dissent. Many weeks of the school term remain, and petitioner may not receive his degree despite respondents' assurances that petitioner will be allowed to complete this term's schooling regardless of our decision. Any number of unexpected events—illness, economic necessity, even academic failure—might prevent his graduation at the end of the term. Were that misfortune to befall, and were petitioner required to register for yet another term, the prospect that he would again face the hurdle of the admissions policy is real, not fanciful; for respondents warn that "Mr. DeFunis would have to take some appropriate action to request continued admission for the remainder of his law school education, and *some discretionary action by the University on such request would have to be taken.*" Respondents' Memorandum on the Question of Mootness 3–4 (emphasis supplied). Thus, respondents' assurances have not dissipated the possibility that petitioner might once again have to run the gantlet of the University's allegedly unlawful admissions policy. The Court therefore proceeds on an erroneous premise in resting its mootness holding on a supposed inability to render any judgment that may affect one way or the other petitioner's completion of his law studies. For surely if we were to reverse the Washington Supreme Court, we could insure that, if for some reason petitioner did not graduate this spring, he would be entitled to re-enrollment at a later time on the same basis as others who have not faced the hurdle of the University's allegedly unlawful admissions policy.

In these circumstances, and because the University's position implies no concession that its admissions policy is unlawful, this controversy falls squarely within the Court's long line of decisions holding that the "[m]ere voluntary cessation of allegedly illegal conduct does not moot a case." United States v. Phosphate Export Assn., 393 U.S. 199, 203 (1968) * * *. Since respondents' voluntary representation to this Court is only that they will permit petitioner to complete this term's studies, respondents have not borne the "heavy burden," United States v. Phosphate Export Assn., *supra,*

---

5. It is suggested in dissent that "[a]ny number of unexpected events—illness, economic necessity, even academic failure— might prevent his graduation at the end of the term." "But such speculative contingencies afford no basis for our passing on the substantive issues [the petitioner] would have us decide," Hall v. Beals, 396 U.S. 45, 49 (1969), in the absence of "evidence that this is a prospect of 'immediacy and reality.'" Golden v. Zwickler, 394 U.S. 103, 109 (1969) * * *.

at 203, of demonstrating that there was not even a "mere possibility" that petitioner would once again be subject to the challenged admissions policy. United States v. W.T. Grant Co., *supra*, at 633. On the contrary, respondents have positioned themselves so as to be "free to return to [their] old ways." *Id.*, at 632.

I can thus find no justification for the Court's straining to rid itself of this dispute. While we must be vigilant to require that litigants maintain a personal stake in the outcome of a controversy to assure that "the questions will be framed with the necessary specificity, that the issues will be contested with the necessary adverseness and that the litigation will be pursued with the necessary vigor to assure that the constitutional challenge will be made in a form traditionally thought to be capable of judicial resolution," Flast v. Cohen, 392 U.S. 83, 106 (1968), there is no want of an adversary contest in this case. Indeed, the Court concedes that, if petitioner has lost his stake in this controversy, he did so only when he registered for the spring term. But petitioner took that action only after the case had been fully litigated in the state courts, briefs had been filed in this Court, and oral argument had been heard. The case is thus ripe for decision on a fully developed factual record with sharply defined and fully canvassed legal issues. *Cf.* Sibron v. New York, 392 U.S. 40, 57 (1968).

Moreover, in endeavoring to dispose of this case as moot, the Court clearly disserves the public interest. The constitutional issues which are avoided today concern vast numbers of people, organizations, and colleges and universities, as evidenced by the filing of twenty-six *amicus curiae* briefs. Few constitutional questions in recent history have stirred as much debate, and they will not disappear. * * * Because avoidance of repetitious litigation serves the public interest, that inevitability counsels against mootness determinations, as here, not compelled by the record. Although the Court should, of course, avoid unnecessary decisions of constitutional questions, we should not transform principles of avoidance of constitutional decisions into devices for sidestepping resolution of difficult cases. *Cf.* Cohens v. Virginia, 6 Wheat. 264, 404–405 (1821) (Marshall, C.J.).

On what appears in this case, I would find that there is an extant controversy and decide the merits of the very important constitutional questions presented.

NOTE ON MOOTNESS: ITS RATIONALE AND APPLICATIONS

(1) The Court in DeFunis viewed the mootness doctrine as a function of the Article III "case" or "controversy" requirement. This view has not gone unchallenged. See, *e.g.*, Honig v. Doe, 108 S.Ct. 592, 607–09 (1988) (Rehnquist, C.J., concurring); Monaghan, *Constitutional Adjudication: The Who and When*, 82 Yale L.J. 1363, 1383–84 (1973). *Cf.* Franks v. Bowman Transp. Co., Inc., 424 U.S. 747, 756 n. 8 (1976) (referring to mootness as one of the rules that "find their source in policy, rather than purely constitutional, considerations"); A.L. Mechling Barge Lines, Inc. v. United States, 368 U.S. 324, 331 (1961) (considerations relevant to mootness militate against discretionary grant of declaratory or injunctive relief).

What policies underlie the rule against deciding a moot case, particularly one that has become moot while an appeal or other review is pending?

The same as those that preclude advisory opinions? What weight should be given to considerations of economy of judicial effort and allocation of scarce judicial resources?

Note the relationship of the doctrine of mootness to those of standing and ripeness. If a controversy is judged not ripe, the court is saying that it is *too early* for a party claiming injury to seek relief, and if it is judged to be moot, the court is saying that it is *too late*—that because the matter has been resolved, or for other reasons, the party no longer has a claim for redress.[1]

(2) Although it may become unnecessary or impossible to grant the primary relief requested in the action, remaining or collateral consequences of the litigation may prevent the case from becoming moot. The cases, however, leave considerable uncertainty about when such consequences will be determined to be present, or how likely of occurrence they must be.[2]

Were there remaining or collateral consequences in DeFunis that kept the case from being moot? What of the possible consequences of a decision on the merits in the event that DeFunis had to withdraw before graduation and to apply for readmission?

(3) As both sides in DeFunis noted, a long line of cases holds that an action for an injunction, or other judgment with continuing force, does not become moot merely because the conduct immediately complained of has terminated, if there is a sufficient possibility of a recurrence that would be barred by the terms of a proper decree.[3] This "voluntary cessation"

1. For further discussion of the relationship of these doctrines, see pp. 267, 269, *infra.* See also Monaghan, Paragraph (1), *supra,* at 1384 (stating that mootness is "the doctrine of standing set in a time frame"); Varat, *Variable Justiciability and the Duke Power Case,* 58 Tex.L.Rev. 273, 296–305 (1980).

2. For cases rejecting claims of mootness, see, *e.g.,* Bowen v. Roy, 476 U.S. 693 (1986) (holding, 7–2, but without a majority for any rationale, that a First Amendment challenge to a statute requiring plaintiffs to "supply" a Social Security number for their child as a precondition to AFDC aid was not moot even though the record showed that the child had received a number at birth); Firefighters Local Union No. 1784 v. Stotts, 467 U.S. 561 (1984) (holding, 6–3, that challenge by union to layoffs of white employees pursuant to preliminary injunction was not moot even though all laid off employees had been reinstated; lower court's determination continued to affect relationships among the parties); Jago v. Van Curen, 454 U.S. 14, 21–22 n. 3 (1981) (claim of right to hearing on withdrawal of parole recommendation was not moot, even though parole had been granted after petition filed; since parole might have been granted earlier, release from conditions of parole might now be an appropriate remedy); Super Tire Engineering Co. v. McCorkle, 416 U.S. 115 (1974) (holding, 5–4, that settlement of a strike did not moot employer's challenge to state regulations entitling striking workers to state welfare assistance).

With these decisions, compare, *e.g.,* Burke v. Barnes, 107 S.Ct. 734 (1987) (challenge to President's pocket veto became moot when bill in question expired by its own terms; questions of failure to publish the bill as an enacted law and of the settlement of accounts do not constitute a "live controversy"); University of Texas v. Camenisch, 451 U.S. 390 (1981) (question whether a preliminary injunction should have issued is moot because the terms of the injunction have been carried out; any remaining question of liability on injunction bond should be resolved not on appeal but at trial on the merits); Local No. 8–6, Oil, Chem. & Atom Workers Union v. Missouri, 361 U.S. 363 (1960) (injunctive relief mooted by termination of strike and government seizure; remaining penalty provisions severable and subject of separate action).

See also the criminal cases discussed in Paragraph (6), *infra.*

3. See, *e.g.,* United States v. Concentrated Phosphate Export Ass'n, 393 U.S. 199, 202–04 (1968); United States v. W.T. Grant Co., 345 U.S. 629 (1953); United States v. Trans-Missouri Freight Ass'n, 166 U.S. 290, 307–09 (1897) (dissolution of al

doctrine has been a frequent cause of controversy in recent years. Thus, in County of Los Angeles v. Davis, 440 U.S. 625 (1979), the Court held moot a challenge to certain proposed local government hiring practices in light of the defendant's compliance with a district court decree over a period of five years, the resulting elimination of any discriminatory effects of the wrong complained of, and the asserted lack of any indication that defendant's hiring practices would change if the district court decree were dissolved.

But the Court, by a 5–4 vote, may have changed direction in Vitek v. Jones, 445 U.S. 480 (1980), a case somewhat similar to Preiser v. Newkirk, note 3, *supra*. Jones, a convicted felon, brought a federal court action challenging (on procedural grounds) his transfer from a prison to a mental hospital. While the case was pending, he was retransferred to prison, placed in the psychiatric ward, paroled on condition that he accept psychiatric treatment at a V.A. hospital, and subsequently returned to prison for violation of parole. The majority agreed with both parties that the case was not moot, stating that against the background of Jones' mental illness, it was not "absolutely clear" that the challenged wrong would not recur (p. 487).

Justice Stewart, for three dissenters, argued that the case was moot because there was "no demonstrated probability" of recurrence, and thus Jones was "simply one of thousands of [state] prisoners with no more standing than any other" (p. 501). Justice Blackmun, dissenting separately, saw the case as presenting less an issue of mootness than of ripeness. See Section 5, *infra*. He argued that the liberal standards of the "voluntary cessation" cases, which were designed to prevent frustration of judicial review through manipulation by the parties, were inapplicable. And he noted the absence of any indicated intention of transferring Jones to a mental hospital during his remaining prison term. He concluded that "the Court's analysis invites the criticism, increasingly voiced, that this Court's decisions on threshold issues 'are concealed decisions on the merits of the underlying constitutional claim.' Tushnet, *The New Law of Standing: A Plea for Abandonment*, 62 Cornell L.Rev. 663, 663 (1977)" (445 U.S. at 504 n. 3).[4]

Both Vitek and DeFunis raised a question of the possible recurrence of the events complained of. Comparing the two cases, doesn't it appear less likely that DeFunis would have had to go through the admissions process again than that Jones would again be transferred to a mental hospital? But should even a slim possibility of recurrence have been enough in

legedly unlawful combination did not moot the case, since a similar combination might be formed in the future). But *cf.* Preiser v. Newkirk, 422 U.S. 395, 402 (1975) (convict's retransfer from maximum to minimum security prison mooted his challenge to the original transfer).

4. With Justice Blackmun's analysis, compare Justice Powell's observation that defendants' jurisdictional statement referred to "a very real expectation" of transfer if the lower court injunction were removed (p. 497 n. 1) (Powell, J., concurring in part).

For cases since Vitek, see Princeton University v. Schmid, 455 U.S. 100, 103 (1982) (change in University's regulations moots its appeal with respect to reversal of trespass conviction based on prior regulation); Iron Arrow Honor Society v. Heckler, 464 U.S. 67 (1983) (case mooted by voluntary act of non-party); City of Mesquite v. Aladdin's Castle, Inc., 455 U.S. 283, 288–89 (1982) (controversy not mooted by city's repeal of challenged provision after decision below; repeal would not preclude reenactment if the judgment were vacated, and the city had "announced just such an intention").

DeFunis, given the completeness of the record, the time and energy expended, and the clear adversity of the parties?[5]

(4) The result in DeFunis effectively postponed for several years a decision on the merits of a question that had stirred considerable public controversy. (The later decision on the merits was Regents of the University of California v. Bakke, 438 U.S. 265 (1978).) For a similar pair of decisions in another area of controversy over the scope of affirmative action, see Boston Firefighters Union, Local 718 v. Boston Chapter, NAACP, 461 U.S. 477 (1983); Firefighters Local Union No. 1784 v. Stotts, 467 U.S. 561 (1984). Commenting on the justiciability issue in these decisions, Professors Fallon and Weiler said there was a "pattern" in cases "presenting hard issues of racial justice: a dubious decision not to decide one case was followed by an equally doubtful conclusion that a later case, presenting the same but now more 'percolated' issue, was fit for judicial resolution. The sequence does not seem coincidental. According to one celebrated argument, justiciability doctrines perform an important function in allowing the Supreme Court to pick its time and its case for decision." Fallon and Weiler, *Firefighters v. Stotts: Conflicting Models of Racial Justice*, 1984 S.Ct.Rev. 1, 7–8. See also Mishkin, *The Uses of Ambivalence: Reflections on the Supreme Court and the Constitutionality of Affirmative Action*, 131 U.Pa.L.Rev. 907, 911–12 (1983) (noting, inter alia, that the Court knew the DeFunis case might become moot before it granted review).

The "celebrated argument" referred to by Fallon and Weiler is that of Professor Bickel, who catalogued a number of techniques for avoiding decision on the merits. See Bickel, The Least Dangerous Branch 111–98 (1962), p. 87, *supra*. If the result in DeFunis can be explained on this ground, do you think that this use of mootness doctrine as an avoidance device is warranted? Are there other devices more appropriate to the task? See generally pp. 735, 739, *infra*.

(5) Closely related to the "voluntary cessation" cases are a group, also discussed in DeFunis, in which the alleged wrong has ceased but the wrong is of a sort that is "capable of repetition, yet evading review."[6] Do these decisions suggest a kind of justiciability by necessity in cases where there may otherwise be no way to obtain Supreme Court review of an important issue? Recent decisions emphasize that, in the absence of a class action, the question in such cases is the possibility of recurrence with respect to the complaining party, see Weinstein v. Bradford, 423 U.S. 147, 149 (1975); Murphy v. Hunt, 455 U.S. 478, 482 (1982);[7] and the relevant time for

---

5. If DeFunis had brought his action as a class action, and all other facts had been the same, would the result have been different? See United States Parole Comm'n v. Geraghty and the following Note, p. 212, *infra*.

6. See, *e.g.*, Globe Newspaper Co. v. Superior Court, 457 U.S. 596 (1982) (order excluding press and public from certain portions of rape trial had expired with the completion of the trial); Nebraska Press Ass'n v. Stuart, 427 U.S. 539 (1976) (short-term judicial orders, restricting press coverage of certain criminal proceedings, had expired prior to Supreme Court review); Moore v. Ogilvie, 394 U.S. 814 (1969) (chal-

lenge to signature requirement on nominating petitions; election had occurred before Supreme Court review); Carroll v. President and Com'rs of Princess Anne, 393 U.S. 175 (1968) (ten-day injunction restraining white supremacist organization from holding public rallies had expired two years before); Southern Pac. Terminal Co. v. ICC, 219 U.S. 498 (1911) (short-term agency cease-and-desist order had expired).

7. This point was given a good deal less emphasis in earlier decisions, however. Thus in Southern Pac. Terminal Co., note 6, *supra*, the Court focused not so much on the complaining party as on the need for guidance of the government in the event

calculating that possibility is the present, see Golden v. Zwickler, 394 U.S. 103 (1969). But the requisite likelihood of recurrence that must be established, by evidence or by inference from the pleadings, is far less clear. The Court has spoken of a "reasonable expectation" or "demonstrated probability" that the controversy would recur, insisting that a "mere physical or theoretical possibility" was insufficient. See, *e.g.,* Murphy v. Hunt, *supra,* at 482.[7a] Yet in Southern Pac. Term. Co. v. ICC, note 6, *supra,* there was no showing that the Commission proposed to issue similar short term orders in the future. And in Roe v. Wade, 410 U.S. 113, 124–25 (1973), a challenge to an abortion statute was held not moot even though the woman who had initiated the action was no longer pregnant. "Pregnancy," the Court said, "often comes more than once to the same woman * * * [and] truly could be 'capable of repetition, yet evading review.'"

Even assuming a sufficient showing of possible recurrence in Roe v. Wade, was the controversy one "evading review" given the fact that in a companion case, the Court upheld the standing of a physician to challenge a similar statute? See Doe v. Bolton, 410 U.S. 179, 188 (1973).[8]

(6) The doctrines discussed in this Note have been applied in criminal as well as civil cases, and indeed some of the cases already cited (like Murphy v. Hunt and Weinstein v. Bradford, Paragraph (5), *supra*) involved complaints by those in criminal custody. But two questions unique to criminal proceedings are worthy of separate discussion: the ability of a convicted defendant to attack his conviction or sentence after serving that sentence, and the effect of the defendant's death on the justiciability of such an attack.

(a) For many years, the general rule in the federal courts was that after a criminal defendant had served his sentence, his case was moot because "there was no longer a subject matter on which the judgment * * * could operate." St. Pierre v. United States, 319 U.S. 41, 42 (1943). But that rule was gradually eroded because of recognition, first, that issues characteristically involving only short sentences might forever escape review [9] and, second, that criminal sentences, even after their expiration, have collateral consequences (recidivism statutes, testimonial impeachment, etc.). The development is described in Sibron v. New York, 392 U.S. 40, 50–58 (1968). As now stated, the rule is that a criminal case is moot "only if it is shown that there is no possibility that any collateral conse-

---

that the issue arose again. See also Dunn v. Blumstein, 405 U.S. 330 (1972), in which the Court considered on the merits a challenge to a durational residency requirement for voting even though Blumstein had satisfied the requirement long before the case reached the Supreme Court. Neither party argued on appeal that the case was moot, and the Court said in a footnote that Blumstein had standing to challenge the requirement "as a member of the class of people affected by the presently written statute" (p. 333 n. 2). Although no class had actually been certified, the case may be seen as a harbinger of Sosna v. Iowa, 419 U.S. 393 (1975), p. 226, *infra.*

7a. *Cf.* Honig v. Doe, Paragraph (1), *supra,* at 601 n. 6 (distinguishing between the two quoted standards and stating that cases have been held not moot "based on expectations that, while reasonable, were hardly demonstrably probable").

8. Since the actions in Doe and in Roe had been brought as class actions, the mootness questions would presumably not be difficult today. See pp. 212–30, *infra.*

9. Note that unless the Court is predicting recidivism (which it has generally declined to do), this recognition is hard to square with the rule that the likelihood of repetition must exist with respect to the complaining party. See Paragraph (5), *supra.*

quences will be imposed on the basis of the challenged conviction" (Sibron, *supra*, at p. 57). *Cf.* Carafas v. LaVallee, 391 U.S. 234 (1968), p. 1570, *infra*.

The defendant's interest in attacking a conviction or sentence surely guarantees the requisite adverseness in most instances.[10] But the Court has sustained claims of mootness in attacks on sentences. See Lane v. Williams, 455 U.S. 624 (1982) (6–3 decision holding that expiration of special parole term mooted petitioner's habeas corpus attack on the validity of that term, since petitioner did not attack the underlying conviction and the only continuing consequences of the parole term itself were "discretionary" and "nonstatutory"); North Carolina v. Rice, 404 U.S. 244 (1971) (habeas corpus attack on higher sentence following appeal and trial de novo remanded; since the higher sentence had been served and the prisoner's claim was directed not to the conviction but only to the sentence, the case would be moot unless it could be shown that collateral consequences flowed from the difference between the two sentences).

Should the stigma of a criminal conviction always be regarded as an answer to the argument that an attack on the conviction is moot, at least while the defendant is alive? *Cf.* Hart, *The Aims of the Criminal Law*, 23 Law & Contemp.Probs. 401, 404 (1958).

(b) The rule has been, and is, that the death of a criminal defendant renders his case moot on direct or collateral review. See, *e.g.*, Singer v. United States, 323 U.S. 338, 346 (1945).[11] And for a brief period, the Court resolved the uncertainty in its own opinions by holding that, at least in a federal criminal proceeding, death abated "not only the appeal but also all proceedings had in the prosecution from its inception," thus requiring dismissal of the indictment. Durham v. United States, 401 U.S. 481, 483 (1971). But in Dove v. United States, 423 U.S. 325 (1976), the Court overruled this holding without discussion and dismissed a petition for certiorari on learning of petitioner's death.[12] Can this action be squared with the practice in civil cases described in Paragraph (7), *infra*?

In Robinson v. California, 370 U.S. 660 (1962), a divided Court held in a novel decision that a law making drug addiction a crime constituted "cruel

---

10. In Pennsylvania v. Mimms, 434 U.S. 106, 108 n. 3 (1977), the Court rejected a claim of mootness, made by a criminal defendant who had completed his sentence, in view of the collateral consequences to the *state* of the judgment of reversal it was seeking to have reviewed. Such consequences included the setting of bail, length of sentence, and availability of probation in any future criminal proceedings against the defendant. Justice Stevens, dissenting, supported his argument that certiorari should have been denied with the observation that the case "barely escapes mootness" (p. 116 n. 4).

11. On the significance of the defendant's flight or escape pending appeal, see Eisler v. United States, 338 U.S. 189 (1949), in which the petitioner fled the country after the case had been submitted on the merits, and the majority held that the case should be removed from the docket and held "pending the return of the fugitive"

(p. 190). Five months later, the Court, in an unexplained order, granted the government's motion to dismiss the writ, over the opposition of Eisler's counsel. 338 U.S. 883 (1949).

Compare Molinaro v. New Jersey, 396 U.S. 365 (1970), in which the Court, per curiam, dismissed the appeal of a defendant who had jumped bail after his conviction. The Court stated that while the escape "does not strip the case of its character as a case or controversy, we believe it disentitles the defendant to call upon the resources of the Court • • •" (p. 366). No reason was given for failing to postpone the appeal pending Molinaro's return.

12. Dove was a case before the Supreme Court on direct review; the procedure was later followed on collateral review as well. Warden v. Palermo, 431 U.S. 911 (1977).

and unusual punishment" in violation of the Eighth and Fourteenth Amendments. Justice Stewart delivered the opinion of the Court; Justice Harlan concurred in the judgment; Justice Clark dissented, as did Justice White. Subsequently, the state informed the Court that the defendant in the case had died ten days before the appeal to the Supreme Court was taken, and petitioned for rehearing and abatement of the judgment. The petition was denied without opinion. 371 U.S. 905 (1962). Justice Clark, joined by Justices Harlan and Stewart, dissented, arguing that the judgment should be vacated as moot.[13]

If the dissenters on the petition for rehearing in Robinson had prevailed, would the precedential force of the original Robinson decision have been affected? Should it be, if the case was treated by all concerned (including Robinson's counsel) on the assumption that Robinson was still alive?

(7) "The established practice of the Court in dealing with a civil case from a court in the federal system which has become moot while on its way here or pending our decision on the merits is to reverse or vacate the judgment below and remand with a direction to dismiss [citing many cases, together with four 'exceptions']." United States v. Munsingwear, Inc., 340 U.S. 36, 39 (1950).[14] The Court in Munsingwear nevertheless held res judicata a district court decision previously dismissed as moot on appeal, because the parties had failed to move in the court of appeals for vacation of the original judgment. What is the purpose of such a formal motion requirement after an appellate ruling of mootness? On what grounds, if any, could such a motion be denied?

Plaintiffs in Diffenderfer v. Central Baptist Church, 404 U.S. 412 (1972), challenged a state statute that had been superseded before their case reached the Supreme Court. The Court held the case moot and vacated the district court judgment. Yet because it found that the plaintiffs might wish to show that the superseded statute retained some continuing force, or might wish to attack its replacement, the Court did not direct dismissal of the action as prescribed by the Munsingwear decision, but remanded the case to the district court with leave to the appellants to amend their complaint. (Is the decision between dismissal and leave to amend in such a case best made at the Supreme Court level?)[15]

Should there be a distinction, for purposes of the res judicata effect of a lower court decision, between a case that becomes moot before the first appeal as of right and a case that becomes moot only after that appeal and before further Supreme Court review? Between the issue preclusive (collateral estoppel) and claim preclusive effect of a case that becomes moot on appeal? And what of the stare decisis effect of the lower court decision in

---

13. *Cf.* Wetzel v. Ohio, 371 U.S. 62 (1962) (6–3 per curiam decision granting motion on appeal in criminal case to substitute deceased appellant's wife as appellant; as administratrix and probable heir of appellant's estate, she had a substantial interest in protecting the estate from costs to be levied against it if conviction stood).

14. In Honig v. Doe, Paragraph (1), *supra*, Chief Justice Rehnquist, concurring, argued for "an additional exception to our present mootness doctrine for those cases where the events which render the case moot have supervened since our grant of certiorari or noting of probable jurisdiction" (108 S.Ct. at 608).

15. *Cf.* Crowell v. Mader, 444 U.S. 505, 506 (1980) (since legislation did not moot the entire case, but only the issues on appeal, the Court directed that the district court judgment "be vacated without prejudice to such further proceedings in the District Court as may be appropriate").

such a case? For a full discussion of these and related issues, see Green-baum, *Mootness on Appeal in Federal Courts: A Reexamination of the Consequences of Appellate Disposition,* 17 U.C. Davis L.Rev. 7 (1983).

(8) If the Supreme Court holds moot a case coming to it from a state court, it dismisses the appeal or writ of certiorari. May it also mandate dismissal of the action? Are state courts bound by the federal doctrine of "case" or "controversy"? Note the disposition in DeFunis, after the Supreme Court remanded "for such proceedings as by [the Washington Supreme Court] may be deemed appropriate." [16] If the state court on remand does render a decision on the merits, will it have any binding effect in subsequent federal litigation, even between the same parties? *Cf.* Tileston v. Ullman, p. 137, *supra.*

If a state court holds moot a case involving a federal question, is Supreme Court review precluded? In Liner v. Jafco, Inc., 375 U.S. 301 (1964), a state court enjoined picketing in a labor dispute, despite a contention that its jurisdiction was federally preempted. Pending decision on appeal, construction at the site was completed, and the state appellate court held that the case had become moot (though it also expressed an opinion on the merits). The Supreme Court unanimously held, per Justice Brennan, that "in this case the question of mootness is itself a question of federal law upon which we must pronounce final judgment" (p. 304). In holding that the case was not moot, the Court pointed to the existence of an indemnity bond requiring payment if the injunction was "wrongfully" sued out, but also relied upon the frustration of federal policy which might result if the state court's ruling on the preemption claim were immunized from review. See also, *e.g.,* Gannett Co., Inc. v. DePasquale, 443 U.S. 368 (1979).

UNITED STATES PAROLE COMMISSION v. GERAGHTY

445 U.S. 388, 100 S.Ct. 1202, 63 L.Ed.2d 479 (1980).
Certiorari to the United States Court of Appeals for the Third Circuit.

[Geraghty was one of two cases involving similar issues that were decided by the Court on the same day. The other, Deposit Guar. Nat'l Bank v. Roper, 445 U.S. 326 (1980), is discussed in the Geraghty opinions; it involved a damage suit for allegedly unlawful finance charges brought by credit card holders who sought to represent themselves as individuals and also to represent a class of similarly situated card holders. After the district court denied a motion to certify the class under Rule 23 of the Federal Rules of Civil Procedure, and an attempt to take an interlocutory appeal of that denial under 28 U.S.C. § 1292(b) was rejected, the defendant tendered to each individual plaintiff the maximum amount he could have recovered, but plaintiffs refused to accept the tender. The district court, on the basis of the tender, entered judgment over plaintiffs' objections and dismissed the action. Plaintiffs then sought review of the class certifica-

16. On remand, DeFunis moved in the Washington Supreme Court to designate the case a class action and to reinstate the trial court judgment. The defendants countered with a motion to reinstate the prior judgment of the state supreme court.

Seven Justices joined in denying the motion to designate the suit as a class action, but no majority could be mustered on the other issues. DeFunis v. Odegaard, 84 Wash.2d 617, 529 P.2d 438 (1974).

tion ruling in the court of appeals and obtained a reversal of that ruling, with the appellate court rejecting the defendant's argument that the entry of judgment had mooted the case. The Supreme Court granted certiorari limited to the question of mootness, and affirmed, 7–2. In an opinion for six Justices (with Justice Blackmun concurring on a broader ground), Chief Justice Burger emphasized that plaintiffs had rejected the offer of settlement and that, even after that offer, they retained "a continuing individual interest in the resolution of the class certification question in their desire to shift part of the costs of litigation [including attorney's fees] to those who will share in its benefits if the class is certified and ultimately prevails" (p. 336). Justice Stevens joined the Court's opinion, but wrote separately to state his view that even if the named plaintiffs had *not* retained a sufficient personal stake in the outcome on the certification issue, the interests of the unnamed members of the class would have sufficed: "[W]hen a proper class-action complaint is filed, the absent members of the class should be considered parties to the case or controversy at least for the limited purpose of the court's Art. III jurisdiction. If the district judge fails to certify the class, I believe they remain parties until a final determination has been made that the action may not be maintained as a class action" (p. 342).

[Dissenting for himself and Justice Stewart, Justice Powell argued that since no class had been certified, only the individual plaintiffs were involved at the time the tender of full relief to them was made, and such a tender "remedies a plaintiff's injuries and eliminates his stake in the outcome" (p. 347).

[On the specific question of attorney's fees, Justice Powell noted that plaintiffs appeared to have entered a "customary type contingent fee" arrangement for payment to counsel of 25% of the final judgment. "[N]o one has explained," he continued, "how [plaintiffs'] obligation to pay 25% of their recovery to counsel could be reduced if a class is certified and its members become similarly obligated to pay 25% of their recovery" (p. 351).

[The Geraghty case, in which the Court was more closely divided, involved a class action by a prospective parolee who was released from prison while his appeal from denial of class certification was pending.]

Mr. Justice Blackmun delivered the opinion of the Court.

This case raises the question whether a trial court's denial of a motion for certification of a class may be reviewed on appeal after the named plaintiff's personal claim has become "moot." The United States Court of Appeals for the Third Circuit held that a named plaintiff, respondent here, who brought a class action challenging the validity of the United States Parole Commission's Parole Release Guidelines, could continue his appeal of a ruling denying class certification even though he had been released from prison while the appeal was pending. We granted certiorari, 440 U.S. 945 (1979), to consider this issue of substantial significance, under Art. III of the Constitution, to class action litigation,[1] and to resolve the conflict in approach among the Courts of Appeals.

---

1. • • •

While the petition for a writ of certiorari was pending, respondent Geraghty filed a motion to substitute as respondents in this Court five prisoners, then incarcerated, who also were represented by Geraghty's attorneys. In the alternative, the prisoners sought to intervene. We deferred our ruling on the motion to the hearing of the case on the merits, 440 U.S. 945 (1979). These prisoners, or most of them, now also have been released from incarceration.

I

In 1973, the United States Parole Board adopted explicit Parole Release Guidelines for adult prisoners. * * *

Respondent John M. Geraghty was convicted in the United States District Court for the Northern District of Illinois of conspiracy to commit extortion, in violation of 18 U.S.C. § 1951, and of making false material declarations to a grand jury, in violation of 18 U.S.C. § 1623. On January 25, 1974, two months after initial promulgation of the release guidelines, respondent was sentenced to concurrent prison terms of four years on the conspiracy count and one year on the false declarations count. * * *

[Later, Geraghty's sentence was reduced by the District Court to 30 months.] Geraghty then applied for release on parole. His first application was denied in January 1976 * * * [with the explanation that under the Parole Release Guidelines, Geraghty should serve between 26 and 36 months]. If the customary release date applicable to respondent under the guidelines were adhered to, he would not be paroled before serving his entire sentence minus good-time credits. Geraghty applied for parole again in June 1976; that application was denied for the same reasons. He then instituted this civil suit as a class action in the United States District Court for the District of Columbia, challenging the guidelines as inconsistent with the PCRA [Parole Commission and Reorganization Act] and the Constitution, and questioning the procedures by which the guidelines were applied to his case.

Respondent sought certification of a class of "all federal prisoners who are or will become eligible for release on parole." Without ruling on Geraghty's motion, the court transferred the case to the Middle District of Pennsylvania, where respondent was incarcerated. Geraghty continued to press his motion for class certification, but the court postponed ruling on the motion until it was prepared to render a decision on cross-motions for summary judgment.

The District Court subsequently denied Geraghty's request for class certification and granted summary judgment for petitioners on all the claims Geraghty asserted. 429 F.Supp. 737 (M.D.Pa.1977). The court regarded respondent's action as a petition for a writ of habeas corpus, to which Fed.Rule Civ.Proc. 23 applied only by analogy. It denied class certification as "neither necessary nor appropriate." * * * On the merits, the court ruled that the guidelines are consistent with the PCRA and do not offend the Ex Post Facto Clause, U.S.Const., Art. I, § 9, cl. 3.

Respondent, individually "and on behalf of a class," appealed to the United States Court of Appeals for the Third Circuit. * * *

[Another prisoner, whose petition to intervene had been denied by the District Court, had apparently also been released by the time the case reached the Supreme Court.] On September 25, 1979, a supplement to the motion to substitute or intervene was filed, proposing six new substitute respondents or intervenors; each of these is a presently incarcerated federal prisoner who, allegedly, has been adversely affected by the guidelines and who is represented by Geraghty's counsel.

Since we hold that respondent may continue to litigate the class certification issue, there is no need for us to consider whether the motion should be granted in order to prevent the case from being moot. We conclude that the District Court initially should rule on the motion.

On June 30, 1977, before any brief had been filed in the Court of Appeals, Geraghty was mandatorily released from prison; he had served 22 months of his sentence, and had earned good-time credits for the rest. Petitioners then moved to dismiss the appeals as moot. The appellate court reserved decision of the motion to dismiss until consideration of the merits.

The Court of Appeals, concluding that the litigation was not moot, reversed the judgment of the District Court and remanded the case for further proceedings. 579 F.2d 238 (CA3 1978). * * *

II

Article III of the Constitution limits federal "Judicial Power," that is, federal court jurisdiction, to "Cases" and "Controversies." This case or controversy limitation serves "two complementary" purposes. Flast v. Cohen, 392 U.S. 83, 95 (1968). It limits the business of federal courts to "questions presented in an adversary context and in a form historically viewed as capable of resolution through the judicial process," and it defines the "role assigned to the judiciary in a tripartite allocation of power to assure that the federal courts will not intrude into the areas committed to the other branches of government." *Ibid.* Likewise, mootness has two aspects: "when the issues presented are no longer 'live' or the parties lack a legally cognizable interest in the outcome." Powell v. McCormack, 395 U.S. 486, 496 (1969).

It is clear that the controversy over the validity of the Parole Release Guidelines is still a "live" one between petitioners and at least some members of the class respondent seeks to represent. This is demonstrated by the fact that prisoners currently affected by the guidelines have moved to be substituted, or to intervene, as "named" respondents in this Court. See n. 1, *supra.* We therefore are concerned here with the second aspect of mootness, that is, the parties' interest in the litigation. The Court has referred to this concept as the "personal stake" requirement. *E.g.,* Franks v. Bowman Transportation Co., 424 U.S. 747, 755 (1976); Baker v. Carr, 369 U.S. 186 (1962).

The personal stake requirement relates to the first purpose of the case or controversy doctrine—limiting judicial power to disputes capable of judicial resolution. * * *

The "personal stake" aspect of mootness doctrine also serves primarily the purpose of assuring that federal courts are presented with disputes they are capable of resolving. One commentator has defined mootness as "the doctrine of standing set in a time frame: The requisite personal interest that must exist at the commencement of the litigation (standing) must continue throughout its existence (mootness)." Monaghan, Constitutional Adjudication: The Who and When, 82 Yale L.J. 1363, 1384 (1973).

III

On several occasions the Court has considered the application of the "personal stake" requirement in the class action context. In Sosna v. Iowa, 419 U.S. 393 (1975), it held that mootness of the named plaintiff's individual claim *after* a class has been duly certified does not render the action moot. It reasoned that "even though appellees * * * might not again enforce the Iowa durational residency requirement against [the class representative], it is clear that they will enforce it against those persons in the class that appellant sought to represent and that the District Court certified." *Id.,* at 400. The Court stated specifically that an Art. III case or controversy "may exist * * * between a named defendant and a member of the class represented by the named plaintiff, even though the claim of the named plaintiff has become moot." *Id.,* at 402.[6]

Although one might argue that Sosna contains at least an implication that the critical factor for Art. III purposes is the timing of class certification, other cases, applying a "relation back" approach, clearly demonstrate that timing is not crucial. When the claim on the merits is "capable of repetition, yet evading review," the named plaintiff may litigate the class certification issue despite loss of his personal stake in the outcome of the litigation. *E.g.,* Gerstein v. Pugh, 420 U.S. 103, 110, n. 11 (1975). The "capable of repetition, yet evading review" doctrine to be sure, was developed outside the class action context. See Southern Pacific Terminal Co. v. ICC, 219 U.S. 498, 514–515 (1911). But it has been applied where the named plaintiff does have a personal stake at the outset of the lawsuit, and where the claim may arise again with respect to that plaintiff; the litigation then may continue notwithstanding the named plaintiff's current lack of a personal stake. See, *e.g.,* Weinstein v. Bradford, 423 U.S. 147, 149 (1975); Roe v. Wade, 410 U.S. 113, 123–125 (1973). Since the litigant faces some likelihood of becoming involved in the same controversy in the future, vigorous advocacy can be expected to continue.

When, however, there is no chance that the named plaintiff's expired claim will reoccur, mootness still can be avoided through certification of a class prior to expiration of the named plaintiff's personal claim, *e.g.,* Franks v. Bowman Transportation Co., 424 U.S., at 752–757. See Kremens v. Bartley, 431 U.S. 119, 129–130 (1977). Some claims are so inherently transitory that the trial court will not have even enough time to rule on a motion for class certification before the proposed representative's individual interest expires. The Court considered this possibility in Gerstein v. Pugh, 420 U.S., at 110, n. 11. Gerstein was an action challenging pretrial detention conditions. The Court assumed that the named plaintiffs were no longer in custody awaiting trial at the time the trial court certified a class of pretrial detainees. There was no indication that the particular named plaintiffs might again be subject to pretrial detention. Nonetheless, the case was held not to be moot because:

"The length of pretrial custody cannot be ascertained at the outset, and it may be ended at any time by release on recognizance, dismissal of the charges, or a guilty plea, as well as by acquittal or conviction after trial. It is by no means certain that any given individual, named as plaintiff, would be in pretrial custody long enough for a district judge to certify the class. Moreover, in this case the constant existence of a class of persons suffering the deprivation is certain. The attorney representing the named respondents is a public defender, and we can

---

6. The claim in Sosna also fit the traditional category of actions that are deemed not moot despite the litigant's loss of personal stake, that is, those "capable of repetition, yet evading review." See Southern Pacific Terminal Co. v. ICC, 219 U.S. 498, 515 (1911). In Franks v. Bowman Trans-portation Co., 424 U.S., at 753–755, however, the Court held that the class action aspect of mootness doctrine does not depend on the class claim's being so inherently transitory that it meets the "capable of repetition, yet evading review" standard.

safely assume that he has other clients with a continuing live interest in the case." *Ibid.*

See also Sosna v. Iowa, 419 U.S., at 402, n. 11.

In two different contexts the Court has stated that the proposed class representative who proceeds to a judgment on the merits may appeal *denial* of class certification. First, this assumption was "an important ingredient," Deposit Guaranty Nat. Bank v. Roper, 445 U.S., at 338, in the rejection of interlocutory appeals, "as of right," of class certification denials. Coopers & Lybrand v. Livesay, 437 U.S. 463, 469, 470, n. 15 (1978). The Court reasoned that denial of class status will not necessarily be the "death knell" of a small claimant action, since there still remains "the prospect of prevailing on the merits and reversing an order denying class certification." *Ibid.*

Second, in United Airlines, Inc. v. McDonald, 432 U.S. 385, 393–395 (1977), the Court held that a putative class member may intervene, for the purpose of appealing the denial of a class certification motion, after the named plaintiffs' claims have been satisfied and judgment entered in their favor. Underlying that decision was the view that "refusal to certify was subject to appellate review after final judgment at the behest of the named plaintiffs." *Id.,* at 393. And today, the Court holds that named plaintiffs whose claims are satisfied through entry of judgment over their objections may appeal the denial of a class certification ruling. Deposit Guaranty Nat. Bank v. Roper, 445 U.S. 326.

Gerstein, McDonald, and Roper are all examples of cases found not to be moot, despite the loss of a "personal stake" in the merits of the litigation by the proposed class representative. The interest of the named plaintiffs in Gerstein was precisely the same as that of Geraghty here. Similarly, after judgment had been entered in their favor, the named plaintiffs in McDonald had no continuing narrow personal stake in the outcome of the class claims. And in Roper the Court points out that an individual controversy is rendered moot, in the strict Art. III sense, by payment and satisfaction of a final judgment. 445 U.S., at 333.

These cases demonstrate the flexible character of the Art. III mootness doctrine.[7] As has been noted in the past, Art. III justiciability is "not a legal concept with a fixed content or susceptible of scientific verification." Poe v. Ullman, 367 U.S. 497, 508 (1961) (plurality opinion). "[T]he justiciability doctrine [is] one of uncertain and shifting contours." Flast v. Cohen, 392 U.S., at 97.

IV

* * * [Petitioners] assert that a proposed class representative who individually prevails on the merits still has a "personal stake" in the

---

7. Three of the Court's cases might be described as adopting a less flexible approach. In Indianapolis School Comm'rs v. Jacobs, 420 U.S. 128 (1975), and in Weinstein v. Bradford, 423 U.S. 147 (1975), dismissal of putative class suits, as moot, was ordered after the named plaintiffs' claims became moot. And in Pasadena City Bd. of Education v. Spangler, 427 U.S. 424, 430 (1976), it was indicated that the action would have been moot, upon expiration of the named plaintiffs' claims, had not the United States intervened as a party plaintiff. Each of these, however, was a case in which there was an attempt to appeal the merits without first having obtained proper certification of a class. * * * Thus we do not find this line of cases dispositive of the question now before us.

outcome of the litigation, while the named plaintiff whose claim is truly moot does not. In the latter situation, where no class has been certified, there is no party before the court with a live claim, and it follows, it is said, that we have no jurisdiction to consider whether a class should have been certified.

We do not find this distinction persuasive. As has been noted earlier, Geraghty's "personal stake" in the outcome of the litigation is, in a practical sense, no different from that of the putative class representatives in Roper. * * *

Similarly, the fact that a named plaintiff's substantive claims are mooted due to an occurrence other than a judgment on the merits does not mean that all the other issues in the case are mooted. A plaintiff who brings a class action presents two separate issues for judicial resolution. One is the claim on the merits; the other is the claim that he is entitled to represent a class. * * *

Application of the personal stake requirement to a procedural claim, such as the right to represent a class, is not automatic or readily resolved. A "legally cognizable interest," as the Court described it in Powell v. McCormack, 395 U.S., at 496, in the traditional sense rarely ever exists with respect to the class certification claim. The justifications that led to the development of the class action include the protection of the defendant from inconsistent obligations, the protection of the interests of absentees, the provision of a convenient and economical means for disposing of similar lawsuits, and the facilitation of the spreading of litigation costs among numerous litigants with similar claims. * * * In order to achieve the primary benefits of class suits, the Federal Rules of Civil Procedure give the proposed class representative the right to have a class certified if the requirements of the rules are met. This "right" is more analogous to the private attorney general concept than to the type of interest traditionally thought to satisfy the "personal stake" requirement. See Roper, 445 U.S., at 338.

As noted above, the purpose of the "personal stake" requirement is to assure that the case is in a form capable of judicial resolution. The imperatives of a dispute capable of judicial resolution are sharply presented issues in a concrete factual setting and self-interested parties vigorously advocating opposing positions. Franks v. Bowman Transportation Co., 424 U.S., at 753–756; Baker v. Carr, 369 U.S., at 204; Poe v. Ullman, 367 U.S., at 503 (plurality opinion). We conclude that these elements can exist with respect to the class certification issue notwithstanding the fact that the named plaintiff's claim on the merits has expired. The question whether class certification is appropriate remains as a concrete, sharply presented issue. In Sosna v. Iowa it was recognized that a named plaintiff whose claim on the merits expires *after* class certification may still adequately represent the class. Implicit in that decision was the determination that vigorous advocacy can be assured through means other than the traditional requirement of a "personal stake in the outcome." Respondent here continues vigorously to advocate his right to have a class certified.

We therefore hold that an action brought on behalf of a class does not become moot upon expiration of the named plaintiff's substantive claim, even though class certification has been denied.[10] The proposed representative retains a "personal stake" in obtaining class certification sufficient to assure that Art. III values are not undermined. If the appeal results in reversal of the class certification denial, and a class subsequently is properly certified, the merits of the class claim then may be adjudicated pursuant to the holding in Sosna.

Our holding is limited to the appeal of the denial of the class certification motion. A named plaintiff whose claim expires may not continue to press the appeal on the merits until a class has been properly certified. See Roper, 445 U.S., at 336–337. If, on appeal, it is determined that class certification properly was denied, the claim on the merits must be dismissed as moot.[11]

10. We intimate no view as to whether a named plaintiff who settles the individual claim after denial of class certification may, consistent with Art. III, appeal from the adverse ruling on class certification. See United Airlines, Inc. v. McDonald, 432 U.S. 385, 393–394, and n. 14 (1977).

11. * * *

The erosion of the strict, formalistic perception of Art. III was begun well before today's decision. For example, the protestations of the dissent are strikingly reminiscent of Mr. Justice Harlan's dissent in Flast v. Cohen, 392 U.S. 83, 116. Mr. Justice Harlan hailed the taxpayer standing rule pronounced in that case as a "new doctrine" resting "on premises that do not withstand analysis." *Id.*, at 117. * * *

Notwithstanding the taxpayers' lack of a formalistic "personal stake," even Justice Harlan felt that the case should be held nonjusticiable on purely prudential grounds. His interpretation of the cases led him to conclude that "it is * * * clear that [plaintiffs in a public action] as such are not *constitutionally* excluded from the federal courts." *Ibid.* (emphasis in original). * * *

* * * [T]he assumption thought to be "[p]ervading the Court's opinion" in [United Airlines, Inc. v.] McDonald, and so vigorously attacked by the dissent [of Mr. Justice Powell] there, is now relegated to "gratuitous" "dictum". Mr. Justice Powell, who [in his dissent] finds the situation presented in the case at hand "fundamentally different" from that in Sosna and Franks, also found the facts of McDonald "sharply distinguishable" from those previous cases. 432 U.S., at 400.

We do not recite these cases for the purpose of showing that our result is mandated by the precedents. We concede that the prior cases may be said to be somewhat confusing, and that some, perhaps, are irreconcilable with others. Our point is that the strict, formalistic view of Art. III juris-

prudence, while perhaps the starting point of all inquiry, is riddled with exceptions. And, in creating each exception, the Court has looked to practicalities and prudential considerations. The resulting doctrine can be characterized, aptly, as "flexible"; it has been developed, not irresponsibly, but "with some care," including the present case.

The dissent is correct that once exceptions are made to the formalistic interpretation of Art. III, principled distinctions and bright lines become more difficult to draw. We do not attempt to predict how far down the road the Court eventually will go toward premising jurisdiction "upon the bare existence of a sharply presented issue in a concrete and vigorously argued case." Each case must be decided on its own facts. We hasten to note, however, that this case does not even approach the extreme feared by the dissent. This respondent suffered actual, concrete injury as a result of the putatively illegal conduct, and this injury would satisfy the formalistic personal stake requirement if damages were sought. See, *e.g.,* Powell v. McCormack, 395 U.S., at 495–500. His injury continued up to and beyond the time the District Court denied class certification. We merely hold that when a District Court erroneously denies a procedural motion, which, if correctly decided, would have prevented the action from becoming moot, an appeal lies from the denial and the corrected ruling "relates back" to the date of the original denial. * * *

* * * The "relation back" principle, a traditional equitable doctrine applied to class certification claims in Gerstein v. Pugh, *supra,* serves logically to distinguish this case from the one brought a day after the prisoner is released. If the named plaintiff has no personal stake in the outcome at the time class certification is denied, relation back of appellate reversal of that denial still would not prevent mootness of the action.

Our conclusion that the controversy here is not moot does not automatically establish that the named plaintiff is entitled to continue litigating the interests of the class. "[I]t does shift the focus of examination from the elements of justiciability to the ability of the named representative to 'fairly and adequately protect the interests of the class.' Rule 23(a)." Sosna v. Iowa, 419 U.S., at 403. We hold only that a case or controversy still exists. The question of who is to represent the class is a separate issue.

We need not decide here whether Geraghty is a proper representative for the purpose of representing the class on the merits. No class as yet has been certified. Upon remand, the District Court can determine whether Geraghty may continue to press the class claims or whether another representative would be appropriate. We decide only that Geraghty was a proper representative for the purpose of appealing the ruling denying certification of the class that he initially defined. Thus, it was not improper for the Court of Appeals to consider whether the District Court should have granted class certification.

V

* * * Our holding that the case is not moot extends only to the appeal of the class certification denial. If the District Court again denies class certification, and that decision is affirmed, the controversy on the merits will be moot. Furthermore, although the Court of Appeals commented upon the merits for the sole purpose of avoiding waste of judicial resources, it did not reach a final conclusion on the validity of the guidelines. Rather, it held only that summary judgment was improper and remanded for further factual development. Given the interlocutory posture of the case before us, we must defer decision on the merits of respondent's case until after it is determined affirmatively that a class properly can be certified.

The judgment of the Court of Appeals is vacated and the case is remanded for further proceedings consistent with this opinion.

It is so ordered.

Mr. Justice POWELL, with whom THE CHIEF JUSTICE, Mr. Justice STEWART and Mr. Justice REHNQUIST join, dissenting.

* * *

The Court's analysis proceeds in two steps. First, it says that mootness is a "flexible" doctrine which may be adapted as we see fit to "nontraditional" forms of litigation. Second, the Court holds that the named plaintiff has a right "analogous to the private attorney general concept" to appeal the denial of class certification even when his personal claim for relief is moot. Both steps are significant departures from settled law that rationally cannot be confined to the narrow issue presented in this case. Accordingly, I dissent.

I

As the Court observes, this case involves the "personal stake" aspect of the mootness doctrine. There is undoubtedly a "live" issue which an appropriate plaintiff could present for judicial resolution. The question is whether respondent, who has no further interest in this action, nevertheless may—through counsel—continue to litigate it.

Recent decisions of this Court have considered the personal stake requirement with some care. When the issue is presented at the outset of litigation as a question of standing to sue, we have held that the personal stake requirement has a double aspect. On the one hand, it derives from Art. III limitations on the power of the federal courts. On the other, it embodies additional, self-imposed restraints on the exercise of judicial power. *E.g.,* Singleton v. Wulff, 428 U.S. 106, 112 (1976); Warth v. Seldin, 422 U.S. 490, 498 (1975). The prudential aspect of standing aptly is described as a doctrine of uncertain contours. But the constitutional minimum has been given definite content: "In order to satisfy Art. III, the plaintiff must show that he personally has suffered some actual or threatened injury as a result of the putatively illegal conduct of the defendant." Gladstone, Realtors v. Village of Bellwood, 441 U.S. 91 (1979). * * *

As the Court notes today, the same threshold requirement must be satisfied throughout the action. * * *

* * * The essential and irreducible constitutional requirement is simply a nonfrivolous showing of continuing or threatened injury at the hands of the adversary.

[The] cases demonstrate, contrary to the Court's view today, that the core requirement of a personal stake in the outcome is not "flexible." * * *

II

* * * These principles were developed outside the class action context. But Art. III contains no exception for class actions. Thus, we have held that a putative class representative who alleges no individual injury "may not seek relief on behalf of himself or any other member of the class." O'Shea v. Littleton, 414 U.S. 488, 494 (1974). Only after a class has been certified in accordance with Rule 23 can it "acquir[e] a legal status separate from the interest asserted by [the named plaintiff]." Sosna v. Iowa, *supra,* 419 U.S. at 399 (1975). "Given a properly certified class," the live interests of unnamed but identifiable class members may supply the personal stake required by Art. III when the named plaintiff's individual claim becomes moot. Franks v. Bowman Transportation Co., 424 U.S. 747, 755–756 (1976); Sosna v. Iowa, *supra,* 419 U.S. at 402.

This case presents a fundamentally different situation. No class has been certified, and the lone plaintiff no longer has any personal stake in the litigation. In the words of his own lawyer, respondent "can obtain absolutely no additional personal relief" in this case. Tr. of Oral Arg., at 25. Even the lawyer has evinced no interest in continuing to represent respondent as named plaintiff, as distinguished from other persons presently incarcerated. Ibid. In these circumstances, Art. III and the precedents of this Court require dismissal. But the Court views the case differently, and constructs new doctrine to breathe life into a lawsuit that has no plaintiff.

The Court announces today for the first time—and without attempting to reconcile the many cases to the contrary—that there are two categories of "the Art. III mootness doctrine": "flexible" and "less flexible." The

Court then relies on cases said to demonstrate the application of "flexible" mootness to class action litigation. The cases principally relied upon are Gerstein v. Pugh, 420 U.S. 103, 110–111, n. 11 (1975), United Airlines, Inc. v. McDonald, 432 U.S. 385 (1977), and today's decision in Deposit Guaranty Nat. Bank v. Roper, 445 U.S. 326. Each case is said to show that a class action is not mooted by the loss of the class representative's personal stake in the outcome of the lawsuit, even though no class has been certified. Sosna itself is cited for the proposition that the requirements of Art. III may be met "through means other than the traditional requirement of a 'personal stake in the outcome.'" In my view, the Court misreads these precedents.

A

In Sosna, the Court simply acknowledged that actual class certification gives legal recognition to additional adverse parties. Cf. Aetna Life Ins. Co. v. Haworth, 300 U.S. 227, 240 (1937).[8] And in Gerstein the Court applied a rule long established, outside the class action context, by cases that never have been thought to erode the requirement of a personal stake in the outcome. Gerstein held that a class action challenging the constitutionality of pretrial detention procedures could continue after the named plaintiffs' convictions had brought their detentions to an end. The Court did not suggest that a personal stake in the outcome on the merits was unnecessary. The action continued only because of the transitory nature of pretrial detention, which placed the claim within "that narrow class of cases" that are "distinctly 'capable of repetition, yet evading review.'" 420 U.S., at 110, n. 11.[9]

McDonald and Roper sanction some appeals from the denial of class certification notwithstanding satisfaction of the class representative's claim on the merits. But neither case holds that Art. III may be satisfied in the absence of a personal stake in the outcome. ∗ ∗ ∗

There is dictum in McDonald that the "refusal to certify was subject to appellate review after final judgment at the behest of the named plaintiffs ∗ ∗ ∗." 432 U.S., at 393. That gratuitous sentence, repeated in Coopers & Lybrand v. Livesay, 437 U.S. 463, 469, 470, n. 15 (1978), apparently is elevated by the Court's opinion in this case to the status of new doctrine. There is serious tension between this new doctrine and the much narrower reasoning adopted today in Roper. In Roper the Court holds that the

8. Certification is no mere formality. It represents a judicial finding that injured parties other than the named plaintiff exist. It also provides a definition by which they can be identified. Certification identifies and sharpens the interests of unnamed class members in the outcome; only thereafter will they be bound by the outcome. After certification, class members can be certain that the action will not be settled or dismissed without appropriate notice. ∗ ∗ ∗ After certification, the case is no different in principle from more traditional representative actions involving, for example, a single party who cannot participate himself because of his incompetence but is permitted to litigate through an appointed fiduciary.

9. The Court's Gerstein analysis, which emphasized that "[p]retrial detention is by nature temporary" and that "[t]he individual could ∗ ∗ ∗ suffer repeated deprivations" with no access to redress, falls squarely within the rule of Southern Pac. Terminal v. ICC, 219 U.S. 498, 515 (1911). See Roe v. Wade, 410 U.S. 113, 125 (1973). In similar cases we have noted that the continuation of the action will depend "'especially [upon] the reality of the claim that otherwise the issue would evade review.'" Swisher v. Brady, 438 U.S. 204, 213, n. 11 (1978), quoting Sosna v. Iowa, 419 U.S. 393, 402, n. 11 (1975). These limitations are inconsistent with the concept of "flexible" mootness and the redefinition of "personal stake" adopted today.

named plaintiffs, who have refused to accept proffered individual settlements, retain a personal stake in sharing anticipated litigation costs with the class. 445 U.S., at 334, n. 6, 336. * * *

It is far from apparent how Roper can be thought to support the decision in this case. Indeed, the opinion by The Chief Justice in Roper reaffirms the obligation of a federal court to dismiss an appeal when the parties no longer retain the personal stake in the outcome required by Art. III. Ibid. Here, there is not even a speculative interest in sharing costs, and respondent affirmatively denies that he retains any stake or personal interest in the outcome of his appeal. Thus, a fact that was critical to the analysis in Roper is absent in this case. One can disagree with that analysis yet conclude that Roper affords no support for the Court's ruling here.

B

The cases cited by the Court as "less flexible"—and therefore less authoritative—apply established Art. III doctrine in cases closely analogous to this one. Indianapolis School Comm'rs v. Jacobs, 420 U.S. 128 (1975) (*per curiam*); Weinstein v. Bradford, 423 U.S. 147 (1975) (*per curiam*); Pasadena City Board of Education v. Spangler, 427 U.S. 424, 430 (1976). As they are about to become second class precedents, these cases are relegated to a footnote. But the cases are recent and carefully considered decisions of this Court. They applied long settled principles of Art. III jurisprudence. And no Justice who participated in them suggested the distinction drawn today. The Court's backhanded treatment of these "less flexible" cases ignores their controlling relevance to the issue presented here. * * *

The Court suggests that Jacobs and Spangler may be distinguished because the plaintiffs there were not appealing the denial of class certification. The Court overlooks the fact that in each case the class representatives were defending a judgment on the merits from which the defendants had appealed. The plaintiff/respondents continued vigorously to assert the claims of the class. They did not take the procedural route of appealing a denial of certification only because the District Court had granted—albeit defectively—class status. We chose not to remand for correction of the oral certification order in Jacobs because we recognized that the putative class representative had suffered no injury that could be redressed by adequate certification. Underlying Jacobs, and Bradford as well, is the elementary principle that no one has a personal stake in obtaining relief for third parties, through the mechanism of class certification or otherwise.[13] The Court rejects that principle today.

III

While the Court's new concept of "flexible" mootness is unprecedented, the content given that concept is even more disturbing. The Court splits the class aspects of this action into two separate "claims": (i) that the action may be maintained by respondent on behalf of a class, and (ii) that the class is entitled to relief on the merits. Since no class has been

---

13. In some circumstances, litigants are permitted to argue the rights of third parties in support of their claims. *E.g.*, Singleton v. Wulff, 428 U.S. 106, 113 (1976); Barrows v. Jackson, 346 U.S. 249, 255–256 (1953). In each such case, however, the Court has identified a concrete, individual injury suffered by the litigant himself.

certified, the Court concedes that the claim on the merits is moot. But respondent is said to have a personal stake in his "procedural claim" despite his lack of a stake in the merits.

The Court makes no effort to identify any injury to respondent that may be redressed by, or any benefit to respondent that may accrue from, a favorable ruling on the certification question.[14] Instead, respondent's "personal stake" is said to derive from two factors having nothing to do with concrete injury or stake in the outcome. First, the Court finds that the Federal Rules of Civil Procedure create a "right," "analogous to the private attorney general concept," to have a class certified. Second, the Court thinks that the case retains the "imperatives of a dispute capable of judicial resolution," which are identified as (i) a sharply presented issue, (ii) a concrete factual setting, and (iii) a self-interested party actually contesting the case.[15]

The Court's reliance on some new "right" inherent in Rule 23 is misplaced. We have held that even Congress may not confer federal court jurisdiction when Art. III does not. Gladstone, Realtors v. Village of Bellwood, 441 U.S., at 100; O'Shea v. Littleton, 414 U.S., at 494, and n. 2; see Marbury v. Madison, 1 Cranch (5 U.S.) 137, 175–177 (1803). Far less so may a rule of procedure which "shall not be construed to extend * * * the jurisdiction of the United States district courts." Fed.Rule Civ.Proc. 82. Moreover, the "private attorney general concept" cannot supply the personal stake necessary to satisfy Art. III. It serves only to permit litigation by a party who has a stake of his own but otherwise might be barred by prudential standing rules. See Warth v. Seldin, 422 U.S., at 501; Sierra Club v. Morton, 405 U.S., at 737–738.

Since neither Rule 23 nor the private attorney general concept can fill the jurisdictional gap, the Court's new perception of Art. III requirements must rest entirely on its tripartite test of concrete adverseness. Although the components of the test are no strangers to our Art. III jurisprudence, they operate only in " 'cases confessedly within [the Court's] jurisdiction.' " Franks v. Bowman Transportation Co., 424 U.S., at 755–756, and n. 8, quoting Flast v. Cohen, 392 U.S. 83, 97 (1968). The Court cites no decision that has premised jurisdiction upon the bare existence of a sharply presented issue in a concrete and vigorously argued case, and I am aware of none. Indeed, each of these characteristics is sure to be present in the typical "private attorney general" action brought by a public spirited citizen.

14. In a footnote, the Court states:

"This respondent suffered actual, concrete injury as a result of the putatively illegal conduct, and this injury would satisfy the formalistic personal stake requirement if damages were sought. See, e.g, Powell v. McCormack, 395 U.S., at 495–500."

This appears to be a categorical claim of the actual, concrete injury our cases have required. Yet, again, the Court fails to identify the injury. The reference to damages is irrelevant here, as respondent sought no damages—only injunctive and declaratory relief. Moreover, counsel for respondent frankly conceded that his client "can obtain absolutely no additional personal relief" in this case. Tr. of Oral Arg. 25. * * *

15. The Court attempts to limit the sweeping consequences that could flow from the application of these criteria by asserting that "[e]ach case must be decided on its own facts" on the basis of "practicalities and prudential considerations." The Court long has recognized a difference between the prudential and constitutional aspects of the standing and mootness doctrines. I am not aware that the Court, until today, ever has merged these considerations for the purpose of eliminating the Art. III requirement of a personal stake in the litigation. * * *

Although we have refused steadfastly to countenance the "public action," the Court's redefinition of the personal stake requirement leaves no principled basis for that practice.[18] * * *

Class actions may advance significantly the administration of justice in appropriate cases. Indeed, the class action is scarcely a new idea. * * * The effect of mootness on the vitality of a device like the class action may be a relevant prudential consideration.[19] But it cannot provide a plaintiff when none is before the Court, for we are powerless to assume jurisdiction in violation of Art. III.

IV

In short, this is a case in which the putative class representative—respondent here—no longer has the slightest interest in the injuries alleged in his complaint. No member of the class is before the Court; indeed, none has been identified. The case therefore lacks a plaintiff with the minimal personal stake that is a constitutional prerequisite to the jurisdiction of an Art. III court. In any realistic sense, the only persons before this Court who appear to have an interest are the defendants and a lawyer who no longer has a client.

I would vacate the decision of the Court of Appeals and remand with instructions to dismiss the action as moot.

NOTE ON MOOTNESS AND CLASS ACTIONS

(1) In 1973, Professor Monaghan wrote: "Marbury's analogy of constitutional litigation to 'ordinary' common law litigation strongly suggested that the occasions for judicial review were limited to the protection of identifiable and concrete personal rights, similar to those protected by the common law courts." Monaghan, *Constitutional Adjudication: The Who and When,* 82 Yale L.J. 1363, 1366 (1973). See p. 79, *supra.* Later in the same piece, he concluded: "Perhaps more than any other single development, the mushrooming of class actions has rendered the private rights model [of Marbury] largely unintelligible" (p. 1383). *Cf.* Fiss, *Foreword: The Forms of Justice,* 92 Harv.L.Rev. 1, 19–21 (1974).

Does the majority opinion in Geraghty, written seven years later, bear out this thesis? Isn't Justice Powell correct that Geraghty had no personal

---

18. The Court's view logically cannot be confined to moot cases. If a plaintiff who is released from prison the day after filing a class action challenging parole guidelines may seek certification of the class, why should a plaintiff who is released the day before filing the suit be barred? As an Art. III matter, there can be no difference.

Even on prudential grounds, there is little difference between this action and one filed promptly after the named plaintiff's release from prison. In the present case, this Court has ruled on neither the merits nor the propriety of the class action. At the same time, it has vacated a judgment by the Court of Appeals that in turn reversed the judgment of the District Court. No determination on any issue is left standing. For every practical purpose the action must begin anew—this time without a plaintiff. The prudential considerations in favor of a finding of mootness could scarcely be more compelling.

19. I do not imply that the result reached today is necessary in any way to the continued vitality of the class-action device. On the contrary, the practical impact of mootness in this case would be slight indeed. See note, 18, *supra.* And this may well be typical of class actions brought under Rule 23(b)(1) or (2) to seek injunctive or declaratory relief. * * *

stake in the outcome of the certification issue?[1] If so, the tenets of the dispute resolution model, pp. 79–82, *supra*, would appear to require dismissal for lack of a case or controversy.

Is that model, then, inconsistent with the recognition of group interests underlying the development of the class action? Or is the Geraghty majority at fault for not recognizing that the major goal of the class action—more vigorous and effective enforcement of group rights—can best be achieved by insistence that the litigation be prosecuted by a representative of the group who continues to share its concerns? Is it an answer, as Justice Stevens suggested in Roper, that in any event the members of the group not themselves before the court have an ongoing dispute? Does the court know whether they do, or what the true dimensions of that dispute are, without at least one of their number at the bar? Should it accept the assurances of their lawyer, on the theory that whether or not there is a "named plaintiff" with a live interest, it is really counsel who controls the litigation in such cases and determines its course?[2]

Geraghty itself was not written on a clean slate, and as the following Paragraphs suggest, was to a significant extent a consequence of earlier decisions.

(2) As the opinions in Geraghty indicate, the evolution of the mootness doctrine in class actions was extraordinarily rapid. Following a brief footnote alluding to the issue in Dunn v. Blumstein, 405 U.S. 330 (1972), the Court in Indiana Employment Sec. Div. v. Burney, 409 U.S. 540, 541–42 (1973), remanded a class action for consideration of the question of mootness after the named plaintiff's claim had been fully settled. Then in Sosna v. Iowa, 419 U.S. 393 (1975), discussed in Geraghty, the Court first announced that certification as a class action could save litigation from mootness even after the named plaintiff no longer had an individual claim. The Court, however, appeared to require that the controversy (over a state durational residency requirement for obtaining a divorce) be within the "capable of repetition yet evading review" category (not for the named plaintiff but for the remaining members of the class) and indicated that the question of the adequacy of representation would have to be looked at closely in light of the mootness of the plaintiff's individual claim.[3]

The first of these requirements crumbled in Franks v. Bowman Transp. Co., 424 U.S. 747 (1976), a class action in which the sole issue before the Supreme Court was a demand for retroactive seniority in employment and in which the plaintiff, the only named representative of the class, had been lawfully discharged by the employer after certification. In holding the case not moot, the Court, which was unanimous on this point, said (pp. 754–56):

1. For forceful criticism of the Geraghty majority's reliance on a Rule 23 right to seek class certification, see Greenstein, *Bridging the Mootness Gap in Federal Court Class Actions*, 35 Stan.L.Rev. 897, 907–08 (1983). Does such reliance raise a question under the Enabling Act? (See Chap. VI, Sec. 1, *infra*.)

2. The court can, of course, seek to communicate with members of the class either before or after certification. But should that technique—which must to some degree operate through counsel—be regarded as a complete substitute for the requirement that the lawyer in such a case have a direct relationship with a live client? See Paragraph (6), *infra*.

3. In Sosna itself, the Court said that "where it is unlikely that segments of the class appellant represents would have interests conflicting with those she has sought to advance, and where the interests of that class have been competently urged at each level of the proceeding, we believe that the [adequate representation] test of Rule 23(a) is met" (p. 403). For further discussion of this issue, see Paragraph (8) of this Note.

"[N]othing in our Sosna * * * [or other] opinions holds or even intimates that the fact the named plaintiff no longer has a personal stake in the outcome of a certified class action renders the class action moot in the absence of an issue 'capable of repetition, yet evading review.' * * *

" * * * Given a properly certified class action, Sosna contemplates that mootness turns on whether, in the specific circumstances of the given case at the time it is before this Court, an adversary relationship sufficient to fulfill this function [of 'concrete adverseness which sharpens the presentation of issues'] exists. In this case, that adversary relationship obviously obtained as to unnamed class members * * *.

"The unnamed members of the class involved are identifiable individuals, individually named in the record. * * * No questions are raised concerning the continuing desire of any of these class members for the seniority relief presently in issue. No questions are raised concerning the tenacity and competence of their counsel in pursuing that mode of legal relief before this Court. It follows that there is no meaningful sense in which a 'live controversy' reflecting the issues before the Court could be found to be absent. * * * "

How significant was it that other members of the class in the Franks case were "individually named in the record" and actively seeking relief? Wouldn't the mootness issue have been obviated if one or more had been added as a named plaintiff? If so, why wasn't that required? *Cf.* n. 1 of the majority opinion in Geraghty.

(3) Even before Geraghty, the significance of class certification in the application of evolving mootness doctrine was in flux. In Board of School Comm'rs v. Jacobs, 420 U.S. 128 (1975), and Weinstein v. Bradford, 423 U.S. 147 (1975), discussed in both opinions in Geraghty, the Court held that the mootness of the named plaintiffs' claims mooted the entire case where class action status had been sought but formal certification had not been granted. Yet in Gerstein v. Pugh, 420 U.S. 103 (1975), relied on by the Geraghty majority, a putative class action challenging pretrial detention procedures was held by a unanimous Court to be not moot even though the named plaintiffs had evidently been tried before the district court certified the class. The Court said (pp. 110–11 n. 11): "Such a showing [that the case was not moot as to all named plaintiffs at the time of certification] ordinarily would be required to avoid mootness under Sosna. But this case is a suitable exception to that requirement. * * * It is by no means certain that any given individual, named as plaintiff, would be in pretrial custody long enough for a district judge to certify the class. Moreover, in this case the constant existence of a class of persons suffering deprivation is certain. The attorney representing the named respondents [plaintiffs] is a public defender, and we can safely assume that he has other clients with a continuing live interest in the case."

(4) Paralleling these decisions were several important cases dealing with appeals from district court denials of class certification motions. In United Airlines, Inc. v. McDonald, 432 U.S. 385 (1977), a class member was held entitled to intervene in order to appeal the denial of class certification, after the named plaintiffs' claims had been fully satisfied. And in Coopers & Lybrand v. Livesay, 437 U.S. 463 (1978), the Court held that a denial of a motion to certify was not an appealable final judgment under 28 U.S.C. § 1291. Both decisions explicitly assumed the appealability of a denial of

class certification, at the behest of the named plaintiff, after final judgment, and both were invoked by the majority in support of the Geraghty result.

(5) If its prior decisions in this area were correct, could the Court responsibly have stopped short of the Geraghty result? Sosna and Franks established that neither constitutional nor prudential considerations invariably required the named plaintiff to have a continuing stake in the outcome. And Gerstein had eliminated formal certification prior to mootness of the named plaintiff's claim as an indispensable requirement. Indeed, is the act of formal certification as significant, either in constitutional or prudential terms, as Sosna suggested and Justice Powell, dissenting in Geraghty, insisted? A class may be certified without any real contest between the parties, since certification may be to the advantage of both sides, and even after certification, other members of the class may be able to opt out (see Fed.R.Civ.P. 23(c)(2)), or to challenge the adequacy of representation and thus the binding effect of the judgment in a collateral proceeding (see Hansberry v. Lee, 311 U.S. 32 (1940)). Moreover, even if certification is critical, despite these considerations, why shouldn't an order of certification relate back, for purposes of determining mootness, when a request for class action status had been improperly denied before the case became moot? Cf. Fed.R.Civ.P. 15(c) (relation back of amended complaint for purposes of the statute of limitations). Wasn't the case for "relation back," and for appealability generally in a case like Geraghty, made even stronger by the Court's own decision in Coopers & Lybrand to bar interlocutory appeals of certification denials as a matter of right?

(6) The constitutional argument for nonjusticiability in a case like Geraghty centers on the lack of an ongoing dispute involving the class member who is before the court. Whether or not that argument is accepted, does the absence of a named plaintiff with a stake in the outcome invoke prudential considerations favoring a refusal to adjudicate on the merits? Without a real, live client, is there sufficient insurance of counsel's competence, tenacity, and orientation? Does the simple fact that there is such a client impose significant limitations on the conduct of counsel?[4] As noted in Paragraph (2), above, there were identified people

---

4. This question and its implications, and the general subject of possible divergence of interests between lawyers and clients, have become increasingly important (and the object of increasing attention) in class action cases and in the growing number of cases involving "public interest" lawyers. See, e.g., Stewart, The Reformation of American Administrative Law, 88 Harv.L.Rev. 1667, 1762–69 (1975), and sources there cited; Bell, Serving Two Masters: Integration Ideals and Client Interests in School Desegregation Litigation, 85 Yale L.J. 470 (1976). See also NAACP v. Button, 371 U.S. 415, 462–63 (1963), in which Justice Harlan, dissenting, discusses some of the ethical problems that may confront an attorney in a school desegregation case.

For a provocative debate, primarily in the context of standing, over the utility and necessity of a "traditional," Hohfeldian plaintiff, see Brilmayer, The Jurispru-

dence of Article III: Perspectives on the "Case or Controversy" Requirement, 93 Harv.L.Rev. 297 (1979) (also discussed at pp. 68–69, supra); Tushnet, The "Case or Controversy" Controversy, 93 Harv.L.Rev. 1698 (1980); Brilmayer, A Reply, 93 Harv. L.Rev. 1727 (1980). See also Simon, Homo Psychologicus: Notes on a New Legal Formalism, 32 Stan.L.Rev. 487, 505 (1980): "Although it appears that the way the disadvantaged can most effectively use the legal system is through organization and through coordination and aggregation of claims, the bar continues to discourage and inhibit this kind of lawyering in the name of 'devotion to the interests of individual clients.' Issues concerning the distribution of power in society are translated into issues of personal relations."

See generally Tribe, American Constitutional Law 67–155 (2d ed. 1988); Vining, Legal Identity (1978).

who might well have come forward as representatives in Franks v. Bowman Transp. Co. (as there were in Geraghty), and they were apparently actively involved in the litigation. But didn't the Court's failure to insist that at least one actually be named as plaintiff make it less likely that in the future the Franks case would be limited to that situation? Why did the Court ignore that available alternative in Geraghty? [5]

(7) What is the answer to the question posed in note 18 of Justice Powell's dissent? Given the relationship between mootness and standing, can the courts turn away, on grounds of nonjusticiability, the plaintiff who is no longer a member of the class when the suit is filed, or who has never been in the class at all?

In Hall v. Beals, 396 U.S. 45 (1969), plaintiffs brought a federal court class action challenging a six-month residency requirement for voting. When the action was filed, they had resided in the state more than two but less than six months. While their appeal from dismissal of their complaint was pending, the election they had wanted to vote in was held, and the state legislature reduced the residency requirement to two months. The Court decided that the case had become moot, and emphasized that the class of voters disqualified by virtue of the new two-month requirement was "a class of which the appellants have *never* been members" (p. 49) (emphasis added).

Is Hall v. Beals still good law? [6] Note that in terms of the interest in self-determination articulated by Professor Brilmayer as one of the policies underlying Article III, p. 69, *supra*, there may well be a difference between a plaintiff who is no longer part of a class and one who has never been a member at all.

(8) Richardson v. Ramirez, 418 U.S. 24 (1974), was a state court action against state election officials challenging a law disenfranchising convicted felons. The Supreme Court concluded that the state courts had treated the case as a class action and that, as such, it presented a justiciable controversy; even though the named plaintiffs had received all the relief they sought from the defendant officials, there was a continuing dispute involving "the unnamed members of the classes represented below by petitioners and respondents" (p. 40). Had the suit been brought in federal court, there "would be serious doubt as to whether it could proceed as a class action * * *. But California is at liberty to prescribe its own rules for class actions" (p. 39). The Court saw strong practical arguments militating against a holding of mootness, especially the fact that were the state judgment for the plaintiffs allowed to stand, the defendant officials would

---

5. In some instances, insistence that the lawyer have an identifiable client with an ongoing interest may lead only to the naming of a class representative with little or no knowledge of the case who will play no role in the course of the litigation. Does it follow that such insistence is always and necessarily a sterile formalism? Or do Simon's concerns, note 4, *supra*, suggest that adherence to the requirement may in some instances temper the single-minded pursuit of some outsider's conception of the interests of the group?

For discussion of ways of increasing counsel's accountability to the class in "plaintiff class actions seeking structural reforms in public and private institutions," see Rhode, *Class Conflicts in Class Actions*, 34 Stan.L.Rev. 1183 (1982).

6. See the last paragraph of footnote 11 of the Court's opinion in Geraghty. *Cf.* Blum v. Yaretsky, 457 U.S. 991, 999 (1982), in which the Court, without citing either Geraghty or Hall v. Beals, held part of a class action claim nonjusticiable, saying: "It is not enough that the conduct of which the plaintiff complains will injure *someone*. The complaining party must show that he is within the class of persons who will be concretely affected."

be "permanently bound by [the state court's] conclusion on a matter of federal constitutional law" (p. 35)—a conclusion that the U.S. Supreme Court went on to reverse.

(9) Though the Court held in Geraghty that the question of class certification was justiciable, it emphasized that it was not deciding "whether Geraghty is a proper representative for the purpose of representing the class on the merits." That question calls for application of the criteria of Rule 23 of the Federal Rules of Civil Procedure, and several Supreme Court decisions have applied those criteria to bar prosecution of a claim by the named plaintiff.[7]

In General Tel. Co. v. Falcon, 457 U.S. 147 (1982), for example, an employee who claimed he had been denied a promotion on the basis of his Mexican-American national origin brought a federal court class action against his employer on behalf of all Mexican-American employees *and* applicants for employment allegedly discriminated against with respect to promotion or hiring. The Supreme Court held, unanimously on this issue, that it was error, on these allegations alone, to certify the case as an "across-the-board" class action. Noting the overlap among the commonality, typicality, and adequacy-of-representation requirements of Rule 23(a), the Court said (pp. 158–59):

"Respondent's complaint provided an insufficient basis for concluding that the adjudication of his claim of discrimination in promotion would require the decision of any common question concerning the failure of petitioner to hire more Mexican-Americans. * * * If one allegation of specific discriminatory treatment were sufficient to support an across-the-board attack, every Title VII case would be a potential companywide class action." [8]

(10) The end result of Sosna and its progeny, on the one hand, and decisions like Falcon, on the other, is apparently to move consideration of issues bearing on the role of courts in certain class action cases from the context of the mootness doctrine to that of Rule 23. Can that move perhaps be justified in terms of Justice Stevens' argument in Roper that Article III is satisfied so long as there is a live dispute between the class and its adversary? Under this argument, the class itself is regarded as a legal entity, not simply as a device for the efficient litigation of many similar individual claims.

Even if such a view is adopted, isn't a question of standing raised with respect to the appropriateness of the named representative as litigator of that dispute? (See Sec. 2, *supra.*) Is that question of standing one of constitutional dimension, or may it be viewed as essentially prudential, to be determined in accordance with the criteria laid down in Rule 23? [9]

---

7. *Cf.* Kremens v. Bartley, 431 U.S. 119 (1977), in which the Court held that changes in the law not only mooted the claims of the named plaintiffs but also served to fragment the original class and required reconsideration of the class definition as well as the substitution of representatives with live claims.

8. The Court also underscored "the potential unfairness to the class members bound by the judgment if the framing of the class is overbroad" (p. 161).

See also East Texas Motor Freight System Inc. v. Rodriguez, 431 U.S. 395 (1977); Satterwhite v. City of Greenville, 578 F.2d 987 (5th Cir.1978) (en banc), *vacated and remanded,* 445 U.S. 940 (1980), *on remand,* 634 F.2d 231 (5th Cir.1981) (en banc).

9. For an able discussion of these issues, see Greenstein, note 1, *supra.*

SECTION 5: ABSTRACT, HYPOTHETICAL, AND CONJECTURAL QUESTIONS: HEREIN OF DECLARATORY JUDGMENTS AND OF "RIPENESS"

NOTE ON THE MUSKRAT CASE AND ON TEST CASES FRAMED BY CONGRESS

(1) In Muskrat v. United States, 219 U.S. 346 (1911), the Court refused to entertain a suit that Congress had specifically authorized in order to determine the constitutionality of prior legislation. In 1902, Congress had provided for the transfer of Cherokee property from tribal to private ownership; every citizen of the Cherokee Nation as of September 1, 1902, was entitled to be enrolled, and upon enrollment, to an allotment equal in value to 110 acres of the average allottable lands of the tribe (plus a proportionate share of any tribal funds on deposit in the U.S. Treasury and, presumably, of any land remaining after the allotments). In 1906, Congress extended the time for completion of the roll by permitting enrollment of minor children living on March 4, 1906. At the same time, it imposed new restraints on alienation by the original allottees. The Secretaries of the Interior and of the Treasury were charged with implementation of various aspects of these statutes.

In 1907, Congress authorized certain named original allottees to bring suit against the United States in the Court of Claims, with a right of appeal by either party to the Supreme Court, "to determine the validity of any acts of Congress" passed after the 1902 act that purported to diminish their rights as allottees. Attorneys' fees for plaintiffs, if they prevailed, were to be paid by the Treasury out of tribal funds.

Pursuant to this statute, a suit challenging the validity of the 1906 Act was brought in the Court of Claims by Muskrat and other allottees. On their appeal to the Supreme Court, the case was remanded with directions to dismiss for want of jurisdiction: The suit was not justiciable before the Supreme Court, and Congress would not have authorized the Court of Claims to entertain the action had it known that the judgment of that court could not constitutionally be reviewed.[1]

After rehearsing the learning of Marbury v. Madison—that the judicial power "is the right to determine actual controversies arising between adverse litigants" and that the right to declare a law unconstitutional is an incident of that power—the Court continued (pp. 361–62):

" * * * It is true the United States is made a defendant to this action, but it has no interest adverse to the claimants. The object is not to assert a property right as against the Government, or to demand compensation for alleged wrongs because of action upon its part. The whole purpose of the law is to determine the constitutional validity of this class of legislation, in a suit not arising between parties concerning a property right necessarily involved in the decision in question, but in a proceeding against the Government in its sovereign capacity, and concerning which

---

1. At the time, the Court of Claims was not regarded as an Article III court.

the only judgment required is to settle the doubtful character of the legislation in question. Such judgment will not conclude private parties, when actual litigation brings to the court the question of the constitutionality of such legislation. In a legal sense the judgment could not be executed, and amounts in fact to no more than an expression of opinion upon the validity of the acts in question. * * *"

(2) Complete the following sentence: "The Supreme Court held that no justiciable controversy was presented in the Muskrat case because * * *".

Was the Court's concern influenced by doubts that a request for a declaratory judgment, without more, was a sufficient basis for the invocation of judicial power? See the following *Note on the Development of the Declaratory Judgment and its Use in Private Litigation.*

As the Court observed in Muskrat, there was pending at the time of decision another case, which was decided by the Supreme Court in the following year. Gritts v. Fisher, 224 U.S. 640 (1912). The complainants were three Cherokees enrolled under the 1902 act. Invoking the general jurisdictional statutes for the District of Columbia courts, they sought to enjoin the Secretaries of the Interior and of the Treasury from carrying into effect the provision of the 1906 acts for the inclusion of after-born children. The Court stated that the later legislation did not affect the individual allotments initially made to the complainants and other enrollees under the 1902 act, but did diminish their participation in the residue left over from those allotments. The defendants, it said, "are respectively charged with important duties in that connection, [and] have taken the position, and are proceeding upon the theory, that * * * the right of the controversy is with the children; and the purpose of this suit is to test the accuracy of that position, and, if it be held untenable, to enjoin those officers from giving effect to it" (p. 641). Without adverting to the Muskrat case or to any jurisdictional problem, the Court affirmed the dismissal of the bill on the merits.

(3) In the Cherokee Intermarriage Cases, 203 U.S. 76 (1906), numerous protests had been filed with the Secretary of the Treasury by full-blooded Cherokees against the inclusion on the rolls (as Cherokee citizens) of white persons who had intermarried with Cherokees. The Secretary of the Treasury had referred the protests to the Court of Claims, in accordance with the Act of March 3, 1883, 22 Stat. 485. Thereafter Congress passed the Act of March 3, 1905, 33 Stat. 1048, 1071, authorizing the Court of Claims to render final judgment in the case, with the right in an aggrieved party to appeal to the Supreme Court of the United States. The Court of Claims entered an elaborate decree stating what classes of intermarried persons were, and what classes were not, entitled to enrollment under the 1902 act. On appeal, the Supreme Court affirmed this decree, without adverting to any jurisdictional problem.

On numerous other occasions, Congress has by special act empowered the Court of Claims or a federal district court, and the Supreme Court on review, to decide a particular case; and the Supreme Court has accepted jurisdiction.

What distinguishes these acts from the Muskrat statute? See, for example, La Abra Silver Mining Co. v. United States, 175 U.S. 423, 455–63

(1899); United States v. Alcea Band of Tillamooks, 329 U.S. 40 (1946); Northern Cheyenne Tribe v. Hollowbreast, 425 U.S. 649 (1976).

(4) The Voting Rights Act of 1965 imposed certain requirements on states or political subdivisions which maintained as of November 1, 1964 "any test or device" as a prerequisite to voting, and in that same month had less than 50% of their voting-age residents registered or actually voting. Section 5 of the Act, 42 U.S.C. § 1973c, provided that whenever any such state or subdivision "shall enact or seek to administer any voting qualification or prerequisite to voting, or standard, practice, or procedure with respect to voting different from that in force or effect on November 1, 1964," it must either submit it to the Attorney General or alternatively "may institute an action in the United States District Court for the District of Columbia for a declaratory judgment that such qualification, prerequisite, standard, practice, or procedure does not have the purpose and will not have the effect of denying or abridging the right to vote on account of race or color." If the Attorney General interposed an objection, the declaratory judgment might still be sought and would have to be obtained before the new law could be put into effect.

In South Carolina v. Katzenbach, 383 U.S. 301 (1966), the Supreme Court sustained the validity of § 5. The Court's opinion, by Chief Justice Warren, disposed of the justiciability question summarily (p. 335): "Nor has Congress authorized the District Court to issue advisory opinions, in violation of the principles of Article III * * *. The Act automatically suspends the operation of voting regulations enacted after November 1, 1964, and furnishes mechanisms for enforcing the suspension. A State or political subdivision wishing to make use of a recent amendment to its voting laws therefore has a concrete and immediate "controversy" with the Federal Government. * * * An appropriate remedy is a judicial determination that continued suspension of the new rule is unnecessary to vindicate rights guaranteed by the Fifteenth Amendment."

Only Justice Black perceived a problem on this point (p. 357): "If it can be said that any case or controversy arises under this section which gives the District Court for the District of Columbia jurisdiction to approve or reject state laws or constitutional amendments, then the case or controversy must be between a State and the United States Government. But it is hard for me to believe that a justiciable controversy can arise in the constitutional sense from a desire by the United States Government or some of its officials to determine in advance what legislative provisions a State may enact or what constitutional amendments it may adopt. If this dispute between the Federal Government and the States amounts to a case or controversy it is a far cry from the traditional constitutional notion of a case or controversy as a dispute over the meaning of enforceable laws or the manner in which they are applied."

Is there any significant difference, with regard to justiciability, between the procedures authorized by § 5 and an action brought by the Attorney General to enforce federal statutory or constitutional restrictions against state officials proceeding to carry out the state law?

(5) The Muskrat decision is occasionally cited in Supreme Court opinions, and with apparent acceptance of its authority, if not actual approval. See, *e.g.,* North Carolina v. Rice, 404 U.S. 244, 246 (1971); Sierra Club v. Morton, 405 U.S. 727, 732 n. 3 (1972); Williams v. Zbaraz, 448 U.S. 358, 368

(1980). In light of the material in this Note, what is the present significance of the Muskrat holding?

NOTE ON THE DEVELOPMENT OF THE DECLARATORY JUDGMENT AND ITS USE IN PRIVATE LITIGATION

(1) In Willing v. Chicago Auditorium Ass'n, 277 U.S. 274 (1928), the
Auditorium Association was the ground lessee, for a term of up to 198
years, of land on which it had constructed a building housing an auditorium, galleries, offices, and other rooms. The building had been used as
planned for forty years, during which the Association paid rent and
interest regularly, but virtually no dividends to its stockholders. To make
the investment remunerative, the Association sought to tear the building
down and construct in its place a "large modern commercial building of
greatly increased height." However, nothing in the leases spoke to the
right of the lessee to take such action. Though advised by counsel that it
had the right to proceed, the Association decided to seek the consent of the
lessors and the trustee for the bondholders. Discussion was had with
Willing, one of the lessors, who reported his counsel's opinion that the
lessees had no right to demolish the existing building without consent.
"Several of the lessors were never approached by anyone on behalf of the
association. Nor was the trustee for the bondholders. After this talk with
Willing, a year passed without further occurrence" (pp. 286–87). The
Association then brought a suit in the Illinois courts, in the nature of a bill
to remove a cloud upon title, against all the lessors and the trustee for the
bondholders. Defendants sought to remove the action to federal court on
the basis of diversity of citizenship. The district court dismissed for want
of jurisdiction, but the court of appeals reversed. The Supreme Court, per
Justice Brandeis, held the case not cognizable in a federal court (pp. 288–
90):

"There is not in the bill, or in the evidence, even a suggestion that any
of the defendants had ever done anything which hampered the full enjoyment of the present use and occupancy of the demised premises authorized
by the leases. There was neither hostile act nor a threat. There is no
evidence of a claim of any kind made by any defendant, except the
expression by Willing, in an amicable, private conversation, of an opinion
on a question of law. Then, he merely declined orally to concur in the
opinion of the association that it has the right asserted. * * *

"Obviously, mere refusal by a landlord to agree with a tenant as to the
meaning and effect of a lease, his mere failure to remove obstacles to the
fulfillment of the tenant's desires, is not an actionable wrong, either at law
or in equity. And the case lacks elements essential to the maintenance in
a federal court of a bill to remove a cloud upon title. The alleged doubt as
to plaintiff's right under the leases arises on the face of the instruments by
which the plaintiff derives title. Because of that fact, the doubt is not in
legal contemplation a cloud, and the bill to remove it as such does not lie.
* * * What the plaintiff seeks is simply a declaratory judgment. To
grant that relief is beyond the power conferred upon the federal judiciary.
Liberty Warehouse Co. v. Grannis, 273 U.S. 70, 74. Compare Liberty
Warehouse Co. v. Burley Tobacco Growers' Ass'n, 276 U.S. 71. * * *

"It is true that this is not a moot case ∗ ∗ ∗ and that there is here no attempt to secure an abstract determination by the court of the validity of a statute, as there was in Muskrat v. United States, 219 U.S. 346, 361, and Texas v. Interstate Commerce Commission, 258 U.S. 158, 162. But still the proceeding is not a case or controversy within the meaning of article 3 of the Constitution. The fact that the plaintiff's desires are thwarted by its own doubts, or by the fears of others, does not confer a cause of action. No defendant has wronged the plaintiff or has threatened to do so. Resort to equity to remove such doubts is a proceeding which was unknown to either English or American courts at the time of the adoption of the Constitution and for more than half a century thereafter. ∗ ∗ ∗

"As the proceeding is not a suit within the meaning of section 28 of the Judicial Code, the motions to remand the cause to the state court should have been granted. ∗ ∗ ∗ "

Justice Stone concurred in the result, but chided the Court: "It suffices to say that the suit is plainly not one within the equity jurisdiction conferred by sections 24, 28, of the Judicial Code. But it is unnecessary, and I am therefore not prepared, to go further and say anything in support of the view that Congress may not constitutionally confer on the federal courts jurisdiction to render declaratory judgments in cases where that form of judgment would be an appropriate remedy, or that this Court is without constitutional power to review such judgments of state courts when they involve a federal question" (pp. 290–91).

When the Willing case was decided, several states had already passed declaratory judgment acts; others were considering them; and a proposal for a federal declaratory judgment act was pending in Congress. As a member of the judiciary committee of the House or the Senate, would you have read Justice Brandeis's opinion as meaning that *any* federal declaratory judgment act would be unconstitutional? Or as saying simply that no actual controversy was presented in the Willing case and that *in such a case* Congress was without power to authorize a declaratory judgment? Compare Paragraphs (2) and (3) of the *Note on Advisory Opinions,* pp. 67–69, *supra.*

(2) The possibility that the Supreme Court would hold that it lacked jurisdiction to review decisions of state courts on federal questions in declaratory judgment proceedings raised special problems. Would such decisions nevertheless operate as res judicata? If so, the ultimate power of decision in federal questions would often be lodged in state courts. If not, an important state procedural reform would be rendered ineffectual in every case in which a federal question was involved.

In Fidelity Nat. Bank & Trust Co. v. Swope, 274 U.S. 123 (1927), landholders brought an action in a federal district court to have certain benefit assessments declared void and to secure the cancellation of tax bills issued to defray the costs of the improvements. The defendants, who were purchasers of the tax bills, set up as a bar the decision of a state court in a prior proceeding declaring the assessments and tax bills to be valid.

The Supreme Court assumed that if this state proceeding did not constitute a case or controversy within its appellate jurisdiction under Article III, so that federal claims could not have been reviewed, the judgment would not be res judicata in later proceedings in a federal court. It held, however, that the proceedings were judicial and the judgment binding. Justice Stone, speaking for a unanimous Court, said (p. 132): "While ordinarily a case or judicial controversy results in a judgment requiring award of process of execution to carry it into effect, such relief is not an indispensable adjunct to the exercise of the judicial function." See also Old Colony Trust Co. v. Commissioner, 279 U.S. 716 (1929); Restatement (Second) of Judgments § 33 (1982).

In Nashville, C. & St. L. Ry. v. Wallace, 288 U.S. 249 (1933), the Court for the first time reviewed a declaratory judgment of a state court. The plaintiff had sued the state taxing officials and the state attorney general alleging that they were demanding payment of a certain tax and asking a declaratory judgment that the tax violated the federal Constitution. Justice Stone, again speaking for a unanimous Court, said that the proceeding had all the elements of a traditional bill for an injunction, except that the plaintiffs sought no coercive decree and had not shown that they would suffer irreparable injury if preventive relief were not given. Neither of these elements, the Court held, was essential to the existence of a controversy in the constitutional sense.

(3) Apparently encouraged by the Wallace decision, Congress passed the Federal Declaratory Judgment Act in 1934. 48 Stat. 955. A year later the act was amended to bar declaratory judgments in federal tax cases. 49 Stat. 1027. For the present provisions, see 28 U.S.C. §§ 2201–02.

In Aetna Life Insurance Co. v. Haworth, 300 U.S. 227 (1937), a unanimous Supreme Court, with Justice Brandeis sitting, upheld the Act's constitutionality.

The insurance company had brought the action to secure a declaration that four policies held by the defendant were void by reason of lapse for nonpayment of premiums, and that the company's only obligation under them was to pay $45 on the insured's death as extended insurance on one policy. The complaint asserted that the defendant claimed to be totally and permanently disabled within the meaning of the policies, in which event, it said, the policies would be in full force and the company presently obliged to pay disability benefits under two of them. It said that the defendant, while making this claim repeatedly, had failed to institute any action in which the company would have a chance to prove its falsity. The complaint pointed to the danger that the company might lose the benefit of evidence through disappearance, illness, or death of witnesses, and to the necessity meanwhile of maintaining reserves against the policies in excess of $20,000.

Chief Justice Hughes, writing the opinion, said (pp. 239–40):

" * * * The Declaratory Judgment Act of 1934, in its limitation to 'cases of actual controversy,' manifestly has regard to the constitutional provision and is operative only in respect to controversies which are such in the constitutional sense. The word 'actual' is one of emphasis rather than of definition. Thus the operation of the Declaratory Judgment Act is procedural only. In providing remedies and defining procedure in relation to cases and controversies in the constitutional sense the Congress is acting within its delegated power over the jurisdiction of the federal courts which the Congress is authorized to establish. * * * Exercising this control of practice and procedure the Congress is not confined to traditional forms or traditional remedies."

After reviewing the earlier constitutional cases, the opinion continued (pp. 242–44):

"There is here a dispute between parties who face each other in an adversary proceeding. The dispute relates to legal rights and obligations arising from the contracts of insurance. The dispute is definite and concrete, not hypothetical or abstract. Prior to this suit, the parties had taken adverse positions with respect to their existing obligations. Their contentions concerned the disability benefits which were to be payable upon prescribed conditions. On the one side, the insured claimed that he had become totally and permanently disabled and hence was relieved of the obligation to continue the payment of premiums and was entitled to the stipulated disability benefits and to the continuance of the policies in force. The insured presented this claim formally, as required by the policies. It was a claim of a present, specific right. On the other side, the company made an equally definite claim that the alleged basic fact did not exist, that the insured was not totally and permanently disabled and had not been relieved of the duty to continue the payment of premiums, that in consequence the policies had lapsed, and that the company was thus freed from its obligation either to pay disability benefits or to continue the insurance in force. Such a dispute is manifestly susceptible of judicial determination. It calls, not for an advisory opinion upon a hypothetical basis, but for an adjudication of present right upon established facts. * * *

"If the insured had brought suit to recover the disability benefits currently payable under two of the policies there would have been no question that the controversy was of a justiciable nature, whether or not the amount involved would have permitted its determination in a federal court. Again, on repudiation by the insurer of liability in such a case and insistence by the insured that the repudiation was unjustified because of his disability, the insured would have 'such an interest in the preservation of the contracts that he might maintain a suit in equity to declare them still in being.' Burnet v. Wells, 289 U.S. 670, 680; Cohen v. New York Life Insurance Co., 50 N.Y. 610, 624; Fidelity National Bank & Trust Co. v. Swope, *supra.* But the character of the controversy and of the issue to be determined is essentially the same whether it is presented by the insured or by the insurer."

(4) If the Willing case had arisen after the Haworth case, would the Court have held that an "actual controversy" was presented?

(5) The Haworth case effectively disposed of a strict view, taken by some lower federal courts, that the statutory grant of jurisdiction to declare "rights and other legal relations" did not warrant a declaration of non-liability. Is this not actually one of the areas in which the declaratory judgment is most useful?

Would it be a safe generalization to say that an actual controversy always exists if either party could maintain an action for coercive relief?

(6) Should a plaintiff be able to secure a declaration concerning a contingent liability?

When an action has been brought against an insured, and the insurance company is under duty to defend and to pay any judgment if the accident is within the scope of the policy, many cases permit either the company or the insured to maintain an action for a declaratory judgment to determine the issue of coverage. *E.g.,* Transit Casualty Co. v. Snow, 584

F.2d 97 (5th Cir.1978); Sears, Roebuck & Co. v. American Mut. Liability Ins. Co., 372 F.2d 435 (7th Cir.1967); *cf.* Provident Tradesmens Bank & Trust Co. v. Patterson, 390 U.S. 102, 125–28 (1968) (suit for declaratory judgment brought by injured party against insurer).

(7) The defendant in the Haworth case had formally assumed an adverse position by filing a written claim. Is it essential to the existence of an "actual controversy" that the defendant have taken an adverse position before the action was filed? Why? To insure an adverse presentation? Or to insure that the resources of private settlement have been exhausted? With what degree of formality must the defendant have announced his position? [1]

(8) The dispute in the Haworth case turned upon the legal consequences of past events which, however controverted, could be determined with formal definiteness so as to pose precise legal issues. Under what circumstances, if any, should a plaintiff be able to obtain a declaration of the legal consequences of future conduct?

This issue sometimes arises when a plaintiff having an established position, or pursuing a continuing course of conduct, wishes to prevent action by the defendant prejudicial to his position. If he seeks an injunction, he must show a definite threat of definite action by the defendant, which gives concreteness to the legal issue and makes the situation analogous to that of a present wrong. *Cf.* Meredith v. Winter Haven, 320 U.S. 228 (1943), involving a prayer both for a declaration and for an injunction. If the prayer is only for a declaration, should the requirement of a definitely formulated threat be dispensed with? *Cf.* Nashville, C. & St. L. Ry. v. Wallace, Paragraph (2), *supra.* If not, wouldn't the significance of the declaratory judgment in this type of case be limited to relieving the plaintiff of the need of showing that his common law remedies are inadequate?

A more difficult question is presented if the plaintiff wishes to embark on a new course of conduct and to prevent the defendant from interfering with it. Here the situation is doubly contingent. Will the plaintiff really take the proposed action and, if so, exactly what action? Will the defendant then really interfere with him, and, if so, exactly how? To what extent should declaratory relief be made available to guide plaintiffs in circumstances of this kind?

The problem often arises when a person who has not yet manufactured or sold a product brings an action against a patentee of the product for a declaratory judgment of invalidity or noninfringement. Here, the courts generally insist on a showing of immediate intention and ability to engage in the activity in question—manufacture, use, or sale of the patented product—as a basis for entertaining the action. Compare International Harvester Co. v. Deere & Co., 623 F.2d 1207 (7th Cir.1980) (action not entertained), with Super Products Corp. v. D P Way Corp., 546 F.2d 748 (7th Cir.1976) (action entertained).

---

1. See Treemond Co. v. Schering Corp., 122 F.2d 702 (3d Cir.1941) (action for a declaratory judgment of patent invalidity and noninfringement; court holds that while notification of claim of infringement is prerequisite to justiciability, notice need not be formal or given directly to plaintiff); Sweetheart Plastics, Inc. v. Illinois Tool Works, Inc., 439 F.2d 871, 874 (1st Cir. 1971) (emphasizing "reasonable apprehension" of an infringement suit as the touchstone of justiciability in such a case).

(9) The statute says that in a "case of actual controversy within its jurisdiction" a federal court "may" give a declaratory judgment. 28 U.S.C. § 2201. (Virtually all state statutes contain similar language.) Because of the discretionary character of the remedy, opinions denying relief often leave it doubtful whether the court thought that a controversy was lacking or simply that declaratory relief was inappropriate. The issue of discretion is frequently posed as one of determining whether a declaration will serve "a useful purpose". Among the factors bearing on this issue are whether a declaration would terminate the uncertainty or controversy giving rise to the proceeding—a factor made explicit in the Uniform Declaratory Judgments Act; the convenience of the parties; the public interest in a settlement; and the availability and relative convenience of other remedies. See generally 10A Wright & Miller, Federal Practice and Procedure §§ 2751, 2759 (1983); Borchard, Declaratory Judgments 293–314 (2d ed. 1941). See also Fed.R.Civ.P. 57.

UNITED PUBLIC WORKERS v. MITCHELL

330 U.S. 75, 67 S.Ct. 556, 91 L.Ed. 754 (1947).
Appeal from the District Court for the District of Columbia.

MR. JUSTICE REED delivered the opinion of the Court. * * *

The present appellants sought an injunction before a statutory three judge district court of the District of Columbia against appellees, members of the United States Civil Service Commission, to prohibit them from enforcing against petitioners the provisions of the second sentence of § 9(a) of the Hatch Act for the reason that the sentence is repugnant to the Constitution of the United States. A declaratory judgment of the unconstitutionality of the sentence was also sought. The sentence referred to reads, "No officer or employee in the executive branch of the Federal Government * * * shall take any active part in political management or in political campaigns."

[The Act imposes a penalty of dismissal from employment for its violation. The act also provides that activities theretofore forbidden to civil service employees by the civil service rules shall be deemed to be within its prohibitions for all federal employees. The relevant part of the applicable Civil Service Rule, 5 C.F.R., Cum.Supp. § 1.1 reads:

["Persons who by the provisions of the rules in this chapter are in the competitive classified service, while retaining the right to vote as they please and to express their opinion on all political subjects, shall take no active part in political management or in political campaigns."]

Various individual employees of the federal executive civil service and the United Public Workers of America,[10] a labor union with these and other executive employees as members, as a representative of all its members, joined in the suit. It is alleged that the individuals desire to engage in acts of political management and in political campaigns. Their purposes are as stated in the excerpt from the complaint set out in the

---

10. No contention that appellant, United Public Workers of America (C.I.O.), lacked capacity to bring this action is made by appellees. We need not consider the question here. McCandless v. Furlaud, 293 U.S. 67, 73, 74. See Fishgold v. Sullivan Drydock & Repair Corp., 328 U.S. 275.

margin.[11] From the affidavits it is plain, and we so assume, that these activities will be carried on completely outside of the hours of employment. Appellants challenge the second sentence of § 9(a) as unconstitutional for various reasons. They are set out below in the language of the complaint.[12]

None of the appellants, except George P. Poole, has violated the provisions of the Hatch Act. They wish to act contrary to its provisions and those of § 1 of the Civil Service Rules and desire a declaration of the legally permissible limits of regulation. Defendants moved to dismiss the complaint for lack of a justiciable case or controversy. The District Court determined that each of these individual appellants had an interest in their claimed privilege of engaging in political activities, sufficient to give them a right to maintain this suit. United Federal Workers of America (C.I.O.) v. Mitchell, D.C., 56 F.Supp. 621, 624. The District Court further determined that the questioned provision of the Hatch Act was valid and that the complaint therefore failed to state a cause of action. It accordingly dismissed the complaint and granted summary judgment to defendants.

* * *

Second. At the threshold of consideration, we are called upon to decide whether the complaint states a controversy cognizable in this Court. We defer consideration of the cause of action of Mr. Poole until section *Three* of this opinion. The other individual employees have elaborated the grounds of their objection in individual affidavits for use in the hearing on the summary judgment. We select as an example one that contains the

11. "In discharge of their duties of citizenship, of their right to vote, and in exercise of their constitutional rights of freedom of speech, of the press, of assembly, and the right to engage in political activity, the individual plaintiffs desire to engage in the following acts: write for publication letters and articles in support of candidates for office; be connected editorially with publications which are identified with the legislative program of UFWA [former name of the present union appellant] and candidates who support it; solicit votes, aid in getting out voters, act as accredited checker, watcher, or challenger; transport voters to and from the polls without compensation therefor; participate in and help in organizing political parades; initiate petitions, and canvass for the signatures of others on such petitions; serve as party ward committeeman or other party official; and perform any and all acts not prohibited by any provision of law other than the second sentence of Section 9(a) and Section 15 of the Hatch Act, which constitute taking an active part in political management and political campaigns."

12. "The second sentence of Section 9(a) of the Hatch Act is repugnant to the Constitution of the United States as a deprivation of freedom of speech, of the press, and of assembly in violation of the First Amendment.

"The second sentence of Section 9(a) of the Hatch Act is repugnant to the Constitution of the United States as a deprivation of the fundamental right of the people of the United States to engage in political activity, reserved to the people of the United States by the Ninth and Tenth Amendments.

"The second sentence of Section 9(a) of the Hatch Act is repugnant to the Constitution of the United States, since it unreasonably prohibits Federal employees from engaging in activities which may be lawfully carried on by persons who are not Federal employees, thus constituting a deprivation of liberty in violation of the Fifth Amendment.

"The second sentence of Section 9(a) of the Hatch Act is repugnant to the Constitution of the United States since it effects an arbitrary and grossly unreasonable discrimination between employees of the Federal Government in the classified civil service subject to its provisions and employees specifically exempted therefrom, in violation of the Fifth Amendment.

"The second sentence of Section 9(a) of the Hatch Act is repugnant to the Constitution of the United States since it is so vague and indefinite as to prohibit lawful activities as well as activities which are properly made unlawful by other provisions of law, in violation of the Fifth Amendment."

essential averments of all the others and print below the portions with significance in this suit.[18] Nothing similar to the fourth paragraph of the printed affidavit is contained in the other affidavits. The assumed controversy between affiant and the Civil Service Commission as to affiant's right to act as watcher at the polls on November 2, 1943, had long been moot when this complaint was filed. We do not therefore treat this allegation separately. The affidavits it will be noticed, follow the generality of purpose expressed by the complaint. See note 11 *supra*. They declare a desire to act contrary to the rule against political activity but not that the rule has been violated. In this respect, we think they differ from the type of threat adjudicated in Railway Mail Association v. Corsi, 326 U.S. 88. In that case, the refusal to admit an applicant to membership in a labor union on account of race was involved. Admission had been refused. 326 U.S. at page 93, note 10. Definite action had also been taken in Hill v. Florida, 325 U.S. 538. In the Hill case an injunction had been sought and allowed against Hill and the union forbidding Hill from acting as the business agent of the union and the union from further functioning as a union until it complied with the state law. The threats which menaced the affiants of these affidavits in the case now being considered are closer to a general threat by officials to enforce those laws which they are charged to administer, compare Watson v. Buck, 313 U.S. 387, 400, than they are to the direct threat of punishment against a named organization for a completed act that made the Mail Association and the Hill cases justiciable.

18. "At this time, when the fate of the entire world is in the balance, I believe it is not only proper but an obligation for all citizens to participate actively in the making of the vital political decisions on which the success of the war and the permanence of the peace to follow so largely depend. For the purpose of participating in the making of these decisions it is my earnest desire to engage actively in political management and political campaigns. I wish to engage in such activity upon my own time, as a private citizen.

"I wish to engage in such activities on behalf of those candidates for public office who I believe will best serve the needs of this country and with the object of persuading others of the correctness of my judgments and of electing the candidates of my choice. This objective I wish to pursue by all proper means such as engaging in discussion, by speeches to conventions, rallies and other assemblages, by publicizing my views in letters and articles for publication in newspapers and other periodicals, by aiding in the campaign of candidates for political office by posting banners and posters in public places, by distributing leaflets, by 'ringing doorbells', by addressing campaign literature, and by doing any and all acts of like character reasonably designed to assist in the election of candidates I favor.

"I desire to engage in these activities freely, openly, and without concealment.

However, I understand that the second sentence of Section 9(a) of the Hatch Act and the Rules of the C.S.C. provide that if I engage in this activity, the Civil Service Commission will order that I be dismissed from federal employment. Such deprivation of my job in the federal government would be a source of immediate and serious financial loss and other injury to me.

"At the last Congressional election I was very much interested in the outcome of the campaign and offered to help the party of my choice by being a watcher at the polls. I obtained a watcher's certificate but I was advised that there might be some question of my right to use the certificate and retain my federal employment. Therefore, on November 1, 1943, the day before the election, I called the regional office of the Civil Service Commission in Philadelphia and spoke to a person who gave his name as * * *. Mr. * * * stated that if I used my watcher's certificate, the Civil Service Commission would see that I was dismissed from my job at the * * * for violation of the Hatch Act. I, therefore, did not use the certificate as I had intended.

"I believe that Congress may not constitutionally abridge my right to engage in the political activities mentioned above. However, unless the courts prevent the Civil Service Commission from enforcing this unconstitutional law, I will be unable freely to exercise my rights as a citizen." [Identifying words omitted.]

As is well known, the federal courts established pursuant to Article III of the Constitution do not render advisory opinions. For adjudication of constitutional issues, "concrete legal issues, presented in actual cases, not abstractions" are requisite. This is as true of declaratory judgments as any other field. These appellants seem clearly to seek advisory opinions upon broad claims of rights protected by the First, Fifth, Ninth and Tenth Amendments to the Constitution. As these appellants are classified employees, they have a right superior to the generality of citizens, compare Fairchild v. Hughes, 258 U.S. 126, but the facts of their personal interest in their civil rights, of the general threat of possible interference with those rights by the Civil Service Commission under its rules, if specified things are done by appellants, does not make a justiciable case or controversy. Appellants want to engage in "political management and political campaigns," to persuade others to follow appellants' views by discussion, speeches, articles and other acts reasonably designed to secure the selection of appellants' political choices. Such generality of objection is really an attack on the political expediency of the Hatch Act, not the presentation of legal issues. It is beyond the competence of courts to render such a decision. State of Texas v. Interstate Commerce Commission, 258 U.S. 158, 162.

The power of courts, and ultimately of this Court to pass upon the constitutionality of acts of Congress arises only when the interests of litigants require the use of this judicial authority for their protection against actual interference. A hypothetical threat is not enough. We can only speculate as to the kinds of political activity the appellants desire to engage in or as to the contents of their proposed public statements or the circumstances of their publication. It would not accord with judicial responsibility to adjudge, in a matter involving constitutionality, between the freedom of the individual and the requirements of public order except when definite rights appear upon the one side and definite prejudicial interferences upon the other.

The Constitution allots the nation's judicial power to the federal courts. Unless these courts respect the limits of that unique authority, they intrude upon powers vested in the legislative or executive branches. * * * Should the courts seek to expand their power so as to bring under their jurisdiction ill-defined controversies over constitutional issues, they would become the organ of political theories. Such abuse of judicial power would properly meet rebuke and restriction from other branches. * * * No threat of interference by the Commission with rights of these appellants appears beyond that implied by the existence of the law and the regulations. * * * These reasons lead us to conclude that the determination of the trial court, that the individual appellants, other than Poole, could maintain this action, was erroneous.

Third. The appellant Poole does present by the complaint and affidavit matters appropriate for judicial determination. The affidavits filed by appellees confirm that Poole has been charged by the Commission with political activity and a proposed order for his removal from his position adopted subject to his right under Commission procedure to reply to the charges and to present further evidence in refutation. We proceed to consider the controversy over constitutional power at issue between Poole and the Commission as defined by the charge and preliminary finding upon one side and the admissions of Poole's affidavit upon the other. Our determination is limited to those facts. This proceeding so limited meets the requirements of defined rights and a definite threat to interfere with a possessor of the menaced rights by a penalty for an act done in violation of the claimed restraint.

Because we conclude hereinafter that the prohibition of § 9 of the Hatch Act and Civil Service Rule 1, * * *, are valid, it is unnecessary to consider, as this is a declaratory judgment action, whether or not this appellant sufficiently alleges that an irreparable injury to him would result from his removal from his position. Nor need we inquire whether or not a court of equity would enforce by injunction any judgment declaring rights. Since Poole admits that he violated the rule against political activity and that removal from office is therefore mandatory under the act, there is no question as to the exhaustion of administrative remedies. * * * Under such circumstances, we see no reason why a declaratory judgment action, even though constitutional issues are involved, does not lie. See Rules of Civil Procedure, Rule 57. Steele v. Louisville & Nashville Railroad Co., 323 U.S. 192, 197, 207; Tunstall v. Brotherhood of Locomotive Firemen & Enginemen, 323 U.S. 210, 212, *et seq.* * * *

[The Court held that Poole had violated the Act, and that the Act as applied to him was valid.

[MR. JUSTICE FRANKFURTER delivered a concurring opinion dealing with a point of appellate procedure.

[MR. JUSTICE BLACK delivered a dissenting opinion, expressing the view that all the complaints stated a case or controversy, and that the Act as applied in all the cases was invalid.]

MR. JUSTICE DOUGLAS, dissenting in part.

I disagree with the Court on two of the four matters decided.

First. There are twelve individual appellants here asking for an adjudication of their rights. The Court passes on the claim of only one of them, Poole. It declines to pass on the claims of the other eleven on the ground that they do not present justiciable cases or controversies. With this conclusion I cannot agree.

* * *

The declaratory judgment procedure is designed "to declare rights and other legal relations of any interested party * * * whether or not further relief is or could be prayed." Judicial Code, § 274d, 28 U.S.C. § 400, 28 U.S.C.A. § 400. The fact that equity would not restrain a wrongful removal of an office holder but would leave the complainant to his legal remedies, White v. Berry, *supra,* is, therefore, immaterial. A judgment which, without more, adjudicates the status of a person is permissible under the Declaratory Judgment Act. Perkins v. Elg, 307 U.S. 325, 349, 350. The "declaration of a status was perhaps the earliest exercise of this procedure." H.R. No. 1264, 73d Cong., 2d Sess., p. 2. The right to hold an office or public position against such threats is a common example of its use. Borchard, Declaratory Judgments (2d ed.), pp. 858 *et seq.* Declaratory relief is the singular remedy available here to preserve the status quo while the constitutional rights of these appellants to make these utterances and to engage in these activities are determined. The threat against them is real not fanciful, immediate not remote. The case is therefore an actual not a hypothetical one. And the present case seems to me to be a good example of a situation where uncertainty, peril, and insecurity result from imminent and immediate threats to asserted rights.

Since the Court does not reach the constitutionality of the claims of these eleven individual appellants, a discussion of them would seem to be premature. * * *

NOTE ON "RIPENESS" IN PUBLIC LITIGATION CHALLENGING THE VALIDITY OR APPLICATION OF STATUTES AND REGULATIONS

(1) In cases like Mitchell, plaintiffs are challenging statutes (or regulations), or their interpretation by government officials. Plaintiffs in these cases generally allege that they intend to violate the law as written, or as interpreted by the defendant officials, or that they have been deterred from engaging in certain activities by the existence of the law or by its interpretation; they commonly seek a declaration of invalidity, or an injunction against enforcement, or both.

In cases of this kind, courts generally examine, under the heading of ripeness, such questions as the extent of any injury presently suffered by plaintiffs, the likelihood that they will engage in future conduct that could expose them to some sanction (or would so engage if not threatened with sanctions), and the probable response of the defendant officials if the conduct occurs. An exhaustive catalogue of these decisions, even limited to those in the Supreme Court, is beyond the scope of this Note. See generally 13A Wright, Miller & Cooper, Federal Practice and Procedure §§ 3532–3532.6 (1984). But a review and analysis of the leading decisions may give some sense of how these factors have been applied. In your study of these materials, consider whether a coherent doctrine has developed, or is emerging, and whether the results have been affected by the Justices' perceptions of the appropriate role of adjudication. See pp. 79–82, *supra*. Consider also the extent to which premature adjudication may increase the risk of an unduly broad opinion, and may expend judicial resources unnecessarily.

The discussion that follows considers separately those actions that do not involve challenges to criminal statutes (Paragraphs (2)–(6)), and those that do (Paragraph (7)). The distinction may be of some analytical value in view of the traditionally greater reluctance of civil courts to interfere in the administration of the criminal law, especially when questions of federal-state relations are involved. See, *e.g.*, Younger v. Harris, p. 1383, *infra*. But you should not attach too much significance to the use of these two categories.

(2) International Longshoremen's Union v. Boyd, 347 U.S. 222 (1954), may be the high water mark of the Court's ripeness decisions. Plaintiff union and some of its resident-alien members sued for an injunction and declaratory judgment against a construction of the Immigration and Nationality Act of 1952 that would treat aliens domiciled in the continental United States, upon their return from temporary work in Alaska, as if they were aliens entering the United States for the first time. (The grounds for exclusion of aliens were much broader than those for deportation.) Plaintiffs also alleged that such a construction would be unconstitutional. The

action was begun before the union members departed from the continental United States, but the record showed that over three thousand union members, including aliens, worked in the canneries in Alaska every summer fishing season. The district court entertained the suit on the merits, but the Supreme Court held that no "case or controversy" had been presented. Justice Frankfurter, for the Court, characterized the action as "not a lawsuit to enforce a right; it is an endeavor to obtain a court's assurance that a statute does not govern hypothetical situations that may or may not make the challenged statute applicable. Determination of the scope and constitutionality of legislation in advance of its immediate adverse effect in the context of a concrete case involves too remote and abstract an inquiry for the proper exercise of the judicial function [citing UPW v. Mitchell; Muskrat; and Alabama State Federation of Labor v. McAdory, 325 U.S. 450 (1945)]" (p. 224). Justice Black, dissenting, noted that the administrator had made clear his position that the statute applied, and that by the time of decision, workers had already gone to Alaska and been processed on return as new entrants.

Do Boyd and Mitchell imply that plaintiff must actually have engaged in the conduct in question in order for the operative facts to be sufficiently definite and specific? If so, their authority has plainly been weakened by the cases discussed in the remainder of this Note.

(3) Adler v. Board of Education, 342 U.S. 485 (1952), was a state court action for a declaratory judgment (that a provision of the New York Civil Service Law, as implemented by the "Feinberg Law," violated the Fourteenth Amendment) and for injunctive relief. The underlying statute required the dismissal of public school teachers who advocated the "doctrine that any government in the United States should be overthrown or overturned by force or violence" or who belonged to any organization so advocating. The implementing Feinberg Law directed the state board of regents to issue regulations for the enforcement of this provision. It also directed the board, after appropriate notice and hearing, to "make a listing of organizations which it finds to be subversive in that they advocate, advise, teach or embrace the doctrine" just referred to. It directed the board, in addition, to provide by rule that any teacher's membership in a listed organization should constitute *prima facie* evidence of disqualification for a teaching position. Listed organizations were given a right of judicial review. Individual teachers, before being dismissed or denied employment, were given a right to a hearing and also to judicial review.

The Board of Regents had issued the required rules, including rules for securing reports on individual teachers; and it appeared that the defendant Board of Education had issued an order—not in the record—elaborating the reporting provisions. The Board of Regents had announced its intention to publish the required list of proscribed organizations; but it did not appear that it had yet done so. The defendant Board of Education was holding enforcement in abeyance pending the outcome of the action.

The plaintiffs were two municipal taxpayers complaining of threatened waste of funds, two parents complaining of the effect on their children's education, and four teachers in city schools. They contended *inter alia* that the statute imposed invalid limitations on freedom of speech, press and assembly; that it constituted a bill of attainder; and that the presumptive significance attached to membership in listed organizations denied due process of law.

The New York Court of Appeals rejected these attacks, finding in the statute "no restriction which exceeds the legislature's constitutional power". 301 N.Y. 476, 495. This judgment the Supreme Court affirmed.

Justice Minton, joined by five other justices, held that the statute and the rules did not deprive persons employed or seeking employment in the New York Schools of "any right to free speech or assembly" (342 U.S. at 492); that the presumption of disqualification based on knowing membership in a listed organization did not offend due process; and that the term "subversive" as used in the statute was not unconstitutionally vague and indefinite. He concluded: "We find no constitutional infirmity * * * in the Feinberg Law * * *" (p. 496).

Justice Douglas, joined by Justice Black, dissented, saying (p. 511):

" * * * The Framers knew the danger of dogmatism; they also knew the strength that comes when the mind is free, when ideas may be pursued wherever they lead. We forget these teachings of the First Amendment when we sustain this law."

Justice Frankfurter was alone on the Court in even noticing a jurisdictional problem. He concluded that the appeal should be dismissed "in accordance with the settled limits upon our jurisdiction", saying *inter alia* (p. 504):

* * *

"The allegations in the present action fall short of those found insufficient in the Mitchell case. These teachers do not allege that they have engaged in proscribed conduct or that they have any intention to do so. They do not suggest that they have been, or are, deterred from supporting causes or from joining organizations for fear of the Feinberg Law's interdict, except to say generally that the system complained of will have this effect on teachers as a group. They do not assert that they are threatened with action under the law, or that steps are imminent whereby they would incur the hazard of punishment for conduct innocent at the time, or under standards too vague to satisfy due process of law. They merely allege that the statutes and Rules permit such action against some teachers. Since we rightly refused in the Mitchell case to hear government employees whose conduct was much more intimately affected by the law there attacked than are the claims of plaintiffs here, this suit is wanting in the necessary basis for our review."

(4) In the Adler case, could the decision on the available record mean any more than that the statute was susceptible of valid applications? If the contestants were prepared to defend the extreme submission that there could be no valid applications, should they be denied a forum for that purpose? [1] Or should the Court resist pressure from litigants to hand down such general pronouncements without being afforded the alternative of limiting its judgment to the validity of particular applications?

1. In Keyishian v. Board of Regents, 385 U.S. 589 (1967), the Court overturned Adler on the merits, holding invalid substantial portions of the Feinberg Law and some amendments to it. Adler was characterized as "a declaratory judgment suit in which the Court held, in effect, that there was no constitutional infirmity in [the New York Civil Service Law] or in the Feinberg Law on their faces and that they were capable of constitutional application" (p. 594).

In Times Film Corp. v. Chicago, 365 U.S. 43 (1961), plaintiff motion picture distributor refused to submit a film to the censorship board. After being denied a permit to show the movie, it sought injunctive relief from a federal court on the grounds that the ordinance was void on its face as a prior restraint. Both lower courts dismissed the suit as unripe. The court of appeals even stated: "In its complaint, plaintiff has limited its statement of the facts in an obvious attempt to so frame its case that the United States Supreme Court will be persuaded to rule upon the question of constitutionality of motion picture censorship, a course from which ∗ ∗ ∗ the Court has carefully abstained." 272 F.2d 90, 91 (7th Cir.1959). The Supreme Court, however, was "satisfied that a justiciable controversy exists. ∗ ∗ ∗ The claim is that this concrete and specific statutory requirement, the production of the film at the office of the Commissioner for examination, is invalid as a previous restraint on freedom of speech. ∗ ∗ ∗ [T]he broad justiciable issue is therefore present as to whether the ambit of constitutional protection includes complete and absolute freedom to exhibit, at least once, any and every kind of motion picture. It is that question alone which we decide" (pp. 45–46). The ordinance was upheld, over sharp dissent on the merits.[2]

(5) After receiving short shrift in Adler, Mitchell may have been further weakened in United States Civil Service Commission v. National Ass'n of Letter Carriers, 413 U.S. 548 (1973), in which the Court, without discussing ripeness, entertained and rejected on the merits anticipatory attacks on § 9(a) of the Hatch Act as facially vague and overbroad. The union plaintiff alleged that its members desired to run for public and party office as well as participate in political campaigns, but were deterred from doing so by Civil Service Commission enforcement or threats of enforcement of the Hatch Act. In addition, one individual plaintiff alleged that he was "compelled to engage" in prohibited activity in order to perform his duties as a Union officer and had in fact engaged in the proscribed conduct. Another alleged that he had resigned from full-time federal employment to run for public office and had been frustrated and delayed in obtaining reemployment with the same federal agency after his political defeat "because of the dispute over his political activities while acting as a consultant" to the government during the campaign (p. 551 n. 3).

The Court reaffirmed the substantive holding in Mitchell (reached there as to plaintiff Poole) that the statute was valid as to "plainly identifiable acts of political management and political campaigning" (p. 567), and held that the Act (as interpreted in Civil Service Commission regulations) was not unconstitutionally vague or overbroad.

Can Letter Carriers be adequately distinguished from Mitchell solely on the basis of the different factual situations presented by the various plaintiffs in the two cases? In the interim between the two cases, there had of course been substantial experience in operation under the statute as

---

2. For a critical analysis of Times Film, see Bickel, The Least Dangerous Branch 133–43 (1962).

For cases allowing facial challenges (and rejecting them on the merits) while reserving questions relating to particular applications, see, e.g., California v. LaRue, 409 U.S. 109, 118–19 (1972); Hodel v. Virginia Surface Mining & Reclamation Ass'n, Inc., 452 U.S. 264 (1981); cf. Dames & Moore v. Regan, 453 U.S. 654, 688–90 (1981) (in Iranian assets case, question whether suspension of claims would constitute a taking is premature, but question whether petitioner would have a remedy in the Court of Claims in that event is ripe for review).

well as continual interpretation and administration of it by the Civil Service Commission (known and apparently accepted by Congress). The Court relied on these facts in deciding the merits. Are they also relevant to the ripeness of the case for decision? [3]

(6) In Buckley v. Valeo, 424 U.S. 1 (1976), for example, the Court upheld the justiciability of an action for declaratory and injunctive relief attacking the constitutionality of all the major elements of the Federal Election Campaign Act of 1971, as amended in 1974: limitation of political contributions and expenditures, requirements of disclosure and recordkeeping of a wide range of such contributions and expenditures, public financing of national party conventions and presidential campaigns, and the constituting of a Federal Election Commission with responsibility for administering the Act. Plaintiffs included a Presidential candidate and a committee organized on his behalf, a United States Senator running for reelection, a potential contributor, and a number of political organizations. The action, which was instituted shortly after enactment of the amending statute, was based in part on § 315(a) of the Act, 2 U.S.C. § 437h, providing that: "The Commission, the national committee of any political party, or any individual eligible to vote in any election for the office of President of the United States may institute such actions in the appropriate district court of the United States, including actions for declaratory judgment, as may be appropriate to construe the constitutionality of any provision of this Act [or related sections of 18 U.S.C., the Criminal Code]." Because of the special expediting provisions of that section, the case was orally argued before the Supreme Court on November 10, 1975, and decided on January 30, 1976, near the beginning of the first national election campaign to be governed by the amended Act.

The Court passed on the merits of all the contentions with only the briefest treatment of justiciability of the case as a whole, concluding (p. 12): "In our view, the complaint in this case demonstrates that at least some of the appellants have a sufficient 'personal stake' in a determination of the constitutional validity of each of the challenged provisions to present 'a real and substantial controversy admitting of specific relief through a decree of conclusive character, as distinguished from an opinion advising what the law would be upon a hypothetical state of facts.' Aetna Life Insurance Co. v. Haworth, supra, 300 U.S. [227], at 241." [4]

3. More recently, in Clemens v. Fashing, 457 U.S. 957 (1982), the Court unanimously upheld the justiciability of a challenge by state judicial officers to state constitutional provisions (a) making them ineligible to run for the state legislature during their term of office and (b) providing that an announcement of candidacy for any other office would result in automatic loss of their judicial post. Each plaintiff alleged that but for (b), he would announce his candidacy for higher judicial office and one said that but for (a), he would run for the legislature during his term. In a brief section of the opinion, the Court said that the challenge to (a) was not abstract or hypothetical and that as to (b): "Unlike the situation in Mitchell, [plaintiff] appellees have alleged in a precise manner that, but for the sanctions of the constitutional provision they seek to challenge, they would engage in the very acts that would trigger the enforcement of the provision" (p. 962).

Is this enough of a distinction? Does the reference to "very acts" in the quoted passage suggest that the applicability of the statute to the conduct in question was clearer than in Mitchell? Note too the self-executing aspect of the statutory provisions.

4. The attack on the validity of the Federal Election Commission's authority to issue regulations and perform other functions assigned by the Act—based upon the fact that its members were not appointed by the President (with or without the consent of the Senate) under Art. II, Sec. 2— gave the Court additional pause. The

How relevant to the Article III issue was Congress' direction for speedy adjudication? Would the consequences of deferring adjudication—possibly until after the 1976 campaign—have been unusually troublesome? If so, should that point have been made explicit?[5]

(7) The problems involved in the consideration of challenges to criminal statutes overlap in many respects those already discussed. Should it suffice, for example, that the plaintiff claims injury by virtue of the law's existence, or must he also show a threat of enforcement by a particular official? Should such a requirement be viewed as only a drily logical corollary of the principle of sovereign immunity—that the quarrel must be with the official and not with the statute book[6]—or should it be seen as serving a function also in assuring that the law does indeed apply and that the controversy is sufficiently concrete? Is this function significant only when the application of the statute to the conduct in question is a matter of some doubt?

Challenges to criminal statutes also confront the traditional doctrine—often honored in the breach—that equity will not enjoin a criminal prosecution. Should there be any special reluctance to entertain preventive attacks on criminal laws? On *state* criminal laws? *Cf.* Note, *Declaratory Relief in the Criminal Law*, 80 Harv.L.Rev. 1401 (1967); Chap. X, Sec. 2(C), *infra*.

In Pierce v. Society of Sisters, 268 U.S. 510 (1925), two private schools were allowed to maintain an action to enjoin the enforcement of a criminal statute requiring parents and guardians to send their children to public school, although the measure was not to be effective for several years. The complaints alleged that the defendant officials had announced their intention to proceed under the law, and that as a result parents were withdraw-

court of appeals had held that the issue relating to the Commission's method of appointment was not "ripe" for decision. The Supreme Court disagreed. Noting that since the judgment of the lower court the Commission had undertaken to issue regulations, and that as to yet unexercised powers, "the date of their all but certain exercise is now closer by several months than it was at the time the Court of Appeals ruled" (pp. 116–17), the Supreme Court held the issue was ripe for decision. The opinion buttressed this conclusion by relying on the finding that Congress was "most concerned with obtaining a final adjudication of as many issues as possible litigated pursuant to the provisions of § 437h" (p. 117). The Court held the Commission invalidly constituted to perform some of the major functions assigned to it, but delayed the effectiveness of that holding to give Congress time to establish a properly appointed body.

5. For other challenges to regulatory statutes, or to their interpretation, since Buckley v. Valeo, see Thomas v. Union Carbide Agr. Prods. Co., 473 U.S. 568, 579–82 (1985); Pacific Gas & Electric Co. v. State Energy Resources Conserv. & Devel. Com'n, 461 U.S. 190, 200–03 (1983); Sea-train Shipbldg. Co. v. Shell Oil Co., 444 U.S. 572, 581–83 (1980); Vance v. Universal Amusement Co., Inc., 445 U.S. 308 (1980). In each of these cases the controversy was held justiciable in whole or in substantial part; in Vance, the issue of ripeness was raised only in the dissent. Compare Williamson County Regional Planning Com'n v. Hamilton Bank, 473 U.S. 172 (1985) (challenge to zoning ordinance, on grounds of taking without just compensation, is not ripe until final state decision has been rendered regarding application of the ordinance); Ohio Civil Rights Com'n v. Dayton Christian Schools, Inc., 477 U.S. 619, 629 (1986) (concurring opinion) (challenge to the constitutionality of an antidiscrimination statute as applied to sectarian schools is not ripe prior to the imposition of any sanction).

See also Paragraph (12), *infra*.

6. See Chap. IX, Secs. 1(B), 2(A), *infra*. For a forceful statement of the close relationship between the "case or controversy" concept and the doctrine of sovereign immunity, with suggestions for the rethinking of both, see Monaghan, *Constitutional Adjudication: The Who and When*, 82 Yale L.J. 1363 (1973) (especially pp. 1386–89).

ing children or refusing to enter them in complainants' schools, to their immediate and irreparable injury.

In Poe v. Ullman, 367 U.S. 497 (1961), married persons and their doctor brought a state court action for a declaratory judgment of the unconstitutionality of the state's law prohibiting the use of contraceptive devices or the giving of medical advice about them. An appeal from the state supreme court's decision upholding the statute was dismissed for nonjusticiability, with the plurality emphasizing the absence of any specific threat of enforcement, as well as the long history of non-enforcement.[7]

Yet only a few years later, in Epperson v. Arkansas, 393 U.S. 97 (1968), the Court held justiciable an attack on a 1928 state law prohibiting the teaching of evolution, even though there was no record of any prosecution under the statute. The law might be "more of a curiosity than a vital fact of life," but it was "properly here [on appeal from a state court], and it is our duty to decide the issues presented" (p. 102).

In Doe v. Bolton, 410 U.S. 179, 188 (1973), the Court allowed physicians consulted by pregnant women to challenge a state anti-abortion statute without any showing that they had been prosecuted or threatened with prosecution; but in Roe v. Wade, 410 U.S. 113, 127–29 (1973), the Court refused to allow a similar challenge by a childless couple who alleged that they feared pregnancy for medical and personal reasons and that the inability to obtain a legal abortion in the state was forcing them to " 'the choice of refraining from normal sexual relations or of endangering [the plaintiff wife's] health through a possible pregnancy' " (p. 128). The Court said that the alleged injury was too speculative in character, resting as it did on possible contraceptive failure, possible pregnancy, and possible future impairment of health.

Six years later, in Babbitt v. United Farm Workers National Union, 442 U.S. 289 (1979), the Court allowed a pre-enforcement challenge to several provisions of a farm labor statute, though there had been no showing of probable prosecution. With respect to one of the provisions, the Court noted that the fear of prosecution was "not imaginary or wholly speculative," and with respect to another, that the state had "not disavowed any intention" of invoking it (p. 302).[8]

Also relevant here is the line of cases allowing advance challenges to criminal statutes on the basis of a First Amendment claim of vagueness or overbreadth. See, e.g., Erznoznik v. City of Jacksonville, 422 U.S. 205 (1975) (holding an ordinance invalid on its face); Brockett v. Spokane Arcades, Inc., 472 U.S. 491 (1985) (holding a statute invalid in part). These and related cases are more fully discussed in the Note on the Scope of the Issue in First Amendment Cases, p. 184, supra.[9]

---

7. Justice Brennan, concurring in the result, said that the "true controversy," not presented by the parties in the case, was "over the opening of birth-control clinics on a large scale" (p. 509). There were four dissents.

8. The Court held that challenges to several other provisions, governing access to employers' property and compulsory arbitration of certain disputes, were premature.

9. For other cases dealing with ripeness in the context of a challenge to a criminal statute, see Boyle v. Landry, 401 U.S. 77 (1971) (summarized at p. 1400, infra;) Lake Carriers' Ass'n v. MacMullan, 406 U.S. 498 (1972) (case presents actual controversy as to the validity of state anti-pollution law; state authorities had indicated they would not bring immediate prosecution but were attempting to obtain compliance as soon as possible); Steffel v. Thompson, 415 U.S. 452 (1974), p. 1406,

Is there any consistent thread running through these cases? In Poe v. Ullman and in Roe v. Wade, was the Court saying that it was not enough for plaintiffs to claim that they were presently deterred from engaging in desired conduct by an existing law? That under the circumstances, their claim was not credible?

(8) Should a distinction be drawn between the injury relevant to the issue of standing, Sec. 3, *infra*, and that relevant to ripeness?

In Duke Power Co. v. Carolina Environmental Study Group, Inc., 438 U.S. 59 (1978), also discussed at pp. 1039–40, *infra*, the Court first held that there was federal question jurisdiction over an action challenging the constitutionality of the Price–Anderson Act's limitation on liability for nuclear accidents at nuclear power plants, and that the plaintiffs had standing to sue. It then turned briefly to the question of the ripeness of plaintiffs' challenge, indicating that any constitutional prerequisite on this score was satisfied by the earlier conclusion as to standing "that appellees will sustain immediate [environmental] injury from the [routine] operation of the disputed power plants and that such injury would be redressed by the relief requested * * *" (p. 81). The Court went on to say (pp. 81–82) that the "prudential considerations" embodied in the ripeness doctrine also militated in favor of resolution of the issues presented, even though no nuclear accident had yet occurred; delayed resolution "would foreclose any relief from the present injury" and "would frustrate one of the key purposes of the Price–Anderson Act—the elimination of doubts concerning the scope of private liability in the event of major nuclear accident."

Of the three separate opinions concurring in the judgment of reversal but disagreeing with the decision to reach the merits, Justice Stevens' focused most squarely on the question of ripeness: "The string of contingencies that supposedly holds this litigation together is too delicate for me. * * * [We are] asked to remedy an alleged due process violation [*i.e.*, the limitation of liability in the event of a nuclear accident] that may possibly occur at some uncertain time in the future and may possibly injure the appellees in a way that has no significant connection with any present injury. It is remarkable that such a series of speculations is considered sufficient either to make this litigation ripe for decision or to establish appellees' standing. * * * The Court's opinion will serve the national interest in removing doubts concerning the constitutionality of the [Act] * * *. But whenever we are persuaded by reasons of expediency to engage in the business of giving legal advice, we chip away a part of the foundation of our independence and our strength" (pp. 102–03).

In a perceptive discussion of Duke Power, Professor Varat concluded that for the first time, the Court had "held the constitutional dimension of ripeness satisfied by the imminence of the injury that gave plaintiff standing [environmental injury from the plant's routine operation], instead of requiring the imminence of injury to the legal rights asserted in the suit

infra; Bowers v. Hardwick, 106 S.Ct. 2841 (1986) (Court entertains plaintiff's challenge to criminal sodomy statute without discussion of question of ripeness; plaintiff had been charged with a violation of the statute, but the matter had not been presented to the grand jury); City of Houston, Texas v. Hill, 107 S.Ct. 2502, 2508 n. 7 (1987) (upholding plaintiff's "standing" to challenge the validity of a city ordinance; plaintiff had been arrested four times and faced a clear "threat of future enforcement"). See generally Laycock, Modern American Remedies 1211 (1985) (concluding that the Court "routinely entertain(s) suits to declare statutes unconstitutional, invoking the ripeness requirement only occasionally").

[injury from a major nuclear accident].   The unacknowledged result was to collapse the article III ripeness inquiry into the article III standing inquiry and to alter the primary policy of ripeness from a concern with the issues to a concern with the plaintiff's cognizable injury in fact."   Varat, *Variable Justiciability and the Duke Power Case,* 58 Tex.L.Rev. 273, 298 (1980).

(9) Do the cases discussed in this Note suggest that a judge's view of the ripeness question may turn on the strength of his view of the merits— that the fewer doubts there seem to be about the merits, the more willing the judge may be to decide on the basis of an abstract record?   If this relation does exist, is it an appropriate one?

Consider the discussion of the Adler case in Scharpf, *Judicial Review and the Political Question: A Functional Analysis,* 75 Yale L.J. 517, 532 (1966): "For [Justice Minton, writing for the majority], the statute was clearly constitutional because it in no way deprived teachers of their freedoms of speech and association—it merely put before them the choice of either exercising these freedoms or continuing their employment in the public school system which, after all, was not a right but merely a privilege.   Justices Black and Douglas, dissenting, also saw no reason to worry about standing or ripeness.   For them the statute was clearly unconstitutional because it penalized teachers for the exercise of their 'absolute' freedoms of speech and association.   The conclusion seems inevitable that Justice Frankfurter alone advocated avoidance because he alone defined the substantive issues in terms of a close balance between the equally legitimate interests of society in its self-preservation and of the teachers in their freedom of thought, inquiry and expression.   Thus, in order to strike this balance in the particular case, Frankfurter would have had to know much more about the actual practices of enforcement and the degree of surveillance to which the teachers would be subjected than the bare text of an unenforced statute permitted him to know."

(10) When the question of ripeness arises, as it often does, in the context of a federal court action for declaratory or injunctive relief, it is clear that the courts have some measure of discretion not to proceed even if the case is justiciable.   Some of the results reached in the cases discussed may be explainable on that ground even though the language of justiciability was used.   Is Mitchell such a case?   If so, why did the Court allow only Poole to litigate the merits?   Did he have more, or less, to gain than did the other plaintiffs in an action for declaratory or prospective relief?   (He had already engaged in arguably prohibited activity; the only question remaining was the consequence of that activity.)

Occasionally, the Court is quite explicit about the "constitutional" and "prudential" aspects of its decision.[10]   In the Duke Power case, Paragraph (7), *supra,* for example, the Court stated that the present injury to the plaintiffs satisfied the constitutional requirement and that prudential considerations also militated in favor of the elimination of doubt as soon as possible.   The Court added that it would not be in a better position later than it was now to decide the case—the actual occurrence of a nuclear

---

10.   See Nichol, *Ripeness and the Constitution,* 54 U.Chi.L.Rev. 153 (1987), for a forceful argument that the "marriage of ripeness and article III is flawed" (p. 156) and that the ripeness doctrine should be "returned in its entirety to its prudential status" (p. 183).

accident would not "significantly advance our ability to deal with the legal issues presented nor aid us in their resolution" (438 U.S. at 82).[11]

(11) Adler, Poe v. Ullman, and Epperson v. Arkansas were all cases that came to the Supreme Court on review of state courts. Is there "discretion" to decline adjudication in those instances if, as was true in each instance, the case arises on appeal and not on certiorari? See pp. 740–48, infra. Note that refusal to adjudicate in federal cases results in dismissal of the entire action, without prejudice as to the merits.[12] Refusal to review state cases leaves the state court's decision standing. If a "case" or "controversy" within Article III is presented, can the state court's decision be denied res judicata effect? Cf. Fidelity Nat. Bank & Trust Co. v. Swope, p. 235, supra. Can the Supreme Court require a state court to dismiss an action for lack of "ripeness"? On what basis could such results be supported? That "ripeness" is part of a "federalized" law of remedies in cases of Supreme Court review because of "the overriding institutional need of the Supreme Court to avoid premature and excessive interventions?" See Gunther, Constitutional Law 1584 n. 6 (11th ed. 1985). Insofar as Congress has made Supreme Court review obligatory, is this an appropriate judgment for the Court? See Chap. V, Sec. 4(C), infra.

(12) Federal statutes creating administrative agencies generally provide for judicial review of final agency orders, and challenges to newly promulgated agency regulations prior to their application against particular individuals have often been entertained. In 1967, in three cases under the Food, Drug, and Cosmetic Act, the Court addressed itself extensively to the "ripeness" of such challenges. Abbott Laboratories v. Gardner, 387 U.S. 136; Toilet Goods Ass'n v. Gardner, 387 U.S. 158; Gardner v. Toilet Goods Ass'n, 387 U.S. 167.

Justice Harlan, who wrote for the Court in all three cases, first determined that there was no statutory bar to pre-enforcement judicial attacks on the regulations, and then noted that "further inquiry" must be made. "The injunctive and declaratory judgment remedies are discretionary, and courts traditionally have been reluctant to apply them to administrative determinations unless these arise in the context of a controversy 'ripe' for judicial resolution" (p. 148). The inquiry to determine whether a challenge to an administrative regulation is ripe for review is, he said, "twofold": "first to determine whether the issues tendered are appropriate for judicial resolution, and second to assess the hardship to the parties if judicial relief is denied at that stage" (p. 162).

Using these dual criteria, the Court found one of the three cases not ripe: Toilet Goods Ass'n v. Gardner. In that case, cosmetic manufacturers challenged the authority of the Commissioner of Food and Drugs to issue regulations under the Color Additive Amendments of 1960, 21 U.S.C. §§ 321–376, which would authorize the Commissioner to suspend certification service (a requirement for sale) to those who denied Food and Drug Administration inspectors free access to manufacturing facilities and data. Acknowledging that the issue framed by the plaintiffs was "a purely legal question: whether the regulation is totally beyond the agency's power

---

11. Professor Varat, Paragraph (8), supra, is strongly critical of the Court's conclusion on this point in Duke Power. 58 Tex.L.Rev. at 305–07.

12. But see Socialist Labor Party v. Gilligan, 406 U.S. 583 (1972), p. 1835, infra.

under the statute," the Court nevertheless found the first criterion not satisfied:

"The regulation serves notice only that the Commissioner *may* under certain circumstances order inspection of certain facilities and data, and that further certification of additives *may* be refused to those who decline to permit a duly authorized inspection until they have complied in that regard. At this juncture we have no idea whether or when such an inspection will be ordered and what reasons the Commissioner will give to justify his order. The statutory authority asserted for the regulation is the power to promulgate regulations 'for the efficient enforcement' of the Act, § 701(a). Whether the regulation is justified thus depends * * * on whether the statutory scheme as a whole justified promulgation of the regulation. * * * This will depend not merely on an inquiry into statutory purpose, but concurrently on an understanding of what types of enforcement problems are encountered by the FDA, the need for various sorts of supervision in order to effectuate the goals of the Act, and the safeguards devised to protect legitimate trade secrets (see 21 CFR § 130.14(c)). We believe that judicial appraisal of these factors is likely to stand on a much surer footing in the context of a specific application of this regulation than could be the case in the framework of the generalized challenge made here" (pp. 163–64).

The same result was further supported in terms of the second criterion: the regulation would have no immediate impact on manufacturers "in conducting their day-to-day affairs. * * * [A] refusal to admit an inspector here would at most lead only to a suspension of certification services to the particular party, a determination that can then be promptly challenged through an administrative procedure, which in turn is reviewable by a court. Such review will provide an adequate forum for testing the regulation in a concrete situation" (pp. 164–65).

The regulations challenged in the other two cases, and found ripe for review, involved a requirement that the "established name" of a drug be printed "every time" the proprietary name was used, Abbott Laboratories v. Gardner, *supra*, as well as an expanded definition of "color additives" (subject to listing and pre-market certification of each batch) to include diluents and other additional items, Gardner v. Toilet Goods Ass'n, *supra*. The majority held that the questions in these cases were "straightforward" legal ones, depending less on specific facts than in the factory access case. Moreover, these regulations had an immediate substantial impact on the manufacturers, involving large expenditures and the risk of serious penalties.

Justice Fortas, joined by Chief Justice Warren and Justice Clark, thought that anticipatory review should be denied in all three cases (p. 200): "Those challenging the regulations have a remedy and there are no special reasons to relieve them of the necessity of deferring their challenge to the regulations until enforcement is undertaken. In this way, and only in this way, will the administrative process have an opportunity to function—to iron out differences, to accommodate special problems, to grant exemptions, etc. The courts do not and should not pass on these complex problems in the abstract and the general—because these regulations peculiarly depend for their quality and substance upon the facts of particular situations. We should confine ourselves—as our jurisprudence dictates—to actual, specific, particularized cases and controversies, in substance as well as in technical analysis."

Should the two criteria formulated by Justice Harlan be considered of equal significance? [13]

(13) Should justiciability requirements be more or less rigorous in constitutional cases than in others? In his opinion in the Food, Drug, and Cosmetic Act cases, Justice Fortas suggested that at least some constitutional attacks might be entertained under a less restrictive standard than otherwise. He also said (p. 187): "Where personal status or liberties are involved, the courts may well insist upon a considerable ease of challenging administrative orders or regulations." But compare Scharpf, Paragraph (9), *supra*, at 528–29: "[T]he public interest in responsible and realistic constitutional decisions is much too serious to be left unprotected against the accidents of ordinary litigation. If this protection cannot be afforded by an enlargement of the Court's jurisdiction to permit the most competent parties to sue, or by an enlargement of the Court's procedural powers to conduct an independent investigation of facts and issues, then it seems reasonable to expect that this protection will be provided by restrictive techniques which will permit the Court to screen the cases in order to select those which provide an adequate basis for the responsible performance of the reviewing function. In order to qualify for the exercise of judicial review, the factual situation of the case would have to illuminate in a concrete fashion the practical implications of the constitutional issue * * *."

It is at times argued that anticipatory actions asserting First Amendment claims should in particular be entertained at an early stage. See, *e.g.*, Note, 83 Harv.L.Rev. 1870 (1970). Indeed, the development of overbreadth doctrine as a means of facilitating such actions appears to have been responsive to these arguments. See *Note on the Scope of the Issue in First Amendment Cases*, p. 184, *supra*.

---

13. For decisions since Abbott holding similar challenges ripe for review, see EPA v. National Crushed Stone Ass'n, 449 U.S. 64, 72–73 n. 12 (1980) (mentioning conflict between the circuits as "yet another reason" in support of the conclusion of ripeness); FCC v. WNCN Listeners Guild, 450 U.S. 582 (1981) (without discussion of the issue). *Cf.* California Bankers Ass'n v. Shultz, 416 U.S. 21, 55–57, 72–75 (1974) (certain aspects of challenge to record-keeping requirements of Bank Secrecy Act held premature); EPA v. Brown, 431 U.S. 99, 104 (1977) (refusal to review regulations "not yet promulgated, the final form of which has been only hinted at").

For general discussions of the issue of ripeness in administrative law, see Jaffe, Judicial Control of Administrative Action 395–417 (1965); 4 Davis, Administrative Law Treatise, Chap. 25 (2d ed. 1983); Vining, *Direct Judicial Review and the Doctrine of Ripeness in Administrative Law*, 69 Mich.L.Rev. 1443 (1971). Note too the related concepts of exhaustion of administrative remedies (Davis, *supra*, Chap. 26) and finality of administrative decision (Davis, *supra*, § 26:10) as prerequisites to the availability of judicial review.

O'SHEA v. LITTLETON

414 U.S. 488, 94 S.Ct. 669, 38 L.Ed.2d 674 (1974).
Certiorari to the United States Court of Appeals for the Seventh Circuit.

MR. JUSTICE WHITE delivered the opinion of the Court.

The respondents are 19 named individuals who commenced this civil rights action, individually and on behalf of a class of citizens of the city of Cairo, Illinois, against the State's Attorney for Alexander County, Illinois, his investigator, the Police Commissioner of Cairo, and the petitioners here, Michael O'Shea and Dorothy Spomer, Magistrate and Associate Judge of the Alexander County Circuit Court, respectively, alleging that they have intentionally engaged in, and are continuing to engage in, various patterns and practices of conduct in the administration of the criminal justice system in Alexander County that deprive respondents of rights secured by the First, Sixth, Eighth, Thirteenth, and Fourteenth Amendments, and by 42 U.S.C. §§ 1981, 1982, 1983, and 1985. The complaint, as amended, alleges that since the early 1960's, black citizens of Cairo, together with a small number of white persons on their behalf, have been actively, peaceably and lawfully seeking equality of opportunity and treatment in employment, housing, education, participation in governmental decisionmaking and in ordinary day-to-day relations with white citizens and officials of Cairo, and have, as an important part of their protest, participated in, and encouraged others to participate in, an economic boycott of city merchants who respondents consider have engaged in racial discrimination. Allegedly, there had resulted a great deal of tension and antagonism among the white citizens and officials of Cairo.

The individual respondents are 17 black and two white residents of Cairo. The class, or classes, which they purport to represent are alleged to include "all those who, on account of their race or creed and because of their exercise of First Amendment rights, have [been] in the past and continue to be subjected to the unconstitutional and selectively discriminatory enforcement and administration of criminal justice in Alexander County," as well as financially poor persons "who, on account of their poverty, are unable to afford bail, or are unable to afford counsel and jury trials in city ordinance violation cases." The complaint charges the State's Attorney, his investigator, and the Police Commissioner with a pattern and practice of intentional racial discrimination in the performance of their duties, by which the state criminal laws and procedures are deliberately applied more harshly to black residents of Cairo and inadequately applied to white persons who victimize blacks, to deter respondents from engaging in their lawful attempt to achieve equality. Specific supporting examples of such conduct involving some of the individual respondents are detailed in the complaint as to the State's Attorney and his investigator.

With respect to the petitioners, the county magistrate and judge, a continuing pattern and practice of conduct, under color of law, is alleged to have denied and to continue to deny the constitutional rights of respondents and members of their class in three respects: (1) petitioners set bond in criminal cases according to an unofficial bond schedule without regard to the facts of a case or circumstances of an individual defendant in violation of the Eighth and Fourteenth Amendments; (2) "on information and belief" they set sentences higher and impose harsher conditions for respondents and members of their class than for white persons, and (3) they require respondents and members of their class when charged with violations of city ordinances which carry fines and possible jail penalties if the fine cannot be paid, to pay for a trial by jury in violation of the Sixth, Eighth, and Fourteenth Amendments. Each of these continuing practices is alleged to have been carried out intentionally to deprive respondents and their class of the protections of the county criminal justice system and to deter them from engaging in their boycott and similar activities. The complaint further alleges that there is no adequate remedy at law and requests that the practices be enjoined. No damages were sought against the petitioners in this case, nor were any specific instances involving the individually named respondents set forth in the claim against these judicial officers.

The District Court dismissed the case for want of jurisdiction to issue the injunctive relief prayed for and on the ground that petitioners were immune from suit with respect to acts done in the course of their judicial duties. The Court of Appeals reversed, holding that Pierson v. Ray, 386 U.S. 547, 554 (1967), on which the District Court relied, did not forbid the issuance of injunctions against judicial officers if it is alleged and proved that they have knowingly engaged in conduct intended to discriminate against a cognizable class of persons on the basis of race. Absent sufficient remedy at law, the Court of Appeals ruled that in the event respondents proved their allegations, the District Court should proceed to fashion appropriate injunctive relief to prevent petitioners from depriving others of their constitutional rights in the course of carrying out their judicial duties in the future.[1] We granted certiorari.

I

We reverse the judgment of the Court of Appeals. The complaint failed to satisfy the threshold requirement imposed by Art. III of the Constitution that those who seek to invoke the power of federal courts must allege an actual case or controversy. * * * Plaintiffs in the federal courts "must allege some threatened or actual injury resulting from the putatively illegal action before a federal court may assume jurisdiction." Linda R. S. v. Richard D., 410 U.S. 614, 617 (1973).[2] There must be a

---

1. While the Court of Appeals did not attempt to specify exactly what type of injunctive relief might be justified, it at least suggested that it might include a requirement of "periodic reports of various types of aggregate data on actions on bail and sentencing." 468 F.2d, at 415. The dissenting judge urged that a federal district court has no power to supervise and regulate by mandatory injunction the discretion which state court judges may exercise within the limits of the powers vested in them by law, and that any relief contemplated by the majority holding which might be applicable to the pattern and practice alleged, if proven, would subject the petitioners to the continuing supervision of the District Court, the necessity of defending their motivations in each instance when the fixing of bail or sentence was challenged by a Negro defendant as inconsistent with the equitable relief granted, and the possibility of a contempt citation for failure to comply with the relief awarded.

2. We have previously noted that "Congress may enact statutes creating legal rights, the invasion of which creates standing, even though no injury would exist without the statute. See, e.g., Trafficante v. Metropolitan Life Ins. Co., 409 U.S. 205, 212 (1972) (White, J., concurring); Hardin v. Kentucky Utilities Co., 390 U.S. 1, 6 (1968)." Linda R. S. v. Richard D., 410 U.S. 614, 617 n. 3 (1973). But such statutes do not purport to bestow the right to sue in the absence of any indication that invasion of the statutory right has occurred or is likely to occur. Title 42 U.S.C. § 1983, in particular, provides for liability to the "party injured" in an action at law,

"personal stake in the outcome" such as to "assure that concrete adverseness which sharpens the presentation of issues upon which the court so largely depends for illumination of difficult constitutional questions." Baker v. Carr, 369 U.S. 186, 204 (1962). Nor is the principle different where statutory issues are raised. * * * Abstract injury is not enough. It must be alleged that the plaintiff "has sustained or is immediately in danger of sustaining some direct injury" as the result of the challenged statute or official conduct. Massachusetts v. Mellon, 262 U.S. 447, 488 (1923). The injury or threat of injury must be both "real and immediate," not "conjectural" or "hypothetical." Golden v. Zwickler, 394 U.S. 103 (1969); * * * United Public Workers v. Mitchell, 330 U.S. 75, 89–91 (1947). Moreover, if none of the named plaintiffs purporting to represent a class establishes the requisite of a case or controversy with the defendants, none may seek relief on behalf of himself or any other member of the class.[3] * * *

In the complaint that began this action, the sole allegations of injury are that petitioners "have engaged in and continue to engage in, a pattern and practice of conduct * * * all of which has deprived and continues to deprive plaintiffs and members of their class of their" constitutional rights and, again, that petitioners "have denied and continue to deny to plaintiffs and members of their class their constitutional rights" by illegal bond-setting, sentencing, and jury-fee practices. None of the named plaintiffs is identified as himself having suffered any injury in the manner specified. In sharp contrast to the claim for relief against the State's Attorney where specific instances of misconduct with respect to particular individuals are alleged, the claim against petitioners alleges injury in only the most general terms. At oral argument, respondents' counsel stated that some of the named plaintiffs-respondents, who could be identified by name if necessary, had actually been defendants in proceedings before petitioners and had suffered from the alleged unconstitutional practices. Past exposure to illegal conduct does not in itself show a present case or controversy regarding injunctive relief, however, if unaccompanied by any continuing, present adverse effects. Neither the complaint nor respondents' counsel suggested that any of the named plaintiffs at the time the complaint was filed were themselves serving an allegedly illegal sentence or were on trial or awaiting trial before petitioners. Indeed, if any of the respondents were then serving an assertedly unlawful sentence, the complaint would inappropriately be seeking relief from or modification of current, existing custody.

suit in equity, or other proper proceeding for redress. Perforce, the constitutional requirement of an actual case or controversy remains. Respondents still must show actual or threatened injury of some kind to establish standing in the constitutional sense.

3. There was no class determination in this case as the complaint was dismissed on grounds which did not require that determination to be made. Petitioners assert that the lack of standing of the named respondents to raise the class claim is buttressed by the incongruous nature of the class respondents seek to represent. The class is variously and incompatibly defined in the complaint as those residents of Cairo, both Negro and white, who have boycotted certain businesses in that city and engaged in similar activities for the purpose of combatting racial discrimination, as a class of all Negro citizens suffering racial discrimination in the application of the criminal justice system in Alexander County (though two white persons are named respondents), and as all poor persons unable to afford bail, counsel, or jury trials in city ordinance cases. The absence of specific claims of injury as a result of any of the wrongful practices charged, in light of the ambiguous and contradictory class definition proffered, bolsters our conclusion that these respondents cannot invoke federal jurisdiction to hear the claims they present in support of their request for injunctive relief.

See Preiser v. Rodriguez, 411 U.S. 475 (1973). Furthermore, if any were then on trial or awaiting trial in state proceedings, the complaint would be seeking injunctive relief that a federal court should not provide. Younger v. Harris, 401 U.S. 37 (1971). We thus do not strain to read inappropriate meaning into the conclusory allegations of this complaint.

Of course, past wrongs are evidence bearing on whether there is a real and immediate threat of repeated injury. But here the prospect of future injury rests on the likelihood that respondents will again be arrested for and charged with violations of the criminal law and will again be subjected to bond proceedings, trial, or sentencing before petitioners. Important to this assessment is the absence of allegations that any relevant criminal statute of the State of Illinois is unconstitutional on its face or as applied or that respondents have been or will be improperly charged with violating criminal law. If the statutes that might possibly be enforced against respondents are valid laws, and if charges under these statutes are not improvidently made or pressed, the question becomes whether any perceived threat to respondents is sufficiently real and immediate to show an existing controversy simply because they anticipate violating lawful criminal statutes and being tried for their offenses, in which event they may appear before petitioners and, if they do, will be affected by the allegedly illegal conduct charged. Apparently, the proposition is that *if* respondents proceed to violate an unchallenged law and *if* they are charged, held to answer, and tried in any proceedings before petitioners, they will be subjected to the discriminatory practices that petitioners are alleged to have followed. But it seems to us that attempting to anticipate whether and when these respondents will be charged with crime and will be made to appear before either petitioner takes us into the area of speculation and conjecture. See Younger v. Harris, *supra,* at 41–42. The nature of respondents' activities is not described in detail and no specific threats are alleged to have been made against them. Accepting that they are deeply involved in a program to eliminate racial discrimination in Cairo and that tensions are high, we are nonetheless unable to conclude that the case-or-controversy requirement is satisfied by general assertions or inferences that in the course of their activities respondents will be prosecuted for violating valid criminal laws. We assume that respondents will conduct their activities within the law and so avoid prosecution and conviction as well as exposure to the challenged course of conduct said to be followed by petitioners.

As in Golden v. Zwickler, we doubt that there is " 'sufficient immediacy and reality' " to respondents' allegations of future injury to warrant invocation of the jurisdiction of the District Court. There, "it was wholly conjectural that another occasion might arise when Zwickler might be prosecuted for distributing the handbills referred to in the complaint." 394 U.S., at 109. Here we can only speculate whether respondents will be arrested, either again or for the first time, for violating a municipal ordinance or a state statute, particularly in the absence of any allegations that unconstitutional criminal statutes are being employed to deter constitutionally protected conduct. *Cf.* Perez v. Ledesma, 401 U.S. 82, 101–102 (1971) (opinion of Brennan, J.). Even though Zwickler attacked a specific statute under which he had previously been prosecuted, the threat of a new prosecution was not sufficiently imminent to satisfy the jurisdictional requirements of the federal courts. Similarly, respondents here have not pointed to any imminent prosecutions contemplated against any of their number and they naturally do not suggest that any one of them expects to violate valid criminal laws. Yet their vulnerability to the alleged threatened injury from which relief is sought is necessarily contingent upon the bringing of prosecutions against one or more of them. Under these circumstances, where respondents do not claim any constitutional right to engage in conduct proscribed by therefore presumably permissible state laws, or indicate that it is otherwise their intention to so conduct themselves, the threat of injury from the alleged course of conduct they attack is simply too remote to satisfy the case-or-controversy requirement and permit adjudication by a federal court.

In Boyle v. Landry, 401 U.S. 77, 81 (1971), the Court ordered a complaint dismissed for insufficiency of its allegations where there was no basis for inferring "that any one or more of the citizens who brought this suit is in any jeopardy of suffering irreparable injury if the State is left free to prosecute under the intimidation statute in the normal manner." The Court expressed the view that "the normal course of state criminal prosecutions cannot be disrupted or blocked on the basis of charges which in the last analysis amount to nothing more than speculation about the future." *Ibid.* A similar element of uncertainty about whether the alleged injury will be likely to occur is present in this case, and a similar reluctance to interfere with the normal operation of state administration of its criminal laws in the manner sought by respondents strengthens the conclusion that the allegations in this complaint are too insubstantial to warrant federal adjudication of the merits of respondents' claim.

II

The foregoing considerations obviously shade into those determining whether the complaint states a sound basis for equitable relief; and even if we were inclined to consider the complaint as presenting an existing case or controversy, we would firmly disagree with the Court of Appeals that an adequate basis for equitable relief against petitioners had been stated. The Court has recently reaffirmed the "basic doctrine of equity jurisprudence that courts of equity should not act, and particularly should not act to restrain a criminal prosecution, when the moving party has an adequate remedy at law and will not suffer irreparable injury if denied equitable relief." Younger v. Harris, 401 U.S. 37, 43–44 (1971). Additionally, recognition of the need for a proper balance in the concurrent operation of federal and state courts counsels restraint against the issuance of injunctions against state officers engaged in the administration of the State's criminal laws in the absence of a showing of irreparable injury which is "'both great and immediate.'" *Id.*, at 46. * * *

Respondents do not seek to strike down a single state statute, either on its face or as applied; nor do they seek to enjoin any criminal prosecutions that might be brought under a challenged criminal law. In fact, respondents apparently contemplate that prosecutions will be brought under seemingly valid state laws. What they seek is an injunction aimed at controlling or preventing the occurrence of specific events that might take place in the course of future state criminal trials. The order the Court of Appeals thought should be available if respondents proved their allegations would be operative only where permissible state prosecutions are pending against one or more of the beneficiaries of the injunction. Apparently the order would contemplate interruption of state proceedings to adjudicate assertions of noncompliance by petitioners. This seems to us nothing less than an ongoing federal audit of state criminal proceedings which would indirectly accomplish the kind of interference that Younger v. Harris, *supra*, and related cases sought to prevent.

A federal court should not intervene to establish the basis for future intervention that would be so intrusive and unworkable. In concluding that injunctive relief would be available in this case because it would not interfere with prosecutions to be commenced under challenged statutes, the Court of Appeals misconceived the underlying basis for withholding federal equitable relief when the normal course of criminal proceedings in the state courts would otherwise be disrupted. The objection is to unwarranted anticipatory interference in the state criminal process by means of continuous or piecemeal interruptions of the state proceedings by litigation in the federal courts; the object is to sustain "[t]he special delicacy of the adjustment to be preserved between federal equitable power and State administration of its own law." Stefanelli v. Minard, 342 U.S. 117, 120 (1951). * * * An injunction of the type contemplated by respondents and the Court of Appeals would disrupt the normal course of proceedings in the state courts via resort to the federal suit for determination of the claim *ab initio*, just as would the request for injunctive relief from an ongoing state prosecution against the federal plaintiff which was found to be unwarranted in Younger. Moreover, it would require for its enforcement the continuous supervision by the federal court over the conduct of the petitioners in the course of future criminal trial proceedings involving any of the members of the respondents' broadly defined class. The Court of Appeals disclaimed any intention of requiring the District Court to sit in constant day-to-day supervision of these judicial officers, but the "periodic reporting" system it thought might be warranted would constitute a form of monitoring of the operation of state court functions that is antipathetic to established principles of comity. *Cf.* Greenwood v. Peacock, 384 U.S. 808 (1966). Moreover, because an injunction against acts which might occur in the course of future criminal proceedings would necessarily impose continuing obligations of compliance, the question arises of how compliance might be enforced if the beneficiaries of the injunction were to charge that it had been disobeyed. Presumably, any member of respondents' class who appeared as an accused before petitioners could allege and have adjudicated a claim that petitioners were in contempt of the federal court's injunction order, with review of adverse decisions in the Court of Appeals and, perhaps, in this Court. Apart from the inherent difficulties in defining the proper standards against which such claims might be measured, and the significant problems of proving noncompliance in individual cases, such a major continuing intrusion of the equitable power of the federal courts into the daily conduct of state criminal proceedings is in sharp conflict with the principles of equitable restraint which this Court has recognized in the decisions previously noted.

Respondents have failed, moreover, to establish the basic requisites of the issuance of equitable relief in these circumstances—the likelihood of substantial and immediate irreparable injury, and the inadequacy of remedies at law. We have already canvassed the necessarily conjectural nature of the threatened injury to which respondents are allegedly subjected. And if any of the respondents are ever prosecuted and face trial, or if they are illegally sentenced, there are available state and federal procedures which could provide relief from the wrongful conduct alleged. * * *

Nor is it true that unless the injunction sought is available federal law will exercise no deterrent effect in these circumstances. Judges who would willfully discriminate on the ground of race or otherwise would willfully deprive the citizen of his constitutional rights, as this complaint alleges, must take account of 18 U.S.C. § 242. See Greenwood v. Peacock, *supra*, at 830 * * *. That section provides:

"Whoever, under color of any law, statute, ordinance, regulation, or custom, willfully subjects any inhabitant of any State * * * to the deprivation of any rights, privileges, or immunities secured or protected by the Constitution or laws of the United States, or to different punishments, pains, or penalties, on account of such inhabitant being an alien, or by reason of his color, or race, than are prescribed for the punishment of citizens, shall be fined * * * or imprisoned * * *."

Whatever may be the case with respect to civil liability generally, see Pierson v. Ray, 386 U.S. 547 (1967) * * *, we have never held that the performance of the duties of judicial, legislative, or executive officers, requires or contemplates the immunization of otherwise criminal deprivations of constitutional rights. *Cf.* Ex parte Virginia, 100 U.S. 339 (1880). On the contrary, the judicially fashioned doctrine of official immunity does not reach "so far as to immunize criminal conduct proscribed by an Act of Congress * * *." Gravel v. United States, 408 U.S. 606, 627 (1972).

Considering the availability of other avenues of relief open to respondents for the serious conduct they assert, and the abrasive and unmanageable intercession which the injunctive relief they seek would represent, we conclude that, apart from the absence of an existing case or controversy presented by respondents for adjudication, the Court of Appeals erred in deciding that the District Court should entertain respondents' claim.

Reversed.

MR. JUSTICE BLACKMUN, concurring in part.

I join the judgment of the Court and Part I of the Court's opinion which holds that the complaint "failed to satisfy the threshold requirement imposed by Art. III of the Constitution that those who seek to invoke the power of federal courts must allege an actual case or controversy."

When we arrive at that conclusion, it follows, it seems to me, that we are precluded from considering any other issue presented for review. Thus, the Court's additional discussion of the question whether a case for equitable relief was stated amounts to an advisory opinion that we are powerless to render. * * *

MR. JUSTICE DOUGLAS, with whom MR. JUSTICE BRENNAN and MR. JUSTICE MARSHALL concur, dissenting.

* * *

This Court now decides for the first time in the course of this litigation that the complaint is deficient because it does not state a "case or controversy" within the meaning of Art. III.

The fact that no party has raised that issue in this closely contested case is no barrier, of course, to our consideration of it. But the reasoning and result reached by the Court are to say the least a *tour de force* and quite inconsistent with the allegations in the complaint, which are within constitutional requirements.

We know from the record and oral argument that Cairo, Illinois, is boiling with racial conflicts. This class action brought under 42 U.S.C. §§ 1981, 1982, 1983, and 1985 is to remedy vast invasions of civil rights. The Court, however, says that it is not a "case or controversy" because none of the named plaintiffs has alleged infringement of his rights and the fact that other members of the class may have been injured is not enough. As to the latter, Bailey v. Patterson, 369 U.S. 31, 32–33, is cited in support. But in Bailey the named persons were given standing to sue, the statement that "[t]hey cannot represent a class of whom they are not a part," *id.,* at 32–33, being dictum and its only authority being McCabe v. Atchison, T. & S.F.R. Co., 235 U.S. 151, 162–163, which was not a class action. * * *

But I do not press the point, for the amended complaint is sufficiently specific to warrant a trial.

As respects O'Shea, the Magistrate, and Spomer, the Circuit Judge, the charges concerning *named plaintiffs* are as follows:

(1) that excessive bonds have been required in violation of the Eighth and Fourteenth Amendments because petitioners follow an unofficial bond schedule without regard to the facts of individual cases;

(2) on information and belief, that petitioners set higher sentences and impose harsher conditions for respondents and members of their class than for white persons;

(3) that, where the named plaintiffs have been fined and at times sentenced to jail and cannot pay the fines, these judges have required them to pay for a trial by jury.

Moreover, the amended complaint alleges that O'Shea and Spomer "continue to engage in a pattern and practice" which "has deprived and continues to deprive" the named plaintiffs and members of their class of their constitutional rights. Moreover, it is alleged that since early in the 1960's the blacks of Cairo and some whites have been actively and peaceably seeking to end discrimination in Cairo and that those activities have generated and continue to generate tension and antagonism in Cairo.

It is also alleged that the police commissioner in Cairo "has denied and continues to deny to plaintiffs and members of their class their constitutional rights in the following ways:

"(a) Defendant has made or caused to be made or cooperated in the making of arrests and the filing of charges against plaintiffs and members of their class where such charges are not warranted and are merely for the purpose of harassment and to discourage and prevent plaintiffs and their class from exercising their constitutional rights.

"(b) Defendant has made or caused to be made or cooperated in the making of arrests and the filing of charges against plaintiffs and members of their class where there may be some colorable basis to the arrest or charge, but the crime defined in the charge is much harsher than is warranted by the facts and is far more severe than like charges would be against a white person."

These allegations support the likelihood that the named plaintiffs as well as members of their class will be arrested in the future and therefore will be brought before O'Shea and Spomer and be subjected to the alleged discriminatory practices in the administration of justice.

These allegations of past and continuing wrongdoings clearly state a case or controversy in the Art. III sense. They are as specific as those alleged in Jenkins v. McKeithen, 395 U.S. 411, and in Doe v. Bolton, 410 U.S. 179, where we held that cases or controversies were presented.

Specificity of proof may not be forthcoming: but specificity of charges is clear.

What has been alleged here is not only wrongs done to named plaintiffs, but a recurring pattern of wrongs which establishes, if proved, that the legal regime under control of the whites in Cairo, Illinois, is used over and over again to keep the blacks from exercising First Amendment rights, to discriminate against them, to keep from the blacks the protection of the law in their lawful activities, to weight the scales of justice repeatedly on the side of white prejudices and against black protests, fears, and suffering. This is a more pervasive scheme for suppression of blacks and their civil rights than I have ever seen. It may not survive a trial. But if this case does not present a "case or controversy" involving the named plaintiffs, then that concept has been so watered down as to be no longer recognizable. This will please the white superstructure, but it does violence to the conception of evenhanded justice envisioned by the Constitution.

Suits under 42 U.S.C. § 1983 are exceptions to the absolute bar against federal injunctions directed at state court proceedings provided in 28 U.S.C. § 2283. * * * It will be much more appropriate to pass on the nature of any equitable relief to be granted after the case has been tried. It may be that when the case is ended, no injunction against any state proceeding will be asked for or will seem appropriate. Or the injunctive relief in final analysis may come down to very narrow and discrete orders prohibiting precise practices. The Court labels this an "ongoing federal audit of state criminal proceedings." That of course is a regime that we do not foster. But the federal Constitution is supreme and if the power of the white power-structure in Cairo, Illinois, is so great as to disregard it, extraordinary relief is demanded. I would cross the bridge of remedies only when the precise contours of the problem have been established after a trial.

* * *

NOTE ON "RIPENESS" IN PUBLIC ACTIONS CHALLENGING PATTERNS OR PRACTICES IN THE ADMINISTRATION OF THE LAW

(1) The line between the matters discussed in the preceding Note and those considered in this one is indistinct. But a case like O'Shea is different from a case like Epperson v. Arkansas, p. 250, *supra,* in several respects. First, in O'Shea there is no challenged statute or regulation but rather a pattern of past events (and their implication for the future) that form the basis of the complaint and of the prayer for equitable relief. Second, in a case like O'Shea, in which the matters complained of consist of official practices in law enforcement, it is especially difficult to identify the individuals who are likely to be harmed by those practices in the future. Such cases frequently involve requests for "structural relief"—for the

shaping of a decree designed to modify significantly the way in which an arm of government (or, in some instances, a private institution) conducts its affairs. The Court's evident reluctance to become enmeshed in those affairs, especially when state institutions are at the bar, has been expressed, in part, in terms of justiciability doctrine—notably ripeness and standing.[1] Is the problem in these cases properly viewed as one of justiciability under Article III?

Consider O'Shea itself. Did the Court take adequate account of plaintiffs' allegation, referred to in the opinion, that the effect of defendants' continuing practices was "to deter them [plaintiffs] from engaging in their boycott and similar activities"? If this allegation was true, and the boycott and related activities had ceased as a result of the challenged practices, should the controversy have been deemed premature?

What considerations do you think were most persuasive to the majority: That plaintiffs had failed to show sufficient need for the requested relief? That the relief sought was too vague and general? That federal courts should not become embroiled with state courts and state officials on a continuing basis?

(2) In Spomer v. Littleton, 414 U.S. 514 (1974), a companion case to O'Shea, the same plaintiffs brought an action in which the original defendant was the state's prosecutor. The complaint alleged numerous instances in which he had violated the constitutional rights of plaintiffs (both named and "unnamed" members of the class) by discriminatory administration of the criminal justice system. While the case was on appeal, a new prosecutor was elected. Noting that the plaintiffs had alleged no misconduct by the successor, the Court remanded the case for a determination of mootness and of "whether [plaintiffs] will want to, and should be permitted to, amend their complaint * * *" (p. 522).

If there had been no change in prosecutors, and the two cases had been taken together, wouldn't the prosecutor's alleged misconduct have created the possibility that plaintiffs would continue to be subjected to the abusive

---

1. See also Rizzo v. Goode, 423 U.S. 362 (1976), in which the Supreme Court, partly on grounds of nonjusticiability, set aside a broad lower court order requiring Philadelphia police authorities to institute comprehensive civilian complaint procedures in accordance with specified guidelines. The order was based on some 19 instances in one year in which the police were found to have violated citizens' constitutional rights. The majority, per Justice Rehnquist, said that the considerations expressed in O'Shea "apply here with even more force, for the individual [plaintiffs'] claim to 'real and immediate' injury rests not upon what the named [defendants] might do to them in the future—such as set a bond on the basis of race—but upon what one of a small, unnamed minority of policemen might do to them in the future because of that unknown policeman's perception of departmental disciplinary procedures" (p. 372).

In Laird v. Tatum, 408 U.S. 1 (1972), plaintiffs sought to enjoin Army surveillance of civilian political activity, claiming they had been the subject of such surveillance and that the practice exerted a "chilling effect" on the exercise of First Amendment rights. The Court, 5–4, held the action not justiciable, stating that "[a]llegations of a subjective 'chill' are not an adequate substitute for a claim of specific present objective harm or a threat of specific future harm. * * *

"Stripped to its essentials, what respondents appear to be seeking is a broad-scale investigation, conducted by themselves * * * to probe into the Army's intelligence-gathering activities, with the district court determining at the conclusion of that investigation the extent to which those activities may or may not be appropriate to the Army's mission. * * *

"Carried to its logical end, this approach would have the federal courts as virtually continuous monitors of the wisdom and soundness of Executive action * * *" (pp. 13–15).

practices charged in O'Shea even though they did not violate any statute? Under those circumstances, should the combined cases have been held ripe? If so, would the cases still have presented difficult questions as to the nature and scope of appropriate relief?

(3) In City of Los Angeles v. Lyons, 461 U.S. 95 (1983), Lyons brought a civil rights action against the city and certain of its police officers in a federal district court, claiming that he had been unconstitutionally subjected to a "chokehold" after being stopped for a traffic violation. He alleged that pursuant to official authorization, chokeholds were routinely applied in situations where they were not warranted, and that many people had been injured as a result. Damages and declaratory and injunctive relief were sought. On the basis of the pleadings, affidavits, depositions, and government records, the district court granted a preliminary injunction against the use of chokeholds "under circumstances which do not threaten death or serious bodily injury"—an injunction that was to continue in effect until an improved training and reporting program had been approved by the court.

Following affirmance of the preliminary injunction by the court of appeals, the Supreme Court reversed on the grounds that Lyons had "failed to demonstrate a case or controversy" that "would justify the equitable relief sought" (p. 105). Noting that only the question of an injunctive remedy was before it, and that the damages claim could be severed on remand, the Court relied on O'Shea and on Rizzo v. Goode, note 1, *supra,* in concluding that there was no jurisdiction to entertain the claim for equitable relief.[2] First, the Court concluded that Lyons was not more immediately threatened than the plaintiffs in those cases:

"[I]t is no more than conjecture to suggest that in every instance of a traffic stop, arrest, or other encounter between the police and a citizen, the police will act unconstitutionally and inflict injury without provocation or legal excuse. And it is surely no more than speculation to assert either that Lyons himself will again be involved in one of those unfortunate instances, or that he will be arrested in the future and provoke the use of a chokehold by resisting arrest, attempting to escape, or threatening deadly force or serious bodily injury" (p. 108).

Second, it decided that O'Shea and Rizzo could not be distinguished on the basis that in those proceedings, unlike the present one, "massive structural relief" had been sought:

"If Lyons has made no showing that he is realistically threatened by a repetition of his experience of October 1976, then he has not met the requirements for seeking an injunction in a federal court, whether the injunction contemplates intrusive structural relief or the cessation of a discrete practice" (pp. 108–09).

Still relying on O'Shea, the Court went on to conclude that even if Lyons' pending damage suit "affords him Article III standing to seek an injunction as a remedy," the showing of irreparable injury prerequisite to that remedy had not been made:

2. The Court summarily rejected a claim of mootness that was based on a six-month moratorium declared by the city on certain uses of the chokehold. The Court said (p. 101): "Intervening events have not 'irrevocably eradicated the effects of the alleged violation.' County of Los Angeles v. Davis, 440 U.S. 625, 631 (1979) [p. 207, *supra*]."

"We decline the invitation to slight the preconditions for equitable relief; for as we have held, recognition of the need for a proper balance between state and federal authority counsels restraint in the issuance of injunctions against state officers engaged in the administration of the States' criminal laws in the absence of irreparable injury which is both great and immediate [Citing O'Shea and Younger v. Harris, p. 1383, *infra*]" (pp. 111–12).

Justice Marshall, for four dissenters, focused on the majority's claim of lack of "standing," [3] and argued that O'Shea and Rizzo were not controlling because the plaintiffs in those cases had not sought damages for past injury:

"By contrast, Lyons' request for prospective relief is coupled with his claim for damages based on past injury. In addition to the risk that he will be subjected to a chokehold in the future, Lyons has suffered past injury. Because he has a live claim for damages, he need not rely solely on the threat of future injury to establish his personal stake in the outcome of the controversy.

* * *

"The Court provides no justification for departing from the traditional treatment of remedial issues and demanding a separate threshold inquiry into each form of relief a plaintiff seeks. It is anomalous to require a plaintiff to demonstrate 'standing' to seek each particular form of relief requested in the complaint when under Rule 54(c) the remedy to which a party may be entitled need not even be demanded in the complaint" (pp. 124, 130–31).

As to the majority's alternative ground—the failure to satisfy the traditional prerequisites for equitable relief—Justice Marshall urged that the question was not properly before the Court on the grant of certiorari. Moreover, he argued, Younger v. Harris was not in point because Lyons did not seek to enjoin state judicial proceedings; under general equitable principles the district court's findings that Lyons had been choked pursuant to city policy and that the policy posed grave risks of injury and death warranted preliminary relief. "The Court's decision," he concluded, "immunizes from prospective equitable relief any policy that authorizes persistent deprivations of constitutional rights as long as no individual can establish with substantial certainty that he will be injured, or injured again, in the future" (p. 137).

(4) Note the substantial overlap, in both O'Shea and Lyons, in the reasons given for lack of justiciability and for the absence of an adequate basis for equitable relief.[4] Note too that although the injunction sought and granted in Lyons was, as the Court conceded, less intrusive in scope

---

3. On the appropriateness of considering the issues in cases like Lyons, Rizzo, and O'Shea in terms of standing, see Fallon, *Of Justiciability, Remedies, and Public Law Litigation: Notes on the Jurisprudence of Lyons,* 59 N.Y.U.L.Rev. 1 (1984). Professor Fallon argues that in cases where past injury has occurred, the justiciability question in an action for equitable relief should be viewed, under the rubric of mootness, as a question of the likelihood of recurrence.

4. In Allee v. Medrano, 416 U.S. 802 (1974), a case decided in the same Term as O'Shea, the Court held that an injunction against continuing police harassment was "an appropriate exercise of the federal court's equitable powers" (p. 814). Plaintiffs were attempting to organize farmworkers in the state and complained of both police reliance on unconstitutional statutes and of police exercise of authority under valid laws in an unconstitutional manner. Without discussing any question

and less "structural" in nature, it was, like the injunctions sought in O'Shea and in Rizzo, designed to effectuate a significant change in the law enforcement and administrative practices of a state government agency. Thus this case, like the other two, raised questions of the judicial role in the context of an effort to reform the operation of government.

Since Lyons had in fact been subjected to a chokehold, and was seeking damages for that injury, would not the Court have been on sounder ground to acknowledge the existence of a concrete justiciable controversy and to have focused on the appropriateness of equitable relief (assuming that question was properly before it)? And in a case like O'Shea, where only an equitable remedy was sought, did the claim of past events, when taken with the allegations of present effect on the plaintiffs themselves (see Paragraph (1), *supra*), similarly satisfy the demands of Article III? (See also Paragraph (5), *infra*, for discussion of the class action aspects of the case.) Did the real issues presented by the prayer for an injunction require a careful weighing of the federal and state interests—as well as consideration of the proper relation between the wrong complained of and the relief sought— more appropriate to the law of remedies than to threshold questions of justiciability under Article III? In the Court's view, would there ever be a time when a claim for equitable relief in cases like these would be justiciable?[5] Has the Court's insistence on examining these issues in Article III terms unduly restricted the power of Congress to deal with remedial questions in public law litigation?[6]

As a way of highlighting the remedial question, consider whether the Court in Lyons or in O'Shea might have taken a different view of the justiciability issue if the plaintiffs had sought only a declaration of the unlawfulness of the conduct engaged in.[7]

of justiciability on this aspect of the case, the Court noted that the record showed not simply "isolated instances of police misconduct under valid statutes" but rather a "persistent pattern" of misconduct (p. 815). Hague v. CIO, 307 U.S. 496 (1939), was cited as a case involving "strikingly similar facts" (*id.*).

5. *Cf.* Kolender v. Lawson, 461 U.S. 352, 355 n. 3 (1983) (individual who had been stopped by police on 15 occasions pursuant to a state law could seek declaratory and injunctive relief; there was a "credible threat" that he might again be detained).

6. See generally Nichol, p. 252, note 10, *supra.* See also Fallon, note 3, *supra.* Professor Fallon argues persuasively that the basic question in Lyons should have been viewed as one of the law of remedies—a law that, properly conceived, affords to plaintiffs a "balancing of the public and private interests unique to the circumstances of their situations" (59 N.Y.U.L. Rev. at 73). Such a question, he contends, can fairly be resolved only on a full record.

For an analysis of substantive and remedial issues in "institutional" or structural reform litigation, with special emphasis on problems of remedial discretion, see Fletcher, *The Discretionary Constitution: Institu-*

tional Remedies and Judicial Legitimacy, 91 Yale L.J. 635 (1982). See generally Mishkin, *Federal Courts as State Reformers,* 35 Wash. & Lee L.Rev. 949 (1978); Nagel, *Separation of Powers and the Scope of Federal Equitable Remedies,* 30 Stan.L. Rev. 661 (1978); authorities cited pp. 79– 82, *supra.*

7. *Cf.* Steffel v. Thompson, 415 U.S. 452 (1974), p. 1406, *infra.* But *cf.* Public Service Com'n v. Wycoff Co., 344 U.S. 237 (1952), in which the complainants had sought a declaratory judgment that their carriage of certain goods between points in Utah constituted interstate commerce and thus lay beyond the regulatory power of the state commission. (A prayer for an injunction had been abandoned, apparently because of lack of proof of irreparable injury.) A divided Court held that the discretionary remedy of declaratory relief should not be given in view of the inappropriateness of interfering with a state's administration of its law in the absence of a clear showing of need. But the Court also rested on a broader ground—based on its perception that the sole purpose of seeking the declaration was to hold it "in readiness for use should the Commission at any future time attempt to apply any part of a compli-

(5) What significance, if any, should attach to the fact that Lyons was not prosecuted as a class action? O'Shea had been brought as a class action, but no class determination had been made, and the Court (in footnote 3) expressed some doubt about the appropriateness of the class claim; at the same time, it indicated that a named plaintiff must establish a case or controversy on his own behalf before he could seek individual or class relief. And in Rizzo, a class had been certified but the Court concluded that no showing had been made of a pattern of misbehavior toward the class as a whole that would warrant equitable relief. (It is noteworthy that in Rizzo the Court discussed the class claim only *after* that portion of the opinion addressed to justiciability, in a section addressed to the appropriateness of an injunctive remedy).

Assuming that Lyons cannot establish a sufficient likelihood that he will be subjected to another chokehold, is there nevertheless a justiciable controversy if he can establish his membership in an identifiable class at least some of whose members are virtually certain to be subjected to chokeholds in the near future? Is the argument for justiciability—for treating the class itself as a legal entity—strengthened if the class has some characteristics (such as race or ethnicity) that distinguish it from the community at large? Do the cases relating to mootness of class claims, especially Roper and Geraghty (p. 212, *supra*), lend some support to this argument? See LaDuke v. Nelson, 762 F.2d 1318, 1325–26 (9th Cir.1985), in which the court (relying in part on the Geraghty case) held justiciable a class action for injunctive relief against Immigration and Naturalization Service checks of migrant housing units without sufficient cause.

For discussion of these and other questions, see generally Meltzer, *Deterring Constitutional Violations By Law Enforcement Officials: Plaintiffs and Defendants as Private Attorneys General*, 88 Colum.L.Rev. 247 (1988).

(6) Both in this Note and elsewhere in this Chapter, relationships between the doctrines of ripeness, mootness, and standing have been suggested. Goldwater v. Carter, 444 U.S. 996 (1979), points toward a possible relation between the doctrine of ripeness and that of the nonjusticiability of political questions. In that case, several Members of Congress brought an action against the President challenging his authority to terminate a treaty with Taiwan without some form of congressional approval. The Court of Appeals for the District of Columbia, reversing the district court, held for the President on the merits, but the Supreme Court granted certiorari and summarily remanded the case to the district court with "directions to dismiss the complaint" (p. 996). Of the six Justices who favored this result, four regarded the basic question as political and therefore nonjusticiable; one concurred without explanation; and one, Justice Powell, focused on the question of ripeness.

Emphasizing that disputes between the executive and legislative branches are "commonplace" and generally "turn on political rather than legal considerations," Justice Powell argued that the judiciary should not

cated regulatory statute to it. If there is any more definite or contemporaneous purpose to this case, neither this record nor the briefs make it clear to us. We think this for several reasons exceeds any permissible discretionary use of the Federal Declaratory Judgment Act" (p. 245).

In the Lyons case itself, Lyons had included a count seeking declaratory relief, but that count was not before the Supreme Court. See 461 U.S. at 98–99.

become involved in such controversies "until the political branches reach a constitutional impasse" (p. 997). In this case, "Congress has taken no official action" with respect to the President's decision to terminate, and "[i]f the Congress chooses not to confront the President, it is not our task to do so" (p. 998). He went on explicitly to disagree with the four Justices who took the position that a controversy of this kind could never be considered by the federal courts.[8]

SECTION 6.   POLITICAL QUESTIONS

BAKER v. CARR

369 U.S. 186, 82 S.Ct. 691, 7 L.Ed.2d 663 (1962).
Appeal from the United States District Court for the
Middle District of Tennessee.

MR. JUSTICE BRENNAN delivered the opinion of the Court.

This civil action was brought under 42 U.S.C. §§ 1983 and 1988 to redress the alleged deprivation of federal constitutional rights. The complaint, alleging that by means of a 1901 statute of Tennessee apportioning the members of the General Assembly among the State's 95 counties, "these plaintiffs and others similarly situated, are denied the equal protection of the laws accorded them by the Fourteenth Amendment to the Constitution of the United States by virtue of the debasement of their votes," was dismissed by a three-judge court * * *. We hold that the dismissal was error, and remand the cause to the District Court for trial and further proceedings consistent with this opinion.

The General Assembly of Tennessee consists of the Senate with 33 members and the House of Representatives with 99 members. * * * Tennessee's standard for allocating legislative representation among her counties is the total number of qualified voters resident in the respective counties, subject only to minor qualifications. * * * In 1901 the General Assembly * * * passed the Apportionment Act here in controversy. In the more than 60 years since that action, all proposals in both Houses of the General Assembly for reapportionment have failed to pass.

Between 1901 and 1961, Tennessee has experienced substantial growth and redistribution of her population. * * * It is primarily the continued application of the 1901 Apportionment Act to this shifted and enlarged voting population which gives rise to the present controversy.

* * * [The complaint alleges] that "because of the population changes since 1900, and the failure of the Legislature to reapportion itself since 1901," the 1901 statute became "unconstitutional and obsolete." Appellants also argue that, because of the composition of the legislature effected by the 1901 Apportionment Act, redress in the form of a state constitutional amendment to change the entire mechanism for reapportioning, or any other change short of that, is difficult or impossible. The

---

8. For further discussion of Justice Powell's opinion, and of the significance of discretion in the determination of questions of justiciability, see Shapiro, *Jurisdiction and Discretion*, 60 N.Y.U.L.Rev. 543, 552–55, 585–86 (1985).

complaint concludes that "these plaintiffs and others similarly situated, are denied the equal protection of the laws accorded them by the Fourteenth Amendment to the Constitution of the United States by virtue of the debasement of their votes." They seek a declaration that the 1901 statute is unconstitutional and an injunction restraining the appellees from acting to conduct any further elections under it. They also pray that unless and until the General Assembly enacts a valid reapportionment, the District Court should either decree a reapportionment by mathematical application of the Tennessee constitutional formulae to the most recent Federal Census figures, or direct the appellees to conduct legislative elections, primary and general, at large. They also pray for such other and further relief as may be appropriate.

I. The District Court's Opinion and Order of Dismissal.

Because we deal with this case on appeal from an order of dismissal granted on appellees' motions, precise identification of the issues presently confronting us demands clear exposition of the grounds upon which the District Court rested in dismissing the case. The dismissal order recited that the court sustained the appellees' grounds "(1) that the Court lacks jurisdiction of the subject matter, and (2) that the complaint fails to state a claim upon which relief can be granted * * *."

In the setting of a case such as this, the recited grounds embrace two possible reasons for dismissal:

First: That the facts and injury alleged, the legal bases invoked as creating the rights and duties relied upon, and the relief sought, fail to come within that language of Article III of the Constitution and of the jurisdictional statutes which define those matters concerning which United States District Courts are empowered to act;

Second: That, although the matter is cognizable and facts are alleged which establish infringement of appellants' rights as a result of state legislative action departing from a federal constitutional standard, the court will not proceed because the matter is considered unsuited to judicial inquiry or adjustment.

We treat the first ground of dismissal as "lack of jurisdiction of the subject matter." The second we consider to result in a failure to state a justiciable cause of action. * * *

* * * [W]e hold today only (a) that the court possessed jurisdiction of the subject matter; (b) that a justiciable cause of action is stated upon which appellants would be entitled to appropriate relief; and (c) because appellees raise the issue before this Court, that the appellants have standing to challenge the Tennessee apportionment statutes. Beyond noting that we have no cause at this stage to doubt the District Court will be able to fashion relief if violations of constitutional rights are found, it is improper now to consider what remedy would be most appropriate if appellants prevail at the trial.

II. Jurisdiction of the Subject Matter.

The District Court was uncertain whether our cases withholding federal judicial relief rested upon a lack of federal jurisdiction or upon the inappropriateness of the subject matter for judicial consideration—what we have designated "nonjusticiability." The distinction between the two grounds is significant. In the instance of nonjusticiability, consideration of the cause is not wholly and immediately foreclosed; rather, the Court's inquiry necessarily proceeds to the point of deciding whether the duty asserted can be judicially identified and its breach judicially determined, and whether protection for the right asserted can be judicially molded. In the instance of lack of jurisdiction the cause either does not "arise under" the federal Constitution, laws or treaties (or fall within one of the other enumerated categories of Art. III, § 2), or is not a "case or controversy" within the meaning of that section; or the cause is not one described by any jurisdictional statute. Our conclusion [*infra*] that this cause presents no nonjusticiable "political question" settles the only possible doubt that it is a case or controversy. Under the present heading of "Jurisdiction of the Subject Matter" we hold only that the matter set forth in the complaint does arise under the Constitution and is within 28 U.S.C. § 1343.

* * * Since the District Court obviously and correctly did not deem the asserted federal constitutional claim unsubstantial and frivolous, it should not have dismissed the complaint for want of jurisdiction of the subject matter. And of course no further consideration of the merits of the claim is relevant to a determination of the court's jurisdiction of the subject matter. * * *

Since the complaint plainly sets forth a case arising under the Constitution, the subject matter is within the federal judicial power defined in Art. III, § 2, and so within the power of Congress to assign to the jurisdiction of the District Courts. Congress has exercised that power in 28 U.S.C. § 1343(3) * * *.

An unbroken line of our precedents sustains the federal courts' jurisdiction of the subject matter of federal constitutional claims of this nature. * * *

III. Standing.

* * * Have the appellants alleged such a personal stake in the outcome of the controversy as to assure that concrete adverseness which sharpens the presentation of issues upon which the court so largely depends for illumination of difficult constitutional questions? This is the gist of the question of standing. It is, of course, a question of federal law. * * *

We hold that the appellants do have standing to maintain this suit. * * *

These appellants seek relief in order to protect or vindicate an interest of their own, and of those similarly situated. * * * The injury which appellants assert is that this classification disfavors the voters in the counties in which they reside, placing them in a position of constitutionally unjustifiable inequality *vis-à-vis* voters in irrationally favored counties. * * *

It would not be necessary to decide whether appellants' allegations of impairment of their votes by the 1901 apportionment will, ultimately, entitle them to any relief, in order to hold that they have standing to seek it. If such impairment does produce a legally cognizable injury, they are among those who have sustained it. They are asserting "a plain, direct and adequate interest in maintaining the effectiveness of their votes," Coleman

v. Miller, 307 U.S. at 438, not merely a claim of "the right possessed by every citizen 'to require that the government be administered according to law' " * * *.

IV. Justiciability.

* * * Of course the mere fact that the suit seeks protection of a political right does not mean it presents a political question. Such an objection "is little more than a play upon words." Nixon v. Herndon, 273 U.S. 536, 540. Rather, it is argued that apportionment cases, whatever the actual wording of the complaint, can involve no federal constitutional right except one resting on the guaranty of a republican form of government, [Art. IV, § 4] and that complaints based on that clause have been held to present political questions which are nonjusticiable.

We hold that the claim pleaded here neither rests upon nor implicates the Guaranty Clause and that its justiciability is therefore not foreclosed by our decisions of cases involving that clause. * * * To show why we reject the argument based on the Guaranty Clause, we must examine the authorities under it. But because there appears to be some uncertainty as to why those cases did present political questions, and specifically as to whether this apportionment case is like those cases, we deem it necessary first to consider the contours of the "political question" doctrine.

Our discussion, even at the price of extending this opinion, requires review of a number of political question cases, in order to expose the attributes of the doctrine—attributes which, in various settings, diverge, combine, appear, and disappear in seeming disorderliness. Since that review is undertaken solely to demonstrate that neither singly nor collectively do these cases support a conclusion that this apportionment case is nonjusticiable, we of course do not explore their implications in other contexts. That review reveals that in the Guaranty Clause cases and in the other "political question" cases, it is the relationship between the judiciary and the coordinate branches of the Federal Government, and not the federal judiciary's relationship to the States, which gives rise to the "political question."

We have said that "In determining whether a question falls within [the political question] category, the appropriateness under our system of government of attributing finality to the action of the political departments and also the lack of satisfactory criteria for a judicial determination are dominant considerations." Coleman v. Miller, 307 U.S. 433, 454–455. The nonjusticiability of a political question is primarily a function of the separation of powers. Much confusion results from the capacity of the "political question" label to obscure the need for case-by-case inquiry. Deciding whether a matter has in any measure been committed by the Constitution to another branch of government, or whether the action of that branch exceeds whatever authority has been committed, is itself a delicate exercise in constitutional interpretation, and is a responsibility of this Court as ultimate interpreter of the Constitution. To demonstrate this requires no less than to analyze representative cases and to infer from them the analytical threads that make up the political question doctrine. We shall then show that none of those threads catches this case.

Foreign relations: There are sweeping statements to the effect that all questions touching foreign relations are political questions. Not only does resolution of such issues frequently turn on standards that defy judicial application, or involve the exercise of a discretion demonstrably committed to the executive or legislature; but many such questions uniquely demand single-voiced statement of the Government's views. Yet it is error to suppose that every case or controversy which touches foreign relations lies beyond judicial cognizance. Our cases in this field seem invariably to show a discriminating analysis of the particular question posed, in terms of the history of its management by the political branches, of its susceptibility to judicial handling in the light of its nature and posture in the specific case, and of the possible consequences of judicial action. For example, though a court will not ordinarily inquire whether a treaty has been terminated, since on that question "governmental action * * * must be regarded as of controlling importance," if there has been no conclusive "governmental action" then a court can construe a treaty and may find it provides the answer. * * * Though a court will not undertake to construe a treaty in a manner inconsistent with a subsequent federal statute, no similar hesitancy obtains if the asserted clash is with state law. * * *

While recognition of foreign governments so strongly defies judicial treatment that without executive recognition a foreign state has been called "a republic of whose existence we know nothing," and the judiciary ordinarily follows the executive as to which nation has sovereignty over disputed territory, once sovereignty over an area is politically determined and declared, courts may examine the resulting status and decide independently whether a statute applies to that area. Similarly, recognition of belligerency abroad is an executive responsibility, but if the executive proclamations fall short of an explicit answer, a court may construe them seeking, for example, to determine whether the situation is such that statutes designed to assure American neutrality have become operative. The Three Friends, 166 U.S. 1, 63, 66. Still again, though it is the executive that determines a person's status as representative of a foreign government, Ex parte Hitz, 111 U.S. 766, the executive's statements will be construed where necessary to determine the court's jurisdiction, In re Baiz, 135 U.S. 403. Similar judicial action in the absence of a recognizedly authoritative executive declaration occurs in cases involving the immunity from seizure of vessels owned by friendly foreign governments. * * *

Dates of duration of hostilities: Though it has been stated broadly that "the power which declared the necessity is the power to declare its cessation, and what the cessation requires," Commercial Trust Co. v. Miller, 262 U.S. 51, 57, here too analysis reveals isolable reasons for the presence of political questions, underlying this Court's refusal to review the political departments' determination of when or whether a war has ended. Dominant is the need for finality in the political determination, for emergency's nature demands "A prompt and unhesitating obedience," Martin v. Mott, 12 Wheat. 19, 30 (calling up of militia). * * * But deference rests on reason, not habit. The question in a particular case may not seriously implicate considerations of finality—*e.g.,* a public program of importance (rent control) yet not central to the emergency effort. Further, clearly definable criteria for decision may be available. In such case the political question barrier falls away * * *. On the other hand, even in private litigation which directly implicates no feature of separation of powers, lack of judicially discoverable standards and the drive for even-handed application may impel reference to the political departments' determination of dates of hostilities' beginning and ending. The Protector, 12 Wall. 700.

Validity of enactments: In Coleman v. Miller, *supra*, this Court held that the questions of how long a proposed amendment to the Federal Constitution remained open to ratification, and what effect a prior rejection had on a subsequent ratification, were committed to congressional resolution and involved criteria of decision that necessarily escaped the judicial grasp. Similar considerations apply to the enacting process: "The respect due to coequal and independent departments," and the need for finality and certainty about the status of a statute contribute to judicial reluctance to inquire whether, as passed, it complied with all requisite formalities. * * * But it is not true that courts will never delve into a legislature's records upon such a quest: If the enrolled statute lacks an effective date, a court will not hesitate to seek it in the legislative journals in order to preserve the enactment. Gardner v. Collector, 6 Wall. 499. The political question doctrine, a tool for maintenance of governmental order, will not be so applied as to promote only disorder.

The status of Indian tribes: This Court's deference to the political departments in determining whether Indians are recognized as a tribe, while it reflects familiar attributes of political questions, United States v. Holliday, 3 Wall. 407, also has a unique element in that "the relation of the Indians to the United States is marked by peculiar and cardinal distinctions which exist no where else. * * * [The Indians are] domestic dependent nations * * * in a state of pupilage. Their relation to the United States resembles that of a ward to his guardian." Cherokee Nation v. Georgia, 5 Pet. 1, 16, 17.[43] Yet, here too, there is no blanket rule.

43. This case, so frequently cited for the broad proposition that the status of an Indian tribe is a matter for the political departments, is in fact a noteworthy example of the limited and precise impact of a political question. The Cherokees brought an original suit in this Court to enjoin Georgia's assertion of jurisdiction over Cherokee territory and abolition of Cherokee government and laws. Unquestionably the case lay at the vortex of most fiery political embroilment. See 1 Warren, The Supreme Court in United States History (Rev. ed.), 729–779. But in spite of some broader language in separate opinions, all that the Court held was that it possessed no original jurisdiction over the suit: for the Cherokees could in no view be considered either a State of this Union or a "foreign state." Chief Justice Marshall treated the question as one of *de novo* interpretation of words in the Constitution. The Chief Justice did say that "The acts of our government plainly recognize the Cherokee nation as a state, and the courts are bound by those acts," but here he referred to their existence "as a state, as a distinct political society, separated from others * * *." From there he went to "A question of much more difficulty * * *. Do the Cherokees constitute a foreign state in the sense of the constitu-

tion?" *Id.,* at 16. Thus, while the Court referred to "the political" for the decision whether the tribe was an entity, a separate polity, it held that whether being an entity the tribe had such status as to be entitled to sue originally was a judicially soluble issue: criteria were discoverable in relevant phrases of the Constitution and in the common understanding of the times. As to this issue, the Court was not hampered by problems of the management of unusual evidence or of possible interference with a congressional program. Moreover, Chief Justice Marshall's dictum that "It savours too much of the exercise of political power to be within the proper province of the judicial department," id. at 20, was not addressed to the issue of the Cherokees' status to sue, but rather to the breadth of the claim asserted and the impropriety of the relief sought. Compare Georgia v. Stanton, 6 Wall. 50, 77. The Chief Justice made clear that if the issue of the Cherokees' rights arose in a customary legal context, "a proper case with proper parties," it would be justiciable. Thus, when the same dispute produced a case properly brought, in which the right asserted was one of protection under federal treaties and laws from conflicting state law, and the relief sought was the voiding of a conviction under that state law, the Court did

While " 'It is for [Congress] * * *, and not for the courts, to determine when the true interests of the Indian require his release from [the] condition of tutelage' * * *, it is not meant by this that Congress may bring a community or body of people within the range of this power by arbitrarily calling them an Indian tribe." * * *

Able to discern what is "distinctly Indian," the courts will strike down any heedless extension of that label. They will not stand impotent before an obvious instance of a manifestly unauthorized exercise of power.

It is apparent that several formulations which vary slightly according to the settings in which the questions arise may describe a political question, although each has one or more elements which identify it as essentially a function of the separation of powers. Prominent on the surface of any case held to involve a political question is found a textually demonstrable constitutional commitment of the issue to a coordinate political department; or a lack of judicially discoverable and manageable standards for resolving it; or the impossibility of deciding without an initial policy determination of a kind clearly for nonjudicial discretion; or the impossibility of a court's undertaking independent resolution without expressing lack of the respect due coordinate branches of government; or an unusual need for unquestioning adherence to a political decision already made; or the potentiality of embarrassment from multifarious pronouncements by various departments on one question.

Unless one of these formulations is inextricable from the case at bar, there should be no dismissal for non-justiciability on the ground of a political question's presence. The doctrine of which we treat is one of "political questions," not one of "political cases." The courts cannot reject as "no law suit" a bona fide controversy as to whether some action denominated "political" exceeds constitutional authority. The cases we have reviewed show the necessity for discriminating inquiry into the precise facts and posture of the particular case, and the impossibility of resolution by any semantic cataloguing.

But it is argued that this case shares the characteristics of decisions that constitute a category not yet considered, cases concerning the Constitution's guaranty, in Art. IV, § 4, of a republican form of government. A conclusion as to whether the case at bar does present a political question cannot be confidently reached until we have considered those cases with special care. We shall discover that Guaranty Clause claims involve those elements which define a "political question," and for that reason and no other, they are nonjusticiable. In particular, we shall discover that the nonjusticiability of such claims has nothing to do with their touching upon matters of state governmental organization.

Republican form of government: Luther v. Borden, 7 How. 1, though in form simply an action for damages for trespass was, as Daniel Webster said in opening the argument for the defense, "an unusual case." The defendants, admitting an otherwise tortious breaking and entering, sought to justify their action on the ground that they were agents of the established

---

void the conviction. Worcester v. Georgia, 6 Pet. 515. There, the fact that the tribe was a separate polity served as a datum contributing to the result, and despite the consequences in a heated federal-state controversy and the opposition of the other branches of the National Government, the judicial power acted to reverse the State Supreme Court. An example of similar isolation of a political question in the decision of a case is Luther v. Borden, 7 How. 1; see *infra*.

lawful government of Rhode Island, which State was then under martial law to defend itself from active insurrection; that the plaintiff was engaged in that insurrection; and that they entered under orders to arrest the plaintiff. The case arose "out of the unfortunate political differences which agitated the people of Rhode Island in 1841 and 1842," 7 How., at 34, and which had resulted in a situation wherein two groups laid competing claims to recognition as the lawful government. The plaintiff's right to recover depended upon which of the two groups was entitled to such recognition; but the lower court's refusal to receive evidence or hear argument on that issue, its charge to the jury that the earlier established or "charter" government was lawful, and the verdict for the defendants, were affirmed upon appeal to this Court. * * *

Clearly, several factors were thought by the Court in Luther to make the question there "political": the commitment to the other branches of the decision as to which is the lawful state government; the unambiguous action by the President, in recognizing the charter government as the lawful authority; the need for finality in the executive's decision; and the lack of criteria by which a court could determine which form of government was republican.[48]

But the only significance that Luther could have for our immediate purposes is in its holding that the Guaranty Clause is not a repository of judicially manageable standards which a court could utilize independently in order to identify a State's lawful government. The Court has since refused to resort to the Guaranty Clause—which alone had been invoked for the purpose—as the source of a constitutional standard for invalidating state action. See Taylor & Marshall v. Beckham (No. 1), 178 U.S. 548 (claim that Kentucky's resolution of contested gubernatorial election deprived voters of republican government held nonjusticiable); Pacific States Tel. & T. Co. v. Oregon, 223 U.S. 118 (claim that initiative and referendum negated republican government held nonjusticiable); * * * Ohio ex rel. Bryant v. Akron Metropolitan Park District, 281 U.S. 74 (claim that rule requiring invalidation of statute by all but one justice of state court negated republican government held nonjusticiable) * * *.

Just as the Court has consistently held that a challenge to state action based on the Guaranty Clause presents no justiciable question so has it held, and for the same reasons, that challenges to congressional action on the ground of inconsistency with that clause present no justiciable question. In Georgia v. Stanton, 6 Wall. 50, the State sought by an original bill to enjoin execution of the Reconstruction Acts, claiming that it already possessed "A republican State, in every political, legal, constitutional, and juridical sense," and that enforcement of the new Acts "Instead of keeping the guaranty against a forcible overthrow of its government by foreign

---

48. Even though the Court wrote of unrestrained legislative and executive authority under this Guaranty, thus making its enforcement a political question, the Court plainly implied that the political question barrier was no absolute: "Unquestionably a military government, established as the permanent government of the State, would not be a republican government, and it would be the duty of Congress to overthrow it." 7 How., at 45. Of course, it does not necessarily follow that if Congress did not act, the Court would. For while the judiciary might be able to decide the limits of the meaning of "republican form," and thus the factor of lack of criteria might fall away, there would remain other possible barriers to decision because of primary commitment to another branch, which would have to be considered in the particular fact setting presented. * * *

invaders or domestic insurgents, * * * is destroying that very government by force." Congress had clearly refused to recognize the republican character of the government of the suing State. It seemed to the Court that the only constitutional claim that could be presented was under the Guaranty Clause, and Congress having determined that the effects of the recent hostilities required extraordinary measures to restore governments of a republican form, this Court refused to interfere with Congress' action at the behest of a claimant relying on that very guaranty.[52] * * *[53]

We come, finally, to the ultimate inquiry whether our precedents as to what constitutes a nonjusticiable "political question" bring the case before us under the umbrella of that doctrine. A natural beginning is to note whether any of the common characteristics which we have been able to identify and label descriptively are present. We find none: The question here is the consistency of state action with the Federal Constitution. We have no question decided, or to be decided, by a political branch of government coequal with this Court. Nor do we risk embarrassment of our government abroad, or grave disturbance at home if we take issue with Tennessee as to the constitutionality of her action here challenged. Nor need the appellants, in order to succeed in this action, ask the Court to enter upon policy determinations for which judicially manageable standards are lacking. Judicial standards under the Equal Protection Clause are well developed and familiar, and it has been open to courts since the enactment of the Fourteenth Amendment to determine, if on the particular facts they must, that a discrimination reflects *no* policy, but simply arbitrary and capricious action.

This case does, in one sense, involve the allocation of political power within a State, and the appellants might conceivably have added a claim under the Guaranty Clause. Of course, as we have seen, any reliance on that clause would be futile. But because any reliance on the Guaranty Clause could not have succeeded it does not follow that appellants may not be heard on the equal protection claim which in fact they tender. True, it must be clear that the Fourteenth Amendment claim is not so enmeshed with those political question elements which render Guaranty Clause claims nonjusticiable as actually to present a political question itself. But we have found that not to be the case here. * * *

We conclude then that the nonjusticiability of claims resting on the Guaranty Clause which arises from their embodiment of questions that were thought "political," can have no bearing upon the justiciability of the equal protection claim presented in this case. Finally, we emphasize that it is the involvement in Guaranty Clause claims of the elements thought to

52. In Mississippi v. Johnson, 4 Wall. 475, the State sought to enjoin the President from executing the Acts, alleging that his role was purely ministerial. The Court held that the duties were in no sense ministerial, and that although the State sought to compel inaction rather than action, the absolute lack of precedent for any such distinction left the case one in which "general principles * * * forbid judicial interference with the exercise of Executive discretion." 4 Wall., at 499. * * *

53. On the other hand, the implication of the Guaranty Clause in a case concerning congressional action does not always preclude judicial action. It has been held that the clause gives Congress no power to impose restrictions upon a State's admission which would undercut the constitutional mandate that the States be on an equal footing. Coyle v. Smith, 221 U.S. 559. And in Texas v. White, 7 Wall. 700, although Congress had determined that the State's government was not republican in form, the State's standing to bring an original action in this Court was sustained.

define "political questions," and no other feature, which could render them nonjusticiable. Specifically, we have said that such claims are not held nonjusticiable because they touch matters of state governmental organization. * * *

We conclude that the complaint's allegations of a denial of equal protection present a justiciable constitutional cause of action upon which appellants are entitled to a trial and a decision. The right asserted is within the reach of judicial protection under the Fourteenth Amendment. * * *

Reversed and remanded.

MR. JUSTICE WHITTAKER did not participate in the decision of this case.

MR. JUSTICE DOUGLAS, concurring.

While I join the opinion of the Court and, like the Court, do not reach the merits, a word of explanation is necessary.[1] * * *

So far as voting rights are concerned, there are large gaps in the Constitution. Yet the right to vote is inherent in the republican form of government envisaged by Article IV, Section 4 of the Constitution. * * * A "republican form" of government is guaranteed each State by Article IV, Section 4, and each is likewise promised protection against invasion.[2] *Ibid.* That the States may specify the qualifications for voters is implicit in Article I, Section 2, Clause 1. * * * It is, however, clear that by reason of the commands of the Constitution there are several qualifications that a State may not require. * * *

The traditional test under the Equal Protection Clause has been whether a State has made "an invidious discrimination," as it does when it selects "a particular race or nationality for oppressive treatment." See Skinner v. Oklahoma, 316 U.S. 535, 541. Universal equality is not the test; there is room for weighting. * * *

It is said that any decision in cases of this kind is beyond the competence of courts. Some make the same point as regards the problem of equal protection in cases involving racial segregation. Yet the legality of claims and conduct is a traditional subject for judicial determination. Adjudication is often perplexing and complicated. An example of the

1. I feel strongly that many of the cases cited by the Court and involving so-called "political" questions were wrongly decided.

In joining the opinion, I do not approve those decisions but only construe the Court's opinion in this case as stating an accurate historical account of what the prior cases have held.

2. The statements in Luther v. Borden, 7 How. 1, 42, that this guaranty is enforceable only by Congress or the Chief Executive is not maintainable. Of course the Chief Executive, not the Court, determines how a State will be protected against invasion. Of course each House of Congress, not the Court, is "the judge of the elections, returns, and qualifications of its own members." Article I, Section 5, Clause 1. But the abdication of all judicial functions respecting voting rights (7 How. at 41), however justified by the peculiarities of the

charter form of government in Rhode Island at the time of Dorr's Rebellion, states no general principle. It indeed is contrary to the cases discussed in the body of this opinion—the modern decisions of the Court that give the full panoply of judicial protection to voting rights. * * *

Moreover, the Court's refusal to examine the legality of the regime of martial law which had been laid upon Rhode Island (id. at 45–46) is indefensible, as Mr. Justice Woodbury maintained in his dissent. * * *

What he wrote was later to become the tradition, as expressed by Chief Justice Hughes in Sterling v. Constantin, 287 U.S. 378, 401: "What are the allowable limits of military discretion, and whether or not they have been overstepped in a particular case, are judicial questions."

extreme complexity of the task can be seen in a decree apportioning water among the several States. Nebraska v. Wyoming, 325 U.S. 589, 565. The constitutional guide is often vague, as the decisions under the Due Process and Commerce Clauses show. The problem under the Equal Protection Clause is no more intricate. See Lewis, Legislative Apportionment and the Federal Courts, 71 Harv.L.Rev. 1057, 1083–1084.

There are, of course, some questions beyond judicial competence. Where the performance of a "duty" is left to the discretion and good judgment of an executive officer, the judiciary will not compel the exercise of his discretion one way or the other (Commonwealth of Kentucky v. Dennison, 24 How. 66, 109), for to do so would be to take over the office. Cf. Federal Communications Comm'n v. Broadcasting Co., 309 U.S. 134, 135.

Where the Constitution assigns a particular function wholly and indivisibly[3] to another department, the federal judiciary does not intervene. Oetjen v. Central Leather Co., 246 U.S. 297, 302. None of those cases is relevant here.

There is no doubt that the federal courts have jurisdiction of controversies concerning voting rights. * * *

The justiciability of the present claims being established, any relief accorded can be fashioned in the light of well-known principles of equity.[5]

MR. JUSTICE CLARK, concurring.

One emerging from the rash of opinions with their accompanying clashing of views may well find himself suffering a mental blindness. The Court holds that the appellants have alleged a cause of action. However, it refuses to award relief here—although the facts are undisputed—and fails to give the District Court any guidance whatever. One dissenting opinion, bursting with words that go through so much and conclude with so little, contemns the majority action as "a massive repudiation of the experience of our whole past." Another describes the complaint as merely asserting conclusory allegations that Tennessee's apportionment is "incorrect," "arbi-

3. The category of the "political" question is, in my view, narrower than the decided cases indicate. * * *

In The Pocket Veto Case, 279 U.S. 655, the Court undertook a review of the veto provisions of the Constitution and concluded that the measure in litigation had not become a law. *Cf.* Coleman v. Miller, 307 U.S. 433.

Georgia v. Stanton, 6 Wall. 50, involved the application of the Reconstruction Acts to Georgia—laws which destroyed by force the internal regime of that State. Yet the Court refused to take jurisdiction. That question was no more "political" than a host of others we have entertained. See, *e.g.,* Pennsylvania v. West Virginia, 262 U.S. 553; Youngstown Sheet & Tube Co. v. Sawyer, 343 U.S. 579; Alabama v. Texas, 347 U.S. 272.

Today would this Court hold nonjusticiable or "political" a suit to enjoin a Governor who, like Fidel Castro, takes every-

thing into his own hands and suspends all election laws?

Georgia v. Stanton, supra, expresses a philosophy at war with Ex parte Milligan, 4 Wall. 2, and Duncan v. Kahanamoku, 327 U.S. 304. The dominance of the civilian authority has been expressed from the beginning. See Wise v. Withers, 3 Cranch 331, 337; Sterling v. Constantin, *supra,* note 2.

5. The recent ruling by the Iowa Supreme Court that a legislature, though elected under an unfair apportionment scheme, is nonetheless a legislature empowered to act * * * is plainly correct.

The District Court need not undertake a complete reapportionment. It might possibly achieve the goal of substantial equality merely by directing respondent to eliminate the egregious injustices. Or its conclusion that reapportionment should be made may in itself stimulate legislative action. * * *

trary," "obsolete," and "unconstitutional." I believe it can be shown that this case is distinguishable from earlier cases dealing with the distribution of political power by a State, that a patent violation of the Equal Protection Clause of the United States Constitution has been shown, and that an appropriate remedy may be formulated. * * *

Although I find the Tennessee apportionment statute offends the Equal Protection Clause, I would not consider intervention by this Court into so delicate a field if there were any other relief available to the people of Tennessee. But the majority of the people of Tennessee have no "practical opportunities for exerting their political weight at the polls" to correct the existing "invidious discrimination." Tennessee has no initiative and referendum. I have searched diligently for other "practical opportunities" present under the law. I find none other than through the federal courts. The majority of the voters have been caught up in a legislative strait jacket. Tennessee has an "informed, civically militant electorate" and "an aroused popular conscience," but it does not sear "the conscience of the people's representatives." This is because the legislative policy has riveted the present seats in the Assembly to their respective constituencies, and by the votes of their incumbents a reapportionment of any kind is prevented. The people have been rebuffed at the hands of the Assembly; they have tried the constitutional convention route, but since the call must originate in the Assembly it, too, has been fruitless. They have tried Tennessee courts with the same result, and Governors have fought the tide only to flounder. It is said that there is recourse in Congress and perhaps that may be, but from a practical standpoint this is without substance. To date Congress has never undertaken such a task in any State. We therefore must conclude that the people of Tennessee are stymied and without judicial intervention will be saddled with the present discrimination in the affairs of their state government.

Finally, we must consider if there are any appropriate modes of effective judicial relief. The federal courts are of course not forums for political debate, nor should they resolve themselves into state constitutional conventions or legislative assemblies. Nor should their jurisdiction be exercised in the hope that such a declaration as is made today may have the direct effect of bringing on legislative action and relieving the courts of the problem of fashioning relief. To my mind this would be nothing less than blackjacking the Assembly into reapportioning the State. If judicial competence were lacking to fashion an effective decree, I would dismiss this appeal. However, like the Solicitor General of the United States, I see no such difficulty in the position of this case. One plan might be to start with the existing assembly districts, consolidate some of them, and award the seats thus released to those counties suffering the most egregious discrimination. Other possibilities are present and might be more effective. But the plan here suggested would at least release the stranglehold now on the Assembly and permit it to redistrict itself. * * *

As John Rutledge (later Chief Justice) said 175 years ago in the course of the Constitutional Convention, a chief function of the Court is to secure the national rights. Its decision today supports the proposition for which our forebears fought and many died, namely, that to be fully conformable to the principle of right, the form of government must be representative. That is the keystone upon which our government was founded and lacking which no republic can survive. It is well for this Court to practice self-restraint and discipline in constitutional adjudication, but never in its history have those principles received sanction where the national rights of so many have been so clearly infringed for so long a time. National respect for the courts is more enhanced through the forthright enforcement of those rights rather than by rendering them nugatory through the interposition of subterfuges. In my view the ultimate decision today is in the greatest tradition of this Court.

MR. JUSTICE STEWART, concurring.

The separate writings of my dissenting and concurring Brothers stray so far from the subject of today's decision as to convey, I think, a distressingly inaccurate impression of what the Court decides. For that reason, I think it appropriate, in joining the opinion of the Court, to emphasize in a few words what the opinion does and does not say.

* * * I repeat, the Court today decides only: (1) that the District Court possessed jurisdiction of the subject matter; (2) that the complaint presents a justiciable controversy; (3) that the appellants have standing.
* * *

MR. JUSTICE FRANKFURTER, whom MR. JUSTICE HARLAN joins, dissenting.

The Court today reverses a uniform course of decision established by a dozen cases, including one by which the very claim now sustained was unanimously rejected only five years ago. The impressive body of rulings thus cast aside reflected the equally uniform course of our political history regarding the relationship between population and legislative representation—a wholly different matter from denial of the franchise to individuals because of race, color, religion or sex. Such a massive repudiation of the experience of our whole past in asserting destructively novel judicial power demands a detailed analysis of the role of this Court in our constitutional scheme. Disregard of inherent limits in the effective exercise of the Court's "judicial Power" not only presages the futility of judicial intervention in the essentially political conflict of forces by which the relation between population and representation has time out of mind been and now is determined. It may well impair the Court's position as the ultimate organ of "the supreme Law of the Land" in that vast range of legal problems, often strongly entangled in popular feeling, on which this Court must pronounce. The Court's authority—possessed of neither the purse nor the sword—ultimately rests on sustained public confidence in its moral sanction. Such feeling must be nourished by the Court's complete detachment, in fact and in appearance, from political entanglements and by abstention from injecting itself into the clash of political forces in political settlements.

A hypothetical claim resting on abstract assumptions is now for the first time made the basis for affording illusory relief for a particular evil even though it foreshadows deeper and more pervasive difficulties in consequence. The claim is hypothetical and the assumptions are abstract because the Court does not vouchsafe the lower courts—state and federal— guidelines for formulating specific, definite, wholly unprecedented remedies for the inevitable litigations that today's umbrageous disposition is bound to stimulate in connection with politically motivated reapportionments in so many States. In such a setting, to promulgate jurisdiction in the abstract is meaningless. It is as devoid of reality as "a brooding omnipresence in the sky," for it conveys no intimation what relief, if any, a District

Court is capable of affording that would not invite legislatures to play ducks and drakes with the judiciary. For this Court to direct the District Court to enforce a claim to which the Court has over the years consistently found itself required to deny legal enforcement and at the same time to find it necessary to withhold any guidance to the lower court how to enforce this turnabout, new legal claim, manifests an odd—indeed an esoteric—conception of judicial propriety. One of the Court's supporting opinions, as elucidated by commentary, unwittingly affords a disheartening preview of the mathematical quagmire (apart from divers judicially inappropriate and elusive determinants) into which this Court today catapults the lower courts of the country without so much as adumbrating the basis for a legal calculus as a means of extrication. Even assuming the indispensable intellectual disinterestedness on the part of judges in such matters, they do not have accepted legal standards or criteria or even reliable analogies to draw upon for making judicial judgments. To charge courts with the task of accommodating the incommensurable factors of policy that underlie these mathematical puzzles is to attribute, however flatteringly, omnicompetence to judges. The Framers of the Constitution persistently rejected a proposal that embodied this assumption and Thomas Jefferson never entertained it.

* * *

We were soothingly told at the bar of this Court that we need not worry about the kind of remedy a court could effectively fashion once the abstract constitutional right to have courts pass on a state-wide system of electoral districting is recognized as a matter of judicial rhetoric, because legislatures would heed the Court's admonition. This is not only a euphoric hope. It implies a sorry confession of judicial impotence in place of a frank acknowledgment that there is not under our Constitution a judicial remedy for every political mischief, for every undesirable exercise of legislative power. The Framers carefully and with deliberate forethought refused so to enthrone the judiciary. In this situation, as in others of like nature, appeal for relief does not belong here. Appeal must be to an informed, civically militant electorate. In a democratic society like ours, relief must come through an aroused popular conscience that sears the conscience of the people's representatives. In any event there is nothing judicially more unseemly nor more self-defeating than for this Court to make *in terrorem* pronouncements, to indulge in merely empty rhetoric, sounding a word of promise to the ear, sure to be disappointing to the hope.

* * *

* * * From its earliest opinions this Court has consistently recognized a class of controversies which do not lend themselves to judicial standards and judicial remedies. To classify the various instances as "political questions" is rather a form of stating this conclusion than revealing of analysis. Some of the cases so labelled have no relevance here. But from others emerge unifying considerations that are compelling.

1. The cases concerning war or foreign affairs, for example, are usually explained by the necessity of the country's speaking with one voice in such matters. While this concern alone undoubtedly accounts for many of the decisions, others do not fit the pattern. It would hardly embarrass the conduct of war were this Court to determine, in connection with private transactions between litigants, the date upon which war is to be deemed terminated. But the Court has refused to do so. * * * It does not suffice

to explain such cases as Ludecke v. Watkins, 335 U.S. 160—deferring to political determination the question of the duration of war for purposes of the Presidential power to deport alien enemies—that judicial intrusion would seriously impede the President's power effectively to protect the country's interests in time of war. Of course, this is true; but the precise issue presented is the duration of the time of war which demands the power. * * * And even for the purpose of determining the extent of congressional regulatory power over the tribes and dependent communities of Indians, it is ordinarily for Congress, not the Court, to determine whether or not a particular Indian group retains the characteristics constitutionally requisite to confer the power. * * * A controlling factor in such cases is that, decision respecting these kinds of complex matters of policy being traditionally committed not to courts but to the political agencies of government for determination by criteria of political expediency, there exists no standard ascertainable by settled judicial experience or process by reference to which a political decision affecting the question at issue between the parties can be judged. Where the question arises in the course of a litigation involving primarily the adjudication of other issues between the litigants, the Court accepts as a basis for adjudication the political departments' decision of it. But where its determination is the sole function to be served by the exercise of the judicial power, the Court will not entertain the action. * * * The dominant consideration is "the lack of satisfactory criteria for a judicial determination" * * *.

This may be, like so many questions of law, a matter of degree. * * * The doctrine of political questions, like any other, is not to be applied beyond the limits of its own logic, with all the quiddities and abstract disharmonies it may manifest. * * *

2. The Court has been particularly unwilling to intervene in matters concerning the structure and organization of the political institutions of the States. * * *

3. The cases involving Negro disfranchisement are no exception to the principle of avoiding federal judicial intervention into matters of state government in the absence of an explicit and clear constitutional imperative. For here the controlling command of Supreme Law is plain and unequivocal. * * *

4. The Court has refused to exercise its jurisdiction to pass on "abstract questions of political power, of sovereignty, of government." Massachusetts v. Mellon, 262 U.S. 447, 485. * * * The crux of the matter is that courts are not fit instruments of decision where what is essentially at stake is the composition of those large contests of policy traditionally fought out in non-judicial forums, by which governments and the actions of governments are made and unmade. * * *

5. The influence of these converging considerations—the caution not to undertake decision where standards meet for judicial judgment are lacking, the reluctance to interfere with matters of state government in the absence of an unquestionable and effectively enforceable mandate, the unwillingness to make courts arbiters of the broad issues of political organization historically committed to other institutions and for whose adjustment the judicial process is ill-adapted—has been decisive of the settled line of cases, reaching back more than a century, which holds that

Art. IV, § 4, of the Constitution, guaranteeing to the States "a Republican Form of Government," is not enforceable through the courts. * * *

The present case involves all of the elements that have made the Guarantee Clause cases non-justiciable. It is, in effect, a Guarantee Clause claim masquerading under a different label. But it cannot make the case more fit for judicial action that appellants invoke the Fourteenth Amendment rather than Art. IV, § 4, where, in fact, the gist of their complaint is the same—unless it can be found that the Fourteenth Amendment speaks with greater particularity to their situation. * * * Art. IV, § 4, is not committed by express constitutional terms to Congress. It is the nature of the controversies arising under it, nothing else, which has made it judicially unenforceable. * * *

At first blush, [appellants'] charge of discrimination based on legislative underrepresentation is given the appearance of a more private, less impersonal claim, than the assertion that the frame of government is askew. * * * However, the discrimination relied on is the deprivation of what appellants conceive to be their proportionate share of political influence. This, of course, is the practical effect of any allocation of power within the institutions of government. * * *

What, then, is this question of legislative apportionment? Appellants invoke the right to vote and to have their votes counted. But they are permitted to vote and their votes are counted. They go to the polls, they cast their ballots, they send their representatives to the state councils. Their complaint is simply that the representatives are not sufficiently numerous or powerful—in short, that Tennessee has adopted a basis of representation with which they are dissatisfied. Talk of "debasement" or "dilution" is circular talk. One cannot speak of "debasement" or "dilution" of the value of a vote until there is first defined a standard of reference as to what a vote should be worth. What is actually asked of the Court in this case is to choose among competing bases of representation— ultimately, really, among competing theories of political philosophy—in order to establish an appropriate frame of government for the State of Tennessee and thereby for all the States of the Union.

In such a matter, abstract analogies which ignore the facts of history deal in unrealities; they betray reason. This is not a case in which a State has, through a device however oblique and sophisticated, denied Negroes or Jews or redheaded persons a vote, or given them only a third or a sixth of a vote. * * * What Tennessee illustrates is an old and still widespread method of representation—representation by local geographical division, only in part respective of population—in preference to others, others, forsooth, more appealing. Appellants contest this choice and seek to make this Court the arbiter of the disagreement. They would make the Equal Protection Clause the charter of adjudication, asserting that the equality which it guarantees comports, if not the assurance of equal weight to every voter's vote, at least the basic conception that representation ought to be proportionate to population, a standard by reference to which the reasonableness of apportionment plans may be judged.

To find such a political conception legally enforceable in the broad and unspecific guarantee of equal protection is to rewrite the Constitution. See Luther v. Borden, *supra*. Certainly, "equal protection" is no more secure a foundation for judicial judgment of the permissibility of varying forms of representative government than is "Republican Form." * * *

The notion that representation proportioned to the geographic spread of population is so universally accepted as a necessary element of equality between man and man that it must be taken to be the standard of a political equality preserved by the Fourteenth Amendment—that it is, in appellants' words "the basic principle of representative government"—is, to put it bluntly, not true. However desirable and however desired by some among the great political thinkers and framers of our government, it has never been generally practiced, today or in the past. It was not the English system, it was not the colonial system, it was not the system chosen for the national government by the Constitution, it was not the system exclusively or even predominantly practiced by the States at the time of adoption of the Fourteenth Amendment, it is not predominantly practiced by the States today. Unless judges, the judges of this Court, are to make their private views of political wisdom the measure of the Constitution— views which in all honesty cannot but give the appearance, if not reflect the reality, of involvement with the business of partisan politics so inescapably a part of apportionment controversies—the Fourteenth Amendment, "itself a historical product," * * * provides no guide for judicial oversight of the representation problem. * * *

Manifestly, the Equal Protection Clause supplies no clearer guide for judicial examination of apportionment methods than would the Guarantee Clause itself. Apportionment, by its character, is a subject of extraordinary complexity, involving—even after the fundamental theoretical issues concerning what is to be represented in a representative legislature have been fought out or compromised—considerations of geography, demography, electoral convenience, economic and social cohesions or divergencies among particular local groups, communications, the practical effects of political institutions like the lobby and the city machine, ancient traditions and ties of settled usage, respect for proven incumbents of long experience and senior status, mathematical mechanics, censuses compiling relevant data, and a host of others. * * * The practical significance of apportionment is that the next election results may differ because of it. Apportionment battles are overwhelmingly party or intra-party contests. It will add a virulent source of friction and tension in federal-state relations to embroil the federal judiciary in them. * * *

Although the District Court had jurisdiction in the very restricted sense of power to determine whether it could adjudicate the claim, the case is of that class of political controversy which, by the nature of its subject, is unfit for federal judicial action. The judgment of the District Court, in dismissing the complaint for failure to state a claim on which relief can be granted, should therefore be affirmed.

Dissenting opinion of MR. JUSTICE HARLAN, whom MR. JUSTICE FRANK- FURTER joins. * * *

Once one cuts through the thicket of discussion devoted to "jurisdiction," "standing," "justiciability," and "political question," there emerges a straightforward issue which in my view, is determinative of this case. Does the complaint disclose a violation of a federal constitutional right, in other words, a claim over which a United States District Court would have jurisdiction under 28 U.S.C. § 1343(3) and 42 U.S.C. § 1983? The majority opinion does not actually discuss this basic question, but, as one concurring Justice observes, seems to decide it "*sub silentio.*" However, in my opinion, appellants' allegations, accepting all of them as true, do not, parsed down or as a whole, show an infringement by Tennessee of any rights assured by the Fourteenth Amendment. Accordingly, I believe the complaint should have been dismissed for "failure to state a claim upon which relief can be granted." * * *

In short, there is nothing in the Federal Constitution to prevent a State, acting not irrationally, from choosing any electoral legislative structure it thinks best suited to the interests, temper, and customs of its people. I would have thought this proposition settled by MacDougall v. Green, 335 U.S. 281, at p. 283, in which the Court observed that to "assume that political power is a function exclusively of numbers is to disregard the practicalities of government" * * *.

The suggestion of my Brother Frankfurter that courts lack standards by which to decide such cases as this, is relevant not only to the question of "justiciability," but also, and perhaps more fundamentally, to the determination whether any cognizable constitutional claim has been asserted in this case. Courts are unable to decide when it is that an apportionment originally valid becomes void because the factors entering into such a decision are basically matters appropriate only for legislative judgment. And so long as there exists a possible rational legislative policy for retaining an existing apportionment, such a legislative decision cannot be said to breach the bulwark against arbitrariness and caprice that the Fourteenth Amendment affords. * * *

From a reading of the majority and concurring opinions one will not find it difficult to catch the premises that underlie this decision. The fact that the appellants have been unable to obtain political redress of their asserted grievances appears to be regarded as a matter which should lead the Court to stretch to find some basis for judicial intervention. While the Equal Protection Clause is invoked, the opinion for the Court notably eschews explaining how, consonant with past decisions, the undisputed facts in this case can be considered to show a violation of that constitutional provision. The majority seems to have accepted the argument, pressed at the bar, that if this Court merely asserts authority in this field, Tennessee and other "malapportioning" States will quickly respond with appropriate political action, so that this Court need not be greatly concerned about the federal courts becoming further involved in these matters. At the same time the majority has wholly failed to reckon with what the future may hold in store if this optimistic prediction is not fulfilled. Thus, what the Court is doing reflects more an adventure in judicial experimentation than a solid piece of constitutional adjudication. * * *

* * * Those observers of the Court who see it primarily as the last refuge for the correction of all inequality or injustice, no matter what its nature or source, will no doubt applaud this decision and its break with the past. Those who consider that continuing national respect for the Court's authority depends in large measure upon its wise exercise of self-restraint and discipline in constitutional adjudication, will view the decision with deep concern. * * *

NOTE ON POLITICAL QUESTIONS—AND SOME COMMENTS ON JUDICIAL "DISCRETION" TO REFUSE TO ADJUDICATE

(1) Every question about official action which is not a judicial question is a political question in the sense that it is a question to be decided by one or the other of the political departments of government, or by the electorate. Consider whether the questions denominated as "political" in the cases have any other element in common than this conclusion that they involve matters as to which the political departments or the electorate ought to have the final say. Consider also the extent to which the various criteria articulated in the Baker case, and explored in this Note, are helpful in deciding whether a particular question is political in this sense.[1]

(2) One of the criteria laid down in the Baker case is whether there is a "textually demonstrable constitutional commitment of the issue to a coordinate political department." In what instances does the "text" of the Constitution make such a commitment? May sources other than the text be consulted in making the determination?

Until Powell v. McCormack, 395 U.S. 486 (1969), one might have thought that a clear instance of such a textual commitment was the provision of Art. I, § 5, that "Each House shall be the Judge of the * * * Qualifications of its own Members." That case involved the question whether Adam Clayton Powell, Jr. was constitutionally entitled to take the seat in the House of Representatives to which he had been elected. It was conceded that he met the age, citizenship, and residence requirements of Art. I, § 2, but he had been denied his seat by a House resolution on the basis of findings by a Select Committee that he "had asserted an unwarranted privilege and immunity from the processes of the courts of New York; that he had wrongfully diverted House funds for the use of others and himself; and that he had made false reports on expenditures of foreign currency to the Committee on House Administration" (p. 492). Together with some voters in his district, he brought suit for a declaration that his exclusion was unconstitutional (and for back salary). The district court dismissed the complaint and the court of appeals affirmed. The Supreme Court reversed (Justice Stewart alone dissenting on the ground that the case was moot). Chief Justice Warren, for the Court, held that the claim did not present a political question. After a lengthy historical examination, he concluded that the provision of Art. I, § 5, is "at most a 'textually demonstrable commitment' to Congress to judge only the qualifications expressly set forth in the Constitution" (p. 548).[2]

As the Powell case shows, the Court's inquiry on the issue of commitment to other branches has included such matters as the precedents of the English Parliament and American colonial assemblies prior to the Constitutional Convention, the debates at that convention, and the debates at state ratifying conventions. The requirement of a "textually demonstrable

---

1. For writings on the political question doctrine, see Redish, *Judicial Review and the Political Question,* 79 Nw.U.L.Rev. 1031 (1985); Henkin, *Is There a Political Question Doctrine?,* 85 Yale L.J. 597 (1976); Scharpf, *Judicial Review and the Political Question: A Functional Analysis,* 75 Yale L.J. 517 (1966); Finkelstein, *Judicial Self-Limitation,* 37 Harv.L.Rev. 338 (1924); Fin-

kelstein, *Further Notes on Judicial Self-Limitation,* 39 Harv.L.Rev. 221 (1925).

2. The Court also rejected several other arguments for concluding that the case presented a political question, including those discussed in Paragraphs (3) and (4), *infra.*

commitment," in other words, is not to be taken literally. Is there any reason why it should be? Shouldn't the issue of constitutional allocation of power to branches other than the judicial be decided on the same basis as all other constitutional issues, using legislative history, judicial precedent, and other relevant material as well as the text of the document? [3]

The Constitution provides that the House has the "sole Power of Impeachment" and the Senate possesses the "sole Power to try all Impeachments" (with the Chief Justice presiding when the trial is of the President). Art. I, § 2, cl. 5, and § 3, cl. 6. Should questions relating to impeachment proceedings be subject to any judicial consideration or review? Should final effectiveness of the judgment have to await such review? In a case involving impeachment or trial of a President? Does the text suggest that Congress has the final word on the meaning of the terms "other high Crimes and Misdemeanors" in Art. II, § 4? Compare Berger, Impeachment: The Constitutional Problems 103–21 (1973) (arguing, primarily in the context of non-Presidential impeachment proceedings, that the scope and content of these terms is a question of law subject to judicial review), with Black, Impeachment: A Handbook 53–55 (1974); Kurland, Watergate and the Constitution 121–30 (1978); Wechsler, *Toward Neutral Principles of Constitutional Law,* 73 Harv.L.Rev. 1, 8 (1959).

(3) A further criterion for identifying political questions was advanced in Baker: "the impossibility of a court's undertaking independent resolution without expressing lack of the respect due coordinate branches of government." Does this criterion add anything to that discussed in Paragraph (2)? Should it? Does it indicate that judicial review may be unavailable even when ordinary processes of constitutional interpretation do *not* yield the conclusion that the matter has been committed to the final discretion of another branch? Does this criterion have more bite when the issue involves a dispute *between* the other two branches? [4]

In Powell v. McCormack, Paragraph (2), *supra,* the Court rejected an argument based on this criterion in conclusory language: "[A]s our interpretation of Art. I, § 5, discloses, a determination of petitioner Powell's right to sit would require no more than an interpretation of the Constitution. Such a determination falls within the traditional role accorded courts to interpret the law, and does not involve a 'lack of respect due [a]

3. For other cases in which this issue was considered, see INS v. Chadha, 462 U.S. 919, 940–43 (1983) (rejecting a claim that the constitutionality of the one-House veto of a suspension of deportation was a political question; the grant of power to Congress to "establish an uniform Rule of Naturalization" did not preclude the Court from considering whether Congress had chosen a permissible means of implementing that power); United States v. Nixon, 418 U.S. 683, 692–97 (1974) (rejecting the argument, in an action to enforce a subpoena against the President, that his claim of executive privilege raised a political question; the question was one arising in the regular course of a federal criminal prosecution and thus was "within the traditional scope of Art. III power"); Gilligan v. Morgan, 413 U.S. 1 (1973), note 7, *infra.*

4. Professor Choper has argued, in Judicial Review and the National Political Process (1980), that questions involving the proper relationship of Congress to the President (as well as questions involving the proper relationship between the states and the federal government) should be nonjusticiable. His theory is that the political process is capable of protecting the relevant interests, and that the courts should preserve their institutional capital for the protection of individual rights.

For criticism of this view, see Monaghan, Book Review, 94 Harv.L.Rev. 296 (1980); Farago, *The Asymmetrical Hermeneutics of Jesse Choper,* 15 Val.U.L.Rev. 603 (1981).

coordinate [branch] of the federal government,' nor does it involve an 'initial policy determination of a kind clearly for nonjudicial discretion.' Our system of government requires that federal courts on occasion interpret the Constitution in a manner at variance with the construction given the document by another branch. The alleged conflict that such an adjudication may cause cannot justify the courts' avoiding their constitutional responsibility" (pp. 548–49).

The criterion of respect for other branches does appear to have played a significant role, however, at least for some Justices in some cases decided before and after Powell. Thus in Coleman v. Miller, 307 U.S. 433 (1939), referred to several times in Baker, the Court "affirmed" a judgment of the Supreme Court of Kansas refusing to restrain the Kansas Secretary of State from certifying that Kansas had ratified the Child Labor Amendment. Chief Justice Hughes, in an opinion for three Justices, said (a) that the question whether Kansas, once having rejected the amendment, could later ratify it was a question that Congress had the ultimate authority to decide, and (b) that while ratification of a proposed amendment must occur within a "reasonable time" after promulgation of the proposal, decision of that question was "essentially political and not justiciable. * * * In determining whether a question falls within that category [of political questions], the appropriateness under our system of government of attributing finality to the action of the political departments and also the lack of satisfactory criteria for a judicial determination are dominant considerations" (pp. 454–55).

Justice Black, in an opinion for four Justices, said that "Congress has sole and complete control over the amending process, subject to no judicial review" (p. 459), and thus no opinion should be expressed even on the question whether ratification must take place within a reasonable time.[5]

Justice Black's view is supported by Scharpf, note 1, *supra*, at 589: "It is one thing for the Court to strike down the Child Labor Law as incompatible with its choice of constitutional values * * * but it would seem to be quite a different matter if the Court could, by a narrow interpretation of the amendment procedures, prevent the ratification of the amendment which was intended to overrule [the Court's decision]. Of course, the amendment process is itself governed by the Constitution, and it is by no means inconceivable that an amendment might be unconstitutional. But this seems to be one instance in which the Court cannot assume responsibility for saying 'what the law is' without, at the same time, undermining the legitimacy of its power to say so."[6]

More recently, in Goldwater v. Carter, 444 U.S. 996 (1979), the Court, summarily and without opinion, vacated a lower court judgment holding, on the merits, that the President had authority to terminate a mutual defense treaty with Taiwan without the approval of either two-thirds of the Senate or a majority of both Houses of Congress. Justice Rehnquist, in an

---

5. Justice Butler, with whom Justice McReynolds joined, thought that mandamus should be granted on the ground that a reasonable time had expired.

6. See also Professor Dellinger's argument for a substantially expanded judicial role in reviewing amending process issues, *The Legitimacy of Constitutional Change:* *Rethinking the Amending Process*, 97 Harv.L.Rev. 386 (1983); Professor Tribe's reply, *A Constitution We Are Amending:* *In Defense of a Restrained Judicial Role*, 97 Harv.L.Rev. 433 (1983); and Professor Dellinger's response, *Constitutional Politics: A Rejoinder*, 97 Harv.L.Rev. 446 (1983).

opinion for four Justices, concurred in the judgment; citing Coleman v. Miller, he argued that since the Constitution spoke only of the ratification of treaties, and not of their termination, the question of the President's power unilaterally to terminate a treaty was a political one. In addition, he emphasized that the question involved the politically sensitive area of foreign affairs and that especially in this area judicial intervention in "a dispute between coequal branches of our Government, each of which has resources available to protect and assert its interests" (p. 1004) was inappropriate.[7] Justice Powell, in a concurring opinion, disagreed with the view that the question was a political one; he argued that the case was not ripe—that prudential considerations militated against judicial involvement in a quarrel between the other two branches until and unless those branches were more at loggerheads than was indicated by the record before the Court.

(4) Still another criterion referred to in Baker, and one frequently discussed in the cases, is the "lack of judicially discoverable and manageable standards for resolving" the controversy.[8] (Note the reference to this factor in the Baker Court's discussion of Luther v. Borden[9] and in Chief Justice Hughes' opinion in Coleman v. Miller, Paragraph (3), *supra*.) If the problem raised by this criterion involves a search for standards for determining invalidity, is the absence of satisfactory standards for making that determination itself a demonstration of validity?

7. See also Gilligan v. Morgan, 413 U.S. 1 (1973), in which officers of the student government at Kent State University, acting in the aftermath of the shootings that occurred there in May 1970, sued for injunctive relief against the Ohio National Guard. The court of appeals had remanded for a determination whether the Guard employed a pattern of weaponry, training, and orders making inevitable the use of lethal force to quell civil disorders. The Supreme Court held that a combination of factors—possible mootness, doubts as to standing, and commitment of military functions to Congress and the Executive—rendered the issue nonjusticiable. In the course of its opinion, the Court agreed with the dissent below that the relief sought would offend every one of the Baker criteria, and noted: "[I]t is difficult to conceive of an area of governmental activity in which the courts have less competence. * * * The ultimate responsibility for these decisions [as to the composition, training, equipping, and control of a military force] is appropriately vested in branches of the government which are periodically subject to electoral accountability" (p. 10). But *cf.* Scheuer v. Rhodes, 416 U.S. 232, 249 (1974) (holding Gilligan v. Morgan not a bar to actions for damages by the estates of students killed at the Kent State demonstration).

8. A similar criterion has been invoked under the rubric of what has sometimes been referred to as "administrative questions". Thus in Federal Radio Com'n v. General Electric Co., 281 U.S. 464 (1930), the Court held that it could not review a decision by the D.C. Circuit reversing the Commission's denial of a license. The relevant statute had given the lower court authority to review the record and the evidence and to "alter or revise the decision appealed from and to enter such judgment as to it may seem just." Review under such a standard, the Court concluded, was an administrative function, and while the D.C. Circuit might perform such a function (*cf.* p. 46, *supra*), the Supreme Court could not.

Following this decision, Congress amended the statute to limit court of appeals review to "questions of law", and the Supreme Court held that it had jurisdiction to review a court of appeals decision under that standard. Federal Radio Com'n v. Nelson Bros. B. & M. Co., 289 U.S. 266 (1933). Subsequent decisions upholding power to review administrative action under broad standards cast doubt on the continued vitality of the General Electric decision. See, *e.g.*, United States v. First City Nat. Bank, 386 U.S. 361 (1967).

9. *Cf.* Note, 100 Harv.L.Rev. 1125, 1128 (1987) (arguing that "despite its claim that it was abstaining from adjudicating the substantive issues, the Luther Court decisively repudiated the idea of a principled competency standard upon which the republican conception of a right to political participation depends").

After the Baker decision, the Court went on to develop the "one person, one vote" rule in apportionment cases. See Reynolds v. Sims, 377 U.S. 533 (1964). (Was this rule in part a result of the inability of a majority to discern or agree on a workable standard short of substantial arithmetical equality?) Two decades after Reynolds, the Court rejected a claim that a challenge to political gerrymandering of legislative districts raised a non-justiciable political question. Davis v. Bandemer, 478 U.S. 109 (1986). The Court in Davis, while conceding that no similar arithmetical resolution could be applied in gerrymandering cases, relied heavily on the Baker line of decisions in rejecting the argument that judicially manageable standards were not available. (The Court also relied on several racial gerrymandering cases, e.g., Rogers v. Lodge, 458 U.S. 613 (1982).) In dissent, Justice O'Connor, for herself and three other Justices, argued that the question was a political one, in large part because of the lack of such standards. She asserted that the claim of discrimination against a political group, if sustained, would inevitably lead to unwarranted judicial superintendence and to a requirement of "some loose form of proportionality" (p. 2822). Thus the claim was qualitatively different from claims involving either numerical malapportionment or discrimination against racial groups.

(5) The Baker Court also referred to "embarrassment of our government abroad, or grave disturbance at home" as grounds for holding an issue to be political. Cases involving recognition of foreign governments and related matters (discussed in the Baker opinion) appear to fall into the first of these categories, but the Court has often passed on similarly sensitive issues even when they touched on our relations with other countries. Thus in Japan Whaling Ass'n v. American Cetacean Society, 106 S.Ct. 2860 (1986), the Court (unanimously on this point) rejected the government's argument that it should not review a decision of the Secretary of Commerce refusing to certify that Japan's whaling practices diminished the effectiveness of an international conservation program. "[U]nder the Constitution'" the Court said," one of the judiciary's characteristic roles is to interpret statutes, and we cannot shirk this responsibility merely because our decision may have significant political overtones" (p. 2866).

Under what circumstances might the fear of "grave disturbance at home" warrant a conclusion of nonjusticiability? Note that in the school desegregation cases beginning with Brown v. Board of Education, the Court was obviously influenced by this concern in formulating guidelines for implementation of its decision, but did not even discuss the matter in its determination of the underlying constitutional claim. Should it have done so? [10]

(6) All of the criteria discussed in Baker and in this Note were put to the test in a series of cases during the late '60s and early '70s attacking the legality of the Vietnam War. These cases included a variety of challenges (by individuals, groups, and even states) to executive actions relating to Vietnam and Cambodia in the absence of a formal declaration of war by the Congress. The Supreme Court never gave plenary consideration to the

---

10. Recent disclosures indicate that several Justices did fear domestic repercussions from the outset and that their decision to join in the Brown decision was aided by the government's argument (as amicus) that the district courts could be given "a reasonable time to work out the details and timing of implementation of the decision." Elman, *The Solicitor General's Office, Justice Frankfurter, and Civil Rights Litigation, 1946–60: An Oral History,* 100 Harv.L.Rev. 817, 827 (1987).

justiciability of any of these challenges, though in one case it summarily affirmed a three-judge court holding of nonjusticiability,[11] and in another summarily denied leave to file an original complaint.[12] But a number of lower courts did pass on this question, and invariably held all or a substantial part of the issues raised to be nonjusticiable.[13] Factors cited included the lack of manageable standards, commitment of final authority to other branches of the federal government, and the difficulty of gaining access to and determining the relevant facts. Several commentators urged, however, that at least some of the challenges did present justiciable issues of the scope of executive power. See, *e.g.,* Henkin, note 1, *supra,* at 623–24.[14]

If it had been held that our actions in Vietnam and Cambodia violated the Constitution, what consequences would have flowed from the decision? Was the Court right in Powell v. McCormack when it described as an "inadmissible suggestion" the risk that "action might be taken in disregard of a judicial determination" (p. 549, n. 86)? Do problems of enforcement and confrontation with other branches loom larger in cases like those challenging executive actions in Vietnam than in a case like Powell? *Cf.* Youngstown Sheet & Tube Co. v. Sawyer, 343 U.S. 579 (1952), p. 1129, *infra.*

(7) Does the political question doctrine have its source in the Constitution, including Article III as well as other provisions, or is it founded on some other base? To what extent does the doctrine permit the courts, in the exercise of their discretion, to decline to resolve an issue that is both justiciable and within their jurisdiction? Consider the following views:

"[A]ll the [political question] doctrine can defensibly imply is that the courts are called upon to judge whether the Constitution has committed to another agency of government the autonomous determination of the issue raised, a finding that itself requires an interpretation. * * * [T]he only proper judgment that may lead to an abstention from decision is that the Constitution has committed the determination of the issue to another agency of government than the courts. Difficult as it may be to make that judgment wisely, whatever factors may be rightly weighed in situations where the answer is not clear, what is involved is in itself an act of constitutional interpretation, to be made and judged by standards that should govern the interpretive process generally. That, I submit, is *toto*

---

11. Atlee v. Richardson, 411 U.S. 911 (1973). Justices Douglas, Brennan, and Stewart would have noted probable jurisdiction.

12. Massachusetts v. Laird, 400 U.S. 886 (1970). Justices Harlan, Stewart, and Douglas dissented; Justice Douglas, in a separate opinion, considered the justiciability issue at some length. In several other cases involving similar challenges, there were dissents from decisions denying certiorari. *E.g.,* Mora v. McNamara, 389 U.S. 934 (1967); Da Costa v. Laird, 405 U.S. 979 (1972).

13. *E.g.,* Mitchell v. Laird, 488 F.2d 611 (D.C.Cir.1973); Orlando v. Laird, 443 F.2d 1039 (2d Cir.1971); Massachusetts v. Laird, 451 F.2d 26 (1st Cir.1971). In Orlando, the court held that there was a manageable standard "imposing on the Congress a duty of mutual participation in the prosecution of war," but that the question of "[t]he form which congressional authorization should take is one of policy, committed to the discretion of Congress and outside the power and competence of the judiciary" (pp. 1042–43).

14. For recent echoes of the Vietnam decisions, see Crockett v. Reagan, 720 F.2d 1355 (D.C.Cir.1983), and Sanchez–Espinoza v. Reagan, 770 F.2d 202 (D.C.Cir.1985), holding nonjusticiable challenges to the Administration's activities in El Salvador and Nicaragua.

caelo different from a broad discretion to abstain or intervene." Wechsler, Principles, Politics and Fundamental Law 11–14 (1961).[15]

"[O]nly by means of a play on words can the broad discretion that the courts have in fact exercised be turned into an act of constitutional interpretation governed by the general standards of the interpretive process. The political-question doctrine simply resists being domesticated in this fashion. There is * * * something different about it, in kind not in degree; something greatly more flexible, something of prudence, not construction and not principle. And it is something that cannot exist within the four corners of Marbury v. Madison. * * *

" * * * Such is the foundation, in both intellect and instinct, of the political-question doctrine: the Court's sense of lack of capacity, compounded in unequal parts of (a) the strangeness of the issue and its intractibility to principled resolution; (b) the sheer momentousness of it, which tends to unbalance judicial judgment; (c) the anxiety, not so much that the judicial judgment will be ignored, as that perhaps it should but will not be; (d) finally ('in a mature democracy'), the inner vulnerability, the self-doubt of an institution which is electorally irresponsible and has no earth to draw strength from." Bickel, The Least Dangerous Branch 125–26, 184 (1962).[16]

The question of judicial discretion not to exercise jurisdiction conferred by the Constitution and by statute has come up before in these materials and will come up again. See, *e.g.,* p. 87, *supra* ; pp. 740, 1839 *infra* ; see generally Shapiro, *Jurisdiction and Discretion,* 60 N.Y.U.L.Rev. 543 (1985). But in the present context, invocation of discretion often goes beyond questions of timing, appropriate forum, and the appropriate form of relief, and may operate to leave a person injured by a constitutional violation effectively without redress. Can such a result be squared with the constitutional duty imposed on the federal courts by Marbury v. Madison?

Note the difference, in this connection, between the opinion of Justice Rehnquist and that of Justice Powell in Goldwater v. Carter, Paragraph (3), *supra.* Justice Rehnquist would hold the question of the President's power to terminate a treaty to be beyond judicial cognizance no matter what the context. Justice Powell's approach is that in a matter of such sensitivity, arising between two other coordinate branches, the courts may not escape ultimate responsibility but should abstain so long as there is any chance that the dispute will be resolved extrajudicially.

---

15. See also Henkin, note 1, *supra,* at 622–23 (arguing that the doctrine is "an unnecessary, deceptive packaging of several established doctrines" whose "proper content" relates to such matters as the obligation of the courts to "accept decisions by the political branches within their constitutional authority" and the ability of the courts to "refuse some (or all) remedies for want of equity").

16. See also Moore, Law and the Indo-China War 574–78 (1972).

Chapter III

THE ORIGINAL JURISDICTION OF THE SUPREME COURT

INTRODUCTORY NOTE ON THE POWER OF CONGRESS TO REGULATE THE JURISDICTION AND TO GIVE CONCURRENT JURISDICTION TO THE DISTRICT AND STATE COURTS

(1) The Constitution specifically defines the original jurisdiction, and the Supreme Court has repeatedly said that it can be exercised without further enabling action by Congress. See, *e.g.*, Kentucky v. Dennison, 24 How. 66, 86 (U.S.1861).[1] (It will be observed, however, that the present statute, 28 U.S.C. § 1251, fails to dispose of the whole of the constitutional grant.)

(2) Does this mean that Congress has no power to contract or qualify the original jurisdiction?

In California v. Arizona, 440 U.S. 59 (1979), the Court held that the United States was an indispensable party to an original action, brought by California against Arizona and the United States, to quiet title to certain land. It held further that the immunity of the United States was not an obstacle to the action because the United States had consented to suit in 28 U.S.C. § 2409a(a), which permits the United States to be named as defendant in certain actions relating to real property. (See further, as to this statute, p. 1155, *infra*.) The Court held the consent effective notwithstanding 28 U.S.C. § 1346(f), which gives the *district* courts "exclusive original jurisdiction" of actions under § 2409a(a). The Court interpreted the legislative history as showing that the purpose of exclusivity was to assure that no such actions could be brought in a state court, and not to divest the Supreme Court of actions otherwise within its original jurisdiction. The Court stated that any other construction would raise constitutional difficulties: "It is clear, of course, that Congress could refuse to waive the Nation's sovereign immunity in all cases or only in some cases but in all courts. Either action would bind this Court even in the exercise of its original jurisdiction. * * * But once Congress has waived the Nation's sovereign immunity, it is far from clear that it can withdraw the constitutional jurisdiction of this Court over such suits. The constitutional grant to this Court of original jurisdiction is limited to cases involving the States and the envoys of foreign nations. The Framers seem to have been concerned with matching the dignity of the parties to the status of the court. * * * Elimination of this Court's original jurisdiction would require those sovereign parties to go to another court, in derogation of this constitutional purpose. Congress has broad powers over the jurisdiction of the federal courts and over the sovereign immunity of the United States, but it is

---

1. See further, as to this case, p. 1191 n. 1, *infra*.

extremely doubtful that they include the power to limit in this manner the original jurisdiction conferred upon this Court by the Constitution" (pp. 65–66).[2]

In South Carolina v. Regan, 465 U.S. 367 (1984), the state brought an action in the original jurisdiction against the Secretary of the Treasury to enjoin the enforcement of the provisions of the federal tax code specifying that interest on bearer bonds issued by a state (unlike interest on registered state bonds) shall be subject to federal income tax. South Carolina alleged that these provisions violated the state's Tenth Amendment rights. The Court held, surprisingly, that the Tax Code's Anti–Injunction Act, 26 U.S.C. § 7421(a), which provides that no suit to restrain the assessment or collection of any federal tax "shall be maintained in any court by any person, whether or not such person is the person against whom such tax was assessed," does not apply to aggrieved parties (such as South Carolina here) who have no alternative forum for litigating the validity of a tax; South Carolina, the Court said, had no effective way to raise its Tenth Amendment claim except by an injunctive or declaratory action. Justice O'Connor, concurring, argued that the Anti–Injunction Act does apply even to plaintiffs who have no alternative remedy. She stated, however, that to read the Act as applicable to original actions brought by a state in the Supreme Court would raise a "grave" constitutional question: "whether Congress constitutionally can impose remedial limitations so jurisdictional in nature that they effectively withdraw the original jurisdiction of this Court" (p. 395). Justice O'Connor stated that to apply the Act would mean that the Court could never exercise its original jurisdiction to pass on a state's Tenth Amendment tax claim. In order to avoid this constitutional problem, she argued that the Act should be construed not to apply to original actions brought by a state in the Supreme Court.

Surely, the proposition that Congress cannot deprive the Supreme Court of original jurisdiction over cases falling within the constitutional boundaries of that jurisdiction should not be deemed to bar Congress from passing general measures, otherwise valid, regulating who may bring federal claims, what remedies they may seek, when these claims may be brought, and what procedures apply to the suit. The constitutional purpose of the original jurisdiction—to afford states and foreign diplomats access to a court having a status appropriate to their "sovereign" character—does not require that the doors of that Court be wider than those of any other federal court; general procedural requirements, such as limitation periods and exhaustion rules, may surely be applied to the Supreme Court like all other federal courts. Thus if Congress has the substantive constitutional authority, apart from Article III, to specify that only taxpayers may litigate the validity of a federal tax and may do so only by way of refund suits, why should the application of that statute to a plaintiff such

2. In South Carolina v. Regan, 465 U.S. 367 (1984), a Supplemental Memorandum filed by the United States stated about California v. Arizona (p. 3 n. 4): "We do not fully understand how granting exclusive jurisdiction to a district court (or any other tribunal) over actions that previously were barred by sovereign immunity in all federal courts can be said to 'withdraw' (440 U.S. at 65) or 'limit' (id. at 66) this Court's original jurisdiction. • • • The Court may wish to reconsider the broad dictum of California v. Arizona • • • before States with claims under the Tucker Act or the Tort Claims Act, or the Internal Revenue Code, are emboldened to invoke this Court's original jurisdiction, notwithstanding provisions of the Judicial Code apparently restricting such suits to lower courts. See 28 U.S.C. §§ 1346(a)(1), 1346(a)(2), 1346(b), 1491; 26 U.S.C. §§ 6213(a), 7422."

as South Carolina be deemed invalid solely because it would result in the failure of a case theretofore maintainable in the original jurisdiction? Justice O'Connor's constitutional analysis works only on the assumption that South Carolina has a *constitutional* right as such to enforce its Tenth Amendment "rights" by judicial action. Does the Tenth Amendment guarantee the states such an action? Should Article III itself be deemed to give the states such a cause of action? *Cf.* General Oil v. Crain, p. 586, *infra.*

Should it be deemed an unconstitutional narrowing of the original jurisdiction to apply statutes such as the Norris LaGuardia Act (see p. 370, *infra*), or the United States Arbitration Act (see p. 810, *infra*), or the anti-injunction provision codified in 28 U.S.C. § 2283 (see p. 1309, *infra*), to cases falling within the original jurisdiction? Are these questions answered by the Court's statement in California v. Arizona, *supra,* that Congress has clear power to insist on the sovereign immunity of the United States "in all courts ∗ ∗ ∗ [including] this Court even in the exercise of its original jurisdiction"?

(3) Although there is dictum to the contrary in Marbury v. Madison, 1 Cranch 137, 174 (U.S.1803), Congress has, ever since the First Judiciary Act, § 13, 1 Stat. 73, 80, assumed the power to make the Supreme Court's original jurisdiction in part concurrent with the jurisdiction of the lower federal courts or with state courts. The two paragraphs of § 1251 show the present division between exclusive and concurrent jurisdiction. Observe, however, that § 1251(b) does not purport itself to confer jurisdiction on any other court, but simply permits a jurisdiction otherwise existing or conferred to operate. *Cf.* 28 U.S.C. § 1351, giving the district courts jurisdiction "of all actions and proceedings against consuls or vice consuls of foreign states", and making that jurisdiction "exclusive of the courts of the States".

A divided circuit court composed of three judges, two of whom were Supreme Court Justices, early approved Congress's assumption that the constitutional grant of original jurisdiction to the Supreme Court was not exclusive. United States v. Ravara, 2 Dall. 297 (Cir.Pa.1793). So apparently did every lower federal court before which the question came in the next 90 years. But it was not until Börs v. Preston, 111 U.S. 252 (1884), and Ames v. Kansas, 111 U.S. 449 (1884), that the Supreme Court finally put the question to rest.

The opinions of the Court lean heavily on the contemporaneous legislative construction and on the unbroken line of judicial authority.

In Börs v. Preston, the Court quoted an observation of Chief Justice Taney on circuit (p. 260):

"∗ ∗ ∗ 'It could hardly have been the intention of the statesmen who framed our Constitution to require that one of our citizens who had a petty claim of even less than five dollars against another citizen, who had been clothed by some foreign government with the consular office, should be compelled to go into the Supreme Court to have a jury summoned in order to enable him to recover it; nor could it have been intended, that the time of that court, with all its high duties to perform, should be taken up with the trial of every petty offence that might be committed by a consul in any part of the United States; that consul, too, being often one of our own citizens.' "

In Ames v. Kansas, involving concurrent jurisdiction of a case removed from a state court to a federal circuit court, the Court said (p. 464): "The evident purpose was to open and keep open the highest court of the nation for the determination, in the first instance, of suits involving a State or a diplomatic or commercial representative of a foreign government. So much was due to the rank and dignity of those for whom the provision was made; but to compel a State to resort to this one tribunal for the redress of all its grievances, or to deprive an ambassador, public minister or consul of the privilege of suing in any court he chose having jurisdiction of the parties and the subject matter of his action, would be, in many cases, to convert what was intended as a favor into a burden."

The concurrent jurisdiction of the state court in Ames v. Kansas did not defeat access to a federal court, since the action could have been brought there by the plaintiff and in fact was removed there by the defendant, and since the decision was subject to review by the Supreme Court. However, in Plaquemines Tropical Fruit Co. v. Henderson, 170 U.S. 511 (1898), the Court upheld, against collateral attack, a judgment of a state court in an action by a state against citizens of another state, although the action could not have been removed to a federal trial court and the judgment was not subject to review by the Supreme Court.

Note also the conclusion of the Supreme Court that it may properly decline to hear a case of which it has original jurisdiction and remit the parties to some other more appropriate forum. Ohio v. Wyandotte Chem. Corp., p. 332 infra.

NOTE ON THE PROCEDURE IN ORIGINAL ACTIONS

Rule 9 of the 1980 Revised Rules of the Supreme Court provides that the "form of pleadings and motions in original actions shall be governed, so far as may be, by the Federal Rules of Civil Procedure, and in other respects those rules, where their application is appropriate, may be taken as a guide to procedure in original actions".[1] (Procedure in applications for extraordinary writs is governed by Rules 26–27; see p. 356, infra.)

Rule 9 states that the "initial pleading in any original action shall be prefaced by a motion for leave to file such pleading". The adverse parties have 60 days to file briefs in opposition to the motion. The Court often disposes of major issues of original jurisdiction in its ruling on the motion to file.[2] That ruling may be based on printed papers or may be preceded by oral argument.

1. See Utah v. United States, 394 U.S. 89, 95 (1969), holding that the FRCP are merely a "guide," and that a party may therefore waive the protections of Rule 19(a) whether or not this would be permissible in an ordinary action in the district courts.

2. In Ohio v. Kentucky, 410 U.S. 641 (1973), the Court denied Ohio's motion for leave to file an amended complaint in a boundary dispute. Noting that "proceedings under this Court's original jurisdiction are basically equitable in nature" (p. 648),

the Court stated that "procedures governing the exercise of our original jurisdiction are not invariably governed by common-law precedent or by current rules of civil procedure. * * * Under our rules, the requirement of a motion for leave to file a complaint, and the requirement of a brief in opposition, permit and enable us to dispose of matters at a preliminary stage" (p. 644). The Court held that Ohio's boundary claim was barred by century-long "acquiescence" in Kentucky's possession of the claimed territory.

"Additional pleadings," says Rule 9, "may be filed, and subsequent proceedings had, as the court may direct".

Since the earliest days, original cases have usually been equitable in character, and invariably the Court has dealt with problems of taking testimony and preparing findings of fact by the procedure of reference to a special master. The Seventh Amendment applies, however, to trials at common law in the Court (as 28 U.S.C. § 1872 recognizes), although no jury trial seems to have been held since the eighteenth century.[3]

SECTION 1. CASES IN WHICH A STATE IS A PARTY

UNITED STATES v. TEXAS

143 U.S. 621, 12 S.Ct. 488, 36 L.Ed. 285 (1892).
Original.

MR. JUSTICE HARLAN delivered the opinion of the Court.

This suit was brought by original bill in this court pursuant to the act of May 2, 1890, providing a temporary government for the territory of Oklahoma. The 25th section recites the existence of a controversy between the United States and the state of Texas as to the ownership of what is designated on the map of Texas as "Greer County," and provides that the act shall not be construed to apply to that county until the title to the same has been adjudicated and determined to be in the United States. In order that there might be a speedy and final judicial determination of this controversy the attorney general of the United States was authorized and directed to commence and prosecute on behalf of the United States a proper suit in equity in this court against the state of Texas, setting forth the title of the United States to the country lying between the North and South Forks of the Red river where the Indian Territory and the state of Texas adjoin, east of the 100th degree of longitude, and claimed by the state of Texas as within its boundary. * * *

The relief asked is a decree determining the true line between the United States and the state of Texas, and whether the land constituting what is called "Greer County" is within the boundary and jurisdiction of the United States or of the state of Texas. The government prays that its rights, as asserted in the bill, be established, and that it have such other relief as the nature of the case may require.

In support of the contention that the ascertainment of the boundary between a territory of the United States and one of the states of the Union is political in its nature and character, and not susceptible of judicial determination, the defendant cites Foster v. Neilson, 2 Pet. 253, 307, 309; Cherokee Nation v. Georgia, 5 Pet. 1, 21; U.S. v. Arredondo, 6 Pet. 691, 711; and Garcia v. Lee, 12 Pet. 511, 517. * * *

---

3. See Georgia v. Brailsford, 3 Dall. 1 (U.S.1794). See also 1 Carson, History of the Supreme Court of the United States 169, n. 1 (1902), describing two other unreported instances of trial by jury, in 1795 and 1797. *Cf.* United States v. Louisiana, 339 U.S. 699, 706 (1950), denying Louisiana's motion for a jury trial.

These authorities do not control the present case. They relate to questions of boundary between independent nations, and have no application to a question of that character arising between the general government and one of the states composing the Union, or between two states of the Union. By the articles of confederation, congress was made "the last resort on appeal in all disputes and differences" then subsisting or which thereafter might arise "between two or more states concerning boundary jurisdiction, or any other cause whatever;" the authority so conferred to be exercised by a special tribunal to be organized in the mode prescribed in those articles, and its judgment to be final and conclusive. Article 9. At the time of the adoption of the constitution, there existed, as this court said in Rhode Island v. Massachusetts, 12 Pet. 657, 723, 724, controversies between 11 states, in respect to boundaries, which had continued from the first settlement of the colonies. The necessity for the creation of some tribunal for the settlement of these and like controversies that might arise, under the new government to be formed, must, therefore, have been perceived by the framers of the constitution; and consequently, among the controversies to which the judicial power of the United States was extended by the constitution, we find those between two or more states. And that a controversy between two or more states, in respect to boundary, is one to which, under the constitution, such judicial power extends, is no longer an open question in this court. The cases of Rhode Island v. Massachusetts, 12 Pet. 657; New Jersey v. New York, 5 Pet. 284, 290; Missouri v. Iowa, 7 How. 660; Florida v. Georgia, 17 How. 478; Alabama v. Georgia, 23 How. 505; Virginia v. West Virginia, 11 Wall. 39, 55; Missouri v. Kentucky, 11 Wall. 395; Indiana v. Kentucky, 136 U.S. 479; and Nebraska v. Iowa, 143 U.S. 359,—were all original suits in this court for the judicial determination of disputed boundary lines between states. * * *

In view of these cases, it cannot with propriety be said that a question of boundary between a territory of the United States and one of the states of the Union is of a political nature, and not susceptible of judicial determination by a court having jurisdiction of such a controversy. The important question, therefore, is whether this court can, under the constitution, take cognizance of an original suit brought by the United States against a state to determine the boundary between one of the territories and such state. Texas insists that no such jurisdiction has been conferred upon this court, and that the only mode in which the present dispute can be peaceably settled is by agreement, in some form, between the United States and that state. Of course, if no such agreement can be reached,—and it seems that one is not probable,—and if neither party will surrender its claim of authority and jurisdiction over the disputed territory, the result, according to the defendant's theory of the constitution, must be that the United States, in order to effect a settlement of this vexed question of boundary, must bring its suit in one of the courts of Texas,—that state consenting that its courts may be opened for the assertion of claims against it by the United States,—or that in the end there must be a trial of physical strength between the government of the Union and Texas. The first alternative is unwarranted both by the letter and spirit of the constitution. Mr. Justice Story has well said: "It scarcely seems possible to raise a reasonable doubt as to the propriety of giving to the national courts jurisdiction of cases in which the United States are a party. It would be a perfect novelty in the history of national jurisprudence, as well as of public law, that a sovereign had no authority to sue in his own courts. Unless this power were given to the United States, the enforcement of all their rights, powers, contracts, and privileges in their sovereign capacity would be at the mercy of the states. They must be enforced, if at all, in the state tribunals." Story, Const. § 1674. The second alternative above mentioned has no place in our constitutional system, and cannot be contemplated by any patriot except with feelings of deep concern.

The cases in this court show that the framers of the constitution did provide by that instrument for the judicial determination of all cases in law and equity between two or more states, including those involving questions of boundary. Did they omit to provide for the judicial determination of controversies arising between the United States and one or more of the states of the Union? This question is, in effect, answered by U.S. v. North Carolina, 136 U.S. 211. That was an action of debt brought in this court by the United States against the state of North Carolina upon certain bonds issued by that state. The state appeared, the case was determined here upon its merits, and judgment was rendered for the state. It is true that no question was made as to the jurisdiction of this court, and nothing was therefore said in the opinion upon that subject. But it did not escape the attention of the court, and the judgment would not have been rendered except upon the theory that this court has original jurisdiction of a suit by the United States against a state. As, however, the question of jurisdiction is vital in this case, and is distinctly raised, it is proper to consider it upon its merits. * * *

It is apparent upon the face of [Article III] that in one class of cases the jurisdiction of the courts of the Union depends "on the character of the cause, whoever may be the parties," and in the other, on the character of the parties, whatever may be the subject of controversy. Cohens v. Virginia, 6 Wheat. 264, 378, 393. The present suit falls in each class; for it is plainly, one arising under the constitution, laws, and treaties of the United States, and also one in which the United States is a party. It is therefore one to which, by the express words of the constitution, the judicial power of the United States extends. That a circuit court of the United States has not jurisdiction, under existing statutes, of a suit by the United States against a state, is clear; for by the Revised Statutes it is declared—as was done by the judiciary act of 1789—that "the supreme court shall have exclusive jurisdiction of all controversies of a civil nature where a state is a party, except between a state and its citizens, or between a state and citizens of other states, or aliens, in which latter cases it shall have original, but not exclusive, jurisdiction." Rev.St. § 687; Act Sept. 24, 1789, c. 20, § 13; 1 St. p. 80. Such exclusive jurisdiction was given to this court because it best comported with the dignity of a state that a case in which it was a party should be determined in the highest, rather than in a subordinate, judicial tribunal of the nation. Why, then, may not this court take original cognizance of the present suit, involving a question of boundary between a territory of the United States and a state?

The words in the constitution, "in all cases * * * in which a state shall be party, the supreme court shall have original jurisdiction," necessarily refer to all cases mentioned in the preceding clause in which a state may be made of right a party defendant, or in which a state may of right be a party plaintiff. It is admitted that these words do not refer to suits brought against a state by its own citizens or by citizens of other states, or by citizens or subjects of foreign states, even where such suits arise under the constitution, laws, and treaties of the United States, because the judicial power of the United States does not extend to suits of individuals against states. Hans v. Louisiana, 134 U.S. 1, and authorities there cited; North Carolina v. Temple, 134 U.S. 22. It is, however, said that the words last quoted refer only to suits in which a state is a party, and in which, also, the opposite party is another state of the Union or a foreign state. This cannot be correct, for it must be conceded that a state can bring an original suit in this court against a citizen of another state. Wisconsin v. Pelican Ins. Co., 127 U.S. 265, 287. Besides, unless a state is exempt altogether from suit by the United States, we do not perceive upon what sound rule of construction suits brought by the United States in this court—especially if they be suits, the correct decision of which depends upon the constitution, laws, or treaties of the United States—are to be excluded from its original jurisdiction as defined in the constitution. That instrument extends the judicial power of the United States "to all cases," in law and equity, arising under the constitution, laws, and treaties of the United States, and to controversies in which the United States shall be a party, and confers upon this court original jurisdiction "in all cases" "in which a state shall be party;" that is, in all cases mentioned in the preceding clause in which a state may of right be made a party defendant, as well as in all cases in which a state may of right institute a suit in a court of the United States. The present case is of the former class. We cannot assume that the framers of the constitution, while extending the judicial power of the United States to controversies between two or more states of the Union, and between a state of the Union and foreign states, intended to exempt a state altogether from suit by the general government. They could not have overlooked the possibility that controversies capable of judicial solution might arise between the United States and some of the states, and that the permanence of the Union might be endangered if to some tribunal was not intrusted the power to determine them according to the recognized principles of law. And to what tribunal could a trust so momentous be more appropriately committed than to that which the people of the United States, in order to form a more perfect Union, establish justice, and insure domestic tranquillity, have constituted with authority to speak for all the people and all the states upon questions before it to which the judicial power of the nation extends? It would be difficult to suggest any reason why this court should have jurisdiction to determine questions of boundary between two or more states, but not jurisdiction of controversies of like character between the United States and a state. * * *

The question as to the suability of one government by another government rests upon wholly different grounds. Texas is not called to the bar of this court at the suit of an individual, but at the suit of the government established for the common and equal benefit of the people of all the states. The submission to judicial solution of controversies arising between these two governments, "each sovereign, with respect to the objects committed to it, and neither sovereign with respect to the objects committed to the other," McCulloch v. State of Maryland, 4 Wheat. 316, 400, 410, but both subject to the supreme law of the land, does no violence to the inherent nature of sovereignty. The states of the Union have agreed, in the constitution, that the judicial power of the United States shall extend to all cases arising under the constitution, laws, and treaties of the United States, without regard to the character of the parties, (excluding, of course, suits against a state by its own citizens or by citizens of other states, or by citizens or subjects of foreign states,) and equally to controversies to which the United States shall be a party, without regard to the subject of such controversies, and that this court may exercise original jurisdiction in all such cases "in which a state shall be party," without excluding those in which the United States may be the opposite party. The exercise, therefore, by this court, of such original jurisdiction in a suit brought by one state against another to determine the boundary line between them, or in a suit brought by the United States against a state to determine the boundary between a territory of the United States and that state, so far from infringing in either case upon the sovereignty, is with the consent of the state sued. Such consent was given by Texas when admitted into the Union upon an equal footing in all respects with the other states.

We are of opinion that this court has jurisdiction to determine the disputed question of boundary between the United States and Texas.

* * *

Demurrer overruled.

MR. CHIEF JUSTICE FULLER, with whom concurred MR. JUSTICE LAMAR, dissenting.

MR. JUSTICE LAMAR and myself are unable to concur in the decision just announced.

This court has original jurisdiction of two classes of cases only,—those affecting ambassadors, other public ministers, and consuls, and those in which a state shall be a party.

The judicial power extends to "controversies between two or more states," "between a state and citizens of another state," and "between a state, or the citizens thereof, and foreign states, citizens, or subjects." Our original jurisdiction, which depends wholly upon the character of the parties, is confined to the cases enumerated in which a state may be a party, and this is not one of them.

The judicial power also extends to controversies to which the United States shall be a party, but such controversies are not included in the grant of original jurisdiction. To the controversy here the United States is a party.

We are of opinion, therefore, that this case is not within the original jurisdiction of the court.

NOTE ON THE SCOPE OF THE JURISDICTION

(1) The constitutional provision for original jurisdiction in "those [cases] in which a State shall be Party" might conceivably have been construed as an independent grant of jurisdiction, empowering the Court to hear *all* such cases—including, for example, an action by a state against one of its own citizens to enforce a claim based on state law.

However, this broadest of the possible constructions of the second clause of Article III, Sec. 2, has been uniformly rejected. "This second clause distributes the jurisdiction conferred upon the Supreme Court in the previous one into original and appellate jurisdiction; but does not profess to confer any." Pennsylvania v. Quicksilver Co., 10 Wall. 553, 556 (U.S.1871).

(2) Does United States v. Texas mean that the original jurisdiction extends to any of the classes of cases enumerated in the first clause in which a state happens to be a party, regardless of whether the case belongs to one of the classes in which a state is mentioned expressly as a party?

In California v. Southern Pacific Co., 157 U.S. 229 (1895), a state brought an action against a citizen of another state but joined also one of its own citizens. In denying jurisdiction the Court said (pp. 257–58):

" * * * The original jurisdiction depends solely on the character of the parties, and is confined to the cases in which are those enumerated parties and those only. Among those in which jurisdiction must be exercised in the appellate form are cases arising under the Constitution and laws of the United States. In one description of cases the character of the parties is everything, the nature of the case nothing. In the other description of cases the nature of the case is everything, the character of the parties nothing."

No claim appears actually to have been made in California v. Southern Pacific Co. that the case arose under the Constitution or laws of the United States. Nevertheless, in a later action by a state which undoubtedly did so arise, the case was relied upon without discussion as a basis for holding that the presence as a defendant of a citizen of the plaintiff state would be fatal to the jurisdiction. Texas v. Interstate Commerce Commission, 258 U.S. 158 (1922). *Cf.* Minnesota v. Northern Securities Co., 184 U.S. 199, 245 (1902); New Mexico v. Lane, 243 U.S. 52 (1917).

Is there any way of reconciling Texas v. Interstate Commerce Commission with United States v. Texas? Is the answer that the jurisdiction distributed in the second clause extends only to those classes of cases in the first clause which are described in terms of parties rather than of subject matter? What would be the justification of such a distinction? Compare Justice Frankfurter's explanation of United States v. Texas in Ex parte Peru, p. 352, *infra.*

(3) If the Court would have jurisdiction of an action by the plaintiff against one or more of the defendants (as, for example, an action by a state against one or more citizens of another state), should the presence of an additional defendant who could not have been sued separately oust the jurisdiction?

In actions by states, the Court seems uniformly to have regarded the presence of a defendant who could not have been sued independently as fatal to jurisdiction. In addition to the Southern Pacific, Northern Securities, Lane, and Interstate Commerce Commission cases, see Louisiana v. Cummins, 314 U.S. 577 (1941).

In the Cummins case, the state's attorney general argued that the prior cases could be distinguished on the ground that the ineligible parties were indispensable. He said that in his case the Louisiana defendant was merely a proper or conditionally necessary party, so that the Court would have jurisdiction to proceed without him, and his joinder should be permitted for the sake of convenience in settling the entire matter in controversy. Ought the grant of original jurisdiction to be construed as forbidding the exercise of an ancillary jurisdiction of this kind? See the views of Justices

Harlan and Brewer, dissenting in California v. Southern Pac. Co., 157 U.S. at 262–71. Compare the doctrines of ancillary jurisdiction applied in district court litigation, Chap. XIII, Sec. 2, *infra.*

In actions by the United States against a state, the Court has repeatedly permitted, without discussion, the joinder of individuals as additional defendants, although, of course, the United States could not have sued them separately in the original jurisdiction. See, *e.g.,* United States v. Wyoming, 331 U.S. 440 (1947), and United States v. West Virginia, 295 U.S. 463 (1935). Are these cases distinguishable?

(4) In a suit against a state by another state or by the United States, would the intervention of a person other than a state as plaintiff violate the Eleventh Amendment? In Maryland v. Louisiana, 451 U.S. 725 (1981), the United States, one of its administrative agencies (FERC), and private pipeline companies were allowed to intervene as plaintiffs in an original action between two states; Eleventh Amendment concerns were summarily waived aside (p. 745 n. 21). In Arizona v. California, 460 U.S. 605 (1983), Indian tribes were allowed to intervene as plaintiffs in a suit by the United States against a state. The Court, citing Maryland v. Louisiana, said that the Eleventh Amendment could not be a bar because the tribes did not seek to raise any independent or new claims; thus "our judicial power is not enlarged" and state sovereign immunity is not "compromised" (p. 614).

NOTE ON ACTIONS BY THE UNITED STATES AGAINST A STATE [1]

(1) For the final decision and decree in the principal case, see United States v. Texas, 162 U.S. 1 (1896). For later phases in the settlement of the disputed boundary, see Oklahoma v. Texas, 256 U.S. 70 (1921); Oklahoma v. Texas, 258 U.S. 574 (1922).

(2) The most spectacular instances of exercise of the jurisdiction sanctioned in United States v. Texas were the famous tidelands cases.[2] In earlier phases of these cases, the Court rejected without opinion earnest efforts to persuade it to overturn the basic holding of United States v. Texas.

(3) Under 28 U.S.C. § 1251(b)(2), the original jurisdiction of the Supreme Court in "controversies between the United States and a State" is not exclusive. Under § 1345, the district courts have jurisdiction of "all" civil actions commenced by the United States; this grant has been held to

1. For a complete list, as of July 1959, of original actions by the United States against a state in which there has been at least one written opinion, see Note, *The Original Jurisdiction of the United States Supreme Court,* 11 Stan.L.Rev. 665, 701–04 (1959).

2. For a sampling of the opinions and decrees in these seemingly endless litigations over title to the submerged coastal lands and the resources under them, see United States v. California, 332 U.S. 19 (1947); United States v. Louisiana, 389 U.S. 155 (1967); Texas Boundary Case, 394 U.S. 1 (1969); Louisiana Boundary Case, 394 U.S. 11 (1969); United States v. Maine, 420 U.S. 515 (1975); Massachusetts Boundary Case, 452 U.S. 429 (1981); Rhode Island and New York Boundary Case, 469 U.S. 504 (1985). Federal common law, not state law, determines the boundary of oceanfront lands owned or patented by the United States. See California v. United States, 457 U.S. 273 (1982).

For another important instance of the jurisdiction see United States v. Arizona, reported *sub nom.* Oregon v. Mitchell, 400 U.S. 112 (1970) (suit to determine the constitutionality of the Voting Rights Act of 1970).

include actions against a state. See, *e.g.,* United States v. California, 328 F.2d 729 (9th Cir.1964) (district court has jurisdiction under § 1345 over suit by U.S. against state to recover damages for injuries to federal property caused by the negligence of state employees). Other special jurisdictional provisions may also give the district courts a concurrent jurisdiction in such cases.[3]

Until 1948, the Supreme Court's jurisdiction of actions by the United States against a state was exclusive, see 28 U.S.C. § 341 (1940), save only as a concurrent jurisdiction might on occasion be given the district courts by special jurisdictional provisions overriding the general provision in § 341. See the discussion in United States v. California, *supra;* Note, 38 N.Y.U.L. Rev. 405 (1963).

(4) In United States v. Nevada and California, 412 U.S. 534 (1973), the doctrine of Massachusetts v. Missouri and Ohio v. Wyandotte Chemicals Corp. (see pp. 332–44, *infra*), giving the Court discretion to deny leave to file in cases within its original jurisdiction if there is a more convenient alternative forum, was for the first time applied to an action brought by the United States. See p. 342, *infra.*[4]

PRINCIPALITY OF MONACO v. MISSISSIPPI

292 U.S. 313, 54 S.Ct. 745, 78 L.Ed. 1282 (1934).
Motion for Leave to File Declaration.

MR. CHIEF JUSTICE HUGHES delivered the opinion of the Court.

The Principality of Monaco asks leave to bring suit in this Court against the State of Mississippi upon bonds issued by the State and alleged to be the absolute property of the Principality. * * *

The State of Mississippi, in its return to the rule to show cause why leave should not be granted, raises the following objections: * * *

* * * We find it necessary to deal with but one, that is, the question whether this Court has jurisdiction to entertain a suit brought by a foreign State against a State without her consent. That question, not hitherto determined, is now definitely presented.

The Principality relies upon the provisions of section 2 of article 3 of the Constitution of the United States that the judicial power shall extend to controversies "between a State, or the Citizens thereof, and foreign States, Citizens or Subjects" (clause 1), and that in cases "in which a State shall be Party" this Court shall have original jurisdiction (clause 2). The absence of qualification requiring the consent of the State in the case of a suit by a foreign State is asserted to be controlling. And the point is stressed that the Eleventh Amendment of the Constitution, providing that the judicial power shall not be construed to extend to any suit against one of the United States "by Citizens of another State, or by Citizens or subjects of

3. See, *e.g.,* United States v. Mississippi, 380 U.S. 128, 138–41 (1965), and United States v. Alabama, 362 U.S. 602 (1960) (both upholding district court suits by United States against state under the Civil Rights Act of 1957, 42 U.S.C. § 1971(c)).

4. Theretofore the United States had apparently been denied leave to file on only one occasion: United States v. Alabama, 282 U.S. 897 (1965). On the same date, however, the Court granted leave in another original action, South Carolina v. Katzenbach, 382 U.S. 898 (1965), which raised the identical questions as to the validity of the Voting Rights Act of 1965.

any Foreign State," contains no reference to a suit brought by a foreign State.

The argument drawn from the lack of an express requirement of consent to be sued is inconclusive. Thus there is no express provision that the United States may not be sued in the absence of consent. Clause 1 of section 2 of article 3 extends the judicial power "to Controversies to which the United States shall be a Party." Literally, this includes such controversies, whether the United States be party plaintiff or defendant. Williams v. United States, 289 U.S. 553, 573. But by reason of the established doctrine of the immunity of the sovereign from suit except upon consent, the provision of clause 1 of section 2 of article 3 does not authorize the maintenance of suits against the United States. Williams v. United States, *supra.* Compare Cohens v. Virginia, 6 Wheat. 264, 411, 412; Minnesota v. Hitchcock, 185 U.S. 373, 384, 386; Kansas v. United States, 204 U.S. 331, 341, 342. And while clause 2 of section 2 of article 3 gives this Court original jurisdiction in those cases in which "a State shall be Party," this Court has no jurisdiction of a suit by a State against the United States in the absence of consent. Kansas v. United States, supra. Clause 2 merely distributes the jurisdiction conferred by clause 1, and deals with cases in which resort may be had to the original jurisdiction of this Court in the exercise of the judicial power as previously given. Duhne v. New Jersey, 251 U.S. 311, 314.

Similarly, neither the literal sweep of the words of clause 1 of section 2 of article 3, nor the absence of restriction in the letter of the Eleventh Amendment, permits the conclusion that in all controversies of the sort described in clause 1, and omitted from the words of the Eleventh Amendment, a State may be sued without her consent. Thus clause 1 specifically provides that the judicial power shall extend "to *all* Cases, in Law and Equity, arising under this Constitution, the Laws of the United States, and Treaties made, or which shall be made, under their Authority." But, although a case may arise under the Constitution and laws of the United States, the judicial power does not extend to it if the suit is sought to be prosecuted against a State, without her consent, by one of her own citizens. Hans v. Louisiana, 134 U.S. 1; Duhne v. New Jersey, supra, page 311 of 251 U.S. The requirement of consent is necessarily implied. The State has the same immunity in case of a suit brought by a corporation created by act of Congress. Smith v. Reeves, 178 U.S. 436. Yet in neither case is the suit within the express prohibition of the Eleventh Amendment. Again, the Eleventh Amendment mentions only suits "in law or equity"; it does not refer to suits in admiralty. But this Court has held that the Amendment does not "leave open a suit against a state in the admiralty jurisdiction by individuals, whether its own citizens or not." Ex parte State of New York, No. 1, 256 U.S. 490, 498.

Manifestly, we cannot rest with a mere literal application of the words of section 2 of article 3, or assume that the letter of the Eleventh Amendment exhausts the restrictions upon suits against nonconsenting States. Behind the words of the constitutional provisions are postulates which limit and control. There is the essential postulate that the controversies, as contemplated, shall be found to be of a justiciable character. There is also the postulate that States of the Union, still possessing attributes of sovereignty, shall be immune from suits, without their consent, save where there has been "a surrender of this immunity in the plan of the convention." The Federalist, No. 81. The question is whether the plan of the Constitution involves the surrender of immunity when the suit is brought against a State, without her consent, by a foreign State.

The debates in the Constitutional Convention do not disclose a discussion of this question. But Madison, in the Virginia Convention, answering objections to the ratification of the Constitution, clearly stated his view as to the purpose and effect of the provision conferring jurisdiction over controversies between States of the Union and foreign States. That purpose was suitably to provide for adjudication in such cases if consent should be given but not otherwise.[2] Madison said: "The next case provides for disputes between a foreign state and one of our states, should such a case ever arise; and between a citizen and a foreign citizen or subject. I do not conceive that any controversy can ever be decided, in these courts, between an American state and a foreign state, without the consent of the parties. If they consent, provision is here made." 3 Elliot's Debates, 533.

Marshall, in the same Convention, expressed a similar view. Replying to an objection as to the admissibility of a suit by a foreign state, Marshall said: "He objects, in the next place, to its jurisdiction in controversies between a state and a foreign state. Suppose, says he, in such a suit, a foreign state is cast; will she be bound by the decision? If a foreign state brought a suit against the commonwealth of Virginia, would she not be barred from the claim if the federal judiciary thought it unjust? The previous consent of the parties is necessary; and, as the federal judiciary will decide, each party will acquiesce." 3 Elliot's Debates, 557.

Hamilton, in the Federalist, No. 81, made the following emphatic statement of the general principle of immunity: "It is inherent in the nature of sovereignty not to be amenable to the suit of an individual without its consent. This is the general sense and the general practice of mankind; and the exemption, as one of the attributes of sovereignty, is now enjoyed by the government of every State in the Union. Unless, therefore, there is a surrender of this immunity in the plan of the convention, it will remain with the States, and the danger intimated must be merely ideal. The circumstances which are necessary to produce an alienation of State sovereignty were discussed in considering the article of taxation and need not be repeated here. A recurrence to the principles there established will satisfy us that there is no color to pretend that the State governments would by the adoption of that plan be divested of the privilege of paying their own debts in their own way, free from every constraint but that which flows from the obligations of good faith. The contracts between a nation and individuals are only binding on the conscience of the sovereign, and have no pretensions to a compulsive force. They confer no right of action independent of the sovereign will. To what purpose would it be to authorize suits against States for the debts they owe? How could recoveries be enforced? It is evident it could not be done without waging war against the contracting State; and to ascribe to the federal courts by mere implication, and in destruction of a pre-existing right of the State govern-

---

2. There is no question but that foreign States may sue private parties in the federal courts. King of Spain v. Oliver, Fed. Cas. No. 7,814, 2 Wash.C.C. 429, 431; The Sapphire, 11 Wall. 164, 167. * * *

ments, a power which would involve such a consequence would be altogether forced and unwarrantable." [4]

It is true that, despite these cogent statements of the views which prevailed when the Constitution was ratified, the Court held, in Chisholm v. Georgia, 2 Dall. 419, over the vigorous dissent of Mr. Justice Iredell, that a State was liable to suit by a citizen of another State or of a foreign country. But this decision created such a shock of surprise that the Eleventh Amendment was at once proposed and adopted. As the Amendment did not in terms apply to a suit against a State by its own citizen, the Court had occasion, when that question was presented in Hans v. Louisiana, supra (a case alleged to arise under the Constitution of the United States), to give elaborate consideration to the application of the general principle of the immunity of States from suits brought against them without their consent. Mr. Justice Bradley delivered the opinion of the Court ＊ ＊ ＊. After quoting the statements of Hamilton, Madison, and Marshall, the Court continued:

"It seems to us that these views of those great advocates and defenders of the constitution were most sensible and just, and they apply equally to the present case as to that then under discussion. The letter is appealed to now, as it was then, as a ground for sustaining a suit brought by an individual against a state. The reason against it is as strong in this case as it was in that. ＊ ＊ ＊

"The suability of a state, without its consent, was a thing unknown to the law. This has been so often laid down and acknowledged by courts and jurists that it is hardly necessary to be formally asserted. It was fully shown by an exhaustive examination of the old law by Mr. Justice Iredell in his opinion in Chisholm v. Georgia; and it has been conceded in every case since, where the question has, in any way, been presented, even in the cases which have gone furthest in sustaining suits against the officers or agents of the states." ＊ ＊ ＊

＊ ＊ ＊ The reasoning of the Court in Hans v. Louisiana with respect to the general principle of sovereign immunity from suits was recently reviewed and approved in Williams v. United States, *supra.*

The question of that immunity, in the light of the provisions of clause 1 of section 2 of article 3 of the Constitution, is thus presented in several distinct classes of cases, that is, in those brought against a State (a) by another State of the Union; (b) by the United States; (c) by the citizens of another State or by the citizens or subjects of a foreign State; (d) by citizens of the same State or by federal corporations; and (e) by foreign States. Each of these classes has its characteristic aspect, from the standpoint of the effect, upon sovereign immunity from suits, which has been produced by the constitutional scheme.

1. The establishment of a permanent tribunal with adequate authority to determine controversies between the States, in place of an inadequate scheme of arbitration, was essential to the peace of the Union. The Federalist, No. 80; Story on the Constitution, § 1679. With respect to such controversies, the States by the adoption of the Constitution, acting "in

---

4. For statements by Madison and Marshall in the Virginia Convention in relation to the nonsuability of States by individuals, see 3 Elliot's Debates, 533, 555.

their highest sovereign capacity, in the convention of the people," waived their exemption from judicial power. The jurisdiction of this Court over the parties in such cases was thus established "by their own consent and delegated authority" as a necessary feature of the formation of a more perfect Union. * * *

2. Upon a similar basis rests the jurisdiction of this Court of a suit by the United States against a State, albeit without the consent of the latter. While that jurisdiction is not conferred by the Constitution in express words, it is inherent in the constitutional plan. * * *

3. To suits against a State, without her consent, brought by citizens of another State or by citizens or subjects of a foreign State, the Eleventh Amendment erected an absolute bar. Superseding the decision in Chisholm v. Georgia, supra, the Amendment established in effective operation the principle asserted by Madison, Hamilton, and Marshall in expounding the Constitution and advocating its ratification. The "entire judicial power granted by the Constitution" does not embrace authority to entertain such suits in the absence of the State's consent. Ex parte State of New York, No. 1, supra, page 497 of 256 U.S.; Missouri v. Fiske, 290 U.S. 18, 25, 26.

4. Protected by the same fundamental principle, the States, in the absence of consent, are immune from suits brought against them by their own citizens or by federal corporations, although such suits are not within the explicit prohibitions of the Eleventh Amendment. * * *

5. We are of the opinion that the same principle applies to suits against a State by a foreign State. The decision in Cherokee Nation v. Georgia, 5 Pet. 1, is not opposed, as it rested upon the determination that the Cherokee nation was not a "foreign State" in the sense in which the term is used in the Constitution. The question now before us necessarily remained an open one. We think that Madison correctly interpreted clause 1 of section 2 of article 3 of the Constitution as making provision for jurisdiction of a suit against a State by a foreign State in the event of the State's consent but not otherwise. In such a case, the grounds of coercive jurisdiction which are present in suits to determine controversies between States of the Union, or in suits brought by the United States against a State, are not present. The foreign State lies outside the structure of the Union. The waiver or consent, on the part of a State, which inheres in the acceptance of the constitutional plan, runs to the other States who have likewise accepted that plan, and to the United States as the sovereign which the Constitution creates. We perceive no ground upon which it can be said that any waiver or consent by a State of the Union has run in favor of a foreign State. As to suits brought by a foreign State, we think that the States of the Union retain the same immunity that they enjoy with respect to suits by individuals whether citizens of the United States or citizens or subjects of a foreign State. The foreign State enjoys a similar sovereign immunity and without her consent may not be sued by a State of the Union.

The question of the right of suit by a foreign State against a State of the Union is not limited to cases of alleged debts or of obligations issued by a State and claimed to have been acquired by transfer. Controversies between a State and a foreign State may involve international questions in relation to which the United States has a sovereign prerogative. * * *

The National Government, by virtue of its control of our foreign relations, is entitled to employ the resources of diplomatic negotiations and to effect such an international settlement as may be found to be appropriate, through treaty, agreement of arbitration, or otherwise. It cannot be supposed that it was the intention that a controversy growing out of the action of a State, which involves a matter of national concern and which is said to affect injuriously the interests of a foreign State, or a dispute arising from conflicting claims of a State of the Union and a foreign State as to territorial boundaries, should be taken out of the sphere of international negotiations and adjustment through a resort by the foreign State to a suit under the provisions of section 2 of article 3. In such a case, the State has immunity from suit without her consent and the National Government is protected by the provision prohibiting agreements between States and foreign powers in the absence of the consent of the Congress. While, in this instance, the proposed suit does not raise a question of national concern, the constitutional provision which is said to confer jurisdiction should be construed in the light of all its applications.

We conclude that * * * the application for leave to sue must be denied.

Rule discharged, and leave denied.

NOTE ON SOVEREIGN IMMUNITY AND THE EFFECT OF ITS WAIVER

(1) The wise words of Chief Justice Hughes—"Behind the words of the constitutional provisions are postulates which limit and control"—are much celebrated and frequently quoted. But note how, in the field under review, opposing implications, sometimes of waiver and sometimes of non-waiver, have been drawn from substantially identical language.

(2) The parent case for the rule that a state may not sue the United States without its consent is Kansas v. United States, 204 U.S. 331 (1907). There the Court, after holding that the claims in suit were actually those of private corporations that Kansas did not have standing to assert, added as an alternative ground of decision that the United States was the real party in interest and, since it had not given its consent, was not subject to suit. The Court said little more than this in explanation (p. 342):

"It does not follow that because a State may be sued by the United States without its consent, therefore the United States may be sued by a State without its consent. Public policy forbids that conclusion."[1]

(3) The United States not being suable, states have not infrequently sought to achieve a similar result by suing federal officials, as citizens of other states, in the original jurisdiction.

For examples of such suits that have been dismissed as in substance against the United States, see Hawaii v. Gordon, 373 U.S. 57 (1963) (action to compel Director of Budget Bureau to take certain actions with respect to

---

1. See further Oregon v. Hitchcock, 202 U.S. 60 (1906); Minnesota v. United States, 305 U.S. 382 (1939). Cf. Arizona v. California, 298 U.S. 558 (1936) (United States an indispensable party and, not having consented, cannot be joined; suit dismissed); compare Idaho v. Oregon, 444 U.S. 380 (1980) (United States not an indispensable party). See also California v. Arizona, p. 295, supra.

land); Oregon v. Hitchcock, *supra* (action to restrain the Secretary of the Interior and the Commissioner of the General Land Office from allotting or patenting certain lands to Indians or other persons, and praying a decree establishing the title of the state); New Mexico v. Lane, p. 304, *supra* (action to enjoin the Secretary of the Interior from issuing a land patent to a New Mexico citizen).

For examples of such suits that were entertained, see South Carolina v. Regan, p. 296, *supra;* Oregon v. Mitchell, 400 U.S. 112 (1970) (suit to enjoin Attorney General from enforcing the 18–year–old–vote provision of the Voting Rights Act of 1970); South Carolina v. Katzenbach, 383 U.S. 301 (1966) (suit to enjoin enforcement of Voting Rights Act of 1965); Ohio v. Helvering, 292 U.S. 360 (1934) (motion for leave to file original bill against Commissioner of Internal Revenue to enjoin him from enforcing against the state certain federal statutes imposing taxes upon dealers in intoxicating liquors; denied on the ground that the state was subject to the taxes).

(4) If Mississippi had given its consent to be sued, would the Court have had jurisdiction? See 28 U.S.C. § 1251; *cf.* p. 297, *supra.* (What, incidentally, would happen if Monaco tried to sue a citizen of one of the States? Is Monaco worse off than its ambassador would be?)

Would there be jurisdiction in the converse situation, if Mississippi were suing Monaco with Monaco's consent?

Unless these questions are answered in the affirmative, how could effect be given to the constitutional grant of jurisdiction in "Controversies * * * between a State * * * and foreign States * * *"?

The question whether the doctrine of sovereign immunity qualifies the constitutional grants of jurisdiction themselves, or simply erects a bar to the exercise of jurisdiction which is removed when consent is given, has been mainly discussed in connection with problems of jurisdiction of actions against the United States. In United States v. Louisiana, 123 U.S. 32 (1887), the Court took jurisdiction, on appeal from the Court of Claims, of an action by a state against the United States. The Court said (p. 35):

" * * * The action before us, being one in which the United States have consented to be sued, falls within those designated, to which the judicial power extends; for, as already stated, both of the demands in controversy arise under laws of the United States."

At first blush the case would also seem to have been a controversy "to which the United States shall be a Party". And in Minnesota v. Hitchcock, 185 U.S. 373, 382–88 (1902), an original action against the Secretary of the Interior to which the United States had consented and which was treated as an action in substance against the United States, the Court examined the question at length and squarely determined that the case was one "to which the United States shall be a Party" within the first clause of Article III, Sec. 2, and, being also one "in which a State shall be a Party", was brought by the second clause within the original jurisdiction. Other expressions of the Court accepted this same simple and natural view.

So the matter stood until Justice Sutherland's opinion in Williams v. United States, 289 U.S. 553 (1933), introduced intellectual chaos. The Court there held that the constitutional provision should be read as if it spoke only of "cases to which the United States shall be a party plaintiff or petitioner", and specifically rejected the contention that jurisdiction attached under Article III once the United States had given its consent. But this and other aspects of Williams would seem to have been repudiated in Glidden Co. v. Zdanok, 370 U.S. 530 (1962), p. 449 *infra.* See, further, Chap. IV, Sec. 1(b), *infra.*

Both before and after the Williams case, the Court has repeatedly entertained on the merits, without notice of any jurisdictional difficulty, appeals from district courts in actions by a state against the United States with its consent. *E.g.,* Florida v. United States, 282 U.S. 194 (1931); Alabama v. United States, 325 U.S. 535 (1945), both successful actions to set aside orders of the Interstate Commerce Commission. See also California v. Arizona, p. 295, *supra,* and, as an example of a consented-to original action, Utah v. United States, 403 U.S. 9 (1971).

(5) Is a different question presented if the suit is against a state? The Eleventh Amendment says that "The Judicial power of the United States shall not be construed to extend to" some such suits. Yet the Supreme Court has consistently assumed that "The immunity from suit belonging to a State, which is respected and protected by the Constitution within the limits of the judicial power of the United States is a personal privilege which it may waive at pleasure". Clark v. Barnard, 108 U.S. 436, 447 (1883). For further consideration of waiver of state sovereign immunity, see pp. 1213–21, *infra.*

(6) In the light of this note, look at what the revisers have done in 28 U.S.C. § 1251.

KENTUCKY v. INDIANA

281 U.S. 163, 50 S.Ct. 275, 74 L.Ed. 784 (1930).
Original.

MR. CHIEF JUSTICE HUGHES delivered the opinion of the Court.

In September, 1928, the commonwealth of Kentucky and the state of Indiana, by their respective highway commissions, entered into a contract for the building of a bridge across the Ohio river between Evansville, Ind., and Henderson, Ky. The contract was approved by the Governor, and as to legality and form, also by the Attorney General, of each state. The contract recited the acts of Congress and of the state Legislatures which were deemed to authorize the enterprise. Acts of Congress of July 11, 1916, 39 Stat. 355, 356; March 2, 1927, 44 Stat. 1337; March 3, 1927, 44 Stat. 1398, Indiana, Act of 1919, c. 53; Act of 1927, c. 10, Kentucky, Acts of 1928, chapters 172 and 174. The state of Indiana immediately began the performance of the covenants of the contract on its part, and thereupon nine citizens and taxpayers of Indiana brought suit in the superior court of Marion county in that state to enjoin the members of the highway commission and other officers of Indiana from carrying out the contract upon the ground that it was unauthorized and void.

The commonwealth of Kentucky then asked leave to file the bill of complaint in this suit against the state of Indiana and the individuals who were plaintiffs in the suit in the state court, seeking to restrain the breach of the contract and the prosecution of that suit, and for specific performance. In its return to the order to show cause why this leave should not be granted the state of Indiana said that it had "no cause to show"; that the state intended ultimately to perform the contract, if performance were permitted or ordered by the courts in which the litigation over the contract was pending, but that it did not intend to do so until after that litigation had finally been disposed of favorably to its performance; that the state of Indiana had entered into the contract by virtue of authority of its own statutes and of the Act of Congress of March 2, 1927; that, as there was no court having complete jurisdiction over the parties and subject-matter, other than this court, the state yielded to the jurisdiction of this court, and that it was in the public interest that an early adjudication be had which would be final and binding upon all parties interested.

Leave being granted, the bill of complaint herein was filed. * * *

Separate answers were filed by the state of Indiana and by the individual defendants. The answer of the state of Indiana admitted that the allegations of the complaint were true. The answer then averred:

"The only excuse which the State of Indiana offers for failure to perform the contract set out in plaintiff's complaint is the litigation, mentioned in the complaint, instituted by her above-named co-defendants against the officers of the State of Indiana whose function it is to perform said contract. The resulting delay in performance of said contract is in breach of its terms, which contemplate immediate and continued perform-ance."

After stating that, as the validity of the contract had been drawn in question in the litigation in the state court, the state did not feel warranted in proceeding until there was a final adjudication establishing its right to perform, the answer added:

"The State of Indiana believes said contract is valid. If this honorable court shall grant the relief prayed against Indiana by plaintiff Common-wealth of Kentucky in either of its paragraphs of complaint, the State of Indiana will thereupon immediately proceed with the performance of said contract and will continue such performance until the objects of said contract shall have been fully attained as contemplated by the terms thereof."

The individual defendants filed an answer and, at the same time, moved to dismiss the complaint * * *.

After hearing argument, the court overruled the motion to dismiss in so far as it questioned the jurisdiction of the court to entertain the bill of complaint and to proceed to a hearing and determination of the merits of the controversy, and directed that all other questions sought to be present-ed by that motion be reserved for further consideration at the hearing upon the merits. * * *

The question of the jurisdiction of this court was determined on the hearing of the motion to dismiss. The state of Indiana, while desiring to perform its contract, is not going on with its performance because of a suit brought by its citizens in its own court. There is thus a controversy between the states, although a limited one.

A state suing, or sued, in this court, by virtue of the original jurisdic-tion over controversies between states, must be deemed to represent all its citizens. The appropriate appearance here of a state by its proper officers, either as complainant or defendant, is conclusive upon this point. Citizens, voters, and taxpayers, merely as such, of either state, without a showing of any further and proper interest, have no separate individual right to contest in such a suit the position taken by the state itself. Otherwise, all the citizens of both states, as one citizen, voter, and taxpayer has as much right as another in this respect, would be entitled to be heard. An individual citizen may be made a party where relief is properly sought as against him, and in such case he should have suitable opportunity to show the nature of his interest and why the relief asked against him individually should not be granted.

If the controversy within the original jurisdiction of this court is over a contract alleged to have been made between two states, to which an individual defendant is not a party, it is manifest that such an individual defendant, merely as a citizen, voter, and taxpayer of the defendant state, is not entitled to enter upon a separate contest in relation to the merits of the controversy so far as it relates to the making of the contract by the two states, and the obligations that the contract imposes upon his state, and does not relate to any separate and proper interest of his own. The fact that an individual citizen in such a case is made a party defendant in order that the complainant may obtain some particular relief against him, which is merely incidental to the complete relief to which the complainant would be entitled if it should prevail as against the defendant state, gives such an individual defendant no standing to litigate on his own behalf the merits of a controversy which, properly viewed, lies solely between the states, but only to contest the propriety of the particular relief sought against him in case the decision on the merits is against his state. This gives an individual defendant in such a suit between states full opportunity to litigate the only question which concerns him individually as distinguished from the questions which concern him only in common with all the citizens of his state.

In the present instance, there is no showing that the individual defendants have any interest whatever with respect to the contract and its performance other than that of the citizens and taxpayers, generally, of Indiana, an interest which that state in this suit fully represents. The individual defendants have presented no defense other than that which they seek to make on behalf of their state with respect to the making of the contract by that state and the obligations thereby imposed upon it. The particular relief asked against them is sought only as an incident to the relief which the commonwealth of Kentucky seeks against the state of Indiana. The individual defendants were made parties solely for the purpose of obtaining an injunction against them restraining the prosecution of the suit in the state court. Such an injunction is not needed, as a decree in this suit would bind the state of Indiana, and, on being shown, would bar any inconsistent proceedings in the courts of that state. As no sufficient ground appears for maintaining the bill of complaint against the individual defendants, it should be dismissed as against them.

The question, then, is as to the case made by the commonwealth of Kentucky against the state of Indiana. By admitting in its answer that the allegations of the complaint are true, the state of Indiana admits the making of the contract and the authority of its officers to make it under the applicable legislation. Not only are the allegations of fact in the complaint conceded to be true, but there is also no dispute as to the legal import of these facts. * * * The only suggestion of a defense for its failure to perform the contract, that is, what the state of Indiana in its answer characterizes as its "only excuse," is the pendency of this litigation in the state court. The state of Indiana avers that it does not feel warranted in proceeding in the absence of a final determination establishing its right to proceed under the contract.

It is manifest that if, in accordance with the pleading of each state, the contract for the building of the bridge is deemed to be authorized and valid, the mere pendency of a suit brought by citizens to restrain performance does not constitute a defense. In that aspect, the question would be, not as to a defense on the merits, but whether this court should withhold a final determination merely because of the fact that such a suit is pending. This question raises important considerations. It cannot be gainsaid that in a controversy with respect to a contract between states, as to which the original jurisdiction of this court is invoked, this court has the authority and duty to determine for itself all questions that pertain to the obligations of the contract alleged. The fact that the solution of these questions may involve the determination of the effect of the local legislation of either state, as well as of acts of Congress, which are said to authorize the contract, in no way affects the duty of this court to act as the final, constitutional arbiter in deciding the questions properly presented. It has frequently been held that, when a question is suitably raised whether the law of a state has impaired the obligation of a contract, in violation of the constitutional provision, this court must determine for itself whether a contract exists, what are its obligations, and whether they have been impaired by the legislation of the state. While this court always examines with appropriate respect the decisions of state courts bearing upon such questions, such decisions do not detract from the responsibility of this court in reaching its own conclusions as to the contract, its obligations and impairment, for otherwise the constitutional guaranty could not properly be enforced. Larson v. South Dakota, 278 U.S. 429, 433, and cases there cited. Where the states themselves are before this court for the determination of a controversy between them, neither can determine their rights inter sese, and this court must pass upon every question essential to such a determination, although local legislation and questions of state authorization may be involved. Virginia v. West Virginia, 11 Wall. 39, 56, 220 U.S. 1, 28. A decision in the present instance by the state court would not determine the controversy here.

It is none the less true that this court might await such a decision, in order that it might have the advantage of the views of the state court, if sufficient grounds appeared for delaying final action.* The question is as to the existence of such grounds in this case. The gravity of the situation cannot be ignored. The injury to the commonwealth of Kentucky by the delay in the performance of the contract by the state of Indiana is definitely alleged and expressly admitted. That injury is concededly irreparable, without adequate remedy at law. It is specifically set forth in the agreed statement of facts that "it is of great interest and concern to the States of Indiana and Kentucky and the United States and the citizens thereof generally who will travel said Route 41" (the highway through the states which will be made continuous by the construction of the bridge) "to

---

* [Ed.] For an example of a case where the Court, having acknowledged jurisdiction, continued an original case pending the resolution of state-law questions in state court litigation, see Arkansas v. Texas, 346 U.S. 368 (1953), dismissed as moot, 351 U.S. 977 (1956).

have as early determination of this litigation as is possible." In these circumstances there would appear to be no adequate ground for withholding the determination of this suit because of objections raised by individuals, merely in their capacity as citizens, voters, and taxpayers of Indiana, objections which the state itself declines to sponsor.

It would be a serious matter, where a state has entered into a contract with another state, the validity of the contract not being questioned by either state, if individual citizens could delay the prompt performance which was admittedly important, not only to the complainant state but to the people of both states, merely by bringing a suit. It is not difficult to institute suits, and contracts between states, of increasing importance as interstate interests grow in complexity, would be at the mercy of individuals, if the action of the latter, without more, unsupported by any proper averments on the part of the state itself questioning its obligations, should lead this court to stay its hand in giving the relief to which the complainant state would otherwise be entitled, and of which it stood seriously in need.

On such a record as we have in this case, it is unnecessary for the court to search the legislation underlying the contract in order to discover grounds of defense which the defendant state does not attempt to assert. The state of Indiana concludes its answer by saying that, if a decree goes against it as prayed for, the state will at once proceed with the performance of the contract and fully complete that performance according to its terms.

Held

We conclude that the controversy between the states is within the original jurisdiction of this court; that the defendant state has shown no adequate defense to this suit; that nothing appears which would justify delay in rendering a decree; and that the commonwealth of Kentucky is entitled to the relief sought against the state of Indiana.

The complainant and the defendant state will be accorded twenty days within which to submit a form of decree to carry these conclusions into effect. Costs will be divided equally between the states.

Dismissed as to individual defendants.

Decree for complainant against the defendant state.

NOTE ON LITIGATION BETWEEN STATES

(1) On the question, in Kentucky v. Indiana, of the state as representative of its citizens, see also Wyoming v. Colorado, 286 U.S. 494, 508–09 (1932), and cases cited. Private interests may be similarly bound when disputes between states are settled by the alternative method of interstate compact. Hinderlider v. La Plata River & Cherry Creek Ditch Co., 304 U.S. 92 (1938). See generally Frankfurter & Landis, *The Compact Clause of the Constitution—A Study in Interstate Adjustments,* 34 Yale L.J. 685 (1925). Compare New Jersey v. New York, 345 U.S. 369 (1953), denying Philadelphia's motion to intervene in a dispute regarding the Delaware River on the ground that Pennsylvania (a party) adequately represents all its citizens, whereas the City represents only a special group.

(2) Actions between states have been the most numerous class of cases in the Supreme Court's original jurisdiction.[1] See Note, 11 Stan.L.Rev. 665, 708–718 (1959); Scott, Judicial Settlement of Controversies Between States of the American Union (1919); Barnes, *Suits Between States in the Supreme Court,* 7 Vand.L.Rev. 494 (1954).

(3) Boundary disputes were the first cases between states in which the Court exercised jurisdiction, and these have remained the most productive source of such litigation. The parent case in which the justiciability of boundary disputes was definitely established was Rhode Island v. Massachusetts, 12 Pet. 657 (U.S.1838). For other examples see Nebraska v. Iowa, 406 U.S. 117 (1972); and New Mexico v. Colorado, 364 U.S. 296 (1960).

Since Kansas v. Colorado, 185 U.S. 125 (1902), conflicting claims to water from interstate streams have become the second most productive source of litigation between states. For an example of controversies of this kind, vividly illustrating the complexity of the task which the Court may assume when it undertakes to apportion water rights, see Arizona v. California, 373 U.S. 546 (1963). *Cf.* Idaho v. Oregon, 444 U.S. 380 (1980) (equitable apportionment between states of migrating anadromous fish(!)).

Other types of disputes which have come before the Court include conflicting claims to escheat (see, *e.g.,* Texas v. New Jersey, 379 U.S. 674 (1965)); suits to enforce interstate compacts (see Texas v. New Mexico, 462 U.S. 554 (1983)); suits on contracts and debts (see, *e.g.,* the principal case, and Virginia v. West Virginia, p. 322, *infra*); and suits to prevent injuries to the citizens of the state (see, *e.g.,* Missouri v. Illinois, 180 U.S. 208 (1901); Pennsylvania v. West Virginia, 262 U.S. 553 (1923)); Maryland v. Louisiana, 451 U.S. 725 (1981)).[2]

---

1. "Evidencing the seriousness of some of these disputes is the fact that in at least four instances—New Jersey v. New York in the 1820's; Missouri v. Iowa in the 1840's; Louisiana v. Mississippi in the 1900's; and Oklahoma v. Texas in very recent years, armed conflicts between the militia or citizens of the contending States had been a prelude to the institution of the suits in the Court. And in several of the other suits, a state of facts was presented which, if arising between independent nations, might well have been a cause for war." Charles Warren, The Supreme Court and Sovereign States 38 (1924). See also Herbert A. Smith, The American Supreme Court as an International Tribunal (1920).

2. The Court has experienced difficulty in determining whether it should exercise its original jurisdiction to resolve conflicting claims by two or more states that a decedent was a domiciliary at the time of death and therefore subject to its estate tax. In Texas v. Florida, 306 U.S. 398 (1939), over the dissent of Justice Frankfurter, it took jurisdiction of such an action, characterizing it as a "bill in the nature of interpleader" (p. 406), and noting that there was a substantial possibility

that the four states claiming jurisdiction to tax the estate of a peripatetic millionaire would levy taxes exceeding the entire estate. But in California v. Texas, 437 U.S. 601 (1978), the Court without opinion or explanation denied California leave to file a suit to determine which state had power to tax the estate of Howard Hughes. Three Justices concurred on the ground that, although the case was indistinguishable from Texas v. Florida, that case was "wrongly decided", and that no "case or controversy" between states existed there—or would exist in the case at bar until both states finally established enforceable claims to estate taxes that in the aggregate clearly exceeded the assets of the decedent. The concurring Justices also suggested that federal interpleader might be available (notwithstanding the Eleventh Amendment) to estates threatened with double death taxation on account of inconsistent adjudications of domicile.

Four years later the Court reversed itself again, and by a 5–4 vote granted California leave to file suit against Texas to secure a determination of Hughes' domicile at death. California v. Texas, 457 U.S. 164 (1982). (It acted on the same day that it decided Cory v. White, 457 U.S. 85 (1982),

NOTE ON THE LAW APPLIED IN
ACTIONS BETWEEN STATES

(1) In Kentucky v. Indiana Chief Justice Hughes says that "this court has the authority and duty to determine for itself all questions that pertain to the obligations of the contract alleged." Does he mean that state law applies, but the Court will determine for itself what the state law is? Or that the applicable law is federal? Does it make a difference? Is the question of the Indiana officials' authority to enter into this contract (in contrast to questions as to the obligations it creates) governed by state law?

Having held that the individual defendants did not have standing in this suit to raise the question of authorization, was it wise for the Court to accept, without any inquiry into the merits, Indiana's concession on this question?

What is the basis for the Chief Justice's statement that an injunction against the individual defendants "is not needed, as a decree in this suit would bind the state of Indiana, and, on being shown, would bar any inconsistent proceedings in the courts of that state"? Are the individual defendants bound by the holding on the merits, itself based on Indiana's concession which they were held not to have standing to contradict? Or is it the holding that they have no standing to raise the issue of authorization which would bar a suit in state court? Is this latter holding itself based on federal or state law? If based on federal law, should it apply to a suit in state court?

(2) West Virginia ex rel. Dyer v. Sims, 341 U.S. 22 (1951), was a mandamus proceeding brought originally in the Supreme Court of Appeals of West Virginia by the West Virginia members of the Ohio River Valley Sanitation Commission against the West Virginia state auditor. The auditor had refused to issue a warrant to pay an appropriation for West Virginia's contribution to the expenses of the Commission, which was formed under the Ohio River Valley Sanitation Compact; and the plaintiffs sought to compel him to do so.

"The West Virginia court found that the 'sole question' before it was the validity of the Act of 1939 approving West Virginia's adherence to the Compact. It found that Act invalid in that (1) the Compact was deemed to delegate West Virginia's police power to other States and to the Federal Government, and (2) it was deemed to bind future legislatures to make appropriations for the continued activities of the Sanitation Commission and thus to violate Art. X, § 4 of the West Virginia Constitution."

On certiorari, the Supreme Court reversed this decision unanimously, but eight Justices found three different grounds for reversal and Justice Black concurred in the result without explanation.

holding that the Eleventh Amendment barred a federal interpleader action brought in a federal district court by the administrator of the Hughes estate against the two states.) The Court said (i) that California's allegation—that the various state and federal tax claims would exceed the estate—established that there was an actual controversy between the states; (ii) that the case was therefore indistinguishable from Texas v. Florida; and (iii) that in light of Cory v. White, exercise of the original jurisdiction would be "appropriate" since there existed no realistic alternative forum. Justice Powell, writing for the four dissenters, argued that as long as it was the law that the Constitution does not itself prohibit several states from taxing the same estate, no ripe controversy existed until both states obtained tax judgments that they were unable to satisfy.

That the questions involved were federal, and so within the competence of the Court to review, Justice Frankfurter said, "needs no discussion after Delaware River Comm'n v. Colburn, 310 U.S. 419, 427."

On the merits Justice Frankfurter, speaking for a majority of six, relied upon Kentucky v. Indiana and Hinderlider v. La Plata River & Cherry Creek Ditch Co., 304 U.S. 92 (1938). In the Hinderlider case, the Court reversed a decision that an interstate compact concerning water rights was invalid because it affected appropriation rights guaranteed by the state's constitution. These cases, Justice Frankfurter said, "make clear, however, that we are free to examine determinations of law by State courts in the limited field where a compact brings in issue the rights of other States and the United States". The opinion then concluded that the compact did not violate the West Virginia constitution in either of the respects in which the state court had said it did. *Cf.* Indiana ex rel. Anderson v. Brand and the *Note on Federal Protection of State–Created Rights,* Chap. V, Sec. 2, pp. 569, 573, *infra.*

Justice Reed, concurring, rejected the suggestion that the Supreme Court was empowered to override a state court's interpretation of its own constitution, "unless it is prepared to say that the interpretation is a palpable evasion to avoid a federal rule". He said:

"Under the Compact Clause, however, the federal questions are the execution, validity and meaning of federally approved state compacts. The interpretation of the meaning of the compact controls over a state's application of its own law through the Supremacy Clause and not by any implied federal power to construe state law".

Justice Jackson, like the majority, thought the questions controlled by state law, but placed his concurrence on the narrow ground that West Virginia was estopped to "raise an issue of *ultra vires,* decide it, and release herself from an interstate obligation", in the absence of "clear notice or fair warning to Congress or other States of any defect in her authority to enter into this Compact".

See also Petty v. Tennessee–Missouri Bridge Comm'n, 359 U.S. 275 (1959), holding that federal law governs the question whether two states, which had set up a bridge commission by an interstate compact approved by Congress, thereby waived sovereign immunity in suits against the commission, and answering the question in the affirmative. Justice Frankfurter, in dissent, distinguished Dyer v. Sims, which, he said, "was a typical controversy among States, a controversy as to the undertaking of a Compact among States, for the peaceful solution of which the Constitution designed Art. III, § 2. * * * Since a Compact comes into being through an Act of Congress, its construction gives rise to a federal question. Delaware River Comm'n v. Colburn, 310 U.S. 419, 427. But a federal question does not require a federal answer by way of a blanket, nationwide substantive doctrine where essentially local interests are at stake. See, *e.g.,* Board of County Comm'rs v. United States, 308 U.S. 343. A Compact is, after all, a contract. Ordinarily, in the interpretation of a contract, the meaning the parties attribute to the words governs the obligations assumed in the agreement. Similarly, since these States had the freedom to waive or to refuse to waive immunity granted by the Eleventh Amendment, the language they employed in the Compact, not modified by Congress, should be limited to the legal significance that these States have placed upon such language, not to avoid the obligations they undertook, but to enforce the meaning of conventional language used in their law" (pp. 284–85).

What would Justice Frankfurter have said if Missouri and Tennessee law differed on the question whether the bridge commission could be sued?

See generally Engdahl, *Construction of Interstate Compacts: A Questionable Federal Question,* 51 Va.L.Rev. 987 (1965).

(3) In Connecticut v. Massachusetts, 282 U.S. 660 (1931), Connecticut brought a bill to enjoin Massachusetts from diverting waters from the watershed of the Connecticut river to provide water for the Boston area. The Court said (pp. 669–71):

"Connecticut suggests that, under the common law in force in both States, each riparian owner has a vested right in the use of the flowing waters and is entitled to have them to flow as they were wont, unimpaired as to quantity and uncontaminated as to quality. It maintains that the taking of waters from the Ware and Swift infringes vested property rights in that State which cannot be taken without its consent against the will of the owners. And it insists that this Court, following the law enforced by each of the States within its own boundaries, should grant injunction against any diversion from the watersheds of these rivers.

"But the laws in respect of riparian rights that happen to be effective for the time being in both States do not necessarily constitute a dependable guide or just basis for the decision of controversies such as that here presented. * * *

"For the decision of suits between States, federal, state and international law are considered and applied by this Court as the exigencies of the particular case may require. The determination of the relative rights of contending States in respect of the use of streams flowing through them does not depend upon the same considerations and is not governed by the same rules of law that are applied in such States for the solution of similar questions of private right. Kansas v. Colorado, 185 U.S. 125, 146. And, while the municipal law relating to like questions between individuals is to be taken into account, it is not to be deemed to have controlling weight. As was shown in Kansas v. Colorado, 206 U.S. 46, 100, such disputes are to be settled on the basis of equality of right. But this is not to say that there must be an equal division of the waters of an interstate stream among the States through which it flows. It means that the principles of right and equity shall be applied having regard to the 'equal level or plane on which all the States stand, in point of power and right, under our constitutional system' and that, upon a consideration of the pertinent laws of the contending States and all other relevant facts, this Court will determine what is an equitable apportionment of the use of such waters. Wyoming v. Colorado, 259 U.S. 419, 465, 470.

"The development of what Mr. Justice Brewer, speaking for the Court in Kansas v. Colorado, 206 U.S. 46, 98, refers to as interstate common law is indicated and its application for the ascertainment of the relative rights of States in respect of interstate waters is illustrated by Missouri v. Illinois, 200 U.S. 496; Kansas v. Colorado, *supra*; Wyoming v. Colorado, *supra*, and Wisconsin v. Illinois, 278 U.S. 367; 281 U.S. 179."

See also Justice Brandeis' statement in Hinderlider v. La Plata River Co., *supra*, at 110, that "whether the water of an interstate stream must be apportioned between the two States is a question of 'federal common law' upon which neither the statutes nor the decisions of either State can be conclusive." This case was decided on the same day as Erie R. R. v. Tompkins, p. 783, *infra.*

For a recent example of the application of the "federal common-law doctrine" of equitable apportionment of interstate waters, see Colorado v. New Mexico, 459 U.S. 176 (1982), 467 U.S. 310 (1984).

(4) In Texas v. New Jersey, 379 U.S. 674 (1965), the question was which state may by escheat take abandoned intangible personal property (unclaimed small debts owed by Sun Oil Company to many unknown creditors). The Court held, as a matter of federal law, that jurisdiction to escheat lies in the "State of the creditor's last known address as shown by the debtor's books and records" (pp. 680–81), rejecting the claims of the state of the debtor's incorporation, the state of the debtor's principal offices, and the state with the most significant "contacts" with the debt. For further refinements of the rule thus fashioned, see Pennsylvania v. New York, 407 U.S. 206 (1972).

NOTE ON THE ENFORCEMENT OF JUDGMENTS AGAINST A STATE

How can a judgment against a state be enforced?

Consider the following instances:

Virginia v. West Virginia

206 U.S. 290 (1907). Bill by Virginia for an accounting to determine the amount due with respect to West Virginia's undertaking, on the separation of the two states, to assume "an equitable proportion of the public debt" of Virginia prior to the separation. The Court overruled a demurrer alleging, *inter alia*, want of jurisdiction and the inability of the Court to enforce a judgment if it should assume jurisdiction. Chief Justice Fuller said (p. 319) that "it is not to be presumed on demurrer that West Virginia would refuse to carry out the decree of this court. If such repudiation should be absolutely asserted we can then consider by what means the decree may be enforced."

209 U.S. 514 (1908). Cases referred to master with statement of conditions under which testimony should be taken.

220 U.S. 1 (1911). The principal sum due tentatively settled, on report of the master, leaving to a conference between the parties the question of interest and certain disputed adjustments. The opinion of Justice Holmes concludes (p. 36):

" * * * But this case is one that calls for forbearance upon both sides. Great States have a temper superior to that of private litigants, and it is to be hoped that enough has been decided for patriotism, the fraternity of the Union, and mutual consideration to bring it to an end."

222 U.S. 17 (1911). Motion by Virginia that the Court proceed with the further hearing and determination of the case denied, on the ground that West Virginia's decision to await the next regular session of the legislature

before conference should not be overridden. Justice Holmes said (pp. 19–20):

"A question like the present should be disposed of without undue delay. But a State cannot be expected to move with the celerity of a private business man; it is enough if it proceeds, in the language of the English chancery, with all deliberate speed. * * *"

231 U.S. 89 (1913). On a renewal of Virginia's motion, decision postponed, in view of West Virginia's representations that a Commission was considering the problem, but case "assigned for final hearing" before the close of the term.

234 U.S. 117 (1914). West Virginia's motion for leave to file supplemental answer asserting new credits to reduce liability granted, and case again referred to master.

238 U.S. 202 (1915). Master's report fixing amount of liability approved, and decree entered.

241 U.S. 531 (1916). Virginia's petition for a writ of execution denied, in a brief opinion by Chief Justice White, on the ground that West Virginia's legislature had not convened since the rendering of the decree.

246 U.S. 565 (1918). Decision after oral argument on West Virginia's return to a rule to show cause why the Court should not grant Virginia's motion for leave to file a petition for a writ of mandamus against the state of West Virginia and the members of her legislature commanding the levy of a tax to satisfy the judgment. Long opinion by Chief Justice White saying definitely and in strong language that the judgment was enforceable but not saying exactly how. Case restored to docket for further argument on this question, with a suggestion of later reference to a master to report on the amount and method of taxation appropriate.

1919 W.Va. Acts (Ext.Sess.) ch. 10, p. 19. Act passed providing for payment of judgment partly in cash and partly by an issue of bonds which Virginia had agreed to accept at par.

Wyoming v. Colorado

259 U.S. 419, 496 (1922). Final decision and decree on bill filed in 1911 (evidence having been taken in 1913 and 1914, and the cause first argued in 1916 and thereafter twice reargued) enjoining Colorado and the two corporate defendants from diverting more than 15,500 acre-feet of water per year from the Laramie River by means of the Laramie-Poudre project.

286 U.S. 494 (1932). New suit to enforce 1922 decree. Colorado's motion to dismiss bill denied, with opinion clarifying former decree in certain respects, and Colorado directed to answer the charges of violation.

298 U.S. 573 (1936). Wyoming's charges of violation of 1922 decree rejected, but injunction broadened to forbid certain other diversions, and jurisdiction retained for a further order in the event the two states were unable to agree on the installation of measuring devices.

309 U.S. 572 (1940). Petition by Wyoming that Colorado be adjudged in contempt for violation of former decree. Decree clarified in certain respects, but Colorado found to be in violation. Petition denied on the basis of Colorado's defense, which Wyoming contested, that the excessive diver-

sion was made with the consent of a Wyoming official. Chief Justice Hughes said (p. 582):

"＊ ＊ ＊ In the light of all the circumstances, we think it sufficiently appears that there was a period of uncertainty and room for misunderstanding which may be considered in extenuation. In the future there will be no ground for any possible misapprehension ＊ ＊ ＊."[1]

Vermont v. New York

417 U.S. 270 (1974). Suit by Vermont against New York and International Paper Co., alleging unlawful pollution of Vermont waters. The Special Master worked out a settlement and presented a proposed consent decree embodying it. The proposed decree included no findings of fact or conclusions of law. It contained elaborate provisions relating to steps to be taken with regard to the pollution problem at issue, and provided for a Special Master to "police the execution of the settlement set forth in the decree" and to "pass on to this Court his proposed resolution of contested issues that the future might bring forth." The Supreme Court declined to approve the proposed decree. Noting that "continuing Court supervision over decrees of equitable apportionment of waters was undesirable" (p. 275), the Court stated (p. 277):

"Such a procedure would materially change the function of the Court in these interstate contests. Insofar as we would be supervising the execution of the Consent Decree, we would be acting more in an arbitral rather than a judicial manner. Our original jurisdiction heretofore has been deemed to extend to adjudications of controversies between States according to principles of law, some drawn from the international field, some expressing a 'common law' formulated over the decades by this Court.

"The proposals submitted by the South Lake Master to this Court might be proposals having no relation to law. Like the present Decree they might be mere settlements by the parties acting under compulsions and motives that have no relation to performance of our Article III functions. Article III speaks of the 'judicial power' of this Court, which embraces application of principles of law or equity to facts, distilled by hearings or by stipulations. Nothing in the Proposed Decree nor in the mandate to be given the South Lake Master speaks in terms of 'judicial power.' "

Compare New Hampshire v. Maine, 426 U.S. 363 (1976), accepting a proposed consent decree finally settling a boundary dispute in accordance with findings made on the basis of the evidence.

NOTE ON A STATE'S STANDING TO SUE AND RELATED PROBLEMS OF JUSTICIABILITY

(1) In New Hampshire v. Louisiana and New York v. Louisiana, 108 U.S. 76 (1883), the plaintiff states sued on defaulted bonds as assignees for collection only in behalf of certain of their citizens. The Court rejected the argument that the original jurisdiction should in this instance be available as a substitute for the traditional methods of enforcement by sovereign

1. A new decree on the merits was subsequently substituted. See 353 U.S. 953 (1957).

states of the claims of their citizens through war or diplomacy. It dismissed the bills as in violation of the substance of the Eleventh Amendment.

Since then it has become settled doctrine that a state, whatever the character of the defendant, has standing to sue only when it is the real party in interest and is not merely sponsoring the claims of individual citizens. See, *e.g.*, Kansas v. United States, 204 U.S. 331 (1907); Oklahoma v. Atchison, T. & S.F. Ry., 220 U.S. 277 (1911) (state may not maintain bill to enjoin unlawful railroad rates where injury is to certain shippers) (but *cf.* Georgia v. Pennsylvania R.R., p. 329, *infra*); North Dakota v. Minnesota, 263 U.S. 365 (1923) (denying claim for damages made by state on behalf of individual farmers injured by flooding caused by neighboring state); Oklahoma ex rel. Johnson v. Cook, 304 U.S. 387 (1938) (where the state had legal title to the assets of a liquidating bank but was found to be trying to enforce a stockholder's liability merely for the benefit of the bank's creditors and depositors). *Cf.* New Jersey v. New York, p. 317, *supra*.

South Dakota learned a lesson from the experience of New Hampshire and New York. She took absolute title (by gift from an individual) to some of North Carolina's defaulted bonds and got judgment on them. South Dakota v. North Carolina, 192 U.S. 286 (1904). Here, as in Kentucky v. Indiana, the state was asserting an interest of precisely the same type that a private litigant might have asserted. Can the boundary and water rights cases be explained in the same terms? See Justice Bradley's view of the boundary cases in Hans v. Louisiana, 134 U.S. 1, 15 (1890).

(2) Note that a *defendant* state's "standing" in the litigation may raise a question just as the plaintiff state's can. In Massachusetts v. Missouri, 308 U.S. 1 (1939), Massachusetts asked for leave to file a complaint against Missouri and others. It alleged that Massachusetts inheritance taxes were due with respect to certain trusts (with Missouri trustees) created by a Massachusetts domiciliary; that Missouri claimed the exclusive right to impose inheritance taxes on these trusts; and that the taxes could not be collected from any person or property in Massachusetts. Massachusetts asked the Court to decide which state had jurisdiction to tax and to issue appropriate injunctive relief.[1] The Court, in an opinion by Chief Justice Hughes, held that "the proposed bill of complaint does not present a justiciable controversy between the States." He stated (pp. 15–16): "To constitute such a controversy, it must appear that the complaining State has suffered a wrong through the action of the other State, furnishing ground for judicial redress, or is asserting a right against the other State which is susceptible of judicial enforcement according to the accepted principles of the common law or equity systems of jurisprudence. Florida v. Mellon, 273 U.S. 12, 16, 17; Texas v. Florida, 306 U.S. 398, 405. Missouri in claiming a right to recover taxes from the respondent trustees, or in taking proceedings for collection, is not injuring Massachusetts. By the allegations, the property held in Missouri is amply sufficient to answer the claims of both States and recovery by either does not impair the exercise of any right the other may have. It is not shown that there is danger of the depletion of a fund or estate at the expense of the complainant's interest. It is not shown that the tax claims of the two States are

---

1. Massachusetts also named the Missouri trustees as defendants. On the   Court's disposition of this aspect of the case, see p. 339, *infra*.

mutually exclusive. On the contrary, the validity of each claim is wholly independent of that of the other and, in the light of our recent decisions, may constitutionally be pressed by each State without conflict in point of fact or law with the decision of the other. Curry v. McCanless, 307 U.S. 357; Graves v. Elliott, 307 U.S. 383. The question is thus a different one from that presented in Texas v. Florida, *supra,* where the controlling consideration was that by the law of the several States concerned only a single tax could be laid by a single State, that of the domicile. This was sufficient basis for invoking the equity jurisdiction of the Court, where it also appeared that there was danger that through successful prosecution of the claims of the several States in independent suits enough of the estate would be absorbed to deprive some State of its lawful tax. Texas v. Florida, *supra,* 405, 406, 408, 410."

Compare Texas v. New Jersey, 379 U.S. 674 (1965), p. 322, *supra;* Western Union Tel. Co. v. Pennsylvania, 368 U.S. 71, 77–80 (1961).

(3) To what extent should the state as *parens patriae* be able to litigate in defense of public or governmental interests that concern the state as a whole? See Note, 11 Stan.L.Rev. 665, 671–80 (1959); Note, 125 U.Pa.L.Rev. 1069 (1977). In the rest of this Note (and in the following *Note on the Standing of a State as Parens Patriae to Sue the Federal Government,* p. 331, *infra*) some of the important cases bearing on this issue are abstracted. In considering them, consider also the question whether the function of the original jurisdiction as a substitute for diplomacy and war justifies a more liberal standard of justiciability in actions between states than in actions by a state against individuals.

(4) Louisiana v. Texas, 176 U.S. 1 (1900), was the first case to pose the issue sharply. Charles Warren, p. 318, note 1, *supra* states the case thus (p. 45):

" * * * The latter State by statute had given to her officials wide powers to enforce very drastic quarantine regulations and to detain vessels, persons and property coming into Texas. In 1899, a health officer of Texas took advantage of a single case of yellow fever in New Orleans to lay an embargo on all commerce between that city and the State of Texas, and this embargo was enforced by armed guards posted at the frontier. Louisiana alleged that the yellow fever case was a mere pretext, that the real motive was to divert commerce from New Orleans to the port of Galveston in Texas, that this was shown by the fact that no embargo was maintained against commerce coming to Galveston from the seriously infested ports of Mexico. Accordingly, Louisiana sought an injunction against Texas and its officials."

The Court dismissed the bill. Later cases have explained the decision as based on the absence of proof that the health officer's action was the act of the state, and on the lack of sufficient allegations of inescapable damage to justify the extraordinary intervention of a court of equity in a controversy between states. See, *e.g.,* Alabama v. Arizona, 291 U.S. 286, 291–92 (1934). But Chief Justice Fuller placed the decision also on broader grounds (pp. 19, 22):

" * * * Inasmuch as the vindication of the freedom of interstate commerce is not committed to the State of Louisiana, and that State is not engaged in such commerce, the cause of action must be regarded not as involving any infringement of the powers of the State of Louisiana, or any special injury to her property, but as asserting that the State is entitled to seek relief in this way because the matters complained of affect her citizens at large. ∗ ∗ ∗

"But in order that a controversy between States, justiciable in this court, can be held to exist, something more must be put forward than that the citizens of one State are injured by the maladministration of the laws of another."

Justice Harlan placed his concurrence squarely on the ground that the words of the Constitution "refer to controversies or cases that are justiciable as between the parties thereto, and not to controversies or cases that do not involve either the property or powers of the State which complains ∗ ∗ ∗." Justice Brown was willing to contemplate the possibility of a suit by Louisiana in behalf of all her citizens, but thought she was not a proper party here because "the controversy is not one in which the citizens of Louisiana generally can be assumed to be interested, but only the citizens of New Orleans".

(5) In the very next year the Court broke new ground in Missouri v. Illinois, 180 U.S. 208 (1901). By a 6 to 3 decision, it sustained against demurrer a bill to enjoin the dumping of Chicago's sewage into a specially constructed canal draining into the Mississippi River which, so it was alleged, was poisoning the water supply in Missouri and injuring its land. The Court said (p. 241):

"An inspection of the bill discloses that the nature of the injury complained of is such that an adequate remedy can only be found in this court at the suit of the State of Missouri. It is true that no question of boundary is involved, nor of direct property rights belonging to the complainant State. But it must surely be conceded that, if the health and comfort of the inhabitants of a State are threatened, the State is the proper party to represent and defend them. If Missouri were an independent and sovereign State all must admit that she could seek a remedy by negotiation, and, that failing, by force. Diplomatic powers and the right to make war having been surrendered to the general government, it was to be expected that upon the latter would be devolved the duty of providing a remedy and that remedy, we think, is found in the constitutional provisions we are considering." [2]

(6) In Georgia v. Tennessee Copper Co., 206 U.S. 230 (1907), the state sought to enjoin the company from discharging noxious gas from its works in Tennessee over Georgia's territory. The state claimed an injury both to lands of its own and to the lands of its citizens generally. In upholding the bill, the Court referred to the proprietary claims as a "make-weight" and placed its decision primarily on the ground of the state's right to protect its interests as a sovereign. Justice Holmes said (p. 237):

" ∗ ∗ ∗ When the States by their union made the forcible abatement of outside nuisances impossible to each, they did not thereby agree to

---

2. For similar decisions, see New York v. New Jersey, 256 U.S. 296 (1921) (bill to enjoin discharge of sewage into New York harbor dismissed on merits because damage was not proved with requisite clarity); North Dakota v. Minnesota, 263 U.S. 365 (1923) (bill to enjoin continued use of system of drainage ditches alleged to have caused overflows injuring North Dakota land dismissed without prejudice for failure to sustain "the peculiar burden" on the complainant state); Wisconsin v. Illinois, 278 U.S. 367 (1929) (successful effort, but with a long aftermath, to enjoin diversion of water from the Great Lakes through a sanitary canal into another watershed).

submit to whatever might be done. They did not renounce the possibility of making reasonable demands on the ground of their still remaining *quasi*-sovereign interests; and the alternative to force is a suit in this court. Missouri v. Illinois, 180 U.S. 208, 241."

Justice Harlan in a separate opinion expressed the view (p. 240) that the Court was not authorized to apply in behalf of a state "any principle or rule of equity that would not be applied, under the same facts, in suits wholly between private parties". He concurred in the decision on the ground that Georgia had met this test.

(7) Four years later Justice Harlan wrote the opinion for a unanimous Court in Oklahoma v. Atchison, T. & S.F. Ry., 220 U.S. 277 (1911), holding that the state could not maintain a bill for an injunction against allegedly unlawful railroad rates which were asserted to be "a hindrance to the growth of the State, as well as an injury to the property rights of its inhabitants". It was doubtful whether the state made any showing of illegality, nor was it clear that it was in need of equitable relief, in view of its legislative power of regulation. But Justice Harlan, relying primarily on Louisiana v. Texas, *supra,* placed the decision on the broader ground that the wrongs complained of were wrongs to "be reached, without the intervention of the State, by suits instituted by the persons directly or immediately injured". He said (p. 289):

"We are of opinion that the words, in the Constitution, conferring original jurisdiction on this court, in a suit 'in which a State shall be a party,' are not to be interpreted as conferring such jurisdiction in every cause in which the State elects to make itself strictly a party plaintiff of record and seeks not to protect its own property, but only to vindicate the wrongs of some of its people or to enforce its own laws or public policy against wrongdoers, generally."

(8) In Pennsylvania v. West Virginia and Ohio v. West Virginia, 262 U.S. 553 (1923), the Court, by a divided vote, granted an injunction forbidding West Virginia to enforce a statute designed to limit the export of natural gas to the excess of output over its own domestic needs. The Court said (pp. 591–92):

"The attitude of the complainant States is not that of mere volunteers attempting to vindicate the freedom of interstate commerce or to redress purely private grievances. Each sues to protect a two-fold interest—one as the proprietor of various public institutions and schools whose supply of gas will be largely curtailed or cut off by the threatened interference with the interstate current, and the other as the representative of the consuming public whose supply will be similarly affected. * * *

"The private consumers in each State not only include most of the inhabitants of many urban communities but constitute a substantial portion of the State's population. Their health, comfort and welfare are seriously jeopardized by the threatened withdrawal of the gas from the interstate stream. This is a matter of grave public concern in which the State, as the representative of the public, has an interest apart from that of the individuals affected. It is not merely a remote or ethical interest but one which is immediate and recognized by law.

"In principle these views have full support in prior decisions * * *."

Did they?

(9) So the cases stood when the Court, in a five to four decision, granted a motion by the state of Georgia to file a bill of complaint against twenty railroads to enjoin an alleged conspiracy to fix arbitrary and noncompetitive rates in restraint of trade and commerce among the states. Georgia v. Pennsylvania R.R., 324 U.S. 439 (1945). The complaint bristled with jurisdictional difficulties, including a question of the primary jurisdiction of the Interstate Commerce Commission. The dissenting opinion by Chief Justice Stone took a wide range of objections to the proceeding, among them the assertion that the state was foreclosed on the issue of standing by the prior cases.

For the majority, Justice Douglas pointed out (p. 443) that Georgia sued in two relevant capacities: "(1) in her capacity as a quasi-sovereign or as agent and protector of her people against a continuing wrong done to them; and (2) in her capacity as a proprietor to redress wrongs suffered by the State as the owner of a railroad and as the owner and operator of various institutions of the State." The claim in the first capacity was supported by allegations (p. 444) that the effect of the rates complained of was "to frustrate and counteract the measures taken by the State to promote * * * the general progress and welfare of its people", and "to hold the Georgia economy in a state of arrested development."

Justice Douglas said (pp. 446–47):

" * * * Nor is this a situation where the United States rather than Georgia stands as *parens patriae* to the citizens of Georgia. This is not a suit like those in Massachusetts v. Mellon, and Florida v. Mellon, *supra,* where a State sought to protect her citizens from the operation of federal statutes. Here Georgia asserts rights based on the anti-trust laws. The fact that the United States may bring criminal prosecutions or suits for injunctions under those laws does not mean that Georgia may not maintain the present suit. * * * Suits by a State, *parens patriae,* have long been recognized. There is no apparent reason why those suits should be excluded from the purview of the anti-trust acts."

The opinion then cited, among other cases, Georgia v. Tennessee Copper Co., Missouri v. Illinois, Kansas v. Colorado, and Pennsylvania v. West Virginia, and continued (pp. 450–52):

"It seems to us clear that under the authority of these cases Georgia may maintain this suit as *parens patriae* acting on behalf of her citizens though here, as in Georgia v. Tennessee Copper Co., * * * we treat the injury to the State as proprietor merely as a 'makeweight'. The original jurisdiction of this Court is one of the mighty instruments which the framers of the Constitution provided so that adequate machinery might be available for the peaceful settlement of disputes between States and between a State and citizens of another State. * * *

"Oklahoma v. Atchison, T. & S.F.R. Co., *supra,* is not opposed to this view. * * * This is not a suit in which a State is a mere nominal plaintiff, individual shippers being the real complainants. This is a suit in which Georgia asserts claims arising out of federal laws and the gravamen of which runs far beyond the claim of damage to individual shippers."

After protracted hearings before a special master and the building of an immense record, the complaint was eventually dismissed, on motion of both parties, by a memorandum order. Georgia v. Pennsylvania R.R., 340 U.S. 889 (1950).[3]

(10) Pennsylvania v. New Jersey and Maine v. New Hampshire, 426 U.S. 660 (1976), were motions for leave to file based on the Supreme Court's decision in Austin v. New Hampshire, 420 U.S. 656 (1975), holding invalid the New Hampshire Commuters Income Tax. Austin had held that New Hampshire violated the privileges and immunities clause when it imposed a 4% income tax on the New Hampshire-derived income of nonresidents, since New Hampshire residents paid no income tax to the state at all.

The State of Maine provided a credit to its residents for income tax paid to other states. Its bill of complaint alleged that, consequently, some $3.5 millions of taxes were "diverted" from Maine to New Hampshire in the form of tax revenues collected by New Hampshire under the invalid statute from Maine residents; Maine sought an accounting for such taxes.

Pennsylvania (which provided a similar tax credit) sued for a declaration that New Jersey's commuter income tax was invalid under Austin, and also sought an accounting for "diverted" taxes.

The Court denied leave to file in both cases. It held, first, that under Massachusetts v. Missouri no showing was made that the defendant states had caused plaintiff states an injury (p. 664): "The injuries to the plaintiffs' fiscs were self-inflicted, resulting from decisions by their respective state legislatures. Nothing required Maine * * * to extend a tax credit to their residents * * * and nothing prevents Pennsylvania from withdrawing that credit * * *." Second, it held further that no state has standing in its own right to complain of violations of the privileges and immunities clause or the equal protection clause: "both Clauses protect people, not States."

Finally, the Court held that Pennsylvania could not sue *parens patriae:* the action is "nothing more than a collectivity of private suits against New Jersey for taxes withheld from private parties" (p. 666).[4]

(11) Finally, in Maryland v. Louisiana, 451 U.S. 725 (1981), the Court permitted eight states to challenge the constitutional validity of Louisiana's tax on the "first use" of previously untaxed natural gas coming into the state (a tax that fell heavily on gas derived from offshore wells passing through Louisiana for eventual sale to consumers in other states). Although the tax was imposed on private pipeline companies, it was passed through to their customers, among whom were the plaintiff states; in any event, the suits could be maintained *parens patriae,* since Louisiana's tax

---

3. Compare Hawaii v. Standard Oil Co., 405 U.S. 251 (1972), a suit brought by the state in a *district* court for treble damages for injuries to the state's "economy and prosperity" caused by violations of Section 4 of the Clayton Act. The Court, reviewing on certiorari, held that a state may not, as *parens patriae,* sue for damages for violations of Section 4 of the Clayton Act; it was said that the State could sue in its "proprietary capacity", but that to allow damages for injury to the state's "general economy" would open the door to duplicate recoveries. See also Comment, *Suits by a State as Parens Patriae,* 48 N.C.L.Rev. 963 (1970).

4. See also Illinois v. Michigan, 409 U.S. 36 (1972), in which the Court denied leave to file in a case involving an alleged violation of the reciprocity provisions of the Uniform Insurers Liquidation Act. In a cursory per curiam, the Court stated that "the problem presented is essentially one between private litigants," and that "while the complaint on its face is within our original, as well as our exclusive, jurisdiction, it seems apparent from the moving papers and the response that Illinois, though nominally a party, is here 'in the vindication of the grievances of particular individuals.'"

visited "substantial economic injury" to "a great many citizens in each of the plaintiff states" (p. 739). The Court said that the suit was "functionally indistinguishable from Pennsylvania v. West Virginia" (p. 738).[5]

NOTE ON THE STANDING OF A STATE AS PARENS PATRIAE TO SUE THE FEDERAL GOVERNMENT

(1) Massachusetts v. Mellon, 262 U.S. 447 (1923), was a companion case to Frothingham v. Mellon, see pp. 138–39, *supra,* in which the Commonwealth sought substantially the same relief as Miss Frothingham. A unanimous Court held that the Commonwealth lacked standing also. Justice Sutherland said (pp. 484–86):

" * * * in so far as the case depends upon the assertion of a right on the part of the State to sue in its own behalf, we are without jurisdiction. In that aspect of the case we are called upon to adjudicate, not rights of person or property, not rights of dominion over physical domain, not quasi-sovereign rights actually invaded or threatened, but abstract questions of political power, of sovereignty, of government. * * *

"We come next to consider whether the suit may be maintained by the State as the representative of its citizens. To this the answer is not doubtful. We need not go so far as to say that a State may never intervene by suit to protect its citizens against any form of enforcement of unconstitutional acts of Congress; but we are clear that the right to do so does not arise here. Ordinarily, at least, the only way in which a State may afford protection to its citizens in such cases is through the enforcement of its own criminal statutes, where that is appropriate, or by opening its courts to the injured persons for the maintenance of civil suits or actions. But the citizens of Massachusetts are also citizens of the United States. It cannot be conceded that a State, as *parens patriae,* may institute judicial proceedings to protect citizens of the United States from the operation of the statutes thereof. While the State, under some circumstances, may sue in that capacity for the protection of its citizens (Missouri v. Illinois, 180 U.S. 208, 241), it is no part of its duty or power to enforce their rights in respect of their relations with the Federal Government. In that field it is the United States, and not the State, which represents them as *parens patriae,* when such representation becomes appropriate; and to the former, and not to the latter, they must look for such protective measures as flow from that status."

See also Florida v. Mellon, 273 U.S. 12, 18 (1927).[1]

---

5. *Cf.* Alfred L. Snapp & Son, Inc. v. Puerto Rico ex rel. Barez, 458 U.S. 592 (1982), upholding an action in a *district* court by Puerto Rico, as *parens patriae,* for a declaration that certain apple growers in the eastern states had violated federal statutes creating a preference for domestic over temporary foreign workers. The Court discussed its original jurisdiction precedents, but noted (p. 603 n. 12) that the special considerations limiting *parens patriae* suits in the original jurisdiction may not apply to suits in the district courts—a

point emphasized by four concurring Justices.

1. In Jones ex rel. Louisiana v. Bowles, 322 U.S. 707 (1944), the governor brought an original action in behalf of the state against the Price Administrator (in the hope of escaping the exclusive jurisdiction provisions of the Emergency Price Control Act of 1942) to enjoin the enforcement of a regulation fixing ceiling prices for strawberries, which were alleged to be a crop of major importance to the economy of the state. The motion for leave to file

(2) South Carolina v. Katzenbach, 383 U.S. 301 (1966), was a suit to enjoin the Attorney General from enforcing the Voting Rights Act of 1965—"the heart of [which] is a complex scheme of stringent remedies aimed at areas where voting discrimination has been most flagrant" (p. 315). The Court, relying on Massachusetts v. Mellon, held that the state could not, as *parens patriae,* invoke the protection of the Fifth Amendment due process and bill of attainder clauses on behalf of its citizens against the federal government. But the Court did, without discussion of the issue of standing, pass on the merits of the state's challenge to the statute, based on the Fifteenth Amendment, "on the fundamental ground" (p. 323) that the statute invades the reserved power of the states to determine voter qualifications and regulate elections, and exceeds the powers of the Congress. Is the handling of the standing questions internally consistent? Consistent with the prior cases? Correct? See Bickel, *The Voting Rights Cases,* 1966 Sup.Ct.Rev. 79, 80–93. Compare the refusal, without opinion or citation, to allow Massachusetts to file an original bill of complaint against the Secretary of Defense to challenge the legality of the Vietnam war: Massachusetts v. Laird, 400 U.S. 886 (1970) (with elaborate dissent by Justice Douglas).[2]

OHIO v. WYANDOTTE CHEMICALS CORP.

401 U.S. 493, 91 S.Ct. 1005, 28 L.Ed.2d 256 (1971).
Original.

MR. JUSTICE HARLAN delivered the opinion of the Court.

By motion for leave to file a bill of complaint, Ohio seeks to invoke this Court's original jurisdiction. Because of the importance and unusual character of the issues tendered we set the matter for oral argument, inviting the Solicitor General to participate and to file a brief on behalf of the United States, as *amicus curiae.* For reasons that follow we deny the motion for leave to file.

The action, for abatement of a nuisance, is brought on behalf of the State and its citizens, and names as defendants Wyandotte Chemicals Corp. (Wyandotte), Dow Chemical Co. (Dow America), and Dow Chemical Company of Canada, Ltd. (Dow Canada). Wyandotte is incorporated in Michigan and maintains its principal office and place of business there. Dow America is incorporated in Delaware, has its principal office and place of business in Michigan, and owns all the stock of Dow Canada. Dow Canada is incorporated, and does business, in Ontario. A majority of Dow Canada's directors are residents of the United States.

the complaint was denied "for want of jurisdiction of this Court to entertain it under Article III, Section 2, of the Constitution."

2. Justices Harlan and Stewart noted their dissent, stating that they would have set the motion for leave to file for argument on "questions of standing and justiciability".

For subsequent proceedings in the lower courts (with individuals joining Massachu-

setts as plaintiffs), see Massachusetts v. Laird, 451 F.2d 26 (1st Cir.1971).

See also Notes, 61 Minn.L.Rev. 691 (1977) and 125 U.Pa.L.Rev. 1069 (1977), both commenting on Pennsylvania v. Kleppe, 533 F.2d 668 (D.C.Cir.1976) (Pennsylvania has no standing to challenge Small Business Administration's designation of state as a Class B disaster area for purpose of distribution of federal disaster relief after 1972 hurricane).

The complaint alleges that Dow Canada and Wyandotte have each dumped mercury into streams whose courses ultimately reach Lake Erie, thus contaminating and polluting that lake's waters, vegetation, fish, and wildlife, and that Dow America is jointly responsible for the acts of its foreign subsidiary. Assuming the State's ability to prove these assertions, Ohio seeks a decree: (1) declaring the introduction of mercury into Lake Erie's tributaries a public nuisance; (2) perpetually enjoining these defendants from introducing mercury into Lake Erie or its tributaries; (3) requiring defendants either to remove the mercury from Lake Erie or to pay the costs of its removal into a fund to be administered by Ohio and used only for that purpose; (4) directing defendants to pay Ohio monetary damages for the harm done to Lake Erie, its fish, wildlife, and vegetation, and the citizens and inhabitants of Ohio.

Original jurisdiction is said to be conferred on this Court by Art. III of the Federal Constitution. Section 2, cl. 1, of that Article, provides: "The judicial Power shall extend * * * to Controversies * * * between a State and Citizens of another State * * * and between a State * * * and foreign * * * Citizens or Subjects." Section 2, cl. 2, provides: "In all Cases * * * in which a State shall be Party, the Supreme Court shall have original Jurisdiction." Finally, 28 U.S.C. § 1251(b) provides: "The Supreme Court shall have original but not exclusive jurisdiction of * * * (3) All actions or proceedings by a State against the citizens of another State or against aliens."

While we consider that Ohio's complaint does state a cause of action that falls within the compass of our original jurisdiction, we have concluded that this Court should nevertheless decline to exercise that jurisdiction.

I

That we have jurisdiction seems clear enough. Beyond doubt, the complaint on its face reveals the existence of a genuine "case or controversy" between one State and citizens of another, as well as a foreign subject. Diversity of citizenship is absolute. Nor is the nature of the cause of action asserted a bar to the exercise of our jurisdiction. While we have refused to entertain, for example, original actions designed to exact compliance with a State's penal laws, Wisconsin v. Pelican Ins. Co., 127 U.S. 265 (1888), or that seek to embroil this tribunal in "political questions," Mississippi v. Johnson, 4 Wall. 475 (1867); Georgia v. Stanton, 6 Wall. 50 (1868), this Court has often adjudicated controversies between States and between a State and citizens of another State seeking to abate a nuisance that exists in one State yet produces noxious consequences in another. See Missouri v. Illinois and The Sanitary Dist. of Chicago, 180 U.S. 208 (1901) (complaint filed), 200 U.S. 496 (1906) (final judgment); Georgia v. Tennessee Copper Co., 206 U.S. 230 (1907); New York v. New Jersey, 256 U.S. 296 (1921); New Jersey v. New York City, 283 U.S. 473 (1931). In short, precedent leads almost ineluctably to the conclusion that we are empowered to resolve this dispute in the first instance.

Ordinarily, the foregoing would suffice to settle the issue presently under consideration: whether Ohio should be granted leave to file its complaint. For it is a time-honored maxim of the Anglo–American common-law tradition that a court possessed of jurisdiction generally must exercise it. Cohens v. Virginia, 6 Wheat. 264, 404 (1821). Nevertheless, although it may initially have been contemplated that this Court would always exercise its original jurisdiction when properly called upon to do so, it seems evident to us that changes in the American legal system and the development of American society have rendered untenable, as a practical matter, the view that this Court must stand willing to adjudicate all or most legal disputes that may arise between one State and a citizen or citizens of another, even though the dispute may be one over which this Court does have original jurisdiction.

As our social system has grown more complex, the States have increasingly become enmeshed in a multitude of disputes with persons living outside their borders. Consider, for example, the frequency with which States and nonresidents clash over the application of state laws concerning taxes, motor vehicles, decedents' estates, business torts, government contracts, and so forth. It would, indeed, be anomalous were this Court to be held out as a potential principal forum for settling such controversies. The simultaneous development of "long-arm jurisdiction" means, in most instances, that no necessity impels us to perform such a role. And the evolution of this Court's responsibilities in the American legal system has brought matters to a point where much would be sacrificed, and little gained, by our exercising original jurisdiction over issues bottomed on local law. This Court's paramount responsibilities to the national system lie almost without exception in the domain of federal law. As the impact on the social structure of federal common, statutory, and constitutional law has expanded, our attention has necessarily been drawn more and more to such matters. We have no claim to special competence in dealing with the numerous conflicts between States and nonresident individuals that raise no serious issues of federal law.

This Court is, moreover, structured to perform as an appellate tribunal, ill-equipped for the task of factfinding and so forced, in original cases, awkwardly to play the role of factfinder without actually presiding over the introduction of evidence. Nor is the problem merely our lack of qualifications for many of these tasks potentially within the purview of our original jurisdiction; it is compounded by the fact that for every case in which we might be called upon to determine the facts and apply unfamiliar legal norms we would unavoidably be reducing the attention we could give to those matters of federal law and national import as to which we are the primary overseers.

Thus, we think it apparent that we must recognize "the need [for] the exercise of a sound discretion in order to protect this Court from an abuse of the opportunity to resort to its original jurisdiction in the enforcement by States of claims against citizens of other States." Massachusetts v. Missouri, 308 U.S. 1, 19 (1939), opinion of Chief Justice Hughes. See also Georgia v. Pennsylvania R. Co., 324 U.S. 439, 464-465 (1945), and *id.*, at 469-471 (dissenting opinion).[3] We believe, however, that the focus of

3. In our view the federal statute, 28 U.S.C. § 1251(b)(3), providing that our original jurisdiction in cases such as these is merely concurrent with that of the federal district courts, reflects this same judgment. However, this particular case cannot be disposed of by transferring it to an appropriate federal district court since this statute by itself does not actually confer juris-diction on those courts, see C. Wright, Federal Courts 502 (2d ed. 1970), and no other statutory jurisdictional basis exists. The fact that there is diversity of citizenship among the parties would not support district court jurisdiction under 28 U.S.C. § 1332 because that statute does not deal with cases in which a State is a party. Nor would federal question jurisdiction ex-

concern embodied in the above-quoted statement of Chief Justice Hughes should be somewhat refined. In our opinion, we may properly exercise such discretion, not simply to shield this Court from noisome, vexatious, or unfamiliar tasks, but also, and we believe principally, as a technique for promoting and furthering the assumptions and value choices that underlie the current role of this Court in the federal system. Protecting this Court *per se* is at best a secondary consideration. What gives rise to the necessity for recognizing such discretion is pre-eminently the diminished societal concern in our function as a court of original jurisdiction and the enhanced importance of our role as the final federal appellate court. A broader view of the scope and purposes of our discretion would inadequately take account of the general duty of courts to exercise that jurisdiction they possess.

Thus, at this stage we go no further than to hold that, as a general matter, we may decline to entertain a complaint brought by a State against the citizens of another State or country only where we can say with assurance that (1) declination of jurisdiction would not disserve any of the principal policies underlying the Article III jurisdictional grant and (2) the reasons of practical wisdom that persuade us that this Court is an inappropriate forum are consistent with the proposition that our discretion is legitimated by its use to keep this aspect of the Court's functions attune with its other responsibilities.

II

In applying this analysis to the facts here presented, we believe that the wiser course is to deny Ohio's motion for leave to file its complaint.

A

Two principles seem primarily to have underlain conferring upon this Court original jurisdiction over cases and controversies between a State and citizens of another State or country. The first was the belief that no State should be compelled to resort to the tribunals of other States for redress, since parochial factors might often lead to the appearance, if not the reality, of partiality to one's own. Chisholm v. Georgia, 2 Dall. 419, 475–476 (1793); Wisconsin v. Pelican Ins. Co., 127 U.S. 265, 289 (1888). The second was that a State, needing an alternative forum, of necessity had to resort to this Court in order to obtain a tribunal competent to exercise jurisdiction over the acts of nonresidents of the aggrieved State.

Neither of these policies is, we think, implicated in this lawsuit. The courts of Ohio, under modern principles of the scope of subject matter and *in personam* jurisdiction, have a claim as compelling as any that can be made out for this Court to exercise jurisdiction to adjudicate the instant controversy, and they would decide it under the same common law of nuisance upon which our determination would have to rest. In essence, the State has charged Dow Canada and Wyandotte with the commission of acts, albeit beyond Ohio's territorial boundaries, that have produced and, it is said, continue to produce disastrous effects within Ohio's own domain. While this Court, and doubtless Canadian courts, if called upon to assess

ist under 28 U.S.C. § 1331. So far as it appears from the present record, an action such as this, if otherwise cognizable in federal district court, would have to be adjudicated under state law. Erie R. Co. v. Tompkins, 304 U.S. 64 (1938).

the validity of any decree rendered against either Dow Canada or Wyandotte, would be alert to ascertain whether the judgment rested upon an even-handed application of justice, it is unlikely that we would totally deny Ohio's competence to act if the allegations made here are proved true. See, *e.g.,* International Shoe Co. v. Washington, 326 U.S. 310 (1945); United States v. Aluminum Co. of America, 148 F.2d 416 (CA2 1945); ALI, Restatement of the Foreign Relations Law of the United States 2d, § 18. And while we cannot speak for Canadian courts, we have been given no reason to believe they would be less receptive to enforcing a decree rendered by Ohio courts than one issued by this Court. Thus, we do not believe exercising our discretion to refuse to entertain this complaint would undermine any of the purposes for which Ohio was given the authority to bring it here.

B

Our reasons for thinking that, as a practical matter, it would be inappropriate for this Court to attempt to adjudicate the issues Ohio seeks to present are several. History reveals that the course of this Court's prior efforts to settle disputes regarding interstate air and water pollution has been anything but smooth. In Missouri v. Illinois, 200 U.S. 496, 520–522 (1906), Justice Holmes was at pains to underscore the great difficulty that the Court faced in attempting to pronounce a suitable general rule of law to govern such controversies. The solution finally grasped was to saddle the party seeking relief with an unusually high standard of proof and the Court with the duty of applying only legal principles "which [it] is prepared deliberately to maintain against all considerations on the other side," *id.,* at 521, an accommodation which, in cases of this kind, the Court has found necessary to maintain ever since. See, *e.g.,* New York v. New Jersey, 256 U.S. 296, 309 (1921). Justice Clarke's closing plea in New York v. New Jersey, *supra,* at 313, strikingly illustrates the sense of futility that has accompanied this Court's attempts to treat with the complex technical and political matters that inhere in all disputes of the kind at hand:

"We cannot withhold the suggestion, inspired by the consideration of this case, that the grave problem of sewage disposal presented by the large and growing populations living on the shores of New York Bay is one more likely to be wisely solved by cooperative study and by conference and mutual concession on the part of representatives of the States so vitally interested in it than by proceedings in any court however constituted."

The difficulties that ordinarily beset such cases are severely compounded by the particular setting in which this controversy has reached us. For example, the parties have informed us, without contradiction, that a number of official bodies are already actively involved in regulating the conduct complained of here. A Michigan circuit court has enjoined Wyandotte from operating its mercury cell process without judicial authorization. The company is, moreover, currently utilizing a recycling process specifically approved by the Michigan Water Resources Commission and remains subject to the continued scrutiny of that agency. Dow Canada reports monthly to the Ontario Water Resources Commission on its compliance with the commission's order prohibiting the company from passing any mercury into the environment.

Additionally, Ohio and Michigan are both participants in the Lake Erie Enforcement Conference, convened a year ago by the Secretary of the Interior pursuant to the Federal Water Pollution Control Act, 62 Stat. 1155, as amended. The Conference is studying all forms and sources of pollution, including mercury, infecting Lake Erie. The purpose of this Conference is to provide a basis for concerted remedial action by the States or, if progress in that regard is not rapidly made, for corrective proceedings initiated by the Federal Government. 333 U.S.C. § 466g (1964 ed. and Supp. V). And the International Joint Commission, established by the Boundary Waters Treaty of 1909 between the United States and Canada, 36 Stat. 2448, issued on January 14, 1971, a comprehensive report, the culmination of a six-year study carried out at the request of the contracting parties, concerning the contamination of Lake Erie. That document makes specific recommendations for joint programs to abate these environmental hazards and recommends that the IJC be given authority to supervise and coordinate this effort.

In view of all this, granting Ohio's motion for leave to file would, in effect, commit this Court's resources to the task of trying to settle a small piece of a much larger problem that many competent adjudicatory and conciliatory bodies are actively grappling with on a more practical basis.

The nature of the case Ohio brings here is equally disconcerting. It can fairly be said that what is in dispute is not so much the law as the facts. And the factfinding process we are asked to undertake is, to say the least, formidable. We already know, just from what has been placed before us on this motion, that Lake Erie suffers from several sources of pollution other than mercury; that the scientific conclusion that mercury is a serious water pollutant is a novel one; that whether and to what extent the existence of mercury in natural waters can safely or reasonably be tolerated is a question for which there is presently no firm answer; and that virtually no published research is available describing how one might extract mercury that is in fact contaminating water. Indeed, Ohio is raising factual questions that are essentially ones of first impression to the scientists. The notion that appellate judges, even with the assistance of a most competent Special Master, might appropriately undertake at this time to unravel these complexities is, to say the least, unrealistic. Nor would it suffice to impose on Ohio an unusually high standard of proof. That might serve to mitigate our personal difficulties in seeking a just result that comports with sound judicial administration, but would not lessen the complexity of the task of preparing responsibly to exercise our judgment, or the serious drain on the resources of this Court it would entail. Other factual complexities abound. For example, the Department of the Interior has stated that eight American companies are discharging, or have discharged, mercury into Lake Erie or its tributaries. We would, then, need to assess the business practices and relative culpability of each to frame appropriate relief as to the one now before us.

Finally, in what has been said it is vitally important to stress that we are not called upon by this lawsuit to resolve difficult or important problems of federal law and that nothing in Ohio's complaint distinguishes it from any one of a host of such actions that might, with equal justification, be commenced in this Court. Thus, entertaining this complaint not only would fail to serve those responsibilities we are principally charged with, but could well pave the way for putting this Court into a quandary whereby we must opt either to pick and choose arbitrarily among similarly situated litigants or to devote truly enormous portions of our energies to such matters.

To sum up, this Court has found even the simplest sort of interstate pollution case an extremely awkward vehicle to manage. And this case is an extraordinarily complex one both because of the novel scientific issues of fact inherent in it and the multiplicity of governmental agencies already involved. Its successful resolution would require primarily skills of factfinding, conciliation, detailed coordination with—and perhaps not infrequent deference to—other adjudicatory bodies, and close supervision of the technical performance of local industries. We have no claim to such expertise or reason to believe that, were we to adjudicate this case, and others like it, we would not have to reduce drastically our attention to those controversies for which this Court is a proper and necessary forum. Such a serious intrusion on society's interest in our most deliberate and considerate performance of our paramount role as the supreme federal appellate court could, in our view, be justified only by the strictest necessity, an element which is evidently totally lacking in this instance.

III

What has been said here cannot, of course, be taken as denigrating in the slightest the public importance of the underlying problem Ohio would have us tackle. Reversing the increasing contamination of our environment is manifestly a matter of fundamental import and utmost urgency. What is dealt with above are only considerations respecting the appropriate role this Court can assume in efforts to eradicate such environmental blights. We mean only to suggest that our competence is necessarily limited, not that our concern should be kept within narrow bounds.

Ohio's motion for leave to file its complaint is denied without prejudice to its right to commence other appropriate judicial proceedings.

It is so ordered.

MR. JUSTICE DOUGLAS, dissenting.

The complaint in this case presents basically a classic type of case congenial to our original jurisdiction. It is to abate a public nuisance. Such was the claim of Georgia against a Tennessee company which was discharging noxious gas across the border into Georgia. Georgia v. Tennessee Copper Co., 206 U.S. 230. The Court said:

"It is a fair and reasonable demand on the part of a sovereign that the air over its territory should not be polluted on a great scale by sulphurous acid gas, that the forests on its mountains, be they better or worse, and whatever domestic destruction they have suffered, should not be further destroyed or threatened by the act of persons beyond its control, that the crops and orchards on its hills should not be endangered from the same source." *Id.*, at 238.

Dumping of sewage in an interstate stream, Missouri v. Illinois, 200 U.S. 496, or towing garbage to sea only to have the tides carry it to a State's beaches, New Jersey v. New York City, 283 U.S. 473, have presented analogous situations which the Court has entertained in suits invoking our original jurisdiction. The pollution of Lake Erie or its tributaries by the discharge of mercury or compounds thereof, if proved, certainly creates a public nuisance of a seriousness and magnitude which a State by our historic standards may prosecute or pursue as *parens patriae.* * * *

Much is made of the burdens and perplexities of these original actions. Some are complex, notably those involving water rights.

The drainage of Lake Michigan with the attendant lowering of water levels, affecting Canadian as well as United States interests, came to us in an original suit in which the Hon. Charles E. Hughes was Special Master. This Court entered a decree, Wisconsin v. Illinois, 278 U.S. 367, and has since that time entered supplementary decrees.

The apportionment of the waters of the Colorado between Arizona and California was a massive undertaking entailing a searching analysis by the Special Master, the Hon. Simon H. Rifkind. Our decision was based on the record made by him and on exceptions to his Report. Arizona v. California, 373 U.S. 546.

The apportionment of the waters of the North Platte River among Colorado, Wyoming, and Nebraska came to us in an original action in which we named as Special Master, Hon. Michael J. Doherty. We entered a complicated decree, which dissenters viewed with alarm, Nebraska v. Wyoming, 325 U.S. 589, but which has not demanded even an hour of the Court's time during the 26 years since it was entered.

If in these original actions we sat with a jury, as the Court once did, there would be powerful arguments for abstention in many cases. But the practice has been to appoint a Special Master which we certainly would do in this case. We could also appoint—or authorize the Special Master to retain—a panel of scientific advisers. The problems in this case are simple compared with those in the water cases discussed above. It is now known that metallic mercury deposited in water is often transformed into a dangerous chemical. This lawsuit would determine primarily the extent, if any, to which the defendants are contributing to that contamination at the present time. It would determine, secondarily, the remedies within reach—the importance of mercury in the particular manufacturing processes, the alternative processes available, the need for a remedy against a specified polluter as contrasted to a basin-wide regulation, and the like.

The problem, though clothed in chemical secrecies, can be exposed by the experts. It would indeed be one of the simplest problems yet posed in the category of cases under the head of our original jurisdiction.

The Department of Justice in a detailed brief tells us there are no barriers in federal law to our assumption of jurisdiction. I can think of no case of more transcending public importance than this one.

NOTE ON THE ORIGINAL JURISDICTION AS AN INAPPROPRIATE FORUM

(1) Massachusetts v. Missouri, 308 U.S. 1 (1939), was the first case within the Court's original jurisdiction that was dismissed squarely on the ground that it was inconvenient for the Court to adjudicate (and that a more convenient forum was available).[1] Having held that Massachusetts

---

1. In Georgia v. Pennsylvania R.R., p. 329, *supra*, the entire Court asserted the existence of power to decline to exercise jurisdiction on the ground that the parties should be remitted to a more convenient forum, although the majority thought the

had no cause of action against Missouri, see p. 325, *supra*, the Court declined to adjudicate Massachusetts' claim against the Missouri trustees for the taxes in question (pp. 18–19): "In the exercise of our original jurisdiction so as truly to fulfill the constitutional purpose we not only must look to the nature of the interest of the complaining State—the essential quality of the right asserted—but we must also inquire whether recourse to that jurisdiction in an action by a State merely to recover money alleged to be due from citizens of other States is necessary for the State's protection. ✻ ✻ ✻ To open this Court to actions by States to recover taxes claimed to be payable by citizens of other States, in the absence of facts showing the necessity for such intervention, would be to assume a burden which the grant of original jurisdiction cannot be regarded as compelling this Court to assume and which might seriously interfere with the discharge by this Court of its duty in deciding the cases and controversies appropriately brought before it. We have observed that the broad statement that a court having jurisdiction must exercise it (see Cohens v. Virginia, 6 Wheat. 264, 404) is not universally true but has been qualified in certain cases where the federal courts may, in their discretion, properly withhold the exercise of the jurisdiction conferred upon them where there is no want of another suitable forum. Canada Malting Co. v. Paterson Co., 285 U.S. 413, 422; Rogers v. Guaranty Trust Co., 288 U.S. 123, 130, 131."

The Court quoted (p. 20) the Missouri Attorney General's statement that Massachusetts could sue in a Missouri state court " 'or in a federal district court in Missouri.' " The latter assertion seems plainly wrong.[2]

Under current jurisdictional standards, could Massachusetts sue the Missouri trustees in a Massachusetts court?

(2) In Louisiana v. Cummins, 314 U.S. 580 (1941), rehearing denied, 314 U.S. 712 (1941), the Court followed Massachusetts v. Missouri in the face of a full-dress attack by the state's attorney general. The action was brought to rescind a contract alleged to have been procured by fraud and to recover its proceeds; and counsel pointed out that, since no federal district court would have jurisdiction, the result of the Court's refusal to act would be to remit the controversy to the courts of whatever state the defendants could be served in. Counsel said (brief in support of petition for rehearing, pp. 36–38):

power should not be exercised in that case. In support of the existence of the power both the majority and minority opinions cited (in addition to Massachusetts v. Missouri) North Dakota v. Chicago & Nw. R.R., 257 U.S. 485 (1922); Georgia v. Chattanooga, 264 U.S. 472, 483 (1924); and Oklahoma ex rel. Johnson v. Cook, 304 U.S. 387, 396 (1938). But in the first case the Court held that the United States was an indispensable party, and that the United States had consented to suit only in the district court. In the second case the Court held that the bill lacked equity because Georgia had an adequate remedy at law in defense of condemnation proceedings in the state court. And in the third case the Court's comments on the inconve-

nience of an exercise of original jurisdiction were made only by way of emphasizing the importance of strict adherence to the doctrine, held to be controlling, that the complaining state must be the real party in interest.

2. Indeed, in most states the former assertion would also have been wrong, since generally states will not, in the absence of a reciprocity statute, enforce each other's revenue laws. Coincidentally, Missouri held, seven years after Massachusetts v. Missouri, that it would accept such a suit. State ex rel. Oklahoma Tax Comm'n v. Rodgers, 238 Mo.App. 1115, 193 S.W.2d 919 (1946).

" * * * This completely defeats the purpose of the judiciary article of the Constitution, and places sovereign states in a worse position than private citizens and creatures of states—*i.e.* corporations—who can in similar circumstances invoke the diversity of citizenship jurisdiction. * * *

" * * * Truly the doctrine of a discretionary original jurisdiction in the Supreme Court has made a veritable '*Through the Looking-glass*' world out of the Judiciary Articles of the Constitution. Everything works backward! What was intended as a favor is turned into a burden. What was intended to give the parties a choice results in giving them no voice in the matter, and all the choice to the Court. The Act that was designed to give them recourse to the federal judiciary ends up in forcing them to accept the state judiciary. And the only practical method by which Congress can vest original jurisdiction in the Supreme Court, if indeed it can at all, is by withdrawing it from every other court. Such a system can not have been the intention either of the Founding Fathers, the Constitution, the Congress or the Court." [3]

(3) Wyandotte was followed in Illinois v. Milwaukee, 406 U.S. 91 (1972), involving a motion by Illinois for leave to file an original action against, *inter alia*, four Wisconsin cities [4] to abate as a nuisance the alleged pollution of Lake Michigan. The Court, first satisfying itself that the case was one "arising under" federal law and therefore maintainable in a federal district court, said that "while this original suit normally might be the appropriate vehicle for resolving this controversy, we exercise our discretion to remit the parties to an appropriate district court * * *" (p. 108). (As to the question whether federal or state law governs, see the discussion of this case in Chap. VII, pp. 898–900, *infra*.)

On the same day, in Washington v. General Motors Corp., 406 U.S. 109 (1972), a unanimous Court applied the doctrine of the Wyandotte case to deny a motion for leave to file a complaint by eighteen states against the

---

3. For an earlier case in which the Court assumed the burden of an ordinary action for the recovery of money by a state against a private person, see Ohio v. Chattanooga Boiler & Tank Co., 289 U.S. 439 (1933) (action for $4,910.64 as reimbursement for payment of workmen's compensation award out of state insurance fund).

The Court in Massachusetts v. Missouri refrained from grounding its decision on the doctrine of Wisconsin v. Pelican Ins. Co., 127 U.S. 265 (1888). In that case the Court upheld a demurrer in an original action brought on a judgment for certain statutory penalties. The original jurisdiction in cases in which a state is a party, the Court said (p. 297), "is limited to controversies of a civil nature".

" * * * The grant is of 'judicial power,' and was not intended to confer upon the courts of the United States jurisdiction of a suit or prosecution by the one State, of such a nature that it could not, on the settled principles of public and international law, be entertained by the judiciary of the other State at all" (p. 289).

The Pelican case was disapproved in part in Milwaukee County v. M.E. White Co., 296 U.S. 268 (1935), which held that a federal district court should take jurisdiction of an action on a judgment for taxes. The Court reserved opinion (pp. 275, 279) as to actions, outside the obligation-creating state, to enforce revenue laws or to enforce judgments "for an obligation created by a penal law, in the international sense".

4. In support of its motion Illinois argued that two of the named defendants, the Sewerage Commissions of the City and County of Milwaukee, were "instrumentalities" of the State of Wisconsin, that the suit was therefore between States within the meaning of § 1251(a)(1), and that the Wyandotte doctrine was therefore inapplicable because the Supreme Court's jurisdiction was exclusive. The Court held that Wisconsin could be but did not have to be joined as a defendant, and that political subdivisions of the state are not "States" within the meaning of § 1251(a)(1).

four major automobile manufacturers and their trade associations, charging a conspiracy in violation of the antitrust laws to restrain the development of automobile air pollution control equipment. The Court stated that the federal district court was an available and more appropriate forum in view of the fact that "as a matter of law as well as practical necessity corrective remedies for air pollution * * * necessarily must be considered in the context of localized situations" (p. 116).

(4) The Court expanded the Wyandotte doctrine to apply to a suit by the United States in United States v. Nevada and California, 412 U.S. 534 (1973), involving a dispute over the waters of the Truckee River. The Court stressed that original jurisdiction over the case was not exclusive, that "[w]e need not employ our original jurisdiction to settle competing claims to water within a single State," and that private users of the disputed waters could participate in a district court litigation whereas they could not intervene in an original action in the Supreme Court (p. 538). The Court recognized that the United States could not join California in an action against Nevada in the Nevada district court, but it characterized the controversy between the United States and California as "remote" and one that could be settled in separate actions in the federal district courts in California (pp. 539–40).

(5) Still another major step was taken when, in Arizona v. New Mexico, 425 U.S. 794 (1976), the Court for the first time asserted that it has discretion not to adjudicate original cases even where its jurisdiction is exclusive. Arizona sought leave to file an action for a declaratory judgment that certain allegedly discriminatory features of New Mexico's electrical energy tax created an unconstitutional burden on interstate commerce and that the tax "denies Arizona citizens due process and equal protection" (p. 795). The tax was already under constitutional challenge in the courts of New Mexico by the Arizona utility companies that generated electricity in New Mexico and were subject to the tax. Arizona sued both as a proprietary consumer of electricity and as *parens patriae* on behalf of its citizens.

The Court in a brief per curiam, after quoting language from Illinois v. Milwaukee, Massachusetts v. Missouri, and Wyandotte, denied leave to file because "we are persuaded that the pending state-court action provides an appropriate forum in which the *issues* tendered here may be litigated. [Emphasis in original.] If on appeal, the New Mexico Supreme Court should hold the electrical energy tax unconstitutional, Arizona will have been vindicated. If, on the other hand, the tax is held to be constitutional, the issues raised now may be brought to this Court by way of direct appeal under 28 U.S.C. § 1257(2).

"In denying the State of Arizona leave to file, we are not unmindful that the legal incidence of the electrical energy tax is upon the utilities" (pp. 797–98).[5]

5. Justice Stevens concurred on the ground that Arizona did not have standing to sue. He added: "However, except to the extent that they apply to Arizona's attempt to litigate on behalf of an entity which has access to another forum, I do not believe the comments which the Court has previously made about its non-exclusive original jurisdiction adequately support an order denying a State leave to file a complaint against another State" (pp. 798–99).

In Arizona Pub. Serv. Co. v. Snead, 441 U.S. 141 (1979), the Court in fact reviewed the state court litigation described in Arizona v. New Mexico, in an appeal from the New Mexico Supreme Court's judgment upholding the validity of the tax. It held

(6) The power to decline jurisdiction over a case within the exclusive original jurisdiction was reasserted, but not exercised, in Maryland v. Louisiana, 451 U.S. 725 (1981). Having held that the plaintiff states had standing to sue, see p. 330, *supra,* the Court cited Illinois v. Milwaukee and Arizona v. New Mexico for the proposition that "we have construed the congressional grant of exclusive jurisdiction under § 1251(a) as requiring resort to our obligatory jurisdiction only in 'appropriate cases' " (p. 739). Justice White, for the Court, concluded that this was such a case, distinguishing Arizona v. New Mexico: (i) although the validity of the Louisiana tax was being litigated in various lower courts, in none of those cases were the plaintiff states adequately represented; (ii) the harm caused to other states by the Louisiana tax was far more severe than the tax involved in the Arizona case; (iii) the Louisiana tax affects the interests of the United States in the outer continental shelf. (In fact the United States had intervened as a plaintiff in the case.) The Court then went on to hold on the merits that the Louisiana "first-use" tax was invalid. Justice Rehnquist dissented on the ground that although the Court has power to adjudicate, the case was not "appropriate" for the exercise of original jurisdiction because the plaintiff states' claims did not involve any relation to their "sovereign" interests "qua States"—the injury was entirely to the states as consumers and as representatives of other consumers. He complained that the Court's opinion "articulates no limiting principles that would prevent this Court from being deluged by original actions brought by States simply in their role as consumers or on behalf of groups of their citizens as consumers" (p. 770).[6]

(7) Reread the Court's words in California v. Arizona, quoted at the outset of this Chapter (p. 295, *supra*), explaining why it would be in "derogation" of the purpose of the framers—"matching the dignity of the parties to the status of the court"—for *Congress* to narrow the Court's original jurisdiction. Why is it any less in derogation of that purpose for the *Court* to require "sovereign parties" to resort to another tribunal?

See, for a general discussion, Shapiro, *Jurisdiction and Discretion,* 60 N.Y.U.L.Rev. 543, 560–61 (1985).

(8) Does the Wyandotte opinion convincingly demonstrate that the Supreme Court is a particularly inconvenient or inappropriate forum for that litigation? Or does it merely point up that *any* court will find it extremely difficult to deal with the case? Is it then the theory of the case that the Supreme Court has other, more significant, uses for its limited time? By what criteria does the Court determine this? Is the doctrine of forum non conveniens properly applied in a case where the convenience being served is that of the court rather than the litigants?

the New Mexico tax inconsistent with a federal tax statute and therefore invalid.

6. Justice Stevens joined the Court's opinion in Maryland v. Louisiana, but a few months later—in a lone dissent to a summary denial of leave to file a suit by California against West Virginia alleging a breach of contract, stated that the Wyandotte "explanation" for discretionary refusals of original jurisdiction is "inapplicable to cases in which our jurisdiction is exclusive. The fact that two sovereign States have been unable to resolve this matter without adding to our burdens ∗ ∗ ∗ does not, in my opinion, justify our refusal to exercise our exclusive jurisdiction under 28 U.S.C. § 1251(a)." California v. West Virginia, 454 U.S. 1027 (1981).

How carefully did the Court in Wyandotte satisfy itself that the suit could be brought in another forum? An appropriate and convenient forum?

(9) Note that in Arizona v. New Mexico, *supra,* the Court did not decide the question whether Arizona had standing or otherwise had a *right* to sue New Mexico. If Arizona had such a right, what is the relevance of the fact that the *issues* it proffered were subject to litigation in the state courts in proceedings in which it was not a party? Shouldn't the Court at least have satisfied itself that Arizona could intervene in the New Mexico action, notwithstanding the Supreme Court's exclusive jurisdiction over suits between states? Or was the Court in effect holding that Arizona had no right to sue, given the "derivative" nature of its claim and the fact that the issue was being litigated by the Arizona utilities?

(10) Consider Justice White's statement in Maryland v. Louisiana, *supra,* that "the congressional grant of exclusive jurisdiction under § 1251(a) requir[es] resort to our obligatory jurisdiction only in 'appropriate cases'." Is it an oxymoron?

(11) Statistically the original docket is not a significant part of the Court's work; it tends to generate only a handful of opinions each year. Nevertheless, many of the cases are disproportionately lengthy and difficult, and often involve elaborate factual rather than legal issues. The Court obviously finds these cases unwelcome, and has as a result significantly expanded its self-assumed power to make general judgments about the most "appropriate" forum to litigate actions seeking to invoke its original jurisdiction. Is the expansion justified?

SECTION 2. CASES AFFECTING AMBASSADORS, OTHER PUBLIC MINISTERS, AND CONSULS

EX PARTE GRUBER

269 U.S. 302, 46 S.Ct. 112, 70 L.Ed. 280 (1925).
Motion for Leave to File Petition for Mandamus.

MR. JUSTICE SUTHERLAND delivered the opinion of the Court.

This is an application for leave to file a petition and for a rule directing Albert Halstead, Consul General of the United States at Montreal, Canada, to show cause why a writ of mandamus should not issue commanding him to visa the passport or the certificate of origin and identity presented to him by one Rosa Porter, a citizen of Russia, who recently arrived in Montreal from Russia and from whom petitioner, a relative, desires a visit in the United States of several months' duration. We do not review the averments of the petition, since, other questions aside, it is clear that this court is without original jurisdiction.

Article III, § 2, cl. 2, of the Constitution provides that this court shall have original jurisdiction "in all cases affecting Ambassadors, other public Ministers and Consuls." Manifestly, this refers to diplomatic and consular representatives accredited to the United States by foreign powers, not to those representing this country abroad. Milward v. McSaul, 17 Fed.Cas. 425, 426, No. 9624. The provision, no doubt, was inserted in view of the important and sometimes delicate nature of our relations and intercourse with foreign governments. It is a privilege, not of the official, but of the sovereign or government which he represents, accorded from high considerations of public policy, considerations which plainly do not apply to the United States in its own territory. See generally Davis v. Packard, 7 Pet. 276, 284; Marshall v. Critico, 9 East 447; Valarino v. Thompson, 7 N.Y. 576, 578; The Federalist, No. 80, Ford's Ed., pp. 531, 532, 533, 537.

The application is denied for want of original jurisdiction.

NOTE ON CASES AFFECTING FOREIGN DIPLOMATIC REPRESENTATIVES

(1) See 28 U.S.C. § 1251(a)(2) and (b)(1), incorporating the Gruber decision.

(2) Remarkably, Gruber and two other cases seem to be the only instances in which this head of the Supreme Court's original jurisdiction has been directly invoked. Jones v. Le Tombe, 3 Dall. 384 (U.S.1798) was a suit against the consul general of France as the drawer of a number of bills of exchange; the case was dismissed without opinion on the ground that the obligation sued on was that of the government and not of the defendant as an individual. Casey v. Galli, 94 U.S. 673 (1877) was an original action in debt against a vice consul; judgment was rendered for the plaintiff without discussion of jurisdiction. For whatever reasons of policy, representatives of foreign nations have not invoked the original jurisdiction as plaintiffs.

(3) The dearth of suits against foreign diplomats is due probably to the wide immunity enjoyed by them. See generally, Wilson, Diplomatic Privileges and Immunities (1967). That immunity has been in part codified ever since the Crimes Act of 1790, 1 Stat. 118, presently 22 U.S.C. §§ 252–54. Note also the further recognition of the immunity, tracing back to the Judiciary Act of 1789, in 28 U.S.C. § 1251(a)(2), giving the Supreme Court only such jurisdiction as is "not inconsistent with the law of nations." See, further, Bergman v. de Sieyes, 170 F.2d 360 (2d Cir.1948), holding that the immunity is broader than 22 U.S.C. § 252. See also Note, 11 Stan.L.Rev. 665, 667–68 (1959).[1]

(4) Given the triple protection accorded foreign diplomats by 22 U.S.C. § 252, the law of nations, and the exclusive jurisdiction of the Supreme Court, litigation against them in the lower courts has been concerned largely with peripheral questions relating to the establishment of these defenses. In only a handful of instances have these cases reached the Court on review.[2]

1. The scope of immunity is also affected by the Convention on Diplomatic Relations (Vienna Convention), see 55 Am.J.Int. L. 1064 (1965), which the United States ratified in 1965.

2. As to who is a diplomat entitled to the immunity, see In re Baiz, 135 U.S. 403 (1890), denying a writ of prohibition to a district court against assuming jurisdiction in a civil action against the Consul General of Guatemala and Honduras who was acting for the Guatemalan minister, in the minister's absence, with the consent of the Department of State, but who had not been

(5) Do the two classes of cases in which diplomats (or consuls, for that matter) are plaintiffs and those in which they are defendants exhaust the constitutional category of cases "affecting" them? Note the assumption of the draftsmen of 28 U.S.C. § 1251 that they do. Compare Justice Frankfurter's comment in Ex parte Peru, p. 350, *infra*. The leading, if inconclusive, case is United States v. Ortega, 11 Wheat. 467 (U.S.1826), holding that an indictment for offering violence to the person of a foreign minister was not a case "affecting" the minister.

(6) Save for the period from 1875 to 1911, the concurrent jurisdiction of the lower federal courts over actions against foreign consuls has been exclusive of that of the state courts. See 28 U.S.C. § 1351. Actions against consuls in the state courts thus raise problems with respect to the defense of exclusive jurisdiction similar to those raised by actions against higher diplomatic officials in the state or lower federal courts. See, *e.g.*, Davis v. Packard, 7 Pet. 276 (U.S.1833), holding that the failure to plead consular status in the state trial court was not a waiver of the defense, where it was insisted upon on appeal, the privilege being that of the foreign government rather than of the official personally.

In Ohio ex rel. Popovici v. Agler, 280 U.S. 379 (1930), the Supreme Court held that the exclusion of state court jurisdiction was not to be construed as extending to a suit for divorce by an American wife against a Rumanian vice-consul, in view of the traditional doctrine that matters of domestic relations are reserved to the courts of the states. See, further, Chap. X, Sec. 2(E), *infra*.

(7) No decision of the Supreme Court casts any direct light on the status of officials of the United Nations and other international organizations or of foreign delegates to them, for the purposes either of the original jurisdiction or of the provisions of the Judicial Code excluding jurisdiction of state courts. Relevant provisions are contained in the United Nations Charter, in the Headquarters Agreement between the United States and the United Nations, 61 Stat. 756, reprinted following 22 U.S.C.A. § 287, and in the International Organizations Immunities Act, 22 U.S.C. § 288 et seq., and various executive orders of the President issued pursuant thereto.[3]

---

recognized by the Department as having diplomatic status. As to the duration of the immunity, see Ex parte Hitz, 111 U.S. 766 (1884).

As to waiver of the immunity, see Davis v. Packard, 7 Pet. 276 (U.S.1833), dealing with the parallel problem of waiver of a

consul's right to be tried only in a federal court.

3. There is an extensive discussion of the immunity of members of U.N. missions in United States ex rel. Casanova v. Fitzpatrick, 214 F.Supp. 425 (S.D.N.Y.1963).

SECTION 3. EXTRAORDINARY WRITS AND THE ORIGINAL JURISDICTION

EX PARTE REPUBLIC OF PERU

318 U.S. 578, 63 S.Ct. 793, 87 L.Ed. 1014 (1943).
Motion for Leave to File Petition for a Writ of Prohibition
and/or a Writ of Mandamus.

MR. CHIEF JUSTICE STONE delivered the opinion of the Court.

This is a motion for leave to file in this Court the petition of the Republic of Peru for a writ of prohibition or of mandamus. The petition asks this Court to prohibit respondent, a judge of the District Court for the Eastern District of Louisiana, and the other judges and officers of that court, from further exercise of jurisdiction over a proceeding in rem, pending in that court against petitioner's steamship Ucayali, and to direct the district judge to enter an order in the proceeding declaring the vessel immune from suit. * * *

[The proceeding was commenced by a libel filed against the ship by a Cuban corporation for its failure to carry a cargo of sugar from a Peruvian port to New York, as required by the terms of a charter party entered into by libelant with a Peruvian corporation acting as agent in behalf of the Peruvian Government. The petitioner procured the release of the vessel by filing a surety release bond in the sum of $60,000, and filed various claims and motions, each time asserting its sovereign immunity and disclaiming any waiver of this defense.]

In the meantime petitioner, following the accepted course of procedure (see Ex parte Muir, 254 U.S. 522; The Navemar, 303 U.S. 68), by appropriate representations, sought recognition by the State Department of petitioner's claim of immunity, and asked that the Department advise the Attorney General of the claim of immunity and that the Attorney General instruct the United States Attorney for the Eastern District of Louisiana to file in the district court the appropriate suggestion of immunity of the vessel from suit. These negotiations resulted in formal recognition by the State Department of the claim of immunity. This was communicated to the Attorney General by the Under Secretary's letter of May 5, 1942. The letter requested him to instruct the United States Attorney to present to the district court a copy of the Ambassador's formal claim of immunity filed with the State Department, and to say that "this Department accepts as true the statements of the Ambassador concerning the steamship Ucayali, and recognizes and allows the claim of immunity".

Pursuant to these instructions the United States Attorney, on June 29th, filed in the district court a formal statement advising the court of the proceedings and communications mentioned, suggesting to the court and praying "that the claim of immunity made on behalf of the said Peruvian Steamship Ucayali and recognized and allowed by the State Department be given full force and effect by this court"; and "that the said vessel proceeded against herein be declared immune from the jurisdiction and process of this court". On July 1st petitioner moved for release of the vessel and that the suit be dismissed. The district court denied the motion on the ground that petitioner had waived its immunity by applying for extensions of time within which to answer, and by taking the deposition of the master—steps which the district court thought constituted a general appearance despite petitioner's attempted reservation of its right to assert its immunity as a defense in the suit. The Ucayali, D.C., 47 F.Supp. 203.

The first question for our consideration is that of our jurisdiction. Section 13 of the Judiciary Act of 1789, 1 Stat. 81, conferred upon this Court "power to issue writs of prohibition to the district courts, when proceeding as courts of admiralty and maritime jurisdiction, and writs of mandamus, in cases warranted by the principles and usages of law, to any courts appointed, or persons holding office, under the authority of the United States". And § 14 provided that this Court and other federal courts "shall have power to issue writs of scire facias, habeas corpus, and all other writs not specially provided for by statute, which may be necessary for the exercise of their respective jurisdictions, and agreeable to the principles and usages of law." 1 Stat. 81. These provisions have in substance been carried over into §§ 234 and 262 of the Judicial Code, 28 U.S.C. §§ 342, 377, and § 751 of the Revised Statutes, 28 U.S.C. § 451.

The jurisdiction of this Court as defined in Article III, § 2 of the Constitution is either "original" or "appellate". Suits brought in the district courts of the United States, not of such character as to be within the original jurisdiction of this Court under the Constitution, are cognizable by it only in the exercise of its appellate jurisdiction. Hence its statutory authority to issue writs of prohibition or mandamus to district courts can be constitutionally exercised only insofar as such writs are in aid of its appellate jurisdiction. Marbury v. Madison, 1 Cranch 137, 173, 180; Ex parte Siebold, 100 U.S. 371, 374, 375.

Under the statutory provisions, the jurisdiction of this Court to issue common law writs in aid of its appellate jurisdiction has been consistently sustained. The historic use of writs of prohibition and mandamus directed by an appellate to an inferior court has been to exert the revisory appellate power over the inferior court. The writs thus afford an expeditious and effective means of confining the inferior court to a lawful exercise of its prescribed jurisdiction, or of compelling it to exercise its authority when it is its duty to do so. Such has been the office of the writs when directed by this Court to district courts, both before the Judiciary Act of 1925, 43 Stat. 936,[1] and since.[2] In all these cases (cited in notes 1 and 2), the appellate, not the original, jurisdiction of this Court was invoked and exercised.[3]

---

1. *E.g.*, Ex parte State of New York, No. 1, 256 U.S. 490; The Western Maid, 257 U.S. 419; In re Simons, 247 U.S. 231; Ex parte Peterson, 253 U.S. 300, 305; Ex parte Hudgings, 249 U.S. 378; Ex parte Uppercu, 239 U.S. 435; Matter of Heff, 197 U.S. 488; Ex parte Siebold, 100 U.S. 371; Ex parte Watkins, 3 Pet. 193; United States v. Peters, 3 Dall. 121.

2. Ex parte United States, 287 U.S. 241; State of Maryland v. Soper (No. 1), 270 U.S. 9, 27, 28; State of Maryland v. Soper (No. 2), 270 U.S. 36; State of Maryland v. Soper (No. 3), 270 U.S. 44; State of Colorado v. Symes, 286 U.S. 510; McCullough v. Cosgrave, 309 U.S. 634; Ex parte Kawato,

317 U.S. 69; see Los Angeles Brush Corp. v. James, 272 U.S. 701.

3. See particularly the discussion in State of Maryland v. Soper (No. 1), 270 U.S. 9, 28–30, and in Ex parte United States, 287 U.S. 241. Compare Ex parte Siebold, 100 U.S. 371.

Ex parte United States, *supra*, was not and could not have been a case of original jurisdiction. The Constitution confers original jurisdiction only in cases affecting ambassadors, other public ministers and consuls, and "those in which a State shall be Party" (Art. III, § 2, cl. 2). No state was made a party to Ex parte United States. The United States has never been

The common law writs, like equitable remedies, may be granted or withheld in the sound discretion of the Court, Ex parte Skinner & Eddy Corp., 265 U.S. 86, 95, 96; Ex parte City of Monterey, 269 U.S. 527; State of Maryland v. Soper (No. 1), 270 U.S. 9, 29; United States v. Dern, 289 U.S. 352, 359, and are usually denied where other adequate remedy is available. Ex parte Baldwin, 291 U.S. 610. And ever since the statute vested in the circuit courts of appeals appellate jurisdiction on direct appeal from the district courts, this Court, in the exercise of its discretion, has in appropriate circumstances declined to issue the writ to a district court, but without prejudice to an application to the circuit court of appeals (Ex parte Apex Mfg. Co., 274 U.S. 725; Ex parte Daugherty, 282 U.S. 809; Ex parte Krentler–Arnold Hinge Last Co., 286 U.S. 533), which likewise has power under § 262 of the Judicial Code to issue the writ. McClellan v. Carland, 217 U.S. 268; Adams v. U.S. ex rel. McCann, 317 U.S. 269.

After a full review of the traditional use of the common law writs by this Court, and in issuing a writ of mandamus, in aid of its appellate jurisdiction, to compel a district judge to issue a bench warrant in conformity to statutory requirements, this Court declared in Ex parte United States, 287 U.S. 241, 248, 249: "The rule deducible from the later decisions, and which we now affirm, is that this court has full power in its discretion to issue the writ of mandamus to a federal District Court, although the case be one in respect of which direct appellate jurisdiction is vested in the Circuit Court of Appeals—this court having ultimate discretionary jurisdiction by certiorari—but that such power will be exercised only where a question of public importance is involved, or where the question is of such a nature that it is peculiarly appropriate that such action by this court should be taken. In other words, application for the writ ordinarily must be made to the intermediate appellate court, and made to this court as the court of ultimate review only in such exceptional cases." [4]

We conclude that we have jurisdiction to issue the writ as prayed. And we think that—unless the sovereign immunity has been waived—the case is one of such public importance and exceptional character as to call for the exercise of our discretion to issue the writ rather than to relegate the Republic of Peru to the circuit court of appeals, from which it might be necessary to bring the case to this Court again by certiorari. The case

held to be a "State" within this provision— and it obviously is not—nor has it any standing to bring an original action in this Court which does not otherwise come within one of the provisions of Article III, § 2, cl. 2. United States v. Texas, 143 U.S. 621, relied upon to sustain a different view, was within the original jurisdiction because the state of Texas was the party defendant. And until now it has never been suggested that necessity, however great, warrants the exercise by this Court of original jurisdiction which the Constitution has not conferred upon it. Moreover, even if Congress had withdrawn this Court's appellate jurisdiction by the 1925 Act, there would have been no necessity in Ex parte United States for inventing an original jurisdiction which the Constitution had withheld, since a writ of mandamus could have been applied for in the circuit court of appeals.

4. The suggestion that the Judiciary Act of 1925 was intended to curtail the jurisdiction previously exercised by this Court in granting such writs to the district courts finds no support in the history or language of the Act. * * * Ex parte United States, and most of the other cases cited in note 2, *supra*, were decided at a time when members of the Court's committee responsible for the 1925 Act were still members of the Court. The Court's unanimous concurrence in the existence of its jurisdiction in the cases subsequent to the 1925 Act establishes a practice (*cf.* Stuart v. Laird, 1 Cranch 299, 309) which would be beyond explanation if there had been any thought that any provision of the Act had placed such a restriction on the Court's jurisdiction to issue the writs.

* * *

involves the dignity and rights of a friendly sovereign state, claims against which are normally presented and settled in the course of the conduct of foreign affairs by the President and by the Department of State. When the Secretary elects, as he may and as he appears to have done in this case, to settle claims against the vessel by diplomatic negotiations between the two countries rather than by continued litigation in the courts, it is of public importance that the action of the political arm of the Government taken within its appropriate sphere be promptly recognized, and that the delay and inconvenience of a prolonged litigation be avoided by prompt termination of the proceedings in the district court. If the Republic of Peru has not waived its immunity, we think that there are persuasive grounds for exercising our jurisdiction to issue the writ in this case and at this time without requiring petitioner to apply to the circuit court of appeals, and that those grounds are at least as strong and urgent as those found sufficient in Ex parte United States, in State of Maryland v. Soper, in State of Colorado v. Symes, and in McCullough v. Cosgrave, all *supra*, note 2. We accordingly pass to the question whether petitioner has waived his immunity. * * *

We cannot say that the Republic of Peru has waived its immunity. * * *

The motion for leave to file is granted. We assume that, in view of this opinion, formal issuance of the writ will be unnecessary, and we direct that the writ issue only on further application by the petitioner.

MR. JUSTICE ROBERTS concurs in the result.

Motion granted.

MR. JUSTICE FRANKFURTER, dissenting.

* * * I put to one side the relation of the Peruvian Ambassador to this litigation. This is not a proceeding falling under the rubric "Cases affecting Ambassadors" and thereby giving us original jurisdiction. My brethren do not so treat it, and our common starting point is that in taking hold of this case the Court is exercising its appellate jurisdiction.

We are also agreed that this Court "can exercise no appellate jurisdiction, except in the cases, and in the manner and form, defined and prescribed by congress". Amer. Const. Co. v. Jacksonville, T. & K.W. Railway Co., 148 U.S. 372, 378. Had this case arisen under the Evarts Act, Act of March 3, 1891, 26 Stat. 826, appeal could have been taken from the district court, since its jurisdiction was in issue, directly to this Court without going to the Circuit Court of Appeals. See, *e.g.*, Wilson v. Republic Iron Co., 257 U.S. 92. And since the case would have been within the immediate appellate jurisdiction of this Court, §§ 13 and 14 of the first Judiciary Act, 1 Stat. 73, 80–82, now 28 U.S.C. §§ 342, 377, 451, would have authorized this Court to issue an appropriate writ to prevent frustration of its appellate power, see Ex parte Crane, 5 Pet. 190, or have enabled it to accelerate its own undoubted reviewing authority where, under very exceptional circumstances, actual and not undefined interests of justice so required. Compare In re Chetwood, 165 U.S. 443; Whitney v. Dick, 202 U.S. 132; Adams v. U.S. ex rel. McCann, 317 U.S. 269.

The power to issue these auxiliary writs is not a qualification or even a loose construction of the strict limits, defined by the Constitution and the Congress, within which this Court must move in reviewing decisions of lower courts. There have been occasional, but not many, deviations from the true doctrine in employing these auxiliary writs as incidental to the right granted by Congress to this Court to review litigation, in aid of which it may become necessary to issue a facilitating writ. The issuance of such a writ is, in effect, an anticipatory review of a case that can in due course come here directly. When the Act of 1891 established the intermediate courts of appeals and gave to them a considerable part of the appellate jurisdiction formerly exercised by the Supreme Court, the philosophy and practice of federal appellate jurisdiction came under careful scrutiny. This Court uniformly and without dissent held that it was without power to issue a writ of mandamus in a case in which it did not otherwise have appellate jurisdiction. In re Commonwealth of Massachusetts, 197 U.S. 482, and In re Glaser, 198 U.S. 171. In these cases rules were discharged because, under the Circuit Court of Appeals Act, appeals could not be brought directly to the Supreme Court but would have to go to the Circuit Court of Appeals, and only thereafter could they come here, if at all, through certiorari. But review could be brought directly to this Court of cases in which the jurisdiction of the district court was in issue, and therefore writs of "prohibition or mandamus or certiorari as ancillary thereto", In re Commonwealth of Massachusetts, *supra*, 197 U.S. at 488, were available. Cases which came here directly, prior to the Judiciary Act of February 13, 1925, 43 Stat. 936, to review the jurisdiction of the district courts, whether on appeal or through the informal procedure of auxiliary writs, are therefore not relevant precedents for the present case. * * *

[The opinion then urges that the Judiciary Act of 1925 should be read as removing the basis for issuance of an ancillary writ directly to a district court, save in the special situations in which direct review was authorized by Section 237. Compare the present provisions for direct review in 28 U.S.C. §§ 1252 and 1253. It cites the general purpose of the Act to remove "the needless clog on the Court's proper business", and the purpose to do this, in particular, by restricting appellate jurisdiction over the district courts.]

Finally, it is urged that practice since the Judicial Act of 1925 sanctions the present assumption of jurisdiction. Cases like Ex parte Northern Pac. R. Co., 280 U.S. 142, ordering a district judge to summon three judges to hear a suit under § 266 of the Judicial Code, 28 U.S.C. § 380, must be put to one side. This is one of the excepted classes under the Act of 1925 in which direct review lies from a district court to the Supreme Court, and it is therefore an orthodox utilization of an ancillary writ within the rule of In re Commonwealth of Massachusetts, *supra*. Of all the other cases in which, since the Act of 1925, a writ was authorized to be issued, none is comparable to the circumstances of the present case. In one, Ex parte Kawato, *supra*, the appellate jurisdiction of this court was invoked only after appellate jurisdiction was denied by a circuit court of appeals. Another, Ex parte United States, 287 U.S. 241, while in form a review of action by a district court, was in fact an independent suit by the United States because no appeal as such lay from the refusal of the district judge in that case to issue a bench warrant in denial of his duty. If the suit was a justiciable controversy through use of the ancillary writ, it was equally justiciable if regarded as an original suit by the United States. While, to be sure, it was not formally such, and while an ordinary suit by the United States to enforce an obligation against one of its citizens properly cannot be brought within the original jurisdiction of this Court, Ex parte United States, *supra*, was quite different. There the United States sought enforcement of a public duty for which no redress could be had in any other court. Therefore, the considerations which led this Court in United States v. Texas, 143 U.S. 621, to allow the United States to initiate an original suit in this Court, although the merely literal language of the Constitution precluded it (as the dissent in that case insisted), might have been equally potent to allow assumption of such jurisdiction in the circumstances of Ex parte United States. But, in any event, merely because there is no other available judicial relief is no reason for taking appellate jurisdiction. For some situations the only appropriate remedy is corrective legislation. Of the same nature were four other cases, three suits by Maryland and one by Colorado. State of Maryland v. Soper (1), 270 U.S. 9; State of Maryland v. Soper (2), 270 U.S. 36; State of Maryland v. Soper (3), 270 U.S. 44; State of Colorado v. Symes, 286 U.S. 510. These cases were not ordinary claims by a state against one of its citizens for which the state courts are the appropriate tribunals, see State of California v. Southern Pacific Co., 157 U.S. 229. They were in effect suits by states against federal functionaries in situations in which the citizenship of these functionaries was irrelevant to the controversy. And so the considerations that made the controversies by Maryland and Colorado justiciable through ancillary writs might have been equally relevant in establishing justiciability for original suits in this Court under Article III, Section 2. It is not without significance that the State of Maryland v. Soper cases and State of Colorado v. Symes, which the Court now regards as precedents for the ruling in Ex parte United States, were not even referred to in the opinion in the latter case.

If Ex parte United States, the State of Maryland v. Soper cases, and State of Colorado v. Symes, *supra*, are not to be supported on the basis of their peculiar circumstances which might have justified the Court in assuming jurisdiction, they should be candidly regarded as deviations from the narrow limits within which our appellate jurisdiction should move. They would then belong with the occasional lapses which occur when technical questions of jurisdiction are not properly presented to the Court and consciously met. * * *

* * * The essence of the Act of 1925 was curtailment of our appellate jurisdiction as a measure necessary for the effective discharge of the Court's functions. It is hardly consonant with this restrictive purpose of the Act of 1925 to enlarge the opportunities to come to this Court beyond the limit recognized and enforced under the Act of 1891—that there can be no ancillary jurisdiction where the litigation on the merits could not directly come here for review. In only one of the cases since the Act of 1925 in which the ancillary writs were invoked in situations in which this Court did not have direct appellate jurisdiction, did counsel call to the attention of this Court the bearing of the Act of 1925 upon the power to issue ancillary writs and the relevance of cases prior to that Act, and in no case did this Court apparently address itself to the problem now canvassed. Authority exercised sub silentio does not establish jurisdiction. * * *

Had the Court jurisdiction, this case would furnish no occasion for its exercise. On whatever technical basis of jurisdiction the availability of these writs may have been founded, their use has been reserved for very special circumstances. * * *

No palpable exigency either of national or international import is made manifest for seeking this extraordinary relief here. * * *

To remit a controversy like this to the circuit court of appeals where it properly belongs is not to be indifferent to claims of importance but to be uncompromising in safeguarding the conditions which alone will enable this Court to discharge well the duties entrusted exclusively to us. The tremendous and delicate problems which call for the judgment of the nation's ultimate tribunal require the utmost conservation of time and energy even for the ablest judges. Listening to arguments and studying records and briefs constitute only a fraction of what goes into the judicial process. For one thing, as the present law reports compared with those of even a generation ago bear ample testimony, the types of cases that now come before the Court to a considerable extent require study of materials outside the technical law books. But more important, the judgments of this Court are collective judgments. Such judgments presuppose ample time and freshness of mind for private study and reflection in preparation for discussions in Conference. Without adequate study there cannot be adequate reflection; without adequate reflection there cannot be adequate discussion; without adequate discussion there cannot be that mature and fruitful interchange of minds which is indispensable to wise decisions and luminous opinions. * * *

MR. JUSTICE REED is of the opinion that this Court has jurisdiction to grant the writ requested, Ex parte United States, 287 U.S. 241, but concurs in this dissent on the ground that application for the writ sought should have been made first to the Circuit Court of Appeals.

———

NOTE ON THE POWER TO ISSUE EXTRAORDINARY WRITS

(1) If the Republic of Peru had intervened in the litigation through its ambassador, would the Supreme Court have had original jurisdiction under the Constitution?

(2) Note that the Constitution gives the Supreme Court appellate jurisdiction "with such Exceptions, and under such Regulations as the Congress shall make". In Durousseau v. United States, 6 Cranch 307 (U.S.1810), the Court construed the Judiciary Act of 1789 as a general and all-inclusive regulation, containing an implied negative of appellate jurisdiction in every situation in which it was not expressly conferred. Hence power to issue one of the extraordinary writs (mandamus, prohibition, common-law certiorari, quo warranto, or habeas corpus) as an exercise of appellate jurisdiction must be found in some statute, which in turn must be authorized by the Constitution.

The original jurisdiction, on the other hand, is conferred directly by the Constitution. See p. 295, *supra.* In any situation in which the issuance of an extraordinary writ would constitute an exercise of original jurisdiction,[1] therefore, no statute is needed to authorize it if the case falls within one of the two enumerated classes in Article III; and if it does not, under Marbury v. Madison, p. 72, *supra,* no statute can authorize it.

---

1. For a discussion of some possible instances, see Oaks, *The "Original" Writ of* *Habeas Corpus in the Supreme Court,* 1962 Sup.Ct.Rev. 153, 156–59.

Do Marbury v. Madison and Ex parte Peru, taken together, yield satisfactory criteria for deciding when the issuance of an extraordinary writ would involve an exercise only of appellate jurisdiction in the constitutional sense, and when of original jurisdiction?

Note that constitutional difficulties in this area could be met either by a broad construction of "appellate jurisdiction" in Article III, or by a decision, overruling Marbury v. Madison, that the enumeration of the heads of original jurisdiction in that article is not exclusive but subject to enlargement by Congress.

(3) The Supreme Court at one time seems to have considered that its power, in the exercise of appellate jurisdiction, to issue mandamus or prohibition existed only when the writ was in aid of the proper disposition of a case then pending in the Supreme Court. Ex parte Warmouth, 17 Wall. 64 (U.S.1872). In re Massachusetts, 197 U.S. 482 (1905), recognized the propriety of issuing the writ in aid of the disposition of a case pending in a lower federal court if the case was one over which the Supreme Court had a power of direct review. Ex parte Peru moves one step further to bring in cases over which power of direct review is vested in an intermediate court.

(4) What of a case involving a federal question pending in a state court? (Note that under § 13 of the Judiciary Act of 1789, writs could be issued only to "courts appointed * * * under the authority of the United States", but that the surviving authority in the all-writs section has never been so restricted). The only decisions are two cases where the Court had already once exercised appellate jurisdiction over the merits of the case; subsequently in each case it granted, without discussion of its own jurisdiction, leave to file a petition for a writ of mandamus ordering the state court to conform its decision to the Supreme Court's previous mandate. Deen v. Hickman, 358 U.S. 57 (1958); General Atomic Co. v. Felter, 436 U.S. 493 (1978); see, further, Chap. V, Sec. 1, p. 519, *infra*.

What of cases, over which a lower federal court has a power of direct review, pending in a federal administrative agency? *Cf.* Civil Aeronautics Board v. American Air Transport, Inc., 344 U.S. 4 (1952), dismissing a certificate from a court of appeals in a case coming from an administrative agency; see also FTC v. Dean Foods Co., 384 U.S. 597 (1966).

What of situations in which a case has not yet been brought in any federal or state court but might be?

(5) Compare the development in the case of habeas corpus. In Ex parte Bollman, 4 Cranch 75 (U.S.1807), the Court, following United States v. Hamilton, 3 Dall. 17 (U.S.1795), and Ex parte Burford, 3 Cranch 448 (U.S.1806), held that granting the writ to pass on the legality of a detention, based on an order committing petitioners to stand trial (after a finding of probable cause) issued by a lower court, involved an exercise of appellate jurisdiction, though no appeal from a conviction had been authorized by Congress. The Court said (p. 101) that "the decision that the individual shall be imprisoned must always precede the application for a writ of *habeas corpus,* and this writ must always be for the purpose of revising that decision, and, therefore, appellate in its nature." See also Ex parte Watkins, 7 Pet. 568 (U.S.1833). Subsequently, in Ex parte Yerger, 8 Wall. 85 (U.S.1868), where application for the writ was made by a prisoner in military custody, the fact that a writ had been granted and thereafter

dismissed by a circuit court was deemed sufficient to establish that the jurisdiction invoked was appellate, not original—and this despite the fact that Congress had repealed the statute authorizing an appeal from the denial of the writ by lower courts.[2] See also Ex parte Siebold, 100 U.S. 371 (1880). But see Ex parte Barry, 2 How. 65 (1844) (no appellate jurisdiction to issue writ to test confinement by a private party in a child custody case). See generally the comprehensive discussion in Oaks, note 1, *supra*, at 154–73.

Does the power of a single Justice of the Supreme Court to issue the writ, granted in the First Judiciary Act and continued ever since, 28 U.S.C. § 2241(a), involve original or appellate jurisdiction? The answer rests in obscurity. *Cf.* In re Kaine, 14 How. 103, 116, 130–31 (U.S.1852); Ex parte Clarke, 100 U.S. 399, 402–03 (1880); Locks v. Commanding General, Sixth Army, 89 S.Ct. 31 (1968) (Douglas, J., sitting as Circuit Justice).

On the present practice of the Court in habeas cases, see Oaks, *supra*, and see further pp. 1471–73, *infra*.

(6) Look at §§ 13 and 14 of the Judiciary Act of 1789, quoted by Chief Justice Stone at p. 348, *supra*. Problems of the relation between these two sections and their successor provisions have given rise to many unresolved doubts. In Ex parte Peru, what did the Court consider the relation to be?

In particular, did the Court consider that its power to issue a writ of prohibition depended, in view of § 13, on the fact that the district court was proceeding as a court of admiralty and maritime jurisdiction? The question was previously an open one. See, *e.g.*, Ex parte Graham, 10 Wall. 541 (U.S.1870) (holding the power limited to admiralty cases); Ex parte United States, 226 U.S. 420 (1913) (issuing the writ, without discussion, in a non-admiralty case); Ex parte Bakelite Corp., 279 U.S. 438 (1929).

In the 1948 revision of the Judicial Code, the successor provision of § 13 was repealed, with the explanation by the revisers that it was "omitted as unnecessary". Thus, the only statutory authority for the issuance of any of the extraordinary writs—apart from habeas corpus, which is specially dealt with in 28 U.S.C. § 2241(a)—is now the successor provision of § 14, the famous all-writs section, 28 U.S.C. § 1651(a).

In LaBuy v. Howes Leather Co., 352 U.S. 249 (1957), Justice Brennan, dissenting, relied on the opinion of Judge Magruder in In re Josephson, 218 F.2d 174 (1st Cir.1954), and argued (pp. 265–66) that the mandamus power granted by the all-writs section (§ 14) is significantly narrower than that formerly granted by § 13. The argument was made, however, in the context of discussing the powers of the courts of appeals (which were never covered by § 13), and Justice Brennan did not have to face the question whether the 1948 revision eliminating § 13 should be interpreted as narrowing the power of the Supreme Court to issue mandamus. The problem

---

2. The present vitality of this conclusion would have been determined in Ex parte Quirin, 317 U.S. 1 (1942) (involving the trial of German saboteurs by a military commission appointed by the President), except that counsel, during argument in the Supreme Court on their motion for leave to file petitions for habeas corpus, perfected appeals from the district court's denial of the writ and petitioned for certiorari before judgment in the circuit court of appeals. The Supreme Court denied the applications for leave to file, but granted the petitions for certiorari and affirmed the district court's denial of the writ on the merits (see 317 U.S. at 19–20). Counsel in the case had earlier considered seeking relief from Justice Black as Circuit Justice as a predicate for Supreme Court action. See Mason, Harlan Fiske Stone 653–64 (1956). See also *Note on the War Crimes Cases*, p. 357, *infra*.

is discussed in Justice Harlan's concurring opinion in Chandler v. Judicial Council of the Tenth Circuit, 398 U.S. 74, 89, 117 n. 15 (1970).[3]

(7) Rules 26–27 of the Supreme Court Rules govern the issuance of extraordinary writs. Issuance of such writs under § 1651 "is not a matter of right, but of discretion sparingly exercised". "[I]t must be shown that

3. The Chandler case raised, but did not answer, important questions about the Court's powers to issue extraordinary writs in connection with the disciplining of lower court judges. The Tenth Circuit Judicial Council, purporting to act on the basis of 28 U.S.C. § 332, found that United States District Judge Chandler was "unable or unwilling" to discharge the duties of his office, and ordered that cases pending before him be reassigned and that no new cases be assigned to him. Judge Chandler filed a motion in the Supreme Court for leave to file a petition for writs of mandamus and/or prohibition, urging that the Council's order was unauthorized by statute and unconstitutional, being an invalid attack on the independence guaranteed by Article III and a usurpation of the impeachment power.

The majority of the Court did not decide the question of its own jurisdiction. The opinion by Chief Justice Burger noted that it would be "no mean feat" to find that the action of the Judicial Council was a "judicial act or decision by a judicial tribunal" and therefore reviewable "without doing violence to the constitutional requirement that [the Court's] review be appellate". But, he went on, it is "an exercise we decline to perform since we conclude that in the present posture of the case other avenues of relief on the merits may yet be open to Judge Chandler" (p. 86). Without clearly specifying what these other avenues were, the Court concluded (p. 89): "Whether the Council's action was administrative action not reviewable in this Court, or whether it is reviewable here, plainly petitioner has not made a case for the extraordinary relief of mandamus or prohibition."

Do you agree that the Court's jurisdiction turns on whether the Judicial Council's order was "administrative" or "judicial"? *Cf.* Prentis v. Atlantic Coast Line Co., p. 1348, *infra,* and District of Columbia Court of Appeals v. Feldman, p. 1632, *infra.*

In an elaborate concurring opinion, Justice Harlan argued: (1) that the Court's conclusion that Judge Chandler had other adequate remedies (and that the jurisdictional issue therefore need not be reached) was unwarranted; (2) that acting on the petition would be an exercise of appellate jurisdiction and therefore valid under Article III; and (3) that 28 U.S.C. § 1651 authorized the Court to entertain the petition

in this case. He concluded that the motion for leave to file should be granted. Turning to the merits, he argued that the action of the Judicial Council should be upheld and the writ should not issue.

In connection with point 2, Justice Harlan made a lengthy analysis of the history and role of Judicial Councils, as a basis for his conclusion that the orders of the Council here were an exercise of judicial power and that the exercise of a mandamus power by the Court would, therefore, be appellate.

In connection with point 3, Justice Harlan wrote (pp. 113, 115): "Each of the prior cases in which this Court has invoked § 1651(a) to issue a writ 'in aid of [its jurisdiction]' has involved a particular lawsuit over which the Court would have statutory review jurisdiction at a later stage. By contrast, petitioner's reliance on this statute is bottomed on the fact that the action of the Judicial Council 'touches, through Judge Chandler's fate, hundreds of cases over which this court has appellate or review jurisdiction.' Petition for Writ of Prohibition and/or Mandamus 13. He argues that the Council's orders, allocating to other judges in his district cases that would otherwise be decided by him, constitute a usurpation of power that cannot adequately be remedied on final review of those cases by certiorari or appeal in this Court. The United States as *amicus curiae* agrees that this claim properly invokes the Court's power to consider whether mandamus or prohibition should be granted. Although this expansive use of § 1651(a) has no direct precedent in this Court, it seems to me wholly in line with the history of that statute and consistent with the manner in which it has been interpreted both here and in the lower courts. * * * It is difficult to see how the very multiplicity of the cases affected by the Council's orders could derogate from the Court's authority under § 1651(a) to issue an extraordinary writ in aid of its appellate jurisdiction over them."

Justice Black and Douglas dissented, each arguing that the Court had jurisdiction and that the Judicial Council's orders were invalid.

The Chandler case evoked copious comment. See, *e.g.,* Kurland, *The Constitution and the Tenure of Federal Judges: Some Notes From History,* 36 U.Chi.L.Rev. 665 (1969).

the writ will be in aid of the Court's appellate jurisdiction, that there are present exceptional circumstances warranting the exercise of the Court's discretionary powers, and that adequate relief cannot be had in any other form or from any other court." The petition for a writ must be prefaced by a motion for leave to file. If the petition seeks issuance of a writ of prohibition or mandamus, "it shall set forth with particularity why the relief sought is not available in any other court". "If the petition seeks issuance of an original writ of habeas corpus," it must comply with 28 U.S.C. § 2242, especially its last paragraph, and must show compliance with exhaustion requirements.

(8) Do you agree with the following conclusion:

"In Ex parte Peru, doubtless as a result of Mr. Justice Frankfurter's scholarly dissent, the Supreme Court was compelled to articulate the criteria delimiting its power. When that was done, the Court found that, with respect to cases coming from the federal courts, its power was practically limitless. Thus, the inquiry into power, which had plagued the judiciary since the establishment of the Republic, was answered, and the conflict moved into the area of discretion. It is true, of course, that the rules relating to power developed in the last hundred and fifty years have been influential in determining whether discretion should be exercised." Wolfson, *Extraordinary Writs in the Supreme Court Since Ex parte Peru,* 51 Colum.L.Rev. 977, 991 (1951).

For further material on the exercise of discretion, see Chap. XV, p. 1841, *infra.*

NOTE ON THE WAR CRIMES CASES

After World War II the Supreme Court was confronted with a series of petitions for writs of habeas corpus, numbering upwards of a hundred, by or in behalf of persons convicted by or held for trial before various American or international military tribunals abroad. Except for the cases cited in note 1, below, in none was relief first sought in a lower federal court. For a comprehensive review of these cases as of 1949, see Fairman, *Some New Problems of the Constitution Following the Flag,* 1 Stan.L.Rev. 587 (1949); see also Oaks, p. 353, note 1, *supra,* at 169–73.

The first group of cases [1] involved both American military personnel complaining of court martial proceedings abroad and American civilians held for offenses in occupied territory. Ex parte Betz, 329 U.S. 672 (1946). The per curiam opinion, on behalf of Chief Justice Vinson and Justices Burton, Douglas, Frankfurter, Jackson [2] and Reed, denied leave to file

1. See also Ex parte Quirin, discussed at p. 355, note 2, *supra.* In re Yamashita, 327 U.S. 1 (1946), like Quirin, did not involve the problem of direct review of military tribunals by the Court, since a lower court had already denied habeas corpus. In Yamashita, a Japanese general, while on trial for war crimes before a military tribunal in the Philippines, sought leave to file petitions for writs of habeas corpus and prohibition in the Supreme Court. Similar relief was sought and denied in the Supreme Court of the Philippines, and the Court stayed its own case, 326 U.S. 693 (1945), pending receipt of the petition for certiorari from that decision. Subsequently the Court heard argument and vacated the stay, denied certiorari, and denied leave to file, with an opinion holding that Yamashita was not entitled to relief on the merits.

2. Justice Jackson disqualified himself from one of the seven cases to which the opinion applied.

petitions for habeas corpus "for want of original jurisdiction." Justices Black and Rutledge would have denied leave without prejudice to the filing of the petitions "in the appropriate District Court." Justice Murphy would have "heard and determined" the questions of jurisdiction and proper procedure.

A year later, in October 1947, the motion of a German general to file a petition for habeas corpus to test the validity of his conviction and sentence to life imprisonment by a Military Tribunal at Nuremberg was denied, without statement of reasons, by an evenly divided Court. Justice Jackson, in view of his participation in the Nuremberg prosecution, took no part. Justices Black, Douglas, Murphy and Rutledge recorded their opinion "that the petition should be set for hearing on the question of the jurisdiction of this Court." Milch v. United States, 332 U.S. 789.[3]

Fourteen other war crimes cases were disposed of in February 1948 by an identical order, Brandt v. United States, 333 U.S. 836, with Justice Douglas, however, back with the majority. But three more cases in April 1948 met simply the response, "Petition denied", without notation of dissent. In re Eichel, 333 U.S. 865.

In May 1948 came a petition, on behalf of 74 Germans convicted by the Military Government Court at Dachau for crimes in connection with the Malmedy massacre, containing serious allegations of prosecution based upon systematic use of third-degree methods. Everett v. Truman, 334 U.S. 824. The per curiam decision in this case is as follows:

"The Court met in Special Term pursuant to a call by The Chief Justice having the approval of all the Associate Justices. The motion for leave to file a petition for an original writ of habeas corpus for relief from sentences upon the verdicts of a General Military Government Court at Dachau, Germany, is denied. The Chief Justice, Mr. Justice Reed, Mr. Justice Frankfurter, and Mr. Justice Burton are of the opinion that there is want of jurisdiction. U.S. Constitution, Article III, § 2, Clause 2; see Ex parte Betz and companion cases, all 329 U.S. 672 (1946); Milch v. United States, 332 U.S. 789 (1947); Brandt v. United States, 333 U.S. 836 (1948); In re Eichel, 333 U.S. 865 (1948). Mr. Justice Black, Mr. Justice Douglas, Mr. Justice Murphy, and Mr. Justice Rutledge are of the opinion that the motion for leave to file the petition should be granted and that the case should be set for argument forthwith. Mr. Justice Jackson took no part in the consideration or decision of the motion."

By identical orders fifteen more petitions were disposed of before the Court rose in June 1948, and another thirteen at the opening of the following term in October and November 1948. See Fairman, supra, at pp. 599–600.

Then on December 6, 1948, the Court set for oral argument motions for leave to file petitions in behalf of a group of Japanese, including former Premier Hirota, who had been convicted by the International Military Tribunal of the Far East. The deadlock had been broken by Justice Jackson who cast his vote in favor of a hearing. In an unusual separate opinion, the Justice recognized that his non-participation had prevented the

3. The Court apparently assumed that it takes a majority of the Court to set such a motion for argument. Why, given the fact that four votes are enough to note probable jurisdiction of an appeal (i.e., set it for oral argument) or to grant a writ of certiorari? See pp. 734, 1869, infra.

resolution of the issues involved, and that this stalemate was embarrassing not only to the Court but to the country in the conduct of its foreign affairs. He explained that, not having had a direct part in the far eastern trials, he felt free to participate in these cases, as he had not in the German cases, at least to the extent of securing full consideration, although he hoped to avoid participation in the final decision. Hirota v. MacArthur, 335 U.S. 876.

The case was argued on December 16–17, 1948, and the decision announced on December 20. Hirota v. MacArthur and companion cases, 338 U.S. 197. The text of the opinion follows:

"PER CURIAM. The petitioners, all residents and citizens of Japan, are being held in custody pursuant to the judgment of a military tribunal in Japan. Two of the petitioners have been sentenced to death, the others to terms of imprisonment. They filed motions in this Court for leave to file petitions for *habeas corpus*. We set all the motions for hearing on the question of our power to grant the relief prayed and that issue has now been fully presented and argued.

"We are satisfied that the tribunal sentencing these petitioners is not a tribunal of the United States. The United States and other allied countries conquered and now occupy and control Japan. General Douglas MacArthur has been selected and is acting as the Supreme Commander for the Allied Powers. The military tribunal sentencing these petitioners has been set up by General MacArthur as the agent of the Allied Powers.

"Under the foregoing circumstances the courts of the United States have no power or authority to review, to affirm, set aside or annul the judgments and sentences imposed on these petitioners and for this reason the motions for leave to file petitions for writs of *habeas corpus* are denied.

"MR. JUSTICE MURPHY dissents.

"MR. JUSTICE RUTLEDGE reserves decision and the announcement of his vote until a later time. [Mr. Justice Rutledge died September 10, 1949, without having announced his vote.]

"MR. JUSTICE JACKSON took no part in the final decision on these motions.

"MR. JUSTICE DOUGLAS concurs in the result for reasons to be stated in an opinion."

Justice Douglas announced his concurring opinion on June 27, 1949. At the outset, he said (pp. 199–200):

"There is an important question of jurisdiction that lies at the threshold of these cases. Respondents contend that the Court is without power to issue a writ of *habeas corpus* in these cases. It is argued that the Court has no original jurisdiction as defined in Art. III, § 2, Cl. 2 of the Constitution, since these are not cases affecting an ambassador, public minister, or consul; nor is a State a party. And it is urged that appellate jurisdiction is absent (1) because military commissions do not exercise judicial power within the meaning of Art. III, § 2 of the Constitution and hence are not agencies whose judgments are subject to review by the Court; and (2) no court of the United States to which the potential appellate jurisdiction of this Court extends has jurisdiction over this cause.

"It is to the latter contention alone that consideration need be given. I think it plain that a District Court of the United States does have jurisdiction to entertain petitions for *habeas corpus* to examine into the cause of the restraint of liberty of the petitioners."

As to this issue, he concluded (p. 203):

"It is therefore clear to me that the District Court of the District of Columbia is the court to hear these motions. The appropriate course would be to remit the parties to it, reserving any further questions until the cases come here by certiorari. But the Court is unwilling to take that course, apparently because it deems the cases so pressing and the issues so unsubstantial that the motions should be summarily disposed of."

In the balance of his opinion, Justice Douglas, apparently acquiescing in this mode of disposition, recorded his objection to the sweep of the Court's decision that jurisdiction was barred by the fact alone that the committing tribunal was international. In his view, the appropriate course was to "ascertain whether, so far as American participation is concerned, there was authority to try the defendants for the precise crimes with which they are charged." Undertaking to do this, he placed his concurrence on the narrower ground that "the capture and control of those who were responsible for the Pearl Harbor incident was a political question on which the President as Commander-in-Chief, and as spokesman for the nation in foreign affairs, had the final say."

Is Justice Douglas assuming that the Supreme Court has "appellate jurisdiction", in the constitutional sense, in any case which is within the potential jurisdiction of a lower federal court? Is such an assumption sound? If it is, why could not the writ of mandamus have issued in Marbury v. Madison as an exercise of appellate jurisdiction? Does the majority opinion imply acceptance of the Douglas assumption? Did the Court, or did it not, actually exercise an original jurisdiction in this case?

Following the Hirota decision at the 1948 term, a series of motions for leave to file petitions in war crimes cases were again denied by an evenly divided Court. Four Justices returned to their pre-Hirota ground of lack of original jurisdiction. The other four Justices amended their notation to state "the opinion that argument should be heard on the motions for leave to file the petitions in order to settle what remedy, if any, the petitioners have". In re Dammann and companion cases, 336 U.S. 922; In re Muhlbauer and companion cases, 336 U.S. 964; In re Steimle, 337 U.S. 913; In re Felsch, 337 U.S. 953.

Meanwhile, however, the Court, acting unanimously, denied an application from an American civilian convicted by a General Provost Court sitting in Japan, "without prejudice to the right to apply to any appropriate court that may have jurisdiction". In re Bush, 336 U.S. 971. Three weeks earlier it had denied "a somewhat comparable case from Germany" without comment. Bickford v. United States, 336 U.S. 950. See the reference to both cases in the concurring opinion of Justice Douglas in Hirota v. MacArthur, 338 U.S. at 201–02.

At the 1949 term, a reconstituted Court denied without explanation three more motions, with the notation that "Mr. Justice Black and Mr. Justice Douglas vote to deny without prejudice to making applications in a District Court". In re Hans, 339 U.S. 976 (1950).

In connection with the question of original jurisdiction, consider the concluding comment of Fairman, *supra,* at p. 603, made after examining the documents in all but the most recent of these cases:

"One can scarcely hope to put in brief compass any adequate summary of the many sorts of contentions set out in these thousands of pages. One defense counsel sent to the Court an 'opinion on the verdict' covering 104 typed pages in the translation. These are *ex parte* statements and should be read with as much reserve as other allegations of error in criminal trials, remembering that one does not expect the petitioner to profess a 'good opinion of the law'. Many of the documents run on and on without form or headings, although some later applications show that German counsel are gaining an idea of how an American legal brief is organized. Many pages devoted to the petitioner's version of factual details must remain quite incomprehensible apart from the record of trial. As one might expect, contentions of want of jurisdiction, appeals for a new trial, assignment of error in law, and pleas for clemency are often mixed together in these applications, which the Supreme Court appropriately treats as petitions for *habeas corpus.* A conception that runs throughout is neatly expressed in the form of address used by one applicant: 'To the Supreme Federal Court of Justice (War Crimes Department) Washington'. If the men convicted of war crimes ought to have further consideration, beyond the administrative reviews that preceded the Military Governor's confirmation of the sentences—and Everett v. Truman showed that that was badly needed in the Malmedy case—very evidently the solution cannot be an original proceeding in the Supreme Court."

For material on the jurisdiction of the District Court of the District of Columbia in cases of aliens and citizens held under American authority abroad, see Chap. IV, sec. 1(a), p. 422, *infra,* and particularly Johnson v. Eisentrager, 339 U.S. 763 (1950).

Chapter IV

CONGRESSIONAL CONTROL OF THE DISTRIBUTION OF JUDICIAL POWER AMONG FEDERAL AND STATE COURTS

SECTION 1. THE JURISDICTION OF FEDERAL COURTS

SUBSECTION A: CONGRESSIONAL RESTRICTION OF JURISDICTION

SHELDON v. SILL

8 How. 441, 12 L.Ed. 1147 (U.S.1850).
Appeal from the Circuit Court for the District of Michigan.

MR. JUSTICE GRIER delivered the opinion of the Court.

The only question which it will be necessary to notice in this case is, whether the Circuit Court had jurisdiction.

Sill, the complainant below, a citizen of New York, filed his bill in the Circuit Court of the United States for Michigan, against Sheldon, claiming to recover the amount of a bond and mortgage, which had been assigned to him by Hastings, the President of the Bank of Michigan.

Sheldon, in his answer, among other things, pleaded that "the bond and mortgage in controversy, having been originally given by a citizen of Michigan to another citizen of the same State, and the complainant being assignee of them, the Circuit Court had no jurisdiction."

The eleventh section of the Judiciary Act, which defines the jurisdiction of the Circuit Courts, restrains them from taking "cognizance of any suit to recover the contents of any promissory note or other chose in action, in favor of an assignee, unless a suit might have been prosecuted in such court to recover the contents, if no assignment had been made, except in cases of foreign bills of exchange."

The third article of the Constitution declares that "the judicial power of the United States shall be vested in one Supreme Court, and such inferior courts as the Congress may, from time to time, ordain and establish." The second section of the same article enumerates the cases and controversies of which the judicial power shall have cognizance, and, among others, it specifies "controversies between citizens of different States."

362

It has been alleged, that this restriction of the Judiciary Act, with regard to assignees of choses in action, is in conflict with this provision of the Constitution, and therefore void.

It must be admitted, that if the Constitution had ordained and established the inferior courts, and distributed to them their respective powers, they could not be restricted or divested by Congress. But as it has made no such distribution, one of two consequences must result,—either that each inferior court created by Congress must exercise all the judicial powers not given to the Supreme Court, or that Congress, having the power to establish the courts, must define their respective jurisdictions. The first of these inferences has never been asserted, and could not be defended with any show of reason, and if not, the latter would seem to follow as a necessary consequence. And it would seem to follow, also, that, having a right to prescribe, Congress may withhold from any court of its creation jurisdiction of any of the enumerated controversies. Courts created by statute can have no jurisdiction but such as the statute confers. No one of them can assert a just claim to jurisdiction exclusively conferred on another, or withheld from all.

The Constitution has defined the limits of the judicial power of the United States, but has not prescribed how much of it shall be exercised by the Circuit Court; consequently, the statute which does prescribe the limits of their jurisdiction, cannot be in conflict with the Constitution, unless it confers powers not enumerated therein.

Such has been the doctrine held by this court since its first establishment. To enumerate all the cases in which it has been either directly advanced or tacitly assumed would be tedious and unnecessary.

In the case of Turner v. Bank of North America, 4 Dall. 10, it was contended, as in this case, that, as it was a controversy between citizens of different States, the Constitution gave the plaintiff a right to sue in the Circuit Court, notwithstanding he was an assignee within the restriction of the eleventh section of the Judiciary Act. But the court said,—"The political truth is, that the disposal of the judicial power (except in a few specified instances) belongs to Congress: and Congress is not bound to enlarge the jurisdiction of the Federal courts to every subject, in every form which the Constitution might warrant." This decision was made in 1799; since that time, the same doctrine has been frequently asserted by this court, as may be seen in McIntire v. Wood, 7 Cranch, 506; Kendall v. United States, 12 Peters, 616; Cary v. Curtis, 3 Howard, 245.

The only remaining inquiry is, whether the complainant in this case is the assignee of a "chose in action," within the meaning of the statute.

* * *

The complainant in this case is the purchaser and assignee of a sum of money, a debt, a chose in action, not of a tract of land. He seeks to recover by this action a debt assigned to him. He is therefore the "assignee of a chose in action," within the letter and spirit of the act of Congress under consideration, and cannot support this action in the Circuit Court of the United States, where his assignor could not.

The judgment of the Circuit Court must therefore be reversed, for want of jurisdiction.

EX PARTE McCARDLE

7 Wall. 506, 19 L.Ed. 264 (U.S.1869).

Appeal from the Circuit Court for the Southern District of Mississippi.

[The petitioner was held in custody by military authority for trial before a military commission upon charges founded upon the publication of articles alleged to be incendiary and libelous in a newspaper of which he was editor. The custody was alleged to be under the authority of certain acts of Congress. The petitioner applied to the Circuit Court for the Southern District of Mississippi for a writ of habeas corpus, basing his application upon the Act of February 5, 1867, authorizing the grant of such writs "in all cases where any person may be restrained of his or her liberty in violation of the Constitution, or of any treaty or law of the United States."

[The petition having been denied and the petitioner having been remanded to military custody, he took an appeal, as authorized by the same act, to the Supreme Court. After the case had been argued but before conference or decision, Congress, over the President's veto, passed the Act of March 27, 1868, 15 Stat. 44, the second section of which provided: *"And be it further enacted,* That so much of the Act approved February 5, 1867, entitled 'An Act to amend an act to establish the judicial courts of the United States, approved September 24, 1789,' as authorized an appeal from the judgment of the Circuit Court to the Supreme Court of the United States, or the exercise of any such jurisdiction by said Supreme Court, on appeals which have been, or may hereafter be taken, be, and the same is hereby repealed."]

The attention of the court was directed to this statute at the last term, but counsel having expressed a desire to be heard in argument upon its effect, and the Chief Justice being detained from his place here, by his duties in the Court of Impeachment, the cause was continued under advisement. Argument was now heard upon the effect of the repealing act.

* * *

The Chief Justice delivered the opinion of the court.

The first question necessarily is that of jurisdiction; for, if the act of March, 1868, takes away the jurisdiction defined by the act of February, 1867, it is useless, if not improper, to enter into any discussion of other questions.

It is quite true, as was argued by the counsel for the petitioner, that the appellate jurisdiction of this court is not derived from acts of Congress. It is, strictly speaking, conferred by the Constitution. But it is conferred "with such exceptions and under such regulations as Congress shall make."

It is unnecessary to consider whether, if Congress had made no exceptions and no regulations, this court might not have exercised general appellate jurisdiction under rules prescribed by itself. For among the earliest acts of the first Congress, at its first session, was the act of September 24th, 1789, to establish the judicial courts of the United States. That act provided for the organization of this court, and prescribed regulations for the exercise of its jurisdiction.

The source of that jurisdiction, and the limitations of it by the Constitution and by statute, have been on several occasions subjects of consideration here. In the case of Durousseau v. The United States,* particularly, the whole matter was carefully examined, and the court held, that while "the appellate powers of this court are not given by the judicial act, but are given by the Constitution," they are, nevertheless, "limited and regulated by that act, and by such other acts as have been passed on the subject." The court said, further, that the judicial act was an exercise of the power given by the Constitution to Congress "of making exceptions to the appellate jurisdiction of the Supreme Court." "They have described affirmatively," said the court, "its jurisdiction, and this affirmative description has been understood to imply a negation of the exercise of such appellate power as is not comprehended within it."

The principle that the affirmation of appellate jurisdiction implies the negation of all such jurisdiction not affirmed having been thus established, it was an almost necessary consequence that acts of Congress, providing for the exercise of jurisdiction, should come to be spoken of as acts granting jurisdiction, and not as acts making exceptions to the constitutional grant of it.

The exception to appellate jurisdiction in the case before us, however, is not an inference from the affirmation of other appellate jurisdiction. It is made in terms. The provision of the act of 1867, affirming the appellate jurisdiction of this court in cases of *habeas corpus* is expressly repealed. It is hardly possible to imagine a plainer instance of positive exception.

We are not at liberty to inquire into the motives of the legislature. We can only examine into its power under the Constitution; and the power to make exceptions to the appellate jurisdiction of this court is given by express words.

What, then, is the effect of the repealing act upon the case before us? We cannot doubt as to this. Without jurisdiction the court cannot proceed at all in any cause. Jurisdiction is power to declare the law, and when it ceases to exist, the only function remaining to the court is that of announcing the fact and dismissing the cause. And this is not less clear upon authority than upon principle. * * *

It is quite clear, therefore, that this court cannot proceed to pronounce judgment in this case, for it has no longer jurisdiction of the appeal; and judicial duty is not less fitly performed by declining ungranted jurisdiction than in exercising firmly that which the Constitution and the laws confer.

Counsel seem to have supposed, if effect be given to the repealing act in question, that the whole appellate power of the court, in cases of *habeas corpus,* is denied. But this is an error. The act of 1868 does not except from that jurisdiction any cases but appeals from Circuit Courts under the act of 1867. It does not affect the jurisdiction which was previously exercised.*

The appeal of the petitioner in this case must be dismissed for want of jurisdiction.[1]

---

* 6 Cranch, 312; Wiscart v. Dauchy, 3 Dallas, 321. Vol. VII.

* Ex parte McCardle, 6 Wallace, 324.

1. [Ed.] The reconstruction legislation involved in the McCardle case was enacted shortly after the decision in Ex parte Milli-

gan, 4 Wall. 2 (U.S.1867), which gave rise to the hope that the Supreme Court would invalidate the military government provisions. See, *e.g.*, Burgess, Reconstruction and the Constitution 197 (1902); 2 Warren, The Supreme Court in United States Histo-

NOTE ON THE POWER OF CONGRESS TO LIMIT THE JURISDICTION OF FEDERAL COURTS

A. The Position of Justice Story

The view that Article III casts an obligation on the Congress to endow federal courts with the full scope of original and appellate federal judicial power was rejected in the framing of the First Judiciary Act. See Casto, *The First Congress's Understanding of its Authority over the Federal Courts' Jurisdiction,* 26 B.C.L.Rev. 1101 (1985). A more limited but still expansive view of the obligation of Congress was expressed by Justice Story in his opinion for the Court in Martin v. Hunter's Lessee, 1 Wheat. 304 (U.S.1816):

" * * * The language of the article throughout is manifestly designed to be mandatory upon the legislature. Its obligatory force is so imperative, that congress could not, without a violation of its duty, have refused to carry it into operation. The judicial power of the United States *shall be vested* (not may be vested) in one supreme court, and in such inferior courts as congress may, from time to time, ordain and establish. Could congress have lawfully refused to create a supreme court, or to vest in it the constitutional jurisdiction? * * *

"If, then, it is a duty of congress to vest the judicial power of the United States, it is a duty to vest the *whole judicial power.* The language, if imperative as to one part, is imperative as to all. If it were otherwise, this anomaly would exist, that congress might successively refuse to vest the jurisdiction in any one class of cases enumerated in the constitution, and thereby defeat the jurisdiction as to all; for the constitution has not singled out any class on which congress are bound to act in preference to others.

"The next consideration is, as to the courts in which the judicial power shall be vested. It is manifest, that a supreme court must be established; but whether it is equally obligatory to establish inferior courts, is a question of some difficulty. If congress may lawfully omit to establish inferior courts, it might follow, that in some of the enumerated cases, the judicial power could nowhere exist. * * * Congress cannot vest any portion of the judicial power of the United States except in courts ordained and established by itself; and if in any of the cases enumerated in the constitution, the state courts did not then possess jurisdiction, the appellate jurisdiction of the supreme court (admitting that it could act on state courts) could not reach those cases, and consequently, the injunction of the

ry 455 (rev. ed. 1935). Test cases failed to produce an adjudication in Mississippi v. Johnson, 4 Wall. 475 (U.S.1867) and Georgia v. Stanton, 6 Wall. 50 (U.S.1867), but the affirmation of jurisdiction when Ex parte McCardle reached the Court (6 Wall. 324) suggested that adverse decision was at hand. The Act withdrawing jurisdiction, though successful to frustrate decision in McCardle's case, was later held to leave intact the power to review denial of the writ on a petition in the Supreme Court for habeas corpus and certiorari. Ex parte Yerger, 8 Wall. 85 (U.S.1868). Decision on

the merits was again prevented, however, this time by releasing Yerger from the challenged military custody. see 2 Warren, *supra,* at 496–97.

See also the splendid accounts of the McCardle case in Van Alstyne, *A Critical Guide to Ex Parte McCardle,* 15 Ariz.L.Rev. 229 (1973), and Fairman, Reconstruction and Reunion, 1864–88, Part One, ch. X (1971) (Volume VI of the Oliver Wendell Holmes Devise History of the Supreme Court of the United States).

constitution, that the judicial power *'shall be vested',* would be disobeyed. It would seem, therefore, to follow, that congress are bound to create some inferior courts, in which to vest all that jurisdiction which, under the constitution, is *exclusively* vested in the United States, and of which the supreme court cannot take original cognizance. They might establish one or more inferior courts; they might parcel out the jurisdiction among such courts, from time to time, at their own pleasure. But the whole judicial power of the United States should be, at all times, vested, either in an original or appellate form, in some courts created under its authority.

"This construction will be fortified by an attentive examination of the second section of the third article. The words are 'the judicial power *shall extend,* ' & c. Much minute and elaborate criticism has been employed upon these words. It has been argued that they are equivalent to the words 'may extend,' and that 'extend' means to widen to new cases not before within the scope of the power. For the reasons which have been already stated, we are of opinion that the words are used in an imperative sense. They import an absolute grant of judicial power" (pp. 330–31).

A few pages later, Justice Story continued his analysis of Article III:

"[T]here are two classes of cases enumerated in the constitution, between which a distinction seems to be drawn. The first class includes cases arising under the constitution, laws, and treaties of the United States; cases affecting ambassadors, other public ministers and consuls, and cases of admiralty and maritime jurisdiction. In this class the expression is, and that the judicial power shall extend to *all cases;* but in the subsequent part of the clause which embraces all the other cases of national cognizance, and forms the second class, the word *'all'* is dropped seemingly *ex industria.* * * * From this difference of phraseology, perhaps, a difference of constitutional intention may, with propriety, be inferred. * * * In respect to the first class, it may well have been the intention of the framers of the constitution imperatively to extend the judicial power either in an original form or appellate form to *all cases;* and in the latter class to leave it to Congress to qualify the jurisdiction, original or appellate, in such manner as public policy might dictate" (pp. 333–34).

Note the three positions suggested in these excerpts. First, Justice Story argues that Congress is obligated to vest all of the judicial power "either in an original or appellate form" in some federal court. Second, he argues that if any cases described in Article III are beyond the jurisdiction of the state courts, and thus not capable of review on appeal from a state court to the Supreme Court, Congress would be obligated to create inferior federal courts in order that these cases might be entertained in some federal court. (The argument assumes that the cases do not fall within the Supreme Court's original jurisdiction.) And third, Justice Story appears to limit his argument of congressional obligation to the first three categories of cases described in Article III—to those in which the Framers used the adjective "all".[1]

---

1. A similar position with respect to the first of these categories—cases "arising under" federal law—was espoused by the Supreme Court reporter, Henry Wheaton, in a series of articles (signed "A Federalist of 1789") in *The New York American* in July and August 1821. (The identification of Wheaton as the author of these articles was made by Professor Gerald Gunther in the course of his research on the Marshall Court.)

Do these three positions differ in their strength and persuasiveness? Congress did not adhere to either the first or the third in the Judiciary Act of 1789, though its departures from the first (for example, with respect to diversity cases falling below the jurisdictional minimum) were more substantial. And the second, to the extent it mandates creation of inferior courts, appears flatly inconsistent with the deliberate compromises of the Constitutional Convention. See pp. 10–11, *supra*.[2]

Would Justice Story have dissented in the Sheldon or McCardle cases? Whatever his view might have been of the obligation of Congress in those cases, White v. Fenner, 1 Mason 520, 29 Fed.Cas. 1015 (No. 17,547) (C.C.R.I. 1818), indicates that he did not consider the constitutional imperative to be self-executing, at least with respect to lower federal court jurisdiction. While declaring that "it is somewhat singular the jurisdiction actually conferred on the courts of the United States should have stopped so far short of the constitutional extent," he dismissed a diversity suit excluded from the statutory grant, holding that the "Court has no jurisdiction which is not given by some statute" (p. 1016). Does this mean that the dicta in Martin were designed only to provide a basis for appeal to Congress?

B. The Klein Case

In United States v. Klein, 13 Wall. 128 (U.S.1871), plaintiff was the administrator of the deceased owner of property sold by agents of the government during the Civil War. He sued for the proceeds of the sale and recovered judgment in the Court of Claims, under legislation according this right of action to noncombatant rebel owners upon proof of loyalty. The Supreme Court had previously held that one who, like the decedent, had received a Presidential pardon must be treated as loyal, and the Court of Claims awarded recovery on this basis. Pending appeal from the judgment by the United States, Congress passed an act providing in effect that no pardon should be admissible as proof of loyalty and, further, that acceptance without written protest or disclaimer of a pardon reciting that the claimant took part in or supported the rebellion should be conclusive evidence of the claimant's disloyalty. The statute directed the Court of Claims and the Supreme Court to dismiss for want of *jurisdiction* any pending claims based on a pardon.[3]

---

2. In a study of the historical materials, Professor Clinton has embraced a variant of the first position; he concludes that "Congress must allocate to the federal judiciary as a whole each and every case or controversy" within the scope of Article III "excluding, possibly, only those cases that Congress deemed to be so trivial that they would pose an unnecessary burden." Clinton, *A Mandatory View of Federal Court Jurisdiction: A Guided Quest for the Original Understanding of Article III*, 132 U.Pa. L.Rev. 741, 749–50 (1984). And in another study, Professor Amar has advocated acceptance of the third position. see Amar, *A Neo-Federalist View of Article III: Separating the Two Tiers of Federal Jurisdiction*, 65 B.U.L.Rev. 205 (1985).

For further discussion of these positions, see pp. 385–87, *infra*.

3. The statute provided, with respect to any pending appeal in which a claimant had prevailed on proof of loyalty other "than such as is above required and provided, * * * the Supreme Court shall, on appeal, have no further jurisdiction of the cause, and shall dismiss the same for want of jurisdiction." Act of July 12, 1870, 16 Stat. 230, 235. Senator Edmonds, in response to a question whether this provision would simply require dismissal of the appeal (leaving the lower court judgment intact) said: "No; * * * we say they shall dismiss the case out of court for want of jurisdiction; not dismiss the appeal, but dismiss the case—everything.

"* * *

"The case is dead and gone; it is in no court whatever." Cong.Globe, 41st Cong., 2d Sess. 3824 (1870).

The Supreme Court held the supervening statute to be unconstitutional and affirmed the judgment of the Court of Claims. The opinion, though brief, is not a model of clarity. But it does emphasize that the "denial of jurisdiction to this court, as well as to the court of claims, is founded solely on the application of a rule of decision, in causes pending, prescribed by Congress. The court has jurisdiction of the cause to a given point; but when it ascertains that a certain state of things exists, its jurisdiction is to cease and it is required to dismiss the cause for want of jurisdiction. * * * It seems to us that this is not an exercise of the acknowledged power of Congress to make exceptions and prescribe regulations to the appellate power" (p. 146). And the rule of decision in question—which purported to determine the significance of a Presidential pardon—impairs the effect of such a pardon and thus "infring[es] the constitutional power of the Executive" (p. 147).[4]

In his dissenting opinion in Glidden Co. v. Zdanok, 370 U.S. 530, 605 n. 11 (1962), Justice Douglas suggests that Klein is in principle inconsistent with McCardle, presumably because Klein invalidated a statute purporting to withdraw Supreme Court jurisdiction over a particular class of cases. But doesn't this suggestion ignore some crucial distinctions? Does Klein in fact do more than hold that it is an unconstitutional invasion of the judicial function when Congress purports, not to withdraw appellate jurisdiction completely, but to bind the Court to reverse a decision below in accordance with a rule of law independently unconstitutional on other grounds? Cf. Yakus v. United States, p. 374, infra, and the Dialogue at pp. 399–407, infra.

For an exhaustive and illuminating analysis of Klein and its significance on a variety of issues, see Young, Congressional Regulation of Federal Courts' Jurisdiction and Processes: United States v. Klein Revisited, 1981 Wis.L.Rev. 1189.[5]

---

4. In addition to the passage quoted in text, Klein contains other broad language questioning the power of Congress to "prescribe rules of decision to the judicial department of the government in cases pending before it" (p. 146). Given the context, such language should surely not be read as casting doubt on the ancient principle, clear since the decision in United States v. Schooner Peggy, 1 Cranch 103 (U.S.1801), that the courts are obligated to apply law (otherwise valid) as they find it at the time of their decision, including when a case is on review, the time of the appellate judgment. See, e.g., Carpenter v. Wabash Ry. Co., 309 U.S. 23 (1940); Vandenbark v. Owens–Illinois Glass Co., 311 U.S. 538 (1941); Huddleston v. Dwyer, 322 U.S. 232 (1944); Cort v. Ash, 422 U.S. 66 (1975). In fact the Supreme Court has, on timely motion, modified its own judgment to permit consideration by the district court of a defense created by Act of Congress after entry of the judgment. See 149 Madison Ave. Corp. v. Asselta, 331 U.S. 795 (1947); for subsequent proceedings, see 79 F.Supp. 413 (S.D.N.Y.1948); 90 F.Supp. 442 (S.D. N.Y.1950).

Compare United States v. Sioux Nation of Indians, 448 U.S. 371 (1980), in which the Court upheld the constitutionality of a statute directing the Court of Claims to review the merits of a Fifth Amendment taking claim by the Sioux Nation, without reference to the res judicata effect of a previous Court of Claims decision favorable to the government. The Court distinguished Klein (over Justice Rehnquist's dissent) on the grounds that (1) in Klein, "Congress was attempting to decide the controversy at issue in the Government's own favor" and (2) "even more important, the proviso at issue in Klein had attempted to 'prescribe a rule for the decision of a cause in a particular way' * * * [while the amendment in the case at bar simply] waived the defense of res judicata so that a legal claim could be resolved on the merits" (p. 405). Shouldn't the Court in Sioux Nation have added to the second distinction the point that the rule of decision prescribed in Klein was itself unconstitutional as an invasion of executive power?

5. The Second Edition of this book (at p. 316) suggested as a further basis of the decision in Klein that the rule of law laid down by Congress was invalid not only as an impairment of executive power but also as an effort "to prescribe how the Court should decide an *issue of fact* (under threat

C. The Norris–LaGuardia Act

The Norris–LaGuardia Act of March 23, 1932, 29 U.S.C. §§ 101–115, narrowly restricted the authority of courts of the United States to issue a restraining order or a temporary or permanent injunction in "a case involving or growing out of a labor dispute", and provided that "yellow-dog" contracts "shall not be enforceable in any court of the United States and shall not afford any basis for the granting of legal or equitable relief by any such court". The term "court of the United States" was defined to mean "any court of the United States whose jurisdiction has been or may be conferred or defined or limited by Act of Congress". The Act throughout was drawn as a limitation of the "jurisdiction" of the courts.

At the time of the enactment, Truax v. Corrigan, 257 U.S. 312 (1921), had found state legislation similarly limiting employers' remedies to be a denial of due process; and Coppage v. Kansas, 236 U.S. 1 (1915), and Adair v. United States, 208 U.S. 161 (1908), had held that the right to condition employment on an undertaking not to join a labor union or on non-membership also was protected by the due process clauses of the Constitution.

Did the fact that the Norris–LaGuardia Act, as interpreted, merely limited federal jurisdiction render these due process arguments (whatever their validity) irrelevant? This was the view of the reports of the Judiciary Committees. S.Rep. No. 163, H.R.Rep. No. 669, 72d Cong., 1st Sess. 10 (1932). See also Frankfurter & Greene, The Labor Injunction 210–11 (1930), and the memorandum by Professor Frankfurter in the Appendix to H.R.Rep. No. 669, *supra*. The position was apparently sustained by the Supreme Court in Lauf v. E.G. Shinner & Co., 303 U.S. 323, 330 (1938), Justice Roberts saying: "There can be no question of the power of Congress thus to define and limit the jurisdiction of the inferior courts of the United States." [6]

Is it fair to say that the theory of the legislation was that the Constitution may impose more stringent limitations on state power to restrict state court jurisdiction than on federal power to restrict federal jurisdiction? Does this make sense? [7]

D. The Price Control Legislation

In the Sheldon case, limitation of federal jurisdiction left the plaintiff free to sue in a state court. So, too, the Norris–LaGuardia Act, though much copied by the states, did not seek to limit the jurisdiction of state

---

of loss of jurisdiction)." Young, 1981 Wis. L.Rev. at 1233–38, argues persuasively that Klein itself contained no holding "which limits Congress' power to govern the fact-finding process," since the parties had in effect stipulated that, absent the pardon, the decedent's conduct required a finding of disloyalty.

Young also notes that the jurisdictional implications of some decisions applying Klein (especially Armstrong v. United States, 13 Wall. 154 (U.S.1872)) may be broader than the significance of Klein itself. 1981 Wis.L.Rev. at 1222–23 n. 179.

For further discussion of Klein, see Sager, *Foreword: Constitutional Limitations on Congress' Authority to Regulate the Jurisdiction of the Federal Courts*, 95 Harv.L. Rev. 17, 29, 70–77, 87–88 (1981).

6. Lauf was an action by an employer to enjoin a union and one of its officials from engaging in picketing and related activities.

7. For other limitations on the power of federal courts to grant injunctions, see Chap. X, *infra*.

courts.[8] When an Act of Congress does purport to limit state as well as federal court jurisdiction, does its validity depend upon a different constitutional standard?

(1) The Emergency Price Control Act of 1942, 56 Stat. 23, created "a court of the United States to be known as the Emergency Court of Appeals," to consist of three Federal District or Circuit Judges, and having "the powers of a district court with respect to the jurisdiction conferred on it" by the Act, except that it had <u>no power to issue any temporary</u> restraining order or interlocutory decree staying the effectiveness of any order, regulation or price schedule issued under the Act. Section 203(a) provided for attack on any order, regulation or price schedule issued under the Act by filing a protest with the Administrator;[9] if the protest was denied, Section 204(a) gave the party aggrieved thirty days to file a complaint with the Emergency Court of Appeals. Section 204(d) provided that the judgments of that court could be reviewed by the Supreme Court on petition for writ of certiorari, with a direction that these cases be expedited.

Section 204(d) also provided:

"The Emergency Court of Appeals, and the Supreme Court upon review of judgments and orders of the Emergency Court of Appeals, shall have exclusive jurisdiction to <u>determine</u> the validity of any regulation or order issued under section 2, of any price schedule effective in accordance with the provisions of section 206, and of any provision of any such regulation, order or price schedule. Except as provided in this section, no court, Federal, State or Territorial, shall have jurisdiction or power to consider the validity of any such regulation, order, or price schedule, or to stay, restrain, enjoin, or set aside, in whole or in part, any provision of this Act authorizing the issuance of such regulations or orders, or making effective any such price schedule, or any provision of any such regulation, order, or price schedule, or to restrain or enjoin the enforcement of any such provision."

Section 205 authorized the Administrator to bring suit for an injunction restraining violations of the Act or an order directing compliance; declared wilful violations criminal; and authorized treble damage suits in case of over-ceiling sales to be brought by a buyer for use and consumption or, in other cases, by the Administrator. Concurrent jurisdiction was conferred upon state courts, except in criminal prosecutions.

As originally enacted, the statute made no provision for a stay of enforcement proceedings either to permit the filing of a protest or to await the disposition of a protest previously filed. The Stabilization Extension Act of June 30, 1944, 58 Stat. 632, however, added a new Section 204(e), which directed a stay of enforcement suits pending action on a protest already filed or review of its denial; it also gave a narrow scope for stays in

---

8. Note, however, that Norris–LaGuardia would seem to come into operation in a case where the defendant is allowed to (and in fact does) remove the case from state to federal court under 28 U.S.C. § 1441. See Avco Corp. v. Aero Lodge 735, 390 U.S. 557 (1968), discussed at pp. 1056–57, *infra.*

9. As originally enacted, the statute required such a protest to be filed within 60 days after the issuance of the regulation or after the grounds of protest had arisen, but this time limit was removed in the Stabilization Extension Act of June 30, 1944, 58 Stat. 632.

certain cases to permit suits to be filed in the Emergency Court of Appeals where no protest had been filed.

(2) Lockerty v. Phillips, 319 U.S. 182 (1943), involved a suit by wholesale meat dealers in a federal district court in New Jersey to restrain the United States Attorney from prosecuting violations of certain price regulations. The regulations and the Act were challenged on constitutional grounds.

The district court dismissed the suit for want of jurisdiction under § 204(d). The Supreme Court affirmed, Chief Justice Stone saying (pp. 187–89):

"By this statute Congress has seen fit to confer on the Emergency Court (and on the Supreme Court upon review of decisions of the Emergency Court) equity jurisdiction to restrain the enforcement of price orders under the Emergency Price Control Act. At the same time it has withdrawn that jurisdiction from every other federal and state court. There is nothing in the Constitution which requires Congress to confer equity jurisdiction on any particular inferior federal court. All federal courts, other than the Supreme Court, derive their jurisdiction wholly from the exercise of the authority to 'ordain and establish' inferior courts, conferred on Congress by Article III, § 1 of the Constitution. Article III left Congress free to establish inferior federal courts or not as it thought appropriate. It could have declined to create any such courts, leaving suitors to the remedies afforded by state courts, with such appellate review by this Court as Congress might prescribe. Kline v. Burke Construction Co., 260 U.S. 226, 234, and cases cited; McIntire v. Wood, 7 Cranch 504, 506. The Congressional power to ordain and establish inferior courts includes the power 'of investing them with jurisdiction either limited, concurrent, or exclusive, and of withholding jurisdiction from them in the exact degrees and character which to Congress may seem proper for the public good.' Cary v. Curtis, 3 How. 236, 245; Lauf v. E.G. Shinner & Co., 303 U.S. 323, 330; Hallowell v. Commons, 239 U.S. 506, 509; Smallwood v. Gallardo, 275 U.S. 56; Toucey v. New York Life Ins. Co., 314 U.S. 118, 129. See also United States v. Hudson and Goodwin, 7 Cranch 32, 33; Mayor v. Cooper, 6 Wall. 247, 252; Stevenson v. Fain, 195 U.S. 165, 167; Kentucky v. Powers, 201 U.S. 1, 24; Chicot County Drainage Dist. v. Baxter Bank, 308 U.S. 371, 376. In the light of the explicit language of the Constitution and our decisions, it is plain that Congress has power to provide that the equity jurisdiction to restrain enforcement of the Act, or of regulations promulgated under it, be restricted to the Emergency Court, and, upon review of its decisions, to this Court. Nor can we doubt the authority of Congress to require that a plaintiff seeking such equitable relief resort to the Emergency Court only after pursuing the prescribed administrative procedure.

* * *

"Appellants also contend that the review in the Emergency Court is inadequate to protect their constitutional rights, and that § 204 is therefore unconstitutional, because § 204(c) prohibits all interlocutory relief by that court. We need not pass upon the constitutionality of this restriction. For, in any event, the separability clause of § 303 of the Act would require us to give effect to the other provisions of § 204, including that withholding from the district courts authority to enjoin enforcement of the Act—a provision which as we have seen is subject to no constitutional infirmity.

"Since appellants seek only an injunction which the district court is without authority to give, their bill of complaint was rightly dismissed. We have no occasion to determine now whether, or to what extent, appellants may challenge the constitutionality of the Act or the Regulation in courts other than the Emergency Court, either by way of defense to a criminal prosecution or in a civil suit brought for some other purpose than to restrain enforcement of the Act or regulations issued under it."

(3) In what court should the plaintiffs in Lockerty have attempted to test the constitutionality, under the Due Process Clause, of the complete prohibition on interlocutory relief in the Act? Given the fact that the jurisdiction of the Emergency Court was itself explicitly defined as not including the power to grant such relief, would their position have been stronger there than it was in the district court? What about applying for an interlocutory injunction in a state court? As the Dialogue below suggests, see p. 423, *infra*, it should be clear in principle that a state court of general jurisdiction cannot be prevented from passing on the constitutionality of any restriction placed on its jurisdiction by the Congress. (As a practical matter, plaintiffs would have faced formidable obstacles to persuading a state court to pass on the question in light of the confusion surrounding the question of state-court power over suits against federal officers, see pp. 488–92, *infra*.) But if a state court would be under an obligation to pass on the validity of the remedial restriction in spite of the Act's provision completely withdrawing jurisdiction from state as well as federal courts, could Congress have conceivably meant the separability clause to deny a similar authority to the federal district courts? In any event does not the foundation for the Chief Justice's holding as to separability collapse?

For cases suggesting that due process requires an opportunity to apply to a court for an interlocutory stay of a state administrative order challenged on constitutional grounds, see Pacific Tel. & Tel. Co. v. Kuykendall, 265 U.S. 196, 204–05 (1924); Porter v. Investors' Syndicate, 286 U.S. 461, 471 (1932).[10]

10. Compare, with the provisions passed on in Lockerty, the Voting Rights Act of 1965, 42 U.S.C. § 1973, which provided that actions to exempt states from the coverage of the Act and actions to permit certain "suspended" state voting regulations to go into effect must be brought in the District Court for the District of Columbia. In South Carolina v. Katzenbach, 383 U.S. 301 (1966), the Court upheld this scheme, saying (pp. 331–32): "Congress might appropriately limit litigation under this provision to a single court in the District of Columbia, pursuant to its constitutional power under Art. III, § 1, to 'ordain and establish' inferior federal tribunals. see Bowles v. Willingham, 321 U.S. 503, 510–512; Yakus v. United States, 321 U.S. 414, 427–431; Lockerty v. Phillips, 319 U.S. 182. At the present time, contractual claims against the United States for more than $10,000 must be brought in the Court of Claims, and, until 1962, the District of Columbia was the sole venue of suits against federal officers officially residing in the Nation's Capital. We have discovered no suggestion that Congress exceeded constitutional bounds in imposing these limitations on litigation against the Federal Government, and the Act is no less reasonable in this respect."

South Carolina v. Katzenbach was an action to enjoin enforcement of various provisions of the Voting Rights Act, brought in the original jurisdiction of the Supreme Court. The parties do not seem to have referred to, and the Court decided the case without discussing, Section 14(b) of the Act, which provided that only the District Court for the District of Columbia "shall have jurisdiction to issue • • • any restraining order or temporary or permanent injunction" against enforcement of any provision of the Act. Did the Court, in deciding the case, sub silentio hold Section 14(b) unconstitutional insofar as it restricted the Supreme Court's original jurisdiction? See Justice Black's dissent, 383 U.S.

(4) Yakus v. United States, 321 U.S. 414 (1944), presented one of the issues reserved in Lockerty: the status of a claim of invalidity of the Price Control Act or of a regulation as a defense to a criminal prosecution for a violation. Section 204(d) was interpreted to bar attack upon a regulation (at least where not invalid on its face) but not upon the Act itself. Thus construed it was sustained against contentions that it involved deprivation of due process, contravened the Sixth Amendment, and worked an unconstitutional legislative interference with judicial power.

On the due process issue, the opinion of the Court by Chief Justice Stone treats as the central question whether the procedure for protest and review in the Emergency Court "affords to those affected a reasonable opportunity to be heard and present evidence" (p. 433). Concluding that it did, the opinion further holds that in "the circumstances of this case" there was "no denial of due process in the statutory prohibition of a temporary stay or injunction. * * * If the alternatives, as Congress could have concluded, were wartime inflation or the imposition on individuals of the burden of complying with a price regulation while its validity is being determined, Congress could constitutionally make the choice in favor of the protection of the public interest from the dangers of inflation" (pp. 437, 439). Upon the other issues, the opinion stated, *inter alia:*

"* * * [W]e are pointed to no principle of law or provision of the Constitution which precludes Congress from making criminal the violation of an administrative regulation, by one who has failed to avail himself of an adequate separate procedure for the adjudication of its validity, or which precludes the practice, in many ways desirable, of splitting the trial for violations of an administrative regulation by committing the determination of the issue of its validity to the agency which created it, and the issue of violation to a court which is given jurisdiction to punish violations. Such a requirement presents no novel constitutional issue * * *" (p. 444).

"Nor has there been any denial in the present criminal proceeding of the right, guaranteed by the Sixth Amendment, to a trial by a jury of the state and district where the crime was committed. Subject to the requirements of due process, which are here satisfied, Congress could make criminal the violation of a price regulation. The indictment charged a violation of the regulation in the district of trial, and the question whether petitioners had committed the crime thus charged in the indictment and defined by Congress, namely, whether they had violated the statute by willful disobedience of a price regulation promulgated by the Administrator, was properly submitted to the jury" (pp. 447–48).

Justice Rutledge, dissenting in an opinion in which Justice Murphy joined, found "the crux" of the case to be in "the question whether Congress can confer jurisdiction upon federal and state courts in the enforcement proceedings, more particularly the criminal suit, and at the same time deny them 'jurisdiction or power to consider the validity' of the regulations for which enforcement is thus sought" (p. 467).

"It is one thing for Congress to withhold jurisdiction. It is entirely another to confer it and direct that it be exercised in a manner inconsistent

at 357 n. 1; see generally Chap. III, p. 295, *supra.*

with constitutional requirements or, what in some instances may be the same thing, without regard to them. * * * There are limits to the judicial power. Congress may impose others. And in some matters Congress or the President has final say under the Constitution. But whenever the judicial power is called into play, it is responsible directly to the fundamental law and no other authority can intervene to force or authorize the judicial body to disregard it. The problem therefore is not solely one of individual right or due process of law. It is equally one of the separation and independence of the powers of government and of the constitutional integrity of the judicial process, more especially in criminal trials" (p. 468).

After questioning the constitutional adequacy of the statutory procedure even in cases where it is pursued and the regulation under protest is declared invalid, Justice Rutledge found a "deeper fault" in a conviction "on a trial in two parts, one so summary and civil and the other criminal or, in the alternative, on a trial which shuts out what may be the most important of the issues material to * * * guilt" (pp. 478, 479). Quoting the guarantee of jury trial in the Sixth Amendment and Article III as well as the definition of the judicial power in Article III, he stated: "By these provisions the purpose hardly is to be supposed to authorize splitting up a criminal trial into separate segments, with some of the issues essential to guilt triable before one court in the state and district where the crime was committed and others, equally essential, triable in another court in a highly summary civil proceeding held elsewhere, or to dispense with trial on them because that proceeding has not been followed. * * * If Congress can remove these questions, it can remove also all questions of validity of the statute, or, it would seem, of law" (pp. 479, 480).[11]

(5) Bowles v. Willingham, 321 U.S. 503 (1944), decided the same day, sustained the exclusion of the validity of the regulation from the scope of a civil action brought by the Administrator to enjoin a landlord from prosecuting in a state court a suit to restrain the issuance of an order reducing certain rentals to conform to the prescribed maximum. In concurring in the result, Justice Rutledge distinguished between such a civil proceeding and enforcement by criminal prosecution, insisting, however, upon the following limitations, satisfied in his judgment in this case: "(1) The order or regulation must not be invalid on its face; (2) the previous opportunity must be adequate for the purpose prescribed, in the constitutional sense; and (3) * * * the circumstances and nature of the substantive problem dealt with by the legislature must be such that they justify both the creation of the special remedy and the requirement that it be followed to the exclusion of others normally available" (p. 526).

---

11. In Adamo Wrecking Co. v. United States, 434 U.S. 275 (1978), the Court dealt with issues similar to those in Yakus by construing the relevant statute to permit a particular defense to be raised in a criminal prosecution. Nine years later, in United States v. Mendoza–Lopez, 107 S.Ct. 2148 (1987), an important constitutional question was confronted and resolved. The Court in Mendoza–Lopez first cited Yakus (along with other cases) for the proposition that "where a determination made in an administrative proceeding is to play a critical role in the subsequent imposition of a criminal sanction, there must be *some* meaningful review of the administrative proceeding" (p. 2154). It then went on to hold that when a prior deportation proceeding "effectively eliminate[d] the right of an alien to obtain judicial review," due process required that the alien be allowed to make a collateral challenge to the use of that proceeding as an element of a subsequent criminal offense (p. 2155).

E. The Portal to Portal Question

The Fair Labor Standards Act of 1938, 29 U.S.C. §§ 201–219, guaranteed employees in industries covered by the Act compensation "at a rate not less than one and one-half times the regular rate" for a "work week longer than forty hours" and prescribed liability for unpaid overtime together with an additional equal amount as liquidated damages.

In Tennessee Coal Co. v. Muscoda Local, 321 U.S. 590 (1944); Jewell Ridge Corp. v. Local No. 6167, 325 U.S. 161 (1945); and Anderson v. Mt. Clemens Pottery Co., 328 U.S. 680 (1946), the Supreme Court held that "work week", which the Act did not define, included underground travel in iron ore mines and similar preliminary and incidental activities of employees in connection with their work, which to a large extent had not theretofore been regarded as compensable unless the parties so agreed.

Actions instituted in the federal courts, based on these decisions, totaled 1,913 between July 1, 1946, and January 31, 1947, claiming in excess of $5,000,000,000. The potential liability of the United States on War Department cost-plus contracts was estimated at $1,400,000,000; and $128,500,000 was claimed in five claims against the Maritime Commission. see H.R.Rep. No. 71, 80th Cong., 1st Sess. 3, 4, 5 (1947).

Moved by these facts, Congress enacted the Portal-to-Portal Act of 1947, 29 U.S.C. §§ 251–62. The Act recited the finding of Congress that the recent decisions created immense, unexpected and retroactive liabilities, which would result in financial ruin for many employers, unexpected windfall payments to employees, and serious financial consequences for the United States Treasury. Sections 2(a) and (b) of the Act then proceeded to wipe out the liabilities substantively by providing that "no employer shall be subject to any liability or punishment" under the Fair Labor Standards Act for failure to compensate the preliminary and incidental work at issue.[12] In addition, Section 2(d) provided:

"No court of the United States, of any State, Territory or possession of the United States, or of the District of Columbia, shall have jurisdiction of any action or proceeding, whether instituted prior to or on or after May 14, 1947, to enforce liability or impose punishment for or on account of the failure of the employer to pay minimum wages or overtime compensation under the Fair Labor Standards Act of 1938, as amended, under the Walsh–Healey Act, or under the Bacon–Davis Act, to the extent that such action or proceeding seeks to enforce any liability or impose any punishment with respect to an activity which was not compensable under subsections (a) and (b) of this section."

It was claimed that the Act, in its retroactive operation, destroyed vested rights in violation of the Fifth Amendment. The contention was universally rejected on the merits. see Thomas v. Carnegie–Illinois Steel Corp., 174 F.2d 711 (3d Cir.1949). But the courts of appeals and most district courts treated it as open to decision, despite the jurisdictional provision and the usual separability clause. Thus Judge Chase, writing for

---

12. An exception was made for work which was compensable by virtue of express contractual agreements or by virtue of custom or practice at a particular establishment.

the Second Circuit in Battaglia v. General Motors Corp., 169 F.2d 254, 257 (2d Cir.1948), said:

"A few of the district court decisions sustaining section 2 of the Portal-to-Portal Act have done so on the ground that since jurisdiction of federal courts other than the Supreme Court is conferred by Congress, it may at the will of Congress be taken away in whole or in part. * * * These district court decisions would, in effect, sustain subdivision (d) of section 2 of the Act regardless of whether subdivisions (a) and (b) were valid. We think, however, that the exercise by Congress of its control over jurisdiction is subject to compliance with at least the requirements of the Fifth Amendment. That is to say, while Congress has the undoubted power to give, withhold, and restrict the jurisdiction of the courts other than the Supreme Court,[a] it must not so exercise that power as to deprive any person of life, liberty, or property without due process of law or to take private property without just compensation. * * * Thus regardless of whether subdivision (d) of section 2 had an independent end in itself, if one of the effects would be to deprive the appellants of property without due process or just compensation, it would be invalid."

Judge Parker, on the other hand, approached decision of the question by sustaining § 2(a) on the merits and then adding: "Whether the denial of jurisdiction would be valid, if the provision striking down the claims were invalid, is a question which does not arise". Seese v. Bethlehem Steel Co., 168 F.2d 58, 65 (4th Cir.1948).

If the jurisdictional issue were considered first and subdivision (d) held separable and valid, without regard to the due process question, would the consequence be that subdivision (a) would escape the due process test entirely or that it could be tested in an action brought in a state court? If the latter, would the judgment of the highest state court be reviewable in the Supreme Court, notwithstanding subdivision (d)?

Assuming that the state courts could not be prevented from passing on the constitutionality of subdivision (a), why didn't the federal courts pass first on the jurisdictional issue and leave the due process question to the state courts? Was it their premise that if Congress could not validly prevent the state courts from passing on the due process question, the Act should not be read as denying the same power to the federal courts?

F. Legislative Efforts to Restrict Federal Jurisdiction: The Last Forty Years

Since the 1940s, well over 100 proposals have been introduced in Congress to eliminate or restrict the jurisdiction of the federal courts. No such proposal directed at a particular Supreme Court decision or group of decisions has been enacted, though some have come close and have been the subject of heated debate.

In the late '50s and in the '60s, the proposals embraced such subjects as: state and federal legislation regulating or restricting subversive activi-

---

a. "It also has the power, of course, to make 'exceptions' to and 'regulations' regarding the Supreme Court's appellate jurisdiction. * * *"

ties,[13] the admissibility of confessions in state criminal cases,[14] and state legislative apportionments. An example of the last of these was H.R. 11926, 88th Cong., 2d Sess. (1964), introduced by Representative Tuck. This bill, which passed the House, would have added the following provisions to Title 28:

§ 1259. "The Supreme Court shall not have the right to review the action of a Federal court or a State court of last resort concerning any action taken upon a petition or complaint seeking to apportion or reapportion any legislature of any State of the Union or any branch thereof."

§ 1331(c). "The district courts shall not have jurisdiction to entertain any petition or complaint seeking to apportion or reapportion the legislature of any State of the Union or any branch thereof * * *." [15]

(3) Beginning in the early 1970s, a number of bills were introduced that were designed to curb the power of the federal courts to use busing as a remedy in school segregation cases,[16] or to prohibit the Justice Department from participating in any school segregation case in which busing would result.[17] Some of these bills were apparently—though ambiguously—grounded in the power to control jurisdiction.

(4) In the 97th Congress (1981 and 1982), two of the major efforts to limit jurisdiction concerned the issues of abortion and school prayer. With respect to abortion,[18] some of the proposals left the Supreme Court's jurisdiction untouched but severely limited the powers of lower federal

---

13. See, *e.g.*, the Jenner bill, S. 2646, 85th Cong., 1st Sess. (1957), which would have deprived the Supreme Court of jurisdiction to review any case where there was drawn in question such matters as: the functions or practices of a congressional committee, any state law or regulation concerning subversive activities, or any state law or regulation relating to admission to the practice of law. The bill was voted down on the Senate floor, 49–41. See 104 Cong.Rec. 18687 (1958).

14. S. 917, 90th Cong., 2d Sess. (1968) contained a provision withdrawing federal court jurisdiction to review in any way a state court ruling "in any criminal prosecution admitting in evidence as voluntarily made an admission or confession of an accused if such ruling has been affirmed or otherwise upheld by the highest court of the State having appellate jurisdiction of the cause." Another provision of the bill was similarly designed to withdraw federal jurisdiction to apply the rule of United States v. Wade, 388 U.S. 218 (1967). These provisions were eliminated when the bill reached the Senate floor. See 114 Cong. Rec. 14171–84 (1968).

15. The Senate rejected the Tuck bill, 56–21. See 110 Cong.Rec. 22104 (1964). This bill was one of more than fifty introduced in 1964 designed either to eliminate jurisdiction in or to "stay" reapportionment cases. None became law. See generally McKay, *Court, Congress, and Reapportionment*, 63 Mich.L.Rev. 255 (1964).

16. For discussion of many of these proposals, see Goldberg, *The Administration's Anti–Busing Proposals—Politics Makes Bad Law*, 67 Nw.U.L.Rev. 319 (1972); Note, *The Nixon Busing Bills and Congressional Power*, 81 Yale L.J. 1542 (1972). For one proposal that was carefully drafted to attain a limited objective, see H.R. 14553, 94th Cong., 2d Sess. (1976). This bill, entitled the "School Desegregation Standards and Assistance Act of 1976," attempted to limit the scope of busing orders to the extent necessary to create the general pattern of integration that probably would have existed had government officials not violated the Constitution.

17. See, *e.g.*, S. 951, 97th Cong., 2d Sess. (1981). This bill also prohibited federal courts from issuing desegregation orders involving busing beyond a neighborhood school. After a ten month debate and filibuster, the Senate passed the bill as a rider to the Justice Department authorization bill. But a petition to dislodge the bill from the House Judiciary Committee failed for lack of signatures and the bill never reached the House floor.

18. *Cf.* Chrisman v. Sisters of St. Joseph of Peace, 506 F.2d 308 (9th Cir.1974), interpreting a provision of the Health Programs Extension Act of 1973. Relying in part on the power of Congress to restrict jurisdiction, the court upheld the dismissal of a suit brought against a hospital for its refusal to permit the sterilization of a woman patient.

courts to grant certain preventive relief.[19] Another proposal deprived *all* federal courts of jurisdiction in any case arising out of any state or local law "which relates to abortion." [20] None of these proposals passed either House.

With respect to school prayer, several bills introduced in the 97th Congress sought to withdraw from the jurisdiction of all federal courts any case arising out of any state or local law or rule "which relates to voluntary prayer in public schools and buildings." [21] Senator Helms attempted to attach one such bill (S. 1742) as a rider to a debt limit bill, but the Senate rejected the effort, after vigorous and extended debate, by a vote of 51–48. No such proposal passed either House. (And three years later, the Senate voted, 62–36, not to consider S. 47, 99th Cong., 1st Sess. (1985), which contained a similar proposal.)

G. The Current Debate

(1) The question of the power of Congress to limit federal court jurisdiction is not a unitary one.[22] There are at least three separate issues: (1) the power of Congress to limit the appellate jurisdiction of the Supreme Court (while leaving untouched the present jurisdiction of the lower federal courts), (2) the power of Congress to limit the jurisdiction of the lower federal courts on matters that continue to be within the jurisdiction of the Supreme Court, and (3) the power of Congress to withdraw certain matters from the jurisdiction of all federal courts. The legislative proposals discussed in Part F, above, raise various combinations of these issues, but an effort will be made in the following paragraphs to consider each of them separately.[23]

Issues of lower court jurisdiction—authority to adjudicate a case at all—are distinct from issues of remedial authority in a case admittedly within the competence of the court to decide. Although the terminology of the governing statute may often be confusing, there is plainly a difference, for example, between a statute withdrawing certain breach of contract actions from judicial cognizance and a statute limiting the remedy in such actions to monetary damages.

This Chapter is concerned primarily with issues of jurisdiction, although questions of the power over remedies are raised at several points. see pp. 372–73, *supra;* pp. 395–98, *infra.* As stated in the Dialogue, p. 395, *infra,* "Congress necessarily has a wide choice in the selection of remedies," and some of the legislative proposals discussed in Part F, above, were cast not in terms of withdrawing jurisdiction over a whole case but rather in terms of limiting available remedies.

19. See, *e.g.,* H.R. 73, 97th Cong., 1st Sess. (1981); H.R. 900, sec. 2, 97th Cong., 1st Sess. (1981).

20. H.R. 867, 97th Cong., 1st Sess. (1981).

21. *E.g.,* H.R. 326, 97th Cong., 1st Sess. (1981); H.R. 865, 97th Cong., 1st Sess. (1981). In 1979, the Senate passed a similar provision, S. 450, § 11, 96th Cong., 1st Sess. (1979), as an attachment to a bill dealing with the Supreme Court's obligatory jurisdiction. The bill died in the House.

22. See Bator, *Congressional Power Over the Jurisdiction of the Federal Courts,* 27 Vill.L.Rev. 1030 (1981–82).

23. Paragraphs (2) and (3) of this Part focus on the power of Congress to limit Supreme Court jurisdiction; Paragraphs (4) and (5) on its power to limit lower court jurisdiction, and Paragraph (6) on its power to withdraw all jurisdiction from the federal courts.

But even assuming broad legislative power over remedies, might there not be times when the unavailability of a particular remedy (especially injunctive relief) would impose such hardship as to raise a serious constitutional issue? The problem was recognized, in a somewhat different context, as long ago as Ex Parte Young, 209 U.S. 123 (1908). In that decision, which allowed a federal court challenge to the validity of a state criminal statute, the Court stated: "[T]o impose upon a party interested the burden of obtaining a judicial decision of such a question ✱ ✱ ✱ only upon the condition that, if unsuccessful, he must suffer imprisonment and pay fines, as provided in these acts, is, in effect, to close up all approaches to the courts, and thus prevent any hearing upon the question ✱ ✱ ✱ [of constitutionality]" (p. 148).[24]

A similar question was raised by the unavailability of interlocutory relief in Lockerty v. Phillips, Part (D), Paragraph (2), *supra*. (Did the Court in that case assume that there was a more appropriate forum than the one in which the action had been brought to raise the constitutional issue? If so, was it correct in that assumption?) And the issue appeared once again in the selective service cases, involving pre-induction challenges to administrative draft classifications during the Vietnam War. See p. 406, note 24, *infra*.

Might not a statutory limitation on the availability of a particular remedy—in desegregation cases, for example—pose such an issue if the inability to grant that remedy prevents any meaningful relief for a constitutional wrong? Indeed, isn't the core of Marbury v. Madison implicated by a grant of jurisdiction that is coupled with a ban on the granting of effective relief?

(2) Professor Ratner, building on a phrase in Professor Hart's Dialogue (p. 394, *infra*), called the Jenner bill, note 13, *supra*, "clearly invalid," on the ground that Congress has no power to make exceptions to the appellate jurisdiction of the Supreme Court which would "negate" the Court's "essential constitutional functions of maintaining the uniformity and supremacy of federal law." Ratner, *Congressional Power Over the Appellate Jurisdiction of the Supreme Court*, 109 U.Pa.L.Rev. 157, 201–02 (1960) ("legislation that precludes Supreme Court review in every case involving a particular subject is an unconstitutional encroachment"). See also Ratner, *Majoritarian Constraints on Judicial Review: Congressional Control of Supreme Court Jurisdiction*, 27 Vill.L.Rev. 929 (1981–82). That theory was endorsed by Attorney General William French Smith in a letter to Senator Strom Thurmond, May 6, 1982, printed in 128 Cong.Rec. S. 4727 (Daily ed., May 6, 1982).[25]

Can this position be reconciled with the constitutional language? Berger, Congress v. The Supreme Court 285–96 (1969), and Merry, *Scope of the Supreme Court's Appellate Jurisdiction: Historical Basis*, 47 Minn.L.

---

24. See also the decisions in the area of First Amendment rights discussed in Monaghan, *First Amendment Due Process*, 83 Harv.L.Rev. 518, 520–32 (1970), and p. 402, note 15, *infra*.

25. In a variant of the "essential functions" argument, Professor Sager stresses the need for some federal court, either the Supreme Court or an inferior court, to be able to review "state court decisions that repudiate federal constitutional claims of right." Sager, *Foreword: Constitutional Limitations on Congress' Authority to Regulate the Jurisdiction of the Federal Courts*, 95 Harv.L.Rev. 17, 44 (1981); see *id.* at 42–60. Thus his position raises questions of the power of Congress to withdraw jurisdiction from all federal courts in certain kinds of cases. See Paragraph (6), *infra*.

Rev. 53 (1962), argued that the power to make exceptions to the appellate jurisdiction was intended exclusively to deal with the problem of appellate review of findings of fact by a jury.[26] But see Wechsler, *The Courts and the Constitution,* 65 Colum.L.Rev. 1001, 1005–06 (1965): "There is, to be sure, a school of thought that argues that 'exceptions' has a narrow meaning, not including cases that have constitutional dimension; or that the supremacy clause or the due process clause of the fifth amendment would be violated by an alteration of the jurisdiction motivated by hostility to the decisions of the Court. I see no basis for this view and think it antithetical to the plan of the Constitution for the courts—which was quite simply that the Congress would decide from time to time how far the federal judicial institution should be used within the limits of the federal judicial power; or, stated differently, how far judicial jurisdiction should be left to the state courts, bound as they are by the Constitution as 'the supreme Law of the Land * * * any Thing in the Constitution or Laws of any State to the Contrary notwithstanding.' Federal courts, including the Supreme Court, do not pass on constitutional questions because there is a special function vested in them to enforce the Constitution or police the other agencies of the government. They do so rather for the reason that they must decide a litigated issue that is otherwise within their jurisdiction and in doing so must give effect to the supreme law of the land. That is, at least, what Marbury v. Madison was all about. I have not heard that it has yet been superseded, though I confess I read opinions on occasion that do not exactly make its doctrine clear."

How would "essential function[s]" be defined if the program of Professor Ratner and others were to be adopted? Is providing uniform application of federal law an essential aspect of the Supreme Court's role? If so, how does one explain the significant gaps in Supreme Court jurisdiction left by the provisions of the Judiciary Act of 1789—especially the lack of jurisdiction to review decisions upholding claims of federal right? And if maintaining the supremacy of federal law is an essential function, is any scope left for the exceptions power in cases where there is an asserted conflict between federal law and state conduct? Does the essential functions position confuse "the familiar with the necessary, the desirable with the constitutionally mandated"? See Gunther, *Congressional Power to Curtail Federal Court Jurisdiction: An Opinionated Guide to the Ongoing Debate,* 36 Stan.L.Rev. 895, 905 (1984). *Cf.* Bator, note 22, *supra,* at 1039, suggesting that a statute depriving the Supreme Court of appellate jurisdiction over an important category of constitutional litigation would "violate the spirit of the Constitution, even if it would not violate its letter * * * because the structure contemplated by the instrument makes sense—and was thought to make sense—only on the premise that there would be a federal Supreme Court with the power to pronounce uniform and authoritative rules of law."

(3) Is it perhaps politically healthy that the limits of congressional power over Supreme Court appellate jurisdiction have never been completely clarified? Does the existence of congressional power of unspecified scope

---

26. Note the grammatical difficulties in limiting the exceptions power to questions of fact. Berger himself has substantially qualified his earlier position, especially with respect to matters arising under the Fourteenth Amendment. See Berger, Death Penalties 153–72 (1982); McAffee, *Berger v. The Supreme Court—The Implications of His Exceptions–Clause Odyssey,* 9 U.Dayton L.Rev. 219 (1984).

contribute to the maintenance of a desirable tension between Court and Congress?[27] In some circumstances, may not attempts to restrict jurisdiction be an appropriate and important way for the political branches to register disagreement with the Court and to channel and focus such contrary opinions in a way that will come to the Court's attention?[28] And is it not enormously significant that, ever since McCardle, such "attempts" have, in the main, been just that—that Congress has not significantly cut back the Supreme Court's jurisdiction in a "vindictive" manner despite the great unpopularity from time to time of some of its rulings?[29]

(4) With respect to the lower federal courts, the Supreme Court, in *Palmore v. United States*, 411 U.S. 389, 400–01 (1973), restated the traditional view. Quoting from *Cary v. Curtis*, 3 How. 236, 245 (U.S.1845), the Court said that Congress "was not constitutionally required to create inferior Art. III courts * * *. Nor, if inferior federal courts were created, was it required to invest them with all the jurisdiction it was authorized to bestow under Art. III."

Revisionist views continue to be expressed, however. See, *e.g.*, Eisenberg, *Congressional Authority to Restrict Federal Court Jurisdiction*, 83 Yale L.J. 498 (1974).[30] Professor Eisenberg asserted that the "national judiciary was intended * * * to be able to hear and to do justice in all cases within its jurisdiction" (p. 506). He then argued that since the Supreme Court can no longer perform this function alone, by reviewing every case that originates in state courts, it is "no longer reasonable to assert that Congress may simply abolish the lower federal courts" (p. 513), and concluded that the "power to curtail [jurisdiction] is limited to prudent steps which help avoid case overloads" (p. 516).

The fundamental premise of Madison's compromise was the perception that the extent to which lower federal courts were needed to assure the effectiveness of federal rights should be a matter for legislative judgment made from time to time rather than a matter for constitutional judgment made once for all time. See Bator, note 22, *supra*, at 1031. Thus the fact that conditions today are different from those in 1789 with respect to the need for and role of lower federal courts seems to support the wisdom of the compromise rather than furnish an excuse for its abandonment.

---

27. For analyses of this tension, see Stumpf, *Congressional Response to Supreme Court Rulings: The Interaction of Law and Politics*, 14 J.Pub.L. 377 (1965); Nagel, *Court–Curbing Periods in American History*, 18 Vand.L.Rev. 925 (1965); see also Murphy, *Congress and the Courts* (1962).

28. See *Hearings on the Supreme Court Before the Subcomm. on Separation of Powers of the Sen. Comm. on the Judiciary*, 90th Cong., 2d Sess. (1968), and especially the remarks of Professor Mishkin at 160–63, 202.

29. It has been suggested that the continuing legitimacy of the Court's role, and especially of judicial review, is greatly buttressed by the very existence of congressional power to curtail jurisdiction. See, *e.g.*, Black, Decision According to Law 18–19, 37–39 (1981); Wechsler, *The Appellate Jurisdiction of the Supreme Court: Reflections on the Law and the Logistics of Direct Review*, 34 Wash. & Lee L.Rev. 1043, 1044–49 (1977). But see Tribe, *Jurisdictional Gerrymandering: Zoning Disfavored Rights Out of the Federal Courts*, 16 Harv. C.R.–C.L.L.Rev. 129, 132–33 (1981).

30. See also Rotunda, *Congressional Power to Restrict the Jurisdiction of the Lower Federal Courts and the Problem of School Busing*, 64 Geo.L.J. 839 (1976) (arguing that Congress does not have unlimited power under Article III to place interstitial restrictions on the jurisdiction of the lower federal courts).

Has Congress in fact done such a poor job over the years in regulating lower court jurisdiction as to call for a major revision in constitutional thinking?

Compare the far narrower argument advanced in Redish & Woods, *Congressional Power to Control the Jurisdiction of Lower Federal Courts: A Critical Review and a New Synthesis,* 124 U.Pa.L.Rev. 45 (1975), discussed at pp. 490–91, *infra.*

(5) Assume, then, that a particular statute withdrawing jurisdiction from the lower federal courts does not violate any provision of Article III. Might it nevertheless violate some other provision of the Constitution? If so, does the court whose jurisdiction has been withdrawn by the invalid law have jurisdiction to declare its invalidity?

(a) If Congress were to add a proviso to § 1331 closing the doors of the federal courts in federal question cases to plaintiffs who were black, or Jewish, the provision would surely violate the equal protection component of the Fifth Amendment Due Process Clause. *Cf.* Bolling v. Sharpe, 347 U.S. 497 (1954). Could a district court then disregard the proviso and accept jurisdiction in such a case? [31] If so, would this rationale extend to a case in which the distinction was based not on a "suspect classification" like race, religion, or national origin but on one that seemed patently irrational, like height or weight?

(b) Following this analysis, suppose that a withdrawal of federal jurisdiction in a category of cases appeared to have—or was indeed intended to have—a disproportionate impact on access to federal courts by members of a class entitled to a high level of equal protection review. What if, for example, Congress were to withdraw federal district court jurisdiction in any case involving the racial composition of all or part of a public school system? Or involving the validity of any state or federal law relating to abortion? [32] Professor Gunther contends that the equal protection argument at this point has moved too easily from the invalidity of certain distinctions among *litigants* to an assault on differentiations based on *subject matter,* and that, as so extended, it threatens to engulf the power of Congress to choose among categories of cases under Article III. Gunther, Paragraph (2), *supra,* at 918–19.

(c) Professor Tribe has argued that any effort to single out cases involving a particular category of constitutional claims for exclusion from the federal courts—cases relating to "voluntary prayer in a public building," for example—constitutes the imposition of an impermissible burden on the underlying constitutional right being asserted in those cases.[33]

---

31. Would it make a difference if Congress, in reenacting § 1331 with the proviso, were to state that the proviso was not severable from the underlying jurisdictional grant?

32. It may be relevant to this question that the Supreme Court has never held that a law affecting the right to an abortion constitutes discrimination on grounds of sex in violation of the equal protection clause. *Cf.* Geduldig v. Aiello, 417 U.S. 484 (1974).

33. See Tribe, note 29, *supra,* at 142–43. A different argument against the singling out of particular constitutional claims for exclusion from federal jurisdiction is developed in Brilmayer & Underhill, *Congressional Obligation to Provide a Forum for Constitutional Claims: Discriminatory Jurisdictional Rules and the Conflict of Laws,* 69 Va.L.Rev. 819 (1983). The authors suggest an analogy to the decisions holding that state courts may not refuse to adjudicate claims on grounds that the claims were created by federal law or by the laws of other states. Similarly, they argue, Congress "cannot single out constitutional issues and exclude them from fed-

This argument rests heavily on the position that being required to litigate a federal question in a state court is a "burden." But given the deliberate decision of the Framers that the allocation of original jurisdiction over federal claims is for Congress to decide, what justifies the assertion that it is a "burden," from a constitutional perspective, to send a case to a state court? [34] There is no substantial question, is there, of the validity of 28 U.S.C. §§ 1341, 1342, precluding the district courts from entertaining certain constitutional challenges to state regulatory and taxing authority? (See Chap. X, Sec. 1, *infra.*) Or of the existing bar to the removal of all but a few state civil and criminal prosecutions on the basis of a federal defense? [35]

Is the burden argument strengthened if it can be shown that the motive behind the withdrawal was to undermine the continuing force of certain Supreme Court or lower court decisions? [36]

Aside from the obvious difficulties that inhere in any effort to establish the "motive" of a legislative act, Professor Gunther points to a "deeper issue"—"whether Congress acts with an unconstitutional motive when it redraws jurisdictional lines in part because it dislikes certain federal court decisions." In Gunther's view, "the basic structure of article III affords precisely that power to Congress * * *. Moreover, disaffection-based jurisdictional statutes have been sustained in the past. The Tax Injunction Act and the Norris–LaGuardia Act, for example, evolved from disagreements with the way federal courts were handling state tax and labor injunction cases, not merely from an abstract preference to have the law in those areas developed by state tribunals. The Supreme Court found no constitutional flaws with those congressional devices." Gunther, Paragraph (2), *supra,* at 919–20.

(6) The fact that Congress has not heretofore abused its power to restrict jurisdiction is no mere accident. There are substantial political

eral court jurisdiction without a sufficient reason" (p. 822).

This argument seems vulnerable to a charge of circularity. It asserts that Congress may not exclude constitutional claims from federal jurisdiction because the Constitution is a higher law than any act of Congress and does not permit exclusion in the absence of a good reason. But what is the source of the constitutional prohibition? And as the authors concede, their argument depends at least in part on the assumption "that Marbury [v. Madison] gives the Supreme Court the license to be the ultimate arbiter of the Constitution and not simply the power to decide cases and controversies before it according to constitutional values" (p. 831 n. 68).

34. Note the implicit assumption of the "burden" argument that state courts invariably, or at least characteristically, give less protection to federal rights than do federal courts—an assumption that not only "[flies] in the face of the original understanding (which viewed the state courts as ordinarily appropriate enforcers of federal law); it also is a questionable generalization today." Gunther, Paragraph (2), *supra,* at 918. See also Bator, *The State Courts and Federal Constitutional Litigation,* 22 Wm. & Mary L.Rev. 605, 606, 629–35 (1981); Tushnet & Jaff, *Why the Debate Over Congress' Power to Restrict the Jurisdiction of the Federal Courts is Unending,* 72 Geo.L.J. 1311, 1324–25 (1984). Compare Neuborne, *The Myth of Parity,* 90 Harv.L. Rev. 1105 (1977).

The question, of course, is a different one if a state court is unavailable. Apart from the issues raised by Tarble's Case, p. 484, *infra,* or by specific congressional attempts to withdraw state court jurisdiction, state court availability may be limited by the reach of process when the relevant events occur overseas. *Cf.* Johnson v. Eisentrager, pp. 422–23, *infra.*

35. For one of the few instances in which removal on the basis of a federal defense is available, see 28 U.S.C. § 1442.

36. See Ely, *Legislative and Administrative Motivation in Constitutional Law,* 79 Yale L.J. 1205, 1306–08 (1970). See also Gressman & Gressman, *Necessary and Proper Roots of Exceptions to Federal Jurisdiction,* 51 Geo.Wash.L.Rev. 495 (1983).

and practical obstacles to a complete withdrawal of jurisdiction: "To begin with, government cannot be run without the use of courts for the enforcement of coercive sanctions and within large areas it will be thought that federal tribunals are essential to administer federal law. Within that area, the opportunity for litigating constitutional defenses is built in and cannot be foreclosed. The same necessity for federal tribunals will be felt in many situations that do not involve proceedings for enforcement; it has led Congress in recent years to expand remedial jurisdiction by such measures as the Federal Declaratory Judgment Act, the Tucker Act, the Administrative Procedure Act and others I could name. The withdrawal of such jurisdiction would impinge adversely on so many varied interests that its durability can be assumed. Beyond this, if the jurisdiction of the Supreme Court alone is withdrawn in a given field, as happened in McCardle, issues are left to final resolution in the lower courts, which may, of course, reach contrary results in different sections of the country. If, in addition, all federal jurisdiction is withdrawn, the resolution is perforce left to the courts of fifty states, with even greater probability of contrariety in their decisions. How long would you expect such inconsistency in the interpretation of the law of the United States to be regarded as a tolerable situation? There is, moreover, still another difficulty. The lower courts or the state courts would still be faced with the decisions of the Supreme Court as precedents—decisions which that Court would now be quite unable to reverse or modify or even to explain. The jurisdictional withdrawal thus might work to freeze the very doctrines that had prompted its enactment, placing an intolerable moral burden on the lower courts.

"These are the reasons why congressional control of jurisdiction has so rarely been exerted as a method of expressing dissidence to constitutional decisions, even when such dissidence has won the sympathy of Congress." Wechsler, Paragraph (2), *supra*, at 1006–07.

(7) Two recent efforts have been made to revive aspects of Justice Story's thesis (see pp. 366–68, *supra*). In the first, Professor Clinton argues that Congress must allocate to the federal judiciary either original or appellate jurisdiction over every case within the scope of Article III "excluding, possibly, only those cases that Congress deemed to be so trivial that they would pose an unnecessary burden on both the federal judiciary and on the parties forced to litigate in federal court." Clinton, *A Mandatory View of Federal Jurisdiction: A Guided Quest for the Original Understanding of Article III,* 132 U.Pa.L.Rev. 741, 749–50 (1984); see also Clinton, *A Mandatory View of Federal Court Jurisdiction: Early Implementation and Departures from the Constitutional Plan,* 86 Colum.L.Rev. 1515 (1986). In the second, Professor Amar argues that "The judicial power of the United States must, as an absolute minimum, comprehend the subject matter jurisdiction to decide finally all cases involving federal questions, admiralty, or public ambassadors," and "may—but need not—extend to cases in the six other, party-defined, jurisdictional categories." Amar, *A Neo–Federalist View of Article III: Separating the Two Tiers of Federal Jurisdiction,* 65 B.U.L.Rev. 205, 229 (1985).[37]

37. Note that a legislative decision to deprive all federal courts of jurisdiction over a particular category of constitutional claims is subject to challenge not only under Article III but also under the "burden" theory outlined in Paragraph 5(c), *supra.* Is the argument stronger when no federal court is open to the assertion of a constitutional claim?

Clinton draws on the records of the Constitutional Convention and the ratification process to support his view that the uses of "shall" in Article III were designed to impose some kind of obligation on the legislature, and not merely to afford it a choice. But the broad scope of the obligation that he infers runs into difficulties in interpreting the Exceptions Clause and in explaining the large gaps left in federal jurisdiction by the Judiciary Act of 1789.[38]

Amar's thesis, which is fully and powerfully presented, is less subject to these difficulties. He places considerable emphasis (as did Story in part of his discussion) on the use of the word "all" in the first three categories of cases listed in Article III. And he supports his argument by pointing to the critical importance of these three categories and to the "structural superiority" of federal judges, whose tenure and salary are constitutionally assured.[39]

Amar argues forcefully that his thesis is the best interpretation of Article III, but admits that it is not "patently self-evident" (p. 230 n. 86). And indeed, it raises difficult questions of its own. If the distinction between the two tiers was so significant, why is there so little evidence of explicit recognition of that distinction in contemporary commentary or in the available history of the 1789 Act?[40] Why did that Act leave some significant gaps in federal court jurisdiction, even in the "mandatory" categories?[41] Why did the drafters of Article III single out cases affecting

38. For an exhaustive study of the history of that Act which challenges Clinton's view of federal jurisdiction, see Casto, *The First Congress's Understanding of its Authority over the Federal Courts' Jurisdiction,* 26 B.C.L.Rev. 1101 (1985). This position is in turn challenged by Clinton's 1986 study in the Columbia Law Review (cited in text), in which he argues that the Act "departed remarkably little from the conception of an independent federal judiciary with constitutionally defined and demarcated jurisdiction" (86 Colum.L.Rev. at 1520). (He argues further in this article that "the notion of congressional power over the scope of federal jurisdiction originated in a peculiar abdication of judicial independence by the Supreme Court, particularly in certain decisions of Chief Justices Taney and Chase that were not fully consistent with prior judicial precedent or thought" (*id.*).)

For Clinton's discussion of the Exceptions Clause, see 132 U.Pa.L.Rev. at 776–78.

39. For similar stress on these factors in support of the view that some federal court must be available for claims of constitutional right, see Sager, note 25, *supra,* at 61–68. But see Redish, *Constitutional Limitations on Congressional Power to Control Federal Jurisdiction: A Reaction to Professor Sager,* 77 Nw.U.L.Rev. 143, 150–54 (1982).

40. One recent study of the history of the 1789 Act reveals no references to the distinction. Casto, note 38, *supra.* More-

over, Justice Story, who at one point in Martin v. Hunter's Lessee appeared to emphasize the distinction, said at another point in the same opinion that "the constitution has not singled out any class [of cases] on which Congress are bound to act in preference to others" (1 Wheat. at 330).

41. Congress provided no general federal question jurisdiction in the lower federal courts, and under section 25, the Supreme Court's appellate jurisdiction over the state courts did not extend to cases in which the federal claim had been *upheld.* Amar struggles valiantly with this gap (65 B.U.L. Rev. at 262–64), but recognizes its difficulty. Moreover the Supreme Court itself appears to have understood that the gap was wholly within Congress's prerogative. See, *e.g.,* Commonwealth Bank v. Griffith, 14 Pet. 56 (U.S. 1840).

In cases involving ambassadors, etc., section 13 of the 1789 Act allowed such a suit to be brought *by* an ambassador in a state court, and once it was, neither side could get it into a federal court by removal or appeal. Why does it suffice for Article III purposes that one of the parties has one opportunity (at the outset) to choose a federal court? Do those purposes in this context relate only to the plaintiff's original choice? (A similar question might be raised about the "saving to suitors" clause of the admiralty provision of section 9 of the 1789 Act.) Moreover, even federal concurrent jurisdiction of actions brought *by* ambassadors, etc., was not coextensive with federal exclusive jurisdiction of actions ambassadors, etc., for mandatory treatment and leave Congress an option in cases in which the United States was a party? And what are the present-day implications of the thesis for the broad scope of the Supreme Court's discretion to deny certiorari? [42] Or for the authority of Congress to delegate certain matters to the final decision of a non-Article III federal tribunal? Even the most ardent advocates of a constitutional right to judicial review have not claimed that any matter that can be considered a "case" within the scope of Article III is for that reason alone beyond the authority of Congress to delegate to an administrative agency for final decision.

CROWELL v. BENSON

285 U.S. 22, 52 S.Ct. 285, 76 L.Ed. 598 (1932).
Certiorari to the Circuit Court of Appeals for the Fifth Circuit.

MR. CHIEF JUSTICE HUGHES delivered the opinion of the Court.

This suit was brought in the District Court to enjoin the enforcement of an award made by petitioner Crowell, as Deputy Commissioner of the United States Employees' Compensation Commission, in favor of the petitioner Knudsen and against the respondent Benson. The award was made under the Longshoremen's and Harbor Workers' Compensation Act (Act of March 4, 1927, c. 509, 44 Stat. 1424, U.S.C. tit. 33, §§ 901–950), and rested upon the finding of the deputy commissioner that Knudsen was injured while in the employ of Benson and performing service upon the navigable waters of the United States. The complainant alleged that the award was contrary to law for the reason that Knudsen was not at the time of his injury an employee of the complainant and his claim was not "within the jurisdiction" of the Deputy Commissioner. An amended complaint charged that the act was unconstitutional upon the grounds that it violated the due process clause of the Fifth Amendment, the provision of the Seventh Amendment as to trial by jury, that of the Fourth Amendment as to unreasonable search and seizure, and the provisions of article 3 with respect to the judicial power of the United States. The District Judge denied motions to dismiss and granted a hearing de novo upon the facts and the law, expressing the opinion that the act would be invalid if not construed to permit such a hearing. The case was transferred to the admiralty docket, answers were filed presenting the issue as to the fact of employment, and, the evidence of both parties having been heard, the District Court decided that Knudsen was not in the employ of the petitioner and restrained the enforcement of the award. 33 F.2d 137; 38 F.2d 306. The decree was affirmed by the Circuit Court of Appeals [45 F.2d 66] and this Court granted writs of certiorari. 283 U.S. 814.

The question of the validity of the act may be considered in relation to (1) its provisions defining substantive rights and (2) its procedural requirements. * * *

brought *against* them (since the latter extended to suits involving their domestic servants).

42. Commentators have raised in other contexts the question whether the Su-

preme Court's present-day certiorari jurisdiction to review state court decisions is sufficient to enable it to fulfill the role contemplated for it by the Framers. See, *e.g.*, Eisenberg, Paragraph (4), *supra*.

[The first part of the opinion sustains the substantive provisions of the Act as a proper exercise of "the general authority of the Congress to alter or revise the maritime law which shall prevail throughout the country".

[The second part of the opinion begins by describing the procedural provisions of the Act and the provisions for judicial review. Awards may be made by a deputy commissioner only after investigation, notice and hearing. They may be enforced by a federal district court, on application of beneficiaries or of the deputy commissioner, if found to have been "made and served in accordance with law". Or they may be suspended or set aside, in whole or in part, on application of a respondent if "not in accordance with law".]

Second. The objections to the procedural requirements of the act relate to the extent of the administrative authority which it confers. * * *

(1) The contention under the due process clause of the Fifth Amendment relates to the determination of questions of fact. Rulings of the deputy commissioner upon questions of law are without finality. * * *

Apart from cases involving constitutional rights to be appropriately enforced by proceedings in court, there can be no doubt that the act contemplates that as to questions of fact, arising with respect to injuries to employees within the purview of the act, the findings of the deputy commissioner, supported by evidence and within the scope of his authority, shall be final. To hold otherwise would be to defeat the obvious purpose of the legislation to furnish a prompt, continuous, expert, and inexpensive method for dealing with a class of questions of fact which are peculiarly suited to examination and determination by an administrative agency specially assigned to that task. The object is to secure within the prescribed limits of the employer's liability an immediate investigation and a sound practical judgment, and the efficacy of the plan depends upon the finality of the determinations of fact with respect to the circumstances, nature, extent, and consequences of the employee's injuries and the amount of compensation that should be awarded. And this finality may also be regarded as extending to the determination of the question of fact whether the injury "was occasioned solely by the intoxication of the employee or by the willful intention of the employee to injure or kill himself or another." While the exclusion of compensation in such cases is found in what are called "coverage" provisions of the act (section 3 [33 U.S.C.A. § 903]), the question of fact still belongs to the contemplated routine of administration, for the case is one of employment within the scope of the act, and the cause of the injury sustained by the employee as well as its character and effect must be ascertained in applying the provisions for compensation. The use of the administrative method for these purposes, assuming due notice, proper opportunity to be heard, and that findings are based upon evidence, falls easily within the principle of the decisions sustaining similar procedure against objections under the due process clauses of the Fifth and Fourteenth Amendments. * * *

(2) The contention based upon the judicial power of the United States, as extended "to all cases of admiralty and maritime jurisdiction" (Const. Art. III), presents a distinct question. * * *

The question in the instant case, in this aspect, can be deemed to relate only to determinations of fact. The reservation of legal questions is to the same court that has jurisdiction in admiralty, and the mere fact that the court is not described as such is unimportant. * * * The Congress did not attempt to define questions of law, and the generality of the description leaves no doubt of the intention to reserve to the Federal court full authority to pass upon all matters which this Court had held to fall within that category. There is thus no attempt to interfere with, but rather provision is made to facilitate, the exercise by the court of its jurisdiction to deny effect to any administrative finding which is without evidence, or "contrary to the indisputable character of the evidence," or where the hearing is "inadequate," or "unfair," or arbitrary in any respect. Interstate Commerce Commission v. Louisville R.R. Co., *supra,* at pages 91, 92 of 227 U.S.; Tagg Bros. & Moorhead v. United States, *supra.*

As to determinations of fact, the distinction is at once apparent between cases of private right and those which arise between the government and persons subject to its authority in connection with the performance of the constitutional functions of the executive or legislative departments. The Court referred to this distinction in Murray's Lessee v. Hoboken Land & Improvement Company, *supra,* pointing out that "there are matters, involving public rights, which may be presented in such form that the judicial power is capable of acting on them, and which are susceptible of judicial determination, but which congress may or may not bring within the cognizance of the courts of the United States, as it may deem proper." Thus the Congress, in exercising the powers confided to it, may establish "legislative" courts (as distinguished from "constitutional courts in which the judicial power conferred by the Constitution can be deposited") which are to form part of the government of territories or of the District of Columbia, or to serve as special tribunals "to examine and determine various matters, arising between the government and others, which from their nature do not require judicial determination and yet are susceptible of it." But "the mode of determining matters of this class is completely within congressional control. Congress may reserve to itself the power to decide, may delegate that power to executive officers, or may commit it to judicial tribunals." Ex parte Bakelite Corporation, 279 U.S. 438, 451. Familiar illustrations of administrative agencies created for the determination of such matters are found in connection with the exercise of the congressional power as to interstate and foreign commerce, taxation, immigration, the public lands, public health, the facilities of the post office, pensions, and payments to veterans.

The present case does not fall within the categories just described, but is one of private right, that is, of the liability of one individual to another under the law as defined. But, in cases of that sort, there is no requirement that, in order to maintain the essential attributes of the judicial power, all determinations of fact in constitutional courts shall be made by judges. On the common-law side of the federal courts, the aid of juries is not only deemed appropriate but is required by the Constitution itself. In cases of equity and admiralty, it is historic practice to call to the assistance of the courts, without the consent of the parties, masters, and commissioners or assessors, to pass upon certain classes of questions, as, for example, to take and state an account or to find the amount of damages. * * *

* * * The statute has a limited application, being confined to the relation of master and servant, and the method of determining the questions of fact, which arise in the routine of making compensation awards to

employees under the act, is necessary to its effective enforcement. The act itself, where it applies, establishes the measure of the employer's liability, thus leaving open for determination the questions of fact as to the circumstances, nature, extent and consequences of the injuries sustained by the employee for which compensation is to be made in accordance with the prescribed standards. Findings of fact by the deputy commissioner upon such questions are closely analogous to the findings of the amount of damages that are made according to familiar practice by commissioners or assessors, and the reservation of full authority to the court to deal with matters of law provides for the appropriate exercise of the judicial function in this class of cases. For the purposes stated, we are unable to find any constitutional obstacle to the action of the Congress in availing itself of a method shown by experience to be essential in order to apply its standards to the thousands of cases involved, thus relieving the courts of a most serious burden while preserving their complete authority to insure the proper application of the law.

③ What has been said thus far relates to the determination of claims of employees within the purview of the act. A different question is presented where the determinations of fact are fundamental or "jurisdictional," [17] in the sense that their existence is a condition precedent to the operation of the statutory scheme. These fundamental requirements are that the injury occur upon the navigable waters of the United States and that the relation of master and servant exist. These conditions are indispensable to the application of the statute, not only because the Congress has so provided explicitly (section 3), but also because the power of the Congress to enact the legislation turns upon the existence of these conditions. * * *

In relation to these basic facts, the question is not the ordinary one as to the propriety of provision for administrative determinations. Nor have we simply the question of due process in relation to notice and hearing. It is rather a question of the appropriate maintenance of the federal judicial power in requiring the observance of constitutional restrictions. It is the question whether the Congress may substitute for constitutional courts, in which the judicial power of the United States is vested, an administrative agency—in this instance a single deputy commissioner—for the final determination of the existence of the facts upon which the enforcement of the constitutional rights of the citizen depend. The recognition of the utility and convenience of administrative agencies for the investigation and finding of facts within their proper province, and the support of their authorized action, does not require the conclusion that there is no limitation of their use, and that the Congress could completely oust the courts of all determinations of fact by vesting the authority to make them with finality in its own instrumentalities or in the executive department. That would be to sap the judicial power as it exists under the federal Constitution, and to establish a government of a bureaucratic character alien to our system, wherever fundamental rights depend, as not infrequently they do depend,

---

17. The term "jurisdictional," although frequently used, suggests analogies which are not complete when the reference is to administrative officials or bodies. See Interstate Commerce Commission v. Humboldt Steamship Co., 224 U.S. 474, 484. In relation to administrative agencies, the question in a given case is whether it falls within the scope of the authority validly conferred.

upon the facts, and finality as to facts becomes in effect finality in law.
* * *

Even where the subject lies within the general authority of the Congress, the propriety of a challenge by judicial proceedings of the determinations of fact deemed to be jurisdictional, as underlying the authority of executive officers, has been recognized. When proceedings are taken against a person under the military law, and enlistment is denied, the issue has been tried and determined de novo upon habeas corpus. In re Grimley, 137 U.S. 147, 154, 155. * * *

In cases brought to enforce constitutional rights, the judicial power of the United States necessarily extends to the independent determination of all questions, both of fact and law, necessary to the performance of that supreme function. The case of confiscation is illustrative, the ultimate conclusion almost invariably depending upon the decisions of questions of fact. This court has held the owner to be entitled to "a fair opportunity for submitting that issue to a judicial tribunal for determination upon its own independent judgment as to both law and facts." Ohio Valley Water Company v. Ben Avon Borough, *supra.* * * * Jurisdiction in the executive to order deportation exists only if the person arrested is an alien, and while, if there were jurisdiction, the findings of fact of the executive department would be conclusive, the claim of citizenship "is a denial of an essential jurisdictional fact" both in the statutory and the constitutional sense, and a writ of habeas corpus will issue "to determine the status." Persons claiming to be citizens of the United States "are entitled to a judicial determination of their claims," said this Court in Ng Fung Ho v. White, *supra*, at page 285 of 259 U.S., and in that case the cause was remanded to the federal District Court "for trial in that court of the question of citizenship." * * *

When the validity of an act of the Congress is drawn in question, and even if a serious doubt of constitutionality is raised, it is a cardinal principle that this Court will first ascertain whether a construction of the statute is fairly possible by which the question may be avoided. We are of the opinion that such a construction is permissible and should be adopted in the instant case. * * *

In the absence of any provision as to the finality of the determination by the deputy commissioner of the jurisdictional fact of employment, the statute is open to the construction that the court in determining whether a compensation order is in accordance with law may determine the fact of employment which underlies the operation of the statute. And, to remove the question as to validity, we think that the statute should be so construed. * * *

Assuming that the federal court may determine for itself the existence of these fundamental or jurisdictional facts, we come to the question, Upon what record is the determination to be made? * * * We think that the essential independence of the exercise of the judicial power of the United States in the enforcement of constitutional rights requires that the federal court should determine such an issue upon its own record and the facts elicited before it. * * *

We are of the opinion that the District Court did not err in permitting a trial de novo on the issue of employment. Upon that issue the witnesses who had testified before the deputy commissioner and other witnesses were heard by the District Court. The writ of certiorari was not granted to review the particular facts, but to pass upon the question of principle. With respect to the facts, the two courts below are in accord, and we find no reason to disturb their decision.

Decree affirmed.

MR. JUSTICE BRANDEIS (dissenting).

[The following excerpt from the long dissenting opinion indicates only one of the grounds of dissent.]

Sixth. Even if the constitutional power of Congress to provide compensation is limited to cases in which the employer-employee relation exists, I see no basis for a contention that the denial of the right to a trial de novo upon the issue of employment is in any manner subversive of the independence of the federal judicial power. Nothing in the Constitution, or in any prior decision of this Court to which attention has been called, lends support to the doctrine that a judicial finding of any fact involved in any civil proceeding to enforce a pecuniary liability may not be made upon evidence introduced before a properly constituted administrative tribunal, or that a determination so made may not be deemed an independent judicial determination. Congress has repeatedly exercised authority to confer upon the tribunals which it creates, be they administrative bodies or courts of limited jurisdiction, the power to receive evidence concerning the facts upon which the exercise of federal power must be predicated, and to determine whether those facts exist. The power of Congress to provide by legislation for liability under certain circumstances subsumes the power to provide for the determination of the existence of those circumstances. It does not depend upon the absolute existence in reality of any fact.

It is true that, so far as Knudsen is concerned, proof of the existence of the employer-employee relation is essential to recovery under the act. But under the definition laid down in Noble v. Union River Logging R. Co., 147 U.S. 165, 173, 174, that fact is not jurisdictional. It is quasi-jurisdictional. The existence of a relation of employment is a question going to the applicability of the substantive law, not to the jurisdiction of the tribunal. Jurisdiction is the power to adjudicate between the parties concerning the subject-matter. Compare Reynolds v. Stockton, 140 U.S. 254, 268. Obviously, the deputy commissioner had not only the power but the duty to determine whether the employer-employee relation existed. * * *

The "judicial power" of article 3 of the Constitution is the power of the federal government, and not of any inferior tribunal. There is in that article nothing which requires any controversy to be determined as of first instance in the federal District Courts. The jurisdiction of those courts is subject to the control of Congress. Matters which may be placed within their jurisdiction may instead be committed to the state courts. If there be any controversy to which the judicial power extends that may not be subjected to the conclusive determination of administrative bodies or federal legislative courts, it is not because of any prohibition against the diminution of the jurisdiction of the federal District Courts as such, but because, under certain circumstances, the constitutional requirement of due process is a requirement of judicial process. An accumulation of precedents, already referred to, has established that in civil proceedings involving property rights determination of facts may constitutionally be made otherwise than judicially; and necessarily that evidence as to such facts may be taken outside of a court. I do not conceive that article 3 has properly any bearing upon the question presented in this case. ＊ ＊ ＊

MR. JUSTICE STONE and MR. JUSTICE ROBERTS join in this opinion.[1]

A DIALOGUE ON THE POWER OF CONGRESS TO LIMIT THE JURISDICTION OF FEDERAL COURTS *

A. Limitations as to Which Court Has Jurisdiction

Q. Does the Constitution give people any right to proceed or be proceeded against, in the first instance, in a federal rather than a state court?

A. It's hard to see how the answer can be anything but no, in view of cases like Sheldon v. Sill and Lauf v. E.G. Shinner & Co., and in view of the language and history of the Constitution itself. Congress seems to have plenary power to limit federal jurisdiction when the consequence is merely to force proceedings to be brought, if at all, in a state court.

Q. But suppose the state court disclaims any jurisdiction?

A. If federal rights are involved, perhaps the state courts are under a constitutional obligation to vindicate them. There are cases, like Testa v. Katt, 330 U.S. 386 (1947), p. 492, *infra,* and General Oil Co. v. Crain, 209 U.S. 211 (1908), p. 586, *infra,* which seem to say so.

Q. But even assuming the obligation, and I gather it's something of an assumption, only the Supreme Court can enforce it if the state courts balk. The McCardle case says that the appellate jurisdiction of the Supreme Court is entirely within Congressional control.

A. You read the McCardle case for all it might be worth rather than the least it has to be worth, don't you?

Q. No, I read it in terms of the language of the Constitution and the antecedent theory that the Court articulated in explaining its decision. This seems to me to lead inevitably to the same result, whatever jurisdiction is denied to the Court.

A. You would treat the Constitution, then, as authorizing exceptions which engulf the rule, even to the point of eliminating the appellate jurisdiction altogether. How preposterous!

Q. If you think an "exception" implies some residuum of jurisdiction, Congress could meet that test by excluding everything but patent cases. This is so absurd, and it is so impossible to lay down any measure of a

---

1. For developments since Crowell on the authority of Congress to allocate power among federal tribunals, see Subsection B, *infra.*

* The text of the late Professor Henry M. Hart's celebrated "Dialogue" has been retained in this edition unchanged from the first edition. The reader must remember that the text speaks as of 1953. Since then, much has happened, and much has been written. Some of these developments are explored in the Note at p. 366, *supra.*

In addition, the editors of this edition have made changes in the footnotes to the Dialogue; some material from the original has been omitted, and much updating material, including references to critical commentary, has been added. (The omissions are not indicated; significant additions are in brackets.) Those interested in the original documentation should consult: Hart, *The Power of Congress to Limit the Jurisdiction of Federal Courts: An Exercise in Dialectic,* 66 Harv.L.Rev. 1362 (1953).

necessary reservation, that it seems to me the language of the Constitution must be taken as vesting plenary control in Congress.

A. It's not impossible for me to lay down a measure. The measure is simply that the exceptions must not be such as will destroy the essential role of the Supreme Court in the constitutional plan. McCardle, you will remember, meets that test. The circuit courts of the United States were still open in habeas corpus. And the Supreme Court itself could still entertain petitions for the writ which were filed with it in the first instance.[1]

Q. The measure seems pretty indeterminate to me.

A. Ask yourself whether it is any more so than the tests which the Court has evolved to meet other hard situations. But whatever the difficulties of the test, they are less, are they not, than the difficulties of reading the Constitution as authorizing its own destruction?

Q. Has the Supreme Court ever done or said anything to suggest that it is prepared to adopt the view you are stating?

A. No, it's never had any occasion to. Congress so far has never tried to destroy the Constitution.

Q. Passing to another question, does the Constitution give people any right to proceed or be proceeded against in one inferior federal constitutional court rather than another?

A. As to civil plaintiffs, no. Congress has plenary power to distribute jurisdiction among such inferior federal constitutional courts as it chooses to establish.

As to civil defendants, the answer almost certainly is also no. To be sure, doubts are occasionally suggested about the validity in all circumstances of nation-wide service of process, but they don't seem to me to have much substance.[2]

As to criminal defendants, of course, the answer is controlled by the express language of the Constitution—Article III, Sec. 2, Par. 3, and the Sixth Amendment.

Q. Does the Constitution give people any right to proceed or be proceeded against, in the first instance, in an inferior federal constitutional court rather than a federal legislative court?

A. As to criminal defendants charged with offenses committed in one of the states, surely.[3] As to others, it's hard to say. The answer may well vary for civil plaintiffs and civil defendants. And it must vary, must it not,

---

1. Ex parte Yerger, 365, note 1, *supra.*

2. See Chap. XIV, Sec. 2, *infra.*

3. [Since 1955, several decisions have significantly narrowed the power of Congress to determine what offenses may be tried (at least in peacetime) by military courts martial. See United States ex rel. Toth v. Quarles, 350 U.S. 11 (1955) (Constitution forbids trial by court martial of a civilian, discharged from the armed forces, for an offense committed while abroad before discharge); Reid v. Covert, 354 U.S. 1 (1957) (civilian dependents may not be subjected to court martial, at least in capital cases, for offenses committed overseas);

Kinsella v. United States ex rel. Singleton, 361 U.S. 234 (1960) (extending Reid to non-capital offenses). A later decision, O'Callahan v. Parker, 395 U.S. 258 (1969) (a soldier may not constitutionally be court martialed for the attempted rape of a civilian allegedly committed while the soldier was on leave in Hawaii), was overruled in Solorio v. United States, 107 S.Ct. 2924 (1987).

[For comment on the first three of these cases, see Bishop, *Court–Martial Jurisdiction Over Military–Civilian Hybrids,* 112 U.Pa.L.Rev. 317 (1964).]

according to the nature of the right in question and the availability and scope of review in a constitutional court? [4]

B. Limitations of Jurisdiction to Give Particular Kinds of Remedies

Q. The power of Congress to regulate jurisdiction gives it a pretty complete power over remedies, doesn't it? To deny a remedy all Congress needs to do is to deny jurisdiction to any court to give the remedy.

A. That question is highly multifarious. If what you are asking is whether the power to regulate jurisdiction isn't, in effect, a power to deny rights which otherwise couldn't be denied, why don't you come right out and ask it?

Before you do, however, I'll take advantage of the question to make a point that may help in the later discussion. The denial of *any* remedy is one thing—that raises the question we're postponing. But the denial of one remedy while another is left open, or the substitution of one for another, is very different. It must be plain that Congress necessarily has a wide choice in the selection of remedies, and that a complaint about action of this kind can rarely be of constitutional dimension. [5]

Q. Why is that plain?

A. History has a lot to do with it. Take, for example, the tradition of our law that preventive relief is the exception rather than the rule. That naturally makes it hard to hold that anybody has a constitutional right to an injunction or a declaratory judgment.

But the basic reason, I suppose, is the great variety of possible remedies and the even greater variety of reasons why in different situations a legislature can fairly prefer one to another. That usually makes it hard to say, when one procedure has been provided, that it was unreasonable to make it exclusive. Witness, for example, the Yakus case and, even more strikingly, the more familiar examples cited in the Yakus opinion.

Q. Please spell that out a little bit.

A. Tax remedies furnish one of the best illustrations.

More than a hundred years ago the Supreme Court distressed Justice Story and many other people by holding that Congress had withdrawn the traditional right of action against a collector of customs for duties claimed to have been exacted illegally. Cary v. Curtis, 3 How. 236 (U.S.1845). Congress soon showed that it had never intended to do this, by restoring the right of action. But meanwhile the misunderstanding of the statute had produced a notable constitutional decision.

Story thought it unconstitutional to abolish the right of action against the collector. The majority opinion by Justice Daniel poses very nicely the apparent dilemma which is the main problem of this discussion. It states the contention that the construction adopted would attribute to Congress

---

4. [Consider the relevance to this question of Crowell v. Benson and of the material on legislative courts, Subsection B, *infra*. See also Jaffe, Judicial Control of Administrative Action 87–94 (1965).]

5. [The law of remedies, especially for invasion of certain constitutionally protected rights, has developed considerably since this sentence was written. See the discussion at pp. 379–80, *supra*, and authorities cited in notes 7, 15, 24, *infra*. As those materials indicate, there may in some circumstances be a right to adjudication in advance of the imposition of any sanction.]

purposes which "would be repugnant to the Constitution, inasmuch as they would debar the citizen of his right to resort to the courts of justice". In a bow to this position, he said:

" * * * The supremacy of the Constitution over all officers and authorities, both of the federal and state governments, and the sanctity of the rights guaranteed by it, none will question. These are *concessa* on all sides."

But then Justice Daniel stated the other horn of the dilemma as if it were an answer:

" * * * The objection above referred to admits of the most satisfactory refutation. This may be found in the following positions, familiar in this and most other governments, viz: that the government, as a general rule, claims an exemption from being sued in its own courts. That although, as being charged with the administration of the laws, it will resort to those courts as means of securing this great end, it will not permit itself to be impleaded therein, save in instances forming conceded and express exceptions. Secondly, in the doctrine so often ruled in this court that the judicial power of the United States, although it has its origin in the Constitution, is (except in enumerated instances, applicable exclusively to this court) dependent for its distribution and organization, and for the modes of its exercise, entirely upon the action of Congress, who possess the sole power of creating tribunals (inferior to the Supreme Court) for the exercise of the judicial power, and of investing them with jurisdiction either limited, concurrent, or exclusive, and of withholding jurisdiction from them in the exact degrees and character which to Congress may seem proper for the public good. To deny this position would be to elevate the judicial over the legislative branch of the government, and to give to the former powers limited by its own discretion merely." 3 How. at 245.

Q. I can't see how to reconcile those two horns. How did Justice Daniel do it?

A. He escaped by way of the power to select remedies. He said:

" * * * The claimant had his option to refuse payment; the detention of the goods for the adjustment of duties, being an incident of probable occurrence, to avoid this it could not be permitted to effect the abrogation of a public law, or a system of public policy essentially connected with the general action of the government. The claimant, moreover, was not without other modes of redress had he chosen to adopt them. He might have asserted his right to the possession of the goods, or his exemption from the duties demanded, either by replevin, or in an action of detinue, or perhaps by an action of trover, upon tendering the amount of duties admitted by him to be legally due. The legitimate inquiry before this court is not whether all right of action has been taken away from the party, and the court responds to no such inquiry." [6]

---

6. 3 How. at 250. Neither did the Court respond to any such question in Murray's Lessee v. Hoboken Land & Improvement Co., 18 How. 272 (U.S.1856). It upheld a summary procedure, without benefit of the courts, for the collection by the United States of moneys claimed to be due from one of its customs collectors. Justice Curtis' opinion has a much-quoted statement carefully limiting the holding, and foreshadowing later developments (p. 284):

"To avoid misconstruction upon so grave a subject, we think it proper to state that we do not consider Congress can either withdraw from judicial cognizance any matter which, from its nature, is the subject of a suit at the common law, or in equity, or admiralty; nor, on the other

Q. Why bother with an old case that ducked the issue that way? What is today's law? Has a taxpayer got a constitutional right to litigate the legality of a tax or hasn't he?

A. Personally, I think he has. But I can't cite any really square decision for the very reason I'm trying to tell you. The multiplicity of remedies, and the fact that Congress has seldom if ever tried to take them all away, has prevented the issue from ever being squarely presented.

For example, history and the necessities of revenue alike make it clear that the government must have constitutional power to make people pay their taxes first and litigate afterward. Summary distraint to compel payment is proper. Springer v. United States, 102 U.S. 586 (1880); Phillips v. Commissioner, 283 U.S. 589 (1931). And injunctions against collection can be forbidden. Snyder v. Marks, 109 U.S. 189 (1883). But these decisions all proceeded on the express assumption that the taxpayer had other remedies.

Correspondingly, a remedy after payment may be denied if the taxpayer had a remedy before, as Cary v. Curtis shows. Or the remedy may be conditioned upon following exactly a prescribed procedure. Rock Island, Arkansas & Louisiana Ry. v. United States, 254 U.S. 141 (1920).

Q. The taxpayer has to watch out, then, or he'll lose his rights.

A. He certainly does. As Justice Holmes said in the Rock Island case, "Men must turn square corners when dealing with the government." That's true of constitutional rights generally. Witness Yakus again, and the cases on proper presentation of federal questions in state courts. There isn't often a constitutional right to a second bite at the apple.

Q. Why do you think there is a right even to one bite in tax cases?

A. For reasons of principle, which I'll develop later. And on the basis of some authority, which you'll find in a footnote.[7]

hand, can it bring under the judicial power a matter which, from its nature, is not a subject for judicial determination. At the same time there are matters, involving public rights, which may be presented in such form that the judicial power is capable of acting on them, and which are susceptible of judicial determination, but which Congress may or may not bring within the cognizance of the courts of the United States, as it may deem proper. * * *"

[For developments since Murray's Lessee on the question of the permissible fora for the adjudication of "public rights," see Crowell v. Benson, *supra; Note on Legislative Courts*, p. 465, *infra.*]

7. Among federal tax decisions the authority consists of several cases which could readily have been disposed of on the ground that the taxpayer had no right to a judicial hearing if the Court had been of that opinion, but in which the Court was at pains to show that a right satisfying the requirements of due process had been accorded. See, in particular, Graham & Foster v. Goodcell, 282 U.S. 409 (1931); and

Anniston Mfg. Co. v. Davis, 301 U.S. 337 (1937).

And the Court has several times held that the due process clause of the Fourteenth Amendment entitles the taxpayer to an opportunity to contest the legality of state taxes. *E.g.*, Central of Georgia Ry. v. Wright, 207 U.S. 127 (1907); Brinkerhoff–Faris Co. v. Hill, 281 U.S. 673 (1930).

[*Cf.* the dictum in Societe Internationale v. Rogers, 357 U.S. 197, 210–11 (1957): "* * * petitioner's position is * * * analogous to that of a defendant, for it belatedly challenges the Government's action by now protesting against a seizure and seeking the recovery of assets which were summarily possessed by the Alien Property Custodian without the opportunity for protest by any party claiming that seizure was unjustified under the Trading with the Enemy Act. Past decisions of this Court emphasize that this summary power to seize property which is believed to be enemy-owned is rescued from constitutional invalidity under the Due Process and Just Compensation Clauses of the Fifth Amendment only by those provisions of the

Q. I can find that unconvincing without even looking at your footnote. Granting the right, you still have to reckon separately with the power of Congress to prevent its vindication by controlling jurisdiction. May I remind you of Sheldon and McCardle?

A. There you go oversimplifying again.

C. The Bearing of Sovereign Immunity

Q. Well, if it's too simple for you, let me complicate it a little bit. Justice Daniel mentioned sovereign immunity in Cary v. Curtis. That gives a double reason, doesn't it, why Congress has an absolute power over legal relations between the government and private persons? If it doesn't want to defeat private rights by regulating the jurisdiction of the federal courts, it can do it by withholding the government's consent to suit.

A. I can't deny that that does complicate things. But the power of withholding consent to suit isn't as absolute as it seems.

Q. What mitigates it?

A. You have to remember, in the first place, that the immunity is only to suits against the government. This isn't the place to go into the question of what constitutes such a suit.[8] My point now is that the possibility remains, as Cary v. Curtis indicates, of a personal action against an official who commits a wrong in the name of the government.[9] Wherever the applicable substantive law allows such a remedy, the government may be forced to protect its officers by providing a remedy against itself. The validity of any protection it tries to give may depend on its doing so—as, indeed, the validity of other parts of its program. Consider, for example, the possibility that summary collection of taxes might be invalid if the government did not waive its immunity to a suit for refund.

Too, the government may be under other kinds of practical pressure not to insist on its immunity. Take government contracts, for example. The law gives no immunity against being branded as a defaulter. The business of the government requires that people be willing to contract with it. You've already read the story of how this pressure made itself felt even before the Civil War and brought about a blanket consent to suit which has stood ever since.[10]

Act which afford a nonenemy claimant a later judicial hearing as to the propriety of the seizure. See Stoehr v. Wallace, 255 U.S. 239, 245–246; Guessefeldt v. McGrath, 342 U.S. 308, 318; *cf.* Russian Volunteer Fleet v. United States, 282 U.S. 481, 489."

[Compare the holdings greatly restricting the right of the government to suppress or seize allegedly obscene materials in advance of an adversary hearing on and judicial determination of the question of obscenity. See, *e.g.,* Blount v. Rizzi, 400 U.S. 410 (1971); Freedman v. Maryland, 380 U.S. 51 (1965); A Quantity of Copies of Books v. Kansas, 378 U.S. 205 (1964); Monaghan, *First Amendment "Due Process,"* 83 Harv.L.Rev. 518, 520–26 (1970). *Cf.* Sniadach v. Family Finance Corp., 395 U.S. 337 (1969) (holding unconstitutional

Wisconsin's prejudgment garnishment procedure where no provision was made for a hearing before the attachment took effect); Goldberg v. Kelly, 397 U.S. 254 (1970) (holding unconstitutional the termination of welfare benefits prior to an administrative hearing).

[For further references bearing on the possible scope and extent of a constitutional right to judicial consideration, see note 27, *infra.*]

8. See Chap. IX, Secs. 1(B), 2(A), *infra.*

9. On the personal responsibility of government officials in damages, see Chap. IX, Sec. 3, *infra.*

10. See Chap. II, Sec. 2, pp. 102–03, *supra.*

Finally, no democratic government can be immune to the claims of justice and legal right. The force of those claims of course varies in different situations. If private property is taken, for example, the claim for just compensation has the moral sanction of an express constitutional guarantee; and it is not surprising that there is a standing consent to that kind of suit. 28 U.S.C. §§ 1346(a)(2), 1491.[10a] And where constitutional rights are at stake the courts are properly astute, in construing statutes, to avoid the conclusion that Congress intended to use the privilege of immunity, or of withdrawing jurisdiction, in order to defeat them. Lynch v. United States, 292 U.S. 571, 586–87 (1934).

D. Limitations on the Jurisdiction of Enforcement Courts and Courts in the Position of Enforcement Courts: The Possibility of Judicial Control

Q. Let's stop beating around the bush and get to the central question. The bald truth is, isn't it, that the power to regulate jurisdiction is actually a power to regulate rights—rights to judicial process, whatever those are, and substantive rights generally? Why, that *must* be so. What can a court do if Congress says it has no jurisdiction, or only a restricted jurisdiction? It's helpless—helpless even to consider the validity of the limitation, let alone to do anything about it if it's invalid.

A. Why, what monstrous illogic! To build up a mere power to regulate jurisdiction into a power to affect rights having nothing to do with jurisdiction! And into a power to do it in contradiction to all the other terms of the very document which confers the power to regulate jurisdiction!

Q. Will you please explain what's wrong with the logic?

A. What's wrong, for one thing, is that it violates a necessary postulate of constitutional government—that a court must always be available to pass on claims of constitutional right to judicial process, and to provide such process if the claim is sustained.

Q. Whose Constitution are you talking about—Utopia's or ours?

A. Ours. It's a perfectly good Constitution if we know how to interpret it.

Q. Have you got the patience to spell out just what my fallacies are?

A. There are so many of them it will take a little time.

Let's start with the most obvious one. Your point, at best, can apply only to plaintiffs. Perhaps a plaintiff *does* have to take what Congress gives him or doesn't give him, although I have my doubts about it. But surely not a defendant. It's only a *limitation* on what a court can do once it has jurisdiction, not a denial of jurisdiction, that can hurt a defendant. And if the court thinks the limitation invalid, it's always in a position to

10a. [In First English Evangelical Lutheran Church of Glendale v. County of Los Angeles, California, 107 S.Ct. 2378, 2386 n. 9 (1987), the Supreme Court rejected an argument that "the prohibitory nature of the Fifth Amendment [Just Compensation Clause], combined with principles of sovereign immunity, establishes that the Amendment itself is only a limitation on the power of the Government to act, not a remedial provision." The "cases make clear," the Court said, "that it is the Constitution that dictates the remedy for interfering with property rights amounting to a taking."]

say so, and either to ignore it or let the defendant go free. Crowell v. Benson and the Yakus case make that clear, don't they?

Q. You're saying, then, that the power to regulate jurisdiction is subject in part to the other provisions of the Constitution?

A. No. It's subject in whole not in part. My point is simply that the difficulty involved in asserting any judicial control in the face of a total denial of jurisdiction doesn't exist if Congress gives jurisdiction but puts strings on it.

I'm also pointing out more than that. Where the *way* of exercising jurisdiction is in question, rather than its denial, the constitutional tests are different.

It's hard, for me at least, to read into Article III any guarantee to a civil litigant of a hearing in a federal constitutional court (outside the original jurisdiction of the Supreme Court), if Congress chooses to provide some alternative procedure. The alternative procedure may be unconstitutional. But, if so, it seems to me it must be because of some other constitutional provision, such as the due process clause.

On the other hand, if Congress directs an Article III court to decide a case, I can easily read into Article III a limitation on the power of Congress to tell the court *how* to decide it. Rutledge makes that point clearly in the Yakus case, as the Court itself made it clear long ago in United States v. Klein, p. 368, *supra*. That's the reason, isn't it, why Hughes invokes Article III as well as the Fifth Amendment in Crowell v. Benson? As he says, the case was one "where the question concerns the proper exercise of the judicial power in enforcing constitutional limitations".

Q. But Crowell v. Benson wasn't an enforcement case. It was a suit by an employer to set aside an award in favor of an employee.

A. Under the Act the award was enforceable only by judicial process. Congress chose to give the employer a chance to challenge an award in advance of enforcement proceedings. The Court was certainly entitled to assume in those circumstances, wasn't it, that whatever would invalidate an award in enforcement proceedings would invalidate it also in an advance challenge?

Q. I guess so. But that brings a lot of cases involving plaintiffs' rights within the sweep of your principle, doesn't it?

A. Yes, when the plaintiffs are prospective defendants. What you have to keep your eye on, when a plaintiff is attacking governmental action, is whether the action plays a part in establishing a duty which later may be judicially enforced against him. If so, the court has to decide as a matter of construction—including possible problems of separability—whether an objection to a limitation on jurisdiction can be raised only in enforcement proceedings or can be asserted in advance.

Because of the wide power of Congress in the selection of remedies, which I spoke of before, the question usually *is* one of construction. But the inference ordinarily should be in favor of making the statute workable and constitutional as a whole. Once that inference is drawn, the court in the advance proceeding is substantially in the position of an enforcement court.

Q. You mean that in an advance challenge the court, regardless of any restriction on its jurisdiction, should consider and decide any question which it thinks the plaintiff would have a right to have it decide if he were a defendant?

A. I think you're hitting it. If the court disposes of the case on the advance challenge, the decision will be res judicata. And so, if the court thinks the restriction invalid, it has only the two choices of disregarding it or else refusing to proceed to a decision and thus forcing the government to bring an enforcement proceeding. Since the purpose of the advance challenge is to make an enforcement proceeding unnecessary, the court ought ordinarily, as a matter of statutory construction, to make the first choice and treat the plaintiff now as if he were a defendant.

Q. Well, I'll admit that all this makes Sheldon and McCardle a little less frightening. But only a little less so. I'm wondering what there is to prevent Congress from by-passing the courts altogether. If a court has no jurisdiction at all, it obviously can't seize on the excuse of merely invalidating a limitation on its jurisdiction.

But before I ask you about that, let's see what Congress would have to gain by it—or the defendants to lose. When you come right down to it, what *are* the rights of a defendant in an enforcement proceeding?

E. Limitations on the Jurisdiction of Enforcement Courts: Their Validity

A. The Yakus case and Crowell v. Benson give you a good starting-point. Most people reading Yakus concentrate on what the Court said Congress *could* do, and reading Crowell concentrate on what it said Congress could *not* do. I hope you won't make those simple mistakes.

Q. You'll have to spell that out for me. Take Crowell first.

1. Civil Defendants

A. Well, the solid or apparently solid thing about Crowell is the holding that administrative findings of non-constitutional and non-jurisdictional facts may be made conclusive upon the courts, if not infected with any error of law, as a basis for judicial enforcement of a money liability of one private person to another.[11]

Q. What's so surprising about that?

A. It's worth thinking about even as a matter of due process and Article III judicial power. But stop and think particularly about the Seventh Amendment.

Q. No right of jury trial in admiralty.

A. Good. But the Seventh Amendment hasn't been treated as standing in the way of the Crowell result even when the admiralty answer wasn't available. Administrative proceedings haven't been regarded as "Suits at common law".[12]

11. [Recall, however, the Chief Justice's careful and repeated insistence in Crowell that sufficiency of the evidence is among the questions of law which the court must pass on; only findings "supported by evidence" are to be final. *Cf.* Jaffe, note 4, *supra,* at 595–99.]

12. See, *e.g.,* Wickwire v. Reinecke, 275 U.S. 101, 105–06 (1927); NLRB v. Jones & Laughlin Steel Corp., 301 U.S. 1, 48–49 (1937). [See further Atlas Roofing Co., Inc. v. Occupational Safety & Health Review Com'n, 430 U.S. 442 (1977) (Seventh Amendment does not require Congress to

Q. My, the Seventh Amendment might have been a major safeguard against bureaucracy with a little different interpretation, mightn't it?

A. Don't build it up too much. How many administrative arrangements can you think of that involve establishment of a money liability?

Q. I'm still interested in what Crowell said Congress could *not* do. Isn't that solid?

A. Not very. So far as the case insists on trial *de novo*, it seems clear it has no germinal significance.[13] Do you think it should have?

Q. But Crowell also spoke of the right to have the independent judgment of a court on constitutional and jurisdictional facts. That's important, isn't it, even if the court is confined to the administrative record?

A. It's a right with very different implications. That was the right insisted on in the Ben Avon case [14] on review of a state court decision, where of course it had to be rested solely on due process.

The Ben Avon part of the Crowell holding was reaffirmed in 1936, although in somewhat less rigorous form, in St. Joseph Stock Yards Co. v. United States, 298 U.S. 38 (1936). That was a case coming from a three-judge district court involving a rate order of the Secretary of Agriculture under the Packers and Stockyards Act. The judgment sustaining the order was affirmed. But Chief Justice Hughes, prompted by the lower court's expression of doubts, went out of his way to emphasize that an "independent judicial judgment on the facts" (which actually had been exercised) was constitutionally necessary. He added, however, that such a judgment "does not require or justify disregard of the weight which may properly attach to findings upon hearing and evidence". Justice Brandeis, concurring in the result with Justices Stone and Cardozo, thought that "no good reason exists for making special exception of issues of fact bearing upon a constitutional right". He said (p. 84):

"The supremacy of law demands that there shall be an opportunity to have some court decide whether an erroneous rule of law was applied; and whether the proceeding in which facts were adjudicated was conducted regularly. To that extent, the person asserting a right, whatever its source, should be entitled to the independent judgment of a court on the ultimate question of constitutionality. But supremacy of law does not demand that the correctness of every finding of fact to which the rule is to be applied shall be subject to review by a court. If it did, the power of courts to set aside findings of fact by an administrative tribunal would be broader than their power to set aside a jury's verdict. The Constitution contains no such command."

Q. Where does the Ben Avon–Crowell–St. Joseph rule stand now?

A. Most commentators question its present vitality, at least in the field of civil liability.[15] Certainly, the recent decisions on rate-making, to

provide jury trial in administrative proceeding for monetary civil penalties for violations of OSHA).]

13. See generally 4 Davis, Administrative Law Treatise §§ 29.08–.09 (1958; Supp.1970; Supp.1982). Compare Jaffe, note 4, *supra*, at 624–53. See also note 30, *infra*.

14. Ohio Valley Water Co. v. Borough of Ben Avon, 253 U.S. 287 (1920).

15. See authorities cited in note 13, *supra*. [Compare, in the area of First Amendment rights, the decisions discussed in Monaghan, note 7, *supra*, at 520–32, especially Bantam Books, Inc. v. Sullivan, 372 U.S. 58 (1963) (holding unconstitution-

which the commentators point, reflect such altered views of the applicable constitutional restraints as to leave little room for the Ben Avon question to arise within its original field.[16] The same thing is true in other areas of administrative action. Putting aside questions of personal liberty where the governing criteria are likely to be more rigorous, constitutionality, as distinguished from statutory authority, will rarely turn upon a concrete factual situation sought to be reviewed.

Q. The Crowell case also has a dictum that questions of law, including the question of the existence of evidence to support the administrative decision, must be open to judicial consideration. And you quoted Brandeis as saying *that* was necessary to the supremacy of law. Have those statements stood up?

A. If I can speak broadly and loosely, I'll say yes—they *have* stood up.

Shutting off the courts from questions of law determinative of enforceable duties was one of the things Yakus assumed that Congress could *not* do. To be sure, that was a criminal case; but there's no reason to suppose the Court would have made a different assumption if the sanction had been civil.

Q. How do you explain cases like Gray v. Powell, 314 U.S. 402 (1941), and National Labor Relations Board v. Hearst Publications, Inc., 322 U.S. 111 (1944)? Or, for that matter, O'Leary v. Brown–Pacific–Maxon Co., 340 U.S. 504 (1951)? Didn't these cases allow the agencies to make final determinations of questions of law?

A. That depends on how you define "law". I think Professor Davis is right in saying that the term "law" in the first sentence I quoted from Justice Brandeis has to be read "as excluding the body of rules and principles that grow out of the exercise of administrative discretion"—at least while the rules are in process of crystallizing. Davis, Administrative Law 34 (1941).

In recent years we've recognized increasingly a permissible range of administrative discretion in the shaping of judicially enforceable duties. How wide that discretion should be, and what are the appropriate ways to control it, are crucial questions in administrative law. But so long as the courts sit to answer the questions, the spirit of Brandeis' statement is maintained. And, since discretion by hypothesis is not law, the letter of it is not in question.[17]

al the activities of a state obscene literature commission partly on grounds that there was no assurance of immediate judicial determination of the validity of any administratively imposed restraint); Freedman v. Maryland, 380 U.S. 51, 58 (1965) (invalidating a state movie censorship statute and stating that "only a procedure requiring a judicial determination suffices to impose a valid final restraint").]

16. See, *e.g.,* FPC v. Hope Natural Gas Co., 320 U.S. 591 (1944).

17. [For criticism of the Dialogue's formulation at this point, see Monaghan, *Marbury and the Administrative State,* 83

Colum.L.Rev. 1, 28–34 (1983). Monaghan argues that "[t]he opposition of 'discretion' to 'law' cannot dissolve Hart's problem," since "the result of the exercise of discretion is, as it was in Hearst, an administrative formulation of a rule of law" (p. 29). He concludes that "there has never been a pervasive notion that limited government mandated an all-encompassing judicial duty to supply all of the relevant meaning of statutes. Rather, the judicial duty is to ensure that the administrative agency stays within the zone of discretion committed to it by its organic act" (p. 33).]

Q. But it's notorious that there are all kinds of administrative decisions that are not reviewable at all. Professor Davis devotes a whole fat chapter to "Unreviewable Action" of administrative agencies.[18]

A. Administrative law is a relatively new subject. Naturally there have been a number of ill-considered decisions. But if you look closely at Professor Davis' cases you'll find that almost all of them are distinguishable. Many of them don't involve judicially enforceable duties of the complaining party at all. Others involve political questions, or administrative questions in the old-fashioned sense. See Chap. II, Sec. 6, *supra*. Still others turn on this point of administrative discretion we were just talking about. The remainder were not themselves enforcement cases, and the opinions simply didn't face up to the question whether the validity of the restriction on jurisdiction should be judged as it would be in an enforcement proceeding.

Name me a single Supreme Court case that has squarely held that, in a civil enforcement proceeding, questions of law can be validly withdrawn from the consideration of the enforcement court where no adequate opportunity to have them determined by a court has been previously accorded.[19] When you do, I'm going back to re-think Marbury v. Madison.

Q. You put a lot of weight on the point of whether an enforceable legal duty is involved, don't you?[20]

A. Yes.

2. Criminal Defendants

Q. You haven't mentioned criminal defendants so far. I suppose that all you've said, and more, applies to them. They have a right to trial by jury that isn't limited to offenses that were crimes at common law—and a lot of other specific guarantees, too.

A. Well, the same basic point certainly ought to apply. I don't believe that courts can be given criminal jurisdiction, and at the same time be told to exercise it in violation of the Constitution. Yakus, at least, went on that basis. It dealt directly with the scope of constitutional rights, with no nonsense about any question being foreclosed by the power to regulate jurisdiction. Whether the courts define the rights too narrowly or too broadly, they are there to declare them—and whenever appropriate to overrule and re-declare.

There is significance, moreover, in the conformities to the traditional pattern of a criminal trial which Yakus assumed to be necessary as well as in the departures which it sanctioned. The departures were the withdrawal from the court or jury of certain questions of legislative fact and from the court of certain questions of law. But these departures were sanctioned only because an alternative procedure had been provided which, in the exigencies of the national situation, the Court found to be adequate.

18. 4 Davis, Administrative Law Treatise ch. 28 (1958); 5 *id.* ch. 28 (2d ed. 1985).

19. [See generally Jaffe, note 4, *supra*, at 353–76, 381–89. But *cf.* Monaghan, note 17, *supra*, at 21–22.]

20. [Professor Monaghan has criticized the distinction drawn in this part of the Dialogue, at least as it relates to the scope of review. See Monaghan, note 17, *supra*, at 22–24: "*So long as the court has general jurisdiction* to render a final judgment, why should the permissible limitation on the court's law-declaring competence vary with whether the private litigant is asserting rights rather than defenses?" (p. 24).]

The alternative procedure for the decision of the questions of law was in a court; and everybody assumed it had to be.

Q. Does Yakus mark the maximum inroad on the rights of a criminal defendant to judicial process?

A. No, unfortunately it doesn't. We have to take account of two World War II selective service cases, Falbo v. United States, 320 U.S. 549 (1944), and Estep v. United States, 327 U.S. 114 (1946). "By the terms of" the selective service legislation, as Justice Douglas put it in Estep, "Congress enlisted the aid of the federal courts only for enforcement purposes." And so the question was sharply presented on what terms that could be done.

The Court held in Falbo, with only Justice Murphy dissenting, that a registrant who was being prosecuted for failure to report for induction (or for work of national importance) could not defend on the ground that he had been wrongly classified and was entitled to a statutory exemption.

Q. Doesn't that pretty well destroy your notion that there has to be some kind of reasonable means for getting a judicial determination of questions of law affecting liability for criminal punishment? All Congress has to do is to authorize an administrative agency to issue an individualized order, make the violation of the order a crime in itself, and at the same time immunize the order from judicial review. On the question of the violation of the order, all the defendant's rights are preserved in the criminal trial, except that they don't mean anything.

A. Whoa! Falbo doesn't go that far. In Estep, after the fighting was over, the case was explained—and perhaps it had actually been decided— on the basis that the petitioner in failing to report for induction had failed to exhaust his administrative remedies. Considering the emergency, the requirement that claims be first presented at the induction center was pretty clearly a reasonable procedure.[21]

Q. How about Estep?

A. The petitioner there went to the end of the administrative road, and was indicted for refusing to submit to induction. The Court held that he was entitled to make the defense that the local board had "acted beyond its jurisdiction". Justice Douglas, speaking for himself and Justices Reed and Black, said (pp. 122–23):

" * * * The provision making the decisions of the local boards 'final' means to us that Congress chose not to give administrative action under this Act the customary scope of judicial review which obtains under other statutes. It means that the courts are not to weigh the evidence to determine whether the classification made by the local boards was justified. The decisions of the local boards made in conformity with the regulations are final even though they may be erroneous. The question of jurisdiction of the local board is reached only if there is no basis in fact for the classification which it gave the registrant." [22]

---

21. [Recent cases indicate that even this "exhaustion" aspect of Falbo will be only selectively enforced, at least at a time when the nation is not fully engaged in war. Compare McKart v. United States, 395 U.S. 185 (1969), with McGee v. United States, 402 U.S. 479 (1971).]

22. [But see Jaffe, note 4, *supra*, at 367: "It has since [Estep] become very clear that an absence of sufficient evidence or an error of law is, in this context, lack of jurisdiction. The judicial review permitted is only a shade, if at all, more narrow than the usual review."]

Justices Murphy and Rutledge concurred specially on the ground that the Court's construction was required by the Constitution. Justice Frankfurter thought the construction wrong but concurred on the ground that there were other errors in the trial. Justice Burton and Chief Justice Stone dissented.

Q. Well, the holding in the end wasn't such a departure after all, was it?

A. Stop and think before you say that.

Except for two Justices who are now dead, the whole Court dealt with the question as if it were merely one of statutory construction. Three Justices of the Supreme Court of the United States were willing to assume that Congress has power under Article I of the Constitution to direct courts created under Article III to employ the judicial power conferred by Article III to convict a man of crime and send him to jail without his ever having had a chance to make his defenses.[23] No decision in 164 years of constitutional history, so far as I know, had ever before sanctioned such a thing.[24]

---

23. Would the force of the objection to a refusal to permit a criminal defendant to show that an order of induction was erroneous in law be destroyed if it were concluded that Congress might have made such an order a matter purely of the board's discretion? Is the power to do that material if the Congress has never exercised it?

Because Congress might have excluded the courts altogether from the process of raising an army in crisis, would it follow that it has also the alternative of using them for the limited purpose of punishing as a civil crime a violation of a purely discretionary determination?

[Some further questions: Even if it is assumed that Congress has power to draft everyone, without exemption, does that logically lead to the conclusion that if it decides not to draft a certain group, the question whether someone falls into that group can be left to the conclusive determination of the executive departments? Does the fact that Congress can set the tax rate where it wills force us to conclude that Congress may leave to the final determination of the Commissioner whether the taxpayer's bill is at the rate the Congress chose? More generally, does the power of the Congress to define the law's content give Congress unlimited discretion to allocate between the judiciary and the executive the power to interpret the law as it is enforced against the citizen's person or property?]

24. In criminal prosecutions of draft evaders during world War I, the question of the finality of the draft board's classifications apparently did not arise. See Bell, *Selective Service and the Courts,* 28 A.B. A.J. 164, 167 (1942). However, the courts were in general agreement that habeas corpus would be granted after induction where the classification was arbitrary or not based on substantial evidence. *E.g.,* Arbitman v. Woodside, 258 Fed. 441 (4th Cir.1919). There was some suggestion that a draftee could only obtain judicial review after induction. See United States ex rel. Roman v. Rauch, 253 Fed. 814 (S.D.N.Y. 1918). But see Angelus v. Sullivan, 246 Fed. 54 (2d Cir.1917) (injunction against issuance of induction order denied because common-law certiorari was available).

[The question of the scope of congressional choice in the selection of remedies arose in a series of challenges to actions of the Selective Service system during the Vietnam War. In 1967, apparently in reaction to a lower federal court decision, Congress added § 10(b)(3) to the Military Selective Service Act of 1967, 50 U.S.C.App. § 460(b) (3):

["No judicial review shall be made of the classification or processing of any registrant ∗ ∗ ∗ except as a defense to a criminal prosecution ∗ ∗ ∗ [for violation of an order to report for induction]."

[Despite this provision, in Oestereich v. Selective Service System Local Board No. 11, 393 U.S. 233 (1968), the Court allowed a registrant (who had been reclassified I–A for turning back his draft card to the government) to test the validity of his reclassification in an action to enjoin his induction. The majority emphasized the "blatantly lawless" action of the local board (p. 238). Justice Harlan, concurring, cited the Dialogue in support of his suggestion that to withhold preinduction review in such a case would raise "serious constitutional problems." These problems, he said, were intensified by the unavailability of a "prompt subsequent hearing" after induction and by the registrant's "nonfrivolous argument" that induction pursuant to the delinquency reclassification proce-

Certainly no such decision was cited. For these three didn't even see it as a problem. There is ground to doubt whether the first three in the majority did either.

Bear in mind that the three dissenters from the Court's construction expressly recognized that the order of induction might have been erroneous in law. They said that the remedy for that was habeas corpus after induction. They seemed to say that the existence of the remedy of habeas corpus saved the constitutionality of the prior procedure. That turns an ultimate safeguard of law into an excuse for its violation. And it strikes close to the heart of one of the main theses of this discussion—that so long at least as Congress feels impelled to invoke the assistance of courts, the supremacy of law in their decisions is assured.[24a]

F. Denial of Jurisdiction: Withholding From Plaintiffs Affirmative Governmental Aid

Q. So much for defendants and prospective defendants. How about other kinds of plaintiffs? Have they any rights?

A. Before we can even start dealing with that question, we'll have to break it down into parts. An initial division which I find useful is between plaintiffs who are simply trying to get the government's help, and those who are trying to protect themselves against extra-judicial governmental coercion—and whose claims thus reach much more closely to the foundations of liberty. Let's take the first group first, breaking it into two subgroups.

dure constituted " 'punishment' * * * without jury trial, right to counsel, and other constitutional requisites" (pp. 243, 244 n. 6). For Justice Stewart, dissenting, no constitutional difficulties were presented because a registrant had the option of refusing induction and raising his claims in a criminal prosecution or of initiating habeas corpus proceedings after induction. With respect to the former, he noted that "persons arrested for criminal offenses are routinely deprived of their liberty—to a greater extent than are military inductees—without any prior opportunity for the adjudication of legal or constitutional claims, and often without any hope of securing release on bail (p. 250 n. 10).

[In Clark v. Gabriel, 393 U.S. 256 (1968), decided the same day, the Court, acting per curiam and without briefs or argument, denied preinduction review to a registrant who objected to denial of his request for conscientious objector status. Oestereich was distinguished as not involving any determination of fact or exercise of judgment; constitutional objections were summarily disposed of by noting the availability of the claim as a basis for habeas corpus after induction, or as a defense in a criminal prosecution for disobeying an induction order.

[For later decisions, see Breen v. Selective Service Local Board No. 16, 396 U.S. 460 (1970) (allowing preinduction judicial review of a registrant's classification); Fein v. Selective Service System Local Board No. 7, 405 U.S. 365 (1972) (refusing to allow a pre-induction challenge to the constitutionality of the selective service statute and regulations). See generally Beytagh, *Judicial Review in Selective Service Cases—Lessons From Vietnam*, 48 Notre Dame Law. 1164 (1973); Monaghan, note 7, *supra*, at 543–51; O'Neil, *Public Employment, Antiwar Protest and Preinduction Review*, 17 U.C.L.A. L.Rev. 1028 (1970).]

24a. [The Supreme Court relied on and extended both Yakus and Estep in United States v. Mendoza-Lopez, 107 S.Ct. 2148 (1987). In this case, the Court held that when a prior deportation proceeding "effectively eliminate[d] the right of an alien to obtain judicial review," due process required that the alien be allowed to make a collateral challenge to the use of that proceeding as an element of a subsequent criminal offense (p. 2155). Thus the Court (without citation of the Dialogue) embraced the argument made in this section.]

1. Plaintiffs Wanting to Enforce Other
Private Persons' Duties

Q. Do men have a constitutional right to judicial assistance against their fellow men?

A. Very possibly, at least when rights of action have already accrued. The portal-to-portal cases illustrate one type of problem of this kind. You will remember that when Congress acted to deprive both state and federal courts of jurisdiction to entertain the bonanza claims under the Fair Labor Standards Act to which previous Supreme Court decisions had unexpectedly given rise, it was careful at the same time to outlaw the substantive liability.

Q. Why was that necessary when no court was left with jurisdiction to enforce the liability?

A. A few district courts looked at it that way, but the courts of appeals were mostly perspicacious enough to see that a total denial of any remedy, in either the state or federal courts, was not a mere regulation of jurisdiction. They applied the act only after they had satisfied themselves that the liability had been validly extinguished.

Q. Then here is a clear case of plaintiffs who *do* have a constitutional right of access to a federal court with jurisdiction to pass on the merits of their claims, isn't it?

A. Not so fast. We can't be sure of that. The Supreme Court never granted certiorari; and perhaps the courts of appeals' decisions are to be explained on grounds of statutory construction, or more accurately of separability. Perhaps the courts were simply unwilling to believe that Congress would have wanted the withdrawal of jurisdiction to be effective if the substantive action were invalid.

Q. You indicated that there was another type of case in this group.

A. Yes. Congress hasn't often tried to take away preexisting rights of action for judicial relief between private persons. The question is more likely to arise when a private plaintiff complains of the refusal of an administrative agency to make an order, favorable to him, against another private person.

A good illustration of this latter type is the situation in Crowell v. Benson itself. Suppose the plaintiff complaining of the administrative decision in that case had been an employee denied an award instead of an employer called upon to pay one. Do you think the Court would have written the same opinion?

Q. Why not?

A. The employer in the actual case was being made to do something to his disadvantage. The employee in the supposed case simply failed to gain a hoped-for advantage. Do the two have an equal warrant to appeal to the courts? The employee, after all, couldn't even prove the soundness of his claim to the agency created for his special protection.

Haven't you noticed how frequently the protected groups in an administrative program pay for their protection by a sacrifice of procedural and litigating rights? The agency becomes their champion and they stand or fall by it. Does this phenomenon reflect a disregard or a recognition of the equities of the situation?[25]

Q. I can see the force of that point if the employee were getting something he never had before—like a consumer under the Federal Food, Drug and Cosmetic Act. But the compensation system was imposed on longshoremen in lieu, at least in part, of prior rights of action at law and in admiralty.

A. Yes, that does seem to make a difference.

I wonder what you would think of Switchmen's Union v. National Mediation Board, 320 U.S. 297 (1943). There the union brought suit under the general federal question jurisdiction to set aside a Board order designating a rival union as the authorized collective bargaining representative. The union said the order was based on a misconstruction of the statutory provisions concerning the appropriate bargaining unit. But the Court collected from the silence of the statute an intention of Congress to preclude judicial review, and held that the alleged error of law could not be examined.

Q. The order, I suppose, resulted in an enforceable duty of the employer to bargain with the designated union?

A. Yes.

Q. Then if the employer had been denied review, the case would have met the challenge with which you ended the last section?

A. That's right. And most of Justice Douglas' opinion would apply to the employer just as readily as to the union. But at the end he expressly reserved the question of "What is open when a court of equity is asked for its affirmative help by granting a decree for the enforcement" of a Board certificate.

Q. I gather that the unsuccessful union did not come under any enforceable duty *not* to bargain?

A. That's right. All it lost was the liberty to bargain with an employer free from an enforceable duty not to bargain with it.

Q. Then the case is a little like your supposititious inversion of Crowell v. Benson. But here the union's interest actually seems more important than the employer's. Don't you think the denial of review is pretty significant?

A. Not very. The opinion seems too weakly reasoned to have much growing power.[26]

25. [For subsequent developments on the issue of agency discretion not to initiate proceedings, compare Heckler v. Chaney, 470 U.S. 821 (1985), with Dunlop v. Bachowski, 421 U.S. 560 (1975). Both cases are discussed in Pierce, Shapiro & Verkeuil, Administrative Law and Process § 6.4 (1985). See also Stewart & Sunstein, *Public Programs and Private Rights*, 95 Harv.L.Rev. 1195, 1205–06, 1267–89 (1982).]

26. [The holding of Switchmen's in fact lost some of its significance when the Court decided Leedom v. Kyne, 358 U.S. 184 (1958) (sustaining jurisdiction to review an NLRB certification similar to the Mediation Board order involved in Switchmen's).

[Recent decades have, in general, seen a reaffirmation in Administrative Law of what Professor Jaffe terms the presumption of judicial review: "[I]n our system of remedies, an individual whose interest is acutely and immediately affected by an administrative action presumptively has a right to secure at some point a judicial determination of its validity." Jaffe, note 4, *supra*, at 336; and see generally Jaffe's chapter 9, on "The Right to Judicial Review." See also Abbott Laboratories v. Gardner, 387 U.S. 136 (1967), where Jus-

Q. Well, you've got me all up in the air now. What's the answer?

A. I don't think anybody, including the Supreme Court, has thought through to one. For present purposes we don't need to exhaust the question of just what constitutional rights of access to courts there are in this kind of situation. Our main interest is in the question of the extent to which the power to control jurisdiction is a power to impair these rights, whatever they may be. On this question I think you'll find that the answer here falls in with that in the remaining groups of problems.

2. Plaintiffs Complaining About Decisions in Connection with Non-Coercive Governmental Programs

Q. What's the next group of problems?

A. It's really a miscellany rather than a group. It's all the cases I can't stop to talk about now if I'm going to avoid occupying the field of administrative law entirely. Broadly, it's the cases of plaintiffs complaining about governmental decisions which do not involve the direct coercion of private persons.

More specifically, the group includes problems with respect to plaintiffs who are *neither* (a) trying to avoid becoming defendants, or (b) complaining about a governmental decision concerning a judicially enforceable duty of another private person, or (c) complaining about extra-judicial governmental coercion of themselves. For example, a plaintiff seeking review of a government contracting officer's decision which he had agreed in the contract should be final. United States v. Moorman, 338 U.S. 457 (1950). Or a plaintiff seeking some statutory benefit from the government.

It's perfectly obvious that final authority to determine even questions of law can be given to executive or administrative officials in many situations not having the direct impact on private persons of a governmentally-created and judicially-enforceable duty, or of an immediate deprivation of liberty or property by extra-judicial action.[27] These cases, by and

tice Harlan for the Court stated that courts should restrict access to judicial review only on "clear and convincing" evidence of a contrary legislative intent, and spoke expressly of the "basic presumption of judicial review" (pp. 140–41); and see note 27, *infra.* Compare Schilling v. Rogers, 363 U.S. 666 (1960); Morris v. Gressette, 432 U.S. 491 (1977) (discussed in 5 Davis, Administrative Law Treatise 314–15 (2d ed. 1984).]

27. [See, *e.g.,* Panama Canal Co. v. Grace Line, Inc. 356 U.S. 309 (1958). See also the following cases upholding the preclusion of judicial review with respect to actions of the Attorney General under the Voting Rights Act of 1965: South Carolina v. Katzenbach, 383 U.S. 301, 332–33 (1966); Briscoe v. Bell, 432 U.S. 404 (1977); Morris v. Gressette, 432 U.S. 491 (1977). *Cf.* United States v. Erika, Inc., 456 U.S. 201, 206–11 and n. 14 (1982) (Court of Claims has no jurisdiction to review private insurance carrier's determination of certain Medicare benefits available under Medicare program; the Court did not address the re-

spondent's claim of a constitutional right to judicial review because the issue had not been properly raised); Block v. Community Nutrition Inst., 467 U.S. 340 (1984) (individual consumers could not obtain judicial review of administrative milk marketing order; the presumption favoring judicial review was overcome by a showing of congressional intent to preclude such review); ICC v. Brotherhood of Locomotive Engineers, 107 S.Ct. 2360 (1987) (ICC order refusing to clarify a prior order and refusing to reconsider is not subject to judicial review); United States v. Fausto, 108 S.Ct. 668 (1988) (Civil Service Reform Act precludes judicial review of employee's claim based on alleged violations of Back Pay Act).

[Note, however, that since the Dialogue, the areas where the Government has the "final authority" have narrowed, as matters traditionally thought to be "of grace" become protected as "rights" and subject to judicial review. For an early illustration, see Harmon v. Brucker, 355 U.S. 579 (1958), in which the Court reviewed the

large, are those falling in the third of Justice Curtis' three classes in Murray's Lessee (p. 396 note 6, *supra*). Some such situations may rise to the dignity of a constitutional problem. But whatever the constitutional rights to judicial process of these plaintiffs may be, the power of Congress to impair them seems to involve no distinctive problems. The problems appear to be the same as those discussed in the next section.

G. Denial of Jurisdiction: Plaintiffs Complaining of Extra-Judicial Governmental Coercion

Q. All right, then, now comes the sixty-four dollar question we've been avoiding. What happens if the government is hurting people and not simply refusing to help them? Suppose Congress authorizes a program of direct action by government officials against private persons or private property. Suppose, further, that it not only dispenses with judicial enforcement but either limits the jurisdiction of the federal courts to inquire into what the officials do or denies it altogether.

1. Relief Under General Jurisdiction

A. You sound as if you thought you finally had me in a corner. But after what we've been through the answer to this one is easy, isn't it—so long as there is any applicable grant of general jurisdiction?

Obviously, the answer is that the validity of the jurisdictional limitation depends on the validity of the program itself, or the particular part of it in question. If the court finds that what is being done is invalid, its duty is simply to declare the jurisdictional limitation invalid also, and then proceed under the general grant of jurisdiction.[28]

validity of a less-than-honorable discharge from the army in spite of the long tradition against judicial interference with military functions and in spite of the relevant statute that made the order of the Army Discharge Review Board "final subject only to review by the Secretary of the Army." The Court stated: "Generally, judicial relief is available to one who has been injured by an act of a government official which is in excess of his express or implied powers" (pp. 581–82).

[A later, important example is Johnson v. Robison, 415 U.S. 361 (1974), a suit challenging the constitutionality of the statutory provision that denied certain veterans' benefits to conscientious objectors. The section in question (38 U.S.C. § 211(a), providing that "decisions of the Administrator on any question of law or fact under any law administered by the Veterans, Administration * * * shall be final and conclusive and no * * * court of the United States shall have power or jurisdiction to review any such decision") was held inapplicable to suits challenging the constitutional validity of legislative classifications enacted by Congress. A construction precluding review in such a case, the Court said, would "raise serious questions concerning the constitutionality of § 211(a)"

(p. 366). See also Northern Pipeline Const. Co. v. Marathon Pipe Line Co., 458 U.S. 50, 69 n. 23 (1982) ("when Congress assigns * * * [certain] matters to administrative agencies, or to legislative courts, it has generally provided, and we have suggested that it may be required to provide, for Art. III judicial review"); Lindahl v. Office of Personnel Management, 470 U.S. 768 (1985) (upholding judicial review of alleged errors of law and procedure in OMB's denial of a request for disability annuity); Bartlett v. Bowen, 816 F.2d 695, 697 (D.C. Cir.1987) (holding, 2–1, that Congress, in providing $1,000 amount in controversy requirement for judicial review of Medicare benefit decisions, did not intend to preclude review of challenges to the underlying Act; such preclusion would constitute "a clear violation of due process").

[For further discussion of the shift from notions of pure "privilege" to notions of entitlement, see Pierce, Shapiro & Verkeuil, Administrative Law and Process 227–48 (1985).]

28. [For discussion and criticism of this paragraph, see Redish & Woods, *Congressional Power to Control the Jurisdiction of Lower Federal Courts: A Critical Review and a New Synthesis*, 124 U.Pa.L.Rev. 45,

Q. That can't be as easy as you make it sound. Is that what the federal courts actually do?

A. That's what they've often done.

Take the clearest case—an attempt by Congress to authorize the administrative imposition of infamous punishment. That, substantially, is Wong Wing v. United States, 163 U.S. 228 (1896), one of the bulwarks of the Constitution. There Congress had directed that any Chinese person adjudged in a summary proceeding by any judge or United States commissioner to be in the country unlawfully should first be imprisoned at hard labor for not more than a year and then deported. In the exercise of its general jurisdiction in habeas corpus, the Court ordered the prisoners discharged from such imprisonment—without prejudice of course to their detention according to law for deportation.

In Lipke v. Lederer, 259 U.S. 557 (1922), the Court found that a payment required by the tax laws was actually a penalty enforceable only by the processes of the criminal law. It exercised general federal question jurisdiction to enjoin summary collection, in spite of the statute prohibiting injunctions against federal taxes.[29]

Q. In those cases the whole extra-judicial procedure was found unconstitutional. That's an unusual situation. What if the party simply says that the executive officers are proceeding erroneously in his particular case?

A. If he has a constitutional right to have that question examined in court, and the court has a general jurisdiction, it can disregard any special jurisdictional limitation and go ahead and examine it.

That's what the Court did, for example, in Ng Fung Ho v. White, 259 U.S. 276 (1922). That case involved an administrative order to deport an asserted alien who claimed to be a citizen. On habeas corpus the Court held that the due process clause entitled the claimant to a trial de novo and an independent judicial judgment on the issue of citizenship; and it directed the district court to give it to him. Crowell, you remember, relied on Ng Fung Ho.

Q. Is Ng Fung Ho any more solid now than Crowell?

A. On the trial de novo point, maybe not, if Congress tried expressly to override it.[30] Possibly not, even on the other point. In recent years Ng Fung Ho has been cited for the proposition that judicial review may be a constitutional requirement, without suggesting that its scope includes an independent judgment on the facts.[31] But I'd be surprised if the deportee

63–66 (1975). The authors argue, inter alia, that "[w]hen Congress limits lower federal court jurisdiction over a particular matter, it necessarily is suspending all available general grants of jurisdiction with respect to that particular matter" (p. 65). For the Dialogue's own recognition of this possibility with respect to the jurisdictional amount limitation as it then existed in federal question cases, see p. 419, infra.]

29. [See also cases discussed in notes 24, 27, supra. On the question of the administrative imposition of penalties and fines, see Gellhorn, Administrative Prescription

and Imposition of Penalties, 1970 Wash. U.L.Q. 265. On the question of jury trial in such cases, see the Atlas Roofing Co. case, note 12, supra.]

30. [Congress codified the rule of Ng Fung Ho in 1961 in 8 U.S.C. § 1105a, which calls for a "hearing de novo of the nationality claim" in deportation cases. See Agosto v. INS, 436 U.S. 748 (1978).]

31. See Estep, supra, 327 U.S. at 120; Frankfurter, J., dissenting in Stark v. Wickard, 321 U.S. 288, 312 (1944).

claiming citizenship were ever denied, on the issue of citizenship, a review at least as broad as that called for, say, by Hughes' formulation in St. Joseph.

Q. What about a claim of citizenship by an applicant for admission to the country?

A. That's an interesting present problem. If United States v. Ju Toy, 198 U.S. 253 (1905), is still law, the applicant for admission has no right to a *de novo* review of his claim of citizenship.[32] But lots of people have doubted whether Ju Toy could stand after Ng Fung Ho.

The Ninth Circuit, in particular, doubts it, at least as to prior residents, and accords them a *de novo* inquiry into citizenship on habeas corpus.[33] In 1940, Congress seemed to recognize the essential justice of this position when it provided a special statutory procedure for a judicial determination of citizenship.[34] The Second Circuit thought that this made it unnecessary to reexamine Ju Toy.[35] But the Immigration and Nationality Act of 1952 abolished the statutory procedure.[36] And so the question whether the Ninth Circuit is right about the scope of review in habeas corpus has taken on new importance, and is likely to come to a head soon.[37]

Q. But even admitted aliens have access to the courts on habeas corpus on the question of their right to enter or remain in the country, don't they?

A. Yes, although the scope of review, of course, falls short of trial *de novo*. Indeed, judicial review in exclusion and deportation cases is one of the most impressive examples of the general point I am making, and currently provides a testing crucible of basic principle.

The structure of review has been developed by the courts in the face of a statutory plan of administrative control which looked neither to their

32. But *cf.* Chin Yow v. United States, 208 U.S. 8 (1908), per Holmes, J., in which the Court, after deciding that an applicant for admission claiming citizenship had been unfairly deprived by the administrative officers of access to evidence to prove his case to them, corrected the wrong by giving him a chance to prove the case to a court.

33. Carmichael v. Delaney, 170 F.2d 239 (9th Cir.1948).

34. Section 503, Nationality Act of Oct. 14, 1940, 54 Stat. 1171.

35. United States ex rel. Chu Leung v. Shaughnessy, 176 F.2d 249 (2d Cir.1949).

36. See 8 U.S.C. § 1503, authorizing the bringing of a declaratory judgment suit to establish citizenship by those "within the United States," but not those whose nationality is in question in "connection with any exclusion proceeding," the latter being remitted to the pre–1940 remedy of habeas corpus. See *Developments in the Law— Immigration and Nationality,* 66 Harv.L. Rev. 643, 673–74, 744–45 (1953).

[In 1962, the Supreme Court nevertheless held, in the teeth of § 1503, that persons outside the United States may, under the Administrative Procedure Act and the Declaratory Judgment Act, sue to establish their American citizenship in the District Court of the District of Columbia; Justice Stewart said that the statutory scheme of § 1503 is not exclusive and that the "broadly remedial" provisions of the APA will be held inapplicable only if there is "clear and convincing evidence" of Congress' intent. Rusk v. Cort, 369 U.S. 367 (1962). That case, however, does not state whether there would be a de novo inquiry into the nationality question in such a suit.]

37. [The question remains an open one in exclusion cases, since the 1961 "judicial review" addition to the Act, Section 106, see note 30, *supra,* specifies a hearing de novo only in deportation cases raising the issue of U.S. nationality. That act remits "aliens" who are excluded to the remedy of habeas corpus, see § 106(b), but says nothing about scope of review in a habeas case if there is a claim of U.S. nationality. See also the discussion of Rusk v. Cort, note 36, *supra.* See generally 2 Gordon & Rosenfield, Immigration Law and Procedure §§ 8.29–.30 (1983).]

help nor interference. For years the statutes have provided that orders in these matters of the Secretary of Labor (now the Attorney General) shall be "final".

Q. How then can aliens have any rights to assert in habeas corpus? I thought they came and stayed only at the pleasure of Congress.

A. The Supreme Court seemed to think so, too, at first. In its earliest decisions the Court started with the premise of plenary legislative power and on that basis seemed to be prepared to take the word "final" in the statutes literally and to decline any review whatever, even in deportation cases.[38]

Before long, however, it began to see that the premise needed to be qualified—that a power to lay down general rules, even if it were plenary, did not necessarily include a power to be arbitrary or to authorize administrative officials to be arbitrary. It saw that, on the contrary, the very existence of a jurisdiction in habeas corpus, coupled with the constitutional guarantee of due process, implied a regime of law. It saw that in such a regime the courts had a responsibility to see that statutory authority was not transgressed, that a reasonable procedure was used in exercising the authority, and—seemingly also—that human beings were not unreasonably subjected, even by direction of Congress, to an uncontrolled official discretion.[39]

38. The Chinese Exclusion Case, 130 U.S. 581 (1889) (admission); Nishimura Ekiu v. United States, 142 U.S. 651 (1892) (admission); Fong Yue Ting v. United States, 149 U.S. 698 (1893) (deportation); Lem Moon Sing v. United States, 158 U.S. 538 (1895) (admission); Li Sing v. United States, 180 U.S. 486 (1901) (deportation); Fok Yong Yo v. United States, 185 U.S. 296 (1902) (admission); Lee Lung v. Patterson, 186 U.S. 168 (1902) (admission).

39. The turning point was The Japanese Immigrant Case (Yamataya v. Fisher), 189 U.S. 86 (1903), involving an immigrant taken into custody for deportation four days after her landing. After referring to earlier cases cited in note 38, *supra*, the Court said (pp. 100–01):

" * * * But this court has never held, nor must we now be understood as holding, that administrative officers, when executing the provisions of a statute involving the liberty of persons, may disregard the fundamental principles that inhere in 'due process of law' as understood at the time of the adoption of the Constitution. One of these principles is that no person shall be deprived of his liberty without opportunity, at some time, to be heard, before such officers, in respect of the matters upon which that liberty depends * * *. * * * No such arbitrary power can exist where the principles involved in due process of law are recognized.

"This is the reasonable construction of the acts of Congress here in question, and they need not be otherwise interpreted.

* * * An act of Congress must be taken to be constitutional unless the contrary plainly and palpably appears."

Compare Justice Holmes' formulation in Chin Yow, an admission case, note 32, *supra:* "The decision of the Department is final, but that is on the presupposition that the decision was after a hearing in good faith, however summary in form."

For other deportation cases, see Low Wah Suey v. Backus, 225 U.S. 460, 468 (1912); Zakonaite v. Wolf, 226 U.S. 272, 274–75 (1912); Bilokumsky v. Tod, 263 U.S. 149, 156–57 (1923); Bridges v. Wixon, 326 U.S. 135, 156 (1945).

On admissions, see Justice Stone's summary of the law in Lloyd Sabaudo Societa v. Elting, 287 U.S. 329, 334–36 (1932). See also Gegiow v. Uhl, 239 U.S. 3 (1915); and see Kwock Jan Fat v. White, 253 U.S. 454, 457–58 (1920), where the Court in setting aside an order excluding a person claiming to be a citizen said:

"It is fully settled that the decision by the Secretary of Labor, of such a question as we have here, is final, and conclusive upon the courts, unless it be shown that the proceedings were 'manifestly unfair,' were 'such as to prevent a fair investigation,' or show 'manifest abuse' of the discretion committed to the executive officers by the statute, Low Wah Suey v. Backus, * * *, or that 'their authority was not fairly exercised, that is, consistently with the fundamental principles of justice embraced within the conception of due pro-

Under the benign influence of these ideas, the law grew and flourished, like Egypt under the rule of Joseph. Thousands of cases were decided whose presence in the courts cannot be explained on any other basis. But what the status of many of these cases is now is not altogether clear.

Q. Why?

A. There arose up new justices in Washington which knew not Joseph. Citing only the harsh precepts of the very earliest decisions, they began to decide cases accordingly, as if nothing had happened in the years between.[40]

In the Knauff case, Justice Minton said (338 U.S. at 543) that, "Whatever the rule may be concerning deportation of persons who have gained entry into the United States, it is not within the province of any court, unless expressly authorized by law, to review the determination of the political branch of the Government to exclude a given alien". Since Congress has never expressly authorized any court to review an exclusion order, this statement either ignores or renders obsolete every habeas corpus case in the books involving an exclusion proceeding.

On the procedural side, Justice Minton went so far as to say (p. 544) that, "Whatever the procedure authorized by Congress is, it is due process as far as an alien denied entry is concerned," a patently preposterous proposition.

Justice Clark repeated and applied both statements in the Mezei case.

Q. Then we're back where we started half a century ago?

A. Oh no. The aberrations have been largely confined to admission cases. In deportations, for the most part, the Court has adhered to the sound and humane philosophy of the middle period. In some respects it has even extended its applications.[41]

cess of law.' Tang Tun v. Edsell, 223 U.S. 673, 681, 682. The decision must be after a hearing in good faith, however summary, Chin Yow v. United States, * * * and it must find adequate support in the evidence. Zakonaite v. Wolf, * * *."

See generally *Developments in the Law*, note 36, *supra*, at 671–76, 681–82, 692–95, and particularly the excellent discussion at 666–70.

40. United States ex rel. Knauff v. Shaughnessy, 338 U.S. 537 (1950), interpreting the War Brides Act as permitting the wife of an American soldier to be excluded without a hearing for security reasons; Shaughnessy v. United States ex rel. Mezei, 345 U.S. 206 (1953).

For the uncontrolled power to deport an alien enemy, even after the cessation of actual hostilities, see the five-to-four decision in Ludecke v. Watkins, 335 U.S. 160 (1948).

The frequently doctrinaire approach of the Court to the general problem is sharply exposed in Harisiades v. Shaughnessy, 342 U.S. 808 (1952), suggesting that the power of Congress to specify grounds for deportation is without limit. [This view was reaf-

firmed in Galvan v. Press, 347 U.S. 522 (1954); see also Kleindienst v. Mandel, 408 U.S. 753 (1972); Fiallo v. Bell, 430 U.S. 787 (1977). But *cf.* Rowoldt v. Perfetto, 355 U.S. 115 (1957); Hampton v. Mow Sun Wong, 426 U.S. 88 (1976).]

41. In Kwong Hai Chew v. Colding, 344 U.S. 590 (1953), the Court decided that, "for purposes of his constitutional right to due process", the position of an alien seaman previously admitted for permanent residence and applying for re-admission after a four months voyage on an American vessel was to be "assimilate[d] * * * to that of an alien continuously residing and physically present in the United States". With his position thus assimilated, the Court held that the Constitution forbade it to construe the regulations permitting exclusion without a hearing for security reasons, under which Knauff and Mezei had been barred, as applying to him.

Cf. note 43, *infra.*

[For later decisions illustrating the propositions in text, see Woodby v. INS, 385 U.S. 276 (1966); Rosenberg v. Fleuti, 374 U.S. 449 (1963); Gastelum-Quinones v. Kennedy, 374 U.S. 469 (1963).

What is happening is what so often happens when there has been a development in the law of which the judges are incompletely aware. Some decisions follow the earlier precedents and some the later, until the conflict of principle becomes intolerable, and it gets ironed out.

Q. Do you mean to say that you don't think there are any material differences between the case of an alien trying to get into the country and the case of one whom the government is trying to put out?

A. No. Of course there are differences in these alien cases—not only those simple ones but many others.[42] But such differences are material only in determining the content of due process in the particular situation. What process is due always depends upon the circumstances, and the due process clause is always flexible enough to take the circumstances into account.

The distinctions the Court has been drawing recently, however, are of a different order. They are distinctions between when the Constitution applies and when it does not apply at all. Any such distinction as that produces a conflict of basic principle, and is inadmissible.

Q. What basic principle?

A. The great and generating principle of this whole body of law—that the Constitution always applies when a court is sitting with jurisdiction in habeas corpus. For then the Court has always to inquire, not only whether the statutes have been observed, but whether the petitioner before it has been "deprived of life, liberty, or property, without due process of law", or injured in any other way in violation of the fundamental law.

[In Landon v. Plasencia, 459 U.S. 21 (1982), a case involving admission to the United States, the Court again distinguished Knauff and Mezei, and at least some doubt was cast on their future scope and application. Then, after a good deal of ferment in the lower courts and in the law reviews, the admission issue came before the Court again in Jean v. Nelson, 472 U.S. 846 (1985). This case involved a claim by "unadmitted aliens" from Haiti that their detention without parole violated certain statutes and regulations, as well as the Constitution. The majority remanded for further consideration of the claims under the statutes and regulations, and declined to consider the constitutional issues. Justice Marshall, joined by Justice Brennan in dissent, said that there was "no principled way to avoid the constitutional question," and on that question concluded that "petitioners have a Fifth Amendment right to parole decisions free from invidious discrimination" (p. 858). Rejecting the "broad dicta" in Knauff and Mezei, Justice Marshall pointed to cases establishing the rights of unadmitted aliens in other contexts, and urged that "any limitations on the applicability of the Constitution within our territorial jurisdiction fly in the face of this Court's long-held and recently reaffirmed commitment to apply the Constitution's due process and equal protection guarantees to all individuals within the reach of our sovereignty" (pp. 868, 874–75). He cited the Dialogue (at p. 876) for the proposition that though the requirements of due process must vary with the circumstances, decisions concerning the parole of unadmitted aliens may not be left entirely to the judgment of Congress.]

42. For example, if the alien is applying for admission, the force of his claim may vary according to whether he is coming for the first time or seeking to resume a permanent residence previously authorized. If he is coming for the first time, it may make a difference whether he is a stowaway or in possession of a duly issued visa. If he has a visa, it may make a difference whether it is one for permanent residence or only for a temporary visit. If he is seeking to resume a previously authorized residence, it may make a difference whether he carries a reentry permit, border crossing card, or other document purporting to facilitate reentry.

Similarly, if the alien is resisting expulsion, the force of his claim may vary according to whether he entered legally or illegally. If he entered legally, it may make a difference whether he was duly admitted for permanent residence or came in only as a seaman, student, or other temporary visitor for business or pleasure.

That is the premise of the deportation cases,[43] and it applies in exactly the same way in admission cases. The harsh early decisions announcing a contrary premise applied the contrary premise without distinction in both deportations and admissions. Indeed, Justice Minton cited early admission and deportation precedents indiscriminately in Knauff, without noticing that the principle which admittedly compelled repudiation of the deportation precedents required repudiation also of the others.[44]

That principle forbids a constitutional court with jurisdiction in habeas corpus from ever accepting as an adequate return to the writ the mere statement that what has been done is authorized by act of Congress. The inquiry remains, if Marbury v. Madison still stands, whether the act of

---

43. See, in addition to the cases cited in notes 39 and 41, *supra*, Heikkila v. Barber, 345 U.S. 229 (1953). Speaking for the Court, Justice Clark there held squarely that judicial review in deportation cases is "required by the Constitution". He said that "Regardless of whether or not the scope of inquiry on habeas corpus has been expanded, the function of the courts has always been limited to the enforcement of due process requirements".

It is to be observed that since the courts in habeas corpus have always enforced statutory requirements, too, Justice Clark must here be understood as saying that the Constitution gives the alien a right, among others, to have the statutes observed. The statement seems to apply equally to admission cases.

The Court gave this sweeping declaration of the constitutional rights of aliens an ironical twist by turning it, in the particular case, against the alien. It said that since review in habeas corpus was required by the Constitution rather than by the statute (the statute making deportation orders in terms "final"), the case was one in which the "statutes preclude judicial review" within the meaning of § 10 of the Administrative Procedure Act. Hence a prospective deportee could not get review of an order for his deportation under that section, and since he had been set at large pending efforts to effectuate his removal he was for the moment without a remedy.

Was it reasonable to read the statute as if Congress had said, "We wish to except from this broad grant of judicial review all cases in which a statute precludes judicial review, even where the statute does so unconstitutionally, and even though the courts for half a century have been according judicial review under the statute, saying as they did so that they were construing the statute to authorize such review in order to save its constitutionality"?

[In 1955 the Court regained lost ground, however, by holding that Heikkila applies only to the term "final" in the Act of 1917, and not to the same term in the Act of

1952, so that a deportation order under the latter may be reviewed in an action for declaratory judgment and injunction pursuant to the general judicial review provisions of the Administrative Procedure Act. Shaughnessy v. Pedreiro, 349 U.S. 48 (1955). And in 1956, Brownell v. Tom We Shung, 352 U.S. 180 (1956), eroded the distinction between deportation and exclusion by holding that under the APA exclusion orders, as well as deportations, were reviewable in declaratory actions as well as by habeas corpus.

[In 1961, Congress reentered the dialogue by adding new § 106 to the Act, 8 U.S.C. § 1105a, which for the first time codified the structure of judicial review. Section 106 creates a new statutory procedure for direct review of deportation orders by petition for review in the Courts of Appeals. This statutory procedure is exclusive, except that habeas corpus is expressly preserved as an available remedy. In exclusion cases, the 1961 statute overturns Tom We Shung by making habeas corpus the exclusive remedy. See also notes 30, 37, *supra*.

[For an extensive and excellent analysis of the 1961 statute and its background, see Comment, 71 Yale L.J. 760 (1962). See also 2 Gordon & Rosenfield, Immigration Law and Procedure Chap. 8 (1986).]

44. Justice Minton cited Nishimura Ekiu and Fong Yue Ting, note 38, *supra*, and Ludecke v. Watkins, note 40, *supra*, three times each. At the end of one string of these three citations, he included an unexplained "*Cf.* Yamataya v. Fisher", note 39, *supra*. He cited no other alien cases.

As will be seen from the cases in note 39 the earlier premise, in substance, had already been repudiated in admission as well as deportation cases. Justice Clark's statement in Heikkila, note 43, *supra*, that the function of courts in habeas corpus cases "has always been limited to the enforcement of due process requirements" makes this unmistakable.

Congress is consistent with the fundamental law. Only upon such a principle could the Court reject, as it surely would, a return to the writ which informed it that the applicant for admission lay stretched upon a rack with pins driven in behind his finger nails pursuant to authority duly conferred by statute in order to secure the information necessary to determine his admissibility. The same principle which would justify rejection of this return imposes responsibility to inquire into the adequacy of other returns.

Granting that the requirements of due process must vary with the circumstances,[45] and allowing them all the flexibility that can conceivably be claimed, it still remains true that the Court is obliged, by the presuppositions of its whole jurisdiction in this area, to decide whether what has been done is consistent with due process—and not simply pass back the buck to an assertedly all-powerful and unimpeachable Congress.

Q. Would it have made any difference in Knauff and Mezei if the Court had said that the aliens were entitled to due process and had got it, instead of saying that they weren't entitled to it at all?

A. At least the opinions in that case might have been intellectually defensible. Whether the results would have been different depends upon subtler considerations. Usually, however, it does make a difference whether a judge treats a question as not properly before him at all or as involving a matter for decision.

Take Knauff, for example. Remember that the War Brides Act was highly ambiguous on the point in issue of whether exclusion without a hearing was authorized. If one approaches such a question on the assumption that it is constitutionally neutral, as Justice Minton declared it to be, it is at least possible to resolve the doubt as he resolved it. But if one sees constitutional overtones, the most elementary principles of interpretation call for the opposite conclusion. Note how crucially important constitutional assumptions have been in the interpretation of statutes throughout this whole area.

Again, take the facts of Mezei, in comparison with its *dicta*. The *dicta* say, in effect, that a Mexican who sneaks successfully across the Rio Grande is entitled to the full panoply of due process in his deportation.[46] But the holding says that a duly admitted immigrant of twenty-five years' standing who has married an American wife and sired American children,

---

45. [This point was explicitly recognized and discussed in Landon v. Plasencia, 459 U.S. 21, 34–35 (1982). "[Plasencia] may lose the right to rejoin her immediate family, a right that ranks high among the interests of the individual. * * * The Government's interest in efficient administration of the immigration laws at the border also is weighty. Further, it must weigh heavily in the balance that control over matters of immigration is a sovereign prerogative, largely within the control of the Executive and the Legislature. * * * Thus, it would be improper simply to impose deportation procedures here because the reviewing court may find them preferable. Instead, the courts must evaluate the particular circumstances and determine what procedures would satisfy the minimum requirements of due process on the reentry of a permanent resident alien." See also *Developments in the Law, Immigration Policy and the Rights of Aliens,* 96 Harv.L.Rev. 1286, 1324–33 (1983).]

46. "It is true that aliens who have once passed through our gates, even illegally, may be expelled only after proceedings conforming to traditional standards of fairness encompassed in due process of law." 345 U.S. at 212. Compare the facts of The Japanese Immigrant Case, note 39, *supra,* Justice Jackson's statement in Wong Yang Sung v. McGrath, note 41, *supra,* and the Court's holding in Kwong Hai Chew v. Colding, note 41, *supra.*

who goes abroad as the law allows to visit a dying parent, and who then returns with passport and visa duly issued by an American consul, is entitled to nothing—and, indeed, may be detained on an island in New York harbor for the rest of his life if no other country can be found to take him.

I cannot believe that judges adequately aware of the foundations of principle in this field would permit themselves to trivialize the great guarantees of due process and the freedom writ by such distinctions. And I cannot believe that judges taking responsibility for an affirmative declaration that due process has been accorded would permit themselves to arrive at such brutal conclusions.

Q. But that is what the Court has held. And so I guess that's that.

A. No, it isn't.

The deepest assumptions of the legal order require that the decisions of the highest court in the land be accepted as settling the rights and wrongs of the particular matter immediately in controversy. But the judges who sit for the time being on the court have no authority to remake by fiat alone the fabric of principle by which future cases are to be decided. They are only the custodians of the law and not the owners of it. The law belongs to the people of the country, and to the hundreds of thousands of lawyers and judges who through the years have struggled, in their behalf, to make it coherent and intelligible and responsive to the people's sense of justice.

And so when justices write opinions in behalf of the Court which ignore the painful forward steps of a whole half century of adjudication, making no effort to relate what then is being done to what the Court has done before, they write without authority for the future. The appeal to principle is still open and, so long as courts of the United States sit with general jurisdiction in habeas corpus, that means an appeal to them and their successors.

2. In Default of Grants of General Jurisdiction

Q. Well, maybe so and maybe not so. In any event, what I thought was the sixty-four dollar question turned out to be only the thirty-two dollar one. You've brought in general grants of jurisdiction, and everything you've just been saying depends on them. What if those grants didn't exist?

A. But they *do* exist. And although they don't quite cover the waterfront, they take care of most of the basic situations. On the crucial matter of personal liberty, there is the habeas corpus statute we've just been talking about. 28 U.S.C. § 2241. There's §§ 1346 and 1491 to assure just compensation for the taking of private property. And, passing other special provisions, there is § 1331 for denials of constitutional right generally. The principal hole is the jurisdictional amount requirement there, which, I admit, may be a big one.[47]

47. [In 1980, Congress eliminated the jurisdictional amount requirement in § 1331.]

Q. But suppose those statutes were repealed. Why wouldn't the executive department then be free to go ahead and violate fundamental rights at will?

A. That's a pretty unlikely situation, isn't it? You're supposing that two of the three branches of the federal government are going to gang up on the third. Congress would need the executive arm to seize persons and property, if it were going to act on an important scale. And the executive arm could be checked by the courts unless Congress had repealed the general grants of jurisdiction. If both of them did get together, it wouldn't be long before the voters had something to say, would it?

Besides, what would be the practical incentive to act that way in any very great number of situations? Remember the *Federalist* papers. Were the framers wholly mistaken in thinking that, as a matter of the hard facts of power, a government needs courts to vindicate its decisions? Is there some new science of government that tells how to do it in some other way?[48]

Q. Granting all that, you can do a lot of things without courts, as the alien laws show. The problem can easily arise by deliberate action directed to some obscure or unpopular group, or even by inadvertence. Suppose Congress says flatly that no court shall have jurisdiction in such and such a situation, even in habeas corpus?

A. The habeas corpus part of it would be in direct violation of the Constitution. Article I, Sec. 9, Cl. 2.[49]

True, the constitution does not explain what happens if the constitutional command is disobeyed. In Ex parte Bollman, 4 Cranch 75 (U.S.1807), Chief Justice Marshall said unequivocally that "the power to award the writ by any of the courts of the United States must be given by written law". And in considering § 14 of the Judiciary Act of 1789 as a source of jurisdiction he observed:

"It may be worthy of remark that this act was passed by the first congress of the United States, sitting under a constitution that had declared 'that the privilege of the writ of habeas corpus should not be suspended, unless when, in cases of rebellion or invasion, the public safety may require it'. Acting under the immediate influence of this injunction, they must have felt, with peculiar force, the obligation of providing effi-

---

48. [Compare the history of Congress's power to punish for contempt: "Since World War II, the Congress has practically abandoned its original practice of utilizing the coercive sanction of contempt proceedings at the bar of the House. The sanction there imposed is imprisonment by the House * * * provided that the incarceration does not extend beyond adjournment. The Congress has instead invoked the aid of the federal judicial system in protecting itself against contumacious conduct. It has become customary to refer these matters to the United States Attorneys for prosecution under criminal law." Watkins v. United States, 354 U.S. 178, 206–07 (1957).]

49. [This would seem to be clear insofar as the attempt is to prevent *both* federal and state courts from issuing the writ. But what if Congress withdraws jurisdiction only from the lower federal courts; is this an unconstitutional suspension if the state courts are left free to issue the writ? (Of course the state courts would be free to do so only on the assumption—surely warranted—that in such an event the dubious rule of Tarble's Case, p. 484, *infra*, that the state courts may not issue the writ to federal prisoners, would not survive.)

[For further discussion of the relation between Tarble's Case and the problems canvassed in the Dialogue, see pp. 490–91, *infra*. See also, with respect to the Suspension Clause, p. 1577, *infra*.]

cient means by which this great constitutional privilege should receive life and activity; for if the means be not in existence, the privilege itself would be lost, although no law for its suspension should be enacted. Under the impression of this obligation, they gave to all the courts the power of awarding writs of habeas corpus."

However, where statutory jurisdiction to issue the writ obtains, but the privilege of it has been suspended in particular circumstances, the Court has declared itself ready to consider the validity of the suspension and, if it is found invalid, of the detention. See Ex parte Milligan, 4 Wall. 2 (U.S.1866); Ex parte Quirin, 317 U.S. 1, 24–25 (1942). In such an event the courts at least may speak, though they may still be helpless to enforce their orders if they are defied.[50]

Q. Habeas corpus has a special constitutional position. But suppose Congress is in dead earnest about withdrawing general jurisdiction in a special class of cases arising under the Constitution. Do you mean that it could only accomplish that by repealing § 1331 *in toto,* on the theory that a mere amendment might be declared unconstitutional and the prior § 1331 then left free to operate? Or that it couldn't accomplish it even by a total repealer, since the repealer could be declared unconstitutional?

A. Well, now, I'll have to stall a little. Habeas corpus aside, I'd hesitate to say that Congress couldn't effect an unconstitutional withdrawal of jurisdiction—that is, a withdrawal to effectuate unconstitutional purposes—if it really wanted to. But the Court should use every possible resource of construction to avoid the conclusion that it did want to.

Q. That's the second or third time you've said something like that. What basis for it have you?

A. Sound principle. Our whole constitutional history shows that Congress generally doesn't intend to violate constitutional rights, and a court ought not readily to assume any sudden departure.

But there's a deeper reason which follows from what we were saying a moment ago. In the end we have to depend on Congress for the effective functioning of our judicial system, and perhaps for any functioning. The primary check on Congress is the political check—the votes of the people. If Congress wants to frustrate the judicial check, our constitutional tradi-

---

50. See the famous opinion of Taney. C.J., in Ex parte Merryman, 17 F.Cas. 144 (No. 9487) (C.C.D.Md.1861): " * * * I have exercised all the power which the constitution and laws confer upon me, but that power has been resisted by a force too strong for me to overcome. It is possible that the officer who has incurred this grave responsibility may have misunderstood his instructions, and exceeded the authority intended to be given him; I shall, therefore, order all the proceedings in this case, with my opinion, to be filed and recorded in the circuit court of the United States for the district of Maryland, and direct the clerk to transmit a copy, under seal, to the president of the United States. It will then remain for that high officer, in fulfillment of his constitutional obligation to 'take care that the laws be faithfully executed' to determine what measures he will take to cause the civil process of the United States to be respected and enforced."

Difficult questions relating to the privileges of the writ and its suspension were raised by the regime of martial law imposed in Hawaii after the attack at Pearl Harbor. See, *e.g.,* Fairman, *The Supreme Court on Military Jurisdiction: Martial Law in Hawaii and the Yamashita Case,* 59 Harv.L.Rev. 833 (1946); Duncan v. Kahanamoku, 327 U.S. 304 (1946). For an account of efforts to prevent the district court from entertaining a petition to test the validity of the suspension, see McColloch, *Judge Metzger and the Military,* 35 A.B.A.J. 365 (1949); *cf.* Houston, *Martial Law in Hawaii: A Defense of the War-Time Military Governor,* 36 A.B.A.J. 825 (1950).

tion requires that it be made to say so unmistakably, so that the people will understand and the political check can operate.

Q. But you still haven't answered the question of what happens if Congress *does* withdraw jurisdiction unmistakably or if, by inadvertence or whatever, there just isn't any grant of jurisdiction.

A. One current situation may present that question. The present habeas corpus statute authorizes courts and judges to issue the writ only "within their respective jurisdictions". Ahrens v. Clark, 335 U.S. 188 (1948), held that the quoted language precluded the district court for the District of Columbia from inquiry into restraint in a New York district. This was held to be so even though the defendant Attorney General had issued the orders involved and had supervision of the custodians. And the defect was held to be one of jurisdiction which could not be waived.[51] The Court reserved the question of possible application of this decision to persons held abroad and so not under restraint in any judicial district.

Q. You mean that such persons might have no access to the writ at all?

A. Exactly. But the Court of Appeals of the District of Columbia considered any such conclusion inadmissible, and held that the case should be entertained regardless. It said, without limitation to the habeas corpus problem, that the provisions of Article III "were compulsory upon Congress to confer the whole of the federal judicial power upon some federal court".[52]

Q. I should think the government would have taken that case up.

A. It did. But the victory it won was equivocal. The petitioners for the writ were German nationals, confined in Germany upon conviction of war crimes by a United States military commission in China. The Supreme Court held that, as enemy aliens, they had failed to state a case. But whether this was for the reason that their confinement was legal or, though illegal, irremediable, the opinion leaves obscure. Johnson v. Eisentrager, 339 U.S. 763 (1950). *Cf.* Ludecke v. Watkins, 335 U.S. 160 (1948). Thus, the position of a citizen imprisoned abroad who states a genuine challenge to the legality, or even the constitutionality, of his detention remains undecided.[53]

---

51. [Ahrens was legislatively modified by 28 U.S.C. § 2255 (federal prisoners must test convictions in "the court which imposed the sentence"), and by 28 U.S.C. § 2241(d) (allowing state prisoners in multi-district states to file petitions in the district of confinement or in the district where the sentencing court sat). The case was then overruled in Braden v. 30th Judicial Circuit Court, 410 U.S. 484, 495–501 (1973).]

52. Eisentrager v. Forrestal, 174 F.2d 961, 965–66 (D.C.Cir.1949).

[Would the decision of the Court of Appeals have been more persuasive if based on the special powers of the courts of the District of Columbia as inheritors of the general jurisdiction of the Virginia and Maryland courts sitting in the lands comprising the District prior to their cession to the federal government?

53. [But in Burns v. Wilson, 346 U.S. 137 (1953), the Supreme Court, without discussing the issue, passed on a habeas corpus petition brought against the Secretary of Defense in the District of Columbia by a soldier held by the military in Japan; see the opinion of Mr. Justice Frankfurter commenting on the denial of rehearing, 346 U.S. at 844, 851–52 ("Petitioners have not discussed the question of jurisdiction, and the Government appears disinclined to argue it"). See also United States ex rel. Toth v. Quarles, 350 U.S. 11 (1955).]

H. Conclusion

Q. At least the Court in Eisentrager didn't squarely accuse Congress of intending to leave constitutional rights without a remedy, where Congress hadn't said that. But it ducked the ultimate question, just as you've done so far.

A. I've given all the important answers to that question, haven't I? I would have thought the rest was clear. Why, it's been clear ever since September 17, 1787.

Q. Not to me.

A. The state courts. In the scheme of the Constitution, they are the primary guarantors of constitutional rights, and in many cases they may be the ultimate ones. If they were to fail, and if Congress had taken away the Supreme Court's appellate jurisdiction and been upheld in doing so,[54] then we really would be sunk.

Q. But Congress can regulate the jurisdiction of state courts, too, in federal matters.

A. Congress can't do it unconstitutionally. The state courts always have a general jurisdiction to fall back on. And the supremacy clause binds them to exercise that jurisdiction in accordance with the Constitution.

Q. But the Supreme Court could reverse their decisions.

A. Not lawfully, if the decisions were in accordance with the Constitution. Congress can't shut the Supreme Court off from the merits and give it jurisdiction simply to reverse. Not, anyway, if I'm right that the implications of Estep were an aberration, and that jurisdiction always is jurisdiction only to decide constitutionally.

CONCLUDING NOTE: PROBLEMS OF ACCESS TO AMERICAN COURTS UNDER PRISONER TRANSFER TREATIES

Intricate questions implicating a right of access to a judicial forum are raised by the Mexican–American Prisoner Transfer Treaty of 1977 and similar treaties entered with other countries.[1] The Treaty with Mexico permits some Americans, held in Mexican prisons for offenses against Mexican criminal law which would also be "generally punishable as

54. The vulnerability of the Supreme Court's appellate jurisdiction to control by Congress has led to various proposals for amendments of the Constitution. One, initiated by the Association of the Bar of the City of New York, supported by former Justice Roberts, and, after some conflict of views, by the American Bar Association, proposed that Article III, Section 2, be amended to provide in substance that the Supreme Court shall have appellate jurisdiction in all cases arising under the Constitution of the United States, both as to law and fact, with such exceptions and under such regulations as the Court shall make. See 34 A.B.A.J. 1072–3 (1948); Roberts, *Now is the Time: Fortifying the Supreme Court's Independence,* 35 A.B.A.J. 1 (1944). See also S.J.Res. 44, 83d Cong., 1st Sess. (1953).

1. The Treaty with Mexico was ratified by the Senate in July 1977, and enabling legislation was enacted in October 1977. 91 Stat. 1212–22 (codified at 10 U.S.C. § 955, 18 U.S.C. §§ 3006A, 3244, 4100–4115).

crimes" in the United States, to elect, with the permission of the authorities of both nations, to serve the remainder of their sentences in federal prisons in the United States. Reciprocal options are given to Mexicans imprisoned in the United States. The Treaty provides that the transferor state has exclusive jurisdiction over "any proceeding" to challenge, set aside or modify the sentence of the transferor court. The Treaty thus on its face prohibits an American court from taking jurisdiction on habeas corpus to determine whether American constitutional rights are in any sense "applicable" to an American held in an American prison after a conviction in a Mexican court. The Treaty also provides that a prisoner must give his express consent before he can be transferred, and must agree to abide by the provision requiring that all attacks on a prisoner's conviction and sentence be made in the courts of the transferor state.

For analysis of the constitutional questions raised by this and similar treaties, see Robbins, *A Constitutional Analysis of the Prohibition Against Collateral Attack in the Mexican–American Prisoner Exchange Treaty,* 26 U.C.L.A.L.Rev. 1 (1978); Note, *Constitutional Problems in the Execution of Foreign Penal Sentences,* 90 Harv.L.Rev. 1500 (1976). A strong case for the constitutional validity of the treaty was made in a memorandum on behalf of the State Department by Professor Detlev Vagts [2] and in testimony by Professor Herbert Wechsler.[3]

Suppose that an American transferred under this Treaty seeks habeas corpus in a federal district court, alleging that his Mexican conviction was based entirely on a confession extracted from him by physical torture. Suppose further that no remedies are now available to challenge that conviction in a Mexican court. Try to formulate all of the questions which a federal district court would have to resolve before it could grant the writ.

For an exploration of some of these questions, see the opinion of Kaufman, J., in Rosado v. Civiletti, 621 F.2d 1179 (2d Cir.1980), stating that the Treaty cannot constitutionally prohibit all access to American courts to test the validity of a prisoner's detention by the United States pursuant to transfer under the Treaty, but concluding that the petitioners' express agreement to refrain from such a challenge, in compliance with the Treaty, created an estoppel against their release on habeas corpus. See also Pfeifer v. United States Bureau of Prisons, 615 F.2d 873 (9th Cir.1980) (rejecting, on waiver grounds, attack on Treaty by transferred prisoner).

---

2. See *Transfer of Offenders and Administration of Foreign Penal Sentences: Hearings on S. 1682 Before the Subcomm. on Penitentiaries and Corrections,* Sen. Comm. on the Judiciary, 95th Cong., 1st Sess. 209 (1977).

3. See *Penal Treaties With Mexico and Canada: Hearings Before the Comm. on Foreign Relations, U.S.Sen.,* 95th Cong., 1st Sess. 93 (1977).

SUBSECTION B: CONGRESSIONAL AUTHORITY TO ALLOCATE JUDICIAL POWER AMONG FEDERAL TRIBUNALS: HEREIN OF LEGISLATIVE COURTS

NORTHERN PIPELINE CONSTRUCTION CO. v. MARATHON PIPE LINE CO.

458 U.S. 50, 102 S.Ct. 2858, 73 L.Ed.2d 598 (1982).
Appeal from the United States District Court for the District of Minnesota.

JUSTICE BRENNAN announced the judgment of the Court and delivered an opinion, in which JUSTICE MARSHALL, JUSTICE BLACKMUN, and JUSTICE STEVENS joined.

The question presented is whether the assignment by Congress to bankruptcy judges of the jurisdiction granted in 28 U.S.C. § 1471 by § 241(a) of the Bankruptcy Act of 1978 violates Art. III of the Constitution.

I

A

In 1978, after almost 10 years of study and investigation, Congress enacted a comprehensive revision of the bankruptcy laws. The Bankruptcy Act of 1978 (Act) made significant changes in both the substantive and procedural law of bankruptcy. It is the changes in the latter that are at issue in this case.

Before the Act, federal district courts served as bankruptcy courts and employed a "referee" system. Bankruptcy proceedings were generally conducted before referees,[2] except in those instances in which the district court elected to withdraw a case from a referee. See Bkrtcy. Rule 102. The referee's final order was appealable to the district court. Bkrtcy. Rule 801. The bankruptcy courts were vested with "summary jurisdiction"— that is, with jurisdiction over controversies involving property in the actual or constructive possession of the court. And, with consent, the bankruptcy court also had jurisdiction over some "plenary" matters—such as disputes involving property in the possession of a third person.

The Act eliminates the referee system and establishes "in each judicial district, as an adjunct to the district court for such district, a bankruptcy court which shall be a court of record known as the United States Bankruptcy Court for the district." 28 U.S.C. § 151(a) (1976 ed., Supp. IV). The judges of these courts are appointed to office for 14-year terms by the President, with the advice and consent of the Senate. §§ 152, 153(a). They are subject to removal by the "judicial council of the circuit" on account of "incompetency, misconduct, neglect of duty or physical or mental disability." § 153(b). In addition, the salaries of the bankruptcy judges are set by

2. Bankruptcy referees were redesignated as "judges" in 1973. Bkrtcy. Rule 901(7). For purposes of clarity, however, we refer to all judges under the old Act as "referees."

statute and are subject to adjustment under the Federal Salary Act, 2 U.S.C. §§ 351–361. 28 U.S.C. § 154.

The jurisdiction of the bankruptcy courts created by the Act is much broader than that exercised under the former referee system. Eliminating the distinction between "summary" and "plenary" jurisdiction, the Act grants the new courts jurisdiction over all "civil proceedings arising under title 11 [the Bankruptcy title] or arising in or *related to* cases under title 11." 28 U.S.C. § 1471(b) (emphasis added). This jurisdictional grant empowers bankruptcy courts to entertain a wide variety of cases involving claims that may affect the property of the estate once a petition has been filed under Title 11. Included within the bankruptcy courts' jurisdiction are suits to recover accounts, controversies involving exempt property, actions to avoid transfers and payments as preferences or fraudulent conveyances, and causes of action owned by the debtor at the time of the petition for bankruptcy. The bankruptcy courts can hear claims based on state law as well as those based on federal law. See 1 W. Collier, Bankruptcy ¶ 3.01, pp. 3–47 to 3–48 (15th ed. 1982).[4]

The judges of the bankruptcy courts are vested with all of the "powers of a court of equity, law, and admiralty," except that they "may not enjoin another court or punish a criminal contempt not committed in the presence of the judge of the court or warranting a punishment of imprisonment." 28 U.S.C. § 1481. In addition to this broad grant of power, Congress has allowed bankruptcy judges the power to hold jury trials, § 1480; to issue declaratory judgments, § 2201; to issue writs of habeas corpus under certain circumstances, § 2256; to issue all writs necessary in aid of the bankruptcy court's expanded jurisdiction, § 451; see 28 U.S.C. § 1651; and to issue any order, process or judgment that is necessary or appropriate to carry out the provisions of Title 11, 11 U.S.C. § 105(a).

The Act also establishes a special procedure for appeals from orders of bankruptcy courts. The circuit council is empowered to direct the chief judge of the circuit to designate panels of three bankruptcy judges to hear appeals. 28 U.S.C. § 160. These panels have jurisdiction of all appeals from final judgments, orders, and decrees of bankruptcy courts, and, with leave of the panel, of interlocutory appeals. § 1482. If no such appeals panel is designated, the district court is empowered to exercise appellate jurisdiction. § 1334. The court of appeals is given jurisdiction over appeals from the appellate panels or from the district court. § 1293. If the parties agree, a direct appeal to the court of appeals may be taken from a final judgment of a bankruptcy court. § 1293(b).[5]

* * *

4. With respect to both personal jurisdiction and venue, the scope of the Act is also expansive. * * * Furthermore, the Act permits parties to remove many kinds of actions to the bankruptcy court. * * * [28 U.S.C.] § 1478(a). The bankruptcy court may, however, remand such actions "on any equitable ground"; the decision to remand or retain an action is unreviewable. § 1478(b).

5. Although no particular standard of review is specified in the Act, the parties in the present cases seem to agree that the appropriate one is the clearly-erroneous standard, employed in old Bankruptcy Rule 810 for review of findings of fact made by a referee. * * *

B

This case arises out of proceedings initiated in the United States *Facts*
Bankruptcy Court for the District of Minnesota after appellant Northern
Pipeline Construction Co. (Northern) filed a petition for reorganization in
January 1980. In March 1980 Northern, pursuant to the Act, filed in that
court a suit against appellee Marathon Pipe Line Co. (Marathon). Appellant sought damages for alleged breaches of contract and warranty, as well
as for alleged misrepresentation, coercion, and duress. Marathon sought *claim*
dismissal of the suit, on the ground that the Act unconstitutionally conferred Art. III judicial power upon judges who lacked life tenure and
protection against salary diminution. The United States intervened to
defend the validity of the statute.

The Bankruptcy Judge denied the motion to dismiss. 6 B.R. 928 (1980).
But on appeal the District Court entered an order granting the motion, on
the ground that "the delegation of authority in 28 U.S.C. § 1471 to the *Dist.*
Bankruptcy Judges to try cases which are otherwise relegated under the *ct.*
Constitution to Article III judges" was unconstitutional. Both the United *held*
States and Northern filed notices of appeal in this Court. We noted
probable jurisdiction. 454 U.S. 1029 (1981).

II

A

Basic to the constitutional structure established by the Framers was
their recognition that "[t]he accumulation of all powers, legislative, executive, and judiciary, in the same hands, whether of one, a few, or many, and
whether hereditary, self-appointed, or elective, may justly be pronounced
the very definition of tyranny." The Federalist No. 47, p. 300 (H. Lodge ed.
1888) (J. Madison). To ensure against such tyranny, the Framers provided
that the Federal Government would consist of three distinct Branches, each
to exercise one of the governmental powers recognized by the Framers as
inherently distinct. "The Framers regarded the checks and balances that
they had built into the tripartite Federal Government as a self-executing
safeguard against the encroachment or aggrandizement of one branch at
the expense of the other." Buckley v. Valeo, 424 U.S. 1, 122 (1976) (per
curiam).

The Federal Judiciary was therefore designed by the Framers to stand
independent of the Executive and Legislature—to maintain the checks and
balances of the constitutional structure, and also to guarantee that the
process of adjudication itself remained impartial. Hamilton explained the
importance of an independent Judiciary:

> "Periodical appointments, however regulated, or by whomsoever made,
> would, in some way or other, be fatal to [the courts'] necessary
> independence. If the power of making them was committed either to
> the Executive or legislature, there would be danger of an improper
> complaisance to the branch which possessed it; if to both, there would
> be an unwillingness to hazard the displeasure of either; if to the
> people, or to persons chosen by them for the special purpose, there
> would be too great a disposition to consult popularity, to justify a

reliance that nothing would be consulted but the Constitution and the laws." The Federalist No. 78, p. 489 (H. Lodge ed. 1888).

* * *

As an inseparable element of the constitutional system of checks and balances, and as a guarantee of judicial impartiality, Art. III both defines the power and protects the independence of the Judicial Branch. It provides that "The judicial Power of the United States, shall be vested in one supreme Court, and in such inferior Courts as the Congress may from time to time ordain and establish." Art. III, § 1. The inexorable command of this provision is clear and definite: The judicial power of the United States must be exercised by courts having the attributes prescribed in Art. III. Those attributes are also clearly set forth:

> "The Judges, both of the supreme and inferior Courts, shall hold their Offices during good Behaviour, and shall, at stated Times, receive for their Services, a Compensation, which shall not be diminished during their Continuance in Office." Art. III, § 1.

The "good Behaviour" Clause guarantees that Art. III judges shall enjoy life tenure, subject only to removal by impeachment. United States ex rel. Toth v. Quarles, 350 U.S. 11, 16 (1955). The Compensation Clause guarantees Art. III judges a fixed and irreducible compensation for their services. United States v. Will, [449 U.S. 200 (1980)] at 218–221. Both of these provisions were incorporated into the Constitution to ensure the independence of the Judiciary from the control of the Executive and Legislative Branches of government.[10] * * *

B

It is undisputed that the bankruptcy judges whose offices were created by the Bankruptcy Act of 1978 do not enjoy the protections constitutionally afforded to Art. III judges. The bankruptcy judges do not serve for life subject to their continued "good Behaviour." Rather, they are appointed for 14–year terms, and can be removed by the judicial council of the circuit in which they serve on grounds of "incompetency, misconduct, neglect of duty, or physical or mental disability." Second, the salaries of the bankruptcy judges are not immune from diminution by Congress. In short, there is no doubt that the bankruptcy judges created by the Act are not Art. III judges.

That Congress chose to vest such broad jurisdiction in non-Art. III bankruptcy courts, after giving substantial consideration to the constitutionality of the Act, is of course reason to respect the congressional conclusion.[12] Palmore v. United States, 411 U.S. 389, 409 (1973). See also

---

10. These provisions serve other institutional values as well. The independence from political forces that they guarantee helps to promote public confidence in judicial determinations. See The Federalist No. 78 (A. Hamilton). The security that they provide to members of the Judicial Branch helps to attract well-qualified persons to the federal bench. *Ibid.* The guarantee of life tenure insulates the individual judge from improper influences not only by other branches but by colleagues as well, and thus promotes judicial individualism.

See Kaufman, *Chilling Judicial Independence,* 88 Yale L.J. 681, 713 (1979). See generally Note, *Article III Limits on Article I Courts: The Constitutionality of the Bankruptcy Court and the 1979 Magistrate Act,* 80 Colum.L.Rev. 560, 583–585 (1980).

12. It should be noted, however, that the House of Representatives expressed substantial doubts respecting the constitutionality of the provisions eventually included in the Act * * *. [S]ee generally Klee, *Legislative History of the New Bank-*

National Ins. Co. v. Tidewater Co., 337 U.S. 582, 655 (1949) (Frankfurter, J., dissenting). But at the same time,

RV
BY
S.Ct

> "[d]eciding whether a matter has in any measure been committed by the Constitution to another branch of government, or whether the action of that branch exceeds whatever authority has been committed, is itself a delicate exercise in constitutional interpretation, and is a responsibility of this Court as ultimate interpreter of the Constitution." Baker v. Carr, 369 U.S. 186, 211 (1962).

With these principles in mind, we turn to the question presented for decision: whether the Bankruptcy Act of 1978 violates the command of Art. III that the judicial power of the United States must be vested in courts whose judges enjoy the protections and safeguards specified in that Article.

appellants
Argue
to
uphold

Appellants suggest two grounds for upholding the Act's conferral of broad adjudicative powers upon judges unprotected by Art. III. First, it is urged that "pursuant to its enumerated Article I powers, Congress may establish legislative courts that have jurisdiction to decide cases to which the Article III judicial power of the United States extends." Brief for United States 9. Referring to our precedents upholding the validity of "legislative courts," appellants suggest that "the plenary grants of power in Article I permit Congress to establish non-Article III tribunals in 'specialized areas having particularized needs and warranting distinctive treatment,'" such as the area of bankruptcy law. *Ibid.,* quoting Palmore v. United States, *supra,* at 408. Second, appellants contend that even if the Constitution does require that this bankruptcy-related action be adjudicated in an Art. III court, the Act in fact satisfies that requirement. "Bankruptcy jurisdiction was vested in the district court" of the judicial district in which the bankruptcy court is located, "and the exercise of that jurisdiction by the adjunct bankruptcy court was made subject to appeal as of right to an Article III court." Brief for United States 12. Analogizing the role of the bankruptcy court to that of a special master, appellants urge us to conclude that this "adjunct" system established by Congress satisfies the requirements of Art. III. We consider these arguments in turn.

III

Congress did not constitute the bankruptcy courts as legislative courts.[13] Appellants contend, however, that the bankruptcy courts could have been so constituted, and that as a result the "adjunct" system in fact chosen by Congress does not impermissibly encroach upon the judicial power. In advancing this argument, appellants rely upon cases in which we have identified certain matters that "congress may or may not bring within the cognizance of [Art. III courts], as it may deem proper." Murray's Lessee v. Hoboken Land & Improvement Co., 18 How. 272, 284 (1856).[14] But when properly understood, these precedents represent no broad departure from the constitutional command that the judicial power

---

ruptcy Law, 28 DePaul L.Rev. 941, 945–949, 951 (1979). * * * The bill that was finally enacted, denying bankruptcy judges the tenure and compensation protections of Art. III, was the result of a series of last-minute conferences and compromises between the managers of both Houses.

13. The Act designates the bankruptcy court in each district as an "adjunct" to the district court. 28 U.S.C. § 151(a). * * *

14. At one time, this Court suggested a rigid distinction between those subjects that could be considered only in Art. III

3 areas where ART. III + BAT Cong. Creation of Legislative Cts

Argument #1

① Territorial courts

of the United States must be vested in Art. III courts.[15] Rather, they reduce to three narrow situations not subject to that command, each recognizing a circumstance in which the grant of power to the Legislative and Executive Branches was historically and constitutionally so exceptional that the congressional assertion of a power to create legislative courts was consistent with, rather than threatening to, the constitutional mandate of separation of powers. These precedents simply acknowledge that the literal command of Art. III, assigning the judicial power of the United States to courts insulated from Legislative or Executive interference, must be interpreted in light of the historical context in which the Constitution was written, and of the structural imperatives of the Constitution as a whole.

Appellants first rely upon a series of cases in which this Court has upheld the creation by Congress of non-Art. III "territorial courts." This exception from the general prescription of Art. III dates from the earliest days of the Republic, when it was perceived that the Framers intended that as to certain geographical areas, in which no State operated as sovereign, Congress was to exercise the general powers of government. For example, in American Ins. Co. v. Canter, 1 Pet. 511 (1828), the Court observed that Art. IV bestowed upon Congress alone a complete power of government over territories not within the States that constituted the United States. The Court then acknowledged Congress' authority to create courts for those territories that were not in conformity with Art. III. Such courts were

> "created in virtue of the general right of sovereignty which exists in the government, or in virtue of that clause which enables Congress to make all needful rules and regulations, respecting the territory belonging to the United States. The jurisdiction with which they are invested * * * is conferred by Congress, in the execution of those general powers which that body possesses over the territories of the United States. Although admiralty jurisdiction can be exercised in the states in those Courts, only, which are established in pursuance of the third article of the Constitution; the same limitation does not extend to the territories. In legislating for them, Congress exercises the combined powers of the general, and of a state government." 1 Pet., at 546.

courts and those that could be considered only in legislative courts. See Williams v. United States, 289 U.S. 553 (1933). But this suggested dichotomy has not withstood analysis. See C. Wright, Law of the Federal Courts 33–35 (3d ed. 1976). Our more recent cases clearly recognize that legislative courts may be granted jurisdiction over some cases and controversies to which the Art. III judicial power might also be extended. *E.g.,* Palmore v. United States, 411 U.S. 389 (1973). See Glidden Co. v. Zdanok, 370 U.S. 530, 549–551 (1962) (opinion of Harlan, J.).

15. Justice White's dissent finds particular significance in the fact that Congress could have assigned all bankruptcy matters to the state courts. But, of course, virtually all matters that might be heard in Art. III courts could also be left by

Congress to state courts. This fact is simply irrelevant to the question before us. Congress has no control over state-court judges; accordingly the principle of separation of powers is not threatened by leaving the adjudication of federal disputes to such judges. See Krattenmaker, *Article III and Judicial Independence: Why the New Bankruptcy Courts are Unconstitutional,* 70 Geo.L.J. 297, 304–305 (1981). The Framers chose to leave to Congress the precise role to be played by the lower federal courts in the administration of justice. See Hart and Wechsler's The Federal Courts and the Federal System, at 11. But the Framers did not leave it to Congress to define the character of those courts—they were to be independent of the political branches and presided over by judges with guaranteed salary and life tenure.

The Court followed the same reasoning when it reviewed Congress' creation of non-Art. III courts in the District of Columbia. It noted that there was in the District

> "no division of powers between the general and state governments. Congress has the entire control over the district for every purpose of government; and it is reasonable to suppose, that in organizing a judicial department here, all judicial power necessary for the purposes of government would be vested in the courts of justice." Kendall v. United States, 12 Pet. 524, 619 (1838).[16]

Appellants next advert to a second class of cases—those in which this Court has sustained the exercise by Congress and the Executive of the power to establish and administer courts-martial. The situation in these cases strongly resembles the situation with respect to territorial courts: It too involves a constitutional grant of power that has been historically understood as giving the political Branches of Government extraordinary control over the precise subject matter at issue. Article I, § 8, cls. 13, 14, confer upon Congress the power "[t]o provide and maintain a Navy," and "[t]o make Rules for the Government and Regulation of the land and naval Forces." The Fifth Amendment, which requires a presentment or indictment of a grand jury before a person may be held to answer for a capital or otherwise infamous crime, contains an express exception for "cases arising in the land or naval forces." And Art. II, § 2, cl. 1, provides that "The President shall be Commander in Chief of the Army and Navy of the United States, and of the Militia of the several States, when called into the actual Service of the United States." Noting these constitutional directives, the Court in Dynes v. Hoover, 20 How. 65 (1857), explained:

> "These provisions show that Congress has the power to provide for the trial and punishment of military and naval offences in the manner then and now practiced by civilized nations; and that the power to do so is given without any connection between it and the 3d article of the Constitution defining the judicial power of the United States; indeed, that the two powers are entirely independent of each other." *Id.*, at 79.[17]

Finally, appellants rely on a third group of cases, in which this Court has upheld the constitutionality of legislative courts and administrative agencies created by Congress to adjudicate cases involving "public rights." [18] The "public rights" doctrine was first set forth in Murray's Lessee v. Hoboken Land & Improvement Co., 18 How. 272 (1856):

16. We recently reaffirmed the principle, expressed in these early cases, that Art. I, § 8, cl. 17, provides that Congress shall have power "[t]o exercise exclusive Legislation in all Cases whatsoever, over" the District of Columbia. Palmore v. United States, 411 U.S., at 397. See also Wallace v. Adams, 204 U.S. 415, 423 (1907) (recognizing Congress' authority to establish legislative courts to determine questions of tribal membership relevant to property claims within Indian territory); In re Ross, 140 U.S. 453 (1891) (same, respecting consular courts established by concession from foreign countries).
· · · ·

17. See also Burns v. Wilson, 346 U.S. 137, 139–140 (1953). But this Court has been alert to ensure that Congress does not exceed the constitutional bounds and bring within the jurisdiction of the military courts matters beyond that jurisdiction, and properly within the realm of "judicial power." See, *e.g.*, Reid v. Covert, [354 U.S. 1 (1957)]; United States ex rel. Toth v. Quarles, 350 U.S. 11 (1955).

18. Congress' power to create legislative courts to adjudicate public rights carries with it the lesser power to create administrative agencies for the same purpose, and to provide for review of those agency decisions in Art. III courts. See,

"[W]e do not consider congress can either withdraw from judicial cognizance any matter which, from its nature, is the subject of a suit at the common law, or in equity, or admiralty; nor, on the other hand, can it bring under the judicial power a matter which, from its nature, is not a subject for judicial determination. At the same time there are matters, *involving public rights,* which may be presented in such form that the judicial power is capable of acting on them, and which are susceptible of judicial determination, but which congress may or may not bring within the cognizance of the courts of the United States, as it may deem proper." *Id.,* at 284 (emphasis added).*

This doctrine may be explained in part by reference to the traditional principle of sovereign immunity, which recognizes that the Government may attach conditions to its consent to be sued. See *id.,* at 283–285; see also Ex parte Bakelite Corp., 279 U.S. 438, 452 (1929). But the public-rights doctrine also draws upon the principle of separation of powers, and a historical understanding that certain prerogatives were reserved to the political Branches of Government. The doctrine extends only to matters arising "between the Government and persons subject to its authority in connection with the performance of the constitutional functions of the executive or legislative departments," Crowell v. Benson, 285 U.S. 22, 50 (1932), and only to matters that historically could have been determined exclusively by those departments, see Ex parte Bakelite Corp., *supra,* at 458. The understanding of these cases is that the Framers expected that Congress would be free to commit such matters completely to nonjudicial executive determination, and that as a result there can be no constitutional objection to Congress' employing the less drastic expedient of committing their determination to a legislative court or an administrative agency. Crowell v. Benson, *supra,* at 50.

The public-rights doctrine is grounded in a historically recognized distinction between matters that could be conclusively determined by the Executive and Legislative Branches and matters that are "inherently * * * judicial." Ex parte Bakelite Corp., *supra,* at 458. See Murray's Lessee v. Hoboken Land & Improvement Co., 18 How., at 280–282. For example, the Court in Murray's Lessee looked to the law of England and the States at the time the Constitution was adopted, in order to determine whether the issue presented was customarily cognizable in the courts. Concluding that the matter had not traditionally been one for judicial determination, the Court perceived no bar to Congress' establishment of summary procedures, outside of Art. III courts, to collect a debt due to the Government from one of its customs agents.[20] On the same premise, the

---

e.g., Atlas Roofing Co. v. Occupational Safety and Health Review Comm'n, 430 U.S. 442, 450 (1977).

* [Ed.] Murray's Lessee involved the validity of summary levy of execution by a federal officer on the property of a former U.S. collector of customs from whom moneys were allegedly due. The statute authorizing such summary process was challenged on the ground that it allowed the executive to exercise judicial power. The Court upheld the validity of the summary process.

20. Doubtless it could be argued that the need for independent judicial determination is greatest in cases arising between the Government and an individual. But the rationale for the public-rights line of cases lies not in political theory, but rather in Congress' and this Court's understanding of what power was reserved to the Judiciary by the Constitution as a matter of historical fact.

Court in Ex parte Bakelite Corp., *supra,* held that the Court of Customs Appeals had been properly constituted by Congress as a legislative court:

> "The *full* province of the court under the act creating it is that of determining matters arising between the Government and others in the executive administration and application of the customs laws. * * * The appeals include nothing which inherently or necessarily requires <u>judicial determination</u>, but only matters the determination of *which may be, and at times has been, committed exclusively to executive officers.*" 279 U.S., at 458 (emphasis added).[21]

The distinction between public rights and private rights has not been definitively explained in our precedents.[22] Nor is it necessary to do so in the present cases, for it suffices to observe that a matter of public rights must at a minimum arise "between the government and others." Ex parte Bakelite Corp., *supra,* at 451.[23] In contrast, "the liability of one individual to another under the law as defined," Crowell v. Benson, *supra,* at 51, is a matter of private rights. Our precedents clearly establish that *only* controversies in the former category may be removed from Art. III courts and delegated to legislative courts or administrative agencies for their determination. See Atlas Roofing Co. v. Occupational Safety and Health Review Comm'n, 430 U.S. 442, 450, n. 7 (1977); Crowell v. Benson, *supra,* at 50–51.[24] Private-rights disputes, on the other hand, lie at the core of the historically recognized judicial power.

In sum, this Court has identified three situations in which Art. III does not bar the creation of legislative courts. In each of these situations, the Court has recognized certain exceptional powers bestowed upon Congress by the Constitution or by historical consensus. Only in the face of such an exceptional grant of power has the Court declined to hold the authority of Congress subject to the general prescriptions of Art. III.[25]

21. See also Williams v. United States, 289 U.S. 553 (1933) (holding that Court of Claims was a legislative court and that salary of a judge of that court could therefore be reduced by Congress).

22. Crowell v. Benson, 285 U.S. 22 (1932), attempted to catalog some of the matters that fall within the public-rights doctrine:

"Familiar illustrations of administrative agencies created for the determination of such matters are found in connection with the exercise of the congressional power as to interstate and foreign commerce, taxation, immigration, the public lands, public health, the facilities of the post office, pensions and payments to veterans." *Id.,* at 51 (footnote omitted).

23. Congress cannot "withdraw from [Art. III] judicial cognizance *any* matter which, *from its nature,* is the subject of a suit at the common law, or in equity, or admiralty." Murray's Lessee v. Hoboken Land & Improvement Co., 18 How. 272, 284 (1856) (emphasis added). It is thus clear that the presence of the United States as a proper party to the proceeding is a necessary but not sufficient means of distinguishing "private rights" from "public

rights." And it is also clear that even with respect to matters that arguably fall within the scope of the "public rights" doctrine, the presumption is in favor of Art. III courts. See Glidden Co. v. Zdanok, 370 U.S., at 548–549, and n. 21 (opinion of Harlan, J.). See also Currie, *The Federal Courts and the American Law Institute,* Part 1, 36 U.Chi.L.Rev. 1, 13–14, n. 67 (1968). Moreover, when Congress assigns these matters to administrative agencies, or to legislative courts, it has generally provided, and we have suggested that it may be required to provide, for Art. III judicial review. See Atlas Roofing Co. v. Occupational Safety and Health Review Comm'n, 430 U.S., at 455, n. 13.

24. Of course, the public-rights doctrine does not extend to any criminal matters, although the Government is a proper party. See, *e.g.,* United States ex rel. Toth v. Quarles, 350 U.S. 11 (1955).

25. The "unifying principle" that Justice White's dissent finds lacking in all of these cases is to be found in the exceptional constitutional grants of power to Congress with respect to certain matters. Although the dissent is correct that these grants are not explicit in the language of

We discern no such exceptional grant of power applicable in the cases before us. * * * Appellants argue that a discharge in bankruptcy is indeed a "public right," similar to such congressionally created benefits as "radio station licenses, pilot licenses, or certificates for common carriers" granted by administrative agencies. See Brief for United States 34. But the restructuring of debtor-creditor relations, which is at the core of the federal bankruptcy power, must be distinguished from the adjudication of state-created private rights, such as the right to recover contract damages that is at issue in this case. The former may well be a "public right," but the latter obviously is not. Appellant Northern's right to recover contract damages to augment its estate is "one of private right, that is, of the liability of one individual to another under the law as defined." Crowell v. Benson, 285 U.S., at 51.[26]

Recognizing that the present cases may not fall within the scope of any of our prior cases permitting the establishment of legislative courts, appellants argue that we should recognize an additional situation beyond the command of Art. III, sufficiently broad to sustain the Act. Appellants contend that Congress' constitutional authority to establish "uniform Laws on the subject of Bankruptcies throughout the United States," Art. I, § 8, cl. 4, carries with it an inherent power to establish legislative courts capable of adjudicating "bankruptcy-related controversies." Brief for United States 14. In support of this argument, appellants rely primarily upon a quotation from the opinion in Palmore v. United States, 411 U.S. 389 (1973), in which we stated that

> "both Congress and this Court have recognized that * * * the requirements of Art. III, which are applicable where laws of national applicability and affairs of national concern are at stake, must in proper circumstances give way to accommodate plenary grants of power to Congress to legislate with respect to specialized areas having particularized needs and warranting distinctive treatment." *Id.*, 407–408.

Appellants cite this language to support their proposition that a bankruptcy court created by Congress under its Art. I powers is constitutional, because the law of bankruptcy is a "specialized area," and Congress has found a "particularized need" that warrants "distinctive treatment." Brief for United States 20–33.

the Constitution, they are nonetheless firmly established in our historical understanding of the constitutional structure. When these three exceptional grants are properly constrained, they do not threaten the Framers' vision of an independent Federal Judiciary. What clearly remains subject to Art. III are all private adjudications in federal courts within the States—matters from their nature subject to "a suit at common law or in equity or admiralty"— and all criminal matters, with the narrow exception of military crimes. There is no doubt that when the Framers assigned the "judicial Power" to an independent Art. III Branch, these matters lay at what they perceived to be the protected core of that power. * * *

26. This claim may be adjudicated in federal court on the basis of its relationship to the petition for reorganization. See Williams v. Austrian, 331 U.S. 642 (1947); Schumacher v. Beeler, 293 U.S. 367 (1934). See also National Ins. Co. v. Tidewater Co., 337 U.S. 582, 611–613 (1949) (Rutledge, J., concurring); Textile Workers v. Lincoln Mills, 353 U.S. 448, 472 (1957) (Frankfurter, J., dissenting). *Cf.* Osborn v. Bank of the United States, 9 Wheat. 738 (1824). But this relationship does not transform the state-created right into a matter between the Government and the petitioner for reorganization. Even in the absence of the federal scheme, the plaintiff would be able to proceed against the defendant on the state-law contractual claims.

Appellants' contention, in essence, is that pursuant to any of its Art. I powers, Congress may create courts free of Art. III's requirements whenever it finds that course expedient. * * *

The flaw in appellants' analysis is that it provides no limiting principle. It thus threatens to supplant completely our system of adjudication in independent Art. III tribunals and replace it with a system of "specialized" legislative courts. True, appellants argue that under their analysis Congress could create legislative courts pursuant only to some "specific" Art. I power, and "only when there is a particularized need for distinctive treatment." Brief for United States 22–23. They therefore assert that their analysis would not permit Congress to replace the independent Art. III Judiciary through a "wholesale assignment of federal judicial business to legislative courts." But these "limitations" are wholly illusory. For example, Art. I, § 8, empowers Congress to enact laws, *inter alia*, regulating interstate commerce and punishing certain crimes. Art. I, § 8, cls. 3, 6. On appellants' reasoning Congress could provide for the adjudication of these and "related" matters by judges and courts within Congress' exclusive control. The potential for encroachment upon powers reserved to the Judicial Branch through the device of "specialized" legislative courts is dramatically evidenced in the jurisdiction granted to the courts created by the Act before us. The broad range of questions that can be brought into a bankruptcy court because they are "related to cases under title 11," 28 U.S.C. § 1471(b), is the clearest proof that even when Congress acts through a "specialized" court, and pursuant to only one of its many Art. I powers, appellants' analysis fails to provide any real protection against the erosion of Art. III jurisdiction by the unilateral action of the political Branches. In short, to accept appellants' reasoning, would require that we replace the principles delineated in our precedents, rooted in history and the Constitution, with a rule of broad legislative discretion that could effectively eviscerate the constitutional guarantee of an independent Judicial Branch of the Federal Government.[28]

28. Justice White's suggested "limitations" on Congress' power to create Art. I courts are even more transparent. Justice White's dissent suggests that Art. III "should be read as expressing one value that must be balanced against competing constitutional values and legislative responsibilities," and that the Court retains the final word on how the balance is to be struck. The dissent would find the Art. III "value" accommodated where appellate review by Art. III courts is provided and where the Art. I courts are "designed to deal with issues likely to be of little interest to the political branches." But the dissent's view that appellate review is sufficient to satisfy either the command or the purpose of Art. III is incorrect. See n. 39, *infra*. And the suggestion that we should consider whether the Art. I courts are designed to deal with issues likely to be of interest to the political Branches would undermine the validity of the adjudications performed by most of the administrative agencies, on which validity the dissent so heavily relies.

In applying its ad hoc balancing approach to the facts of this case, the dissent rests on the justification that these courts differ from standard Art. III courts because of their "extreme specialization." As noted above, "extreme specialization" is hardly an accurate description of bankruptcy courts designed to adjudicate the entire range of federal and state controversies. Moreover, the special nature of bankruptcy adjudications is in no sense incompatible with performance of such functions in a tribunal afforded the protection of Art. III. As one witness pointed out to Congress:

"Relevant to that question of need, it seems worth noting that Article III itself permits much flexibility; so long as tenure during good behavior is granted, much room exists as regards other conditions. Thus it would certainly be possible to create a special bankruptcy court under Article III and there is no reason why the judges of that court would have to be paid the same salary as district judges or any other existing judges. It would also be permissible to provide that when a judge of

Appellants' reliance upon Palmore for such broad legislative discretion is misplaced. * * * Palmore was concerned with the courts of the District of Columbia, a unique federal enclave over which "Congress has * * * entire control * * * for every purpose of government." Kendall v. United States, 12 Pet., at 619. The "plenary authority" under the District of Columbia Clause, Art. I, § 8, cl. 17, was the subject of the quoted passage and the powers granted under that Clause are obviously different in kind from the other broad powers conferred on Congress: Congress' power over the District of Columbia encompasses the *full* authority of government, and thus, necessarily, the Executive and Judicial powers as well as the Legislative. This is a power that is clearly possessed by Congress only in limited geographic areas. Palmore itself makes this limitation clear. The quoted passage distinguishes the congressional powers at issue in Palmore from those in which the Art. III command of an independent Judiciary must be honored: where "laws of national applicability and affairs of national concern are at stake." 411 U.S., at 408. Laws respecting bankruptcy, like most laws enacted pursuant to the national powers cataloged in Art. I, § 8, are clearly laws of national applicability and affairs of national concern. Thus our reference in Palmore to "specialized areas having particularized needs" referred only to *geographic* areas, such as the District of Columbia or territories outside the States of the Federal Union. In light of the clear commands of Art. III, nothing held or said in Palmore can be taken to mean that in every area in which Congress may legislate, it may also create non-Art. III courts with Art. III powers.

In sum, Art. III bars Congress from establishing legislative courts to exercise jurisdiction over all matters related to those arising under the bankruptcy laws. The establishment of such courts does not fall within any of the historically recognized situations in which the general principle of independent adjudication commanded by Art. III does not apply. Nor can we discern any persuasive reason, in logic, history, or the Constitution, why the bankruptcy courts here established lie beyond the reach of Art. III.

IV

Appellants advance a second argument for upholding the constitutionality of the Act: that "viewed within the entire judicial framework set up by Congress," the bankruptcy court is merely an "adjunct" to the district court, and that the delegation of certain adjudicative functions to the bankruptcy court is accordingly consistent with the principle that the judicial power of the United States must be vested in Art. III courts. See Brief for United States 11–13, 37–45. As support for their argument, appellants rely principally upon Crowell v. Benson, 285 U.S. 22 (1932), and United States v. Raddatz, 447 U.S. 667 (1980), cases in which we approved the use of administrative agencies and magistrates as adjuncts to Art. III courts. Brief for United States 40–42. The question to which we turn, therefore, is whether the Act has retained "the essential attributes of the judicial power," Crowell v. Benson, *supra,* at 51, in Art. III tribunals.

that court retired pursuant to statute, a vacancy for a new appointment would not automatically be created. And it would be entirely valid to specify that the judges of that court could not be assigned to sit, even temporarily, on the general district courts or courts of appeals." Hearings on H.R. 31 and H.R. 32 before the Subcommittee on Civil and Constitutional Rights of the House Committee on the Judiciary, 94th Cong., 2d Sess., 2697 (1976) (letter of Paul Mishkin).

The essential premise underlying appellants' argument is that even where the Constitution denies Congress the power to establish legislative courts, Congress possesses the authority to assign certain factfinding functions to adjunct tribunals. It is, of course, true that while the power to adjudicate "private rights" must be vested in an Art. III court, see Part III, *supra,*

> "this Court has accepted factfinding by an administrative agency, * * * as an adjunct to the Art. III court, analogizing the agency to a jury or a special master and permitting it in admiralty cases to perform the function of the special master. Crowell v. Benson, 285 U.S. 22, 51–65 (1932)." Atlas Roofing Co. v. Occupational Safety and Health Review Comm'n, 430 U.S., at 450, n. 7.

The use of administrative agencies as adjuncts was first upheld in Crowell v. Benson, *supra.* * * *

Crowell involved the adjudication of congressionally created rights. But this Court has sustained the use of adjunct factfinders even in the adjudication of constitutional rights—so long as those adjuncts were subject to sufficient control by an Art. III district court. In United States v. Raddatz, *supra,* the Court upheld the 1978 Federal Magistrates Act, which permitted district court judges to refer certain pretrial motions, including suppression motions based on alleged violations of constitutional rights, to a magistrate for initial determination. The Court observed that the magistrate's proposed findings and recommendations were subject to *de novo* review by the district court, which was free to rehear the evidence or to call for additional evidence. Moreover, it was noted that the magistrate considered motions only upon reference from the district court, and that the magistrates were appointed, and subject to removal, by the district court. (Blackmun, J., concurring).[30] In short, the ultimate decisionmaking authority respecting all pretrial motions clearly remained with the district court. Under these circumstances, the Court held that the Act did not violate the constraints of Art. III.[31]

Together these cases establish two principles that aid us in determining the extent to which Congress may constitutionally vest traditionally judicial functions in non-Art. III officers. First, it is clear that when Congress creates a substantive federal right, it possesses substantial discretion to prescribe the manner in which that right may be adjudicated—including the assignment to an adjunct of some functions historically performed by judges.[32] * * * Second, the functions of the adjunct must be limited in such a way that "the essential attributes" of judicial power

30. Thus in Raddatz there was no serious threat that the exercise of the judicial power would be subject to incursion by other branches. * * *

31. Appellants and Justice White's dissent also rely on the broad powers exercised by the bankruptcy referees immediately before the Bankruptcy Act of 1978. But those particular adjunct functions, which represent the culmination of years of gradual expansion of the power and authority of the bankruptcy referee, see 1 Collier, Bankruptcy ¶ 1.02 (15th ed. 1982), have never been explicitly endorsed by this Court. * * *

32. Contrary to Justice White's suggestion, we do not concede that "Congress may provide for initial adjudications by Art. I courts or administrative judges of all rights and duties arising under otherwise valid federal laws." Rather we simply reaffirm the holding of Crowell—that Congress may assign to non-Art. III bodies some adjudicatory functions. Crowell itself spoke of "specialized" functions. These cases do not require us to specify further any limitations that may exist with respect to Congress' power to create adjuncts to assist in the adjudication of federal statutory rights.

are retained in the Art. III court. Thus in upholding the adjunct scheme challenged in Crowell, the Court emphasized that "the reservation of full authority to the court to deal with matters of law provides for the appropriate exercise of the judicial function in this class of cases." And in refusing to invalidate the Magistrates Act at issue in Raddatz, the Court stressed that under the congressional scheme " '[t]he authority—and the responsibility—to make an informed, final determination * * * remains with the judge,' " 447 U.S. at 682, * * *.

These two principles assist us in evaluating the "adjunct" scheme presented in these cases. * * * [W]hile Crowell certainly endorsed the proposition that Congress possesses broad discretion to assign factfinding functions to an adjunct created to aid in the adjudication of congressionally created statutory rights, Crowell does not support the further proposition necessary to appellants' argument—that Congress possesses the same degree of discretion in assigning traditionally judicial power to adjuncts engaged in the adjudication of rights *not* created by Congress. Indeed, the validity of this proposition was expressly denied in Crowell, when the Court rejected "the untenable assumption that the constitutional courts may be deprived in all cases of the determination of facts upon evidence even though a *constitutional* right may be involved," 285 U.S., at 60–61 (emphasis added),[33] and stated that

> "the essential independence of the exercise of the judicial power of the United States in the enforcement of *constitutional* rights requires that the Federal court should determine * * * an issue [of agency jurisdiction] upon its own record and the facts elicited before it." *Id.,* at 64 (emphasis added).[34]

* * *

Although Crowell and Raddatz do not explicitly distinguish between rights created by Congress and other rights, such a distinction underlies in part Crowell's and Raddatz' recognition of a critical difference between rights created by federal statute and rights recognized by the Constitution. Moreover, such a distinction seems to us to be necessary in light of the delicate accommodations required by the principle of separation of powers reflected in Art. III. * * * [W]hen Congress creates a statutory right, it clearly has the discretion, in defining that right, to create presumptions, or assign burdens of proof, or prescribe remedies; it may also provide that persons seeking to vindicate that right must do so before particularized tribunals created to perform the specialized adjudicative tasks related to that right. Such provisions do, in a sense, affect the exercise of judicial power, but they are also incidental to Congress' power to define the right that it has created. No comparable justification exists, however, when the right being adjudicated is not of congressional creation. In such a situa-

---

33. The Court in Crowell found that the requirement of *de novo* review as to certain facts was not "simply the question of due process in relation to notice and hearing," but was "rather a question of the appropriate maintenance of the Federal judicial power." 285 U.S., at 56. The dissent agreed that some factual findings cannot be made by adjuncts, on the ground that "under certain circumstances, the constitutional requirement of due process is a requirement of [Art. III] judicial process." *Id.,* at 87 (Brandeis, J., dissenting).

34. Crowell's precise holding, with respect to the review of "jurisdictional" and "constitutional" facts that arise within ordinary administrative proceedings, has been undermined by later cases. See St. Joseph Stock Yards Co. v. United States, 298 U.S. 38, 53 (1936). See generally 4 K. Davis, Administrative Law Treatise §§ 29.08, 29.09 (1st ed. 1958). * * *

tion, substantial inroads into functions that have traditionally been performed by the Judiciary cannot be characterized merely as incidental extensions of Congress' power to define rights that it has created. Rather, such inroads suggest unwarranted encroachments upon the judicial power of the United States, which our Constitution reserves for Art. III courts.

We hold that the Bankruptcy Act of 1978 carries the possibility of such an unwarranted encroachment. Many of the rights subject to adjudication by the Act's bankruptcy courts, like the rights implicated in Raddatz, are not of Congress' creation. Indeed, the cases before us, which center upon appellant Northern's claim for damages for breach of contract and misrepresentation, involve a right created by *state* law, a right independent of and antecedent to the reorganization petition that conferred jurisdiction upon the Bankruptcy Court.[36] Accordingly, Congress' authority to control the manner in which that right is adjudicated, through assignment of historically judicial functions to a non-Art. III "adjunct," plainly must be deemed at a minimum. Yet it is equally plain that Congress has vested the "adjunct" bankruptcy judges with powers over Northern's state-created right that far exceed the powers that it has vested in administrative agencies that adjudicate only rights of Congress' own creation.

Unlike the administrative scheme that we reviewed in Crowell, the Act vests all "essential attributes" of the judicial power of the United States in the "adjunct" bankruptcy court. First, the agency in Crowell made only specialized, narrowly confined factual determinations regarding a particularized area of law. In contrast, the subject-matter jurisdiction of the bankruptcy courts encompasses not only traditional matters of bankruptcy, but also "all civil proceedings arising under title 11 or arising in or *related to* cases under title 11." 28 U.S.C. § 1471(b) (emphasis added). Second, while the agency in Crowell engaged in statutorily channeled factfinding functions, the bankruptcy courts exercise "*all* of the jurisdiction" conferred by the Act on the district courts, § 1471(c) (emphasis added). Third, the agency in Crowell possessed only a limited power to issue compensation orders pursuant to specialized procedures, and its orders could be enforced only by order of the district court. By contrast, the bankruptcy courts exercise all ordinary powers of district courts * * *. Fourth, while orders issued by the agency in Crowell were to be set aside if "not supported by the evidence," the judgments of the bankruptcy courts are apparently subject to review only under the more deferential "clearly erroneous" standard. Finally, the agency in Crowell was required by law to seek enforcement of its compensation orders in the district court. In contrast, the bankruptcy courts issue final judgments, which are binding and enforceable even in the absence of an appeal. In short, the "adjunct" bankruptcy courts created by the Act exercise jurisdiction behind the facade of a grant to the district courts, and are exercising powers far greater than those lodged in the adjuncts approved in either Crowell or Raddatz.[39]

---

36. Of course, bankruptcy adjudications themselves, as well as the manner in which the rights of debtors and creditors are adjusted, are matters of federal law. Appellant Northern's state-law contract claim is now in federal court because of its relationship to Northern's reorganization petition. See n. 26, *supra*. But Congress has not purported to prescribe a rule of decision for the resolution of Northern's contractual claims.

39. Appellants suggest that Crowell and Raddatz stand for the proposition that Art. III is satisfied so long as some degree of appellate review is provided. But that

We conclude that 28 U.S.C. § 1471, as added by § 241(a) of the Bankruptcy Act of 1978, has impermissibly removed most, if not all, of "the essential attributes of the judicial power" from the Art. III district court, and has vested those attributes in a non-Art. III adjunct. Such a grant of jurisdiction cannot be sustained as an exercise of Congress' power to create adjuncts to Art. III courts.

V

Having concluded that the broad grant of jurisdiction to the bankruptcy courts contained in 28 U.S.C. § 1471 is unconstitutional, we must now determine whether our holding should be applied retroactively to the effective date of the Act.[40] Our decision in Chevron Oil Co. v. Huson, 404 U.S. 97 (1971), sets forth the three considerations recognized by our precedents as properly bearing upon the issue of retroactivity. They are, first, whether the holding in question "decid[ed] an issue of first impression whose resolution was not clearly foreshadowed" by earlier cases, id., at 106; second, "whether retrospective operation will further or retard [the] operation" of the holding in question, id., at 107; and third, whether retroactive application "could produce substantial inequitable results" in individual cases, ibid. In the present cases, all of these considerations militate against the retroactive application of our holding today. It is plain that Congress' broad grant of judicial power to non-Art. III bankruptcy judges presents an unprecedented question of interpretation of Art. III. It is

suggestion is directly contrary to the text of our Constitution: "The Judges, both of the supreme and inferior Courts, shall hold their Offices during good Behaviour, and shall * * * receive [undiminished] Compensation." Art. III, § 1 (emphasis added). Our precedents make it clear that the constitutional requirements for the exercise of the judicial power must be met at all stages of adjudication, and not only on appeal, where the court is restricted to considerations of law, as well as the nature of the case as it has been shaped at the trial level. * * *

Justice White's dissent views the function of the Third Branch as interpreting the Constitution in order to keep the other two Branches in check, and would accordingly find the purpose, if not the language, of Art. III satisfied where there is an appeal to an Art. III court. But in the Framers' view, Art. III courts would do a great deal more than, in an abstract way, announce guidelines for the other two Branches. While "expounding" the Constitution was surely one vital function of the Art. III courts in the Framers' view, the tasks of those courts, for which independence was an important safeguard, included the mundane as well as the glamorous, matters of common law and statute as well as constitutional law, issues of fact as well as issues of law. * * *

40. It is clear that, at the least, the new bankruptcy judges cannot constitutionally

be vested with jurisdiction to decide this state-law contract claim against Marathon. As part of a comprehensive restructuring of the bankruptcy laws, Congress has vested jurisdiction over this and all matters related to cases under Title 11 in a single non-Art. III court, and has done so pursuant to a single statutory grant of jurisdiction. In these circumstances we cannot conclude that if Congress were aware that the grant of jurisdiction could not constitutionally encompass this and similar claims, it would simply remove the jurisdiction of the bankruptcy court over these matters, leaving the jurisdictional provision and adjudicatory structure intact with respect to other types of claims, and thus subject to Art. III constitutional challenge on a claim-by-claim basis. Indeed, we note that one of the express purposes of the Act was to ensure adjudication of all claims in a single forum and to avoid the delay and expense of jurisdictional disputes. See H.R.Rep. No. 95–595, pp. 43–48 (1977); S.Rep. No. 95–989, p. 17 (1978). Nor can we assume, as The Chief Justice suggests, that Congress' choice would be to have these cases "routed to the United States district court of which the bankruptcy court is an adjunct." We think that it is for Congress to determine the proper manner of restructuring the Bankruptcy Act of 1978 to conform to the requirements of Art. III in the way that will best effectuate the legislative purpose.

equally plain that retroactive application would not further the operation of our holding, and would surely visit substantial injustice and hardship upon those litigants who relied upon the Act's vesting of jurisdiction in the bankruptcy courts. We hold, therefore, that our decision today shall apply only prospectively.

The judgment of the District Court is affirmed. However, we stay our judgment until October 4, 1982. This limited stay will afford Congress an opportunity to reconstitute the bankruptcy courts or to adopt other valid means of adjudication, without impairing the interim administration of the bankruptcy laws. * * *

It is so ordered.

JUSTICE REHNQUIST, with whom JUSTICE O'CONNOR joins, concurring in the judgment.

Were I to agree with the plurality that the question presented by these cases is "whether the assignment by Congress to bankruptcy judges of the jurisdiction granted in 28 U.S.C. § 1471 by § 241(a) of the Bankruptcy Act of 1978 violates Art. III of the Constitution," I would with considerable reluctance embark on the duty of deciding this broad question. But appellee Marathon Pipe Line Co. has * * * simply been named defendant in a lawsuit about a contract, a lawsuit initiated by appellant Northern after having previously filed a petition for reorganization under the Bankruptcy Act. Marathon may object to proceeding further with this lawsuit on the grounds that if it is to be resolved by an agency of the United States, it may be resolved only by an agency which exercises "[t]he judicial power of the United States" described by Art. III of the Constitution. But resolution of any objections it may make on this ground to the exercise of a different authority conferred on bankruptcy courts by the 1978 Act, should await the exercise of such authority. * * *

From the record before us, the lawsuit in which Marathon was named defendant seeks damages for breach of contract, misrepresentation, and other counts which are the stuff of the traditional actions at common law tried by the courts at Westminster in 1789. There is apparently no federal rule of decision provided for any of the issues in the lawsuit; the claims of Northern arise entirely under state law. No method of adjudication is hinted, other than the traditional common-law mode of judge and jury. The lawsuit is before the Bankruptcy Court only because the plaintiff has previously filed a petition for reorganization in that court.

The cases dealing with the authority of Congress to create courts other than by use of its power under Art. III do not admit of easy synthesis. * * * I need not decide whether these cases in fact support a general proposition and three tidy exceptions, as the plurality believes, or whether instead they are but landmarks on a judicial "darkling plain" where ignorant armies have clashed by night, as Justice White apparently believes them to be. None of the cases has gone so far as to sanction the type of adjudication to which Marathon will be subjected against its will under the provisions of the 1978 Act. To whatever extent different powers granted under that Act might be sustained under the "public rights" doctrine of Murray's Lessee v. Hoboken Land & Improvement Co., 18 How. 272 (1856), and succeeding cases, I am satisfied that the adjudication of Northern's lawsuit cannot be so sustained.

I am likewise of the opinion that the extent of review by Art. III courts provided on appeal from a decision of the bankruptcy court in a case such as Northern's does not save the grant of authority to the latter under the rule espoused in Crowell v. Benson, 285 U.S. 22 (1932). All matters of fact and law in whatever domains of the law to which the parties' dispute may lead are to be resolved by the bankruptcy court in the first instance, with only traditional appellate review by Art. III courts apparently contemplated. Acting in this manner the bankruptcy court is not an "adjunct" of either the district court or the court of appeals.

I would, therefore, hold so much of the Bankruptcy Act of 1978 as enables a Bankruptcy Court to entertain and decide Northern's lawsuit over Marathon's objection to be violative of Art. III of the United States Constitution. Because I agree with the plurality that this grant of authority is not readily severable from the remaining grant of authority to bankruptcy courts under § 1471, I concur in the judgment. I also agree with the discussion in Part V of the plurality opinion respecting retroactivity and the staying of the judgment of this Court.

CHIEF JUSTICE BURGER, dissenting.

I join Justice White's dissenting opinion, but I write separately to emphasize that, notwithstanding the plurality opinion, the Court does *not* hold today that Congress' broad grant of jurisdiction to the new bankruptcy courts is generally inconsistent with Art. III of the Constitution. Rather, the Court's holding is limited to the proposition stated by Justice Rehnquist in his concurrence in the judgment—that a "traditional" state common-law action, not made subject to a federal rule of decision, and related only peripherally to an adjudication of bankruptcy under federal law, must, absent the consent of the litigants, be heard by an "Art. III court" if it is to be heard by any court or agency of the United States. This limited holding, of course, does not suggest that there is something inherently unconstitutional about the new bankruptcy courts; nor does it preclude such courts from adjudicating all but a relatively narrow category of claims "arising under" or "arising in or related to cases under" the Bankruptcy Act.

It will not be necessary for Congress, in order to meet the requirements of the Court's holding, to undertake a radical restructuring of the present system of bankruptcy adjudication. The problems arising from today's judgment can be resolved simply by providing that ancillary common-law actions, such as the one involved in these cases, be routed to the United States district court of which the bankruptcy court is an adjunct.

JUSTICE WHITE, with whom THE CHIEF JUSTICE and JUSTICE POWELL join, dissenting.

Article III, § 1, of the Constitution is straightforward and uncomplicated on its face:

* * *

Any reader could easily take this provision to mean that although Congress was free to establish such lower courts as it saw fit, any court that it did establish would be an "inferior" court exercising "judicial Power of the United States" and so must be manned by judges possessing both life tenure and a guaranteed minimal income. This would be an eminently sensible reading and one that, as the plurality shows, is well founded in both the documentary sources and the political doctrine of separation of powers that stands behind much of our constitutional structure.

If this simple reading were correct and we were free to disregard 150 years of history, these would be easy cases and the plurality opinion could end with its observation that "[i]t is undisputed that the bankruptcy judges whose offices were created by the Bankruptcy Act of 1978 do not enjoy the protections constitutionally afforded to Art. III judges." The fact that the plurality must go on to deal with what has been characterized as one of the most confusing and controversial areas of constitutional law itself indicates the gross oversimplification implicit in the plurality's claim that "our Constitution unambiguously enunciates a fundamental principle—that the 'judicial Power of the United States' must be reposed in an independent Judiciary [and] provides clear institutional protections for that independence." While this is fine rhetoric, analytically it serves only to put a distracting and superficial gloss on a difficult question.

That question is what limits Art. III places on Congress' ability to create adjudicative institutions designed to carry out federal policy established pursuant to the substantive authority given Congress elsewhere in the Constitution. Whether fortunate or unfortunate, at this point in the history of constitutional law that question can no longer be answered by looking only to the constitutional text. This Court's cases construing that text must also be considered. In its attempt to pigeonhole these cases, the plurality does violence to their meaning and creates an artificial structure that itself lacks coherence.

I

There are, I believe, two separate grounds for today's decision. First, non-Art. III judges, regardless of whether they are labeled "adjuncts" to Art. III courts or "Art. I judges," may consider only controversies arising out of federal law. Because the immediate controversy in these cases— Northern Pipeline's claim against Marathon—arises out of state law, it may only be adjudicated, within the federal system, by an Art. III court.[2] Second, regardless of the source of law that governs the controversy, Congress is prohibited by Art. III from establishing Art. I courts, with three narrow exceptions. Adjudication of bankruptcy proceedings does not fall within any of these exceptions. I shall deal with the first of these contentions in this section.

The plurality concedes that Congress may provide for initial adjudications by Art. I courts or administrative judges of all rights and duties arising under otherwise valid federal laws. There is no apparent reason why this principle should not extend to matters arising in federal bankruptcy proceedings. The plurality attempts to escape the reach of prior decisions by contending that the bankrupt's claim against Marathon arose under state law. Non–Article III judges, in its view, cannot be vested with authority to adjudicate such issues. It then proceeds to strike down 28 U.S.C. § 1471 on this ground. For several reasons, the Court's judgment is unsupportable.

First, clearly this ground alone cannot support the Court's invalidation of § 1471 on its face. The plurality concedes that in adjudications and

---

2. Because this is the sole ground relied upon by the Justices concurring in the judgment this is the effective basis for today's decision.

discharges in bankruptcy, "the restructuring of debtor-creditor relations, which is at the core of the federal bankruptcy power," and "the manner in which the rights of debtors and creditors are adjusted," are matters of federal law. Under the plurality's own interpretation of the cases, therefore, these matters could be heard and decided by Art. I judges. But because the bankruptcy judge is also given authority to hear a case like that of appellant Northern against Marathon, which the Court says is founded on state law, the Court holds that the section must be stricken down on its face. This is a grossly unwarranted emasculation of the scheme Congress has adopted. Even if the Court is correct that such a state-law claim cannot be heard by a bankruptcy judge, there is no basis for doing more than declaring the section unconstitutional as applied to the claim against Marathon, leaving the section otherwise intact. In that event, cases such as these would have to be heard by Art. III judges or by state courts—unless the defendant consents to suit before the bankruptcy judge—just as they were before the 1978 Act was adopted. But this would remove from the jurisdiction of the bankruptcy judge only a tiny fraction of the cases he is now empowered to adjudicate and would not otherwise limit his jurisdiction.[3]

Second, the distinction between claims based on state law and those based on federal law disregards the real character of bankruptcy proceedings. The routine in ordinary bankruptcy cases now, as it was before 1978, is to stay actions against the bankrupt, collect the bankrupt's assets, require creditors to file claims or be forever barred, allow or disallow claims that are filed, adjudicate preferences and fraudulent transfers, and make pro rata distributions to creditors, who will be barred by the discharge from taking further actions against the bankrupt. The crucial point to be made is that in the ordinary bankruptcy proceeding the great bulk of creditor claims are claims that have accrued under state law prior to bankruptcy—claims for goods sold, wages, rent, utilities, and the like. * * * Every such claim must be filed and its validity is subject to adjudication by the bankruptcy court. The existence and validity of such claims recurringly depend on state law. Hence, the bankruptcy judge is constantly enmeshed in state-law issues.

The new aspect of the Bankruptcy Act of 1978, in this regard, therefore, is not the extension of federal jurisdiction to state-law claims, but its extension to particular kinds of state-law claims, such as contract cases against third parties or disputes involving property in the possession of a third person. Prior to 1978, a claim of a bankrupt against a third party, such as the claim against Marathon in this case, was not within the jurisdiction of the bankruptcy judge. The old limits were based, of course, on the restrictions implicit within the concept of *in rem* jurisdiction; the new extension is based on the concept of *in personam* jurisdiction. * * *

3. The plurality attempts to justify its sweeping invalidation of § 1471, because of its inclusion of state-law claims, by suggesting that this statutory provision is nonseverable. The Justices concurring in the judgment specifically adopt this argument as the reason for their decision to join the judgment of the Court. The basis for the conclusion of nonseverability, however, is nothing more than a presumption * * *. I had not thought this to be the contemporary approach to the problem of severability, particularly when dealing with federal statutes. I would follow the approach taken by the Court in Buckley v. Valeo, 424 U.S. 1, 108 (1976): " 'Unless it is evident that the Legislature would not have enacted those provisions which are within its power, independently of that which is not, the invalid part may be dropped if what is left is fully operative as a law.' " * * *

The majority at no place explains why this distinction should have constitutional implications. * * *

    * * *

In theory and fact, therefore, I can find no basis for that part of the majority's argument that rests on the state-law character of the claim involved here. Even if, prior to 1978, the referee could not generally participate in cases aimed at collecting the assets of a bankrupt estate, he nevertheless repeatedly adjudicated issues controlled by state law. There is very little reason to strike down § 1471 on its face on the ground that it extends, in a comparatively minimal way, the referees' authority to deal with state-law questions. To do so is to lose all sense of proportion.

II

The plurality unpersuasively attempts to bolster its case for facial invalidity by asserting that the bankruptcy courts are now "exercising powers far greater than those lodged in the adjuncts approved in either Crowell or Raddatz." * * *

I * * * believe that the major premise of the plurality's argument is wholly unsupported: There is no explanation of why Crowell v. Benson, 285 U.S. 22 (1932), and United States v. Raddatz, 447 U.S. 667 (1980), define the outer limits of constitutional authority. Much more relevant to today's decision are, first, the practice in bankruptcy prior to 1978, which neither the majority nor any authoritative case has questioned, and, second, the practice of today's administrative agencies. Considered from this perspective, all of the plurality's arguments are unsupportable abstractions, divorced from the realities of modern practice. * * *

    * * *

Even if there are specific powers now vested in bankruptcy judges that should be performed by Art. III judges, the great bulk of their functions are unexceptionable and should be left intact. Whatever is invalid should be declared to be such; the rest of the 1978 Act should be left alone. I can account for the majority's inexplicably heavy hand in this case only by assuming that the Court has once again lost its conceptual bearings when confronted with the difficult problem of the nature and role of Art. I courts. To that question I now turn.

III

A

The plurality contends that the precedents upholding Art. I courts can be reduced to three categories. First, there are territorial courts, which need not satisfy Art. III constraints because "the Framers intended that as to certain geographical areas * * * Congress was to exercise the general powers of government." Second, there are courts-martial, which are exempt from Art. III limits because of a constitutional grant of power that has been "historically understood as giving the political Branches of Government extraordinary control over the precise subject matter at issue." Finally, there are those legislative courts and administrative agencies that adjudicate cases involving public rights—controversies between the Government and private parties—which are not covered by Art. III because the controversy could have been resolved by the executive alone without judicial review. Despite the plurality's attempt to cabin the domain of Art.

I courts, it is quite unrealistic to consider these to be only three "narrow," limitations on or exceptions to the reach of Art. III. In fact, the plurality itself breaks the mold in its discussion of "adjuncts" in Part IV, when it announces that "when Congress creates a substantive federal right, it possesses substantial discretion to prescribe the manner in which that right may be adjudicated." Adjudications of federal rights may, according to the plurality, be committed to administrative agencies, as long as provision is made for judicial review.

The first principle introduced by the plurality is geographical: Art. I courts presumably are not permitted within the States.[8] The problem, of course, is that both of the other exceptions recognize that Art. I courts can indeed operate within the States. The second category relies upon a new principle: Art. I courts are permissible in areas in which the Constitution grants Congress "extraordinary control over the precise subject matter." Preliminarily, I do not know how we are to distinguish those areas in which Congress' control is "extraordinary" from those in which it is not. Congress' power over the Armed Forces is established in Art. I, § 8, cls. 13, 14. There is nothing in those Clauses that creates congressional authority different in kind from the authority granted to legislate with respect to bankruptcy. But more importantly, in its third category, and in its treatment of "adjuncts," the plurality itself recognizes that Congress can create Art. I courts in virtually all the areas in which Congress is authorized to act, regardless of the quality of the constitutional grant of authority. At the same time, territorial courts or the courts of the District of Columbia, which are Art. I courts, adjudicate private, just as much as public or federal, rights.

Instead of telling us what it is Art. I courts can and cannot do, the plurality presents us with a list of Art. I courts. When we try to distinguish those courts from their Art. III counterparts, we find—apart from the obvious lack of Art. III judges—a series of nondistinctions. By the plurality's own admission, Art. I courts can operate throughout the country, they can adjudicate both private and public rights, and they can adjudicate matters arising from congressional actions in those areas in which congressional control is "extraordinary." I cannot distinguish this last category from the general "arising under" jurisdiction of Art. III courts.

The plurality opinion has the appearance of limiting Art. I courts only because it fails to add together the sum of its parts. Rather than limiting each other, the principles relied upon complement each other; together they cover virtually the whole domain of possible areas of adjudication. Without a unifying principle, the plurality's argument reduces to the proposition that because bankruptcy courts are not sufficiently like any of these three exceptions, they may not be either Art. I courts or adjuncts to Art. III courts. But we need to know why bankruptcy courts cannot qualify as Art. I courts in their own right.

8. Had the plurality cited only the territorial courts, the principle relied on perhaps could have been the fact that power over the Territories is provided Congress in Art. IV. However, Congress' power over the District of Columbia is an Art. I power. As such, it does not seem to have any greater status than any of the other powers enumerated in Art. I, § 8.

B

The plurality opinion is not the first unsuccessful attempt to articulate a principled ground by which to distinguish Art. I from Art. III courts. The concept of a legislative, or Art. I, court was introduced by an opinion authored by Chief Justice Marshall. Not only did he create the concept, but at the same time he started the theoretical controversy that has ever since surrounded the concept:

> "The Judges of the Superior Courts of Florida hold their offices for four years. These Courts, then, are not constitutional Courts, in which the judicial power conferred by the Constitution on the general government, can be deposited. They are incapable of receiving it. They are legislative Courts, created in virtue of the general right of sovereignty which exists in the government, or in virtue of that clause which enables Congress to make all needful rules and regulations, respecting the territory belonging to the United States. The jurisdiction with which they are invested, is not a part of that judicial power which is defined in the 3d article of the Constitution, but is conferred by Congress, in the execution of those general powers which that body possesses over the territories of the United States." American Insurance Co. v. Canter, 1 Pet. 511, 546 (1828).

The proposition was simple enough: Constitutional courts exercise the judicial power described in Art. III of the Constitution; legislative courts do not and cannot.

There were only two problems with this proposition. First, Canter itself involved a case in admiralty jurisdiction, which is specifically included within the "judicial power of the United States" delineated in Art. III. How, then, could the territorial court not be exercising Art. III judicial power? Second, and no less troubling, if the territorial courts could not exercise Art. III power, how could their decisions be subject to appellate review in Art. III courts, including this one, that can exercise only Art. III "judicial" power? Yet from early on this Court has exercised such appellate jurisdiction. Benner v. Porter, 9 How. 235, 243 (1850); Clinton v. Englebrecht, 13 Wall. 434 (1872); Reynolds v. United States, 98 U.S. 145, 154 (1879); United States v. Coe, 155 U.S. 76, 86 (1894); Balzac v. Porto Rico, 258 U.S. 298, 312–313 (1922). The attempt to understand the seemingly unexplainable was bound to generate "confusion and controversy." This analytic framework, however—the search for a principled distinction—has continued to burden the Court.

The first major elaboration on the Canter principle was in Murray's Lessee v. Hoboken Land & Improvement Co., 18 How. 272 (1856). The plaintiff in that case argued that a proceeding against a customs collector for the collection of moneys claimed to be due to the United States was an exercise of "judicial power" and therefore had to be carried out by Art. III judges. The Court accepted this premise: "It must be admitted that, if the auditing of this account, and the ascertainment of its balance, and the issuing of this process, was an exercise of the judicial power of the United States, the proceeding was void; for the officers who performed these acts could exercise no part of that judicial power." Having accepted this premise, the Court went on to delineate those matters which could be determined only by an Art. III court, *i.e.*, those matters that fall within the nondelegable "judicial power" of the United States. The Court's response to this was twofold. First, it suggested that there are certain matters which are inherently "judicial": "[W]e do not consider congress can either withdraw from judicial cognizance any matter which, from its nature, is the subject of a suit at the common law, or in equity, or admiralty." Second, it suggested that there is another class of issues that, depending upon the form in which Congress structures the decisionmaking process, may or may not fall within "the cognizance of the courts of the United States." This latter category consisted of the so-called "public rights." Apparently, the idea was that Congress was free to structure the adjudication of "public rights" without regard to Art. III.

Having accepted the plaintiff's premise, it is hard to see how the Court could have taken too seriously its first contention. The Court presented no examples of such issues that are judicial "by nature" and simply failed to acknowledge that Art. I courts already sanctioned by the Court—*e.g.*, territorial courts—were deciding such issues all the time. The second point, however, contains implicitly a critical insight; one that if openly acknowledged would have undermined the entire structure. That insight follows from the Court's earlier recognition that the term "judicial act" is broad enough to encompass all administrative action involving inquiry into facts and the application of law to those facts. If administrative action can be characterized as "judicial" in nature, then obviously the Court's subsequent attempt to distinguish administrative from judicial action on the basis of the manner in which Congress structures the decision cannot succeed. There need be no Art. III court involvement in any adjudication of a "public right," which the majority now interprets as any civil matter arising between the Federal Government and a citizen. In that area, whether an issue is to be decided by an Art. III court depends, finally, on congressional intent.

Although Murray's Lessee implicitly undermined Chief Justice Marshall's suggestion that there is a difference in kind between the work of Art. I and that of Art. III courts, it did not contend that the Court must always defer to congressional desire in this regard. The Court considered the plaintiff's contention that removal of the issue from an Art. III court must be justified by "necessity." Although not entirely clear, the Court seems to have accepted this proposition: "[I]t seems to us that the just inference from the entire law is, that there was such a necessity for the warrant."

The Court in Murray's Lessee was precisely right: Whether an issue can be decided by a non-Art. III court does not depend upon the judicial or nonjudicial character of the issue, but on the will of Congress and the reasons Congress offers for not using an Art. III court. This insight, however, was completely disavowed in the next major case to consider the distinction between Art. I and Art. III courts, Ex parte Bakelite Corp., 279 U.S. 438 (1929), in which the Court concluded that the Court of Customs Appeals was a legislative court. The Court there directly embraced the principle also articulated in Murray's Lessee that Art. I courts may not consider any matter "which inherently or necessarily requires judicial determination," but only such matters as are "susceptible of legislative or executive determination." 279 U.S., at 453. It then went on effectively to bury the critical insight of Murray's Lessee, labeling as "fallacious" any argument that "assumes that whether a court is of one class or the other depends on the intention of Congress, whereas the true test lies in the power under which the court was created and in the jurisdiction conferred." 279 U.S., at 459.

The distinction between public and private rights as the principle delineating the proper domains of legislative and constitutional courts respectively received its death blow, I had believed, in Crowell v. Benson, 285 U.S. 22 (1932). In that case, the Court approved an administrative scheme for the determination, in the first instance, of maritime employee compensation claims. Although acknowledging the framework set out in Murray's Lessee and Ex parte Bakelite Corp., the Court specifically distinguished the case before it: "The present case does not fall within the categories just described but is one of private right, that is, of the liability of one individual to another under the law as defined." 285 U.S., at 51. Nevertheless, the Court approved of the use of an Art. I adjudication mechanism on the new theory that "there is no requirement that, in order to maintain the essential attributes of the judicial power, all determinations of fact in constitutional courts shall be made by judges." Article I courts could deal not only with public rights, but also, to an extent, with private rights. The Court now established a distinction between questions of fact and law: "[T]he reservation of full authority to the court to deal with matters of law provides for the appropriate exercise of the judicial function in this class of cases." *Id.,* at 54.

Whatever sense Crowell may have seemed to give to this subject was exceedingly short-lived. One year later, the Court returned to this subject, abandoning both the public/private and the fact/law distinction and replacing both with a simple literalism. In O'Donoghue v. United States, 289 U.S. 516 (1933), considering the courts of the District of Columbia, and in Williams v. United States, 289 U.S. 553 (1933), considering the Court of Claims, the Court adopted the principle that if a federal court exercises jurisdiction over cases of the type listed in Art. III, § 2, as falling within the "judicial power of the United States," then that court must be an Art. III court * * *.[13]

In order to apply this same principle and yet hold the Court of Claims to be a legislative court, the Court found it necessary in Williams, *supra,* to conclude that the phrase "Controversies to which the United States shall be a party" in Art. III must be read as if it said "Controversies to which the United States shall be a party plaintiff or petitioner."[14] * * *

[Justice White here discusses National Insurance Co. v. Tidewater Co., 337 U.S. 582 (1949); see, as to this case, *Note on the Tidewater Problem,* p. 473, *infra.*]

Another chapter in this somewhat dense history of a constitutional quandary was provided by Justice Harlan's plurality opinion in Glidden Co. v. Zdanok, 370 U.S. 530 (1962), in which the Court, despite Bakelite and Williams—and relying on an Act of Congress enacted since those deci-

---

13. O'Donoghue does not apply this principle wholly consistently: It still recognizes a territorial court exception to Art. III's requirements. It now bases this exception, however, not on any theoretical difference in principle, but simply on the "transitory character of the territorial governments." 289 U.S., at 536.

14. See P. Bator, P. Mishkin, D. Shapiro, & H. Wechsler, Hart and Wechsler's The Federal Courts and The Federal System 399 (2d ed. 1973) (reviewing the problems of the Williams case and characterizing it as an "intellectual disaster").

sions—held the Court of Claims and the Court of Customs and Patent Appeals to be Art. III courts. Justice Harlan continued the process of intellectual repudiation begun by Chief Justice Vinson in [his dissent in] Tidewater. First, it was clear to him that Chief Justice Marshall could not have meant what he said in Canter on the inability of Art. I courts to consider issues within the jurisdiction of Art. III courts: "Far from being 'incapable of receiving' federal-question jurisdiction, the territorial courts have long exercised a jurisdiction commensurate in this regard with that of the regular federal courts and have been subjected to the appellate jurisdiction of this Court precisely because they do so." 370 U.S., at 545, n. 13. Second, exceptions to the requirements of Art. III, he thought, have not been founded on any principled distinction between Art. I issues and Art. III issues; rather, a "confluence of practical considerations" accounts for this Court's sanctioning of Art. I courts:

> "The touchstone of decision in all these cases has been the need to exercise the jurisdiction then and there and for a transitory period. Whether constitutional limitations on the exercise of judicial power have been held inapplicable has depended on the particular local setting, the practical necessities, and the possible alternatives." *Id.*, at 547–548.

Finally, recognizing that there is frequently no way to distinguish between Art. I and Art. III courts on the basis of the work they do, Justice Harlan suggested that the only way to tell them apart is to examine the "establishing legislation" to see if it complies with the requirements of Art. III. This, however, comes dangerously close to saying that Art. III courts are those with Art. III judges; Art. I courts are those without such judges. One hundred and fifty years of constitutional history, in other words, had led to a simple tautology.

IV

The complicated and contradictory history of the issue before us leads me to conclude that Chief Justice Vinson and Justice Harlan reached the correct conclusion: There is no difference in principle between the work that Congress may assign to an Art. I court and that which the Constitution assigns to Art. III courts. Unless we want to overrule a large number of our precedents upholding a variety of Art. I courts—not to speak of those Art. I courts that go by the contemporary name of "administrative agencies"—this conclusion is inevitable. It is too late to go back that far; too late to return to the simplicity of the principle pronounced in Art. III and defended so vigorously and persuasively by Hamilton in The Federalist Nos. 78–82.

To say that the Court has failed to articulate a principle by which we can test the constitutionality of a putative Art. I court, or that there is no such abstract principle, is not to say that this Court must always defer to the legislative decision to create Art. I, rather than Art. III, courts. Article III is not to be read out of the Constitution; rather, it should be read as expressing one value that must be balanced against competing constitutional values and legislative responsibilities. This Court retains the final word on how that balance is to be struck.

Despite the principled, although largely mistaken, rhetoric expanded by the Court in this area over the years, such a balancing approach stands

behind many of the decisions upholding Art. I courts. Justice Harlan
suggested as much in Glidden, although he needlessly limited his consideration to the "temporary" courts that Congress has had to set up on a variety
of occasions. In each of these instances, this Court has implicitly concluded
that the legislative interest in creating an adjudicative institution of
temporary duration outweighed the values furthered by a strict adherence
to Art. III. Besides the territorial courts approved in American Insurance
Co. v. Canter, 1 Pet. 511 (1828), these courts have included the Court of
Private Land Claims, United States v. Coe, 155 U.S. 76 (1894), the Choctaw
and Chickasaw Citizenship Court, Stephens v. Cherokee Nation, 174 U.S.
445 (1899), and consular courts established in foreign countries, In re Ross,
140 U.S. 453 (1891). This same sort of "practical" judgment was voiced,
even if not relied upon, in Crowell with respect to the Employees' Compensation Claims Commission, which was not meant to be of limited duration:
"[W]e are unable to find any constitutional obstacle to the action of the
Congress in availing itself of a method shown by experience to be essential
in order to apply its standards to the thousands of cases involved." 285
U.S., at 54. And even in Murray's Lessee, there was a discussion of the
"necessity" of Congress' adopting an approach that avoided adjudication in
an Art. III court. 18 How., at 285.

This was precisely the approach taken to this problem in Palmore v.
United States, 411 U.S. 389 (1973), which, contrary to the suggestion of the
plurality, did not rest on any theory of territorial or geographical control.*
Rather, it rested on an evaluation of the strength of the legislative interest
in pursuing in this manner one of its constitutionally assigned responsibilities—a responsibility not different in kind from numerous other legislative
responsibilities. Thus, Palmore referred to the wide variety of Art. I
courts, not just territorial courts. It is in this light that the critical
statement of the case must be understood:

> "[T]he requirements of Art. III, which are applicable where laws of
> national applicability and affairs of national concern are at stake, must
> in proper circumstances give way to accommodate plenary grants of
> power to Congress to legislate with respect to specialized areas having
> particularized needs and warranting distinctive treatment." 411 U.S.,
> at 407–408.

I do not suggest that the Court should simply look to the strength of
the legislative interest and ask itself if that interest is more compelling
than the values furthered by Art. III. The inquiry should, rather, focus
equally on those Art. III values and ask whether and to what extent the
legislative scheme accommodates them or, conversely, substantially undermines them. The burden on Art. III values should then be measured
against the values Congress hopes to serve through the use of Art. I courts.

To be more concrete: Crowell, supra, suggests that the presence of
appellate review by an Art. III court will go a long way toward insuring a
proper separation of powers. Appellate review of the decisions of legislative courts, like appellate review of state-court decisions, provides a firm
check on the ability of the political institutions of government to ignore or
transgress constitutional limits on their own authority. Obviously, therefore, a scheme of Art. I courts that provides for appellate review by Art. III

* [Ed.] The opinion in Palmore was written by Justice White.

courts should be substantially less controversial than a legislative attempt entirely to avoid judicial review in a constitutional court.

Similarly, as long as the proposed Art. I courts are designed to deal with issues likely to be of little interest to the political branches, there is less reason to fear that such courts represent a dangerous accumulation of power in one of the political branches of government. * * *

V

I believe that the new bankruptcy courts established by the Bankruptcy Act of 1978, 28 U.S.C. § 1471 (1976 ed., Supp. IV), satisfy this standard.

First, ample provision is made for appellate review by Art. III courts. Appeals may in some circumstances be brought directly to the district courts. 28 U.S.C. § 1334. Decisions of the district courts are further appealable to the court of appeals. § 1293. In other circumstances, appeals go first to a panel of bankruptcy judges, § 1482, and then to the court of appeals. § 1293. In still other circumstances—when the parties agree—appeals may go directly to the court of appeals. In sum, there is in every instance a right of appeal to at least one Art. III court. Had Congress decided to assign all bankruptcy matters to the state courts, a power it clearly possesses, no greater review in an Art. III court would exist. Although I do not suggest that this analogy means that Congress may establish an Art. I court wherever it could have chosen to rely upon the state courts, it does suggest that the critical function of judicial review is being met in a manner that the Constitution suggests is sufficient.

Second, no one seriously argues that the Bankruptcy Act of 1978 represents an attempt by the political branches of government to aggrandize themselves at the expense of the third branch or an attempt to undermine the authority of constitutional courts in general. Indeed, the congressional perception of a lack of judicial interest in bankruptcy matters was one of the factors that led to the establishment of the bankruptcy courts: Congress feared that this lack of interest would lead to a failure by federal district courts to deal with bankruptcy matters in an expeditious manner. H.R.Rep.No. 95–595, p. 14 (1977). Bankruptcy matters are, for the most part, private adjudications of little political significance. Although some bankruptcies may indeed present politically controversial circumstances or issues, Congress has far more direct ways to involve itself in such matters than through some sort of subtle, or not so subtle, influence on bankruptcy judges. Furthermore, were such circumstances to arise, the Due Process Clause might very well require that the matter be considered by an Art. III judge: Bankruptcy proceedings remain, after all, subject to all of the strictures of that constitutional provision.

Finally, I have no doubt that the ends that Congress sought to accomplish by creating a system of non-Art. III bankruptcy courts were at least as compelling as the ends found to be satisfactory in Palmore v. United States, 411 U.S. 389 (1973), or the ends that have traditionally justified the creation of legislative courts. The stresses placed upon the old bankruptcy system by the tremendous increase in bankruptcy cases were well documented and were clearly a matter to which Congress could respond. I do not believe it is possible to challenge Congress' further determination that it was necessary to create a specialized court to deal with bankruptcy matters. This was the nearly uniform conclusion of all those that testified before Congress on the question of reform of the bankruptcy system, as well as the conclusion of the Commission on Bankruptcy Laws established by Congress in 1970 to explore possible improvements in the system.

The real question is not whether Congress was justified in establishing a specialized bankruptcy court, but rather whether it was justified in failing to create a specialized, Art. III bankruptcy court. My own view is that the very fact of extreme specialization may be enough, and certainly has been enough in the past,[18] to justify the creation of a legislative court. Congress may legitimately consider the effect on the federal judiciary of the addition of several hundred specialized judges: We are, on the whole, a body of generalists. The addition of several hundred specialists may substantially change, whether for good or bad, the character of the federal bench. Moreover, Congress may have desired to maintain some flexibility in its possible future responses to the general problem of bankruptcy. There is no question that the existence of several hundred bankruptcy judges with life tenure would have severely limited Congress' future options. Furthermore, the number of bankruptcies may fluctuate, producing a substantially reduced need for bankruptcy judges. Congress may have thought that, in that event, a bankruptcy specialist should not as a general matter serve as a judge in the countless nonspecialized cases that come before the federal district courts. It would then face the prospect of large numbers of idle federal judges. Finally, Congress may have believed that the change from bankruptcy referees to Art. I judges was far less dramatic, and so less disruptive of the existing bankruptcy and constitutional court systems, than would be a change to Art. III judges.

For all of these reasons, I would defer to the congressional judgment. Accordingly, I dissent.*

---

18. Consider, for example, the Court of Customs Appeals involved in Ex parte Bakelite Corp., 279 U.S. 438 (1929), or the variety of specialized administrative agencies that engage in some form of adjudication.

* [Ed.] After the Marathon decision (and after a short period during which an emergency rule, drafted by the Judicial Conference, was in effect in most districts, see Chap. 6, Sec. 1, p. 754, *infra*), Congress in 1984 enacted a new Bankruptcy Act to deal with the problems created by that decision. Act of July 10, 1984, 98 Stat. 333. The new statute makes the bankruptcy judges "units" of the district court. It amended 28 U.S.C. § 157 to provide that each district court "may provide" that "any or all" cases or proceedings arising under Title 11, or arising in or related to a case under Title 11, shall be referred to the bankruptcy judges of the district. If the matter is a "core" proceeding—corresponding, roughly, to the pre–1978 bankruptcy court's "summary" jurisdiction—the bankruptcy judge may "hear and determine." But if the matter is a non-core proceeding, the bankruptcy judge makes only proposed findings and conclusions, and the final order is entered by the district judge after "reviewing de novo" all matters as to which an objection was made. "Personal injury tort and wrongful death claims" must be adjudicated in the district court. The bankruptcy judges are appointed by the courts of appeals for 14–year terms. See generally Countryman, *Scrambling to Define Bankruptcy Jurisdiction: The Chief Justice, the Judicial Conference, and the Legislative Process*, 22 Harv.J.Legis. 1 (1985); Snider, Rochkind, Grew, Stein & Welford, *The Bankruptcy Amendments and Federal Judgeship Act of 1984*, 83 Mich.L. Rev. 775 (1984).

COMMODITY FUTURES TRADING COMM'N v. SCHOR

478 U.S. 833, 106 S.Ct. 3245, 92 L.Ed.2d 675 (1986).
Certiorari to the United States Court of Appeals for the
District of Columbia Circuit.

JUSTICE O'CONNOR delivered the opinion of the Court.

The question presented is whether the Commodity Exchange Act (CEA or Act), 7 U.S.C. § 1 *et seq.,* empowers the Commodity Futures Trading Commission (CFTC or Commission) to entertain state law counterclaims in reparation proceedings and, if so, whether that grant of authority violates Article III of the Constitution.

I

The CEA broadly prohibits fraudulent and manipulative conduct in connection with commodity futures transactions. In 1974, Congress "overhaul[ed]" the Act in order to institute a more "comprehensive regulatory structure to oversee the volatile and esoteric futures trading complex." H.R.Rep. No. 93–975, p. 1 (1974). See Pub.L. 93–463, 88 Stat. 1389. Congress also determined that the broad regulatory powers of the CEA were most appropriately vested in an agency which would be relatively immune from the "political winds that sweep Washington." H.R.Rep. No. 93–975, pp. 44, 70. It therefore created an independent agency, the CFTC, and entrusted to it sweeping authority to implement the CEA.

Among the duties assigned to the CFTC was the administration of a reparations procedure through which disgruntled customers of professional commodity brokers could seek redress for the brokers' violations of the Act or CFTC regulations. Thus, § 14 of the CEA, 7 U.S.C.A. § 18 (Supp.1986), provides that any person injured by such violations may apply to the Commission for an order directing the offender to pay reparations to the complainant and may enforce that order in federal district court. Congress intended this administrative procedure to be an "inexpensive and expeditious" alternative to existing fora available to aggrieved customers, namely, the courts and arbitration. * * *

In conformance with the congressional goal of promoting efficient dispute resolution, the CFTC promulgated a regulation in 1976 which allows it to adjudicate counterclaims "aris[ing] out of the transaction or occurrence or series of transactions or occurrences set forth in the complaint." 17 CFR § 12.23(b)(2) (1983). This permissive counterclaim rule leaves the respondent in a reparations proceeding free to seek relief against the reparations complainant in other fora.

The instant dispute arose in February 1980, when respondents Schor and Mortgage Services of America invoked the CFTC's reparations jurisdiction by filing complaints against petitioner ContiCommodity Services, Inc. (Conti), a commodity futures broker, and Richard L. Sandor, a Conti employee. Schor had an account with Conti which contained a debit balance because Shor's net futures trading losses and expenses, such as commissions, exceeded the funds deposited in the account. Schor alleged that this debit balance was the result of Conti's numerous violations of the CEA.

Before receiving notice that Schor had commenced the reparations proceeding, Conti had filed a diversity action in Federal District Court to recover the debit balance. Schor counterclaimed in this action, reiterating his charges that the debit balance was due to Conti's violations of the CEA. Schor also moved on two separate occasions to dismiss or stay the district court action, arguing that the continuation of the federal action would be a waste of judicial resources and an undue burden on the litigants in view of the fact that "[t]he reparations proceedings * * * will fully * * * resolve and adjudicate all the rights of the parties to this action with respect to the transactions which are the subject matter of this action."

Although the District Court declined to stay or dismiss the suit, Conti voluntarily dismissed the federal court action and presented its debit balance claim by way of a counterclaim in the CFTC reparations proceeding. Conti denied violating the CEA and instead insisted that the debit balance resulted from Schor's trading, and was therefore a simple debt owed by Schor. Schor v. Commodity Futures Trading Comm'n, 740 F.2d 1262, 1265 (1984).

After discovery, briefing and a hearing, the Administrative Law Judge (ALJ) in Schor's reparations proceeding ruled in Conti's favor on both Schor's claims and Conti's counterclaims. After this ruling, Schor for the first time challenged the CFTC's statutory authority to adjudicate Conti's counterclaim. The ALJ rejected Schor's challenge, stating himself "bound by agency regulations and published agency policies." The Commission declined to review the decision and allowed it to become final, at which point Schor filed a petition for review with the Court of Appeals for the District of Columbia Circuit. Prior to oral argument, the Court of Appeals, *sua sponte,* raised the question of whether CFTC could constitutionally adjudicate Conti's counterclaims in light of Northern Pipeline Construction Co. v. Marathon Pipe Line Co., 458 U.S. 50 (1982) (Northern Pipeline), in which this Court held that "Congress may not vest in a non-Article III court the power to adjudicate, render final judgment, and issue binding orders in a traditional contract action arising under state law, without consent of the litigants, and subject only to ordinary appellate review." Thomas v. Union Carbide Agricultural Products Co., 473 U.S. 568, 584 (1985) (Thomas).

After briefing and argument, the Court of Appeals upheld the CFTC's decision on Schor's claim in most respects, but ordered the dismissal of Conti's counterclaims on the ground that "the CFTC lacks authority (subject matter competence) to adjudicate" common law counterclaims. In support of this latter ruling, the Court of Appeals reasoned that the CFTC's exercise of jurisdiction over Conti's common law counterclaim gave rise to "[s]erious constitutional problems" under Northern Pipeline. The Court of Appeals therefore concluded that, under well-established principles of statutory construction, the relevant inquiry was whether the CEA was " 'fairly susceptible' of [an alternative] construction," such that Article III objections, and thus unnecessary constitutional adjudication, could be avoided, *Ibid.*

After examining the CEA and its legislative history, the court concluded that Congress had no "clearly expressed" or "explicit" intention to give the CFTC constitutionally questionable jurisdiction over state common law counterclaims. The Court of Appeals therefore "adopt[ed] the construction of the Act that avoids significant constitutional questions," reading the CEA to authorize the CFTC to adjudicate only those counterclaims alleging violations of the Act or CFTC regulations. Because Conti's counterclaims did not allege such violations, the Court of Appeals held that the CFTC exceeded its authority in adjudicating those claims, and ordered that the ALJ's decision on the claims be reversed and the claims dismissed for lack of jurisdiction.

The Court of Appeals denied rehearing en banc by a divided vote. * * * This Court granted the CFTC's petition for certiorari, vacated the court of appeals' judgment, and remanded the case for further consideration in light of Thomas [v. Union Carbide Agricultural Products Co., 473 U.S. 568 (1985)]. We had there ruled that the arbitration scheme established under the Federal Insecticide, Fungicide, and Rodenticide Act (FIFRA), 7 U.S.C. § 136 *et seq.*, does not contravene Article III and, more generally, held that "Congress, acting for a valid legislative purpose pursuant to its constitutional powers under Article I, may create a seemingly 'private' right that is so closely integrated into a public regulatory scheme as to be a matter appropriate for agency resolution with limited involvement by the Article III judiciary."

On remand, the Court of Appeals reinstated its prior judgment. * * * We again granted certiorari, 474 U.S. 1018 (1985), and now reverse.

II

* * * Assuming that the Court of Appeals correctly discerned a "serious" constitutional problem in the CFTC's adjudication of Conti's counterclaim, we nevertheless believe that the court was mistaken in finding that the CEA could fairly be read to preclude the CFTC's exercise of jurisdiction over that counterclaim. * * *

Congress' assumption that the CFTC would have the authority to adjudicate counterclaims is evident on the face of the statute. * * * Accordingly, the court below did not seriously contest that Congress intended to authorize the CFTC to adjudicate *some* counterclaims in reparations proceedings. Rather, the court read into the facially unqualified reference to counterclaim jurisdiction a distinction between counterclaims arising under the Act or CFTC regulations and all other counterclaims. While the court's reading permitted it to avoid a potential Article III problem, it did so only by doing violence to the CEA, for its distinction cannot fairly be drawn from the language or history of the CEA, nor reconciled with the congressional purposes motivating the creation of the reparation proceeding.

We can find no basis in the language of the statute or its legislative history for the distinction posited by the Court of Appeals. * * *

Moreover, quite apart from congressional statements of intent, the broad grant of power in § 12a(5) clearly authorizes the promulgation of regulations providing for adjudication of common law counterclaims arising out of the same transaction as a reparations complaint because such jurisdiction is necessary, if not critical, to accomplish the purposes behind the reparations program.

Reference to the instant controversy illustrates the crippling effect that the Court of Appeals' restrictive reading of the CFTC's counterclaim jurisdiction would have on the efficacy of the reparations remedy. The dispute between Schor and Conti is typical of the disputes adjudicated in reparations proceedings: a customer and a professional commodities broker agree that there is a debit balance in the customer's account, but the customer attributes the deficit to the broker's alleged CEA violations and the broker attributes it to the customer's lack of success in the market. The customer brings a reparations claim; the broker counterclaims for the amount of the debit balance. In the usual case, then, the counterclaim "arises out of precisely the same course of events" as the principal claim and requires resolution of many of the same disputed factual issues.

Under the Court of Appeals' approach, the entire dispute may not be resolved in the administrative forum. Consequently, the entire dispute will typically end up in court, for when the broker files suit to recover the debit balance, the customer will normally be compelled either by compulsory counterclaim rules or by the expense and inconvenience of litigating the same issues in two fora to forgo his reparations remedy and to litigate his claim in court. * * * In sum, as Schor himself aptly summarized, to require a bifurcated examination of the single dispute "would be to emasculate if not destroy the purposes of the Commodity Exchange Act to provide an efficient and relatively inexpensive forum for the resolution of disputes in futures trading." * * *

As our discussion makes manifest, the CFTC's longheld position that it has the power to take jurisdiction over counterclaims such as Conti's is eminently reasonable and well within the scope of its delegated authority. * * *

III

* * *

Schor claims that [Article III] prohibit[s] Congress from authorizing the initial adjudication of common law counterclaims by the CFTC, an administrative agency whose adjudicatory officers do not enjoy the tenure and salary protections embodied in Article III.

Although our precedents in this area do not admit of easy synthesis, they do establish that the resolution of claims such as Schor's cannot turn on conclusory reference to the language of Article III. Rather, the constitutionality of a given congressional delegation of adjudicative functions to a non-Article III body must be assessed by reference to the purposes underlying the requirements of Article III. This inquiry, in turn, is guided by the principle that "practical attention to substance rather than doctrinaire reliance on formal categories should inform application of Article III." Thomas, *supra*.

A

Article III, § 1 serves both to protect "the role of the independent judiciary within the constitutional scheme of tripartite government," Thomas, *supra*, at 582–83, and to safeguard litigants' "right to have claims decided before judges who are free from potential domination by other branches of government." United States v. Will, 449 U.S. 200, 218 (1980). Although our cases have provided us with little occasion to discuss the nature or significance of this latter safeguard, our prior discussions of Article III, § 1's guarantee of an independent and impartial adjudication by the federal judiciary of matters within the judicial power of the United States intimated that this guarantee serves to protect <u>primarily personal, rather than structural, interest</u>s. * * *

Our precedents also demonstrate, however, that Article III does not confer on litigants an absolute right to the plenary consideration of every nature of claim by an Article III court. Moreover, as a personal right, Article III's guarantee of an impartial and independent federal adjudication is subject to waiver, just as are other personal constitutional rights that dictate the procedures by which civil and criminal matters must be tried. See, *e.g.,* Boykin v. Alabama, 395 U.S. 238 (1969) (waiver of criminal trial by guilty plea); Duncan v. Louisiana, 391 U.S. 145, 158 (1968) (waiver of right to trial by jury in criminal case); Fed.Rule of Civ.Proc. 38(d) (waiver of right to trial by jury in civil cases). Indeed, the relevance of concepts of waiver to Article III challenges is demonstrated by our decision in Northern Pipeline, in which the absence of consent to an initial adjudication before a non-Article III tribunal was relied on as a significant factor in determining that Article III forbade such adjudication. * * *

In the instant case, Schor indisputably waived any right he may have possessed to the full trial of Conti's counterclaim before an Article III court. Schor expressly demanded that Conti proceed on its counterclaim in the reparations proceeding rather than before the District Court, and was content to have the entire dispute settled in the forum he had selected until the ALJ ruled against him on all counts; it was only after the ALJ rendered a decision to which he objected that Schor raised any challenge to the CFTC's consideration of Conti's counterclaim.

Even were there no evidence of an express waiver here, Schor's election to forgo his right to proceed in state or federal court on his claim and his decision to seek relief instead in a CFTC reparations proceeding constituted an effective waiver. * * *

B

As noted above, our precedents establish that Article III, § 1 not only preserves to litigants their interest in an impartial and independent federal adjudication of claims within the judicial power of the United States, but also serves as "an inseparable element of the constitutional system of checks and balances." Northern Pipeline, 458 U.S. at 58. * * * To the extent that this structural principle is implicated in a given case, the parties cannot by consent cure the constitutional difficulty for the same reason that the parties by consent cannot confer on federal courts subject matter jurisdiction beyond the limitations imposed by Article III, § 2. See, *e.g.,* United States v. Griffin, 303 U.S. 226, 229 (1938). When these Article III limitations are at issue, notions of consent and waiver cannot be dispositive because the limitations serve institutional interests that the parties cannot be expected to protect.

In determining the extent to which a given congressional decision to authorize the adjudication of Article III business in a non-Article III tribunal impermissibly threatens the institutional integrity of the Judicial Branch, the Court has declined to adopt formalistic and unbending rules. Thomas, 473 U.S., at 583. Although such rules might lend a greater degree of coherence to this area of the law, they might also unduly constrict Congress' ability to take needed and innovative action pursuant to its Article I powers. Thus, in reviewing Article III challenges, we have weighed a number of factors, none of which has been deemed determinative, with an eye to the practical effect that the congressional action will have on the constitutionally assigned role of the federal judiciary. Among the factors upon which we have focused are the extent to which the "essential attributes of judicial power" are reserved to Article III courts, and, conversely, the extent to which the non-Article III forum exercises the range of jurisdiction and powers normally vested only in Article III courts, the origins and importance of the right to be adjudicated, and the concerns that drove Congress to depart from the requirements of Article III.

* * *

An examination of the relative allocation of powers between the CFTC and Article III courts in light of the considerations given prominence in our precedents demonstrates that the congressional scheme does not impermissibly intrude on the province of the judiciary. The CFTC's adjudicatory powers depart from the traditional agency model in just one respect: the CFTC's jurisdiction over common law counterclaims. While wholesale importation of concepts of pendent or ancillary jurisdiction into the agency context may create greater constitutional difficulties, we decline to endorse an absolute prohibition on such jurisdiction out of fear of where some hypothetical "slippery slope" may deposit us. Indeed, the CFTC's exercise of this type of jurisdiction is not without precedent. Thus, in Reconstruction Finance Corp. v. Bankers Trust Co., 318 U.S. 163, 168–171 (1943), we saw no constitutional difficulty in the initial adjudication of a state law claim by a federal agency, subject to judicial review, when that claim was ancillary to a federal law dispute. Similarly, in Katchen v. Landy, 382 U.S. 323 (1966), this Court upheld a bankruptcy referee's power to hear and decide state law counterclaims against a creditor who filed a claim in bankruptcy when those counterclaims arose out of the same transaction. We reasoned that, as a practical matter, requiring the trustee to commence a plenary action to recover on its counterclaim would be a "meaningless gesture." *Id.,* at 334.

In the instant case, we are likewise persuaded that there is little practical reason to find that this single deviation from the agency model is fatal to the congressional scheme. Aside from its authorization of counterclaim jurisdiction, the CEA leaves far more of the "essential attributes of judicial power" to Article III courts than did that portion of the Bankruptcy Act found unconstitutional in Northern Pipeline. The CEA scheme in fact hews closely to the agency model approved by the Court in Crowell v. Benson.

The CFTC, like the agency in Crowell, deals only with a "particularized area of law," Northern Pipeline, *supra,* 458 U.S., at 85, whereas the jurisdiction of the bankruptcy courts found unconstitutional in Northern Pipeline extended to broadly "all civil proceedings arising under title 11 or arising in or *related to* cases under title 11." 28 U.S.C. § 1471(b). CFTC orders, like those of the agency in Crowell, but unlike those of the bankruptcy courts under the 1978 Act, are enforceable only by order of the District Court. See 7 U.S.C.A. § 18(f) (Supp.1986); Northern Pipeline, *supra,* at 85–86. CFTC orders are also reviewed under the same "weight of the evidence" standard sustained in Crowell, rather than the more deferential standard found lacking in Northern Pipeline. The legal rulings of the CFTC, like the legal determinations of the agency in Crowell, are subject to *de novo* review. Finally, the CFTC, unlike the bankruptcy courts under the 1978 Act, does not exercise "all ordinary powers of district courts," and thus may not, for instance, preside over jury trials or issue writs of habeas corpus. 458 U.S., at 85.

Of course, the nature of the claim has significance in our Article III analysis quite apart from the method prescribed for its adjudication. The counterclaim asserted in this case is a "private" right for which state law provides the rule of decision. It is therefore a claim of the kind assumed to be at the "core" of matters normally reserved to Article III courts. * * * Yet this conclusion does not end our inquiry; just as this Court has rejected any attempt to make determinative for Article III purposes the distinction between public rights and private rights, Thomas, *supra,* at 585–86, there is no reason inherent in separation of powers principles to accord the state law character of a claim talismanic power in Article III inquiries. * * *

[T]he state law character of a claim is significant for purposes of determining the effect that an initial adjudication of those claims by a non-Article III tribunal will have on the separation of powers for the simple reason that private, common law rights were historically the types of matters subject to resolution by Article III courts. * * * Accordingly, where private, common law rights are at stake, our examination of the congressional attempt to control the manner in which those rights are adjudicated has been searching. In this case, however, "[l]ooking beyond form to the substance of what" Congress has done, we are persuaded that the congressional authorization of limited CFTC jurisdiction over a narrow class of common law claims as an incident to the CFTC's primary, and unchallenged, adjudicative function does not create a substantial threat to the separation of powers.

It is clear that Congress has not attempted to "withdraw from judicial cognizance" the determination of Conti's right to the sum represented by the debit balance in Schor's account. Congress gave the CFTC the authority to adjudicate such matters, but the decision to invoke this forum is left entirely to the parties and the power of the federal judiciary to take jurisdiction of these matters is unaffected. In such circumstances, separation of powers concerns are diminished, for it seems self-evident that just as Congress may encourage parties to settle a dispute out of court or resort to arbitration without impermissible incursions on the separation of powers, Congress may make available a quasi-judicial mechanism through which willing parties may, at their option, elect to resolve their differences. This is not to say, of course, that if Congress created a phalanx of non-Article III tribunals equipped to handle the entire business of the Article III courts without any Article III supervision or control and without evidence of valid and specific legislative necessities, the fact that the parties had the election to proceed in their forum of choice would necessarily save the scheme from constitutional attack. But this case obviously bears no resemblance to such a scenario, given the degree of judicial control saved to the federal courts, as well as the congressional purpose behind the jurisdictional delegation, the demonstrated need for the delegation, and the limited nature of the delegation.

When Congress authorized the CFTC to adjudicate counterclaims, its primary focus was on making effective a specific and limited federal regulatory scheme, not on allocating jurisdiction among federal tribunals. Congress intended to create an inexpensive and expeditious alternative forum through which customers could enforce the provisions of the CEA against professional brokers. Its decision to endow the CFTC with jurisdiction over such reparations claims is readily understandable given the perception that the CFTC was relatively immune from political pressures, see H.R.Rep. No. 93–975, pp. 44, 70, and the obvious expertise that the Commission possesses in applying the CEA and its own regulations. This reparations scheme itself is of unquestioned constitutional validity. See, *e.g.,* Thomas, *supra;* Northern Pipeline; Crowell v. Benson. It was only to ensure the effectiveness of this scheme that Congress authorized the CFTC to assert jurisdiction over common law counterclaims. Indeed, as was explained above, absent the CFTC's exercise of that authority, the purposes of the reparations procedure would have been confounded.

It also bears emphasis that the CFTC's assertion of counterclaim jurisdiction is limited to that which is necessary to make the reparations procedure workable. See 7 U.S.C. § 12a(5). The CFTC adjudication of common law counterclaims is incidental to, and completely dependent upon, adjudication of reparations claims created by federal law, and in actual fact is limited to claims arising out of the same transaction or occurrence as the reparations claim.

In such circumstances, the magnitude of any intrusion on the Judicial Branch can only be termed *de minimis.* Conversely, were we to hold that the Legislative Branch may not permit such limited cognizance of common law counterclaims at the election of the parties, it is clear that we would "defeat the obvious purpose of the legislation to furnish a prompt, continuous, expert and inexpensive method for dealing with a class of questions of fact which are peculiarly suited to examination and determination by an administrative agency specially assigned to that task." Crowell v. Benson, 285 U.S., at 46. We do not think Article III compels this degree of prophylaxis. * * * We conclude that the limited jurisdiction that the CFTC asserts over state law claims as a necessary incident to the adjudication of federal claims willingly submitted by the parties for initial agency adjudication does not contravene separation of powers principles or Article III.

C

Schor asserts that Article III, § 1, constrains Congress for reasons of federalism, as well as for reasons of separation of powers. He argues that the state law character of Conti's counterclaim transforms the central question in this case from whether Congress has trespassed upon the judicial powers of the Federal Government into whether Congress has invaded the prerogatives of state governments.

At the outset, we note that our prior precedents in this area have dealt only with separation of powers concerns, and have not intimated that principles of federalism impose limits on Congress' ability to delegate adjudicative functions to non-Article III tribunals. This absence of discussion regarding federalism is particularly telling in Northern Pipeline, where the Court based its analysis solely on the separation of powers principles inherent in Article III despite the fact that the claim sought to be adjudicated in the bankruptcy court was created by state law.

Even assuming that principles of federalism are relevant to Article III analysis, however, we are unpersuaded that those principles require the invalidation of the CFTC's counterclaim jurisdiction. The sole fact that Conti's counterclaim is resolved by a *federal* rather than a *state* tribunal could not be said to unduly impair state interests, for it is established that a federal court could, without constitutional hazard, decide a counterclaim such as the one asserted here under its ancillary jurisdiction, even if an independent jurisdictional basis for it were lacking. * * * Given that the federal courts can and do exercise ancillary jurisdiction over counterclaims such as the one at issue here, the question becomes whether the fact that a federal agency rather than a federal Article III court initially hears the state law claim gives rise to a cognizably greater impairment of principles of federalism.

Schor argues that those framers opposed to diversity jurisdiction in the federal courts acquiesced in its inclusion in Article III only because they were assured that the federal judiciary would be protected by the tenure and salary provisions of Article III. He concludes, in essence, that to protect this constitutional compact, Article III should be read to absolutely preclude any adjudication of state law claims by federal decisionmakers that do not enjoy the Article III salary and tenure protections. We are unpersuaded by Schor's novel theory, which suffers from a number of flaws, the most important of which is that Schor identifies no historical support for the critical link he posits between the provisions of Article III that protect the independence of the federal judiciary and those provisions that define the extent of the judiciary's jurisdiction over state law claims.

The judgment of the Court of Appeals for the District of Columbia Circuit is reversed and the case remanded for further proceedings consistent with this opinion.

It is so ordered.

JUSTICE BRENNAN, with whom JUSTICE MARSHALL joins, dissenting.

* * *

[The] important functions of Article III are too central to our constitutional scheme to risk their incremental erosion. The exceptions we have recognized for territorial courts, courts martial, and administrative courts were each based on "certain exceptional powers bestowed upon Congress by the Constitution or by historical consensus." Northern Pipeline, 458 U.S., at 70 (opinion of Brennan, J.). Here, however, there is no equally forceful reason to extend further these exceptions to situations that are distinguishable from existing precedents. *Cf.* Currie, *Bankruptcy Judges and the Independent Judiciary*, 16 Creighton L.Rev. 441, 445 (1983). The Court, however, engages in just such an extension. By sanctioning the adjudication of state-law counterclaims by a federal administrative agency, the Court far exceeds the analytic framework of our precedents.

* * *

The Court attempts to support the substantial alteration it works today in our Article III jurisprudence by pointing, *inter alia*, to legislative convenience; to the fact that Congress does not altogether eliminate federal court jurisdiction over ancillary state-law counterclaims; and to

Schor's "consent" to CFTC adjudication of ContiCommodity's counter-claims. In my view, the Court's effort fails.

II

* * * Were we to hold that the CFTC's authority to decide common-law counterclaims offends Article III, the Court declares, "it is clear that we would 'defeat the obvious purpose of the legislation.' " Article III, the Court concludes, does not "compel[ ] this degree of prophylaxis."

I disagree—Article III's prophylactic protections were intended to prevent just this sort of abdication to claims of legislative convenience. The Court requires that the legislative interest in convenience and efficiency be weighed against the competing interest in judicial independence. In doing so, the Court pits an interest the benefits of which are immediate, concrete, and easily understood against one, the benefits of which are almost entirely prophylactic, and thus often seem remote and not worth the cost in any single case. Thus, while this balancing creates the illusion of objectivity and ineluctability, in fact the result was foreordained, because the balance is weighted against judicial independence. See Redish, *Legislative Courts, Administrative Agencies, and the Northern Pipeline Decision*, 1983 Duke L.J. 197, 221–222. The danger of the Court's balancing approach is, of course, that as individual cases accumulate in which the Court finds that the short-term benefits of efficiency outweigh the long-term benefits of judicial independence, the protections of Article III will be eviscerated.

Perhaps the resolution of reparations claims such as respondent's may be accomplished more conveniently under the Court's decision than under my approach, but the Framers foreswore this sort of convenience in order to preserve freedom. As we explained in INS v. Chadha, 462 U.S. 919, 959 (1983):

> "The choices we discern as having been made in the Constitutional Convention impose burdens on governmental processes that often seem clumsy, inefficient, even unworkable, but those hard choices were consciously made by men who had lived under a form of government that permitted arbitrary governmental acts to go unchecked.
>
> * * *."

Moreover, in Bowsher v. Synar, 478 U.S. 714 (1986), we rejected the appellant's argument that legislative convenience saved the constitutionality of the assignment by Congress to the Comptroller General of essentially executive functions, stating that " 'the fact that a given law or procedure is efficient, convenient, and useful in facilitating functions of government, standing alone, will not save it if it is contrary to the Constitution. Convenience and efficiency are not the primary objectives—or the hallmarks—of democratic government * * *' " *Id.*, at 736 (quoting Chadha, *supra*, at 944).

It is impossible to reconcile the radically different approaches the Court takes to separation of powers in this case and in Bowsher. The Framers established *three* coequal branches of government and intended to preserve *each* from encroachment by either of the others. The Constitution did not grant Congress the general authority to bypass the judiciary whenever Congress deems it advisable, any more than it granted Congress the authority to arrogate to itself executive functions.

III

According to the Court, the intrusion into the province of the federal judiciary caused by the CFTC's authority to adjudicate state-law counter-claims is insignificant, both because the CFTC *shares* in, rather than displaces, federal district court jurisdiction over these claims and because only a very narrow class of state-law issues are involved. The "sharing" justification fails under the reasoning used by the Court to support the CFTC's authority. If the administrative reparations proceeding is so much more convenient and efficient than litigation in federal district court that abrogation of Article III's commands is warranted, it seems to me that complainants would rarely, if ever, choose to go to district court in the first instance. Thus, any "sharing" of jurisdiction is more illusory than real.

More importantly, the Court, in emphasizing that *this case* will permit solely a narrow class of state-law claims to be decided by a non-Article III court, ignores the fact that it establishes a broad principle. The decision today may authorize the administrative adjudication only of state-law claims that stem from the same transaction or set of facts that allow the customer of a professional commodity broker to initiate reparations pro-ceedings before the CFTC, but the *reasoning* of this decision strongly suggests that, given "legislative necessity" and party consent, any federal agency may decide state-law issues that are ancillary to federal issues within the agency's jurisdiction. Thus, while in this case "the magnitude of intrusion on the judicial branch" may conceivably be characterized as "*de minimis*," the potential impact of the Court's decision on federal court jurisdiction is substantial. * * *

IV

The Court's reliance on Schor's "consent" to a non-Article III tribunal is also misplaced. The Court erroneously suggests that there is a clear division between the separation of powers and the impartial adjudication functions of Article III. The Court identifies Article III's structural, or separation of powers, function as preservation of the judiciary's domain from encroachment by another branch. The Court identifies the impartial adjudication function as the protection afforded by Article III to individual litigants against judges who may be dominated by other branches of government.

In my view, the structural and individual interests served by Article III are inseparable. The potential exists for individual litigants to be deprived of impartial decisionmakers only where federal officials who exercise judicial power are susceptible to congressional and executive pressure. That is, individual litigants may be harmed by the assignment of judicial power to non-Article III federal tribunals only where the Legislative or Executive Branches have encroached upon judicial authority and have thus threatened the separation of powers. The Court correctly recognizes that to the extent that Article III's structural concerns are implicated by a grant of judicial power to a non-Article III tribunal, "the parties cannot by consent cure the constitutional difficulty for the same reason that the parties by consent cannot confer on federal courts subject-matter jurisdic-tion beyond the limitations imposed by Article III, § 2." Because the individual and structural interests served by Article III are coextensive, I do not believe that a litigant may ever waive his right to an Article III tribunal where one is constitutionally required. In other words, consent is irrelevant to Article III analysis.

V

Our Constitution unambiguously enunciates a fundamental principle—that the "judicial power of the United States" be reposed in an independent judiciary. It is our obligation zealously to guard that independence so that our tripartite system of government remains strong and that individuals continue to be protected against decisionmakers subject to majoritarian pressures. Unfortunately, today the Court forsakes that obligation for expediency. I dissent.

NOTE ON LEGISLATIVE COURTS

(1) As indicated in the Schor opinions, between Northern Pipeline and Schor the Court had also faced the issue of the validity of special Article I tribunals in Thomas v. Union Carbide Agricultural Products Co., 473 U.S. 568 (1985), involving a challenge to a statute requiring private parties under certain circumstances to arbitrate a dispute arising under federal law. The Federal Insecticide, Fungicide, and Rodenticide Act (FIFRA), 7 U.S.C. § 136 et seq., requires manufacturers of pesticides, as a precondition for obtaining the registration necessary to market a pesticide, to submit extensive research data to EPA concerning the product's health and environmental effects. In order to streamline the registration process and make it less costly, the statute permits the EPA in certain situations to use data previously submitted by another registrant in considering the registration application of a later (so-called "me-too" or "follow-on") registrant. The Act authorizes the EPA to consider previously submitted data, however, only if the later registrant offers to compensate the original data submitter. If the original and follow-up registrants cannot agree on the terms of compensation, the issue must be submitted to binding arbitration before a private arbitrator; the arbitrator's decision is subject to judicial review only for "fraud, misrepresentation, or other misconduct." See 7 U.S.C. § 136a(c)(1)(D)(ii).

Justice O'Connor's opinion for the Court upheld this statute against the contention that it violated Article III. The Court stated that "an absolute construction of Article III is not possible," and that "the Court has long recognized that Congress is not barred from acting pursuant to its powers under Article I to vest decisionmaking authority in tribunals that lack the attributes of Article III courts" (p. 583). It continued:

"The Court's most recent pronouncement on the meaning of Article III is Northern Pipeline. A divided Court was unable to agree on the precise scope and nature of Article III's limitations. The Court's holding in that case establishes only that Congress may not vest in a non-Article III court the power to adjudicate, render final judgment, and issue binding orders in a traditional contract action arising under state law, without consent of the litigants, and subject only to ordinary appellate review. * * *

"[A]ppellees contend that FIFRA confers a 'private right' to compensation, requiring either Article III adjudication or review by an Article III court sufficient to retain 'the essential attributes of the judicial power.' Northern Pipeline Co., 458 U.S., at 77, 85–86 (plurality opinion). This 'private right' argument rests on the distinction between public and private rights drawn by the plurality in Northern Pipeline. * * *

"This theory that the public rights/private rights dichotomy of Crowell and Murray's Lessee provides a bright-line test for determining the requirements of Article III did not command a majority of the Court in Northern Pipeline. Insofar as appellees interpret that case and Crowell as establishing that the right to an Article III forum is absolute unless the Federal Government is a party of record, we cannot agree. * * *

"Crowell held that Congress could replace a seaman's traditional negligence action in admiralty with a statutory scheme of strict liability. In response to practical concerns, Congress rejected adjudication in Article III courts and instead provided that claims for compensation would be determined in an administrative proceeding by a deputy commissioner appointed by the United States Employees' Compensation Commission. '[T]he findings of the deputy commissioner, supported by evidence and within the scope of his authority' were final with respect to injuries to employees within the purview of the statute. Although such findings clearly concern obligations among private parties, this fact did not make the scheme invalid under Article III. Instead, after finding that the administrative proceedings satisfied due process, Crowell concluded that the judicial review afforded by the statute, including review of matters of law, 'provides for the appropriate exercise of the judicial function in this class of cases.'

"The enduring lesson of Crowell is that practical attention to substance rather than doctrinaire reliance on formal categories should inform application of Article III. *Cf.* Glidden Co. v. Zdanok, 370 U.S., at 547–548. The extent of judicial review afforded by the legislation reviewed in Crowell does not constitute a minimal requirement of Article III without regard to the origin of the right at issue or the concerns guiding the selection by Congress of a particular method for resolving disputes" (pp. 584–87).

The Court noted that the Crowell legislation, unlike FIFRA, displaced a traditional common law cause of action, and thus required broader Article III review. And it went on expressly to repudiate the suggestion that suits that determined the liabilities of individuals could not be "public rights" suits, since the result would be to raise doubts about the validity of "many quasi-adjudicative activities involving claims between individuals" (p. 587).

Finally, the Court turned to the FIFRA scheme itself and concluded that Congress acted within permissible bounds in providing for arbitration of FIFRA compensation disputes and severely limiting judicial review of the arbitrator's award. "Use of a registrant's data to support a follow-on registration serves a public purpose as an integral part of a program safeguarding the public health. Congress has the power, under Article I, to authorize an agency administering a complex regulatory scheme to allocate costs and benefits among voluntary participants in the program without providing an Article III adjudication." "The 1978 amendments represent a pragmatic solution to the difficult problem of spreading the costs of generating adequate information * * *. * * * Given the nature of the right at issue and the concerns motivating the Legislature, we do not think this system threatens the independent role of the Judiciary in our constitutional scheme." "The danger of Congress or the Executive encroaching on the Article III judicial powers is at a minimum when no unwilling defendant is subjected to judicial enforcement * * *." "FIFRA limits, but does not preclude review of the arbitration proceeding by an Article III court," since awards can be set aside for "fraud, misconduct or misrepresentation" and "review of constitutional error is preserved." "FIFRA, therefore, does not obstruct whatever judicial review might be required by due process" (pp. 589–92).

Justice Brennan, joined by Justices Blackman and Marshall, concurred in the judgment in a separate opinion. He recalled that the Northern Pipeline plurality had disclaimed any intent to create "a generally applicable definition of 'public rights' but concluded that at a minimum public rights disputes must arise 'between the government and others' " (p. 597). But, here, Justice Brennan was prepared to switch gears: "I agree with the Court that the determinative factor with respect to the proper characterization of the nature of the dispute in this case should not be the presence or absence of the Government as a party. * * * Properly understood, the analysis elaborated by the plurality in Northern Pipeline does not place the Federal Government in an Article III straitjacket whenever a dispute technically is one between private parties" (p. 598–99). Justice Brennan continued:

"Though the issue before us in this case is not free of doubt, in my judgment the FIFRA compensation scheme challenged in this case should be viewed as involving a matter of public rights as that term is understood in the line of cases culminating in Northern Pipeline. In one sense the question of proper compensation for a follow-on registrant's use of test data is, under the FIFRA scheme, a dispute about 'the liability of one individual to another under the law as defined', Crowell v. Benson, at 51 (defining matters of private right). But the dispute arises in the context of a federal regulatory scheme that virtually occupies the field. Congress has decided that effectuation of the public policies of FIFRA demands not only a requirement of compensation from follow-on registrants in return for mandatory access to data but also an administrative process—mandatory negotiation followed by binding arbitration—to ensure that unresolved compensation disputes do not delay public distribution of needed products. This case, in other words, involves not only the congressional prescription of a federal rule of decision to govern a private dispute but also the active participation of a federal regulatory agency in resolving the dispute. Although a compensation dispute under FIFRA ultimately involves a determination of the duty owed one private party by another, at its heart the dispute involves the exercise of authority by a Federal Government arbitrator in the course of administration of FIFRA's comprehensive regulatory scheme" (pp. 600–01).

(2) What continuing authority does the plurality opinion in Northern Pipeline have after Thomas and Schor?

(3) All of the Justices now seem to agree that a congressional decision allocating some of the federal judicial business enumerated in Article III to a legislative court does not in itself change the inherent character of that business, and that it is therefore impossible to distinguish constitutional from legislative courts on the ground that the former exercise the exclusive

power to adjudicate the judicial business enumerated in Article III whereas the latter exercise judicial power in another class of cases. (This is made plain not only by the many instances, noted in the opinions, of concurrent jurisdiction between legislative and constitutional courts, but by the fact that the Supreme Court freely reviews the judgments of legislative courts, treating the review as a conventional instance of "appellate jurisdiction" in the constitutional sense.)

The most notorious instance of an attempt to act on the contrary view—that legislative courts may not adjudicate any of the cases and controversies enumerated in Article III—was the Williams case, referred to in the Northern Pipeline opinion, holding that the salaries of the judges of the Court of Claims were subject to reduction under the Economy Act of 1933. In Williams, Justice Sutherland, after setting forth the holding in Ex parte Bakelite Corp., 279 U.S. 438 (1929) (Court of Customs and Patent Appeals is an Article I court), said (289 U.S. at 571):

"We might well rest the present case upon that determination; but must not do so without considering another view of the question, which seems to find support in some expressions of this court, namely, that when the United States consents to be sued, the judicial power of Article III at once attaches to the court upon which jurisdiction is conferred in virtue of the clause which in comprehensive terms extends the judicial power to 'controversies to which the United States shall be a party'."

The opinion appeared to accept without question the premise of this argument—namely, that if cases in the Court of Claims are "controversies to which the United States shall be a party," in the constitutional sense, the court would have to be a constitutional court. And after elaborate consideration it rejected the argument on the sole ground that the constitutional provision must be treated "as though it read, 'controversies to which the United States shall be a party plaintiff or petitioner' ".

Among other things wrong with Justice Sutherland's reasoning, note (a) his failure to explain how the Supreme Court can have original jurisdiction of an action by a state against the United States when the United States consents, Minnesota v. Hitchcock, 185 U.S. 373 (1902), p. 312, *supra;* (b) the unexamined difficulties with the corollary of his conclusion that in other consented actions against the United States, the district courts, and the Supreme Court on appeal, must be exercising some other judicial power than "the judicial power defined by Article III"; and (c) his failure even to consider the question why cases in the Court of Claims, at least, are not "Cases * * * arising under * * * the Laws of the United States".

Are not cases in the Court of Claims, the Customs Court, and the Court of Customs and Patent Appeals—whether or not these courts are constitutional or legislative—all cases arising under the laws of the United States? What of cases in the territorial and District of Columbia courts that would be outside the jurisdiction of an ordinary district court? If they do not arise under the laws of the United States, what law do they arise under? Upon what other basis could decisions in such cases be reviewed by the Supreme Court?

It is hard to explain how the intellectual disaster of the Williams case could have been perpetrated within a year of Crowell v. Benson.

(4) Now consider the approach of the Northern Pipeline plurality to the problems of Article I courts. The plurality asserts that if cases to

which the federal judicial power extends are to be adjudicated by a federal tribunal, they must be adjudicated in an Article III court (or at least a properly constituted "adjunct" of an Article III court), *except* in the "three narrow situations" discussed by Justice Brennan—situations deemed to be "exceptional".

This assertion raises two questions: (i) In what respects are the three named categories justifiedly "exceptional"? (ii) Are the exceptions "narrow"?

(a) Does Justice Brennan give a persuasive reason why Article I courts are justified in the territories (and the District of Columbia), in cases subject to courts martial, and in "public rights" cases, but not in any other situation? Are the "independence" guarantees of Article III less relevant in some or all of these three categories of cases than in cases involving bankruptcy? Why do the grants of power to Congress to legislate with respect to these three matters suggest that they alone should be deemed to include the power to constitute tribunals not subject to the rules of Article III?

(b) The "courts martial" and "territorial court" categories are reasonably confined. But what are cases within the "public rights" exception? Does this category have any intelligible content after Justice Brennan gets through with it in Northern Pipeline, Thomas and Schor? Particularly given the concurrence in Thomas, does this category give the judge less discretion to evaluate particular circumstances than the balancing test espoused by Justices White and O'Connor?

Is it possible, in the modern administrative state, with its elaborate statutory schemes that characteristically create complex interdependencies between public and private enforcement, to maintain rigid distinctions between public and private rights? Is it an intelligent enterprise to try to do so? Is there anything about the structure and philosophy of Article III that is illuminated by asking whether an action to set aside a bankruptcy preference or to allocate the costs of a FIFRA registration should be deemed a matter of "public" or "private" right?

See, for a splendid history and analysis of the "public rights" doctrine, Young, *Public Rights and the Federal Judicial Power: From Murray's Lessee Through Crowell to Schor*, 35 Buff.L.Rev. 765 (1986).

(5) Now turn to the proposition on which a majority of the Court agreed in Northern Pipeline: that Congress is, in any event, precluded from authorizing a non-Article III court or agency to adjudicate a case arising under *state* law.

Why should this be so?

It seems clear that Congress may not authorize a legislative court or agency to adjudicate a *diversity* case presenting no issues of federal law. (Do you see why?)

But suppose that, as in Northern Pipeline and in Schor, the adjudication of the state law question by a federal tribunal is itself justified by a substantive grant of power to Congress to regulate matters of federal concern, so that the *case* in question can be deemed a case arising under federal law.[1] It seems clear that the diversity-jurisdiction analysis does not

---

1. As Justice White's dissent points out, long before the passage of the new bank- ruptcy act, referees in bankruptcy were routinely adjudicating state-law issues in

automatically carry over to such a case; additional considerations must be marshalled to compel the conclusion that here, too, Congress is limited to a choice between a state court and a full-blown Article III court. (Do you see why?)

What are these additional considerations?

Was Justice O'Connor right in Schor to dismiss so quickly the argument that special federalism concerns arise when Congress authorizes a federal tribunal not constituted in accordance with Article III to adjudicate pendent or ancillary state-law claims?

Consider these questions after reading the *Note on the Tidewater Problem,* p. 473, *infra,* and the materials on protective jurisdiction at pp. 975–89, *infra.*

(6) After Thomas and Schor, the black-letter law would appear to be not very distant from what it was before Northern Pipeline—that the validity of statutes giving legislative or administrative tribunals the power to adjudicate cases arising under federal law will depend on a "balancing" of the concerns that animated Congress in choosing such a tribunal against the values embodied in the "independence" guarantees of Article III.

It is evident that this test gives Congress considerable latitude, in connection with its legislative enterprises, to conclude that in a specific context resort to the initial jurisdiction of an Article III court is, simply, ill-adapted to the achievement of some legitimate substantive end. Thomas and Schor—like Crowell and Palmore before them—appear to be based ultimately on the notion that the choice of a legislative or administrative tribunal is valid if Congress has made a reasoned judgment that it is necessary and proper, in connection with a valid statutory enterprise, to delegate an adjudicative function to a special or temporary tribunal or agency that is constituted without regard to the restrictions and guarantees of Article III.

Is Justice White correct, that specialization is itself a good reason for creating an Article I tribunal rather than setting up a specialized Article III court?

Is there any relevant distinction, in this connection, between administrative agencies and legislative courts?

Is Justice Brennan correct in his criticism, that the Court's approach empties Article III's constraints of all meaning? Does it give Congress wholesale power to delegate the initial adjudication of the federal judicial business to agencies and special Article I tribunals?

(7) Almost all the judges (and commentators) who discuss the problem of legislative courts—even Justice White—appear to assume that the *text* of Article III gives a *clear* direction that cases to which the federal judicial

connection with the ordinary bankruptcy tasks of allowing and disallowing claims against the bankruptcy estate. These were conceptualized as proceedings "in rem", however, whereas the new act expanded the bankruptcy court's jurisdiction to actions in personam brought by the trustee against the bankrupt's debtors. Justice White asks why this should make a constitutional difference. Why should it? See, in this connection, Katchen v. Landy, 382 U.S. 323 (1966), ruling that a bankruptcy court had power to adjudicate whether a payment to a creditor was a preference and to order the payment disgorged—these being, normally, "in personam" claims that the trustee had to bring in state court. The holding that the bankruptcy court had jurisdiction was based on the fact that the creditor had himself filed a claim in bankruptcy, thus giving the bankruptcy court "constructive possession" of the preference.

power extends must be tried, as a matter of original jurisdiction, in a court constituted as an Article III court if it is to be tried at all in a federal tribunal. And, if this is so, it follows that the development of legislative and administrative tribunals must be seen as problematic and anomalous, an example of "exceptions" based on expediency being read into the clear text of the Constitution.

But is the text clear? It provides that the "judicial Power of the United States shall be vested" in the courts specified therein. But what is the "federal judicial power"? More precisely, just what "counts" as its exercise?

Reflection will show that the answers to these questions are elusive and that the concept of the "judicial power" is a slippery one, not easily cabined in any rigid table of organization. As the opinions in Crowell and Marathon make clear, the cast of characters who may properly share in the exercise of the judicial power includes many persons who are not judges at all: jurors, masters, magistrates. The text of Article III does not itself in any way specify what their share may or may not be. That question must be answered, not by reference to the text, but by reference to custom and history understood in the light of the purposes of Article III.

More fundamentally, the concept of "the judicial power" *cannot* be defined so as to draw a bright-line around it and thus to create a monopoly for the judges in the adjudicatory task of finding facts and determining the meaning and applicability of provisions of law. See Bator, *The Constitution as Architecture: Legislative and Administrative Courts Under Article III*, 64 Ind.L.J. —— (1988): "Every time an official of the executive branch, in determining how faithfully to execute the laws, goes through the process of finding facts and determining the meaning and application of the relevant law, he is doing something which functionally is akin to the exercise of judicial power. Every time the Commissioner of Internal Revenue makes a determination that, on X facts, the Tax Code requires the collection of Y tax, and issues a tax assessment on that basis, or the Immigration Service determines that Z is a deportable alien and issues an order to deport, an implicit adjudicatory process is going on. Of course, many such executive determinations are informal. But it is only a step— and one quite consistent with the ideal of 'faithful' execution of the laws— from informal, implicit adjudication to the notion that in making these determinations the official should hear the parties, make a record of the evidence, and give explicit formulations to his interpretation of the law. It follows, therefore, that determinations by the executive to apply law and judicial adjudication have a symbiotic relationship and flow naturally from and into each other. There is no *a priori* wall between them. * * * It is history and custom and expediency, rather than logic—or the text of the Constitution—that determine what needs to be the participation of the judges in the adjudicatory enterprise. * * * The judicial power is neither a platonic essence nor a pre-existing empirical classification. It is a purposive institutional concept, whose content is a product of history and custom distilled in the light of experience and expediency."

(8) See Bator, *supra*, for the further argument that, in light of these considerations, the concept of "the judicial Power of the United States" should be formulated, not in terms of the Article III courts' *original* (or trial) jurisdiction—or indeed, in terms of any "table of organization"

categories—but *in terms of ultimate judicial control*: the essence of the federal judicial power—and a sufficient guarantee of its independence—lies not in any question of trial jurisdiction, but in a power of judicial review that assures that an Article III court will have the final say in determining whether the law was correctly applied and the findings of fact had reasoned support in the evidence.

Bator asserts that the opinions of Justices Hughes and Brandeis in Crowell gave this reformulation a powerful intellectual start: Brandeis, in his insistence that Article III does not guarantee access to any Article III *trial* court, and Hughes in his specific assertion that access to judicial review touches on the proper exercise of the judicial power of the United States.

(9) As explored in the Dialogue, the Due Process Clause imposes certain requirements of access to judicial review in some "court", but of course does not in any way suggest that that court must be an Article III court. (Due process does, however, limit the power of the legislature to undermine the disinterestedness of that court.) What, precisely, does Article III add to this? Should Article III be read as creating independent rules guaranteeing access to an Article III appellate system? Is Congress *less* free to create specialized Article I appellate courts than Article I trial courts? (Note that in the territories and the District of Columbia, there have always existed complete systems of Article I courts, subject to Article III review only by way of certiorari or appeal to the Supreme Court.) Suppose Congress were to create an Article I social security court to adjudicate the thousands of social security disability cases, and were also to constitute an Article I "Social Security Court of Appeals" to review these; suppose further that the judgments of the latter were final subject only to the certiorari jurisdiction of the Supreme Court. Should this be deemed to satisfy Article III?

What is the relationship of this question to the thesis discussed at pp. 385–87, *supra,* that Congress is required to vest jurisdiction in *"all"* cases arising under federal law in some Article III court?

May Congress create an Article I court to review the judgments of state courts in cases involving questions of federal law?

(10) Does the consent of the parties eliminate objections to a non-Article III federal tribunal? What light does Schor cast on this question? Is it a useful question whether Article III is "structural" or protects individual rights?

The courts of appeals have been unanimous in upholding the validity of 28 U.S.C. § 636(c), permitting magistrates to adjudicate any civil case brought in a federal district court if both parties consent. See, *e.g.,* K.M.C. Co., Inc. v. Irving Trust Co., 757 F.2d 752, 755 (6th Cir.1985); Gairola v. Virginia Dept. of General Services, 753 F.2d 1281 (4th Cir.1985); Geras v. Lafayette Display Fixtures, Inc., 742 F.2d 1037 (7th Cir.1984); and cases cited. But see the powerful dissent of Judge Posner in the Geras case, at 1045, maintaining that § 636(c) is invalid. Judge Posner argues that "consent" does not dispose of the problem, because Article III was designed to guarantee to the "citizens of the nation," and to the states, as well as to the particular litigants in the case, a quality of justice that can be obtained only from judges who are guaranteed independence.

See generally Whitten, *Consent, Caseload and Other Justifications for Non-Article III Courts and Judges: A Comment on Commodity Futures Trading Comm'n v. Schor*, 20 Creighton L.Rev. 11 (1986).

(11) Note that the question of the use of magistrates and other judicial auxiliaries within the Article III system is analytically distinct from the issue of the validity of legislative and administrative tribunals. The use of magistrates does not depend on a congressional judgment that it wants a new and different *institution* to adjudicate the case. Magistrates are, institutionally, just like judges—except that they do not have tenure and salary protections. Congress has given them judicial functions, not because it sees the need for a different institution, but because it wants to relieve the judges of an overwhelming caseload.

Does this make a difference?

See, as to this, Silberman, *Masters and Magistrates*, 50 N.Y.U.L.Rev. 1070 (*Part I: The English Model*), 1297 (*Part II: The American Analogue*) (1975).

(12) For a wide variety of views on the problems explored in this section, see, *e.g.*, Baird, *Bankruptcy Procedure and State–Created Rights: The Lessons of Gibbons and Marathon*, 1982 Sup.Ct.Rev. 25; Baker, *Is the United States Claims Court Constitutional?*, 32 Cleve.St.L.Rev. 55 (1983); Currie, *Bankruptcy Judges and the Independent Judiciary*, 16 Creighton L.R. 441 (1983); Redish, *Legislative Courts, Administrative Agencies, and the Northern Pipeline Decision*, 1983 Duke L.J. 197.

NOTE ON THE TIDEWATER PROBLEM

(1) What are the limits on the scope of the jurisdiction that Congress may vest in an Article III court? An extraordinary debate on this issue occurred in National Mutual Insurance Co. v. Tidewater Transfer Co., Inc., 337 U.S. 582 (1949). This case arose out of an action by a District of Columbia citizen against a citizen of Maryland on an insurance contract involving only issues of Maryland law. The suit was brought in the federal district court in Maryland, under a 1940 statute that gave the district courts jurisdiction in actions between citizens of the states and citizens of the District. The question was whether this statute was valid.

(a) In the venerable Hepburn case [1] Chief Justice Marshall had ruled that a citizen of the District was not a citizen of a "State" within the meaning of the Diversity Clause. In Tidewater, a majority of the Court (with Justices Rutledge and Murphy, dissenting) declined to overrule this holding.

(b) Justice Jackson, joined by Justices Black and Burton, wrote the plurality opinion upholding the statute on another ground. His opinion is remarkably brilliant and remarkably perverse; it is not easily captured in summary form. Justice Jackson noted that Congress has extensive power under Article I to legislate with respect to the affairs of the District of Columbia. This power provides Congress with authority to constitute tribunals to adjudicate cases involving District citizens even if these cases are not diversity cases, do not arise under federal law, and do not fall

---

1. Hepburn & Dundas v. Ellzey, 2 Cranch 445 (U.S.1805).

within any other category of case or controversy to which the federal judicial power extends. Further, Justice Jackson opined—and this was the critical and hotly controversial step—Article I gives Congress power to authorize *Article III courts* to adjudicate such non-Article III cases; the Article III courts "can also exercise judicial power conferred by Congress pursuant to Article I" (p. 592).

Justice Jackson claimed that the cases upholding the validity of legislative courts supported his proposition that, in connection with its Article I powers, Congress may authorize Article III courts to adjudicate cases not falling within the Article III enumeration. He pointed out that, in many cases (*e.g.,* consented suits against the United States), the district courts have traditionally exercised a jurisdiction concurrent with that of legislative courts. But since legislative courts are "incapable of receiving" Article III judicial power, it must be that both the legislative courts and the district courts are, in such cases, exercising an Article I judicial power entirely outside the scope of Article III. Justice Jackson cited the Williams case, p. 468, *supra,* in support of this proposition.

Justice Jackson also cited Schumacher v. Beeler, 293 U.S. 367 (1934) and Williams v. Austrian, 331 U.S. 642 (1947), for the proposition that "Congress had power to authorize an Art. III court to entertain a non-Art. III suit because such judicial power was conferred under Art. I." In these cases the Court had upheld provisions authorizing a district court to entertain non-diversity suits by bankruptcy trustees against debtors of the bankrupt based on state-law causes of action. Objecting to the view that these actions could be viewed as cases "arising under" federal law,[2] Justice Jackson said that "the fact that the congressional power over bankruptcy granted by Art. I could open the court to the trustee does not mean that such suits arise under the laws of the United States; but it does mean that Art. I can supply a source of judicial power for their adjudication" (p. 599).

Justice Jackson stated that, although Congress is free to give the federal courts Article I judicial business that lies outside the enumeration of Article III, it must be *judicial* business: separation of powers postulates require that the jurisdiction conferred be "limited to controversies of a justiciable nature" (p. 591).

(c) The remaining six Justices objected violently to Justice Jackson's opinion. Justice Rutledge called it a "dangerous doctrine" (p. 626). Chief Justice Vinson, joined by Justice Douglas, also disagreed, and dissented from the Court's judgment upholding the validity of the statute. His opinion is remarkable chiefly for prefiguring the clearly established modern doctrine, that legislative and constitutional courts may share in the exercise of the federal judicial power—that is, that both sorts of courts *do* adjudicate cases and controversies arising under federal law (see pp. 467–68, *supra*).

(d) The remaining dissent was a passionate essay by Justice Frankfurter, joined by Justice Reed, reaffirming the classical proposition that the federal courts are courts of limited jurisdiction with no authority to adjudicate except in the instances specifically enumerated in Article III. For "if courts established under Article III can exercise wider jurisdiction

---

2. Here Justice Jackson cited cases such as Gully v. First National Bank, discussed in Chap. VIII, Sec. 3, *infra,* construing the statutory grant of "arising under" jurisdiction to the district courts.

than that defined and confined by Article III, and if they are available to effectuate the various substantive powers of Congress, such as the power to legislate for the District of Columbia, what justification is there for interpreting Article III as imposing one restriction in the exercise of those other powers of the Congress—the restriction to the exercise of 'judicial power'— yet not interpreting it as imposing the restrictions that are most explicit, namely, the particularization of the 'cases' to which 'the judicial Power shall extend'?" (p. 648).

Justice Frankfurter continued (pp. 650–53): "We are here concerned with the power of the federal courts to adjudicate merely because of the citizenship of the parties. Power to adjudicate between citizens of different states, merely because they are citizens of different states, has no relation to any substantive rights created by Congress. When the sole source of the right to be enforced is the law of a State, the right to resort to a federal court is restricted to 'Citizens of different States.' The right to enforce such State-created obligations derives its sole strength from Article III. No other provision of the Constitution lends support. But for Article III, the judicial enforcement of rights which only a State, not the United States, creates would be confined to State courts. It is Article III and nothing outside it that authorizes Congress to treat federal courts as 'only another court of the State,' Guaranty Trust Co. v. York, 326 U.S. 99, 108 (1945), and Article III allows it to do so only when the parties are citizens of different 'States.' If Congress, in its lawmaking power over the District of Columbia, created some right for the inhabitants of the District, it could choose to provide for the enforcement of that right in any court of the United States, because the case would be one arising under 'the Laws of the United States.' But here the controversy is one arising not under the laws of the United States but under the laws of Maryland. By the command of the Constitution, this Maryland-created right can be enforced in a federal court only if the controversy is between 'Citizens of different States' in relation to the State in which the federal court is sitting.

"The diversity jurisdiction of the federal courts was probably the most tenuously founded and most unwillingly granted of all the heads of federal jurisdiction which Congress was empowered by Article III to confer. It is a matter of common knowledge that the jurisdiction of the federal courts based merely on diversity of citizenship has been more continuously under fire than any other. * * *

"[T]he dislocation of the Constitutional scheme for the establishment of the federal judiciary and the distribution of jurisdiction among its tribunals so carefully formulated in Article III is too heavy a price to pay for whatever advantage there may be to a citizen of the District, natural or artificial, to go to a federal court in a particular State instead of to the State court in suing a citizen of that State. Nor is it merely a dislocation for the purpose of accomplishing a result of trivial importance in the practical affairs of life. The process of reasoning by which this result is reached invites a use of the federal courts which breaks with the whole history of the federal judiciary and disregards the wise policy behind that history. It was because Article III defines and confines the limits of jurisdiction of the courts which are established under Article III that the first Court of Claims Act fell, Gordon v. United States, 2 Wall. 561, 17 U.S. 921.

"To find a source for 'the judicial Power,' therefore, which may be exercised by courts established under Article III of the Constitution outside that Article would be to disregard the distribution of powers made by the Constitution. The other alternative—to expand 'the judicial Power' of Article III to include a controversy between a citizen of the District of Columbia and a citizen of one of the States by virtue of the provision extending 'the judicial Power' to controversies 'between Citizens of different States'—would disregard an explicit limitation of Article III. For a hundred and fifty years 'States' as there used meant 'States'—the political organizations that form the Union and alone have power to amend the Constitution. * * *

"A substantial majority of the Court agrees that each of the two grounds urged in support of the attempt by Congress to extend diversity jurisdiction to cases involving citizens of the District of Columbia must be rejected—but not the same majority. And so, conflicting minorities in combination bring to pass a result—paradoxical as it may appear—which differing majorities of the Court find insupportable."

(2) What does Justice Jackson mean by "judicial power conferred by Congress pursuant to Article I"?

All the lower federal constitutional courts are created by Congress pursuant not only to Article III but also to the power in Article I, Sec. 8, Cl. 9, "To constitute Tribunals inferior to the Supreme Court". In some sense, therefore, they all derive their power from Article I. Where else does Congress get authority to regulate their jurisdiction, or that of the state courts? Where, for example, does it get authority, in such a statute as the Emergency Price Control Act, to confer jurisdiction on courts to enforce the rights of action the Act creates? Do such jurisdictional provisions stand on a different constitutional footing from the instances of "Article I jurisdiction" which Justice Jackson cites? Is there a category of cases that Congress is authorized to empower courts to decide but that do not arise under the laws of the United States nor fit any other of the classes of cases described in Article III?

The framers of the Constitution declared their intention of authorizing a judicial power at least coextensive with the legislative. See pp. 3–5, 13, 23, *supra*. Must not Article III have at least that content? Note that in some respects, such as the diversity clause, the judicial power under Article III seems to be broader than the legislative power under Article I.

The historical instrument for matching the two powers was the grant of jurisdiction in cases arising under the laws of the United States. Is this instrument inadequate?

(3) Do the opinions in Tidewater adequately canvass the question whether jurisdiction could rest on the ground that the case arose under the laws of the United States?

Consider the soundness of the following line of argument:

(a) All the parties and judges in Tidewater assumed as common ground that the Congress has wide power to regulate and protect the activities of the citizens of the District of Columbia. This assumption was the basis of counsel's concession that Congress could provide for nationwide service in actions by District citizens in District courts against out-of-District defendants, as well as of Justice Jackson's further point that Congress could establish legislative courts outside the District to hear the cases authorized by the act. Indeed, Congress may even have power to establish a substantive law governing legal relations between residents of the District of Columbia and residents of the states. An action under such substantive legislation would clearly arise under the laws of the United States.

(b) But must Congress actually enact such a substantive law in order for an action so to arise? May not Congress have power to protect citizens of the District of Columbia from discrimination, or the possibility of it, by means falling short of declaring a substantive law to govern their legal relations—*i.e.,* by affording them a federal haven for litigation?

(c) Justice Jackson seems to assume that a case cannot arise under the laws of the United States within the meaning of the Constitution, unless the substantive law in accordance with which it is to be decided is established by federal statute. But this is a position not supported by principle or precedent (see, *e.g.,* the great case of Osborn v. Bank of the United States, 9 Wheat. 738 (U.S.1824), p. 967, *infra*). The Austrian and Beeler cases are clear examples where jurisdiction is validly conferred in order to protect a substantive federal interest (the interest in bankruptcy proceedings) and the cases therefore "arise" under federal law for jurisdictional purposes, even though substantive rights and liabilities continue to be governed by state law.

(d) To summarize, then, consider the soundness of the following thesis: *first,* that Article III courts can be given jurisdiction only in Article III classes of cases; *second,* that cases arising under the laws of the United States, within the meaning of Article III, include not only those which are governed on the merits, in whole or in part, by validly established federal rules of decision, statutory or otherwise, but also those brought pursuant to a valid federal statute enacted to prevent the possibility of discrimination against federally-protectible interests.

(4) Consider the following objections to the above line of argument:

(a) The diversity clause, and the other "party" clauses of Article III, exhaust the instances where the Framers made federal jurisdiction available solely for the purpose of protecting parties against discrimination in state courts, without a federal substantive interest to be protected. The purpose of the "arising under" clause was not to protect parties against discrimination but to allow federal courts to protect substantive federal interests and to decide questions of federal law.

(b) Thus, even if a case can arise under federal law without being governed by substantive federal law, to justify federal jurisdiction there must be some substantive federal regulatory policy to be protected by the grant of jurisdiction, other than a mere fear of "party" discrimination in the state courts. Beeler and Austrian meet this test, but Tidewater does not.

(c) The argument is in any event circular. It assumes that a case can arise under federal law where the only federal law involved is a naked grant of federal jurisdiction. If accepted, it would give Congress virtually limitless power to channel to the federal courts controversies between co-citizens governed wholly by state law on the basis of some remote connection with an unexpressed federal interest.

(5) Should the thesis advanced in paragraph (3)(d) be limited to situations where Congress clearly has substantive power to enact the rules of decision governing the specific case? What would such a limit do to the Austrian and Beeler cases? Does Congress have power under the bankruptcy clause to provide that the validity of all claims by and against the bankrupt's estate be decided by some uniform federal rule? Should the validity of the Austrian–Beeler jurisdiction under the "arising under" clause depend on the answer to that question?

(6) Should the thesis be limited to areas where Congress has in fact expressed a federal interest by enacting substantive legislation at least partly occupying a given field? Such regulation could then be "filled in" by conferring jurisdiction over some cases within that field in which the substantive rules of decision have been left to be governed by state law. The Tidewater decision could not stand under such a rule, could it? What about Austrian and Beeler?

(7) The materials relevant to these arguments are examined in detail in Chap. VIII, Sec. 2, pp. 975–89, *infra*.

(8) Notice how central to Justice Jackson's reasoning is the untenable proposition of the Williams case, discussed in the *Note on Legislative Courts*, p. 468, *supra*, that suits against the United States cannot be within the federal judicial power as described in Article III. Given such a parentage, it is not surprising that his opinion—albeit characteristically lively and interesting—is so contrived.

(9) If Justice Jackson's view in Tidewater had prevailed and a majority had ruled that Article III courts may be given jurisdiction over cases not enumerated in Article III, what are the resulting possibilities of extension of federal jurisdiction? By what criteria would the validity of the extensions be judged? Would the criteria be different from those which would be involved in applying the second part of the thesis stated in paragraph (3)(d) above?

(10) May Congress confer jurisdiction on the federal courts in state-law-based actions between aliens? In Hodgson v. Bowerbank, 5 Cranch 303 (U.S.1809), the Court, in a short opinion by Marshall, held that jurisdiction may not be exercised in such a case notwithstanding the provision of the First Judiciary Act conferring jurisdiction in "all suits" in which an alien is a party. For a persuasive argument that this was a statutory, not a constitutional, holding, see Mahoney, *A Historical Note on Hodgson v. Bowerbank*, 49 U.Chi.L.Rev. 725 (1982). See also the Verlinden case, discussed at p. 986, *infra*, holding that such a case may, under certain circumstances, be deemed a case "arising under" federal law.

SECTION 2. FEDERAL AUTHORITY AND STATE COURT JURISDICTION

THE FEDERALIST, NO. 82

This paper is reprinted in Chap. I, pp. 28–30, *supra.*

NOTE ON CONGRESSIONAL EXCLUSION OF STATE COURT JURISDICTION

(1) A jurisdiction in the lower federal courts "exclusively of the courts of the several States" (1 Stat. 76) has always been defined by act of Congress, though the area of exclusivity has varied through the years.

Originally the area included only "crimes and offenses cognizable under the authority of the United States," "seizures" on land or water, "suits for penalties and forfeitures, incurred under the laws of the United States," "suits against consuls or vice-consuls" and "civil causes of admiralty and maritime jurisdiction * * * saving to suitors, in all cases, the right of a common law remedy, where the common law is competent to give it". Act of Sept. 24, 1789, §§ 9, 11, 1 Stat. 76, 78.

Important surviving additions include prize cases, proceedings in bankruptcy, antitrust actions, actions "arising under" patent or copyright laws, and most of the remedies against the United States or federal agencies or officials that have been specially defined by statute.

Section 256 of the former Judicial Code (28 U.S.C. § 371, 1940 ed.) purported to enumerate the areas from which state courts had been excluded, but the enumeration was incomplete and the section was repealed in the 1948 revision. For exclusivity to be found, it must be either expressly stated (see, *e.g.,* 28 U.S.C. §§ 1333, 1338, 1346(b), 1351, 1355, 1356; 15 U.S.C. § 78aa; 18 U.S.C. § 3231; 40 U.S.C. § 270b(b)), or implied (see, *e.g.,* 28 U.S.C. §§ 1346(a), 1491(a)(1), 2321–22; 15 U.S.C. §§ 15, 26), in the provisions granting jurisdiction.[1]

(2) The power of Congress to make exclusive any valid grant of jurisdiction has hardly been in issue. (The early doubt was rather whether there are areas in which Article III itself makes the federal jurisdiction "unavoidably * * * exclusive." See Martin v. Hunter's Lessee, 1 Wheat. 304, 337 (U.S.1816); *cf.* 3 Story, Commentaries on the Constitution 533, n. 3 (1833).) Definitive adjudication seems, however, to have been delayed until The Moses Taylor, 4 Wall. 411 (1867), where the Supreme Court reversed a state court judgment sustaining an *in rem* proceeding against a vessel, holding that such relief is not a "common law" remedy preserved by the saving clause in the exclusive grant of admiralty jurisdiction.[2]

With respect to the constitutional question Justice Field said (pp. 429, 430):

1. On the exclusive original jurisdiction of the Supreme Court, see Chap. III, p. 295, *supra.*

2. But *cf.* C.J. Hendry Co. v. Moore, 318 U.S. 133 (1943) (sustaining a state forfei-

ture proceeding, with an illuminating historical discussion).

" * * * The Judiciary Act of 1789, in its distribution of jurisdiction to the several federal courts, recognizes and is framed upon the theory that in all cases to which the judicial power of the United States extends, Congress may rightfully vest exclusive jurisdiction in the Federal courts. It declares that in some cases, from their commencement, such jurisdiction shall be exclusive; in other cases it determines at what stage of procedure such jurisdiction shall attach, and how long and how far concurrent jurisdiction of the State courts shall be permitted. * * *

"The constitutionality of these provisions cannot be seriously questioned, and is of frequent recognition by both State and Federal courts."

For similar affirmations, see Houston v. Moore, 5 Wheat. 1, 25–26 (U.S.1820); Lockerty v. Phillips, p. 372, *supra;* Bowles v. Willingham, p. 375, *supra;* Brown v. Gerdes, 321 U.S. 178 (1944).

Would these decisions support an act of Congress declaring the diversity jurisdiction exclusive? *Cf.* Hamilton in The Federalist, No. 82.

(3) The broad authority of Congress to establish exclusive jurisdiction has been exercised with restraint—but not without posing impressive problems of interpretation and of policy. See, *e.g.,* pp. 984, 999, 1071, *infra.* And see generally Currie, Federal Courts 201–06, 248–51 (3d ed. 1982); Redish and Muench, *Adjudication of Federal Causes of Action in State Court,* 75 Mich.L.Rev. 311 (1977); Note, *Exclusive Jurisdiction of the Federal Courts in Private Civil Actions,* 70 Harv.L.Rev. 509 (1957).

(4) The Supreme Court has, in general, applied a rebuttable presumption that when Congress is silent on the question, state courts have concurrent jurisdiction of claims arising under federal law. See, *e.g.,* Claflin v. Houseman, 93 U.S. 130 (1876); [3] Martinez v. California, 444 U.S. 277, 283 n. 7 (1980) (claim for relief under 42 U.S.C. § 1983); Gulf Offshore Co. v. Mobil Oil Corp., 453 U.S. 473, 477–78 (1981) (cause of action under Outer Continental Shelf Lands Act). But *cf.* Tarble's Case, p. 484, *infra.*

Occasionally, jurisdiction has been held to be exclusive in the federal courts even when Congress's purpose has not been clearly spelled out in the jurisdictional statute. See, *e.g.,* General Investment Co. v. Lake Shore & M.S. Ry. Co., 260 U.S. 261, 286–88 (1922) (Sherman and Clayton Acts). In determining whether a grant of jurisdiction is impliedly exclusive, courts appear to consider such factors as the need for uniformity in interpretation and application of the law, the novelty and difficulty of the issues likely to be presented, and the possibility of state court hostility to the objectives of the statute.[4] If both parties have access to a federal court (originally or on

---

3. The Court in Claflin, in upholding the right of an assignee in bankruptcy to sue in a state court to recover assets of the bankrupt, said: "[W]here jurisdiction may be conferred on the United States Courts, it may be made exclusive where not so by the Constitution itself; but, if exclusive jurisdiction be neither express nor implied, the State Courts have concurrent jurisdiction whenever, by their own Constitution, they are competent to take it" (p. 136).

4. See Charles Dowd Box Co. v. Courtney, 368 U.S. 502 (1962) (concluding,

after examination of the legislative history of § 301 of the Labor Management Relations Act, that Congress did not intend the grant of federal jurisdiction over certain contract actions to preclude the exercise of jurisdiction by state courts); Gulf Offshore Co. v. Mobil Oil Corp., *supra* (upholding concurrent state court jurisdiction in part because the governing federal rules were to be borrowed from state law).

removal),[5] is there any federal interest in precluding a state court from proceeding when the parties are content to be there?

TENNESSEE v. DAVIS

Look @ Removal Statutes 28 USC 1441

100 U.S. 257, 25 L.Ed. 648 (1880).

Certificate from the Circuit Court for the Middle District of Tennessee.

[The defendant, James M. Davis, was indicted for murder in the Circuit Court of Grundy County, Tennessee. Before the trial of the indictment he presented to the Circuit Court of the United States for the proper district a petition for removal of the case from the state court. On the hearing of the motion, the judges were divided in opinion, and certified to the Supreme Court the following three questions:

[*First,* Whether an indictment of a revenue officer (of the United States) for murder, found in a State court, under the facts alleged in the petition for removal in this case, is removable to the Circuit Court of the United States, under § 643 of the Revised Statutes. * * * *]

Mr. Justice Strong delivered the opinion of the court.

The first of the questions certified is one of great importance, bringing as it does into consideration the relation of the general government to the government of the States, and bringing also into view not merely the construction of an act of Congress, but its constitutionality. That in this case the defendant's petition for removal of the cause was in the form prescribed by the act of Congress admits of no doubt. It represented that * * * he was acting by and under the authority of the internal-revenue laws of the United States; that what he did was done under and by right of his office, to wit, as deputy collector of internal revenue; that it was his duty to seize illicit distilleries and the apparatus that is used for the illicit and unlawful distillation of spirits; and that while so attempting to enforce the revenue laws of the United States, as deputy collector as aforesaid, he was assaulted and fired upon by a number of armed men, and that in defence of his life he returned the fire. * * * The language of the statute (so far as it is necessary at present to refer to it) is as follows: "When any civil suit or criminal prosecution is commenced in any court of a State against any officer appointed under, or acting by authority of, any revenue law of the United States, now or hereafter enacted, or against any person acting by or under authority of any such officer, on account of any act done under color of his office or of any such law, or on account of any right, title, or authority claimed by such officer or other person under any such law," the case may be removed into the Federal court. * * *

We come, then, to the inquiry, most discussed during the argument, whether sect. 643 is a constitutional exercise of the power vested in Congress. * * *

By the last clause of the eighth section of the first article of the Constitution, Congress is invested with power to make all laws necessary

---

[5.] In a few instances, Congress has precluded removal of a federal question case when it is brought in a state court. See 28 U.S.C. § 1445. And when a federal issue arises defensively in a state court action, it must ordinarily be adjudicated in the state court even though it falls into an area of exclusive federal jurisdiction. See, *e.g.,* Lear, Inc. v. Adkins, 395 U.S. 653 (1969) (state court may not award damages for breach of a patent license agreement if the patent is invalid).

and proper for carrying into execution not only all the powers previously specified, but also all other powers vested by the Constitution in the government of the United States, or in any department or officer thereof. Among these is the judicial power of the government. That is declared by the second section of the third article to "extend to all cases in law and equity arising under the Constitution, the laws of the United States, and treaties made or which shall be made under their authority," & c. This provision embraces alike civil and criminal cases arising under the Constitution and laws. Cohens v. Virginia, 6 Wheat. 264. Both are equally within the domain of the judicial powers of the United States, and there is nothing in the grant to justify an assertion that whatever power may be exerted over a civil case may not be exerted as fully over a criminal one. And a case arising under the Constitution and laws of the United States may as well arise in a criminal prosecution as in a civil suit. What constitutes a case thus arising was early defined in the case cited from 6 Wheaton. It is not merely one where a party comes into court to demand something conferred upon him by the Constitution or by a law or treaty. A case consists of the right of one party as well as the other, and may truly be said to arise under the Constitution or a law or a treaty of the United States whenever its correct decision depends upon the construction of either. Cases arising under the laws of the United States are such as grow out of the legislation of Congress, whether they constitute the right or privilege, or claim or protection, or defence of the party, in whole or in part, by whom they are asserted. * * *

The constitutional right of Congress to authorize the removal before trial of civil cases arising under the laws of the United States has long since passed beyond doubt. It was exercised almost contemporaneously with the adoption of the Constitution, and the power has been in constant use ever since. The Judiciary Act of Sept. 24, 1789, was passed by the first Congress, many members of which had assisted in framing the Constitution; and though some doubts were soon after suggested whether cases could be removed from State courts before trial, those doubts soon disappeared. Whether removal from a State to a Federal court is an exercise of appellate jurisdiction, as laid down in Story's Commentaries on the Constitution, sect. 1745, or an indirect mode of exercising original jurisdiction, as intimated in Railway Company v. Whitton (13 Wall. 270), we need not now inquire. Be it one or the other, it was ruled in the case last cited to be constitutional. But if there is power in Congress to direct a removal before trial of a civil case arising under the Constitution or laws of the United States, and direct its removal because such a case has arisen, it is impossible to see why the same power may not order the removal of a criminal prosecution, when a similar case has arisen in it. * * *

The argument so much pressed upon us, that it is an invasion of the sovereignty of a State to withdraw from its courts into the courts of the general government the trial of prosecutions for alleged offences against the criminal laws of a State, even though the defence presents a case arising out of an act of Congress, ignores entirely the dual character of our government. It assumes that the States are completely and in all respects sovereign. But when the national government was formed, some of the attributes of State sovereignty were partially, and others wholly, surrendered and vested in the United States. Over the subjects thus surrendered the sovereignty of the States ceased to extend. Before the adoption of the

Constitution, each State had complete and exclusive authority to administer by its courts all the law, civil and criminal, which existed within its borders. Its judicial power extended over every legal question that could arise. But when the Constitution was adopted, a portion of that judicial power became vested in the new government created, and so far as thus vested it was withdrawn from the sovereignty of the State. Now the execution and enforcement of the laws of the United States, and the judicial determination of questions arising under them, are confided to another sovereign, and to that extent the sovereignty of the State is restricted. The removal of cases arising under those laws, from State into Federal courts, is, therefore, no invasion of State domain. On the contrary, a denial of the right of the general government to remove them, to take charge of and try any case arising under the Constitution or laws of the United States, is a denial of the conceded sovereignty of that government over a subject expressly committed to it. * * *

It follows that the first question certified to us from the Circuit Court of Tennessee must be answered in the affirmative. * * *

MR. JUSTICE CLIFFORD, with whom concurred MR. JUSTICE FIELD, dissenting. * * *

NOTE ON THE POWER OF CONGRESS TO PROVIDE FOR REMOVAL FROM STATE TO FEDERAL COURTS

(1) In Martin v. Hunter's Lessee, 1 Wheat. 304 (U.S.1816), counsel conceded the authority of Congress to provide for a removal before final judgment of a case within the ambit of the federal judicial power, confining their attack to the review by the Supreme Court upon writ of error after judgment, provided by Section 25 of the Judiciary Act of 1789. See Chap. V, Sec. 1, *infra*. Justice Story's theory of removal as a mode of exercising an "appellate jurisdiction" (1 Wheat. at 347–51) thus used counsels' concession to refute their attack.

But the validity of a removal before judgment, though declared to be beyond doubt in The Moses Taylor, 4 Wall. 411, 429–30 (1867), was not directly determined in a civil action until The Mayor v. Cooper, 6 Wall. 247 (U.S.1868). This was a suit for trespass and conversion challenging a seizure under claim of federal authority during the Civil War, removed under the Act of March 3, 1863, 12 Stat. 756, p. 961, *infra*. Railway Co. v. Whitton, 13 Wall. 270 (U.S.1872), reaffirmed this decision in a case where the removal rested on diversity of citizenship. See also City of Greenwood v. Peacock, 384 U.S. 808, 833 (1966) ("We may assume that Congress has constitutional power to provide that all federal issues be tried in the federal courts, that all be tried in the courts of the States, or that jurisdiction of such issues be shared. And in the exercise of that power, we may assume that Congress is constitutionally fully free to establish the conditions under which civil or criminal proceedings involving federal issues may be removed from one court to another.").

Unlike most removal statutes, the Act of 1863 applied after as well as before judgment in the state court, providing that the Circuit Court "shall thereupon proceed to try and determine the facts and law in such action in the same manner as if the same had been there originally commenced, the judgment in such case notwithstanding".[1] In The Justices v. Murray, 9 Wall. 274 (U.S.1870), an action for assault and battery and false imprisonment removed after a jury trial and verdict for the plaintiff, the Court held that the Seventh Amendment governed and that "so much of the Act of Congress * * * as provides for the removal of a judgment in a State court, and in which the cause was tried by a jury, to the Circuit Court of the United States for a retrial on the facts and law, is not in pursuance of the Constitution, and is void". See also McKee v. Rains, 10 Wall. 22 (U.S.1870).

(2) Congress has since 1815 provided for the removal of state actions or prosecutions against federal officials likely to encounter sectional or state hostility. For an account of these statutes, see pp. 1057–59, infra. The current statute, 28 U.S.C. § 1442, extending removal to any action or prosecution against any "officer" or "agency" or "person acting under him" for "any act under color of such office", was broadly construed in Willingham v. Morgan, 395 U.S. 402 (1969). See also 28 U.S.C. § 1442a.

Since the Force Act (Act of March 2, 1833, sec. 7, 4 Stat. 634), an alternative to removal has been the power of the federal courts to *release* on habeas corpus persons confined for an act or omission "in pursuance of" a federal statute or a federal court order. See 28 U.S.C. § 2241(c)(2). However, this latter power has been exercised most sparingly; for the relevant materials, see pp. 1557–58, infra.

(3) For additional materials on removal, see pp. 1052–71, 1767–88, infra.

TARBLE'S CASE
13 Wall. 397, 20 L.Ed. 597 (U.S.1872).
Error to the Supreme Court of Wisconsin.

This was a proceeding on habeas corpus for the discharge of one Edward Tarble, held in the custody of a recruiting officer of the United States as an enlisted soldier, on the alleged ground that he was a minor, under the age of eighteen years at the time of his enlistment, and that he enlisted without the consent of his father.

The writ was issued on the 10th of August, 1869, by a court commissioner of Dane County, Wisconsin, an officer authorized by the laws of that State to issue the writ of habeas corpus upon the petition of parties imprisoned or restrained of their liberty, or of persons on their behalf. It was issued in this case upon the petition of the father of Tarble, in which he alleged that his son, who had enlisted under the name of Frank Brown, was confined and restrained of his liberty by Lieutenant Stone, of the United States army, in the city of Madison, in that State and county * * *.

[The Supreme Court of Wisconsin affirmed] * * * the order of the commissioner discharging the prisoner. This judgment was now before this

---

1. At present, removal of a civil action must ordinarily be effected within thirty days after receipt of the initial pleading (28 U.S.C. § 1446(b)), and removal of a criminal proceeding must be effected within thirty days after arraignment "or at any time before trial, whichever is earlier, except that for good cause shown the * * * [federal] court may enter an order granting the petitioner leave to file the [removal] petition at a later time" (28 U.S.C. § 1446(c)(1)).

court for examination on writ of error prosecuted by the United States.

* * *

MR. JUSTICE FIELD, after stating the case, delivered the opinion of the court, as follows:

The important question is presented by this case, whether a State court commissioner has jurisdiction, upon habeas corpus, to inquire into the validity of the enlistment of soldiers into the military service of the United States, and to discharge them from such service when, in his judgment, their enlistment has not been made in conformity with the laws of the United States. The question presented may be more generally stated thus: Whether any judicial officer of a State has jurisdiction to issue a writ of habeas corpus, or to continue proceedings under the writ when issued, for the discharge of a person held under the authority, or claim and color of the authority, of the United States, by an officer of that government.

* * *

The decision of this court in the two cases which grew out of the arrest of Booth, that of Ableman v. Booth, and that of The United States v. Booth,* disposes alike of the claim of jurisdiction by a State court, or by a State judge, to interfere with the authority of the United States, whether that authority be exercised by a Federal officer or be exercised by a Federal tribunal. * * *

For a review in this court of the judgments in both of these cases, writs of error were prosecuted. * * * The cases were afterwards heard and considered together, and the decision of both was announced in the same opinion. In that opinion the Chief Justice details the facts of the two cases at length, and comments upon the character of the jurisdiction asserted by the State judge and the State court * * *.

And in answer to this assumption of judicial power by the judges and by the Supreme Court of Wisconsin thus made, the Chief Justice said as follows: If they "possess the jurisdiction they claim, they must derive it either from the United States or the State. It certainly has not been conferred on them by the United States; and it is equally clear it was not in the power of the State to confer it, even if it had attempted to do so; for no State can authorize one of its judges or courts to exercise judicial power, by habeas corpus or otherwise, within the jurisdiction of another and independent government. And although the State of Wisconsin is sovereign within its territorial limits to a certain extent, yet that sovereignty is limited and restricted by the Constitution of the United States. And the powers of the General government and of the State, although both exist and are exercised within the same territorial limits, are yet separate and distinct sovereignties, acting separately and independently of each other, within their respective spheres. And the sphere of action appropriated to the United States, is as far beyond the reach of the judicial process issued

---

* 21 Howard 506.

[Ed.] This decision, handed down in 1859, involved two habeas corpus petitions filed in Wisconsin state courts by Booth, a federal prisoner charged with aiding in the escape of a fugitive slave. In the first petition, Booth challenged his arrest and detention on the grounds, *inter alia*, of the unconstitutionality of the Fugitive Slave

Act. The state courts held in his favor and ordered his release. Following that release, he was tried and convicted in a federal court for violation of the Act, and was again imprisoned. He then filed his second petition in state court attacking the act on the same grounds, and the state court again ordered his discharge.

by a State judge or a State court, as if the line of division was traced by landmarks and monuments visible to the eye. And the State of Wisconsin had no more power to authorize these proceedings of its judges and courts, than it would have had if the prisoner had been confined in Michigan, or in any other State of the Union, for an offence against the laws of the State in which he was imprisoned."

It is in the consideration of this distinct and independent character of the government of the United States, from that of the government of the several States, that the solution of the question presented in this case, and in similar cases, must be found. There are within the territorial limits of each State two governments, restricted in their spheres of action, but independent of each other, and supreme within their respective spheres.
*   *   *

Such being the distinct and independent character of the two governments, within their respective spheres of action, it follows that neither can intrude with its judicial process into the domain of the other, except so far as such intrusion may be necessary on the part of the National government to preserve its rightful supremacy in cases of conflict of authority. In their laws, and mode of enforcement, neither is responsible to the other. How their respective laws shall be enacted; how they shall be carried into execution; and in what tribunals, or by what officers; and how much discretion, or whether any at all shall be vested in their officers, are matters subject to their own control, and in the regulation of which neither can interfere with the other.

Now, among the powers assigned to the National government, is the power "to raise and support armies," and the power "to provide for the government and regulation of the land and naval forces." The execution of these powers falls within the line of its duties; and its control over the subject is plenary and exclusive. *   *   * Probably in every county and city in the several States there are one or more officers authorized by law to issue writs of habeas corpus on behalf of persons alleged to be illegally restrained of their liberty; and if soldiers could be taken from the army of the United States, and the validity of their enlistment inquired into by any one of these officers, such proceeding could be taken by all of them, and no movement could be made by the National troops without their commanders being subjected to constant annoyance and embarrassment from this source. The experience of the late rebellion has shown us that, in times of great popular excitement, there may be found in every State large numbers ready and anxious to embarrass the operations of the government, and easily persuaded to believe every step taken for the enforcement of its authority illegal and void. Power to issue writs of habeas corpus for the discharge of soldiers in the military service, in the hands of parties thus disposed, might be used, and often would be used, to the great detriment of the public service. In many exigencies the measures of the National government might in this way be entirely bereft of their efficacy and value. An appeal in such cases to this court, to correct the erroneous action of these officers, would afford no adequate remedy. Proceedings on habeas corpus are summary, and the delay incident to bringing the decision of a State officer, through the highest tribunal of the State, to this court for review, would necessarily occupy years, and in the meantime, where the soldier was discharged, the mischief would be accomplished. It is manifest that the powers of the National government could not be exercised with energy and efficiency at all times, if its acts could be interfered with and controlled for any period by officers or tribunals of another sovereignty.

It is true similar embarrassment might sometimes be occasioned, though in a less degree, by the exercise of the authority to issue the writ possessed by judicial officers of the United States, but the ability to provide a speedy remedy for any inconvenience following from this source would always exist with the National legislature. * * *

This limitation upon the power of State tribunals and State officers furnishes no just ground to apprehend that the liberty of the citizen will thereby be endangered. The United States are as much interested in protecting the citizen from illegal restraint under their authority, as the several States are to protect him from the like restraint under their authority, and are no more likely to tolerate any oppression. Their courts and judicial officers are clothed with the power to issue the writ of habeas corpus in all cases, where a party is illegally restrained of his liberty by an officer of the United States, whether such illegality consists in the character of the process, the authority of the officer, or the invalidity of the law under which he is held. And there is no just reason to believe that they will exhibit any hesitation to exert their power, when it is properly invoked. Certainly there can be no ground for supposing that their action will be less prompt and efficient in such cases than would be that of State tribunals and State officers.

It follows, from the views we have expressed, that the court commissioner of Dane County was without jurisdiction to issue the writ of habeas corpus for the discharge of the prisoner in this case, it appearing, upon the application presented to him for the writ, that the prisoner was held by an officer of the United States, under claim and color of the authority of the United States, as an enlisted soldier mustered into the military service of the National government; and the same information was imparted to the commissioner by the return of the officer. The commissioner was, both by the application for the writ and the return to it, apprised that the prisoner was within the dominion and jurisdiction of another government, and that no writ of habeas corpus issued by him could pass over the line which divided the two sovereignties.

The conclusion we have reached renders it unnecessary to consider how far the declaration of the prisoner as to his age, in the oath of enlistment, is to be deemed conclusive evidence on that point on the return to the writ.

Judgment reversed.

THE CHIEF JUSTICE [CHASE], dissenting.

I cannot concur in the opinion just read. I have no doubt of the right of a State court to inquire into the jurisdiction of a Federal court upon habeas corpus, and to discharge when satisfied that the petitioner for the writ is restrained of liberty by the sentence of a court without jurisdiction. If it errs in deciding the question of jurisdiction, the error must be corrected in the mode prescribed by the 25th section of the Judiciary Act; not by denial of the right to make inquiry.

I have still less doubt, if possible, that a writ of habeas corpus may issue from a State court to inquire into the validity of imprisonment or detention, without the sentence of any court whatever, by an officer of the

United States. The State court may err; and if it does, the error may be corrected here. The mode has been prescribed and should be followed.

To deny the right of State courts to issue the writ, or, what amounts to the same thing, to concede the right to issue and to deny the right to adjudicate, is to deny the right to protect the citizen by habeas corpus against arbitrary imprisonment in a large class of cases; and, I am thoroughly persuaded, was never within the contemplation of the Convention which framed, or the people who adopted, the Constitution. That instrument expressly declares that "the privilege of the writ of habeas corpus shall not be suspended, unless when, in case of rebellion or invasion, the public safety may require it."

NOTE ON TARBLE'S CASE AND STATE COURT PROCEEDINGS AGAINST FEDERAL OFFICIALS

(1) Prior to the Booth case and Tarble's Case, state courts "for a period of eighty years, continued to assert a right, through the issue of writs of *habeas corpus,* to take persons out of the custody of federal officials". Warren, *Federal and State Court Interference,* 43 Harv.L.Rev. 345, 353 (1930). However, there were also notable instances of refusal to interfere with federal enforcement of the Fugitive Slave Law—even in areas where its validity was most contested. See, *e.g.,* Passmore Williamson's Case, 26 Pa. 9 (1855); Warren, *supra,* at 356.

Moreover, "such was the tenacity with which the state courts maintained their authority to issue writs of *habeas corpus,* that, for twelve years after the Booth decision, they continued to issue such writs against federal officials, on the ground that the Booth case only applied to instances where the prisoner was held under actual judicial federal process. Thus, during the Civil War, New York, Ohio, Iowa and Maine judges granted *habeas corpus* for persons serving in the United States Army. And as late as 1871, one Massachusetts court said that this power was so well settled by judicial opinion and long practice that it was not 'to be now disavowed, unless in obedience to an express act of congress or to a direct adjudication of the supreme court of the United States'." Warren, *supra,* at 357, quoting Gray, J., in McConologue's Case, 107 Mass. 154, 160 (1871).

(2) To what extent is the decision in Tarble's Case based on (a) the Constitution; (b) the acts of Congress with respect to federal habeas corpus; (c) the acts of Congress with respect to the raising and government of the Army; (d) a federal common law of state-federal relations, developed by the courts but subject to control by Congress?

Should the Court have attached significance to the fact that Congress had not legislated against state court assumption of the challenged jurisdiction? *Cf.* Claflin v. Houseman and other authorities cited, p. 480, *supra.* Is habeas corpus for persons in federal custody one of the rare instances of implied exclusivity and, if so, what is the source of the implication? Would the Court's concern over the threat to federal interests inherent in the exercise of state court jurisdiction have been alleviated by removal provisions like those now contained in 28 U.S.C. §§ 1442 and 1442a?

Note that Tarble's Case, unlike the Booth cases, did not involve state court interference with federal judicial processes,[1] but rather with executive action. Should that matter? Note also that the case involved state court interference with the "government and regulation of the land and naval forces." Is this an area of greater sensitivity than that affected by an application for habeas corpus filed by a federal prisoner.[2]

(3) Is it a premise of the holding in Tarble's Case that the federal courts were open on habeas corpus to determine the legality of the enlistment? If the statute empowering the district courts to issue writs of habeas corpus, 28 U.S.C. § 2241, were now repealed, would it be clear that the state courts would have jurisdiction? That Congress could not deprive them of such a jurisdiction? Compare pp. 420–23, *supra*, and pp. 1577–78, *infra*.

(4) How far does or should the rationale of Tarble's Case exclude other types of state proceedings challenging the legality of federal official action?

(a) *Mandamus.* State court jurisdiction was denied in McClung v. Silliman, 6 Wheat. 598 (U.S.1821), a suit for mandamus to compel the register of a land office of the United States to take action on the plaintiff's claim of a pre-emptive interest in alleged federal public land. The decision was based on the ground that the United States had denied its own courts authority to issue such a mandamus to an executive official, warranting the inference "that parties should be referred to the ordinary mode of obtaining justice, instead of resorting to the extraordinary and unprecedented mode of trying such questions on a motion for a mandamus" (p. 605). The ruling has been interpreted, however, to exclude state mandamus under any circumstances. See, *e.g.*, Armand Schmoll, Inc. v. Federal Reserve Bank, 286 N.Y. 503, 37 N.E.2d 225 (1941); Ex parte Schockley, 17 F.2d 133 (N.D.Ohio 1926); and see generally Arnold, note 2 *supra*, at 1391–92.[3]

(b) *Damage Actions.* State court jurisdiction, on the other hand, has been routinely sustained in damage actions against federal officials, averring tortious conduct unsupported by the claimed authority. See, *e.g.*, Teal v. Felton, 12 How. 284 (U.S.1852); Buck v. Colbath, 3 Wall. 334 (U.S.1866). But *cf.* Davis v. Passman, 442 U.S. 228, 245 n. 23 (1979) (p. 927, *infra*); Chap. IX, Sec. 3, *infra*, on the scope of substantive immunity.

(c) *Actions at Law for Specific Relief.* Slocum v. Mayberry, 2 Wheat. 1 (U.S.1817), sustained an action for replevin of a cargo seized and held by customs officers, where the statutes gave no right to hold the cargo with the vessel. Chief Justice Marshall said that "the act of congress neither expressly, nor by implication, forbids the state courts to take cognizance of suits instituted for property in possession of an officer of the United States, not detained under some law of the United States; consequently their jurisdiction remains" (p. 11). It has also been assumed that state courts may try ejectment actions against federal officers. See, *e.g.*, Scranton v.

---

1. *Cf.* Donovan v. City of Dallas, 377 U.S. 408 (1964), discussed at p. 1331, *infra*.

2. Compare the "striking" case of Houston v. Moore, 5 Wheat. 1 (U.S.1820), holding that a state court had jurisdiction to try a militiaman for a violation of *federal* military law. See Arnold, *The Power of State Courts to Enjoin Federal Officers*, 73 Yale L.J. 1385, 1399–1401 (1964).

3. But in at least one case the Supreme Court has decided on the merits a state-court mandamus action against a federal officer. Northern Pac. Ry. Co. v. North Dakota ex rel. Langer, 250 U.S. 135 (1919).

Original jurisdiction to issue mandamus against federal officers was granted to the *federal* district courts by the Act of October 5, 1962, see 28 U.S.C. § 1361.

Wheeler, 179 U.S. 141 (1900), an action for ejectment brought against the superintendent of a government canal and pier, alleging that the Fifth Amendment was infringed by the uncompensated deprivation of the plaintiff's access to a navigable river. But *cf.* Malone v. Bowdoin, p. 1126, *infra.*

(d) *Injunctions.* The Supreme Court has not yet decided whether state courts have jurisdiction to entertain injunction actions against federal officers.[4] Other courts are divided on the question. Compare, *e.g.,* Alabama ex rel. Gallion v. Rogers, 187 F.Supp. 848 (M.D.Ala.1960), *aff'd per curiam,* 285 F.2d 430 (5th Cir.1961); and Pennsylvania Turnpike Comm'n v. McGinnes, 179 F.Supp. 578 (E.D.Pa.1959), *aff'd per curiam,* 278 F.2d 330 (3d Cir.1960), with, *e.g.,* Perez v. Rhiddlehoover, 247 F.Supp. 65 (E.D.La.1965); and McNally v. Jackson, 7 F.2d 373 (E.D.La.1925).[5]

Note that a decision against state court jurisdiction, whether in an injunction or other type of suit, may mean that the plaintiff has no remedy at all against the defendant.[6] In the McGinnes case, *supra,* plaintiff first sued in a federal district court, seeking an injunction to prevent the Director of Internal Revenue from making a tax refund to a third party, who had allegedly obtained money from the plaintiff by fraud. The suit was dismissed for lack of original jurisdiction on the ground that the plaintiff's case raised no federal question. See 268 F.2d 65 (3d Cir.1958). When plaintiff subsequently sued in state court, defendant removed to federal court under 28 U.S.C. § 1442(a), and then obtained dismissal on the basis of the rule (then in force) that on removal a federal court cannot take jurisdiction over a case if the state court had none to begin with. And the holding in McClung v. Silliman, *supra,* came after the Supreme Court had already held that there was no original federal jurisdiction over the case. McIntire v. Wood, 7 Cranch 504 (U.S.1813).

For a full discussion of the issue of state court jurisdiction and a powerful argument in favor of jurisdiction, see Arnold, note 2, *supra.* See also 1 Moore, Federal Practice ¶ 0.6[5] (2d ed. 1986); Warren, *Federal and State Court Interference,* 43 Harv.L.Rev. 345 (1930); Note, 53 Cornell L.Rev. 916, 926–29 (1968).

(5) Redish & Woods, note 5, *supra,* read Tarble's Case as standing for the broad proposition that "state courts have no power to control directly the acts of federal officers" (124 U.Pa.L.Rev. at 93). The authors argue (in agreement with the Dialogue) that there is a due process right of access to some court for judicial review when a government official invades a citizen's constitutional rights (at least if coercion is involved). They then

<hr>

4. A dictum in Keely v. Sanders, 99 U.S. 441, 443 (1878) stated that "no state court could, by injunction or otherwise, prevent federal officers from collecting federal taxes." The government could have, but did not, raise the question in Tennessee Elec. Power Co. v. TVA, 306 U.S. 118 (1939), though other issues of state court jurisdiction (prior to removal) were raised. See Freund, On Understanding the Supreme Court 96–97 (1949). The issue was raised in Brooks v. Dewar, 313 U.S. 354 (1941), but the Court was unwilling to resolve "asserted conflict touching issues of so grave consequence" where there was no case for injunction on the merits.

5. Redish & Woods, *Congressional Power to Control the Jurisdiction of Lower Federal Courts: A Critical Review and a New Synthesis,* 124 U.Pa.L.Rev. 45, 89 (1975), conclude that "[t]he weight of reasoned opinion emanating from the state and lower federal courts supports the general denial of state court power" to enjoin federal officers.

6. Until the amendments to 28 U.S.C. § 1331 in 1976 and 1980, there was a jurisdictional amount limitation on general federal question jurisdiction, and of course until 1875, there was no general federal question jurisdiction at all.

argue that because the rule of Tarble's Case bars a state court from providing such review when a federal officer would be the defendant, it would violate the Fifth Amendment to prevent the federal courts from hearing these cases. Thus they conclude that Congress's power to control the jurisdiction of the lower federal courts must be limited by the Fifth Amendment obligation to provide a federal forum to protect constitutional rights in cases where Tarble's Case prevents a state court from acting.

Do you agree? Why should the dubious tail of Tarble's Case wag such a large dog?[7] Tarble's Case can be criticized as wrong (at least in theory) even on its facts—even when Congress *has* provided a full and adequate remedy in a federal court, must it be presumed that a state court should not "interfere" with federal officials? Why then should the error be compounded by reading the meandering and poorly reasoned Tarble opinion as creating a generic barrier to state-court actions to control the acts of federal officials when there exists no remedy in federal court? Is there anything in the constitutional plan to justify the notion that the Framers regarded state courts of general jurisdiction as *incapable* of passing on the legality of official action by federal officers—at a time when it was a more than plausible possibility that lower federal courts would not be created at all? Indeed, might there not be occasions in which the state courts would provide a more disinterested forum than the federal courts for adjudicating disputes between individuals and the federal government?[8]

Consider whether the argument of the Dialogue is more consistent with the constitutional plan: Congress may foreclose access to a lower federal court to test the constitutional validity of a deprivation of life, liberty, or property by a federal official, but if it does so it cannot prevent a state court from taking jurisdiction.

(6) Wasservogel v. Meyerowitz, 300 N.Y. 125, 89 N.E.2d 712 (1949), was a summary proceeding in the New York City Municipal Court to evict a tenant for non-payment of rent. The rent demanded was in excess of the maximum permitted by the Federal Housing and Rent Act for the months in question but the Housing Expediter, without notice or hearing, had, pursuant to a regulation, increased the ceiling retroactively. The owner based his claim upon this order. The tenant defended by challenging the validity of the order and regulation under the Fifth Amendment, for want of notice and hearing.

---

7. In a subsequent passage Redish and Woods suggest a "potentially severe limitation on the reach of the new synthesis"— that "Congress can probably circumvent the difficulties created by Tarble's Case by *explicitly* authorizing state court jurisdiction over the acts of federal officials" (p. 106) (emphasis added). It is unclear what this concession does to the previous constitutional argument. And in a later piece Redish plainly waters down the argument: "[A]ll my reading of Tarble's Case does is require that, before it excludes federal jurisdiction to review the alleged invasion of constitutional rights by federal officers, Congress be aware that (1) *some* judicial forum independent of congressional control will have to remain available to enforce constitutional rights, and that (2) with the federal courts removed from the picture, that forum will be the courts of the fifty states, with all the risks inherent in that avenue." Redish, *Constitutional Limitations on Congressional Limitations on Congressional Power to Control Federal Jurisdiction: A Reaction to Professor Sager*, 77 Nw.U.L.Rev. 143, 159 (1982).

8. See Bator, *The State Courts and Federal Constitutional Litigation*, 22 Wm. & Mary L.Rev. 605, 632 n. 64 (1981). And see generally, on the values of parallel jurisdiction, Cover, *The Uses of Jurisdictional Redundancy: Interest, Ideology, and Innovation*, 22 Wm. & Mary L.Rev. 639 (1981).

While the Court of Appeals rejected this contention on the merits, an alternative ground of decision was that the "state courts have no jurisdiction to review federal administrative orders", with the consequence that the Municipal Court "when shown the federal expediter's determination was bound to accept and act upon it, and could not review or overrule it for supposed invalidity". It was said to be immaterial that Congress had omitted from the 1947 and 1948 Housing and Rent Acts the provision of the Emergency Price Control Act of 1942, vesting exclusive jurisdiction in the Emergency Court of Appeals (see p. 371, *supra*), since this conferred no jurisdiction on state courts, or that the district court might have no jurisdiction to review the challenged order, the jurisdictional amount not being involved. And it was added that: "not only have our courts, under our own decisions, no power to revise or invalidate this federal determination, but we are, by the Supremacy Clause (Art. VI) of the Federal Constitution, put under a positive duty to enforce it, in these appropriate proceedings", citing Testa v. Katt, immediately below.

Did the Court of Appeals subordinate the Constitution to a housing regulation in its view of the requirements of the Supremacy Clause? See Note, 51 Colum.L.Rev. 84, 95–96 (1951).

TESTA v. KATT

330 U.S. 386, 67 S.Ct. 810, 91 L.Ed. 967 (1947).
Certiorari to the Superior Court for Providence
and Bristol Counties, Rhode Island.

MR. JUSTICE BLACK delivered the opinion of the Court.

Section 205(e) of the Emergency Price Control Act provides that a buyer of goods above the prescribed ceiling price may sue the seller "in any court of competent jurisdiction" for not more than three times the amount of the overcharge plus costs and a reasonable attorney's fee. Section 205(c) provides that federal district courts shall have jurisdiction of such suits "concurrently with State and Territorial courts." Such a suit under § 205(e) must be brought "in the district or county in which the defendant resides or has a place of business ＊ ＊ ＊."

The respondent was in the automobile business in Providence, Providence County, Rhode Island. In 1944 he sold an automobile to petitioner Testa, who also resides in Providence, for $1100, $210 above the ceiling price. The petitioner later filed this suit against respondent in the State District Court in Providence. Recovery was sought under § 205(e). The court awarded a judgment of treble damages and costs to petitioner. On appeal to the State Superior Court, where the trial was de novo, the petitioner was again awarded judgment, but only for the amount of the overcharge plus attorney's fees. Pending appeal from this judgment, the Price Administrator was allowed to intervene. On appeal, the State Supreme Court reversed, 71 R.I. 472, 47 A.2d 312. It interpreted § 205(e) to be "a penal statute in the international sense." It held that an action for violation of § 205(e) could not be maintained in the courts of that State. The State Supreme Court rested its holding on its earlier decision in Robinson v. Norato, 1945, 71 R.I. 256, 43 A.2d 467, 468 (1945), in which it had reasoned that: A state need not enforce the penal laws of a government which is "foreign in the international sense"; § 205(e) is treated by

State ct Reasoning

Rhode Island as penal in that sense; the United States is "foreign" to the State in the "private international" as distinguished from the "public international" sense; hence Rhode Island courts, though their jurisdiction is adequate to enforce similar Rhode Island "penal" statutes, need not enforce § 205(e). Whether state courts may decline to enforce federal laws on these grounds is a question of great importance. For this reason, and because the Rhode Island Supreme Court's holding was alleged to conflict with this Court's previous holding in Mondou v. New York, N.H. & H.R. Co., 223 U.S. 1, we granted certiorari.

For the purposes of this case, we assume, without deciding, that § 205(e) is a penal statute in the "public international," "private international," or any other sense. So far as the question of whether the Rhode Island courts properly declined to try this action, it makes no difference into which of these categories the Rhode Island court chose to place the statute which Congress has passed. For we cannot accept the basic premise on which the Rhode Island Supreme Court held that it has no more obligation to enforce a valid penal law of the United States than it has to enforce a penal law of another state or a foreign country. Such a broad assumption flies in the face of the fact that the States of the Union constitute a nation. It disregards the purpose and effect of Article VI, § 2 of the Constitution which provides: "This Constitution, and the Laws of the United States which shall be made in Pursuance thereof; and all Treaties made, or which shall be made, under the Authority of the United States, shall be the supreme Law of the Land; and the Judges in every State shall be bound thereby, any Thing in the Constitution or Laws of any State to the Contrary notwithstanding."

Supremacy clause

It cannot be assumed, the supremacy clause considered, that the responsibilities of a state to enforce the laws of a sister state are identical with its responsibilities to enforce federal laws. Such an assumption represents an erroneous evaluation of the statutes of Congress and the prior decisions of this Court in their historic setting. Those decisions establish that state courts do not bear the same relation to the United States that they do to foreign countries. The first Congress that convened after the Constitution was adopted conferred jurisdiction upon the state courts to enforce important federal civil laws,[4] and succeeding Congress conferred on the states jurisdiction over federal crimes and actions for penalties and forfeitures.[5]

Enforcement of federal laws by state courts did not go unchallenged. Violent public controversies existed throughout the first part of the Nineteenth Century until the 1860's concerning the extent of the constitutional supremacy of the Federal Government. During that period there were instances in which this Court and state courts broadly questioned the power and duty of state courts to exercise their jurisdiction to enforce United States civil and penal statutes or the power of the Federal Govern-

---

4. Judiciary Act of 1789, 1 Stat. 73, 77 (suits by aliens for torts committed in violation of federal laws and treaties; suits by the United States).

5. 1 Stat. 376, 378 (1794) (fines, forfeitures and penalties for violation of the License Tax on Wines and Spirits); 1 Stat. 373, 375 (1794) (the Carriage Tax Act); 1 Stat. 452 (penalty for purchasing guns from Indians); 1 Stat. 733, 740 (1799) (criminal and civil actions for violation of the postal laws). See Warren, *Federal Criminal Laws and the State Courts*, 38 Harv.L.Rev. 545; Barnett, *The Delegation of Federal Jurisdiction to State Courts*, 3 Selected Essays on Constitutional Law 1202 (1938).

ment to require them to do so. But after the fundamental issues over the extent of federal supremacy had been resolved by war, this Court took occasion in 1876 to review the phase of the controversy concerning the relationship of state courts to the Federal Government. Claflin v. Houseman, 93 U.S. 130. The opinion of a unanimous court in that case was strongly buttressed by historic references and persuasive reasoning. It repudiated the assumption that federal laws can be considered by the states as though they were laws emanating from a foreign sovereign. Its teaching is that the Constitution and the laws passed pursuant to it are the supreme laws of the land, binding alike upon states, courts, and the people, "anything in the Constitution or Laws of any State to the contrary notwithstanding." It asserted that the obligation of states to enforce these federal laws is not lessened by reason of the form in which they are cast or the remedy which they provide. And the Court stated that "If an act of Congress gives a penalty to a party aggrieved, without specifying a remedy for its enforcement, there is no reason why it should not be enforced, if not provided otherwise by some act of Congress, by a proper action in a state court." *Id.* 93 U.S. at page 137.

The Claflin opinion thus answered most of the arguments theretofore advanced against the power and duty of state courts to enforce federal penal laws. And since that decision, the remaining areas of doubt have been steadily narrowed. There have been statements in cases concerned with the obligation of states to give full faith and credit to the proceedings of sister states which suggested a theory contrary to that pronounced in the Claflin opinion.[9] But when in Mondou v. New York, N.H. & H.R. Co., *supra*, this Court was presented with a case testing the power and duty of states to enforce federal laws, it found the solution in the broad principles announced in the Claflin opinion.

The precise question in the Mondou case was whether rights arising under the Federal Employers' Liability Act, 36 Stat. 291, could "be enforced, as of right, in the courts of the states when their jurisdiction, as prescribed by local laws, is adequate to the occasion. * * *" *Id.* 223 U.S. at page 46. The Supreme Court of Connecticut had decided that they could not. Except for the penalty feature, the factors it considered and its reasoning were strikingly similar to that on which the Rhode Island Supreme Court declined to enforce the federal law here involved. But this Court held that the Connecticut court could not decline to entertain the action. The contention that enforcement of the congressionally created right was contrary to Connecticut policy was answered as follows:

"The suggestion that the act of Congress is not in harmony with the policy of the State, and therefore that the courts of the state are free to decline jurisdiction, is quite inadmissible, because it presupposes what in legal contemplation does not exist. When Congress, in the exertion of the power confided to it by the Constitution, adopted that act, it spoke for all the people and all the states, and thereby established a policy for all. That policy is as much the policy of Connecticut as if the act had emanated from its own legislature, and should be respected accordingly in the courts of the state." Mondou v. New York, N.H. & H.R. Co., *supra*, 223 U.S. at page 57.

So here, the fact that Rhode Island has an established policy against enforcement by its courts of statutes of other states and the United States

9. See n. 10, *infra.*

which it deems penal, cannot be accepted as a "valid excuse." Cf. Douglas v. New York, N.H. & H.R. Co., 279 U.S. 377, 388.[10] For the policy of the federal Act is the prevailing policy in every state. Thus, in a case which chiefly relied upon the Claflin and Mondou precedents, this Court stated that a state court cannot "refuse to enforce the right arising from the law of the United States because of conceptions of impolicy or want of wisdom on the part of Congress in having called into play its lawful powers." Minneapolis & St. L.R. Co. v. Bombolis, 241 U.S. 211, 222.

The Rhode Island court in its Robinson decision on which it relies cites cases of this Court which have held that states are not required by the full faith and credit clause of the Constitution to enforce judgments of the courts of other states based on claims arising out of penal statutes. But those holdings have no relevance here, for this case raises no full faith and credit question. Nor need we consider in this case prior decisions to the effect that federal courts are not required to enforce state penal laws. Compare State of Wisconsin v. Pelican Ins. Co., 127 U.S. 265, with Commonwealth of Massachusetts v. State of Missouri, 308 U.S. 1, 20.

For whatever consideration they may be entitled to in the field in which they are relevant, those decisions did not bring before us our instant problem of the effect of the supremacy clause on the relation of federal laws to state courts. Our question concerns only the right of a state to deny enforcement to claims growing out of a valid federal law.

It is conceded that this same type of claim arising under Rhode Island law would be enforced by that State's courts. Its courts have enforced claims for double damages growing out of the Fair Labor Standards Act, 29 U.S.C.A. § 201 et seq. Thus the Rhode Island courts have jurisdiction adequate and appropriate under established local law to adjudicate this action. Under these circumstances the State courts are not free to refuse enforcement of petitioners' claim. See McKnett v. St. Louis & S.F.R. Co., 292 U.S. 230; and compare Herb v. Pitcairn, 324 U.S. 117; 325 U.S. 77. The case is reversed and the cause is remanded for proceedings not inconsistent with this opinion.

Reversed.

NOTE ON THE OBLIGATION OF STATE COURTS TO ENFORCE FEDERAL LAW

(1) In Douglas v. New York, N.H. & H.R.R., 279 U.S. 377 (1929), the New York courts had dismissed an action under the Federal Employers' Liability Act brought by a Connecticut resident against a Connecticut corporation based on an accident occurring in Connecticut. A New York

---

10. It has been observed that the historic origin of the concept first expressed in this country by Chief Justice Marshall in The Antelope, 10 Wheat. 66, 123, that "The Courts of no country execute the penal laws of another • • •" lies in an earlier English case, Folliott v. Ogden, 1 H.Bl. 124 (1789), aff'd., Ogden v. Folliott, 3 T.R. 726 (1790), 4 Bro.P.C. 111. In that case the English courts refused to enforce an American Revolutionary statute confiscating property of loyal British subjects on the ground that English courts must refuse to enforce such penal statutes of a foreign enemy. It has been observed of this case that "of course they could as well have spoken of local public policy, and have reached the same result as surely." Leflar, *Extrastate Enforcement of Penal and Governmental Claims,* 46 Harv.L.Rev. 193, 195 (1932).

statute permitted actions by a nonresident against a foreign corporation only in certain classes of cases, of which this was not one. On appeal, plaintiff attacked the statute as a violation of the privileges and immunities clause of Article IV of the Federal Constitution. Justice Holmes, for the Court, rejected this attack on the ground that the statute applied equally to citizens of New York who were nonresidents of the state,[1] and then said (pp. 387–88):

"As to the grant of jurisdiction in the Employers' Liability Act, that statute does not purport to require State Courts to entertain suits arising under it, but only to empower them to do so, so far as the authority of the United States is concerned. It may very well be that if the Supreme Court of New York were given no discretion, being otherwise competent, it would be subject to a duty. But there is nothing in the Act of Congress that purports to force a duty upon such Courts as against an otherwise valid excuse. Second Employers' Liability Cases, 223 U.S. 1, 56, 57."

In McKnett v. St. Louis & S.F. Ry., 292 U.S. 230 (1934), an Alabama statute had opened the doors of Alabama courts to suits against foreign corporations arising under the laws of other states. This statute superseded a previous rule of decision that no Alabama court had jurisdiction of any suit against a foreign corporation unless the cause of action arose in Alabama. The Alabama Supreme Court had dismissed an action based on an out-of-state accident arising under the Federal Employers' Liability Act, holding that the statute lifted the prior bar only for causes of action arising under the laws of sister states. The Supreme Court reversed, Justice Brandeis saying (pp. 233–34):

"While Congress has not attempted to compel states to provide courts for the enforcement of the Federal Employers' Liability Act, Douglas v. New York, N.H. & H.R. Co., 279 U.S. 377, 387, the Federal Constitution prohibits state courts of general jurisdiction from refusing to do so solely because the suit is brought under a federal law. The denial of jurisdiction by the Alabama court is based solely upon the source of law sought to be enforced. The plaintiff is cast out because he is suing to enforce a federal act. A state may not discriminate against rights arising under federal laws."

Does the theory of these decisions suffice to support Testa v. Katt? Cf. Holmes, J., in Kenney v. Supreme Lodge, 252 U.S. 411, 415 (1920): " * * * it is plain that a State cannot escape its constitutional obligations [under the Full Faith and Credit Clause] by the simple device of denying jurisdiction in such cases to courts otherwise competent." See also Broderick v. Rosner, 294 U.S. 629 (1935).

In Missouri ex rel. Southern Ry. v. Mayfield, 340 U.S. 1 (1950), the Missouri Supreme Court had quashed writs of mandamus to compel a state trial judge to exercise his discretion, on a plea of forum non conveniens, to dismiss actions brought by nonresidents under the Federal Employers' Liability Act. Justice Frankfurter, speaking for the Court, reiterated the statement of the Douglas case that there is nothing in the Act "which

1. But cf. Hicklin v. Orbeck, 437 U.S. 518, 524 n. 8 (1978). The Court in Hicklin, in invalidating a state law requiring preferential hiring of qualified state residents, said: "Although this Court has not always equated state residency with state citizenship * * * [citing Douglas and other cases], it is now established that the terms 'citizen' and 'resident' are 'essentially interchangeable' * * * for purposes of analysis of most cases under the Privileges and Immunities Clause of Art. IV, § 2."

purported to 'force a duty' upon the State courts to entertain or retain Federal Employers' Liability litigation 'against an otherwise valid excuse'." He made clear that the doctrine of forum non conveniens, if applied without discrimination to all nonresidents, constitutes a valid excuse. In the view that the state court might have acted under a misapprehension of a federal duty, its judgment was vacated and the cause remanded for further proceedings.

(2) In Brown v. Gerdes, 321 U.S. 178, 188 (1944), Justice Frankfurter, concurring, said:

"Since 1789, rights derived from federal law could be enforced in state courts unless Congress confined their enforcement to the federal courts. This has been so precisely for the same reason that rights created by the British Parliament or by the Legislature of Vermont could be enforced in New York courts. Neither Congress nor the British Parliament nor the Vermont Legislature has power to confer jurisdiction upon the New York courts. But the jurisdiction conferred upon them by the only authority that has power to create them and to confer jurisdiction upon them— namely the law-making power of the State of New York—enables them to enforce rights no matter what the legislative source of the right may be. See, for instance, United States v. Jones, 109 U.S. 513, 520."

Is Testa v. Katt consistent with the views of Justice Frankfurter as to the basis of state jurisdiction to enforce federal rights of action? Are those views tenable in light of the possibility that Congress may choose not to create lower federal courts at all?[2]

Is there greater compulsion on state courts to hear federal defenses than to take jurisdiction of causes of action that arise under federal law and, if so, why?[3]

Consider also the question of Congress's power (and the appropriateness of using it) not only to force state courts to hear federal claims, but

2. See Neuborne, *Toward Procedural Parity in Constitutional Litigation*, 22 Wm. & Mary L.Rev. 725, 753–66 (1981); Redish & Muench, *Adjudication of Federal Causes of Action in State Court*, 75 Mich.L.Rev. 311, 340–61 (1976); Sandalow, *Henry v. Mississippi and the Adequate State Ground: Proposals for a Revised Doctrine*, 1965 Sup.Ct.Rev. 187, 203–09. See also Warren, *New Light on the History of the Federal Judiciary Act of 1789*, 37 Harv.L. Rev. 49 (1923); Warren, *Federal Criminal Laws and the State Courts*, 38 Harv.L.Rev. 545 (1925); Note, 73 Harv.L.Rev. 1551 (1960).

3. In Lynbrook Gardens, Inc. v. Ullmann, 291 N.Y. 472, 53 N.E.2d 353 (1943), the buyer in a suit for specific performance of a land contract set up a defense of lack of marketable title grounded on a doubt of the constitutionality of the tax statutes under which the seller had previously purchased the land. The New York Court of Appeals sustained the defense, without passing on the question of constitutionality under the Federal Constitution, saying (291 N.Y. at 477, 53 N.E.2d at 354–55):

"The question of the validity of the statute has been challenged on substantial grounds. This court can authoritatively determine whether or not the statute violates the provisions of the Constitution of the State of New York; only the Supreme Court of the United States can ultimately determine whether the statute violates the provisions of the Constitution of the United States. Even though this court were to sustain the validity of the statute, the Supreme Court of the United States might still reach a different conclusion. A subsequent purchaser could at any time reject title on that ground and litigate that question in a different forum. A title which can be challenged in that manner is not marketable and decree of specific performance may not be rendered under such circumstances."

Do you agree with the reasoning or the result? If the court had passed on the question of validity, would its ruling on that question have been subject to Supreme Court review? See pp. 559–63, *infra*.

also to use federal procedural and quasi-procedural rules in doing so.[4] See *Dice v. Akron, C. & Y.R.R.*, 342 U.S. 359 (1952), and the *Note on "Substance" and "Procedure" in the Enforcement of Federal Rights of Action in State Courts*, pp. 628–38, *infra*. See generally Meltzer, *State Court Forfeitures of Federal Rights*, 99 Harv.L.Rev. 1130 (1986).

(3) In National League of Cities v. Usery, 426 U.S. 833 (1976), a divided Court invalidated amendments to the Fair Labor Standards Act that extended the statute's minimum wage and maximum hours provisions to most state employees. The Court held that the Tenth Amendment limited federal authority to act under such constitutional provisions as the Commerce Clause of Article I, and that the statute constituted an undue interference with state sovereignty, in violation of that amendment.

Did Usery cast doubt on the validity of Testa?

The Usery decision, highly controversial from the date of its birth, was itself overruled by a divided Court in Garcia v. San Antonio Metropolitan Transit Auth., 469 U.S. 528 (1985). "[We] continue to recognize," the majority said, "that the States occupy a special and specific position in our constitutional system and that the scope of Congress' authority under the Commerce Clause must reflect that position. But the principal and basic limit on the federal commerce power is that inherent in all congressional action—the built-in restraints that our system provides through state participation in federal government action" (p. 556).

During the decade of Usery's tenure, an important case exemplifying the tension between the Usery rationale and that of Testa was Federal Energy Regulatory Com'n v. Mississippi, 456 U.S. 742 (1982). In the Public Utilities Regulatory Policies Act of 1978 (PURPA), 16 U.S.C. §§ 2601 *et seq.*, Congress, *inter alia*, directed state utility regulatory authorities to implement certain federal rules, to "consider" the adoption and implementation of certain rate design and regulatory standards, and to follow certain procedures when considering these proposed standards. In the FERC case, the Court, relying heavily on Testa, upheld these requirements against a Tenth Amendment challenge based on Usery. The Court stressed that the area of public utility regulation was one that Congress could choose to preempt altogether, and that the states could opt not to regulate.

Justice O'Connor, dissenting in part with two other Justices, argued that "[a]pplication of Testa to legislative power [such as that exercised by state utility regulatory commissions] * * * vastly expands the scope of that decision. Because trial courts of general jurisdiction do not choose the cases that they hear, the requirement that they evenhandedly adjudicate state and federal claims falling within their jurisdiction does not infringe any sovereign authority to set an agenda. * * * [But] the power to choose subjects for legislation is a fundamental attribute of legislative

---

4. Compare the issues raised by Section 811 of the Fair Debt Collection Practices Act of 1977, 15 U.S.C. § 1692i. That section provides, *inter alia*, that "any debt collector who brings any legal action on a debt against any consumer" (other than an action to enforce an interest in real property) may bring the action "only in the judicial district or similar legal entity (A) in which such consumer signed the contract sued upon; or (B) in which such consumer resides * * *." The statute was specifically designed to encompass the regulation of consumer debt actions arising under state law and brought in the state courts. Does Congress have the power in matters such as this to regulate the venue of state-law actions in the state courts? *Cf.* Mercantile National Bank v. Langdeau, 371 U.S. 555 (1963) (upholding federal limitations on venue in state court actions against national banks).

power, and interference with this power unavoidably undermines state sovereignty" (pp. 784–85).[5]

Is the FERC decision a significant expansion of Testa? Does the overruling of Usery cut the ground from under the FERC dissents?[6]

(4) State courts have concurrent jurisdiction over claims brought under 42 U.S.C. § 1983 to redress the deprivation of rights secured by federal law. See Martinez v. California, 444 U.S. 277 (1980). And though the Supreme Court has left the question open, Testa and the cases discussed in this Note strongly support the conclusion that state courts are obligated to entertain such claims. But in view of the policy underlying the Tax Injunction Act, 28 U.S.C. § 1341, may a state court refuse to entertain a § 1983 claim challenging a state tax statute so long as there is a "plain, speedy and efficient remedy" under state law? The issue was presented in Spencer v. South Carolina Tax Comm'n, but the decision below was affirmed without opinion by an equally divided Court. 471 U.S. 82 (1985). See also Arkansas Writers' Project, Inc. v. Ragland, 107 S.Ct. 1722, 1730 (1987), p. 1345, *infra*. See generally Note, 95 Yale L.J. 414 (1985).

(5) Would it constitute a "valid excuse" under Testa v. Katt for a state court to refuse to entertain a federal action on the ground that the state courts do not currently enforce any analogous forum-created rights? Unlike a state door-closing rule rooted in the doctrine of forum non conveniens, wouldn't allowance of such an excuse pose a serious threat that a state court might reject a case because of disagreement with the policy underlying the federal law? See Redish & Muench, note 2, *supra*, at 350–59.

What if a state court's refusal to entertain a federal claim against a state official or agency is based on the state's law of sovereign immunity? See General Oil Co. v. Crain, 209 U.S. 211 (1908), discussed at p. 586, *infra*.

(6) If jurisdiction of federal criminal prosecutions were not made exclusive in the federal district courts, see 18 U.S.C. § 3231, could a United States Attorney prosecute criminal violations in a state court of general criminal jurisdiction? If the state court should hold its jurisdiction limited to crimes under state law, would its excuse be "valid" under Testa v. Katt?

See Note, 60 Harv.L.Rev. 966 (1947); *cf.* p. 493, note 5, *supra*.

The possibility of utilizing the state courts for criminal enforcement of federal price regulations was considered in preliminary stages of the drafting of the Emergency Price Control Act of 1942, but the validity of any mandate to the states was deemed too questionable for proposal. There were, however, strong efforts to secure state and local legislation declaring violation of federal regulations punishable in state courts, and many

---

5. Justice Powell, writing separately, expressed sympathy with the concerns voiced in Justice O'Connor's opinion. But he limited his own dissent to that part of the majority opinion upholding the power of Congress to prescribe the "administrative and judicial *procedures* that States must follow" (p. 771) (emphasis added). On this issue, see pp. 632–38, *infra*.

6. A contemporaneous discussion of FERC in the Harvard Law Review suggests that the case goes well beyond Testa because it upholds "a federally mandated commingling of federal and state policies in the development of state law." *The Supreme Court, 1981 Term,* 96 Harv.L.Rev. 62, 193 (1982). The Note goes on to argue that the implications of FERC are in turn limited not only by Usery but by other decisions, and that the Court might well refuse to uphold "federal directives that impose on the states more onerous burdens of consideration than those of PURPA or that address more integral concerns" than those involved in FERC itself (p. 194).

dispositions were effected on this basis. See Mermin, *"Cooperative Federalism" Again: State and Municipal Legislation Penalizing Violation of Existing and Future Federal Requirements,* 57 Yale L.J. 1, 201 (1974): *cf.* Frankfurter & Landis, The Business of the Supreme Court 293 (1928) (suggesting use of the state courts for trying such offenses as liquor violations, thefts in interstate freight, and "schemes to defraud essentially local in their operation but involving a minor use of the mails").

What are the principal objections to attempts to enforce federal criminal law through the state courts?

(7) How would you analyze the problem faced by Congress in determining when federal jurisdiction should be exclusive in the district courts, when concurrent with state courts, with or without removal; and when original jurisdiction should be left to the states, with or without review by the Supreme Court?

This is the underlying legislative issue to be kept in mind in working through the chapters that follow. What objectives should be sought in fashioning the distribution of the jurisdiction that Congress has the power to control? To what extent is the prevailing law adapted to these ends? What better means, if any, can be found? For a preview of these issues, see Wechsler, *Federal Jurisdiction and the Revision of the Judicial Code,* 13 Law & Contemp.Prob. 216 (1948); for one set of solutions, see the ALI Study.

Chapter V

REVIEW OF STATE COURT DECISIONS BY THE SUPREME COURT

SECTION 1. THE ESTABLISHMENT OF THE JURISDICTION

DEVELOPMENT OF THE STATUTORY PROVISIONS

1. *The Judiciary Act of 1789 and the Amendments of 1867.* The following text, with accompanying footnotes, shows the original form of Section 25 of the Judiciary Act of 1789 (1 Stat. 73, 85), and the changes made by the Act of February 5, 1867 (14 Stat. 385, 386): [1]

"Sec. 25. And be it further enacted, That a final judgment or decree in any suit, in the highest court [of law or equity] [2] of a State in which a decision in the suit could be had, where is drawn in question the validity of a treaty or statute of, or an authority exercised under the United States, and the decision is against their validity; or where is drawn in question the validity of a statute of, or an authority exercised under any State, on the ground of their being repugnant to the constitution, treaties or laws of the United States, and the decision is in favour of such their validity, [or where is drawn in question the construction of any clause of the constitution, or of a treaty, or statute of, or commission held under the United States,] [3] and the decision is against the title, right, privilege or [exemption] [4] specially set up or claimed by either party, under such [clause of the said] [2] Constitution, treaty, statute [or] commission, [5] may be re-examined and reversed or affirmed in the Supreme Court of the United States upon a writ of error, the citation being signed by the chief justice, or judge or chancellor of the court rendering or passing the judgment or decree complained of, or by a justice of the Supreme Court of the United States, in the same manner and under the same regulations, and the writ shall have the same effect, as if the judgment or decree complained of had been rendered or passed in a [Circuit Court] [6] and the proceeding upon the reversal shall also be the same, except that the Supreme Court, [instead of remanding the cause for a

1. The text is reproduced from Frankfurter & Shulman, Cases on Federal Jurisdiction and Procedure 627–28 (Rev. ed. 1937). For the full text of the successive jurisdictional enactments see Robertson & Kirkham, Jurisdiction of the Supreme Court of the United States, Appendix A, 931–41 (Wolfson & Kurland ed. 1951).

2. The amendatory Act of Feb. 5, 1867, deleted these words.

3. The act of 1867 substituted the following: "or where any title, right, privilege, or immunity is claimed under the constitution, or any treaty or statute of or commission held, or authority exercised under the United States."

4. The Act of 1867 substituted "immunity."

5. The Act of 1867 added "or authority."

6. The Act of 1867 substituted "court of the United States."

501

final decision as before provided,] [2] may at their discretion, [if the cause shall have been once remanded before,] [2] proceed to a final decision of the same, and award execution. [7] [But no other error shall be assigned or regarded as a ground of reversal in any such case as aforesaid, than such as appears on the face of the record, and immediately respects the before mentioned questions of validity or construction of the said constitution, treaties, statutes, commissions, or authorities in dispute.] [2]"

2. *The Judiciary Act of 1914.* The provisions of the First Judiciary Act, as amended in 1867, were re-enacted in substantially the same form as § 709 of the Revised Statutes (1874) and § 237 of the Judicial Code (1911). The Act of December 23, 1914, c. 2, 38 Stat. 790, authorized the Supreme Court to require to be certified for its review ("by certiorari or otherwise") any case within § 237, although the decision of the state court "may have been in favor of the validity of the treaty or statute or authority exercised under the United States" or "against the validity of the State statute or authority claimed to be repugnant to the Constitution, treaties, or laws of the United States" or "in favor of the title, right, privilege, or immunity claimed under the Constitution, treaty, statute, commission, or authority of the United States."

The amendment was prompted largely by the decision in Ives v. South Buffalo Ry., 201 N.Y. 271, 94 N.E. 431 (1911), holding the first American workmen's compensation act in conflict with the due process guaranties of both the Federal and state constitutions. See Frankfurter & Landis, The Business of the Supreme Court 188–98 (1928).

3. *The Judiciary Act of 1916.* The Act of September 6, 1916, c. 448, § 2, 39 Stat. 726, provided for review only on certiorari in cases where "any title, right, privilege or immunity is claimed under the Constitution, or any treaty or statute of, or commission held or authority exercised under the United States, and the decision is either in favor of or against the title, right, privilege, or immunity especially set up or claimed." Review on writ of error otherwise remained the same.

4. *The Judiciary Act of 1925.* Under the 1916 Act review by writ of error was retained in cases in which there was drawn in question "the validity of * * * an authority exercised under the United States" and the decision was against validity, or in which there was drawn in question "the validity of * * * an authority exercised under any State" as "repugnant to the Constitution, treaties, or laws of the United States" and the decision was in favor of validity. Cases involving the validity of claims asserted under an "authority," as distinguished from the validity of the authority itself, were reviewable only on certiorari. See, *e.g.,* Philadelphia & Reading Coal & Iron Co. v. Gilbert, 245 U.S. 162 (1917); Yazoo & Mississippi Valley R.R. v. Clarksdale, 257 U.S. 10, 15–16 (1921).

Difficulty with this subtle distinction (see Frankfurter & Landis, *supra,* at 265) led to its abandonment on the enactment of the Judges' Bill (Act of February 13, 1925, 43 Stat. 936). Obligatory review of state judgments was preserved only for decisions against the validity of a treaty or Act of Congress or in favor of the validity of a statute of a state attacked upon federal grounds. Section 237(c) was added, however, providing that when writ of error was improperly sought or allowed in a certiorari case, the

7. The Act of 1867 added "or remand the same to an inferior court."

papers shall be treated by the Supreme Court as a petition for a writ of certiorari in the cause. The Act of January 31, 1928, c. 14, 45 Stat. 54, as amended, substituted an appeal for writ of error in all cases reviewable as of right.

5. *The Revised Judicial Code of 1948.* This revision of the Judicial Code made no substantial change in § 237. The basic provisions conferring jurisdiction to review state court decisions were re-formulated in 28 U.S.C. § 1257.[8]

Three of the clauses of § 237 are now separate sections of Chapter 133 of Title 28, collecting miscellaneous procedural provisions relating to Supreme Court review: § 2103 (formerly § 237(c)[9]); § 2104 (appeal from state court to be taken in same manner and with same effect as if judgment rendered by court of the United States); § 2106 (power to affirm, modify, vacate, reverse, remand, direct entry of judgment or require further proceedings).

Under § 2101(c), the time in which to appeal or apply for certiorari in civil cases from state courts is ninety days, with power in a justice of the Supreme Court within this period to extend the time to apply for certiorari, but not the time to appeal, for not more than sixty days. Section 2101(d) defines the time in criminal cases as that "prescribed by rules of the Supreme Court." Supreme Court Rule 11.1 specifies ninety days for appeals from state courts in criminal cases; Rule 20.1 sets the time limit for filing a petition for certiorari in criminal cases at sixty days, extendable for another thirty by a justice for good cause.

Procedure on appeal is prescribed by Supreme Court Rules 10–16. Included is the requirement of Rule 15.1(h) that the jurisdictional statement must include "A statement of the reasons why the questions presented are so substantial as to require plenary consideration, with briefs on the merits and oral argument, for their resolution." (See Section 4(B) of this Chapter, p. 724, *infra.*) Procedure on petition for certiorari is set out in Rules 17–23. The "character of reasons that will be considered" in passing on petitions for certiorari, indicated in Rule 17.1, include: "When a state court of last resort has decided a federal question in a way in conflict with the decision of another state court of last resort or of a federal court of appeals", and "When a state court ✽ ✽ ✽ has decided an important question of federal law which has not been, but should be, settled by this Court, or has decided a federal question in a way in conflict with applicable decisions of this Court." These rules should be examined in detail. See also Chap. XV, Sec. 3, *infra.*

An authoritative work on Supreme Court practice is Stern, Gressman & Shapiro, Supreme Court Practice (6th ed. 1986). A useful reference is volumes 1 and 1A of West's Federal Forms, by Bennett Boskey (3d ed. 1982).

---

8. In 1970 a provision was added to § 1257 that "For the purposes of this section, the term 'highest court of a State' includes the District of Columbia Court of Appeals." Act of July 29, 1970, § 172(a)(1), 84 Stat. 590.

In 1961, separate provisions precisely parallel to § 1257 were adopted for review of the Supreme Court of the Commonwealth of Puerto Rico. See 28 U.S.C. § 1258.

9. Amended in 1962 to apply to appeals "improvidently taken" from federal courts of appeals as well. Act of Sept. 19, 1962, § 1, 76 Stat. 556.

MARTIN v. HUNTER'S LESSEE

1 Wheat. 304, 4 L.Ed. 97 (1816).
Error to the Court of Appeals of Virginia.

This was an action of ejectment instituted by Hunter in the Superior Court at Winchester, Virginia, in 1791 against Denny Martin Fairfax, devisee of Thomas, Lord Fairfax.[1] The land involved was a portion of the "waste and ungranted land" of a large tract known as the Northern Neck, owned by Lord Fairfax, a citizen of Virginia, at his death in 1781. The plaintiff claimed under a grant from the State of Virginia made in 1789; the defendant, a British subject resident in England, claimed as the devisee of the Fairfax estate.

In 1779 Virginia had enacted legislation purporting to declare the escheat or forfeiture of property then belonging to British subjects, prescribing a proceeding on inquest of office for escheat. An act of 1782, dealing specifically with the Northern Neck, recited that "there is reason to suppose" that the proprietorship has "descended upon alien enemies", and required that persons holding land in the Neck sequester and retain quit-rents then due and pay such rents thereafter to the public treasury. Another act of 1782 provided that entries made with the surveyors of the Northern Neck after the death of Lord Fairfax should be as valid as those made previously, under his direction. An act of 1785 directed the removal of land records relating to the Neck to the register's office; provided for issuing grants for surveys under entries made during the life of the proprietor or thereafter with the surveyors; exonerated landholders from composition and quit-rents; and declared unappropriated lands within the district subject to grant in the same manner as other unappropriated lands belonging to the commonwealth.

Hunter's grant was made under this last act. The land, however, had not been the subject of any inquest of office or other proceeding for escheat.

The Treaty of Peace with Great Britain of 1783 provided that "no future confiscations shall be made"; and the Jay Treaty of 1794 provided that "British subjects who now hold lands in the territories of the United States, and American citizens who now hold lands in the dominions of his majesty, shall continue to hold them, according to the nature and tenure of their respective estates and titles therein; and may grant, sell or devise the same to whom they please, in like manner as if they were natives", and "neither they nor their heirs or assigns shall, so far as respects the said lands and the legal remedies incident thereto, be considered as aliens."

The case was submitted in the Superior Court on an agreed statement and that court decided against Hunter, April 24, 1794. An appeal to the Court of Appeals of Virginia was argued in May 1796. No decision appears to have been rendered by November 15, 1803, when the appeal abated by reason of the death of the appellee. Revived against Martin by consent, Hunter's appeal was reargued in the Virginia Court of Appeals in October 1809 before Judges Roane and Fleming, who in April, 1810 joined in reversal of the judgment of the Superior Court.

In 1793 or 1794, a syndicate including John Marshall and his brother James had contracted for the purchase of the main part of the Fairfax

---

1. Statement of facts by the editors.

estate from Denny Martin Fairfax. Partial payment was made by James Marshall in January 1797 (2 Beveridge, Life of John Marshall 210 (1911)); and in August 1797, Fairfax conveyed to James Marshall all the Fairfax lands in Virginia "save and except * * * the manor of Leeds," a conveyance probably including the land claimed by Hunter. 4 Beveridge, *supra,* at 150, n. 2. The deed for the balance, conveyed to both Marshalls and Rawleigh Colston, was filed in 1806 (2 Beveridge, *supra,* at 211, n. 1); and there was a partition in 1808 and 1809.

In 1796, however, the Virginia legislature, after petitions of more than two hundred settlers occupying other parts of the Fairfax lands, passed a resolution proposing to relinquish "all claim to any lands specifically appropriated by * * * Lord Fairfax to his own use either by deed or actual survey * * * if the devises [*sic*] of Lord Fairfax, or those claiming under them, will relinquish all claims to lands * * * which were waste and unappropriated at the time of the death of Lord Fairfax." Prior to passage of the resolution John Marshall, describing himself as "one of the purchasers of the lands of Mr. Fairfax, and authorized to act for all of them", wrote to the Speaker of the House of Delegates that he had "determined to accede to the proposition" if the act passed. 2 Beveridge *supra,* at 208–09.

On the reargument in the Virginia Court of Appeals, Hunter relied upon the act of compromise, as well as on the propositions that Denny Martin Fairfax as an alien was incapable of holding land in Virginia and that there had, in any case, been an escheat of the land under the Virginia legislation. The appellee contended that Martin was capable of holding until his title was divested by inquest of office or some equivalent act, that no such act had taken place before the Treaty of Peace, and that the act of compromise, passed after judgment in the case, did not affect it and could not be introduced. Separate opinions were rendered, Judge Roane—Marshall's political enemy, see 4 Beveridge, *supra,* at 146; Note, 66 Harv.L.Rev. 1242 (1953))—holding that Martin had acquired at best a defeasible title, that the Act of 1782 vested the title in the commonwealth before any treaty and, finally, that the compromise was binding, having been "intended to settle and determine this among other suits." Judge Fleming concurred solely on the basis of the compromise, disagreeing on the other points. Hunter v. Fairfax's Devisee, 15 Va. (1 Munf.) 218.

The Supreme Court on writ of error, Judge Fleming as presiding judge having certified the record, reversed the judgment. Fairfax's Devisee v. Hunter's Lessee, 7 Cranch 603 (U.S.1813).

Justice Story, writing the opinion for reversal, held that an alien has the capacity to take title to land by devise, subject to divestiture by the sovereign on office found; that none of the Virginia acts altered the common law requirement of inquest of office to vest title in the state but at the most proceeded on the erroneous belief that title had already vested in the commonwealth; and, therefore, that the treaty of 1794 confirmed the undivested Fairfax title. "It was once in the power of the commonwealth of Virginia, by an inquest of office or its equivalent, to have vested the estate completely in itself, or its grantee. But it has not so done, and its inchoate title (and of course, the derivative title, if any, of its grantee) has, by the operation of the treaty, become ineffectual and void" (p. 627).

Justice Johnson dissented on the ground that the "interest acquired under the devise was a mere *scintilla juris,* and that *scintilla* was extinguished by the grant of the state," the legislature being competent to dispense with inquest of office. He agreed, however, that under § 25 of the Judiciary Act an inquiry into "the title of the parties litigant" was necessary and "must, in the nature of things, precede the consideration how far the law, treaty and so forth, is applicable to it; otherwise an appeal to this court would be worse than nugatory" (p. 632).

Neither the majority nor the dissenting opinion mentioned the act of compromise relied upon by the Virginia court.

Chief Justice Marshall did not participate. Justice Washington was absent on the argument, and Justice Todd on delivery of judgment.

The Supreme Court mandate directed to "the Honorable the Judges of the Court of Appeals in and for the Commonwealth of Virginia," reciting that the "Court is of opinion that there is error in the judgment of the Court of Appeals," "adjudged and ordered, that the judgment of the Court of Appeals * * * in this case be, and the same is hereby reversed and annulled, and that the judgment of the District Court of Winchester be affirmed, with costs; and it is further ordered, that the said cause be remanded to the said Court of Appeals * * * with instructions to enter judgment for the appellant." It ended with the formal provision: "You therefore are hereby commanded that such proceedings be had in said cause, as according to right and justice, and the laws of the United States, and agreeably to said judgment and instructions of said Supreme Court ought to be had, the said writ of error notwithstanding". Hunter v. Martin, Devisee of Fairfax, 18 Va. (4 Munf.) 2–3.

"The question, whether this mandate should be obeyed, excited all that attention from the bench and bar, which its great importance truly merited; and, at the request of the Court, was solemnly argued by Leigh and Wirt, for Martin, devisee of Fairfax, and by Williams, Nicholas and Hay, on the other side". (Nicholas and Hay "expressed their sentiments in consequence of a request from the Court to the members of the bar generally".) On December 16, 1815, the judges (Cabell, Brooke, Roane and Fleming) expressed their separate opinions *seriatim,* joining in the following conclusion (pp. 58–59):

"The court is unanimously of opinion that the appellate power of the Supreme Court of the United States, does not extend to this court, under a sound construction of the constitution of the United States;—that so much of the 25th section of the act of Congress * * * as extends the appellate jurisdiction of the Supreme Court to this court, is not in pursuance of the constitution of the United States; that the writ of error in this case was improvidently allowed under the authority of that act; that proceedings thereon in the Supreme Court were *coram non judice* in relation to this court; and that obedience to its mandate be declined by this court."

The common grounds set forth for this conclusion are indicated by the following extracts from the opinion of Judge Cabell (pp. 8, 9, 12, 13):

" * * * The present government of the United States, grew out of the weakness and inefficacy of the confederation, and was intended to remedy its evils. Instead of a government of requisition, we have a government of power. But how does the power operate? On individuals in their individual capacity. No one presumes to contend, that the state governments can operate compulsively on the general government or any of its departments, even in cases of unquestionable encroachment on state authority. * * * Such encroachment of jurisdiction could neither be prevented nor redressed by the state government, or any of its departments, by any procedure acting on the Federal Courts. I can perceive nothing in the constitution which gives to the Federal Courts any stronger claim to prevent or redress, by any procedure acting on the state courts, an equally obvious encroachment on the Federal jurisdiction. The constitution of the United States contemplates the independence of both governments and regards the residuary sovereignty of the states, as not less inviolable, than the delegated sovereignty of the United States. It must have been foreseen that controversies would sometimes arise as to the boundaries of the two jurisdictions. Yet the constitution has provided no umpire, has erected no tribunal by which they shall be settled. The omission proceeded, probably, from the belief, that such a tribunal would produce evils greater than those of the occasional collisions which it would be designed to remedy. * * *

"If this Court should now proceed to enter a judgment in this case, according to instructions of the Supreme Court, the Judges of this Court, in doing so, must act either as Federal or as State Judges. But we cannot be made Federal Judges without our consent, and without commissions. Both these requisites being wanting, the act could not, therefore, be done by us, constitutionally, as Federal Judges. We must, then, in obeying this mandate, be considered still as State Judges. We are required, as State Judges to enter up a judgment, not our own, but dictated and prescribed to us by another Court. * * * But, before one Court can dictate to another, the judgment it shall pronounce, it must bear, to that other, the relation of an appellate Court. The term appellate, however, necessarily includes the idea of superiority. But one Court cannot be correctly said to be superior to another, unless both of them belong to the same sovereignty. It would be a misapplication of terms to say that a Court of Virginia is superior to a Court of Maryland, or vice versa. The Courts of the United States, therefore, belonging to one sovereignty, cannot be appellate Courts in relation to the State Courts, which belong to a different sovereignty—and, of course, their commands or instructions impose no obligation.

" * * * But the act of Congress now under consideration, attempts, in fact, to make the State Courts Inferior Federal Courts, and to exercise through them, jurisdiction over the subjects of federal cognizance.

" * * * If, therefore, I am correct in this position, the appellate jurisdiction of the Supreme Court of the United States [under the constitution], must have reference to the inferior Courts of the United States, and not to the State Courts. * * * It has been contended that the constitution contemplated only the objects of appeal, and not the tribunals from which the appeal is to be taken; and intended to give to the Supreme Court of the United States appellate jurisdiction in all the cases of federal cognizance. But this argument proves too much, and what is utterly inadmissible. It would give appellate jurisdiction, as well over the courts of England or France, as over the State courts; for, although I do not think the State Courts are foreign Courts in relation to the Federal Courts, yet I consider them not less independent than foreign Courts."

To the argument that without the appellate jurisdiction "there will be no other mode by which congress can extend the judicial power of the

United States to the cases of federal cognizance; that there will, consequently be no uniformity of decision", Judge Cabell replied: "All the purposes of the constitution of the United States will be answered by the erection of Federal Courts, into which any party, plaintiff or defendant, concerned in a case of federal cognizance, may carry it for adjudication" (pp. 15–16). Judges Brooke and Fleming apparently shared this opinion (pp. 23, 58), on which Judge Roane expressed no view. Judges Roane and Fleming advanced as a further ground of their decision that the case was not embraced within the 25th section of the Judiciary Act since the record did not show that the decision turned upon the treaty; and if the Supreme Court "had held itself at liberty, to go outside of the record, and resort to those reports, which are deemed authentic evidences of the decisions therein contained" the report would have shown "that the decision of this Court was rendered upon another, and ordinary ground of jurisdiction—the act of compromise * * *" (pp. 49, 50).

In the Supreme Court—

STORY, J., delivered the opinion of the court,—This is a writ of error from the court of appeals of Virginia, founded upon the refusal of that court to obey the mandate of this court, requiring the judgment rendered in this very cause, at February term 1813, to be carried into due execution.

* * *

Before proceeding to the principal questions, it may not be unfit to dispose of some preliminary considerations which have grown out of the arguments at the bar.

The constitution of the United States was ordained and established, not by the states in their sovereign capacities, but emphatically, as the preamble of the constitution declares, by "the People of the United States." * There can be no doubt, that it was competent to the people to invest the general government with all the powers which they might deem proper and necessary; to extend or restrain these powers according to their own good pleasure, and to give them a paramount and supreme authority. As little doubt can there be, that the people had a right to prohibit to the states the exercise of any powers which were, in their judgment, incompatible with the objects of the general compact; to make the powers of the state governments, in given cases, subordinate to those of the nation, or to reserve to themselves those sovereign authorities which they might not choose to delegate to either. The constitution was not, therefore, necessarily carved out of existing state sovereignties, nor a surrender of powers already existing in state institutions, for the powers of the states depend upon their own constitutions; and the people of every state had the right to modify and restrain them, according to their own views of policy or principle. On the other hand, it is perfectly clear, that the sovereign powers vested in the state governments, by their respective constitutions, remained unaltered and unimpaired, except so far as they were granted to the government of the United States. These deductions do not rest upon general reasoning, plain and obvious as they seem to be. They have been positively recognized by one of the articles in amendment of the constitution, which declares, that "the powers not delegated to the United States by

* The preamble to the Constitution is constantly referred to, by statesmen and jurists, to aid them in the exposition of its provisions. On the proper construction of the words quoted in the opinion of the court, the two great political parties into which the country is divided, have based their respective principles of government.

the constitution, nor prohibited by it to the states, are reserved to the states respectively, or to the people." * * *

The third article of the constitution is that which must principally attract our attention.[2] * * *

This leads us to the consideration of the great question as to the nature and extent of the appellate jurisdiction of the United States. We have already seen that appellate jurisdiction is given by the constitution to the supreme court in all cases where it has not original jurisdiction; subject, however, to such exceptions and regulations as congress may prescribe. It is, therefore, capable of embracing every case enumerated in the constitution, which is not exclusively to be decided by way of original jurisdiction. But the exercise of appellate jurisdiction is far from being limited by the terms of the constitution to the supreme court. There can be no doubt that congress may create a succession of inferior tribunals, in each of which it may vest appellate as well as original jurisdiction. The judicial power is delegated by the constitution in the most general terms, and may, therefore, be exercised by congress under every variety of form, of appellate or original jurisdiction. * * *

As, then, by the terms of the constitution, the appellate jurisdiction is not limited as to the supreme court, and as to this court it may be exercised in all other cases than those of which it has original cognizance, what is there to restrain its exercise over state tribunals in the enumerated cases? The appellate power is not limited by the terms of the third article to any particular courts. The words are, "the judicial power (which includes appellate power) shall extend *to all cases*," &c., and "in all other cases before mentioned the supreme court shall have appellate jurisdiction." It is the *case*, then, and not *the court*, that gives the jurisdiction. If the judicial power extends to the case, it will be in vain to search in the letter of the constitution for any qualification as to the tribunal where it depends. It is incumbent, then, upon those who assert such a qualification to show its existence by necessary implication. * * *

If the constitution meant to limit the appellate jurisdiction to cases pending in the courts of the United States, it would necessarily follow that the jurisdiction of these courts would, in all cases enumerated in the constitution, be exclusive of state tribunals. How otherwise could the jurisdiction extend to *all* cases arising under the constitution, laws, and treaties of the United States, or *to all cases* of admiralty and maritime jurisdiction? If some of these cases might be entertained by state tribunals, and no appellate jurisdiction as to them should exist, then the appellate power would not extend to *all*, but to *some*, cases. If state tribunals might exercise concurrent jurisdiction over all or some of the other classes of cases in the constitution without control, then the appellate jurisdiction of the United States might, as to such cases, have no real existence, contrary to the manifest intent of the constitution. Under such circumstances, to give effect to the judicial power, it must be construed to be exclusive; and this not only when the *casus foederis* should arise directly, but when it should arise, incidentally, in cases pending in state courts. This construction would abridge the jurisdiction of such court far more than has been ever contemplated in any act of congress.

---

2. [Ed.] In the omitted portion of the opinion the view that the language of Arti- cle III is "designed to be mandatory" upon Congress is developed. See p. 366, *supra*.

On the other hand, if, as has been contended, a discretion be vested in congress to establish, or not to establish, inferior courts at their own pleasure, and congress should not establish such courts, the appellate jurisdiction of the supreme court would have nothing to act upon, unless it could act upon cases pending in the state courts. Under such circumstances it must be held that the appellate power would extend to state courts; for the constitution is peremptory that it shall extend to certain enumerated cases, which cases could exist in no other courts. Any other construction, upon this supposition, would involve this strange contradiction, that a discretionary power vested in congress, and which they might rightfully omit to exercise, would defeat the absolute injunctions of the constitution in relation to the whole appellate power.

But it is plain that the framers of the constitution did contemplate that cases within the judicial cognizance of the United States not only might but would arise in the state courts, in the exercise of their ordinary jurisdiction. With this view the sixth article declares, that "this constitution, and the laws of the United States which shall be made in pursuance thereof, and all treaties made, or which shall be made, under the authority of the United States, shall be the supreme law of the land, and the judges in every state shall be bound thereby, any thing in the constitution or laws of any state to the contrary notwithstanding." It is obvious that this obligation is imperative upon the state judges in their official, and not merely in their private, capacities. * * *

A moment's consideration will show us the necessity and propriety of this provision in cases where the jurisdiction of the state courts is unquestionable. Suppose a contract for the payment of money is made between citizens of the same state, and performance thereof is sought in the courts of that state; no person can doubt that the jurisdiction completely and exclusively attaches, in the first instance, to such courts. Suppose at the trial the defendant sets up in his defence a tender under a state law, making paper money a good tender, or a state law, impairing the obligation of such contract, which law, if binding, would defeat the suit. The constitution of the United States has declared that no state shall make anything but gold or silver coin a tender in payment of debts, or pass a law impairing the obligation of contracts. If congress shall not have passed a law providing for the removal of such a suit to the courts of the United States, must not the state court proceed to hear and determine it? Can a mere plea in defence be of itself a bar to further proceedings, so as to prohibit an inquiry into its truth or legal propriety, when no other tribunal exists to whom judicial cognizance of such cases is confided? Suppose an indictment for a crime in a state court, and the defendant should allege in his defence that the crime was created by an *ex post facto* act of the state, must not the state court, in the exercise of a jurisdiction which has already rightfully attached, have a right to pronounce on the validity and sufficiency of the defence? It would be extremely difficult, upon any legal principles, to give a negative answer to these inquiries. Innumerable instances of the same sort might be stated, in illustration of the position; and unless the state courts could sustain jurisdiction in such cases, this clause of the sixth article would be without meaning or effect, and public mischiefs, of a most enormous magnitude, would inevitably ensue.

It must, therefore, be conceded that the constitution not only contemplated, but meant to provide for cases within the scope of the judicial power of the United States, which might yet depend before state tribunals. It was foreseen that in the exercise of their ordinary jurisdiction, state courts would incidentally take cognizance of cases arising under the constitution, the laws, and treaties of the United States. Yet to all these cases the judicial power, by the very terms of the constitution, is to extend. It cannot extend by original jurisdiction if that was already rightfully and exclusively attached in the state courts, which (as has been already shown) may occur; it must, therefore, extend by appellate jurisdiction, or not at all. It would seem to follow that the appellate power of the United States must, in such cases, extend to state tribunals; and if in such cases, there is no reason why it should not equally attach upon all others within the purview of the constitution. * * *

It is further argued, that no great public mischief can result from a construction which shall limit the appellate power of the United States to cases in their own courts: first, because state judges are bound by an oath to support the constitution of the United States, and must be presumed to be men of learning and integrity; and, secondly, because congress must have an unquestionable right to remove all cases within the scope of the judicial power from the state courts to the courts of the United States, at any time before final judgment, though not after final judgment. As to the first reason—admitting that the judges of the state courts are, and always will be, of as much learning, integrity, and wisdom, as those of the courts of the United States, (which we very cheerfully admit,) it does not aid the argument. It is manifest that the constitution has proceeded upon a theory of its own, and given or withheld powers according to the judgment of the American people, by whom it was adopted. We can only construe its powers, and cannot inquire into the policy or principles which induced the grant of them. The constitution has presumed (whether rightly or wrongly we do not inquire) that state attachments, state prejudices, state jealousies, and state interests, might sometimes obstruct, or control, or be supposed to obstruct or control, the regular administration of justice. Hence, in controversies between states; between citizens of different states; between citizens claiming grants under different states; between a state and its citizens, or foreigners, and between citizens and foreigners, it enables the parties, under the authority of congress, to have the controversies heard, tried, and determined before the national tribunals. No other reason than that which has been stated can be assigned, why some, at least, of those cases should not have been left to the cognizance of the state courts. In respect to the other enumerated cases—the cases arising under the constitution, laws, and treaties of the United States, cases affecting ambassadors and other public ministers, and cases of admiralty and maritime jurisdiction—reasons of a higher and more extensive nature, touching the safety, peace, and sovereignty of the nation, might well justify a grant of exclusive jurisdiction.

This is not all. A motive of another kind, perfectly compatible with the most sincere respect for state tribunals, might induce the grant of appellate power over their decisions. That motive is the importance, and even necessity of *uniformity* of decisions throughout the whole United States, upon all subjects within the purview of the constitution. Judges of equal learning and integrity, in different states, might differently interpret a statute, or a treaty of the United States, or even the constitution itself: If there were no revising authority to control these jarring and discordant judgments, and harmonize them into uniformity, the laws, the treaties, and the constitution of the United States would be different in different states, and might, perhaps, never have precisely the same construction, obligation, or efficacy, in any two states. The public mischiefs that would attend such a state of things would be truly deplorable; and it cannot be believed that they could have escaped the enlightened convention which formed the constitution. What, indeed, might then have been only prophecy, has now become fact; and the appellate jurisdiction must continue to be the only adequate remedy for such evils.

There is an additional consideration, which is entitled to great weight. The constitution of the United States was designed for the common and equal benefit of all the people of the United States. The judicial power was granted for the same benign and salutary purposes. It was not to be exercised exclusively for the benefit of parties who might be plaintiffs, and would elect the national forum, but also for the protection of defendants who might be entitled to try their rights, or assert their privileges, before the same forum. Yet, if the construction contended for be correct, it will follow, that as the plaintiff may always elect the state court, the defendant may be deprived of all the security which the constitution intended in aid of his rights. Such a state of things can, in no respect, be considered as giving equal rights. To obviate this difficulty, we are referred to the power which it is admitted congress possess to remove suits from state courts to the national courts; and this forms the second ground upon which the argument we are considering has been attempted to be sustained.

This power of removal is not to be found in express terms in any part of the constitution; if it be given, it is only given by implication, as a power of removal is certainly not, in strictness of language, an exercise of original jurisdiction; it presupposes an exercise of original jurisdiction to have attached elsewhere. The existence of this power of removal is familiar in courts acting according to the course of the common law in criminal as well as civil cases, and it is exercised before as well as after judgment. But this is always deemed in both cases an exercise of appellate, and not of original jurisdiction. If, then, the right of removal be included in the appellate jurisdiction, it is only because it is one mode of exercising that power, and as congress is not limited by the constitution to any particular mode, or time of exercising it, it may authorize a removal either before or after judgment. The time, the process, and the manner, must be subject to its absolute legislative control. A writ of error is, indeed, but a process which removes the record of one court to the possession of another court, and enables the latter to inspect the proceedings, and give such judgment as its own opinion of the law and justice of the case may warrant. * * *

The remedy, too, of removal of suits would be utterly inadequate to the purposes of the constitution, if it could act only on the parties, and not upon the state courts. In respect to criminal prosecutions, the difficulty seems admitted to be insurmountable; and in respect to civil suits, there would, in many cases, be rights without corresponding remedies. If state courts should deny the constitutionality of the authority to remove suits from their cognizance, in what manner could they be compelled to relinquish the jurisdiction? In respect to criminal cases, there would at once be an end of all control, and the state decisions would be paramount to the constitution; and though in civil suits the courts of the United States might act upon the parties, yet the state courts might act in the same way; and this conflict of jurisdictions would not only jeopardise private rights, but bring into imminent peril the public interests.

On the whole, the court are of opinion, that the appellate power of the United States does extend to cases pending in the state courts; and that the 25th section of the judiciary act, which authorizes the exercise of this jurisdiction in the specified cases, by a writ of error, is supported by the letter and spirit of the constitution. We find no clause in that instrument which limits this power; and we dare not interpose a limitation where the people have not been disposed to create one.

Strong as this conclusion stands upon the general language of the constitution, it may still derive support from other sources. It is an historical fact, that this exposition of the constitution, extending its appellate power to state courts, was, previous to its adoption, uniformly and publicly avowed by its friends, and admitted by its enemies, as the basis of their respective reasonings, both in and out of the state conventions. It is an historical fact, that at the time when the judiciary act was submitted to the deliberations of the first congress, composed, as it was, not only of men of great learning and ability, but of men who had acted a principal part in framing, supporting, or opposing that constitution, the same exposition was explicitly declared and admitted by the friends and by the opponents of that system. It is an historical fact, that the supreme court of the United States have, from time to time, sustained this appellate jurisdiction in a great variety of cases, brought from the tribunals of many of the most important states in the union, and that no state tribunal has ever breathed a judicial doubt on the subject, or declined to obey the mandate of the supreme court, until the present occasion. This weight of contemporaneous exposition by all parties, this acquiescence of enlightened state courts, and these judicial decisions of the supreme court through so long a period, do, as we think, place the doctrine upon a foundation of authority which cannot be shaken, without delivering over the subject to perpetual and irremediable doubts.

The next question which has been argued, is, whether the case at bar be within the purview of the 25th section of the judiciary act, so that this court may rightfully sustain the present writ of error. * * *

That the present writ of error is founded upon a judgment of the court below, which drew in question and denied the validity of a statute of the United States, is incontrovertible, for it is apparent upon the face of the record. That this judgment is final upon the rights of the parties is equally true; for if well founded, the former judgment of that court was of conclusive authority, and the former judgment of this court utterly void. The decision was, therefore, equivalent to a perpetual stay of proceedings upon the mandate, and a perpetual denial of all the rights acquired under it. The case, then, falls directly within the terms of the act. It is a final judgment in a suit in a state court, denying the validity of a statute of the United States; and unless a distinction can be made between proceedings under a mandate, and proceedings in an original suit, a writ of error is the proper remedy to revise that judgment. In our opinion no legal distinction exists between the cases. * * *

But it is contended, that the former judgment of this court was rendered upon a case not within the purview of this section of the judicial act, and that as it was pronounced by an incompetent jurisdiction, it was utterly void, and cannot be a sufficient foundation to sustain any subsequent proceedings. * * * [I]n ordinary cases a second writ of error has never been supposed to draw in question the propriety of the first judgment, and it is difficult to perceive how such a proceeding could be sustained upon principle. * * *

In this case, however, from motives of a public nature, we are entirely willing to waive all objections, and to go back and re-examine the question of jurisdiction as it stood upon the record formerly in judgment. * * *

The objection urged at the bar is, that this court cannot inquire into the title, but simply into the correctness of the construction put upon the treaty by the court of appeals; and that their judgment is not re-examinable here, unless it appear on the face of the record that some construction was put upon the treaty. If, therefore, that court might have decided the case upon the invalidity of the title, (and, *non constat*, that they did not,) independent of the treaty, there is an end of the appellate jurisdiction of this court. In support of this objection much stress is laid upon the last clause of the section, which declares, that no other cause shall be regarded as a ground of reversal than such as appears *on the face* of the record and *immediately* respects the construction of the treaty, &c., in dispute.

If this be the true construction of the section, it will be wholly inadequate for the purposes which it professes to have in view, and may be evaded at pleasure. But we see no reason for adopting this narrow construction; and there are the strongest reasons against it, founded upon the words as well as the intent of the legislature. What is the case for which the body of the section provides a remedy by writ of error? The answer must be in the words of the section, a suit where is drawn in question the construction of a treaty, and the decision is against *the title set up by the party.* It is, therefore, the decision against the title set up with reference to the treaty, and not the mere abstract construction of the treaty itself, upon which the statute intends to found the appellate jurisdiction. * * *

The restraining clause was manifestly intended for a very different purpose. It was foreseen that the parties might claim under various titles, and might assert various defences, altogether independent of each other. The court might admit or reject evidence applicable to one particular title, and not to all, and in such cases it was the intention of congress to limit what would otherwise have unquestionably attached to the court, the right of revising all the points involved in the cause. It therefore restrains this right to such errors as respect the questions specified in the section; and in this view, it has an appropriate sense, consistent with the preceding clauses. We are, therefore, satisfied, that, upon principle, the case was rightfully before us, and if the point were perfectly new, we should not hesitate to assert the jurisdiction. * * *

It has been asserted at the bar that, in point of fact, the court of appeals did not decide either upon the treaty or the title apparent upon the record, but upon a compromise made under an act of the legislature of Virginia. If it be true (as we are informed) that this was a private act, to take effect only upon a certain condition, *viz.* the execution of a deed of release of certain lands, which was matter *in pais,* it is somewhat difficult to understand how the court could take judicial cognizance of the act, or of the performance of the condition, unless spread upon the record. At all events, we are bound to consider that the court did decide upon the facts actually before them. The treaty of peace was not necessary to have been stated, for it was the supreme law of the land, of which all courts must take notice. And at the time of the decision in the court of appeals and in this court, another treaty had intervened, which attached itself to the title in controversy, and, of course, must have been the supreme law to govern the decision, if it should be found applicable to the case. It was in this view that this court did not deem it necessary to rest its former decision upon the treaty of peace, believing that the title of the defendant was, at all events, perfect under the treaty of 1794. * * *

We have thus gone over all the principal questions in the cause, and we deliver our judgment with entire confidence, that it is consistent with the constitution and laws of the land.

We have not thought it incumbent on us to give any opinion upon the question, whether this court have authority to issue a writ of mandamus to the court of appeals to enforce the former judgments, as we do not think it necessarily involved in the decision of this cause.

It is the opinion of the whole court, that the judgment of the court of appeals of Virginia, rendered on the mandate in this cause, be reversed, and the judgment of the district court, held at Winchester, be, and the same is hereby affirmed.

JOHNSON, J., * * * In this act I can see nothing which amounts to an assertion of the inferiority or dependence of the state tribunals. The presiding judge of the state court is himself authorized to issue the writ of error, if he will, and thus give jurisdiction to the supreme court: and if he thinks proper to decline it, no compulsory process is provided by law to oblige him. The party who imagines himself aggrieved is then at liberty to apply to a judge of the United States, who issues the writ of error, which (whatever the form) is, in substance, no more than a mode of compelling the opposite party to appear before this court, and maintain the legality of his judgment obtained before the state tribunal. An exemplification of a record is the common property of every one who chooses to apply and pay for it, and thus the case and the parties are brought before us; and so far is the court itself from being brought under the revising power of this court, that nothing but the case, as presented by the record and pleadings of the parties, is considered, and the opinions of the court are never resorted to unless for the purpose of assisting this court in forming their own opinions.

The absolute necessity that there was for congress to exercise something of a revising power over cases and parties in the state courts, will appear from this consideration.

Suppose the whole extent of the judicial power of the United States vested in their own courts, yet such a provision would not answer all the ends of the constitution, for two reasons:

1st. Although the plaintiff may, in such case, have the full benefit of the constitution extended to him, yet the defendant would not; as the plaintiff might force him into the court of the state at his election.

2dly. Supposing it possible so to legislate as to give the courts of the United States original jurisdiction in all cases arising under the constitution, laws, &c., in the words of the 2d section of the 3d article, (a point on which I have some doubt, and which in time might, perhaps, under some *quo minus* fiction, or a willing construction, greatly accumulate the jurisdiction of those courts,) yet a very large class of cases would remain unprovided for. Incidental questions would often arise, and as a court of competent jurisdiction in the principal case must decide all such questions, whatever laws they arise under, endless might be the diversity of decisions throughout the union upon the constitution, treaties, and laws, of the United States; a subject on which the tranquillity of the union, internally and externally, may materially depend.

I should feel the more hesitation in adopting the opinions which I express in this case, were I not firmly convinced that they are practical, and may be acted upon without compromitting the harmony of the union, or bringing humility upon the state tribunals. God forbid that the judicial power in these states should ever, for a moment, even in its humblest departments, feel a doubt of its own independence. Whilst adjudicating on a subject which the laws of the country assign finally to the revising power of another tribunal, it can feel no such doubt. An anxiety to do justice is ever relieved by the knowledge that what we do is not final between the parties. And no sense of dependence can be felt from the knowledge that the parties, not the court, may be summoned before another tribunal. With this view, by means of laws, avoiding judgments obtained in the state courts in cases over which congress has constitutionally assumed jurisdiction, and inflicting penalties on parties who shall contumaciously persist in infringing the constitutional rights of others—under a liberal extension of the writ of injunction and the *habeas corpus ad subjiciendum,* I flatter myself that the full extent of the constitutional revising power may be secured to the United States, and the benefits of it to the individual, without ever resorting to compulsory or restrictive process upon the state tribunals; a right which, I repeat again, congress has not asserted, nor has this court asserted, nor does there appear any necessity for asserting.

* * *

NOTE ON THE ATTACKS UPON THE JURISDICTION

(1) "Between 1789 and 1860 the courts of seven States denied the constitutional right of the United States Supreme Court to decide cases on writs of error to State courts—Virginia, Ohio, Georgia, Kentucky, South Carolina, California and Wisconsin. The Legislatures of all these states (except California), and also of Pennsylvania and Maryland, formally adopted resolutions or statutes against this power of the Supreme Court. Bills were introduced in Congress on at least ten occasions to deprive the Court of its jurisdiction—in 1821, 1822, 1824, 1831, 1846, 1867, 1868, 1871, 1872 and 1882." Warren, *Legislative and Judicial Attacks on the Supreme Court of the United States—A History of the Twenty–Fifth Section of the Judiciary Act,* 47 Am.L.Rev. 1, 161 at 3–4 (1913).

The arguments advanced in these attacks ranged from the relatively narrow grounds adduced against the jurisdiction in the Hunter case to the extreme position, culminating in the doctrines of secession, that each state had an equal right to stand on its interpretation of the Constitution.

The latter view, tracing its origin to the Kentucky and Virginia resolutions of 1798 (4 Elliot's Debates 540, 528), was forcefully stated in Hayne's speech on Foot's resolution (6 Reg. Debates in Congress, 21st Cong.,

1st Sess., 56–58, 86–92) and the South Carolina Ordinance of Nullification, 1 S.C.Stat. 329 (1832). For memorable answers, see replies of the states to the Kentucky and Virginia resolutions (4 Elliot's Debates 532–539); Webster's reply to Hayne, 6 Reg. Debates in Congress, 73–80, 92–93; President Jackson's Proclamation to the People of South Carolina (1832), 2 Richardson, Messages and Papers of the Presidents 640. The course of the debate is summarized in Warren, *supra;* Haines, The Role of the Supreme Court in American Government and Politics 499–577 (1944). See also Corwin, *National Power and State Interposition,* 10 Mich.L.Rev. 535 (1912); Reference Note, *Interposition vs. Judicial Power—A Study of Ultimate Authority in Constitutional Questions,* 1 Race Rel.L.Rep. 465 (1956).

The dissident remedies proposed included the repeal of the 25th section of the Judiciary Act, *e.g.,* H.R.Rep. No. 43, 21st Cong., 2d Sess. (1831), and constitutional amendment depriving the courts of authority to annul legislation, or vesting jurisdiction in the Senate, or establishing a new tribunal, differently composed, to mediate between the Nation and the States. See Ames, The Proposed Amendments to the Constitution of the United States During the First Century of its History 158–63 (1897).

The Court's position, as defined by Justice Story, did not change throughout the period of controversy. It was strongly reaffirmed, Chief Justice Marshall writing, in Cohens v. Virginia, 6 Wheat. 264 (U.S.1821), a writ of error to review a criminal conviction. The judgment was affirmed upon the merits but the Court denied a motion to dismiss the writ, rejecting two additional contentions urged against the jurisdiction: (1) that the Eleventh Amendment barred the writ of error as a suit against the State; and (2) that the review was inconsistent with the constitutional grant of original jurisdiction where a state is party.[1]

In Craig v. Missouri, 4 Pet. 410 (U.S.1830), the Court reversed a civil judgment obtained by the State, holding the loan certificate in suit, issued under a state statute, a forbidden "bill of credit." And in Worcester v. Georgia, 6 Pet. 515 (U.S.1832), it set aside a criminal conviction based upon a statute held in conflict with the treaties with the Cherokees and implementing acts of Congress. Significant as these decisions were, especially in view of Georgia's defiance of the mandate,[2] the opinions covered no new ground upon the issue of the jurisdiction. See also Tarble's Case, p. 484, *supra.*[3]

1. Another possible argument, that the Court's jurisdiction under § 25 did not extend to criminal cases, was not advanced by counsel for Virginia and apparently not noted by the Court. According to one critic of the decision, Virginia counsel "were especially instructed to place the case upon the ground of the constitution alone," but the Court should have noticed the statutory question on its own. Hammond, Hampden Essays, No. X (1821).

2. See 1 Warren, The Supreme Court in United States History 768 (1935 ed.). In 1830 Georgia had executed Corn Tassel, a Cherokee, despite a writ of error issued by the Supreme Court and the service of the citation on the Governor. See Warren, *supra,* 47 Am.L.Rev. at 167; Burke, *The Cherokee Cases: A Study in Law, Politics, and Morality,* 21 Stan.L.Rev. 500 (1969).

3. It is curious, in view of the issues drawn by the South prior to the Civil War, that the "judicial power" of the Confederate States extended to "cases arising under this Constitution, the laws of the Confederate States, and treaties made, or which shall be made under this authority", and that the Judiciary Act conferred an even broader jurisdiction on the Supreme Court to review state decisions than § 25 of the act of the United States. Hostility to this provision played a major part, however, in preventing the organization of a Confederate Supreme Court. See Robinson, Justice in Grey 48, 437–91 (1941).

(2) The constitutional validity of the Court's jurisdiction to review state court decisions has not been seriously challenged in the contemporary era. The decision outlawing racial segregation in public schools (Brown v. Board of Educ., 347 U.S. 483 (1954)) did provoke attacks on the authoritativeness of Court decisions, including "interposition" resolutions by state legislatures reminiscent of the pre-Civil War pattern. See, *e.g.,* the "Southern Manifesto" signed by Congressmen and Senators, and the 1956 legislative resolutions of five Southern states reprinted at 1 Race Rel.L.Rep. 435–47 (1956). For Supreme Court responses to such positions, see Cooper v. Aaron, 358 U.S. 1 (1958), p. 84, *supra;* Bush v. Orleans Parish Sch. Bd., 364 U.S. 803 (1960) (summarily rejecting the assertion that certain state statutes should be sustained on the ground that Louisiana "has interposed itself in the field of public education over which it has exclusive control"). And there have been numerous attempts—none successful—to restrict the Court's jurisdiction over specific controversial subjects (*e.g.,* reapportionment, school prayer, abortion). As to these attempts, see Chap. IV, Section 1A, pp. 377–79, *supra.* Various constitutional amendments to overturn Supreme Court decisions have, of course, also been frequently proposed.[4] A proposed amendment, advanced under the auspices of the Council of State Governments and echoing a similar scheme of the pre-Civil War era, would have created a "Court of the Union", composed of the chief justices of the fifty states, with power to review "any judgment of the Supreme Court relating to the rights reserved to the states or to the people by this Constitution." *Amending the Constitution to Strengthen the States in the Federal System,* 36 State Gov't 10, 13 (1963).[5]

NOTE ON ENFORCEMENT OF THE MANDATE

(1) When the Supreme Court reverses the judgment of a state court, it normally remands the cause for proceedings "not inconsistent" with the Court's opinion. This mandate leaves the state court free to pass on any other undetermined questions, or even to alter its determination of underlying state law. The reversal may not, therefore, be decisive of the final judgment. See, *e.g.,* Georgia Ry. & Elec. Co. v. Decatur, 297 U.S. 620 (1936); Schuylkill Trust Co. v. Pennsylvania, 302 U.S. 506 (1938).

Compare the mandate given upon the first review in Fairfax's Devisee v. Hunter's Lessee. Would a more satisfactory result have been achieved if the mandate had been in usual form?

When it is claimed that the state court has deviated from the Supreme Court's mandate, the proper remedy is to seek a new review of the judgment, as in Martin v. Hunter's Lessee. So long as such review is

---

4. One proposal would have supplemented an exclusion of state legislative apportionment from constitutional control with a constitutional restriction on federal "judicial power" over that subject. See Auerbach, *Proposal II and the National Interest in State Legislative Apportionment,* 39 Notre Dame Lawyer 628 (1964).

5. See also Kurland, *The Court of the Union or Julius Caesar Revised,* 39 Notre Dame Lawyer 636 (1964). The "Court of

the Union" plan was accompanied by two additional proposals: the legislative apportionment amendment, note 4, *supra,* and an amendment to facilitate state initiation of constitutional amendments through the Article V convention process. See Black, *The Proposed Amendment of Article V: A Threatened Disaster,* 72 Yale L.J. 957 (1963). See generally Oberst, *The Genesis of the Three States–Rights Amendments of 1963,* 39 Notre Dame Lawyer 644 (1964).

possible, whether by appeal or certiorari, mandamus has been considered inappropriate. In re Blake, 175 U.S. 114 (1899).

Whether the Court has power to issue mandamus when immediate review is precluded by the absence of a final judgment in the state court was argued but undecided in Ex parte Texas, 315 U.S. 8 (1942). *Cf.* Chap. III, Sec. 3, *supra.* Attempts to obtain mandamus in these circumstances have generally been met by denial of leave to file the petition, without explanation. Lavender v. Clark, 329 U.S. 674 (1946); Ex parte Kedroff, 346 U.S. 893 (1953); International Ass'n of Machinists v. Duckworth, 368 U.S. 982 (1962). However, in Deen v. Hickman, 358 U.S. 57 (1958), after determining that the Texas courts were treating as open an issue it considered foreclosed by its prior decision, the Supreme Court granted leave to file a petition for mandamus; the writ itself was not issued, since the Court assumed that the Texas court "will of course conform to the disposition we now make." The opinion did not discuss the question of the Court's power to issue mandamus to a state court. See also NAACP v. Alabama, 360 U.S. 240, 245 (1959) (granting certiorari and reversing state judgment inconsistent with prior mandate; leave to file petition for mandamus denied on the assumption state court will comply).

In General Atomic Co. v. Felter, 436 U.S. 493 (1978), the Supreme Court, on motion for leave to file a petition for mandamus, determined that a state trial court "has again done precisely what we held [when the case was previously before the Court] that it lacked the power to do: interfere with attempts by [plaintiff] to assert in federal forums what it views as its entitlement to arbitration" (p. 496). Invoking the principle that if "a lower court" fails to "give full effect" to the Court's mandate, its action may be controlled by writ of mandamus, the Court, acting summarily, granted the motion for leave to file. As in Deen, however, the Court did not issue the "formal writ" on the assumption that "the Santa Fe court will now conform to our previous judgment" (pp. 497–98). The Court did not discuss its assumption that the state courts were "lower court[s]" subject to control by mandamus.

Certiorari would not have been immediately available in the General Atomic case. *Cf.* Stanton v. Stanton, 429 U.S. 501 (1977) (review by appeal of Utah Supreme Court judgment violating previous Supreme Court mandate).

(2) The First Judiciary Act authorized the Supreme Court to enter judgment and award execution if the case had previously been remanded once. See pp. 501–02, *supra.* The requirement of one remand was eliminated in 1867. *Cf.* Judicial Code § 237(a), 28 U.S.C. § 344(a) (1940). In combination, 28 U.S.C. §§ 2106 and 1651(a) would presumably confer no less authority than the Court had before the 1948 revision.

Thus state recalcitrance can be met by entry of judgment, as in Martin v. Hunter's Lessee; McCulloch v. Maryland, 4 Wheat. 316, 437 (U.S.1819); Gibbons v. Ogden, 9 Wheat. 1, 239 (U.S.1824); Williams v. Bruffy, 102 U.S. 248 (1880); an award of execution, as in Tyler v. Magwire, 17 Wall. 253 (U.S.1873); or by remanding with directions to enter a specific judgment, as

1. On the same day, the Court summarily denied a petition for certiorari in the same case "in view of the order entered this day" in the mandamus proceeding. Deen v. Gulf, C. & S.F. Ry., 358 U.S. 874 (1958).

in Stanley v. Schwalby, 162 U.S. 255 (1896); and Poindexter v. Greenhow, 114 U.S. 270 (1885).

In NAACP v. Alabama ex rel. Flowers, 377 U.S. 288 (1964), after eight years of litigation (including four separate considerations by the Supreme Court) and obvious recalcitrance in the state courts, the Court still refused to formulate its own decree for entry in the state courts, as had been requested "[i]n view of the history of this case". Accepting that it "undoubtedly" has the power to do this, the Court said that "we prefer to follow our usual practice and remand the case to the Supreme Court of Alabama for further proceedings not inconsistent with this opinion." The opinion concluded: "Should we unhappily be mistaken in our belief that the Supreme Court of Alabama will promptly implement this disposition, leave is given the Association to apply to this Court for further appropriate relief" (p. 310). This proved not to be necessary; see 277 Ala. 89, 167 So.2d 171 (1964).

(3) If a mandate to enter a specific judgment should be issued and defied, which of the following procedures, if any, might be pursued: (a) recall of mandate and entry of judgment with award of execution or other process (28 U.S.C. §§ 569, 672, 1651, 2241); (b) mandamus to the state court to enter the proper judgment; (c) punishment for contempt for disobedience to "lawful * * * order * * * or command" under 18 U.S.C. § 401?

In United States v. Shipp, 203 U.S. 563 (1906), 214 U.S. 386 (1909), 215 U.S. 580 (1909), the Attorney General of the United States filed an information charging a contempt of the Supreme Court. The information alleged that Shipp, a state sheriff, and the other defendants combined to lynch a prisoner in the sheriff's custody, after the Supreme Court had allowed an appeal from the federal circuit court's denial of a petition for habeas corpus and had, to the defendants' knowledge, ordered a stay of the prisoner's execution pending the appeal. The Court sustained the information, appointed a commissioner to take testimony, rendered judgments of conviction, and imposed sentences of imprisonment.

See also In re Herndon, 394 U.S. 399 (1969), where appellants in an election case moved the Supreme Court for a show-cause order to initiate contempt proceedings against the local probate judge, as the state official responsible for preparing the ballot, for disobedience of a temporary restraining order granting interim relief. The order had been entered originally by a three-judge district court (which later dissolved it) and reinstated by the Supreme Court pending appeal. The Court postponed decision on the motion until after completion of proceedings in the district court to determine whether the judge's actions constituted contempt of that court's original order. Justice Douglas, joined by Justice Harlan, dissented on the ground that there was probable cause to believe there had been purposeful disobedience of the Supreme Court's order and prosecution for that contempt should not be postponed until after the district court's adjudication because it might then be barred by the Double Jeopardy clause.

Should state judges (in their judicial role) be shielded against a contempt sanction in a case of clear defiance any more than sheriffs or other officials? Does the story of Martin v. Hunter's Lessee have any bearing on the issue? See also the opinion of Justice Baldwin in Holmes v. Jennison, 14 Pet. (Appendix) 614, 632 (U.S.1840).

MURDOCK v. CITY OF MEMPHIS

20 Wall. 590, 22 L.Ed. 429 (U.S.1875).
Error to the Supreme Court of Tennessee.

* * *

Murdock filed a bill in one of the courts of chancery of Tennessee, against the city of Memphis, in that State. The bill and its exhibits made this case:

In July, 1844,—Congress having just previously authorized the establishment of a naval depot in that city, and appropriated a considerable sum of money for the purpose—the ancestors of Murdock—by ordinary deed of bargain and sale, without any covenants or declaration of trust on which the land was to be held by the city, but referring to the fact of "the location of the naval depot lately established by the United States at said town"— conveyed to the city certain land described in and near its limits "for the location of the naval depot aforesaid."

By the same instrument (a quadrupartite one) both the grantors and the city conveyed the same land to one Wheatley, in fee, in trust for the grantors and their heirs "in case the same shall not be appropriated by the United States for that purpose."

On the 14th of September, 1844, the city of Memphis, in consideration of the sum of $20,000 paid by the United States, conveyed the said land to the United States with covenant of general warranty; there being, however, in this deed to the United States no designation of any purpose to which the land was to be applied, nor any conditions precedent or subsequent, or of any kind whatsoever.

The United States took possession of the land for the purpose of the erection of a naval depot upon it, erected buildings, and made various expenditures and improvements for the said purpose; but in about ten years after, by an act of August 5th, 1854, transferred the land back to the city. The act was in these words:

"All the grounds and appurtenances thereunto belonging, known as the Memphis Navy Yard, in Shelby County, Tennessee, be, and the same is hereby, ceded to the mayor and aldermen of the city of Memphis, *for the use and benefit of said city.*"

There was no allegation in the bill that the city was in any way instrumental in procuring this transfer or the abandonment of the site as a naval depot; on the contrary, it is averred that the city authorities endeavored to prevent both.

The bill charged that by the failure of the United States to appropriate the land for a naval depot, and the final abandonment by the United States of any intention to do so, the land came within the clause of the deed of July 1844, conveying it to Wheatley in trust; or if not, that it was held by the city in trust for the original grantors, and the prayer sought to subject it to said trusts.

The answer, denying the construction put upon the deed of 1844, which established a trust, asserted that the land had been appropriated by the United States as a naval depot within the meaning and intent of the deed of July, 1844, and that the subsequent perpetual occupation of it was not a condition subsequent; and consequently that the abandonment of it as a naval depot was not a breach of a condition such as divested the title so conveyed by the deed.

It pleaded the statute of limitations. It also demurred to the bill as seeking to enforce a forfeiture for breach of condition subsequent.

The court sustained the demurrer, and also decreed that the city had a perfect title to the property against the complainants both under the act of Congress and the statute of limitations, and dismissed the bill. The Supreme Court of Tennessee affirmed this decree.

That court was also of opinion, and so declared itself to be, that the act of Congress "cedes the property in controversy in this cause to the mayor and aldermen of the city of Memphis, for the use of the city only, and not in trust for the complainant; and that the complainant takes no benefit under the said act."

The complainant thereupon sued out a writ of error to this court.

* * *

MR. JUSTICE MILLER * * * delivered the opinion of the court.

In the year 1867 Congress passed an act, approved February 5th, entitled an act to amend "An act to establish the judicial courts of the United States, approved September the 24th, 1789." This act consisted of two sections, the first of which conferred upon the Federal courts and upon the judges of those courts additional power in regard to writs of habeas corpus, and regulated appeals and other proceedings in that class of cases. The second section was a reproduction, with some changes, of the twenty-fifth section of the act of 1789, to which, by its title, the act of 1867 was an amendment, and it related to the appellate jurisdiction of this court over judgments and decrees of State courts.[1] * * *

The proposition is that by a fair construction of the act of 1867 this court must, when it obtains jurisdiction of a case decided in a State court, by reason of one of the questions stated in the act, proceed to decide every other question which the case presents which may be found necessary to a final judgment on the whole merits. To this has been added the further suggestion that in determining whether the question on which the jurisdiction of this court depends has been raised in any given case, we are not limited to the record which comes to us from the State court—the record proper of the case as understood at common law—but we may resort to any such method of ascertaining what was really done in the State court as this court may think proper, even to *ex parte* affidavits.

When the case standing at the head of this opinion came on to be argued, it was insisted by counsel for defendants in error that none of the questions were involved in the case necessary to give jurisdiction to this court, either under the act of 1789 or of 1867, and that if they were, there were other questions exclusively of State court cognizance which were

---

1. [Ed.] The changes effected by the Act of 1867 are indicated *supra*, pp. 501–02. Counsel relied particularly on the elimina- tion of the last sentence of section 25 of the Act of 1789.

sufficient to dispose of the case, and that, therefore, the writ of error should be dismissed.

Counsel for plaintiffs in error, on the other hand, argued that not only was there a question in the case decided against them which authorized the writ of error from this court under either act, but that this court having for this reason obtained jurisdiction of the case, should re-examine all the questions found in the record, though some of them might be questions of general common law or equity, or raised by State statutes, unaffected by any principle of Federal law, constitutional or otherwise.

When, after argument, the court came to consider the case in consultation, it was found that it could not be disposed of without ignoring or deciding some of these propositions, and it became apparent that the time had arrived when the court must decide upon the effect of the act of 1867 on the jurisdiction of this court as it had been supposed to be established by the twenty-fifth section of the act of 1789.

That we might have all the aid which could be had from discussion of counsel, the court ordered a reargument of the case on three distinct questions which it propounded, and invited argument, both oral and written, from any counsel interested in them. This reargument was had, and the court was fortunate in obtaining the assistance of very eminent and very able jurists.[2] The importance of the proposition under discussion justified us in delaying a decision until the present term, giving the judges the benefit of ample time for its most mature examination.

With all the aid we have had from counsel, and with the fullest consideration we have been able to give the subject, we are free to confess that its difficulties are many and embarrassing, and in the results we are about to announce we have not been able to arrive at entire harmony of opinion.

The questions propounded by the court for discussion by counsel were these:

1. Does the second section of the act of February 5th, 1867, repeal all or any part of the twenty-fifth section of the act of 1789, commonly called the Judiciary Act?[3]

2. Is it the true intent and meaning of the act of 1867, above referred to, that when this court has jurisdiction of a case, by reason of any of the questions therein mentioned, it shall proceed to decide all the questions presented by the record which are necessary to a final judgment or decree?

3. If this question be answered affirmatively, does the Constitution of the United States authorize Congress to confer such a jurisdiction on this court? * * *

2. The affirmative of the second question propounded above is founded upon the effect of the omission or repeal of the last sentence of the twenty-fifth section of the act of 1789. That clause in express terms limited the power of the Supreme Court in reversing the judgment of a State court, to errors apparent on the face of the record and which

2. [Ed.] Among counsel who argued in support of the extended jurisdiction was former Justice Benjamin R. Curtis, who filed a printed brief amicus curiae summarized at 20 Wall. 602–606 and printed in Curtis, Jurisdiction, Practice and Peculiar Jurisprudence of the Courts of the United States 54–58 (1880).

3. [Ed.] The Court answered the first question in the affirmative.

respected questions, that for the sake of brevity, though not with strict verbal accuracy, we shall call Federal questions, namely, those in regard to the validity or construction of the Constitution, treaties, statutes, commissions, or authority of the Federal government.

The argument may be thus stated: 1. That the Constitution declares that the judicial power of the United States shall extend to *cases* of a character which includes the questions described in the section, and that by the word *case* is to be understood all of the cases in which such a question arises. 2. That by the fair construction of the act of 1789 in regard to removing those cases to this court, the power and the duty of re-examining the whole case would have been devolved on the court, but for the restriction of the clause omitted in the act of 1867; and that the same language is used in the latter act regulating the removal, but omitting the restrictive clause. And, 3. That by re-enacting the statute in the same terms as to the removal of cases from the State courts, without the restrictive clause, Congress is to be understood as conferring the power which that clause prohibited.

We will consider the last proposition first.

What were the precise motives which induced the omission of this clause it is impossible to ascertain with any degree of satisfaction. In a legislative body like Congress, it is reasonable to suppose that among those who considered this matter at all, there were varying reasons for consenting to the change. No doubt there were those who, believing that the Constitution gave no right to the Federal judiciary to go beyond the line marked by the omitted clause, thought its presence or absence immaterial; and in a revision of the statute it was wise to leave it out, because its presence implied that such a power was within the competency of Congress to bestow. There were also, no doubt, those who believed that the section standing without that clause did not confer the power which it prohibited, and that it was, therefore, better omitted. It may also have been within the thought of a few that all that is now claimed would follow the repeal of the clause. But if Congress, or the framers of the bill, had a clear purpose to enact affirmatively that the court *should consider* the class of errors which that clause forbids, nothing hindered that they should say so in positive terms; and in reversing the policy of the government from its foundation in one of the most important subjects on which that body could act, it is reasonably to be expected that Congress would use plain, unmistakable language in giving expression to such intention.

There is, therefore, no sufficient reason for holding that Congress, by repealing or omitting this restrictive clause, intended to enact affirmatively the thing which that clause had prohibited. * * *

There is * * * nothing in the language of the act, as far as we have criticized it, which in express terms defines the extent of the re-examination which this court shall give to such cases.

But we have not yet considered the most important part of the statute, namely, that which declares that it is only upon the existence of certain questions in the case that this court can entertain jurisdiction at all. Nor is the mere existence of such a question in the case sufficient to give jurisdiction—the question must have been *decided* in the State court. Nor is it sufficient that such a question was raised and was decided. It must have been decided in a certain way, that is, against the right set up under the Constitution, laws, treaties, or authority of the United States. The Federal question may have been erroneously decided. It may be quite apparent to this court that a wrong construction has been given to the Federal law, but if the right claimed under it by plaintiff in error has been conceded to him, this court cannot entertain jurisdiction of the case, so very careful is the statute, both of 1789 and of 1867, to narrow, to limit, and define the jurisdiction which this court exercises over the judgments of the State courts. Is it consistent with this extreme caution to suppose that Congress intended, when those cases came here, that this court should not only examine those questions, but all others found in the record?—questions of common law, of State statutes, of controverted facts, and conflicting evidence. Or is it the more reasonable inference that Congress intended that the case should be brought here that *those questions* might be decided and *finally* decided by the court established by the Constitution of the Union, and the court which has always been supposed to be not only the most appropriate but the only proper tribunal for their final decision? No such reason nor any necessity exists for the decision by this court of other questions in those cases. The jurisdiction has been exercised for nearly a century without serious inconvenience to the due administration of justice. The State courts are the appropriate tribunals, as this court has repeatedly held, for the decision of questions arising under their local law, whether statutory or otherwise. And it is not lightly to be presumed that Congress acted upon a principle which implies a distrust of their integrity or of their ability to construe those laws correctly.

Let us look for a moment into the effect of the proposition contended for upon the cases as they come up for consideration in the conference-room. If it is found that no such question is raised or decided in the court below, then all will concede that it must be dismissed for want of jurisdiction. But if it is found that the Federal question was raised and was decided against the plaintiff in error, then the first duty of the court obviously is to determine whether it was correctly decided by the State court. Let us suppose that we find that the court below was right in its decision on that question. What, then, are we to do? Was it the intention of Congress to say that while you can only bring the case here on account of this question, yet when it is here, though it may turn out that the plaintiff in error was wrong on that question, and the judgment of the court below was right, though he has wrongfully dragged the defendant into this court by the allegation of an error which did not exist, and without which the case could not rightfully be here, he can still insist on an inquiry into all the other matters which were litigated in the case? This is neither reasonable nor just.

In such case both the nature of the jurisdiction conferred and the nature and fitness of things demand that, no error being found in the matter which authorized the re-examination, the judgment of the State court should be affirmed, and the case remitted to that court for its further enforcement.

The whole argument we are combating, however, goes upon the assumption that when it is found that the record shows that one of the questions mentioned has been decided against the claim of the plaintiff in error, this court has jurisdiction, and that jurisdiction extends to the whole case. If it extends to the whole case then the court must re-examine the whole case, and if it re-examines it must decide the whole case. It is difficult to escape the logic of the argument if the first premise be conceded. But it is here the error lies. We are of opinion that upon a fair construction of the whole language of the section the jurisdiction conferred is limited to the decision of the questions mentioned in the statute, and, as a necessary consequence of this, to the exercise of such powers as may be necessary to cause the judgment in that decision to be respected.

We will now advert to one or two considerations apart from the mere language of the statute, which seem to us to give additional force to this conclusion.

It has been many times decided by this court, on motions to dismiss this class of cases for want of jurisdiction, that if it appears from the record that the plaintiff in error raised and presented to the court by pleadings, prayer for instruction, or other appropriate method, one of the questions specified in the statute, and the court ruled against him, the jurisdiction of this court attached, and we must hear the case on its merits. Heretofore these merits have been held to be to determine whether the propositions of law involved in the specific Federal question were rightly decided, and if not, did the *case* of plaintiff in error, on the pleadings and evidence, come within the principle ruled by this court. This has always been held to be the exercise of the jurisdiction and re-examination of the case provided by the statute. But if when we once get jurisdiction, everything in the case is open to re-examination, it follows that every case tried in any State court, from that of a justice of the peace to the highest court of the State, may be brought to this court for final decision on all the points involved in it.

* * *

It is impossible to believe that Congress intended this result, and equally impossible that they did not see that it would follow if they intended to open the cases that are brought here under this section to re-examination on all the points involved in them and necessary to a final judgment on the merits.

The twenty-fifth section of the act of 1789 has been the subject of innumerable decisions, some of which are to be found in almost every volume of the reports from that year down to the present. These form a system of appellate jurisprudence relating to the exercise of the appellate power of this court over the courts of the States. That system has been based upon the fundamental principle that this jurisdiction was limited to the correction of errors relating solely to Federal law. And though it may be argued with some plausibility that the reason of this is to be found in the restrictive clause of the act of 1789, which is omitted in the act of 1867, yet an examination of the cases will show that it rested quite as much on the conviction of this court that without that clause and on general principles the jurisdiction extended no further. It requires a very bold reach of thought, and a readiness to impute to Congress a radical and hazardous change of a policy vital in its essential nature to the independence of the State courts, to believe that that body contemplated, or intended, what is claimed, by the mere omission of a clause in the substituted statute, which may well be held to have been superfluous, or nearly so, in the old one.

Another consideration, not without weight in seeking after the intention of Congress, is found in the fact that where that body has clearly shown an intention to bring the whole of a case which arises under the constitutional provision as to its subject-matter under the jurisdiction of a Federal court, it has conferred its cognizance on Federal courts of original jurisdiction and not on the Supreme Court.

* * * It was no doubt the purpose of Congress to secure to every litigant whose rights depended on any question of Federal law that that question should be decided for him by the highest Federal tribunal if he desired it, when the decisions of the State courts were against him on that question. That rights of this character, guaranteed to him by the Constitution and laws of the Union, should not be left to the exclusive and final control of the State courts.

There may be some plausibility in the argument that these rights cannot be protected in all cases unless the Supreme Court has final control of the whole case. But the experience of eighty-five years of the administration of the law under the opposite theory would seem to be a satisfactory answer to the argument. It is not to be presumed that the State courts, where the rule is clearly laid down to them on the Federal question, and its influence on the case fully seen, will disregard or overlook it, and this is all that the rights of the party claiming under it require. Besides, by the very terms of this statute, when the Supreme Court is of opinion that the question of Federal law is of such relative importance to the whole case that it should control the final judgment, that court is authorized to render such judgment and enforce it by its own process. It cannot, therefore, be maintained that it is in any case necessary for the security of the rights claimed under the Constitution, laws, or treaties of the United States that the Supreme Court should examine and decide other questions not of a Federal character.

And we are of opinion that the act of 1867 does not confer such a jurisdiction.

This renders unnecessary a decision of the question whether if Congress had conferred such authority, the act would have been constitutional. It will be time enough for this court to inquire into the existence of such a power when that body has attempted to exercise it in language which makes such an intention so clear as to require it. * * *.

It is proper, in this first attempt to construe this important statute as amended, to say a few words on another point. What shall be done by this court when the question has been found to exist in the record, and to have been decided against the plaintiff in error, and *rightfully* decided, we have already seen, and it presents no difficulties.

But when it appears that the Federal question was decided erroneously against the plaintiff in error, we must then reverse the case undoubtedly, if there are no other issues decided in it than that. It often has occurred, however, and will occur again, that there are other points in the case than those of Federal cognizance, on which the judgment of the court below may stand; those points being of themselves sufficient to control the case.

Or it may be, that there are other issues in the case, but they are not of such controlling influence on the whole case that they are alone sufficient to support the judgment.

It may also be found that notwithstanding there are many other questions in the record of the case, the issue raised by the Federal question is such that its decision must dispose of the whole case.

In the two latter instances there can be no doubt that the judgment of the State court must be reversed, and under the new act this court can either render the final judgment or decree here, or remand the case to the State court for that purpose.

But in the other cases supposed, why should a judgment be reversed for an error in deciding the Federal question, if the same judgment must be rendered on the other points in the case? And why should this court reverse a judgment which is right on the whole record presented to us; or where the same judgment will be rendered by the court below, after they have corrected the error in the Federal question?

We have already laid down the rule that we are not authorized to examine these other questions for the purpose of deciding whether the State court ruled correctly on them or not. We are of opinion that on these subjects not embraced in the class of questions stated in the statute, we must receive the decision of the State courts as conclusive.

But when we find that the State court has decided the Federal question erroneously, then to prevent a useless and profitless reversal, which can do the plaintiff in error no good, and can only embarrass and delay the defendant, we must so far look into the remainder of the record as to see whether the decision of the Federal question alone is sufficient to dispose of the case, or to require its reversal; or on the other hand, whether there exist other matters in the record actually decided by the State court which are sufficient to maintain the judgment of that court, notwithstanding the error in deciding the Federal question. In the latter case the court would not be justified in reversing the judgment of the State court.

But this examination into the points in the record other than the Federal question is not for the purpose of determining whether they were correctly or erroneously decided, but to ascertain if any such have been decided, and their sufficiency to maintain the final judgment, as decided by the State court.

Beyond this we are not at liberty to go, and we can only go this far to prevent the injustice of reversing a judgment which must in the end be reaffirmed, even in this court, if brought here again from the State court after it has corrected its error in the matter of Federal law.

Finally, we hold the following propositions on this subject as flowing from the statute as it now stands:

1. That it is essential to the jurisdiction of this court over the judgment of a State court, that it shall appear that one of the questions mentioned in the act must have been raised, and presented to the State court.

2. That it must have been decided by the State court, or that its decision was necessary to the judgment or decree, rendered in the case.

3. That the decision must have been against the right claimed or asserted by plaintiff in error under the Constitution, treaties, laws, or authority of the United States.

4. These things appearing, this court has jurisdiction and must examine the judgment so far as to enable it to decide whether this claim of right was correctly adjudicated by the State court.

5. If it finds that it was rightly decided, the judgment must be affirmed.

6. If it was erroneously decided against plaintiff in error, then this court must further inquire, whether there is any other matter or issue adjudged by the State court, which is sufficiently broad to maintain the judgment of that court, notwithstanding the error in deciding the issue raised by the Federal question. If this is found to be the case, the judgment must be affirmed without inquiring into the soundness of the decision on such other matter or issue.

7. But if it be found that the issue raised by the question of Federal law is of such controlling character that its correct decision is necessary to any final judgment in the case, or that there has been no decision by the State court of any other matter or issue which is sufficient to maintain the judgment of that court without regard to the Federal question, then this court will reverse the judgment of the State court, and will either render such judgment here as the State court should have rendered, or remand the case to that court, as the circumstances of the case may require.

Applying the principles here laid down to the case now before the court, we are of opinion that this court has jurisdiction, and that the judgment of the Supreme Court of Tennessee must be affirmed. * * *

* * * The complainants, in their bill, and throughout the case, insisted that the effect of the act of 1854 was to vest the title in the mayor or aldermen of the city in trust for them.

It may be very true that it is not easy to see anything in the deed by which the United States received the title from the city, or the act by which they ceded it back, which raises such a trust, but the complainants claimed a right under this act of the United States, which was decided against them by the Supreme Court of Tennessee, and this claim gives jurisdiction of that question to this court.

But we need not consume many words to prove that neither by the deed of the city to the United States, which is an ordinary deed of bargain and sale for a valuable consideration, nor from anything found in the act of 1854, is there any such trust to be inferred. The act, so far from recognizing or implying any such trust, cedes the property to the mayor and aldermen *for the use of the city.* We are, therefore, of opinion that this, the only Federal question in the case, was rightly decided by the Supreme Court of Tennessee.

But conceding this to be true, the plaintiffs in error have argued that the court having jurisdiction of the case must now examine it upon all the questions which affect its merits; and they insist that the conveyance by which the city of Memphis received the title previous to the deed from the city to the government, and the circumstances attending the making of the former deed are such, that when the title reverted to the city, a trust was raised for the benefit of plaintiffs.

After what has been said in the previous part of this opinion, we need discuss this matter no further. The claim of right here set up is one to be determined by the general principles of equity jurisprudence, and is unaffected by anything found in the Constitution, laws, or treaties of the United States. Whether decided well or otherwise by the State court, we have no authority to inquire. According to the principles we have laid down as applicable to this class of cases, the judgment of the Supreme Court of Tennessee must be

Affirmed.

MR. JUSTICE CLIFFORD, with whom concurred MR. JUSTICE SWAYNE, dissenting:

I dissent from so much of the opinion of the court as denies the jurisdiction of this court to determine the whole case, where it appears that the record presents a Federal question and that the Federal question was erroneously decided to the prejudice of the plaintiff in error; as in that state of the record it is, in my judgment, the duty of this court, under the recent act of Congress, to decide the whole merits of the controversy, and to affirm or reverse the judgment of the State court. * * *

MR. JUSTICE BRADLEY, dissenting: I feel obliged to dissent from the conclusion to which a majority of the court has come on the public question in this cause, but shall content myself with stating briefly the grounds of that dissent, without entering into any prolonged argument on the subject.

Meantime, however, it is proper to say that I deem it very doubtful whether the court has any jurisdiction at all over this particular case. The complainants claim the property in question under the terms, and what they regard as the true construction, of the trust-deed of July, 1844 * * *.

* * * Proving that the government did not appropriate the land for a navy yard is a very different thing from setting up a claim to the land under an act of Congress.

I think, therefore, that in this case there was no title or right claimed by the appellants under any statute of, or authority exercised under, the United States; and consequently that there was no decision against any such title; and, therefore, that this court has no jurisdiction.

But supposing, as the majority of the court holds, that it has jurisdiction, I cannot concur in the conclusion that we can only decide the Federal question raised by the record. If we have jurisdiction at all, in my judgment we have jurisdiction of the *case,* and not merely of a *question* in it. * * *

* * * The clause by its presence in the original act meant something, and effected something. It had the effect of restricting the consideration of the court to a certain class of questions as a ground of reversal, which restriction would not have existed without it. The omission of the clause, according to a well-settled rule of construction, must necessarily have the effect of removing the restriction which it effected in the old law.

In my judgment, therefore, if the court had jurisdiction of the case, it was bound to consider not only the Federal question raised by the record, but the whole case. As the court, however, has decided otherwise, it is not proper that I should express any opinion on the merits.

The case having been reargued, as well as argued originally, before the appointment of the CHIEF JUSTICE, he took no part in the judgment.

NOTE ON MURDOCK v. MEMPHIS

① On the constitutional question, the Curtis brief (note 2, *supra*) asserted: "Unless, therefore, some distinction can be made between the power of Congress to confer original and appellate jurisdiction, and neither the Constitution nor the decisions of this court permit this distinction, it is clear that Congress may confer appellate power over all cases to which the judicial power of the United States extends, and is not restricted by the Constitution to particular questions, by reason of which the cases are brought within the judicial power * * *." [1]

Note that where a federal court exercises original jurisdiction, it must necessarily decide the entire case, including state-law questions, in order to come to judgment on the case. When the Supreme Court exercises appellate jurisdiction, however, the highest state court has, by hypothesis, already decided the state law question (or will on remand), and Supreme Court decision of the question is not necessary for complete adjudication. There is, therefore, a fundamental structural difference between original and appellate adjudication that the Curtis syllogism ignores.

(2) Suppose Murdock had been decided the other way, so that the Supreme Court would be free (in a case otherwise within its appellate jurisdiction) to review and reverse a state Supreme Court on an issue of state law. What would be the future authority of such a Supreme Court determination, if the identical issue of state law arose:

(a) in the state courts of that state, in a case that did not involve any issue of federal law and was not otherwise a case within the federal judicial power?

(b) in the state courts of that state, in a case where there was a federal question, so that the case would potentially be subject to the appellate jurisdiction of the Supreme Court?

(c) in the state courts of that state, in a case in which there was no federal question, but was between citizens of different states?

(d) in a federal district court of that state, in a diversity case arising before Erie R.R. Co. v. Tompkins, 304 U.S. 64 (1938) see p. 783, *infra*)?

(e) in a federal district court of that state, in a diversity case arising after Erie?

(f) in a federal district court in a diversity case that also involved an issue of federal law?

(g) in a state court of a second state, in a case where under applicable conflicts principles the rule of decision was to be furnished by the law of the first state, and in which there was not (or, alternatively, there was) also a federal question in the case?

Do these questions shed light on the correctness of Murdock? On its constitutional underpinnings?

(3) The Court's clear recognition in Murdock that it does not have the authority to review and reverse a state court on issues of state law should be contrasted with its conclusion in Swift v. Tyson, p. 771, *infra,* that the federal courts sitting in diversity do not have to follow state court decisions on issues of common law.

What explains the two different developments?

(4) Do Justice Miller's seven propositions (see pp. 528–29) continue to represent the current law and the Court's contemporary practice? Return

---

1. *Cf.* 2 Crosskey, Politics and the Constitution in the History of the United States 711–817 (1953), arguing on a much broader base for the Court's power to decide state law. But see Hart, *The Relations Between State and Federal Law,* 54 Colum.L.Rev. 489, 499–506 (1954).

to this question after considering Section 2 of this Chapter, which explores the implications of Murdock v. Memphis.

(5) In Murdock v. Memphis the state law issue was logically (and functionally) quite independent of any issue of federal law; answering the state law question was not a necessary antecedent to any question of federal law. In Martin, the state law question (when did escheat vest title in the State?) was an essential antecedent to the application of the federal provision giving federal protection to certain titles in existence when the Jay Treaty of 1794 was concluded.

The distinction between these two types of cases is critical to an understanding of this area of the law. Where the state issue is wholly independent, is there any plausible argument that the Supreme Court has power to review the "adequacy" of the state ruling? On the other hand, it has been plain from the decision in Martin itself that if a ruling of state law serves as an antecedent for determining whether or not a federal right has been violated, some review of the "adequacy" of the state court's determination of the state-law question is essential if the federal right is to be protected from evasion and discrimination. See Wechsler, *The Appellate Jurisdiction of the Supreme Court: Reflections on the Law and Logistics of Direct Review*, 34 Wash. & Lee L.Rev. 1043, 1050–56 (1977).

In evaluating revisionist suggestions that the "independent state ground" rule of Murdock be abandoned, consider whether the proposals do not make the fundamental mistake of overlooking or slighting this distinction—assuming that *all* rulings on state law in cases where there is a federal question fall into the Martin category? See, *e.g.*, Matasar & Bruch, *Procedural Common Law, Federal Jurisdictional Policy, and Abandonment of the Adequate and Independent State Grounds Doctrine*, 86 Colum.L.Rev. 1291 (1986). Indeed, consider whether more systematic emphasis on this point would not help illumine many opinions and discussions of the relations between state law (substantive and procedural) and federal law.

Finally, in studying the materials in Section 2 of this Chapter, consider whether the law lends itself to any general theory of or formulation as to what is the proper scope of review when the Supreme Court is reviewing the "adequacy" of a state ground of decision by a state court where federal rights do depend on the answer to a state-law question. Is the scope of review different depending on what federal right or interest is in play? On whether the antecedent state law ground is substantive or procedural?

SECTION 2. THE RELATION BETWEEN STATE AND FEDERAL LAW

SUBSECTION A: SUBSTANTIVE LAW

INTRODUCTORY NOTE: THE INTERSTITIAL CHARACTER OF FEDERAL LAW

Federal law is generally interstitial in its nature. It rarely occupies a legal field completely, totally excluding all participation by the legal systems of the states. This was plainly true in the beginning when the federal legislative product (including the Constitution) was extremely small. It is significantly true today, despite the volume of Congressional enactments, and even within areas where Congress has been very active. Federal legislation, on the whole, has been conceived and drafted on an *ad hoc* basis to accomplish limited objectives. It builds upon legal relationships established by the states, altering or supplanting them only so far as necessary for the special purpose. Congress acts, in short, against the background of the total *corpus juris* of the states in much the way that a state legislature acts against the background of the common law, assumed to govern unless changed by legislation.

That this is so was partially affirmed in § 34 of the First Judiciary Act, now 28 U.S.C. § 1652, but an attentive canvass of the total product of the Congress would establish its surprising generality and force. Indeed, the strength of the conception of the central government as one of delegated, limited authority is most significantly manifested on this mundane plane of working, legislative practice.

The point involved is vital to appreciation of the legal issues posed by the materials in this and later chapters (especially Chapters VI and VII), concerned with the relationship between the law of the United States and of the states. It explains why frequently in litigation federal law bears only partially upon the case: the basis of a right asserted by the plaintiff which is open to defenses grounded in state law, the basis of a defense when a state-created right has been advanced, the foundation of a replication to a state defense or only of the rejoinder to a replication that would otherwise be good. It explains why federal law often embodies concepts that derive their content, or some portion of their content, from the states. It makes it less anomalous, at least, that substantive rights may be defined by Congress but the remedies for their enforcement left undefined or relegated wholly to the states; or that *per contra* national law may do no more than formulate remedies for vindicating rights that have their source and definition in state law.

See generally, Hart, *The Relations Between State and Federal Law*, 54 Colum.L.Rev. 489 (1954). For analysis of relevant institutional factors, see Wechsler, *The Political Safeguards of Federalism: The Role of the States in the Composition and Selection of the National Government*, 54 Colum.L. Rev. 543 (1954). And consider, again, the point made in paragraph (5) of the immediately preceding note.

The diversity of the relationships between federal and state law is shown most plainly in cases that reach the Supreme Court from the authorized expositors of state law, the state courts.

FOX FILM CORP. v. MULLER

296 U.S. 207, 56 S.Ct. 183, 80 L.Ed. 158 (1935).
Certiorari to the Supreme Court of Minnesota.

MR. JUSTICE SUTHERLAND delivered the opinion of the Court.

This is an action brought in a Minnesota state court of first instance by the Film Corporation against Muller, to recover damages for an alleged breach of two contracts by which Muller was licensed to exhibit certain moving picture films belonging to the corporation. Muller answered, setting up the invalidity of the contracts under the Sherman Anti–Trust Act (15 U.S.C.A. §§ 1–7, 15 note). It was and is agreed that these contracts are substantially the same as the one involved in United States v. Paramount Famous Lasky Corporation et al., (D.C.) 34 F.2d 984, affirmed 282 U.S. 30; that petitioner was one of the defendants in that action; and that the "arbitration clause," paragraph 18 of each of the contracts sued upon, is the same as that held in that case to be invalid. In view of the disposition which we are to make of this writ, it is not necessary to set forth the terms of the arbitration clause or the other provisions of the contract.

The court of first instance held that each contract sued upon violated the Sherman Anti–Trust Act, and dismissed the action. In a supplemental opinion, that court put its decision upon the grounds, first, that the arbitration plan is so connected with the remainder of the contract that the entire contract is tainted; and, second, that the contract violates the Sherman Anti–Trust law. The state Supreme Court affirmed. 192 Minn. 212, 255 N.W. 845. We granted certiorari, 293 U.S. 550; but, when the case was called for argument, it appeared that no final judgment had been entered, and the writ was dismissed as improvidently granted. 294 U.S. 696. The case was then remanded to the state Supreme Court; and, the judgment having been made final, and again affirmed by the state Supreme Court on the authority of its previous opinion, (Minn.) 260 N.W. 320, we allowed the present writ. 295 U.S. 730.

In its opinion, the state Supreme Court, after a statement of the case, said: "The question presented on this appeal is whether the arbitration clause is severable from the contract, leaving the remainder of the contract enforceable or not severable, permeating and tainting the whole contract with illegality and making it void." That court then proceeded to refer to and discuss a number of decisions of state and federal courts, some of which took the view that the arbitration clause was severable, and others that it was not severable, from the remainder of the contract. After reviewing the opinion and decree of the federal District Court in the Paramount Case, the lower court reached the conclusion that the holding of the federal court was that the entire contract was illegal; and upon that view and upon what it conceived to be the weight of authority, held the arbitration plan was inseparable from the other provisions of the contract. Whether this conclusion was right or wrong we need not determine. It is enough that it is, at least, not without fair support.

Respondent contends that the question of severability was alone decided and that no federal question was determined by the lower court. This contention petitioner challenges, and asserts that a federal question was involved and decided. We do not attempt to settle the dispute; but, assuming for present purposes only that petitioner's view is the correct one, the case is controlled by the settled rule that where the judgment of a state court rests upon two grounds, one of which is federal and the other nonfederal in character, our jurisdiction fails if the nonfederal ground is independent of the federal ground and adequate to support the judgment. This rule had become firmly fixed at least as early as Klinger v. State of Missouri, 13 Wall. 257, 263, and has been reiterated in a long line of cases since that time. It is enough to cite, in addition to the Klinger Case, the following: Enterprise Irr. Dist. v. Farmers' Mut. Canal Co., 243 U.S. 157, 163–165; Petrie v. Nampa etc., Irr. Dist., 248 U.S. 154, 157; McCoy v. Shaw, 277 U.S. 302; Eustis v. Bolles, 150 U.S. 361.

Whether the provisions of a contract are nonseverable, so that if one be held invalid the others must fall with it, is clearly a question of general and not of federal law. The invalidity of the arbitration clause which the present contracts embody is conceded. It was held invalid by the federal District Court in the Paramount Case, and its judgment was affirmed here. The question, therefore, was foreclosed; and was not the subject of controversy in the state courts. In that situation, the primary question to be determined by the court below was whether the concededly invalid clause was separable from the other provisions of the contract. The ruling of the state Supreme Court that it was not, is sufficient to conclude the case without regard to the determination, if, in fact, any was made, in respect of the federal question. It follows that the nonfederal ground is adequate to sustain the judgment.

The rule announced in Enterprise Irr. Dist. v. Farmers' Mut. Canal Co., supra, and other cases, to the effect that our jurisdiction attaches where the nonfederal ground is so interwoven with the other as not to be an independent matter, does not apply. The construction put upon the contracts did not constitute a preliminary step which simply had the effect of bringing forward for determination the federal question, but was a decision which automatically took the federal question out of the case if otherwise it would be there. The nonfederal question in respect of the construction of the contracts and the federal question in respect of their validity under the Anti–Trust Act were clearly independent of one another. See Allen v. Southern Pacific Railroad Co., 173 U.S. 479, 489–492. The case, in effect, was disposed of before the federal question said to be involved was reached. Chouteau v. Gibson, 111 U.S. 200; Chapman v. Goodnow, 123 U.S. 540, 548. A decision of that question then became unnecessary; and whether it was decided or not, our want of jurisdiction is clear.

Writ dismissed for want of jurisdiction.

The CHIEF JUSTICE took no part in the consideration or decision of this case.

PRELIMINARY NOTE ON THE INDEPENDENT AND
ADEQUATE STATE GROUND

(1) The "settled rule" referred to in Fox Film—that the Court's jurisdiction to review a federal question fails if the state court's judgment also rested on a nonfederal ground that is itself "independent of the federal ground and adequate to support the judgment"—would seem to follow necessarily from Murdock's holding that the Court has no power to review nonfederal grounds of decision. Ruling on a federal question in such a case by hypothesis cannot affect the judgment.

In the earlier cases decided after Murdock, the rule was apparently regarded as resting on prudential principles (why should the Court do useless work?); but this was soon replaced by recognition that it rests on principles that are strictly jurisdictional. See, e.g., Enterprise Irrigation District v. Farmers' Mutual Canal Co., 243 U.S. 157, 164 (1917) (where a nonfederal ground is sufficient to sustain the judgment, "we have no power to disturb it"); Herb v. Pitcairn, 324 U.S. 117, 126 (1945) ("our power is to correct wrong judgments, not to revise opinions. * * * [I]f the same judgment would be rendered by the state court after we corrected its view of federal laws, our review could amount to nothing more than an advisory opinion"); see also Harlan, J., dissenting in Fay v. Noia, 372 U.S. 391, 463–67 (1963) (pp. 1493, 1544, infra). It follows from this, in turn, that where a state-court judgment is found to rest on an independent and adequate state-law ground, the proper mandate is to dismiss for lack of jurisdiction (rather than to affirm); and this has been the Court's practice since Eustis v. Bolles, 150 U.S. 361 (1893).

(2) The rule just stated has been, in principle, quite uncontroversial. But its application and administration have engendered impressive difficulties. See, generally, Hill, The Inadequate State Ground, 65 Colum.L.Rev. 943 (1965); Wechsler, The Appellate Jurisdiction of the Supreme Court: Reflections on the Law and Logistics of Direct Review, 4 Wash. & Lee L.Rev. 1043 (1977); Note, The Untenable Nonfederal Ground in the Supreme Court, 74 Harv.L.Rev. 1375 (1961).

Suppose, for example, that a state tax statute is challenged, in a state-court action for refund, on the ground that it violates both the federal and state constitutions. If the state supreme court holds the tax invalid solely under the state constitution, refusing to reach the federal question, there is clearly no jurisdiction to review. Similarly, if the state supreme court holds that the tax is invalid under the federal constitution, and is also, quite independently, invalid under the state constitution, there is no jurisdiction to review. (Of course if the state court holds the tax statute valid under both constitutions, the state ground cannot independently support the judgment, and the federal-law ruling is subject to review.)

But suppose the state court holds that the tax statute is invalid under the federal constitution and fails to consider the state-law issue of validity? It is the settled rule that the Supreme Court has jurisdiction in such a case to review and decide the federal issue: its jurisdiction depends on the state court's actual grounds of decision rather than on possible grounds. For instances of review where the state court explicity relied on federal grounds (although possible state-law grounds also existed), see Grayson v. Harris, 267 U.S. 352, 358 (1925); Indiana ex rel. Anderson v. Brand, p. 569, *infra;* Poafpybitty v. Skelly Oil Co., 390 U.S. 365, 375–76 (1968); Zacchini v. Scripps–Howard Broadcasting Co., 433 U.S. 562, 565–68 (1977) ("if the state court erred in its understanding [of the federal law] * * * we should so declare, leaving the state court free to decide the privilege issue solely as a matter of Ohio law"); Regents of the Univ. of California v. Bakke, 438 U.S. 265, 279–80 (1978); Ferri v. Ackerman, 444 U.S. 193 (1979); Orr v. Orr, 440 U.S. 268, 274–77 (1979); Caldwell v. Mississippi, 472 U.S. 320 (1985).[1]

In such a case, if the Supreme Court reverses the state court with respect to the federal question, the proper disposition is to remand, to give the state court an opportunity to pass on the undetermined state-law issue. See, *e.g.,* California v. Ramos, 463 U.S. 992, 997–98 n. 7 (1983); see also p. 518, *supra.* The state court is, of course, free to reinstate its prior judgment on that state-law ground. See, *e.g.,* Washington v. Chrisman, 455 U.S. 1 (1982), *reinstated on remand* 100 Wash.2d 814, 676 P.2d 419 (1984) (original decision on federal ground; decision on remand based explicitly on state constitution); South Dakota v. Neville, 459 U.S. 553 (1983), *reinstated on remand* 346 N.W.2d 425 (S.D.1984).

Is the freedom of the state court to reinstate its judgment on the basis of the unconsidered state ground problematic? Has the Supreme Court's opinion become, *ex post,* advisory? In Paschall v. Christie–Stewart, Inc., note 1, below, the Court decided not to review a state court decision resting squarely on the Due Process Clause, and remanded instead, on the ground that the running of the state statute of limitations might have provided a state ground for decision; it said that "[i]f that should prove to be the case, any decision by this Court would be advisory and beyond our jurisdiction" (pp. 101–02). Do you agree? Is an opinion always advisory if, at the end of the day, it turns out that it has not had a decisive effect on the final judgment? Even though, at the time it is rendered, it is decisive in eliminating the erroneous ground for decision that the state court in fact made decisive and that will stand unless corrected? Would it be possible to administer a rule against advisory opinions that depended on advance knowledge of the final outcome of the case?

When a state court is faced with alternative grounds of decision—one federal, one state—does it have a federal obligation—at least in a case involving the federal Constitution—to decide the state-law issue first? Where would such an obligation come from? May the Supreme Court impose it? May Congress? See Wechsler, *supra,* at 1056. How would such an obligation be enforced? (Presumably, the Court would vacate the state court judgment and remand, with directions to decide the state law ground.[2] But note that the Court cannot, in such a case, itself enter judgment as a way of enforcing the mandate.)

1. Occasionally the Supreme Court has vacated a state court judgment based on federal grounds and remanded for consideration of possible state grounds whose decision might obviate the necessity for resolution of a federal constitutional question. See Kirkpatrick v. Christian Homes of Abilene, Inc., 460 U.S. 1074 (1983); Paschall v. Christie–Stewart, Inc., 414 U.S. 100 (1973); Musser v. Utah, 333 U.S. 95 (1948).

What would justify the Court's use of this technique in some cases but not others?

2. *Cf.* Massachusetts v. Upton, 466 U.S. 727 (1984), where Justice Stevens concurred specially in a judgment reversing a state court on the merits of a Fourth Amendment question, emphasizing that the Massachusetts Supreme Judicial Court had committed "an error of a more fundamental character than the one this Court corrects today. It rested its decision on the Fourth Amendment to the United States Constitution without telling us whether the warrant was valid as a matter of Massachusetts law" (p. 735).

In the event, the accepted rule—that the Court is free to pass on federal questions actually decided (and made decisive) by the state court even where there are other undetermined, and possibly dispositive, state law grounds in the case—has not given rise to severe problems of administration.[3] For techniques available to ensure that the state courts do not on remand evade the obligation of the mandate, see p. 518, *supra*.

(3) The remaining, more formidable, difficulties created by the adequate and independent state ground rule are explored in the remaining materials in this section. The difficulties are of three different sorts, and are compounded if these are intermixed:

(a) Murdock v. Memphis, and the jurisdictional rule it reaffirmed, evidently makes the Court's jurisdiction turn on characterization and choice of law: on whether a given issue in the case is properly to be regarded as one of federal or state law. The rule thus connects this subject to important choices about the respective spheres of state and federal lawmaking power. (Thus, in Fox Film itself, the jurisdictional rule operated on the antecedent characterization of the issue of separability as an issue purely of state law. Was this question as obvious as the Court seemed to think?[4])

(b) Once questions of choice of law are untangled, and the various issues properly characterized as issues of federal or state law, the further question is whether the logical relationship between the two is such that the state law ground is "independent" of the federal for purposes of the Court's appellate jurisdiction. (Recall, in this connection, the fundamental distinction between independent and antecedent state law rulings, outlined in paragraph (5) of the *Note on Murdock v. Memphis*, p. 530, *supra*.) Thus, in the tax example in Paragraph (2), *supra*, suppose that the state court holds that the state tax statute violates the state constitution, but in so doing interprets its constitution as identical to the parallel federal constitutional limit? Is the state court's holding reviewable?

(c) Superimposed on all of these difficulties is the possibility of ambiguity in the state grounds of decision. The Court's jurisdictional rule turns on what the state court in fact did (or intended to do): did its judgment "rest" on an independent state-law ground? This is not always easy to unravel. State court opinions are frequently ambiguous (when they exist at all). State practice on whether it is the opinion or the syllabus that is

---

3. For analysis from the point of view of state courts' responsibilities, see Linde, *First Things First: Rediscovering the States' Bills of Rights,* 9 U.Balt.L.Rev. 379 (1980); Roberts, *The Adequate and Independent State Ground: Some Practical Considerations,* 19 Land & Water L.Rev. 647 (1984). For an instance and discussion of how failure to address state issues first may cause problems for the administration of the state courts, see State v. Kennedy, 295 Or. 260, 666 P.2d 1316, 1319 (1983).

4. Even if the ruling of *inseparability* is correctly characterized as a ruling of state law, would a contrary ruling—that the rest of the contract was *severable* from the federally-invalid arbitration clause—be immune from review? Note that, on this

hypothesis, the federal validity of the rest of the contract would not be independent from the severability issue and would in any event be reviewable. But suppose the Supreme Court agrees with a state court holding that the rest of the contract, independently viewed, is valid under the Sherman Act. Surely it would not be foreclosed from determining whether, given the conceded invalidity of the arbitration clause, enforcing the rest of the contract violates the remedial policies of the Sherman Act. The point shows that this is a field where principles of reversibility do not always hold: a holding one way may be a "pure" state law holding, but if the holding is the other way, federal law problems immediately enter the scene.

authoritative varies. How should the Court deal with these uncertainties, which depend on its understanding of the meanings and intentions of the state court?

It is this last problem that is the chief focus of the next case and the following Note.

MICHIGAN v. LONG

463 U.S. 1032, 103 S.Ct. 3469, 77 L.Ed.2d 1201 (1983).
Certiorari to the Supreme Court of Michigan.

JUSTICE O'CONNOR delivered the opinion of the Court.

In Terry v. Ohio, 392 U.S. 1 (1968), we upheld the validity of a protective search for weapons in the absence of probable cause to arrest because it is unreasonable to deny a police officer the right "to neutralize the threat of physical harm," *id.*, at 24, when he possesses an articulable suspicion that an individual is armed and dangerous. We did not, however, expressly address whether such a protective search for weapons could extend to an area beyond the person in the absence of probable cause to arrest. In the present case, respondent David Long was convicted for possession of marihuana found by police in the passenger compartment and trunk of the automobile that he was driving. The police searched the passenger compartment because they had reason to believe that the vehicle contained weapons potentially dangerous to the officers. We hold that the protective search of the passenger compartment was reasonable under the principles articulated in Terry and other decisions of this Court. We also examine Long's argument that the decision below rests upon an adequate and independent state ground, and we decide in favor of our jurisdiction.

I

[The opinion here provides a detailed statement of the facts.]

The Barry County Circuit Court denied Long's motion to suppress the marihuana taken from both the interior of the car and its trunk. He was subsequently convicted of possession of marihuana. The Michigan Court of Appeals affirmed Long's conviction, holding that the search of the passenger compartment was valid as a protective search under Terry, and that the search of the trunk was valid as an inventory search under South Dakota v. Opperman, 428 U.S. 364 (1976). See 94 Mich.App. 338, 288 N.W.2d 629 (1979). The Michigan Supreme Court reversed. The court held that "the sole justification of the Terry search, protection of the police officers and others nearby, cannot justify the search in this case." 413 Mich., at 472, 320 N.W.2d, at 869. The marihuana found in Long's trunk was considered by the court below to be the "fruit" of the illegal search of the interior, and was also suppressed.

We granted certiorari in this case to consider the important question of the authority of a police officer to protect himself by conducting a Terry-type search of the passenger compartment of a motor vehicle during tʰ' lawful investigatory stop of the occupant of the vehicle. 459 U.S. (1982).

II

Before reaching the merits, we must consider Long's argument that we are without jurisdiction to decide this case because the decision below rests on an adequate and independent state ground. The court below referred twice to the State Constitution in its opinion, but otherwise relied exclusively on federal law.[3] Long argues that the Michigan courts have provided greater protection from searches and seizures under the State Constitution than is afforded under the Fourth Amendment, and the references to the State Constitution therefore establish an adequate and independent ground for the decision below.

It is, of course, "incumbent upon this Court * * * to ascertain for itself * * * whether the asserted non-federal ground independently and adequately supports the judgment." Abie State Bank v. Bryan, 282 U.S. 765, 773 (1931). Although we have announced a number of principles in order to help us determine whether various forms of references to state law constitute adequate and independent state grounds,[4] we openly admit that we have thus far not developed a satisfying and consistent approach for resolving this vexing issue. In some instances, we have taken the strict view that if the ground of decision was at all unclear, we would dismiss the case. See, e.g., Lynch v. New York ex rel. Pierson, 293 U.S. 52 (1934). In other instances, we have vacated, see, e.g., Minnesota v. National Tea Co., 309 U.S. 551 (1940), or continued a case, see, e.g., Herb v. Pitcairn, 324 U.S. 117 (1945), in order to obtain clarification about the nature of a state court decision. See also California v. Krivda, 409 U.S. 33 (1972). In more recent cases, we have ourselves examined state law to determine whether state courts have used federal law to guide their application of state law or to provide the actual basis for the decision that was reached. See Texas v. Brown, 460 U.S. 730, 732–733, n. 1 (1983) (plurality opinion). Cf. South Dakota v. Neville, 459 U.S. 553, 569 (1983) (Stevens, J., dissenting). In Oregon v. Kennedy, 456 U.S. 667, 670–671 (1982), we rejected an invitation to remand to the state court for clarification even when the decision rested in part on a case from the state court, because we determined that the state case itself rested upon federal grounds. We added that "[e]ven if the case

3. On the first occasion, the court merely cited in a footnote both the State and Federal Constitutions. On the second occasion, at the conclusion of the opinion, the court stated: "We hold, therefore, that the deputies' search of the vehicle was proscribed by the Fourth Amendment to the United States Constitution and art. 1, § 11 of the Michigan Constitution."

4. For example, we have long recognized that "where the judgment of a state court rests upon two grounds, one of which is federal and the other non-federal in character, our jurisdiction fails if the non-federal ground is independent of the federal ground and adequate to support the judgment." Fox Film Corp. v. Muller, 296 U.S. 207, 210 (1935). We may review a state case decided on a federal ground even if it is clear that there was an available state ground for decision on which the state court could properly have relied.

Beecher v. Alabama, 389 U.S. 35, 37, n. 3 (1967). Also, if, in our view, the state court "'felt compelled by what it understood to be federal constitutional considerations to construe * * * its own law in the manner it did,'" then we will not treat a normally adequate state ground as independent, and there will be no question about our jurisdiction. Delaware v. Prouse, 440 U.S. 648, 653 (1979) (quoting Zacchini v. Scripps–Howard Broadcasting Co., 433 U.S. 562, 568 (1977)). See also South Dakota v. Neville, 459 U.S. 553, 556–557, n. 3 (1983). Finally, "where the non-federal ground is so interwoven with the [federal ground] as not to be an independent matter, or is not of sufficient breadth to sustain the judgment without any decision of the other, our jurisdiction is plain." Enterprise Irrigation District v. Farmers Mutual Canal Co., 243 U.S. 157, 164 (1917).

admitted of more doubt as to whether federal and state grounds for decision were intermixed, the fact that the state court relied to the extent it did on federal grounds requires us to reach the merits." *Id.,* at 671.

This ad hoc method of dealing with cases that involve possible adequate and independent state grounds is antithetical to the doctrinal consistency that is required when sensitive issues of federal-state relations are involved. Moreover, none of the various methods of disposition that we have employed thus far recommends itself as the preferred method that we should apply to the exclusion of others, and we therefore determine that it is appropriate to reexamine our treatment of this jurisdictional issue in order to achieve the consistency that is necessary.

The process of examining state law is unsatisfactory because it requires us to interpret state laws with which we are generally unfamiliar, and which often, as in this case, have not been discussed at length by the parties. Vacation and continuance for clarification have also been unsatisfactory both because of the delay and decrease in efficiency of judicial administration, see Dixon v. Duffy, 344 U.S. 143 (1952),[5] and, more important, because these methods of disposition place significant burdens on state courts to demonstrate the presence or absence of our jurisdiction. See Philadelphia Newspapers, Inc. v. Jerome, 434 U.S. 241, 244 (1978) (Rehnquist, J., dissenting); Department of Motor Vehicles v. Rios, 410 U.S. 425, 427 (1973) (Douglas, J., dissenting). Finally, outright dismissal of cases is clearly not a panacea because it cannot be doubted that there is an important need for uniformity in federal law, and that this need goes unsatisfied when we fail to review an opinion that rests primarily upon federal grounds and where the *independence* of an alleged state ground is not apparent from the four corners of the opinion. We have long recognized that dismissal is inappropriate "where there is strong indication * * * that the federal constitution as judicially construed controlled the decision below." National Tea Co., *supra,* at 556.

Respect for the independence of state courts, as well as avoidance of rendering advisory opinions, have been the cornerstones of this Court's refusal to decide cases where there is an adequate and independent state ground. It is precisely because of this respect for state courts, and this desire to avoid advisory opinions, that we do not wish to continue to decide issues of state law that go beyond the opinion that we review, or to require state courts to reconsider cases to clarify the grounds of their decisions. Accordingly, when, as in this case, a state court decision fairly appears to rest primarily on federal law, or to be interwoven with the federal law, and when the adequacy and independence of any possible state law ground is not clear from the face of the opinion, we will accept as the most reasonable explanation that the state court decided the case the way it did because it believed that federal law required it to do so. If a state court chooses merely to rely on federal precedents as it would on the precedents of all other jurisdictions, then it need only make clear by a plain statement in its judgment or opinion that the federal cases are being used only for the

---

5. Indeed, Dixon v. Duffy is also illustrative of another difficulty involved in our requiring state courts to reconsider their decisions for purposes of clarification. In Dixon, we continued the case on two occasions in order to obtain clarification, but none was forthcoming: "[T]he California court advised petitioner's counsel informally that it doubted its jurisdiction to render such a determination." 344 U.S., at 145. We then vacated the judgment of the state court, and remanded.

purpose of guidance, and do not themselves compel the result that the court has reached. In this way, both justice and judicial administration will be greatly improved. If the state court decision indicates clearly and expressly that it is alternatively based on bona fide separate, adequate, and independent grounds, we, of course, will not undertake to review the decision.

This approach obviates in most instances the need to examine state law in order to decide the nature of the state court decision, and will at the same time avoid the danger of our rendering advisory opinions.[6] It also avoids the unsatisfactory and intrusive practice of requiring state courts to clarify their decisions to the satisfaction of this Court. We believe that such an approach will provide state judges with a clearer opportunity to develop state jurisprudence unimpeded by federal interference, and yet will preserve the integrity of federal law. "It is fundamental that state courts be left free and unfettered by us in interpreting their state constitutions. But it is equally important that ambiguous or obscure adjudications by state courts do not stand as barriers to a determination by this Court of the validity under the federal constitution of state action." National Tea Co., *supra*, at 557.

The principle that we will not review judgments of state courts that rest on adequate and independent state grounds is based, in part, on "the limitations of our own jurisdiction." Herb v. Pitcairn, 324 U.S. 117, 125 (1945).[7] The jurisdictional concern is that we not "render an advisory opinion, and if the same judgment would be rendered by the state court after we corrected its views of federal laws, our review could amount to nothing more than an advisory opinion." *Id.*, at 126. Our requirement of a "plain statement" that a decision rests upon adequate and independent state grounds does not in any way authorize the rendering of advisory opinions. Rather, in determining, as we must, whether we have jurisdiction to review a case that is alleged to rest on adequate and independent state grounds, see Abie State Bank v. Bryan, 282 U.S., at 773, we merely assume that there are no such grounds when it is not clear from the opinion itself that the state court relied upon an adequate and independent state ground and when it fairly appears that the state court rested its decision primarily on federal law.[8]

---

6. There may be certain circumstances in which clarification is necessary or desirable, and we will not be foreclosed from taking the appropriate action.

7. In Herb v. Pitcairn, 324 U.S., at 128, the Court also wrote that it was desirable that state courts "be asked rather than told what they have intended." It is clear that we have already departed from that view in those cases in which we have examined state law to determine whether a particular result was guided or compelled by federal law. Our decision today departs further from Herb insofar as we disfavor further requests to state courts for clarification, and we require a clear and express statement that a decision rests on adequate and independent state grounds. However, the "plain statement" rule protects the integrity of state courts for the reasons discussed above. The preference for clarifica-

tion expressed in Herb has failed to be a completely satisfactory means of protecting the state and federal interests that are involved.

8. It is not unusual for us to employ certain presumptions in deciding jurisdictional issues. For instance, although the petitioner bears the burden of establishing our jurisdiction, Durley v. Mayo, 351 U.S. 277, 285 (1956), we have held that the party who alleges that a controversy before us has become moot has the "heavy burden" of establishing that we lack jurisdiction. County of Los Angeles v. Davis, 440 U.S. 625, 631 (1979). That is, we presume in those circumstances that we have jurisdiction until some party establishes that we do not for reasons of mootness.

We also note that the rule that we announce today was foreshadowed by our

Our review of the decision below under this framework leaves us unconvinced that it rests upon an independent state ground. Apart from its two citations to the State Constitution, the court below relied *exclusively* on its understanding of Terry and other federal cases. Not a single state case was cited to support the state court's holding that the search of the passenger compartment was unconstitutional. Indeed, the court declared that the search in this case was unconstitutional because "[t]he Court of Appeals erroneously applied the principles of Terry v. Ohio * * * to the search of the interior of the vehicle in this case." The references to the state constitution in no way indicate that the decision below rested on grounds in any way *independent* from the state court's interpretation of federal law. Even if we accept that the Michigan constitution has been interpreted to provide independent protection for certain rights also secured under the Fourth Amendment, it fairly appears in this case that the Michigan Supreme Court rested its decision primarily on federal law.

Rather than dismissing the case, or requiring that the state court reconsider its decision on our behalf solely because of a mere possibility that an adequate and independent ground supports the judgment, we find that we have jurisdiction in the absence of a plain statement that the decision below rested on an adequate and independent state ground. It appears to us that the state court "felt compelled by what it understood to be federal constitutional considerations to construe * * * its own law in the manner it did." Zacchini v. Scripps–Howard Broadcasting Co., 433 U.S. 562, 568 (1977).[10]

opinions in Delaware v. Prouse, 440 U.S. 648 (1979), and Zacchini v. Scripps–Howard Broadcasting Co., 433 U.S. 562 (1977). In these cases, the state courts relied on both state and federal law. We determined that we had jurisdiction to decide the cases because our reading of the opinions led us to conclude that each court "felt compelled by what it understood to be federal constitutional considerations to construe and apply its own law in the manner it did." Zacchini, *supra*, at 568; Delaware, *supra*, at 653. In Delaware, we referred to prior state decisions that confirmed our understanding of the opinion in that case, but our primary focus was on the face of the opinion. In Zacchini, we relied entirely on the syllabus and opinion of the state court.

In dissent, Justice Stevens proposes the novel view that this Court should never review a state court decision unless the Court wishes to vindicate a federal right that has been endangered. The rationale of the dissent is not restricted to cases where the decision is arguably supported by adequate and independent state grounds. Rather, Justice Stevens appears to believe that even if the decision below rests exclusively on federal grounds, this Court should not review the decision as long as there is no federal right that is endangered.

The state courts handle the vast bulk of all criminal litigation in this country. In 1982, more than 12 million criminal actions (excluding juvenile and traffic charges) were filed in the 50 state court systems and the District of Columbia. See 7 State Court Journal, No. 1, p. 18 (1983). By comparison, approximately 32,700 criminal suits were filed in federal courts during that same year. See Annual Report of the Director of the Administrative Office of the United States Courts 6 (1982). The state courts are required to apply federal constitutional standards, and they necessarily create a considerable body of "federal law" in the process. It is not surprising that this Court has become more interested in the application and development of federal law by state courts in the light of the recent significant expansion of federally created standards that we have imposed on the States. * * *

10. There is nothing unfair about requiring a plain statement of an independent state ground in this case. Even if we were to rest our decision on an evaluation of the state law relevant to Long's claim, as we have sometimes done in the past, our understanding of Michigan law would also result in our finding that we have jurisdiction to decide this case. Under state search and seizure law, a "higher standard" is imposed under art. 1, § 11 of the 1963 Michigan Constitution. See People v. Secrest, 413 Mich. 521, 525, 321 N.W.2d 368, 369 (1982). If, however, the item seized is, *inter alia*, a "narcotic drug * * * seized by a peace officer outside

III

[The Court here ruled that the police action in the case was valid under Terry.]

*   *   *

V

The judgment of the Michigan Supreme Court is reversed, and the case is remanded for further proceedings not inconsistent with this opinion.

It is so ordered.

JUSTICE BLACKMUN, concurring in part and concurring in the judgment.

I join Parts I, III, IV, and V of the Court's opinion. While I am satisfied that the Court has jurisdiction in this particular case, I do not join the Court, in Part II of its opinion, in fashioning a new presumption of jurisdiction over cases coming here from state courts. Although I agree with the Court that uniformity in federal criminal law is desirable, I see little efficiency and an increased danger of advisory opinions in the Court's new approach.

[JUSTICE BRENNAN, whom JUSTICE MARSHALL joined, agreed that the Court had jurisdiction, but dissented on the merits.]

*   *   *

JUSTICE STEVENS, dissenting.

The jurisprudential questions presented in this case are far more important than the question whether the Michigan police officer's search of respondent's car violated the Fourth Amendment. The case raises profoundly significant questions concerning the relationship between two sovereigns—the State of Michigan and the United States of America.

The Supreme Court of the State of Michigan expressly held "that the deputies' search of the vehicle was proscribed by the Fourth Amendment to the United States Constitution and *art 1, § 11 of the Michigan Constitution.*" (Emphasis added). The state law ground is clearly adequate to support the judgment, but the question whether it is independent of the Michigan Supreme Court's understanding of federal law is more difficult. Four possible ways of resolving that question present themselves: (1) asking the Michigan Supreme Court directly, (2) attempting to infer from all possible sources of state law what the Michigan Supreme Court meant, (3) presuming that adequate state grounds are independent unless it clearly appears otherwise, or (4) presuming that adequate state grounds are *not* independent unless it clearly appears otherwise. This Court has, on different occasions, employed each of the first three approaches; never until today has it even hinted at the fourth. In order to "achieve the consistency that is necessary," the Court today undertakes a reexamination of all the possibilities. It rejects the first approach as inefficient and unduly burdensome for state courts, and rejects the second approach as an inappropriate expenditure of our resources. Although I find both of those decisions defensible in themselves, I cannot accept the Court's decision to

the curtilage of any dwelling house in this state," art. 1, § 11 of the 1963 Michigan Constitution, then the seizure is governed by a standard identical to that imposed by the Fourth Amendment. See People v. Moore, 391 Mich. 426, 435, 216 N.W.2d 770, 775 (1974). *   *   *

choose the fourth approach over the third—to presume that adequate state grounds are intended to be dependent on federal law unless the record plainly shows otherwise. I must therefore dissent.

If we reject the intermediate approaches, we are left with a choice between two presumptions: one in favor of our taking jurisdiction, and one against it. Historically, the latter presumption has always prevailed. See, *e.g.*, Durley v. Mayo, 351 U.S. 277, 285 (1956); Stembridge v. Georgia, 343 U.S. 541, 547 (1952); Lynch v. New York, 293 U.S. 52 (1934). The rule, as succinctly stated in Lynch, was as follows:

> "Where the judgment of the state court rests on two grounds, one involving a federal question and the other not, or if it does not appear upon which of two grounds the judgment was based, and the ground independent of a federal question is sufficient in itself to sustain it, this Court will not take jurisdiction. Allen v. Arguimbau, 198 U.S. 149, 154, 155; Johnson v. Risk, [137 U.S. 300, 306, 307]; Wood Mowing & Reaping Machine Co. v. Skinner, [139 U.S. 293, 295, 297]; Consolidated Turnpike Co. v. Norfolk & Ocean View Ry. Co., 228 U.S. 596, 599; Cuyahoga River Power Co. v. Northern Realty Co., 244 U.S. 300, 302, 304." *Id.*, at 54–55.

The Court today points out that in several cases we have weakened the traditional presumption by using the other two intermediate approaches identified above. Since those two approaches are now to be rejected, however, I would think that *stare decisis* would call for a return to historical principle. Instead, the Court seems to conclude that because some precedents are to be rejected, we must overrule them all.[1]

Even if I agreed with the Court that we are free to consider as a fresh proposition whether we may take presumptive jurisdiction over the decisions of sovereign States, I could not agree that an expansive attitude makes good sense. It appears to be common ground that any rule we adopt should show "respect for state courts, and [a] desire to avoid advisory opinions." And I am confident that all Members of this Court agree that there is a vital interest in the sound management of scarce federal judicial resources. All of those policies counsel against the exercise of federal jurisdiction. They are fortified by my belief that a policy of judicial restraint—one that allows other decisional bodies to have the last word in legal interpretation until it is truly necessary for this Court to intervene— enables this Court to make its most effective contribution to our federal system of government.

The nature of the case before us hardly compels a departure from tradition. These are not cases in which an American citizen has been deprived of a right secured by the United States Constitution or a federal statute. Rather, they are cases in which a state court has upheld a citizen's assertion of a right, finding the citizen to be protected under both federal and state law. The attorney for the complaining party is an officer of the State itself, who asks us to rule that the state court interpreted federal rights too broadly and "overprotected" the citizen.

Such cases should not be of inherent concern to this Court. The reason may be illuminated by assuming that the events underlying this case had arisen in another country, perhaps the Republic of Finland. If the Finnish

---

1. A sampling of the cases may be found in the footnotes to my dissenting opinion in South Dakota v. Neville, 459 U.S. 553, 566 (1983). • • •

police had arrested a Finnish citizen for possession of marihuana, and the Finnish courts had turned him loose, no American would have standing to object. If instead they had arrested an American citizen and acquitted him, we might have been concerned about the arrest but we surely could not have complained about the acquittal, even if the Finnish court had based its decision on its understanding of the United States Constitution. That would be true even if we had a treaty with Finland requiring it to respect the rights of American citizens under the United States Constitution. We would only be motivated to intervene if an American citizen were unfairly arrested, tried, and convicted by the foreign tribunal.

In this case the State of Michigan has arrested one of its citizens and the Michigan Supreme Court has decided to turn him loose. The respondent is a United States citizen as well as a Michigan citizen, but since there is no claim that he has been mistreated by the State of Michigan, the final outcome of the state processes offended no federal interest whatever. Michigan simply provided greater protection to one of its citizens than some other State might provide or, indeed, than this Court might require throughout the country.

I believe that in reviewing the decisions of state courts, the primary role of this Court is to make sure that persons who seek to *vindicate* federal rights have been fairly heard. That belief resonates with statements in many of our prior cases. In Abie State Bank v. Bryan, 282 U.S. 765 (1931), the Supreme Court of Nebraska had rejected a federal constitutional claim, relying in part on the state law doctrine of laches. Writing for the Court in response to the Nebraska Governor's argument that the Court should not accept jurisdiction because laches provided an independent ground for decision, Chief Justice Hughes concluded that this Court must ascertain for itself whether the asserted nonfederal ground independently and adequately supported the judgment "in order that constitutional guaranties may appropriately be enforced." He relied on our earlier opinion in Union Pacific R. Co. v. Public Service Comm'n of Missouri, 248 U.S. 67 (1918), in which Justice Holmes had made it clear that the Court engaged in such an inquiry so that it would not "be possible for a State to impose an unconstitutional burden" on a private party. * * *

Until recently we had virtually no interest in cases of this type. Thirty years ago, this Court reviewed only one. Nevada v. Stacher, 346 U.S. 906 (1953). Indeed, that appears to have been the only case during the entire 1953 Term in which a State even sought review of a decision by its own judiciary. Fifteen years ago, we did not review any such cases, although the total number of requests had mounted to three.[2] Some time during the past decade, perhaps about the time of the 5-to-4 decision in Zacchini v. Scripps–Howard Broadcasting Co., 433 U.S. 562 (1977), our

---

2. In Commonwealth v. Dell Publications, Inc., 427 Pa. 189, 233 A.2d 840 (1967), the Supreme Court of Pennsylvania held that the First and Fourteenth Amendments protected the defendant's right to publish and distribute the book "Candy." The Commonwealth petitioned to this Court, and we denied certiorari. 390 U.S. 948 (1968). In People v. Noroff, 67 Cal.2d 791, 433 P.2d 479 (1967), the Supreme Court of California held that the First and Fourteenth Amendments protected the de-fendant's right to distribute a magazine called "International Nudist Sun." The State petitioned to this Court, and we denied certiorari. 390 U.S. 1012 (1968). In State v. Franc, 165 Colo. 69, 437 P.2d 48 (1968), the Supreme Court of Colorado held that under Colorado law title in a certain piece of property should be quieted in a citizen. The State petitioned to this Court, and we denied certiorari. 392 U.S. 928 (1968).

priorities shifted. The result is a docket swollen with requests by States to reverse judgments that their courts have rendered in favor of their citizens.[3] I am confident that a future Court will recognize the error of this allocation of resources. When that day comes, I think it likely that the Court will also reconsider the propriety of today's expansion of our jurisdiction.

The Court offers only one reason for asserting authority over cases such as the one presented today: "an important need for uniformity in federal law [that] goes unsatisfied when we fail to review an opinion that rests primarily upon federal grounds and where the independence of an alleged state ground is not apparent from the four corners of the opinion" (emphasis omitted). Of course, the supposed need to "review an opinion" clashes directly with our oft-repeated reminder that "our power is to correct wrong judgments, not to revise opinions." Herb v. Pitcairn, 324 U.S. 117, 126 (1945). The clash is not merely one of form: the "need for uniformity in federal law" is truly an ungovernable engine. That same need is no less present when it is perfectly clear that a state ground is both independent and adequate. In fact, it is equally present if a state prosecutor announces that he believes a certain policy of nonenforcement is commanded by federal law. Yet we have never claimed jurisdiction to correct such errors, no matter how egregious they may be, and no matter how much they may thwart the desires of the state electorate. We do not sit to expound our understanding of the Constitution to interested listeners in the legal community; we sit to resolve disputes. If it is not apparent that our views would affect the outcome of a particular case, we cannot presume to interfere.

Finally, I am thoroughly baffled by the Court's suggestion that it must stretch its jurisdiction and reverse the judgment of the Michigan Supreme Court in order to show "[r]espect for the independence of state courts."

Would we show respect for the Republic of Finland by convening a special sitting for the sole purpose of declaring that its decision to release an American citizen was based upon a misunderstanding of American law?

I respectfully dissent.

NOTE ON AMBIGUOUS STATE DECISIONS AND TECHNIQUES FOR CLARIFYING THEM

(1) As Justice Stevens' dissent points out, when it is uncertain whether the state decision rested on a federal ground, a state ground, or both, the Court can adopt the following approaches: (a) it can seek a clarification from the state court, either by obtaining a certificate from the state court, or by vacating and remanding with a request for clarification; (b) it can try

---

3. This Term, we devoted argument time to Florida v. Royer, 460 U.S. 491 (1983); Illinois v. Gates, 462 U.S. 213 (1983) (argued twice); Connecticut v. Johnson, 460 U.S. 73 (1983); Missouri v. Hunter, 459 U.S. 359 (1983); South Dakota v. Neville, 459 U.S. 553 (1983); Texas v. Brown, 460 U.S. 730 (1983); California v. Ramos, *ante*, p. 992; Florida v. Casal, 462 U.S. 637 (1983); City of Revere v. Massachusetts General Hospital, *ante*, p. 239; Oregon v. Bradshaw, 462 U.S. 1039 (1983); Illinois v. Andreas, *ante*, p. 765; Illinois v. Lafayette, 462 U.S. 640 (1983), as well as this case. And a cursory survey of the United States Law Week index reveals that so far this Term at least 80 petitions for certiorari to state courts were filed by the States themselves.

to resolve the ambiguity itself by examination of the relevant state-law materials; (c) it can dismiss, on the ground that, in view of the ambiguity, the obligation affirmatively to establish the Court's jurisdiction to review has not been satisfied; or (d) it can create a presumption (which can itself be strong or weak) that the decision rested on a federal ground. (Note that the contrary presumption is the equivalent of alternative "c".)

In its administration of the independent state-ground rule, the Court over the years oscillated among the first three of these alternatives.

(2) In the earliest cases, the Court took the view that jurisdiction would fail when there was ambiguity about the grounds of decision. See, e.g., Klinger v. Missouri, 80 U.S. (13 Wall.) 257 (1871); Eustis v. Bolles, 150 U.S. 361 (1893). But as early as Johnson v. Risk, 137 U.S. 300 (1890), the Court itself examined the prior Tennessee decisions before it concluded that a state court judgment (rendered without opinion) could plausibly have rested on the state statute of limitations; it added, further, that the plaintiff in error, "if he wished to claim that this cause was disposed of by the decision of a federal question, should have obtained the certificate of the [State] Supreme Court to that effect * * *" (p. 307).

(3) Uncertainty could thus be resolved by a certificate from the state court stating what it had decided. For illustrations of the use of a certificate, see Whitney v. California, 274 U.S. 357, 361 (1927), and McGoldrick v. Gulf Oil Corp., 309 U.S. 2, 692, 414 (1940) (both dismissed for want of jurisdiction; petition for rehearing granted after amendment of order by state court; decided then on merits); Lynumn v. Illinois, 368 U.S. 908 (1961), 372 U.S. 528, 535–36 (1963) (consideration of certiorari petition deferred, over dissent contending that opinion below rested purely on state grounds; certificate treated as conclusive to establish jurisdiction).

Herb v. Pitcairn, 324 U.S. 117 (1945), involved an action in a city court of Illinois under the Federal Employers' Liability Act. While the action was pending, the Supreme Court of Illinois held that a city court lacked jurisdiction of a cause of action arising outside the city. The plaintiff thereupon moved for a change of venue to the circuit court, a court of general jurisdiction. The motion was granted.

The two-year period of limitations prescribed by the federal act had expired, however, prior to the transfer. The defendant, appearing specially, moved to dismiss upon this ground, contending that no action was commenced within the two-year period; that the change of venue was unauthorized by the state venue statute; and that if the venue statute authorized the change it would violate the state constitution. The motion to dismiss was granted and the Supreme Court of Illinois affirmed.

On certiorari, the Supreme Court deemed it uncertain whether the state decision rested on the ground that no action was pending as a matter of Illinois law, or on the ground that even though pending (because transferable) the suit was barred by the federal limitation, or on both grounds.

After reviewing the Court's practice in dealing with ambiguities, Justice Jackson said (pp. 127–28):

"It is no criticism of a state court that we are unable to say in a case where both state and federal questions are presented, discussed, and perhaps decided, that the judgment would have been the same had only one of the grounds been present. Those courts may adjudicate both kinds of questions and because it is not necessary to their functions to make a sharp separation of the two their discussion is often interlaced. But we cannot perform our duty to refrain from interfering in state law questions and also to review federal ones without making a determination whether the one or the other controls the judgment. And in cases where the answer is not clear to us, it seems consistent with the respect due the highest courts of states of the Union that they be asked rather than told what they have intended. If this imposes an unwelcome burden it should be mitigated by the knowledge that it is to protect their jurisdiction from unwitting interference as well as to protect our own from unwitting renunciation.

"It is our purpose scrupulously to observe the long standing rule that we will not review a judgment of a state court that rests on an adequate and independent ground in state law. Nor will we review one until the fact that it does not do so appears of record. But because we will not proceed with a review while our jurisdiction is conjectural it does not follow that we should not take steps to protect our jurisdiction when we are given reasonable grounds to believe it exists. We think the simplest procedure to do so, where the record is deficient, is to hold the case pending application to the state court for clarification or amendment. It need not be elaborate or formal if it is clear and decisive in stating whether a federal question, and if so, what federal question, was decided as a necessary ground for reaching the judgment under review. In proper cases we may grant counsel's request for continuance for the purpose. In proper cases we will impose the duty of applying for it upon petitioners or appellants upon our own motion.

"These causes are continued for such period as will enable counsel for petitioners with all convenient speed to apply to the Supreme Court of Illinois for amendment, or certificate, which will show whether it intended to rest the judgments herein on an adequate and independent state ground or whether decision of the federal question was necessary to the judgment rendered."

④ Minnesota v. National Tea Co., 309 U.S. 551 (1940), was a state-court action for refund of taxes; the plaintiff's contention that the tax was invalid rested on both the Equal Protection Clause of the federal Constitution and the "uniformity" clause of the state constitution. The Supreme Court analyzed the state court's opinion, and concluded that "there is considerable uncertainty as to the precise grounds for the decision." It continued (pp. 555-57): "That is sufficient reason for us to decline at this time to review the federal question asserted to be present, Honeyman v. Hanan, 300 U.S. 14, consistently with the policy of not passing upon questions of a constitutional nature which are not clearly necessary to a decision of the case.

"But that does not mean that we should dismiss the petition. This Court has frequently held that in the exercise of its appellate jurisdiction it has the power not only to correct errors of law in the judgment under review but also to make such disposition of the case as justice requires. State Tax Commission v. Van Cott, 306 U.S. 511; Patterson v. Alabama, 294 U.S. 600. That principle has been applied to cases coming from state courts where supervening changes had occurred since entry of the judgment, where the record failed adequately to state the facts underlying a decision of the federal question, and where the grounds of the state decision were obscure. * * *

"The procedure in those cases was to vacate the judgment and to remand the cause for further proceedings, so that the federal question might be dissected out or the state and federal questions clearly separated.

"In this type of case we deem it essential that this procedure be followed. It is possible that the state court employed the decisions under the federal constitution merely as persuasive authorities for its independent interpretation of the state constitution. If that were true, we would have no jurisdiction to review. State Tax Commission v. Van Cott, *supra*. On the other hand we cannot be content with a dismissal of the petition where there is strong indication, as here, that the federal constitution as judicially construed controlled the decision below. * * *

"It is important that this Court not indulge in needless dissertations on constitutional law. It is fundamental that state courts be left free and unfettered by us in interpreting their state constitutions. But it is equally important that ambiguous or obscure adjudications by state courts do not stand as barriers to a determination by this Court of the validity under the federal constitution of state action. Intelligent exercise of our appellate powers compels us to ask for the elimination of the obscurities and ambiguities from the opinions in such cases. Only then can we ascertain whether or not our jurisdiction to review should be invoked. Only by that procedure can the responsibility for striking down or upholding state legislation be fairly placed. For no other course assures that important federal issues, such as have been argued here, will reach this Court for adjudication; that state courts will not be the final arbiters of important issues under the federal constitution; and that we will not encroach on the constitutional jurisdiction of the states. This is not a mere technical rule nor a rule for our convenience. It touches the division of authority between state courts and this Court and is of equal importance to each. Only by such explicitness can the highest courts of the states and this Court keep within the bounds of their respective jurisdictions.

"For these reasons we vacate the judgment of the Supreme Court of Minnesota and remand the cause to that court for further proceedings. It is so ordered." [1]

① On remand, the Minnesota Supreme Court reinstated its judgment, stating that "we conclude that our prior decision was right. * * * We think that the * * * statute * * * is violative of the uniformity clause of our own constitution." 208 Minn. 607, 608, 294 N.W. 230 (1940). Does this response show that the Supreme Court's decision was unwise?

In Department of Motor Vehicles v. Rios, 410 U.S. 425, 427 (1973), the California Supreme Court had issued a writ of mandate requiring a hearing before a driver's license could be suspended, but left unclear whether that decision rested only on federal grounds or on state grounds as well. The Supreme Court vacated and remanded to allow clarification. Justice Douglas (who wrote the Court's opinion in Minnesota v. National Tea) dissented, arguing that when a state court judgment arguably rests on both state and federal grounds, the Court should not take jurisdiction unless the federal basis for decision is clearly demonstrated.

Justice Rehnquist, joined by Justice Stevens, took essentially the same position in his dissent in Philadelphia Newspapers, Inc. v. Jerome, 434 U.S. 241 (1978). In that case newspapers had sought mandamus and other original relief from the Pennsylvania Supreme Court to gain access to pre-trial evidence-suppression hearings; that court had denied relief without opinion. On appeal, finding that the record did not disclose whether the state court had passed on appellant's federal claims or had denied mandamus on a state ground, the Supreme Court summarily vacated and remanded to allow further proceedings "to

(5) What ends can be achieved by vacating a state judgment that cannot be served by a certificate? In Dixon v. Duffy, 344 U.S. 143 (1952), judgment was vacated after a continuance because the California Supreme Court maintained that it had no power to issue a formal clarification. Justice Jackson dissented, doubting the power to vacate under the circumstances.

In Department of Mental Hygiene v. Kirchner, 380 U.S. 194 (1965), the Court, anticipating the difficulty which developed in Dixon v. Duffy, immediately vacated the judgment and at the same time gave the parties leave to file a new certiorari petition, incorporating by reference the record and briefs already filed, if the state court should hold that its judgment did not rest on the non-federal ground.

Kirchner involved the validity of a statute imposing liability for support of indigent state mental patients on specified relatives. The California Supreme Court had held the statute invalid, without making clear whether its decision rested on the federal or the California constitution, or both. Forty-two states, Puerto Rico, and the District of Columbia had similar statutes. Certiorari had been granted and eight states had filed amicus briefs. The Supreme Court concluded (pp. 200–01): "While the ambiguity of the opinion might normally lead us to dismiss the writ of certiorari as improvidently granted, we think the preferable course is to leave the way open for obtaining clarification from the California Supreme Court (Minnesota v. National Tea Co., *supra*), in view of the importance of and widespread interest in the case." [2]

(6) Vacation and remand—like continuances for the obtaining of a certificate—gave the parties an opportunity to obtain further clarification from the state courts. But the Court did not always provide that opportunity. For cases where it simply proceeded on its own to resolve doubts on the basis of the relevant state-law materials, see, *e.g.,* Jankovich v. Indiana Toll Road Com'n, 379 U.S. 487 (1965) (state court ruling determined to rest on state constitutional grounds; two dissenters argued for vacating on the basis of National Tea); Konigsberg v. State Bar of California, 353 U.S. 252, 254–58 (1957) (state grounds proferred to justify California Supreme Court's refusal, without opinion, to review denial of bar admission were insubstantial; jurisdiction taken). For cases where the Court reverted to its earliest tradition and simply dismissed, without resolving ambiguities, on the ground that if the judgment below might have rested on a nonfederal ground, petitioner or appellant had not sustained the burden of establish-

clarify the record" (p. 242). Justice Rehnquist would have acquiesced in a delay to allow counsel an opportunity to seek a certificate from the Pennsylvania court. But he contended that when a state court judgment arguably rests on both state and federal grounds, the Court should not take jurisdiction absent clear demonstration that the decision was federally based.

2. On remand, the California Supreme Court in banc held that it had been "independently constrained" to the result by the state constitutional provision. 62 Cal.2d 586, 400 P.2d 321 (1965).

Cf. Musser v. Utah, 333 U.S. 95 (1948), where a judgment was vacated, Justice Jackson writing, on the ground that argument in the Supreme Court disclosed that a vagueness challenge to a state conspiracy statute involved problems of interpretation of the statute "not presented to or considered by the Utah Supreme Court" and possibly "waived or lost" for lack of timely or sufficient assignment. On remand, the state court held the statute void upon this ground, though it noted that "the question here presented was never specifically assigned or argued in any court until inquiries from the bench suggested it during the argument before the United States Supreme Court." State v. Musser, 118 Utah 537, 223 P.2d 193, 194 (1950).

ing jurisdiction, see Lynch v. New York *ex rel.* Pierson, 293 U.S. 52 (1934) ("It may be surmised * * * that the affirmance by the [New York] Court of Appeals went upon the [federal] ground * * *. But jurisdiction cannot be founded upon surmise" (p. 54)); Memphis Natural Gas Co. v. Beeler, 315 U.S. 649 (1942); Stembridge v. Georgia, 343 U.S. 541 (1952); Durley v. Mayo, 351 U.S. 277 (1956); *cf.* Black v. Cutter Laboratories, 351 U.S. 292 (1956). On the other hand, for cases where the Court concluded, on the basis of rather aggressive readings of the state court opinions, that the decisions below rested on a federal ground, see Zacchini v. Scripps–Howard Broadcasting Co., 433 U.S. 562 (1977) (concluding that Ohio judgment rejecting celebrated "human cannonball's" claim for damages for invasion of the "right to publicity" rested on First Amendment grounds; Justice Stevens would have preferred remand); Delaware v. Prouse, 440 U.S. 648 (1979); South Dakota v. Neville, 459 U.S. 553 (1983).

⑦ So the law stood when Michigan v. Long was decided. Will it change the law significantly? Note that the application of Long's presumption depends on a whole series of "soft" requirements: the state decision must "fairly appear" to rest "primarily" on federal law or be "interwoven" with federal law, and the independence of the state ground must be "not clear" from the face of the state opinion. These are not self-applying concepts. Further, note that the Court carefully reserved the right to seek clarification from the state court where this is "necessary or desirable" (see p. 542, note 6, *supra*). The Court was clearly impatient with the indeterminacies of the previous practice; but it is quite possible that the underlying policy tensions that created those indeterminacies will overcome the effort to work out a uniform approach.

Since Michigan v. Long the Court has often relied on it, and accepted jurisdiction in the face of ambiguities in the state court opinion in, *e.g.,* California v. Ramos, 463 U.S. 992 (1983) (state court reversed death sentence on federal ground and also found a state-law error in admission of evidence; in absence of explicit statement that latter error warranted reversal, Court assumed jurisdiction); Maine v. Thornton, 466 U.S. 170 (1984) (state court "did not articulate an independent state ground with the clarity required by Michigan v. Long"); Florida v. Meyers, 466 U.S. 380 (1984) (there was "hardly a clear indication" that the state ground was an adequate basis for reversing a criminal conviction; dissent by Justice Stevens); Ohio v. Johnson, 467 U.S. 493 (1984) (three dissents); Delaware v. Van Arsdall, 475 U.S. 673 (1986) (dissent by Stevens, J., pointing out that in this case Long was being used to review a state court's holding, arguably based on state law, that the proper *remedy* for violation of a federal right was automatic reversal (without inquiry into questions of prejudice)).

But in Capital Cities Media, Inc. v. Toole, 466 U.S. 378 (1984), the Court reverted to the practice of vacating and remanding. Here the trial judge had imposed severe restrictions on media access to various aspects of a criminal trial. The Supreme Court of Pennsylvania, without opinion, denied a media petition for writ of prohibition. The Supreme Court, per curiam, stated: "[T]he record does not disclose whether the Supreme Court of Pennsylvania passed on petitioners' federal claims or whether it denied their petition * * * on an adequate and independent state ground. For this reason, we grant the petition for writ of certiorari, vacate the judgment * * * and remand the cause to that court for such further proceedings as it may deem appropriate to clarify the record * * *" (pp. 378–79).

Does the Long presumption not apply where the state court has written no opinion?

(8) The reaction of some commentators to Long has been hostile.[3] But some of the hostility is directed not to the use of the presumption as a technique for dealing with genuine ambiguities about the roles of state and federal law in the state court opinion, but to two other (and distinct) issues lurking behind Michigan v. Long: (1) The appropriateness of Supreme Court review of state rulings *upholding* claims of federal right, even if the ruling is squarely based on federal law. (This is one of the issues raised in Justice Stevens' dissent in Long, and is considered in the Note immediately following, p. 554, *infra*.) (2) The question whether a state court decision that adopts federal law as a measure of a state-law obligation or limitation involves a genuine "federal question" at all. (This issue is considered in the *Note on State Incorporation of or Reference to Federal Law*, p. 559, *infra*.)

Apart from misgivings about these two distinct issues, what are the objections to the "presumption" approach of Long? Many years' experience had persuaded the Court that it would not and could not stick rigorously to the hard-nosed line that jurisdiction will fail whenever there is ambiguity in the state court disposition.[4] The possibility that, under Long, at the end of the day the Supreme Court's decision of the federal question will turn out not to be decisive, because the state court on remand will reinstate its judgment on an unmistakably state-law ground, has always attended the Court's jurisdictional practice (see p. 536, *supra*); the characterization of this as resulting in an "advisory" opinion seems wrong. And the fact that the state courts do continue to have the power, after the Court's decision, to consider independent state-law issues and to base ultimate judgment on them shows that the Court's new approach does not in any serious way undermine the states' power to apply their own law.

On the other hand, the Court's protestations—that its presumption shows greater respect for state courts than asking them to clarify their opinions—ring hollow: Long simply puts the burden of clarification on the state court in advance.

The real objection to Long is the serious concern that it will cause the Supreme Court to waste its limited resources by reaching out to make

---

3. See, *e.g.*, Welsh, *Reconsidering the Constitutional Relationship Between State and Federal Courts: A Critique of Michigan v. Long*, 59 Notre Dame L.Rev. 1118 (1984); Seid, *Schizoid Federalism, Supreme Court Power and Inadequate Adequate State Ground Theory: Michigan v. Long*, 18 Creighton L.Rev. 1 (1984). For more favorable treatments, see Althouse, *How to Build a Separate Sphere: Federal Courts and State Power*, 100 Harv.L.Rev. 1485 (1987); Baker, *The Ambiguous Independent and Adequate State Ground in Criminal Cases: Federalism Along a Möbius Strip*, 19 Ga.L.Rev. 799 (1985); Redish, *Supreme Court Review of State Court "Federal" Decisions: A Study in Interactive Federalism*, 19 Ga.L.Rev. 861 (1985).

4. Normally, a party invoking the jurisdiction of a federal court has the burden of establishing the court's jurisdiction. See Philadelphia Newspapers, Inc. v. Jerome, 434 U.S. 241, 244 (1978) (Rehnquist, J., dissenting). But note that this rule usually applies where it is within the *party's* control (in the complaint or the petition for removal) to meet the burden. In the context of Supreme Court review of state court decisions, the parties have no ultimate control over the state court's choices for grounding decision; if the court's opinion is ambiguous, or the court writes no opinion, there is often nothing the losing party can do (or could have done) to meet the "burden" of establishing jurisdiction. It may be quite appropriate, therefore, to place the obligation of meeting the burden—which can be satisfied with a short statement by the court—on the state court.

unnecessary decisions on grave and difficult federal questions. The countervailing risk is that the Court will be prevented from correcting a serious and important misapplication of federal law that has in fact misled a state court and that may engender disuniformity, confusion, and instability in the law. But doesn't vacation and remand adequately guard against that risk?

Note that most of the cases using the Long presumption involved situations where the Court wished to correct state-court overenforcement of federal constitutional restrictions on the enforcement of the criminal law—an area in which the Court has been active in changing the underlying substantive rules. (Compare Capital Cities, where the Court reverted to the technique of vacation and remand of a state decision that did not recognize a federal right.) Michigan v. Long thus illustrates a general principle: jurisdictional rules tend to move in the direction of allowing more intense supervision in areas of the law where the Supreme Court is in the process of changing the relevant substantive rules and wants to assure itself that the state courts are complying with the new dispensation.

In any event, the practical significance of Michigan v. Long should not be exaggerated: the likelihood is that the case will not do much more than to create a modest expansion in the Supreme Court's discretion in dealing with ambiguous and indeterminate state-court decisions.[5]

NOTE ON REVIEW OF STATE DECISIONS UPHOLDING CLAIMS OF FEDERAL RIGHT

(1) Justice Stevens' dissent in Long raises an underlying issue that is quite separate from the problem of ambiguity. He argues that the Court should not review and revise state-court judgments (even if they clearly rest on federal grounds) when those judgments *uphold* claims of federal right.)[1]

Justice Stevens returned to this theme in his dissent in Delaware v. Van Arsdall, p. 552, *supra,* where the Court on certiorari reviewed the Delaware Supreme Court's holding that certain limitations placed by the trial court on defense counsel's cross examination of a witness violated the Confrontation Clause of the Sixth Amendment. The Supreme Court agreed that the Sixth Amendment had been violated, but vacated the state court's judgment reversing the conviction. It concluded that (a) as a matter of federal law, the violation was not grounds for automatic reversal of the conviction if the error was "harmless," (b) the state court's reversal did not clearly rest on a state-law "automatic reversal" rule; and (c) the case should therefore be remanded to allow the state court to determine whether the error was "harmless" under federal standards.

---

5. See, for an example, Pennsylvania v. Finley, 107 S.Ct. 1990 (1987) (no federal constitutional right to counsel in post conviction proceedings; three Justices argue that case rested on state procedural ground).

1. See also Minnesota v. Clover Leaf Creamery, 449 U.S. 456 (1981), and City of

Revere v. Massachusetts General Hospital, 463 U.S. 239 (1983), in both of which Justice Stevens objected to the Court's review of state court judgments upholding claims of federal right.

Justice Stevens objected that this disposition "operates to expand this Court's review of state remedies that overcompensate for violations of federal constitutional rights" (p. 695). Pointing out that such rulings were entirely unreviewable until 1914, Justice Stevens said that "the claim of these cases on our docket is secondary to the need to scrutinize judgments disparaging those rights" (p. 697). Justice Stevens also complained that reviewing such cases puts pressure on the state courts to confine *state* constitutional protections to the level required by the federal Constitution. He added that on remand the Delaware courts should be deemed free to impose the automatic reversal rule on the basis of state law. (Justice Marshall also made this latter point in a separate dissent. Is it clearly correct? Does a state court always have unreviewable power to add state-law remedies to violations of *federal* constitutional norms? Isn't the question whether violation of a federal constitutional rule should be deemed *per se* prejudicial, or whether a harmless error rule is applicable, itself a function of the policies underlying the basic federal rule? On the other hand, in the specific circumstances of Van Arsdall, there does not appear to be any strong federal interest in requiring a state to deal with noncompliance with the Confrontation Clause by adopting a "harmless error" rather than an absolute standard. *Cf.* Dice v. Akron, Canton & Youngstown RR., p. 628, infra.)

(2) As Justice Stevens acknowledged in Van Arsdall (but did not acknowledge in Long), the Court's *power* to review and revise state court determinations that uphold claims of federal right was explicitly conferred by Congress in the Judiciary Act of 1914. See p. 502, *supra*. Given that statute, should the Court adopt a systematic policy (as against the normal case-by-case operations of the certiorari practice) disfavoring review in such cases?[2] Would such a "low priority" policy be different than other policies—some reflected in the Court's formal rules—that govern priorities in managing petitions for certiorari (*e.g.*, cases involving conflicts among the lower courts have a higher priority than cases where there is no conflict) (see generally pp. 1873–74, *infra*)? If Justice Stevens' "low priority" approach is justified, should the Court's rules state that this is a relevant factor in determining whether certiorari should be denied? If the answer to this is no, does this bear on the question whether a systematic "low-priority" approach is justified?

Justice Stevens' position—that no important constitutional interests are threatened when a state court upholds an individual's claim of federal constitutional rights—rejects the Court's view that important uniformity concerns are undermined if state court judgments overenforcing federal restrictions on state power are left unreviewed.[3] Beyond the uniformity

---

2. In Van Arsdall, Justice Stevens stated that the purpose of the 1914 amendment was to allow the Court to review "Lochner-style" overenforcement of supposed federal limits on the states' power to enact social legislation. Is this a principled distinction?

3. In this connection, consider Justice Stevens' remarkable assertion in Long that Michigan's overenforcement of the Fourth Amendment (under a mistaken assumption about the federal Constitution's requirements) creates no different problem than when a court in Finland overprotects a United States citizen on the same mistaken assumption. Is it tolerable in the long run for the Fourth Amendment to be deemed to give different protections to citizens of Michigan than to those of other states? As stressed by Hamilton in Federalist No. 82, see p. 28, *supra*, and by Justice Story in Martin, see p. 511, *supra*, it was a significant purpose of Article III to permit the United States Supreme Court to unify federal law by review of state-court decisions of federal questions. Section 1257

problems lie other, deeper issues. Justice Stevens' arguments obviously assume that the Constitution's guarantees of individual rights represent the only *significant* constitutional norms. But even if this is true of the Bill of Rights and the other amendments viewed in isolation, can it be meaningfully asserted about the Constitution as a whole? See Bator, *The State Courts and Federal Constitutional Litigation,* 22 Wm. & Mary L.Rev. 605, 631–633 (1981): "[T]he Constitution contains other sorts of values as well. It gives the federal government powers, but also enacts limitations on those powers. *The limitations, too, count as setting forth constitutional values.* * * * When a court upholds a state criminal statute against the claim that it violates the first amendment, it is rejecting one sort of constitutional claim, but it is also upholding principles of separation of powers and federalism which themselves have constitutional status." Compare Sager, *Fair Measure: The Legal Status of Underenforced Constitutional Norms,* 91 Harv.L.Rev. 1212 (1978), (*inter alia*) urging the Stevens position.

(3) If a state supreme court construes its own statutes and constitution more expansively than required by federal constitutional norms, the state retains political power to disagree and correct the decision by amending the state statute or constitution; the fact that the decision is not reviewed by the United States Supreme Court does not block the possibility of change. But if a state court holds that the federal Constitution bars the state government from action, its judgment—if unreviewable by the Supreme Court—effectively freezes the law in that state (subject only to an amendment of the United States Constitution): neither state statute nor state constitutional amendment can overcome the decision. (The possibility of the state court having the opportunity in a subsequent case itself to reconsider and reverse its own judgment on the issue is remote.) Is this a tolerable institutional situation? [4]

(4) The Court has repeatedly adhered to the classical position, that it has both the power and responsibility to review state court decisions (meeting the normal standards for certiorari) that uphold individual claims of federal right. See, *e.g.,* in addition to Michigan v. Long and cases cited in the Note at p. 552, *supra,* Fare v. Michael C., 442 U.S. 707, 716 (1979) (reviewing state court's extension of Miranda rule); Oregon v. Hass, 420 U.S. 714, 719–20 (1975) ("a State is free *as a matter of its own law* to impose greater restrictions on police activity than those this Court holds to be necessary upon federal constitutional standards. * * * But * * * a State may not impose such greater restrictions as a matter of *federal constitutional law* * * *. [A] holding that, for constitutional reasons, the

---

enacts that purpose into law. Is Justice Stevens entitled to dismiss this out of hand?

In any event, hasn't Justice Stevens overlooked the Supremacy Clause? Erroneous over-extensions of the Fourth Amendment are not adopted by Finland under the supposed compulsion of the U.S. Constitution; and even if they were, this could hardly be deemed to threaten any of *our* constitutional values. In the case of Michigan, an erroneous over-extension is always based on supposed compulsion, and if uncorrected implicates important consti-

tutional concerns regarding the automony of the states.

4. In Bice, *Anderson and the Adequate State Ground,* 45 S.Calif.L.Rev. 750 (1972), these problems lead the author to propose that the Supreme Court should review a state court's federal-law decision even when the judgment also rests on an independent alternative state-law ground. For an answer to Bice, see Falk, *The State Constitution: A More than "Adequate" Nonfederal Ground,* 61 Calif.L.Rev. 273 (1973).

prosecution may not utilize otherwise relevant evidence makes the State an aggrieved party for purposes of review") (emphasis in original).

STANDARD OIL CO. OF CALIFORNIA v. JOHNSON

316 U.S. 481, 62 S.Ct. 1168, 86 L.Ed. 1611 (1942).
Appeal from the Supreme Court of California.

MR. JUSTICE BLACK delivered the opinion of the Court.

The California Motor Vehicle Fuel License Tax Act imposes a license tax, measured by gallonage, on the privilege of distributing any motor vehicle fuel. Section 10 states that the Act is inapplicable "to any motor vehicle fuel sold to the government of the United States or any department thereof for official use of said government." The appellant, a "distributor" within the meaning of the Act, sold gasoline to the United States Army Post Exchanges in California. The State levied a tax, and the appellant paid it under protest. The appellant then filed this suit in the Superior Court of Sacramento County seeking to recover the payment on two grounds: ① That sales to the Exchanges were exempt from tax under Section 10; ② that if construed and applied to require payment of the tax on such sales the Act would impose a burden upon instrumentalities or agencies of the United States contrary to the federal constitution. Holding against the appellant on both grounds, the trial court rendered judgment for the State. The Supreme Court of California affirmed. 19 Cal.2d 104, 119 P.2d 329. Since validity of the State statute as construed was drawn in question on the ground of its being repugnant to the Constitution, we think the case is properly here on appeal under Section 237(a) of the Judicial Code, 28 U.S.C.A. § 344(a).

Since Section 10 of the California Act made the tax inapplicable "to any motor vehicle fuel sold to the government of the United States or any department thereof", it was necessary for the Supreme Court of California to determine whether the language of this exemption included sales to post exchanges. If the court's construction of Section 10 of the Act had been based purely on local law, this construction would have been conclusive, and we should have to determine whether the statute so construed and applied is repugnant to the federal constitution. But in deciding that post exchanges were not "the government of the United States or any department thereof", the court did not rely upon the law of California. On the contrary, it relied upon its determination concerning the relationship between post exchanges and the government of the United States, a relationship which is controlled by federal law. For post exchanges operate under regulations of the Secretary of War pursuant to federal authority. These regulations and the practices under them establish the relationship between the post exchange and the United States government, and together with the relevant statutory and constitutional provisions from which they derive, afford the data upon which the legal status of the post exchange may be determined. It was upon a determination of a federal question, therefore, that the Supreme Court of California rested its conclusion that, by Section 10, sales to post exchange were not exempted from the tax. Since this determination of a federal question was by a state court, we are not bound by it. We proceed to consider whether it is correct.

On July 25, 1895, the Secretary of War, under authority of Congressional enactments promulgated regulations providing for the establishment of post exchanges. These regulations have since been amended from time to time and the exchange has become a regular feature of Army posts. That the establishment and control of post exchanges have been in accordance with regulations rather than specific statutory directions does not alter their status, for authorized War Department regulations have the force of law.

Congressional recognition that the activities of post exchanges are governmental has been frequent. Since 1903, Congress has repeatedly made substantial appropriations to be expended under the direction of the Secretary of War for construction, equipment, and maintenance of suitable buildings for post exchanges. In 1933 and 1934, Congress ordered certain moneys derived from disbanded exchanges to be handed over to the Federal Treasury. And in 1936, Congress gave consent to state taxation of gasoline sold by or through post exchanges, when the gasoline was not for the exclusive use of the United States.

The commanding officer of an Army Post, subject to the regulations and the commands of his own superior officers, has complete authority to establish and maintain an exchange. He details a post exchange officer to manage its affairs. This officer and the commanding officers of the various company units make up a council which supervises exchange activities. None of these officers receives any compensation other than his regular salary. The object of the exchanges is to provide convenient and reliable sources where soldiers can obtain their ordinary needs at the lowest possible prices. Soldiers, their families, and civilians employed on military posts here and abroad can buy at exchanges. The government assumes none of the financial obligations of the exchange. But government officers, under government regulations, handle and are responsible for all funds of the exchange which are obtained from the companies or detachments composing its membership. Profits, if any, do not go to individuals. They are used to improve the soldiers' mess, to provide various types of recreation, and in general to add to the pleasure and comfort of the troops.

From all of this, we conclude that post exchanges as now operated are arms of the government deemed by it essential for the performance of governmental functions. They are integral parts of the War Department, share in fulfilling the duties entrusted to it, and partake of whatever immunities it may have under the constitution and federal statutes. In concluding otherwise the Supreme Court of California was in error.

Whether the California Supreme Court would have construed the Motor Vehicle Fuel License Act as applicable to post exchanges if it had decided the issue of legal status of post exchanges in accordance with this opinion, we have no way of knowing. Hence, a determination here of the constitutionality of such an application of the Act is not called for by the state of the record. Cf. State of Minnesota v. National Tea Co., 309 U.S. 551, 557. Accordingly, we reverse the judgment and remand the cause to the court below for further proceedings not inconsistent with this opinion.

Reversed.

NOTE ON STATE INCORPORATION OF OR REFERENCE TO FEDERAL LAW

(1) In State Tax Commission v. Van Cott, 306 U.S. 511 (1939), a Utah income tax law exempted "wages from the United States * * * for services rendered in connection with the exercise of an essential governmental function." An attorney for the Reconstruction Finance Corporation and the Regional Agricultural Credit Corporation claimed exemption for the salaries paid him by those federal agencies, relying both upon the statute and upon the constitutional immunity declared in Rogers v. Graves, 299 U.S. 401 (1937). The Supreme Court of Utah sustained the exemption, stating: "We shall have to be content to follow, as we think we must, the doctrine of the Graves Case, until such time as a different rule is laid down by the courts, the Congress, or the people through amendment to the Constitution."

The Supreme Court granted certiorari and, prior to decision, overruled the Graves decision, repudiating the view that any federal salaries are constitutionally immune from state taxation. Graves v. O'Keefe, 306 U.S. 466 (1939). The respondent argued that the change was immaterial since the Utah decision rested on construction of the taxing statute.

Rejecting this contention, the Supreme Court said (pp. 514–15): "If the [state] court were only incidentally referring to decisions of this Court in determining the meaning of the state law, and had concluded therefrom that the statute was itself intended to grant exemption to respondent, this Court would have no jurisdiction to review that question. But, if the state court did in fact intend alternatively to base its decision upon the state statute and upon an immunity it thought granted by the Constitution as interpreted by this Court, these two grounds are so interwoven that we are unable to conclude that the judgment rests upon an independent interpretation of the state law. Whatever exemptions the Supreme Court of Utah may find in the terms of this statute, its opinion in the present case only indicates that 'it thought the Federal Constitution [as construed by this Court] required' it to hold respondent not taxable.

" * * * Whether the Utah income tax, by its terms, exempts respondent, can now be decided by the state's highest court apart from any question of Constitutional immunity, and without the necessity, so far as the Federal Constitution is concerned, of attempting to divide functions of government into those which are essential and those which are non-essential."

The judgment was vacated "so that the state court may be free to act."

On remand the Utah court adhered to its decision in the view that it "correctly interpreted the intent of the Legislature in using the phrase 'essential governmental functions'" and that "such interpretation is still correct regardless of any change in decision of the United States Supreme Court." Van Cott v. State Tax Comm., 98 Utah 264, 96 P.2d 740 (1939).

(2) In Minnesota v. National Tea Co., p. 549, supra, the Court said (pp. 556–57): "If a state court merely said that the Fourteenth Amendment, as construed by this Court, is the 'supreme law of the land' to which obedience must be given, our jurisdiction would seem to be inescapable. And that would follow though the state court might have given, if it had chosen, a different construction to an identical provision in the state constitution.

But the Minnesota Supreme Court did not take such an unequivocal position. On the other hand, it did not declare its independence of the decisions of this Court, when the state constitutional provision avowedly had identity of scope with the relevant clause of the Fourteenth Amendment. * * * The instant case therefore presents an intermediate situation to which an application of the procedure followed in State Tax Commission v. Van Cott, *supra,* is peculiarly appropriate."

Does the decision in Johnson follow from Van Cott? From Minnesota v. National Tea? Does National Tea follow from Van Cott? Would it have altered the result in any of these cases if the claim asserted under state law had not been accompanied by an independent claim of federal immunity?

(3) A provision of the Alabama Unemployment Compensation Act of 1935, as amended, declared that "in the event the Supreme Court of the United States shall hold the Federal 'Social Security Act' * * * unconstitutional or inoperative for any reason whatsoever, then this Act shall become void, inoperative and of no effect * * *." (The federal statute had included financial incentives encouraging the states to enact state compensation systems.) The Alabama Supreme Court interpreted this provision to mean that the statute was operative only if the federal act was constitutional and concluded that in a suit challenging the state act it was, therefore, obliged to pass on the contention that the act of Congress was invalid. Beeland Wholesale Co. v. Kaufman, 234 Ala. 249, 260, 174 So. 516 (1937).

Would its judgment on the latter point have been subject to review by the Supreme Court?

Flournoy v. Wiener, 321 U.S. 253 (1944), posed a similar problem. Section 402(b)(2) of the Revenue Act of 1942 included in the gross estate of a decedent for purposes of the federal estate tax property "to the extent of the interest therein held as community property by the decedent and surviving spouse under the law of any State, Territory, or possession of the United States * * *." A Louisiana statute levied an estate transfer tax on all estates subject to taxation under the federal act in the amount of the difference between inheritance, succession and estate taxes paid to any other states and 80% of the tax payable to the United States.

In a suit by a taxpayer resisting the inclusion in the decedent's estate of the interest of the widow in the community, the Supreme Court of Louisiana held that the construction of the state act by the tax collector "would render it violative of the due process guaranteed by the 14th amendment * * * since such interpretation would result in the imposition of a tax upon those succeeding to the estate of a decedent measured in part by the property comprising the estate of another, to which the estate of the decedent is in no way related." It also held that if § 402(b) of the federal tax, invoked by the collector as the measure of the state tax, is interpreted to tax the whole community, it violates the Fifth Amendment.

On appeal, the Supreme Court dismissed for want of jurisdiction on the ground that the petitioner had assigned as error only the state court's ruling on the validity of § 402(b), omitting an assignment with respect to the court's ruling on the state act. "Any determination which we might make of the Fifth Amendment question would thus leave unaffected the state court's judgment brought here for review" (p. 261).

If proper assignment had been made, would the validity of the federal provision have been drawn in question because the state employed it as the measure of its tax?

Justice Frankfurter, dissenting, joined by Justice Roberts and Justice Jackson, thought the answer governed by the Johnson case. He said (pp. 270–72): "Much is to be said for the reasoning of Mr. Justice Holmes [dissenting] in the Kansas City Title case [Smith v. Kansas City Title & Trust Co., 255 U.S. 180 (1921), p. 992, *infra*] in urging that the incorporation of a federal act into a state law nevertheless makes the suit, for purposes of our jurisdiction, one arising under the state and not under the federal law. But his view was rejected. In the recent Standard Oil case we had an opportunity to adopt his view and reject that of the Court in the Kansas City Title case. Instead, we unanimously applied the reasoning of the Kansas City Title case that where a decision under state law necessarily involves the construction or validity of federal law the determination of such federal law in the application of state law gives rise to a federal question for review here."

Compare cases involving actions in state courts to recover damages for negligence where state law treats the violation of a statutory safety standard—whether federal or state—as negligence *per se*. If the violation claimed is of an act of Congress, there is no doubt that state construction of the federal provision presents a federal question. See, *e.g.*, Moore v. Chesapeake & O. Ry., 291 U.S. 205, 214 (1934); St. Louis, I.M. & S. Ry. v. Taylor, 210 U.S. 281, 293 (1908). This is true though it remains entirely clear that the federal act does not create the cause of action. See Crane v. Cedar Rapids & I.C. Ry., 395 U.S. 164 (1969). *Cf.* Holmes, J., in Schlemmer v. Buffalo, R. & P. Ry., 205 U.S. 1, 11 (1907): "if it is evident that a ruling purporting to deal only with local law has for its premise or necessary concomitant a cognizable mistake, that may be sufficient to warrant a review." [1]

(4) In California v. Byers, 402 U.S. 424 (1971), a driver involved in an automobile accident was prosecuted for violation of the state "hit and run" statute. After a demurrer to the charge was overruled, he sought a writ of prohibition against the prosecution on the ground that the statutory obligation to stop and identify himself following the accident was a violation of his privilege against self-incrimination. The California Supreme

---

1. The entire line of decisions in the text would seem to cast doubt on the Court's holding in Miller's Executors v. Swann, 150 U.S. 132 (1893) (dismissing for want of a federal question a case in which a railroad's power to convey was limited by a state statute that simply incorporated the limits imposed by federal statute). But see Shapiro, *Jurisdiction and Discretion,* 60 N.Y.U.L.R. 543, 564–65 (1985) (arguing that Swann shows that where "decision of a question of state law turns on a question of federal law," the Court has an "implicit power to choose" whether the case is reviewable in light of "the strength of the federal interest").

See also St. Martin Evangelical Lutheran Church v. South Dakota, 451 U.S. 772 (1981), dealing with South Dakota's unemployment statute, which (like the unemployment statutes of all fifty states) was specifically drafted to meet the conditions of the Federal Unemployment Tax Act for allowing the states to recapture 90% of the tax that would otherwise be payable to the federal government. The Supreme Court reviewed a state court determination, based explicitly on interpretations of the federal statute and the First Amendment, that church schools were not subject to the state statute. It does not matter, the Court concluded, that the decision "literally" concerned the coverage of the state tax statute; the South Dakota courts "deserve to be made aware of the proper and, here, significant interpretation of the intertwined federal law" (p. 780 n. 9).

Court held that if disclosure compelled by the statute could be subsequently used for evidence in a traffic offense (or other) prosecution, the statute would violate the federal Constitution. It therefore read into the statute a prohibition on such use of the required disclosures, and upheld the statute with that restriction. It then went on nevertheless to restrain the prosecution in this case on the ground that it would be "unfair" to punish someone for violation when he could not reasonably have anticipated the judicial promulgation of the use restriction.

The Supreme Court granted the state's petition for certiorari and vacated the state court judgment, holding that the statute would be valid even without a use restriction. No jurisdictional issue was discussed.

Did the Court properly assume jurisdiction to decide the self-incrimination question?

What if the state court had construed the statute to include a use restriction, without actually deciding that its absence would make the statute invalid, but solely in order to avoid the *question* of constitutionality?

United Air Lines v. Mahin, 410 U.S. 623 (1973), involved an Illinois use tax applied to fuel stored in the state and then loaded onto United's airplanes there, for consumption in interstate flight. Before 1963 the state Department of Revenue had construed the tax as applicable only to such fuel as was presumably "burned off" over Illinois (based on a plane-consumption formula). In that year, the Department reinterpreted the law so as to make taxable all fuel stored in the state and loaded there for use by the receiving plane anywhere. The new interpretation was upheld by the Illinois Supreme Court. Only three of the seven members of that court, however, held that the new interpretation was the correct one purely as a state-law matter. Two others joined in that result on the ground that the older "burn off" rule was federally unconstitutional under Helson v. Kentucky, 279 U.S. 245 (1929). The two dissenters took the position that the older "burn off" interpretation was correct as a matter of state law and was valid federally. (All members of the court agreed that the new interpretation was consistent with the federal Constitution.)

The Supreme Court considered the validity under the federal Constitution of both the new interpretation and the "burn off" rule. In reaching the latter issue, the Court noted that the two determining votes were premised on a construction of the federal Constitution regarding it and held that "[t]his basis for construing a state statute creates a federal question" (p. 630), even though the state court might have reached the same conclusion purely as a matter of state law. Holding that either state rule would be constitutional, the Court vacated the judgment and remanded for further proceedings.[2]

See also Three Affiliated Tribes v. Wold Engineering, P.C., 467 U.S. 138 (1984) (correcting state court's misconceptions as to federal law that apparently caused it to decline jurisdiction over a case involving claims by an Indian Tribe; remand to enable state court to pass on state-law issues).

2. On remand, the Illinois Supreme Court reaffirmed its prior judgment because "[t]he conclusion of those [concurring] justices is that the current interpretation of the Act and the application of it by the Department are not improper * * *." 54 Ill.2d 431, 432, 298 N.E.2d 161 (1973).

(5) California, like a number of other states, provides by statute that its courts may exercise long-arm jurisdiction in any case permitted by the Federal Constitution. See California Code Civil Proc. § 410.10; see also, e.g., Rhode Island Gen.Laws Ann. § 9–5–33. Does this mean that every case where the California courts hold that jurisdiction cannot be obtained under the state statute presents a federal question subject to Supreme Court review?

(6) In Delaware v. Prouse, 440 U.S. 648 (1979), the state supreme court reversed a conviction on the ground that illegally seized evidence was used, in violation of the Fourth Amendment and the Delaware constitution. On certiorari, the Supreme Court held it had jurisdiction: "As we understand the opinion below, Art I, § 6, of the Delaware Constitution will automatically be interpreted at least as broadly as the Fourth Amendment; that is, every police practice authoritatively determined to be contrary to the Fourth and Fourteenth Amendments will, without further analysis, be held to be contrary to Art. I, § 6. This approach * * * was followed in this case. The court * * * concluded that the Fourth Amendment foreclosed spot checks of automobiles, and summarily held that the State Constitution was therefore also infringed" (pp. 652–53).

In order to fit Prouse into the prevailing case law, wasn't the Court also required to find that the Delaware provision was interpreted by the state court as prohibiting *only* those searches prohibited by the Fourth Amendment?

(7) If a state imposes its own tax on taxable income as defined by federal law, is every state court decision regarding its income tax reviewable by the Supreme Court? If a state were to adopt the Federal Rules of Civil Procedure and provide that state courts should follow the interpretation of the federal rules by the Supreme Court, would every procedural question arising in civil cases in the state courts present a federal question?

(8) Consider the suggestion of Greene, *Hybrid State Law in the Federal Courts,* 83 Harv.L.Rev. 289, 309 (1969), that in determining Supreme Court jurisdiction to review federal questions made relevant by state law, the "touchstone * * * is whether the federal law is itself operative in the circumstances of the case—whether Supreme Court jurisdiction could effect the coordination of two coextensive and possibly conflicting obligations."

Would it, as Greene suggests, support Supreme Court review of a case arising out of a private contract under state law that is conditioned on some federal question—for example, an action on a lease for a suburban Washington home expressly contingent upon the lessor's holding federal office, in which the issue is the validity of the statute under which the lessor was discharged from federal employ? *Cf.* Skelly Oil Co. v. Phillips Petrol. Co., 339 U.S. 667 (1950) (involving district court "federal question" jurisdiction), pp. 1032, 1039, *infra.* See also Mishkin, *The Federal "Question" in the District Courts,* 53 Colum.L.Rev. 157, 183–84 (1953).

RECONSTRUCTION FINANCE CORP. v. BEAVER COUNTY

328 U.S. 204, 66 S.Ct. 992, 90 L.Ed. 1172 (1946).
Appeal from the Supreme Court of Pennsylvania.

MR. JUSTICE BLACK delivered the opinion of the Court.

By Section 10 of the Reconstruction Finance Corporation Act, as amended, 47 Stat. 5, 9, 55 Stat. 248, 15 U.S.C.A. § 610, Congress made it clear that it did not permit states and local governments to impose taxes of any kind on the franchise, capital, reserves, surplus, income, loans, and personal property of the Reconstruction Finance Corporation or any of its subsidiary corporations.[1] Congress provided in the same section that "any real property" of these governmental agencies "shall be subject to State, Territorial, county, municipal, or local taxation to the same extent according to its value as other real property is taxed." The Supreme Court of Pennsylvania sustained the imposition of a tax on certain machinery owned and used in Beaver County, Pennsylvania, by the Defense Plant Corporation, an RFC subsidiary. The question presented on this appeal from the Supreme Court judgment is whether the Supreme Court's holding that this machinery is "subject to" a local "real property" tax means that the Pennsylvania tax statute, 72 Purdon's Pennsylvania Stat. § 5020–201, as applied conflicts with Section 10 of the Reconstruction Finance Corporation Act. This appeal, thus, challenges the validity of a state statute sustained by the highest court of the state and raises a substantial federal question. We have jurisdiction under 28 U.S.C. § 344(a), and appellee's motion to dismiss is denied.

In 1941 Defense Plant Corporation[3] acquired certain land in Beaver County. It erected buildings on the property and equipped them with machinery and attachments necessary and essential to the existence and operation of a manufacturing plant for aircraft propellers. The plant, thus fully equipped, was leased to Curtiss–Wright Corporation, to carry out its war contracts with the government for the manufacture of propellers. Most of the machinery was heavy, not attached to the buildings, and was held in place by its own weight. Other portions of the machinery were attached by easily removable screws and bolts, and some of the equipment and fixtures could be moved from place to place within the plant. The lease contract with Curtiss–Wright authorized the government to receive and to replace existing equipment, and parts of the machinery appear to have been frequently interchanged and replaced as the convenience of the government required. The lease contract also provided that the machinery should "remain personalty notwithstanding the fact it may be affixed or attached to realty."

The government contends that under these circumstances the machinery was not "real" but was "personal" property, and that therefore its taxation was forbidden by Congress. The "real property" which Congress made "subject" to state taxation, should in the Government's view be limited to "land and buildings and those fixtures which are so integrated

1. As to the Constitutional tax immunity of governmental properties see United States v. County of Allegheny, 322 U.S. 174. * * *

3. By joint resolution of Congress, Ch. 215, Public Law 109, June 30, 1945, 79th

Congress, 15 U.S.C.A. § 606b note, Defense Plant Corporation was dissolved and all of its functions, powers, duties and liabilities were transferred to Reconstruction Finance Corporation.

with the buildings as to be uniformly, or, at most, generally, regarded as real property." "Real property", within this definition would include buildings and "fixtures essential to a building's operations" but would not include fixtures, movable machinery, or equipment, which though essential to applicant's operations as a plant, are not essential to a building's operation as a building.

The county would, for tax purposes, define real property so as to treat machinery, equipment, fixtures, and the land on which a manufacturing establishment is located as an integral real property unit. This is in accord with the view of the state's supreme court which made the following statement in sustaining the tax here involved [350 Pa. 520, 39 A.2d 714]: "It has long been the rule in Pennsylvania that 'Whether fast or loose, therefore, all the machinery of a manufactory which is necessary to constitute it, and without which it would not be a manufactory at all, must pass for a part of the freehold.' * * * Appellant's machinery, being an integrated part of the manufactory, and so, of the freehold, was therefore taxable" under Pennsylvania's definition of real property. This interpretation of Pennsylvania's tax law is of course binding on us. But Pennsylvania's definition of "real property" cannot govern if it conflicts with the scope of that term as used in the federal statute. What meaning Congress intended is a federal question which we must determine.

The 1941 Act does not itself define real property. Nor do the legislative reports or other relevant data provide any single decisive piece of evidence as to Congressional intent. Obviously, it could have intended either, as the government argues, that content be given to the term "real property" as a matter of federal law, under authoritative decisions of this Court, or, as the county contends, that the meaning of the term should be its meaning under local tax laws so long as those tax laws were not designed to discriminate against the government.

In support of its contention that a federal definition of real property should be applied, the government relies on the generally accepted principle that Congress normally intends that its laws shall operate uniformly throughout the nation so that the federal program will remain unimpaired. Jerome v. United States, 318 U.S. 101, 104; Commissioner v. Tower, 327 U.S. 280. But Congress in permitting local taxation of the real property, made it impossible to apply the law with uniform tax consequences in each state and locality. For the several states, and even the localities within them, have diverse methods of assessment, collection, and refunding. Tax rates vary widely. To all of these variable tax consequences Congress has expressly subjected the "real property" of the Defense Plant Corporation. In view of this express provision the normal assumption that Congress intends its law to have the same consequences throughout the nation cannot be made. Furthermore, Congress, had it desired complete nationwide uniformity as to tax consequences, could have stipulated for fixed payments in lieu of taxes, as it has done in other statutes. Nor can we see how application of a local rule governing what is "real property" for tax purposes would impair the Congressional program for the production of war materials any more than the program would be impaired by the action of Congress in leaving the fixing of rates of taxation to local communities.

We think the Congressional purpose can best be accomplished by application of settled state rules as to what constitutes "real property" so long as it is plain, as it is here, that the state rules do not effect a discrimination against the government, or patently run counter to the terms of the Act. Concepts of real property are deeply rooted in state traditions, customs, habits, and laws. Local tax administration is geared to those concepts. To permit the states to tax, and yet to require them to alter their long-standing practice of assessments and collections, would create the kind of confusion and resultant hampering of local tax machinery, which we are certain Congress did not intend. The fact that Congress subjected Defense Plant Corporation's properties to local taxes "to the same extent according to its value as other real property is taxed" indicated an intent to integrate Congressional permission to tax with established local tax assessment and collection machinery.

Affirmed.

MR. JUSTICE JACKSON took no part in the consideration or decision of this case.

NOTE ON FEDERAL INCORPORATION BY REFERENCE OF STATE LAW

(1) State incorporation of federal legal terms or standards sometimes gives the Supreme Court the final word as to their meaning. But when federal law adopts state terms or standards, the state courts do not have the final word: the Supreme Court has authority to supervise the construction of state law adopted by the state court, to assure that the purposes of federal law have not been evaded or undermined. (See, *e.g.*, the care with which Justice Black makes this point in the "so long as" clause of the first sentence of the last paragraph of Beaver County.) The state cannot be allowed to manipulate the state-law definition so as to discriminate against the federal policy. (Consider by what techniques such manipulations could be accomplished.) Furthermore, an aberrant state definition, even if not discriminatory, may fall outside of Congress' understanding of what it was accomplishing. (Consider a state that treats automobiles garaged at the plant as "real property" for purposes of real estate tax.)

In United States v. Nardello, 393 U.S. 286 (1969), the Court held that 18 U.S.C. § 1952, prohibiting interstate travel with intent to carry on "extortion, bribery, or arson in violation of the laws of the State in which committed," included conduct classified as "blackmail" rather than "extortion" under Pennsylvania statutes. Pennsylvania followed the common-law definition making "extortion" applicable only to the conduct of public officials; it denominated private conduct of the same kind "blackmail." Chief Justice Warren, for the Court, said (pp. 293–95):

"Appellees argue that Congress' decision not to define extortion combined with its decision to prohibit only extortion in violation of state law compels the conclusion that peculiar versions of state terminology are controlling. Since in Pennsylvania a distinction is maintained between extortion and blackmail with only the latter term covering appellees' activities, it follows that the Travel Act does not reach the conduct charged. The fallacy of this contention lies in its assumption that, by defining extortion with reference to state law, Congress also incorporated state labels for particular offenses. Congress' intent was to aid local law enforcement officials, not to eradicate only those extortionate activities which any given State denominated extortion. * * * We can discern no reason why Congress would wish to have § 1952 aid local law enforcement efforts in [another State] but to deny that aid to Pennsylvania when both States have statutes covering the same offense. We therefore conclude that the inquiry is not the manner in which States classify their criminal prohibitions but whether the particular State involved prohibits the extortionate activity charged." [1]

(2) Whether Congress in a particular enactment did in fact intend to adopt state law, rather than to impose a uniform federal standard or definition, is of course itself a question of federal law. It arises most frequently in litigation in the lower federal courts; for that reason, the materials relevant to this issue are canvassed in Chapter VII in connection with Federal Common Law, at p. 849, *infra.*

Problems analogous to that presented in the Beaver County case are legion in connection with the federal criminal law, the federal tax law, and other areas that are concerned with legal relations and property interests created and defined by state law.[2] Sometimes (as in Beaver County) Congress does not specify whether it intends to refer to state law; sometimes the direction to refer to state law is explicit (see, *e.g.*, the Federal Tort Claims Act, discussed at p. 1147, *infra*). The "substantive" choice of law issues raised by these questions of interpretation can present formidable difficulties. But, as Beaver County shows, the scope of the Court's review when these questions come to it from the state courts has not been problematic.

NOTE ON THE REVIEW OF STATE DECISIONS CONCERNING TRANSACTIONS OR RIGHTS OF THE UNITED STATES, ITS AGENCIES OR OFFICERS

(1) Jurisdiction in the Beaver County case rested on what is now 28 U.S.C. § 1257(2), the validity of the Pennsylvania tax statute having been "drawn in question" and sustained by the state court. Note that § 1257 does not confer jurisdiction on the Supreme Court to review state judgments on the ground that the United States or a federal agency or officer is party to the litigation. These litigants, like any others, may challenge the validity of state legislation on federal grounds. In addition to Beaver County, see, *e.g.*, United States v. Burnison, 339 U.S. 87 (1950); United

---

1. See also, *e.g.*, Aloha Airlines, Inc. v. Director of Taxation of Hawaii, 464 U.S. 7 (1983): A federal statute prohibits states from taxing "gross receipts" derived from air transportation, but allows them to impose property taxes on airlines. Hawaii imposed a tax on the gross receipts of airlines, but provided specifically that the tax "is a means of taxing the personal property of the airline." The Court was unanimous in invalidating the tax: "The manner in which the state legislature has described and categorized § 239–6 cannot mask the fact that the purpose and effect of the provision is to impose a levy upon the gross receipts of airlines."

2. For a sampling of important cases on the question, see, *e.g.*, Morgan v. Commissioner, 309 U.S. 78, 80 (1940) (definition of "general power of appointment" under tax statute); Helvering v. Stuart, 317 U.S. 154 (1942) (whether there is "power to revest" title to trust corpus in grantor); Jerome v. United States, 318 U.S. 101 (1943) (Bank Robbery Act; meaning of term "felony"); Richards v. United States, 369 U.S. 1 (1962) (Federal Tort Claims Act); De Sylva v. Ballentine, 351 U.S. 570 (1956) (definition of author's "children" under Copyright Act).

States v. County of Allegheny, 322 U.S. 174 (1944). Or they may assert rights or immunities based on the Constitution, treaties, laws or federal commissions or authorities. *Cf.* United States v. Ansonia Brass & Copper Co., 218 U.S. 452 (1910); United States v. Pink, 315 U.S. 203 (1942). But if their rights admittedly rest on state law alone, does the Supreme Court have jurisdiction to review an adverse state adjudication and, if so, what is its statutory source?

In United States v. Thompson, 93 U.S. 586, 588 (1876), the Court declared that judgments "in the State courts against the United States cannot be brought here for re-examination upon a writ of error, except in cases where the same relief would be afforded to private parties". It dismissed a writ of error to review a judgment, resting upon "principles of general law alone", that a debt to the United States had been extinguished. See also United States v. Fox, 94 U.S. 315 (1876) (New York construction of state statute of wills to bar devise of realty to United States held "conclusive" on Supreme Court).

But in Stanley v. Schwalby, 147 U.S. 508 (1893), 162 U.S. 255 (1896), a Texas judgment in a trespass action against officers in charge of the San Antonio military reservation, awarding the plaintiff an undivided one-third interest in the land and the right to joint possession, was reversed upon the ground that the state court erroneously held that the United States took a deed from the City of San Antonio with notice of a previous conveyance. Holding the evidence insufficient "in fact and in law" to establish notice, the Court said (pp. 278–79):

" * * * so far as the judgment of the state court against the validity of an authority set up by the defendants under the United States necessarily involves the decision of a question of law, it must be reviewed by this court, whether that question depends upon the Constitution, laws or treaties of the United States, or upon the local law, or upon principles of general jurisprudence. For instance, if a marshal of the United States takes personal property upon attachment on mesne process issued by a court of the United States, and is sued in an action of trespass in a state court by one claiming title in the property, and sets up his authority under the United States, and judgment is rendered against him in the highest court of the State, he may bring the case by writ of error to this court; and, as his justification depends upon the question whether the title to the property was in the defendant in attachment, or in the plaintiff in the action of trespass, this court, upon the writ of error, has the power to decide that question, so far as it is one of law, even if it depends upon local law, or upon general principles."

(2) The question posed in the previous paragraph has tended to lose importance in light of the developing jurisprudence that holds that questions touching on the legal relations of the United States are questions of federal common law (although the answer may incorporate state law by reference). See, *e.g.,* cases such as Silas Mason Co. v. Tax Comm'n, 302 U.S. 186, 197 (1937); Wilson v. Cook, 327 U.S. 474, 486 (1946); and see the *Note on Choice of Law in Cases Involving the Legal Relations of the United States: Herein of Federal Government Litigation,* p. 863, *infra.*

Consider, nevertheless, whether the jurisdictional statutes should be amended to provide in terms for Supreme Court review of federal government litigation arising in the state courts. If so, how?

INDIANA ex rel. ANDERSON v. BRAND

303 U.S. 95, 58 S.Ct. 443, 82 L.Ed. 685 (1938).
Certiorari to the Supreme Court of Indiana.

MR. JUSTICE ROBERTS delivered the opinion of the Court.

The petitioner sought a writ of mandate to compel the respondent to continue her in employment as a public school teacher. Her complaint alleged that as a duly licensed teacher she entered into a contract in September, 1924, to teach in the township schools and, pursuant to successive contracts, taught continuously to and including the school year 1932–1933; that her contracts for the school years 1931–1932 and 1932–1933 contained this clause: "It is further agreed by the contracting parties that all of the provisions of the Teachers' Tenure Law, approved March 8, 1927, shall be in full force and effect in this contract"; and that by force of that act she had a contract, indefinite in duration, which could be canceled by the respondent only in the manner and for the causes specified in the act. She charged that in July, 1933, the respondent notified her he proposed to cancel her contract for cause; that, after a hearing, he adhered to his decision and the county superintendent affirmed his action; that, despite what occurred in July, 1933, the petitioner was permitted to teach during the school year 1933–1934 and the respondent was presently threatening to terminate her employment at the end of that year. The complaint alleged the termination of her employment would be a breach of her contract with the school corporation. The respondent demurred on the grounds that (1) the complaint disclosed the matters pleaded had been submitted to the respondent and the county superintendent who were authorized to try the issues and had lawfully determined them in favor of the respondent; and (2) the Teachers' Tenure Law, Acts Ind.1927, c. 97, had been repealed in respect of teachers in township schools. The demurrer was sustained and the petitioner appealed to the state Supreme Court which affirmed the judgment. The court did not discuss the first ground of demurrer relating to the action taken in the school year 1932–1933, but rested its decision upon the second, that, by an act of 1933, Acts Ind.1933, c. 116, the Teachers' Tenure Law had been repealed as respects teachers in township schools; and held that the repeal did not deprive the petitioner of a vested property right and did not impair her contract within the meaning of the Constitution. * * *

The court below holds that in Indiana teachers' contracts are made for but 1 year; that there is no contractual right to be continued as a teacher from year to year; that the law grants a privilege to one who has taught 5 years and signed a new contract to continue in employment under given conditions; that the statute is directed merely to the exercise of their powers by the school authorities and the policy therein expressed may be altered at the will of the Legislature; that in enacting laws for the government of public schools, the Legislature exercises a function of sovereignty and the power to control public policy in respect of their management and operation cannot be contracted away by one Legislature so as to create a permanent public policy unchangeable by succeeding Legislatures. In the alternative the court declares that if the relationship be considered as controlled by the rules of private contract the provision for re-employment from year to year is unenforceable for want of mutuality.

As in most cases brought to this court under the contract clause of the Constitution, the question is as to the existence and nature of the contract and not as to the construction of the law which is supposed to impair it. The principal function of a legislative body is not to make contracts but to make laws which declare the policy of the state and are subject to repeal when a subsequent Legislature shall determine to alter that policy. Nevertheless, it is established that a legislative enactment may contain provisions which, when accepted as the basis of action by individuals, become contracts between them and the State or its subdivisions within the protection of article 1, § 10. If the people's representatives deem it in the public interest they may adopt a policy of contracting in respect of public business for a term longer than the life of the current session of the Legislature. This the petitioner claims has been done with respect to permanent teachers. The Supreme Court has decided, however, that it is the state's policy not to bind school corporations by contract for more than 1 year.

On such a question, one primarily of state law, we accord respectful consideration and great weight to the views of the state's highest court but, in order that the constitutional mandate may not become a dead letter, we are bound to decide for ourselves whether a contract was made, what are its terms and conditions, and whether the State has, by later legislation, impaired its obligation. This involves an appraisal of the statutes of the State and the decisions of its courts.

The courts of Indiana have long recognized that the employment of school teachers was contractual and have afforded relief in actions upon teachers' contracts. * * *

In 1927, the State adopted the Teachers' Tenure Act under which the present controversy arises. * * * By this act it was provided that a teacher who has served under contract for 5 or more successive years, and thereafter enters into a contract for further service with the school corporation, shall become a permanent teacher and the contract, upon the expiration of its stated term, shall be deemed to continue in effect for an indefinite period, shall be known as an indefinite contract, and shall remain in force unless succeeded by a new contract or canceled as provided in the Act. The corporation may cancel the contract, after notice and hearing, for incompetency, insubordination, neglect of duty, immorality, justifiable decrease in the number of teaching positions, or other good or just cause, but not for political or personal reasons. The teacher may not cancel the contract during the school term nor for a period 30 days previous to the beginning of any term (unless by mutual agreement) and may cancel only upon 5 days' notice.

By an amendatory act of 1933 township school corporations were omitted from the provisions of the Act of 1927. The court below construed this act as repealing the act of 1927 so far as township schools and teachers are concerned and as leaving the respondent free to terminate the petitioner's employment. But we are of opinion that the petitioner had a valid contract with the respondent, the obligation of which would be impaired by the termination of her employment.

Where the claim is that the state's policy embodied in a statute is to bind its instrumentalities by contract, the cardinal inquiry is as to the terms of the statute supposed to create such a contract. The State long prior to the adoption of the Act of 1927 required the execution of written contracts between teachers and school corporations, specified certain subjects with which such contracts must deal, and required that they be made a matter of public record. These were annual contracts, covering a single school term. The Act of 1927 announced a new policy that a teacher who had served for 5 years under successive contracts, upon the execution of another was to become a permanent teacher and the last contract was to be indefinite as to duration and terminable by either party only upon compliance with the conditions set out in the statute. The policy which induced the legislation evidently was that the teacher should have protection against the exercise of the right, which would otherwise inhere in the employer, of terminating the employment at the end of any school term without assigned reasons and solely at the employer's pleasure. The state courts in earlier cases so declared.

The title of the Act is couched in terms of contract. It speaks of the making and canceling of indefinite contracts. In the body the word "contract" appears ten times in section 1, defining the relationship; eleven times in section 2, relating to the termination of the employment by the employer, and four times in section 4, stating the conditions of termination by the teacher.

The tenor of the act indicates that the word "contract" was not used inadvertently or in other than its usual legal meaning. By section 6 it is expressly provided that the act is a supplement to that of March 7, 1921, supra, requiring teachers' employment contracts to be in writing. By section 1 it is provided that the written contract of a permanent teacher "shall be deemed to continue in effect for an indefinite period and shall be known as an indefinite contract." Such an indefinite contract is to remain in force unless succeeded by a new contract signed by both parties or canceled as provided in section 2. No more apt language could be employed to define a contractual relationship. By section 2 it is enacted that such indefinite contracts may be canceled by the school corporation only in the manner specified. The admissible grounds of cancellation, and the method by which the existence of such grounds shall be ascertained and made a matter of record, are carefully set out. Section 4 permits cancellation by the teacher only at certain times consistent with the convenient administration of the school system and imposes a sanction for violation of its requirements. Examination of the entire act convinces us that the teacher was by it assured of the possession of a binding and enforceable contract against school districts.

Until its decision in the present case the Supreme Court of the State had uniformly held that the teacher's right to continued employment by virtue of the indefinite contract created pursuant to the act was contractual. * * *

[The opinion here reviews four decisions of the Indiana Supreme Court explicitly referring to teachers' contractual rights while also indicating that mandamus to compel reinstatement had been available.]

We think the decision in this case runs counter to the policy evinced by the Act of 1927, to its explicit mandate and to earlier decisions construing its provisions. * * *

The respondent urges that every contract is subject to the police power and that in repealing the Teachers' Tenure Act the Legislature validly exercised that reserved power of the State. The sufficient answer is found in the statute. By section 2 of the Act of 1927 power is given to the school corporation to cancel a teacher's indefinite contract for incompetency, insubordination (which is to be deemed to mean willful refusal to obey the school laws of the State or reasonable rules prescribed by the employer), neglect of duty, immorality, justifiable decrease in the number of teaching positions, or other good and just cause. The permissible reasons for cancellation cover every conceivable basis for such action growing out of a deficient performance of the obligations undertaken by the teacher, and diminution of the school requirements. Although the causes specified constitute in themselves just and reasonable grounds for the termination of any ordinary contract of employment, to preclude the assumption that any other valid ground was excluded by the enumeration, the Legislature added that the relation might be terminated for any other good and just cause. Thus in the declaration of the state's policy, ample reservations in aid of the efficient administration of the school system were made. * * * It is significant that the act of 1933 left the system of permanent teachers and indefinite contracts untouched as respects school corporations in cities and towns of the State. * * *

Our decisions recognize that every contract is made subject to the implied condition that its fulfillment may be frustrated by a proper exercise of the police power but we have repeatedly said that, in order to have this effect, the exercise of the power must be for an end which is in fact public and the means adopted must be reasonably adapted to that end, and the Supreme Court of Indiana has taken the same view in respect of legislation impairing the obligation of the contract of a state instrumentality. The causes of cancellation provided in the Act of 1927 and the retention of the system of indefinite contracts in all municipalities except townships by the act of 1933 are persuasive that the repeal of the earlier act by the later was not an exercise of the police power for the attainment of ends to which its exercise may properly be directed.

As the court below has not passed upon one of the grounds of demurrer which appears to involve no federal question, and may present a defense still open to the respondent, we reverse the judgment and remand the cause for further proceedings not inconsistent with this opinion.

So ordered.

MR. JUSTICE CARDOZO took no part in the consideration or decision of this case.

MR. JUSTICE BLACK, dissenting. * * *

The Indiana Supreme Court has consistently held, even before its decision in this case, that the right of teachers, under the 1927 Act, to serve until removed for cause, was *not given by contract, but by statute.* Such

was the express holding in the two cases cited in the majority opinion:
* * *

These cases demonstrate that the Supreme Court of Indiana has uniformly held that teachers did not hold their "indefinite" tenure under *contract,* but by grant of a repealable statute. In order to hold in this case that a contract was impaired, it is necessary to create a contract unauthorized by the Indiana Legislature and declared to be nonexistent by the Indiana Supreme Court. * * *

The clear purport of Indiana law is that its Legislature cannot surrender any part of its plenary constitutional right to repeal, alter or amend existing legislation relating to the school system whenever the conditions demand change for the public good. Under Indiana law the Legislature can neither barter nor give away its constitutional investiture of power. It can make no contract in conflict with this sovereign power. The construction of the constitution of Indiana by the Supreme Court of Indiana *must be accepted as correct.* That court holds that Indiana's Constitution invests Indiana's Legislature with *continuing* power to change Indiana's educational policies. It has here held that the Legislature did not attempt or intend to surrender its constitutional power by authorizing *definite* contracts which would prevent the future exercise of this continuing, constitutional power. If the Constitution and statutes of Indiana, as construed by its Supreme Court, prohibit the Legislature from making a contract which is inconsistent with a continuing power to legislate, there could have been no *definite* contracts to be impaired. * * *

Merits of a policy establishing a permanent teacher tenure law are not for consideration here. We are dealing with the constitutional right of the people of a sovereign state to control their own public school system as they deem best for the public welfare. This Court should neither make it impossible for states to experiment in the matter of security of tenure for their teachers, nor deprive them of the right to change a policy if it is found that it has not operated successfully. * * *

NOTE ON FEDERAL PROTECTION OF STATE–CREATED RIGHTS

A. The Contract Clause

(1) The opinion in the Brand case refers to the question "as to the existence and nature of the contract" claimed to be impaired as one "primarily of state law". Was it not *exclusively* a question of the law of Indiana? Is not the obligation that the contract clause protects against impairment normally created by state law? For explicit statements of this view, see, *e.g.,* Ogden v. Saunders, 12 Wheat. 213, 256–59, 326 (U.S.1827); Appleby v. City of New York, 271 U.S. 364 (1926); R.L. Hale, *The Supreme Court and the Contract Clause,* 57 Harv.L.Rev. 512, 621, 852 (1944).

Justice Jackson has, however, pointed to the contract clause as "an example of the part the common law must play in our system" in a context which suggests that he may have viewed the issue as one calling for the application of a federal common law. D'Oench, Duhme & Co. v. Federal Deposit Ins. Corp., 315 U.S. 447, 470 (1942), p. 858, *infra.* Can this position be defended?   Does it imply that the contract clause itself creates the contract obligation, the impairment of which it forbids?

(2) Even though the obligation is created by state law, the inquiry does not concern what state law *is* but rather what it *was*. The contract clause prohibits only impairment by legislation, not by alteration of judicial decision.   Tidal Oil Co. v. Flanagan, 263 U.S. 444 (1924); Fleming v. Fleming, 264 U.S. 29 (1924); see Frankfurter & Landis, The Business of the Supreme Court 199–202 (1928). It would seem, therefore, that the time at which to estimate the obligation is when the allegedly impairing legislation was enacted.   The Supreme Court appears, however, to have emphasized the date of the agreement. See, *e.g.,* El Paso v. Simmons, 379 U.S. 497, 506 (1965); Appleby v. New York, *supra;* Taney, C.J., in Ohio Life Ins. & Trust Co. v. Debolt, 16 How. 416, 431 (U.S.1854). In either case, does the fact that the relevant state law antedates the state court's judgment in the case under review explain why that judgment does not foreclose the issue in the Supreme Court?   Is the state court less authoritative an expositor of what the state law was than of what it now is?

(3) In the Brand case, the state court enforced the allegedly impairing statute; its judgment that there was no contract operated only to deny the claim of invalidity.   In Bacon v. Texas, 163 U.S. 207 (1896), the state recovered judgment for possession of 300,000 acres of public land.   The defendant claimed to have acquired title under a statute of 1877, alleging that his tender of payment had been illegally refused. The statute was repealed in 1883, and the defendant challenged the repeal as an impairment. The state court held the tender ineffective (1) because defendant did not comply with the requirements of the act of 1877, and (2) because the tender was not made until after the repeal. The Supreme Court dismissed a writ of error, holding that the first ground gave no effect to the challenged legislation and was broad enough to sustain the judgment.

Other decisions, however, suggest a duty in the Supreme Court to inquire whether, given an acceptable determination as to the existence or the meaning of the contract, the state court could have rendered judgment without resting on impairing legislation. See, *e.g.,* Terre Haute & Indianapolis R.R. v. Indiana ex rel. Ketcham, 194 U.S. 579 (1904); Columbia Ry. v. South Carolina, 261 U.S. 236 (1923); *cf.* Long Sault Dev. Co. v. Call, 242 U.S. 272 (1916). Should this inquiry be undertaken and, if so, should the scope of review be any different than it is when the state has admittedly enforced a later statute?

④ In affirming the "independent judgment" rule, the Supreme Court usually has avowed a disposition to accord respectful weight to the state court's determination.   The Court has said that with regard to "the effect and meaning of the contract as well as its existence * * * we lean toward agreement with the courts of the state, and accept their judgment as to such matters unless manifestly wrong."   Hale v. State Board, 302 U.S. 95, 101 (1937).   See also, *e.g.,* Rapid Transit Corp. v. New York, 303 U.S. 573, 593 (1938); Atlantic Coast Line v. Phillips, 332 U.S. 168, 171 (1947).

With this qualification, is the scope of review under the contract clause broader than in other situations where the existence of a federal right turns on preliminary questions of state law? See, *e.g.,* pp. 575–81, *infra.* Should it be? Can a state court be held "manifestly wrong" on a matter of state law in the absence of explicit, earlier decisions setting forth a different view?   Was the state court "manifestly wrong" in Brand? Is it psychologically possible for the Supreme Court to do any more than ask itself whether it clearly would have judged the issue differently, on the available materials of decision, if it were the state's highest court? Compare the scope of review in West Virginia ex rel. Dyer v. Sims, p. 319, *supra.*

(5) In United States Mortgage Co. v. Matthews, 293 U.S. 232 (1934), the state court affirmed a contract obligation and invalidated the alleged impairment. The Supreme Court, on certiorari, reversed, disagreeing as to the existence of the obligation. Should the scope of review have been narrower because the claimed federal right was sustained rather than denied? *Cf.* Municipal Investors v. Birmingham, 316 U.S. 153 (1942), where the state court assumed, without deciding, that there was a contract right but sustained the validity of its impairment. The Supreme Court affirmed upon the ground that no contract existed, saying (p. 157): "While this approach forces us to decide the meaning of Michigan legislation without the assistance of the courts of that State, it is necessary to do so because of the obligation of this Court to determine for itself the basic assumptions upon which interpretations of the Federal Constitution rest." Was this disposition "necessary"? Proper?

(6) Contrast, with the problems presented above, issues as to whether a particular kind of obligation is protected from impairment by the contract clause or whether a particular impairment is forbidden. Such questions plainly involve nothing but interpretation of the Constitution. See, *e.g.,* El Paso v. Simmons, 379 U.S. 497, 506–08 (1965). See, generally, Wright, The Contract Clause of the Constitution (1938); Hale, *supra;* Note, *The Contract Clause of the Federal Constitution,* 32 Colum.L.Rev. 476 (1932); Kauper, *What is a "Contract" Under the Contracts Clause of the Federal Constitution?,* 31 Mich.L.Rev. 187 (1932).

B. Due Process

A huge body of law addresses the question whether, and to what extent, state law controls in determining whether a challenged state deprivation constitutes an invasion of "property" or "liberty" interests within the meaning of the Due Process Clause.

(1) The earlier cases involved traditional ("old") property interests. For an example, see Demorest v. City Bank Farmers Trust Co., 321 U.S. 36 (1944): A New York statute prescribed a rule for apportionment between life tenants and remaindermen under a will or trust of the proceeds of mortgage salvage operations uncompleted at the date of the enactment, where the instrument is silent on apportionment. The remaindermen contended that the statutory rule was less favorable to their interests than the decisional doctrines that it supplanted. They urged, therefore, that its retroactive application constituted a deprivation of property without due process. The New York Court of Appeals held, however, that its earlier decisions did not lay down fixed rules on the subject, as distinguished from tentative guides to the discretion of trustees. Affirming the state judgment sustaining the statute, Justice Jackson said (pp. 42–43):

"In thus rejecting appellants' version of its previous decisions the Court of Appeals disposed of their cases on the ground that appellants have never possessed under New York law such a property right as they claim has been taken from them. If this is the case, appellants have no question for us under the Due Process Clause. Decisions of this Court as to its province in such circumstances were summarized in Broad River Power Co. v. South Carolina, 281 U.S. 537, 540, as follows: 'Whether the state court has denied to rights asserted under local law the protection which the Constitution guarantees is a question upon which the petitioners are entitled to invoke the judgment of this Court. Even though the constitutional protection invoked be denied on non-federal grounds, it is the province of this Court to inquire whether the decision of the state court rests upon a fair or substantial basis. If unsubstantial, constitutional obligations may not be thus evaded. But if there is no evasion of the constitutional issue, and the nonfederal ground of decision has fair support, this Court will not inquire whether the rule applied by the state court is right or wrong, or substitute its own view of what should be deemed the better rule, for that of the state court.'[1]

"Despite difference of opinion within the Court of Appeals as to the effect of its earlier cases, we think that the decision of the majority that they did not amount to a rule of property does rest on a fair and substantial basis."

Is this a different measure of the scope of Supreme Court review than in the contract clause cases? If so, is there a basis for distinction?

(2) The recent cases on this subject are devoted almost exclusively to the question whether asserted deprivations of "new" property interests— claims for government benefits; claims for continuation of or access to advantageous relations with the government (e.g., government employment); claims by students or prisoners that the government has acted

---

1. In the Broad River case, quoted by Justice Jackson, the state court awarded mandamus to compel the Power Company and its subsidiary to continue operation of a street railway system that produced an operating loss, on the ground that the franchise was inseparable from a profitable franchise for electric light and power that the defendants did not offer to surrender. An otherwise confiscatory mandate was, in short, sustained as the enforcement of a valid contract. The Supreme Court on certiorari dismissed the writ, finding that "the judgment below is supported by a state ground which we may rightly accept as substantial."

On petition for rehearing counsel argued, inter alia, that "where it becomes necessary to consider whether a State is depriving, or attempting to deprive, a litigant of property without due process of law in violation of the Fourteenth Amendment, and the question turns on the existence and terms of an asserted contract, this Court determines for itself whether there is a contract and what are its terms". 282 U.S. 187, 191 (1930). The petition was denied, Chief Justice Hughes, Justices Holmes, Brandeis, and Stone adhering to the views expressed in the original opinion. Justices Van Devanter, McReynolds, Sutherland and Butler retreated from the opinion, concurring only because of a finding by the state court that petitioners "did not make a bona fide effort to make the street railway business a success." In view of this finding they saw "no present need" to consider whether the franchises were unified or separate (pp. 192–93). Justice Roberts did not participate.

In Muhlker v. Harlem R.R., 197 U.S. 544 (1905), a New York statute directed the railroad to elevate its tracks above the level of the street. Abutting owners, claiming an invasion of their easements of light and air, sued to enjoin use of the elevated structure, challenging the statute as a deprivation of their property in violation of the Fourteenth Amendment. They also argued that their easements had been recognized by state decisions prior to the acquisition of their title and that the statute, therefore, impaired the obligation of the contract embodied in their deeds. The Court of Appeals held for the defendant. What scope of review should the Supreme Court have accorded each contention? See also Sauer v. New York, 206 U.S. 536 (1907); Fox River Paper Co. v. Railroad Comm., 274 U.S. 651 (1927). Compare the treatment of the title issue in Fairfax's Devisee v. Hunter's Lessee, p. 505, supra.

Compare also Webb's Fabulous Pharmacies, Inc. v. Beckwith, 449 U.S. 155 (1980).

arbitrarily or unfairly—involve a deprivation of "liberty" or "property" within the meaning of the Due Process Clause, and the antecedent question whether and to what extent state law is determinative of that question.

This burgeoning body of case law started with Board of Regents v. Roth, 408 U.S. 564 (1972), and Perry v. Sindermann, 408 U.S. 593 (1972). In Roth, a state university teacher was not reappointed at the end of his one-year term. He alleged that the failure to renew without statement of reasons or a hearing constituted a deprivation of property without due process of law. The district court and the court of appeals held that such procedures were required. The Supreme Court reversed. Justice Stewart, for the Court, pointed out (p. 577): "Property interests, of course, are not created by the Constitution. Rather they are created and their dimensions are defined by existing rules or understandings that stem from an independent source such as state law * * *." In the present case, he said, "the terms of the respondent's appointment secured absolutely no interest in re-employment for the next year. They supported absolutely no possible claim of entitlement to re-employment. Nor, significantly, was there any state statute or University rule or policy that secured his interest in re-employment or that created any legitimate claim to it. In these circumstances, * * * he did not have a *property* interest sufficient to require the University authorities to give him a hearing * * *" (p. 578). Justices Douglas, Brennan and Marshall dissented. Justice Marshall's dissent took the position that "every citizen who applies for a government job is entitled to it unless the government can establish some reason for denying the employment. This is the 'property' right that I believe is protected by the Fourteenth Amendment * * *. And it is also liberty—liberty to work—which is * * * secured by the Fourteenth Amendment" (pp. 588–89).

In Perry, a state college teacher made a similar claim concerning the nonrenewal of his appointment. In this case Justice Stewart, for the Court, held that the teacher's allegations did "raise a genuine issue as to his interest in continued employment at [the particular] College. He alleged that this interest, though not secured by a formal contractual tenure provision, was secured by a no less binding understanding fostered by the college administration" (p. 599). The case was remanded for a hearing to allow the teacher to show a "legitimate claim of entitlement to continued employment absent 'sufficient cause'" (p. 602).

Detailed study of developments since Roth and Perry belongs primarily to the courses in Administrative Law and Constitutional Law and is beyond our scope. The cases generally take the view that the question whether a "property" interest exists is governed by state law. The relevance of state law to the question whether a constitutionally-protected "liberty" interest exists is more controversial, with the weight of the authority being that, although there exist "liberty" interests as a matter of federal law without regard to state law, state law can create "liberty" interests. (The law is now also clear that if the case involves "property" or "liberty," the question whether due process has been afforded is a matter of federal constitutional law.) A flavor of these developments can be gleaned by considering the cases cited in the margin; [2] see also pp. 1268–69, *infra.*

2. See, *e.g.,* Arnett v. Kennedy, 416 U.S. 134 (1974) (plurality opinion, representing three Justices, suggests that where state law determines whether there is any "property" interest in state employment, state is also free to define what procedures must be followed for termination; plaintiff must "take the bitter with the sweet");

Since almost all the recent cases in this line have come to the Court from the lower federal courts (usually in actions under 42 U.S.C. § 1983), no special jurisprudence has emerged with respect to the Court's scope of review of state-court holdings as to whether the particular interest in question involved an "entitlement" under state law that qualified as a property or liberty interest under the Fourteenth Amendment.[3] Roth and Perry themselves were instituted in the federal district courts. (If the Perry case had been brought in state court, what would have been the scope of review of a state supreme court's determination as to whether there existed a "binding understanding" or "claim of entitlement" under state law?)

In Bishop v. Wood, 426 U.S. 341 (1976), a policeman who had been designated a permanent employee claimed that his discharge without a hearing deprived him of property in violation of the Fourteenth Amendment. Justice Stevens, for the Court, stated that "the sufficiency of the claim of entitlement must be decided by reference to state law. The North Carolina Supreme Court has held that an enforceable expectation of continued public employment in that State can exist only if the employer, by statute or contract, has actually granted some form of guarantee. [Citing one case.] Whether such a guarantee has been given can be determined only by an examination of the particular statute or ordinance in question.

"On its face the ordinance * * * may fairly be read as conferring such a guarantee. However, such a reading is not the only possible

Goss v. Lopez, 419 U.S. 565 (1975) ("on the basis of state law, appellees plainly had legitimate claims of entitlement to a public education"); Meachum v. Fano, 427 U.S. 215 (1976) (transfer of prisoner to maximum security facility; question whether "liberty" is implicated turns on "expectations" generated by state law); Ingraham v. Wright, 430 U.S. 651 (1977) (right to be free from unjustified corporal punishment involves "liberty;" no reference to state law); Greenholtz v. Inmates of Nebraska Penal and Correctional Complex, 442 U.S. 1 (1979) (refusal to grant parole does not implicate a protected "liberty," but Nebraska state law makes it a protected "property" interest); Vitek v. Jones, 445 U.S. 480 (1980) (transfer of prisoner to mental institution implicates "liberty" as a matter of federal law and also because of "objective expectations" created by state law); Logan v. Zimmerman Brush Co., 455 U.S. 422 (1982) (state law held to have created a "property" interest in the administrative enforcement of a state statute prohibiting employment discrimination); Youngberg v. Romeo, 457 U.S. 307 (1982) (liberty interest in conditions of confinement for the mentally ill; no reference to state law); Cleveland Board of Education v. Loudermill, 470 U.S. 532 (1985) (state law created a "property" entitlement in state employment; Arnett's "bitter with the sweet" analysis, collapsing the question of what procedures are due into the state's

definition of the entitlement, repudiated); Board of Pardons v. Allen, 107 S.Ct. 2415, 2418 n. 3 (1987) (parole; follows Greenholtz).

For a sampling of the extensive secondary comment, see Monaghan, Of "Liberty" and "Property," 62 Cornell L.Rev. 405 (1977); Van Alstyne, Cracks in "The New Property": Adjudicative Due Process in the Administrative State, 62 Cornell L.Rev. 445 (1977); Herman, The New Liberty, 59 N.Y. U.L.Rev. 482 (1984). For a more elaborate survey of the literature and cases, see the perceptive treatments in Breyer & Stewart, Administrative Law and Regulatory Policy 718–772 (2d ed. 1985), and Gellhorn, Byse, Strauss, Rakoff & Schotland, Administrative Law: Cases and Comments 562–656 (8th ed. 1987).

3. The few cases coming to the Court from state courts cast no special light on any distinctive scope of review. See, e.g., Hicks v. Oklahoma, 447 U.S. 343 (1980) (where state law provides for sentencing by a jury, Fourteenth Amendment protects, as a liberty interest, defendant's expectation that jury discretion will be determinative; Court makes its own evaluation of state requirements); Webb's Fabulous Pharmicies, Inc. v. Beckwith, 449 U.S. 155 (1980). Logan v. Zimmerman Brush Co., note 2, supra, exhibits a striking absence of deference to the state courts on the nature of the state-law interest involved in the case.

interpretation; the ordinance may also be construed as granting no right to continued employment but merely conditioning an employee's removal on compliance with certain specified procedures. We do not have any authoritative interpretation of this ordinance by a North Carolina state court. We do, however, have the opinion of the United States District Judge who, of course, sits in North Carolina and practiced law there for many years. * * * In this case, as the District Court construed the ordinance, * * * the employee is merely given certain procedural rights which the District Court found not to have been violated in this case. The District Court's reading of the ordinance is tenable; it derives some support from a decision of the North Carolina Supreme Court [cite]; and it was accepted by the Court of Appeals for the Fourth Circuit [by an equally divided court]. These reasons are sufficient to foreclose our independent examination of the state-law issue" (pp. 344–47).[4]

Does the Court's acceptance of the lower federal courts' finding and characterization of state law so long as it was "tenable" imply that the same standard of review would have governed if the case had come up through the North Carolina state courts?

(3) Is there any reason why the Court's general approach to this question should develop differently from the approach exemplified in both Beaver County and Brand: where a determination of state law is necessarily antecedent to the enforcement of a federal right, privilege or immunity (as where a Due Process Clause violation turns on whether state law has created a "property" or "liberty" interest), the opinion of the state courts on the question of state law will govern so long as there is fair support in the state law for that court's characterization, and so long as the state definition is not so aberrational or surprising that it subverts the purposes of the constitutional guarantee? (Note that the latter limitation suggests that substantive choice of law issues can reappear under the guise of scope-of-review issues.)

(4) Claims of deprivation of "liberty" on account of an unexpected and retroactive change in state law (see Bouie v. City of Columbia, p. 680, *infra*) may also raise questions as to the scope of review of state-court determinations with respect to what the pre-existing state law actually was.

In Splawn v. California, 431 U.S. 595 (1977), defendant was prosecuted for selling obscene films. He contended (a) that a decision of the California Supreme Court in effect at the time of the conduct for which he was convicted had held that evidence of "pandering" was inadmissible, (b) that a statute enacted thereafter had changed the law to allow evidence of "pandering" as probative of guilt, and (c) that this change was in violation of the prohibition against ex post facto laws and of the requirements of due process enunciated in Bouie.

4. Justices Brennan, White, Marshall, and Blackmun dissented. Justice Brennan, asserting (p. 353) that "[t]here is certainly a federal dimension to the definition of 'property' in the Federal Constitution * * *," contended that the relevant inquiry should be whether it was objectively reasonable for the employee to believe that under state law he could rely on continued employment. Justice White took the view that the ordinance "plainly grants" a right to the job, and that it then follows that the federal Constitution determines the process for discharge. Justice Blackmun took the position that the North Carolina law was not as held by the district court and accepted by the majority.

The Supreme Court affirmed the conviction, noting that defendant's arguments depended upon his contention regarding the prior state law. It pointed out that the state court in this case had rejected that contention, and said that, "since it is a contention which must in the last analysis turn on a proper reading of the California decisions, such a determination by the California Court of Appeal is entitled to great weight in evaluating petitioner's constitutional contentions" (p. 600). Quoting from the court of appeals opinion, and without explicit statement indicating independent verification, the opinion went on to accept the conclusion of that state court. The dissenters' position on the ex post facto issue was based on an independent assessment of state law.

C. Full Faith and Credit

(1) The full faith and credit clause and implementing legislation (Article IV, Sec. 1; 28 U.S.C. § 1738) accord federal protection to state-created rights when they are asserted in another state. The forum state is called upon to judge the existence and nature of the right in the state of its creation, and its judgment is reviewable by the Supreme Court. See, e.g., Clark v. Williard, 292 U.S. 112 (1934); Adam v. Saenger, 303 U.S. 59 (1938); Titus v. Wallick, 306 U.S. 282, 287–88 (1939); Barber v. Barber, 323 U.S. 77 (1944); Union National Bank v. Lamb, 337 U.S. 38 (1949); Johnson v. Muelberger, 340 U.S. 581 (1951); Ford v. Ford, 371 U.S. 187 (1962).

In Adam v. Saenger, *supra*, where the issue was whether a California judgment on which suit was brought in Texas had been rendered by a court with jurisdiction under California law, Justice Stone described the scope of Supreme Court review as follows (p. 64):

"While this Court reexamines such an issue with deference after its determination by a state court, it cannot, if the laws and Constitution of the United States are to be observed, accept as final the decision of the state tribunal as to matters alleged to give rise to the asserted federal right. This is especially the case where the decision is rested, not on local law or matters of fact of the usual type, which are peculiarly within the cognizance of the local courts, but upon the law of another state, as readily determined here as in a state court."

How much deference does the Supreme Court owe to Texas on a question of the law of California? Compare United States v. Pink, 315 U.S. 203 (1942), where New York's interpretation of a Soviet decree was held reviewable by the Supreme Court since the interpretation governed the rights of the United States as successor under the Litvinoff assignment to causes of action under New York law.

(2) Though there may be no doubt about the Supreme Court's power to resolve questions of one state's law in the context of a full-faith-and-credit proceeding in the courts of another state, it may at times be possible to secure answers to those questions from the highest court of the original state. To what extent should the Supreme Court then seek to have that state court answer those questions? In Aldrich v. Aldrich, 378 U.S. 540 (1964), a case from the West Virginia courts involving a question about the effect in Florida of a prior Florida decree, the Supreme Court held the case before it while it certified questions to the Florida Supreme Court under then established state procedures for such certification from a federal court (see p. 1381, *infra*). But see Hanson v. Denckla, 357 U.S. 235 (1958), which

also involved a key issue of Florida law; the certification procedure was not yet available at that time, but the Court had before it concurrently the original Florida case as well as the Delaware case in which full faith and credit for the Florida judgment was being sought. The Court specifically refused (over three dissents) to hold the Delaware proceeding while allowing the Florida Supreme Court to resolve the question in the Florida proceeding. Asserting that the state law was clear, the Supreme Court itself resolved the issue of Florida law at that point. Because this allowed the Delaware judgment to be entered while the Florida proceeding was still pending, the apparent result was effectively to bind the Florida courts on that issue of Florida law in the Florida litigation. Criticizing the wisdom of this disposition, see Comment, 107 U.Pa.L.Rev. 261 (1958).

WARD v. LOVE COUNTY

253 U.S. 17, 40 S.Ct. 419, 64 L.Ed. 751 (1920).
Certiorari to the Supreme Court of Oklahoma.

Mr. Justice Van Devanter delivered the opinion of the Court.

This is a proceeding by and on behalf of Coleman J. Ward and sixty-six other Indians to recover moneys alleged to have been coercively collected from them by Love county, Oklahoma, as taxes on their allotments, which under the laws and Constitution of the United States were nontaxable. The county commissioners disallowed the claim and the claimants appealed to the district court of the county. There the claimants' petition was challenged by a demurrer, which was overruled and the county elected not to plead further. A judgment for the claimants followed, and this was reversed by the Supreme Court. Board of Com'rs of Love County v. Ward, 173 Pac. 1050. The case is here on writ of certiorari. 248 U.S. 556.

The claimants, who were members of the Choctaw Tribe and wards of the United States, received their allotments out of the tribal domain under a congressional enactment of 1898, which subjected the right of alienation to certain restrictions and provided that "the lands allotted shall be nontaxable while the title remains in the original allottee, but not to exceed twenty-one years from date of patent." Chapter 517, 30 Stat. 507. In the act of 1906, enabling Oklahoma to become a state, Congress made it plain that no impairment of the rights of property pertaining to the Indians was intended, chapter 3335, § 1, 34 Stat. 267; and the state included in its Constitution a provision exempting from taxation "such property as may be exempt by reason of treaty stipulations, existing between the Indians and the United States government, or by federal laws, during the force and effect of such treaties or federal laws." Article 10, § 6. Afterwards Congress, by an act of 1908, removed the restrictions on alienation as to certain classes of allottees, including the present claimants, and declared that all land from which the restrictions were removed "shall be subject to taxation, * * * as though it were the property of other persons than allottees." Chapter 199, §§ 1, 4, 35 Stat. 312.

Following the last enactment the officers of Love and other counties began to tax the allotted lands from which restrictions on alienation were removed, and this met with pronounced opposition on the part of the Indian allottees, who insisted, as they had been advised, that the tax exemption was a vested property right which could not be abrogated or destroyed consistently with the Constitution of the United States. Suits were begun in the state courts to maintain the exemption and enjoin the threatened taxation, one of the suits being prosecuted by some 8,000 allottees against the officers of Love and other counties. The suits were resisted, and the state courts, being of opinion that the exemption had been repealed by Congress, sustained the power to tax. * * * The cases were then brought here, and this court held that the exemption was a vested property right which Congress could not repeal consistently with the Fifth Amendment, that it was binding on the taxing authorities in Oklahoma, and that the state courts had erred in refusing to enjoin them from taxing the lands. Choate v. Trapp, 224 U.S. 665; Gleason v. Wood, 224 U.S. 679; English v. Richardson, 224 U.S. 680.

While those suits were pending the officers of Love county, with full knowledge of the suits, and being defendants in one, proceeded with the taxation of the allotments, demanded of these claimants that the taxes on their lands be paid to the county, threatened to advertise and sell the lands unless the taxes were paid, did advertise and sell other lands similarly situated, and caused these claimants to believe that their lands would be sold if the taxes were not paid. So, to prevent such a sale and to avoid the imposition of a penalty of eighteen per cent., for which the local statute provided, these claimants paid the taxes. They protested and objected at the time that the taxes were invalid, and the county officers knew that all the allottees were pressing the objection in the pending suits.

As a conclusion from these facts the claimants asserted that the taxes were collected by Love county by coercive means, that their collection was in violation of a right arising out of a law of Congress and protected by the Constitution of the United States, and that the county was accordingly bound to repay the moneys thus collected. The total amount claimed is $7,833.35, aside from interest. * * *

In reversing the judgment which the district court had given for the claimants the Supreme Court held, first, that the taxes were not collected by coercive means, but were paid voluntarily, and could not be recovered back as there was no statutory authority therefor; and, secondly, that there was no statute making the county liable for taxes collected and then paid over to the state and municipal bodies other than the county—which it was assumed was true of a portion of these taxes—and that the petition did not show how much of the taxes was retained by the county, or how much paid over to the state and other municipal bodies, and therefore it could not be the basis of any judgment against the county.

The county challenges our jurisdiction by a motion to dismiss the writ of certiorari and by way of supporting the motion insists that the Supreme Court put its judgment entirely on independent nonfederal grounds which were broad enough to sustain the judgment.

As these claimants had not disposed of their allotments and twenty-one years had not elapsed since the date of the patents, it is certain that the lands were nontaxable. This was settled in Choate v. Trapp, supra, and the other cases decided with it; and it also was settled in those cases that the exemption was a vested property right arising out of a law of Congress and protected by the Constitution of the United States. This being so, the state and all its agencies and political subdivisions were bound to give effect to the exemption. It operated as a direct restraint on Love county, no matter what was said in local statutes. The county did not respect it, but, on the contrary, assessed the lands allotted to these claimants, placed them on the county tax roll, and there charged them with taxes like other property. If a portion of the taxes was to go to the state and other municipal bodies after collection—which we assume was the case—it still was the county that charged the taxes against these lands and proceeded to collect them. Payment of all the taxes was demanded by the county, and all were paid to it in the circumstances already narrated.

We accept so much of the Supreme Court's decision as held that, if the payment was voluntary, the moneys could not be recovered back in the absence of a permissive statute, and that there was no such statute. But we are unable to accept its decision in other respects. *Analysis*

The right to the exemption was a federal right, and was specially set up and claimed as such in the petition. Whether the right was denied, or not given due recognition, by the Supreme Court is a question as to which the claimants were entitled to invoke our judgment, and this they have done in the appropriate way. It therefore is within our province to inquire not only whether the right was denied in express terms, but also whether it was denied in substance and effect, as by putting forward nonfederal grounds of decision that were without any fair or substantial support. Union Pacific R.R. Co. v. Public Service Commission, 248 U.S. 67; Leathe v. Thomas, 207 U.S. 93, 99; Vandalia R.R. Co. v. South Bend, 207 U.S. 359, 367; Gaar, Scott & Co. v. Shannon, 223 U.S. 468; Creswill v. Knights of Pythias, 225 U.S. 246, 261; Enterprise Irrigation District v. Farmers' Mutual Canal Co., 243 U.S. 157, 164. * * * Of course, if nonfederal grounds, plainly untenable, may be thus put forward successfully, our power to review easily may be avoided. Terre Haute, etc., R.R. Co. v. Indiana, 194 U.S. 579, 589. With this qualification, it is true that a judgment of a state court, which is put on independent nonfederal grounds broad enough to sustain it, cannot be reviewed by us. But the qualification is a material one and cannot be disregarded without neglecting or renouncing a jurisdiction conferred by law and designed to protect and maintain the supremacy of the Constitution and the laws made in pursuance thereof.

The facts set forth in the petition, all of which were admitted by the demurrer whereon the county elected to stand, make it plain, as we think, that the finding or decision that the taxes were paid voluntarily was without any fair or substantial support. The claimants were Indians just emerging from a state of dependency and wardship. Through the pending suits and otherwise they were objecting and protesting that the taxation of their lands was forbidden by a law of Congress. But, notwithstanding this, the county demanded that the taxes be paid, and by threatening to sell the lands of these claimants and actually selling other lands similarly situated made it appear to the claimants that they must choose between paying the taxes and losing their lands. To prevent a sale and to avoid the imposition of a penalty of eighteen per cent, they yielded to the county's demand and paid the taxes, protesting and objecting at the time that the same were illegal. The moneys thus collected were obtained by coercive means—by compulsion. The county and its officers reasonably could not have regarded it otherwise; much less the Indian claimants. Atchison, Topeka & Santa Fé Ry. Co. v. O'Connor, 223 U.S. 280; Gaar, Scott & Co. v. Shannon, supra, 223 U.S. 471; Union Pacific R.R. Co. v. Public Service Commission, supra; Swift Co. v. United States, 111 U.S. 22; Robertson v. Frank Bros.

Co., 132 U.S. 17, 23; Oceanic Steam Navigation Co. v. Stranahan, 214 U.S. 320, 329. The county places some reliance on Lamborn v. County Commissioners, 97 U.S. 181, and Railroad v. Commissioners, 98 U.S. 541; but those cases are quite distinguishable in their facts, and some of the general observations therein to which the county invites attention must be taken as modified by the later cases just cited.

As the payment was not voluntary, but made under compulsion, no statutory authority was essential to enable or require the county to refund the money. It is a well-settled rule that "money got through imposition" may be recovered back; and, as this court has said on several occasions, "the obligation to do justice rests upon all persons, natural and artificial, and if a county obtains the money or property of others without authority, the law, independent of any statute, will compel restitution or compensation." Marsh v. Fulton County, 10 Wall. 676, 684; City of Louisiana v. Wood, 102 U.S. 294, 298, 299; Chapman v. County of Douglas, 107 U.S. 348, 355. To say that the county could collect these unlawful taxes by coercive means and not incur any obligation to pay them back is nothing short of saying that it could take or appropriate the property of these Indian allottees arbitrarily and without due process of law. Of course this would be in contravention of the Fourteenth Amendment, which binds the county as an agency of the state.

If it be true, as the Supreme Court assumed, that a portion of the taxes was paid over, after collection, to the state and other municipal bodies, we regard it as certain that this did not alter the county's liability to the claimants. The county had no right to collect the money, and it took the same with notice that the rights of all who were to share in the taxes were disputed by these claimants and were being contested in the pending suits. In these circumstances it could not lessen its liability by paying over a portion of the money to others whose rights it knew were disputed and were no better than its own. Atchison, Topeka & Santa Fé Ry. Co. v. O'Connor, supra, 223 U.S. 287. In legal contemplation it received the money for the use and benefit of the claimants and should respond to them accordingly.

The county calls attention to the fact that in the demurrer to the petition the statute of limitation (probably meaning section 1570, Rev.Laws 1910) was relied on. This point was not discussed by the Supreme Court and we are not concerned with it beyond observing that when the case is remanded it will be open to that court to deal with the point as to the whole claim or any item in it as any valid local law in force when the claim was filed may require.

Motion to dismiss denied.

Judgment reversed.

NOTE ON STATE REMEDIES FOR FEDERAL RIGHTS

(1) The act of Congress in the Ward case would have furnished a defense in a proceeding to collect the tax, but did not explicitly create a right of action to recover taxes paid under compulsion. Did it create such a right by implication, or was the issue relegated to state law? Is the Supreme Court's determination that no statutory authority was "essential"

for recovery against the county based upon the law of Oklahoma? Assuming that the absence of a remedy would vitiate the tax collection under the Fourteenth Amendment, can a right to the recovery be drawn from the Amendment? If so, would it be enforceable in federal district courts as well as the state courts? [1]

(2) Iowa–Des Moines National Bank v. Bennett, 284 U.S. 239 (1931), involved an action for mandamus to compel county officers to refund *ad valorem* taxes levied on the plaintiffs' stock at a higher rate than was applied to the shares of domestic competing corporations. It was claimed that the discrimination was illegal under state law, the equal protection clause of the Fourteenth Amendment, and, in the case of a national bank, § 5219 of the Revised Statutes (consenting to state taxation of national bank shares at no greater rate "than is assessed upon other moneyed capital in the hands of individual citizens of such State").

The Supreme Court of Iowa found or assumed that there was systematic discrimination but nonetheless affirmed a judgment denying relief. It held that the auditor, responsible for the reduction of the taxes on competitors, acted in violation of state law; that the competitors were liable for the higher tax; and that the plaintiffs' remedy was to await collection of the higher tax from their competitors or to initiate proceedings to compel collection.

The Supreme Court reversed, in an opinion by Justice Brandeis. The discrimination by the auditor was held no less forbidden by the Constitution and the act of Congress because it also was illegal under the state law. "When a state official, acting under color of state authority, invades, in the course of his duties, a private right secured by the federal Constitution, that right is violated, even if the state officer not only exceeded his authority but disregarded special commands of state law" (p. 246). With respect to the remedy, the Court said (p. 247):

"The fact that the State may still have power to equalize the treatment of the petitioners and the competing domestic corporations by compelling the latter to pay hereafter the unpaid balance of the amounts assessed against them in 1919, 1920, 1921 and 1922 is not material. The petitioners' rights were violated, and the causes of action arose, when taxes at the lower rate were collected from their competitors. It may be assumed that all ground for a claim for refund would have fallen if the State, promptly upon discovery of the discrimination, had removed it by collecting the additional taxes from the favored competitors. By such collection the petitioners' grievances would have been redressed; for these are not primarily over-assessment. The right invoked is that to equal treatment; and such treatment will be attained if either their competitors' taxes are increased or their own reduced. But it is well settled that a taxpayer who

1. See further, as to enforcement in a federal court, Chap. IX, Sec. 2, *infra*.

Ward v. Love County was followed in Carpenter v. Shaw, 280 U.S. 363 (1930), Justice Stone remarking (p. 369): "The Supreme Court of Oklahoma also rested its denial to petitioners of the right to recover the 1926 tax upon the ground that, having failed to pay the tax for the year when due, they were barred by [Oklahoma statutes providing that only those who have timely paid a tax may sue] • • •. But the petitioners' allegations • • • are that the tax was paid under duress and compulsion • • •. These allegations are sufficient to bring the case within the ruling of this Court in Ward v. Love County • • • that a denial by a state court of a recovery of taxes exacted in violation of the laws or Constitution of the United States by compulsion is itself in contravention of the 14th Amendment."

has been subjected to discriminatory taxation through the favoring of others in violation of federal law, cannot be required himself to assume the burden of seeking an increase of the taxes which the others should have paid. Cumberland Coal Co. v. Board of Revision, 284 U.S. 23; Greene v. Louisville & Interurban R.R. Co., 244 U.S. 499, 514–518; Chicago Great Western Ry. Co. v. Kendall, 266 U.S. 94, 98; Sioux City Bridge Co. v. Dakota County, 260 U.S. 441, 446. Nor may he be remitted to the necessary of awaiting such action by the state officials upon their own initiative. Montana National Bank v. Yellowstone County, 276 U.S. 499, 504, 505.

"The petitioners are entitled to obtain in these suits refund of the excess of taxes exacted from them." [2]

(3) In General Oil Co. v. Crain, 209 U.S. 211 (1908), a suit was brought in Tennessee to enjoin a state official from enforcing a tax for the inspection of certain oils within the state. The bill challenged the tax as a burden upon interstate commerce, asserted that the tax was excessive for inspection purposes, and also charged a violation of the constitution of the state. The penalties for violation, coupled with a doubt that payments under protest could be recovered and the multiplicity of suits that would be necessary for recovery, were relied on as a basis for relief in equity.

The Supreme Court of Tennessee held the state courts without jurisdiction to grant an injunction in the view that the suit was one against the state. On appeal to the U.S. Supreme Court, Tennessee urged that the judgment "involved no Federal question, but only the powers and jurisdiction of the courts of the State of Tennessee, in respect to which the Supreme Court of Tennessee is the final arbiter." The appellant argued that by dismissing the bill the state court gave effect to the challenged statute and, further, that a state statute that denies injunctive relief for the federal rights asserted is itself in conflict with the Constitution.

The Supreme Court sustained the tax upon the merits but affirmed its jurisdiction, on the same day it decided Ex parte Young, 209 U.S. 123, p. 1173, infra, holding a similar suit in a federal circuit court not barred by the Eleventh Amendment. Justice McKenna said (p. 226):

"* * * Necessarily to give adequate protection to constitutional rights a distinction must be made between valid and invalid state laws, as determining the character of the suit against state officers. And the suit at bar illustrates the necessity. If a suit against state officers is precluded in the national courts by the Eleventh Amendment to the Constitution, and may be forbidden by a state to its courts, as it is contended in the case at

---

2. In Allied Stores v. Bowers, 358 U.S. 522 (1959), an Ohio resident taxpayer sought redetermination of a tax assessed on his stored merchandise; he argued that he was being denied equal protection under the Fourteenth Amendment because the statute exempted similar property of nonresidents. The Ohio Supreme Court held that it lacked power to extend the exemption to residents; that, consequently, if the taxpayer's contention was valid, equal protection could be achieved only by eliminating the nonresident's exemption; that the taxpayer would then remain liable for the tax assessed on him; and that

therefore he was in any event not entitled to relief in this proceeding. The United States Supreme Court interpreted the Ohio court's ground as being that the taxpayer "lacked standing to raise the constitutional questions presented." It considered this a federal issue, and held that so long as the state court was allowing the exemption for non-residents to remain in the statute "it is quite immaterial that appellant's claim necessarily would fall if it were out. It follows that appellant does have standing to prosecute its constitutional claim" (pp. 525–26). The Court then upheld the tax on the merits.

bar that it may be, without power of review by this court, it must be evident that an easy way is open to prevent the enforcement of many provisions of the Constitution, and the Fourteenth Amendment, which is directed at state action could be nullified as to much of its operation. * * *

"It being then the right of a party to be protected against a law which violates a constitutional right, whether by its terms or the manner of its enforcement, it is manifest that a decision which denies such protection gives effect to the law, and the decision is reviewable by this court. Wilmington & W.R. Co. v. Alsbrook, 146 U.S. 279 (1892)".

Justice Harlan, disagreeing as to jurisdiction, said (209 U.S. at 232–33):

"The oil company seeks a reversal of the decree of the state court, contending that it was denied a right arising under the commerce clause of the Constitution. But back of any question of that kind was the question before the Supreme Court of Tennessee whether the inferior state court, under the law of its organization, that is, under the law of Tennessee, could entertain jurisdiction of the suit. The question, we have seen, was determined adversely to jurisdiction. That certainly is a state, not a Federal question. Surely, Tennessee has the right to say of what class of suits its own courts may take cognizance, and it was peculiarly the function of the Supreme Court of Tennessee to determine such a question. When, therefore, its highest court has declared that the Tennessee statute referred to in argument did not allow the inferior state court to take cognizance of a suit like this, that decision must be accepted as the interpretation to be placed on the local statute. Otherwise, this court will adjudge that the Tennessee court *shall* take jurisdiction of a suit of which the highest court of the State adjudges that it cannot do consistently with the laws of the State which created it and which established its jurisdiction. It seems to me that this court, accepting the decision of the highest court of Tennessee, as to the meaning of the Tennessee statute in question, as I think it must, has no alternative but to affirm the judgment, on the ground simply that the ground upon which it is placed is broad enough to support the judgment without reference to any question raised or discussed by counsel."

(4) Ward, Bennett, and Crain are the three leading cases usually thought to stand for the proposition that the state courts may, under some circumstances, be obligated (notwithstanding state remedial and jurisdictional rules) to provide a remedy for violations of federal rights. The cases leave open a host of questions, however, about the nature and scope of this obligation. (a) Is the right to sue for a refund in Bennett, or for an injunction in Crain, itself a creation of federal law? Are these rights of action implied directly "from" the Constitution? Compare the Bivens case and the *Note on the Implication of Private Remedies for the Violation of Constitutional Norms,* Chap. VII, pp. 917, 926, *infra.* (b) Is the obligation an inchoate one, to be imposed only if for some reason no adequate remedy to repair the violation is available in a federal court?[2] (c) What is the

2. In this connection, compare Crain with Georgia R.R. & Banking Co. v. Musgrove, 335 U.S. 900 (1949): The Georgia Supreme Court had dismissed an action for injunctive relief against certain state property taxes on the ground that the suit was an unconsented action against the state; the opinion suggested that other (unspecified) state remedies might be available. The Supreme Court dismissed the appeal on the ground that there was an adequate nonfederal ground for decision. (A later Supreme Court decision affirmed that an injunction *was* available in federal court.

content of the obligation? Not to deny any effective remedy? Not to deny the most effective remedy? What are the roles of federal and state law in determining exactly when a remedy may or may not be refused? (See further, as to this, McCoy v. Shaw, 277 U.S. 302 (1928) (affirming a state's denial of anticipatory equitable relief against a state tax on the ground that the state could properly require payment and a suit for refund)).

All of these questions are left open by the three leading cases. And note further that the scope of the obligation is contained by the limiting principle, exemplified in a host of cases, that ordinary state remedial and procedural principles may continue (at least presumptively) to operate in state-court cases complaining of federal constitutional violations. (Thus note the Court's statement in Ward that the application of the state's statute of limitations is open on remand. Would the state statute of limitations, if it otherwise applied, similarly be a bar in Bennett, Bowers and Crain?) See, e.g., Utley v. City of St. Petersburg, 292 U.S. 106 (1934) (laches is an adequate state ground); [3] Enterprise Irrigation District v. Farmers' Mutual Canal Co., 243 U.S. 157 (1917) (estoppel is an adequate state ground); Wood v. Chesborough, 228 U.S. 672 (1913) (limitations is an adequate state ground); Coombes v. Getz, 217 Cal. 320, 18 P.2d 939 (1933), upon remand after reversal by the Supreme Court, 285 U.S. 434 (1932); cf. Holmberg v. Armbrecht, 327 U.S. 392 (1946), p. 950, infra; Edelman v. California, 344 U.S. 357 (1953) (wrong remedy chosen in state court).

Compare the materials dealing with Congress' power to require state courts to hear federal causes of action, considered in Testa v. Katt and the Note on the Obligation of State Courts to Enforce Federal Law, pp. 492, 495, supra.

Compare also the cases that appear to hold that the Compensation Clause of the Fifth Amendment itself requires that the states provide a damages remedy for takings (permanent or temporary) of private property. See the discussion and cases cited in First English Evangelical Lutheran Church of Glendale v. County of Los Angeles, 107 S.Ct. 2378 (1987). Is the Compensation Clause special in this respect? If so, why? [4]

(5) In American Trucking Associations, Inc. v. Conway, 107 S.Ct. 3262 (1987), the Supreme Court was asked to grant certiorari to review a challenge to the constitutional validity of Vermont statutes imposing various taxes on interstate motor carriers. The litigation started with a suit in the Vermont federal district court to enjoin collection of the taxes; this suit was dismissed pursuant to the Tax Injunction Act, 28 U.S.C. § 1341 (see p. 1339, infra), on the ground that a "plain, speedy and efficient remedy" was available in the courts of Vermont. 514 F.Supp. 1341 (D.Vt.1981). Plaintiffs promptly renewed their constitutional challenge in the state courts. A preliminary injunction to enjoin collection was denied by the trial court on the ground that an adequate remedy at law

Georgia R.R. & Banking Co. v. Redwine, 342 U.S. 299 (1952).) Does Musgrove mean that the Crain obligation will not be enforced unless it is first demonstrated that no federal court remedy exists? Should the state's obligation to grant a remedy be contingent on the hypothetical availability of a federal action?

3. Cf. Creswill v. Knights of Pythias, 225 U.S. 246 (1912).

4. Compare North Carolina State Board v. Swann, 402 U.S. 43 (1971) (statute prohibiting student assignments on the basis of race held invalid under Brown v. Board of Education). Is there a distinction between a state attempt to curtail administrative remedies and judicial? Or should the standards be the same?

existed pursuant to the state's statutory refund mechanism. The action then went forward as an action for refund of the taxes being collected. After elaborate proceedings on the merits, the Vermont Supreme Court held that the state taxes violated the Commerce Clause. But the court refused to order refunds of the taxes exacted from the plaintiffs during the litigation, ruling that, as a matter of state law, sovereign immunity barred a damages remedy against the state for return of taxes illegally exacted, and that the state refund statute did not encompass this type of suit. 508 A.2d 405, 408 (1986). Having earlier held, in a case from Pennsylvania, that taxes similar to the Vermont statutes discriminated against interstate commerce (see American Trucking Ass'ns, Inc. v. Scheiner, 107 S.Ct. 2829 (1987)), the Supreme Court denied certiorari (55 L.W. 3871).

Suppose the Court had granted the writ, and suppose that the state taxes were found to be in violation of the Commerce Clause. How should the jurisdictional and remedial aspects of the case be analyzed and decided? Is Vermont required to provide a damages remedy? Must it do so at least where the Vermont courts have themselves ruled out preventive relief on the very ground that a refund remedy exists? Is it relevant whether any form of refund relief would now be available in the federal district court? (Would it be? Note that a suit in the federal courts against the *state* for refund would almost certainly be barred by the Eleventh Amendment. A suit for refund against individual state officials, although not barred by the Eleventh Amendment, would probably fail on substantive and remedial grounds. See further Chap. IX, Sec. 2(A), *infra*.)

The petition in ATA asked the Court squarely to hold that the Constitution required Vermont to order a refund of the taxes illegally collected, notwithstanding the state law of sovereign immunity. Under Ward and Crain, could the Court have rejected that submission?

(6) Is a state obligated by the Due Process Clause of the Fourteenth Amendment to provide a post-conviction "corrective process" to remedy denial of federal rights, at least when those rights could not have been effectively asserted in the original conviction proceedings? The view that there is such an obligation derives from language in Frank v. Mangum, 237 U.S. 309, 335 (1915) (mob domination); Moore v. Dempsey, 261 U.S. 86, 91 (1923) (same); and Mooney v. Holohan, 294 U.S. 103, 113 (1935) (knowing use of perjured testimony); and has been reiterated since, see cases cited in Case v. Nebraska, 381 U.S. 336, 343 n. 5 (1965). In the contingency that there is no available state remedy, however, these decisions unanimously affirmed that the prisoner's recourse is to apply for a writ of habeas corpus in the appropriate *federal* district court. See, *e.g.*, Jennings v. Illinois, 342 U.S. 104 (1951). Is this defensible? See, generally, Bator, *Finality in Criminal Law and Federal Habeas Corpus for State Prisoners*, 76 Harv.L. Rev. 441, 459–60, 491–93 (1963); Note, *Effect of the Federal Constitution in Requiring State Post–Conviction Remedies*, 53 Colum.L.Rev. 1143 (1953). See also p. 1560, *infra*.[4]

In Case v. Nebraska, 381 U.S. 336 (1965), the prisoner applied for habeas corpus in a state court, alleging an unconstitutional denial of the assistance of counsel in connection with his plea of guilty to a burglary

---

4. Compare the thoughtful discussion of the proper roles of federal and state remedial law with respect to the arbitrability of certain kinds of contract disputes under the Federal Arbitration Act, in Justice Stevens' separate opinion in Southland Corp. v. Keating, 465 U.S. 1, 17 (1984).

charge in that same court. The Nebraska Supreme Court held that habeas corpus was not available so long as the original court "had jurisdiction of the offense and of the person charged" and the sentence did not exceed its power. The Supreme Court granted certiorari "to decide whether the Fourteenth Amendment requires that the States afford state prisoners some adequate corrective process for the hearing and determination of claims of violation of federal constitutional guarantees." Thereafter, but before oral argument, Nebraska by statute adopted a broad post-conviction hearing procedure, including claims of denial of federal constitutional rights. The Court vacated the state judgment and remanded the case, leaving the constitutional issue unresolved.

SUBSECTION B: PROCEDURAL REQUIREMENTS

HERNDON v. GEORGIA

295 U.S. 441, 55 S.Ct. 794, 79 L.Ed. 1530 (1935).
Appeal from the Supreme Court of Georgia.

MR. JUSTICE SUTHERLAND delivered the opinion of the Court.

Appellant was sentenced to a term of imprisonment upon conviction by a jury in a Georgia court of first instance of an attempt to incite insurrection by endeavoring to induce others to join in combined resistance to the authority of the state to be accomplished by acts of violence, in violation of section 56 of the Penal Code of Georgia.[1] The supreme court of the state affirmed the judgment. 178 Ga. 832, 174 S.E. 597, rehearing denied, 179 Ga. 597, 176 S.E. 620, 622. On this appeal, the statute is assailed as contravening the due process clause of the Fourteenth Amendment in certain designated particulars. We find it unnecessary to review the points made, since this court is without jurisdiction for the reason that no federal question was seasonably raised in the court below or passed upon by that court.

It is true that there was a preliminary attack upon the indictment in the trial court on the ground, among others, that the statute was in violation "of the Constitution of the United States," and that this contention was overruled. But, in addition to the insufficiency of the specification, the adverse action of the trial court was not preserved by exceptions pendente lite or assigned as error in due time in the bill of exceptions, as the settled rules of the state practice require. In that situation, the state supreme court declined to review any of the rulings of the trial court in respect of that and other preliminary issues, and this determination of the state court is conclusive here. John v. Paullin, 231 U.S. 583, 585; Atlantic Coast Line R. Co. v. Mims, 242 U.S. 532, 535; Nevada–California–Oregon Ry. v. Burrus, 244 U.S. 103, 105; Brooks v. Missouri, 124 U.S. 394, 400;

---

1. "§ 56. Any attempt, by persuasion or otherwise, to induce others to join in any combined resistance to the lawful authority of the State shall constitute an attempt to incite insurrection."

"Insurrection" is defined by the preceding section. "§ 55. Insurrection shall con-

sist in any combined resistance to the lawful authority of the State, with intent to the denial thereof, when the same is manifested, or intended to be manifested, by acts of violence."

Central Union Co. v. Edwardsville, 269 U.S. 190, 194, 195; Erie R. Co. v. Purdy, 185 U.S. 148, 154; Mutual Life Ins. Co. v. McGrew, 188 U.S. 291, 308.

The federal question was never properly presented to the state supreme court unless upon motion for rehearing; and that court then refused to consider it. The long-established general rule is that the attempt, to raise a federal question after judgment, upon a petition for rehearing, comes too late, unless the court actually entertains the question and decides it. Texas, etc., R. Co. v. Southern Pacific Co., 137 U.S. 48, 54; Loeber v. Schroeder, 149 U.S. 580, 585; Godchaux Co. v. Estopinal, 251 U.S. 179, 181; Rooker v. Fidelity Trust Co., 261 U.S. 114, 117; Tidal Oil Co. v. Flanagan, 263 U.S. 444, 454, 455, and cases cited.

Petitioner, however, contends that the present case falls within an exception to the rule—namely, that the question respecting the validity of the statute as applied by the lower court first arose from its unanticipated act in giving to the statute a new construction which threatened rights under the Constitution. There is no doubt that the federal claim was timely if the ruling of the state court could not have been anticipated and a petition for rehearing presented the first opportunity for raising it. Saunders v. Shaw, 244 U.S. 317, 320; Ohio v. Akron Park District, 281 U.S. 74, 79; Missouri v. Gehner, 281 U.S. 313, 320; Brinkerhoff–Faris Co. v. Hill, 281 U.S. 673, 677–678; American Surety Co. v. Baldwin, 287 U.S. 156, 164; Great Northern R. Co. v. Sunburst Co., 287 U.S. 358, 367. The whole point, therefore, is whether the ruling here assailed should have been anticipated.

The trial court instructed the jury that the evidence would not be sufficient to convict the defendant if it did not indicate that his advocacy would be acted upon immediately; and that: "In order to convict the defendant, * * * it must appear clearly by the evidence that immediate serious violence against the State of Georgia was to be expected or was advocated." Petitioner urges that the question presented to the state supreme court was whether the evidence made out a violation of the statute as thus construed by the trial court, while the supreme court construed the statute as not requiring that an insurrection should follow instantly or at any given time, but that "it would be sufficient that he [the defendant] intended it to happen at any time, as a result of his influence, by those whom he sought to incite," and upon that construction determined the sufficiency of the evidence against the defendant. If that were all, the petitioner's contention that the federal question was raised at the earliest opportunity well might be sustained; but it is not all.

The verdict of the jury was returned on January 18, 1933, and judgment immediately followed. On July 5, 1933, the trial court overruled a motion for new trial. The original opinion was handed down and the judgment of the state supreme court entered May 24, 1934, the case having been in that court since the preceding July.

On March 18, 1933, several months prior to the action of the trial court on the motion for new trial, the state supreme court had decided Carr v. State, 176 Ga. 747, 169 S.E. 201. In that case section 56 of the Penal Code, under which it arose, was challenged as contravening the Fourteenth Amendment. The court in substance construed the statute as it did in the present case. In the course of the opinion it said: "It [the state] cannot reasonably be required to defer the adoption of measures for its own peace and safety until the revolutionary utterances lead to actual disturbances of the public peace or imminent and immediate danger of its own destruction; but it may, in the exercise of its judgment, suppress the threatened danger in its incipiency. * * * 'Manifestly, the legislature has authority to forbid the advocacy of a doctrine designed and intended to overthrow the government, without waiting until there is a present and imminent danger of the success of the plan advocated. If the State were compelled to wait until the apprehended danger became certain, then its right to protect itself would come into being simultaneously with the overthrow of the government, when there would be neither prosecuting officers nor courts for the enforcement of the law.' "

The language contained in the subquotation is taken from People v. Lloyd, 304 Ill. 23, 35, 136 N.E. 505, and is quoted with approval by this court in Gitlow v. New York, 268 U.S. 652, 669.

In the present case, following the language quoted at an earlier point in this opinion to the effect that it was sufficient if the defendant intended an insurrection to follow *at any time,* etc., the court below, in its original opinion added: "It was the intention of this law to arrest at its incipiency any effort to overthrow the state government, where it takes the form of an actual attempt to incite others to insurrection." The phrase "at any time" is not found in the foregoing excerpt from the Carr Case, but it is there in effect, when the phrase is given the meaning disclosed by the context, as that meaning is pointed out by the court below in its opinion denying the motion for a rehearing, when it said that the phrase was necessarily intended to mean within a reasonable time—"that is, within such time as one's persuasion or other adopted means might reasonably be expected to be directly operative in causing an insurrection."

Appellant, of course, cannot plead ignorance of the ruling in the Carr Case, and was therefore bound to anticipate the probability of a similar ruling in his own case, and preserve his right to a review here by appropriate action upon the original hearing in the court below. It follows that his contention that he raised the federal question at the first opportunity is without substance, and the appeal must be dismissed for want of jurisdiction.

It is so ordered.

Mr. Justice Cardozo. * * *

I hold the view that the protection of the Constitution was seasonably invoked and that the court should proceed to an adjudication of the merits.

* * *

We are told by the state that the securities of the Constitution should have been invoked upon the trial. The presiding judge should have been warned that a refusal to accept the test of clear and present danger would be a rejection of the restraints of the Fourteenth Amendment. But the trial judge had not refused to accept the test proposed; on the contrary, he had accepted it and even gone a step beyond. In substance he had charged that even a present "danger" would not suffice, if there was not also an expectation, and one grounded in reason, that the insurrection would begin at once. It is novel doctrine that a defendant who has had the benefit of all he asks, and indeed of a good deal more, must place a statement on the record that if some other court at some other time shall read the statute differently, there will be a denial of liberties that at the moment of the protest are unchallenged and intact. Defendants charged with crime are as slow as are men generally to borrow trouble of the future.

We are told, however, that protest, even if unnecessary at the trial, should have been made by an assignment of error or in some other appropriate way in connection with the appeal, and this for the reason that by that time, if not before, the defendant was chargeable with knowledge as a result of two decisions of the highest court of Georgia that the statute was destined to be given another meaning. The decisions relied upon are Carr v. State (No. 1), 176 Ga. 55, 166 S.E. 827, 167 S.E. 103, and Carr v. State (No. 2), 176 Ga. 747, 169 S.E. 201. The first of these cases was decided in November, 1932, before the trial of the appellant, which occurred in January, 1933. The second was decided in March, 1933, after the appellant had been convicted, but before the denial or submission of his motion for a new trial. Neither is decisive of the question before us now.

Carr v. State, No. 1, came up on demurrer to an indictment. The prosecution was under section 58 of the Penal Code, which makes it a crime to circulate revolutionary documents. All that was held was that upon the face of the indictment there had been a wilful incitement to violence, sufficient, if proved, to constitute a crime. The opinion contains an extract covering about four pages from the opinion of this court in Gitlow v. New York, supra. Imbedded in that long quotation are the words now pointed to by the state as decisive of the case at hand. ⁕ ⁕ ⁕

⁕ ⁕ ⁕ There is no reason to believe that the Supreme Court of Georgia, when it quoted from the opinion in Gitlow's case, rejected the restraints which the author of that opinion had placed upon his words. For the decision of the case before it there was no need to go so far. Circulation of documents with intent to incite to revolution had been charged in an indictment. The state had the power to punish such an act as criminal, or so the court had held. How close the nexus would have to be between the attempt and its projected consequences was matter for the trial.

Carr v. State, No. 2, like the case under review, was a prosecution under Penal Code, § 56 (not § 58), and like Carr v. State, No. 1, came up on demurrer. All that the court held was that when attacked by demurrer the indictment would stand. This appears from the headnote, drafted by the court itself. After referring to this headnote, the court states that it may be "useful and salutary" to repeat what it had written in Carr v. State, No. 1. Thereupon it quotes copiously from its opinion in that case including the bulk of the same extracts from Gitlow v. New York. The extracts show upon their face that they have in view a statute denouncing a particular doctrine and prohibiting attempts to teach it. They give no test of the bond of union between an idea and an event.

What has been said as to the significance of the opinions in the two cases against Carr has confirmation in what happened when appellant was brought to trial. The judge who presided at that trial had the first of those opinions before him when he charged the jury, or so we may assume. He did not read it as taking from the state the burden of establishing a clear and present danger that insurrection would ensue as a result of the defendant's conduct. This is obvious from the fact that in his charge he laid that very burden on the state with emphasis and clarity. True, he did not have before him the opinion in prosecution No. 2, for it had not yet been handed down, but if he had seen it, he could not have gathered from its quotation of the earlier case that it was announcing novel doctrine.

From all this it results that Herndon, this appellant, came into the highest court of Georgia without notice that the statute defining his offense was to be given a new meaning. There had been no rejection, certainly no unequivocal rejection, of the doctrine of Schenck v. United States, which had been made the law of the case by the judge presiding at his trial. For all that the record tells us, the prosecuting officer acquiesced in the charge, and did not ask the appellate court to apply a different test. In such a situation the appellant might plant himself as he did on the position that on the case given to the jury his guilt had not been proved. He was not under a duty to put before his judges the possibility of a definition less favorable to himself, and make an argument against it, when there had been no threat of any change, still less any forecast of its form or measure. He might wait until the law of the case had been rejected by the reviewing court before insisting that the effect would be an invasion of his constitutional immunities. If invasion should occur, a motion for rehearing diligently pressed thereafter would be seasonable notice. This is the doctrine of Missouri v. Gehner and Brinkerhoff–Faris Co. v. Hill. It is the doctrine that must prevail if the great securities of the Constitution are not to be lost in a web of procedural entanglements.

New strength is given to considerations such as these when one passes to a closer view of just what the Georgia court did in its definition of the statute. We have heard that the meaning had been fixed by what had been held already in Carr v. State, and that thereby the imminence of the danger had been shown to be unrelated to innocence or guilt. But if that is the teaching of those cases, it was discarded by the very judgment now subjected to review. True, the Georgia court, by its first opinion in the case at hand, did prescribe a test that, if accepted, would bar the consideration of proximity in time. * * * It would not be "necessary to guilt that the alleged offender should have intended that an insurrection should follow instantly or at any given time, but it would be sufficient that he intended it to happen at any time, as a result of his influence, by those whom he sought to incite." On the motion for a rehearing the Georgia court repelled with a little heat the argument of counsel that these words were to be taken literally, without "the usual reasonable implications." "The phrase 'at any time' as criticized in the motion for rehearing was not intended to mean at any time in the definite future, or at any possible later time, however remote." "On the contrary, the phrase 'at any time' was necessarily intended, and should have been understood, to mean within a reasonable time; that is, within such time as one's persuasion or other adopted means might reasonably be expected to be directly operative in causing an insurrection." "Under the statute as thus interpreted, we say, as before, that the evidence was sufficient to authorize the conviction."

Here is an unequivocal rejection of the test of clear and present danger, yet a denial also of responsibility without boundaries in time. True, in this rejection, the court disclaimed a willingness to pass upon the question as one of constitutional law, assigning as a reason that no appeal to the Constitution had been made upon the trial or then considered by the judge. * * * Such a rule of state practice may have the effect of attaching a corresponding limitation to the jurisdiction of this court where fault can fairly be imputed to an appellant for the omission to present the question sooner. * * * No such consequence can follow where the ruling of the trial judge has put the Constitution out of the case and made an appeal to its provisions impertinent and futile. *Cf.* Missouri v. Gehner, *supra*; Rogers v. Alabama, 192 U.S. 226, 230. In such circumstances, the power does not reside in a state by any rule of local practice to restrict the jurisdiction of this court in the determination of a constitutional question brought into the case thereafter. Davis v. Wechsler, 263 U.S. 22, 24. If the rejection of the test of clear and present danger was a denial of fundamental liberties, the path is clear for us to say so.

What was brought into the case upon the motion for rehearing was a standard wholly novel, the expectancy of life to be ascribed to the persuasive power of an idea. The defendant had no opportunity in the state court to prepare his argument accordingly. He had no opportunity to argue from the record that guilt was not a reasonable inference, or one permitted by the Constitution, on the basis of that test any more than on the basis of others discarded as unfitting. *Cf.* Fiske v. Kansas, *supra*. The argument thus shut out is submitted to us now. * * *

MR. JUSTICE BRANDEIS and MR. JUSTICE STONE join in this opinion.

MICHEL v. LOUISIANA

350 U.S. 91, 76 S.Ct. 158, 100 L.Ed. 83 (1955).
Certiorari to the Supreme Court of Louisiana.

MR. JUSTICE CLARK delivered the opinion of the Court.

Louisiana requires that objections to a grand jury be raised before the expiration of the third judicial day following the end of the grand jury's term or before trial, whichever is earlier. In these cases we are asked to decide whether this statute as applied violates the Fourteenth Amendment. The three petitioners, all Negroes sentenced to death for aggravated rape, make no attack on the composition of the petit jury nor on the fairness of their trials but challenge the composition of the grand juries which indicted them on the ground that there was a systematic exclusion of Negroes from the panels. No hearing was held on these allegations because the lower courts found that the question had been waived. In each case the Supreme Court of Louisiana affirmed, 225 La. 1040, 74 So.2d 207 and 226 La. 201, 75 So.2d 333, and we granted certiorari, 348 U.S. 936 and 348 U.S. 950, because of the importance of the issues involved.

Grand juries in Orleans Parish are impaneled in September and March to serve for six months. Since § 202 of the Louisiana Criminal Code, as interpreted, requires a defendant to object to the grand jury before three judicial days after its term, the time to raise such objections may vary from a minimum of three days—if the defendant is indicted on the last day of the term—to a much longer period if he is indicted during the term. Section 284 of the Louisiana Code of Criminal Procedure provides that in any case such objections must be made before arraignment.

We do not find that this requirement on its face raises an insuperable barrier to one making claim to federal rights. The test is whether the defendant has had "a reasonable opportunity to have the issue as to the claimed right heard and determined by the state court." Parker v. Illinois, 333 U.S. 571, 574; Davis v. Wechsler, 263 U.S. 22; Central Union Tel. Co. v.

Edwardsville, 269 U.S. 190; Paterno v. Lyons, 334 U.S. 314. See Carter v. Texas, 177 U.S. 442. In Avery v. Alabama, 308 U.S. 444, this Court held that a lapse of three days between the appointment of counsel and the date of trial was not of itself a denial of due process. In Louisiana a motion to quash is a short, simple document, easily prepared in a single afternoon. In the light of Avery, a three-day minimum for such a motion is not unreasonable. Wilson v. Louisiana, 320 U.S. 714. But in the circumstances of a particular case, the application of such a rule may not give a reasonable opportunity to raise the federal question. See Reece v. Georgia, decided this day [see p. 605, *infra*]. Accordingly we pass to a consideration of the facts in each of these cases.

No. 32. John Michel.—Michel was indicted by the grand jury on February 19, 1953, and was presented to the court for arraignment on February 23. He appeared without counsel and the arraignment was continued for one week. During that week, the trial judge talked with Mr. Schreiber, a former assistant district attorney with wide experience in local criminal practice. He asked Mr. Schreiber whether he would take the case if private counsel was not retained. The judge indicated that if Mr. Schreiber accepted, additional counsel would be appointed.

The term of the grand jury which indicted Michel expired March 2, 1953. On that same date Michel appeared again for arraignment without counsel. Mr. Schreiber was also present in court on other business and the trial judge then appointed him counsel for Michel. Whereupon Mr. Schreiber asked the court to give him an opportunity to look it over and continue the matter for one week. No mention of co-counsel was made, and the continuance was granted.

Thereafter, on March 5, Mr. Schreiber received a formal notice of his appointment which, though not required by Louisiana law, appears at times to have been served in appointment cases. On March 6, Mr. Fust was appointed co-counsel. The motion to quash the indictment was filed on March 9—four days after Mr. Schreiber received the formal notice of appointment, and five judicial days (7 calendar days) after the expiration of the term of the grand jury. The State demurred on the ground that it came too late.

The determination of a single question of fact is decisive in this case: the precise date of appointment of counsel for Michel. It is contended that Mr. Schreiber was not appointed as counsel until March 5, the date of his formal notice; that he was not aware that he was to be chief counsel until after Mr. Fust told him on the 7th of his appointment to "assist" Mr. Schreiber; and that even if he assumed that he was appointed on March 2, he was unfamiliar with the case and thought the week's continuance held open for that period all of petitioner's rights. The record, however, shows without contradiction that Mr. Schreiber was appointed in open court, in the presence of petitioner, on March 2. The trial judge so found and the Supreme Court of Louisiana explicitly upheld this finding. While such findings are not conclusive on this Court, Rogers v. Alabama, 192 U.S. 226, they are entitled to great weight, Fay v. New York, 332 U.S. 261, 272. On a question of state practice with which we are unfamiliar, we will not ordinarily overturn the findings of two courts on the mere assertion of counsel that he did not consider himself appointed on the date of record. Since we find that counsel, a lawyer experienced in state criminal practice, had adequate time to file the motion after his appointment, we hold that the application of § 202 in this case was not unreasonable.

No. 36. Poret and Labat.—These codefendants were also convicted of rape and sentenced to death. Neither made any attack on the composition of the petit jury, but both filed motions to quash their indictments claiming discrimination in the selection of the grand-jury panel. The facts in each case will be considered separately.

Poret.—Shortly after the crime was committed, Poret eluded police officers and fled the State of Louisiana. He was indicted on December 11, 1950, but he was not arrested and nothing was known of his whereabouts until late 1951 when Louisiana authorities discovered that he was in prison in Tennessee. That State refused to release him until he had served his term. Louisiana filed a detainer against him, and he was returned to New Orleans on October 3, 1952. At his arraignment on October 27, 1952, he was assisted by counsel of his own selection. He pleaded not guilty to the indictment and was granted additional time to file a motion for severance. On November 7, after denial of his motion for severance, he moved—for the first time—to quash the indictment because of systematic exclusion of Negroes from the grand jury. After a hearing at which it was determined that Poret was a fugitive from justice, this motion was denied by the trial court on the ground that it was filed more than a year and a half too late. Under § 202, the time for filing had expired in March 1951, and the trial court held that the provisions of § 202 would not be "suspended or nullified for the benefit of a fugitive from justice who, by his own conduct" was unable to assert his right. The holding was affirmed on this ground by the Supreme Court of Louisiana.

It is beyond question that under the Due Process Clause of the Fourteenth Amendment Louisiana may attach reasonable time limitations to the assertion of federal constitutional rights. More particularly, the State may require prompt assertion of the right to challenge discriminatory practices in the make-up of a grand jury. The problem here is whether such a limitation may be avoided by Poret simply on the showing that he was a fugitive from prosecution throughout the entire period provided him.

Petitioner argues that he has had no opportunity to make his challenge to the grand jury, since the time allowed him by § 202 had expired before he was returned to Louisiana. But the record shows that he was not sentenced in Tennessee until five months after that period had expired, and nothing appears to have intervened during this period except his own voluntary flight. Thus Poret's claim is, in effect, that a flight which itself is a violation of federal law, 18 U.S.C. § 1073, is converted into a federal immunity from the operation of a valid state rule. We do not believe that the mere fugitive status existing here excuses a failure to resort to Louisiana's established statutory procedure available to all who wish to assert claimed constitutional rights. This is not to say that the act of fleeing and becoming a fugitive deprives one of federal rights. We hold only that due regard for the fair as well as effective administration of criminal justice gives the State a legitimate interest in requiring reasonable attacks on its inquisitorial process [5] and that the present case is not one

---

5. Not only may the prompt determination of such preliminary matters avoid the necessity of a second trial, but a long delay in its determination, such as here, makes it extremely difficult in this class of case for the State to overcome the prima facie claim which may be established by a defendant. Material witnesses and grand jurors

this interest must bow to essential considerations of fairness to defendants.

said that Poret had no lawyer, either before he fled the State the 87-day period from his indictment to the expiration of his time to file under § 202. However, during all of this time he remained a fugitive, and there is no showing that he could not have filed in time had he not elected to flee. * * * We, therefore, conclude that Poret, by his own action, failed to avail himself of Louisiana's adequate remedies. * * *

Poret's case affords a perfect illustration of the necessity for prompt determination of claims such as he raises here. Five years have now elapsed since the crime was committed, and the delay has been largely caused by Poret's own actions. Even if available, and memory permitted, the victim and chief witness would be reluctant to retell the sordid story of her unfortunate experience. Poret's conviction by a petit jury whose composition he did not attack has been affirmed by Louisiana's highest court and no constitutional challenge is made here to the fairness of that trial.

Furthermore, it may be added that after being returned to Louisiana on October 3, and employing his personal lawyer on October 26, Poret still did not file his motion to quash until November 7. * * * Rather than asserting his federal claim at the first opportunity, he delayed the filing of his motion until 12 days after his selection of counsel. This is four times the period we upheld in Michel. We, therefore, find no violation of due process in denying this motion as out of time.

Labat.—Edgar Labat was Poret's codefendant. He was apprehended the evening of the crime, and implicated Poret. Labat was indicted December 11, 1950, and arraigned on January 3, 1951, and he pleaded not guilty. On January 5 the court appointed Mr. E.I. Mahoney as counsel for petitioner. Thereafter the status of the case remained unchanged for more than a year. The next entry is dated January 29, 1952, when Mr. Mahoney asked leave to withdraw. Mr. Gill was thereafter employed, and on June 12, 1952, moved for a continuance. After a hearing, the motion was granted and the case was again continued. In October the codefendant Poret was returned to the State. Labat filed his motion to quash the indictment on November 7. The term of the grand jury that indicted Labat had expired in March 1951.

Petitioner now contends that he was denied effective representation of counsel. Powell v. Alabama, 287 U.S. 45. Mr. Mahoney had a reasonable time in which to file his motion to quash, but did not do so. It was stated on oral argument that he was 76 or 77 years old when he took the case, and was ill in bed during several months of the year. The trial court and the Supreme Court of Louisiana held that the facts did not show a lack of effective counsel. As in No. 32, Michel's case, we accept these findings. There is little support for the opposite conclusion in the record. Mr. Mahoney was a well-known criminal lawyer with nearly fifty years' experience at the bar. There is no evidence of incompetence. The mere fact that

may die or leave the jurisdiction, and memories as to intent or specific practices relating to the selection of a particular grand jury may lose their sharpness. Furthermore, a successful attack on a grand jury that sat several years earlier may affect other convictions based on indictments returned by the same grand jury.

a timely motion to quash was not filed does not overcome the presumption of effectiveness. * * * The delay might be considered sound trial strategy, particularly since the codefendant could not be found. We cannot infer lack of effective counsel from this circumstance alone. Such an inference would vitiate state rules of procedure designed to require preliminary objections to be disposed of before trial.

At argument, petitioners for the first time raised the contention that the requirements of § 202 had been applied by the district attorney only when Negro defendants attempted to attack the composition of the grand jury. They cited two cases in which the district attorney had failed to file demurrers to such motions and the indictments were quashed after the time set out in the statute. The present district attorney, who had been in office some eighteen months but was not serving at the time of these prosecutions, stated that it was his policy to apply § 202 whenever possible. Petitioners' contention was not raised below, and we do not believe it has been properly put in issue. Pennsylvania R. Co. v. Illinois Buick Co., 297 U.S. 447, 463. If such an allegation had been presented and preserved, and found support in the record, we might have a very different case here. See Rogers v. Alabama, 192 U.S. 226.

For the reasons stated the judgments of the Supreme Court of Louisiana are

Affirmed.

MR. JUSTICE BLACK with whom THE CHIEF JUSTICE [WARREN] and MR. JUSTICE DOUGLAS concur, dissenting.

Petitioners, who are colored, were indicted, convicted and sentenced to death in a Louisiana state court. The grand jury indicting the petitioners was drawn from the parish of Orleans where 32% of the population is colored. Only once within the memory of people living in that parish had a colored person been selected as a grand juror. That juror, who happened to look like a white man, was selected under the mistaken idea that he was one. The foregoing facts are not disputed here.

* * * The Court holds, however, that these petitioners had a reasonable opportunity to challenge the composition of the grand jury indicting them but failed to do so, thereby waiving their constitutional and statutory rights to have the charges against them considered by a fair and legal grand jury. Without going into the facts of each particular case, I think that the record shows that there was no such reasonable opportunity afforded to petitioners Michel and Poret or their counsel. I shall add a few words, however, about the supposed opportunity of petitioner Poret to challenge the validity of the indicting grand jury.

* * * It is true that if Poret had not fled and had been arrested and had the benefit of counsel early enough he could have challenged the grand jury's composition. For this reason the Court holds that he forfeited his federally guaranteed right to have his case considered by an unpacked grand jury. I cannot agree that the right to the kind of fair trial guaranteed by the Federal Constitution and congressional enactment can be thus denied by a State. If Poret can be denied this constitutional right, why not others? Could a state statute of limitations like this one declare that anyone under indictment who flees the State has thereby waived his right to counsel or his right to be tried by an unbiased judge? Cf. Re Murchison, 349 U.S. 133.

Court's opinion here appears to me to give far too little weight ....utional and statutory rights of an accused to be indicted and juries selected without racial discrimination.

I would reverse the convictions of Poret and Michel. Since Labat and Poret were jointly indicted by the same unconstitutionally selected grand jury, I would vacate the conviction of Poret's codefendant Labat. * * *

MR. JUSTICE DOUGLAS, with whom THE CHIEF JUSTICE and MR. JUSTICE BLACK concur, dissenting.

I do not think that petitioners were accorded the opportunity, guaranteed by due process of law, to challenge the constitutionality of the composition of the grand juries that indicted them.

As to Michel, the trial judge found that counsel was appointed on March 2, 1953, three days before the deadline for filing a motion to quash. * * *

The crucial question in this case is not what the trial judge thought, but what the effect of the misunderstanding between him and counsel had upon the constitutional rights of Michel. If counsel on March 2 believed that he was not yet appointed and rendered no service to the petitioner during this critical three-day period, the appointment was not an effective appointment. * * * Without counsel, of course, he had no effective opportunity to raise the constitutional question. * * *

Petitioner Poret apparently fled Louisiana shortly after the crime was committed. He was apprehended in Tennessee, but long after the indictment had been returned and the statutory period for filing a motion to quash had expired. The opportunity to raise the constitutional objection, therefore, was foreclosed before he was arraigned and, as far as the record shows, before he had any knowledge that the indictment was pending against him. It's as if the grand jury had been impaneled before the commission of the offense, and the time for raising objections to it expired with the impaneling, as was the case of Carter v. Texas, 177 U.S. 442, 447. Under these circumstances Poret had no real opportunity to challenge the constitutionality of the composition of the grand jury. * * *

I would reverse both convictions[1] * * *.

NOTE ON THE PRESENTATION AND PRESERVATION OF FEDERAL QUESTIONS: HEREIN OF THE ADEQUACY OF STATE PROCEDURAL GROUNDS

(1) In Cardinale v. Louisiana, 394 U.S. 437 (1969), a state statute required that confessions be admitted into evidence in their entirety. A defendant convicted of murder and sentenced to death objected to the admission of allegedly irrelevant and prejudicial parts of his confession and challenged the statute as unconstitutional. Justice White, for the Court, said (pp. 438–39):

1. The conviction of Labat should be vacated because he was jointly indicted with Poret by the same grand jury whose composition is challenged on constitutional grounds. Cf. Ashcraft v. Tennessee, 322 U.S. 143.

"Although certiorari was granted to consider this question, the fact emerged in oral argument that the sole federal question argued here had never been raised, preserved, or passed upon in the state courts below. It was very early established that the Court will not decide federal constitutional issues raised here for the first time on review of state court decisions. In Crowell v. Randell, 10 Pet. 368 (U.S.1836), Justice Story reviewed the earlier cases commencing with Owings v. Norwood's Lessee, 5 Cranch 344 (1809), and came to the conclusion that the Judiciary Act of 1789, c. 20, § 25, 1 Stat. 85, vested this Court with no jurisdiction unless a federal question was raised and decided in the state court below. * * * The Court has consistently refused to decide federal constitutional issues raised here for the first time on review of state court decisions both before the Crowell opinion, Miller for Use of U.S. v. Nicholls, 4 Wheat. 311, 315 (U.S.1819), and since *e.g.,* Safeway Stores, Inc. v. Oklahoma Retail Grocers Ass'n, Inc., 360 U.S. 334, 342, n. 7 (1959); State Farm Mutual Automobile Ins. Co. v. Duel, 324 U.S. 154, 160–163 (1945); McGoldrick v. Compagnie Generale Transatlantique, 309 U.S. 430, 434–435 (1940); Whitney v. California, 274 U.S. 357, 362–363 (1927); Dewey v. Des Moines, 173 U.S. 193, 197–201 (1899); Murdock v. City of Memphis, 20 Wall. 590 (U.S.1874).

"In addition to the question of jurisdiction arising under the statute controlling our power to review final judgments of state courts, 28 U.S.C. § 1257, there are sound reasons for this. Questions not raised below are those on which the record is very likely to be inadequate, since it certainly was not compiled with those questions in mind. And in a federal system it is important that state courts be given the first opportunity to consider the applicability of state statutes in light of constitutional challenge, since the statutes may be construed in a way which saves their constitutionality. Or the issue may be blocked by an adequate state ground. Even though States are not free to avoid constitutional issues on inadequate state grounds, O'Connor v. Ohio, 385 U.S. 92 (1966), they should be given the first opportunity to consider them."

Certiorari was dismissed for want of jurisdiction. Justices Black, Douglas and Fortas concurred in dismissal of the writ, "believing it to have been improvidently granted."

(2) For additional authority for the conventional proposition that the Court will not consider federal questions coming from the state courts unless the question was properly raised in the state courts, see, *e.g.,* Webb v. Webb, 451 U.S. 493 (1981); Illinois v. Gates, 462 U.S. 213, 217–24 and cases cited (1983); and see 16 Wright, Miller & Cooper, Federal Practice and Procedure § 4022 (1977; 1987 Supp.).[1] There has, however, been considerable variation in how strictly this rule is applied. Thus in Vachon v. New Hampshire, 414 U.S. 478 (1974), p. 677, *infra,* the Court reached out to decide that a conviction violated the Due Process Clause

---

1. See also Supreme Court Rule 21.1(h), stating that a petition for certiorari to a state court shall "specify the stage in the proceedings, both in the court of first instance and in the appellate court, at which the federal questions sought to be reviewed were raised; the method or manner of raising them and the way in which they were passed upon by the court; such pertinent quotation of specific portions of the record, or summary thereof, with specific reference to the places in the record where the matter appears (*e.g.,* ruling on exception, portion of court's charge and exception thereto, assignment of errors) as will show that the federal question was timely and properly raised so as to give this Court jurisdiction to review the judgment on writ of certiorari." Rule 15.1(g) has a parallel requirement for appeals.

because there was no evidence of an element of the crime ("wilfulness"), even though no federal constitutional issue had been raised as to this point in the state courts. In dissent, Justice Rehnquist protested (pp. 482–84) that "[a] litigant seeking to preserve a constitutional claim for review in this Court must not only make clear to the lower courts the nature of his claim, but he must also make it clear that the claim is constitutionally grounded. The closest that appellant came in his brief on appeal to the Supreme Court of New Hampshire to discussing the issue on which this Court's opinion turns is in the sixth section, which is headed: 'The State's failure to introduce any evidence of scienter should have resulted in dismissal of the charge following the presentation of the State's case.' Appellant in that section makes the customary appellate arguments of insufficiency of the evidence and does not so much as mention either the United States Constitution or a single case decided by this Court. The Supreme Court of New Hampshire treated these arguments as raising a classic state law claim of insufficient evidence of scienter; nothing in that court's opinion remotely suggests that it was treating the claim as having a basis other than in state law. * * * Since the Supreme Court of New Hampshire was not presented with a federal constitutional challenge to the sufficiency of the evidence, resolution of this question by the Court is inconsistent with the congressional limitation on our jurisdiction to review the final judgment of the highest court of a State."

See also Terminiello v. Chicago, 337 U.S. 1 (1949);[2] Batson v. Kentucky, 476 U.S. 79 (1986) (passing on Equal Protection claim that, according to three dissenters, was explicitly disclaimed by petitioners); Eddings v. Oklahoma, 455 U.S. 104 (1982) (passing on a claim in a death penalty case that four dissenters said was not properly raised); Williams v. Florida, 465 U.S. 1109 (1984) (certiorari denied; dissent by Marshall, J.: "[w]hen the record in a case has revealed plain error, this Court has enforced federal constitutional standards despite the petitioner's failure to raise clearly his federal constitutional claim below. See, e.g., Vachon v. New Hampshire * * *"); Taylor v. Illinois, 108 S.Ct. 646, 651 n.9 (1988); compare Wood v. Georgia, 450 U.S. 261 (1981) (where question is whether petitioner's lawyer had divided loyalties, failure of that lawyer to raise a question not dispositive).

2. In Terminiello, the petitioner, convicted of violating a disorderly conduct ordinance for making a speech, took no exception to a statement in the trial court's charge to the jury that "misbehavior may constitute a breach of the peace if it stirs the public to anger, invites dispute, brings about a condition of unrest * * *". He did, however, move for a directed verdict on the ground that "what he said was protected by the first amendment" and that "to charge this defendant with committing a misdemeanor because he gave the speech in question is a contravention of the First Amendment" (Petition for Certiorari, pp. 4–5). Both in the state courts and in the Supreme Court, the argument focused wholly on the character of the petitioner's address under the circumstances shown.

The Supreme Court reversed, holding that the ordinance, as construed in the portion of the charge quoted above, was invalid, and that the question had been adequately raised by the petitioner's contention that "inclusion of his speech within the ordinance was a violation of the Constitution". (337 U.S. at 6).

Chief Justice Vinson, Justices Frankfurter, Jackson and Burton dissented.

Justice Frankfurter observed (pp. 8–9): "For the first time in the course of the 130 years in which State prosecutions have come here for review, this Court is today reversing a sentence imposed by a State court on a ground that was urged neither here nor below and that was explicitly disclaimed on behalf of the petitioner at the bar of this Court."

(3) The requirement of presenting the federal question to the state courts is sometimes spoken of as if it were tested by federal-law standards: "There are various ways in which the validity of a state statute may be drawn in question on the ground that it is repugnant to the Constitution of the United States. No particular form of words or phrases is essential, but only that the claim of invalidity and the ground therefor be brought to the attention of the state court with fair precision and in due time. And if the record as a whole shows either expressly or by clear intendment that this was done, the claim is to be regarded as having been adequately presented." Justice Van Devanter in New York ex rel. Bryant v. Zimmerman, 278 U.S. 63, 67 (1928). And the Court seems to make up its own mind about what is to be deemed to have been subsumed in questions put to and decided by the state courts, and how much variation and expansion of such questions is to be allowed. See, *e.g.,* Bailey v. Anderson, 326 U.S. 203 (1945) (argument presented in state-law terms cannot be converted, in the Supreme Court, into a federal constitutional question); compare Vachon v. New Hampshire, *supra.*

In Street v. New York, 394 U.S. 576 (1969), Justice Harlan, writing for the Court, said: "The issue whether a federal question was sufficiently and properly raised in the state courts is itself ultimately a federal question, as to which this Court is not bound by the decision of the state courts. However, it is not entirely clear whether in such cases the scope of our review is limited to determining whether the state court has 'by-passed the federal right under forms of local procedure' or whether we should decide the matter '*de novo* for ourselves.' Ellis v. Dixon, 349 U.S. 458, 463 (1955)" (p. 583). Justice Harlan stated that when the highest state court fails to pass on a federal question, "it will be assumed that the omission was due to want of proper presentation" and that the burden is on appellant "affirmatively [to] show the contrary" (p. 582). He concluded, however, that in this case the burden had been met both as a matter of federal law and under the New York authorities, which do not "require that an issue be raised in the trial court with greater specificity than occurred here" (p. 583).[3]

(3.) In Chambers v. Mississippi, 410 U.S. 284 (1973), the Supreme Court decided that due process had been denied by the strict application of the Mississippi common-law evidence rule preventing cross-examination or impeachment of one's own witness, even though the state supreme court had not addressed that question. Defendant had, in his motion for new trial (after the verdict), asserted the evidence rulings as error and argued generally that the trial "was not in accord with fundamental fairness guaranteed by the Fourteenth Amendment of the Constitution." Justice Powell, for the Court, held that the federal claim, based upon the cumulative effect of evidentiary rulings, could not practicably have been raised prior to the close of defendant's evidence, and he accepted as sufficient the general allegations in the motion and in the Mississippi Supreme Court (particularly on petition for rehearing there). He stressed that the state in this case did not assert that the questions were not properly reviewable (p. 290 n. 3). Justice Rehnquist dissented on the jurisdictional issue. Justice White concurred specially on the point.

In Taylor v. Kentucky, 436 U.S. 478, 482 n. 10 (1978), refusal to give a jury instruction on the presumption of innocence was held a violation of due process; the Court treated defendant's objection that the refusal conflicted with "fundamental principles of judicial fair play" as sufficient to raise the federal contention at the trial level. See also Martinez v. California, 444 U.S. 277, 283 n. 6 (1980) (assertion of "a federally protected right to life under the Constitution of the United States" sufficient challenge to validity of paroling authority's absolute immunity in action for damages for releasing prisoner who later committed murder).

(4) On the other hand, as Herndon v. Georgia indicates, there is also no doubt that state practice presumptively determines both the time when and the mode by which federal claims must be asserted and preserved in the state courts—*e.g.*, pleading, motion or objection at the trial, exception, renewal, presentation on appeal. See, *e.g.*, Edelman v. California, 344 U.S. 357 (1953); Beck v. Washington, 369 U.S. 541, 549–54 (1962); Parker v. North Carolina, 397 U.S. 790, 798–99 (1970); Exxon Corp. v. Eagerton, 462 U.S. 176 (1983); and see generally Stern, Gressman & Shapiro, Supreme Court Practice 149–58 (6th ed. 1986). Thus, if Herndon's attack on the indictment had been preserved in the bill of exceptions, as required by state practice, the requirement that the federal question be properly raised in the state proceedings would presumably have been met.

Does the requirement that federal questions be raised in the state court in accordance with state procedure derive from: (a) 28 U.S.C. § 1257 ("drawn in question," "specially set up and claimed"), *cf.* Amalgamated Food Emp. Union Local 590 v. Logan Valley Plaza, Inc., 391 U.S. 308, 334–36 (1968) (Harlan, J., dissenting); (b) constitutional requirements, including proscriptions against advisory opinions; (c) inherent necessities of the federal system; (d) general standards of appellate practice; (e) special standards formulated by the Supreme Court to facilitate its work?

(5) If the highest state court actually decides the merits of a federal question, it is irrelevant how and when the question was raised in the state court system, and the Supreme Court's jurisdiction is secure. See, *e.g.*, Whitney v. California, 274 U.S. 357, 360–63 (1927); Raley v. Ohio, 360 U.S. 423, 436 (1959); Coleman v. Alabama, 377 U.S. 129 (1964); Orr v. Orr, 440 U.S. 268, 274–75 (1979); Payton v. New York, 445 U.S. 573, 582 n. 19 (1980).

The federal questions that the Supreme Court declined to review in Herndon v. Georgia were subsequently considered and decided by the Georgia courts on an application for a writ of habeas corpus. The judgment of the Supreme Court of Georgia sustaining the validity of the statute was reviewed and reversed by the Supreme Court in Herndon v. Lowry, 301 U.S. 242 (1937). Justice Roberts said (p. 247): "The scope of a *habeas corpus* proceeding in the circumstances disclosed is a state and not a federal question and since the state courts treated the proceeding as properly raising issues of federal constitutional right, we have jurisdiction and all such issues are open here."

See generally Stern, Gressman & Shapiro, *supra,* at 158–60.

(6) Suppose that a state court refuses to decide a federal question on the ground that the litigant failed to comply with a state rule of procedure specifying how and when that question must be raised. As Herndon and Michel indicate, the resulting judgment is deemed to rest on an adequate and independent state ground, foreclosing Supreme Court review, unless the state procedural ground for the judgment is "inadequate." As the foregoing and following materials show, however, the Court has not had an easy time defining the content of "inadequacy."

(7) If the right to raise the federal claim was forfeited on account of noncompliance with a state procedural rule that, on its face or as applied, violates the Due Process Clause, it is plain that Supreme Court review cannot be foreclosed.

In Saunders v. Shaw, 244 U.S. 317 (1917), the highest state court on rehearing rendered judgment on a finding as to fact that the trial court, in

accordance with appellant's contention, had held immaterial. In Brinkerhoff–Faris Trust & Savings Co. v. Hill, 281 U.S. 673 (1930), relief was
denied by the state appellate court for failure to resort to an administrative
remedy that earlier decisions held the state administrative body lacked the
power to award and that it was then too late to pursue. In both cases the
Supreme Court viewed the action of the highest state court as a deprivation
of the right to hearing, constituting a denial of due process. The point was
raised in Brinkerhoff on petition for rehearing in the state court, in
Saunders by the assignment of errors in the Supreme Court, state rules
precluding a second petition for rehearing.

Missouri v. Gehner, 281 U.S. 313 (1930), involved a judgment sustaining a state tax on the property of domestic insurance companies in
excess of legal reserves and unpaid claims. In fixing the assessment the
board of equalization excluded the company's United States bonds, holding
them nontaxable. In sustaining the assessment on an independent compu-
tation, the Missouri Supreme Court included the bonds. On motion for
rehearing, the company challenged the statute as applied, contending that
the bonds were immune under the Constitution and an act of Congress.
The motion was overruled with an irrelevant change in the opinion but
without adverting to the federal claim. The Supreme Court reversed on
the merits on appeal, holding that "it may not reasonably be held that the
company was bound to anticipate such a construction or in advance to
invoke federal protection against the taxation of its United States bonds"
(p. 320).

Was there a denial of due process in the Gehner case in denying a
hearing on the issue of immunity?

In Reece v. Georgia, 350 U.S. 85 (1955), decided the same day as Michel
(and referred to therein), the Court accepted the general validity of the
Georgia rule requiring challenges to the grand jury to be made before
indictment, finding that the "rule goes back to 1882, * * * and has been
consistently followed in that State," but nevertheless, per Justice Clark,
unanimously held the rule invalid as applied, violating due process in this
case (pp. 89–90): "Reece is a semi-illiterate Negro of low mentality. We
need not decide whether, with the assistance of counsel, he would have had
an opportunity to raise his objection during the two days he was in jail
before indictment. But it is utterly unrealistic to say that he had such
opportunity when counsel was not provided for him until the day after he
was indicted. * * * The effective assistance of counsel in such a [capital]
case is a constitutional requirement of due process which no member of the
Union may disregard. Georgia should have considered Reece's motion to
quash on its merits."[4]

Note that the validity of a state procedural rule under the Due Process
Clause raises an independent federal question that the Court has jurisdiction to review apart from any other federal issues in the case. And note,

4. Cf. Cole v. Arkansas, 333 U.S. 196
(1948), p. 680, infra, where convictions of
violating one statutory section, challenged
as unconstitutional, were sustained by the
state supreme court under another section
of the statute without consideration of the
federal constitutional question. Defendants petitioned for rehearing, urging that
the affirmance violated the Due Process
Clause. The petition was denied and the
Supreme Court granted certiorari and reversed, holding that the Due Process
Clause had been violated, that defendant
was entitled to notice of the charge against
him and to be tried, judged and have his
conviction reviewed on the basis of that
charged offense. See also Cole v. Arkansas, 338 U.S. 345 (1949).

such a rule is invalid, presumably it may not be applied to
to litigate a state-law claim any more than a federal claim.
Or is it possible that the Due Process Clause imposes more stringent
requirements on the right to be heard with respect to a federal constitutional claim than a claim based on state law?)

(8) The Michel opinion appears to assume that if the state procedural
ruling is valid under the Due Process Clause, Supreme Court review is
barred.   In this respect, however, that opinion is highly unusual.   As
Herndon itself indicates, a large body of authority rests on the assumption
that a state procedural ground may be found "inadequate" for purposes of
Supreme Court review without the necessity of finding that the state's
procedures violated the Due Process Clause.   See generally Harlan, J.,
dissenting in Fay v. Noia, 372 U.S. 391, 448, 465–66 (1963) (see pp. 1544–45,
infra); Meltzer, *State Court Forfeitures of Federal Rights,* 99 Harv.L.Rev.
1128, 1137–45, 1159–60 (1986); Hart, *Foreword: The Time Chart of the
Justices,* 73 Harv.L.Rev. 84, 116 (1959); Note, *The Untenable Nonfederal
Ground in the Supreme Court,* 74 Harv.L.Rev. 1375 (1961); but *cf.* Hill, *The
Inadequate State Ground,* 65 Colum.L.Rev. 943, 971–80 (1965).

In a much-quoted passage in Davis v. Wechsler, 263 U.S. 22, 24 (1923),
Justice Holmes said: "Whatever springes the State may set for those who
are endeavoring to assert rights that the State confers, the assertion of
federal rights, when plainly and reasonably made, is not to be defeated
under the name of local practice."

In Lawrence v. State Tax Com'n, 286 U.S. 276, 282 (1932), Justice Stone
observed that "Even though the claimed constitutional protection be denied
on non-federal grounds, it is the province of this Court to inquire whether
the decision of the state court rests upon a fair or substantial basis.   If
unsubstantial, constitutional obligations may not thus be avoided.   See
Ward v. Love County * * *.   [C]onstitutional rights [may be] denied as
well by the refusal of the state court to decide the question, as by an
erroneous decision of it."

Compare Justice Clark's formulation in Williams v. Georgia, 349 U.S.
375, 399 (1955) (dissenting opinion): "A purported state ground is not
independent and adequate in two instances.   *First,* where the circumstances give rise to an inference that the state court is guilty of an
evasion—an interpretation of state law with the specific intent to deprive a
litigant of a federal right.   *Second,* where the state law, honestly applied
though it may be, and even dictated by the precedents, throws such
obstacles in the way of enforcement of federal rights that it must be struck
down as unreasonably interfering with the vindication of such rights." [5]

(9) Underneath these general formulations, the cases finding state
procedural grounds "inadequate" break down into several categories:

   (a) *The Due Process cases.*   These are described in Paragraph (7), *supra.*

   (b) *The state procedural ground is not fairly supported by state law
because the requirement is novel or has been inconsistently applied.*

---

5. Appended to the sentence beginning
"First" is the following footnote (n. 3):
"This charge upon the integrity of a State
Supreme Court is so serious that this Court
has restricted such findings to cases where
the state court decision lacked 'fair support' in the state law.   See Rogers v. Alabama, 192 U.S. 226.   *Cf.* Fox Film Corp. v.
Muller, 296 U.S. 207, 209."

In NAACP v. Alabama ex rel. Patterson, 357 U.S. 449 (1958), the NAACP had been held in contempt for failure to produce its membership lists, as required by the trial court, despite its contention that this order was unconstitutional. It thereupon petitioned the Alabama Supreme Court for certiorari to review the contempt judgment. That court held that it could not consider the constitutional issues in this proceeding, and that the only proper recourse was mandamus to quash the discovery order prior to the contempt adjudication.

The Supreme Court held that it had jurisdiction to entertain the federal claim. The Court examined previous Alabama authority and held that it could not reconcile the ground below with the Alabama court's "past unambiguous holdings as to the scope of review available upon a writ of certiorari addressed to a contempt judgment." It recognized that under existing Alabama authority an order requiring production of evidence could be reviewed on petition for mandamus. Justice Harlan, for a unanimous Court, continued (pp. 457–58): "But we can discover nothing in the prior state cases which suggests that mandamus is the *exclusive* remedy for reviewing court orders after disobedience of them has led to contempt judgments. Nor, so far as we can find, do any of these prior decisions indicate that the validity of such orders can be drawn in question by way of certiorari only in instances where a defendant had no opportunity to apply for mandamus. * * * Even if that is indeed the rationale of the Alabama Supreme Court's present decision, such a local procedural rule, although it may now appear in retrospect to form a part of a consistent pattern of procedures to obtain appellate review, cannot avail the State here, because petitioner could not fairly be deemed to have been apprised of its existence. Novelty in procedural requirements cannot be permitted to thwart review in this Court applied for by those who, in justified reliance upon prior decisions, seek vindication in state courts of their federal constitutional rights. *Cf.* Brinkerhoff–Faris Co. v. Hill, 281 U.S. 673."

Inadequacy is also established by a demonstration that the state courts had not previously applied their stated rule "with the pointless severity" shown in regard to the federal issue. See, *e.g.*, Rogers v. Alabama, 192 U.S. 226 (1904) (two-page motion to quash indictment stricken as prolix); NAACP v. Alabama ex rel. Flowers, 377 U.S. 288, 294–302 (1964) (formal arrangement of points in brief); Barr v. City of Columbia, 378 U.S. 146, 149–50 (1964) (generality of stated exceptions; same form accepted in other cases).

See also James v. Kentucky, 466 U.S. 341, 345–48 (1984) (state rule requiring that a request for a jury charge be labeled as a request for a jury "instruction" rather than an "admonition" not consistently applied in prior cases); Hathorn v. Lovorn, 457 U.S. 255 (1982).[6]

Is the result in Herndon consistent with these cases? On Justice Sutherland's opinion, what should Herndon's lawyer have done to preserve the constitutional issue?

6. See Meltzer, *supra*, at 1138–39, for a discussion of the cases resting on a finding of inconsistency or novelty. Meltzer points out (at 1139 n. 44) that a state ruling that is novel or inconsistent could be characterized either as an impermissible misapplica-tion of state law, or as an impermissible implicit revision of state law; if it is characterized as the latter, it may presumably be applied to future cases "once notice of the new interpretation is provided."

Consider whether the cases finding state procedural rulings "inadequate" on the ground that they are novel or inconsistent with past practice are of a piece with the cases finding "inadequate" a state ruling on a substantive state law question that is a predicate for or antecedent to passing on a federal claim (see, *e.g.,* Indiana ex rel. Anderson v. Brand and the cases discussed in the Note following it, pp. 569–81, *supra*).

(c) *The state procedural requirement is unacceptably burdensome.*

In Davis v. Wechsler, 263 U.S. 22 (1923), a federal official defending a state court action entered a general denial and also pleaded a special federal jurisdictional objection. The official's successor, substituting as defendant, entered an appearance and adopted the previous pleadings; but the state court ruled that the appearance, coming just before the adoption of the pleadings, was a general one and waived the jurisdictional objection. The Supreme Court found the state ground unduly burdensome and therefore inadequate.

See also Douglas v. Alabama, 380 U.S. 415, 422–23 (1965) (failure to repeat, after every question put to a witness, a constitutional objection that had been thrice made and whose repetition would have been futile and strategically harmful; state forfeiture ruling held inadequate); Staub v. City of Baxley, 355 U.S. 313, 319–20 (1958) (failure to specify the section-numbers of the ordinance whose validity plaintiff had clearly challenged; state forfeiture ruling, "forc[ing] resort to an arid ritual of meaningless form," held inadequate); Shuttlesworth v. City of Birmingham, 376 U.S. 339 (1964) (failure to use proper paper for petition to review criminal conviction; state forfeiture ruling held inadequate); Brown v. Western Ry., 338 U.S. 294 (1949) (discussed further at p. 635, *infra*).[7]

(10) What is the basis for the Supreme Court's power to review a case where the state judgment rests on a procedural ruling that the Court finds "inadequate" to support the judgment—even though that ruling has not been found unconstitutional?

Is this assertion of power more problematic than the Court's assertion of power, ever since Martin v. Hunter's Lessee, to review the "adequacy" of state substantive rulings where the decision of the state law question is antecedent to a claim of federal right? See pp. 532 and 569–90, *supra*. Are not all state procedural rulings that determine whether a federal question has been seasonably raised in the state courts, "antecedent" in the relevant sense? Could Supreme Court review of federal questions be adequately effectuated if state procedural rulings with respect to the litigation of federal questions, once found constitutional, were insulated from review? See Wechsler, *The Appellate Jurisdiction of the Supreme Court: Reflections on the Law and Logistics of Direct Review,* 34 Wash. & Lee L.Rev. 1043, 1053–56 (1977).

Do the "burdensome" cases present a special problem in this regard? Doesn't it make sense to read into § 1257, as informed by the Supremacy Clause, a requirement that state courts be reasonably hospitable to the litigation of federal claims? See Hart, p. 606, *supra*, at 117–18.

7. The categories overlap. In James v. Kentucky, *supra*, the Court plainly regarded the state ruling, insisting that the word "instruction," rather than the word "admonition," be used, as unjustifiably burdensome as well as inconsistent with prior state law.

(11) Meltzer, p. 606, *supra*, at 1158–85, suggests that the law of procedural "inadequacy" should be recharacterized as requiring the application of a "federal common law" to the question of when noncompliance with state procedural rules may lead to the forfeiture of the right to raise a federal claim. He then uses the reformulation as the basis for advocating a more permissive standard for excusing state procedural defaults. *Id.* at 1208 *et seq.* Compare Wechsler, *supra*, at 1054 ("The problem of federal-state relations is the same * * * whether the antecedent state law issue is substantive or procedural. It is difficult to understand, therefore, why there should be a difference in the nature or the scope of the Supreme Court's examination of the state determination"). Compare also Hart, *supra*, and consider whether the traditional formulation—that the question of forfeiture is an issue of state law subject to federal limits—is adequate to the task of insuring that federal claims are treated hospitably by state courts.

(12) Professor Meltzer also argues that, if the question of forfeiture is characterized as an issue of federal common law, this would also make it clear that a federal ruling, to the effect that a particular state procedural default may not lead to forfeiture, must be applied in the future in the state courts, and should not be regarded simply as a ruling governing federal jurisdiction to review.

This question—whether a finding of "inadequacy" should bind the state courts in future cases—has divided the commentators, see Meltzer, *supra*, at 1150–52, 1202 n. 70. For a survey of the state cases responding both to Supreme Court findings of "inadequacy" on direct review and to analogous federal court findings in habeas corpus cases, see *id.* at 1154–58.

(13) Tileston v. Ullman, 318 U.S. 44 (1943), see pp. 137–38, *supra*, involved a state court action by a physician for a declaratory judgment that the Connecticut statute prohibiting the use of contraceptives and the giving of assistance or counsel in their use was unconstitutional. The Connecticut Supreme Court upheld the applicability and validity of the statute, and the plaintiff appealed. The Supreme Court, per curiam, held that the plaintiff had no standing to raise this question, since neither his liberty nor his property was at stake; citing federal cases, it dismissed the appeal.

The Supreme Court's disposition—leaving the state court judgment standing—made it clear that the state court's ruling that the plaintiff had standing, albeit not binding on the Supreme Court, was valid as a matter of state law. This case therefore stands as an exception, doesn't it, to the general principle described in Paragraph (5), *supra*, that if a state court actually decides a federal question, the Supreme Court has jurisdiction to review? The federal law of standing and justiciability—deriving as it does from Article III—binds the federal courts but (apparently) not the state courts. Thus state court adjudication of federal questions may turn out to be unreviewable if the state law characterizes as justiciable a case that the federal courts regard as nonjusticiable. Is this a necessary institutional relationship? A desirable one?

Suppose that the Connecticut state court had invalidated the Connecticut statute. Would it be wise to conclude that the Supreme Court does not have jurisdiction to review the judgment?

If Connecticut, after the Tileston case, prosecuted Dr. Tileston for violating the statute, would the issue of validity be res judicata in the

Connecticut courts? If those courts so hold, would this be an adequate state ground foreclosing the Supreme Court from reviewing the merits? For a clear indication that the answer to the latter question is no, see Fidelity National Bank & Trust Co. v. Swope, 274 U.S. 123 (1927), discussed at p. 235, *supra.*

Waiver

————

HENRY v. MISSISSIPPI
379 U.S. 443, 85 S.Ct. 564, 13 L.Ed.2d 408 (1965).
Certiorari to the Supreme Court of Mississippi.

MR. JUSTICE BRENNAN delivered the opinion of the Court.

Petitioner was convicted of disturbing the peace, by indecent proposals to and offensive contact with an 18–year-old hitchhiker to whom he is said to have given a ride in his car. The trial judge charged the jury that "you cannot find the defendant guilty on the unsupported and uncorroborated testimony of the complainant alone." The petitioner's federal claim derives from the admission of a police officer's testimony introduced to corroborate the hitchhiker's testimony. The Mississippi Supreme Court held that the officer's testimony was improperly admitted as the fruit of "an unlawful search and was in violation of § 23, Miss.Constitution 1890." 154 So.2d 289, 294. The tainted evidence tended to substantiate the hitchhiker's testimony by showing its accuracy in a detail which could have been seen only by one inside the car. In particular, it showed that the right-hand ashtray of the car in which the incident took place was full of Dentyne chewing gum wrappers, and that the cigarette lighter did not function. The police officer testified that after petitioner's arrest he had returned to the petitioner's home and obtained the permission of petitioner's wife to look in petitioner's car. The wife provided the officer with the keys, with which the officer opened the car. He testified that he tried the lighter and it would not work, and also that the ashtray "was filled with red dentyne chewing gum wrappers."

The Mississippi Supreme Court first filed an opinion which reversed petitioner's conviction and remanded for a new trial. The court held that the wife's consent to the search of the car did not waive petitioner's constitutional rights, and noted that the "[t]estimony of the State's witness * * * is, in effect, uncorroborated without the evidence disclosed by the inspection of defendant's automobile." 154 So.2d, at 296 (advance sheet). Acting in the belief that petitioner had been represented by nonresident counsel unfamiliar with local procedure, the court reversed despite petitioner's failure to comply with the Mississippi requirement that an objection to illegal evidence be made at the time it is introduced. The court noted that petitioner had moved for a directed verdict at the close of the State's case, assigning as one ground the use of illegally obtained evidence; it did not mention petitioner's renewal of his motion at the close of all evidence.

After the first opinion was handed down, the State filed a Suggestion of Error, pointing out that petitioner was in fact represented at his trial by competent local counsel, as well as by out-of-state lawyers. Thereupon the Mississippi Supreme Court withdrew its first opinion and filed a new opinion in support of a judgment affirming petitioner's conviction. The new opinion is identical with the first save for the result, the statement that petitioner had local counsel, and the discussion of the effect of failure for whatever reason to make timely objection to the evidence. "In such circumstances, even if honest mistakes of counsel in respect to policy or strategy or otherwise occur, they are binding upon the client as a part of the hazards of courtroom battle." 154 So.2d, at 296 (bound volume). Moreover, the court reasoned, petitioner's cross-examination of the State's witness before the initial motion for directed verdict, and introduction of other evidence of the car's interior appearance afterward, "cured" the original error and estopped petitioner from complaining of the tainted evidence. We granted certiorari, 376 U.S. 904. We vacate the judgment of conviction and remand for a hearing on the question whether the petitioner is to be deemed to have knowingly waived decision of his federal claim when timely objection was not made to the admission of the illegally seized evidence.

It is, of course, a familiar principle that this Court will decline to review state court judgments which rest on independent and adequate state grounds, even where those judgments also decide federal questions. The principle applies not only in cases involving state substantive grounds, Murdock v. City of Memphis, 20 Wall. 590, but also in cases involving state procedural grounds. Compare Herb v. Pitcairn, 324 U.S. 117, 125–126, with Davis v. Wechsler, 263 U.S. 22. But it is important to distinguish between state substantive grounds and state procedural grounds. Where the ground involved is substantive, the determination of the federal question cannot affect the disposition if the state court decision on the state law question is allowed to stand. Under the view taken in Murdock of the statutes conferring appellate jurisdiction on this Court, we have no power to revise judgments on questions of state law. Thus, the adequate nonfederal ground doctrine is necessary to avoid advisory opinions.

These justifications have no application where the state ground is purely procedural. A procedural default which is held to bar challenge to a conviction in state courts, even on federal constitutional grounds, prevents implementation of the federal right. Accordingly, we have consistently held that the question of when and how defaults in compliance with state procedural rules can preclude our consideration of a federal question is itself a federal question. *Cf.* Lovell v. City of Griffin, 303 U.S. 444, 450. As Mr. Justice Holmes said:

"When as here there is a plain assertion of federal rights in the lower court, local rules as to how far it shall be reviewed on appeal do not necessarily prevail. * * * Whether the right was denied or not given due recognition by the [state court] * * * is a question as to which the plaintiffs are entitled to invoke our judgment." Love v. Griffith, 266 U.S. 32, 33–34.

Only last Term, we reaffirmed this principle, holding that a state appellate court's refusal, on the ground of mootness, to consider a federal claim, did not preclude our independent determination of the question of mootness; that is itself a question of federal law which this Court must ultimately decide. Liner v. Jafco, Inc., 375 U.S. 301. These cases settle the proposition that a litigant's procedural defaults in state proceedings do not prevent vindication of his federal rights unless the State's insistence on compliance with its procedural rule serves a legitimate state interest. In every case we must inquire whether the enforcement of a procedural forfeiture serves such a state interest. If it does not, the state procedural rule ought not be permitted to bar vindication of important federal rights.[3]

The Mississippi rule requiring contemporaneous objection to the introduction of illegal evidence clearly does serve a legitimate state interest. By immediately apprising the trial judge of the objection, counsel gives the court the opportunity to conduct the trial without using the tainted evidence. If the objection is well taken the fruits of the illegal search may be excluded from jury consideration, and a reversal and new trial avoided. But on the record before us it appears that this purpose of the contemporaneous-objection rule may have been substantially served by petitioner's motion at the close of the State's evidence asking for a directed verdict because of the erroneous admission of the officer's testimony. For at this stage the trial judge could have called for elaboration of the search and seizure argument and, if persuaded, could have stricken the tainted testimony or have taken other appropriate corrective action. For example, if there was sufficient competent evidence without his testimony to go to the jury, the motion for a directed verdict might have been denied, and the case submitted to the jury with a properly worded appropriate cautionary instruction.[4] In these circumstances, the delay until the close of the State's case in presenting the objection cannot be said to have frustrated the State's interest in avoiding delay and waste of time in the disposition of the case. If this is so, and enforcement of the rule here would serve no substantial state interest, then settled principles would preclude treating the state ground as adequate; giving effect to the contemporaneous-objection rule for its own sake "would be to force resort to an arid ritual of meaningless form." Staub v. City of Baxley, 355 U.S. 313, 320; see also Wright v. Georgia, 373 U.S. 284, 289–291.[5]

We have no reason, however, to decide that question now or to express any view on the merits of petitioner's substantial constitutional claim. For even assuming that the making of the objection on the motion for a directed verdict satisfied the state interest served by the contemporaneous-objection rule, the record suggests a possibility that petitioner's counsel deliberately bypassed the opportunity to make timely objection in the state court, and thus that the petitioner should be deemed to have forfeited his

---

3. This will not lead inevitably to a plethora of attacks on the application of state procedural rules; where the state rule is a reasonable one and clearly announced to defendant and counsel, application of the waiver doctrine will yield the same result as that of the adequate nonfederal ground doctrine in the vast majority of cases.

4. The view of the Mississippi court in its first opinion seems to have been that there was insufficient evidence apart from the tainted testimony to support the conviction. Hence, appropriate corrective action as a matter of state law might have included granting petitioner's motion. We have not overlooked the fact that the first opinion remanded for a new trial, although the usual practice of the Mississippi Supreme Court where a motion for directed verdict, renewed at the close of all the evidence, is improperly denied is to dismiss

the prosecution. ⁎ ⁎ ⁎ The opinion offers no explanation of the mandate; the answer is probably that the court refers only to the motion at the end of the State's case, 154 So.2d, at 294, 295, and overlooks the fact that it was renewed at the close of all the evidence, just as it overlooks the presence of local counsel. If the motion were not renewed, the appellate court could not dismiss the prosecution. See Smith v. State, *supra.*

5. We do not rely on the principle that our review is not precluded when the state court has failed to exercise discretion to disregard the procedural default. See Williams v. Georgia, 349 U.S. 375. We read the second Mississippi Supreme Court opinion as holding that there is no such discretion where it appears that petitioner was represented by competent local counsel familiar with local procedure.

state court remedies. Although the Mississippi Supreme Court characterized the failure to object as an "honest mistake," 154 So.2d, at 296 (bound volume), the State, in the brief in support of its Suggestion of Error in the Supreme Court of Mississippi asserted its willingness to agree that its Suggestion of Error "should not be sustained if either of the three counsel [for petitioner] participating in this trial would respond hereto with an affidavit that he did not know that at some point in a trial in criminal court in Mississippi that an objection to such testimony must have been made." The second opinion of the Mississippi Supreme Court does not refer to the State's proposal and thus it appears that the Court did not believe that the issue was properly presented for decision. Another indication of possible waiver appears in an affidavit attached to the State's brief in this Court; there, the respondent asserted that one of petitioner's lawyers stood up as if to object to the officer's tainted testimony, and was pulled down by co-counsel. Again, this furnishes an insufficient basis for decision of the waiver questions at this time. But, together with the proposal in the Suggestion of Error, it is enough to justify an evidentiary hearing to determine whether petitioner "after consultation with competent counsel or otherwise, understandingly and knowingly forewent the privilege of seeking to vindicate his federal claims in the state courts, whether for strategic, tactical, or any other reasons that can fairly be described as the deliberate by-passing of state procedures * * *." Fay v. Noia, 372 U.S. 391, 439.

The evidence suggests reasons for a strategic move. Both the complaining witness and the police officer testified that the cigarette lighter in the car did not work. After denial of its motion for a directed verdict the defense called a mechanic who had repaired the cigarette lighter. The defense might have planned to allow the complaining witness and the officer to testify that the cigarette lighter did not work, and then, if the motion for directed verdict were not granted, to discredit both witnesses by showing that it did work, thereby persuading the jury to acquit. Or, by delaying objection to the evidence, the defense might have hoped to invite error and lay the foundation for a subsequent reversal. If either reason motivated the action of petitioner's counsel, and their plans backfired, counsel's deliberate choice of the strategy would amount to a waiver binding on petitioner and would preclude him from a decision on the merits of his federal claim either in the state courts or here. Although trial strategy adopted by counsel without prior consultation with an accused will not, where the circumstances are exceptional, preclude the accused from asserting constitutional claims, see Whitus v. Balkcom, 333 F.2d 496 (C.A.5th Cir.1964), we think that the deliberate bypassing by counsel of the contemporaneous-objection rule as a part of trial strategy would have that effect in this case.

Only evidence extrinsic to the record before us can establish the fact of waiver, and the State should have an opportunity to establish that fact. In comparable cases arising in federal courts we have vacated the judgments of conviction and remanded for a hearing, suspending the determination of the validity of the conviction pending the outcome of the hearing. See United States v. Shotwell Mfg. Co., 355 U.S. 233; Campbell v. United States, 365 U.S. 85. We recently adopted a similar procedure to determine an issue essential to the fairness of a state conviction. See Jackson v. Denno, 378 U.S. 368, 393–394; Boles v. Stevenson, 379 U.S. 43. We think a similar course is particularly desirable here, since a dismissal on the basis of an adequate state ground would not end this case; petitioner might still pursue vindication of his federal claim in a federal habeas corpus proceeding in which the procedural default will not alone preclude consideration of his claim, at least unless it is shown that petitioner deliberately bypassed the orderly procedure of the state courts. Fay v. Noia, *supra,* at 438.

Of course, in so remanding we neither hold nor even remotely imply that the State must forgo insistence on its procedural requirements if it finds no waiver. Such a finding would only mean that petitioner could have a federal court apply settled principles to test the effectiveness of the procedural default to foreclose consideration of his constitutional claim. If it finds the procedural default ineffective, the federal court will itself decide the merits of his federal claim, at least so long as the state court does not wish to do so. By permitting the Mississippi courts to make an initial determination of waiver, we serve the causes of efficient administration of criminal justice, and of harmonious federal-state judicial relations. Such a disposition may make unnecessary the processing of the case through federal courts already laboring under congested dockets, or it may make unnecessary the relitigation in a federal forum of certain issues. See Townsend v. Sain, 372 U.S. 293, 312–319. The Court is not blind to the fact that the federal habeas corpus jurisdiction has been a source of irritation between the federal and state judiciaries. It has been suggested that this friction might be ameliorated if the States would look upon our decisions in Fay v. Noia, *supra,* and Townsend v. Sain, *supra,* as affording them an opportunity to provide state procedures, direct or collateral, for a full airing of federal claims. That prospect is better served by a remand than by relegating petitioner to his federal habeas remedy. Therefore, the judgment is vacated and the case is remanded to the Mississippi Supreme Court for further proceedings not inconsistent with this opinion.

It is so ordered.

MR. JUSTICE BLACK, dissenting.

Petitioner contends that his conviction was based in part on evidence obtained by an allegedly unlawful search in violation of the United States Constitution. I would decide this federal question here and now. I do not believe that the Mississippi procedural trial rule relied on by the State can shut off this Court's review, nor do I find a particle of support for the Court's suggestion that petitioner knowingly waived his right to have this constitutional question decided by the state trial court.

As far as the issue of waiver is concerned, I agree with the Mississippi Supreme Court, which considered the failure to object one of the "honest mistakes" which any lawyer might make, since I believe that the record is completely barren of evidence to support a finding of a conscious and intentional waiver of petitioner's due process right to have the trial court decide whether evidence used against him had been unconstitutionally seized. Therefore I would not remand for a hearing by the State Supreme Court or the trial court on the issue of waiver. And even if I considered that a real issue of waiver had been shown and was properly before us, I would decide it here. I cannot agree to the Court's judgment remanding the case to the state courts for a hearing on that issue alone, thereby giving the State a chance to supplement the trial record to save its conviction from constitutional challenge in a summary hearing before a court without a jury. * * *

Nor do I believe that Mississippi's procedural rule concerning the stage of a trial at which constitutional objections should be made is the kind of rule that we should accept as an independent, adequate ground for the State Supreme Court's refusal to decide the constitutional question raised by petitioner. In Williams v. Georgia, 349 U.S. 375, this Court held that where a State allows constitutional questions "to be raised at a late stage and be determined by its courts as a matter of discretion, we are not concluded from assuming jurisdiction and deciding whether the state court action in the particular circumstances is, in effect, an avoidance of the federal right." No Mississippi court opinions or state statutes have been called to our attention that I read as denying *power* of the State Supreme Court, should that court wish to do so, to consider and determine constitutional questions presented at the time this one was. * * *

[T]his Court now apparently holds that the state court may, if it chooses to do so, depart from its prior cases and apply a new, stricter rule against this defendant and thereby prevent this Court from reviewing the case to see that his federal constitutional rights were safeguarded. I do not believe the cherished federal constitutional right of a defendant to object to unconstitutionally seized evidence offered against him can be cut off irrevocably by state-court discretionary rulings which might be different in particular undefined circumstances in other cases. I think such a procedural device for shutting off our review of questions involving constitutional rights is too dangerous to be tolerated.

For these reasons I dissent from the disposition of this case.

MR. JUSTICE HARLAN, with whom MR. JUSTICE CLARK and MR. JUSTICE STEWART join, dissenting.

Flying banners of federalism, the Court's opinion actually raises storm signals of a most disquieting nature. While purporting to recognize the traditional principle that an adequate procedural, as well as substantive, state ground of decision bars direct review here of any federal claim asserted in the state litigation, the Court, unless I wholly misconceive what is lurking in today's opinion, portends a severe dilution, if not complete abolition, of the concept of "adequacy" as pertaining to state procedural grounds.

In making these preliminary observations I do not believe I am seeing ghosts. For I cannot account for the remand of this case in the face of what is a demonstrably adequate state procedural ground of decision by the Mississippi Supreme Court except as an early step toward extending in one way or another the doctrine of Fay v. Noia, 372 U.S. 391, to direct review. In that case, decided only two Terms ago, the Court turned its back on history (see dissenting opinion of this writer, at 448 *et seq.*), and did away with the adequate state ground doctrine in federal habeas corpus proceedings.

Believing that any step toward extending Noia to direct review should be flushed out and challenged at its earliest appearance in an opinion of this Court, I respectfully dissent.

I.

The Mississippi Supreme Court did not base its ultimate decision upon petitioner's federal claim that his wife's consent could not validate an otherwise improper police search of the family car, but on the procedural ground that petitioner (who was represented by three experienced lawyers) had not objected at the time the fruits of this search were received in evidence. This Court now strongly implies, but does not decide (in view of its remand on the "waiver" issue) that enforcement of the State's "contemporaneous-objection" rule was inadequate as a state ground of decision because the petitioner's motion for a directed verdict of acquittal afforded the trial judge a satisfactory opportunity to take "appropriate corrective action" with reference to the allegedly inadmissible evidence. Thus, it is suggested, this may be a situation where "giving effect to the contemporaneous-objection rule for its own sake 'would be to force resort to an arid ritual of meaningless form.'"

From the standpoint of the realities of the courtroom, I can only regard the Court's analysis as little short of fanciful. The petitioner's motion for a verdict could have provoked one of three courses of action by the trial judge, none of which can reasonably be considered as depriving the State's contemporaneous-objection rule of its capacity to serve as an adequate state ground.

1. The trial judge might have granted the directed verdict. But had this action been appropriate, the Supreme Court of Mississippi, in its first opinion, would have ordered the prosecution dismissed. Since it did not, and the matter is entirely one of state law, further speculation by this Court should be foreclosed.

2. The trial judge might have directed a mistrial. The State's interest in preventing mistrials through the contemporaneous-objection requirement is obvious.

3. The remaining course of action is the example given by the Court; the trial judge could have denied the motion for a directed verdict, but, *sua sponte,* called for elaboration of the argument, determined that the search of the automobile was unconstitutional, and given cautionary instructions to the jury to disregard the inadmissible evidence when the case was submitted to it.

The practical difficulties with this approach are manifestly sufficient to show a substantial state interest in their avoidance, and thus to show an "adequate" basis for the State's adherence to the contemporaneous-objection rule. To make my point I must quote the motion for directed verdict in full. [The motion, which Justice Harlan here sets out, occupies a page and a half of the U.S. Reports. The Justice then points out that only one sentence in this lengthy motion referred to the search and seizure question, and that that question was not referred to at all when the motion was renewed at the completion of the defense.] * * *

As every trial lawyer of any experience knows, motions for directed verdicts are generally made as a matter of course at the close of the prosecution's case, and are generally denied without close consideration unless the case is clearly borderline. It is simply unrealistic in this context to have expected the trial judge to pick out the single vague sentence from the directed verdict motion and to have acted upon it with the refined imagination the Court would require of him. Henry's three lawyers apparently regarded the search and seizure claim as makeweight. They had not mentioned it earlier in the trial and gave no explanation for their laxity in raising it. And when they did mention it, they did so in a cursory and conclusional sentence placed in a secondary position in a directed verdict motion. The theory underlying the search and seizure argument— that a wife's freely given permission to search the family car is invalid—is subtle to say the very least, and as the matter was presented to the trial judge it would have been extraordinary had he caught it, or even realized that there was a serious problem to catch. But this is not all the Court would require of him. He must, in addition, realize that despite the inappropriateness of granting the directed verdict requested of him, he could partially serve the cause of the defense by taking it upon himself to frame and give cautionary instructions to the jury to disregard the evidence obtained as fruits of the search.[2]

Contrast with this the situation presented by a contemporaneous objection. The objection must necessarily be directed to the single question of admissibility; the judge must inevitably focus on it; there would be no doubt as to the appropriate form of relief, and the effect of the trial judge's decision would be immediate rather than remote. Usually the proper timing of an objection will force an elaboration of it. Had objection been made in this case during the officer's testimony about the search, it would have called forth of its own force the specific answer that the wife had given her permission and, in turn, the assertion that the permission was ineffective. The issue, in short, would have been advertently faced by the trial judge and the likelihood of achieving a correct result maximized.

Thus the state interest which so powerfully supports the contemporaneous-objection rule is that of maximizing correct decisions and concomitantly minimizing errors requiring mistrials and retrials. The alternative for the State is to reverse a trial judge who, from a long motion, fails to pick out and act with remarkable imagination upon a single vague sentence relating to admissibility of evidence long since admitted. A trial judge is a decision-maker, not an advocate. To force him out of his proper role by requiring him to coax out the arguments and imaginatively reframe the requested remedies for the counsel before him is to place upon him more responsibility than a trial judge can be expected to discharge.

There was no "appropriate corrective action" that could have realistically satisfied the purposes of the contemporaneous-objection rule. Without question the State had an interest in maintaining the integrity of its procedure, and thus without doubt reliance on the rule in question is "adequate" to bar direct review of petitioner's federal claim by this Court.[3]

---

2. Furthermore, even if counsel had fully elaborated the argument and had made it in the context of a motion to strike rather than a motion for directed verdict, the trial judge could properly have exercised his discretion (as the Mississippi Supreme Court did) and denied any relief. This power is recognized in trial judges in the federal system in order to prevent the "ambushing" of a trial through the withholding of an objection that should have been made when questionable evidence was first introduced. Federalism is turned upside down if it is denied to judges in the state systems. See Fed.Rules Crim.Proc. 41(e) and 26; United States v. Milanovich, 303 F.2d 626, cert. denied 371 U.S. 876; Hollingsworth v. United States, 321 F.2d 342, 350; Isaacs v. United States, 301 F.2d 706, 734–735, cert. denied 371 U.S. 818; United States v. Murray, 297 F.2d 812, 818, cert. denied 369 U.S. 828; Metcalf v. United States, 195 F.2d 213, 216–217.

3. As the first opinion by the Mississippi Supreme Court shows, there is discre-

II.

The real reason for remanding this case emerges only in the closing pages of the Court's opinion. It is pointed out that even were the contemporaneous-objection rule considered to be an adequate state ground, this would not, under Fay v. Noia, preclude consideration of Henry's federal claim in federal habeas corpus unless it were made to appear that Henry had deliberately waived his federal claim in the state proceedings. It is then said that in the interest of "efficient administration of criminal justice" and "harmonious" relations between the federal and state judiciaries the Mississippi courts should be given the opportunity to pass, in the first instance, on the waiver issue; the prospect is entertained that such action on the part of this Court will encourage the States to grasp the "opportunity" afforded by Fay v. Noia and Townsend v. Sain by providing "state procedures, direct or collateral, for a full airing of federal claims." It is "suggested" that were this to be done "irritation" and "friction" respecting the exercise of federal habeas corpus power *vis-a-vis* convictions "might be ameliorated."

What does all this signify? The States are being invited to voluntarily obliterate all state procedures, however conducive they may be to the orderly conduct of litigation, which might thwart state-court consideration of federal claims. But what if the States do not accept the invitation? Despite the Court's soft-spoken assertion that "settled principles" will be applied in the future, I do not think the intimation will be missed by any discerning reader of the Court's opinion that at the least a substantial dilution of the adequate state-ground doctrine may be expected. A contrary prediction is belied by the implication of the opinion that under "settled principles," the contemporaneous-objection rule relied upon in this case could be declared inadequate.

To me this would not be a move toward "harmonious" federalism; any further disrespect for state procedures, no longer cognizable at all in federal habeas corpus, would be the very antithesis of it. While some may say that, given Fay v. Noia, what the Court is attempting to do is justifiable as a means of promoting "efficiency" in the administration of criminal justice, it is the sort of efficiency which, though perhaps appropriate in some watered-down form of federalism, is not congenial to the kind of federalism I had supposed was ours. I venture to say that to all who believe the federal system as we have known it to be a priceless aspect of our Constitutionalism, the spectre implicit in today's decision will be no less disturbing than what the Court has already done in Fay v. Noia.

Believing that the judgment below rests on an adequate independent state ground, I would dismiss the writ issued in this case as improvidently granted.

---

tion in certain circumstances to lower the procedural bar. It does not follow that this Court is completely free to exercise that discretion. Even in cases from lower federal courts we do so only if there has been an abuse. If, in order to insulate its decisions from reversal by this Court, a state court must strip itself of the discretionary power to differentiate between different sets of circumstances, the rule operates in a most perverse way.

NOTE ON HENRY v. MISSISSIPPI AND ITS AFTERMATH

(1) As indicated in the Henry opinions, two years before Henry the Court had ruled in Fay v. Noia, 372 U.S. 391 (1963), that a state criminal judgment resting on the application of an adequate and independent state procedural rule could be collaterally attacked in a federal habeas corpus proceeding; the federal habeas court was free to reach the merits of the federal question not passed on by the state courts because of noncompliance with the state procedural rule. The only restriction on this principle, according to Noia, was that the habeas court should not decide a federal claim that the state defendant had "waived"—with only a "deliberate bypass" by the defendant himself counting as waiver.[1]

In Noia, the Court reasoned that substantial differences between habeas and direct review justify a ruling that a conviction that may not be reversed by the Supreme Court on appeal may nevertheless be set aside by a federal district court on collateral attack. On the other hand, in Henry, the Court asserted that the availability of habeas is a reason for widening the availability of direct review.

The antecedents and aftermath of Fay v. Noia are recounted in Wainwright v. Sykes, and the Note immediately following it, which are set out at pp. 1524, 1539, infra, but which should be read directly after this Note. In considering these materials, reflect on whether they don't show that attempts to maintain a wide gulf between the rules of forfeiture applicable on direct review and those applicable on collateral review create an unstable institutional system. Henry dealt with the instability by trying to widen access to direct review; later cases deal with it by narrowing access to collateral review. See Wechsler, p. 608, infra, at 1054–55.

Which resolution is preferable?

Meltzer, p. 606, supra, at 1188–89, argues that the rules for direct and collateral review should have the same content.

(2) On remand in the Henry case, on the record of a hearing before a state trial judge, the Supreme Court of Mississippi found that Henry had knowingly waived his right to object to the evidence; that court presented this finding in the form of a report to the United States Supreme Court in response to the latter's request, denying that the case as such was properly before the state court. 198 So.2d 213 (1967). A motion by the State that the Supreme Court reinstate the judgment of conviction was denied with

[1] In Noia the Court noted that "we wish it clearly understood that the standard here put forth depends on the considered choice of the petitioner. * * * A choice made by counsel not participated in by the petitioner does not automatically bar relief." Henry, on the other hand, declared that "[a]lthough trial strategy adopted by counsel without prior consultation with an accused will not, where the circumstances are exceptional, preclude the accused from asserting constitutional claims, * * * we think that the deliberate bypassing of counsel of the contemporaneous objection rule as a part of trial strategy would have that effect in this case." H. & W.—Fed.Cts. & Sys. 3d Ed. UCB—16

Did Henry intend to retreat from the personal waiver standard applied in Fay v. Noia? See Brookhart v. Janis, 384 U.S. 1 (1966); McMann v. Richardson, 397 U.S. 759 (1970); Humphrey v. Cady, 405 U.S. 504, 514–17 (1972); White, Federal Habeas Corpus: The Impact of the Failure to Assert a Constitutional Claim at Trial, 58 V. L.Rev. 67 (1972); Comment, 54 Calif.L.Rev. 1262 (1966).

Does footnote 3 of the Henry opinion suggest an equivalence between waiver and adequate-state-ground concepts? In light of the rest of the opinion, is such a suggestion tenable?

the statement that further proceedings "should be addressed to any new final judgment which may be entered by the Mississippi Courts." 388 U.S. 901 (1967). After further proceedings in the state court, the conviction was reinstated, 202 So.2d 40 (1967); a petition for certiorari to the Supreme Court was then denied "without prejudice to the bringing of a proceeding for relief in federal habeas corpus." 392 U.S. 931 (1968). On the basis of the state court records plus further evidence presented before it, the federal district court held that there had been no waiver, upheld the constitutional claim on the merits and granted habeas corpus. Henry v. Williams, 299 F.Supp. 36 (N.D.Miss.1969).

(3) The Henry formulation—that a state procedural rule, to be accepted as a basis for forfeiting a federal claim, must affirmatively be shown to serve a legitimate state interest—was itself novel; consider whether it was harmonious with the spirit of the preexisting law.

But the most radical element in Henry was the Court's further excursion into the question whether a failure to comply with a rule (such as the contemporaneous objection rule) that undoubtedly serves such an interest should be overlooked because, in the particular case, that interest could have been "substantially served" by some *other* procedure.

When a trial court has to decide whether to enforce a general time limit or other procedural device, should it have to consider in every case whether noncompliance should be excused because an appellate court might later conclude that an alternative procedure could safeguard the interests served by the rule? Is it feasible for a trial court to make such judgments during trial? Isn't there a legitimate state interest in enforcing the rule as a *rule*? If that rule allows a reasonable and fair opportunity for the federal claim to be presented, why isn't that sufficient? Should the states be precluded from concluding that they wish to rely on general rules, generally enforced, as a method for organizing their procedural systems— even when dealing with federal questions? [2]

2. Compare Walker v. Birmingham, 388 U.S. 307 (1967). Here city officials sued to enjoin a civil rights march planned for Good Friday. The state court issued an *ex parte* temporary injunction the preceding Wednesday. Without moving to dissolve the injunction, defendants proceeded with the march, and were cited for contempt. At the hearing on that charge, they sought to attack the constitutionality of the injunction. The state trial judge held that the only questions open were whether the court had jurisdiction to issue the temporary injunction and whether the defendants had knowingly violated it. Convictions of contempt were affirmed by the Supreme Court of Alabama, which also refused to consider the constitutional contentions.

The Supreme Court affirmed, citing, *inter alia*, the federal authority holding that an injunction must be obeyed, even if there is question of its validity, until it is challenged and overturned in court. "In the present case, however, we are asked to hold that this rule of law, upon which the Alabama courts relied, was constitutionally impermissible. . . .

"This case would arise in quite a different constitutional posture if the petitioners, before disobeying the injunction, had challenged it in the Alabama courts, and had been met with delay or frustration of their constitutional claims. But there is no showing that such would have been the fate of a timely motion to modify or dissolve the injunction. There was an interim of two days between the issuance of the injunction and the Good Friday march. The petitioners give absolutely no explanation of why they did not make some application to the state court during that period. The injunction had issued *ex parte*; if the court had been presented with the petitioners' contentions, it might well have dissolved or at least modified its order in some respects. If it had not done so, Alabama procedure would have provided for an expedited process of appellate review. It cannot be presumed that the Alabama courts would have ignored the petitioners' constitutional claims. . . .

"The rule of law upon which the Alabama courts relied in this case was one firmly established by previous precedents.

The Henry case generated an important literature. See, in particular, Hill, *The Inadequate State Ground*, 65 Colum.L.Rev. 943 (1965); Sandalow, *Henry v. Mississippi and the Adequate State Ground: Proposals for a Revised Doctrine*, 1965 Sup.Ct.Rev. 187; Wechsler, p. 608, *supra*, at 1053–56.

(4) The procedural rule involved in Henry—requiring contemporaneous objections to the admission of evidence—is a commonplace of American procedure, and, as Justice Harlan pointed out (see footnote 2 of his opinion, *supra*), is fully applicable in the federal courts.

What is the justification for concluding that a rule of procedure that would be enforced in a federal court is "inadequate" when enforced by a state court? See Meltzer, p. 606, *supra*, at 1202–08, for the argument that the rules for excusing procedural defaults in the state courts should not be more forgiving than the rules enforced in the federal courts. Compare, in this connection, the default standards enforced in collateral challenges to state and federal convictions; and see in particular Davis v. United States, 411 U.S. 233 (1973), and Francis v. Henderson, 425 U.S. 536 (1976), both discussed in Wainwright v. Sykes, applying parallel forfeiture standards for failures to make timely challenges to the composition of the grand jury in federal and state trials.

(5) The Henry case, when first announced, was widely thought to portend a radical change in the law of adequate state procedural grounds. Even during the hegemony of Fay v. Noia on the habeas side, however, Henry appeared to have little effect on the standards governing the Court's jurisdiction on direct review. Some opinions failed to cite Henry, though it would have supported the decision. See Douglas v. Alabama, 380 U.S. 415 (1965) (counsel's failure to continue making "a patently futile objection, already thrice rejected," to prosecution's piecemeal reading of an accomplice's confession was not an adequate state ground barring Supreme Court review); Parrot v. Tallahassee, 381 U.S. 129 (1965) (failure to obtain certification of lower court record for review in higher state court, described as a "nonjurisdictional defect," was not an adequate non-federal ground); Chambers v. Mississippi, p. 603, note 3, *supra*.[3]

* * * This is not a case where a procedural requirement has been sprung upon an unwary litigant when prior practice did not give him fair notice of its existence" (pp. 315–19). Chief Justice Warren and Justices Brennan, Douglas and Fortas dissented.

Why didn't the Court examine whether enforcement of the rule served a legitimate state interest in the circumstances of the particular case? Was it too obvious to merit discussion?

When the defendants in Walker were imprisoned for contempt, could they have raised their constitutional contentions on federal habeas?

Also compare, with Henry, the Court's approach in Taylor v. Illinois, 108 S.Ct. 646, 654–57 (1988), upholding a state decision prohibiting a defense witness from testifying (as a sanction for defendant's failure to include the witness' name in a list provided to the prosecutor in response to the latter's pretrial discovery request). The Court concluded that the state's interests may not be adequately served by less severe sanctions.

3. *Cf.* Camp v. Arkansas, 404 U.S. 69 (1971), an embezzlement conviction in which the defendant had raised, for the first time on appeal to the state supreme court, an objection to "certain arguments made by the prosecuting attorney in his jury summation". 249 Ark. 1075, 1080, 467 S.W.2d 707, 710 (1971). The Arkansas court held that failure to object when the arguments were made precluded raising the issue on appeal. The Supreme Court, in a brief per curiam, held: "Petitioner's alleged procedural default does not bar consideration of his constitutional claim in the circumstances of this case. See Henry v. Mississippi, 379 U.S. 443, 447–449 (1965)," and summarily reversed the judgment with a single citation to Griffin v. California, 380 U.S. 609 (1965) (holding

Other cases, also without citation of Henry, found state grounds adequate where Henry might have suggested the opposite. See Johnson v. New Jersey, 384 U.S. 719 (1966) (state rule precluding reconsideration of issue adjudicated in prior litigation was adequate to bar that issue on Supreme Court review of state post-conviction proceedings); Parker v. North Carolina, 397 U.S. 790 (1970) (failure to object to grand jury composition prior to entry of guilty plea, as required by state rule, was adequate non-federal ground).

In Monger v. Florida, 405 U.S. 958 (1972), the state supreme court, in a 4–3 decision, dismissed an appeal from an obscenity conviction on the ground that petitioner filed his notice of appeal before judgment and therefore too *soon*. The notice had been filed on January 12, the day the trial judge pronounced an oral judgment and imposed sentence. The written judgment, "*nunc pro tunc* January 12", was entered on January 18.

The Supreme Court entered the following per curiam order: "Certiorari denied, it appearing that judgment of the Supreme Court of Florida rests upon an adequate state ground."

Justice Douglas, joined by Justices Brennan and Stewart, dissented: "I can fathom no state interest which would be served by rejecting a notice of appeal filed after an oral pronouncement of judgment but before a written order. This is not a case where the orderly progress of the trial was disrupted by a dilatory interlocutory appeal or where an appeal was sought before some vital aspect of the trial was completed. * * * Under such circumstances Henry v. Mississippi teaches that we are free to consider petitioner's federal claims" (pp. 962–63).

Can this case be reconciled with Henry?

(6) The effective repudiation of Fay v. Noia in Wainwright v. Sykes, *infra,* had direct implications for Henry. In Wainwright the Court said (pp. 86–87): "Florida procedure did, consistently with the United States Constitution, require that respondent's confession be challenged at trial or not at all, and thus his failure to timely object to its admission amounted to an independent and adequate state procedural ground which would have prevented direct review here. See Henry v. Mississippi, 379 U.S. 443 (1965)." While the opinion stated the general holding of Henry in a footnote (p. 83 n. 8), the Court in Wainwright clearly did not follow the Henry approach. It engaged in a full discussion of the *general* utility of contemporaneous objection rules, and expressed strong approval of their legitimacy and wisdom. It did not focus on the specific circumstances of the case, or on the particular Florida rule. There was no sign of interest in conceivably effective alternatives, as in Henry.[4]

that comment by the prosecution on the defendant's failure to testify violates his privilege against self-incrimination).

4. A similar, more restrictive view of Henry is indicated by Justice Stewart's opinion for the Court in Michigan v. Tyler, 436 U.S. 499, 512 n. 7 (1978): "Failure to present a federal question in conformance with state procedure constitutes an adequate and independent ground of decision barring review in this Court, so long as the State has a legitimate interest in enforcing its procedural rule. [Citing Henry and two other cases.] The petitioner does not claim that Michigan's procedural rule serves no legitimate purpose."

Compare James v. Kentucky, p. 607, *supra,* where the Court cited Henry for the proposition that a requirement that a request be labeled as one for an "instruction" rather than an "admonition," would further "no perceivable state interest."

(7) It is clear, over-all, that Henry's special suggestion—that an "adequate" state rule may become "inadequate" if the Supreme Court finds that in the particular circumstance the trial judge should have found a substitute for achieving the purposes of the rule and thus excused noncompliance—has not taken hold in the law. Nor has Henry's suggestion, that the Noia "waiver" standard should infuse direct review, taken hold. The law has reverted generally to the pre-Henry approach, with Henry itself assimilated to the mainstream of the law by general references to its "legitimate state interest" formulation.

(8) Note Justice Black's suggestion in Henry, that where a state court has discretion, under state law, to excuse noncompliance with a state procedural rule, a refusal to adjudicate should not foreclose Supreme Court jurisdiction; and note Justice Harlan's comment on this in footnote 3 of his opinion. In connection with this issue, consider the following cases:

(a) In Patterson v. Alabama, 294 U.S. 600 (1935) the defendant, convicted of rape and sentenced to death on a third trial—see Powell v. Alabama, 287 U.S. 45 (1932)—contended that blacks had been systematically excluded from the grand and petit juries. The Supreme Court of Alabama declined to consider the contention on the ground that the motion for a new trial had been filed after expiration of the term of court and the bill of exceptions more than ninety days after "judgment," which counsel had erroneously thought to be the date of sentence rather than of verdict. In a companion case, presenting the same federal point on the same evidence but without these procedural difficulties, the state court affirmed upon the merits. Granting certiorari in both cases, the Supreme Court held in Norris v. Alabama, 294 U.S. 587 (1935), p. 642, *infra,* that discrimination was established. In Patterson's case, the Court examined the procedural determinations, found them supported by earlier Alabama decisions but vacated the judgment for the following reasons (294 U.S. at 606–07):

"* * * * The state court decided the constitutional question against Norris, and it was manifestly with that conclusion in mind that the court approached the decision in the case of Patterson and struck his bill of exceptions. We are not satisfied that the court would have dealt with the case in the same way if it had determined the constitutional question as we have determined it. We are not convinced that the court, in the presence of such a determination of constitutional right, confronting the anomalous and grave situation which would be created by a reversal of the judgment against Norris, and an affirmance of the judgment of death in the companion case of Patterson, who had asserted the same right, and having regard to the relation of the two cases and the other circumstances disclosed by the record, would have considered itself powerless to entertain the bill of exceptions or otherwise to provide appropriate relief. It is always hazardous to apply a judicial ruling, especially in a matter of procedure, to a serious situation which was not in contemplation when the ruling was made. At least the state court should have an opportunity to examine its powers in the light of the situation which has now developed. We should not foreclose that opportunity.

"We have frequently held that in the exercise of our appellate jurisdiction we have power not only to correct error in the judgment under review but to make such disposition of the case as justice requires. And in determining what justice does require, the Court is bound to consider any change, either in fact or in law, which has supervened since the judgment was entered. We may recognize such a change, which may affect the result, by setting aside the judgment and remanding the case so that the state court may be free to act. We have said that to do this is not to review, in any proper sense of the term, the decision of the state court upon a non-federal question, but only to deal appropriately with a matter arising since its judgment and having a bearing upon the right disposition of the case."

A new trial was thereafter granted and a conviction sustained in Patterson v. State, 234 Ala. 342, 175 So. 371, *cert. denied,* 302 U.S. 733 (1937).

(b) Williams v. Georgia, 349 U.S. 375 (1955), involved the conviction of a black for murder of a white man, in which the jury array was selected from a box containing names of whites on white tickets and names of blacks on yellow tickets; no blacks actually served on the jury. The Georgia Supreme Court had ten months previously disapproved the colored-ticket practice in Avery v. Georgia, another case from the same county, but had refused to upset Avery's conviction. The United States Supreme Court reversed Avery, 345 U.S. 559 (1953), on the basis of the unconstitutionality of the jury selection procedure, after Williams' trial but a month before he filed an amended motion for a new trial. Williams' counsel did not raise the federal question, however, until six months later, in an extraordinary motion for a new trial. This motion was dismissed by the state courts on the ground that state procedure allowed a challenge to the array only before trial, and that there had not been the due diligence required to justify the later extraordinary motion. On petition for certiorari, Justice Frankfurter, writing for the Court, said: "A state procedural rule which forbids the raising of federal questions at late stages in the case, or by any other than a prescribed method, has been recognized as a valid exercise of state power. The principle is clear enough. But the unique aspects of the never-ending new cases that arise require its individual application to particular circumstances. Thus, we would have a different question from that before us if the trial court had no power to consider Williams' constitutional objection at the belated time he raised it. But, where a State allows questions of this sort to be raised at a later stage and be determined by its courts as a matter of discretion, we are not concluded from assuming jurisdiction and deciding whether the state court action in the particular circumstances is, in effect, an avoidance of the federal right. A state court may not, in the exercise of its discretion, decline to entertain a constitutional claim while passing upon kindred issues raised in the same manner" (pp. 382–83).

The Court then examined the Georgia cases at length, and found that extraordinary motions challenging individual jurors had been granted in a substantial number of cases. Seeing no reason why the same procedure would not be applicable to an attack on the whole jury panel, and finding confirmation for that view in the Georgia Supreme Court's consideration of the "due diligence" issue in this case, the opinion continued:

"We conclude that the trial court and the State Supreme Court declined to grant Williams' motion though possessed of power to do so under state law. Since his motion was based upon a constitutional objection, and one the validity of which has in principle been sustained here, the discretionary decision to deny the motion does not deprive this Court of jurisdiction to find that the substantive issue is properly before us.

"But the fact that we have jurisdiction does not compel us to exercise it. In Patterson v. Alabama, 294 U.S. 600, we remanded a case to the highest court of the State, even though that court had affirmed on state procedural grounds, because after that affirmance we had reversed on constitutional grounds a case having identical substantive facts. * * *

"In the instant case, there is an important factor which has intervened since the affirmance by the Georgia Supreme Court which impels us to remand for that court's further consideration. This is the acknowledgment by the State before this Court that, as a matter of substantive law, Williams has been deprived of his constitutional rights. * * *

"The facts of this case are extraordinary, particularly in view of the use of yellow and white tickets by a judge of the Fulton County Superior Court almost a year after the State's own Supreme Court had condemned the practice in the Avery case. That life is at stake is of course another important factor in creating the extraordinary situation. The difference between capital and non-capital offenses is the basis of differentiation in law in diverse ways in which the distinction becomes relevant. We think that orderly procedure requires a remand to the Supreme Court for reconsideration of the case. Fair regard for the principles which the Georgia courts have enforced in numerous cases and for the constitutional commands binding on all courts compels us to reject the assumption that the courts of Georgia would allow this man to go to his death as the result of a conviction secured from a jury which the State admits was unconstitutionally impaneled" (pp. 389–91).[5]

Did the Williams majority hold the state grounds inadequate? Or was it seeking "to cajole the Georgia court into reversing itself where the United States Supreme Court lacked grounds to do so?" Note, 69 Harv.L. Rev. 158, 160 (1955).

On remand, the Georgia Supreme Court refused to reconsider and "[a]dhered to" its earlier judgment. 211 Ga. 763, 88 S.E.2d 376 (1955). The United States Supreme Court denied certiorari. 350 U.S. 950 (1956).

(c) Sullivan v. Little Hunting Park, Inc., 396 U.S. 229 (1969), was an action in state court for damages and an injunction under the Civil Rights Acts, 42 U.S.C. §§ 1981, 1982, for alleged racial discrimination in use of community facilities. The Virginia trial court dismissed petitioners' complaints and the Supreme Court of Appeals of Virginia denied the appeals saying that they were not perfected "in the manner provided by law in that opposing counsel was not given reasonable written notice of the time and place of tendering the transcript and a reasonable opportunity to examine the original or a true copy of it" under that court's Rule 5:1, § 3(f). On a remand for reconsideration in light of an intervening Supreme Court decision, the highest state court restated its holding that it had "no jurisdiction in the cases". The Supreme Court reversed, in an opinion by Justice Douglas; on the jurisdictional point he wrote (pp. 233–34):

---

5. Compare Justice Frankfurter, dissenting in Daniels v. Allen, 344 U.S. 443, 554–58 (1953), p. 1540, *infra*. See also Hill,   *The Inadequate State Ground,* 65 Colum.L. Rev. 943, 984–85 n. 174 (1965).

"Petitioners' counsel does not urge—nor do we suggest—that the Virginia Supreme Court of Appeals has fashioned a novel procedural requirement for the first time in this case; *cf.* NAACP v. Alabama, 357 U.S. 449, 457–458; past decisions of the state court refute any such notion. * * * But those same decisions do not enable us to say that the Virginia court has so consistently applied its notice requirement as to amount to a self-denial of the *power* to entertain the federal claim here presented if the Supreme Court of Appeals desires to do so. See Henry v. Mississippi, 379 U.S. 443, 455–57 (Black, J., dissenting). Such a rule, more properly deemed discretionary than jurisdictional, does not bar review here by certiorari."

Justice Harlan, joined by Chief Justice Burger and Justice White, dissented, arguing that certiorari should be dismissed because of the possible, still undecided impact of the very recently enacted Fair Housing Law. On the adequacy of the state ground, he said (pp. 243–45):

"I agree with the majority's conclusion that there is no adequate state ground shown, but I find myself unable to subscribe to the majority's reasoning * * *.

"I am not certain what the majority means in its apparent distinction between rules that it deems 'discretionary' and those that it deems 'jurisdictional.' Perhaps the majority wishes to suggest that the dismissals of petitioners' writs of error by the Supreme Court of Appeals were simply *ad hoc* discretionary refusals to accept plenary review of the lower court's decisions, analogous to this Court's denial of certiorari. If this were all the Virginia Supreme Court of Appeals had done, review of a federal question properly raised below would of course not be barred here. * * * In such circumstances, the decision of the lower court, rather than the order of the highest court refusing review, becomes the judgment of the 'highest court of a State in which a decision could be had' for purposes of 28 U.S.C. § 1257, our jurisdictional statute.

"But this case clearly does not present this kind of discretionary refusal of a state appellate court to accept review. * * * When a state appellate court's refusal to consider the merits of a case is based on the failure to conform to a state rule of practice, review by this Court is barred unless this Court is able to find that application of the state rule of practice to the case at hand does not constitute an adequate state ground. This is so quite irrespective of whether the state appellate court had the power to refuse review for no reason at all.

"The majority might have another meaning in mind when it describes the State's procedural rule as 'discretionary.' It may be suggesting that 'reasonable written notice,' and 'reasonable opportunity to examine' are such flexible standards that the Virginia Supreme Court of Appeals has the 'discretion' to decide a close case either of two ways without creating an obvious conflict with earlier decisions. If this is what the majority means by 'discretionary rule,' then I must register my disagreement. This kind of 'discretion' is nothing more than 'the judicial formulation of law,' for a court has an obligation to be reasonably consistent and 'to explain the decision, including the reason for according different treatment to the instant case.' Surely a state ground is no less adequate simply because it involves a standard that requires a judgment of what is reasonable, and because the result may turn on a close analysis of the facts of a particular case in light of competing policy considerations.

"Although the majority's loose use of the word 'discretionary' may suggest that any decision made pursuant to a broad standard cannot provide an adequate state ground, I think examination of the earlier opinions of the Virginia Supreme Court of Appeals, several of which are cited by the majority, provides the proper foundation for the result reached by the majority, under the principle of NAACP v. Alabama, 357 U.S. 449 (1958).

"The finding of the Virginia Supreme Court of Appeals of a violation of Rule 5:1, § 3(f), in this case was in my view based on a standard of reasonableness much stricter than that which could have been fairly extracted from the earlier Virginia cases applying the rule and its predecessor statute."

Cf. Wolfe v. North Carolina, 364 U.S. 177, 191–92 (1960), in which the Court, rejecting an argument based upon the opinion in Williams v. Georgia, *supra,* concluded that even if the state court "has power to make independent inquiry as to evidence proffered in the trial court but not included in the case on appeal, its decisions make clear that it has without exception refused to do so. This is not a case, therefore, where the state court failed to exercise discretionary power on behalf of appellants' 'federal rights' which it had on other occasions exercised in favor of 'kindred issues.' "

(6) Should the fact that the state courts have "power" to hear a federal claim always render their refusal to do so an inadequate ground? Excepting only the situations where they have "without exception" refused to exercise that "power"? Isn't it often true that "discretion" may be "a power of reasoned elaboration"—in Justice Harlan's terms, "the judicial formulation of law"—rather than simply and continually *ad hoc?* When a state court's refusal to entertain a federal claim is based on the former kind of "discretionary rule", should it be automatically considered as resting on an inadequate ground? Why should such a refusal be treated any differently from any other based on a general state procedural rule? On the other hand, where the state court's discretion is truly *ad hoc,* isn't there a much stronger argument that refusal to entertain the federal claim does not constitute an adequate state ground? Or, at least, should not the Supreme Court in such a case be able to make its own discretionary choice? See Meltzer, p. 606, *supra,* at 1139–42; Sandalow, p. 621, *supra,* at 225–26; *cf.* Hill, p. 621, *supra,* at 984–85 n. 174.

———————

WAINWRIGHT v. SYKES

[The report of this case appears at p. 1524, *infra*.]

NOTE ON FEDERAL HABEAS CORPUS AND STATE PROCEDURAL DEFAULT

[This Note appears at p. 1539, *infra*.]

DICE v. AKRON, CANTON & YOUNGSTOWN R.R.

342 U.S. 359, 72 S.Ct. 312, 96 L.Ed. 398 (1952).
Certiorari to the Supreme Court of Ohio.

MR. JUSTICE BLACK delivered the opinion of the Court.

Petitioner, a railroad fireman, was seriously injured when an engine in which he was riding jumped the track. Alleging that his injuries were due to respondent's negligence, he brought this action for damages under the Federal Employers' Liability Act, 45 U.S.C. § 51 et seq., in an Ohio court of common pleas. Respondent's defenses were (1) a denial of negligence and (2) a written document signed by petitioner purporting to release respondent in full for $924.63. Petitioner admitted that he had signed several receipts for payments made him in connection with his injuries but denied that he had made a full and complete settlement of all his claims. He alleged that the purported release was void because he had signed it relying on respondent's deliberately false statement that the document was nothing more than a mere receipt for back wages.

After both parties had introduced considerable evidence the jury found in favor of petitioner and awarded him a $25,000 verdict. The trial judge later entered judgment notwithstanding the verdict. In doing so he reappraised the evidence as to fraud, found that petitioner had been "guilty of supine negligence" in failing to read the release, and accordingly held that the facts did not "sustain either in law or in equity the allegations of fraud by clear, unequivocal and convincing evidence." [1] This judgment notwithstanding the verdict was reversed by the Court of Appeals of Summit County, Ohio, on the ground that under federal law, which controlled, the jury's verdict must stand because there was ample evidence to support its finding of fraud. The Ohio Supreme Court, one judge dissenting, 155 Ohio St. 185, 98 N.E.2d 301, reversed the Court of Appeals' judgment and sustained the trial court's action, holding that: (1) Ohio, not federal, law governed; (2) under that law petitioner, a man of ordinary intelligence who could read, was bound by the release even though he had been induced to sign it by the deliberately false statement that it was only a receipt for back wages; and (3) under controlling Ohio law factual issues as to fraud in the execution of this release were properly decided by the judge rather than by the jury. We granted certiorari because the decision of the

1. The trial judge had charged the jury that petitioner's claim of fraud must be sustained "by clear and convincing evidence," but since the verdict was for peti-tioner, he does not here challenge this charge as imposing too heavy a burden under controlling federal law.

Supreme Court of Ohio appeared to deviate from previous decisions of this Court that federal law governs cases arising under the Federal Employers' Liability Act.

First. We agree with the Court of Appeals of Summit County, Ohio, and the dissenting judge in the Ohio Supreme Court and hold that validity of releases under the Federal Employers' Liability Act raises a federal question to be determined by federal rather than state law. Congress in § 51 of the Act granted petitioner a right to recover against his employer for damages negligently inflicted. State laws are not controlling in determining what the incidents of this federal right shall be. * * * Manifestly the federal rights affording relief to injured railroad employees under a federally declared standard could be defeated if states were permitted to have the final say as to what defenses could and could not be properly interposed to suits under the Act. Moreover, only if federal law controls can the federal Act be given that uniform application throughout the country essential to effectuate its purposes. See Garrett v. Moore–McCormack Co., 317 U.S. 239, 244, and cases there cited. Releases and other devices designed to liquidate or defeat injured employees' claims play an important part in the federal Act's administration. Compare Duncan v. Thompson, 315 U.S. 1. Their validity is but one of the many interrelated questions that must constantly be determined in these cases according to a uniform federal law.

Second. In effect the Supreme Court of Ohio held that an employee trusts his employer at his peril, and that the negligence of an innocent worker is sufficient to enable his employer to benefit by its deliberate fraud. Application of so harsh a rule to defeat a railroad employee's claim is wholly incongruous with the general policy of the Act to give railroad employees a right to recover just compensation for injuries negligently inflicted by their employers. And this Ohio rule is out of harmony with modern judicial and legislative practice to relieve injured persons from the effect of releases fraudulently obtained. * * * We hold that the correct federal rule is that announced by the Court of Appeals of Summit County, Ohio, and the dissenting judge in the Ohio Supreme Court—a release of rights under the Act is void when the employee is induced to sign it by the deliberately false and material statements of the railroad's authorized representatives made to deceive the employee as to the contents of the release. The Trial Court's charge to the jury correctly stated this rule of law.

Third. Ohio provides and has here accorded petitioner the usual jury trial of factual issues relating to negligence. But Ohio treats factual questions of fraudulent releases differently. It permits the judge trying a negligence case to resolve all factual questions of fraud "other than fraud in the factum." The factual issue of fraud is thus split into fragments, some to be determined by the judge, others by the jury.

It is contended that since a state may consistently with the Federal Constitution provide for trial of cases under the Act by a nonunanimous verdict, Minneapolis & St. Louis R. Co. v. Bombolis, 241 U.S. 211, Ohio may lawfully eliminate trial by jury as to one phase of fraud while allowing jury trial as to all other issues raised. The Bombolis case might be more in point had Ohio abolished trial by jury in all negligence cases including those arising under the federal Act. But Ohio has not done this. It has provided jury trials for cases arising under the federal Act but seeks to single out one phase of the question of fraudulent releases for determination by a judge rather than by a jury. Compare Testa v. Katt, 330 U.S. 386.

We have previously held that "The right to trial by jury is 'a basic and fundamental feature of our system of federal jurisprudence' " and that it is "part and parcel of the remedy afforded railroad workers under the Employers' Liability Act." Bailey v. Central Vermont R. Co., 319 U.S. 350, 354. We also recognized in that case that to deprive railroad workers of the benefit of a jury trial where there is evidence to support negligence "is to take away a goodly portion of the relief which Congress has afforded them." It follows that the right to trial by jury is too substantial a part of the rights accorded by the Act to permit it to be classified as a mere "local rule of procedure" for denial in the manner that Ohio has here used. Brown v. Western R. Co., 338 U.S. 294.

The trial judge and the Ohio Supreme Court erred in holding that petitioner's rights were to be determined by Ohio law and in taking away petitioner's verdict when the issues of fraud had been submitted to the jury on conflicting evidence and determined in petitioner's favor. The judgment of the Court of Appeals of Summit County, Ohio, was correct and should not have been reversed by the Supreme Court of Ohio. The cause is reversed and remanded to the Supreme Court of Ohio for further action not inconsistent with this opinion.

Reversed and remanded with directions. It is so ordered.

MR. JUSTICE FRANKFURTER, whom MR. JUSTICE REED, MR. JUSTICE JACKSON and MR. JUSTICE BURTON join, concurring for reversal but dissenting from the Court's opinion.

Ohio, as do many other States, maintains the old division between law and equity even though the same judge administers both. The Ohio Supreme Court has told us what, on one issue, is the division of functions in all negligence actions brought in the Ohio courts: "Where it is claimed that a release was induced by fraud (other than fraud in the factum) or by mistake, it is * * * necessary, before seeking to enforce a cause of action which such release purports to bar, that equitable relief from the release be secured." 155 Ohio St. 185, 186, 98 N.E.2d 301, 304. Thus, in all cases in Ohio the judge is the trier of fact on this issue of fraud, rather than the jury. It is contended that the Federal Employers' Liability Act requires that Ohio courts send the fraud issue to a jury in the cases founded on that Act. To require Ohio to try a particular issue before a different fact-finder in negligence actions brought under the Employers' Liability Act from the fact-finder on the identical issue in every other negligence case disregards the settled distribution of judicial power between Federal and State courts where Congress authorizes concurrent enforcement of federally-created rights.

It has been settled ever since the Second Employers' Liability Cases (Mondou v. New York, N.H. & H.R. Co.) 223 U.S. 1, that no State which gives its courts jurisdiction over common law actions for negligence may deny access to its courts for a negligence action founded on the Federal Employers' Liability Act. Nor may a State discriminate disadvantageously against actions for negligence under the Federal Act as compared with local causes of actions in negligence. McKnett v. St. Louis & S.F. R. Co., 292 U.S. 230, 234; Missouri ex rel. Southern R. Co. v. Mayfield, 340 U.S. 1,

4. Conversely, however, simply because there is concurrent jurisdiction in Federal and State courts over actions under the Employers' Liability Act, a State is under no duty to treat actions arising under that Act differently from the way it adjudicates local actions for negligence, so far as the mechanics of litigation, the forms in which law is administered, are concerned. This surely covers the distribution of functions as between judge and jury in the determination of the issues in a negligence case.

In 1916 the Court decided without dissent that States in entertaining actions under the Federal Employers' Liability Act need not provide a jury system other than that established for local negligence actions. States are not compelled to provide the jury required of Federal courts by the Seventh Amendment. Minneapolis & St. L. R. Co. v. Bombolis, 241 U.S. 211. In the thirty-six years since this early decision after the enactment of the Federal Employers' Liability Act, 35 Stat. 65 (1908), the Bombolis case has often been cited by this Court but never questioned. Until today its significance has been to leave to States the choice of the fact-finding tribunal in all negligence actions, including those arising under the Federal Act. * * *

Although a State must entertain negligence suits brought under the Federal Employers' Liability Act if it entertains ordinary actions for negligence, it need conduct them only in the way in which it conducts the run of negligence litigation. The Bombolis case directly establishes that the Employers' Liability Act does not impose the jury requirements of the Seventh Amendment on the States *pro tanto* for Employers' Liability litigation. If its reasoning means anything the Bombolis decision means that if a State chooses not to have a jury at all, but to leave questions of fact in all negligence actions to a court, certainly the Employers' Liability Act does not require a State to have juries for negligence actions brought under the Federal Act in its courts. Or, if a State chooses to retain the old double system of courts, common law and equity—as did a good many States until the other day, and as four States still do—surely there is nothing in the Employers' Liability Act that requires traditional distribution of authority for disposing of legal issues as between common law and chancery courts to go by the board. And if States are free to make a distribution of functions between equity and common law courts, it surely makes no rational difference whether a State chooses to provide that the same judge preside on both the common law and the chancery sides in a single litigation, instead of in separate rooms in the same building. So long as all negligence suits in a State are treated in the same way, by the same mode of disposing equitable, non-jury, and common law, jury issues, the State does not discriminate against Employers' Liability suits nor does it make any inroad upon substance.

Ohio and her sister States with a similar division of functions between law and equity are not trying to evade their duty under the Federal Employers' Liability Act; nor are they trying to make it more difficult for railroad workers to recover, than for those suing under local law. The States merely exercise a preference in adhering to historic ways of dealing with a claim of fraud; they prefer the traditional way of making unavailable through equity an otherwise valid defense. The State judges and local lawyers who must administer the Federal Employers' Liability Act in State courts are trained in the ways of local practice; it multiplies the difficulties and confuses the administration of justice to require, on purely theoretical grounds, a hybrid of State and Federal practice in the State courts as to a single class of cases. Nothing in the Employers' Liability Act or in the judicial enforcement of the Act for over forty years forces such judicial hybridization upon the States. The fact that Congress authorized actions under the Federal Employers' Liability Act to be brought in State as well as in Federal courts seems a strange basis for the inference that Congress overrode State procedural arrangements controlling all other negligence suits in a State, by imposing upon State courts to which plaintiffs choose to go the rules prevailing in the Federal courts regarding juries. Such an inference is admissible, so it seems to me, only on the theory that Congress included as part of the right created by the Employers' Liability Act an assumed likelihood that trying all issues to juries is more favorable to plaintiffs. At least, if a plaintiff's right to have all issues decided by a jury rather than the court is "part and parcel of the remedy afforded railroad workers under the Employers Liability Act," the Bombolis case should be overruled explicitly instead of left as a derelict bound to occasion collisions on the waters of the law. We have put the questions squarely because they seem to be precisely what will be roused in the minds of lawyers properly pressing their clients' interests and in the minds of trial and appellate judges called upon to apply this Court's opinion. It is one thing not to borrow trouble from the morrow. It is another thing to create trouble for the morrow.

Even though the method of trying the equitable issue of fraud which the State applies in all other negligence cases governs Employers' Liability cases, two questions remain for decision: Should the validity of the release be tested by a Federal or a State standard? And if by a Federal one, did the Ohio courts in the present case correctly administer the standard? If the States afford courts for enforcing the Federal Act, they must enforce the substance of the right given by Congress. They cannot depreciate the legislative currency issued by Congress—either expressly or by local methods of enforcement that accomplish the same result. Davis v. Wechsler, 263 U.S. 22, 24. In order to prevent diminution of railroad workers' nationally-uniform right to recover, the standard for the validity of a release of contested liability must be federal. * * *

NOTE ON "SUBSTANCE" AND "PROCEDURE" IN THE ENFORCEMENT OF FEDERAL RIGHTS OF ACTION IN STATE COURTS

(1) Minneapolis & St. Louis R.R. v. Bombolis, 241 U.S. 211 (1916), involved a Minnesota provision for a civil verdict by five-sixths of the jury, after failure for twelve hours to achieve unanimity. Companion cases involved verdicts by three-fourths, St. Louis & San Francisco R.R. v. Brown, 241 U.S. 223 (1916); Louisville & Nashville R.R. v. Stewart, 241 U.S. 261 (1916), and trial to a jury of seven, Chesapeake & Ohio Ry. v. Carnahan, 241 U.S. 241 (1916). The contention which these decisions rejected, as Chief Justice White put it, was that state courts can enforce federal rights of action only if "such courts in enforcing the Federal right are to be treated as Federal courts and be subjected *pro hac vice* to the limitations of the Seventh Amendment". 241 U.S. at 221. See also Justice Holmes in Louisville & Nashville R.R. v. Stewart, *supra*, at 263.

Prior to these decisions, however, the Court had held inapplicable to an F.E.L.A. action in a state court the state rule that the plaintiff was obliged to prove his freedom from contributory negligence. Central Vermont Ry. v. White, 238 U.S. 507 (1915). The "general principle that matters respecting the remedy—such as the form of action, sufficiency of the pleadings, rules of evidence, and the statute of limitations—depend upon the law of the place where the suit is brought" was affirmed. But Justice Lamar called it a "misnomer to say that the question as to the burden of proof as to contributory negligence is a mere matter of state procedure." Noting that "the United States courts have uniformly held that as a matter of general law the burden of proving contributory negligence is on the defendant" and that the "Federal courts have enforced that principle even in trials in States which hold that the burden is on the plaintiff," he concluded: "Congress in passing the Federal Employers' Liability Act evidently intended that the Federal statute should be construed in the light of these and other decisions of the Federal courts" (pp. 511–12).

Was there a stronger argument that Congress intended to displace state rules as to the burden of proof than state rules as to non-unanimous jury verdicts?

(2) The Bombolis decision does not prevent the Supreme Court from reversing a state court judgment directing a verdict for the railroad, where the Court deems the evidence sufficient to create an issue for the jury although it would not overturn a jury verdict in defendant's favor. See, *e.g.*, Bailey v. Central Vermont Ry., 319 U.S. 350 (1943); Wilkerson v. McCarthy, 336 U.S. 53 (1949); Rogers v. Missouri Pac. R.R., 352 U.S. 500 (1957), p. 1864, *infra; cf.* Arnold v. Panhandle & S.F. Ry., 353 U.S. 360 (1957). The Court deals with this issue in such cases as it would if the case had been tried in a federal district court.

In Brady v. Southern Ry., 320 U.S. 476, 479 (1943), where the direction of a verdict was sustained, Justice Reed said: "Only by a uniform federal rule as to the necessary amount of evidence may litigants under the federal act receive similar treatment in all states. * * * It is true that this Court has held that a state need not provide in F.E.L.A. cases any trial by jury according to the requirements of the Seventh Amendment. * * * But when a state's jury system requires the court to determine the sufficiency of the evidence to support a finding of a federal right to recover, the correctness of its ruling is a federal question."

Why? If the plaintiff has no federal right to have the facts determined by a jury, what federal right, as distinguished from rights under local practice, is denied if they are determined by the court, assuming the determination is supported by the evidence? *Cf.* Holmes, J., in Chicago, R.I. & Pac. Ry. v. Cole, 251 U.S. 54 (1919). Is there a general federal right to have the local practice properly applied in the adjudication of federal claims?

(3) Is the Bombolis decision still law? Is there a valid distinction, as Justice Black suggests, between state failure to provide a jury trial as to "one phase of fraud" and failure to provide such trial on any issue? Can Congress have intended to displace the former practice but to leave the latter undisturbed? If state procedure diminishes a federal right when it denies a jury trial on one issue, would it not do so *a fortiori* if it abolished jury trial on all issues? On the other hand, wouldn't it be more of an

imposition on state courts to compel them to convene juries if they otherwise have none (or perhaps even merely juries larger than otherwise employed in the state [1]) than to require submission of an additional issue to a jury already convened and functioning? Would a unanimous verdict requirement be more like the former or the latter? [2]

What would have been the result in Dice if it had arisen in the courts of a state which maintained in full the traditional separation of law and equity (and which regarded fraud as an equitable issue)?

(4) In what sense is jury trial "part and parcel of the remedy afforded railroad workers under the Employers Liability Act"? The F.E.L.A. makes no explicit grant of a right to trial by jury; [3] it refers to jury trial only in the context of providing that contributory negligence shall not bar a recovery "but the damages shall be diminished by the jury in proportion to the amount of negligence" attributable to the employee. 45 U.S.C. § 53. As indicated by the cases cited previously, this language has certainly not been taken to mean that every F.E.L.A. case must be submitted to the jury and indeed has not even been cited by the Supreme Court in support of holdings regarding jury trials in state courts. On what, then, does the Court's conclusion rest? Compare the other statement in Bailey v. Central Vermont Ry., *supra,* referred to in the same paragraph of the Dice opinion: "To deprive these workers of the benefit of a jury trial in close or doubtful cases is to take away a goodly portion of the relief which Congress has afforded them." Why is this true? On the premise that juries tend strongly to favor injured railroad workers? See Hill, *Substance and Procedure in State FELA Actions—The Converse of the Erie Problem?,* 17 Ohio St. L.J. 384, 397 (1956). There is some historical evidence to support the conclusion that Congressional policy favored jury trials in F.E.L.A. cases, and possibly for plaintiff-favoring reasons, but it is far from conclusive. See Tiller v. Atlantic Coast Line R.R., 318 U.S. 54, 58–67 (1943); Rogers v. Missouri Pac. R.R., 352 U.S. 500, 508–9 (1957), and sources cited. Consider also the possible relevance of the fact that Congress has given F.E.L.A. plaintiffs an absolute option of maintaining suit in either state or federal court, denying railroads the usual right of defendants on federal claims to remove such state court actions to federal court. 28 U.S.C. §§ 1441, 1445(a).

If the federal rule with respect to the jury's role in F.E.L.A. is seen as implementing Congressional policy regarding risk-distribution and compensation for railroad work injuries—in other words, as having substantive as well as procedural functions—doesn't it follow that the Court was correct in imposing that rule on the state courts? Isn't the same true of Bailey and the cases following it on sufficiency of evidence for submission to the jury?

1. *Cf.* Williams v. Florida, 399 U.S. 78 (1970), holding that the Sixth Amendment does not require a jury of twelve in state criminal cases.

2. *Cf.* Apodaca v. Oregon, 406 U.S. 404 (1972), holding that a unanimous verdict is not constitutionally required in state criminal cases. Five justices expressed the view that unanimity is required by the Sixth Amendment in federal criminal cases.

3. The Jones Act, 46 U.S.C. § 688, which extends the benefits of the F.E.L.A. to seamen, expressly confers a right of "action for damages at law, with the right of trial by jury". Under the "saving clause," an action under the act may be maintained in a state court. See p. 1079, *infra.* Assuming the Bombolis case is still law, what, if any, application would it have in a state court action under the Jones Act?

(5) To the extent that the Court's holdings are based on invoking the "plaintiff-mindedness" of juries, what would this imply about the continued vitality of Bombolis and the other non-unanimous verdict cases? [4]

(6) What is the basis for the Court's unanimous conclusion in the Dice case that the standard governing the validity of the release is federal? Is this necessarily true of any release of federal rights of action? Garrett v. Moore–McCormack Co., 317 U.S. 239 (1942), cited by the Court, involved a seaman's admiralty claim. Is it significant that both the Jones Act and the F.E.L.A. expressly create a cause of action enforceable in state as well as federal courts?

(7) In Brown v. Western Ry. of Alabama, 338 U.S. 294 (1949), the complaint in an F.E.L.A. case in Georgia alleged, in substance, that the railroad had allowed "clinkers" and other debris "to collect in" the "yards along the side of the tracks"; that such debris made the "yards unsafe"; that the railroad thus failed to supply the plaintiff a reasonably safe place to work; that it was necessary for him "to cross over all such material and debris"; that in performing his duties he "ran around" an engine and "stepped on a large clinker lying beside the tracks as aforesaid which caused" him "to fall and be injured"; that his injuries were "directly and proximately caused in whole or in part by the negligence of the defendant * * * (a) In failing to furnish plaintiff with a reasonably safe place in which to work as herein alleged. (b) In leaving clinkers * * * and other debris along the side of the track in its yards as aforesaid, well knowing that said yards in such condition were dangerous for use by brakemen, working therein and that petitioner would have to perform his duties with said yards in such condition."

The trial court sustained a demurrer and its judgment was sustained by the Court of Appeals of Georgia which, construing the complaint "most strongly against the pleader," in accordance with the Georgia rule of practice, held that the complaint failed to allege that the clinker was present due to the defendant's negligence or that the sole cause of the accident was not the act of plaintiff in stepping on a clinker he could see and could have avoided.

The Supreme Court granted certiorari and reversed. Justice Black, holding the allegations sufficient, said (pp. 296–98):

" * * * To what extent rules of practice and procedure may themselves dig into 'substantive rights' is a troublesome question at best as is shown in the very case on which respondent relies. Central Vermont R. Co. v. White, 238 U.S. 507. Other cases in this Court point up the impossibility of laying down a precise rule to distinguish 'substance' from 'procedure.' Fortunately, we need not attempt to do so. A long series of cases previously decided, from which we see no reason to depart, makes it our duty to construe the allegations of this complaint ourselves in order to determine whether petitioner has been denied a right of trial granted him by Congress. This federal right cannot be defeated by the forms of local practice. * * * And we cannot accept as final a state court's interpretation of allegations in a complaint asserting it. * * * This rule applies to F.E.L.A. cases no less than to other types. * * *

4. At least so long as the Seventh Amendment is not held applicable to state trials generally (and even then if it is not held always to require unanimous verdicts).

"Strict local rules of pleading cannot be used to impose unnecessary burdens upon rights of recovery authorized by federal laws."

Justice Frankfurter, joined by Justice Jackson, dissented (pp. 300–02):

" * * * One State may cherish formalities more than another, one State may be more responsive than another to procedural reforms. If a litigant chooses to enforce a Federal right in a State court, he cannot be heard to object if he is treated exactly as are plaintiffs who press like claims arising under State law with regard to the form in which the claim must be stated—the particularity, for instance, with which a cause of action must be described. Federal law, though invoked in a State court, delimits the Federal claim—defines what gives a right to recovery and what goes to prove it. But the form in which the claim must be stated need not be different from what the State exacts in the enforcement of like obligations created by it, so long as such a requirement does not add to, or diminish, the right as defined by Federal law, nor burden the realization of this right in the actualities of litigation. * * *

"These decisive differences are usually conveyed by the terms 'procedure' and 'substance.' The terms are not meaningless even though they do not have fixed undeviating meanings. They derive content from the functions they serve here in precisely the same way in which we have applied them in reverse situations—when confronted with the problem whether the Federal courts respected the substance of State-created rights, as required by the rule in Erie R. Co. v. Tompkins, 304 U.S. 64, or impaired them by professing merely to enforce them by the mode in which the Federal courts do business. * * * Congress has authorized State courts to enforce Federal rights, and Federal courts State-created rights. Neither system of courts can impair these respective rights, but both may have their own requirements for stating claims (pleading) and conducting litigation (practice).

"In the light of these controlling considerations, I cannot find that the Court of Appeals of Georgia has either sought to evade the law of the United States or did so unwittingly. * * * All that the Georgia court did was conscientiously to apply its understanding of what is necessary to set forth a claim of negligence according to the local requirement of particularity." [5]

5. In Norfolk & Western Ry. Co. v. Liepelt, 444 U.S. 490 (1980), a wrongful death action under the F.E.L.A. brought in an Illinois court, the Supreme Court held that a state trial court must (a) allow the defendant to introduce evidence to show the effect of income taxes on the decedent's projected future earnings, and (b) on request, instruct the jury that their award will not be subject to federal income taxes. Justice Stevens, for the Court, held that both issues were governed by federal law. Saying simply, "It has long been settled that questions concerning the measure of damages in an FELA action are federal in character," (p. 493), he treated both issues on the merits without reference to what the state law might be.

Justice Blackmun, joined by Justice Marshall, dissented on both issues. On the issue of instructing the jury regarding the non-taxability of their award, he contended that the law of Illinois should govern. Characterizing such instructions as "purely cautionary" in nature, he argued that the necessity of giving such instructions should be governed by state law when an F.E.L.A. action is brought in state court. Recognizing that "state rules that interfere with federal policy are to be rejected, even if they might be characterized as 'procedural'," he said that he could not conclude "that a purely cautionary instruction to the jury not to misbehave implicates any federal interest" (pp. 502–04).

Does it implicate any state interest?

See also St. Louis Southwestern Ry. Co. v. Dickerson, 470 U.S. 409 (1985) (federal law determines whether jury should, in an

Consider the suggestion of Professor Hill, p. 634, *supra*, that "whatever the troubles [Brown] may have encountered in the state courts, they were not due to excessively burdensome pleading rules as such." Pointing out that Brown had ample opportunity under Georgia law to amend his complaint and failed to do so, he notes: "Presumably it would have been easy for Brown to amend his complaint to set forth the more particularized allegations, but this would have been improvident if these allegations would have been difficult of proof *and* if as a matter of law he really did not have to adduce such proof to win. * * * This would suggest that the problem below was not the local pleading rules as such but rather a misconception concerning the minimum quantum of evidence needed in an FELA case" (p. 407 & n. 143).

Compare the analysis in Meltzer, p. 606, *supra*, at 1142–43, noting that on Hill's view the proper disposition would have been a remand to permit the state courts to decide, whether, on a proper understanding of federal law, the plaintiff had complied with state pleading rules, rather than a direction to the state courts to treat the plaintiff as having complied.

(8) The extent to which there should be federal control over state procedures where a state court is adjudicating a federal cause of action [6] is a question that has generated controversy. See, for a range of the relevant opinions, Meltzer, p. 606, *supra;* Redish & Muench, *Adjudication of Federal Causes of Action in State Court*, 75 Mich.L.Rev. 311 (1976); Neuborne, *Toward Procedural Parity in Constitutional Litigation*, 22 Wm. & Mary L.Rev. 725 (1981).[7] Compare Hart, *The Relations Between State and Federal Law*, 54 Colum.L.Rev. 489, 508 (1954):

F.E.L.A. case, be instructed that its award should reflect the present value of future losses). Compare Morgan v. Monessen Southwestern Ry. Co., 513 Pa. 86, 518 A.2d 1171 (1986), *prob. juris. noted*, 108 S.Ct. 63 (1987) (are state rules as to prejudgment interest and as to "total offset" for present value of future damages applicable in state-court F.E.L.A. action?).

6. Compare the debate between Justice Black, for the Court, and Justice Harlan, dissenting, about whether state or federal law should govern the question whether a criminal conviction may stand, notwithstanding a federal constitutional error in the proceedings, because the error was "harmless." Chapman v. California, 386 U.S. 18 (1967). Justice Black said that "[w]hether a conviction for crime should stand when a State has failed to accord federal constitutionally guaranteed rights is every bit as much of a federal question as what particular federal constitutional provisions themselves mean, what they guarantee, and whether they have been denied" (p. 21). Justice Harlan said (pp. 46, 49): "I would hold that a state appellate court's reasonable application of a constitutionally proper state harmless-error rule to sustain a state conviction constitutes an independent and adequate state

ground of judgment. * * * The challenged decision has no direct relation to federal constitutional provisions, rather it is an analysis of the question whether this admittedly improper comment had any significant impact on the outcome of the trial."

Note that a harmless error rule not only measures the degree of risk that a particular error actually had an adverse effect; it also defines the extent to which such a risk is accepted as permissible. Isn't this latter judgment a function of the importance attached to vindicating the underlying constitutional right? See Stewart, J., concurring separately in Chapman; *cf.* Justice Brennan dissenting in Harrington v. California, 395 U.S. 250, 255 (1969). If so, is not the definition of "harmless error" inseparable from the task of defining the scope of that constitutional right?

For further development of this question, see Delaware v. Van Arsdall, 475 U.S. 673 (1986), pp. 552, 554, *supra.*

7. For an examination of how claims under 42 U.S.C. § 1983 fare in the state courts, see Steinglass, *The Emerging State Court § 1983 Action: A Procedural Review*, 38 U.Miami L.Rev. 381 (1984).

"The general rule, bottomed deeply in belief in the importance of state control of state judicial procedure, is that federal law takes the state courts as it finds them. * * * The Supreme Court in recent years has been disturbed by the recognition that differences between state and federal procedure may sometimes lead to different results in actions to enforce federally-created rights of which state and federal courts have concurrent jurisdiction. [Here citing Dice and Brown, noting explicitly that they are F.E.L.A. cases.] * * * Some differences in remedy and procedure are inescapable if the different governments are to retain a measure of independence in deciding how justice should be administered. If the differences become so conspicuous as to affect advance calculations of outcome, and so to induce an undesirable shopping between forums, the remedy does not lie in the sacrifice of the independence of either government. It lies rather in provision by the federal government, confident of the justice of its own procedure, of a federal forum equally accessible to both litigants."

(9) In Federal Energy Regulatory Comm'n v. Mississippi, 456 U.S. 742 (1982), the Court upheld provisions of the Public Utility Regulatory Policies Act of 1978 that imposed important federal procedural requirements on state commissions regulating energy. The Act, passed during a period of energy shortages, was designed to encourage conservation of oil and gas and the development of alternative energy sources. To this end the Act required state regulatory authorities to "consider" the adoption of a wide range of regulations relating to utility rates and services. It then imposed mandatory procedural requirements for this "consideration": the state commissions were required to hold public hearings after notice, to provide written explanations, to allow a wide range of interventions in the proceedings, to issue various findings and reports, to allow discovery, to provide transcripts, to allow attorneys' fees in certain cases, etc.

The Court upheld the Act, by a 5–4 vote, against a challenge based on the Tenth Amendment. With respect to the procedural provisions,[8] although acknowledging that they are "more intrusive" than the "hortatory" substantive provisions, the Court simply said: "If Congress can require a state administrative body to consider proposed regulations as a condition to its continued involvement in a pre-emptible field—and we hold today that it can—there is nothing unconstitutional about Congress' requiring certain procedural minima as that body goes about undertaking its tasks" (p. 771). Justice Powell's dissent stated that "I know of no other attempt by the Federal Government to supplant state prescribed procedures that in part define the nature of their administrative agencies" (p. 774). Justice O'Connor's dissent said that "[s]tate legislative and administrative bodies are not field offices of the national bureaucracy" (p. 777). Neither the Court nor the dissenters alluded to Dice or the other F.E.L.A. cases.[9]

(10) Should there be equivalence between the concepts of "procedure" when used to measure the applicability of state rules to litigation in state courts arising under federal law and the applicability of federal rules to cases in the district courts arising under state law? Compare Dice with the cases discussed in Chap. VI, Sec. 4, *infra*.

---

8. See Chap. IV, Sec. 2, p. 498, *supra*, for discussion of other aspects of the case.

9. See also Felder v. Casey, 139 Wis.2d 614, 408 N.W.2d 19 (1987), *cert. granted*, 108 S.Ct. 326 (1987), holding that litigants who bring § 1983 actions in the state court are required to comply with the state notice of claim statute.

SUBSECTION C: APPLICATION OF LAW TO FACT

FISKE v. KANSAS

274 U.S. 380, 47 S.Ct. 655, 71 L.Ed. 1108 (1927).
Error to the Supreme Court of Kansas.

MR. JUSTICE SANFORD delivered the opinion of the Court.

The plaintiff in error was tried and convicted in the District Court of Rice County, Kansas, upon an information charging him with violating the Criminal Syndicalism Act of that State. The judgment was affirmed by the Supreme Court of the State, 117 Kan. 69, 230 P. 88; and this writ of error was allowed by the Chief Justice of that court.

The only substantial Federal question presented to and decided by the State court, and which may therefore be re-examined by this Court, is whether the Syndicalism Act as applied in this case is repugnant to the due process clause of the Fourteenth Amendment.

The relevant provisions of the Act are:

"Section 1. 'Criminal syndicalism' is hereby defined to be the doctrine which advocates crime, physical violence, arson, destruction of property, sabotage, or other unlawful acts or methods, as a means of accomplishing or effecting industrial or political ends, or as a means of effecting industrial or political revolution, or for profit. * * *

"Sec. 3. Any person who, by word of mouth, or writing, advocates, affirmatively suggests or teaches the duty, necessity, propriety or expediency of crime, criminal syndicalism, or sabotage, * * * is guilty of a felony. * * *"

The information charged that the defendant did "by word of mouth and by publicly displaying and circulating certain books and pamphlets and written and printed matter, advocate, affirmatively suggest and teach the duty, necessity, propriety and expediency of crime, criminal syndicalism, and sabotage by * * * knowingly and feloniously persuading, inducing and securing" certain persons "to sign an application for membership in * * * and by issuing to" them "membership cards" in a certain Workers' Industrial Union, "a branch of and component part of the Industrial Workers of the World organization, said defendant then and there knowing that said organization unlawfully teaches, advocates and affirmatively suggests: 'That the working class and the employing class have nothing in common, and that there can be no peace so long as hunger and want are found among millions of working people and the few who make up the employing class have all the good things of life.' And that 'Between these two classes a struggle must go on until the workers of the World organize as a class, take possession of the earth and the machinery of production and abolish the wage system.' And that: 'Instead of the conservative motto, "A fair day's wages for a fair day's work," we must inscribe on our banner the revolutionary watchword, "Abolition of the wage system." By organizing industrially we are forming the structure of the new society within the shell of the old.'"

The defendant moved to quash the information as insufficient, for the reason, among others, that it failed to specify the character of the organization in which he was alleged to have secured members. This was overruled.

On the trial the State offered no evidence as to the doctrines advocated, suggested or taught by the Industrial Workers of the World organization other than a copy of the preamble to the constitution of that organization containing the language set forth and quoted in the information. The defendant, who testified in his own behalf, stated that he was a member of that organization and understood what it taught; that while it taught the matters set forth in this preamble it did not teach or suggest that it would obtain industrial control in any criminal way or unlawful manner, but in a peaceful manner; that he did not believe in criminal syndicalism or sabotage, and had not at any time advocated, suggested or taught the duty, necessity, propriety and expediency of crime, criminal syndicalism or sabotage, and did not know that they were advocated, taught or suggested by the organization; and that in taking the applications for membership in the organization, which contained the preamble to the constitution, he had explained the principles of the organization so far as he knew them by letting the applicants read this preamble.

The jury was instructed that before the defendant could be convicted they must be satisfied from the evidence, beyond a reasonable doubt, that the Industrial Workers of the World was an organization that taught criminal syndicalism as defined by the Syndicalism Act.

The defendant moved in arrest of judgment upon the ground, among others, that the evidence and the facts stated did not constitute a public offense and substantiate the charges alleged in the information. And he also moved for a new trial upon the grounds, among others, that the verdict was contrary to the law and the evidence and wholly unsupported by the evidence. Both of these motions were overruled.

On the appeal to the Supreme Court of the State, among the errors assigned were, generally, that the court erred in overruling his motions to quash the information, his demurrer to the evidence—which does not appear in the record—and his motions in arrest of judgment and for a new trial; and specifically, that the "court erred in refusing to quash the information, in overruling the demurrer to the evidence, and in overruling the motion in arrest of judgment, because the information and the cause of action attempted to be proved were based upon" the Kansas Syndicalism Act, "which, in so far as it sustains this prosecution is in violation * * * of the Constitution of the United States and especially of the Fourteenth Amendment" including the due process clause thereof.

The Supreme Court of the State, in its opinion, said:

The information "does not in set phrase allege that the association known as the Industrial Workers of the World advocates, affirmatively suggests or teaches criminal syndicalism, but when read as a whole it clearly signifies this, and also that the language quoted (which the evidence shows to be taken from the preamble of the constitution of that organization) was employed to express that doctrine. * * * The language quoted from the I.W.W. preamble need not—in order to sustain the judgment—be held necessarily and as a matter of law, to advocate, teach or even affirmatively suggest physical violence as a means of accomplishing industrial or political ends. It is open to that interpretation and is capable of use to convey that meaning. * * * The jury were not required to accept the defendant's testimony as a candid and accurate statement. There was room for them to find, as their verdict shows they did, that the equivocal language of the preamble and of the defendant in explaining it to his prospects was employed to convey and did convey the sinister meaning attributed to it by the state. A final contention is that the statute * * * is obnoxious to the due process of law clause of the Fourteenth Amendment to the Federal Constitution. Statutes penalizing the advocacy of violence in bringing about governmental changes do not violate constitutional guarantees of freedom of speech."

A decision of a State court applying and enforcing a State statute of general scope against a particular transaction as to which there was a distinct and timely insistence that if so applied, the statute was void under the Federal Constitution, necessarily affirms the validity of the statute as so applied, and the judgment is, therefore, reviewable by writ of error under section 237 of the Judicial Code. Dahnke–Walker Co. v. Bondurant, 257 U.S. 282, 288. The inquiry then is whether the statute is constitutional as applied and enforced in respect of the situation presented. * * * Ward & Gow v. Krinsky, 259 U.S. 503, 510; Cudahy Co. v. Parramore, 263 U.S. 418, 422. And see St. Louis, etc., R. Co. v. Wynne, 224 U.S. 354, 359.

And this Court will review the finding of facts by a State court where a Federal right has been denied as the result of a finding shown by the record to be without evidence to support it; or where a conclusion of law as to a Federal right and a finding of fact are so intermingled as to make it necessary, in order to pass upon the Federal question, to analyze the facts. Northern Pacific R. v. North Dakota, 236 U.S. 585, 593; Ætna Life Ins. Co. v. Dunken, 266 U.S. 389, 394, and cases cited.

Here the State court held the Syndicalism Act not to be repugnant to the due process clause as applied in a case in which the information in effect charged the defendant with violation of the Act in that he had secured members in an organization which taught, advocated and affirmatively suggested the doctrines set forth in the extracts from the preamble to its constitution, and in which there was no evidence that the organization, taught, advocated or suggested any other doctrines. No substantial inference can, in our judgment, be drawn from the language of this preamble, that the organization taught, advocated or suggested the duty, necessity, propriety, or expediency of crime, criminal syndicalism, sabotage, or other unlawful acts or methods. There is no suggestion in the preamble that the industrial organization of workers as a class for the purpose of getting possession of the machinery of production and abolishing the wage system, was to be accomplished by any other than lawful methods; nothing advocating the overthrow of the existing industrial or political conditions by force, violence or unlawful means. And standing alone, as it did in this case, there was nothing which warranted the court or jury in ascribing to this language, either as an inference of law or fact, "the sinister meaning attributed to it by the state." In this respect the language of the preamble is essentially different from that of the manifesto involved in Gitlow v. New York, 268 U.S. 652, 665, and lacks the essential elements which brought that document under the condemnation of the law. And it is not as if the preamble were shown to have been followed by further statements or declarations indicating that it was intended to mean, and to be understood as advocating, that the ends outlined therein would be accomplished or brought about by violence or other related unlawful acts or methods. Compare Whitney v. California, 274 U.S. 357, and Burns v. United States, 274 U.S. 328, this day decided.

The result is that the Syndicalism Act has been applied in this case to sustain the conviction of the defendant, without any charge or evidence that the organization in which he secured members advocated any crime, violence or other unlawful acts or methods as a means of effecting industrial or political changes or revolution. Thus applied the Act is an arbitrary and unreasonable exercise of the police power of the State, unwarrantably infringing the liberty of the defendant in violation of the due process clause of the Fourteenth Amendment. The judgment is accordingly reversed, and the case is remanded for further proceedings not inconsistent with this opinion.

Reversed.

NORRIS v. ALABAMA
294 U.S. 587, 55 S.Ct. 579, 79 L.Ed. 1074 (1935).
Certiorari to the Supreme Court of Alabama.

MR. CHIEF JUSTICE HUGHES delivered the opinion of the Court.

Petitioner, Clarence Norris, is one of nine negro boys who were indicted in March, 1931, in Jackson county, Ala., for the crime of rape. On being brought to trial in that county, eight were convicted. The Supreme Court of Alabama reversed the conviction of one of these and affirmed that of seven, including Norris. This Court reversed the judgments of conviction upon the ground that the defendants had been denied due process of law in that the trial court had failed in the light of the circumstances disclosed and of the inability of the defendants at that time to obtain counsel, to make an effective appointment of counsel to aid them in preparing and presenting their defense. Powell v. Alabama, 287 U.S. 45.

After the remand, a motion for change of venue was granted and the cases were transferred to Morgan county. Norris was brought to trial in November, 1933. At the outset, a motion was made on his behalf to quash the indictment upon the ground of the exclusion of negroes from juries in Jackson county where the indictment was found. A motion was also made to quash the trial venire in Morgan county upon the ground of the exclusion of negroes from juries in that county. In relation to each county, the charge was of long-continued, systematic, and arbitrary exclusion of qualified negro citizens from service on juries, solely because of their race and color, in violation of the Constitution of the United States. The state joined issue on this charge and after hearing the evidence, which we shall presently review, the trial judge denied both motions, and exception was taken. The trial then proceeded and resulted in the conviction of Norris who was sentenced to death. On appeal the Supreme Court of the state considered and decided the federal question which Norris had raised and affirmed the judgment. 156 So. 556. We granted a writ of certiorari, 293 U.S. 552.

First. There is no controversy as to the constitutional principle involved. That principle, long since declared, was not challenged, but was expressly recognized, by the Supreme Court of the state. Summing up precisely the effect of earlier decisions, this Court thus stated the principle in Carter v. Texas, 177 U.S. 442, 447, in relation to exclusion from service on grand juries: "Whenever by any action of a state, whether through its Legislature, through its courts, or through its executive or administrative officers, all persons of the African race are excluded, solely because of their race or color, from serving as grand jurors in the criminal prosecution of a person of the African race, the equal protection of the laws is denied to him, contrary to the Fourteenth Amendment of the Constitution of the United States. Strauder v. West Virginia, 100 U.S. 303; Neal v. Delaware, 103 U.S. 370; Gibson v. Mississippi, 162 U.S. 565." This statement was repeated in the same terms in Rogers v. Alabama, 192 U.S. 226, 231, and again in Martin v. Texas, 200 U.S. 316, 319. The principle is equally applicable to a similar exclusion of negroes from service on petit juries. Strauder v. West Virginia, *supra;* Martin v. Texas, *supra.* And although the state statute defining the qualifications of jurors may be fair on its face, the constitutional provision affords protection against action of the state through its administrative officers in effecting the prohibited discrimination. Neal v. Delaware, *supra;* Carter v. Texas, *supra.* Compare Virginia v. Rives, 100 U.S. 313, 322, 323; In re Wood, 140 U.S. 278, 285; Thomas v. Texas, 212 U.S. 278, 282, 283.

The question is of the application of this established principle to the facts disclosed by the record. That the question is one of fact does not relieve us of the duty to determine whether in truth a federal right has been denied. When a federal right has been specially set up and claimed in a state court, it is our province to inquire not merely whether it was denied in express terms but also whether it was denied in substance and effect. If this requires an examination of evidence, that examination must be made. Otherwise, review by this Court would fail of its purpose in safeguarding constitutional rights. Thus, whenever a conclusion of law of a state court as to a federal right and findings of fact are so intermingled that the latter control the former, it is incumbent upon us to analyze the facts in order that the appropriate enforcement of the federal right may be assured. Creswill v. Knights of Pythias, 225 U.S. 246, 261; Northern Pacific Railway Co. v. North Dakota, 236 U.S. 585, 593; Ward v. Board of Com'rs of Love County, 253 U.S. 17, 22; Davis, Director General, v. Wechsler, 263 U.S. 22, 24; Fiske v. Kansas, 274 U.S. 380, 385, 386; Ancient Egyptian Order v. Michaux, 279 U.S. 737, 745.

Second. *The evidence on the motion to quash the indictment.* In 1930, the total population of Jackson county, where the indictment was found, was 36,881, of whom 2,688 were negroes. The male population over twenty-one years of age numbered 8,801, and of these 666 were negroes.

The qualifications of jurors were thus prescribed by the state statute (Alabama Code 1923, § 8603): "The jury commission shall place on the jury roll and in the jury box the names of all male citizens of the county who are generally reputed to be honest and intelligent men, and are esteemed in the community for their integrity, good character and sound judgment, but no person must be selected who is under twenty-one or over sixty-five years of age, or, who is an habitual drunkard, or who, being afflicted with a permanent disease or physical weakness is unfit to discharge the duties of a juror, or who cannot read English, or who has ever been convicted of any offense involving moral turpitude. If a person cannot read English and has all the other qualifications prescribed herein and is a freeholder or house-holder, his name may be placed on the jury roll and in the jury box." See Gen.Acts Alabama 1931, No. 47, p. 59, § 14.

Defendant adduced evidence to support the charge of unconstitutional discrimination in the actual administration of the statute in Jackson county. The testimony, as the state court said, tended to show that "in a long number of years no negro had been called for jury service in that county." It appeared that no negro had served on any grand or petit jury in that county within the memory of witnesses who had lived there all their lives. Testimony to that effect was given by men whose ages ran from fifty to seventy-six years. Their testimony was uncontradicted. It was supported by the testimony of officials. The clerk of the jury commis-sion and the clerk of the circuit court had never known of a negro serving on a grand jury in Jackson county. The court reporter, who had not missed a session in that county in twenty-four years, and two jury commis-sioners testified to the same effect. One of the latter, who was a member of the commission which made up the jury roll for the grand jury which found the indictment, testified that he had "never known of a single instance where any negro sat on any grand or petit jury in the entire history of that county."

That testimony in itself made out a prima facie case of the denial of the equal protection which the Constitution guarantees. See Neal v. Delaware, *supra*. The case thus made was supplemented by direct testimo-ny that specified negroes, thirty or more in number, were qualified for jury service. Among these were negroes who were members of school boards, or trustees, of colored schools, and property owners and householders. It also appeared that negroes from that county had been called for jury service in the federal court. Several of those who were thus described as qualified were witnesses. While there was testimony which cast doubt upon the qualifications of some of the negroes who had been named, and there was also general testimony by the editor of a local newspaper who gave his opinion as to the lack of "sound judgment" of the "good negroes" in Jackson county, we think that the definite testimony as to the actual qualifications of individual negroes, which was not met by any testimony equally direct, showed that there were negroes in Jackson county qualified for jury service.

The question arose whether names of negroes were in fact on the jury roll. The books containing the jury roll for Jackson county for the year 1930–31 were produced. They were produced from the custody of a member of the jury commission which, in 1931, had succeeded the commis-sion which had made up the jury roll from which the grand jury in question had been drawn. On the pages of this roll appeared the names of six negroes. They were entered, respectively, at the end of the precinct lists which were alphabetically arranged. The genuineness of these entries was disputed. It appeared that after the jury roll in question had been made up, and after the new jury commission had taken office, one of the new commissioners directed the new clerk to draw lines after the names which had been placed on the roll by the preceding commission. These lines, on the pages under consideration, were red lines, and the clerk of the old commission testified that they were not put in by him. The entries made by the new clerk, for the new jury roll, were below these lines.

The names of the six negroes were in each instance written immediately above the red lines. An expert of long experience testified that these names were superimposed upon the red lines, that is, that they were written after the lines had been drawn. The expert was not cross-examined and no testimony was introduced to contradict him.[1] In denying the motion to quash, the trial judge expressed the view that he would not "be authorized to presume that somebody had committed a crime" or to presume that the jury board "had been unfaithful to their duties and allowed the books to be tampered with." His conclusion was that names of negroes were on the jury roll.

We think that the evidence did not justify that conclusion. The Supreme Court of the state did not sustain it. That court observed that the charge that the names of negroes were fraudulently placed on the roll did not involve any member of the jury board, and that the charge "was, by implication at least, laid at the door of the clerk of the board." The court, reaching its decision irrespective of that question, treated that phase of the matter as "wholly immaterial" and hence passed it by "without any expression of opinion thereon."

The state court rested its decision upon the ground that even if it were assumed that there was no name of a negro on the jury roll, it was not established that race or color caused the omission. The court pointed out that the statute fixed a high standard of qualifications for jurors (Green v. State, 73 Ala. 26; State v. Curtis, 210 Ala. 1, 97 So. 291) and that the jury commission was vested with a wide discretion. The court adverted to the fact that more white citizens possessing age qualifications had been omitted from the jury roll than the entire negro population of the county, and regarded the testimony as being to the effect that "the matter of race, color, politics, religion or fraternal affiliations" had not been discussed by the commission and had not entered into their consideration, and that no one had been excluded because of race or color.

The testimony showed the practice of the jury commission. One of the commissioners who made up the jury roll in question, and the clerk of that commission, testified as to the manner of its preparation. The other two commissioners of that period did not testify. It was shown that the clerk, under the direction of the commissioners, made up a preliminary list which was based on the registration list of voters, the polling list and the tax list, and apparently also upon the telephone directory. The clerk testified that he made up a list of all male citizens between the ages of twenty-one and sixty-five years without regard to their status or qualifications. The commissioner testified that the designation "col." was placed after the names of those who were colored. In preparing the final jury roll, the preliminary list was checked off as to qualified jurors with the aid of men whom the commissioners called in for that purpose from the different precincts. And the commissioner testified that in the selections for the jury roll no one was "automatically or systematically" excluded, or excluded on account of race or color; that he "did not inquire as to color," that was not discussed.

---

1. The books containing the jury roll in question were produced on the argument at this bar and were examined by the Court. [Ed. See the dramatic account of this incident in Schmidt, *Juries, Jurisdiction, and Race Discrimination: The Lost Promise of Strauder v. West Virginia*, 61 Texas L.Rev. 1401, 1476–79 (1983).]

But, in appraising the action of the commissioners, these statements cannot be divorced from other testimony. As we have seen, there was testimony, not overborne or discredited, that there were in fact negroes in the county qualified for jury service. That testimony was direct and specific. After eliminating those persons as to whom there was some evidence of lack of qualifications, a considerable number of others remained. The fact that the testimony as to these persons, fully identified, was not challenged by evidence appropriately direct, cannot be brushed aside. There is no ground for an assumption that the names of these negroes were not on the preliminary list. The inference to be drawn from the testimony is that they were on that preliminary list, and were designated on that list as the names of negroes, and that they were not placed on the jury roll. There was thus presented a test of the practice of the commissioners. Something more than mere general asseverations was required. Why were these names excluded from the jury roll? Was it because of the lack of statutory qualifications? Were the qualifications of negroes actually and properly considered?

The testimony of the commissioner on this crucial question puts the case in a strong light. That testimony leads to the conclusion that these or other negroes were not excluded on account of age, or lack of esteem in the community for integrity and judgment, or because of disease or want of any other qualification. The commissioner's answer to specific inquiry upon this point was that negroes were "never discussed." We give in the margin quotations from his testimony.[2]

We are of the opinion that the evidence required a different result from that reached in the state court. We think that the evidence that for a generation or longer no negro had been called for service on any jury in Jackson county, that there were negroes qualified for jury service, that according to the practice of the jury commission their names would normally appear on the preliminary list of male citizens of the requisite age but that no names of negroes were placed on the jury roll, and the testimony

2. "Q. Did you ever exclude from the jury rolls any negroes because you found first, he was a man under twenty-one years old or over sixty-five, and he was excluded by reason of his age; secondly because he was a person who wasn't esteemed in the community for being a decent and honorable citizen, for good sound common sense and judgment, did you ever see or hear of them not going to take that negro because he wasn't esteemed in the community for good sense and judgment? A. No, sir.

"Q. Did you ever have occasion to say, I can't take that negro because he is a fellow that has a disease which may affect or does affect, his mentality, did you ever say that to yourself, with reference to any particular negro? A. No, sir, negroes was never discussed.

"Q. Did you ever say to yourself as a jury commissioner in compiling those lists, I am not going to take that negro because he has been convicted before of a crime involving moral turpitude, have you ever excluded a negro on that ground, did you

ever find any negro that came within that category, under your personal knowledge in Jackson County? A. I couldn't recall any, no, sir, I don't know.

"Q. Have you ever known of any negro in Jackson County who was excluded by reason of the fact that he could not read English, and that negro at the same time wasn't a free holder or house holder, did you ever say I can't take that negro because he is prohibited under the rules from serving by reason of that provision? A. No, sir.

"Q. Or anybody in your presence? A. It never was discussed.

"Q. You had been a jury commissioner how long? A. I was on it under Bibb Graves administration, 1928, 1929, 1930.

"Q. Three years? A. Yes, sir.

"Q. And you never had occasion to exclude any negro in Jackson County by reason of the disqualifying provisions I have just called to your attention? A. Not to my personal knowledge, no, sir."

with respect to the lack of appropriate consideration of the qualifications of negroes, established the discrimination which the Constitution forbids. The motion to quash the indictment upon that ground should have been granted.

Third. *The evidence on the motion to quash the trial venire.* The population of Morgan county, where the trial was had, was larger than that of Jackson county, and the proportion of negroes was much greater. The total population of Morgan county in 1930 was 46,176, and of this number 8,311 were negroes.

Within the memory of witnesses, long resident there, no negro had ever served on a jury in that county or had been called for such service. Some of these witnesses were over fifty years of age and had always lived in Morgan county. Their testimony was not contradicted. A clerk of the circuit court, who had resided in the county for thirty years, and who had been in office for over four years, testified that during his official term approximately 2,500 persons had been called for jury service and that not one of them was a negro; that he did not recall "ever seeing any single person of the colored race serve on any jury in Morgan County."

There was abundant evidence that there were a large number of negroes in the county who were qualified for jury service. Men of intelligence, some of whom were college graduates, testified to long lists (said to contain nearly 200 names) of such qualified negroes, including many business men, owners of real property and householders. When defendant's counsel proposed to call many additional witnesses in order to adduce further proof of qualifications of negroes for jury service, the trial judge limited the testimony, holding that the evidence was cumulative.

We find no warrant for a conclusion that the names of any of the negroes as to whom this testimony was given, or of any other negroes, were placed on the jury rolls. No such names were identified. The evidence that for many years no negro had been called for jury service itself tended to show the absence of the names of negroes from the jury rolls, and the state made no effort to prove their presence. The trial judge limited the defendant's proof "to the present year, the present jury roll." The sheriff of the county, called as a witness for defendants, scanned the jury roll and after "looking over every single name on that jury roll, from A to Z," was unable to point out "any single negro on it."

For this long-continued, unvarying, and wholesale exclusion of negroes from jury service we find no justification consistent with the constitutional mandate. We have carefully examined the testimony of the jury commissioners upon which the state court based its decision. One of these commissioners testified in person and the other two submitted brief affidavits. By the state act (Gen.Acts Ala.1931, No. 47, p. 55), in force at the time the jury roll in question was made up, the clerk of the jury board was required to obtain the names of all male citizens of the county over twenty-one and under sixty-five years of age, and their occupation, place of residence, and place of business. *Id.,* p. 58, § 11. The qualifications of those who were to be placed on the jury roll were the same as those prescribed by the earlier statute which we have already quoted. *Id.,* p. 59, § 14. The member of the jury board, who testified orally, said that a list was made up which included the names of all male citizens of suitable age; that black residents were not excluded from this general list; that in compiling the jury roll he did not consider race or color; that no one was excluded for that reason; and that he had placed on the jury roll the names of persons possessing the qualifications under the statute. The affidavits of the other members of the board contained general statements to the same effect.

We think that this evidence failed to rebut the strong prima facie case which defendant had made. That showing as to the long-continued exclusion of negroes from jury service, and as to the many negroes qualified for that service, could not be met by mere generalities. If, in the presence of such testimony as defendant adduced, the mere general assertions by officials of their performance of duty were to be accepted as an adequate justification for the complete exclusion of negroes from jury service, the constitutional provision—adopted with special reference to their protection—would be but a vain and illusory requirement. The general attitude of the jury commissioner is shown by the following extract from his testimony: "I do not know of any negro in Morgan County over twenty-one and under sixty-five who is generally reputed to be honest and intelligent and who is esteemed in the community for his integrity, good character and sound judgment, who is not an habitual drunkard, who isn't afflicted with a permanent disease or physical weakness which would render him unfit to discharge the duties of a juror, and who can read English, and who has never been convicted of a crime involving moral turpitude." In the light of the testimony given by defendant's witnesses, we find it impossible to accept such a sweeping characterization of the lack of qualifications of negroes in Morgan county. It is so sweeping, and so contrary to the evidence as to the many qualified negroes, that it destroys the intended effect of the commissioner's testimony.

In Neal v. Delaware, *supra,* decided over fifty years ago, this Court observed that it was a "violent presumption," in which the state court had there indulged, that the uniform exclusion of negroes from juries, during a period of many years, was solely because, in the judgment of the officers, charged with the selection of grand and petit jurors, fairly exercised, "the black race in Delaware were utterly disqualified by want of intelligence, experience, or moral integrity, to sit on juries." Such a presumption at the present time would be no less violent with respect to the exclusion of the negroes of Morgan county. And, upon the proof contained in the record now before us, a conclusion that their continuous and total exclusion from juries was because there were none possessing the requisite qualifications, cannot be sustained.

We are concerned only with the federal question which we have discussed, and in view of the denial of the federal right suitably asserted, the judgment must be reversed and the cause remanded for further proceedings not inconsistent with this opinion.

It is so ordered.

Mr. Justice McReynolds did not hear the argument and took no part in the consideration and decision of this case.

––––––––

COX v. LOUISIANA

379 U.S. 536, 85 S.Ct. 453, 13 L.Ed.2d 471 (1965).
Appeal from the Supreme Court of Louisiana.

MR. JUSTICE GOLDBERG delivered the opinion of the Court.

Appellant, the Reverend Mr. B. Elton Cox, the leader of a civil rights demonstration, was arrested and charged with four offenses under Louisiana law—criminal conspiracy, disturbing the peace, obstructing public passages and picketing before a courthouse. In a consolidated trial before a judge without a jury, and on the same set of facts, he was acquitted of criminal conspiracy but convicted of the other three offenses. He was sentenced to serve four months in jail and pay a $200 fine for disturbing the peace, to serve five months in jail and pay a $500 fine for obstructing public passages, and to serve one year in jail and pay a $5,000 fine for picketing before a courthouse. The sentences were cumulative.

In accordance with Louisiana procedure the Louisiana Supreme Court reviewed the "disturbing the peace" and "obstructing public passages" convictions on certiorari and the "courthouse picketing" conviction on appeal. The Louisiana court, in two judgments, affirmed all three convictions. 244 La. 1087, 156 So.2d 448; 245 La. 303, 158 So.2d 172. Appellant filed two separate appeals to this Court from these judgments contending that the three statutes under which he was convicted were unconstitutional on their face and as applied. We noted probable jurisdiction of both appeals, 377 U.S. 921. This case, No. 24, involves the convictions for disturbing the peace and obstructing public passages, and No. 49 [379 U.S. 559] concerns the conviction for picketing before a courthouse.

I. The Facts.

On December 14, 1961, 23 students from Southern University, a Negro college, were arrested in downtown Baton Rouge, Louisiana, for picketing stores that maintained segregated lunch counters. This picketing, urging a boycott of those stores, was part of a general protest movement against racial segregation, directed by the local chapter of the Congress of Racial Equality, a civil rights organization. The appellant, an ordained Congregational minister, the Reverend Mr. B. Elton Cox, a Field Secretary of CORE, was an advisor to this movement. On the evening of December 14, appellant and Ronnie Moore, student president of the local CORE chapter, spoke at a mass meeting at the college. The students resolved to demonstrate the next day in front of the courthouse in protest of segregation and the arrest and imprisonment of the picketers who were being held in the parish jail located on the upper floor of the courthouse building.

The next morning about 2,000 students left the campus, which was located approximately five miles from downtown Baton Rouge. Most of them had to walk into the city since the drivers of their busses were arrested. Moore was also arrested at the entrance to the campus while parked in a car equipped with a loudspeaker, and charged with violation of an antinoise statute. Because Moore was immediately taken off to jail and the vice president of the CORE chapter was already in jail for picketing, Cox felt it his duty to take over the demonstration and see that it was carried out as planned. He quickly drove to the city "to pick up this leadership and keep things orderly."

When Cox arrived, 1,500 of the 2,000 students were assembling at the site of the old State Capitol building, two and one-half blocks from the courthouse. Cox walked up and down cautioning the students to keep to one side of the sidewalk while getting ready for their march to the courthouse. The students circled the block in a file two or three abreast occupying about half of the sidewalk. The police had learned of the proposed demonstration the night before from news media and other sources. Captain Font of the City Police Department and Chief Kling of the Sheriff's office, two high-ranking subordinate officials, approached the group and spoke to Cox at the northeast corner of the capitol grounds. Cox identified himself as the group's leader, and, according to Font and Kling, he explained that the students were demonstrating to protest "the illegal arrest of some of their people who were being held in jail." The version of Cox and his witnesses throughout was that they came not "to protest just the arrest but ∗ ∗ ∗ [also] to protest the evil of discrimination." Kling asked Cox to disband the group and "take them back from whence they came." Cox did not acquiesce in this request but told the officers that they would march by the courthouse, say prayers, sing hymns, and conduct a peaceful program of protest. The officer repeated his request to disband, and Cox again refused. Kling and Font then returned to their car in order to report by radio to the Sheriff and Chief of Police who were in the immediate vicinity; while this was going on, the students, led by Cox, began their walk toward the courthouse.

They walked in an orderly and peaceful file, two or three abreast, one block east, stopping on the way for a red traffic light. In the center of this block they were joined by another group of students. The augmented group now totaling about 2,000[1] turned the corner and proceeded south, coming to a halt in the next block opposite the courthouse.

As Cox, still at the head of the group, approached the vicinity of the courthouse, he was stopped by Captain Font and Inspector Trigg and brought to Police Chief Wingate White, who was standing in the middle of St. Louis Street. The Chief then inquired as to the purpose of the demonstration. Cox, reading from a prepared paper, outlined his program to White, stating that it would include a singing of the Star Spangled Banner and a "freedom song," recitation of the Lord's Prayer and the Pledge of Allegiance, and a short speech. White testified that he told Cox that "he must confine" the demonstration "to the west side of the street." White added, "This, of course, was not—I didn't mean it in the import that I was giving him any permission to do it, but I was presented with a situation that was accomplished, and I had to make a decision." Cox testified that the officials agreed to permit the meeting. James Erwin, news director of radio station WIBR, a witness for the State, was present and overheard the conversation. He testified that "My understanding was that they would be allowed to demonstrate if they stayed on the west side of the street and stayed within the recognized time,"[2] and that this was "agreed to" by White.[3]

1. Estimates of the crowd's size varied from 1,500 to 3,800. Two thousand seems to have been the consensus and was the figure accepted by the Louisiana Supreme Court.

2. There were varying versions in the record as to the time the demonstration would take. The State's version was that Cox asked for seven minutes. Cox's version was that he said his speech would take seven minutes but that the whole program would take between 17 and 25 minutes.

3. The "permission" granted the students to demonstrate is discussed at

The students were then directed by Cox to the west sidewalk, across the street from the courthouse, 101 feet from its steps. They were lined up on this sidewalk about five deep and spread almost the entire length of the block. The group did not obstruct the street. It was close to noon and, being lunch time, a small crowd of 100 to 300 curious white people, mostly courthouse personnel, gathered on the east sidewalk and courthouse steps, about 100 feet from the demonstrators. Seventy-five to eighty policemen, including city and state patrolmen and members of the Sheriff's staff, as well as members of the fire department and a fire truck were stationed in the street between the two groups. Rain fell throughout the demonstration.

Several of the students took from beneath their coats picket signs similar to those which had been used the day before. These signs bore legends such as "Don't buy discrimination for Christmas," "Sacrifice for Christ, don't buy," and named stores which were proclaimed "unfair." They then sang "God Bless America," pledged allegiance to the flag, prayed briefly, and sang one or two hymns, including "We Shall Overcome." The 23 students, who were locked in jail cells in the courthouse building out of the sight of the demonstrators, responded by themselves singing; this in turn was greeted with cheers and applause by the demonstrators. Appellant gave a speech, described by a State's witness as follows:

"He said that in effect that it was a protest against the illegal arrest of some of their members and that other people were allowed to picket * * * and he said that they were not going to commit any violence,[4] that if anyone spit on them, they would not spit back on the person that did it." [5]

Cox then said:

"All right. It's lunch time. Let's go eat. There are twelve stores we are protesting. A number of these stores have twenty counters; they accept your money from nineteen. They won't accept it from the twentieth counter. This is an act of racial discrimination. These stores are open to the public. You are members of the public. We pay taxes to the Federal Government and you who live here pay taxes to the State." [6]

In apparent reaction to these last remarks, there was what state witnesses described as "muttering" and "grumbling" by the white onlookers.[7]

---

greater length in No. 49, where its legal effect is considered.

4. A few days before, Cox had participated with some of the demonstrators in a "direct non-violent clinic" sponsored by CORE and held at St. Mark's Church.

5. Sheriff Clemmons had no objection to this part of the speech. He testified on cross-examination as follows:

"Q. Did you have any objection to that part of his talk?

"A. None whatever. If he would have done what he said, there would have been no trouble at all. The whole thing would have been over and done with.

"Q. Did you have any objection to them being assembled on that side of the street while he was making that speech, sir?

"A. I had no objection to it."

6. Sheriff Clemmons objected strongly to these words. He testified on cross-examination as follows:

"Q. Now, what part of his speech became objectionable to him being assembled there?

"A. The inflammatory manner in which he addressed that crowd and told them to go on up town, go to four places on the protest list, sit down and if they don't feed you, sit there for one hour."

7. The exact sequence of these events is unclear from the record, being described

The Sheriff, deeming, as he testified, Cox's appeal to the students to sit in at the lunch counters to be "inflammatory," then took a power microphone and said, "Now, you have been allowed to demonstrate. Up until now your demonstration has been more or less peaceful, but what you are doing now is a direct violation of the law, a disturbance of the peace, and it has got to be broken up immediately." The testimony as to what then happened is disputed. Some of the State's witnesses testified that Cox said, "don't move"; others stated that he made a "gesture of defiance." It is clear from the record, however, that Cox and the demonstrators did not then and there break up the demonstration. Two of the Sheriff's deputies immediately started across the street and told the group, "You have heard what the Sheriff said, now, do what he said." A state witness testified that they put their hands on the shoulders of some of the students "as though to shove them away."

Almost immediately thereafter—within a time estimated variously at two to five minutes—one of the policemen exploded a tear gas shell at the crowd. This was followed by several other shells. The demonstrators quickly dispersed, running back towards the State Capitol and the downtown area; Cox tried to calm them as they ran and was himself one of the last to leave.

No Negroes participating in the demonstration were arrested on that day. The only person then arrested was a young white man, not a part of the demonstration, who was arrested "because he was causing a disturbance." The next day appellant was arrested and charged with the four offenses above described.

II. The Breach of the Peace Conviction.

Appellant was convicted of violating a Louisiana "disturbing the peace" statute, which provides:

"Whoever with intent to provoke a breach of the peace, or under circumstances such that a breach of the peace may be occasioned thereby * * * crowds or congregates with others * * * in or upon * * * a public street or public highway, or upon a public sidewalk, or any other public place or building * * * and who fails or refuses to disperse and move on * * * when ordered so to do by any law enforcement officer of any municipality, or parish, in which such act or acts are committed, or by any law enforcement officer of the state of Louisiana, or any other authorized person * * * shall be guilty of disturbing the peace." LSA—Rev. Stat. § 14:103.1 (Cum.Supp.1962).

It is clear to us that on the facts of this case, which are strikingly similar to those present in Edwards v. South Carolina, 372 U.S. 229, and Fields v. South Carolina, 375 U.S. 44, Louisiana infringed appellant's rights of free speech and free assembly by convicting him under this statute. * * * We hold that Louisiana may not constitutionally punish appellant under this statute for engaging in the type of conduct which this record reveals, and also that the statute as authoritatively interpreted by the Louisiana Supreme Court is unconstitutionally broad in scope.

differently not only by the State and the defense, but also by the state witnesses themselves. It seems reasonably certain, however, that the response to the singing from the jail, the end of Cox's speech, and the "muttering" and "grumbling" of the white onlookers all took place at approximately the same time.

The Louisiana courts have held that appellant's conduct constituted a breach of the peace under state law, and, as in Edwards, "we may accept their decision as binding upon us to that extent," Edwards v. South Carolina, *supra*, at 235; but our independent examination of the record, which we are required to make,[8] shows no conduct which the State had a right to prohibit as a breach of the peace.

Appellant led a group of young college students who wished "to protest segregation" and discrimination against Negroes and the arrest of 23 fellow students. They assembled peaceably at the State Capitol building and marched to the courthouse where they sang, prayed and listened to a speech. A reading of the record reveals agreement on the part of the State's witnesses that Cox had the demonstration "very well controlled," and until the end of Cox's speech, the group was perfectly "orderly." Sheriff Clemmons testified that the crowd's activities were not "objectionable" before that time. They became objectionable, according to the Sheriff himself, when Cox, concluding his speech, urged the students to go uptown and sit in at lunch counters. The Sheriff testified that the sole aspect of the program to which he objected was "[t]he inflammatory manner in which he [Cox] addressed that crowd and told them to go on up town, go to four places on the protest list, sit down and if they don't feed you, sit there for one hour." Yet this part of Cox's speech obviously did not deprive the demonstration of its protected character under the Constitution as free speech and assembly. See Edwards v. South Carolina, *supra;* Cantwell v. State of Connecticut, 310 U.S. 296; Thornhill v. State of Alabama, 310 U.S. 88; Garner v. State of Louisiana, 368 U.S. 157, 185 (concurring opinion of Mr. Justice Harlan).

The State argues, however, that while the demonstrators started out to be orderly, the loud cheering and clapping by the students in response to the singing from the jail converted the peaceful assembly into a riotous one.[9] The record, however, does not support this assertion. It is true that the students, in response to the singing of their fellows who were in custody, cheered and applauded. However, the meeting was an outdoor meeting and a key state witness testified that while the singing was loud, it was not disorderly. There is, moreover, no indication that the mood of the students was ever hostile, aggressive, or unfriendly. Our conclusion that the entire meeting from the beginning until its dispersal by tear gas was

8. Because a claim of constitutionally protected right is involved, it "remains our duty in a case such as this to make an independent examination of the whole record." Edwards v. South Carolina, 372 U.S. 229, 235; Blackburn v. State of Alabama, 361 U.S. 199, 205, n. 5; Pennekamp v. State of Florida, 328 U.S. 331, 335; Fiske v. State of Kansas, 274 U.S. 380, 385–386. In the area of First Amendment freedoms as well as areas involving other constitutionally protected rights, "we cannot avoid our responsibilities by permitting ourselves to be 'completely bound by state court determination of any issue essential to decision of a claim of federal right, else federal law could be frustrated by distorted fact finding.'" Haynes v. State of Washington, 373 U.S. 503, 515–516; Stein v. People of State of New York, 346 U.S. 156, 181.

9. The cheering and shouting were described differently by different witnesses, but the most extravagant descriptions were the following: "a jumbled roar like people cheering at a football game," "loud cheering and spontaneous clapping and screaming and a great hullabaloo," "a great outburst," a cheer of "conquest • • • much wilder than a football game," "a loud reaction, not disorderly, loud," "a shout, a roar," and an emotional response "in jubilation and exhortation." Appellant agreed that some of the group "became emotional" and "tears flowed from young ladies' eyes."

orderly [10] and not riotous is confirmed by a film of the events taken by a television news photographer, which was offered in evidence as a state exhibit. We have viewed the film, and it reveals that the students, though they undoubtedly cheered and clapped, were well-behaved throughout. My Brother BLACK, concurring in this opinion and dissenting in No. 49, *post,* agrees "that the record does not show boisterous or violent conduct or indecent language on the part of the * * *" students. The singing and cheering do not seem to us to differ significantly from the constitutionally protected activity of the demonstrators in Edwards,[11] who loudly sang "while stamping their feet and clapping their hands." Edwards v. South Carolina, *supra,* 372 U.S., at 233.[12]

10. There is much testimony that the demonstrators were well controlled and basically orderly throughout. G. Dupre Litton, an attorney and witness for the State, testified, "I would say that it was an orderly demonstration. It was too large a group, in my opinion, to congregate at that place at that particular time, which is nothing but my opinion * * * but generally * * * it was orderly." Robert Durham, a news photographer for WBRZ, a state witness, testified that although the demonstration was not "quiet and peaceful," it was basically "orderly." James Erwin, news director of WIBR, a witness for the State, testified as follows:

"Q. Was the demonstration generally orderly?

"A. Yes, Reverend Cox had it very well controlled."

On the other hand, there is some evidence to the contrary: Erwin also stated:

"Q. Was it orderly up to the point of throwing the tear gas?

"A. No, there was one minor outburst after he called for the sit-ins, and then a minor reaction, and then a loud reaction, not disorderly, loud * * *. A loud reaction when the singing occurred upstairs."

And James Dumigan, a police officer, thought that the demonstrators showed a certain disorder by "hollering loud, clapping their hands." But this latter evidence is surely not sufficient, particularly in face of the film, to lead us to conclude that the cheering was so disorderly as to be beyond that held constitutionally protected in Edwards v. South Carolina, *supra.*

11. Moreover, there are not significantly more demonstrators here than in Fields v. South Carolina, *supra,* which involved more than 1,000 students.

12. Witnesses who concluded that a breach of the peace was threatened or had occurred based their conclusions, not upon the shouting or cheering, but upon the fact that the group was demonstrating at all, upon Cox's suggestion that the group sit in, or upon the reaction of the white onlookers across the street. Rush Biossat, a state witness, testified that while appellant "didn't say anything of a violent nature," there was "emotional upset," "a feeling of disturbance in the air," and "agitation"; he thought, however, that all this was caused by Cox's remarks about "black and white together." James Erwin, a state witness, and news director of WIBR, testified that there was "considerable stirring" and a "restiveness," but among the white group. He also stated that the reaction of the white group to Cox's speech "was electrifying." "You could hear grumbling from the small groups of white people, some total of two hundred fifty, perhaps * * * and there was a definite feeling of ill will that had sprung up." He was afraid that "violence was about to erupt" but also thought that Cox had his group under control and did not want violence. G.L. Johnston, a police officer and a witness for the State, felt that the disorderly part of the demonstration was Cox's suggestion that the group sit in. Vay Carpenter, and Mary O'Brien, legal secretaries and witnesses for the State, thought that the mood of the crowd changed at the time of Cox's speech and became "tense." They thought this was because of the sit-in suggestion. Chief Kling of the Sheriff's office, testifying for the State, said that the situation became one "that was explosive and one that had gotten to the point where it had to be handled or it would have gotten out of hand"; however, he based his opinion upon "the mere presence of these people in downtown Baton Rouge * * * in such great numbers." Police Captain Font also testified for the State that the situation was "explosive"; he based this opinion on "how they came, such a large group like that, just coming out of nowhere, just coming, filling the streets, filling the sidewalks. We are prepared—we have traffic officers. We can handle traffic situations if we are advised that we are going to have a traffic situation, if the sidewalk is going to be blocked, if the street is going to be blocked, but we wasn't advised of it. They just came and blocked it." He added that he feared "bloodshed," but based this fear upon

Our conclusion that the record does not support the contention that the students' cheering, clapping and singing constituted a breach of the peace is confirmed by the fact that these were not relied on as a basis for conviction by the trial judge, who, rather, stated as his reason for convicting Cox of disturbing the peace that "[i]t must be recognized to be inherently dangerous and a breach of the peace to bring 1,500 people, colored people, down in the predominantly white business district in the City of Baton Rouge and congregate across the street from the courthouse and sing songs as described to me by the defendant as the CORE national anthem carrying lines such as 'black and white together' and to urge those 1,500 people to descend upon our lunch counters and sit there until they are served. That has to be an inherent breach of the peace, and our statute 14:103.1 has made it so."

Finally, the State contends that the conviction should be sustained because of fear expressed by some of the state witnesses that "violence was about to erupt" because of the demonstration. It is virtually undisputed, however, that the students themselves were not violent and threatened no violence. The fear of violence seems to have been based upon the reaction of the group of white citizens looking on from across the street. One state witness testified that "he felt the situation was getting out of hand" as on the courthouse side of St. Louis Street "were small knots or groups of white citizens who were muttering words, who seemed a little bit agitated." A police officer stated that the reaction of the white crowd was not violent, but "was rumblings." Others felt the atmosphere became "tense" because of "mutterings," "grumbling," and "jeering" from the white group. There is no indication, however, that any member of the white group threatened violence. And this small crowd estimated at between 100 and 300 was separated from the students by "seventy-five to eighty" armed policemen, including "every available shift of the City Police," the "Sheriff's Office in full complement," and "additional help from the State Police," along with a "fire truck and the Fire Department." As Inspector Trigg testified, they could have handled the crowd.

"when the Sheriff requested them to move, they didn't move; when they cheered in a conquest type of tone; their displaying of the signs; the deliberate agitation that twenty-five people had been arrested the day before, and then they turned right around and just agitated the next day in the same prescribed manner." He also felt that the students displayed their signs in a way which was "agitating." Inspector Trigg testified for the State that "from their actions, I figured they were going to try to storm the Courthouse and take over the jail and try to get the prisoners that they had come down here to protest." However, Trigg based his conclusions upon the students having marched down from the Capitol and paraded in front of the courthouse; he thought they were "violent" because "they continued to march around this Courthouse, and they continued to march down here and do things that disrupts our way of living down here."

Sheriff Clemmons testified that the assembly "became objectionable" at the time of Cox's speech. The Sheriff objected to "the inflammatory manner in which he addressed that crowd and told them to go on up town, go to four places on the protest list, sit down and if they don't feed you, sit there for one hour. Prior to that, though, out from under these coats, some signs of—picketing signs. I don't know what's coming out of there next. It could be anything under a coat. It became inflammatory, and when he gestured, go on up town and take charge of these places • • • of business. That is what they were trying to do is take charge of this Courthouse."

A close reading of the record seems to reveal next to no evidence that anyone thought that the shouting and cheering were what constituted the threatened breach of the peace.

* * * Here again, as in Edwards, this evidence "showed no more than that the opinions which [the students] were peaceably expressing were sufficiently opposed to the views of the majority of the community to attract a crowd and necessitate police protection." Edwards v. South Carolina, *supra*, at 237. Conceding this was so, the "compelling answer * * * is that constitutional rights may not be denied simply because of hostility to their assertion or exercise." Watson v. City of Memphis, 373 U.S. 526, 535.

There is an additional reason why this conviction cannot be sustained. The statute at issue in this case, as authoritatively interpreted by the Louisiana Supreme Court, is unconstitutionally vague in its overly broad scope. The statutory crime consists of two elements: (1) congregating with others "with intent to provoke a breach of the peace, or under circumstances such that a breach of the peace may be occasioned," and (2) a refusal to move on after having been ordered to do so by a law enforcement officer. While the second part of this offense is narrow and specific, the first element is not. The Louisiana Supreme Court in this case defined the term "breach of the peace" as "to agitate, to arouse from a state of repose, to molest, to interrupt, to hinder, to disquiet." In Edwards, defendants had been convicted of a common-law crime similarly defined by the South Carolina Supreme Court. Both definitions would allow persons to be punished merely for peacefully expressing unpopular views. Yet, a "function of free speech under our system of government is to invite dispute. It may indeed best serve its high purpose when it induces a condition of unrest, creates dissatisfaction with conditions as they are, or even stirs people to anger. Speech is often provocative and challenging. It may strike at prejudices and preconceptions and have profound unsettling effects as it presses for acceptance of an idea. That is why freedom of speech * * * is * * * protected against censorship or punishment * * *. There is no room under our Constitution for a more restrictive view. For the alternative would lead to standardization of ideas either by legislatures, courts, or dominant political or community groups." Terminiello v. City of Chicago, 337 U.S. 1, 4–5. In Terminiello convictions were not allowed to stand because the trial judge charged that speech of the defendants could be punished as a breach of the peace " 'if it stirs the public to anger, invites dispute, brings about a condition of unrest, or creates a disturbance, or if it molests the inhabitants in the enjoyment of peace and quiet by arousing alarm.' " *Id.*, at 3. The Louisiana statute, as interpreted by the Louisiana court, is at least as likely to allow conviction for innocent speech as was the charge of the trial judge in Terminiello. Therefore, as in Terminiello and Edwards the conviction under this statute must be reversed as the statute is unconstitutional in that it sweeps within its broad scope activities that are constitutionally protected free speech and assembly. Maintenance of the opportunity for free political discussion is a basic tenet of our constitutional democracy. As Chief Justice Hughes stated in Stromberg v. People of State of California, 283 U.S. 359, 369: "A statute which upon its face, and as authoritatively construed, is so vague and indefinite as to permit the punishment of the fair use of this opportunity is repugnant to the guaranty of liberty contained in the Fourteenth Amendment."

For all these reasons we hold that appellant's freedoms of speech and assembly, secured to him by the First Amendment, as applied to the States by the Fourteenth Amendment, were denied by his conviction for disturbing the peace. The conviction on this charge cannot stand.

III. The Obstructing Public Passages Conviction.

We now turn to the issue of the validity of appellant's conviction for violating the Louisiana statute, LSA—Rev.Stat. § 14:100.1 (Cum.Supp. 1962), which provides:

"Obstructing Public Passages

"No person shall wilfully obstruct the free, convenient and normal use of any public sidewalk, street, highway, bridge, alley, road, or other passageway, or the entrance, corridor or passage of any public building, structure, watercraft or ferry, by impeding, hindering, stifling, retarding or restraining traffic or passage thereon or therein. [* * *]"

Appellant was convicted under this statute, not for leading the march to the vicinity of the courthouse, which the Louisiana Supreme Court stated to have been "orderly," but for leading the meeting on the sidewalk across the street from the courthouse. In upholding appellant's conviction under this statute, the Louisiana Supreme Court thus construed the statute so as to apply to public assemblies which do not have as their specific purpose the obstruction of traffic. There is no doubt from the record in this case that this far sidewalk was obstructed, and thus, as so construed, appellant violated the statute.

Appellant, however, contends that as so construed and applied in this case, the statute is an unconstitutional infringement on freedom of speech and assembly. * * *

We have no occasion in this case to consider the constitutionality of the uniform, consistent, and nondiscriminatory application of a statute forbidding all access to streets and other public facilities for parades and meetings. Although the statute here involved on its face precludes all street assemblies and parades, it has not been so applied and enforced by the Baton Rouge authorities. City officials who testified for the State clearly indicated that certain meetings and parades are permitted in Baton Rouge, even though they have the effect of obstructing traffic, provided prior approval is obtained. This was confirmed in oral argument before this Court by counsel for the State. He stated that parades and meetings are permitted, based on "arrangements * * * made with officials." The statute itself provides no standards for the determination of local officials as to which assemblies to permit or which to prohibit. Nor are there any administrative regulations on this subject which have been called to our attention. From all the evidence before us it appears that the authorities in Baton Rouge permit or prohibit parades or street meetings in their completely uncontrolled discretion.

The situation is thus the same as if the statute itself expressly provided that there could only be peaceful parades or demonstrations in the unbridled discretion of the local officials. * * *

* * * It is clearly unconstitutional to enable a public official to determine which expressions of view will be permitted and which will not or to engage in invidious discrimination among persons or groups either by use of a statute providing a system of broad discretionary licensing power

or, as in this case, the equivalent of such a system by selective enforcement of an extremely broad prohibitory statute.   *   *   *

For the reasons discussed above the judgment of the Supreme Court of Louisiana is reversed.

Reversed.

[A companion case (No. 49) was Cox's appeal from his conviction for violating the Louisiana statute providing: "Whoever, with the intent of interfering with, obstructing, or impeding the administration of justice, or with the intent of influencing any judge, juror, witness, or court officer, in the discharge of his duty pickets or parades in or near a building housing a court of the State of Louisiana * * * shall be fined not more than five thousand dollars or imprisoned not more than one year, or both." La.Rev. Stat. § 14:401 (Cum.Supp.1962). The Court, again per Justice Goldberg, first rejected Cox's contention that the statute was "invalid on its face as an unjustifiable restriction upon freedoms guaranteed by the First and Fourteenth Amendments." Finding the statute "narrowly drawn to punish specific conduct that infringes a substantial state interest in protecting the judicial process," the Court concluded that "this statute on its face is a valid law dealing with conduct subject to regulation so as to vindicate important interests of society."

[The Court also rejected Cox's claim that there was no evidence of intent to influence any judicial official. The Court found, however, that though the "lack of specificity in a word such as 'near', * * * may not render the statute unconstitutionally vague, at least as applied to a demonstration within the sight and hearing of those in the courthouse, it is clear that the statute, with respect to the determination of how near the courthouse a particular demonstration can be, foresees a degree of on-the-spot administrative interpretation by officials charged with responsibility for administering and enforcing it." The Court assumed that reliance on such an interpretation would be justifiable and found that in this case: "The record here clearly shows that the officials present gave permission for the demonstration to take place across the street from the courthouse.[†] * * * Thus, the highest police officials of the city * * * in effect told the demonstrators that they could meet where they did, * * * but could not meet closer to the courthouse. In effect, [Cox] was advised that a demonstration at the place it was held would not be one 'near' the courthouse within the terms of the statute." The Court said that to uphold a conviction under such circumstances "would be to sanction an indefensible sort of entrapment by the state."]

MR. JUSTICE BLACK, concurring in No. 24 and dissenting in No. 49. * * * *

I agree with that part of the Court's opinion holding that the Louisiana breach-of-the-peace statute on its face and as construed by the State Supreme Court is so broad as to be unconstitutionally vague under the First and Fourteenth Amendments. See Winters v. People of State of New York, 333 U.S. 507, 509–510.   *   *   *

---

† [Ed.] To a quotation of Police Chief White's testimony (see opinion, *supra*) in support of this statement, the Court appended the following footnote: "It is true that the Police Chief testified that he did not subjectively intend to grant permission, but there is no evidence at all that this subjective state of mind was ever communicated to appellant, or in fact to anyone else present" (p. 570, n. 4).

* * *

I would sustain the conviction of appellant for violation of LSA—Rev. Stat. § 14:401 (Cum.Supp.1962), which makes it an offense for anyone, under any conditions, to picket or parade near a courthouse, residence or other building used by a judge, juror, witness, or court officer, "with the intent of influencing" any of them. * * * The Court attempts to support its holding by its inference that the Chief of Police gave his consent to picketing the courthouse. But quite apart from the fact that a police chief cannot authorize violations of his State's criminal laws, there was strong, emphatic testimony that if any consent was given it was limited to telling Cox and his group to come no closer to the courthouse than they had already come without the consent of any official, city, state, or federal.

* * *

MR. JUSTICE CLARK, concurring in No. 24 and dissenting in No. 49.

According to the record, the opinions of all of Louisiana's courts and even the majority opinion of this Court, the appellant, in an effort to influence and intimidate the courts and legal officials of Baton Rouge and procure the release of 23 prisoners being held for trial, agitated and led a mob of over 2,000 students in the staging of a modern Donnybrook Fair across from the courthouse and jail. * * *

Louisiana's statute, § 14:401, under attack here, was taken *in haec verba* from a bill which became 18 U.S.C. § 1507 (1958 ed.). The federal statute was enacted by the Congress in 1950 to protect federal courts from demonstrations similar to the one involved in this case. It applies to the Supreme Court Building where this Court sits. I understand that § 1507 was written by members of this Court after disturbances similar to the one here occurred at buildings housing federal courts. Naturally, the Court could hardly be expected to hold its progeny invalid either on the ground that the use in the statute of the phrase "in or near a building housing a court" was vague or that it violated free speech or assembly. It has been said that an author is always pleased with his own work.

But the Court excuses Cox's brazen defiance of the statute—the validity of which the Court upholds—on a much more subtle ground. It seizes upon the acquiescence of the Chief of Police arising from the laudable motive to avoid violence and possible bloodshed to find that he made an on-the-spot administrative determination that a demonstration confined to the west side of St. Louis Street—101 feet from the courthouse steps—would not be "near" enough to the court building to violate the statute. * * *

With due deference, the record will not support this novel theory. * * * This mob of young Negroes led by Cox—2,000 strong—was not only within sight but in hearing distance of the courthouse. The record is replete with evidence that the demonstrators with their singing, cheering, clapping and waving of banners drew the attention of the whole courthouse square as well as the occupants and officials of the court building itself. Indeed, one judge was obliged to leave the building. The 23 students who had been arrested for sit-in demonstrations the day before and who were in custody in the building were also aroused to such an extent that they sang and cheered to the demonstrators from the jail which was in the courthouse and the demonstrators returned the notice with like activity. The law enforcement officials were confronted with a direct obstruction to the orderly administration of their duties as well as an interference with the courts. One hardly needed an on-the-spot administrative decision that the demonstration was "near" the courthouse with the disturbance being conducted before the eyes and ringing in the ears of court officials, police officers and citizens throughout the courthouse.

Moreover, the Chief testified that when Cox and the 2,000 Negroes approached him on the way to the courthouse he was faced with a "situation that was accomplished." From the beginning they had been told not to proceed with their march; twice officers had requested them to turn back to the school; on each occasion they had refused. Finding that he could not stop them without the use of force the Chief told Cox that he must confine the demonstration to the west side of St. Louis Street across from the courthouse.

All the witnesses, including the appellant, state that the time for the demonstration was expressly limited. The State's witnesses say seven minutes, while Cox claims his speech was to be seven minutes but the program would take from 17 to 25 minutes. Regardless of the amount of time agreed upon, it is a novel construction of the facts to say that the grant of permission to demonstrate for a limited period of time was an administrative determination that the west side of the street was not "near" the courthouse. * * *

Because I am unable to agree that the word "near," when applied to the facts of this case, required an administrative interpretation, and since I feel that the record refutes the conclusion that it was made, I must respectfully dissent from such a finding. * * *

I must, therefore, respectfully dissent from this action and join my Brother Black on this facet of the case. I also agree with him that the statute prohibiting obstruction of public passages is invalid under the Equal Protection Clause. And, as will be seen, I arrive at the same conclusion for the same reason on the question regarding the breach of the peace statute. However, I cannot agree that the latter Act is unconstitutionally vague.

The statute declares congregating "with intent to provoke a breach of the peace" and refusing to disperse after being ordered so to do by an officer to be an offense. Each of these elements is set out in clear and unequivocal language. * * *

MR. JUSTICE WHITE, with whom MR. JUSTICE HARLAN joins, concurring in part and dissenting in part.

In No. 49 I agree with the dissent filed by my Brother BLACK in [the last part] of his opinion. In No. 24, although I do not agree with everything the Court says concerning the breach of peace conviction, particularly its statement concerning the unqualified protection to be extended to Cox's exhortations to engage in sit-ins in restaurants, I agree that the conviction for breach of peace is governed by Edwards v. South Carolina, 372 U.S. 229, and must be reversed.

Regretfully, I also dissent from the reversal of the conviction for obstruction of public passages. The Louisiana statute is not invalidated on its face but only in its application. But this remarkable emasculation of a prohibitory statute is based on only very vague evidence that other meetings and parades have been allowed by the authorities. The sole indication in the record from the state court that such has occurred was contained in the testimony of the Chief of Police who, in the process of pointing out that Cox and his group had not announced the fact or purpose of their meeting, said "most organizations that want to hold a parade or a meeting of any kind, they have no reluctance to evidence their desires at the start." There is no evidence in the record that other meetings of this magnitude had been allowed on the city streets, had been allowed in the vicinity of the courthouse or had been permitted completely to obstruct the sidewalk and to block access to abutting buildings. Indeed, the sheriff testified that "we have never had such a demonstration since I have been in law enforcement in this parish." He also testified that "any other organization" would have received the same treatment if it "had conducted such a demonstration in front of the Parish Courthouse," whether it had been "colored or white, Protestant, Catholic, Jewish, any kind of organization, if they had conducted this same type of demonstration * * *." Similarly the trial judge noted that although Louisiana respects freedom of speech and the right to picket, Louisiana courts "have held that picketing is unlawful when it is mass picketing."

At the oral argument in response to Mr. Justice Goldberg's question as to whether parades and demonstrations are allowed in Baton Rouge, counsel said, "arrangements are usually made depending on the size of the demonstration, of course, arrangements are made with the officials and their cooperation is not only required it is needed where you have such a large crowd." In my view, however, all of this evidence together falls far short of justification for converting this prohibitory state statute into an open-ended licensing statute invalid under prior decisions of this Court as applied to this case. This is particularly true since the Court's approach is its own invention and has not been urged or litigated by the parties either in this Court or the courts below. Certainly the parties have had no opportunity to develop or to refute the factual basis underlying the Court's rationale. * * *

NOTE ON CONTROL OF FACTFINDING AND OF APPLICATION OF LAW TO FACT

A. Introduction

(1) Judicial review, to be effective, must include some control over the factfinding function; if the factfinder (jury, agency, lower court) is free to act at will, control over the lawfulness of decisions is lost. That is why in our legal system the question whether there is sufficient evidence to justify a finding is consistently regarded as a question of law, for the reviewing court to decide. (See the illuminating general discussion in Jaffe, Judicial Control of Administrative Action 546–623 (1967).) The point is, of course, not limited to—but does hold in—a federal system, and has been apparent since Martin v. Hunter's Lessee: if review is to be effective where a federal claim was presented to a state court, the Supreme Court, must, in principle, possess the power to assure itself that the claim was not undermined or discriminated against by misuse of the factfinding function.

Article III explicitly legitimates this power by specifying that the Supreme Court shall have appellate jurisdiction "both as to Law and Fact." (Note, however, that in the early practice the Court's power to review facts was limited or nonexistent because of Congress's statutory choice in Section 25 to limit review to the writ of error. See generally Gibbons, *Federal Law and the State Courts, 1790–1860,* 36 Rutgers L.Rev. 399 (1984).)

(2) Where the federal question in the case is the validity of a rule of law "on its face"—*e.g.,* Cox's challenge to the "court-house picketing" statute on its face; challenges to statutes as construed by the highest state court, as in Herndon v. Georgia, p. 590, *supra,* and Cole v. Arkansas, 333 U.S. 196 (1948) (see p. 680, *infra);* or challenges to statutes as construed by the trial court (often in charging the jury), as in Terminiello v. Chicago, 337 U.S. 1 (1949) and Stromberg v. California, 283 U.S. 359 (1931)—the scope of review with respect to adjudicative facts is not problematic. Such a challenge puts into issue an explicit rule of law, as formulated by the legislature or the court, and involves the facts only insofar as it is necessary to establish that the rule served as a basis of decision.

as applied

Challenges to the validity of a statute as applied to specific facts, on the other hand, turn necessarily on a determination of what the adjudicative facts were, and call on the court to judge the statute with its scope defined by the concrete situation to which it has been applied. Indeed, the application point can always be rephrased simply as an assertion of a federal right or immunity with respect to the operative facts. (Casting the point as a challenge to the statute as applied makes appeal rather than certiorari available, see Section 4 of this Chapter, pp. 711–20, *infra,* but does not in any way affect the problem of scope of review.)

(3) If the question is the validity of the statute as applied, and there is no dispute as to what are the underlying operative facts, the Court's power to reexamine and correct the state court's conclusion is beyond question. (See, *e.g.,* the many cases overruling state courts on whether a given book or movie is "obscene" within the meaning of the First Amendment, discussed at pp. 667–71, *infra.)* Was Fiske such a case? When the Court has before it undisputed testimony as to the circumstances leading to a confession, and must determine whether it is the product of unconstitutional coercion, is it making a judgment of fact or is it applying a legal standard to undisputed facts? See Miller v. Fenton, 474 U.S. 104 (1985) ("the ultimate issue of 'voluntariness' is a legal question requiring independent federal determination").[1]

How far the Court can—and should—attempt to exercise meaningful supervision over individual instances of law application, where the process

1. The problem of distinguishing issues of "fact" from issues of "application of law to fact" have come to the forefront recently in habeas corpus litigation, where the distinction is relevant to the important question whether 28 U.S.C. § 2254(d), with its elaborate rules of deference to state court findings of fact, is applicable. The Supreme Court's confusing decisions in this context include Maggio v. Fulford, 462 U.S. 111 (1983) (competency to stand trial); Wainright v. Witt, 469 U.S. 412 (1985) (questions relating to juror impartiality); Sumner v. Mata I, and II, 449 U.S. 539 (1981) and 455 U.S. 591 (1982) (whether a lineup procedure is impermissibly sugges-

tive). See further Chap. XI, pp. 1565–66, *infra.*

The most sophisticated discussion of the general problem continues to be Jaffe, Judicial Control of Administrative Action 546–64, 595–99 (1967). It is complicated by the fact that many legal rules require the decisionmaker to make *simultaneous* judgments about (i) empirical phenomena (what was the juror's state of mind?) that themselves require the drawing of factual inferences, and (ii) the legal consequence to be attached to the factual conclusion (is such a juror *impermissibly* biased?).

is not accompanied by any development in general rules and standards, has been an important problem of judicial administration for the Court; it is discussed further in this Note in Paragraphs (11)–(14), *infra*. But if there is no dispute as to the underlying facts, the problem of supervising the factfinding function as such is not, strictly speaking, in play.

B.　Scope of Review Over Disputes With Respect to Historical Facts

(4) Because of the technical nature of the writ of error, the Court in the nineteenth century had ruled that it had no power to review state court findings of fact. See, *e.g.*, Egan v. Hart, 165 U.S. 188 (1897). But in this century this position soon eroded, and it was accepted that where there is a dispute over a question of historical fact bearing on a federal claim, the Court has authority to assure itself that there was "fair" or "substantial" support for the state court's finding. (See, *e.g.*, the conclusion of the Court that the state-court finding in Ward v. Love County, p. 581, *supra*, that the tax payments made by the plaintiffs were voluntary, was "without any fair or substantial support.")

Should the Court's role in this respect be different from its role in reviewing cases coming from the lower federal courts?

(5) When there is substantial evidence on *both* sides of a factual issue, the traditional view has been that the Court looks to the evidence adduced to support the state finding, and assesses the case on the basis of those facts.[2] In General Motors v. Washington, 377 U.S. 436, 444–42 (1964), the Court said: "[W]e have power to examine the whole record to arrive at an independent judgment as to whether constitutional rights have been invaded, but this does not mean that we will reexamine, as a court of first instance, findings of fact supported by substantial evidence." In Taylor v. Mississippi, 319 U.S. 583, 585–86 (1943), Justice Roberts said: "The evidence was contradictory and conflicting but the juries resolved the conflict against the appellants. We must, therefore, examine the questions presented on the basis of the proofs submitted by the State." (After such examination, the statute was held invalid as applied.) *Cf.* Feiner v. New York, 340 U.S. 315, 316 (1951), where the trial was by the court: "Our appraisal of the facts is ＊ ＊ ＊ based upon the uncontroverted facts and, where controversy exists, upon that testimony which the trial judge did reasonably conclude to be true." See also Container Corp. of America v. Franchise Tax Bd., 463 U.S. 159 (1983).

Compare Harlan, J., in Beck v. Ohio, 379 U.S. 89, 100–01 (1964) (dissenting opinion) on "the appropriate standards of appellate review": " '[T]here has been complete agreement that any conflict in testimony as to what actually led to a contested confession [or to a contested arrest] is not this Court's concern. Such conflict comes here authoritatively resolved by the State's adjudication.' Watts v. Indiana, 338 U.S. 49, 51–52 (1949). See also Gallegos v. Nebraska, 342 U.S. 55, 60–61 (1951); Haley v. Ohio, 332 U.S. 596, 597–598 (1948). It is equally clear that in cases involving asserted violations of constitutional rights the Court is free to draw its own infer-

---

2. Note, however, the crucial subsidiary proposition implicit in Norris v. Alabama: even though there is *testimony* on one side of the case that has apparently been accepted by the factfinder, the Court will assert the power to examine whether the testimony is credible; the mere fact of testimony that "X" existed is not automatically "substantial" evidence.

ences from established facts, giving due weight to the conclusions of the state court, but not being conclusively bound by them, Ker v. California, 374 U.S. 23 (1963); Spano v. New York, 360 U.S. 315 (1959).

"A distinction between facts and inferences may often be difficult to draw, but the guiding principle for this Court should be that when a question is in doubt and demeanor and credibility of witnesses, or contemporaneous understandings of the parties, have a part to play in its resolution, this Court should be extremely slow to upset a state court's inferential findings. The impetus for our exercising *de novo* review of the facts comes from the attitude that unless this Court can fully redetermine the facts of each case for itself, it will be unable to afford complete protection for constitutional rights. But when the 'feel' of the trial may have been a proper element in resolving an issue which is unclear on the record, our independent judgment should give way to the greater capability of the state trial court in determining whether a constitutional right has been infringed. Proper regard for the duality of the American judicial system demands no less." [3]

Should state court findings of historical fact based on credibility determinations be treated differently than findings based on inferences derived from physical or documentary evidence? Compare Anderson v. City of Bessemer City, 470 U.S. 564 (1985), involving review of a federal court, and holding that, although Rule 52(a)'s "clearly erroneous" standard applies to both, it "demands even greater deference to the trial court's findings" where credibility determinations are involved (p. 575). See also Resnik, *Tiers*, 57 So.Cal.L.Rev. 837, 998–1005 (1984).

(6) The Court's approach in Cox, in the face of sharp disputes about the basic historical facts,[4] obviously manifests a far more independent approach to the question of what happened than is described by the traditional view. (In fact the Court's opinion in Cox, far from exhibiting deference, does not even refer to any state-court findings, either with respect to whether there was a breach of the peace, or whether the police chief had given permission to demonstrate.)

Is the departure from the traditional approach justified? [5]

The news film of the events seems to have played a significant role in the Court's review of the breach-of-the-peace conviction in Cox. Was this

---

3. Note that Justice Harlan's formulation, if read with precision (and particularly in light of his second paragraph), does not contradict the central assumption of the traditional approach, that findings must have some support in the evidence: that premise is by hypothesis met in cases in which there is a "conflict in testimony." But *cf.* Norris v. Alabama, *supra*.

4. Compare, *e.g.*, the sequence of events described in the Court's opinion with that set forth by the state supreme court in reviewing the breach-of-peace conviction (156 So.2d at 452): "There were silent prayers and a display of signs"; "Cox *then* made a speech"; "the crowd *then* sang songs, answered by the prisoners in the jailhouse, and this *in turn* evoked loud and frenzied outbursts and 'wild yells' from the demonstrators"; "*[w]hereupon* 'grumbling'

was heard among the white people"; "*[a]t this time*, the prisoners in jail were 'hollering'" (italics added). *Cf.* also footnote 7 of Justice Goldberg's opinion.

Compare also Justice Clark's statement of the facts with that in the majority opinion.

5. For another example of an aggressive approach by the Court to redetermining issues of basic fact, see Moore v. Michigan, 355 U.S. 155 (1957) in which the majority relied heavily on evidence (corroborating petitioner's story about how he came to waive his right to counsel) that the trial judge had found "insignificant", and apparently squarely overruled the trial judge on his assessment of petitioner's own credibility. See also N.A.A.C.P. v. Claiborne Hardware Co., 458 U.S. 886 (1982).

appropriate? Though a movie may convey a great sense of verisimilitude, its import and credibility inevitably depend upon the perspective and choices of the photographer and editor. Does the fact that the film was offered in evidence by the prosecution justify the Court's reliance upon it?

In the obstructing-public-passages case, the ground of the Court's decision made material the question of what kind of street assemblies and parades were permitted by the Baton Rouge police. Did the differences between the opinion of the Court and Justice White's dissent on this point relate to the applicable law or to the facts? Should the Court have determined the issue as it did on the record before it?

Suppose Cox had been tried to a jury which was impeccably charged with respect to what findings must be made if the defendants' conduct is to be deemed punishable under the Constitution. Should—and would—the Court have reversed a resulting conviction on the ground that the evidence did not provide fair support for the conclusion that the defendants' conduct was not constitutionally immune?

And again: should the Court's role with respect to a case like Cox be different than in a case coming to it from a lower federal court? *Cf.* Hill, *The Adequate State Ground,* 65 Colum.L.Rev. 943, 946–47 n. 18 (1965).

(7) When factual issues are unclear on the record and involve demeanor and credibility of witnesses or other elements that may depend on the "feel" of the trial, Justice Harlan suggested in Beck v. Ohio, *supra,* that "[f]ederal habeas corpus, which allows a federal court in appropriate circumstances to develop a fresh record * * * provides a far more satisfactory vehicle [than Supreme Court review] for resolving such unclear issues, for the judge can evaluate for himself the on-the-spot considerations which no appellate court can estimate with assurance on a cold record" (p. 101). See further 28 U.S.C. § 2254(d), and the *Note on Relitigating the Facts on Habeas Corpus,* p. 1561, *infra.*

Federal habeas corpus is generally available to try constitutional contentions in state criminal cases. It is virtually never available in civil cases. See, further, Chaps. XI, XII, *infra.* If one reaches the conclusion that federal interests are seriously jeopardized by state-court factfinding processes, would a federal trial forum in the first instance, either by original federal question jurisdiction or removal, be more satisfactory than an expanded scope of appellate review?

C. Techniques for Controlling the Factfinding and Law-Applying Functions

(8) Where the Court has misgivings in a given case about the integrity and adequacy of the state court's factfindings relevant to a federal claim, it may (as in Cox) redetermine the facts on the basis of its own conclusions drawn from the record; of course it may (or must) also draw its own conclusions with respect to the (federal) legal significance of these facts.

Suppose the Court, however, comes to feel that the problem is broader and does not simply infect the case at hand? What if the Court comes to the conclusion that there is a significant danger of systemic erosion of a certain sort of federal claim, because the state courts (and perhaps even the lower federal courts) are resisting (or misunderstanding) the relevant claim? Must the Court review more and more specific cases to control the factfinding and law-applying functions in such an area?

(9) In the period 1940–1965, the Court reviewed—and usually reversed—a large number of state court holdings admitting into evidence confessions alleged to be coerced. The Court's decisions were typically heavily fact-bound, detailing the particular circumstances and concluding that the specific confession was coerced; the opinions failed to develop or articulate any new constitutional standards for determining admissibility. (Indeed, the Court typically was unable to isolate with precision just what was the "error" below.) The Court itself was severely split in most of these cases. See, *e.g.,* Chambers v. Florida, 309 U.S. 227 (1940); Ashcraft v. Tennessee, 322 U.S. 143 (1944); Lyons v. Oklahoma, 322 U.S. 596 (1944); Haley v. Ohio, 332 U.S. 596 (1948); Watts v. Indiana, 338 U.S. 49 (1949); Haynes v. Washington, 373 U.S. 503 (1963).

In Miranda v. Arizona, 384 U.S. 436 (1966), a narrow majority of the Court announced a new set of rules that would in most cases eliminate the necessity of reviewing the "voluntariness" of confessions introduced in trials thereafter. Miranda held that, in the absence of other equivalent safeguards against compulsory self-incrimination, a prisoner must be warned that he has the right to remain silent, that anything he says can be used against him, that he has the right to the presence of an attorney, and that if he cannot afford one, an attorney would be appointed for him; if these procedures were not observed, a confession given in response to "custodial interrogation" would be inadmissible in a criminal prosecution.

Compare the evolution of the due process right to counsel from Powell v. Alabama, 287 U.S. 45 (1932) and Betts v. Brady, 316 U.S. 455 (1942) (counsel must be appointed when circumstances make such assistance fundamental to fair trial) to Gideon v. Wainwright, 372 U.S. 335 (1963) and Scott v. Illinois, 440 U.S. 367 (1979) (counsel required in any case resulting in imprisonment). See Wechsler, The Nationalization of Civil Liberties and Civil Rights 18–19 (1969): "[T]here can be no doubt but that the administration of a standard of due process calling for the closest scrutiny of records to appraise essential fairness has proved to be increasingly intractable and burdensome, and to exert too little impact on the grave abuse in our practice so frequently revealed by the cases in the Court. The pressure to decree more rigid rules more easily applied has grown accordingly apace."

(10) Miranda and Gideon are examples of changes in substantive law, designed to protect federal rights against erosion by adoption of per se rules that minimize the need for case-by-case consideration of all the various specific circumstances relevant to a more open-ended standard.

Can the Court accomplish some of the same results by making changes in those federal legal rules that are avowedly directed to the fact-finding process: rules of evidence governing matters such as burden of proof, presumptions, and scope of review?

Consider, in this connection, Norris v. Alabama. Is Norris merely a fact-bound review of a single set of circumstances? Or should it be seen as creating a new legal rule, in the form of a rebuttable presumption ("prima facie case") of unconstitutional discrimination when the statistical evidence shows disparities that have not been otherwise explained? Is this not, then, an example of "protecting" federal claims of right against erosion in the fact-finding process by surrounding them with the protective shield of special rules with respect to burdens of proof and standards of evidence? For other examples, see New York Times v. Sullivan, 376 U.S. 254 (1964), holding that the evidence of "actual malice" required by the Constitution to support certain libel actions must be shown with "convincing clarity" (pp. 285–86), and Bose Corp. v. Consumer Union, 466 U.S. 485 (1984), holding that, with respect to such a finding of actual malice, appellate review must include an "independent judgment" by an appellate court. See further pp. 671–72, *infra.*

In considering the materials in this Note, reflect on the question whether the Court has been sufficiently inventive in its use of such evidentiary rules in dealing with its problems in supervising the processes of fact-finding and law application in the state courts.

D. The Problem of Ad Hoc Review

(11) What can and should the Court do when the above-discussed techniques are unavailable—when the Court has mustered all of the relevant general rules and standards it is able or minded to develop (including any relevant new per se rules and evidentiary norms) and yet lacks confidence that the state courts (or the lower federal courts) are applying these standards "correctly"? The most vivid example of this problem of judicial administration comes from the intractable field of obscenity.

(12) The general constitutional standards for what materials may be suppressed as "obscene" under the First Amendment have been defined in a small number of well-known cases, starting with Roth v. United States, 354 U.S. 476 (1957); refined in Memoirs v. Massachusetts, 383 U.S. 413 (1966) (plurality opinion) (all three Roth factors—dominant appeal to prurient interest, patent offensiveness, and utter lack of redeeming social value—must coalesce to justify suppression); Ginzburg v. United States, 383 U.S. 463 (1966) (intent to pander relevant to whether materials are obscene); and Ginsberg v. New York, 390 U.S. 629 (1968) ("variable obscenity" standard for juveniles). The general standard was then substantially modified in Miller v. California, 413 U.S. 15 (1973) (see paragraph (c), *infra*).[6] The governing standards are notoriously vague and open-ended. The question that has bedeviled the Court is whether it must or should review individual applications of these standards.

(a) In Jacobellis v. Ohio, 378 U.S. 184 (1964) (involving Louis Malle's important film, *Les Amants*), the Court reversed a conviction for possessing and exhibiting an obscene film. There was no opinion of the Court. The Court split sharply on the content of the constitutional standard for punishable "obscenity", and even more so on the issue of whether the Court should make its own determination of whether a particular film is "obscene". Justice Brennan, joined by Justice Goldberg in the first plurality opinion, noted (pp. 188–96):

" * * * Since it is only 'obscenity' that is excluded from the constitutional protection, the question whether a particular work is obscene

---

6. For further, later, refinements, see also, *e.g.,* Jenkins v. Georgia, 418 U.S. 153, 157 (1974); Pinkus v. United States, 436 U.S. 293 (1978); New York v. Ferber, 458 U.S. 747 (1982); Brockett v. Spokane Arcades, Inc., 472 U.S. 491 (1985); Pope v. Illinois, 107 S.Ct. 1918 (1987).

necessarily implicates an issue of constitutional law. See Roth v. United States, *supra*, 354 U.S. [476,] 497–498 (separate opinion). Such an issue, we think, must ultimately be decided by this Court. Our duty admits of no 'substitute for facing up to the tough individual problems of constitutional judgment involved in every obscenity case.' *Id.*, at 498 * * *. [W]e reaffirm the principle that, in 'obscenity' cases as in all others involving rights derived from the First Amendment guarantees of free expression, this Court cannot avoid making an independent constitutional judgment on the facts of the case as to whether the material involved is constitutionally protected.

"The question of the proper standard for making this determination has been the subject of much discussion and controversy since our decision in Roth seven years ago. Recognizing that the test for obscenity enunciated there—'whether to the average person, applying contemporary community standards, the dominant theme of the material taken as a whole appeals to prurient interest,' 354 U.S., at 489—is not perfect, we think any substitute would raise equally difficult problems, and we therefore adhere to that standard * * *.

"It has been suggested that the 'contemporary community standards' aspect of the Roth test implies a determination of the constitutional question of obscenity in each case by the standards of the particular local community from which the case arises. * * * We do not see how any 'local' definition of the 'community' could properly be employed in delineating the area of expression that is protected by the Federal Constitution. * * * It is, after all, a national Constitution we are expounding.

" * * * We have viewed the film, in light of the record made in the trial court, and we conclude that it is not obscene within the standards enunciated in Roth * * *."

Justice Black, joined by Justice Douglas, in a concurring opinion maintained the position that the First Amendment permits all films to be shown, reiterating that "If despite the Constitution * * * this Nation is to embark on the dangerous road of censorship * * * this Court is about the most inappropriate Supreme Board of Censors that could be found" (p. 196).

Justice Stewart concurred on the basis of a standard of obscenity limited to "hard-core pornography." Attempting no further definition, he nevertheless felt that "I know it when I see it, and the motion picture involved in this case is not that" (p. 197). Justice White concurred without opinion.

Chief Justice Warren, joined in dissent by Justice Clark, had a different view of the Supreme Court's role: "This Court hears cases such as the instant one not merely to rule upon the alleged obscenity of a specific film or book but to establish principles for the guidance of lower courts and legislatures. Yet most of our decisions since Roth have been given without opinion and have thus failed to furnish such guidance. Nor does the Court in the instant case—which has now been twice argued before us—shed any greater light on the problem. * * *

"For all the sound and fury that the Roth test has generated, it has not been proved unsound, and I believe that we should try to live with it—at least until a more satisfactory definition is evolved. * * * It is my belief that when the Court said in Roth that obscenity is to be defined by reference to 'community standards,' it meant community standards—not a national standard, as is sometimes argued. I believe that there is no provable 'national standard' and perhaps there should be none. At all events, this Court has not been able to enunciate one, and it would be unreasonable to expect local courts to divine one. * * *

" * * * I would commit the enforcement of this [Roth] rule to the appropriate state and federal courts, and I would accept their judgments made pursuant to the Roth rule, limiting myself to a consideration only of whether there is sufficient evidence in the record upon which a finding of obscenity could be made. * * * [O]nce a finding of obscenity has been made below under a proper application of the Roth test, I would apply a 'sufficient evidence' standard of review—requiring something more than merely any evidence but something less than 'substantial evidence on the record [including the allegedly obscene material] as a whole.' * * * This is the only reasonable way I can see to obviate the necessity of this Court's sitting as the Super Censor of all the obscenity purveyed throughout the Nation" (pp. 200–03).

Justice Harlan filed a separate dissent: "The application of any general constitutional tests must thus necessarily be pricked out on a case-by-case basis, but as a point of departure I would apply to the Federal Government the Roth standards. * * * As to the States, I would make the federal test one of rationality. I would not prohibit them from banning any material which, taken as a whole, has been reasonably found in state judicial proceedings to treat with sex in a fundamentally offensive manner, under rationally established criteria for judging such material. On this basis, having viewed the motion picture in question, I think the state acted within permissible limits in condemning the film" (pp. 203–04).

(b) In Redrup v. New York, 386 U.S. 767 (1967), see p. 1850, *infra*, the Court returned to the matter but again failed to achieve a consensus on developing further general standards for obscenity. The decision, rendered per curiam, noted that the case did *not* involve pandering or juveniles, but "can and should be decided upon a common and controlling fundamental constitutional basis * * *. We have concluded, in short, that the distribution of the publications in each of these cases is protected by the First and Fourteenth Amendments from governmental suppression, whether criminal or civil, *in personam* or *in rem* " (p. 770). After reviewing the differing approaches the members of the Court took to review of obscenity cases, the opinion simply stated that "[w]hichever of these constitutional views is brought to bear upon the cases before us, it is clear that the judgments cannot stand" (p. 771).

In addition, between 1966 and 1973 (when Miller substantially modified the Roth standard), the Court summarily reviewed a substantial number of obscenity cases and disposed of them per curiam, most often simply reversing with a citation to Redrup. See, *e.g.*, the cases cited in Justice Harlan's concurrence in Ginsberg, *supra*, 390 U.S. at 707 n. 11; Cain v. Kentucky, 397 U.S. 319 (1970); Walker v. Ohio, 398 U.S. 434 (1970); Hoyt v. Minnesota, 399 U.S. 524 (1970); Childs v. Oregon, 401 U.S. 1006 (1971); Bloss v. Michigan, 402 U.S. 938 (1971). The per curiams do not identify or describe the film or written material being passed upon.

(c) In Miller itself, Chief Justice Burger said: "In resolving the inevitably sensitive questions of fact and law, we must continue to rely on the jury system, accompanied by the safeguards that judges, rules of evidence, presumption of innocence, and other protective features provide * * *" (p. 26). And a footnote appended to this sentence continued: "The mere fact juries may reach different conclusions as to the same material does not mean that constitutional rights are abridged" (p. 26 n. 9). But Justice Brennan, dissenting (also on behalf of Justices Stewart and Marshall), argued that statutes seeking to prohibit distribution of obscene material to adults should be held unconstitutionally vague and overbroad, *inter alia* on account of the unpredictability, ineffectiveness, and inordinate burdens stemming from reliance upon case-by-case Supreme Court review for protection of First Amendment rights. He contended that independent factual review would continue to be necessary under the Court's new standard.

(d) Justice Brennan's prediction appeared to be borne out when the Court, in the year after Miller, reviewed and reversed a state conviction for showing Mike Nichols' movie "Carnal Knowledge." Jenkins v. Georgia, 418 U.S. 153 (1974). Justice Rehnquist wrote for the majority: "Our own viewing of the film satisfies us that 'Carnal Knowledge' could not be found under the Miller standards to depict sexual conduct in a patently offensive way. * * * While the subject matter of the picture is, in a broader sense, sex, and there are scenes in which sexual conduct including 'ultimate sexual acts' is to be understood to be taking place, the camera does not focus on the bodies of the actors at such times. There is no exhibition whatever of the actors' genitals, lewd or otherwise, during these scenes. There are occasional scenes of nudity, but nudity alone is not enough to make material legally obscene under the Miller standards" (p. 161). Justice Brennan wrote: "Today's decision confirms my observation in Paris Adult Theatre I v. Slaton, 413 U.S. 49 (1973) [the opinion that incorporated Justice Brennan's dissent in Miller], that the Court's new [Miller] formulation does not extricate us from the mire of case-by-case determination of obscenity. * * * After the Court's decision today, there can be no doubt that Miller requires appellate courts—including this Court—to review independently the constitutional fact of obscenity. * * * In order to make the review mandated by Miller, the Court was required to screen the film "Carnal Knowledge" and make an independent determination of obscenity *vel non*. * * * Thus it is clear that as long as the Miller test remains in effect 'one cannot say with certainty that material is obscene until at least five members of this Court, applying inevitably obscure standards, have pronounced it so' [quoting Slaton]" (pp. 162–65).

Since Jenkins the Court has, however, tended simply to decline *ad hoc* review of obscenity cases by denying certiorari or (less frequently) dismissing appeals for want of a substantial federal question. See, *e.g.*, Pendleton v. California, 423 U.S. 1068 (1976) (appeal dismissed; dissent by Justice Brennan complains that Court is not discharging its responsibility to review facts independently).

(13) Is there a satisfactory solution to the sort of dilemma presented to the Court by the obscenity cases? If the Court is unable to define a federal constitutional standard—particularly in connection with the First Amendment—with sufficient precision to permit reliable law application by lower courts and juries, is the answer to review a large number of cases and dispose of them per curiam? Do these summary dispositions help to delineate and strengthen the constitutional standard? If not, do they represent a wise use of the Court's limited time?

Why in principle is the Court the "best" decider for these issues? Are juries especially suspect in this area?[7] What about state courts? Should obscenity cases involving First Amendment claims be made removable to federal court?

Note that there are limits on the Court's power to protect itself against having to review obscenity cases by denying certiorari: many of these cases can, if carefully pleaded, be turned into appeals, so that even summary dispositions import a judgment "on the merits." See further Section 4 of this Chapter, p. 711, *infra*.

(14) Problems analogous to the obscenity question have arisen in connection with the "actual malice" standard of New York Times v. Sullivan, 376 U.S. 254 (1976), in which the Court conducted an extensive independent review of the facts and determined for itself that the evidence could not support a libel judgment consistent with the Constitution. See, further, Time, Inc. v. Pape, 401 U.S. 279 (1971), involving another extensive review of "the specific facts of this case" to determine whether there was a permissible jury issue under the Constitution. Justice Harlan, dissenting in Pape, said (p. 294):

"While it is true, of course, that this Court is free to re-examine for itself the evidentiary bases upon which rest decisions that allegedly impair or punish the exercise of Fourteenth Amendment freedoms, this does not mean that we are of necessity always, or even usually, compelled to do so. Indeed, it is almost impossible to conceive how this Court might continue to function effectively were we to resolve afresh the underlying factual disputes in all cases containing constitutional issues. Nor can I discern in those First Amendment considerations that led us to restrict the States' powers to regulate defamation of public officials any additional interest that is not served by the actual malice rule of New York Times, but is substantially promoted by utilizing this Court as the ultimate arbiter of factual disputes in those libel cases where no unusual factors, such as allegations of harassment or the existence of a jury verdict resting on erroneous instructions, cf. New York Times, are present. While I am confident that the Court does not intend its decision to have any such broad reach, I fear that what is done today may open a door that will prove difficult to close.

"Having determined that the court below properly defined the quality of proof required of Pape by New York Times and that it applied the correct standard of review in passing upon the trial judge's decision to grant a directed verdict—determinations that I do not think my Brethren dispute—I would stop the inquiry at this point and affirm the judgment of the Court of Appeals."[8]

7. For an argument that the evolution of the First Amendment from a guarantee of majority criticism of unrepresentative government to a guarantee protecting unpopular speech against majority standards requires a "reevaluation of the assumption that the jury is a reliable factfinder in free speech cases," see Monaghan, *First Amendment "Due Process"*, 83 Harv.L.Rev. 518, 527–29 (1970).

8. In Rosenbloom v. Metromedia, Inc., 403 U.S. 29 (1971), two dissents argued for a change in one aspect of the relevant constitutional standard, in part to avoid case-by-case review and "constitutionalizing the fact-finding process." Gertz v. Robert Welch, Inc., 418 U.S. 323 (1974) adopted in part the rule proposed by the dissenters in Rosenbloom: "We must lay down broad rules of general application"; to scrutinize the competing interests in every libel case "would lead to unpredictable results and uncertain expectations, and * * * could

In Bose Corp. v. Consumers Union, 466 U.S. 485 (1984), the Court emphatically reaffirmed the necessity for independent judicial redetermination of the central New York Times factor of "actual malice." Bose came to the Court from the lower federal courts, and involved an action for "product disparagement." The Court held that, in reviewing a trial judge's finding that the defendant acted with "actual malice," the courts of appeals are not limited by Federal Rule of Civil Procedure 52(a)'s "clearly erroneous" standard, but "must exercise independent judgment and determine whether the record establishes actual malice with convincing clarity" (p. 514). "[T]he rule of independent review assigns to judges a constitutional responsibility that cannot be delegated to the trier of fact, whether the factfinding function be performed in the particular case by a jury or by a trial judge" (p. 501). "When the standard governing the decision of a particular case is provided by the Constitution, this Court's role in marking out the limits of the standard through the process of case-by-case adjudication is of special importance. This process has been vitally important in cases involving restrictions on the freedom of speech protected by the First Amendment, particularly in those cases in which it is contended that the communication in issue is within one of the few classes of 'unprotected speech' " (p. 503) (citing, inter alia, the obscenity cases). "The requirement of independent appellate review * * * reflects a deeply held conviction that judges—and particularly Members of this Court—must exercise such review in order to preserve the precious liberties established and ordained by the Constitution" (pp. 510–11).

Note that the actual rule of decision in Bose does not specify any special role for the Supreme Court as such; it imposes a duty on appellate judges (presumably state as well as federal) reviewing the findings of the factfinder. It is thus not formally inconsistent with the approach of Justice Harlan in Time Inc. v. Pape. But the rhetoric of the opinion stands in sharp contrast with the spirit of the Harlan approach.

Further: Bose itself involved a federal bench trial with express findings of fact, including an explicit statement by the trial judge that he did not believe a particular witness. But how should the Bose requirement operate in the face of a general jury verdict in a libel case where there are credibility and demeanor issues? Is it possible for an appellate court to engage in independent review of the facts while not disturbing these credibility and demeanor findings? In this context is the traditional approach—that appellate courts should defer to the finder, presumably by assuming that the jury discredited witnesses for the verdict-loser—consistent with Bose's requirement of independent review of historical facts?

For an excellent discussion of Bose, and of the problems canvassed in this Note, see Monaghan, *Constitutional Fact Review*, 85 Colum.L.Rev. 229 (1985).

(15) The command of the Seventh Amendment that "no fact tried by a jury, shall be otherwise reexamined in any Court of the United States, than according to the rules of the common law," is applicable to Supreme Court review of state courts. See Chicago, B. & Q. R. R. v. Chicago, 166 U.S. 226, 242–43 (1897). Is the scope of review exercised by the Supreme Court in First Amendment cases, and specifically in civil (private) libel actions,

render our duty to supervise the lower
courts unmanageable" (pp 343–44).

consistent with that Amendment? See Henderson, *The Background of the Seventh Amendment,* 80 Harv.L.Rev. 289 (1966).

THOMPSON v. LOUISVILLE

362 U.S. 199, 80 S.Ct. 624, 4 L.Ed.2d 654 (1960).
Certiorari to the Police Court of Louisville, Kentucky.

MR. JUSTICE BLACK delivered the opinion of the Court.

Petitioner was found guilty in the Police Court of Louisville, Kentucky, of two offenses—loitering and disorderly conduct. The ultimate question presented to us is whether the charges against petitioner were so totally devoid of evidentiary support as to render his conviction unconstitutional under the Due Process Clause of the Fourteenth Amendment. Decision of this question turns not on the sufficiency of the evidence, but on whether this conviction rests upon any evidence at all.

The facts as shown by the record are short and simple. Petitioner, a long-time resident of the Louisville area, went into the Liberty End Cafe about 6:20 on Saturday evening, January 24, 1959. In addition to selling food the cafe was licensed to sell beer to the public and some 12 to 30 patrons were present during the time petitioner was there. When petitioner had been in the cafe about half an hour, two Louisville police officers came in on a "routine check." Upon seeing petitioner "out there on the floor dancing by himself," one of the officers, according to his testimony, went up to the manager who was sitting on a stool nearby and asked him how long petitioner had been in there and if he had bought anything. The officer testified that upon being told by the manager that petitioner had been there "a little over a half-hour and that he had not bought anything," he accosted Thompson and "asked him what was his reason for being in there and he said he was waiting on a bus." The officer then informed petitioner that he was under arrest and took him outside. This was the arrest for loitering. After going outside, the officer testified, petitioner "was very argumentative—he argued with us back and forth and so then we placed a disorderly conduct charge on him." Admittedly the disorderly conduct conviction rests solely on this one sentence description of petitioner's conduct after he left the cafe.

The foregoing evidence includes all that the city offered against him, except a record purportedly showing a total of 54 previous arrests of petitioner. Before putting on his defense, petitioner moved for a dismissal of the charges against him on the ground that a judgment of conviction on this record would deprive him of property and liberty without due process of law under the Fourteenth Amendment in that (1) there was no evidence to support findings of guilt and (2) the two arrests and prosecutions were reprisals against him because petitioner had employed counsel and demanded a judicial hearing to defend himself against prior and allegedly baseless charges by the police. This motion was denied.

Petitioner then put in evidence on his own behalf, none of which in any way strengthened the city's case. He testified that he bought, and one of the cafe employees served him, a dish of macaroni and a glass of beer and that he remained in the cafe awaiting for a bus to go home.[3] Further evidence showed without dispute that at the time of his arrest petitioner gave the officers his home address; that he had money with him, and a bus schedule showing that a bus to his home would stop within half a block of the cafe at about 7:30; that he owned two unimproved lots of land; that in addition to work he had done for others, he had regularly worked one day or more a week for the same family for 30 years; that he paid no rent in the home where he lived and that his meager income was sufficient to meet his needs. The cafe manager testified that petitioner had frequently patronized the cafe, and that he had never told petitioner that he was unwelcome there. The manager further testified that on this very occasion he saw petitioner "standing there in the middle of the floor and patting his foot," and that he did not at any time during petitioner's stay there object to anything he was doing. There is no evidence that anyone else in the cafe objected to petitioner's shuffling his feet in rhythm with the music of the jukebox or that his conduct was boisterous or offensive to anyone present. At the close of his evidence, petitioner repeated his motion for dismissal of the charges on the ground that a conviction on the foregoing evidence would deprive him of liberty and property without due process under the Fourteenth Amendment. The court denied the motion, convicted him of both offenses, and fined him $10 on each charge. A motion for new trial, on the same grounds, also was denied, which exhausted petitioner's remedies in the police court.

Since police court fines of less than $20 on a single charge are not appealable or otherwise reviewable in any other Kentucky court, petitioner asked the police court to stay the judgments so that he might have an opportunity to apply for certiorari to this Court (before his case became moot)[5] to review the due process contentions he raised. The police court suspended judgment for 24 hours during which time petitioner sought a longer stay from the Kentucky Circuit Court. That court, after examining the police court's judgments and transcript, granted a stay concluding that "there appears to be merit" in the contention that "there is no evidence upon which conviction and sentence by the Police Court could be based" and that petitioner's "Federal Constitutional claims are substantial and not frivolous." On appeal by the city, the Kentucky Court of Appeals held that the Circuit Court lacked the power to grant the stay it did, but nevertheless went on to take the extraordinary step of granting its own stay, even though petitioner had made no original application to that court for such a stay. Explaining its reason, the Court of Appeals took occasion to agree with the Circuit Court that petitioner's "federal constitutional claims are substantial and not frivolous." The Court of Appeals then went on to say that petitioner "appears to have a real question as to whether he has been denied due process under the Fourteenth Amendment of the Federal Constitution, yet this substantive right cannot be tested unless we grant

---

3. The officer's previous testimony that petitioner had bought no food or drink is seriously undermined, if not contradicted, by the manager's testimony at trial. There the manager stated that the officer "asked me *I had* [sic] sold him any thing to eat and I said no and he said any beer and I said no ● ● ●." (Emphasis supplied.) And the manager acknowledged that petitioner might have bought something and

been served by a waiter or waitress without the manager noticing it. Whether there was a purchase or not, however, is of no significance to the issue here.

5. Without a stay and bail pending application for review petitioner would have served out his fines in prison in 10 days at the rate of $2 a day. Taustine v. Thompson, 322 S.W.2d 100 (Ky.1959).

him a stay of execution because his fines are not appealable and will be satisfied by being served in jail before he can prepare and file his petition for certiorari. Appellee's substantive right of due process is of no avail to him unless this court grants him the ancillary right whereby he may test same in the Supreme Court."

Our examination of the record presented in the petition for certiorari convinced us that although the fines here are small, the due process questions presented are substantial and we therefore granted certiorari to review the police court's judgments. 360 U.S. 916. Compare Yick Wo v. Hopkins, 118 U.S. 356 (San Francisco Police Judges Court judgment imposing a $10 fine, upheld by state appellate court, held invalid as in contravention of the Fourteenth Amendment).

The city correctly assumes here if there is no support for these convictions in the record they are void as denials of due process.[10] The pertinent portion of the city ordinance under which petitioner was convicted of loitering reads as follows:

"It shall be unlawful for any person * * *, without visible means of support, or who cannot give a satisfactory account of himself, * * * to sleep, lie, loaf, or trespass in or about any premises, building, or other structure in the City of Louisville, without first having obtained the consent of the owner or controller of said premises, structure, or building; * * *."

In addition to the fact that petitioner proved he had "visible means of support," the prosecutor at trial said "This is a loitering charge here. There is no charge of no visible means of support." Moreover, there is no suggestion that petitioner was sleeping, lying or trespassing in or about this cafe. Accordingly he could only have been convicted for being unable to give a satisfactory account of himself while loitering in the cafe, without the consent of the manager. Under the words of the ordinance itself, if the evidence fails to prove all three elements of this loitering charge, the conviction is not supported by evidence, in which event it does not comport with due process of law. The record is entirely lacking in evidence to support any of the charges.

Here, petitioner spent about half an hour on a Saturday evening in January in a public cafe which sold food and beer to the public. When asked to account for his presence there, he said he was waiting for a bus. The city concedes that there is no law making it an offense for a person in such a cafe to "dance," "shuffle" or "pat" his feet in time to music. The undisputed testimony of the manager, who did not know whether petitioner had bought macaroni and beer or not but who did see the patting, shuffling or dancing, was that petitioner was welcome there. The manager testified that he did not at any time during petitioner's stay in the cafe object to anything petitioner was doing and that he never saw petitioner do anything that would cause any objection. Surely this is implied consent, which the city admitted in oral argument satisfies the ordinance. The arresting officer admitted that there was nothing in any way "vulgar" about what he called petitioner's "ordinary dance," whatever relevance, if any, vulgarity

10. For illustration, the city's brief in this Court states that the questions presented are "1. Whether the evidence was sufficient to support the convictions, and therefore meets the requirements of the due process clause of the Fourteenth Amendment. * * *"

might have to a charge of loitering. There simply is no semblance of evidence from which any person could reasonably infer that petitioner could not give a satisfactory account of himself or that he was loitering or loafing there (in the ordinary sense of the words) without "the consent of the owner or controller" of the cafe.

Petitioner's conviction for disorderly conduct was under § 85–8 of the city ordinance which, without definition, provides that "[w]hoever shall be found guilty of disorderly conduct in the City of Louisville shall be fined * * *." etc. The only evidence of "disorderly conduct" was the single statement of the policeman that after petitioner was arrested and taken out of the cafe he was very argumentative. There is no testimony that petitioner raised his voice, used offensive language, resisted the officers or engaged in any conduct of any kind likely in any way to adversely affect the good order and tranquillity of the City of Louisville. The only information the record contains on what the petitioner was "argumentative" about is his statement that he asked the officers "what they arrested me for." We assume, for we are justified in assuming, that merely "arguing" with a policeman is not, because it could not be, "disorderly conduct" as a matter of the substantive law of Kentucky. See Lanzetta v. New Jersey, 306 U.S. 451. Moreover, Kentucky law itself seems to provide that if a man wrongfully arrested fails to object to the arresting officer, he waives any right to complain later that the arrest was unlawful. Nickell v. Commonwealth, 285 S.W.2d 495, 496.

Thus we find no evidence whatever in the record to support these convictions. Just as "Conviction upon a charge not made would be sheer denial of due process," [12] so is it a violation of due process to convict and punish a man without evidence of his guilt.[13]

The judgments are reversed and the cause is remanded to the Police Court of the City of Louisville for proceedings not inconsistent with this opinion.

Reversed and remanded.

NOTE ON REVIEW FOR "ANY" EVIDENCE AND OTHER CONTROLS ON ARBITRARINESS

(1) Garner v. Louisiana, 368 U.S. 157 (1961), dealt with three "sit-in" cases. The facts in the three cases followed a pattern: a group of black students entered a segregated lunch counter and in an orderly and quiet manner, awaited service. In each case there was a denial of service or a request to leave, followed by the arrest of the demonstrators. The students were convicted of violating the Louisiana disturbing the peace statute. On appeal, the Louisiana Supreme Court denied relief, with an oral unreported opinion pointing out that it was without jurisdiction to review the facts but continuing, "The rulings of the district judge on matters of law are not erroneous."

12. De Jonge v. Oregon, 299 U.S. 353, 362. See also Cole v. Arkansas, 333 U.S. 196, 201.

13. See Schware v. Board of Bar Examiners, 353 U.S. 232; United States ex rel. Vajtauer v. Commissioner, 273 U.S. 103, 106; Moore v. Dempsey, 261 U.S. 86; Yick Wo v. Hopkins, 118 U.S. 356. Cf. Akins v. Texas, 325 U.S. 398, 402; Tot v. United States, 319 U.S. 463, 473 (concurring opinion); Mooney v. Holohan, 294 U.S. 103.

On certiorari in the United States Supreme Court, petitioners raised a number of constitutional objections to their convictions, including claimed denials of freedom of speech and equal protection; the Court chose to rest its reversal on the no-evidence doctrine. Chief Justice Warren, for the majority, began his analysis of the case by determining "the type of conduct proscribed by this statute and the elements of guilt which the evidence must prove to support a criminal conviction thereunder." Recognizing that "We of course are bound by a State's interpretation of its own statute," the Chief Justice looked to Louisiana authority. Relying heavily on a particular Louisiana Supreme Court case, he concluded that the statute was not intended to cover peaceful and orderly conduct, even if it might be offensive to others. Accepting that "the Louisiana courts have the final authority to interpret and, where they see fit, to reinterpret that State's legislation," the opinion saw "no indication that the Louisiana Supreme Court has changed" its interpretation in the previous case "and we will not infer that an inferior Louisiana court intended to overrule a long-standing and reasonable interpretation of a state statute by that State's highest court. * * * However, because this case comes to us from a state court and necessitates a delicate involvement in federal-state relations, we are willing to assume with the respondent that the Louisiana courts might construe the statute more broadly to encompass the traditional common-law concept of disturbing the peace. Thus construed, it might permit the police to prevent an imminent public commotion even though caused by peaceful and orderly conduct on the part of the accused." In any event, the Court held, "these records contain [1] no evidence to support a finding that petitioners disturbed the peace, either by outwardly boisterous conduct or by passive conduct likely to cause a public disturbance," and reversed the convictions as denials of due process (pp. 165–66, 169, 173–74).

Justices Frankfurter, Douglas, and Harlan each concurred separately in the judgment.[2] But Justice Harlan, with the support of Justice Douglas, specifically rejected the applicability of the Thompson "no evidence" doctrine. In his view, "the State Supreme Court's refusal to review these convictions, taken in light of its assertion that the 'rulings of the district judge on matters of law are not erroneous,' must be accepted as an authoritative and binding state determination that the petitioners' activities, as revealed in these records, did violate the statute * * *. More basically, established principles of constitutional adjudication require us to consider that the Louisiana Supreme Court's refusal to review these cases signifies a holding that the breach of the peace statute which controls these cases does embrace the conduct of the petitioners, peaceful though it was" (pp. 187–88).

(2) In Vachon v. New Hampshire, 414 U.S. 478 (1974), the Court summarily reversed, on the basis of the jurisdictional papers, an appeal from a conviction affirmed (with opinion) by the New Hampshire Supreme Court, on the ground that there was no evidence of one element of the

1. [Ed.] The majority also held that the lower court could not rely upon judicial notice to supply a finding of likelihood of public disturbance.

2. Justice Frankfurter differed principally on the construction of state law. Justice Douglas concluded that the conviction constituted "state action" and denied petitioners equal protection of the laws. Justice Harlan thought that the statute was unconstitutionally vague and that (in two of the cases) its application violated petitioners' freedom of expression.

crime. (This issue was apparently raised by the Court on its own initiative. See p. 601, *supra*.) The Court described the case as follows:

"A 14–year–old girl bought a button inscribed 'Copulation Not Masturbation' at the Head Shop in Manchester, New Hampshire. In consequence, appellant, operator of the shop, was sentenced to 30 days in jail and fined $100 after conviction upon a charge of 'wilfully' contributing to the delinquency of a minor in violation of New Hampshire's Rev.Stat.Ann. § 169:32 (Supp.1972). In affirming the conviction, the New Hampshire Supreme Court held that the 'wilfully' component of the offense required that the State prove that the accused acted ' "voluntarily and intentionally and not because of mistake or accident or other innocent reason." ' 113 N.H. 239, 242, 306 A.2d 781, 784 (1973). Thus, the State was required to produce evidence that appellant, knowing the girl to be a minor, personally sold her the button, or personally caused another to sell it to her. Appellant unsuccessfully sought dismissal of the charge at the close of the State's case on the ground that the State had produced no evidence to meet this requirement, and unsuccessfully urged the same ground as a reason for reversal in the State Supreme Court. We have reviewed the transcript of the trial on this issue, pursuant to Rule 40(1)(d)(2) of the Rules of this Court.

"Our independent examination of the trial record discloses that evidence is completely lacking that appellant personally sold the girl the button or even that he was aware of the sale or present in the store at the time. The girl was the State's only witness to the sale. She testified that she and a girl friend entered the store and looked around until they saw 'a velvet display card on a counter' from which they 'picked out [the] pin.' She went to some person in the store with the button 'cupped in [her] hand' and paid that person 25 cents for the button. She did not say that appellant was that person, or even that she saw him in the store. Rather, she testified that she could not identify who the person was. We therefore agree with Justice Grimes, dissenting, that 'there is no evidence whatever that the defendant sold the button, that he knew it had been sold to a minor, that he authorized such sales to minors or that he was even in the store at the time of the sale.' This fatal void in the State's case was not filled by appellant's concession at trial that he 'controlled the premises on July 26.' That concession was evidence at most that he operated the shop; it was in no way probative of the crucial element of the crime that he personally sold the minor the button or personally caused it to be sold to her.

"In these circumstances, the conviction must be reversed. 'It is beyond question, of course, that a conviction based on a record lacking any relevant evidence as to a crucial element of the offense charged * * * violate[s] due process.' Harris v. United States, 404 U.S. 1232, 1233 (1971) (Douglas, J., in chambers); Thompson v. Louisville, * * *" (pp. 479–80).

Justice Rehnquist's dissent, joined by Chief Justice Burger and Justice White, responded (pp. 484–87): "In Thompson [v. Louisville], the only state court proceedings reaching the merits of the case were in the Louisville Police Court from which there was no right of appeal to any higher state court, and there was therefore no state court opinion written which construed the statute under which Thompson was convicted. * * *.

"Here, however, the Supreme Court of New Hampshire construed the state statute defining contributing to the delinquency of a minor, and held that the evidence adduced at the trial was sufficient to support a finding on each element of that offense. While the Supreme Court of New Hampshire did say, as the Court indicates, that the State was required to prove that the accused acted ' "voluntarily and intentionally and not because of mistake or accident or other innocent reason," ' it said this in a context of several paragraphs of treatment of the elements of the offense. * * *

"The Court simply casts aside this authoritative construction of New Hampshire law, seizes one phrase out of context, and concludes that there was no evidence to establish that the appellant '[knew] the girl to be a minor, personally sold her the button, or personally caused another to sell it to her.' The word 'personally' is the contribution of this Court to the New Hampshire statute; it is not contained in the statute, and is not once used by the Supreme Court of New Hampshire in its opinion dealing with the facts of this very case. Indeed, the entire thrust of the opinion of the Supreme Court of New Hampshire is that appellant need not *personally,* have sold the button to the minor nor *personally* have authorized its sale to a minor in order to be guilty of the statutory offense. * * *.

"This may seem to us a somewhat broad construction of the language 'wilfully' or 'knowingly,' though our own cases make it clear that we are dealing with words which may be given a variety of meanings by their context: * * *.

"But since our authority to review state court convictions is limited to the vindication of claims of federal rights, we must take the meaning of the statute, and of the words 'wilfully' and 'knowingly' which it uses, as given to us by the Supreme Court of New Hampshire. I would have thought such a proposition well settled by our prior decisions * * *."

(3) The question of what acts are in fact prohibited by a state criminal statute is a question solely of state law: the answer is necessarily a function of interpreting that statute. Where a state supreme court has held that the evidence in a particular case supports a finding that that statute has been violated, why isn't its judgment conclusive? If the Supreme Court overrules that judgment, is it not necessarily overruling the state court's interpretation of state law? See Note, *No Evidence to Support a Conviction,* 110 U.Pa.L.Rev. 1137 (1962). Did the court in Thompson v. Louisville overlook the crucial question whether this state law issue was antecedent to the application of a proposition of federal law (see p. 532, *supra*)?

Are these problems solved by the notion that a judgment based on a finding of fact for which there is no supporting evidence is a denial of procedural due process?

Note, too, that these objections to the Thompson reasoning do not dispose of other possible constitutional objections to the conviction. The substantive argument that the state has no power to punish the conduct that the record reveals, as well as the argument that the state statute fails to provide adequate warning because it misdescribes what conduct is punishable (vagueness), remain open, as do other possible lines of argument (see further Paragraphs (5)–(7), *infra*).

Does the situation change where the state appellate courts have not reviewed at all (as in Thompson), or where there is no relevant state court opinion (as in Garner)? Most of the scattered cases relying on the Thompson "no evidence" rule have involved judgments without a state supreme court construction of the statute. See, *e.g.*, Barr v. Columbia, 378 U.S. 146 (1964); Shuttlesworth v. Birmingham, 382 U.S. 87 (1965); Johnson v. Florida, 391 U.S. 596 (1968) (state supreme court considered constitutionality of statute only). The danger of an arbitrary singling-out of a defendant is especially acute in such circumstances. But in Vachon there was an explicit state court opinion on the issue: the case thus obviously breaks new ground in exposing state law to Supreme Court reexamination.

(4) Can the Thompson rule be restricted to cases of "*no*" evidence? Was there "*no*" evidence in Thompson? See Stewart, J., dissenting from denial of certiorari in Freeman v. Zahradnick, 429 U.S. 1111 (1977).

(5) Compare with the above cases the approach adopted in Cole v. Arkansas, 333 U.S. 196 (1948), referred to in both Thompson and Garner. Defendants were convicted on a charge of violating § 2 of a 1943 statute declaring it "unlawful for any person acting in concert with one or more other persons, to assemble at or near any place where a 'labor dispute' exists and by force or violence prevent * * * any person from engaging in any lawful vocation, or for any person acting * * * in concert with one or more other persons, to promote, encourage or aid any such unlawful assemblage." The conviction was affirmed under § 1 of the same statute which made it a crime "for any person by the use of force or violence, or the threat of the use of force or violence, to prevent or attempt to prevent any person from engaging in any lawful vocation within this State." Federal constitutional challenges to § 2 were not considered on appeal. The Supreme Court reversed. "To conform to due process of law, petitioners were entitled to have the validity of their convictions appraised on consideration of the case as it was tried and as the issues were determined in the trial court" (p. 202). See also Cole v. Arkansas, 338 U.S. 345, 347–52 (1949).

Does Cole's rationale help to explain Thompson and Garner? If the actions of the state courts redefined or extended state law in Thompson and Garner, was the change of such a magnitude that there was not fair notice of the charges so that defendants could properly defend themselves?

Would a holding on the Cole basis allow re-trial of defendants on proper charges with new notice? Would that seem an appropriate course of action following remand in Thompson or Garner?

(6) Compare Bouie v. Columbia, 378 U.S. 347 (1964), another "sit-in" case. On March 14, 1960 two black college students entered the restaurant section of a large drug store in Columbia, South Carolina, and took seats in an available booth. Blacks were invited to patronize all departments in the store except the lunch counter. There were no signs announcing this exclusionary policy, though it seems to have been well understood. Shortly after the students sat down, a store employee put up a chain with a "no trespassing" sign hanging from it. The store owner then twice asked the students to leave. They refused and were arrested, and were subsequently convicted of criminal trespass.

The criminal trespass charge was based on section 16–386 of the South Carolina Code of 1952: "Every entry upon the lands of another * * * after notice from the owner or tenant prohibiting such entry shall be a misdemeanor." Though the defendants entered the lunch counter area before any notice was given, the lower state courts were untroubled by the statutory language. They apparently relied on the notion that the state common law definition of civil trespass had been incorporated into the statute. By the time the Bouie case reached the South Carolina Supreme Court, there was another basis for affirming conviction. In December 1960—after Bouie's trial—the State Supreme Court decided Mitchell v. City of Charleston, affirming convictions based on section 16–386 for another sit-in demonstration, and construing the statutory language "entry * * * after notice" to encompass remaining after notice. Thus in Bouie that court was able to affirm simply on the authority of Mitchell.

The United States Supreme Court granted certiorari and reversed. Justice Brennan's opinion for the Court rested on the basis that a criminal statute must give fair warning of the conduct that it makes a crime; unforeseeable retroactive expansion of a criminal statute operates like an ex post facto law in that it makes conduct, innocent when done, criminal and thus violates the Due Process Clause. The due process concept was analogized to that involved in cases holding that an "unforeseeable and unsupported" state procedural decision will not be considered an adequate, independent state ground of decision precluding Supreme Court review of a case. See pp. 606–08, supra.

Justice Black, joined by Justices Harlan and White, dissented; without quarreling directly with the majority's general thesis, he concluded: "We cannot believe that either the petitioners or anyone else could have been misled by the language of this statute into believing that it would permit them to stay on the property of another over the owner's protest without being guilty of trespass" (pp. 366–67).[3]

(7) Another doctrine obviously relevant to problems of discriminatory and arbitrary enforcement of state criminal statutes is that of "vagueness": if a state statute is so ill-defined that it does not give fair warning about what conduct is prohibited, it is void. See, e.g., Lanzetta v. New Jersey, 306 U.S. 451 (1939) (statute made it a crime to be a member of a "gang"; case cited in Thompson); Giaccio v. Pennsylvania, 382 U.S. 399 (1966) ("the law must be one that carries an understandable meaning with legal standards"); Papachristou v. Jacksonville, 405 U.S. 156, 162 (1972) (vagrancy ordinance too vague); Village of Hoffman Estates v. Flipside, Hoffman Estates, Inc., 455 U.S. 489 (1982); cf. Rabe v. Washington, 405 U.S. 313 (1972) (retroactive state court expansion of criminal obscenity statute

---

3. With Bouie compare Hamling v. United States, 418 U.S. 87, 115–16 (1974) (particular retroactive reinterpretation of federal obscenity statute following Miller v. California held not an expansion of liability and therefore not within the Bouie principle); Ward v. Illinois, 431 U.S. 767 (1977) (similar holding re Illinois obscenity statute); Rose v. Locke, 423 U.S. 48 (1975) (broad definition of "crimes against nature" adequately signalled by prior state decisions and therefore not within Bouie).

See also Marks v. United States, 430 U.S. 188 (1977), holding that, to the extent that the decision in Miller v. California expanded criminal liability, constitutionally and in construction of the federal obscenity statute, due process bars retroactive application of the new construction to conduct not punishable under preexisting authority (citing Bouie).

Cf. Douglas v. Buder, 412 U.S. 430 (1973), in which the Court put its holding on "no evidence" grounds, pointed out that neither the trial court nor the state supreme court had specifically construed state law to cover the facts of the case, and said that if there had been such a specific holding, "we would have to conclude that under the rationale of Bouie v. City of Columbia, * * * the unforeseeable application of that interpretation in the case before us deprived petitioner of due process" (p. 432).

rendered the statute "impermissibly vague"). Compare the overbreadth doctrine at issue in Cox. See generally Monaghan, *Overbreadth,* 1981 Sup. Ct.Rev. 1; Amsterdam, *The Void-for-Vagueness Doctrine in the Supreme Court,* 109 U.Pa.L.Rev. 67 (1960); Note, *The First Amendment Overbreadth Doctrine,* 83 Harv.L.Rev. 844 (1970).

Could Thompson (and Garner) have been disposed of on the ground that application of the state criminal statute to the conduct in the case had the effect of rendering that statute unconstitutionally vague?

JACKSON v. VIRGINIA

443 U.S. 307, 99 S.Ct. 2781, 61 L.Ed.2d 560 (1979).
Certiorari to the United States Court of Appeals for the Fourth Circuit.

MR. JUSTICE STEWART delivered the opinion of the Court. * * *

I

The petitioner was convicted after a bench trial in the Circuit Court of Chesterfield County, Va., of the first-degree murder of a woman named Mary Houston Cole. Under Virginia law, murder is defined as "the unlawful killing of another with malice aforethought." Stapleton v. Commonwealth, 123 Va. 825, 96 S.E. 801. Premeditation, or specific intent to kill, distinguishes murder in the first from murder in the second degree; proof of this element is essential to conviction of the former offense, and the burden of proving it clearly rests with the prosecution. [Citing two Virginia cases.]

That the petitioner had shot and killed Mrs. Cole was not in dispute at the trial. * * * [The opinion here reviews the evidence at some length, concluding with defendant's postarrest statement (introduced by the prosecution) that the shooting had been accidental and that he had been "pretty high" but not drunk at the time.] At the trial, his position was that he had acted in self-defense. Alternatively, he claimed that in any event the State's own evidence showed that he had been too intoxicated to form the specific intent necessary under Virginia law to sustain a conviction of murder in the first degree.[2]

The trial judge, declaring himself convinced beyond a reasonable doubt that the petitioner had committed first-degree murder, found him guilty of that offense. The petitioner's motion to set aside the judgment as contrary to the evidence was denied, and he was sentenced to serve a term of 30 years in the Virginia state penitentiary. A petition for writ of error to the Virginia Supreme Court on the ground that the evidence was insufficient to support the conviction was denied.

The petitioner then commenced this habeas corpus proceeding in the United States District Court for the Eastern District of Virginia, raising the same basic claim. Applying the "no evidence" criterion of Thompson v. Louisville, 362 U.S. 199, the District Court found the record devoid of evidence of premeditation and granted the writ. The Court of Appeals for

---

2. Under Virginia law, voluntary intoxication—although not an affirmative defense to second-degree murder—is material to the element of premeditation and may be found to have negated it. Hatcher v. Commonwealth, 218 Va. 811, 241 S.E.2d 756.

the Fourth Circuit reversed the judgment. [That] court was of the view that some evidence that the petitioner had intended to kill the victim could be found in the facts that the petitioner had reloaded his gun after firing warning shots, that he had had time to do so, and that the victim was then shot not once but twice. The court also concluded that the state trial judge could have found that the petitioner was not so intoxicated as to be incapable of premeditation.

We granted certiorari * * *.

II

Our inquiry in this case is narrow. The petitioner has not seriously questioned any aspect of Virginia law governing the allocation of the burden of production or persuasion in a murder trial. See Mullaney v. Wilbur, 421 U.S. 684; Patterson v. New York, 432 U.S. 197. As the record demonstrates, the judge sitting as factfinder in the petitioner's trial was aware that the State bore the burden of establishing the element of premeditation, and stated that he was applying the reasonable-doubt standard in his appraisal of the State's evidence. The petitioner, moreover, does not contest the conclusion of the Court of Appeals that under the "no evidence" rule of Thompson v. Louisville, *supra*, his conviction of first-degree murder is sustainable. And he has not attacked the sufficiency of the evidence to support a conviction of second-degree murder. His sole constitutional claim, based squarely upon [In re] Winship, [397 U.S. 358,] is that the District Court and the Court of Appeals were in error in not recognizing that the question to be decided in this case is whether any rational factfinder could have concluded beyond a reasonable doubt that the killing for which the petitioner was convicted was premeditated.
* * *

III

A

This is the first of our cases to expressly consider the question whether the due process standard recognized in Winship constitutionally protects an accused against conviction except upon evidence that is sufficient fairly to support a conclusion that every element of the crime has been established beyond a reasonable doubt. Upon examination of the fundamental differences between the constitutional underpinnings of Thompson v. Louisville, *supra*, and of In re Winship, *supra*, the answer to that question, we think, is clear.

It is axiomatic that a conviction upon a charge not made or upon a charge not tried constitutes a denial of due process. * * * These standards no more than reflect a broader premise that has never been doubted in our constitutional system: that a person cannot incur the loss of liberty for an offense without notice and a meaningful opportunity to defend. * * * A meaningful opportunity to defend, if not the right to a trial itself, presumes as well that a total want of evidence to support a charge will conclude the case in favor of the accused. Accordingly, we held in the Thompson case that a conviction based upon a record wholly devoid of any relevant evidence of a crucial element of the offense charged is constitutionally infirm. * * * The "no evidence" doctrine of Thompson v.

Louisville thus secures to an accused the most elemental of due process rights: freedom from a wholly arbitrary deprivation of liberty.

The Court in Thompson explicitly stated that the due process right at issue did not concern a question of evidentiary "sufficiency." 362 U.S., at 199. The right established in In re Winship, however, clearly stands on a different footing. Winship involved an adjudication of juvenile delinquency made by a judge under a state statute providing that the prosecution must prove the conduct charged as delinquent—which in Winship would have been a criminal offense if engaged in by an adult—by a preponderance of the evidence. Applying that standard, the judge was satisfied that the juvenile was "guilty," but he noted that the result might well have been different under a standard of proof beyond a reasonable doubt. In short, the record in Winship was not totally devoid of evidence of guilt.

The constitutional problem addressed in Winship was thus distinct from the stark problem of arbitrariness presented in Thompson v. Louisville. In Winship, the Court held for the first time that the Due Process Clause of the Fourteenth Amendment protects a defendant in a criminal case against conviction "except upon proof beyond a reasonable doubt of every fact necessary to constitute the crime with which he is charged." 397 U.S., at 364. In so holding, the Court emphasized that proof beyond a reasonable doubt has traditionally been regarded as the decisive difference between criminal culpability and civil liability. *Id.*, at 358–362. * * * The standard of proof beyond a reasonable doubt, said the Court, "plays a vital role in the American scheme of criminal procedure," because it operates to give "concrete substance" to the presumption of innocence, to ensure against unjust convictions, and to reduce the risk of factual error in a criminal proceeding. 397 U.S., at 363. At the same time, by impressing upon the factfinder the need to reach a subjective state of near certitude of the guilt of the accused, the standard symbolizes the significance that our society attaches to the criminal sanction and thus to liberty itself. *Id.*, at 372 (Harlan, J., concurring).

The constitutional standard recognized in the Winship case was expressly phrased as one that protects an accused against a conviction except on "*proof* beyond a reasonable doubt * * *." In subsequent cases discussing the reasonable-doubt standard, we have never departed from this definition of the rule or from the Winship understanding of the central purposes it serves. * * * In short, Winship presupposes as an essential of the due process guaranteed by the Fourteenth Amendment that no person shall be made to suffer the onus of a criminal conviction except upon sufficient proof—defined as evidence necessary to convince a trier of fact beyond a reasonable doubt of the existence of every element of the offense.

B

* * * [T]he Federal Courts of Appeals have generally assumed that so long as the reasonable-doubt instruction has been given at trial, the no-evidence doctrine of Thompson v. Louisville remains the appropriate guide for a federal habeas corpus court to apply in assessing a state prisoner's challenge to his conviction as founded upon insufficient evidence. * * * We cannot agree.

The Winship doctrine requires more than simply a trial ritual. A doctrine establishing so fundamental a substantive constitutional standard must also require that the factfinder will rationally apply that standard to the facts in evidence. A "reasonable doubt," at a minimum, is one based upon "reason." Yet a properly instructed jury may occasionally convict even when it can be said that no rational trier of fact could find guilt beyond a reasonable doubt, and the same may be said of a trial judge sitting as jury. In a federal trial, such an occurrence has traditionally been deemed to require reversal of the conviction. * * * Under Winship, which established proof beyond a reasonable doubt as an essential of Fourteenth Amendment due process, it follows that when such a conviction occurs in a state trial, it cannot constitutionally stand.

A federal court has a duty to assess the historic facts when it is called upon to apply a constitutional standard to a conviction obtained in a state court. For example, on direct review of a state-court conviction, where the claim is made that an involuntary confession was used against the defendant, this Court reviews the facts to determine whether the confession was wrongly admitted in evidence. Blackburn v. Alabama, 361 U.S. 199, 205–210. The same duty obtains in federal habeas corpus proceedings. See Townsend v. Sain, 372 U.S. 293, 318; Brown v. Allen, 344 U.S. 443, 506–507 (opinion of Frankfurter, J.).

After Winship the critical inquiry on review of the sufficiency of the evidence to support a criminal conviction must be not simply to determine whether the jury was properly instructed, but to determine whether the record evidence could reasonably support a finding of guilt beyond a reasonable doubt. But this inquiry does not require a court to "ask itself whether *it* believes that the evidence at the trial established guilt beyond a reasonable doubt." Woodby v. INS, 385 U.S., at 282 (emphasis added). Instead, the relevant question is whether, after viewing the evidence in the light most favorable to the prosecution, *any* rational trier of fact could have found the essential elements of the crime beyond a reasonable doubt. See Johnson v. Louisiana, 406 U.S., at 362. This familiar standard gives full play to the responsibility of the trier of fact fairly to resolve conflicts in the testimony, to weigh the evidence, and to draw reasonable inferences from basic facts to ultimate facts. Once a defendant has been found guilty of the crime charged, the factfinder's role as weigher of the evidence is preserved through a legal conclusion that upon judicial review *all of the evidence* is to be considered in the light most favorable to the prosecution. The criterion thus impinges upon "jury" discretion only to the extent necessary to guarantee the fundamental protection of due process of law.

That the Thompson "no evidence" rule is simply inadequate to protect against misapplications of the constitutional standard of reasonable doubt is readily apparent. "[A] mere modicum of evidence may satisfy a 'no evidence' standard * * *." Jacobellis v. Ohio, 378 U.S. 184, 202 (Warren, C.J., dissenting). Any evidence that is relevant—that has any tendency to make the existence of an element of a crime slightly more probable than it would be without the evidence, *cf.* Fed.Rule Evid. 401—could be deemed a "mere modicum." But it could not seriously be argued that such a "modicum" of evidence could by itself rationally support a conviction beyond a reasonable doubt. The Thompson doctrine simply fails to supply a workable or even a predictable standard for determining whether the due process command of Winship has been honored.

C

Under 28 U.S.C. § 2254, a federal court must entertain a claim by a state prisoner that he or she is being held in "custody in violation of the Constitution or laws or treaties of the United States." Under the Winship decision, it is clear that a state prisoner who alleges that the evidence in support of his state conviction cannot be fairly characterized as sufficient to have led a rational trier of fact to find guilt beyond a reasonable doubt has stated a federal constitutional claim. Thus, assuming that state remedies have been exhausted, see 28 U.S.C. § 2254(b), and that no independent and adequate state ground stands as a bar, see Estelle v. Williams, 425 U.S. 501; Francis v. Henderson, 425 U.S. 536; Wainwright v. Sykes, 433 U.S. 72; Fay v. Noia, 372 U.S. 391, 438, it follows that such a claim is cognizable in a federal habeas corpus proceeding. The respondents have argued, nonetheless, that a challenge to the constitutional sufficiency of the evidence should not be entertained by a federal district court under 28 U.S.C. § 2254.

In addition to the argument that a Winship standard invites replication of state criminal trials in the guise of § 2254 proceedings—an argument that simply fails to recognize that courts can and regularly do gauge the sufficiency of the evidence without intruding into any legitimate domain of the trier of fact—the respondents have urged that any departure from the Thompson test in federal habeas corpus proceedings will expand the number of meritless claims brought to the federal courts, will duplicate the work of the state appellate courts, will disserve the societal interest in the finality of state criminal proceedings, and will increase friction between the federal and state judiciaries. In sum, counsel for the State urges that this type of constitutional claim should be deemed to fall within the limit on federal habeas corpus jurisdiction identified in Stone v. Powell, 428 U.S. 465, with respect to Fourth Amendment claims. We disagree.

First, the burden that is likely to follow from acceptance of the Winship standard has, we think, been exaggerated. Federal-court challenges to the evidentiary support for state convictions have since Thompson been dealt with under § 2254. * * * A more stringent standard will expand the contours of this type of claim, but will not create an entirely new class of cases cognizable on federal habeas corpus. Furthermore, most meritorious challenges to constitutional sufficiency of the evidence undoubtedly will be recognized in the state courts, and, if the state courts have fully considered the issue of sufficiency, the task of a federal habeas court should not be difficult. Cf. Brown v. Allen, 344 U.S., at 463.[15] And this type of claim can almost always be judged on the written record without need for an evidentiary hearing in the federal court.

Second, the problems of finality and federal-state comity arise whenever a state prisoner invokes the jurisdiction of a federal court to redress an alleged constitutional violation. A challenge to a state conviction brought

15. The Virginia Supreme Court's order denying Jackson's petition for writ of error does not make clear what criterion was applied to the petitioner's claim that the evidence in support of his first-degree murder conviction was insufficient. * * * [W]e decline to speculate as to the criterion that the state court applied. The fact that a state appellate court invoked the proper standard, however, although entitled to great weight, does not totally bar a properly presented claim of this type under § 2254.

on the ground that the evidence cannot fairly be deemed sufficient to have established guilt beyond a reasonable doubt states a federal constitutional claim. Although state appellate review undoubtedly will serve in the vast majority of cases to vindicate the due process protection that follows from Winship, the same could also be said of the vast majority of other federal constitutional rights that may be implicated in a state criminal trial. It is the occasional abuse that the federal writ of habeas corpus stands ready to correct. Brown v. Allen, *supra,* at 498–501 (opinion of Frankfurter, J.).

The respondents have argued nonetheless that whenever a person convicted in a state court has been given a "full and fair hearing" in the state system—meaning in this instance state appellate review of the sufficiency of the evidence—further federal inquiry—apart from the possibility of discretionary review by this Court—should be foreclosed. * * * The duty of a federal habeas corpus court to appraise a claim that constitutional error did occur—reflecting as it does the belief that the "finality" of a deprivation of liberty through the invocation of the criminal sanction is simply not to be achieved at the expense of a constitutional right—is not one that can be so lightly abjured.

The constitutional issue presented in this case is far different from the kind of issue that was the subject of the Court's decision in Stone v. Powell, *supra.* The question whether a defendant has been convicted upon inadequate evidence is central to the basic question of guilt or innocence. The constitutional necessity of proof beyond a reasonable doubt is not confined to those defendants who are morally blameless. *E.g.,* Mullaney v. Wilbur, 421 U.S., at 697–698 (requirement of proof beyond a reasonable doubt is not "limit[ed] to those facts which, if not proved, would wholly exonerate" the accused). Under our system of criminal justice even a thief is entitled to complain that he has been unconstitutionally convicted and imprisoned as a burglar.

We hold that in a challenge to a state criminal conviction brought under 28 U.S.C. § 2254—if the settled procedural prerequisites for such a claim have otherwise been satisfied—the applicant is entitled to habeas corpus relief if it is found that upon the record evidence adduced at the trial no rational trier of fact could have found proof of guilt beyond a reasonable doubt.[16]

IV

Turning finally to the specific facts of this case, we reject the petitioner's claim that under the constitutional standard dictated by Winship his conviction of first-degree murder cannot stand. A review of the record in the light most favorable to the prosecution convinces us that a rational factfinder could readily have found the petitioner guilty beyond a reasonable doubt of first-degree murder under Virginia law. * * *

For these reasons, the judgment of the Court of Appeals is affirmed.

16. The respondents have suggested that this constitutional standard will invite intrusions upon the power of the States to define criminal offenses. Quite to the contrary, the standard must be applied with explicit reference to the substantive elements of the criminal offense as defined by state law. Whether the State could constitutionally make the conduct at issue criminal at all is, of course, a distinct question. See Papachristou v. Jacksonville, 405 U.S. 156; Robinson v. California, 370 U.S. 660.

MR. JUSTICE POWELL took no part in the consideration or decision of this case.

MR. JUSTICE STEVENS with whom THE CHIEF JUSTICE and MR. JUSTICE REHNQUIST join, concurring in the judgment.

The Constitution prohibits the criminal conviction of any person except upon proof *sufficient to convince the trier of fact* of guilt beyond a reasonable doubt. This rule has prevailed in our courts "at least from our early years as a Nation." In re Winship, 397 U.S. 358, 361.

Today the Court creates a new rule of law—one that has never prevailed in our jurisprudence. According to the Court, the Constitution now prohibits the criminal conviction of any person—including, apparently, a person against whom the facts have already been found beyond a reasonable doubt by a jury, a trial judge, and one or more levels of state appellate judges—except upon proof sufficient to convince a *federal judge* that a "rational trier of fact could have found the essential elements of the crime beyond a reasonable doubt."

The adoption of this novel constitutional rule is not necessary to the decision of this case. Moreover, I believe it is an unwise act of lawmaking. Despite its chimerical appeal as a new counterpart to the venerable principle recognized in Winship, I am persuaded that its precipitous adoption will adversely affect the quality of justice administered by federal judges. For that reason I shall analyze this new brainchild with some care.

I shall begin by explaining why neither the record in this case, nor general experience with challenges to the sufficiency of the evidence supporting criminal convictions, supports, much less compels, the conclusion that there is *any* need for this new constitutional precept. I shall next show that it is not logically compelled by either the holding or the analysis in In re Winship, *supra*. Finally, I shall try to demonstrate why the Court's new rule—if it is not just a meaningless shibboleth—threatens serious harm to the quality of our judicial system.

I

* * * Most significantly, the Court has announced its new constitutional edict in a case in which it has absolutely no bearing on the outcome. The only factual issue at stake is whether petitioner intended to kill his victim. If the evidence is viewed "in the light most favorable to the prosecution," * * * there can be only one answer to that question no matter *what* standard of appellate review is applied. In Part IV of its opinion, the Court accepts this conclusion. There is, therefore, no need to fashion a broad new rule of constitutional law to dispose of this squalid but rather routine murder case. Under any view, the evidence is sufficient.

The Court's new rule is adopted simply to forestall some hypothetical evil that has not been demonstrated, and in my view is not fairly demonstrable. Although the Judiciary has received its share of criticism—principally because of the delays and costs associated with litigation—I am aware of no general dissatisfaction with the accuracy of the factfinding process or the adequacy of the rules applied by state appellate courts when reviewing claims of insufficiency.

What little evidence the Court marshals in favor of a contrary conclusion is unconvincing. The Court is simply incorrect in implying that there

are a significant number of occasions when federal convictions are overturned on appeal because no rational trier of fact could have found guilt
beyond a reasonable doubt. The two opinions of this Court cited *ante* stand
for no such proposition. * * *

Moreover, a study of the 127 federal criminal convictions that were
reviewed by the various Courts of Appeals and reported in the most recent
hardbound volume of the Federal Reporter, Second Series, Volume 589,
reveals that only 3 were overturned on sufficiency grounds. And of those,
one was overturned under a "no evidence" standard, while the other two,
in which a total of only 3 out of 36 counts were actually reversed, arguably
involved legal issues masquerading as sufficiency questions. It is difficult
to believe that the federal courts will turn up more sufficiency problems
than this on habeas review when, instead of acting as the first level of
review, as in the cases studied, they will be acting as the second, third, or
even fourth level of appellate review. In short, there is simply no reason to
tinker with an elaborate mechanism that is now functioning well.

II

* * * In distinct contrast to the circumstances of this case, the facts
of Winship presented "a case where the choice of the standard of proof has
made a difference: the [trial] judge below forthrightly acknowledged that
he believed by a preponderance of the evidence, but was not convinced
beyond a reasonable doubt," of the juvenile's guilt. 397 U.S., at 369
(Harlan, J., concurring). Because the trier of fact entertained such a doubt,
this Court held that the juvenile was constitutionally entitled to the same
verdict that an adult defendant in a criminal case would receive. In so
holding, the Court merely extended to juveniles a protection that had
traditionally been available to defendants in criminal *trials* in this Nation.
Id., at 361.

But nothing in the Winship opinion suggests that it also bore on
appellate or habeas corpus procedures. Although it repeatedly emphasized
the function of the reasonable-doubt standard as describing the requisite
"subjective state of certitude" of the "*factfinder*," it never mentioned the
question of how appellate judges are to know whether the trier of fact
really was convinced beyond a reasonable doubt, or, indeed, whether the
factfinder was a "rational" person or group of persons.

Moreover, the mode of analysis employed in Winship finds no counterpart in the Court's opinion in this case. For example, in Winship, the
Court pointed out the breadth of both the historical and the current
acceptance of the reasonable-doubt *trial* standard. In this case, by contrast, the Court candidly recognizes that the Federal Courts of Appeals
have "generally" *rejected* the habeas standard that it adopts today.

The Winship court relied on nine prior opinions of this Court that bore
directly on the issue presented. * * * As the Court itself notes, we have
instead repeatedly endorsed the "no evidence" test, and have continued to
do so after Winship was decided. * * *

The primary reasoning of the Court in Winship is also inapplicable
here. The Court noted in that case that the reasonable-doubt standard has
the desirable effect of significantly reducing the risk of an inaccurate
factfinding and thus of erroneous convictions, as well as of instilling
confidence in the criminal justice system. 397 U.S., at 363–364. See also

id., at 370–372 (Harlan, J., concurring). In this case, however, it would be impossible (and the Court does not even try), to demonstrate that there is an appreciable risk that a factfinding made by a jury beyond a reasonable doubt, and twice reviewed by a trial judge in ruling on directed verdict and post-trial acquittal motions and by one or more levels of appellate courts on direct appeal, as well as by two federal habeas courts under the Thompson "no evidence" rule, is likely to be erroneous. * * *

Having failed to identify the evil against which the rule is directed, and having failed to demonstrate how it follows from the analysis typically used in due process cases of this character, the Court places all of its reliance on a dry, and in my view incorrect, syllogism: If Winship requires the factfinder to apply a reasonable-doubt standard, then logic requires a reviewing judge to apply a like standard. * * *

Time may prove that the rule the Court has adopted today is the wisest compromise between one extreme that maximizes the protection against the risk that innocent persons will be erroneously convicted and the other extreme that places the greatest faith in the ability of fair procedures to produce just verdicts. But the Court's opinion should not obscure the fact that its new rule is not logically compelled by the analysis or the holding in Winship or in any other precedent, or the fact that the rule reflects a new policy choice rather than the application of a pre-existing rule of law.

III

The Court cautions against exaggerating the significance of its new rule. It is true that in practice there may be little or no difference between a record that does not contain at least some evidence tending to prove every element of an offense and a record containing so little evidence that no rational factfinder could be persuaded of guilt beyond a reasonable doubt. Moreover, I think the Court is quite correct when it acknowledges that "most meritorious challenges to constitutional sufficiency of the evidence undoubtedly will be recognized in the state courts." But this only means that the new rule will seldom, if ever, provide a convicted state prisoner with any tangible benefits. It does not mean that the rule will have no impact on the administration of justice. On the contrary, I am persuaded that it will be seriously harmful both to the state and federal judiciaries.

The Court indicates that the new standard to be applied by federal judges in habeas corpus proceedings may be substantially the same as the standard most state reviewing courts are already applying. The federal district courts are therefore being directed simply to duplicate the reviewing function that is now being performed adequately by state appellate courts. * * * [T]o assign a single federal district judge the responsibility of directly reviewing, and inevitably supervising, the most routine work of the highest courts of a State can only undermine the morale and the esteem of the state judiciary—particularly when the stated purpose of the additional layer of review is to determine whether the State's factfinder is "rational." [9] Such consequences are intangible but nonetheless significant.

9. In the past, collateral review of state proceedings has been justified largely on the grounds (1) that federal judges have special expertise in the federal issues that regularly arise in habeas corpus proceed- ing, and (2) that they are less susceptible than state judges to political pressures against applying constitutional rules to overturn convictions. See, *e.g.,* Bartels, *Avoiding a Comity of Errors,* 29 Stan.L.

The potential effect on federal judges is even more serious. Their burdens are already so heavy that they are delegating to staff assistants more and more work that we once expected judges to perform. The new standard will invite an unknown number of state prisoners to make sufficiency challenges that they would not have made under the old rule. Moreover, because the "rational trier of fact" must certainly base its decisions on *all* of the evidence, the Court's broader standard may well require that the entire transcript of the state trial be read whenever the factfinders' rationality is challenged under the Court's rule. Because this task will confront the courts of appeals as well as district courts, it will surely impose countless additional hours of unproductive labor on federal judges and their assistants.[12] The increasing volume of work of this character has already led some of our most distinguished lawyers to discontinue or reject service on the federal bench. The addition of a significant volume of pointless labor can only impair the quality of justice administered by federal judges and thereby undermine "the respect and confidence of the community in applications of the * * * law." * * *

NOTE ON JACKSON v. VIRGINIA

(1) Jackson was a habeas corpus case. But there is no doubt that its holding applies to cases coming to the Court on direct review of state decisions. The sufficiency of the evidence to support such a conviction is now a question of federal constitutional law reviewable under § 1257.

Is the availability of collateral review on habeas corpus relevant to whether the issue is one of federal constitutional law at all? If direct review had been the only way to bring the issue before a federal court, would the Supreme Court have ruled as it did in Jackson?

Are there answers to the institutional concerns expressed by Justice Stevens? Did the Court in Jackson make a persuasive case that the question of sufficiency in every state criminal proceeding requires federal oversight?

In Norris and Cox the Court asserted a broad power to engage in searching (and even independent) review of facts relevant to a claim of federal right. In Jackson, the Court asserted that the question whether the evidence supports a finding that a state law has been violated *is* a question of federal right. Do you understand the difference? Was the additional step justified?

Rev. 27, 30 n. 9 (1976). * * * But neither of these justifications has any force in the present context. State judges are more familiar with the elements of state offenses than are federal judges and should be better able to evaluate sufficiency claims. Moreover, of all decisions overturning convictions, the least likely to be unpopular and thus to distort state decisionmaking processes are ones based on the inadequacy of the evidence. Indeed, once federal courts were divested of authority to second-guess state courts on Fourth Amendment issues, which are far

more likely to generate politically motivated state-court decisions, see Stone v. Powell, 428 U.S. 465, a like result in this case would seem to be *a fortiori*.

12. Professor Bator has persuasively explained how the law of diminishing returns inevitably makes it unwise to have duplicative review processes on the "merits" in criminal cases: [The opinion here quotes extensively from Bator, *Finality in Criminal Law and Federal Habeas Corpus for State Prisoners*, 76 Harv.L.Rev. 441, 450–451 (1963).]

(2) Is Jackson required by Winship? Is it inevitably the case that, where a federal constitutional standard governs the standard of persuasion (or burden of proof) imposed on the factfinder, the question whether the evidence supports the factfinder's conclusions in a specific case must itself be a question of federal constitutional law?

(3) Does Jackson swallow the doctrine of Thompson v. Louisville in the criminal area?[1] Should the "no evidence" rule be retained for application to civil actions? (Recall that all that was at stake in Thompson itself was $20 in fines.)

(4) Note that Jackson applies to those issues as to which Winship requires proof beyond a reasonable doubt. The question of what those issues are is itself a matter of grave difficulty in light of the fact that it is state law that defines what are the elements of a crime (in contrast to matters of defense or mitigation). See Martin v. Ohio, 107 S.Ct. 1098 (1987) (5–4 decision holding that state may place burden of proof as to self-defense on the defendant). These problems are explored in an illuminating article, Jeffries & Stephan, *Defenses, Presumptions and Burden of Proof in the Criminal Law,* 88 Yale L.J. 1325 (1979).

SECTION 3. FINAL JUDGMENTS AND THE HIGHEST STATE COURT

COX BROADCASTING CORP. v. COHN

420 U.S. 469, 95 S.Ct. 1029, 43 L.Ed.2d 328 (1975).
Appeal from the Supreme Court of Georgia.

MR. JUSTICE WHITE delivered the opinion of the Court.

[In 1971, the appellee's daughter was raped and murdered. During criminal proceedings against several youths charged with the crime, a television reporter learned the name of the victim from records publicly available at the court, and subsequently broadcast a news story reporting the victim's identity. Georgia Code Ann. § 26–9901 made the publication or broadcast of the identity of a rape victim a misdemeanor. Relying on § 26–9901, appellee brought an action for damages against the reporter and the television station for invasion of his right to privacy. Despite the defendants' assertion that the imposition of civil liability would violate the First Amendment, the state trial court held that § 26–9901 implicitly created a civil remedy and granted summary judgment for the appellee.]

* * *

On appeal, the Georgia Supreme Court, in its initial opinion, held that the trial court had erred in construing § 26–9901 to extend a civil cause of action for invasion of privacy and thus found it unnecessary to consider the constitutionality of the statute. 231 Ga. 60, 200 S.E.2d 127 (1973). The court went on to rule, however, that the complaint stated a cause of action "for the invasion of the appellee's right of privacy, or for the tort of public

---

1. See, *e.g.,* in addition to Jackson itself, Pilon v. Bordenkircher, 444 U.S. 1 (1979). But *cf.* Comment, *Federal Review of the*   *Evidence Supporting State Convictions: Jackson v. Virginia,* 79 Colum.L.Rev. 1577 (1979).

disclosure"—a "common law tort exist[ing] in this jurisdiction without the help of the statute that the trial judge in this case relied on." Although the privacy invaded was not that of the deceased victim, the father was held to have stated a claim for invasion of his own privacy by reason of the publication of his daughter's name. The court explained, however, that liability did not follow as a matter of law and that summary judgment was improper; whether the public disclosure of the name actually invaded appellee's "zone of privacy," and if so, to what extent, were issues to be determined by the trier of fact. Also, "in formulating such an issue for determination by the fact-finder, it is reasonable to require the appellee to prove that the appellants invaded his privacy with wilful or negligent disregard for the fact that reasonable men would find the invasion highly offensive." The Georgia Supreme Court did agree with the trial court, however, that the First and Fourteenth Amendments did not, as a matter of law, require judgment for appellants. * * *

Upon motion for rehearing the Georgia court countered the argument that the victim's name was a matter of public interest and could be published with impunity by relying on § 26–9901 as an authoritative declaration of state policy that the name of a rape victim was not a matter of public concern. This time the court felt compelled to determine the constitutionality of the statute and sustained it as a "legitimate limitation on the right of freedom of expression contained in the First Amendment." The court could discern "no public interest or general concern about the identity of the victim of such a crime as will make the right to disclose the identity of the victim rise to the level of First Amendment protection."

We postponed decision as to our jurisdiction over this appeal to the hearing on the merits. 415 U.S. 912 (1974). We conclude that the Court has jurisdiction, and reverse the judgment of the Georgia Supreme Court.

II

Appellants invoke the appellate jurisdiction of this Court under 28 U.S.C. § 1257(2) and, if that jurisdictional basis is found to be absent, through a petition for certiorari under 28 U.S.C. § 2103. Two questions concerning our jurisdiction must be resolved: (1) whether the constitutional validity of § 26–9901 was "drawn in question," with the Georgia Supreme Court upholding its validity, and (2) whether the decision from which this appeal has been taken is a "[f]inal judgment or decree."

A

Appellants clearly raised the issue of the constitutionality of § 26–9901 in their motion for rehearing in the Georgia Supreme Court. In denying that motion that court held: "A majority of this court does not consider this statute to be in conflict with the First Amendment." Since the court relied upon the statute as a declaration of the public policy of Georgia that the disclosure of a rape victim's name was not to be protected expression, the statute was drawn in question in a manner directly bearing upon the merits of the action, and the decision in favor of its constitutional validity invokes this Court's appellate jurisdiction. *Cf.* Garrity v. New Jersey, 385 U.S. 493, 495–496 (1967).

B

Since 1789, Congress has granted this Court appellate jurisdiction with respect to state litigation only after the highest state court in which judgment could be had has rendered a "[f]inal judgment or decree." Title 28 U.S.C. § 1257 retains this limitation on our power to review cases coming from state courts. The Court has noted that "[c]onsiderations of English usage as well as those of judicial policy" would justify an interpretation of the final-judgment rule to preclude review "where anything further remains to be determined by a State court, no matter how dissociated from the only federal issue that has finally been adjudicated by the highest court of the State." Radio Station WOW, Inc. v. Johnson, 326 U.S. 120, 124 (1945). But the Court there observed that the rule had not been administered in such a mechanical fashion and that there were circumstances in which there has been "a departure from this requirement of finality for federal appellate jurisdiction." *Ibid.*

These circumstances were said to be "very few," *ibid.;* but as the cases have unfolded, the Court has recurringly encountered situations in which the highest court of a State has finally determined the federal issue present in a particular case, but in which there are further proceedings in the lower state courts to come. There are now at least four categories of such cases in which the Court has treated the decision on the federal issue as a final judgment for the purposes of 28 U.S.C. § 1257 and has taken jurisdiction without awaiting the completion of the additional proceedings anticipated in the lower state courts. In most, if not all, of the cases in these categories, these additional proceedings would not require the decision of other federal questions that might also require review by the Court at a later date,[6] and immediate rather than delayed review would be the best way to avoid "the mischief of economic waste and of delayed justice," Radio Station WOW, Inc. v. Johnson, *supra,* at 124, as well as precipitate interference with state litigation.[7] In the cases in the first two categories considered below, the federal issue would not be mooted or otherwise affected by

6. Eminent domain proceedings are of the type that may involve an interlocutory decision as to a federal question with another federal question to be decided later. "For in those cases the federal constitutional question embraces not only a taking, but a taking on payment of just compensation. A state judgment is not final unless it covers both aspects of that integral problem." North Dakota State Board of Pharmacy v. Snyder's Drug Stores, Inc., 414 U.S. 156, 163 (1973). * * *

7. Gillespie v. United States Steel Corp., 379 U.S. 148 (1964), arose in the federal courts and involved the requirement of 28 U.S.C. § 1291 that judgments of district courts be final if they are to be appealed to the courts of appeals. In the course of deciding that the judgment of the District Court in the case had been final, the Court indicated its approach to finality requirements:

"And our cases long have recognized that whether a ruling is 'final' within the meaning of § 1291 is frequently so close a question that decision of that issue either way can be supported with equally forceful arguments, and that it is impossible to devise a formula to resolve all marginal cases coming within what might well be called the 'twilight zone' of finality. Because of this difficulty this Court has held that the requirement of finality is to be given a 'practical rather than a technical construction.' Cohen v. Beneficial Industrial Loan Corp., [337 U.S. 541, 546]. See also Brown Shoe Co. v. United States, 370 U.S. 294, 306; Bronson v. Railroad Co., 2 Black 524, 531; Forgay v. Conrad, 6 How. 201, 203. Dickinson v. Petroleum Conversion Corp., 338 U.S. 507, 511, pointed out that in deciding the question of finality the most important competing considerations are 'the inconvenience and costs of piecemeal review on the one hand and the danger of denying justice by delay on the other.'" 379 U.S., at 152–153.

the proceedings yet to be had because those proceedings have little substance, their outcome is certain, or they are wholly unrelated to the federal question. In the other two categories, however, the federal issue would be mooted if the petitioner or appellant seeking to bring the action here prevailed on the merits in the later state-court proceedings, but there is nevertheless sufficient justification for immediate review of the federal question finally determined in the state courts.

In the first category are those cases in which there are further proceedings—even entire trials—yet to occur in the state courts but where for one reason or another the federal issue is conclusive or the outcome of further proceedings preordained. In these circumstances, because the case is for all practical purposes concluded, the judgment of the state court on the federal issue is deemed final. In Mills v. Alabama, 384 U.S. 214 (1966), for example, a demurrer to a criminal complaint was sustained on federal constitutional grounds by a state trial court. The State Supreme Court reversed, remanding for jury trial. This Court took jurisdiction on the reasoning that the appellant had no defense other than his federal claim and could not prevail at trial on the facts or any nonfederal ground. To dismiss the appeal "would not only be an inexcusable delay of the benefits Congress intended to grant by providing for appeal to this Court, but it would also result in a completely unnecessary waste of time and energy in judicial systems already troubled by delays due to congested dockets." *Id.*, at 217–218 (footnote omitted).[8]

Second, there are cases such as Radio Station WOW, *supra*, and Brady v. Maryland, 373 U.S. 83 (1963), in which the federal issue, finally decided by the highest court in the State, will survive and require decision regardless of the outcome of future state-court proceedings. In Radio Station WOW, the Nebraska Supreme Court directed the transfer of the properties of a federally licensed radio station and ordered an accounting, rejecting the claim that the transfer order would interfere with the federal license. The federal issue was held reviewable here despite the pending accounting on the "presupposition * * * that the federal questions that could come here have been adjudicated by the State court, and that the accounting which remains to be taken could not remotely give rise to a federal question * * * that may later come here * * *." 326 U.S., at 127. The judgment rejecting the federal claim and directing the transfer was deemed "dissociated from a provision for an accounting even though that is decreed in the same order." *Id.*, at 126. Nothing that could happen in the course of the accounting, short of settlement of the case, would foreclose or make unnecessary decision on the federal question. Older cases in the Court had reached the same result on similar facts. Carondelet Canal & Nav. Co. v. Louisiana, 233 U.S. 362 (1914); Forgay v. Conrad, 6 How. 201 (1848). In the latter case, the Court, in an opinion by Mr. Chief Justice Taney, stated that the Court had not understood the final-judgment rule "in this strict and technical sense, but has given [it] a more liberal, and, as we think, a more reasonable construction, and one more consonant to the intention of the legislature."[9]

8. Other cases from state courts where this Court's jurisdiction was sustained for similar reasons include: Organization for a Better Austin v. Keefe, 402 U.S. 415, 418 n. (1971); Construction Laborers v. Curry, 371 U.S. 542, 550–551 (1963); Pope v. Atlantic C.L.R. Co., 345 U.S. 379, 382 (1953); Richfield Oil Corp. v. State Board, 329 U.S. 69, 73–74 (1946). * * *

9. In Brady v. Maryland, 373 U.S. 83 (1963), the Maryland courts had ordered a

In the third category are those situations where the federal claim has been finally decided, with further proceedings on the merits in the state courts to come, but in which later review of the federal issue cannot be had, whatever the ultimate outcome of the case. Thus, in these cases, if the party seeking interim review ultimately prevails on the merits, the federal issue will be mooted; if he were to lose on the merits, however, the governing state law would not permit him again to present his federal claims for review. The Court has taken jurisdiction in these circumstances prior to completion of the case in the state courts. California v. Stewart, 384 U.S. 436 (1966) (decided with Miranda v. Arizona), epitomizes this category. There the state court reversed a conviction on federal constitutional grounds and remanded for a new trial. Although the State might have prevailed at trial, we granted its petition for certiorari and affirmed, explaining that the state judgment was "final" since an acquittal of the defendant at trial would preclude, under state law, an appeal by the State.

A recent decision in this category is North Dakota State Board of Pharmacy v. Snyder's Drug Stores, Inc., 414 U.S. 156 (1973), in which the Pharmacy Board rejected an application for a pharmacy operating permit relying on a state statute specifying ownership requirements which the applicant did not meet. The State Supreme Court held the statute unconstitutional and remanded the matter to the Board for further consideration of the application, freed from the constraints of the ownership statute. The Board brought the case here, claiming that the statute was constitutionally acceptable under modern cases. After reviewing the various circumstances under which the finality requirement has been deemed satisfied despite the fact that litigation had not terminated in the state courts, we entertained the case over claims that we had no jurisdiction. The federal issue would not survive the remand, whatever the result of the state administrative proceedings. The Board might deny the license on state-law grounds, thus foreclosing the federal issue, and the Court also ascertained that under state law the Board could not bring the federal issue here in the event the applicant satisfied the requirements of state law except for the invalidated ownership statute. Under these circumstances, the issue was ripe for review.[10]

Lastly, there are those situations where the federal issue has been finally decided in the state courts with further proceedings pending in which the party seeking review here might prevail on the merits on nonfederal grounds, thus rendering unnecessary review of the federal issue by this Court, and where reversal of the state court on the federal issue would be preclusive of any further litigation on the relevant cause of action rather than merely controlling the nature and character of, or determining

new trial in a criminal case but on punishment only, and the petitioner asserted here that he was entitled to a new trial on guilt as well. We entertained the case, saying that the federal issue was separable and would not be mooted by the new trial on punishment ordered in the state courts.

10. Cohen v. Beneficial Industrial Loan Corp., 337 U.S. 541 (1949), was a diversity action in the federal courts in the course of which there arose the question of the validity of a state statute requiring plaintiffs in stockholder suits to post security for costs

as a prerequisite to bringing the action. The District Court held the state law inapplicable, the Court of Appeals reversed, and this Court, after granting certiorari, held that the issue of security for costs was separable from and independent of the merits and that if review were to be postponed until the termination of the litigation, "it will be too late effectively to review the present order, and the rights conferred by the statute, if it is applicable, will have been lost, probably irreparably."

the admissibility of evidence in, the state proceedings still to come. In these circumstances, if a refusal immediately to review the state-court decision might seriously erode federal policy, the Court has entertained and decided the federal issue, which itself has been finally determined by the state courts for purposes of the state litigation.

In Construction Laborers v. Curry, 371 U.S. 542 (1963), the state courts temporarily enjoined labor union picketing over claims that the National Labor Relations Board had exclusive jurisdiction of the controversy. The Court took jurisdiction for two independent reasons. First, the power of the state court to proceed in the face of the preemption claim was deemed an issue separable from the merits and ripe for review in this Court, particularly "when postponing review would seriously erode the national labor policy requiring the subject matter of respondents' cause to be heard by the * * * Board, not by the state courts." Second, the Court was convinced that in any event the union had no defense to the entry of a permanent injunction other than the preemption claim that had already been ruled on in the state courts. Hence the case was for all practical purposes concluded in the state tribunals.

In Mercantile National Bank v. Langdeau, 371 U.S. 555 (1963), two national banks were sued, along with others, in the courts of Travis County, Tex. The claim asserted was conspiracy to defraud an insurance company. The banks as a preliminary matter asserted that a special federal venue statute immunized them from suit in Travis County and that they could properly be sued only in another county. Although trial was still to be had and the banks might well prevail on the merits, the Court, relying on Curry, entertained the issue as a "separate and independent matter, anterior to the merits and not enmeshed in the factual and legal issues comprising the plaintiff's cause of action." Moreover, it would serve the policy of the federal statute "to determine now in which state court appellants may be tried rather than to subject them * * * to long and complex litigation which may all be for naught if consideration of the preliminary question of venue is postponed until the conclusion of the proceedings."

Miami Herald Publishing Co. v. Tornillo, 418 U.S. 241 (1974), is the latest case in this category. There a candidate for public office sued a newspaper for refusing, allegedly contrary to a state statute, to carry his reply to the paper's editorial critical of his qualifications. The trial court held the act unconstitutional, denying both injunctive relief and damages. The State Supreme Court reversed, sustaining the statute against the challenge based upon the First and Fourteenth Amendments and remanding the case for a trial and appropriate relief, including damages. The newspaper brought the case here. We sustained our jurisdiction, relying on the principles elaborated in the North Dakota case and observing:

> "Whichever way we were to decide on the merits, it would be intolerable to leave unanswered, under these circumstances, an important question of freedom of the press under the First Amendment; an uneasy and unsettled constitutional posture of § 104.38 could only further harm the operation of a free press. Mills v. Alabama, 384 U.S. 214, 221–222 (1966) (DOUGLAS, J., concurring). See also Organization for a Better Austin v. Keefe, 402 U.S. 415, 418 n. (1971)." 418 U.S., at 247 n. 6.

In light of the prior cases, we conclude that we have jurisdiction to review the judgment of the Georgia Supreme Court rejecting the challenge under the First and Fourteenth Amendments to the state law authorizing damage suits against the press for publishing the name of a rape victim whose identity is revealed in the course of a public prosecution. The Georgia Supreme Court's judgment is plainly final on the federal issue and is not subject to further review in the state courts. Appellants will be liable for damages if the elements of the state cause of action are proved. They may prevail at trial on nonfederal grounds, it is true, but if the Georgia court erroneously upheld the statute, there should be no trial at all. Moreover, even if appellants prevailed at trial and made unnecessary further consideration of the constitutional question, there would remain in effect the unreviewed decision of the State Supreme Court that a civil action for publishing the name of a rape victim disclosed in a public judicial proceeding may go forward despite the First and Fourteenth Amendments. Delaying final decision of the First Amendment claim until after trial will "leave unanswered * * * an important question of freedom of the press under the First Amendment," "an uneasy and unsettled constitutional posture [that] could only further harm the operation of a free press." Tornillo, *supra*, at 247 n. 6. On the other hand, if we now hold that the First and Fourteenth Amendments bar civil liability for broadcasting the victim's name, this litigation ends. Given these factors—that the litigation could be terminated by our decision on the merits [13] and that a failure to decide the question now will leave the press in Georgia operating in the shadow of the civil and criminal sanctions of a rule of law and a statute the constitutionality of which is in serious doubt—we find that reaching the merits is consistent with the pragmatic approach that we have followed in the past in determining finality. * * *

[The Court proceeded to invalidate § 26–9901 and the common-law privacy action on the merits, holding that the First and Fourteenth Amendments preclude states from barring the publication of truthful information contained in official court records open to public inspection.]

Reversed.

Mr. Chief Justice Burger concurs in the judgment.

Mr. Justice Powell, concurring.

---

13. Mr. Justice Rehnquist, is correct in saying that this factor involves consideration of the merits in determining jurisdiction. But it does so only to the extent of determining that the issue is substantial and only in the context that if the state court's final decision on the federal issue is incorrect, federal law forecloses further proceedings in the state court. That the petitioner who protests against the state court's decision on the federal question might prevail on the merits on nonfederal grounds in the course of further proceedings anticipated in the state court and hence obviate later review of the federal issue here is not preclusive of our jurisdiction. Curry, Langdeau, North Dakota State Board of Pharmacy, California v. Stewart, 384 U.S. 436 (1966) (decided with Miranda v. Arizona), and Miami Herald Publishing Co. v. Tornillo, 418 U.S. 241 (1974), make this clear. In those cases, the federal issue having been decided, arguably wrongly, and being determinative of the litigation if decided the other way, the finality rule was satisfied.

The author of the dissent, a member of the majority in Tornillo, does not disavow that decision. He seeks only to distinguish it by indicating that the First Amendment issue at stake there was more important and pressing than the one here. This seems to embrace the thesis of that case and of this one as far as the approach to finality is concerned, even though the merits and the avoidance doctrine are to some extent involved.

I join in the Court's opinion, as I agree with the holding and most of its supporting rationale. * * *.

MR. JUSTICE DOUGLAS, concurring in the judgment.

I agree that the state judgment is "final," and I also agree in the reversal of the Georgia court. * * *.

MR. JUSTICE REHNQUIST, dissenting.

Because I am of the opinion that the decision which is the subject of this appeal is not a "final" judgment or decree, as that term is used in 28 U.S.C. § 1257, I would dismiss this appeal for want of jurisdiction.

Radio Station WOW, Inc. v. Johnson, 326 U.S. 120 (1945), established that in a "very few" circumstances review of state-court decisions could be had in this Court even though something "further remain[ed] to be determined by a State court." Over the years, however, and despite vigorous protest by Mr. Justice Harlan,[1] this Court has steadily discovered new exceptions to the finality requirement, such that they can hardly any longer be described as "very few." Whatever may be the unexpressed reasons for this process of expansion, see, *e.g.*, Hudson Distributors v. Eli Lilly, 377 U.S. 386, 401 (1964) (Harlan, J., dissenting), it has frequently been the subject of no more formal an express explanation than cursory citations to preceding cases in the line. Especially is this true of cases in which the Court, as it does today, relies on Construction Laborers v. Curry, 371 U.S. 542 (1963).[2] Although the Court's opinion today does accord detailed consideration to this problem, I do not believe that the reasons it expresses can support its result.

I

The Court has taken what it terms a "pragmatic" approach to the finality problem presented in this case. In so doing, it has relied heavily on Gillespie v. United States Steel Corp., 379 U.S. 148 (1964). As the Court acknowledges, Gillespie involved 28 U.S.C. § 1291, which restricts the appellate jurisdiction of the federal courts of appeals to "final decisions of the district courts." Although acknowledging this distinction, the Court accords it no importance and adopts Gillespie's approach without any consideration of whether the finality requirement for this Court's jurisdiction over a "judgment or decree" of a state court is grounded on more serious concerns than is the limitation of court of appeals jurisdiction to final "decisions" of the district courts. I believe that the underlying concerns are different, and that the difference counsels a more restrictive approach when § 1257 finality is at issue.

According to Gillespie, the finality requirement is imposed as a matter of minimizing "the inconvenience and costs of piecemeal review." This proposition is undoubtedly sound so long as one is considering the administration of the federal court system. Were judicial efficiency the only interest at stake there would be less inclination to challenge the Court's

---

1. See Construction Laborers v. Curry, 371 U.S. 542, 553 (1963); Mercantile National Bank v. Langdeau, 371 U.S. 555, 572 (1963); Hudson Distributors v. Eli Lilly, 377 U.S. 386, 395 (1964); Organization for a Better Austin v. Keefe, 402 U.S. 415, 420 (1971).

2. See, *e.g.*, American Radio Assn. v. Mobile S.S. Assn., 419 U.S. 215, 217 n. 1 (1974); Hudson Distributors v. Eli Lilly, *supra*, at 389 n. 4.

resolution in this case, although, as discussed below, I have serious reservations that the standards the Court has formulated are effective for achieving even this single goal. The case before us, however, is an appeal from a state court, and this fact introduces additional interests which must be accommodated in fashioning any exception to the literal application of the finality requirement. I consider § 1257 finality to be but one of a number of congressional provisions reflecting concern that uncontrolled federal judicial interference with state administrative and judicial functions would have untoward consequences for our federal system. This is by no means a novel view of the § 1257 finality requirement. In Radio Station WOW, Inc. v. Johnson, 326 U.S., at 124, Mr. Justice Frankfurter's opinion for the Court explained the finality requirement as follows:

> "This requirement has the support of considerations generally applicable to good judicial administration. It avoids the mischief of economic waste and of delayed justice. Only in very few situations, where intermediate rulings may carry serious public consequences, has there been a departure from this requirement of finality for federal appellate jurisdiction. *This prerequisite to review derives added force when the jurisdiction of this Court is invoked to upset the decision of a State court.* Here we are in the realm of potential conflict between the courts of two different governments. And so, ever since 1789, Congress has granted this Court the power to intervene in State litigation only after 'the highest court of a State in which a decision in the suit could be had' has rendered a 'final judgment or decree.' § 237 of the Judicial Code, 28 U.S.C. § 344(a). *This requirement is not one of those technicalities to be easily scorned. It is an important factor in the smooth working of our federal system.*" (Emphasis added.)
>
>   *   *   *

That comity and federalism are significant elements of § 1257 finality has been recognized by other members of the Court as well, perhaps most notably by Mr. Justice Harlan. See, *e.g.,* Hudson Distributors v. Eli Lilly, 377 U.S., at 397–398 (dissenting); Mercantile National Bank v. Langdeau, 371 U.S. 555, 572 (1963) (dissenting). In the latter dissent, he argued that one basis of the finality rule was that it foreclosed "this Court from passing on constitutional issues that may be dissipated by the final outcome of a case, thus helping to keep to a minimum undesirable federal-state conflicts." One need cast no doubt on the Court's decision in such cases as Langdeau to recognize that Mr. Justice Harlan was focusing on a consideration which should be of significance in the Court's disposition of this case.

"Harmonious state-federal relations" are no less important today than when Mr. Justice Frankfurter penned Radio Station WOW * * *. Indeed, we have in recent years emphasized and re-emphasized the importance of comity and federalism in dealing with a related problem, that of district court interference with ongoing state judicial proceedings. See Younger v. Harris, 401 U.S. 37 (1971); Samuels v. Mackell, 401 U.S. 66 (1971). Because these concerns are important, and because they provide "added force" to § 1257's finality requirement, I believe that the Court has erred by simply importing the approach of cases in which the only concern is efficient judicial administration.

II

But quite apart from the considerations of federalism which counsel against an expansive reading of our jurisdiction under § 1257, the Court's holding today enunciates a virtually formless exception to the finality requirement, one which differs in kind from those previously carved out. * * * [At this point, Justice Rehnquist indicates his agreement with the first three categories described in the majority opinion.]

* * * While the totality of these exceptions certainly indicates that the Court has been willing to impart to the language "final judgment or decree" a great deal of flexibility, each of them is arguably consistent with the intent of Congress in enacting § 1257, if not with the language it used, and each of them is relatively workable in practice.

To those established exceptions is now added one so formless that it cannot be paraphrased, but instead must be quoted:

"Given these factors—that the litigation could be terminated by our decision on the merits and that a failure to decide the question now will leave the press in Georgia operating in the shadow of the civil and criminal sanctions of a rule of law and a statute the constitutionality of which is in serious doubt—we find that reaching the merits is consistent with the pragmatic approach that we have followed in the past in determining finality."

There are a number of difficulties with this test. One of them is the Court's willingness to look to the merits. It is not clear from the Court's opinion, however, exactly how great a look at the merits we are to take. On the one hand, the Court emphasizes that if we reverse the Supreme Court of Georgia the litigation will end, and it refers to cases in which the federal issue has been decided "arguably wrongly." On the other hand, it claims to look to the merits "only to the extent of determining that the issue is substantial." If the latter is all the Court means, then the inquiry is no more extensive than is involved when we determine whether a case is appropriate for plenary consideration; but if no more is meant, our decision is just as likely to be a costly intermediate step in the litigation as it is to be the concluding event. If, on the other hand, the Court really intends its doctrine to reach only so far as cases in which our decision in all probability will terminate the litigation, then the Court is reversing the traditional sequence of judicial decisionmaking. Heretofore, it has generally been thought that a court first assumed jurisdiction of a case, and then went on to decide the merits of the questions it presented. But henceforth in determining our own jurisdiction we may be obliged to determine whether or not we agree with the merits of the decision of the highest court of a State.

Yet another difficulty with the Court's formulation is the problem of transposing to any other case the requirement that "failure to decide the question now will leave the press in Georgia operating in the shadow of the civil and criminal sanctions of a rule of law and a statute the constitutionality of which is in serious doubt." Assuming that we are to make this determination of "serious doubt" at the time we note probable jurisdiction of such an appeal, is it enough that the highest court of the State has ruled against any federal constitutional claim? If that is the case, then because § 1257 by other language imposes that requirement, we will have completely read out of the statute the limitation of our jurisdiction to a "final judgment or decree." Perhaps the Court's new standard for finality is limited to cases in which a First Amendment freedom is at issue. The language used by Congress, however, certainly provides no basis for preferring the First Amendment, as incorporated by the Fourteenth Amendment, to the various other Amendments which are likewise "incorporated," or indeed for preferring any of the "incorporated" Amendments over the due process and equal protection provisions which are embodied literally in the Fourteenth Amendment.

Another problem is that in applying the second prong of its test, the Court has not engaged in any independent inquiry as to the consequences of permitting the decision of the Supreme Court of Georgia to remain undisturbed pending final state-court resolution of the case. This suggests that in order to invoke the benefit of today's rule, the "shadow" in which an appellant must stand need be neither deep nor wide. In this case nothing more is at issue than the right to report the name of the victim of a rape. No hindrance of any sort has been imposed on reporting the fact of a rape or the circumstances surrounding it. Yet the Court unquestioningly places this issue on a par with the core First Amendment interest involved in Miami Herald Publishing Co. v. Tornillo, 418 U.S. 241 (1974), and Mills v. Alabama, *supra*, that of protecting the press in its role of providing uninhibited political discourse.

But the greatest difficulty with the test enunciated today is that it totally abandons the principle that constitutional issues are too important to be decided save when absolutely necessary, and are to be avoided if there are grounds for decision of lesser dimension. The long line of cases which established this rule makes clear that it is a principle primarily designed, not to benefit the lower courts, or state-federal relations, but rather to safeguard this Court's own process of constitutional adjudication. * * *.

In this case there has yet to be an adjudication of liability against appellants, and unlike the appellant in Mills v. Alabama, they do not concede that they have no nonfederal defenses. Nonetheless, the Court rules on their constitutional defense. Far from eschewing a constitutional holding in advance of the necessity for one, the Court construes § 1257 so that it may virtually rush out and meet the prospective constitutional litigant as he approaches our doors.

III

This Court is obliged to make preliminary determinations of its jurisdiction at the time it votes to note probable jurisdiction. At that stage of the proceedings, prior to briefing on the merits or oral argument, such determinations must of necessity be based on relatively cursory acquaintance with the record of the proceedings below. The need for an understandable and workable application of a jurisdictional provision such as § 1257 is therefore far greater than for a similar interpretation of statutes dealing with substantive law. * * * It is thus especially disturbing that the rule of this case, unlike the more workable and straightforward exceptions which the Court has previously formulated, will seriously compound the already difficult task of accurately determining at a preliminary stage, whether an appeal from a state-court judgment is a "final judgment or decree." * * *

* * *

Although unable to persuade my Brethren that we do not have in this case a final judgment or decree of the Supreme Court of Georgia, I nonetheless take heart from the fact that we are concerned here with an area in which "*stare decisis* has historically been accorded considerably less than its usual weight." Gonzalez v. Employees Credit Union, 419 U.S. 90, 95 (1974). I would dismiss for want of jurisdiction.

NOTE ON THE FINAL JUDGMENT RULE AND THE HIGHEST STATE COURT REQUIREMENT

(1) Section 25 of the Judiciary Act of 1789 limited Supreme Court review of state courts to "final judgment[s] or decree[s] in any suit, in the highest court of law or equity of a State in which a decision in the suit could be had." (The full text of Section 25 is reproduced at p. 501, *supra*.) The present version, 28 U.S.C. § 1257, uses almost identical language.

As Cox indicates, out of this deceptively simple finality requirement the Supreme Court has spun a complicated web. For many years, the Court construed the requirement to permit review only when litigation on the merits of the case in the state court had proceeded to the point where nothing was left to be done except entry or execution of judgment. See, *e.g.*, Houston v. Moore, 3 Wheat. 433 (U.S.1818). The first major inroad came with Carondelet Canal & Nav. Co. v. Louisiana, 233 U.S. 362 (1914), where the Court reviewed a judgment of the Louisiana Supreme Court ordering the transfer of the canal company's property despite its claim of federal protection. The Court found the judgment final even though the case had been remanded by the state court for an accounting, because the remaining dispute was narrow and because the state judgment disposed of the federal right asserted. As the doctrine further evolved, a "penumbral area" developed within which non-final judgments were nevertheless deemed final. Radio Station WOW, Inc. v. Johnson, 326 U.S. 120, 124 (1945). The holdings often involved state court judgments that in effect resolved the merits of the federal question in a manner threatening immediate and irreparable harm to a party. "In effect, such a controversy is a multiple litigation allowing review of the adjudication which is concluded because it is independent of, and unaffected by, another litigation with which it happens to be entangled" (p. 126); see also Clark v. Williard, 292 U.S. 112 (1934).

In 1963, the Court decided Curry and Langdeau, both discussed in Cox. These cases substantially expanded the penumbra of finality; Curry's formulation included cases where "postponing review would seriously erode" national policy. Local No. 438 and General Laborers' Union v. Curry, 371 U.S. 542, 550 (1963). The erosion standard now forms the central justification for the fourth Cox category and represents the loosest interpretation of the final judgment requirement.

(2) With respect to the first Cox category—cases where, despite a remand to the lower state court, the federal question finally decided by the state court is likely to be completely decisive—see, in addition to the Mills case discussed in the opinion, Richfield Oil Corp. v. State Board of Equalization, 329 U.S. 69 (1946), holding final a judgment of the California Supreme Court reversing the trial court and remanding for a new trial. The Court

determined that the issues that could be presented at a new trial were sharply restricted by a state statute whose effect the state supreme court had already addressed. See also Abood v. Detroit Bd. of Education, 431 U.S. 209, 216 n. 8 (1977) (remand to state trial court characterized as "ministerial").

The finality of a case falling under the first Cox category can of course be affected by the parties' procedural steps and stipulations. See Philadelphia v. New Jersey, 437 U.S. 617 (1978) (appellants dismissed with prejudice several counts so that there would be a final judgment). Indeed, if a party represents that no further evidence will be offered below, that party may be precluded from adducing additional evidence on remand. See NAACP v. Alabama ex rel. Patterson, 360 U.S. 240 (1959). *Cf.* Minnick v. California Dept. of Corrections, 452 U.S. 105 (1981), Paragraph (7), *infra.* Should such a representation be required to establish finality in this kind of case?

(3) The second Cox category allows review of federal claims that will eventually require decision no matter what happens during further state court proceedings. This category, based on the notion that the further state proceedings (*i.e.*, an accounting) seem completely separate from the merits of the already adjudicated federal issues, represents the most traditional incursion into the finality requirement.

Should all such cases be deemed final automatically? Consider the suggestion that each of the cases cited by the Court in support of this second category "arguably involved elements of hardship in addition to the simple burden of proceedings that might prove unnecessary, and this category of finality would be more convincing if it were restricted to such situations." 16 Wright, Miller & Cooper, Federal Practice and Procedure § 4010, at 589 (1977).

(4) The third Cox exception allows immediate review where further proceedings may moot the federal question so that it becomes effectively unreviewable. Typical are criminal cases, where the state court has decided a federal question in favor of the defendant and remanded for new trial. If the new trial again results in a conviction, the defendant (having won on the federal issue) may of course no longer raise that federal issue. If, on the other hand, the defendant is acquitted, the state normally cannot appeal because of double jeopardy. *Cf.* 18 U.S.C. § 3731, expressly permitting interlocutory review in certain circumstances in federal criminal cases in order to protect the government from being bound by an acquittal that resulted from an otherwise unreviewable preliminary decision in the defendant's favor.

For examples of the third exception in a different context, see North Dakota State Bd. of Pharmacy v. Snyder's Drug Stores, Inc., 414 U.S. 156 (1973); Pennsylvania v. Ritchie, 107 S.Ct. 989 (1987).

Is the federal interest in reviewing such cases less pressing than in a case where the state court judgment is concededly final because the state court has definitively reversed a state criminal conviction on the basis of an erroneous ruling of federal law? (Compare the discussion in the *Note on Review of State Decisions Upholding Claims of Federal Right,* and the *Note on State Incorporation of or Reference to Federal Law,* at pp. 554, 559, *supra.*)

Note that, although a failure to provide immediate review may preclude review of a federal question in a particular case falling within this category, the *issue* will not necessarily escape review forever. In California v. Stewart, 384 U.S. 436 (1966), the Court held final a decision of the California Supreme Court suppressing a confession on federal constitutional grounds and remanding for trial. Even under a strict view of finality, if in another case a motion to suppress on that federal constitutional ground were denied, and the defendant convicted, that conviction would of course be subject to review. (This in fact happened in Miranda v. Arizona, 384 U.S. 436 (1966), a companion case to Stewart.) The confession issue would have escaped Supreme Court review only if every state court in the land had followed the California Supreme Court ruling in Stewart and ruled against the state. If every state court did so, would there be an urgent need for Supreme Court review?

Nevertheless, state court decisions to suppress evidence on federal constitutional grounds are now routinely reviewed by the Supreme Court before prosecution proceeds. See, *e.g.*, New York v. Quarles, 467 U.S. 649 (1984) (state court suppressed evidence for failure to give Miranda warnings); California v. Trombetta, 467 U.S. 479 (1984) (state court suppressed evidence of results of intoxilyzer breath test); Florida v. Meyers, 466 U.S. 380 (1984) (state court suppressed evidence obtained in allegedly unlawful car search); South Dakota v. Neville, 459 U.S. 553 (1983) (state court suppressed evidence of defendant's refusal to take blood test).

(5) The fourth Cox category embodies two requirements: reversal of the state court on the federal issue must have the effect of ending the litigation, and a refusal to review the federal issue immediately must threaten serious erosion of a significant federal policy. The range of policies encompassed by this category has been broad. See, *e.g.*, Bullington v. Missouri, 451 U.S. 430 (1981) and Harris v. Washington, 404 U.S. 55 (1971) (constitutional policy against double jeopardy threatened if review postponed and defendant tried a second time); Southland Corp. v. Keating, 465 U.S. 1 (1984) (United States Arbitration Act's policy of preempting state-court jurisdiction eroded if state court decision (ordering state proceedings) not immediately reviewed); Belknap, Inc. v. Hale, 463 U.S. 491 (1983) (same with respect to NLRB's claim to exclusive jurisdiction); Shaffer v. Heitner, 433 U.S. 186, 195–96 n. 12 (1977), and Calder v. Jones, 465 U.S. 783, (1984) (state court holdings upholding state territorial jurisdiction against due process objections reviewed even though state trials were to follow; other cases in this line cited at 465 U.S. 788 n. 8). But see Gillette Co. v. Miner, 459 U.S. 86 (1982) (state court ruled that it had territorial jurisdiction over plaintiff class-members without minimum contacts with the state and remanded for trial; Supreme Court granted certiorari but, after argument, dismissed the writ, "there being no final judgment").

(6) It is in First Amendment cases that the Court has been especially eager to relax finality requirements in order to protect speech interests against the erosion that can attend delay. In Organization for a Better Austin v. Keefe, 402 U.S. 415 (1971), the Court held that a "temporary" injunction granted by a state court prohibiting leafletting was, in effect, final, with further proceedings "a formality." It noted that "the temporary injunction here, which has been in effect for over three years, has already had marked impact on petitioners' First Amendment rights" (p. 418 n.*). In Nebraska Press Ass'n v. Stuart, 423 U.S. 1319, 1327 (1975), Justice

Blackmun, in chambers, granted a stay of a Nebraska trial court "gag" order on the local media. The Nebraska Supreme Court had taken the case but delayed review. Although the order, which prohibited media dissemination of certain materials relating to a pending criminal case, was not "the final one in the matter," Justice Blackmun found that each day of delay by the Nebraska court was itself a final decision, thus giving the Court jurisdiction to grant a stay. Despite the fact that the Nebraska Supreme Court had done nothing on the merits of the case, "[w]hen a reasonable time in which to review the restraint has passed, as here, we may properly regard the state court as having finally decided that the restraint should remain in effect during the period of delay" (p. 1330).[1]

In National Socialist Party v. Skokie, 432 U.S. 43 (1977), the petitioners were enjoined by an Illinois trial court from marching or parading. An appellate court denied a stay of the injunction pending appeal, as did the Illinois Supreme Court. Defendants sought a stay from the United States Supreme Court. "Treating the application as a petition for certiorari from the order of the Illinois Supreme Court [denying a stay]," the Court granted certiorari and reversed: "The order is a final judgment for purposes of our jurisdiction * * *. It finally determined the merits of petitioners' claim that the outstanding injunction will deprive them of rights protected by the First Amendment during the period of appellate review which, in the normal course, may take a year or more to complete. If a State seeks to impose a restraint of this kind, it must provide strict procedural safeguards * * * including immediate appellate review * * *" (p. 44). Three Justices dissented, distinguishing Cox on the ground that there the state supreme court had, at least, finally decided the federal claim.

Note the irony of the proposition that the Constitution requires the states to provide for "immediate appellate review" of certain restraints imposed on freedom of speech, given the "finality" rule of § 1257. Does the Court's reasoning suggest that interlocutory review may sometimes be a matter of constitutional right? (Would that suggest that access to interlocutory review by the Supreme Court could become a constitutional right?)

See also M.I.C. Ltd. v. Bedford Township, 463 U.S. 1341 (1983) (Brennan, J., in chambers) (application for stay of preliminary injunction prohibiting exhibition of allegedly obscene films; stay granted; state court refusal to lift injunction or to provide immediate appellate review "indicates" finality); Seattle Times Co. v. Rhinehart, 467 U.S. 20 (1984) (pretrial discovery protective order reviewed and sustained); Oklahoma Publishing Co. v. District Court for Oklahoma County, Oklahoma, 429 U.S. 967 (1976) (application for stay of gag order granted).[2]

1. The Court's subsequent opinion on the merits expressed no judgment on Justice Blackmun's approach. Nebraska Press Ass'n v. Stuart, 427 U.S. 539 (1976).

2. Note that the cases in this line assume that the power of the Court (or of a Justice) to grant a stay is limited to cases where the state decision is "final." This assumption is plainly correct where the stay is sought pursuant to 28 U.S.C. § 2101(f), providing that "[i]n any case in which the final judgment or decree of any court is subject to review by the Supreme

Court on writ of certiorari," execution or enforcement of the judgment or decree may be stayed. But there is no analogous statute with respect to appeals; and Rule 44 of the Supreme Court rules simply provides that a "stay may be granted by a Justice of this Court as permitted by law; and a writ of injunction may be granted by any Justice in a case where it might be granted by the Court."

Would the All–Writs Act, 28 U.S.C. § 1651, provide an independent basis for the Court to stay the effectiveness of a

Should § 1257 be interpreted to allow immediate Supreme Court review of every injunction restricting the present exercise of First Amendment rights unless the state courts grant a stay?

Note that Cox itself did not involve an injunction against speech. Was there any special urgency in Cox? It is of course true that, if the broadcaster in Cox prevailed on state-law grounds, "there would remain in effect the unreviewed decision of the State Supreme Court that a civil action for publishing the name of a rape victim disclosed in a public judicial proceeding may go forward despite the First and Fourteenth Amendments." But this is true in any case in which a party makes a First Amendment claim that is rejected but there also exists an alternative ground for decision. And note, too, that where a state court enters a *final* judgment rejecting a First Amendment defense but simultaneously upholding a decisive state-law defense, the decision is plainly unreviewable (because it rests on an independent state law ground), and yet there "remains in effect" the unreviewed state-court opinion on the First Amendment issue. Does this differ from Cox?

Despite its sweeping language, Cox apparently does not cover all cases in which First Amendment claims are made. Consider Flynt v. Ohio, 451 U.S. 619 (1981) (per curiam). The state courts had denied defendants' motion to dismiss a prosecution for disseminating obscenity; defendants had claimed that this was a selective prosecution violating the First Amendment. Over four dissents, the United States Supreme Court held the case not final. The Court found that the case could arguably fall within the fourth Cox category. "But the question remains whether delaying review until petitioners are convicted, if they are, would seriously erode federal policy within the meaning of our prior cases. * * * Here there is no identifiable federal policy that will suffer if the state criminal proceeding goes forward. * * * The resolution of this question can await final judgment without any adverse effect upon important federal interests. A contrary conclusion would permit the fourth exception [of Cox] to swallow the rule" (p. 622). The four dissenters found an identifiable federal policy in the First Amendment designed to prevent this sort of prosecution.

(7) In Minnick v. California Dep't of Corrections, 452 U.S. 105 (1981), plaintiffs claimed that the defendants' affirmative action program unlawfully discriminated against white males. The state trial court struck down some aspects of the program, relying on the California Supreme Court's opinion in Bakke v. Regents of the University of California. Bakke was subsequently reversed by the United States Supreme Court, see p. 208, *supra,* and a state appellate court consequently reversed the Minnick trial court. The appellate court's opinion, however, left open certain issues for "examination if the case is to be retried." Moreover, the trial court's factual findings were ambiguous and confusing. The Supreme Court granted certiorari, but dismissed the writ after argument, rejecting plaintiffs' contention that the case was final under the first Cox category. Justice Stevens' opinion for the majority began by analyzing the plaintiffs' contention in light of two factors: the specifics of the particular litigation, and

state-court temporary injunction which is concededly non-final? Would such a stay be "in aid of" the Court's jurisdiction within the meaning of § 1651? See the discussion in Stern, Gressman & Shapiro, Supreme Court Practice 675–81 (6th ed. 1986); compare also the materials at pp. 347–61, *supra,* and 1841–45, *infra.*

"the extent to which the 'policy of strict necessity in disposing of constitutional issues' * * * is implicated" (p. 122) (quoting Rescue Army v. Municipal Court, 331 U.S. 549, 568 (1947), p. 735, *infra*). "In this case our analysis of the question whether the federal constitutional issues may be affected by additional proceedings in the state courts—and therefore take the case out of the first category of final judgments described in Cox—is * * * affected by ambiguities in the record, both as to the character of the petitioners' prima facie case and as to the character of the respondents' justification for their program" (p. 123). "Accordingly, because of significant developments in the law—and perhaps in the facts as well—and because of significant ambiguities in the record concerning both the extent to which race or sex has been used as a factor in making promotions and the justification for such use, we conclude that we should not address the constitutional issues until the proceedings in the trial court are finally concluded and the state appellate courts have completed their review of the trial court record" (p. 127).

Although the Court's opinion never specifies the precise basis for the dismissal, Justice Rehnquist's concurrence explicitly describes it as based on want of jurisdiction.[3] Do ambiguities in findings and developments in the law mean that the Court has no jurisdiction because there is no "final" judgment? Or merely that it should not hear a case for prudential reasons?

(8) What is left of the final judgment requirement as a jurisdictional *rule*? Does Cox—particularly in light of Flynt and Minnick—provide any principled basis for determining when cases will and will not be deemed final? (Note that even the four Cox categories may not exhaust the exceptions to the rule; Justice White speaks of "at least" four categories of exceptions.[4])

The Court acts as if it has wide-ranging discretion to create exceptions to the statutory finality rule; it reads the statute as embodying a *proviso* that non-final judgments may be reviewed where serious policy considerations indicate that it would be desirable to do so. Can this be justified, even if it is conceded that the policy considerations against a rigid application of the finality rule may, in a given case, be urgent?

Justice Rehnquist concluded his dissent in Cox Broadcasting by saying that he "take[s] heart from the fact that we are concerned here with an area in which 'stare decisis has historically been accorded considerably less than its usual weight'" (p. 512). Should *stare decisis* carry reduced weight with regard to the statutory rules that govern the Court's jurisdiction to review state court judgments?

(9) In Cox, Justice Rehnquist argued that the finality rule of § 1257 should be more strictly construed than the analogous finality requirement in § 1291, governing review of district court decisions in the courts of appeals. (As to the latter, see Chap. XV, Sec. 1, *infra*.) The tradition has been to draw no distinction between the two statutes, and cases arising under them are apparently cited interchangably. Thus, in Cox, Justice

---

3. And Justice Brennan's separate concurrence clearly establishes that the dismissal was not on the basis that certiorari had been "improvidently granted."

4. For a particularly mysterious holding that a state judgment is final, even

though it is hard to fit in any of the Cox categories, see American Export Lines, Inc. v. Alvez, 446 U.S. 274 (1980), fully discussed in 16 Wright, Miller & Cooper, Federal Practice and Procedure § 4010, at 533–36 (1987 Supp.).

White cited Forgay v. Conrad, 6 How. 201 (U.S.1848), a federal case, in the same breath with Carondelet Canal & Nav. Co. v. Louisiana, 233 U.S. 362 (1914), a case from a state court, for the proposition that the final judgment rule is to be given a liberal, non-technical construction; and he relied heavily on Gillespie v. United States Steel Corp., 379 U.S. 148 (1964), a federal case. (See further the discussion of Gillespie at p. 1810, *infra*.) In Radio Station WOW, Inc. v. Johnson, 326 U.S. 120, 125–27 (1945), Justice Frankfurter also relied on Forgay in finding a case from the Nebraska Supreme Court final.

Are there good reasons to distinguish between the finality rules of § 1257 and § 1291? If so, do they cut in favor of a "stricter" construction of § 1257?

(10) Since the time within which to appeal or to petition for certiorari runs from the date of final judgment, failure to seek review at an intermediate stage in the proceeding may result in forfeiture of the right to review.

In Rio Grande Western R. Co. v. Stringham, 239 U.S. 44 (1915), the trial court found for the defendants, but on appeal to the state supreme court, the judgment was reversed, and the court ordered partial judgment for the plaintiff. After the trial court entered judgment as directed, plaintiff again appealed, challenging so much of the judgment as was entered for the defendants. The state supreme court denied relief, holding its prior opinion the law of the case. Plaintiff filed two writs of error in the Supreme Court, seeking to review both the first and second judgments. Deciding that the entry of judgment by the trial court constituted a mere ministerial act, so that the first decision of the state supreme court formed the final judgment, the Court dismissed the first writ as filed too late. It then dismissed the second writ, apparently because the state court's decision that the first judgment itself constituted the law of the case was an adequate state ground precluding Supreme Court review. See also Department of Banking v. Pink, 317 U.S. 264 (1942); Cole v. Violette, 319 U.S. 581 (1943).

In light of the lack of definition of the final judgment rule, such a forfeiture seems unfair and imprudent. See Dyk, *Supreme Court Review of Interlocutory State–Court Decisions: "The Twilight Zone of Finality"*, 18 Stan.L.Rev. 907, 929–34 (1967); Frank, *Requiem For The Final Judgment Rule*, 45 Texas L.Rev. 292, 317–18 (1966). If litigants act at their peril, they can be expected to—indeed, to be safe, they must—seek review at every stage possible. This can only have an undesirable effect on the already overcrowded docket of the Supreme Court. For this reason, as well as fairness to litigants, if the question of finality is in doubt, the litigant should be given the option of choosing his time. *Cf.* Corey v. United States, 375 U.S. 169 (1963), pp. 1812–13, *infra.*

(11) If the judgment of the highest state court is not final for purposes of Supreme Court review, the federal questions it determines will (if not mooted) be open in the Supreme Court on later review of the final judgment, whether or not under state law that adjudication is the law of the case on the second state review. See, *e.g.*, Great Western Tel. Co. v. Burnham, 162 U.S. 339 (1896). The power of the Court "to probe issues disposed of on appeals prior to the one under review is, in the last analysis, a 'necessary correlative' of the rule which limits it to the examination of final judgments." Urie v. Thompson, 337 U.S. 163, 172–73 (1949). "Be-

cause we cannot review a state court judgment until it is final, a contrary rule would insulate interlocutory state court rulings on important federal questions from our consideration." Hathorn v. Lovorn, 457 U.S. 255, 262 (1982).

(12) Finality is unaffected by the reservation of authority in the state court to grant a petition for rehearing, though if a timely petition is filed, the date of final judgment is the date of its denial or of the expiration of power to grant it, or, if rehearing is granted, of the new judgment. See Market Street Ry. Co. v. Railroad Commission, 324 U.S. 548, 551–52 (1945). By the same token, the denial of a petition for habeas corpus is a final judgment notwithstanding the authority of other courts to entertain a new petition; and the existence of postconviction remedies does not preclude direct review of a conviction.

In New York ex rel. Bryant v. Zimmerman, 278 U.S. 63 (1928), the relator, held in custody to answer a criminal charge, successfully employed habeas corpus to test the validity of the statute on which the charge was based. The state court judgment denying the writ was held final by the Supreme Court, despite the fact that under the state's judgment the accused still had to stand trial. Is there a difference between such a judgment in a collateral proceeding and a determination overruling a demurrer to the indictment or information, based on the claim of invalidity? See also Madruga v. Superior Court, 346 U.S. 556 (1954) (prohibition); Rescue Army v. Municipal Court, 331 U.S. 549 (1947), p. 735, *infra* (same).

(13) The "highest court of a State in which a decision could be had" (28 U.S.C. § 1257) may be the lowest court in the state system (*e.g.,* the city's Police Court in Thompson v. City of Louisville, 362 U.S. 199 (1960) p. 673, *supra*); or the order of a judge in chambers, as in Betts v. Brady, 316 U.S. 455 (1942). The sole criterion is whether further appellate review is possible within the state. If so, even though such review is discretionary, it must have been sought to confer jurisdiction on the Supreme Court.[5]

R.J. Reynolds Tobacco Co. v. Durham County, 107 S.Ct. 499, 505–06 (1986), involved a decision by the North Carolina Court of Appeals upholding a North Carolina ad valorem tax. Reynolds' petition for discretionary review to the North Carolina Supreme Court was denied for lack of a substantial constitutional question. The decision of the North Carolina Supreme Court could have been interpreted as a decision on the merits affirming the lower court (thus making the former the relevant "highest" court), or as a determination that it lacked jurisdiction over the appeal (making the lower court the relevant "highest" court). The Supreme Court decided that, "[i]n the absence of positive assurance to the contrary," the state court's dismissal of Reynolds' appeal should be deemed "a decision on the merits" (citing Michigan v. Long, p. 539, *supra*). It noted that this interpretation conformed to the Court's treatment of its own summary dispositions (citing Hicks v. Miranda, p. 730, *infra*).

---

5. See, *e.g.,* Costarelli v. Massachusetts, 421 U.S. 193 (1975); Gotthilf v. Sills, 375 U.S. 79 (1963) (leave to appeal on certified questions must be sought); Gorman v. Washington University, 316 U.S. 98 (1942) (review of judgment of division of state highest court by the court *en banc* is available and must be applied for); Matthews v. Huwe, 269 U.S. 262, 265 (1925) (discretionary review must be sought even though writ of error had been denied on the ground that the question was frivolous); but *cf.* Teamsters Local 174 v. Lucas Flour Co., 369 U.S. 95 (1962) (petitioner need not apply for review *en banc* where such review is discretionary and treated as a rehearing, and state law makes the division's actions the judgment of whole court).

Suppose that no interlocutory review had been available within the state court system in Cox, but that the relevant issue would have been open to state review later after the trial court's final judgment. Would the trial court decision be subject to immediate review in the Supreme Court? *Cf.* Organization for a Better Austin v. Keefe, 402 U.S. 415, 420 (1971) (Harlan, J., dissenting); Kentucky v. Powers, 201 U.S. 1, 37–39 (1906). For a discussion of the relationship between the highest state court requirement and finality, see the opinion of Brennan, J., dissenting from denial of certiorari, in Sprading v. Texas, 455 U.S. 971 (1982).

(14) See generally, Stern, Gressman & Shapiro, Supreme Court Practice 120–44 (6th ed. 1986); Dyk, p. 709, *supra;* Frank, p. 709, *supra;* Note, *The Finality Rule for Supreme Court Review of State Court Orders,* 91 Harv. L.Rev. 1004 (1978); Note, *The Requirement of a Final Judgment or Decree for Supreme Court Review of State Courts,* 73 Yale L.J. 515 (1964).

SECTION 4. OBLIGATORY OR DISCRETIONARY REVIEW

SUBSECTION A: APPEAL OR CERTIORARI

DAHNKE–WALKER MILLING CO. v. BONDURANT
257 U.S. 282, 42 S.Ct. 106, 66 L.Ed. 239 (1921).
Error to the Court of Appeals of Kentucky.

MR. JUSTICE VAN DEVANTER delivered the opinion of the Court.

This was an action to recover damages for the breach of a contract for the sale and delivery of a crop of wheat estimated at 14,000 bushels. The plaintiff was a Tennessee corporation engaged in operating a flour and feed mill at Union City, in that state. The defendant was a resident of Hickman, Ky., and extensively engaged in farming in that vicinity. They were the parties to the contract. It was made at Hickman and the wheat was to be delivered and paid for there. But the delivery was to be on board the cars of a common carrier, and the plaintiff intended to ship the wheat to its mill in Tennessee. A small part of the crop was delivered as agreed, but delivery of the rest was refused, although the plaintiff was prepared and expecting to receive and pay for it. A payment advanced on the crop more than covered what was delivered. At the time for delivery wheat had come to be worth several cents per bushel more than the price fixed by the contract. The action was brought in a state court in Kentucky.

The principal defense interposed—the only one which we have occasion to notice—was to the effect that the plaintiff had not complied, as was the fact, with a statute of Kentucky (Ky.Stats.1915, § 571) prescribing the conditions on which corporations of other states might do business in that state, and that the contract was therefore not enforceable. To this the plaintiff replied that the only business done by it in Kentucky consisted in purchasing wheat and other grain in that state for immediate shipment to its Tennessee mill and then shipping the same there; that the contract in question was made in the course of this business and with the purpose of forwarding the wheat to the mill as soon as it was delivered on board the cars; that this transaction was in interstate commerce, and as to it the statute of Kentucky whose application was invoked by the defendant was invalid because in conflict with the commerce clause of the Constitution of the United States.

The cause was tried twice. On the first trial the plaintiff obtained a verdict and judgment, the court ruling that the statute could not constitutionally be applied to the transaction in question. But the Court of Appeals of the state, while conceding the invalidity of the statute as respects transactions in interstate commerce, held the transaction in question was not in such commerce, declared the statute valid and properly enforceable as to that transaction, and reversed the judgment with a direction for a new trial. That court proceeded on the theory that, as the contract was made in Kentucky, related to property then in that state, and was to be wholly performed therein, the transaction was strictly intrastate, and not within the reach or protection of the commerce clause of the Constitution of the United States; and this although the wheat was to be delivered on board the cars of a public carrier and the plaintiff intended to ship it to Tennessee as soon as it was so delivered. Bondurant v. Dahnke–Walker Milling Co., 175 Ky. 774, 195 S.W. 139. On the second trial a verdict for the defendant was directed because the plaintiff had not complied with the statute. The jury conformed to the direction, judgment was entered on the verdict, and that judgment was affirmed by the Court of Appeals on the authority of its former decision. 185 Ky. 386, 215 S.W. 76.

The case is here on a writ of error and our jurisdiction is challenged. The objection is not that we are without power to review the judgment, but that it can be reviewed only on a writ of certiorari. The controlling statute is section 237 of the Judicial Code, as amended by the Act of September 6, 1916, c. 448, § 2, 39 Stat. 726 (Comp.St. § 1214). Besides confining our power of review in cases litigated in the state courts to those in which the decision of a federal question is involved, this jurisdictional section provides that the review in cases falling within certain classes may be on writ of error and in others on writ of certiorari, the distinguishing or dividing line being drawn according to the nature of the federal question and the way in which the state court decides it. Some cases may fall on both sides of the line, but with this we are not now concerned. Among those in which the review may be on writ of error the section includes—

"any suit * * * where is drawn in question the validity of a statute of, or an authority exercised under any state, on the ground of their being repugnant to the Constitution, treaties, or laws of the United States, and the decision is in favor of their validity."

Among those in which the review may be on writ of certiorari are—

"any cause * * * where is drawn in question the validity of a statute of, or an authority exercised under any state, on the ground of their being repugnant to the Constitution, treaties, or laws of the United States, and the decision is against their validity," and "any cause * * * where any title, right, privilege, or immunity is claimed under the Constitution, or any treaty or statute of, or commission held or authority exercised under the United States, and the decision is either in favor of or against the title, right, privilege or immunity especially set up or claimed, by either party, under such Constitution, treaty, statute, commission, or authority."

In the state court the plaintiff did not simply claim a right or immunity under the Constitution of the United States, but distinctly insisted that as to the transaction in question the Kentucky statute was void, and therefore unenforceable, because in conflict with the commerce clause of the Constitution. The court did not accede to the insistence, but applied and enforced the statute. Of course, that was an affirmation of its validity when so applied. * * * The case is therefore of the class described in the first of the provisions which we have quoted from the jurisdictional section. That the statute was not claimed to be invalid in toto and for every purpose does not matter. A statute may be invalid as applied to one state of facts and yet valid as applied to another. Poindexter v. Greenhow, 114 U.S. 270, 295; St. Louis, Iron Mountain & Southern Ry. Co. v. Wynne, 224 U.S. 354; Kansas City Southern Ry. Co. v. Anderson, 233 U.S. 325. Besides, a litigant can be heard to question a statute's validity only when and so far as it is being or is about to be applied to his disadvantage. Yazoo & Mississippi R.R. Co. v. Jackson Vinegar Co., 226 U.S. 217; Jeffrey Manufacturing Co. v. Blagg, 235 U.S. 571, 576. Neither does it matter on what ground the court upheld and enforced the statute. The provisions quoted from the jurisdictional section show that in cases where the validity of a state statute is drawn in question because of the alleged repugnance to the Constitution the mode of review depends on the way in which the state court resolves the question. If it be resolved in favor of the validity of the statute, the review may be on writ of error; and if it be resolved against the validity the review can only be on writ of certiorari. The provisions take no account of the particular grounds or reasons on which the decision is put.

It is loosely said in one of the briefs for the plaintiff that the "sole question for decision" is whether the contract was a part of interstate commerce; but we attach no importance to this, because it not only is said in the same brief that the plaintiff "maintained in the state court, and it maintains here, that the Kentucky statute, as construed and applied in this case by the state court, is unconstitutional under the commerce clause," but much of that brief and of another is devoted to an effort to show the invalidity of the statute in that regard.

Our conclusion on the jurisdictional question is that, as the state court applied and enforced to the plaintiff's disadvantage a state statute which the plaintiff seasonably insisted as so applied and enforced was repugnant to the Constitution and void, the case is rightly here on writ of error. * * *

There is no controversy about the facts bearing on the character of the transaction in question. It had been the practice of the plaintiff to go into Kentucky to purchase grain to be transported to and used in its mill in Tennessee. On different occasions it had purchased from the defendant— at one time 13,000—bushels of corn. This contract was made in continuance of that practice, the plaintiff intending to forward the grain to its mill as soon as the delivery was made. In keeping with that purpose the delivery was to be on board the cars of a public carrier. Applying to these facts the principles before stated, we think the transaction was in interstate commerce. The state court, stressing the fact that the contract was made in Kentucky and was to be performed there, put aside the further facts that the delivery was to be on board the cars and that the plaintiff, in continuance of its prior practice, was purchasing the grain for shipment to its mill in Tennessee. We think the facts so neglected had a material bearing and should have been considered. They showed that what otherwise seemed an intrastate transaction was a part of interstate commerce. * * * The state court also attached some importance to the fact that after the grain was delivered on the cars the plaintiff might have changed its mind and have sold the grain at the place of delivery or have shipped it to another point in Kentucky. No doubt this was possible, but it also was improbable. With equal basis it could be said that a shipment of merchandise billed to a point beyond the state of its origin might be halted by the shipper in the exercise of the right of stoppage in transitu before it got out of that state. The essential character of the transaction as otherwise fixed is not changed by a mere possibility of that sort. * * *

For these reasons we are of opinion that the transaction was a part of interstate commerce, in which the plaintiff lawfully could engage without any permission from the state of Kentucky, and that the statute in question, which concededly imposed burdensome conditions, was as to that transaction invalid because repugnant to the commerce clause.

Judgment reversed.

MR. JUSTICE BRANDEIS, dissenting.

The writ of error should, in my opinion, be dismissed. The obstacle to our assuming jurisdiction is not procedural, as it is in those cases where a plaintiff fails because the claim was not made seasonably or in appropriate form. Here the obstacle is the nature of the constitutional question sought to be reviewed. It involves a state statute. But the validity of the statute is not actually drawn in question. Only the propriety of the application or use of the statute is questioned. Since the Act of September 6, 1916, c. 448, § 2, 39 Stat. 726, such questions are not reviewable in this court as of right. They may now be reviewed only in the court's discretion; and exercise of the discretion must be invoked by a petition for a writ of certiorari.

This court has now, as it had before that act, jurisdiction under section 237 of the Judicial Code to review a final judgment of the highest court of a state whenever a right under the federal Constitution duly claimed has been denied in applying a state statute. And in no case involving a state statute can jurisdiction attach unless the statute has been applied. For, unless it was applied, there could not have been an invasion of the party's constitutional right; and, unless there was such invasion, the constitutional question presented, whatever its nature, would be moot. But the act of 1916 made the nature of the constitutional question raised in applying the statute a matter of importance. If the question is a denial of the power of the Legislature to enact the statute as construed, a review may be had as of right. If the question concerns merely the propriety of the particular use of the statute or of the manner of applying or administering it the review may be had only in this court's discretion. The classification thus introduced rests upon broad considerations of policy. The steady increase of the business of this court had made it necessary to limit the appellate jurisdiction in cases arising under section 237. To this end Congress determined in 1916 that even cases involving constitutional questions should be reviewed here only where the public interest appeared to demand it. Congress left parties a review as of right where the validity of a state statute had been drawn in question; because the decision of such a question is usually a matter of general interest.   But whether a valid state statute has in a particular case been so used as to violate a constitutional guaranty is ordinarily a matter of merely private interest.   Hence Congress provided that, where the validity of the statute is not assailed, the denial of a claim that in applying it a right, privilege, or immunity had been violated should not be reviewed, unless this court, in its discretion to be exercised upon petition for a writ of certiorari, should direct the review; that is, Congress treated a right, privilege, or immunity claimed to have been violated by the courts' erroneously applying a confessedly valid statute to the particular facts of a case just as it treated a claim that the right, privilege, or immunity had been violated by a decision erroneous in some other respect.

In considering whether in this case the validity of the state statute was drawn in question, it is necessary to bear in mind that, in every case involving a statute, the state court must perform (aside from the consideration of any constitutional questions) two functions essentially different. First the court must construe the statute; that is, determine its meaning and scope.   Then it must apply the statute, as so construed, to the facts of the case.[2]   In this case the construction of the statute was never in controversy.   It had been settled by earlier decisions that the statute referred only to corporations when transacting business in intrastate commerce.   Here the only controversy concerned the character of the particular transaction to which defendant sought to have the statute applied. Was it interstate commerce?   If so, the transaction was not within the scope of the statute.   To decide that controversy two determinations had to be made.   One was of fact—whether the wheat was sold and bought for shipment to Tennessee.   The other was of law—whether the fact that the wheat was so sold and bought makes the transaction one in interstate commerce.   Did that controversy over the character of the commerce draw in question the validity of the statute or did it draw in question merely the propriety, that is, the constitutionality, of its application?   What the character of the controversy was must be decided upon the record presented here.

The validity of a statute, as was said in Baltimore & Potomac R.R. Co. v. Hopkins, 130 U.S. 210, 224, is drawn in question whenever the power to enact it "as it is by its terms or is made to read by construction, is fairly open to denial and denied."   The power to enact section 571, Kentucky Statutes, as construed by the highest court of the state, was not fairly open to denial; for the statute was construed as affecting only intrastate transactions of foreign corporations.   *   *   * A writ of error which rested solely upon the challenge of the statute so construed would have presented no substantial claim and must have been dismissed as frivolous.   *   *   * Nor was the power to enact section 571 as construed actually denied.   The question decided below and presented for review here is merely whether this valid statute has been so used—not construed—as to deny to the

---

2.   The word "apply" is used in connection with statutes in two senses.   When construing a statute, in describing the class of persons, things or functions which are within its scope; as that the statute does not "apply" to transactions in interstate commerce.   When discussing the use made of a statute, in referring to the process by which the statute is made operative; as where the jury is told to "apply" the statute of limitation if they find that the cause of action arose before a given date.   In this opinion it is used in the latter sense.

plaintiff a privilege or immunity guaranteed by the federal Constitution.
* * *

Since 1903 it had been the settled law of the state, as then declared by
its highest court, that section 571 did not affect transactions in interstate
commerce, Commonwealth v. Hogan, McMorrow & Tieke Co. (Ky.) 74 S.W.
737. Thus, before this action was begun, it was the settled law that such
transactions of foreign corporations were not within the scope of the
statute. In 1915, after this action was begun, but before the first trial, that
rule was again applied in Louisville Trust Co. v. Bayer Co., 166 Ky. 744,
746, 179 S.W. 1034. When, therefore, this case was before the Circuit
Court at the second trial and when it was before the Court of Appeals for
the second time, there clearly was no actual controversy over the validity of
the statute. It is true that plaintiff had used in pleading language which
imported not only a claim of immunity because the transaction was
interstate commerce, but also an assertion that section 571, if construed so
as to affect it, was invalid. But a review by this court as of right cannot be
acquired by inaccurately describing, or by disguising, the nature of the
constitutional claim actually made. * * *

If jurisdiction upon writ of error can be obtained by the mere claim in
words that a state statute is invalid, if so construed as to "apply" to a given
state of facts, the right to review will depend, in large classes of cases, not
upon the nature of the constitutional question involved, but upon the skill
of counsel. The result would be particularly regrettable, because the
decision of such cases often depends not upon the determination of important questions of law (which should in the main engage the attention of this
court), but upon the appreciation of evidence frequently voluminous. Thus,
in proceedings under state Workmen's Compensation Acts or state Employers' Liability Acts, the question whether a carrier is liable depends often
upon the question whether at the time of the accident the employee was
engaged in interstate or in intrastate commerce. Since the Act of September 6, 1916, certiorari is the proper means of reviewing a judgment
involving that question. Southern Pacific Co. v. Industrial Commission,
251 U.S. 259. If the rule now insisted upon obtains, the carrier could in
every such case secure a review on writ of error by simply claiming that
the state statute is invalid under the commerce clause if construed so as to
apply to the special facts of the case. Yet it was pre-eminently the decision
of the questions like these from which Congress sought to relieve this court
by the act of September 6, 1916.[4] Likewise in cases involving state
taxation the validity of the tax often depends upon the question whether
the specific thing taxed was property within or property without the taxing
state—a question which, as held in Dana v. Dana, 250 U.S. 220, and
Anderson v. Durr, 257 U.S. 99, can be reviewed here only on writ of
certiorari. If the rule now insisted upon should prevail, jurisdiction in such
cases could be secured on writ of error by the simple device of claiming that
the taxing statute is invalid under the Fourteenth Amendment if construed
so as to apply to the specific property involved. So, in suits in state courts
against foreign corporations, the question whether there is jurisdiction
depends often upon the question whether the corporation was doing busi-

4. See Report of Judiciary Committee,
House Doc. No. 794, 64th Cong., 1st Sess.,
House Rep. vol. 3. Of the cases on the
docket for the preceding term of this court
37 presented the question whether the employee was engaged in interstate or intrastate commerce. * * *

ness within the state and had expressly or impliedly consented to be sued there. The correctness of the decision of a state court of this question has been held to be reviewable here only upon certiorari. Philadelphia & Reading Coal & Iron Co. v. Gilbert, 245 U.S. 162. But, if the rule now insisted upon should prevail, jurisdiction on writ of error may be secured by simply making the claim that the state statute is invalid under the Fourteenth Amendment if construed so as to apply to the facts of the case.

Plaintiff relies upon a number of cases, assumed to be similar, in which, after the Act of September 6, 1916, jurisdiction was (mainly without discussion) taken on writ of error. They are not in point. In some of them orders of railroad commissions were challenged as violating the Constitution. Such an order, unlike decisions of courts, being legislative in its nature and made by an instrumentality of the state, is a state law within the meaning of the Constitution of the United States and the laws of Congress regulating our jurisdiction. Lake Erie & Western R.R. Co. v. Public Utilities Commission, 249 U.S. 422, 424. In each of these cases, therefore, attacking the validity of the order was drawing in question the validity of a law. In others the validity of state statutes as construed was actually drawn in question. * * *

It is, of course, permissible to make the claim that a statute is invalid, and also that, as administered or applied, it violates a right of immunity under the Constitution. In such a case the writ of error is clearly appropriate. But in the case at bar there never has been a real claim that the statute as construed by the highest court of Kentucky is invalid. The actual claim was and is that a confessedly valid statute was misapplied, and thereby a constitutional guaranty was violated. A review as of right is not to be obtained by misdescribing the question in controversy. When Congress declared that there should be a review as of right only where the validity of the statute was drawn in question, it did not provide for securing the right by the use of a form of words—a potent formula which should operate as an "open sesame." It was dealing with substance. It legislated to relieve an overburdened court.

NOTE ON THE SCOPE AND LIMITS OF THE DAHNKE-WALKER DOCTRINE

(1) Do you understand Justice Brandeis' position to be that appeal will lie only if a statute is invalidated *in toto?*

In Nashville, C. & St. L. Ry. v. Walters, 294 U.S. 405 (1935), a statute authorized a state commission to require the elimination of grade crossings when necessary to protect the traveling public, and provided that when such elimination was ordered the railroad should pay half the cost. Ordered to remove a crossing, the railroad challenged both the order and the statute as applied, contending that under the special circumstances the requirement that it pay half the cost was so arbitrary as to constitute denial of due process. The state court declined to examine the special circumstances and sustained the order and the statute. The Supreme Court reversed, Justice Brandeis writing, holding that a "statute valid as to one set of facts may be invalid as to another" (p. 415); and that the railroad, therefore, was entitled to a hearing on its claim. Review was by appeal.

If Justice Brandeis' view in the Dahnke–Walker case had prevailed, could this case have been appealed? Would it make sense to allow an appeal in such a case and to deny it in Dahnke–Walker or in Fiske v. Kansas, p. 639, *supra?*

(2) Justice Brandeis' prediction that under the Dahnke–Walker rule "the right to a review will depend, in large classes of cases, not upon the nature of the constitutional question involved but upon the skill of counsel" seems amply sustained by events. See, *e.g.,* Memphis Natural Gas Co. v. Beeler, 315 U.S. 649, 650–51 (1942); Raley v. Ohio, 360 U.S. 423, 434–35 (1959).

Thus, compare Gillespie v. Oklahoma, 257 U.S. 501 (1922), with Indian Territory Illuminating Oil Co. v. Board of Equalization, 287 U.S. 573, 288 U.S. 325 (1933); Citizens National Bank v. Durr, 257 U.S. 99 (1921), with Senior v. Braden, 295 U.S. 422 (1935), and Dahnke–Walker, *supra;* Edwards v. South Carolina, 372 U.S. 229 (1963), and Gregory v. Chicago, 394 U.S. 111 (1969), with Cox v. Louisiana, p. 649, *supra.*

As Chief Justice Stone said in the Beeler case, where a taxpayer contended that the levy of the tax infringed its rights under the commerce clause: "It is not enough that an appellant could have launched his attack upon the validity of the statute itself as applied; if he has failed to do so we are without jurisdiction over the appeal." 315 U.S. at 650–51. See also Hanson v. Denckla, 357 U.S. 235, 244 (1958) (appellants did not explicitly object to state long-arm statute; appeal dismissed and certiorari granted); Richmond Newspapers, Inc. v. Virginia, 448 U.S. 555, 562 n. 4 (1980) ("validity of Va.Code § 19.2–266 was not sufficiently drawn in question by appellants" to invoke appellate jurisdiction; certiorari granted). But if the state statute is "squarely" challenged, appellees will not be permitted to recharacterize the case as involving merely a claim of federal immunity against state action. See Japan Line, Ltd. v. County of Los Angeles, 441 U.S. 434 (1979).

Is there any substantial difference between the assertion of a federal immunity to application of a statute on the facts of record and the contention that the statute is invalid as applied? *Cf.* p. 662, *supra.* Why should the Court accord significance to how the point is made?

(3) Consider the possible relevance to the original decision in Dahnke–Walker of the fact that at the time, an attempted appeal held not to qualify under the statute was dismissed. Under present law, an appeal "improvidently taken" is treated as a petition for certiorari, giving the Court discretion to review or not, as it chooses. 28 U.S.C. § 2103. But the forerunner of this provision did not appear until 1925.

In view of the present provision, if Dahnke–Walker was wrongly decided and if (as Brandeis predicted and may well be true) its doctrine adds a significant number of relatively unimportant cases to the obligatory jurisdiction of an already overburdened Court, is there any reason why it should not be overruled?

Consider also the possibility that the inclusion of such cases in the category of appeals may generate pressure on the Court to dispose of cases in the obligatory jurisdiction with less than full consideration of the merits. *Cf.* subsections (b), (c) of this section, *infra.*

(4) What are the limits—if any—to the possibilities of stating a claim of immunity to an abusive application of a statute as a claim of *pro tanto* invalidity?

Jett Bros. Distilling Co. v. City of Carrollton, 252 U.S. 1 (1920), is often cited as a case where no appeal could lie. There the defendant resisted payment of a tax upon the ground that the assessment was discriminatory and a denial of equal protection. No challenge was leveled at the taxing statute or the authority of the assessors (the statute prior to 1925 including questions as to the "validity" of an "authority"—see p. 502, *supra*). The writ of error was accordingly dismissed. Is there any reason under Dahnke–Walker why the point could not have been made as an attack upon the taxing statute as applied, as distinguished from the assessment or the "tax"? *Cf.* Charleston Federal Savings & Loan Assn. v. Alderson, 324 U.S. 182 (1945);   Rohr Air–Craft Corp. v. San Diego, 362 U.S. 628 (1960). Does Iowa–Des Moines National Bank v. Bennett, p. 585, *supra,* present a different problem?

In Shelley v. Kraemer, 334 U.S. 1 (1948), the Supreme Court held that a state court injunction restraining violation of a racially restrictive covenant worked a denial of equal protection. No statute of the state declared the covenant enforceable, and review was on certiorari. Is there any way in which the petitioner could have provided a basis for appeal? Is it impossible to do so when the subject of the challenge is the court's rule of decision and the only statute that can be involved is that vesting jurisdiction in the court?

Pennsylvania v. Board of Directors of City Trusts, 353 U.S. 230 (1957), involved the will of Stephen Girard, probated in 1831, which had left property in trust for a "college" for "poor white male orphans." The will named the City of Philadelphia trustee. In 1869, a state statute established a "Board of Directors of City Trusts of the City of Philadelphia" to administer the trust and the college. An action was brought to compel the Board to admit Negroes to the college. The state courts rejected the petition. Review in the Supreme Court was sought by appeal, on the theory that the judgment sustaining the exclusion of Negroes involved unconstitutional application of the statute creating the Board. The Supreme Court dismissed the appeal. Certiorari was granted, pursuant to 28 U.S.C. § 2103, and the judgment was reversed. See also Pennsylvania v. Board of Directors of City Trusts, 357 U.S. 570 (1958) (dismissing a subsequent appeal, and denying certiorari). *Cf.* Philadelphia & Reading C. & I. Co. v. Gilbert, 245 U.S. 162, 166, (1917); Union National Bank v. Lamb, 337 U.S. 38 (1949).

In the Lamb case, Justice Douglas said: "Certiorari, not appeal, is the route by which the question whether or not full faith and credit has been given a foreign judgment is brought here." 337 U.S. at 39. See also Morris v. Jones, 329 U.S. 545 (1947); Roche v. McDonald, 275 U.S. 449 (1928). However, in Hughes v. Fetter, 341 U.S. 609 (1951), where Wisconsin's refusal to take jurisdiction of an Illinois wrongful death action was based upon a statute, challenged as a denial of full faith and credit to the Illinois wrongful death statute, review was by appeal. Would not the same result be necessary if the action had been based upon a judgment? If so, the statement in the Lamb case must have reference to situations where no statute gives the state's rule of decision with respect to the enforcement of the judgment. So far as appears, no one has attempted to state the contention as a challenge to the application of the statute vesting general jurisdiction in the court. If that were done, should it succeed?

Under Jackson v. Virginia, p. 682, *supra*, if a state criminal defendant claims that the evidence was not sufficient to support a conviction and adds the assertion that the criminal statute, as applied on the basis of such insufficient evidence, is unconstitutional, will appeal lie?

(5) Kulko v. Superior Court of California, 436 U.S. 84 (1978), and Calder v. Jones, 465 U.S. 783, 787 n. 7 (1984), involved the California long-arm statute, which confers territorial jurisdiction on the state courts in any case permitted by the United States Constitution. California upheld its jurisdiction in both cases; in both the United States Supreme Court dismissed appeals and granted certiorari. In Calder the Court said: "[P]etitioners argued below that the California statute as applied to them would be unconstitutional. We are unpersuaded by this shift in emphasis. * * * As in Kulko, the opinion below does not purport to determine the constitutionality of the California jurisdictional statute. Rather, the question decided was whether the Constitution itself would permit the assertion of jurisdiction. Under the circumstances, we find an appeal improper regardless of the terminology in which the petitioners couch their jurisdictional defense."

Can these cases be reconciled with Dahnke–Walker? What is the relevance of the fact that the state has incorporated the federal constitutional standard into its statute, so that there is a sense in which the statute cannot be "invalid"? Of the fact that the California statute, by creating a mirror image of the federal constitutional standard, exerts no independent policy-force of its own (valid or invalid)? Should not the case be treated as if no state statute existed at all?[1]

(6) There seems to be no disposition on the Court to reopen the Dahnke–Walker doctrine. For a case reaffirming it on essentially similar facts (and indeed citing it on the merits of the substantive issue), see Allenberg Cotton Co., Inc. v. Pittman, 419 U.S. 20 (1974). See also Marcus v. Search Warrants, 367 U.S. 717, 721 (1961); Japan Line, Ltd. v. County of Los Angeles, 441 U.S. 434, 440–41 (1979); McCarty v. McCarty, 453 U.S. 210, 219–20 n. 12 (1981); Fidelity Federal Savings & Loan Ass'n v. de la Cuesta, 458 U.S. 141 (1982); Rotary International v. Rotary Club of Duarte, 107 S.Ct. 1940 n. 3 (1987). *Cf.* Spencer v. Texas, 385 U.S. 554, 557 n. 3 (1967) ("The question of whether Spencer is properly here as an appeal * * * is a tangled one. Rather than undertake to resolve it, we think it more profitable to dismiss this appeal, treat it as a petition for certiorari, 28 U.S.C. § 2103, and grant the petition").[2]

---

1. See also Burger King Corp. v. Rudzewicz, 471 U.S. 462, 470 n. 12 (1985) (involving state long-arm statute in a case on appeal from a federal court; appeal under 28 U.S.C. § 1254(2) dismissed and certiorari granted).

2. See also Lerner v. Casey, 357 U.S. 468 (1958), involving a challenge to the New York Security Risk Law by a subway conductor fired after he refused to disclose whether he was a member of the Communist Party. The Court itself stated (p. 475) that his "major constitutional claim * * * goes to the manner in which the Security Risk Law was applied to him. It is contended that the administrative finding of reasonable grounds for belief [based on his refusal to answer] that he was 'of doubtful trust and reliability,' and therefore a security risk, offends due process." The contention had been presented in state court also on the basis that the statute "as written and applied" violated due process.

(7) An appeal is also provided when there "is drawn in question the validity of a treaty or statute of the United States and the decision is against its validity." 28 U.S.C. § 1257(1). Dahnke–Walker apparently governs when a state court holds an act of Congress invalid as applied. See Wissner v. Wissner, 338 U.S. 655 (1950) (allowing appeal).

(8) If a case presents a question that provides the basis for appeal, the appellant may include in his jurisdictional statement any other federal questions, though in themselves reviewable only on certiorari. He may also file a separate petition for certiorari addressed to the latter points. See Prudential Ins. Co. v. Cheek, 259 U.S. 530, 547 (1922); Flournoy v. Wiener, 321 U.S. 253, 263 (1944).

The normal order accepting an appeal for plenary consideration, "probable jurisdiction noted," brings before the Court all the federal questions presented. But the Court has held that it may treat included nonappealable questions "as if contained in a petition for writ of certiorari" and make restricted notations of probable jurisdiction for the appealable issues only. Mishkin v. New York, 383 U.S. 502, 512–13 (1966); Gent v. Arkansas, 384 U.S. 937 (1966). See also Fisher v. City of Berkeley, 471 U.S. 1124 (1985), and Westinghouse Elec. Corp. v. Tully, 459 U.S. 1144 (1983), in both of which the Court noted probable jurisdiction with respect to one question presented, and dismissed for want of a substantial federal question with respect to another. Justice Stevens in Tully said he did "not believe a court of law has the power simultaneously to dismiss and to accept jurisdiction of a single appeal from a single judgment." Compare Brown–Forman Distillers Corp. v. New York State Liquor Authority, 474 U.S. 814 (1985), where the New York Court of Appeals had held that the state alcoholic price-control statute did not, as applied, violate the Commerce Clause, and was also valid on its face. The Supreme Court noted probable jurisdiction "limited to Question 2 presented"—the question of facial violation. Nothing was said about the "as applied" challenge.

Compare the increasing use of limited grants of certiorari, see p. 1852, *infra*. Are these practices consistent with the jurisdictional statute's provision for review of "judgments or decrees"? With Marbury v. Madison?

NOTE ON THE MEANING OF "STATUTE" IN 28 U.S.C. § 1257

(1) In King Mfg. Co. v. Augusta, 277 U.S. 100 (1928), a municipal rate-fixing ordinance for a municipally-owned canal, challenged by a consumer as an impairment of contract obligations, was held a "statute of any state" within the meaning of the jurisdictional provision. The issue was deemed settled by authority—see, *e.g.,* Williams v. Bruffy, 96 U.S. 176 (1877); Zucht v. King, 260 U.S. 174 (1922)—and unaffected by the Act of 1925's excision of the validity of "an authority exercised under any State" as a basis for review on writ of error. See pp. 502–03, *supra*.

The Supreme Court, nevertheless, said (p. 473):

"We consider that the constitutional questions before us relate primarily, and more substantially, to the propriety of the findings made by appellees rather than to the validity of the provisions of the Security Risk Law. Accordingly, we think it the better course to dismiss the appeal, and to treat the papers as a petition for a writ of certiorari, which is hereby granted."

Justices Brandeis and Holmes dissented. Denying that the question was foreclosed by earlier decisions and pointing to other situations where "statute" was given a restricted meaning, they argued that the change made by the 1925 Act was intended to relieve the already heavily-laden Court from the press of cases involving municipal ordinances that were not only numerous but "entailed a burden out of all proportion to their number" (p. 130).

In Jamison v. Texas, 318 U.S. 413 (1943), the Court saw "no reason" for reconsidering the King decision, as requested by the appellee. That precedent now seems well ensconced. See, *e.g.*, Poulos v. New Hampshire, 345 U.S. 395, 402 (1953); Coates v. Cincinnati, 402 U.S. 611 (1971); Metromedia, Inc. v. City of San Diego, 453 U.S. 490 (1981).

(2) Sultan Ry. & Timber Co. v. Department of Labor, 277 U.S. 135 (1928), decided the same day as the King case, held an order of a state board, requiring a report of the wages of employees and the payment of assessments for the workmen's compensation fund, to be a "statute" of the state. Holmes and Brandeis, JJ., dissented.

This holding extends to all orders "legislative" in character. See, *e.g.*, Hamilton v. Regents of Univ. of Calif., 293 U.S. 245 (1934) (order of regents of state university); La Crosse Telephone Corp. v. Wisconsin Employment Relations Bd., 336 U.S. 18 (1949) (state board certification of union as bargaining agency); Lathrop v. Donohue, 367 U.S. 820 (1961) (court order establishing integrated bar); Mayer v. Chicago, 404 U.S. 189 (1971) (court rule regarding provision of free transcripts); Chandler v. Florida, 449 U.S. 560 (1981) (court rule governing telecast of state trials); Zauderer v. Office of Disciplinary Counsel, 471 U.S. 626 (1985) (disciplinary rules governing conduct of attorneys). But *cf.* Bellotti v. Connolly, 460 U.S. 1057 (1983) (attack on validity of rule issued by Massachusetts Democratic Party, characterized by state court as "augmenting" and "supplementing" state election code; appeal dismissed; 3 dissents).

(3) In view of Dahnke–Walker, have the King and Sultan decisions independent importance? If the ordinance or order were not itself a "statute," could not the appeal be based upon a challenge to the statutory delegation of authority, as applied by the delegated body? *Cf.* United Bldg. & Constr. Trades Council v. Mayor & Council of Camden, 465 U.S. 208 (1984) (challenge to municipal ordinance couched as attack on action of state official in approving the ordinance; appeal allowed).

(4) A state constitutional provision is, of course, a "statute" within the meaning of § 1257(2). Railway Express Agency, Inc. v. Virginia, 282 U.S. 440 (1931); Adamson v. California, 332 U.S. 46 (1947); Pruneyard Shopping Center v. Robins, 447 U.S. 74 (1980).

If a New Jersey court holds a New York statute applicable and sustains it against a federal challenge, should the case be appealable? See Young v. Masci, 289 U.S. 253 (1933). Compare the interesting discussion by Justice Field in Williams v. Bruffy, 96 U.S. 176 (1877) (confederate statute qualifies as a statute of Virginia for purposes of Supreme Court jurisdiction).

(5) There is no decision whether "statute of the United States" in § 1257(1) includes administrative orders, insofar as they may be attacked in the state courts. Should they be included? Does "treaty" include an

executive agreement? *Cf.* B. Altman & Co. v. United States, 224 U.S. 583 (1912); United States v. Pink, 315 U.S. 203 (1942).

(6) In Palmore v. United States, 411 U.S. 389, 394–96 (1973), the Court held that the District of Columbia Code is not a "statute of any state" within the meaning of § 1257(2), so that—although the District's Court of Appeals is explicitly deemed a "highest court of a State" for purposes of § 1257—a decision by that court sustaining the validity of a Code provision is not subject to appeal. In Key v. Doyle, 434 U.S. 59 (1977), the Court (5–4) closed the circle by holding that such a Code provision is not a "statute of the United States" for purposes of § 1257(1), either, so that a judgment invalidating a Code provision is not subject to appeal.

NOTE ON STATE DECISIONS IMPROPERLY IGNORING THE ISSUE OF VALIDITY

(1) When the validity of a state statute is drawn in question on federal grounds, the "decision" of the state court must be "in favor of its validity" for an appeal to lie. If the state court fails to pass upon the issue of validity, and the decision does not rest on an adequate state ground, the Supreme Court treats failure or refusal to decide as equivalent to a determination of validity. See, *e.g.,* Lawrence v. State Tax Com'n, 286 U.S. 276, 282 (1932), p. 606, *supra.*

(2) A more difficult problem is presented when the state court refuses to rule on validity on the basis of an arguably adequate state jurisdictional, remedial, or procedural ground (*e.g.,* the state court holds that plaintiff does not have standing, under state law, to attack the validity of the state statute). If the state standing rule is nonstatutory, can the resulting judgment be appealed? For an example, see United Artists Corp. v. Board of Censors, 189 Tenn. 397, 225 S.W.2d 550 (1949). Here a Board of Censors refused to license exhibition of a motion picture distributed by United Artists, which thereupon petitioned for review, challenging the ordinance on constitutional grounds. United Artists' practice was to ship the film to a Memphis office, submit it for approval, and contract with a local exhibitor for exhibition from outside the state when approval was obtained. The state courts dismissed the petition without passing on the claim of invalidity, holding that United Artists was engaged in intrastate business in Tennessee without having qualified to do so and was therefore barred from access to the courts. A petition for certiorari was filed, seeking review of the validity of the ordinance and urging that the business was interstate and immune to state qualification requirements under the commerce clause. The petition was denied. 339 U.S. 952 (1950).

Could the case have been taken up on an appeal? Is there a distinction between mere refusal to decide validity and a refusal to decide on grounds presenting a federal question itself reviewable only on certiorari?

Garrity v. New Jersey, 385 U.S. 493 (1967), was a prosecution of police officers for conspiracy involving fixing of traffic tickets. Introduced in evidence were statements made by each defendant during a prior general investigation. Defendants contended that the statements had been coerced by a threat of losing their jobs if they refused to testify. On appeal from their convictions, they challenged (*inter alia*) the constitutionality of a state statute that provided for removal from office for such a refusal to testify. The New Jersey Supreme Court upheld the convictions, but refused to pass on the validity of the statute on the ground that the threatened dismissal would be proper as a matter of common law, even if there were no statute. Defendants appealed to the Supreme Court, which, after postponing the question of jurisdiction to the hearing on the merits, dismissed the appeal on the basis that the statute whose validity was sought to be "drawn in question" was the one providing for forfeiture of office that the New Jersey Supreme Court had refused to reach, and that that statute "is therefore too tangentially involved to satisfy 28 U.S.C. § 1257(2)" (p. 496). Treating the papers as a petition for certiorari (under 28 U.S.C. § 2103), the Court granted certiorari and decided (5–4) that the statements were involuntary and the convictions therefore invalid.

(3) When the validity of a treaty or statute of the United States is drawn in question, appeal lies only if the state decision is "against its validity." Viewing refusal to decide as an affirmation of validity does not, accordingly, result in the allowance of appeal. Nor does the denial of rights claimed on the basis of the treaty or the statute necessarily affirm its invalidity; the denial may be based upon interpretation only, in which event review must be by certiorari. This is true even if the state interpretation is motivated by doubts as to constitutionality. See Hopkins Federal Sav. & Loan Ass'n v. Cleary, 296 U.S. 315, 332 (1935). Hence, absent an explicit state court holding of invalidity, it is difficult to see how an appeal will lie.

SUBSECTION B: THE REQUIREMENT OF SUBSTANTIALITY

ZUCHT v. KING

260 U.S. 174, 43 S.Ct. 24, 67 L.Ed. 194 (1922).
Error to the Court of Civil Appeals, Fourth Supreme Judicial District of the State of Texas.

MR. JUSTICE BRANDEIS delivered the opinion of the Court.

Ordinances of the city of San Antonio, Texas, provide that no child or other person shall attend a public school or other place of education without having first presented a certificate of vaccination. Purporting to act under these ordinances, public officials excluded Rosalyn Zucht from a public school because she did not have the required certificate and refused to submit to vaccination. They also caused her to be excluded from a private school. Thereupon Rosalyn brought this suit against the officials in a court of the state. The bill charges that there was then no occasion for requiring vaccination; that the ordinances deprive plaintiff of her liberty without due process of law, by, in effect, making vaccination compulsory; and also that they are void, because they leave to the board of health discretion to determine when and under what circumstances the requirement shall be enforced, without providing any rule by which that board is to be guided in its action, and without providing any safeguards against partiality and oppression. The prayers were for an injunction against enforcing the ordinances, for a writ of mandamus to compel her admission to the public school, and for damages. A general demurrer to the bill of complaint was sustained by the trial court; and, plaintiff having declined to amend, the bill was dismissed. This judgment was affirmed by the Court of Civil Appeals for the Fourth Supreme Judicial District. 225 S.W. 267. A motion for rehearing was overruled, and an application for a writ of error to the Supreme Court of Texas was denied by that court. A petition for a writ of certiorari filed in this court was dismissed for failure to comply with Rule 37. 257 U.S. 650. The case is now here on writ of error granted by the Chief Justice of the Court of Civil Appeals. It is assigned as error that the ordinances violate the due process and equal protection clauses of the Fourteenth Amendment, and that as administered they denied to plaintiff equal protection of the laws.

The validity of the ordinances under the federal Constitution was drawn in question by objections properly taken below. A city ordinance is a law of the state, within the meaning of section 237 of the Judicial Code, as amended, which provides a review by writ of error where the validity of a law is sustained by the highest court of the state in which a decision in the suit could be had. Atlantic Coast Line v. Goldsboro, 232 U.S. 548, 555. But, although the validity of a law was formally drawn in question, it is our duty to decline jurisdiction whenever it appears that the constitutional question presented is not, and was not at the time of granting the writ, substantial in character. Sugarman v. United States, 249 U.S. 182, 184. Long before this suit was instituted, Jacobson v. Massachusetts, 197 U.S. 11, had settled that it is within the police power of a state to provide for compulsory vaccination. That case and others had also settled that a state may, consistently with the federal Constitution, delegate to a municipality authority to determine under what conditions health regulations shall become operative. Laurel Hill Cemetery v. San Francisco, 216 U.S. 358. And still others had settled that the municipality may vest in its officials broad discretion in matters affecting the application and enforcement of a health law. Lieberman v. Van de Carr, 199 U.S. 552. A long line of decisions by this court had also settled that in the exercise of the police power reasonable classification may be freely applied, and that regulation is not violative of the equal protection clause merely because it is not all-embracing. Adams v. Milwaukee, 228 U.S. 572; Miller v. Wilson, 236 U.S. 373, 384. In view of these decisions we find in the record no question as to the validity of the ordinance sufficiently substantial to support the writ of error. Unlike Yick Wo v. Hopkins, 118 U.S. 356, these ordinances confer not arbitrary power, but only that broad discretion required for the protection of the public health.

The bill contains also averments to the effect that in administering the ordinance the officials have discriminated against the plaintiff in such a way as to deny to her equal protection of the laws. These averments do present a substantial constitutional question. Neal v. Delaware, 103 U.S. 370. But the question is not of that character which entitles a litigant to a review by this court on writ of error. The question does not go to the validity of the ordinance; nor does it go to the validity of the authority of the officials. Compare United States v. Taft, 203 U.S. 461; Champion Lumber Co. v. Fisher, 227 U.S. 445; Yazoo & Mississippi Valley R.R. Co. v. Clarksdale, 257 U.S. 10, 16. This charge is of an unconstitutional exercise of authority under an ordinance which is valid. Compare Stadelman v.

Miner, 246 U.S. 544. Unless a case is otherwise properly here on writ of error, questions of that character can be reviewed by this court only on petition for a writ of certiorari.

Writ of error dismissed.

NOTE ON THE PRELIMINARY DETERMINATION OF SUBSTANTIALITY; HEREIN ALSO OF THE PER CURIAM PRACTICE

(1) The view that federal questions must be substantial to confer jurisdiction on the Supreme Court developed late in the Court's history. See New Orleans v. New Orleans Waterworks, 142 U.S. 79 (1891); Richardson v. Louisville & N.R.R., 169 U.S. 128 (1898); Equitable Life Assurance Society v. Brown, 187 U.S. 308 (1902). Compare Pennywit v. Eaton, 15 Wall. 380 (U.S.1872); Amory v. Amory, 91 U.S. 356 (1875); Murdock v. Memphis, p. 521, *supra*.

The issue, however, was of small consequence so long as all questions, including those of jurisdiction, were determined only on full argument. When the case had been heard and was considered unsubstantial on the merits, dismissal or affirmance hardly made a difference to the unsuccessful party.

In 1872, the Court amended its rules to provide for the disposition of a motion to dismiss a writ of error on the printed brief, unless the Court expressed a wish for oral argument. 13 Wall. xi. This change was supplemented in 1876 by provision that a motion to dismiss might be accompanied by "a motion to affirm, on the ground that, although the record may show that this court has jurisdiction, it is manifest the writ was taken for delay only, or that the question on which the jurisdiction depends is so frivolous as not to need further argument". 91 U.S. vii. Once these rules were established, treatment of the question of substantiality as jurisdictional laid the foundation for summary disposition on motion to dismiss or to dismiss or affirm. *Cf.* Spies v. Illinois, 123 U.S. 131 (1887) (one of the few cases where the Court heard oral argument on the question of "substantiality"). See generally Ulman & Spears, *"Dismissed for Want of a Substantial Federal Question"*, 20 B.U.L.Rev. 501 (1940).

Unless the defendant in error made the motion, however, there was no procedure for eliminating unfounded or frivolous invocations of jurisdiction without time-consuming oral argument. Zucht v. King, for example, was dismissed only after plenary hearing by the Court.

In 1928 a new rule was fashioned to surmount this difficulty. To "prevent baseless appeals for which there is no jurisdiction, before they are reached for hearing" (Supreme Court Journal, October 15, 1928, p. 64), the rule required the appellant within 30 days of docketing the case to file a printed statement establishing jurisdiction and indicated that the Court would note probable jurisdiction or dismiss upon the showing made and the printed reply. Though appeals were dismissed from the beginning under this rule for want of a substantial federal question, the rule, as promulgated, did not articulate the point that substantiality was jurisdictional in cases from state courts. This was remedied in 1936 by an amendment calling expressly for a "statement of the grounds upon which it is contended the questions involved are substantial". 297 U.S. at 733.[1]

In 1954, to provide "a warning to counsel that an appeal as of right does not ensure oral argument" (Chief Justice Warren to the American Law Institute, May 19, 1954), Rule 15(1)(e) (now 15.1(h)) was adopted, imposing the requirement that all appeals be docketed with a statement of "the reasons why the questions presented are so substantial as to require plenary consideration, with briefs on the merits and oral argument, for their resolution." The notion that, in order to dispose of a case without oral argument, the disposition must be "jurisdictional," was thus frankly abandoned. Nevertheless, it is still the fact that in cases coming from the state courts, dismissal for want of a substantial federal question is the standard technique for dealing on the merits with an appeal that is frivolous. In cases on review from the lower federal courts, the tradition of such quasi-jurisdictional dismissals never developed, and cases not deserving oral argument are simply affirmed.

Motions to dismiss or affirm are permissible under Rule 16 and are commonly included in the reply to a jurisdictional statement, but it is questionable whether they serve a meaningful purpose under present practice. Milheim v. Moffat Tunnel District, 262 U.S. 710, 716–17 (1923), took the position that even in cases coming from the state courts affirmance rather than dismissal is appropriate where the federal question "requires analysis and exposition for its decision, is not frivolous" but is "so wanting in substance as not to need further argument." It seems clear that today the Court dismisses state appeals that fall within this category, except when an appeal originally presented an arguable question that was foreclosed by the decision in another case after the filing of the papers. Cases from the federal courts are affirmed if it is "manifest" that the questions presented "are so unsubstantial as not to need further argument" (Rule 16.1(c)).

(2) As this history demonstrates, the Court must have some method of protecting itself against having to hear argument and consider plenary briefs in frivolous appeals from the state and federal courts. But dismissals of state-court appeals for want of a substantial federal question, and summary affirmance of federal-court appeals, now comprise only two parts of a more general "summary per curiam practice"—cases that the Court decides on the merits without full briefing and oral argument.[2] These include appeals from state and federal courts that are summarily reversed,

---

1. For discussion of this rule and of its operation, see the incisive series of studies, Frankfurter & Landis, *The Business of the Supreme Court at October Term, 1928*, 43 Harv.L.Rev. 33, 43–44 (1929); • • • *October Term, 1929*, 44 *id.* 1, 11–14 (1930); • • • *October Term, 1930*, 45 *id.* 271, 283–85, 292 (1931); • • • *October Term, 1931*, 46 *id.* 226, 231–36 (1932); Frankfurter & Hart, • • • *October Term, 1932*, 47 *id.* 245, 260–68 (1933); • • • *October Term, 1933*, 48 *id.* 238, 246–60 (1934); • • • *October Term, 1934*, 49 *id.* 68, 71–74, 77–82 (1935); Frankfurter & Fisher, • • • *October Terms, 1935 and 1936*, 51 *id.* 577, 582–92 (1938); Hart, • • • *October Terms, 1937 and 1938*, 53 *id.* 579, 595–

606 (1940); Ulman & Spears, *supra*, at 520; Willey, *Jurisdictional Statements on Appeals to U.S. Supreme Court*, 31 A.B.A.J. 239 (1945); Note, *The Insubstantial Federal Question*, 62 Harv.L.Rev. 488 (1949).

2. Since 1980 the Supreme Court's Rules have explicitly provided that both appeals and certiorari cases may be dealt with by "summary disposition on the merits." Rules 16.7, 23.1. Before 1980 the Rules did not warn of the possibility of summary reversal, and created a risk that an unwary appellee, not wishing to waste resources on a motion to dismiss or affirm, would be greeted with a summary reversal without having filed any brief whatever.

and cases where the Court grants certiorari and without further ado summarily affirms, reverses or otherwise disposes of the case. Per curiam dispositions sometimes merely dispose of the case ("affirmed"; "reversed"; "dismissed"); sometimes include some citations of authority; and sometimes are accompanied by short explanations of the grounds for the disposition. The per curiam practice now constitutes a significant portion of the Court's work.[3] (See, further, the *Note on the Business of the Supreme Court*, p. 57, *supra*, and the materials on Supreme Court review of the federal courts, at p. 1829, *infra*.)

Is the extension of the summary per curiam practice to reversals and to cases on the certiorari docket justified? Necessary? Is the Supreme Court's practice in this regard different in principle than the practice in the courts of appeals? See p. 57, *supra*; and see further pp. 1872–78, *infra*.

Summary reversals of state and federal courts are not uncommon notwithstanding the substantial questions of propriety and fairness raised by the practice. See, *e.g.*, United States v. Benchimol, 471 U.S. 453, 457 (1985), in which Justice Brennan, complaining of the "unsettling practice of summarily reversing decisions rendered in favor of criminal defendants," noted that there had been 27 such summary reversals in four Terms, 24 of which went against the defendant.[4]

Professor Hart has characterized the summary reversal practice as "impossible to reconcile with conventional conceptions of due process of law." Hart, *Foreword: The Time Chart of the Justices*, 73 Harv.L.Rev. 84, 89 n. 13 (1959). See also the detailed study and devastating criticism of the parallel practice on certiorari in Brown, *Foreword: Process of Law*, 72 Harv.L.Rev. 77 (1958), and Sacks, *Foreword: The Supreme Court, 1953 Term*, 68 Harv.L.Rev. 96 (1954), and the sharp response to such a reversal in State v. Funicello, 60 N.J. 60, 69, 286 A.2d 55, 59 (1972) (concurring opinion of Weintraub, C.J.).

(3) The labeling of dismissals for want of a substantial federal question as "jurisdictional" has engendered confusion over the years about what are

3. The Court now consistently dismisses approximately twenty appeals per Term for want of a substantial federal question on the opening day of the Term. See 16 Wright, Miller & Cooper, Federal Practice and Procedure § 4004, at 509–16 (1987 Supp.). In the 1986 Term, the Court dismissed at least 57 appeals altogether for want of a substantial federal question. The Harvard Law Review reports that in 1985, the Court acted by *per curiam* or memorandum decision in 118 of 290 cases decided on the merits; in 1984, 91 of 226; 1983, 81 of 265; 1982, 119 of 301; 1981, 126 of 340; and in 1980, 115 of 274. See the statistical tables in the Harvard Law Review's review of the Supreme Court Term in Volumes 95 through 100. These *per curiam* decisions include cases where certiorari was granted and the case was summarily affirmed or reversed and cases on appeal summarily affirmed or reversed. It is unclear, however, whether these statistics include cases on appeal dismissed for want of a substantial federal question.

4. For examples of reversals of state courts, many of them over objections voiced by dissenting Justices, see, *e.g.*, Gelling v. Texas, 343 U.S. 960 (1952) (appeal); Chamberlin v. Dade County Bd. of Pub. Instruction, 377 U.S. 402 (1964) (appeal); Vachon v. New Hampshire, 414 U.S. 478 (1974) (appeal); Eaton v. City of Tulsa, 415 U.S. 697 (1974) (certiorari); Diamond Nat. Corp. v. State Bd. of Equalization, 425 U.S. 268 (1976) (appeal); Pennsylvania v. Mimms, 434 U.S. 106 (1977) (certiorari); Stone v. Graham, 449 U.S. 39 (1980) (certiorari); Illinois v. Batchelder, 463 U.S. 1112 (1983) (certiorari); Florida v. Meyers, 466 U.S. 380 (1984) (certiorari). It should be noted that in some of the cases cited the Court included in its per curiam an indication of the grounds of its decision on the merits. *Cf.* Metropolitan Life Ins. Co. v. Ward, 470 U.S. 869, 896 n. 2 (1985) (O'Connor, J., dissenting) ("a reversal and remand is more enigmatic even than a summary affirmance").

the appropriate considerations in making the determination of "substantiality."

Whether the question presented for decision on appeal is "substantial" obviously involves judgments that are not wholly determinate. But the resulting "discretion" properly goes to only one issue: whether the case should be decided with or without plenary briefing and oral argument; it does not relieve the Court of its statutory obligation to decide the appeal on the merits.

The Court's "discretion" to deny certiorari is sharply different: it legitimately involves judgments on whether the case should be decided at all (rather than what procedures are appropriate for decision).

The distinction has been subject to slippage for many years. "Plainly, the criterion of substantiality is neither rigid nor narrow. The play of discretion is inevitable, and wherever discretion is operative in the work of the Court the pressure of its docket is bound to sway its exercise. To the extent that there are reasonable differences of opinion as to the solidity of a question presented for decision or the conclusiveness of prior rulings, the administration of [the rule for appeals] operates to subject the obligatory jurisdiction of the Court to discretionary considerations not unlike those governing certiorari." Frankfurter & Landis, *The Business of the Supreme Court at October Term, 1929,* 44 Harv.L.Rev. 1, 12–14 (1930). "It is only accurate to a degree to say that our jurisdiction in cases on appeal is obligatory as distinguished from discretionary on certiorari. As regards appeals from state courts our jurisdiction is limited to those cases which present substantial federal questions. In the absence of what we consider substantiality in the light of prior decisions, the appeal will be dismissed without opportunity for oral argument." Warren, C.J., speaking to the American Law Institute, quoted in Wiener, *The Supreme Court's New Rules,* 68 Harv.L.Rev. 20, 51 (1954). See also Justice Brennan's reference, in his dissent from denial of certiorari in Sidle v. Majors, 429 U.S. 945, 949 (1976), to "the desirable latitude each of us formerly had [prior to Hicks v. Miranda, 422 U.S. 332 (1975) (see Paragraph (4), *infra*)] to weigh, as in the case of petitions for certiorari, whether the issue presented is sufficiently important to merit plenary review, and whether in any event the question might better be addressed after we have had the benefit of the views of other courts." [5]

5. The slippage is accentuated by the use of certiorari-style formulas in notations of probable jurisdiction of appeals. See Wieman v. Updegraff, 344 U.S. 183, 186 (1952) ("we noted probable jurisdiction because of the public importance of this type of legislation and the recurring serious constitutional questions which it presents"); Redrup v. New York, 386 U.S. 767, 772 (1967) (and two cases consolidated with it) (Harlan J. dissenting) ("I prefer to cast my vote to dismiss the writs [of certiorari] in Redrup and Austin as improvidently granted and, in the circumstances, to dismiss the appeal in Gent for lack of a substantial federal question. I deem it more appropriate to defer an expression of my own views on the questions brought here until an occasion when the Court is prepared to come to grips with such issues"); Ward v. Illinois, 431 U.S. 767, 770–71 (1977) ("we noted probable jurisdiction * * * to resolve a conflict with a decision of a three-judge District Court"); Webb's Fabulous Pharmacies, Inc. v. Beckwith, 449 U.S. 155, 159 (1980) ("Because it had been held elsewhere that a county's appropriation of the interest earned on private funds deposited in court in an interpleader action is an unconstitutional taking, * * * we noted probable jurisdiction"); Transcontinental Gas Pipe Line Corp. v. State Oil & Gas Bd., 474 U.S. 409 (1986) ("Because of the importance of the issues * * * we noted probable jurisdiction").

In 1975, retired Justice Tom Clark wrote that during the eighteen Terms in which he sat on the Supreme Court, "appeals from state court decisions received treatment similar to that accorded petitions for certiorari and were given about the same precedential weight." Hogge v. Johnson, 526 F.2d 833, 836 (4th Cir.1975) (concurring opinion; sitting by designation). Note Professor Wechsler's response: "If that was so, and I well know, of course, that others have asserted that it was, the Court simply disregarded its statutory duty to decide appealed cases on the merits. It may be hoped the practice now has changed. It is simply inadmissible that the highest court of law should be lawless in relation to its own jurisdiction." Wechsler, *The Appellate Jurisdiction of the Supreme Court: Reflections on the Law and the Logistics of Direct Review,* 34 Wash. & Lee L.Rev. 1043, 1061 (1977). See also Griswold, *Equal Justice Under Law,* 33 Wash. & Lee L. Rev. 813, 818–21 (1976).

(4) The illegitimacy of equating "discretion" to dismiss an appeal for want of a substantial federal question with "discretion" to deny certiorari is plainly demonstrated by the Court's affirmance, in Hicks v. Miranda, 422 U.S. 332 (1975), of the proposition that a dismissal for want of a substantial federal question is an authoritative decision on the merits that binds the lower courts. In Miller v. California, 418 U.S. 915 (1974) (Miller II), the Court had dismissed, for want of a substantial federal question, an appeal from a state court judgment upholding against constitutional attack the precise statute being challenged in Hicks. The three-judge federal district court in Hicks nevertheless held itself not bound by the dismissal in Miller II and reaffirmed its earlier judgment that the statute was invalid. The Supreme Court reversed. Justice White, for the Court, said (pp. 343–44): "[T]he District Court was in error in holding that it could disregard the decision in Miller II. That case was an appeal from a decision by a state court upholding a state statute against federal constitutional attack. A federal constitutional issue was properly presented, it was within our appellate jurisdiction under 28 U.S.C. § 1257(2), and we had no discretion to refuse adjudication of the case on the merits as would have been true had the case been brought here under our certiorari jurisdiction. We were not obligated to grant the case plenary consideration, and we did not; but we were required to deal with its merits. We did so by concluding that the appeal should be dismissed because the constitutional challenge to the California statute was not a substantial one. The three-judge court was not free to disregard this pronouncement."

(5) The proposition affirmed in Hicks, dealing with the lower courts, must be sharply distinguished from the question addressed in Edelman v. Jordan, 415 U.S. 651 (1974): the weight the Supreme Court itself should give to its summary dispositions. In Edelman the Court said (pp. 670–71): "This case * * * is the first opportunity the Court has taken to fully explore and treat the Eleventh Amendment aspects [of this case] in a written opinion. * * * [T]hree summary affirmances [of lower courts] obviously are of precedential value in support of the contention that the Eleventh Amendment does not bar the relief awarded by the District Court in this case. Equally obviously, they are not of the same precedential value as would be an opinion of this Court treating the question on the merits. Since we deal with a constitutional question, we are less constrained by the principle of *stare decisis* than we are in other areas of the law. Having now had an opportunity to more fully consider the Eleventh Amendment

issue after briefing and argument, we disapprove the Eleventh Amendment holdings of those cases to the extent that they are inconsistent with our holding today." See also Davis v. Bandemer, 106 S.Ct. 2797, 2804 (1986) (issue deserves "further consideration"); Washington v. Confederated Bands and Tribes of Yakima Indian Nation, 439 U.S. 463, 477 n. 20 (1979) ("It is not at all unusual for the Court to find it appropriate to give full consideration to a question that has been the subject of a previous summary action"); Caban v. Mohammed, 441 U.S. 380, 390 n. 9 (1979) (summary disposition not entitled to "same deference").[6]

What does the Court's practice of treating its own summary decisions with reduced deference tell us about the quality of justice obtained by the litigants in the original case?

(6) Hicks requires lower courts to identify the principle or proposition that is to be deemed settled by a previous Supreme Court summary disposition. This is by no means always easy.

In Mandel v. Bradley, 432 U.S. 173 (1977), the Court vacated the decision of a three-judge federal district court, and remanded for reconsideration on the merits, because it found that the lower court had incorrectly considered itself bound by a Supreme Court summary affirmance in a previous case materially distinguishable on its facts. In a per curiam opinion, the Court said (p. 176): "Because a summary affirmance is an affirmance of the judgment only, the rationale of the affirmance may not be gleaned solely from the opinion below. * * * Summary affirmances and dismissals for want of a substantial federal question without doubt reject the specific challenges presented in the statement of jurisdiction and do leave undisturbed the judgment appealed from. They do prevent lower courts from coming to opposite conclusions on the precise issues presented and necessarily decided by those actions. * * * Summary actions, however, * * * should not be understood as breaking new ground but as applying principles established by prior decisions to the particular facts involved."

Justice Brennan, concurring, said (p. 180): "After today, judges of the state and federal systems are on notice that, before deciding a case on the authority of a summary disposition by this Court in another case, they must (a) examine the jurisdictional statement in the earlier case to be certain that the constitutional questions presented were the same and, if they were, (b) determine that the judgment in fact rests upon decision of those questions and not even arguably upon some alternative non-constitutional ground. The judgment should not be interpreted as deciding the constitutional questions unless no other construction of the disposition is plausible. In other words, after today, 'appropriate, but not necessarily conclusive, weight' is to be given this Court's summary dispositions."

---

6. Despite the admonition in Hicks, a few lower courts continue to be confused about the distinction between a summary per curiam's authority in the lower courts and its authority in the Supreme Court. See, *e.g.,* Potter v. Murray City, 760 F.2d 1065, 1070 n. 7 (10th Cir.1985) (citing Edelman for the proposition that a dismissal for lack of a substantial federal question is entitled to less deference than a ruling after plenary consideration). And see Lecates v. Justice of Peace Court, 637 F.2d 898, 902–05 (3d Cir.1980) (lower courts "are not absolutely precluded from considering the merits of contentions that are similar to issues raised in a summarily affirmed case," especially if there are "indications that there have been doctrinal developments since the summary action").

Is this an accurate characterization?[7]

The history of Doe v. Commonwealth's Attorney for Richmond, 425 U.S. 901 (1976), *summarily aff'g* 403 F.Supp. 1199 (E.D.Va.1975), is a vivid illustration of the persistent difficulties created by per curiam dispositions of sensitive issues. In Doe a three-judge district court rejected a claim for a declaratory judgment and injunctive relief to invalidate a Virginia statute making sodomy a crime. The plaintiffs (homosexuals) in Doe had neither been arrested nor threatened with arrest before they brought their attack; the case thus raised preliminary questions of justiciability. Nonetheless the district court addressed the constitutional question: "Our decision is that on its face and in the circumstances here it is not unconstitutional" (p. 1200). The Supreme Court's summary affirmance, however, was far from uniformly understood as supporting the constitutionality of the statute. Indeed, the Court itself fueled this uncertainty in Carey v. Population Services International, 431 U.S. 678, 688 n. 5 (1977), by repeating and confirming the lower court's statement in the case that "the Court has not definitively answered the difficult question whether and to what extent the Constitution prohibits state statutes regulating [private consensual sexual] behavior among adults."

In Dronenburg v. Zech, 741 F.2d 1388 (D.C.Cir.1984), *rehearing en banc denied,* 746 F.2d 1579 (1984), four sets of judges expressed different views with respect to the impact of the affirmance in Doe. See 741 F.2d at 1392 (Bork, J., for 3 judges) ("we doubt that a court of appeals ought to distinguish a Supreme Court precedent on the speculation that the Court might possibly have had * * * [lack of standing] in mind"); 746 F.2d at 1580 (Robinson, J., for 4 judges) ("[w]e find completely unconvincing the suggestion that Doe * * * controls this case"); *id.* at 1582 (Ginsburg, J.) ("Doe controls"); *id.* at 1584 (Starr, J.) ("the panel's moving beyond Doe * * * [was] necessary"). In the event the Court itself finally granted certiorari in another case and addressed the issue in a full dress opinion, upholding the validity of the sodomy statute. Bowers v. Hardwick, 478 U.S. 186 (1986).[8]

(7) In Colorado Springs Amusements, Ltd. v. Rizzo, 428 U.S. 913, 916–19, 922 (1976), Justice Brennan, dissenting from a dismissal for want of a substantial federal question, said: "[T]he same reasons that lead us to deny conclusive precedential value in this Court to our summary dispositions require that we allow the same latitude to state and lower federal courts. We accord summary dispositions less precedential value than dispositions by opinion after full briefing and oral argument, because jurisdictional statements, and motions to affirm or dismiss addressed to them, rarely contain more than brief discussions of the issues presented * * *. [T]he

---

7. In Illinois State Bd. of Elections v. Socialist Workers Party, 440 U.S. 173 (1979), the Court affirmed a district court injunction against an Illinois law whose validity had been sustained in an earlier case that was summarily affirmed by the Supreme Court. The Court emphasized that, although the validity of the same law was at issue, a different constitutional violation had been alleged. And although the constitutional claim now being pressed may have been presented to the *district court* in the earlier case, it had not formed the basis of that court's opinion, nor had it been directly asserted in the jurisdictional statement filed on appeal. See also Sporhase v. Nebraska ex rel. Douglas, 458 U.S. 941 (1982).

8. See also Mississippi Republican Executive Committee v. Brooks, 469 U.S. 1002 (1984) (Justice Stevens concurring) (criticizing the dissenters from a summary affirmance for distorting the parties' jurisdictional statement and unfairly characterizing the district court opinion).

function of the jurisdictional statement and motion to dismiss or affirm is very limited: It is to apprise the Court of issues believed by the appellant to warrant, and by the appellee not to warrant, this Court's plenary review and decision. * * * This treatment is fully in compliance with our Rules * * *. Thus, the nature of materials before us when we vote summarily to dispose of a case rarely suffices as a basis for regarding the summary disposition as a conclusive resolution of an important constitutional question, and we therefore do not treat it as such. For the same reason we should not require that the district courts, courts of appeals, and state courts do so. * * *

"Resolution of important issues, in my view, ought not be made solely on the basis of a single jurisdictional statement, without the benefit of other court decisions and the helpful commentary that follows significant developments in the law. One factor that affects the exercise of our discretionary jurisdiction is a desire to let some complex and significant issues be considered by several courts before granting certiorari. Although this discretionary factor cannot be given weight as to cases on our appellate docket, the effect of Hicks * * * is to prevent this Court from obtaining the views of state and lower federal courts on important issues; after dismissal * * * no court will again consider the merits of the question presented to this Court. * * *

"Moreover, summary dispositions are rarely supported even by a brief opinion identifying the federal questions presented or stating the reasons or authority upon which the disposition rests. * * * When presented with the contention that our unexplained dispositions are conclusively binding, puzzled state and lower court judges are left to guess as to the meaning and scope of our unexplained dispositions. * * *

"Even if the Court rejects my view that Hicks should be modified, at a minimum we have the duty to provide some explanation of the issues presented in the case and the reasons and authorities supporting our summary dispositions. This surely should be the practice in cases presenting novel issues or where there is a disagreement among us as to the grounds of the disposition, and I think it should be the practice in every case. In addition, we ought to distinguish in our dispositions of appeals from state courts between those grounded on the insubstantiality of the federal questions presented and those grounded on agreement with the state court's decision of substantial federal questions."

Assuming agreement with Justice Brennan's diagnosis—that summary dispositions may be inadequately considered and may constitute ambiguous precedent—should the diagnosis lead to his prescription: no *authoritative* effect to be given to such a disposition? The Hicks rule imposes some discipline on the Court's summary rulings on the merits of cases. Without it, wouldn't the problem of ill-considered summary dispositions become worse? Are the parties in the original case—who have a statutory right to appeal and receive an adjudication on the merits—fairly treated if their case is disposed of not only without briefs and arguments but also without the incentives for care in adjudication created by the rules of *stare decisis?*

Is Justice Brennan's proposal consistent with the letter and spirit of the obligatory jurisdiction?

(8) Are there cures to the problems engendered by the per curiam practice?

(a) What about the suggestion of Justice Brennan in Colorado Springs, *supra*, that per curiams should at least be accompanied by a minimal explanation of the grounds of decision?

(b) At present, the practice of the Court with respect to noting probable jurisdiction is akin to the Court's "rule of four" on certiorari (see further Chap. XV, Sec. 3, *infra*): it takes four Justices to put an appeal on the oral argument calendar. See Brennan, J., in Ohio ex rel. Eaton v. Price, 360 U.S. 246, 246–47 (1959). As a result, a substantial number of appeals are dismissed for want of a substantial federal question over the dissent of one, two or even three Justices; similarly, there are frequent dissents to summary grants and dispositions in certiorari cases. See 16 Wright, Miller & Cooper, *supra*, §§ 4004, 4014, at 510 n. 65, 553 n. 28 (1987 Supp.). Are these practices justified? Should all appeals where the Justices are not unanimous be fully heard?

(c) The Court's evident assumption that it needs to engage in a substantial summary per curiam practice is a product not only of its sense of what business (obligatory and discretionary) it must do in order to perform its essential functions, but also of its commitment to the practice of not falling severely behind in its work by allowing a long waiting-queue to develop before cases are heard and decided.

If the Court wanted seriously to narrow its practice of doing summary justice (for instance by restricting summary dispositions to cases where the Court was unanimous), and *also* determined that it would be unwise to cut back on the number of cases where certiorari is granted, it could accomplish both of these goals by allowing a longer queue to develop before merits cases are heard and disposed of. Would this be unacceptable? Would it have the advantage of making the Court's workload problems visible?

(d) Abolition of the Court's obligatory jurisdiction would certainly alleviate the problems of the per curiam practice. A large body of respectable opinion—including, when last heard from, all of the members of the Court—supports this proposal.[9] See also pp. 43–45, *supra*, and 1872–78, *infra*. Congress has, so far, been unwilling to make the change. Should it?

---

9. In 1972 all the Justices joined a letter to Senator DeConcini urging enactment of legislation abolishing the obligatory jurisdiction. See Gressman, *Requiem for the Supreme Court's Obligatory Jurisdiction*, 65 A.B.A.J. 1325, 1328 (1979). For the relevant legislative proposals and secondary literature, see the materials cited in, *e.g.*, Estreicher & Sexton, Redefining the Supreme Court's Role 117 (1986); Hellman, *The Proposed Intercircuit Tribunal: Do We Need It? Will It Work?*, 11 Hastings Const'l L.Q. 375, 389–92 (1984); The Needs of the Federal Courts (Report of the Dep't of Justice Committee on Revision of the Federal Judicial System) at 11 (1977); Simpson, *Turning Over the Reins: The Abolition of the Mandatory Appellate Jurisdiction of the Supreme Court*, 6 Hastings Const'l L.Q. 297 (1978). Compare Tushnet, *The Mandatory Jurisdiction of the Supreme Court—Some Recent Developments*, 46 U.Cin.L.Rev. 347 (1977).

SUBSECTION C: OTHER DISCRETIONARY ELEMENTS IN OBLIGATORY REVIEW

RESCUE ARMY v. MUNICIPAL COURT OF LOS ANGELES

331 U.S. 549, 67 S.Ct. 1409, 91 L.Ed. 1666 (1947).
Appeal from the Supreme Court of California.

MR. JUSTICE RUTLEDGE delivered the opinion of the Court.

On the merits this appeal presents substantial questions concerning the constitutional validity of ordinances of the City of Los Angeles governing the solicitation of contributions for charity. First and Fourteenth Amendments grounds are urged as nullifying them chiefly in the view that they impose prior restraints upon and unduly abridge appellants' rights in the free exercise of their religion. * * *

Similar, but also distinct, questions were involved in Gospel Army v. City of Los Angeles, dismissed today for jurisdictional reasons. 331 U.S. 543. This case, however, arose procedurally in a different fashion, so that it is not subject to the same jurisdictional defect. And the procedural difference is important, not merely for our jurisdiction but also for determining the propriety of exercising it in the special circumstances presented by this appeal.

The California Supreme Court heard and determined the Gospel Army case several months in advance of this one. It sustained the regulations in both instances * * *. But the attack upon the city ordinances in the Gospel Army case covered a much wider range than here, and the court's principal opinion was rendered in that cause. Hence in this case it disposed of overlapping issues merely by reference a fortiori to its "approval" of the challenged provisions in the Gospel Army opinion.

As will more fully appear, this mode of treatment, together with interlacing relationships between provisions involved here and others in the Gospel Army case, has combined with the necessitated dismissal of that appeal to create for us difficult problems in determining exactly how much of the regulatory scheme approved in the Gospel Army opinion, and hence also how much of that decision, must be taken as having been incorporated in the disposition of this cause. * * *

This suit is one for a writ of prohibition. The appeal is from the California Supreme Court's judgment denying appellants' application for such a writ. 28 Cal.2d 460, 171 P.2d 8. * * * Its object was to test the jurisdiction of the respondent Municipal Court of Los Angeles to proceed with a pending criminal prosecution against Murdock, who is an officer of the Rescue Army. In that court he had been charged with violating three provisions of the city ordinances, had been twice convicted, and twice the convictions had been reversed by the Superior Court of Los Angeles County.

While the case was pending in the Municipal Court after the second reversal, appellants filed their petition in this cause * * * [and] set forth grounds held sufficient under the state procedure to present for adjudication the question of the Municipal Court's jurisdiction. * * * As in the Gospel Army case, the Supreme Court, with three of the seven justices dissenting, decided the issues on the merits against the appellants. It therefore denied the writ, * * *. Probable jurisdiction was duly noted here, and the cause was assigned for argument immediately following the Gospel Army case.

Apparently Murdock was charged in the Municipal Court with violating three sections of the Municipal Code. These were §§ 44.09(a), 44.09(b), and 44.12 of Article 4, Chapter IV. * * *

The issue of the Municipal Court's jurisdiction therefore, insofar as it concerns us, turns upon the validity of §§ 44.09(a), 44.09(b) and 44.12, together with the other provisions necessarily incorporated in them by reference; * * *. Moreover the jurisdictional question arises substantially as upon demurrer to the charges, * * *. Hence only the validity of the provisions on their face, not as applied to proven circumstances, is called in question.

The Gospel Army case, on the other hand, was an injunction suit, in which attack was projected on a broad front, against the ordinances and the scheme of regulation they embody as a whole. For some reason § 44.09(a) was not attacked in that suit. But § 44.09(b) was involved indirectly through its relation to § 44.05 and § 44.12 directly, as well as numerous other provisions both of Article 4, Chapter IV, and outside it. That article, as we have noted above, consists of Code §§ 44.01–44.19, entitled "Charities and Relief," and thus includes all of the sections involved here as well as many others which were in issue in the Gospel Army case.

It is this setting of dovetailed legislative enactments and judicial decisions which creates the primary problem for our disposition. Those interrelations, of the cases and of the ordinances they involve, will be better understood in the setting of a summary of the general scheme.

The Municipal Code regulates both charitable and other solicitations, as well as pawnbrokers, secondhand dealers, junk dealers, etc. * * * Article 4 * * * is designed primarily, though not exclusively, to secure a maximum of information and publicity for the public. It seeks to make available to all persons solicited detailed information concerning the persons soliciting, the causes or organizations on behalf of which they act, and the uses to which the donations will be put. The plan also undertakes, in other ways, to assure responsibility, both moral and financial, on the part of soliciting individuals and agencies; and to see to it that the funds collected are applied to their appropriate purposes. * * *

[The opinion at this point reviews at length the details of the ordinance, stressing the interrelationship of the various provisions.]

The Gospel Army case we have dismissed for the technical, nevertheless important, reason that under California law the state Supreme Court's reversal, without more, contemplates further proceedings in the trial court. Consequently that judgment is not final for the purposes of our jurisdiction on appeal, within the meaning of § 237(a) of the Judicial Code, 28 U.S.C. § 344(a), 331 U.S. 543.

On the other hand, this appeal is not subject to that particular infirmity. The effect of the California Supreme Court's judgment, of course, will be to permit further proceedings by the Municipal Court. But under the rule of Bandini Petroleum Co. v. Superior Court, 284 U.S. 8, this prohibition proceeding would be an independent suit, in relation to that criminal prosecution, "and the judgment finally disposing of it," as did the state Supreme Court's judgment, "is a final judgment within the meaning of section 237(a) of the Judicial Code." 284 U.S., at 14.

* * *

While therefore we are unable to conclude that there is no jurisdiction in this cause, nevertheless compelling reasons exist for not exercising it.

From Hayburn's Case, 2 Dall. 409, to * * * the Hatch Act case decided this term [United Public Workers v. Mitchell, 330 U.S. 75, p. 239, *supra*], this Court has followed a policy of strict necessity in disposing of constitutional issues. The earliest exemplifications, too well known for repeating the history here, arose in the Court's refusal to render advisory opinions and in applications of the related jurisdictional policy drawn from the case and controversy limitation. U.S. Const. Art. III. The same policy has been reflected continuously not only in decisions but also in rules of court and in statutes made applicable to jurisdictional matters including the necessity for reasonable clarity and definiteness, as well as for timeliness, in raising and presenting constitutional questions. Indeed perhaps the most effective implement for making the policy effective has been the certiorari jurisdiction conferred upon this Court by Congress. *E.g.*, Judicial Code, §§ 237, 240.

The policy, however, has not been limited to jurisdictional determinations. For, in addition, "the Court [has] developed, for its own governance in the cases confessedly within its jurisdiction, a series of rules under which it has avoided passing upon a large part of all the constitutional questions pressed upon it for decision." [31] Thus, as those rules were listed in support of the statement quoted, constitutional issues affecting legislation will not be determined in friendly, nonadversary proceedings; in advance of the necessity of deciding them; in broader terms than are required by the precise facts to which the ruling is to be applied; if the record presents some other ground upon which the case may be disposed of; at the instance of one who fails to show that he is injured by the statute's operation, or who has availed himself of its benefits; or if a construction of the statute is fairly possible by which the question may be avoided.

Some, if not indeed all, of these rules have found "most varied applications." And every application has been an instance of reluctance, indeed of refusal, to undertake the most important and the most delicate of the Court's functions, notwithstanding conceded jurisdiction, until necessity compels it in the performance of constitutional duty.

Moreover the policy is neither merely procedural nor in its essence dependent for applicability upon the diversities of jurisdiction and procedure, whether of the state courts, the inferior federal courts, or this Court. Rather it is one of substance, grounded in considerations which transcend all such particular limitations. Like the case and controversy limitation itself and the policy against entertaining political questions, it is one of the rules basic to the federal system and this Court's appropriate place within that structure.

Indeed in origin and in practical effects, though not in technical function, it is a corollary offshoot of the case and controversy rule. And

31. Brandeis, J., with whom Stone, Roberts and Cardozo, JJ., concurred, in Ashwander v. Tennessee Valley Authority, 297 U.S. 288, concurring opinion at 346, 56 S.Ct. 466, 482, 80 L.Ed. 688.

often the line between applying the policy or the rule is very thin.[37]   They work, within their respective and technically distinct areas, to achieve the same practical purposes for the process of constitutional adjudication, and upon closely related considerations.

The policy's ultimate foundations, some if not all of which also sustain the jurisdictional limitation, lie in all that goes to make up the unique place and character, in our scheme, of judicial review of governmental action for constitutionality.   They are found in the delicacy of that function, particularly in view of possible consequences for others stemming also from constitutional roots; the comparative finality of those consequences; the consideration due to the judgment of other repositories of constitutional power concerning the scope of their authority; the necessity, if government is to function constitutionally, for each to keep within its power, including the courts; the inherent limitations of the judicial process, arising especially from its largely negative character and limited resources of enforcement; withal in the paramount importance of constitutional adjudication in our system.

All these considerations and perhaps others, transcending specific procedures, have united to form and sustain the policy.   Its execution has involved a continuous choice between the obvious advantages it produces for the functioning of government in all its coordinate parts and the very real disadvantages, for the assurance of rights, which deferring decision very often entails.   On the other hand it is not altogether speculative that a contrary policy, of accelerated decision, might do equal or greater harm for the security of private rights, without attaining any of the benefits of tolerance and harmony for the functioning of the various authorities in our scheme.   For premature and relatively abstract decision, which such a policy would be most likely to promote, have their part too in rendering rights uncertain and insecure.

As with the case and controversy limitation, however, the choice has been made long since.   Time and experience have given its sanction.   They also have verified for both that the choice was wisely made.   Any other indeed might have put an end to or seriously impaired the distinctively American institution of judicial review.[38]   And on the whole, in spite of inevitable exceptions, the policy has worked not only for finding the appropriate place and function of the judicial institution in our governmental system but also for the preservation of individual rights.

Most recently both phases of its operation have been exemplified in declaratory judgment proceedings.   Despite some seemingly widespread misconceptions,[40] the general introduction of that procedure in both state

37. Indeed more than once the policy has been applied in order to avoid the necessity of deciding the "case or controversy" jurisdictional question, when constitutional issues were at stake on the merits, *e.g.*, recently in declaratory judgment proceedings.   See American Federation of Labor, Metal Trades Dept. v. Watson, 327 U.S. 582; United Public Workers v. Mitchell, 330 U.S. 75.   Compare Alabama State Federation of Labor v. McAdory, 325 U.S. 450, and Congress of Industrial Organizations v. McAdory, 325 U.S. 472, which arose under state declaratory judgment acts.

38. It is not without significance for the policy's validity that the periods when the power has been exercised most readily and broadly have been the ones in which this Court and the institution of judicial review have had their stormiest experiences.   See, *e.g.*, Brant, Storm Over the Constitution (1936).

40. As the cases cited in note 37 illustrate, the procedure has been utilized to

and federal spheres has not reversed or modified the policy's general direction or effects.[41]

One aspect of the policy's application, it has been noted, has been by virtue of the presence of other grounds for decision. But when such alternatives are absent, as in this case, application must rest upon considerations relative to the manner in which the constitutional issue itself is shaped and presented.

These cannot be reduced to any precise formula or complete catalogue. But in general, as we have said, they are of the same nature as those which make the case and controversy limitation applicable, differing only in degree. To the more usual considerations of timeliness and maturity, of concreteness, definiteness, certainty, and of adversity of interests affected, are to be added in cases coming from state courts involving state legislation those arising when questions of construction, essentially matters of state law, remain unresolved or highly ambiguous. They include, of course, questions of incorporation by reference and severability, such as this case involves. Necessarily whether decision of the constitutional issue will be made must depend upon the degree to which uncertainty exists in these respects. And this inevitably will vary with particular causes and their varying presentations.

Accordingly the policy's applicability can be determined only by an exercise of judgment relative to the particular presentation, though relative also to the policy generally and to the degree in which the specific factors rendering it applicable are exemplified in the particular case. It is largely a question of enough or not enough, the sort of thing precisionists abhor but constitutional adjudication nevertheless constantly requires. * * * Here relief is neither sought nor needed beyond adjudication of the jurisdictional issue. The suit seeks only, in substance, a judicial declaration that jurisdiction does not exist in the Municipal Court. But for a variety of reasons the shape in which the underlying constitutional issues have reached this Court presents, we think, insuperable obstacles to any exercise of jurisdiction to determine them.

Those reasons comprise not only obstacles of prematurity and comparative abstractness arising from the nature of the proceeding in prohibition and the manner in which the parties have utilized it for presenting the constitutional questions. They also include related considerations growing out of uncertainties resulting from the volume of legislative provisions possibly involved, their intricate interlacing not only with each other on their face but also in the California Supreme Court's disposition of them, and especially from its treatment of this case by reference in considerable part to the Gospel Army case, difficulties all accentuated for us of course by

bring for decision challenges to an entire array of statutory provisions alleged to violate rights secured by an almost equal array of constitutional provisions. The strategic conception seems to have been that the declaratory judgment suit furnishes a ready vehicle for presenting and securing decision of constitutional matters solely upon the pleadings, in highly abstract or premature, if not hypothetical states of fact, and en masse. Such a notion of course is essentially contradictory of the policy and, if accepted, would go far toward nullifying it.

41. * * * Indeed the discretionary element characteristic of declaratory jurisdiction, and imported perhaps from equity jurisdiction and practice without the remedial phase, offers a convenient instrument for making the policy effective, quite to the contrary effect of the conception discussed in note 40 above. But that element, for application of the policy, is only one of convenience, not one of necessity. * * *

the necessity for dismissal of that cause here. Because the application of the policy must be relative to the factors specifically dictating such action, a statement of our particular reasons follows.

[The opinion points out the highly abstract form in which the constitutional issues appear; the lack of clarity, on the record in this case, of the actual charges made; the many questions of construction of the ordinance, including severability, which the Gospel Army decision had left uncertain and which, when resolved by the state courts, would obviate some constitutional issues and narrow those which remained; and the fact that the prosecution of Murdock could not proceed to a conclusion without clarifying these matters (or obviating the need to do so).] * * *

We are not unmindful that our ruling will subject the petitioner Murdock to the burden of undergoing a third trial or that this burden is substantial. Were the uncertainties confronting us in relation to this Court's historic policy less in number, and resolving them not so far from our appropriate function in cases coming from state courts, the inconvenience of undergoing trial another time might justify exercising jurisdiction in this cause. But, consistently with the policy, jurisdiction here should be exerted only when the jurisdictional question presented by the proceeding in prohibition tenders the underlying constitutional issues in clean-cut and concrete form, unclouded by any serious problem of construction relating either to the terms of the questioned legislation or to its interpretation by the state courts.

Our decision of course should be without prejudice to any rights which may arise upon final determination of the Municipal Court proceeding, relative to review in this Court of that determination. With that reservation we think the only course consistent, upon this record, at once with preservation of appellants' rights and with adherence to our long-observed policy, is to decline to exercise jurisdiction in this cause.

Accordingly, the appeal is dismissed, without prejudice to the determination in the future of any issues arising under the Federal Constitution from further proceedings in the Municipal Court.

Mr. Justice Black concurs in the result.

Mr. Justice Murphy, with whom Mr. Justice Douglas concurs, dissenting.

It is difficult for me to believe that the opinion of the Supreme Court of California is so ambiguous that the precise constitutional issues in this case have become too blurred for our powers of discernment. * * *

NOTE ON DISMISSAL FOR WANT OF A "PROPERLY PRESENTED" QUESTION AND OTHER REFUSALS TO ADJUDICATE APPEALS

(1) Poe v. Ullman, 367 U.S. 497 (1961), was an action by married persons and their doctor for a declaratory judgment of the unconstitutionality of a Connecticut statute prohibiting the use of contraceptive devices or the giving of medical advice about them. The state courts upheld the statute, even as applied to married couples and despite allegations that conception would pose a serious threat to the health or lives of the plaintiff-wives. After plenary consideration in the Supreme Court, the appeal was

dismissed. There was no opinion of the Court. Justice Frankfurter, joined by Chief Justice Warren and Justices Clark and Whittaker, found the case not meet for adjudication. He stressed the absence of any specific threat of enforcement, noting that it was only alleged that the State's Attorney "in the course of his public duty * * * intends to prosecute any offenses against Connecticut law" (p. 501). Pointing also to the long history of non-enforcement of the statute (with one exception, in 1940) and the open and well-known sale of contraceptives in drug stores in the state, he found the controversy inappropriate for constitutional adjudication (pp. 502–09):

"The restriction of our jurisdiction to cases and controversies within the meaning of Article III of the Constitution, see Muskrat v. United States, 219 U.S. 346, is not the sole limitation on the exercise of our appellate powers, especially in cases raising constitutional questions. The policy reflected in numerous cases and over a long period was thus summarized in the oft-quoted statement of Mr. Justice Brandeis: 'The Court [has] developed, for its own governance in the cases confessedly within its jurisdiction, a series of rules under which it has avoided passing upon a large part of all the constitutional questions pressed upon it for decision.' Ashwander v. Tennessee Valley Authority, 297 U.S. 288, 341, 346 (concurring opinion). In part the rules summarized in the Ashwander opinion have derived from the historically defined, limited nature and function of courts and from the recognition that, within the framework of our adversary system, the adjudicatory process is most securely founded when it is exercised under the impact of a lively conflict between antagonistic demands, actively pressed, which make resolution of the controverted issue a practical necessity. * * * In part they derive from the fundamental federal and tripartite character of our National Government and from the role—restricted by its very responsibility—of the federal courts, and particularly this Court, within that structure. * * * These considerations press with special urgency in cases challenging legislative action or state judicial action as repugnant to the Constitution. * * *

"The Court has been on the alert against use of the declaratory judgment device for avoiding the rigorous insistence on exigent adversity as a condition for evoking Court adjudication. This is as true of state court suits for declaratory judgments as of federal. By exercising their jurisdiction, state courts cannot determine the jurisdiction to be exercised by this Court. * * * It was with respect to a state-originating declaratory judgment proceeding that we said, in Alabama State Federation of Labor v. McAdory, 325 U.S. 450, 471, that 'The extent to which the declaratory judgment procedure may be used in the federal courts to control state action lies in the sound discretion of the Court. * * *' Indeed, we have recognized, in such cases, that ' * * * the discretionary element characteristic of declaratory jurisdiction, and imported perhaps from equity jurisdiction and practice without the remedial phase, offers a convenient instrument for making * * * effective * * *' the policy against premature constitutional decision. Rescue Army v. Municipal Court, 331 U.S. 549, 573, n. 41. * * *

"Justiciability is of course not a legal concept with a fixed content or susceptible of scientific verification. Its utilization is the resultant of many subtle pressures, including the appropriateness of the issues for decision by this Court and the actual hardship to the litigants of denying them the relief sought. Both these factors justify withholding adjudication of the constitutional issue raised under the circumstances and in the manner in which they are now before the Court."

Justice Brennan concurred in the result (p. 509):

"The true controversy in this case is over the opening of birth-control clinics on a large scale; it is that which the State has prevented in the past, not the use of contraceptives by isolated and individual married couples. It will be time enough to decide the constitutional questions urged upon us when, if ever, that real controversy flares up again."

Justices Black, Douglas, Harlan and Stewart each dissented separately.

Compare Epperson v. Arkansas, 393 U.S. 97 (1968), a declaratory and injunction action challenging the validity of a 1928 law prohibiting the teaching of evolution. Justice Fortas, for the Court, disposed of any "justiciability" problem curtly (pp. 101–02): "There is no record of any prosecutions in Arkansas under its statute. It is possible that the statute is presently more of a curiosity than a vital fact of life in [Arkansas, Mississippi, and Tennessee]. Nevertheless, the present case was brought, the appeal as of right is properly here, and it is our duty to decide the issues presented." Only Justice Black dissented on this point.

(2) Epperson apparently confirms what Justice Frankfurter's opinion clearly implies—that the Poe disposition was not compelled by the "case or controversy" requirements of Article III. See also Chap. II, Sec. 5, *supra.* That is also true of Rescue Army. What justifies such refusals to adjudicate appeals?

Expressions of the Rescue Army approach are articulated in various forms. See, *e.g.,* International Bhd. of Teamsters v. Denver Milk Producers, Inc., 334 U.S. 809 (1948) ("Because of the inadequacy of the record, we decline to decide the constitutional issues involved"); DeBacker v. Brainard, 396 U.S. 28, 29–30 (1969) ("Because we find that resolution of the constitutional issues presented by appellant would not be appropriate in the circumstances of this case, the appeal is dismissed"); Simmons v. West Haven Housing Auth., 399 U.S. 510, 511 (1970) ("Because of an ambiguity in the record * * * we now conclude that this appeal should be dismissed"). The result is often summed up in the conclusion that the federal issue was not "properly presented", see, *e.g.,* Naim v. Naim, 350 U.S. 891 (1955), 985 (1956), paragraph (6), *infra;* not uncommonly, cases are disposed of with nothing more than the notation, "Appeal dismissed for want of a properly presented federal question." See, *e.g.,* Cleveland Elec. Illuminating Co. v. Public Util. Com'n, 459 U.S. 1094 (1983); Doe v. Delaware, 450 U.S. 382 (1981) (two Justices, dissenting, argued that the federal question was in fact presented to the state courts in full compliance with state procedure and was decided by those courts; they characterized the Court's disposition as "unprecedented and inexplicable"); Vincent v. Texas, 449 U.S. 199 (1980); and see the further authorities cited in 16 Wright, Miller & Cooper, Federal Practice and Procedure § 4015, at 647–48 (1976) and 556–57 (1987 Supp.).

Presumably these cases are not ones where a federal question has been presented "improperly" in the sense that there has not been compliance with statutory and procedural requirements; if this were the case, the appropriate disposition would be to dismiss for want of jurisdiction. And if the problem is simply that the record is inadequate or ambiguous, isn't the proper course in an appeal to remand the case for further proceedings? If the technical requirements have been met, and the validity of a state statute "drawn in question" within the meaning of the jurisdictional provision, is it appropriate to dismiss an appeal because the questions have not been "properly presented" in some other sense?

(3) The principal opinions in both Rescue Army and Poe place substantial reliance on Justice Brandeis' famous statement in Ashwander v. Tennessee Valley Authority, 297 U.S. 288, 346 (1936), regarding the rules the Court had developed "for its own governance in the cases confessedly within its jurisdiction." Professor Gunther has stated that the Brandeis statement is "sound and of principled content; it is not an assertion of a vague Court discretion to deny a decision on the merits in a case within the statutory and constitutional bounds of jurisdiction. The Brandeis rules are a far cry from the neo-Brandeisian fallacy that there is a general 'Power To Decline the Exercise of Jurisdiction Which Is Given,' that there is a general discretion not to adjudicate though statute, Constitution, and remedial law present a 'case' for decision and confer no discretion. [The 'Power to Decline' quotation is from Bickel, The Least Dangerous Branch 127 (1962).]

"Of course the Court often may and should avoid 'passing upon a large part of all of the constitutional questions pressed upon it for decision.' Four of the seven Brandeis rules involve well-known instances of such avoidance—avoidance only of some or all of the *constitutional* questions argued, *not* avoidance of all decision on the merits of the case. *   *   * The remaining rules given by Brandeis deal with situations in which there is no 'case' or 'controversy' in terms of the jurisdictional content of Article III— as with the 'non-adversary' proceeding of his first rule—or where there is a lack of what Bickel calls 'pure' standing in the constitutional sense, or where the state of the remedial law prevents a 'case' from arising. In these Brandeis categories, decision on the merits is precluded because the jurisdictional requirements of Article III are not met; in the earlier ones, the jurisdiction to decide the merits is in fact exercised and all that is avoided is decision on some or all of the constitutional issues presented.

"The only possible Brandeis contribution to the fallacy lies in his reference to all of the categories as 'cases confessedly within' the Court's jurisdiction. But that referred to the fact that all of the jurisdictional requirements added by the statute had been met; and adjudication on the merits did in fact result in all of his categories, except where a jurisdictional requirement originating in the Constitution had not been satisfied. There is a sad irony in the transformation of the Brandeis passage into a veritable *carte blanche* for Court discretion as to jurisdiction; and there is sad irony too in the invocation of Brandeis' principled concern with threshold questions by members and appraisers of the Court who would assert a virtually unlimited choice in deciding whether to decide. The neo-Brandeisian fallacy has fortunately not yet gained a firm, persistent foothold on the Court." Gunther, *The Subtle Vices of the "Passive Virtues"—A Comment on Principle and Expediency in Judicial Review*, 64 Colum.L.Rev. 1, 16–17 (1964).

(4) Many of the authorities cited to support the policy advanced in Rescue Army and Poe involved the justiciability of actions, principally for injunctive or declaratory relief, brought originally in federal courts. As the opinions indicate, those holdings drew support from the concepts of judicial discretion in the awarding of equitable relief, which had also been

carried over to declaratory actions. See pp. 244–55, *supra*. When invoked, this discretion led to dismissal of the entire case.

Do the same considerations apply to appeals to the Supreme Court from state courts? Note that the dismissal of an appeal leaves the judgment of the state court standing. What is the res judicata effect of such a judgment in a subsequent state court proceeding against the same person whose prior appeal was dismissed? Assuming that the state court, applying issue preclusion, refuses to reexamine any issues of federal law determined in the prior proceeding, is there an adequate state ground barring direct review by the Supreme Court? Is it more difficult to get past the state ground in this case than it is in a case where the dismissal of the original appeal was based on lack of justiciability under Article III? See Fidelity Nat. Bank & Trust Co. v. Swope, 274 U.S. 123 (1927), p. 235, *supra*. See also 28 U.S.C. § 1738.

In any event, it is clear that the Court in Rescue Army and in Poe anticipated that the federal questions involved would not be foreclosed, but would be open for later resolution, even as to the parties in the case before it.

(5) It is significant that Rescue Army and Poe were both actions seeking preventive relief against actual or potential criminal prosecution. Assuming that res judicata was inapplicable, the result in each case was only that the state was not prevented from prosecuting if it chose to do so, but that if it did, the federal questions presented in the anticipatory action could still be asserted as defenses to the prosecution. Moreover, if convicted, defendant would have a right of appeal to the Supreme Court on those federal questions.

In Mattiello v. Connecticut, 395 U.S. 209 (1969), appellant was a 17–year–old girl who had been found to be "in manifest danger of falling into habits of vice," Conn.Gen.Stats. § 17–379, and committed to the State Farm for Women until the age of 21. Her objection to the statute as unconstitutionally vague had been rejected by the Appellate Division of the Connecticut Circuit Court. 225 A.2d 507 (1966). That decision rested in substantial part upon the ground that the statute was not penal but merely protective of juveniles, and therefore not subject to the constitutional restrictions against vagueness. (But *cf.* In re Gault, 387 U.S. 1 (1967).) The Connecticut Supreme Court of Errors declined her petition for appeal, 154 Conn. 737, 225 A.2d 201 (1966). On review in the Supreme Court, the appeal was dismissed after argument, without explanation, "for want of a properly presented federal question."

Can this result be supported on the ground that federal habeas corpus would be available to test the same constitutional contention? Is there any justification for the Supreme Court declining an appeal in its "discretion" when the result is to permit a state to act coercively against a person who is asserting a federal constitutional defense against that action? If there is in such cases "justice at the discretion of the Court," what is the significance of the Act of Congress creating appeal jurisdiction? Indeed, what is left of Marbury v. Madison?

(6) Naim v. Naim, 350 U.S. 891 (1955), 985 (1956), was a suit to annul a marriage on the ground that it violated Virginia's miscegenation statute. The marriage had been performed in North Carolina, but the Virginia statute specifically applied to couples leaving the state for the purpose of

marriage and intending to return. The Virginia trial court found that Mrs. Naim was a Virginia resident at the time of the marriage and Mr. Naim was not, that the couple was inter-racial within the statutory proscription, that they had left Virginia for the purpose of being married and had intended to and did return to cohabit there as man and wife; it decreed annulment, rejecting a challenge to the constitutionality of the statute. In the year following the first decision in the School Segregation Cases, the Supreme Court of Appeals of Virginia affirmed. On appeal to the United States Supreme Court, the judgment was vacated on the following opinion: "*Per Curiam* : The inadequacy of the record as to the relationship of the parties to the Commonwealth of Virginia at the time of the marriage in North Carolina and upon their return to Virginia, and the failure of the parties to bring here all questions relevant to the disposition of the case, prevents the constitutional issue of the validity of the Virginia statute on miscegenation tendered here being considered 'in clean-cut and concrete form, unclouded' by such problems. Rescue Army v. Municipal Court, 331 U.S. 549, 584. The judgment is vacated and the case remanded to the Supreme Court of Appeals in order that the case may be returned to the Circuit Court of the City of Portsmouth for action not inconsistent with this opinion" (p. 891).

On remand, the Virginia court reiterated the facts that had been established, and reinstated the annulment. (197 Va. 734, 90 S.E.2d 849, (1956)): "[T]he material facts were not * * * in dispute. The record showed that the complainant in the suit, a white woman, was an actual bona fide resident of, and domiciled in, Virginia, and had been for more than a year next preceding the commencement of the suit; that the defendant was a Chinese and a non-resident of Virginia at the time of the institution of the suit; that they had gone to North Carolina to be married for the purpose of evading the Virginia law which forbade their marriage, were married in North Carolina and immediately returned to and lived in Virginia as husband and wife. * * *

"The record before the Circuit Court of the City of Portsmouth was adequate for a decision of the issues presented to it. The record before this court was adequate for deciding the issues on review. The decision of the Circuit Court adjudicated the issues presented to that court. The decision of this court adjudicated the issues presented to it. The decree of the trial court and the decree of this court affirming it have become final so far as these courts are concerned.

"We have no provision either under the rules of practice and procedure of this Court or under the statute law of this Commonwealth by which this court may send the cause back to the Circuit Court with directions to reopen the cause so decided, gather additional evidence and render a new decision."

A motion in the Supreme Court to recall the earlier mandate was denied with the following opinion:

"Appeal from the Supreme Court of Appeals of Virginia. The motion to recall the mandate and to set the case down for oral argument upon the merits, or, in the alternative, to recall and amend the mandate is denied. The decision of the Supreme Court of Appeals of Virginia of January 18, 1956, 197 Va. 734, 90 S.E.2d 849, in response to our order of November 14,

1955, 350 U.S. 891, leaves the case devoid of a properly presented federal question" (p. 985).

Note that the result of Naim was to permit the state, over constitutional objection, affirmatively to dissolve a marriage on the basis of the miscegenation statute. Professor Wechsler has described this as "wholly without basis in the law". *Toward Neutral Principles of Constitutional Law*, in Principle, Politics, and Fundamental Law 47 (1961).[1] Compare Professor Alexander Bickel on Naim v. Naim: "[T]he Court, discounting the interest of the moving party, dismissed outright a case raising the constitutionality of state antimiscegenation statutes. Perhaps Virginia, whose statute was in question, had a 'right' to a decision, although the clamor from those quarters has been something short of deafening. Actually a judgment legitimating such statutes would have been unthinkable, given the principle of the School Segregation Cases and of decisions made in their aftermath. But would it have been wise, at a time when the Court had just pronounced its new integration principle, when it was subject to scurrilous attack by men who predicted that integration of the schools would lead directly to 'mongrelization of the race' and that this was the result the Court had really willed, would it have been wise, just then, in the first case of its sort on an issue that the Negro community as a whole can hardly be said to be pressing hard at the moment, to declare that the states may not prohibit racial intermarriage?" The Least Dangerous Branch: The Supreme Court at the Bar of Politics 174 (1962).

Isn't Professor Bickel's reference to "Virginia's" right to an adjudication patently irrelevant? What about the right of the person against whom Virginia was exercising coercion?

On Bickel's argument, what content is left to the obligatory nature of appeal jurisdiction? Professor Bickel has argued that there is none, and that there is a general "power to decline the exercise of jurisdiction which is given" (p. 127)—pointing to Naim v. Naim as an example in support. Is his view consistent with the Court's obligation of fidelity to law?[2]

---

1. In his dissent to the dismissal in Doe v. Delaware, *supra*, 450 U.S. at 387 n. 11, Justice Brennan summarily brushed aside Naim v. Naim by quoting the Court's statement in the first appeal about the "failure of the parties to bring here all questions relevant to the disposition."

2. See also the private memorandum of Mr. Justice Frankfurter on Naim v. Naim, read at the Court's conference on Nov. 4, 1955, reprinted as Appendix D to Hutchinson, *Unanimity and Desegregation: Decisionmaking in the Supreme Court, 1948–58*, 68 Georgetown L.J. 1, 95–96 (1979):

"So far as I recall, this is the first time since I've been here that I am confronted with the task of resolving a conflict between moral and technical legal considerations. If the question came up on a petition for certiorari, I would have no hesitation in denying the petition. Not because I think petitions for certiorari may be granted or denied as a matter of caprice, but because due consideration of important public consequences is relevant to the exercise of discretion in passing on such petitions.

"But in this case we have an appeal, and Congress has provided for appeals in a few categories of cases including the one here. If it were the settled practice of the Court, since the Judiciary Act of 1925 came in force, that jurisdiction is to be taken as a matter of course where an appeal formally appears, I would bow to the inevitable. But this is not the Court's established practice. The opposite is the practice. I have not made a count of it, but my impression is strong that numerically we do *not* take most of the cases which are formally appeals. Indeed, so strong is this tendency that it has been frequently said, both at the Conference table and by learned commentators, that the Court's practice has assimilated appeals to certiorari.

"The criteria for determining whether a question raised by the jurisdictional statement is so obviously 'substantial' as to preclude an exercise of discretion, are of course not self-defining or automatically

If the Court believed that under the conditions of the time it had to avoid deciding Naim v. Naim without regard to cost, and had to violate the law to do so, it is perhaps preferable to accept that rather than to seek to rationalize and thus generalize the breach. See Gunther, *supra,* at 12: "The Court, to be sure, has sometimes honored the appeal statute in the breach: the miscegenation case is on the books, and there are a very few dismissals similarly indefensible in law. But these are still only aberrations, and surely more can be expected of Bickel than to exaggerate them to the level of the commonplace and to elevate them to the level of the desirable and the acceptable."

(7) In a celebrated dictum, Chief Justice Marshall said: "It is most true that this Court will not take jurisdiction if it should not: but it is equally true, that it must take jurisdiction, if it should. The judiciary cannot, as the legislature may, avoid a measure, because it approaches the confines of the constitution. * * * We have no more right to decline the exercise of jurisdiction which is given, than to usurp that which is not given. The one or the other would be treason to the constitution". Cohens v. Virginia, 6 Wheat. 264, 404 (U.S.1821).

Does Marshall's dictum correctly state the law? Professor Shapiro, in *Jurisdiction and Discretion,* 60 N.Y.U.L.Rev. 543 (1985), demonstrates (in discussing a wide range of traditional and contemporary doctrines) that it cannot, at least, be taken at face value: on many jurisdictional issues,

determinative. There have been a number of striking instances in which this Court on successive occasions declined to entertain an appeal, where eventually the question was entertained and was found to present a claim having constitutional validity. This was true of the question decided in Lovell v. Griffin, 303 U.S. 444; it was true of the Flag Salute issue. See Board of Education v. Barnette, 319 U.S. 624, 664.

"I do not imply that the question in this case is obviously insubstantial. I do say that a Court containing Holmes, Brandeis, Hughes, Stone and Cardozo would only the other day have dismissed the appeal as such. And I further say that even as of today, considering the body of legislation involved, both North and South, and the reach of the problem, namely, divers assumptions by legislatures affecting the regulation of marriage, indicate such a momentum of history, deep feeling, moral and psychological presuppositions, that as of today one can say without wrenching his conscience that the issue has not reached that compelling demand for consideration which precludes refusal to consider it.

"Even if one regards the issue, as I do, of a seriousness that cannot be rejected as frivolous, I candidly face the fact that what I call moral considerations far outweigh the technical considerations in noting jurisdiction. The moral considerations are, of course, those raised by the bearing of adjudicating this question to the Court's responsibility in not thwarting or seriously handicapping the enforcement of its deci-

sion in the segregation cases. I assume, of course, serious division here on the merits. For I find it difficult to believe that there is a single member of this Court who does not think that to throw a decision of this Court other than validating this legislation into the vortex of the present disquietude would not seriously, I believe very seriously, embarrass the carrying-out of the Court's decree of last May.

"The foregoing assumes that the main issue in this case is presented of the record free from the subsidiary or preliminary questions. Such is not my reading of the record. I believe the contrary is true."

Is Justice Frankfurter correct in characterizing Mr. Naim's claim, that Virginia has no power to annul his marriage if the federal Constitution forbids it (a claim he acknowledged to be not insubstantial), as resting on a "technical legal," rather than a "moral," consideration? Is the Court's duty to adjudicate questions Congress has required it to adjudicate "technical" rather than "moral"?

Note Justice Frankfurter's slippery usage when he states that the Court does not "take" appeals that are insubstantial. Is the Court's practice of dismissing insubstantial appeals without oral argument the equivalent of the notion that the Court is free not to "take" any issue about which one can say "without wrenching his conscience" that it "has not reached that compelling demand for consideration which precludes refusal to consider it"?

discretionary considerations have always been legitimately relevant and can be brought to bear in a principled and justifiable manner. But can the cases considered in this section be brought within any notion of a principled or lawful discretion? Or do they rest on a claim for a further discretion, beyond "law", to determine whether a case should be adjudicated? See *id.* at 553–54 & n. 65, 578–79 & nn. 215, 216.

Chapter VI

THE LAW APPLIED IN CIVIL ACTIONS IN THE DISTRICT COURTS

SECTION 34, JUDICIARY ACT OF 1789

1 Stat. 92, Rev.Stat. § 721, 28 U.S.C. § 725 (1940 ed.)

That the laws of the several states, except where the constitution, treaties, or statutes of the United States shall otherwise require or provide, shall be regarded as rules of decision in trials at common law in the courts of the United States in cases where they apply.

---

28 U.S.C. § 1652

The laws of the several states, except where the Constitution or treaties of the United States or Acts of Congress otherwise require or provide, shall be regarded as rules of decision in civil actions in the courts of the United States, in cases where they apply.

SECTION 1.   PROCEDURE

NOTE ON THE HISTORICAL DEVELOPMENT OF THE STATUTES AND RULES OF COURT

The same plan for the regulation of procedure is now in effect in each of the major fields of federal court jurisdiction: bankruptcy, other civil actions (including admiralty), and criminal actions. Some matters in each field are controlled directly by statute or constitutional provision. Primarily, however, procedure in each field is governed by a set of general rules that have been promulgated by the Supreme Court under authority of Congress and that remain continuously subject to revision by the Court. In addition, there is a single set of rules governing the procedure in all cases in the courts of appeals. These general rules are supplemented by special rules dealing with matters of detail, issued and from time to time revised by the district and appellate courts.

The Supreme Court and all courts established by act of Congress are given general authority to prescribe rules for the conduct of their own business by 28 U.S.C. § 2071. The Supreme Court is given specific authority to prescribe rules of procedure for the lower federal courts in bankruptcy by 28 U.S.C. § 2075, in other civil actions by 28 U.S.C. § 2072, and in criminal actions by 18 U.S.C. §§ 3402 (trials before magistrates), 3771,

749

3772. It is given authority to prescribe rules of evidence by 28 U.S.C. § 2076.[1]

Implicit in the decision to make use of the technique of court rule was the decision that federal procedure ought to be uniform rather than conforming to the diverse practices in the state courts. In equity, admiralty, and bankruptcy this decision was readily arrived at. In criminal actions and, more notably, in civil actions at law, the solution made its way much more slowly. Here is another phase, and one of the most instructive ones, of the pervasive problem of federalism: the choice between uniformity and diversity—or, more accurately in this situation, between federal uniformity and federal conformity to state diversities.

A. Equity Before Merger

The story of equity is now merged in that of law. But for nearly a century and a half it had its own history as a distinctive branch of federal practice.

From the beginning federal equity has had to administer the substantive law of the states as well as of the United States. Particularly where rights under state law were in issue, state procedure, in principle, had a claim for acceptance. But in 1789 equity was either non-existent or undeveloped in the courts of many of the states. Federal procedure was thus able to establish and maintain itself without serious challenge.

Even the Rules of Decision Act—the famous thirty-fourth section of the Judiciary Act of 1789—was not made to apply in terms to equity. Not until the 1948 revision, 28 U.S.C. § 1652, was the language broadened to cover all "civil actions".[2]

When the first Congress moved in the Process Act of September 29, 1789 (1 Stat. 93, 94) to deal directly with judicial procedure, it provided that "the forms and modes of proceedings in causes of equity * * * shall be according to the course of the civil law". The second Congress replaced this avowedly stop-gap measure with a formulation that lasted until law and equity were merged in 1938 (Act of May 8, 1792, § 2, 1 Stat. 275, 276). The forms of process in equity, except their style, and the forms and modes

---

1. Section 2071 traces its origin to § 7 of The Act of March 2, 1793, 1 Stat. 333, 335 (giving authority to the several courts of the United States to "make rules and orders for their respective courts directing the returning of writs and processes, the filing of declarations and other pleadings, * * * and otherwise in a manner not repugnant to the laws of the United States, to regulate the practice of the said courts respectively, as shall be fit and necessary for the advancement of justice"). Section 2072, generally known as the Enabling Act, was originally enacted in 1934.

In addition to other rules discussed in this Note, the Supreme Court has prescribed the Copyright Rules, 17 U.S.C. following § 501.

Congress has also conferred certain rulemaking powers on the judicial councils of the circuits in connection with com-plaints of judicial misconduct and disability. See 28 U.S.C. § 372(c)(11); Burbank, *Procedural Reform Under the Judicial Conduct and Disability Act of 1980*, 131 U.Pa. L.Rev. 283 (1982).

2. The change was less significant than it might appear, in view of the often reiterated doctrine that the Rules of Decision Act "is merely declarative of the rule which would exist in the absence of the statute." See Guaranty Trust Co. v. York, p. 800, *infra*. Professor Crosskey argues, however, that the doctrine is incorrect—that the omission of equity and admiralty from the thirty-fourth section of the Judiciary Act meant that the very limited adoption of state law in actions at common law was not extended to those two areas. See 2 Crosskey, Politics and the Constitution in the History of the United States 870–74 (1953).

of proceedings were to be "according to the principles, rules and usages which belong to courts of equity * * *, as contradistinguished from courts of common law".

This formulation got its power of survival from the qualification which was added to it:

" * * * subject however to such alterations and additions as the said courts respectively shall in their discretion deem expedient, or to such regulations as the supreme court of the United States shall think proper from time to time by rule to prescribe to any circuit or district court concerning the same".

The Supreme Court's rulemaking power was affirmed, in language sweeping beyond the confines of equity (and admiralty), in § 6 of the Act of August 23, 1842 (5 Stat. 516, 518):

"That the Supreme Court shall have full power and authority, from time to time, to prescribe, and regulate, and alter, the forms of writs and other process to be used and issued in the district and circuit courts of the United States, and the forms and modes of framing and filing libels, bills, answers, and other proceedings and pleadings, *in suits at common law or in admiralty and in equity* pending in the said courts, and also the forms and modes of taking and obtaining evidence, and of obtaining discovery, and generally the forms and modes of proceeding to obtain relief, and the forms and modes of drawing up, entering, and enrolling decrees, and the forms and modes of proceeding before trustees appointed by the court, and generally to regulate the whole practice of the said courts, so as to prevent delays, and to promote brevity and succinctness in all pleadings and proceedings therein, and to abolish all unnecessary costs and expenses in any suit therein." (Italics supplied).

See also Rev.Stat. §§ 913, 917, 918 (1878).

The Supreme Court first exercised its power to prescribe rules for lower federal courts in 1822 when it promulgated thirty-three Equity Rules (7 Wheat. xvii). Twenty years later these were replaced with ninety-two rules (1 How. xli). Neither the 1822 nor the 1842 rules, however, were comprehensive codes. They assumed the existence of traditional chancery practice, and undertook only *ad hoc* modification or clarification of points of detail. The 1842 rules nevertheless lasted for seventy years, long after they had become archaic.

At length the Supreme Court undertook a comprehensive revision; the Equity Rules of 1912, effective February 1, 1913 (226 U.S. 627) effected a major reform. Three years later Congress took a hand in the Law and Equity Act of 1915 (38 Stat. 956), making equitable defenses available in actions at law and providing for the transfer of cases brought on the wrong side of the court.

The Court itself made only three amendments to the 1912 rules—only three before they were finally superseded in 1938 by the Rules of Civil Procedure, merging the procedure in law and equity. See Rule 70½, 281 U.S. 773 (1930); Rule 75(b), 286 U.S. 570; Rule 61½, 286 U.S. 571 (1932); Rule 70½, 296 U.S. 671 (1935). A practitioner writing in 1933, while expressing general satisfaction with the operation of the rules, criticized the failure of the Court either by amendment or judicial decision to clarify points of uncertainty as they arose. See Lane, *Twenty Years Under the Federal Equity Rules,* 46 Harv.L.Rev. 638 (1933).

See also Talley, *The New and the Old Federal Equity Rules Compared,* 18 Va.L.Reg. 663 (1913); Lane, *Federal Equity Rules,* 35 Harv.L.Rev. 276 (1922); Griswold & Mitchell, *The Narrative Record in Federal Equity Appeals,* 42 Harv.L.Rev. 483 (1929).

B. Admiralty

(1) The story in admiralty parallels that in equity.

Admiralty was thought of in 1789 as a distinct body of law, quasi-international in character. This traditional corpus comprised not only distinctive principles of liability and distinctive remedies but a distinctive practice. From the beginning the principle of federal uniformity both in substance and procedure was thus unquestioned.

State law, to be sure, had played a significant role in relation to admiralty. But this was by virtue of the famous provision in § 9 of the First Judiciary Act (1 Stat. 73, 76) conferring on the district courts "exclusive original cognizance of all civil causes of admiralty and maritime jurisdiction", but "saving to suitors, in all cases, the right of a common law remedy, where the common law is competent to give it". The saving clause preserved remedies in the state courts and on the law side of the federal court. But it did not affect the federal character of proceedings on the admiralty side of the federal court.

As in the case of equity, the first Congress provided (1 Stat. 93, 94) that the forms and modes of proceedings in admiralty "shall be according to the course of the civil law", and the second Congress provided that they should be "according to the principles, rules and usages which belong * * * to courts of admiralty * * *, as contradistinguished from courts of common law". Given content by exercise of the same rulemaking powers that applied in equity, this formulation survived until 1948 when it was swallowed entirely by the general rulemaking authorizations in 28 U.S.C. §§ 2071 and 2073.[3]

For more than half a century after the 1792 act, the Supreme Court left rulemaking in admiralty to the district courts, and divergent practices developed. Spurred apparently by the reaffirmation of its rulemaking authority in § 6 of the Act of August 23, 1842, *supra,* the Court in 1844 promulgated forty-seven "Rules of Practice of the Courts of the United States in Causes of Admiralty and Maritime Jurisdiction on the Instance Side of the Court" (3 How. ix). Like the first Equity Rules, the Admiralty Rules, while introducing certain simplifications, presupposed the traditional framework of admiralty practice.

The 1844 rules remained in effect, with rather frequent amendments and additions, until they were superseded in 1921 (254 U.S. 671). These rules, in turn, were frequently amended until in 1966 admiralty procedure was merged with civil procedure (383 U.S. 1029). The Federal Rules of Civil Procedure now apply in admiralty as well as in other civil cases, but there are a number of special provisions and "supplemental rules for

---

3. In 1966, The general Enabling Act provision, § 2072, was extended to admiralty, and § 2073 was repealed.

certain admiralty and maritime claims"; [4] and the Advisory Committee on Admiralty Rules, created in 1960, did not complete its work until 1971.

(2) An interesting illustration of the interplay between the rulemaking power and the Supreme Court's adjudicatory functions is Fitzgerald v. United States Lines Co., 374 U.S. 16 (1963). The plaintiff, a seaman, brought an action for personal injuries under the Jones Act, on which he had a jury trial right under 46 U.S.C. § 688, and joined with it admiralty claims for unseaworthiness and maintenance and cure, on which no jury trial right existed under the Constitution or the Admiralty Rules. The trial judge submitted the unseaworthiness claim to the jury along with the Jones Act claim, but held the maintenance and cure question in abeyance to try himself. The Supreme Court held that when such claims were joined and arose out of the same set of facts, considerations of trial convenience required that the maintenance and cure claim be submitted to the jury along with the Jones Act claim. Justice Harlan, dissenting, stated that while the result was a desirable one, it should be effectuated through a change in the Admiralty Rules themselves in view of its procedural character. Such a change, he argued, ought not to be made effective until reported to Congress in accordance with the Court's rulemaking authority.

C. Bankruptcy

The power of Congress under the Constitution is a power to pass "uniform laws on the subject of Bankruptcies throughout the United States". In view of this constitutional requirement of uniformity and the absence of any applicable state court procedure, the need for a uniform federal procedure has been unquestioned. The need has been met, as in equity and admiralty, by authorizing the Supreme Court to promulgate general rules. 28 U.S.C. § 2075.

Within five months of the enactment of the Bankruptcy Act of July 1, 1898 (30 Stat. 544), the Court adopted the first "General Orders and Forms in Bankruptcy" (172 U.S. 653). These rules were completely revised in 1939 (305 U.S. 677) following enactment of the Chandler Act of 1938 (52 Stat. 840), and new rules were once again promulgated in the 1970s as a result of the work of the Advisory Committee on Bankruptcy Rules over a period of many years.

In 1978, Congress enacted a comprehensive statute (92 Stat. 2549), which codified bankruptcy law under Title 11 of the U.S.Code. At that time, Congress provided that existing bankruptcy rules, to the extent not inconsistent with the new law, were to remain effective until "repealed or superseded" by new rules. Id. § 405(d).

The judges of the bankruptcy courts established by this act were to be appointed for fourteen year terms. They thus lacked life tenure, as well as other protections guaranteed to federal judges appointed under Article III. The act's broad grant of jurisdiction to these judges was held to violate Article III in Northern Pipeline Const. Co. v. Marathon Pipe Line Co., 458 U.S. 50 (1982), see p. 425, supra. Bankruptcy procedure was, to some extent, left in limbo by this decision.

4. See Fed.Rules 9(h), 14(a), 14(c), 38(e), 82, and Supplemental Rules A–F. Fed. Rule 81(a) provides that the civil rules do not apply to prize proceedings governed by 10 U.S.C. §§ 7651–81.

When Congress failed to fill the gap left by the Northern Pipeline decision, the Administrative Office of the United States Courts, acting under direction of the Judicial Conference, drafted a proposed rule for adoption by all the district courts.[5] On the recommendation of the Judicial Council of each circuit, the rule was promptly adopted, in substantially the form proposed, by every district court. The rule—which was to remain in effect "until Congress enacts appropriate remedial legislation * * * or until March 31, 1984, whichever occurs first"—purported to delegate to the bankruptcy judges much of the authority vested in them by the 1978 Act. (In certain matters, however, the rule provided that judgment would be entered by the district court on review of recommendations by the bankruptcy judge.)

Every court of appeals to consider the question rejected challenges to the validity of this rule. See, *e.g.,* White Motor Corp. v. Citibank, N.A., 704 F.2d 254 (6th Cir.1983). In 1984, the Rule was superseded by substantive and procedural changes in the bankruptcy laws enacted as part of the Bankruptcy Amendments and Federal Judgeship Act of 1984. See p. 49, *supra.* In 1985, an Advisory Committee proposed extensive amendments to the bankruptcy rules to conform to those statutory changes and for other purposes (107 F.R.D. 403 (1985)), and in March 1987, the Supreme Court ordered that amendments based on those proposals would take effect on August 1 (114 F.R.D. 193 (1987)).

D. Criminal Prosecutions

Promulgation of the Rules of Criminal Procedure was encouraged and speeded by the success of the Rules of Civil Procedure. Because their story can be quickly told, however, it is here given out of chronological order.

To attempt a detailed description of federal criminal procedure before the rules would be unprofitable. It was a hodgepodge. Primarily it was a uniform federal procedure. But the federal practices established by judicial elaboration of common law practice, constitutional provisions, and *ad hoc* legislation were interspersed with references to state law, called for by specific statutory direction or judicial interpretation.

The first move that Congress made to bring order out of this wilderness by the technique of court rule was restricted to proceedings after verdict. The Supreme Court was authorized to prescribe rules as to such proceedings by the Act of February 24, 1933, 47 Stat. 904, as amended by the Act of March 8, 1934, 48 Stat. 399. (See 18 U.S.C. § 3772.) The Court issued the first rules in 1934. 292 U.S. 661.

In the Act of June 29, 1940, 54 Stat. 688, Congress enlarged the Court's authority to include the prescription of rules of procedure for criminal proceedings prior to and including verdict. (See 18 U.S.C. § 3771.) The

---

5. This proposal, prepared in the fall of 1982, is reprinted in Vihon, *Delegation of Authority and the Model Rule: The Con-* *tinuing Saga of Northern Pipeline,* 88 Comm.L.J. 64, 77 (1983).

Court determined to exercise this authority in 1944, Justices Black and Frankfurter withholding approval of the decision. 323 U.S. 821.[6]

The Rules of Criminal Procedure, which became effective on March 21, 1946, merged the 1934 post-verdict rules with the new rules. 327 U.S. 821 (1946).

Since then, they have been amended on a number of occasions; as the pace of rulemaking has increased and the subjects of rulemaking have become more controversial, Congress itself has become more deeply enmeshed in the process. See, *e.g.,* Pub.L. No. 93–361, 88 Stat. 397 (1974) (postponing effective date of certain amendments); Pub.L. No. 94–64, 89 Stat. 370 (1975) (approving amendments, with significant changes); Pub.L. No. 94–349, 90 Stat. 822 (1976) (allowing certain amendments to go into effect and postponing effective date of others); Pub.L. No. 95–78, 91 Stat. 319 (1977) (approving certain amendments without change, approving others in modified form, and disapproving still others); Pub.L. No. 96–42, 93 Stat. 326 (1979) (postponing effective date of certain amendments and approving others).

In addition to the criminal rules, the Supreme Court has promulgated rules governing habeas corpus and other collateral proceedings under 28 U.S.C. §§ 2254 and 2255—which became effective, with a number of changes by Congress, in 1977, see pp. 1475–77, *infra* —as well as rules for the trial of misdemeanors before United States magistrates. (The latter are authorized by 18 U.S.C. § 3402. See 445 U.S. 975 (1980).) And the Federal Rules of Evidence, discussed in Part F, below, are applicable to criminal as well as civil cases.

E. Actions at Law Before Merger

(1) Section 34 of the First Judiciary Act (the Rules of Decision Act) blocked out a wide area of application of state law in actions at law in federal courts but left uncertain whether this area included procedure. The Process Act immediately following it (Act of Sept. 29, 1789), however, was unequivocal:

"That until further provision shall be made, and except where by this act or other statutes of the United States is otherwise provided, the forms of writs and executions, except their style, and modes of process and rates of fees, except fees to judges, in the circuit and district courts, in suits at common law, shall be the same in each state respectively as are now used or allowed in the supreme courts of the same."

The Act of May 8, 1792, reaffirmed this provision but made it subject to the same rulemaking power, both in the Supreme Court and the lower courts, that applied in equity and admiralty. See also the Act of March 2, 1793, § 7, 1 Stat. 333, 335, note 1, *supra*.

---

6. Justice Black stated without explanation that he did not approve of the adoption of the rules. Justice Frankfurter explained that his objections went not to the rules on their merits but to the remoteness of the Supreme Court from the day-to-day problems of the district courts, to the undesirability of appearing to prejudge questions that might come before the Court in litigation, and to the heavy burden that the Court was assuming in taking responsibility for the rules.

(2) The peculiarities of the conformity exacted by these provisions did not at once meet the eye. It was a static conformity. And, save for the rulemaking power, the provisions had no application to federal courts sitting in states that entered the union after 1789. As time passed, state procedure changed. It changed notably, in many states, in favor of debtors. In Wayman v. Southard, 10 Wheat. 1 (U.S.1825), the Court was confronted with the question whether a federal court sitting in Kentucky should apply a Kentucky statute requiring a judgment plaintiff either to accept Kentucky bank notes in payment of the judgment or else to take a replevin bond from the defendant for the debt. The case evoked a notable, and notably difficult, constitutional opinion and projected the problem of the law governing federal procedure into the forefront of national politics.

The Court decided, in an opinion by Chief Justice Marshall, that the procedure on executions in the federal courts, as well as the procedure before judgment, was governed by the Process Act of 1792, which continued the Process Act of 1789. These acts adopted the state law "as it existed in September, 1789, * * * not as it might afterwards be made" (p. 32).

The Court recognized that the Rules of Decision Act, by contrast, called for a dynamic rather than a static conformity. But it rejected the claim that the section applied to executions (pp. 24–26):

"* * * This section has never, so far as is recollected, received a construction in this court; but it has, we believe, been generally considered by gentlemen of the profession, as furnishing a rule to guide the court in the formation of its judgment; not one for carrying that judgment into execution. It is 'a rule of decision,' and the proceedings after judgment are merely ministerial. It is, too, 'a rule of decision in trials at common law;' a phrase which presents clearly to the mind the idea of litigation in court, and could never occur to a person intending to describe an execution, or proceedings after judgment, or the effect of those proceedings * * *. The 34th section, then, has no application to the practice of the court, or to the conduct of its officer, in the service of an execution."

The Court also rejected the alternative suggestion that Congress was without power to regulate executions on federal court judgments, and that state laws were independently operative. At the outset of its opinion, it said (pp. 21–22):

"* * * The court cannot accede to this novel construction. The constitution concludes its enumeration of granted powers, with a clause authorizing congress to make all laws which shall be necessary and proper for carrying into execution the foregoing powers, and all other powers vested by this constitution in the government of the United States, or in any department or officer thereof. The judicial department is invested with jurisdiction in certain specified cases, in all which it has power to render judgment. That a power to make laws for carrying into execution all the judgments which the judicial department has power to pronounce, is expressly conferred by this clause, seems to be one of those plain propositions which reasoning cannot render plainer."

Had this been all, no question need have arisen as to the propriety of Congress's exercising this power by providing that the federal courts should follow current state procedure as it existed from time to time. But the opinion proceeded to throw doubt on this. The Court recognized that its holding that the process acts were applicable involved the conclusion that the matters in issue could be regulated by rule of court. Then, in a pioneer discussion of delegation of legislative power, it went out of its way to consider and sustain the validity of this rulemaking authority. At the end of the opinion came this passage (pp. 48–50):

"[T]he question respecting the right of the courts to alter the modes of proceeding in suits at common law, established in the process act, does not arise in this case. That is not the point on which the judges at the circuit were divided, and which they have adjourned to this court. The question really adjourned is, whether the laws of Kentucky respecting executions, passed subsequent to the process act, are applicable to executions which issue on judgments rendered by the federal courts. If they be, their applicability must be maintained, either in virtue of the 34th section of the judiciary act, or in virtue of an original inherent power in the state legislatures, independent of any act of congress, to control the modes of proceeding in suits depending in the courts of the United States, and to regulate the conduct of their officers in the service of executions issuing out of those courts.

"That the power claimed for the state is not given by the 34th section of the judiciary act, has been fully stated in the preceding part of this opinion. That it has not an independent existence in the state legislatures, is, we think, one of those political axioms, an attempt to demonstrate which, would be a waste of argument, not to be excused * * *. Its utter inadmissibility will at once present itself to the mind, if we imagine an act of a state legislature for the direct and sole purpose of regulating proceedings in the courts of the Union, or of their officers in executing their judgments. No gentleman, we believe, will be so extravagant as to maintain the efficacy of such an act. It seems not much less extravagant, to maintain, that the practice of the federal courts, and the conduct of their officers, can be indirectly regulated by the state legislatures, by an act professing to regulate the proceedings of the state courts, and the conduct of the officers who execute the process of those courts. It is a general rule, that what cannot be done directly, from defect of power, cannot be done indirectly. The right of congress to delegate to the courts the power of altering the modes (established by the process act) of proceedings in suits, has been already stated; but, were it otherwise, we are well satisfied that the state legislatures do not possess that power."

Marshall's result was politically unacceptable, and Congress overrode it. In apparent deference to his reasoning, however, it did so by providing not for dynamic conformity but for static conformity brought, in part, up to date. The Process Act of May 19, 1828, 4 Stat. 278, required federal courts to follow, on writs of execution and other final process issued on judgments, the procedure of the state courts in force on the day the act became effective. State procedure in force on the same date was also made the rule for proceedings before judgment in federal courts sitting in states admitted after 1789. But for the original states the 1789 procedure remained the rule. Later legislation made parallel provision for states admitted after 1828. See, *e.g.*, the Act of Aug. 1, 1842, 5 Stat. 499.

Both the Supreme Court and the lower courts retained their rulemaking authority throughout the period of static conformity; the authority, indeed, was reiterated with fresh emphasis in the Act of Aug. 23, 1842, p. 751, *supra*. But the courts were reluctant to use the power. The adoption of the Field Code by New York in 1848 and the spread of the code system to other states complicated the problem; and the situation became increasingly unsatisfactory.

(3) At length, in the Conformity Act of June 1, 1872, 17 Stat. 196, Congress withdrew the unused rulemaking authority, and adopted, with qualifications, the principle of dynamic conformity. Section 5 of the Act provided:

"That the practice, pleadings, and forms and modes of proceeding, in other than equity and admiralty causes in the circuit and district courts of the United States shall conform, as near as may be, to the practice, pleadings, and forms and modes of proceeding existing at the time in like causes in the courts of record of the State within which such circuit or district courts are held, any rule of court to the contrary notwithstanding: *Provided, however,* That nothing herein contained shall alter the rules of evidence under the laws of the United States, and as practiced in the courts thereof."

The Conformity Act eliminated the anachronism of federal adherence to no-longer-existent state practice. On more matters than not a lawyer could now follow in the federal courts the procedure currently prevailing in the courts of his state—an advantage particularly appreciated in the code states. But this conformity, of course, was confined to actions at law. And even as to such actions exceptions and qualifications soon began to appear.

A specific statute on a point of procedure, of which there were many, of course overrode state law. See, *e.g.,* Henkel v. Chicago, St.P., M. & O. Ry., 284 U.S. 444 (1932) (holding that federal statute on costs occupied the field, excluding the operation of state law on a point on which statute was silent). The Conformity Act, moreover, applied only if there were "like causes" triable in the state courts. Was an action for patent infringement, which was within the exclusive jurisdiction of the federal courts, "like" an ordinary action on the case for damages? See, *e.g.,* National Cash–Register Co. v. Leland, 94 Fed. 502 (1st Cir.1899). Contra: Myers v. Cunningham, 44 Fed. 346 (C.C.N.D.Ohio 1890). The earlier process acts, in addition, had been held not to affect "jurisdiction," and the Conformity Act was similarly construed. See, *e.g.,* Davenport v. County of Dodge, 105 U.S. 237 (1881) (holding inapplicable a state statute permitting mandamus as an original proceeding). Finally, even when the Act plainly applied, its terms required the federal courts to conform to state procedure only "as near as may be", a phrase which opened a wide door for adherence to distinctive federal practices. See generally Clark & Moore, *A New Federal Civil Procedure,* 44 Yale L.J. 387, 401–11 (1935).

Partly in reliance on this latter phrase and partly by a restrictive interpretation of the three categories of "practice, pleadings, and forms and modes of proceedings", the Court withdrew from the operation of the Act a wide area of particularly important matters affecting the administration of federal justice. For example, in McDonald v. Pless, 238 U.S. 264 (1915), the district court, on a motion to set aside the verdict as having been reached by compromise, had refused to permit one of the jurors to testify about proceedings in the jury room. The Supreme Court approved the lower court's ruling, saying (pp. 266–67):

"On the argument here it was suggested that it was not necessary to consider the question involved as an original proposition, since the decision of the Federal court was in accordance with the rule in North Carolina (Purcell v. Southern R. Co., 119 N.C. 739, 26 S.E. 161), and therefore binding under Rev.Stat. § 914, Comp.Stat.1913, § 1537, * * *. But neither in letter nor in spirit does the conformity act apply to the power of the court to inquire into the conduct of jurors who had been summoned to perform a duty in the administration of justice and who, for the time being, were officers of the court. The conduct of parties, witnesses and counsel in a case, as well as the conduct of the jurors and officers of the court may be of such a character as not only to defeat the rights of litigants, but it may directly affect the administration of public justice. In the very nature of things the courts of each jurisdiction must each be in a position to adopt and enforce their own self-preserving rules."

See also Herron v. Southern Pacific Co., 283 U.S. 91 (1931), p. 817, *infra.*

F. The Enabling Act, Merger, and Beyond

(1) The movement to reform federal procedure was prompted partly by the need to dispel the confusion created by the uneasy co-existence of several systems of procedure in the same forum. It was also motivated by the conviction that effective reform could be achieved only through the device of court rules, drafted with the assistance of bench and bar. The requisite assistance was likely to be commanded only by a project for rules of nationwide application.

Conformity, it was hoped, would not have to be sacrificed, if the states could be induced to copy the federal model. See, generally, Sunderland, *The Grant of Rule–Making Power to the Supreme Court of the United States,* 32 Mich.L.Rev. 1116 (1934).[7]

Clark & Moore, *supra,* at 388–89, thus summarize the history of the proposal that became the Act of June 19, 1934, 48 Stat. 1064 (*cf.* 28 U.S.C. § 2072):

"The manner of passage of the act disclosed some of the ironies which seem to accompany reform movements. It was the culmination of one of the most persistent and sustained campaigns for law improvement conducted in this country, one sponsored by the American Bar Association since 1912, under the militant leadership of Mr. Thomas W. Shelton and his Committee on Uniform Judicial Procedure, and supported by some of the most distinguished of the legal profession. * * *

"As originally sponsored by the American Bar Association, the act authorized merely uniform rules in procedure in federal actions at law. But in 1922 Mr. Chief Justice Taft addressed the Association shortly before the rendering of his decision in Liberty Oil Company v. Condon National Bank and urged the union of law and equity in the proposed new procedure. Thereafter there was added a second section to the bill providing for such union, and from that time on, the bill was pressed in substantially the same form that it had when finally passed. It should be noted, however, that the draftsmen apparently considered the union of law and equity a more drastic step than the establishment of uniform rules for law actions;

---

7. The federal model has in fact had a major impact on judicial procedure in virtually every state. Indeed, more than half of the states have adopted the federal rules of civil procedure with, at most, only minor changes. See Wright, Federal Courts 406 (4th ed. 1983).

for under the act the latter may become effective six months after their promulgation, while the 'united rules' may not take effect 'until they shall have been reported to Congress by the Attorney General at the beginning of a regular session thereof and until after the close of such session.' * * * "[8]

The actual enactment of the bill was astonishingly casual. On March 1, 1934, Attorney General Cummings wrote identical letters to the chairmen of the House and Senate judiciary committees, as follows:

"I enclose herewith a draft of a bill to empower the Supreme Court of the United States to prescribe rules to govern the practice and procedure in civil actions at law in the District Courts of the United States and the courts of the District of Columbia. The enactment of the bill would bring about uniformity and simplicity in the practice in actions at law in Federal courts and thus relieve the courts and the bar of controversies and difficulties which are continually arising wholly apart from the merits of the litigation in which they are interested. It seems to me that there can be no substantial objection to the result, which, apart from its inherent merit, would also, it is believed, contribute to a reduction in the cost of litigation in the Federal courts.

"I request that you introduce the enclosed bill and hope that you may be able to give it your support."

The favorable Reports of the Senate and House Committees were brief (see S.Rep. No. 1048, H.R.Rep. No. 1829, 73d Cong., 2d Sess. (1934)), and the discussion in the two houses consumed only a few minutes each. In each house the floor manager paraphrased the Attorney General's letter and referred to what was said to be the unanimous approval of bar associations. In each the objection that lawyers would have to learn two systems of practice was made by one member but was quickly withdrawn, and the bill was passed by unanimous consent. 78 Cong.Rec. 9362–63 (Senate); *id.* 10866 (House).[9]

(2) Under the leadership of Chief Justice Hughes the Court made vigorous and effective use of the new power. On May 9, 1935, the Chief Justice announced to the American Law Institute the Court's decision to act under the second section of the statute. 13 Am.Law.Inst.Proc. 61. On

---

8. For an exhaustive and informative study of the pre–1934 efforts at reform, with special emphasis on the period 1912–1930, see Burbank, *The Rules Enabling Act of 1934*, 130 U.Pa.L.Rev. 1015, 1035–98 (1982).

9. The Act provided as follows:

"That the Supreme Court of the United States shall have the power to prescribe, by general rules, for the district courts of the United States and for the courts of the District of Columbia, the forms of process, writs, pleadings, and motions, and the practice and procedure in civil actions at law. Said rules shall neither abridge, enlarge, nor modify the substantive rights of any litigant. They shall take effect six months after their promulgation, and thereafter all laws in conflict therewith shall be of no further force or effect.

"SEC. 2. The court may at any time unite the general rules prescribed by it for cases in equity with those in actions at law so as to secure one form of civil action and procedure for both: *Provided, however,* That in such union of rules the right of trial by jury as at common law and declared by the seventh amendment to the Constitution shall be preserved to the parties inviolate. Such united rules shall not take effect until they shall have been reported to Congress by the Attorney General at the beginning of a regular session thereof and until after the close of such session." Act of June 19, 1934, 48 Stat. 1064 (the present version is 28 U.S.C. § 2072).

June 3, 1935, this decision was embodied in a formal order, and a distinguished Advisory Committee appointed to draw up proposed rules. 295 U.S. 774. The Committee's proposals were subjected to widespread and intensive scrutiny and criticism, through the medium, among others, of special committees of the bench and bar established in the various circuits and districts. With minor changes, the final proposals were approved by the Court, and the rules became effective September 16, 1938. See 308 U.S. 645–766.[10]

From 1938 to 1951, the rules were amended several times with the aid of the Advisory Committee. See 308 U.S. 642 (1939); 329 U.S. 839 (1947); 335 U.S. 919 (1948); 341 U.S. 959 (1951). In 1955, additional amendments were recommended by the Advisory Committee but the Court took no action on them, and in 1956 the Committee was discharged.

In 1958, in an amendment to 28 U.S.C. § 331, Congress instructed the Judicial Conference of the United States to "carry on a continuous study of the operation and effect of the general rules of practice and procedure now or hereafter in use as prescribed by the Supreme Court for the other courts of the United States pursuant to law. Such changes in and additions to those rules as the Conference may deem desirable * * * shall be recommended by the Conference from time to time to the Supreme Court for its consideration and adoption, modification or rejection, in accordance with law."

Pursuant to this provision, a Standing Committee of the Judicial Conference on Rules of Practice and Procedure was established in 1960, together with five Advisory Committees. The task of an Advisory Committee is to draft proposals, solicit public comment on them, and submit a report to the Standing Committee. The Standing Committee in turn reports to the Conference, which makes its recommendations to the Supreme Court.

The results of the work of the Advisory Committees on the Admiralty, Bankruptcy, Criminal and Appellate [11] Rules have already been referred to. The Advisory Committee on the Civil Rules (which, like the Criminal Rules Committee, is regarded as a continuing body) has originated a number of important amendments dealing, among other topics, with service of process, judgment notwithstanding the verdict, multi-party litigation, discovery, and the responsibility of attorneys. See, e.g., 368 U.S. 1009 (1961); 374 U.S. 861 (1963); 383 U.S. 1029 (1966); 389 U.S. 1121 (1968); 398 U.S. 977 (1970); 446 U.S. 995 (1980); 97 F.R.D. 165 (1982).[12]

---

10. For an extensive review and report of previously ignored materials relating to the work of the original Advisory Committee, see Burbank, note 8, *supra*, at 1131–84.

11. 28 U.S.C. § 2072, the present successor to the Enabling Act of 1934, was amended in 1966 (80 Stat. 1323) to add a specific reference to the power to make rules for the "courts of appeals of the United States in civil actions, including admiralty and maritime cases, and appeals therein, and the practice and procedure in proceedings for review by the courts of appeals [of Tax Court and other administrative decisions] * * *." At the same time, 28 U.S.C. § 2073, dealing with admi-

ralty and maritime cases, and § 2074, relating to review of Tax Court decisions, were repealed.

12. For discussion of the major changes in the Civil Rules during this period, see *Appendix A to the Report of the Standing Committee on Rules of Practice and Procedure,* 85 F.R.D. 538 (1980); *Advisory Committee's Explanatory Statement Concerning Amendments of the Discovery Rules,* 48 F.R.D. 487 (1970); Kaplan, *Continuing Work of the Civil Committee: 1966 Amendments of the Federal Rules of Civil Procedure,* 81 Harv.L.Rev. 356, 591 (1967, 1968); Kaplan, *Amendments of the Federal Rules*

(3) In 1965, an Advisory Committee on Rules of Evidence was appointed, and after several drafts were submitted for public comment (see 46 F.R.D. 161 (1969); 51 F.R.D. 315 (1971)), the Supreme Court transmitted the Federal Rules of Evidence to Congress in November 1972. 56 F.R.D. 183 (1972). Justice Douglas, dissenting, argued that rules of evidence did not fall within the scope of authority delegated by Congress, that the Court had had little to do with drafting the rules, and that it was "so far removed from the trial arena that we have no special insight, no meaningful oversight to contribute" (p. 185).

Almost immediately, congressional opposition to the proposed rules surfaced, centering both on the substantive content of certain of the rules and on the question whether the Court was empowered by the Rules Enabling Act to promulgate rules of evidence at all.[13] This opposition culminated in an enactment staying the effectiveness of the proposed rules until they should be affirmatively approved by Congress. Pub.L. No. 93–12, 87 Stat. 9 (1973). Following this resolution, House, Senate, and ultimately, Conference Committees of the Congress redrafted the rules. Although much of the original Court text was left substantially unchanged through this process, significant changes were made, *inter alia*, in the rules relating to privileges and presumptions. Finally, the Federal Rules of Evidence were enacted in statutory form, to become effective on July 1, 1975. Pub.L. No. 93–595, 88 Stat. 1926 (1975).[14]

At the same time that Congress passed the Federal Rules of Evidence, it enacted a new "Enabling Act" to govern amendments to those rules. 28 U.S.C. § 2076. In Conf.Comm.Rep. No. 93–1597, 93d Cong., 2d Sess. (1974), explaining the new requirements, Congress recognized "the continuing role of the Supreme Court in promulgating rules of evidence," but in § 2076 the time allowed for Congressional review of Supreme Court amendments to those rules was extended from the ninety days of § 2072 (the general Enabling Act) to one hundred eighty days, and a provision allowing *either* House of Congress to disapprove or defer a Supreme Court amendment was adopted.[15] Moreover, amendments affecting privileges were not to be effective without approval by act of Congress.

For contemporary comments on, and criticisms of, the balance struck by Congress in this area see 21 Wright & Graham, Federal Practice and Procedure §§ 5006, 5007 (1977); Moore & Bendix, *Congress, Evidence and Rulemaking*, 84 Yale L.J. 9 (1974); Friedenthal, *The Rulemaking Power of*

---

of Civil Procedure, 1961–63, 77 Harv.L.Rev. 601, 801 (1964).

The Supreme Court, in 1982, approved amendments to Rule 4 of the Federal Rules of Civil Procedure which made important changes in the method of process service. See 93 F.R.D. 255 (1982). These amendments were substantially revised by Congress before they went into effect in February 1983. See Pub.L. No. 97–462, 96 Stat. 2527 (1982); Siegel, *Practice Commentary on Amendment of Federal Rule 4 (Eff. Feb. 26, 1983) with Special Statute of Limitations Precautions,* 96 F.R.D. 88 (1983).

13. Professor Burbank has concluded, on the basis of his study of pre–1934 mater-

ials, that rules relating to the admissibility of evidence—as distinguished from rules relating to the mode of taking and obtaining evidence—do lie outside the scope of the 1934 Enabling Act. See Burbank, note 8, *supra,* at 1129–30, 1137–43.

14. As enacted by Congress, several of the rules of evidence refer to state law in cases in which state law supplies the rule of decision. See Rule 302 (presumptions); Rule 501 (privileges).

15. See Paragraph (6), *infra,* for discussion of the effect of INS v. Chadha on this provision.

the Supreme Court: A Contemporary Crisis, 27 Stan.L.Rev. 673 (1975); Note, 76 Mich.L.Rev. 1177 (1978).

(4) Although the pace of the Supreme Court's rulemaking activities since 1938 has been increasing, the Court has not been unanimous in its approval of those activities. The disagreements of Justices Black and Frankfurter with the promulgation of criminal rules, and of Justice Douglas with the rules of evidence, have already been mentioned. Justice Brandeis stated without explanation that he did not approve of the adoption of the civil rules. See 308 U.S. at 643. And Justice Black and Douglas together on several occasions voiced objection to the rulemaking process, both in general and as applied. See, *e.g.,* 368 U.S. 1012 (1961); 374 U.S. 865 (1963); 383 U.S. 1032 (1966); 383 U.S. 1089 (1966); 398 U.S. 979 (1970); 401 U.S. 1019 (1971). Thus in dissenting from certain amendments to the civil rules adopted in 1963, Justices Black and Douglas stated (374 U.S. at 865–66, 869–70):

" * * * We believe that while some of the Rules of Civil Procedure are simply housekeeping details, many determine matters so substantially affecting the rights of litigants in lawsuits that in practical effect they are the equivalent of new legislation which, in our judgment, the Constitution requires to be initiated in and enacted by the Congress and approved by the President. The Constitution, as we read it, provides that all laws shall be enacted by the House, the Senate, and the President, not by the mere failure of Congress to reject proposals of an outside agency * * *.

"Instead of recommending changes to the present rules, we recommend that the statute authorizing this Court to prescribe Rules of Civil Procedure, if it is to remain a law, be amended to place the responsibility upon the Judicial Conference rather than upon this Court. * * * It is [the Conference and its Committees] * * * who do the work, not we, and the rules have only our imprimatur. * * * Transfer of the function to the Judicial Conference would relieve us of the embarrassment of having to sit in judgment on the constitutionality of rules which we have approved and which as applied in given situations might have to be declared invalid." [16]

(5) Criticism of the present rulemaking procedure has also been voiced outside the Supreme Court, and has extended to the promulgation of local as well as national rules. With respect to the national rules, this criticism has embraced the involvement of the Supreme Court, the Chief Justice, and the Judicial Conference; the composition of the Advisory Committees; and the lack of sufficient opportunity for public participation. Proposals for change, however, have not gone so far as to urge elimination of Congress's delegation of rule-making authority. See, *e.g.,* Weinstein, Reform of Court Rule–Making Procedures (1977); Lesnick, *The Federal Rule–Making Process: A Time for Reexamination,* 61 A.B.A.J. 579 (1975); Hazard, *Undemocratic Legislation,* 87 Yale L.J. 1284 (1978) (reviewing Judge Weinstein's

16. See also Justice Powell, dissenting for himself and Justices Stewart and Rehnquist, from certain amendments to the discovery rules in 1980: "Congress should bear in mind that our approval of proposed Rules is more a certification that they are the products of proper procedures than a considered judgment on the merits of the proposals themselves. * * * Congress'

acceptance of these tinkering changes will delay for years the adoption of genuinely effective reforms" (446 U.S. 996, 998 n. 1, 1000 (1980)).

Substantial additional changes in the discovery rules were in fact made some three years later. See note 12, *supra.*

book). See generally Brown, Federal Rulemaking: Problems and Possibilities (1981).

In response to some of these criticisms, the Standing Committee on Rules of Practice and Procedure of the Judicial Conference adopted a statement of operating procedures. See 98 F.R.D. 337 (1983). This statement provides, *inter alia,* for Advisory Committee publication of proposed rule changes and for public hearings on those proposed changes. And in 1985, Civil Rule 83 was amended to require notice and opportunity for comment in the promulgation and modification of local rules. See 105 F.R.D. 225 (1983).

(6) In INS v. Chadha, 462 U.S. 919 (1983), the Supreme Court invalidated a section of the Immigration and Nationality Act, 8 U.S.C. § 244(c)(2), which provided that a decision by the Attorney General to suspend deportation of an alien could be nullified by a resolution of either House of Congress. Such nullification, the Court held, was legislative in character and thus under the Constitution could not take effect without the concurrence of both Houses and presentment to the President. (The Court further held that § 244(c)(2) was severable from the other provisions of the statute, and thus the Attorney General's statutory authority to suspend deportation remained intact.)

What is the effect of this decision—which was rendered after many years of controversy over the validity of the "legislative veto"—on the various Enabling Acts discussed in this Note? It seems clear that the provision of the Rules of Evidence Enabling Act, 28 U.S.C. § 2076, which authorizes either House to reject Supreme Court amendments to those rules, does not survive after Chadha. If the remainder of § 2076 would be valid without that authorization, is the invalid portion severable, or must the entire section fall? The Court in Chadha reaffirmed the doctrine that the invalid portion of a statute should be held severable unless it is evident that the valid portion would not have been independently enacted, and under this test it seems likely that the remainder of § 2076 would survive.

But what of the provision in both § 2072 (the general Rules Enabling Act) and § 2076 that no changes in the rules shall go into effect until they have been reported to Congress and until the expiration of a specified period? Since these provisions in terms require only a report of any rule changes to Congress, and since Congress itself evidently cannot take action with respect to those changes without the concurrence of both Houses and presentment to the President,[17] the Chadha decision would not appear to put the provisions in jeopardy.[18]

(7) Concern with a number of issues discussed in the preceding paragraphs has led to proposals to amend the Enabling Act and related provisions. One proposal, which passed the House in the 99th Congress (H.R. 3550, 99th Cong., 1st Sess. (1985)), but which did not reach the floor of the Senate, would have:

17. At least Congress has consistently proceeded on this understanding. See, *e.g.,* statutes cited at p. 762, *supra.*

18. As noted in Paragraph (3), *supra,* § 2076 also contains a provision that any change in the rules relating to privileges "shall have no force or effect until it shall be approved by Act of Congress." In this instance, the Supreme Court's "rulemaking" function amounts only to the recommendation of legislation to Congress.

- consolidated the Supreme Court's rulemaking power under the present provisions of §§ 2072, 2075 (bankruptcy), and 2076 (evidence), eliminating the legislative veto in § 2076;

- provided that rules prescribed by the Supreme Court "shall not supersede any provision of a law of the United States"; [19]

- specified procedures to be followed by the Judicial Conference and its committees (including the holding of open meetings by committees);

- provided for the compilation and review of local rules by the Judicial Conference; and

- required notice and opportunity for comment in the rulemaking processes of the district court and judicial councils.[20]

SIBBACH v. WILSON & CO., INC.
312 U.S. 1, 61 S.Ct. 422, 85 L.Ed. 479 (1940).
Certiorari to the Circuit Court of Appeals for the Seventh Circuit.

MR. JUSTICE ROBERTS delivered the opinion of the Court.

This case calls for decision as to the validity of Rules 35 and 37 of the Rules of Civil Procedure for District Courts of the United States.

In an action brought by the petitioner in the District Court for Northern Illinois to recover damages for bodily injuries, inflicted in Indiana, respondent answered denying the allegations of the complaint, and moved for an order requiring the petitioner to submit to a physical examination by one or more physicians appointed by the court to determine the nature and extent of her injuries. The court ordered that the petitioner submit to such an examination by a physician so appointed.

Compliance having been refused, the respondent obtained an order to show cause why the petitioner should not be punished for contempt. In response the petitioner challenged the authority of the court to order her to submit to the examination, asserting that the order was void. It appeared that the courts of Indiana, the state where the cause of action arose, hold such an order proper, whereas the courts of Illinois, the state in which the trial court sat, hold that such an order cannot be made. Neither state has any statute governing the matter.

The court adjudged the petitioner guilty of contempt, and directed that she be committed until she should obey the order for examination or otherwise should be legally discharged from custody. The petitioner appealed.

The Circuit Court of Appeals decided that Rule 35, which authorizes an order for a physical examination in such a case, is valid, and affirmed the judgment. The writ of certiorari was granted because of the importance of the question involved. * * * [The opinion here quotes from the act

19. This provision, which differed from existing law (see p. 770, note 3, *infra*), contained a grandfather clause applicable to any rule in effect at the time of enactment.

20. Similar legislation was introduced in the 100th Congress.

authorizing the Rules of Civil Procedure, p. 759, *supra*, and from Rules 35(a) and 37(b).]

The contention of the petitioner, in final analysis, is that Rules 35 and 37 are not within the mandate of Congress to this court. This is the limit of permissible debate, since argument touching the broader questions of Congressional power and of the obligation of federal courts to apply the substantive law of a state is foreclosed.

Congress has undoubted power to regulate the practice and procedure of federal courts,[6] and may exercise that power by delegating to this or other federal courts authority to make rules not inconsistent with the statutes or Constitution of the United States; but it has never essayed to declare the substantive state law, or to abolish or nullify a right recognized by the substantive law of the state where the cause of action arose, save where a right or duty is imposed in a field committed to Congress by the Constitution. On the contrary it has enacted that the state law shall be the rule of decision in the federal courts.

Hence we conclude that the Act of June 19, 1934, was purposely restricted in its operation to matters of pleading and court practice and procedure. Its two provisos or caveats emphasize this restriction. The first is that the court shall not "abridge, enlarge, nor modify the substantive rights", in the guise of regulating procedure. The second is that if the rules are to prescribe a single form of action for cases at law and suits in equity, the constitutional right to jury trial inherent in the former must be preserved. There are other limitations upon the authority to prescribe rules which might have been, but were not mentioned in the Act; for instance, the inability of a court, by rule, to extend or restrict the jurisdiction conferred by a statute.

Whatever may be said as to the effect of the Conformity Act while it remained in force, the rules, if they are within the authority granted by Congress, repeal that statute, and the District Court was not bound to follow the Illinois practice respecting an order for physical examination. On the other hand if the right to be exempt from such an order is one of substantive law, the Rules of Decision Act required the District Court, though sitting in Illinois, to apply the law of Indiana, the state where the cause of action arose, and to order the examination. To avoid this dilemma the petitioner admits, and, we think, correctly, that Rules 35 and 37 are rules of procedure. She insists, nevertheless, that by the prohibition against abridging substantive rights, Congress has banned the rules here challenged. In order to reach this result she translates "substantive" into "important" or "substantial" rights. And she urges that if a rule affects such a right, albeit the rule is one of procedure merely, its prescription is not within the statutory grant of power embodied in the Act of June 19, 1934. She contends that our decisions and recognized principles require us so to hold.

* * * [Discussion of Union Pac. Ry. v. Botsford, 141 U.S. 250 (1891), and Camden & S.Ry. v. Stetson, 177 U.S. 172 (1900), omitted.]

We are thrown back, then, to the arguments drawn from the language of the Act of June 19, 1934. Is the phrase "substantive rights" confined to rights conferred by law to be protected and enforced in accordance with the

---

6. Wayman v. Southard, 10 Wheat. 1, 21; Bank of United States v. Halstead, 10 Wheat. 51, 53; Beers v. Haughton, 9 Pet. 329, 359, 361.

adjective law of judicial procedure? It certainly embraces such rights. One of them is the right not to be injured in one's person by another's negligence, to redress infraction of which the present action was brought. The petitioner says the phrase connotes more; that by its use Congress intended that in regulating procedure this court should not deal with important and substantial rights theretofore recognized. Recognized where and by whom? The state courts are divided as to the power in the absence of statute to order a physical examination. In a number such an order is authorized by statute or rule. The rules in question accord with the procedure now in force in Canada and England.

The asserted right, moreover, is no more important than many others enjoyed by litigants in District Courts sitting in the several states, before the Federal Rules of Civil Procedure altered and abolished old rights or privileges and created new ones in connection with the conduct of litigation. The suggestion that the rule offends the important right to freedom from invasion of the person ignores the fact that as we hold, no invasion of freedom from personal restraint attaches to refusal so to comply with its provisions. If we were to adopt the suggested criterion of the importance of the alleged right we should invite endless litigation and confusion worse confounded. The test must be whether a rule really regulates procedure,—the judicial process for enforcing rights and duties recognized by substantive law and for justly administering remedy and redress for disregard or infraction of them. That the rules in question are such is admitted.

Finally, it is urged that Rules 35 and 37 work a major change of policy and that this was not intended by Congress. Apart from the fact already stated, that the policy of the states in this respect has not been uniform, it is to be noted that the authorization of a comprehensive system of court rules was a departure in policy, and that the new policy envisaged in the enabling act of 1934 was that the whole field of court procedure be regulated in the interest of speedy, fair and exact determination of the truth. The challenged rules comport with this policy. Moreover, in accordance with the Act, the rules were submitted to the Congress so that that body might examine them and veto their going into effect if contrary to the policy of the legislature.

The value of the reservation of the power to examine proposed rules, laws and regulations before they become effective is well understood by Congress. It is frequently, as here, employed to make sure that the action under the delegation squares with the Congressional purpose. Evidently the Congress felt the rule was within the ambit of the statute as no effort was made to eliminate it from the proposed body of rules, although this specific rule was attacked and defended before the committees of the two Houses. The Preliminary Draft of the rules called attention to the contrary practice indicated by the Botsford case, as did the Report of the Advisory Committee and the Notes prepared by the Committee to accompany the final version of the rules. That no adverse action was taken by Congress indicates, at least, that no transgression of legislative policy was found. We conclude that the rules under attack are within the authority granted.

The District Court treated the refusal to comply with its order as a contempt and committed the petitioner therefor. Neither in the Circuit Court of Appeals nor here was this action assigned as error. We think, however, that in the light of the provisions of Rule 37 it was plain error of such a fundamental nature that we should notice it. Section (b)(2)(iv) of Rule 37 exempts from punishment as for contempt the refusal to obey an order that a party submit to a physical or mental examination. The District Court was in error in going counter to this express exemption. The remedies available under the rule in such a case are those enumerated in Section (b)(2)(i)(ii) and (iii). For this error we reverse the judgment and remand the cause to the District Court for further proceedings in conformity to this opinion.

Reversed and remanded.

* * *

MR. JUSTICE FRANKFURTER (dissenting). * * *

Speaking with diffidence in support of a view which has not commended itself to the Court, it does not seem to me that the answer to our question is to be found by an analytic determination whether the power of examination here claimed is a matter of procedure or a matter of substance, even assuming that the two are mutually exclusive categories with easily ascertainable contents. The problem seems to me to be controlled by the policy underlying the Botsford decision. Its doctrine was not a survival of an outworn technicality. It rested on considerations akin to what is familiarly known in the English law as the liberties of the subject. To be sure, the immunity that was recognized in the Botsford case has no constitutional sanction. It is amenable to statutory change. But the "inviolability of a person" was deemed to have such historic roots in Anglo–American law that it was not to be curtailed "unless by clear and unquestionable authority of law". In this connection it is significant that a judge as responsive to procedural needs as was Mr. Justice Holmes, should, on behalf of the Supreme Judicial Court of Massachusetts, have supported the Botsford doctrine on the ground that "the common law was very slow to sanction any violation of or interference with the person of a free citizen". Stack v. New York, etc., R. Co., 177 Mass. 155, 157, 58 N.E. 686.

So far as national law is concerned, a drastic change in public policy in a matter deeply touching the sensibilities of people or even their prejudices as to privacy, ought not to be inferred from a general authorization to formulate rules for the more uniform and effective dispatch of business on the civil side of the federal courts. I deem a requirement as to the invasion of the person to stand on a very different footing from questions pertaining to the discovery of documents, pre-trial procedure and other devices for the expeditious, economic and fair conduct of litigation. That disobedience of an order under Rule 35 cannot be visited with punishment as for contempt does not mitigate its intrusion into an historic immunity of the privacy of the person. Of course the Rule is compulsive in that the doors of the federal courts otherwise open may be shut to litigants who do not submit to such a physical examination.

In this view little significance attaches to the fact that the Rules, in accordance with the statute, remained on the table of two Houses of Congress without evoking any objection to Rule 35 and thereby automatically came into force. Plainly the Rules are not acts of Congress and can not be treated as such. Having due regard to the mechanics of legislation and the practical conditions surrounding the business of Congress when the Rules were submitted, to draw any inference of tacit approval from non-action by Congress is to appeal to unreality. And so I conclude that to make the drastic change that Rule 35 sought to introduce would require explicit legislation.

Ordinarily, disagreement with the majority on so-called procedural matters is best held in silence. Even in the present situation I should be loath to register dissent did the issue pertain merely to diversity litigation. But Rule 35 applies to all civil litigation in the federal courts, and thus concerns the enforcement of federal rights and not merely of state law in the federal courts.

MR. JUSTICE BLACK, MR. JUSTICE DOUGLAS, and MR. JUSTICE MURPHY agree with these views.

NOTE ON CHALLENGES TO THE VALIDITY OF THE FEDERAL RULES

(1) In Mississippi Publishing Corp. v. Murphree, 326 U.S. 438 (1946), a federal district court had held that Rule 4(f), permitting service of process anywhere within the state in which the district court sits, rather than within the district only, was invalid as in excess of the authority granted by the Enabling Act. The Supreme Court, while upholding the rule, was at pains to point out (p. 444) that "The fact that this Court promulgated the rules as formulated and recommended by the Advisory Committee does not foreclose consideration of their validity, meaning or consistency".[1]

On several occasions the Court has had trouble interpreting the civil rules, and the results in some cases are difficult to square with the language of the rule involved. See, *e.g.,* Palmer v. Hoffman, 318 U.S. 109 (1943) (Fed.Rule 8(c)); Anderson v. Yungkau, 329 U.S. 482 (1947) (Fed.Rules 6(b) and 25(a)); Hickman v. Taylor, 329 U.S. 495 (1947) (former Fed.Rules 26, 30(b), 33, and 34); Ragan v. Merchants Transfer & Warehouse Co., 337 U.S. 530 (1949) (Fed.Rule 3); Walker v. Armco Steel Corp., 446 U.S. 740 (1980) (Fed.Rule 3). But to date the Court has never squarely held a provision of the civil rules to be invalid on its face or as applied.

(2) Observe the clear recognition both in the Enabling Act and in the Sibbach opinion of the power of Congress to override court-issued rules. Compare the elaborate dictum in Winberry v. Salisbury, 5 N.J. 240, 74 A.2d 406 (1950), that legislative power over practice and procedure was ousted by a provision of the state constitution that the state supreme court "shall make rules governing the administration of all courts in the State and, subject to law, the practice and procedure in all such courts * * *." Is the resulting disposition of power a wise one? See Kaplan & Greene, *The Legislature's Relation to Judicial Rule–Making: An Appraisal of Winberry v. Salisbury,* 65 Harv.L.Rev. 234 (1951); Levin & Amsterdam, *Legislative Control Over Judicial Rulemaking: A Problem in Constitutional Revision,* 107 U.Pa.L.Rev. 1 (1958).[2]

---

1. For criticism of the rationale in Murphree, and an argument that the Court's rulemaking authority in matters of personal jurisdiction and venue is quite limited, see Whitten, *Separation of Powers Restrictions on Rule Making: A Case Study of Federal Rule 4,* 40 Me.L.Rev. 41 (1988).

2. In Columbia Lumber & Millwork Co. v. DeStefano, 12 N.J. 117, 95 A.2d 914 (1953), the New Jersey Supreme Court applied the Winberry rule to hold a 1949 statute of no effect to the extent that it conflicted with a 1948 court rule. See gen-

The Winberry court found support for its conclusion in the intention of the constitutional provision to establish a continuous rulemaking power and in the danger, under a contrary construction, of an endless merry-go-round of statutes overriding rules and rules superseding statutes. Does the Supreme Court's rulemaking power allow it to supersede acts of Congress passed after the rules became effective? If Congress overrode a particular rule, could the Court thereafter reinstate the rule? Alter in any way the practice established by the overriding statute? (Note that the Court in Sibbach characterized the Enabling Act as giving the courts only the authority "to make rules not inconsistent with the statutes or Constitution of the United States".) [3]

How substantial are the fears expressed by the Winberry court? Isn't it significant that there are no holdings on any of the questions set forth in the preceding paragraph?

(3) The substantive right asserted in the Sibbach case was state-created. What, if any, are the constitutional limits upon the power of Congress to regulate practice and procedure in actions for the enforcement of such rights? Does the Sibbach opinion yield a satisfactory test of what constitutes practice and procedure? Compare Erie R.R. v. Tompkins and succeeding materials in Sections 2 and 3, *infra.* Do you agree with the Court's statement that if the right asserted were one of "substantive law" the Rules of Decision Act would require the application of Indiana law? Compare Klaxon Co. v. Stentor Elec. Mfg. Co., p. 791, *infra.*

(4) In Schlagenhauf v. Holder, 379 U.S. 104 (1964), the Court held that Rule 35 applies to the physical or mental examination of defendants as well as plaintiffs, and as so applied is constitutional and authorized by the Enabling Act. As in Sibbach, the substantive rights asserted in Schlagenhauf were state-created, but the Court did not discuss the impact of its ruling on those rights. It simply stated (p. 113) that it saw "no basis under the Sibbach holding" for a distinction between plaintiffs and defendants.

(5) The tension between the rulemaking authority and the legislative authority of Congress was highlighted by the controversy in Marek v. Chesny, 473 U.S. 1 (1985). In that case the plaintiff, after prevailing in a civil rights action under 42 U.S.C. § 1983, moved for an award of attorney's fees as authorized by 42 U.S.C. § 1988. The district court denied the motion with respect to attorney's fees incurred after an offer of settlement had been made by the defendant, since the amount ultimately recovered after trial was less than the amount of the offer and since Rule 68 provides

erally Levin & Amsterdam, *supra*, at 6–9, 24–29.

Cf. Knight v. Margate, 86 N.J. 374, 389–90, 431 A.2d 833, 841 (1981) (upholding validity of legislation in situation "where the judicial power has not been exercised or fully implemented, and where such action by [the legislature] serves a legitimate governmental purpose and, concomitantly, does not interfere with judicial prerogative or only indirectly or incidentally touches upon the judicial domain").

3. For arguments that the Enabling Act's delegation of authority to abrogate or alter statutes is unconstitutional, see Clin-

ton, *Rule 9 of the Federal Habeas Corpus Rules: A Case Study on the Need for Reform of the Rules Enabling Acts,* 63 Iowa L.Rev. 15, 64–77 (1977); *Hearings on H.R. 3550 Before the Subcomm. on Courts, Civil Liberties, and the Administration of Justice of the House Comm. on the Judiciary,* 99th Cong., 2d Sess. 7–23 (1985) (testimony of Stephen Burbank). Professor Burbank's arguments rely in substantial part on the Chadha case, see p. 764, *supra.*

In 1978, Congress, without explanation, repealed a similar delegation of authority in § 2075 as part of its revision of the bankruptcy laws. See p. 753, *supra.*

that in such circumstances "the offeree must pay the costs incurred after the making of the offer." The Supreme Court agreed with the district court, holding that (a) the term "costs" in Rule 68 included attorney's fees whenever the underlying statute (here § 1988) defined costs to include those fees, and (b) as so construed Rule 68's policy of encouraging settlements was wholly consistent with § 1988's policy of encouraging meritorious civil rights suits.

Justice Brennan (joined by Justices Marshall and Blackmun) dissented on both grounds. He argued that the automatic provisions of Rule 68, if applied to attorney's fees, would put severe pressure on civil rights plaintiffs to settle even meritorious suits without adequate information and were thus wholly inconsistent with the broad discretion conferred by § 1988. He concluded that "[a]s construed by the Court ＊ ＊ ＊ Rule 68 surely will operate to 'abridge' and to 'modify' [the] statutory right to reasonable attorney's fees. ＊ ＊ ＊ [Thus] the Rules Enabling Act requires that the Court's interpretation give way." 473 U.S. at 36–37.[4]

SECTION 2. THE POWERS OF THE FEDERAL COURTS IN DEFINING PRIMARY LEGAL OBLIGATIONS THAT FALL WITHIN THE LEGISLATIVE COMPETENCE OF THE STATES

SWIFT v. TYSON

16 Pet. 1, 10 L.Ed. 865 (U.S.1842).
Certificate of Division from the Circuit Court for the Southern
District of New York.

STORY, JUSTICE, delivered the opinion of the court.—This cause comes before us from the circuit court of the southern district of New York, upon a certificate of division of the judges of that court. The action was brought by the plaintiff, Swift, as indorsee, against the defendant, Tyson, as acceptor, upon a bill of exchange dated at Portland, Maine, on the first day of May 1836, for the sum of $1540.30, payable six months after date, and grace, drawn by one Nathaniel Norton and one Jairus S. Keith upon and accepted by Tyson, at the city of New York, in favor of the order of Nathaniel Norton, and by Norton indorsed to the plaintiff. The bill was dishonored at maturity.

At the trial, the acceptance and indorsement of the bill were admitted, and the plaintiff there rested his case. The defendant then introduced in evidence the answer of Swift to a bill of discovery, by which it appeared,

---

4. Justice Brennan's position finds support in Professor Burbank's study of the history of the 1934 Rules Enabling Act and earlier efforts at reform. See Burbank, *The Rules Enabling Act of 1934*, 130 U.Pa. L.Rev. 1015 (1982), discussed in more detail at p. 827, note 3, *infra*. Applying that study in the context of sanctions for party or attorney misconduct or default, Professor Burbank concludes that while the rules may *authorize* the award of fees and other costs in such circumstances, they may not

require their imposition without running afoul of the Enabling Act. Burbank, *Sanctions in the Proposed Amendments to the Federal Rules of Civil Procedure: Some Questions About Power*, 11 Hofstra L.Rev. 997 (1983).

Justice Brennan also noted the extensive debate over proposals to amend Rule 68 so that it would expressly include attorney's fees and would apply equally to plaintiffs and defendants.

that Swift took the bill, before it became due, in payment of a promissory note due to him by Norton & Keith; that he understood, that the bill was accepted in part payment of some lands sold by Norton to a company in New York; that Swift was a *bona fide* holder of the bill, not having any notice of anything in the sale or title to the lands, or otherwise impeaching the transaction, and with the full belief that the bill was justly due. The particular circumstances are fully set forth in the answer in the record; but it does not seem necessary further to state them. The defendant then offered to prove, that the bill was accepted by the defendant, as part consideration for the purchase of certain lands in the state of Maine, which Norton & Keith represented themselves to be the owners of, and also represented to be of great value, and contracted to convey a good title thereto; and that the representations were in every respect fraudulent and false, and Norton & Keith had no title to the lands, and that the same were of little or no value. The plaintiff objected to the admission of such testimony, or of any testimony, as against him, impeaching or showing a failure of the consideration, on which the bill was accepted, under the facts admitted by the defendant, and those proved by him, by reading the answer of plaintiff to the bill of discovery. The judges of the circuit court thereupon divided in opinion upon the following point or question of law— Whether, under the facts last mentioned, the defendant was entitled to the same defence to the action, as if the suit was between the original parties to the bill, that is to say, Norton, or Norton & Keith, and the defendant; and whether the evidence so offered was admissible as against the plaintiff in the action. And this is the question certified to us for our decision.

* * *

In the present case, the plaintiff is a *bona fide* holder, without notice, for what the law deems a good and valid consideration, that is, for a pre-existing debt; and the only real question in the cause is, whether, under the circumstances of the present case, such a pre-existing debt constitutes a valuable consideration, in the sense of the general rule applicable to negotiable instruments. We say, under the circumstances of the present case, for the acceptance having been made in New York, the argument on behalf of the defendant is, that the contract is to be treated as a New York contract, and therefore, to be governed by the laws of New York, as expounded by its courts, as well upon general principles, as by the express provisions of the 34th section of the judiciary act of 1789, ch. 20. And then it is further contended, that by the law of New York, as thus expounded by its courts, a pre-existing debt does not constitute, in the sense of the general rule, a valuable consideration applicable to negotiable instruments.

In the first place, then, let us examine into the decisions of the courts of New York upon this subject. * * * [The opinion expresses doubt whether the doctrine asserted can "be treated as finally established" by the New York cases.]

But, admitting the doctrine to be fully settled in New York, it remains to be considered, whether it is obligatory upon this court, if it differs from the principles established in the general commercial law. It is observable, that the courts of New York do not found their decisions upon this point, upon any local statute, or positive, fixed or ancient local usage; but they deduce the doctrine from the general principles of commercial law. It is, however, contended, that the 34th section of the judiciary act of 1789, ch. 20, furnishes a rule obligatory upon this court to follow the decisions of the

state tribunals in all cases to which they apply. That section provides
"that the laws of the several states, except where the constitution, treaties
or statutes of the United States shall otherwise require or provide, shall be
regarded as rules of decision, in trials at common law, in the courts of the
United States, in cases where they apply." In order to maintain the
argument, it is essential, therefore, to hold, that the word "laws," in this
section, includes within the scope of its meaning, the decisions of the local
tribunals. In the ordinary use of language, it will hardly be contended,
that the decisions of courts constitute laws. They are, at most, only
evidence of what the laws are, and are not, of themselves, laws. They are
often re-examined, reversed and qualified by the courts themselves, whenever they are found to be either defective, or ill-founded, or otherwise
incorrect. The laws of a state are more usually understood to mean the
rules and enactments promulgated by the legislative authority thereof, or
long-established local customs having the force of laws. In all the various
cases, which have hitherto come before us for decision, this court have
uniformly supposed, that the true interpretation of the 34th section limited
its application to state laws, strictly local, that is to say, to the positive
statutes of the state, and the construction thereof adopted by the local
tribunals, and to rights and titles to things having a permanent locality,
such as the rights and titles to real estate, and other matters immovable
and intraterritorial in their nature and character. It never has been
supposed by us, that the section did apply, or was designed to apply, to
questions of a more general nature, not at all dependent upon local statutes
or local usages of a fixed and permanent operation, as, for example, to the
construction of ordinary contracts or other written instruments, and especially to questions of general commercial law, where the state tribunals are
called upon to perform the like functions as ourselves, that is, to ascertain,
upon general reasoning and legal analogies, what is the true exposition of
the contract or instrument, or what is the just rule furnished by the
principles of commercial law to govern the case. And we have not now the
slightest difficulty in holding, that this section, upon its true intendment
and construction, is strictly limited to local statutes and local usages of the
character before stated, and does not extend to contracts and other instruments of a commercial nature, the true interpretation and effect whereof
are to be sought, not in the decisions of the local tribunals, but in the
general principles and doctrines of commercial jurisprudence. Undoubtedly, the decisions of the local tribunals upon such subjects are entitled to,
and will receive, the most deliberate attention and respect of this court;
but they cannot furnish positive rules, or conclusive authority, by which
our own judgments are to be bound up and governed. The law respecting
negotiable instruments may be truly declared in the language of Cicero,
adopted by Lord Mansfield in Luke v. Lyde, 2 Burr. 883, 887, to be in a
great measure, not the law of a single country only, but of the commercial
world. *Non erit alia lex Romae, alia Athenis; alia nunc, alia posthac; sed
et apud omnes gentes, et omni tempore una eademque lex obtinebit.*

It becomes necessary for us, therefore, upon the present occasion, to
express our own opinion of the true result of the commercial law upon the
question now before us. And we have no hesitation in saying, that a pre-
existing debt does constitute a valuable consideration, in the sense of the
general rule already stated, as applicable to negotiable instruments. Assuming it to be true (which, however, may well admit of some doubt from

the generality of the language), that the holder of a negotiable instrument is unaffected with the equities between the antecedent parties, of which he has no notice, only where he receives it in the usual course of trade and business, for a valuable consideration, before it becomes due; we are prepared to say, that receiving it in payment of, or as security for, a pre-existing debt, is according to the known usual course of trade and business. And why, upon principle, should not a pre-existing debt be deemed such a valuable consideration? It is for the benefit and convenience of the commercial world, to give as wide an extent as practicable to the credit and circulation of negotiable paper, that it may pass not only as security for new purchases and advances, made upon the transfer thereof, but also in payment of, and as security for, pre-existing debts. The creditor is thereby enabled to realize or to secure his debt, and thus may safely give a prolonged credit, or forbear from taking any legal steps to enforce his rights. The debtor also has the advantage of making his negotiable securities of equivalent value to cash. But establish the opposite conclusion, that negotiable paper cannot be applied in payment of, or as security for, pre-existing debts, without letting in all the equities between the original and antecedent parties, and the value and circulation of such securities must be essentially diminished, and the debtor driven to the embarrassment of making a sale thereof, often at a ruinous discount, to some third person, and then, by circuity, to apply the proceeds to the payment of his debts. What, indeed, upon such a doctrine, would become of that large class of cases, where new notes are given by the same or by other parties, by way of renewal or security to banks, in lieu of old securities discounted by them, which have arrived at maturity? Probably, more than one-half of all bank transactions in our country, as well as those of other countries, are of this nature. The doctrine would strike a fatal blow at all discounts of negotiable securities for pre-existing debts.

This question has been several times before this court, and it has been uniformly held, that it makes no difference whatsoever, as to the rights of the holder, whether the debt, for which the negotiable instrument is transferred to him, is a pre-existing debt, or is contracted at the time of the transfer. * * * In England, the same doctrine has been uniformly acted upon. * * *

In the American courts, so far as we have been able to trace the decisions, the same doctrine seems generally, but not universally, to prevail. * * * We are all, therefore, of opinion, that the question on this point, propounded by the circuit court for our consideration, ought to be answered in the negative; and we shall, accordingly, direct it so to be certified to the circuit court.

CATRON, JUSTICE, said:—Upon the point of difference between the judges below, I concur, that the extinguishment of a debt, and the giving a past consideration, such as the record presents, will protect the purchaser and assignee of a negotiable note from the infirmity affecting the instrument before it was negotiated. But I am unwilling to sanction the introduction into the opinion of this court, a doctrine aside from the case made by the record, or argued by the counsel, assuming to maintain, that a negotiable note or bill, pledged as collateral security for a previous debt, is taken by the creditor in the due course of trade; and that he stands on the foot of him who purchases in the market for money, or takes the instrument in extinguishment of a previous debt. State courts of high authority on commercial questions have held otherwise; and that they will yield to a mere expression of opinion of this court, or change their course of decision in conformity to the recent English cases referred to in the principal opinion, is improbable; whereas, if the question was permitted to rest until it fairly arose, the decision of it either way by this court, probably, would, and I think ought to settle it. * * *

NOTE ON SWIFT v. TYSON, ITS ANTECEDENTS AND RISE, AND THE INTIMATIONS OF ITS FALL

(1) Was the problem of Swift v. Tyson one only of statutory interpretation? What guides to decision would there have been if the Rules of Decision Act had never been enacted? What were the relevant postulates to limit and control the Act's interpretation?

(2) Recall that the first volume of American law reports was Kirby's Connecticut reports, published in 1789. In view of the paucity of reported decisions and the difficulties of establishing the grounds of unreported ones, the problem of the authority of state decisions arose infrequently in the early years. See the account of the antecedents of Swift v. Tyson in 2 Crosskey, Politics and the Constitution in the History of the United States 822–62 (1953).

In Brown v. Van Braam, 3 Dall. 344 (U.S.1797), the plaintiff had brought an action on bills of exchange in the United States Circuit Court for Rhode Island. He obtained judgment—on the ground of default in the court proceedings—for the principal, plus interest, protest charges, and (pursuant to a 1743 Rhode Island statute) damages of 10 per cent of the principal. On the defendant's appeal to the Supreme Court, it was argued that the default had been improperly entered, that there was no right to damages under the state statute because timely protest had not been made, and that the damages—if authorized—should have been assessed by a jury. The Court affirmed the judgment with a brief statement that the result was warranted "under the laws, and the practical construction of the courts, of Rhode Island", and with the following footnote (p. 356): "Chase, Justice, observed, that he concurred in the opinion of the court; but that it was on common law principles, and not in compliance with the laws and practice of the state." 2 Crosskey, *supra*, at 823–24, argues that two of the three points in the case were matters of procedure and thus governed by the Process Acts of 1789 and 1792, while the third, though substantive, dealt with a question traditionally delegated to local law and in this instance governed by a state statute enacted before 1789. But whatever the significance of the holding, the argument of the appellee, quoted in part in the margin, is of particular interest.[1]

---

1. In a general introduction to his argument, the appellee said (p. 352): "This adoption of the State laws [in the Rules of Decision Act], extends as well to the unwritten, as to the written law;—to the law arising from established usage and judicial determinations, as well as to the law created by positive acts of the Legislature. And the act for regulating process, in language equally general adopts 'in each State respectively, such forms and modes as are used or allowed in the Supreme Courts of the same.' The only question, therefore, to ascertain the legal correctness of the present record, is—what are the laws and modes adopted by the State of Rhode Island, in relation to the controverted points? It is immaterial, how far the answer shall be inconsistent with certain dogma of the English common law; it is enough to show that such are the laws and modes of Rhode Island, and that they are competent to all the purposes of justice."

In Sim's Lessee v. Irvine, 3 Dall. 425, 457 (U.S.1799), the Court followed a pre-1789 practice of the Pennsylvania courts concerning the right to maintain ejectment, saying, "The right once having become an established legal right, and having incorporated itself as such, with property and tenures, it remains a legal right notwithstanding any new distribution of judicial powers, and must be regarded by the common law courts of the United States, in Pennsylvania, as a rule of decision."

In Robinson v. Campbell, 3 Wheat. 212, 222–23 (U.S.1818), however, the Court said that an equitable defense could not be set up in an action at law for ejectment brought in a federal court sitting in Tennessee, even if it were assumed that the defense would have been allowed under the usage of the Tennessee courts.

Five years later, in Daly's Lessee v. James, 8 Wheat. 495 (U.S.1823), the Court deferred to an earlier Pennsylvania decision construing the same provision of the same will, but in terms (p. 535) which left open the possibility that deference was due only because of the difficulty of the point.

In Jackson v. Chew, 12 Wheat. 153 (U.S.1827), the Court for the first time squarely recognized an obligation to conform to post–1789 decisions of state courts on matters of unwritten law, the question being whether a testamentary limitation over was good as an executory devise. Justice Thompson said (p. 167):

"After such a settled course of decisions, and two of them in the highest court of law in the state, upon the very clause in the will now under consideration, * * * a contrary decision by this court would present a conflict between the state courts and those of the United States, productive of incalculable mischief. * * * And it will be seen, by reference to the decisions of this court, that to establish a contrary doctrine here, would be repugnant to the principles which have always governed this court in like cases.

"It has been urged, however, at the bar, that this court applies this principle only to state constructions of their own statutes. * * * But the same rule has been extended to other cases; and there can be no good reason assigned, why it should not be, when it is applying settled rules of real property. This court adopts the state decisions, because they settle the law applicable to the case; and the reasons assigned for this course, apply as well to rules of construction growing out of the common law, as the statute law of the state, when applied to the title of lands. And such a course is indispensable, in order to preserve uniformity; otherwise, the peculiar constitution of the judicial tribunals of the states and of the United States, would be productive of the greatest mischief and confusion."

In the early case of Huidekoper's Lessee v. Douglass, 3 Cranch 1 (U.S. 1805), Chief Justice Marshall, speaking for a unanimous Court, had decided an important question of title to lands in western Pennsylvania turning upon the construction of a 1792 Pennsylvania statute without reference to two earlier decisions of the Supreme Court of Pennsylvania which were flatly to the contrary. Professor Crosskey, in an elaborate review of the context of this decision, concludes that it is evidence of an original understanding not only that the Supreme Court was to be free to disregard state court decisions of any kind, but that Supreme Court decisions of any kind, once given, were to be binding thereafter upon the state courts. 2 Crosskey, *supra,* at 719–53. But as he himself recognizes, the Supreme Court of Pennsylvania was not the highest court of the state in 1805; and other scholars have persuasively argued that the state law at the time was unsettled.[2] Moreover, while the Pennsylvania judges continued to reach results consistent with the Huidekoper decision, they never followed its reasoning nor acknowledged its authority.

Meanwhile, as noted by Justice Thompson in Jackson v. Chew, the Supreme Court of the United States began more and more clearly to acknowledge the authority of state court decisions construing state statutes. See, particularly, Marshall, in Elmendorf v. Taylor, 10 Wheat. 152, 159–60 (U.S.1825). The question came to a head in its most difficult form in Green v. Neal's Lessee, 6 Pet. 291 (U.S.1832), in which the Court held itself obliged to abandon two of its own former decisions construing a state statute affecting land titles in order to conform to intervening decisions to the contrary by the Tennessee state courts. After reviewing earlier cases, Justice McLean said (pp. 298–301):

"The same reason which influences this court to adopt the construction given to the local law, in the first instance, is not less strong in favor of following it, in the second, if the state tribunals should change the construction. A reference is here made, not to a single adjudication, but to a series of decisions which shall settle the rule. * * * A refusal in the one case, as well as in the other, has the effect to establish in the state two rules of property.

"Would not a change in the construction of a law of the United States, by this tribunal, be obligatory on the state courts? The statute, as last expounded, would be the law of the Union; and why may not the same effect be given to the last exposition of a local law, by the state court? * * * It is emphatically the law of the state; which the federal court, while sitting within the state, and this court, when a case is brought before them, are called to enforce. * * *

"If the construction of the highest judicial tribunal of a state form a part of its statute law, as much as an enactment by the legislature, how can this court make a distinction between them? There could be no hesitation in so modifying our decisions as to conform to any legislative alteration in a statute; and why should not the same rule apply, where the judicial branch of the state government, in the exercise of its acknowledged functions, should, by construction, give a different effect to a statute from what had at first been given to it? * * *

"* * * Here is a judicial conflict, arising from two rules of property in the same state, and the consequences are not only deeply injurious to the citizens of the state, but calculated to engender the most lasting discontents. It is, therefore, essential to the interests of the country, and to the harmony of the judicial action of the federal and state governments, that there should be but one rule of property in a state."

Finally, in Wheaton v. Peters, 8 Pet. 591 (U.S.1834), a federal court copyright action in which the plaintiff relied in part on a claim of right under the common law, the majority opinion of the Court said: "It is clear, there can be no common law of the United States. The federal government is composed of twenty-four sovereign and independent states; each of which

2. Bridwell & Whitten, The Constitution and the Common Law 101–05 (1977).

may have its local usages, customs and common law. There is no principle which pervades the Union and has the authority of law, that is not embodied in the constitution or laws of the Union. The common law could be made a part of our federal system, only by legislative adoption. When, therefore, a common law right is asserted, we must look to the state in which the controversy originated" (pp. 657–58).[3]

(3) Viewed against this background, was the meaning that Justice Story attributed to the term "law" in the Rules of Decision Act an intelligible and defensible one? Notice that his conception of the common law as a single system, and of the law merchant as "a branch of the law of nations" which had been received into that system, had a substantial foundation in the thinking of his time and an even more substantial foundation in eighteenth century thought. See, *e.g.,* Hoffman, Course of Legal Study (2 vols., 2d ed. 1836), particularly Vol. I, pp. 415–16; and the materials in Crosskey, *supra,* particularly Chap. XVIII. See also Fletcher, *The General Common Law and Section 34 of the Judiciary Act of 1789: The Example of Marine Insurance,* 97 Harv.L.Rev. 1513 (1984). In 1842, however, the problems of conflicting applications of common law principles were already fully apparent. Did Story take adequate account of them?

Consider the basic character of those rules of law that guide people in everyday affairs, advising them, in advance of any dispute, of their primary duties and powers and of their corresponding rights and vulnerabilities. Is it consistent with the presuppositions of law to leave people in uncertainty about such matters—to tell them that the rules by which they are to be judged, with respect even to basic obligations and powers, will depend upon the unpredictable circumstance of what court they can get into, or may be haled into? Does the problem in this aspect vary significantly as between questions of property, or commercial law, or other types of obligations?

Is it consistent with the purposes of the Constitution to have two sets of rules about these basic and primary matters—one for co-citizens and diverse citizens who cannot get into a federal court, and the other for diverse citizens who can?

Is it consistent with the theory of the Constitution to have the federal courts declaring primary law, in disregard of state court decisions, with respect to matters as to which the state legislatures rather than Congress have legislative competence?

3. Several contemporary writers expressed a very different view, however. Thus in A Dissertation on the Nature and Extent of the Jurisdiction of the Courts of the United States (1824), DuPonceau wrote:

"I think, then, I can lay it down as a correct principle, that the common law of England, as it was at the time of the declaration of independence, still continues to be the national law of this country, so far as it is applicable to our present state, and subject to the modifications it has received here in the course of near half a century" (pp. 89–90).

"It appears to me also that by the words 'the laws of the United States,' the framers of the Constitution only meant the statutes which should be enacted by the national Legislature * * *

"On the whole, therefore, I think I may venture to assert * * * that when the federal Courts are sitting in or for the States, they can, it is true, derive no jurisdiction from the common law, because the people of the United States, in framing their Constitution, have thought proper to restrict them within certain limits; but that whenever by the Constitution or the laws made in pursuance of it, jurisdiction is given to them either over the person or subject matter, they are bound to take the common law as their rule of decision whenever other laws, national or local, are not applied" (pp. 99, 101).

Did Swift v. Tyson itself necessarily involve the difficulties these questions suggest? Under the judiciary acts as they then stood? Under the Constitution?

Would Congress have had power to authorize the Supreme Court to review such a case as Swift v. Tyson in the light of the principles of general jurisprudence, if it had been brought in a state court? Should the actual decision have been regarded as authoritative, under the Constitution, in later cases in the state courts? Between persons of diverse citizenship? Between co-citizens?

Would Congress have had power to enact the holding of Swift v. Tyson as a rule of decision in the federal courts? As a rule of decision in diverse citizenship cases in the state courts? As a rule of conduct between diverse citizens? As a general rule of conduct?

Would a federal court sitting in New York have been free to disregard a New York statute enacting a rule contrary to Swift v. Tyson?

Professor Crosskey appears to answer all the questions in the last three paragraphs in the affirmative. See 1 Crosskey, *supra*, Part III, entitled "A Unitary View of the National Governing Powers". He reads the Constitution, in other words, as providing for a national legislature with plenary powers to pass laws for the general welfare and a national judiciary with plenary powers to establish justice, and not as contemplating a federal system at all. (In support of this reading he argues that the "laws of the United States" referred to in the jurisdictional provisions of Article III include the common law, and that Congress should have provided for the exercise of jurisdiction in all common-law cases.)

(4) Recent years have seen a revival of interest among legal historians in the rationale and significance of the Swift decision. And these issues are in turn part of a larger debate about the nature of law and the role played by judges in nineteenth century American society.

Professor Horwitz, in The Transformation of American Law, 1780–1860 (1977), argues that the Swift decision is a leading example of the cases in which Justice Story and other judges of the period employed judicial powers as an instrument to aid in the redistribution of wealth and to promote commercial and industrial growth. Justice Story, he suggests, was well aware that the common law was not a brooding omnipresence—an awareness demonstrated by the approach taken in his treatise on Conflict of Laws in 1834—but was anxious to provide the shelter of the federal courts against the application of state policies hostile to commercial interests (see pp. 245–52).

In response, Professors Bridwell and Whitten, in The Constitution and the Common Law (1977), argue that Professor Horwitz' thesis misconstrues both the Swift decision and the perceptions of its author. They suggest that in the first half of the nineteenth century, Story and his contemporaries viewed the law of commercial transactions and contracts not as the command of the sovereign, but rather as the embodiment of prevailing customs and practices and as a process for applying them to the case at hand. To allow local customs to prevail over general practice, in the absence of some strong reason for doing so, would frustrate the understandings on which the transaction was based. Swift v. Tyson, they conclude, is "a prime example of how the diversity jurisdiction operated to preserve the intentions and expectations of the parties intact when their dealings had taken place against the assumed background of general commercial practice" (p. 90).

Finally, Professor Freyer, in Harmony and Dissonance: The Swift and Erie Cases in American Federalism (1981), after considering the "antebellum credit system, the role of the federal courts in this system, the character of the legal profession during the period, and prevalent jurisprudential assumptions" concludes that "Swift was thoroughly consistent with antebellum notions of American constitutionalism and federalism" (p. xiii). The unanimity of the Swift Court on the critical issues, he suggests, shows that even its Jacksonian members did not regard Story's approach as a threat to the interests of the states or to the principles of federalism (p. 26).[4]

(5) After Swift, the Court continued to adhere, in general, to the doctrine of Green v. Neal's Lessee in matters of construction of state statutes. See, *e.g.,* Leffingwell v. Warren, 2 Black 599, 603 (U.S.1862); Bucher v. Cheshire R.R., 125 U.S. 555 (1888); Chicago, M., St.P. & P.R.R. v. Risty, 276 U.S. 567, 570 (1928); Note, 37 Harv.L.Rev. 1129 (1924). But there were some notable exceptions, *e.g.,* Watson v. Tarpley, 18 How. 517, 521 (U.S.1855), in which the Court said: "[A]ny state law or regulation, the effect of which would be to impair the rights [under and defined by the general commercial law] * * * or to devest the federal courts of cognizance thereof, * * * must be nugatory and unavailing."[5]

Among the most controversial of the Court's actions during the regime of Swift v. Tyson was the rule developed with respect to federal court actions on defaulted municipal bonds.[6] In Gelpcke v. City of Dubuque, 1 Wall. 175 (U.S. 1863), the Court declined to follow a state court construction of the state constitution that would have had the effect of invalidating the bonds, in view of the fact that the construction overruled decisions outstanding at the time the bonds were issued. Justice Swayne said for the Court (pp. 206–07):

"We are not unmindful of the importance of uniformity in the decisions of this court, and those of the highest local courts, giving constructions to the laws and constitutions of their own States. It is the settled rule of this court in such cases, to follow the decisions of the State courts.

---

4. See also Fletcher, Paragraph (3), *supra*; LaPiana, *Swift v. Tyson and the Brooding Omnipresence in the Sky: An Investigation of the Idea of Law in Antebellum America,* 20 Suffolk U.L.Rev. 771 (1986). Professor Fletcher draws on diversity cases involving marine insurance during the period 1800–1820 to show that well before Swift, state and federal courts succeeded in developing a uniform system of common law in the adjudication of these commercial disputes under the law merchant. He argues that § 34, and the lex loci principle it was thought to embody, were never seen as precluding the application of general common law in such cases.

Professor LaPiana concludes that "Whatever its relationship to federalism, it seems clear that Story's approach to section 34 reflected a view of the nature of law widespread in his time. Law was a system of principles which could be discovered through the investigation of the cases which reflected the principles. * * * The process was much like that involved in the investigation of the natural sciences: inductive discovery of principles and deductive application" (20 Suffolk U.L.Rev. at 830).

5. For fuller discussion of this case, *see* Bridwell & Whitton, Paragraph (4), *supra,* at 77–78; Freyer, Paragraph (4), *supra,* at 51–55.

6. See Freyer, Paragraph (4), *supra,* at 58–61. According to one report, "the total of defaulted bonds across the nation amounted to between $100,000,000 and $150,000,000." *Id.* at 60. Thus it was not surprising that some 300 bond cases came to the Supreme Court in the thirty years after the Dubuque decision. *Id.*

But there have been heretofore, in the judicial history of this court, as doubtless there will be hereafter, many exceptional cases. We shall never immolate truth, justice, and the law, because a State tribunal has erected the altar and decreed the sacrifice."

Suppose the question had come to the Supreme Court on review of the state court's overruling decision? *Cf.* Railroad Co. v. McClure, 10 Wall. 511 (U.S.1871); see Tidal Oil Co. v. Flanagan, 263 U.S. 444, 451–52 (1924); Great N. Ry. v. Sunburst Co., 287 U.S. 358, 364 (1932).

Again, in Burgess v. Seligman, 107 U.S. 20 (1883), the Court declined to follow a state court's construction of statutes imposing stockholder liability rendered in connection with the same insolvency involved in the case before it. Justice Bradley's opinion noted that the conflicting state court construction was handed down after the decision of the court below and concluded (p. 34):

" * * * [Since] the very object of giving to the national courts jurisdiction to administer the laws of the States in controversies between citizens of different States was to institute independent tribunals which it might be supposed would be unaffected by local prejudices and sectional views, it would be a dereliction of their duty not to exercise an independent judgment in cases not foreclosed by previous adjudication. * * * "

Note the important differences between the reasoning of the Gelpcke and Burgess decisions and that of Story in Swift v. Tyson.

(6) The principle of Swift v. Tyson held sway for nearly a century in a wide area of commercial law, marked off only with difficulty from property and other matters of "local" law. Consistently with the language of Swift, the Court also looked to general principles, rather than to state precedents, in "the construction of ordinary contracts or other written instruments" like deeds and wills. *E.g.,* Lane v. Vick, 3 How. 464 (U.S.1845). And in an extension of the rationale much criticized even by Swift's present-day defenders,[7] it was held applicable in a tort case as early as 1862. Chicago v. Robbins, 2 Black 418 (U.S.1862). Its use in Baltimore & O.R.R. v. Baugh, 149 U.S. 368 (1893), to uphold the fellow-servant defense in a federal court action, evoked a strenuous dissent by Justice Field.[8]

In Kuhn v. Fairmont Coal Co., 215 U.S. 349 (1910), the Court applied in a common law case a doctrine akin to that applied in Gelpcke and Burgess in statutory fields. With Holmes, White, and McKenna dissenting, it held itself free to take its own view of the legal effect of a deed of land when the state decisions had been unsettled at the time of the conveyance.

Finally, in Black & White Taxicab & Transfer Co. v. Brown & Yellow Taxicab & Transfer Co., 276 U.S. 518 (1928), the Court declined to follow state decisions holding that a railroad's agreement to give exclusive taxicab privileges was contrary to public policy, declaring the question to be one of general law. The outcry against the decision was enhanced by the circumstance that the successful company had reincorporated itself in another state in order to establish diversity of citizenship with its rival and thus

7. *E.g.,* Bridwell & Whitten, Paragraph (4), *supra,* at 119–27.

8. Excerpts from the dissent, which was an eloquent challenge to the validity of the concept of "general law," appear in the Court's Erie opinion, p. 786, *infra.* For a

suggestion that this dissent was motivated more by dislike of the fellow-servant rule than by considerations of jurisprudential theory, see Freyer, Paragraph (4), *supra,* at 173 n. 41.

take advantage of the federal rule. Justice Holmes dissenting with Justices Brandeis and Stone said (pp. 532–34):

" *   *   * [I]n my opinion the prevailing doctrine has been accepted upon a subtle fallacy that never has been analyzed. If I am right the fallacy has resulted in an unconstitutional assumption of powers by the Courts of the United States which no lapse of time or respectable array of opinion should make us hesitate to correct. Therefore I think it proper to state what I think the fallacy is—The often repeated proposition of this and the lower Courts is that the parties are entitled to an independent judgment on matters of general law. By that phrase is meant matters that are not governed by any law of the United States or by any statute of the State—matters that in States other than Louisiana are governed in most respects by what is called the common law. It is through this phrase that what I think the fallacy comes in.

"Books written about any branch of the common law treat it as a unit, cite cases from this Court, from the Circuit Courts of Appeals, from the State Courts, from England and the Colonies of England indiscriminately, and criticise them as right or wrong according to the writer's notions of a single theory. It is very hard to resist the impression that there is one august corpus, to understand which clearly is the only task of any Court concerned. If there were such a transcendental body of law outside of any particular State but obligatory within it unless and until changed by statute, the Courts of the United States might be right in using their independent judgment as to what it was. But there is no such body of law. The fallacy and illusion that I think exist consist in supposing that there is this outside thing to be found. Law is a word used with different meanings, but law in the sense in which courts speak of it today does not exist without some definite authority behind it. The common law so far as it is enforced in a State, whether called common law or not, is not the common law generally but the law of that State existing by the authority of that State without regard to what it may have been in England or anywhere else. *   *   *"

Consider whether it is necessary to accept this theory of law to justify rejection of Swift v. Tyson.

(7) In the decade following the Black & White case there was a perceptible erosion of Swift v. Tyson.[9]

In Hawks v. Hamill, 288 U.S. 52 (1933), the Court declined to take an independent view of the validity of an exclusive bridge franchise under the state constitution, although the state courts had not spoken when the franchise was granted.

In Burns Mortgage Co. v. Fried, 292 U.S. 487 (1934), the circuit court of appeals had held that the construction by a state court of last resort of a state statute that was merely declaratory of the common law or law merchant did not bind the federal courts, and hence refused to follow a decision interpreting the Uniform Negotiable Instruments Law. The Su-

---

9. For a discussion of legislative efforts in 1928 and 1929 to overrule Swift, see Burbank, *The Rules Enabling Act of 1934*, 130 U.Pa.L.Rev. 1015, 1109–10 n. 433 (1982). Professor Burbank notes that one of the bills introduced was "drafted by *   *   * [then Professor Frankfurter] and sent to Senator Walsh at the suggestion of Justice Brandeis."

preme Court, granting certiorari because of a conflict among the circuits, said (p. 495):

"We think the better view is that there is no valid distinction * * * between an act which alters the common law and one which codifies or declares it. Both are within the letter of § 34 of the Judiciary Act * * *. And a declaratory act is no less an expression of the legislative will because the rule it prescribes is the same as that announced in prior decisions of the courts of the state. Nor is there a difference in this respect between a statute prescribing rules of commercial law and one concerned with some other subject of narrower scope."

And in Mutual Life Ins. Co. v. Johnson, 293 U.S. 335 (1934), Justice Cardozo built up some prior expressions of the Court into an eroding principle of large if indeterminate potentialities. The question was whether the failure to give notice of disability before default in premium was excused by the physical and mental condition of the insured. The opinion said (pp. 339–40):

"In this situation we are not under a duty to make a choice for ourselves between alternative constructions as if the courts of the place of the contract were silent or uncertain. Without suggesting an independent preference either one way or the other, we yield to the judges of Virginia expounding a Virginia policy and adjudging its effect. * * * No question is here as to any general principle of the law of contracts of insurance * * * with consequences broader than those involved in the construction of a highly specialized condition. All that is here for our decision is the meaning, the tacit implications, of a particular set of words, which, as experience has shown, may yield a different answer to this reader and to that one. With choice so 'balanced with doubt', we accept as our guide the law declared by the state where the contract had its being."

(8) On April 24, 1938, the day before the Erie decision, it is doubtful whether an intelligible and principled formulation could have been put forward with respect to the power and duty of federal judges to disregard decisions of a state's highest court on questions of state law.

ERIE RAILROAD CO. v. TOMPKINS
304 U.S. 64, 58 S.Ct. 817, 82 L.Ed. 1188 (1938).
Certiorari to the Circuit Court of Appeals for the Second Circuit.

MR. JUSTICE BRANDEIS delivered the opinion of the Court.

The question for decision is whether the oft-challenged doctrine of Swift v. Tyson shall now be disapproved.

Tompkins, a citizen of Pennsylvania, was injured on a dark night by a passing freight train of the Erie Railroad Company while walking along its right of way at Hughestown in that state. He claimed that the accident occurred through negligence in the operation, or maintenance, of the train; that he was rightfully on the premises as licensee because on a commonly used beaten footpath which ran for a short distance alongside the tracks; and that he was struck by something which looked like a door projecting from one of the moving cars. To enforce that claim he brought an action in the federal court for Southern New York, which had jurisdiction because the company is a corporation of that state. It denied liability; and the case was tried by a jury.

The Erie insisted that its duty to Tompkins was no greater than that owed to a trespasser. It contended, among other things, that its duty to Tompkins, and hence its liability, should be determined in accordance with the Pennsylvania law; that under the law of Pennsylvania, as declared by its highest court, persons who use pathways along the railroad right of way—that is, a longitudinal pathway as distinguished from a crossing—are to be deemed trespassers; and that the railroad is not liable for injuries to undiscovered trespassers resulting from its negligence, unless it be wanton or willful. Tompkins denied that any such rule had been established by the decisions of the Pennsylvania courts; and contended that, since there was no statute of the state on the subject, the railroad's duty and liability is to be determined in federal courts as a matter of general law.

The trial judge refused to rule that the applicable law precluded recovery. The jury brought in a verdict of $30,000; and the judgment entered thereon was affirmed by the Circuit Court of Appeals, which held (2 Cir., 90 F.2d 603, 604), that it was unnecessary to consider whether the law of Pennsylvania was as contended, because the question was one not of local, but of general, law, and that "upon questions of general law the federal courts are free, in absence of a local statute, to exercise their independent judgment as to what the law is; and it is well settled that the question of the responsibility of a railroad for injuries caused by its servants is one of general law. * * * Where the public has made open and notorious use of a railroad right of way for a long period of time and without objection, the company owes to persons on such permissive pathway a duty of care in the operation of its trains. * * * It is likewise generally recognized law that a jury may find that negligence exists toward a pedestrian using a permissive path on the railroad right of way if he is hit by some object projecting from the side of the train."

The Erie had contended that application of the Pennsylvania rule was required, among other things, by section 34 of the Federal Judiciary Act of September 24, 1789 * * *.

Because of the importance of the question whether the federal court was free to disregard the alleged rule of the Pennsylvania common law, we granted certiorari, 302 U.S. 671.

First. Swift v. Tyson, 16 Pet. 1, 18, held that federal courts exercising jurisdiction on the ground of diversity of citizenship need not, in matters of general jurisprudence, apply the unwritten law of the state as declared by its highest court; that they are free to exercise an independent judgment as to what the common law of the state is—or should be * * *.

The Court in applying the rule of section 34 to equity cases, in Mason v. United States, 260 U.S. 545, 559, said: "The statute, however, is merely declarative of the rule which would exist in the absence of the statute." The federal courts assumed, in the broad field of "general law," the power to declare rules of decision which Congress was confessedly without power to enact as statutes. Doubt was repeatedly expressed as to the correctness of the construction given section 34, and as to the soundness of the rule which it introduced. But it was the more recent research of a competent scholar, who examined the original document, which established that the construction given to it by the Court was erroneous; and that the purpose of the section was merely to make certain that, in all matters except those in which some federal law is controlling, the federal courts exercising jurisdiction in diversity of citizenship cases would apply as their rules of decision the law of the state unwritten as well as written.[5]

Criticism of the doctrine became widespread after the decision of Black & White Taxicab & Transfer Co. v. Brown & Yellow Taxicab & Transfer Co., 276 U.S. 518 [see p. 781, *supra*] * * *.

Second. Experience in applying the doctrine of Swift v. Tyson, had revealed its defects, political and social; and the benefits expected to flow from the rule did not accrue. Persistence of state courts in their own opinions on questions of common law prevented uniformity; and the impossibility of discovering a satisfactory line of demarcation between the province of general law and that of local law developed a new well of uncertainties.[8]

On the other hand, the mischievous results of the doctrine had become apparent. Diversity of citizenship jurisdiction was conferred in order to prevent apprehended discrimination in state courts against those not citizens of the state. Swift v. Tyson introduced grave discrimination by noncitizens against citizens. It made rights enjoyed under the unwritten "general law" vary according to whether enforcement was sought in the state or in the federal court; and the privilege of selecting the court in which the right should be determined was conferred upon the noncitizen.[9] Thus, the doctrine rendered impossible equal protection of the law. In attempting to promote uniformity of law throughout the United States, the doctrine had prevented uniformity in the administration of the law of the state.

The discrimination resulting became in practice far-reaching. This resulted in part from the broad province accorded to the so-called "general law" as to which federal courts exercised an independent judgment. In addition to questions of purely commercial law, "general law" was held to include the obligations under contracts entered into and to be performed within the state, the extent to which a carrier operating within a state may stipulate for exemption from liability for his own negligence or that of his employee; the liability for torts committed within the state upon persons resident or property located there, even where the question of liability depended upon the scope of a property right conferred by the state; and the right to exemplary or punitive damages. Furthermore, state decisions, construing local deeds, mineral conveyances, and even devises of real estate, were disregarded.

5. Charles Warren, New Light on the History of the Federal Judiciary Act of 1789 (1923) 37 Harv.L.Rev. 49, 51–52, 81–88, 108.

8. Compare 2 Warren, The Supreme Court in United States History, Rev.Ed. 1935, 89: "Probably no decision of the Court has ever given rise to more uncertainty as to legal rights; and though doubtless intended to promote uniformity in the operation of business transactions, its chief effect has been to render it difficult for business men to know in advance to what particular topic the Court would apply the doctrine. * * *". The Federal Digest through the 1937 volume, lists nearly 1,000 decisions involving the distinction between questions of general and of local law.

9. It was even possible for a nonresident plaintiff defeated on a point of law in the highest court of a State nevertheless to win out by taking a nonsuit and renewing the controversy in the federal court. Compare Gardner v. Michigan Cent. R.R. Co., 150 U.S. 349; * * *.

In part the discrimination resulted from the wide range of persons held entitled to avail themselves of the federal rule by resort to the diversity of citizenship jurisdiction. Through this jurisdiction individual citizens willing to remove from their own state and become citizens of another might avail themselves of the federal rule. And, without even change of residence, a corporate citizen of the state could avail itself of the federal rule by reincorporating under the laws of another state, as was done in the Taxicab Case.

The injustice and confusion incident to the doctrine of Swift v. Tyson have been repeatedly urged as reasons for abolishing or limiting diversity of citizenship jurisdiction. Other legislative relief has been proposed. If only a question of statutory construction were involved, we should not be prepared to abandon a doctrine so widely applied throughout nearly a century. But the unconstitutionality of the course pursued has now been made clear, and compels us to do so.

Third. Except in matters governed by the Federal Constitution or by acts of Congress, the law to be applied in any case is the law of the state. And whether the law of the state shall be declared by its Legislature in a statute or by its highest court in a decision is not a matter of federal concern. There is no federal general common law. Congress has no power to declare substantive rules of common law applicable in a state whether they be local in their nature or "general," be they commercial law or a part of the law of torts. And no clause in the Constitution purports to confer such a power upon the federal courts. As stated by Mr. Justice Field when protesting in Baltimore & Ohio R.R. Co. v. Baugh, 149 U.S. 368, 401, against ignoring the Ohio common law of fellow-servant liability: "I am aware that what has been termed the general law of the country—which is often little less than what the judge advancing the doctrine thinks at the time should be the general law on a particular subject—has been often advanced in judicial opinions of this court to control a conflicting law of a state. I admit that learned judges have fallen into the habit of repeating this doctrine as a convenient mode of brushing aside the law of a state in conflict with their views. And I confess that, moved and governed by the authority of the great names of those judges, I have, myself, in many instances, unhesitatingly and confidently, but I think now erroneously, repeated the same doctrine. But, notwithstanding the great names which may be cited in favor of the doctrine, and notwithstanding the frequency with which the doctrine has been reiterated, there stands, as a perpetual protest against its repetition, the constitution of the United States, which recognizes and preserves the autonomy and independence of the states,—independence in their legislative and independence in their judicial departments. Supervision over either the legislative or the judicial action of the states is in no case permissible except as to matters by the constitution specifically authorized or delegated to the United States. Any interference with either, except as thus permitted, is an invasion of the authority of the state, and, to that extent, a denial of its independence."

The fallacy underlying the rule declared in Swift v. Tyson is made clear by Mr. Justice Holmes. The doctrine rests upon the assumption that there is "a transcendental body of law outside of any particular State but obligatory within it unless and until changed by statute," that federal courts have the power to use their judgment as to what the rules of common law are; and that in the federal courts "the parties are entitled to an independent judgment on matters of general law":

"But law in the sense in which courts speak of it today does not exist without some definite authority behind it. The common law so far as it is enforced in a State, whether called common law or not, is not the common law generally but the law of that State existing by the authority of that State without regard to what it may have been in England or anywhere else. ＊ ＊ ＊

"The authority and only authority is the State, and if that be so, the voice adopted by the State as its own [whether it be of its Legislature or of its Supreme Court] should utter the last word."

Thus the doctrine of Swift v. Tyson is, as Mr. Justice Holmes said, "an unconstitutional assumption of powers by the Courts of the United States which no lapse of time or respectable array of opinion should make us hesitate to correct." In disapproving that doctrine we do not hold unconstitutional section 34 of the Federal Judiciary Act of 1789 or any other act of Congress. We merely declare that in applying the doctrine this Court and the lower courts have invaded rights which in our opinion are reserved by the Constitution to the several states.

Fourth. The defendant contended that by the common law of Pennsylvania as declared by its highest court in Falchetti v. Pennsylvania R. Co., 307 Pa. 203, 160 A. 859, the only duty owed to the plaintiff was to refrain from willful or wanton injury. The plaintiff denied that such is the Pennsylvania law. In support of their respective contentions the parties discussed and cited many decisions of the Supreme Court of the state. The Circuit Court of Appeals ruled that the question of liability is one of general law; and on that ground declined to decide the issue of state law. As we hold this was error, the judgment is reversed and the case remanded to it for further proceedings in conformity with our opinion.

Reversed.

[JUSTICE REED delivered a concurring opinion joining "in the conclusions reached in this case, in the disapproval of the doctrine of Swift v. Tyson, and in the reasoning of the majority opinion except in so far as it relies upon the unconstitutionality of the 'course pursued' by the federal courts." JUSTICE BUTLER dissented in an opinion in which JUSTICE McREYNOLDS joined. JUSTICE CARDOZO did not participate.]

NOTE ON THE RATIONALE OF THE ERIE DECISION

(1) Under the heading *"First "*, the Court refers to, and relies heavily on, Warren, *New Light on the History of The Federal Judiciary Act of 1789,* 37 Harv.L.Rev. 49, 51–52, 81–88, 108 (1923). In that article Warren notes that section 34 was "not contained in the Draft Bill, as introduced in the Senate, but was proposed, probably by [Senator, later Chief Justice] Ellsworth, as an amendment ＊ ＊ ＊." Warren's examination of the records of the Senate revealed a slip of paper, believed to be in Ellsworth's handwriting, on which an earlier version of the amendment was written:

"And be it further enacted, That the Statute law of the several states in force for the time being and their unwritten or common law now in use, whether by adoption from the common law of England, the ancient statutes of the same or otherwise, except where the Constitution, Treaties or Statutes of the United States shall otherwise require or provide, shall be regarded as rules of decision in the trials at common law in the courts of the United States in cases where they apply."

Warren's conclusion, endorsed by the Court in Erie, was that in light of the earlier draft the phrase "laws of the several states" was plainly designed to cover unwritten law. Do you agree? Even if you accept Warren's conclusion, could you still defend the result of Swift v. Tyson? See Friendly, *In Praise of Erie—And of the New Federal Common Law,* 39 N.Y.U.L.Rev. 383, 389–91 (1964); *cf.* Hill, *The Erie Doctrine and the Constitution,* 53 Nw.U.L.Rev. 427, 442–45 (1958).

(2) In discussing the mischievous results of Swift v. Tyson, under the heading *"Second"*, the Court emphasized the "grave discrimination by noncitizens against citizens" introduced by the decision. The Court seems to be suggesting that only noncitizens of a state have access to a federal court in that state on diversity grounds. This is true of removal but not of original jurisdiction. And as to removal, the problem could be resolved by broadening the removal right. Should the Court's point about discrimination have been phrased differently?

Is the Erie holding and rationale limited to issues arising in litigation between citizens of different states? Plainly, it does not extend to all such issues, even of a wholly substantive character, since federal law may be controlling on particular questions in a diversity case. See, *e.g.,* Gertz v. Robert Welch, Inc., 418 U.S. 323 (1974). But what of questions of state law arising in a nondiversity case? See Maternally Yours v. Your Maternity Shop, 234 F.2d 538, 540–51 n. 1 (2d Cir.1956), where the court said, with respect to a pendent state law claim in a federal question case: "[I]t is the *source* of the right sued upon, and not the ground on which federal jurisdiction is founded, that determines the governing law. ✳ ✳ ✳ Thus, the Erie doctrine applies, whatever the ground for federal jurisdiction, to any issue or claim which has its source in state law." (Emphasis in original.) See also Chap. VII, Sec. 1, p. 861, *infra.*

(3) In a letter to Justice Reed written before the Erie decision was handed down, Justice Brandeis insisted that his opinion did not "pass upon or discuss the constitutionality of section 34 as construed in Swift v. Tyson"; rather the *"Third"* section of the opinion was "addressed to showing that the action of the Court in disregarding state law is unconstitutional." Quoted in Freyer, Harmony and Dissonance: The Swift and Erie Cases in American Federalism 136 (1981). What is the distinction?

From the time of its rendition to the present day, controversy has surrounded the scope and meaning of Erie as a constitutional holding. See Wright, Federal Courts § 56 and authorities cited nn. 15, 16 (4th ed. 1983); ALI Study 442; Ely, *The Irrepressible Myth of Erie,* 87 Harv.L.Rev. 693, 703 (1974); Mishkin, *Some Further Last Words on Erie—The Thread,* 87 Harv. L.Rev. 1682 (1974); Jay, *Origins of Federal Common Law: Part Two,* 133 U.Pa.L.Rev. 1231, 1310–11 (1985)

(4) Under its heading *"Fourth,"* why did the Court assume that Pennsylvania law controlled when the action had been brought in a New York federal court?

NOTE ON THE WAYS OF ASCERTAINING STATE LAW

(1) With what attitude should a federal district court approach a question of state law not plainly resolved by the state's highest court? With the same sense of responsibility for the creative development of law that a state court would have—or that the district court would have itself if the question were federal?

Should the federal court entertain an argument that a prior decision of the highest state court should be overruled? That it should be narrowly distinguished? Should it honor the state court's dicta?

What weight should be given to decisions of an intermediate state appellate court? Or a state trial court? The same weight that would be given by the court that rendered the decision? Or by a coordinate state court? Or by the highest state court?

Should a federal court of appeals, or the Supreme Court itself, exercise any greater freedom in these respects than a district court?

(2) Before Erie, in situations in which the decisions of the highest court of a state were controlling, the Court frequently said that the absence of any such decision at the time of the transaction in question or at the time of trial left the federal court free to form an independent judgment. See pp. 775–78, *supra. A fortiori* this was true when the highest state court still had not spoken at the time of final decision. What was meant by an "independent" judgment, however, was seldom subjected to close analysis.

(3) The lower federal courts did not at first read Erie as restricting their latitude in dealing with decisions of lower state courts. But the Supreme Court brought them up sharply in a series of cases at the 1940 term. Fidelity Union Trust Co. v. Field, 311 U.S. 169 (1940); Six Companies v. Joint Highway District No. 13, 311 U.S. 180 (1940); West v. American Tel. & Tel. Co., 311 U.S. 223 (1940); Stoner v. New York Life Ins. Co., 311 U.S. 464 (1940).

The Field case held that a federal court in New Jersey was bound to follow a decision of the New Jersey Court of Chancery, a trial court of state wide jurisdiction, "in the absence of more convincing evidence of what the state law is". 311 U.S. at 178. The Court recognized that the decision might not be followed by the Court of Errors and Appeals or by the Court of Chancery itself.[1] But it called this "merely a matter of conjecture" (p. 179). Nor did it seem to regard arguments against the soundness of the decision, however persuasive, as "convincing evidence".

The Six Companies, West, and Stoner cases applied the Field principle to decisions of intermediate appellate courts. The Six Companies case emphasized the reluctance of the state's highest court to disturb rulings of the intermediate court; but in the West case, where there was no such showing, this factor seemed to be treated as immaterial.

Eight years after the Field group of cases the Supreme Court granted certiorari in King v. Order of United Commercial Travelers, 333 U.S. 153 (1948), in which the court of appeals had declined to follow an unreported decision of a South Carolina court of common pleas, a trial court of limited

---

1. Indeed, the decision was not followed. See Clark, *State Law in The Federal Courts: The Brooding Omnipresence of Erie v. Tompkins,* 55 Yale L.J. 267, 291–92 (1946).

territorial jurisdiction. The Court unanimously upheld this refusal, stating in its opinion (p. 161) that "a Common Pleas decision does not exact conformity from either the same court or lesser courts within its territorial jurisdiction" and that locating unreported common pleas decisions would entail "laboriously searching the judgment rolls in all of South Carolina's forty-six counties".

The pendulum swing continued, perhaps in an effort to get back to dead center, in Bernhardt v. Polygraphic Co., 350 U.S. 198 (1956). One of the issues in this diversity case was whether a 1910 Vermont Supreme Court decision represented the state law on the question in 1956. The United States Supreme Court held that it did, stating (p. 205):

"＊ ＊ ＊ Were the question in doubt or deserving further canvass, we would of course remand the case to the Court of Appeals to pass on this question of Vermont law. But, as we have indicated, there appears to be no confusion in the Vermont decisions, no developing line of authorities that casts a shadow over the established ones, no dicta, doubts or ambiguities in the opinions of Vermont judges on the question, no legislative development that promises to undermine the judicial rule."

Later, in a federal estate tax case, Commissioner v. Estate of Bosch, 387 U.S. 456, 465 (1967), the Court discussed the question of ascertaining state law under Erie and concluded: "Thus, under some conditions, federal authority may not be bound even by an intermediate state appellate court ruling. ＊ ＊ ＊ If there be no decision by ＊ ＊ ＊ [the State's highest] court then federal authorities must apply what they find to be the state law after giving 'proper regard' to relevant rulings of other courts of the State."

Note one difference between a federal court and an intermediate state court: a decision of the latter can be directly reversed by the state's highest court while a decision of the former cannot. (Compare the process of certification, referred to in Paragraph (5), below.) How does this difference affect your view of the issues raised in this Note?

(4) Consider the following, from Corbin, *The Laws of the Several States*, 50 Yale L.J. 762, 775–76 (1941):

"When the rights of a litigant are dependent on the law of a particular state, the court of the forum must do its best (not its worst) to determine what that law is. It must use its judicial brains, not a pair of scissors and a paste pot. Our judicial process is not mere syllogistic deduction, except at its worst. At its best, it is the wise and experienced use of many sources in combination—statutes, judicial opinions, treatises, prevailing mores, custom, business practices; it is history and economics and sociology, and logic, both inductive and deductive. Shall a litigant, by the accident of diversity of citizenship, be deprived of the advantages of this judicial process? Shall the Supreme Court, by what superficially appears to be an unselfish and self-denying ordinance, foreclose the use of such a process by federal judges? It is in fact a denial of justice to those for whom a court exists. We must not forget that a litigant has only one day in court. When forced into a federal court, that is his only court. If he is denied life, liberty, or property by the narrow syllogistic use of a state judge's worded doctrine, he is not restored by the fact that intelligent state judges later refuse to apply that doctrine to other litigants. ＊ ＊ ＊

"If the federal judges use the customary judicial process in determining and applying state law with respect to the litigating parties before them, it is quite possible that conflict may exist between a federal decision and a state decision. * * * We may not like such conflict; but it is an inevitable part of our judicial process, or of any other. It is by such variation as this that the evolutionary growth of law is possible. Each litigant, whether in the federal or the state courts, has a right that his case shall be a part of this evolution—a live cell in the tree of justice. * * * "

See also McKenna v. Ortho Pharmaceutical Corp., 622 F.2d 657, 662–63 (3d Cir.1980); Essex Universal Corp. v. Yates, 305 F.2d 572, 580–82 (2d Cir. 1962) (concurring opinion); Pomerantz v. Clark, 101 F.Supp. 341 (D.Mass. 1951).

Professor Wright, summarizing the current state of the law, says that a federal judge "need no longer be a ventriloquist's dummy. Instead he is free, just as his state counterpart is, to consider all the data the highest court of the state would use in an effort to determine how the highest court of the state would decide." Wright, Federal Courts 373 (4th ed. 1983).[2]

(5) Under what circumstances may a federal district court refuse to determine a question of state law because of its uncertainty and difficulty? In the event of such a refusal, should the court dismiss the action? Or should it retain jurisdiction, and if so, for what purpose? Do the considerations change if a state has a statute or rule authorizing the state's highest court to answer questions certified to it by a federal court in the course of litigation?[3]

For materials throwing some light on these questions, see Chap. X, Sec. 2, *infra.*

KLAXON CO. v. STENTOR ELECTRIC MANUFACTURING CO., INC.

313 U.S. 487, 61 S.Ct. 1020, 85 L.Ed. 1477 (1941).
Certiorari to the Circuit Court of Appeals for the Third Circuit.

MR. JUSTICE REED delivered the opinion of the Court.

The principal question in this case is whether in diversity cases the federal courts must follow conflict of laws rules prevailing in the states in which they sit. We left this open in Ruhlin v. New York Life Insurance Company, 304 U.S. 202, 208, note 2. The frequent recurrence of the problem, as well as the conflict of approach to the problem between the Third Circuit's opinion here and that of the First Circuit in Sampson v. Channell, 110 F.2d 754, 759–762, led us to grant certiorari.

In 1918 respondent, a New York corporation, transferred its entire business to petitioner, a Delaware corporation. Petitioner contracted to use its best efforts to further the manufacture and sale of certain patented devices covered by the agreement, and respondent was to have a share of

---

2. In Factors Etc., Inc. v. Pro Arts, Inc., 652 F.2d 278 (2d Cir.1981), a divided court held that if the controlling law is that of a state in another circuit, and if the question of state law is a novel and difficult one, the prediction of that other circuit as to the course of state law is entitled to deference.

3. For discussion of certification procedures, see p. 1381, *infra.* For diversity cases in which the Supreme Court urged resort to certification, see Clay v. Sun Ins. Office Ltd., 363 U.S. 207 (1960) (substantial constitutional questions hinged on construction of relevant state statute); Lehman Bros. v. Schein, 416 U.S. 386 (1974) (question involved unsettled law of a state located in a different circuit from the one in which suit was brought).

petitioner's profits. The agreement was executed in New York, the assets were transferred there, and petitioner began performance there although later it moved its operations to other states. Respondent was voluntarily dissolved under New York law in 1919. Ten years later it instituted this action in the United States District Court for the District of Delaware, alleging that petitioner had failed to perform its agreement to use its best efforts. Jurisdiction rested on diversity of citizenship. In 1939 respondent recovered a jury verdict of $100,000, upon which judgment was entered. Respondent then moved to correct the judgment by adding interest at the rate of six percent from June 1, 1929, the date the action had been brought. The basis of the motion was the provision in section 480 of the New York Civil Practice Act directing that in contract actions interest be added to the principal sum "whether theretofore liquidated or unliquidated." The District Court granted the motion, taking the view that the rights of the parties were governed by New York law and that under New York law the addition of such interest was mandatory. 30 F.Supp. 425, 431. The Circuit Court of Appeals affirmed, 3 Cir., 115 F.2d 268, 275, and we granted certiorari, limited to the question whether section 480 of the New York Civil Practice Act is applicable to an action in the federal court in Delaware.

The Circuit Court of Appeals was of the view that under New York law the right to interest before verdict under section 480 went to the substance of the obligation, and that proper construction of the contract in suit fixed New York as the place of performance. It then concluded that section 480 was applicable to the case because "it is clear by what we think is undoubtedly the better view of the law that the rules for ascertaining the measure of damages are not a matter of procedure at all, but are matters of substance which should be settled by reference to the law of the appropriate state according to the type of case being tried in the forum. The measure of damages for breach of a contract is determined by the law of the place of performance; Restatement, Conflict of Laws § 413." The court referred also to section 418 of the Restatement, which makes interest part of the damages to be determined by the law of the place of performance. Application of the New York statute apparently followed from the court's independent determination of the "better view" without regard to Delaware law, for no Delaware decision or statute was cited or discussed.

We are of opinion that the prohibition declared in Erie Railroad v. Tompkins, 304 U.S. 64, against such independent determinations by the federal courts extends to the field of conflict of laws. The conflict of laws rules to be applied by the federal court in Delaware must conform to those prevailing in Delaware's state courts.[2] Otherwise the accident of diversity of citizenship would constantly disturb equal administration of justice in coordinate state and federal courts sitting side by side. See Erie Railroad v. Tompkins, *supra*, 304 U.S. at 74–77. Any other ruling would do violence to the principle of uniformity within a state upon which the Tompkins decision is based. Whatever lack of uniformity this may produce between federal courts in different states is attributable to our federal system, which leaves to a state, within the limits permitted by the Constitution, the

---

2. An opinion in Sampson v. Channell, 110 F.2d 754, 759–762, reaches the same conclusion, as does an opinion of the Third Circuit handed down subsequent to the case at bar, Waggaman v. General Finance Co., 116 F.2d 254, 257. See, also, Goodrich, Conflict of Laws, § 12.

right to pursue local policies diverging from those of its neighbors. It is not for the federal courts to thwart such local policies by enforcing an independent "general law" of conflict of laws. Subject only to review by this Court on any federal question that may arise, Delaware is free to determine whether a given matter is to be governed by the law of the forum or some other law. This Court's views are not the decisive factor in determining the applicable conflicts rule. And the proper function of the Delaware federal court is to ascertain what the state law is, not what it ought to be.

Besides these general considerations, the traditional treatment of interest in diversity cases brought in the federal courts points to the same conclusion. Section 966 of the Revised Statutes, 28 U.S.C. § 811, relating to interest on judgments, provides that it be calculated from the date of judgment at such rate as is allowed by law on judgments recovered in the courts of the state in which the court is held. In Massachusetts Benefit Association v. Miles, 137 U.S. 689, page 691, this Court held that section 966 did not exclude the allowance of interest on verdicts as well as judgments, and the opinion observed that "the courts of the state and the federal courts sitting within the state should be in harmony upon this point".

Looking then to the Delaware cases, petitioner relies on one group to support his contention that the Delaware state courts would refuse to apply section 480 of the New York Civil Practice Act, and respondent on another to prove the contrary. We make no analysis of these Delaware decisions, but leave this for the Circuit Court of Appeals when the case is remanded.

Respondent makes the further argument that the judgment must be affirmed because, under the full faith and credit clause of the Constitution, Art. 4, § 1, the state courts of Delaware would be obliged to give effect to the New York statute. The argument rests mainly on the decision of this Court in John Hancock Mutual Life Insurance Company v. Yates, 299 U.S. 178, where a New York statute was held such an integral part of a contract of insurance that Georgia was compelled to sustain the contract under the full faith and credit clause. Here, however, section 480 of the New York Civil Practice Act is in no way related to the validity of the contract in suit, but merely to an incidental item of damages, interest, with respect to which courts at the forum have commonly been free to apply their own or some other law as they see fit. Nothing in the Constitution ensures unlimited extraterritorial recognition of all statutes or of any statute under all circumstances. Pacific Employers Insurance Co. v. Industrial Accident Comm., 306 U.S. 493; Kryger v. Wilson, 242 U.S. 171. The full faith and credit clause does not go so far as to compel Delaware to apply section 480 if such application would interfere with its local policy.

Accordingly, the judgment is reversed and the case remanded to the Circuit Court of Appeals for decision in conformity with the law of Delaware.

Reversed and remanded.

NOTE ON CHOICE OF LAW IN CASES INVOLVING STATE–CREATED RIGHTS

(1) Judged by Klaxon, was Erie wrongly decided?

For pre-Erie cases similarly using federal choice-of-law rules, as a matter of course, in the selection of the applicable state law, see Burns Mortgage Co. v. Fried, 292 U.S. 487, 493–94 (1934); Boseman v. Connecticut Gen. Life Ins. Co., 301 U.S. 196 (1937); and other cases collected in Note, 41 Colum.L.Rev. 1403, n. 3 (1941).

(2) Is it possible to think soundly about the question Justice Reed states in his opening sentence, and purports to decide, as a single question?

What did Justice Reed mean by speaking of "the right" of a state "to pursue local policies diverging from those of its neighbors"? In a federal system, does this "right" have the same claim to recognition with respect to all who find themselves within the state's borders? The same claim with respect to matters primarily connected with another state as with respect to matters primarily connected with the forum state? The same claim with respect to matters of plainly substantive law as with respect to matters procedural or quasi-procedural?

(3) If the Court in Klaxon proceeded on the assumption that, as in Erie, the result was constitutionally compelled, it was plainly mistaken.

The question in Klaxon was whether New York or Delaware law determined the date from which interest was to be awarded in connection with a judgment. Even assuming that the right to interest is substantive and thus to be governed by state law under Erie, the choice of *which* state's law applies in a federal court is clearly a matter of federal concern. The vesting of jurisdiction in the federal courts in a category of cases carries with it the inherent authority (within the limits set by the Tenth Amendment, the Due Process Clause, and any other relevant provisions of the Constitution) to choose the applicable law. Moreover, even if it could not have legislated the substantive decisional rule for all diversity cases encompassed by Erie, surely Congress, acting under its power to make laws "necessary and proper" to the exercise of jurisdiction under Article III, could authorize the formulation of federal choice-of-law rules for the federal courts, or indeed require a federal court to apply the New York statute on interest in a case like Klaxon. See ALI Study 442–48.

The point is proved by the fact that at least in civil cases, the Constitution does not prohibit the territorial jurisdiction of the federal district courts from cutting across state boundaries. If Congress were to eliminate the district courts of New York and Delaware, and to create a single "Federal District Court for the Middle Atlantic States," the Klaxon rule could not operate on the facts of the case itself. See Hill, *The Erie Doctrine and the Constitution,* 53 Nw.U.L.Rev. 541, 558 (1958).

Indeed, Congress has authority under the full faith and credit clause to federalize choice of law by enacting conflicts rules binding on state as well as federal courts. See Friendly, *In Praise of Erie—And of the New Federal Common Law,* 39 N.Y.U.L.Rev. 383, 401–02 (1964); Jackson, *Full Faith and Credit—The Lawyer's Clause of the Constitution,* 45 Colum.L.Rev. 1 (1945).[1]

---

1. Horowitz, *Toward a Federal Common Law of Choice of Law,* 14 U.C.L.A.L.Rev.   1191 (1967), points to the Full Faith and Credit Clause, the Rules of Decision Act, 28

Is this authority relevant to the issue posed by Justice Reed in his opening sentence?

Note that these points go no further than to criticize the rather simplistic extension of Erie in the Klaxon opinion. They do not make an affirmative case for a contrary result, since it may be desirable, even though not constitutionally compelled, to apply the choice-of-law rules of the forum state.

(4) In the First Edition of this book (pp. 634–35), the authors marshaled the arguments against Klaxon as follows:

"Consider the application of Erie and of Klaxon to problems of the choice of plainly substantive rules of decision, such as those involved in Erie itself and in Swift v. Tyson.

"Notice again that these rules do much more than provide the underlying premises of a decision on the merits when litigation occurs. They help to organize and guide people's everyday lives. Notice that confusion and uncertainty about the rules of law which are relevant at this stage of primary private activity is far more serious than uncertainty about rules which become material only if litigation eventuates. This is so, if for no other reason, because the number of instances of the application of law at the primary stage bears to the number of instances of its application in litigation the ratio of thousands or hundreds of thousands to one.

"As applied in non-conflicts situations, Erie might have been regarded, might it not, as based at least in significant part on the proposition that it is intolerable to have two different systems of courts deciding questions of 'plainly substantive' law differently, where it is unpredictable which system will acquire jurisdiction, since that not only introduces an element of retroactivity into every judicial disposition of such disputes as develop but confuses basic legal relations throughout the area of primary activity affected by the overlap? Notice that it was in the context of questions of this kind that Justice Brandeis spoke of the 'unconstitutionality' of the course which the federal courts had pursued. See Hill, *The Erie Doctrine in Bankruptcy,* 66 Harv.L.Rev. 1013, 1031–35 (1953).

"If this view of Erie had been taken, the problem of marking out the scope of its application in non-conflicts situations would have reduced itself, would it not, to one of distinguishing between (a) those rules of law which characteristically and reasonably affect people's conduct at the stage of primary private activity and should therefore be classified as substantive or quasi-substantive, and (b) those rules which are not of significant importance at the primary stage and should therefore be regarded as quasi-procedural or procedural?

"Consider the bearing which such an analysis of Erie would have had in situations involving state-versus-state conflicts of plainly substantive law.

"Notice that Swift v. Tyson had solved the problem of uncertainty about the applicable substantive law for people who could anticipate access to a federal court. Erie destroyed this assurance, but mitigated the damage with an alternative assurance of the uniform enforcement in any federal

U.S.C. § 1652 (especially the words "in cases where they apply"), and such decisions as Banco Nacional de Cuba v. Sabba- tino, 376 U.S. 398 (1964), p. 901, *infra,* as providing authority for the development of federal common law in this field.

court of whatever state law was applicable. Klaxon destroyed the mitigation, did it not?

"Erie must largely have proceeded upon the assumption, must it not, that the prime need was for an assurance of state-federal conformity in the interest of people who could not be sure of a federal forum? Klaxon cut down the value of this new assurance, did it not, largely to those situations in which it is possible to foresee the state in which litigation will take place? In what proportion of situations *is* this possible, when the people involved are of diverse citizenship?

"Would it be accurate to conclude that Klaxon, in effect, treats Erie as if it had been unconcerned with the problem of uncertainty about the applicable substantive law at the stage of primary private activity? Was it necessary to do this? Why should forum-shopping between different courts in the same state have been regarded as the *summum malum* of diversity litigation while forum-shopping among courts in different geographical areas was dismissed as an inescapable weakness of a federal system? Did the Rules of Decision Act have to be read as authorizing the plaintiff, and the courts of the state he selects, to decide which state's laws are the laws which 'apply', rather than the federal court?"

Are the foregoing assumptions about uniformity—that uniformity among federal courts is more important than uniformity between state and federal courts in a given state—warranted? How certain can one be, at the "stage of primary private activity" of access to a federal forum when the plaintiff can prevent removal by suing the defendant in his home state? Is it more likely that forum shopping for a favorable choice-of-law rule would occur within a given state or among states? Even in controversies between diverse citizens, the defendant is not likely to be subject to suit in a number of states. Further, neither the plaintiff nor his lawyer is likely to be indifferent about the choice of the state in which to sue even if there is no choice-of-law question.

(5) Consider the argument that the federal courts in diversity cases are in a special and strategic position, as a disinterested forum, to work out solutions of problems of interstate conflict of laws which are consistent with the presupposition of a federal judicial system. See Hart, *The Relations Between State and Federal Law*, 54 Colum.L.Rev. 489, 513–15 (1954).

This argument rests on the premise that a state's choice-of-law rules are likely to discriminate (unfairly, even if not unconstitutionally) against out-of-staters and that this is precisely the kind of prejudice that the diversity jurisdiction was designed to prevent. To paraphrase one commentator, allowing the state in which the action happens to be brought to resolve a conflict with another state is like allowing the pitcher to call balls and strikes whenever he manages to beat the batter to the call.[2]

Such an argument suggests that all choice-of-law questions in actions between diverse citizens should be federal questions whether they arise in state or federal courts.[3] But whether or not the argument must carry us

2. See Baxter, *Choice of Law and the Federal System*, 16 Stan.L.Rev. 1, 23 (1963).

3. Indeed, if Erie was rightly decided, how else would you explain the fact that Article III appears in terms to authorize review by the Supreme Court of *state court* decisions in diversity cases? On the basis that a special exception for diversity cases would have been too awkward to draft?

that far, it raises some problems about the supremacy of state policy in matters of essentially state concern. Consider a case in which a product made in State X is sold in State Y, where a consumer is injured in the course of using it.[4] State X holds manufacturers liable only on a showing of negligence, or privity of warranty, while State Y holds them strictly liable for personal injuries caused by a defective product. If litigation occurs in State Y, should Y's rule of liability apply? What is the relevance of state court decisions in Y holding that the rule should have "extra-territorial" application in such a case? Can a federal court in State Y disregard the state's choice of its own law without seriously undermining a substantive state policy? See Hill, Paragraph (3), *supra*, at 546–68. Bear in mind that an out-of-state defendant would undoubtedly remove a state court action if there were any advantage in doing so. Suppose the legislature of Y had enacted a statute explicitly imposing strict liability on all manufacturers, wherever located, whose products cause personal injury within the state. If a federal court in Y were to choose X's law in such a case would that not, in effect, be a holding that, as a matter of federal law, Y could not afford this substantive protection to those injured within its borders?

Is it an answer to these arguments that if the Y federal court disregards X's law limiting the manufacturer's liability in such a case, it is also frustrating a significant state policy? In considering this question, bear in mind that the suit in this hypothetical case is almost certain to take place in Y if the state has a long-arm statute permitting out-of-state service of process. Note too that the decisions upholding the constitutionality of the reach of state process in such a case are themselves a recognition of the substantiality of Y's interest. Do they also suggest the appropriateness of applying Y's laws? See International Shoe Co. v. Washington, 326 U.S. 310 (1945); Martin, *Personal Jurisdiction and Choice of Law,* 78 Mich.L.Rev. 872 (1982); *cf.* Hanson v. Denckla, 357 U.S. 235, 253 (1958) (concluding that a state interest that may be sufficient to justify the state's choice of its own law is too "unsubstantial" a connection to establish personal jurisdiction over a nonresident defendant). See generally Von Mehren & Trautman, Jurisdiction to Adjudicate: A Suggested Analysis, 79 Harv.L.Rev. 1121, 1128–34, 1176–77 (1966).

How different is the situation if the forum state in our hypothetical diversity action is Z, a state having no connection whatever with the events in suit? Would any impairment of Z's policies result from a federal court's refusal to follow Z's choice-of-law rule on the issue of absolute liability? And what if Z chooses to follow its own law on burden of proof, for instance, on the ground that the matter is "procedural": should a federal court be free to disregard the choice? Indeed, should the federal court have that freedom whenever a state looks to its own law simply on the ground that the matter is procedural and thus lex fori applies? The cases hold otherwise. *E.g.,* Wells v. Simonds Abrasive Co., 345 U.S. 514 (1953); Sampson v. Channell, 110 F.2d 754 (1st Cir.1940). Are these cases perhaps justified because it is extremely rare that the forum state is totally disinterested (and sometimes hard to tell whether it is or not), because under a state's "procedural" label there may lurk a significant substantive policy, and

That the question didn't occur to the draft-   4. See Baxter, *supra,* note 2, at 7–11.
ers at all?

because there is in any event an independent value in discouraging forum shopping within a state?

An effort by the Fifth Circuit to develop an exception to Klaxon was rejected by the Supreme Court in Day & Zimmerman, Inc. v. Challoner, 423 U.S. 3 (1975). It held that a Texas federal court must apply Texas choice-of-law rules in a diversity case even if, in the federal court's view, the rationale of those rules was "not operative" under the facts and the case was one in which those rules would lead to the application of the law of a jurisdiction with "no interest * * *, no policy at stake" (p. 4). See Currie, *The Supreme Court and Federal Jurisdiction: 1975 Term,* 1976 Sup. Ct.Rev. 183, 217 (raising a question of the constitutionality of the particular Texas choice-of-law rule involved in the case).[5]

(6) The ALI, after full consideration, recommended retention of the Klaxon rule in standard diversity litigation. ALI Study 153, 379, 461–64. In an article supporting this conclusion, *The Changing Choice-of-Law Process and the Federal Courts,* 28 Law & Contemp.Probs. 732 (1963), Professor Cavers emphasized the emergence of a "policy-oriented, issue-by-issue process for choosing law" (p. 734 n. 8), noted the constructive contribution to this approach that can be made by the federal courts on an ad hoc basis within the Klaxon framework, and expressed concern about the inroads on state authority that a rejection of Klaxon would entail. He further pointed out the difficulties that would lie in the path of creating uniform federal choice-of-law rules, given the many other demands on the time and attention of the Supreme Court. See also Ely, *The Irrepressible Myth of Erie,* 87 Harv.L.Rev. 693, 714–15 n. 125 (arguing, *inter alia,* that the Klaxon result is required by the Rules of Decision Act).

But Klaxon has its contemporary critics too. See, *e.g.,* Bridwell & Whitten, The Constitution and the Common Law 135 (1977) ("The Rules of Decision Act itself embodies a direction to the federal courts to determine when a particular state's law will 'apply' under international conflict of laws rules, which the early cases indicate would have controlled even if the Act itself had never been passed"); Trautman, *The Relation Between American Choice of Law and Federal Common Law,* 41 Law & Contemp. Probs. No. 2, at 105, 120 n. 58 (Spring 1977) (Klaxon reintroduced some of the uncertainty that Erie was designed to eliminate).

(7) The Due Process and Full Faith and Credit Clauses have been held to place some limits on the free choice of law by state courts, though recent decisions indicate that those limits are quite broad. See Allstate Ins. Co. v. Hague, 449 U.S. 302 (1981), and cases cited therein. But see Phillips Petroleum Co. v. Shutts, 472 U.S. 797, 821–22 (1985) (state lacks "significant contact or significant aggregation of contacts" with respect to claims of some members of plaintiff class; thus application of that state's law to those claims is "sufficiently arbitrary and unfair as to exceed constitutional limits").[6] Federal courts are, of course, controlled by the same limitations

---

5. For an extraordinary effort to remain within the Klaxon framework and at the same time to apply a "federal law or national consensus law" of liability in a diversity case, see Judge Weinstein's opinion in In re Agent Orange Product Liability Litigation, 580 F.Supp. 690, 706 (E.D. N.Y.1984), discussed in Schuck, Agent Orange on Trial 128–31 (1986).

6. See also Leflar, *Constitutional Limits on Free Choice of Law,* 28 Law & Contemp. Probs. 706 (1963); Brilmayer, *Legitimate Interests in Multistate Problems: As Between State and Federal Law,* 79 Mich.L. Rev. 1315 (1981). For a persuasive historical and analytical argument that the Full Faith and Credit Clause had a far more limited purpose than that accorded to it by

in administering the Klaxon doctrine. Do these limitations give adequate protection to federal interests by assuring against excessive provincialism in state choice-of-law rules?

(8) Whatever the merits of the Klaxon doctrine on the facts there presented, should the rule be different when a federal court in a diversity case is exercising jurisdiction over one who is beyond the reach of process issuing from the forum state's own courts? (Examples of cases in which, by statute or rule, federal process in diversity cases may reach further than that of the forum state include interpleader actions under 28 U.S.C. § 2361, and actions in which additional parties across state lines but within 100 miles of the federal courthouse are brought in under Fed.Rule 4(f).) Note that in the vast bulk of cases the reach of federal process in a diversity action does not exceed that of the forum state,[7] and thus application of the forum state's choice-of-law rules does not alter the resolution of conflicting interests among states that would be arrived at if there were no federal diversity jurisdiction. But the balance may be significantly affected if the federal court applies the forum state's rules in a case that is beyond that state's power to adjudicate. See Hill, Paragraph (3), *supra,* at 557–58, 566–68.

In Griffin v. McCoach, 313 U.S. 498 (1941), decided the same day as Klaxon, the Court held that the forum state's choice of law rules must be applied in a statutory interpleader case. No reference was made to the fact that at least one of the claimants to the fund was almost certainly beyond the reach of the forum state's process, nor was there any reference to any of the arguments suggested here.

But if the Court in Griffin had taken account of these arguments, and had authorized a federal choice-of-law rule in such cases, another problem would have arisen. Whenever the question of choice of law arose in an interpleader case, for example, it might have been necessary to determine at the outset whether the forum state would have been able to exercise jurisdiction over all the claimants. Changing concepts of personal jurisdiction might have made such a task a burdensome one. Would the extra work have been worth the resulting benefits? Bear in mind that venue choices in interpleader are not unlimited, see 28 U.S.C. § 1397, and that the plaintiff stakeholder will frequently have little incentive to shop for a favorable choice-of-law rule.

(9) Given Klaxon, what choice-of-law rule is to be applied in an action that is transferred to another federal court under 28 U.S.C. § 1404? Under 28 U.S.C. § 1406?

In Van Dusen v. Barrack, 376 U.S. 612 (1964), p. 1732, *infra,* the Court said that in such a case the law to be applied was the law that the courts of the transferor state would apply. The defendants in that case were seeking the transfer, and the law of the transferee state would have been more

---

the Supreme Court, see Whitten, *The Constitutional Limitations on State–Court Jurisdiction: A Historical–Interpretative Reexamination of the Full Faith and Credit and Due Process Clauses* (Part One), 14 Creighton L.Rev. 499 (1981). In a later article, Professor Whitten argues forcefully that the Due Process Clause places a restriction on state choice of law that is "far

narrower than even the 'modest check on state power' currently enforced by the Court." Whitten, *The Constitutional Limitations on State Choice of Law: Due Process,* 9 Hastings Const.L.Q. 851, 853 (1982).

7. See Fed.Rule 4(d)–(f). *Cf.* Arrowsmith v. United Press Int'l, 320 F.2d 219 (2d Cir.1963), p. 1727, *infra.*

favorable to them. "The legislative history of § 1404(a)," the Court said, "certainly does not justify the rather startling conclusion that one might 'get a change of law as a bonus for a change of venue'" (pp. 635–36).

Does the very existence of the issue raised in Van Dusen, which is discussed more fully at pp. 1738–46, *infra,* cast doubt on the soundness of the Klaxon result? Given Klaxon, was the Van Dusen holding the best of the available alternatives?

(10) The Federal Rules of Evidence raise a number of horizontal choice-of-law questions, especially when, as in Rules 302, 501, and 601, the rules refer to state law but give no guide governing a choice among the laws of different states. Is a federal court bound by the choice the forum state would make? "[T]he decisions to date have all but unanimously endorsed this method." 23 Wright & Graham, Federal Practice and Procedure § 5435, at 868, and cases cited n. 24 (1980). Professor Berger has argued, however, that Klaxon should not control, even in a pure diversity case, because a federal choice-of-law rule would be constitutional and would better effectuate the intent of Congress in its references to state law in the rules as enacted. Berger, *Privileges, Presumptions and Competency of Witnesses in the Federal Court: A Federal Choice-of-Laws Rule,* 42 B'klyn L.Rev. 417 (1976). *Cf.* Seidelson, *The Federal Rules of Evidence: Rule 501, Klaxon and the Constitution,* 5 Hofstra L.Rev. 21 (1976) (suggesting significant constitutional limits on state choice of law); Wellborn, *The Federal Rules of Evidence and the Application of State Law in the Federal Courts,* 55 Tex.L.Rev. 371, 448–50 (1977) (whether or not Professor Berger's thesis is sound as it relates to Rules 302, 501, and 601, "there is no reason to regard Klaxon as modified, at least for determinations of relevancy" under Rules 401, 402, and 403).

If Klaxon controls, what if the question of evidence arises in a deposition in a federal court in State A in connection with an action pending in a federal court in State B? When the question is one of privilege, Wright & Graham, *supra,* at 884–85, conclude that "the better rule would seem to be that the deposition state should not require disclosure if the matter is privileged either under local law or the law that will be applied at trial." Do you agree?

SECTION 3. ENFORCING STATE–CREATED OBLIGATIONS—EQUITABLE REMEDIES AND PROCEDURE

GUARANTY TRUST CO. v YORK

326 U.S. 99, 65 S.Ct. 1464, 89 L.Ed. 2079 (1945).
Certiorari to the Circuit Court of Appeals for the Second Circuit.

MR. JUSTICE FRANKFURTER delivered the opinion of the Court.   *   *   *

In May, 1930, Van Sweringen Corporation issued notes to the amount of $30,000,000. Under an indenture of the same date, petitioner, Guaranty Trust Co., was named trustee with power and obligations to enforce the rights of the noteholders in the assets of the Corporation and of the Van Sweringen brothers. In October, 1930, petitioner, with other banks, made large advances to companies affiliated with the Corporation and wholly controlled by the Van Sweringens. In October, 1931, when it was apparent that the Corporation could not meet its obligations, Guaranty co-operated in a plan for the purchase of the outstanding notes on the basis of cash for 50% of the face value of the notes and twenty shares of Van Sweringen Corporation's stock for each $1,000 note. This exchange offer remained open until December 15, 1931.

Respondent York received $6,000 of the notes as a gift in 1934, her donor not having accepted the offer of exchange. In April, 1940, three accepting noteholders began suit against petitioner, charging fraud and misrepresentation. Respondent's application to intervene in that suit was denied, Hackner v. Guaranty Trust Co., 2 Cir., 117 F.2d 95, and summary judgment in favor of Guaranty was affirmed. Hackner v. Morgan, 2 Cir., 130 F.2d 300. After her dismissal from the Hackner litigation, respondent, on January 22, 1942, began the present proceedings.

The suit, instituted as a class action on behalf of non-accepting noteholders and brought in a federal court solely because of diversity of citizenship, is based on an alleged breach of trust by Guaranty in that it failed to protect the interests of the noteholders in assenting to the exchange offer and failed to disclose its self-interest when sponsoring the offer. Petitioner moved for summary judgment, which was granted, upon the authority of the Hackner case. On appeal, the Circuit Court of Appeals, one Judge dissenting, * * * held that in a suit brought on the equity side of a federal district court that court is not required to apply the State statute of limitations that would govern like suits in the courts of a State where the federal court is sitting even though the exclusive basis of federal jurisdiction is diversity of citizenship. 143 F.2d 503. The importance of the question for the disposition of litigation in the federal courts led us to bring the case here.

In view of the basis of the decision below, it is not for us to consider whether the New York statute would actually bar this suit were it brought in a State court. Our only concern is with the holding that the federal courts in a suit like this are not bound by local law. * * *

In exercising their jurisdiction on the ground of diversity of citizenship, the federal courts, in the long course of their history, have not differentiated in their regard for State law between actions at law and suits in equity. Although § 34 of the Judiciary Act of 1789 directed that the "laws of the several States * * * shall be regarded as rules of decision in trials of common law * * *", this was deemed, consistently for over a hundred years, to be merely declaratory of what would in any event have governed the federal courts and therefore was equally applicable to equity suits. See Hawkins v. Barney's Lessee, 5 Pet. 457, 464; Mason v. United States, 260 U.S. 545, 559; Erie R. Co. v. Tompkins, *supra*, 304 U.S. at page 72. Indeed, it may fairly be said that the federal courts gave greater respect to State-created "substantive rights", Pusey & Jones Co. v. Hanssen, 261 U.S. 491, 498, in equity than they gave them on the law side, because rights at law were usually declared by State courts and as such increasingly flouted by extension of the doctrine of Swift v. Tyson, while rights in equity were frequently defined by legislative enactment and as such known and respected by the federal courts. See, *e.g.*, Clark v. Smith, 13 Pet. 195; Scott v. Neely, 140 U.S. 106; Louisville & Nash. R.R. v. West Un. Tel. Co., 234 U.S. 369, 374–376; Pusey & Jones Co. v. Hanssen, *supra,* 261 U.S. at page 498.

Partly because the States in the early days varied greatly in the manner in which equitable relief was afforded and in the extent to which it was available, * * * Congress provided that "the forms and modes of proceeding in suits * * * of equity" would conform to the settled uses of courts of equity. Section 2, 1 Stat. 275, 276. But this enactment gave the federal courts no power that they would not have had in any event when courts were given "cognizance", by the first Judiciary Act, of suits "in equity". From the beginning there has been a good deal of talk in the cases that federal equity is a separate legal system. And so it is, properly understood. The suits in equity of which the federal courts have had "cognizance" ever since 1789 constituted the body of law which had been transplanted to this country from the English Court of Chancery. But this system of equity "derived its doctrines, as well as its powers, from its mode of giving relief". Langdell, Summary of Equity Pleading (1877) xxvii. In giving federal courts "cognizance" of equity suits in cases of diversity jurisdiction, Congress never gave, nor did the federal courts ever claim, the power to deny substantive rights created by State law or to create substantive rights denied by State law.

This does not mean that whatever equitable remedy is available in a State court must be available in a diversity suit in a federal court, or conversely, that a federal court may not afford an equitable remedy not available in a State court. Equitable relief in a federal court is of course subject to restrictions: the suit must be within the traditional scope of equity as historically evolved in the English Court of Chancery, Payne v. Hook, 7 Wall. 425, 430; Atlas Life Ins. Co. v. W.I. Southern, Inc., 306 U.S. 563, 568; Sprague v. Ticonic Bank, 307 U.S. 161, 164, 165; a plain, adequate and complete remedy at law must be wanting, § 16, 1 Stat. 73, 82, 28 U.S.C. § 384; explicit Congressional curtailment of equity powers must be respected, see, e.g., Norris–LaGuardia Act, 47 Stat. 70, 29 U.S.C. § 101 et seq.; the constitutional right to trial by jury cannot be evaded, Whitehead v. Shattuck, 138 U.S. 146. That a State may authorize its courts to give equitable relief unhampered by any or all such restrictions cannot remove these fetters from the federal courts. See Clark v. Smith, 13 Pet. 195, 203; In re Broderick's Will, 21 Wall. 503, 519, 520; * * *. State law cannot define the remedies which a federal court must give simply because a federal court in diversity jurisdiction is available as an alternative tribunal to the State's courts.[3] Contrariwise, a federal court may afford an equita-

3. In Pusey & Jones Co. v. Hanssen, *supra,* the Court had to decide whether a Delaware statute had created a new right appropriate for enforcement in accordance with traditional equity practice or whether the statute had merely given the Delaware Chancery Court a new kind of remedy. * * * [T]he Court construed the Delaware statute merely to extend the power to an equity court to appoint a receiver on the application of an ordinary contract creditor. By conferring new discretionary authority upon its equity court, Delaware could not modify the traditional equity rule in the federal courts that only someone with a defined interest in the estate of an insolvent person, *e.g.,* a judgment creditor, can protect that interest through receivership. But the Court recognized that if the Delaware statute had been one not regulating the powers of the Chancery Court of Delaware but creating a new interest in a contract creditor, the federal court would have had power to grant a receivership at the behest of such a simple

ble remedy for a substantive right recognized by a State even though a State court cannot give it. Whatever contradiction or confusion may be produced by a medley of judicial phrases severed from their environment, the body of adjudications concerning equitable relief in diversity cases leaves no doubt that the federal courts enforced State-created substantive rights if the mode of proceeding and remedy were consonant with the traditional body of equitable remedies, practice and procedure, and in so doing they were enforcing rights created by the States and not arising under any inherent or statutory federal law.[4]

Inevitably, therefore, the principle of Erie R. Co. v. Tompkins, an action at law, was promptly applied to a suit in equity. Ruhlin v. New York Life Ins. Co., 304 U.S. 202.

And so this case reduces itself to the narrow question whether, when no recovery could be had in a State court because the action is barred by the statute of limitations, a federal court in equity can take cognizance of the suit because there is diversity of citizenship between the parties. Is the outlawry, according to State law, of a claim created by the States a matter of "substantive rights" to be respected by a federal court of equity when that court's jurisdiction is dependent on the fact that there is a State-created right, or is such statute of "a mere remedial character", Henrietta Mills v. Rutherford Co., supra, 281 U.S. at page 128, which a federal court may disregard?

Matters of "substance" and matters of "procedure" are much talked about in the books as though they defined a great divide cutting across the whole domain of law. But, of course, "substance" and "procedure" are the same key-words to very different problems. Neither "substance" nor "procedure" represents the same invariants. Each implies different variables depending upon the particular problem for which it is used. See Home Ins. Co. v. Dick, 281 U.S. 397, 409. And the different problems are only distantly related at best, for the terms are in common use in connection with situations turning on such different considerations as those that are relevant to questions pertaining to ex post facto legislation, the impairment of the obligations of contract, the enforcement of federal rights in the State courts and the multitudinous phases of the conflict of laws. * * *

Here we are dealing with a right to recover derived not from the United States but from one of the States. When, because the plaintiff happens to be a non-resident, such a right is enforceable in a federal as well as in a State court, the forms and mode of enforcing the right may at times, naturally enough, vary because the two judicial systems are not identic. But since a federal court adjudicating a state-created right solely because of

---

contract creditor, as much so as in the case of a secured creditor. * * *

4. "It is true that where a state statute creates a new equitable right of a substantive character, which can be enforced by proceedings in conformity with the pleadings and practice appropriate to a court of equity, such enforcement may be had in a Federal court provided a ground exists for invoking the Federal jurisdiction. * * * But the enforcement in the Federal courts of new equitable rights created by States is subject to the qualification that such en-

forcement must not impair any right conferred, or conflict with any inhibition imposed, by the Constitution or laws of the United States. * * * Whatever uncertainty may have arisen because of expressions which did not fully accord with the rule as thus stated, the distinction, with respect to the effect of state legislation, has come to be clearly established between substantive and remedial rights." Henrietta Mills v. Rutherford Co., [281 U.S. 121] at 127-128.

the diversity of citizenship of the parties is for that purpose, in effect, only another court of the State, it cannot afford recovery if the right to recover is made unavailable by the State nor can it substantially affect the enforcement of the right as given by the State.

And so the question is not whether a statute of limitations is deemed a matter of "procedure" in some sense. The question is whether such a statute concerns merely the manner and the means by which a right to recover, as recognized by the State, is enforced, or whether such statutory limitation is a matter of substance in the aspect that alone is relevant to our problem, namely does it significantly affect the result of a litigation for a federal court to disregard a law of a State that would be controlling in an action upon the same claim by the same parties in a State court?

It is therefore immaterial whether statutes of limitation are characterized either as "substantive" or "procedural" in State court opinions in any use of those terms unrelated to the specific issue before us. Erie R. Co. v. Tompkins was not an endeavor to formulate scientific legal terminology. It expressed a policy that touches vitally the proper distribution of judicial power between State and federal courts. In essence, the intent of that decision was to insure that, in all cases where a federal court is exercising jurisdiction solely because of the diversity of citizenship of the parties, the outcome of the litigation in the federal court should be substantially the same, so far as legal rules determine the outcome of a litigation, as it would be if tried in a State court. The nub of the policy that underlies Erie R. Co. v. Tompkins is that for the same transaction the accident of a suit by a nonresident litigant in a federal court instead of in a State court a block away, should not lead to a substantially different result. And so, putting to one side abstractions regarding "substance" and "procedure", we have held that in diversity cases the federal courts must follow the law of the State as to burden of proof, Cities Service Oil Co. v. Dunlap, 308 U.S. 208, as to conflict of laws, Klaxon Co. v. Stentor Co., 313 U.S. 487, as to contributory negligence, Palmer v. Hoffman, 318 U.S. 109, 117. And see Sampson v. Channell, 1 Cir., 110 F.2d 754. Erie R. Co. v. Tompkins has been applied with an eye alert to essentials in avoiding disregard of State law in diversity cases in the federal courts. A policy so important to our federalism must be kept free from entanglements with analytical or terminological niceties.

Plainly enough, a statute that would completely bar recovery in a suit if brought in a State court bears on a State-created right vitally and not merely formally or negligibly. As to consequences that so intimately affect recovery or nonrecovery a federal court in a diversity case should follow State law. * * *

Prior to Erie R. Co. v. Tompkins it was not necessary, as we have indicated, to make the critical analysis required by the doctrine of that case of the nature of jurisdiction of the federal courts in diversity cases. But even before Erie R. Co. v. Tompkins, federal courts relied on statutes of limitations of the States in which they sat. In suits at law State limitations statutes were held to be "rules of decision" within § 34 of the Judiciary Act of 1789 and as such applied in "trials at common law". McClung v. Silliman, 3 Pet. 270, 277; President and Directors of Bank of Alabama v. Dalton, 9 How. 522; Leffingwell v. Warren, 2 Black 599; Bauserman v. Blunt, 147 U.S. 647. While there was talk of freedom of equity from such State statutes of limitations, the cases generally refused recovery where suit was barred in a like situation in the State courts, even if only by way of analogy. See, *e.g.,* Godden v. Kimmell, 99 U.S. 201; Alsop v. Riker, 155 U.S. 448; Benedict v. City of New York, 250 U.S. 321, 327, 328. However in Kirby v. Lake Shore & M.S. Co., 120 U.S. 130, the Court disregarded a State statute of limitations where the Court deemed it inequitable to apply it.

To make an exception to Erie R. Co. v. Tompkins on the equity side of a federal court is to reject the considerations of policy which, after long travail, led to that decision. Judge Augustus N. Hand thus summarized below the fatal objection to such inroad upon Erie R. Co. v. Tompkins: "In my opinion it would be a mischievous practice to disregard state statutes of limitation whenever federal courts think that the result of adopting them may be inequitable. Such procedure would promote the choice of United States rather than of state courts in order to gain the advantage of different laws. The main foundation for the criticism of Swift v. Tyson was that a litigant in cases where federal jurisdiction is based only on diverse citizenship may obtain a more favorable decision by suing in the United States courts." 2 Cir., 143 F.2d 503, 529, 531.

Diversity jurisdiction is founded on assurance to non-resident litigants of courts free from susceptibility to potential local bias. The Framers of the Constitution, according to Marshall, entertained "apprehensions" lest distant suitors be subjected to local bias in State courts, or, at least, viewed with "indulgence the possible fears and apprehensions" of such suitors. Bank of the United States v. Deveaux, 5 Cranch 61, 87. And so Congress afforded out-of-State litigants another tribunal, not another body of law. The operation of a double system of conflicting laws in the same State is plainly hostile to the reign of law. Certainly, the fortuitous circumstance of residence out of a State of one of the parties to a litigation ought not to give rise to a discrimination against others equally concerned but locally resident. The source of substantive rights enforced by a federal court under diversity jurisdiction, it cannot be said too often, is the law of the States. Whenever that law is authoritatively declared by a State, whether its voice be the legislature or its highest court, such law ought to govern in litigation founded on that law, whether the forum of application is a State or a federal court and whether the remedies be sought at law or may be had in equity.

Dicta may be cited characterizing equity as an independent body of law. To the extent that we have indicated, it is. But insofar as these general observations go beyond that, they merely reflect notions that have been replaced by a sharper analysis of what federal courts do when they enforce rights that have no federal origin. And so, before the true source of law that is applied by the federal courts under diversity jurisdiction was fully explored, some things were said that would not now be said. But nothing that was decided, unless it be the Kirby case, needs to be rejected.

* * *

Reversed.

MR. JUSTICE ROBERTS and MR. JUSTICE DOUGLAS took no part in the consideration or decision of this case.

MR. JUSTICE RUTLEDGE.

I dissent. * * *

If any characteristic of equity jurisprudence has descended unbrokenly from and within "the traditional scope of equity as historically evolved in the English Court of Chancery," it is that statutes of limitations, often in terms applying only to actions at law, have never been deemed to be rigidly applicable as absolute barriers to suits in equity as they are to actions at law. That tradition, it would seem, should be regarded as having been incorporated in the various Acts of Congress which have conferred equity jurisdiction upon the federal courts. So incorporated it has been reaffirmed repeatedly by the decisions of this and other courts. It is now excised from those Acts. If there is to be excision, Congress, not this Court, should make it. * * *

* * * [T]his case arises from what are in fact if not in law interstate transactions. It involves the rights of security holders in relation to securities which were distributed not in New York or Ohio alone but widely throughout the country. They are the kind of rights which Congress acted to safeguard when it adopted the Securities and Exchange legislation. Specific provisions of that legislation are not involved in this litigation. The broad policies underlying it may be involved or affected, namely, by the existence of adequate federal remedies, whether judicial or legislative, for the protection of security holders against the misconduct of issuers or against the breach of rights by trustees. Even though the basic rights may be controlled by state law, in such situations the question is often a difficult one whether the law of one state or another applies; and this is true not only of rights clearly substantive but also of those variously characterized as procedural or remedial and substantive which involve the application of statutes of limitations.

Applicable statutes of limitations in state tribunals are not always the ones which would apply if suit were instituted in the courts of the state which creates the substantive rights for which enforcement is sought. The state of the forum is free to apply its own period of limitations, regardless of whether the state originating the right has barred suit upon it. * * *

It is not clear whether today's decision puts it into the power of corporate trustees, by confining their jurisdictional "presence" to states which allow their courts to give equitable remedies only within short periods of time, to defeat the purpose and intent of the law of the state creating the substantive right. If so, the "right" remains alive, with full-fledged remedy, by the law of its origin, and because enforcement must be had in another state, which affords refuge against it, the remedy and with it the right are nullified. I doubt that the Constitution of the United States requires this or that the Judiciary Acts permit it. A good case can be made, indeed has been made, that the diversity jurisdiction was created to afford protection against exactly this sort of nullifying state legislation.[10]

In my judgment this furnishes added reason for leaving any change, if one is to be made, to the judgment of Congress. The next step may well be to say that in applying the doctrine of laches a federal court must

---

10. Frankfurter, Distribution of Judicial Power Between United States and State Courts (1928), 13 Corn.L.Q. 499, 520. See Corwin, The Progress of Constitutional Theory (1925), 30 Am.Hist.Rev. 511, 514. See also Friendly, The Historic Basis of Diversity Jurisdiction (1928), 41 Harv.L. Rev. 483, 495–497. That the motivating desire was or may have been to protect creditors who were men of business does not make the policy less applicable when the creditor is a customer of such men.

surrender its own judgment and attempt to find out what a state court sitting a block away would do with that notoriously amorphous doctrine.

MR. JUSTICE MURPHY joins in this opinion.

NOTE ON STATE LAW AND FEDERAL EQUITY

(1) In Guffey v. Smith, 237 U.S. 101 (1915), lessees under an oil and gas lease brought a federal diversity action to enjoin operations under a later lease and to obtain discovery and an accounting. The complainants' lease gave them an option to surrender it at any time, and though this provision did not, under state law, render the lease "void as wanting in mutuality," the holder of such a lease would have been unable to bring an action of ejectment at law or a suit in equity for injunctive relief in the state's courts. Those courts would have regarded the lease as "so lacking in mutuality" that the lessee's only remedy would have been one at law for damages.

The Supreme Court, in a meticulous opinion by Justice Van Devanter, held that equitable relief was available in a federal court. After noting that the lease was not void as a matter of state substantive law, and that an action of ejectment at law would not be available in a federal court in light of the Conformity Act, he turned to the state decisions denying equitable relief in such a case:

" * * * These decisions, it is insisted, should have been accepted and applied by the Circuit Court. To this we cannot assent. By the legislation of Congress and repeated decisions of this court it has long been settled that the remedies afforded and modes of proceeding pursued in the Federal courts, sitting as courts of equity, are not determined by local laws or rules of decision, but by general principles, rules and usages of equity having uniform operation in those courts wherever sitting. Rev.Stat. §§ 913, 917; Neves v. Scott, 13 How. 268, 272; Payne v. Hook, 7 Wall. 425, 430; Dodge v. Tulleys, 144 U.S. 451, 457; Mississippi Mills v. Cohn, 150 U.S. 202, 204. As was said in the first of these cases: 'Wherever a case in equity may arise and be determined, under the judicial power of the United States, the same principles of equity must be applied to it, and it is for the courts of the United States, and for this court in the last resort, to decide what those principles are, and to apply such of them to each particular case, as they may find justly applicable' " (p. 114).

The Court then went on to consider whether, under "the general principles and rules of equity administered in the Federal courts" (*id.*), there were grounds for denying equitable relief, and concluded that there were not. Finally, after determining that the lessee's failure to make certain payments on time did not constitute a forfeiture of the lease under state law, the Court modified the decree for an accounting and, in doing so, relied on its own prior decisions in other equitable proceedings.

Can Guffey stand after Erie? Does York save it?

Note that the end of the sentence in the York opinion following footnote 3 would have been a good place to cite Guffey, if it had been thought to be alive. But neither Guffey nor any other case is cited. What kind of case might the Court have had in mind? What are the relevant considerations in deciding when "a federal court may afford an equitable remedy for a substantive right recognized by a State even though a State court cannot give it"?

(2) Does Justice Frankfurter account adequately for all of the "talk in the cases that federal equity is a separate legal system"?

In Payne v. Hook, 7 Wall. 425, 430 (U.S.1869), cited in Guffey, the Court said:

"We have repeatedly held 'that the jurisdiction of the courts of the United States over controversies between citizens of different States, cannot be impaired by the laws of the States, which prescribe the modes of redress in their courts, or which regulate the distribution of their judicial power.' If legal remedies are sometimes modified to suit the changes in the laws of the States, and the practice of their courts, it is not so with equitable. The equity jurisdiction conferred on the Federal courts is the same that the High Court of Chancery in England possesses; is subject to neither limitation or restraint by State legislation and is uniform throughout the different States of the Union."

Recall that, as Justice Frankfurter mentions, many states had no separate systems of equity at all in 1789, and often only rudimentary equitable doctrines. Recall that the first Congress, in this context, not only gave the circuit courts diversity jurisdiction in suits "in equity" (Act of Sept. 24, 1789, § 11, 1 Stat. 73, 78), but refrained from making the Rules of Decision Act (§ 34) applicable in such proceedings, laying down only an independent federal limitation (§ 16), which later became § 267 of the Judicial Code of 1911 and which was repealed in 1948, that "suits in equity shall not be sustained in either of the courts of the United States, in any case where plain, adequate and complete remedy may be had at law".

Recall also that traditional equity was not, as the quotation in York from Langdell's *Summary of Equity Pleading* might be thought to imply, a system merely of distinctive remedies without distinctive substantive consequences. In the paragraph before the one from which the opinion quotes, Dean Langdell pointed out (pp. xxv–xxvi) that "of course, * * * it must not be supposed that equity in modern times is simply a different system of remedies from those administered in courts of law; for there are many extensive doctrines in equity, and some whole branches of law, which are unknown to the common-law courts". And he went on to give familiar examples, such as trusts, the mortgagee's equity of redemption, and the doctrine of equitable election, in which equity, because of its distinctive remedies, was able to recognize and enforce an interest which the law entirely denied. Compare also the many equitable defenses, enforced by separate bill in equity, by which the chancellor, having as always the last word, destroyed interests which the law did recognize, so as to reach a wholly different substantive result.

In this context it is likely that federal courts sitting in states lacking courts of equity jurisdiction did claim, and were intended to claim, "the power to deny substantive rights created by State law or to create substantive rights denied by State law". See 2 Crosskey, Politics and the Constitution in the History of the United States 877–902 (1953), so contending. See also Morse, *The Substantive Equity Historically Applied by the U.S. Courts*, 54 Dick.L.Rev. 10 (1949). Nevertheless, the cases are inconclusive. Compare, *e.g.*, Neves v. Scott, 13 How. 268, 272 (U.S.1851) (dictum), with, *e.g.*,

Meade v. Beale, 16 Fed.Cas.No.9,371, at 1291 (C.C.Md.1850) (Taney, C.J., on circuit).

See Hill, *The Erie Doctrine in Bankruptcy,* 66 Harv.L.Rev. 1013, 1024–35 (1953), concluding that the federal equitable jurisdiction was not regarded as a special source of authority to override state substantive law; that insofar as the federal courts overrode state substantive law in equity they did so on the basis of assumptions concerning the nature of law and the nature of federal judicial power which were common both to law and equity; and that for these reasons the implications of Erie have been essentially the same in both law and equity.

(3) The Court in Guffey took great pains to acknowledge the underlying substantive interests recognized by state law, both decisional and statutory, and then carefully distinguished between substantive right and legal remedy, on the one hand, and equitable remedy on the other.

Guffey might be defended on the ground that the federal court was merely giving a fuller and fairer remedy in the enforcement of state-created rights—a kind of "juster justice." But in doing so, is the federal court undercutting the state's purpose to give a *lessor* an option to break a lease and pay damages if the lease itself gives the *lessee* an option to withdraw at any time? At least since the insights of Holmes, should we not hesitate to draw bright lines between right and remedy?

Suppose the legislature or courts of a state decide that the market in land will function more efficiently if specific performance of land contracts is denied except in extraordinary cases. Should a federal court in that state grant specific performance in "ordinary" cases?

(4) May a federal court, sitting in a state that does not authorize declaratory judgments, properly exercise jurisdiction in a diversity case under the Declaratory Judgments Act? Compare Skelly Oil Co. v. Phillips Petroleum Co., 339 U.S. 667, 674 (1950) (the Court stated, in a diversity case, that the fact that "the declaratory remedy which may be given by the federal courts may not be available in the State courts is immaterial"); Allstate Ins. Co. v. Charneski, 286 F.2d 238 (7th Cir.1960) (action by insurance company for declaratory judgment of nonliability with respect to accident dismissed: to allow declaratory relief would undercut state policy favoring direct actions against insurance company in which all questions of the rights of the injured, the insured, and the insurer are resolved in a single suit).

(5) In Bernhardt v. Polygraphic Co., 350 U.S. 198 (1956), the plaintiff brought a breach of contract action in a Vermont state court. The defendant removed to a federal court on diversity grounds and moved to stay the proceedings pending arbitration, pursuant to an arbitration clause in the contract. The district court denied the motion on the ground that under Vermont law an agreement to arbitrate is revocable at any time prior to an award and is therefore not enforceable. The Second Circuit reversed, but the Supreme Court agreed with the district court, saying (p. 203):

" * * * If the federal court allows arbitration where the state court would disallow it, the outcome of litigation might depend on the courthouse where suit is brought. For the remedy by arbitration, whatever its merits or shortcomings, substantially affects the cause of action created by the

State. The nature of the tribunal where suits are tried is an important part of the parcel of rights behind a cause of action."

The Court held, as a matter of statutory construction, that the provisions for judicial enforcement of certain agreements to arbitrate in the United States Arbitration Act, 9 U.S.C. §§ 1–14,[1] did not apply to the case at hand, noting (p. 202) that "If respondent's contention [that the Act applied] is correct, a constitutional question might be presented. Erie R. Co. v. Tompkins indicated that Congress does not have the constitutional authority to make the law that is applicable to controversies in diversity of citizenship cases."

Was anything left of Guffey after Bernhardt?[2] What "constitutional question" was the Court referring to in Bernhardt? How should it be resolved? See Ely, *The Irrepressible Myth of Erie,* 87 Harv.L.Rev. 693, 705–06 (1974); Hirshman, *The Second Arbitration Trilogy: The Federalization of Arbitration Law,* 71 Va.L.Rev. 1305, 1309–20 (1985).

(6) The constitutional question raised in Bernhardt was answered, in part, in Prima Paint Corp. v. Flood & Conklin Mfg. Co., 388 U.S. 395 (1967). In this diversity action, Prima sought rescission of a consulting agreement on the basis of fraudulent inducement, and Flood & Conklin, relying on the Arbitration Act, filed a motion to stay the action pending arbitration of the issue of fraud under an arbitration clause in the contract. The Supreme Court held, 6–3, that the stay was properly granted under the Act, even though such a stay (for arbitration of the issue of fraud) might not have been obtainable had the action been brought in a state court. The Arbitration Act applied because, unlike the contract at issue in Bernhardt, the contract in Prima was one "evidencing a transaction involving commerce" within the meaning of § 2 of the Act. Application of the Act was constitutionally permissible because the question in the case was "not whether Congress may fashion federal substantive rules to govern questions arising in simple diversity cases"; rather it was "whether Congress may prescribe how federal courts are to conduct themselves with respect to subject matter [interstate commerce] over which Congress plainly has power to legislate". The answer, the Court concluded, "can only be in the affirmative" (p. 405). But the Court carefully avoided any explicit endorsement of the view that the Arbitration Act embodied substantive policies that were to be applied to all contracts within its scope, whether sued on in state or federal courts.

1. The Arbitration Act, originally enacted in 1925, provides in § 2 that a written arbitration provision "in any maritime transaction or a contract evidencing a transaction involving commerce * * * shall be valid, irrevocable, and enforceable, save upon such grounds as exist at law or in equity for the revocation of any contract"; in § 3 that when suit is brought "in any of the courts of the United States" on an issue referable to arbitration by an arbitration agreement, the court must stay its own proceedings pending arbitration once it has decided that the issue is arbitrable under the agreement; and in § 4 that a "United States district court" whose assistance is properly invoked by a party to an arbitration agreement shall order arbitration.

2. See Stern v. South Chester Tube Co., 390 U.S. 606, 609–10 (1968): "We need not decide whether this [diversity action] is a case where such a federal remedy can be provided even in the absence of a similar state remedy, Skelly Oil Co. v. Phillips Co., 339 U.S. 667, 674 (1950); *cf.* Guffey v. Smith, 237 U.S. 101 (1915), because it is clear that state law here also provides for enforcement of the shareholder's right [to inspect corporate records] by a compulsory judicial order."

How stable was the result in the Prima Paint case if it contemplated different remedies in federal and state courts for breach of the same contract? (Compare the demise of a similar, but converse, distinction between state and federal remedies in Boys Markets, Inc. v. Retail Clerk's Union, Local 770, 398 U.S. 235 (1970).) In Moses H. Cone Memorial Hospital v. Mercury Construction Corp., 460 U.S. 1, 26 (1983), the Court moved at least part way toward the imposition of the Arbitration Act's remedial provisions on the state courts when it said, in dicta, that "state courts, as much as federal courts, are obliged to grant stays of litigation under § 3 of the Arbitration Act." [3] Then in Southland Corp. v. Keating, 465 U.S. 1 (1984), the Court held that a state law rendering certain claims in franchise agreements not arbitrable was in direct conflict with § 2 of the Act and therefore could not be applied by a state court to a contract within the scope of that Act.[4]

For discussion of these decisions, and their choice-of-law implications, see Hirshman, Paragraph (5), *supra.*

(7) Are considerations different from those in Guffey and Bernhardt involved when state law, and particularly the availability of an equitable remedy in the state courts, is urged not as a reason for denying federal equitable relief but for granting it? To what extent do Erie–Klaxon–York require federal courts to mirror state courts in this respect also?

In Pusey & Jones Co. v. Hanssen, 261 U.S. 491 (1923), a Delaware statute authorizing the appointment of a receiver upon the application of a simple contract creditor was denied enforcement. In a much-cited opinion for the Court, Justice Brandeis said (pp. 497–99):

"That this suit could not be maintained in the absence of the statute is clear. A receiver is often appointed upon application of a secured creditor who fears that his security will be wasted. Kountze v. Omaha Hotel Co., 107 U.S. 378, 395. A receiver is often appointed upon application of a judgment creditor who has exhausted his legal remedy. See White v. Ewing, 159 U.S. 36. But an unsecured simple contract creditor has, in the absence of statute, no substantive right, legal or equitable, in or to the property of his debtor. This is true, whatever the nature of the property; and although the debtor is a corporation and insolvent. The only substantive right of a simple contract creditor is to have his debt paid in due course. His adjective right is, ordinarily, at law. He has no right whatsoever in equity until he has exhausted his legal remedy. After execution upon a judgment recovered at law has been returned unsatisfied, he may proceed in equity by a creditor's bill. Hollins v. Brierfield Coal & Iron Co., 150 U.S. 371 * * *. He may, by such a bill, remove any obstacle to

---

3. The Court went on to say, however, that it was "less clear * * * whether the same is true of an order to compel arbitration under § 4 of the Act" (p. 26). It noted the difference between the language of § 3 ("any of the courts of the United States") and that of § 4 ("United States District Court"). See note 1, *supra.* But it observed that at least one state court had held that it was required by § 4 to order arbitration in an appropriate case. *Id.* at n. 35.

4. The Court ruled, over Justice Stevens' dissent on this point, that the Califor-

nia statute did not come under the savings clause of § 2 as "grounds * * * for the revocation of any contract." (Justices O'Connor and Rehnquist dissented more broadly, arguing that the Arbitration Act was directed only to the federal courts.)

Although the Court in Southland disclaimed direct reliance on § 4 of the Act, its reversal of the state court's judgment effectively required that court to compel arbitration.

satisfying his execution at law; or may reach assets equitable in their nature; or he may provisionally protect his debtor's property from misappropriation or waste, by means either of an injunction or a receiver. Whether the debtor be an individual or a corporation, the appointment of a receiver is merely an ancillary and incidental remedy. A receivership is not final relief. The appointment determines no substantive right; nor is it a step in the determination of such a right. It is a means of preserving property which may ultimately be applied toward the satisfaction of substantive rights.

"That a remedial right to proceed in a federal court sitting in equity cannot be enlarged by a state statute is likewise clear. Scott v. Neely, 140 U.S. 106; Cates v. Allen, 149 U.S. 451. Nor can it be so narrowed. Mississippi Mills v. Cohn, 150 U.S. 202; Guffey v. Smith, 237 U.S. 101, 114. The federal court may therefore be obliged to deny an equitable remedy which the plaintiff might have secured in a state court. Hanssen's contention is that the statute does not enlarge the equitable jurisdiction or remedies; and that it confers upon creditors of a Delaware corporation, if the company is insolvent, a substantive equitable right to have a receiver appointed. If this were true, the right conferred could be enforced in the federal courts, Scott v. Neely, 140 U.S. 106, 109; since the proceeding is in pleading and practice conformable to those commonly entertained by a court of equity. But it is not true that this statute confers upon the creditor a substantive right. * * * Insolvency is made a condition of the Chancellor's jurisdiction; but it does not give rise to any substantive right in the creditor. Jones v. Maxwell Motor Co. (Del.Ch.) 115 Atl. 312, 314, 315. It makes possible a new remedy because it confers upon the Chancellor a new power. Whether that power is visitorial (as the petitioner insists), or whether it is strictly judicial, need not be determined in this case. Whatever its exact nature, the power enables the Chancellor to afford a remedy which theretofore would not have been open to an unsecured simple contract creditor. But because that which the statute confers is merely a remedy, the statute cannot affect proceedings in the federal courts sitting in equity." [5]

For differing views of the impact of Erie on such decisions as Pusey & Jones, see the opinions in Mintzer v. Arthur L. Wright & Co., 263 F.2d 823 (3d Cir.1959). See also Note, *The Equitable Remedial Rights Doctrine: Past and Present*, 67 Harv.L.Rev. 836 (1954).

(8) Is there any objection that can be raised on the score of Erie policy if the federal courts, without passing on the merits, simply close their doors to the complainant seeking equitable relief? Does it matter whether the federal door-closing policy is based on decisional law, a federal rule of civil procedure, or an act of Congress (like the anti-injunction provisions of the Norris–LaGuardia Act)? Or whether the policy is stated in terms of a limitation on subject-matter jurisdiction, as in the case of the jurisdictional

5. With Pusey & Jones, compare Guardian Sav. & Trust Co. v. Road Improvement Dist. No. 7, 267 U.S. 1 (1925), which held that the power to appoint a receiver to collect taxes, in order to pay the money due on certain bonds, could be exercised by a federal court in a diversity case. Similar power had been conferred on the state courts, and the state law was "not merely an enlargement of the remedial powers of a local court * * * [as in Pusey & Jones], it recognizes the inadequacy of the remedy at law and is an attempt to give to purchasers of bonds the assurance of adequate relief against shortcomings that experience has taught the business world to apprehend" (pp. 6–7).

amount requirement?   See Cohen v. Beneficial Ind. Loan Corp., 337 U.S. 541, 556 (1949); Comment, 20 U.Chi.L.Rev. 304 (1953).

A door-closing rule creates special problems if the defendant is able to remove a state court action and then have the case dismissed.   In Cates v. Allen, 149 U.S. 451 (1893), it was held that a federal court sitting in equity in a removed diversity case should not enforce a state statute permitting a simple contract creditor to set aside a fraudulent conveyance.[6]   The Court concluded that the proper disposition was not to dismiss but rather to remand, since the case had been improperly removed.   Compare Venner v. Great Northern Ry., 209 U.S. 24 (1908) (upholding the existence of federal jurisdiction but affirming dismissal of the bill for "want of equity").   *Cf.* Section 4, *infra.*

NOTE ON THE "OUTCOME" TEST AND ITS EVOLUTION TO HANNA v. PLUMER

(1) Wasn't the point raised by Justice Rutledge in the last four paragraphs of his dissent in York answered by the Court four years earlier, in Klaxon?

(2) What did Justice Frankfurter mean in York by "outcome" when he said that it was the intent of Erie that in diversity cases "the outcome of the litigation in the federal court should be substantially the same, so far as legal rules determine the outcome of a litigation, as it would be if tried in a State court"?

(a) Did he mean only that a federal decision finally settling the rights of the parties with respect to the transactions and occurrences in question ought not to be predicated upon a different view of their primary legal relations than the state court would take if it were similarly making a final decision?

(b) Or did he mean that a federal court should not only avoid using different premises about primary legal relations but should refrain also from giving any different kind of relief, on the basis of those premises, than the state court would give if it were finally adjudicating the right to that kind of relief?

(c) Or did he mean to say, in addition, that the federal court should refrain from acting at all on the controversy if the state court would refuse to act, even though the state court's refusal would be without prejudice?

(d) Did he mean to say also that the federal court ought not to refuse to act on the controversy, even though it does so without prejudice, if the state court would be willing to act?

(3) What did Justice Frankfurter mean by "legal rules" which "determine" the outcome of a litigation?

(a) Did he mean to include legal rules, such as that which empowers the federal judge to comment on the evidence, which may determine the outcome of the litigation as a practical matter but do not purport to do so?

---

6. It was noted in this case that to use state law to expand the remedies available on the equity side of the federal court would be to curtail the right of jury trial under the Seventh Amendment.   Would this objection serve as a valid basis today— under a merged procedure—for refusal to enforce the state statute?

(b) Did he mean to include all legal rules which purport to direct, in given circumstances, the final decision? *E.g.*, a rule of evidence which calls for reversal if it is violated? Or a rule of procedure which calls for dismissal if an indispensable party has not been joined? Or a rule of pleading which permits dismissal if an answer is not filed in time?

(c) Or did he mean to exclude all rules which depend for their application upon what the parties or counsel do after litigation is begun and which might have been done differently under different rules of procedure? (In other words, housekeeping rules?)

(d) Did he mean to include at least all rules which purport to control the final judgment upon due proof or failure of proof of given pre-litigation circumstances? Only those rules?

(4) Is the outcome test a material improvement upon the ancient dichotomy between substance and procedure?

(5) The questions raised in the preceding paragraphs have perplexed the federal courts at all levels ever since the York decision. During the first 13 years after the decision the Court disposed of a number of important cases without suggesting a stopping place for the outcome test or even hinting, in the majority opinions, at any limitation on the rationale. Of particular interest are three cases decided on the same day: Ragan v. Merchants Transfer & Warehouse Co., 337 U.S. 530 (1949); Woods v. Interstate Realty Co., 337 U.S. 535 (1949); and Cohen v. Beneficial Indus. Loan Corp., 337 U.S. 541 (1949). Only four members of the Court joined in all three decisions.

In Cohen, a stockholder in a Delaware corporation (who owned about .0125% of the stock, worth less than $10,000) had brought a derivative action in a New Jersey federal court against the corporation and various officers and directors, alleging mismanagement. Jurisdiction was based on diversity of citizenship. The question was whether the federal court should apply a New Jersey statute the general effect of which was "to make a plaintiff having so small an interest liable for the reasonable expenses and attorney's fees of the defense if he fails to make good his complaint and to entitle the corporation to indemnity before the case can be prosecuted" (pp. 544–45).

The Court held, 6–3, that the statute should be applied. It rejected a contention that the statute conflicted with Fed. Rule 23 (now 23.1) and stated (pp. 555–56):

"Even if we were to agree that the New Jersey statute is procedural, it would not determine that it is not applicable. Rules which lawyers call procedural do not always exhaust their effect by regulating procedure. But this statute is not merely a regulation of procedure. With it or without it the main action takes the same course. However, it creates a new liability where none existed before, for it makes a stockholder who institutes a derivative action liable for the expense to which he puts the corporation and other defendants, if he does not make good his claims. Such liability is not usual and it goes beyond payment of what we know as 'costs.' If all the Act did was to create this liability, it would clearly be substantive. But this new liability would be without meaning and value in many cases if it resulted in nothing but a judgment for expenses at or after the end of the case. Therefore, a procedure is prescribed by which the liability is insured by entitling the corporate defendant to a bond of indemnity before the outlay is incurred. We do not think a statute which so conditions the stockholder's action can be disregarded by the federal court as a mere procedural device."

The dissent argued that the statute "merely prescribes the method by which stockholders may enforce [a cause of action] * * *. This New Jersey statute, like statutes governing security for costs * * * need not be applied in this diversity suit in the federal court. Rule 23 of the Federal Rules of Civil Procedure defines that procedure for the federal courts" (p. 557).

In Woods, a Tennessee corporation had brought a diversity action in a Mississippi federal court against a Mississippi resident for a broker's commission allegedly due for the sale of real estate in Mississippi. The defense was based on the argument that since the plaintiff had not qualified to do business in the state, the action had to be dismissed under a state statute providing that any foreign corporation failing to qualify "shall not be permitted to bring or maintain any action or suit in any of the courts of this state." The Court held, 6–3, that the defense should be sustained, stating (p. 538):

"* * * The York case was premised on the theory that a right which local law creates but which it does not supply with a remedy is no right at all for purposes of enforcement in a federal court in a diversity case; that where in such cases one is barred from recovery in the state court, he should likewise be barred in the federal court."

No mention was made in the opinion of Fed. Rule 17(b). Was it relevant? [1]

In Ragan, a diversity action for injuries suffered in a highway accident had been brought in a Kansas federal court. Kansas had a two-year statute of limitations; the action was filed within two years of the accident, but the summons and complaint were not served until after the two-year period had run. The Court held, 8–1, that summary judgment for the defendant should have been granted, despite the provisions of Fed. Rule 3, because of a state statute providing "An action shall be deemed commenced within the meaning of this article, as to each defendant, at the date of the summons which is served on him * * *." In a brief opinion that referred to but did not discuss the apparent conflict with Rule 3, the Court noted the holding of the court below that the Kansas statute was "an integral part" of its statute of limitations and said (pp. 533–34):

"We can draw no distinction [from York] in this case because local law brought the cause of action to an end after, rather than before, suit was started in the federal court. * * * We cannot give it longer life in the federal court than it would have had in the state court without adding something to the cause of action. We may not do that consistently with Erie R. Co. v. Tompkins." [2]

(6) The first sign of a change of direction appeared in Byrd v. Blue Ridge Rural Elec. Cooperative, Inc., 356 U.S. 525 (1958). In a diversity action brought in a South Carolina federal court for injuries resulting from

---

1. See the discussion of the effect of state door-closing rules on federal jurisdiction, Sec. 4, *infra.*

Armco Steel Corp., 446 U.S. 740 (1980), p. 828, *infra.*

2. The problem raised in Ragan was again considered by the Court in Walker v.

alleged negligence, the defendant asserted that it was the plaintiff's employer under South Carolina law, and that the plaintiff's exclusive remedy therefore lay before the state's Industrial Commission under the state's Workmen's Compensation Law. Although the state supreme court had made it clear that such a defense was to be passed on by the judge alone, the United States Supreme Court held that issues of fact relevant to the defense were to be tried to the jury in the federal proceeding.

The Court first addressed itself to the basis for the state supreme court's decision that the issue was one for the judge and noted that no reasons for that result had been given. It continued (pp. 535–38):

" * * * The decisions cited to support the holding [of the state supreme court] * * * are concerned solely with defining the scope and method of judicial review of the Industrial Commission. * * * The conclusion is inescapable that the * * * [state supreme court's] holding is grounded in the practical consideration that the question had theretofore come before the South Carolina courts from the Industrial Commission and the courts had become accustomed to deciding the factual issue of immunity without the aid of juries. We find nothing to suggest that this rule was announced as an integral part of the special relationship created by the statute. Thus the requirement appears to be merely a form and mode of enforcing the immunity, Guaranty Trust Co. v. York, 326 U.S. 99, 108, and not a rule intended to be bound up with the definitions of the rights and obligations of the parties. * * *

" * * * But cases following Erie have evinced a broader policy to the effect that the federal courts should conform as near as may be—in the absence of other considerations—to state rules even of form and mode where the state rules may bear substantially on the question whether the litigation would come out one way in the federal court and another way in the state court if the federal court failed to apply a particular local rule. *E.g.,* Guaranty Trust Co. v. York, *supra;* Bernhardt v. Polygraphic Co., 350 U.S. 198. Concededly the nature of the tribunal which tries issues may be important in the enforcement of the parcel of rights making up a cause of action or defense, and bear significantly upon achievement of uniform enforcement of the right. It may well be that in the instant personal-injury case the outcome would be substantially affected by whether the issue [in question] * * * is decided by a judge or a jury. Therefore, were 'outcome' the only consideration, a strong case might appear for saying that the federal court should follow the state practice.

"But there are affirmative countervailing considerations at work here. The federal system is an independent system for administering justice to litigants who properly invoke its jurisdiction. An essential characteristic of that system is the manner in which, in civil common-law actions, it distributes trial functions between judge and jury and, under the influence—if not the command—of the Seventh Amendment, assigns the decisions of disputed questions of fact to the jury. Jacob v. New York, 315 U.S. 752. The policy of uniform enforcement of state-created rights and obligations, see, *e.g.,* Guaranty Trust Co. v. York, *supra,* cannot in every case exact compliance with a state rule—not bound up with rights and obligations—which disrupts the federal system of allocating functions between judge and jury. Herron v. Southern Pacific Co., 283 U.S. 91. Thus the inquiry here is whether the federal policy favoring jury decisions of disputed fact questions should yield to the state rule in the interest of furthering the objective that the litigation should not come out one way in the federal court and another way in the state court.

"We think that in the circumstances of this case the federal court should not follow the state rule. It cannot be gainsaid that there is a strong federal policy against allowing state rules to disrupt the judge-jury relationship in the federal courts. ＊ ＊ ＊"

(7) Note that in Byrd, perhaps for the first time since Erie, the Court looked to the state rule in an effort to determine whether the policy behind that rule would be frustrated if the federal court were not to follow it. At the same time, the Court recognized that even a state rule relating only to "form and mode"—if it might bear substantially on the outcome—ought not to be disregarded in the absence of "affirmative countervailing considerations". Why not? Because there is no reason to adopt a rule that encourages forum shopping but serves no other purpose?

How successful was the Court in analyzing the state's reasons for assigning the issue in question to a judge rather than a jury? Should the state supreme court's failure to give any reasons mean that it has failed to satisfy its "burden of proof" with respect to the policies underlying the rule? [3] Or should the federal courts conduct a more sympathetic search for those policies? In Byrd itself, the state rule might be supported by arguments (a) that only a judge would be able to view the company's defense as an aspect of a comprehensive statutory scheme of liability without fault for industrial accidents, and (b) that a jury could not articulate the basis for its findings in a way that would help to assure predictability and consistency of decisions for litigants faced with many lawsuits raising the same issue. If such considerations might have led to the state's assignment of the issue to the judge, wouldn't the state's policy be undermined if it were disregarded in the federal courts?

With respect to the "affirmative countervailing considerations" referred to by the Supreme Court, would it not have been simpler, and correct, to rest the result squarely on the Seventh Amendment? [4] The only hint on this point in the Byrd opinion is at p. 537 n. 10, where the Court states that it leaves open the question whether "the Seventh Amendment embraces the factual issue of statutory immunity when asserted, as here, as an affirmative defense in a common-law negligence action".

If the Seventh Amendment does not apply to the trial of a particular issue, is there nevertheless a federal policy favoring trial by jury on that issue? If so, what is the source of the policy?

(8) The Court's reliance on Herron v. Southern Pac. Co., 283 U.S. 91 (1931), in its opinion in Byrd was surprising to many observers. In that case, a pre-Erie diversity action, the Court held that neither the Conformity Act nor the Rules of Decision Act precluded a directed verdict against the plaintiff on the issue of contributory negligence, despite a state constitu-

---

3. In Magenau v. Aetna Freight Lines, Inc., 360 U.S. 273 (1959), a case similar to Byrd in many respects, the majority held that certain issues should be tried to the jury because "We have been given no reason for the distinction in the Pennsylvania practice of trying such disputed factual issues to the court" (p. 278).

4. The Seventh Amendment plainly applies in diversity cases in the federal courts. See Simler v. Conner, 372 U.S. 221 (1963); Scott v. Neely, 140 U.S. 106 (1891). (In Simler, decided after Byrd, the Court held that a jury trial was required without any discussion of the policy behind the contrary state rule.)

tional provision that the defense of contributory negligence "shall, in all cases whatsoever, be a question of fact and shall, at all times, be left to the jury". "[S]tate laws," the Court said (p. 94), "cannot alter the essential character or function of a federal court."

If Herron were to arise today for the first time, how would you argue for application of the state constitutional provision? Do you think you should win? [5]

(9) For discussions of the Erie doctrine during the period covered by this Note, see, e.g., Smith, *Blue Ridge and Beyond: A Byrd's–Eye View of Federalism in Diversity Litigation*, 36 Tul.L.Rev. 443 (1962); Vestal, *Erie R.R. v. Tompkins: A Projection*, 48 Iowa L.Rev. 248 (1963); Note, *Of Lawyers and Laymen: A Study of Federalism, the Judicial Process, and Erie*, 71 Yale L.J. 344 (1961).

HANNA v. PLUMER

380 U.S. 460, 85 S.Ct. 1136, 14 L.Ed.2d 8 (1965).
Certiorari to the United States Court of Appeals for the First Circuit.

MR. CHIEF JUSTICE WARREN delivered the opinion of the Court.

The question to be decided is whether, in a civil action where the jurisdiction of the United States district court is based upon diversity of citizenship between the parties, service of process shall be made in the manner prescribed by state law or that set forth in Rule 4(d)(1) of the Federal Rules of Civil Procedure.

On February 6, 1963, petitioner, a citizen of Ohio, filed her complaint in the District Court for the District of Massachusetts, claiming damages in excess of $10,000 for personal injuries resulting from an automobile accident in South Carolina, allegedly caused by the negligence of one Louise Plumer Osgood, a Massachusetts citizen deceased at the time of the filing of the complaint. Respondent, Mrs. Osgood's executor and also a Massachusetts citizen, was named as defendant. On February 8, service was made by leaving copies of the summons and the complaint with respondent's wife at his residence, concededly in compliance with Rule 4(d)(1), which provides:

"The summons and complaint shall be served together. The plaintiff shall furnish the person making service with such copies as are necessary. Service shall be made as follows:

"(1) Upon an individual other than an infant or an incompetent person, by delivering a copy of the summons and of the complaint to him

---

5. Is the question in Herron any different from the question whether there should be an independent federal standard generally applicable to rulings on the sufficiency of the evidence in diversity cases? On the latter question, see 9 Wright & Miller, Federal Practice and Procedure § 2525 (1971 and 1986 Supp.), and authorities there cited. See also Annot., 10 A.L.R. Fed. 451 (1972). In Wratchford v. S.J. Groves & Sons Co., 405 F.2d 1061, 1065–66 (4th Cir.1969), the court stated: "As in Byrd, the rule as to the sufficiency of the evidence is not bound up with the primary rights and obligations of the parties. * * * For such reasons and in keeping with Byrd's concern for the perpetuation of an independent federal judicial system through maintenance of those rules fundamental to it, we adhere to our earlier holdings that the federal standard was the appropriate one for application here." But see, e.g., Illinois State Trust Co. v. Terminal R.R. Ass'n, 440 F.2d 497 (7th Cir.1971). Compare Dice v. Akron, C. & Y.R.R., 342 U.S. 359 (1952), p. 628, *supra*.

personally or by leaving copies thereof at his dwelling house or usual place of abode with some person of suitable age and discretion then residing therein * * *."

Respondent filed his answer on February 26, alleging, inter alia, that the action could not be maintained because it had been brought "contrary to and in violation of the provisions of Massachusetts General Laws (Ter.Ed.) Chapter 197, Section 9." That section provides:

"Except as provided in this chapter, an executor or administrator shall not be held to answer to an action by a creditor of the deceased which is not commenced within one year from the time of his giving bond for the performance of his trust, or to such an action which is commenced within said year unless before the expiration thereof the writ in such action has been served by delivery in hand upon such executor or administrator or service thereof accepted by him or a notice stating the name of the estate, the name and address of the creditor, the amount of the claim and the court in which the action has been brought has been filed in the proper registry of probate. * * *." Mass.Gen.Laws Ann., c. 197, § 9 (1958).

On October 17, 1963, the District Court granted respondent's motion for summary judgment, citing Ragan v. Merchants Transfer & Warehouse Co., 337 U.S. 530, and Guaranty Trust Co. of New York v. York, 326 U.S. 99, in support of its conclusion that the adequacy of the service was to be measured by § 9, with which, the court held, petitioner had not complied. On appeal, petitioner admitted noncompliance with § 9, but argued that Rule 4(d)(1) defines the method by which service of process is to be effected in diversity actions. The Court of Appeals for the First Circuit, finding that "[r]elatively recent amendments [to § 9] evince a clear legislative purpose to require personal notification within the year," [1] concluded that the conflict of state and federal rules was over "a substantive rather than a procedural matter," and unanimously affirmed. 331 F.2d 157. * * *

We conclude that the adoption of Rule 4(d)(1), designed to control service of process in diversity actions, neither exceeded the congressional mandate embodied in the Rules Enabling Act nor transgressed constitutional bounds, and that the Rule is therefore the standard against which the District Court should have measured the adequacy of the service. Accordingly, we reverse the decision of the Court of Appeals.

* * * Under the cases construing the scope of the Enabling Act, Rule 4(d)(1) clearly passes muster. Prescribing the manner in which a defendant

---

1. Section 9 is in part a statute of limitations, providing that an executor need not "answer to an action * * * which is not commenced within one year from the time of his giving bond * * *." This part of the statute, the purpose of which is to speed the settlement of estates, * * * is not involved in this case, since the action clearly was timely commenced. * * *

Section 9 also provides for the manner of service. *Generally,* service of process must be made by "delivery in hand," although there are two alternatives: acceptance of service by the executor, or filing of a notice of claim, the components of which are set out in the statute, in the appropriate probate court. The purpose of this part of the statute, which *is* involved here, is, as the court below noted, to insure that executors will receive actual notice of claims. Parker v. Rich, 297 Mass. 111, 113–114, 8 N.E.2d 345, 347 (1937). Actual notice is of course also the goal of Rule 4(d)(1); however, the Federal Rule reflects a determination that this goal can be achieved by a method less cumbersome than that prescribed in § 9. In this case the goal seems to have been achieved; although the affidavit filed by respondent in the District Court asserts that he had not been served in hand nor had he accepted service, it does not allege lack of actual notice.

is to be notified that a suit has been instituted against him, it relates to the "practice and procedure of the district courts." * * *

"The test must be whether a rule really regulates procedure,—the judicial process for enforcing rights and duties recognized by substantive law and for justly administering remedy and redress for disregard or infraction of them." Sibbach v. Wilson & Co., 312 U.S. 1, 14.

In Mississippi Pub. Corp. v. Murphree, 326 U.S. 438, this Court upheld Rule 4(f), which permits service of a summons anywhere within the State (and not merely the district) in which a district court sits:

"We think that Rule 4(f) is in harmony with the Enabling Act * * *. Undoubtedly most alterations of the rules of practice and procedure may and often do affect the rights of litigants. Congress' prohibition of any alteration of substantive rights of litigants was obviously not addressed to such incidental effects as necessarily attend the adoption of the prescribed new rules of procedure upon the rights of litigants who, agreeably to rules of practice and procedure, have been brought before a court authorized to determine their rights. Sibbach v. Wilson & Co., 312 U.S. 1, 11–14. The fact that the application of Rule 4(f) will operate to subject petitioner's rights to adjudication by the district court for northern Mississippi will undoubtedly affect those rights. But it does not operate to abridge, enlarge or modify the rules of decision by which that court will adjudicate its rights." Id., at 445–446.

Thus were there no conflicting state procedure, Rule 4(d)(1) would clearly control. * * * However, respondent, focusing on the contrary Massachusetts rule, calls to the Court's attention another line of cases, a line which—like the Federal Rules—had its birth in 1938. Erie R. Co. v. Tompkins, 304 U.S. 64, * * * held that federal courts sitting in diversity cases, when deciding questions of "substantive" law, are bound by state court decisions as well as state statutes. The broad command of Erie was therefore identical to that of the Enabling Act: federal courts are to apply state substantive law and federal procedural law. However, as subsequent cases sharpened the distinction between substance and procedure, the line of cases following Erie diverged markedly from the line construing the Enabling Act. Guaranty Trust Co. of New York v. York, 326 U.S. 99, made it clear that Erie-type problems were not to be solved by reference to any traditional or common-sense substance-procedure distinction:

"And so the question is not whether a statute of limitations is deemed a matter of 'procedure' in some sense. The question is * * * does it significantly affect the result of a litigation for a federal court to disregard a law of a State that would be controlling in an action upon the same claim by the same parties in a State court?" 326 U.S., at 109.

Respondent, by placing primary reliance on York and Ragan, suggests that the Erie doctrine acts as a check on the Federal Rules of Civil Procedure, that despite the clear command of Rule 4(d)(1), Erie and its progeny demand the application of the Massachusetts rule. Reduced to essentials, the argument is: (1) Erie, as refined in York, demands that federal courts apply state law whenever application of federal law in its stead will alter the outcome of the case. (2) In this case, a determination that the Massachusetts service requirements obtain will result in immediate victory for respondent. If, on the other hand, it should be held that Rule 4(d)(1) is applicable, the litigation will continue, with possible victory for petitioner. (3) Therefore, Erie demands application of the Massachusetts rule. The syllogism possesses an appealing simplicity, but is for several reasons invalid.

In the first place, it is doubtful that, even if there were no Federal Rule making it clear that in-hand service is not required in diversity actions, the Erie rule would have obligated the District Court to follow the Massachusetts procedure. "Outcome-determination" analysis was never intended to serve as a talisman. Byrd v. Blue Ridge Rural Elec. Cooperative, 356 U.S. 525, 537. Indeed, the message of York itself is that choices between state and federal law are to be made not by application of any automatic, "litmus paper" criterion, but rather by reference to the policies underlying the Erie rule. * * *

The Erie rule is rooted in part in a realization that it would be unfair for the character or result of a litigation materially to differ because the suit had been brought in a federal court. * * *

The decision was also in part a reaction to the practice of "forum-shopping" which had grown up in response to the rule of Swift v. Tyson. 304 U.S., at 73–74. That the York test was an attempt to effectuate these policies is demonstrated by the fact that the opinion framed the inquiry in terms of "substantial" variations between state and federal litigation. 326 U.S., at 109. Not only are nonsubstantial, or trivial, variations not likely to raise the sort of equal protection problems which troubled the Court in Erie; they are also unlikely to influence the choice of a forum. The "outcome-determination" test therefore cannot be read without reference to the twin aims of the Erie rule: discouragement of forum-shopping and avoidance of inequitable administration of the laws.[9]

The difference between the conclusion that the Massachusetts rule is applicable, and the conclusion that it is not, is of course at this point "outcome-determinative" in the sense that if we hold the state rule to apply, respondent prevails, whereas if we hold that Rule 4(d)(1) governs, the litigation will continue. But in this sense *every* procedural variation is "outcome-determinative." For example, having brought suit in a federal court, a plaintiff cannot then insist on the right to file subsequent pleadings in accord with the time limits applicable in state courts, even though enforcement of the federal timetable will, if he continues to insist that he must meet only the state time limit, result in determination of the controversy against him. So it is here. Though choice of the federal or

---

9. The Court of Appeals seemed to frame the inquiry in terms of how "important" § 9 is to the State. In support of its suggestion that § 9 serves some interest the State regards as vital to its citizens, the court noted that something like § 9 has been on the books in Massachusetts a long time, that § 9 has been amended a number of times and that § 9 is designed to make sure that executors receive actual notice. The apparent lack of relation among these three observations is not surprising, because it is not clear to what sort of question the Court of Appeals was addressing itself. One cannot meaningfully ask how important something is without first asking "important for what purpose?" Erie and its progeny make clear that when a federal court sitting in a diversity case is faced with a question of whether or not to apply state law, the importance of a state rule is indeed relevant, but only in the context of asking whether application of the rule would make so important a difference to the character or result of the litigation that failure to enforce it would unfairly discriminate against citizens of the forum State, or whether application of the rule would have so important an effect upon the fortunes of one or both of the litigants that failure to enforce it would be likely to cause a plaintiff to choose the federal court.

state rule will at this point have a marked effect upon the outcome of the litigation, the difference between the two rules would be of scant, if any, relevance to the choice of a forum. Petitioner, in choosing her forum, was not presented with a situation where application of the state rule would wholly bar recovery; rather, adherence to the state rule would have resulted only in altering the way in which process was served. Moreover, it is difficult to argue that permitting service of defendant's wife to take the place of in-hand service of defendant himself alters the mode of enforcement of state-created rights in a fashion sufficiently "substantial" to raise the sort of equal protection problems to which the Erie opinion alluded.

There is, however, a more fundamental flaw in respondent's syllogism: the incorrect assumption that the rule of Erie R. Co. v. Tompkins constitutes the appropriate test of the validity and therefore the applicability of a Federal Rule of Civil Procedure. The Erie rule has never been invoked to void a Federal Rule. It is true that there have been cases where this Court has held applicable a state rule in the face of an argument that the situation was governed by one of the Federal Rules. But the holding of each such case was not that Erie commanded displacement of a Federal Rule by an inconsistent state rule, but rather that the scope of the Federal Rule was not as broad as the losing party urged, and therefore, there being no Federal Rule which covered the point in dispute, Erie commanded the enforcement of state law.

"Respondent contends in the first place that the charge was correct because of the fact that Rule 8(c) of the Rules of Civil Procedure makes contributory negligence an affirmative defense. We do not agree. Rule 8(c) covers only the manner of pleading. The question of the burden of establishing contributory negligence is a question of local law which federal courts in diversity of citizenship cases * * * must apply." Palmer v. Hoffman, 318 U.S. 109, 117.[12]

(Here, of course, the clash is unavoidable; Rule 4(d)(1) says—implicitly, but with unmistakable clarity—that in-hand service is not required in federal courts.) At the same time, in cases adjudicating the validity of Federal Rules, we have not applied the York rule or other refinements of Erie, but have to this day continued to decide questions concerning the scope of the Enabling Act and the constitutionality of specific Federal Rules in light of the distinction set forth in Sibbach. *E.g.,* Schlagenhauf v. Holder, 379 U.S. 104.

Nor has the development of two separate lines of cases been inadvertent. The line between "substance" and "procedure" shifts as the legal context changes. * * * When a situation is covered by one of the Federal Rules, the question facing the court is a far cry from the typical, relatively unguided Erie choice: the court has been instructed to apply the Federal Rule, and can refuse to do so only if the Advisory Committee, this Court, and Congress erred in their prima facie judgment that the Rule in question transgresses neither the terms of the Enabling Act nor constitutional restrictions.

We are reminded by the Erie opinion that neither Congress nor the federal courts can, under the guise of formulating rules of decision for

---

12. To the same effect, see Ragan v. Merchants Transfer & Warehouse Co., *supra;* Cohen v. Beneficial Indus. Loan Corp., 337 U.S. at 556 (Douglas, J., dissenting) * * *.

federal courts, fashion rules which are not supported by a grant of federal authority contained in Article I or some other section of the Constitution; in such areas state law must govern because there can be no other law. But the opinion in Erie, which involved no Federal Rule and dealt with a question which was "substantive" in every traditional sense (whether the railroad owed a duty of care to Tompkins as a trespasser or a licensee), surely neither said nor implied that measures like Rule 4(d)(1) are unconstitutional. For the constitutional provision for a federal court system (augmented by the Necessary and Proper Clause) carries with it congressional power to make rules governing the practice and pleading in those courts, which in turn includes a power to regulate matters which, though falling within the uncertain area between substance and procedure, are rationally capable of classification as either. Cf. M'Culloch v. State of Maryland, 4 Wheat. 316, 421. Neither York nor the cases following it ever suggested that the rule there laid down for coping with situations where no Federal Rule applies is coextensive with the limitation on Congress to which Erie had adverted. Although this Court has never before been confronted with a case where the applicable Federal Rule is in direct collision with the law of the relevant State,[15] courts of appeals faced with such clashes have rightly discerned the implications of our decisions.

* * *

Erie and its offspring cast no doubt on the long-recognized power of Congress to prescribe housekeeping rules for federal courts even though some of those rules will inevitably differ from comparable state rules. *Cf.* Herron v. Southern Pacific Co., 283 U.S. 91. * * * Thus, though a court, in measuring a Federal Rule against the standards contained in the Enabling Act and the Constitution, need not wholly blind itself to the degree to which the Rule makes the character and result of the federal litigation stray from the course it would follow in state courts, Sibbach v. Wilson & Co., *supra,* 312 U.S. at 13–14, it cannot be forgotten that the Erie rule, and the guidelines suggested in York, were created to serve another purpose altogether. To hold that a Federal Rule of Civil Procedure must cease to function whenever it alters the mode of enforcing state-created rights would be to disembowel either the Constitution's grant of power over federal procedure or Congress' attempt to exercise that power in the Enabling Act. Rule 4(d)(1) is valid and controls the instant case.

Reversed.

MR. JUSTICE BLACK concurs in the result.

MR. JUSTICE HARLAN, concurring.

It is unquestionably true that up to now Erie and the cases following it have not succeeded in articulating a workable doctrine governing choice of law in diversity actions. I respect the Court's effort to clarify the situation in today's opinion. However, in doing so I think it has misconceived the constitutional premises of Erie and has failed to deal adequately with those past decisions upon which the courts below relied.

---

15. In Sibbach v. Wilson & Co., *supra,* the law of the forum State (Illinois) forbade the sort of order authorized by Rule 35. However, Sibbach was decided before Klaxon Co. v. Stentor Electric Mfg. Co., *supra,* and the Sibbach opinion makes clear that the Court was proceeding on the assumption that if the law of any State was relevant, it was the law of the State where the tort occurred (Indiana), which, like Rule 35, made provision for such orders. 312 U.S., at 6–7, 10–11.

Erie was something more than an opinion which worried about "forum-shopping and avoidance of inequitable administration of the laws," although to be sure these were important elements of the decision. I have always regarded that decision as one of the modern cornerstones of our federalism, expressing policies that profoundly touch the allocation of judicial power between the state and federal systems. Erie recognized that there should not be two conflicting systems of law controlling the primary activity of citizens, for such alternative governing authority must necessarily give rise to a debilitating uncertainty in the planning of everyday affairs.[1] And it recognized that the scheme of our Constitution envisions an allocation of law-making functions between state and federal legislative processes which is undercut if the federal judiciary can make substantive law affecting state affairs beyond the bounds of congressional legislative powers in this regard. Thus, in diversity cases Erie commands that it be the state law governing primary private activity which prevails.

The shorthand formulations which have appeared in some past decisions are prone to carry untoward results that frequently arise from oversimplification. The Court is quite right in stating that the "outcome-determinative" test of Guaranty Trust Co. of New York v. York, 326 U.S. 99, if taken literally, proves too much, for any rule, no matter how clearly "procedural," can affect the outcome of litigation if it is not obeyed. In turning from the "outcome" test of York back to the unadorned forum-shopping rationale of Erie, however, the Court falls prey to like oversimplification, for a simple forum-shopping rule also proves too much; litigants often choose a federal forum merely to obtain what they consider the advantages of the Federal Rules of Civil Procedure or to try their cases before a supposedly more favorable judge. To my mind the proper line of approach in determining whether to apply a state or a federal rule, whether "substantive" or "procedural," is to stay close to basic principles by inquiring if the choice of rule would substantially affect those primary decisions respecting human conduct which our constitutional system leaves to state regulation.[2] If so, Erie and the Constitution require that the state rule prevail, even in the face of a conflicting federal rule.

The Court weakens, if indeed it does not submerge, this basic principle by finding, in effect, a grant of substantive legislative power in the constitutional provision for a federal court system (compare Swift v. Tyson, 16 Pet. 1), and through it, setting up the Federal Rules as a body of law inviolate. * * * So long as a reasonable man could characterize any duly adopted federal rule as "procedural," the Court, unless I misapprehend what is said, would have it apply no matter how seriously it frustrated a State's substantive regulation of the primary conduct and affairs of its citizens. Since the members of the Advisory Committee, the Judicial Conference, and this Court who formulated the Federal Rules are presumably reasonable men, it follows that the integrity of the Federal Rules is absolute. Whereas the unadulterated outcome and forum-shopping tests may err too far toward honoring state rules, I submit that the Court's

---

1. Since the rules involved in the present case are parellel rather than conflicting, this first rationale does not come into play here.

2. See Hart and Wechsler, The Federal Courts and the Federal System 678. Byrd v. Blue Ridge Rural Elec. Coop., Inc., 356

U.S. 525, 536–540, indicated that state procedures would apply if the State had manifested a particularly strong interest in their employment. Compare Dice v. Akron, C. & Y.R. Co., 342 U.S. 359. However, this approach may not be of constitutional proportions.

"arguably procedural, *ergo* constitutional" test moves too fast and far in the other direction.

The courts below relied upon this Court's decisions in Ragan v. Merchants Transfer & Warehouse Co., 337 U.S. 530, and Cohen v. Beneficial Indus. Loan Corp., 337 U.S. 541. Those cases deserve more attention than this Court has given them, particularly Ragan which, if still good law, would in my opinion call for affirmance of the result reached by the Court of Appeals. Further, a discussion of these two cases will serve to illuminate the "diversity" thesis I am advocating.

* * * I think that the [Ragan] decision was wrong. At most, application of the Federal Rule would have meant that potential Kansas tort defendants would have to defer for a few days the satisfaction of knowing that they had not been sued within the limitations period. The choice of the Federal Rule would have had no effect on the primary stages of private activity from which torts arise, and only the most minimal effect on behavior following the commission of the tort. In such circumstances the interest of the federal system in proceeding under its own rules should have prevailed.

* * * The proper view of Cohen is in my opinion, that the statute was meant to inhibit small stockholders from instituting "strike suits," and thus it was designed and could be expected to have a substantial impact on private primary activity. Anyone who was at the trial bar during the period when Cohen arose can appreciate the strong state policy reflected in the statute. I think it wholly legitimate to view Federal Rule 23 as not purporting to deal with the problem. But even had the Federal Rules purported to do so, and in so doing provided a substantially less effective deterrent to strike suits, I think the state rule should still have prevailed. That is where I believe the Court's view differs from mine; for the Court attributes such overriding force to the Federal Rules that it is hard to think of a case where a conflicting state rule would be allowed to operate, even though the state rule reflected policy considerations which, under Erie, would lie within the realm of state legislative authority.

It remains to apply what has been said to the present case. The Massachusetts rule provides that an executor need not answer suits unless in-hand service was made upon him or notice of the action was filed in the proper registry of probate within one year of his giving bond. The evident intent of this statute is to permit an executor to distribute the estate which he is administering without fear that further liabilities may be outstanding for which he could be held personally liable. If the Federal District Court in Massachusetts applies Rule 4(d)(1) of the Federal Rules of Civil Procedure instead of the Massachusetts service rule, what effect would that have on the speed and assurance with which estates are distributed? As I see it, the effect would not be substantial. It would mean simply that an executor would have to check at his own house or the federal courthouse as well as the registry of probate before he could distribute the estate with impunity. As this does not seem enough to give rise to any real impingement on the vitality of the state policy which the Massachusetts rule is intended to serve, I concur in the judgment of the Court.

———

NOTE ON "FORUM SHOPPING" AND ON THE FEDERAL RULES

(1) The passage in the First Edition of this book that Justice Harlan was apparently referring to in his concurrence read as follows:

"Is it too late to return to a test which would seek to distinguish between (a) those rules of law which characteristically and reasonably affect people's conduct at the stage of primary private activity and should therefore be classified as substantive or quasi-substantive, and (b) those rules which are not of significant importance at the primary stage and should therefore be regarded as procedural or quasi-procedural?"[1]

If such a distinction were to be adopted, how would you classify a rule of state law allowing rescission or reformation of a contract for a mutual mistake of fact? Shifting the burden of proof with respect to the issue of contributory negligence? Allowing the recovery of reliance damages for breach of a contract within the statute of frauds? Do any such rules characteristically affect people's conduct at the stage of primary private activity? If not, should they be regarded as "quasi-procedural"—as rules that need not be followed in federal diversity actions?

In view of the importance of Erie as a statement about the allocation of law-making power between states and nation, is it perhaps a mistake to ask simply whether a particular state rule in fact affects people's conduct at the planning stage? Is not the more critical question whether that state rule embodies a significant state policy with respect to primary conduct and its effects?

(2) The Court in Hanna suggests that when the matter is not governed by a federal statute or Federal Rule of Civil Procedure, the question is whether failure to follow the state rule would make such an important difference as to "discriminate against citizens of the forum State" or as to lead the "plaintiff to choose the federal court." What if the discrimination is against a *non-citizen* of the forum state? If the failure to follow the state rule leads the *defendant* to choose the federal court?

In any event, doesn't the Court's emphasis on forum-shopping make too short shrift of the Byrd analysis of the impact of state and federal policies? Can't there be affirmative considerations that might justify a uniform federal rule even in the absence of a statute or a Federal Rule of Civil Procedure? Consider, for example, the standard for determining the sufficiency of the evidence to take a case to the jury, p. 818, note 5, *supra*.

Sharply contrasting views on these issues have been expressed by Ely, *The Irrepressible Myth of Erie,* 87 Harv.L.Rev. 693 (1974), and Redish &

---

1. In discussing this question, the text of the first edition referred to the case of Levinson v. Deupree, 345 U.S. 648 (1953), a libel in admiralty to enforce a state-created right of action for wrongful death. The Court held in that case that an amendment to the complaint alleging the appointment of the plaintiff as administrator was authorized under the Admiralty Rules, although the state courts would have held the amendment barred by the statute of limitations. Justice Frankfurter, speaking for the Court, said (p. 652): "Whether, if this were a diversity case, we would consider that we are here dealing with 'forms and modes' or with matters more seriously affecting the enforcement of the right, it is clear that we are not dealing with an integral part of the right created by [the state] * * *." What do you think of the implication that there should be one analysis for diversity cases and another for the other situations in which federal courts enforce rights created by state law? Does this implication survive Byrd and Hanna?

Phillips, *Erie and The Rules of Decision Act: In Search of the Appropriate Dilemma,* 91 Harv.L.Rev. 356 (1977). Arguing that the Rules of Decision Act was designed to mark out enclaves of exclusive state concern, Ely concludes that the Act requires state law to be followed whenever disregard of that law would be "likely to generate an outcome different from that which would result were the case litigated in the state court system and the state rules followed" (87 Harv.L.Rev. at 714). "[I]n light of [the Act's] fairness rationale—or, for that matter in light of a desire either to minimize forum shopping or to avoid 'uncertainty in the planning of everyday affairs'—it becomes clear that there is no place in the analysis for the sort of balancing of federal and state interests contemplated by the Byrd opinion" (p. 717 n. 130).

Redish and Phillips disagree. They see Erie and the Rules of Decision Act as warranting consideration not only of the interests of litigants in uniformity of outcome but of the state's interest in enforcement of its substantive policies and of the federal interest in the fair and efficient administration of justice. Thus they urge a "refined balancing test" that considers, *inter alia,* the federal interest in "doing justice" and in the avoidance of unnecessary cost or inconvenience (91 Harv.L.Rev. at 384–94).[2]

(3) Justice Harlan criticizes the majority for clothing the Federal Rules of Civil Procedure with absolute immunity by adopting an "arguably procedural, ergo constitutional" test. That test is surely appropriate for measuring the constitutionality of a rule of procedure laid down for the federal courts by Congress. And Sibbach seems to require that essentially the same test be applied in determining the validity under the Enabling Act of a rule promulgated by the Supreme Court. Did Hanna continue to apply this test? If so, the fault (if fault is to be found) may well lie with the Sibbach opinion. Was that opinion sufficiently sensitive to state interests, and to the language and purpose of the Enabling Act?[3]

2. For other, contrasting views of the Rules of Decision Act, see Westen & Lehman, *Is There Life for Erie After the Death of Diversity?,* 78 Mich.L.Rev. 311 (1980) (arguing that the Rules of Decision Act itself imposes no limitation, in diversity cases or in other cases, on the authority of federal courts to develop federal common law); Note, 85 Yale L.J. 678 (1976) (arguing that the Rules of Decision Act refers to state substantive *and* procedural law and that the Constitution allows federal replacement of state law in diversity cases only to the extent that state law is not an element of the parties' legal rights).

3. Ely, Paragraph (2), *supra,* argues that the Court in Sibbach failed to give adequate scope to the second sentence of the Enabling Act. That sentence, in his view, does not require evisceration of the Federal Rules of Civil Procedure; it does require, however, that they yield in the face of a state rule that does not merely represent a procedural disagreement but embodies a substantive policy. Such a policy, he argues, may be found whenever the purpose of a rule, in whole or in part, relates to matters other than the fairness or efficiency of the litigation process. See 87 Harv.L.Rev. at 718–27. (For discussion of the difficulties of applying these criteria, and of the means of avoiding conflicts between federal rules and state policies, see Chayes, *The Bead Game,* 87 Harv.L.Rev. 741 (1974). See also Ely's reply, *The Necklace,* 87 Harv.L.Rev. 753 (1974).)

Professor Burbank, in *The Rules Enabling Act of 1934,* 130 U.Pa.L.Rev. 1015 (1982), also objects to the interpretation of the Enabling Act in Sibbach and Hanna, but on quite different grounds. On the basis of his study of the pre–1934 history of the Act, he concludes that the first two sentences "were intended to allocate power between the Supreme Court as rulemaker and Congress and thus to circumscribe the delegation of legislative power, that they were thought to be equally relevant in all actions brought in a federal court, and that the protection of state law was deemed a probable effect, rather than the primary purpose, of the allocation scheme established by the Act" (pp. 1025–26). The second sentence of the Act, he suggests, has no independent meaning (pp. 1107–08) but does serve to underscore the test for the

The majority in Hanna recognized, however, that federal rules and federal statutes must be interpreted by the courts applying them, and that the process of interpretation can and should reflect an awareness of legitimate state interests. Indeed, the existence of that awareness may account for the fact that the Court did not squarely confront the issue posed in Hanna until 27 years after Erie and 25 years after Sibbach.[4]

(4) The Supreme Court has continued since Hanna to interpret the federal rules to avoid conflict with important state regulatory policies.[5] Thus in Walker v. Armco Steel Corp., 446 U.S. 740 (1980), the Court unanimously decided that Ragan was still good law, and that state law rather than Rule 3 determined when a diversity action was commenced for the purpose of tolling the statute of limitations. The Court noted at the outset (p. 749) that the doctrine of stare decisis "weighs heavily" in favor of adherence to Ragan; it then observed that significant state policy interests would be frustrated if Rule 3 operated to supersede the state rule requiring actual service on the defendant in order to stop the running of the statute. The Court did not reach the question of the validity of Rule 3 in this context because the lack of any reference in the rule to the tolling of state limitations statutes meant that there was no "direct conflict between the Federal Rule and the state law" (pp. 750, 752).[6]

validity of a rule: "[Matters classified as substantive] involve at their core, either potential effects on 'rights' recognized by the 'substantive law' that are *predictable and identifiable*, or the creation of remedial rights that *predictably and identifiably* affect personal liberty or the use and enjoyment of property" (p. 1128).

Even if this standard is supported by the pre–1934 history, is it a workable one in the administration of the Act? As Burbank himself concedes in his concluding remarks, the drafters of the pre–1934 proposals "failed * * * to articulate fully and consistently the standards envisioned. Few if any of those individuals were imbued with the Realists' counsel to think functionally. Moreover, the difficulty and essentially reactive nature of the enterprise shaped its content" (p. 1188).

4. In Bangor Punta Operations, Inc. v. Bangor & A.R.R. Co., 417 U.S. 703, 708 n. 4 (1974), the Court recognized that there was a question of the validity, in a diversity case in which state law differed, of the "contemporaneous ownership" requirement of Federal Rule 23.1 in shareholder derivative actions. See Harbrecht, *The Contemporaneous Ownership Rule in Shareholders' Derivative Suits*, 25 U.C. L.A.L.Rev. 1041 (1978); 7C Wright & Miller, Federal Practice and Procedure § 1829 (1986).

If Rule 23.1 does not survive a challenge under the Enabling Act in a diversity case, in the face of conflicting state law, can it survive in a federal question case as a "codification" of a federal decisional rule? (See Hawes v. Oakland, 104 U.S. 450

(1881).) Is it relevant that the rule of Hawes v. Oakland had been incorporated in the former equity rules? (See Equity Rule 27, 226 U.S. 656 (1912).) Is the question a trivial one because the Court could fall back on the Hawes precedent if the rule were invalid? See Burbank, note 3, *supra*, at 1149–53.

5. But *cf.* Burlington N.R.R. v. Woods, 107 S.Ct. 967 (1987). In this federal diversity case, the defendant had appealed from a judgment for the plaintiff; the question was whether the federal appellate court should follow a state rule imposing a fixed penalty on any appellant who obtains a stay of a money judgment pending appeal, if the judgment is affirmed without substantial modification. The Supreme Court held that the state rule should not apply, since it conflicted with the discretion to award damages for frivolous appeals under Rule 38 of the Federal Rules of Appellate Procedure. (The question of the constitutionality of the state rule is raised in Bankers Life & Cas. Co. v. Crenshaw, 483 So.2d 254 (Miss.1985), *probable juris. noted*, 107 S.Ct. 1367 (1987).)

6. The Court also stated, in a footnote: "We do not here address the role of Rule 3 as a tolling provision for a statute of limitations, whether set by federal law or borrowed from state law, if the cause of action is based on federal law (p. 751 n. 11). The question was addressed in West v. Conrail, 107 S.Ct. 1538 (1987); the Court held that "when the underlying cause of action is based on federal law and the absence of an express federal statute of limitations makes it necessary to borrow a limitations

Does the Walker decision cast some doubt on the Hanna result? If the state law at issue in Hanna was essentially a provision for determining when and how the statute of limitations was tolled, should it have prevailed even though it went beyond the requirements of Rule 4(d)(1)? See Burbank, note 3, *supra*, at 1173–76.

(5) To a significant extent, the result of Hanna's permissive standards for measuring the validity of the Federal Rules has been to remit important issues of federalism from the Court as a decider of cases to the Court (and its advisers) as a promulgator of rules, and to Congress in its review of those rules. Doesn't this result increase the significance of the rulemaking process and of the effective allocation of power within that process? (See pp. 759–65, *supra*.)

A case in point is the evolution of the rules relating to privilege in the Federal Rules of Evidence. As proposed by the Advisers and promulgated by the Supreme Court, the rules set out a federally-defined set of privileges for all civil and criminal litigation in the federal courts. In answer to the argument that at least in cases governed by state substantive law these rules might run afoul of Erie and the Enabling Act, the Advisers argued that Hanna gave a large measure of choice to the rulemakers, that state privileges had at most a "tenuous" substantive aspect, that they would have to give way in federal question cases in any event, and that the practical dimensions of the problem were not great. See Revised Draft of Proposed Rules of Evidence, 51 F.R.D. 315, 358–60 (1971). Compare Korn, *Continuing Effect of the State Rules of Evidence in the Federal Courts*, 48 F.R.D. 65, 74–77 (1969).[7]

Congress refused to accept this approach. Moved by concern for privacy interests and by a desire to safeguard substantive state policies, Congress provided in Federal Rule of Evidence 501 that federal "common law" was to control on matters of privilege only with respect to claims or defenses governed by federal substantive law. When the claim or defense was governed by state law, the state law of privilege was to be applied. For the relevant legislative history, see H.R.Rep. No. 93–650, 93d Cong., 1st Sess. (1973); S.Rep. No. 93–1277, 93d Cong., 2d Sess. (1974); Conf.Comm. Rep. No. 93–1597, 93d Cong., 2d Sess. 1974. See also authorities cited at pp. 763–64, *supra*.[8]

----

period from another statute, the action is not barred if it has been 'commenced' in compliance with Rule 3 within the borrowed period" (p. 1541).

7. Ely, Paragraph (2), *supra*, concluded that the proposed privilege rules would have violated the Enabling Act, though he thought they would pass muster under the Constitution if enacted by Congress (87 Harv.L.Rev. at 738–40). He did not indicate any distinction, with respect to either prong of this conclusion, between federal

question and diversity litigation. For a broader attack on the validity of the proposed evidence rules, see Burbank, note 3, *supra*, at 1137–43.

8. How should Rule 501 be applied in a case in which a state claim is pendent to a federal claim, and a question of privilege arises that is relevant to both claims? See, *e.g.*, William T. Thompson Co. v. General Nutrition Corp., Inc., 671 F.2d 100 (3d Cir. 1982) (federal rule favoring admissibility controls).

SECTION 4. THE EFFECT OF STATE LAW (AND OF PRIVATE AGREEMENT) ON THE EXERCISE OF FEDERAL JURISDICTION

RAILWAY CO. v. WHITTON'S ADMINISTRATOR

13 Wall. 270, 20 L.Ed. 571 (U.S.1871).

Writ of Error to the Circuit Court for the Eastern District of Wisconsin.

[Henry Whitton, as administrator of the estate of his wife in Wisconsin, brought suit in a Wisconsin state court to recover damages for the death of his wife which was alleged to have been caused by the carelessness and culpable mismanagement of the defendant railroad. The action was brought under a Wisconsin statute which, after creating a right of action in favor of the decedent's personal representative, subjected it to the proviso that "such action shall be brought for a death caused in this State, and, in some court established by the constitution and laws of the same".

[While the case was pending, Congress passed the Act of March 2, 1867, 14 Stat. 558, which provided that in any suit then pending or later brought in a state court "in which there is a controversy between a citizen of the State in which the suit is brought and a citizen of another State, and the matter in dispute exceeds the sum of $500, exclusive of costs, such citizen of another State, whether he be plaintiff or defendant, if he will make and file in such State court an affidavit stating that he has reason to, and does believe that, from prejudice or local influence, he will not be able to obtain justice in such State court, may, at any time before the final hearing or trial of the suit", remove the case to the federal circuit court.

[The plaintiff removed the case to the federal court under this act and ultimately got judgment for $5,000. The excerpt from the opinion which follows deals with one only of three grounds upon which the jurisdiction of the circuit court was challenged on writ of error.]

Mr. Justice Field, having stated the case, delivered the opinion of the court as follows: * * *

Second; as to the limitation to the State court of the remedy given by the statute of Wisconsin. That statute, after declaring a liability by a person or a corporation to an action for damages when death ensues from a wrongful act, neglect, or default of such person or corporation, contains a proviso "that such action shall be brought for a death caused in this State, and, in some court established by the constitution and the laws of the same." This proviso is considered by the counsel of the defendant as in the nature of a condition, upon a compliance with which the remedy given by the statute can only be enforced.

It is undoubtedly true that the right of action exists only in virtue of the statute, and only in cases where the death was caused within the State. The liability of the party, whether a natural or an artificial person, extends only to cases where, from certain causes, death ensues within the limits of the State. But when death does thus ensue from any of those causes, the relatives of the deceased named in the statute can maintain an action for damages. The liability within the conditions specified extends to all parties through whose wrongful acts, neglect, or default death ensues, and the right of action for damages occasioned thereby is possessed by all persons within the description designated. In all cases, where a general right is thus conferred, it can be enforced in any Federal court within the State having jurisdiction of the parties. It cannot be withdrawn from the cognizance of such Federal court by any provision of State legislation that it shall only be enforced in a State court. The statutes of nearly every State provide for the institution of numerous suits, such as for partition, foreclosure, and the recovery of real property in particular courts and in the counties where the land is situated, yet it never has been pretended that limitations of this character could affect, in any respect, the jurisdiction of the Federal court over such suits where the citizenship of one of the parties was otherwise sufficient. Whenever a general rule as to property or personal rights, or injuries to either, is established by State legislation, its enforcement by a Federal court in a case between proper parties is a matter of course, and the jurisdiction of the court, in such case, is not subject to State limitation. * * *

NOTE ON AGREEMENTS NOT TO RESORT TO THE FEDERAL COURTS

(1) The Supreme Court early and consistently held that an agreement by a foreign corporation, exacted by a state statute, not to remove to a federal court any case brought against it in a state court was ineffectual to oust jurisdiction when the corporation later removed a case in defiance of the agreement. The agreement was condemned independently of the statute on the basis of the common law doctrine that "agreements in advance to oust the courts of the jurisdiction conferred by law are illegal and void". And it was held that the statute gave the agreement no added force, since the state was without power to impose conditions repugnant to the Constitution and laws of the United States. Home Ins. Co. v. Morse, 20 Wall. 445 (U.S.1874). In Barron v. Burnside, 121 U.S. 186 (1887), the Court held that a statute attempting to exact such an agreement was void, so that the penalties it provided for employees of non-complying corporations could not be enforced. Then in Terral v. Burke Const. Co., 257 U.S. 529 (1922), the Court, overruling several earlier decisions, held that a state lacked power to revoke a foreign corporation's license to engage in intrastate business on the grounds that it had violated a state statute by removing a case to federal court:

"The principle established by the more recent decisions of this court is that a state may not, in imposing conditions upon the privilege of a foreign corporation's doing business in the state, exact from it a waiver of the exercise of its constitutional right to resort to the federal courts, or thereafter withdraw the privilege of doing business because of its exercise of such right, whether waived in advance or not. The principle does not depend for its application on the character of the business the corporation does, whether state or interstate, although that has been suggested as a distinction in some cases. It rests on the ground that the Federal Constitution confers upon citizens of one state the right to resort to federal courts in another, that state action, whether legislative or executive, necessarily calculated to curtail the free exercise of the right thus secured is void because the sovereign power of a state in excluding foreign corporations, as in the exercise of all others of its sovereign powers, is subject to the limitations of the supreme fundamental law." (pp. 532–33).

(2) What is the status of a private agreement, not exacted by state law, which precludes suit from being brought in a federal court originally or on removal?[1] The courts of appeals had adopted differing approaches to this question and the matter came before the Supreme Court in The Bremen v. Zapata Off–Shore Co., 407 U.S. 1 (1972). Zapata, an American corporation, had entered a contract with Unterweser, a German corporation, for towage of Zapata's ocean-going drilling rig from Louisiana to the Adriatic Sea. The contract contained a clause providing: "Any dispute arising must be treated before the London Court of Justice." The rig was severely damaged during a storm in the Gulf of Mexico, and Zapata commenced a suit in admiralty in a Florida federal court seeking damages against Unterweser in personam and against Unterweser's deep sea tug, The Bremen, in rem. Unterweser moved to dismiss on the basis of the forum selection clause of the contract or on forum non conveniens grounds, or in the alternative to stay the action pending submission of the dispute to the London Court of Justice. (Unterweser had subsequently commenced an action against Zapata for breach of the towage contract in the London court.) The federal district court, and the Fifth Circuit en banc, refused to dismiss or stay the action and instead enjoined Unterweser from prosecuting its action in the London court. The majority in the Fifth Circuit concluded that a forum selection clause should not be upheld unless the forum so selected would be more convenient than the one in which suit was brought, and in this case it was not.

The Supreme Court reversed, 8–1. The view that "such clauses are prima facie valid and should be enforced unless enforcement is shown by the resisting party to be 'unreasonable' under the circumstances * * * is the correct doctrine to be followed by federal district courts sitting in admiralty" (p. 10). The Court noted that much undesirable uncertainty in international transactions can be eliminated by an advance agreement as to forum and that the party seeking to avoid its impact on such grounds as fraud, undue influence, "overweening bargaining power", or, perhaps, serious inconvenience should have a heavy burden of proof.

A further argument made by Zapata was that enforcement of the forum selection clause would violate public policy because the contract also contained a clause exculpating Unterweser from liability—a clause that an English court would honor but a federal court sitting in admiralty presumably would not. See Bisso v. Inland Waterways Corp., 349 U.S. 85 (1955). This argument was rejected on the ground that, though it might be improper for an American tower contracting with an American towee to avoid the Bisso policy by providing for an exclusive foreign forum to resolve disputes, that policy did not reach "a freely negotiated international commercial transaction between a German and an American corporation for towage of a vessel from the Gulf of Mexico to the Adriatic Sea" (p. 17).

1. The focus of discussion in text is on an agreement that suit may be brought only in the court of another forum (*i.e.,* a court of a state or of another country). Agreements to submit disputes to arbitration, though once disfavored, are now gen-erally enforced under a variety of state and federal statutes. See pp. 809–11, *supra;* Hirschman, *The Second Arbitration Trilogy: The Federalization of Arbitration Law,* 71 Va.L.Rev. 1305, 1309–12 (1985).

Finally, the decision in Home Ins. Co. v. Morse, Paragraph (1), *supra,* was explained by the Court as "one in which a state statutory requirement was viewed as imposing an unconstitutional condition on the exercise of the federal right of removal" (pp. 9–10, n. 10).

Should the rationale of The Bremen extend beyond contracts involving international transactions? In diversity of citizenship cases, what is the bearing of the law of the forum state? [2] Are special considerations applicable to a private agreement allowing suit in a state court but precluding resort to a federal court? For discussion of this last question in the particular context of an action for a labor injunction, see Aaron, *The Strike and the Injunction—Problems of Remand and Removal,* in Proceedings of N.Y.U. 18th Ann.Conf. on Labor 93, 102–03 (1966).

(3) On the special problem of agreements, before and after injury, restricting the plaintiff's choice of venue under the Federal Employers' Liability Act, see Boyd v. Grand Trunk Western R.R., 338 U.S. 263 (1949), and cases cited, particularly the concurring opinion of Chief Judge Learned Hand in Krenger v. Pennsylvania R.R., 174 F.2d 556, 560 (2d Cir.1949).

CHICAGO, R.I. & P.R.R. v. STUDE

346 U.S. 574, 74 S.Ct. 290, 98 L.Ed. 317 (1954).
Certiorari to the United States Court of Appeals for the Eighth Circuit.

MR. JUSTICE MINTON delivered the opinion of the Court.

The petitioner, a Delaware corporation, owns and operates its railroad through Pottawattamie County, Iowa. It was authorized by the Interstate Commerce Commission to improve its line of railway in that county and by the Iowa State Commerce Commission to acquire by condemnation any land necessary for the improvement.

On January 18, 1952, pursuant to the Iowa Code, the petitioner filed with the sheriff of the county its application to condemn certain lands in the county owned by respondent Stude. The sheriff appointed a commission of six resident freeholders to assess damages. Notice was given by the sheriff to the respondent owner and others interested in the land, and an award of damages in the sum of $23,888.60 was allowed to the owner and $1,000 to the tenant. The amount of the assessment was paid by the petitioner to the sheriff and the petitioner took possession of the land. Such appraisal became final unless appealed from.

On March 6, 1952, the petitioner filed with the sheriff of the county a notice of appeal from the commission's award. The Iowa Code provides for appeal as follows:

"472.18 Appeal. Any party interested may, within thirty days after the assessment is made, appeal therefrom to the district court, by giving the adverse party, his agent or attorney, and the sheriff, written notice that such appeal has been taken.

* * *

2. See Stewart Organization, Inc. v. Ricoh Corp., 810 F.2d 1066 (11th Cir.) *cert. granted,* 108 S.Ct. 225 (1987) (en banc decision in a diversity case holding, over five dissents, that a forum-selection clause will be enforced as a matter of federal law even if the clause is unenforceable under the law of the forum state).

"474.21 Appeals—how docketed and tried. The appeal shall be docketed in the name of the owner of the land, or of the party otherwise interested and appealing, as plaintiff, and in the name of the applicant for condemnation as defendant, and be tried as in an action by ordinary proceedings." Code of Iowa 1950, I.C.A.

The petitioner then filed a complaint in the United States District Court for the Southern District of Iowa against the respondents in which it alleged diversity of citizenship, jurisdictional amount, authority to make improvements and to condemn therefor, together with a description of the land and that respondent Stude was the owner, and that the assessment proceedings had been instituted in the sheriff's office, resulting in the assessment of damages of $23,888.60, which was alleged to be excessive, and that appeal was taken by notice duly given. This notice was referred to as Exhibit A to the complaint, which exhibit recited that the appeal was taken to the Federal District Court for the Southern District of Iowa, and a transcript of the sheriff's proceeding was filed in that court. The prayer was that the damages for the taking of the land be fixed at not more than $10,000. On this complaint, a summons was issued and served upon the respondents.

The petitioner also filed an appeal from this assessment in the state court, the District Court for Pottawattamie County. The case was docketed there with the landowner as the plaintiff and the petitioner-condemnor as defendant, as required by the Iowa Code. Thereafter, a petition to remove the cause to the federal court was filed by the petitioner. The respondents filed in the Federal District Court a motion to dismiss the complaint filed therein and a motion to remand the case removed from the state court.

The federal court granted the motion to dismiss and dismissed the complaint but denied the motion to remand. 107 F.Supp. 895. The petitioner appealed from the judgment dismissing its complaint. The respondents gave notice of appeal from the order of the District Court denying the motion to remand. The Court of Appeals affirmed the District Court's judgment dismissing the complaint and reversed the District Court's denial of the motion to remand, and ordered the cause remanded to the state court. 204 F.2d 116; 204 F.2d 954. We granted certiorari.

The Order Denying the Motion to Remand. * * *

The question on this motion is whether the petitioner was a defendant nonresident of Iowa and therefore authorized to remove to the Federal District Court as provided by statute, 28 U.S.C. § 1441(a).

The proceeding before the sheriff is administrative until the appeal has been taken to the district court of the county. Then the proceeding becomes a civil action pending before "those exercising judicial functions" for the purpose of reviewing the question of damages. Myers v. Chicago & N.W.R. Co., 118 Iowa 312, 315–316, 91 N.W. 1076, 1078. When the proceeding has reached the stage of a perfected appeal and the jurisdiction of the state district court is invoked, it then becomes in its nature a civil action and subject to removal by the defendant to the United States District Court. Mississippi & Rum River Boom Co. v. Patterson, 98 U.S. 403, 407.

Is the petitioner such a defendant? The petitioner contends it is because the Code of Iowa, § 472.21, I.C.A., provides that on appeal, the case shall be docketed in the district court with the landowner as the plaintiff and the condemnor as the defendant and thereafter tried as in an original proceeding. * * *

For the purpose of removal, the federal law determines who is plaintiff and who is defendant. It is a question of the construction of the federal statute on removal, and not the state statute. The latter's procedural provisions cannot control the privilege of removal granted by the federal statute. * * * Here the railroad is the plaintiff under 28 U.S.C. § 1441(a), and cannot remove. The remand was proper.

The Motion to Dismiss. We think it was properly granted, and the original complaint in the Federal District Court correctly dismissed. The steps taken by the petitioner were those to perfect an appeal to the Federal District Court. The notice said it was the intention of the petitioner to docket the appeal in the federal court. The transcript on appeal was filed in the federal court, and the complaint filed sought a review of the commission's assessment of damages. The proceeding makes no sense on any other basis, for the action is brought not by the person injured, namely, the landowner, but by the railroad that inflicted the damage. It will be noticed further that there is no prayer for damages but only for a review of the assessment, in keeping with the Iowa Code, § 472.23, I.C.A., which provides "no judgment shall be rendered except for costs * * *." In short, it was an attempt of the petitioner to review the state proceedings on appeal to the Federal District Court.

The petitioner, after giving notice of appeal by filing notice with the sheriff, etc., could not perfect that appeal to any court but the court which the statute of Iowa directed, which was the District Court of that State for the County of Pottawattamie. The United States District Court for the Southern District of Iowa does not sit to review on appeal action taken administratively or judicially in a state proceeding. A state "legislature may not make a federal district court, a court of original jurisdiction, into an appellate tribunal or otherwise expand its jurisdiction * * *." Burford v. Sun Oil Co., 319 U.S. 315, 317. The Iowa Code does not purport to authorize such an appeal, Congress has provided none by statute, and the Federal Rules of Civil Procedure, 28 U.S.C.A., make no such provision.

We cannot ignore this plain attempt to appeal and treat the complaint as initiating an original action, as if the parties had agreed that the petitioner could take the land, leaving only a controversy as to the amount of compensation. In that instance, there would be an implied agreement that the petitioner would pay the landowner the fair value of the land. Either party might in that posture of the case ask for a declaration as to the amount of compensation owing. The claim for damages would arise in that case from the substantive rights given by the implied contract, and the suit would be one to enforce that contract. We have no such case here. The right to take the land and the ensuing right to damages here spring from the exercise of the power of eminent domain. The petitioner here seems to ignore the means by which it obtained the land and seeks to review only the question of damages. It may not separate the question of damages and try it apart from the substantive right from which the claim for damages arose. Nor can it be said that petitioner has fully exercised its power of eminent domain, leaving nothing to be determined but the question of damages. Petitioner has possession but not title to the land. The land does not belong to the petitioner until the damages are paid. The sheriff, or the clerk of the state district court in case of appeal, must file in the county recorder's office all the papers filed in the proceeding. Code of Iowa 1950, §§ 472.35, 472.36, I.C.A. The Iowa Code, § 472.41, I.C.A., makes this record presumptive evidence of title in the condemnor. Petitioner is still in the process of trying to get the land by virtue of its power of eminent domain. But obviously the complaint here was not filed to invoke the jurisdiction of the federal court in an eminent domain proceeding.

The Federal Rules of Civil Procedure do have elaborate provisions for procedure in the federal court in condemnation proceedings. It is obvious that the petitioner was not proceeding under these Rules. Whether it could so proceed as an original action in the United States District Court for the Southern District of Iowa is not before us.

The judgment is affirmed.

Affirmed.

Mr. Justice Black, dissenting.

I think the railroad has a right to have its case tried in the United States District Court. Congress has given such courts power to try any case that is (1) a "civil" action, (2) between "Citizens of different States", (3) a "controversy," and (4) involves a matter which "exceeds the sum or value of $3,000 exclusive of interests and costs". 28 U.S.C. § 1332. If a complaint alleges these four things a district court has jurisdiction. Here the railroad's complaint shows all four. * * * A point is made of the railroad's reference to certain prior state proceedings as though it had a right to "appeal" to the federal court from these proceedings. But assuming that the railroad confidently believed it had a right to appeal from the state commission, and therefore put a wrong label on its civil action, the District Court was still under a duty to try the case. After all, the railroad simply asked the court to fix damages for the property taken at "not to exceed $10,000," and for "such further relief as may be just and proper under the circumstances." And the pendency of a similar condemnation proceeding in the state court certainly did not destroy the federal court's jurisdiction. Nor did the District Court lose its jurisdiction because the railroad failed to invoke Rule 71A or to observe its procedure. In trying the case, the court should of course require observance of the Rule, if applicable, but failure of the railroad to comply with it is no sufficient reason for the court's refusal to settle the controversy. All of the alleged procedural mistakes attributed to the railroad could easily have been cured; none could possibly justify a final, unconditional dismissal of its cause of action. * * *

Mr. Justice Frankfurter, dissenting.

Stripped of irrelevant and beclouding elements, this is a suit brought in a federal court for the ascertainment of the value of land, acquired by eminent domain under the prescribed Iowa procedure.

If the Rock Island had decided to initiate this suit in the United States District Court for the Southern District of Iowa, as it was unquestionably entitled to do since there was diversity of citizenship, Madisonville Traction Co. v. St. Bernard Mining Co., 196 U.S. 239, the procedure defined by the Iowa Code would, under Rule 71A(k) of the Rules of Civil Procedure, have had to be followed. For that Rule provides that in an eminent domain proceeding the state procedure for determination of the value of the condemned land by a jury or commission, or both, must be followed. The sole difference, therefore, between the initiation of such an original condemnation proceeding in the federal court, regarding which no jurisdictional question could have been raised, and what was done here is that the railroad went directly to the sheriff's commissioners instead of having the District Court send it there, or itself employ the same kind of fact-finding procedure.

Once the sheriff's commissioners had found the value of the land, there came into operation the Iowa law authorizing reconsideration of the amount by a court. This marks the beginning of the judicial phase of the proceedings, "appeal" though it loosely be called. One is entitled to ask what considerations bar access at this point to the Federal District Court in Iowa "sitting ∗ ∗ ∗ [as] a court of that state", Madisonville Traction Co. v. St. Bernard Mining Co., *supra*, 196 U.S. at page 255, when all the statutory requirements for diversity jurisdiction are present. Can it be that there is something inexorable about the Iowa eminent domain procedure whereby it must run its full course in the Iowa courts, thus preventing the railroad from pursuing its first judicial remedy in the federal court of the State? But there is nothing in the Iowa Code or in the United States Judicial Code which ousts the federal court of its statutory jurisdiction simply because the Rock Island complied literally with the Iowa condemnation procedure.

Looked at from another aspect, this case may be seen simply as a suit for a declaration of money owed, satisfying the requirements of diversity jurisdiction. ∗ ∗ ∗ As is spelled out in Mr. Justice Black's opinion, with which I substantially agree, this case presents a dispute over some $13,000—only that and nothing more—and as such is within the scope of 28 U.S.C. § 1332.

I am not astute to find grounds for sustaining diversity jurisdiction. But while exercises in procedural dialectics so rampant in the early nineteenth century still hold for me intellectual interest, I do not think they should determine litigation in the middle of the twentieth, even when based merely on diversity of citizenship. I had supposed that the Rules of Civil Procedure for the district courts were to a considerable degree designed as a liberation from these wasteful and fettering niceties. The history of this litigation and its disposition will hardly be cited as an illustration of the fulfillment of the hope with which Congress allowed these Rules to take effect: "It is confidently expected that the adoption of the new rules will materially reduce the uncertainty, delay, expense, and the likelihood that cases may be decided on technical points of procedure which had no relation to the just determination of the controversy on its merits." H.R.Rep. No. 2743, 75th Cong., 3d Sess. 3.

NOTE ON THE VARIED EFFECTS OF STATE LAW ON FEDERAL JURISDICTION

(1) The following statement in 32 Am.Jur.2d, Federal Practice and Procedure § 5, p. 606 (1982), is typical of innumerable others:

"Although federal laws can affect state court jurisdiction, state law cannot affect federal court jurisdiction. State legislation may neither confer jurisdiction on federal courts nor abridge or impair federal court jurisdiction."

The Stude case, and the material in this Note, raise the question whether this statement is tenable. In considering this question, note also cases like Smith v. Reeves, 178 U.S. 436 (1900), which held that in view of the Eleventh Amendment, a state may "give its consent to be sued in its own courts by private persons or by corporations in respect of any cause of action against it and at the same exclude the jurisdiction of the Federal courts" (p. 445).[1]

(2) In Madisonville Traction Co. v. Saint Bernard Mining Co., 196 U.S. 239 (1905), relied on by Justice Frankfurter in his dissent in Stude, the traction company had filed an application in a Kentucky county court to condemn certain lands belonging to the mining company. Pursuant to state law, commissioners were appointed, who awarded $100 as damages, and the county court issued an order to show cause why the commissioners' report should not be confirmed. State law gave either party a right of appeal to the state circuit court, and to a trial de novo, but the mining company sought instead to remove to the federal court, alleging diversity of citizenship and more than $2,000 in controversy. Jurisdiction on removal was upheld by the Supreme Court. Justice Harlan, speaking for the majority, held that the proceeding in the county court was a "judicial" one that could have been brought originally in a federal court. The law to be applied in such a case (subject to constitutional limitations) was state law, but the state could not confine the determination of the questions involved to its own judicial tribunals. The opinion recognized that the state might have chosen to establish a nonjudicial process for determining the issue of condemnation, thus excluding concurrent federal diversity jurisdiction, but suggested that the state could not constitutionally do so with respect to the issue of compensation. Compare Prentis v. Atlantic Coast Line Co., 211 U.S. 210 (1908), p. 1348, *infra;* District of Columbia Court of Appeals v. Feldman, 460 U.S. 462 (1983) (proceedings before D.C. Court of Appeals for waiver of bar admission rule were "judicial"; federal district court lacked jurisdiction of independent action challenging the result in those proceedings).

For Justice Holmes, dissenting in Madisonville, the question of condemnation (as distinguished from compensation) was one involving "a prerogative of the State, which on the one hand may be exercised in any way that the State thinks fit, and on the other may not be exercised except by an authority which the State confers" (p. 257). Since the state had provided that the issue be determined in its own courts, "the United States has no constitutional right to intervene and to substitute other machinery" (p. 258). Can this view be squared with Whitton, p. 830, *supra?*

(3) Given the result in the Madisonville case, the state court appeal in Stude would evidently have been removable by Stude and the other

---

1. The Court went on to state, however, that such exclusion was "subject always to the condition, arising out of the supremacy of the Constitution of the United States and the laws made in pursuance thereof, that the final judgment of the highest court of the State in any action brought against it with its consent may be reviewed or reexamined, as prescribed by the act of Congress, if it denies to the plaintiff any right, title, privilege or immunity secured to him and specially claimed under the Constitution or laws of the United States" (*id.*).

For fuller discussion of Smith and related decisions, see p. 1214, *infra.*

respondents, as the Stude opinion assumes. (In Mason City & F.D.R.R. v. Boynton, 204 U.S. 570 (1907), quoted in Stude, the Court sustained removal by the condemnee under an earlier version of the same Iowa statute.)

But since removal jurisdiction depends on the existence of concurrent original jurisdiction, how could the Court in Stude have found jurisdiction to be lacking in the original action? Was the railroad's failure in that action due only to a mistake of form in designating its complaint an "appeal"? How should the complaint have been designated? Note that the only case cited by the Court on this branch of the discussion is Burford v. Sun Oil Co., 319 U.S. 315 (1943), p. 1364, *infra.* Is it in point? Why can't a federal court review action taken administratively in a state proceeding?

What of the question left open at the end of the Stude opinion—could the railroad have initiated the condemnation proceeding in the federal court, bypassing state procedures altogether? For differing views on this question, compare Note, *The Mystery of Rule 71A(k): The Elusive Right to Federal Diversity Jurisdiction Over Condemnation Actions Authorized by State Statute,* 64 Yale L.J. 600, 607–09 (1955), with Note, *The Supreme Court, 1953 Term,* 68 Harv.L.Rev. 96, 177–79 (1954).

(4) Does the Stude case suggest that, in the Supreme Court's view, federal courts should not be handling condemnation cases arising under state law?[2] Compare Louisiana Power & Light Co. v. City of Thibodaux, 360 U.S. 25 (1959) (upholding a district court decision to abstain in an eminent domain proceeding; majority quotes with approval the dissent in Madisonville), and Kaiser Steel Corp. v. W.S. Ranch Co., 391 U.S. 593 (1968) (endorsing federal abstention in case involving appropriation of water rights under state law), with County of Allegheny v. Frank Mashuda Co., 360 U.S. 185 (1959) (holding it erroneous to abstain in a federal diversity action challenging a taking under state law). These cases are discussed in greater detail at pp. 1369–74, *infra.*

(5) Federal courts have had difficulty over the years distinguishing between a "civil action," which may properly be brought in, or removed to, a federal court, and an administrative proceeding, which may not. Often the outcome will turn on a careful analysis of the precise questions to be decided by the tribunal under the governing state law, as well as of the character of the tribunal contemplated by that law. See, *e.g.,* Upshur County v. Rich, 135 U.S. 467, 472 (1890) (appeal to "county court" from an assessment for taxation is "not a suit within the meaning of the removal act"); Commissioners of Road Improvement Dist. No. 2 v. St. Louis S.W. Ry. Co., 257 U.S. 547 (1922) (proceeding before "county court" to review assessment on railroad for benefits from projected improvements may be removed to a federal court); Range Oil Supply Co. v. Chicago, R.I. & P.R. Co., 248 F.2d 477 (8th Cir.1957) (proceeding for review of administrative denial of application became "civil action" when filed in state court and may be removed); Tool & Die Makers, Lodge No. 78 v. General Elec. Co., 170 F.Supp. 945 (E.D.Wis.1959) (proceeding before Wisconsin Employment Relations Board for breach of collective bargaining agreement may be removed to federal court).

---

2. Compare the policy of the federal courts with respect to traditional types of claims in the fields of decedents' estates and domestic relations—matters thought to be of such peculiar concern to the states as to be inappropriate for determination by any separate even though coordinate system of courts. See Chap. X, Sec. 2(E), *infra.*

(6) The Supreme Court found the Stude case easily distinguishable in Horton v. Liberty Mut. Ins. Co., 367 U.S. 348 (1961). In holding that an action to determine workers' compensation benefits under state law was properly brought in a federal court, the Court said (pp. 354–55):

"* * * Aside from many other relevant distinctions which need not be pointed out, the Stude case is without weight here because, as shown by the Texas Supreme Court's interpretation of its compensation act: 'The suit to set aside an award of the board is in fact a suit, not an appeal * * *.' [T]he trial in court is not an appellate proceeding. It is a trial *de novo* wholly without reference to what may have been done by the Board." Note that in Range Oil, Paragraph (5), *supra,* there was no trial de novo; review was on the record before the state agency and the federal courts upheld the state agency's findings as not unlawful or unreasonable.

How would you react to a proposed statute excluding from the diversity jurisdiction all actions for review of state administrative determinations? *Cf.* 28 U.S.C. § 1445(c), prohibiting removal of state court actions arising under the workers' compensation laws of that state.

(7) In the two principal cases in this section so far—Whitton and Stude—state laws authorized certain litigation in state tribunals. Different considerations arise when the doors of the state tribunal would themselves be closed and the claim in federal court is that a federal doctrine, rule, or statute referring to state law (notably the Rules of Decision Act) requires that the doors of the federal court must also be closed. This problem has already been explored in cases like Guaranty Trust, Ragan, and Woods (pp. 800, 814–15, *supra*). It is pursued further in the materials that follow, and the section concludes with a discussion of the use of special tribunals—such as screening panels in malpractice cases—an issue that brings together a number of themes developed throughout this chapter.

SZANTAY v. BEECH AIRCRAFT CORPORATION

United States Court of Appeals for the Fourth Circuit.
349 F.2d 60 (1965).

Before SOBELOFF and J. SPENCER BELL, CIRCUIT JUDGES, and BARKSDALE, DISTRICT JUDGE.

SOBELOFF, CIRCUIT JUDGE.

These are interlocutory appeals, pursuant to 28 U.S.C.A. § 1292(b). Beech Aircraft Corporation appeals from the denial of its motion to quash the service of process made upon it and to dismiss the complaints for want of jurisdiction.

The complaints alleged that Elmer Szantay purchased a Beech aircraft in Nebraska and flew it to Miami, Florida, and thence to Columbia, South Carolina, where he arrived on the evening of March 31, 1962. During the stopover the plane was serviced by the Dixie Aviation Co., a South Carolina corporation. Szantay and his passengers left Columbia the next morning bound for Chicago but the plane travelled only as far as Tennessee where it crashed, killing all of its occupants.

Companion wrongful death actions were brought by the personal representatives of the victims, all citizens of Illinois, against Dixie and

Beech in the United States District Court for the Eastern District of South Carolina. The complaints charged that the deaths were caused by Beech's negligent manufacture and design of the aircraft, and Dixie's negligent servicing.

Beech is incorporated under the laws of Delaware and has its principal place of business in Kansas. The District Judge found that Beech had sufficient contacts with South Carolina through its local dealer to permit service on it under South Carolina law pursuant to Rule 4(d)(7), Fed.R.Civ. P. The evidence amply justifies the ruling. * * *

The plaintiffs being citizens of Illinois, the defendant Beech being a corporation of Delaware and Dixie of South Carolina, and the amount in controversy exceeding $10,000, all the prerequisites of federal diversity jurisdiction specified in the Constitution and implementing legislation are satisfied. It is conceded that all federal venue requirements are satisfied.

Beech, however, moved for dismissal on the ground that a federal diversity court sitting in South Carolina lacks jurisdiction over Beech because of South Carolina's "door-closing" statute, section 10–214, Code of Laws of South Carolina (1962). That statute provides that:

"An action against a corporation created by or under the laws of any other state, government or country may be brought in the circuit court: (1) By any resident of this State for any cause of action; or (2) By a plaintiff not a resident of this State when the cause of action shall have arisen or the subject of the action shall be situated within this State."

It is conceded that South Carolina state courts do not have jurisdiction over a suit brought by a nonresident against a foreign corporation on a foreign cause of action. The principal question posed is whether this state rule restricts the jurisdiction of the federal courts in South Carolina in diversity cases.

For many years it was generally understood that federal jurisdiction was not affected by state statutes limiting the jurisdiction of their own courts.[4] In recent years, however, this absolute approach has been modified. The change may be said to have begun with Erie R. Co. v. Tompkins, 304 U.S. 64 (1938) * * *.

In 1947 the Court held that a Virginia plaintiff could not sue a North Carolina defendant for a deficiency judgment in a North Carolina federal court because of North Carolina's express statutory policy against such actions. Angel v. Bullington, 330 U.S. 183 (1947). Two years later it held that a Tennessee corporate plaintiff could not sue a Mississippi defendant on a Mississippi cause of action in a Mississippi federal court when that state would not allow the corporation to sue in its courts because of its failure to register as a foreign corporation doing business there. Woods v. Interstate Realty Co., 337 U.S. 535 (1949). The opinion declared that a federal court cannot enforce a state-created right when that state provides no remedy.

A decade later in a case arising in this circuit, the Supreme Court reconsidered the meaning of Erie and refined the "outcome-determinative" test. * * * Byrd v. Blue Ridge Cooperative, 356 U.S. 525, 536 (1958). The spirit of these decisions makes it appropriate for a court attempting to

---

4. See David Lupton's Sons Co. v. Automobile Club of America, 225 U.S. 489 (1912); Barrow Steamship Co. v. Kane, 170 U.S. 100 (1898).

resolve a federal-state conflict in a diversity case to undertake the following analysis:

1. If the state provision, whether legislatively adopted or judicially declared, is the substantive right or obligation at issue, it is constitutionally controlling.

2. If the state provision is a procedure intimately bound up with the state right or obligation, it is likewise constitutionally controlling.[5]

3. If the state procedural provision is not intimately bound up with the right being enforced but its application would substantially affect the outcome of the litigation, the federal diversity court must still apply it unless there are affirmative countervailing federal considerations. This is not deemed a constitutional requirement but one dictated by comity.

A like test was recently applied in Arrowsmith v. United Press International, 320 F.2d 219 (2d Cir.1963). There the court was concerned with the extent to which state or federal rules should control in the service of process on foreign corporations in diversity cases. The Second Circuit, speaking through Judge Friendly, decided first that the state service of process statute was not substantive, nor was it a procedure intimately bound up with the state right being enforced. The decision implied that this exhausted the constitutionally compulsive aspects of the Erie doctrine. The court then ruled that state procedure should be adopted in that case because there were no affirmative countervailing federal considerations. Judge Clark agreed that the constitutionally compulsive aspects of Erie were not there controlling but he dissented upon his view that a countervailing federal policy did exist. *Supra*, 320 F.2d at 242.

In the case before us the parties are in agreement that the South Carolina "door-closing" statute is procedural. And, as the right asserted is one arising under the laws of Tennessee, it cannot be contended that the South Carolina rule is intimately bound up with that right. It follows from this that the constitutional compulsions of the Erie doctrine are not applicable here.

The conclusion is fortified by the recent decision in Hanna v. Plumer, 380 U.S. 460 (1965). * * * Here no contention is made that rejection of the "door-closing" statute will result in a discrimination against South Carolina citizens. South Carolina plaintiffs will remain jurisdictionally free to assert a foreign cause of action against a foreign defendant in either a state or federal court in South Carolina regardless of the decision in this case.[6] At the heart of Erie was the intention to prevent different legal treatment of parties merely because of a variation in the residence of their opponent. See Note, 56 Yale L.J. 1037, 1045 (1947). The adoption in this case of the South Carolina "door-closing" statute would result in just such a variation because the relief available in the federal court to the foreign residents, in this case the Illinois plaintiffs, would then turn on the state of incorporation of the defendant.

5. Such was the case in Cohen v. Beneficial Industrial Loan Corp., 337 U.S. 541 (1949); Ragan v. Merchants Transfer & Warehouse Co., 337 U.S. 530 (1949); and Guaranty Trust Co. v. York, 326 U.S. 99 (1945).

6. Of course, in the rare case where the plaintiff is a nonresident South Carolina citizen a rejection of the state statute would permit him to bring suit in a South Carolina federal court but not in a state court, the same treatment sought by the nonresident noncitizen.

As above indicated, however, this analysis does not exhaust the question. It is necessary to go on and inquire whether the South Carolina rule embodies important policies that would be frustrated by the application of a different federal jurisdictional rule and, if so, is this policy to be overriden because of a stronger federal policy?

We are inhibited in our search for the state policy underlying the South Carolina "door-closing" statute by the unavailability of any legislative history. Furthermore, no South Carolina state court has, to our knowledge, shed any light on the problem. The language of the statute could support several possible explanations. It could be regarded as a statutory formulation of the doctrine of forum non conveniens. If so, the restriction would not be binding on the federal court since federal cognizance of the case would in no way frustrate state policy. A related consideration, to be treated in the same manner, is the suggested possibility that the statute was designed to relieve docket congestion, though there is nothing to indicate that this was a problem in 1870 when the statute was passed.

Beech tenders the hypothesis that the legislation was designed to encourage foreign corporations to do business in South Carolina. This explanation is attenuated by the fact that the same session of the legislature provided that any South Carolina agent of a foreign corporation was to be considered an agent for the service of process no matter where the cause of action arose and irrespective of the plaintiff's residence. See section 10–423, Code of Laws of South Carolina (1962). Furthermore, South Carolina qualification laws indicate that foreign corporations are to be given a status generally comparable to that of domestic corporations. See section 12–705, Code of Laws of South Carolina (1962). The most that can be said for Beech's argument is that it demonstrates that the state's reason for enacting its "door-closing" statute is uncertain.

The countervailing federal considerations, however, are explicit, and they are numerous. The most fundamental is that expressed in the constitutional extension of subject-matter jurisdiction to the federal courts in suits between citizens of different states. U.S. Const. Art. III, § 2. The purpose of this jurisdictional grant was to avoid discrimination against nonresidents. See The Federalist No. 80 (Hamilton); Martin v. Hunter's Lessee, 14 U.S. (1 Wheat.) 304, 347 (1816). The South Carolina "door-closing" statute permits its residents to sue foreign corporations on foreign causes of action yet denies this privilege to nonresidents. While such discrimination may not be unconstitutional,[8] it is the role of diversity jurisdiction, as pointed out for this court by Judge Haynsworth, to make certain that:

"[a] nonresident litigant in resorting to the federal diversity jurisdiction should obtain the same relief a resident litigant asserting the same cause of action would receive in the state courts." Markham v. City of Newport News, 292 F.2d 711, 718 (4th Cir.1961).

A further federal consideration, likewise expressed in the Constitution itself, is that underlying the Full Faith and Credit Clause. U.S. Const. Art.

---

8. "There are manifest reasons for preferring residents in access to often overcrowded Courts, both in convenience and in the fact that broadly speaking it is they who pay for maintaining the Courts concerned." Douglas v. New York, New Haven R. Co., 279 U.S. 377, 387 (1929).

IV, § 1. That clause expresses a national interest "looking toward maximum enforcement in each state of the obligations or rights created or recognized by the statutes of sister states." Hughes v. Fetter, 341 U.S. 609 (1951). While the South Carolina "door-closing" statute may not directly violate the demands of this constitutional principle, it is contrary to its implicit policy in that it prevents enforcement of the Tennessee Wrongful Death Action in the South Carolina state courts.[11]

The plaintiffs' choice of a South Carolina forum was not frivolous. One of the defendants, Dixie, could be served only in that state. It is a federal policy to encourage efficient joinder in multi-party actions, and at least one commentator has suggested that this federal interest is sufficient to override an explicit conflicting state policy. Note, 77 Harv.L.Rev. 559 (1964). Furthermore, if the plaintiffs had brought suit against Beech alone in the federal forum where the accident occurred, the District Judge there would have been free to transfer the case to a South Carolina District Court pursuant to the federal doctrine of forum non conveniens, 28 U.S.C.A. § 1404(a), even though South Carolina law denies the plaintiffs access to its state courts. Van Dusen v. Barrack, 376 U.S. 612 (1964).

Our case is not controlled by Angel v. Bullington, 330 U.S. 183, (1947), or Woods v. Interstate Realty Co., 337 U.S. 535 (1949), referred to above. Each of these decisions paid deference to a clear state policy that would have been frustrated by permitting suit in a federal court. In Angel North Carolina forbade any deficiency judgments, thereby expressing a clear policy in favor of debtors and against enforcement by anyone of such causes of action. In Woods Mississippi's clear purpose was to encourage foreign corporations doing business in Mississippi to register. Furthermore, the cause of action sued on in Woods was created by the forum state, so the measure of it was to be found in the law of that state.[13] See Ragan v. Merchants Transfer & Warehouse Co., 337 U.S. 530, 533 (1949). Neither case involved discrimination against nonresidents, nor were there multiple defendants who could be sued only in the contested forum.

South Carolina has no policy against the particular plaintiffs, as Mississippi had against nonregistered foreign corporations in Woods; nor does it discourage the type of action, as North Carolina did in respect to deficiency judgments in Angel. The superficiality of the South Carolina policy is demonstrated in this case by the fact that the plaintiffs could have gained access to a South Carolina court by simply qualifying as administrators under South Carolina law.

Therefore we hold that the conflict here between federal and state policies, if in fact one exists, is to be resolved in favor of the federal interest

11. It is proper to consider also the duty imposed on federal courts in diversity cases to hear and adjudicate the issues before it. Meredith v. City of Winter Haven, 320 U.S. 228 (1943); *see* County of Allegheny v. Frank Mashuda Co., 360 U.S. 185 (1959).

13. The holding in Hanna v. Plumer, that "[t]he broad command of Erie was * * * identical to that of the Enabling Act; federal courts are to apply state substantive law and federal procedural law," 380 U.S. 460 (1965), makes relevant a reference to earlier Supreme Court cases dealing with the permissible scope of the federal rules. Rule 4(f), permitting service of process anywhere in the state, was upheld since it did not "operate to abridge, enlarge or modify the rules of decision by which that court will adjudicate its rights." Mississippi Publishing Corp. v. Murphree, 326 U.S. 438, 446 (1946). Such is the case here. The federal jurisdictional and venue statutes do not affect the rules of decision by which the parties' rights will be adjudicated; they only determine the forum.

in providing a convenient forum for the adjudication of the plaintiffs' actions.

Affirmed.

NOTE ON THE EFFECT OF STATE DOOR–CLOSING AND "SCREENING" RULES

(1) Suppose that a South Carolina state court, in discussing section 10–214 of the Code, had said: "The clear purpose of this provision is to encourage foreign corporations to do business in this state without fear of being subjected to lawsuits brought by nonresidents on foreign causes of action." What effect, if any, should such a statement be given by a federal court on the Szantay facts? [1]

(2) Does it matter whether the state door-closing rule is operating on a right created under the laws of another jurisdiction, as in Szantay, or on a right created by the forum? In David Lupton's Sons Co. v. Automobile Club, 225 U.S. 489 (1912), a Pennsylvania corporation had brought an action in a New York federal court for breach of a contract entered into and to be partially performed in New York. A New York statute provided that a foreign corporation that had not qualified to do business in the state was disabled from bringing suit in the state. (The statute, as construed by the New York Court of Appeals, did not purport to render void the local contracts of such a corporation.) The Court held that the statute did not preclude the federal action, saying (p. 500): "The State could not prescribe the qualifications of suitors in the courts of the United States, and could not deprive of their privileges those who were entitled under the Constitution and laws of the United States to resort to the federal courts for the enforcement of a valid contract."

In Angel v. Bullington, 330 U.S. 183 (1947), referred to in the Szantay opinion, a statute of North Carolina forbade deficiency judgments in favor of a mortgagee who had resorted to a foreclosure sale of the mortgaged property, and a North Carolina state court had refused to award such a judgment to a Virginia plaintiff in connection with a sale of Virginia land. (The state court had said: "The statute operates upon the adjective law of the State, which pertains to the practice and procedure, or legal machinery by which the substantive law is made effective, and not upon the substantive law itself. It is a limitation of the jurisdiction of the courts of this State." 220 N.C. 18, 20, 16 S.E.2d 411, 412 (1941).) [2] The plaintiff then tried to obtain a similar judgment in a diversity action brought in a North Carolina federal court. Although the matter was complicated by the question of the res judicata effect of the prior state action, the Supreme Court made it clear that by virtue of Erie, North Carolina's rule was applicable in a federal court sitting in that state.[3] "Cases like Lupton's

---

1. On several occasions, most recently in Piper Aircraft Co. v. Reyno, 454 U.S. 235, 248 n. 13 (1981), the Supreme Court has expressly left open the question whether "state or federal law of *forum non conveniens* applies in a diversity case."

2. The point was made in response to a challenge to the constitutionality of apply-

ing the statute to the case at hand. See note 3, *infra*.

3. The Court did not consider the question whether North Carolina could constitutionally apply its rule to a case involving a contract with a Virginia citizen for the sale of Virginia land.

Sons Co. v. Automobile Club, 225 U.S. 489, are obsolete insofar as they are based on a view of diversity jurisdiction which came to an end with Erie Railroad v. Tompkins, 304 U.S. 64. That decision drastically limited the power of federal district courts to entertain suits in diversity cases that could not be brought in the respective State courts or were barred by defenses controlling in the State courts" (p. 192).

Whatever was left of Lupton's appeared to have been buried in Woods v. Interstate Realty Co., pp. 814–15, *supra*. Can Szantay be reconciled with these cases, or is it an indication that some of Erie's progeny are not enduring?[4] Is Angel v. Bullington a case in which a significant state substantive policy may have been involved, though it was not articulated by the state court?

(3) Rule 17(b) of the Federal Rules of Civil Procedure requires that a corporation's capacity to sue be determined by the law of the state of incorporation. This provision may be viewed as a pro tanto modification of Klaxon—as the statement, in other words, of a uniform federal choice-of-law rule on the question of capacity. Can it be squared with the result in Woods? Several district courts have directly faced the issue on facts similar to Woods and rejected the application of Rule 17(b) in a case involving a forum-created right. *E.g.*, Power City Communications, Inc. v. Calaveras Tel. Co., 280 F.Supp. 808 (E.D.Cal.1968). A comment on this case, 82 Harv.L.Rev. 708, 711 (1969), suggests that the result is correct, not because the California door-closing statute prevails over the federal rule, but because the federal rule should be restricted to questions of capacity in a "narrower sense" than the matters dealt with by the California law. See also 6 Wright & Miller, Federal Practice and Procedure 1569 (1971). But see Little, *Out of Woods and Into the Rules*, 72 Va.L.Rev. 767 (1986).[5]

(4) Having taken jurisdiction in the Szantay case, should the federal court interpret Klaxon as requiring it to apply South Carolina's choice-of-law rules in determining Beech's liability? If not, what rules should govern?[6]

---

4. In Poitra v. Demarrias, 502 F.2d 23 (8th Cir.1974), the court upheld diversity jurisdiction in an action between Indians living on a reservation, although a state court in the forum state could not have entertained the case. The reason for the state's lack of power over the case was that the Tribe had not given the consent required for the exercise of such jurisdiction by 25 U.S.C. § 1322(a). The court of appeals reasoned that assumption of federal jurisdiction would not undermine any state policy. It noted further that § 1322(a) was intended not to deprive Indians of state-created rights but to prevent the states from interfering with Indian affairs.

Dissenting from the denial of certiorari in the Poitra case, 421 U.S. 934 (1975), Justice White argued that there was a conflict with certain decisions of the Ninth Circuit which, in denying jurisdiction, had relied in part on Woods v. Interstate Realty.

In several decisions after Szantay, the Fourth Circuit applied South Carolina's door-closing statute, noting in each instance that there was an alternative forum where the plaintiff could obtain full relief. *E.g.*, Proctor & Schwartz, Inc. v. Rollins, 634 F.2d 738 (4th Cir.1980). But *cf.* Atkins v. Schmutz Mfg. Co., 435 F.2d 527 (4th Cir. 1970), where the court relied heavily on the Szantay analysis in refusing to be bound by state law.

5. *Cf.* Tolson v. Hodge, 411 F.2d 123 (4th Cir.1969); Avondale Shipyards, Inc. v. Propulsion Systems, Inc., 53 F.R.D. 341 (E.D.La.1971). Both cases held that counterclaims could be filed by federal defendants under Fed.Rule 13(a) even if the defendants would have lacked capacity to do so in a state court.

6. For further discussion of Szantay, and its relation to Arrowsmith v. United Press Int'l (cited in the Szantay opinion), see *Note on Bringing Corporations and Unincorporated Organizations into Court*, p. 1725, *infra*.

(5) A contentious question in recent years has been the applicability in federal diversity actions of state statutes mandating resort to "screening" or "arbitration" panels. These statutes, which are an aspect of a larger effort to develop alternative means of dispute resolution, vary considerably in their terms. Some require resort as a condition to suit, while others constitute the panel as an arm of the court itself—akin to a master in the federal courts. Though one purpose of these panels is to relieve court congestion, it is clear that another purpose—in medical malpractice cases, for example—is to cut back on large jury verdicts and resulting high insurance costs. It is also clear that plaintiffs have often invoked federal diversity jurisdiction in such cases in order to avoid the necessity of submission to a panel before trial.

An example of a screening statute is Mass.Gen.Laws ch. 231, § 60B, which provides for a panel consisting of a state judge, a physician, and an attorney. The panel is required to determine whether "the evidence presented if properly substantiated is sufficient to raise a legitimate question of liability appropriate for judicial inquiry * * *." A plaintiff wishing to sue for medical malpractice may do so even in the event of a negative determination, but the determination is admissible in evidence, and the plaintiff must post a $2000 bond for costs and attorney's fees, payable to defendant "if the plaintiff does not prevail in the final judgment."

In Feinstein v. Massachusetts General Hospital, 643 F.2d 880 (1st Cir. 1981), the court held that in a diversity action for malpractice filed in a Massachusetts federal court, this procedure must be followed.[7] After concluding that the state law was designed to serve substantive policy objectives that would be undermined if the law were not observed in a federal diversity action, the court rejected the argument that the Whitton case, p. 830, *supra*, precludes the use of Section 60B. Section 60B, the court said, does not attempt to confine medical malpractice actions to state courts: "Rather, [it] creates a screening mechanism through which every malpractice claim must proceed before being pursued in court. No ouster of federal jurisdiction results when, by reason of the policies expressed in Erie, a federal court requires that a state's rule barring an action from proceeding in its courts must be applied to bar the action from the federal court. This principle is exemplified by Woods v. Interstate Realty Co. * * *" (p. 888).

The court went on to hold (1) that the state procedures were not inherently unfair to out of staters, (2) that the bond requirement was not so oppressive for a non-indigent litigant[8] as to interfere with the Seventh Amendment right to a jury trial, and (3) that the question of the admissibility in evidence of the panel's determination, and its effect on the jury trial

7. The particular procedure followed by the district court, and upheld on appeal, was to refer the action to the state Superior Court for a § 60B hearing. This was done after the state supreme court, in response to a question certified to it by a federal judge, had said that if a screening panel was to be used, "the Federal court should not fashion its own tribunal" but should refer the matter to the Superior Court for appointment of the tribunal, "af-

ter which its findings will be transmitted to the clerk of the Federal court." Austin v. Boston University Hospital, 372 Mass. 654, 660, 363 N.E.2d 515, 519 (1977).

8. The plaintiff in the Feinstein case did not claim to be indigent. Under the state law, if the plaintiff is found to be indigent, the court "may reduce the amount of the bond but may not eliminate the requirement thereof."

right, need not then be decided in light of the severability provision in the state law.

Accepting the principle of the Feinstein decision, is there a point at which mandatory resort to a state-created tribunal runs afoul of the Whitton principle? Does the availability of a de novo judicial proceeding resolve all doubts? What if the state law provided that the determination of the screening tribunal was not just admissible but was "prima facie evidence" of the conclusions reached? What if the tribunal had authority not only to make a determination of probable cause but to decide on liability and to award damages? To what extent should federal courts follow state screening or arbitration procedures when it appears that the sole purpose of those procedures is to relieve court congestion and to provide a speedier, more efficient alternative to litigants? To what extent are federal courts free to adopt such procedures in diversity cases without reference to state law? Such questions will grow in importance as efforts increase to channel disputes away from overcrowded courts.

For further discussion of these issues as they relate to malpractice screening panels, see Edelson v. Soricelli, 610 F.2d 131 (3d Cir.1979) (requiring resort to state arbitration procedures as a condition to suit); Alexander, *State Medical Malpractice Screening Panels in Federal Diversity Actions,* 21 Ariz.L.Rev. 959 (1979); Note, 66 Cornell L.Rev. 337 (1981); Case Comment, 93 Harv.L.Rev. 1562 (1980).

Chapter VII

FEDERAL COMMON LAW

INTRODUCTION: THE SCOPE OF THIS CHAPTER

Does a federal common law exist? If it does, is its existence legitimate? What is its nature, source, and scope? These questions, which have often given rise to vigorous debate, frame the subject of this Chapter.

The proposition that the corpus of federal law legitimately includes a body of judge-made law—law that cannot fairly be described as simply constituting the application of federal statutory and constitutional norms—is, today, no longer in serious dispute. Indeed, our legal culture assumes that the existence of such a body of law is a necessary and desirable adjunct of any functioning legal system, and much recent scholarship has sought to justify expanding the frontiers of the sphere of federal common law. But interesting and perplexing problems continue to surround the question of the proper scope and methodology of federal judicial lawmaking.

This Chapter does not attempt an exhaustive consideration of all the possible areas in which power to create federal common law might be asserted. Rather, it focuses on some of the major areas of federal law-making activity in actions in the federal district courts. The materials serve not only as a study in choice of law but as a prelude to investigation of federal question jurisdiction in the district courts in the Chapter that follows.

The Chapter seeks to draw a rough organizational distinction between federal court exercise of substantive common law authority to define primary legal obligations (Section 1) and the exercise of remedial authority to enforce those obligations (Section 2). While this distinction does serve an organizational purpose, the boundary is a difficult one to maintain. The shape and scope of the remedy may have much to do with determining the significance and, at least as a practical matter, the very existence of the right. Indeed, some questions—like capacity to sue or the availability of a right of contribution or indemnity—are hard to place on either side of the boundary. Further, some cases and developments are noted in passing whenever they seem most relevant, even at the risk of straining the distinction.[1]

---

1. Since the Chapter centers on actions in the district courts, it does not consider the relevance of federal common law principles in the review of state court decisions. See, e.g., Note on State Remedies for Federal Rights, p. 584, supra; Meltzer, State Court Forfeitures of Federal Rights, 99 Harv.L.Rev. 1128 (1986) (proposing recognition and development of a federal common law of procedural default, applicable in state courts and on direct and collateral federal review).

SECTION 1. DEFINING PRIMARY OBLIGATIONS

SUBSECTION A: CRIMINAL PROSECUTIONS

UNITED STATES v. HUDSON & GOODWIN
7 Cranch 32, 3 L.Ed. 259 (U.S.1812).

This was a case certified from the Circuit Court for the district of Connecticut, in which, upon argument of a general demurrer to an indictment for a libel on the president and congress of the United States, contained in the Connecticut Currant, of the 7th of May 1806, charging them with having in secret voted $2,000,000 as a present to Bonaparte, for leave to make a treaty with Spain, the judges of that court were divided in opinion upon the question, whether the circuit court of the United States had a common-law jurisdiction in cases of libel?

Pinkney, Attorney–General, in behalf of the United States, and *Dana,* for the defendants, declined arguing the case.

The Court, having taken time to consider, the following opinion was delivered (on the last day of the term, all the judges being present) by JOHNSON, J.

The only question which this case presents is, whether the Circuit Courts of the United States can exercise a common-law jurisdiction in criminal cases. We state it thus broadly, because a decision on a case of libel will apply to every case in which jurisdiction is not vested in those Courts by statute.

Although this question is brought up now for the first time to be decided by this Court, we consider it as having been long since settled in public opinion. In no other case for many years has this jurisdiction been asserted; and the general acquiescence of legal men shows the prevalence of opinion in favor of the negative of the proposition.

The course of reasoning which leads to this conclusion is simple, obvious, and admits of but little illustration. The powers of the general Government are made up of concessions from the several states—whatever is not expressly given to the former, the latter expressly reserve. The judicial power of the United States is a constituent part of those concessions—that power is to be exercised by Courts organized for the purpose, and brought into existence by an effort of the legislative power of the Union. Of all the Courts which the United States may, under their general powers, constitute, one only, the Supreme Court, possesses jurisdiction derived immediately from the constitution, and of which the legislative power cannot deprive it. All other Courts created by the general Government possess no jurisdiction but what is given them by the power that creates them, and can be vested with none but what the power ceded to the general Government will authorize them to confer.

It is not necessary to inquire, whether the general Government, in any and what extent, possesses the power of conferring on its Courts a jurisdiction in cases similar to the present; it is enough that such jurisdiction has not been conferred by any legislative act, if it does not result to those Courts as a consequence of their creation.

And such is the opinion of the majority of this Court: For, the power which congress possess to create Courts of inferior jurisdiction, necessarily implies the power to limit the jurisdiction of those Courts to particular objects; and when a Court is created, and its operations confined to certain specific objects, with what propriety can it assume to itself a jurisdiction—much more extended—in its nature very indefinite—applicable to a great variety of subjects—varying in every state in the Union—and with regard to which there exists no definite criterion of distribution between the district and Circuit Courts of the same district?

The only ground on which it has ever been contended that this jurisdiction could be maintained is, that, upon the formation of any political body, an implied power to preserve its own existence and promote the end and object of its creation, necessarily results to it. But, without examining how far this consideration is applicable to the peculiar character of our constitution, it may be remarked that it is a principle by no means peculiar to the common law. It is coeval, probably, with the first formation of a limited Government; belongs to a system of universal law, and may as well support the assumption of many other powers as those more peculiarly acknowledged by the common law of England.

But if admitted as applicable to the state of things in this country, the consequence would not result from it, which is here contended for. If it may communicate certain implied powers to the general Government, it would not follow that the Courts of that Government are vested with jurisdiction over any particular act done by an individual, in supposed violation of the peace and dignity of the sovereign power. The legislative authority of the Union must first make an act a crime, affix a punishment to it, and declare the Court that shall have jurisdiction of the offence.

Certain implied powers must necessarily result to our Courts of justice from the nature of their institution. But jurisdiction of crimes against the state is not among those powers. To fine for contempt—imprison for contumacy—enforce the observance of order, & c., are powers which cannot be dispensed with in a Court, because they are necessary to the exercise of all others: and so far our Courts no doubt possess powers not immediately derived from statute; but all exercise of criminal jurisdiction in common-law cases, we are of opinion, is not within their implied powers.

UNITED STATES v. COOLIDGE

1 Wheat. 415, 4 L.Ed. 124 (U.S.1816).

This was an indictment in the circuit court for the district of Massa-chusetts, against the defendants, for forcibly rescuing a prize, which had been captured and taken possession of by two American privateers. The captured vessel was on her way, under the direction of a prizemaster and crew, to the port of Salem for adjudication. The indictment laid the offence as committed upon the high seas. The question made was, whether the circuit court has jurisdiction over common law offences against the United States? on which the judges of that court were divided in opinion.

The *Attorney–General* stated that he had given to this case an anxious attention; as much so, he hoped, as his public duty, under whatever view of it, rendered necessary. That he had also examined the opinion of the court, delivered at February term, 1813, in the case of the United States v. Hudson and Goodwin. That considering the point as decided in that case, whether with or without argument on the part of those who had preceded him as the representative of the government in this court, he desired respectfully to state, without saying more, that it was not his intention to argue it now.

STORY, J. I do not take the question to be settled by that case.

JOHNSON, J. I consider it to be settled by the authority of that case.

WASHINGTON, J. Whenever counsel can be found ready to argue it, I shall divest myself of all prejudice arising from that case.

LIVINGSTON, J. I am disposed to hear an argument on the point. This case was brought up for that purpose, but until the question is re-argued, the case of the United States v. Hudson and Goodwin must be taken as law.

JOHNSON, J., delivered the opinion of the court.

Upon the question now before the court a difference of opinion has existed, and still exists, among the members of the court. We should, therefore, have been willing to have heard the question discussed upon solemn argument. But the attorney-general has declined to argue the cause; and no counsel appears for the defendant. Under these circumstances the court would not choose to review their former decision in the case of the United States v. Hudson and Goodwin, or draw it into doubt. They will, therefore, certify an opinion to the circuit court in conformity with that decision.

Certificate for the defendant.

NOTE ON THE HUDSON AND COOLIDGE CASES

(1) In upholding the indictment in the Coolidge case at circuit, Justice Story said (1 Gall. 488, 491, Fed.Cas. No. 14,857):

"I would ask then, what are crimes and offences against the United States, under the construction of its limited sovereignty, by the rules of the common law? Without pretending to enumerate them in detail, I will venture to assert generally, that all offences against the sovereignty, the public rights, the public justice, the public peace, the public trade and the public police of the United States, are crimes and offences against the United States. From the nature of the sovereignty of the United States, which is limited and circumscribed, it is clear that many common law offences, under each of these heads, will still remain cognizable by the states; but whenever the offence is directed against the sovereignty or powers confided to the United States, it is cognizable under its authority. Upon these principles and independent of any statute, I presume that treasons, and conspiracies to commit treason, embezzlement of the public records, bribery and resistance of the judicial process, riots and misdemeanors on the high seas, frauds and obstructions of the public laws of trade, and robbery and embezzlement of the mail of the United States, would be offences against the United States. At common law, these are clearly public offences, and when directed *against the United States*, they must upon principle be deemed *offences against the United States.*"

Earlier prosecutions for common law crimes, yielding some unreviewed convictions, are described in Goebel, History of the Supreme Court of the United States: Antecedents and Beginnings to 1801, at 623 *et seq.* (1971). See, *e.g.*, United States v. Worrall, 2 Dall. 384 (C.C.Pa.1798) (attempt to bribe Commissioner of Revenue).

On the crucial importance of the Hudson and Coolidge cases in the development of the conception of the nature of federal law, and the part which they played in the struggle between the Federalists and the Jeffersonians, see 2 Crosskey, Politics and the Constitution in the History of the United States 767–84 (1953); Jay, *Origins of Federal Common Law*, 133 U.Pa.L.Rev. 1003 (1985) (Part I); 133 U.Pa.L.Rev. 1231 (1985) (Part II).[1]

(2) In defining the criminal jurisdiction of the district and circuit courts, the Judiciary Act of 1789, §§ 9, 11, 1 Stat. 73, 76, 79, used the phrase "all crimes and offences cognizable under the authority of the United States". From the manuscript of the original draft bill, Charles Warren draws interesting inferences as to the intended scope of this jurisdiction. See *New Light on the History of the Federal Judiciary Act of 1789*, 37 Harv.L.Rev. 49, 73 (1923):

" * * * The Draft Bill gave to the District Courts, 'cognizance of all crimes and offences that shall be cognizable under the authority of the United States *and defined by the laws of the same.*' The italicized words make it clear that the framers of the Bill meant to confine criminal jurisdiction to crimes specifically defined by Congress, and to them only. * * * It now appears, on comparison of the Draft Bill with the Act as passed, that by an amendment introduced in and adopted by the Senate, the restrictive clause—'and defined by the laws of the same'—was deliberately stricken out, thus leaving the District Courts with jurisdiction over crimes 'cognizable under the authority of the United States,' without any limitation. The only rational meaning that can be given to this action striking out the restrictive words is, that Congress did not intend to limit criminal jurisdiction to crimes specifically defined by it. Had the Supreme Court consulted these Senate Files, it is probable that the decisions in United States v. Hudson, in 1812, and United States v. Coolidge, in 1816, might have been otherwise than they were."

(3) In principle, was there a stronger case for upholding the indictment in Coolidge than in Hudson?

(4) "Although 'judge-made' or nonstatutory federal crimes disappeared after the Coolidge decision, federal courts continued [through use of the contempt power] to exercise common law power to enforce law and order within their own precincts and continued to employ a variety of common law techniques, forms, and writs in the enforcement of congressionally

---

1. Professor Jay argues that because of the intensity of the political controversy surrounding the Hudson decision, reliance on that decision to justify present restrictions on the scope of federal common law is misplaced. "Hudson was decided in a peculiar setting of partisan disturbance, and grew out of a fear that we can scarcely appreciate today—the belief that there was a scheme afoot to install a consolidated national government through incorporation of the British common law" (p. 1323). Moreover, he asserts, a "survey of jurisdictional theory from the Hudson period" shows a general awareness that "federal courts had what we would term significant common-law powers" (*id.*).

defined crimes. * * * By its 'supervisory powers' over lower federal courts and, through them, over federal law enforcement officers, the Supreme Court can still be said, loosely, to exercise an interstitial common law authority with respect to federal crimes." Levy, *Federal Common Law of Crimes*, 4 Encyclopedia of the American Constitution 693 (1986).

Note that many of the aspects of "common law authority" referrred to in this passage relate not to the definition of legal rights and duties, but to methods of enforcement and remediation. See, *e.g.,* Marshall v. United States, 360 U.S. 310 (1959) (setting aside a jury verdict, in exercise of the "supervisory power," because the jurors had been exposed to potentially prejudicial publicity); *cf.* Mapp v. Ohio, 367 U.S. 643 (1961) (exclusionary rule). See generally Section 2, *infra*. Is the exercise of such law making power easier to defend against a charge of usurpation of the legislative prerogative?

SUBSECTION B: CIVIL ACTIONS

CLEARFIELD TRUST CO. v. UNITED STATES

318 U.S. 363, 63 S.Ct. 573, 87 L.Ed. 838 (1943).
Certiorari to the Circuit Court of Appeals for the Third Circuit.

MR. JUSTICE DOUGLAS delivered the opinion of the Court.

On April 28, 1936, a check was drawn on the Treasurer of the United States through the Federal Reserve Bank of Philadelphia to the order of Clair A. Barner in the amount of $24.20. It was dated at Harrisburg, Pennsylvania and was drawn for services rendered by Barner to the Works Progress Administration. The check was placed in the mail addressed to Barner at his address in Mackeyville, Pa. Barner never received the check. Some unknown person obtained it in a mysterious manner and presented it to the J.C. Penney Co. store in Clearfield, Pa., representing that he was the payee and identifying himself to the satisfaction of the employees of J.C. Penney Co. He endorsed the check in the name of Barner and transferred it to J.C. Penney Co. in exchange for cash and merchandise. Barner never authorized the endorsement nor participated in the proceeds of the check. J.C. Penney Co. endorsed the check over to the Clearfield Trust Co. which accepted it as agent for the purpose of collection and endorsed it as follows: "Pay to the order of Federal Reserve Bank of Philadelphia, Prior Endorsements Guaranteed." [1] Clearfield Trust Co. collected the check from the United States through the Federal Reserve Bank of Philadelphia and paid the full amount thereof to J.C. Penney Co. Neither the Clearfield Trust Co. nor J.C. Penney Co. had any knowledge or suspicion of the forgery. Each acted in good faith. On or before May 10, 1936, Barner advised the timekeeper and the foreman of the W.P.A. project on which he was employed that he had not received the check in question. This information was duly communicated to other agents of the United States and on November 30, 1936, Barner executed an affidavit alleging

---

1. Guarantee of all prior endorsements on presentment for payment of such a check to Federal Reserve banks or member bank depositories is required by Treasury Regulations. 31 Code of Federal Regulations § 202.32, § 202.33.

that the endorsement of his name on the check was a forgery. No notice was given the Clearfield Trust Co. or J.C. Penney Co. of the forgery until January 12, 1937, at which time the Clearfield Trust Co. was notified. The first notice received by Clearfield Trust Co. that the United States was asking reimbursement was on August 31, 1937.

This suit was instituted in 1939 by the United States against the Clearfield Trust Co., the jurisdiction of the federal District Court being invoked pursuant to the provisions of § 24(1) of the Judicial Code, 28 U.S.C. § 41(1). The cause of action was based on the express guaranty of prior endorsements made by the Clearfield Trust Co. J.C. Penney Co. intervened as a defendant. The case was heard on complaint, answer and stipulation of facts. The District Court held that the rights of the parties were to be determined by the law of Pennsylvania and that since the United States unreasonably delayed in giving notice of the forgery to the Clearfield Trust Co., it was barred from recovery under the rule of Market Street Title & Trust Co. v. Chelten T. Co., 296 Pa. 230, 145 A. 848. It accordingly dismissed the complaint. On appeal the Circuit Court of Appeals reversed. 3 Cir., 130 F.2d 93. The case is here on a petition for a writ of certiorari which we granted, 317 U.S. 619, because of the importance of the problems raised and the conflict between the decision below and Security–First Nat. Bank v. United States, 103 F.2d 188, from the Ninth Circuit.

We agree with the Circuit Court of Appeals that the rule of Erie R. Co. v. Tompkins, 304 U.S. 64, does not apply to this action. The rights and duties of the United States on commercial paper which it issues are governed by federal rather than local law. When the United States disburses its funds or pays its debts, it is exercising a constitutional function or power. This check was issued for services performed under the Federal Emergency Relief Act of 1935, 49 Stat. 115, 15 U.S.C. §§ 721–728. The authority to issue the check had its origin in the Constitution and the statutes of the United States and was in no way dependent on the laws of Pennsylvania or of any other state. *Cf.* Board of Commissioners v. United States, 308 U.S. 343; Royal Indemnity Co. v. United States, 313 U.S. 289. The duties imposed upon the United States and the rights acquired by it as a result of the issuance find their roots in the same federal sources.[2] *Cf.* Deitrick v. Greaney, 309 U.S. 190; D'Oench, Duhme & Co. v. Federal Deposit Ins. Corp., 315 U.S. 447. In absence of an applicable Act of Congress it is for the federal courts to fashion the governing rule of law according to their own standards. United States v. Guaranty Trust Co., 293 U.S. 340, is not opposed to this result. That case was concerned with a conflict of laws rule as to the title acquired by a transferee in Yugoslavia under a forged endorsement. Since the payee's address was Yugoslavia, the check had "something of the quality of a foreign bill" and the law of Yugoslavia was applied to determine what title the transferee acquired.

In our choice of the applicable federal rule we have occasionally selected state law. See Royal Indemnity Co. v. United States, *supra.* But reasons which may make state law at times the appropriate federal rule

---

2. Various Treasury Regulations govern the payment and endorsement of government checks and warrants and the reimbursement of the Treasurer of the United States by Federal Reserve banks and member bank depositories on payment of checks or warrants bearing a forged endorsement. See 31 Code of Federal Regulations §§ 202.0, 202.32–202.34. Forgery of the check was an offense against the United States. Criminal Code § 148, 18 U.S.C. § 262.

are singularly inappropriate here. The issuance of commercial paper by the United States is on a vast scale and transactions in that paper from issuance to payment will commonly occur in several states. The application of state law, even without the conflict of laws rules of the forum, would subject the rights and duties of the United States to exceptional uncertainty. It would lead to great diversity in results by making identical transactions subject to the vagaries of the laws of the several states. The desirability of a uniform rule is plain. And while the federal law merchant developed for about a century under the regime of Swift v. Tyson, 16 Pet. 1, represented general commercial law rather than a choice of a federal rule designed to protect a federal right, it nevertheless stands as a convenient source of reference for fashioning federal rules applicable to these federal questions.

United States v. National Exchange Bank, 214 U.S. 302, falls in that category. The Court held that the United States could recover as drawee from one who presented for payment a pension check on which the name of the payee had been forged, in spite of a protracted delay on the part of the United States in giving notice of the forgery. * * *

The National Exchange Bank case went no further than to hold that prompt notice of the discovery of the forgery was not a condition precedent to suit. It did not reach the question whether lack of prompt notice might be a defense. We think it may. If it is shown that the drawee on learning of the forgery did not give prompt notice of it and that damage resulted, recovery by the drawee is barred. See Ladd & Tilton Bank v. United States, 9 Cir., 30 F.2d 334; United States v. National Rockland Bank, D.C., 35 F.Supp. 912; United States v. National City Bank, D.C., 28 F.Supp. 144. The fact that the drawee is the United States and the laches those of its employees are not material. Cooke v. United States, 91 U.S. 389, 398. The United States as drawee of commercial paper stands in no different light than any other drawee. As stated in United States v. National Exchange Bank, 270 U.S. 527, 534, "The United States does business on business terms." It is not excepted from the general rules governing the rights and duties of drawees "by the largeness of its dealings and its having to employ agents to do what if done by a principal in person would leave no room for doubt." Id., 270 U.S. at page 535. But the damage occasioned by the delay must be established and not left to conjecture. Cases such as Market St. Title & Trust Co. v. Chelten Trust Co., supra, place the burden on the drawee of giving prompt notice of the forgery—injury to the defendant being presumed by the mere fact of delay. See London & River Plate Bank v. Bank of Liverpool, [1896] 1 Q.B. 7. But we do not think that he who accepts a forged signature of a payee deserves that preferred treatment. It is his neglect or error in accepting the forger's signature which occasions the loss. See Bank of Commerce v. Union Bank, 3 N.Y. 230, 236. He should be allowed to shift that loss to the drawee only on a clear showing that the drawee's delay in notifying him of the forgery caused him damage. See Woodward, Quasi Contracts (1913) § 25. No such damage has been shown by Clearfield Trust Co. who so far as appears can still recover from J.C. Penney Co. The only showing on the part of the latter is contained in the stipulation to the effect that if a check cashed for a customer is returned unpaid or for reclamation a short time after the date on which it is cashed, the employees can often locate the person who cashed it. It is further stipulated that when J.C. Penney Co. was notified of the forgery in the present case none of its employees was able to remember anything about the transaction or check in question. The inference is that the more prompt the notice the more likely the detection of the forger. But that falls short of a showing that the delay caused a manifest loss. Third Nat. Bank v. Merchants' Nat. Bank, 76 Hun 475, 27 N.Y.S. 1070. It is but another way of saying that mere delay is enough.

Affirmed.

MR. JUSTICE MURPHY and MR. JUSTICE RUTLEDGE did not participate in the consideration or decision of this case.

INTRODUCTORY NOTE ON THE EXISTENCE, SOURCES AND SCOPE OF A FEDERAL COMMON LAW

(1) Friendly, *In Praise of Erie—And of the New Federal Common Law,* 39 N.Y.U.L.Rev. 383, 405, 421–22 (1964): [1] "In one of his last essays Judge Clark expressed the belief that the Erie decision ran counter to the 'trend of nationalism [that] was happily developing in 1938' and that it caused an 'extreme resurgence of state law in the federal courts.' My view is that, by banishing the spurious uniformity of Swift v. Tyson—what Mr. Justice Frankfurter was to call 'the attractive vision of a uniform body of federal law' but a vision only—and by leaving to the states what ought to be left to them, Erie led to the emergence of a federal decisional law in areas of national concern that is truly uniform because, under the supremacy clause, it is binding in every forum, and therefore is predictable and useful as its predecessor, more general in subject matter but limited to the federal courts, was not. The clarion yet careful pronouncement of Erie, 'There is no federal general common law,' opened the way to what, for want of a better term, we may call specialized federal common law. I doubt that we sufficiently realize how far this development has gone—let alone where it is likely to go. * * *

"So, as it seems to me, the Supreme Court, in the years since Erie, has been forging a new centripetal tool incalculably useful to our federal system. It has employed a variety of techniques—spontaneous generation as in the cases of government contracts or interstate controversies, implication of a private federal cause of action from a statute providing other sanctions, construing a jurisdictional grant as a command to fashion federal law, and the normal judicial filling of statutory interstices. * * *

"The complementary concepts—that federal courts must follow state decisions on matters of substantive law appropriately cognizable by the states whereas state courts must follow federal decisions on subjects within national legislative power where Congress has so directed or the basic scheme of the Constitution demands—seem so beautifully simple, and so simply beautiful, that we must wonder why a century and a half was needed to discover them, and must wonder even more why anyone should want to shy away once the discovery was made. We may not yet have achieved the best of all possible worlds with respect to the relationship between state and federal law. But the combination of Erie with Clearfield

---

1. This paper is also printed in Friendly, Benchmarks 155 (1967), and in 19 Record of N.Y.C.B.A. 64 (1964).

and Lincoln Mills [see p. 878, *infra*] has brought us to a far, far better one than we have ever known before. * * *" [2]

(2) In D'Oench, Duhme & Co. v. Federal Deposit Ins. Corp., 315 U.S. 447 (1942), the respondent brought action in a federal district court in Missouri to recover on a note executed by petitioner in 1933 and payable to an Illinois state bank. The note was given to replace certain past due bonds the petitioner had sold the bank so that the bonds would not appear as assets of the bank, and "with the understanding it will not be called for payment". Respondent insured the bank in 1934. Since 1935 the note had been among the bank's charged off assets. The respondent acquired it in 1938 as collateral for a loan made in connection with the assumption of the bank's deposit liabilities by another bank.

The circuit court of appeals applied general conflicts rules to determine that the note was an Illinois contract, and decided that under Illinois law the respondent was the equivalent of a holder in due course and entitled to recover. The petitioner claimed that Missouri's conflict of laws rules should have been applied. The Supreme Court said (p. 456):

" * * * Whether the rule of the Klaxon case applies where federal jurisdiction is not based on diversity of citizenship, we need not decide. For we are of the view that the liability of petitioner on the note involves decision of a federal, not a state, question under the rule of Deitrick v. Greaney, 309 U.S. 190." [3]

The Court found in various federal statutes "a federal policy to protect respondent, and the public funds which it administers, against misrepresentations as to the securities or other assets in the portfolios of the banks which respondent insures or to which it makes loans" (p. 457).

In the course of an illuminating concurring opinion, Justice Jackson said (pp. 467–69, 470–73):

2. The Erie doctrine is sometimes spoken of as applying only in cases in which jurisdiction is based on diversity of citizenship. This view is erroneous: Erie applies, whatever the basis of jurisdiction, to any issue in the case which is governed by state law operating of its own force. (Consider, for example, a state claim that is within federal competence solely because it is pendent to a federal claim.) And it is equally clear that Erie is inapplicable with respect to issues governed by federal law, even if jurisdiction does rest on diversity of citizenship. See generally Hill, *The Erie Doctrine in Bankruptcy*, 66 Harv.L.Rev. 1013 (1953); Sola Elec. Co. v. Jefferson Elec. Co., 317 U.S. 173, 175–77 (1942).

The intersection of these two ideas was explored in DelCostello v. International Brotherhood of Teamsters, 462 U.S. 151, 159–61 n. 13 (1983). The Court in that case rejected the argument that the Erie doctrine and the Rules of Decision Act required application of state statutes of limitations to federal causes of action whenever Congress had failed to provide one, stating broadly that neither Erie nor the statute "can now be taken as establish-ing a *mandatory* rule that we apply state law in federal interstices." For disagreement with the breadth of this statement, see Burbank, *Interjurisdictional Preclusion and Federal Common Law: Toward a General Approach*, 70 Cornell L.Rev. 625, 631 (1985).

3. In this case the receiver of a national bank brought an action against one of the bank's directors upon a note which the director had given the bank, in violation of the National Bank Act, upon the understanding that it was not to be paid and as a substitute for shares of its own stock illegally purchased and retained by the bank. The Court said (pp. 200–01) that it was immaterial "whether, by Massachusetts law respondent is precluded from setting up the illegality of the transaction as a defense to his own note. * * * [I]t is the federal statute which condemns as unlawful respondent's acts. The extent and nature of the legal consequences of this condemnation, though left by the statute to judicial determination, are nevertheless to be derived from it and the federal policy which it has adopted."

"This case is not entertained by the federal courts because of diversity of citizenship. It is here because a federal agency brings the action, and the law of its being provides, with exceptions not important here, that: 'All suits of a civil nature at common law or in equity to which the Corporation shall be a party shall be deemed to arise under the laws of the United States: * * *' That this provision is not merely jurisdictional is suggested by the presence in the same section of the Act of the separate provision that the Corporation may sue and be sued 'in any court of law or equity, State or Federal.'

"Although by Congressional command this case is to be deemed one arising under the laws of the United States, no federal statute purports to define the Corporation's rights as a holder of the note in suit or the liability of the maker thereof. There arises, therefore, the question whether in deciding the case we are bound to apply the law of some particular state or whether, to put it bluntly, we may make our own law from materials found in common-law sources.

"This issue has a long historical background of legal and political controversy as to the place of the common law in federal jurisprudence. As the matter now stands, it seems settled that the federal courts may not resort to the common law to punish crimes not made punishable by Act of Congress; and that, apart from special statutory or constitutional provision, they are not bound in other fields by English precedents existing at any particular date. The federal courts have no *general* common law, as in a sense they have no general or comprehensive jurisprudence of any kind, because many subjects of private law which bulk large in the traditional common law are ordinarily within the province of the states and not of the federal government. But this is not to say that wherever we have occasion to decide a federal question which cannot be answered from federal statutes alone we may not resort to all the source materials of the common law, or that when we have fashioned an answer it does not become a part of the federal non-statutory or common law. * * *

"Were we bereft of the common law, our federal system would be impotent. This follows from the recognized futility of attempting all-complete statutory codes, and is apparent from the terms of the Constitution itself. * * *

"A federal court sitting in a non-diversity case such as this does not sit as a local tribunal. In some cases it may see fit for special reasons to give the law of a particular state highly persuasive or even controlling effect, but in the last analysis its decision turns upon the law of the United States, not that of any state. Federal law is no juridical chameleon, changing complexion to match that of each state wherein lawsuits happen to be commenced because of the accidents of service of process and of the application of the venue statutes. It is found in the federal Constitution, statutes, or common law. Federal common law implements the federal Constitution and statutes, and is conditioned by them. Within these limits, federal courts are free to apply the traditional common-law technique of decision and to draw upon all the sources of the common law in cases such as the present. Board of Commissioners v. United States, 308 U.S. 343, 350.

"The law which we apply to this case consists of principles of established credit in jurisprudence, selected by us because they are appropriate to effectuate the policy of the governing Act. The Corporation was created and financed in part by the United States to bolster the entire banking and credit structure. ＊ ＊ ＊ Under the Act, the Corporation has a dual relation of creditor or potential creditor and of supervising authority toward insured banks. The immunity of such a corporation from schemes concocted by the cooperative deceit of bank officers and customers is not a question to be answered from considerations of geography. That a particular state happened to have the greatest connection, in the conflict of laws sense, with the making of the note involved, or that the subsequent conduct happened to be chiefly centered there, is not enough to make us subservient to the legislative policy or the judicial views of that state.

"I concur in the Court's holding because I think that the defense asserted is nowhere admissible against the Corporation and that we need not go to the law of any particular state as our authority for so holding."

(3) The Clearfield case and the materials that follow explore in a variety of settings the issues raised by Judge Friendly and Justice Jackson. In considering these materials, you should keep two important sets of questions in mind. First, do the federal courts have authority to declare and apply a federal common law rule in the particular context? What is the source of that authority?[4] What is the role played by necessity, as described by Justice Jackson in D'Oench, Duhme, or by "spontaneous generation," as described by Judge Friendly? What is the significance of the general direction in the Rules of Decision Act, 28 U.S.C. § 1652, which makes no explicit exception for federal common law?

Second, if the authority exists, is its exercise appropriate? Note two significant limiting constraints: the constraint of federalism—respect for the role of the states and of state law in the constitutional plan; and the constraint of separation of powers—respect for the central role of the legislature in the formulation of federal policy. The first of these is not a factor in the exercise by state courts of their common law powers, but the second is. Is the relationship between the judicial and legislative branches significantly different at the federal and state levels?[5]

(4) Justice Jackson, concurring in D'Oench, Duhme, Paragraph (2), *supra,* noted the possible relevance of state law to the case at hand before he concluded that state law did not control on the particular issue:

"I hardly suppose that Congress intended to set us completely adrift from state law with regard to all questions as to which it has not provided a statutory answer. An intention to give persuasive or binding effect to state law has been found to exist in a number of cases similar in that they arose under a law of the United States but were not governed by any specific statutory provision. No doubt many questions as to the liability of parties to commercial paper which comes into the hands of the Corporation will best be solved by applying the local law with reference to which the makers and the insured bank presumably contracted. The Corporation would

---

4. Only rarely does Congress explicitly direct the federal courts to declare and apply common law rules. For an example, see Federal Rule of Evidence 501: "Except as otherwise required ＊ ＊ ＊ [by federal law], the privilege of a witness, person, government, State, or political subdivision thereof shall be governed by the principles of the common law as they may be interpreted by the courts of the United States in the light of reason and experience."

5. For criticism of the two-step process described in text, see Field, *Sources of Law: The Scope of Federal Common Law,* 99 Harv.L.Rev. 881, 950–53 (1986).

succeed only to the rights which the bank itself acquired where ordinary and good-faith commercial transactions are involved. But petitioners' conduct here was not intended to confer any right on the bank itself, for as to it the note was agreed to be a nullity. Petitioners' conduct was intended to and did have a direct and independent effect on unknown third parties, among whom the Corporation now appears. The policy of the federal Act does not seem to me to leave dependent on local law the question whether one may plead his own scheme to deceive a bank's creditors and supervising authorities as against the Corporation" (315 U.S. at 473–75).

(5) Note that a complex spectrum of different assumptions about the authoritativeness of state law can be hidden under the surface of the general proposition that state rather than federal law should "apply" as the rule of decision governing a given issue in a federal (or, for that matter, a state) court.

(a) It may be asserted that, as a matter of constitutional allocation of power, the question at issue is entirely beyond the competence of the federal government (Congress as well as federal court), so that state law *must* apply.

(b) The question may arise within the vast area where Congress has constitutional power to legislate, but has not done so, and where state law, judge-made and legislative, continues to operate of its own force. (An example would be the question in Erie itself: the liability of an interstate railroad to a trespasser is subject to potential federal legislative definition; but it is settled that the mere fact that interstate commerce is involved does not automatically lead to displacement of the ordinary state law of torts (or contracts) with federal judge-made law.) Supporting this category is the fundamental political assumption that normally the basic decision to exercise powers granted to the federal government and to displace state law (when not done directly by the Constitution itself) should be in the hands of Congress rather than the courts. See Mishkin, *The Variousness of "Federal Law": Competence and Discretion in the Choice of National and State Rules for Decision*, 105 U.Pa.L.Rev. 797, 799–800 (1957); Mishkin, *Some Further Last Words on Erie—The Thread*, 87 Harv.L.Rev. 1682, 1683–86 (1974). See generally Wechsler, *The Political Safeguards of Federalism: The Role of the States in the Composition and Selection of the National Government*, 54 Colum.L.Rev. 543 (1954). In light of the materials that follow, consider whether (and to what extent) this fundamental assumption has been modified, and, if so, when and with what justification.

(c) State law may operate as a rule of decision because valid federal legislation calls, explicitly or by implication, for the application of state law. See, *e.g.*, the Federal Tort Claims Act, 28 U.S.C. § 1346(b) ("law of the place where the act or omission occurred" is controlling);[6] RFC v. Beaver County, 328 U.S. 204 (1946), p. 564, *supra*. Notice that in such cases state law does not operate of its own authority, but solely by virtue of an authoritative federal legislative command; state law has been "incorporated" to furnish the content of a federal rule of decision.

---

6. See also the Social Security Act, 42 U.S.C. § 416(h)(1)(A), explicitly calling for reference to the law of the state with respect to who is a "wife, husband, widow, or widower" of an insured, but with a complex escape clause creating a "federal" exception.

(d) The federal "command" to incorporate state law may be a judicial rather than a legislative command; that is, it may be determined as a matter of choice of law, even in the absence of statutory command or implication, that, although federal law should "govern" a given question, state law furnishes an appropriate and convenient measure of the content of this federal law. See, *e.g.,* Board of County Commissioners v. United States, p. 865, *infra.*

Does any of this matter? Does anything turn on what "source of authority" is ascribed to applicable state law?

The answer is surely yes. Most obviously, whether the power to change the relevant rule of decision lies in Congress or the state legislatures (or both, as was true to some extent in the Erie case itself) will turn on who has legislative competence in the area. But the inquiry may be relevant in a number of more subtle ways. Consider the extent to which the answer to the following questions may turn on what "type" of state law is involved in the case: (1) To what extent does state law apply not only to the immediate question at issue but to other more-or-less closely adjoining issues? Thus, if a state statute of limitations "applies," does that state's law automatically apply on what serves to toll that statute? (2) Does the state-law answer to the question at issue (assuming of course that it is constitutional) have to be accepted without regard to its particular content? Or is state law to be applied only if its content accords with federal criteria of acceptability? (Thus consider an aberrational state law classifying automobiles as "fixtures" and thus "real property" in the Beaver County case, *supra.*) (3) If more than one state's law is potentially applicable, does the federal court make an independent choice among state laws, or is it bound by Klaxon to the choice of law rules of the forum state? (4) When state law "applies" because federal law refers to it, or because federal legal consequences turn on a characterization that state law supplies, do the rules for "finding" state law developed under Erie, pp. 789–91, *supra,* control? [7]

See, generally, on the problems of this paragraph, von Mehren & Trautman, The Law of Multistate Problems 1049–59 (1965); Mishkin, *supra,* at 802–10. For a critique of this approach, see Field, note 5, *supra.*

---

7. Commissioner v. Bosch's Estate, 387 U.S. 456 (1967), involved the question whether a certain gift in trust qualified for the marital deduction allowed by the federal estate tax. This in turn depended on whether a "release" of certain powers under the trust was valid under state law. (If it was, the deduction was unavailable.) The majority held that a state trial court's determination of the invalidity of the release was not binding on the tax question, even though the state proceeding was adversary in nature. The Court said that in the context of the availability of a federal tax deduction, the state trial court's ruling should not be controlling since it could undermine federal tax policy to bind federal authority in this fashion. It then noted that even in cases governed by Erie, "federal authority may not be bound even by an

intermediate state appellate court ruling" (p. 465). Thus the Court's conclusion was "but an application" of the Erie rule. For Justice Harlan, in dissent, federal courts were obligated to attribute conclusiveness to state court judgments "in cases in which state-adjudicated property rights are contended to have federal tax consequences * * * unless the litigation from which the judgment resulted does not bear the indicia of a genuinely adversary proceeding" (p. 481).

On the basis of the Bosch case, how would you answer question (4) in text? For further discussion of the case, see Wolfman, *Bosch, Its Implications and Aftermath,* 3d Ann.Inst. on Estate Planning ch. 69–2 (Univ. Miami Law Center 1969).

(6) For several decades following Clearfield, the development of federal common law was explosive. That trend has been slowed by Supreme Court decisions of the past ten years, but the field remains an unruly one, with both issues and answers as diverse as the substantive fields touched by federal regulation and federal government activity. Indeed, the very term "federal *common law*" is not analytically precise. The demarcation between "statutory interpretation" or "constitutional interpretation," on the one hand, and judge-made law on the other, is not a sharp line. Statutory interpretation shades into judicial lawmaking on a spectrum, as specific evidence of legislative purpose with respect to the issue at hand attenuates. We will use the term, federal common law, loosely, as most judges and commentators do, to refer generally to federal rules of decision whose content cannot be traced by traditional methods of interpretation to federal statutory or constitutional command.[8]

(7) On the general problems introduced in this Note, see, in addition to the articles already cited, Merrill, *The Common Law Powers of the Federal Courts,* 52 U.Chi.L.Rev. 1 (1985); Stewart & Sunstein, *Public Programs and Private Rights,* 95 Harv.L.Rev. 1193 (1982); Monaghan, *Foreword: Constitutional Common Law,* 89 Harv.L.Rev. 1 (1975); Hill, *The Law–Making Power of the Federal Courts: Constitutional Preemption,* 67 Colum.L.Rev. 1024 (1967); Note, 82 Harv.L.Rev. 1512 (1969); Comment, 74 Yale L.J. 325 (1960).

NOTE ON CHOICE OF LAW IN CASES INVOLVING THE LEGAL RELATIONS OF THE UNITED STATES: HEREIN OF FEDERAL GOVERNMENT LITIGATION

(1) Early cases involving proprietary and other interests asserted by the United States focused on the question whether the federal government has the power to institute civil suits in the absence of explicit congressional authorization.[1] The extent to which state or federal law governed in such suits was not subjected to precise analysis; it was simply assumed or asserted that the case was to be brought under "local law." Characteristic is Cotton v. United States, 11 How. 229 (U.S.1850), an action in trespass *q.c.f.* brought by the United States in a federal district court, charging the defendant with cutting and removing trees from federal land. The Court upheld a refusal to charge the jury that "the United States have no common law remedy for private wrongs." Justice Grier said (p. 231): "Although as a sovereign the United States may not be sued, yet as a corporation or body politic they may bring suits to enforce their contracts and protect their property, in the state courts, or in their own tribunals administering the same laws. As an owner of property in almost every State of the Union, they have the same right to have it protected by the local laws that other persons have."

(2) The tradition of recourse to "local law", at least in connection with federal land litigation, was maintained in Mason v. United States, 260 U.S. 545 (1923), a bill in equity by the United States to quiet title and regain possession of public lands in Louisiana, upon which defendants were

---

8. For an even broader definition along the same lines, see Posner, The Federal Courts: Crisis and Reform 299–300 (1985).

1. See pp. 906–16, *infra,* for materials on the implied right of the United States to bring civil suits.

claimed to have made wrongful locations, and to secure an accounting for oil and gas which defendants had removed. The defendants had acted in the face of an executive order withdrawing the lands from location. The Court upheld the validity of this order, and the remaining question concerned the measure of damages. As to this, the Court held that the defendants "were in moral good faith, within the meaning of the Louisiana Code and decisions", that this being so they were entitled by Louisiana law to deduct the costs of production from the value of the oil produced and converted, and that the Louisiana law was applicable.

Speaking for a unanimous Court, Justice Sutherland said (pp. 558–59):

"Here, while the suit is one in equity, the [state] statute and decisions relied upon have nothing to do with the general principles of equity or with the federal equity jurisdiction, but simply establish a measure of damages applicable alike to actions at law and suits in equity. * * * The enforcement of such a statute in an equity suit in no manner trammels or impairs the equity jurisdiction of the national courts.

"It was urged upon the argument that § 721 of the Revised Statutes, which provides that the laws of the several States shall be regarded as rules of decision in trials *at common law* in the courts of the United States, by implication excludes such laws as rules of decision in equity suits. The statute, however, is merely declarative of the rule which would exist in the absence of the statute. * * * And it is not to be narrowed because of an affirmative legislative recognition in terms less broad than the rule."

While the Court thus rejected the claim that federal law applied because the suit was in equity, it did not refer to the possibility that federal law applied because the suit had been brought by the United States and related to public lands.[2]

(3) The brief for the United States in the Clearfield case stated (pp. 11–12):

" * * * It had been settled prior to Swift v. Tyson that the liability of parties on a bond to the United States was not governed by the law of the state where the bond was executed but by the 'rules of the common law'. Cox v. United States, 6 Pet. 172, 204; Duncan v. United States, 7 Pet. 435, 449. The question was particularly acute in those cases, since if local law had been applied it would have been the civil law of Louisiana. 'In contemplation of law,' the Court said, the contract is made where the principal powers of government are exercised (7 Pet. 449); this was the locution employed to reject Louisiana law in favor of the 'principles of the common law' (*Id.* 446).

"Under the regime of Swift v. Tyson, since the law of commercial contracts and negotiable instruments was of course regarded as 'general law', the courts found it unnecessary to consider separately the applicabili-

---

2. This question had in fact been argued by the appellants, although without citation of authority. They recognized the power of Congress under the Constitution to make regulations respecting the public lands; but then said (brief for appellants, p. 45):

" * * * [E]ven if the United States has the right * * * to give to land which it owns in Louisiana incidents which are different from those which inhere in all other lands within the state, this right has not been exercised. The legislative power is the only one which could have acted and it has not acted."

One page in a 16–page brief for the United States (pp. 14–15) was devoted to the proposition that "The United States, with respect to the measure of damages, is not bound by State law or decisions".

ty of state decisional law to contracts or negotiable instruments involving the United States. The law merchant as interpreted by the federal courts was as a rule applied without discussion. Prior to Erie R. Co. v. Tompkins, an issue in regard to governing law insofar as the United States was concerned could have arisen only where the state law took the form of a state statute or state decisions interpreting such statutes. Such an issue seems to have been rarely presented and cannot be said to have been clearly considered or determined. In National Bank of Commerce of Seattle v. United States, 224 Fed. 679, 681 (C.C.A. 9), *cert. denied,* 241 U.S. 658, local statutory law was held not to apply to government checks. However, the more usual practice apparently was to apply federal substantive law without considering state statutes."

The brief did not attempt a comprehensive analysis of the development of the law governing the legal relations between the United States and private persons outside the field of commercial contracts.

The brief for the trust company relied strongly on United States v. Guaranty Trust Co., referred to in the opinion, but otherwise was pitched almost wholly in post-Erie terms.

(4) The first of the post-Erie cases in the Supreme Court to consider the Clearfield problem was Board of County Commissioners v. United States, 308 U.S. 343 (1939). The question was whether a judgment for the United States in an action to recover tax payments illegally exacted from an Indian should include interest. In an opinion for the Court, Justice Frankfurter said (pp. 349–52):

"The issue is uncontrolled by any formal expression of the will of Congress. The United States urges that we must be indifferent to the law of the state * * *. Jackson County, on the other hand, urges that the law of Kansas controls. It is settled doctrine there that a taxpayer may not recover from a county interest upon taxes wrongfully collected. * * *

"We deem neither the juristic theory urged by the Government nor that of Jackson County entirely appropriate for the solution of our problem. The starting point for relief in this case is the Treaty of 1861, exempting M–Ko–Quah–Wah's property from taxation. Effectuation of the exemption is, of course, entirely within Congressional control. But Congress has not specifically provided for the present contingency, that is, the nature and extent of relief in case loss is suffered through denial of exemption. It has left such remedial details to judicial implications. * * * *

"Having left the matter at large for judicial determination within the framework of familiar remedies equitable in their nature, * * * Congress has left us free to take into account appropriate considerations of 'public convenience'. * * * Nothing seems to us more appropriate than due regard for local institutions and local interests. We are concerned with the interplay between the rights of Indians under federal guardianship and the local repercussion of those rights. * * * With reference to other federal rights, the state law has been absorbed, as it were, as the governing federal rule not because state law was the source of the right but because recognition of state interests was not deemed inconsistent with federal policy. * * * In the absence of explicit legislative policy cutting across state interests, we draw upon a general principle that the beneficiaries of federal rights are not to have a privileged position over other aggrieved taxpayers in their relation with the states or their political subdivisions. To respect the law of interest prevailing in Kansas in no wise impinges upon the exemption which the Treaty of 1861 has commanded Kansas to respect and the federal courts to vindicate."

Other post-Erie pre-Clearfield cases are Deitrick v. Greaney, and D'Oench, Duhme & Co. v. Federal Deposit Ins. Corp., both described at p. 858, *supra*.

(5) Was Clearfield itself correctly decided? Judge Friendly, in his article on federal common law (39 N.Y.U.L.Rev. 383, 410) says: "Clearfield decided not one issue but two. The first, to which most of the opinion was devoted and on which it is undeniably sound, is that the right of the United States to recover for conversion of a government check is a federal right, so that the courts of the United States may formulate a rule of decision. The second, over which the Supreme Court jumped rather quickly and not altogether convincingly, is whether, having this opportunity, the federal courts should adopt a uniform nation-wide rule or should follow state law. * * * [T]he question persists why it is more important that federal fiscal officials rather than Pennsylvanians dealing in commercial paper should have the solace of uniformity."

And a footnote (n. 130) continues: "Although the direct consequence of the Government's victory in Clearfield was to impose liability on the paying bank in accordance with the 'uniform' federal rule, this would necessarily lead to an action by the bank against the endorser. If that action were held to be governed by state law, which would excuse the endorser because of the delay, this would destroy the whole substantive basis of the Clearfield decision, namely, that the bank did not suffer from the delay since, under federal law, it could recover from the endorser, and, as has been noted, 'the burden of financial loss will merely be shifted from the Government to the particular endorser whom it chooses to sue.' Mishkin, [105 U.Pa.L.Rev. 797] at 831. On the other hand, if, as would seem more sensible, decision in the action by the bank against the endorser must reflect the result of applying the federal rule in the Government's action against the bank, a rather nice distinction of the Bank of America case is required.[3] See *id.* at 831–32."[4]

---

3. The reference is to Bank of America Nat. Trust & Savings Ass'n v. Parnell, 352 U.S. 29 (1956). In this case, the bank had sued Parnell in a federal court (basing jurisdiction on diversity of citizenship) to recover funds he had obtained by cashing certain United States bonds that had been stolen from the bank. Two issues in the case were whether the bonds were overdue and whether Parnell had taken them in good faith. The Supreme Court held that the first issue was controlled by federal law: "Federal law of course governs the interpretation of the nature of the rights and obligations created by the Government bonds themselves" (p. 34). But the second was not; distinguishing the Clearfield case, the Court emphasized that "[t]he present litigation is purely between private parties and does not touch the rights and duties of

the United States. The only possible interest of the United States in a situation like the one here * * * is that the floating of securities of the United States might somehow or other be adversely affected by the local rule of a particular State regarding the liability of a converter. This is far too speculative * * * to justify the application of federal law to transactions essentially of local concern" (pp. 33–34).

4. For decisions coming on the heels of, and following the result in Clearfield, see National Metropolitan Bank v. United States, 323 U.S. 454 (1945) (commercial paper issued by United States); Priebe & Sons v. United States, 332 U.S. 407 (1947) (government contracts); United States v. Standard Rice Co., 323 U.S. 106 (1944) (government contracts).

(6) That Clearfield did not require the application of uniform federal law to all questions in federal government litigation, even in cases involving government contracts, was made plain in United States v. Yazell, 382 U.S. 341 (1966) (state law may operate to exempt a married woman's separate property from attachment to satisfy a defaulted federal loan to her and her husband). The approach of Yazell was followed, and developed, in United States v. Kimbell Foods, Inc., 440 U.S. 715 (1979), which held that, while federal law governs the question whether contractual liens arising from certain federal loan programs take precedence over certain private liens, nondiscriminatory state laws should be adopted to answer that question. In a unanimous opinion by Justice Marshall, the Court stressed that adopting state law would not interfere with efficient administrative practice or conflict with the purposes of the federal programs. And since "businessmen depend on state commercial law to provide the stability essential for reliable evaluation of the risks involved, * * * subjecting federal contractual liens to the doctrines developed in the tax lien area could undermine that stability. Creditors who justifiably rely on state law to obtain superior liens would have their expectations thwarted whenever a federal contractual security interest suddenly appeared and took precedence. * * * Thus, the prudent course is to adopt the readymade body of state law as the federal rule of decision until Congress strikes a different accommodation" (pp. 739–40).

Note that Kimbell provides a textbook lesson in how the opinion in Clearfield might have been written.[5]

(7) Choice between state and federal law must also be exercised in tort litigation involving the United States and its officers.

(a) In tort suits against the United States, the Federal Tort Claims Act, 28 U.S.C. § 1346(b), makes the government liable for the negligent and wrongful acts and omissions of its employees "under circumstances where the United States, if a private person, would be liable to the claimant in accordance with the law of the place where the act or omission occurred"; important "federal" exceptions are, however, stated in 28 U.S.C. § 2680. See also 28 U.S.C. § 2674. (For materials on the Tort Claims Act, see Chap. IX, Sec. 1, infra.)

In Richards v. United States, 369 U.S. 1 (1962), the Court held that the "law of the place where the act or omission occurred" includes not only that state's internal law but also its choice of law rules: "Certainly there is nothing in the legislative history that even remotely supports the argument that Congress did not intend state conflict rules to apply to multistate tort actions brought against the Government" (p. 14).

Tort suits against federal government officers are discussed at pp. 1147–53, infra.

---

5. Cf. Wilson v. Omaha Indian Tribe, 442 U.S. 653 (1979) (borrowing state law as the rule of decision on certain questions relating to the rights and titles of Indian tribes for which the United States is trustee).

With Yazell and Kimbell, compare United States v. 93.970 Acres of Land, 360 U.S. 328 (1959) (Illinois law on "election of remedies" is inapplicable to bar United States, as landlord, from simultaneously seeking to obtain immediate possession by condemning the lessee's interest and, by relying on its claimed right to revoke, to eject the lessee without liability); United States v. Little Lake Misere Land Co., Inc., 412 U.S. 580, 594–97 (1973) (rejecting state law in connection with mineral rights reserved in federal government contracts, partly on the ground that the specific state law was "hostile to the interests of the United States").

(b) United States v. Standard Oil Co., 332 U.S. 301 (1947), was a tort action brought by the United States, in which (as Justice Rutledge described it) the Court was "asked to create a new substantive legal liability without legislative aid and as at the common law" (p. 302).

An oil truck had injured a soldier, and the United States had lost his services during convalescence and been put to expense for his hospitalization. It sought to recover damages from the tortfeasor, asserting a right of action by analogy to "the master's rights of recovery for loss of the services of his servant or apprentice; the husband's similar action for interference with the marital relation, including loss of consortium as well as the wife's services; and the parent's right to indemnity for loss of a child's services, including his action for a daughter's seduction" (p. 312).

Justice Rutledge's opinion for the Court began by agreeing (p. 305) with "the Government's view that the creation or negation of such a liability is not a matter to be determined by state law," relying on Clearfield and similar cases. Then, recognizing as in Clearfield that " 'in our choice of the applicable federal rule we have occasionally selected state law' ", it rejected any such reference (pp. 309–11). Having thus found that the matter was federal and that the federal rule with respect to it should be uniform, the opinion came finally to the question of what the content of that rule should be. Seemingly without passing judgment upon the merit of the Government's analogies, it concluded that the question was one of "fiscal policy" for determination by Congress rather than by a federal court. The opinion said (pp. 313–16):

"We would not deny the Government's basic premise of the law's capacity for growth, or that it must include the creative work of judges. Soon all law would become antiquated strait jacket and then dead letter, if that power were lacking. And the judicial hand would stiffen in mortmain if it had no part in the work of creation. But in the federal scheme our part in that work, and the part of the other federal courts, outside the constitutional area is more modest than that of state courts, particularly in the freedom to create new common-law liabilities, as Erie R. Co. v. Tompkins itself witnesses. See also United States v. Hudson, 7 Cranch 32.

"Moreover, * * * we have not here simply a question of creating a new liability in the nature of a tort. For grounded though the argument is in analogies drawn from that field, the issue comes down in final consequence to a question of federal fiscal policy, coupled with considerations concerning the need for and the appropriateness of means to be used in executing the policy sought to be established. The tort law analogy is brought forth, indeed, not to secure a new step forward in expanding the recognized area for applying settled principles of that law as such, or for creating new ones. It is advanced rather as the instrument for determining and establishing the federal fiscal and regulatory policies which the Government's executive arm thinks should prevail in a situation not covered by traditionally established liabilities.

"Whatever the merits of the policy, its conversion into law is a proper subject for congressional action, not for any creative power of ours. Congress, not this Court or the other federal courts, is the custodian of the national purse. By the same token it is the primary and most often the exclusive arbiter of federal fiscal affairs. And these comprehend, as we have said, securing the treasury or the government against financial losses however inflicted, including requiring reimbursement for injuries creating them, as well as filling the treasury itself. * * *

"When Congress has thought it necessary to take steps to prevent interference with federal funds, property or relations, it has taken positive action to that end. We think it would have done so here, if that had been its desire. This it still may do, if or when it so wishes."

Justice Jackson alone dissented, saying (p. 318):

" * * * If there is one function which I should think we would feel free to exercise under a Constitution which vests in us judicial power, it would be to apply well-established common law principles to a case whose only novelty is in facts. The courts of England, whose scruples against legislating are at least as sensitive as ours normally are, have not hesitated to say that His Majesty's Treasury may recover outlay to cure a British soldier from injury by a negligent wrongdoer and the wages he was meanwhile paid. Attorney General v. Valle–Jones, [1935] 2 K.B. 209. I think we could hold as much without being suspected of trying to usurp legislative function."

In what respect was the question in Standard Oil one of federal fiscal policy which was not equally true of the question in Cotton v. United States, Paragraph (1), *supra?*

Note that a decision that a given matter is governed by federal law operates to preclude both state courts and state legislatures from contributing to a solution of the problems involved. If the federal courts then woodenly shift the responsibility to Congress, the consequence is that creative development by the judicial process is wholly prevented in the area in question.

Does legal history suggest that it is wise and practicable to place so complete a reliance on the legislative method of lawmaking? Is Congress equipped, with respect to matters of the order of magnitude involved in Standard Oil, to assume sole responsibility for the constructive elaboration and application of legal principles? [6] See generally Hart & Sacks, The Legal Process: Basic Problems in the Making and Application of Law 541–46 (tent. ed. 1958). See also Texas Industries, Inc. v. Radcliff Materials, Inc. and the following note, pp. 938–50, *infra.*

MIREE v. DeKALB COUNTY, GEORGIA

433 U.S. 25, 97 S.Ct. 2490, 53 L.Ed.2d 557 (1977).
Certiorari to the United States Court of Appeals for the Fifth Circuit.

MR. JUSTICE REHNQUIST delivered the opinion of the Court.

These consolidated cases arise out of the 1973 crash of a Lear Jet shortly after takeoff from the DeKalb–Peachtree Airport. The United States Court of Appeals for the Fifth Circuit, en banc, affirmed the

6. For cases involving similar diffidence in the fashioning of rules of decision, see United States v. Gilman, 347 U.S. 507 (1954) (United States as employer may not seek indemnity from an employee whose negligence resulted in a judgment for damages against the United States under the Federal Tort Claims Act); Francis v. Southern Pacific Co., 333 U.S. 445 (1948) (federal law governs and precludes interstate railroad's liability for ordinary negligence in an action by a railroad employee who was killed while riding on a free pass).

dismissal of petitioners' complaint against respondent DeKalb County (hereafter respondent), holding that principles of federal common law were applicable to the resolution of petitioners' breach-of-contract claim. We granted certiorari to consider whether federal or state law should have been applied to that claim; we conclude that the latter should govern.

I

Petitioners are, respectively, the survivors of deceased passengers, the assignee of the jet aircraft owner, and a burn victim. They brought separate lawsuits, later consolidated, against respondent in the United States District Court for the Northern District of Georgia.[1] The basis for federal jurisdiction was diversity of citizenship, 28 U.S.C. § 1332, and the complaints asserted that respondent was liable on three independent theories: negligence, nuisance, and breach of contract. The District Court granted respondent's motion to dismiss each of these claims. The courts below have unanimously agreed that the negligence and nuisance theories are without merit; only the propriety of the dismissal of the contract claims remains in the cases.

Petitioners seek to impose liability on respondent as third-party beneficiaries of contracts between it and the Federal Aviation Administration (FAA). Their complaints allege that respondent entered into six grant agreements with the FAA. Under the terms of the contracts respondent agreed to

"take action to restrict the use of land adjacent to or in the immediate vicinity of the Airport to activities and purposes compatible with normal airport operations including landing and takeoff of aircraft."

Petitioners assert that respondent breached the FAA contracts by owning and maintaining a garbage dump adjacent to the airport, and that the cause of the crash was the ingestion of birds swarming from the dump into the jet engines of the aircraft.

Applying Georgia law, the District Court found that petitioners' claims as third-party beneficiaries under the FAA contracts were barred by the county's governmental immunity, and dismissed the complaints under Fed. Rule Civ.Proc. 12(b)(6). A divided panel of the Court of Appeals decided that under state law petitioners could sue as third-party beneficiaries and that governmental immunity would not bar the suit. Miree v. United States, 526 F.2d 679 (C.A.5 1976). The dissenting judge argued that the court should have applied federal rather than state law; he concluded that under the principles of federal common law the petitioners in this case did not have standing to sue as third-party beneficiaries of the contracts. Sitting en banc, the Court of Appeals reversed the panel on the breach-of-contract issue and adopted the panel dissent on this point as its opinion. Miree v. United States, 538 F.2d 643 (C.A.5 1976). Judge Morgan, who had written the panel opinion, argued for five dissenters that there was no identifiable federal interest in the outcome of this diversity case, and thus that federal common law had no applicability.

---

1. Petitioners also sued the United States under the Federal Tort Claims Act. See 28 U.S.C. §§ 1346(b), 2671 et seq. The litigation before us arises out of the District Court's granting of respondent DeKalb County's motion to dismiss and the entry of final judgment under Fed.Rule Civ.Proc. 54(b). The United States has made no similar motion, and is not a party to the cases in this Court.

II

Since the only basis of federal jurisdiction alleged for petitioners' claim against respondent is diversity of citizenship, the case would unquestionably be governed by Georgia law, Erie Railroad Co. v. Tompkins, 304 U.S. 64 (1938), but for the fact that the United States is a party to the contracts in question, entered into pursuant to federal statute. See Airport and Airway Development Act of 1970, 84 Stat. 219, as amended, 49 U.S.C. § 1701 *et seq.* (1970 ed. and Supp. V). The en banc majority of the Court of Appeals adopted, by reference, the view that, given these factors, application of federal common law was required * * *

We do not agree with the conclusion of the Court of Appeals. The litigation before us raises no question regarding the liability of the United States or the responsibilities of the United States under the contracts. The relevant inquiry is a narrow one: whether petitioners as third-party beneficiaries of the contracts have standing to sue respondent. While federal common law may govern even in diversity cases [3] where a uniform national rule is necessary to further the interests of the Federal Government, Clearfield Trust Co. v. United States, 318 U.S. 363 (1943), the application of federal common law to resolve the issue presented here would promote no federal interests even approaching the magnitude of those found in Clearfield Trust * * *.

* * * [I]n this case, the resolution of petitioners' breach-of-contract claim against respondent will have no direct effect upon the United States or its Treasury.[4] The Solicitor General, waiving his right to respond in these cases advised us:

> "In the course of the proceedings below, the United States determined that its interests would not be directly affected by the resolution of these issue[s] and therefore did not participate in briefing or argument in the court of appeals. In view of these considerations, the United States does not intend to respond to the petitions unless it is requested to do so by the Court.

The operations of the United States in connection with FAA grants such as these are undoubtedly of considerable magnitude. However, we see no reason for concluding that these operations would be burdened or subjected to uncertainty by variant state-law interpretations regarding whether those with whom the United States contracts might be sued by third-party beneficiaries to the contracts. Since only the rights of private litigants are at issue here, we find the Clearfield Trust rationale inapplicable.

We think our conclusion that these cases do not fit within the Clearfield Trust rule follows from the Court's later decision in Bank of America National Trust & Savings Assn. v. Parnell, 352 U.S. 29 (1956), [p. 866, note 3, *supra*], in which the Court declined to apply that rule in a fact situation analogous to this one. * * *

---

3. The Clearfield Trust rule may apply in diversity cases. See Sola Electric Co. v. Jefferson Electric Co., 317 U.S. 173 (1942); Bank of America National Trust & Savings Association v. Parnell, 352 U.S. 29 (1956); Wallis v. Pan American Petroleum Corporation, 384 U.S. 63 (1966).

4. There is no indication that petitioners' tort claim against the United States, see n. 1, *supra,* will be affected by the resolution of this issue. Indeed, the Federal Tort Claims Act itself looks to state law in determining liability. 28 U.S.C. § 1346(b).

The parallel between Parnell and these cases is obvious. The question of whether petitioners may sue respondent does not require decision under federal common law since the litigation is among private parties and no substantial rights or duties of the United States hinge on its outcome. On the other hand, nothing we say here forecloses the applicability of federal common law in interpreting the rights and duties of the United States under federal contracts.

Nor is the fact that the United States has a substantial interest in regulating aircraft travel and promoting air travel safety sufficient, given the narrow question before us, to call into play the rule of Clearfield Trust. * * *

The question of whether private parties may, as third-party beneficiaries, sue a municipality for breach of the FAA contracts involves this federal interest only insofar as such lawsuits might be thought to advance federal aviation policy by inducing compliance with FAA safety provisions. However, even assuming the correctness of this notion, we adhere to the language in [Wallis v. Pan American Petroleum Corp., 384 U.S. 63, 68 (1966)], stating that the issue of whether to displace state law on an issue such as this is primarily a decision for Congress. Congress has chosen not to do so in this case.[5] Actually the application of federal common law, as interpreted by the Court of Appeals here would frustrate this federal interest *pro tanto*, since that court held that this breach-of-contract lawsuit would not lie under federal law. On the other hand, at least in the opinion of the majority of the panel below, Georgia law would countenance the action. Even assuming that a different result were to be reached under federal common law, we think this language from Wallis all but forecloses its application to these cases:

"Apart from the highly abstract nature of [the federal] interest, there has been no showing that state law is not adequate to achieve it." *Id.*, at 71.

We conclude that any federal interest in the outcome of the question before us "is far too speculative, far too remote a possibility to justify the application of federal law to transactions essentially of local concern." Parnell, 352 U.S., at 33–34.

Although we have determined that Georgia law should be applied to the question raised by respondent's motion to dismiss, we shall not undertake to decide the correct outcome under Georgia law. * * * We therefore vacate the judgment and remand to the Court of Appeals for consideration of the claim under applicable Georgia law.*

* * *

MR. CHIEF JUSTICE BURGER, concurring in the judgment.

There is language in the Court's opinion which might be misinterpreted as rigidly limiting the application of "federal common law" to only those

---

5. The Congress has considered, but not passed, a bill to provide for a federal cause of action arising out of aircraft disasters. See Hearings on S. 961 before the Subcommittee on Improvements in Judicial Machinery of the Senate Committee on the Judiciary, pt. 2, 91st Cong., 1st Sess. (1969).

* [Ed.] On remand, the Fifth Circuit held (on the basis of the Georgia Supreme Court's answers to certified questions) that the plaintiffs could not bring suit as third party beneficiaries under Georgia law. 588 F.2d 453 (5th Cir.1979).

situations where the rights and obligations of the Federal Government are at issue. I do not agree with such a restrictive approach.

I cannot read Clearfield Trust Co. v. United States, 318 U.S. 363 (1943), and Bank of America National Trust and Savings Assn. v. Parnell, 352 U.S. 29 (1956) as, in all circumstances, precluding the application of "federal common law" to all matters involving only the rights of private citizens. Certainly, in a diversity action, state substantive law should not be ousted on the basis of " 'an amorphous doctrine of national sovereignty' divorced from any specific constitutional or statutory provision and premised solely on the argument 'that every authorized activity of the United States represents an exercise of its governmental power.' " United States v. Little Lake Misere Land Co., 412 U.S. 580, 592 n. 10 (1973), quoting United States v. Burnison, 339 U.S. 87, 91, and 92 (1950). However, I am not prepared to foreclose, at this point, the possibility that there may be situations where the rights and obligations of private parties are so dependent on a specific exercise of congressional regulatory power that "the Constitution or Acts of Congress 'require' otherwise than that state law govern of its own force." United States v. Little Lake Misere Land Co., *supra*, 412 U.S., at 592–593.

In such a situation, I would not read Wallis v. Pan American Petroleum Corporation, 384 U.S. 63, 68 (1966), to preclude a choice of "federal common law" simply because there is no specific federal legislation governing the particular transaction at issue. Once it has been determined that it would be inappropriate to apply state law and that federal law must govern, "the inevitable incompleteness presented by all legislation means that interstitial federal lawmaking is a basic responsibility of the federal courts." United States v. Little Lake Misere Land Co., supra, 412 U.S., at 593. In short, although federal courts will be called upon to invoke it infrequently, there must be " 'federal judicial competence to declare the governing law in an area comprising issues substantially related to an established program of government operation.' " *Ibid.*, quoting Mishkin, The Variousness of "Federal Law": Competence and Discretion in the Choice of National and State Rules for Decision, 105 U.Pa.L.Rev. 797, 800 (1957).

Although in my view the issue is close, I conclude, on balance, that the cause of action asserted by the plaintiffs is not so intimately related to the purpose of the Airport and Airway Development Act of 1970, 84 Stat. 219, as amended, 49 U.S.C. § 1701 *et seq.* (1970 ed. and Supp. V), as to require the application of federal law in this case. Accordingly, the rule of Erie R. Co. v. Tompkins, 304 U.S. 64, applies, and I join the judgment of the Court remanding the cases for a determination of the correct outcome under Georgia law.

NOTE ON CHOICE OF LAW IN PRIVATE LITIGATION INVOLVING INTERESTS CREATED BY FEDERAL LAW

(1) The Court in Miree did not use the two-step technique of holding that federal law governs but that state law is adopted as its measure. Compare, *e.g.*, United States v. Kimbell Foods, Inc., 440 U.S. 715 (1979), p. 867, *supra*. Should it have?

Is it difficult to understand how state law can govern the question whether the plaintiffs have standing to sue as third-party beneficiaries of a federal government contract? Note that this question of standing invokes issues of both general contract law (under what circumstances, if any, does a third-party beneficiary of a contract have a right to sue for breach?) and of contract interpretation (does the contract at issue confer such a right?). Is the Court in Miree holding that state law governs on all these issues?

(2) For discussion of the many cases holding that in private litigation involving land, federal law does not generally govern merely because the chain of title includes a patent or grant from the United States, see Chap. VIII, p. 1003, *infra*.[1] Similarly, the fact that patent and copyright interests are the creation of federal law does not automatically mean that contractual arrangements concerning these interests are governed by federal law.

In line with this tradition is Wallis v. Pan American Petroleum Corp., 384 U.S. 63 (1966), quoted in Miree. Wallis raised the question "whether in general federal or state law should govern the dealings of private parties in an oil and gas lease validly issued [by the United States] under the Mineral Leasing Act of 1920" (p. 67). The specific issue was the validity of an oral contract and the interpretation of a written contract allegedly assigning a share in the lease. The Court held that state law governed (pp. 69–71): "If there is a federal statute dealing with the general subject, it is a prime repository of federal policy and a starting point for federal common law. See Deitrick v. Greaney, 309 U.S. 190; Reitmeister v. Reitmeister, 162 F.2d 691. We find nothing in the Mineral Leasing Act of 1920 expressing policies inconsistent with state law in the area that concerns us here. * * *

* * * [After rejecting several claims of conflict between federal policy and specific provisions of state law, the Court concluded:] Finally, it is said that because the leases are issued by the United States and concern federal lands, there is a federal interest in having private disputes over them justly resolved. Apart from the highly abstract nature of this interest, there has been no showing that state law is not adequate to achieve it."

Note that the Court in Wallis, and in Miree, did not invoke the Rules of Decision Act, 28 U.S.C. § 1652, in support of the result reached. The Act mandates reference to state law "except where the Constitution or treaties of the United States or acts of Congress otherwise require or provide," and some have read this language to restrict federal court lawmaking. *E.g.,* Kurland, Politics, The Constitution, and the Warren Court 62 (1970); Merrill, *The Common Law Powers of The Federal Courts,* 52 U.Chi.L.Rev. 1, 27–32 (1985). But the phrase "in cases where they apply" can surely be read to mean "in cases in which there is no federal common law preempting state rules of decision." See Redish, Federal Jurisdiction: Tensions in the Allocation of Judicial Power 81 (1980); Meltzer, *State Court Forfeitures of Federal Rights,* 99 Harv.L.Rev. 1128, 1168 (1986).

(3) The Court has had difficulty choosing between state and federal law in matters involving claims of family members to federal pensions or

---

1. But see Hughes v. Washington, 389 U.S. 290 (1967), holding that federal rather than state law governs the ownership of "rights in accretion" to ocean-front lands, conveyed by the United States to a private owner prior to statehood. The case makes the important point that the scope of the original grant from the United States continues to be governed by federal law even in private litigation.

retirement pay, to the proceeds of federal insurance, or to federal bonds. In a number of instances state law has, to a significant extent, been required to yield.[2] In Wissner v. Wissner, 338 U.S. 655 (1950), Major Wissner had bought a National Service Life Insurance Policy and designated his mother as beneficiary. Premiums were paid out of Wissner's army pay. Under California law, half of the proceeds of the policy were payable to the Major's widow as community property. The Court held, however, that the provision of the governing federal statute which stated that the insured "shall have the right to designate the beneficiary * * * and shall * * * at all times have the right to change the beneficiary," prevented the application of the state's community property law (pp. 658–59). "The National Service Life Insurance Act is the congressional mode of affording a uniform and comprehensive system of life insurance for members and veterans of the armed forces of the United States. A liberal policy toward the serviceman and his named beneficiary is everywhere evident in the comprehensive statutory plan. * * * Congress has spoken with force and clarity in directing that the proceeds belong to the named beneficiary and no other" (p. 658). Justice Minton, joined by Justices Frankfurter and Jackson, dissented: "I am not persuaded that * * * the choice of beneficiary * * * provision should carry the implication of wiping out family property rights, which traditionally have been defined by state law. * * * I cannot believe that Congress intended to say to a serviceman, 'You may take your wife's property and purchase a policy of insurance payable to your mother, and we will see that your defrauded wife gets none of the money'" (pp. 663–64).

Two later decisions involved claims to federal bonds. Free v. Bland, 369 U.S. 663 (1962), held that federal law governed survivorship rights to federal bonds bought with community property, on the ground that the state probate law conflicted with the federal interest in making the bonds attractive to investors. State law fared somewhat better in Yiatchos v. Yiatchos, 376 U.S. 306 (1964), where the Court held that (a) federal law governs on the question whether a person who purchased federal bonds and designated a beneficiary had "defrauded" his wife of property interests protected by state property law, but (b) "in applying the federal standard we shall be guided by state law insofar as the property interests of the widow created by state law are concerned" (p. 309).

Wissner was followed and Yiatchos distinguished in Ridgway v. Ridgway, 454 U.S. 46 (1981). At the time of Sergeant Ridgway's divorce from his first wife, the state court's decree ordered him to keep in force, for the benefit of his children, a life insurance policy issued pursuant to the Serviceman's Group Life Insurance Act (SGLIA).[3] Ridgway subsequently

---

2. In addition to the cases discussed in text, see Hisquierdo v. Hisquierdo, 439 U.S. 572 (1979) (federal law prohibits a state from treating as community property a divorcing husband's expectancy interest in pension benefits under the Railroad Retirement Act); McCarty v. McCarty, 453 U.S. 210 (1981) (federal law precludes a state court from dividing military retirement pay pursuant to state community property laws). For Congress's response to the McCarty decision, see the amendments to Title 10 of the U.S. Code in the Uniformed Services Former Spouses' Protection Act, Pub.L. No. 97–252, §§ 1001–1006, 96 Stat. 718, 730 (1982) (substantially overruling McCarty and permitting division of retirement or retainer pay in accordance with state law).

3. The state decree also provided that if the policy was terminated for any reason, Ridgway "shall immediately replace it with other life insurance of equal amount for the benefit of the children" (p. 48).

remarried and changed the beneficiary designation in favor of his second wife. After his death, the state supreme court held that the second wife should receive the policy proceeds as constructive trustee for the benefit of the children. The U.S. Supreme Court reversed, concluding that the constructive trust conflicted with the provisions of the SGLIA and implementing regulations giving the insured service member the right to designate and change the beneficiary at any time, and also conflicted with the provision exempting policy proceeds "from the claims of creditors" and from any "attachment, levy, or seizure by or under any legal or equitable process whatever" (p. 61). Yiatchos was not controlling because the fraud alleged in that case was committed by the husband " 'while acting in his capacity as manager of the general community property.' * * * In this case, by way of contrast, Sergeant Ridgway misdirected property over which he had exclusive control. In doing so, of course, he deprived the [first wife and the children] of benefits to which they were entitled under state law. But that is precisely what transpired in Wissner * * *" (p. 59 n. 8).

Justice Powell, joined by Justice Rehnquist in dissent, argued that the reference to " 'exclusive control' over the property begs the very question before us: whether Richard [Ridgway] retained this control despite his conduct" (p. 69). He and Justice Stevens, in a separate dissent, argued that Congress had not supplanted state law relating to a breach of trust and that the imposition of the constructive trust by the state court did not damage any federal interest.

Do the decisions discussed in this Paragraph (3) support the position taken by Chief Justice Burger in his concurrence in Miree? Or do they turn entirely on the interpretation of particular federal statutes? Viewed either as federal common law or as statutory construction, didn't the Ridgway decision neglect the essentially interstitial character of federal law by being too quick to discern a federal interest in conflict with an agreed upon division of property under state law? If such insurance policies cannot serve as the subject of binding family settlements, isn't their value to servicemen reduced, and if so, isn't that a result Congress would want to avoid? [4]

(4) The question whether Congress intends to refer to, or incorporate, state law may also arise under other legislation defining and regulating federal property interests. A characteristic example is DeSylva v. Ballentine, 351 U.S. 570 (1956). The copyright statute then in effect allowed

---

The SGLIA is similar in many respects to the National Service Life Insurance Act involved in Wissner, except that under the SGLIA, coverage is not offered by the government itself but rather is purchased by the government from commercial insurers.

4. In Rose v. Rose, 107 S.Ct. 2029 (1987), the Court upheld the power of a state court to order a veteran to pay child support out of the benefits paid to him for a service-connected disability. The relevant federal statute contained language similar to that in the SGLIA, exempting disability benefits from the claims of creditors, but Ridgway was distinguished on the ground that in the present case "Congress

has not made [the serviceman] the exclusive beneficiary of the disability benefits. * * * [T]hese benefits are intended to support not only the veteran, but the veteran's family as well" (p. 2038).

In a concurring opinion, Justice O'Connor (joined by Justice Stevens) said: "[W]hile *stare decisis* concerns may counsel against overruling Ridgway's interpretation of the [SGLIA], I see no reason whatever to extend Ridgway's equation of business debts with family-support obligations absent the clearest congressional direction to do so." (p. 2039).

Only Justice White dissented.

"children" of a deceased author to renew the copyright; the question was whether illegitimates were included; the Court held that the question should be answered by reference to state law (pp. 580–82): "The scope of a federal right is, of course, a federal question, but that does not mean that its content is not to be determined by state, rather than federal law. *Cf.* Reconstruction Finance Corp. v. Beaver County, 328 U.S. 204; Board of County Commissioners v. United States, 308 U.S. 343, 351–352. This is especially true where a statute deals with a familial relationship; there is no federal law of domestic relations, which is primarily a matter of state concern.

"If we look at the other persons who, under this section of the Copyright Act, are entitled to renew the copyright after the author's death, it is apparent that this is the general scheme of the statute. To decide who is the widow or widower of a deceased author, or who are his executors or next of kin, requires a reference to the law of the State which created those legal relationships. The word 'children,' although it to some extent describes a purely physical relationship, also describes a legal status not unlike the others. To determine whether a child has been legally adopted, for example, requires a reference to state law. We think it proper, therefore, to draw on the ready-made body of state law to define the word 'children' in § 24. This does not mean that a State would be entitled to use the word 'children' in a way entirely strange to those familiar with its ordinary usage, but at least to the extent that there are permissible variations in the ordinary concept of 'children' we deem state law controlling.

"This raises two questions: first, to what State do we look, and second, given a particular State, what part of that State's law defines the relationship. The answer to the first question, in this case, is not difficult, since it appears from the record that the only State concerned is California, and both parties have argued the case on that assumption. The second question, however, is less clear. * * * This is really a question of the descent of property, and we think the controlling question under state law should be whether the child would be an heir of the author." [5]

---

5. As part of a complete revision of the Copyright Act in 1976, Congress provided that "[a] person's 'children' are that person's immediate offspring, whether legitimate or not, and any children legally adopted by that person." 17 U.S.C. § 101. Does this revision indicate that Justice Douglas was right when he said in his concurrence in DeSylva: "[T]he statutory policy of protecting dependents would be better served by uniformity, rather than by the diversity which would flow from incorporating into the Act the laws of forty-eight States" (p. 583)? Or was this a judg-ment whose desirability and precise content the Court properly left to Congress?

Does the 1976 revision entirely eliminate the DeSylva problem? Given the advances of modern medicine, can't there be a serious question of who is an "offspring" of whom, even when the facts are not disputed? If such a question should arise, is resort to state law precluded by the revision? (Note also the relevance of state law in determining when and whether a child has been "legally adopted.")

TEXTILE WORKERS UNION v. LINCOLN MILLS
353 U.S. 448, 77 S.Ct. 912, 1 L.Ed.2d 972 (1957).
Certiorari to the United States Court of Appeals for the Fifth Circuit.

Mr. Justice Douglas delivered the opinion of the Court.

Petitioner-union entered into a collective bargaining agreement in 1953 with respondent-employer, the agreement to run one year and from year to year thereafter, unless terminated on specified notices. The agreement provided that there would be no strikes or work stoppages and that grievances would be handled pursuant to a specified procedure. The last step in the grievance procedure—a step that could be taken by either party—was arbitration.

This controversy involves several grievances that concern work loads and work assignments. The grievances were processed through the various steps in the grievance procedure and were finally denied by the employer. The union requested arbitration, and the employer refused. Thereupon the union brought this suit in the District Court to compel arbitration.

The District Court concluded that it had jurisdiction and ordered the employer to comply with the grievance arbitration provisions of the collective bargaining agreement. The Court of Appeals reversed by a divided vote. 230 F.2d 81. It held that, although the District Court had jurisdiction to entertain the suit, the court had no authority founded either in federal or state law to grant the relief. The case is here on a petition for a writ of certiorari which we granted because of the importance of the problem and the contrariety of views in the courts.

The starting point of our inquiry is § 301 of the Labor Management Relations Act of 1947, 29 U.S.C. § 185, which provides:

"(a) Suits for violation of contracts between an employer and a labor organization representing employees in an industry affecting commerce as defined in this chapter, or between any such labor organizations, may be brought in any district court of the United States having jurisdiction of the parties, without respect to the amount in controversy or without regard to the citizenship of the parties.

"(b) Any labor organization which represents employees in an industry affecting commerce as defined in this chapter and any employer whose activities affect commerce as defined in this chapter shall be bound by the acts of its agents. Any such labor organization may sue or be sued as an entity and in behalf of the employees whom it represents in the courts of the United States. Any money judgment against a labor organization in a district court of the United States shall be enforceable only against the organization as an entity and against its assets, and shall not be enforceable against any individual member or his assets."

There has been considerable litigation involving § 301 and courts have construed it differently. There is one view that § 301(a) merely gives federal district courts jurisdiction in controversies that involve labor organizations in industries affecting commerce, without regard to diversity of citizenship or the amount in controversy. Under that view § 301(a) would not be the source of substantive law; it would neither supply federal law to resolve these controversies nor turn the federal judges to state law for answers to the questions. Other courts—the overwhelming number of them—hold that § 301(a) is more than jurisdictional—that it authorizes federal courts to fashion a body of federal law for the enforcement of these collective bargaining agreements and includes within that federal law specific performance of promises to arbitrate grievances under collective bargaining agreements. Perhaps the leading decision representing that point of view is the one rendered by Judge Wyzanski in Textile Workers Union of America (C.I.O.) v. American Thread Co., D.C., 113 F.Supp. 137. That is our construction of § 301(a), which means that the agreement to arbitrate grievance disputes, contained in this collective bargaining agreement, should be specifically enforced.

From the face of the Act it is apparent that § 301(a) and § 301(b) supplement one another. Section 301(b) makes it possible for a labor organization, representing employees in an industry affecting commerce, to sue and be sued as an entity in the federal courts. Section 301(b) in other words provides the procedural remedy lacking at common law. Section 301(a) certainly does something more than that. Plainly, it supplies the basis upon which the federal district courts may take jurisdiction and apply the procedural rule of § 301(b). The question is whether § 301(a) is more than jurisdictional.

The legislative history of § 301 is somewhat cloudy and confusing. But there are a few shafts of light that illuminate our problem.

The bills, as they passed the House and the Senate, contained provisions which would have made the failure to abide by an agreement to arbitrate an unfair labor practice. S.Rep. No. 105, 80th Cong., 1st Sess., pp. 20–21, 23; H.R.Rep. No. 245, 80th Cong., 1st Sess., p. 21. This feature of the law was dropped in Conference. As the Conference Report stated, "Once parties have made a collective bargaining contract, the enforcement of that contract should be left to the usual processes of the law and not to the National Labor Relations Board." H.R.Conf.Rep. No. 510, 80th Cong., 1st Sess., p. 42.

Both the Senate and the House took pains to provide for "the usual processes of the law" by provisions which were the substantial equivalent of § 301(a) in its present form. Both the Senate Report and the House Report indicate a primary concern that unions as well as employees should be bound to collective bargaining contracts. But there was also a broader concern—a concern with a procedure for making such agreements enforceable in the courts by either party. At one point the Senate Report, *supra,* p. 15, states, "We feel that the aggrieved party should also have a right of action in the Federal courts. Such a policy is completely in accord with the purpose of the Wagner Act which the Supreme Court declared was 'to compel employers to bargain collectively with their employees to the end that an employment contract, binding on both parties, should be made * * *.'"

Congress was also interested in promoting collective bargaining that ended with agreements not to strike. The Senate Report, *supra,* p. 16 states:

"If unions can break agreements with relative impunity, then such agreements do not tend to stabilize industrial relations. The execution of an agreement does not by itself promote industrial peace. The chief advantage which an employer can reasonably expect from a collective labor agreement is assurance of uninterrupted operation during the term of the agreement. Without some effective method of assuring freedom from economic warfare for the term of the agreement, there is little reason why an employer would desire to sign such a contract.

"Consequently, to encourage the making of agreements and to promote industrial peace through faithful performance by the parties, collective agreements affecting interstate commerce should be enforceable in the Federal courts. Our amendment would provide for suits by unions as legal entities and against unions as legal entities in the Federal courts in disputes affecting commerce."

Thus collective bargaining contracts were made "equally binding and enforceable on both parties." *Id.,* p. 15. As stated in the House Report, *supra,* p. 6, the new provision "makes labor organizations equally responsible with employers for contract violations and provides for suit by either against the other in the United States district courts." To repeat, the Senate Report, *supra,* p. 17, summed up the philosophy of § 301 as follows: "Statutory recognition of the collective agreement as a valid, binding, and enforceable contract is a logical and necessary step. It will promote a higher degree of responsibility upon the parties to such agreements, and will thereby promote industrial peace."

Plainly the agreement to arbitrate grievance disputes is the *quid pro quo* for an agreement not to strike. Viewed in this light, the legislation does more than confer jurisdiction in the federal courts over labor organizations. It expresses a federal policy that federal courts should enforce these agreements on behalf of or against labor organizations and that industrial peace can be best obtained only in that way.

To be sure, there is a great medley of ideas reflected in the hearings, reports, and debates on this Act. Yet, to repeat, the entire tenor of the history indicates that the agreement to arbitrate grievance disputes was considered as *quid pro quo* of a no-strike agreement. And when in the House the debate narrowed to the question whether § 301 was more than jurisdictional, it became abundantly clear that the purpose of the section was to provide the necessary legal remedies. * * *

It seems, therefore, clear to us that Congress adopted a policy which placed sanctions behind agreements to arbitrate grievance disputes, by implication rejecting the common-law rule, discussed in Red Cross Line v. Atlantic Fruit Co., 264 U.S. 109, against enforcement of executory agreements to arbitrate. We would undercut the Act and defeat its policy if we read § 301 narrowly as only conferring jurisdiction over labor organizations.

The question then is, what is the substantive law to be applied in suits under § 301(a)? We conclude that the substantive law to apply in suits under § 301(a) is federal law, which the courts must fashion from the policy of our national labor laws. See Mendelsohn, Enforceability of Aribtration Agreements Under Taft–Hartley Section 301, 66 Yale L.J. 167. The Labor Management Relations Act expressly furnishes some substantive law. It points out what the parties may or may not do in certain situations. Other problems will lie in the penumbra of express statutory mandates. Some will lack express statutory sanction but will be solved by looking at the policy of the legislation and fashioning a remedy that will effectuate that policy. The range of judicial inventiveness will be determined by the nature of the problem. See Board of Commissioners of Jackson County v.

United States, 308 U.S. 343, 351. Federal interpretation of the federal law will govern, not state law. But state law, if compatible with the purpose of § 301, may be resorted to in order to find the rule that will best effectuate the federal policy. See Board of Commissioners v. United States, *supra,* at 351–352. Any state law applied, however, will be absorbed as federal law and will not be an independent source of private rights.

It is not uncommon for federal courts to fashion federal law where federal rights are concerned. See Clearfield Trust Co. v. United States, 318 U.S. 363, 366–367; National Metropolitan Bank v. United States, 323 U.S. 454. Congress has indicated by § 301(a) the purpose to follow that course here. There is no constitutional difficulty. Article III, § 2, extends the judicial power to cases "arising under * * * the Laws of the United States * * *." The power of Congress to regulate these labor-management controversies under the Commerce Clause is plain. * * * A case or controversy arising under § 301(a) is, therefore, one within the purview of judicial power as defined in Article III.

The question remains whether jurisdiction to compel arbitration of grievance disputes is withdrawn by the Norris–LaGuardia Act, 47 Stat. 70, 29 U.S.C. § 101. Section 7 of that Act prescribes stiff procedural requirements for issuing an injunction in a labor dispute. The kinds of acts which had given rise to abuse of the power to enjoin are listed in § 4. The failure to arbitrate was not a part and parcel of the abuses against which the Act was aimed. * * * The congressional policy in favor of the enforcement of agreements to arbitrate grievance disputes being clear, there is no reason to submit them to the requirements of § 7 of the Norris–LaGuardia Act.

* * *

The judgment of the Court of Appeals is reversed and the cause is remanded to that court for proceedings in conformity with this opinion.

Reversed.

MR. JUSTICE BLACK took no part in the consideration or decision of this case.

MR. JUSTICE BURTON, whom MR. JUSTICE HARLAN joins, concurring in the result.

* * *

MR. JUSTICE FRANKFURTER, dissenting.

The Court has avoided the difficult problems raised by § 301 of the Taft–Hartley Act, by attributing to the section an occult content. This plainly procedural section is transmuted into a mandate to the federal courts to fashion a whole body of substantive federal law appropriate for the complicated and touchy problems raised by collective bargaining. I have set forth in my opinion in Association of Westinghouse Salaried Employees v. Westinghouse Electric Corp. the detailed reasons why I believe that § 301 cannot be so construed, even if constitutional questions cannot be avoided. 348 U.S. 437, 441–449, 452–459. But the Court has a "clear" and contrary conclusion emerge from the "somewhat," to say the least, "cloudy and confusing legislative history." This is more than can be fairly asked even from the alchemy of construction. Since the Court relies on a few isolated statements in the legislative history which do not support its conclusion, however favoringly read, I have deemed it necessary to set forth in an appendix the entire relevant legislative history of the Taft–Hartley Act and its predecessor, the Case Bill. This legislative history reinforces the natural meaning of the statute as an exclusively procedural provision, affording, that is, an accessible federal forum for suits on agreements between labor organizations and employers, but not enacting federal law for such suits. See also Wollett and Wellington, *Federalism and Breach of the Labor Agreement,* 7 Stan.L.Rev. 445.

I have also set forth in my opinion in the Westinghouse case an outline of the vast problems that the Court's present decision creates by bringing into conflict state law and federal law, state courts and federal courts. 348 U.S. at pages 454–455; see also Judge Wyzanski's opinion in Textile Workers Union of America (C.I.O.) v. American Thread Co., D.C., 113 F.Supp. 137, 140. These problems are not rendered non-existent by disregard of them. It should also be noted that whatever may be a union's *ad hoc* benefit in a particular case, the meaning of collective bargaining for labor does not remotely derive from reliance on the sanction of litigation in the courts. Restrictions made by legislation like the Clayton Act of 1914, 38 Stat. 738, §§ 20, 22, and the Norris–LaGuardia Act of 1932, 47 Stat. 70, upon the use of familiar remedies theretofore available in the federal courts, reflected deep fears of the labor movement of the use of such remedies against labor. But a union, like any other combatant engaged in a particular fight, is ready to make an ally of an old enemy, and so we also find unions resorting to the otherwise much excoriated labor injunction. Such intermittent yielding to expediency does not change the fact that judicial intervention is ill-suited to the special characteristics of the arbitration process in labor disputes; nor are the conditions for its effective functioning thereby altered. * * *

* * * Arbitration agreements are for specific terms, generally much shorter than the time required for adjudication of a contested lawsuit through the available stages of trial and appeal. Renegotiation of agreements cannot await the outcome of such litigation; nor can the parties' continuing relation await it. Cases under § 301 will probably present unusual rather than representative situations. A "rule" derived from them is more likely to discombobulate than to compose. A "uniform corpus" cannot be expected to evolve, certainly not within a time to serve its assumed function.

The prickly and extensive problems that the supposed grant would create further counsel against a finding that the grant was made. They present hazardous opportunities for friction in the regulation of contracts between employers and unions. They involve the division of power between State and Nation, between state courts and federal courts, including the effective functioning of this Court. Wisdom suggests self-restraint in undertaking to solve these problems unless the Court is clearly directed to do so. Section 301 is not such a direction. The legislative history contains no suggestion that these problems were considered; the terms of the section do not present them.

One word more remains to be said. The earliest declaration of unconstitutionality of an act of Congress—by the Justices on circuit—involved a refusal by the Justices to perform a function imposed upon them by Congress because of the non-judicial nature of that function. Hayburn's Case, 2 Dall. 409. Since then, the Court has many times declared legislation unconstitutional because it imposed on the Court powers or functions that were regarded as outside the scope of the "judicial power" lodged in the Court by the Constitution. See, *e.g.*, Marbury v. Madison, 1 Cranch 137. * * *

The Court, however, sees no problem of "judicial power" in casting upon the federal courts, with no guides except "judicial inventiveness," the task of applying a whole industrial code that is as yet in the bosom of the judiciary. There are severe limits on "judicial inventiveness" even for the most imaginative judges. The law is not a "brooding omnipresence in the sky," (Mr. Justice Holmes, dissenting, in Southern Pacific Co. v. Jensen, 244 U.S. 205, 222), and it cannot be drawn from there like nitrogen from the air. These problems created by the Court's interpretation of § 301 cannot "be solved by resort to the established canons of construction that enable a court to look through awkward or clumsy expression, or language wanting in precision, to the intent of the legislature. For the vice of the statute here lies in the impossibility of ascertaining, by any reasonable test, that the legislature meant one thing rather than another * * *." Connally v. General Construction Co., 269 U.S. 385, 394. But the Court makes § 301 a mountain instead of a molehill and, by giving an example of "judicial inventiveness," it thereby solves all the constitutional problems that would otherwise have to be faced.

Even on the Court's attribution to § 301 of a direction to the federal courts to fashion, out of bits and pieces elsewhere to be gathered, a federal common law of labor contracts, it still does not follow that Congress has enacted that an agreement to arbitrate industrial differences be specifically enforceable in the federal courts. On the contrary, the body of relevant federal law precludes such enforcement of arbitration clauses in collective-bargaining agreements. * * *

* * * Thus, even assuming that § 301 contains directions for some federal substantive law of labor contracts, I see no justification for translating the vague expectation concerning the remedies to be applied into an overruling of previous federal common law and, more particularly, into the repeal of the previous congressional exemption of collective-bargaining agreements from the class of agreements in which arbitration clauses were to be enforced.

The second ground of my dissent from the Court's action is more fundamental. * * *

[The remaining portion of the dissent, dealing with the constitutionality of § 301 (on the assumption that it is merely a jurisdictional grant), as well as the concurring opinion of Justice Burton, will be found in Chap. VIII, Sec. 2, p. 975, *infra*.]

NOTE ON FEDERAL COMMON LAW IMPLIED BY JURISDICTIONAL GRANTS

(1) Three of the most celebrated instances of assumption of law-making power by the federal courts are based on jurisdictional grants.[1] Perhaps

---

1. For discussion of areas other than the three referred to in text, see the thoughtful treatment of federal habeas corpus jurisdiction in Brilmayer, *State Forfeiture Rules and Federal Review of State Criminal Convictions*, 49 U.Chi.L.Rev. 741 (1982), especially at 765–70; see also the materials on federal equity, pp. 807–13, *supra*. *Compare* the materials on "protective" jurisdiction, Chap. VIII, Sec. 2, pp. 983–89, *infra*.

the most dramatic of these is the power to create federal admiralty law implied by Article III's grant of admiralty jurisdiction—dramatic because the implication is the source not only of power to create judge-made law but also of Congress' power to legislate on admiralty matters. See, as to this, Moragne v. States Marine Lines, Inc., and the following *Note on the Sources of Law in Admiralty*, p. 892, *infra.*

A second well-known instance is the law governing litigation between states: law-making power is inferred from the jurisdictional grant over interstate controversies and justified by the inappropriateness of using any one state's law. See *Note on the Law Applied in Actions Between States*, Chap. III, p. 319, *supra.*[2]

Finally there is the command to fashion federal law governing labor contracts, read into § 301 of the Taft-Hartley Act in Lincoln Mills. While Lincoln Mills itself raised only the question of the enforceability of an undertaking in a collective agreement, its reasoning has been followed in other decisions raising issues of the character and existence of those undertakings. *E.g.*, Local 174 v. Lucas Flour Co., 369 U.S. 95 (1962) (holding, as a matter of federal law, that a union that agreed to a compulsory arbitration provision was contractually obligated not to strike over an arbitrable dispute). For further discussion of Lincoln Mills and its aftermath, see Bickel & Wellington, *Legislative Purpose and the Judicial Process: the Lincoln Mills Case*, 71 Harv.L.Rev. 1 (1957); Shapiro, *Of Institutions and Decisions*, 22 Stan.L.Rev. 657, 663–66 (1970); Note, 28 U.Chi.L.Rev. 707 (1961); Note, 82 Harv.L.Rev. 1512, 1531–35 (1969).

(2) In Texas Industries, Inc. v. Radcliff Materials, Inc., 451 U.S. 630, 640–41 (1981), the Court stated that "[t]he vesting of jurisdiction in the federal courts does not in and of itself give rise to authority to formulate federal common law * * *." United States v. Little Lake Misere Land Co., Inc., 412 U.S. 580, 591 (1973), the only authority cited for this proposition, made a much more limited statement: "The federal jurisdictional grant over suits brought by the United States is not in itself a mandate for applying federal law in all circumstances."

The point that a jurisdictional grant does not necessarily—or even ordinarily—imply a power to formulate substantive rules of decision, is commonplace. The fact, for instance, that a state court has jurisdiction to adjudicate a case does not automatically carry with it the application of the forum's substantive law. Even if not so intended by its creator, the rule of Swift v. Tyson may be thought of as having become an aberrational exception to this principle. (See, *e.g.*, cases such as Gelpcke v. City of Dubuque, and Burgess v. Seligman, pp. 780–81, *supra.*) Are the three instances referred to above also aberrational? Or do special factors serve to distinguish them?

(3) In Charles Dowd Box Co. v. Courtney, 368 U.S. 502 (1962), the Court held that § 301 does not by implication divest state courts of concurrent jurisdiction over suits falling within its scope. And in Lucas Flour, Paragraph (1), *supra*, the Court held that the federal common law governs in suits within the scope of § 301 whether they are brought in state or federal court. Justice Stewart stated (369 U.S. at 103–04): "[T]he subject

---

2. These controversies, and the terms of their settlement, may also affect private interests. See Hinderlider v. La Plata Riv- er & Cherry Creek Ditch Co., 304 U.S. 92 (1938).

matter of § 301(a) 'is peculiarly one that calls for uniform law.' Pennsylvania R. Co. v. Public Service Comm'n, 250 U.S. 566, 569; see Cloverleaf Butter Co. v. Patterson, 315 U.S. 148, 167–169. The possibility that individual contract terms might have different meanings under state and federal law would inevitably exert a disruptive influence upon both the negotiation and administration of collective agreements. * * *

"The importance of the area which would be affected by separate systems of substantive law makes the need for a single body of federal law particularly compelling. The ordering and adjusting of competing interests through a process of free and voluntary collective bargaining is the keystone of the federal scheme to promote industrial peace. State law which frustrates the effort of Congress to stimulate the smooth functioning of that process thus strikes at the very core of federal labor policy."

MORAGNE v. STATES MARINE LINES, INC.

398 U.S. 375, 90 S.Ct. 1772, 26 L.Ed.2d 339 (1970).
Certiorari to the United States Court of Appeals for the Fifth Circuit.

Mr. Justice Harlan delivered the opinion of the Court.

We brought this case here to consider whether The Harrisburg, 119 U.S. 199, in which this Court held in 1886 that maritime law does not afford a cause of action for wrongful death, should any longer be regarded as acceptable law.

The complaint sets forth that Edward Moragne, a longshoreman, was killed while working aboard the vessel Palmetto State on navigable waters within the State of Florida. Petitioner, as his widow and representative of his estate, brought this suit in a state court against respondent States Marine Lines, Inc., the owner of the vessel, to recover damages for wrongful death and for the pain and suffering experienced by the decedent prior to his death. The claims were predicated upon both negligence and the unseaworthiness of the vessel.

States Marine removed the case to Federal District Court for the Middle District of Florida on the basis of diversity of citizenship, and there filed a third-party complaint against respondent Gulf Florida Terminal Company, the decedent's employer, asserting that Gulf had contracted to perform stevedoring services on the vessel in a workmanlike manner and that any negligence or unseaworthiness causing the accident resulted from Gulf's operations.

Both States Marine and Gulf sought dismissal of the portion of petitioner's complaint that requested damages for wrongful death on the basis of unseaworthiness. They contended that maritime law provided no recovery for wrongful death within a State's territorial waters, and that the statutory right of action for death under Florida law, Florida Statutes § 768.01 (1965), did not encompass unseaworthiness as a basis of liability. The District Court dismissed the challenged portion of the complaint on this ground, citing this Court's decision in The Tungus v. Skovgaard, 358 U.S. 588 (1959), and cases construing the state statute, but made the certification necessary under 28 U.S.C. § 1292(b) to allow petitioner an interlocutory appeal to the Court of Appeals for the Fifth Circuit.

The Court of Appeals took advantage of a procedure furnished by state law, Florida Statutes § 25.031 (1965), to certify to the Florida Supreme Court the question whether the state wrongful death statute allowed recovery for unseaworthiness as that concept is understood in maritime law. After reviewing the history of the Florida Act, the state court answered this question in the negative. 211 So.2d 161 (Fla.1968). On return of the case to the Court of Appeals, that court affirmed the District Court's order, rejecting petitioner's argument that she was entitled to reversal under federal maritime law without regard to the scope of the state statute. 409 F.2d 32 (1969). The court stated that its disposition was compelled by our decision in The Tungus. We granted certiorari, and invited the United States to participate as *amicus curiae,* to reconsider the important question of remedies under federal maritime law for tortious deaths on state territorial waters.

In The Tungus this Court divided on the consequences that should flow from the rule of maritime law that "in the absence of a statute there is no action for wrongful death," first announced in The Harrisburg. All members of the Court agreed that where a death on state territorial waters is left remediless by the general maritime law and by federal statutes, a remedy may be provided under any applicable state law giving a right of action for death by wrongful act. However, four Justices dissented from the Court's further holding that "when admiralty adopts a State's right of action for wrongful death, it must enforce the right as an integrated whole, with whatever conditions and limitations the creating State has attached." 358 U.S., at 592. The dissenters would have held that federal maritime law could utilize the state law to "supply a remedy" for breaches of federally imposed duties, without regard to any substantive limitations contained in the state law. *Id.,* at 597, 599.

The extent of the role to be played by state law under The Tungus has been the subject of substantial debate and uncertainty in this Court, see Hess v. United States, 361 U.S. 314 (1960); Goett v. Union Carbide Corp., 361 U.S. 340 (1960), with opinions on both sides of the question acknowledging the shortcomings in the present law. See 361 U.S., at 314–315, 338–339. On fresh consideration of the entire subject, we have concluded that the primary source of the confusion is not to be found in The Tungus, but in The Harrisburg, and that the latter decision, somewhat dubious even when rendered, is such an unjustifiable anomaly in the present maritime law that it should no longer be followed. We therefore reverse the judgment of the Court of Appeals.

I

The Court's opinion in The Harrisburg acknowledged that the result reached had little justification except in primitive English legal history—a history far removed from the American law of remedies for maritime deaths. * * * [The Court] relied primarily on its then recent decision in Insurance Co. v. Brame, 95 U.S. 754 (1878), in which it had held that in American common law, as in English, "no civil action lies for an injury which results in death." *Id.,* at 756.[2] In The Harrisburg, as in Brame, the Court did not examine the justifications for this common-law rule; rather,

---

2. Brame was decided, of course, at a time when the federal courts under Swift v. Tyson, 41 U.S. 1 (1842), expounded a general federal common law.

it simply noted that "we know of no country that has adopted a different rule on this subject for the sea from that which it maintains on the land," and concluded, despite contrary decisions of the lower federal courts both before and after Brame, that the rule of Brame should apply equally to maritime deaths. 119 U.S., at 213.

Our analysis of the history of the common-law rule indicates that it was based on a particular set of factors that had, when The Harrisburg was decided, long since been thrown into discard even in England, and that had never existed in this country at all. Further, regardless of the viability of the rule in 1886 as applied to American land-based affairs, it is difficult to discern an adequate reason for its extension to admiralty, a system of law then already differentiated in many respects from the common law.
* * *

II

We need not, however, pronounce a verdict on whether The Harrisburg, when decided, was a correct extrapolation of the principles of decisional law then in existence. A development of major significance has intervened, making clear that the rule against recovery for wrongful death is sharply out of keeping with the policies of modern American maritime law. This development is the wholesale abandonment of the rule in most of the areas where it once held sway, quite evidently prompted by the same sense of the rule's injustice that generated so much criticism of its original promulgation.

To some extent this rejection has been judicial. The English House of Lords in 1937 emasculated the rule without expressly overruling it. Rose v. Ford, [1937] A.C. 826. * * *

Much earlier, however, the legislatures both here and in England began to evidence unanimous disapproval of the rule against recovery for wrongful death. * * *

In the United States, every State today has enacted a wrongful-death statute. * * * The Congress has created actions for wrongful deaths of railroad employees, Federal Employers' Liability Act, 45 U.S.C. §§ 51–59; of merchant seamen, Jones Act, 46 U.S.C. § 688; and of persons on the high seas, Death on the High Seas Act, 46 U.S.C. §§ 761, 762. Congress has also, in the Federal Tort Claims Act, 28 U.S.C. § 1346(b), made the United States subject to liability in certain circumstances for negligently caused wrongful death to the same extent as a private person. See, *e.g.,* Richards v. United States, 369 U.S. 1 (1962).

These numerous and broadly applicable statutes, taken as a whole, make it clear that there is no present public policy against allowing recovery for wrongful death. The statutes evidence a wide rejection by the legislatures of whatever justifications may once have existed for a general refusal to allow such recovery. This legislative establishment of policy carries significance beyond the particular scope of each of the statutes involved. The policy thus established has become itself a part of our law, to be given its appropriate weight not only in matters of statutory construction but also in those of decisional law. See Landis, Statutes and the Sources of Law, in Harvard Legal Essays 213, 226–227 (1934). * * *

The legislature does not, of course, merely enact general policies. By the terms of a statute, it also indicates its conception of the sphere within which the policy is to have effect. In many cases the scope of a statute may reflect nothing more than the dimensions of the particular problem that came to the attention of the legislature, inviting the conclusion that the legislative policy is equally applicable to other situations in which the mischief is identical. This conclusion is reinforced where there exists not one enactment but a course of legislation dealing with a series of situations, and where the generality of the underlying principle is attested by the legislation of other jurisdictions. *Id.*, at 215–216, 220–222. On the other hand the legislature may, in order to promote other, conflicting interests, prescribe with particularity the compass of the legislative aim, erecting a strong inference that territories beyond the boundaries so drawn are not to feel the impact of the new legislative dispensation. We must, therefore, analyze with care the congressional enactments that have abrogated the common-law rule in the maritime field, to determine the impact of the fact that none applies in terms to the situation of this case. See Part III, *infra.* However, it is sufficient at this point to conclude, as Mr. Justice Holmes did 45 years ago, that the work of the legislatures has made the allowance of recovery for wrongful death the general rule of American law, and its denial the exception. Where death is caused by the breach of a duty imposed by federal maritime law, Congress has established a policy favoring recovery in the absence of a legislative direction to except a particular class of cases.

III

Our undertaking, therefore, is to determine whether Congress has given such a direction in its legislation granting remedies for wrongful deaths in portions of the maritime domain. We find that Congress has given no affirmative indication of an intent to preclude the judicial allowance of a remedy for wrongful death to persons in the situation of this petitioner.

From the date of The Harrisburg until 1920, there was no remedy for death on the high seas caused by breach of one of the duties imposed by federal maritime law. For deaths within state territorial waters, the federal law accommodated the humane policies of state wrongful-death statutes by allowing recovery whenever an applicable state statute favored such recovery. Congress acted in 1920 to furnish the remedy denied by the courts for deaths beyond the jurisdiction of any State, by passing two landmark statutes. The first of these was the Death on the High Seas Act, 46 U.S.C. § 761 *et seq.* * * *

The second statute was the Jones Act, 46 U.S.C. § 688, which, by extending to seamen the protections of the Federal Employers' Liability Act, provided a right of recovery against their employers for negligence resulting in injury or death. This right follows from the seamen's employment status and is not limited to injury or death occurring on the high seas.[11]

11. In 1927 Congress passed the Longshoremen's and Harbor Workers' Compensation Act, 33 U.S.C. §§ 901–950, granting to longshoremen the right to receive workmen's compensation benefits from their employers for accidental injury or death arising out of their employment. These benefits are made exclusive of any other liability for employers who comply with the Act. The Act does not, however, affect the longshoreman's remedies against persons other than his employer, such as a

The United States, participating as *amicus curiae*, contended at oral argument that these statutes, if construed to forbid recognition of a general maritime remedy for wrongful death within territorial waters, would perpetuate three anomalies of present law. The first of these is simply the discrepancy produced whenever the rule of The Harrisburg holds sway: Within territorial waters, identical conduct violating federal law (here the furnishing of an unseaworthy vessel) produces liability if the victim is merely injured, but frequently not if he is killed. As we have concluded, such a distinction is not compatible with the general policies of federal maritime law.

The second incongruity is that identical breaches of the duty to provide a seaworthy ship, resulting in death, produce liability outside the three-mile limit—since a claim under the Death on the High Seas Act may be founded on unseaworthiness, see Kernan v. American Dredging Co., 355 U.S. 426, 430, n. 4 (1958)—but not within the territorial waters of a State whose local statute excludes unseaworthiness claims. The United States argues that since the substantive duty is federal, and federal maritime jurisdiction covers navigable waters within and without the three-mile limit, no rational policy supports this distinction in the availability of a remedy.

The third, and assertedly the "strangest" anomaly is that a true seaman—that is, a member of a ship's company, covered by the Jones Act—is provided no remedy for death caused by unseaworthiness within territorial waters, while a longshoreman, to whom the duty of seaworthiness was extended only because he performs work traditionally done by seamen, does have such a remedy when allowed by a state statute.[12]

There is much force to the United States' argument that these distinctions are so lacking in any apparent justification that we should not, in the absence of compelling evidence, presume that Congress affirmatively intended to freeze them into maritime law. There should be no presumption that Congress has removed this Court's traditional responsibility to vindicate the policies of maritime law by ceding that function exclusively to the States. However, respondents argue that an intent to do just that is manifested by the portions of the Death on the High Seas Act quoted above.

The legislative history of the Act suggests that respondents misconceive the thrust of the congressional concern. * * *

Read in light of the state of maritime law in 1920, we believe this legislative history indicates that Congress intended to ensure the continued

shipowner, and therefore does not bear on the problem before us except perhaps to serve as yet another example of congressional action to allow recovery for death in circumstances where recovery is allowed for nonfatal injuries.

12. A joint contributor to this last situation, in conjunction with the rule of The Harrisburg, is the decision in Gillespie v. United States Steel Corp., 379 U.S. 148 (1964), where the Court held that the Jones Act, by providing a claim for wrongful death based on negligence, precludes any state remedy for wrongful death of a seaman in territorial waters—whether based on negligence or unseaworthiness. * * *

[T]he remedy under general maritime law that will be made available by our overruling today of The Harrisburg seems to be beyond the preclusive effect of the Jones Act as interpreted in Gillespie. The existence of a maritime remedy for deaths of seamen in territorial waters will further, rather than hinder, "uniformity in the exercise of admiralty jurisdiction"; and, of course, no question of preclusion of a *federal* remedy was before the Court in Gillespie or its predecessor, Lindgren v. United States, 281 U.S. 38 (1930), since no such remedy was thought to exist at the time those cases were decided. * * *

availability of a remedy, historically provided by the States, for deaths in territorial waters; its failure to extend the Act to cover such deaths primarily reflected the lack of necessity for coverage by a federal statute, rather than an affirmative desire to insulate such deaths from the benefits of any federal remedy that might be available independently of the Act. The void that existed in maritime law up until 1920 was the absence of any remedy for wrongful death on the high seas. Congress, in acting to fill that void, legislated only to the three-mile limit because that was the extent of the problem. The express provision that state remedies in territorial waters were not disturbed by the Act ensured that Congress' solution of one problem would not create another by inviting the courts to find that the Act pre-empted the entire field, destroying the state remedies that had previously existed.

The beneficiaries of persons meeting death on territorial waters did not suffer at that time from being excluded from the coverage of the Act. To the contrary, the state remedies that were left undisturbed not only were familiar but also may actually have been more generous than the remedy provided by the new Act. * * * Congress in 1920 * * * legislated against a backdrop of state laws that imposed a standard of behavior generally the same as—and in some respects perhaps more favorable than—that imposed by federal maritime law.

Since that time the equation has changed drastically, through this Court's transformation of the shipowner's duty to provide a seaworthy ship into an absolute duty not satisfied by due diligence. See, *e.g.,* Mahnich v. Southern S.S. Co., *supra;* Mitchell v. Trawler Racer, Inc., 362 U.S. 539 (1960). The unseaworthiness doctrine has become the principal vehicle for recovery by seamen for injury or death, overshadowing the negligence action made available by the Jones Act, and it has achieved equal importance for longshoremen and other harbor workers to whom the duty of seaworthiness was extended because they perform work on the vessel traditionally done by seamen. Seas Shipping Co. v. Sieracki, 328 U.S. 85 (1946). The resulting discrepancy between the remedies for deaths covered by the Death on the High Seas Act and for deaths that happen to fall within a state wrongful death statute not encompassing unseaworthiness could not have been foreseen by Congress. Congress merely declined to disturb state remedies at a time when they appeared adequate to effectuate the substantive duties imposed by general maritime law. That action cannot be read as an instruction to the federal courts that deaths in territorial waters, caused by breaches of the evolving duty of seaworthiness, must be *damnum absque injuria* unless the States expand their remedies to match the scope of the federal duty.

To put it another way, the message of the Act is that it does not by its own force abrogate available state remedies; no intention appears that the Act have the effect of foreclosing any nonstatutory federal remedies that might be found appropriate to effectuate the policies of general maritime law.

* * * Our recognition of a right to recover for wrongful death under general maritime law will assure uniform vindication of federal policies, removing the tensions and discrepancies that have resulted from the necessity to accommodate state remedial statutes to exclusively maritime substantive concepts. *E.g.,* Hess v. United States, 361 U.S. 314 (1960);

Goett v. Union Carbide Corp., 361 U.S. 340 (1960).[15] Such uniformity not only will further the concerns of both of the 1920 Acts but also will give effect to the constitutionally based principle that federal admiralty law should be "a system of law coextensive with, and operating uniformly in, the whole country." The Lottawanna, 88 U.S. 558, 575 (1875).

We conclude that the Death on the High Seas Act was not intended to preclude the availability of a remedy for wrongful death under general maritime law in situations not covered by the Act. Because the refusal of maritime law to provide such a remedy appears to be jurisprudentially unsound and to have produced serious confusion and hardship, that refusal should cease * * *. * * *

[In the remaining portions of the opinion, Justice Harlan first concludes that the policies behind *stare decisis* do not in this case militate strongly against overruling The Harrisburg. He then turns to the argument "that overruling The Harrisburg will necessitate a long course of decisions to spell out the elements of the new 'cause of action.'" He continues, "these fears are exaggerated, because our decision does not require the fashioning of a whole new body of federal law, but merely removes a bar to access to the existing general maritime law. In most respects the law applied in personal-injury cases will answer all questions that arise in death cases." With respect to the most difficult question, the determination of the beneficiaries entitled to recover—most difficult because general maritime law, "which denied any recovery for wrongful death, found no need to specify which dependents should receive such recovery"—Justice Harlan described the suggestion of the government, that the courts "borrow" the schedule of beneficiaries specified in the Death on the High Seas Act; he concluded that the issue need not be now determined, but that "its existence affords no sufficient reason" for not overruling The Harrisburg.]

We accordingly overrule The Harrisburg, and hold that an action does lie under general maritime law for death caused by violation of maritime duties. The judgment of the Court of Appeals is reversed, and the case is remanded to that court for further proceedings consistent with this opinion. It is so ordered.

Reversed and remanded.

MR. JUSTICE BLACKMUN took no part in the consideration or decision of this case.*

---

15. The incongruity of forcing the States to provide the sole remedy to effectuate duties that have no basis in state policy is highlighted in this case. The Florida Supreme Court ruled that the state wrongful-death act was concerned only with "traditional common-law concepts," and not with "concepts peculiar to maritime law such as 'unseaworthiness' and the comparative negligence rule." It found no reason to believe that the Florida Legislature intended to cover, or even considered, the "completely foreign" maritime duty of seaworthiness. 211 So.2d, at 164, 166. Federal law, rather than state, is the more appropriate source of a remedy for viola-tion of the federally imposed duties of maritime law. *Cf.* Hill, The Law–Making Power of the Federal Courts: Constitutional Preemption, 67 Col.L.Rev. 1024 (1967); Note, The Federal Common Law, 82 Harv. L.Rev. 1512, 1523–1526 (1969).

* * *

*[Ed.] For commentary on Moragne, see Posner, *Legal Formalism, Legal Realism, and the Interpretation of Statutes and the Constitution*, 37 Case W.Res.L.Rev. 179, 201–04 (1986) (criticizing both the Court's analysis and its conclusion); Note, 82 Yale L.J. 258 (1972) (praising the Court's use of "analogical reasoning from statutes").

NOTE ON THE SOURCES OF LAW IN ADMIRALTY

(1) Moragne, as indicated in the Court's opinion at footnote 15, raised the question whether federal or state law was "the more appropriate source of a remedy for violation of the federally imposed duties of maritime law." Thus it should perhaps have been included in the next section of this chapter, dealing with issues of remedy. But the significance and scope of the question in the case, and of the Court's answer, are difficult to understand without some appreciation of the sources of substantive rights and obligations in admiralty and of the complex relationship between state and federal law in this field.

This Note, on the sources of law in admiralty, is designed to be no more than a brief introduction. For extensive accounts of the development of the law and for citation to the voluminous literature, see Robertson, Admiralty and Federalism (1970); Currie, *Federalism and the Admiralty: "The Devil's Own Mess,"* 1960 Sup.Ct.Rev. 158; Currie, Federal Courts 440–48 (3d ed. 1982); Redish, Federal Jurisdiction: Tensions in the Allocation of Judicial Power 97–105 (1980).[1] For a theoretical overview, see von Mehren & Trautman, The Law of Multistate Problems 1049–73 (1965); and see *Note on the Admiralty Jurisdiction,* p. 1071, *infra.*

(2) For a splendid account of the historical development which found in the jurisdictional grant of the admiralty clause a source of substantive federal law-making power—both judicial and legislative—see Note, 67 Harv.L.Rev. 1214 (1954). And see Robertson, Paragraph (1), *supra,* Ch. IX, for a detailed analysis of the nineteenth century cases; he challenges as an oversimplification the conventional view that until the Jensen case, *infra,* the federal admiralty courts applied uniform maritime law, whereas state courts and federal courts (on the "law side") applied state law when acting under the celebrated saving clause.[2]

(3) The modern doctrine, which holds that admiralty is a uniform body of substantive federal law applicable not only in admiralty courts but also in the state courts and on the "law side" of the federal courts, stems from the decisions in Southern Pac. Co. v. Jensen, 244 U.S. 205 (1917), and Chelentis v. Luckenbach S.S. Co., 247 U.S. 372 (1918).[3]

The Jensen case involved a stevedore killed while loading a vessel in the port of New York. Relying on the saving clause, his next of kin obtained an award of compensation under the New York [Workers'] Compensation Law, and the award was sustained by the state courts. The Supreme Court reversed. Recognizing that "it would be difficult, if not impossible, to define with exactness just how far the general maritime law may be changed, modified, or affected by state legislation" but that "this may be done to some extent," Justice McReynolds declared that "no such legislation is valid if it * * * works material prejudice to the characteristic features of the general maritime law or interferes with the proper

---

1. Other valuable sources include Benedict on Admiralty (7th ed.); Gilmore & Black, The Law of Admiralty (2d ed. 1975); Baer, Admiralty Law of the Supreme Court (3d ed. 1979); Lucas, Admiralty: Cases and Materials (3d ed. 1987).

2. See 28 U.S.C. § 1333 for the current version.

3. For an argument that the modern doctrine should be abandoned and that "with the possible exception of cases on the high seas" the regime of federal common law should be "replaced by applicable state legal principles," see Redish, Paragraph (1), *supra,* at 97–105.

harmony and uniformity of that law in its international or interstate relations." 244 U.S. at 216. Without explaining why a workers' compensation law would be more destructive of "harmony and uniformity" than state wrongful death statutes (which could be relied on to remedy some maritime deaths, see The Hamilton, 207 U.S. 398 (1907)), he concluded that "freedom of navigation between the States and with foreign countries would be seriously hampered and impeded" if the statute could apply (p. 217). Justice Holmes, disagreeing, thought "it is too late to say that the mere silence of Congress excludes the statute or common law of a state from supplementing the wholly inadequate maritime law of the time of the Constitution * * *" (p. 223). His strong dissent and that of Justice Pitney were approved by Justices Brandeis and Clarke.

Chelentis involved a seaman injured on board his vessel while at sea. Instead of pursuing a maritime remedy (*i.e.,* maintenance and cure), he brought a negligence action against his employer in a state court. There being diversity, the case was removed to federal court. The Court held that the negligence action could not be maintained. Justice McReynolds said (247 U.S. at 382): "Under the doctrine approved in Southern Pacific Co. v. Jensen, no state has power to abolish the well recognized maritime rule concerning measure of recovery and substitute therefor the full indemnity rule of the common law. Such a substitution would distinctly and definitely change or add to the settled maritime law; and it would be destructive of the 'uniformity and consistency at which the Constitution aimed on all subjects of a commercial character affecting the intercourse of the States with each other or with foreign states' ".

With a brief lapse in Caldarola v. Eckert, 332 U.S. 155 (1947), it has been clear since Chelentis that, to the extent that the "uniformity" doctrine applies, it does so whether the case is litigated in admiralty or in a common law court; the doubts raised as to this in Caldarola were laid to rest in Pope & Talbot, Inc. v. Hawn, 346 U.S. 406 (1953) ("the substantial rights of an injured person are not to be determined differently whether his case is labelled 'law side' or 'admiralty side' " (p. 411)).

(4) One of the most puzzling areas has been the one dealt with in the Jensen case itself—the availability of workers' compensation for longshoremen and harbor workers.[4] After Jensen, Congress twice sought to fill the gap created by that holding, by explicitly authorizing state law to furnish compensation; each time it was told by the Court that it had exceeded its powers because it is the Constitution which prevents state law from operating. See Knickerbocker Ice Co. v. Stewart, 253 U.S. 149 (1920); Washington v. W.C. Dawson & Co., 264 U.S. 219 (1924).[5] Simultaneously, however, the Court limited the sweep of the Jensen doctrine, holding that if the injury involved was "maritime but local", state compensation law could operate.[6] In 1927 Congress passed a federal compensation statute (the

---

4. See generally Robertson, paragraph (1), *supra,* ch. XII, and the authorities cited, *id.* at 213 n. 45.

5. It is of course doubtful that the doctrine of these cases would be accepted today as a measure of Congress's authority. *Cf.* Wilburn Boat Co. v. Fireman's Fund Ins. Co., 348 U.S. 310, 321 n. 29 (1955); Askew v. American Waterways Operators Inc., 411 U.S. 325, 344 (1973).

6. See Grant Smith–Porter Ship Co. v. Rohde, 257 U.S. 469 (1922) (injury to a carpenter engaged in building a vessel lying in navigable water is compensable under state law); State Industrial Com'n v. Nordenholt Corp., 259 U.S. 263 (1922) (compensation statute may be applied to claim of mother of a longshoreman killed on the dock while unloading a vessel).

Longshoremen's and Harbor Workers' Compensation Act, see 33 U.S.C. §§ 901 *et seq.*), but apparently preserved the "maritime but local" rule by providing in § 903(a) that federal compensation shall be payable only "if recovery for the disability or death through workmen's compensation proceedings may not validly be provided by State law." A tangled and difficult series of distinctions defined the line between federal and state compensability under this provision, see Gilmore & Black, note 1, *supra*, at 418–20. A further complexity was added in Davis v. Department of Labor, 317 U.S. 249 (1942), where the Court—though not denying that state and federal coverage are in theory mutually exclusive—tempered the effect of exclusivity by saying that there exists a "twilight zone" where either a federal or a state award could be upheld on the basis of a "presumption" of validity. See Lucas, note 1, *supra*, at 1002–03.

In 1962 the Court greatly simplified the law by the technique of repealing by fiat the proviso limiting federal compensation to cases which could not "validly" be compensable under state law; it held, with Justices Stewart and Harlan dissenting, that the federal remedy was available for all injuries on navigable waters, even those which state law could validly compensate under the "maritime but local" rubric. Calbeck v. Travelers Ins. Co., 370 U.S. 114 (1962). Commentary on the case was predominantly hostile, on the ground that it constituted high-handed judicial legislation; see Robertson, Paragraph (1), *supra*, at 212–19 and 304–18, for a full citation of authorities and for a valiant attempt at a defense.

In 1972, Congress approved Calbeck by deleting the limitation in § 903(a); it also extended the coverage of the Act by defining "navigable waters" to include piers and other areas where loading, unloading, repairing, or building of vessels is customarily performed. See 86 Stat. 1251.

Given this extension of federal coverage and the provision of § 905 that liability under the federal act is "exclusive * * * of all other liability * * * to the employee," may state compensation be awarded when the injury is "local" for purposes of the Jensen rule? See Sun Ship, Inc. v. Pennsylvania, 447 U.S. 715, 719–22 (1980), answering this question in the affirmative. (The Court held that the 1972 amendments were not intended to preempt state remedies, and that § 905 was not germane because it predated those amendments.)

(5) The problem of wrongful death dealt with in Moragne has also had a troublesome and complex history. Western Fuel Co. v. Garcia, 257 U.S. 233 (1921), reaffirmed the proposition that notwithstanding Jensen an admiralty action could be brought on the basis of a state wrongful death statute;[7] Just v. Chambers, 312 U.S. 383 (1941), confirmed that state survival statutes could also be applied in admiralty. But in the late '50s and early '60s a sorely divided Court proved unable to create stable and intelligible law on the issue of the precise scope and relevance state law should have in these actions. The leading cases, all apparently—and happily—rendered obsolete by Moragne, are discussed in Gilmore & Black, note 1, *supra*, at 365–67.[8]

---

7. The Court also held that the state statute of limitations applied and barred the action. See further pp. 950–57, *infra*.

8. For a particularly interesting decision after Moragne, in which the Court divided sharply on the nature of its role in the development of rules governing wrongful death actions, see Sea–Land Services, Inc. v. Gaudet, 414 U.S. 573 (1974) (recovery by decedent in his lifetime does not bar subsequent wrongful death action by his widow).

Other admiralty remedies for wrongful death are, as Moragne points out, purely federal: the Death on the High Seas Act, now 46 U.S.C. §§ 761–68, and the Jones Act, now 46 U.S.C. § 688, both passed in 1920. Footnote 12 of the Moragne opinion indicates that another happy effect of that decision is to render irrelevant the doctrine first announced in Lindgren v. United States, 281 U.S. 38 (1930), and reaffirmed in Gillespie v. United States Steel Corp., 379 U.S. 148 (1964), that the Jones Act precludes recovery under state wrongful death statutes for the death of a seaman in territorial waters whether the claim is based on negligence or unseaworthiness.

(6) Beginning with Chelentis itself, a strong line of authority affirms the proposition that in personal injury litigation not involving death it is the uniform maritime law, and not state law, that governs the rights and liabilities of the parties. See, *e.g.,* Garrett v. Moore–McCormack Co., 317 U.S. 239 (1942); Pope & Talbot, Inc. v. Hawn, 346 U.S. 406 (1953).[9] And the impact of this line of authority has been magnified by the Court's expansions of the maritime remedy of unseaworthiness. See, *e.g.,* Mahnich v. Southern S.S. Co., 321 U.S. 96 (1944); Mitchell v. Trawler Racer, Inc., 362 U.S. 539 (1960).[10]

In the field of marine insurance, however, see the much-criticized[11] decision in Wilburn Boat Co. v. Fireman's Fund Ins. Co., 348 U.S. 310 (1955), holding that state law governs the question whether breach by plaintiff of warranties in a marine insurance contract precludes recovery on the contract.

FURTHER NOTE ON FEDERAL COMMON LAW GENERATED BY FEDERAL STATUTES

(1) A broad category of cases involving choice between federal and state law—and one which overlaps a good deal of the material already discussed—raises the general question whether, in "filling in" the interstices and gaps left open by federal statutory regulation, or in interpreting general statutory phrases, the federal courts should fashion federal "common law" or should resort to state law. And note that this question shades

Following Gaudet, the Court held in Mobil Oil Corp. v. Higginbotham, 436 U.S. 618 (1978), that damages for loss of society, approved in Gaudet for a death in territorial waters under the general maritime law announced in Moragne, were precluded for a death on the high seas by the Death on the High Seas Act, which limits damages to pecuniary losses. In Offshore Logistics, Inc. v. Tallentire, 477 U.S. 207 (1986), it was further held that a recovery under the Death on the High Seas Act could not be supplemented by nonpecuniary damages under a state wrongful death statute.

9. The counter-indications in Justice Frankfurter's ambiguous opinion for the Court in Caldarola v. Eckert, 332 U.S. 155 (1947), were deprived of continuing effectiveness by the Court's opinion (and indeed to some extent by Justice Frankfurter's

own concurrence) in the Pope & Talbot case.

10. The Court extended the unseaworthiness remedy to longshoremen in Seas Shipping Co. v. Sieracki, 328 U.S. 85 (1946). But Congress effectively overruled this decision in its 1972 amendments to the Longshoremen's and Harbor Workers' Compensation Act. See 33 U.S.C. § 905(b); Friendly, Federal Jurisdiction: A General View 131–32 (1973).

11. For criticism of the decision, see, *e.g.,* Gilmore & Black, note 1, *supra,* at 48–49, 68–71; von Mehren & Trautman, The Law of Multistate Problems 1057 (1965) (arguing that the issue is federal but that the old federal rule needs to be overhauled).

into—and is often indistinguishable from—the pervasive question of the extent to which federal regulation displaces or preempts pre-existing state law within (and adjacent to) the field of federal regulation.

Examples of choice-of-law problems arising within the ambits of federal regulatory programs could be multiplied indefinitely.[1] Only a few illustrative cases will, therefore, be noted here.

(2) The general proposition that state law cannot contradict or impede or violate a valid federal regulatory program is, of course, easily stated. Whether under the circumstances a contradiction really exists may, however, raise difficult and subtle problems.[2] Consider, for example, Farmers Educ. & Coop. Union v. WDAY, Inc., 360 U.S. 525 (1959). Section 315 of the Federal Communications Act, 47 U.S.C. § 315(a), provides that a radio or television licensee which permits a political candidate to use its facilities must give "equal opportunities" to all other candidates for the same office, "*Provided,* That such licensee shall have no power of censorship over the material broadcast under the provisions of this section * * *." WDAY, acting under the compulsion of § 315, allowed one Townley to broadcast a speech in reply to previous speeches made over the station by rival candidates. The question in the case (which came to the Court from a state court) was whether WDAY was liable for defamatory statements made by Townley. The Court held that the implication of the "no censorship" provision of the statute was to immunize broadcasters from liability for defamation occurring in the course of "equal time" broadcasts; the contrary holding, said the Court (p. 531), would "sanction the unconscionable result of permitting civil and perhaps criminal liability to be imposed for the very conduct the statute demands of the licensee." Further (pp. 534–35), "if a licensee could protect himself from liability in no other way but by refusing to broadcast [all] candidates' speeches, the necessary effect would be to hamper the congressional plan to develop broadcasting as a political outlet * * *."

In the course of his dissent, Justice Frankfurter said (pp. 542, 545–46): "The most harmonious deduction to be drawn from the many cases in which the claim has been made that state action cannot survive some contradictory command of Congress is that state action has not been set aside on mere generalities about Congress having 'occupied the field,' or on the basis of loose talk instead of demonstrations about 'conflict' between

---

1. See generally Countryman, *The Use of State Law in Bankruptcy Cases,* 47 N.Y. U.L.Rev. 407, 631 (1972); Hill, *The Law-Making Power of the Federal Courts: Constitutional Preemption,* 67 Colum.L.Rev. 1024 (1967); Note, 75 Harv.L.Rev. 1395 (1962).

2. The cases range over the whole field of federal regulation, and involve varying degrees of congressional disclosure of a purpose to preempt or preserve state law. For recent decisions upholding a preemption claim on grounds of conflict with federal law, see *e.g.,* Capital Cities Cable, Inc. v. Crisp, 467 U.S. 691 (1984) (preemption of state regulation of retransmission by cable television systems); Toll v. Moreno, 458 U.S. 1 (1982) (preemption of state law denying in-state tuition status to certain non-

immigrant aliens domiciled in the state); Fidelity Federal S. & L. Ass'n v. de la Cuesta, 458 U.S. 141 (1982) (preemption of state law limiting ability of federal savings and loan association to invoke "due-on-sale" clause in a mortgage). For a case involving three asserted grounds of federal invalidation of state law—that the state law impermissibly burdened interstate commerce, that it was a "direct" regulation of interstate commerce, and that it conflicted with the objectives of a federal statute, see Edgar v. MITE Corp., 457 U.S. 624 (1982). The majority relied on the first ground in invalidating a state's business takeover statute; two members of the majority—Justices Powell and Stevens—relied on the second and third grounds as well.

state and federal action. We are in the domain of government and practical affairs, and this Court has not stifled state action unless what the State has required, in the light of what Congress has ordered, would truly entail contradictory duties or make actual, not argumentative, inroads on what Congress has commanded or forbidden. * * *

"In discussing in the Federalist Papers the respective areas of federal and state constitutional powers, Hamilton wrote that state powers would be superseded by federal authority if continued authority in the States would be 'absolutely and totally *contradictory* and *repugnant.*' 'I use these terms,' he wrote, 'to distinguish this * * * case from another which might appear to resemble it, but which would, in fact, be essentially different; I mean where the exercise of a concurrent jurisdiction might be productive of occasional interferences in the *policy* of any branch of administration, but would not imply any direct contradiction or repugnancy in point of constitutional authority.' The Federalist, No. 32, at 200 (Van Doren ed. 1945).
* * *

"Hamilton's suggestion, emanating from the contest of constitutional creation, is disregarded in the approach taken by the Court today on a precisely analogous if not identical question, for there exists here not an explicit conflict but, at the very most, an interference with policy.
* * * "

(3) Federal regulation may displace not only contradictory but also parallel state law.[3] In Sears, Roebuck & Co. v. Stiffel Co., 376 U.S. 225 (1964), and Compco Corp. v. Day–Brite Lighting, Inc., 376 U.S. 234 (1964), the question was whether the state law of unfair competition could validly make actionable the copying of products not entitled to patent protection under federal law. The Court held that state-law liability was impliedly barred by federal law (pp. 230–33): "[T]he patent system is one in which uniform federal standards are carefully used to promote invention while at the same time preserving free competition. Obviously a State could not, consistently with the Supremacy Clause of the Constitution, extend the life of a patent beyond its expiration date or give a patent on an article which lacked the level of invention required for federal patents. To do either would run counter to the policy of Congress of granting patents only to true inventions, and then only for a limited time. Just as a State cannot encroach upon the federal patent laws directly, it cannot, under some other law, such as that forbidding unfair competition, give protection of a kind that clashes with the objectives of the federal patent laws.

"* * * To allow a State by use of its law of unfair competition to prevent the copying of an article which represents too slight an advance to

---

3. See, *e.g.*, Garner v. Teamsters Union, 346 U.S. 485 (1953) (state courts may not grant injunctions against activities prohibited by the National Labor Relations Act); Local 926, IUOE v. Jones, 460 U.S. 669 (1983) (state law damage action by supervisory employee against union for tortious interference with his contract of employment was preempted because conduct was arguably prohibited by N.L.R.A.).

Garner was extended to the limit of its logic—or beyond—by Guss v. Utah Labor Board, 353 U.S. 1 (1957), holding that state courts could not give remedies for acts technically violating the federal statute even when the NLRB has declined jurisdiction because of the minor impact of the case on interstate commerce. The problem of the resulting "gap" was cured by legislation, see 29 U.S.C. § 164(c).

See also Pennsylvania v. Nelson, 350 U.S. 497 (1956) (federal Smith Act preempts substantially identical state law against subverting the national government); In re Second Employers' Liability Cases, 223 U.S. 1 (1912) (FELA preempts state law personal injury actions by covered employees).

be patented would be to permit the State to block off from the public something which federal law has said belongs to the public. The result would be that while federal law grants only 14 or 17 years' protection to genuine inventions, see 35 U.S.C. §§ 154, 173, States could allow perpetual protection to articles too lacking in novelty to merit any patent at all under federal constitutional standards. This would be too great an encroachment on the federal patent system to be tolerated."

See also Lear, Inc. v. Adkins, 395 U.S. 653 (1969) (a state may not award damages for breach of a contract licensing the use of a patented product if the patent is invalid).

Recent cases have limited the rationale of these decisions. See, e.g., Kewanee Oil Co. v. Bicron Corp., 416 U.S. 470 (1974) (state's trade secret law is not preempted by federal patent law); Aronson v. Quick Point Pencil Co., 440 U.S. 257 (1979) (enforcement of royalty contract under state law is allowed, even though patent application for product covered by the contract had been rejected). In the area of copyright, account must now be taken of the Copyright Act enacted in 1976, 17 U.S.C. §§ 101–702, and especially of § 301, which deals explicitly with the scope of federal preemption.[4]

(4) The Court has traveled up the hill and down on the role of federal common law in the complex and heavily regulated area of pollution of interstate waters. In a rather casual dictum in Ohio v. Wyandotte Chemicals Corp., 401 U.S. 493, 498–99 n. 3 (1971), the Court suggested that state law would govern in an action by a state to abate, as a nuisance, the pollution of Lake Erie by the dumping of mercury. But a year later, in an action by Illinois against four Wisconsin cities and two sewerage commissions to enjoin alleged polution of Lake Michigan, the Court held that the case was governed by federal common law and that accordingly the federal district court had subject matter jurisdiction. Illinois v. Milwaukee, 406 U.S. 91 (1972). Justice Douglas, for the Court, pointed out that Congress had in a variety of statutes asserted an interest in the problem. His opinion continued (pp. 102–04):

"The Federal Water Pollution Control Act in § 1(b) declares that it is federal policy 'to recognize, preserve, and protect the primary responsibilities and rights of the States in preventing and controlling water pollution.' But the Act makes clear that it is federal, not state, law that in the end controls the pollution of interstate or navigable waters. * * *

"The remedy sought by Illinois is not within the precise scope of remedies prescribed by Congress. Yet the remedies which Congress provides are not necessarily the only federal remedies available. * * * When we deal with air or water in their ambient or interstate aspects, there is a federal common law * * *.

"The application of federal common law to abate a public nuisance in interstate or navigable waters is not inconsistent with the Water Pollution Control Act. Congress provided in § 10(b) of that Act that, save as a court may decree otherwise in an enforcement action, '[s]tate and interstate action to abate pollution of interstate and navigable waters shall be

---

4. For an important decision in the copyright field, see Goldstein v. California, 412 U.S. 546 (1973) (California statute proscribing "record or tape piracy" is not preempted by federal copyright law). See generally Goldstein, Copyright, Patent, Trademark and Related State Doctrines 128–40, 175–96, 213–32 (2d ed. 1981); Brown, Kaplan & Brown's Copyright 504–46 (3d ed. 1978).

encouraged and shall not ＊ ＊ ＊ be displaced by federal enforcement action.' "

In reaching its result the Court relied on Georgia v. Tennessee Copper Co., 206 U.S. 230 (1907), p. 327, *supra*, which was, of course, a pre-Erie case. It relied also on the cases holding that federal law governs questions relating to the apportionment among states of the waters of interstate streams. Do you find the citation of authorities persuasive? The Court might also have cited cases such as Sanitary Dist. of Chicago v. United States, 266 U.S. 405 (1925), discussed in Sec. 2, pp. 912–13, *infra.*

After this decision, Congress enacted the extensive Water Pollution Control Amendments of 1972, 33 U.S.C. § 1311 *et seq.*, which, among other things, made it illegal for anyone to discharge pollutants into the Nation's waters without a permit. Pursuant to this law and regulations issued under it, permits were issued to the defendants in the Illinois case, who by this time had been duly served in an action by Illinois in an Illinois federal district court.[5]

After trial of the claim in 1977, the district court held that a nuisance had been established under federal common law and issued an elaborate decree, and the court of appeals affirmed in part, ruling that the 1972 amendments had not preempted the federal law of nuisance.[6]

The Supreme Court reversed, 6–3. Milwaukee v. Illinois, 451 U.S. 304 (1981). Justice Rehnquist, for the majority, held that:

"[A]t least so far as concerns the claims of respondents, Congress has not left the formulation of appropriate federal standards to the courts through application of often vague and indeterminate nuisance concepts and maxims of equity jurisprudence, but rather has occupied the field through the establishment of a comprehensive regulatory program supervised by an expert administrative agency. The 1972 Amendments to the Federal Water Pollution Control Act were not merely another law 'touching interstate waters' of the sort surveyed in Illinois v. Milwaukee, and found inadequate to supplant federal common law. Rather, the Amendments were viewed by Congress as a 'total restructuring' and 'complete rewriting' of the existing water pollution legislation considered in that case" (p. 317).

The 1972 amendments had explicitly preserved more stringent remedies under state law, 33 U.S.C. § 1370, but for the majority the question of remedies under federal common law was quite different (pp. 316–17):

"[T]he appropriate analysis in determining if federal statutory law governs a question previously the subject of federal common law is not the same as that employed in deciding if federal law pre-empts state law. In considering the latter question 'we start with the assumption that the

---

5. When these defendants did not fully comply with the requirements of their permits, the responsible Wisconsin state agency (as contemplated by the 1972 Act) brought an enforcement action in a Wisconsin state court. In 1977, the state court entered a decree imposing certain requirements and establishing a timetable for additional construction.

6. The district court decree was considerably more restrictive than the terms of

defendants' previously issued permits and the enforcement order of the Wisconsin state court (note 5, *supra*) with respect to both "overflows" of sewage and "effluent limitations." See Milwaukee v. Illinois, 451 U.S. 304, 312 (1981). The court of appeals affirmed with respect to the order to eliminate overflows but reversed "insofar as the effluent limitations ＊ ＊ ＊ were more stringent than those in the permits and applicable EPA regulations" (*id.*).

historic police powers of the States were not to be superseded by the Federal Act unless that was the clear and manifest purpose of Congress.' * * * (quoting Rice v. Santa Fe Elevator Corp., 331 U.S. 218, 230 (1947)). While we have not hesitated to find pre-emption of state law, whether express or implied, when Congress has so indicated, * * * or when enforcement of state regulations would impair 'federal superintendence of the field,' Florida Lime & Avocado Growers, Inc. v. Paul, 373 U.S. 132, 142 (1963), our analysis has included 'due regard for the presuppositions of our embracing federal system, including the principle of diffusion of power not as a matter of doctrinaire localism but as a promoter of democracy.' San Diego Building Trades Council v. Garmon, 359 U.S. 236, 243 (1959). Such concerns are not implicated in the same fashion when the question is whether federal statutory or federal common law governs, and accordingly the same sort of evidence of a clear and manifest purpose is not required. Indeed, as noted, in cases such as the present 'we start with the assumption' that it is for Congress, not federal courts, to articulate the appropriate standards to be applied as a matter of federal law."

Justice Blackmun, for the dissenters, analyzed the 1972 amendments at length and concluded (p. 339): "In my view, the language and structure of the Clean Water Act leave no doubt that Congress intended to preserve the federal common law of nuisance." As a parting shot, he noted an ironic aspect of the result (p. 353):

"There is one final disturbing aspect to the Court's decision. By eliminating the federal common law of nuisance in this area, the Court in effect is encouraging recourse to state law wherever the federal statutory scheme is perceived to offer inadequate protection against pollution from outside the State, either in its enforcement standards or in the remedies afforded. This recourse is now inevitable under a statutory scheme that accords a significant role to state as well as federal law. But in the present context it is also unfortunate, since it undermines the Court's prior conclusion that it is federal rather than state law that should govern the regulation of *inter* state water pollution. Illinois v. Milwaukee, 406 U.S., at 102. Instead of promoting a more uniform federal approach to the problem of alleviating interstate pollution, I fear that today's decision will lead States to turn to their own courts for statutory or common-law assistance in filling the interstices of the federal statute. Rather than encourage such a prospect, I would adhere to the principles clearly enunciated in Illinois v. Milwaukee, and affirm the judgment of the Court of Appeals."

It is difficult to judge the merits of the dispute between the majority and the dissent without a good deal more information about the statute and the scope of regulation than can be presented here. But consider carefully the majority's suggestion that the Court should always be more reluctant to conclude that state law is preempted by a federal regulatory program than to determine that federal common law has been preempted by a federal statute. Note in contrast the point, urged by Justice Blackmun (pp. 333–34 n. 2), that while state law may operate to frustrate the national purpose in regulation, "participation by the federal courts is often desirable, and indeed necessary, if federal policies developed by Congress are to be fully effectuated."

(5) Just as the presence of a clearly declared federal legislative policy has often resulted in the displacement of state law, so the absence of such a

declaration has led to a refusal to displace state law, even under circumstances where strong arguments of uniquely federal interests could be made. Of special note is Jackson v. Johns–Manville Sales Corp., 750 F.2d 1314 (5th Cir.1985), in which a sharply divided court, sitting en banc, rejected an appeal for the development of federal common law governing liability for asbestos-related injuries. In answer to arguments that federal common law was required because of the nationwide impact of "a sequence of massive tort claims that has unparalleled geographic and financial dimension" (dissent, p. 1330), the majority emphasized that "Congress itself has yet to make policy on this issue," that many "practical problems would attend the displacement of state law," and that there was not available "any governing principle of easy application for the imposition of federal common law in the asbestos context" (pp. 1325–27). See also, *e.g.,* In re "Agent Orange" Product Liability Litigation, 635 F.2d 987 (2d Cir.1980) (holding, 2–1, that veterans' personal injury action against herbicide suppliers for injuries incurred during Vietnam War was not governed by federal common law);[7] *cf.* Silkwood v. Kerr–McGee Corp., 464 U.S. 238 (1984) (award of punitive damages under state law, in action for plutonium contamination injuries, not preempted by federal law).

A number of commentators have urged the creation of a federal common law of torts in the mass accident context. See Mullenix, *Class Resolution of the Mass–Tort Case: A Proposed Federal Procedure Act,* 64 Texas L.Rev. 1039, 1077–79 and authorities cited at n. 201 (1986). In addition, there have been numerous proposals for congressional action dealing with specific or general issues of product liability, but so far, none has been enacted into law.

NOTE ON SABBATINO AND THE FEDERAL LAW OF INTERNATIONAL RELATIONS

(1) Still another category of federal common law emerged in Banco Nacional de Cuba v. Sabbatino, 376 U.S. 398 (1964), in which "the dispositive issue" was "whether the so-called act of state doctrine serves to sustain petitioner's claims" to recover the proceeds of a shipload of sugar; the act of state doctrine "in its traditional formulation precludes the courts of this country from inquiring into the validity of the public acts a recognized foreign sovereign power committed within its own territory" (pp. 400–01). Defendant, a New York corporation, had contracted to buy the sugar in Cuba from its former owners, who were American citizens. While the sugar was still in Cuba, and before payment or passage of title, the sugar was expropriated by a decree of the Cuban government;[1] title to the sugar under the decree passed to plaintiff-petitioner, a Cuban governmental agency. Defendant secured an export license for the sugar by promising to

---

7. For a vivid and informative description of this litigation, see Schuck, Agent Orange on Trial: Mass Toxic Disasters in the Courts (1986).

1. Under the decree of expropriation, although "a system of compensation was formally provided, the possibility of payment * * * may well be deemed illusory. Our State Department has described the Cuban law as 'manifestly in violation of those principles of international law which have long been accepted by the free countries of the West. It is in its essence discriminatory, arbitrary and confiscatory.' " 376 U.S. at 402–03.

The statement of the case in the text is simplified in minor and irrelevant respects.

pay the proceeds to the petitioner; but after export it refused to honor this promise and proposed to pay them to the former owners. Thereupon the petitioner brought an action for conversion of the proceeds in a New York federal district court, basing jurisdiction on diversity of citizenship. Both the district court and the court of appeals held that the Cuban expropriation violated international law and therefore did not convey good title to the petitioner. The Supreme Court reversed, holding for plaintiff. The rule of decision announced was "that the Judicial Branch will not examine the validity of a taking of property within its own territory by a foreign sovereign government, extant and recognized by this country at the time of suit, in the absence of a treaty or other unambiguous agreement regarding controlling legal principles, even if the complaint alleges that the taking violates customary international law" (p. 428).

In his opinion for the Court Justice Harlan discussed "the foundations on which we deem the act of state doctrine to rest, and more particularly the question of whether state or federal law governs its application in a federal diversity case" (p. 421).[2]

The Court took the view that compliance with the act of state doctrine is itself neither dictated nor limited by international law, but is, rather, governed by the internal law of each country. Nor does the Constitution "require the act of state doctrine; it does not irrevocably remove from the judiciary the capacity to review the validity of foreign acts of state." But the doctrine does "have 'constitutional' underpinnings. It arises out of the basic relationships between branches of government in a system of separation of powers. * * * The doctrine as formulated in past decisions expresses the strong sense of the Judicial Branch that its engagement in the task of passing on the validity of foreign acts of state may hinder rather than further this country's pursuit of goals both for itself and for the community of nations as a whole in the international sphere. Many commentators disagree with this view; they have striven by means of distinguishing and limiting past decisions and by advancing various considerations of policy to stimulate a narrowing of the apparent scope of the rule. Whatever considerations are thought to predominate, it is plain that the problems involved are uniquely federal in nature. If federal authority, in this instance this Court, orders the field of judicial competence in this area for the federal courts, and the state courts are left free to formulate their own rules, the purposes behind the doctrine could be as effectively undermined as if there had been no federal pronouncement on the subject" (pp. 423–24).

The Court went on to "make it clear that an issue concerned with a basic choice regarding the competence and function of the Judiciary and the National Executive in ordering our relationships with other members of the international community must be treated exclusively as an aspect of federal law. It seems fair to assume that the Court did not have rules like the act of state doctrine in mind when it decided Erie R. Co. v. Tompkins. Soon thereafter, Professor Philip C. Jessup, now a judge of the Internation-

---

2. The courts of many states had, prior to Sabbatino, been accustomed to applying various doctrines of international law as part of their own law, and the Supreme Court had never determined how far the states were free to take independent views on these matters. In particular, Supreme Court precedents relating to the act of state doctrine were all pre-Erie diversity cases and thus were ambiguous on the choice of law question.

al Court of Justice, recognized the potential dangers were Erie extended to legal problems affecting international relations [citing Jessup, *The Doctrine of Erie Railroad v. Tompkins Applied to International Law,* 33 Am.J.Int'l Law 740 (1939)]. He cautioned that rules of international law should not be left to divergent and perhaps parochial state interpretations. His basic rationale is equally applicable to the act of state doctrine" (p. 425).

The Court pointed out (pp. 426–27) that there are precedents for creating "enclaves of federal judge-made law which bind the States", citing as instances Lincoln Mills; D'Oench, Duhme & Co.; and Clearfield. "Perhaps more directly in point are the bodies of law applied between States over boundaries and in regard to the apportionment of interstate waters. * * * The problems surrounding the act of state doctrine are, albeit for different reasons, as intrinsically federal as are those involved in water apportionment or boundary disputes. The considerations supporting exclusion of state authority here are much like those which led the Court in United States v. California, 332 U.S. 19, to hold that the Federal Government possessed paramount rights in submerged lands though within the three-mile limit of coastal States. We conclude that the scope of the act of state doctrine must be determined according to federal law." [3]

Justice White's long dissent did not challenge the holding that federal law governed.[4]

(2) To what extent does Sabbatino make the question of the applicability of any rule of international law a federal question? What about the content of any such rule: is it a "federal" question for purposes of federal-state relations? Does Sabbatino operate only with respect to questions involving the foreign relations of the United States? [5] What is the relation-

---

3. At this point Justice Harlan has a footnote: "Various constitutional and statutory provisions indirectly support this determination, see U.S. Const., Art. I, § 8, cls. 3, 10; Art. II, §§ 2, 3; Art. III, § 2; 28 U.S.C. §§ 1251(a)(2), (b)(1), (b)(3), 1332(a)(2), 1333, 1350–1351, by reflecting a concern for uniformity in this country's dealings with foreign nations and indicating a desire to give matters of international significance to the jurisdiction of federal institutions. See Comment, 62 Col.L.Rev. 1278, 1297, n. 123 * * *."

4. Shortly after Sabbatino Congress enacted overriding legislation, see 22 U.S.C. § 2370(e), barring the judicial invocation of the act of state doctrine except under stated circumstances. This amendment was held to be retroactive, and served to defeat Cuba's claim, on the remand of the Sabbatino case. See Banco Nacional v. Farr, 383 F.2d 166 (2d Cir.1967).

For subsequent views on the act of state doctrine, see First Nat'l City Bank v. Banco Nacional de Cuba, 406 U.S. 759 (1972); Alfred Dunhill of London, Inc., v. Republic of Cuba, 425 U.S. 682 (1976).

5. In Zschernig v. Miller, 389 U.S. 429 (1968), the Court held that, as interpreted and administered, an Oregon statute, barring a foreigner from inheriting if his country does not grant U.S. citizens reciprocal rights, is invalid as "an intrusion by the State into the field of foreign affairs which the Constitution entrusts to the President and the Congress" (p. 432). "The statute as construed seems to make unavoidable judicial criticism of nations established on a more authoritarian basis than our own. * * * The several States, of course, have traditionally regulated the descent and distribution of estates. But those regulations must give way if they impair the effective exercise of the Nation's foreign policy" (p. 440).

Justice Harlan dissented on the issue of constitutionality: "Essentially, the Court's basis for decision appears to be that alien inheritance laws afford state court judges an opportunity to criticize in dictum the policies of foreign governments, and that these dicta may adversely affect our foreign relations" (p. 461).

The Court purported to leave standing Clark v. Allen, 331 U.S. 503 (1947), upholding a similar California "reciprocity" statute, saying that such statutes were not unconstitutional "on their face" but only if, as interpreted and administered, they involved the state courts in an appraisal of the quality of the administration of justice by the foreign state.

ship of the federal courts' law-making authority in this field to the power of
the federal political branches? These and similar questions are left largely
unanswered by the post-Sabbatino case law, but have been extensively
discussed in scholarly commentary. In an especially interesting passage,
Henkin, Foreign Affairs and the Constitution 219–20 (1972), writes that
after Sabbatino:

"There ought to be little doubt * * * that in the established areas of
judicial law-making, law that is substantially related to foreign affairs—the
determination of customary international law and comity for judicial
purposes; guidelines for the interpretation of treaties and the meaning of
particular treaty provisions; the principles of (international) conflicts-of-
laws; rules as to access of foreign governments to domestic courts and the
treatment of foreign judgments—the federal courts can make law for their
own guidance and can decide also whether federal interests require that
the States conform to them. * * *

"Later cases will have to answer the more difficult question, whether
and which new subjects are also within the legislative power of the federal
courts. * * * [O]ne may expect that without limiting their power in
principle, they will legislate sparingly.

" * * * Judge-made law, the courts must recognize, can only serve
foreign policy grossly and spasmodically; their attempts to draw lines and
make exceptions must be bound in doctrine and justified in reasoned
opinions, and they cannot provide flexibility, completeness, and comprehensive coherence." [6]

(3) The Sabbatino Court, in support of its conclusion that federal law
governed, cited a number of constitutional and statutory provisions, including 28 U.S.C. § 1350. See note 3, *supra*. That provision, which confers
jurisdiction in a "civil action by an alien for a tort only, committed in
violation of the law of nations * * *," has itself been the source of
considerable controversy in the years since Sabbatino. Does the provision
do more than confer jurisdiction in cases in which some other source of
federal law creates a cause of action? Does the provision itself create a
cause of action and refer to a source of federal law for its implementation?
If so, is that source of federal law an aspect of federal common law akin to
that declared and applied in Sabbatino? Should it matter whether the
controversy involves the United States or one of its citizens, or whether the
relevant events occurred on U.S. territory?

In Filartiga v. Pena–Irala, 630 F.2d 876 (2d Cir.1980), the court held
that § 1350 afforded jurisdiction over a claim brought by Paraguayan
citizens against a former Paraguayan official for acts of torture allegedly
committed in Paraguay. "The constitutional basis for the Alien Tort
Statute," the court said, "is the law of nations, which has always been part
of the federal common law" (p. 885).

For discussion of Zschernig and its implications, see Henkin, Foreign Affairs and
the Constitution 238–41 (1972).

6. See also Restatement (Revised) of the
Foreign Relations Law of the United States
§§ 111 (and Comment d), 112 (and Comment a) (1987); Edwards, *The Erie Doctrine*
in Foreign Affairs Cases, 42 N.Y.U.L.Rev.
674 (1967); Hill, *The Law–Making Power*
of the Federal Courts: Constitutional Pre-
emption, 67 Colum.L.Rev. 1024 (1967);
Moore, *Federalism and Foreign Relations,*
1965 Duke L.J. 248.

In Tel–Oren v. Libyan Arab Republic, 726 F.2d 774 (D.C.Cir.1984), the panel of three judges agreed only that the action should be dismissed. Plaintiffs in that case, primarily Israeli citizens, brought suit against the Palestine Liberation Organization and others for alleged acts of terrorism committed in Israel. For Judge Edwards, who endorsed the approach in Filartiga, § 1350 itself conferred a right to sue for an offense against the law of nations, but that body of law did not extend to terrorist acts by individuals not acting under color of any recognized state's law. For Judge Bork, concurring, § 1350 did not create a private cause of action, nor did the relevant principles of international law, which "typically does not authorize individuals to vindicate rights by bringing actions in either international or municipal tribunals" (p. 817). Moreover, he urged, the very separation of powers principles that animated Sabbatino counseled against recognition of a cause of action that "would raise substantial problems of judicial interference with * * * the conduct of foreign relations" (p. 804). For Judge Robb, also concurring, the case was controlled by the political question doctrine, since it involved standards that defied application, and touched on sensitive matters of diplomacy historically within the exclusive jurisdiction of the other branches.

(4) One of Justice White's objections to the Sabbatino decision was that "[t]his backward looking [act of state] doctrine, never before declared in this Court, is carried a disconcerting step further: not only are the courts powerless to question acts of state proscribed by international law but they are likewise powerless to refuse to adjudicate the claim founded upon a foreign law; they must render judgment and thereby validate the lawless act." 376 U.S. at 439.

Suppose that a state court were to dismiss a case exactly like Sabbatino on the ground that, as a matter of state law, it has no power to render an affirmative judgment for a claimant without considering the lawfulness of his claim, and that Sabbatino precludes it from such consideration since it bars examination of the validity of the expropriation. Ignoring the legislation enacted by Congress after Sabbatino, do you think the decision would be reviewable by the Supreme Court? If so, should it be reversed?

(5) If there had been no diversity jurisdiction in Sabbatino—if, for example, the defendant had been an alien—would there have been federal jurisdiction under 28 U.S.C. § 1331? Or did the federal issues come into the case only by way of defense? See generally Chap. VIII, Sec. 3, *infra*.

SECTION 2. ENFORCING PRIMARY OBLIGATIONS

SUBSECTION A: CIVIL ACTIONS BY THE FEDERAL GOVERNMENT

UNITED STATES v. SAN JACINTO TIN CO.
125 U.S. 273, 8 S.Ct. 850, 31 L.Ed. 747 (1888).
Appeal from the Circuit Court for the District of California.

MR. JUSTICE MILLER delivered the opinion of the Court.

The suit in this case, which was a bill in chancery filed April 10, 1883, in the Circuit Court for the District of California, purports to be brought by the Attorney General on behalf of the United States against the San Jacinto Tin Company, the Riverside Canal Company, and the Riverside Land & Irrigating Company. These corporations are alleged to be in possession of a large body of land, nearly eleven square leagues in extent, for which a patent was issued by the United States on the 26th day of October, 1867, to Maria del Rosario Estudillo de Aguirre, and her heirs and assigns. The object of the bill is to set aside this patent, and have it declared void, upon the ground that the land described in the survey, which description is a part of the patent, is not the land granted by the Mexican government to said Maria, nor that which was confirmed to her under the proceedings before the land commission, and by the judgment of the District Court of the United States, and by this court also on appeal. The essential feature of the grievance relied on by the complainant is, that this survey was thus located by fraud to include different and more valuable land than that granted by Mexico, and confirmed by the courts, and on account of this fraud it is prayed that the survey and patent be set aside and annulled. * * *

It is alleged that throughout the whole transaction, from the beginning of the effort to have this survey made until its final completion and the issue of the patent, all the proceedings were dictated by fraud, and all the officers of the government below the Secretary of the Interior who had anything to do with it were parties to that fraud, and to be benefited by it. * * *

* * *

Another question, however, is raised by counsel for the defendant, which is earnestly insisted upon by them, and which received the serious consideration of the judges in the Circuit Court; namely, the right of the Attorney General of the United States to institute this suit.

The question as presented is one surrounded by some embarrassment. But as it is in some form or other of frequent recurrence recently, and if decided in favor of the appellees will require the dismissal of the case without a judgment by this court upon its merits, we feel called upon to give the matter our attention. It is denied that the Attorney General has any general authority under the Constitution and laws of the United States to commence a suit in the name of the United States to set aside a patent, or other solemn instrument issued by proper authority.

It is quite true that the Revised Statutes, in the title which establishes and regulates the Department of Justice, simply declares, in section 346, that "there shall be at the seat of government an Executive Department to be known as the Department of Justice, and an Attorney General, who shall be the head thereof." There is no very specific statement of the general duties of the Attorney General, but it is seen from the whole chapter referred to that he has the authority, and it is made his duty, to supervise the conduct of all suits brought by or against the United States, and to give advice to the President and the heads of the other departments of the government. There is no express authority vested in him to authorize suits to be brought against the debtors of the government, or upon bonds, or to begin criminal prosecutions, or to institute proceedings in any of the numerous cases in which the United States is plaintiff; and yet he is invested with the general superintendence of all such suits, and all the district attorneys who do bring them in the various courts in the country are placed under his immediate direction and control. And notwithstanding the want of any specific authority to bring an action in the name of the United States to set aside and declare void an instrument issued under its apparent authority, we cannot believe that where a case exists in which this ought to be done it is not within the authority of that officer to cause such action to be instituted and prosecuted. He is undoubtedly the officer who has charge of the institution and conduct of the pleas of the United States, and of the litigation which is necessary to establish the rights of the government.

If the United States in any particular case has a just cause for calling upon the judiciary of the country, in any of its courts, for relief by setting aside or annulling any of its contracts, its obligations, or its most solemn instruments, the question of the appeal to the judicial tribunals of the country must primarily be decided by the Attorney General of the United States. That such a power should exist somewhere, and that the United States should not be more helpless in relieving itself from frauds, impostures, and deceptions than the private individual, is hardly open to argument. The Constitution itself declares that the judicial power shall extend to all cases to which the United States shall be a party, and that this means mainly where it is a party plaintiff is a necessary result of the well-established proposition that it cannot be sued in any court without its consent. There must, then, be an officer or officers of the government to determine when the United States shall sue, to decide for what it shall sue, and to be responsible that such suits shall be brought in appropriate cases. The attorneys of the United States in every judicial district are officers of this character, and they are by statute under the immediate supervision and control of the Attorney General. How, then, can it be argued that if the United States has been deceived, entrapped, or defrauded into the making, under the forms of law, of an instrument which injuriously affects its rights of property, or other rights, it cannot bring a suit to avoid the effect of such instrument, thus fraudulently obtained, without a special act of Congress in each case, or without some special authority applicable to this class of cases, while all other just grounds of suing in a court of justice concededly belong to the Department of Justice, and are in use every day? The judiciary act of 1789, in its third section, which first created the office of Attorney General, without any very accurate definition of his powers, in using the words that "there shall also be appointed a meet person, learned in the law, to act as Attorney General for the United States," 1 Stat. 93, c. 21, § 35, must have had reference to the similar office with the same designation existing under the English law. And though it has been said that there is no common law of the United States, it is still quite true that when acts of Congress use words which are familiar in the law of England, they are supposed to be used with reference to their meaning in that law. In all this, however, the Attorney General acts as the head of one of the Executive departments, representing the authority of the President in the class of subjects within the domain of that department, and under his control. * * *

We are not insensible to the enormous power and its capacity for evil thus reposed in that department of the government. Since the title to all of the land in more than half of the States and Territories of the Union depends upon patents from the government of the United States, it is to be seen what a vast power is confided to the officer who may order the institution of suits to set aside every one of these patents; and if the doctrine that the United States in bringing such actions is not controlled by any statute of limitations, or governed by the rule concerning *laches* be sound, of which we express no opinion at present, then the evil which may result would seem to be endless as well as enormous. But it has often been said that the fact that the exercise of power may be abused is no sufficient reason for denying its existence, and if restrictions are to be placed upon the exercise of this authority by the Attorney General, it is for the legislative body which created the office to enact them.

We do not think, therefore, that it can be successfully denied that there exists in the Attorney General, as the head of the Department of Justice, the right to institute, in the name of the United States, a suit to abrogate, annul, or set aside a patent for land which has been issued by the government in a case where such an instrument if permitted to stand would work serious injury to the United States, and prejudice its interests, and where it has been obtained by fraud, imposture, or mistake.

     * * *

But we are of opinion that since the right of the government of the United States to institute such a suit depends upon the same general principles which would authorize a private citizen to apply to a court of justice for relief against an instrument obtained from him by fraud or deceit, or any of those other practices which are admitted to justify a court in granting relief, the government must show that, like the private individual, it has such an interest in the relief sought as entitles it to move in the matter. If it be a question of property a case must be made in which the court can afford a remedy in regard to that property; if it be a question of fraud which would render the instrument void, the fraud must operate to the prejudice of the United States; and if it is apparent that the suit is brought for the benefit of some third party, and that the United States has no pecuniary interest in the remedy sought, and is under no obligation to the party who will be benefited to sustain an action for his use; in short, if there does not appear any obligation on the part of the United States to the public, or to any individual, or any interest of its own, it can no more sustain such an action than any private person could under similar circumstances.

In all the decisions to which we have just referred it is either expressed or implied that this interest or duty of the United States must exist as the foundation of the right of action. Of course this interest must be made to appear in the progress of the proceedings, either by pleading or evidence, and if there is a want of it, and the fact is manifest that the suit has actually been brought for the benefit of some third person, and that no obligation to the general public exists which requires the United States to bring it, then the suit must fail. In the case before us the bill itself leaves a fair implication that if this patent is set aside the title to the property will revert to the United States, together with the beneficial interest in it. It is argued in the brief that this is not true; that in fact the government is but the instrument of one Baker, who married the widow of Abel Stearns; and that Stearns contested the correctness of this survey with others before the land department very actively and energetically, because he had such an interest in the land covered by it that if it was defeated he would become the equitable or beneficial owner of the land. This view is supported by some pretty strong testimony and by the fact that Baker was the man at whose instance the action was begun.

* * * *

But we are not so entirely satisfied of the want of interest of the United States in the whole or a part of the land which is covered by this patent as to justify us in saying that the bill in the present case ought to be dismissed on that ground. * * *

[Upon consideration of the merits, the decree was affirmed.]

MR. JUSTICE FIELD, concurring: I concur in affirming the decree of the court below dismissing the bill in this case. * * *

But * * * I cannot assent to the position announced in the opinion of the court, that the Attorney General has unlimited authority by virtue of his office to institute suits to set aside patents issued by the government. * * * Whenever Congress has felt it important that patents for lands should be revoked, either because of fraud in their issue, or of breach of conditions in them, it has not failed to authorize legal proceedings for that purpose. In a multitude of cases titles to lands, upon which whole communities live, rest upon patents of the United States. In several instances, cities having more than a hundred thousand people residing within their limits are built on land patented by the government. I cannot believe that it is within the power of the Attorney General, to be exercised at any time in the future, this generation or the next—as no statute of limitations runs against the government—to institute suits to unsettle the title founded upon such patents, even where there are allegations of fraud in obtaining them. There must be a time when such allegations will not be heeded. * * * If, without the authority of Congress, such proceedings may be instituted by him upon the repetition, as in this case, of old charges, or upon the unsupported statements of interested parties, a cloud may at any moment be cast upon the titles of a whole people and there would be in his hands a tremendous weapon of vexation and oppression. I can never assent to the position that there exists in any officer of the government a power so liable to abuse and so dangerous to the peace of many communities.

I do not recognize the doctrine that the Attorney General takes any power by virtue of his office except what the Constitution and the laws confer. The powers of the executive officers of England are not vested in the executive officers of the United States government, simply because they are called by similar names. It is the theory, and I may add, the glory of our institutions, that they are founded upon law, that no one can exercise any authority over the rights and interests of others except pursuant to and in the manner authorized by law.

* * *

Aside from the qualifications thus expressed to the views of the court, there is much in the opinion which gives me great satisfaction. It holds that in suits brought by the government for relief against an instrument alleged to have been obtained by fraud or deceit, or any practice which would justify a court in granting relief, the government must show, like a private individual, that it has such an interest in the relief sought as entitles it to move in the matter. If it be a question of property, a case must be made in which the court can afford a remedy in regard to that property; if it be a question of fraud, which would render the instrument void, the fraud must operate to the prejudice of the United States; and if it is apparent that the suit is brought for the benefit of some third party, and that the United States have no pecuniary interest in the remedy sought, and are under no obligation to the party who will be benefited, to sustain an action for his use; in short, if there does not appear any obligation on the part of the United States to the public, or to any individual, or any interest of their own, they can no more sustain such an action than any private person could under similar circumstances.

From this ruling some degree of peace and security may come to holders of titles derived by patent from the government. * * *

NOTE ON THE IMPLICATION OF RIGHTS OF ACTION BY THE UNITED STATES

(1) The right of the United States to bring an action on contract without benefit of statute was asserted in Dugan v. United States, 3 Wheat. 172 (U.S.1818), recognized in United States v. Buford, 3 Pet. 12, 28 (U.S.1830), and reasserted in United States v. Tingey, 5 Pet. 115, 127–28 (U.S.1831). In that case Justice Story said that the right of the United States "to enter into a contract, or to take a bond, in cases not previously provided by some law * * * is, in our opinion, an incident to the general right of sovereignty." [1]

From this the right of the United States to maintain an action on the contract in its own name followed as a necessary corollary. As the Court said in Jessup v. United States, 106 U.S. 147, 152 (1882), "It would be absurd to hold a bond to be valid on which a suit in the name of the obligee could not be maintained."

The capacity of the United States to own property had express constitutional recognition, and the conclusion that actions could be maintained, without special statutory provision, to protect the property of the United States followed even more readily. See Benton v. Woolsey, 12 Pet. 27

---

1. See also United States v. Bradley, 10 Pet. 343, 359–60 (U.S.1836); United States v. Linn, 15 Pet. 290 (U.S.1841); United States v. Fitzgerald, 15 Pet. 407, 421 (U.S.1841) (recognizing right to seek rescission of contract in equity); United States v. Hodson, 10 Wall. 395 (U.S.1870).

(U.S.1838) (mortgage foreclosure suit, disapproving adherence to state practice of having district attorney sue in his name); United States v. Gear, 3 How. 120 (U.S.1845) (injunction to restrain waste on public land).

Thus, the holding in Cotton v. United States, 11 How. 229 (U.S.1850), permitting an action of trespass *quare clausum fregit* without special statutory authorization, merely rounded out a picture already fully sketched of a legal entity capable by force of the Constitution alone, so long as it was acting within its constitutional powers, of claiming in its contractual and proprietary relations the same protection of general law, at least, that belonged to any other legal person.

The process by which the Court came to recognize the largely federal elements of this law has already been reviewed. See p. 863, *supra*.[2]

(2) Did the San Jacinto case imply that non-statutory rights of action of the United States were confined to rights of action which could be analogized to those of private persons?

In United States v. American Bell Telephone Co., 128 U.S. 315 (1888), the Court upheld the right of the United States, at the direction of the Solicitor General acting because of the disability of the Attorney General, to maintain without special statutory authorization a bill in equity to vacate a patent for an invention as fraudulently obtained. Referring to the San Jacinto opinion, the Court said (pp. 367–68):

"This language is construed by counsel for the appellee in this case to limit the relief granted at the instance of the United States to cases in which it has a direct pecuniary interest. But it is not susceptible of such construction. It was evidently in the mind of the court that the case before it was one where the property right to the land in controversy was the matter of importance, but it was careful to say that the cases in which the instrumentality of the court cannot thus be used are those where the United States has no pecuniary interest in the remedy sought, and is also under no obligation to the party who will be benefited to sustain an action for his use, and also where it does not appear that any obligation existed on the part of the United States to the public or to any individual. The essence of the right of the United States to interfere in the present case is its obligation to protect the public from the monopoly of the patent which was procured by fraud, and it would be difficult to find language more aptly used to include this in the class of cases which are not excluded from the jurisdiction of the court by want of interest in the government of the United States."

Compare the grounds upon which the Court upheld the interposition of the United States in the Pullman strike of 1894, In re Debs, 158 U.S. 564 (1895):

The United States Attorney for the Northern District of Illinois, acting under the direction of the Attorney General, had filed suit in the United

---

2. A striking example in this century of the assertion of proprietary rights of the United States—an example illustrating the magnitude of the interests that may be involved—is the much disputed tidelands controversy. See p. 305, *supra*.

Closely related to the proprietary cases are those in which the United States has

established its status as guardian of the Indian tribes and its standing in litigation to vindicate Indian rights. See, *e.g.,* Heckman v. United States, 224 U.S. 413 (1912); United States v. Board of Com'rs of Osage County, 251 U.S. 128 (1919).

States circuit court to enjoin the strike, alleging a conspiracy forcibly to obstruct the carriage of the mails and processes of interstate transportation. The circuit court granted relief, relying mainly on the Sherman Act. Adjudications of contempt and sentences of imprisonment led to an application for a writ of habeas corpus in the Supreme Court. The petition was denied.

Justice Brewer, speaking for a unanimous Court, declined to determine whether the circuit court was right or wrong in relying on the Sherman Act to sustain its jurisdiction. "We prefer to rest our judgment on a broader ground," he said (p. 600), "believing it of importance that the principles underlying it should be fully stated and affirmed." The following summary, from the Court's opinion (p. 599) indicates the ground taken:

" * * * Summing up our conclusions, we hold that the government of the United States is one having jurisdiction over every foot of soil within its territory, and acting directly upon each citizen; that while it is a government of enumerated powers, it has within the limits of those powers all the attributes of sovereignty; that to it is committed power over interstate commerce and the transmission of the mail; that the powers thus conferred upon the national government are not dormant, but have been assumed and put into practical exercise by the legislation of Congress; that in the exercise of those powers it is competent for the nation to remove all obstructions upon highways, natural or artificial, to the passage of interstate commerce or the carrying of the mail; that while it may be competent for the government (through the executive branch and in the use of the entire executive power of the nation) to forcibly remove all such obstructions, it is equally within its competency to appeal to the civil courts for an inquiry and determination as to the existence and character of the alleged obstructions, and if such are found to exist, or threaten to occur, to invoke the powers of those courts to remove or restrain such obstructions; that the jurisdiction of courts to interfere in such matters by injunction is one recognized from ancient times and by indubitable authority * * *." [3]

In Sanitary District of Chicago v. United States, 266 U.S. 405 (1925), the United States brought suit in a federal district court to enjoin the Sanitary District, an Illinois corporation, from diverting water from Lake Michigan in excess of 250,000 cubic feet per minute, the amount authorized by the Secretary of War. An injunction issued, and the Supreme Court affirmed.

Justice Holmes' opinion described the charges in the bill of obstruction of the navigable capacity of many waterways, and said (pp. 425–26):

"This is not a controversy between equals. The United States is asserting its sovereign power to regulate commerce and to control the navigable waters within its jurisdiction. It has a standing in this suit not only to remove obstruction to interstate and foreign commerce, the main ground, which we will deal with last, but also to carry out treaty obligations to a foreign power bordering upon some of the Lakes concerned, and, it may be, also on the footing of an ultimate sovereign interest in the Lakes. The Attorney General by virtue of his office may bring this proceeding and no statute is necessary to authorize the suit. United States v. San Jacinto Tin Co., * * *. With regard to the second ground, the

3. For a summary account of the controversy stirred by the injunction in the   Pullman strike, see Frankfurter & Greene, The Labor Injunction 17–20 (1930).

Treaty of January 11, 1909, with Great Britain, expressly provides against uses 'affecting the natural level or flow of boundary waters' without the authority of the United States or the Dominion of Canada within their respective jurisdictions and the approval of the International Joint Commission agreed upon therein. As to its ultimate interest in the Lakes the reasons seem to be stronger than those that have established a similar standing for a State, as the interests of the nation are more important than those of any State. In re Debs, 158 U.S. 564, 584, 585, 599. Georgia v. Tennessee Copper Co., 206 U.S. 230. * * *

"The main ground is the authority of the United States to remove obstructions to interstate and foreign commerce. There is no question that this power is superior to that of the States to provide for the welfare or necessities of their inhabitants. In matters where the States may act the action of Congress overrides what they have done. * * * But in matters where the national importance is imminent and direct even where Congress has been silent the States may not act at all. Kansas City Southern Ry. Co. v. Kaw Valley Drainage District, 233 U.S. 75, 79. Evidence is sufficient, if evidence is necessary, to show that a withdrawal of water on the scale directed by the statute of Illinois threatens and will affect the level of the Lakes, and that is a matter which cannot be done without the consent of the United States, even were there no international covenant in the case." [4]

(3) In New York Times Co. v. United States, 403 U.S. 713 (1971) (the case of the "Pentagon Papers"), the Attorney General brought suit on behalf of the United States to enjoin the New York Times (and in a companion case, the Washington Post) from publishing classified material on Vietnam. Copies of the material had been delivered to the newspapers by a person who had no authority to do so.

The government initially contended that the publication would violate the Espionage Act, particularly 18 U.S.C. § 793(e). In the Supreme Court, however, it placed no reliance on the statute, arguing that the constitutional authority of the President in foreign affairs and as Commander-in-Chief entitled the government to an injunction restraining a publication posing a grave and irreparable danger to national security, specifically the conduct of delicate diplomatic negotiations and the prosecution and settlement of the Vietnam War.

The Times did not dispute the "standing" of the government "to come into a Federal Court to protect its functional interest in the integrity of an established rule of law, whether it is established by statute or by the Constitution" (Brief for Petitioner, p. 37). It contended that the publication was not forbidden by an Act of Congress; that neither the President nor the Court was empowered to fashion a rule of law forbidding publication; and that the publication was protected by the First Amendment, since

---

4. The Court relied on the San Jacinto and Sanitary District cases in awarding remedies to the United States (in addition to those provided by statute) against violations of the Rivers and Harbors Act of 1899. United States v. Republic Steel Corp., 362 U.S. 482 (1960) (injunctive order to restore depth of river decreased by deposit of industrial solids); Wyandotte Transp. Co. v. United States, 389 U.S. 191 (1967) (reimbursement for expenses incurred by the government in exercising statutory right to remove sunken barge loaded with dangerous liquid chlorine). Note that the circumstances in both cases were unusual and difficult to anticipate in the framing of statutory remedies.

nothing in the documents presented a grave and immediate danger of the kind that alone might justify a prior restraint.

In a brief *per curiam* the Court held only that the government had failed to meet the "heavy burden" under the First Amendment "of showing justification for the imposition of" prior restraint. In separate opinions Justice Black noted and Justice Stewart emphasized that the government did not rely on any Act of Congress; Justices Douglas and Marshall were of the view that the relevant penal statutes did not forbid publication and attributed importance to the fact that Congress had not authorized injunctive relief and had, indeed, rejected proposals to authorize the President to prohibit publication of "information relating to the national defense which, in his judgment, * * * might be useful to the enemy." Justice White accorded significance to the latter fact, though he considered that the publication might violate the penal statutes. Chief Justice Burger and Justices Harlan and Blackmun dissented, favoring the remand of the cause for further hearing. Among the questions which Justice Harlan thought "should have been faced" was whether "the Attorney General is authorized to bring these suits in the name of the United States," as to which he added "Compare In re Debs * * * with Youngstown Sheet & Tube Co. v. Sawyer" (p. 1129, *infra*) and also said: "This issue involves as well the construction and validity of a singularly opaque statute—The Espionage Act, 18 U.S.C. § 793(e)" (403 U.S. at 753–54).

Was the concession of the New York Times as to the "standing" of the United States necessary or too broad? Did the government gain or lose by attempting to prevail without reliance on a violation of the statutes? First Amendment considerations apart, was the congressional rejection of presidential authority to prohibit publication an insuperable barrier to the injunction? Does the decision imply that if the government could make a stronger showing of the dangers threatened by a publication, an injunction might be proper, whether or not the publication was forbidden by a statute?

(4) The opinion in the Debs case declared that "it is not the province of the Government to interfere in any mere matter of private controversy between individuals, or to use its great powers to enforce the rights of one against another," as distinguished from "wrongs * * * such as affect the public at large * * * and concerning which the Nation owes the duty to all the citizens of securing to them their common rights * * *" (158 U.S. at 586). This was a reflection of the view of Attorney General Olney that the right asserted by the government to an order forbidding the obstruction of rail commerce and delivery of the mail was analogous to and derivative from the traditional action either at law or in equity to abate a public nuisance. Is the analogy compatible with the doctrine (Sec. 1(A), *supra*) that there are no common law crimes against the United States?

Congress has in a number of instances provided that the Attorney General may institute civil actions by the United States to redress deprivations of the rights of private individuals,[5] though such authority is sometimes conditioned on receipt of a complaint from an aggrieved individual

---

5. See, *e.g.,* 42 U.S.C. §§ 1973(d) (voting rights), 1973bb (voting rights), 1997 (rights of institutionalized persons), 2000a–5 (segregation and discrimination in public schools, facilities and places of public accommodation).

For decisions rejecting challenges to the power of Congress to confer such authority, see, *e.g.,* United States v. Raines, 362 U.S. 17, 27 (1960); United Steelworkers v. United States, 361 U.S. 39, 43, 60–61 (1959).

and the Attorney General's certification that the complainant would be unable to initiate and maintain appropriate legal proceedings.[6] Does the principle of Debs render such statutory authority unnecessary in suits for injunction or other specific relief whenever the President or the Attorney General considers that there is an important public interest in the deprivation alleged?

This question has arisen in a number of cases in recent years, but as yet no clear consensus has emerged in the lower federal courts. Compare, *e.g.,* United States v. Brand Jewelers, Inc., 318 F.Supp. 1293 (S.D.N.Y.1970) (U.S. may seek to enjoin widespread use of "sewer process"—false returns and affidavits—because of the burden on interstate commerce and because of the government's authority to correct widespread deprivations of property without due process); United States v. Brittain, 319 F.Supp. 1058 (N.D. Ala.1970) (U.S. may seek to enjoin state miscegenation law that had been invoked against military personnel); United States v. Marchetti, 466 F.2d 1309 (4th Cir.1972) (U.S. may seek to enjoin publication that would allegedly endanger national security), with, *e.g.,* United States v. Mattson, 600 F.2d 1295 (9th Cir.1979) (holding, prior to enactment of 42 U.S.C. § 1997, note 5, *supra,* that U.S. may not sue to protect the constitutional rights of the mentally retarded in state hospital); United States v. City of Philadelphia, 644 F.2d 187 (3d Cir.1980) (U.S. may not sue to challenge allegedly unconstitutional practices of city police department). As these cases indicate, however, the broad approach to Fourteenth Amendment violations suggested in Brand Jewelers has not generally been followed by other courts. See generally Note, 61 B.U.L.Rev. 1159 (1981).

(5) Do the decisions with respect to non-statutory actions by the government suggest an answer to the questions whether and when the United States, without being expressly named, should have the benefit of rights of action created by regulatory statutes in favor of "any person"?

In United States v. Cooper Corp., 312 U.S. 600 (1941), the question was whether the United States, as a purchaser of goods allegedly sold to it at collusive and monopolistic prices, could maintain an action under § 7 of the Sherman Act, which authorizes suit for treble damages by "any person who shall be injured in his person or property" by reason of any violation of the Act. The majority, without reference to any preexisting legal policy or principle, concluded that the government could not sue, that the "natural and ordinary sense" of the text "makes against the extension of the term 'person' to include the United States" (p. 614). The opinion relied on the "common usage" of the term and pointed out that it could not include the United States in other parts of the statute; stressed the negative implied in the express establishment of criminal sanctions and of a public right of action for an injunction; found support in the legislative history and the provisions of other statutes; and put special weight on the failure of Attorneys General for fifty years to assert the right of action. Three Justices, dissenting, argued that the case was but an instance of the general rule that the government may seek all the legal remedies that others may seek, "both at common law and under statutes, unless there is something in a statute or in its history to indicate an intent to deprive the United States of that right" (p. 620).

6. *E.g.,* 42 U.S.C. § 2000c–6 (public schools and facilities).

In the light of San Jacinto and the other cases discussed in this Note, does the "natural and ordinary sense" of the term "person," when used in relation to proprietary rights of action, exclude the United States? Is it significant that when Congress in 1955 amended the antitrust law to authorize a damage action by the government (15 U.S.C. § 15(a)), it confined the remedy to actual rather than treble damages?

(6) In some instances, the United States comes into court not simply on a par with private litigants, but with a number of advantages, court-made as well as statutory. There is, for example, a doctrine that the United States is not bound by statutes of limitations (or by laches) unless expressly provided by statute. See United States v. Summerlin, 310 U.S. 414 (1940). (In 1966, Congress enacted a general statute of limitations, 28 U.S.C. §§ 2415, 2416, applicable to most actions brought by the United States or by a federal officer or agency.) Another judge-made rule gives the United States the benefit of a special exception from the usual principle that "he who seeks equity must do equity" in suits to rescind land grants alleged to have been obtained by fraud; the government in such cases need not offer to return the consideration it had received. Causey v. United States, 240 U.S. 399, 402 (1916). See generally Note, 55 Colum.L.Rev. 1177 (1955).

An even broader principle was suggested in Chief Justice Vinson's opinion in United States v. United Mine Workers, 330 U.S. 258, 272 (1947)—an "old and well-known rule that statutes which in general terms divest pre-existing rights or privileges will not be applied to the sovereign without express words to that effect."

The five cases cited in support of this rule, however, did not lend it unqualified support. Two, relying on part on the English rule that bankruptcy proceedings do not discharge debts due to the Crown, had held that the United States was not bound by the Bankruptcy Act of 1867. United States v. Herron, 20 Wall. 251, 263 (U.S.1873); Lewis v. United States, 92 U.S. 618, 622 (1875). These decisions had been been overridden in result, if not in reasoning, by decisions under the altered language of the Bankruptcy Act of 1898. See Guarantee Title & Trust Co. v. Title Guaranty & Surety Co., 224 U.S. 152, 155–60 (1912).

The other three decisions simply refused to find a repeal by implication of a remedy previously available to the United States. None involved general language which, if held to include the United States as a legal person, would have directly barred the old remedy.[7]

The United Mine Workers case itself involved the question whether the general language of the Norris–LaGuardia Act, limiting the jurisdiction of the district courts to grant injunctions in labor disputes, applied to an action by the United States to enjoin a coal strike; the government brought the suit in the capacity of an employer, after it had seized the coal mines under the War Disputes Act. The entire Court agreed that the Act would have applied were the government suing only as sovereign, in view of the

---

7. Dollar Savings Bank v. United States, 19 Wall. 227, 238–40 (U.S.1873) (certain taxes could still be collected in an action of debt, although the taxing statute provided another remedy); United States v. American Bell Tel. Co., 159 U.S. 548, 553–55 (1895) (allowing the government to appeal in a case in which it was arguable that a statute made the judgment below reviewable only by certiorari); United States v. Stevenson, 215 U.S. 190, 197 (1909) (refusing to read language authorizing the United States or any other person to bring a civil action for a statutory penalty as by implication barring prosecution for a misdemeanor).

many indications that the Act was designed to prevent injunctions of the type granted in In re Debs, Paragraph (2), *supra.* But Chief Justice Vinson (here joined by four other Justices) posited as an alternative ground for upholding a contempt conviction that Congress "did not intend that the Act should apply to situations in which the United States appears as an employer" (p. 276). Justices Frankfurter, Jackson, Murphy and Rutledge disagreed vigorously.

Did the prior cases point toward the Chief Justice's conclusion or against it? *Cf.* Unexcelled Chemical Corp. v. United States, 345 U.S. 59 (1953) (United States held subject to a short statute of limitations because the actions described in the statute included one that could only be instituted by the government).

(7) For general discussion of district court jurisdiction over civil (and criminal) actions instituted by the federal government, see Chap. VIII, Sec. 6(B), *infra.*

SUBSECTION B: PRIVATE CIVIL ACTIONS

BIVENS v. SIX UNKNOWN NAMED AGENTS OF FEDERAL BUREAU OF NARCOTICS

403 U.S. 388, 91 S.Ct. 1999, 29 L.Ed.2d 619 (1971).
Certiorari to the United States Court of Appeals for the Second Circuit.

MR. JUSTICE BRENNAN delivered the opinion of the Court.

The Fourth Amendment provides that

"The right of the people to be secure in their persons, houses, papers, and effects, against unreasonable searches and seizures, shall not be violated. * * *"

In Bell v. Hood, 327 U.S. 678 (1946), we reserved the question whether violation of that command by a federal agent acting under color of his authority gives rise to a cause of action for damages consequent upon his unconstitutional conduct. Today we hold that it does.

This case has its origin in an arrest and search carried out on the morning of November 26, 1965. Petitioner's complaint alleged that on that day respondents, agents of the Federal Bureau of Narcotics acting under claim of federal authority, entered his apartment and arrested him for alleged narcotics violations. The agents manacled petitioner in front of his wife and children, and threatened to arrest the entire family. They searched the apartment from stem to stern. Thereafter petitioner was taken to the federal courthouse in Brooklyn, where he was interrogated, booked, and subjected to a visual strip search.

On July 7, 1967, petitioner brought suit in Federal District Court. In addition to the allegations above, his complaint asserted that the arrest and search were effected without a warrant, and that unreasonable force was employed in making the arrest; fairly read, it alleges as well that the arrest was made without probable cause. Petitioner claimed to have suffered great humiliation, embarrassment, and mental suffering as a result of the agents' unlawful conduct, and sought $15,000 damages from each of them. The District Court, on respondents' motion, dismissed the complaint on the ground, *inter alia,* that it failed to state a cause of action. 276 F.Supp. 12 (EDNY 1967). The Court of Appeals, one judge concurring specially, affirmed on that basis. 409 F.2d 718 (CA2 1969). We granted certiorari. 399 U.S. 905 (1970). We reverse.

I

Respondents do not argue that petitioner should be entirely without remedy for an unconstitutional invasion of his rights by federal agents. In respondents' view, however, the rights which petitioner asserts—primarily rights of privacy—are creations of state and not of federal law. Accordingly, they argue, petitioner may obtain money damages to redress invasion of these rights only by an action in tort, under state law, in the state courts. In this scheme the Fourth Amendment would serve merely to limit the extent to which the agents could defend the state law tort suit by asserting that their actions were a valid exercise of federal power: if the agents were shown to have violated the Fourth Amendment, such a defense would be lost to them and they would stand before the state law merely as private individuals. Candidly admitting that it is the policy of the Department of Justice to remove all such suits from the state to the federal courts for decision,[4] respondents nevertheless urge that we uphold dismissal of petitioner's complaint in federal court, and remit him to filing an action in the state courts in order that the case may properly be removed to the federal court for decision on the basis of state law.

We think that respondents' thesis rests upon an unduly restrictive view of the Fourth Amendment's protection against unreasonable searches and seizures by federal agents, a view that has consistently been rejected by this Court. Respondents seek to treat the relationship between a citizen and a federal agent unconstitutionally exercising his authority as no different from the relationship between two private citizens. In so doing, they ignore the fact that power, once granted, does not disappear like a magic gift when it is wrongfully used. An agent acting—albeit unconstitutionally—in the name of the United States possesses a far greater capacity for harm than an individual trespasser exercising no authority other than his own. *Cf.* Amos v. United States, 255 U.S. 313, 317 (1921); United States v. Classic, 313 U.S. 299, 326 (1941). Accordingly, as our cases make clear, the Fourth Amendment operates as a limitation upon the exercise of federal power regardless of whether the State in whose jurisdiction that power is exercised would prohibit or penalize the identical act if engaged in by a private citizen. It guarantees to citizens of the United States the absolute right to be free from unreasonable searches and seizures carried out by virtue of federal authority. And "where federally protected rights have been invaded, it has been the rule from the beginning that courts will be alert to adjust their remedies so as to grant the necessary relief." Bell v. Hood, 327 U.S., at 684. * * *

First. Our cases have long since rejected the notion that the Fourth Amendment proscribes only such conduct as would, if engaged in by private persons, be condemned by state law. * * * In light of these cases,

---

4. * * * In light of this, it is difficult to understand our Brother Blackmun's complaint that our holding today "opens the door for another avalanche of new federal cases." * * *

respondents' argument that the Fourth Amendment serves only as a limitation on federal defenses to a state law claim, and not as an independent limitation upon the exercise of federal power, must be rejected.

Second. The interests protected by state laws regulating trespass and the invasion of privacy, and those protected by the Fourth Amendment's guarantee against unreasonable searches and seizures, may be inconsistent or even hostile. Thus, we may bar the door against an unwelcome private intruder, or call the police if he persists in seeking entrance. The availability of such alternative means for the protection of privacy may lead the State to restrict imposition of liability for any consequent trespass. A private citizen, asserting no authority other than his own, will not normally be liable in trespass if he demands, and is granted, admission to another's house. See W. Prosser, The Law of Torts § 18, at 109–110 (3d ed. 1964); 1 F. Harper & F. James, The Law of Torts § 1.11 (1956). But one who demands admission under a claim of federal authority stands in a far different position. Cf. Amos v. United States, 255 U.S. 313, 317 (1921). The mere invocation of federal power by a federal law enforcement official will normally render futile any attempt to resist an unlawful entry or arrest by resort to the local police; and a claim of authority to enter is likely to unlock the door as well. * * *

Nor is it adequate to answer that state law may take into account the different status of one clothed with the authority of the Federal Government. For just as state law may not authorize federal agents to violate the Fourth Amendment, * * * neither may state law undertake to limit the extent to which federal authority can be exercised. In re Neagle, 135 U.S. 1 (1890). The inevitable consequence of this dual limitation on state power is that the federal question becomes not merely a possible defense to the state law action, but an independent claim both necessary and sufficient to make out the plaintiff's cause of action. * * *

Third. That damages may be obtained for injuries consequent upon a violation of the Fourth Amendment by federal officials should hardly seem a surprising proposition. Historically, damages have been regarded as the ordinary remedy for an invasion of personal interests in liberty. See Nixon v. Condon, 286 U.S. 73 (1932); Nixon v. Herndon, 273 U.S. 536, 540 (1927); Swafford v. Templeton, 185 U.S. 487 (1902); Wiley v. Sinkler, 179 U.S. 58 (1900); J. Landynski, Search and Seizure and the Supreme Court 28ff. (1966); N. Lasson, History and Development of the Fourth Amendment to the United States Constitution 43ff. (1937); Katz, The Jurisprudence of Remedies: Constitutional Legality and the Law of Torts in Bell v. Hood, 117 U.Pa.L.Rev. 1, 8–33 (1968); cf. West v. Cabell, 153 U.S. 78 (1894); Lammon v. Feusier, 111 U.S. 17 (1884). Of course the Fourth Amendment does not in so many words provide for its enforcement by an award of money damages for the consequences of its violation. But "it is also well settled that where legal rights have been invaded, and a federal statute provides for a general right to sue for such invasion, federal courts may use any available remedy to make good the wrong done." Bell v. Hood, 327 U.S., at 684 (1946) (footnote omitted). The present case involves no special factors counselling hesitation in the absence of affirmative action by Congress. We are not dealing with a question of "federal fiscal policy," as in United States v. Standard Oil Co., 332 U.S. 301, 311 (1947) * * * Nor are we asked in this case to impose liability upon a congressional employee for actions contrary to no constitutional prohibition, but merely said to be in excess of the authority delegated to him by the Congress. Wheeldin v. Wheeler, 373 U.S. 647 (1963). Finally, we cannot accept respondents' formulation of the question as whether the availability of money damages is necessary to enforce the Fourth Amendment. For we have here no explicit congressional declaration that persons injured by a federal officer's violation of the Fourth Amendment may not recover money damages from the agents, but must instead be remitted to another remedy, equally effective in the view of Congress. The question is merely whether petitioner, if he can demonstrate an injury consequent upon the violation by federal agents of his Fourth Amendment rights, is entitled to redress his injury through a particular remedial mechanism normally available in the federal courts. "The very essence of civil liberty certainly consists in the right of every individual to claim the protection of the laws whenever he receives an injury." Marbury v. Madison, 1 Cranch 137, 163 (1803). Having concluded that petitioner's complaint states a cause of action under the Fourth Amendment, we hold that petitioner is entitled to recover money damages for any injuries he has suffered as a result of the agents' violation of the Amendment.

II

In addition to holding that petitioner's complaint had failed to state facts making out a cause of action, the District Court ruled that in any event respondents were immune from liability by virtue of their official position. This question was not passed upon by the Court of Appeals, and accordingly we do not consider it here. The judgment of the Court of Appeals is reversed and the case is remanded for further proceedings consistent with this opinion.

So ordered.

Judgment reversed and case remanded.

MR. JUSTICE HARLAN, concurring in the judgment.

My initial view of this case was that the Court of Appeals was correct in dismissing the complaint, but for reasons stated in this opinion I am now persuaded to the contrary. Accordingly, I join in the judgment of reversal.

*   *   *

For the reasons set forth below, I am of the opinion that federal courts do have the power to award damages for violation of "constitutionally protected interests" and I agree with the Court that a traditional judicial remedy such as damages is appropriate to the vindication of the personal interests protected by the Fourth Amendment.

I

I turn first to the contention that the constitutional power of federal courts to accord Bivens damages for his claim depends on the passage of a statute creating a "federal cause of action." Although the point is not entirely free of ambiguity, I do not understand either the Government or my dissenting Brothers to maintain that Bivens' contention that he is entitled to be free from the type of official conduct prohibited by the Fourth Amendment depends on a decision by the State in which he resides to accord him a remedy. Such a position would be incompatible with the presumed availability of federal equitable relief, if a proper showing can be made in terms of the ordinary principles governing equitable remedies. See Bell v. Hood, 327 U.S. 678, 684 (1946). However broad a federal court's discretion concerning equitable remedies, it is absolutely clear—at least after Erie R. Co. v. Tompkins, 304 U.S. 64 (1938)—that in a nondiversity suit a federal court's power to grant even equitable relief depends on the presence of a substantive right derived from federal law. Compare Guaranty Trust Co. v. York, 326 U.S. 99, 105–107 (1945), with Holmberg v. Armbrecht, 327 U.S. 392, 395 (1946). See also H. Hart and H. Wechsler, The Federal Courts and the Federal System 818–819 (1953).

Thus the interest which Bivens claims—to be free from official conduct in contravention of the Fourth Amendment—is a federally protected interest.[3] Therefore, the question of judicial *power* to grant Bivens damages is not a problem of the "source" of the "right"; instead, the question is whether the power to authorize damages as a judicial remedy for the vindication of a federal constitutional right is placed by the Constitution itself exclusively in Congress' hands.

II

The contention that the federal courts are powerless to accord a litigant damages for a claimed invasion of his federal constitutional rights until Congress explicitly authorizes the remedy cannot rest on the notion that the decision to grant compensatory relief involves a resolution of policy considerations not susceptible of judicial discernment. Thus, in suits

3. The Government appears not quite ready to concede this point. Certain points in the Government's argument seem to suggest that the "state-created right—federal defense" model reaches not only the question of the power to accord a federal damages remedy, but also the claim to any judicial remedy in any court. Thus, we are pointed to Lasson's observation concerning Madison's version of the Fourth Amendment as introduced into the House:

"The observation may be made that the language of the proposal did not purport to create the right to be secure from unreasonable search and seizures but merely stated it as a right which already existed." N. Lasson, The History and Development of the Fourth Amendment to the United States Constitution, 100 n. 77 (1937), quoted in Govt. Brief at 11 n. 7. And, on the problem of federal equitable vindication of constitutional rights without regard to the presence of a "state-created right," see Hart, The Relations Between State and Federal Law, 54 Colum.L.Rev. 489, 523–524 (1954), quoted in Govt.Br., at 17.

On this point, the choice of phraseology in the Fourth Amendment itself is singularly unpersuasive. The leading argument against a "Bill of Rights" was the fear that individual liberties not specified expressly would be taken as excluded. See generally, Lasson, *supra*, at 79–105. This circumstance alone might well explain why the authors of the Bill of Rights would opt for language which presumes the existence of a fundamental interest in liberty, albeit originally derived from the common law. See Entick v. Carrington, 19 How.St.Tr. 1029, 95 Eng.Rep. 807 (1765).

In truth, the legislative record as a whole behind the Bill of Rights is silent on the rather refined doctrinal question whether the framers considered the rights therein enumerated as dependent in the first instance on the decision of a State to accord legal status to the personal interests at stake. That is understandable since the Government itself points out that general federal question jurisdiction was not extended to the federal district courts until 1875. Act of March 3, 1875, § 1, 18 Stat. 470. The most that can be drawn from this historical fact is that the authors of the Bill of Rights assumed the adequacy of common law remedies to vindicate the federally protected interest. One must first combine this assumption with contemporary modes of jurisprudential thought which appeared to link "rights" and "remedies" in a 1:1 correlation, *cf.*, Marbury v. Madison, 1 Cranch 137, 163, 2 L.Ed. 60 (1803), before reaching the conclusion that the framers are to be understood today as having created no federally protected interests. And, of course, that would simply require the conclusion that federal equitable relief would not lie to protect those interests guarded by the Fourth Amendment. • • •

for damages based on violations of federal statutes lacking any express authorization of a damage remedy, this Court has authorized such relief where, in its view, damages are necessary to effectuate the congressional policy underpinning the substantive provisions of the statute. J.I. Case Co. v. Borak, 377 U.S. 426 (1964); Tunstall v. Brotherhood of Locomotive Firemen & Enginemen, 323 U.S. 210, 213 (1944). Cf. Wyandotte Transportation Co. v. United States, 389 U.S. 191, 201–204 (1967).[4]

If it is not the nature of the remedy which is thought to render a judgment as to the appropriateness of damages inherently "legislative," then it must be the nature of the legal interest offered as an occasion for invoking otherwise appropriate judicial relief. But I do not think that the fact that the interest is protected by the Constitution rather than statute or common law justifies the assertion that federal courts are powerless to grant damages in the absence of explicit congressional action authorizing the remedy. Initially, I note that it would be at least anomalous to conclude that the federal judiciary—while competent to choose among the range of traditional judicial remedies to implement statutory and common-law policies, and even to generate substantive rules governing primary behavior in furtherance of broadly formulated policies articulated by statute or Constitution, see Textile Workers Union v. Lincoln Mills, 353 U.S. 448 (1957); United States v. Standard Oil Co., 332 U.S. 301, 304–311 (1947); Clearfield Trust Co. v. United States, 318 U.S. 363 (1943)—is powerless to accord a damage remedy to vindicate social policies which, by virtue of their inclusion in the Constitution, are aimed predominantly at restraining the Government as an instrument of the popular will.

More importantly, the presumed availability of federal equitable relief against threatened invasions of constitutional interests appears entirely to negate the contention that the status of an interest as constitutionally protected divests federal courts of the power to grant damages absent express congressional authorization. * * *

If explicit congressional authorization is an absolute prerequisite to the power of a federal court to accord compensatory relief regardless of the necessity or appropriateness of damages as a remedy simply because of the status of a legal interest as constitutionally protected, then it seems to me that explicit congressional authorization is similarly prerequisite to the exercise of equitable remedial discretion in favor of constitutionally protected interests. Conversely, if a general grant of jurisdiction to the federal courts by Congress is thought adequate to empower a federal court to grant

---

4. The Borak case [p. 935, *infra*] is an especially clear example of the exercise of federal judicial power to accord damages as an appropriate remedy in the absence of any express statutory authorization of a federal cause of action. There we "implied"—from what can only be characterized as an "exclusively procedural provision" affording access to a federal forum,— a private cause of action for damages for violation of § 14(a) of the Securities Act of 1934, 15 U.S.C. § 78n(a). See § 27, 15 U.S.C. § 78a(a). We did so in an area where federal regulation has been singularly comprehensive and elaborate administrative enforcement machinery had been provided. The exercise of judicial power involved in Borak simply cannot be justified in terms of statutory construction, see Hill, Constitutional Remedies, 69 Columbia 1109, 1120–1121 (1969); nor did the Borak Court purport to do so. See Borak, *supra*, 377 U.S. at 432–434. The notion of "implying" a remedy, therefore, as applied to cases like Borak, can only refer to a process whereby the federal judiciary exercises a choice among *traditionally available* judicial remedies according to reasons related to the substantive social policy embodied in an act of positive law. See *ibid.*, and Bell v. Hood, *supra*, 327 U.S., at 684.

equitable relief for all areas of subject-matter jurisdiction enumerated therein, see 28 U.S.C. § 1331(a), then it seems to me that statute is sufficient to empower a federal court to grant a traditional remedy at law. Of course, the special historical traditions governing the federal equity system, see Sprague v. Ticonic National Bank, 307 U.S. 161 (1939), might still bear on the comparative appropriateness of granting equitable relief as opposed to money damages. That possibility, however, relates not to whether the federal courts have the power to afford one type of remedy as opposed to the other, but rather to the criteria which should govern the exercise of our power. To that question, I now pass.

III

The major thrust of the Government's position is that, where Congress has not expressly authorized a particular remedy, a federal court should exercise its power to accord a traditional form of judicial relief at the behest of a litigant, who claims a constitutionally protected interest has been invaded, only where the remedy is "essential," or "indispensable for vindicating constitutional rights." Govt.Brief, 19, 24. * * *

These arguments for a more stringent test to govern the grant of damages in constitutional cases seem to be adequately answered by the point that the judiciary has a particular responsibility to assure the vindication of constitutional interests such as those embraced by the Fourth Amendment. To be sure, "it must be remembered that legislatures are ultimate guardians of the liberties and welfare of the people in quite as great a degree as the courts." Missouri, Kansas & Texas R. Co. of Texas v. May, 194 U.S. 267, 270 (1904). But it must also be recognized that the Bill of Rights is particularly intended to vindicate the interests of the individual in the face of the popular will as expressed in legislative majorities; at the very least, it strikes me as no more appropriate to await express congressional authorization of traditional judicial relief with regard to these legal interests than with respect to interests protected by federal statutes.

The question then, is, as I see it, whether compensatory relief is "necessary" or "appropriate" to the vindication of the interest asserted. * * * In resolving that question, it seems to me that the range of policy considerations we may take into account are at least as broad as those a legislature would consider with respect to an express statutory authorization of a traditional remedy. In this regard I agree with the Court that the appropriateness of according Bivens compensatory relief does not turn simply on the deterrent effect liability will have on federal official conduct.[8]

* * *

8. And I think it follows from this point that today's decision has little, if indeed any, bearing on the question whether a federal court may properly devise remedies—other than traditionally available forms of judicial relief—for the purpose of enforcing substantive social policies embodied in constitutional or statutory policies. Compare today's decision with Mapp v. Ohio, 367 U.S. 643 (1961), and Weeks v. United States, 232 U.S. 383 (1914). The Court today simply recognizes what has long been implicit in our decisions concern-

ing equitable relief and remedies implied from statutory schemes; i.e., that a court of law vested with jurisdiction over the subject matter of a suit has the power—and therefore the duty—to make principled choices among traditional judicial remedies. Whether special prophylactic measures—which at least arguably the exclusionary rule exemplifies, see Hill, The Bill of Rights and the Supervisory Power, 69 Col.L.Rev. 181, 182–185 (1969)—are supportable on grounds other than a court's competence to select among traditional ju-

*   *   * I think it is clear that Bivens advances a claim of the sort that, if proved, would be properly compensable in damages. The personal interests protected by the Fourth Amendment are those we attempt to capture by the notion of "privacy"; while the Court today properly points out that the type of harm which officials can inflict when they invade protected zones of an individual's life are different from the types of harm private citizens inflict on one another, the experience of judges in dealing with private trespass and false imprisonment claims supports the conclusion that courts of law are capable of making the types of judgment concerning causation and magnitude of injury necessary to accord meaningful compensation for invasion of Fourth Amendment rights.

On the other hand, the limitations on state remedies for violation of common law rights by private citizens argue in favor of a federal damage remedy. The injuries inflicted by officials acting under color of law, while no less compensable in damages than those inflicted by private parties, are substantially different in kind, as the Court's opinion today discusses in detail. See Monroe v. Pape, 365 U.S. 167, 195 (1961) (Harlan, J., concurring). It seems to me entirely proper that these injuries be compensable according to uniform rules of federal law, especially in light of the very large element of federal law which must in any event control the scope of official defenses to liability. See Wheeldin v. Wheeler, 373 U.S. 647, 652 (1963); Monroe v. Pape, 365 U.S. 167, 194–195 (Harlan, J., concurring); Howard v. Lyons, 360 U.S. 593 (1959). Certainly, there is very little federalism interest in preserving different rules of liability for federal officers dependent on the State where the injury occurs. *Cf.,* United States v. Standard Oil Co., 332 U.S. 301, 305–311 (1947).

Putting aside the desirability of leaving the problem of federal official liability to the vagaries of common law actions, it is apparent that damages in some form is the only possible remedy for someone in Bivens' alleged position. It will be a rare case indeed in which an individual in Bivens' position will be able to obviate the harm by securing injunctive relief from any court. However desirable a direct remedy against the Government might be as a substitute for individual official liability, the Sovereign still remains immune to suit. Finally, assuming Bivens' innocence of the crime charged, the "exclusionary rule" is simply irrelevant. For people in Bivens' shoes, it is damages or nothing.

The only substantial policy consideration advanced against recognition of a federal cause of action for violation of Fourth Amendment rights by federal officials is the incremental expenditure of judicial resources that will be necessitated by this class of litigation. There is, however, something ultimately self-defeating about this argument. For if, as the Government contends, damages will rarely be realized by plaintiffs in these cases because of jury hostility, the limited resources of the official concerned, etc., then I am not ready to assume that there will be a significant increase in the expenditure of judicial resources on these claims. Few responsible lawyers and plaintiffs are likely to choose the course of litigation if the statistical chances of success are truly *de minimis.* And I simply cannot agree with my Brother Black that the possibility of "frivolous" claims—if defined simply as claims with no legal merit—warrants closing the court-

dicial remedies to make good the wrong done, *cf.* Bell v. Hood, *supra,* 327 U.S. at 684, is a separate question.

house doors to people in Bivens' situation. There are other ways, short of that, of coping with frivolous lawsuits.

On the other hand, if—as I believe is the case with respect, at least, to the most flagrant abuses of official power—damages to some degree will be available when the option of litigation is chosen, then the question appears to be how Fourth Amendment interests rank on a scale of social values compared with, for example, the interests of stockholders defrauded by misleading proxies. See J.I. Case Co. v. Borak, *supra*. Judicial resources, I am well aware, are increasingly scarce these days. Nonetheless, when we automatically close the courthouse door solely on this basis, we implicitly express a value judgment on the comparative importance of classes of legally protected interests. And current limitations upon the effective functioning of the courts arising from budgetary inadequacies should not be permitted to stand in the way of the recognition of otherwise sound constitutional principles.

Of course, for a variety of reasons, the remedy may not often be sought. See generally, Foote, Tort Remedies for Police Violations of Individual Rights, 39 Minn.L.Rev. 493 (1955). And the countervailing interests in efficient law enforcement of course argue for a protective zone with respect to many types of Fourth Amendment violations. *Cf.* Barr v. Matteo, 360 U.S. 564 (1959) (opinion of Harlan, J.). But, while I express no view on the immunity defense offered in the instant case, I deem it proper to venture the thought that at the very least such a remedy would be available for the most flagrant and patently unjustified sorts of police conduct. Although litigants may not often choose to seek relief, it is important, in a civilized society, that the judicial branch of the Nation's government stand ready to afford a remedy in these circumstances. It goes without saying that I intimate no view on the merits of petitioner's underlying claim.

For these reasons, I concur in the judgment of the Court.

MR. CHIEF JUSTICE BURGER, dissenting.

I dissent from today's holding which judicially creates a damage remedy not provided for by the Constitution and not enacted by Congress. We would more surely preserve the important values of the doctrine of separation of powers—and perhaps get a better result—by recommending a solution to the Congress as the branch of government in which the Constitution has vested the legislative power. Legislation is the business of the Congress, and it has the facilities and competence for that task—as we do not.   *   *   *

MR. JUSTICE BLACK, dissenting.

In my opinion for the Court in Bell v. Hood, 327 U.S. 678 (1946), we did as the Court states, reserve the question whether an unreasonable search made by a federal officer in violation of the Fourth Amendment gives the subject of the search a federal cause of action for damages against the officers making the search. There can be no doubt that Congress could create a federal cause of action for damages for an unreasonable search in violation of the Fourth Amendment. Although Congress has created such a federal cause of action against *state* officials acting under color of state law, it has never created such a cause of action against federal officials. If it wanted to do so, Congress could, of course, create a remedy against federal officials who violate the Fourth Amendment in the performance of their duties. But the point of this case and the fatal weakness in the

Court's judgment is that neither Congress nor the State of New York has enacted legislation creating such a right of action. For us to do so is, in my judgment, an exercise of power that the Constitution does not give us.

Even if we had the legislative power to create a remedy, there are many reasons why we should decline to create a cause of action where none has existed since the formation of our Government. The courts of the United States as well as those of the States are choked with lawsuits. * * *

We sit at the top of a judicial system accused by some of nearing the point of collapse. Many criminal defendants do not receive speedy trials and neither society nor the accused are assured of justice when inordinate delays occur. Citizens must wait years to litigate their private civil suits. Substantial changes in correctional and parole systems demand the attention of the lawmakers and the judiciary. If I were a legislator I might well find these and other needs so pressing as to make me believe that the resources of lawyers and judges should be devoted to them rather than to civil damage actions against officers who generally strive to perform within constitutional bounds. There is also a real danger that such suits might deter officials from the *proper* and honest performance of their duties.

All of these considerations make imperative careful study and weighing of the arguments both for and against the creation of such a remedy under the Fourth Amendment. I would have great difficulty for myself in resolving the competing policies, goals, and priorities in the use of resources, if I thought it were my job to resolve those questions. But that is not my task. The task of evaluating the pros and cons of creating judicial remedies for particular wrongs is a matter for Congress and the legislatures of the States. * * *

MR. JUSTICE BLACKMUN, dissenting.

I, too, dissent. I do so largely for the reasons expressed in Chief Judge Lumbard's thoughtful and scholarly opinion for the Court of Appeals. But I also feel that the judicial legislation, which the Court by its opinion today concededly is effectuating, opens the door for another avalanche of new federal cases. * * *

NOTE ON THE IMPLICATION OF PRIVATE REMEDIES FOR THE VIOLATION OF CONSTITUTIONAL NORMS

(1) The Constitution is singularly bare of remedial specification: it lays down a multitude of substantive rules but says virtually nothing about what is to happen if these are violated (or about who is to decide what is to happen if they are).[1]

The Bivens case and the materials in this Note deal with a variety of questions raised by this absence of constitutional direction. What are the respective roles of Congress and judiciary in formulating a remedial system? Should the federal courts regard themselves as freer, or under a greater duty, to create a federal remedy for the violation of constitutional rights and duties than to imply a federal remedy for the violation of

1. Section 5 of the Fourteenth Amendment, in its specific grant of authority to Congress, is a notable exception.

statutory obligations?[2]   To what extent should the federal courts take into account such factors as (a) the availability of a state law remedy for the particular violation,[3] (b) the effect on federal district court jurisdiction of the recognition of a federal remedy, (c) the nature of the remedy sought (damages or declaratory or injunctive relief), and (d) the availability of other federal remedies under applicable statutes and regulations?

(2) The question of the availability of a damage remedy for violation of a constitutional right had been much mooted ever since the celebrated decision in Bell v. Hood, 327 U.S. 678 (1946), p. 1022, *infra*. (The Court in Bell held that the federal district court had jurisdiction under § 1331 of a claim for damages against federal officers for allegedly unconstitutional searches, seizures, and arrests, but reserved the question on the merits whether such a claim in fact stated a good cause of action under federal (as opposed to state) law.) Is it surprising that the question was not resolved until the Bivens decision in 1971? Does the explanation lie in part in the availability of state damage remedies for a substantial range of violations and of federal statutory remedies (under such statutes as the Tort Claims Act) for others? Note that state authority to issue *injunctions* against federal officers is not clearly established—see Chap. IV, Sec. 2, *supra*, a fact that may help to account for the much earlier development of federal equitable remedies for constitutional violations. See Ex parte Young, 209 U.S. 123 (1908).

In answering the question in Bivens, what significance should the Court have attached to the absence of any broad statutory authorization of private remedies comparable to 42 U.S.C. § 1983 (for violations under color of *state* law)?

(3) Between 1971 and 1979, development of the Bivens doctrine was left to the lower courts. Then in Davis v. Passman, 442 U.S. 228 (1979), the Court held that a damages remedy "can also be implied directly under the the Constitution when the Due Process Clause of the Fifth Amendment is violated" (p. 230). Davis itself was a damage action brought against Congressman Otto Passman by Shirley Davis, an administrative assistant who alleged that she had lost her job because she was a woman and claimed that the discharge violated her Fifth Amendment rights. The lower courts declined to recognize a private cause of action under the Constitution, and the Supreme Court reversed.

Justice Brennan, writing for the majority, said that "Our inquiry proceeds in three stages. We hold first that, pretermitting the question whether [Passman's] conduct is shielded by the Speech or Debate Clause, petitioner [Davis] asserts a constitutionally protected right; second, that petitioner has stated a cause of action which asserts this right; and third, that relief in damages constitutes an appropriate form of remedy" (p. 234).

On the first of these points, the Court was brief, concluding that "The Equal Protection component of the Due Process Clause * * * confers on petitioner a federal constitutional right to be free from gender discrimina-

---

2. See *Note on the Implication of Private Remedies for Statutory Violations*, p. 943, *infra*.

3. *Cf.* Ward v. Love County and the following Note, Chap. V, pp. 581–90, *supra*

(dealing with the obligation of state courts to furnish an adequate remedy for violation of federal rights).

tion which cannot meet these requirements [of substantial relationship to the achievement of important governmental objectives]" (p. 235).

On the second, the Court spoke at greater length, saying that "the question whether a litigant has a 'cause of action' is analytically distinct from and prior to the question of what relief, if any, a litigant may be entitled to receive. The concept of a 'cause of action' is employed specifically to determine who may judicially enforce the statutory rights or obligations" (p. 239).[4]

"Statutory rights and obligations," the Court continued (pp. 241–44), "are established by Congress, and it is entirely appropriate for Congress, in creating these rights and obligations, to determine in addition, who may enforce them and in what manner. For example, statutory rights and obligations are often embedded in complex regulatory schemes, so that if they are not enforced through private causes of action, they may nevertheless be enforced through alternative mechanisms, such as criminal prosecutions, or other public causes of actions. * * * In each case, however, the question is the nature of the legislative intent informing a specific statute * * *.

"The Constitution, on the other hand, does not 'partake of the prolixity of a legal code.' M'Culloch v. Maryland, 17 U.S. 316, 407 (1819). It speaks instead with a majestic simplicity. One of 'its important objects,' *ibid.*, is the designation of rights. And in 'its great outlines,' *ibid.*, the judiciary is clearly discernible as the primary means through which these rights may be enforced. * * *.

"At least in the absence of "a textually demonstrable constitutional commitment of [an] issue to a coordinate political department,' Baker v. Carr, 369 U.S. at 217, we presume that justiciable constitutional rights are to be enforced through the courts. And, unless such rights are to become merely precatory, the class of those litigants who allege that their own constitutional rights have been violated, and who at the same time have no effective means other than the judiciary to enforce these rights, must be able to invoke the existing jurisdiction of the courts for the protection of their justiciable constitutional rights. * * *

* * *

" * * * [P]etitioner rests her claim directly on the Due Process Clause of the Fifth Amendment. She claims that her rights under the Amendment have been violated, and that she has no effective means other than the judiciary to vindicate these rights. We conclude, therefore, that

---

4. At this point, the Court dropped the following footnote:

"Thus it may be said that *jurisdiction* is a question of whether a federal court has the power, under the Constitution or laws of the United States, to hear a case * * *; *standing* is a question of whether a plaintiff is sufficiently adversary to a defendant to create an Art. III case or controversy, or at least to overcome prudential limitations on federal court jurisdiction, * * *; *cause of action* is a question of whether a particular plaintiff is a member of the class of litigants that may, as a matter of law, appropriately invoke the power of the court; and *relief* is a question of the various remedies a federal court may make available. A plaintiff may have a cause of action even though he be entitled to no relief at all, as, for example, when a plaintiff sues for declaratory or injunctive relief although his case does not fulfill the 'preconditions' for such equitable remedies. * * *

" * * * Whether petitioner has asserted a cause of action * * * depends not on the quality or extent of her injury, but on whether the class of litigants of which petitioner is a member may use the courts to enforce the right at issue. The focus must therefore be on the nature of the right petitioner asserts."

she is an appropriate party to invoke the general federal question jurisdiction of the District Court to seek relief. She has a cause of action under the Fifth Amendment."

On the third issue (the availability of a damages remedy), the Court noted that since Passman was no longer a Congressman, "for Davis, as for Bivens, 'it is damages or nothing' " (p. 245). With respect to the argument that Congress had excluded a damage remedy in such a case by exempting federal legislative employees from the scope of Title VII, the Court said (p. 247):

"When § 717 was added to Title VII to protect federal employees from discrimination, it failed to extend this protection to congressional employees such as petitioner who are not in the competitive service. See 42 U.S.C. § 2000e–16(a). There is no evidence, however, that Congress meant § 717 to foreclose alternative remedies available to those not covered by the statute. Such silence is far from 'the clearly discernible will of Congress' perceived by the Court of Appeals. * * * On the contrary, § 717 leaves undisturbed whatever remedies petitioner might otherwise possess."

Four Justices dissented, writing three separate opinions. Chief Justice Burger (joined by Justices Powell and Rehnquist) emphasized the "grave questions of separation of powers" that are presented when the courts interfere with the decisions of Members of Congress on how to fill their staff positions (pp. 249–51). For Justice Stewart (joined by Justice Rehnquist), the Court had erred in failing to address at the outset the question of immunity under the Speech or Debate Clause. And for Justice Powell (joined by Chief Justice Burger and Justice Rehnquist), the Court had misinterpreted its own precedents and had failed to recognize the proper criteria to be applied (pp. 252, 254):

"The Court's analysis starts with the general proposition that 'the judiciary is clearly discernible as the primary means through which [constitutional] rights may be enforced.' It leaps from this generalization, unexceptionable itself, to the conclusion that individuals who have suffered an injury to a constitutionally protected interest, and who lack an 'effective' alternative, '*must* be able to invoke the existing jurisdiction of the courts for the protection of their justiciable constitutional rights.' (Emphasis supplied.) Apart from the dubious logic of this reasoning, I know of no precedent of this Court that supports such an absolute statement of the federal judiciary's obligation to entertain private suits that Congress has not authorized. On the contrary, I have thought it clear that federal courts must exercise a principled discretion when called upon to infer a private cause of action directly from the language of the Constitution. In the present case, for reasons well summarized by The Chief Justice, principles of comity and separation of powers should require a federal court to stay its hand.

* * *

"The foregoing would seem self-evident even if Congress had not indicated an intention to reserve to its Members the right to select, employ and discharge staff personnel without judicial interference. But Congress unmistakably has made clear its view on this subject. It took pains to exempt itself from the coverage of Title VII. Unless the Court is abandoning or modifying *sub silentio* our holding in Brown v. General Services Administration, 425 U.S. 820 (1976), that Title VII as amended 'provides the exclusive judicial remedy for claims of discrimination in federal employment,' *id.*, at 835, the exemption from this statute for congressional employees should bar all judicial relief."

(4) The Court in Davis v. Passman barely touched on the statutory framework surrounding the case. Since they are outside the competitive Civil Service, personal staff of members of Congress serve at will. See, *e.g.*, 2 U.S.C. § 92 ("subject to removal at any time * * * with or without cause"). When passing Title VII of the Civil Rights Act of 1964, Congress in § 701 excluded the federal government from the definition of "employers" covered by the Act. See 42 U.S.C. § 2000e(b). In 1972, Congress amended Title VII by adding § 717, which created a detailed separate administrative remedy for certain federal employees who are victims of discrimination. *Id.* § 2000e–16. Among those covered were employees of the "legislative and judicial branches of the federal government having positions in the competitive service." [5] The statute thus explicitly ruled out statutory coverage for persons not in the competitive service, such as Davis. And, as the legislative history clearly showed, that decision was made on the premise that, *apart* from Title VII, no remedies were available for federal-employee victims of discrimination.[6]

Did the Court in Davis give adequate weight to the congressional purpose expressed by the exclusion of personal staff assistants (and, by the way, of judicial law clerks, who also do not have positions in the competitive service) from the coverage of Title VII? If Congress wishes to leave the criteria for hiring confidential assistants entirely at the discretion of an employer, how should it express its intention?

The ironic result of Davis is that it grants federal employees in noncompetitive positions, whom Congress did not intend to protect, a more direct and forceful remedy than Congress provided for employees in the competitive service whom Congress did intend to protect, since the latter are bound by the ruling (in Brown v. General Services Adm'n, 425 U.S. 820 (1976)), that Title VII is the "exclusive, pre-emptive administrative and judicial scheme for the redress of federal employment discrimination" (p. 829); persons in the competitive service must therefore proceed through the administrative mechanism of Title VII; moreover, any monetary remedy is ordinarily limited to back pay.[7]

The ultimate question in Davis would seem to be whether, in the absence of a statute authorizing suit, a complaint seeking damages for injuries caused by a federal official's violation of the plaintiff's rights under the Due Process Clause of the Fifth Amendment states a claim upon which relief can be granted (or, to use the more old-fashioned shorthand, states a good cause of action). Is this as complex a question linguistically as the Court seems to have made it? (See Paragraph (3), note 4, *supra*.) Is it meaningful to think of plaintiffs having a cause of action apart from the question whether they are entitled to relief?

5. The § 717 remedy is, after various administrative steps, eventually a suit for reinstatement and back pay.

6. See the account of the legislative history on this point in Brown v. General Services Adm'n, 425 U.S. 820, 824–29 (1976).

7. Note, however, that the plaintiff's burden of proof is different, and heavier, in a case resting solely on the Constitution than in a case under Title VII. See Washington v. Davis, 426 U.S. 229 (1976).

Note the extraordinary divergence in approach to the case between Justice Brennan and Justice Powell. Justice Powell's approach, calling for "principled discretion", rests on the notion, also made explicit in Justice Harlan's opinion in Bivens, that in framing an appropriate remedial scheme for constitutional interests the Court should consider a range of policy considerations "at least as broad" as that which a legislature considers—that is, that the Court should in effect adopt the perspective of a common-law court.

Now note the factors weighing against the creation of a damage action in Davis *if* there is any discretion in the matter at all: (a) the action was against a high official of a coordinate branch making personnel decisions with respect to his personal staff of confidential advisors; (b) Congress had decided (about as explicitly as it could) that such officials should retain plenary discretion with respect to this small group of intimate advisors and that therefore no legal remedies should be available to them; (c) allowing the action to go forward would make necessary the resolution of difficult and sensitive constitutional issues under the Speech and Debate Clause. Are there many cases which would present *more* difficult obstacles to the inferring of a cause of action?

Given these factors, it is understandable why the Court in arriving at its result avoided questions of discretion (principled or unprincipled) and refrained from asking whether, in light of all the circumstances, a cause of action *should* be judicially created in this context. Does this help to explain the extraordinary extent to which the opinion formalizes the issues of the case by suggesting that the "cause of action", rather than being judicially created in this case, is simply the automatic consequence of an already existing set of postulates?

(5) Within a year after Davis, the Court issued a second major opinion on the subject in Carlson v. Green, 446 U.S. 14 (1980). Carlson was a damage action against federal prison officials alleging that their failure to provide medical attention to plaintiff's deceased son constituted cruel and unusual punishment in violation of the Eighth Amendment. The Court, again per Justice Brennan, held that a Bivens remedy was available. The Court stated flatly that "the victims of a constitutional violation by a federal agent have a right to recover damages against the official in federal court despite the absence of any statute conferring such a right," unless (1) the defendant demonstrates "special factors counselling hesitation," or (2) "Congress has provided an alternative remedy which it explicitly declared to be a *substitute* for recovery directly under the Constitution and viewed as equally effective" (pp. 18–19) (emphasis in original). It dismissed with a few words the question of "special factors", finding none. The second problem caused more difficulty in light of the passage by Congress in 1974 of an amendment to the Federal Tort Claims Act (FTCA) to allow recovery against the United States for intentional torts of the kind at issue in Bivens and in Carlson. See p. 1151, *infra*. The Court rejected the argument that this amendment was designed to supersede the Bivens remedy against the individual official. It found nothing in the text or its legislative history to indicate that the amendment was to be a substitute rather than an alternative remedy; and it suggested four ways in which the Bivens remedy might be more effective than the FTCA remedy: (a) an action against the individual wrongdoer is a more effective deterrent than an action against the government; (b) the Bivens remedy could include puni-

tive damages, whereas the FTCA bars punitive damages; (c) a Bivens plaintiff can opt for jury trial, unavailable under the FTCA; (d) the FTCA remedy exists only for acts which would be actionable under state law if committed by a private person (see 28 U.S.C. § 1346(b)), whereas uniform federal rules govern the extent of Bivens liability. "Plainly FTCA is not a sufficient protector of the citizens' constitutional rights," concluded Justice Brennan (p. 23).

Justice Powell, concurring with Justice Stewart, reiterated the view that the question whether a Bivens remedy should be inferred was a question of "principled discretion," and criticized the Court for "dramatically" restricting that discretion. "The Court now volunteers the view that defendant cannot defeat a Bivens action simply by showing that there are adequate alternative avenues for relief. The defendant also must show that Congress 'explicitly declared [its remedy] to be a *substitute* for recovery directly under the Constitution and viewed [it] as equally effective.' These are unnecessarily rigid conditions" (pp. 26–27).

Justice Powell agreed, however, that in fact the FTCA was not an adequate substitute remedy, and that no good reasons existed why the Bivens remedy should be unavailable on the particular facts.

Chief Justice Burger dissented, on the ground that the FTCA provided an "adequate" remedy and therefore there was no warrant for inferring an additional one. In a separate and elaborate dissent, Justice Rehnquist objected to the "formalistic" approach of the Court, which he said "highlights the wrong turn this Court took in Bivens" (pp. 31–32). Relying on Justice Black's dissent in Bivens, Justice Rehnquist took the view that the Court has no authority to infer private civil damage remedies from the Constitution.

(6) The Bivens, Davis, and Carlson cases raised, but did not resolve, some difficult questions about the respective roles of Congress and the Court in the articulation of a remedial system for constitutional violations.

Further light was cast on these questions by two unanimous decisions in the 1982 Term. In Chappell v. Wallace, 462 U.S. 296 (1983), Navy enlisted men brought an action against their superior officers for racial discrimination, alleging that the discrimination violated their rights under the Constitution and under federal civil rights legislation. The Court held that the claim for violation of constitutional rights could not be maintained, and stated that "the unique disciplinary structure of the Military Establishment and Congress' activity in the field constitute 'special factors' [a phrase quoted from Bivens and Carlson] which dictate that it would be inappropriate to provide enlisted military personnel a Bivens-type remedy against their superior officers" (p. 304). The activity of Congress that the Court referred to embraced "a comprehensive internal system of justice to regulate military life," which included procedures "for the review and remedy of complaints and grievances such as those presented by respondents" (p. 302). The Court also noted that "Congress, the constitutionally authorized source of authority over the military system of justice, has not provided a damages remedy for claims by military personnel that constitutional rights have been violated by superior officers" (p. 304).[8]

8. The Court left it to the lower court on remand to consider whether an action could be maintained for damages resulting from an alleged conspiracy in violation of 42 U.S.C. § 1985(3).

"Special factors counselling hesitation" were also found in Bush v. Lucas, 462 U.S. 367 (1983). Bush, an aerospace engineer employed by the federal government, brought a damage action against his superior for defamation and retaliatory demotion, claiming that the demotion violated his First Amendment rights. The lower courts held that the superior was absolutely immune from liability for defamation under Barr v. Matteo, 360 U.S. 564 (1959), and that an action for damages for the alleged constitutional deprivation could not be maintained. On the latter point, the Supreme Court affirmed.

Bush had previously been restored to his former position and awarded back pay by the Civil Service Commission's Appeals Review Board. Assuming that a federal right had been violated and that the civil service remedy was "less than complete" (because it did not provide attorney's fees or compensation for alleged emotional and dignitary harms), the Court nevertheless held that in this matter of "federal personnel policy" the "elaborate remedial system" constructed by Congress should not be "augmented by the creation of a new judicial remedy" (pp. 373, 380–81, 388). Relying in part on the Standard Oil and Gilman cases, pp. 868–69, *supra,* the Court said: "[W]e decline 'to create a new substantive legal liability without legislative aid and as at the common law' * * * because we are convinced that Congress is in a better position to decide whether or not the public interest would be served by creating it" (p. 390).[9]

Note that in neither Bush nor Chappell had Congress "explicitly" declared a statutory remedy to be a substitute for a judicially created one. Is a requirement of explicitness in this context tenable? Sound?

(7) The Chappell holding was in turn extended in United States v. Stanley, 107 S.Ct. 3054 (1987), in which a former serviceman brought suit against military officers and civilians for injuries resulting from the administration of the drug LSD to him, without his consent, as part of an army experiment. The Supreme Court held, 5–4, that a Bivens action could not be maintained. (An earlier dismissal of Stanley's claim under the Federal Tort Claims Act was held not subject to appeal.) The Court said (p. 3063) that the special factors found in Chappell "extend beyond the situation in which an officer-subordinate relationship exists, and require abstention in the inferring of Bivens actions as extensive as the exception to the FTCA established by Feres [v. United States, 340 U.S. 135 (1950), p. 1152, *infra*] * * *. We hold that no Bivens remedy is available for injuries that 'arise out of or are in the course of activity incident to [military] service.'"

Justice O'Connor, dissenting in part, said that in her view "conduct of the type alleged in this case is so far beyond the bounds of human decency that as a matter of law it simply cannot be considered a part of the military mission" (p. 3065). Justice Brennan, in a lengthy dissent joined by Justice Marshall and (in part) by Justice Stevens, argued that: (1) the question of the availability of a Bivens action should not be different from the question of the scope of official immunity (see Chap. IX, Sec. 3, *infra*), and thus the case should be remanded to see whether the defendants can show "that absolute immunity was necessary to the effective performance of their functions" (p. 3072), (2) the Chappell decision was not in point because "the

---

9. For a case raising problems similar to those raised in Bush, but in the context of an action for due process violations in the denial of social security disability bene- fits, see Schweiker v. Chilicky, 108 S.Ct. 64 (1987) (granting certiorari). The case had been argued but not decided as this edition went to press.

defendants are not alleged to be Stanley's superior officers" (p. 3073), and (3) in contrast to the situation in Chappell, no intramilitary system " 'provides for the * * * remedy' of Stanley's complaint" (p. 3076).

Has the Court, in Chappell, Bush, and Stanley, implicitly embraced Justice Powell's view that the question of the availability of a Bivens remedy is one calling for the exercise of principled discretion? If so, can you articulate the principle(s) guiding that discretion?

(8) Would Congress have constitutional power to eliminate the remedy created in Bivens? In Davis?

The Court in Bush v. Lucas, Paragraph (6), *supra,* stated that the remedy afforded by Congress was "constitutionally adequate" even though it was not an "equally effective substitute" for the judicial remedy sought (462 U.S. at 378 & n. 14). Thus, the Court said, it "need not reach the question whether the Constitution itself requires a judicially fashioned damages remedy in the absence of any other remedy to vindicate the underlying right, unless there is an express textual command to the contrary" (*id.*).[10] Justice Marshall, joined by Justice Blackmun, concurred in the opinion but wrote separately to emphasize that in his view "a different case would be presented if Congress had not created a comprehensive scheme that was specifically designed to provide full compensation * * * and that affords a remedy that is substantially as effective as a damage action" (p. 390).

In the context of the Fifth Amendment requirement of just compensation, the Court has said that "it is the Constitution that dictates the remedy for interference with property rights amounting to a taking." First English Evangelical Lutheran Church of Glendale v. County of Los Angeles, California, 107 S.Ct. 2378, 2386 n. 9 (1987). On the other hand, in Chappell v. Wallace, Paragraph (6), *supra,* the Court avoided discussion of the effectiveness or adequacy of the alternative "internal" remedy available to the plaintiffs. Rather, it stressed the unique structure and special needs of the Military Establishment. And as Justice Brennan noted in his dissent in United States v. Stanley, Paragraph (7), *supra,* no alternative remedy of any kind existed in that case.

The Supreme Court has recognized in a series of opinions that official liability in damages under Bivens and its successors is subject to various immunity defenses—sometimes qualified and sometimes absolute. Is the implication of Justice Marshall's approach in Bush v. Lucas that Congress could not decide to confer absolute immunity on an officer who had only qualified immunity under the Court's existing decisions?

See generally Monaghan, *Foreword: Constitutional Common Law,* 89 Harv.L.Rev. 1 (1975) (endorsing the development of "constitutionally inspired common law" with Congress playing a coordinate role), criticized in Schrock & Welsh, *Reconsidering the Constitutional Common Law,* 91 Harv. L.Rev. 1117 (1978); Amar, *Of Sovereignty and Federalism,* 96 Yale L.J. 1425, 1484–92 (1987) (arguing that there is a "remedial imperative of government liability" for the violation of constitutional rights).

---

10. *Cf.* Spagnola v. Mathis, 809 F.2d 16 (D.C.Cir.1986) (holding that an administrative remedy available to a federal employee for alleged retaliation against "whistle-blowing" was not constitutionally adequate and that, in view of this inadequacy, Congress did not intend to foreclose a private civil remedy).

(9) The availability of a remedy under federal law for a claimed violation of a constitutionally protected interest arises in a variety of contexts other than damages, and may frequently be determinative of the existence of federal question jurisdiction under § 1331. See *e.g.,* the discussion of federal jurisdiction in actions for a declaratory judgment, Chap. VIII, Sec. 3, pp. 1027–40, *infra.*

J.I. CASE CO. v. BORAK

377 U.S. 426, 84 S.Ct. 1555, 12 L.Ed.2d 423 (1964).
Certiorari to the United States Court of Appeals for the Seventh Circuit.

MR. JUSTICE CLARK delivered the opinion of the Court.

This is a civil action brought by respondent, a stockholder of petitioner J.I. Case Company, charging deprivation of the pre-emptive rights of respondent and other shareholders by reason of a merger between Case and the American Tractor Corporation. It is alleged that the merger was effected through the circulation of a false and misleading proxy statement by those proposing the merger. The complaint was in two counts, the first based on diversity and claiming a breach of the directors' fiduciary duty to the stockholders. The second count alleged a violation of § 14(a)[1] of the Securities Exchange Act of 1934 with reference to the proxy solicitation material. The trial court held that as to this count it had no power to redress the alleged violations of the Act but was limited solely to the granting of declaratory relief thereon under § 27 of the Act.[2] The court held Wis.Stat., 1961, § 180.405(4), which requires posting security for expenses in derivative actions, applicable to both counts, except that portion of Count 2 requesting declaratory relief. It ordered the respondent to furnish a bond in the amount of $75,000 thereunder and, upon his failure to do so, dismissed the complaint, save that part of Count 2 seeking a declaratory judgment. On interlocutory appeal the Court of Appeals reversed on both counts, holding that the District Court had the power to grant remedial relief and that the Wisconsin statute was not applicable. 317 F.2d 838. We granted certiorari. We consider only the question of

1. Section 14(a) of the Securities Exchange Act of 1934, 48 Stat. 895, 15 U.S.C. § 78n(a), provides: "It shall be unlawful for any person, by the use of the mails or by any means or instrumentality of interstate commerce or of any facility of any national securities exchange or otherwise to solicit or to permit the use of his name to solicit any proxy or consent or authorization in respect of any security (other than an exempted security) registered on any national securities exchange in contravention of such rules and regulations as the [Securities and Exchange] Commission may prescribe as necessary or appropriate in the public interest or for the protection of investors."

2. Section 27 of the Act, 48 Stat. 902–903, 15 U.S.C. § 78aa, provides in part: "The district courts of the United States, the Supreme Court of the District of Columbia, and the United States courts of any Territory or other place subject to the jurisdiction of the United States shall have exclusive jurisdiction of violations of this title or the rules and regulations thereunder, and of all suits in equity and actions at law brought to enforce any liability or duty created by this title or the rules and regulations thereunder. Any criminal proceeding may be brought in the district wherein any act or transaction constituting the violation occurred. Any suit or action to enforce any liability or duty created by this title or rules and regulations thereunder, or to enjoin any violation of such title or rules and regulations, may be brought in any such district or in the district wherein the defendant is found or is an inhabitant or transacts business, and process in such cases may be served in any other district of which the defendant is an inhabitant or wherever the defendant may be found."

whether § 27 of the Act authorizes a federal cause of action for rescission or damages to a corporate stockholder with respect to a consummated merger which was authorized pursuant to the use of a proxy statement alleged to contain false and misleading statements violative of § 14(a) of the Act. This being the sole question raised by petitioners in their petition for certiorari, we will not consider other questions subsequently presented.

* * *

II.

It appears clear that private parties have a right under § 27 to bring suit for violation of § 14(a) of the Act. Indeed, this section specifically grants the appropriate District Courts jurisdiction over "all suits in equity and actions at law brought to enforce any liability or duty created" under the Act. The petitioners make no concessions, however, emphasizing that Congress made no specific reference to a private right of action in § 14(a); that, in any event, the right would not extend to derivative suits and should be limited to prospective relief only. In addition, some of the petitioners argue that the merger can be dissolved only if it was fraudulent or non-beneficial, issues upon which the proxy material would not bear. But the causal relationship of the proxy material and the merger are questions of fact to be resolved at trial, not here. We therefore do not discuss this point further.

III.

While the respondent contends that his Count 2 claim is not a derivative one, we need not embrace that view, for we believe that a right of action exists as to both derivative and direct causes.

The purpose of § 14(a) is to prevent management or others from obtaining authorization for corporate action by means of deceptive or inadequate disclosure in proxy solicitation. The section stemmed from the congressional belief that "[f]air corporate suffrage is an important right that should attach to every equity security bought on a public exchange." H.R.Rep. No. 1383, 73d Cong., 2d Sess., 13. It was intended to "control the conditions under which proxies may be solicited with a view to preventing the recurrence of abuses which * * * [had] frustrated the free exercise of the voting rights of stockholders." *Id.,* at 14. "Too often proxies are solicited without explanation to the stockholder of the real nature of the questions for which authority to cast his vote is sought." S.Rep. No. 792, 73d Cong., 2d Sess., 12. These broad remedial purposes are evidenced in the language of the section which makes it "unlawful for any person * * * to solicit or to permit the use of his name to solicit any proxy or consent or authorization in respect of any security * * * registered on any national securities exchange in contravention of such rules and regulations as the Commission may prescribe as necessary or appropriate in the public interest *or for the protection of investors.*" (Italics supplied.) While this language makes no specific reference to a private right of action, among its chief purposes is "the protection of investors," which certainly implies the availability of judicial relief where necessary to achieve that result.

The injury which a stockholder suffers from corporate action pursuant to a deceptive proxy solicitation ordinarily flows from the damage done the corporation, rather than from the damage inflicted directly upon the stockholder. The damage suffered results not from the deceit practiced on him alone but rather from the deceit practiced on the stockholders as a group. To hold that derivative actions are not within the sweep of the section would therefore be tantamount to a denial of private relief. Private enforcement of the proxy rules provides a necessary supplement to Commission action. As in anti-trust treble damage litigation, the possibility of civil damages or injunctive relief serves as a most effective weapon in the enforcement of the proxy requirements. The Commission advises that it examines over 2,000 proxy statements annually and each of them must necessarily be expedited. Time does not permit an independent examination of the facts set out in the proxy material and this results in the Commission's acceptance of the representations contained therein at their face value, unless contrary to other material on file with it. Indeed, on the allegations of respondent's complaint, the proxy material failed to disclose alleged unlawful market manipulation of the stock of ATC, and this unlawful manipulation would not have been apparent to the Commission until after the merger.

We, therefore, believe that under the circumstances here it is the duty of the courts to be alert to provide such remedies as are necessary to make effective the congressional purpose. As was said in Sola Electric Co. v. Jefferson Electric Co., 317 U.S. 173, 176 (1942):

> "When a federal statute condemns an act as unlawful, the extent and nature of the legal consequences of the condemnation, though left by the statute to judicial determination, are nevertheless federal questions, the answers to which are to be derived from the statute and the federal policy which it has adopted."

* * * Section 27 grants the District Courts jurisdiction "of all suits in equity and actions at law brought to enforce any liability or duty created by this title * * *." In passing on almost identical language found in the Securities Act of 1933, the Court found the words entirely sufficient to fashion a remedy to rescind a fraudulent sale, secure restitution and even to enforce the right to restitution against a third party holding assets of the vendor. Deckert v. Independence Shares Corp., 311 U.S. 282 (1940). This significant language was used:

> "The power *to enforce* implies the power to make effective the right of recovery afforded by the Act. And the power to make the right of recovery effective implies the power to utilize any of the procedures or actions normally available to the litigant according to the exigencies of the particular case." At 288 of 311 U.S.

Nor do we find merit in the contention that such remedies are limited to prospective relief. * * *

Moreover, if federal jurisdiction were limited to the granting of declaratory relief, victims of deceptive proxy statements would be obliged to go into state courts for remedial relief. And if the law of the State happened to attach no responsibility to the use of misleading proxy statements, the whole purpose of the section might be frustrated. Furthermore, the hurdles that the victim might face (such as separate suits, security for expenses statutes, bringing in all parties necessary for complete relief, etc.) might well prove insuperable to effective relief.

IV.

Our finding that federal courts have the power to grant all necessary remedial relief is not to be construed as any indication of what we believe to be the necessary and appropriate relief in this case. We are concerned here only with a determination that federal jurisdiction for this purpose does exist. Whatever remedy is necessary must await the trial on the merits.

The other contentions of the petitioners are denied.

Affirmed.

TEXAS INDUSTRIES, INC. v. RADCLIFF MATERIALS, INC.

451 U.S. 630, 101 S.Ct. 2061, 68 L.Ed.2d 500 (1981).
Certiorari to the United States Court of Appeals for the Fifth Circuit.

CHIEF JUSTICE BURGER delivered the opinion of the Court.

This case presents the question whether the federal antitrust laws allow a defendant, against whom civil damages, costs, and attorney's fees have been assessed, a right to contribution from other participants in the unlawful conspiracy on which recovery was based. We granted certiorari to resolve a conflict in the Circuits. 449 U.S. 949 (1980). We affirm.

I

Petitioner and the three respondents manufacture and sell ready-mix concrete in the New Orleans, La., area. In 1975, the Wilson P. Abraham Construction Corp., which had purchased concrete from petitioner, filed a civil action in the United States District Court for the Eastern District of Louisiana naming petitioner as defendant; the complaint alleged that petitioner and certain unnamed concrete firms had conspired to raise prices in violation of § 1 of the Sherman Act, 26 Stat. 209, as amended, 15 U.S.C. § 1 * * *.

The complaint sought treble damages plus attorney's fees under § 4 of the Clayton Act, 15 U.S.C. § 15 * * *.

Through discovery, petitioner learned that Abraham believed respondents were the other concrete producers that had participated in the alleged price-fixing scheme. Petitioner then filed a third-party complaint against respondents seeking contribution from them should it be held liable in the action filed by Abraham. The District Court dismissed the third-party complaint for failure to state a claim upon which relief could be granted, holding that federal law does not allow an anti-trust defendant to recover in contribution from co-conspirators. The District Court also determined there was no just reason for delay with respect to that aspect of the case and entered final judgment under Federal Rule of Civil Procedure 54(b).

On appeal, the Court of Appeals for the Fifth Circuit affirmed, holding that, although the Sherman and the Clayton Acts do not expressly afford a right to contribution, the issue should be resolved as a matter of federal common law. Wilson P. Abraham Construction Corp. v. Texas Industries, Inc., 604 F.2d 897 (1979). The court then examined what it perceived to be the benefits and the difficulties of contribution and concluded that no common-law rule of contribution should be fashioned by the courts.

II

The common law provided no right to contribution among joint tortfeasors. * * * In part, at least, this common-law rule rested on the idea that when several tortfeasors have caused damage, the law should not lend its aid to have one tortfeasor compel others to share in the sanctions imposed by way of damages intended to compensate the victim. * * * Since the turn of the century, however, 39 states and the District of Columbia have fashioned rules of contribution in one form or another, 10 initially through judicial action and the remainder through legislation. * * * Because courts generally have acknowledged that treble-damages actions under the antitrust laws are analogous to common-law actions sounding in tort, we are urged to follow this trend and adopt contribution for antitrust violators.

The parties and amici representing a variety of business interests—as well as a legion of commentators—have thoroughly addressed the policy concerns implicated in the creation of a right to contribution in antitrust cases. With potentially large sums at stake, it is not surprising that the numerous and articulate amici disagree strongly over the basic issue raised: whether sharing of damages liability will advance or impair the objectives of the antitrust laws.

Proponents of a right to contribution advance concepts of fairness and equity in urging that the often massive judgments in antitrust actions be shared by all the wrongdoers. In the abstract, this position has a certain appeal: collective fault, collective responsibility. But the efforts of petitioner and supporting amici to invoke principles of equity presuppose a legislative intent to allow parties violating the law to draw upon equitable principles to mitigate the consequences of their wrongdoing. Moreover, traditional equitable standards have something to say about the septic state of the hands of such a suitor in the courts, and, in the context of one wrongdoer suing a co-conspirator, these standards similarly suggest that parties generally in pari delicto should be left where they are found.

The proponents of contribution also contend that, by allowing one violator to recover from co-conspirators, there is a greater likelihood that most or all wrongdoers will be held liable and thus share the consequences of the wrongdoing. It is argued that contribution would thus promote more vigorous private enforcement of the antitrust laws and thereby deter violations, one of the important purposes of the treble-damages action under § 4 of the Clayton Act. * * * Independent of this effect, a right to contribution may increase the incentive of a single defendant to provide evidence against co-conspirators so as to avoid bearing the full weight of the judgment. Realization of this possibility may also deter one from joining an antitrust conspiracy.

Respondents and amici opposing contribution point out that an even stronger deterrent may exist in the possibility, even if more remote, that a single participant could be held fully liable for the total amount of the judgment. In this view, each prospective co-conspirator would ponder long and hard before engaging in what may be called a game of "Russian roulette." Moreover, any discussion of this problem must consider the problem of "overdeterrence," *i.e.,* the possibility that severe antitrust penalties will chill wholly legitimate business agreements. ✳ ✳ ✳

The parties and amici also discuss at length how a right to contribution should be structured and, in particular, how to treat problems that may arise with the allocation of damages among the wrongdoers and the effect of settlements. Dividing or apportioning damages among a cluster of co-conspirators presents difficult issues, for the participation of each in the conspiracy may have varied. ✳ ✳ ✳ In addition to the question of allocation, a right to contribution may have a serious impact on the incentive of defendants to settle. Some amici and commentators have suggested that the total amount of the plaintiff's claim should be reduced by the amount of any settlement with any one co-conspirator; others strongly disagree. Similarly, vigorous arguments can be made for and against allowing a losing defendant to seek contribution from co-conspirators who settled with the plaintiff before trial. Regardless of the particular rule adopted for allocating damages or enforcing settlements, the complexity of the issues involved may result in additional trial and pretrial proceedings, thus adding new complications to what already is complex litigation. ✳ ✳ ✳

III

The contentions advanced indicate how views diverge as to the "unfairness" of not providing contribution, the risks and trade-offs perceived by decisionmakers in business, and the various patterns for contribution that could be devised. In this vigorous debate over the advantages and disadvantages of contribution and various contribution schemes, the parties, amici, and commentators have paid less attention to a very significant and perhaps dispositive threshold question: whether courts have the power to create such a cause of action absent legislation and, if so, whether that authority should be exercised in this context.

Earlier this Term, in Northwest Airlines, Inc. v. Transport Workers, 451 U.S. 77 (1981), we addressed the similar question of a right to contribution under the Equal Pay Act of 1963, 29 U.S.C. § 206(d), and Title VII of the Civil Rights Act of 1964, 42 U.S.C. § 2000e *et seq.* We concluded that a right to contribution may arise in either of two ways: first, through the affirmative creation of a right of action by Congress, either expressly or by clear implication; or, second, through the power of federal courts to fashion a federal common law of contribution. 451 U.S., at 90–91.[10]

A

There is no allegation that the antitrust laws expressly establish a right of action for contribution. Nothing in these statutes refers to contribution, and if such a right exists it must be by implication. Our focus, as it is in any case involving the implication of a right of action, is on the intent of Congress. ✳ ✳ ✳ Congressional intent may be discerned by looking to the legislative history and other factors: e.g., the identity of the class for whose benefit the statute was enacted, the overall legislative scheme, and the traditional role of the States in providing relief. See ✳ ✳ ✳; Cort v. Ash, 422 U.S. 66 (1975).

---

10. In Northwest Airlines, we decided that no such right exists under the Equal Pay Act or Title VII, and we declined to fashion such a right from federal common law.

Petitioner readily concedes that "there is nothing in the legislative history of the Sherman Act or the Clayton Act to indicate that Congress considered whether contribution was available to defendants in antitrust actions." Brief for Petitioner 10. Moreover, it is equally clear that the Sherman Act and the provision for treble-damages actions under the Clayton Act were not adopted for the benefit of the participants in a conspiracy to restrain trade. On the contrary, petitioner "is a member of the class whose activities Congress intended to regulate for the protection and benefit *of an entirely distinct class*," Piper v. Chris–Craft Industries, Inc., 430 U.S. 1, 37 (1977) (emphasis added). The very idea of treble damages reveals an intent to punish past, and to deter future, unlawful conduct, not to ameliorate the liability of wrongdoers. The absence of any reference to contribution in the legislative history or of any possibility that Congress was concerned with softening the blow on joint wrongdoers in this setting makes examination of other factors unnecessary. * * * Touche Ross & Co. v. Redington, 442 U.S. 560, 574–576 (1979). We therefore conclude that Congress neither expressly nor implicitly intended to create a right to contribution.[11] If any right to contribution exists, its source must be federal common law.

B

There is, of course, "no federal general common law." Erie R. Co. v. Tompkins, 304 U.S. 64, 78 (1938). Nevertheless, the Court has recognized the need and authority in some limited areas to formulate what has come to be known as "federal common law." See United States v. Standard Oil Co., 332 U.S. 301, 308 (1947). These instances are "few and restricted," Wheeldin v. Wheeler, 373 U.S. 647, 651 (1963), and fall into essentially two categories: those in which a federal rule of decision is "necessary to protect uniquely federal interests," Banco Nacional de Cuba v. Sabbatino, 376 U.S. 398, 426 (1964), and those in which Congress has given the courts the power to develop substantive law, Wheeldin v. Wheeler, *supra,* at 652.

(1)

The vesting of jurisdiction in the federal courts does not in and of itself give rise to authority to formulate federal common law, United States v. Little Lake Misere Land Co., 412 U.S. 580, 591 (1973), nor does the existence of congressional authority under Art. I mean that federal courts are free to develop a common law to govern those areas until Congress acts. Rather, absent some congressional authorization to formulate substantive rules of decision, federal common law exists only in such narrow areas as those concerned with the rights and obligations of the United States, interstate and international disputes implicating the conflicting rights of States or our relations with foreign nations, and admiralty cases. In these instances, our federal system does not permit the controversy to be resolved under state law, either because the authority and duties of the United States as sovereign are intimately involved or because the interstate or international nature of the controversy makes it inappropriate for state law to control.

11. That Congress knows how to define a right to contribution is shown by the express actions for contribution under § 11(f) of the Securities Act of 1933, 15 USC § 77k(f), and §§ 9(e) and 18(b) of the Securities Exchange Act of 1934, 15 USC §§ 78i(e) and 78r(b). * * *

In areas where federal common law applies, the creation of a right to contribution may fall within the power of the federal courts. For example, in Cooper Stevedoring Co. v. Fritz Kopke, Inc., 417 U.S. 106 (1974), we held that contribution is available among joint tortfeasors for injury to a longshoreman. But that claim arose within admiralty jurisdiction, one of the areas long recognized as subject to federal common law, see Edmonds v. Compagnie Generale Transatlantique, 443 U.S. 256, 259 (1979); our decision there was based, at least in part, on the traditional division of damages in admiralty not recognized at common law, see 417 U.S., at 110. Cooper Stevedoring thus does not stand for a general federal common-law right to contribution. See Northwest Airlines, Inc. v. Transport Workers, *supra*, at 96–97.

The antitrust laws were enacted pursuant to the power of Congress under the Commerce Clause, Art. I, § 8, cl. 3, to regulate interstate and foreign trade, and the case law construing the Sherman Act now spans nearly a century. Nevertheless, a treble-damages action remains a private suit involving the rights and obligations of private parties. Admittedly, there is a federal interest in the sense that vindication of rights arising out of these congressional enactments supplements federal enforcement and fulfills the objects of the statutory scheme. Notwithstanding that nexus, contribution among antitrust wrongdoers does not involve the duties of the Federal Government, the distribution of powers in our federal system, or matters necessarily subject to federal control even in the absence of statutory authority. Cf. Bank of America v. Parnell, 352 U.S. 29, 33 (1956). In short, contribution does not implicate "uniquely federal interests" of the kind that oblige courts to formulate federal common law.

(2)

Federal common law also may come into play when Congress has vested jurisdiction in the federal courts and empowered them to create governing rules of law. In this vein, this Court has read § 301(a) of the Labor Management Relations Act, 29 U.S.C. § 185(a), not only as granting jurisdiction over defined areas of labor law but also as vesting in the courts the power to develop a common law of labor-management relations within that jurisdiction. Textile Workers v. Lincoln Mills, 353 U.S. 448 (1957). A similar situation arises with regard to the first two sections of the Sherman Act, which in sweeping language forbid "[e]very contract, combination * * *, or conspiracy, in restraint of trade" and "monopoliz[ing], or attempt[ing] to monopolize, * * * any part of the trade or commerce. * * *" 15 U.S.C. §§ 1, 2. * * *

* * *

It does not necessarily follow, however, that Congress intended to give courts as wide discretion in formulating remedies to enforce the provisions of the Sherman Act or the kind of relief sought through contribution. The intent to allow courts to develop governing principles of law, so unmistakably clear with regard to substantive violations, does not appear in debates on the treble-damages action created in § 7 of the original Act, 26 Stat. 210.

* * *

In contrast to the sweeping language of §§ 1 and 2 of the Sherman Act, the remedial provisions defined in the antitrust laws are detailed and specific: (1) violations of §§ 1 and 2 are crimes; (2) Congress has expressly authorized a private right of action for treble damages, costs, and reasonable attorney's fees; (3) other remedial sections also provide for suits by the United States to enjoin violations or for injury to its "business or property." and parens patriae suits by state attorneys general; (4) Congress has provided that a final judgment or decree of an antitrust violation in one proceeding will serve as prima facie evidence in any subsequent action or proceeding; and (5) the remedial provisions in the antimerger field, not at issue here, are also quite detailed.

"The presumption that a remedy was deliberately omitted from a statute is strongest when Congress has enacted a comprehensive legislative scheme including an integrated system of procedures for enforcement." Northwest Airlines, Inc. v. Transport Workers *supra*, at 97. That presumption is strong indeed in the context of antitrust violations; the continuing existence of this statutory scheme for 90 years without amendments authorizing contribution is not without significance. There is nothing in the statute itself, in its legislative history, or in the overall regulatory scheme to suggest that Congress intended courts to have the power to alter or supplement the remedies enacted.

* * *

We are satisfied that neither the Sherman Act nor the Clayton Act confers on federal courts the broad power to formulate the right to contribution sought here.

IV

The policy questions presented by petitioner's claimed right to contribution are far reaching. In declining to provide a right to contribution, we neither reject the validity of those arguments nor adopt the views of those opposing contribution. Rather, we recognize that, regardless of the merits of the conflicting arguments, this is a matter for Congress, not the courts, to resolve.

The range of factors to be weighed in deciding whether a right to contribution should exist demonstrates the inappropriateness of judicial resolution of this complex issue. Ascertaining what is "fair" in this setting calls for inquiry into the entire spectrum of antitrust law, not simply the elements of a particular case or category of cases. Similarly, whether contribution would strengthen or weaken enforcement of the antitrust laws, or what form a right to contribution should take, cannot be resolved without going beyond the record of a single lawsuit. * * *

Because we are unable to discern any basis in federal statutory or common law that allows federal courts to fashion the relief urged by petitioner, the judgment of the Court of Appeals is affirmed.

NOTE ON THE IMPLICATION OF PRIVATE REMEDIES FOR STATUTORY VIOLATIONS

(1) When Congress imposes a duty, it may say nothing about sanctions or remedies in the event of violation; it may provide criminal sanctions but be silent as to the availability of civil remedies; or it may specify particular administrative or judicial remedies and say nothing about others. In each of these instances, the federal courts may be asked to determine (a)

whether, and to what extent, *state* remedies are available to redress violations, and (b) whether, and to what extent, the courts should recognize a *federal* remedy not expressly authorized by the governing statute.

The Borak and Texas Industries cases represent very different approaches to these questions. To some degree, the cases differ because they dealt with different problems. But they also reflect a dramatic change in the Court's thinking about the nature of its role in the implication of remedies. This Note seeks to explore and to criticize the content and direction of that change.

(2) Allowing a private plaintiff to sue for a violation of a federal statute always adds force to the deterrent effect of a statutory prohibition. Since Congress must have meant the prohibition to be taken seriously, does it follow that recognition of a private remedy not explicitly provided by statute should always be deemed consistent with, and in furtherance of, the statutory purpose?

Note the difficulties with this argument. First, it assumes that a statutory prohibition is motivated by a simple one-dimensional purpose to deter or require certain kinds of conduct. In fact, a statute is often the product of a pitched battle between competing interest groups, and one outcome of that battle may well have been a tacit understanding that the available remedies would be limited—that full compliance was neither desired nor desirable.[1]

Second, even when full compliance with the prohibition is the statutory goal, private enforcement through the courts may create serious problems of overinclusion or excessive deterrence—may discourage socially productive conduct outside the scope of the prohibition. For this reason, Congress may have created an administrative scheme to coordinate enforcement and sharpen the boundaries of proscribed conduct. Recognition of a private remedy in such an instance—especially one that does more than compensate an individual for the particular harm done to him—may be counterproductive.[2]

Third, judicial recognition of a private remedy not authorized by Congress may raise institutional questions about the role of the courts. Should Congress, having spoken on a subject, be presumed to have spoken on it completely? Would recognition of a private remedy require the working out of many difficult questions that would unduly tax the ingenuity and capacity of the federal courts? Would recognition of a private remedy, carrying in its wake an expansion of the number and kinds of

1. See Posner, The Federal Courts: Crisis and Reform 270–72 (1985); Easterbrook, *Foreword: The Court and the Economic System*, 98 Harv.L.Rev. 4, 45–51 (1984).

2. For a fuller development of this and related ideas, see Stewart and Sunstein, *Public Programs and Private Rights*, 95 Harv.L.Rev. 1193 (1982). The authors consider the private right of action as one of several available forms of private initiative in the operation of various regulatory programs. They suggest that such a private remedy is of greatest worth in a program emphasizing "entitlement values"—for example, the value of being treated with respect and without invidious discrimination—and is considerably more problematic when a program is designed primarily to increase productive efficiency. In the latter instance, however, they note that the likelihood of overdeterrence is significantly less when the remedy is limited to damages for the injuries suffered than it is when the remedy extends to a broad injunction, or to damages not directly tied to actual harm.

For other valuable studies see Frankel, *Implied Rights of Action*, 67 Va.L.Rev. 553 (1981); Dooley, *The Effects of Civil Liability on Investment Banking and the New Issues Market*, 58 Va.L.Rev. 776 (1972).

cases that could be filed in federal court, constitute an unwarranted expansion of federal jurisdiction?

Even if private remedies are thought desirable, an important issue of federalism remains: Is a *federal* remedy, enforceable in a federal court, necessary or appropriate? If state remedies may be sought, are they adequate to the task?

Consider the discussion in the following paragraphs in the light of these questions.

(3) One of the earliest issues to arise was the availability of a private damage remedy for employees injured as a result of violations of the Federal Safety Appliance Act. The wavering course of decisions on this issue led to the apparent conclusion that no such remedy was created by federal law, although violations were in this instance redressable as a matter of state law.[3]

Before 1964, implied federal remedies were recognized in limited statutory contexts, primarily those relating to regulation of railroad labor relations. See, *e.g.*, Texas & N.O.R. Co. v. Brotherhood of Railway & S.S. Clerks, 281 U.S. 548 (1930); Steele v. Louisville & N.R. Co., 323 U.S. 192 (1944); *cf.* International Ass'n of Machinists, AFL–CIO v. Central Airlines, Inc., 372 U.S. 682 (1963).[4] Then in 1964, the Borak case was decided; Borak was in turn relied on in both the majority and concurring opinions in Bivens, and its broad rationale—emphasizing the value of private enforcement as a "necessary supplement" to [SEC] action—was followed by a number of similar Supreme Court and lower court holdings in other statutory settings.[5]

(4) A decade after Borak the Court in a trio of cases rebuffed attempts to extend the Borak principle. See National R.R. Passenger Corp. v. National Ass'n of R.R. Passengers (the Amtrak case), 414 U.S. 453 (1974) (Amtrak Act provides exclusive remedies for breaches of obligations created by Act, and no additional private actions to enforce compliance may be inferred); Securities Investor Protection Corp. v. Barbour, 421 U.S. 412 (1975) (customers of broker-dealers do not have implied right of action under Securities Investor Protection Act to compel Securities Investor Protection Corp. to exercise its statutory authority for their benefit); Cort v. Ash, 422 U.S. 66 (1975) (no private cause of action for damages may be inferred from Federal Election Campaign Act). Cort v. Ash was doctrinally significant in particular because the Court in its opinion attempted to

---

3. The problem arose with respect to employees covered by the FSAA but not so directly involved in interstate commerce as to be covered by the Federal Employers Liability Act. See Minneapolis, St. P., & S. St. M. Ry. Co. v. Popplar, 237 U.S. 369 (1915); Texas & P. Ry. Co. v. Rigsby, 241 U.S. 33 (1916); Moore v. Chesapeake & O. Ry. Co., 291 U.S. 205 (1934); Jacobson v. New York, N.H. & H.R. Co., 206 F.2d 153 (1st Cir.1953), *affirmed per curiam*, 347 U.S. 909 (1954).

4. The Court during this period also upheld the implication of a civil remedy in favor of the federal government in United States v. Republic Steel Corp., 362 U.S. 482 (1960). See also Wyandotte Transp. Co. v.

United States, 389 U.S. 191 (1967). Private remedies were denied in Wheeldin v. Wheeler, 373 U.S. 647 (1963), and T.I.M.E. Inc. v. United States, 359 U.S. 464 (1959) (holding that the federal statute involved in that case (the Motor Carrier Act) did not contemplate either an implied right of action or retention of a common-law right to recover).

5. See, *e.g.*, Allen v. State Bd. of Elections, 393 U.S. 544 (1969) (allowing private litigants to sue to enforce the preclearance provisions of § 5 of the Voting Rights Act of 1965); Superintendent of Ins. v. Bankers Life & Cas. Co., 404 U.S. 6, 13 n. 9 (1971) (upholding availability of private actions for violation of SEC Rule 10b–5).

harmonize and rationalize the law in this entire area by formulating a four-part test for determining whether private remedies were available for violations of statutes not expressly providing them.[6]

In several post–1975 cases the Court, applying the four criteria of Cort v. Ash, held that no private rights of action were to be inferred from various federal statutes; none of the cases created new doctrinal formulations.[7] A doctrinal shift was apparent, however, in Cannon v. University of Chicago, 441 U.S. 677 (1979), holding that a private right of action was to be inferred from § 901(a) of Title IX of the Education Amendments of 1972, 20 U.S.C. § 1681 (providing that: "No person * * * shall, on the basis of sex, be excluded from participation in, be denied the benefits of, or be subjected to discrimination under any education program or activity receiving Federal financial assistance * * * "). The Cort v. Ash criteria were again used as the governing standard, but the Court clearly regarded all of them as subsidiary to—and, basically, relevant as guidelines to—discovering legislative "intent". Thus the Court described the case as turning on a "question of statutory construction," and said that "before concluding that Congress intended to make a remedy available to a special class of litigants, a court must carefully analyze the four factors that Cort identifies as indicative of such an intent" (p. 688). The Court's conclusion that plaintiff (who alleged that she had been denied admission to medical school on account of her sex) had a cause of action was in turn based primarily on two findings: (a) the statutory language, which expressly identified a class of persons to be protected (rather than merely barring discriminatory behavior), reflected a legislative intent to benefit members of that particular class; and (b) the legislative history specifically indicated that Congress intended the statute to create private causes of action.

The view that no private right of action can be inferred unless it is shown that the legislature "intended" it to exist was expressed even more clearly in Justice Rehnquist's concurrence (joined by Justice Stewart), which concluded with an unusual "warning" to Congress:

"I fully agree with the Court's statement that '[w]hen Congress intends private litigants to have a cause of action to support their statutory rights, the far better course is for it to specify as much when it creates those rights.' * * * It seems to me that the factors to which I have here briefly adverted apprise the lawmaking branch of the Federal Government that the ball, so to speak, may well now be in its court. * * * [T]his Court in

6. The Court stated the test as follows (422 U.S. at 78):

"First, is the plaintiff 'one of the class for whose *especial* benefit the statute was enacted,' Texas & Pacific R. Co. v. Rigsby, 241 U.S. 33, 39 (1916) (emphasis supplied)—that is, does the statute create a federal right in favor of the plaintiff? Second, is there any indication of legislative intent, explicit or implicit, either to create such a remedy or to deny one? See, *e.g.*, National Railroad Passenger Corp. v. National Assn. of Railroad Passengers, 414 U.S. 453, 458, 460 (1974) (Amtrak). Third, is it consistent with the underlying purposes of the legislative scheme to imply such a remedy for the plaintiff? See, *e.g.*, Amtrak, *supra*; Securities Investor Protec-

tion Corp. v. Barbour, 421 U.S. 412, 423 (1975). And finally, is the cause of action one traditionally relegated to state law, in an area basically the concern of the States, so that it would be inappropriate to infer a cause of action based solely on federal law? See Wheeldin v. Wheeler, 373 U.S. 647, 652 (1963); *cf.* J.I. Case Co. v. Borak, 377 U.S. 426, 434 (1964); Bivens v. Six Unknown Federal Narcotics Agents, 403 U.S. 388, 394–395 (1971); *id.*, at 400 (Harlan, J., concurring in judgment)."

7. See, *e.g.*, Piper v. Chris–Craft Indus., Inc., 430 U.S. 1 (1977) (Section 14(e) of the Securities Exchange Act); Santa Clara Pueblo v. Martinez, 436 U.S. 49 (1978) (Indian Civil Rights Act of 1968).

the future should be extremely reluctant to imply a cause of action absent such specificity on the part of the Legislative Branch" (p. 718).

Justice Powell, in an elaborate dissent clearly intended to break new paths and stimulate reconsideration of the entire area, stated that the "mode of analysis we have applied in the recent past cannot be squared with the doctrine of separation of powers. * * * In recent history the Court has tended to stray from the Art. III and separation-of-powers principle of limited jurisdiction. This, I believe, is evident from a review of the more or less haphazard line of cases that led to our decision in Cort v. Ash * * *. The 'four factor' analysis of that case is an open invitation to federal courts to legislative causes of action not authorized by Congress. It is an analysis not faithful to constitutional principles and should be rejected. Absent the most compelling evidence of affirmative congressional intent, a federal court should not infer a private cause of action" (pp. 730–31). A detailed review of the cases led Justice Powell to the conclusion that, until Cort v. Ash, the inferring of a private cause of action was a highly exceptional occurrence. Quoting the celebrated words of Erie about the "unconstitutionality of the course pursued" (p. 742), he concluded that the need to "restrain courts" and to "encourage Congress to confront its obligation to resolve crucial policy questions created by the legislation it enacts" calls for a fresh start and a refusal to infer private rights of action absent compelling evidence of congressional intent (p. 749).

(5) In the period since Cannon, the Court has continued to reject claims of implied federal remedies, relying primarily on its construction of legislative intent.[8] In Merrill Lynch, Pierce, Fenner & Smith, Inc. v. Curran, 456 U.S. 353, 381 (1982)—one of the few instances in which an implied remedy was found—the Court by a 5–4 vote inferred a private cause of action under the Commodity Exchange Act primarily on the

---

8. In addition to the Texas Industries case, and Northwest Airlines, Inc. v. Transport Workers Union, 451 U.S. 77 (1981), discussed in Texas Industries, see, *e.g.,* California v. Sierra Club, 451 U.S. 287 (1981) (Section 10 of Rivers and Harbors Appropriation Act of 1899); Universities Research Ass'n, Inc. v. Coutu, 450 U.S. 754 (1981) (Davis–Bacon Act); Touche Ross & Co. v. Redington, 442 U.S. 560 (1979) (Section 17(a) of Securities Act of 1934); Thompson v. Thompson, 108 S.Ct. 513 (1988) (Parental Kidnaping Prevention Act); *cf.* Transamerica Mortgage Advisors, Inc. (Tama) v. Lewis, 444 U.S. 11 (1979) (Section 215 of the Investment Advisors Act of 1940, which renders "void" any contract made in violation of the Act, implies a private remedy for rescission and restitution with respect to a contract coming within its terms, but no private cause of action for damages is available for violation of § 206, which makes it unlawful for an investment adviser to "employ any device, scheme, or artifice to defraud").

The Court's opinion in the Touche Ross case, *supra,* is representative of its willingness to follow through on Justice Rehnquist's warning in Cannon. "Here," said,

the Court in Touche Ross (now speaking through Justice Rehnquist), "the statute by its terms grants no private rights to any identifiable class and proscribes no conduct as unlawful. And * * * the legislative history of the 1934 Act simply does not speak to the issue of private remedies under § 17(a). At least in such a case as this, the inquiry ends there * * *" (442 U.S. at 576).

Justice Scalia, in his concurring opinion in Thompson v. Thompson, *supra,* spelled out his view of the significance of legislative intent in some detail. In Part I (where he was joined by Justice O'Connor), he argued that Touche Ross had "effectively overruled the Cort v. Ash analysis," and he then criticized the majority for examining "the 'context' of the [Parental Kidnaping Prevention Act] for indication of an intent to create a private right of action, after having found no such indication in either text or legislative history" (108 S.Ct. at 521). In Part II, speaking for himself alone, he urged the adoption of "a flat rule that private rights of action will not be implied in statutes hereafter enacted" (p. 523).

theory that such a remedy was part of the "contemporary legal context" that was preserved when Congress undertook a comprehensive revision of the Act in 1974. The case thus resembled Cannon in its grudging recognition that certain statutes were enacted during a period when the legislature's expectations with respect to implied remedies were influenced by the Borak line of decisions.

The Court during this period also resisted efforts to rely on 42 U.S.C. § 1983 as a means of bypassing its restrictive approach when the plaintiffs were challenging action under color of state law. In Middlesex County Sewerage Auth. v. National Sea Clammers Ass'n, 453 U.S. 1 (1981), plaintiffs sought relief against state and federal officials under the Federal Water Pollution Control Act and related statutes. The Court held that the remedies prescribed in those statutes were exclusive, and since the plaintiffs had failed to comply with the statutory notice provisions, they could not sue. Moreover, "Congress [not only] intended to foreclose implied private actions but also * * * intended to supplant any remedy that could otherwise be available under § 1983" (p. 21). See also Pennhurst State School and Hosp. v. Halderman, 451 U.S. 1, 28 (1981).

(6) The Court in its recent decisions has insisted that the question whether a private plaintiff injured by a statutory violation may sue for damages or other relief should be regarded as essentially a pure (or conventional) question of statutory interpretation viewed in terms of "legislative intent". Doesn't that insistence—especially if it relies heavily on the absence of textual warrant for an implied remedy—create a danger that effectuation of congressional purpose, more broadly and sympathetically viewed, will be thwarted?

Justice Powell is correct, isn't he, that the fundamental issue is whether, and to what extent, a federal court may exercise powers akin to those of a common-law court in adjusting a particular statute to the general remedial framework and in developing the "equity" of a statute to serve its purposes and those of the surrounding legal regime? Do you find his answer to this question satisfactory? (Review, in this connection, the words of Justice Jackson in the D'Oench, Duhme case, pp. 858–60, supra.) In particular, why is it appropriate for the federal courts to exercise "principled discretion" in creating a remedial framework for constitutional violations and wholly inappropriate for them to do so in connection with statutory violations?

Note that a broader inquiry into legislative purpose might itself lead to a rejection of any private remedy, especially when Congress has established a comprehensive scheme for administration of a regulatory program. Thus while Stewart and Sunstein, note 2, supra, are quite critical of the Court's tendency to engage in simplistic analysis of statutory text and legislative intent, they regard the Court's retrenchment since 1974 as, in the main, consistent with their view of the values and policies at stake.

(7) In one significant instance, Congress has responded critically to the Court's new approach to the implication of remedies. The House Committee Report on the Small Business Investment Incentive Act of 1980, Pub.L. No. 96–477, 94 Stat. 2294, states:

"The rationale for implying private rights of action under the securities laws * * * had been well articulated by the Supreme Court when it observed that implied private rights of action * * * would significantly assist the congressional goal of promoting fair corporate suffrage. But in recent years, the Supreme Court turned its focus toward a strict construction of statutory language and expressed intent.

"The Committee wishes to make plain that it expects the courts to imply private rights of action under this legislation, where the plaintiff falls within the class of persons protected by the statutory provision in question [—where] [s]uch a right would be consistent with and further Congress' intent in enacting that provision, and where such actions would not improperly occupy an area traditionally the concern of state law." H.R.Rep. No. 1341, 96th Congress, 2d Sess. 28–29 (1980).

What bearing should this history have on the construction of the statute? On the construction of other securities laws? On the construction of federal legislation in other spheres? See Ashford, *Implied Causes of Action Under Federal Laws: Calling the Court Back to Borak*, 79 Nw.U.L. Rev. 227, 313–41 (1984) (arguing that the House Report's reformulation of the test of Cort v. Ash (note 6, *supra*) should lead to adoption of that test in connection with all federal legislation).

(8) The Court in Texas Industries took a restrictive view not only of the proper approach to statutory construction, but also of the power of the federal courts to declare the governing law. On this latter question— which is the principal focus of this chapter—was the Court in Texas Industries implying that since Congress had not dealt with the issue of contribution in antitrust cases, the matter must be governed by *state* law? Surely the Court did not intend that result; indeed a reference of the contribution question to the laws of the fifty states would cause difficulties in the determination of which state's law to apply in a multi-state controversy, as well as in the selection of an appropriate state rule to govern in a case within exclusive federal jurisdiction. Moreover, application of differing contribution rules on identical facts, depending on the locus of the forum or of the place where the events occurred, might interfere with effective enforcement of antitrust goals.

Once it is clear that state law is displaced (as it plainly was in Texas Industries), then the Court's emphasis on a lack of "power" to deal effectively with the merits of the contribution question is especially puzzling. If state law is preempted, should the federal courts regard themselves as less capable of filling the void—of formulating a rule which will best advance the regulatory goal—than would a state court in similar circumstances? Is there any particular aspect of the judicial-legislative balance at the federal level that explains why only Congress can address this issue? The question is similar to that raised in connection with United States v. Standard Oil, p. 868, *supra,* and much the same criticism can be leveled at the Court's refusal to accept responsibility for the development of a coherent system of rights and remedies.

Of course, recognition of such responsibility does not mandate the adoption of a contribution scheme. Nor does it exclude the possibility that institutional considerations may persuade the Court that the legislative scheme is complete or that the contribution thicket is too hazardous to enter without more legislative guidance.[9] Note that while such institution-

9. In Northwest Airlines, Inc. v. Transport Workers Union, 451 U.S. 77 (1981), such institutional considerations did lead the Court not to recognize a right of contribution in an employment discrimination case. Given the comprehensive statutory

al considerations were discussed by the Court in Texas Industries, its concentration on the question of power seemed to blind it to the fact that its decision was not neutral—that the result was effectively to *deny* the existence of a right of contribution.

HOLMBERG v. ARMBRECHT

327 U.S. 392, 66 S.Ct. 582, 90 L.Ed. 743 (1946).
Certiorari to the Circuit Court of Appeals for the Second Circuit.

MR. JUSTICE FRANKFURTER delivered the opinion of the Court.

This is a suit in equity by petitioners on behalf of themselves and all other creditors of the Southern Minnesota Joint Stock Land Bank of Minneapolis to enforce the liability imposed upon shareholders of the Bank by § 16 of the Federal Farm Loan Act, equal to one hundred per cent of their holdings. 12 U.S.C. § 812. The Bank closed its doors in May, 1932. Its debts exceeded its assets by more than $3,000,000, the amount of its outstanding stock. Suit was accordingly brought in the United States District Court for the District of Minnesota for determining and collecting the assessment due under § 16. Holmberg v. Southern Minnesota Joint Stock Land Bank of Minnesota, D.C., 10 F.Supp. 795. Armbrecht, a New York stockholder, was sued there. The suit failed on procedural grounds and was dismissed without prejudice to further action. Holmberg v. Anchell, D.C., 24 F.Supp. 594, 598. Not until 1942, so it is alleged, did petitioners learn that Jules S. Bache had concealed his ownership of one hundred shares of the Bank stock under the name of Charles Armbrecht. The present action against Armbrecht and Bache was begun in the Southern District of New York in November, 1943. Bache died during pendency of the suit and his executors were substituted as parties.

The respondents made two defenses: (1) They invoked a New York statute of limitation barring such an action after ten years, New York Civil Practice Act, § 53; (2) they urged laches, claiming that petitioners had unduly delayed commencement of the suit. Neither defense was sustained in the District Court, and judgment went against the respondents. The judgment was reversed by the Circuit Court of Appeals. 2 Cir., 150 F.2d 829. That court did not reach the defense of laches because it held, relying on Guaranty Trust Co. v. York, 326 U.S. 99, that the New York statute of limitation was controlling and that the mere lapse of ten years barred the action. Since the case raises a question of considerable importance in enforcing liability under federal equitable enactments, we brought it here for review.

In Guaranty Trust Co. v. York, *supra*, we ruled that when a State statute bars recovery of a suit in a State court on a State-created right, it likewise bars recovery of such a suit on the equity side of a federal court brought there merely because it was "between citizens of different States" under Art. III, § 2 of the Constitution. The amenability of such a federal suit to a State statute of limitation cannot be regarded as a problem in terminology, whereby the practical effect of a statute of limitation would turn on the content which abstract analysis may attribute to "substance"

scheme of remedies, the Court said, the "judiciary may not • • • fashion new remedies that might upset carefully considered legislative programs" (p. 97).

and "procedure." We held, on the contrary, that a statute of limitation is a significant part of the legal rules which determine the outcome of a litigation. As such, it is as significant in enforcing a State-created right by an exclusively equitable remedy as it is in an action at law. But in the York case we pointed out with almost wearisome reiteration, in reaching this result, that we were there concerned solely with State-created rights. For purposes of diversity suits a Federal court is, in effect, "only another court of the State." Guaranty Trust Co. v. York, *supra,* 326 U.S. at page 108. The considerations that urge adjudication by the same law in all courts within a State when enforcing a right created by that State are hardly relevant for determining the rules which bar enforcement of an equitable right created not by a State legislature but by Congress.

If Congress explicitly puts a limit upon the time for enforcing a right which it created, there is an end of the matter. The Congressional statute of limitation is definitive. See, *e.g.,* Herget v. Central Nat. Bank & Trust Co., 324 U.S. 4. The rub comes when Congress is silent. Apart from penal enactments, Congress has usually left the limitation of time for commencing actions under national legislation to judicial implications. As to actions at law, the silence of Congress has been interpreted to mean that it is federal policy to adopt the local law of limitation. See Campbell v. City of Haverhill, 155 U.S. 610; Chattanooga Foundry & Pipe Works v. City of Atlanta, 203 U.S. 390; Rawlings v. Ray, 312 U.S. 96. The implied absorption of State statutes of limitation within the interstices of the federal enactments is a phase of fashioning remedial details where Congress has not spoken but left matters for judicial determination within the general framework of familiar legal principles. See Board of Cm'rs of the County of Jackson, Kansas, v. United States, 308 U.S. 343, 349, 350, 351, 352.

The present case concerns not only a federally-created right but a federal right for which the sole remedy is in equity. Wheeler v. Greene, 280 U.S. 49; Christopher v. Brusselback, 302 U.S. 500; Russell v. Todd, 309 U.S. 280, 285. And so we have the reverse of the situation in Guaranty Trust Co. v. York, *supra.* We do not have the duty of a federal court, sitting as it were as a court of a State, to approximate as closely as may be State law in order to vindicate without discrimination a right derived solely from a State. We have the duty of federal courts, sitting as national courts throughout the country, to apply their own principles in enforcing an equitable right created by Congress. When Congress leaves to the federal courts the formulation of remedial details, it can hardly expect them to break with historic principles of equity in the enforcement of federally-created equitable rights.

Traditionally and for good reasons, statutes of limitation are not controlling measures of equitable relief. Such statutes have been drawn upon by equity solely for the light they may shed in determining that which is decisive for the chancellor's intervention, namely, whether the plaintiff has inexcusably slept on his rights so as to make a decree against the defendant unfair. See Russell v. Todd, *supra,* 309 U.S. at page 289. "There must be conscience, good faith, and reasonable diligence, to call into action the powers of the court." McKnight v. Taylor, 1 How. 161, 168. A federal court may not be bound by a State statute of limitation and yet that court may dismiss a suit where the plaintiffs' "lack of diligence is wholly unexcused; and both the nature of the claim and the situation of the parties was such as to call for diligence." Benedict v. City of New York,

250 U.S. 321, 328. A suit in equity may fail though "not barred by the act of limitations." McKnight v. Taylor, *supra;* Alsop v. Riker, 155 U.S. 448.

Equity eschews mechanical rules; it depends on flexibility. Equity has acted on the principle that "laches is not, like limitation, a mere matter of time; but principally a question of the inequity of permitting the claim to be enforced,—an inequity founded upon some change in the condition or relations of the property or the parties." Galliher v. Cadwell, 145 U.S. 368, 373; see Southern Pacific Co. v. Bogert, 250 U.S. 483, 488, 489. And so, a suit in equity may lie though a comparable cause of action at law would be barred. If want of due diligence by the plaintiff may make it unfair to pursue the defendant, fraudulent conduct on the part of the defendant may have prevented the plaintiff from being diligent and may make it unfair to bar appeal to equity because of mere lapse of time.

Equity will not lend itself to such fraud and historically has relieved from it. It bars a defendant from setting up such a fraudulent defense, as it interposes against other forms of fraud. And so this Court long ago adopted as its own the old chancery rule that where a plaintiff has been injured by fraud and "remains in ignorance of it without any fault or want of diligence or care on his part, the bar of the statute does not begin to run until the fraud is discovered, though there be no special circumstances or efforts on the part of the party committing the fraud to conceal it from the knowledge of the other party." Bailey v. Glover, 21 Wall. 342, 348.

This equitable doctrine is read into every federal statute of limitation. If the Federal Farm Loan Act had an explicit statute of limitation for bringing suit under § 16, the time would not have begun to run until after petitioners had discovered, or had failed in reasonable diligence to discover, the alleged deception by Bache which is the basis of this suit. Bailey v. Glover, *supra.* It would be too incongruous to confine a federal right within the bare terms of a State statute of limitation unrelieved by the settled federal equitable doctrine as to fraud, when even a federal statute in the same terms would be given the mitigating construction required by that doctrine.

We conclude that the decision in the York case is inapplicable to the enforcement of federal equitable rights. The federal doctrine applied in Bailey v. Glover, *supra,* and in the series of cases following it, governs. When the liability, if any, accrued in this case, and whether the petitioners are chargeable with laches, are questions as to which we imply no views. We leave them for determination by the Circuit Court of Appeals to which the case is remanded.

Reversed and remanded.

MR. JUSTICE JACKSON took no part in the consideration or decision of this case.

MR. JUSTICE RUTLEDGE, concurring.

I agree with the result and with the opinion, reserving however any intimation, explicit or implied, as to the full scope to which the doctrine of Guaranty Trust Co. v. York, 326 U.S. 99, may be applied in diversity cases. Many of the considerations now stated by the Court for refusing to extend that doctrine to cases concerning federally created rights, relating to the flexibility of remedies in equity either to cut down or to extend the state statutory period of limitations, seemed to me to be applicable whenever a federal court might be asked to extend the aid of its equity arm, whether in its diversity jurisdiction or other. The ruling in the York case however may be accepted generally for diversity cases and, moreover, rejected for extension to cases of this sort, without indicating that there may not be some cases even of diversity jurisdiction to which federal courts may not be required to apply it. With this reservation I join in the Court's action.

NOTE ON STATE STATUTES OF LIMITATIONS AND OTHER QUASI-PROCEDURAL RULES IN LITIGATION INVOLVING FEDERAL MATTERS

(1) Congress has never seen fit to enact a general statute of limitations applicable to all federal civil causes of action not governed by a specific federal limitations period. Moreover, it has frequently neglected to provide a limitations period when creating a particular cause of action. (And sometimes, the courts have inferred the existence of a federal right of action when the question was not directly addressed by those who drafted the relevant legislation.)

As the Holmberg opinion indicates, the custom in such cases has been to "adopt" a state limitations period. But adoptions of this kind raise a welter of hard questions. Are there times when the federal concerns are so special that a federal time limitation must be found somewhere in order to assure uniformity of administration and to avoid dependence on inapt state provisions? When state law is adopted, how is the applicable state selected, and which of that state's limitations periods shall be applied? Must the state period be accepted even if it seems unduly short, or long? And is the federal court to be bound by all of the state's judicial gloss on its own limitations law?

These issues pose in a particular context the more general questions raised earlier (p. 862, *supra*) about the process of applying state law for purposes of enforcing federal rights.

(2) In Johnson v. Railway Express Agency, Inc., 421 U.S. 454 (1975), the Court once again confronted the question whether there was a federal interest sufficient to suspend the running of a state limitations period. Johnson had filed a charge of employment discrimination with the federal Equal Employment Opportunity Commission, and several years later, the Commission told him that there was reasonable cause to believe his charges and that he had thirty days to bring an action under Title VII of the 1964 Civil Rights Act. He did so, and joined with it a claim under 42 U.S.C. § 1981,[1] but the federal district court dismissed the latter claim as barred by the applicable one year state statute of limitations. The Supreme Court agreed, holding that the filing of a Title VII charge with the EEOC did not suspend the running of the statute on the separate § 1981 claim. The Court noted that no basis for suspension could be found in state law; it

1. This section, originally part of the Civil Rights Act of 1866, provides, *inter alia*, that all persons within the jurisdiction of the United States "shall have the same right • • • to make and enforce contracts • • • and to the full and equal benefits of all laws and proceedings for the security of persons and property as is en-joyed by white citizens • • •." Before addressing the problem discussed in text, the Court held that Title VII does not supersede or preempt a claim under § 1981 and that an action under that section does not have to await the outcome of a Title VII administrative proceeding.

then conceded that the result might press a civil rights complainant who valued his § 1981 claim to take it to court before the EEOC had completed its work under Title VII but concluded that this was the product of Congress's decision to retain that section as a remedy "separate from and independent of the more elaborate and time-consuming procedures of Title VII. * * * [In] a very real sense, petitioner has slept on his § 1981 rights" (p. 466).

Justice Marshall dissented, joined by Justices Douglas and Brennan. For them, suspending the running of the statute under these circumstances would not have frustrated any of the state's purposes in enacting the statute and would have protected "the federal interest in preserving multiple remedies for employment discrimination" (p. 474). Refusal to suspend, they concluded, imposed on a complainant "the draconian choice of losing the benefits of [EEOC] conciliation or giving up the right to sue" (p. 476).

Johnson v. Railway Express Agency was followed by Board of Regents v. Tomanio, 446 U.S. 478 (1980). The Court in Tomanio, relying both on Johnson and on 42 U.S.C. § 1988, held that in a New York federal court action under 42 U.S.C. § 1983 alleging violations of federal constitutional rights, the court must adopt New York's statute of limitations and must also apply that state's tolling rule, which would not suspend the running of the statute during the pendency of a prior state court proceeding involving the same occurrences as those in suit.[2] The Court found no inconsistency between the state rule and federal policy.

Although the dissent in Johnson cited and relied upon Holmberg, that case was not even mentioned by the majority in Johnson or in Tomanio. Nor was there any discussion in either case of the legal or equitable character of the plaintiff's complaint. Is Holmberg, then, still good law? Or has it been replaced by a strong presumption that in all cases in which a state statute of limitations is adopted, the state's interpretation of its statute will govern unless there is some clear and specific inconsistency with federal statutory policy?[3]

2. Section 1988 provides, in part, that in certain civil rights actions where the laws of the United States are not "adapted to the object, or are deficient in the provisions necessary to furnish suitable remedies * * *, the common law, as modified and changed by the constitution and statutes of the [forum] state * * *, so far as not inconsistent with [federal law] * * *, shall be extended to and govern the said [federal] courts in the trial and disposition of the cause." The Court in Tomanio held that since § 1988 is itself "deficient" in not including a federal statute of limitations, that section requires resort to the state law of limitations unless it is inconsistent with federal law. The Court's method of analysis under § 1988 did not diverge significantly, however, from its approach in a case like Johnson, where the matter was deemed to be a problem for judge-made law.

In an important article on § 1988, Professor Eisenberg argues that it has been widely misunderstood by the courts and that, properly viewed, it is relevant only to state-created causes of action removed from state to federal court under the civil rights removal provision (28 U.S.C. § 1443). Eisenberg, *State Law in Federal Civil Rights Cases: The Proper Scope of Section 1988*, 128 U.Pa.L.Rev. 499 (1980). For another provocative interpretation, see Kreimer, *The Source of Law in Civil Rights Actions: Some Old Light on Section 1988*, 133 U.Pa.L.Rev. 601 (1985) (arguing *inter alia* that § 1988 expressly provides for development of *federal* common law except where modified by state enactments not inconsistent with federal legislation).

3. Note that the Holmberg doctrine was always limited in its scope and application. Thus in Russell v. Todd, 309 U.S. 280, 287–89 (1940), the opinion indicates that in the absence of special circumstances such as fraud, a federal court acting in equity has usually permitted its conscience to be controlled quite exactly by the state statutory

(3) When Congress has not specified a limitations period, an argument frequently made against the application of state law is the injustice and complexity of subjecting plaintiffs in different states to different statutory provisions and interpretations. This argument has generally been rejected, as it was in UAW v. Hoosier Cardinal Corp. 383 U.S. 696 (1966). In that case—a suit for violation of a collective bargaining agreement under § 301 of the Taft–Hartley Act—the majority recognized the difficulty of applying state law but held that course preferable to "the drastic sort of judicial legislation that is urged upon us" (p. 703).

In several cases, however, the Court has refused to apply a state limitations period. In McAllister v. Magnolia Petroleum Co., 357 U.S. 221 (1958), McAllister brought a state court action for negligence under the Jones Act and for unseaworthiness, and the state supreme court held the unseaworthiness claim barred by the Texas two-year statute for personal injury cases. The Supreme Court reversed, holding that "where an action of unseaworthiness is combined with an action under the Jones Act a [state or federal] court cannot apply to the former a shorter period of limitations than Congress has prescribed for the latter. * * * Since the seaman must sue for both unseaworthiness and Jones Act negligence in order to make full utilization of his remedies for personal injury, and since that can be accomplished only in a single proceeding, a time limitation on the unseaworthiness claim effects in substance a similar limitation on the right of action under the Jones Act" (pp. 224–25).

A more recent decision adopting a uniform federal limitations period is DelCostello v. International Brotherhood of Teamsters, 462 U.S. 151 (1983). In DelCostello, the Court held that the six-month limitations period in the National Labor Relations Act for filing unfair labor practice charges applied to an employee's action against his employer for breach of the collective bargaining agreement and against his union for breach of the duty of fair representation. Such an action, the Court reasoned, had no close analogy in state law, and the analogies that had been suggested raised problems of "legal substance" and "practical application" (p. 165).

Justice Stevens, in dissent, relied heavily on the reference to state law in the Rules of Decision Act, 28 U.S.C. § 1652. But the majority, in a lengthy footnote (pp. 159–61 n. 13) said that since "the choice of a limitations period for a federal cause of action is itself a question of federal law[,] * * * the Rules of Decision Act is inapplicable by its own terms. * * * [A]s Holmberg recognizes, neither Erie nor the Rules of Decision Act can now be taken as establishing a *mandatory* rule that we apply state law in federal interstices."

Justice O'Connor, dissenting separately, noted that she "agree[d] with the Court that the Rules of Decision Act * * * only puts the question, for it simply requires application of state law unless federal law applies.

period. Moreover, it has never been clear whether the Holmberg doctrine applied with respect to fraudulent concealment in an action at law to enforce a federal right, though Moviecolor Ltd. v. Eastman Kodak Co., 288 F.2d 80 (2d Cir.1961) (cited by Justice Marshall in his dissent in Johnson) held that it did.

For an argument that the Holmberg doctrine should continue to apply on the issue

of fraudulent concealment in actions based on federal law, see Marcus, *Fraudulent Concealment in Federal Court: Toward a More Disparate Standard?*, 71 Geo.L.J. 829 (1983).

What if state law provides that the statute of limitations continues to run until actual service of process, and is not tolled by filing of the complaint? See West v. Conrail, 107 S.Ct. 1538 (1987), p. 828, *supra.*

* * * My disagreement with the Court arises because I do not think that federal law implicitly rejects the practice of borrowing state periods of limitation in this situation" (pp. 174–75 n. 1).[4]

(4) The rationale of DelCostello was extended, over the strong objection of Justice Scalia, in Agency Holding Corp. v. Malley–Duff & Associates, Inc., 107 S.Ct. 2759 (1987). This case involved a civil suit under the Racketeer Influenced and Corrupt Organizations Act (RICO), an Act that contains no express statute of limitations for the bringing of private actions. The Court decided that "[t]he federal policies at stake and the practicalities of litigation" supported the conclusion that the four-year limitations period of the Clayton Anti–Trust Act was "a significantly more appropriate statute of limitations than any state limitations period" (p. 2765). Among the "practicalities" cited were: "RICO cases commonly involve interstate transactions"; "the use of state statutes would present the danger of forum shopping"; and application of a uniform federal period would avoid the possibility of application of "unduly short state statutes" (p. 2766).

Justice Scalia, in an opinion concurring in the judgment, argued that the early federal decisions in this area reflected the view that state limitations statutes applied of their own force unless preempted by federal law; the later treatment of congressional silence as an affirmative directive to "borrow" state law was, in his view, an analytical error. This error, he urged, was now compounded by the Court's willingness, without any showing of congressional intent, to depart from the practice of borrowing state statutes and to "prowl[ ] hungrily through the Statutes at Large for an appetizing federal limitations period" (p. 2772). He concluded that "if [as in the case at hand] we determine that the state limitations period that would apply under state law is pre-empted because it is inconsistent with the federal statute, that is the end of the matter, and there is no limitation on the federal cause of action" (p. 2771). Cf. Occidental Life Ins. Co. v. EEOC, note 4, supra.

Is the decision in the Agency Holding case a natural outgrowth of prior decisions, or does it reflect a new willingness to treat congressional failure to write in a limitations period as a blank check to the federal courts to find the most suitable period in any available source?

(5) When the federal courts do decide to borrow a state limitations period, they have frequently been troubled by the question of which statute to select. In Hoosier Cardinal Corp., Paragraph (3), supra, the Court decided that (a) Indiana would apply its six-year statute governing contracts not in writing, and (b) this choice was acceptable as a matter of federal law. "[T]here is no reason to reject the characterization that state

4. See also Occidental Life Ins. Co. v. EEOC, 432 U.S. 355 (1977) (EEOC enforcement actions under Title VII are not subject to state limitations periods; courts have discretion to deny retrospective relief if there is inordinate delay in filing an action); Oscar Mayer & Co. v. Evans, 441 U.S. 750 (1979) (though Age Discrimination in Employment Act requires resort to certain state proceedings before bringing federal court action, the statute does not require the state proceeding to be commenced within the time limits specified by state law(!)); County of Oneida v. Oneida Indian Nation, 470 U.S. 226 (1985) (borrowing of state limitations period would be inconsistent with federal policy against the application of state statutes of limitations in the context of Indian claims). But cf. South Carolina v. Catawba Indian Tribe, Inc., 476 U.S. 498 (1986) (applying state limitations period to action seeking possession of former tribal lands).

law would impose unless that characterization is unreasonable or otherwise inconsistent with national labor policy" (p. 706). The Court added that "Other questions would be raised if this case presented a state law characterization of a § 301 suit that reasonably described the nature of the cause of action, but required application of an unusually short or long limitations period" (p. 707 n. 9).

Later decisions on this question have centered on the prosecution of civil rights claims under 42 U.S.C. §§ 1981 and 1983. In Burnett v. Grattan, 468 U.S. 42 (1984), an action against state officers for race and gender discrimination in employment, the Court unanimously decided that the appropriate state limitations period was the three-year period specified by statute for all civil actions not otherwise provided for, rather than the six-month period for filing discrimination complaints with a state administrative agency. The majority emphasized the practical differences between the litigation and an administrative proceeding, as well as the different goals of the Civil Rights Act and the state administrative process. Three concurring Justices argued that the majority's approach relied too heavily on its perception of federal policies and paid too little attention to the state's "legislative intent" in enacting the various limitations periods.

One year later, in Wilson v. Garcia, 471 U.S. 261 (1985), a divided Court held that (1) as a matter of federal law, "a simple, broad characterization of all § 1983 claims best fits the statute's remedial purpose" and (2) such claims are "best characterized as personal injury actions" for purposes of selecting the applicable statute of limitations (pp. 1945, 1949). Justice O'Connor, the sole dissenter, argued that the Court's effort to legislate uniformity was inconsistent with a century of precedent and was at odds with the long standing obligation under § 1983 (and § 1988) to "identify and apply the statute of limitations of the state claim most closely analogous to the *particular* § 1983 claim" (p. 1949) (emphasis added).

Note the tendency in these cases to derive results not from a close examination of state law but rather from the Court's perceptions of governing federal policies. Is this tendency consistent with the Court's attitude towards questions of tolling in Johnson and Tomanio?

(6) Apart from statutes of limitations and their incidents, to what extent do other state "procedural" and "quasi-procedural" rules, particularly those which may affect outcome or which relate to the availability or scope of the remedy, play a role in federal question litigation? The question has arisen infrequently, and the relevant authorities are sparse. One area that has caused difficulty is the applicability of state law in stockholders' derivative actions brought to enforce a federal right. See, *e.g.*, Burks v. Lasker, 441 U.S. 471 (1979) (in derivative action alleging violations of federal law, federal courts should adopt state law on the question whether independent directors have the authority to terminate the action, provided that the relevant state law does not interfere with federal policy); Fielding v. Allen, 181 F.2d 163 (2d Cir.1950) (New York "security-for-costs" statute is inapplicable in a derivative action to enforce a claimed federal right).[5]

Robertson v. Wegmann, 436 U.S. 584 (1978), raised a difficult issue: what law governs on the question whether a civil rights action against state

---

5. And see the cryptic reference to the security-for-costs problem in the context of suits under the Securities Act in J.I. Case Co. v. Borak, p. 935, *supra*.

officials survives if the plaintiff dies during the action and his executor is substituted as plaintiff. The lower courts had held that under 42 U.S.C. § 1988, note 2, *supra*, the federal civil rights laws were "deficient" in not providing for survival of actions; but they nevertheless refused to apply the relevant Louisiana law (which in this type of action would allow survival only if the decedent is survived by spouse, children, parents, or siblings), finding it inconsistent with federal law. In place of state law the lower courts announced a federal common-law rule of survival of civil rights actions in favor of the personal representative of the deceased. The Supreme Court, per Justice Marshall, reversed, holding that § 1988 requires that the Louisiana law should be adopted and that the action must therefore abate. The Court found no inconsistency between the policies of the federal statute and Louisiana's determination that certain actions should survive only if the deceased is survived by relatives: the compensatory goals of the federal statute are unaffected by the Louisiana rule, and its deterrent policies are adequately safeguarded—at least where there is no allegation that the defendants' illegal acts caused the plaintiff's death— by the fact that most Louisiana actions do survive.

Justice Blackmun, joined by Justices Brennan and White, dissented, arguing that a uniform federal rule assuring the survival of all § 1983 actions would better serve the purposes of the federal act. Justice Blackmun further argued that a federal rule is required by analogy to the many cases holding that the question whether a state official in a § 1983 action is entitled to an absolute or qualified immunity by way of defense is governed by federal law. See, *e.g.,* Pierson v. Ray, 386 U.S. 547 (1967); Imbler v. Pachtman, 424 U.S. 409 (1976). Do you think the analogy is persuasive?

The Court's reliance on § 1988 as relevant to the choice of law problem in Robertson is criticized in Eisenberg, note 2, *supra.*

In Carey v. Piphus, 435 U.S. 247 (1978), the Court in a civil rights action under § 1983 fashioned a federal rule with respect to the measure of damages in a case alleging that defendant state officials deprived the plaintiffs of procedural rights in violation of the Due Process Clause; the Court did not inquire into the question of analogous state law.[6] Do you think the case is distinguishable from Robertson?

The Court declined to follow Robertson in Carlson v. Green, 446 U.S. 14 (1980), p. 931, *supra,* holding that a complaint alleging that defendant federal officials violated the Eighth Amendment by imposing cruel and unusual punishment (causing death) on a federal prisoner (plaintiff's son) stated a good cause of action. The Court ruled that the question of the survival of the administratrix' action in a Bivens-type suit should be governed by a federal common-law rule assuring that the action survives. Robertson was distinguished on several grounds: (a) § 1988 does not apply to Bivens actions against federal officials; (b) the liability of federal (as against state) officials should be uniform; (c) here the death itself was caused, allegedly, by the defendants' violations, so effective deterrence

---

6. See also Smith v. Wade, 461 U.S. 30 (1983), holding, as a matter of federal law, that punitive damages are available in a § 1983 action when the defendant's conduct involves reckless or callous indifference to the plaintiff's federally protected rights. The dissenters did not disagree with the conclusion that federal law controlled, and indeed Justice Rehnquist in his dissent was especially critical of the majority's willingness to rely on state court decisions rendered after the enactment of § 1983 in 1871.

requires survival; (d) the power to transfer prisoners among federal facilities would invite manipulation of survival laws.

(7) When federal law adopts state law, or when state law rights are enforced by federal courts in the context of federal regulatory purposes (as is the case in bankruptcy), does the Klaxon rule, p. 791, *supra,* determine how a federal court decides *which* state's law to apply? This question has been reserved a number of times, see, *e.g.,* UAW v. Hoosier Cardinal Corp., Paragraph (3), *supra,* at 705 n. 8 ("no occasion to consider whether such a choice of law should be made in accord with the [Klaxon] principle, or by operation of a different federal conflict of laws rule"); De Sylva v. Ballentine, p. 876, *supra;* McKenzie v. Irving Trust Co., 323 U.S. 365, 371 n. 2 (1945); D'Oench, Duhme & Co. v. Federal Deposit Ins. Co., p. 858, *supra,* at 456.[7] See also Richards v. United States, p. 867, *supra,* and the excellent Note, 68 Harv.L.Rev. 1212 (1955).[8]

7. Statutes of limitations present a special problem in this regard. Traditionally, the federal courts followed the limitations statute of the forum, whether jurisdiction was based on diversity of citizenship, Bauserman v. Blunt, 147 U.S. 647 (1893), or on the presence of a federal question, Campbell v. Haverhill, 155 U.S. 610 (1895). But no case seems squarely to have faced the problem.

In Cope v. Anderson, 331 U.S. 461, 466 (1947), Justice Black mentioned that "limitations on federally created rights to sue have similarly been considered to be governed by the limitations law of the state where the crucial combination of events transpired." But he got to the obviously appropriate statute of Kentucky, where the insolvent national bank had been located, only by the hard route of construction of the forum state's "borrowing statute."

8. *Cf.* Oil, Chemical and Atomic Workers v. Mobil Oil Corp., 426 U.S. 407 (1976) (under § 14(b) of the NLRA, allowing states to prohibit the union shop as a "condition of employment in any State," a federal standard controls in determining whether a state may apply its right-to-work laws to a particular employment relationship).

Chapter VIII

THE FEDERAL QUESTION JURISDICTION OF THE DISTRICT COURTS

SECTION 1. INTRODUCTION

This chapter surveys the federal question ("arising under") jurisdiction of the federal district courts. Section 2 deals with the constitutional scope of the jurisdiction. Section 3 studies the development of the statutory grant of original jurisdiction to the federal district courts. (Since a defendant's right to remove a federal question case from state to federal court is generally conditioned on whether the federal court would have had original jurisdiction over the case, see 28 U.S.C. § 1441, some of the important cases dealing with the scope of the original jurisdiction are removal cases, and these are freely intermixed with cases invoking the original jurisdiction.)

Section 4 is concerned with pendent jurisdiction. Section 5 is devoted to the distinctive problems of removal jurisdiction in the context of federal question litigation. It surveys "federal defense removal": special jurisdictional grants allowing removal of cases not within the original jurisdiction (*e.g.*, removal by federal officials; civil rights removal), and also cases that seek to stretch the borderline of original jurisdiction in order to allow the defendant independent access to the federal courts. (More general problems of removal are studied in Chap. XIV, Sec. 4, *infra*.)

Section 6 is a brief survey of jurisdictional categories that are functionally closely tied to and frequently overlap the "arising under" jurisdiction: admiralty, and litigation instituted by the United States. (Suits against the federal government and its agencies and officials are studied in Chapter IX.)

NOTE ON THE STATUTORY DEVELOPMENT OF THE JURISDICTION

Although the protection of federally-granted rights was a primary purpose of the establishment of a system of federal courts, the principle established by the first Judiciary Act was that private litigants must look to the state tribunals in the first instance for vindication of federal claims, subject to limited review by the United States Supreme Court.[1] In the course of time, exceptions were made in the case of matters of a peculiarly federal nature or where political exigencies demanded. But it was not until the consolidation of national sentiment after the Civil War that the

1. Act of Sept. 24, 1789, § 25, 1 Stat. 73, 85. See Chap. I, pp. 30–34, *supra*.

basic change was made whereby the national courts became the primary forum for the vindication of federal rights.[2]

The early Congresses used most sparingly their authority to vest the federal courts with jurisdiction of cases "arising under" the Constitution, laws and treaties of the United States. The Judiciary Act of 1789, besides the grant of jurisdiction of suits for "penalties and forfeitures ∗ ∗ ∗ incurred" under federal laws,[3] gave the national courts cognizance only of cases "where an alien sues for a tort only in violation of the law of nations or a treaty of the United States."[4] The first patent law imposed only limited duties on the district courts in proceedings to revoke wrongfully secured patents,[5] though subsequently jurisdiction was extended to infringement suits.[6] Certain functions were likewise to be performed by the federal courts under the 1792 pension law.[7] But it was only when the Federalist Party was beaten at the polls and driven to refuge in the judicial branch[8] that the national courts were first vested with their constitutional jurisdiction in this area.[9] The Federalist statute, however, lasted barely more than a year.[10]

The story of the early removal acts for the protection of federal interests from hostile state action, which began with the Non–Intercourse Act of 1815, is told below.[11] Primarily these statutes were concerned with state court proceedings against federal officers, but they extended also to actions against private persons for acts done under federal authority.

Until the second half of the nineteenth century no other important additions were made to federal jurisdiction of federal questions. Jurisdiction was continued in patent cases,[12] and in 1846 the federal courts were empowered to enforce awards made by consuls under our treaty with Prussia.[13] But the Civil War brought on a great surge of national feeling and national power,[14] which resulted in the vesting of a large part of the constitutionally-authorized jurisdiction in the federal courts.

The process began during the war, when removal was authorized of all suits and prosecutions against any one "for any arrest or imprisonment made, or other trespasses or wrongs done or committed ∗ ∗ ∗ [during the rebellion], by virtue or under color of any authority derived from ∗ ∗ ∗ the President of the United States, or any Act of Congress ∗ ∗ ∗."[15] In the period that followed, Congress freely invoked the federal courts to secure

2. See Frankfurter & Landis, The Business of the Supreme Court 64–65 (1928).

3. For this and other grants of jurisdiction in actions by the United States or federal officials, see pp. 1080–81, *infra.*

4. Act of Sept. 24, 1789, § 9, 1 Stat. 73, 77. This jurisdiction was exclusive in the district courts. It is now concurrent. 28 U.S.C. § 1350.

5. Act of April 10, 1790, § 5, 1 Stat. 109, 111.

6. Act of Feb. 21, 1793, § 6, 1 Stat. 318, 322; see also, Act of Feb. 15, 1819, 3 Stat. 481. The jurisdiction was concurrent. It is now exclusive. 28 U.S.C. § 1338(a).

7. Act of March 23, 1792, §§ 2, 3, 1 Stat. 243, 244. See Hayburn's Case, p. 89, *supra.*

8. See 3 Beveridge, Life of John Marshall, chs. 1, 2 (1919).

9. Act of Feb. 13, 1801, § 11, 2 Stat. 89, 92. The statute used virtually the language of the Constitution and required no jurisdictional amount. It also provided for removal of such suits. *Id.* § 13.

10. It was repealed by the Act of March 8, 1802, 2 Stat. 132.

11. See pp. 1057–60, *infra.*

12. Act of July 4, 1836, 5 Stat. 117.

13. Act of Aug. 8, 1846, 9 Stat. 78.

14. See Frankfurter & Landis, *supra* note 2, at 56 *et seq.*

15. Act of March 3, 1863, § 5, 12 Stat. 755, 756, amended by Act of May 11, 1866, 14 Stat. 46. See p. 1058 *infra.*

blacks' newly granted civil rights, and there was enacted a series of jurisdictional and remedial provisions most of which have lasted to this day.[16] The first Civil Rights Act gave the federal courts cognizance, both original and by removal, of "all causes, civil and criminal, affecting persons who are denied or cannot enforce in the courts * * * of the state or locality where they may be any of the rights secured to them by the first section of this act * * *."[17] Any one could remove his case if he were sued or prosecuted "for any arrest or imprisonment, trespasses, or wrongs done * * * under color of authority derived from this act * * * or for refusing to do any act upon the ground that it would be inconsistent with this act. * * *"[18] The Act of 1870 provided for federal jurisdiction of "all causes, civil and criminal, arising under" it.[19] The following year Congress went further by adding a remedy in damages[20] and giving the federal courts cognizance of suits for their recovery.[21] Removal was as usual authorized where any one was brought into court for an act done under color of the statute.[22] The last Civil Rights Act of that series, that of 1875, extended the remedies and again provided complete federal jurisdiction.[23]

Civil rights cases were not the only new federal question litigation coming to the federal judiciary during this period. Jurisdiction was given in 1864 of suits against national banks,[24] and four years later Congress authorized removal of suits against "any corporation, organized under a law of the United States. * * *"[25] The Act of 1874, which imposed certain obligations (such as non-discrimination in rates) on the Pacific railroads, gave the federal courts cognizance of treble damage suits for injuries resulting from violations of the statute.[26]

The culmination of the movement came with the passage of the 1875 Judiciary Act. Although this legislation in a very real sense revolutionized the concept of the federal judiciary, it passed almost unnoticed inside or outside the halls of Congress.[27] It gave the circuit courts concurrent jurisdiction, subject to a $500 amount requirement, of "all suits of a civil nature, at common law or in equity, * * * arising under the Constitution or laws of the United States, or treaties made, or which shall be made,

---

16. See 28 U.S.C. §§ 1343, 1344, 1443. See also 42 U.S.C. § 1983, discussed at pp. 1229–77, *infra*.

17. Act of April 9, 1866, § 3, 14 Stat. 27.

18. *Id.* These provisions are now found in 28 U.S.C. § 1443, except that original jurisdiction of such cases is omitted.

19. Act of May 31, 1870, § 8, 16 Stat. 140, 142.

20. Act of Feb. 28, 1871, § 15, 16 Stat. 433, 438.

21. Act of April 20, 1871, §§ 2, 6, 17 Stat. 13, 14, 15.

22. Act of Feb. 28, 1871, § 16, 16 Stat. 433, 439.

23. Act of March 1, 1875, §§ 2, 3, 18 Stat. 335, 336.

24. Act of June 3, 1864, § 57, 13 Stat. 99, 116.

25. Act of July 27, 1868, § 2, 15 Stat. 226, 227.

26. Act of June 20, 1874, 18 Stat. 111, 112. See also Act of Feb. 8, 1875, § 12, 18 Stat. 307, 309, providing for district court jurisdiction of actions on bonds posted by deputy revenue collectors (and see also, Act of March 1, 1879, § 12, 20 Stat. 327, 329); an Act of Jan. 22, 1869, 15 Stat. 267, allowing removal of suits against carriers for losses caused by acts of the Rebel or Union forces; and section 8 of an Act of March 3, 1875, 18 Stat. 371, 401, permitting removal of suits against Congressional officers discharging official duties.

27. The Act started as a bill to expand diversity jurisdiction. The main body of the law was added by amendment and the original provision was stricken out before the bill passed. See Frankfurter & Landis, *supra* note 2, at 64–68.

under their authority * * *." [28] Such cases were also made removable by either party.[29] In its one cautionary note, Section 5 of the Act directed the federal court to dismiss or remand if it appeared at any time "that such suit does not really and substantially involve a dispute or controversy properly within [its] jurisdiction. * * *" [30]

The flood of litigation to which the federal courts were now subjected, especially after the decision of the Pacific Removal Cases,[31] moved Congress to pare down the federal question jurisdiction. In 1887 the jurisdictional amount was raised to $2000, removal by plaintiffs was eliminated, and orders remanding removed cases to the state courts were made non-appealable.[32] Prior to that, Congress had begun the long process of reducing jurisdiction based solely on federal incorporation to cases in which the United States owns more than half the corporation's stock.[33]

The history of federal question jurisdiction between 1875 and 1980 revolves largely around the creation by Congress of myriad new federal rights and provision for their enforcement in the national courts without regard to jurisdictional amount. The federal courts were opened to damage and injunction suits under regulatory measures such as the old Interstate Commerce Act [34] and the Sherman Act,[35] under the copyright [36] and trademark [37] laws,[38] and under the Employers' Liability Act.[39] The Judicial Code of 1911 [40] listed the types of cases where no jurisdictional amount was required. In addition to those already mentioned, it included [41] internal revenue [42] and postal [43] matters, suits under any act regulating commerce,[44] and immigration and naturalization proceedings.[45] Existing removal provisions were codified as well.[46]

The codification, however, proved to be but a momentary convenience, for Congress persisted in embodying new jurisdictional provisions in the particular substantive statutes without amending the Judicial Code. In 1948 the Revisers found 158 such provisions in various parts of the United

---

28. Act of March 3, 1875, § 1, 18 Stat. 470.

29. Act of March 3, 1875, § 2, 18 Stat. 470, 471.

30. *Id.,* § 5, 18 Stat. at 472.

31. 115 U.S. 1 (1885), pp. 976, 996, *infra.*

32. Act of March 3, 1887, 24 Stat. 552, corrected by Act of Aug. 13, 1888, 25 Stat. 433. Section 24 of the first Judicial Code [Act of March 3, 1911, 36 Stat. 1087, 1091] raised the amount to $3000, and the Act of July 25, 1958, 72 Stat. 415, to $10,000, where it stood until removed in 1980. 28 U.S.C. §§ 1331, 1441(a). Removal is still limited to defendants. 28 U.S.C. § 1441(a). And remanding orders are still non-reviewable, except in cases removed under 28 U.S.C. § 1443, dealing with civil rights. 28 U.S.C. § 1447(d).

33. See p. 996, note 2, *infra.*

34. Act of Feb. 4, 1887, § 8, 24 Stat. 379, 382, 49 U.S.C. § 8.

35. Act of July 2, 1890, § 7, 26 Stat. 209, 210. 15 U.S.C. § 15.

36. Act of Jan. 6, 1897, 29 Stat. 481.

37. Act of Feb. 20, 1905, 33 Stat. 724. The jurisdiction under this law extended to all civil actions respecting registered trademarks, "arising under the present Act. * * *"

38. See 28 U.S.C. § 1338(a) for the present provision. Jurisdiction is exclusive in copyright cases, concurrent in trademark cases.

39. Act of April 22, 1908, 35 Stat. 65, as amended by Act of April 5, 1910, 36 Stat. 291, 45 U.S.C. § 56. Jurisdiction was concurrent.

40. Act of March 3, 1911, § 24, 36 Stat. 1087, 1091.

41. *Id.,* 36 Stat. at 1092–94.

42. Now 28 U.S.C. § 1340.

43. Now 28 U.S.C. § 1339.

44. Now 28 U.S.C. § 1337.

45. This provision appeared as 28 U.S.C. § 41(22) (1940), but was repealed by section 39 of the Act of June 25, 1948, 62 Stat. 869, 992, 996.

46. Act of March 3, 1911, §§ 28, 33, 36 Stat. 1087, 1094–97.

States Code.[47] Most of these concern controversies between private parties and the government or its officers or agencies under various regulatory laws.[48] But many of them authorized private suits without regard to amount in controversy. The major acts regulating commerce, such as the Clayton Act [49] and the Federal Communications Act [50] provided for damage suits in the district courts. Also under this head were actions to enforce liabilities and duties created by the various statutes regulating security issues and holding companies,[51] as well as private suits to enforce orders of the Civil Aeronautics Board [52] and awards of the Railway Labor [53] and Railroad Retirement Boards.[54] The Fair Labor Standards Act provided for employee suits to recover minimum wages and overtime pay,[55] and the Jones Act gave maritime workers damage and wrongful death actions similar to those provided for railroad employees under the Federal Employers' Liability Act.[56] During World War II, the district courts had jurisdiction of suits for injunctions and damages for violation of the Emergency Price Control Act.[57]

Special removal provisions—or rather, provisions prohibiting removal in certain cases—were also enacted. The Federal Employers' Liability Act, in order to secure to employees the exclusive choice of forum, declared that damage suits under it were non-removable.[58] The Jones Act followed suit in the maritime field.[59] Railroads sued under federal law for damages to

---

47. Reviser's Notes to 28 U.S.C. § 1332.

48. Some concern suits by the United States or its officers, of which jurisdiction without regard to amount is already provided by § 1345. Some provide for suits against the United States itself, thus constituting exceptions to the general lack of jurisdiction derived from the doctrine of sovereign immunity. The other provisions in this category concern suits against federal officials or agencies. See Chap. IX, Sec. 1, *infra.*

49. Act of Oct. 15, 1914, §§ 4, 16, 38 Stat. 730, 731, 737, 15 U.S.C. §§ 15, 26. The present language of 15 U.S.C. § 15 is typical: "Any person who shall be injured in his business or property by reason of anything forbidden in the antitrust laws may sue therefor in any district court of the United States in the district in which the defendant resides or is found or has an agent, without respect to the amount in controversy, and shall recover threefold the damages by him sustained and the cost of suit, including a reasonable attorney's fee."

Jurisdiction without regard to amount would have obtained, even in the absence of special provision, under the general grant of jurisdiction of cases arising under any act regulating commerce, now found in 28 U.S.C. § 1337. This is true of many of the statutes cited in this paragraph.

50. Act of June 19, 1934, § 207, 48 Stat. 1064, 1073, 47 U.S.C. § 207.

51. Act of May 27, 1933, § 22(a), 48 Stat. 74, 86, 15 U.S.C. § 77v; Act of June 6,

1934, § 27, 48 Stat. 881, 902, 15 U.S.C. § 78aa; Act of Aug. 26, 1935, § 317, 49 Stat. 803, 862, 16 U.S.C. § 825p; Act of Aug. 3, 1939, § 322(b), 53 Stat. 1149, 1176, 15 U.S.C. § 77vvv; Act of Aug. 22, 1940, § 44, 54 Stat. 789, 844, 15 U.S.C. § 80a–43.

52. Act of June 23, 1938, § 1007, 52 Stat. 973, 1025, amended to include Federal Aviation Administration by Act of Aug. 23, 1958, 72 Stat. 737, 796, 49 U.S.C. § 1487.

53. Act of May 20, 1926, § 9, 44 Stat. 577, 585, 45 U.S.C. § 159.

54. Act of Aug. 29, 1935, § 9, 49 Stat. 967, 973, 45 U.S.C. § 231f.

55. Act of June 25, 1938, § 16(b), 52 Stat. 1060, 1069, 29 U.S.C. § 216.

56. Act of June 5, 1920, § 33, 41 Stat. 988, 1007, as amended by the Act of Dec. 29, 1982, 96 Stat. 1955, now 46 U.S.C. § 688.

57. Act of Jan. 30, 1942, § 205, 56 Stat. 23, 33; 50 U.S.C. § 925 (App.).

58. Act of April 22, 1908, 35 Stat. 65, as amended by Act of April 5, 1910, 36 Stat. 291. Now 28 U.S.C. § 1445(a).

59. See 46 U.S.C. § 688. The Act made the Federal Employers' Liability Act applicable to seamen by generic reference, and there is conflict in the decisions as to whether the reference included the removal prohibition. Compare Ramos v. H.E. Butt Grocery Co., 632 F.Supp. 342 (S.D.Tex. 1986) with Bintrim v. Bruce–Merilees Elec. Co., 520 F.Supp. 1026 (W.D.Pa.1981).

goods shipped were prevented from removing, although they might be sued originally in the district courts, unless the claim was at least $3000.[60] In 1933 certain corporations of the Farm Credit Administration were likewise denied the right to remove, except where a federal official or a receiver of the corporation was a party,[61] and all suits under the Securities Act of 1933 were made non-removable.[62]

The Judicial Code of 1948 did not attempt a new codification of these numerous provisions, nor did it purport to make more than a few significant changes in the district courts' jurisdiction.[63] One new jurisdictional section was added, allowing suits in the district courts on bonds "executed under any law of the United States."[64] Section 1338(b) seemed on its face to expand the pendent jurisdiction in patent, copyright and trademark cases, though the Reviser's note declares the purpose to be merely that of codifying the rule of Hurn v. Oursler.[65] And two important changes were made in removal jurisdiction.[66] The privilege of removal was extended to all federal officers and agencies sued or prosecuted "for any act under color of * * * office."[67] And the revisers, while purporting to narrow the old "separable controversy" provision which had before applied only in diversity cases, expanded it confusingly so as to include some cases in which a removable federal claim was joined with a non-removable claim.[68]

The creation of a large number of special jurisdictional grants outside the corners of the Judicial Code[69] continued in the 50s and accelerated in the period of intense federal legislative activity in the late 60s and 70s. For discussion of this development (and supporting references), see Friendly, Federal Jurisdiction: A General View, 22–26 & n. 53 (1973); Leventhal, Book Review, 75 Colum.L.Rev. 1009, 1018 and n. 41 (1975). For a general

Some courts have construed the Fair Labor Standards Act [Act of June 25, 1938, § 16, 52 Stat. 1060, 1069, 29 U.S.C. § 216] as denying removal of employee suits for unpaid minimum wages and overtime. See, *e.g.,* Johnson v. Butler Bros., 162 F.2d 87, especially at 89, n. 3 (8th Cir.1947); but see, *e.g.,* Asher v. Wm. L. Crow Constr. Co., 118 F.Supp. 495 (S.D.N.Y.1953).

60. Act of Jan. 20, 1914, 38 Stat. 278. Now 28 U.S.C. § 1445(b).

61. Act of June 16, 1933, § 60, 48 Stat. 257, 267, 12 U.S.C. § 1138.

62. Act of May 27, 1933, § 22(a), 48 Stat. 74, 87, 15 U.S.C. § 77v.

63. The provisions relating to original jurisdiction in the district courts are found in 28 U.S.C. §§ 1331–1366.

64. 28 U.S.C. § 1352.

65. 289 U.S. 238 (1933). See p. 1047, *infra.*

66. The removal provisions are 28 U.S.C. §§ 1441–1445.

67. 28 U.S.C. § 1442(a)(1). Other parts of this section retain old provisions for removal of suits against particular officials. See pp. 1057–60, *infra.*

68. 28 U.S.C. § 1441(c). The problem is discussed in Chap. XIV, Sec. 4, pp. 1782–86, *infra.*

69. Within the Judicial Code some changes have been: (1) the addition of a new subsection, of uncertain import, providing for jurisdiction over civil actions "under any Act of Congress providing for the protection of civil rights, including the right to vote" (28 U.S.C. § 1343(4)); a provision for jurisdiction without a required amount in controversy for actions by certain Indian tribes (28 U.S.C. § 1362); a provision for actions to enforce Senate subpoenas (28 U.S.C. § 1364); a provision for actions for the "protection of jurors' employment" under 28 U.S.C. § 1875 (28 U.S.C. § 1363); and provisions for jurisdiction over controversies involving foreign states and foreign diplomats (28 U.S.C. §§ 1330, 1332(a)(2)–(4), 1364; see further pp. 986, 988, *infra*).

Counter to the general trend in the federal question area, a new jurisdictional amount requirement was imposed in 1978 for original freight damage actions against rail or motor carriers under the Interstate Commerce Act (and the existing requirement raised in removal cases). 28 U.S.C. §§ 1337, 1445(b), as amended by Pub.L. No. 95–486 (1978).

survey of the various substantive heads of federal question jurisdiction, see 13B Wright, Miller & Cooper, Federal Practice and Procedure §§ 1368–85 (1984).

The same period, however, saw the development of a movement that eventually deprived these specific jurisdictional grants of their principal significance: the movement eroding, and eventually eliminating, the jurisdictional amount requirement in the context of the general federal-question jurisdiction. The forerunner statute was a 1962 provision conferring jurisdiction of actions "in the nature of mandamus" to compel federal officials to carry out their duties, together with special venue and process for such actions. See 28 U.S.C. §§ 1361, 1391(e). This was overtaken by the amendment in 1976 of § 1331—the general federal question statute—to eliminate the jurisdictional amount requirement in any civil action "brought against the United States, any agency thereof, or any officer or employee thereof in his official capacity." Act of October 21, 1976, 90 Stat. 2721.[70] And, finally, on December 1, 1980, § 1331 was amended by eliminating—for the first time since the passage of the original act in 1875—any jurisdictional amount requirement in "all civil actions arising under the Constitution, laws, or treaties of the United States." (The requirement was expressly preserved for suits under the Consumer Product Safety Act, 15 U.S.C. § 2072(a); and it presumably continues in effect under other substantive statutes that explicitly require a minimum amount in controversy.[71])

Does the 1980 amendment make the numerous specific grants of federal question jurisdiction in the various substantive statutes irrelevant? Caution must be exercised. Some of those provisions provide for exclusive jurisdiction in the federal courts; section 1331 has always been read as a grant of concurrent jurisdiction. And other questions of interpretation may also arise. Section 1331 is encrusted with a complex gloss of interpretive doctrines, as the materials in this Chapter demonstrate. Whether and how some or all of these glosses apply in the context of specific substantive jurisdictional grants is, itself, a question of interpretation that can raise substantial difficulties. See, e.g., Aldinger v. Howard, 427 U.S. 1 (1976) (problem of "pendent party" jurisdiction in the specific context of actions against municipalities under 42 U.S.C. § 1983 (discussed further at pp. 1050–51, infra)); cf. Merrell Dow Pharmaceuticals Inc. v. Thompson, 478 U.S. 804 (1986) (meaning of § 1331 in specific context of Congress's decision not to create a private federal right of action for violation of Food, Drug and Cosmetic Act) (see p. 1007, infra).

---

70. The Supreme Court relied in part on the passage of this statute in holding that the judicial review provisions of the Administrative Procedure Act did not provide a basis for original jurisdiction in the district courts independent of the general federal question provision. See Califano v. Sanders, 430 U.S. 99 (1977).

71. E.g., the proviso added in 1978 to 28 U.S.C. § 1337, note 69, supra; see Pillsbury Co. v. Atchison, Topeka and Santa Fe Ry. Co., 548 F.Supp. 28 (D.Kan.1982).

SECTION 2. THE SCOPE OF THE CONSTITUTIONAL GRANT OF FEDERAL QUESTION JURISDICTION

OSBORN v. BANK OF THE UNITED STATES

9 Wheat. 738, 6 L.Ed. 204 (U.S.1824).
Appeal from the Circuit Court of Ohio.

The bill filed in this cause, was exhibited in the court below, at September term 1819, in the name of the respondents, * * * praying an injunction to restrain Ralph Osborn, auditor of the state of Ohio, from proceeding against the complainants, under an act of the legislature of that state, passed February the 8th, 1819, entitled, "an act to levy and collect a tax from all banks, and individuals, and companies and associations of individuals, that may transact business in this state, without being allowed to do so by the laws thereof."

This act, after reciting that the Bank of the United States pursued its operations contrary to a law of the state, enacted, that if, after the 1st day of the following September, the said bank, or any other, should continue to transact business in the state, it should be liable to an annual tax of $50,000 on each office of discount and deposit. * * *

[Soon thereafter a writ of injunction was issued, as prayed, and was served upon Osborn and upon Harper, who was alleged to have been employed by Osborn to collect the tax.

[An amended bill charged that Harper, after service of the injunction and a subpoena, proceeded by violence to the office of the bank at Chillicothe and took therefrom $100,000 in specie and bank-notes belonging to or on deposit with the plaintiffs. It appeared that $98,000 of this money was being held separately, with notice of the circumstances, by Sullivan, the present state treasurer, who was also made a defendant.

[After a hearing upon the defendants' answers and upon the decrees nisi against Osborn and Harper, the circuit court pronounced a decree directing them to restore to the bank the sum of $100,000, with interest on $19,830, the amount of specie in the hands of Sullivan.]

MARSHALL, CHIEF JUSTICE, delivered the opinion of the court and after stating the case, proceeded as follows:—At the close of the argument, a point was suggested, of such vital importance, as to induce the court to request that it might be particularly spoken to. That point is the right of the bank to sue in the courts of the United States. It has been argued, and ought to be disposed of, before we proceed to the actual exercise of jurisdiction, by deciding on the rights of the parties.

The appellants contest the jurisdiction of the court on two grounds: 1st. That the act of congress has not given it. 2d. That, under the constitution, congress cannot give it.

1. The first part of the objection depends entirely on the language of the act. The words are, that the bank shall be "made able and capable in law,"—"to sue and be sued, plead and be impleaded, answer and be answered, defend and be defended, in all state courts having competent

jurisdiction, and in any circuit court of the United States." These words seem to the court to admit of but one interpretation; they cannot be made plainer by explanation. They give, expressly, the right "to sue and be sued," "in every circuit court of the United States," and it would be difficult to substitute other terms which would be more direct and appropriate for the purpose. The argument of the appellants is founded on the opinion of this court, in the Bank of the United States v. Deveaux (5 Cranch 85). In that case, it was decided, that the former Bank of the United States was not enabled, by the act which incorporated it, to sue in the federal courts. The words of the 3d section of that act are, that the bank may "sue and be sued," & c., "in courts of record, or any other place whatsoever." The court was of opinion, that these general words, which are usual in all acts of incorporation, gave only a general capacity to sue, not a particular privilege to sue in the courts of the United States; * * * Whether this decision be right or wrong, it amounts only to a declaration, that a general capacity in the bank to sue, without mentioning the courts of the Union, may not give a right to sue in those courts. To infer from this, that words expressly conferring a right to sue in those courts, do not give the right, is surely a conclusion which the premises do not warrant. The act of incorporation, then, confers jurisdiction on the circuit courts of the United States, if congress can confer it.

2. We will now consider the constitutionality of the clause in the act of incorporation, which authorizes the bank to sue in the federal courts. In support of this clause, it is said, that the legislative, executive and judicial powers of every well-constructed government, are co-extensive with each other; that is, they are potentially co-extensive. The executive department may constitutionally execute every law which the legislature may constitutionally make, and the judicial department may receive from the legislature the power of construing every such law. All governments which are not extremely defective in their organization, must possess, within themselves, the means of expounding, as well as enforcing, their own laws. If we examine the constitution of the United States, we find that its framers kept this great political principle in view. The 2d article vests the whole executive power in the president; and the 3d article declares, "that the judicial power shall extend to all cases in law and equity, arising under this constitution, the laws of the United States, and treaties made, or which shall be made, under their authority." This clause enables the judicial department to receive jurisdiction to the full extent of the constitution, laws and treaties of the United States, when any question respecting them shall assume such a form that the judicial power is capable of acting on it. That power is capable of acting only when the subject is submitted to it by a party who asserts his rights in the form prescribed by law. It then becomes a case, and the constitution declares, that the judicial power shall extend to all cases arising under the constitution, laws and treaties of the United States.

The suit of the Bank of the United States v. Osborn and others, is a case, and the question is, whether it arises under a law of the United States? The appellants contend, that it does not, because several questions may arise in it, which depend on the general principles of the law, not on any act of congress. If this were sufficient to withdraw a case from the jurisdiction of the federal courts, almost every case, although involving the construction of a law, would be withdrawn; and a clause in the constitution, relating to a subject of vital importance to the government, and expressed in the most comprehensive terms, would be construed to mean almost nothing. There is scarcely any case, every part of which depends on the constitution, laws or treaties of the United States. The questions, whether the fact alleged as the foundation of the action, be real or fictitious; whether the conduct of the plaintiff has been such as to entitle him to maintain his action; whether his right is barred; whether he has received satisfaction, or has in any manner released his claims, are questions, some or all of which may occur, in almost every case; and if their existence be sufficient to arrest the jurisdiction of the court, words which seem intended to be as extensive as the constitution, laws and treaties of the Union—which seem designed to give the courts of the government the construction of all its acts, so far as they affect the rights of individuals—would be reduced to almost nothing.

In those cases in which original jurisdiction is given to the supreme court, the judicial power of the United States cannot be exercised in its appellate form. In every other case, the power is to be exercised in its original or appellate form, or both, as the wisdom of congress may direct. With the exception of these cases, in which original jurisdiction is given to this court, there is none to which the judicial power extends, from which the original jurisdiction of the inferior courts is excluded by the constitution. Original jurisdiction, so far as the constitution gives a rule, is co-extensive with the judicial power. We find, in the constitution, no prohibition to its exercise, in every case in which the judicial power can be exercised. It would be a very bold construction, to say, that this power could be applied in its appellate form only, to the most important class of cases to which it is applicable. The constitution establishes the supreme court, and defines its jurisdiction. It enumerates cases in which its jurisdiction is original and exclusive; and then defines that which is appellate, but does not insinuate, that in any such case, the power cannot be exercised in its original form, by courts of original jurisdiction. It is not insinuated, that the judicial power, in cases depending on the character of the cause, cannot be exercised, in the first instance, in the courts of the Union, but must first be exercised in the tribunals of the state; tribunals over which the government of the Union has no adequate control, and which may be closed to any claim asserted under a law of the United States. We perceive, then, no ground on which the proposition can be maintained, that congress is incapable of giving the circuit courts original jurisdiction, in any case to which the appellate jurisdiction extends.

We ask, then, if it can be sufficient to exclude this jurisdiction, that the case involves questions depending on general principles? A cause may depend on several questions of fact and law. Some of these may depend on the construction of a law of the United States; others on principles unconnected with that law. If it be a sufficient foundation for jurisdiction, that the title or right set up by the party, may be defeated by one construction of the constitution or law of the United States, and sustained by the opposite construction, provided the facts necessary to support the action be made out, then all the other questions must be decided as incidental to this, which gives that jurisdiction. Those other questions cannot arrest the proceedings. Under this construction, the judicial power of the Union extends, effectively and beneficially, to that most important class of cases, which depend on the character of the cause. On the opposite construction, the judicial power never can be extended to a whole case, as expressed by the constitution, but to those parts of cases only which present the particular question involving the construction of the constitution or the law. We say, it never can be extended to the whole case, because, if the circumstance that other points are involved in it, shall disable congress from authorizing the courts of the Union to take jurisdiction of the original cause, it equally disables congress from authorizing those courts to take jurisdiction of the whole cause, on an appeal, and thus will be restricted to a single question in that cause; and words obviously intended to secure to those who claim rights under the constitution, laws or treaties of the United States, a trial in the federal courts, will be restricted to the insecure remedy of an appeal, upon an insulated point, after it has received that shape against his will. We think, then, that when a question to which the judicial power of the Union is extended by the constitution, forms an ingredient of the original cause, it is in the power of congress to give the circuit courts jurisdiction of that cause, although other questions of fact or of law may be involved in it.

The case of the bank is, we think, a very strong case of this description. The charter of incorporation not only creates it, but gives it every faculty which it possesses. The power to acquire rights of any description, to transact business of any description, to make contracts of any description, to sue on those contracts, is given and measured by its charter, and that charter is a law of the United States. This being can acquire no right, make no contract, bring no suit, which is not authorized by a law of the United States. It is not only itself the mere creature of a law, but all its actions and all its rights are dependent on the same law. Can a being, thus constituted, have a case which does not arise literally, as well as substantially, under the law?

Take the case of a contract, which is put as the strongest against the bank. When a bank sues, the first question which presents itself, and which lies at the foundation of the cause, is, has this legal entity a right to sue? Has it a right to come, not into this court particularly, but into any court? This depends on a law of the United States. The next question is, has this being a right to make this particular contract? If this question be decided in the negative, the cause is determined against the plaintiff; and this question, too, depends entirely on a law of the United States. These are important questions, and they exist in every possible case. The right to sue, if decided once, is decided forever; but the power of congress was exercised antecedently to the first decision on that right, and if it was constitutional then, it cannot cease to be so, because the particular question is decided. It may be revived at the will of the party, and most probably would be renewed, were the tribunal to be changed. But the question respecting the right to make a particular contract, or to acquire a particular property, or to sue on account of a particular injury, belongs to every particular case, and may be renewed in every case. The question forms an original ingredient in every cause. Whether it be, in fact, relied on or not, in the defence, it is still a part of the cause, and may be relied on. The right of the plaintiff to sue cannot depend on the defence which the defendant may choose to set up. His right to sue is anterior to that defence, and must depend on the state of things when the action is brought. The question which the case involved, then, must determine its character, whether those questions be made in the cause or not.

The appellants say, that the case arises on the contract; but the validity of the contract depends on a law of the United States, and the plaintiff is compelled, in every case, to show its validity. The case arises emphatically under the law; the act of congress is its foundation. The contract could never have been made, but under the authority of that act. The act itself is the first ingredient in the case—is its origin—is that from which every other part arises. That other questions may also arise, as the execution of the contract, or its performance, cannot change the case, or give it any other origin than the charter of incorporation. The action still originates in, and is sustained by, that charter. ∗ ∗ ∗.

It is said, that a clear distinction exists between the party and the cause; that the party may originate under a law with which the cause has no connection; and that congress may with the same propriety, give a naturalized citizen, who is the mere creature of law, a right to sue in the courts of the United States, as give that right to the bank. This distinction is not denied; and if the act of congress was a simple act of incorporation, and contained nothing more, it might be entitled to great consideration. But the act does not stop with incorporating the bank. It proceeds to bestow upon the being it has made, all the faculties and capacities which that being possesses. Every act of the bank grows out of this law, and is tested by it. To use the language of the constitution, every act of the bank arises out of this law. A naturalized citizen is, indeed, made a citizen under an act of congress, but the act does not proceed to give, to regulate, or to prescribe his capacities. He becomes a member of the society, possessing all the rights of a native citizen, and standing, in the view of the constitution, on the footing of a native. The constitution does not authorize congress to enlarge or abridge those rights. The simple power of the national legislature is, to prescribe a uniform rule of naturalization, and the exercise of this power exhausts it, so far as respects the individual. The constitution then takes him up, and, among other rights, extends to him the capacity of suing in the courts of the United States, precisely under the same circumstances under which a native might sue. He is distinguishable in nothing from a native citizen, except so far as the constitution makes the distinction; the law makes none. There is, then, no resemblance between the act incorporating the bank, and the general naturalization law.

Upon the best consideration we have been able to bestow on this subject, we are of opinion, that the clause in the act of incorporation, enabling the bank to sue in the courts of the United States, is consistent with the constitution, and to be obeyed in all courts.

We will now proceed to consider the merits of the cause. ∗ ∗ ∗.

We think, then, that there is no error in the decree of the circuit court for the district of Ohio, so far as it directs restitution of the specific sum of $98,000, which was taken out of the bank unlawfully, and was in the possession of the defendant, Samuel Sullivan, when the injunction was awarded, in September 1820, to restrain him from paying it away, or in any manner using it; and so far as it directs the payment of the remaining sum of $2000 by the defendants, Ralph Osborn and John L. Harper; but that the same is erroneous, so far as respects the interest on the coin, part of the said $98,000, it being the opinion of this court, that, while the parties were restrained by the authority of the circuit court from using it, they ought not to be charged with interest. The decree of the circuit court for the district of Ohio is affirmed, as to the said sums of $98,000 and $2000; and reversed as to the residue.

JOHNSON, JUSTICE. (Dissenting.)—The argument in this cause presents three questions: 1. Has congress granted to the Bank of the United States, an unlimited right of suing in the courts of the United States? 2. Could congress constitutionally grant such a right? 3. Has the power of the court been legally and constitutionally exercised in this suit?

I have very little doubt, that the public mind will be easily reconciled to the decision of the court here rendered: for, whether necessary or unnecessary, originally, a state of things has now grown up, in some of the states, which renders all the protection necessary, that the general government can give to this bank. The policy of the decision is obvious, that is, if the bank is to be sustained; and few will bestow upon its legal correctness, the reflection that it is necessary to test it by the constitution and laws, under which it is rendered.

The Bank of the United States is now identified with the administration of the national government. It is an immense machine economically and beneficially applied to the fiscal transactions of the nation. Attempts have been made to dispense with it, and they have failed; serious and very weighty doubts have been entertained of its constitutionality, but they have been abandoned; and it is now become the functionary that collects, the depository that holds, the vehicle that transports, the guard that protects, and the agent that distributes and pays away, the millions that pass annually through the national treasury; and all this, not only without expense to the government, but after paying a large *bonus,* and sustaining actual annual losses to a large amount; furnishing the only possible means of embodying the most ample security for so immense a charge.

Had its effects, however, and the views of its framers, been confined exclusively to its fiscal uses, it is more than probable, that this suit, and the laws in which it originated, would never have had existence. But it is well known, that with that object was combined another, of a very general, and not less important character. The expiration of the charter of the former bank, led to state creations of banks; each new bank increased the facilities of creating others; and the necessities of the general government, both to make use of the state banks for their deposits, and to borrow largely of all who would lend to them, produced that rage for multiplying banks, which, aided by the emoluments derived to the states in their creation, and the many individual incentives which they developed, soon inundated the country with new description of bills of credit, against which, it was obvious, that the provisions of the constitution opposed no adequate inhibition. A specie-paying bank, with an overwhelming capital, and the whole aid of the government deposits, presented the only resource to which the government could resort, to restore that power over the currency of the country, which the framers of the constitution evidently intended to give to congress alone. But this necessarily involved a restraint upon individual cupidity, and the exercise of state power; and in the nature of things, it was hardly possible, for the mighty effort necessary to put down an evil, spread so wide, and arrived to such maturity, to be made, without embodying against it an immense moneyed combination, which could not fail of making its influence to be felt, wherever its claimances could reach, or its industry and wealth be brought to operate.

I believe, that the good sense of a people, who know that they govern themselves, and feel that they have no interests distinct from those of their government, would readily concede to the bank, thus circumstanced, some, if not all the rights here contended for. But I cannot persuade myself, that they have been conceded in the extent which this decision affirms. Whatever might be proper to be done by an amendment of the constitution, this court is only, at present, expounding its existing provisions. In the present instance, I cannot persuade myself, that the constitution sanctions the vesting of the right of action in this bank, in cases in which the privilege is exclusively personal, or in any case, merely on the ground that a question might possibly be raised in it, involving the constitution, or constitutionality of a law of the United States.

When laws were heretofore passed for raising a revenue by a duty on stamped paper, the tax was quietly acquiesced in, notwithstanding it entrenched so closely on the questionable power of the states over the law of contracts; but had the same law which declared void contracts not written upon stamped paper, declared, that every person holding such paper should be entitled to bring his action "in any circuit court" of the United States, it is confidently believed, that there could have been but one opinion on the constitutionality of such a provision. The whole jurisdiction over contracts, might thus have been taken from the state courts, and conferred upon those of the United States. Nor would the evil have rested there; by a similar exercise of power, imposing a stamp on deeds, generally, jurisdiction over the territory of the state, whoever might be parties, even between citizens of the same state—jurisdiction of suits instituted for the recovery of legacies or distributive portions of intestates' estates—jurisdiction, in fact, over almost every possible case, might be transferred to the courts of the United States. Wills might be required to be executed on stamped paper; taxes may be, and have been, imposed upon legacies and distributions, and in all such cases, there is not only a possibility, but a probability, that a question may arise, involving the constitutionality, construction, &c., of a law of the United States. If the circumstance, that the questions which the case involves, are to determine its character, whether those questions be made in the case or not, then, every case here alluded to, may as well be transferred to the jurisdiction of the United States, as those to which this bank is a party. But still further, as was justly insisted in argument, there is not a tract of land of the United States, acquired under laws of the United States, whatever be the number of mesne transfers that it may have undergone, over which the jurisdiction of the court of the United States might not be extended by congress, upon the very principle on which the right of suit in this bank is here maintained. Nor is the case of the alien, put in argument, at all inapplicable. The one acquires its character of individual property, as the other does his political existence, under a law of the United States; and there is not a suit which may be instituted to recover the one, nor an action of ejectment to be brought by the other, in which a right acquired under a law of the United States, does not lie as essentially at the basis of the right of action, as in the suits brought by this bank. It is no answer to the argument, to say, that the law of the United States is but ancillary to the constitution, as to the alien; for the constitution could do nothing for him, without the law: and whether the question be upon law or constitution, still, if the possibility of its arising, be a sufficient circumstance to bring it within the jurisdiction of the United States courts, that possibility exists with regard to every suit affected by alien disabilities; to real actions, in time of peace—to all actions, in time of war.

I cannot persuade myself, then, that, with these palpable consequences in view, congress ever could have intended to vest in the Bank of the United States the right of suit to the extent here claimed. * * *

* * * I next proceed to consider, more distinctly, the constitutional question, on the right to vest the jurisdiction to the extent here contended for. And here I must observe, that I altogether misunderstood the counsel, who argued the cause for the plaintiff in error, if any of them contended against the jurisdiction, on the ground, that the cause involved questions depending on general principles. No one can question, that the court which has jurisdiction of the principal question, must exercise jurisdiction over every question. Neither did I understand them as denying, that if congress could confer on the circuit courts appellate, they could confer original, jurisdiction. The argument went to deny the right to assume jurisdiction, on a mere hypothesis. It was one of description, identity, definition; they contended, that until a question involving the construction or administration of the laws of the United States did actually arise, the *casus foederis* was not presented, on which the constitution authorized the government to take to itself the jurisdiction of the cause. That until such a question actually arose, until such a case was actually presented, *non constat*, but the cause depended upon general principles, exclusively cognisable in the state courts; that neither the letter nor the spirit of the constitution sanctioned the assumption of jurisdiction on the part of the United States, at any previous stage.

And this doctrine has my hearty concurrence in its general application. A very simple case may be stated, to illustrate its bearing on the question of jurisdiction between the two governments. By virtue of treaties with Great Britain, aliens holding lands were exempted from alien disabilities, and made capable of holding, aliening and transmitting their estates, in common with natives. But why should the claimants of such lands, to all eternity, be vested with the privilege of bringing an original suit in the courts of the United States? It is true, a question might be made, upon the effect of the treaty, on the rights claimed by or through the alien; but until that question does arise, nay, until a decision against the right takes place, what end has the United States to subserve, in claiming jurisdiction of the cause? * * *

Efforts have been made to fix the precise sense of the constitution, when it vests jurisdiction in the general government, in "cases arising under the laws of the United States." To me, the question appears susceptible of a very simple solution; that all depends upon the identity of the case supposed; according to which idea, a case may be such, in its very existence, or may become such, in its progress. An action may "live, move and have its being," in a law of the United States; such is that given for the violation of a patent-right, and four or five different actions given by this act of incorporation; particularly that against the president and directors for over-issuing; in all of which cases, the plaintiff must count upon the law itself as the ground of his action. And of the other description, would have been an action of trespass, in this case, had remedy been sought for an actual levy of the tax imposed. Such was the case of the former bank against Deveaux, and many others that have occurred in this court, in which the suit, in its form, was such as occur in ordinary cases, but in which the pleadings or evidence raised the question on the law or constitution of the United States. In this class of cases, the occurrence of a question makes the case, and transfers it, as provided for under the 25th section of the judiciary act, to the jurisdiction of the United States. And this appears to me to present the only sound and practical construction of the constitution on this subject; for no other cases does it regard as necessary to place under the control of the general government. It is only when the case exhibits one or the other of these characteristics, that it is acted upon by the constitution. Where no question is raised, there can be no contrariety of construction; and what else had the constitution to guard against? As to cases of the first description, *ex necessitate rei,* the courts of the United States must be susceptible of original jurisdiction; and as to all other cases, I should hold them also susceptible of original jurisdiction, if it were practicable, in the nature of things, to make out the definition of the case, so as to bring it under the constitution judicially, upon an original suit. But until the plaintiff can control the defendant in his pleadings, I see no practical mode of determining when the case does occur, otherwise than by permitting the cause to advance, until the case for which the constitution provides shall actually arise. If it never occurs, there can be nothing to complain of; and such are the provisions of the 25th section. The cause might be transferred to the circuit court, before an adjudication takes place; but I can perceive no earlier stage at which it can possibly be predicated of such a case, that it is one within the constitution; nor any possible necessity for transferring it then, or until the court has acted upon it to the prejudice of the claims of the United States. It is not, therefore, because congress may not vest an *original* jurisdiction, where they can constitutionally vest in the circuit courts *appellate* jurisdiction, that I object to this general grant of the right to sue; but because that the peculiar nature of this jurisdiction is such, as to render it impossible to exercise it, in a strictly original form, and because the principle of a possible occurrence of a question, as a ground of jurisdiction, is transcending the bounds of the constitution, and placing it on a ground which will admit of an enormous accession, if not an unlimited assumption, of jurisdiction.

* * * *

Upon the whole, I feel compelled to dissent from the court, on the point of jurisdiction; and this renders it unnecessary for me to express my sentiments on the residue of the points in the cause.

TEXTILE WORKERS UNION v. LINCOLN MILLS

353 U.S. 448, 77 S.Ct. 912, 1 L.Ed.2d 972 (1957).
Certiorari to the United States Court of Appeals for the Fifth Circuit.

[The Opinion of the Court appears at pp. 878–881, *supra.*]

MR. JUSTICE BURTON, whom MR. JUSTICE HARLAN joins, concurring in the result. * * *

* * * * I do not subscribe to the conclusion of the Court that the substantive law to be applied in a suit under § 301 [of the Taft–Hartley

Act] is federal law. At the same time, I agree with Judge Magruder in International Brotherhood v. W.L. Mead, Inc., 230 F.2d 576, that some federal rights may necessarily be involved in a § 301 case, and hence that the constitutionality of § 301 can be upheld as a congressional grant to Federal District Courts of what has been called "protective jurisdiction."

MR. JUSTICE FRANKFURTER, dissenting. * * *

[The first portion of this opinion appears at pp. 881–83, *supra*.]

The second ground of my dissent from the Court's action is more fundamental. Since I do not agree with the Court's conclusion that federal substantive law is to govern in actions under § 301, I am forced to consider the serious constitutional question that was adumbrated in the Westinghouse case, 348 U.S., at 449–452, the constitutionality of a grant of jurisdiction to federal courts over contracts that came into being entirely by virtue of state substantive law, a jurisdiction not based on diversity of citizenship, yet one in which a federal court would, as in diversity cases, act in effect merely as another court of the State in which it sits. The scope of allowable federal judicial power that this grant must satisfy is constitutionally described as "Cases, in Law and Equity, arising under this Constitution, the Laws of the United States, and Treaties made, or which shall be made, under their Authority." Art. III, § 2. While interpretive decisions are legion under general statutory grants of jurisdiction strikingly similar to this constitutional wording, it is generally recognized that the full constitutional power has not been exhausted by these statutes. See, *e.g.*, Mishkin, *The Federal "Question" in the District Courts*, 53 Col.L.Rev. 157, 160; Shulman and Jaegerman, *Some Jurisdictional Limitations on Federal Procedure*, 45 Yale L.J. 393, 405, n. 47; Wechsler, *Federal Jurisdiction and the Revision of the Judicial Code*, 13 Law & Contemp.Prob., 216, 224–225.

Almost without exception, decisions under the general statutory grants have tested jurisdiction in terms of the presence, as an integral part of plaintiff's cause of action, of an issue calling for interpretation or application of federal law. * * * The litigation-provoking problem has been the degree to which federal law must be in the forefront of the case and not collateral, peripheral or remote.

In a few exceptional cases, arising under special jurisdictional grants, the criteria by which the prominence of the federal question is measured against constitutional requirements have been found satisfied under circumstances suggesting a variant theory of the nature of these requirements. The first, and the leading case in the field, is Osborn v. Bank of United States, 9 Wheat. 738.

There, Chief Justice Marshall sustained federal jurisdiction in a situation—hypothetical in the case before him but presented by the companion case of Bank of United States v. Planters' Bank, 9 Wheat. 904—involving suit by a federally incorporated bank upon a contract. Despite the assumption that the cause of action and the interpretation of the contract would be governed by state law, the case was found to "arise under the laws of the United States" because the propriety and scope of a federally granted authority to enter into contracts and to litigate might well be challenged. This reasoning was subsequently applied to sustain jurisdiction in actions against federally chartered railroad corporations. Pacific Railroad Removal Cases, 115 U.S. 1. The traditional interpretation of this series of cases is that federal jurisdiction under the "arising" clause of the Constitution, though limited to cases involving potential federal questions, has such flexibility that Congress may confer it whenever there exists in the background some federal proposition that might be challenged, despite the remoteness of the likelihood of actual presentation of such a federal question.[4]

The views expressed in Osborn and the Pacific Railroad Removal Cases were severely restricted in construing general grants of jurisdiction. But the Court later sustained this jurisdictional section of the Bankruptcy Act of 1898:

"The United States district courts shall have jurisdiction of all controversies at law and in equity, as distinguished from proceedings in bankruptcy, between trustees as such and adverse claimants concerning the property acquired or claimed by the trustees, in the same manner and to the same extent only as though bankruptcy proceedings had not been instituted and such controversies had been between the bankrupts and such adverse claimants." § 23, sub. a, as amended, 44 Stat. 664, 11 U.S.C. § 46, sub. a.

Under this provision the trustee could pursue in a federal court a private cause of action arising under and wholly governed by state law. Schumacher v. Beeler, 293 U.S. 367; Williams v. Austrian, 331 U.S. 642 (Chandler Act of 1938, 52 Stat. 840, 11 U.S.C.A. § 1 et seq.). To be sure, the cases did not discuss the basis of jurisdiction. It has been suggested that they merely represent an extension of the approach of the Osborn case; the trustee's right to sue might be challenged on obviously federal grounds—absence of bankruptcy or irregularity of the trustee's appointment or of the bankruptcy proceedings. National Mutual Ins. Co. of Dist. of Col. v. Tidewater Transfer Co., 337 U.S. 582, 611–613 (Rutledge, J., concurring). So viewed, this type of litigation implicates a potential federal question.

Apparently relying on the extent to which the bankruptcy cases involve only remotely a federal question, Mr. Justice Jackson concluded in National Mutual Insurance Co. of Dist. of Col. v. Tidewater Transfer Co., 337 U.S. 582, that Congress may confer jurisdiction on the District Courts as incidental to its powers under Article I. No attempt was made to reconcile this view with the restrictions of Article III; a majority of the Court recognized that Article III defined the bounds of valid jurisdictional legislation and rejected the notion that jurisdictional grants can go outside these limits.

With this background, many theories have been proposed to sustain the constitutional validity of § 301. In Textile Workers Union of America v. American Thread Co., 113 F.Supp. 137, 140, Judge Wyzanski suggested, among other possibilities, that § 301 might be read as containing a direction that controversies affecting interstate commerce should be governed by federal law incorporating state law by reference, and that such controversies would then arise under a valid federal law as required by Article III. Whatever may be said of the assumption regarding the validity of federal jurisdiction under an affirmative declaration by Congress that state law should be applied as federal law by federal courts to contract disputes affecting commerce, we cannot argumentatively legislate for Congress

---

4. Osborn might possibly be limited on the ground that a federal instrumentality, the Bank of the United States, was in- volved, see note 5, *infra*, but such an explanation could not suffice to narrow the holding in the Pacific Railroad Removal Cases.

when Congress has failed to legislate. To do so disrespects legislative responsibility and disregards judicial limitations.

Another theory, relying on Osborn and the bankruptcy cases, has been proposed which would achieve results similar to those attainable under Mr. Justice Jackson's view, but which purports to respect the "arising" clause of Article III. See Hart and Wechsler, The Federal Courts and the Federal System, pp. 744–747 [1st ed. 1953]; Wechsler, *Federal Jurisdiction and the Revision of the Judicial Code,* 13 Law & Contemp. Prob. 216, 224–225; International Brotherhood of Teamsters, etc. v. W.L. Mead, Inc., 230 F.2d 576. Called "protective jurisdiction," the suggestion is that in any case for which Congress has the constitutional power to prescribe federal rules of decision and thus confer "true" federal question jurisdiction, it may, without so doing, enact a jurisdictional statute, which will provide a federal forum for the application of state statute and decisional law. Analysis of the "protective jurisdiction" theory might also be attempted in terms of the language of Article III—construing "laws" to include jurisdictional statutes where Congress could have legislated substantively in a field. This is but another way of saying that because Congress could have legislated substantively and thereby could give rise to litigation under a statute of the United States, it can provide a federal forum for state-created rights although it chose not to adopt state law as federal law or to originate federal rights.

Surely the truly technical restrictions of Article III are not met or respected by a beguiling phrase that the greater power here must necessarily include the lesser. In the compromise of federal and state interests leading to distribution of jealously guarded judicial power in a federal system, see 13 Cornell L.Q. 499, it is obvious that very different considerations apply to cases involving questions of federal law and those turning solely on state law. It may be that the ambiguity of the phrase "arising under the laws of the United States" leaves room for more than traditional theory could accommodate. But, under the theory of "protective jurisdiction," the "arising under" jurisdiction of the federal courts would be vastly extended. For example, every contract or tort arising out of a contract affecting commerce might be a potential cause of action in the federal courts, even though only state law was involved in the decision of the case. At least in Osborn and the bankruptcy cases, a substantive federal law was present somewhere in the background. See 353 U.S. 470–472, *supra,* and 353 U.S. 480–484, *infra.* But this theory rests on the supposition that Congress could enact substantive federal law to govern the particular case. It was not held in those cases, nor is it clear, that federal law could be held to govern the transactions of all persons who subsequently become bankrupt, or of all suits of a Bank of the United States. See Mishkin, *The Federal "Question" in the District Courts,* 53 Col.L.Rev. 157, 189.

"Protective jurisdiction," once the label is discarded, cannot be justified under any view of the allowable scope to be given to Article III. "Protective jurisdiction" is a misused label for the statute we are here considering. That rubric is properly descriptive of safeguarding some of the indisputable, staple business of the federal courts. It is a radiation of an existing jurisdiction. See Adams v. United States ex rel. McCann, 317 U.S. 269; 28 U.S.C. § 2283. "Protective jurisdiction" cannot generate an independent source for adjudication outside of the Article III sanctions and what Congress has defined. The theory must have as its sole justification a belief in the inadequacy of state tribunals in determining state law. The

Constitution reflects such a belief in the specific situation within which the Diversity Clause was confined. The intention to remedy such supposed defects was exhausted in this provision of Article III.[5] That this "protective" theory was not adopted by Chief Justice Marshall at a time when conditions might have presented more substantial justification strongly suggests its lack of constitutional merit. Moreover, Congress in its consideration of § 301 nowhere suggested dissatisfaction with the ability of state courts to administer state law properly. Its concern was to provide access to the federal courts for easier enforcement of state-created rights.

Another theory also relies on Osborn and the bankruptcy cases as an implicit recognition of the propriety of the exercise of some sort of "protective jurisdiction" by the federal courts. Mishkin, op. cit. *supra*, 53 Col.L. Rev. 157, 184 *et seq.* Professor Mishkin tends to view the assertion of such a jurisdiction, in the absence of any exercise of substantive powers, as irreconcilable with the "arising" clause since the case would then arise only under the jurisdictional statute itself, and he is reluctant to find a constitutional basis for the grant of power outside Article III. Professor Mishkin also notes that the only purpose of such a statute would be to insure impartiality to some litigant, an objection inconsistent with Article III's recognition of "protective jurisdiction" only in the specified situation of diverse citizenship. But where Congress has "an articulated and active federal policy regulating a field, the 'arising under' clause of Article III apparently permits the conferring of jurisdiction on the national courts of all cases in the area—including those substantively governed by state law." *Id.,* at 192. In such cases, the protection being offered is not to the suitor, as in diversity cases, but to the "congressional legislative program." Thus he supports § 301: "even though the rules governing collective bargaining agreements continue to be state-fashioned, nonetheless the mode of their application and enforcement may play a very substantial part in the labor-management relations of interstate industry and commerce—an area in which the national government has labored long and hard." *Id.,* at 196.

Insofar as state law governs the case, Professor Mishkin's theory is quite similar to that advanced by Professors Hart and Wechsler and followed by the Court of Appeals for the First Circuit: The substantive power of Congress, although not exercised to govern the particular "case," gives "arising under" jurisdiction to the federal courts despite governing state law. The second "protective jurisdiction" theory has the dubious advantage of limiting incursions on state judicial power to situations in which the State's feelings may have been tempered by early substantive federal invasions.

Professor Mishkin's theory of "protective jurisdiction" may find more constitutional justification if there is not merely an "articulated and

---

5. To be sure, the Court upheld the removal statute for suits or prosecutions commenced in a state court against federal revenue officers on account of any act committed under color of office. State of Tennessee v. Davis, 100 U.S. 257, 25 L.Ed. 648. The Court, however, construed the action of Congress in defining the powers of revenue agents as giving them a substantive defense against prosecution under state law for commission of acts "warranted by the Federal authority they possess." *Id.,* 100 U.S. at page 263. That put federal law in the forefront as a defense. In any event, the fact that officers of the Federal Government were parties may be considered sufficient to afford access to the federal forum. See In re Debs, 158 U.S. 564, 584–586; Mishkin, 53 Col.L.Rev., at 193: "Without doubt, a federal forum should be available for all suits involving the Government, its agents and instrumentalities, regardless of the source of the substantive rule."

active" congressional policy regulating the labor field but also federal rights existing in the interstices of actions under § 301. See Wollett and Wellington, *Federalism and Breach of the Labor Agreement,* 7 Stan.L.Rev. 445, 475–479. * * *

Legislation must, if possible, be given a meaning that will enable it to survive. This rule of constitutional adjudication is normally invoked to narrow what would otherwise be the natural but constitutionally dubious scope of the language. * * * Here the endeavor of some lower courts and of this Court has resulted in adding to the section substantive congressional regulation even though Congress saw fit not to exercise such power or to give the courts any concrete guidance for defining such regulation.

To be sure, the full scope of a substantive regulation is frequently in dispute and must await authoritative determination by courts. Congress declares its purpose imperfectly or partially, and compatible judicial construction completes it. But in this case we start with a provision that is wholly jurisdictional and as such bristles with constitutional problems under Article III. To avoid them, interpolation of substantive regulation has been proposed. From what materials are we to draw a determination that § 301 is something other than what it declares itself? Is the Court justified in creating all the difficult problems of choice within a sphere of delicate policy without any direction from Congress and merely for the sake of giving effect to a provision that seems to deal with a different subject? * * * The suggestion that the section permits the federal courts to work out, without more, a federal code governing collective-bargaining contracts must, for reasons that have already been stated, be rejected. Likewise the suggestion that § 301 may be viewed as a congressional authorization to the federal courts to work out a concept of the nature of the collective-bargaining contract, leaving detailed questions of interpretation to state law. * * *.

There is a point, however, at which the search may be ended with less misgiving regarding the propriety of judicial infusion of substantive provisions into § 301. The contribution of federal law might consist in postulating the right of a union, despite its amorphous status as an unincorporated association, to enter into binding collective-bargaining contracts with an employer. The federal courts might also give sanction to this right by refusing to comply with any state law that does not admit that collective bargaining may result in an enforceable contract. It is hard to see what serious federal-state conflicts could arise under this view. At most, a state court might dismiss the action, while a federal court would entertain it. Moreover, such a function of federal law is closely related to the removal of the procedural barriers to suit. * * *

Even if this limited federal "right" were read into § 301, a serious constitutional question would still be present. It does elevate the situation to one closely analogous to that presented in Osborn v. Bank of United States, 9 Wheat. 738. Section 301 would, under this view, imply that a union is to be viewed as a juristic entity for purposes of acquiring contract rights under a collective-bargaining agreement, and that it has the right to enter into such a contract and to sue upon it. This was all that was immediately and expressly involved in the Osborn case, although the historical setting was vastly different and the juristic entity in that case was completely the creature of federal law, one engaged in carrying out essential governmental functions. Most of these special considerations had disappeared, however, at the time and in the circumstances of the decision of the Pacific Railroad Removal Cases, 115 U.S. 1. There is force in the view that regards the latter as a "sport" and finds that the Court has so viewed it. See Mishkin, 53 Col.L.Rev., at 160, n. 24, citing Gully v. First National Bank, 299 U.S. 109, 113–114 ("Only recently we said after full consideration that the doctrine of the charter cases was to be treated as exceptional, though within their special field there was no thought to disturb them."), and People of Puerto Rico v. Russell & Co., 288 U.S. 476, 485; see also Mr. Justice Holmes, in Smith v. Kansas City Title & Trust Co., 255 U.S. 180, 214–215 (dissenting opinion). The question is whether we should now so consider it and refuse to apply its holding to the present situation.

I believe that we should not extend the precedents of Osborn and the Pacific Railroad Removal Cases to this case even though there be some elements of analytical similarity. Osborn, the foundation for the Removal Cases, appears to have been based on premises that today, viewed in the light of the jurisdictional philosophy of Gully v. First National Bank, *supra,* are subject to criticism. The basic premise was that every case in which a federal question might arise must be capable of being commenced in the federal courts, and when so commenced it might, because jurisdiction must be judged as the outset, be concluded there despite the fact that the federal question was never raised. Marshall's holding was undoubtedly influenced by his fear that the bank might suffer hostile treatment in the state courts that could not be remedied by an appeal on an isolated federal question. There is nothing in Article III that affirmatively supports the view that original jurisdiction over cases involving federal questions must extend to every case in which there is the potentiality of appellate jurisdiction. We also have become familiar with removal procedures that could be adapted to alleviate any remaining fears by providing for removal to a federal court whenever a federal question was raised. In view of these developments, we would not be justified in perpetuating a principle that permits assertion of original federal jurisdiction on the remote possibility of presentation of a federal question. Indeed, Congress, by largely withdrawing the jurisdiction that the Pacific Railroad Removal Cases recognized, and this Court, by refusing to perpetuate it under general grants of jurisdiction, see Gully v. First National Bank, *supra,* have already done much to recognize the changed atmosphere.

Analysis of the bankruptcy power also reveals a superficial analogy to § 301. The trustee enforces a cause of action acquired under state law by the bankrupt. Federal law merely provides for the appointment of the trustee, vests the cause of action in him, and confers jurisdiction on the federal courts. Section 301 similarly takes the rights and liabilities which under state law are vested distributively in the individual members of a union and vests them in the union for purposes of actions in federal courts, wherein the unions are authorized to sue and be sued as an entity. While the authority of the trustee depends on the existence of a bankrupt and on the propriety of the proceedings leading to the trustee's appointment, both of which depend on federal law, there are similar federal propositions that may be essential to an action under § 301. Thus, the validity of the contract may in any case be challenged on the ground that the labor organization negotiating it was not the representative of the employees concerned, a question that has been held to be federal, La Crosse Telephone Corp. v. Wisconsin Employment Relations Board, 336 U.S. 18, or on the ground that subsequent change in the representative status of the union has affected the continued validity of the agreement. Perhaps also the qualifications imposed on a union's right to utilize the facilities of the National Labor Relations Board, dependent on the filing of non-Communist affidavits required by § 9(h), 29 U.S.C.A. § 159(h), and the information and reports required by § 9(f) and (g), might be read as restrictions on the right of the union to sue under § 301, again providing a federal basis for challenge to the union's authority. Consequently, were the bankruptcy cases to be viewed as dependent solely on the background existence of federal questions, there would be little analytical basis for distinguishing actions under § 301. But the bankruptcy decisions may be justified by the scope of the bankruptcy power, which may be deemed to sweep within its scope interests analytically outside the "federal question" category, but sufficiently related to the main purpose of bankruptcy to call for comprehensive treatment. See National Mutual Ins. Co. v. Tidewater Transfer Co., 337 U.S. 582, 652, Note 3 (concurring in part, dissenting in part). Also, although a particular suit may be brought by a trustee in a district other than the one in which the principal proceedings are pending, if all the suits by the trustee, even though in many federal courts, are regarded as one litigation for the collection and apportionment of the bankrupt's property, a particular suit by the trustee, under state law, to recover a specific piece of property might be analogized to the ancillary or pendent jurisdiction cases in which, in the disposition of a cause of action, federal courts may pass on state grounds for recovery that are joined to federal grounds. See Hurn v. Oursler, 289 U.S. 238; Siler v. Louisville & Nashville R. Co., 213 U.S. 175; but see Mishkin, 53 Col.L.Rev., at 194, n. 161.

If there is in the phrase "arising under the laws of the United States" leeway for expansion of our concepts of jurisdiction, the history of Article III suggests that the area is not great and that it will require the presence of some substantial federal interest, one of greater weight and dignity than questionable doubt concerning the effectiveness of state procedure. The bankruptcy cases might possibly be viewed as such an expansion. But even so, not merely convenient judicial administration but the whole purpose of the congressional legislative program—conservation and equitable distribution of the bankrupt's estate in carrying out the constitutional power over bankruptcy—required the availability of federal jurisdiction to avoid expense and delay. Nothing pertaining to § 301 suggests vesting the federal courts with sweeping power under the Commerce Clause comparable to that vested in the federal courts under the bankruptcy power.

In the wise distribution of governmental powers, this Court cannot do what a President sometimes does in returning a bill to Congress. We cannot return this provision to Congress and respectfully request that body to face the responsibility placed upon it by the Constitution to define the jurisdiction of the lower courts with some particularity and not to leave these courts at large. Confronted as I am, I regretfully have no choice. For all the reasons elaborated in this dissent, even reading into § 301 the limited federal rights consistent with the purposes of that section, I am impelled to the view that it is unconstitutional in cases such as the present ones where it provides the sole basis for exercise of jurisdiction by the federal courts.

NOTE ON THE SCOPE OF THE CONSTITUTIONAL GRANT
AND THE VALIDITY OF A PROTECTIVE JURISDICTION

(1) In a companion case to the Osborn case, in which the jurisdiction also was sustained, the Bank of the United States had brought suit in a federal circuit court as the bearer of negotiable notes made by a state bank. Bank of the United States v. Planter's Bank of Georgia, 9 Wheat. 904 (U.S.1824). Was the Court right in treating the two cases as raising the same question?

The Bank's existence as a federal corporation was only a remote premise of its claim for relief in both cases. But in the Osborn case, unlike the other, the immediate premise was also federal—namely, the right under the Constitution and laws of the United States to be free from state taxation. Compare Justice Johnson's description of the type of case in which, in his view, a "strictly original" jurisdiction is proper.

(2) Consider Marshall's proposition that original jurisdiction "is coextensive with judicial power" and that Congress is capable of "giving the Circuit Courts original jurisdiction, in any case to which the appellate jurisdiction extends." Can this be right? Does it also suggest that appellate jurisdiction may be exercised in any case over which there would have been original jurisdiction? Can that be right?

Osborn apparently holds that Congress has the constitutional authority to endow the federal district courts with original "arising under" jurisdiction in any case where any proposition of federal law might be an "ingredient" of the cause, even though the proposition is unchallenged and unchallengeable. Even if this is correct, however, should it lead to the conclusion that if such a case is litigated in a state court, and no question of federal law is in any way raised or decided in fact, the Supreme Court could constitutionally be given appellate jurisdiction over the case? *Per contra*, assume that the Osborn proposition is too broad in suggesting that the mere theoretical possibility of a federal issue is sufficient to justify a grant of original jurisdiction. Isn't it clear that if such a case is litigated in a state court, and, unexpectedly, a federal question does in fact arise, the Supreme Court would have appellate jurisdiction even though (by hypothesis) there could not have been original jurisdiction?

The important point is that appellate jurisdiction can be tailored to the case as it actually developed: whether there is a federal "ingredient" is known by the time the appeal is taken. The original jurisdiction must, on the other hand, be based on conjecture: it cannot be known with certainty what issues will turn out to be decisive. Doesn't this difference have implications for the question whether the constitutional scope of the appellate jurisdiction is wholly congruent with the original jurisdiction? See also the *Note on Murdock v. Memphis*, p. 530, *supra*.

(3) Justice Frankfurter, noting that Osborn's premises have been "subject to criticism," asserts that "we would not be justified in perpetuating a principle that permits assertion of original federal jurisdiction on the remote possibility of presentation of a federal question." Is there an answer to this? If the Osborn proposition is taken at face value, is there any case not within the constitutional scope of the "arising under" jurisdiction? On any theory of the purposes of the constitutional grant, should it be deemed to include cases where the only federal interest is the entirely

theoretical possibility that some federal issue could conceivably arise in the litigation?

(4) What are those purposes? Justice Johnson's view was that federal tribunals must be available as expositors of federal law. If this is the sole purpose of the constitutional grant, it can be fully exploited by (a) authorizing federal appellate review of state court decisions upon determinative points of federal law and (b) giving federal trial courts (i) original jurisdiction only in cases necessarily involving federal law, and (ii) removal jurisdiction in such cases and in other cases when and if a determinative federal issue has been framed.

In addition, it would be universally conceded that a further constitutional function of federal courts is to enforce federal law—to establish the facts determinative of the application of federal law even if the law's content and applicability are undisputed, and to enter and enforce the appropriate judgment. What additions to the original and removal jurisdiction would be required fully to exploit this constitutional function?

(5) Do these two functions fulfill all of the purposes of the framers "to make the judicial power coextensive with the legislative"? Does Justice Frankfurter present a persuasive case that the federal concerns animating the constitutional grant of "arising under" jurisdiction are not implicated simply because the issues in the law suit involve the exposition and application of state law?

Take the case of the Bank. Congress had power to incorporate it and to provide for its continuing functioning. Should Congress be held to have power to provide a federal forum for litigation in which the Bank might become involved only to the extent that the outcome of the litigation depends upon exposition and application of substantive federal law? Is the only risk of the Bank's litigating in state courts that those courts might hold that the Bank did not have capacity to sue or to contract? If Congress' concern extended beyond that, to the ways in which state courts might handle other issues in Bank cases, should it not be deemed to have power to bring such litigation into the federal courts? Should it have to enact federal substantive law to govern all those other issues—or even be sure of its power to do so—in order to bring those cases before a federal forum?

May not a basis for a protective jurisdiction exist to prevent discrimination against federal instrumentalities or interests even though there is no need to enact an encompassing federal substantive law? Cf. Tennessee v. Davis, 100 U.S. 257 (1879), p. 481, supra; Strauder v. West Virginia, 100 U.S. 303 (1879). Isn't protection of congressionally created or recognized interests an essential purpose of extending the judicial power to cases "arising under * * * the Laws of the United States"? May not that purpose be served by the grant of federal jurisdiction in situations like that of the Bank—where an active and articulated congressional legislative program is at stake—even though the particular cases may involve state substantive law only? In terms of the purposes of the Article III provision, do not such cases truly "arise under" the federal laws creating the program?

See also the Note on the Tidewater Problem, p. 473, supra.

(6) The Bankruptcy Act of 1867, 14 Stat. 517, as construed in Lathrop v. Drake, 91 U.S. 516 (1875), gave the district courts two distinct classes of

jurisdiction: "first, jurisdiction as a court of bankruptcy over the proceedings in bankruptcy initiated by the petition, and ending in the distribution of assets amongst the creditors, and the discharge or refusal of a discharge of the bankrupt; secondly, jurisdiction, as an ordinary court, of suits at law or in equity brought by or against the assignee in reference to alleged property of the bankrupt, or to claims alleged to be due from or to him". The latter jurisdiction, the Court held, could be exercised, without regard to the citizenship of the parties, and was not confined to the court in which the bankruptcy proceedings were initiated. The Court also construed the act as giving the circuit courts concurrent jurisdiction, similarly without regard to citizenship, of any action "brought by the assignee in bankruptcy against any person claiming an adverse interest".

Without directly adverting to the question of the validity of this protective jurisdiction, the Court said (p. 518):

" * * * The State courts may undoubtedly be resorted to in cases of ordinary suits for the possession of property or the collection of debts; and it is not to be presumed that embarrassments would be encountered in those courts in the way of a prompt and fair administration of justice. But a uniform system of bankruptcy, national in its character, ought to be capable of execution in the national tribunals, without dependence upon those of the States in which it is possible that embarrassments might arise."

The Bankruptcy Act of 1898 adopted a sharply different policy with respect to independent suits by the trustee in bankruptcy. Section 23 of the Act, as amended, 44 Stat. 664 (1926), 11 U.S.C. § 46, laid down the general rule that the federal courts should have jurisdiction of "controversies at law and in equity, as distinguished from proceedings in bankruptcy, between trustees as such and adverse claimants concerning the property acquired or claimed by the trustees, in the same manner and to the same extent only as though bankruptcy proceedings had not been instituted and such controversies had been between the bankrupts and such adverse claimants". See Bardes v. Hawarden Bank, 178 U.S. 524 (1900).

Among other exceptions to this general rule in the case of suits by the trustee, however, was the clause "unless by consent of the proposed defendant". This provision was construed in Schumacher v. Beeler, 293 U.S. 367 (1934), as relating to jurisdiction and not venue and as restoring in cases of consent the general jurisdiction of the district courts over plenary suits by the trustee which had existed under the 1867 act. On the issue of power, Chief Justice Hughes said shortly (p. 374): "The Congress, by virtue of its constitutional authority over bankruptcies, could confer or withhold jurisdiction to entertain such suits and could prescribe the conditions upon which the federal courts should have jurisdiction".

In Williams v. Austrian, 331 U.S. 642 (1947), the Court again found that Congress had authorized a similar protective jurisdiction of actions by the trustee, in the case of reorganizations under the Chandler Act of 1938, 52 Stat. 840. The Justices divided sharply over the issue of construction, but none doubted the constitutional power.[1]

1. See also the cryptic reference to the basis for "arising under" jurisdiction over state-law cases brought in connection with bankruptcy, in footnote 26 of the Northern Pipeline case, p. 434, supra.

(7) In 1976 Congress enacted the Foreign Sovereign Immunities Act (FSIA),[2] a comprehensive statute designed to set forth the substantive standards and procedural rules governing suits brought against foreign nations in the federal and state courts. The Act provides broadly that the federal district courts "shall have original jurisdiction without regard to amount in controversy of any nonjury civil action against a foreign state * * * as to any claim * * * with respect to which the foreign state is not entitled to immunity" either under the terms of the FSIA itself or under any applicable international agreement. 28 U.S.C. § 1330(a). Any such claim brought in a state court may be removed by the foreign state to a federal court. Section 1441(d). The Act sets forth detailed standards for determining when foreign states are or are not immune from suit in courts in the United States; no such immunity exists, *inter alia,* when immunity has been waived, when the claim arises from specified commercial activities of the foreign state carried on or causing effects in the United States, when certain rights in property taken in violation of international law are at issue, when rights in specified property located in the United States are at issue, or when certain tortious injuries to persons or property within the United States are at issue. Sections 1604, 1605. When immunity does not apply, "the foreign state shall be liable in the same manner and to the same extent as a private individual under like circumstances." Section 1606. The Act specifies rules as to punitive damages (§ 1606), attachment and execution (§§ 1609–11), venue (§ 1391(f)), process (§ 1607), counterclaims (§ 1607), and default judgment (§ 1608(e)).

Verlinden B.V. v. Central Bank of Nigeria, 461 U.S. 480 (1983), involved a suit by a Dutch corporation against an instrumentality of the Government of Nigeria for breach of a contract allegedly having effects within the United States within the meaning of one of the FSIA provisions abrogating foreign sovereign immunity. The court of appeals held that, although the FSIA applies to suits by foreign plaintiffs against foreign states, it was unconstitutional insofar as it permits the federal courts to entertain such actions when the substantive claim is not itself based on federal law. 647 F.2d 320 (2d Cir.1981). The court concluded that Osborn should be limited to its facts; that the FSIA was merely jurisdictional and that a federal case or controversy could not arise under such a law; and that the cases narrowly construing the "arising under" language in the *statutory* grant of federal question jurisdiction governed the interpretation of the constitutional text.

The Supreme Court reversed in a unanimous opinion by Chief Justice Burger. Agreeing that the Act applies to foreign plaintiffs (and thus cannot be justified as an instance of diversity jurisdiction), the Court stated that the "controlling decision" is Osborn, which "reflects a broad conception of 'arising under' jurisdiction, according to which Congress may confer on the federal courts jurisdiction over any case or controversy that might call for the application of federal law." The Court continued (pp. 492–97): "The breadth of that conclusion has been questioned. It has been observed that, taken at its broadest, Osborn might be read as permitting 'assertion of original federal jurisdiction on the remote possibility of presentation of a federal question.' Textile Workers Union v. Lincoln Mills, 353 U.S. 448, 482 (1957) (Frankfurter, J., dissenting). See, *e.g.,* P. Bator, P. Mishkin, D.

---

2. Act of October 21, 1976, 90 Stat. 2891–98. The FSIA is codified at 28 U.S.C. §§ 1330, 1332(a)(2)–1332(a)(4), 1391(f), 1441(d), and 1602–1611.

Shapiro, & H. Wechsler, Hart & Wechsler's The Federal Courts and the Federal System 866–867 (2d ed. 1973). We need not now resolve that issue or decide the precise boundaries of Art. III jurisdiction, however, since the present case does not involve a mere speculative possibility that a federal question may arise at some point in the proceeding. Rather, a suit against a foreign state under this Act necessarily raises questions of substantive federal law at the very outset, and hence clearly 'arises under' federal law, as that term is used in Art. III.

"By reason of its authority over foreign commerce and foreign relations, Congress has the undisputed power to decide, as a matter of federal law, whether and under what circumstances foreign nations should be amenable to suit in the United States. Actions against foreign sovereigns in our courts raise sensitive issues concerning the foreign relations of the United States, and the primacy of federal concerns is evident. See, *e.g.,* Banco Nacional De Cuba v. Sabbatino, 376 U.S. 398, 423–425 (1964); Zschernig v. Miller, 389 U.S. 429, 440–441 (1968).

"To promote these federal interests, Congress exercised its Art. I powers by enacting a statute comprehensively regulating the amenability of foreign nations to suit in the United States. The statute must be applied by the district courts in every action against a foreign sovereign, since subject-matter jurisdiction in any such action depends on the existence of one of the specified exceptions to foreign sovereign immunity, 28 U.S.C. § 1330(a). At the threshold of every action in a district court against a foreign state, therefore, the court must satisfy itself that one of the exceptions applies—and in doing so it must apply the detailed federal law standards set forth in the Act. Accordingly, an action against a foreign sovereign arises under federal law, for purposes of Art. III jurisdiction.

"In reaching a contrary conclusion, the Court of Appeals relied heavily upon decisions construing 28 U.S.C. § 1331, the statute which grants district courts general federal-question jurisdiction over any case that 'arises under' the laws of the United States. The court placed particular emphasis on the so-called 'well-pleaded complaint' rule, which provides, for purposes of *statutory* 'arising under' jurisdiction, that the federal question must appear on the face of a well-pleaded complaint and may not enter in anticipation of a defense. * * *

"Although the language of § 1331 parallels that of the 'Arising Under' Clause of Art. III, this Court never has held that statutory 'arising under' jurisdiction is identical to Art. III 'arising under' jurisdiction. Quite the contrary is true. * * * Art. III 'arising under' jurisdiction is broader than federal-question jurisdiction under § 1331, and the Court of Appeals' heavy reliance on decisions construing that statute was misplaced. * * *

"Congress, pursuant to its unquestioned Art. I powers, has enacted a broad statutory framework governing assertions of foreign sovereign immunity. In so doing, Congress deliberately sought to channel cases against foreign sovereigns away from the state courts and into federal courts, thereby reducing the potential for a multiplicity of conflicting results among the courts of the 50 States. The resulting jurisdictional grant is within the bounds of Art. III, since every action against a foreign sovereign necessarily involves application of a body of substantive federal law, and accordingly 'arises under' federal law, within the meaning of Art. III."

(8) The Diplomatic Relations Act of 1978, Pub.L. No. 95–393, added the following provision to the Judicial Code (28 U.S.C. § 1364):

> "(a) The district courts shall have original and exclusive jurisdiction, without regard to the amount in controversy, of any civil action commenced by any person against an insurer who by contract has insured an individual, who is a member of a mission (as defined in the Vienna Convention on Diplomatic Relations) or a member of the family of such a member of a mission * * * against liability for personal injury, death, or damage to property.

> "(b) Any direct action brought against an insurer under subsection (a) shall be tried without a jury, but shall not be subject to the defense that the insured is immune from suit, that the insured is an indispensable party, or in the absence of fraud or collusion, that the insured has violated a term of the contract, unless the contract was cancelled before the claim arose."

The purpose of this provision was to provide a means of recovering damages, particularly for automobile accident injuries, caused by foreign diplomats who are themselves immune from suit. The Senate Judiciary Committee Report accompanying the bill said (S.Rep. No. 1108, 95th Cong., 2d Sess. 5 (1978)):

> "The substantive tort law to be applied by Federal courts in direct actions against insurers under [this section] of the bill will be State law (*i.e.*, the law of the place where the tortious act or omission occurs. *Cf.* 28 U.S.C. § 1364(b)). Resort to State law will also be made to determine the applicable statute of limitations."

It seems most unlikely that all actions within this section could be considered "Cases affecting Ambassadors, other public Ministers and Consuls" within Art. III, Sec. 2 of the Constitution.[3] If not within that provision, is there any basis other than the "arising under" clause on which jurisdiction in these direct actions may properly be predicated?

See also 28 U.S.C. § 1350, conferring jurisdiction over "any civil action by an alien for a tort only, committed in violation of the law of nations or a treaty of the United States," discussed in Casto, *The Federal Courts' Protective Jurisdiction Over Torts Committed in Violation of the Law of Nations,* 18 Conn.L.Rev. 467 (1986). See further pp. 904–05, *supra.*

(9) Issues of "protective jurisdiction" may also arise under Section 304 of the Clean Air Act, 42 U.S.C. § 7604 which authorizes private civil actions against any person alleged to be in violation of any "emission standard or limitation" issued under the Act, and provides for district court jurisdiction over such actions without regard to citizenship. "Emission standards" presumably include standards contained in state-promulgated "State Implementation Plans"; these plans must meet federal minimums and be approved by EPA, but otherwise constitute detailed programs of

---

3. See S.Rep. 95–1108, pp. 6–7, indicating that many members of missions within the Vienna Convention or statutory definition would not be of the level of ambassadors, ministers or consuls, and would thus be outside the scope of the Article III provision regarding them. The discussion of the Report at that point is directed to another provision of the statute, amending 28 U.S.C. § 1351 so as to give the district courts exclusive jurisdiction over all civil actions against members of a diplomatic mission or their families. Is this jurisdictional provision valid?

implementation, maintenance and enforcement of air quality standards as a matter of state law.[4]

SECTION 3. THE SCOPE OF THE STATUTORY GRANT OF FEDERAL QUESTION JURISDICTION

LOUISVILLE & NASHVILLE R. CO. v. MOTTLEY

211 U.S. 149, 29 S.Ct. 42, 53 L.Ed. 126 (1908).
Appeal From the Circuit Court of the United States for the
Western District of Kentucky.

MR. JUSTICE MOODY delivered the opinion of the Court.

[Appellees, husband and wife and citizens of Kentucky, brought this suit in equity for specific performance of a contract against the railroad, a Kentucky corporation. The contract provided that the Mottleys would release the railroad from all claims for damages arising from a certain train collision; in return the railroad agreed to issue free passes to the Mottleys during the rest of their lives. The bill alleged that, beginning in 1907, the railroad declined to renew the passes, relying on the Act of Congress of June 29, 1906, forbidding the giving of free passes. The bill further alleged that the statute properly construed did not prohibit free passes pursuant to contracts entered into before its passage; but that if construed retroactively to invalidate the Mottleys' contract, it violated the Fifth Amendment. The federal circuit court overruled the railroad's demurrer and entered a decree of specific performance; the railroad appealed to the Supreme Court.]

Two questions of law * * * have been argued before us. They are, first, whether that part of the act of Congress of June 29, 1906 (34 Stat. 584), which forbids the giving of free passes or the collection of any different compensation for transportation of passengers than that specified in the tariff filed, makes it unlawful to perform a contract for transportation of persons, who in good faith, before the passage of the act, had accepted such contract in satisfaction of a valid cause of action against the railroad; and, second, whether the statute, if it should be construed to render such a contract unlawful, is in violation of the Fifth Amendment of the Constitution of the United States. We do not deem it necessary, however, to consider either of these questions, because, in our opinion, the court below was without jurisdiction of the cause. Neither party has questioned that jurisdiction, but it is the duty of this court to see to it that the jurisdiction of the Circuit Court, which is defined and limited by statute, is not exceeded. This duty we have frequently performed of our

---

4. For a decision upholding jurisdiction in an analogous situation under the Truth in Lending Act, 15 U.S.C. § 1640, although without discussion of the issue, see Ives v. W.T. Grant Co., 522 F.2d 749 (2d Cir.1975), commented on in Note, 89 Harv.L.Rev. 998 (1976).

For discussions of protective jurisdiction, see Goldberg–Ambrose, *The Protective Jurisdiction of the Federal Courts*, 30 U.C. L.A.L.Rev. 542 (1983); Note, *The Theory of Protective Jurisdiction*, 57 N.Y.U.L.Rev. 933 (1982).

own motion. Mansfield, & c. Railway Company v. Swan, 111 U.S. 379, 382; King Bridge Company v. Otoe County, 120 U.S. 225; Blacklock v. Small, 127 U.S. 96, 105; Cameron v. Hodges, 127 U.S. 322, 326; Metcalf v. Watertown, 128 U.S. 586, 587; Continental National Bank v. Buford, 191 U.S. 119.

There was no diversity of citizenship and it is not and cannot be suggested that there was any ground of jurisdiction, except that the case was a "suit * * * arising under the Constitution and laws of the United States." It is the settled interpretation of these words, as used in this statute, conferring jurisdiction, that a suit arises under the Constitution and laws of the United States only when the plaintiff's statement of his own cause of action shows that it is based upon those laws or that Constitution. It is not enough that the plaintiff alleges some anticipated defense to his cause of action and asserts that the defense is invalidated by some provision of the Constitution of the United States. Although such allegations show that very likely, in the course of the litigation, a question under the Constitution would arise, they do not show that the suit, that is, the plaintiff's original cause of action, arises under the Constitution. In Tennessee v. Union & Planters' Bank, 152 U.S. 454, the plaintiff, the State of Tennessee, brought suit in the Circuit Court of the United States to recover from the defendant certain taxes alleged to be due under the laws of the State. The plaintiff alleged that the defendant claimed an immunity from the taxation by virtue of its charter, and that therefore the tax was void, because in violation of the provision of the Constitution of the United States, which forbids any State from passing a law impairing the obligation of contracts. The cause was held to be beyond the jurisdiction of the Circuit Court, the court saying, by Mr. Justice Gray (p. 464), "a suggestion of one party, that the other will or may set up a claim under the Constitution or laws of the United States, does not make the suit one arising under that Constitution or those laws." * * *

The interpretation of the act which we have stated was first announced in Metcalf v. Watertown, 128 U.S. 586, and has since been repeated and applied in * * * [citing 17 cases]. The application of this rule to the case at bar is decisive against the jurisdiction of the Circuit Court.

It is ordered that the *judgment be reversed and the case remitted to the Circuit Court with instructions to dismiss the suit for want of jurisdiction.*

AMERICAN WELL WORKS CO. v. LAYNE & BOWLER CO.

241 U.S. 257, 36 S.Ct. 585, 60 L.Ed. 987 (1916).
Error to the District Court of the United States for the
Eastern District of Arkansas.

MR. JUSTICE HOLMES delivered the opinion of the Court.

This is a suit begun in a state court, removed to the United States court, and then, on motion to remand by the plaintiff, dismissed by the latter court, on the ground that the cause of action arose under the patent laws of the United States, that the state court had no jurisdiction, and that therefore the one to which it was removed had none. There is a proper certificate and the case comes here direct from the district court.

Of course the question depends upon the plaintiff's declaration. The Fair v. Kohler Die & Specialty Co., 228 U.S. 22, 25. That may be summed up in a few words. The plaintiff alleges that it owns, manufactures, and sells a certain pump, has or has applied for a patent for it, and that the pump is known as the best in the market. It then alleges that the defendants have falsely and maliciously libeled and slandered the plaintiff's title to the pump by stating that the pump and certain parts thereof are infringements upon the defendants' pump and certain parts thereof, and that without probable cause they have brought suits against some parties who are using the plaintiff's pump, and that they are threatening suits against all who use it. The allegation of the defendants' libel or slander is repeated in slightly varying form, but it all comes to statements to various people that the plaintiff was infringing the defendants' patent, and that the defendant would sue both seller and buyer if the plaintiff's pump was used. Actual damage to the plaintiff in its business is alleged to the extent of $50,000, and punitive damages to the same amount are asked.

It is evident that the claim for damages is based upon conduct; or, more specifically, language, tending to persuade the public to withdraw its custom from the plaintiff, and having that effect to its damage. Such conduct, having such effect, is equally actionable whether it produces the result by persuasion, by threats, or by falsehood (Moran v. Dunphy, 177 Mass. 485, 487), and it is enough to allege and prove the conduct and effect, leaving the defendant to justify if he can. If the conduct complained of is persuasion, it may be justified by the fact that the defendant is a competitor, or by good faith and reasonable grounds. If it is a statement of fact, it may be justified, absolutely or with qualifications, by proof that the statement is true. But all such justifications are defenses, and raise issues that are no part of the plaintiff's case. In the present instance it is part of the plaintiff's case that it had a business to be damaged; whether built up by patents or without them does not matter. It is no part of it to prove anything concerning the defendants' patent, or that the plaintiff did not infringe the same—still less to prove anything concerning any patent of its own. The material statement complained of is that the plaintiff infringes,—which may be true notwithstanding the plaintiff's patent. That is merely a piece of evidence. Furthermore, the damage alleged presumably is rather the consequence of the threat to sue than of the statement that the plaintiff's pump infringed the defendants' rights.

A suit for damages to business caused by a threat to sue under the patent law is not itself a suit under the patent law. And the same is true when the damage is caused by a statement of fact,—that the defendant has a patent which is infringed. What makes the defendants' act a wrong is its manifest tendency to injure the plaintiff's business; and the wrong is the same whatever the means by which it is accomplished. But whether it is a wrong or not depends upon the law of the state where the act is done, not upon the patent law, and therefore the suit arises under the law of the state. A suit arises under the law that creates the cause of action. The fact that the justification may involve the validity and infringement of a patent is no more material to the question under what law the suit is brought than it would be in an action of contract. If the state adopted for civil proceedings the saying of the old criminal law: the greater the truth, the greater the libel, the validity of the patent would not come in question at all. In Massachusetts the truth would not be a defense if the statement was made from disinterested malevolence. Rev.Laws, chap. 173, § 91. The state is master of the whole matter, and if it saw fit to do away with actions of this type altogether, no one, we imagine, would suppose that they still could be maintained under the patent laws of the United States.

Judgment reversed.

MR. JUSTICE MCKENNA dissents, being of opinion that the case involves a direct and substantial controversy under the patent laws.

SMITH v. KANSAS CITY TITLE & TRUST CO.

255 U.S. 180, 41 S.Ct. 243, 65 L.Ed. 577 (1921).
Appeal from the District Court of the United States for the
Western District of Missouri.

MR. JUSTICE DAY delivered the opinion of the Court.

A bill was filed in the United States District Court for the Western Division of the Western District of Missouri by a shareholder in the Kansas City Title & Trust Company to enjoin the company, its officers, agents and employees, from investing the funds of the company in farm loan bonds issued by Federal Land Banks or Joint–Stock Land Banks under authority of the Federal Farm Loan Act of July 17, 1916, c. 245, 39 Stat. 360, as amended by Act Jan. 18, 1918, c. 9, 40 Stat. 431.

The relief was sought on the ground that these acts were beyond the constitutional power of Congress. The bill avers that the board of directors of the company are about to invest its funds in the bonds to the amount of $10,000 in each of the classes described, and will do so unless enjoined by the court in this action. * * *

Section 27 of the act provides that farm loan bonds issued under the provisions of the act by Federal Land Banks or Joint–Stock Land Banks shall be a lawful investment for all fiduciary and trust funds, and may be accepted as security for all public deposits. The bill avers that the defendant Trust Company is authorized to buy, invest in and sell government, state and municipal and other bonds, but it cannot buy, invest in or sell any such bonds, papers, stocks or securities which are not authorized to be issued by a valid law or which are not investment securities, but that nevertheless it is about to invest in farm loan bonds; that the Trust Company has been induced to direct its officers to make the investment by reason of its reliance upon the provisions of the Farm Loan Acts, especially sections 21, 26 and 27, by which the farm loan bonds are declared to be instrumentalities of the government of the United States, and as such, with the income derived therefrom, are declared to be exempt from federal, state, municipal and local taxation, and are further declared to be lawful investments for all fiduciary and trust funds. The bill further avers that the acts by which it is attempted to authorize the bonds are wholly illegal, void and unconstitutional, and of no effect, because unauthorized by the Constitution of the United States.

The bill prays that the acts of Congress authorizing the creation of the banks, especially sections 26 and 27 thereof, shall be adjudged and decreed to be unconstitutional, void and of no effect, and that the issuance of the farm loan bonds, and the taxation exemption feature thereof, shall be adjudged and decree to be invalid.

The First Joint-Stock Land Bank of Chicago and the Federal Land Bank of Wichita, Kan., were allowed to intervene and became parties defendant to the suit. The Kansas City Title & Trust Company filed a motion to dismiss in the nature of a general demurrer, and upon hearing the District Court entered a decree dismissing the bill. From this decree appeal was taken to this court.

No objection is made to the federal jurisdiction, either original or appellate, by the parties to this suit, but that question will be first examined. The company is authorized to invest its funds in legal securities only. The attack upon the proposed investment in the bonds described is because of the alleged unconstitutionality of the acts of Congress undertaking to organize the banks and authorize the issue of the bonds. No other reason is set forth in the bill as a ground of objection to the proposed investment by the board of directors acting in the company's behalf. As diversity of citizenship is lacking, the jurisdiction of the District Court depends upon whether the cause of action set forth arises under the Constitution or laws of the United States. Judicial Code, § 24 (Comp.St. § 991).

The general rule is that, where it appears from the bill or statement of the plaintiff that the right to relief depends upon the construction or application of the Constitution or laws of the United States, and that such federal claim is not merely colorable, and rests upon a reasonable foundation, the District Court has jurisdiction under this provision.

At an early date, considering the grant of constitutional power to confer jurisdiction upon the federal courts, Chief Justice Marshall said:

"A case in law or equity consists of the right of the one party, as well as of the other, and may truly be said to arise under the Constitution or a law of the United States, whenever its correct decision depends upon the construction of either," Cohens v. Virginia, 6 Wheat. 264, 379; and again, when "the title or right set up by the party, may be defeated by one construction of the Constitution or law of the United States, and sustained by the opposite construction." Osborn v. Bank of the United States, 9 Wheat. 738, 822. * * *

The jurisdiction of this court is to be determined upon the principles laid down in the cases referred to. In the instant case the averments of the bill show that the directors were proceeding to make the investments in view of the act authorizing the bonds about to be purchased, maintaining that the act authorizing them was constitutional and the bonds valid and desirable investments. The objecting shareholder avers in the bill that the securities were issued under an unconstitutional law, and hence of no validity. It is therefore apparent that the controversy concerns the constitutional validity of an act of Congress which is directly drawn in question. The decision depends upon the determination of this issue.

The general allegations as to the interest of the shareholder, and his right to have an injunction to prevent the purchase of the alleged unconstitutional securities by misapplication of the funds of the corporation, gives jurisdiction under the principles settled in Pollock v. Trust Company [157 U.S. 429] and Brushaber v. Union Pacific Company [240 U.S. 1], *supra.* We are therefore of the opinion that the District Court had jurisdiction under the averments of the bill and that a direct appeal to this court upon constitutional grounds is authorized. * * *

Affirmed [on merits].

MR. JUSTICE BRANDEIS took no part in the consideration or decision of this case.

MR. JUSTICE HOLMES, dissenting.

No doubt it is desirable that the question raised in this case should be set at rest, but that can be done by the Courts of the United States only within the limits of the jurisdiction conferred upon them by the Constitution and the laws of the United States. As this suit was brought by a citizen of Missouri against a Missouri corporation the single ground upon which the jurisdiction of the District Court can be maintained is that the suit "arises under the Constitution or laws of the United States" within the meaning of section 24 of the Judicial Code. I am of opinion that this case does not arise in that way and therefore that the bill should have been dismissed.

It is evident that the cause of action arises not under any law of the United States but wholly under Missouri law. The defendant is a Missouri corporation and the right claimed is that of a stockholder to prevent the directors from doing an act, that is, making an investment, alleged to be contrary to their duty. But the scope of their duty depends upon the charter of their corporation and other laws of Missouri. If those laws had authorized the investment in terms the plaintiff would have had no case, and this seems to me to make manifest what I am unable to deem even debatable, that, as I have said, the cause of action arises wholly under Missouri law. If the Missouri law authorizes or forbids the investment according to the determination of this Court upon a point under the Constitution or Acts of Congress, still that point is material only because the Missouri law saw fit to make it so. The whole foundation of the duty is Missouri law, which at its sole will incorporated the other law as it might incorporate a document. The other law or document depends for its relevance and effect not on its own force but upon the law that took it up, so I repeat once more the cause of action arises wholly from the law of the State.

But it seems to me that a suit cannot be said to arise under any other law than that which creates the cause of action. It may be enough that the law relied upon creates a part of the cause of action although not the whole, as held in Osborn v. Bank of United States, 9 Wheat. 738, 819–823, which perhaps is all that is meant by the less guarded expressions in Cohens v. Virginia, 6 Wheat. 264, 379. I am content to assume this to be so, although the Osborn Case has been criticized and regretted. But the law must create at least a part of the cause of action by its own force, for it is the suit, not a question in the suit, that must arise under the law of the United States. The mere adoption by a State law of a United States law as a criterion or test, when the law of the United States has no force proprio vigore, does not cause a case under the State law to be also a case under the law of the United States, and so it has been decided by this Court again and again. Miller v. Swann, 150 U.S. 132, 136, 137; Louisville & Nashville R.R. Co. v. Western Union Telegraph Co., 237 U.S. 300, 303. See, also, Shoshone Mining Co. v. Rutter, 177 U.S. 505, 508, 509.

I find nothing contrary to my views in Brushaber v. Union Pacific R.R. Co., 240 U.S. 1, 10. It seems to me plain that the objection that I am considering was not before the mind of the Court or the subject of any of its observations, if open. I am confirmed in my view of that case by the fact that in the next volume of reports is a decision, reached not without discussion and with but a single dissent, that "a suit arises under the law that creates the cause of action." That was the ratio decidendi of American Well Works Co. v. Layne & Bowler Co., 241 U.S. 257, 260. I know of no decisions to the contrary and see no reason for overruling it now.

MR. JUSTICE MCREYNOLDS concurs in this dissent. In view of our opinion that this Court has no jurisdiction we express no judgment on the merits.

NOTE ON THE MEANING OF "ARISING UNDER" IN THE FEDERAL QUESTION STATUTE: THE TRADITIONAL LEARNING

(1) In light of the three cases above, and the remaining materials in this Note, consider whether the following "Restatement" accurately summarized the state of the law as of 1985, just before Merrell Dow (p. 1007, *infra*) was decided:

Proposition A. A case "arises under" federal law for purposes of the general federal question statute if it is brought to enforce a right of action created by federal law.

Proposition B. A case also "arises under" federal law for the same purposes if it is brought to enforce a right of action created by state law, if under orderly rules of pleading and proof the plaintiff, as part of his case in chief, must establish the correctness and applicability of a proposition of federal law in order to prevail.

Proposition C. No case other than those described in Propositions A and B "arises under" federal law within the meaning of the general federal question statute.

A. The Effect of the Statutory Adoption of the Constitutional Language

(2) What is the significance of the fact that the 1875 Act and its successors have always used the language of the Constitution to describe the statutory jurisdiction?[1]

The Act was a Senate amendment to a House bill relating only to the removal jurisdiction, and was hurriedly enacted at the close of a session without substantial debate. See Frankfurter & Landis, The Business of the Supreme Court 65–69 (1928); Chadbourn & Levin, *Original Jurisdiction of Federal Questions,* 90 U.Pa.L.Rev. 639, 642–45 (1942); Forrester, *The Na-*

---

1. The only possibly significant departure from the language of the constitution was the use of the word "suits" instead of "cases". Justice Miller, dissenting in Railroad Co. v. Mississippi, 102 U.S. 135, 143 (1880), seized upon this difference as the basis for his argument that, under the statute, jurisdiction depended on the law under which the plaintiff claimed and could not rest on a federal defense. The conclusion, though not the argument, was adopted in Tennessee v. Union & Planters' Bank, 152 U.S. 454 (1894), and it has not been affected by the substitution of the phrase, "matter in controversy," in 1911. Act of March 3, 1911, § 24, 36 Stat. 1087, 1091.

The current statute (§ 1331) substitutes "civil actions" for the term "suits of a civil nature, at common law or in equity."

ture of a "Federal Question", 16 Tulane L.Rev. 362 (1942). The most significant bit in the legislative history was a statement of Senator Carpenter, who was in charge of the bill. Speaking of the bill as a whole rather than of the federal question section, he first presented as authoritative the views of Justice Story discussed in Chap. IV, Sec. 1, pp. 366–68, *supra*, and then said:

" * * * The act of 1789 did not confer the whole power which the Constitution conferred; it did not do what the Supreme Court has said Congress ought to do; it did not perform what the Supreme Court has declared to be the duty of Congress. This bill does. * * * This bill gives precisely the power which the Constitution confers—nothing more, nothing less."

Relying on this incident and on the identity of language, Dean Forrester argued that the statutory provision and the constitutional provision should be "considered synonymous".

(3) Professors Chadbourn and Levin agree with Dean Forrester that the 1875 act should be read as conferring, in the first instance, the whole of the federal question jurisdiction permissible under the Constitution, or at least the whole of it permissible under the Osborn opinion. But, they say, the draftsmen recognized that "if this radical legislation was to prove practicable * * *, provision had to be made to protect the lower federal courts from a flood of litigation technically within the broad limits staked out by Marshall, but actually unrelated to the purpose of the Act". Such a provision they find in § 5 of the act, p. 963, *supra*, requiring dismissal or remand if "it shall appear * * * at any time after such suit has been brought or removed * * * that such suit does not really and substantially involve a dispute or controversy properly within the jurisdiction of said circuit court". See Chadbourn & Levin, *supra*, at 650.

In only one case does the Supreme Court seem to have applied the act in this fashion. Robinson v. Anderson, 121 U.S. 522, 524 (1887). This was an action in the nature of ejectment by a plaintiff claiming under a United States patent of the land against defendants who were alleged also to be claiming under a patent. The defendants' answers, however, either denied possession or justified under an alleged license from the plaintiff. The Supreme Court affirmed a judgment of dismissal for want of jurisdiction.

(4) As pointed out in Justice Frankfurter's opinion in Lincoln Mills, in the Pacific Railroad Removal Cases, 115 U.S. 1 (1885), the Court held that federal incorporation of a party *ipso facto* made a case one "arising under" national law within the 1875 Act. At the time of the decision the requirements for removal jurisdiction were not tied to those for original jurisdiction, the 1875 Act permitting removal by either party of any suit, involving the requisite amount, "arising under the Constitution or laws of the United States".[2]

The Pacific Railroad Removal Cases go farther than any case decided before[3] or since to suggest that the 1875 Act filled the whole of the

---

2. Congress has overruled the Pacific Railroad Removal Cases, save as to corporations in which the United States is the owner of more than one-half the capital stock. 28 U.S.C. § 1349. The steps by which this overruling was effected are traced in Frankfurter, *Distribution of Ju-* *dicial Power Between United States and State Courts*, 13 Corn.L.Q. 499, 509–11 (1928).

3. For cases antedating the Pacific Railroad Removal Cases that appeared to construe the 1875 removal provision more nar-

constitutional space provided for "arising under" cases. In light of the cases already considered and to be considered in this Chapter, it would seem clear that they can no longer be regarded as authoritative in this regard. In addition to the discussions in Lincoln Mills and Verlinden, *supra,* see Shoshone Mining Co. v. Rutter, 177 U.S. 505, 506 (1900) ("the question, therefore, is not one of the power of Congress, but of its intent"); Romero v. International Terminal Operating Co., 358 U.S. 354, 379 n. 51 (1959) ("the many limitations which have been placed on jurisdiction under § 1331 are not limitations on the constitutional power of Congress to confer jurisdiction on the federal courts"); Zwickler v. Koota, 389 U.S. 241, 246 n. 8 (1967); Franchise Tax Board v. Construction Laborers Vacation Trust, 463 U.S. 1, 8 n. 8 (1983), p. 1029, *infra;* Merrell Dow Pharmaceuticals Inc. v. Thompson, 478 U.S. 804 (1986), p. 1007, *infra.*

In light of the manifest differences between the functions of the constitutional grant and the statutory grant, would it be appropriate to treat the language in the two provisions as encompassing identical territory? Would the expansive approach of Osborn be tenable if it were to define the scope of the statutory jurisdiction?

Note in particular the significance of the fact that "[a] case in law or equity consists of the right of the one party, as well as of the other, and may truly be said to arise under the constitution or a law of the United States, whenever its correct decision depends on the construction of either." Marshall, C.J., in Cohens v. Virginia, 6 Wheat. 264, 379 (U.S.1821). If the statutory grant of original federal question jurisdiction were deemed to encompass all cases within the scope of the constitutional grant, would not all cases where a federal defense *might* be an "ingredient" of the defendant's case be maintainable by the plaintiff in a federal court? Would this be manageable?

The Mottley case, subsequent to the Supreme Court's decision, was adjudicated in the state courts; the federal issues were the only decisive questions. It was then reviewed by the United States Supreme Court. 219 U.S. 467 (1911). What lesson does this teach?

B. The Well-Pleaded Complaint Rule

(5) The principle of the Mottley case—that a case does not "arise under" federal law for purposes of original jurisdiction under the Act of 1875 and its successors unless an assertion as to federal law is part of the plaintiff's well-pleaded complaint—might be regarded as a technical rule of convenience, designed to avoid making original jurisdiction turn on speculation as to what issues will be decisive in the litigation. But the rule has a wide ranging policy impact as well, as a consequence of the fact that, ever since 1887, the general removal statute has been limited to cases falling within the original jurisdiction of the district court. See p. 1052, *infra.* Thus, cases like the Mottley case, if brought in a state court, could not be

rowly (and which the Court continued to treat as authoritative), see, *e.g.,* Little York Gold–Washing & Water Co. v. Keyes, 96 U.S. 199 (1878) (defense to injunction action grounded on claim that mining titles from the United States conferred a federal right to do the complained-of acts; removal denied); Albright v. Teas, 106 U.S. 613

(1883) (suit by patentee for royalties under an assignment; held not removable). Compare also Provident Savings Life Assurance Society v. Ford, 114 U.S. 635 (1885) (decided on same day as Pacific Railroad Removal Cases; suit on a judgment obtained in a federal court does not, for that reason alone, "arise under" federal law).

removed to federal court—even though the federal defenses raised by the railroad were the sole decisive issues in the litigation.

The wisdom of the policy barring federal-defense cases from the trial jurisdiction of the federal courts is further considered in the *Note on The General Removal Statute and the Problem of Federal Defense Removal,* p. 1052, *infra.* The continued vitality of the well pleaded complaint rule is, however, not in doubt. See, *e.g.,* the Franchise Tax Board case, p. 1027, *infra;* and see the authorities collected in 13B Wright, Miller & Cooper, Federal Practice and Procedure § 3566 (1984).

(6) Closely related to federal defense cases, and perhaps analytically identical, are actions maintainable only if they fall within the scope of a federal permission. In such cases the plaintiff may or may not assert compliance with the permission in his complaint, and the issue of compliance may or may not be drawn by the defendant.

The leading case is Gully v. First National Bank in Meridian, 299 U.S. 109 (1936). There a state tax collector sued a national bank to recover state taxes assessed upon the shares of a predecessor national bank, counting upon a contract by the defendant to assume its predecessor's debts. The taxes were permissible only by virtue of Rev.Stat. § 5219, 12 U.S.C. § 548. Speaking for a unanimous Court, Justice Cardozo said (p. 116):

"The argument for the respondent [the bank, which was trying to justify removal] proceeds on the assumption that because permission at times is preliminary to action the two are to be classed as one. But the assumption will not stand. A suit does not arise under a law renouncing a defense, though the result of the renunciation is an extension of the area of legislative power which will cause the suitor to prevail. Let us suppose an amendment of the Constitution by which the states are left at liberty to levy taxes on the income derived from federal securities, or to lay imposts and duties at their pleasure upon imports and exports. If such an amendment were adopted, a suit to recover taxes or duties imposed by the state law would not be one arising under the Constitution of the United States, though in the absence of the amendment the duty or the tax would fail. We recur to the test announced in Puerto Rico v. Russell & Co. [288 U.S. 476 (1933)]: 'The federal nature of the right to be established is decisive— not the source of the authority to establish it.' Here the right to be established is one created by the state. If that is so, it is unimportant that federal consent is the source of state authority. To reach the underlying law we do not travel back so far. By unimpeachable authority, a suit brought under a state statute does not arise under an act of Congress or the Constitution of the United States because prohibited thereby. Louisville & Nashville R. Co. v. Mottley, *supra.* With no greater reason can it be said to arise thereunder because permitted thereby."

Elsewhere in the Gully opinion, Justice Cardozo repeats a much-quoted statement from Shulthis v. McDougal, 225 U.S. 561, 569 (1912), the equivalent of which may be found in many other cases:

"A suit to enforce a right which takes its origin in the laws of the United States is not necessarily, or for that reason alone, one arising under those laws, for a suit does not so arise unless it really and substantially involves a dispute or controversy respecting the validity, construction or effect of such a law, upon the determination of which the result depends."

The latter statement has been the source of much confusion. It seems impossible to reconcile with the principle of the well-pleaded complaint rule: the complaint by itself can hardly be expected to demonstrate whether an issue of federal law will turn out to be "really and substantially" in dispute. And the formulation is inconsistent with the well settled proposition that if the plaintiff's action is brought to enforce a federally-created right, it "arises under" federal law even though it turns out, at the end of the day, that the only issues "really and substantially" in dispute are issues of state law, or issues of fact. Mishkin, *The Federal "Question" in the District Courts*, 53 Colum.L.Rev. 157, 170 (1953), suggests that Justice Cardozo's formulation represents "an uncritical transference to the lower federal courts of a standard developed for the exercise of the Supreme Court's appellate jurisdiction." But *cf.* Trautman, *Federal Right Jurisdiction and the Declaratory Remedy*, 7 Vand.L.Rev. 445 (1954).

(7) The well pleaded complaint rule has led to many complex refinements turning on the niceties of pleading lore, much of it deservedly forgotten today. See, *e.g.*, Hopkins v. Walker, 244 U.S. 486, 490 (1917) (bill to remove a cloud on title; jurisdiction upheld where the validity of the competing title depended on federal law, since "the facts showing the plaintiff's title and the existence and invalidity of the instrument or record sought to be eliminated as a cloud upon the title are essential parts of the plaintiff's cause of action" both as a matter of "general" and of Montana law); compare Shulthis v. McDougal, 225 U.S. 561 (1912) (jurisdiction denied, since in actions to quiet title allegations with respect to competing claims are not properly part of plaintiff's complaint), and Joy v. St. Louis, 201 U.S. 332 (1906) (action for ejectment; jurisdiction denied since, in an action for ejectment by a plaintiff not in possession, allegations with respect to plaintiff's title (which was allegedly based on a federal grant) are not properly part of the plaintiff's pleading); *cf.* Oneida Indian Nation v. County of Oneida, 414 U.S. 661 (1974), p. 1004, *infra* (general rule as to actions in ejectment not applicable to actions by Indian tribe to recover possession of lands because of the uniquely and continuously federal nature of the Indians' rights).

C. The Holmes Test: "A Suit Arises Under the Law That Creates the Cause of Action"

(8) As a principle of inclusion, the proposition that an action arises under federal law if the plaintiff asserts a federally created cause of action should be uncontroversial. The problem of jurisdiction when such a case involves only disputes as to the facts has bemused some commentators, but few courts (notwithstanding the previously quoted formulation of Justice Cardozo in Gully requiring a "dispute" about federal law). See, *e.g.*, McGoon v. Northern Pac. Ry., 204 Fed. 998 (D.N.D.1913), and the approving opinion in Peyton v. Railway Express Agency, Inc., 316 U.S. 350 (1942). *Cf.* Chadbourn and Levin, p. 995, *supra.* See also Note, *Proposed Revision of Federal Question Jurisdiction*, 40 Ill.L.Rev. 387 (1945).

(9) The scope of the Holmes proposition is illustrated by many cases under the patent and copyright laws. The current statute governing

jurisdiction in such cases is 28 U.S.C. § 1338; [4] but the governing concepts of what cases "arise under" these laws appear interchangeable with those developed under § 1331. Note, however, that the jurisdiction granted over cases arising under the patent and copyright laws by § 1338 is exclusive, so that a holding that a case is within that section is equally a holding that that case may not be brought in a state court—and vice versa.

(a) The federal right created by the patent and copyright statutes is the right to the monopoly, enforceable by an action for infringement. Many cases hold that there is federal jurisdiction over such an action even though plaintiff could have based his suit on a breach of a contract to license the patent, and even though the defendant's only defense may rest on such a licensing contract. See, *e.g.,* White v. Rankin, 144 U.S. 628 (1892) (jurisdiction not defeated by plea that allegedly infringing acts were justified by contract of license); Excelsior Wooden Pipe Co. v. Pacific Bridge Co., 185 U.S. 282 (1902) (exclusive licensee of patent brought suit for damages for infringement; plaintiff set up license only to show title to patent; jurisdiction sustained); The Fair v. Kohler Die & Specialty Co., 228 U.S. 22 (1913) (action by patentee to enjoin retailer from selling below specified minimum price, in alleged violation of patent law; "good or bad, the cause of action alleged is a cause of action under the laws of the United States"; the "party who brings a suit is master to decide what law he will rely upon"); Healy v. Sea Gull Specialty Co., 237 U.S. 479 (1915) (upholding jurisdiction over infringement action even though the bill (anticipating a defense) alleged a license and its termination, and used the license royalty to measure damages for infringement).

(b) It is equally clear that if the patentee bases his action on rights created by a contract, or on the common law of torts, the case is not one "arising under" federal law (at least for purposes of inclusion within the Holmes proposition). See, *e.g.,* (in addition to the American Well Works case, and Albright v. Teas, note 3, *supra*), New Marshall Engine Co. v. Marshall Engine Co., 223 U.S. 473 (1912) (state court has jurisdiction of suit for specific performance of contract to assign patent); Geneva Furniture Mfg. Co. v. S. Karpen & Bros., 238 U.S. 254 (1915) (upholding federal jurisdiction over part of bill charging contributory infringement; rest of bill not sustainable because based on contract); Becher v. Contoure Laboratories, Inc., 279 U.S. 388 (1929) (explaining why state court has jurisdiction over bill to compel assignment of a patent tortiously secured by patentee).

In Luckett v. Delpark, Inc., 270 U.S. 496 (1926), the Court summed up the law as follows (pp. 510–11): " * * * where a patentee complainant makes his suit one for recovery of royalties under a contract of license or assignment, or for damages for a breach of its covenants, or for a specific performance thereof, or asks the aid of the Court in declaring a forfeiture of the license or in restoring an unclouded title to the patent, he does not give the federal district court jurisdiction of the cause as one arising under the patent laws. Nor may he confer it in such a case by adding to his bill an averment that after the forfeiture shall be declared, or the title to the patent shall be restored, he fears the defendant will infringe and therefore asks an injunction to prevent it. * * * If * * * the patentee complainant had based his action on his patent right and had sued for infringement,

---

4. For a summary of the statutory development since 1790, see Chisum, *The Allocation of Jurisdiction Between State and*   *Federal Courts in Patent Litigation,* 46 Wash.L.Rev. 633, 634–38 (1971).

and by anticipation of a defense of the assignment had alleged a forfeiture by his own declaration without seeking aid of the court, jurisdiction under the patent laws would have attached, and he would have had to meet the claim by the defendant that forfeiture of the license or assignment and restoration of title could not be had except by a decree of a court, which if sustained, would have defeated his prayer for an injunction on the merits. But when the patentee exercises his choice and bases his action on the contract and seeks remedies thereunder, he may not give the case a double aspect, so to speak, and make it a patent case conditioned on his securing equitable relief as to the contract. *   *   *"

(c) Note that the result of these jurisdictional rules is that in some cases within exclusive federal court jurisdiction the dispute will be entirely about issues of state law (as where the question of liability for infringement turns entirely on the interpretation of a licensing contract); *per contra,* some cases within the exclusive jurisdiction of the state courts will turn out to depend entirely on federal questions involving the patent and copyright laws.

In Pratt v. Paris Gaslight & Coke Co., 168 U.S. 255 (1897), an action brought in a state court by a patentee-manufacturer for the purchase price of a patented machine, the Court held that the state court did not err in entertaining a defense of frustration based on the claim that the patent was void and that the use of the machine would infringe another patent. The Court said (p. 259):

"*   *   * Section 711 [the predecessor of § 1338(a)] does not deprive the state courts of the power to determine *questions* arising under the patent laws, but only of assuming jurisdiction of *'cases'* arising under those laws. There is a clear distinction between a case and a question arising under the patent laws. The former arises when the plaintiff in his opening pleading—be it a bill, complaint or declaration—sets up a right under the patent laws as ground for a recovery. Of such the state courts have no jurisdiction. The latter may appear in the plea or answer or in the testimony. The determination of such a question is not beyond the competency of the state tribunals."

In MacGregor v. Westinghouse Electric & Mfg. Co., 329 U.S. 402 (1947), a patentee-licensor sued a licensee in a state court for royalties under a licensing agreement that also contained a price-fixing covenant. The licensee defended on the ground, among others, that the patent was invalid, that the price-fixing covenant was therefore outside the protection of any lawful patent monopoly and in violation of the federal antitrust laws, and that the illegality of the covenant infected the whole licensing agreement. The state court, holding that the defendant was estopped to challenge the validity of his licensor's patent and rejecting other defenses, gave judgment for the plaintiff. This judgment the Supreme Court reversed, without any discussion of the state court's jurisdiction. It held that the state court was wrong, as a matter of federal law, in holding the licensee estopped, and directed "that the cause be remanded for a new trial to determine the validity of Westinghouse's patent".

Lear, Inc. v. Adkins, 395 U.S. 653 (1969), involved a patentee's state court action for royalties under a licensing agreement not involving a price-fixing term or alleged antitrust violation. The state supreme court held that the defendant was estopped to deny the validity of his licensor's patent. Reconsidering the general estoppel rule in light of "the strong federal policy favoring free competition in ideas which do not merit patent protection" (p. 656), the Supreme Court reversed and remanded, holding that the validity of the patent was open to attack in this proceeding and arguments to that effect should first be considered by the state courts.

(d) Does the wide power of state courts to pass on "patent questions" undermine the justification for exclusive federal jurisdiction of "patent cases"? Suggesting that it does, even before the Lear decision, *supra,* see Note, *The Enforcement of Rights Against Patent Infringers,* 72 Harv.L.Rev. 328, 330 (1958). Consider also Chisum, note 4, *supra,* at 663–64:

"The Court's decision in Lear has caused a decisive shift in the division of jurisdiction over patent questions between state and federal courts. The question of a patent's validity is now a potential issue in literally every action brought in state court for breach of a patent license or assignment.

"State court jurisdiction over patent validity questions is much less acceptable than state court jurisdiction over infringement questions, because the former does greater damage to the congressional policy of confining patent cases to the federal courts. Validity adjudications require a greater sensitivity to national policy—a sensitivity that only the national judiciary can be assumed to possess. Also, validity adjudications, unlike infringement adjudications, have a direct impact beyond the rights of parties involved. While a decision upholding a patent is res judicata only as to the particular defendant, that decision will significantly deter others from challenging the patent monopoly. Furthermore, in Blonder–Tongue Laboratories, Inc. v. University of Illinois Foundation [402 U.S. 313 (1971)], the Supreme Court held that a decision holding a patent invalid is binding in rem, that is, in favor of all whom the patentee might sue for infringement." [5]

Solutions suggested include legislation providing for enlargement of original federal jurisdiction to include all cases involving the licensing or assignment of patent rights or for removal, at the option of either party, whenever an issue of patent validity or infringement appears at any pleading stage. Note, *supra,* 72 Harv.L.Rev. at 330–31. See also Cooper, *State Law of Patent Exploitation,* 56 Minn.L.Rev. 313 (1972).

As to declaratory judgments in patent and copyright matters, see further the Franchise Tax Board case, p. 1027, *infra,* and the *Note on the Jurisdictional Significance of the Declaratory Judgment Act,* p. 1038, *infra.*

(e) For a masterly exposition of the jurisdictional rules governing copyright cases, see the opinion of Judge Henry Friendly in T.B. Harms Co. v. Eliscu, 339 F.2d 823 (2d Cir.1964). Here the complaint contained formal allegations of copyright infringement. The district court nevertheless dismissed the action for want of jurisdiction, on the ground that none of the acts charged in the complaint constituted acts of infringement and that the real controversy in the case turned upon whether defendant had executed an agreement assigning his rights in the specific copyrights. In affirming, Judge Friendly pointed out (p. 824): "A layman would doubtless be surprised to learn that an action wherein the purported sole owner of a copyright alleged that persons claiming partial ownership had recorded

5. In Blonder–Tongue, the previous determination of invalidity had been made by a federal court. Would a ruling by a state court have an identical estoppel effect? See the discussion in Chap. XII, pp. 1627–29, *infra.*

their claim in the Copyright Office and had warned his licensees against disregarding their interests was not one 'arising under any Act of Congress relating to * * * copyrights' over which 28 U.S.C. § 1338 gives the federal courts exclusive jurisdiction. Yet precedents going back for more than a century teach that lesson and lead us to affirm [the district court's] dismissal of the complaint." Compare De Sylva v. Ballentine, 351 U.S. 570 (1956), pp. 876–77, *supra* (declaratory judgment regarding interests in copyright renewals addressed on merits in non-diversity case; no discussion of district court's jurisdiction).

(10) Cases involving disputes about land in which the chain of title includes a grant or patent from the United States have generated some of the most confusing and difficult cases under the "arising under" language of § 1331 and its predecessors. Many—but not all—of these cases are excluded from federal court by the well pleaded complaint rule, see Paragraphs (5)–(7), *supra;* in most others, it is clear that the plaintiff's right of action is a creation of state, rather than federal law, so that federal jurisdiction, if available at all, cannot be justified on the basis of the Holmes test.

But a problematic (and perhaps anomalous) case is Shoshone Mining Co. v. Rutter, 177 U.S. 505 (1900). In Rev.Stat. §§ 2325–26, Congress laid down the conditions for issuance of patents for mining claims by the Commissioner of the General Land Office. The law provided that if, after notice of an application, an adverse claim were filed, "it shall be the duty of the adverse claimant, within thirty days after filing his claim, to commence proceedings in a court of competent jurisdiction, to determine the question of the right of possession, and prosecute the same with reasonable diligence to final judgment"; and directed that the patent should issue in accordance with the judgment. Rev.Stat. §§ 2319, 2324, and 2332 provided that this right of possession could be determined by "local customs or rules of miners in the several mining districts, so far as the same are applicable and not inconsistent with the laws of the United States", or "by the statute of limitations for mining claims of the State or Territory where the same may be situated."

In the Shoshone case, the Court reaffirmed its previous holding in Blackburn v. Portland Gold-Mining Co., 175 U.S. 571 (1900), that such an adverse suit was not within the general grant of federal question jurisdiction. It said (p. 509):

"Inasmuch, therefore, as the 'adverse suit' to determine the right of possession may not involve any question as to the construction or effect of the Constitution or laws of the United States, but may present simply a question of fact as to the time of the discovery of the mineral, the location of the claim on the ground, or a determination of the meaning and effect of certain local rules and customs prescribed by the miners of the district, or the effect of state statutes, it would seem to follow that it is not one which necessarily arises under the Constitution and laws of the United States."

Earlier in its opinion the Court had said (p. 507): " * * * [It is] well settled that a suit to enforce a right which takes its origin in the laws of the United States is not necessarily one arising under the Constitution or laws of the United States, within the meaning of the jurisdiction clauses, for if it did every action to establish title to real estate (at least in the newer States) would be such a one, as all titles in those States come from the United States or by virtue of its laws."

Note the ambiguity of the phrase "a suit to enforce a right which takes its origin in the laws of the United States." The "for if it did" clause in the rest of that sentence shows that the Court was thinking here of a vast range of cases where the chain of title includes a federal grant but there is no federal question in the forefront of the case and the right of action is entirely state-created. But in Shoshone itself the right to sue was arguably created by Congress itself. Why wasn't that decisive? Does the case stand as an exception to the inclusive aspect of the Holmes rule? If so, was the exception justified? (For arguments that it was, see Shapiro, *Jurisdiction and Discretion*, 60 N.Y.U.L.Rev. 543, 569–70 (1985).) See also the reference to Shoshone in Justice Stevens' opinion in Merrell Dow Pharmaceuticals, Inc. v. Thompson, p. 1011, n. 12, *infra*.)

(11) With Shoshone, compare Oneida Indian Nation v. County of Oneida, 414 U.S. 661 (1974), in which the Court found that it was federal, not state, law that gave the Indian Nation "a current right to possession" of certain lands, so that its action of ejectment "arose under" federal law for purposes of Section 1331. The Court relied on the long, unique and continuous federal concern for Indian lands. The assertion of jurisdiction "rests on the not insubstantial claim that federal law now protects, and has continuously protected from the time of the formation of the United States, possessory right to tribal lands, wholly apart from the application of state law principles which normally and separately protect a valid right of possession" (p. 677).

D. The Rule of Smith v. Kansas City Title & Trust Co.

(12) "It has come to be realized that Mr. Justice Holmes' formula [a suit arises under the law that creates the cause of action] is more useful for inclusion than for the exclusion for which it was intended. Even though the claim is created by state law, a case may 'arise under' a law of the United States if the complaint discloses a need for determining the meaning or application of such a law. The path-breaking opinion to this effect was Smith v. Kansas City Title & Trust Co., 255 U.S. 180 (1921), pointedly rendered over a dissent by Mr. Justice Holmes, 255 U.S. at 213–215 * * *." Friendly, J., in T.B. Harms Co. v. Eliscu, 339 F.2d 823, 827 (2d Cir.1964).

Supreme Court cases applying the Smith rule are, however, rare. One interesting case prior to Smith is Hopkins v. Walker, 244 U.S. 486 (1917), p. 999, *supra*, a suit to remove a cloud on title where federal law governed many of the issues with respect to the validity of the competing claims that constituted the alleged cloud. Without referring to the undoubted fact that the underlying right to have a title free from cloud and the right of action to enforce it both came from state law, the Supreme Court upheld jurisdiction after satisfying itself that, as a matter of proper pleading, the federal issues were part of the plaintiff's complaint.

See also De Sylva v. Ballentine, 351 U.S. 570 (1956), p. 1003, *supra*, where the Supreme Court decided on the merits—without discussing any jurisdictional question [6]—a claim to partial ownership of copyright renewal

---

6. Although the parties did not question federal jurisdiction and the Court did not mention it, the issue had been sharply raised by a dissent in the Court of Appeals,

terms. "Since there was no diversity of citizenship, and no infringement, the only, and a sufficient, explanation for the taking of jurisdiction was the existence of two major questions of construction of the Copyright Act." T.B. Harms Co. v. Eliscu, *supra,* at 827.

For lower court authority, see 13B Wright, Miller & Cooper, Federal Practice and Procedure § 3562 at 43–44 nn. 51, 52 (1984).

(13) Note Holmes' statement, in his dissent, that "the law of the United States has no force proprio vigore " in the Smith case. Was he suggesting that there was no "real" federal question in the case at all? In every situation where a state cause of action incorporates an element of federal law, an antecedent question is whether the incorporation is such that the so-called "federal" issue can properly be characterized as a real question of federal law. This question can be tested by asking whether a state court decision of the case would, because of this "federal" element, be subject to Supreme Court review. See *Note on State Incorporation of or Reference to Federal Law,* p. 559, *supra.* If the answer is yes, the further, distinct question is whether the role the federal question plays in the case is such that it supports original "arising under" jurisdiction in the district courts under § 1331.

Would a decision by the Missouri Supreme Court granting plaintiff the relief he sought in Smith be reviewable by the Supreme Court?

(14) In Moore v. Chesapeake & Ohio Ry., 291 U.S. 205 (1934), the specific issue was one of venue—namely, whether, for the purposes of the predecessor of 28 U.S.C. § 1391(a), jurisdiction in an action in a federal district court was "founded only on diversity of citizenship", or whether the action was also one arising under the Federal Safety Appliance Act. In the claim in question the plaintiff employee alleged injuries received while he was engaged in *intrastate* commerce and sought recovery under the Employers' Liability Act of Kentucky. But the claim also set forth asserted violations of the Federal Safety Appliance Act which, as amended in 1903, 32 Stat. 943, prescribes certain equipment for all cars used on any railroad which is a highway of interstate commerce, and thus applies even while a particular car is being used in intrastate commerce.

The Kentucky Act provided that no employee should be held "to have been guilty of contributory negligence" or "to have assumed the risk of his employment" in any case "where the violation by such common carrier of any statute, state or federal, enacted for the safety of employees contributed to the injury or death of such employee". As the Supreme Court stated (p. 213), "the Federal Safety Appliance Acts were manifestly embraced in this description."

The Court held that jurisdiction rested solely on diversity of citizenship. It said (pp. 214–17):

"* * * Questions arising in actions in state courts to recover for injuries sustained by employees in intrastate commerce and relating to the scope or construction of the Federal Safety Appliance Acts are, of course, federal questions which may appropriately be reviewed in this Court. * * * But it does not follow that a suit brought under the state statute which defines liability to employees who are injured while engaged in

see 226 F.2d 623, 634 (9th Cir.1955), and can hardly have passed unnoticed.

intrastate commerce, and brings within the purview of the statute a breach of the duty imposed by the federal statute, should be regarded as a suit arising under the laws of the United States and cognizable in the federal court in the absence of diversity of citizenship. The Federal Safety Appliance Acts, while prescribing absolute duties, and thus creating correlative rights in favor of injured employees, did not attempt to lay down rules governing actions for enforcing these rights. The original Act of 1893 made no provision for suits, except for penalties. That Act did impliedly recognize the employee's right of action by providing in section 8 that he should not be deemed to have assumed the risk of injury occasioned by the breach of duty. But the Act made no provision as to the place of suit or the time within which it should be brought, or as to the right to recover, or as to those who should be the beneficiaries of recovery, in case of the death of the employee. While dealing with assumption of risk, the statute did not affect the defense of contributory negligence and hence that defense was still available according to the applicable state law. * * * In these respects the amended Act of 1903 made no change, notwithstanding the enlargement of the scope of the statutory requirements. The Act of 1910, by a proviso in section 4 relating to penalties (36 Stat. 299 [45 U.S.C.A. § 13]), provided that nothing in that section should 'be construed to relieve such carrier from liability in any remedial action for the death or injury of any railroad employee' caused by the use of the prohibited equipment.

"The Safety Appliance Acts having prescribed the duty in this fashion, the right to recover damages sustained by the injured employee through the breach of duty sprang from the principle of the common law (Texas & Pacific R.R. Co. v. Rigsby, *supra*, at pages 39, 40 of 241 U.S.) and was left to be enforced accordingly, or, in case of the death of the injured employee, according to the applicable statute * * *. When the Federal Employers' Liability Act was enacted, it drew to itself the right of action for injuries or death of the employees within its purview who were engaged in interstate commerce, including those cases in which injuries were due to a violation of the Safety Appliance Acts. Such an action must be brought as prescribed in the Federal Employers' Liability Act, and, if brought in the state court, it cannot be removed to the federal court, although violation of the Safety Appliance Acts is involved. See St. Joseph & G.I.R. Co. v. Moore, 243 U.S. 311. With respect to injuries sustained in intrastate commerce, nothing in the Safety Appliance Acts precluded the State from incorporating in its legislation applicable to local transportation the paramount duty which the Safety Appliance Acts imposed as to the equipment of cars used on interstate railroads. As this Court said in Minneapolis, St. Paul & Sault Ste. Marie R. Co. v. Popplar [237 U.S. 369], as to an action for injuries sustained in intrastate commerce: 'The action fell within the familiar category of cases involving the duty of a master to his servant. This duty is defined by the common law, except as it may be modified by legislation. The federal statute, in the present case, touched the duty of the master at a single point and, save as provided in the statute, the right of the plaintiff to recover was left to be determined by the law of the State.'"

Can Moore be reconciled with the Smith case? See the elaborate footnote war as to this in the opinions in the Merrell Dow case, immediately following. But isn't there a simple explanation? In Moore, the state statute did not give the plaintiff a remedy for violation of the federal statute; it merely said that such a violation will negate the defenses of contributory negligence and assumption of risk. Moore thus fails the well-pleaded complaint rule: the federal issue, as in Mottley, comes in by way of reply to a defense. If this analysis is correct—and if Smith v. Kansas City is good law—the Moore outcome might be different if the state statute had provided that violation of the Federal Act was actionable or constituted negligence for purposes of a state negligence action.

(15) Return now to the three propositions of paragraph (1). Do they correctly state the law in light of the materials heretofore canvassed?

Compare the description of the law of "arising under" in the opinion of Justice Brennan, for a unanimous Supreme Court, in Franchise Tax Board v. Construction Laborers Vacation Trust, 463 U.S. 1, 8–9 (1983), p. 1029, *infra*, in which the Court characterized it as "well-settled" and "often held" that a case "arises under" federal law for purposes of Section 1331 "where the vindication of a right under state law necessarily turned on some construction of federal law."

So things stood when the Court issued its opinion in Merrell Dow, immediately following.

MERRELL DOW PHARMACEUTICALS, INC. v. THOMPSON
478 U.S. 804, 106 S.Ct. 3229, 92 L.Ed.2d 650 (1986).
Certiorari to the United States Court of Appeals for the Sixth Circuit.

JUSTICE STEVENS delivered the opinion of the Court.

The question presented is whether the incorporation of a federal standard in a state-law private action, when Congress has intended that there not be a federal private action for violations of that federal standard, makes the action one "arising under the Constitution, laws, or treaties of the United States," 28 U.S.C. § 1331.

I

The Thompson respondents are residents of Canada and the MacTavishes reside in Scotland. They filed virtually identical complaints against petitioner, a corporation, that manufactures and distributes the drug Bendectin. The complaints were filed in the Court of Common Pleas in Hamilton County, Ohio. Each complaint alleged that a child was born with multiple deformities as a result of the mother's ingestion of Bendectin during pregnancy. In five of the six counts, the recovery of substantial damages was requested on common-law theories of negligence, breach of warranty, strict liability, fraud, and gross negligence. In Count IV, respondents alleged that the drug Bendectin was "misbranded" in violation of the Federal Food, Drug, and Cosmetic Act (FDCA), 21 U.S.C. § 301 et seq. (1982 ed., Supp. II), because its labeling did not provide adequate warning that its use was potentially dangerous. Paragraph 26 alleged that the violation of the FDCA "in the promotion" of Bendectin "constitutes a rebuttable presumption of negligence." Paragraph 27 alleged that the "violation of said federal statutes directly and proximately caused the injuries suffered" by the two infants.

Petitioner filed a timely petition for removal from the state court to the Federal District Court alleging that the action was "founded, in part, on an alleged claim arising under the laws of the United States." After removal, the two cases were consolidated. Respondents filed a motion to remand to the state forum on the ground that the federal court lacked subject-matter jurisdiction. Relying on our decision in Smith v. Kansas City Title & Trust Co., 255 U.S. 180 (1921), the District Court held that Count IV of the complaint alleged a cause of action arising under federal law and denied the motion to remand. It then granted petitioner's motion to dismiss on *forum non conveniens* grounds.

The Court of Appeals for the Sixth Circuit reversed. 766 F.2d 1005 (1985). After quoting one sentence from the concluding paragraph in our recent opinion in Franchise Tax Board v. Construction Laborers Vacation Trust, 463 U.S. 1 (1983),* and noting "that the FDCA does not create or imply a private right of action for individuals injured as a result of violations of the Act," it explained:

> "Federal question jurisdiction would, thus, exist only if plaintiffs' right to relief *depended necessarily* on a substantial question of federal law. Plaintiffs' causes of action referred to the FDCA merely as one available criterion for determining whether Merrell Dow was negligent. Because the jury could find negligence on the part of Merrell Dow without finding a violation of the FDCA, the plaintiffs' causes of action did not depend necessarily upon a question of federal law. Consequently, the causes of action did not arise under federal law and, therefore, were improperly removed to federal court." 766 F.2d at 1006.

We granted certiorari, 474 U.S. 1004 (1985), and we now affirm.

II

Article III of the Constitution gives the federal courts power to hear cases "arising under" federal statutes. That grant of power, however, is not self-executing, and it was not until the Judiciary Act of 1875 that Congress gave the federal courts general federal-question jurisdiction. Although the constitutional meaning of "arising under" may extend to all cases in which a federal question is "an ingredient" of the action, Osborn v. Bank of the United States, 9 Wheat. 738, 823 (1824), we have long construed the statutory grant of federal-question jurisdiction as conferring a more limited power. Verlinden B.V. v. Central Bank of Nigeria, 461 U.S. 480, 494–495 (1983); Romero v. International Terminal Operating Co., 358 U.S. 354, 379 (1959).

Under our longstanding interpretation of the current statutory scheme, the question whether a claim "arises under" federal law must be determined by reference to the "well-pleaded complaint." Franchise Tax Board, 463 U.S., at 9–10. A defense that raises a federal question is inadequate to confer federal jurisdiction. Louisville & Nashville R. Co. v. Mottley, 211 U.S. 149 (1908). Since a defendant may remove a case only if the claim could have been brought in federal court, 28 U.S.C. § 1441(b),

---

* [Ed.] The Franchise Tax Board opinion is printed at p. 1027, *infra,* since its holding and analysis are most significant in connection with the problems of declaratory judgments and of federal defense removal, which are considered later in this Chapter. Its general account of "arising under" jurisdiction, already referred to p. 1007, *supra,* is frequently referred to in the opinions in Merrell Dow, however; the reader might, therefore, wish to read Part II of the Franchise Tax Board opinion at this point.

moreover, the question for removal jurisdiction must also be determined by reference to the "well-pleaded complaint."

As was true in Franchise Tax Board, *supra,* the propriety of the removal in this case thus turns on whether the case falls within the original "federal question" jurisdiction of the federal courts. There is no "single, precise definition" of that concept; rather, "the phrase 'arising under' masks a welter of issues regarding the interrelation of federal and state authority and the proper management of the federal judicial system." *Id.,* 463 U.S., at 8.

This much, however, is clear. The "vast majority" of cases that come within this grant of jurisdiction are covered by Justice Holmes' statement that a " 'suit arises under the law that creates the cause of action.' " *Id.,* at 8–9, quoting American Well Works Co. v. Layne & Bowler Co., 241 U.S. 257, 260 (1916). Thus, the vast majority of cases brought under the general federal-question jurisdiction of the federal courts are those in which federal law creates the cause of action.

We have, however, also noted that a case may arise under federal law "where the vindication of a right under state law necessarily turned on some construction of federal law." Franchise Tax Board, 463 U.S., at 9.[5] Our actual holding in Franchise Tax Board demonstrates that this statement must be read with caution; the central issue presented in that case turned on the meaning of the Employment Retirement Income Security Act of 1974, 29 U.S.C. § 1001 *et seq.* (1982 ed. and Supp. II), but we nevertheless concluded that federal jurisdiction was lacking.

This case does not pose a federal question of the first kind; respondents do not allege that federal law creates any of the causes of action that they have asserted.[6] This case thus poses what Justice Frankfurter called the "litigation-provoking problem," Textile Workers v. Lincoln Mills, 353 U.S. 448, 470 (1957) (dissenting opinion)—the presence of a federal issue in a state-created cause of action.

In undertaking this inquiry into whether jurisdiction may lie for the presence of a federal issue in a nonfederal cause of action, it is, of course, appropriate to begin by referring to our understanding of the statute conferring federal-question jurisdiction. We have consistently emphasized that, in exploring the outer reaches of § 1331, determinations about federal jurisdiction require sensitive judgments about congressional intent, judicial power, and the federal system. "If the history of the interpretation of judiciary legislation teaches us anything, it teaches the duty to reject treating such statutes as a wooden set of self-sufficient words. * * * The Act of 1875 is broadly phrased, but it has been continuously construed and limited in the light of the history that produced it, the demands of reason and coherence, and the dictates of sound judicial policy which have

---

5. The case most frequently cited for that proposition is Smith v. Kansas City Title & Trust Co., 255 U.S. 180 (1921). In that case the Court upheld federal jurisdiction of a shareholder's bill to enjoin the corporation from purchasing bonds issued by the federal land banks under the authority of the Federal Farm Loan Act on the ground that the federal statute that authorized the issuance of the bonds was unconstitutional. * * *

6. Jurisdiction may not be sustained on a theory that the plaintiff has not advanced. See Healy v. Sea Gull Specialty Co., 237 U.S. 479, 480 (1915) ("[T]he plaintiff is absolute master of what jurisdiction he will appeal to"); The Fair v. Kohler Die and Specialty Co., 228 U.S. 22, 25 (1913) ("[T]he party who brings a suit is master to decide what law he will rely upon"). * * *

emerged from the Act's function as a provision in the mosaic of federal judiciary legislation." Romero v. International Terminal Operating Co., 358 U.S., at 379. In Franchise Tax Board, we forcefully reiterated this need for prudence and restraint in the jurisdictional inquiry: "We have always interpreted what Skelly Oil [Co. v. Phillips Petroleum Co., 339 U.S. 667, 673 (1950)] called 'the current of jurisdictional legislation since the Act of March 3, 1875 * * * with an eye to practicality and necessity.' " 463 U.S., at 20.

In this case, both parties agree with the Court of Appeals' conclusion that there is no federal cause of action for FDCA violations. For purposes of our decision, we assume that this is a correct interpretation of the FDCA. Thus, as the case comes to us, it is appropriate to assume that, under the settled framework for evaluating whether a federal cause of action lies, some combination of the following factors is present: (1) the plaintiffs are not part of the class for whose special benefit the statute was passed; (2) the indicia of legislative intent reveal no congressional purpose to provide a private cause of action; (3) a federal cause of action would not further the underlying purposes of the legislative scheme; and (4) the respondents' cause of action is a subject traditionally relegated to state law.[7] In short, Congress did not intend a private federal remedy for violations of the statute that it enacted.

This is the first case in which we have reviewed this type of jurisdictional claim in light of these factors. That this is so is not surprising. The development of our framework for determining whether a private cause of action exists has proceeded only in the last 11 years, and its inception represented a significant change in our approach to congressional silence on the provision of federal remedies.[8]

The recent character of that development does not, however, diminish its importance. Indeed, the very reasons for the development of the modern implied remedy doctrine—the "increased complexity of federal legislation and the increased volume of federal litigation," as well as "the desirability of a more careful scrutiny of legislative intent," Merrill Lynch, Pierce, Fenner & Smith v. Curran, 456 U.S. 353, 377 (1982) (footnote omitted)—are precisely the kind of considerations that should inform the concern for "practicality and necessity" that Franchise Tax Board advised for the construction of § 1331 when jurisdiction is asserted because of the presence of a federal issue in a state cause of action.

The significance of the necessary assumption that there is no federal private cause of action thus cannot be overstated. For the ultimate import of such a conclusion, as we have repeatedly emphasized, is that it would flout congressional intent to provide a private federal remedy for the violation of the federal statute.[9] We think it would similarly flout, or at

---

7. See California v. Sierra Club, 451 U.S. 287, 293 (1981); Cannon v. University of Chicago, 441 U.S. 677, 689–709 (1979); Cort v. Ash, 422 U.S. 66, 78 (1975).

8. See Merrill Lynch, Pierce, Fenner & Smith v. Curran, 456 U.S. 353, 377 (1982) ("In 1975 the Court unanimously decided to modify its approach to the question whether a federal statute includes a private right of action"). * * *

9. See, *e.g.*, Daily Income Fund, Inc. v. Fox, 464 U.S. 523, 535–536 (1984) ("In evaluating such a claim, our focus must be on the intent of Congress when it enacted the statute in question"); Middlesex County Sewerage Authority v. National Sea Clammers Assn., 453 U.S. 1, 13 (1981) ("The key to the inquiry is the intent of the Legislature"); Texas Industries, Inc. v. Radcliff Materials, Inc., 451 U.S. 630, 639 (1981) ("Our focus, as it is in any case involving

least undermine, congressional intent to conclude that the federal courts might nevertheless exercise federal-question jurisdiction and provide remedies for violations of that federal statute solely because the violation of the federal statute is said to be a "rebuttable presumption" or a "proximate cause" under state law, rather than a federal action under federal law.

III

Petitioner advances three arguments to support its position that, even in the face of this congressional preclusion of a federal cause of action for a violation of the federal statute, federal-question jurisdiction may lie for the violation of the federal statute as an element of a state cause of action.

First, petitioner contends that the case represents a straightforward application of the statement in Franchise Tax Board that federal-question jurisdiction is appropriate when "it appears that some substantial, disputed question of federal law is a necessary element of one of the well-pleaded state claims." 463 U.S., at 13. Franchise Tax Board, however, did not purport to disturb the long-settled understanding that the mere presence of a federal issue in a state cause of action does not automatically confer federal-question jurisdiction.[11] Indeed, in determining that federal-question jurisdiction was not appropriate in the case before us, we stressed Justice Cardozo's emphasis on principled, pragmatic distinctions: " 'What is needed is something of that common-sense accommodation of judgment to kaleidoscopic situations which characterizes the law in its treatment of causation * * * a selective process which picks the substantial causes out of the web and lays the other ones aside.' " *Id.*, at 20–21 (quoting Gully v. First National Bank, 299 U.S. 109, 117–118 (1936)).

Far from creating some kind of automatic test, Franchise Tax Board thus candidly recognized the need for careful judgments about the exercise of federal judicial power in an area of uncertain jurisdiction. Given the significance of the assumed congressional determination to preclude federal private remedies, the presence of the federal issue as an element of the state tort is not the kind of adjudication for which jurisdiction would serve congressional purposes and the federal system. This conclusion is fully consistent with the very sentence relied on so heavily by petitioner. We simply conclude that the congressional determination that there should be no federal remedy for the violation of this federal statute is tantamount to a congressional conclusion that the presence of a claimed violation of the statute as an element of a state cause of action is insufficiently "substantial" to confer federal-question jurisdiction.[12]

the implication of a right of action, is on the intent of Congress"); * * *.

11. See, *e.g.*, Textile Workers v. Lincoln Mills, 353 U.S. 448, 470 (1957) (Frankfurter, J., dissenting) (defining inquiry as "the degree to which federal law must be in the forefront of the case and not collateral, peripheral or remote"); Gully v. First National Bank, 299 U.S. 109, 115 (1936) ("Not every question of federal law emerging in a suit is proof that a federal law is the basis of the suit"); *id.*, at 118 ("If we follow the ascent far enough, countless claims of right can be discovered to have their source or their operative limits in the provisions of a

federal statute or in the Constitution itself with its circumambient restrictions upon legislative power. To set bounds to the pursuit, the courts have formulated the distinction between controversies that are basic and those that are collateral, between disputes that are necessary and those that are merely possible. We shall be lost in a maze if we put that compass by").

12. Several commentators have suggested that our § 1331 decisions can best be understood as an evaluation of the *nature* of the federal interest at stake. See, *e.g.*, Shapiro, *Jurisdiction and Discretion*, 60 N.Y.U.L.Rev. 543, 568 (1985); C. Wright,

Second, petitioner contends that there is a powerful federal interest in seeing that the federal statute is given uniform interpretations, and that federal review is the best way of insuring such uniformity. In addition to the significance of the congressional decision to preclude a federal remedy, we do not agree with petitioner's characterization of the federal interest and its implications for federal-question jurisdiction. To the extent that petitioner is arguing that state use and interpretation of the FDCA pose a threat to the order and stability of the FDCA regime, petitioner should be arguing, not that federal courts should be able to review and enforce state FDCA–based causes of action as an aspect of federal-question jurisdiction, but that the FDCA pre-empts state-court jurisdiction over the issue in dispute. Petitioner's concern about the uniformity of interpretation, moreover, is considerably mitigated by the fact that, even if there is no original district court jurisdiction for these kinds of action, this Court retains power to review the decision of a federal issue in a state cause of action.[14]

Finally, petitioner argues that, whatever the general rule, there are special circumstances that justify federal-question jurisdiction in this case. Petitioner emphasizes that it is unclear whether the FDCA applies to sales

Federal Courts 96 (4th ed.1983); Cohen, *The Broken Compass: The Requirement That A Case Arise 'Directly' Under Federal Law*, 115 U.Pa.L.Rev. 890, 916 (1967).

* * *

Focusing on the nature of the federal interest, moreover, suggests that the widely perceived "irreconcilable" conflict between the finding of federal jurisdiction in Smith v. Kansas City Title & Trust Co., 255 U.S. 180 (1921) and the finding of no jurisdiction in Moore v. Chesapeake & Ohio R. Co., 291 U.S. 205 (1934), see, *e.g.*, M. Redish, Federal Jurisdiction: Tensions in the Allocation of Judicial Power 67 (1980), is far from clear. For the difference in results can be seen as manifestations of the differences in the nature of the federal issues at stake. In Smith, as the Court emphasized, the issue was the constitutionality of an important federal statute. See 255 U.S., at 201 ("It is * * * apparent that the controversy concerns the constitutional validity of an act of Congress which is directly drawn in question. The decision depends upon the determination of this issue"). In Moore, in contrast, the Court emphasized that the violation of the federal standard as an element of state tort recovery did not fundamentally change the state tort nature of the action. See 291 U.S., at 216–217 (" 'The action fell within the familiar category of cases involving the duty of a master to his servant. This duty is defined by the common law, except as it may be modified by legislation. The federal statute, in the present case, touched the duty of the master at a single point and, save as provided in the statute, the right of the plaintiff to recover was left to be determined by the law of the State' ") (quoting Minneapolis, St. P. & S.S.M.R. Co. v. Popplar, 237 U.S. 369, 372 (1915)).

The importance of the nature of the federal issue in federal question jurisdiction is highlighted by the fact that, despite the usual reliability of the Holmes test as an inclusionary principle, this Court has sometimes found that formally federal causes of action were not properly brought under federal-question jurisdiction because of the overwhelming predominance of state-law issues. See Shulthis v. McDougal, 225 U.S. 561, 569–570 (1912) ("A suit to enforce a right which takes its origin in the laws of the United States is not necessarily, or for that reason alone, one arising under those laws, for a suit does not so arise unless it really and substantially involves a dispute or controversy respecting the validity, construction or effect of such a law, upon the determination of which the result depends. This is especially so of a suit involving rights to land acquired under a law of the United States. If it were not, every suit to establish title to land in the central and western States would so arise, as all titles in those States are traceable back to those laws"); Shoshone Mining Co. v. Rutter, 177 U.S. 505, 507 (1900) ("We pointed out in the former opinion that it was well settled that a suit to enforce a right which takes its origin in the laws of the United States is not necessarily one arising under the Constitution or laws of the United States, within the meaning of the jurisdiction clauses, for if it did every action to establish title to real estate (at least in the newer States) would be such a one, as all titles in those States come from the United States or by virtue of its laws").

14. See Moore v. Chesapeake & Ohio R. Co., 291 U.S. 205, 214–215 (1934) * * *.

in Canada and Scotland; there is, therefore, a special reason for having a federal court answer the novel federal question relating to the extraterritorial meaning of the Act. We reject this argument. We do not believe the question whether a particular claim arises under federal law depends on the novelty of the federal issue. Although it is true that federal jurisdiction cannot be based on a frivolous or insubstantial federal question, "the interrelation of federal and state authority and the proper management of the federal judicial system," Franchise Tax Board, 463 U.S., at 8 would be ill-served by a rule that made the existence of federal-question jurisdiction depend on the district court's case-by-case appraisal of the novelty of the federal question asserted as an element of the state tort. The novelty of an FDCA issue is not sufficient to give it status as a federal cause of action; nor should it be sufficient to give a state-based FDCA claim status as a jurisdiction-triggering federal question.[15]

IV

We conclude that a complaint alleging a violation of a federal statute as an element of a state cause of action, when Congress has determined that there should be no private, federal cause of action for the violation, does not state a claim "arising under the Constitution, laws, or treaties of the United States." 28 U.S.C. § 1331.

The judgment of the Court of Appeals is affirmed.

JUSTICE BRENNAN, with whom JUSTICE WHITE, JUSTICE MARSHALL, and JUSTICE BLACKMUN join, dissenting.

Article III, § 2 of the Constitution provides that the federal judicial power shall extend to "all Cases, in Law and Equity, arising under this Constitution, the Laws of the United States, and Treaties made, or which shall be made, under their Authority." We have long recognized the great breadth of this grant of jurisdiction, holding that there is federal jurisdiction whenever a federal question is an "ingredient" of the action, Osborn v. Bank of the United States, 9 Wheat. 738, 823 (1824), and suggesting that there may even be jurisdiction simply because a case involves "potential federal questions," Textile Workers v. Lincoln Mills, 353 U.S. 448, 471 (1957) (Frankfurter, J., dissenting); see also, Osborn, *supra*, 9 Wheat. at 824; Martin v. Hunter's Lessee, 1 Wheat. 304 (1816); Pacific Railroad Removal Cases, 115 U.S. 1 (1885); Verlinden B.V. v. Central Bank of Nigeria, 461 U.S. 480, 492–493 (1983).

28 U.S.C. § 1331 provides, in language that parrots the language of Article III, that the district courts shall have original jurisdiction "of all civil actions arising under the Constitution, laws or treaties of the United States." Although this language suggests that Congress intended in § 1331 to confer upon federal courts the full breadth of permissible "federal

---

15. Petitioner also contends that the Court of Appeals opinion rests on a view that federal question jurisdiction was inappropriate because, whatever the role of the federal issue in the FDCA–related count, the plaintiff could recover on other, strictly state law claims. See 766 F.2d, at 1006 (noting that "the jury could find negligence on the part of Merrell Dow without finding a violation of the FDCA"). To the extent that the opinion can be read to express

such a view, we agree that it was erroneous. If the FDCA–related count presented a sufficient federal question, its relationship to the other, state-law claims would be determined by the ordinary principles of pendent jurisdiction described in Mine Workers v. Gibbs, 383 U.S. 715 (1966). For the reasons that we have stated, however, there is no federal-question jurisdiction even with that possible error corrected.

question" jurisdiction (an inference that is supported by the contemporary evidence, see Franchise Tax Board v. Construction Laborers Vacation Trust, 463 U.S. 1, 8, n. 8 (1983); Forrester, The Nature of a "Federal Question", 16 Tul.L.Rev. 362, 374–376 (1942); Shapiro, Jurisdiction and Discretion, 60 N.Y.U.L.Rev. 543, 568 (1985)), § 1331 has been construed more narrowly than its constitutional counterpart. See Verlinden B.V., *supra,* 461 U.S., at 494–495; Romero v. International Terminal Operating Co., 358 U.S. 354, 379 (1959). Nonetheless, given the language of the statute and its close relation to the constitutional grant of federal question jurisdiction, limitations on federal question jurisdiction under § 1331 must be justified by careful consideration of the reasons underlying the grant of jurisdiction and the need for federal review. *Ibid.* I believe that the limitation on federal jurisdiction recognized by the Court today is inconsistent with the purposes of § 1331. Therefore, I respectfully dissent.

I

While the majority of cases covered by § 1331 may well be described by Justice Holmes' adage that "a suit arises under the law that creates the cause of action," ＊ ＊ ＊ it is firmly settled that there may be federal question jurisdiction even though both the right asserted and the remedy sought by the plaintiff are state created. See C. Wright, Federal Courts § 17, pp. 95–96 (4th ed. 1983) (hereinafter Wright); M. Redish, Federal Jurisdiction: Tensions in the Allocation of Judicial Power 64–71 (1980) (hereinafter Redish). The rule as to such cases was stated in what Judge Friendly described as "[t]he path-breaking opinion" in Smith v. Kansas City Title & Trust Co., 255 U.S. 180 (1921). T.B. Harms Co. v. Eliscu, 339 F.2d 823, 827 (CA2 1964). ＊ ＊ ＊

The continuing vitality of Smith is beyond challenge. We have cited it approvingly on numerous occasions, and reaffirmed its holding several times—most recently just three Terms ago by a unanimous Court in Franchise Tax Board v. Construction Laborers Vacation Trust, 463 U.S., at 9. ＊ ＊ ＊ Moreover, in addition to Judge Friendly's authoritative opinion in T.B. Harms v. Eliscu, *supra,* at 827, Smith has been widely cited and followed in the lower federal courts. ＊ ＊ ＊ Furthermore, the principle of the Smith case has been recognized and endorsed by most commentators as well. Redish 67, 69; American Law Institute, Study of the Division of Jurisdiction Between State and Federal Courts 178 (1969) (hereinafter ALI); Wright § 17, p. 96; P. Bator; P. Mishkin, D. Shapiro, & H. Wechsler, Hart & Wechsler's The Federal Courts and the Federal System 889 (2d ed. 1973); Mishkin, The Federal "Question" in the District Courts, 53 Colum.L.Rev. 157, 166 (1953); Wechsler, Federal Jurisdiction and the Revision of the Judicial Code, 13 Law & Contemp.Prob. 216, 225 (1948).[1]

1. Some commentators have argued that the result in Smith conflicts with our decision in Moore v. Chesapeake & Ohio Ry., 291 U.S. 205 (1934). See, *e.g.,* Greene, Hybrid State Law in the Federal Courts, 83 Harv.L.Rev. 289, 323 (1969). ＊ ＊ ＊

The Court suggests that Smith and Moore may be reconciled if one views the question whether there is jurisdiction under § 1331 as turning upon "an evaluation of the nature of the federal interest at stake." *Ante,* n. 12 (emphasis in original). Thus, the Court explains, while in Smith the issue was the constitutionality of "an important federal statute," in Moore the federal interest was less significant in that "the violation of the federal standard as an element of state tort recovery did not fundamentally change the state tort nature of the action." *Ibid.*

In one sense, the Court is correct in asserting that we can reconcile Smith and

There is, to my mind, no question that there is federal jurisdiction over the respondents' fourth cause of action under the rule set forth in Smith and reaffirmed in Franchise Tax Board. Respondents pleaded that petitioner's labeling of the drug Bendectin constituted "misbranding" in violation of §§ 201 and 502(f)(2), and (j) of the Federal Food, Drug, and Cosmetics Act (FDCA), 21 U.S.C. § 301 *et seq.* (1982 ed. Supp. II), and that this violation "directly and proximately caused" their injuries. Respondents asserted in the complaint that this violation established petitioner's negligence *per se* and entitled them to recover damages without more. No other basis for finding petitioner negligent was asserted in connection with this claim. As pleaded, then, respondents' "right to relief depend[ed] upon the construction or application of the Constitution or laws of the United States." Smith, 255 U.S., at 199; see also, Franchise Tax Board, 463 U.S., at 28 (there is federal jurisdiction under § 1331 where the plaintiff's right to relief "necessarily depends" upon resolution of a federal question).[2] Furthermore, although petitioner disputes its liability under the FDCA, it concedes that respondents' claim that petitioner violated the FDCA is "colorable, and rests upon a reasonable foundation." Smith, *supra,* 255 U.S., at 199.[3] Of course, since petitioner must make this concession to

Moore on the ground that the "nature" of the federal interest was more significant in Smith than in Moore. Indeed, as the Court appears to believe, *ibid.,* we could reconcile many of the seemingly inconsistent results that have been reached under § 1331 with such a test. But this is so only because a test based upon an ad hoc evaluation of the importance of the federal issue is infinitely malleable: at what point does a federal interest become strong enough to create jurisdiction? What principles guide the determination whether a statute is "important" or not? Why, for instance, was the statute in Smith so "important" that direct review of a state court decision (under our mandatory appellate jurisdiction) would have been inadequate? Would the result in Moore have been different if the federal issue had been a more important element of the tort claim? The point is that if one makes the test sufficiently vague and general, virtually any set of results can be "reconciled." However, the inevitable—and undesirable—result of a test such as that suggested in the Court's footnote 12 is that federal jurisdiction turns in every case on an appraisal of the federal issue, its importance and its relation to state law issues. Yet it is precisely because the Court believes that federal jurisdiction would be "ill-served" by such a case-by-case appraisal that it rejects petitioners' claim that the difficulty and importance of the statutory issue presented by their claim suffices to confer jurisdiction under § 1331. The Court cannot have it both ways.

My own view is in accord with those commentators who view the results in Smith and Moore as irreconcilable. See, *e.g.,* Redish 67; Currie, Federal Jurisdiction in a Nutshell 109 (2d ed. 1981). That fact does not trouble me greatly, however, for I view Moore as having been a "sport" at the time it was decided and having long been in a state of innocuous desuetude. Unlike the jurisdictional holding in Smith, the jurisdictional holding in Moore has never been relied upon or even cited by this Court. Moore has similarly borne little fruit in the lower courts, leading Professor Redish to conclude after comparing the vitality of Smith and Moore that "the principle enunciated in Smith is the one widely followed by modern lower federal courts." Redish 67. Finally, as noted in text, the commentators have also preferred Smith. Moore simply has not survived the test of time; it is presently moribund, and, to the extent that it is inconsistent with the well-established rule of the Smith case, it ought to be overruled.

2. As the Court correctly notes, the Court of Appeals erred in holding that respondents' right to relief did not depend upon the resolution of a federal question because respondents might prevail on one of their other, wholly state law claims. The fourth cause of action presents an independent and independently sufficient claim for relief. Whether it "arises under" federal law within the meaning of § 1331 must therefore be determined without reference to any other claims, as if only that claim was asserted. If, after such consideration, it is determined that there is jurisdiction, the plaintiff may join additional state law claims meeting the test for pendent jurisdiction set forth in Mine Workers v. Gibbs, 383 U.S. 715 (1966).

3. Franchise Tax Board states that the plaintiff's right to relief must necessarily

prevail in this Court, it need not be accepted at face value. However, independent examination of respondents' claim substantiates the conclusion that it is neither frivolous nor meritless. * * * Thus, the statutory question is one which "discloses a need for determining the meaning or application of [the FDCA]," T.B. Harms v. Eliscu, 339 F.2d, at 827, and the claim raised by the fourth cause of action is one "arising under" federal law within the meaning of § 1331.

II

The Court apparently does not disagree with any of this—except, of course, for the conclusion. According to the Court, if we assume that Congress did not intend for there to be a private federal cause of action under a particular federal law (and, presumably, *a fortiori* if Congress' decision not to create a private remedy is express), we must also assume that Congress did not intend for there to be federal jurisdiction over a state cause of action that is determined by that federal law. Therefore, assuming—only because the parties have made a similar assumption—that there is no private cause of action under the FDCA,[4] the Court holds that there is no federal jurisdiction over the plaintiff's claim * * *.

The Court nowhere explains the basis for this conclusion. Yet it is hardly self-evident. Why should the fact that Congress chose not to create a private federal *remedy* mean that Congress would not want there to be federal *jurisdiction* to adjudicate a state claim that imposes liability for violating the federal law? Clearly, the decision not to provide a private federal remedy should not affect federal jurisdiction unless the reasons Congress withholds a federal remedy are also reasons for withholding federal jurisdiction. Thus, it is necessary to examine the reasons for Congress' decisions to grant or withhold both federal jurisdiction and private remedies, something the Court has not done.

A

In the early days of our Republic, Congress was content to leave the task of interpreting and applying federal laws in the first instance to the state courts; with one shortlived exception, Congress did not grant the inferior federal courts original jurisdiction over cases arising under federal law until 1875. Judiciary Act of 1875, ch. 137, § 1, 18 Stat. 470. The reasons Congress found it necessary to add this jurisdiction to the district

---

depend upon resolution of a "substantial" federal question. 463 U.S., at 28. In context, however, it is clear that this was simply another way of stating that the federal question must be colorable and have a reasonable foundation. This understanding is consistent with the manner in which the Smith test has always been applied, as well as with the way we have used the concept of a "substantial" federal question in other cases concerning federal jurisdiction. See, *e.g.,* Hagans v. Lavine, 415 U.S. 528, 536–37 (1974); Bell v. Hood, 327 U.S. 678, 682 (1946).

4. It bears emphasizing that the Court does *not* hold that there is no private cause of action under the FDCA. Rather, it expressly states that "[f]or purposes of our decision, we assume that this is a correct interpretation of the FDCA." The Court simply holds petitioner to its concession that the FDCA provides no private remedy, and decides petitioner's claim on the basis of this concession. I shall do the same. Under the Court's analysis, however, if a party persuaded a court that there is a private cause of action under the FDCA, there would be federal jurisdiction under Smith and Franchise Tax Board over a state cause of action making violations of the FDCA actionable. Such jurisdiction would apparently exist even if the plaintiff did not seek the federal remedy.

courts are well known. First, Congress recognized "the importance, and even necessity of *uniformity* of decisions throughout the whole United States, upon all subjects within the purview of the constitution." Martin v. Hunter's Lessee, 1 Wheat., at 347–348 (Story, J.) (emphasis in original). See also, Comment, Federal Preemption, Removal Jurisdiction, and the Well–Pleaded Complaint Rule, 51 U.Chi.L.Rev. 634, 636 (1984) (hereinafter Comment); D. Currie, Federal Courts 160 (3d ed. 1982) (hereinafter Currie). Concededly, because federal jurisdiction is not always exclusive and because federal courts may disagree with one another, absolute uniformity has not been obtained even under § 1331. However, while perfect uniformity may not have been achieved, experience indicates that the availability of a federal forum in federal question cases has done much to advance that goal. This, in fact, was the conclusion of the American Law Institute's Study of the Division of Jurisdiction Between State and Federal Courts. ALI 164–168.

In addition, § 1331 has provided for adjudication in a forum that specializes in federal law and that is therefore more likely to apply that law correctly. Because federal question cases constitute the basic grist for federal tribunals, "the federal courts have acquired a considerable expertise in the interpretation and application of federal law." ALI 164–165. By contrast, "it is apparent that federal question cases must form a very small part of the business of [state] courts." ALI 165. As a result, the federal courts are comparatively more skilled at interpreting and applying federal law, and are much more likely correctly to divine Congress' intent in enacting legislation.[6] * * *

These reasons for having original federal question jurisdiction explain why cases like this one and Smith—*i.e.*, cases where the cause of action is a creature of state law, but an essential element of the claim is federal— "arise under" federal law within the meaning of § 1331. Congress passes laws in order to shape behavior; a federal law expresses Congress' determination that there is a federal interest in having individuals or other entities conform their actions to a particular norm established by that law. Because all laws are imprecise to some degree, disputes inevitably arise over what specifically Congress intended to require or permit. It is the duty of courts to interpret these laws and apply them in such a way that

_____

6. Another reason Congress conferred original federal question jurisdiction on the district courts was its belief that state courts are hostile to assertions of federal rights. See Hornstein 564–565; Comment 636; Redish 71. Although this concern may be less compelling today than it once was, the American Law Institute reported as recently as 1969 that "it is difficult to avoid concluding that federal courts are more likely to apply federal law sympathetically and understandingly than are state courts." ALI 166. In any event, this rationale is, like the rationale based on the expertise of the federal courts, simply an expression of Congress' belief that federal courts are more likely to interpret federal law correctly.

One might argue that this Court's appellate jurisdiction over state court judgments in cases arising under federal law can be depended upon to correct erroneous state court decisions and to insure that federal law is interpreted and applied uniformly. However, as any experienced observer of this Court can attest, "Supreme Court review of state courts, limited by docket pressures, narrow review of the facts, the debilitating possibilities of delay, and the necessity of deferring to adequate state grounds of decision, cannot do the whole job." Currie 160. Indeed, having served on this Court for 30 years, it is clear to me that, realistically, it cannot even come close to "doing the whole job" and that § 1331 is essential if federal rights are to be adequately protected.

the congressional purpose is realized. As noted above, Congress granted the district courts power to hear cases "arising under" federal law in order to enhance the likelihood that federal laws would be interpreted more correctly and applied more uniformly. In other words, Congress determined that the availability of a federal forum to adjudicate cases involving federal questions would make it more likely that federal laws would shape behavior in the way that Congress intended.

By making federal law an essential element of a state law claim, the State places the federal law into a context where it will operate to shape behavior: the threat of liability will force individuals to conform their conduct to interpretations of the federal law made by courts adjudicating the state law claim. It will not matter to an individual found liable whether the officer who arrives at his door to execute judgment is wearing a state or a federal uniform; all he cares about is the fact that a sanction is being imposed—and may be imposed again in the future—because he failed to comply with the federal law. Consequently, the possibility that the federal law will be incorrectly interpreted in the context of adjudicating the state law claim implicates the concerns that led Congress to grant the district courts power to adjudicate cases involving federal questions in precisely the same way as if it was federal law that "created" the cause of action. It therefore follows that there is federal jurisdiction under § 1331.

B

The only remaining question is whether the assumption that Congress decided not to create a private cause of action alters this analysis in a way that makes it inappropriate to exercise original federal jurisdiction. According to the Court, "the very reasons for the development of the modern implied remedy doctrine" support the conclusion that, where the legislative history of a particular law shows (whether expressly or by inference) that Congress intended for there to be no private federal remedy, it must also mean that Congress would not want federal courts to exercise jurisdiction over a state law claim making violations of that federal law actionable. These reasons are " 'the increased complexity of federal legislation,' " " 'the increased volume of federal litigation,' " and " 'the desirability of a more careful scrutiny of legislative intent.' " * * *

These reasons simply do not justify the Court's holding. Given the relative expertise of the federal courts in interpreting federal law, the increased complexity of federal legislation argues rather strongly in *favor* of recognizing federal jurisdiction. And, while the increased volume of litigation may appropriately be considered in connection with reasoned arguments that justify limiting the reach of § 1331, I do not believe that the day has yet arrived when this Court may trim a statute solely because it thinks that Congress made it too broad.[7]

---

7. *Cf.* Cohens v. Virginia, 6 Wheat. 264, 404 (1821) (Marshall, C.J.) ("It is most true that this Court will not take jurisdiction if it should not but it is equally true that it must take jurisdiction if it should. * * * We have no more right to decline the exercise of jurisdiction which is given, than to usurp that which is not given. * * * "). The narrow exceptions we have recognized to Chief Justice Marshall's famous dictum have all been justified by compelling judicial concerns of comity and federalism. See, *e.g.,* Younger v. Harris, 401 U.S. 37 (1971); Burford v. Sun Oil Co., 319 U.S. 315 (1943). It would be wholly illegitimate, however, for this Court to determine that there was no jurisdiction over a class of cases simply because the Court thought that there were too many cases in the federal courts.

This leaves only the third reason: " 'the desirability of a more careful scrutiny of legislative intent.' " *Ibid.* I certainly subscribe to the proposition that the Court should consider legislative intent in determining whether or not there is jurisdiction under § 1331. But the Court has not examined the purposes underlying either the FDCA or § 1331 in reaching its conclusion that Congress' presumed decision not to provide a private federal remedy under the FDCA must be taken to withdraw federal jurisdiction over a private state remedy that imposes liability for violating the FDCA. Moreover, such an examination demonstrates not only that it is consistent with legislative intent to find that there is federal jurisdiction over such a claim, but, indeed, that it is the Court's contrary conclusion that is inconsistent with congressional intent.

The enforcement scheme established by the FDCA is typical of other, similarly broad regulatory schemes. Primary responsibility for overseeing implementation of the Act has been conferred upon a specialized administrative agency, here the Food and Drug Administration (FDA). Congress has provided the FDA with a wide-ranging arsenal of weapons to combat violations of the FDCA, including authority to obtain an ex parte court order for the seizure of goods subject to the Act, see 21 U.S.C. § 334, authority to initiate proceedings in a federal district court to enjoin continuing violations of the FDCA, see *id.* § 332, and authority to request a United States Attorney to bring criminal proceedings against violators, see *id.* § 333. See generally, 1 J. O'Reilly, Food and Drug Administration chs. 6–10 (1985). Significantly, the FDA has no independent enforcement authority; final enforcement must come from the federal courts, which have exclusive jurisdiction over actions under the FDCA. See §§ 332(a), 333, 334(a)(1). Thus, while the initial interpretive function has been delegated to an expert administrative body whose interpretations are entitled to considerable deference, final responsibility for interpreting the statute in order to carry out the legislative mandate belongs to the federal courts. *Cf.* Chevron U.S.A. Inc. v. Natural Resources Defense Council, 467 U.S. 837, 843, n. 9 (1984) ("The judiciary is the final authority on issues of statutory construction and must reject administrative constructions which are contrary to clear congressional intent").

Given that Congress structured the FDCA so that all express remedies are provided by the federal courts, it seems rather strange to conclude that it either "flout[s]" or "undermine[s]" congressional intent for the federal courts to adjudicate a private state law remedy that is based upon violating the FDCA. That is, assuming that a state cause of action based on the FDCA is not preempted, it is entirely consistent with the FDCA to find that it "arises under" federal law within the meaning of § 1331. Indeed, it is the Court's conclusion that such a state cause of action must be kept *out* of the federal courts that appears contrary to legislative intent inasmuch as the enforcement provisions of the FDCA quite clearly express a preference for having federal courts interpret the FDCA and provide remedies for its violation.

It may be that a decision by Congress not to create a private remedy is intended to preclude all private enforcement. If that is so, then a state cause of action that makes relief available to private individuals for violations of the FDCA is pre-empted. But if Congress' decision not to provide a private federal remedy does *not* pre-empt such a state remedy, then, in light of the FDCA's clear policy of relying on the federal courts for enforcement, it also should not foreclose federal jurisdiction over that state remedy. Both § 1331 and the enforcement provisions of the FDCA reflect Congress' strong desire to utilize the federal courts to interpret and enforce the FDCA, and it is therefore at odds with both these statutes to recognize a private state law remedy for violating the FDCA but to hold that this remedy cannot be adjudicated in the federal courts. * * *

* * * Congress' decision to withhold a private right of action and to rely instead on public enforcement reflects congressional concern with obtaining more accurate implementation and more coordinated enforcement of a regulatory scheme. See * * * Stewart & Sunstein, *Public Programs and Private Rights*, 95 Harv.L.Rev. 1193, 1208–1209 (1982). These reasons are closely related to the Congress' reasons for giving federal courts original federal question jurisdiction. Thus, if anything, Congress' decision not to create a private remedy *strengthens* the argument in favor of finding federal jurisdiction over a state remedy that is not preempted.

NOTE ON MERRELL DOW AND ON THE DISCRETIONARY ELEMENT IN ARISING UNDER JURISDICTION

(1) The court carefully refrained from overruling Smith in Merrell Dow. Rather, it purported to find, in Congress's (hypothesized) decision not to create a federal cause of action for violations of the Food, Drug, and Cosmetics Act, special reasons militating against jurisdiction.

But in most cases where the Smith rule is in play, it will be the case that no federal right of action will be available. Won't the Merrell Dow analysis—that federal court adjudication would undermine the policy that animated the decision not to have a substantive federal cause of action—be applicable in most such situations? What then is left of Smith—except the unusual case where a federal right of action exists but plaintiff chooses to sue only on a state cause of action with a federal ingredient? (Note that in the latter situation the defendant may remove if the suit is brought in a state court.)

(2) Justice Stevens' opinion is replete with hints that the Court wishes to reserve a wide discretion to tailor the "arising under" jurisdiction to the practical needs of the particular situation. In note 12, he cites Cohen, *The Broken Compass: The Requirement That a Case Arise "Directly" Under Federal Law*, 115 U.Pa.L.Rev. 890 (1967), which argued against the use of any analytic formula for determining when a case "arises under" federal law for purposes of § 1331, and in favor of "pragmatic standards for a pragmatic problem."[1] He also cites Shapiro, *Jurisdiction and Discretion*, 60 N.Y.U.L.Rev. 543 (1985). Professor Shapiro said (pp. 568–70):

"My own view is that no formulation can possibly explain or even begin to account for the variety of outcomes unless it accords sufficient room for the federal courts to make a range of choices based on considerations of judicial administration and the degree of federal concern. * * * [The] cases suggest that the Court's authority, but not its obligation, is very

---

1. Cohen suggests (p. 916) that the relevant "pragmatic" considerations should include "the extent of the caseload increase" if jurisdiction is recognized; the extent to which cases "of this class" turn on federal versus state law; "the extent of the necessity for an expert federal tribunal"; and the "extent of the necessity for a sympathetic federal tribunal."

broad indeed. In Smith, the presence of a federal ingredient made relevant by state law was sufficient to confer jurisdiction, but in Shoshone [p. 1003, supra], a federally created claim that turned on issues of state law was not. Both cases, however, may be better understood if viewed in terms of the federal interest at stake and the effect on the federal docket. Cases like Smith arise infrequently, but the issue—the ability of a party to invest in federally authorized securities—was a matter of great federal moment. Cases like Shoshone must have arisen with monotonous regularity at the turn of the century, but the degree of federal interest in an outcome dependent on local custom was marginal at best."

(3) What is the proper role of "discretion" in determining whether § 1331 jurisdiction is proper? Professor Cohen's position appears to be that the *district* courts should exercise an ad hoc case-by-case discretion, unguided by any "formulation", in determining whether jurisdiction is justified by "pragmatic" factors.

Would such a regime be tolerable? (Note that its effect would be both to narrow and complicate Supreme Court supervision of this area. See *Note on Control of Factfinding and of Application of Law to Fact*, p. 661, supra.)

Professor Shapiro's position is different.[2] He acknowledges that the Supreme Court has developed general standards for applying § 1331; but, finding anomalous cases at the margin, he explains them by surmising that the Court was influenced by factors of "federal interest" and "effect on the federal docket." Approving this, he argues that the Supreme Court should feel free to create exceptions to the general § 1331 standards to reflect these concerns.

Would it be desirable to add the following, fourth, proposition to the three listed on p. 995, supra: "*Proposition D*. The rules stated in propositions A and B shall not apply to [categories of] cases where the court concludes that considerations of judicial administration and the degree of federal concern justify a refusal to exercise federal jurisdiction"? (Should the bracketed words be included?)

Except in footnote 12 of Merrell Dow, the Court has not explicitly indicated approval of any notion of "discretion" in interpreting § 1331. Rather, it has based decisions such as Franchise Tax Board and Merrell Dow on statutory interpretation, finding in a particular substantive statute a Congressional intent to create a special exception to the usual § 1331 rules.

Is this approach likely to lead to results that differ significantly from that advocated by Professor Shapiro?

For a powerful argument that rules of subject matter jurisdiction should be subject to a "bright line" test, see Chaffee, Some Problems of Equity (1950), especially at pp. 1–102, discussing the mischief created by the "unclean hands" doctrine in equity. See also Hirshman, *Whose Law Is It*

2. Professor Shapiro carefully disassociated himself from the *ad hoc* approach of Professor Cohen, stressing that the range of discretion under § 1331, "though extremely broad at the outset, has been significantly narrowed by the course of decisions since the jurisdictional statute was enacted" (p. 568 n. 149). He concluded:

"The discretion I advocate relates primarily to the existence of a range of permissible choices under the relevant grants of jurisdiction. It is entirely consistent with this view for judicial precedent to narrow the scope of discretion and even to generate predictable rules" (pp. 588–89).

Anyway? A Reconsideration of Federal Question Jurisdiction Over Cases of Mixed State and Federal Law, 60 Ind.L.J. 17 (1984) supporting a return to the Holmes test; Note, 54 N.Y.U.L.Rev. 978 (1979).

(4) The American Law Institute decided not to recommend changes in or an attempt to create a further statutory specification of the term "arising under," considering it "the safer course to follow the traditional language, with only minor change, and thus to make it clear that the subsection preserves [the existing] body of law." See ALI Study 178–79, proposed § 1311. The significance of this judgment was greatly diminished by the much more controversial recommendation to end the rule that a federal defense does not generally give rise to district court jurisdiction. As to this issue, see further pp. 1052–57, *infra.*

NOTE ON CASES ARISING UNDER FEDERAL COMMON LAW

(1) The holding in Merrell Dow, that jurisdiction should not be upheld on the basis of Smith v. Kansas City Title & Trust, rests on the antecedent premise—not disputed in the case—that no federal common-law cause of action may properly be "implied" from the federal Food, Drug and Cosmetics Act. The case does not cast doubt on the distinct proposition—now well settled (as the materials in this Note will show)—that causes of action that are properly "implied" from federal statutes or the federal Constitution, or that are otherwise a creation of federal common law, do "arise under" federal law within the meaning of § 1331 and its predecessors.

(2) The Court's approach to this proposition began with cases where the substantive question—whether a federal cause of action could be maintained—was itself in doubt when the lawsuit was commenced.

The foundation case was Bell v. Hood, 327 U.S. 678 (1946). This was a suit against FBI agents, brought in a federal district court under the predecessor of § 1331, seeking damages for violations of the Fourth and Fifth Amendments. The complaint alleged unconstitutional arrests, searches, and seizures. The district court dismissed the action for want of jurisdiction on the ground that it was not one which "arises under the Constitution or laws of the United States"; the Circuit Court of Appeals affirmed. The Supreme Court reversed, deciding the jurisdictional issue only.

After stating that it was undoubtedly "the pleaders' purpose to make violation of these Constitutional provisions the basis of this suit," the Court, per Justice Black, held that "the federal court, but for two possible exceptions later noted, must entertain the suit. * * * The reason for this is that the court must assume jurisdiction to decide whether the allegations state a cause of action on which the court can grant relief as well as to determine issues of fact arising in the controversy.

"Jurisdiction, therefore, is not defeated as respondents seem to contend, by the possibility that the averments might fail to state a cause of action on which petitioners could actually recover. For it is well settled that the failure to state a proper cause of action calls for a judgment on the merits and not for a dismissal for want of jurisdiction. Whether the complaint states a cause of action on which relief could be granted is a question of law and just as issues of fact it must be decided after and not before the court has assumed jurisdiction over the controversy. If the court does later exercise its jurisdiction to determine that the allegations in the complaint do not state a ground for relief, then dismissal of the case would be on the merits, not for want of jurisdiction. * * * The previously carved out exceptions are that a suit may sometimes be dismissed for want of jurisdiction where the alleged claim under the Constitution or federal statutes clearly appears to be immaterial and made solely for the purpose of obtaining jurisdiction or where such a claim is wholly insubstantial and frivolous. * * *

" * * * Respondents contend that the Constitutional provisions here involved are prohibitions against the federal government as a government and that 28 U.S.C. § 41(1) [now § 1331] does not authorize recovery in money damages in suits against unauthorized officials who according to respondents are in the same position as individual trespassers.

"Respondents' contention does not show that petitioners' cause is insubstantial or frivolous, and the complaint does in fact raise serious questions, both of law and fact, which the district court can decide only after it has assumed jurisdiction over the controversy. The issue of law is whether federal courts can grant money recovery for damages said to have been suffered as a result of federal officers violating the Fourth and Fifth Amendments. That question has never been specifically decided by this Court. * * * Whether the petitioners are entitled to recover depends upon an interpretation of 28 U.S.C. § 41(1), and on a determination of the scope of the Fourth and Fifth Amendments' protection from unreasonable searches and deprivations of liberty without due process of law. Thus, the right of the petitioners to recover under their complaint will be sustained if the Constitution and laws of the United States are given one construction and will be defeated if they are given another. For this reason the district court has jurisdiction. Gully v. First National Bank, 299 U.S. 109, 112, 113; Smith v. Kansas City Title & Trust Co., 255 U.S. 180, 199, 200. Reversed."

Chief Justice Stone and Justice Burton dissented.[1]

(3) Wheeldin v. Wheeler, 373 U.S. 647 (1963), was a federal court action alleging that defendant—an investigator for the House Un–American Activities Committee—had, without lawful authority, subpoenaed plaintiff to appear before the Committee for the sole purpose of subjecting him to public stigma as a disloyal person. The question was "whether a federal claim for damages is stated." The Supreme Court, in an opinion by Justice Douglas, held that, under Bell v. Hood, the federal court had jurisdiction to determine that question, but concluded that, on the merits, "no federal cause of action can be made out."[2] The Court said it did not have to decide whether a federal cause of action for damages may be based

---

1. Upon the remand in Bell v. Hood the district court took jurisdiction, and "being of the opinion that neither the Constitution nor the statutes of the United States give rise to any cause of action in favor of plaintiffs upon the facts alleged," granted the defendants' motion to dismiss the complaint for failure to state a claim upon which relief could be granted. Bell v. Hood, 71 F.Supp. 813, 820–21 (S.D.Calif. 1947). The case went no further.

Did the eventual judgment have any different effect from the judgment which the Supreme Court reversed?

As to the problem of pendent jurisdiction over a joined claim under state law, see Section 4, infra.

2. The Court said that plaintiffs did not attempt to state a claim under state law, and therefore no question of pendent jurisdiction was before it.

directly on the Fourth Amendment, because there was here no search or seizure within the meaning of that Amendment. And the Court rather briskly rejected the argument that a federal right of action could be implied from the statutes governing the issuance of subpoenas, or could be created as a matter of federal common law:

"When it comes to suits for damages for abuse of power, federal officials are usually governed by local law. See, *e.g.,* Slocum v. Mayberry, 2 Wheat. 1, 10, 12. Federal law, however, supplies the defense, if the conduct complained of was done pursuant to a federally imposed duty (see, *e.g.,* Mayor v. Cooper, 6 Wall. 247; *cf.* Tennessee v. Davis, 100 U.S. 257), or immunity from suit. See Barr v. Matteo, [360 U.S. 564]; Howard v. Lyons, [360 U.S. 593]. Congress could, of course, provide otherwise, but it has not done so. Over the years Congress has considered the problem of state civil and criminal actions against federal officials many times. See Hart and Wechsler, The Federal Courts and the Federal System, 1147–1150 [1st ed. 1953]. But no general statute making federal officers liable for acts committed 'under color,' but in violation, of their federal authority has been passed. Congress has provided for removal to a federal court of any state action, civil or criminal, against '[a]ny officer of the United States * * *, or person acting under him, for any act under color of such office * * *.' 28 U.S.C. § 1442(a)(1). That state law governs the cause of action alleged is shown by the fact that removal is possible in a nondiversity case such as this one only because the interpretation of a federal defense makes the case one 'arising under' the Constitution or laws of the United States. See Tennessee v. Davis, supra; Gay v. Ruff, 292 U.S. 25, 34. We conclude, therefore, that it is not for us to fill any *hiatus* Congress has left in this area" (p. 652).

Justice Brennan's dissent urged that the case should be remanded for further consideration by the court of appeals of questions not adequately briefed and argued. He said that the complaint, properly read, did state a common law claim of abuse of process, and that federal jurisdiction might, therefore, be sustainable either on the basis of pendent jurisdiction or under Smith v. Kansas City Title & Trust. He also suggested "in a deliberately tentative manner" that the complaint might be upheld as a federal right of action implied from the federal statutes specifying the authority to issue subpoenas, or as a federal common law action. "[W]here, as here, it is alleged that a federal officer acting under color of federal law has so abused his federal powers as to cause unjustifiable injury to a private person, I see no warrant for concluding that state law must be looked to as the sole basis for liability" (p. 664).

Justice Brennan added: "[O]nce the federal common-law cause of action is recognized, the much-mooted problem remains whether such a cause arises under federal law within the meaning of 28 U.S.C. § 1331(a). This Court has never decided that question" (pp. 664–65).

(4) As Wheeldin indicates, the doctrine of Bell v. Hood is well established.[3] See also Montana–Dakota Util. Co. v. Northwestern Pub. Serv. Co.,

---

[3]. In a number of cases the Court has exploited the Bell v. Hood distinction between rulings on "jurisdiction" and rulings on the "merits" to limit the reach of the so-called "Mansfield principle"—the principle that, even if neither party objects to feder-al jurisdiction, the courts must on their own dismiss a case if there is no subject matter jurisdiction. (See Chap. XIV, Sec. 1.) Thus, in Mt. Healthy City Sch. Dist. Bd. of Educ. v. Doyle, 429 U.S. 274, 277–79 (1977), the Court first held that the federal

341 U.S. 246, 249 (1951). That doctrine supported district court jurisdiction in the Wheeldin case itself. Would there be original federal question jurisdiction over another case on identical facts brought following the Supreme Court decision in Wheeldin?

Wheeldin clearly holds that federal law does not create a right to recover damages on these facts. A claim for such damages brought shortly thereafter presumably would not present a substantial federal question. At the same time, if a claim for such relief is asserted under state law, will not federal law still govern key issues such as the scope of authority and immunity (and possibly even incidents of the remedy, such as punitive damages)? See Hill, *Constitutional Remedies*, 69 Colum.L.Rev. 1109, 1143–46 (1969); Katz, *The Jurisprudence of Remedies*, 117 U.Pa.L.Rev. 1, 51–58 (1968).

Was Justice Brennan correct in suggesting that there would be original jurisdiction in such a case under Smith v. Kansas City Title & Trust Co., p. 992, *supra*? After Merrell Dow, could jurisdiction be upheld on such a theory?

Damage suits in state courts against federal officers for acts done under color of their office are removable by the officers to federal court. See 28 U.S.C. § 1442(a). Are the reasons for a federal trial forum in such cases limited to protection of the defendants, or should federal jurisdiction be available at the option of the plaintiff as well? See Wechsler, *Federal Jurisdiction and the Revision of the Judicial Code*, 13 Law & Contemp. Prob. 216, 220–21 (1948). See further pp. 1057–60, *infra*.

claim asserted in the complaint was not frivolous, and that under Bell the federal court therefore had subject matter jurisdiction. The Court then turned around and held that the defendant's failure to challenge the asserted right of action on the merits permitted the court to proceed on the assumption that there was such a federal right of action, without in fact deciding that difficult point. See also Duke Power Co. v. Carolina Environmental Study Group, Inc., 438 U.S. 59, 69–72 (1978); Burks v. Lasker, 441 U.S. 471, 475–76 & n. 5 (1979); *cf.* Lake Country Estates, Inc. v. Tahoe Regional Planning Agency, 440 U.S. 391, 398 (1979).

Consider also Jackson Transit Authority v. Local Div. 1285, 457 U.S. 15 (1982). Section 13(c) of the Urban Mass Transportation Act of 1964, 49 U.S.C. § 1609(c), provides that, as a condition of federal financial aid for the acquisition of private transit companies, state and local governments must make "arrangements" to preserve existing collective bargaining rights. The city of Jackson bought a private bus company with federal aid, and, under § 13(c), entered into a contract with the union guaranteeing existing collective bargaining rights. It later repudiated that contract. The union brought an action for damages and an injunction in a federal court "under" § 13(c). The court of ap-

peals held that there was § 1331 jurisdiction under Bell v. Hood, and that § 13(c) implicitly provides a federal right of action. The Supreme Court reversed. Agreeing that, "strictly speaking", the district court had jurisdiction under Bell "for the purpose of determining whether the union stated a cause of action" (p. 21 n. 6), the Court nevertheless concluded that § 13(c) was not intended to generate a federal right to enforce such contracts in a federal court: "The legislative history indicates that Congress intended those contracts to be governed by state law applied in state courts" (p. 29).

Doesn't this case show that, notwithstanding Bell, there is often a complete functional congruence between the question whether the plaintiff states a valid claim of federal right and the question whether, for jurisdictional purposes, the case "arises under" federal law?

In a dissent from a denial of certiorari, Justice Rehnquist criticized and called for reexamination of the "cryptic" decision in Bell v. Hood, which he said requires a "three tiered analysis" of motions to dismiss; he said that this requirement contradicts Rule 12 of the Federal Rules of Civil Procedure. Yazoo County Industrial Development Corp. v. Suthoff, 454 U.S. 1157 (1982).

(5) Even at the time that Bell v. Hood left uncertain the source of any right to damages for violation of the Fourth and Fifth Amendments, it was settled law (as the district court on remand in that case recognized) that a suit in equity to enjoin officials from threatened actions alleged to be in excess of authority under the Constitution or federal statute was one arising under federal law within the jurisdictional statute. See Bell v. Hood, 71 F.Supp., at 818–19, and cases there cited. See also Chap. IX, pp. 1179–80, *infra.*

Twenty-five years after Bell v. Hood, the Supreme Court addressed the issue left open there, rejected the concept that the Fourth Amendment operates solely to limit possible federal defenses against state law liability, and held that the Amendment gives rise to an action for damages against federal officers who violated it. Bivens v. Six Unknown Named Agents of the Federal Bureau of Narcotics, 403 U.S. 388 (1971). See p. 917, *supra.*

(6) The question that Justice Brennan in Wheeldin described as "much mooted"—whether a case arising under federal common law falls within the scope of § 1331—was in fact controversial principally in the special context of admiralty litigation, where much debate surrounded the issue whether, in the absence of diversity, certain admiralty cases could be brought on the "law" side of the federal court under § 1331. (As to this, see Romero v. International Terminal Operating Co., 358 U.S. 354 (1959), discussed in the *Note on the Admiralty Jurisdiction,* p. 1071, *infra;* see also Kurland, *The Romero Case and Some Problems of Federal Jurisdiction,* 73 Harv.L.Rev. 817, 831–33 (1960).) Apart from admiralty, no plausible reason was ever advanced why—once a claim was determined to be a creation of federal, rather than state, law—the appropriateness and need for a federal forum should turn on whether the case arose under a federal statute or under federal common law.

The Court finally came to that unsurprising conclusion in Illinois v. Milwaukee, 406 U.S. 91 (1972). See pp. 341, 898, *supra.* The Court denied a motion for leave to file an original action in the Supreme Court seeking to enjoin pollution of Lake Michigan, on the ground that a district court would be a more appropriate forum. As a predicate for its action, the Court determined that pollution of interstate and navigable waters is governed by federal common law (as well as by statutes), that cases asserting such common law rights are actions arising under the "laws" of the United States within § 1331, and that the district courts thus had jurisdiction of such cases. See also National Farmers Union Ins. Cos. v. Crow Tribe of Indians, 471 U.S. 845 (1985), holding that § 1331 supports jurisdiction over an action in federal court to enjoin the execution of a default judgment rendered by an Indian tribal court, where the plaintiff alleged that federal law divested the tribal court of jurisdiction. "The question whether an Indian tribe retains the power to compel a non-Indian property owner to submit to the civil jurisdiction of a tribal court is one that must be answered by reference to federal law and is a 'federal question' under § 1331" (p. 852). "Federal common law as articulated in rules that are fashioned by court decisions are 'laws' as that term is used in § 1331" (p. 850) (citing, *inter alia,* Erie).[4]

---

4. *Cf.* Southland Corp. v. Keating, 465 U.S. 1 (1984), holding (in a case coming from a state court) that the United States Arbitration Act preempts a California stat- ute that rendered certain claims unarbi- trable. In a footnote the Court said: "While the Federal Arbitration Act creates federal substantive law requiring the par-

(7) Suppose plaintiff sues a state official for violations of constitutional rights under 42 U.S.C. § 1983, and is unsuccessful in that action. Would a suit by the former defendant against the former plaintiff for malicious prosecution "arise under" federal law within the meaning of § 1331? Note that, unless the answer is "yes", the former plaintiff could not, under § 1441, remove such a case from state to federal court. Would that be a sound result? See Sweeney v. Abramovitz, 449 F.Supp. 213 (D.Conn.1978), upholding jurisdiction on removal, a result supported by Note, 54 N.Y.U.L. Rev. 978 (1979).

FRANCHISE TAX BOARD OF CALIFORNIA v. CONSTRUCTION LABORERS VACATION TRUST

463 U.S. 1, 103 S.Ct. 2841, 77 L.Ed.2d 420 (1983).
Appeal from the United States Court of Appeals for the Ninth Circuit.

JUSTICE BRENNAN delivered the opinion of the Court.

The principal question in dispute between the parties is whether the Employee Retirement Income Security Act of 1974 (ERISA), 88 Stat. 829, as amended, 29 U.S.C. § 1001 *et seq.* (1976 ed. and Supp. V), permits state tax authorities to collect unpaid state income taxes by levying on funds held in trust for the taxpayers under an ERISA-covered vacation benefit plan. The issue is an important one, which affects thousands of federally regulated trusts and all nonfederal tax collection systems, and it must eventually receive a definitive, uniform resolution. Nevertheless, for reasons involving perhaps more history than logic, we hold that the lower federal courts had no jurisdiction to decide the question in the case before us, and we vacate the judgment and remand the case with instructions to remand it to the state court from which it was removed.

I

None of the relevant facts is in dispute. Appellee Construction Laborers Vacation Trust for Southern California (CLVT) is a trust established by an agreement between four associations of employers active in the construction industry in southern California and the Southern California District Council of Laborers, an arm of the District Council and affiliated locals of the Laborers' International Union of North America. The purpose of the agreement and trust was to establish a mechanism for administering the provisions of a collective-bargaining agreement that grants construction workers a yearly paid vacation. The trust agreement expressly proscribes any assignment, pledge, or encumbrance of funds held in trust by CLVT. The Plan that CLVT administers is unquestionably an "employee welfare benefit plan" within the meaning of § 3 of ERISA, 29 U.S.C. § 1002(1), and

ties to honor arbitration agreements, it does not create any independent federal-question jurisdiction under 28 U.S.C. § 1331 or otherwise" (p. 15 n. 9).

The Court is apparently reading the Arbitration Act—which makes agreements to arbitrate "valid, irrevocable, and enforceable" (9 U.S.C. § 2)—as a substantive provision (negativing a defense of unenforceabil-ity) rather than one that creates or authorizes the implication of a federal right of action.

The Court relied on the provisions of §§ 3 and 4 of the Act as indicating Congress' contemplation that suits to enforce promises to arbitrate will continue to be litigated in state court absent an independent basis of federal jurisdiction.

CLVT and its individual trustees are thereby subject to extensive regulation under Titles I and III of ERISA.

Appellant Franchise Tax Board is a California agency charged with enforcement of that State's personal income tax law. California law authorizes appellant to require any person in possession of "credits or other personal property or other things of value, belonging to a taxpayer" "to withhold * * * the amount of any tax, interest, or penalties due from the taxpayer * * * and to transmit the amount withheld to the Franchise Tax Board." Cal.Rev. & Tax.Code Ann. § 18817 (West Supp.1983). Any person who, upon notice by the Franchise Tax Board, fails to comply with its request to withhold and to transmit funds becomes personally liable for the amounts identified in the notice. § 18818.

In June 1980, the Franchise Tax Board filed a complaint in state court against CLVT and its trustees. Under the heading "First Cause of Action," appellant alleged that CLVT had failed to comply with three levies issued under § 18817, concluding with the allegation that it had been "damaged in a sum * * * not to exceed $380.56 plus interest from June 1, 1980." Under the heading "Second Cause of Action," appellant incorporated its previous allegations and added:

> "There was at the time of the levies alleged above and continues to be an actual controversy between the parties concerning their respective legal rights and duties. The Board [appellant] contends that defendants [CLVT] are obligated and required by law to pay over to the Board all amounts held * * * in favor of the Board's delinquent taxpayers. On the other hand, defendants contend that section 514 of ERISA preempts state law and that the trustees lack the power to honor the levies made upon them by the State of California.

> "[D]efendants will continue to refuse to honor the Board's levies in this regard. Accordingly, a declaration by this court of the parties' respective rights is required to fully and finally resolve this controversy."

In a prayer for relief, appellant requested damages for defendants' failure to honor the levies and a declaration that defendants are "legally obligated to honor all future levies by the Board."

CLVT removed the case to the United States District Court for the Central District of California, and the court denied the Franchise Tax Board's motion for remand to the state court. On the merits, the District Court ruled that ERISA did not pre-empt the State's power to levy on funds held in trust by CLVT. CLVT appealed, and the Court of Appeals reversed. 679 F.2d 1307 (CA9 1982). On petition for rehearing, the Franchise Tax Board renewed its argument that the District Court lacked jurisdiction over the complaint in this case. The petition for rehearing was denied, and an appeal was taken to this Court. We postponed consideration of our jurisdiction pending argument on the merits. We now hold that this case was not within the removal jurisdiction conferred by 28 U.S.C. § 1441, and therefore we do not reach the merits of the preemption question.[6]

---

6. At least for purposes of determining whether the courts below had jurisdiction over this case, we have appellate jurisdiction under 28 U.S.C. § 1254(2).

II

The jurisdictional structure at issue in this case has remained basically unchanged for the past century. * * * For this case—as for many cases where there is no diversity of citizenship between the parties—the propriety of removal turns on whether the case falls within the original "federal question" jurisdiction of the United States district courts * * *.

Since the first version of § 1331 was enacted, Act of Mar. 3, 1875, ch. 137, § 1, 18 Stat. 470, the statutory phrase "arising under the Constitution, laws, or treaties of the United States" has resisted all attempts to frame a single, precise definition for determining which cases fall within, and which cases fall outside, the original jurisdiction of the district courts. Especially when considered in light of § 1441's removal jurisdiction, the phrase "arising under" masks a welter of issues regarding the interrelation of federal and state authority and the proper management of the federal judicial system.[8]

The most familiar definition of the statutory "arising under" limitation is Justice Holmes' statement, "A suit arises under the law that creates the cause of action." American Well Works Co. v. Layne & Bowler Co., 241 U.S. 257, 260 (1916). However, it is well settled that Justice Holmes' test is more useful for describing the vast majority of cases that come within the district courts' original jurisdiction than it is for describing which cases are beyond district court jurisdiction. We have often held that a case "arose under" federal law where the vindication of a right under state law necessarily turned on some construction of federal law, see, e.g., Smith v. Kansas City Title & Trust Co., 255 U.S. 180 (1921); Hopkins v. Walker, 244 U.S. 486 (1917), and even the most ardent proponent of the Holmes test has admitted that it has been rejected as an exclusionary principle, see Flournoy v. Wiener, 321 U.S. 253, 270–272 (1944) (Frankfurter, J., dissenting). See also T.B. Harms Co. v. Eliscu, 339 F.2d 823, 827 (CA2 1964) (Friendly, J.). Leading commentators have suggested that for purposes of § 1331 an action "arises under" federal law "if in order for the plaintiff to secure the relief sought he will be obliged to establish both the correctness and the applicability to his case of a proposition of federal law." P. Bator, P. Mishkin, D. Shapiro, & H. Wechsler, Hart and Wechsler's The Federal Courts and the Federal System 889 (2d ed. 1973) (hereinafter Hart & Wechsler); cf. T.B. Harms Co., supra, at 827 ("a case may 'arise under' a law of the United States if the complaint discloses a need for determining the meaning or application of such a law").

One powerful doctrine has emerged, however—the "well-pleaded complaint" rule—which as a practical matter severely limits the number of cases in which state law "creates the cause of action" that may be initiated

---

8. The statute's "arising under" language tracks similar language in Art. III, § 2, of the Constitution, which has been construed as permitting Congress to extend federal jurisdiction to any case of which federal law potentially "forms an ingredient," see Osborn v. Bank of United States, 9 Wheat. 738, 823 (1824), and its limited legislative history suggests that the 44th Congress may have meant to "confer the whole power which the Constitution conferred," 2 Cong.Rec. 4986 (1874) (remarks of Sen. Carpenter). Nevertheless, we have only recently reaffirmed what has long been recognized—that "Art. III 'arising under' jurisdiction is broader than federal-question jurisdiction under § 1331." Verlinden B.V. v. Central Bank of Nigeria, 461 U.S. 480, 495 (1983).

in or removed to federal district court, thereby avoiding more-or-less automatically a number of potentially serious federal-state conflicts.

    * * * For better or worse, under the present statutory scheme as it has existed since 1887, a defendant may not remove a case to federal court unless the *plaintiff's* complaint establishes that the case "arises under" federal law.[9] "[A] right or immunity created by the Constitution or laws of the United States must be an element, and an essential one, of the plaintiff's cause of action." Gully v. First National Bank in Meridian, 299 U.S. 109, 112 (1936).

    For many cases in which federal law becomes relevant only insofar as it sets bounds for the operation of state authority, the well-pleaded complaint rule makes sense as a quick rule of thumb. * * *

    The rule, however, may produce awkward results, especially in cases in which neither the obligation created by state law nor the defendant's factual failure to comply are in dispute, and both parties admit that the only question for decision is raised by a federal pre-emption defense. Nevertheless, it has been correctly understood to apply in such situations.[11] As we said in Gully: "By unimpeachable authority, a suit brought upon a state statute does not arise under an act of Congress or the Constitution of the United States because prohibited thereby." *Id.*, at 116.[12]

III

    Simply to state these principles is not to apply them to the case at hand. Appellant's complaint sets forth two "causes of action," one of

---

    9. The well-pleaded complaint rule applies to the original jurisdiction of the district courts as well as to their removal jurisdiction. See Phillips Petroleum Co. v. Texaco Inc., 415 U.S. 125, 127 (1974) (*per curiam*) (case brought originally in federal court); Pan American Petroleum Corp. v. Superior Court, 366 U.S. 656, 663 (1961) (attack on jurisdiction of state court).

    It is possible to conceive of a rational jurisdictional system in which the answer as well as the complaint would be consulted before a determination was made whether the case "arose under" federal law, or in which original and removal jurisdiction were not coextensive. Indeed, until the 1887 amendments to the 1875 Act, Act of Mar. 3, 1887, ch. 373, 24 Stat. 552, as amended by Act of Aug. 13, 1888, ch. 866, 25 Stat. 433, the well-pleaded complaint rule was not applied in full force to cases removed from state court; the defendant's petition for removal could furnish the necessary guarantee that the case necessarily presented a substantial question of federal law. See Railroad Co. v. Mississippi, 102 U.S. 135, 140 (1880); Gold–Washing & Water Co. v. Keyes, 96 U.S. 199, 203–204 (1878). Commentators have repeatedly proposed that some mechanism be established to permit removal of cases in which a federal defense may be dispositive. See, *e.g.*, American Law Institute, Study of the

Division of Jurisdiction Between State and Federal Courts § 1312, pp. 188–194 (1969) (ALI Study); Wechsler, *Federal Jurisdiction and the Revision of the Judicial Code,* 13 Law & Contemp. Prob. 216, 233–234 (1948). But those proposals have not been adopted.

    11. *E.g.*, Trent Realty Associates v. First Federal Savings & Loan Assn., 657 F.2d 29, 34–35 (CA3 1981); First National Bank of Aberdeen v. Aberdeen National Bank, 627 F.2d 843, 850–852 (CA8 1980); Washington v. American League of Professional Baseball Clubs, 460 F.2d 654, 660 (CA9 1972); *cf.* First Federal Savings & Loan Assn. of Boston v. Greenwald, 591 F.2d 417, 422–423 (CA1 1979).

    12. Note, however, that a claim of federal pre-emption does not always arise as a defense to a coercive action. See n. 20, *infra.* And, of course, the absence of original jurisdiction does not mean that there is no federal forum in which a pre-emption defense may be heard. If the state courts reject a claim of federal pre-emption, that decision may ultimately be reviewed on appeal by this Court. See, *e.g.*, Fidelity Federal Savings & Loan Assn. v. De la Cuesta, 458 U.S. 141 (1982) (deciding pre-emption question at issue in Trent Realty, *supra*).

which expressly refers to ERISA; if either comes within the original jurisdiction of the federal courts, removal was proper as to the whole case. See 28 U.S.C. § 1441(c). Although appellant's complaint does not specifically assert any particular statutory entitlement for the relief it seeks, the language of the complaint suggests (and the parties do not dispute) that appellant's "first cause of action" states a claim under Cal.Rev. & Tax.Code Ann. § 18818 (West Supp.1983), and its "second cause of action" states a claim under California's Declaratory Judgment Act, Cal.Civ.Proc.Code Ann. § 1060 (West 1980). As an initial proposition, then, the "law that creates the cause of action" is state law, and original federal jurisdiction is unavailable unless it appears that some substantial, disputed question of federal law is a necessary element of one of the well-pleaded state claims, or that one or the other claim is "really" one of federal law.

A

Even though state law creates appellant's causes of action, its case might still "arise under" the laws of the United States if a well-pleaded complaint established that its right to relief under state law requires resolution of a substantial question of federal law in dispute between the parties. For appellant's first cause of action—to enforce its levy, under § 18818—a straightforward application of the well-pleaded complaint rule precludes original federal-court jurisdiction. California law establishes a set of conditions, without reference to federal law, under which a tax levy may be enforced; federal law becomes relevant only by way of a defense to an obligation created entirely by state law, and then only if appellant has made out a valid claim for relief under state law. The well-pleaded complaint rule was framed to deal with precisely such a situation. * * *

Appellant's declaratory judgment action poses a more difficult problem. Whereas the question of federal pre-emption is relevant to appellant's first cause of action only as a potential defense, it is a necessary element of the declaratory judgment claim. Under Cal.Civ.Proc.Code Ann. § 1060 (West 1980), a party with an interest in property may bring an action for a declaration of another party's legal rights and duties with respect to that property upon showing that there is an "actual controversy relating to the legal rights and duties" of the parties. The only questions in dispute between the parties in this case concern the rights and duties of CLVT and its trustees under ERISA. Not only does appellant's request for a declaratory judgment under California law clearly encompass questions governed by ERISA, but appellant's complaint identifies no other questions as a subject of controversy between the parties. Such questions must be raised in a well-pleaded complaint for a declaratory judgment. Therefore, it is clear on the face of its well-pleaded complaint that appellant may not obtain the relief it seeks in its second cause of action ("[t]hat the court declare defendants legally obligated to honor all future levies by the Board upon [CLVT],") without a construction of ERISA and/or an adjudication of its pre-emptive effect and constitutionality—all questions of federal law.

Appellant argues that original federal-court jurisdiction over such a complaint is foreclosed by our decision in Skelly Oil Co. v. Phillips Petroleum Co., 339 U.S. 667 (1950). As we shall see, however, Skelly Oil is not directly controlling.

In Skelly Oil, Skelly Oil and Phillips had a contract, for the sale of natural gas, that entitled the seller—Skelly Oil—to terminate the contract at any time after December 1, 1946, if the Federal Power Commission had not yet issued a certificate of convenience and necessity to a third party, a pipeline company to whom Phillips intended to resell the gas purchased from Skelly Oil. Their dispute began when the Federal Power Commission informed the pipeline company on November 30 that it would issue a conditional certificate, but did not make its order public until December 2. By this time Skelly Oil had notified Phillips of its decision to terminate their contract. Phillips brought an action in United States District Court under the federal Declaratory Judgment Act, 28 U.S.C. § 2201, seeking a declaration that the contract was still in effect.

There was no diversity between the parties, and we held that Phillips' claim was not within the federal-question jurisdiction conferred by § 1331. We reasoned:

" '[T]he operation of the Declaratory Judgment Act is procedural only.' Aetna Life Ins. Co. v. Haworth, 300 U.S. 227, 240. Congress enlarged the range of remedies available in the federal courts but did not extend their jurisdiction. When concerned as we are with the power of the inferior federal courts to entertain litigation within the restricted area to which the Constitution and Acts of Congress confine them, 'jurisdiction' means the kinds of issues which give right of entrance to federal courts. Jurisdiction in this sense was not altered by the Declaratory Judgment Act. Prior to that Act, a federal court would entertain a suit on a contract only if the plaintiff asked for an immediately enforceable remedy like money damages or an injunction, but such relief could only be given if the requisites of jurisdiction, in the sense of a federal right or diversity, provided foundation for resort to the federal courts. The Declaratory Judgment Act allowed relief to be given by way of recognizing the plaintiff's right even though no immediate enforcement of it was asked. But the requirements of jurisdiction—the limited subject matters which alone Congress had authorized the District Courts to adjudicate—were not impliedly repealed or modified." 339 U.S., at 671–672.

We then observed that, under the well-pleaded complaint rule, an action by Phillips to enforce its contract would not present a federal question. Skelly Oil has come to stand for the proposition that "if, but for the availability of the declaratory judgment procedure, the federal claim would arise only as a defense to a state created action, jurisdiction is lacking." 10A C. Wright, A. Miller, & M. Kane, Federal Practice and Procedure § 2767, pp. 744–745 (2d ed. 1983). Cf. Public Service Comm'n of Utah v. Wycoff Co., 344 U.S. 237, 248 (1952) (dictum).[14]

14. In Wycoff Co., a company that transported films between various points within the State of Utah sought a declaratory judgment that a state regulatory commission had no power to forbid it to transport over routes authorized by the Interstate Commerce Commission. However, "[i]t offered no evidence whatever of any past, pending or threatened action by the Utah Commission." 344 U.S., at 240. We held that there was no jurisdiction, essentially because the dispute had "not matured to a point where we can see what, if any, concrete controversy will develop." Id., at 245. We also added:

"Where the complaint in an action for declaratory judgment seeks in essence to assert a defense to an impending or threatened state court action, it is the character of the threatened action, and not of the defense, which will determine whether there is federal-question jurisdiction in the District Court. If the cause of action,

1. As an initial matter, we must decide whether the doctrine of Skelly Oil limits original federal-court jurisdiction under § 1331—and by extension removal jurisdiction under § 1441—when a question of federal law appears on the face of a well-pleaded complaint for a state-law declaratory judgment. Apparently, it is a question of first impression. As the passage quoted above makes clear, Skelly Oil relied significantly on the precise contours of the federal Declaratory Judgment Act as well as of § 1331. *Cf.* 339 U.S., at 674 (stressing the need to respect "the limited procedural purpose of the Declaratory Judgment Act"). The Court's emphasis that the Declaratory Judgment Act was intended to affect only the remedies available in a federal district court, not the court's jurisdiction, was critical to the Court's reasoning. Our interpretation of the federal Declaratory Judgment Act in Skelly Oil does not apply of its own force to *state* declaratory judgment statutes, many of which antedate the federal statute, see Developments in the Law—Declaratory Judgments—1941–1949, 62 Harv.L.Rev. 787, 790–791 (1949). * * *

Yet while Skelly Oil itself is limited to the federal Declaratory Judgment Act, fidelity to its spirit leads us to extend it to state declaratory judgment actions as well. If federal district courts could take jurisdiction, either originally or by removal, of state declaratory judgment claims raising questions of federal law, without regard to the doctrine of Skelly Oil, the federal Declaratory Judgment Act—with the limitations Skelly Oil read into it—would become a dead letter. For any case in which a state declaratory judgment action was available, litigants could get into federal court for a declaratory judgment despite our interpretation of § 2201, simply by pleading an adequate state claim for a declaration of federal law. Having interpreted the Declaratory Judgment Act of 1934 to include certain limitations on the jurisdiction of federal district courts to entertain declaratory judgment suits, we should be extremely hesitant to interpret the Judiciary Act of 1875 and its 1887 amendments in a way that renders the limitations in the later statute nugatory. Therefore, we hold that under the jurisdictional statutes as they now stand [17] federal courts do not have original jurisdiction, nor do they acquire jurisdiction on removal, when a federal question is presented by a complaint for a state declaratory judgment, but Skelly Oil would bar jurisdiction if the plaintiff had sought a federal declaratory judgment.

2. The question, then, is whether a federal district court could take jurisdiction of appellant's declaratory judgment claim had it been brought

which the declaratory defendant threatens to assert, does not itself involve a claim under federal law, it is doubtful if a federal court may entertain an action for a declaratory judgment establishing a defense to that claim. This is dubious even though the declaratory complaint sets forth a claim of federal right, if that right is in reality in the nature of a defense to a threatened cause of action. Federal courts will not seize litigations from state courts merely because one, normally a defendant, goes to federal court to begin his federal-law defense before the state court begins the case under state law." *Id.*, at 248.

17. It is not beyond the power of Congress to confer a right to a declaratory judgment in a case or controversy arising under federal law—within the meaning of the Constitution or of § 1331—without regard to Skelly Oil's particular application of the well-pleaded complaint rule. The 1969 ALI report strongly criticized the Skelly Oil doctrine: "If no other changes were to be made in federal question jurisdiction, it is arguable that such language, and the historical test it seems to embody, should be repudiated." ALI Study § 1311, at 170–171. Nevertheless, Congress has declined to make such a change. At this point, any adjustment in the system that has evolved under the Skelly Oil rule must come from Congress.

under 28 U.S.C. § 2201.[18] The application of Skelly Oil to such a suit is somewhat unclear. Federal courts have regularly taken original jurisdiction over declaratory judgment suits in which, if the declaratory judgment defendant brought a coercive action to enforce its rights, that suit would necessarily present a federal question.[19] Section 502(a)(3) of ERISA specifically grants trustees of ERISA–covered plans like CLVT a cause of action for injunctive relief when their rights and duties under ERISA are at issue, and that action is exclusively governed by federal law.[20] If CLVT could have sought an injunction under ERISA against application to it of state regulations that require acts inconsistent with ERISA,[21] does a declaratory judgment suit by the State "arise under" federal law?

We think not. We have always interpreted what Skelly Oil called "the current of jurisdictional legislation since the Act of March 3, 1875," 339 U.S., at 673, with an eye to practicality and necessity. "What is needed is something of that common-sense accommodation of judgment to kaleidoscopic situations which characterizes the law in its treatment of problems of causation * * * a selective process which picks the substantial causes out of the web and lays the other ones aside." Gully v. First National Bank in Meridian, 299 U.S., at 117–118. There are good reasons why the

18. It may seem odd that, for purposes of determining whether removal was proper, we analyze a claim brought under state law, in state court, by a party who has continuously objected to district court jurisdiction over its case, as if that party had been trying to get original federal-court jurisdiction all along. That irony, however, is a more-or-less constant feature of the removal statute, under which a case is removable if a federal district court could have taken jurisdiction had the same complaint been filed. See Wechsler, *Federal Jurisdiction and the Revision of the Judicial Code,* 13 Law & Contemp.Prob. 216, 234 (1948).

19. For instance, federal courts have consistently adjudicated suits by alleged patent infringers to declare a patent invalid, on the theory that an infringement suit by the declaratory judgment defendant would raise a federal question over which the federal courts have exclusive jurisdiction. See E. Edelmann & Co. v. Triple–A Specialty Co., 88 F.2d 852 (CA7 1937); Hart & Wechsler 896–897. Taking jurisdiction over this type of suit is consistent with the dictum in Public Service Comm'n of Utah v. Wycoff Co., 344 U.S. 237, 248 (1952), see n. 14, *supra,* in which we stated only that a declaratory judgment plaintiff could not get original federal jurisdiction if the anticipated lawsuit by the declaratory judgment defendant would *not* "arise under" federal law. It is also consistent with the nature of the declaratory remedy itself, which was designed to permit adjudication of either party's claims of right. See E. Borchard, Declaratory Judgments 15–18, 23–25 (1934).

20. Section 502(a)(3) provides:

"[A civil action may be brought] by a participant, beneficiary, or fiduciary (A) to enjoin any act or practice which violates any provision of this subchapter or the terms of the plan, or (B) to obtain other appropriate equitable relief (i) to redress such violations or (ii) to enforce any provision of this subchapter. * * *" 29 U.S.C. § 1132(a) (3).

See also n. 26, *infra* (federal jurisdiction over suits under § 502 is exclusive, and they are governed entirely by federal common law).

Even if ERISA did not expressly provide jurisdiction, CLVT might have been able to obtain federal jurisdiction under the doctrine applied in some cases that a person subject to a scheme of federal regulation may sue in federal court to enjoin application to him of conflicting state regulations, and a declaratory judgment action by the same person does not necessarily run afoul of the Skelly Oil doctrine. See, *e.g.,* Lake Carriers' Assn. v. MacMullan, 406 U.S. 498, 506–508 (1972); Rath Packing Co. v. Becker, 530 F.2d 1295, 1303–1306 (CA9 1975), aff'd *sub nom.* Jones v. Rath Packing Co., 430 U.S. 519 (1977); First Federal Savings & Loan Assn. of Boston v. Greenwald, 591 F.2d, at 423, and n. 8.

21. We express no opinion, however, whether a party in CLVT's position could sue under ERISA to enjoin or to declare invalid a state tax levy, despite the Tax Injunction Act, 28 U.S.C. § 1341. See California v. Grace Brethren Church, 457 U.S. 393 (1982). To do so, it would have to show either that state law provided no "speedy and efficient remedy" or that Congress intended § 502 of ERISA to be an exception to the Tax Injunction Act.

federal courts should not entertain suits by the States to declare the validity of their regulations despite possibly conflicting federal law. States are not significantly prejudiced by an inability to come to federal court for a declaratory judgment in advance of a possible injunctive suit by a person subject to federal regulation. They have a variety of means by which they can enforce their own laws in their own courts, and they do not suffer if the pre-emption questions such enforcement may raise are tested there.[22] The express grant of federal jurisdiction in ERISA is limited to suits brought by certain parties, see *infra,* as to whom Congress presumably determined that a right to enter federal court was necessary to further the statute's purposes.[23] It did not go so far as to provide that any suit *against* such parties must also be brought in federal court when they themselves did not choose to sue. The situation presented by a State's suit for a declaration of the validity of state law is sufficiently removed from the spirit of necessity and careful limitation of district court jurisdiction that informed our statutory interpretation in Skelly Oil and Gully to convince us that, until Congress informs us otherwise, such a suit is not within the original jurisdiction of the United States district courts. Accordingly, the same suit brought originally in state court is not removable either.

B

CLVT also argues that appellant's "causes of action" are, in substance, federal claims. Although we have often repeated that "the party who brings a suit is master to decide what law he will rely upon," The Fair v. Kohler Die & Specialty Co., 228 U.S. 22, 25 (1913), it is an independent corollary of the well-pleaded complaint rule that a plaintiff may not defeat removal by omitting to plead necessary federal questions in a complaint, see Avco Corp. v. Aero Lodge No. 735, Int'l Assn. of Machinists, 376 F.2d 337, 339–340 (CA6 1967), aff'd, 390 U.S. 557 (1968).

CLVT's best argument stems from our decision in Avco Corp. v. Aero Lodge No. 735. In that case, the petitioner filed suit in state court alleging simply that it had a valid contract with the respondent, a union, under which the respondent had agreed to submit all grievances to binding arbitration and not to cause or sanction any "work stoppages, strikes, or slowdowns." The petitioner further alleged that the respondent and its officials had violated the agreement by participating in and sanctioning work stoppages, and it sought temporary and permanent injunctions against further breaches. App., O.T.1967, No. 445, pp. 2–9. It was clear that, had petitioner invoked it, there would have been a federal cause of

---

22. Indeed, as appellant's strategy in this case shows, they may often be willing to go to great lengths to avoid federal-court resolution of a pre-emption question. Realistically, there is little prospect that States will flood the federal courts with declaratory judgment actions; most questions will arise, as in this case, because a State has sought a declaration in state court and the defendant has removed the case to federal court. Accordingly, it is perhaps appropriate to note that considerations of comity make us reluctant to snatch cases which a State has brought from the courts of that State, unless some clear rule demands it.

23. *Cf.* nn. 19 and 20, *supra.* Alleged patent infringers, for example, have a clear interest in swift resolution of the federal issue of patent validity—they are liable for damages if it turns out they are infringing a patent, and they frequently have a delicate network of contractual arrangements with third parties that is dependent on their right to sell or license a product. Parties subject to conflicting state and federal regulatory schemes also have a clear interest in sorting out the scope of each government's authority, especially where they face a threat of liability if the application of federal law is not quickly made clear.

action under § 301 of the Labor Management Relations Act, 1947 (LMRA), 29 U.S.C. § 185, see Textile Workers v. Lincoln Mills, 353 U.S. 448 (1957), and that, even in state court, any action to enforce an agreement within the scope of § 301 would be controlled by federal law, see Teamsters v. Lucas Flour Co., 369 U.S. 95, 103–104 (1962). It was also clear, however, under the law in effect at the time, that independent limits on federal jurisdiction made it impossible for a federal court to grant the injunctive relief petitioner sought. See Sinclair Refining Co. v. Atkinson, 370 U.S. 195 (1962) (later overruled in Boys Markets, Inc. v. Retail Clerks, 398 U.S. 235 (1970)).

The Court of Appeals held, and we affirmed, that the petitioner's action "arose under" § 301, and thus could be removed to federal court, although the petitioner had undoubtedly pleaded an adequate claim for relief under the state law of contracts and had sought a remedy available *only* under state law. The necessary ground of decision was that the pre-emptive force of § 301 is so powerful as to displace entirely any state cause of action "for violation of contracts between an employer and a labor organization." [25] Any such suit is purely a creature of federal law, notwithstanding the fact that state law would provide a cause of action in the absence of § 301. Avco stands for the proposition that if a federal cause of action completely pre-empts a state cause of action any complaint that comes within the scope of the federal cause of action necessarily "arises under" federal law.

CLVT argues by analogy that ERISA, like § 301, was meant to create a body of federal common law, and that "any state court action which would require the interpretation or application of ERISA to a plan document 'arises under' the laws of the United States." Brief for Appellees 20–21. ERISA contains provisions creating a series of express causes of action in favor of participants, beneficiaries, and fiduciaries of ERISA–covered plans, as well as the Secretary of Labor. § 502(a), 29 U.S.C. § 1132(a).[26] It may be that, as with § 301 as interpreted in Avco, any state action coming within the scope of § 502(a) of ERISA would be removable to federal district court, even if an otherwise adequate state cause of action were pleaded without reference to federal law. It does not follow, however, that either of appellant's claims in this case comes within the scope of one of ERISA's causes of action.

25. To similar effect is Oneida Indian Nation v. County of Oneida, 414 U.S. 661, 677 (1974), in which we held that—unlike all other ejectment suits in which the plaintiff derives its claim from a federal grant, *e.g.*, Taylor v. Anderson, 234 U.S. 74 (1914)—an ejectment suit based on Indian title is within the original "federal question" jurisdiction of the district courts, because Indian title creates a federal possessory right to tribal lands, "wholly apart from the application of state law principles which normally and separately protect a valid right of possession." *Cf.* 414 U.S., at 682–683 (Rehnquist, J., concurring).

26. The statute further states that "the district courts of the United States shall have exclusive jurisdiction of civil actions under this subchapter brought by the Secretary or by a participant, beneficiary, or fiduciary," except for actions by a participant or beneficiary to recover benefits due, to enforce rights under the terms of a plan, or to clarify rights to future benefits, over which state courts have concurrent jurisdiction. § 502(e)(1), 29 U.S.C. § 1132(e)(1). In addition, ERISA's legislative history indicates that, in light of the Act's virtually unique pre-emption provision, see § 514, 29 U.S.C. § 1144, "a body of Federal substantive law will be developed by the courts to deal with issues involving rights and obligations under private welfare and pension plans." 120 Cong.Rec. 29942 (1974) (remarks of Sen. Javits).

The phrasing of § 502(a) is instructive. Section 502(a) specifies which persons—participants, beneficiaries, fiduciaries, or the Secretary of Labor—may bring actions for particular kinds of relief. It neither creates nor expressly denies any cause of action in favor of state governments, to enforce tax levies or for any other purpose. It does not purport to reach every question relating to plans covered by ERISA.[28] Furthermore, § 514(b)(2)(A) of ERISA, 29 U.S.C. § 1144(b)(2)(A), makes clear that Congress did not intend to pre-empt entirely every state cause of action relating to such plans. With important, but express limitations, it states that "nothing in this subchapter shall be construed to exempt or relieve any person from any law of any State which regulates insurance, banking, or securities."

Against this background, it is clear that a suit by state tax authorities under a statute like § 18818 does not "arise under" ERISA. Unlike the contract rights at issue in Avco, the State's right to enforce its tax levies is not of central concern to the federal statute. For that reason, as in Gully, on the face of a well-pleaded complaint there are many reasons completely unrelated to the provisions and purposes of ERISA why the State may or may not be entitled to the relief it seeks.[29] Furthermore, ERISA does not provide an alternative cause of action in favor of the State to enforce its rights, while § 301 expressly supplied the plaintiff in Avco with a federal cause of action to replace its pre-empted state contract claim. Therefore, even though the Court of Appeals may well be correct that ERISA precludes enforcement of the State's levy in the circumstances of this case, an action to enforce the levy is not itself pre-empted by ERISA.

Once again, appellant's declaratory judgment cause of action presents a somewhat more difficult issue. The question on which a declaration is sought—that of the CLVT trustees' "power to honor the levies made upon them by the State of California,"—is undoubtedly a matter of concern under ERISA. It involves the meaning and enforceability of provisions in CLVT's trust agreement forbidding the trustees to assign or otherwise to alienate funds held in trust, and thus comes within the class of questions for which Congress intended that federal courts create federal common law.[30] Under § 502(a)(3)(B) of ERISA, a participant, beneficiary, or fiduciary of a plan covered by ERISA may bring a declaratory judgment action in federal court to determine whether the plan's trustees may comply with a state levy on funds held in trust.[31] Nevertheless, CLVT's argument that

---

28. In contrast, § 301(a) of the LMRA applies to all "[s]uits for violation of contracts between an employer and a labor organization representing employees in an industry affecting commerce * * * or between any such labor organizations." * * * But even under § 301 we have never intimated that any action merely relating to a contract within the coverage of § 301 arises exclusively under that section. For instance, a state battery suit growing out of a violent strike would not arise under § 301 simply because the strike may have been a violation of an employer-union contract. *Cf.* Automobile Workers v. Russell, 356 U.S. 634, 640–642 (1958).

29. In theory (looking only at the complaint), it may turn out that the levy was improper under state law, or that in fact the defendant had complied with the levy. * * * Furthermore, a levy on CLVT might be for something like property taxes on real estate it owned. CLVT's trust agreement authorizes its trustees to pay such taxes. Art. V, ¶ 5.21(k), App. 29.

30. See *supra*, n. 26. * * *

31. See n. 19, *supra*. Section 502(a)(3)(B) of ERISA has been interpreted as creating a cause of action for a declaratory judgment. See Cutaiar v. Marshall, 590 F.2d 523, 527 (CA3 1979). We repeat, however, the caveat expressed in n. 21, *supra*, as to the effect of the Tax Injunction Act.

appellant's second cause of action arises under ERISA fails for the second reason given above. ERISA carefully enumerates the parties entitled to seek relief under § 502; it does not provide anyone other than participants, beneficiaries, or fiduciaries with an express cause of action for a declaratory judgment on the issues in this case. A suit for similar relief by some other party does not "arise under" that provision.

IV

Our concern in this case is consistent application of a system of statutes conferring original federal-court jurisdiction, as they have been interpreted by this Court over many years. Under our interpretations, Congress has given the lower federal courts jurisdiction to hear, originally or by removal from a state court, only those cases in which a well-pleaded complaint establishes either that federal law creates the cause of action or that the plaintiff's right to relief necessarily depends on resolution of a substantial question of federal law. We hold that a suit by state tax authorities both to enforce its levies against funds held in trust pursuant to an ERISA–covered employee benefit plan, and to declare the validity of the levies notwithstanding ERISA, is neither a creature of ERISA itself nor a suit of which the federal courts will take jurisdiction because it turns on a question of federal law. Accordingly, we vacate the judgment of the Court of Appeals and remand so that this case may be remanded to the Superior Court of the State of California for the County of Los Angeles.

It is so ordered.

NOTE ON THE JURISDICTIONAL SIGNIFICANCE OF THE DECLARATORY JUDGMENT ACT

(1) Note, *Developments in the Law: Declaratory Judgments—1941–1949*, 62 Harv.L.Rev. 787, 802–03 (1949), suggests that there are three possible views of the jurisdictional effect of the Declaratory Judgment Act: (1) that jurisdiction exists if the federal question is properly set forth in the complaint, even though the question would have arisen only as a defense in a coercive action between the same parties; (2) that jurisdiction exists only if it would exist in a coercive action by the plaintiff against the defendant; and (3) that jurisdiction exists if it would exist in a coercive action by either party against the other. The Note urges adoption of the third view.

The Skelly Oil case—discussed and quoted in Franchise Tax—cited the Harvard Note with apparent approval, but its language looked toward the more restrictive "second" alternative.[1]

Where does Franchise Tax Board leave this question? The Court's opinion says that "federal courts" have "regularly" assumed jurisdiction over declaratory judgment suits where the declaratory defendant could have brought a coercive federal action against the declaratory plaintiff; and footnote 19 seems to approve the large body of decisions holding (notwithstanding Skelly Oil) that an alleged patent infringer may bring an

---

1. Skelly stressed the notion that the Declaratory Judgment Act was "procedural only" and was not meant to enlarge the federal courts' jurisdiction. But see Mishkin, *The Federal "Question" in the* District Courts, 53 Colum.L.Rev. 157, 178 n. 99 (1953) (arguing that these concerns related to fears that the Act might assign to the federal courts controversies that were not justiciable under Article III).

action for a declaration of non-infringement or of the invalidity of the patent in a federal district court. (The leading case holding that such an action "arises under" the patent laws, cited in Franchise Tax Board n. 19, is the Edelman case in the Seventh Circuit (88 F.2d 852 (1937)), which has been followed in a large body of cases. The Supreme Court has passed on the merits of such actions for a declaratory judgment without raising any question of jurisdiction. See, *e.g.,* Calmar, Inc. v. Cook Chem. Co., decided *sub nom.* Graham v. John Deere Co., 383 U.S. 1 (1966); Jungersen v. Ostby & Barton Co., 335 U.S. 560 (1949).)

(2) In the Skelly Oil case, Chief Justice Vinson expressed "real doubts whether there is a federal question here at all" (p. 679). Were these doubts well founded? Did the fact that federal law was "incorporated" into the case by private contract differentiate the case from Standard Oil v. Johnson, p. 557, *supra,* and Smith v. Kansas City Title & Trust, p. 992, *supra?*

(3) Shaw v. Delta Air Lines, Inc., 463 U.S. 85 (1983), decided on the same day as Franchise Tax Board, was an action by employees and employers for an injunction and declaratory judgment that certain provisions of New York's Human Rights Law and Disability Benefits Law were preempted by ERISA (the statute also at issue in Franchise Tax Board). The Court decided the case on the merits. In footnote 14, the opinion states (p. 96): "The Court's decision today in Franchise Tax Board v. Construction Laborers Vacation Trust does not call into question the lower courts' jurisdiction to decide these cases. Franchise Tax Board was an action seeking a declaration that state laws were *not* preempted by ERISA. Here, in contrast, companies subject to ERISA regulation seek injunctions against enforcement of state laws they claim *are* pre-empted by ERISA, as well as declarations that those laws are pre-empted.

"It is beyond dispute that federal courts have jurisdiction over suits to enjoin state officials from interfering with federal rights. See Ex parte Young, 209 U.S. 123, 160–162 (1908). A plaintiff who seeks injunctive relief from state regulation, on the ground that such regulation is pre-empted by a federal statute which, by virtue of the Supremacy Clause of the Constitution, must prevail, thus presents a federal question which the federal courts have jurisdiction under 28 U.S.C. § 1331 to resolve. See * * * Note, *Federal Jurisdiction Over Declaratory Suits Challenging State Action,* 79 Colum.L.Rev. 983 (1979). This Court, of course, frequently has resolved preemption disputes in a similar jurisdictional posture * * *." [2]

See also Duke Power Co. v. Carolina Environmental Study Group, Inc., 438 U.S. 59 (1978), involving a declaratory judgment action against, *inter alia,* the Nuclear Regulatory Commission for a declaration of the invalidity of the Price Anderson Act, 42 U.S.C. § 2210, which limits the liability of nuclear plants for nuclear accidents. Reading the complaint as stating a claim against the Commission "directly under" the Due Process Clause of the Fifth Amendment, the Court upheld § 1331 jurisdiction. Justice Rehnquist, dissenting, argued that the complaint involved a claim of "taking" and was subject to the special jurisdiction statutes limiting district court jurisdiction in favor of the Court of Claims. He also argued that, under

---

2. Shaw involved a suit seeking injunctive as well as declaratory relief. But in dictum in Lawrence County v. Lead–Deadwood School Dist., No. 40–1, 469 U.S. 256, 259 n. 6 (1985), the Court cited Shaw as upholding the existence of jurisdiction over a suit seeking a declaratory judgment that a state statute was preempted by federal law. Accord, Schneidewind v. ANR Pipeline Co., 108 S.Ct. 1145 (1988).

Mottley, there was no § 1331 jurisdiction over the action against co-defendant Duke Power Company—a point not addressed by the majority.

(4) The American Law Institute proposed that the district courts should have jurisdiction "of all civil actions, including those for a declaratory judgment, in which the initial pleading sets forth a substantial claim arising under the Constitution, laws, or treaties of the United States." ALI Study, proposed § 1311(a). How would Franchise Tax be decided under this provision?

(5) In Merrell Dow the Court concluded that what might otherwise be a general rule allowing § 1331 jurisdiction is trumped if, in a particular statutory context, the Court discerns a congressional purpose not to give access to the federal courts. Justice Brennan's dissent appears to cast doubt on the appropriateness of this approach. But isn't it exactly this approach that he adopted in Franchise Tax?

SECTION 4. PENDENT JURISDICTION

UNITED MINE WORKERS OF AMERICA v. GIBBS

383 U.S. 715, 86 S.Ct. 1130, 16 L.Ed.2d 218 (1966).
Certiorari to the United States Court of Appeals for the Sixth Circuit.

MR. JUSTICE BRENNAN delivered the opinion of the Court.

Respondent Paul Gibbs was awarded compensatory and punitive damages in this action against petitioner United Mine Workers of America (UMW) for alleged violations of § 303 of the Labor Management Relations Act, 1947, 61 Stat. 158, as amended, and of the common law of Tennessee. The case grew out of the rivalry between the United Mine Workers and the Southern Labor Union over representation of workers in the southern Appalachian coal fields. Tennessee Consolidated Coal Company, not a party here, laid off 100 miners of the UMW's Local 5881 when it closed one of its mines in southern Tennessee during the spring of 1960. Late that summer, Grundy Company, a wholly owned subsidiary of Consolidated, hired respondent as mine superintendent to attempt to open a new mine on Consolidated's property at nearby Gray's Creek through use of members of the Southern Labor Union. As part of the arrangement, Grundy also gave respondent a contract to haul the mine's coal to the nearest railroad loading point.

On August 15 and 16, 1960, armed members of Local 5881 forcibly prevented the opening of the mine, threatening respondent and beating an organizer for the rival union. * * * [At that point the UMW international union intervened.] There was no further violence at the mine site; a picket line was maintained there for nine months; and no further attempts were made to open the mine during that period.

Respondent lost his job as superintendent, and never entered into performance of his haulage contract. He testified that he soon began to lose other trucking contracts and mine leases he held in nearby areas. Claiming these effects to be the result of a concerted union plan against him, he sought recovery * * * against petitioner, the international union.

The suit was brought in the United States District Court for the Eastern District of Tennessee, and jurisdiction was premised on allegations of secondary boycotts under § 303. The state law claim, for which jurisdiction was based upon the doctrine of pendent jurisdiction, asserted "an unlawful conspiracy and an unlawful boycott aimed at him and [Grundy] to maliciously, wantonly and willfully interfere with his contract of employment and with his contract of haulage."

The trial judge refused to submit to the jury the claims of pressure intended to cause mining firms other than Grundy to cease doing business with Gibbs; he found those claims unsupported by the evidence. The jury's verdict was that the UMW had violated both § 303 and state law. Gibbs was awarded $60,000 as damages under the employment contract and $14,500 under the haulage contract; he was also awarded $100,000 punitive damages. On motion, the trial court set aside the award of damages with respect to the haulage contract on the ground that damage was unproved. It also held that union pressure on Grundy to discharge respondent as supervisor would constitute only a primary dispute with Grundy, as respondent's employer, and hence was not cognizable as a claim under § 303. Interference with the employment relationship was cognizable as a state claim, however, and a remitted award was sustained on the state law claim. 220 F.Supp. 871. The Court of Appeals for the Sixth Circuit affirmed. 343 F.2d 609. We granted certiorari. 382 U.S. 809. We reverse.

I.

A threshold question is whether the District Court properly entertained jurisdiction of the claim based on Tennessee law. * * *

The Court held in Hurn v. Oursler, 289 U.S. 238, that state law claims are appropriate for federal court determination if they form a separate but parallel ground for relief also sought in a substantial claim based on federal law. The Court distinguished permissible from nonpermissible exercises of federal judicial power over state law claims by contrasting "a case where two distinct grounds in support of a single cause of action are alleged, one only of which presents a federal question, and a case where two separate and distinct causes of action are alleged, one only of which is federal in character. In the former, where the federal question averred is not plainly wanting in substance, the federal court, even though the federal ground be not established, may nevertheless retain and dispose of the case upon the non-federal *ground;* in the latter it may not do so upon the non-federal *cause of action.*" 289 U.S., at 246. The question is into which category the present action fell.

Hurn was decided in 1933, before the unification of law and equity by the Federal Rules of Civil Procedure. At the time, the meaning of "cause of action" was a subject of serious dispute; the phrase might "mean one thing for one purpose and something different for another." United States v. Memphis Cotton Oil Co., 288 U.S. 62, 67–68. The Court in Hurn identified what it meant by the term by citation of Baltimore S.S. Co. v. Phillips, 274 U.S. 316, a case in which "cause of action" had been used to identify the operative scope of the doctrine of *res judicata.* In that case the Court had noted that " 'the whole tendency of our decisions is to require a plaintiff to try his whole cause of action and his whole case at one time.' " 274 U.S., at 320. * * * Had the Court found a jurisdictional bar to reaching the state claim in Hurn, we assume that the doctrine of *res judicata* would not have been applicable in any subsequent state suit. But the citation of Baltimore S.S. Co. shows that the Court found that the weighty policies of judicial economy and fairness to parties reflected in *res judicata* doctrine were in themselves strong counsel for the adoption of a rule which would permit federal courts to dispose of the state as well as the federal claims.

With the adoption of the Federal Rules of Civil Procedure and the unified form of action, Fed.Rule Civ.Proc. 2, much of the controversy over "cause of action" abated. The phrase remained as the keystone of the Hurn test, however, and, as commentators have noted, has been the source of considerable confusion. Under the Rules, the impulse is toward entertaining the broadest possible scope of action consistent with fairness to the parties; joinder of claims, parties and remedies is strongly encouraged. Yet because the Hurn question involves issues of jurisdiction as well as convenience, there has been some tendency to limit its application to cases in which the state and federal claims are, as in Hurn, "little more than the equivalent of different epithets to characterize the same group of circumstances." 289 U.S., at 246.

This limited approach is unnecessarily grudging. Pendent jurisdiction, in the sense of judicial *power*, exists whenever there is a claim "arising under [the] Constitution, the Laws of the United States, and Treaties made, or which shall be made, under their Authority * * *," U.S. Const., Art. III, § 2, and the relationship between that claim and the state claim permits the conclusion that the entire action before the court comprises but one constitutional "case." The federal claim must have substance sufficient to confer subject matter jurisdiction on the court. Levering & Garrigues Co. v. Morrin, 289 U.S. 103. The state and federal claims must derive from a common nucleus of operative fact. But if, considered without regard to their federal or state character, a plaintiff's claims are such that he would ordinarily be expected to try them all in one judicial proceeding, then, assuming substantiality of the federal issues, there is *power* in federal courts to hear the whole.[13]

That power need not be exercised in every case in which it is found to exist. It has consistently been recognized that pendent jurisdiction is a doctrine of discretion, not of plaintiff's right. Its justification lies in considerations of judicial economy, convenience and fairness to litigants; if these are not present a federal court should hesitate to exercise jurisdiction over state claims, even though bound to apply state law to them, Erie R. Co. v. Tompkins, 304 U.S. 64. Needless decisions of state law should be avoided both as a matter of comity and to promote justice between the parties, by procuring for them a surer-footed reading of applicable law. Certainly, if the federal claims are dismissed before trial, even though not insubstantial in a jurisdictional sense, the state claims should be dismissed as well. Similarly, if it appears that the state issues substantially predominate, whether in terms of proof, of the scope of the issues raised, or of the

---

13. *Cf.* Armstrong Co. v. Nu–Enamel Corp., 305 U.S. 315, 325. Note, *Problems of Parallel State and Federal Remedies,* 71 Harv.L.Rev. 513, 514 (1958). While it is commonplace that the Federal Rules of Civil Procedure do not expand the jurisdiction of federal courts, they do embody "the whole tendency of our decisions * * * to require a plaintiff to try his * * * whole case at one time," Baltimore S.S. Co. v. Phillips, *supra,* and to that extent emphasize the basis of pendent jurisdiction.

comprehensiveness of the remedy sought, the state claims may be dismissed without prejudice and left for resolution to state tribunals. There may, on the other hand, be situations in which the state claim is so closely tied to questions of federal policy that the argument for exercise of pendent jurisdiction is particularly strong. In the present case, for example, the allowable scope of the state claim implicates the federal doctrine of pre-emption; while this interrelationship does not create statutory federal question jurisdiction, Louisville & N.R. Co. v. Mottley, 211 U.S. 149, its existence is relevant to the exercise of discretion. Finally, there may be reasons independent of jurisdictional considerations, such as the likelihood of jury confusion in treating divergent legal theories of relief, that would justify separating state and federal claims for trial, Fed.Rule Civ.Proc. 42(b). If so, jurisdiction should ordinarily be refused.

The question of power will ordinarily be resolved on the pleadings. But the issue whether pendent jurisdiction has been properly assumed is one which remains open throughout the litigation. Pretrial procedures or even the trial itself may reveal a substantial hegemony of state law claims, or likelihood of jury confusion, which could not have been anticipated at the pleading stage. Although it will of course be appropriate to take account in this circumstance of the already completed course of the litigation, dismissal of the state claim might even then be merited. For example, it may appear that the plaintiff was well aware of the nature of his proofs and the relative importance of his claims; recognition of a federal court's wide latitude to decide ancillary questions of state law does not imply that it must tolerate a litigant's effort to impose upon it what is in effect only a state law case. Once it appears that a state claim constitutes the real body of a case, to which the federal claim is only an appendage, the state claim may fairly be dismissed.

We are not prepared to say that in the present case the District Court exceeded its discretion in proceeding to judgment on the state claim. We may assume for purposes of decision that the District Court was correct in its holding that the claim of pressure on Grundy to terminate the employment contract was outside the purview of § 303. Even so, the § 303 claims based on secondary pressures on Grundy relative to the haulage contract and on other coal operators generally were substantial. Although § 303 limited recovery to compensatory damages based on secondary pressures, Teamsters Union v. Morton, *supra*, and state law allowed both compensatory and punitive damages, and allowed such damages as to both secondary and primary activity, the state and federal claims arose from the same nucleus of operative fact and reflected alternative remedies. Indeed, the verdict sheet sent in to the jury authorized only one award of damages, so that recovery could not be given separately on the federal and state claims.

It is true that the § 303 claims ultimately failed and that the only recovery allowed respondent was on the state claim. We cannot confidently say, however, that the federal issues were so remote or played such a minor role at the trial that in effect the state claim only was tried. Although the District Court dismissed as unproved the § 303 claims that petitioner's secondary activities included attempts to induce coal operators other than Grundy to cease doing business with respondent, the court submitted the § 303 claims relating to Grundy to the jury. The jury returned verdicts against petitioner on those § 303 claims, and it was only on petitioner's motion for a directed verdict and a judgment *n.o.v.* that the verdicts on those claims were set aside. The District Judge considered the claim as to the haulage contract proved as to liability, and held it failed only for lack of proof of damages. Although there was some risk of confusing the jury in joining the state and federal claims—especially since, as will be developed, differing standards of proof of UMW involvement applied—the possibility of confusion could be lessened by employing a special verdict form, as the District Court did. Moreover, the question whether the permissible scope of the state claim was limited by the doctrine of pre-emption afforded a special reason for the exercise of pendent jurisdiction; the federal courts are particularly appropriate bodies for the application of pre-emption principles. We thus conclude that although it may be that the District Court might, in its sound discretion, have dismissed the state claim, the circumstances show no error in refusing to do so. * * *

[The judgment was reversed because, even if the state-law claim was not pre-empted by the Labor–Management Relations Act, the proof of defendant's responsibility had not met the requirements imposed by § 6 of the Norris–LaGuardia Act, 29 U.S.C. § 106.]

NOTE ON PENDENT JURISDICTION

(1) The Gibbs opinion focuses on the question whether pendent jurisdiction is within the scope of the judicial power conferred by Article III, and simply assumes that, within that boundary, the federal courts have "discretion" to entertain or refuse the case. But this elides the question of the scope of § 1331. Should § 1331 be read to authorize the federal courts to exercise pendent jurisdiction over state-law claims? (Consider the relevance of the fact that § 1331 uses the phrase "civil actions," not "cases.")

(2) Hurn v. Oursler, referred to in Gibbs, was a suit to enjoin production of a play on the grounds of copyright infringement and unfair competition. The action originally involved only the plagiarizing of a copyrighted play. The bill was subsequently amended to allege also unfair competition with a revised, uncopyrighted version of the same play. The Court held that the two original claims were "but different grounds asserted in support of the same cause of action", and could thus both be adjudicated in federal court; the claim with regard to the uncopyrighted play asserted a "separate and distinct" cause of action "entirely outside the federal jurisdiction".

The Hurn opinion supported jurisdiction to decide some state claims joined with federal claims on the basis, *inter alia,* of Osborn v. Bank of the United States, p. 967, *supra.* It also relied upon Siler v. Louisville & Nashville R. Co., 213 U.S. 175 (1909), an action to enjoin the enforcement of an order made by the Railroad Commission of Kentucky fixing intrastate rates of transportation upon the railroad. The validity of the order was assailed on the ground that the Kentucky statute under which the commission assumed to act was violative of the federal Constitution in several particulars, and upon the further ground that such order was unauthorized by the state statute. The Court held that a claim that the rate order under attack violated state law did not undermine the basis of the parallel claim that the order violated federal law. See p. 1226, *infra.* But the Court went further and held that, even in the absence of diversity of citizenship, the case should be disposed of, if possible, on state grounds without reaching the federal question. Justice Peckham said (213 U.S. at 191–93):

"The Federal questions, as to the invalidity of the state statute * * * gave the Circuit Court jurisdiction, and, having properly obtained it, that court had the right to decide all the questions in the case, even though it decided the Federal questions adversely to the party raising them, or even if it omitted to decide them at all, but decided the case on local or state questions only. * * *

"The character of some of the Federal questions raised is such as to show that they are not merely colorable, and have not been fraudulently raised for the purpose of attempting to give jurisdiction to a Federal court. * * *

"Where a case in this court can be decided without reference to questions arising under the Federal Constitution, that course is usually pursued and is not departed from without important reasons. In this case we think it much better to decide it with regard to the question of a local nature, involving the construction of the state statute and the authority therein given to the commission to make the order in question, rather than to unnecessarily decide the various constitutional questions appearing in the record."

The Court then went on to hold that the broad power asserted by the state commission to fix general maximum rates for the transportation of all commodities upon all railroads to and from points within the state ought not to be recognized in the absence of an express grant, and that the commission's power should be construed as limited to the fixing of particular rates upon appropriate challenge.

(3) The original edition of this book raised the following issues:

"Notice that a federal trial court would often be unable to function as a court at all, in the absence of the jurisdiction over state questions which Marshall asserted in Osborn v. Bank of the United States. At stake there was the ability of such a court, ever, to be sure of being able to decide a whole case.

"No such justification, obviously, is available for the ancillary jurisdiction asserted in Siler. The justification there, is it not, is different and twofold: namely, the policy in favor of avoiding avoidable decisions of federal constitutional questions, plus the policy in favor of having one lawsuit, if possible, instead of two?

"Hurn, however, is supported only by the single policy against piecemeal litigation. How strong is this policy? How far does it warrant stretching the constitutional concept of a 'case'?"

The last questions of course apply equally well to Gibbs, which indeed explicitly asserts the justification for its conclusion in terms of "judicial economy, convenience and fairness to litigants." But beyond their intrinsic value, are these considerations—and the policy against piecemeal litigation—not relevant to jurisdictional issues, even when perceived in terms of distribution of power? Consider the effect of a rule contrary to Hurn and Gibbs. If in order to invoke a federal forum for a federal claim, a party who also has related, even overlapping, state claims will have to litigate those claims separately, might he not be deterred from going to federal court? Where federal jurisdiction is exclusive, this may effectively attenuate the value of the federal claim. Where federal and state courts have concurrent jurisdiction, such a party could litigate his claims without duplication of effort and cost only in the state tribunals.

Shakman, *The New Pendent Jurisdiction of the Federal Courts,* 20 Stan.L.Rev. 262 (1968), contends that these considerations argue against the Gibbs outcome, at least where federal jurisdiction is not exclusive. He takes the position that a broad holding such as Gibbs is undesirable precisely "because it will place many cases in the federal courts that would otherwise be decided in state courts" (p. 265). If the choice is between allowing a suitor with a federal claim to invoke a federal forum, which may then have to adjudicate a state claim, or relegating him to a state tribunal even for his federal claim, how is that choice to be made? The statutory grant of federal question jurisdiction certainly implies a judgment by Congress that federal claims should be litigable in a federal court if a party wishes. Doesn't Gibbs ultimately rest on the premise that it would be inconsistent with that judgment for a federal claimant to be deterred from seeking access to federal jurisdiction? See generally Mishkin, *The Federal "Question" in the District Courts,* 53 Colum.L.Rev. 157, 167, 172–73 (1953).

If the problem of pendent jurisdiction is analyzed in terms of effectuating such a policy of nondeterrence, rather than simply economy and convenience, the focus of inquiry would be on those factors which would be significant to a prospective litigant of a federal claim. Would this produce a rule different from that of Gibbs?

(4) Is any particular rule of pendent jurisdiction required by res judicata doctrines? Is not Justice Brennan correct in assuming that if a state claim is held to be outside the "case" or "civil action" which is the subject of federal court jurisdiction, no state court would later hold that consideration of the merits of that claim is barred by the federal adjudication? Indeed, would any other result be consistent with the due process clause? With Article III and the Supremacy Clause?

(5) The Gibbs, Hurn, and Siler cases all stress the point that pendent jurisdiction attaches, if at all, only when the federal claim asserted is "substantial". See also Bell v. Hood, 327 U.S. 678 (1946), p. 1022, *supra.* In Levering & Garrigues Co. v. Morrin, 289 U.S. 103 (1933), cited in the Gibbs opinion, the Court said (p. 105):

" *   *   * And the federal question averred may be plainly unsubstantial either because obviously without merit, or 'because its unsoundness so clearly results from the previous decisions of this court as to foreclose the subject and leave no room for the inference that the questions sought to be raised can be the subject of controversy.' "

The wisdom of the doctrine that an insubstantial federal question does not confer jurisdiction has been questioned. See, *e.g.,* Rosado v. Wyman, 397 U.S. 397, 404 (1970) ("a maxim more ancient than analytically sound"). But it serves as a useful barrier against efforts to manufacture federal jurisdiction over state claims. In most cases, early dismissal of the federal claim on the merits would result in refusal to entertain the joined state questions, as a matter of discretion if not of power.

The rule that an insubstantial federal question does not provide a basis for jurisdiction was considerably diluted, however, in Hagans v. Lavine, 415 U.S. 528 (1974). The Court there had first determined that there was pendent jurisdiction to decide a federal statutory claim under 28 U.S.C.

§ 1343(3) if there existed a "substantial" constitutional claim as well. It then concluded that the constitutional claim actually presented—an attack on the validity of state regulations allowing the state to make certain deductions from AFDC payments—was not so frivolous or insubstantial as to be beyond the jurisdiction of the district court: "[It is not] immediately obvious to us from the face of the complaint that recouping emergency rent payments from future welfare disbursements, which petitioners argue deprived needy children because of parental default, was so patently rational [sic] as to require no meaningful consideration. * * * Nor can we say that petitioners' claim is 'so insubstantial, implausible, foreclosed by prior decisions of this Court or otherwise completely devoid of merit as not to involve a federal controversy within the jurisdiction of the District Court, whatever may be the ultimate resolution of the federal issues on the merits.' Oneida Indian Nation v. County of Oneida, 414 U.S. 661, 666–67 (1974)" (pp. 539–41, 543). The dissent argued that pendent jurisdiction requires a constitutional claim that has more than a "glimmer of merit" (p. 552); "the one clear fact is that the [constitutional] claim is not very good" (p. 561); "under today's rationale it appears sufficient for jurisdiction that a plaintiff is able to plead his claim with a straight face" (p. 564); "this seems to be a classic case of the statutory tail wagging the constitutional dog" (p. 564).

(6) The 1948 revision of the Judicial Code conferred jurisdiction over "a claim of unfair competition when joined with a substantial and related claim under the copyright, patent or trade-mark laws". 28 U.S.C. § 1338(b).[1]

The Reviser's Notes on this provision stated: "Subsection (b) is added and is intended to avoid 'piecemeal' litigation to enforce common-law and statutory copyright, patent, and trade-mark rights by specifically permitting such enforcement in a single civil action in the district court. While this is the rule under federal decisions, this section would enact it as statutory authority. The problem is discussed at length in Hurn v. Oursler. * * *"

Did the revisers fairly represent to Congress what they were doing? What was their warrant for singling out the unfair competition aspect of the Siler–Hurn doctrine for special statutory mention? They apparently forgot that Hurn itself was based on Siler. Note that while cases under the copyright and patent laws are exclusively in federal jurisdiction, trademark cases are not.

The lower courts struggled with the relationship between § 1338(b) and the Hurn doctrine, generally moving toward a wider definition of the term "related" in the statute, though certainly not with ease or unanimity. Since Gibbs, however, § 1338(b) has been more and more ignored, and the doctrine of pendent jurisdiction treated as a general judge-made gloss on the federal question jurisdiction. See 13B Wright, Miller & Cooper, Federal Practice and Procedure § 3567 (1984).

(7) The Hurn test was exceedingly difficult to apply. Gibbs sought to meet this problem by an expansive definition of power, combined with a wide district court discretion after the case is in the court. For a survey of

---

1. In 1970, claims under plant variety protection laws were added to § 1338(b) as well as to the categories of exclusive jurisdiction in § 1338(a). Dec. 24, 1970, 84 Stat. 1559.

the lower court authority applying this approach, see 13B Wright, Miller & Cooper, *supra*, § 3567.1.

Compare the proposal of the American Law Institute, that the federal and state claims must "arise out of the same transaction or occurrence" and have a common "substantial question of fact." See ALI Study, proposed § 1313(a). This approach was said to be consistent with Gibbs, but couched in "terms familiar in procedural rules". *Id.* at 210.

(8) The ALI's proposed standard resembles that of Federal Rule 13(a) for identifying compulsory counterclaims. Hurn relied in part on Moore v. New York Cotton Exchange, 270 U.S. 593 (1926), holding that federal jurisdiction extended to a compulsory counterclaim even though it arose under state law and even after the basic federal anti-trust claim had been dismissed on the merits. Are the considerations regarding parallel claims (as in Hurn and Gibbs) and counterclaims the same?

Lower court authority is unanimous that compulsory counterclaims are within pendent jurisdiction, but that permissive counterclaims—at least those amounting to more than a set-off—must be supported by independent jurisdictional grounds. See 6 Wright & Miller, Federal Practice and Procedure §§ 1414, 1422 (1971; 1987 Supp.). Could Gibbs be the basis for extending ancillary jurisdiction to permissive counterclaims? See Friendly, J., concurring, in United States ex rel. D'Agostino Excavators, Inc. v. Heyward–Robinson Co., 430 F.2d 1077, 1088 (2d Cir.1970).

(9) Is discretion to dismiss pendent claims when the basic federal claim had been disposed of consistent with Chief Justice Marshall's view that a federal court had "no more right to decline the exercise of jurisdiction which is given, than to usurp that which is not given" (Cohens v. Virginia, 6 Wheat. 264, 404 (U.S.1821))? Compare Shapiro, *Jurisdiction and Discretion,* 60 N.Y.U.L.Rev. 543 (1985).[2]

(10) Consider the statement in Gibbs, "Certainly, if the federal claims are dismissed before trial [even though on the merits], the state claims should be dismissed as well." Always? Suppose the statute of limitations has run on the state claim in the interim? Doesn't the rationale of pendent jurisdiction require that a party properly invoking it be assured that he will not be hurt by the attempt? *Cf.* ALI Study, proposed § 1313(c), (d), conditioning discretion not to adjudicate the state claim upon a specific finding that "determination of such claims in a State court is in the interest of justice and not prejudicial to the parties".

(11) Pendent jurisdiction widens the plaintiff's opportunity to join overlapping state and federal claims in one action. By creating that opportunity, pendent jurisdiction also generates new res judicata pitfalls for the plaintiff who does not in fact raise both claims in the first action. In Federated Dep't Stores, Inc. v. Moitie, 452 U.S. 394 (1981), plaintiff's antitrust action was dismissed on the merits by a federal court; no appeal was taken. The Supreme Court held that a second federal antitrust suit was barred even though in the interim the Court had, in another case, made a ruling that demonstrated that the original dismissal had been wrong. The Court declined, however, to decide the question whether the

---

2. The courts have, under Gibbs, assumed that they have discretion to dismiss even those pendent claims falling within § 1338(b) (see par. (6), *supra*). See, *e.g.*, Pate Co. v. RPS Corp., 685 F.2d 1019 (7th Cir.1982). Is this justified? See also Carnegie-Mellon Univ. v. Cohill, 108 S.Ct. 614 (1988), p. 1788, *infra*.

first case was also res judicata with respect to state-law issues (unfair competition, fraud, restitution) raised in the second action. Justice Blackmun, concurring, stated that he "would flatly hold that [the first case] is res judicata as to respondents' state-law claims. * * * Since there is no reason to believe that it was clear at the outset of this litigation that the District Court would have declined to exercise pendent jurisdiction over state claims, respondents were obligated to plead those claims if they wished to preserve them" (p. 404). On the question whether the preclusive effect of the first litigation is governed by state or federal law, see the complex rulings in Marrese v. American Academy of Orthopaedic Surgeons, 470 U.S. 373 (1985), and Parsons Steel, Inc. v. First Alabama Bank, 474 U.S. 518 (1986), further discussed in Chapter XII, at pp. 1627–29, *infra.*

(12) The scope of the Siler–Hurn–Gibbs doctrine was significantly affected by the Court's ruling in Pennhurst State School & Hospital v. Halderman, 465 U.S. 89 (1984), p. 1195, *infra,* which held that the Eleventh Amendment prohibits the federal courts from ordering state officials to conform their conduct to state law, and thereby bars the exercise of pendent jurisdiction over claims against state officials arising under state law where the relief sought "has an impact directly on the State itself" (p. 117). The Court acknowledged that Siler, and the numerous cases in its line, had approved the exercise of pendent jurisdiction in such cases (and had even held that the state-law issue should be adjudicated first); [3] but stated that none of those cases had discussed the problem of the Eleventh Amendment. Pendent jurisdiction is a "judge-made doctrine of expediency and efficiency"; it should not override the constitutional barriers the Eleventh Amendment creates against the adjudication of state-law injunction actions against state officials (pp. 120–21). The resulting problem of "bifurcation of claims" (p. 122) raises a policy consideration that cannot outweigh the ban of the Eleventh Amendment. Justice Stevens' strong dissent (on behalf also of three other justices) complained that the Siler rule has "an impressive historical pedigree" and is also "strongly supported by the interest in avoiding duplicative litigation and the unnecessary decision of federal constitutional questions" (p. 162).

The Eleventh Amendment aspect of the ruling in the Pennhurst case is fully discussed at pp. 1195–1204, *infra.* The case presumably leaves open the adjudication of pendent state-law claims against state officials where state consent has eliminated an Eleventh Amendment objection; and the ruling of course has no effect on cases where the Eleventh Amendment is inapplicable (*e.g.,* suits against local governments and their officials).

(13) Suppose that plaintiff makes a pendent state-law claim against the original defendant and seeks, for purposes of that claim, to add defendants who are not liable under the federal claim and who could not otherwise be sued in a federal court. May he do so? "Until approximately 10 years ago, pendent party jurisdiction was rejected. Then, as the Gibbs doctrine broadened and as ancillary jurisdiction [see Chap. XIII, Sec. 2, *infra*] became more commonly applied, lower federal courts began to accept pendent party jurisdiction because they satisfied the common nucleus of

---

3. This latter rule had been reaffirmed as recently as 1982, the Court holding per curiam that it was abuse of discretion under Gibbs for the court of appeals not to resolve a pendent state-law question (whether an affirmative action plan was invalid under state law), resolution of which might moot a federal constitutional question. Schmidt v. Oakland Unified School District, 457 U.S. 594 (1982).

operative fact test and because ancillary jurisdiction already allowed the bringing in of new parties, under Rules 13(h) and 14(a). * * * Pendent party jurisdiction was justified as a combination of the pendency test and the expansion of ancillarity." Miller, *Ancillary and Pendent Jurisdiction*, 26 So.Texas L.Rev. 1, 11 (1985).

Supreme Court cases restricting notions of ancillary jurisdiction in the context of class actions (*e.g.*, Zahn v. International Paper Co., 414 U.S. 291 (1973), p. 1764, *infra*) were thought to indicate that the Supreme Court would not view the notion of pendent party jurisdiction with favor. See Currie, *Pendent Parties*, 45 U.Chi.L.Rev. 753 (1978). This prediction proved accurate when the Court finally addressed the issue directly. Aldinger v. Howard, 427 U.S. 1 (1976), was an action under 42 U.S.C. § 1983 against county officials for violating the plaintiff's constitutional rights. Jurisdiction was founded on 28 U.S.C. § 1343(3), the jurisdictional portion of the Civil Rights Act that had created these federal claims. The established rule at that time (since overruled, see p. 1251, *infra*) was that cities and counties were not "persons" suable under § 1983, and thus could not be sued in a federal court under § 1343(3).[4] In Aldinger, however, plaintiff also asserted a pendent state-law claim against the defendant officials, and named the county as a defendant in that state-law claim.

The Supreme Court held that the claim against the county must be dismissed. Since Congress had determined that local governmental entities should not be liable as a matter of federal law in a federal court under §§ 1343(3) and 1983, the Court concluded that it would undermine that determination to allow them to be sued in federal court under the judge-made doctrine of pendent jurisdiction. "In Osborn and Gibbs Congress was silent on the extent to which the defendant, already properly in federal court under a statute, might be called upon to answer nonfederal questions or claims; the way was thus left open for the Court to fashion its own rules under the general language of Article III. But the extension of Gibbs [here] * * * must be decided, not in the context of congressional silence or tacit encouragement, but in quite the opposite context" (pp. 15–16).

The holding of Aldinger is that if Congress makes a deliberate decision that a certain claim should not give rise to a federal cause of action and should be excluded from federal court, that claim should not be propelled back into the federal judicial power by the doctrine of pendent jurisdiction. (Note that the reasoning is similar to that used in Merrell Dow and Franchise Tax Board.) The case is not, therefore, determinative of the question whether pendent party jurisdiction is ever proper. But in its opinion the Court, without wholly closing the door, spoke negatively on this more general question:

"From a purely factual point of view, it is one thing to authorize two parties, already present in federal court by virtue of a case over which the court has jurisdiction, to litigate in addition to their federal claim a state-law claim over which there is no independent basis of federal jurisdiction. But it is quite another thing to permit a plaintiff, who has asserted a claim against one defendant with respect to which there is federal jurisdiction, to join an entirely different defendant on the basis of a state-law claim over

4. See Monroe v. Pape, 365 U.S. 167 (1961); Moor v. County of Alameda, 411 U.S. 693 (1973); Kenosha v. Bruno, 412 U.S. 507 (1973). The stated doctrine was overruled in Monell v. Department of Social Services, 436 U.S. 658 (1978).

which there is no independent basis of federal jurisdiction, simply because his claim against the first defendant and his claim against the second defendant 'derive from a common nucleus of operative fact.' * * * But the addition of a completely new party would run counter to the well-established principle that federal courts, as opposed to state trial courts of general jurisdiction, are courts of limited jurisdiction marked out by Congress (pp. 14–15). * * *

"[W]e decide here only the issue of so-called 'pendent party' jurisdiction with respect to a claim brought under §§ 1343(3) and 1983. Other statutory grants and other alignments of parties and claims might call for a different result. When the grant of jurisdiction to a federal court is exclusive, for example, as in the prosecution of tort claims against the United States under 28 U.S.C. § 1346, the argument of judicial economy and convenience can be coupled with the additional argument that *only* in a federal court may all of the claims be tried together. As we indicated at the outset of this opinion, the question of pendent-party jurisdiction is 'subtle and complex,' and we believe that it would be as unwise as it would be unnecessary to lay down any sweeping pronouncement upon the existence or exercise of such jurisdiction. Two observations suffice for the disposition of the type of case before us. If the new party sought to be joined is not otherwise subject to federal jurisdiction, there is a more serious obstacle to the exercise of pendent jurisdiction than if parties already before the court are required to litigate a state-law claim. Before it can be concluded that such jurisdiction exists, a federal court must satisfy itself not only that Art. III permits it, but that Congress in the statutes conferring jurisdiction has not expressly or by implication negated its existence" (pp. 17–18).

Justice Brennan, joined by Justices Marshall and Blackmun, dissented, arguing that the majority's inference as to congressional intent in the civil rights provisions was untenable.

The plaintiff in Aldinger did not rely on § 1331 as a basis of jurisdiction, only on the special grant of jurisdiction over civil rights cases in § 1343(3). But the result would surely have been the same had § 1331 jurisdiction been invoked.

But would Aldinger apply if there were diversity between the plaintiff and the defendant county and the state law claim involved more than $10,000?

For a survey of the post-Aldinger lower court opinions with respect to pendent party jurisdiction, see 13B Wright, Miller & Cooper, Federal Practice and Procedure § 3567.2 (1984; 1987 Supp.). Encouraged to do so by the Court in Aldinger, most courts allow pendent party jurisdiction when the jurisdiction of the federal court over the federal claims is exclusive; otherwise the cases "do not fall into any single pattern" (*id.* at 156).[5]

---

5. Aldinger's analytical approach has been employed to reach the conclusion that Title VII of the Civil Rights Act of 1964 evidences an implied congressional purpose to restrict federal jurisdiction and thus negates pendent jurisdiction over state-law claims that overlap Title VII claims; but there is authority to the contrary. There is also a split of authority on whether pendent jurisdiction applies to cases under the Age Discrimination in Employment Act. See Wright, Miller & Cooper, *supra,* at 13 (1987 Supp.).

(14) The term "pendent jurisdiction" has been applied where the issue involved, not state claims joined to federal, but two federal claims normally handled differently within the federal court system. See, *e.g.*, Romero v. International Term. Oper. Co., 358 U.S. 354, 380–81 (1959) (maritime claims joined with a Jones Act claim on "the law side" of federal court); Rosado v. Wyman, 397 U.S. 397, 402–05 (1970) (federal statutory claim joined with a constitutional claim that would have required a three-judge court).

Are the relevant considerations in such cases the same as those in Gibbs and other state-claim cases? Do they present issues of jurisdiction or simply of appropriateness? See generally Kurland, *The Romero Case and Some Problems of Federal Jurisdiction,* 73 Harv.L.Rev. 817, 833–50 (1960). As to the maritime law questions, see B. Currie, *The Silver Oar and All That,* 27 U.Chi.L.Rev. 1, 41–58 (1959). As to three-judge courts, compare Rosado v. Wyman, *supra,* with Florida Lime & Avocado Growers v. Jacobsen, 362 U.S. 73 (1960) and with Perez v. Ledesma, 401 U.S. 82, 86–88 (1971).[6]

There is also, obviously, a close relationship between the doctrine of pendent jurisdiction and other doctrines of "ancillary jurisdiction" that permit the federal courts sometimes to adjudicate elements of a "case" that are not, independently viewed, within the court's jurisdiction. These latter doctrines are examined in Chap. XIII, Sec. 3, *infra.* See generally Freer, *A Principled Statutory Approach to Supplemental Jurisdiction,* 1987 Duke L.J. 34 (1987).

SECTION 5. FEDERAL QUESTION REMOVAL

NOTE ON THE GENERAL REMOVAL STATUTE AND THE PROBLEM OF FEDERAL DEFENSE REMOVAL

(1) As in the case of original jurisdiction, no general grant of removal jurisdiction in "arising under" cases was enacted until 1875: Congress contented itself in the 1789–1875 period with a series of specific statutes (prompted by occasions of sharp conflict with state authority) allowing removal by federal officials and persons acting under them. (As to these statutes, see the immediately following Note.)

The Act of March 3, 1875, 18 Stat. 470, went to the opposite extreme: subject to a $500 jurisdictional amount requirement, virtually every case removable under Article III was made removable by either a plaintiff or a defendant. See pp. 960–63, *supra.*

The existing statutory pattern for federal question removal was created by the Judiciary Act of March 3, 1887, 24 Stat. 552, corrected by the Act of August 13, 1888, 25 Stat. 433. The key element was (and is) to tie removal jurisdiction to original jurisdiction: removal was restricted to cases in

---

6. May a claim under the Magnuson–Moss Warranty Act that does not meet the amount-in-controversy requirement ($50,000) for federal jurisdiction over actions under that Act be appended to state-law claims over which there exists diversity jurisdiction? The authorities are divided. See Wright, Miller & Cooper, *supra,* at 13–14.

which "the circuit courts of the United States are given original jurisdiction." (The statute also limited removal to defendants.) The present general removal statute, 28 U.S.C. § 1441(a), states the identical rule: the action must be one "of which the district courts of the United States have original jurisdiction." On removal generally, see further Chap. XIV, Sec. 4, p. 1767, *infra.* For a detailed discussion of the background of federal question removal, see Collins, *The Unhappy History of Federal Question Removal,* 71 Iowa L.Rev. 717 (1986).

(2) The requirement tying removal to original jurisdiction, seemingly technical, has had a profound impact on the jurisdictional structure, and even on our ways of thinking about that structure. Debates about the "need for a federal forum" are frequently carried on as if the only issue were whether plaintiffs with a claim of federal right should have access to a federal court; defendants with a claim of federal immunity are characteristically forgotten about. See Bator, *The State Courts and Federal Constitutional Litigation,* 22 Wm. & Mary L.Rev. 605, 608–11 (1981). But what justifies the distinction? Why should defendants with a claim of federal right or privilege be forced to litigate in a state court? Is the point that, where the federal ingredient is in the plaintiff's case, it is likely to be the predominant element in the case, whereas a federal defense is more likely to be only one element in a case dominated by state-law issues? (But what about cases like Mottley, where the only issues actually in contention are federal?) Or is the point the more profound one, that where the claimant seeks to enforce state law, and the contention based on federal law is that the state law may not be validly enforced, federalistic considerations make it appropriate to give the state court—the "enforcement" court—first crack? [1]

1. *Cf.* Wechsler, *Federal Jurisdiction and the Revision of the Judicial Code,* 13 Law & Contemp.Prob. 216, 233–34 (1948), commenting on 28 U.S.C. § 1441 before its enactment:

"The bill retains the rule of present law that a defendant may remove a case in a state court founded on a federal 'claim or right'—provided it is one 'of which the district courts have original jurisdiction.' The rule has quite anomalous implications. Though the plaintiff who puts forth the federal claim is content to seek its vindication in the state tribunals, the defendant may insist upon an initial federal forum. When, on the other hand, the plaintiff's reliance is on state law and the defendant claims a federal defense, neither party may remove—except, of course, the special case, to which attention has been called, of actions against federal officials. * * *

"It would, it seems to me, be far more logical to shape the rule precisely in reverse, granting removal to defendants when they claim a federal defense against the plaintiff's state-created claim and to the plaintiff when, as the issues have developed, he relies by way of replication on assertion of a federal right. The need is to remember that the reason for providing the initial federal forum is the fear that

state courts will view the federal right ungenerously. That reason is quite plainly absent in the only situation where, apart from federal officers, removal now obtains: the case where the *defendant* may remove because the *plaintiff's* case is federal. If in any case the reason can be present, it is only in the situations where removal is denied.

"The statute ought to be reshaped in terms of a consistent theory that permits removal by the party who puts forth the federal right, or else removal should be dropped entirely in cases where the jurisdiction is based on federal question. To drop it seems to me the better course, for reasons indicated in the discussion of the state-action cases. When the defendant claims a federal defense to an asserted right founded on state law, his assertion is, in substance, that there is *pro tanto* invalidity in the demanded application of that law. The same is true when federal grounds are first advanced to push aside a state defense to a state cause of action. In both these situations, therefore, the matter should be viewed in terms of principles appropriate to state-action cases. And since there is no doubt in either case of adequacy of state remedy, the statute should confine the litigation to state

Note, however, that federal immunities can frequently be recast as affirmative claims of federal right; and it is the case that we frequently open the doors of the federal courthouse to plaintiffs whose "affirmative" claim consists of a prayer to enjoin the enforcement of state law on the ground of federal invalidity. See, *e.g.*, the line of cases flowing from Ex parte Young, 209 U.S. 123 (1908), discussed in Chap. IX, Section 2, *infra*. It is thus not the case that the existing law generally excludes from federal court all litigants whose claim is that state-law claims are rendered *pro tanto* invalid by federal law: if the relevant federal remedial law (express or implied) gives the claimant a federal cause of action, and the claimant reaches the federal courthouse first, federal jurisdiction is usually upheld. On the other hand, if the state claim is raised first, in state court, the defendant may not remove on the basis of a claim of *pro tanto* invalidity (He is also normally precluded from thereafter transforming himself into a plaintiff and bringing a separate federal action to enjoin or otherwise abort the pending state proceeding (see Chap. X, *infra*).)

Isn't the underlying difficulty that litigants do not come labeled as "plaintiffs" and "defendants" as a matter of preexisting Platonic reality: whether one is a plaintiff or a defendant—when is the law a sword? when a shield?—is itself contingent, a product of our remedial and substantive rules?

In light of these considerations, do the existing jurisdictional lines reflect a sensible accommodation of policies in tension? Or are they merely an *ad hoc* patchwork?

(3) The only serious challenge to the fundamental structure tying removal to original jurisdiction has come from the American Law Institute's 1968 Study. The ALI proposed that removal—by plaintiffs or defendants—should be allowed where "a substantial defense arising under the Constitution, laws, or treaties of the United States is properly asserted that, if sustained, would be dispositive of the action." ALI Study proposed § 1312.

The ALI tempered its proposal by excluding from removal jurisdiction eminent domain proceedings, and cases in which the federal defense was based on constitutional objections to service of process or on the Full Faith and Credit Clause.[2] More significantly, the Institute excepted from removal those cases involving state and local government law enforcement.

The ALI proposal raised serious concerns—primarily its impact on swollen federal dockets. See Friendly, Federal Jurisdiction: A General View 124–27 (1972), expressing "serious question how far it is advisable to introduce federal defense removal in civil cases on a broad scale * * * when the federal courts are under such severe pressure," and suggesting that removal should be allowed only where the defense is based on a

courts. No one would urge that criminal cases in state courts should be removable generally because a federal defense is interposed. The reason holds for civil litigation too. There is no need for the original jurisdiction when litigants rely on federal rights to furnish them a shield but not a sword.

"What has been said is not intended to refer to actions against federal officers founded on official conduct. Such cases are, as has been said, of special federal interest because they constitute, in substance, suits against the national Government. The bill correctly deals with them in separate sections, providing a removal on that ground."

2. The ALI proposed that removal be limited to cases involving $10,000 (at the same time that it proposed removing the then-existing $10,000 jurisdictional amount limit in original federal question cases).

federal statute rather than the federal Constitution.[3] And consider the views of Judge Posner: "Under present law the defendant is not allowed to remove the case to federal court just because he has a federal defense (a right he would have if the complaint were based on federal law), although if the same federal issue were the basis of a claim made by him he could sue in federal court. The distinction is not quite so arbitrary as it sounds. It would be a serious mistake to make all cases in which a federal defense was asserted removable as a matter of right. In many the federal defense would have little merit—would, indeed, have been concocted purely to confer federal jurisdiction—yet this fact might be impossible to determine, with any confidence, without having a trial before the trial. Of course, frivolous federal claims are also a problem when only plaintiffs can use them to get into court, but a less serious problem. If the plaintiff gets thrown out of federal court because his claim is frivolous, and must start over in state court, he has lost time; and the loss may be fatal if meanwhile the statute of limitations has run. But the defendant may be delighted to see the plaintiff's case thrown out of federal court when the court discovers that the federal defense is frivolous. This is why it would not be a complete answer to the problem of the frivolous federal defense to allow removal on the basis of a federal question first raised by way of defense but give the district court discretion to remand the case back to the state court. (There would be an analogy to the well-recognized discretion of a federal district court to dismiss a state law claim even though it is so closely related to the plaintiff's federal claim that it is within the court's pendent jurisdiction.)" Posner, The Federal Courts: Crisis and Reform 190–91 (1985).

(4) The ALI proposal never came near enactment, and it continues to be the fundamental feature of federal question removal that it is restricted to cases where the plaintiff—subject to the well-pleaded complaint rule and all the other restrictions on original "arising under" jurisdiction surveyed in Sections 3 and 4, *supra*—could have sued in federal court.

The effect of this is, of course, to tell prospective defendants with a claim of federal immunity to the enforcement of state law claims to turn themselves into plaintiffs if they can and if they wish to resort to federal court. As to the use of declaratory judgment actions in this connection, see the Franchise Tax Board case and the following Note, p. 1027, *supra*; and in particular compare Public Service Comm'n v. Wycoff Co., 344 U.S. 237 (1952), discussed in notes 14 and 19 of the Court's opinion in Franchise Tax Board, with Shaw v. Delta Air Lines, Inc., p. 1039, *supra*. But, even apart from declaratory judgments, federal defenses are sometimes made the basis of affirmative federal claims in actions for damages or injunction. Whether such a claim *may* be maintained as a federal action is, of course, dependent on whether the federal remedial law—express or implied—gives the claimant a federal cause of action. For examples of cases where a claim of federal immunity from state regulation becomes the basis of an "affirmative" federal action, see Shaw v. Delta Airlines, Inc., p. 1039, *supra*; Jones v. Rath Packing Co., 430 U.S. 519 (1977); Ray v. Atlantic Richfield

---

3. Judge Friendly expressed the fear that, given the open-ended nature of the Constitution, "imaginative defense lawyers" could too easily contrive federal constitutional defenses as a basis for removal. He predicted that many state libel, privacy, eviction, civil commitment and civil contempt cases would become removable under the ALI proposal.

Co., 435 U.S. 151 (1978); and see the discussion of ERISA § 502(a)(3) in Franchise Tax Board (text at note 20).

(5) A claim of federal preemption is usually a defense to a state-law coercive action, and thus typically does not furnish the basis for removal. See generally 14A Wright, Miller & Cooper, Federal Jurisdiction and Procedure § 3722, at 244–50 (1985); Note, 62 Texas L.Rev. 893 (1984); Comment, 51 U.Chi.L.Rev. 634 (1984); and see text at and note 12 of Franchise Tax Board, p. 1030, *supra*. But if the plaintiff's claim, albeit cast as a state-law claim, is itself "really" a federal claim, removal will be permitted on the ground that the plaintiff should not, by artful pleading, be allowed to negate the defendant's removal rights. The leading case for this proposition is Avco Corp. v. Aero Lodge No. 735, IAM, 390 U.S. 557 (1968) (discussed in Franchise Tax Board), holding that a claim that defendant had violated a collective bargaining agreement, although labeled as a state contract claim, "necessarily" arose under § 301 of the Taft Hartley Act and was therefore removable by the defendant.[4] In Caterpillar Inc. v. Williams, 107 S.Ct. 2425 (1987), the Supreme Court described this doctrine as the "'complete preemption' doctrine," under which, "once an area of state law has been completely preempted, any claim purportedly based on that preempted state law is considered, from its inception, a federal claim, and therefore arises under federal law" (p. 2430). Caterpillar itself held the complete preemption doctrine inapplicable to a claim for breach of individual employment contracts, concluding that § 301 did not wholly absorb such claims; removal was consequently denied.

(6) In Franchise Tax Board itself the Court rejected the application of the "complete preemption" theory to California's claims, but stated that "[i]t may be that, as with § 301 as interpreted in Avco, any state [court] action coming within the scope of § 502(a) of ERISA would be removable to federal district court, even if an otherwise adequate state cause of action were pleaded without reference to federal law" (p. 1036, *supra*). The question thus prefigured in Franchise Tax Board came before the Court in Metropolitan Life Insurance Co. v. Taylor, 107 S.Ct. 1542 (1987), involving common-law tort and contract claims brought in a state court by an employee complaining that his employer had illegally terminated disability benefits due under an ERISA-covered salaried employee benefit plan. The defendants removed the case to federal court, and the Supreme Court upheld removal. Relying on Pilot Life Ins. Co. v. Dedeaux, 107 S.Ct. 1549 (1987), decided on the same day as Taylor, the Court first concluded that the common-law contract and tort claims were preempted by ERISA's substantive preemption provision, 29 U.S.C. § 1144(a). Turning to the question whether the common-law claims are "not only preempted" but are "also displaced by ERISA's civil enforcement provision, § 502(a)(1)(B)" (p. 1544), the Court indicated that it "was reluctant to find that extraordinary preemptive power, such as has been found with respect to § 301 of the LMRA, that converts an ordinary state common law complaint into one stating a federal claim for purposes of the well-pleaded complaint rule." But the Court found strong indications in the legislative history of ERISA that Congress intended the preemptive sweep of the statute to replicate that of § 301, showing that Congress wished "to make § 502(a)(1)(B) suits

4. See also Federated Dep't Stores, Inc. v. Moitie, 452 U.S. 394, 397 n. 2 (1981), approving removal of an antitrust action where plaintiffs had "artfully" cast their "essentially federal law claims" as state-law claims.

brought by participants or beneficiaries federal questions for the purposes of federal court jurisdiction in like manner as § 301 of the LMRA" (p. 1547).

How do you distinguish cases like Avco and Taylor from Mottley? In Mottley, the federal defense was that Congress had completely superseded the plaintiffs' contract action by rendering the contract illegal. In Avco and Taylor, the defense was that Congress had completely superseded the plaintiffs' common law actions by creating an exclusive federal remedy. Why should a state court have exclusive jurisdiction to adjudicate the first defense but not the second? Is the point that in the second situation, Congress intended not only to provide a shield but created an "exclusive" federal sword as well, thus signifying an incremental intention to give access to the federal courts? Is this a sufficient distinction? Does it suggest that whenever Congress provides for federal jurisdiction over a new federal cause of action, the question whether state remedies can continue to coexist with the new federal cause of action may be litigated in a federal court?

NOTE ON REMOVAL STATUTES FOR THE PROTECTION OF FEDERAL OFFICERS AND AGENCIES

(1) The Revised Judicial Code, 28 U.S.C. § 1442(a)(1), provides in sweeping terms for the removal of any civil action or criminal prosecution commenced in a state court against "any officer of the United States or any agency thereof, or person acting under him, for any act under color of such office or on account of any right, title or authority claimed under any Act of Congress for the apprehension or punishment of criminals or the collection of the revenue".

The first part of this provision was an innovation, concerning which the Reviser's notes said only this in explanation:

"The revised subsection (a)(1) is extended to apply to all officers and employees of the United States or any agency thereof. Section 76 of title 28, U.S.C., 1940 ed., was limited to revenue officers engaged in the enforcement of the criminal or revenue laws."

No argument apparently was needed to induce Congress to generalize a principle of federal protection which was first invoked in times of crisis and thereafter always limited to special situations deemed to present special needs.

In view of the breadth of the new language at the beginning of paragraph (1), what purpose is served by the more specialized grants of jurisdiction in the last clause of the paragraph and the following three paragraphs?

(2) These four specialized grants of jurisdiction in § 1442(a) are the residue of a long series of enactments.

The series begins in 1815. Prompted by New England's resistance to the War of 1812, Congress inserted in an act for the collection of customs duties a provision—of limited duration—for the removal to the federal circuit court of any suit or prosecution begun in a state court against federal officers or other persons as a result of enforcement of the act.[1]

The first permanent legislation in the series—and the antecedent of the last clause of § 1442(a)(1)—was the "Force Bill" of 1833, passed in response to South Carolina's threats of nullification. This authorized the removal of all suits or prosecutions against officers of the United States or other persons on account of any acts done under the customs laws.[2]

Then, with the Civil War, came a wave of removal acts. In 1863, Congress authorized, for the period only of the rebellion, the removal of cases brought against United States officers or others for acts committed during the rebellion and justified under the authority of the President or Congress.[3]

Soon afterward, permanent legislative policy was further developed by the extension of the removal provisions of the "Force Bill" to cases involving the collection of internal revenue as well as import duties.[4] What is now the last clause of § 1442(a)(1) continued through successive codifications to be thus limited to cases growing out of the revenue laws[5] until 1948, when the revisers, with no other notice to Congress than that above quoted, added the reference to acts "for the apprehension or punishment of criminals".[6]

Paragraph (2) of § 1442(a), providing for the removal of cases brought against a property holder claiming under a federal officer, where the case affects the validity of an act of Congress, grew out of the same group of Civil War revenue acts. Before 1948 it was similarly limited to cases involving the validity of a revenue law. Again without notice to Congress, the revisers struck out the limitation to revenue laws.

The provisions of paragraph (4) of § 1442(a) for the removal of cases brought against an officer of either House of Congress for an act done under an order of the House originated in an appropriation bill in 1875.[7]

---

1. Act of Feb. 4, 1815, § 8, 3 Stat. 195, 198. See also Act of March 3, 1815, § 6, 3 Stat. 231, 233, extended for one year by the Act of April 27, 1816, § 3, 3 Stat. 315, and for another four years by the Act of March 3, 1817, § 2, 3 Stat. 396.

2. Act of March 2, 1833, 4 Stat. 632, 633–34. The act referred to "revenue" laws but, as explained in The Assessors v. Osbornes, note 4, *infra*, no laws for the collection of internal revenue duties were in existence in 1833, and the Court in that case treated the act as limited to cases involving import duties.

3. Act of March 3, 1863, § 5, 12 Stat. 756, amended by Act of May 11, 1866, §§ 3–4, 14 Stat. 46, and the Act of Feb. 5, 1867, 14 Stat. 385. See The Mayor v. Cooper, 6 Wall. 247 (U.S.1868). See also the Act of July 28, 1866, § 8, 14 Stat. 328, 329; and the Act of July 27, 1868, § 1, 15 Stat. 243.

4. This was the net of a confusing series of enactments from 1864 to 1866. See Act

of March 7, 1864, § 9, 13 Stat. 14, 17; Act of June 30, 1864, § 50, 13 Stat. 241; Act of July 13, 1866, §§ 67–68, 14 Stat. 98, 171–72. See Philadelphia v. The Collector, 5 Wall. 720 (U.S.1867); The Assessors v. Osbornes, 9 Wall. 567 (U.S.1869); Frankfurter & Landis, The Business of the Supreme Court 61–62 (1928).

5. See Rev.Stat. § 643; Judicial Code of 1911, Act of March 3, 1911, § 33, 36 Stat. 1087, 1097; 28 U.S.C. (1940 ed.) § 76. See Venable v. Richards, 105 U.S. 636, 637–38 (1882).

6. *Cf.* Willingham v. Morgan, 395 U.S. 402, 406–07 (1969): "The federal officer removal statute is not 'narrow' or 'limited' * * *. At the very least, it is broad enough to cover all cases where federal officers can raise a colorable defense arising out of their duty to enforce federal law."

7. Act of March 3, 1875, § 8, 18 Stat. 371, 401.

The provisions of paragraph (3) of the subsection, authorizing the removal of proceedings against an officer of a United States court for acts done under color of office, were added in 1916.[8]

A few days later, in an enactment which in substance is still in effect, Congress extended similar protection to any member of the armed forces when proceeded against "on account of any act done under color of his office or status, or in respect to which he claims any right, title, or authority under any law of the United States respecting the military forces thereof, or under the law of war".[9]

Now only of historical importance were comparable provisions, enacted in 1919, for the protection of persons engaged in enforcement of the National Prohibition Act.[10]

In 1961, the remedy against the United States under the Federal Tort Claims Act for damages resulting from "the operation by any employee of the Government of any motor vehicle while acting within the scope of his employment" was declared to be "exclusive of any other civil action * * * by reason of the same subject against the employee or his estate." State court actions certified by the Attorney General to arise from such incidents were made removable by him and the proceedings thereafter "deemed a tort action brought against the United States." [11]

(3) The peculiar grant of removal jurisdiction of personal actions brought by an alien against a nonresident who is, or was at the time the action accrued, a civil officer of the United States, in which the state court got jurisdiction by personal service of process, now embodied in 28 U.S.C. § 1442(b), originated in a brief enactment of 1872.[12] The revisers accepted this provision substantially *in haec verba*.

What purpose, if any, did it serve, in view of 28 U.S.C. §§ 1332(a)(2), and 1441(b)? Escape from the requirement of a jurisdictional amount in this class of cases? [13] The protection of former officers?

If it were not for the diversity aspect, would the provision be constitutional?

(4) Deriving also from the Civil War period are the civil rights removal provisions of 28 U.S.C. § 1443. While this section has a broader application, subsection (2) covers proceedings against federal officers or persons acting under them, and the original statutes referred expressly to such

---

8. Act of Aug. 23, 1916, 39 Stat. 532. For a discussion of this act and prior related statutes, see Gay v. Ruff, 292 U.S. 25 (1934). The Court referred to the House committee report stating that the amendment was designed to give United States marshals the same protection in the execution of process in any case that they already had in cases under the revenue laws. See Davis v. South Carolina, 107 U.S. 597 (1882). It held that the act did not authorize removal of an action against a railroad receiver appointed by a federal court to recover damages caused by the negligence of railroad employees after the appointment. *Cf.* Barnette v. Wells Fargo Nevada Nat. Bank, 270 U.S. 438, 441, 450 (1926).

9. Act of Aug. 29, 1916, § 3, Art. 117, 39 Stat. 619, 669; Act of June 4, 1920, Art. 117, 41 Stat. 759, 811; Act of June 24, 1948, § 242, 62 Stat. 642; Act of May 5, 1950, § 9, 64 Stat. 145, 146, 50 U.S.C. § 738, superseded by Act of Aug. 10, 1956, 70A Stat. 626, 28 U.S.C. § 1442a.

10. Act of Oct. 28, 1919, § 28, 41 Stat. 305, 316. See Maryland v. Soper (No. 1), 270 U.S. 9, 31–32 (1926).

11. Act of Sept. 21, 1961, 75 Stat. 539, 28 U.S.C. § 2679(d).

12. Act of March 30, 1872, 17 Stat. 44.

13. See Matarazzo v. Hustis, 256 Fed. 882, 887 (N.D.N.Y.1919).

cases.[14] See *Note on Civil Rights Removal Under 28 U.S.C. § 1443*, p. 1067, *infra*.

(5) Note that the broad language of § 1442(a)(1) refers to any "officer of the United States or any agency thereof," etc. Can the language be read to authorize removal if the action is against the agency rather than an officer thereof?[15] If not, is there a basis in policy for the distinction? *Cf.* Davis, *Suing the Government by Falsely Pretending to Sue an Officer*, 29 U.Chi.L.Rev. 435 (1962).

(6) On the constitutionality of removal of state criminal proceedings against federal officers, see Tennessee v. Davis, p. 481, *supra*. For the full disclosure which the Court has enforced as a condition of such removal, notwithstanding the privilege against self-incrimination, see Maryland v. Soper (No. 1), note 10, *supra;* and Colorado v. Symes, 286 U.S. 510 (1932).

On the requirement of action under color of office, see Willingham v. Morgan, 395 U.S. 402 (1969); *cf.* Maryland v. Soper (No. 2), 270 U.S. 36 (1926), with which compare Cleveland, Columbus, etc. R.R. v. McClung, 119 U.S. 454 (1886).[16]

GEORGIA v. RACHEL

384 U.S. 780, 86 S.Ct. 1783, 16 L.Ed.2d 925 (1966).
Certiorari to the United States Court of Appeals for the Fifth Circuit.

MR. JUSTICE STEWART delivered the opinion of the Court. * * *

The case arises from a removal petition filed by Thomas Rachel and 19 other defendants seeking to transfer to the United States District Court for the Northern District of Georgia criminal trespass prosecutions pending against them in the Superior Court of Fulton County, Georgia. The petition stated that the defendants had been arrested on various dates in the spring of 1963 when they sought to obtain service at privately owned restaurants open to the general public in Atlanta, Georgia. The defendants alleged: "their arrests were effected for the sole purpose of aiding, abetting, and perpetuating customs, and usages which have deep historical and psychological roots in the mores and attitudes which exist within the City of Atlanta with respect to serving and seating members of the Negro race in such places of public accommodation and convenience upon a racially discriminatory basis and upon terms and conditions not imposed upon members of the so-called white or Caucasian race. Members of the so-called white or Caucasian race are similarly treated and discriminated against when accompanied by members of the Negro race."

---

14. Act of April 9, 1866, § 3, 14 Stat. 27; and Act of May 31, 1870, § 18, 16 Stat. 144. See also Rev.Stat. § 641 (1874).

15. See Lance Int'l, Inc. v. Aetna Cas. & Sur. Co., 264 F.Supp. 349 (S.D.N.Y.1967); Harlem River Produce Co. v. Aetna Cas. & Sur. Co., 257 F.Supp. 160 (S.D.N.Y.1965). But see James River Apartments v. FHA, 136 F.Supp. 24 (D.C.Md.1955).

16. For recent cases on the "color of office" requirement, see, *e.g.,* California v. Mesa, 813 F.2d 960 (9th Cir.1987) (prosecu-

tion of federal postal employee for misdemeanor manslaughter, after her mailtruck killed a bicyclist, held not removable); Swett v. Schenk, 792 F.2d 1447 (9th Cir. 1986) (civil contempt action against federal investigator for refusal to answer deposition questions, where refusal was allegedly ordered by his superior; held removable); Lepucki v. Van Wormer, 765 F.2d 86 (7th Cir.1985) (libel action against IRS agent held removable).

Each defendant, according to the petition, was then indicted under the Georgia statute making it a misdemeanor to refuse to leave the premises of another when requested to do so by the owner or the person in charge. On these allegations, the defendants maintained that removal was authorized under both subsections of 28 U.S.C. § 1443. the defendants maintained broadly that they were entitled to removal under the First Amendment and the Due Process Clause of the Fourteenth Amendment. Specifically invoking the language of subsection (1), the "denied or cannot enforce" clause, their petition stated: "petitioners are denied and/or cannot enforce in the Courts of the State of Georgia rights under the Constitution and Laws of the United States providing for the equal rights of citizens of the United States * * * in that, among other things, the State of Georgia by statute, custom, usage, and practice supports and maintains a policy of racial discrimination."

Invoking the language of subsection (2), the "color of authority" clause, the petition stated: "petitioners are being prosecuted for acts done under color of authority derived from the constitution and laws of the United States and for refusing to do an act which was, and is, inconsistent with the Constitution and Laws of the United States."

On its own motion and without a hearing, the Federal District Court remanded the cases to the Superior Court of Fulton County, Georgia, finding that the petition did not allege facts sufficient to sustain removal under the federal statute. The defendants appealed to the Court of Appeals for the Fifth Circuit.

While the case was pending in that court, two events of critical significance took place. The first of these was the enactment into law by the United States Congress of the Civil Rights Act of 1964, 78 Stat. 241. The second was the decision of this Court in Hamm v. City of Rock Hill, 379 U.S. 306. That case held that the Act precludes state trespass prosecutions for peaceful attempts to be served upon an equal basis in establishments covered by the Act, even though the prosecutions were instituted prior to the Act's passage. In view of these intervening developments in the law, the Court of Appeals reversed the District Court. * * *

We granted certiorari to consider the applicability of the removal statute to the circumstances of this case. 382 U.S. 808. No issues touching the constitutional power of Congress are involved. We deal only with questions of statutory construction.

The present statute is a direct descendant of a provision enacted as part of the Civil Rights Act of 1866. 14 Stat. 27. The subsection that is now § 1443(1) was before this Court in a series of decisions beginning with Strauder v. West Virginia, 100 U.S. 303, and Com. of Virginia v. Rives, 100 U.S. 313, in 1880 and ending with Kentucky v. Powers, 201 U.S. 1. The Court has not considered the removal statute since then, one reason being that an order remanding a case sought to be removed under § 1443 was not appealable after the year 1887. In § 901 of the Civil Rights Act of 1964, however, Congress specifically provided for appeals from remand orders in § 1443 cases, so as to give the federal reviewing courts a new opportunity to consider the meaning and scope of the removal statute. 78 Stat. 266, 28 U.S.C. § 1447(d) (1964 ed.). The courts of appeals in four circuits have now had occasion to give extensive consideration to various aspects of the removal statute.[8] In the case before us, the Court of Appeals for the Fifth Circuit dealt only with issues arising under the first subsection of § 1443, and we confine our review to those issues.

Section 1443(1) entitles the defendants to remove these prosecutions to the federal court only if they meet both requirements of that subsection. They must show both that the right upon which they rely is a "right under any law providing for * * * equal civil rights," and that they are "denied or cannot enforce" that right in the courts of Georgia.

The statutory phrase "any law providing for * * * equal civil rights" did not appear in the original removal provision in the Civil Rights Act of 1866. That provision allowed removal only in cases involving the express statutory rights of racial equality guaranteed in the Act itself. The first section of the 1866 Act secured for all citizens the "same" rights as were "enjoyed by white citizens" in a variety of fundamental areas. Section 3, the removal section of the 1866 Act, provided for removal by "persons who are denied or cannot enforce * * * the rights secured to them by the first section of this act * * *."

The present language "any law providing for * * * equal civil rights" first appeared in § 641 of the Revised Statutes of 1874. When the Revised Statutes were compiled, the substantive and removal provisions of the Civil Rights Act of 1866 were carried forward in separate sections. Hence, Congress could no longer identify the rights for which removal was available by using the language of the original Civil Rights Act—"rights secured to them by the first section of this act." The new language it chose, however, does not suggest that it intended to limit the scope of removal to rights recognized in statutes existing in 1874. On the contrary, Congress' choice of the open-ended phrase "any law providing for * * * equal civil rights" was clearly appropriate to permit removal in cases involving "a right under" both existing and future statutes that provided for equal civil rights.

There is no substantial indication, however, that the general language of § 641 of the Revised Statutes was intended to expand the kinds of "law" to which the removal section referred. In spite of the potential breadth of the phrase "any law providing for * * * equal civil rights," it seems clear that in enacting § 641, Congress intended in that phrase only to include laws comparable in nature to the Civil Rights Act of 1866. * * *

* * * As originally proposed in the Senate, § 1 of the bill that became the 1866 Act did not contain the phrase "as is enjoyed by white citizens." That phrase was later added in committee in the House, apparently to emphasize the racial character of the rights being protected. More important, the Senate bill did contain a general provision forbidding "discrimination in civil rights or immunities," preceding the specific enumeration of rights to be included in § 1. Objections were raised in the legislative debates to the breadth of the rights of racial equality that might be encompassed by a prohibition so general as one against "discrimination in civil rights or immunities." There was sharp controversy in the Senate,

<hr/>

8. * * * The statistics on the number of criminal cases of all kinds removed from state to federal courts in recent years are revealing. For the fiscal years 1962, 1963, 1964, and 1965, there were 18, 14, 43, and 1,192 such cases, respectively. Of the total removed criminal cases for 1965, 1,079 were in the Fifth Circuit. See Annual Report of the Director of the Administrative Office of the United States Courts 213–217 (1965).

but the bill passed. After similar controversy in the House, however, an amendment was accepted striking the phrase from the bill.

On the basis of the historical material that is available, we conclude that the phrase "any law providing for * * * equal civil rights" must be construed to mean any law providing for specific civil rights stated in terms of racial equality. Thus, the defendants' broad contentions under the First Amendment and the Due Process Clause of the Fourteenth Amendment cannot support a valid claim for removal under § 1443, because the guarantees of those clauses are phrased in terms of general application available to all persons or citizens, rather than in the specific language of racial equality that § 1443 demands. * * *

But the defendants in the present case did not rely solely on these broad constitutional claims in their removal petition. They also made allegations calling into play the Civil Rights Act of 1964. That Act is clearly a law conferring a specific right of racial equality, for in § 201(a) it guarantees to all the "full and equal enjoyment" of the facilities of any place of public accommodation without discrimination on the ground of race. By that language the Act plainly qualifies as a "law providing for * * * equal civil rights" within the meaning of 28 U.S.C. § 1443(1).

Moreover, it is clear that the right relied upon as the basis for removal is a "right under" a law providing for equal civil rights. The removal petition may fairly be read to allege that the defendants will be brought to trial solely as the result of peaceful attempts to obtain service at places of public accommodation. The Civil Rights Act of 1964 endows the defendants with a right not to be prosecuted for such conduct. As noted, § 201(a) guarantees to the defendants the equal access they sought. Section 203 then provides that, "No person shall * * * (c) punish or *attempt to punish* any person for exercising or attempting to exercise any right or privilege secured by section 201 or 202." (Emphasis supplied.) 78 Stat. 244. In Hamm v. City of Rock Hill, 379 U.S. 306, 311, the Court held that this section of the Act "prohibits prosecution of any person for seeking service in a covered establishment, because of his race or color." Hence, if the facts alleged in the petition are true, the defendants not only are immune from conviction under the Georgia trespass statute, but they have a "right under" the Civil Rights Act of 1964 not even to be brought to trial on these charges in the Georgia courts.

The question remaining, then, is whether within the meaning of § 1443(1), the defendants are "denied or cannot enforce" that right "in the courts of" Georgia. That question can be answered only after consideration of the legislative and judicial history of this requirement.

When Congress adopted the first civil rights removal provisions in § 3 of the Civil Rights Act of 1866, it incorporated by reference the procedures for removal established in § 5 of the Habeas Corpus Suspension Act of 1863, 12 Stat. 756. The latter section, in turn, permitted removal either at the pre-trial stage of the proceedings in the state court or after final judgment in that court. There can be no doubt that post-judgment removal was a practical remedy for civil rights defendants invoking either the "denied or cannot enforce" clause or the "color of authority" clause of the

1866 removal provision, in order to vindicate rights that had actually been denied at the trial. The scope of pre-trial removal, however, was unclear.[24]

Congress eliminated post-judgment removal when it enacted § 641 of the Revised Statutes of 1874. The compilation of the Revised Statutes coincided with the end of the Reconstruction period. During Reconstruction itself, removal under § 3 of the Civil Rights Act of 1866 had been but one measure established by Congress for the enforcement of the numerous statutory rights created under the Civil War Amendments. In other enactments, Congress had taken relatively more drastic steps to enforce those rights. But by the end of the Reconstruction period, many of these measures had expired, and by eliminating post-judgment removal, Congress had substantially truncated the original civil rights removal provision. Pre-trial removal was retained, but the scope of the provision had never been clarified. It was in this historic setting that the Court examined the scope of § 641. In a series of cases commencing with Strauder v. West Virginia, *supra*, and Virginia v. Rives, *supra*, decided on the same day in the 1879 Term, the Court established a relatively narrow, well-defined area in which pre-trial removal could be sustained under the "denied or cannot enforce" clause of that section.

In Strauder, the removal petition of a Negro indicted for murder pointed to a West Virginia statute that permitted only white male persons to serve on a grand or petit jury. Since Negroes were excluded from jury service pursuant to that statute, the defendant claimed that the "probabilities" were great that he would suffer a denial of his right to the "full and equal benefit of all laws and proceedings in the State of West Virginia. * * *" 100 U.S., at 304. The state court denied removal, however, and the defendant was convicted. This Court held that pre-trial removal should have been granted because, in the language of § 641, it appeared

---

24. * * * The obscure legislative history of § 3 of the Civil Rights Act of 1866 indicates only that the Reconstruction Congress did not intend the language of the "denied or cannot enforce" clause of § 3 to be read to its fullest possible extent. In his veto message accompanying the bill President Johnson construed the clause so broadly as to give the federal courts jurisdiction over all cases affecting a person who was denied any of the various rights conferred by § 1, whether or not the right in question was in issue in the particular case. For example, in the President's view, a state court defendant under indictment for murder, who happened to be denied a contractual right under § 1, would be able to remove his case for trial in the federal court. In urging passage of the bill over the President's veto, Senator Trumbull, the floor manager of the bill, rejected the President's construction of the "denied or cannot enforce" clause:

"* * * So in reference to this third section, the jurisdiction is given to the Federal courts of a case affecting the person that is discriminated against. Now, he is not necessarily discriminated against, because there may be a custom in the community discriminating against him, nor because a Legislature may have passed a statute discriminating against him; that statute is of no validity if it comes in conflict with a statute of the United States; and it is not to be presumed that any judge of a State court would hold that a statute of a State discriminating against a person on account of color was valid when there was a statute of the United States with which it was in direct conflict, and the case would not therefore rise in which a party was discriminated against until it was tested, and then if the discrimination was held valid he would have a right to remove it to a Federal court—or, if undertaking to enforce his right in a State court he was denied that right, then he could go into the Federal court; but it by no means follows that every person would have a right in the first instance to go to the Federal court because there was on the statute-book of the State a law discriminating against him, the presumption being that the judge of the court, when he came to act upon the case, would, in obedience to the paramount law of the United States, hold the State statute to be invalid." Cong.Globe, 39th Cong., 1st Sess., p. 1759. * * *

even before trial that the defendant would be denied or could not enforce a right secured to him by a "law providing for ✶ ✶ ✶ equal civil rights." The law specifically invoked by the Court was § 1977 of the Revised Statutes, now 42 U.S.C. § 1981. That law, the Court held, conferred upon the defendant the right to have his jurors selected without discrimination on the ground of race. Because of the direct conflict between the West Virginia statute and § 1977, the Court in Strauder held that the defendant would be the victim of "a denial by the statute law of the State." 100 U.S., at 312.

In Com. of Virginia v. Rives, however, the defendants could point to no such state statute as the basis for removal. Their petition alleged that strong community racial prejudice existed against them, that the grand and petit jurors summoned to try them were all white, that Negroes had never been allowed to serve on county juries in cases in which a Negro was involved in any way, and that the judge, the prosecutor, and the assistant prosecutor had all rejected their request that Negroes be included in the petit jury. Hence, the defendants maintained, they could not obtain a fair trial in the state court. But the only relevant Virginia statute to which the petition referred imposed jury duty on *all* males within a certain age range. Thus, the law of Virginia did not, on its face, sanction the discrimination of which the defendants complained. This Court held that the petition stated no ground for removal. Critical to its holding was the Court's observation that § 641 of the Revised Statutes authorized only pre-trial removal. The Court concluded: "the denial or inability to enforce in the judicial tribunals of a State, rights secured to a defendant by any law providing for ✶ ✶ ✶ equal civil rights ✶ ✶ ✶ of which sect. 641 speaks, is primarily, if not exclusively, a denial of such rights, or an inability to enforce them, resulting from the Constitution or laws of the State, rather than a denial first made manifest at the trial of the case. In other words, the statute has reference to a legislative denial or an inability resulting from it. ✶ ✶ ✶ "

The Court acknowledged that even though Virginia's statute did not authorize discrimination in jury selection, the officer in charge of the selection might nevertheless bring it about.

"But when a subordinate officer of the State, in violation of State law, undertakes to deprive an accused party of a right which the statute law accords to him, as in the case at bar, it can hardly be said that he is denied, or cannot enforce, 'in the judicial tribunals of the State' the rights which belong to him. In such a case it ought to be presumed the court will redress the wrong." 100 U.S., at 321–322.

The Court distinguished the situation in Strauder:

"It is to be observed that [§ 641] gives the right of removal only to a person 'who is denied, or cannot enforce, in *the judicial tribunals of the State* his equal civil rights.' And this is to appear before trial. When a statute of the State denies his right, or interposes a bar to his enforcing it, in the judicial tribunals, the presumption is fair that they will be controlled by it in their decisions; and in such a case a defendant may affirm on oath what is necessary for a removal. Such a case is clearly within the provisions of sect. 641." 100 U.S., at 321. (Emphasis in original.)

Strauder and Rives thus teach that removal is not warranted by an assertion that a denial of rights of equality may take place and go uncorrected at trial. Removal is warranted only if it can be predicted by reference to a law of general application that the defendant will be denied or cannot enforce the specified federal rights in the state courts. A state statute authorizing the denial affords an ample basis for such a prediction. * * * [Discussion of subsequent cases, in which, the Court states, the Strauder–Rives doctrine was "consistently applied", is omitted.]

In Rives itself, however, the Court noted that the denial of which the removal provision speaks "is primarily, *if not exclusively,* a denial * * * resulting from the Constitution or laws of the State * * *." 100 U.S., at 319. (Emphasis supplied.) * * * The Court thereby gave some indication that removal might be justified, even in the absence of a discriminatory state enactment, if an equivalent basis could be shown for an equally firm prediction that the defendant would be "denied or cannot enforce" the specified federal rights in the state court. Such a basis for prediction exists in the present case.

In the narrow circumstances of this case, *any* proceedings in the courts of the State will constitute a denial of the rights conferred by the Civil Rights Act of 1964, as construed in Hamm v. City of Rock Hill, if the allegations of the removal petition are true. The removal petition alleges, in effect, that the defendants refused to leave facilities of public accommodation, when ordered to do so solely for racial reasons, and that they are charged under a Georgia trespass statute that makes it a criminal offense to refuse to obey such an order. The Civil Rights Act of 1964, however, as Hamm v. City of Rock Hill, 379 U.S. 306, made clear, protects those who refuse to obey such an order not only from conviction in state courts, but from *prosecution* in those courts. Hamm emphasized the precise terms of § 203(c) that prohibit any "attempt to punish" persons for exercising rights of equality conferred upon them by the Act. The explicit terms of that section compelled the conclusion that "nonforcible attempts to gain admittance to or remain in establishments covered by the Act, are immunized from prosecution * * *." 379 U.S., at 311. The 1964 Act therefore "substitutes a right for a crime." 379 U.S., at 314. Hence, if as alleged in the present removal petition, the defendants were asked to leave solely for racial reasons, then the mere pendency of the prosecutions enables the federal court to make the clear prediction that the defendants will be "denied or cannot enforce in the courts of [the] State" the right to be free of any "attempt to punish" them for protected activity. It is no answer in these circumstances that the defendants might eventually prevail in the state court. The burden of having to defend the prosecutions is itself the denial of a right explicitly conferred by the Civil Rights Act of 1964 as construed in Hamm v. City of Rock Hill, *supra.*

Since the Federal District Court remanded the present case without a hearing, the defendants as yet have had no opportunity to establish that they were ordered to leave the restaurant facilities solely for racial reasons. If the Federal District Court finds that allegation true, the defendants' right to removal under § 1443(1) will be clear. The Strauder–Rives doctrine requires no more, for the denial in the courts of the State then clearly appears without any detailed analysis of the likely behavior of any particular state court. Upon such a finding it will be apparent that the conduct of the defendants is "immunized from prosecution" in any court, and the Federal District Court must then sustain the removal and dismiss the prosecutions.

For these reasons, the judgment is affirmed.

Affirmed.

MR. JUSTICE DOUGLAS, with whom THE CHIEF JUSTICE, MR. JUSTICE BRENNAN and MR. JUSTICE FORTAS join, concurring. * * *

It is the right to equal service in restaurants and the right to be free of prosecution for asserting that right—not the right to have a trespass conviction reversed—that the present prosecutions threaten. It is this right which must be vindicated by complete insulation from the State's criminal process if it is to be wholly vindicated. It is this right which the defendants are "denied" so long as the present prosecutions persist.

Georgia claims that Hamm v. City of Rock Hill, *supra*, does not cover cases of sit-ins prosecuted for disorderly conduct or other unlawful acts. Of course that is true. But one of the functions of the hearing on the allegations of the removal petition will be to determine whether the defendants were ejected on racial grounds or for some other, valid reason. The Court of Appeals correctly ruled that "in the event it is established that the removal of the appellants from the various places of public accommodation was done *for racial reasons*, then under authority of the Hamm case it would become the duty of the district court to order a dismissal of the prosecutions without further proceedings." 342 F.2d 336, 343. (Emphasis added.)

If service was denied for other reasons, no case for removal has been made out. And if, as is intimated, any doubt remains as to whether the restaurants in question were covered by the 1964 Act, that too should be left open in the hearing to be held before the District Court—a procedure to which the defendants do not object.

NOTE ON CIVIL RIGHTS REMOVAL UNDER 28 U.S.C. § 1443

(1) City of Greenwood v. Peacock, 384 U.S. 808 (1966), was decided on the same day as Rachel. Alleging that they were civil rights workers engaged in a drive to encourage black voter registration in Mississippi, 29 defendants in state criminal proceedings sought to remove those proceedings to a federal court under § 1443(1) and (2). In their removal petitions, they claimed that the courts and law enforcement officers of the state were prejudiced against them because of their race or their association with blacks, that their arrests and prosecutions were for the sole purpose of harassing them and of punishing them for and deterring them from the exercise of their constitutional rights to protest racial discrimination, that they would be tried in segregated courtrooms, that blacks would be excluded from the juries, that the judges and prosecutors had gained office at elections at which black voters had been excluded, and that the statutes and ordinances under which they were charged were unconstitutionally vague and were unconstitutional as applied to their conduct.

The Supreme Court, reversing the Fifth Circuit, held the cases nonremovable. As to § 1443(2), the Court stated, the first phrase allowed removal only by "federal officers or agents and those authorized to act with or for them in affirmatively executing duties under any federal law providing for equal civil rights"; [1] the second phrase, plainly inapplicable in Peacock, "is available only to state officers" (p. 824).

Turning to subsection (1), the Court said (384 U.S. at 826–28):

" * * * [In Rachel] the Civil Rights Act of 1964 * * * specifically and uniquely conferred upon the defendants an absolute right to 'violate' the explicit terms of the state criminal trespass law with impunity under the conditions alleged in the * * * removal petition, and any attempt by the State to make them answer in a court for this conceded 'violation' would directly deny their federal right 'in the courts of [the] State.' The present case differs from Rachel in two significant respects. First, no federal law confers an absolute right on private citizens—on civil rights advocates, or Negroes, or on anybody else—to obstruct a public street, to contribute to the delinquency of a minor, to drive an automobile without a license, or to bite a policeman. [These were among the offenses charged.] Second, no federal law confers immunity from state prosecution on such charges. * * * It is *not* enough to support removal under § 1443(1) to allege or show that the defendant's federal equal civil rights have been illegally and corruptly denied by state administrative officials in advance of trial, that the charges against the defendants are false, or that the defendant is unable to obtain a fair trial in a particular state court. The motives of the officers bringing the charges may be corrupt, but that does not show that the state trial court will find the defendant guilty if he is innocent, or that in any other manner the defendant will be 'denied or cannot enforce in the courts' of the State any right under a federal law providing for equal civil rights. The civil rights removal statute does not require and does not permit the judges of the federal courts to put their brethren of the state judiciary on trial."

The Court noted that remedies other than removal—including, in appropriate cases, injunctions, actions for damages under 42 U.S.C. § 1983, and habeas corpus—were available to defendants for vindicating their constitutional rights, and expressed apprehension that a broad construction of § 1443 would lead to an explosion of state criminal litigation in the federal courts. (See footnote 8 of the opinion in Rachel.) Such a change raised fundamental issues of policy for Congress to consider: "Has the historic practice of holding state criminal trials in state courts * * * been such a failure that the relationship of the state and federal courts should now be revolutionized? Will increased responsibility of the state courts in the area of federal civil rights be promoted and encouraged by denying those courts any power at all to exercise that responsibility?" (p. 834).

Justice Douglas, writing for himself and two other dissenters, argued that the cases were removable: "A defendant 'is denied' his federal right when 'disorderly conduct' statutes, 'breach of the peace' ordinances, and the like are used as the instrument to suppress his promotion of civil rights. * * * The examples are numerous. First is the case of prosecution under a law which is valid on its face but applied discriminatorily. Second is a prosecution under, say, a trespass law for conduct which is privileged under federal law. Third is an unwarranted charge brought against a civil rights worker to intimidate him for asserting those rights, or to suppress or discourage their promotion * * * " (pp. 842–43).

---

1. In light of this holding, is any case removable under the first phrase of § 1443(2) that is not also removable under § 1442?

(2) A decade after Rachel and Peacock, the Court returned to the "murky language" of § 1443(1) and again construed it narrowly. In Johnson v. Mississippi, 421 U.S. 213 (1975), after a detailed review of the Rachel and Peacock cases, the Court held that the provision of the 1968 Civil Rights Act, 18 U.S.C. § 245, which prohibits interference with certain federal rights "by force or threat of force," did not confer upon petitioners a right under § 1443(1) to remove a state criminal prosecution for conspiracy and unlawful boycott. (The petitioners had been picketing and urging the boycott of certain Vicksburg, Mississippi, merchants for alleged racial discrimination in their hiring practices.) "Whether or not § 245 * * * provides for 'specific civil rights stated in terms of racial equality' [within the meaning of Rachel] * * * it evinces no intention to interfere in any manner with state criminal prosecutions." Rather, its central purpose was to "prevent and punish *violent* interferences with the exercise of specified rights" (pp. 223–24). Since "a state prosecution, proceeding as it does in a court of law, cannot be characterized as an application of 'force or threat of force' within the meaning of § 245" (p. 227), the Court concluded that, as in Peacock, there was no federal statutory right that the state not prosecute. The allegation that there was "no basis in fact" for the prosecution was of no assistance to the petitioners.

Justices Marshall and Brennan, dissenting in Johnson, argued that "[t]he use of force or the threat of force to intimidate or interfere with persons engaged in protected activity fairly describes an 'attempt to punish' the same persons" by arrest and prosecution (p. 236). Commenting on the Court's observation that "varied avenues of relief" still lay open for vindication of any federal rights which might actually be violated in the state prosecution, the dissent, citing Younger v. Harris, p. 1383, *infra*, concluded: "I only hope that the recent instances in which this Court has emphasized the values of comity and federalism in restricting the issuance of federal injunctions against state criminal * * * proceedings will not mislead the district courts into forgetting that at times these values must give way to the need to protect federal rights from being irremediably trampled" (p. 239).

(3) Writing before the Rachel and Peacock decisions, Professor Amsterdam urged a broader construction of § 1443(1) and (2) than the Court adopted in these cases, though not so broad as the language of the statute might arguably permit. Amsterdam, *Criminal Prosecutions Affecting Federally Guaranteed Civil Rights: Federal Removal and Habeas Corpus Jurisdiction to Abort State Court Trial,* 113 U.Pa.L.Rev. 793 (1965). Describing the section as "a text of exquisite obscurity" (p. 843), Amsterdam explored in depth the history and interpretation of the statute, and found support for his arguments in the deep distrust of state courts as protectors of civil rights on the part of "bad Tad Stevens and his rads" (p. 830)—the principal architects of the 1866 legislation. His article also emphasized the harm to the civil rights movement that could be caused by groundless and discriminatory prosecutions, even if all convictions were ultimately set aside.

See also Redish, *Revitalizing Civil Rights Removal Jurisdiction,* 64 Minn.L.Rev. 523 (1980), also arguing for a broader (though different) reading of § 1443.

(4) What is included in the Rachel Court's formulation that a law providing for "equal civil rights" is any law providing for "specific civil rights stated in terms of racial equality"? Is the Equal Protection Clause itself excluded? What of a law designed to protect a racial minority that is not stated in terms of equality? Is the right to equal employment opportunity under Title VII of the Civil Rights Act of 1964 a "civil right" or some other kind of right?

The lower court authorities are collected in 14A Wright, Miller & Cooper, Federal Practice and Procedure § 3728 (1985 & 1987 Supp.).

(5) After Congress eliminated the possibility of post-judgment removal, was the language "is denied or cannot enforce in the courts of the State" meaningful at all? Note, however, that in a 1977 amendment to 28 U.S.C. § 1446(c), Congress authorized removal even after the commencement of trial in a criminal case "for good cause shown." In doing so, did it, perhaps inadvertently, breathe new life into § 1443 by allowing for post-judgment removal when the results of the state judicial proceeding have established that the claimed right was in fact denied or could not be enforced? In any event, must all state court remedies first be exhausted? Even so, might removal be available in such a case as a substitute, or supplement, to a petition for certiorari in the Supreme Court or for habeas corpus in the district court? Or is the "good cause" provision designed to serve a narrower purpose? The legislative history does not address these questions. Does this silence suggest that a change of this dimension is beyond the scope of the revision?

Absent the possibility of post-judgment removal, if the task of the federal court is to find some basis for a "firm prediction" of denial of federal rights, what relevance does the existence of a state law invalid on its face have to the making of such a prediction? Even if relevant, should it be either sufficient or necessary? *Cf.* Amsterdam, *supra,* at 857–58, 861.

(6) Consider the meaning and significance of the first ground of distinction from Rachel drawn by the Court in Peacock, Paragraph (1) *supra.* Does it mean that a case is not removable unless the conduct *charged to be a violation of state law* (rather than merely the conduct engaged in) is protected by a federal law providing for equal civil rights? If so, does this leave any room for the removal statute to operate? See Judge Brown's exhaustive dissent in Perkins v. Mississippi, 455 F.2d 7, 11–58 (5th Cir. 1972).

(7) Note that the second ground of distinction advanced in Peacock—that "no federal law confers immunity from prosecution"—was the one further elaborated in Johnson v. Mississippi, Paragraph (2), *supra.* The Court in Johnson insisted that the federal "right" in question be a statutory right not to be proceeded against in the state courts at all. Did Rachel itself meet this test?

(8) Section 1443 is not limited to criminal actions, and instances of removal of civil actions, though rare, may be found in the reports. See, *e.g.,* Thompson v. Brown, 434 F.2d 1092 (5th Cir.1970).

(9) Among the other possible remedies alluded to by the Court in Peacock were federal injunction against state proceedings, see Chap. X, *infra,* and federal habeas corpus, see Chap. XI, *infra.* What are the relative advantages and disadvantages of these remedies as devices for interfering with the state's administration of justice? What obstacles are

placed in the path of a state defendant seeking to obtain an injunction, or to obtain a writ of habeas corpus before or after trial?

The ALI Study proposed leaving the civil rights removal provision almost unchanged, see proposed § 1312(c), but would have authorized an injunction against state proceedings "to restrain a criminal prosecution that should not be permitted to continue either because the statute or other law that is the basis of the prosecution plainly cannot constitutionally be applied to the party seeking the injunction or because the prosecution is so plainly discriminatory as to amount to a denial of the equal protection of the laws" (proposed § 1372(7)).

SECTION 6. RELATED HEADS OF JURISDICTION

SUBSECTION A: ADMIRALTY JURISDICTION

NOTE ON THE ADMIRALTY JURISDICTION

(1) This Note provides only a quick survey of the admiralty jurisdiction. For comprehensive accounts, reference may be made to Gilmore & Black, The Law of Admiralty (2d ed. 1975) and to Jhirad, Sann, Chase & Chynsky, Benedict on Admiralty (7th ed. 1985).

(2) "Section 9 of the First Judiciary Act granted the District Courts maritime jurisdiction [exclusive of the courts of the states]. This jurisdiction has remained unchanged in substance to the present day. Indeed it was recognition of the need for federal tribunals to exercise admiralty jurisdiction that was one of the controlling considerations for the establishment of a system of lower federal courts. * * *

"Section 9 not only established federal courts for the administration of maritime law; it recognized that some remedies in matters maritime had been traditionally administered by common-law courts of the original States. This role of the States * * * was preserved in the famous 'savings clause'—'saving to suitors, in all cases, the right of a common-law remedy, where the common law is competent to give it.' Since the original Judiciary Act also endowed the federal courts with diversity jurisdiction, common-law remedies for maritime causes could be enforced by the then Circuit Courts when the proper diversity of parties afforded access." Romero v. International Terminal Operating Co., 358 U.S. 354, 361–62 (1959).

(3) The current provision granting admiralty jurisdiction, 28 U.S.C. § 1333(1), maintains the traditional language: "The district courts shall have original jurisdiction, exclusive of the courts of the States, of * * * [a]ny civil case of admiralty or maritime jurisdiction, saving to suitors in all cases all other remedies to which they are otherwise entitled."

(4) What is the relationship between the jurisdiction of the federal courts sitting in admiralty and their "law" jurisdiction to decide cases "arising under" federal law? This was the issue in the celebrated case of

Romero v. International Terminal Operating Co., *supra.* Romero, a Spanish seaman, was injured aboard the S.S. Guadalupe while it was docked in New Jersey. He filed an action for damages in district court against the ship's Spanish owners, Compania Trasatlantica (among others). His complaint asserted a statutory claim against Compania under the Jones Act, 46 U.S.C. § 688, and claims under general judge-made maritime law for unseaworthiness and maintenance and cure. Romero did not, however, invoke the admiralty jurisdiction; he claimed the district court had jurisdiction under the Jones Act and 28 U.S.C. §§ 1331.[1]

Justice Frankfurter, writing for a majority of the Supreme Court, concluded that § 1331 did not give the district courts federal question jurisdiction (as distinct from admiralty jurisdiction) over claims arising out of judge-made maritime law (pp. 362–72):

"Up to the passage of the Judiciary Act of 1875 [the grant of admiralty jurisdiction in § 9 of the Judiciary Act, and the grant of diversity jurisdiction to adjudicate common-law claims] * * * provided the only claim for jurisdiction in the federal courts in maritime matters. [On the admiralty side], [t]his jurisdiction was exercised according to the historic procedure in admiralty, by a judge without a jury. * * * Except in diversity cases, maritime litigation brought in state courts could not be removed to the federal courts.

"The Judiciary Act of 1875 effected an extensive enlargement of the jurisdiction of the lower federal courts. For the first time their doors were opened to 'all suits of a civil nature at common law or in equity, * * * arising under the Constitution or laws of the United States * * *.' From 1875 to 1950 there is not to be found a hint or suggestion to cast doubt on the conviction that the language of that statute was taken straight from Art. III, § 2, cl. 1, * * *. Indeed what little legislative history there is affirmatively indicates that this was the source. Thus the Act of 1875 drew on the scope of this provision of Clause 1, just as the Judiciary Act of 1789 reflected the constitutional authorization of Clause 1 of Section 2, which extended the judicial power 'to all Cases of admiralty and maritime Jurisdiction.'

"These provisions of Article III are two of the nine separately enumerated classes of cases to which 'judicial power' was extended by the Constitution and which thereby authorized grants by Congress of 'judicial Power' to the 'inferior' federal courts. The vast stream of litigation which has flowed through these courts from the beginning has done so on the assumption that, in dealing with a subject as technical as the jurisdiction of the courts, the Framers, predominately lawyers, used precise, differentiating and not redundant language. This assumption, reflected in The Federalist Papers, was authoritatively confirmed by Mr. Chief Justice Marshall in American Ins. Co. v. Canter, 1 Pet. 511, 544:

'We are therefore to inquire, whether cases in admiralty, and cases arising under the laws and Constitution of the United States, are identical.

'If we have recourse to that pure fountain from which all the jurisdiction of the Federal Courts is derived, we find language employed which

---

1. The Jones Act explicitly confers jurisdiction on the district courts in the action "at law" that it provides for a seaman's death or injury. See Paragraph (5), *infra,* for discussion of the possible reasons for Romero's decision not to invoke the admiralty jurisdiction.

cannot well be misunderstood. The Constitution declares, that "the judicial power shall extend to all cases in law and equity, arising under this Constitution, the laws of the United States, and treaties made, or which shall be made, under their authority; to all cases affecting ambassadors, or other public ministers, and consuls; to all cases of admiralty and maritime jurisdiction."

'The Constitution certainly contemplates these as three distinct classes of cases; and if they are distinct, the grant of jurisdiction over one of them does not confer jurisdiction over either of the other two. The discrimination made between them, in the Constitution, is, we think, conclusive against their identity.' See also The Sarah, 8 Wheat. 391.

"This lucid principle of constitutional construction * * * was part of the realm of legal ideas in which the authors of the Act of 1875 moved. Certainly the accomplished lawyers who drafted the Act of 1875 drew on the language of the constitutional grant on the assumption that they were dealing with a distinct class of cases, that the language incorporated in their enactment precluded 'identity' with any other class of cases contained in Article III. * * *

" * * * The provision of the Act of 1875 with which we are concerned was designed to give a new content of jurisdiction to the federal courts, not to reaffirm one long-established, smoothly functioning since 1789. We have uncovered no basis for finding the additional design of changing the method by which federal courts had administered admiralty law from the beginning. The federal admiralty courts had been completely adequate to the task of protecting maritime rights rooted in federal law. There is not the slightest indication of any intention, or of any professional or lay demands for a change in the time-sanctioned mode of trying suits in admiralty without a jury, from which it can be inferred that by the new grant of jurisdiction of cases 'arising under the Constitution or laws' a drastic innovation was impliedly introduced in admiralty procedure, whereby Congress changed the method by which federal courts had administered admiralty law for almost a century. To draw such an inference is to find that a revolutionary procedural change had undesignedly come to pass. If we are now to attribute such a result to Congress the sole remaining justification for the federal admiralty courts which have played such a vital role in our federal judicial system for 169 years will be to provide a federal forum for the small number of maritime claims which derive from state law, and to afford the ancient remedy of a libel *in rem* in those limited instances when an *in personam* judgment would not suffice to satisfy a claim. * * *

"[Moreover,] the infusion of general maritime jurisdiction into the Act of 1875 * * * would have a disruptive effect on the traditional allocation of power over maritime affairs in our federal system.

"Thus the historic option of a maritime suitor pursuing a common-law remedy to select his forum, state or federal, would be taken away by an expanded view of § 1331, since saving-clause actions would then be freely removable under § 1441 of Title 28. * * * [Further,] [b]y making maritime cases removable to the federal courts it would make considerable inroads into the traditionally exercised concurrent jurisdiction of the state courts in admiralty matters—a jurisdiction which it was the unquestioned aim of the saving clause of 1789 to preserve. * * *

"Although the corpus of admiralty law is federal in the sense that it derives from the implications of Article III evolved by the courts, to claim that all enforced rights pertaining to matters maritime are rooted in federal law is a destructive oversimplification of the highly intricate interplay of the States and the National Government in their regulation of maritime commerce. It is true that state law must yield to the needs of a uniform federal maritime law when this Court finds inroads on a harmonious system. But this limitation still leaves the States a wide scope. State-created liens are enforced in admiralty. State remedies for wrongful death and state statutes providing for the survival of actions, both historically absent from the relief offered by the admiralty, have been upheld when applied to maritime causes of action. Federal courts have enforced these statutes. State rules for the partition and sale of ships, state laws governing the specific performance of arbitration agreements, state laws regulating the effect of a breach of warranty under contracts of maritime insurance—all these laws and others have been accepted as rules of decision in admiralty cases, even, at times, when they conflicted with a rule of maritime law which did not require uniformity. ＊ ＊ ＊

"＊ ＊ ＊ If jurisdiction of maritime claims were allowed to be invoked under § 1331, it would become necessary for courts to decide whether the action 'arises under federal law,' and this jurisdictional decision would largely depend on whether the governing law is state or federal. Determinations of this nature are among the most difficult and subtle that federal courts are called upon to make. ＊ ＊ ＊ "

The Court held, on the other hand, that Romero's "assertion [of a substantial claim that the Jones Act affords him a right of recovery for the negligence of his employer] was sufficient to empower the District Court to assume jurisdiction over the case and determine whether, in fact, the Act does provide the claimed rights" (p. 359). Further, though the Court rejected the argument that § 1331 provided "law" jurisdiction over the unseaworthiness and maintenance and cure claims, it saw no barrier to the district court exercising jurisdiction over these claims *pendent* to its Jones Act jurisdiction. (It did not decide "whether the District Court may submit to the jury the 'pendent' claims under the general maritime law" (p. 381).) Turning then to the merits, the Court held the Jones Act and unseaworthiness and maintenance and cure doctrines inapplicable to a foreign seaman on the facts before it.

Justice Brennan, writing for four dissenters, argued that the district court had jurisdiction under § 1331 (pp. 391–403):

"In a long series of decisions tracing from Southern Pacific Co. v. Jensen, 244 U.S. 205, this Court has made it clear that, in a seaman's action to recover damages for a maritime tort from his employer, the substantive law to be applied is federal maritime law made applicable as part of the laws of the United States by the Constitution itself, and that the right of recovery, if any, is a federally created right. ＊ ＊ ＊

"Since petitioner's causes of action for unseaworthiness and for maintenance and cure are created by federal law, his case arises under 'the laws ＊ ＊ ＊ of the United States' within the meaning of § 1331, for it is clear that 'a suit arises under the law that creates the cause of action.' Holmes, J., in American Well Works Co. v. Layne & Bowler Co., 241 U.S. 257, 260. ＊ ＊ ＊

" * * * [A]ny argument that § 1333 is an exclusive grant of jurisdiction would be false to the history of enactments allocating the judicial power of the United States. The fact that, in a diversity case under § 1332, the claimant is free to proceed on the law side of the federal court to enforce rights created by the federal maritime law, Seas Shipping Co. v. Sieracki, 328 U.S. 85, 88–89, clearly runs counter to any theory that the federal courts, because of § 9 of the Judiciary Act of 1789, can adjudicate maritime claims only while sitting in admiralty. There is no compelling reason why § 1333, which does not exclude maritime actions from being brought at law in a federal court under § 1332, should exclude them from being so brought under § 1331. Indeed, I find it a gross anomaly to hold, as the Court holds today, that an action rooted in federal law can be brought on the law side of a federal court only if the diversity jurisdiction, usually a vehicle for the enforcement of state-created rights, can be invoked. * * *

" * * * The issue before us is not whether all cases 'of admiralty and maritime jurisdiction' are *per se* encompassed in the statutory 'arising under' jurisdiction. A suit seeking the sort of remedy that the common law is not competent to give could not be fairly contended to lie under § 1331; it would clearly be the sort of suit in which the jurisdictional grant of § 1333 was intended to be exclusive. The issue before us concerns only actions maintainable in some forum 'at law' under the Saving Clause. And again, the issue is not even the narrower one whether Saving Clause actions are *per se* cognizable under § 1331. The tests of jurisdiction under § 1331 must still be met, and there is no contention that they are met merely by a showing that an action is one maintainable under the Saving Clause and involving the requisite jurisdictional amount. The plaintiff's right to recovery must still be one rooted in federal substantive law, and it has quite recently been made clear that there are Saving Clause actions that do not meet that test. Wilburn Boat Co. v. Fireman's Fund Ins. Co., 348 U.S. 310. The issue before us is only whether the fact that an action is a Saving Clause action excludes it from § 1331 where it would otherwise be maintainable thereunder. * * *

" * * * The fact that the jurisdictional categories are separate and distinct * * * does not mean that a particular action could not come under the heading of more than one of them. Everyone recognizes that this is the case in a maritime matter in which the parties are of diverse citizenship. I see no reason why it should not be true here of Romero's general maritime law claims against his employer. * * * "

(5) Why didn't Romero invoke the admiralty jurisdiction? In the hope that by not doing so, he would be able to have a jury on his claims under general maritime law? What was the significance of the Court's finding of "pendent jurisdiction" over the maritime law claims if it did not mean that those claims would go to the jury? On pendent jurisdiction generally, see Sec. 4, *supra.*

In Fitzgerald v. United States Lines, 374 U.S. 16 (1963), the Court held that when (as is the usual case) a seaman's claims for unseaworthiness and for maintenance and cure are joined in his action under the Jones Act on the "law side" of the district court, the general maritime claims must be submitted to the jury with the Jones Act claim as a matter of trial convenience.

In view of this, what is the ultimate significance of the Romero decision? Is the elaborateness of treatment explained by the suggestion that its question "wakes echoes in the deepest metaphysics of admiralty"? Gilmore & Black, The Law of Admiralty, 33 n. 118 (1st ed. 1957). Or does the case have other practical implications?

For thorough analyses, see Currie, *The Silver Oar and All That: A Study of the Romero Case,* 27 U.Chi.L.Rev. 1 (1959); Kurland, *The Romero Case and Some Problems of Jurisdiction,* 73 Harv.L.Rev. 817 (1960). See also ALI Study 250–54, and proposed § 1319.

(6) Romero held that claims resting on the general federal maritime law do not come within § 1331. Would the same be true of a claim founded on a federal maritime statute? See Wethering, *Jurisdictional Bases of Maritime Claims Founded on Acts of Congress,* 18 U.Miami L.Rev. 163 (1963) (arguing that Romero does not apply to statutory claims).

(7) What interests are served by making admiralty an area of federal jurisdiction? The original decision to do so was undoubtedly influenced by concern about international relations; consider, *e.g.,* the possible implications of prize cases, involving adjudication of the rights and status of foreign claimants and nations, neutral and belligerent. See The Federalist, No. 80. The value of uniformity in maritime law was also advanced to support federal jurisdiction. This notion of uniformity reflects the traditional view of the law of the sea as an independent and international body of rules transcending the power of territorial jurisdictions. Related to that but going beyond it, and of more contemporary significance, may be a general federal interest in furthering maritime commerce. Are any of these or all in combination sufficient to support exclusive federal jurisdiction? Concurrent jurisdiction? Could the interests be adequately protected by Supreme Court review of state court decisions?

(8) Historically, admiralty's powers have been limited to the high seas and to certain other waters within the country. The limits of those waters were defined by the Supreme Court in The Daniel Ball, 10 Wall. 557, 563 (U.S.1871), a case involving federal inspection and licensing of steam vessels operating in the navigable waters of the United States. "The doctrine of the common law as to the navigability of waters has no application in this country. Here the ebb and flow of the tide [the English common law limitation] do not constitute the usual test * * *. Those rivers must be regarded as public navigable rivers in law which are navigable in fact. And, they are navigable in fact when they are used, or are susceptible of being used, in their ordinary condition, as highways for commerce * * *. And they constitute navigable waters of the United States * * * where they form in their ordinary condition by themselves, or by uniting with other waters, a continued highway over which commerce is or may be carried on with other States or foreign countries * * *." For additional discussion of waters within the jurisdiction, see 1 Benedict on Admiralty, Paragraph (1), *supra,* ch. IX.

(9) The traditional view of admiralty tort jurisdiction turned on the locality of the tort. Maritime law governed torts occurring on navigable waters. See The Plymouth, 3 Wall. 20 (U.S.1866). The distinction produced anomalous results: if a vessel collided with a bridge, the bridge owner could not proceed against the ship by a libel in admiralty since the damage to the bridge was considered to be on land. Similarly, docks and

piers were viewed as extensions of the land and injuries occurring on them were outside the admiralty jurisdiction. See, *e.g.,* State Industrial Comm'n v. Nordenholt Corp., 259 U.S. 263, 275 (1922); T. Smith & Son, Inc. v. Taylor, 276 U.S. 179, 182 (1928). Dissatisfaction with these results led Congress to enact the Admiralty Extension Act of 1948, 46 U.S.C. § 740, providing that "[t]he admiralty and maritime jurisdiction of the United States shall extend to and include all cases of damage or injury, to person or property, caused by a vessel on navigable water, notwithstanding that such damage or injury be done or consummated on land." [2]

The Extension Act did not entirely eliminate the question whether the injury must occur on waters within the jurisdiction. In Victory Carriers v. Law, 404 U.S. 202 (1971), a longshoreman was injured by a defective forklift truck, owned by his stevedore employer, as he transferred cargo from a dock to a place on the pier where it would be picked up and stowed by the ship's equipment. He brought an action invoking the admiralty jurisdiction of the district court on a claim of unseaworthiness against the vessel and Victory Carriers, its owner. The Supreme Court, Justices Brennan and Douglas dissenting, held that federal maritime law did not govern the suit because the injury did not occur on waters within the jurisdiction and was not cognizable under the Extension Act because the ship's equipment had not been involved. See also Rodrigue v. Aetna Casualty & Surety Co., 395 U.S. 352 (1969) (recovery for death on artificial island oil drilling platform not within Death on the High Seas Act, which permits an action for wrongful death occurring on the high seas).

(10) Recent cases have modified the rule that the locality of a tort alone is enough to sustain admiralty jurisdiction. In Executive Jet Aviation, Inc. v. City of Cleveland, 409 U.S. 249 (1972), the tort claim arose out of the crash into the navigable waters of Lake Erie of a jet on a domestic flight. Writing for a unanimous Court, Justice Stewart recognized that admiralty jurisdiction in tort cases "has traditionally depended upon the locality of the wrong" (p. 253). But noting that "there has existed over the years a judicial, legislative, and scholarly recognition that * * * reliance on the relationship of the wrong to a traditional maritime activity is often more sensible and more consonant with the purposes of maritime law than is a purely mechanical application of the locality test" (p. 261), he concluded that "claims arising from airplane accidents are not cognizable in admiralty" unless "the wrong bear[s] a significant relationship to traditional maritime activity" (p. 268). The mere fact that aircraft falling into navigable waters may pose problems similar to those arising out of the sinking of a ship did not constitute such a relationship.

The opinion specifically left open the question of jurisdiction with respect to a transoceanic airliner, and the question whether the fact that particular commerce by air would previously have been carried on by water borne vessels is a "significant relationship to traditional maritime activity." It also noted that the holding as to land-based aircraft on domestic flights would not extend to circumstances where there is federal legislation

2. Constitutional attacks on the statute failed in lower federal courts, *e.g.,* United States v. Matson Navigation Co., 201 F.2d 610, 614–16 (9th Cir.1953), and in Gutierrez v. Waterman Steamship Corp., 373 U.S. 206 (1963), the Supreme Court took jurisdiction under the Extension Act of a longshoreman's suit for injuries sustained when he slipped on beans spilled from a defective shipboard container onto a pier. The constitutionality of the Extension Act was not discussed in the Court's opinion.

providing for jurisdiction—as a possible example, the Death on the High Seas Act.

In Foremost Insurance Co. v. Richardson, 457 U.S. 668 (1982), the issue was whether the collision of two pleasure boats on navigable United States waters falls within the admiralty jurisdiction. All members of the Court agreed that the Executive Jet requirement that the wrong have a significant connection with traditional maritime activity was controlling, thus ending doubts as to whether the requirement was limited to the aviation context. But the Court split upon the application of the test. For a majority of five, Justice Marshall held that because the wrong "involves the negligent operation of a vessel on navigable waters, * * * it has a sufficient nexus to traditional maritime activity" (p. 674). The majority rejected an argument that, "because commercial shipping is at the heart of * * * traditional maritime activity," a nexus with commerce was required for jurisdiction: "The federal interest in protecting maritime commerce cannot be adequately served if admiralty jurisdiction is restricted to those individuals actually *engaged* in commercial maritime activity. This interest can be fully vindicated only if *all* operators of vessels on navigable waters are subject to uniform rules of conduct" (pp. 674–75). The minority would have denied jurisdiction, stating that since neither craft was engaged in commercial activity, there was "no connection with any historic federal admiralty interest," pleasure boating being "basically a new phenomenon" (pp. 680–81).[3]

It is not yet settled whether the Executive Jet nexus requirement will be applied in cases where the tort occurred on the high seas. See East River S.S. Corp. v. Transamerica Delaval, Inc., 476 U.S. 858 (1986), involving a products liability claim relating to turbines that failed while ships were on the high seas. The Court noted that Executive Jet and Foremost involved torts that occurred on navigable waters within the United States, and stated that it did not need to reach the question "whether a maritime nexus also must be established when a tort occurs on the high seas" because "were there such a requirement, it was clearly met" in East River.

For a collection of lower court cases applying the Executive Jet test, see 14 Wright, Miller & Cooper, Federal Practice & Procedure § 3676 (1985 & 1987 Supp.).

(11) Admiralty jurisdiction over contract cases "depends upon the subject-matter—the nature and character of the contract * * * as to whether it have reference to maritime service or maritime transaction." North Pacific S.S. Co. v. Hall Bros. Co., 249 U.S. 119, 125 (1919). The application of this generalization has produced rather blurred jurisdictional lines. For example, a contract to build a ship is not within the admiralty jurisdiction, People's Ferry Co. v. Beers, 20 How. 393 (U.S.1857), while a contract to reconstruct or repair a ship may be litigated in admiralty, The Jack–O–Lantern, 258 U.S. 96 (1922). For examples of maritime contracts, see Gilmore & Black, Paragraph (1), *supra*, at 22. Professor Black has said of the pattern, "[T]here is about as much 'principle' as there is in a list of irregular verbs." Black, *Admiralty Jurisdiction: Critique and Suggestion*, 50 Colum.L.Rev. 259, 264 (1950). Gilmore & Black (paragraph (1), *supra*, at

---

3. See generally on this issue Stolz, *Pleasure Boating and Admiralty: Erie at Sea*, 51 Calif.L.Rev. 661 (1963).

31) suggest that the correct line may be drawn to include "those things principally connected with maritime transportation," and that on this view the courts have been under-inclusive as to contracts. For an attempt to formulate a general rule from the cases, see Moore & Pelaez, *Admiralty Jurisdiction—The Sky's the Limit,* 33 J.Air Law 3, 5 (1967) (contracts enforced in admiralty all concerned a "vessel").

(12) The grant of exclusive jurisdiction to the district courts in § 1333 is honeycombed with actions maintainable in state courts by virtue of the saving clause. The current interpretation allows a plaintiff to institute an action in personam in federal admiralty court, in state court, or, if federal jurisdiction is otherwise supported, on the "law side" of the federal court. See 14 Wright, Miller & Cooper, *supra,* at 430–33. Only a maritime action in rem must be brought in a federal admiralty court. See The Moses Taylor, 4 Wall. 411 (U.S.1867).

The original saving clause ("saving to suitors, in all cases, the right of a common law remedy, where the common law is competent to give it") was interpreted to permit a state court to order specific performance of a maritime contract—an equitable remedy unknown to the common law courts of 1789. See Red Cross Line v. American Fruit Co., 264 U.S. 109 (1924). The 1948 revision ("saving to suitors * * * all other remedies to which they are otherwise entitled") has been taken as intended to conform to the Red Cross decision, and, other than this change, has been read as preserving the meaning of the original language. See Madruga v. Superior Court, 346 U.S. 556, 560 n. 12 (1954).

(13) Certain maritime actions are committed by statute to exclusive federal jurisdiction. *E.g.,* suits against the United States arising from the operation of government vessels, 46 U.S.C. §§ 741–42, 781–82; proceedings under the Limitation of Liability Act, 46 U.S.C. §§ 183–89; actions under the Ship Mortgage Act, 46 U.S.C. § 951.[4] The ALI proposed exclusive federal jurisdiction in only three classes of cases: in rem proceedings, Limitation of Liability Act actions, and suits against the United States and its agencies. See ALI Study 238. On the utility of state court jurisdiction under the saving clause, consider Justice Brennan's dissent in Romero (pp. 409–10): "[I]n the five-year period 1953 to 1957 inclusive only about 150 decisions in Saving Clause actions have been rendered in the state courts of the country. * * * Saving Clause suitors seem long ago to have deserted the state courts." Compare the reasons advanced in support of concurrent jurisdiction by the Romero majority (p. 372) and in the ALI Study (p. 236). See also the proposal of Professor Black, Paragraph (11), *supra,* 50 Colum.L. Rev. at 276–80 (exclusive federal jurisdiction in maritime industry contract and commercial matters; exclusive state court jurisdiction of all personal injury claims).

(14) On the roles of federal and state law in maritime matters, see the *Note on the Sources of Law in Admiralty,* p. 892, *supra.*

---

4. Some lower courts had held the Death on the High Seas Act, 46 U.S.C. § 761, to confer exclusive federal jurisdiction, but in dicta in Offshore Logistics, Inc. v. Tallentire, 477 U.S. 207 (1986), the Court stated that DOHSA jurisdiction was concurrent.

SUBSECTION B: ACTIONS BROUGHT BY THE FEDERAL GOVERNMENT

NOTE ON CIVIL ACTIONS INSTITUTED BY THE FEDERAL GOVERNMENT *

(1) The present general grant of jurisdiction to the federal courts for civil litigation instituted by the United States is 28 U.S.C. § 1345. This provision had its roots in the First Judiciary Act, which gave the district courts jurisdiction, concurrent with the state courts, "of all suits at common law where the United States shall sue", subject to a jurisdictional amount requirement of $100. (Act of Sept. 24, 1789, § 9, 1 Stat. 73, 77.) It gave the circuit courts jurisdiction, also concurrent, "of all suits at common law or in equity," subject to a jurisdictional amount requirement of $500. (*Id.* § 11, 1 Stat. 78.)

In 1815 both the district courts and the circuit courts were given jurisdiction of "all suits at common law" where either "the United States, or any officer thereof, under the authority of an act of Congress, shall sue"; and the requirement of a jurisdictional amount was dropped. (Act of March 3, 1815, § 4, 3 Stat. 244, 245.)

The Judiciary Act of 1875 restored the jurisdictional amount requirement of $500 in the circuit courts in suits at common law as well as in equity "in which the United States are plaintiffs or petitioners," and for the first time authorized removal in such cases. (Act of March 3, 1875, §§ 1, 2, 18 Stat. 470.) Twelve years later removal was limited to nonresident defendants, and the requirement of a jurisdictional amount was permanently eliminated. (Act of March 3, 1887, 24 Stat. 552, as corrected by Act of August 13, 1888, 25 Stat. 433.) (If there is no basis for federal question jurisdiction, removal is evidently still limited to nonresident defendants under 28 U.S.C. § 1441(b). Does this make sense?)

When the circuit courts were abolished in 1911, their jurisdiction in these cases was transferred to the district courts, and to it was added cognizance of all civil actions brought by federal officers "authorized by law to sue". (Act of March 3, 1911, § 24, 36 Stat. 1087, 1091.) Thus was removed the last obstacle to federal access to the national courts. The general grant in § 1345, which includes actions by "any agency" as well as officers of the United States, remains a concurrent jurisdiction.[1]

The First Judiciary Act also gave the district courts cognizance "of all seizures on land, or [on non-navigable waters] * * *, and of all suits for penalties and forfeitures incurred, under the laws of the United States." (Act of Sept. 24, 1789, § 9, 1 Stat. 73, 77.) The jurisdiction survives today in 28 U.S.C. §§ 1355–1356 and, like its predecessor in 1789, is exclusive.

---

* Problems of actions against the United States and its agencies and officers—including the statutory bases of jurisdiction in such actions, and doctrines of sovereign and official immunity—are dealt with in Chapter IX. Implied causes of action for constitutional violations against federal officials are discussed in Chapter VII, Sec. 2, p. 917, *supra*. Implied causes of action on behalf of the United States are discussed in Chapter VII, Sec. 2, p. 906, *supra*.

1. Note also the provision for counterclaims in suits against the United States, 28 U.S.C. § 1346(c).

In addition to the general grants of jurisdiction, there are a number of specific grants in the Judicial Code. *E.g.*, §§ 1336 (ICC orders), 1339 (postal matters), 1340 (internal revenue; customs duties), and 1358 (eminent domain). (With the elimination of any jurisdictional amount requirement in suits brought by the government and in all federal question suits under § 1331, do these provisions serve any function?) And the other titles of the Code abound in specific provisions, embedded in substantive statutes, authorizing particular officers or agencies to bring actions, and frequently including an express grant of federal jurisdiction as part of the authorization.

For general discussion of the United States as plaintiff, see 14 Wright, Miller & Cooper, Federal Practice and Procedure §§ 3651–53 (1985; 1987 Supp.).

(2) Most rights of action by the United States or federal agencies rest on a statutory basis,[2] but the statutes vary greatly in how explicitly and comprehensively they delineate the rights and remedies involved. (For a selective catalogue of such statutes, see 14 Wright, Miller & Cooper, Paragraph (1), *supra*, § 3653.)

The simplest kind of statutory formulation is illustrated by § 4 of the Sherman Act and § 15 of the Clayton Act (15 U.S.C. §§ 4, 25). The district courts are "invested with" jurisdiction "to prevent and restrain" violations of the statutes, and it is declared to be the "duty" of the United States "under the direction of the Attorney General, to institute proceedings in equity to prevent and restrain such violations."

Simplicity yields to complexity, however, when restrictive practices challenged by the Antitrust Division as a violation occur in regulated industries. For the regime of regulation may itself condemn, or authorize an administrative agency to condemn, the challenged practice; it may authorize the agency to approve or disapprove the practice, with or without consideration of antitrust norms; and administrative approval may or may not immunize the practice from antitrust condemnation. In such situations the doctrine of "primary jurisdiction" (see Texas & Pacific Ry. Co. v. Abilene Cotton Oil Co., 204 U.S. 426 (1907)) may require the United States to apply to the administrative agency for relief before instituting action to enjoin. For discussion of this complex and important doctrine, see Pierce, Shapiro & Verkuil, Administrative Law and Process 206–18 (1985).

(3) What is the significance of a statutory right of action like § 4 of the Sherman Act? Would a right of action exist anyway under the San Jacinto and Debs cases, pp. 906–17, *supra* (both of which recognize, in the particular circumstances, an implied right of action on behalf of the United States)? Are there material differences between such a "common law" remedy and a statutory remedy?

The cases are replete with statements that a statutory jurisdiction to grant injunctions is to be administered in the light of general equitable principles. *E.g.*, Appalachian Coals, Inc. v. United States, 288 U.S. 344, 377 (1933); Hecht Co. v. Bowles, 321 U.S. 321 (1944); De Beers Consolidated Mines, Ltd. v. United States, 325 U.S. 212, 218–23 (1945). And some of these statements may have been motivated by Article III concerns over the

---

2. For discussion of the scope of implied rights of action by the United States, see Chap. VII, Sec. 2, pp. 906–17, *supra*.

integrity of judicial processes. See Shreve, *Federal Injunctions and the Public Interest,* 51 Geo.Wash.L.Rev. 382, 397–405 (1983).

But should not a statutory grant be read as dispensing in some degree with the usual prerequisites of equity jurisdiction? *Cf.* United Steelworkers v. United States, 361 U.S. 39 (1959), holding an 80–day injunction mandatory under § 208 of the Labor–Management Relations Act, 29 U.S.C. § 178, when statutory findings of fact are made by the court. And see generally Shreve, *supra,* at 405: "[T]he essentials of equitable restraint are rarely sacrificed in the face of the so-called mandatory injunction [provided for by a specific statutory provision]. Judicial reservations concerning substantiality, adequacy, and irreparability give way, as they should, in the face of special law-enforcement authority and the needs of the governmental plaintiff. Judicial reservations concerning imminence [of threatened harm] and manageability, in contrast, do not. They must be addressed in each case." [3]

(4) To what extent do district courts have authority to decline to exercise jurisdiction in actions brought by the United States or federal officers on the ground that they assert rights more appropriately asserted in state courts? See United States v. Bank of New York & Trust Co., 296 U.S. 463, 479–81 (1936); Markham v. Allen, p. 1454, *infra; cf.* Colorado River Water Conserv. Dist. v. United States, p. 1438, *infra.*

(5) When the United States or a federal agency seeks to intervene as of right in a private action, should it be required to satisfy the conditions ordinarily imposed by Rule 24(a) of the Federal Rules of Civil Procedure—a sufficient "interest relating to the property or transaction which is the subject of the action" and a lack of adequate representation by existing parties? And what of third-party intervention in a civil action brought by the United States; is it more restricted than intervention in private civil actions? See generally Shapiro, *Some Thoughts on Intervention Before Courts, Agencies, and Arbitrators,* 81 Harv.L.Rev. 721 (1968); Note, 65 Harv.L.Rev. 319 (1951).

Rule 24(b) was amended in 1948 to give the district courts discretion to permit intervention by a governmental officer or agency when a party to an action relies on a statute, order, regulation, requirement, or agreement issued or administered by that officer or agency. See 7C Wright, Miller & Kane, Federal Practice and Procedure § 1912 (1986). And the government has an absolute right to intervene in any private action "wherein the constitutionality of any Act of Congress affecting the public interest is drawn in question." 28 U.S.C. § 2403.[4]

(6) In addition to certain judge-made doctrines favoring the United States as a party in civil litigation, see p. 916 *supra,* there are a number of special statutory and rule provisions affecting the government as a litigant.

---

3. For an interesting case involving the construction of a statutory grant of remedial authority, see Porter v. Warner Holding Co., 328 U.S. 395 (1946). The majority in this case held that a provision of the Emergency Price Control Act of 1942, authorizing the Administrator to bring a civil action "for a permanent or temporary injunction, temporary restraining order, *or other order*" (emphasis added) permitted him to obtain equitable restitution from a landlord to the tenants who had been overcharged. In the view of the dissenters, the elaborate statutory scheme of remedies precluded such an exercise of "the creative resources of a court of equity" (p. 408).

4. The right was acquired as salvage from the 1937 court-packing proposal. See the discussion of the predecessor to § 2403, former § 401, in Note, 51 Harv.L.Rev. 148 (1937).

Thus there is a general statute of limitations, 28 U.S.C. § 2415, that applies to most actions brought by the government or a federal officer or agency. See also 28 U.S.C. § 2404 (no abatement of damage action on death of defendant); § 2405 (garnishment); § 2407 (delinquents for public money); § 2408 (security not required); § 2413 (executions in favor of the United States).[5]

(7) The question of the control of government litigation is more complex on the civil side than it is on the criminal side. (As to the latter, see p. 1088, *infra*.)

(a) The Gray Jacket, 5 Wall. 370, 371 (U.S.1866) was a Civil War prize case in which, following an appearance by Assistant Attorney General Ashton in support of the captors, Caleb Cushing sought to appear in behalf of the Treasury Department to support the opposing position of the claimants. The Court treated the case as an exception and heard Mr. Cushing, but Chief Justice Chase announced:

"The court * * * has instructed me to say that in causes where the United States is a party, and is represented by the Attorney–General or the Assistant Attorney–General, or special counsel employed by the Attorney–General, no counsel can be heard in opposition on behalf of any other of the departments of the government."

This ruling has in effect been codified in 28 U.S.C. § 516, which states that, except as otherwise provided by law, the conduct of litigation involving the United States and its interests is "reserved to officers of the Department of Justice, under the direction of the Attorney General." Thus the Attorney General and the Department of Justice have been vested with large power and responsibility in resolving conflicts of opinion within the government concerning the positions to be presented to the courts.[6]

(b) In addition to the Attorney General, many officers and agencies are expressly authorized to sue (as well as to be sued) in their own names. See, *e.g.*, 47 U.S.C. § 401(b) (authorizing suit by the FCC or by the Attorney General); 15 U.S.C. §§ 77t(b), 78u(e) (SEC); 29 U.S.C. §§ 160(e), 160(j), 160(l) (NLRB); 15 U.S.C. §§ 45(l), 45(m), 53, 56, 57b (giving the FTC exclusive authority to represent itself in certain actions and discretion to represent itself in others, as well as discretion to represent itself before the Supreme Court).

The steady trend away from concentration of litigating authority in the Department of Justice led Attorney General Griffin Bell, in 1978, to urge the development of a more rational system for the conduct of government

---

5. Some statutory provisions permit the award of attorney's fees to prevailing private parties in actions by or against the United States in situations in which the generally accepted common law rule in this country would not permit such an award. See Chap. IX, pp. 1113–14, *infra*.

6. *Cf.* United States v. San Francisco, 310 U.S. 16 (1940), an injunction action against the city (to enjoin the disposal of municipally generated power to a private utility) brought by the Attorney General at the request of the Secretary of the Interior. The granting statute provided that in certain circumstances, "upon written request

of the Secretary of the Interior, it is made the duty of the Attorney General" to bring all necessary proceedings to carry out the provisions of the Act.

What are the respective duties of the Secretary and the Attorney General under this not uncommon type of statute? Is it proper to oblige the Attorney General to institute litigation, at the direction of a layman, if his professional conscience and sense of obligation as a sworn officer of the court tell him the litigation ought not to be instituted? To prevent him, in the absence of a request, from bringing an action he believes ought to be brought?

litigation. See Bell, *The Attorney General: The Government's Chief Lawyer and Chief Litigator, or One Among Many?*, 46 Fordham L.Rev. 1049 (1978). As a result, on July 18, 1979, the President issued Exec.Order No. 12146, 44 Fed.Reg. 42657, entitled "Management of Federal Legal Resources." This Order established a Federal Legal Council, chaired by the Attorney General, whose duties would include promoting coordination among federal legal offices; the Order also "encourages" executive branch agencies to submit legal disputes to the Attorney General for resolution.

(c) In some instances, the diffusion of authority has meant that both the Department of Justice and a concerned agency may present their views in the same case, and those views may be opposed. See, *e.g.*, Mitchell v. United States, 313 U.S. 80 (1941); *cf.* St. Regis Paper Co. v. United States, 368 U.S. 208, 217 (1961); Note, 78 Yale L.J. 1443, 1465 (1969). In other instances, in which both the agency and the United States are formal parties, the Department of Justice may be actively espousing the conflicting views of another government agency. Do these cases raise problems of justiciability when the only contesting parties are both agencies or officers of the United States? See Chap. II, Sec. 2, p. 94, *supra*. Is the judicial process an appropriate way of resolving differences of opinion between different executive departments of the same government? Between an executive department and an "independent" agency? Between two independent agencies? To the extent that the dispute involves a conflict between major statutory schemes, may there not be special value in resorting to the courts to determine how the schemes should be adjusted? See ICC v. Jersey City, 322 U.S. 503 (1944).

See generally Bell, *supra*, at 1058; Stern, *"Inconsistency" in Government Litigation*, 64 Harv.L.Rev. 759 (1951); Note, 76 Mich.L.Rev. 324 (1977); Note, 62 Harv.L.Rev. 1050 (1949).

(d) Incident to the authority to conduct government litigation, the Attorney General has almost plenary power to settle or compromise government cases. See In re Confiscation Cases, 7 Wall. 454 (U.S.1868); New York v. New Jersey, 256 U.S. 296 (1921). Congress has rarely undertaken to reduce that authority, though some control has been asserted over particular controversies, such as prescribing the procedure for compromise or limiting the amount that may be paid in settlement. See, *e.g.*, 28 U.S.C. § 2672 (tort claims); 10 U.S.C. § 224(b) (claims against the FBI).

What standards ought to guide the Attorney General in approving or disapproving proposed settlements? Should government attorneys feel as free as private counsel to accept a compromise based on a prudent estimate of the probability of failure and success? When another government department or agency is involved, how far should the Department of Justice defer to its opinion?

(e) Compare with the foregoing the anachronistic preservation of a qui tam action by 31 U.S.C. §§ 231–34. These sections first declare certain efforts to defraud the government to be criminal. They then provide that whoever commits any of the prohibited acts shall pay $2,000 plus double the amount of damages sustained, together with costs of the suit, and authorize "any" person in behalf of the government to bring a suit for forfeiture and damages, with half the recovery to be paid to the government and half to the relator.

See United States ex rel. Marcus v. Hess, 317 U.S. 537, 545–47 (1943) (holding that such an action could be maintained in spite of the previous conviction of the offenders and in spite of the fact that the relator might have "received his information not by his own investigation, but from the previous indictment").

(f) Title VII of the Ethics in Government Act of 1978 (codified at 2 U.S.C. §§ 288–288m; 28 U.S.C. § 1364) establishes the Office of Senate Legal Counsel. The Counsel is charged, inter alia, to represent the Senate, its committees, subcommittees, members, officers, or employees in a wide variety of civil actions. The Attorney General is relieved of responsibility for representation in certain actions but retains any existing right to intervene or appear as amicus.

The rationale for this legislation is fully set forth in S.Rep. No. 95–170, 95th Cong., 1st Sess. 8–16 (1977). The Report concluded that the result of reliance on the Department of Justice (and occasionally on private counsel) for representation had been that congressional interests were "often inadequately represented or [were] not represented at all." [7]

NOTE ON CRIMINAL PROSECUTIONS INSTITUTED BY THE FEDERAL GOVERNMENT

(1) The First Judiciary Act, §§ 9, 11, 1 Stat. 73, 76, 79, gave the district and circuit courts jurisdiction (exclusive of the state courts) over crimes and offenses "cognizable under the authority of the United States"; the district courts were restricted to prosecutions "where no other punishment than whipping, not exceeding thirty stripes, a fine not exceeding one hundred dollars, or a term of imprisonment not exceeding six months, is to be inflicted." (For discussion of United States v. Hudson & Goodwin, 7 Cranch 32 (U.S.1812), refusing to recognize a common-law jurisdiction in criminal cases, see pp. 850–54, *supra.*)

In 1794, however, Congress provided in the Carriage Tax Act for concurrent jurisdiction in the state courts to award all "fines, penalties, and forfeitures" under that Act.[1] Subsequent federal criminal legislation occasionally authorized state court enforcement, although federal court enforcement remained the rule. See generally Warren, *Federal Criminal Laws and the State Courts*, 38 Harv.L.Rev. 545 (1925), who also discusses the power of Congress to require state courts to enforce federal penal laws; on that question, see generally Chap. IV, Sec. 2, *supra.*

The present jurisdiction is codified at 18 U.S.C. § 3231, and gives the district courts exclusive jurisdiction "of all offenses against the laws of the United States."

(2) Most federal prosecutions involve the enforcement of general statutes, enacted in the exercise of constitutionally defined powers of Congress, that criminalize conduct without regard to its specific location within the United States. In an important article in 1948, Professor Louis Schwartz suggested that "federal criminal jurisdiction is being employed in three

---

7. The bill as reported out by the Senate would have established an office of legal counsel to represent Congress as a whole, but those provisions were not approved by the House.

1. Act of June 5, 1794, ch. 45, § 10, 1 Stat. 373.

different ways: (1) to punish anti-social conduct of distinctively, if not exclusively, federal concern; (2) to punish conduct of local concern, with which local enforcement authorities are unable or unwilling to cope; and (3) to secure compliance with federal administrative regulations." *Federal Criminal Jurisdiction and Prosecutor's Discretion,* 13 L. & Contemp.Prob. 64, 66–67 (1948). Yet as Professor Schwartz notes, many of the most important federal crimes employ criteria (such as use of the mails, use of means of interstate commerce, or conduct involving interstate transportation of some kind) that relate imperfectly to these categories. Consider Friendly, Federal Jurisdiction: A General View 58–59 (1973): "Why should it make a difference that a New York pimp chooses Newark, N.J., rather than Nyack, N.Y., as the place where his employees transact their business? * * * Why should the federal government be concerned with a $100 robbery from a federally insured savings bank although it is not if someone burned down Macy's?"

Just when should federal authority and resources be used to hunt out and punish conduct that has already been denounced as criminal by the states? In addition to the purposes suggested by Schwartz, should federal criminal jurisdiction be used in order (i) to protect interstate channels or federal instrumentalities, (ii) adequately to combat interstate crimes that state officials with limited territorial authority have difficulty pursuing, or (iii) to respond to the public's indignation against particular types of crime and its greater confidence in the efficiency of federal law enforcement?

For a fuller discussion of "non-territorial" federal criminal offenses, see Abrams, Federal Criminal Law And Its Enforcement, chs. 3, 5–12 (1986).

(3) The Supreme Court has repeatedly held to the controversial position that parallel prosecutions by federal and state governments for the same conduct do not constitute double jeopardy. See, *e.g.,* Bartkus v. Illinois, 359 U.S. 121 (1959); Abbate v. United States, 359 U.S. 187 (1959).[2] Consequently, federal criminal liability usually poses the theoretical risk, at least, of double liability.[3] A memorandum issued by Attorney General Rogers to United States Attorneys after the Abbate case, however, declared a department policy against federal prosecution following state prosecution for "substantially the same act or acts," unless "the reasons are compelling." (The policy is known as the "Petite policy,"[4] and is codified in U.S. Dep't of Justice, U.S. Attorneys' Manual § 9–2.142). For a collection of lower court decisions holding that this policy may not be invoked against the government to bar prosecution, see Abrams, Paragraph (2), *supra,* at 779–80. See also Note, 66 Geo.L.J. 1137 (1978); Note, note 3, *supra,* at 488–94.

(4) In some areas federal criminal law bears the whole burden of maintaining public order. These include: (i) the District of Columbia and

---

2. For discussion, see, *e.g.,* Miller, Double Jeopardy and the Federal System (1968); Fisher, *Double Jeopardy and Federalism,* 50 Minn.L.Rev. 607 (1966); Note, 80 Harv.L.Rev. 1538 (1967); Note, 66 Nw.U.L. Rev. 248 (1971); Comment, 44 Minn.L.Rev. 534 (1960).

3. A few federal statutes bar prosecution after a state acquittal or conviction. See, *e.g.,* 18 U.S.C. §§ 659–60, 1992, 2117. Some state statutes or constitutional provisions similarly prohibit a state prosecution following a federal prosecution for the same conduct. See generally Abrams, Paragraph (2), *supra,* at 748–49; Note, 31 Stan. L.Rev. 477, 494–96 (1979).

4. So named for Petite v. United States, 361 U.S. 529 (1960), in which the Supreme Court granted the government's motion to vacate a judgment of conviction below and to dismiss the indictment because the federal prosecution violated this policy.

the territories; (ii) the admiralty and maritime jurisdiction that falls outside the territorial jurisdiction of any state; and (iii) federal enclaves—areas within the territorial jurisdiction of the states over which the federal government has acquired exclusive jurisdiction, such as military reservations or national parks.

The Criminal Code now deals with the last two of these areas by defining a distinct group of acts that constitute federal crimes when committed within the "special maritime and territorial jurisdiction" of the United States.[5] That jurisdiction is defined in 18 U.S.C. § 7 to include the high seas and waters within the admiralty and maritime jurisdiction and outside any state's jurisdiction (including any American aircraft in flight over these areas), as well as lands reserved or acquired for the use of the United States.

(a) As long ago as 1790, Congress provided for the punishment of "wilful murder" and manslaughter "within any fort, arsenal, dock-yard, magazine, or in any other place or district of country, under the sole and exclusive jurisdiction of the United States." See Act of April 30, 1790, §§ 3, 7, 1 Stat. 112, 113. Even today, Title 18 includes a number of provisions making it a federal crime to engage in specified conduct "within the special maritime and territorial jurisdiction of the United States." *E.g.,* 18 U.S.C. §§ 113 (assault), 661 (larceny), 662 (receiving stolen property), 1111–13 (murder and manslaughter), 2241–45 (rape).

But the need soon arose for more complete specification of conduct occuring within these areas of federal jurisdiction that should be criminally punished. Recognition of this need led to the enactment of § 3 of the Federal Crimes Act of March 3, 1825, 4 Stat. 115, known as the Assimilative Crimes Act, and today codified at 18 U.S.C. § 13. The Act makes it a federal crime to engage, in any place falling within the scope of § 7, in conduct "not made punishable by any enactment of Congress" that would be a crime if committed within the jurisdiction of the state (or territory or the District of Columbia) in which that place is located.[6]

Presumably to avoid constitutional doubts, the Act was originally construed as adopting only the state criminal laws in force at the time of its enactment, United States v. Paul, 6 Pet. 141 (U.S.1832)—a limitation that necessitated a series of re-enactments to bring the Act up to date. See Note, 101 U.Pa.L.Rev. 124, 133–34 (1952). In the 1948 revision of the Criminal Code, Congress for the first time adopted the principle that the Act incorporates subsequent modifications in state criminal laws, and the constitutionality of this approach was upheld (over the dissents of Justices Douglas and Black) in United States v. Sharpnack, 355 U.S. 286 (1958).

(b) In most of the vast area of lands belonging to the United States, the federal interest is limited to ownership. Only a small fraction of these

---

5. Criminal offenses within the District of Columbia are governed by the D.C. Code, which includes a plenary set of criminal prohibitions enacted by (or pursuant to delegation of authority from) the Congress. Jurisdiction over such offenses is vested in the local D.C. Superior Court, see D.C. Code § 11–923, but the United States District Court for the District of Columbia has jurisdiction over D.C. offenses that are joined in the same information or indict-ment with a federal criminal offense, see *id.* § 11–502. On the constitutionality of these provisions, see Palmore v. United States, p. 451, *supra.*

6. On the difficulties of determining when conduct is "not made punishable by any enactment of Congress," see Williams v. United States, 327 U.S. 711 (1946); Abrams, Paragraph (2), *supra,* at 673–87; Note, 70 Harv.L.Rev. 685 (1957).

lands is thought by the government agencies concerned to be within exclusive federal jurisdiction, or even within its concurrent or partial jurisdiction (presumably encompassing territorial criminal jurisdiction). The problem of determining when the United States possesses special governmental powers in such areas has had a long history and can raise intricate questions.[7]

(5) Though most federal crimes—territorial and non-territorial alike—are codified in Title 18, that title is not an integrated criminal code but rather a collection of diverse offenses enacted over the years. In 1970, the National Commission on Reform of the Federal Criminal Laws published a Study Draft (as well as two volumes of Working Papers), and in 1971 a Final Report draft, proposing a comprehensive revision of Title 18. Though the Commission's work has been the basis of many bills to reform the federal criminal code,[8] none has been enacted. Nonetheless, that work, and the commentary it generated,[9] remains a valuable source of analysis of the problems discussed in this Note.

(6) The Attorney General has traditionally maintained unified control of the initiation of federal criminal prosecutions. See 28 U.S.C. §§ 509, 515–516; cf. 28 U.S.C. § 547 (United States Attorneys). Appointment of the Watergate Special Prosecutor—whose almost autonomous position was created by an order of the Attorney General—qualified this control, but as the Supreme Court emphasized in United States v. Nixon, 418 U.S. 683, 696 (1974), the Attorney General had not rescinded that departmental order.

In Title VI of the Ethics in Government Act of 1978, 92 Stat. 1875, now codified (as amended) at 28 U.S.C. §§ 591–99, Congress established a new procedure for temporary appointment of "special prosecutors" (since renamed "independent counsel") with limited jurisdiction.

The Attorney General is charged with undertaking a preliminary investigation when specific information is received that a violation of federal criminal law has been committed by the President, Vice President, or various high federal officials.[10] He is then required, unless he "finds

7. See generally, on these questions, Twitty, The Respective Powers of the Federal and Local Governments Within Lands Owned or Occupied by the United States (1944); Report of the Interdepartmental Committee for the Study of Jurisdiction over Federal Areas Within the States, pt. II (1956); Abrams, Comment on Assimilated Offenses, 1 National Commission on Reform of Federal Criminal Laws, Working Papers 77, 82 (1970); Note, 101 U.Pa.L. Rev. 124 (1952); Note, 58 Yale L.J. 1402 (1949); Note, 18 Geo.W.L.Rev. 500 (1950).

On the special problems of federal criminal jurisdiction in the "Indian Country," see 18 U.S.C. §§ 1151–1153, 1162; see generally Cohen, Handbook of Federal Indian Law 358–65 (1941).

8. For discussion of early bills, see Schwartz, Reform of the Federal Criminal Laws: Issues, Tactics, and Prospects, 41 L. & Contemp.Prob. 1 (1977).

9. See, e.g., Brown & Schwartz, New Federal Criminal Code Is Submitted, 56

A.B.A.J. 844, Sentencing Under the Draft Criminal Code, id. at 935, Offenses Redefined Under Proposed Federal Criminal Code, id. at 1181 (1970); McClellan, Codification, Reform and Revision: The Challenge of a Modern Federal Criminal Code, 1971 Duke L.J. 663. For criticism of the proposed code as too expansive, see Liebmann, Chartering a National Police Force, 56 A.B.A.J. 1070, 1176 (1970). See also Dobbyns, A Proposal for Changing the Jurisdictional Provisions of the New Federal Criminal Code, 57 Corn.L.Q. 198 (1972); Note, 47 N.Y.U.L.Rev. 320 (1972).

10. These include cabinet officials, certain high-level employees of the Executive Office of the President, Department of Justice, CIA, and IRS, and in some instances persons who formerly held these offices. Also covered are officers of the President's "principal national campaign committee" (§ 591).

that there are no reasonable grounds to believe that further investigation is warranted" (§ 592), to apply to a three-judge division of the U.S. Court of Appeals for the D.C. Circuit, specially designated by the Chief Justice pursuant to 28 U.S.C. § 49, for the appointment of an independent counsel.[11] That division in turn is empowered to name an individual to serve as independent counsel, and to define his "prosecutorial jurisdiction," subject to possible future expansion by the division upon the application of the Attorney General (§ 593). While in office the independent counsel has, with minor exceptions, all the powers and authority of the Attorney General and the Department of Justice with respect to matters within his prosecutorial jurisdiction (§ 594).

An independent counsel may be removed, other than by impeachment and conviction, only by "personal action" of the Attorney General for "good cause" or substantial disabilities, subject to judicial review in a civil action in the district court for the District of Columbia for reinstatement or other "appropriate relief" (§ 596(a)). The office of a particular independent counsel terminates when either the independent counsel or the three-judge division determines that the independent counsel's investigations and prosecutions are "completed" or "substantially completed" (§ 596(b)).

The statute has been challenged on constitutional grounds, relating to assertions that it (i) interferes with the President's appointment and removal power, (ii) confers upon federal judges duties that fall outside of Article III's judicial power, or (iii) otherwise violates the separation of powers. See generally Tribe, American Constitutional Law §§ 4–9 to 4–11 (2d ed. 1988). The court of appeals for the D.C. Circuit has held the statute unconstitutional, and the Supreme Court has agreed to review that decision during the 1987 Term. In re Sealed Case, 56 Law Week 2421 (1988). Other challenges to the statute have been deflected by the Attorney General's decision to delegate by regulation his own investigative and prosecutorial power to an independent counsel on whom the division had previously conferred prosecutorial jurisdiction over the same matter. See In re Sealed Case, 829 F.2d 50 (D.C.Cir.1987) (finding the delegation to be valid, and to make unnecessary the court's consideration of the validity of an appointment under the statute alone).

(7) Beginning with the passage of the Federal Magistrates Act of October 17, 1968, 82 Stat. 1107, federal magistrates have been authorized, upon the election of the defendant, to try prosecutions for minor offenses. The pertinent provisions, as amended and now codified in 18 U.S.C. § 3401, extend this authority to any misdemeanor offense.[12] Appeal from a conviction before a magistrate may be taken to the district court. *Id.* § 3402.

The Act extends only to serious offenses, however; it excludes infractions and minor misdemeanors.

11. Upon his determination that a conflict of interest might otherwise exist, the Attorney General may also apply for appointment of an independent counsel to investigate other federal officials.

Members of the Judiciary Committees may also request that the Attorney General apply for appointment of an independent counsel. The Attorney General must then report to the requesting committee reasons for his decision whether to begin a preliminary investigation (§ 591(e)).

12. Section § 3401(f) permits removal of a prosecution from the magistrate to the district court on the court's own motion, or on the government's motion for "good cause shown" (defined as including "the novelty, importance or complexity of the case").

Chapter IX

SUITS CHALLENGING OFFICIAL ACTION

SECTION 1. SUITS CHALLENGING FEDERAL OFFICIAL ACTION

INTRODUCTORY NOTE

A lawsuit challenging federal official action implicates a variety of related doctrines. Such a suit may be filed only in a court that possesses subject matter jurisdiction, a point of special importance given the limited jurisdiction of the federal courts. The litigant bringing the lawsuit must also surmount the barrier of sovereign immunity, which, unless waived by Congress, generally bars suit against the United States *eo nomine* or its agencies and departments, and also bars some actions nominally against federal officials. Finally, the litigant must establish an entitlement to the particular remedy sought.

Though distinct, these doctrines are closely related. For example, one may ordinarily assume that Congress, by vesting a federal court with subject matter jurisdiction over particular suits against the United States, meant to provide a concomitant waiver of the United States' immunity from suit. Similarly, the doctrine of sovereign immunity is closely related to the evolution of remedies in suits nominally against federal officers: in practice, both damages and specific relief have often been available in such lawsuits, thereby providing methods of reviewing official action thought to be consistent with any concept of sovereign immunity. Finally, the appropriateness of a particular remedy may depend heavily upon whether Congress has waived sovereign immunity and thus made available an alternative form of relief.

This Section is divided into three parts. Subsection A provides an overview of the evolution of remedies available in suits against federal officials and agencies. Subsection B then considers the doctrine of sovereign immunity, and related questions raised by Youngstown Sheet & Tube Co. v. Sawyer (the Steel Seizure case). Finally, Subsection C reviews the most important congressional enactments waiving the sovereign immunity of the United States.

SUBSECTION A: REMEDIES

NOTE ON THE DEVELOPMENT OF REMEDIES IN ACTIONS AGAINST FEDERAL OFFICIALS AND FEDERAL AGENCIES

The development of remedies against federal officials and agencies follows two important paths. The first, nonstatutory review, involves the system of remedies generally available against any defendant in judicial proceedings. The remedies may be derived from the common law (as with damage actions, injunctions, or the prerogative writs) or from a statute (as with the declaratory judgment). The second path, statutory review, involves more specialized remedies created by Congress for the distinctive purpose of reviewing the actions of federal officers or agencies.

1. *Nonstatutory Review of Federal Official Action* [1]

(1) Nonstatutory review of the action of federal officials draws upon the English heritage, which provided a variety of remedies against an officer or agency of the Crown. While the King enjoyed sovereign immunity, his officers did not. They could be required, for example, to pay damages to private persons injured by illegal acts, on the theory that officials, like other wrongdoers, were subject to the law.

In this country, until recently "the basic judicial remedy for the protection of the individual against illegal official action [was] a private action for damages against the official in which the court determine[d], in the usual common-law manner and with the aid of a jury, whether or not the officer was legally authorized to do what he did in the particular case. The plaintiff [could not] sue to redress merely any unauthorized action by an officer. To maintain the suit the plaintiff [had to] allege conduct by the officer which, if not justified by his official authority, [was] a private wrong to the plaintiff, entitling the latter to recover damages." Attorney General's Committee on Administrative Procedure, Administrative Procedure in Government Agencies, S.Doc. No. 8, 77th Cong, 1st Sess. 81 (1941). (On whether officials can today assert a qualified or absolute immunity from personal liability in damages, see Sec. 3, *infra.*)

(2) A litigant seeking specific relief against federal officials could similarly avail himself of the usual common law remedies, like ejectment or replevin, in appropriate cases. See, *e.g.,* United States v. Lee, Sec. 1(B), *infra.* Also available were the prerogative writs—quo warranto, habeas corpus, prohibition, certiorari, and mandamus—that were issued by the King's Bench in England. As a result of the highly creative development of the English law, these writs were available against royal officers notwithstanding the sovereign immunity of the King.[2] In this country, too,

---

1. See generally Byse, *Proposed Reforms in Federal "Nonstatutory" Judicial Review: Sovereign Immunity, Indispensable Parties, Mandamus,* 75 Harv.L.Rev. 1479 (1962); Jaffe, *Suits Against Governments and Officers: Sovereign Immunity,* 77 Harv.L.Rev. 1 (1963); Note, *Developments in the Law—Remedies Against the* *United States and Its Officials,* 70 Harv.L. Rev. 827 (1957).

2. See generally Gellhorn, *et al.,* Administrative Law: Cases and Comments 989–95 (8th ed. 1986); Jaffe, Judicial Control of Administrative Action 165–93 (1965); Smith, *The Prerogative Writs,* 11 Camb.L.J. 40 (1951).

the prerogative writs provided an important means of controlling official action, though each was subject to distinctive limitations.

The writ of quo warranto is ordinarily limited to testing the right to an office, as when an official has been unlawfully appointed or attempts to continue in office beyond his term.

The writ of habeas corpus is available to test the legality of official detention or custody. Its contemporary uses include challenges to the custody of aliens, of individuals in military service, and of persons confined pursuant to arrest or criminal conviction. For detailed discussion, see Chap. XI, *infra*.

The writ of prohibition is usually directed to an inferior judicial or quasi-judicial body, to bar it from exceeding its jurisdiction. This writ generally does not permit review of actions (even if unlawful) of a tribunal that does have jurisdiction, or of actions that are deemed to be purely administrative or ministerial. Moreover, the writ is discretionary, and is not to be awarded if another remedy is available. For these reasons, prohibition has been of limited importance in reviewing action by federal officials.

The writ of certiorari directs a lower tribunal to certify its record to a superior court (in England, the King's Bench) for review. It is generally limited to review of judicial or quasi-judicial action, and it too is available as a matter of discretion rather than right. Congress has never authorized its use in the federal district courts, and even in the District of Columbia courts—long regarded as common law courts—certiorari fell into disuse as a means of reviewing administrative action. See Degge v. Hitchcock, 229 U.S. 162 (1913).

(3) A remedy of more general applicability in suits seeking specific relief against officials is the writ of mandamus, which, under the conventional formulation, is available to compel an official to perform a ministerial (but not a discretionary) duty. An aggrieved party, however, has to find a court with jurisdiction to award the writ. By 1838 it was established that, largely as the result of historical accident, neither the state courts nor the federal courts generally, but only the Circuit Court for the District of Columbia, possessed that jurisdiction. See Kendall v. United States ex rel. Stokes, 12 Pet. 524, 619–26 (U.S.1838).[3]

(4) Early Supreme Court decisions adhered to the conventional formulation of the circumstances in which mandamus would issue.[4] In Work v.

---

3. Section 13 of the First Judiciary Act, 1 Stat. 73, 81, purported to vest in the Supreme Court an original jurisdiction "to issue * * * writs of *mandamus*, * * * in cases warranted by the principles and usages of law, to * * * any * * * persons holding office, under the authority of the United States." That provision was held unconstitutional in Marbury v. Madison, p. 72, *supra*.

Efforts to obtain mandamus in the inferior federal courts also failed. In McIntire v. Wood, 7 Cranch 504 (U.S.1813), the Supreme Court held that § 11 of the Judiciary Act did not authorize a federal circuit court to issue mandamus to a local federal official, and, subsequently, in McClung v.

Silliman, 6 Wheat. 598, 604–05 (U.S.1821), p. 489, *supra*, the Court held that the state courts did not possess power to issue writs of mandamus to federal officials that Congress had not given to the federal courts. See generally Byse, note 1, *supra*, at 1499–1502; Brill, *The Citizen's Relief Against Inactive Federal Officials: Case Studies in Mandamus, Actions "In The Nature of Mandamus," and Mandatory Injunctions*, 16 Akron L.Rev. 339, 349–63 (1983).

4. Thus, in Kendall v. United States, Paragraph (3), *supra*, the Court upheld issuance of a writ of mandamus to the Postmaster General, compelling him to allow certain credits (for carriage of the mails) that had been upheld by the Solicitor of

United States ex rel. Rives, 267 U.S. 175 (1925), Chief Justice Taft reformulated the ministerial-discretionary distinction by transforming its general concern with the existence of executive discretion into a particularistic concern with the construction of the specific enactment alleged to have been violated (pp. 177–78):

"Mandamus issues to compel an officer to perform a purely ministerial duty. It can not be used to compel or control a duty in the discharge of which by law he is given discretion. The duty may be discretionary within limits. He can not transgress those limits, and if he does so, he may be controlled by injunction or mandamus to keep within them. The power of the court to intervene, if at all, thus depends upon what statutory discretion he has. * * * [There] are decisions in which the discretion is greater than in the Kendall Case and less than in the Decatur Case,[5] and its extent and the scope of judicial action in limiting it depend upon a proper interpretation of the particular statute and congressional purpose. * * *"

How useful is the distinction between the exercise of discretion and the performance of a ministerial duty in the modern administrative state—in which most official decisions involve an element of discretion without being wholly unbounded? See Jaffe, note 2, *supra*, at 181; Byse and Fiocca, *Section 1361 of the Mandamus and Venue Act of 1962 and "Nonstatutory" Judicial Review of Federal Administrative Action*, 81 Harv.L.Rev. 308, 333–35 (1967).

(5) Though mandamus is a legal remedy, it is governed by equitable principles. In its "equitable" discretion, a court may decline to issue mandamus "to compel the doing of an idle act, * * * or to give a remedy which would work a public injury or embarrassment," United States ex rel. Greathouse v. Dern, 289 U.S. 352, 359–60 (1933), or when other avenues of relief have not been exhausted, see Heckler v. Ringer, 466 U.S. 602, 616–17

the Treasury. Congress had authorized the Solicitor to decide such claims, and the defendant was said to have no discretion to deny them. The Court rejected the defendant's argument that the courts lacked power to issue the requested order: though the President in the exercise of constitutionally derived powers was "beyond the reach of any other departments" except via impeachment, executive officers are not under the President's exclusive direction, and Congress may impose official duties that "are subject to the control of the law * * *. * * * [T]his is emphatically the case, where the duty enjoined is of a mere ministerial character." 12 Pet. at 610, 612–13.

Two years later, in Decatur v. Paulding, 14 Pet. 497 (U.S.1840), the Court (per Taney, C.J.) affirmed the refusal to issue mandamus to the Secretary of the Navy (who was by law trustee of a navy pension fund) to compel him to pay a pension claim. The Court accepted but distinguished Kendall, finding that the Secretary did not have a merely ministerial

duty to pay the claim (pp. 514–16): the official duties of the head of an executive department are generally discretionary; he must exercise judgment in expounding the law; "he has a right to call on the Attorney General to assist him with his counsel; and it would be difficult to imagine why a legal adviser was provided by law for the heads of departments, as well as for the President, unless their duties were regarded as executive in which judgment and discretion were to be exercised.

"If a suit should come before this Court, which involved the construction of any of these laws, the Court certainly would not be bound to adopt the construction given by the head of a department. * * * But their judgment upon the construction of a law must be given in a case in which they have jurisdiction, and in which it is their duty to interpret the act of Congress, in order to ascertain the rights of the parties in the cause before them."

5. [Ed.] On Kendall and Decatur, see note 4, *supra*.

(1984); United States ex rel. Girard Trust Co. v. Helvering, 301 U.S. 540, 543–44 (1937). See also Brill, note 3, *supra*, at 355 n. 115.

(6) The Mandamus and Venue Act of 1962, 28 U.S.C. § 1361, gave jurisdiction, without regard to amount in controversy, to all federal district courts (rather than just those of the District of Columbia) over actions "in the nature of mandamus" to compel a federal officer to perform his duty.[6] See generally Byse, note 1, *supra;* Byse & Fiocca, Paragraph (4), *supra*.[7] In response to this enactment and to a more general movement toward expanded review of administrative action, two differing views of mandamus came to be articulated in the case law: the "orthodox" view that the writ "is intended to provide a remedy for a plaintiff * * * only if the defendant owes him a clear nondiscretionary duty," Heckler v. Ringer, 466 U.S. 602, 616 (1984), and the "reformed" view that mandamus is a more flexible remedy available whenever an official acts beyond the scope of his lawful authority.[8]

(7) The unavailability of mandamus relief outside the District of Columbia before 1962, and uncertainty even after 1962 about its scope, made it a highly imperfect remedy for review of official action. Particularly after the advent of general federal question jurisdiction in 1875, equitable remedies like the injunction (and, later, the declaratory judgment) came to be the predominant nonstatutory remedies for obtaining specific relief from unlawful action by federal officials. The injunction "rests on the same theory [as a private action for damages, see Paragraph (1), *supra*], namely, the answerability of a Government officer as a private individual for conduct injurious to another, and depends upon the assumption that unless enjoined, the officer will commit acts which will entitle the plaintiff to maintain an action for damages." Attorney General's Committee on Administrative Procedure, Paragraph (1), *supra*, at 81.

The issuance of "negative injunctions" was relatively straightforward in cases meeting the requisites for equitable relief and not otherwise barred. Prior to 1962, however, it was uncertain whether federal courts outside the District of Columbia could issue "mandatory injunctions" which, in compelling an official to take action in fulfillment of his duty, resembled a writ of mandamus, which those courts lacked jurisdiction to issue.[9] The Mandamus and Venue Act clearly permits all federal district courts to issue orders in the nature of mandamus. The question remained, however, whether a plaintiff could obtain broader relief in a suit for a mandatory injunction than would have been available in an action seeking an order in the nature of mandamus.

The Supreme Court suggested in Panama Canal Co. v. Grace Line, Inc., 356 U.S. 309, 318 (1958), that a suit for a mandatory injunction should be

---

6. In 1938, Fed.R.Civ.Proc. 81(b) abolished the separate writ of mandamus in the district courts, providing that relief previously available by mandamus "may be obtained by appropriate action or by appropriate motion under the practice prescribed in these rules."

7. For discussion of the Act's impact on questions of process and venue, see pp. 1716–17, *infra*.

8. See generally 4 Davis, Administrative Law Treatise §§ 23:12–13 (2d ed.

1983); Byse and Fiocca, Paragraph (4), *supra*, at 336–37; Brill, note 3, *supra*, at 355–63; Note, 1973 Duke L.J. 207, 209–11.

9. In Smith v. Bourbon County, 127 U.S. 105 (1888), the Supreme Court intimated that the power did not exist. Nonetheless, the Court never squarely resolved the issue, and the lower courts were divided. See generally Byse & Fiocca, Paragraph (4), *supra*, at 312–13.

judged by the same principles as mandamus, and lower courts have generally followed that lead.[10] The significance of Panama Canal depends, of course, upon whether the orthodox or the reformed view of mandamus (see Paragraph (6) *supra*) is used as the measure of the scope of mandatory injunctive relief.[11]

Before 1976, a litigant whose claim was worth less than $10,000 could not bring a simple action for an injunction under 28 U.S.C. § 1331, and if he resorted to § 1361, he would encounter all of the traditional limitations upon mandamus. But in 1976 Congress eliminated the minimum jurisdictional amount in suits under § 1331 against any federal official in his official capacity. Pub.L. No. 94–574. Professor Davis has suggested that "[t]he best way to compel agency action unlawfully withheld is by injunction or declaratory judgment or both, but without the word 'mandatory' before 'injunction.' Jurisdiction under § 1331 always suffices; mention of § 1361 unnecessarily risks judicial advertence to mandamus technicalities." 4 Davis, note 8, *supra*, § 23.11, at 169.[12]

The provision of specific relief against federal official action often raises peculiarly sensitive questions of separation of powers and judicial role, particularly when the President or other high officials are involved. For exploration of these questions, see Youngstown Sheet & Tube Co. v. Sawyer, p. 1129, *infra*, and the Notes following that case.

2. Statutory Review of Federal Official Action

(8) Statutory review, largely a development of the twentieth century, has become the predominant method of reviewing federal official action. Although nonstatutory review remains important with regard to the older executive departments (*e.g.*, State, Defense, Treasury, Justice, Interior, and Agriculture), Congress usually makes action taken by new agencies or under new programs subject to statutory review, through a variety of mechanisms.

(9) In many instances an administrative order is not self-operative, and becomes binding only when the agency brings an action, as authorized in its governing statute, to enforce its order. The statute may provide for enforcement in an action in a federal court of appeals (as is true, for example, of orders of the National Labor Relations Board, see 29 U.S.C. § 160(e)), or in a federal district court (as is often true of agency reparation orders, see, *e.g.*, 49 U.S.C. § 16(2) (orders of the Interstate Commerce Commission); 7 U.S.C. §§ 210(f), 499g(b) (certain orders of the Secretary of Agriculture)). In such a proceeding, the court will ensure that the order is within the scope of the agency's delegated authority and is otherwise valid

---

10. See, *e.g.*, National Wildlife Federation v. United States, 626 F.2d 917, 918 n. 1, 923 (D.C.Cir.1980); Fallini v. Hodel, 783 F.2d 1343, 1345 (9th Cir.1986).

See also Marshall v. Crotty, 185 F.2d 622 (1st Cir.1950), refusing a declaratory judgment where the court thought that mandamus would be improper even if, as in the District of Columbia, there were jurisdiction to award the writ.

11. For cases importing the orthodox view of mandamus into decisions concerning mandatory injunctions, see M. Stein-

thal & Co. v. Seamans, 455 F.2d 1289, 1303 (D.C.Cir.1971); Vann v. Housing Auth. of Kansas City, 87 F.R.D. 642, 668–69 (W.D. Mo.1980); Sodus Central School Dist. v. Kreps, 468 F.Supp. 884, 885 (W.D.N.Y. 1978).

12. Mandamus jurisdiction remains important in certain actions under the Social Security Act, in which all other routes (including suit under § 1331) are specifically foreclosed by statute. See Ellis v. Blum, 643 F.2d 68 (2d Cir.1981).

before ordering enforcement. See generally Attorney General's Committee on Administrative Procedure, Paragraph (1), *supra*, at 82–83; pp. 370–75, 401–07, *supra*.

(10) Regulatory statutes often authorize judicial review at the instance of a private person who wishes to take the initiative in challenging official action. Though these statutory review provisions vary widely,[13] probably most common are provisions that authorize a petition in a federal court of appeals to set aside an administrative order of a particular agency. Thus, the National Labor Relations Act specifies that final orders of the NLRB may be reviewed in an appropriate court of appeals, see 29 U.S.C. § 160(f), and similar provisions govern other agencies.[14] Other statutes authorize review in a federal district court.[15] An important example is section 205(g) of the Social Security Act, 42 U.S.C. § 405(g), which provides for district court review of final and adverse administrative decisions on claims for social security benefits.

(11) In addition to specific statutory review provisions, Congress in 1946 enacted the Administrative Procedure Act (APA), which in section 10, 5 U.S.C. §§ 701–06, generally authorizes judicial review at the behest of a person who suffers legal wrong because of final agency action or who is adversely affected by such action.[16] Though review under the APA may be denied, *inter alia*, when (1) the action is committed to agency discretion, (2) the governing regulatory statute expressly or impliedly precludes judicial review, (3) the challenge is not ripe, (4) the petitioner lacks standing, or (5) the petitioner has failed to exhaust administrative remedies, the decisions have established a strong presumption that federal agency action is reviewable.[17]

(12) The various statutory review provisions differ as to matters like the timing of review and the weight to be attached to administrative determinations. Some provisions prescribe a new form for the action seeking review, such as a "petition to modify or set aside" an order.[18] Absent this kind of specification, any appropriate nonstatutory method of review may be used, unless Congress is found to have intended no further review. See Section 10(b) of the APA, 5 U.S.C. § 703.

---

13. See generally 4 Davis, note 8, *supra*, §§ 23:4–5; Developments Note, note 1, *supra*, at 909–11.

14. See, *e.g.,* 15 U.S.C. § 77i (Securities & Exchange Commission); 47 U.S.C. § 402 (Federal Communications Commission). See also Friendly, Federal Jurisdiction: A General View 34–35 (1973), listing a number of little known statutes authorizing direct review by the courts of appeals of specialized administrative actions.

For discussion of *which* circuit court may entertain a review proceeding, see Note, 93 Harv.L.Rev. 1735 (1980).

15. For discussion of the choice between review in the district courts and courts of appeals, see 4 Davis, note 8, *supra*, § 23:5; Currie & Goodman, *Judicial Review of Federal Administrative Action: Quest for the Optimum Forum*, 75 Colum.L.Rev. 1 (1975) Note, 88 Harv.L.Rev. 980 (1975).

16. Resolving a dispute among the lower courts, in 1977 the Supreme Court held that the Act does not give the federal courts subject matter jurisdiction. Califano v. Sanders, 430 U.S. 99 (1977). But (as the Court noted in Califano) Congress had amended § 1331 the year before to eliminate the amount in controversy requirement in suits against federal agencies or a federal official in his official capacity. See Paragraph (7), *supra*. Thus, there is now virtually always subject matter jurisdiction under § 1331 for a review proceeding under the APA. But see Ellis v. Blum, note 12, *supra*.

17. For an introduction to review under the APA, see Gellhorn, *et al.,* note 2, *supra*, at 995–1149.

18. See McAllister, *Statutory Roads to Review of Federal Administrative Orders*, 28 Calif.L.Rev. 129, 130–39 (1940).

(13) Without much discussion, courts generally have assumed that statutes creating statutory review mechanisms also contain corresponding waivers of sovereign immunity. See, *e.g.*, Huie v. Bowen, 788 F.2d 698, 705 (11th Cir.1986) ("42 U.S.C. § 405(g) operates as a waiver of sovereign immunity by giving the federal courts the right to review and modify or reverse the Secretary's decisions.") The assumption seems wholly justified, since it would have been futile for Congress to have established a statutory review mechanism that was barred by sovereign immunity.

The lower courts were long divided, however, on whether the APA constituted a waiver of sovereign immunity. See the cases compiled in S.Rep. No. 94–996, 94th Cong., 2d Sess at 10 n. 33 (1976). In 1976, Congress amended § 702 so as to effect a broad waiver of immunity in federal court suits seeking relief other than money damages against federal agencies. See Subsection 1(C)(3), *infra*.

(14) The many provisions enacted by Congress that have waived sovereign immunity as to particular kinds of actions may themselves be viewed as constituting a form of statutory review, providing remedies that would have been unavailable absent specific congressional action. Of these provisions, three stand out: (1) the 1976 amendment to the APA described in Paragraph (13), *supra;* (2) the Tucker Act, generally permitting suit against the United States on non-tort monetary claims; and (3) the Federal Tort Claims Act, generally permitting suit against the United States for common law torts committed by its employees. There are important exceptions and limitations to each of these three statutory schemes, which are discussed in Subsection 1(C), *infra*.

SUBSECTION B: THE SOVEREIGN IMMUNITY OF THE UNITED STATES AND ASSOCIATED REMEDIAL PROBLEMS

UNITED STATES v. LEE

106 U.S. 196, 1 S.Ct. 240, 27 L.Ed. 171 (1882).
Appeal from the Circuit Court for the Eastern District of Virginia.

[The United States purchased the Arlington, Virginia estate of General Robert E. Lee's wife, after an alleged failure to pay a $92 assessment under a tax to support the Civil War. The tax commissioners had refused a proffer of payment on behalf of the owner, under a rule (later held invalid) that only the owner in person could pay overdue taxes. The United States proceeded to use part of the estate for the Arlington Cemetery and a fort.

The Lees' son (who claimed title under his grandfather's will) filed an ejectment action in state court against the two federal officers who, under authority of the Secretary of War, had charge of the property. The defendants removed the action to the Circuit Court of the United States for the Eastern District of Virginia. Though the United States was not a party, the Attorney General filed a pleading in the Circuit Court seeking dismissal of the suit, stating that the United States possessed the property in the exercise of its sovereign and constitutional powers, and that "the court has no jurisdiction of the subject in controversy." Plaintiff's demurrer to this pleading was sustained, and after a jury trial, judgment for the plaintiff was entered.

Both the individual defendants and the United States filed a writ of error in the Supreme Court. The Solicitor General argued the case for the individual defendants and for the United States.]

MR. JUSTICE MILLER delivered the opinion of the Court.

[The Court expressed doubt that the United States, a non-party, could file a writ of error, but noted that the defendants' writ raised all the issues pressed by the United States. After upholding the jury's determination that the United States did not acquire valid title under the tax sale proceeding because of the illegal refusal to accept payment on behalf of the owner, the Court turned to the question of sovereign immunity.]

* * *

The counsel for plaintiffs in error and in behalf of the United States assert the proposition, that though it has been ascertained by the verdict of the jury, in which no error is found, that the plaintiff has the title to the land in controversy, and that what is set up in behalf of the United States is no title at all, the court can render no judgment in favor of the plaintiff against the defendants in the action, because the latter hold the property as officers and agents of the United States, and it is appropriated to lawful public uses.

This proposition rests on the principle that the United States cannot be lawfully sued without its consent in any case, and that no action can be maintained against any individual without such consent, where the judgment must depend on the right of the United States to property held by such persons as officers or agents for the government.

The first branch of this proposition is conceded to be the established law of this country and of this court at the present day; the second, as a necessary or proper deduction from the first, is denied.

In order to decide whether the inference is justified from what is conceded, it is necessary to ascertain, if we can, on what principle the exemption of the United States from a suit by one of its citizens is founded, and what limitations surround this exemption. In this, as in most other cases of like character, it will be found that the doctrine is derived from the laws and practices of our English ancestors; and * * * it is beyond question that from the time of Edward the First until now the King of England was not suable in the courts of that country, except where his consent had been given on petition of right * * *.

It is believed that this petition of right, as it has been practised and observed in the administration of justice in England, has been as efficient in securing the rights of suitors against the crown in all cases appropriate to judicial proceedings, as that which the law affords to the subjects of the King in legal controversies among themselves. * * *

There is in this country, however, no such thing as the petition of right, as there is no such thing as a kingly head to the nation, or to any of the States which compose it. There is vested in no officer or body the authority to consent that the State shall be sued except in the law-making power, which may give such consent on the terms it may choose to impose. Congress has created a court in which it has authorized suits to be brought against the United States, but has limited such suits to those arising on contract, with a few unimportant exceptions.

What were the reasons which forbid that the King should be sued in his own court, and how do they apply to the political body corporate which we call the United States of America? As regards the King, one reason given by the old judges was the absurdity of the King's sending a writ to himself to command the King to appear in the King's court. No such reason exists in our government, as process runs in the name of the President, and may be served on the Attorney–General, as was done in Chisholm v. Georgia, 2 Dall. 419. Nor can it be said that the government is degraded by appearing as a defendant in the courts of its own creation, because it is constantly appearing as a party in such courts, and submitting its rights as against the citizen to their judgment.

Mr. Justice Gray, of the Supreme Court of Massachusetts, in an able and learned opinion which exhausts the sources of information on this subject, says: "The broader reason is, that it would be inconsistent with the very idea of supreme executive power, and would endanger the performance of the public duties of the sovereign, to subject him to repeated suits as a matter of right, at the will of any citizen, and to submit to the judicial tribunals the control and disposition of his public property, his instruments and means of carrying on his government in war and in peace, and the money in his treasury." Briggs & Another v. Light Boats, 11 Allen (Mass.), 157. As no person in this government exercises supreme executive power, or performs the public duties of a sovereign, it is difficult to see on what solid foundation of principle the exemption from liability to suit rests. It seems most probable that it has been adopted in our courts as a part of the general doctrine of publicists, that the supreme power in every State, wherever it may reside, shall not be compelled, by process of courts of its own creation, to defend itself from assaults in those courts.

It is obvious that in our system of jurisprudence the principle is as applicable to each of the States as it is to the United States, except in those cases where by the Constitution a State of the Union may be sued in this court.

That the doctrine met with a doubtful reception in the early history of this court may be seen from the opinions of two of its justices in the case of Chisholm v. Georgia, where Mr. Justice Wilson, a member of the convention which framed the Constitution, after a learned examination of the laws of England and other states and kingdoms, sums up the result by saying: "We see nothing against, but much in favor of, the jurisdiction of this court over the State of Georgia, a party to this cause." Mr. Chief Justice Jay also considered the question as affected by the difference between a republican State like ours and a personal sovereign, and held that there is no reason why a state should not be sued, though doubting whether the United States would be subject to the same rule.

The first recognition of the general doctrine by this court is to be found in the case of Cohens v. Virginia, 6 Wheat. 264.

The terms in which Mr. Chief Justice Marshall there gives assent to the principle does not add much to its force. "The counsel for the defendant," he says, "has laid down the general proposition that a sovereign independent State is not suable except by its own consent." This general proposition, he adds, will not be controverted.

And while the exemption of the United States and of the several States from being subjected as defendants to ordinary actions in the courts has since that time been repeatedly asserted here, the principle has never been discussed or the reasons for it given, but it has always been treated as an established doctrine. United States v. Clarke, 8 Pet. 436; United States v. McLemore, 4 How. 286; Hill v. United States, 9 *id.* 386; Nations v. Johnson, 24 *id.* 195; The Siren, 7 Wall. 152; The Davis, 10 *id.* 15.

On the other hand, while acceding to the general proposition that in no court can the United States be sued directly by original process as a defendant, there is abundant evidence in the decisions of this court that the doctrine, if not absolutely limited to cases in which the United States are made defendants by name, is not permitted to interfere with the judicial enforcement of the established rights of plaintiffs when the United States is not a defendant or a necessary party to the suit.

But little weight can be given to the decisions of the English courts on this branch of the subject, for two reasons:—

1. In all cases where the title to property came into controversy between the crown and a subject, whether held in right of the person who was king or as representative of the nation, the petition of right presented a judicial remedy,—a remedy which this court, on full examination in a case which required it, held to be practical and efficient. There has been, therefore, no necessity for suing the officers or servants of the King who held possession of such property, when the issue could be made with the King himself as defendant.

2. Another reason of much greater weight is found in the vast difference in the essential character of the two governments as regards the source and the depositaries of power.

Notwithstanding the progress which has been made since the days of the Stuarts in stripping the crown of its powers and prerogatives, it remains true today that the monarch is looked upon with too much reverence to be subjected to the demands of the law as ordinary persons are, and the king-loving nation would be shocked at the spectacle of their Queen being turned out of her pleasure-garden by a writ of ejectment against the gardener.   *   *   *

Under our system the *people,* who are there called *subjects,* are the sovereign. Their rights, whether collective or individual, are not bound to give way to a sentiment of loyalty to the person of a monarch. The citizen here knows no person, however near to those in power, or however powerful himself, to whom he need yield the rights which the law secures to him when it is well administered. When he, in one of the courts of competent jurisdiction, has established his right to property, there is no reason why deference to any person, natural or artificial, not even the United States, should prevent him from using the means which the law gives him for the protection and enforcement of that right.

   *   *   *

The earliest case in this court in which the true rule is laid down, and which, bearing a close analogy to the one before us, seems decisive of it, is United States v. Peters, 5 Cranch, 115. In an admiralty proceeding, *   *   * the District Court of the United States for Pennsylvania *   *   * had decided that the libellants were entitled to the proceeds of the sale of a vessel condemned as prize of war, which had come to the possession of

David Rittenhouse as treasurer of Pennsylvania. The district judge had declined to issue any process to enforce his decree against the representatives of Rittenhouse, on the ground that the funds were held as the property of that State, and that as she could not be subjected to judicial process, neither could the officer who held the money in her right. * * * But, on an application therefor, a writ of *mandamus* to compel the judge of the District Court to proceed in the execution of his decree was granted. In delivering the opinion, Mr. Chief Justice Marshall says: "The State cannot be made a defendant to a suit brought by an individual, but it remains the duty of the courts of the United States to decide all cases brought before them by citizens of one State against citizens of a different State, when a State is not necessarily a defendant. In this case, the suit was not instituted against the State or its treasurer, but against the executrixes of David Rittenhouse, for the proceeds of a vessel condemned in the Court of Admiralty, which were admitted to be in their possession. If these proceeds had been the actual property of Pennsylvania, however wrongfully acquired, the disclosure of that fact would have presented a case on which it was unnecessary to give an opinion; *but it certainly can never be alleged that a mere suggestion of title in a State to property in possession of an individual must arrest the proceedings of the court, and prevent their looking into the suggestion and examining the validity of the title.*"

* * *

It may be said—in fact it is said—that the present case differs from the one in 5 Cranch, because the officers who are sued assert no personal possession, but are holding as the mere agents of the United States, while the executors of Rittenhouse held the money until a better right was established. But the very next case in this court of a similar character, Meigs v. McClung's Lessee, 9 Cranch, 11, shows that this distinction was not recognized as sound. The property sued for in that case was land on which the United States had a garrison erected at a cost of $30,000, and the defendants were the military officers in possession; and the very question now in issue was raised by these officers, who, according to the bill of exceptions, insisted that the action could not be maintained against them, "because the land was occupied by the United States troops, and the defendants as officers of the United States, for the benefit of the United States and by their direction." * * * The court below overruled these objections, and held that the title being in plaintiff he might recover, and that "if the land was private property the United States could not have intended to deprive the individual of it without making him compensation therefor."

Although the judgment of the Circuit Court was in favor of the plaintiff, and its result was to turn the soldiers and officers out of possession and deliver it to plaintiff, Mr. Chief Justice Marshall concludes his opinion in this emphatic language: "This court is unanimously and clearly of opinion that the Circuit Court committed no error in instructing the jury that the Indian title was extinguished to the land in controversy, *and that the plaintiff below might sustain his action.*"

We are unable to discover any difference whatever in regard to the objection we are now considering between this case and the one before us.

* * * *

Osborn v. Bank of United States, 9 Wheat. 738, is a leading case, remarkable in many respects, and in none more than in those resembling the one before us.

It was this: The State of Ohio having levied a tax upon the branch of the Bank of the United States located in that State, which the bank refused to pay, Osborn, auditor of the State, was about to proceed to collect said tax by a seizure of the money of the bank in its vaults, and an amended bill alleged that he had so seized $100,000, and while aware that an injunction had been issued by the Circuit Court of the United States on the prayer of the bank, the money so seized had been delivered to the treasurer of the State, Curry, and afterwards came to the possession of Sullivan, who had succeeded Curry as treasurer. Both Curry and Sullivan were made defendants as well as Osborn and his assistant, Harper.

One of the objections pressed with pertinacity all through the case to the jurisdiction of the court was the conceded fact that the State of Ohio, though not made a defendant to the bill, was the real party in interest. That all the parties sued were her officers,—her auditor, her treasurer, and their agents,—concerning acts done in their official character, and in obedience to her laws. It was conceded that the State could not be sued, and it was earnestly argued there, as here, that what could not be done directly could not be done by suing her officers. And it was insisted that while the State could not be brought before the court, it was a necessary party to the relief sought, namely, the return of the money and obedience to the injunction, and that the bill must be dismissed.

A few citations from the opinion of Mr. Chief Justice Marshall will show the views entertained by the court on the question thus raised.
* * *

[Marshall stated]: "The process is substantially, though not in form, against the State, * * * and the direct interest of the State in the suit as brought is admitted; and had it been in the power of the bank to make it a party, perhaps no decree ought to have been pronounced in the cause until the State was before the court. But this was not in the power of the bank, * * * and the very difficult question is to be decided, whether, in such a case, the court may act upon agents employed by the State and on the property in their hands." In answering this question he says: "A denial of jurisdiction forbids all inquiry into the nature of the case. It applies to cases perfectly clear in themselves; to cases where the government is in the exercise of its best-established and most essential powers, as well as to those which may be deemed questionable. It asserts that the agents of a State, alleging the authority of a law void in itself because repugnant to the Constitution, may arrest the execution of any law in the United States." Again: "The bank contends that in all cases in which jurisdiction depends on the character of the party, reference is made to the party on the record, not to one who may be interested, but is not shown by the record to be a party." "If this question were to be determined on the authority of English decisions, it is believed that no case can be adduced where any person can be considered as a party who is not made so in the record." Again: "In cases where a State is a party on the record, the question of jurisdiction is decided by inspection. If jurisdiction depend not on this plain fact, but on the interest of the State, what rule has the Constitution given by which this interest is to be measured? If no rule is given, is it to be settled by the court? If so, the curious anomaly is presented of a court examining the whole testimony of a cause, inquiring into and deciding on the extent of a State's interest, without having a right to exercise any jurisdiction in the case. Can this inquiry be made without the exercise of jurisdiction?"

The decree of the Circuit Court ordering a restitution of the money was affirmed.

* * *

* * * [A]s late as the case of Davis v. Gray, 16 Wall. 203, the case of Osborn v. Bank of United States is cited with approval as establishing these among other propositions: "Where the State is concerned, the State should be made a party, if it can be done. That it cannot be done, is a sufficient reason for the omission to do it, and the court may proceed to decree against the officers of the State in all respects as if the State were a party to the record. In deciding who are parties to the suit, the court will not look beyond the record. Making a State officer a party does not make the State a party, *although her law may have prompted his action, and the State may stand behind him as a real party in interest.* A State can be made a party only by shaping the bill expressly with that view, as where individuals or corporations are intended to be put in that relation to the case."

Though not prepared to say now that the court can proceed against the officer in "all respects" as if the State were a party, this may be taken as intimating in a general way the views of the court at that time.

* * *

This examination of the cases in this court establishes clearly this result: that the proposition that when an individual is sued in regard to property which he holds as officer or agent of the United States, his possession cannot be disturbed when that fact is brought to the attention of the court, has been overruled and denied in every case where it has been necessary to decide it, and that in many others where the record shows that the case as tried below actually and clearly presented that defence, it was neither urged by counsel nor considered by the court here, though, if it had been a good defence, it would have avoided the necessity of a long inquiry into plaintiff's title and of other perplexing questions, and have quickly disposed of the case. * * *

* * *

The fact that the property which is the subject of this controversy is devoted to public uses, is strongly urged as a reason why those who are so using it under the authority of the United States shall not be sued for its possession even by one who proves a clear title to that possession. In this connection many cases of imaginary evils have been suggested, if the contrary doctrine should prevail. Among these are a supposed seizure of vessels of war, and invasions of forts and arsenals of the United States. Hypothetical cases of great evils may be suggested by a particularly fruitful imagination in regard to almost every law upon which depend the rights of the individual or of the government, and if the existence of laws is to depend upon their capacity to withstand such criticism, the whole fabric of the law must fail.

The cases already cited * * * necessarily involved this question, for the property recovered by the plaintiff in the case of Meigs v. McClung was a garrison and barracks then in use for such purposes by the officers of the United States who were sued. * * *

The objection is also inconsistent with the principle involved in the last two clauses of article 5 of the amendments to the Constitution of the United States, whose language is: "That no person * * * shall be deprived of life, liberty, or property without due process of law, nor shall private property be taken for public use without just compensation."

Conceding that the property in controversy in this case is devoted to a proper public use, and that this has been done by those having authority to establish a cemetery and a fort, the verdict of the jury finds that it is and was the private property of the plaintiff, and was taken without any process of law and without any compensation. Undoubtedly those provisions of the Constitution are of that character which it is intended the courts shall enforce, when cases involving their operation and effect are brought before them. The instances in which the life and liberty of the citizen have been protected by the judicial writ of *habeas corpus* are too familiar to need citation, and many of these cases, indeed almost all of them, are those in which life or liberty was invaded by persons assuming to act under the authority of the government. Ex parte Milligan, 4 Wall. 2.

If this constitutional provision is a sufficient authority for the court to interfere to rescue a prisoner from the hands of those holding him under the asserted authority of the government, what reason is there that the same courts shall not give remedy to the citizen whose property has been seized without due process of law, and devoted to public use without just compensation?

Looking at the question upon principle, and apart from the authority of adjudged cases, we think it still clearer that this branch of the defence cannot be maintained. It seems to be opposed to all the principles upon which the rights of the citizen, when brought in collision with the acts of the government, must be determined. In such cases there is no safety for the citizen, except in the protection of the judicial tribunals, for rights which have been invaded by the officers of the government, professing to act in its name. * * *

* * *

No man in this country is so high that he is above the law. No officer of the law may set that law at defiance with impunity. All the officers of the government, from the highest to the lowest, are creatures of the law, and are bound to obey it.

* * *

Courts of justice are established, not only to decide upon the controverted rights of the citizens as against each other, but also upon rights in controversy between them and the government; and the docket of this court is crowded with controversies of the latter class.

Shall it be said, in the face of all this, and of the acknowledged right of the judiciary to decide in proper cases, statutes which have been passed by both branches of Congress and approved by the President to be unconstitutional, that the courts cannot give a remedy when the citizen has been deprived of his property by force, his estate seized and converted to the use of the government without lawful authority, without process of law, and without compensation, because the President has ordered it and his officers are in possession?

If such be the law of this country, it sanctions a tyranny which has no existence in the monarchies of Europe, nor in any other government which has a just claim to well-regulated liberty and the protection of personal rights.

* * *

The evils supposed to grow out of the possible interference of judicial action with the exercise of powers of the government essential to some of its most important operations, will be seen to be small indeed compared to this evil, and much diminished, if they do not wholly disappear, upon a recurrence to a few considerations.

One of these, of no little significance, is, that during the existence of the government for now nearly a century under the present Constitution, with this principle and the practice under it well established, no injury from it has come to that government. During this time at least two wars, so serious as to call into exercise all the powers and all the resources of the government, have been conducted to a successful issue. * * *

Another consideration is, that since the United States cannot be made a defendant to a suit concerning its property, and no judgment in any suit against an individual who has possession or control of such property can bind or conclude the government, * * * the government is always at liberty, notwithstanding any such judgment, to avail itself of all the remedies which the law allows to every person, natural or artificial, for the vindication and assertion of its rights. Hence, taking the present case as an illustration, the United States may proceed by a bill in chancery to quiet its title, in aid of which, if a proper case is made, a writ of injunction may be obtained. Or it may bring an action of ejectment, in which, on a direct issue between the United States as plaintiff, and the present plaintiff as defendant, the title of the United States could be judicially determined. Or, if satisfied that its title has been shown to be invalid, and it still desires to use the property, or any part of it, for the purposes to which it is now devoted, it may purchase such property by fair negotiation, or condemn it by a judicial proceeding, in which a just compensation shall be ascertained and paid according to the Constitution.

If it be said that the proposition here established may subject the property, the officers of the United States, and the performance of their indispensable functions to hostile proceedings in the State courts, the answer is, that no case can arise in a State court, where the interests, the property, the rights, or the authority of the Federal government may come in question, which cannot be removed into a court of the United States under existing laws. * * *

* * *

The Circuit Court was competent to decide the issues in this case between the parties that were before it; in the principles on which these issues were decided no error has been found; and its judgment is

Affirmed.

MR. JUSTICE GRAY, with whom concurred MR. CHIEF JUSTICE WAITE, MR. JUSTICE BRADLEY, and MR. JUSTICE WOODS, dissenting.

* * * The case so deeply affects the sovereignty of the United States, and its relations to the citizen, that it is fit to announce the grounds of our dissent.

* * *

This is not an action of trespass to recover damages only. Nor is it an action to recover property violently and suddenly wrested from the owner by officers of the government without its directions and without color of title in the government. But it is brought to recover possession of land which the United States have for years held, and still hold, for military and other public purposes, claiming title under a certificate of sale for direct taxes, which is declared by the act of Congress of June 7, 1862, c. 98, sect. 7, to be *prima facie* evidence of the regularity and validity of the sale and of the title of the purchaser * * *.

The principles upon which we are of opinion that the court below had no authority to try the question of the validity of the title of the United States in this action, and that this court has therefore no authority to pass upon that question, may be briefly stated.

The sovereign is not liable to be sued in any judicial tribunal without its consent. The sovereign cannot hold property except by agents. To maintain an action for the recovery of possession of property held by the sovereign through its agents, not claiming any title or right in themselves, but only as the representatives of the sovereign and in its behalf, is to maintain an action to recover possession of the property against the sovereign; and to invade such possession of the agents, by execution or other judicial process, is to invade the possession of the sovereign, and to disregard the fundamental maxim that the sovereign cannot be sued.

That maxim is not limited to a monarchy, but is of equal force in a republic. In the one, as in the other, it is essential to the common defence and general welfare that the sovereign should not, without its consent, be dispossessed by judicial process of forts, arsenals, military posts, and ships of war, necessary to guard the national existence against insurrection and invasion; of custom-houses and revenue cutters, employed in the collection of the revenue; or of light-houses and light-ships, established for the security of commerce with foreign nations and among the different parts of the country.

These principles appear to us to be axioms of public law, which would need no reference to authorities in their support, were it not for the exceeding importance and interest of the case, the great ability with which it has been argued, and the difference of opinion that has been manifested as to the extent and application of the precedents.

The exemption of the United States from being impleaded without their consent is, as has often been affirmed by this court, as absolute as that of the Crown of England or any other sovereign. * * *

The English authorities from the earliest to the latest times show that no action can be maintained to recover the title or possession of land held by the crown by its officers or servants, and leave no doubt that in a case like the one before us the proceedings would be stayed at the suggestion of the Attorney–General in behalf of the crown.

* * *

It was argued at the bar that the petition of right in England was in effect a suit against the crown. But the petition of right could never be maintained except after an application to the King and his consent granted. * * * The granting of the royal consent as a matter of course is but of very modern introduction in England. * * *

The English remedies of petition of right *monstrans de droit,* and traverse of office, were never introduced into this country as part of our common law; but in the American Colonies and States claims upon the government were commonly made by petition to the legislature. The inadequacy or the want of those remedies is no reason for maintaining a suit against the sovereign, in a form which is usual between private citizens, but which has not been expressly granted to them as against the sovereign. * * *

* * *

To maintain this action, independently of any legislation by Congress, is to declare that the exemption of the United States from being impleaded without their consent does not embrace lands held by a disputed title; to defeat the exemption from judicial process in the very cases in which it is of the utmost importance to the public that it should be upheld; and to compel the United States to submit to the determination of courts and juries the validity of their title to any land held and used for military, naval, commercial, revenue, or police purposes.

[Justice Gray then argued that several precedents relied upon by the plaintiff were distinguishable. Chisholm v. Georgia, 2 Dall. 419 (U.S.1793), which held that under the original Constitution a state could be sued by a citizen of another state in the Supreme Court's original jurisdiction, did not control because the opinions declined to affirm that the United States could be sued without its consent, and because Chisholm's holding had been set aside by the Eleventh Amendment. Peters, Osborn, and Davis v. Gray were all cases in which (i) the money was in the personal possession of the defendants rather than of the state, and/or (ii) the suit was one to enjoin federal constitutional violations. Finally, "[i]n the case on which the plaintiff principally relies," Meigs v. M'Clung's Lessee, 9 Cranch 11 (U.S.1815), "[n]o objection to the exercise of jurisdiction was made by the defendants or by the United States, or noticed by the Court"; "[h]ad the decision covered the question of jurisdiction," Chief Justice Marshall would surely have referred to it in Osborn.]

* * *

In the case of The Siren, 7 Wall. 152, the court said: "It is a familiar doctrine of the common law, that the sovereign cannot be sued in his own courts without his consent. The doctrine rests upon reasons of public policy; the inconvenience and danger which would follow from any different rule. It is obvious that the public service would be hindered, and the public safety endangered, if the supreme authority could be subjected to suit at the instance of every citizen, and consequently controlled in the use and disposition of the means required for the proper administration of the government. The exemption from direct suit is therefore without exception. This doctrine of the common law is equally applicable to the supreme authority of the nation,—the United States. They cannot be subjected to legal proceedings at law or in equity without their consent; and whoever institutes such proceedings must bring his case within the authority of some act of Congress." * * *

* * *

The view on which this court appears to have constantly acted, which reconciles all its decisions, and is in accord with the English authorities, is this: The objection to the exercise of jurisdiction over the sovereign or his property, in an action in which he is not a party to the record, is in the nature of a personal objection, which, if not suggested by the sovereign, may be presumed not to be intended to be insisted upon. If ejectment is brought by one citizen against another, the court *prima facie* has jurisdiction of the subject-matter and of the parties, and, if no objection is interposed in behalf of the sovereign, proceeds to judgment between the parties before it. If the property is in the possession of the defendants and not of the sovereign, an informal suggestion that it belongs to the sovereign will not defeat the action. But if the sovereign, in proper form and by sufficient proof, makes known to the court that he insists upon his exemption from suit, and that the property sued for is held by the nominal defendants exclusively for him and on his behalf as public property, the right of the plaintiff to prosecute the suit and the authority of the court to exercise jurisdiction over it cease, and all further proceedings must be stayed.

* * *

* * * [W]e are of opinion that the court had no authority to proceed to trial and judgment * * *.

PRELIMINARY NOTE ON THE SOVEREIGN IMMUNITY OF THE UNITED STATES

(1) What is the basis of the doctrine that bars suit against the United States in its own courts without its consent? [1] The traditional immunity of the sovereign, which survives by implication the grant of judicial power in Article III? See The Federalist, No. 81. The inability of the courts to enforce a judgment? See Jay, C.J., in Chisholm v. Georgia, 2 Dall. 419, 478 (U.S.1793), p. 1159, *infra*. The "logical and practical ground that there can be no legal right as against the authority that makes the law on which the right depends"? See Holmes, J., in Kawananakoa v. Polyblank, 205 U.S. 349, 353 (1907). The avoidance of interference with governmental functions and with the government's control over its instrumentalities, funds, and property? See Justice Gray's dissent in Lee.

Consider to what extent each of these purposes (a) is persuasive, (b) squares with the decided cases, or (c) might not better be served through other doctrines. Consider, also, whether the Supreme Court has misunderstood the historical foundations of sovereign immunity, and has given it too broad a scope, while professing at times to regard it with disfavor.

(2) Many scholars have argued that the doctrine of sovereign immunity, as it had evolved in England prior to 1789, was less about *whether* the Crown or its agents could be sued than about *how*. In some instances, officers could be sued for damages, enjoined from doing wrong, or compelled to perform their duty. In other cases, relief could be obtained through resort to the petition of right, which permitted suits directly against the

---

1. See generally Davis, *Suing the Government by Falsely Pretending to Sue an Officer*, 29 U.Chi.L.Rev. 435 (1962); Byse, *Proposed Reforms in Federal "Nonstatutory" Judicial Review: Sovereign Immunity, Indispensable Parties, Mandamus*, 75 Harv.L.Rev. 1479 (1962); Jaffe, *Suits Against Governments and Officers: Sovereign Immunity*, 77 Harv.L.Rev. 1 (1963); Cramton, *Nonstatutory Review of Federal Administrative Action: The Need for Statutory Reform of Sovereign Immunity, Subject Matter Jurisdiction, and Parties Defendant*, 68 Mich.L.Rev. 387 (1970); Engdahl, *Immunity and Accountability for Positive Government Wrongs*, 44 U.Colo.L.Rev. 1 (1972).

Crown; this remedy was cumbersome and required consent by the sovereign, but according to Professor Jaffe, "when it was necessary to sue the Crown *eo nomine* consent apparently was given as of course." Jaffe, note 1, *supra*, at 1; see also Borchard, *Governmental Responsibility in Tort, VI*, 36 Yale L.J. 1, 17–36 (1926). Professor Jaffe concluded that the "so-called doctrine of sovereign immunity was largely an abstract idea without determinative impact on the subject's right to relief against government illegality," and that "[t]he one serious deficiency [in English law] was the nonliability of the government for torts of its servants." Jaffe, *supra*, at 18–19.

Despite the Constitution's silence on immunity (and, indeed, Article III's grant of jurisdiction over "Controversies to which the United States shall be a Party"),[2] early Supreme Court decisions assumed that the United States could not be sued *eo nomine* absent congressional consent. Yet the doctrine developed largely in dicta,[3] without careful scrutiny of its underpinnings.

The earliest cases upholding a plea of immunity by the United States appear to be United States v. McLemore, 4 How. 286 (U.S.1846), and Hill v. United States, 9 How. 386 (U.S.1850). Both rejected bills in equity to enjoin the enforcement of judgments at law in favor of the United States, though the first pointed out that the relief sought could be obtained in the law action, and the second suggested that it might have been. Still, in 1882 Justice Miller could state in Lee that "the principle has never been discussed or the reasons for it given, but it has always been treated as an established doctrine."

Consider also Justice Millers' doubts about the doctrine's justification, especially in a constitutional republic. Do the lack of a monarch, the existence of a written constitution, and the institution of judicial review suggest a different role for sovereign immunity in this country than in England? See Chisholm v. Georgia, 2 Dall. 419, 453–66 (U.S.1793) (Wilson, J.).

(3) Sovereign immunity may play a more limited role in "takings" cases. In First English Evangelical Lutheran Church of Glendale v. County of Los Angeles, 107 S.Ct. 2378 (1987), the county had adopted an interim flood control measure prohibiting construction in an area that included land owned by the plaintiff church. The church sought damages in a state court inverse condemnation action. That suit was dismissed on the ground that a landowner may not obtain damages for a "regulatory taking" until the challenged regulation has been held invalid and the government has nevertheless decided that it should remain in effect. The Supreme Court reversed, 6–3, holding that the Fifth Amendment's Just Compensation Clause, as applied to the states through the Fourteenth Amendment, requires the provision of damages for harm suffered even before a challenged regulation has been judicially determined to constitute a "taking" of property. In an important footnote, the Court said (p. 2386 n. 9): "The

---

2. But *cf.* the discredited decision in Williams v. United States, p. 468 *supra*, which interpreted this language to apply only when the United States is a plaintiff.

3. Lee refers to a number of the early cases with such statements, including Chisholm v. Georgia, 2 Dall. 419, 478

(U.S.1793) (Jay, C.J.), Cohens v. Virginia, 6 Wheat. 264, 383, 392, 411–12 (U.S.1821), United States v. Clarke, 8 Pet. 436, 443 (U.S.1834), and Nations v. Johnson, 24 How. 195, 204–05 (U.S.1860). See also note 4, *infra*.

Solicitor General urges that the prohibitory nature of the Fifth Amendment, combined with principles of sovereign immunity, establishes that the Amendment itself is only a limitation on the power of the Government to act, not a remedial provision. The cases cited in the text, we think, refute the argument of the United States that 'the Constitution does not, of its own force, furnish a basis for a court to award money damages against the government.' Though arising in various factual and jurisdictional settings, these cases make clear that it is the Constitution that dictates the remedy for interference with property rights amounting to a taking."

In determining whether the United States is immune from damages liability, is there a basis in the constitutional text or in other considerations for treating actions under the Just Compensation Clause differently from actions under other constitutional provisions? See Young, *Congressional Regulation of Federal Courts' Jurisdiction and Processes: United States v. Klein Revisited*, 1981 Wis.L.Rev. 1189, 1224–33.

(4) As noted in the Lee case, the English practice of royal consent was transformed in this country into the notion that the government is immune from suit absent consent of the legislature. When Lee was decided, congressional consent was limited to certain money claims against the United States cognizable in the Court of Claims.[4] Today, the scope of various congressional consents is far broader, though the courts have generally insisted that a waiver by Congress be unmistakably expressed. See generally Sec. 1(C), *infra*.

(5) In The Siren, 7 Wall. 152 (U.S.1868), a ship captured by the United States rammed another ship while sailing under a navy crew. The United States filed its libel in prize against the captured ship, which was condemned, and the sale proceeds were deposited with the assistant treasurer of the United States. The owners of the other ship then asserted a claim for a maritime tort against the prize ship. The Supreme Court held that the captured vessel was guilty of a maritime tort and subject to a lien for damages extending also to its proceeds, but that the lien could not be enforced against the United States without its consent. By seeking a judicial decree of sale, however, the government had consented to an adjudication of the tort claim and to its payment out of the sale proceeds.[5]

Note that the theory of The Siren—that the tort claim was valid, but unenforceable against the United States until its suit put the claimed property into issue—is inconsistent with Justice Holmes' conception, Paragraph (1), *supra*, that sovereign immunity flows from the absence of any underlying obligation of the sovereign. Evidently recognizing this inconsistency, Justice Holmes later stated that the discussion in The Siren of unenforceable liens was just a means of stating that any claims against the sovereign were "ethical only," but that when the sovereign came into court it consented to see justice done with regard to the subject matter of the suit. The Western Maid, 257 U.S. 419, 433–34 (1922). In United States v. The Thekla, 266 U.S. 328, 339–40 (1924), also involving a collision of two ships, Holmes wrote: "The trial of such cases in the ordinary course is upon libel and cross libel, consolidated under authority of statute. * * *

4. Many of the early dicta asserting the immunity of the sovereign are found in cases advocating strict construction of the Court of Claims Act. See Lee, 106 U.S. at 227 (Gray, J., dissenting).

5. For a similar holding, see The Davis, 10 Wall. 15 (U.S.1869).

[T]he subject matter is the collision, rather than the vessel first libelled. * * * The libel in such a case is like a bill for an account, which imports an offer to pay the balance if it should turn out against the party bringing the bill."

Is it useful or realistic to view the substantive law applied in rendering a judgment against the United States as having been created retroactively by the waiver of sovereign immunity? Is this conception tenable when the waiver of immunity in The Siren arose from a government official's presentation of a claim in court?

(6) When the United States sues as plaintiff, does sovereign immunity bar a defensive credit in favor of the defendant? In 1797, Congress provided that, with certain exceptions, in actions by the United states "no claim for a credit shall be admitted, upon trial" unless previously presented for examination to the accounting officers of the government and by them disallowed. Act of March 3, 1797, § 4, 1 Stat. 512, 515, which survives in substance in 28 U.S.C. § 2406. A series of Supreme Court cases held that, this procedural requirement being satisfied, the defendant was entitled to at least a purely defensive credit against any judgment for the United States as plaintiff.[6]

Though some language in Supreme Court cases could be read to interpret § 2406 as itself a waiver of sovereign immunity, see, *e.g.,* United States v. Shaw, 309 U.S. 495, 501 (1940), the Court in United States v. United States Fidelity & Guaranty Co., 309 U.S. 506, 511 (1940) noted the government's concession of the validity of a claim "upon the theory that a defendant may, without statutory authority, recoup on a counterclaim an amount equal to the principal claim."

Yet not all counterclaims may qualify for a defensive credit. Despite some broad language in dictum in United States v. Shaw, *supra,* that "cross-claims are allowed to the amount of the government's claim, where the government voluntarily sues," 309 U.S. at 501, the courts have permitted a defensive claim in recoupment, which arises out of the same transaction,[7] while refusing to permit a counterclaim (including a set-off) that arises from a distinct transaction.[8]

What underlies the cases allowing a defensive credit? The need for economical resolution of an entire dispute? A sense of injustice that only one party may litigate a claim arising from the transaction? Are these justifications consistent with the courts' routine insistence that immunity

6. See, *e.g.,* United States v. Wilkins, 6 Wheat. 135, 143–45 (U.S.1821); United States v. Ringgold, 8 Pet. 150, 163–64 (U.S.1834).

7. See, *e.g.,* United States v. Industrial Crane & Mfg. Corp., 492 F.2d 772, 774 (5th Cir.1974); Federal Sav. & Loan Ins. Corp. v. Williams, 599 F.Supp. 1184, 1209–10 (D.Md.1984).

8. See, *e.g.,* United States v. Timmons, 672 F.2d 1373, 1379–80 (11th Cir.1982); EEOC v. First Nat. Bank of Jackson, 614 F.2d 1004, 1008 (5th Cir.1980). But see United States v. Buchanan, 8 How. 83, 105 (U.S.1850) (the statute extends "to matters even distinct from the cause of action, if

only such as the defendant is entitled to a credit on, whether equitable or legal. * * * But any wrongs or torts done, and any unliquidated damages claimed, have never been permitted as a set-off"). See generally Comment, 11 U.Mich.J.L.Ref. 110 (1977).

Also barred, no doubt because not truly defensive in nature, are counterclaims seeking relief different in kind from that sought by the United States. United States v. 2,116 Boxes of Boned Beef, 726 F.2d 1481, 1490–91 (10th Cir.1984); United States v. Ameco Electronic Corp., 224 F.Supp. 783, 786 (E.D.N.Y.1963). See Paragraph (7), *infra.*

can be waived only by Congress, not by an officer of the United States? Compare the rule that, even absent waiver by Congress, the United States as defendant can waive venue requirements in the same way as any other litigant. Industrial Addition Ass'n v. Commissioner, 323 U.S. 310, 313–14 (1945).

(7) A defensive credit requires no affirmative enforcement against the United States. But may a court enter judgment for the defendant if a balance is found due the defendant on his counterclaim? United States v. Eckford, 6 Wall. 484 (U.S.1867), found such a judgment improper and hence unenforceable, but that decision appeared to conflict with The Thekla, Paragraph (5), *supra*. The conflict was resolved in United States v. Shaw, 309 U.S. 495 (1940), in which Michigan courts allowed a claim by the United States against an estate and a larger cross-claim by the estate against the United States, and entered a judgment (on which enforcement might later have been sought in the Court of Claims) against the United States for the difference. The Supreme Court reversed the judgment, rejecting the estate's argument that when the United States seeks judicial aid, it assumes the position of a private suitor subject to the full jurisdiction of the court (p. 502): "It is not our right to extend the waiver of sovereign immunity more broadly than has been directed by the Congress. * * * Against the background of complete immunity we find no Congressional action modifying the immunity rule in favor of cross-actions beyond the amount necessary as a set-off.

"The Thekla turns upon a relationship characteristic of claims for collision in admiralty but entirely absent in claims and cross-claims in settlement of estates. * * * Libels and cross-libels for collision are one litigation and give rise to one liability. * * *"

Note the interaction of Shaw and the Federal Rules of Civil Procedure. Rule 13(a) provides for compulsory counterclaims; Rule 13(d) provides: "These rules shall not be construed to enlarge beyond the limits now fixed by law the right to assert counterclaims or to claim credits against the United States or an officer or agency thereof." These provisions, together with Shaw, seem to require a defendant to split a compulsory counterclaim that exceeds the amount of the United States' primary claim, using part as a defensive credit and seeking the balance in (for example) the United States Claims Court pursuant to a congressional waiver of immunity. In the subsequent action, could the claimant be barred by the doctrine of claim preclusion? See Shaw, *supra*, at 504–05, and United States v. United States Fidelity & Guaranty Co., 309 U.S. 506 (1940), which imply not. Could the United States be precluded from relitigating issues on which it lost in the first action? See Hahn v. United States, p. 1155 note 27, *infra*.

(8) May a defendant obtain an affirmative judgment against the United States on a counterclaim that would be within the jurisdiction of the district court, pursuant to a congressional waiver of sovereign immunity, had it been brought as an original action? Many courts said no, asserting that the consent to sue is expressly limited to direct actions, and that some statutes deal explicitly with counterclaims by, but not against, the United States. Recent cases have tended to permit counterclaims and third party claims to the extent that the court would have had jurisdiction over them had they been filed as direct actions. The cases are collected in 14 Wright, Miller, and Cooper, Federal Practice & Procedure § 3654, at 203–06 (1985).

The ALI Study 38–39, 255–59 (1969) not only endorsed the latter view, but also proposed that courts be permitted by statute to enter affirmative relief on any claim arising from the same transaction or occurrence "of which any court of the United States would have jurisdiction"—a step that the courts had been unwilling to take on their own without legislative authorization. See, *e.g.,* Nassau Smelting & Refining Works, Ltd. v. United States, 266 U.S. 101 (1924). See generally Comment, note 8, *supra.* Is the government's filing a lawsuit sufficient reason to transfer to the district courts jurisdiction that would otherwise be vested exclusively in the United States Claims Court, see Sec. 1(C), *infra?*

(9) In United States v. Alcea Band of Tillamooks, 341 U.S. 48, 49 (1951), the Court said:

"It is the 'traditional rule' that interest on claims against the United States cannot be recovered in the absence of an express provision to the contrary in the relevant statute or contract. This rule precludes an award of interest even though a statute should direct an award of 'just compensation' for a particular taking. The only exception arises when the taking entitles the claimant to just compensation under the Fifth Amendment."

Since a suit seeking to compel the payment of treasury funds will almost surely be considered to be against the United States, the question of liability for interest usually arises in construing a statute that waives immunity with respect to a particular claim. When Congress has provided that justice should be done in the main matter, is there any persuasive reason for assuming an intention to deny the usual incidents of justice? A few cases have exhibited this liberal attitude, see, *e.g.,* Standard Oil Co. v. United States, 267 U.S. 76, 79 (1925) (rule against interest inapplicable where government assumed the status of a private commercial enterprise); United States v. The Thekla, Paragraph (5), *supra* (award permitted with little explanation), but the contrary approach is well-entrenched, particularly in recent cases, see, *e.g.,* Library of Congress v. Shaw, 106 S.Ct. 2957, 2960 (1986); Boston Sand & Gravel Co. v. United States, 278 U.S. 41 (1928).

In some instances, Congress has reinforced the traditional rule by expressly precluding interest awards. See 28 U.S.C. § 2516, prohibiting the allowance of interest on a judgment of the United States Claims Court; *id.* § 2674, governing actions under the Federal Tort Claims Act. In many others, Congress has expressly authorized the allowance of interest.[9]

(10) In the absence of an authorizing statute, the United States is never liable for costs or attorney's fees.[10] Here, too, once the United States may be sued, why isn't a court warranted in treating it like any other litigant?

In 1966 an amendment to 28 U.S.C. § 2412 permitted costs (other than attorney's fees) to be awarded in any civil action "brought by or against the United States or any agency of any official * * * acting in his official capacity," except as "otherwise specifically provided by statute."[11]

---

9. See, *e.g.,* 28 U.S.C. §§ 2411 (tax refund suits), 2516(b) (post-judgment interest on Claims Court judgments); 41 U.S.C. § 611 (interest on claims under the Contract Disputes Act).

10. See, *e.g.,* United States v. Bodcaw Co., 440 U.S. 202, 203–04 n. 3 (1979) (per curiam). The early cases laid down the rule without explanation, see, *e.g.,* United States v. Hooe, 3 Cranch 73, 90–91 (U.S.1805), but by the mid-nineteenth century it was regarded as a corollary of sovereign immunity, see, *e.g.,* United States v. McLemore, 4 How. 286, 288 (U.S.1846).

11. Allowable costs are set forth in 28 U.S.C. § 1920.

The rule as to attorney's fees has also been changed by statute. See the Equal Access to Justice Act of 1980, codified at 28 U.S.C. § 2412. Section 2412(b) authorizes the award of attorney's fees against the United States in the same circumstances in which courts would award fees against private parties. In addition, § 2412(d) provides that courts *shall* award attorney's fees (ordinarily not to exceed $75/hour) to certain persons who prevail against the United States in non-tort, non-tax civil actions, unless the United States' position was "substantially justified" or "special circumstances make an award unjust." There are, moreover, many specific statutory provisions authorizing the award of attorney's fees in particular kinds of actions. See generally Bennett, Winning Attorneys' Fees From the U.S. Government (1986).

(11) See generally, on the interpretation of statutes consenting to suits against the United States or its instrumentalities, Sec. 1(C), *infra*.

NOTE ON SOVEREIGN IMMUNITY IN SUITS AGAINST FEDERAL OFFICERS

(1) Despite the doctrine of sovereign immunity, the idea of official responsibility to law has received extensive judicial development. As had been true in England, many suits in the federal courts in which the nominal defendant was an officer, rather than the government or an executive agency, were deemed to be against the individual and not the sovereign—even though the suit challenged the legality of official action, and the relief granted required him to take action affecting the government.

Many decisions, like Lee, referred interchangeably to decisions in suits against federal officials and suits against state officials brought in federal court. The history of these cases in the nineteenth century is not easily described, as the disagreements between Justices Miller and Gray show. And there may be differences between suits against a state and against the United States; at a minimum, in the former context, one must consider the pertinence of the Eleventh Amendment, which has been interpreted as embodying a principle of state sovereign immunity in federal court actions. See generally Sec. 2(A), *infra*.

(2) In Little v. Barreme, 2 Cranch 170, 179 (U.S.1804), the Supreme Court affirmed a damage judgment against an American naval captain who, in seizing a Danish vessel, had acted under presidential orders issued through the Secretary of Navy and purportedly pursuant to an act of Congress. The Court (per Marshall, C.J.) found that the orders had been based upon a misconstruction of the statute, and that the seizure was thus a trespass unauthorized by federal law. Despite the presidential direction, the need for military obedience, and the harshness of holding the officer personally liable, the Court ruled that the captain's claim of official authority could not shield an act that, absent lawful authorization, constituted a simple trespass.

The same principle of official accountability was applied by Chief Justice Marshall in Meigs v. McClung's Lessee, 9 Cranch 11 (U.S.1815), United States v. Peters, 5 Cranch 115 (U.S.1809), and Osborn v. Bank of the United States, 9 Wheat. 738 (U.S.1824), all discussed in Lee. In these cases, the claimant was permitted, in a suit against an officer, to recover property to which the government claimed title. (Peters and Osborn were suits against state officials.)

In Osborn, the Chief Justice admitted that the state was an interested party in the suit,[1] but said that since the Eleventh Amendment deprived the Bank of power to name Ohio as a defendant, the case could proceed without the state as a party (pp. 846–47). Marshall ruled, however, that the Eleventh Amendment was not implicated (p. 856): "It may, we think, be laid down as a rule which admits of no exception, that, in all cases where jurisdiction depends upon the party, it is the party named in the record. Consequently, the 11th amendment * * * is, of necessity, limited to those suits in which a state is a party on the record." As late as Davis v. Gray, 83 U.S. 203, 220 (1872), the Court suggested adherence to the party of record rule.[2]

Lee, while finding no barrier to suit, suggests that immunity may not be "absolutely limited to cases in which the United States are made defendants by name." The Court clearly rejected the party of record test in In re Ayers, 123 U.S. 443, 487 (1887), p. 1180, *infra*, and in this respect has followed Ayers ever since.

(3) Rejection of the party of record rule, however, left in place a broad scope for suits against officers, so long as it could be shown that the officer himself had committed an actionable wrong. The officials in Lee, Peters, Osborn, and Little v. Barreme committed acts that would have been trespasses at common law. That the act was committed under color of office was not an automatic defense. The Court explained the underlying theory in Philadelphia Co. v. Stimson, 223 U.S. 605 (1912), in which a property owner sued to enjoin the Secretary of War from prosecuting him criminally for constructing a wharf beyond a harbor line that the defendant was authorized by Congress to fix, and that the plaintiff alleged had been unlawfully established (pp. 619–20) (citations omitted):

"The exemption of the United States from suit does not protect its officers from personal liability to persons whose rights of property they have wrongfully invaded. And in case of any injury threatened by his illegal action, the officer cannot claim immunity from injunction process. The principle has frequently been applied with respect to state officers seeking to enforce unconstitutional enactments. And it is equally applicable to a Federal officer acting in excess of his authority or under an authority not validly conferred.

"The complainant did not ask the court to interfere with the official discretion of the Secretary of War, but challenged his authority to do the things of which complaint was made. The suit rests upon the charge of abuse of power, and its merits must be determined accordingly; it is not a suit against the United States."

The officer could not only be enjoined from causing harm (as in Philadelphia Co.), but could even be compelled to perform affirmative acts if he was shown to be required by law to discharge some duty. See, *e.g.*,

1. Doesn't this admission undercut Justice Gray's effort in Lee to distinguish Osborn?

2. At the same time, Marshall had signaled a retreat from the broad party of record rule in the complicated proceedings in Governor of Georgia v. Madrazo, 1 Pet. 110 (U.S.1828), p. 1162, *infra*.

Wilbur v. United States ex rel. Krushnic, 280 U.S. 306 (1930); Tindal v. Wesley, 167 U.S. 204 (1897).

Does Philadelphia Co. import into the law of sovereign immunity the ministerial/discretionary distinction of mandamus jurisprudence? See pp. 1092–95, *supra.*

In contrast to the liability of officers engaging in tortious conduct, officers agreeing to contracts on behalf of the government would not, under principles of the general law, be personally liable if the government committed a breach. Thus, suit for breach of contract could be brought only against the government—and such an action was barred by immunity. See, *e.g.,* Wells v. Roper, 246 U.S. 335 (1918); Louisiana ex rel. Elliott v. Jumel, 107 U.S. 711, 721, 727 (1883), p. 1179, infra. See generally Engdahl, *Immunity and Accountability for Positive Government Wrongs,* 44 U.Colo.L. Rev. 1, 1–21 (1972). The particular sensitivity of suits involving breach of government contracts was clear from the resistance to such suits brought by bondholders of state governments following both the Revolutionary and Civil Wars. The Eleventh Amendment was enacted, and later interpreted, to protect state governments from federal jurisdiction to impose just such liability. See pp. 1159–66, 1179–82, *infra.*

(4) After surveying the evolution of suits against officers, Professor Jaffe concluded that "the sensitive areas—the areas where consent to suit [was] likely to be required—[were] those involving the enforcement of contracts, treasury liability for tort, and the adjudication of interests in property which [had] come unsullied by tort into the bosom of the government." Jaffe, *Suits Against Governments and Officers: Sovereign Immunity,* 77 Harv.L.Rev. 1, 29 (1963). The cases are by no means easy to square. For helpful discussions, see, in addition to Jaffe, *supra,* Cramton, *Nonstatutory Review of Federal Administrative Action: The Need for Statutory Reform of Sovereign Immunity, Subject Matter Jurisdiction, and Parties Defendant,* 68 Mich.L.Rev. 387, 402–04 (1970), and Engdahl, Paragraph (3), *supra,* at 20–21, 32–34.

Is it useful to ask whether a particular action against government officials is "really" against the government? Government interests are fully implicated in Lee and other actions not barred by sovereign immunity. Isn't it a fiction that such suits against officers are not against the state—in the sense of implicating important government interests? Or is the fiction that there ever existed a broad doctrine of sovereign immunity that, outside of a few specific areas, barred relief at the behest of individuals complaining of government illegality?

(5) In Ex parte Young, 209 U.S. 123 (1908), p. 1173, *infra,* the Supreme Court upheld the authority of a federal circuit court to enjoin a state attorney general from instituting any suits to impose sanctions for violation of a state statute that allegedly conflicted with the Fourteenth Amendment. Although the threatened conduct of the defendant would not have been an actionable wrong under general principles of the common law, the court in effect found that there was a judicially created federal right of action for equitable relief from violations of the Constitution. The Court also held that such an action was not barred by the Eleventh Amendment. See generally pp. 1173–94, *infra.*

Young remains a pivotal decision in the interpretation of the Eleventh Amendment and *state* sovereign immunity. And its principle has been easily absorbed in suits challenging *federal* official action as unconstitutional. See, *e.g.*, Shields v. Utah Idaho Central R.R., 305 U.S. 177, 183–84 (1938); Rickert Rice Mills, Inc. v. Fontenot, 297 U.S. 110 (1936).

(6) The Supreme Court has held that an action seeking the writ of mandamus is not barred by sovereign immunity. See Houston v. Ormes, 252 U.S. 469, 472–74 (1920); Minnesota v. Hitchcock, 185 U.S. 373, 386 (1902). Why should this be?[3] In Vishnevsky v. United States, 581 F.2d 1249, 1255–56 (7th Cir.1978), the court, in approving a writ of mandamus to compel IRS officials to credit plaintiffs with an overpayment of taxes, noted a long line of Supreme Court and lower cases issuing mandamus to compel payment of funds out of the federal treasury, even absent consent by Congress.

NOTE ON THE LARSON CASE AND SUBSEQUENT DECISIONS CONCERNING SOVEREIGN IMMUNITY IN SUITS CHALLENGING FEDERAL OFFICIAL ACTION

(1) In Larson v. Domestic & Foreign Commerce Corp., 337 U.S. 682 (1949), the Supreme Court rendered an important decision, much-criticized ever since, on the sovereign immunity of the United States. The facts were described in Justice Frankfurter's dissenting opinion as follows (pp. 706–07):

"The Government had some surplus coal at an Army camp in Texas. On March 11, 1947, the War Assets Administration, through the Regional Office in Dallas, Texas, invited a bid from the plaintiff, respondent here, for purchase of the coal. The Dallas office expressed thus its approval of the bid submitted by the plaintiff: ' * * * your terms of placing $17,500 with the First National Bank, Dallas, Texas, for payment upon presentation of our invoices to said bank are accepted.' Thereupon the plaintiff arranged for resale of the coal and its shipment abroad. On April 1, 1947, the Dallas office wired the plaintiff that unless the sum of $17,500 was deposited in the First National Bank in Dallas by noon April 4, 'the sale will be cancelled and other disposition made.' Though claiming that this demand was in the teeth of the contract, the plaintiff arranged for an irrevocable letter of credit payable through the First National Bank of Dallas to the War Assets Administration. The Dallas office now insisted that unless cash was deposited 'the sale of 10,000 tons of coal * * * will be cancelled ten days from this date.' That office disregarded further endeavors by the plaintiff to adjust the matter, and on April 16 it informed the plaintiff that the contract was cancelled. Having learned that the coal was to be sold to another concern, the plaintiff, asserting ownership in the coal and the threat of irreparable damage, brought this suit in the District Court of the United States for the District of Columbia to restrain the War Assets Administrator and those under his control from transferring the coal to any other person than the plaintiff."

The district court granted a motion to dismiss the complaint on the ground, among others, that the court did not have jurisdiction because the

---

3. Recall that in England mandamus and the other prerogative writs were issued by the King's Bench, over which the King once presided. His presence eventually became only a fiction, but the writ was still regarded as an indirect command of the sovereign himself. See Developments Note, p. 1091 note 1, *supra*, at 846.

suit was one against the United States. The court of appeals reversed, holding that the jurisdiction of the court depended on whether or not title to the coal had passed. The Supreme Court, with Justice Rutledge concurring only in the result and Justices Frankfurter, Burton, and Jackson dissenting, reversed "with directions that the complaint be dismissed".

Chief Justice Vinson, speaking for the Court, said (p. 695):

"We hold that if the actions of an officer do not conflict with the terms of his valid statutory authority, then they are the actions of the sovereign, whether or not they are tortious under general law, if they would be regarded as the actions of a private principal under the normal rules of agency. A Government officer is not thereby necessarily immunized from liability, if his action is such that a liability would be imposed by the general law of torts. But the action itself cannot be enjoined or directed, since it is also the action of the sovereign."

"The relief sought in this case," the Court explained (pp. 688–89), "was not the payment of damages by the individual defendant. To the contrary, it was asked that the court order the War Assets Administrator, his agents, assistants, deputies and employees and all persons acting under their direction, not to sell the coal involved and not to deliver it to anyone other than the respondent.[9] The district court held that this was relief against the sovereign and therefore dismissed the suit. We agree."

The plaintiff contended, in the Court's words, that "[i]f an officer of the Government wrongly takes or holds specific property to which the plaintiff has title, then his taking or holding is a tort, and illegal as a matter of general law, whether or not it be within his delegated powers. He may therefore be sued individually to prevent the illegal taking or to recover the property illegally held" (p. 692). The Court responded that this theory was "erroneous," and "confuse[d] the doctrine of sovereign immunity with the requirement that a plaintiff state a cause of action. It is a prerequisite to the maintenance of any action for specific relief that the plaintiff claim an invasion of his legal rights, either past or threatened. He must, therefore, allege conduct which is illegal in the sense that the respondent suggests. * * * But, in a suit against an agency of the sovereign, it is not sufficient that he make such a claim. Since the sovereign may not be sued, it must also appear that the action to be restrained or directed is not action of the sovereign. The mere allegation that the officer, acting officially, wrongfully holds property to which the plaintiff has title does not meet that requirement. * * *" (p. 693).

Chief Justice Vinson recognized that the plaintiff would be entitled to maintain its action if it were asserting either that the defendant were seeking to enforce an unconstitutional enactment or "acting in excess of his

---

"9. The complaint also asked for declaratory relief even more clearly directed at the sovereign. It was asked that the court declare that the sale of this coal * * * is still valid and in effect. The Administrator, an agent for a disclosed principal, was not a party to the contract of sale. See 2 Restatement, Agency (1933) § 320. The request for an adjudication of the validity of the sale was thus, even in form, a request for an adjudication against the sovereign. Such a declaration of the rights of the respondent vis-a-vis the United States would clearly have been beyond the court's jurisdiction. See Stanley v. Schwalby, 162 U.S. 255 (1896). We do not rest our conclusion here on the request for such a declaration, since the district court could have granted only the injunctive relief requested."

authority or under an authority not validly conferred [11]." Here, however, he said (p. 703):

"* * * The very basis of the respondent's action is that the Administrator was an officer of the Government, validly appointed to administer its sales program and therefore authorized to enter, through his subordinates, into a binding contract concerning the sale of the Government's coal. There is no allegation of any statutory limitation on his powers as a sales agent. In the absence of such a limitation he, like any other sales agent, had the power and the duty to construe such contracts and to refuse delivery in cases in which he believed that the contract terms had not been complied with. His action in so doing in this case was, therefore, within his authority even if, for purposes of decision here, we assume that his construction was wrong and that title to the coal had, in fact, passed to the respondent under the contract. There is no claim that his action constituted an unconstitutional taking.[27] It was, therefore, inescapably the action of the United States and the effort to enjoin it must fail as an effort to enjoin the United States."

The Chief Justice explained United States v. Lee as resting on "the assumed lack of the defendants' constitutional authority to hold the land against the plaintiff" and the further assumption "that if title had been in the plaintiff the taking of the property by the defendants would be a taking without just compensation and, therefore, an unconstitutional action." [17] And he added (pp. 697–702):

"* * * The cases which followed Lee's do not require a different result. There are a great number of such cases and, as this Court has itself remarked, it is not 'an easy matter to reconcile all the decisions of the court in this class of cases.' With only one possible exception, however, specific relief in connection with property held or injured by officers of the sovereign acting in the name of the sovereign has been granted only where there was a claim that the taking of the property or the injury to it was not the action of the sovereign because unconstitutional or beyond the officer's statutory powers. Certainly, the Court has repeatedly stated these to be the cases in which such relief could be granted. A contrary doctrine was stated in Goltra v. Weeks, 271 U.S. 536 (1926). In that case the United States had leased barges to the plaintiff under a contract which gave it a right to repossess under certain conditions. Believing that those conditions existed, officers of the Government attempted to repossess the barges. The

"11. Of course, a suit may fail, as one against the sovereign, even if it is claimed that the officer being sued has acted unconstitutionally or beyond his statutory powers, if the relief requested can not be granted by merely ordering the cessation of the conduct complained of but will require affirmative action by the sovereign or the disposition of unquestionably sovereign property. North Carolina v. Temple, 134 U.S. 22 (1890)."

"27. There could not be since the respondent admittedly has a remedy, in a suit for breach of contract, in the Court of Claims. Such a suit, indeed, would be based on the theory that the action of the Administrator in refusing to deliver *was* the action of the United States and thus

created a cause of action against it for breach of contract. Only if the Administrator's action was within his authority could such a suit be maintained. Hooe v. United States, 218 U.S. 322 (1910). It has never been suggested that a suit in the Court of Claims for breach of an express contract could be defeated because the action of the officer in breaching it constituted a tort and was therefore 'unauthorized.' "

"17. The Lee case was decided in 1882. At that time there clearly was no remedy available by which he could have obtained compensation for the taking of his land. Whether compensation could be obtained today in such a case is, of course, not the issue here."

Court held that a suit to enjoin them from doing so was not a suit against the United States. The Court said that the taking of the barges was alleged to be a trespass and hence 'illegal.' Therefore, the actions of the officers were personal actions, not the actions of the United States, and injunction against them would not be injunction against the United States. 271 U.S. at 544. For this conclusion the Court relied entirely upon the opinion of Mr. Justice Hughes in Philadelphia Co. v. Stimson, 223 U.S. 605 (1912). The reliance was misplaced, since the opinion in that case clearly and specifically rested on the claim that there was a lack of statutory power to act, not simply on a claim of tortious injury to the plaintiff.

"Opposed to the rationale of the Goltra opinion is the decision, by Mr. Justice Holmes, in Goldberg v. Daniels, 231 U.S. 218 (1913). There, as here, the question concerned the effect of a claimed sale of Government surplus property. The plaintiff submitted a sealed bid for a surplus war vessel, accompanied in that case by a certified check as payment in advance. When the bids were opened his was the highest. The Secretary of the Navy, however, determined not to accept the bid and refused to deliver the vessel. The plaintiff brought mandamus. He alleged that the sale was complete when the bids were opened and that the ownership of the vessel was therefore in him, and he asked that the Secretary be compelled to deliver it. The lower courts examined the details of the transaction and concluded that the sale was not complete until the Secretary announced his acceptance of the bid. On appeal here, it was expressly held that it was not necessary to decide whether the lower courts were correct. The suit must fail as one against the United States, the Court said, whether or not the sale was complete. In so holding the Court said, in effect, that the question of title was immaterial to the court's jurisdiction. Wrongful the Secretary's conduct might be, but a suit to relieve the wrong by obtaining the vessel would interfere with the sovereign behind its back and hence must fail.

"Both cases are pressed upon us. The petitioner argues, and correctly, that the result in the Goldberg case calls for a similar result in this case—a dismissal of the suit for want of jurisdiction. The respondent argues, with equal correctness, that the theory of the Goltra opinion—that an allegation that the actions of Government officers are wrongful under general law is sufficient to show that they are 'unauthorized'—calls for an affirmance of the decision below. Since we must therefore resolve the conflict in doctrine we adhere to the rule applied in the Goldberg case and to the principle which has been frequently repeated by this Court, both before and after the Goltra case: the action of an officer of the sovereign (be it holding, taking or otherwise legally affecting the plaintiff's property) can be regarded as so 'illegal' as to permit a suit for specific relief against the officer as an individual only if it is not within the officer's statutory powers or, if within those powers, only if the powers, or their exercise in the particular case, are constitutionally void.[26] "

"26. In addition to Goltra v. Weeks, *supra*, three other cases are argued to be inconsistent with this principle [, of which one was Land v. Dollar, 330 U.S. 731 (1947).]

* * *

"In Land v. Dollar, where the plaintiffs alleged that they were entitled to stock held by the Maritime Commission because the stock was received by the Commission only as a pledge, it was contended that any other kind of acquisition would constitute a violation of § 207 of the Merchant Marine Act, which allegedly gave the Commission authority to acquire stock only as collateral. The complaint therefore al-

Concluding, the Chief Justice said (pp. 703–05):

"It is argued that the principle of sovereign immunity is an archaic hangover not consonant with modern morality and that it should therefore be limited wherever possible. There may be substance in such a viewpoint as applied to suits for damages. The Congress has increasingly permitted such suits to be maintained against the sovereign and we should give hospitable scope to that trend. But the reasoning is not applicable to suits for specific relief. For, it is one thing to provide a method by which a citizen may be compensated for a wrong done to him by the Government. It is a far different matter to permit a court to exercise its compulsive powers to restrain the Government from acting, or to compel it to act. There are the strongest reasons of public policy for the rule that such relief cannot be had against the sovereign. The Government, as representative of the community as a whole, cannot be stopped in its tracks by any plaintiff who presents a disputed question of property or contract right.

* * *

"There are limits, of course. Under our constitutional system, certain rights are protected against governmental action and, if such rights are infringed by the actions of officers of the Government, it is proper that the courts have the power to grant relief against those actions. But in the absence of a claim of constitutional limitation, the necessity of permitting the Government to carry out its functions unhampered by direct judicial intervention outweighs the possible disadvantage to the citizen in being relegated to the recovery of money damages after the event.

"It is argued that a sales agency, such as the War Assets Administration, is not the type of agency which requires the protection from direct judicial interference which the doctrine of sovereign immunity confers. We do not doubt that there may be some activities of the Government which do not require such protection. There are others in which the necessity of immunity is apparent. But it is not for this Court to examine the necessity in each case. That is a function of the Congress. The Congress has, in many cases, entrusted the business of the Government to agencies which may contract in their own names and which are subject to suit in their own names. In other cases it has permitted suits for damages, but, significantly, not for specific relief, in the Court of Claims. The differentiations as to remedy which the Congress has erected would be rendered nugatory if the basis on which they rest—the assumed immunity of the sovereign from suit in the absence of consent—were undermined by an unwarranted extension of the Lee doctrine."

Justice Douglas concurred in Larson (337 U.S. at p. 705) on the ground "that the principles announced by the Court are the ones which should govern the selling of government property. Less strict applications of those principles would cause intolerable interference with public administration.

leged that the members of the Commission acted in excess of their authority as public officers. 330 U.S. at 738."

[Ed.] Consider whether this description of Land v. Dollar is accurate in light of the following statement of the Court in that case (pp. 735–36): "The allegations of the complaint, if proved, would establish that [defendant officials] are unlawfully withholding [plaintiffs'] property under the claim that it belongs to the United States. That conclusion would follow if either of [plaintiffs'] contentions were established: (1) that the Commission had no authority to purchase the shares or acquire them outright; or (2) that, even though such authority existed, the * * * contract resulted not in an outright transfer but in a pledge of the shares."

To make the right to sue the officer turn on whether by the law of sales title had passed to the buyer would clog this governmental function with intolerable burdens."

In a dissenting opinion more than matching in length the long opinion of the Chief Justice, Justice Frankfurter undertook a comprehensive analysis of the cases against governmental agents, both state and federal, in which the defense of sovereign immunity was raised. He put them in four groups, as follows (pp. 709–10):

"(1) Cases in which the plaintiff seeks an interest in property which concededly, even under the allegation of the complaint, belongs to the government, or calls for an assertion of what is unquestionably official authority.

"(2) Cases in which action to the legal detriment of a plaintiff is taken by an official justifying his action under an unconstitutional statute.

"(3) Cases in which a plaintiff suffers a legal detriment through action of an officer who has exceeded his statutory authority.

"(4) Cases in which an officer seeks shelter behind statutory authority or some other sovereign command for the commission of a common-law tort."

On the point directly in issue, Justice Frankfurter said, *inter alia* (pp. 716–18, 726–27):

"The fourth category of cases brings us to the controversy immediately before the Court and demands detailed analysis. These are the cases, it will be recalled, in which an official seeks to screen himself behind the sovereign in a suit against him based on the commission of a common-law tort. * * * A plaintiff's right 'under general law to recover possession of specific property wrongfully withheld' may be enforced against an official and he cannot plead the sovereign's immunity against the court's power to afford a remedy. Land v. Dollar, 330 U.S. 731, 736; Belknap v. Schild, 161 U.S. 10, 18–20; Hopkins v. Clemson Agricultural College, 221 U.S. 636, 643.

"The starting point of this line of cases is United States v. Lee, 106 U.S. 196. * * *

"While there was some talk in the Lee opinion, as well as in some of the cases which followed that decision, about taking property without compensation, the basis of the action was that the defendants were ordinary tortfeasors, not immunized for their wrongful invasion of the plaintiff's property by the fact that they claimed to have acted on behalf of the Government. This group of cases is quite different from those in which the plaintiff claimed that the defendant, purporting to act in an official capacity, exceeded the authority which a statute conferred upon him, or that the statute under which he justified his action exceeded the power of the legislature to confer such authority. In this class of cases the governmental agent had valid statutory authority but he determined erroneously the condition which had to exist before he could exercise it. The basis of action in this class of cases is the defendant's personal responsibility for the commission of a tort, which makes it irrelevant that by waiving the case against the governmental agent the plaintiff might choose to sue the Government as for a contract. * * *

" * * * When a pleading raises a substantial claim that the defendant is wrongfully withholding from the plaintiff property belonging to him, the defendant has not heretofore been permitted to shield himself behind the immunity of the sovereign. Only after the preliminary question of ownership is decided against the plaintiff does the claim of sovereign immunity come into play. Only then can it be said that the decree will affect property of the sovereign.

"The Court tries to explain away Land v. Dollar, [see footnote 26 of the Court's opinion] by suggesting that it was a case where the officers acted in excess of their authority, although the opinion in that case makes clear that, even if the officers had authority, there still remained the issue whether the shares of stock were sold or pledged to the United States. If the latter, to hold after satisfaction of the pledge would be tortious, and the stock could be recovered in the suit against the defendants. The Court seeks to avoid the decision in Ickes v. Fox, [300 U.S. 82 (1937)], by saying that the ground of decision is not made clear. But not even these most dubious arguments can explain away Goltra v. Weeks, 271 U.S. 536. Accordingly, the Court impliedly overrules that decision. No reason of policy is vouchsafed for overruling a decision that carries the authority that the Goltra case does. * * * The Goltra case is now thrown into the discard because it did not cite Goldberg v. Daniels, 231 U.S. 218. * * *

"* * * Goldberg was not cited in Goltra for the conclusive reason that Goldberg had nothing to do with Goltra. In the Goldberg case the Court, on the basis of the pleadings before it, was dealing with a suit where 'the United States is the owner in possession of the vessel.' 231 U.S. 218, 221–222. Accordingly, the suit was not for a tortious withholding of the plaintiff's property and the Government's immunity barred suit. In Goltra, on the contrary, the claim was for the delivery of property allegedly belonging to the plaintiff and tortiously in possession of the individual defendants, and the Court held that the plaintiff is entitled to establish such a claim as he can, 'even though the United States for whom they [the defendants] may profess to act is not a party and can not be made one.' 271 U.S. at 544. That is this case."

(2) Observe that historically the most plainly permissible of all types of actions against government officials, federal or state, are those in which (a) the plaintiff seeks to enjoin conduct or threatened conduct which, if not officially justified, would constitute a common law tort, and (b) the relief sought can be given by simply directing the defendant to abstain from what he is doing or threatening to do. Notice how the majority opinion in Larson succeeds in obscuring the rationale even of this heretofore clear type of action. Is "the Government, as representative of the community as a whole" any the less "stopped in its tracks" in such cases than it would have been in Larson?

Has it ever been thought relevant to inquire in such cases whether the action of the representative is action for which the government would be held responsible, if it were subject to suit? Indeed, is there in the whole domain of the law any support for the repeated assumption of the Larson opinion that the responsibility of the agent and of the principal for wrongful action are somehow mutually exclusive categories?

Upon what ground of reason or history can the question whether an action is, in substance, against the government be made to depend upon whether the law under which an official's conduct is wrongful is statutory or judge-made? Notice the effort in the Chief Justice's opinion to derive a kind of implied exception to the implied constitutional prohibition of suits against the government in cases in which other constitutional guarantees are at stake. But notice that at this point the opinion has forgotten about cases involving only "excess of statutory authority".

(3) Apart from cases in which the United States is named as a party defendant, the clearest class of cases open to the defense of sovereign immunity under the pre-Larson law were actions to establish an interest in, or satisfy a claim out of, property of the United States, where the United States admittedly had title and the property was in possession of its officers or agents.[1] Should the Larson situation have been assimilated to these property cases, as Justice Douglas suggested? Is there ground for saying that the action, in substance, was one to enforce a merely equitable claim for fulfillment of the contract of sale and hence in principle governed by these decisions, as well as by the cases holding that the United States' consent to be sued for damages in contract actions does not extend to specific relief?

Or might the case have been more successfully handled as presenting, not a question of immunity, but a question only of the propriety of the remedy sought as a matter of sound exercise of the chancellor's discretion?

(4) Notice that the Larson decision not only limits United States v. Lee but overrides a whole series of pre-Lee cases holding that a claim of legal title to property may be tried in an action against a United States officer holding the property under a claim of title of the United States. In many of these cases it would have been difficult, would it not, to dig up a pretense of an issue either of constitutional power or statutory authority? Were these cases, and the post-Lee cases discussed in the Larson dissent, unsound in principle?

(5) Notice that Justice Frankfurter, in the first category of his Larson dissent, commingles the property cases with "cases in which the plaintiff * * * calls for an assertion of what is unquestionably official authority." To what extent should an action be deemed to be in substance against the United States because the relief sought requires the affirmative exercise of official authority? Consider the history of mandamus against federal officials. See pp. 1091–95, *supra*.

What of footnote 11 in Larson? Isn't Professor Jaffe correct that it can be reconciled with prior cases only by reading "may" in that footnote "as *may* and not as *must* "? Jaffe, *Suits Against Governments and Officers: Sovereign Immunity*, 77 Harv.L.Rev. 1, 34 (1963). Is the footnote nonetheless misleading? Consider Hawaii v. Gordon, Paragraph (9), *infra*.

(6) Actions against federal officers have often been dismissed on the ground, easily confused with sovereign immunity, that the United States was an indispenable party and could not be joined.[2] Whether anything of substance hinges on the difference in stated grounds for dismissal has been

---

1. See, *e.g.*, The Siren, p. 1110, *supra*, 7 Wall. at 154; Stanley v. Schwalby, 162 U.S. 255, 272 (1896); Oregon v. Hitchcock, 202 U.S. 60, 69 (1906); Cummings v. Deutsche Bank, 300 U.S. 115 (1937); Minnesota v. United States, 305 U.S. 382 (1939); United States v. Alabama, 313 U.S. 274, 282 (1941); Maricopa County v. Valley Nat. Bank, 318 U.S. 357, 362 (1943).

Compare, with these cases, Carr v. United States, 98 U.S. 433 (1878), much of the language of which was disapproved in United States v. Lee.

2. See, *e.g.*, Mine Safety Appliances Co. v. Forrestal, 326 U.S. 371, 374–75 (1945); Louisiana v. Garfield, 211 U.S. 70, 77–78 (1908).

a controverted point.[3] The debate has been preempted by a 1976 congressional enactment broadly waiving sovereign immunity, and providing that the United States may but need not be named as a party defendant in suits seeking relief other than money damages. (See Sec. 1(C), *infra*).[4]

(7) Is it material in determining whether an action is in substance against the United States that the United States will be bound by the judgment? As the Lee case notes, the traditional rule held that the United States is not bound by a judgment in an in personam suit against one of its officers. See, *e.g.,* Carr v. United States, 98 U.S. 433 (1878); Hussey v. United States, 222 U.S. 88 (1911); *cf.* Tait v. Western Maryland Ry., 289 U.S. 620, 627 (1933).[5]

Under modern preclusion law, an interested person who is active in the conduct of litigation is ordinarily bound by the judgment, at least by way of issue preclusion, even though he is not a party. Applying this rule in a case in which the government had employed special counsel to prosecute an action concerning title to Indian lands, the Eighth Circuit held that "the United States is as effectually concluded as if it were a party to the judgment." United States v. Candelaria, 16 F.2d 559, 562–63 (8th Cir. 1926), following United States v. Candelaria, 271 U.S. 432, 444 (1926). Accord, Montana v. United States, 440 U.S. 147 (1979) (United States is bound, in its federal court challenge to a state tax, by a state court judgment in a suit filed by a private party but in which the United States had the "laboring oar"); see also Drummond v. United States, 324 U.S. 316, 318 (1945).

There appears to be no reason why sovereign immunity should bar the application of this rule to bind the United States to a judgment in a prior action against one of its officers, when (as is customary) the government employed counsel to defend or assist in the officer's defense. See 28 U.S.C. §§ 517–18 (authorizing the Attorney General to direct Justice Department lawyers to conduct any federal court case in which the United States is interested). In Duncan v. United States, 667 F.2d 36, 38 (Ct.Cl.1981), the court held that plaintiffs, having previously obtained a federal court injunction forbidding unlawful action of the Secretary of the Interior, could estop the United States, in a separate suit for damages in the Court of Claims, from denying the illegality of the action. That result is especially

---

3. Would courts promote clarity by not referring to the indispensable party rule in suits against government officers when the essential objection is that the suit is substantially against the United States? See Block, *Suits Against Government Officers and the Sovereign Immunity Doctrine,* 59 Harv.L.Rev. 1060, 1064–66 (1946). Or, as the Second Edition of this book responded, would it be preferable "to return to Marshall's position in [Osborn] and [Madrazo, see p. 1162, *infra*,] * * * that the only actions against the United States are actions in which the United States is named as a party defendant or in which the court is asked to enter a judgment affecting the title to property admitted or found to belong to the United States and in its possession, or compelling the expenditure of public funds, while recognizing that there may be other instances in which the interests of the United States are so intimately involved that the action cannot in justice proceed in its absence?"

4. A different and nettlesome problem of parties defendant, involving the substitution of successors in office, appears to have been cured by a 1961 amendment to Rule 25(d) of the Federal Rules of Civil Procedure. See generally 7C Wright, Miller & Kane, Federal Practice & Procedure §§ 1959–61 (1986).

5. There appears to be little doubt that a subordinate federal official may be precluded by a prior judgment either against another federal official (with whom the defendant in the subsequent action is deemed to be in privity), see Tait, *supra,* or against the United States or one of its agencies, see Sunshine Anthracite Coal Co. v. Adkins, 310 U.S. 381, 402–03 (1940).

appropriate in view of the 1976 statute mentioned in Paragraph (6), *supra*, which treats suits for specific relief nominally against officers as indistinguishable from suits against the United States.

(8) The Supreme Court has revisited the question of sovereign immunity in several decisions since Larson. In Malone v. Bowdoin, 369 U.S. 643 (1962), the plaintiffs sought to eject a federal forest service officer from certain land to which both plaintiffs and the federal government claimed title. The Supreme Court held that sovereign immunity barred the action (pp. 646–48):

"In a number of later cases, arising over the years in a variety of factual situations, the principles of the Lee case were approved. But in several other cases which came to the Court during the same period, it was held that suits against government agents, specifically affecting property in which the United States claimed an interest, were barred by the doctrine of sovereign immunity. ∗ ∗ ∗

"∗ ∗ ∗ [I]n Larson the Court, aware that it was called upon to 'resolve the conflict in doctrine' (337 U.S., at 701), thoroughly reviewed the many prior decisions, and made an informed and carefully considered choice between the seemingly conflicting precedents. ∗ ∗ ∗

"While not expressly overruling United States v. Lee, *supra*, the Court in Larson ∗ ∗ ∗ interpreted Lee as simply 'a specific application of the constitutional exception to the doctrine of sovereign immunity.' 337 U.S., at 696. So construed, the Lee case has continuing validity only 'where there is a claim that the holding constitutes an unconstitutional taking of property without just compensation.' *Id.*, at 697.

"No such claim has been advanced in the present case. Nor has it been asserted that the petitioner was exceeding his delegated powers as an officer of the United States in occupying the land in question, or that he was in possession of the land in anything other than his official capacity. This suit, therefore, is not within the class of cases in which, under Larson, specific relief can be obtained against a government officer. ∗ ∗ ∗ "

Justice Douglas in dissent argued that Lee controlled (pp. 650–53):

"[T]he Larson case was a suit for specific performance of a contract to sell coal, a matter that courts had long left to damage suits. As I said in my separate concurrence in that case, any other rule would 'clog' government procurement 'with intolerable burdens.' 337 U.S., at 705.

"Ejectment, on the other hand, is the classic form of action to try title. It takes place in the locality where the land is located. No judges are better qualified to try it than the local judges. ∗ ∗ ∗ If the [United States] is aggrieved by the state or federal court ruling on title, it can bring its arsenal of power into play. Eminent domain—with the power immediately to take possession—is available.

"If, however, the citizen must bow to the doctrine of sovereign immunity, he is precluded from any relief except a suit for damages ∗ ∗ ∗. This places the advantage with an all-powerful Government, not with the citizen. He may, as the Court says, go into court and get the value of his property. But he does not get his property, even though we assume, as we must, that the Government is not the rightful claimant.

∗ ∗ ∗

"The balance between the convenience of the citizen and the management of public affairs is a recurring consideration in suits determining when and where a citizen can sue a government official. The balance is, in my view, on the side of the citizen where he claims realty in the Government's possession and where there are ready means of adjudicating the title. If legal title is actually in the claimant, if the action of the official in taking possession under authority of the United States is *ultra vires,* what objectionable interference with governmental functions can be said to exist?"

Since the government claimed no authority to condemn the property if it belonged to the plaintiffs, was not their assertion of title an "assertion that the officer was exceeding his delegated powers"? Is it conceivable that the case turned merely on the plaintiffs' failure to make this allegation in terms? Is the result of the decision to force the government to pay compensation for property it has no wish to occupy unless its claim of title is well founded?[6]

(9) Hawaii v. Gordon, 373 U.S. 57 (1963), concerned the Hawaii Statehood Act, which in § 5(e) required the President to determine whether certain federal properties were no longer needed by the United States, and, if not, to convey them to the State of Hawaii. The President's designee, the Director of the Bureau of the Budget, decided that § 5(e) did not apply to lands obtained by the United States through purchase, condemnation, or gift. He therefore did not determine whether any such land was "needed." Hawaii brought an original action in the Supreme Court seeking to obtain an order requiring the Director to withdraw his decision, to exercise his discretion in determining whether certain land acquired through condemnation was needed and, if not needed, to convey it to Hawaii. The Court in a brief per curiam opinion held that the complaint should be dismissed as a suit against the United States.

Does the judgment rest upon the premise that the nature of the decision called for by the statute precluded its interpretation to confer a legal right? Can the disposition on immunity grounds mean that that question never was considered? Are there other reasons why Hawaii should be made to seek its remedy from Congress rather than from the Court? [7]

(10) Dugan v. Rank, 372 U.S. 609 (1963), was a suit to enjoin the United States and officers of the Bureau of Reclamation from impounding water behind Friant Dam, a part of the Central Valley Project in California, on the ground that this retention interfered with the plaintiffs' rights to the use of the water downstream.

6. Compare, *e.g.,* Udall v. Tallman, 380 U.S. 1 (1965), an action "in the nature of mandamus" to compel the Secretary of the Interior to issue oil and gas leases on certain federal lands, the plaintiffs claiming to be entitled to the leases as the first qualified applicant under 30 U.S.C. § 226. The Secretary's rejection of the claim on the ground that prior leases had been validly granted was sustained by the Supreme Court after an elaborate review of the legal issues involved. No claim of sovereign immunity was advanced or considered. Scalia, *Sovereign Immunity and Nonstatu-* *tory Review of Federal Administrative Action: Some Conclusions From the Public-Lands Cases,* 68 Mich.L.Rev. 867 (1970), suggests that the case is distinguishable from Malone only in terms of the long tradition of judicial review in public land grant cases. Is it not sufficient explanation that the statute conferred a right to the lease if the claimant was the first applicant?

7. Is the decision consistent with the explanation of Udall v. Tallman suggested in Scalia, note 6, *supra?*

The Supreme Court unanimously held that the suit against the officers was barred by sovereign immunity. In the Court's view, Congress had authorized physical seizure of the water and had limited the relief available to affected persons to a suit against the United States under the Tucker Act. The Court continued (pp. 620–21): "The general rule is that a suit is against the sovereign if 'the judgment sought would expend itself on the public treasury or domain, or interfere with the public administration,' [citing Land v. Dollar], or if the effect of the judgment would be 'to restrain the Government from acting, or to compel it to act.' * * * To require the full natural flow of the river to go through the dam would force the abandonment of this portion of a project which has not only been fully authorized by the Congress but paid for through its continuing appropriations. Moreover, it would prevent the fulfillment of the contracts made by the United States with the Water and Utility Districts. * * * The Government would, indeed, be 'stopped in its tracks. . . . ' [citing Larson]."

Discussing an alternative form of relief requiring federal construction of additional dams to meet the plaintiffs' needs, the Court said (pp. 621–23): "The physical solution has no less direct effect. The Secretary of the Interior, the President and the Congress have authorized the Project as now constructed and operated. Its plans do not include the 10 additional dams required by the physical solution to be built at government expense. The judgment, therefore, would not only 'interfere with the public administration' but also 'expend itself on the public treasury. . . . ' [citing Land v. Dollar]. Moreover, the decree would require the United States—contrary to the mandate of the Congress—to dispose of valuable irrigation water and deprive it of the full use and control of its reclamation facilities. It is therefore readily apparent that the relief granted operates against the United States.

"* * * The power to seize which was granted here had no limitation placed upon it by the Congress. * * * It follows that if any part of respondents' claimed water rights were invaded it amounted to an interference therewith and a taking thereof—not a trespass."

What was the significance of the finding of immunity if its existence turned on the antecedent conclusions that Congress had authorized the seizure, subject to suit under the Tucker Act for just compensation, and that the seizure on these terms was constitutional?

Remember when you read the Youngstown case, which follows this Note, Dugan's "general rule" that a suit is against the sovereign if the judgment sought would interfere with the public administration, etc. Far from explaining the decisions, does the formulation even describe them?

(11) The Supreme Court's decision in Pennhurst State School & Hosp. v. Halderman, 465 U.S. 89 (1984), pp. 1195–1204, *infra*, involved a state's Eleventh Amendment immunity, but it relied heavily upon Larson. The opinion in Pennhurst characterized as a fiction the view that an injunction against an officer (even when he is acting outside his constitutional or statutory authority) does not run against the government, and said "it may well be wondered what principled basis there is to the ultra vires doctrine as it was set forth in Larson * * *. * * * For present purposes, we do no more than question the continued vitality of the ultra vires doctrine in the Eleventh Amendment context" (pp. 114–15 n. 25). The Court held that

the doctrine was in any event a narrow one that did not permit the suit in question.

Should this language be read as calling into question even the limited scope for equitable relief against government officers that Larson and subsequent decisions seemed to permit?

YOUNGSTOWN SHEET & TUBE CO. v. SAWYER

343 U.S. 579, 72 S.Ct. 863, 96 L.Ed. 1153 (1952).
Certiorari to the United States Court of Appeals for the
District of Columbia Circuit.

MR. JUSTICE BLACK delivered the opinion of the Court.

We are asked to decide whether the President was acting within his constitutional power when he issued an order directing the Secretary of Commerce to take possession of and operate most of the Nation's steel mills. The mill owners argue that the President's order amounts to lawmaking, a legislative function which the Constitution has expressly confided to the Congress and not to the President. The Government's position is that the order was made on findings of the President that his action was necessary to avert a national catastrophe which would inevitably result from a stoppage of steel production, and that in meeting this grave emergency the President was acting within the aggregate of his constitutional powers as the Nation's Chief Executive and the Commander in Chief of the Armed Forces of the United States. The issue emerges here from the following series of events:

In the latter part of 1951, a dispute arose between the steel companies and their employees over terms and conditions that should be included in new collective bargaining agreements. Long-continued conferences failed to resolve the dispute. On December 18, 1951, the employees' representative, United Steelworkers of America, C.I.O., gave notice of an intention to strike when the existing bargaining agreements expired on December 31. The Federal Mediation and Conciliation Service then intervened in an effort to get labor and management to agree. This failing, the President on December 22, 1951, referred the dispute to the Federal Wage Stabilization Board to investigate and make recommendations for fair and equitable terms of settlement. This Board's report resulted in no settlement. On April 4, 1952, the Union gave notice of a nation-wide strike called to begin at 12:01 a.m. April 9. The indispensability of steel as a component of substantially all weapons and other war materials led the President to believe that the proposed work stoppage would immediately jeopardize our national defense and that governmental seizure of the steel mills was necessary in order to assure the continued availability of steel. Reciting these considerations for his action, the President, a few hours before the strike was to begin, issued Executive Order 10340 * * *. The order directed the Secretary of Commerce to take possession of most of the steel mills and keep them running. The Secretary immediately issued his own possessory orders, calling upon the presidents of the various seized companies to serve as operating managers for the United States. They were directed to carry on their activities in accordance with regulations and directions of the Secretary. The next morning the President sent a message to Congress reporting his action. Cong.Rec., April 9, 1952, p. 3962.

Twelve days later he sent a second message. Cong.Rec., April 21, 1952, p. 4192. Congress has taken no action.

Obeying the Secretary's orders under protest, the companies brought proceedings against him in the District Court. Their complaints charged that the seizure was not authorized by an act of Congress or by any constitutional provisions. The District Court was asked to declare the orders of the President and the Secretary invalid and to issue preliminary and permanent injunctions restraining their enforcement. Opposing the motion for preliminary injunction, the United States asserted that a strike disrupting steel production for even a brief period would so endanger the well-being and safety of the Nation that the President had "inherent power" to do what he had done—power "supported by the Constitution, by historical precedent, and by court decisions." The Government also contended that in any event no preliminary injunction should be issued because the companies had made no showing that their available legal remedies were inadequate or that their injuries from seizure would be irreparable. Holding against the Government on all points, the District Court on April 30 issued a preliminary injunction restraining the Secretary from "continuing the seizure and possession of the plants ＊ ＊ ＊ and from acting under the purported authority of Executive Order No. 10340." 103 F.Supp. 569. On the same day the Court of Appeals stayed the District Court's injunction. 197 F.2d 582. Deeming it best that the issues raised be promptly decided by this Court, we granted certiorari on May 3 and set the cause for argument on May 12. 343 U.S. 937.

Two crucial issues have developed: *First.* Should final determination of the constitutional validity of the President's order be made in this case which has proceeded no further than the preliminary injunction stage? *Second.* If so, is the seizure order within the constitutional power of the President?

I.

It is urged that there were nonconstitutional grounds upon which the District Court could have denied the preliminary injunction and thus have followed the customary judicial practice of declining to reach and decide constitutional questions until compelled to do so. On this basis it is argued that equity's extraordinary injunctive relief should have been denied because (a) seizure of the companies' properties did not inflict irreparable damages, and (b) there were available legal remedies adequate to afford compensation for any possible damages which they might suffer. While separately argued by the Government, these two contentions are here closely related, if not identical. Arguments as to both rest in large part on the Government's claim that should the seizure ultimately be held unlawful, the companies could recover full compensation in the Court of Claims for the unlawful taking. Prior cases in this Court have cast doubt on the right to recover in the Court of Claims on account of properties unlawfully taken by government officials for public use as these properties were alleged to have been. See, *e.g.,* Hooe v. United States, 218 U.S. 322, 335–336; United States v. North American Transportation & Trading Co., 253 U.S. 330, 333. But see Larson v. Domestic & Foreign Commerce Corp., 337 U.S. 682, 701–702. Moreover, seizure and governmental operation of these going businesses were bound to result in many present and future damages of such nature as to be difficult, if not incapable, of measurement. Viewing the case this way, and in the light of the facts presented, the District Court saw no reason for delaying decision of the constitutional validity of the orders. We agree with the District Court and can see no reason why that question was not ripe for determination on the record presented. We shall therefore consider and determine that question now.

II.

The President's power, if any, to issue the order must stem either from an act of Congress or from the Constitution itself. There is no statute that expressly authorizes the President to take possession of property as he did here. Nor is there any act of Congress to which our attention has been directed from which such a power can fairly be implied. Indeed, we do not understand the Government to rely on statutory authorization for this seizure. There are two statutes which do authorize the President to take both personal and real property under certain conditions.[2] However, the Government admits that these conditions were not met and that the President's order was not rooted in either of the statutes. The Government refers to the seizure provisions of one of these statutes (§ 201(b) of the Defense Production Act) as "much too cumbersome, involved, and time-consuming for the crisis which was at hand."

Moreover, the use of the seizure technique to solve labor disputes in order to prevent work stoppages was not only unauthorized by any congressional enactment; prior to this controversy, Congress had refused to adopt that method of settling labor disputes. When the Taft–Hartley Act was under consideration in 1947, Congress rejected an amendment which would have authorized such governmental seizures in cases of emergency. Apparently it was thought that the technique of seizure, like that of compulsory arbitration, would interfere with the process of collective bargaining. Consequently, the plan Congress adopted in that Act did not provide for seizure under any circumstances. Instead, the plan sought to bring about settlements by use of the customary devices of mediation, conciliation, investigation by boards of inquiry, and public reports. In some instances temporary injunctions were authorized to provide cooling-off periods. All this failing, unions were left free to strike after a secret vote by employees as to whether they wished to accept their employers' final settlement offer.

It is clear that if the President had authority to issue the order he did, it must be found in some provision of the Constitution. And it is not claimed that express constitutional language grants this power to the President. The contention is that presidential power should be implied from the aggregate of his powers under the Constitution. Particular reliance is placed on provisions in Article II which say that "the executive Power shall be vested in a President * * *"; that "he shall take Care that the Laws be faithfully executed"; and that he "shall be Commander in Chief of the Army and Navy of the United States."

The order cannot properly be sustained as an exercise of the President's military power as Commander in Chief of the Armed Forces. The Government attempts to do so by citing a number of cases upholding broad

2. The Selective Service Act of 1948, 62 Stat. 604, 625–627, 50 U.S.C.App. (Supp.IV) § 468; the Defense Production Act of 1950, Tit. II, 64 Stat. 798, as amended, 65 Stat. 132.

powers in military commanders engaged in day-to-day fighting in a theater of war. Such cases need not concern us here. Even though "theater of war" be an expanding concept, we cannot with faithfulness to our constitutional system hold that the Commander in Chief of the Armed Forces has the ultimate power as such to take possession of private property in order to keep labor disputes from stopping production. This is a job for the Nation's lawmakers, not for its military authorities.

Nor can the seizure order be sustained because of the several constitutional provisions that grant executive power to the President. In the framework of our Constitution, the President's power to see that the laws are faithfully executed refutes the idea that he is to be a lawmaker. The Constitution limits his functions in the lawmaking process to the recommending of laws he thinks wise and the vetoing of laws he thinks bad. And the Constitution is neither silent nor equivocal about who shall make laws which the President is to execute. The first section of the first article says that "All legislative Powers herein granted shall be vested in a Congress of the United States ＊ ＊ ＊." After granting many powers to the Congress, Article I goes on to provide that Congress may "make all Laws which shall be necessary and proper for carrying into Execution the foregoing Powers and all other Powers vested by this Constitution in the Government of the United States, or in any Department or Officer thereof."

The President's order does not direct that a congressional policy be executed in a manner prescribed by Congress—it directs that a presidential policy be executed in a manner prescribed by the President. The preamble of the order itself, like that of many statutes, sets out reasons why the President believes certain policies should be adopted, proclaims these policies as rules of conduct to be followed, and again, like a statute, authorizes a government official to promulgate additional rules and regulations consistent with the policy proclaimed and needed to carry that policy into execution. The power of Congress to adopt such public policies as those proclaimed by the order is beyond question. It can authorize the taking of private property for public use. It can make laws regulating the relationships between employers and employees, prescribing rules designed to settle labor disputes, and fixing wages and working conditions in certain fields of our economy. The Constitution did not subject this law-making power of Congress to presidential or military supervision or control.

It is said that other Presidents without congressional authority have taken possession of private business enterprises in order to settle labor disputes. But even if this be true, Congress has not thereby lost its exclusive constitutional authority to make laws necessary and proper to carry out the powers vested by the Constitution "in the Government of the United States, or in any Department or Officer thereof."

The Founders of this Nation entrusted the lawmaking power to the Congress alone in both good and bad times. It would do no good to recall the historical events, the fears of power and the hopes for freedom that lay behind their choice. Such a review would but confirm our holding that this seizure order cannot stand.

The judgment of the District Court is affirmed.

––––––––

NOTE ON THE CONCURRING AND DISSENTING OPINIONS
IN THE STEEL CASE

(1) Justices Frankfurter, Douglas, Jackson, Burton, and Clark each delivered separate concurring opinions; Chief Justice Vinson, joined by Justices Reed and Minton, dissented.

Of the concurring Justices, all went with unhesitance directly to the merits except Justice Frankfurter, who observed (pp. 595–96):

"So here our first inquiry must be not into the powers of the President, but into the powers of a District Judge to issue a temporary injunction in the circumstances of this case. Familiar as that remedy is, it remains an extraordinary remedy. To start with a consideration of the relation between the President's powers and those of Congress—a most delicate matter * * *—is to start at the wrong end. A plaintiff is not entitled to an injunction if money damages would fairly compensate him for any wrong he may have suffered. The same considerations by which the Steelworkers, in their brief *amicus*, demonstrate, from the seizure here in controversy, consequences that cannot be translated into dollars and cents, preclude a holding that only compensable damage for the plaintiffs is involved. Again, a court of equity ought not to issue an injunction, even though a plaintiff otherwise makes out a case for it, if the plaintiff's right to an injunction is overborne by a commanding public interest against it. One need not resort to a large epigrammatic generalization that the evils of industrial dislocation are to be preferred to allowing illegality to go unchecked. To deny inquiry into the President's power in a case like this, because of the damage to the public interest to be feared from upsetting its exercise by him, would in effect always preclude inquiry into challenged power, which presumably only avowed great public interest brings into action. And so, with the utmost unwillingness, with every desire to avoid judicial inquiry into the powers and duties of the other two branches of the government, I cannot escape consideration of the legality of Executive Order No. 10340."

(2) On the merits Justice Douglas agreed with Justice Black that the President had exercised legislative power. Instead, however, of merely asserting this, he gave two reasons why he thought the power exercised *was* legislative. He said (pp. 630, 631):

"The method by which industrial peace is achieved is of vital importance not only to the parties but to society as well. A determination that sanctions should be applied, that the hand of the law should be placed upon the parties, and that the force of the courts should be directed against them, is an exercise of legislative power. * * *

"The President has no power to raise revenues. * * * The President might seize and the Congress by subsequent action might ratify the seizure. But until and unless Congress acted, no condemnation would be lawful. The branch of government that has the power to pay compensation for a seizure is the only one able to authorize a seizure or make lawful one that the President has effected. That seems to me to be the necessary result of the condemnation provision in the Fifth Amendment."

The other concurring Justices all pinned their agreement on the merits to congressional enactments that in their view impliedly forbade the President to take the course he had chosen.

(3) Chief Justice Vinson, joined by Justices Reed and Minton, dissented. Initially, they noted (pp. 677–78) that "we assume that defendant Charles Sawyer is not immune from judicial restraint and that plaintiffs are entitled to equitable relief if we find the Executive Order under which defendant acts is unconstitutional." In urging the legality of the seizure, the dissenters stressed, *inter alia,* the legislative programs for increased production of military equipment and for economic stabilization which the President was engaged in executing and his duty to execute them; the gravity of the threat to those programs; the need for recognition of executive power to act in the face of emergency; the absence of any statute prohibiting seizure; and the temporary character of the taking and the right to just compensation for it. In the concluding section, the opinion said (pp. 708–10):

"The broad executive power granted by Article II to an officer on duty 365 days a year cannot, it is said, be invoked to avert disaster. Instead, the President must confine himself to sending a message to Congress recommending action. Under this messenger-boy concept of the Office, the President cannot even act to preserve legislative programs from destruction so that Congress will have something left to act upon. There is no judicial finding that the executive action was unwarranted because there was in fact no basis for the President's finding of the existence of an emergency for, under this view, the gravity of the emergency and the immediacy of the threatened disaster are considered irrelevant as a matter of law. * * *

" * * * There is no question that the possession was other than temporary in character and subject to congressional direction—either approving, disapproving or regulating the manner in which the mills were to be administered and returned to the owners. The President immediately informed Congress of his action and clearly stated his intention to abide by the legislative will. No basis for claims of arbitrary action, unlimited powers or dictatorial usurpation of congressional power appears from the facts of this case."

NOTE ON THE REMEDIAL ASPECTS OF THE STEEL CASE

(1) The steel case is not strictly about the sovereign immunity of the United States. However, the award of equitable relief contrasts sharply with Larson's ruling that an injunction of far smaller dimension was not merely inappropriate but wholly beyond the judicial power. The steel case thus raises the question of the relationship between sovereign immunity and the traditions of equity in shaping the appropriate scope of relief against federal officials.

(2) The steel case began on April 9, 1952, the day after the President's seizure order, when counsel representing several major steel producers appeared before Judge Holtzoff of the District Court for the District of Columbia on motions for a temporary restraining order. After hearing argument by plaintiffs' counsel and by Assistant Attorney General Baldridge on behalf of Secretary Sawyer, Judge Holtzoff denied the motions. He emphasized the gravity of restraining the President through the Secretary, the concessions of the Secretary's counsel that an action for just compensation would lie in the Court of Claims, and the absence of any

showing of immediate threat of irreparable injury. 1 The Steel Seizure Case 263–66 (82d Cong., 2d Sess., H.Doc. No. 534, Pt. I). He said:

"True, plaintiffs fear that other drastic steps may be taken which would displace the management or which would supersede its control over labor relations. * * * If these possibilities arise, applications for restraining orders, if they are proper and well-founded, may be renewed and considered."

Following this decision the plants continued in operation at the preexisting wage scale. Then on April 20 Secretary Sawyer indicated in a television appearance an intention to grant an interim wage increase, pending completion of negotiations between the companies and the union. On April 24 counsel representing the bulk of basic steel production appeared before District Judge Pine on what Mr. Theodore Kiendl, speaking first on behalf of the United States Steel Company, described as "an application * * * primarily for an injunction restraining what we consider to be the imminent threatened changes in the terms and conditions of employment of a steel employee."

After the argument had proceeded a while, it appeared that this really was all that Mr. Kiendl was asking, and that he did not contemplate an immediate order of dispossession. Exhibiting some perturbation, Judge Pine asked whether "the preservation of the status quo" was all the other companies were asking, too, and the reply seemed to be in the affirmative. When the judge shortly afterward repeated the question, however, Mr. Bruce Bromley rose on behalf of the Bethlehem Steel Company, and said that "We have filed a motion for a preliminary injunction and our position is 'the whole hog'".

Judge Pine then precipitately called a short recess. As Mr. Kiendl resumed thereafter, the judge interrupted to ask whether he did not "have an announcement to make". When Mr. Kiendl said he had no announcement, the judge asked counsel for all the other plaintiffs to rise and state their position. All the others thereupon said that, like Bethlehem, they wanted "the whole hog", thus leaving Mr. Kiendl alone in his request for a simple preservation of the status quo pending "a full trial on the merits", a position which drew from Judge Pine several barbed comments. 1 The Steel Seizure Case 285, 311–18, 353, 360–61.

On April 29 Judge Pine handed down an opinion announcing his readiness to issue an interlocutory injunction giving all the plaintiffs except the United States Steel Company the whole hog. Youngstown Sheet & Tube Co. v. Sawyer, 103 F.Supp. 569 (D.D.C.1952). The more limited relief asked by United States Steel he said he could not "consistently" give because of its "stultifying implications", since it "would contemplate a possible basis for the validity of defendant's acts". He stated, however, that "if the United States Steel Company wishes to withdraw its verbal amendment and proceed on the basis of its original motion, leave will be granted for that purpose".

The next morning, in the proceedings to settle the form of the preliminary injunction, the United States Steel Company accepted this suggestion.

At this hearing on April 30 Judge Pine denied the Secretary's motion for a stay of the preliminary injunction pending appeal. On the same day the court of appeals granted a temporary stay, an action which it explained in a memorandum opinion on May 2. 197 F.2d 582 (D.C.Cir.1952).

On May 2 cross petitions for writ of certiorari before judgment in the court of appeals were filed in the Supreme Court, and on May 3 were granted. In its order granting certiorari, the Supreme Court continued the stay of the preliminary injunction granted by the court of appeals, but with the proviso that the Secretary "take no action to change any term or condition of employment while this stay is in effect unless such change is mutually agreed upon by the steel companies * * * and the bargaining representatives of the employees". 343 U.S. 937, 938 (1952).

Was the Supreme Court wise in attaching this condition?

Were counsel for the other steel companies wise in abandoning Mr. Kiendl and asking for more than this prior to "a full trial on the merits"?

(3) In the initial proceedings on April 9, Judge Holtzoff raised the question whether an injunction would not "in essence and in spirit * * * be an injunction against the President". 1 The Steel Seizure Case 247. In his opinion denying a temporary injunction he cited Mississippi v. Johnson, 4 Wall. 475 (U.S.1866), in which the State filed an original action in the Supreme Court to restrain the President from executing the provisions of the Reconstruction Acts.[1] In that case, after referring to cases on mandamus against executive officers, and expressly reserving the question whether the President may be ordered to perform a purely ministerial act, Chief Justice Chase said (pp. 499–501):

"It is true that in the instance before us the interposition of the court is not sought to enforce action by the Executive under constitutional legislation, but to restrain such action under legislation alleged to be unconstitutional. But we are unable to perceive that this circumstance takes the case out of the general principles which forbid judicial interference with the exercise of Executive discretion. * * *

* * *

"The impropriety of such interference will be clearly seen upon consideration of its possible consequences.

"Suppose the bill filed and the injunction prayed for allowed. If the President refuse obedience, it is needless to observe that the court is without power to enforce its process. If, on the other hand, the President complies with the order of the court and refuses to execute the acts of Congress, is it not clear that a collision may occur between the executive and legislative departments of the government? May not the House of Representatives impeach the President for such refusal? And in that case could this court interfere, in behalf of the President, thus endangered by compliance with its mandate, and restrain by injunction the Senate of the United States from sitting as a court of impeachment? Would the strange spectacle be offered to the public world of an attempt by this court to arrest proceedings in that court? * * * *"[2]

Judge Holtzoff concluded that the consideration that a court "should not do by indirection what it could not do directly, irrespective of whether the Court has the power to do so * * * is a consideration that should affect the exercise of the Court's discretion". 1 The Steel Seizure Case 265.

1. Mississippi also sued the district military commander, a fact whose significance is not discussed in the Court's opinion.

the Supreme Court: Civil War and Reconstruction, 1865–73, 51 U.Chi.L.Rev. 131, 147–50 (1984).

2. For discussion and criticism of the decision, see Currie, The Constitution in

In the hearing fifteen days later before Judge Pine, Assistant Attorney General Baldridge, appearing for Secretary Sawyer, picked up Judge Holtzoff's suggestion and enlarged upon it. He said flatly (*id.* at 362):

"Our position is that there is no power in the Courts to restrain the President and, as I say, Secretary Sawyer is the alter ego of the President and not subject to injunctive order of the Court."

Developing the theme of the *alter ego,* Mr. Baldridge said later (*id.* at 372):

"Suppose your Honor could enjoin Mr. Sawyer. The President could immediately appoint somebody else to operate the steel mills, or he could undertake that himself."

The interrelation of the argument on the merits and on the remedy was summarized in the following exchange with Judge Pine (*id.* at 371–72):

"The Court: So you contend the Executive has unlimited power in time of an emergency?

"Mr. Baldridge: He has the power to take such action as is necessary to meet the emergency.

"The Court: If the emergency is great, it is unlimited, is it?

"Mr. Baldridge: I suppose if you carry it to its logical conclusion, that is true. But I do want to point out that there are two limitations on the Executive power. One is the ballot box and the other is impeachment.

"The Court: Then, as I understand it, you claim that in time of emergency the Executive has this great power.

"Mr. Baldridge: That is correct.

"The Court: And that the Executive determines the emergencies and the Courts cannot even review whether it is an emergency.

"Mr. Baldridge: That is correct.

"The Court: Do you have any case that sustains such a proposition as that?

"Mr. Baldridge: Yes, indeed, your Honor", citing Mississippi v. Johnson.

The next morning Mr. Baldridge drew a somewhat different argument from Mississippi v. Johnson (*id.* at 379):

"I mean this: We do not say that it is an unconsented suit against the United States, but we do say that the President is an indispensable party and, because the President cannot be enjoined as a defendant, he is immune from judicial process."

The brief for the Secretary in the Supreme Court reduced Mississippi v. Johnson to a footnote, using it only as a basis for a suggestion "that the courts should consider the inappropriateness of issuing what is in effect a mandatory injunction to the President", and "the difficulties implicit" therein, as "a sound reason for denying the injunction sought on other grounds, if it is possible to do so." 2 The Steel Seizure Case 760. Was the case worth more than this?

Would Mississippi v. Johnson have prevented an injunction against the President in the steel situation? Is the problem different when the President is off in a corner by himself, and the Court is not confronted with the possibility of precipitating a conflict between him and Congress which it could not resolve?

(4) In United States v. Nixon, 418 U.S. 683 (1974), the Supreme Court unanimously affirmed an order requiring President Nixon to respond to a grand jury subpoena *duces tecum* seeking, *inter alia*, tape recordings of presidential conversations. The Court stressed the special importance of the government's demonstrated need for evidence in a criminal trial. It did not cite Mississippi v. Johnson, and the question of presidential immunity from process was submerged in a discussion of the merits of the President's claim of executive privilege.[3]

Nixon v. Fitzgerald, 457 U.S. 731, 748 n. 27, 757 (1982), held that the President is absolutely immune from damages liability for all acts "within the outer perimeter" of his official responsibilities—at least absent "explicit affirmative action by Congress," a matter not reached in the case. Plaintiff, a dismissed federal employee, sued President Nixon (who was alleged to share responsibility for the dismissal) and other officials for damages, pleading implied rights of action under the First Amendment and two federal statutes. Justice Powell's majority opinion cited Mississippi v. Johnson as evidencing a tradition of judicial restraint in actions involving presidential responsibilities, and stated (pp. 753–54): "It is settled law that the separation-of-powers doctrine does not bar every exercise of jurisdiction over the President of the United States. See, *e.g.*, United States v. Nixon ＊ ＊ ＊; *cf.* Youngstown Sheet & Tube Co. v. Sawyer ＊ ＊ ＊. But our cases also have established that a court, before exercising jurisdiction, must balance the constitutional weight of the interest to be served against the dangers of intrusion on the authority and functions of the Executive Branch. ＊ ＊ ＊ When judicial action is needed to serve broad public interests—as when the Court acts, not in derogation of the separation of powers, but to maintain their proper balance, *cf.* Youngstown Sheet & Tube Co. v. Sawyer, *supra,* or to vindicate the public interest in an ongoing criminal prosecution, see United States v. Nixon, *supra* —the exercise of jurisdiction has been held warranted. In the case of this merely private suit for damages based on a President's official acts, we hold it is not." Justice White's dissent (joined by Justices Brennan, Marshall, and Blackmun) objected to the Court's conferring absolute immunity upon the office of the President, rather than upon only those functions deemed to require it. He distinguished Mississippi v. Johnson and Kendall v. United States, pp. 1092–93, note 4, *supra,* as resting on the limited scope of mandamus jurisdiction (*i.e.*, the "ministerial-discretionary" distinction).

Is the implication of the two Nixon decisions that the President has no distinctive immunity from process in a civil suit seeking specific relief

---

3. A different issue that was much mooted during the Watergate affair is whether an incumbent President is immune from criminal prosecution. Article I, Sec. 3 of the Constitution provides that an official convicted in an impeachment proceeding "shall nevertheless be liable and subject to Indictment, Trial, Judgment, and Punishment, according to Law." Can one infer from this language, or from the constitutional structure, that impeach- ment must precede criminal prosecution of the President? Compare Kurland, Watergate and the Constitution 131–36 (1978) (yes), with Berger, *The President, Congress, and the Courts,* 83 Yale L.J. 1111, 1123–36 (1974) (no). Compare Art. I, Sec. 6, the Speech or Debate Clause, which limits the power of a grand jury and a criminal court to inquire into a member of Congress's legislative acts or the motivations therefor. See pp. 1303–05, *infra.*

against allegedly unlawful executive conduct?[4] Can one fairly argue that President Johnson had discretion to enforce the Reconstruction Acts if, as Mississippi alleged, the legislation was unconstitutional? Or after the two Nixon decisions, is Mississippi v. Johnson a dead letter?

(5) Were government counsel in Youngstown wise in failing to press the objection that the suit was in substance against the United States? Is Larson plainly distinguishable? In terms of the rationale of sovereign immunity set forth in Larson?

(6) In the Supreme Court, the government argued that the steel companies had an adequate remedy at law in the Court of Claims, which had jurisdiction "upon any claim against the United States * * * founded upon the Constitution" [or] "any regulation of an executive department." 28 U.S.C. §§ 1491(1), 1491(3). That section, counsel said, "does not add that the regulation must be valid or authorized." 2 The Steel Seizure Case 777–78.

Though a temporary taking is clearly compensable, United States v. General Motors Corp., 323 U.S. 373 (1945), doubts that the companies could obtain monetary relief in the Court of Claims were based primarily on the two cases cited by Justice Black—Hooe v. United States, 218 U.S. 322 (1910), and United States v. North American Transp. & Trading Co., 253 U.S. 330 (1920).

In the Hooe case, the Civil Service Commission, having already committed itself to pay rent for a part of a building up to the amount of its appropriation, occupied other parts of it, in violation of statutes expressly forbidding contracts for the lease of buildings until an appropriation had been made. In the opinion denying recovery, Justice Harlan said (218 U.S. at 335–36):

"* * * If an officer of the United States assumes, by virtue alone of his office, and *without the authority of Congress,* to take such matters under his control, he will not, in any legal or constitutional sense, represent the United States, and what he does or omits to do, without the authority of the Congress, cannot create a claim against the Government 'founded upon the Constitution'. It would be a claim having its origin in a violation of the Constitution. The constitutional prohibition against taking private property for public use without just compensation is directed against the Government, and not against individual or public officers proceeding without the authority of legislative enactment. The taking of private property by an officer of the United States for public use, without being authorized, expressly or by necessary implication, to do so by some act of Congress, is not the act of the Government."

4. Compare National Treasury Employees Union v. Nixon, 492 F.2d 587 (D.C.Cir. 1974), which, six months before United States v. Nixon, ruled that President Nixon was not immune from a suit seeking a writ of mandamus to compel him, in accordance with an Act of Congress, either to implement a pay increase for federal employees or to submit an alternative plan to Congress. However, "in order to show the utmost respect to the office of the Presidency" and to avoid an inter-branch conflict, the court deemed it appropriate "at this time" to issue only declaratory relief, thereby giving the President an opportunity to implement the law or to seek further judicial review (p. 616).

See generally Karst & Horowitz, *Presidential Prerogative and Judicial Power,* 22 U.C.L.A.L.Rev. 47, 49–51 (1974). But *cf.* Carter, *The Political Aspects of Judicial Power: Some Notes on the Presidential Immunity Decision,* 131 U.Pa.L.Rev. 1341 (1983) (court has authority to issue but not to enforce subpoena against the President; compliance is secured by the political process, not judicial sanctions).

In the North American case, a commanding general, who lacked statutory authority, had taken possession of land for an army post, and the Secretary of War, who had the authority, had not ratified until later. If the claim for compensation arose at the time of the initial occupation, it was barred by the statute of limitations, but not otherwise. In this context Justice Brandeis said (253 U.S. at 333):

"When the Government without instituting condemnation proceedings appropriates for a public use under legislative authority private property to which it asserts no title, it impliedly promises to pay therefor. * * * In order that the Government shall be liable it must appear that the officer who has physically taken possession of the property was duly authorized so to do, either directly by Congress or by the official upon whom Congress conferred the power." The Court treated the claim as resting, however, only on an "implied contract" and not upon the Fifth Amendment, and hence denied interest (p. 1113, *supra*) as well as compensation for use and occupancy. *Cf.* Seaboard Air Line Ry. v. United States, 261 U.S. 299, 305 (1923). See Anderson, *Tort and Implied Contract Liability of the Federal Government,* 30 Minn.L.Rev. 133, 156–64 (1946). Later cases, however, made it unmistakably clear that, at least where the taking was *in invitum,* the claim for just compensation was founded not only upon a benevolently hypothesized contract but upon the Constitution; and that it made no difference that the government proceeded by "informal eminent domain" rather than by formal condemnation proceedings or order of requisition. Jacobs v. United States, 290 U.S. 13, 16 (1933); United States v. Dickinson, 331 U.S. 745, 747–48 (1947).

A number of decisions prior to Youngstown involved direct action taken by government officers that was authorized but, because of the mistaken belief that what was being done did not constitute a compensable taking, did not follow appropriate procedures. In such cases, the Court overlooked the procedural defects and permitted compensation, at least where the project in which the officers were engaged was an authorized one. See, *e.g.,* United States v. Lynah, 188 U.S. 445, 465–66 (1903); Hurley v. Kincaid, 285 U.S. 95 (1932). In other cases, authority for the officer's direct action might have been but was not challenged, and the Court upheld compensation while ignoring the problem. United States v. Causby, 328 U.S. 256 (1946) (low flights of military aircraft over a chicken farm); United States v. Pewee Coal Co., 341 U.S. 114 (1951) (war-time plant seizure—lack of specific statutory authority disclosed in government's brief).

These cases may have assumed, if they did not decide, that the constitutional and statutory right to recover just compensation results, irrespective of the taking officer's authority, from the facts alone of an unbargained taking and of retention by the government of the property taken. Would such a principle be sound? (Note that Malone v. Bowdoin, p. 1126, *supra,* appears to have accepted it.)

Compare the argument made to the Supreme Court by counsel for the steel companies, content apparently with the reflection that the evil of the day was sufficient thereto. After distinguishing such cases as Hurley v. Kincaid on the ground that "that type of illegality 'does not go to the essence of the taking'", the brief continued (2 The Steel Seizure Case 661–62):

" * * * But where the taking itself is utterly devoid of authority, the very illegality of which the plaintiffs complain also deprives them of any remedy in a suit for just compensation under the Fifth Amendment.

"This clear and repeatedly asserted rule is a basic proposition in a legal system, such as ours, in which private rights are not at the mercy of unfettered executive action. For were the rule otherwise—were compensation at law available for a wholly unauthorized taking, and the doors of equity thereby closed to the private interest—not only would the Federal Treasury be exposed to incalculable expense, but citizens would be exposed to arbitrary action by governmental officials to an extent altogether startling in its consequences."

Is preventive equitable relief sometimes less intrusive than an obligation to compensate for past harms? *Cf.* 5 U.S.C. § 702, Sec. 1(C)(3), *infra;* Edelman v. Jordan, p. 1182, *infra.*

Would it have been relevant in the steel case for the Supreme Court to have resolved the doubt about the right to just compensation for the taking? To guide judgment in weighing the conflicting interests on the issue of an interlocutory injunction? Of a final injunction? To guide judgment in weighing the probability that Congress had impliedly forbidden a seizure?

By contrast, do the doubts expressed in Youngstown about the availability of Tucker Act relief invite courts to draw a line, much like that drawn in Larson, between acts that are merely illegal (for which the Tucker Act is an available, and likely the exclusive, remedy) and acts that are in some relevant sense ultra vires (for which equitable relief is the only possible remedy)? Can such a line be drawn with sufficient clarity that litigants can make reliable judgments whether to seek monetary relief in the Claims Court or equitable relief in a district court?

For an example of the difficulties resulting from Youngstown's approach, consider Ramirez de Arellano v. Weinberger, 745 F.2d 1500 (D.C. Cir.1984) (en banc), *vacated on other grounds,* 471 U.S. 1113 (1985), in which a United States citizen sought equitable relief against the Secretaries of Defense and State, alleging that an American military facility for training Salvadoran soldiers had been established, without authority under federal law, on plaintiff's cattle ranch in Honduras. Reversing the district court, the court of appeals, per Wilkey, J., found the suit justiciable. Then, relying on Youngstown and Hooe, the court ruled that no Tucker Act remedy would be available (pp. 1523–24): "[W]hen an officer acts wholly outside the scope of the powers granted to him by statute or constitutional provision, the official's actions have been considered to be unauthorized for the purposes of a damages remedy under the Tucker Act. * * * Whether or not a Tucker Act claim will lie depends upon facts not yet ascertained and the nature of the congressional and constitutional grants of power to these defendants to make military acquisitions."[5] Therefore, dismissal was inappropriate.

5. The court also held that even if a damages remedy were available in the Claims Court, an injunction might be appropriate if, under traditional equitable principles, the remedy at law was inade-quate. To this, Judge Scalia responded in dissent (p. 1552): "That 'money alone [may] not constitute just compensation' for purposes of the Fifth Amendment is a principle of breathtaking novelty."

Judge Scalia's dissent, joined by Judges Bork and Starr, argued that "the question whether a government officer was acting sufficiently within his authorized powers to permit a Tucker Act remedy is precisely the same as the question whether he was acting sufficiently within his authorized powers to preclude injunctive relief against him" (p. 1554). Under Larson and Malone, the question "is not whether these defendants are authorized to 'make military acquisitions,' but whether they are authorized to conduct military training exercises abroad, with no specific limitation upon trespass or unlawful taking in the process" (p. 1555). Finding such authority to exist, he argued that the suit for injunctive relief should be dismissed because there was a Tucker Act remedy.

See also Southern California Financial Corp. v. United States, 634 F.2d 521 (Ct.Cl.1980) (because Air Force's use of plaintiff's land was not authorized, plaintiffs were not entitled to Tucker Act remedy for alleged taking).

(7) Assuming (i) that statutory authority for the seizure existed, even though the statutory procedure had not been followed, and (ii) that the failure to follow the statutory procedure did not bar an action for just compensation in the Court of Claims, should the existence of this remedy at law have been held to oust the jurisdiction of equity?

The Secretary's counsel argued that on this issue, Hurley v. Kincaid, 285 U.S. 95, 104 (1932), was directly controlling. 2 The Steel Seizure Case 769. There, a landowner sought to enjoin construction of a water project that threatened to flood his land, claiming that the government was required by statute to acquire his land before construction could begin. The Court denied the injunction, reasoning that "even if the defendants are acting illegally, * * * the illegality, on complainant's own contention, is confined to the failure to compensate him for the taking, and affords no basis for an injunction if such compensation may be procured in an action at law." 285 U.S. at 104.

Can the Court's failure in Youngstown even to mention the Secretary's argument be justified, except on the assumption that one or the other of its two premises was rejected?

In what respect did the companies suffer irreparable injury from the failure to follow the statutory procedure for seizure, if the procedure was available and the failure to follow it had no bearing on the right to compensation?

Was there a difference in the two cases in terms of the public interest in the observance of law? Notice that in Hurley v. Kincaid, the government officers did not purport to be "taking" property, were violating in their view no procedural restrictions, and indeed in their view had no alternative procedure. Is it material that in the steel case the fact of taking was admitted; that an authorized means of taking did exist; and that, if equity could not interpose, even an open violation of a recognized restriction might go without restraint?

(8) Granting the jurisdiction of equity, was a case made which should have moved the Chancellor to grant relief?

Alone on the Court, Justice Frankfurter sought to relate his analysis of the merits to his analysis of the problem of the exercise of equity jurisdiction. He said (343 U.S. at 609–10):

"The legislative history here canvassed is relevant to yet another of the issues before us, namely, the Government's argument that overriding public interest prevents the issuance of the injunction despite the illegality of the seizure. I cannot accept that contention. 'Balancing the equities' when considering whether an injunction should issue, is lawyers' jargon for choosing between conflicting public interests. When Congress itself has struck the balance, has defined the weight to be given the competing interests, a court of equity is not justified in ignoring that pronouncement under the guise of exercising equitable discretion."

In what sense had Congress "struck the balance" and "defined the weight to be given the competing interests" other than by forbidding seizure, impliedly, in the Taft–Hartley Act? Does Justice Frankfurter mean that upon a finding alone that the seizure was unlawful, an injunction should issue, without regard to the public damage or the importance of the private interests to be protected?

(9) If it had been thought that the Court had a function of examining the competing private and public interests and striking a balance among them, would a case for relief have been made? On an interlocutory hearing, on mere affidavits of irreparable injury, without opportunity for cross-examination, upon the undocumented findings of a single trial judge, and without the usual assistance in clarifying the issues of review by a court of three appellate judges?

Consider, first, the private interests involved, from the vantage point of hindsight.

On the eve of the seizure the companies were faced with a strike. As a result of the seizure the companies received the profits of two months of operation at a high rate of production. These profits were unimpaired by any wage increase, as a result of the condition attached by the Supreme Court to its stay of Judge Pine's injunction. As a result of the Supreme Court's final decision, there ensued a two-months strike, during which there were no profits. At the end of the strike the companies granted a wage increase approximating, if not exceeding, the amount that would have produced an agreement in the beginning, and at the same time received an increase in ceiling prices, very probably exceeding that which they could have secured in the beginning.

Upon what suppositions as to what might otherwise have happened can it be concluded in retrospect that the seizure caused the companies irreparable injury from which the Supreme Court's decision relieved them?

Did the variables in the situation defy analysis as of the time when the issue of an interlocutory injunction was before the courts? Did the evidence and argument by which the Supreme Court permitted itself to be persuaded reflect as careful a scrutiny of plausible claims of irreparable damage as it is reasonable to expect in the judicial process?

Consider, on the other hand, the public interests at stake. Do the opinions suggest that the Court took at something less than face value the statements of the President and Secretary concerning the public dangers implicit in the situation? Should the Court as an institution resist impulses of skepticism toward the representations of another branch of the government to which, as individuals, the Justices might reasonably yield?

Nine months after the steel decision there were recurrent reports, recurrently denied, that the effects of the steel strike were being felt in Korea in a grave shortage of artillery ammunition. Does the soundness of the decision depend upon the assumption that these reports were ill-founded?

(10) Consider the bearing of Justice Frankfurter's statement, just quoted, upon the problem of court and counsel in resolving remedial issues at the interlocutory stage. The Justice's remedial conclusion is plainly a function, is it not, of the certitude of his ultimate judgment on the merits? [6]

Suppose the Secretary's counsel had succeeded in laying bare at the beginning of the proceeding the actual difficulties of the problems that the companies' application for an injunction had thrust upon the courts—instead of merely mesmerizing the whole country with the provocative unreasonableness of extreme claims. Would not the full gamut of remedial doctrines that are of principal concern here have then stopped being dead formulas and suddenly come to life?

Is the moral of this that all doctrines of judicial self-limitation are relative—relative to the judge's sense of the difficulties of his substantive problem—and that the task of counsel at the interlocutory stage is to give the judge an adequate sense of what lies ahead? [7]

SUBSECTION C: CONGRESSIONAL ENACTMENTS WAIVING THE SOVEREIGN IMMUNITY OF THE FEDERAL GOVERNMENT

NOTE ON FEDERAL LEGISLATION WAIVING THE SOVEREIGN IMMUNITY OF THE UNITED STATES

The importance of federal sovereign immunity has declined substantially over time as Congress has enacted a variety of measures authorizing federal courts to hear suits that would otherwise be barred. It has been

---

6. *Cf.* Thornburgh v. American College of Obstetricians and Gynecologists, 476 U.S. 747 (1986), in which the district court denied preliminary injunctive relief in a suit challenging state restrictions on abortion, finding no likelihood of success on the merits. The court of appeals reversed and rendered a final decision finding several statutory provisions unconstitutional. While agreeing with the state that ordinarily the court of appeals should limit its review of the denial of preliminary relief to determining whether there was an abuse of discretion, the Supreme Court noted that Youngstown had deviated from that approach. Because here the record was complete and the appropriateness of relief depended upon a clear issue of constitutional law, the Court held that plenary appellate review was appropriate. The dissents of Justice White and Justice O'Connor (each joined by Justice Rehn-

quist) both questioned this procedural ruling; Justice O'Connor distinguished the "highly unusual" situation in Youngstown on the grounds that there time was of the essence and the government had had an adequate opportunity to present the facts.

7. See, generally, Corwin, *The Steel Seizure Case: A Judicial Brick Without Straw,* 53 Colum.L.Rev. 53 (1953); Freund, *Foreword: The Year of the Steel Case,* 66 Harv.L.Rev. 89 (1952); Lea, *The Steel Case: Presidential Seizure of Private Industry,* 47 Nw.L.Rev. 289 (1952); Kauper, *The Steel Seizure Case: Congress, the President and the Supreme Court,* 51 Mich.L.Rev. 141 (1952); Marcus, Truman and the Steel Seizure Case: The Limits of Presidential Power (1977); Note, *The Steel Seizure Cases,* 41 Geo.L.J. 45 (1952); Westin, The Anatomy of a Constitutional Law Case (1958).

taken for granted that specific statutory review mechanisms contained in particular regulatory statutes constitute pro tanto waivers of sovereign immunity. See p. 1097, *supra.* There are also, however, more general enactments, not tied to review of a particular regulatory program, in which Congress has waived the United States' immunity. Discussed below are the three most important schemes: the Tucker Act, governing non-tort monetary claims against the United States; the Federal Tort Claims Act, governing tort suits against the United States; and a 1976 statute governing all claims against the United States for relief other than money damages.[1] In reviewing the system that has arisen, consider whether it lives up to reasonable standards of rationality and comprehensiveness.

1. The United States Claims Court and the Tucker Act[2]

(1) Before 1855, no statute gave consent to suit against the United States on claims for money damages; such claims were disposed of, if at all, by private act. Because reliance on private acts had proved burdensome and inequitable, the Court of Claims was created in that year. It was authorized to hear and determine all claims against the government founded upon any statute, executive regulation, or express or implied contract with the United States.[3]

(2) In 1887, the Tucker Act broadened the Court of Claims' jurisdiction to include all "claims founded upon the Constitution of the United States or any law of Congress, except for pensions, or upon any regulation of an Executive Department, or upon any contract, expressed or implied, with the Government of the United States, or for damages, liquidated or unliquidated, in cases not sounding in tort, in respect of which claims the party would be entitled to redress against the United States either in a court of law, equity, or admiralty if the United States were suable." Act of March 3, 1887, 24 Stat. 505. Concurrent jurisdiction of claims not exceeding $1,000 was given to the district courts, and of claims of $1,000 to $10,000 to the circuit courts. The basic structure established by the Tucker Act, now codified at 28 U.S.C. §§ 1346(a)(2), 1491(a)(1), remains. (On the history of the Court of Claims' Article III status, and the problem of legislative revision of its judgments, see pp. 102–06, *supra*).

(3) In 1982, the United States Claims Court, an Article I court, was established to assume the trial jurisdiction formerly possessed by the Court of Claims. The Claims Court thus has jurisdiction over all claims governed

---

1. Other important measures consenting to suit against the United States include legislation authorizing district court jurisdiction over specified land disputes, see 28 U.S.C. §§ 2409–2410; Paragraph (14)(a), *infra,* and provisions authorizing jurisdiction of the United States Claims Court over (i) patent and copyright infringement cases, *id.* § 1498, (ii) disputes with government contractors arising under the Contract Disputes Act of 1978, see 28 U.S.C. § 1491(a)(2), and (iii) specified claims of Indian tribes, see *id.* § 1505. See generally *id.* §§ 1491–1509; Steadman, Schwartz, & Jacoby, Litigation With the Federal Government (2d ed. 1983); 14 Wright, Miller & Cooper, Federal Practice and Procedure § 3656 (1985).

For a summary of the statutory provisions consenting to suit against the United States in maritime cases, see Currie, Federal Courts 587–90 (3d ed. 1982).

Recall, also, the general provisions discussed at pp. 1113–14, *supra,* providing for the award of costs and attorney's fees against the United States.

2. See generally Steadman, Schwartz, & Jacoby, note 1, *supra,* at 147–232; Wright, Miller & Cooper, note 1, *supra,* § 4101.

3. Act of Feb. 24, 1855, 10 Stat. 612, as amended by Act of March 3, 1863, 12 Stat. 765, Act of March 17, 1866, 14 Stat. 9, and Act of June 25, 1868, 15 Stat. 75.

by the Tucker Act; its jurisdiction over claims (other than for a tax refund) in excess of $10,000 is exclusive,[4] while the district courts have concurrent jurisdiction of claims not exceeding $10,000. There is no right in either forum to jury trial under the Tucker Act. 28 U.S.C. § 2402.

(4) The Tucker Act is merely a grant of jurisdiction and a concomitant waiver of sovereign immunity; it does not itself create any substantive rights. A suit under the Tucker Act must establish not only a violation of a federal enactment, but must also "demonstrate that the source of substantive law [the plaintiff] relies upon 'can fairly be interpreted as mandating compensation by the Federal Government for the damage sustained.' " United States v. Mitchell, 463 U.S. 206, 216–17 (1983), quoting United States v. Testan, 424 U.S. 392, 400 (1976). (The claimant need not, however, demonstrate a separate waiver of immunity in the substantive provision relied upon.)[5] Constitutional claims founded on the Just Compensation Clause have been held to satisfy this standard. See, *e.g.*, United States v. Causby, 328 U.S. 256 (1946); *cf.* First English Evangelical Lutheran Church of Glendale v. County of Los Angeles, 107 S.Ct. 2378 (1987) (Just Compensation Clause, as incorporated against a local government by the Fourteenth Amendment, by its own force authorizes award of money damages).[6] The lower courts have consistently rejected Tucker Act suits based on violations of other constitutional provisions, however, on the ground that these provisions do not "expressly grant a money remedy," Featheringill v. United States, 217 Ct.Cl. 24, 33 (1978) (First Amendment claim); accord, *e.g.*, Hohri v. United States, 782 F.2d 227, 244–45 (D.C.Cir. 1986) (claims based on, *inter alia*, Fourth Amendment, Due Process Clause, Sixth Amendment's counsel and fair trial provisions, and Cruel and Unusual Punishment Clause), *vacated on other grounds*, 107 S.Ct. 2246 (1987). The Act also does not extend to claims based on contracts implied-in-law (*i.e.*, quasi-contract or restitution claims). See generally Jacoby, Steadman, and Schwartz, note 1, *supra*, §§ 9.120–9.121.

The Tucker Act is strictly limited to claims for money. It gives no jurisdiction to hear claims for specific performance, delivery of property in kind, or equitable relief,[7] although other provisions give the Claims Court a limited power to award equitable relief.[8]

---

4. This exclusivity has given rise to difficult questions about district court jurisdiction under provisions other than the Tucker Act. See Paragraph (14)(c), *infra*.

5. United States v. Mitchell, 463 U.S. 206, 213–19 (1983) reaffirmed this view, and disavowed contrary intimations in United States v. Testan, 424 U.S. 392, 398 (1976) and United States v. Mitchell, 445 U.S. 535, 538 (1980).

6. On the scope of Tucker Act relief in inverse condemnation actions, see Note on Remedial Aspects of the Steel Seizure Case, p. 1134, *supra*.

7. See Richardson v. Morris, 409 U.S. 464 (1973) (per curiam) (refusing injunctive relief); United States v. King, 395 U.S. 1 (1969) (Declaratory Judgment Act inapplicable); United States v. Jones, 131 U.S. 1 (1889) (refusing to order issuance of land

patent). See generally United States v. Mitchell, 463 U.S. 206, 218 (1983).

8. To limit the need for claimants to bring two actions, one in district court seeking specific relief and one in the Claims Court seeking monetary relief, the latter has authority, in cases in which a judgment for damages is entered under the Tucker Act, to provide incidental and collateral relief "directing restoration to office or position, placement in appropriate duty or retirement status, and correction of applicable records." 28 U.S.C. § 1491(a) (2). On whether this jurisdiction is exclusive, see Hahn v. United States, 757 F.2d 581, 589–90 (3d Cir.1985). See also 28 U.S.C. § 1491(a)(3) (Claims Court has exclusive jurisdiction to provide "complete relief on any contract claim brought before the contract is awarded), discussed in Comment, 16 Pub.Contract L.J. 530 (1987); 28

(5) Judgments in cases under the Tucker Act, both in the United States Claims Court and (except for cases based on the internal revenue laws) in the district courts are appealable only to the Court of Appeals for the Federal Circuit, an Article III tribunal established in 1982. See 28 U.S.C. § 1295(a); United States v. Hohri, note 29, *infra.*

2. The Federal Tort Claims Act [9]

(6) The exclusion of tort claims from coverage under the Tucker Act left tort victims without any general remedy against the government itself (rather than against individual officers) until 1946, when Congress enacted the Federal Tort Claims Act (FTCA).[10] The Act establishes district court jurisdiction and waives sovereign immunity in suits against the United States "for injury or loss of property, or personal injury or death caused by the negligent or wrongful act or omission of any employee of the Government while acting within the scope of his office or employment, under circumstances where the United States, if a private person, would be liable to the claimant in accordance with the law of the place where the act or omission occurred." 28 U.S.C. § 1346(b). Though it contains significant exceptions and limitations, the FTCA for the first time recognized the general principle of governmental liability in tort.[11]

(7) Procedure under the FTCA differs from ordinary tort suits in important respects.[12] No suit may be filed unless the claimant has made a timely application to the involved agency for administrative settlement, and the claim has been denied or not acted upon for six months. 28 U.S.C. § 2675.[13] Trial is de novo, however, and is to the court. Relief is limited to money damages,[14] and punitive damages are barred.[15]

U.S.C. § 1507 (Claims Court may issue declaratory judgment under section 7428 of the Internal Revenue Code of 1954).

9. See generally Steadman, Schwartz & Jacoby, note 1, *supra,* at 243–78; Jayson, Handling Federal Tort Claims (1984 & Supp.1986); Davis, 5 Administrative Law Treatise §§ 27:5–27:17 (1984).

10. 60 Stat. 842 (1946). The FTCA's grant of jurisdiction is codified in 28 U.S.C. § 1346(b); procedures for tort claims are set forth in *id.* §§ 1402, 2401–02, 2412, 2671–79; exceptions to the rule of liability are contained in *id.* § 2680.

There are dozens of other statutes that provide remedies against the government in particular circumstances for the tortious conduct of its employees. See 1 Jayson, note 9, *supra,* § 55.

11. Most courts have not permitted the government to defend an FTCA action on the basis of the immunity that the officer would have had in a tort action brought against him individually. See, *e.g.,* Arnsberg v. United States, 549 F.Supp. 55, 57–58 (D.Or.1982), *rev'd on other grounds,* 757 F.2d 971 (9th Cir.1985); Townsend v. Carmel, 494 F.Supp. 30, 36 (D.D.C.1979). See also Comment, 47 Geo.Wash.L.Rev. 651 (1979). *Cf.* Owen v. City of Independence, 445 U.S. 622, 650–56 (1980), p. 1253, *infra,*

H. & W.—Fed.Cts. & Sys. 3d Ed. UCB—27

holding that a local government, when liable in damages in a constitutional tort action under 42 U.S.C. § 1983, may not avail itself of the qualified immunity that its officers would enjoy had they been sued. (On the scope of an officer's immunity, see Sec. 3, *infra.*)

12. See generally 1 Jayson, note 9, *supra,* §§ 134–44.

13. Approval of the Attorney General is required for settlements in excess of $25,000. See 28 U.S.C. § 2672. On administrative settlement of tort claims, see generally Bermann, *Federal Tort Claims at the Agency Level: The FTCA Administrative Process,* 35 Case W.Res.L.Rev. 509, 515 (1985).

14. See Hatahley v. United States, 351 U.S. 173 (1956). The courts have divided on whether a declaratory judgment of liability is permissible as one step toward a money judgment. See 1 Jayson, note 9, *supra,* § 211.02. *Cf.* United States v. King, note 7, *supra.*

15. 28 U.S.C. § 2674. For exploration of the complications that have arisen under this prohibition, see Levin, *The Tail Wags the Dog: Judicial Misinterpretation of the Punitive Damages Ban in the Federal Tort Claims Act,* 27 Wm. & Mary L.Rev. 245 (1986).

(8) There are a number of express exceptions to the FTCA. The most important of these, and one that from the outset has been difficult to apply, excludes any claim "based upon the exercise or performance or the failure to exercise or perform a discretionary function or duty on the part of a federal agency or an employee of the Government, whether or not the discretion involved be abused." 28 U.S.C. § 2680(a).[16]

The "discretionary function" exception was first interpreted by the Supreme Court in Dalehite v. United States, 346 U.S. 15 (1953).

Pursuant to a high level government decision, a program was developed to manufacture and ship to occupied Germany, Japan and Korea large quantities of an ammonium nitrate fertilizer as a means of increasing food production. The material was being loaded on ships at Texas City when spontaneous combustion led to an explosion that killed 560 people, injured some 3,000 and leveled a portion of the City.

The District Court awarded damages in the test case, finding negligence in the manufacture, coating and packaging of the fertilizer as well as in the failure to give warning of the danger of fire and explosion. Sustaining a reversal of the judgment by the Court of Appeals, Justice Reed relied upon the fact that the entire program, including the aspects of the operation held to involve negligence, had been planned "at a high level under a direct delegation of plan-making authority from the apex of the Executive Department" (p. 40). The "discretionary function or duty" exception "includes more than the initiation of programs and activities. It also includes determinations made by executives or administrators in establishing plans, specifications or schedules of operations. Where there is room for policy judgment and decision there is discretion. It necessarily follows that acts of subordinates in carrying out the operations of government in accordance with official directions cannot be actionable. If this were not so, the protection of § 2680(a) would fail at the time it would be needed, that is, when a subordinate performs or fails to perform a causal step, each action or nonaction being directed by the superior, exercising, perhaps abusing, discretion" (pp. 35–36).

Justice Jackson, joined by Justices Black and Frankfurter, filed a powerful dissent. He dealt with the "discretionary function" defense as follows:

"We do not predicate liability on any decision taken at 'Cabinet level' or on any other high-altitude thinking. Of course, it is not a tort for government to govern, and the decision to aid foreign agriculture by making and delivering fertilizer is no actionable wrong. Nor do we find that in these deliberations any decision was made to take a calculated risk of doing what was done, in the way it was done, on the chance that what did happen might not happen. Therefore, we are not deterred by fear that governmental liability in this case would make the discretion of executives and administrators timid and restrained. However, if decisions are being made at Cabinet levels as to the temperature of bagging explosive fertilizers, whether paper is suitable for bagging hot fertilizer, and how the bags should be labeled, perhaps an increased sense of caution and responsibility

16. See generally 2 Jayson, note 9, supra, §§ 245–49; Reynolds, *The Discretionary Function Exception of the Federal Tort Claims Act,* 57 Geo.L.J. 81 (1968); Kratzke, *The Convergence of the Discretionary Function Exception to the Federal Tort Claims Act with Limitations of Liability in Common Law Negligence,* 60 St. John's L.Rev. 221 (1986).

even at that height would be wholesome. The common sense of this matter is that a policy adopted in the exercise of an immune discretion was carried out carelessly by those in charge of the detail. We cannot agree that all the way down the line there is immunity for every balancing of care against cost, of safety against production, of warning against silence.

" * * * When an official exerts governmental authority in a manner which legally binds one or many he is acting in a way no private person could. Such activities do and are designed to affect, often deleteriously, the affairs of individuals, but courts have long recognized the public policy that such official shall be controlled solely by the statutory or administrative mandate and not by the added threat of private damage suits. * * * The exception clause of the Tort Claims Act protects the public treasury where the common law would protect the purse of the acting public official.

"But many acts of government officials deal only with the housekeeping side of federal activities. The Government, as landowner, as manufacturer, as shipper, as warehouseman, as shipowner and operator, is carrying on activities indistinguishable from those performed by private persons. In this area, there is no good reason to stretch the legislative text to immunize the Government or its officers from responsibility for their acts, if done without appropriate care for the safety of others. Many official decisions even in this area may involve a nice balancing of various considerations, but this is the same kind of balancing which citizens do at their peril and we think it is not within the exception of the statute" (pp. 57–58, 59–60).[17]

Two years later, the Court divided 5–4 in deciding Indian Towing Co. v. United States, 350 U.S. 61 (1955). The action was for damage to a barge caused by the Coast Guard's negligent failure to check and discover defects, make repairs or give warning that a light in a government operated lighthouse had gone out. The government contended that in imposing liability "in the same manner and to the same extent as a private individual under like circumstances," the statute excluded liability for the performance of activities that private persons do not perform. Rejecting analogies to the "casuistries of municipal liability for torts," Justice Frankfurter's opinion for the Court said:

" * * * The Government reads the statute as if it imposed liability to the same extent as would be imposed on a private individual 'under the same circumstances.' But the statutory language is 'under like circumstances' and it is hornbook tort law that one who undertakes to warn the public of danger and thereby induces reliance must perform his 'good Samaritan' task in a careful manner" (pp. 64–65).

The government conceded that the "discretionary function" exception, which it described as relieving from liability for negligent "exercise of

---

17. On a different theory, the Court found no liability for the Coast Guard's negligence in fighting the fire. "The Act did not create new causes of action where none existed before," and "if anything is doctrinally sanctified in the law of torts it is the immunity of communities and other public bodies for injuries due to fighting fire" (pp. 43, 44). This part of Dalehite was overruled four years later in Rayonier Inc. v. United States, 352 U.S. 315 (1957), holding that the United States could be liable for the Forest Service's negligence in fighting a fire, and viewing "the very purpose of the Tort Claims Act" to be "to establish novel and unprecedented governmental liability" (p. 319). See also United States v. Muniz, 374 U.S. 150 (1963), holding that the FTCA permits a prisoner's suit for personal injuries caused by the negligence of prison employees, and rejecting the government's argument that it could not be liable because private actors do not operate prisons.

judgment," did not apply. The Court agreed with that conclusion but simply on the ground that the negligence alleged was at "the operational level" of governmental activity (p. 64). As the opinion elsewhere said, the government "need not undertake the lighthouse service" but having done so, the Coast Guard was obliged to use due care to keep the light in working order or give warning that it was not functioning (p. 69).

Justice Reed, joined by Justices Burton, Clark and Minton, dissented, relying in part on Dalehite as a controlling precedent impliedly approved by Congress in its failure to amend the Act.

The Court returned to the discretionary function exception in United States v. S.A. Empresa de Viacao Aerea Rio Grandense (Varig Airlines), 467 U.S. 797 (1984), in which victims of airplane accidents alleged that the planes did not meet federal safety standards, and that the Federal Aviation Administration (FAA) had been negligent in certificating the planes for commercial use. As authorized by statute, the FAA had delegated certain inspection and certification responsibilities to employees of aircraft manufacturers, whose work was subject to spot checks by FAA employees. There was no record that an FAA inspector had checked the aircraft at issue in the suit.

The court of appeals found the claims cognizable under the FTCA, holding that inspection for compliance with air safety regulations did not entail the kind of policymaking discretion exempted by § 2680(a). The Supreme Court unanimously reversed. While admitting that its decisions "ha[d] not followed a straight line," the Court rejected the plaintiffs' contention that, after Indian Towing, Dalehite "no longer represents a valid interpretation of the discretionary function exception" (pp. 811–12). The Court then offered this explanation (pp. 813–14): "First, it is the nature of the conduct, rather than the status of the actor, that governs whether the discretionary function exception applies in a given case. * * * Thus, the basic inquiry concerning the application of the * * * exception is whether the challenged acts of a Government employee— whatever his or her rank—are of the nature and quality that Congress intended to shield from tort liability.

"Second, whatever else the discretionary function exception may include, it plainly was intended to encompass the discretionary acts of the Government acting in its role as a regulator of the conduct of private individuals. Time and again the legislative history refers to the acts of regulatory agencies as examples of those covered by the exception * * *. Congress wished to prevent judicial 'second-guessing' of legislative and administrative decisions grounded in social, economic, and political policy through the medium of an action in tort."

In light of this second observation, the Court had little difficulty holding that the FAA's decision to delegate inspection responsibility to the manufacturers was a discretionary function exempt from liability.

Doesn't the Chief Justice's first factor reduce to a perfect circularity? Does the second factor clarify the exception's scope outside the context of regulation of private enterprise?

More generally, do Dalehite, Indian Towing, and Varig create a clear pattern? Is it helpful to consider whether the exception's rationale is similar to that underlying (i) the doctrine of sovereign immunity itself, (ii) traditional limitations on the scope of mandamus, see pp. 1091–95, *supra*,

(iii) the scope of review of administrative actions under the Administrative Procedure Act, see p. 1096, *supra,* (iv) the political question doctrine, see Chap. II, Sec. 6, *supra,* or (v) historic notions of officers' immunity in tort, see Sec. 3, *infra?* [18] Does the United States require more or less protection from damage actions in tort than from suits for specific relief? *Cf.* the discussion of the Steel Seizure case, pp. 1134–44, *supra.* Is the discretionary function exception more likely to be found applicable when (as in Dalehite but not in Indian Towing) the potential liability in tort is enormous? [18a]

(9) Of the numerous other exceptions to the FTCA,[19] four should be highlighted.

(a) Section 2680(a) excludes, in addition to claims arising from discretionary functions, those based upon the action of a government employee "exercising due care, in the execution of a statute or regulation, whether or not * * * valid." Note the contrasting rule of Monell v. Department of Social Services, 436 U.S. 658 (1978), p. 1251, *infra,* under which local government bodies are liable under 42 U.S.C. § 1983 for constitutional torts of their employees only when the allegedly unconstitutional conduct "implements or executes a policy statement, ordinance, regulation, or decision officially adopted and promulgated by that body's officers" (p. 690).

(b) Section 2680(h) excludes liability for any claim arising out of assault, battery, false imprisonment, false arrest, malicious prosecution, abuse of process, libel, slander, misrepresentation, deceit, or interference with contract rights. The legislative history sheds little light on the reason for exclusion of these intentional torts.[20] Compare Daniels v. Williams, p. 1269, *infra,* holding that an allegation that state officials acted negligently (rather than intentionally) in depriving the plaintiff of liberty or property without due process does not state a cause of action.

In 1974, Congress enacted the Intentional Tort Amendments Act, Pub. L. 93–253, 88 Stat. 50, the effect of which is to permit recovery for assault, battery, false imprisonment, false arrest, abuse of process, and malicious prosecution (but not libel, slander, misrepresentation, deceit, or interference with contract rights) when the suit is based upon acts or omissions of investigative or law enforcement officers. See Boger, Gitenstein and Verkuil, *The Federal Tort Claims Act Intentional Torts Amendment: An Interpretative Analysis,* 54 N.C.L.Rev. 497 (1976).

(c) In Laird v. Nelms, 406 U.S. 797 (1972), the plaintiff brought suit for property damage suffered as a result of a sonic boom caused by military aircraft. The Court held that a tort suit based on a theory of strict liability

18. For some discussion of these and other analogies, see 2 Jayson, note 9, *supra,* § 248.03.

18a. See also Berkovitz by Berkovitz v. United States, 822 F.2d 1322 (3d Cir. 1987) (discretionary function exception bars suit, by child paralyzed by polio vaccine, alleging that federal officials were negligent in approving the vaccine's marketing), *cert. granted,* 108 S.Ct. 692 (1988).

19. See generally 28 U.S.C. § 2680; 2 Jayson, note 9, *supra,* §§ 255–60.

20. In United States v. Shearer, 473 U.S. 52, 54–57 (1985), four Justices, in an alternative holding, rejected the view taken by some lower courts that the FTCA encompasses suits alleging that a federal employee's intentional tort resulted from a superior's *negligent* supervision; four other Justices concurred in the judgment on other grounds; Justice Powell did not participate. The lower courts have since divided on this issue, which is presented in Sheridan v. United States, 823 F.2d 820 (4th Cir. 1987), *cert. granted,* 108 S.Ct. 747 (1988).

for ultrahazardous activity could not be brought under the FTCA. Does any provision in the Act justify that result?

(d) Numerous cases have considered the FTCA's application to injuries suffered by military personnel. In Brooks v. United States, 337 U.S. 49 (1949), the Court interpreted the Act as permitting suit by a soldier injured, while on furlough, by the civilian driver of a military truck. The following year, however, the Court unanimously held the Act inapplicable to injuries to servicemen that "arise out of or are in the course of activity incident to service," notwithstanding the absence of any statutory language supporting that result. Feres v. United States, 340 U.S. 135, 146 (1950).[21] The Court later explained this doctrine as based primarily upon three considerations: the distinctively federal character of military relationships, the existence of alternative compensation systems, and the deleterious effect that tort suits could have upon military discipline. Stencel Aero Engineering Corp. v. United States, 431 U.S. 666, 673 (1977). More recently, the Court stressed that the last of these considerations is the most important,[22] and that "[t]he Feres doctrine cannot be reduced to a few bright-line rules." United States v. Shearer, 473 U.S. 52, 57 (1985).

This emphasis on case-by-case application of Feres led some lower courts to chip away at the doctrine where the tortious conduct was quite divorced from military command relationships. In United States v. Johnson, 107 S.Ct. 2063 (1987), for example, a divided court of appeals held that a wrongful death claim filed by the widow of a Coast Guard pilot, alleging negligence by civilian FAA personnel under whose control the pilot had been flying, was not barred by Feres; the suit, the court reasoned, would not threaten military discipline. The Supreme Court reversed, 5–4. Justice Powell stated broadly that "the Feres doctrine has been applied consistently to bar all suits on behalf of service members against the Government based on service-related injuries. We decline to modify the doctrine at this late date" (p. 2067). He reiterated the three concerns underlying the doctrine, and argued that any service-related suit "necessarily implicates the military judgments and decisions that are inextricably intertwined with the conduct of the military mission" (p. 2069).

Justice Scalia, joined by Justices Brennan, Marshall, and Stevens, dissented. In his view, the Feres decision was simply unjustified; Congress had created numerous express exceptions to the FTCA's general rule of governmental liability, and there was no adequate basis for judicial implication of an additional exception. He argued that whether or not Feres should be overruled in a proper case, it should not be extended to injuries caused by civilian conduct.

An expansive interpretation of Feres was again adopted in United States v. Stanley, 107 S.Ct. 3054 (1987), which held that a former serviceman could not maintain a Bivens action against military officers and civilians who had administered the drug LSD to him, without his consent, as part of an army experiment. Justice Scalia, now speaking for the Court,

21. In United States v. Brown, 348 U.S. 110 (1954), affirming that Feres did not disapprove Brooks, the Court held that a discharged veteran may sue under the FTCA for negligent treatment in a Veterans' Administration hospital for a service-connected disability.

22. Note that the first rationale is in some tension with Rayonier v. United States and United States v. Muniz, note 17, *supra*, while the second cannot explain the differing outcomes of Feres and Brooks.

applied the approach of Chappell v. Wallace, p. 932, *supra,* which was held to require "abstention in the inferring of Bivens actions as extensive as the exception to the FTCA established by Feres and United States v. Johnson"—*i.e.,* whenever the injury is "incident to [military] service" (p. 3063). (The court of appeals had ruled that Stanley's injury was incident to service, and the Court refused to reexamine that ruling.)

Justice Brennan (joined by Justices Marshall and Stevens) and Justice O'Connor dissented. In Justice O'Connor's view, "conduct of the type alleged in this case is so far beyond the bounds of human decency that as a matter of law it simply cannot be considered a part of the military mission" (p. 3065).[23]

(10) Carlson v. Green, p. 931, *supra,* held that the FTCA does not preclude a Bivens action against individual officers.[24] However, the FTCA does not in terms create liability for conduct in violation of the Constitution. Such conduct may be the basis for an FTCA claim if suit is not barred by some limitation upon FTCA liability and if the conduct violates the applicable tort law; liability and damages are determined, however, under state law, not under constitutionally derived standards. See, *e.g.,* Birnbaum v. United States, 588 F.2d 319, 322, 327–28 (2d Cir.1978); Van Schaick v. United States, 586 F.Supp. 1023 (D.S.C.1983).[25]

3. Suits for Relief Other Than Money Damages

(11) In 1976, Congress enacted an important statute designed to eliminate three barriers to federal court actions seeking specific relief against federal official action. Pub.L. No. 94–574, 90 Stat. 2721. First, the statute amended 28 U.S.C. § 1331 to eliminate any jurisdictional minimum in suits thereunder "brought against the United States, any agency thereof, or any officer or employee thereof in his official capacity." Second, the statute waived sovereign immunity in federal court suits seeking relief other than money damages against federal agencies or officials. And third, it provided that the United States may be named as a defendant and have judgment entered against it, providing that any mandatory or injunctive order specify the officer(s) responsible for compliance.

(12) The language waiving sovereign immunity is codified as the last three sentences of section 10(b) of the Administrative Procedure Act, 5 U.S.C. § 702, and reads as follows:

"An action in a court of the United States seeking relief other than money damages and stating a claim that an agency or an officer or employee thereof acted or failed to act in an official capacity or under color of legal authority shall not be dismissed nor relief therein be denied on the ground that it is against the United States or that the United States is an

---

23. The Feres doctrine is criticized in Note, 77 Mich.L.Rev. 1099 (1979). See also 1 Jayson, note 9, § 155.04; Jacoby, *The Feres Doctrine,* 24 Hastings L.J. 1281, 1284–85 (1973).

24. Efforts to imply a Bivens remedy against the United States itself have been rejected on grounds of sovereign immunity. See Arnsberg v. United States, 757 F.2d 971, 980 (9th Cir.1985), and cases cited. But *cf.* Davis, note 9, *supra,* § 27.26.

25. Note, however, that a judgment against the United States under the FTCA bars further suit against individual tortfeasors. 28 U.S.C. § 2676; see Arevalo v. Woods, 811 F.2d 487 (9th Cir.1987) (district court entered $1000 judgment under the FTCA against the United States for false imprisonment and battery, and $1500 judgment under Bivens against the federal officer involved; court of appeals reversed judgment against officer, finding it barred by § 2676).

indispensable party. The United States may be named as a defendant in any such action, and a judgment or decree may be entered against the United States: *Provided,* That any mandatory or injunctive decree shall specify the Federal officer or officers (by name or by title), and their successors in office, personally responsible for compliance. Nothing herein (1) affects other limitations on judicial review or the power or duty of the court to dismiss any action or deny relief on any other appropriate legal or equitable ground; or (2) confers authority to grant relief if any other statute that grants consent to suit expressly or impliedly forbids the relief which is sought."

The House Report accompanying that legislation remarks:

" * * * [T]he amendment to 5 U.S.C. section 702 is not intended to permit suit in circumstances where statutes forbid or limit the relief sought. Clause (2) of the third new sentence added to section 702 contains a second proviso concerned with situations in which Congress has consented to suit and the remedy provided is intended to be the exclusive remedy. For example, in the Court of Claims Act, Congress created a damage remedy for contract claims with jurisdiction limited to the Court of Claims except in suits for less than $10,000. The measure is intended to foreclose specific performance of government contracts. In the terms of the proviso, a statute granting consent to suit, *i.e.,* the Tucker Act, 'impliedly forbids' relief other than the remedy provided by the act. Thus, the partial abolition of sovereign immunity brought about by this bill does not change existing limitations on specific relief, if any, derived from statutes dealing with such matters as government contracts, as well as patent infringement, tort claims, and tax claims.

" * * *

" * * * The proviso as amended also emphasizes that the requisite intent can be implied as well as expressed." H.R.Rep. No. 94–1656, 94th Cong., 2d Sess. 9, 12–13 (1976).

(13) How complete is this statute's waiver of sovereign immunity in suits for specific relief? Though codified in the APA, the waiver applies to any suit, whether under the APA, § 1331, § 1361, or any other statute.[26] Note, however, that § 702 applies only to suits in federal court, and that it covers only actions of an "agency" of the United States as that term is defined in 5 U.S.C. § 701(b)(1), thereby excluding, for example, suits against Congress, the federal courts, the District of Columbia, and the territories. See, *e.g.,* Clark v. Library of Congress, 750 F.2d 89, 102 (D.C.Cir.1984), finding § 702 inapplicable in a discrimination suit filed by an employee of the Library of Congress.

26. See, *e.g.,* Sea–Land Serv., Inc. v. Alaska R.R., 659 F.2d 243, 244 (D.C.Cir. 1981) (suit under § 1331); Doe v. Casey, 601 F.Supp. 581, 585–86 (D.D.C.1985) (suit under § 1361).

In Estate of Watson v. Blumenthal, 586 F.2d 925, 932 (2d Cir.1978), the court advanced as an alternative holding the surprising conclusion that § 702's waiver does not affect sovereign immunity in suits under § 1331. Since the APA is not itself a grant of jurisdiction, see p. 1096, note 16, *supra,* this view would have left the amendment to § 702 with no effect on immunity. Other circuits disagreed, see, *e.g.,* Jaffee v. United States, 592 F.2d 712 (3d Cir.1979); Sea–Land Serv. Inc. v. Alaska R.R., *supra,* as did a subsequent Second Circuit panel that included the author of Watson, see B.K. Instrument, Inc. v. United States, 715 F.2d 713, 724–25 (2d Cir. 1983).

(14) Does § 702 overrule Malone v. Bowdoin, p. 1126, *supra?* Dugan v. Rank, p. 1127, *supra?* The Larson decision?

(a) A case like Malone v. Bowdoin would today be permitted under a 1972 statute that (subject to some exceptions) authorizes suit against the United States in the district courts "to adjudicate a disputed title to real property in which the United States claims an interest." Pub.L. 92–562, 86 Stat. 1176, codified in 28 U.S.C. §§ 1346(f), 1402(d), 2409a. This statute has been held to be the exclusive remedy for real property actions to which it pertains, and thus, under the second proviso of § 702, it constitutes an implied preclusion of relief. Block v. North Dakota ex rel. Bd. of Univ. & School Lands, 461 U.S. 273, 280–86 & n. 22 (1983).

(b) In South Delta Water Agency v. United States Dept. of Interior, 767 F.2d 531 (9th Cir.1985), users of water from the same federal reclamation project at issue in Dugan v. Rank sued state and federal agencies, alleging that the defendants were operating their respective water facilities in violation of plaintiffs' rights under state and federal law. The court of appeals upheld the district court's jurisdiction under § 702 to award equitable relief, and found that the Tucker Act did not impliedly preclude non-monetary relief under the second proviso of § 702.

(c) Would that proviso be pertinent, however, if a suit like Larson were brought today? In Spectrum Leasing Corp. v. United States, 764 F.2d 891 (D.C.Cir.1985), a supplier who had leased computer hardware to the government encountered difficulties meeting contractual commitments to provide computer software. The government invoked the contract's liquidated damages clause, collecting those damages by withholding regular lease payments for the hardware. The contractor sued in district court for an injunction requiring the United States to make the payments, the withholding of which was claimed to violate the Debt Collection Act of 1982 (DCA). The court of appeals concluded that the existence of district court jurisdiction "turns upon whether Spectrum's claim is a contract dispute subject to the jurisdiction of the Claims Court under the Tucker Act, or a request for review of agency action under the APA and section 1331" (p. 893). After determining that the DCA itself provides no right to the payment, the court concluded that Spectrum was seeking "the classic contractual remedy of specific performance," and that the Tucker Act impliedly precludes contractual remedies other than money damages (p. 894). *Cf.* Mine Safety Appliances Co. v. Forrestal, 326 U.S. 371, 374–75 (1945).

Will it always be easy to distinguish specific performance from review of the legality of administrative action? [27]

---

27. See, *e.g.,* Megapulse, Inc. v. Lewis, 672 F.2d 959, 968–70 (D.C.Cir.1982) (permitting district court action to enjoin, as a violation of the Trade Secrets Act, disclosure of information, claimed to be proprietary, that the government had acquired under a contract with plaintiff). Compare Hahn v. United States, 757 F.2d 581 (3d Cir.1985) (district court suit to enjoin the denial of certain "constructive service credits" in computing pay levels of Public Health Service officers; court of appeals concedes that Claims Court's exclusive jurisdiction may not be evaded by disguising a monetary claim as a claim for an injunction, and that a district court injunction might ultimately require the expenditure of federal funds, but refuses to dismiss the suit, as the relief would also affect plaintiffs who were considering joining the PHS; the court rejected the government's argument that, because a district court judgment might have preclusive effect in the Claims Court in a separate suit for back pay, under § 702 jurisdiction is impliedly precluded) with Matthews v. United States, 810 F.2d 109 (6th Cir.1987) (per curiam) (dismissing, as within the Claims Court's exclusive jurisdiction, a district court action for reinstatement by air traffic con-

(15) How should the phrase "money damages" in § 702 be construed? In Maryland Dept. of Human Resources v. Department of HHS, 763 F.2d 1441 (D.C.Cir.1985), the state sued to enjoin a threatened reduction of federal funding on the ground of alleged misspending by the plaintiff of federal grants-in-aid. The court held that the effort to compel payment of money by the federal government was not a claim for "money damages," and hence fell within § 702's waiver of sovereign immunity (p. 1446): "Damages are given to the plaintiff to *substitute* for a suffered loss, whereas specific remedies 'are not substitute remedies at all, but attempt to give the plaintiff the very thing to which he was entitled.' D. Dobbs, *Handbook on the Law of Remedies* 135 (1973)." Maryland was not seeking damages for losses suffered from the withholding, but rather funds to which it claimed a legal entitlement.[28] Compare New Mexico v. Regan, 745 F.2d 1318, 1321 n. 3 (10th Cir.1984), barring a state's suit to recover alleged underpayment by the federal government of mineral royalties. The court held that § 702's waiver does not extend to claims for money, whether damages or otherwise. The First Circuit followed the New Mexico case in Commonwealth of Massachusetts v. Departmental Grant Appeals Bd., 815 F.2d 778, 782–84 (1st Cir. 1987). But in Commonwealth of Massachusetts v. Secretary of HHS, 816 F.2d 796 (1st Cir. 1987), *cert. granted sub nom.* Bowen v. Massachusetts, 108 S.Ct. 693 (1988), it ruled that where a grant-in-aid dispute revolves around not only a past denial of funds but also an issue of law that will affect future funding decisions, § 702 permits the award of injunctive or declaratory relief (but not of relief for the past denial).

If § 702 were interpreted to bar relief for past denials of funds in cases like these, could a court provide relief in the nature of mandamus without running afoul of sovereign immunity? See p. 1117, *supra*. The court in the New Mexico case found mandamus inappropriate because of the existence of an adequate remedy under the Tucker Act in the Claims Court.

(16) Note, in connection with the previous two Paragraphs, that a key purpose of the Federal Rules of Civil Procedure was to replace the forms of action and separate systems of law and equity with a single civil action in the district courts. Litigants suing the government face, however, a far more complex system. Will it always be clear whether a suit seeking specific relief should be filed in district court, or, because it is "really" a disguised suit for specific performance of a contract, in the Claims Court? Whether a suit for monetary relief is for money damages, and thus outside § 702 (though perhaps cognizable in the Claims Court), or for some other kind of monetary relief, and therefore within the district court's jurisdiction under § 702? Whether a damage claim in excess of $10,000 lies under a contract (and thus within the Claims' Court's exclusive jurisdiction under the Tucker Act), in tort (and thus within the district courts' FTCA jurisdic-

---

trollers; provision of injunctive relief would effectively dispose of all issues pertinent to a back pay action except the amount, and would thus effectively require payments by the United States in excess of $10,000 per plaintiff).

See also North Side Lumber Co. v. Block, 474 U.S. 931 (1985) (White, J., dissenting from the denial of certiorari) (questioning court of appeals' decision that the Tucker Act impliedly precludes district court jurisdiction over suit seeking a declaration that plaintiffs' contracts with the United States are void).

28. The Court refused to interpret § 702 in light of the Tucker Act's line between monetary relief (whether or not damages), which can be awarded, and non-monetary relief, which cannot. See Paragraph (4), *supra*.

tion), or both? Whether an official's taking of property worth more than $10,000 was "authorized," so that damages are available under the Tucker Act, or was not, so that only equitable relief in the district courts is available? See pp. 1139–42, *supra.*[29]

To eliminate such problems, should Congress abolish the Claims Court, and give the district courts jurisdiction to entertain all claims against the United States under the Tucker Act, the FTCA, and every other statute consenting to suit? Should it instead expand the Claims Court's jurisdiction? Compare 28 U.S.C. § 1631 (permitting, in the interest of justice, transfer of a civil action from a court without jurisdiction to one in which the case could have been filed.).

4. The Interpretation of Statutes Consenting to Suit

(17) The view that statutes waiving immunity should be strictly construed seems to have been established in the early cases under the Court of Claims Act. See, *e.g.,* Borchard, *Government Liability in Tort,* 34 Yale L.J. 1, 28–41 (1924). Should not the waiver of immunity be construed, if not liberally, at least sensibly—with a sympathetic assumption of a congressional intention to introduce, in the area in question, a regime of law infused with a spirit of equity? Why shouldn't a court find an implied consent to suit when Congress has authorized the government to incur debts or to make contracts, or to engage in activity that might cause harm of the kind that normally is actionable when caused by private actors? Consider in this connection the numerous state judicial decisions attenuating or rejecting sovereign immunity in actions under state law. See, *e.g.,* the cases collected in S.Rep. 94–996, 94th Cong., 2d. Sess. 4 n. 11 (1976), and Keeton, *et al.,* Prosser & Keeton on The Law of Torts § 131 (5th ed. 1984).

(18) In Keifer & Keifer v. Reconstruction Finance Corp., 306 U.S. 381 (1939), the defendant was a regional government corporation. The Court found that the corporation was not protected by sovereign immunity, even though its authorizing legislation contained no "sue-and-be-sued" clause, reasoning that since the parent corporation and many similarly situated entities lacked immunity, Congress could not have intended a different result for the regional corporation. Justice Frankfurter wrote (pp. 388–89): "the government does not become the conduit of its immunity in suits against its agents or instrumentalities merely because they do its work," and the immunity is not readily implied. Accord, Federal Housing Admin-

---

29. Similar jurisdictional uncertainties can arise on appeal. In United States v. Hohri, 107 S.Ct. 2246 (1987), Japanese–American citizens placed in internment camps during World War II brought damage actions against the United States in district court, alleging both Tucker Act claims (apparently not exceeding $10,000) and FTCA claims. The D.C. Circuit found that it did have appellate jurisdiction under 28 U.S.C. § 1291 to review the district court's dismissal of the suit. The United States Court of Appeals for the Federal Circuit has exclusive jurisdiction over an appeal from a decision of a district court whose jurisdiction "was based, in whole or in part, on [28 U.S.C. § 1346], except that jurisdiction of an appeal in a case brought in a district court under [28 U.S.C. § 1346(b)] * * * shall be governed by [28 U.S.C. § 1291] * * *." 28 U.S.C. § 1295(a)(2). The D.C. Circuit read the "except" clause to apply to "mixed" cases—those based on both § 1346(b) (the FTCA) and § 1346(a)(2) (the Tucker Act). The Supreme Court unanimously reversed, finding the statutory language ambiguous but more easily interpreted to give the Federal Circuit exclusive jurisdiction over "mixed" cases, a view supported by the desirability of enabling the Federal Circuit to promote uniformity by exercising jurisdiction over every Tucker Act appeal.

istration, Region No. 4 v. Burr, 309 U.S. 242 (1940) (no immunity from garnishment and execution from state court against funds in hands of agency; at least in cases involving federal instrumentalities, "waivers by Congress of governmental immunity * * * should be liberally construed"); Franchise Tax Bd. of California v. United States Postal Service, 467 U.S. 512, 520 (1984) (Postal Service subject to state administrative tax levies on employees' wages; "Congress has 'launched [the Postal Service] into the commercial world'" and hence the Court must "liberally construe the sue-and-be-sued clause" and "must presume that the Service's liability is the same as that of any other business." [30]

(19) Cases like Keifer & Keifer and Burr reflected doubts about sovereign immunity even outside the context of specialized government agencies or corporations. Keifer & Keifer spoke of the "present climate of opinion which has brought governmental immunity from suit into disfavor," 306 U.S. at 391; accord, Burr, 309 U.S. at 245. The Supreme Court has continued to voice such misgivings, albeit in a halting and irregular fashion. In United States v. Yellow Cab Co., 340 U.S. 543 (1951), for example, in holding that the United States could be impleaded under the FTCA as a third party defendant and required to answer the claim of a joint tortfeasor for contribution, the Court said (p. 550): "Recognizing such a clearly defined breadth of purpose for the bill as a whole, and the general trend toward increasing the scope of the waiver by the United States of its sovereign immunity from suit, it is inconsistent to whittle it down by refinements." [31] Interspersed with such statements, however, have been regular reiterations in other cases of the conventional position. [32]

Recent Supreme Court decisions appear to have adhered to the conventional position. See, e.g., Library of Congress v. Shaw, 106 S.Ct. 2957, 2963, 2965 (1986) (the Court "must construe waivers strictly in favor of the sovereign"; "policy, no matter how compelling, is insufficient, standing alone, to waive this immunity"); United States v. Mottaz, 476 U.S. 834, 851 (1986), quoting United States v. Mitchell, 445 U.S. 535, 538 (1980) (notwithstanding traditional solicitude for Indian plaintiffs, "[a] waiver of sovereign immunity 'cannot be lightly implied, but must be unequivocally expressed'").

---

30. In Loeffler v. Tisch, 806 F.2d 817 (8th Cir.1986), cert. granted, 107 S.Ct. 3227 (1987), the en banc court of appeals ruled, 6–5, that in an action against the Postal Service brought under Title VII of the Civil Rights Act of 1964 rather than under the sue-and-be-sued clause at issue in Franchise Tax Board, the defendant was immune from an award of prejudgment interest.

31. See also, e.g., Canadian Aviator, Ltd. v. United States, 324 U.S. 215, 222 (1945); National City Bank of New York v. Republic of China, 348 U.S. 356, 359 (1955).

32. See, e.g., United States v. Sherwood, 312 U.S. 584, 590 (1941); McMahon v. United States, 342 U.S. 25, 27 (1951).

SECTION 2. SUITS CHALLENGING STATE OFFICIAL ACTION

SUBSECTION A: THE ELEVENTH AMENDMENT AND STATE SOVEREIGN IMMUNITY

NOTE ON THE ORIGIN, MEANING, AND SCOPE OF THE ELEVENTH AMENDMENT

(1) In Chisholm v. Georgia, 2 Dall. 419 (U.S.1793), a South Carolina citizen filed an assumpsit claim against the State of Georgia as an original action in the Supreme Court. Rejecting Georgia's protest that an unconsenting state was immune from suit, the Supreme Court upheld its jurisdiction as consistent with Article III's grant of judicial power over controversies "between a State and Citizens of another State." Each of the five Justices wrote separately. Justices Blair and Cushing both relied on the clear language of Article III, noting that its grant of jurisdiction over controversies between two states contemplated that an unconsenting state could be a defendant (pp. 450–53, 466–69). Chief Justice Jay likewise relied on Article III's language, but argued in addition that the "feudal" doctrine of sovereign immunity was incompatible with popular sovereignty. Troubled, though, that this argument implied that the United States itself could be sued, notwithstanding the difficulty of enforcing a judgment against it, he ultimately left that question open (pp. 472–79). Justice Wilson argued most fully that the doctrine of sovereign immunity was incompatible with principles of public law and with a republican form of government, reasoning that a state was no more sovereign, and no less subject to the law, than a free man (pp. 453–58).

Justice Iredell's lone dissent stressed that the Supreme Court could exercise only that jurisdiction conferred by Congress. He contended that the First Judiciary Act's grant of original jurisdiction should be interpreted in light of common law principles. English law would have permitted an action like Chisholm's only by petition of right, with the sovereign's consent; [1] when the Constitution and First Judiciary Act took effect, no state permitted "a compulsory suit for the recovery of money against a State" (pp. 434–35). Though acknowledging (pp. 449–50) that he strongly opposed "any construction of [the Constitution] which will admit, under any circumstances, a compulsive suit against a State for the recovery of money," he rested only on statutory grounds, and conceded (pp. 432, 435) that the outcome might differ in a suit arising under federal law.[2]

---

1. On the petition of right, see pp. 1098–99, 1106–07, 1110, *supra.*

2. For an illuminating account of Chisholm in historical context, arguing that assertion of federal jurisdiction over suits against the states was necessary to enforce the Peace Treaty of 1783 with Britain, see Gibbons, *The Eleventh Amendment* and *State Sovereign Immunity: A Reinterpretation,* 83 Colum.L.Rev. 1889, 1895–1941 (1983). See also Mathis, *Chisholm v. Georgia: Background and Settlement,* 54 J.Am. Hist. 19 (1967); Mathis, *The Eleventh Amendment: Adoption and Interpretation,* 2 Ga.L.Rev. 207 (1968).

(2) Chisholm "created such a shock of surprise" that the Eleventh Amendment was soon enacted. Hans v. Louisiana, 134 U.S. 1, 11 (1890), Paragraph (6), *infra;* see also, *e.g.,* Monaco v. Mississippi, 292 U.S. 313, 325 (1934), p. 306, *supra;* 1 C. Warren, The Supreme Court in United States History 96 (1924).[3] A constitutional amendment to overrule Chisholm was introduced in the Senate only two days after the decision.[4] As finally adopted and ratified, the Eleventh Amendment provides:

"The Judicial power of the United States shall not be construed to extend to any suit in law or equity, commenced or prosecuted against one of the United States by Citizens of another State, or by Citizens or Subjects of any Foreign State."

(3) Before the Civil War, the Supreme Court faced relatively few cases involving the Eleventh Amendment. And until 1875 there was, of course, no general federal question jurisdiction.

In Cohens v. Virginia, 6 Wheat. 264 (U.S.1821), defendants convicted in state court in Virginia for selling District of Columbia lottery tickets, in violation of Virginia law, sought review in the Supreme Court, asserting that under the Supremacy Clause they were immune from prosecution for selling tickets because the lottery was authorized by Congress. The Court affirmed the convictions on the merits, but only after rejecting the state's contention that it was being sued without its consent for a writ of error in the Supreme Court, in violation of the Eleventh Amendment.[5] Chief Justice Marshall's opinion argued, first, that under the Constitution, the states had surrendered a portion of their sovereignty to the Union. He stated (p. 383) that "a case arising under the constitution or laws of the United States, is cognizable in the courts of the Union, whoever may be the parties to that case." Marshall appealed to the "political axiom" that "the judicial power of every well-constructed government must be co-extensive with the legislative," arguing that otherwise each of the states "will possess a *veto* on the will of the whole" (pp. 384–85; see The Federalist, No. 80, p. 23, *supra*). The Eleventh Amendment was designed to quiet apprehension about suits on the states' debts by barring federal jurisdiction in actions by those likely to be creditors, not "to strip the government of the means of protecting, by the instrumentality of its courts, the constitution and laws from active violation" (p. 407).

Marshall also asserted that a writ of error, which acts on the record, not the parties, was not a "suit" within the meaning of the Amendment. He added that if "we in this be mistaken, the error does not affect the case now before the Court," as the defendants were citizens of Virginia (pp. 407–12). (In Worcester v. Georgia, 6 Pet. 515 (U.S.1832), the party seeking a

---

3. But see Gibbons, note 2, *supra,* at 1926 (contending that "Congress's initial reaction to the Chisholm decision hardly demonstrates the sort of outrage so central to the profound shock thesis"). For other commentary on the history, see, *e.g.,* Jacobs, The Eleventh Amendment and Sovereign Immunity 67–74 (1972); Amar, *Of Federalism and Sovereignty,* 96 Yale L.J. 1425, 1481–84 (1987); Fletcher, *A Historical Interpretation of the Eleventh Amendment: A Narrow Construction of an Affirmative Grant of Jurisdiction Rather* than a Prohibition Against Jurisdiction, 35 Stan.L.Rev. 1033, 1058–59 (1983).

4. See Gibbons, note 2, *supra,* at 1926–27 & n. 186.

5. In three prior decisions, the Court had reviewed suits between states and private citizens without discussion of the Amendment. See McCulloch v. Maryland, 4 Wheat. 316 (U.S.1819); New Jersey v. Wilson, 7 Cranch 164 (U.S.1812); Smith v. Maryland, 6 Cranch 286 (U.S.1810).

writ of error was a noncitizen; the Supreme Court exercised jurisdiction without discussing the Eleventh Amendment issue).

Should Cohens be read as recognizing an exception to the Eleventh Amendment limited to appellate review of state court judgments—an exception demanded by the need to ensure the supremacy of federal law? See Tribe, *Intergovernmental Immunities in Litigation, Taxation, and Regulation: Separation of Powers Issues in Controversies About Federalism*, 89 Harv.L.Rev. 682, 685 (1976). Is there any historical or textual basis for holding that the Amendment's impact on the federal courts' original jurisdiction differs from its impact on the appellate jurisdiction? See Gibbons, note 2, *supra*, at 1946 & n. 310, arguing no; *cf.* Osborn v. Bank of the United States, p. 967, *supra*. How significant is the fact that Cohens, unlike Chisholm, was a federal question case?

(4) In Osborn v. Bank of the United States, 9 Wheat. 738 (U.S.1824), after the federal circuit court enjoined state officials from collecting an unconstitutional tax from the plaintiff Bank, an official seized $100,000 from a Bank office. The Supreme Court upheld a second decree ordering one official to return the $98,000 held in his possession but credited to the state, and ordering two others to repay the remaining $2000 (the location of which was not discussed in the opinion), all over defendants' objection that the order violated the Eleventh Amendment.[6] Chief Justice Marshall stated for the Court (pp. 846–47): "The direct interest of the state in the suit, as brought, is admitted; and, had it been in the power of the bank to make it a party, perhaps no decree ought to have been pronounced in the cause, until the state was before the court. But this was not in the power of the bank. The eleventh amendment of the constitution has exempted a state from the suits of citizen of other states, or aliens * * *." That provision, however, did not bar suit against the officers (pp. 857–58): "It may, we think, be laid down as a rule which admits of no exception, that, in all cases where jurisdiction depends on the party, it is the party named in the record. Consequently, the 11th amendment * * * is, of necessity, limited to those suits in which a state is a party on the record. The amendment has its full effect, if the constitution be construed as it would have been construed, had the jurisdiction of the Court never been extended to suits brought against a state, by the citizens of another state, or by aliens."

Does the first quotation from Osborn concede, albeit in dictum, that the Eleventh Amendment bars suit against an unconsenting state even in a federal question case? See Gibbons, note 2, *supra*, at 1958 n. 370, reading the quoted language as a paraphrase of defense counsel's position. Does the second quotation suggest merely that the Amendment bars the exercise of judicial power only in cases, like Chisholm, in which jurisdiction over a defendant state is based entirely on party status?

(5) The Marshall Court was able to dispose of several admiralty cases without deciding whether the Eleventh Amendment applied to that head of jurisdiction. In United States v. Peters, 5 Cranch 115 (U.S.1809), a Connecticut sailor and the State of Pennsylvania both claimed proceeds of an admiralty prize sale, which had been paid to the state treasurer, since

6. While a state has no immunity from suit brought by the United States, see Paragraph (7), *infra*, the Bank was treated as a private party rather than as an arm of the United States.

deceased, and were held by his personal representatives. The Supreme Court ruled that an order requiring the representatives to pay the proceeds to the sailor did not violate the Amendment, because the suit was against the officer (or his representatives), not the State. Chief Justice Marshall noted (p. 139) that "if these proceeds had been the actual property of Pennsylvania, however wrongfully acquired, the disclosure of that fact would have presented a case on which it is unnecessary to give an opinion * * *." [7]

In Governor of Georgia v. Madrazo, 1 Pet. 110 (U.S.1828), the Court dismissed a libel in admiralty brought in federal district court by Madrazo against the governor for possession of certain slaves (and the proceeds of the sale of others) seized under a state statute after allegedly having been imported in violation of federal law. The Court reasoned that the suit could be justified neither as an in rem action (because the slaves—which the Court treated as "property"—were not in the possession of the court) nor as an in personam action against the governor (because he was sued "not by his name, but by his title" and "[t]he demand made upon him, is not made personally, but officially") (p. 123). Therefore, "the state itself may be considered as a party on the record" (pp. 123–24). Even if the governor were treated as if he had been sued personally, "no case is made which justifies a decree against him personally" since he "acted in obedience to a law of the state, made for the purpose of giving effect to an Act of Congress; and has done nothing in violation of any law of the United States" (p. 124). Because the suit was against the state, it fell within the Supreme Court's, rather than the district court's, original jurisdiction.[8]

Madrazo subsequently filed a libel in admiralty against the state of Georgia as an original action in the Supreme Court. In a one paragraph opinion, Chief Justice Marshall dismissed the suit: it was not within the admiralty jurisdiction, as the property was not in the custody of either the court or any private person. "It is a mere personal suit against a state to recover proceeds in its possession, and in such a case no private person has a right to commence an original suit in this court against a state." Ex parte Madrazzo, 7 Pet. 627, 632 (U.S.1833).

Note that Ex parte Madrazzo—the only case prior to the Civil War in which the Court's opinion based a dismissal on Eleventh Amendment grounds—involved no federal cause of action.

(6) Hans v. Louisiana, 134 U.S. 1 (1890), was a major turning point in Eleventh Amendment doctrine. Hans had purchased bonds issued in 1874 by the state of Louisiana, of which he was a citizen. The state defaulted on interest payments due in 1880. Hans then filed suit against Louisiana in

---

7. Pennsylvania's Governor subsequently instructed a militia officer to guard the treasurer's home to prevent the enforcement of the district court's decree. When the officer was prosecuted for interfering with federal judicial process, the federal circuit court, per Justice Washington, rejected his contention that the Eleventh Amendment barred issuance of the original decree. Justice Washington reiterated the basis for decision in Peters, but added that the Amendment did not extend to admiralty, pointing to the text's limitation to suits at law or in equity, and noting that

in an admiralty in rem proceeding, the "delicate" issue of enforcement against a state does not arise. United States v. Bright, 24 F.Cas. 1232, 1236 (C.C.D.Pa. 1809) (No. 14,647). Over a century later, the Supreme Court rejected his view. See Paragraph (7), *infra.*

8. For a thorough discussion of Madrazo, see Gibbons, note 2, *supra,* at 1961–68; see also Jaffe, *Suits Against Governments and Officers: Sovereign Immunity,* 77 Harv.L.Rev. 1, 21–24 (1963).

federal circuit court, alleging a violation of the Contracts Clause. Writing for a unanimous Court, Justice Bradley found that the state was immune from suit in a federal court.

To plaintiff's argument that Louisiana could claim no immunity in a federal question action, the Court responded (p. 10): "That a State cannot be sued by a citizen of another State, or of a foreign state, on the mere ground that the case is one arising under the Constitution or laws of the United States, is clearly established by the decisions of this court in several recent cases. Louisiana v. Jumel, 107 U.S. 711; Hagood v. Southern, 117 U.S. 52; In Re Ayers, 123 U.S. 443. * * *

"In the present case the plaintiff in error contends that he, being a citizen of Louisiana, is not embarrassed by the obstacle of the Eleventh Amendment, inasmuch as that amendment only prohibits suits against a State which are brought by the citizens of another State, or by citizens or subjects of a foreign State.

"It is true, the amendment does so read: and if there were no other reason or ground for abating his suit, it might be maintainable; and then we should have this anomalous result, that in cases arising under the Constitution or laws of the United States, a State may be sued in the federal courts by its own citizens, though it cannot be sued for a like cause of action by the citizens of other States, or of a foreign state; and may be thus sued in the federal courts, although not allowing itself to be sued in its own courts. If this is the necessary consequence of the language of the Constitution and the law, the result is no less startling and unexpected than was the original decision of this court, that under the language of the Constitution and of the judiciary act of 1789, a State was liable to be sued by a citizen of another State, or of a foreign country. That decision was made in the case of Chisholm v. Georgia, 2 Dall. 419, and created such a shock of surprise throughout the country that, at the first meeting of Congress thereafter, the Eleventh Amendment to the Constitution was almost unanimously proposed, and was in due course adopted by the legislatures of the States. This amendment, expressing the will of the ultimate sovereignty of the whole country, superior to all legislatures and all courts, actually reversed the decision of the Supreme Court. It did not in terms prohibit suits by individuals against the States, but declared that the Constitution should not be construed to import any power to authorize the bringing of such suits.

"* * *

"* * * [O]n this question of the suability of the States by individuals, the highest authority of this country was in accord rather with the minority than with the majority of the court in the decision of the case of Chisholm v. Georgia; and this fact lends additional interest to the able opinion of Mr. Justice Iredell on that occasion. The other justices were more swayed by a close observance of the letter of the Constitution, without regard to former experience and usage * * *. Justice Iredell, on the contrary, contended that it was not the intention to create new and unheard of remedies, by subjecting sovereign States to actions at the suit of individuals, (which he conclusively showed was never done before,) but only, by proper legislation, to invest the federal courts with jurisdiction to hear and determine controversies and cases, between the parties designated, that were properly susceptible of litigation in courts.

"Looking back from our present standpoint at the decision in Chisholm v. Georgia, we do not greatly wonder at the effect which it had upon the country. Any such power as that of authorizing the federal judiciary to entertain suits by individuals against the States, had been expressly disclaimed, and even resented, by the great defenders of the Constitution whilst it was on its trial before the American people. * * *

"The eighty-first number of the Federalist, written by Hamilton, has the following profound remarks:

"'It has been suggested that an assignment of the public securities of one State to the citizens of another, would enable them to prosecute that State in the federal courts for the amount of those securities; a suggestion which the following considerations prove to be without foundation:

"'It is inherent in the nature of sovereignty not to be amenable to the suit of an individual *without its consent*. This is the general sense and the general practice of mankind; and the exemption, as one of the attributes of sovereignty, is now enjoyed by the government of every State in the Union. Unless, therefore, there is a surrender of this immunity in the plan of the convention, it will remain with the States, and the danger intimated must be merely ideal. The circumstances which are necessary to produce an alienation of state sovereignty were discussed in considering the article of taxation, and need not be repeated here. A recurrence to the principles there established will satisfy us, that there is no color to pretend that the state governments would, by the adoption of that plan, be divested of the privilege of paying their own debts in their own way, free from every constraint but that which flows from the obligations of good faith. The contracts between a nation and individuals are only binding on the conscience of the sovereign, and have no pretension to a compulsive force. They confer no right of action independent of the sovereign will. To what purpose would it be to authorize suits against States for the debts they owe? How could recoveries be enforced? It is evident that it could not be done without waging war against the contracting State; and to ascribe to the federal courts by mere implication, and in destruction of a pre-existing right of the state governments, a power which would involve such a consequence, would be altogether forced and unwarrantable.'

"The obnoxious clause to which Hamilton's argument was directed, and which was the ground of the objections which he so forcibly met, was that which declared that "the judicial power shall extend to all * * * controversies between a State and citizens of another State, * * * and between a State and foreign states, citizens or subjects." It was argued by the opponents of the Constitution that this clause would authorize jurisdiction to be given to the federal courts to entertain suits against a State brought by the citizens of another State, or of a foreign state. Adhering to the mere letter, it might be so; and so, in fact, the Supreme Court held in Chisholm v. Georgia; but looking at the subject as Hamilton did, and as Mr. Justice Iredell did, in the light of history and experience and the established order of things, the views of the latter were clearly right,—as the people of the United States in their sovereign capacity subsequently decided.

"But Hamilton was not alone in protesting against the construction put upon the Constitution by its opponents. In the Virginia convention the same objections were raised by George Mason and Patrick Henry, and were met by Madison and Marshall as follows. Madison said: * * * 'It is not in the power of individuals to call any State into court. The only operation it can have is that, if a State should wish to bring a suit against a citizen, it must be brought before the federal court. This will give satisfaction to individuals, as it will prevent citizens on whom a State may have a claim being dissatisfied with the state courts. * * * It appears to me that this [clause] can have no operation but this—to give a citizen a right to be heard in the federal courts; and if a State should condescend to be a party, this court may take cognizance of it.' 3 Elliott's Debates, 2d ed. 533. Marshall, in answer to the same objection, said: ' * * * It is not rational to suppose that the sovereign power should be dragged before a court. The intent is to enable States to recover claims of individuals residing in other States. * * * But, say they, there will be partiality in it if a State cannot be defendant—if an individual cannot proceed to obtain judgment against a State, though he may be sued by a State. It is necessary to be so, and cannot be avoided. I see a difficulty in making a State defendant which does not prevent its being plaintiff.' *Ib.* 555.

"It seems to us that these views of those great advocates and defenders of the Constitution were most sensible and just; and they apply equally to the present case as to that then under discussion. The letter is appealed to now, as it was then, as a ground for sustaining a suit brought by an individual against a State. The reason against it is as strong in this case as it was in that. It is an attempt to strain the Constitution and the law to a construction never imagined or dreamed of. Can we suppose that, when the Eleventh Amendment was adopted, it was understood to be left open for citizens of a State to sue their own state in the federal courts, whilst the idea of suits by citizens of other states, or of foreign states, was indignantly repelled? Suppose that Congress, when proposing the Eleventh Amendment, had appended to it a proviso that nothing therein contained should prevent a State from being sued by its own citizens in cases arising under the Constitution or laws of the United States: can we imagine that it would have been adopted by the States? The supposition that it would is almost an absurdity on its face.

"The truth is, that the cognizance of suits and actions unknown to the law, and forbidden by the law, was not contemplated by the Constitution when establishing the judicial power of the United States. * * * "

The Court also held that the federal courts had no statutory jurisdiction over the action, reading Congress's grant of federal question jurisdiction, "concurrent with the courts of the several States," to preclude the federal courts from entertaining suits against unconsenting states when the state courts lacked such power. The same qualification existed in the First Judiciary Act, and the Court reasoned that in light of the reaction to Chisholm, it was "at liberty to prefer Justice Iredell's views [in dissent] in this regard" (pp. 18–19).

Justice Bradley then dismissed as "extra judicial" the statements in Cohens v. Virginia, Paragraph (3), *supra,* that the Eleventh Amendment does not extend to cases arising under federal law, instead viewing Cohens as resting on the ground that a writ of error was not a suit against a state. He concluded (pp. 20–21):

"To avoid misapprehension it may be proper to add that, although the obligations of a State rest for their performance upon its honor and good faith, and cannot be made the subjects of judicial cognizance unless the State consents to be sued, or comes itself into court; yet where property or rights are enjoyed under a grant or contract made by a State, they cannot wantonly be invaded. Whilst the State cannot be compelled by suit to perform its contracts, any attempt on its part to violate property or rights acquired under its contracts, may be judicially resisted; and any law impairing the obligation of contracts under which such property or rights are held is void and powerless to affect their enjoyment.

"It is not necessary that we should enter upon an examination of the reason or expediency of the rule which exempts a sovereign State from prosecution in a court of justice at the suit of individuals. This is fully discussed by writers on public law. It is enough for us to declare its existence. The legislative department of a State represents its polity and its will; and is called upon by the highest demands of natural and political law to preserve justice and judgment, and to hold inviolate the public obligations. Any departure from this rule, except for reasons most cogent, (of which the legislature, and not the courts, is the judge,) never fails in the end to incur the odium of the world, and to bring lasting injury upon the State itself. But to deprive the legislature of the power of judging what the honor and safety of the State may require, even at the expense of a temporary failure to discharge the public debts, would be attended with greater evils than such failure can cause." [9]

(7) Since Hans v. Louisiana, the Court has continued to depart from the text in construing the Eleventh Amendment, reading it more "as if it were a precedent to the opposite of Chisholm v. Georgia." Hart & Sacks, The Legal Process: Basic Problems in the Making and Application of Law 807 (tent. ed. 1958). The Court thus has held, despite earlier dicta to the contrary, see, *e.g.,* Cherokee Nation v. Georgia, 5 Pet. 1, 15–16 (U.S.1831); Cohens v. Virginia, Paragraph (3), *supra,* 19 U.S. at 406, that the Amendment bars suit against a state by a foreign country, Principality of Monaco v. Mississippi, 292 U.S. 313 (1934), p. 306, *supra,* asserting that "behind the words of the constitutional provisions are postulates which limit and control." In Ex parte New York, No. 1, 256 U.S. 490 (1921), the Court held the Amendment applicable to suits in admiralty, despite the textual limitation to suits "in law or equity"; accord, Florida Dept. of State v. Treasure Salvors, Inc., 458 U.S. 670, 683 n. 17 (1982). But see United States v. Bright, note 7, *supra.*

However, the Amendment bars neither suits against a state by another state, see, *e.g.,* Kansas v. Colorado, 206 U.S. 46, 83 (1907); p. 318, *supra,*[10] nor by the United States, see, *e.g.,* United States v. Mississippi, 380 U.S. 128, 140–41 (1965); United States v. Texas, 143 U.S. 621, 642–46 (1892); p. 299, *supra.* In Monaco v. Mississippi, the Court explained that the former holding "was essential to the peace of the Union" and "a necessary feature of the formation of a more perfect Union," while the latter was "inherent in the constitutional plan" (292 U.S. at 328–29).

9. Justice Harlan's brief concurring opinion agreed that the judicial power does not extend to suit against an unconsenting state by one of its citizens, but refused to embrace all of the majority's reasoning, noting in particular his belief that Chisholm "was based upon a sound interpretation of the Constitution as that instrument then was" (p. 21).

10. But *cf.* New Hampshire v. Louisiana, 108 U.S. 76 (1883), discussed at p. 324, *supra,* and p. 1180, note 3, *infra.*

(8) Is the immunity recognized by cases like Hans, Monaco v. Mississippi, and Ex parte New York a *constitutional* immunity? If so, is it derived from the Eleventh Amendment itself, notwithstanding its wording? Many modern decisions seem to so hold. See, *e.g.*, Florida Dept. of State v. Treasure Salvors, Inc., 458 U.S. 670, 683 n. 17 (1982); Edelman v. Jordan, 415 U.S. 651, 662–63 (1974), p. 1182, *infra*. Or does the Amendment simply undo a mistake made in Chisholm, and restore the (implicit) understanding that Article III's judicial power does not extend to a suit against an unconsenting state by any plaintiff other than the United States or another State? See, *e.g.*, Employees of Dept. of Pub. Health & Welfare v. Department of Pub. Health & Welfare, 411 U.S. 279, 291–92 (1973) (Marshall, J., concurring in the result); Poindexter v. Greenhow, 114 U.S. 270, 337–38 (1885) (Bradley, J., dissenting).

At one time, Justice Brennan advanced the view that the Eleventh Amendment did create a constitutional immunity, but only in suits by citizens of other states or by aliens; Hans, he argued, recognized only a nonconstitutional immunity from suit by a state's own citizens, which could be overcome by congressional enactments. See, *e.g.*, Employees of Dept. of Pub. Health & Welfare, *supra*, 411 U.S. at 309–22 (Brennan, J., dissenting); Edelman v. Jordan, *supra*, at 687–88 (Brennan, J., dissenting). Professor Field takes that argument one step further: she contends that the original Constitution neither imposed nor abrogated state sovereign immunity, but simply left a common law immunity in place; the Eleventh Amendment returned, after Chisholm, to that understanding; and Hans recognizes only that common law immunity. Field, *The Eleventh Amendment and Other Sovereign Immunity Doctrines: Part I*, 126 U.Pa.L.Rev. 515 (1978) (Field I); Field, *The Eleventh Amendment and Other Sovereign Immunity Doctrines: Congressional Imposition of Suit Upon the States*, 126 U.Pa.L.Rev. 1203 (1978) (Field II).

Does the question whether the Constitution "imposes" sovereign immunity create a semantic confusion? State sovereign immunity is quite plainly a "common-law" doctrine in the sense that it can be breached by a statute enacted by the state legislature. Whether immunity can also be breached by a federal statute raises an independent issue of federalism. Can that issue be resolved by arguing that the immunity should be conceptualized as a "common law" rather than a "constitutional" doctrine?

Consider, further, whether Field's view rests upon a strained reading of Hans and of the constitutional text. Under her view, it appears that Congress could authorize the federal courts to entertain an action against an unconsenting state by a citizen of another state, even when the only basis of jurisdiction under Article III was the status of the parties. How can one square such a result with the text of the Amendment? [11]

Professor Field also suggests that "in an era of freewheeling federal common law, the federal judiciary might itself make desired modifications" in sovereign immunity. Field I, *supra*, at 545 n. 98. But *cf.* Field II, *supra*, at 1262–65 (federal courts may *modify* immunity but judicial *abrogation* not to be expected). Is it conceivable that the purpose of the Eleventh Amend-

---

11. Field reads the language "The Judicial power of the United States shall not be construed to extend to ∗ ∗ ∗" to mean that the judicial power should not be deemed, of its own force, "affirmatively to allow" such cases to be heard. Is that plausible, especially when Article III uses the words "extend to" to mean simply "reach"?

ment was merely to overturn Chisholm for as long as, or to whatever extent that, federal judges thought desirable?

(9) The Supreme Court still follows the understanding set forth in Hans that the Eleventh Amendment embodies (or reinstates) a general constitutional principle of state sovereign immunity in federal court actions. In Atascadero State Hosp. v. Scanlon, 473 U.S. 234 (1985), p. 1204, *infra*, however, Justice Brennan presented a powerful revisionist view of the meaning of the Amendment. Drawing on the work of several recent commentators,[12] his dissent (which Justices Marshall, Blackmun, and Stevens joined) argued that the Amendment had nothing to do with sovereign immunity. Rather, it was designed to regulate the scope of federal judicial power: it barred jurisdiction in suits against an unconsenting state brought under the state-citizen diversity clause; but it did not restrict suits against an unconsenting state brought under the admiralty or federal question jurisdiction. Even in suits against a state by a noncitizen, the Amendment creates no constitutional barrier; it simply requires that jurisdiction be based upon subject matter (the existence of a federal question) rather than party status.

According to Justice Brennan, "in most of the States in 1789, the doctrine of sovereign immunity formally forbade the maintenance of suits against States in state courts" (p. 261). To permit federal court jurisdiction based on party status "was a particularly troublesome prospect to the States that had incurred debts, some of which dated back to the Revolutionary War. The debts would naturally find their way into the hands of noncitizens and aliens, who at the first sign of default could be expected promptly to sue the State in federal court. The State's effort to retain its sovereign immunity in its own courts would turn out to be futile" (p. 262).[13]

After concluding that neither the records of the Constitutional Convention nor the language of Article III provide much guidance as to the Amendment's intended scope, Justice Brennan reviewed at length the ratification debates over Article III, including the comments of Hamilton, Madison, and Marshall discussed in Hans v. Louisiana (pp. 263–64):

"The various references to state sovereign immunity all appear in discussions of the state-citizen diversity clause. Virtually all of the comments were addressed to the problem created by state debts that predated the Constitution, when the State's creditors may often have had meager judicial remedies in the case of default. Yet, even in this sensitive context, a number of participants in the debates welcomed the abrogation of sovereign immunity that they thought followed from the state-citizen and state-alien clauses.[14] The debates do not directly address the question of

---

12. See, *e.g.*, Fletcher, note 3, *supra*; Gibbons, note 2, *supra*; Orth, *The Interpretation of the Eleventh Amendment, 1798–1908: A Case Study of Judicial Power*, 1983 U.Ill.L.Rev. 423. See also the subsequent article by Amar, note 3, *supra*.

13. [Ed.] For contrasting views of the doctrine's status in the Colonies, compare Jacobs, note 3, *supra*, at 12 (sovereign immunity and limitations on its scope were well-established), with Gibbons, note 2, *supra*, at 1895–99 (governmental immunity was not an accepted doctrine) and Orth, The Judicial Power of the United States:

The Eleventh Amendment in American History 23–24 (1987) (same).

14. [Ed.] The view that the Constitution abrogated immunity was advanced as an argument against ratification by some opponents (such as George Mason and Patrick Henry in Virginia) and various anti-Federalist publicists, but the view was also held by proponents of ratification (like Edmund Pendleton and Edmund Randolph of Virginia and Timothy Pickering and James Wilson of Pennsylvania). 473 U.S. at 263–80. See generally Gibbons, note 2, *supra*, at 1902–08.

suits against States in admiralty or federal question cases, where federal law and not state law would govern.[15] Nonetheless, the apparent willingness of many delegates to read the state-citizen clause as abrogating sovereign immunity in state-law causes of action suggests that they would have been even more willing to permit suits against States in federal question cases, where Congress had authorized such suits in the exercise of its Article I or other powers."

Justice Brennan then examined the drafting of the Eleventh Amendment by Congress. He concluded that the language chosen "would have been a particularly cryptic way to embody" in the Constitution a consensus that the doctrine of state sovereign immunity would apply in federal court. Had the drafters wished that result, they could have "merely omitted the last fourteen words" of the Amendment. The language chosen—"The Judicial power of the United States shall not be construed to extend * * *"—parallels the phrasing of Article III, and was meant merely to abandon the construction of Article III in Chisolm, which permitted federal court suit against a state based simply upon party status. The Amendment, accordingly, singles out suits against a State by aliens or citizens of another state, in order to track (and restrict) the party-based jurisdiction in Article III (pp. 286–87).

Finally, Justice Brennan considered the Marshall Court's decisions in Cohens, Osborn, Peters, and both Madrazo cases. He argued that they were consistent with his interpretation of the Amendment, for in none of them did the Court decline jurisdiction in a suit against a state based upon federal law.[16] And he relied particularly on the statement in Osborn that " '[t]he amendment has its full effect, if the constitution be construed as it would have been construed, had the jurisdiction of the Court never been extended to suits brought against a state, by the citizens of another state, or by aliens' " (p. 298, quoting 9 Wheat. at 857–58).

Recall that Chisholm was an assumpsit action. In drafting a provision to overrule it, the Framers of the Eleventh Amendment gave little if any explicit consideration to the question of an unconsenting state's liability under federal law. Are the justifications for the sovereign immunity of the United States, see p. 1108, *supra,* as weighty when offered in support of a state's claim of immunity in a system in which federal law is supreme and federal power may be invoked to enforce judgments against recalcitrant states? Compare the argument of then Professor Scalia that a state's immunity from federal court suit is an aspect of "foreign" sovereign immunity, which is "essential to the security and dignity" of that state, and therefore entitled to more protection than the United States' own immunity from suit in its own courts. Scalia, *Sovereign Immunity and Nonstatuto-*

---

15. [Ed.] Later in his opinion, Justice Brennan observed (p. 282 n. 33): "Most likely, Chisholm could not have been brought directly under the Contracts Clause of the Constitution. Prior to Fletcher v. Peck, 6 Cranch 87 (1810), it was not at all clear that the Contracts Clause applied to contracts to which a state was a party. Moreover, the case involved a simple breach of contract, not a law impairing the obligation of the contract to which the Clause would have applied. Finally, it was certainly not clear at the time of Chisholm that the Contracts Clause provided a plaintiff with a private right of action for damages."

16. Consider, the relationship of Justice Brennan's argument to that of Professor Amar, p. 385, *supra.* Recall that Amar argues that Congress is obliged to vest jurisdiction in some federal court over cases that fall within the subject matter clauses, but not the party clauses, of Article III's definition of judicial power.

ry Review of Federal Administrative Action: Some Conclusions from the Public–Lands Cases, 68 Mich.L.Rev. 867, 886–88 (1970).

The Atascadero case involved a claim that a state was liable in damages under a federal statute, while Hans involved a claim for a judicially-implied remedy directly under the Constitution. Justice Brennan's dissent did not specifically address the question whether the federal courts' power to imply damage remedies for violations of federal constitutional provisions (as in the Bivens line of cases) or of federal statutes should extend to remedies against the states themselves. (He did suggest, however, that the *result* in Hans, denying relief, might be justified. See note 15, *supra.*) Should the Amendment be viewed as resting on the theory that federal judges (who are far less politically responsive to state interests than are federal legislators) should not on their own hold states liable in damages—a theory that necessarily would preclude holding states liable under modern judically-fashioned damages remedies? Can that theory be squared with Justice Washington's view (see United States v. Bright, note 7, *supra*) that the Amendment did not extend to admiralty cases, which apply judge-made law? Is it sometimes imperative that unconsenting states be held liable in federal court suits in order adequately to redress violations of constitutional rights? See Amar, note 3, *supra,* at 1484–92, so arguing; and recall the more limited holding in First English Evangelical Lutheran Church of Glendale v. County of Los Angeles, 107 S.Ct. 2378, 2386 n. 9 (1987), that the Fifth Amendment's Just Compensation Clause, as applied to the states by the Fourteenth Amendment, "of its own force, furnish[es] a basis for a court to award money damages against the government."

If Justice Brennan's view—that the *Amendment* merely restricts party-based jurisdiction—were adopted, might the states nonetheless enjoy some form of immunity (derived from the common law rather than the Constitution) in federal court actions?

(10) The question whether Hans correctly interpreted the Eleventh Amendment as giving rise to a general rule of state sovereign immunity, and the further question whether that interpretation is in any event too well-established to warrant reconsideration, were debated in Welch v. Texas Dept. of Highways and Pub. Transp., 107 S.Ct. 2941 (1987). There the Court held that the Amendment barred a suit in admiralty, for damages under the Jones Act, 46 U.S.C. § 688, brought against the State of Texas by an employee of a state-owned ferry. Justice Brennan's dissent, again joined by Justices Marshall, Blackmun, and Stevens, largely reiterated the views he expressed in his Atascadero dissent. In Welch, however, he stressed that the Amendment applied only to suits in law and equity, not to suits in admiralty (pp. 2958–60). He added that the Court's contrary ruling in Ex Parte New York, No. 1, Paragraph (7), *supra,* was distinguishable because that admiralty action, unlike Welch, was based on federal common law rather than on a federal statute.

Justice Powell, writing for a plurality of four, responded at length to the dissent, arguing (as had the Court in Hans) that Madison, Hamilton, and John Marshall all took the position that Article III did not subject unconsenting states to federal court suit, whatever the basis of federal jurisdiction, and that their representations "may have been essential to ratification" (p. 2951). He also asserted that "the delicate problem of enforcing judgments against the States * * * would have arisen in cases presenting a federal question as well as in other cases" (p. 2950). Justice Powell disputed the claim that the decisions of the Marshall Court called into question the applicability of the Amendment to admiralty. And he concluded that "the fundamental principle enunciated in Hans has been among the most stable in our constitutional jurisprudence," and that the Court did not "write on a clean slate; Hans had been followed for 97 years and in at least 17 other cases" (pp. 2952, 2956).

Justice Scalia, concurring in part and concurring in the judgment, cast the deciding vote in favor of dismissing the action. For him, "both the correctness of Hans as an original matter, and the feasibility, if it was wrong, of correcting it without distorting what we have done in tacit reliance upon it, [are] complex enough questions that I am unwilling to address them in a case whose presentation focused on other matters" (pp. 2957–58). But even if Hans had been wrong in holding that unconsenting states cannot be sued on federal causes of action in federal court, that understanding "clearly underlay the Jones Act," and "we could not, in reason, interpret the statute[ ] as though the assumption never existed." Thus, he did not read the Jones Act, which by its terms applies to common carriers by water, to impose liability upon the states (p. 2958).

Unlike Justice Scalia, the plurality reserved the question whether the Jones Act affords a remedy to a seaman employed by a state. If such a remedy exists, where could it be enforced?

(11) The Eleventh Amendment applies by its terms only in the federal courts. The question whether a state is free to subject sister states to damage liability in its own courts was faced in Nevada v. Hall, 440 U.S. 410 (1979). There, a California plaintiff, who had been involved in a California automobile accident with an employee of the state of Nevada driving a state-owned car, sued Nevada in a California court. Service of process was made on Nevada under the California long-arm statute permitting service on nonresidents whose agents use California highways and are involved in an accident there. The Supreme Court affirmed a $1.15 million verdict against Nevada, holding that nothing in the federal Constitution requires California to accord Nevada immunity, and that consequently California has the same discretion as a sovereign nation would have in deciding whether to provide immunity in its courts to other sovereigns.[17] In dissent, Justice Rehnquist argued that, even though nothing in the text of the Constitution speaks directly to this issue, cases like Hans and Principality of Monaco "recognized that Art. III and the Eleventh Amendment are built on important concepts of sovereignty" that are "of constitutional dimension because their derogation would undermine the logic of the constitutional scheme" (p. 439).[18]

17. The Court was urged to hold that the Constitution directly gives Nevada immunity in the California courts, or, in the alternative, that the Full Faith and Credit Clause requires California to resort to Nevada law in determining whether Nevada was amenable to suit. In connection with the second argument, the Court was asked to limit recovery against Nevada to $25,000, that being the limit Nevada law places on tort recoveries against Nevada in the Nevada courts. The Court rejected all these arguments; it met the Full Faith and Credit contention with the conventional doctrine that the Clause does not force a state to apply a sister state's laws in violation of its own public policy (pp. 421–24).

18. The Chief Justice and Justice Blackmun also dissented.

On what theory can one justify holding that Nevada can be sued in California state court but not in a federal district court in California, when the latter is presumably less likely to favor parochial interests? That Nevada's sovereign interest in avoiding suit is no more compelling than California's sovereign interest in deciding whether to extend comity to a friendly sovereign? That, especially in view of Nevada's power to "retaliate" against California if the roles were reversed, California's interference with Nevada's sovereignty is likely to be less threatening than federal court jurisdiction over California would be?

Does Justice Rehnquist's view require a greater stretch of the constitutional text than Hans or Monaco because he would draw inferences about *state court* jurisdiction from provisions regulating *federal* judicial power?

Suppose Hall wishes to bring suit against Nevada to enforce her California judgment. Could she do so in federal court in Nevada, notwithstanding the Eleventh Amendment? If she filed instead in a Nevada state court, would it be obliged to give the California judgment full faith and credit, notwithstanding a plea of sovereign immunity by the state? See Brilmayer, An Introduction to Jurisdiction in the American Federal System 183–84 (1986).

(12) A suit against a statewide agency is considered a suit against the state under the Eleventh Amendment. See, *e.g.*, Edelman v. Jordan, 415 U.S. 651 (1974); Ford Motor Co. v. Dept. of Treasury of Indiana, 323 U.S. 459 (1945). However, Lincoln County v. Luning, 133 U.S. 529 (1890), decided the same day as Hans, held that the Eleventh Amendment does not bar an individual's suit in federal court against a county for nonpayment of a debt. The unanimous Court noted its "general acquiescence" in such suits over the prior thirty years (p. 530). The Court has adhered to this position as to local government bodies ever since. See, *e.g.*, Mount Healthy City School Dist. Bd. of Educ. v. Doyle, 429 U.S. 274, 280–81 (1977) (school board); Workman v. New York, 179 U.S. 552, 563–66 (1900) (city).

Since a local government body is a creature of the state, it is hard to see any functional basis for distinguishing the two. See Note, 1979 Duke L.J. 1042. But *cf.* Moor v. Alameda County, 411 U.S. 693, 717–21 (1973) (county is a citizen of a state for purposes of diversity jurisdiction). Professor Fletcher explains the different treatment on the ground that in the nineteenth century, a municipal corporation was viewed as more closely analogous to a private corporation than to a state government. Fletcher, note 3, *supra*, at 1099–1107. Professor Orth explains the opposing outcomes in Hans and Lincoln County as resting on the limits of judicial power: in Hans and other cases against debt-ridden Southern states, the Court chose not to issue orders that, in the post-Reconstruction political environment, could never have been enforced; by contrast, enforcement of court orders was far easier against counties, especially Western counties (like Lincoln County, Nevada) that depended upon maintaining their credit to permit further borrowing. See Orth, note 13, *supra*, at 110–20; accord, Gibbons, note 2, *supra*, at 1973–2002.[19]

---

19. In dicta in Pennhurst State School & Hosp. v. Halderman, 465 U.S. 89, 123 (1984) p. 1195, *infra*, the Court, per Powell, J., may have cast some doubt on the continuing suability of local bodies. "Even assuming that these [county] officials are not immune from suit," the Court said, "we have applied the Amendment to bar relief against county officials 'in order to protect the state treasury from liability that would have had essentially the same practical consequences as a judgment

Note how important the distinction between an arm of the state and a local government body has become after the decision in Monell v. Department of Social Services, 436 U.S. 658 (1978), p. 1251, *infra*, that local government bodies are in some instances liable in damages under 42 U.S.C. § 1983. By what criteria does one determine whether, for purposes of the Eleventh Amendment, a governmental unit such as a school board or county welfare department—which may administer state laws, be subject to some control by state authorities, and share fiscal responsibility for its operations with the state—should be deemed to be an arm of the state (and hence immune), or a separate political subdivision (and hence not immune)? See, *e.g.*, Martinez v. Board of Educ. of Taos Muni. School Dist., 748 F.2d 1393 (10th Cir.1984); Holley v. Lavine, 605 F.2d 638 (2d Cir.1979); Note, 55 Fordham L.Rev. 101 (1986). What is the pertinence of federal and state law in answering that question?

EX PARTE YOUNG

209 U.S. 123, 28 S.Ct. 441, 52 L.Ed. 714 (1908).
Petition for Writs of Habeas Corpus and Certiorari.

[Shareholders of various railroads brought derivative actions in federal circuit court in Minnesota, alleging that state legislation regulating railroad rates was confiscatory and violated the Fourteenth Amendment. The companies' managements, plaintiffs alleged, had refused their demands that the companies not comply with the legislation.

[The trial court entered a temporary restraining order prohibiting Edward Young, the state's Attorney General, from enforcing the legislation, and after denying Young's motion under the Eleventh Amendment to dismiss, entered a preliminary injunction to the same effect. Young then defied the injunction by filing a state court action seeking to enforce the legislation against the railroads.

[The circuit court held Young in contempt, again rejecting his Eleventh Amendment defense. He then filed an application in the Supreme Court for leave to file a petition for writs of habeas corpus and certiorari.]

Mr. Justice Peckham * * * delivered the opinion of the court.

[The Court first concluded that the circuit court had "arising under" jurisdiction, as the suit raised several federal questions: (i) whether enforcement of the rates would take property without due process of law, (ii) whether the penalties for violation were so enormous as to deny equal protection and due process, and (iii) whether the legislation interfered with interstate commerce.]

against the State itself'" (p. 123 n. 34, quoting Lake Country Estates, Inc. v. Tahoe Regional Planning Agency, 440 U.S. 391, 401 (1979)). In the Lake Tahoe case, the Court held that a bi-state regional agency created by an interstate compact between California and Nevada to coordinate development of the Lake Tahoe area was not immune from suit in federal court: "Unless there is good reason to believe that the States structured the new agency to enable it to enjoy the special constitu-tional protection of the States themselves, and that Congress concurred in that purpose, there would appear to be no justification for reading additional meaning into the limited language of the Amendment" (p. 401). Doesn't the Lake Tahoe case undercut rather than support the proposition for which it is cited in Pennhurst? Compare Welch, Paragraph (10), *supra*, at 2953 (plurality opinion of Powell, J.) ("Municipalities and other local government agencies may be sued under 42 U.S.C. § 1983").

* * *

Coming to the inquiry regarding the alleged invalidity of these acts, we take up the contention that they are invalid on their face on account of the penalties. For disobedience to the freight act the officers, directors, agents and employés of the company are made guilty of a misdemeanor, and upon conviction each may be punished by imprisonment in the county jail for a period not exceeding ninety days. Each violation would be a separate offense, and, therefore, might result in imprisonment of the various agents of the company who would dare disobey for a term of ninety days each for each offense. Disobedience to the passenger rate act renders the party guilty of a felony and subject to a fine not exceeding five thousand dollars or imprisonment in the state prison for a period not exceeding five years, or both fine and imprisonment. The sale of each ticket above the price permitted by the act would be a violation thereof. * * * The company, in order to test the validity of the acts, must find some agent or employé to disobey them at the risk stated. The necessary effect and result of such legislation must be to preclude a resort to the courts (either state or Federal) for the purpose of testing its validity. * * * It may therefore be said that when the penalties for disobedience are by fines so enormous and imprisonment so severe as to intimidate the company and its officers from resorting to the courts to test the validity of the legislation, the result is the same as if the law in terms prohibited the company from seeking judicial construction of laws which deeply affect its rights.

It is urged that there is no principle upon which to base the claim that a person is entitled to disobey a statute at least once, for the purpose of testing its validity without subjecting himself to the penalties for disobedience provided by the statute in case it is valid. This is not an accurate statement of the case. Ordinarily a law creating offenses in the nature of misdemeanors or felonies relates to a subject over which the jurisdiction of the legislature is complete in any event. In the case, however, of the establishment of certain rates without any hearing, the validity of such rates necessarily depends upon whether they are high enough to permit at least some return upon the investment (how much it is not now necessary to state), and an inquiry as to that fact is a proper subject of judicial investigation. If it turns out that the rates are too low for that purpose, then they are illegal. Now, to impose upon a party interested the burden of obtaining a judicial decision of such a question (no prior hearing having ever been given) only upon the condition that if unsuccessful he must suffer imprisonment and pay fines as provided in these acts, is, in effect, to close up all approaches to the courts, and thus prevent any hearing upon the question whether the rates as provided by the acts are not too low, and therefore invalid. * * *

We hold, therefore, that the provisions of the acts relating to the enforcement of the rates, either for freight or passengers, by imposing such enormous fines and possible imprisonment as a result of an unsuccessful effort to test the validity of the laws themselves, are unconstitutional on their face, without regard to the question of the insufficiency of those rates.

* * *

* * *

* * * The question that arises is whether there is a remedy that the parties interested may resort to, by going into a Federal court of equity, in a case involving a violation of the Federal Constitution, and obtaining a judicial investigation of the problem, and pending its solution obtain freedom from suits, civil or criminal, by a temporary injunction, and if the question be finally decided favorably to the contention of the company, a permanent injunction restraining all such actions or proceedings.

This inquiry necessitates an examination of the most material and important objection made to the jurisdiction of the Circuit Court, the objection being that the suit is, in effect, one against the State of Minnesota * * *. This objection is to be considered with reference to the Eleventh and Fourteenth Amendments to the Federal Constitution. * * *

The case before the Circuit Court proceeded upon the theory that the orders and acts heretofore mentioned would, if enforced, violate rights of the complainants protected by the latter Amendment. We think that whatever the rights of complainants may be, they are largely founded upon that Amendment, but a decision of this case does not require an examination or decision of the question whether its adoption in any way altered or limited the effect of the earlier Amendment. We may assume that each exists in full force, and that we must give to the Eleventh Amendment all the effect it naturally would have, without cutting it down or rendering its meaning any more narrow than the language, fairly interpreted, would warrant. It applies to a suit brought against a State by one of its own citizens as well as to a suit brought by a citizen of another State. Hans v. Louisiana, 134 U.S. 1. It was adopted after the decision of this court in Chisholm v. Georgia (1793), 2 Dall. 419 where it was held that a State might be sued by a citizen of another State. Since that time there have been many cases decided in this court involving the Eleventh Amendment, among them being Osborn v. United States Bank (1824), 9 Wheat. 738, 846, 857, which held that the Amendment applied only to those suits in which the State was a party on the record. In the subsequent case of Governor of Georgia v. Madrazo (1828), 1 Pet. 110, 122, 123, that holding was somewhat enlarged, and Chief Justice Marshall, delivering the opinion of the court, while citing Osborn v. United States Bank, *supra,* said that where the claim was made, as in the case then before the court, against the Governor of Georgia as governor, and the demand was made upon him, not personally, but officially (for moneys in the treasury of the State and for slaves in possession of the state government), the State might be considered as the party on the record (page 123), and therefore the suit could not be maintained.

* * *

The cases upon the subject were reviewed, and it was held, In re Ayers, 123 U.S. 443, that a bill in equity brought against officers of a State, who, as individuals, have no personal interest in the subject-matter of the suit, and defend only as representing the State, where the relief prayed for, if done, would constitute a performance by the State of the alleged contract of the State, was a suit against the State (page 504), following in this respect Hagood v. Southern, [117 U.S. 52, 67].

A suit of such a nature was simply an attempt to make the State itself, through its officers, perform its alleged contract, by directing those officers to do acts which constituted such performance. The State alone had any interest in the question, and a decree in favor of plaintiff would affect the treasury of the State.

[The Court then discussed a number of its recent decisions which it viewed as "ample justification" for the assertion that a state official who is about to commence civil or criminal proceedings to enforce unconstitutional state legislation may be enjoined from such action by a federal court of equity. Those cases included Reagan v. Farmers' Loan & Trust Co., 154 U.S. 362 (1894) and Smyth v. Ames, 169 U.S. 466, 518 (1898). The Court continued:]

* * * In those cases the only wrong or injury or trespass involved was the threatened commencement of suits to enforce the statute as to rates, and the threat of such commencement was in each case regarded as sufficient to authorize the issuing of an injunction to prevent the same. The threat to commence those suits under such circumstances was therefore necessarily held to be equivalent to any other threatened wrong or injury to the property of a plaintiff which had theretofore been held sufficient to authorize the suit against the officer.

* * * It is contended that the complainants do not complain and they care nothing about any action which Mr. Young might take or bring as an ordinary individual, but that he was complained of as an officer, to whose discretion is confided the use of the name of the State of Minnesota so far as litigation is concerned, and that when or how he shall use it is a matter resting in his discretion and cannot be controlled by any court.

The answer to all this is the same as made in every case where an official claims to be acting under the authority of the State. The act to be enforced is alleged to be unconstitutional, and if it be so, the use of the name of the State to enforce an unconstitutional act to the injury of complainants is a proceeding without the authority of and one which does not affect the State in its sovereign or governmental capacity. It is simply an illegal act upon the part of a state official in attempting by the use of the name of the State to enforce a legislative enactment which is void because unconstitutional. If the act which the state Attorney General seeks to enforce be a violation of the Federal Constitution, the officer in proceeding under such enactment comes into conflict with the superior authority of that Constitution, and he is in that case stripped of his official or representative character and is subjected in his person to the consequences of his individual conduct. The State has no power to impart to him any immunity from responsibility to the supreme authority of the United States. * * *

It is further objected (and the objection really forms part of the contention that the State cannot be sued) that a court of equity has no jurisdiction to enjoin criminal proceedings, by indictment or otherwise, under the state law. This, as a general rule, is true. But there are exceptions. When such indictment or proceeding is brought to enforce an alleged unconstitutional statute, which is the subject matter of inquiry in a suit already pending in a Federal court, the latter court having first obtained jurisdiction over the subject matter, has the right, in both civil and criminal cases, to hold and maintain such jurisdiction, to the exclusion of all other courts, until its duty is fully performed. But the Federal court cannot, of course, interfere in a case where the proceedings were already pending in a state court.

* * *

It is proper to add that the right to enjoin an individual, even though a state official, from commencing suits under circumstances already stated, does not include the power to restrain a court from acting in any case brought before it, either of a civil or criminal nature, nor does it include power to prevent any investigation or action by a grand jury. The latter body is part of the machinery of a criminal court, and an injunction against a state court would be a violation of the whole scheme of our Government.

* * *

* * *

It is further objected that there is a plain and adequate remedy at law open to the complainants and that a court of equity, therefore, has no jurisdiction in such case. It has been suggested that the proper way to test the constitutionality of the act is to disobey it, at least once, after which the company might obey the act pending subsequent proceedings to test its validity. But in the event of a single violation the prosecutor might not avail himself of the opportunity to make the test, as obedience to the law was thereafter continued, and he might think it unnecessary to start an inquiry. If, however, he should do so while the company was thereafter obeying the law, several years might elapse before there was a final determination of the question, and if it should be determined that the law was invalid the property of the company would have been taken during that time without due process of law, and there would be no possibility of its recovery.

Another obstacle to making the test on the part of the company might be to find an agent or employé who would disobey the law, with a possible fine and imprisonment staring him in the face if the act should be held valid. Take the passenger rate act, for instance: A sale of a single ticket above the price mentioned in that act might subject the ticket agent to a charge of felony, and upon conviction to a fine of five thousand dollars and imprisonment for five years. It is true the company might pay the fine, but the imprisonment the agent would have to suffer personally. It would not be wonderful if, under such circumstances, there would not be a crowd of agents offering to disobey the law. The wonder would be that a single agent should be found ready to take the risk.

* * *

* * * [I]t must be remembered that jurisdiction of this general character has, in fact, been exercised by Federal courts from the time of Osborn v. United States Bank up to the present; the only difference in regard to the case of Osborn and the case in hand being that in this case the injury complained of is the threatened commencement of suits, civil or criminal, to enforce the act, instead of, as in the Osborn case, an actual and direct trespass upon or interference with tangible property. A bill filed to prevent the commencement of suits to enforce an unconstitutional act, under the circumstances already mentioned, is no new invention, as we have already seen. The difference between an actual and direct interference with tangible property and the enjoining of state officers from enforcing an unconstitutional act, is not of a radical nature, and does not extend, in truth, the jurisdiction of the courts over the subject matter. * * * The sovereignty of the State is, in reality, no more involved in one case than in the other. The State cannot in either case impart to the official immunity from responsibility to the supreme authority of the United States. See In re Ayers, 123 U.S. 507.

This supreme authority, which arises from the specific provisions of the Constitution itself, is nowhere more fully illustrated than in the series of decisions under the Federal *habeas corpus* statute (§ 753, Rev.Stat.), in some of which cases persons in the custody of state officers for alleged crimes against the State have been taken from that custody and discharged by a Federal court or judge, because the imprisonment was adjudged to be in violation of the Federal Constitution. The right to so discharge has not been doubted by this court, and it has never been supposed there was any suit against the State by reason of serving the writ upon one of the officers of the State in whose custody the person was found. * * *

* * *

The rule to show cause is discharged and the petition for writs of *habeas corpus* and certiorari is dismissed.

So ordered.

MR. JUSTICE HARLAN, dissenting.

* * *

Let it be observed that the suit * * * in the Circuit Court of the United States was, as to the defendant Young, one against him *as, and only because he was,* Attorney General of Minnesota. No relief was sought against him individually but only in his capacity *as* Attorney General. And the manifest, indeed the avowed and admitted, object of seeking such relief was *to tie the hands* of the *State* so that it could not in any manner or by any mode of proceeding, *in its own courts,* test the validity of the statutes and orders in question. It would therefore seem clear that within the true meaning of the Eleventh Amendment the suit brought in the Federal court was one, in legal effect, against the State—as much so as if the State had been formally named on the record as a party—and therefore it was a suit to which, under the Amendment, so far as the State or its Attorney General was concerned, the judicial power of the United States did not and could not extend.

* * * [T]he intangible thing, called a State, however extensive its powers, can never appear or be represented or known in any court in a litigated case, except by and through its officers. When, therefore, the Federal court forbade the defendant Young, as Attorney General of Minnesota, from taking any action, suit, step or proceeding whatever looking to the enforcement of the statutes in question, it said in effect to the State of Minnesota: "* * * the Federal court adjudges that you, the State, although a sovereign for many important governmental purposes, shall not appear in your own courts, by your law officer, with the view of enforcing, or even for determining the validity of the state enactments which the Federal court has, upon a preliminary hearing, declared to be in violation of the Constitution of the United States."

This principle, if firmly established, would work a radical change in our governmental system. It would inaugurate a new era in the American judicial system and in the relations of the National and state governments. It would enable the subordinate Federal courts to supervise and control the official action of the States as if they were "dependencies" or provinces. It would place the States of the Union in a condition of inferiority never dreamed of when the Constitution was adopted or when the Eleventh Amendment was made a part of the Supreme Law of the Land. * * * Too little consequence has been attached to the fact that the courts of the

States are under an obligation equally strong with that resting upon the courts of the Union to respect and enforce the provisions of the Federal Constitution as the Supreme Law of the Land, and to guard rights secured or guaranteed by that instrument. We must assume—a decent respect for the States requires us to assume—that the state courts will enforce every right secured by the Constitution. If they fail to do so, the party complaining has a clear remedy for the protection of his rights; for, he can come by writ of error, in an orderly, judicial way, from the highest court of the State to this tribunal for redress in respect of every right granted or secured by that instrument and denied by the state court. * * *

NOTE ON THE ELEVENTH AMENDMENT AND SUITS AGAINST STATE OFFICERS

(1) Osborn v. Bank of United States, 9 Wheat. 738 (U.S.1824), p. 1161, *supra*, held that the Eleventh Amendment was simply inapplicable to suits in which the state was not a party of record. Although the decision in Governor of Georgia v. Madrazo, 1 Pet. 110 (U.S.1828), p. 1162 *supra*, cast some doubt on the party of record rule, the rule was reiterated in Davis v. Gray, 16 Wall. 203 (U.S.1872), in which the Governor of Texas was enjoined from disturbing the plaintiff's possession of certain land previously granted by the state, on the ground that the new state constitution, which deemed the land forfeited, violated the Contracts Clause.

Was the party of record rule consistent with the historical development of suits against officers as a means of ensuring official accountability? See pp. 1114–17, *supra*. What of Professor Currie's observation that "[p]eople are not likely to amend constitutions just to change captions on complaints"? Currie, *State Sovereign Immunity and Suits Against Government Officers,* 1984 Sup.Ct.Rev. 149, 151 n. 11.

(2) The scope of the Eleventh Amendment in suits against state officers was shaped largely in cases involving the repudiation of bond obligations by southern states after Reconstruction. Recent accounts have stressed the political context in which those cases arose, in particular the so-called Compromise of 1877, which made it unlikely that a federal judgment recognizing such obligations would have proved enforceable. See Orth, The Judicial Power of the United States: The Eleventh Amendment in American History 47–120 (1987); Gibbons, *The Eleventh Amendment and State Sovereign Immunity: A Reinterpretation,* 83 Colum.L.Rev. 1978–2002 (1983).[1]

Louisiana ex rel. Elliott v. Jumel, 17 Otto 711 (U.S.1883), held that the Eleventh Amendment barred a suit by Louisiana bondholders seeking to require state officials to honor contractual obligations to collect a property tax and devote its proceeds to paying state bonds. The Court stressed that the officials were not personally liable on the contract,[2] and expressed its

---

1. Two years before the Compromise, the Court had barred Louisiana officials who were carrying out a bond refunding from diluting a previous issue in violation of law; the unanimous decision cited Osborn and Davis and stressed the nondiscretionary duty involved. Board of Liquidation v. McComb, 92 U.S. 531 (1875).

2. See the similar holding in Cunningham v. Macon & Brunswick R.R., 109 U.S. 446 (1883), dismissing, on the ground that the state was an indispensable party, a suit against state officials by bondholders who asserted a superior right to assets that had been seized by the state.

unwillingness to assume "the control of the administration of the fiscal affairs of the State to the extent that may be necessary" (p. 722).[3]

The Virginia Coupon Cases involved a Virginia statute that flatly repudiated prior legislation authorizing the payment of state taxes with the interest coupons on state bonds. The Supreme Court upheld an award of restitution, damages, and injunctive relief against state officials who had seized or threatened to seize taxpayers' property in satisfaction of taxes that had already been paid by such coupons. See Poindexter v. Greenhow, 114 U.S. 270 (1885) (discussing the bearing of the Eleventh Amendment even though the case had been prosecuted in *state* court); White v. Greenhow, 114 U.S. 307 (1885); Allen v. Baltimore & O.R.R., 114 U.S. 311 (1885). In Poindexter, the Court said (p. 288) that because any law purporting to authorize the conduct violated the Contract Clause, the official "stands * * * stripped of his official character; and, confessing a personal violation of the plaintiff's rights for which he must personally answer, he is without defence." Justice Bradley, joined by Chief Justice Waite and Justices Gray and Miller, dissented in Poindexter and the companion cases, contending that the suits were "virtually" suits against the state to compel specific performance of its contractual obligations (p. 330).

(3) The State of Virginia responded by passing legislation ordering state officials to bring suit to recover taxes from taxpayers who had used the coupons as payment. In such actions, the coupons were to be considered *prima facie* counterfeit; the taxpayer had the burden of establishing their genuineness, but was barred from introducing expert testimony on that issue, and to prevail was required to produce the bond from which the coupons were cut. Some British bondholders sued in federal court to enjoin officials from bringing such actions, alleging that the legislation violated the Contracts Clause. The Supreme Court, in In re Ayers, 123 U.S. 443 (1887), held that the Eleventh Amendment barred the lower court's award of injunctive relief. The Virginia Coupon Cases were distinguishable: there, "the defendants, though professing to act as officers of the State, [were] threatening a violation of the personal or property rights of the complainant, for which they [were] personally and individually liable" (p. 500). But "a bill, the object of which is by injunction, indirectly, to compel the specific performance of the contract, by forbidding all those acts and doings which constitute breaches of the contract [instead of requiring the acts that would constitute performance] must also, necessarily, be a suit against the State. In such a case, though the State be not nominally a party on the record, if the defendants are its officers and agents, through whom alone it can act in doing and refusing to do the things which constitute a breach of its contract, the suit is still, in substance, though not in form, a suit against the State. * * *

"* * * The acts alleged in the bill as threatened by the defendants * * * are violations of the assumed contract between the State of Virginia and the complainants, only as they are considered to be the acts of the State of Virginia. The defendants, as individuals, not being parties to that

---

3. Louisiana bondholders also failed to obtain relief when the States of New York and New Hampshire, having agreed to take assignment from their citizens of unpaid bonds, tried to bring what was in effect a parens patriae action suit against Louisiana in the Supreme Court's original jurisdiction. New Hampshire v. Louisiana, 108 U.S. 76 (1883), p. 324, *supra.*

contract, are not capable in law of committing a breach of it.[4] * * * In a certain sense and in certain ways the Constitution of the United States protects contracts against laws of a State subsequently passed impairing their obligation, and this provision is recognized as extending to contracts between an individual and a State; but this, as is apparent, is subject to the other constitutional principle, of equal authority, contained in the 11th Amendment, which secures to the State an immunity from suit. Wherever the question arises in a litigation between individuals, which does not involve a suit against a State, the contract will be judicially recognized as of binding force, notwithstanding any subsequent law of the State impairing its obligation. But this right is incidental to the judicial proceeding in the course of which the question concerning it arises. It is not a positive and substantive right of an absolute character, secured by the Constitution of the United States against every possible infraction, or for which redress is given as against strangers to the contract itself, for the injurious consequences of acts done or omitted by them" (pp. 502–04).[5]

(4) Attorney General Young's conduct was probably not tortious under traditional common law concepts. See Jacobs, The Eleventh Amendment and Sovereign Immunity 138–42 (1972). Is it not plain that in Ex parte Young the Court abandoned the use of general principles of common law liability as the exclusive measure of the appropriateness of injunctive relief, and recognized a judicially implied federal cause of action for injunctive relief under the Fourteenth Amendment? Indeed, since the parties in Young were not diverse, on what other basis could federal court jurisdiction have been predicated? Cf. Louisville & Nashville R.R. v. Mottley, p. 989, supra.[6]

What justified the departure from common law principles of liability? The felt exigencies of effective constitutional administration? In deciding whether to recognize a federal right of action for "wrongful individual action" in the use of purported state authority, what criteria should the Court use once it has departed from traditional common law principles? See Chap. VII, pp. 917–50, supra.

(5) If Ex parte Young recognizes a judicially implied right to injunctive relief under the Fourteenth Amendment, why couldn't the Court in Ayers have recognized a judicially implied right to injunctive relief under the Contracts Clause? See Georgia R.R. & Banking Co. v. Redwine, 342 U.S. 299 (1952), holding that the Eleventh Amendment does not bar a federal court action, based on the Contracts Clause, seeking to enjoin the state revenue commissioner from imposing taxes upon property claimed to be exempt pursuant to a state charter. The Court purported to distinguish Ayers on the ground that there the "complainant had not alleged that officers threatened to tax its property in violation of its constitutional rights," while in Redwine the plaintiff sought "to enjoin [the commissioner] from a threatened and allegedly unconstitutional invasion of its property"

---

4. [Ed.] Should the plaintiffs in Ayers have argued that the defendants, though not liable for breach of contract, could be sued as individuals in tort for interfering with the performance of the contract?

5. Justice Field concurred in the judgment, id. at 506; Justice Harlan dissented, id. at 510–16.

6. Under modern understandings of federal question jurisdiction, could cases like White v. Greenhow, 114 U.S. 307 (1885) and Allen v. Baltimore & O.R.R., 114 U.S. 311 (1885), Paragraph (2), supra, which purported to be common law actions in which the federal Constitution operated to strip the defendant of a state law defense, be filed in federal court?

(p. 305). Shouldn't the Redwine opinion have acknowledged that Ex parte Young had undermined the basis of In re Ayers?

(6) What would have been the effect upon the protection of constitutional rights generally of adherence to the doctrine of In re Ayers?

Observe that claimants of such rights would still have been able (a) to present federal claims defensively in the state courts, or in any federal court having jurisdiction, in any situation in which the state chose to provide for enforcement of the questioned arrangement through judicial proceedings; (b) to present federal claims offensively in a federal (or state) court in any situation in which the defendant official was threatening extra-judicial enforcement under circumstances which would give rise to common-law liability in the absence of official justification; (c) to present federal claims offensively in a state court, or in a federal court having jurisdiction, in any situation in which the state was under a federal constitutional obligation to provide a remedy for a denial of federal right; and (d) to present such claims in any such court in any other situation in which the state chose as a matter of grace to provide a remedy.

Would such protection have been adequate?

Consider the much more far-reaching consequences of a doctrine recognizing any claim of color of official authority, advanced in good faith, as an absolute defense.

(7) On the history of suits against officers up to and including Ex parte Young, see generally Orth, Paragraph (2), *supra;* Engdahl, *Immunity and Accountability for Positive Governmental Wrongs,* 44 U.Colo.L.Rev. 1 (1972); Gibbons, Paragraph (2), *supra.*

EDELMAN v. JORDAN

415 U.S. 651, 94 S.Ct. 1347, 39 L.Ed.2d 662 (1974).
Certiorari to the United States Court of Appeals for the Seventh Circuit.

MR. JUSTICE REHNQUIST delivered the opinion of the Court.

Respondent John Jordan filed a complaint in the United States District Court for the Northern District of Illinois, individually and as a representative of a class, seeking declaratory and injunctive relief against two former directors of the Illinois Department of Public Aid, the director of the Cook County Department of Public Aid, and the comptroller of Cook County. Respondent alleged that these state officials were administering the federal-state programs of Aid to the Aged, Blind, or Disabled (AABD) in a manner inconsistent with various federal regulations and with the Fourteenth Amendment to the Constitution.

AABD is one of the categorical aid programs administered by the Illinois Department of Public Aid pursuant to the Illinois Public Aid Code, Ill.Rev.Stat., c. 23, §§ 3–1 through 3–12 (1973). Under the Social Security Act, the program is funded by the State and the Federal Governments. 42 U.S.C. §§ 1381–1385. The Department of Health, Education, and Welfare (HEW), which administers these payments for the Federal Government, issued regulations prescribing maximum permissible time standards within which States participating in the program had to process AABD applications. Those regulations, originally issued in 1968, required, at the time of the institution of this suit, that eligibility determinations must be made by the States within 30 days of receipt of applications for aid to the aged and blind, and within 45 days of receipt of applications for aid to the disabled. For those persons found eligible, the assistance check was required to be received by them within the applicable time period. 45 CFR § 206.10(a)(3).

During the period in which the federal regulations went into effect, Illinois public aid officials were administering the benefits pursuant to their own regulations as provided in the Categorical Assistance Manual of the Illinois Department of Public Aid. Respondent's complaint charged that the Illinois defendants, operating under those regulations, were improperly authorizing grants to commence only with the month in which an application was approved and not including prior eligibility months for which an applicant was entitled to aid under federal law. The complaint also alleged that the Illinois defendants were not processing the applications within the applicable time requirements of the federal regulations; specifically, respondent alleged that his own application for disability benefits was not acted on by the Illinois Department of Public Aid for almost four months. Such actions of the Illinois officials were alleged to violate federal law and deny the equal protection of the laws. Respondent's prayer requested declaratory and injunctive relief, and specifically requested "a permanent injunction enjoining the defendants to award to the entire class of plaintiffs all AABD benefits wrongfully withheld."

In its judgment of March 15, 1972, the District Court declared § 4004 of the Illinois Manual to be invalid insofar as it was inconsistent with the federal regulations found in 45 CFR § 206.10(a)(3), and granted a permanent injunction requiring compliance with the federal time limits for processing and paying AABD applicants. The District Court, in paragraph 5 of its judgment, also ordered the state officials to "release and remit AABD benefits wrongfully withheld to all applicants for AABD in the State of Illinois who applied between July 1, 1968 [the date of the federal regulations] and April 16, 197[1] [the date of the preliminary injunction issued by the District Court] and were determined eligible * * *."

On appeal to the United States Court of Appeals for the Seventh Circuit, the Illinois officials contended, *inter alia*, that the Eleventh Amendment barred the award of retroactive benefits, that the judgment of inconsistency between the federal regulations and the provisions of the Illinois Categorical Assistance Manual could be given prospective effect only, and that the federal regulations in question were inconsistent with the Social Security Act itself. The Court of Appeals rejected these contentions and affirmed the judgment of the District Court. Jordan v. Weaver, 472 F.2d 985 (1973). * * *

* * * Because we believe the Court of Appeals erred in its disposition of the Eleventh Amendment claim, we reverse that portion of the Court of Appeals decision which affirmed the District Court's order that retroactive benefits be paid by the Illinois state officials.

* * *

While the Amendment by its terms does not bar suits against a State by its own citizens, this Court has consistently held that an unconsenting State is immune from suits brought in federal courts by her own citizens as well as by citizens of another State. Hans v. Louisiana, 134 U.S. 1 (1890); Duhne v. New Jersey, 251 U.S. 311 (1920); Great Northern Life Insurance

Co. v. Read, 322 U.S. 47 (1944); Parden v. Terminal R. Co., 377 U.S. 184 (1964); Employees v. Department of Public Health and Welfare, 411 U.S. 279 (1973). It is also well established that even though a State is not named a party to the action, the suit may nonetheless be barred by the Eleventh Amendment. In Ford Motor Co. v. Department of Treasury, 323 U.S. 459 (1945), the Court said:

"[W]hen the action is in essence one for the recovery of money from the state, the state is the real, substantial party in interest and is entitled to invoke its sovereign immunity from suit even though individual officials are nominal defendants." *Id.*, at 464.

Thus the rule has evolved that a suit by private parties seeking to impose a liability which must be paid from public funds in the state treasury is barred by the Eleventh Amendment. Great Northern Life Insurance Co. v. Read, *supra;* Kennecott Copper Corp. v. State Tax Comm'n, 327 U.S. 573 (1946).

The Court of Appeals in this case, while recognizing that the Hans line of cases permitted the State to raise the Eleventh Amendment as a defense to suit by its own citizens, nevertheless concluded that the Amendment did not bar the award of retroactive payments of the statutory benefits found to have been wrongfully withheld. The Court of Appeals held that the above-cited cases, when read in light of this Court's landmark decision in Ex parte Young, 209 U.S. 123 (1908), do not preclude the grant of such a monetary award in the nature of equitable restitution.

Petitioner concedes that Ex parte Young, *supra,* is no bar to that part of the District Court's judgment that prospectively enjoined petitioner's predecessors from failing to process applications within the time limits established by the federal regulations. Petitioner argues, however, that Ex parte Young does not extend so far as to permit a suit which seeks the award of an accrued monetary liability which must be met from the general revenues of a State, absent consent or waiver by the State of its Eleventh Amendment immunity, and that therefore the award of retroactive benefits by the District Court was improper.

Ex parte Young was a watershed case in which this Court held that the Eleventh Amendment did not bar an action in the federal courts seeking to enjoin the Attorney General of Minnesota from enforcing a statute claimed to violate the Fourteenth Amendment of the United States Constitution. This holding has permitted the Civil War Amendments to the Constitution to serve as a sword, rather than merely as a shield, for those whom they were designed to protect. But the relief awarded in Ex parte Young was prospective only; the Attorney General of Minnesota was enjoined to conform his future conduct of that office to the requirement of the Fourteenth Amendment. Such relief is analogous to that awarded by the District Court in the prospective portion of its order under review in this case.

But the retroactive portion of the District Court's order here, which requires the payment of a very substantial amount of money which that court held should have been paid, but was not, stands on quite a different footing. These funds will obviously not be paid out of the pocket of petitioner Edelman. Addressing himself to a similar situation in Rothstein v. Wyman, 467 F.2d 226 (C.A.2 1972), Judge McGowan observed for the court:

"It is not pretended that these payments are to come from the personal resources of these appellants. Appellees expressly contemplate that they will, rather, involve substantial expenditures from the public funds of the state. * * *

"It is one thing to tell the Commissioner of Social Services that he must comply with the federal standards for the future if the state is to have the benefit of federal funds in the programs he administers. It is quite another thing to order the Commissioner to use state funds to make reparation for the past. The latter would appear to us to fall afoul of the Eleventh Amendment if that basic constitutional provision is to be conceived of as having any present force." 467 F.2d, at 236–237.

We agree with Judge McGowan's observations. The funds to satisfy the award in this case must inevitably come from the general revenues of the State of Illinois, and thus the award resembles far more closely the monetary award against the State itself, Ford Motor Co. v. Department of Treasury, *supra*, than it does the prospective injunctive relief awarded in Ex parte Young.

The Court of Appeals, in upholding the award in this case, held that it was permissible because it was in the form of "equitable restitution" instead of damages, and therefore capable of being tailored in such a way as to minimize disruptions of the state program of categorical assistance. But we must judge the award actually made in this case, and not one which might have been differently tailored in a different case, and we must judge it in the context of the important constitutional principle embodied in the Eleventh Amendment.[11]

We do not read Ex parte Young or subsequent holdings of this Court to indicate that any form of relief may be awarded against a state officer, no matter how closely it may in practice resemble a money judgment payable out of the state treasury, so long as the relief may be labeled "equitable" in nature. The Court's opinion in Ex parte Young hewed to no such line. Its citation of Hagood v. Southern, 117 U.S. 52 (1886), and In re Ayers, 123 U.S. 443 (1887), which were both actions against state officers for specific performance of a contract to which the State was a party, demonstrate that equitable relief may be barred by the Eleventh Amendment.

As in most areas of the law, the difference between the type of relief barred by the Eleventh Amendment and that permitted under Ex parte Young will not in many instances be that between day and night. The injunction issued in Ex parte Young was not totally without effect on the State's revenues, since the state law which the Attorney General was enjoined from enforcing provided substantial monetary penalties against

---

11. It may be true, as stated by our Brother Douglas in dissent, that "[m]ost welfare decisions by federal courts have a financial impact on the States." But we cannot agree that such a financial impact is the same where a federal court applies Ex parte Young to grant prospective declaratory and injunctive relief, as opposed to an order of retroactive payments as was made in the instant case. It is not necessarily true that "[w]hether the decree is prospective only or requires payments for the weeks or months wrongfully skipped over by the state officials, the nature of the impact on the state treasury is precisely the same." This argument neglects the fact that where the State has a definable allocation to be used in the payment of public aid benefits, and pursues a certain course of action such as the processing of applications within certain time periods as did Illinois here, the subsequent ordering by a federal court of retroactive payments to correct delays in such processing will invariably mean there is less money available for payments for the continuing obligations of the public aid system. * * *

railroads which did not conform to its provisions. Later cases from this Court have authorized equitable relief which has probably had greater impact on state treasuries than did that awarded in Ex parte Young. In Graham v. Richardson, 403 U.S. 365 (1971), Arizona and Pennsylvania welfare officials were prohibited from denying welfare benefits to otherwise qualified recipients who were aliens. In Goldberg v. Kelly, 397 U.S. 254 (1970), New York City welfare officials were enjoined from following New York State procedures which authorized the termination of benefits paid to welfare recipients without prior hearing. But the fiscal consequences to state treasuries in these cases were the necessary result of compliance with decrees which by their terms were prospective in nature. State officials, in order to shape their official conduct to the mandate of the Court's decrees, would more likely have to spend money from the state treasury than if they had been left free to pursue their previous course of conduct. Such an ancillary effect on the state treasury is a permissible and often an inevitable consequence of the principle announced in Ex parte Young, *supra*.

But that portion of the District Court's decree which petitioner challenges on Eleventh Amendment grounds goes much further than any of the cases cited. It requires payment of state funds, not as a necessary consequence of compliance in the future with a substantive federal-question determination, but as a form of compensation to those whose applications were processed on the slower time schedule at a time when petitioner was under no court-imposed obligation to conform to a different standard. While the Court of Appeals described this retroactive award of monetary relief as a form of "equitable restitution," it is in practical effect indistinguishable in many aspects from an award of damages against the State. It will to a virtual certainty be paid from state funds, and not from the pockets of the individual state officials who were the defendants in the action. It is measured in terms of a monetary loss resulting from a past breach of a legal duty on the part of the defendant state officials.

Were we to uphold this portion of the District Court's decree, we would be obligated to overrule the Court's holding in Ford Motor Co. v. Department of Treasury, *supra*. There a taxpayer, who had, under protest, paid taxes to the State of Indiana, sought a refund of those taxes from the Indiana state officials who were charged with their collection. The taxpayer claimed that the tax had been imposed in violation of the United States Constitution. The term "equitable restitution" would seem even more applicable to the relief sought in that case, since the taxpayer had at one time had the money, and paid it over to the State pursuant to an allegedly unconstitutional tax exaction. Yet this Court had no hesitation in holding that the taxpayer's action was a suit against the State, and barred by the Eleventh Amendment. We reach a similar conclusion with respect to the retroactive portion of the relief awarded by the District Court in this case.

The Court of Appeals held in the alternative that even if the Eleventh Amendment be deemed a bar to the retroactive relief awarded respondent in this case, the State of Illinois had waived its Eleventh Amendment immunity and consented to the bringing of such a suit by participating in the federal AABD program. The Court of Appeals relied upon our holdings in Parden v. Terminal R. Co., 377 U.S. 184 (1964), and Petty v. Tennessee–Missouri Bridge Comm'n, 359 U.S. 275 (1959), and on the dissenting opinion of Judge Bright in Employees v. Department of Public Health and Welfare, 452 F.2d 820, 827 (C.A.8 1971). While the holding in the latter case was ultimately affirmed by this Court in 411 U.S. 279 (1973), we do not think that the answer to the waiver question turns on the distinction between Parden, *supra*, and Employees, *supra*. Both Parden and Employees involved a congressional enactment which by its terms authorized suit by designated plaintiffs against a general class of defendants which literally included States or state instrumentalities. Similarly, Petty v. Tennessee–Missouri Bridge Comm'n, *supra*, involved congressional approval, pursuant to the Compact Clause, of a compact between Tennessee and Missouri, which provided that each compacting State would have the power "to contract, to sue, and be sued in its own name." The question of waiver or consent under the Eleventh Amendment was found in those cases to turn on whether Congress had intended to abrogate the immunity in question, and whether the State by its participation in the program authorized by Congress had in effect consented to the abrogation of that immunity.

But in this case the threshold fact of congressional authorization to sue a class of defendants which literally includes States is wholly absent. Thus respondent is not only precluded from relying on this Court's holding in Employees, but on this Court's holdings in Parden and Petty as well.

The Court of Appeals held that as a matter of federal law Illinois had "constructively consented" to this suit by participating in the federal AABD program and agreeing to administer federal and state funds in compliance with federal law. Constructive consent is not a doctrine commonly associated with the surrender of constitutional rights, and we see no place for it here. In deciding whether a State has waived its constitutional protection under the Eleventh Amendment, we will find waiver only where stated "by the most express language or by such overwhelming implications from the text as [will] leave no room for any other reasonable construction." Murray v. Wilson Distilling Co., 213 U.S. 151, 171 (1909). We see no reason to retreat from the Court's statement in Great Northern Life Insurance Co. v. Read, 322 U.S., at 54:

"[W]hen we are dealing with the sovereign exemption from judicial interference in the vital field of financial administration a clear declaration of the state's intention to submit its fiscal problems to other courts than those of its own creation must be found."

The mere fact that a State participates in a program through which the Federal Government provides assistance for the operation by the State of a system of public aid is not sufficient to establish consent on the part of the State to be sued in the federal courts. And while this Court has, in cases such as J.I. Case Co. v. Borak, 377 U.S. 426 (1964), authorized suits by one private party against another in order to effectuate a statutory purpose, it has never done so in the context of the Eleventh Amendment and a state defendant. Since Employees, *supra*, where Congress had expressly authorized suits against a general class of defendants and the only thing left to implication was whether the described class of defendants included States, was decided adversely to the putative plaintiffs on the waiver question, surely this respondent must also fail on that issue. The only language in the Social Security Act which purported to provide a federal sanction against a State which did not comply with federal requirements for the distribution of federal monies was found in former 42 U.S.C. § 1384 (now replaced by substantially similar provisions in 42 U.S.C. § 804), which provided for termination of future allocations of federal funds when a participating State failed to conform with federal law. This provision by its terms did not authorize suit against anyone, and standing alone, fell far short of a waiver by a participating State of its Eleventh Amendment immunity.

Our Brother Marshall argues in dissent, and the Court of Appeals held, that although the Social Security Act itself does not create a private cause of action, the cause of action created by 42 U.S.C. § 1983, coupled with the enactment of the AABD program, and the issuance by HEW of regulations which require the States to make corrective payments after successful "fair hearings" and provide for federal matching funds to satisfy federal court orders of retroactive payments, indicate that Congress intended a cause of action for public aid recipients such as respondent. It is, of course, true that Rosado v. Wyman, 397 U.S. 397 (1970), held that suits in federal court under § 1983 are proper to secure compliance with the provisions of the Social Security Act on the part of participating States. But it has not heretofore been suggested that § 1983 was intended to create a waiver of a State's Eleventh Amendment immunity merely because an action could be brought under that section against state officers, rather than against the State itself. * * *

Respondent urges that since the various Illinois officials sued in the District Court failed to raise the Eleventh Amendment as a defense to the relief sought by respondent, petitioner is therefore barred [19] from raising the Eleventh Amendment defense in the Court of Appeals or in this Court. The Court of Appeals apparently felt the defense was properly presented, and dealt with it on the merits. We approve of this resolution, since it has been well settled since the decision in Ford Motor Co. v. Department of Treasury, *supra,* that the Eleventh Amendment defense sufficiently partakes of the nature of a jurisdictional bar so that it need not be raised in the trial court. * * *

For the foregoing reasons we decide that the Court of Appeals was wrong in holding that the Eleventh Amendment did not constitute a bar to that portion of the District Court decree which ordered retroactive payment of benefits found to have been wrongfully withheld. The judgment of the Court of Appeals is therefore reversed and the cause remanded for further proceedings consistent with this opinion.

So ordered.

MR. JUSTICE DOUGLAS, dissenting.

* * *

MR. JUSTICE BRENNAN, dissenting.

This suit is brought by Illinois citizens against Illinois officials. In that circumstance, Illinois may not invoke the Eleventh Amendment, since that Amendment bars only federal court suits against States by citizens of other States. Rather the question is whether Illinois may avail itself of the nonconstitutional but ancient doctrine of sovereign immunity as a bar to

---

19. Respondent urges that the State of Illinois has abolished its common-law sovereign immunity in its state courts, and appears to argue that suit in a federal court against the State may thus be maintained. Brief for Respondent 23. Petitioner contends that sovereign immunity has not been abolished in Illinois as to this type of case. Brief for Petitioner 31–36. Whether Illinois permits such a suit to be brought against the State in its own courts is not determinative of whether Illinois has relinquished its Eleventh Amendment immunity from suit in the federal courts. Chandler v. Dix, 194 U.S. 590, 591–592 (1904).

respondent's claim for retroactive AABD payments. In my view Illinois may not assert sovereign immunity for the reason I expressed in dissent in Employees v. Department of Public Health and Welfare, 411 U.S. 279, 298 (1973): the States surrendered that immunity in Hamilton's words, "in the plan of the Convention," that formed the Union, at least insofar as the States granted Congress specifically enumerated powers. See *id.,* at 319 n. 7; Parden v. Terminal R. Co., 377 U.S. 184 (1964). Congressional authority to enact the Social Security Act, of which AABD is a part, former 42 U.S.C. §§ 1381–1385 (now replaced by similar provisions in 42 U.S.C. §§ 801–804 (1970 ed., Supp. II)), is to be found in Art. I, § 8, cl. 1, one of the enumerated powers granted Congress by the States in the Constitution. I remain of the opinion that "because of its surrender, no immunity exists that can be the subject of a congressional declaration or a voluntary waiver," 411 U.S., at 300, and thus have no occasion to inquire whether or not Congress authorized an action for AABD retroactive benefits, or whether or not Illinois voluntarily waived the immunity by its continued participation in the program against the background of precedents which sustained judgments ordering retroactive payments.

I would affirm the judgment of the Court of Appeals.

MR. JUSTICE MARSHALL, with whom MR. JUSTICE BLACKMUN joins, dissenting.

The Social Security Act's categorical assistance programs, including the Aid to the Aged, Blind, or Disabled (AABD) program involved here, are fundamentally different from most federal legislation. Unlike the Fair Labor Standards Act involved in last Term's decision in Employees v. Department of Public Health and Welfare, 411 U.S. 279 (1973), or the Federal Employers' Liability Act at issue in Parden v. Terminal R. Co., 377 U.S. 184 (1964), the Social Security Act does not impose federal standards and liability upon all who engage in certain regulated activities, including often-unwilling state agencies. Instead, the Act seeks to induce state participation in the federal welfare programs by offering federal matching funds in exchange for the State's voluntary assumption of the Act's requirements. I find this basic distinction crucial: it leads me to conclude that by participation in the programs, the States waive whatever immunity they might otherwise have from federal court orders requiring retroactive payment of welfare benefits.

In its contacts with the Social Security Act's assistance programs in recent years, the Court has frequently described the Act as a "scheme of cooperative federalism." See, *e.g.,* King v. Smith, 392 U.S. 309, 316 (1968); Jefferson v. Hackney, 406 U.S. 535, 542 (1972). While this phrase captures a number of the unique characteristics of these programs, for present purposes it serves to emphasize that the States' decision to participate in the programs is a voluntary one. In deciding to participate, however, the States necessarily give up their freedom to operate assistance programs for the needy as they see fit, and bind themselves to conform their programs to the requirements of the federal statute and regulations.   *   *   *

In agreeing to comply with the requirements of the Social Security Act and HEW regulations, I believe that Illinois has also agreed to subject itself to suit in the federal courts to enforce these obligations. I recognize, of course, that the Social Security Act does not itself provide for a cause of action to enforce its obligations. As the Court points out, the only sanction expressly provided in the Act for a participating State's failure to comply with federal requirements is the cutoff of federal funding by the Secretary of HEW. Former 42 U.S.C. § 1384 (now 42 U.S.C. § 804 (1970 ed., Supp. II)).

But a cause of action is clearly provided by 42 U.S.C. § 1983, which in terms authorizes suits to redress deprivations of rights secured by the "laws" of the United States. And we have already rejected the argument that Congress intended the funding cutoff to be the sole remedy for noncompliance with federal requirements. In Rosado v. Wyman, 397 U.S. 397, 420–423 (1970), we held that suits in federal court under § 1983 were proper to enforce the provisions of the Social Security Act against participating States.

* * *

I believe that Congress also intended the full panoply of traditional judicial remedies to be available to the federal courts in these § 1983 suits. There is surely no indication of any congressional intent to restrict the courts' equitable jurisdiction. Yet the Court has held that "[u]nless a statute in so many words, or by a necessary and inescapable inference, restricts the court's jurisdiction in equity, the full scope of that jurisdiction is to be recognized and applied." Porter v. Warner Holding Co., 328 U.S. 395, 398 (1946).

* * *

In particular, I am firmly convinced that Congress intended the restitution of wrongfully withheld assistance payments to be a remedy available to the federal courts in these suits. Benefits under the categorical assistance programs "are a matter of statutory entitlement for persons qualified to receive them." Goldberg v. Kelly, 397 U.S. 254, 262 (1970). Retroactive payment of benefits secures for recipients this entitlement which was withheld in violation of federal law. Equally important, the courts' power to order retroactive payments is an essential remedy to insure future state compliance with federal requirements. See Porter v. Warner Holding Co., 328 U.S., at 400. No other remedy can effectively deter States from the strong temptation to cut welfare budgets by circumventing the stringent requirements of federal law. The funding cutoff is a drastic sanction, one which HEW has proved unwilling or unable to employ to compel strict compliance with the Act and regulations. See Rosado v. Wyman, *supra*, 397 U.S., at 426. Moreover, the cutoff operates only prospectively; it in no way deters the States from even a flagrant violation of the Act's requirements for as long as HEW does not discover the violation and threaten to take such action.

* * *

I have no quarrel with the Court's view that waiver of constitutional rights should not lightly be inferred. But I simply cannot believe that the State could have entered into this essentially contractual agreement with the Federal Government without recognizing that it was subjecting itself to the full scope of the § 1983 remedy provided by Congress to enforce the terms of the agreement.

* * *

A finding of waiver here is also consistent with the reasoning of the majority in Employees, which relied on a distinction between "governmental" and "proprietary" functions of state government. This distinction apparently recognizes that if sovereign immunity is to be at all meaningful, the Court must be reluctant to hold a State to have waived its immunity simply by acting in its sovereign capacity—*i.e.*, by merely performing its "governmental" functions. On the other hand, in launching a profitmaking enterprise, "a State leaves the sphere that is exclusively its own," Parden v. Terminal R. Co., 377 U.S., at 196, and a voluntary waiver of sovereign immunity can more easily be found. While conducting an assistance program for the needy is surely a "governmental" function, the State here has done far more than operate its own program in its sovereign capacity. It has voluntarily subordinated its sovereignty in this matter to that of the Federal Government, and agreed to comply with the conditions imposed by Congress upon the expenditure of federal funds. In entering this federal-state cooperative program, the State again "leaves the sphere that is exclusively its own," and similarly may more readily be found to have voluntarily waived its immunity. * * *

NOTE ON THE KINDS OF RELIEF PERMITTED IN SUITS AGAINST STATE OFFICERS

(1) Consider the Court's statement that officers have always been immune from suits "seeking to impose a liability which must be paid from public funds in the state treasury." Prior cases had ordered state officials to perform ministerial duties—the traditional office of the writ of mandamus[1]—and some writs of mandamus issued against federal officials had required payments from the federal treasury.[2] Should Edelman be read to bar mandamus requiring state officers to perform ministerial duties that involve the payment of public funds? Why should a state have an immunity that is broader in this respect than that of the United States?

Would Edelman permit a bondholder to obtain an order, under the Contracts Clause, requiring officials of a state that passed legislation unconstitutionally repudiating bonds to make payments due *in the future?* Cf. Georgia R.R. & Banking Co. v. Redwine, 342 U.S. 299 (1952), p. 1181, *supra;* Papasan v. Allain, note 3, *infra.*

(2) A suit nominally against an unconsenting state itself (rather than an officer) is barred regardless of the kind of relief sought. See, *e.g.,* Alabama v. Pugh, 438 U.S. 781 (1978) (per curiam). What justifies making federal court jurisdiction over the claim for injunctive relief in Edelman depend on whether the named defendant is the Illinois Department of Public Aid or its director?

(3) The prospective/retrospective line has been a difficult one to apply. In Milliken v. Bradley, 433 U.S. 267 (1977) (Milliken II), after the Supreme

---

1. See, *e.g.,* Board of Liquidation v. Mc-Comb, 2 Otto 531 (U.S.1875), p. 1179 note 1, *supra;* Tindal v. Wesley, 167 U.S. 204 (1897); Rolston v. Missouri Fund Com'rs, 120 U.S. 390 (1887).

However, in Kentucky v. Dennison, 24 How. 66, 107 (U.S.1860), the Court refused to issue mandamus to compel the Governor of Ohio to extradite to Kentucky a black free man accused of trying to help slaves escape. Though the Governor's refusal violated a mandatory duty created by the Extradition Clause, the Court concluded that he had only "a moral duty"; "the Federal Government * * * has no power to impose on a State officer, as such, any duty whatever, and compel him to perform it * * *." That this decision could only be understood in light of its extraordinary circumstances was confirmed when it was overruled in Puerto Rico v. Branstad, 107 S.Ct. 2802 (1987).

2. See, *e.g.,* Kendall v. United States, p. 1092, note 4, *supra;* Roberts v. United States ex rel. Valentine, 176 U.S. 221 (1900); pp. 1091–95, *supra.*

Court had disapproved an interdistrict busing remedy to desegregate the Detroit schools, the district court ordered the provision of remedial education for pupils and in-service training for teachers and administrators, as well as the hiring of more counselors. The state, which shared responsibility for the segregation, was ordered to pay half the cost of these programs; though the order ran only against state officials, it contemplated payment from the state treasury. The Supreme Court unanimously held that the decree "fits squarely within the prospective-compliance exception reaffirmed by Edelman. * * * The educational components * * * are plainly designed to wipe out continuing conditions of inequality produced by the inherently unequal dual school system long maintained by Detroit.

"These programs were not, and as a practical matter could not be, intended to wipe the slate clean by one bold stroke, as could a retroactive award of money in Edelman. * * * Reading and speech deficiencies cannot be eliminated by judicial fiat; they will require time, patience, and the skills of specially trained teachers. That the programs are also 'compensatory' in nature does not change the fact that they are part of a plan that operates *prospectively* to bring about the delayed benefits of a unitary school system" (pp. 289–90).

Wasn't the decree in Milliken II just as much an effort to redress past violations as the retroactive benefits in Edelman? Is Milliken distinguishable because the order required the state to purchase services for (rather than to pay cash to) the plaintiffs? Because the payments in Milliken would be made over a long period, giving more time for budgetary planning? Because of the continuing effects of past violations?[3] (Might not indigent beneficiaries in Edelman have been suffering continuing effects of previous denials of benefits?)

Does it help, in understanding Milliken II, to recall the history of the Supreme Court's efforts to eradicate school desegregation? Is it pertinent that the order that was upheld took the place of an earlier multidistrict busing order? Would that earlier order have been "prospective"?

(4) In Hutto v. Finney, 437 U.S. 678 (1978), after finding that the Arkansas penal system constituted cruel and unusual punishment and issuing various injunctive orders over the course of seven years, the district court ruled that defendant officials had acted in bad faith and ordered them to pay $20,000 "out of Department of Correction funds" to plaintiffs' attorneys. In upholding that fee award, the Supreme Court stressed the

---

3. In Papasan v. Allain, 106 S.Ct. 2932 (1986), Mississippi officials were sued for allegedly underfunding certain public schools. One theory of suit was that federal land grants had created a perpetual trust, with the state as trustee, to benefit the schools; the state was alleged long ago to have breached the trust; and current officials were said to be violating a continuing obligation under federal common law to meet their trust responsibilities. The Supreme Court held this claim barred by the Eleventh Amendment (pp. 2941–42): "The distinction between a continuing obligation on the part of the trustee and an ongoing liability for past breach of trust is essentially a formal distinction of the sort we rejected in Edelman." However, plain-tiffs' second theory—that the state's current school funding methods denied Equal Protection—was not barred: "A remedy to eliminate this current disparity, even a remedy that might require the expenditure of state funds, would ensure ' "compliance *in the future* with a substantive federal-question determination" ' rather than bestow an award for accrued monetary liability" (p. 2942, quoting Milliken and Edelman). Justice Brennan, joined by Justices Marshall, Blackmun and Stevens, dissented from the first holding, based on Justice Brennan's dissenting opinion in Atascadero State Hosp. v. Scanlon, 473 U.S. 234 (1985), p. 1168, *supra;* Justice Blackmun also dissented separately from the first holding.

importance of enforcing federal court orders, and held (p. 691) that "[t]he power to impose a fine is properly treated as ancillary to the federal court's power to impose injunctive relief. In this case, the award of attorney's fees for bad faith served the same purpose as a remedial fine imposed for civil contempt. It vindicated the District Court's authority over a recalcitrant litigant." The Court also observed that the compensatory effect of the award did not distinguish it from a fine for civil contempt, and the award was not so large "that it interfered with the State's budgeting process" (p. 691 & n. 17). In a footnote (p. 692 n. 19), the Court added: "We do not understand the Attorney General to urge that the fees should have been awarded against the officers personally; that would be a remarkable way to treat individuals who have relied on the Attorney General to represent their interests throughout this litigation." In dissent, Justice Rehnquist (joined by Justice White) argued that the injunction could have been enforced by fining the defendant officials personally, and noted that state law provided for reimbursement at least in some cases.

Hutto also upheld a second award of attorneys' fees on the distinct theory that Congress, in authorizing fee awards to plaintiffs prevailing in actions under federal civil rights legislation, had abrogated any Eleventh Amendment immunity. See p. 1217, *infra*. But in so ruling, the Court noted that "[c]osts have traditionally been awarded without regard for the States' Eleventh Amendment immunity," and though the precedents predate Edelman, such awards "do not seriously strain" the retrospective/prospective distinction; "[w]hen a State defends a suit for prospective relief, it is not exempt from the ordinary discipline of the courtroom" (p. 695 & n. 24).

Is Hutto consistent with Edelman? With the treatment (see pp. 1113–14, *supra*) of attorney's fees in suits against the United States?

(5) After the Edelman case was remanded, the defendant state officials were ordered "to send a mere explanatory notice to members of the plaintiff class advising them that there are state administrative procedures available by which they are entitled to past welfare benefits." In Quern v. Jordan, 440 U.S. 332 (1979), the Supreme Court unanimously held (pp. 347–49) that "this relief falls on the Ex Parte Young side of the Eleventh Amendment line rather than on the Edelman side. Petitioner makes no issue of the incidental administrative expense connected with preparing and mailing the notice. Instead, he argues that giving the proposed notice will lead inexorably to the payment of state funds for retroactive benefits and therefore it, in effect, amounts to a monetary award. But the chain of causation which petitioners seek to establish is by no means unbroken * * *. The notice * * * simply apprises plaintiff class members of the existence of whatever administrative procedures may already be available under state law * * *. * * * Whether a recipient of notice decides to take advantage of those available state procedures is left completely to [his] discretion * * *. And whether or not the class member will receive retroactive benefits rests entirely with the State, * * * not with the federal court.

"The notice * * * is more properly viewed as ancillary to the prospective relief already ordered by the court. See Milliken v. Bradley * * *. The notice in effect simply informs class members that their federal suit is at an end, that the federal court can provide them with no further relief, and that there are existing state administrative procedures which they may wish to pursue."

(6) Green v. Mansour, 474 U.S. 64 (1985), was an action very similar to Edelman. In Green, the plaintiff class sued the state Director of Social Services, alleging underpayment of AFDC benefits in violation of federal law. While the suit was pending in the district court, Congress modified the program and the state came into compliance with federal law. In these circumstances, the Supreme Court, per Rehnquist, J., ruled that plaintiffs' request for a declaratory judgment that the defendant's past conduct violated federal law, and for notice relief (as in Quern), was barred by the Eleventh Amendment (p. 427): "a request for a limited notice order will escape the Eleventh Amendment bar if the notice is ancillary to the grant of some other appropriate relief that can be 'noticed.'" Injunctive relief could no longer be issued, the Court noted, because the state had come into compliance with the statute as amended; consequently, notice relief could be granted only as ancillary to a declaratory judgment. Stressing the discretionary character of declaratory relief, the Court held that it should not be awarded: because there was no dispute about present compliance with federal law, a declaration "would be useful in resolving the dispute over the past lawfulness of respondent's action only if it might be offered in state court proceedings as res judicata on the issue of liability," leaving to the state courts the question of damages. But to issue a federal court declaratory judgment as a step toward a state court damage remedy would be an " 'end run' around our decision in Edelman v. Jordan" (p. 428).

Justice Brennan, joined by Justices Marshall, Blackmun and Stevens, dissented, arguing that in Green, as in Quern, any "use of the declaratory judgment in the State's courts is * * * left completely to the discretion of individual notice recipients and the award of retroactive benefits 'rests entirely with the State * * *' " (p. 430, quoting Quern, 440 U.S. at 348). Nor could Quern be distinguished as involving notice relief ancillary to an injunction, for (as the Court in Quern had recognized) that injunction had been mooted by Congress's abolition of the program at issue in Quern three years before the notice relief was issued. Justices Marshall and Blackmun also filed dissenting opinions.

In light of the decisions since Edelman, how stable or coherent is the line between permissible and impermissible relief in suits against state officers? See generally Currie, *Sovereign Immunity and Suits Against Government Officers*, 1984 Sup.Ct.Rev. 149.

(7) The Eleventh Amendment does not apply to actions in state courts. See Maine v. Thiboutot, 448 U.S. 1, 9 n. 7 (1980); Nevada v. Hall, p. 1171, *supra*. Is it the implication of the Court's opinion in Quern, and of the dissenting opinions in Green, that the state courts were free to refuse, on the ground of state sovereign immunity, to award retroactive benefits even if a claimant could establish that their denial violated federal law?[4] Would such a refusal be consistent with General Oil v. Crain and Ward v. Love County, pp. 581–87, *supra*?

---

4. After the decision in Quern v. Jordan, class members who filed for past benefits in the state court of claims obtained a judgment in their favor and were ultimately paid. See Lichtenstein, *Retroactive Re*- *lief in the Federal Courts Since Edelman v. Jordan: A Trip Through the Twilight Zone*, 32 Case W.L.Rev. 364, 375 n. 73 (1982).

Is it possible to view the Eleventh Amendment as being, in effect, a forum choice provision, which merely permits the states to resist *federal court* jurisdiction over suits (even if nominally against officials) seeking retrospective relief—while leaving the state courts obliged, under the Supremacy Clause, to provide such relief in suits under federal law? See, *e.g.,* Employees of Dept. of Pub. Health & Welfare v. Department of Pub. Health & Welfare, 411 U.S. 279, 291–94 (1973) (Marshall, J., concurring in the result), p. 1215, *infra; cf.* footnote 2 in Atascadero State Hosp. v. Scanlon, p. 1204, *infra.*[5] See generally Wolcher, *Sovereign Immunity and the Supremacy Clause: Damages Against States in Their Own Courts for Constitutional Violations,* 69 Calif.L.Rev. 189 (1981).

(8) Under Edelman, the Eleventh Amendment does not bar judgments for monetary relief to be paid by an official personally. (Distinct doctrines establishing official immunities, however, will make such relief difficult to obtain. See Sec. 3, *infra.*) Can the state, by providing for indemnification of officials for such judgments, transform such actions into suits against the state that are barred by the Eleventh Amendment? Most courts have held not. See, *e.g.,* Demery v. Kupperman, 735 F.2d 1139, 1146–48 (9th Cir. 1984), and cases cited.

NOTE ON THE PENNHURST CASE AND THE BEARING OF THE ELEVENTH AMENDMENT ON FEDERAL COURT RELIEF FOR VIOLATIONS OF STATE LAW

(1) In Pennhurst State School & Hosp. v. Halderman, 465 U.S. 89 (1984), the Supreme Court sharply restricted the reach of federal court jurisdiction in suits against state officials for violations of state law. In this case, a resident of a Pennsylvania state institution for the mentally retarded (Pennhurst) filed a federal class action against the institution and various state and county officials, alleging that conditions at Pennhurst violated federal statutory and constitutional requirements, as well as the state's Mental Health and Mental Retardation Act of 1966 (the "MH/MR Act").[1] The district judge held that conditions at Pennhurst contravened state law, federal statutory requirements, and the federal Constitution, and that the mentally retarded who were cared for by the state were constitutionally entitled to live in "the least restrictive setting" consistent with their rehabilitative needs. The defendants were ordered, among other things, to close Pennhurst as soon as practicable and to provide "suitable

---

5. Under this view, would a state that legislatively repudiates a bond be obliged, under the Contracts Clause, to provide a damage remedy in its own courts? See Hans v. Louisiana, p. 1162, *supra,* 134 U.S. at 18 ("[t]he state courts have no power to entertain suits • • • against a State without its consent. Then how does the [federal] Circuit Court, having only concurrent jurisdiction, acquire any such power?") Is it possible that the Contracts Clause does not provide a federal cause of action for damages, and thus, unlike other federal enactments, cannot give rise to any state court obligation to provide damage

relief? See Field, *The Eleventh Amendment and Other Sovereign Immunity Doctrines: Congressional Imposition of Suit Upon the States,* 126 U.Pa.L.Rev. 1203, 1265–68 (1978); Liberman, *State Sovereign Immunity in Suits to Enforce Federal Rights,* 1977 Wash.U.L.Q. 195, 229; *cf.* Carter v. Greenhow, 114 U.S. 317, 322 (1885).

1. The statement of facts is derived from Shapiro, *Wrong Turns: The Eleventh Amendment and the Pennhurst Case,* 98 Harv.L.Rev. 61 (1984).

community living arrangements" for the residents. A special master was appointed to implement the decision.

The Third Circuit upheld the decision on the merits, but rested its conclusion that treatment must be afforded in the least restrictive setting exclusively on the federal Developmentally Disabled Assistance and Bill of Rights Act. It also affirmed the district court's remedial order except insofar as it decreed that Pennhurst itself be closed.

On its initial review in 1981, the Supreme Court held that the federal statutory provisions relied on by the courts below did not create any substantive rights. Pennhurst State School & Hosp. v. Halderman, 451 U.S. 1 (1981). The case was remanded for a determination whether the remedial order could be supported under other provisions of state or federal law. On remand, the Third Circuit en banc affirmed its prior judgment, ruling that the state's MH/MR Act required placement of residents in the least restrictive setting.

In 1984, the Supreme Court again reversed, holding (5–4) that the Eleventh Amendment barred relief based on state law. 465 U.S. 89. Justice Powell wrote for the Court (pp. 101–06; some paragraphing omitted):

"The Eleventh Amendment bars a suit against state officials when 'the state is the real substantial party in interest.' * * * Thus, '[t]he general rule is that relief sought nominally against an officer is in fact against the sovereign if the decree would operate against the latter.' Hawaii v. Gordon, 373 U.S. 57, 58 (1963) (per curiam) [p. 1127, *supra*].[11]

"The Court has recognized an important exception to this general rule: a suit challenging the constitutionality of a state official's action is not one against the State. This was the holding in Ex parte Young, 209 U.S. 123 (1908) * * *. The theory of the case was that an unconstitutional enactment is 'void' and therefore does not 'impart to [the officer] any immunity from responsibility to the supreme authority of the United States.' *Id.*, at 160. Since the State could not authorize the action, the officer was 'stripped of his official or representative character and [was] subjected to the consequences of his individual conduct.' *Ibid.* * * * [T]he Young doctrine has been accepted as necessary to permit the federal courts to vindicate federal rights and hold state officials responsible to 'the supreme authority of the United States.' Young, *supra*, 209 U.S., at 160.
* * * *

"The Court also has recognized, however, that the need to promote the supremacy of federal law must be accommodated to the constitutional immunity of the States. This is the significance of Edelman v. Jordan

"11. * * * Respondents * * * suggest * * * that the suit here should not be considered to be against the State * * * because * * * petitioners were acting ultra vires their authority. Respondents rely largely on Florida Dept. of State v. Treasure Salvors, Inc., 458 U.S. 670 (1982) [p. 1198, note 3, *infra*], which in turn was founded upon Larson v. Domestic & Foreign Commerce Corp., 337 U.S. 682 (1949) [p. 1117, *supra*]. * * * These and other modern cases make clear that a state officer may be said to act ultra vires only when he acts 'without any authority whatever.' Treasure Salvors, 458 U.S., at 697. * * * 'A claim of error in the exercise of [delegated] power is * * * not sufficient.' Larson, *supra*, at 690. Petitioners' actions in operating this mental health institution plainly were not beyond their delegated authority in this sense. The MH/MR Act gave them broad discretion to provide 'adequate' mental health services. * * * The essence of respondents' claim is that petitioners have not provided such services adequately. * * *"

* * * [, where] we declined to extend the fiction of Young to encompass retroactive relief, for to do so would effectively eliminate the constitutional immunity of the States. * * *

"This need to reconcile competing interests is wholly absent, however, when a plaintiff alleges that a state official has violated *state* law. * * * [Relief in such a case] does not vindicate the supreme authority of federal law. On the contrary, it is difficult to think of a greater intrusion on state sovereignty than when a federal court instructs state officials on how to conform their conduct to state law. Such a result conflicts directly with the principles of federalism that underlie the Eleventh Amendment. We conclude that Young and Edelman are inapplicable in a suit against state officials on the basis of state law."

According to Justice Powell, the view of the dissenters that in Pennhurst, as in Ex parte Young, the officer's wrong stripped him of his official character, making the suit one against him personally rather than against the state, "would make the law a pretense. * * * And the dissent's underlying view that the named defendants here were acting beyond and contrary to their authority cannot be reconciled with reality—or with the record. The District Court in this case held that the individual defendants 'acted in the utmost good faith * * * *within the sphere of their official responsibilities*' and therefore were entitled to immunity from damages" (p. 107).

Justice Powell then considered a wealth of nineteenth and early twentieth century precedents on which the dissenters relied. Most, he argued, were distinguishable: they either did not in fact rest on the Eleventh Amendment, involved allegations of federal constitutional as well as state law violations, or sought damages against the individual officer personally rather than relief that affected the state. Two other cases alleged only common law torts, not violations of state statutes, and "were explicitly" overruled in Larson v. Domestic & Foreign Commerce Corp., p. 1117, *supra*. Only one decision, he concluded, clearly held injunctive relief against state officials for failing to carry out their duties under state statutes to be consistent with the Eleventh Amendment—Rolston v. Missouri Fund Com'rs, 120 U.S. 390 (1887)—and that case ordered compliance with a plain ministerial duty. In Justice Powell's view, analogous cases involving the sovereign immunity of the United States, though far from uniform, "make clear that suit may not be predicated on violations of state statutes that command purely discretionary duties. Since it cannot be doubted that the statutes at issue here gave petitioners broad discretion in operating Pennhurst, see n. 11, *supra*, * * * the conduct alleged in this case would not be ultra vires even under the standards of the dissent's cases" (pp. 109–11 & nn. 18–20). He continued (pp. 111–14):

"Thus, while there is language in the early cases that advances the authority-stripping theory advocated by the dissent, this theory had never been pressed as far as Justice Stevens would do in this case. And when the expansive approach of the dissent was advanced, this Court plainly and explicitly rejected it. In Larson v. Domestic & Foreign Commerce Corp., 337 U.S. 682 (1949), the Court was faced with the argument that an allegation that a government official committed a tort sufficed to distinguish the official from the sovereign. * * * The Court rejected the argument, noting that it would make the doctrine of sovereign immunity

superfluous. A plaintiff would need only to 'claim an invasion of his legal rights' in order to override sovereign immunity. *Id.,* at 693. In the court's view the argument 'confuse[d] the doctrine of sovereign immunity with the requirement that a plaintiff state a cause of action.' *Id.,* at 692–93.
* * *[25]"

The Court then discussed the impact of its ruling on the doctrine of pendent jurisdiction:

"As the Court of Appeals noted, in Siler [v. Louisville & N.R.R., 213 U.S. 175 (1909)] and subsequent cases concerning pendent jurisdiction, relief was granted against state officials on the basis of state-law claims that were pendent to federal constitutional claims. In none of these cases, however, did the Court so much as mention the Eleventh Amendment in connection with the state-law claim" (p. 118). As for plaintiffs' argument that the Court's ruling "may cause litigants to split causes of action between state and federal courts" and could undercut the policy of constitutional avoidance by denying federal courts the opportunity to premise relief on state law grounds, Justice Powell responded that pendent jurisdiction was a "judge-made doctrine of expediency and efficiency," and that "neither pendent jurisdiction nor any other basis of jurisdiction may override the Eleventh Amendment" (pp. 120–21).[2]

Justice Stevens, joined by Justices Brennan, Marshall, and Blackmun, filed an unusually long and bitter dissent. He noted (p. 126) that the Court was reversing the Third Circuit for having done, on remand from Pennhurst I, "precisely what this Court ordered it to do"—*i.e.,* for having premised its remedial order on state law. After asserting (p. 127) that the Court's decision repudiated "at least 28 cases, spanning well over a century of this Court's jurisprudence," he continued (pp. 130–32):

"The majority proceeds as if this Court has not had previous occasion to consider the Eleventh Amendment argument made by petitioners, and contends that Ex parte Young, 209 U.S. 123 (1908), has no application to a suit seeking injunctive relief on the basis of state law. That is simply not the case. The Court rejected the argument that the Eleventh Amendment precludes injunctive relief on the basis of state law twice only two Terms ago. In Florida Dept. of State v. Treasure Salvors, Inc., 458 U.S. 670 (1982), four Justices concluded that a suit for possession of property in the hands of state officials was not barred by the Eleventh Amendment inasmuch as the State did not have even a colorable claim to the property under state law. See *id.,* at 696–697 (opinion of Stevens, J., joined by Burger, C.J., and Marshall and Blackmun, JJ.)[3] Four additional Justices accepted the proposition that if the state officers' conduct had been in violation of a state

---

"25. * * * We have noted that the authority-stripping theory of Young is a fiction that has been narrowly construed. In this light, it may well be wondered what principled basis there is to the ultra vires doctrine as it was set forth in Larson and Treasure Salvors [p. 1198, note 3, *infra*]. * * * For present purposes, however, we do no more than question the continued vitality of the ultra vires doctrine in the Eleventh Amendment context. We hold only that to the extent the doctrine is consistent with the analysis of this opinion, it is a very narrow exception that will

allow suit only under the standards set forth in n. 11, *supra.*"

2. [Ed.] The Court stated, however, that "[n]othing in our decision is meant to cast doubt on the desirability of applying the Siler principle in cases where the federal court has jurisdiction to decide the state-law issues" (p. 119 n. 28).

3. [Ed.] In this case, after a salvor discovered a wrecked vessel, it entered into a contract with the State of Florida, predicated on the assumed validity of Florida's claim under state law to own the vessel,

statute, the Eleventh Amendment would not bar the action. *Id.,* at 714 (White, J., concurring in the judgment in part and dissenting in part, joined by Powell, Rehnquist, and O'Connor, JJ.). And in just one short paragraph in Cory v. White, 457 U.S. 85 (1982), the Court thrice restated the settled rule that the Eleventh Amendment does not bar suits against state officers when they are 'alleged to be acting against federal or state law.'[4] These are only the two most recent in an extraordinarily long line of cases."

Justice Stevens then reviewed a number of prior decisions that he viewed as establishing that the Eleventh Amendment does not bar suits alleging that state officials have acted tortiously as a matter of state law, or in violation of state statutes (pp. 134–38, 145–50, 153–56):

"* * * [I]n Rolston v. Missouri Fund Commissioners, 120 U.S. 390 (1887), the Court rejected the argument that a suit to enjoin a state officer to comply with state law violated the Eleventh Amendment. The Court wrote: 'Here the suit is to get a state officer to do what a statute requires of him. The litigation is with the officer, not the state.' *Id.,* at 411.[5]

"* * * The appellants in Scully v. Bird, 209 U.S. 481 (1908), brought a diversity suit seeking injunctive relief against the dairy and food commissioner of the State of Michigan, on the ground that 'under cover of his office' he had maliciously engaged in a course of conduct designed to ruin plaintiff's business in the State. [Rejecting an Eleventh Amendment objection], * * * [t]his Court * * * noted that the complaint alleged action 'in dereliction of duties enjoined by the statutes of the State,' and concluded that it was 'manifest from this summary of the allegations of the bill that this is not a suit against the State.' *Id.,* at 490.[6]

"Finally, in Greene v. Louisville & Interurban R. Co., 244 U.S. 499 (1917), and its companion cases, * * * the plaintiffs challenged the conduct of state officials under both federal and state law. The Court,

that permitted the salvor to undertake salvage operations and to retain 75% of the value of material recovered.

In unrelated proceedings between Florida and the United States, the Supreme Court ruled that Florida's boundary was landward of the site of the wreck. The salvor then filed an admiralty in rem action in federal court, naming the vessel as defendant and claiming title to all property recovered from the wreck. The district court issued, on plaintiff's motion, a "warrant of arrest" directing the United States Marshal to take custody of artifacts in the possession of state officials that had already been recovered from the wreck. The officials contended that execution of the warrant was barred by the Eleventh Amendment.

The Supreme Court rejected the claim of immunity; four Justices held that the officials' continued possession of the artifacts was beyond their statutory authority; four Justices disagreed; the deciding vote was cast by Justice Brennan, who reasoned that the Eleventh Amendment is inapplicable to suits against a state by a citizen thereof, see p. 1167, *supra.*

4. [Ed.] There, the administrator of Howard Hughes' estate filed a statutory interpleader action against officials of California and Texas, alleging that each state sought to tax the estate. The Court ruled that Edelman v. Jordan had not overruled Worcester County Trust Co. v. Riley, 302 U.S. 292 (1937), which, in holding a nearly identical action to be barred, stated that "generally suits to restrain action of state officials can * * * be prosecuted only when the action sought to be restrained is without the authority of state law or contravenes the statutes or Constitution of the United States" (p. 297). There being no violation of state or federal law alleged, Edelman provided no basis for injunctive relief. Justice Powell, joined by Justices Marshall and Stevens, dissented.

5. [Ed.] Recall Justice Powell's distinction of Rolston as involving a nondiscretionary duty. Is it persuasive?

6. [Ed.] The majority characterized Scully as involving only a common law tort, and hence as having been overruled by Larson. 465 U.S. at 110 n. 19.

citing, *inter alia,* Young * * *, held that the Eleventh Amendment did not bar injunctive relief on the basis of state law, noting that the plaintiffs' federal claim was sufficiently substantial to justify the exercise of pendent jurisdiction over plaintiffs' state-law claims, and that since violations of federal and state law had been alleged, it was appropriate for the federal court to issue injunctive relief on the basis of state law without reaching the federal claims, despite the strictures of the Eleventh Amendment. In short, the Greene Court approved of precisely the methodology employed by the Court of Appeals in this case.[7]

"* * * [A]ll of [these cases] explicitly consider and reject the claim that the Eleventh Amendment prohibits federal courts from issuing injunctive relief based on state law * * *. The Court tries to explain away these cases by arguing that the applicable state statutes gave petitioners such 'broad discretion' over Pennhurst that their actions were not *ultra vires* * * *. The Court, however, does not dispute the Court of Appeals' conclusion that these state statutes gave petitioners *no discretion whatsoever* to disregard their duties with respect to institutionalization of the retarded as they did. Petitioners acted outside of their lawful discretion every bit as much as did the government officials in the cases I have discussed, which hold that when an official commits an act prohibited by law, he acts beyond his authority and is not protected by sovereign immunity. * * *

"The majority states that the holding of Ex parte Young is limited to cases in which relief is provided on the basis of federal law, and that it rests entirely on the need to protect the supremacy of federal law. That position overlooks the foundation of the rule of Young * * *.

"The pivotal consideration in Young was that it was not conduct of the sovereign that was at issue. The rule that unlawful acts of an officer should not be attributed to the sovereign has deep roots in the history of sovereign immunity and makes Young reconcilable with the principles of sovereign immunity found in the Eleventh Amendment, rather than merely an unprincipled accommodation between federal and state interests that ignores the principles contained in the Eleventh Amendment.

"This rule plainly applies to conduct of state officers in violation of state law. Young states that the significance of the charge of unconstitutional conduct is that it renders the state official's conduct 'simply an illegal act,' and hence the officer is not entitled to the sovereign's immunity. Since a state officer's conduct in violation of state law is certainly no less illegal than his violation of federal law, in either case the official, by committing an illegal act, is 'stripped of his official or representative character.' * * *

"* * * The majority criticizes this approach as being 'out of touch with reality' because it ignores the practical impact of an injunction on the State though directed at its officers. * * * Yet that criticism cannot account for Young, since an injunction has the same effect on the State whether it is based on federal or state law. * * * In the final analysis the distinction between the State and its officers, realistic or not, is one firmly embedded in the doctrine of sovereign immunity. * * *

7. [Ed.] The majority argued that in these cases, the Court had rejected an Eleventh Amendment defense only in connection with the federal law, but not the state law, claim. 465 U.S. at 118 & n. 28.

"That the doctrine of sovereign immunity does not protect conduct which has been prohibited by the sovereign is clearly demonstrated by the case on which petitioners chiefly rely, Larson v. Domestic & Foreign Commerce Corp., 337 U.S. 682 (1949). The Larson opinion teaches that the actions of state officials are not attributable to the state—are *ultra vires* — in two different types of situations: (1) when the official is engaged in conduct that the sovereign has not authorized, and (2) when he has engaged in conduct that the sovereign has forbidden. A sovereign, like any other principal, cannot authorize its agent to violate the law. * * *

" * * * Under the second track of the Larson analysis, petitioners were acting *ultra vires*, because they were acting in a way that the sovereign, by statute, had forbidden."

Finally, Justice Stevens objected to the overruling of Siler and similar cases exercising pendent jurisdiction over state law claims against state officials. Such jurisdiction, he argued, not only serves the policy of constitutional avoidance, but "enhances the decisionmaking autonomy of the States. Siler directs the federal court to turn first to state law, which the State is free to modify or repeal." By contrast, under the Court's opinion, "federal courts are required to resolve cases on federal grounds that no state authority can undo" (p. 163).

(2) Pennhurst can be viewed as extending Larson to cases where an official's conduct is not merely tortious under the common law, but violates a state statute—an extension of which Justice Stevens was sharply critical. But however powerful his arguments against that extension, shouldn't Justice Stevens have admitted that the implications of Larson for a case like Pennhurst were far more ambiguous than he suggested? And rather than accepting Larson as a given, should he have stressed that Larson itself was poorly reasoned and was a major departure from precedent?

On the other hand, Justice Stevens clearly demonstrates the difficulties with the majority's argument that the outcome in Pennhurst was consistent with the Court's prior decisions and was compelled by Larson.

(3) What accounts for the majority's strained reading and repudiation of so many precedents?[8]

The Pennhurst lawsuit implicated questions about the appropriate scope of federal equitable relief in cases seeking to restructure institutions of state government. There are perils in such actions, especially when relief is based upon an interpretation of unsettled state law. But aren't "the eleventh amendment and sovereign immunity * * * inappropriately blunt instruments for dealing with these delicate matters," especially when "[o]ther, more precise * * * nonconstitutional doctrines of restraint" are available? See Shapiro, note 1, *supra*, at 79. (On those doctrines more generally, see pp. 267–68, *supra*; Chap. X, Secs. 2(B)–2(D), *infra*).

It is argued in Dwyer, *Pendent Jurisdiction and the Eleventh Amendment*, 75 Calif.L.Rev. 129 (1987), that Pennhurst should be read as barring only intrusive relief, such as structural injunctions, but not declaratory relief or even negative injunctions. Is that an attractive reading? A well-supported one?

8. Among the problems created by the Pennhurst decision is whether, since the Eleventh Amendment is treated as a jurisdictional defect, federal court consent judg-ments based upon state law that were entered prior to Pennhurst are now subject to being reopened. See Lelsz v. Kavanagh, 807 F.2d 1243 (5th Cir.1987), so holding.

Assuming that the decision reaches more broadly, consider the options open after Pennhurst to a litigant like Halderman who has plausible claims under both state and federal law for equitable relief against a course of ongoing state action.

She is free, of course, to file in state court under both state and federal law—but to do so she must forgo her right under § 1331 to a federal forum for her federal cause of action.

She may instead file the federal claim in federal court.[9] But to do so, she must either forgo her state law claim altogether, or file a second lawsuit in state court asserting the state law claim. Even if she can afford to file two separate lawsuits, the result is patently inefficient for the judicial system and the litigants, and it may deprive the federal court of the chance to avoid a constitutional decision.[10] And it raises further complications:

(a) Should one court stay its hand while the other proceeds? See generally Chap. X, Sec. 2(D), *infra*. If so, what standards govern whether the federal court, or the state court, should abstain? See Werhan, *Pullman Abstention After Pennhurst: A Comment on Judicial Federalism,* 27 Wm. & Mary L.Rev. 449 (1986).

(b) Suppose the state court action comes to judgment first. At a minimum, the doctrine of issue preclusion may prevent the plaintiff from obtaining an independent federal court adjudication of issues in her federal lawsuit. It is also possible that the entire federal action might be barred by a plea of claim preclusion. See Chap. XII, pp. 1615–27, *infra*.

Is any of the options left open after Pennhurst satisfactory?[11]

(4) Absent consent, does Pennhurst foreclose the exercise of diversity jurisdiction in suits against state officials seeking injunctive relief under state law?

(5) Will it always be clear whether a federal injunction should be characterized as resting on state law (and hence barred by Pennhurst) or federal law (and hence permissible under Young and Edelman)? Consider, for example, the Education of the Handicapped Act, 20 U.S.C. §§ 1400–61, which conditions federal assistance upon a state's adopting a plan (that must be federally approved) for ensuring handicapped children the right to a free public education. May a district court award prospective relief upon a finding that state officials have not complied with state law requirements in a federally-approved plan, even if that plan provides greater protection

---

9. This is the only option available, of course, if the federal claim falls within the exclusive jurisdiction of the federal courts—for example, a patent or copyright claim.

10. Consider Rogers v. Okin, 738 F.2d 1, 3–5 (1st Cir.1984). Pennhurst was decided after the court of appeals had obtained from the state supreme court answers to certified issues of state law, indicating that state law provided broader protection of the rights of plaintiffs (involuntarily committed mental patients) than did the federal Constitution. The federal court then refused to abstain on the federal issues because there was no pending state court

proceeding, but likewise refused to enjoin state officials under federal law to meet lower standards than those established by state law (with which the court assumed the defendants would comply.)

11. A rare good word for Pennhurst is found in Althouse, *How to Build A Separate Sphere: Federal Courts and State Power,* 100 Harv.L.Rev. 1485 (1987). The author argues that Pennhurst forestalls the misinterpretation of state law and encourages the states to provide mechanisms for reform of their own institutions in order to obtain independence from federal supervision.

to handicapped pupils than is minimally required under federal law? See, *e.g.,* Geis v. Board of Educ. of Parsippany-Troy Hills, 774 F.2d 575 (3d Cir. 1985) (permitting such relief).

(6) Does Pennhurst permit a suit under state law against a state official for damages to be paid by the officer personally rather than by the state? In a footnote, Justice Powell distinguished several cases in which relief had been awarded against federal officials on the ground that the actions sought damages in tort against the individual officer, and stated that because such relief does not run directly against the government, "nothing in our opinion touches these cases" (p. 111 n. 21). Could the judgment in such a case have preclusive effect in a subsequent state court action against a state official, or the state itself, seeking injunctive relief under state law? *Cf.* Duncan v. United States, p. 1125, *supra.*

Does a suit seeking a declaratory judgment that official action violates state law "operate against the sovereign"? Recall the argument of Dwyer, Paragraph (3), *supra,* that Pennhurst should not be read to bar unintrusive relief like negative injunctions or declaratory judgments. But what purpose would be served by such a declaration "if [the federal court] cannot back up its decision with an injunctive decree if the decision is disregarded."? Shapiro, note 1, *supra,* at 82; *cf.* Green v. Mansour, p. 1194, *supra.* See generally Chap. X, Sec. 2(C), pp. 1426–28, *infra.*[12]

(7) Though local governments and their officials have no Eleventh Amendment immunity, see p. 1172 *supra,* the Court in Pennhurst refused to leave standing a judgment against the defendant county officials: "[e]ven assuming" that they have no immunity, the relief ordered relates to an institution run and funded by the state; the state law under which relief had been ordered "contemplates that the state and county officials will cooperate in operating mental retardation programs"; and any relief against the county officials would be partial and incomplete (465 U.S. at 123–24).

The lower courts have not read Pennhurst as casting general doubt upon their authority to award relief under state law against county officials absent some significant effect on the state treasury. See, *e.g.,* Crane v. Texas, 759 F.2d 412 (5th Cir.1985); Greater Los Angeles Council of Deafness, Inc. v. Zolin, 607 F.Supp. 175, 178 n. 5 (D.Cal.1984), *aff'd in pertinent part,* 812 F.2d 1103, 1110 (9th Cir.1987).[13]

(8) Given Justice Powell's view that Ex parte Young was really a suit against the State—one justified by the need to enforce federal supremacy— what reason is there for following the rule (see p. 1191, *supra*) that a suit nominally against the State, but, like Young, seeking only prospective relief under federal law, is barred by the Eleventh Amendment?

12. Declaratory relief was refused in Everett v. Schramm, 587 F.Supp. 228, 235 n. 11 (D.Del.1984), *aff'd,* 772 F.2d 1114 (3d Cir.1985). *Cf.* Wohl Shoe Co. v. Wirtz, 246 F.Supp. 821 (E.D.Mo.1965), and Tejidos Konfort, Inc. v. McAuliffe, 290 F.Supp. 748 (D.P.R.1968), both holding a declaratory judgment against a federal official barred by the United States' sovereign immunity. *Cf.,* also, Hawaii v. Gordon, p. 1127, *supra;* footnote 9 of Larson v. Domestic & Foreign Commerce Corp., p. 1117, *supra.*

13. Suppose that a local government defendant claims, in a case seeking prospective relief under federal law, that the state is an indispensable party, because of its authority or responsibility under *state law* over the subject matter in question. Would joinder of state officials in such a case violate the Eleventh Amendment?

(9) Pennhurst is not novel in assuming that the Eleventh Amendment may immunize the state from federal court suit on a state law cause of action, even if state law provides no immunity.[14] But wholly apart from the Eleventh Amendment, a decision by Pennsylvania to give state officials or agencies immunity from a state law cause of action would, under the Erie doctrine, be binding in a federal court. See, *e.g.*, Zeidner v. Wulforst, 197 F.Supp. 23 (E.D.N.Y.1961); *cf.* Martinez v. California, 444 U.S. 277, 280–83 (1980). Is there then any need in such cases for *additional* protection under the Eleventh Amendment—for protection that is broader than the state's Eleventh Amendment immunity from suit on a *federal* cause of action?[15]

(10) For discussion of Pennhurst, in addition to the articles already cited, see Brown, *Beyond Pennhurst—Protective Jurisdiction, the Eleventh Amendment, and the Power of Congress to Enlarge Federal Jurisdiction in Response to the Burger Court,* 71 Va.L.Rev. 343 (1985); Rudenstine, *Pennhurst and the Scope of Federal Judicial Power to Reform Social Institutions,* 6 Cardozo L.Rev. 71 (1984).

ATASCADERO STATE HOSPITAL v. SCANLON

473 U.S. 234, 105 S.Ct. 3142, 87 L.Ed.2d 171 (1985).
Certiorari to the United States Court of Appeals for the Ninth Circuit.

JUSTICE POWELL delivered the opinion of the Court.

This case presents the question whether States and state agencies are subject to suit in federal court by litigants seeking retroactive monetary relief under § 504 of the Rehabilitation Act of 1973, 29 U.S.C. § 794, or whether such suits are proscribed by the Eleventh Amendment.

I

Respondent, Douglas James Scanlon, suffers from diabetes mellitus and has no sight in one eye. In November 1979, he filed this action against petitioners, Atascadero State Hospital and the California Department of Mental Health, in the United States District Court for the Central District of California, alleging that in 1978 the hospital denied him employment as a graduate student assistant recreational therapist solely because of his physical handicaps. Respondent charged that the hospital's discriminatory refusal to hire him violated § 504 of the Rehabilitation Act of 1973, 87 Stat. 394, as amended, 29 U.S.C. § 794, and certain state fair employment laws. Respondent sought compensatory, injunctive, and declaratory relief.

---

14. Professor Field argues that since Erie was decided, state law does govern in such cases. Field, *The Eleventh Amendment and Other Sovereign Immunity Doctrines: Part I,* 126 U.Pa.L.Rev. 515, 520 n. 24 (1978); Field, *The Eleventh Amendment and Other Sovereign Immunity Doctrines: Congressional Imposition of Suit Upon the States,* 126 U.Pa.L.Rev. 1203, 1254 n. 240, 1264 n. 272 (1978). Compare Shapiro, note 1, *supra,* at 70 n. 55 ("Perhaps it should, but neither Pennhurst nor most of the cases [Field] cites * * * lend much support to that view.")

15. There is one "advantage" to the state of an Eleventh Amendment immunity; under existing law, the state may waive immunity in its own courts without waiving its Eleventh Amendment immunity in federal court. See Smith v. Reeves, p. 1214, *infra.* If in the Pennhurst case the state had no Eleventh Amendment immunity, it might have to either create a substantive state law immunity, which would bar relief in state as well as federal court, or provide no immunity at all, which would leave it subject to suit in federal court.

* * *

* * * [The Court of Appeals] held that "the Eleventh Amendment does not bar [respondent's] action because the State, if it has participated in and received funds from programs under the Rehabilitation Act, has implicitly consented to be sued as a recipient under 29 U.S.C. § 794." 735 F.2d 359, 362 (1984). Although noting that the Rehabilitation Act did not expressly abrogate the States' Eleventh Amendment immunity, the court reasoned that a State's consent to suit in federal court could be inferred from its participation in programs funded by the Act. The court based its view on the fact that the Act provided remedies, procedures, and rights against "any recipient of Federal assistance" while implementing regulations expressly defined the class of recipients to include the States. Quoting our decision in Edelman v. Jordan, 415 U.S. 651, 672 (1974), the court determined that the " 'threshold fact of congressional authorization to sue a class of defendants which literally includes [the] States' " was present in this case. 735 F.2d, at 361.

The court's decision in this case is in conflict with those of the Courts of Appeals for the First and Eighth Circuits. See Ciampa v. Massachusetts Rehabilitation Comm'n, 718 F.2d 1 (CA1 1983); Miener v. Missouri, 673 F.2d 969 (CA8), cert. denied, 459 U.S. 909 (1982). We granted certiorari to resolve this conflict, 469 U.S. 1032 (1984), and we now reverse.

II

* * *

There are * * * certain well-established exceptions to the reach of the Eleventh Amendment. For example, if a State waives its immunity and consents to suit in federal court, the Eleventh Amendment does not bar the action. See, e.g., Clark v. Barnard, 108 U.S. 436, 447 (1883). Moreover, the Eleventh Amendment is "necessarily limited by the enforcement provisions of § 5 of the Fourteenth Amendment," that is, by Congress' power "to enforce, by appropriate legislation, the substantive provisions of the Fourteenth Amendment." Fitzpatrick v. Bitzer, 427 U.S. 445, 456 (1976). As a result, when acting pursuant to § 5 of the Fourteenth Amendment, Congress can abrogate the Eleventh Amendment without the States' consent. Ibid.

But because the Eleventh Amendment implicates the fundamental constitutional balance between the Federal Government and the States,[2] this Court consistently has held that these exceptions apply only when certain specific conditions are met. Thus, we have held that a State will be deemed to have waived its immunity "only where stated 'by the most express language or by such overwhelming implication from the text as [will] leave no room for any other reasonable construction.' " Edelman v. Jordan, supra, at 673, quoting Murray v. Wilson Distilling Co., 213 U.S.

---

2. * * *

Justice Brennan's dissent * * * argues that in the absence of jurisdiction in the federal courts, the States are "exemp[t] . . . from compliance with laws that bind every other legal actor in our Nation." This claim wholly misconceives our federal system. As Justice Marshall has noted, "the issue is not the general immunity of the States from private suit * * * but

merely the susceptibility of the States to suit before *federal tribunals*." Employees v. Missouri Dept. of Public Health and Welfare, [411 U.S. 279, 293–94 (1973)] (concurring in result) (emphasis added). It denigrates the judges who serve on the state courts to suggest that they will not enforce the supreme law of the land. See Martin v. Hunter's Lessee, 1 Wheat. 304, 341–344 (1816).

151, 171 (1909). Likewise, in determining whether Congress in exercising its Fourteenth Amendment powers has abrogated the States' Eleventh Amendment immunity, we have required "an unequivocal expression of congressional intent to 'overturn the constitutionally guaranteed immunity of the several States.'" Pennhurst II, 465 U.S., at 99, quoting Quern v. Jordan, 440 U.S. 332, 342 (1979).

In this case, we are asked to decide whether the State of California is subject to suit in federal court for alleged violations of § 504 of the Rehabilitation Act. Respondent makes three arguments in support of his view that the Eleventh Amendment does not bar such a suit: first, that the State has waived its immunity by virtue of Art. III, § 5, of the California Constitution; second, that in enacting the Rehabilitation Act, Congress has abrogated the constitutional immunity of the States; third, that by accepting federal funds under the Rehabilitation Act, the State has consented to suit in federal court. Under the prior decisions of this Court, none of these claims has merit.

III

Respondent argues that the State of California has waived its immunity to suit in federal court, and thus the Eleventh Amendment does not bar this suit. See Clark v. Barnard, 108 U.S. 436 (1883). Respondent relies on Art. III, § 5, of the California Constitution, which provides: "Suits may be brought against the State in such manner and in such courts as shall be directed by law." In respondent's view, unless the California Legislature affirmatively imposes sovereign immunity, the State is potentially subject to suit in any court, federal as well as state.

The test for determining whether a State has waived its immunity from federal-court jurisdiction is a stringent one. Although a State's general waiver of sovereign immunity may subject it to suit in state court, it is not enough to waive the immunity guaranteed by the Eleventh Amendment. Florida Dept. of Health v. Florida Nursing Home Assn., 450 U.S. 147, 150 (1981) (*per curiam*). As we explained just last Term, "a State's constitutional interest in immunity encompasses not merely whether it may be sued, but *where* it may be sued." Pennhurst II, *supra*, at 99. Thus, in order for a state statute or constitutional provision to constitute a waiver of Eleventh Amendment immunity, it must specify the State's intention to subject itself to suit in *federal court*. See Smith v. Reeves, 178 U.S. 436, 441 (1900); Great Northern Life Insurance Co. v. Read, 322 U.S. 47, 54 (1944). In view of these principles, we do not believe that Art. III, § 5, of the California Constitution constitutes a waiver of the State's constitutional immunity. This provision does not specifically indicate the State's willingness to be sued in federal court. Indeed, the provision appears simply to authorize the legislature to waive the State's sovereign immunity. In the absence of an unequivocal waiver specifically applicable to federal-court jurisdiction, we decline to find that California has waived its constitutional immunity.

IV

Respondent also contends that in enacting the Rehabilitation Act, Congress abrogated the States' constitutional immunity. In making this argument, respondent relies on the pre- and post-enactment legislative history of the Act and inferences from general statutory language. To reach respondent's conclusion, we would have to temper the requirement, well established in our cases, that Congress unequivocally express its intention to abrogate the Eleventh Amendment bar to suits against the States in federal court. Pennhurst II, *supra*, at 99; Quern v. Jordan, *supra*, at 342–345. We decline to do so, and affirm that Congress may abrogate the States' constitutionally secured immunity from suit in federal court only by making its intention unmistakably clear in the language of the statute. The fundamental nature of the interests implicated by the Eleventh Amendment dictates this conclusion.

Only recently the Court reiterated that "the States occupy a special and specific position in our constitutional system. * * *" Garcia v. San Antonio Metropolitan Transit Authority, 469 U.S. 528, 547 (1985). The "constitutionally mandated balance of power" between the States and the Federal Government was adopted by the Framers to ensure the protection of "our fundamental liberties." *Id.*, at 572 (Powell, J., dissenting). By guaranteeing the sovereign immunity of the States against suit in federal court, the Eleventh Amendment serves to maintain this balance. * * *

Congress' power to abrogate a State's immunity means that in certain circumstances the usual constitutional balance between the States and the Federal Government does not obtain. "Congress may, in determining what is 'appropriate legislation' for the purpose of enforcing the provisions of the Fourteenth Amendment, provide for private suits against States or state officials which are constitutionally impermissible in other contexts." Fitzpatrick, 427 U.S., at 456. In view of this fact, it is incumbent upon the federal courts to be certain of Congress' intent before finding that federal law overrides the guarantees of the Eleventh Amendment. The requirement that Congress unequivocally express this intention in the statutory language ensures such certainty.

It is also significant that in determining whether Congress has abrogated the States' Eleventh Amendment immunity, the courts themselves must decide whether their own jurisdiction has been expanded. Although it is of course the duty of this Court "to say what the law is," Marbury v. Madison, 1 Cranch 137, 177 (1803), it is appropriate that we rely only on the clearest indications in holding that Congress has enhanced our power. See American Fire & Cas. Co. v. Finn, 341 U.S. 6, 17 (1951) ("The jurisdiction of the federal courts is carefully guarded against expansion by judicial interpretation * * *").

For these reasons, we hold—consistent with Quern, Edelman, and Pennhurst II—that Congress must express its intention to abrogate the Eleventh Amendment in unmistakable language in the statute itself.

In light of this principle, we must determine whether Congress, in adopting the Rehabilitation Act, has chosen to override the Eleventh Amendment.[4] Section 504 of the Rehabilitation Act provides in pertinent part:

---

4. Petitioners assert that the Rehabilitation Act of 1973 does not represent an exercise of Congress' Fourteenth Amendment authority, but was enacted pursuant to the Spending Clause, Art. I, § 8, cl. 1. Petitioners conceded below, however, that the Rehabilitation Act was passed pursuant to § 5 of the Fourteenth Amendment. Thus, we first analyze § 504 in light of Congress' power under the Fourteenth Amendment to subject unconsenting States to federal court jurisdiction. See Fitzpatrick v. Bitzer, 427 U.S. 445 (1976). In Part V, infra, we address the reasoning of the

"No otherwise qualified handicapped individual in the United States, as defined in section 706(7) of this title, shall, solely by reason of his handicap, be excluded from the participation in, be denied the benefits of, or be subjected to discrimination under any program or activity receiving Federal financial assistance or under any program or activity conducted by any Executive agency or by the United States Postal Service." 87 Stat. 394, as amended and as set forth in 29 U.S.C. § 794.

Section 505, which was added to the Act in 1978, as set forth in 29 U.S.C. § 794a, describes the available remedies under the Act, including the provisions pertinent to this case:

"(a)(2) The remedies, procedures, and rights set forth in title VI of the Civil Rights Act of 1964 [42 U.S.C. 2000d et seq.] shall be available to any person aggrieved by any act or failure to act by any recipient of Federal assistance or Federal provider of such assistance under section 794 of this title.

"(b) In any action or proceeding to enforce or charge a violation of a provision of this subchapter, the court, in its discretion, may allow the prevailing party, other than the United States, a reasonable attorney's fee as part of the costs."

The statute thus provides remedies for violations of § 504 by "*any* recipient of Federal assistance." There is no claim here that the State of California is not a recipient of federal aid under the statute. But given their constitutional role, the States are not like any other class of recipients of federal aid. A general authorization for suit in federal court is not the kind of unequivocal statutory language sufficient to abrogate the Eleventh Amendment. When Congress chooses to subject the States to federal jurisdiction, it must do so specifically. Pennhurst II, 465 U.S., at 99, citing Quern v. Jordan, 440 U.S. 332 (1979). Accordingly, we hold that the Rehabilitation Act does not abrogate the Eleventh Amendment bar to suits against the States.

V

Finally, we consider the position adopted by the Court of Appeals that the State consented to suit in federal court by accepting funds under the Rehabilitation Act.[5] 735 F.2d, at 361–362. In reaching this conclusion, the Court of Appeals relied on "the extensive provisions [of the Act] under which the states are the express intended recipients of federal assistance." *Id.*, at 360. It reasoned that "this is a case in which a 'congressional enactment * * * by its terms authorized suit by designated plaintiffs against a general class of defendants which literally included States or state instrumentalities,' and 'the State by its participation in the program authorized by Congress had in effect consented to the abrogation of that immunity,'" *id.*, at 361, citing Edelman v. Jordan, 415 U.S., at 672.
* * *

Court of Appeals and conclude that by accepting funds under the Act, the State did not "implicitly consen[t] to be sued. * * *" 735 F.2d 359, 362 (1984).

5. Although the Court of Appeals seemed to state that the Rehabilitation Act was adopted pursuant to § 5 of the Fourteenth Amendment, by focusing on whether the State consented to federal jurisdiction it engaged in analysis relevant to Spending Clause enactments.

* * * The court erred, however, in concluding that because various provisions of the Rehabilitation Act are addressed to the States, a State necessarily consents to suit in federal court by participating in programs funded under the statute. We have decided today that the Rehabilitation Act does not evince an unmistakable congressional purpose, pursuant to § 5 of the Fourteenth Amendment, to subject unconsenting States to the jurisdiction of the federal courts. The Act likewise falls far short of manifesting a clear intent to condition participation in the programs funded under the Act on a State's consent to waive its constitutional immunity. Thus, were we to view this statute as an enactment pursuant to the Spending Clause, Art. I, § 8, see n. 4, *supra*, we would hold that there was no indication that the State of California consented to federal jurisdiction.

VI

The provisions of the Rehabilitation Act fall far short of expressing an unequivocal congressional intent to abrogate the States' Eleventh Amendment immunity. Nor has the State of California specifically waived its immunity to suit in federal court. In view of these determinations, the judgment of the Court of Appeals must be reversed.

It is so ordered.

JUSTICE BRENNAN, with whom JUSTICE MARSHALL, JUSTICE BLACKMUN, and JUSTICE STEVENS join, dissenting.

* * * I believe that the Court should take advantage of the opportunity provided by this case to reexamine the [Eleventh Amendment's] historical and jurisprudential foundations. Such an inquiry would reveal that the Court, in Professor Shapiro's words, has taken a wrong turn.[1] Because the Court today follows this mistaken path, I respectfully dissent.

I

I first address the Court's holding that Congress did not succeed in abrogating the States' sovereign immunity when it enacted § 504 of the Rehabilitation Act, 29 U.S.C. § 794. * * *

Section 504 imposes an obligation not to discriminate against the handicapped in "any program or activity receiving Federal financial assistance." This language is general and unqualified, and contains no indication whatsoever that an exemption for the States was intended. Moreover, state governmental programs and activities are undoubtedly the recipients of a large percentage of federal funds. Given this widespread state dependence on federal funds, it is quite incredible to assume that Congress did not intend that the States should be fully subject to the strictures of § 504.

The legislative history confirms that the States were among the primary targets of § 504. In introducing the predecessor of § 504 as an amendment to Title VI of the Civil Rights Act of 1964, 42 U.S.C. § 2000d, Representative Vanik clearly indicated that governments would be among the primary targets of the legislation: "Our Governments tax [handicapped] people, their parents and relatives, but fail to provide services for

1.　See Shapiro, *Wrong Turns: The Eleventh Amendment and the Pennhurst Case,* 98 Harv.L.Rev. 61 (1984).

them. * * * The opportunities provided by the Government almost always exclude the handicapped." 117 Cong.Rec. 45974 (1971). He further referred approvingly to a federal-court suit against the State of Pennsylvania raising the issue of educational opportunities for the handicapped. See *id.*, at 45974–45975 (citing Pennsylvania Assn. for Retarded Children v. Pennsylvania, 343 F.Supp. 279 (ED Pa 1972), and characterizing it as a "suit against the State"). Two months later, Representative Vanik * * * pointed out that "the States are unable to define and deal with" the illnesses of the handicapped child, and that "[e]xclusion of handicapped children [from public schools] is illegal in some States, but the States plead lack of funds." [118 Cong.Rec. 4341 (1972).] Similarly, Senator Humphrey, the bill's sponsor in the Senate, focused particularly on a suit against a state-operated institution for the mentally retarded as demonstrating the need for the bill. See *id.*, at 9495, 9502.

The language used in the statute ("any program or activity receiving Federal financial assistance") has long been used to impose obligations on the States under other statutory schemes. For example, Title VI, enacted in 1964, bans discrimination on the basis of race, color, or national origin by "any program or activity receiving Federal financial assistance." 42 U.S.C. § 2000d. Soon after its enactment, seven agencies promulgated regulations that defined a recipient of federal financial assistance to include "any State, political subdivision of any State or instrumentality of any State or political subdivision." See, *e.g.*, 29 Fed.Reg. 16274, § 15.2(e) (1964). * * *

Similarly Title IX of the Education Amendments of 1972, 20 U.S.C. § 1681(a), prohibits discrimination on the basis of sex by "any education program or activity receiving Federal financial assistance." The regulations governing Title IX use the same definition of "recipient"—which explicitly includes the States—as do the Title VI regulations. See 34 CFR § 106.2(h) (1985). The Congress that enacted § 504 had the examples of Titles VI and IX before it, and plainly knew that the language of the statute would include the States.

Implementing regulations promulgated for § 504 included the same definition of "recipient" that had previously been used to implement Title VI and Title IX. See 45 CFR § 84.3(f) (1984). In 1977, Congress held hearings on the implementation of § 504, and subsequently produced amendments to the statute enacted in 1978. Pub.L. 95–602, 92 Stat. 2982, § 505(a)(2), 29 U.S.C. § 794a. The Senate Report accompanying the amendments explicitly approved the implementing regulations. S.Rep. No. 95–890, p. 19 (1981). No Member of Congress questioned the reach of the regulations. * * *

The 1978 amendments also addressed the remedies for violations of § 504:

"The remedies, procedures, and rights set forth in title VI of the Civil Rights Act of 1964 [42 U.S.C. 2000d et seq.] shall be available to any person aggrieved by any act or failure to act by any recipient of Federal assistance or Federal provider of such assistance under section 794 of this title." 29 U.S.C. § 794a(a)(2).

Again, the amendment referred in general and unqualified terms to "any recipient of Federal assistance." * * *

Given the unequivocal legislative history, the Court's conclusion that Congress did not abrogate the States' sovereign immunity when it enacted § 504 obviously cannot rest on an analysis of what Congress intended to do or on what Congress thought it was doing. Congress intended to impose a legal obligation on the States not to discriminate against the handicapped. In addition, Congress fully intended that whatever remedies were available against *other* entities—including the Federal Government itself after the 1978 amendments—be equally available against the States. There is simply not a shred of evidence to the contrary.

II

Rather than an interpretation of the intent of Congress, the Court's decision rests on the Court's current doctrine of Eleventh Amendment sovereign immunity, which holds that "the fundamental principle of sovereign immunity limits the grant of judicial authority in Art. III" of the Constitution. Pennhurst State School and Hospital v. Halderman, 465 U.S. 89, 98 (1984). * * *

The Court acknowledges that the supposed lack of judicial power may be remedied, either by the State's consent,[5] or by express congressional abrogation pursuant to the Civil War Amendments, see Fitzpatrick v. Bitzer, 427 U.S. 445 (1976); City of Rome v. United States, 446 U.S. 156 (1980), or perhaps pursuant to other congressional powers. But the Court has raised formidable obstacles to congressional efforts to abrogate the States' immunity; the Court has put in place a series of special rules of statutory draftsmanship that Congress must obey before the Court will accord recognition to its act. Employees v. Missouri Dept. of Public Health and Welfare, 411 U.S. 279 (1973), held that Congress must make its intention "clear" if it sought to lift the States' sovereign immunity conditional on their participation in a federal program. *Id.*, at 285. Edelman v. Jordan, 415 U.S. 651 (1974), made it still more difficult for Congress to act, stating that "we will find waiver only where stated by the most express

5. The "stringent" test that the Court applies to purported state waivers of sovereign immunity is a mirror image of the test it applies to congressional abrogation of state sovereign immunity. Just as the Court today decides that Congress, if it desires effectively to abrogate a State's sovereign immunity, must do so expressly in the statutory language, so the Court similarly decides that a State's waiver, to be effective, must be "specifically applicable to federal-court jurisdiction." In the Court's words, "[a]lthough a State's general waiver of sovereign immunity may subject it to suit in state court, it is not enough to waive the immunity guaranteed by the Eleventh Amendment." Ordinarily, a federal court is expected faithfully to decide state-law questions before it as the courts of a State would. I would think that a federal court deciding the scope of a state waiver of sovereign immunity should attempt to construe the state law of sovereign immunity as a state court would, making use of relevant legislative history and legal precedents. Yet, despite the absence of any identifiable federal interest that would justify a departure from state law, the Court eschews any effort to construe California's constitutional waiver requirement in accordance with California law. See, e.g., Muskopf v. Corning Hospital Dist., 55 Cal.2d 211, 216, 359 P.2d 457, 460 (1961) (abrogating state sovereign immunity for all tort cases and holding it to be an "anachronism, without rational basis, and exist[ing] only by the force of inertia"). *Id.*, at 216, 359 P.2d, at 460. Instead, the Court seems to believe that the Eleventh Amendment justifies the Court in imposing on the state legislatures, as well as Congress, special rules of statutory draftsmanship if they would make a waiver of state sovereign immunity in federal court successful. Apparently, even States that want to make a federal forum available for the fair adjudication of grievances arising under federal law ought to be deterred from doing so.

language or by such overwhelming implications from the text as will leave no room for any other reasonable construction." *Id.*, at 673. * * * Finally, the Court today tightens the noose by requiring "that Congress must express its intention to abrogate the Eleventh Amendment in unmistakable language *in the statute itself.*"

These special rules of statutory drafting are not justified (nor are they justifiable) as efforts to determine the genuine intent of Congress; no reason has been advanced why ordinary canons of statutory construction would be inadequate to ascertain the intent of Congress. Rather, the special rules are designed as hurdles to keep the disfavored suits out of the federal court. In the Court's words, the test flows from need to maintain "the usual constitutional balance between the States and the Federal Government." The doctrine is thus based on a fundamental policy decision, vaguely attributed to the Framers of Article III or the Eleventh Amendment, that the federal courts ought not to hear suits brought by individuals against States. This Court executes the policy by making it difficult, but not impossible, for Congress to create private rights of action against the States.[7]

Reliance on this supposed constitutional policy reverses the ordinary role of the federal courts in federal-question cases. Federal courts are instruments of the National Government, seeing to it that constitutional limitations are obeyed while interpreting the will of Congress in enforcing the federal laws. In the Eleventh Amendment context, however, the Court instead relies on a supposed constitutional policy disfavoring suits against States as justification for ignoring the will of Congress; the goal seems to be to obstruct the ability of Congress to achieve ends that are otherwise constitutionally unexceptionable and well within the reach of its Article I powers.

* * *

[In the remainder of his dissent, Justice Brennan advanced the view that Hans v. Louisiana, p. 1162, *supra,* was wrongly decided, and that the Amendment had nothing to do with sovereign immunity. He contended, instead, that the Amendment simply barred jurisdiction, in suits against an unconsenting state, that was based merely on party status, but did not restrict suits against an unconsenting state brought under the admiralty or federal question jurisdiction. For excerpts of that argument, see pp. 1168–70, *supra.*]

JUSTICE BLACKMUN, with whom JUSTICE BRENNAN, JUSTICE MARSHALL, and JUSTICE STEVENS join, dissenting.

* * *

* * * The shield against just legal obligations afforded the States by the Court's prevailing construction of the Eleventh Amendment as an "exemplification" of the rule of sovereign immunity simply cannot be reconciled with the federal system envisioned by our Basic Document and its Amendments.

Indeed, though of more mature vintage, the Court's Eleventh Amendment cases spring from the same soil as the Tenth Amendment jurispru-

---

7. In this case, the Court's decision relentlessly to apply its "clear-statement rule" demonstrates how that rule serves no purpose other than obstructing the will of Congress. When Congress enacted § 504, it could have had no idea that it must obey the extreme clear-statement rule adopted by the Court for the first time today. * * *

dence recently abandoned in Garcia v. San Antonio Metropolitan Transit Authority, 469 U.S. 528 (1985). Both in its modern reading of Hans, *supra*, and in National League of Cities v. Usery, 426 U.S. 833 (1976), the Court, in derogation of otherwise unquestioned congressional power, gave broad scope to circumscribed language by reference to principles of federalism said to inform that language. The intuition underlying Hans and its contemporary progeny is no truer to the federal structure or to a proper view of congressional power than was that underlying National League of Cities.

But I would dissent from the Court's spare opinion and predictable result on other grounds as well. There is no need to expatiate on them here, where so much already has been written. It suffices to say that I adhere to the views expressed in the dissenting opinion in Edelman v. Jordan, 415 U.S. 651, 688 (1974). See also Florida Dept. of Health v. Florida Nursing Home Assn., 450 U.S. 147, 151 (1981) (dissenting statement). Thus, I would affirm the judgment here on the ground that California, as a willing recipient of federal funds under the Rehabilitation Act, consented to suit when it accepted such assistance. And a fair reading of the statute and its legislative history indicates for me that Congress produced the Act in exercise of its power under § 5 of the Fourteenth Amendment and thereby abrogated any claim of immunity the State otherwise might raise.

JUSTICE STEVENS, dissenting.

* * *

NOTE ON WAIVER AND CONGRESSIONAL ABROGATION OF ELEVENTH AMENDMENT IMMUNITY

(1) There has never been any doubt that Article III's judicial power extends to suits against *consenting* states. See, *e.g.*, Petty v. Tennessee–Missouri Bridge Com'n, 359 U.S. 275 (1959); Clark v. Barnard, 108 U.S. 436, 447 (1883). Is this an anomaly (however well-established) in light of the ordinary rule that the parties lack power to confer jurisdiction on the federal courts? Or does that rule depend upon why jurisdiction is limited in the first instance?

Less clear is what constitutes a valid waiver on the part of a state. Enactment of a state statute (or constitutional provision) consenting to suit is the clearest example of a valid waiver. On the other hand, the failure of attorneys representing the state to assert the defense does not waive it; indeed, the defect is deemed to be jurisdictional, as Edelman v. Jordan, p. 1182, *supra*, made clear.[1] Note, however, that in Clark v. Barnard, *supra*, the state was held to have waived its immunity after its officials filed an

---

1. But later, in Patsy v. Board of Regents, 457 U.S. 496 (1982), the Supreme Court, in holding that the district court had erred in dismissing a § 1983 action on the ground that plaintiff had not exhausted administrative remedies, refused to reach a colorable Eleventh Amendment issue. That issue was first raised (but not vigorously pressed) before the court of appeals, which had not addressed it. Before the Supreme Court, the defendant had not briefed or argued the immunity issue (though it was mentioned in opposing the petition for certiorari). The Court denied that the Eleventh Amendment "is jurisdictional in the sense that it must be raised and decided by this Court on its own motion," and left the issue to the district court on remand (p. 515 n. 19).

appearance by the state as a claimant to a fund.[2] Compare the similar holdings in federal sovereign immunity cases, p. 1110, *supra*.

What justifies the Supreme Court's insistence in Atascadero that a *state* legislature's waiver be unmistakable? See Note, 17 Ga.L.Rev. 513 (1983). Is a policy of clear statement appropriate when a federal court is construing a state rather than a federal statute?[3]

(2) Smith v. Reeves, 178 U.S. 436, 441 (1900), held that a state may waive sovereign immunity as to suits for tax refunds in its own courts, while retaining its Eleventh Amendment immunity from such lawsuits in federal court. Earlier cases looked the other way, see Reagan v. Farmers' Loan & Trust Co., 154 U.S. 362, 391 (1894); Davis v. Gray, 16 Wall. 203, 221 (U.S.1872), but Smith reasoned that a limitation upon tax refund actions could not be seen as "hostile to the General Government, or as touching upon any right granted or secured by the Constitution of the United States" (p. 445). *Cf.* the Tax Injunction Act, 28 U.S.C. § 1341, Chap. X, Sec. 1(B), *infra*. Subsequent cases have permitted selective waiver by the state without regard to Smith's qualifications. See, *e.g.,* Edelman v. Jordan, *supra;* Murray v. Wilson Distilling Co., 213 U.S. 151, 172 (1909). Should they have, especially when other efforts by states to restrict lawsuits to the state courts have been held unlawful? See, *e.g.,* Chicago & N.W. Ry. v. Whitton's Adm'r, 13 Wall. 270 (U.S.1871), p. 830, *supra,* holding that a state statute purporting to permit enforcement of a state wrongful death action only in state court could not prevent the exercise of federal diversity jurisdiction. See also Tribe, *Intergovernmental Immunities in Litigation, Taxation, and Regulation: Separation of Powers Issues in Controversies About Federalism,* 89 Harv.L.Rev. 682, 698–99 n. 80 (1976); Shapiro, *Wrong Turns: The Eleventh Amendment and the Pennhurst Case,* 98 Harv.L.Rev. 61, 76–78 (1984). Or is the whole point of the Eleventh Amendment not to exempt the state from suit altogether, but to give it a forum choice? See pp. 1194–95, *supra*.

(3) In Parden v. Terminal Ry., 377 U.S. 184 (1964), the Supreme Court (per Brennan, J.) held that Alabama had constructively consented to a federal court negligence action under the Federal Employees Liability Act (FELA) brought by an employee of a state-owned railway. In the Court's view, the case presented two questions (p. 187): "(1) Did Congress in enacting the FELA intend to subject a State to suit in these circumstances? (2) Did it have power to do so, as against the State's claim of immunity?"

On the first question, the Court ruled that the FELA, which provides a damage action against "every" railroad in interstate commerce, "meant what it said," and refused to "read a 'sovereign immunity exception' " into the statute: "we should not presume to say, in the absence of express provision to the contrary, that [Congress] intended to exclude a particular group of such workers from the benefits conferred by the Act" (pp. 187–90).

---

2. This waiver doctrine has not been extended to counterclaims against a state that do not arise from the same transaction as the state's claim, or that seek not merely a setoff or recoupment but rather an affirmative judgment against the state. See, *e.g.,* Maryland Port Admin. v. SS American Legend, 453 F.Supp. 584, 590 (D.Md.1978); Burgess v. M/V Tamano, 382 F.Supp. 351, 355–56 (D.Me.1974), *aff'd,* 559 F.2d 1200 (1st Cir.1977).

3. *Cf.* Della Grotta v. State of Rhode Island, 781 F.2d 343 (1st Cir.1986) (state is subject to federal court suit where state statute that did not expressly subject the state to *federal court* suit had previously been interpreted by the state supreme court to waive immunity in federal court).

On the second question, the Court stated that "the States surrendered a portion of their sovereignty when they granted Congress the power to regulate commerce. * * * Since imposition of the FELA right of action upon interstate railroads is within the congressional regulatory power, it must follow that application of the Act to such a railroad cannot be precluded by sovereign immunity" (pp. 191–92). The Eleventh Amendment, the Court insisted, was not being overridden (p. 192): "Our conclusion is simply that Alabama, when it began operation of an interstate railroad approximately 20 years after enactment of the FELA, necessarily consented to such suit as was authorized by that Act." That the Alabama constitution barred any waiver of immunity was immaterial, as "the question whether the State's act constitutes the alleged consent is one of federal law" (p. 196).

Justice White, joined by Justices Douglas, Harlan, and Stewart, dissented, arguing that "[o]nly when Congress has clearly considered the problem and expressly declared that any State which undertakes given regulable conduct will be deemed thereby to have waived its immunity should courts disallow the invocation of this defense" (pp. 198–99).

Is Parden "schizophrenic" in arguing both that the states had ceded part of their sovereignty in the constitutional plan and that Alabama could be subjected to suit only if it waived its immunity? See Tribe, Paragraph (2), *supra*, at 688. Did the Court unconstitutionally condition Alabama's operation of a railroad on surrender of its Eleventh Amendment immunity? *Cf.* Terral v. Burke Construction Co., 257 U.S. 529, 532–33 (1922), p. 831, *supra*.

In Employees of Dept. of Pub. Health and Welfare v. Department of Pub. Health & Welfare, 411 U.S. 279 (1973), employees of Missouri state hospitals and schools brought suit under the Fair Labor Standards Act for overtime compensation. Though the Act initially excluded all state employees, a 1966 amendment extended coverage to employees of state schools and hospitals. The Supreme Court held Missouri immune from federal court suit, distinguishing Parden as involving a "for profit" operation of the kind normally run by private parties (p. 284); "[t]he dramatic circumstances of the Parden case, which involved a rather isolated state activity, can be put to one side" (p. 285). Though § 16(b) of the Act, which predated the 1966 amendment, made "[a]ny employer" suable for damages "in any court of competent jurisdiction," it would be "surprising * * * to infer that Congress deprived Missouri of her constitutional immunity without changing the old § 16(b) * * * or indicating in some way by clear language that the constitutional immunity was swept away" (p. 285), especially as § 16(b) provided for double damages. The Court contended that its ruling would not leave plaintiffs unprotected; the Act provided other remedies against state employers, including suits by the Secretary of Labor for unpaid compensation or injunctive relief.[4]

Justice Marshall (joined by Justice Stewart) concurred in the result. In his view, the Act gave the plaintiffs all of § 16(b)'s remedies, but the Eleventh Amendment barred the federal courts from providing them. (Parden, he said, approached the "outer limit" of constructive waiver, and

---

4. Is it clear that a suit by the Secretary as parens patriae would be deemed a suit by the United States, as to which the amendment does not apply? *Cf.* New Hampshire v. Louisiana, p. 1180, note 3, *supra*.

could not be extended to state operations, like these, that predated the enactment of federal regulation). The Eleventh Amendment, however, was "nothing more than a regulation of the forum in which these petitioners may seek a remedy," and the state's courts "have an independent constitutional obligation to entertain employee actions to enforce [their] rights" (p. 298).[5]

Recall that Edelman v. Jordan, in holding that Illinois did not consent to federal court suit by participating in a federally-funded cooperative welfare program, stated: "Constructive consent is not a doctrine commonly associated with the surrender of constitutional rights." The question whether Parden's approach survived Employees, Edelman, and Atascadero was resolved in Welch v. State Dept. of Highways & Pub. Transp., 107 S.Ct. 2941 (1987), p. 1170, *supra*. The plaintiff, an employee of a Texas agency that operated a ferry, sought damages under the Jones Act for injuries suffered on the ferry dock. (Section 33 of that Act, 46 U.S.C. § 688, provides that "[a]ny seaman who shall suffer personal injury in the course of his employment" may bring a personal injury action under the provisions of the FELA.) After finding that the question of express waiver by the State had not been presented for review, Justice Powell (speaking for a plurality of four) said that the plaintiff's remaining argument for jurisdiction rested upon congressional abrogation. Assuming without deciding that Congress's power to subject unconsenting states to federal court suit is not confined to § 5 of the Fourteenth Amendment, the plurality concluded that "Congress has not expressed in unmistakable statutory language its intention to allow States to be sued in federal court under the Jones Act" (p. 2947). The decision in Parden, Justice Powell said (p. 2948), failed to recognize that "the constitutional role of the States sets them apart from other employers." He declared that to the extent that Parden is inconsistent with the requirement that Congress express its intent to abrogate "in unmistakably clear language, it is overruled" (p. 2948).

Justice Scalia, concurring in part and concurring in the judgment, agreed that Parden should be overruled, but on the more limited ground that, in light of the general acceptance of Hans v. Louisiana when the FELA and the Jones Act were enacted, they should not be interpreted as providing a cause of action against a state employer. (Could a state employee bring an FELA action in state court under Justice Scalia's view? Under the plurality's view?) Justices Brennan, Marshall, Blackmun, and Stevens dissented; for a discussion of their position, see pp. 1168–70, *supra*.

(4) A shift away from the theory of constructive consent had taken place in Fitzpatrick v. Bitzer, 427 U.S. 445 (1976), a Title VII action alleging that Connecticut's retirement plan discriminated against male employees. (Title VII regulates any "person" employing the requisite number of employees in interstate commerce; in 1972 Congress amended the definition of "person" to include state and local "governments, governmental agencies, [and] political subdivisions.") The Supreme Court, per Rehnquist, J., held that the Eleventh Amendment did not bar an award of retroactive retirement benefits and attorney's fees as allowed by Title VII.

---

5. Justice Brennan dissented, finding Parden indistinguishable. He argued, in addition, that in a suit against a State by one of its own citizens, the Eleventh Amendment is simply inapplicable; the state has only a nonconstitutional sovereign immunity, which can be overcome by congressional regulation under the Commerce Clause. See p. 1167, *supra*.

Here, as in Parden but not in Employees and Edelman, "the 'threshold fact of congressional authorization' * * * is clearly present," and "factual differences between the type of state activity involved in Parden and that involved in this case * * * [are not] material for our purposes" (p. 452).

The 1972 amendment was enacted, the Court noted, pursuant to Congress's power under § 5 of the Fourteenth Amendment. The Amendment as a whole represented a "shift in the federal-state balance [that] has been carried forward by more recent decisions of this Court," and past decisions had "sanctioned intrusions by Congress, acting under the Civil War Amendments, into the judicial, executive, and legislative spheres of autonomy previously preserved to the States" (p. 455). Justice Rehnquist continued (p. 456):

"It is true that none of these previous cases presented the question of the relationship between the Eleventh Amendment and the enforcement power granted to Congress under § 5 of the Fourteenth Amendment. But we think that the Eleventh Amendment, and the principle of state sovereignty which it embodies, are necessarily limited by the enforcement provisions of § 5 of the Fourteenth Amendment. In that section Congress is expressly granted authority to enforce 'by appropriate legislation' the substantive provisions of the Fourteenth Amendment, which themselves embody significant limitations on state authority. When Congress acts pursuant to § 5, not only is it exercising legislative authority that is plenary within the terms of the constitutional grant, it is exercising that authority under one section of a constitutional Amendment whose other sections by their own terms embody limitations on state authority. We think that Congress may, in determining what is 'appropriate legislation' for the purpose of enforcing the provisions of the Fourteenth Amendment, provide for private suits against States or state officials which are constitutionally impermissible in other contexts."

(5) Fitzpatrick was applied in Hutto v. Finney, 437 U.S. 678 (1978), also discussed at p. 1192, *supra*, a lawsuit under 42 U.S.C. § 1983 in which the Arkansas penal system was found to impose cruel and unusual punishment, and in which injunctive relief against state officials had been awarded. Plaintiffs sought attorney's fees under the Civil Rights Attorney's Fees Awards Act of 1976, 42 U.S.C. § 1988, which provides that in actions to enforce certain federal civil rights statutes (including § 1983), a court may award prevailing parties reasonable attorney's fees "as part of the costs". (On § 1988, see p. 1248, *infra.*) The Act does not specify that fees may be awarded against a state, but the Senate and House reports did say that fees may be collected, *inter alia,* "from the State," and the House report cited Fitzpatrick. The Court concluded that Congress intended to make states vulnerable to liability for attorney's fees in § 1983 actions, and that because § 1983 enforces the Fourteenth Amendment, the case fell within the principle of Fitzpatrick. To the argument that, if Congress wished to abrogate the states' immunity, Employees and Edelman required it to "enact express statutory language making the States liable," the Court responded (pp. 694–95): "these cases concern retroactive liability for prelitigation conduct rather than expenses incurred in litigation seeking only prospective relief." The Court argued that costs had traditionally been imposed upon states without regard to the Eleventh Amendment, that attorney's fees are not infrequently treated as allowable costs, and that the purpose of requiring an express statement—to ensure "that Congress has

not imposed 'enormous fiscal burdens on the States' without careful thought"—was not implicated by a limited award of fees (pp. 696–97 & nn. 24, 27).[6]

Justice Powell's dissent argued that a provision overriding immunity must be "in statutory language sufficiently clear to alert every voting Member of Congress" (p. 705). He suggested that the committee reports were ambiguous because the states as such cannot themselves be made defendants and are not liable for damages in § 1983 actions.[7] That argument in turn evoked a concurrence from Justice Brennan, who argued that Fitzpatrick, in combination with Monell v. Department of Social Services, 436 U.S. 658 (1978), p. 1251, *infra* (holding that cities and counties may in some circumstances be sued under § 1983), had "seriously undermined" Edelman's conclusion that Congress did not, in § 1983, intend to override the states' Eleventh Amendment immunity.

The issue thus raised by Justice Brennan came to the forefront in Quern v. Jordan, 440 U.S. 332 (1979), p. 1193, *supra*. Though it there ruled that the particular relief ordered did not violate the Eleventh Amendment, the Court, in a lengthy dictum, rejected Justice Brennan's argument that § 1983 should now be interpreted to make states suable in federal court: "[W]e simply are unwilling to believe, on the basis of such slender 'evidence', that Congress intended by the general language of § 1983 to override the traditional sovereign immunity of the States. * * * § 1983 does not explicitly and by clear language indicate on its face an intent to sweep away the immunity of the States; nor does it have a history which focuses directly on the question of state liability and which shows that Congress considered and firmly decided to abrogate the Eleventh Amendment immunity of the States" (pp. 341, 345).[8]

(6) What do Fitzpatrick and Atascadero (and other precedents) imply about whether Congress may abrogate immunity under powers other than § 5 of the Fourteenth Amendment? Consider the persuasiveness of these possible distinctions: (a) the Fourteenth Amendment itself (in § 1) restricts state power; (b) the Fourteenth Amendment (in § 5) grants Congress plenary and exceptional legislative authority; (c) the Fourteenth Amendment is unique because *both* (a) and (b) are true; (d) statutes enacted under § 5 are unusually important; (e) the Fourteenth Amendment, unlike Article I, was enacted after the Eleventh Amendment. As to point (a), consider, first, whether it implies that a state should be subject to suit in federal court, even absent congressional action, in a suit under the Bivens line of cases seeking a judicially implied damages remedy under the Fourteenth

---

6. The ruling in Hutto was deemed to be controlling in Maher v. Gagne, 448 U.S. 122 (1980), allowing an award of attorney's fees against a state in an action under § 1983 that alleged violations by state officials of plaintiff's federal statutory as well as constitutional rights. The power of Congress under § 5 of the Fourteenth Amendment to subject states to liability for attorney's fees was said to extend to cases where a statutory claim is joined to a substantial claim that the Fourteenth Amendment was violated.

7. Justices Rehnquist and White also dissented, embracing Justice Powell's rea-

sons while also expressing doubt that Congress's power to enforce rights incorporated by the Fourteenth Amendment (here, rights under the Eighth Amendment's Cruel and Unusual Punishment Clause) is as broad as its power to enforce rights in the Fourteenth Amendment itself.

8. Justices Brennan and Marshall dissented. They viewed the majority's opinion as ruling that a state is not a "person" made liable to suit by § 1983. Isn't that an unnecessarily broad characterization of the Quern dictum? See p. 1258, *infra*.

Amendment; and second, whether the so-called "negative" Commerce Clause doesn't also restrict state power absent congressional action.

Several commentators have argued that Congress, acting under any of its enumerated powers, may abrogate Eleventh Amendment immunity, which is said to confer an immunity "against the federal judiciary [rather than] * * * against Congress." Tribe, Paragraph (2), *supra*, at 693; accord, Nowak, *The Scope of Congressional Power to Create Causes of Action Against State Government and the History of the Eleventh and Fourteenth Amendments*, 75 Colum.L.Rev. 1413, 1441–42 (1975). The argument rests upon the political safeguards of federalism inherent in congressional representation, and, in Professor Nowak's view (pp. 1430, 1440–41), evidence that the framers of both Article III and the Eleventh Amendment feared life-tenured federal judges rather than politically accountable legislators.

Is it plausible to read the Amendment as providing the *states* with a constitutional immunity, but one that the *federal* legislature can override? Is this view consistent with Marbury v. Madison's holding that Congress lacks power to expand the jurisdiction of the federal courts? [9]

Four months before deciding Atascadero, the Supreme Court, dividing 5–4, overruled its decision in National League of Cities v. Usery, 426 U.S. 833 (1976), and held that Congress may require state and local employers to pay overtime wages under the Fair Labor Standards Act. Garcia v. San Antonio Metro. Transit Auth., 469 U.S. 528 (1985). The Court did not quite say that there were *no* limits on congressional regulation of the states under an enumerated power. But it stressed (pp. 550, 552) that "[w]ith rare exceptions, like the guarantee, in Article IV, § 3, of state territorial integrity, the Constitution does not carve out express elements of state sovereignty that Congress may not employ its delegated powers to displace"; "[s]tate sovereign interests * * * are more properly protected by procedural safeguards inherent in the structure of the federal system than by judicially created limitations on federal power."

After Garcia, is it sensible to find that Congress has plenary power to impose substantive regulation on the states (and *perhaps* to require the state courts to enforce such regulation, see pp. 492–500, *supra*), but that Congress may not fully enforce such regulation in federal court? *Cf.* Fletcher, *A Historical Interpretation of the Eleventh Amendment: A Narrow Construction of an Affirmative Grant of Jurisdiction Rather than a Prohibition Against Jurisdiction*, 35 Stan.L.Rev. 1033, 1109–13 (1983). Isn't immunity from retrospective relief in federal court an odd place for the last stand of state sovereignty?

9. A number of decisions (most of them pre-dating Atascadero) have upheld Congress's power to abrogate (and thereby make retroactive relief available in federal court) under powers other than the enforcement clauses of the post-Civil War amendments. See, *e.g.*, United States v. Union Gas Co., 832 F.2d 1343 (3d Cir.1987) (environmental legislation under the commerce power), *cert. granted sub nom.* Pennsylvania v. Union Gas Co., 108 S.Ct. 1219 (1988); In re McVey Trucking, Inc., 812 F.2d 311 (7th Cir.1987) (bankruptcy power); Jennings v. Illinois Office of Educ., 589 F.2d 935, 941 (7th Cir.1979) (enactment under war powers giving veterans the right to reemployment after military service); County of Monroe v. Florida, 678 F.2d 1124, 1128–35 (2d Cir.1982) (extradition power); Mills Music, Inc. v. Arizona, 591 F.2d 1278, 1285 (9th Cir.1979) (copyright act, enacted under Article I's specific authority to regulate copyrights). But see Richard Anderson Photography v. Radford Univ., 633 F.Supp. 1154, 1158 (W.D.Va. 1986) (no abrogation under copyright power; power to abrogate limited to § 5 of Fourteenth Amendment).

Recall the portion of Justice Brennan's dissent in Atascadero that was discussed at pp. 1168–70, *supra*, which views the Eleventh Amendment as having nothing to do with sovereign immunity, but simply as forbidding the exercise of federal subject matter jurisdiction based exclusively on party status over an individual's suit against a nonconsenting state. Note that this theory, though different from that advocated by Professors Tribe and Nowak, would often lead to similar results: under either theory, Congress would have power to subject unconsenting states to federal court suit (and to retrospective relief) on federal statutory causes of action.

(7) What justifies the Court's insistence that Congress state with special clarity its intent to subject the states to suit in federal court? Is this policy of clear statement a corollary of the political safeguards of federalism: "If Congress is the only source of protection of the states' interests, it does not seem unfair for the Court to force Congress to do its job." Brown, *State Sovereignty Under the Burger Court—How the Eleventh Amendment Survived the Death of the Tenth: Some Broader Implications of Atascadero State Hospital v. Scanlon*, 74 Geo.L.J. 363, 390 (1985). If ordinary techniques of statutory interpretation lead to the conclusion that Congress intended to subject the states to suit, why should a court presume that Congress was not doing its job? See Note, 86 Colum.L.Rev. 1436 (1986).[10] Would it make more sense to require a policy of clear statement on the question whether Congress meant to subject the states to regulation than on the question whether such regulation is fully enforceable in federal court? *Cf.* Scalia, J., in Welch v. State Dep't of Highways & Pub. Transp., Paragraph (3), *supra*. Or is retroactive relief for a violation of federal law more appropriately provided by state courts sensitive to state fiscal interests? See Brown, *supra*, at 391.

Does it matter, in answering these questions, whether state sovereign immunity is viewed as having common law or constitutional status? Whether, if federal court relief is barred, the state courts would be obliged to provide all relief authorized by the federal statute?

Even assuming some policy of clear statement is appropriate, does Atascadero articulate that policy with undue severity? In neither Hutto nor Fitzpatrick did the statute unequivocally express Congress's intention to subject the states to suit in *federal court*. And in both Employees and Quern, the Court consulted legislative history to help determine whether abrogation was intended.

Does Atascadero impose an unjustified burden upon an already heavily-burdened Congress?[11] Consider, for example, Atascadero's implications for the federal copyright law, which provides that an infringer (defined as "anyone who violates * * * the exclusive rights of the copyright owner")

---

10. Compare also David D. v. Dartmouth School Comm., 775 F.2d 411, 422 (1st Cir.1985) (finding abrogation under the Education for All Handicapped Children Act, in large part because the Act is directed "to one class of actors: states and their political subdivisions responsible for providing public education"), with Gary A. v. New Trier High School Dist. No. 203, 796 F.2d 940 (7th Cir.1986) (per curiam) (reaching a contrary result as to state governments, though noting that local governments may be sued under the Act in federal court).

11. The year after the decision in Atascadero, Congress enacted legislation providing that "A State shall not be immune under the Eleventh Amendment * * * from suit in federal court for a violation [occurring after the date of the legislation] of section 504 * * * or any other Federal statute prohibiting discrimination by recipients of Federal financial assistance." Pub.L. 99–506, § 1003, Oct. 21, 1986.

is liable for damages, and gives the federal courts exclusive jurisdiction over infringement actions. No provision expressly subjects states to federal court suit. On a strict reading of Atascadero, if a state agency infringes a copyright, has Congress created a liability to the copyright owner that cannot be enforced in any forum? [12]

(8) Suppose Congress viewed the Pennhurst decision, p. 1195, *supra*, as having unduly discouraged litigants with parallel federal and state law claims against state officials from seeking relief in federal court. Does it have power to abrogate the state's Eleventh Amendment immunity as to all state law claims that fall within the federal courts' pendent jurisdiction? For an affirmative answer, see Brown, *Beyond Pennhurst—Protective Jurisdiction, the Eleventh Amendment, and the Power of Congress to Enlarge Federal Jurisdiction in Response to the Burger Court,* 71 Va.L.Rev. 343 (1985).

_____

SUBSECTION B: FEDERAL CONSTITUTIONAL PROTECTION AGAINST STATE OFFICIAL ACTION

_____

HOME TELEPHONE & TELEGRAPH CO. v. CITY OF LOS ANGELES

227 U.S. 278, 33 S.Ct. 312, 57 L.Ed. 510 (1913).
Appeal from the United States District Court for the Southern District of California.

MR. CHIEF JUSTICE WHITE delivered the opinion of the Court.

The appellant, a California corporation furnishing telephone service in the city of Los Angeles, sued the city and certain of its officials to prevent the putting into effect of a city ordinance establishing telephone rates for the year commencing July 1, 1911.

It was alleged that by the Constitution and laws of the state the city was given a right to fix telephone rates, and had passed the assailed ordinance in the exercise of the general authority thus conferred. It was charged that the rates fixed were so unreasonably low that their enforcement would bring about the confiscation of the property of the corporation, and hence the ordinance was repugnant to the due process clause of the 14th Amendment. The averments as to the confiscatory character of the rates were as ample as they could possibly have been made. ＊ ＊ ＊

Being of the opinion that no jurisdiction was disclosed by the bill, the court refused to grant a restraining order or allow a preliminary injunction, and thereafter, on the filing of a formal plea to the jurisdiction the bill was dismissed for want of power as a Federal court to consider it. This direct appeal was then taken.

12. See, *e.g.,* Woelffer v. Happy States of America, Inc., 626 F.Supp. 499 (N.D.Ill. 1985), and Richard Anderson Photography, note 9, *supra,* finding no abrogation under the copyright act; compare Mills Music, note 9, *supra,* finding abrogation prior to Atascadero.

The plea to the jurisdiction was as follows:

"* * * that this court ought not to take jurisdiction of this suit for that the said suit does not really or substantially involve a dispute or controversy properly within the jurisdiction of this court, forasmuch as the Constitution of the state of California, in article 1, § 13 thereof, provides that 'no person shall be * * * deprived of life, liberty, or property without due process of law'; that this complainant, a citizen of the state of California, has never invoked the aid or protection of its said state to prevent the alleged taking of its property, nor has complainant appealed to the courts of said state, nor to any of them, to enforce the law of said state."

The ground of challenge to the jurisdiction advanced by the plea may be thus stated: As the acts of the state officials (the city government) complained of were alleged to be wanting in due process of law, and therefore repugnant to the 14th Amendment,—a ground which, on the face of the bill, if well founded, also presumptively caused the action complained of to be repugnant to the due-process clause of the state Constitution,— there being no diversity of citizenship, there was no Federal jurisdiction. In other words, the plea asserted that where, in a given case, taking the facts averred to be true, the acts of state officials violated the Constitution of the United States, and likewise, because of the coincidence of a state constitutional prohibition, were presumptively repugnant to the state Constitution, such acts could not be treated as acts of the state within the 14th Amendment, and hence no power existed in a Federal court to consider the subject until, by final action of an appropriate state court, it was decided that such acts were authorized by the state, and were therefore not repugnant to the state Constitution. * * *

Coming to consider the real significance of this doctrine, we think it is so clearly in conflict with the decisions of this court as to leave no doubt that plain error was committed in announcing and applying it. In view, however, of the fact that the proposition was sanctioned by the court below, and was by it deemed to be supported by the persuasive authority of two opinions of the circuit court of appeals for the ninth circuit, before coming to consider the decided cases we analyze some of the conceptions upon which the proposition must rest, in order to show its inherent unsoundness, to make its destructive character manifest, and to indicate its departure from the substantially unanimous view which has prevailed from the beginning.

In the first place, the proposition addresses itself not to the mere distribution of the judicial power granted by the Constitution, but substantially denies the existence of power under the Constitution over the subject with which the proposition is concerned. It follows that the limitation which it imposes would be beyond possible correction by legislation. Its restriction would, moreover, attach to the exercise of Federal judicial power under all circumstances, whether the issue concerned original jurisdiction or arose in the course of a controversy to which otherwise jurisdiction would extend. Thus, being applicable equally to all Federal courts, under all circumstances, in every stage of a proceeding, the enforcement of the doctrine would hence render impossible the performance of the duty with which the Federal courts are charged under the Constitution. Such paralysis would inevitably ensue, since the consequence would be that, at least in every case where there was a coincidence between a national safeguard or prohibition and a state one, the power of the Federal court to afford protection to a claim of right under the Constitution of the United States, as against the action of a state or its officers, would depend on the ultimate determination of the state courts, and would therefore require a stay of all action to await such determination. While this would be obviously true as to cases where there was a coincident constitutional guaranty, in reason it is clear that the principle, if sound, could not be confined to a case of coincident Federal and state guaranty or prohibition, since, as the Constitution of the United States is the paramount law, as much applicable to states or their officers as to others, it would come to pass that in every case where action of a state officer was complained of as violating the Constitution of the United States, the Federal courts, in any form of procedure, or in any stage of the controversy, would have to await the determination of a state court as to the operation of the Constitution of the United States. It is manifest that, in necessary operation, the doctrine which was sustained would, in substance, cause the state courts to become the primary source for applying and enforcing the constitution of the United States in all cases covered by the 14th Amendment.

It would certainly be open to controversy if the proposition were carried to its logical result, whether the only right under the 14th Amendment, which the proposition admits, to exert Federal judicial power growing out of wrongful acts of state officers, would not be unavailing. This naturally suggests itself, since, if there be no right to exert such power until, by the final action of a state court of last resort, the act of a state officer has been declared rightful and to be the lawful act of the state as a governmental entity, the inquiry naturally comes whether, under such circumstances, a suit against the officer would not be a suit against the state, within the purview of the 11th Amendment. The possibility of such a result, moreover, at once engenders a further inquiry; that is, whether the effect of the proposition would not be to cause the 14th Amendment to narrow Federal judicial power instead of enlarging it and making it more efficacious. It must be borne in mind, also, that the limitations which the proposition, if adopted, would impose upon Federal judicial power, would not be in reason solely applicable to an exertion of such power as to the persons and subjects covered by the 14th Amendment, but would equally govern controversies concerning the contract and possibly other clauses of the Constitution.

The vice which not only underlies but permeates the proposition is not far to seek. It consists, first, in causing by an artificial construction the provisions of the 14th Amendment not to reach those to whom they are addressed when reasonably construed; and, second, in wholly misconceiving the scope and operation of the 14th Amendment, thereby removing from the control of that Amendment the great body of rights which it was intended it should safeguard, and in taking out of reach of its prohibitions the wrongs which it was the purpose of the Amendment to condemn.

Before demonstrating the accuracy of the statement just made as to the essential result of the proposition relied upon by a reference to decided cases, in order that the appreciation of the cases may be made more salient, we contrast the meaning as above stated, which the 14th Amendment would have if the proposition was maintained, with the undoubted significance of that Amendment as established by many decisions of this court.

By the proposition the prohibitions and guaranties of the Amendment are addressed to and control the states only in their complete governmental capacity, and as a result give no authority to exert Federal judicial power until, by the decision of a court of last resort of a state, acts complained of under the 14th Amendment have been held valid, and therefore state acts in the fullest sense. To the contrary, the provisions of the Amendment as conclusively fixed by previous decisions are generic in their terms, are addressed, of course, to the states, but also to every person, whether natural or juridical, who is the repository of state power. By this construction the reach of the Amendment is shown to be coextensive with any exercise by a state of power, in whatever form exerted. * * *

To speak broadly, the difference between the proposition insisted upon and the true meaning of the Amendment is this: that the one assumes that the Amendment virtually contemplates alone wrongs authorized by a state, and gives only power accordingly, while in truth the Amendment contemplates the possibility of state officers abusing the powers lawfully conferred upon them by doing wrongs prohibited by the Amendment. In other words, the Amendment, looking to the enforcement of the rights which it guarantees and to the prevention of the wrongs which it prohibits, proceeds not merely upon the assumption that states, acting in their governmental capacity, in a complete sense, may do acts which conflict with its provisions, but, also conceiving, which was more normally to be contemplated, that state powers might be abused by those who possessed them, and as a result might be used as the instrument for doing wrongs, provided against all and every such possible contingency. Thus, the completeness of the Amendment in this regard is but the complement of its comprehensive inclusiveness from the point of view of those to whom its prohibitions are addressed. Under these circumstances it may not be doubted that where a state officer, under an assertion of power from the state, is doing an act which could only be done upon the predicate that there was such power, the inquiry as to the repugnancy of the act to the 14th Amendment cannot be avoided by insisting that there is a want of power. That is to say, a state officer cannot, on the one hand, as a means of doing a wrong forbidden by the Amendment, proceed upon the assumption of the possession of state power, and at the same time, for the purpose of avoiding the application of the Amendment, deny the power, and thus accomplish the wrong. * * *

Let us consider the decided cases in order to demonstrate how plainly they refute the contention here made by the court below, and how clearly they establish the converse doctrine which we have formulated in the two propositions previously stated. * * *

Although every contention pressed and authority now relied upon in favor of affirmance is disposed of by the general principles which we have previously stated, before concluding we specially advert to some of the contentions urged to the contrary. 1. Much reliance is placed upon the decisions in Barney v. New York, [193 U.S. 430], and Memphis v. Cumberland Teleph. & Teleg. Co., 218 U.S. 624. The latter we at once put out of view with the statement that, on its face, the question involved was one of pleading, and in no sense of substantive Federal power. As to the other,— the Barney Case,—it might suffice to say, as we have already pointed out, was considered in [Raymond v. Chicago Union Traction Co., 207 U.S. 20], and if it conflicted with the doctrine in that case and the doctrine of the subsequent and leading case of Ex parte Young, is now so distinguished or qualified as not to be here authoritative or even persuasive. But on the face of the Barney Case it is to be observed that however much room there may be for the contention that the facts in that case justified a different conclusion, as the doctrine which we have stated in this case was plainly recognized in the Barney Case, and the decision there rendered proceeded upon the hypothesis that the facts presented took the case out of the established rule, there is no ground for saying that that case is authority for overruling the settled doctrine which, abstractly, at least, it recognized. If there were room for such conclusion, in view of what we have said, it would be our plain duty to qualify and restrict the Barney Case in so far as it might be found to conflict with the rule here applied. * * *

Reversed.

NOTE ON THE SCOPE OF FEDERAL CONSTITUTIONAL PROTECTION AGAINST UNAUTHORIZED STATE ACTION

(1) Is the Home Telephone construction of the Fourteenth Amendment inconsistent with the construction of the Eleventh Amendment in Ex parte Young?[1]

(2) Barney v. City of New York, 193 U.S. 430 (1904), was a suit to enjoin the city from proceeding with construction of the Park Avenue subway tunnel, which was adjacent to plaintiff's premises. The bill alleged that the construction deprived plaintiff of his property without due process in violation of the Fourteenth Amendment. It also asserted that the construction was not in accordance with the plan approved by the local authorities, and hence was forbidden under state law. The federal circuit court dismissed the bill for want of jurisdiction. The Supreme Court affirmed, with Chief Justice Fuller writing (pp. 437–38, 441):

"Controversies over violations of the laws of New York are controversies to be dealt with by the courts of the State. Complainant's grievance was that the law of the State had been broken, and not a grievance inflicted by action of the legislative or executive or judicial department of the State; and the principle is that it is for the state courts to remedy acts of state officers done without the authority of, or contrary to, state law. Missouri v. Dockery, 191 U.S. 165; Civil Rights Cases, 109 U.S. 3; Virginia v. Rives, 100 U.S. 313. * * *

"In the present case defendants were proceeding, not only in violation of provisions of the state law, but in opposition to plain prohibitions."

The bill of complaint seems to have been framed principally upon the theory that the acts of the defendants constituted a taking of the complainant's property without due process of law, in violation of the Fourteenth

---

1. With the Home Telephone case, compare Iowa–Des Moines Nat. Bank v. Bennett, 284 U.S. 239 (1931), p. 585, supra (holding that a state court was obliged to provide a tax refund to plaintiffs who were subjected to discriminatory taxation in violation of the Fourteenth Amendment, even if the plaintiffs were liable under state law for the taxes paid and the state auditor had acted in violation of state law when he had collected taxes from plaintiffs' competitors at a lower rate than that applied to plaintiffs). But cf. Hooe v. United States, 218 U.S. 322, 335–36 (1910), p. 1139, supra (holding that the owner of private property that was occupied by federal officers acting without the authority of Congress does not state a claim against the federal government under the Just Compensation Clause).

Amendment, not because of their intrinsic nature but simply because they were a violation of state law. Can the quoted passages in the Chief Justice's opinion be read as construing the bill in this way? If so, the Court's substantive interpretation of the Fourteenth Amendment would be unexceptionable, would it not?

However, the bill also alleged (p. 433) that "said rapid transit act, so far as it purports to authorize the construction of a tunnel and railway in said Park avenue without the consent of abutting owners or compensation therefor, is void, because it deprives your orator of his property without due process of law, in violation of the provisions of the said amendment." Whether this allegation raised a substantial federal question may be doubted. The appellees pointed out that the subway affected neither light nor air nor access of abutters, and argued (p. 436) that "the alleged impairment of the comfort to be enjoyed in the plaintiff's premises through the acts of the city and its Rapid Transit Board underneath the surface of its own streets is not a taking of property within the meaning of the Fourteenth Amendment". The opinion does not discuss this question.

(3) In Siler v. Louisville & N.R.R., 213 U.S. 175 (1909), the railroad sought to enjoin the enforcement of a state administrative order fixing maximum rates, on the grounds that it was unauthorized under state law and that it violated various provisions of the federal Constitution. Relying upon Barney, the defendants argued that if the order was unauthorized as had been alleged, it was "not the action of the State" and hence there could be no constitutional violation (p. 192). To this, the Supreme Court responded that if the bill alleged *only* "that the order was invalid because it was not authorized by the State * * * the objection might be good, but the bill sets up several Federal questions. * * * The various questions are entirely separate from each other. Under these circumstances there can be no doubt that the Circuit Court obtained jurisdiction over the case by virtue of the Federal questions set up in the bill * * *" (pp. 192–93).[2]

(4) Justice Frankfurter attempted a resuscitation of the Barney doctrine in his concurrence in Snowden v. Hughes, 321 U.S. 1 (1944). There, an Illinois citizen sued the members of the State Primary Canvassing Board for damages under the Civil Rights Act of 1871, 42 U.S.C. § 1983, alleging that defendants had maliciously and arbitrarily refused to file a certificate of plaintiff's selection as a Republican candidate for election to the state legislature. The certificate was necessary for plaintiff to be included on the ballot, and in the particular circumstances, certification would have been tantamount to final election. The complaint alleged that defendants had violated Illinois law and the Privileges and Immunities and Equal Protection Clauses of the Fourteenth Amendment.

The Court held that plaintiff had failed to state a cause of action. Chief Justice Stone's opinion focused on the equal protection claim. He stressed (pp. 11, 13) that the plaintiff "disclaimed any contention that class

---

2. For the lower courts' persistent misunderstanding of the Barney case as reinterpreted in Home Telephone and Siler, see Isseks, *Jurisdiction of the Lower Federal Courts to Enjoin Unauthorized Action of State Officials,* 40 Harv.L.Rev. 969 (1927). See also Mosher v. City of Phoenix, 287 U.S. 29 (1932).

Cf. United States v. Raines, 362 U.S. 17, 25–26 (1960) (discriminatory voting practices that violated state law were unlawful under the Fifteenth Amendment and federal civil rights legislation; "Barney must be regarded as having 'been worn away by the erosion of time' * * * and of contrary authority").

or racial discrimination is involved," and reasoned that "not every denial of a right conferred by state law involves a denial of the equal protection of the laws, even though the denial of the right to one person may operate to confer it to another." The statutory distinction between successful and unsuccessful candidates was permissible. "And where the official action purports to be in conformity to the statutory classification, an erroneous or mistaken performance of the statutory duty ＊ ＊ ＊ is not without more a denial of the equal protection of the laws.

"The unlawful administration by state officers of a state statute fair on its face, resulting in its unequal application to those who are entitled to be treated alike, is not a denial of equal protection unless there is shown to be present in it an element of intentional or purposeful discrimination. ＊ ＊ ＊

"If the action of the Board is official action it is subject to constitutional infirmity to the same but no greater extent than if the action were taken by the state legislature. Its illegality under the state statute can neither add to nor subtract from its constitutional validity. Mere violation of a state statute does not infringe the federal Constitution. Compare Owensboro Water Works Co. v. City of Owensboro, 200 U.S. 38, 47. And state action, even though illegal under state law, can be no more and no less constitutional under the Fourteenth Amendment than if it were sanctioned by the state legislature. A state statute which provided that one nominee rather than two should be certified in a particular election district would not be unconstitutional on its face and would be open to attack only if it were shown, as it is not here, that the exclusion of one and the election of another were invidious and purposely discriminatory. ＊ ＊ ＊

"As we conclude that the right asserted by petitioner is not one secured by the Fourteenth Amendment and affords no basis for a suit brought under the sections of the Civil Rights Acts relied upon, we find it unnecessary to consider whether the action by the State Board of which petitioner complains is state action within the meaning of the Fourteenth Amendment. The authority of Barney v. City of New York, *supra,* on which the court below relied, has been so restricted by our later decisions, see Raymond v. Chicago Union Traction Co., 207 U.S. 20, 37; Home Tel. & Tel. Co. v. City of Los Angeles, 227 U.S. 278, 294; Iowa–Des Moines Nat. Bank v. Bennett, *supra,* 284 U.S. at pages 246, 247; *cf.* United States v. Classic, 313 U.S. 299, 326, that our determination may be more properly and more certainly rested on petitioner's failure to assert a right of a nature such as the Fourteenth Amendment protects against state action."

Justices Douglas and Murphy dissented on the "narrow ground" that the complaint sufficiently charged "an invidious, purposeful discrimination", and that the plaintiff should be given a chance to prove the claim.

Justice Frankfurter apparently agreed with the dissenters on this point but concurred with the majority on another ground. He said (pp. 15–17):

"＊ ＊ ＊ [I]n forbidding a state to 'deny to any person within its jurisdiction the equal protection of the laws', the Fourteenth Amendment does not permit a state to deny the equal protection of its laws because such denial is not wholesale. ＊ ＊ ＊ Speaking of a situation in which conscious discrimination by a state touches 'the plaintiff alone', this Court tersely expressed the governing principle by observing that 'we suppose that no one would contend that the plaintiff was given the equal protection of the laws.' McFarland v. American Sugar Refining Co., 241 U.S. 79, 86, 87. * * *

"But to constitute such unjust discrimination the action must be that of the state. Since the state, for present purposes, can only act through functionaries, the question naturally arises what functionaries, acting under what circumstances, are to be deemed the state for purposes of bringing suit in the federal courts on the basis of illegal state action. The problem is beset with inherent difficulties and not unnaturally has had a fluctuating history in the decisions of the Court. Compare Barney v. City of New York, 193 U.S. 430, with Raymond v. Chicago Union Traction Co., 207 U.S. 20, City of Memphis v. Cumberland Tel. & Tel. Co., 218 U.S. 624, with Home Tel. & Tel. Co. v. City of Los Angeles, 227 U.S. 278. It is not to be resolved by abstract considerations such as the fact that every official who purports to wield power conferred by a state is pro tanto the state. Otherwise every illegal discrimination by a policeman on the beat would be state action for purpose of suit in a federal court.

"Our question is not whether a remedy is available for such an illegality, but whether it is available in the first instance in a federal court. Such a problem of federal judicial control must be placed in the historic context of the relationship of the federal courts to the states, with due regard for the natural sensitiveness of the states and for the appropriate responsibility of state courts to correct the action of lower state courts and state officials. See, e.g., Ex parte Royall, 117 U.S. 241, 251. * * *

"I am clear * * * that the action of the Canvassing Board taken, as the plaintiff himself acknowledges, in defiance of the duty of that Board under Illinois law, cannot be deemed the action of the State, certainly not until the highest court of the State confirms such action and thereby makes it the law of the State. I agree, in a word, with' the court below that Barney v. City of New York, 193 U.S. 430, is controlling. See Isseks, *Jurisdiction of the Lower Federal Courts to Enjoin Unauthorized Action of State Officials,* 40 Harv.L.Rev. 969. Neither the wisdom of its reasoning nor its holding has been impaired by subsequent decisions. A different problem is presented when a case comes here on review from a decision of a state court as the ultimate voice of state law. See for instance Iowa–Des Moines Nat. Bank v. Bennett, 284 U.S. 239. And the case is wholly unlike Lane v. Wilson, 307 U.S. 268, in which the election officials acted not in defiance of a statute of a state but under its authority."

(5) Observe that the difficulties of administering a principle that constitutional prohibitions are addressed to all actions of state officials taken under color of state authority, without superseding the corrective processes of state law and assuming an impossible burden of federal supervision, are most sharply presented in the equal protection situation. Are they, however, insuperable?

Could Justice Frankfurter's effort to escape from these difficulties by way of the jurisdictional doctrine suggested by the broad language of the Barney opinion have been accepted without rethinking the whole course of constitutional history since the Home Telephone case?

Would the guarantees of the Fourteenth Amendment be adequately protected by a constitutional interpretation that treated the prohibitions of the Amendment as addressed only to the state as a whole after it has spoken with its final judicial voice?

(6) The question whether federal law should be construed to regulate the conduct of state officials acting without authorization under or contrary to state law has proven to be a persistent one. In the next subsection, dealing with the scope of federal *statutory* protection against unauthorized state action, this question (or some variant of it) resurfaces in two contexts: (i) as a question of the proper interpretation of the Civil Rights Act of 1871, 42 U.S.C. § 1983, see Monroe v. Pape, which follows immediately; Monell v. Department of Social Services, p. 1251, *infra;* and (ii) in cases considering whether the existence of state-law remedies to redress a state official's deprivation of liberty or property provide "due process of law" so as to preclude any constitutional claim under the Due Process Clause, see Parratt v. Taylor, p. 1259, *infra,* and the subsequent *Note on the Relationship Between Common Law Torts and Constitutional Torts in Actions Against State and Local Officials.*

SUBSECTION C: FEDERAL STATUTORY PROTECTION AGAINST STATE OFFICIAL ACTION: HEREIN OF 42 U.S.C. § 1983

MONROE v. PAPE

365 U.S. 167, 81 S.Ct. 473, 5 L.Ed.2d 492 (1961).
Certiorari to the United States Court of Appeals for the Seventh Circuit.

MR. JUSTICE DOUGLAS delivered the opinion of the Court.

This case presents important questions concerning the construction of R.S. § 1979, 42 U.S.C. § 1983, which reads as follows:

> "Every person who, under color of any statute, ordinance, regulation, custom, or usage, of any State or Territory, subjects, or causes to be subjected, any citizen of the United States or other person within the jurisdiction thereof to the deprivation of any rights, privileges, or immunities secured by the Constitution and laws, shall be liable to the party injured in an action at law, suit in equity, or other proper proceeding for redress."

The complaint alleges that 13 Chicago police officers broke into petitioners' home in the early morning, routed them from bed, made them stand naked in the living room, and ransacked every room, emptying drawers and ripping mattress covers. It further alleges that Mr. Monroe was then taken to the police station and detained on "open" charges for 10 hours, while he was interrogated about a two-day-old murder, that he was not taken before a magistrate, though one was accessible, that he was not permitted to call his family or attorney, that he was subsequently released without criminal charges being preferred against him. It is alleged that the officers had no search warrant and no arrest warrant and that they acted "under color of the statutes, ordinances, regulations, customs and usages" of Illinois and of the City of Chicago. Federal jurisdiction was asserted under [§ 1983], which we have set out above, and 28 U.S.C. § 1343 and 28 U.S.C. § 1331.

The City of Chicago moved to dismiss the complaint on the ground that it is not liable under the Civil Rights Acts nor for acts committed in performance of its governmental functions. All defendants moved to dismiss, alleging that the complaint alleged no cause of action under those Acts or under the Federal Constitution. The District Court dismissed the complaint. The Court of Appeals affirmed * * *.

I.

Petitioners claim that the invasion of their home and the subsequent search without a warrant and the arrest and detention of Mr. Monroe without a warrant and without arraignment constituted a deprivation of their "rights, privileges, or immunities secured by the Constitution" within the meaning of [§ 1983]. * * *

Section [1983] came onto the books as § 1 of the Ku Klux Act of April 20, 1871. 17 Stat. 13. * * *

Its purpose is plain from the title of the legislation, "An Act to enforce the Provisions of the Fourteenth Amendment to the Constitution of the United States, and for other Purposes." 17 Stat. 13. Allegation of facts constituting a deprivation under color of state authority of a right guaranteed by the Fourteenth Amendment satisfies to that extent the requirement of [§ 1983]. See Douglas v. Jeannette, 319 U.S. 157, 161–162. So far petitioners are on solid ground. For the guarantee against unreasonable searches and seizures contained in the Fourth Amendment has been made applicable to the States by reason of the Due Process Clause of the Fourteenth Amendment. Wolf v. Colorado, 338 U.S. 25 * * *.

II.

There can be no doubt at least since Ex parte Virginia, 100 U.S. 339, 346–347, that Congress has the power to enforce provisions of the Fourteenth Amendment against those who carry a badge of authority of a State and represent it in some capacity, whether they act in accordance with their authority or misuse it. See Home Tel. & Tel. Co. v. Los Angeles, 227 U.S. 278, 287–296. The question with which we now deal is the narrower one of whether Congress, in enacting § [1983], meant to give a remedy to parties deprived of constitutional rights, privileges and immunities by an official's abuse of his position. Cf. Williams v. United States, 341 U.S. 97; Screws v. United States, 325 U.S. 91; United States v. Classic, 313 U.S. 299. We conclude that it did so intend.

It is argued that "under color of" enumerated state authority excludes acts of an official or policeman who can show no authority under state law, state custom, or state usage to do what he did. In this case it is said that these policemen, in breaking into petitioners' apartment, violated the Constitution and laws of Illinois. It is pointed out that under Illinois law a simple remedy is offered for that violation and that, so far as it appears, the courts of Illinois are available to give petitioners that full redress which the common law affords for violence done to a person; and it is earnestly argued that no "statute, ordinance, regulation, custom or usage" of Illinois bars that redress.

* * *

The legislation—in particular the section with which we are now concerned—had several purposes. * * * One who reads [the debates] in their entirety sees that the present section had three main aims.

First, it might, of course, override certain kinds of state laws. Mr. Sloss of Alabama, in opposition, spoke of that object and emphasized that it was irrelevant because there were no such laws:

"The first section of this bill prohibits any invidious legislation by States against the rights or privileges of citizens of the United States. The object of this section is not very clear, as it is not pretended by its advocates on this floor that any State has passed any laws endangering the rights or privileges of the colored people."

Second, it provided a remedy where state law was inadequate. That aspect of the legislation was summed up as follows by Senator Sherman of Ohio:

" * * * it is said the reason is that any offense may be committed upon a negro by a white man, and a negro cannot testify in any case against a white man, so that the only way by which any conviction can be had in Kentucky in those cases is in the United States courts, because the United States courts enforce the United States laws by which negroes may testify."

But the purposes were much broader. The *third* aim was to provide a federal remedy where the state remedy, though adequate in theory, was not available in practice. * * *

This Act of April 20, 1871, sometimes called "the third 'force bill,'" was passed by a Congress that had the Klan "particularly in mind." The debates are replete with references to the lawless conditions existing in the South in 1871. * * * It was not the unavailability of state remedies but the failure of certain States to enforce the laws with an equal hand that furnished the powerful momentum behind this "force bill." Mr. Lowe of Kansas said:

"While murder is stalking abroad in disguise, while whippings and lynchings and banishment have been visited upon unoffending American citizens, the local administrations have been found inadequate or unwilling to apply the proper corrective. * * * Immunity is given to crime, and the records of the public tribunals are searched in vain for any evidence of effective redress."
* * *

There was, it was said, no quarrel with the state laws on the books. It was their lack of enforcement that was the nub of the difficulty. Speaking of conditions in Virginia, Mr. Porter of that State said:

"The outrages committed upon loyal men there are under the forms of law."
* * *

Senator Pratt of Indiana spoke of the discrimination against Union sympathizers and Negroes in the actual enforcement of the laws:

"Plausibly and sophistically it is said the laws of North Carolina do not discriminate against them; that the provisions in favor of rights and liberties are general; that the courts are open to all; that juries, grand and petit, are commanded to hear and redress without distinction as to color, race, or political sentiment.

"But it is a fact, asserted in the report, that of the hundreds of outrages committed upon loyal people through the agency of this Ku Klux organization not one has been punished. This defect in the administration of the laws does not extend to other cases. Vigorously enough are the laws enforced against Union people. They only fail in efficiency when a man of known Union sentiments, white or black, invokes their aid. Then Justice closes the door of her temples."

It was precisely that breadth of the remedy which the opposition emphasized. Mr. Kerr of Indiana referring to the section involved in the present litigation said:

"This section gives to any person who may have been injured in any of his rights, privileges, or immunities of person or property, a civil action for damages against the wrongdoer in the Federal courts. The offenses committed against him may be the common violations of the municipal law of his State. * * * It is a covert attempt to transfer another large portion of jurisdiction from the State tribunals, to which it of right belongs, to those of the United States. * * *
* * *

The debates were long and extensive. It is abundantly clear that one reason the legislation was passed was to afford a federal right in federal courts because, by reason of prejudice, passion, neglect, intolerance or otherwise, state laws might not be enforced and the claims of citizens to the enjoyment of rights, privileges, and immunities guaranteed by the Fourteenth Amendment might be denied by the state agencies.
* * *

Although the legislation was enacted because of the conditions that existed in the South at that time, it is cast in general language and is as applicable to Illinois as it is to the States whose names were mentioned over and again in the debates. It is no answer that the State has a law which if enforced would give relief. The federal remedy is supplementary to the state remedy, and the latter need not be first sought and refused before the federal one is invoked. Hence the fact that Illinois by its constitution and laws outlaws unreasonable searches and seizures is no barrier to the present suit in the federal court.

We had before us in United States v. Classic, *supra*, § 20 of the Criminal Code, 18 U.S.C. § 242, which provides a criminal punishment for anyone who "under color of any law, statute, ordinance, regulation, or custom" subjects any inhabitant of a State to the deprivation of "any rights, privileges, or immunities secured or protected by the Constitution or laws of the United States." Section 242 first came into the law as § 2 of the Civil Rights Act, Act of April 9, 1866, 14 Stat. 27. After passage of the Fourteenth Amendment, this provision was re-enacted and amended by §§ 17, 18, Act of May 31, 1870, 16 Stat. 140, 144. The right involved in the Classic case was the right of voters in a primary to have their votes counted. The laws of Louisiana required the defendants "to count the ballots, to record the result of the count, and to certify the result of the election." United States v. Classic, *supra*, 325–326. But according to the indictment they did not perform their duty. In an opinion written by Mr. Justice (later Chief Justice) Stone, in which Mr. Justice Roberts, Mr. Justice Reed, and Mr. Justice Frankfurter joined, the Court ruled, "Misuse of power, possessed by virtue of state law and made possible only because the wrongdoer is clothed with the authority of state law, is action taken 'under color of' state law." *Id.,* 326. There was a dissenting opinion; but the ruling as to the meaning of "under color of" state law was not questioned.

That view of the meaning of the words "under color of" state law, 18 U.S.C. § 242, was reaffirmed in Screws v. United States, *supra,* * * * [and] in Williams v. United States, *supra,* * * *.

Mr. Shellabarger, reporting out the bill which became the Ku Klux Act, said of the provision with which we now deal:

"The model for it will be found in the second section of the act of April 9, 1866, known as the 'civil rights act.' * * * This section of this bill, on the same state of facts, not only provides a civil remedy for persons whose former condition may have been that of slaves, but also to all people where, under color of State law, they or any of them may be deprived of rights. * * * "

Thus, it is beyond doubt that this phrase should be accorded the same construction in both statutes—in § [1983] and in 18 U.S.C. § 242.

* * *

In the Screws case we dealt with a statute that imposed criminal penalties for acts "wilfully" done. We construed that word in its setting to mean the doing of an act with "a specific intent to deprive a person of a federal right." 325 U.S., at 103. We do not think that gloss should be placed on § [1983] which we have here. The word "wilfully" does not appear in § [1983]. Moreover, § [1983] provides a civil remedy, while in the Screws case we dealt with a criminal law challenged on the ground of vagueness. Section [1983] should be read against the background of tort liability that makes a man responsible for the natural consequences of his actions.

So far, then, the complaint states a cause of action. There remains to consider only a defense peculiar to the City of Chicago.

III.

The City of Chicago asserts that it is not liable under § [1983]. We do not stop to explore the whole range of questions tendered us on this issue at oral argument and in the briefs. For we are of the opinion that Congress did not undertake to bring municipal corporations within the ambit of § [1983].

When the bill that became the Act of April 20, 1871, was being debated in the Senate, Senator Sherman of Ohio proposed an amendment which would have made "the inhabitants of the county, city, or parish" in which certain acts of violence occurred liable "to pay full compensation" to the person damaged or his widow or legal representative. The amendment was adopted by the Senate. The House, however, rejected it. The Conference Committee reported another version.[41] The House rejected the Conference

41. "That if any house, tenement, cabin, shop, building, barn, or granary shall be unlawfully or feloniously demolished, pulled down, burned, or destroyed, wholly or in part, by any persons riotously and tumultuously assembled together; or if any person shall unlawfully and with force and violence be whipped, scourged, wounded, or killed by any persons riotously and tumultuously assembled together, with intent to deprive any person of any right conferred upon him by the Constitution and laws of the United States, or to deter him or punish him for exercising such right, or by reason of his race, color, or previous condition of servitude, in every such case the county, city, or parish in which any of the said offenses shall be committed shall be

report. In a second conference the Sherman amendment was dropped and in its place § 6 of the Act of April 20, 1871, was substituted. This new section, which is now R.S. § 1981, 42 U.S.C. § 1986, dropped out all provision for municipal liability and extended liability in damages to "any person or persons, having knowledge that any" of the specified wrongs are being committed. Mr. Poland, speaking for the House Conferees about the Sherman proposal to make municipalities liable, said:

> "We informed the conferees on the part of the Senate that the House had taken a stand on that subject and would not recede from it; that that section imposing liability upon towns and counties must go out or we should fail to agree."

The objection to the Sherman amendment stated by Mr. Poland was that "the House had solemnly decided that in their judgment Congress had no constitutional power to impose any obligation upon county and town organizations, the mere instrumentality for the administration of state law." The question of constitutional power of Congress to impose civil liability on municipalities was vigorously debated with powerful arguments advanced in the affirmative.

Much reliance is placed on the Act of February 25, 1871, 16 Stat. 431, entitled "An Act prescribing the Form of the enacting and resolving Clauses of Acts and Resolutions of Congress, and Rules for the Construction thereof." Section 2 of this Act provides that "the word 'person' may extend and be applied to bodies politic and corporate." It should be noted, however, that this definition is merely an allowable, not a mandatory, one. It is said that doubts should be resolved in favor of municipal liability because private remedies against officers for illegal searches and seizures are conspicuously ineffective, and because municipal liability will not only afford plaintiffs responsible defendants but cause those defendants to eradicate abuses that exist at the police level. We do not reach those policy considerations. Nor do we reach the constitutional question whether Congress has the power to make municipalities liable for acts of its officers that violate the civil rights of individuals.

The response of the Congress to the proposal to make municipalities liable for certain actions being brought within federal purview by the Act of April 20, 1871, was so antagonistic that we cannot believe that the word "person" was used in this particular Act to include them. Accordingly we hold that the motion to dismiss the complaint against the City of Chicago was properly granted. But since the complaint should not have been dismissed against the officials the judgment must be and is reversed.

Mr. Justice Harlan, whom Mr. Justice Stewart joins, concurring.

Were this case here as one of first impression, I would find the "under color of any statute" issue very close indeed. However, in Classic and Screws this Court considered a substantially identical statutory phrase to have a meaning which, unless we now retreat from it, requires that issue to go for the petitioners here.

* * *

Those aspects of Congress' purpose which are quite clear in the earlier congressional debates, as quoted by my Brothers Douglas and Frankfurter

liable to pay full compensation to the person or persons damnified by such offense
* * *."

in turn, seem to me to be inherently ambiguous when applied to the case of an isolated abuse of state authority by an official. One can agree with the Court's opinion that:

> "It is abundantly clear that one reason the legislation was passed was to afford a federal right in federal courts because, by reason of prejudice, passion, neglect, intolerance or otherwise, state laws might not be enforced and the claims of citizens to the enjoyment of rights, privileges, and immunities guaranteed by the Fourteenth Amendment might be denied by the state agencies. * * *"

without being certain that Congress meant to deal with anything other than abuses so recurrent as to amount to "custom, or usage." One can agree with my Brother Frankfurter, in dissent, that Congress had no intention of taking over the whole field of ordinary state torts and crimes, without being certain that the enacting Congress would not have regarded actions by an official, made possible by his position, as far more serious than an ordinary state tort, and therefore as a matter of federal concern. If attention is directed at the rare specific references to isolated abuses of state authority, one finds them neither so clear nor so disproportionately divided between favoring the positions of the majority or the dissent as to make either position seem plainly correct.

* * * *

The dissent considers that the "under color of" provision of § 1983 distinguishes between unconstitutional actions taken without state authority, which only the State should remedy, and unconstitutional actions authorized by the State, which the Federal Act was to reach. If so, then the controlling difference for the enacting legislature must have been either that the state remedy was more adequate for unauthorized actions than for authorized ones or that there was, in some sense, greater harm from unconstitutional actions authorized by the full panoply of state power and approval than from unconstitutional actions not so authorized or acquiesced in by the State. I find less than compelling the evidence that either distinction was important to that Congress.

I.

If the state remedy was considered adequate when the official's unconstitutional act was unauthorized, why should it not be thought equally adequate when the unconstitutional act was authorized? * * *

Since the suggested narrow construction of § 1983 presupposes that state measures were adequate to remedy unauthorized deprivations of constitutional rights and since the identical state relief could be obtained for state-authorized acts with the aid of Supreme Court review, this narrow construction would reduce the statute to having merely a jurisdictional function, shifting the load of federal supervision from the Supreme Court to the lower courts and providing a federal tribunal for fact findings in cases involving authorized action. Such a function could be justified on various grounds. It could, for example, be argued that the state courts would be less willing to find a constitutional violation in cases involving "authorized action" and that therefore the victim of such action would bear a greater burden in that he would more likely have to carry his case to this Court, and once here, might be bound by unfavorable state court findings. But the legislative debates do not disclose congressional concern about the burdens of litigation placed upon the victims of "authorized" constitutional violations contrasted to the victims of unauthorized violations. Neither did Congress indicate an interest in relieving the burden placed on this Court in reviewing such cases.

The statute becomes more than a jurisdictional provision only if one attributes to the enacting legislature the view that a deprivation of a constitutional right is significantly different from and more serious than a violation of a state right and therefore deserves a different remedy even though the same act may constitute both a state tort and the deprivation of a constitutional right. This view, by no means unrealistic as a common-sense matter,[5] is, I believe, more consistent with the flavor of the legislative history than is a view that the primary purpose of the statute was to grant a lower court forum for fact findings. * * *

* * *

II.

I think [the] limited interpretation of § 1983 fares no better when viewed from the other possible premise for it, namely that state-approved constitutional deprivations were considered more offensive than those not so approved. For one thing, the enacting Congress was not unaware of the fact that there was a substantial overlap between the protections granted by state constitutional provisions and those granted by the Fourteenth Amendment. * * * I hesitate to assume that the proponents of the present statute, who regarded it as necessary even though they knew that the provisions of the Fourteenth Amendment were self-executing, would have thought the remedies unnecessary whenever there were self-executing provisions of state constitutions also forbidding what the Fourteenth Amendment forbids. * * *

These difficulties in explaining the basis of a distinction between authorized and unauthorized deprivations of constitutional rights fortify my view that the legislative history does not bear the burden which *stare decisis* casts upon it. For this reason and for those stated in the opinion of the Court, I agree that we should not now depart from the holdings of the Classic and Screws cases.

MR. JUSTICE FRANKFURTER, dissenting except insofar as the Court holds that this action cannot be maintained against the City of Chicago.

* * *

5. There will be many cases in which the relief provided by the state to the victim of a use of state power which the state either did not or could not constitutionally authorize will be far less than what Congress may have thought would be fair reimbursement for deprivation of a constitutional right. I will venture only a few examples. There may be no damage remedy for the loss of voting rights or for the harm from psychological coercion leading to a confession. And what is the dollar value of the right to go to unsegregated schools? Even the remedy for such an unauthorized search and seizure as Monroe was allegedly subjected to may be only the nominal amount of damages to physical property allowable in an action for trespass to land. It would indeed be the purest coincidence if the state remedies for violations of common-law rights by private citizens were fully appropriate to redress those injuries which only a state official can cause and against which the Constitution provides protection.

III.

* * * [A]lthough this Court has three times found that conduct of state officials which is forbidden by state law may be "under color" of state law for purposes of the Civil Rights Acts, it is accurate to say that that question has never received here the consideration which its importance merits. * * *

* * * * *

* * * The issue in the present case concerns directly a basic problem of American federalism: the relation of the Nation to the States in the critically important sphere of municipal law administration. In this aspect, it has significance approximating constitutional dimension. * * * This imposes on this Court a corresponding obligation to exercise its power within the fair limits of its judicial discretion. * * *

* * * * *

IV.

* * * [Plaintiffs] assert that they have been deprived of due process of law and of equal protection of the laws under color of state law, although from all that appears the courts of Illinois are available to give them the fullest redress which the common law affords for the violence done them, nor does any "statute, ordinance, regulation, custom, or usage" of the State of Illinois bar that redress. Did the enactment by Congress of § 1 of the Ku Klux Act of 1871 encompass such a situation?

That section, it has been noted, was patterned on the similar criminal provision of § 2, Act of April 9, 1866 [18 U.S.C. § 242]. The earlier Act had as its primary object the effective nullification of the Black Codes, those statutes of the Southern legislatures which had so burdened and disqualified the Negro as to make his emancipation appear illusory. The Act had been vetoed by President Johnson, whose veto message describes contemporary understanding of its second section; the section, he wrote,

> "seems to be designed to apply to some existing or future law of a State or Territory which may conflict with the provisions of the bill. * * * It provides for counteracting such forbidden legislation by imposing fine and imprisonment upon the legislators who may pass such conflicting laws, or upon the officers or agents who shall put, or attempt to put, them into execution. It means an official offense, not a common crime committed against law upon the persons or property of the black race. Such an act may deprive the black man of his property, but not of the right to hold property. It means a deprivation of the right itself, either by the State judiciary or the State Legislature."

And Senator Trumbull, then Chairman of the Senate Judiciary Committee, in his remarks urging its passage over the veto, expressed the intendment of the second section as those who voted for it read it:

> "If an offense is committed against a colored person simply because he is colored, in a State where the law affords him the same protection as if he were white, this act neither has nor was intended to have anything to do with his case, because he has adequate remedies in the State courts; but if he is discriminated against under color of State

laws because he is colored, then it becomes necessary to interfere for his protection."

*   *   *

The original text of the present § [1983] contained words, left out in the Revised Statutes, which clarified the objective to which the provision was addressed:

"That any person who, under color of any law, statute, ordinance, regulation, custom, or usage of any State, shall subject, or cause to be subjected, any person within the jurisdiction of the United States to the deprivation of any rights, privileges, or immunities secured by the Constitution of the United States, shall, *any such law, statute, ordinance, regulation, custom, or usage of the State to the contrary notwithstanding,* be liable to the party injured. *   *   * "

*   *   *

The Court now says, however, that "It was not the unavailability of state remedies but the failure of certain States to enforce the laws with an equal hand that furnished the powerful momentum behind this 'force bill.'" Of course, if the notion of "unavailability" of remedy is limited to mean an absence of statutory, paper right, this is in large part true. Insofar as the Court undertakes to demonstrate—as the bulk of its opinion seems to do—that § [1983] was meant to reach some instances of action not specifically authorized by the avowed, apparent, written law inscribed in the statute books of the States, the argument knocks at an open door. No one would or could deny this, for by its express terms the statute comprehends deprivations of federal rights under color of any "statute, ordinance, regulation, *custom, or usage* " of a State. (Emphasis added.) The question is, *what* class of cases other than those involving state statute law were meant to be reached. And, with respect to this question, the Court's conclusion is undermined by the very portions of the legislative debates which it cites. For surely the misconduct of individual municipal police officers, subject to the effective oversight of appropriate state administrative and judicial authorities, presents a situation which differs *toto coelo* from one in which "Immunity is given to crime, and the records of the public tribunals are searched in vain for any evidence of effective redress," or in which murder rages while a State makes "no successful effort to bring the guilty to punishment or afford protection or redress," or in which the "State courts *   *   * [are] unable to enforce the criminal laws *   *   * or to suppress the disorders existing," or in which, in a State's "judicial tribunals one class is unable to secure that enforcement of their rights and punishment for their infraction which is accorded to another," or "of *   *   * hundreds of outrages *   *   * not one [is] punished," or "the courts of the *   *   * States fail and refuse to do their duty in the punishment of offenders against the law," or in which a "class of officers charged under the laws with their administration permanently and as a rule refuse to extend [their] protection." These statements indicate that Congress—made keenly aware by the post-bellum conditions in the South that States through their authorities could sanction offenses against the individual by settled practice which established state law as truly as written codes—designed § [1983] to reach, as well, official conduct which, because engaged in "permanently and as a rule," or "systematically," came through acceptance by law-administering officers to constitute "custom, or usage" having the cast of law. They do not indicate an attempt to reach, nor does the statute by its terms include, instances of acts in defiance of state law and which no settled state practice, no systematic pattern of official action or inaction, no "custom, or usage, of any State," insulates from effective and adequate reparation by the State's authorities.

   * * * [A]ll the evidence converges to the conclusion that Congress by § [1983] created a civil liability enforceable in the federal courts only in instances of injury for which redress was barred in the state courts because some "statute, ordinance, regulation, custom, or usage" sanctioned the grievance complained of. This purpose, manifested even by the so-called "Radical" Reconstruction Congress in 1871, accords with the presuppositions of our federal system. The jurisdiction which Article III of the Constitution conferred on the national judiciary reflected the assumption that the state courts, not the federal courts, would remain the primary guardians of that fundamental security of person and property which the long evolution of the common law had secured to one individual as against other individuals. The Fourteenth Amendment did not alter this basic aspect of our federalism.

Its commands were addressed to the States. Only when the States, through their responsible organs for the formulation and administration of local policy, sought to deny or impede access by the individual to the central government in connection with those enumerated functions assigned to it, or to deprive the individual of a certain minimal fairness in the exercise of the coercive forces of the State, or without reasonable justification to treat him differently than other persons subject to their jurisdiction, was an overriding federal sanction imposed. * * *

  * * *

  * * * Suppose that a state legislature or the highest court of a State should determine that within its territorial limits no damages should be recovered in tort for pain and suffering, or for mental anguish, or that no punitive damages should be recoverable. Since the federal courts went out of the business of making "general law," Erie R. Co. v. Tompkins, 304 U.S. 64, such decisions of local policy have admittedly been the exclusive province of state lawmakers. Should the civil liability for police conduct which can claim no authority under local law, which is actionable as common-law assault or trespass in the local courts, comport different rules? Should an unlawful intrusion by a policeman in Chicago entail different consequences than an unlawful intrusion by a hoodlum? These are matters of policy in its strictly legislative sense, not for determination by this Court. And if it be, as it is, a matter for congressional choice, the legislative evidence is overwhelming that § [1983] is not expressive of that choice. * * *

[Justice Frankfurter concluded that the general allegation that the police intrusion was under color of Illinois law failed to state a claim under § 1983 in the face of Illinois decisions holding such intrusions unlawful. However, the averment that it was the "custom or usage" of the Chicago police department to detain individuals for long periods on "open charges" did state a valid claim of unlawful detention.]

NOTE ON 42 U.S.C. § 1983

(1) *The Meaning of "Under Color of Law".*

(a) *The Relationship of Monroe to Home Telephone and Telegraph.*
Monroe establishes two overlapping but distinct propositions: (1) § 1983
creates a federal remedy, cognizable in federal court, against state officials
for violation of federal rights; and (2) that remedy is available even if the
officials' conduct is wholly unauthorized under state law. In the view of
some, the primary significance of § 1983 is procedural—*i.e.*, even when it
affords no substantive relief that could not also be obtained under state
law, the *federal* remedy permits the exercise of federal court jurisdiction.
See Chevigny, *Section 1983 Jurisdiction: A Reply*, 83 Harv.L.Rev. 1352
(1970); Whitman, *Constitutional Torts*, 79 Mich.L.Rev. 5, 22–25 (1980).

Note that Justice Frankfurter's position in Monroe (which permits
immediate resort to federal court when the defendant's acts have formal
sanction in state law) gives a greater role to the federal courts than they
would have had under the apparent argument of the defendants in the
Home Telephone case (under which there is no state action until the
particular defendant's acts in the very case have been passed on by the
highest state court).[1] Consider the question raised by Justice Harlan: if
state court remedies are deemed adequate to redress federal constitutional
violations when the officer's acts violate state law, why should immediate
resort to a federal court be allowed—as Justice Frankfurter concedes it is—
when the officer's act is formally sanctioned by a state law or practice?
Recall that in the latter case, too, the state courts are obliged under the
Supremacy Clause to disregard the state law if it conflicts with the federal,
and that failure to do so is subject to review in the Supreme Court. Why
should the adequacy of this mode of redress be deemed to depend on
whether the conduct at issue violated state law?

Note also the possibly awkward inquiry that Justice Frankfurter's test
would force on the federal courts in determining whether state "custom or
usage" sanctions the defendant's unconstitutional acts. This same determination must be made today in ruling, under decisions limiting Monroe's
ban on municipal liability, whether a city is liable as such under § 1983; it
has not proved easy to make. See pp. 1251–57, *infra*. Do the difficulties of
such an inquiry argue for the reading of § 1983 in Monroe—a reading that
makes the inquiry unnecessary? But see Zagrans, *"Under Color of" What
Law: A Reconstructed Model of Section 1983 Liability*, 71 Va.L.Rev. 499
(1985), arguing that the legislative history of the Civil Rights Act of 1871
supports Justice Frankfurter's interpretation.

(b) *State Action and Private Conduct.* To recover under § 1983 for a
constitutional tort in violation of the Fourteenth Amendment, the plaintiff
must establish that the violation resulted from "state action." See, *e.g.*,
Flagg Bros., Inc. v. Brooks, 436 U.S. 149 (1978). In a suit against a
government official, the state action requirement is identical to § 1983's
requirement of conduct under color of state law; satisfying the former

---

1. *Cf.* City of Columbus v. Leonard, 443
U.S. 905, 910–11 (1979) (Rehnquist, J., dissenting) (suggesting reconsideration of
Monroe's holding that the state remedy
"need not be first sought and refused before the federal one is invoked").

necessarily satisfies the latter. Lugar v. Edmondson Oil Co., 457 U.S. 922, 928, 930 (1982).[2]

On the extent of state involvement needed, in a suit against private persons, to establish state action under the Constitution, and conduct under color of law, custom or usage for purposes of § 1983, see Lugar v. Edmondson Oil Co., *supra;* Pennzoil Co. v. Texaco, Inc., 107 S.Ct. 1519 (1987), p. 1437, *infra;* Adickes v. S.H. Kress & Co., 398 U.S. 144, 162–69 (1970). See also Note, 80 Colum.L.Rev. 802 (1980).

(c) *Under Color of Whose Law?* Section 1983 does not extend to conduct of federal officers, Wheeldin v. Wheeler, 373 U.S. 647, 650 & n. 2 (1963), unless they are acting in concert with others who are acting under color of state law, Dombrowski v. Eastland, 387 U.S. 82 (1967).[3] Judicial decisions established that conduct under color of the law of Puerto Rico was governed by § 1983, which by its terms extends to "Territories" as well as states, see Examining Bd. of Engineers, Architects and Surveyors v. Flores de Otero, 426 U.S. 572 (1976), while conduct under color of the law of the District of Columbia was not, see District of Columbia v. Carter, 409 U.S. 418 (1973). The latter holding was overturned by a 1979 amendment to § 1983, extending its coverage to conduct under any law of the District (including any Act of Congress applicable exclusively thereto).

(2) *Jurisdiction Over Section 1983 Actions.* Section 1 of the Civil Rights Act of 1871 contained not only a substantive provision, now codified as § 1983, but also a grant of jurisdiction to the federal courts, without regard to amount in controversy, over suits brought under the section (now codified as 28 U.S.C. § 1343(3)). Before 1980, the general federal question jurisdiction, 28 U.S.C. § 1331, extended only to suits in which there was more than $10,000 in controversy; smaller disputes under § 1983 could thus be brought in federal court only under § 1343(3). During this period, § 1343(3) was particularly important in cases involving rights whose valuation was difficult, such as freedom of speech. See Hague v. CIO, 307 U.S. 496, 531–32 (1939) (Stone, J., concurring); Lynch v. Household Finance Corp., 405 U.S. 538 (1972); Hagans v. Lavine, 415 U.S. 528 (1974). But the elimination in 1980 of the amount in controversy requirement under § 1331 has rendered § 1343(3) superfluous.

Nothing in § 1983 or § 1343(3) disturbs the normal presumption that state courts have concurrent jurisdiction over federal causes of action. See Martinez v. California, 444 U.S. 277, 283–84 n. 7 (1980); Maine v. Thiboutot, 448 U.S. 1, 3 n. 1 (1980); see generally Steinglass, *The Emerging State Court § 1983 Analysis: A Procedural Review,* 38 U.Miami L.Rev. 381 (1984); Note, 95 Yale L.J. 414 (1985). On the question whether state courts are *obliged* to entertain such suits, see pp. 492, 500, *supra.*

2. But *cf.* Polk County v. Dodson, 454 U.S. 312 (1981), where the Court held (without considering whether state action was present) that a state public defender was not acting under color of law because she undertook an "essentially • • • private function • • • for which state office and authority are not needed" (p. 319).

In the Lugar case, the Court noted that in § 1983 actions based upon violations of constitutional provisions (or federal statutes) containing no state action require-

ment (such as the Thirteenth Amendment, see, *e.g.,* Jones v. Alfred H. Mayer Co., 392 U.S. 409 (1968)), the "under color of state law" requirement would remain a distinct element of the § 1983 cause of action. 457 U.S. at 935 n. 18.

3. *Cf.* Ellis v. Blum, 643 F.2d 68, 83 n. 17 (2d Cir.1981) (state officials who administer the federal disability program, in which the funding is 100% federal, function solely as *federal* agents, and hence do not act under color of *state* law).

(3) *The Growth in § 1983 Litigation.* Prior to Monroe, litigation under § 1983 was infrequent; one commentator reports that there were only 19 cases in the U.S.C.A. annotations under § 1983 in its first 65 years. See Note, 82 Harv.L.Rev. 1486, 1486 n. 4 (1969). However, many suits that might have been brought under § 1983 as interpreted by Monroe were treated instead as actions for a remedy (usually an injunction) implied directly under the Constitution.[4]

Since Monroe, § 1983 litigation has grown rapidly. According to oft-cited statistics gathered by the Administrative Office of the United States Courts, in 1961 there were 296 civil rights cases filed (the 1961 records do not indicate whether the plaintiff was a prisoner); in 1986 there were over 40,000: 20,842 filed by prisoners, and 20,128 filed by nonprisoners. These data, however, include many civil rights cases not filed under § 1983; more refined analysis reveals a less striking pattern of increase in § 1983 suits, particularly in nonprisoner cases. For a revealing empirical study of § 1983 litigation, see Eisenberg & Schwab, *The Reality of Constitutional Tort Litigation,* 72 Cornell L.Rev. 101 (1987).[5]

The variety of official activities subjected to suit under § 1983 is enormous, ranging from the question whether state officials denied a constitutional right by requiring someone to cut his hair, to matters of more profound significance, sometimes with far-reaching inquiries into areas previously untouched by the law, such as the constitutional rights of the mentally ill. One study showed that by far the largest single subject of actions by nonprisoner plaintiffs is alleged police misconduct, with employment-related suits a distant second. Eisenberg & Schwab, *supra,* at 151.

The general perception that constitutional tort actions are less likely to prove meritorious than civil litigation in general has been confirmed as to both prisoner and nonprisoner actions by Professors Eisenberg & Schwab, *supra,* at 136–48, although it is in the former class that the general lack of substance is most striking. Prisoners are also far less likely to have counsel, making the winnowing process especially difficult.

Overall, Justice Frankfurter's prediction that Monroe would open the floodgates of § 1983 litigation in federal court has proved correct (although the increase is attributable in part to the vast expansion in the scope of federal constitutional rights themselves). The desirability of this development is, of course, a subject of intense controversy. It has, however,

---

4. See, *e.g.,* General Oil v. Crain, p. 586, *supra;* Ex parte Young, p. 1173, *supra;* Iowa Des Moines Nat'l Bank v. Bennett, p. 585, *supra* (refund of taxes collected in violation of the Constitution); Ward v. Love County, p. 581, *supra* (same).

5. Based on a detailed review of one federal judicial district, this article concludes that (i) only 50% of the Administrative Office's "civil rights cases" are constitutional tort actions brought under § 1983 or the *Bivens* line of cases (p. 669); (ii) a good measure of the increase reflected in the Administrative Office's data is attributable to the rise of other kinds of actions, such as those under Title VII (pp. 662–65); (iii) from 1975–84, the number of nonprisoner civil rights cases outside the employment area increased by 94%, while the number of all other civil cases increased more rapidly, by 125% (p. 666); and (iv) though prisoner civil rights cases rose by nearly 200% between 1975 and 1984, from 6,606 to 18,856, when one adjusts for increases in prison population, the rate of increase was only 101%, compared to a 119% increase in all civil cases other than prisoner civil rights actions (p. 667).

Other useful empirical information is found in Eisenberg, *Section 1983: Doctrinal Foundations and an Empirical Study,* 67 Cornell L.Rev. 482 (1982); Turner, *When Prisoners Sue: A Study of Prisoner Section 1983 Suits in the Federal Courts,* 92 Harv.L.Rev. 610 (1979); Project, *Suing the Police in Federal Court,* 88 Yale L.J. 781 (1979).

frequently been noted by various Justices, at times with dismay.[6] Consider to what extent concerns about the burdens of § 1983 litigation on state and local governments and on the federal courts have (and should have) influenced (i) the doctrines discussed in this Note and the following Note, which give shape to § 1983; (ii) the interpretation of the Fourteenth Amendment in Parratt v. Taylor, p. 1259, *infra;* (iii) doctrines of official immunity discussed in Section 3, *infra;* and (iv) doctrines restricting federal court jurisdiction in civil rights cases, see Chapter X, *infra.* Are the concerns properly directed at § 1983 itself? At the interpretations given the substantive rights for which § 1983 provides a remedy? Are the concerns especially forceful in suits seeking damages rather than equitable relief? See Whitman, Paragraph (1), *supra,* at 10–11.

(4) *Violation of Federal Statutes.*

(a) *Maine v. Thiboutot.* Section 1983 extends to any deprivation of rights secured by the Constitution "and laws," without restriction, while its jurisdictional counterpart, 28 U.S.C. § 1343(3), is limited to rights secured by the Constitution or "by any Act of Congress *providing for equal rights.*" In Chapman v. Houston Welfare Rights Org., 441 U.S. 600 (1979), the Court interpreted § 1343(3) as not extending to a federal court suit challenging the deprivation of welfare benefits as unlawful under the federal Social Security Act.

The question whether § 1983 itself should also be interpreted as limited to actions claiming violations of "equal rights" statutes was resolved in Maine v. Thiboutot, 448 U.S. 1 (1980), a similar challenge to the denial of welfare benefits, but one filed in state court, to which § 1343(3) had no application.[7] The Supreme Court, per Brennan J., held that the complaint (which asserted no denial of equal rights) stated a good claim under § 1983. The Court reasoned that prior decisions had upheld provision of relief in such cases, and that there was no contrary legislative history sufficiently clear to warrant departure from the plain statutory language.[8]

Justice Powell (joined by Burger, C.J., and Rehnquist, J.) wrote a lengthy dissent, arguing that the legislative history showed an intention to encompass only rights secured by the Constitution and laws providing for

6. See, *e.g.,* Cleavinger v. Saxner, 474 U.S. 193, 210–11 (1985) (Rehnquist, J., dissenting); Maine v. Thiboutot, 448 U.S. 1, 23 (1980) (Powell, J., dissenting).

7. As noted in Paragraph (2), *supra,* since 1980 § 1343(3) has been superfluous even in federal court actions.

8. The Chapman case had held that the Supremacy Clause does not itself secure or provide a "right, privilege or immunity" within the meaning of § 1343(3); a contrary holding, the Court pointed out, would undercut the equal rights limitation. The question has arisen whether § 1983, with its broader language, extends to suits alleging that under the Supremacy Clause, state laws are preempted by federal regulation. (A similar question is whether § 1983 extends to suits alleging that state laws are preempted by the dormant Commerce Clause. See Note, 86 Mich.L.Rev.

157 (1987).) Most courts have held that § 1983 does not encompass these claims, as they pertain not to individual rights but to the distribution of power between federal and state governments. See, *e.g.,* Gould, Inc. v. Wisconsin Dept. of Industry, Labor & Human Relations, 750 F.2d 608 (7th Cir. 1984) (preemption by federal regulation), *aff'd on other grounds,* 475 U.S. 282 (1986); *cf.* Consolidated Freightways Corp. of Del. v. Kassel, 730 F.2d 1139, 1144 (8th Cir. 1984) (Commerce Clause). These holdings do not prevent a federal court from hearing preemption claims. However, a ruling that such claims fall outside § 1983 (i) bars reliance on 42 U.S.C. § 1988, which entitles a prevailing plaintiff in a § 1983 action to an award of attorneys fees, see Paragraph (6), *infra,* and (ii) may affect application of the Anti–Injunction Act, 28 U.S.C. § 2283, see p. 1324, note 7, *infra.*

equal rights. The original limitation on the coverage of statutory rights was, he argued, left out of a predecessor to § 1983 by accident in the process of recodifying the United States statutes (pp. 15–16). Justice Powell also criticized the Court for imposing upon state and local governments and officials "liability whenever a person believes he has been injured by the administration of *any* federal-state cooperative program * * *. * * * [L]iterally hundreds of cooperative regulatory and social welfare enactments may be affected" (p. 22). An appendix to his opinion suggested the potential reach of Thiboutot, by listing a large number of federal statutes that are administered in part by state and local officials, but that do not expressly provide for private enforcement.[9]

(b) *Pennhurst State School & Hosp. v. Halderman.* Subsequent decisions have limited the broadest implications of Thiboutot. In Pennhurst State School and Hosp. v. Halderman, 451 U.S. 1 (1981), a class action challenging conditions at a state institution for the mentally retarded, see p. 1195, *supra,* the court of appeals had upheld a sweeping injunctive order issued by the district court as an appropriate remedy for violation of the federal Developmentally Disabled Assistance and Bill of Rights Act. That Act provides federal grants for state programs serving the developmentally disabled. The Supreme Court reversed, holding that the particular provisions relied on below did not confer any private rights enforceable under § 1983. The case was remanded for consideration whether the state had violated other provisions in the Act, which impose conditions on the receipt of federal funds, and, if so, whether plaintiffs could obtain relief for those violations under § 1983. In dictum, however, the Court stated that the "typical remedy for state noncompliance with federally imposed conditions is not a private cause of action for noncompliance" but a cut-off of federal funds. Whether Thiboutot permitted relief under § 1983 would depend on whether the fund cut-off remedy expressly provided by the Act was exclusive—a question deemed "unclear" (p. 28).

(c) *Middlesex County Sewerage Auth. v. National Sea Clammers Ass'n.* The implication of Pennhurst's dictum—that some federal remedial schemes might be read to preclude additional remedies under § 1983— became the holding of Middlesex County Sewerage Auth. v. National Sea Clammers Ass'n, 453 U.S. 1 (1981). The case involved a § 1983 action for an injunction and damages brought by commercial fishermen against state and local governments and their officials. Plaintiffs alleged that defendants' discharge of sewage and pollutants violated the Federal Water Pollution Control Act (FWPCA) and the Marine Protection, Research, and Sanctuaries Act of 1972 (MPRSA). Both statutes provided what the Court termed "elaborate enforcement provisions," expressly authorizing suits by federal administrators to impose sanctions, suits by private persons to obtain judicial review of federal administrative decisions, and citizen suits against polluters for injunctive relief. (Injunctive relief under the two statutes' citizen suit provisions was unavailable in the actual case because the plaintiffs had not given the requisite 60–day notice to federal and state officials).

9. For the view that the historical record, though not unambiguous, favors the majority's interpretation, see Sunstein, *Section 1983 and the Private Enforcement of Federal Law,* 49 U.Chi.L.Rev. 394, 396– 411 (1982); for criticism of the majority, see Brown, *Whither Thiboutot? Section 1983, Private Enforcement, and the Damages Dilemma,* 33 De Paul L.Rev. 31, 36–40 (1983).

The Supreme Court ruled that the plaintiffs could not obtain remedies other than those expressly provided in the two regulatory statutes. The Court first rejected plaintiffs' argument that they were entitled to implied remedies under the two Acts: "it cannot be assumed that Congress intended to authorize implication of" additional remedies in suits by private citizens (p. 14). The Court then ruled that Congress intended, in providing these "quite comprehensive enforcement mechanisms," not only to foreclose implied private actions, but also "to supplant any remedy that otherwise would be available under § 1983" (pp. 20–21).[10] However, the majority denied the charge made by the dissenters that the decision placed on plaintiffs, in § 1983 actions based on rights created by Congress, the burden of demonstrating congressional intent to preserve the § 1983 remedy (p. 20 n. 31).[11]

For an application of Middlesex, see Wright v. City of Roanoke Redevelop. & Hous. Auth., 107 S.Ct. 766 (1987), a damage action under § 1983 by tenants of a federally-funded public housing project against the municipal housing authority. The tenants alleged that the charges for utility service violated a rent ceiling governing the project that was set by a federal statute and implementing regulations. The Court ruled that the suit could go forward: federal law created enforceable rights in the tenants, and HUD's powers to audit its contract with the public housing authority and to cut off funds were insufficient to indicate congressional intent to foreclose enforcement under § 1983: "§ 1983 provides a remedial cause of action unless the state actor demonstrates by express provision or other specific evidence from the statute itself that Congress intended to foreclose such private enforcement. 'We do not lightly conclude that Congress intended to preclude reliance on § 1983 as a remedy' for the deprivation of a federally secured right" (p. 771, quoting Smith v. Robinson, note 10, *supra*). The four dissenters expressed uncertainty about whether § 1983 permitted suit for violation of federal administrative regulations, but argued that in any event neither the statute nor the regulations conferred judicially enforceable rights.[12]

10. The Court has applied this reasoning to find that congressional programs can impliedly preclude relief under § 1983 even for constitutional violations. See Smith v. Robinson, 468 U.S. 992 (1984), holding that a handicapped child could not bypass the detailed and comprehensive administrative system established under the Education of the Handicapped Act by suing local school officials under § 1983 for an alleged denial of equal protection.

11. Both statutes in Middlesex contained savings clauses stating that the remedies provided by statute shall not "restrict any right which any persons (or class of persons) may have under any statute or common law to seek enforcement [of any standard or limitation] or to seek any other relief * * *." These provisions, the Court held, preserved only remedies for violations of other regulatory statutes or of state common law, not a remedy under § 1983 for a violation of the FWCPA or MPRSA itself. Alternatively, the Court ruled that the savings clauses related only

to the effect of the citizen suit provisions, and therefore did not bar a finding that the overall remedial schemes precluded relief under § 1983.

Justice Stevens, joined by Justice Blackmun, dissented, arguing that the plaintiffs' "right to proceed under § 1983 * * * could have been made more plain only had Congress substituted the citation '42 U.S.C. § 1983' for the words 'any statute' in the savings clauses" (p. 29).

12. Note that permitting a § 1983 action for violation of conditions governing the award of federal funds via a grant or contract may divert funds from the program itself to damage awards, while the threat of liability may deter state participation. There may also be special problems with judicial enforcement of these conditions, which are likely to be vague, pointless, or unduly complex—problems that can be alleviated if enforcement is left to the discretion of the federal administrators who dispense the funds. Finally, it is

(d) *The Implications of Thiboutot and Middlesex.* In its decision in Thiboutot, the Court did not consider the relationship between its construction of § 1983 and case law on whether to imply a private right of action under a federal statute that does not expressly provide one. See generally Chap. VII, Sec. 2, *supra.* Suppose that, in the absence of § 1983, no private remedy would be implied under a particular federal statute—as is generally the case under the recent implied right of action precedents. Did Thiboutot announce or imply the proposition that § 1983 is available to supply the missing remedy whenever the offender is a state official?

Did Middlesex (or the dictum in Pennhurst) subsequently suggest that the express private right of action under § 1983 for violation of an Act of Congress is preempted whenever a right of action would not have been inferred under the Act? [13] Doesn't Thiboutot (even after Middlesex) mean that there is a presumption that § 1983 provides a private remedy, in contrast to the implied right of action cases, in which the presumption appears to be quite the opposite? See Victorian v. Miller, 813 F.2d 718, 721 (5th Cir.1987) (en banc).

Recall the virtues and vices of implied private rights of action that make the federal courts front-line enforcers of federal statutes. On the one hand, private suits may help to deter violations of federal law, to compensate victims of federal violations, and to provide a federal forum for the enforcement of federal law. On the other hand, they may lead to overdeterrence, undercut congressional compromises about the desired level or means of enforcement, displace political control of policy decisions, and bypass the expertise of federal agencies as well as their ability to fashion a coordinated regulatory policy. Aren't the benefits and risks of private enforcement the same whether the plaintiff claims an express remedy under § 1983 or a judicially implied right of action? Does the mere invocation of § 1983 provide a satisfactory answer to the complicated question of regulatory policy?

argued that private enforcement exacerbates the tendency of these federal programs to undercut the political accountability of state and local governments. See Stewart, *Federalism and Rights,* 19 Ga.L. Rev. 917, 959 (1985).

On the other hand, if the only remedy under the statute is that of cutting off funding—one so drastic as almost never to be used—private enforcement may be particularly important.

Is any of this relevant to the interpretation of § 1983 as applied to these kinds of programs?

In Guardians Ass'n v. Civil Serv. Com'n, 463 U.S. 582 (1983), minority police officers sued a local government whose acceptance of federal funds rendered it subject to the anti-discrimination provisions of Title VI of the Civil Rights Act of 1964. A badly-fractured Court ruled, without a majority opinion, that the plaintiffs were entitled only to noncompensatory, injunctive relief, but not to the compensatory relief (including constructive seniority) that the district

court had awarded. The Justices divided on (i) whether in view of the express remedy of a funding cut-off, there should be a private right of action for Title VI violations, either as an implied remedy under Title VI or under § 1983; and (ii) if so, whether private plaintiffs could obtain retrospective, compensatory relief or only prospective injunctive relief, for a deprivation of rights created by a Spending Clause statute. These issues were intertwined with disagreements about whether a violation of Title VI could be found absent proof of intentional discrimination.

The Guardians case was not cited in Wright, *supra.*

13. Note that even if § 1983 were limited to instances in which a remedy was available directly under the regulatory statute, the applicability of § 1983 would have the important consequence of permitting a prevailing plaintiff to obtain legal fees under 42 U.S.C. § 1988. See Paragraph (6), *infra.*

Is a court capable of determining, on a case-by-case basis, whether the drawbacks of private enforcement actions in a particular regulatory setting argue for implied preemption of an otherwise presumptively available § 1983 remedy? Compare Sunstein, note 9, *supra*, at 418–38, attempting to provide a framework to guide courts in these cases, with Brown, note 9, *supra*, at 33, doubting the feasibility of such an enterprise, and arguing that lower courts have rendered "a crazy quilt of decisions in which one can find support for virtually any proposition about statutory claims under section 1983." (Is the lack of uniformity less troublesome when it goes not to the existence or scope of statutory duties governing primary conduct, but only to remedies for violations of those duties?)

Note, finally, how far Thiboutot (even as narrowed) takes § 1983 from its historical origins, in the Civil Rights Act of 1871, as a remedy for abuses directed at blacks (and their white supporters) in the South during Reconstruction. Has the added breadth of § 1983 perhaps led to a loss of depth in its protection against invidious discrimination? Consider, for example, whether it is possible, had the statute remained more closely limited to its historical context, that the Supreme Court might have held that § 1983 *was* intended to make individuals fully liable without any defense of official immunity, and to make local and state governments fully liable on a respondeat superior theory without any possible defense of governmental immunity. See *Further Note on 42 U.S.C. § 1983: Individual Officers, Local Governments, and States as Defendants,* pp. 1249–58, *infra.* See generally Eisenberg, note 5, *supra*, at 484–87.

(5) *Remedial and Procedural Doctrines in § 1983 Actions.* Section 1983 provides a barebones cause of action, without specifying such important matters as the measure of damages, the immunities of official defendants, and the statute of limitations. From what sources should the courts fashion rules of decision to govern issues like these?

One approach, which the Court has followed in fashioning doctrines governing official immunities and the measure of damages in § 1983 actions, is to establish a federal common law rule of decision that is designed to promote the statutory purposes.[14] A second approach—borrowing analogous rules of decisions of the applicable state (at least so long as those rules do not interfere with federal purposes)—has been followed in deciding whether a § 1983 action survives if the plaintiff dies during the lawsuit and his executor is substituted, see Robertson v. Wegmann, 436 U.S. 584 (1978), and in selecting the appropriate statute of limitations for § 1983 actions, see Board of Regents v. Tomanio, 446 U.S. 478 (1980); Wilson v. Garcia, 471 U.S. 261 (1985).[15] A third possible approach, which the Court has not taken, is to borrow analogous doctrines from other federal civil rights statutes. See, *e.g.,* Smith v. Wade, note 14, *supra*, at 90–91 n. 17 (Rehnquist, J., dissenting) (advocating this approach).

---

14. See, *e.g.,* Memphis Community School Dist. v. Stachura, 477 U.S. 299 (1986) (rules governing the measure of compensatory damages); Smith v. Wade, 461 U.S. 30 (1983) (punitive damages may be awarded on a showing of recklessness by an official defendant); Sec. 3, *infra* (on official immunity doctrines).

15. These last three decisions found that language now codified in 42 U.S.C. § 1988 instructed the courts to resort to state law. For discussion of the relevance, or arguable irrelevance, of § 1988, see p. 954 note 2, *supra.*

Is the Court's decision to follow quite different approaches as to different issues intelligible? For more detailed discussion of these questions, see Chap. VII, Sec. 2, *supra*.

(6) *Attorney's Fees.* In the Civil Rights Attorney's Fees Awards Act of 1976, codified in 42 U.S.C. § 1988, Congress provided that a court "in its discretion, may allow the prevailing party, other than the United States, a reasonable attorney's fee as part of the costs." This provision is applicable to § 1983 actions seeking vindication of statutory as well as constitutional rights, and applies in state as well as federal courts. Maine v. Thiboutot, 448 U.S. 1, 8–11 (1980). And despite the statutory language, it is established that (i) awards to plaintiffs who prevail (by settlement as well as by judgment, Maher v. Gagne, 448 U.S. 122 (1980)) are required absent special circumstances—a very narrow category perhaps limited to *pro se* plaintiffs;[16] and (ii) defendants may not automatically recover whenever they prevail, but only when the plaintiff's action was frivolous or vexatious, see Hughes v. Rowe, 449 U.S. 5 (1980) (per curiam).

Plaintiffs clearly have an incentive to try to fit a claim for relief under § 1983 in order to obtain fees, and the essentially one-way shifting of fees presumably has increased the number of § 1983 actions filed. See Rowe, *Predicting the Effects of Attorney Fee Shifting,* 47 Law & Contemp.Prob. 139, 147 (1984); but *cf.* Eisenberg and Schwab, Paragraph (3), *supra,* at 149–50. Is the subsidy justified by the importance of the rights asserted in § 1983 actions? By the presumed impecuniousness of many plaintiffs? By the fact that relief in § 1983 suits often provides benefits to non-parties? See Miller and Percival, *The Role of Attorney Fee Shifting in Public Interest Litigation,* 47 Law & Contemp.Prob. 233 (1984). Or does it merely exacerbate problems associated with the increase in § 1983 litigation?

Section 1988 has generated considerable litigation over circumstances in which fees should be awarded and the calculation of particular awards.[17] For a survey of decisional law under § 1988 and other statutes providing for attorney's fees, see Derfner & Wolf, Court Awarded Attorney Fees (1986).

(7) *Other Federal Civil Rights Statutes.* For surveys of other federal civil rights statutes, which often overlap with § 1983, see, *e.g.,* Eisenberg, Federal Civil Rights Legislation 487–1134 (2d ed. 1987); Gunther, Constitutional Law 855–971 (11th ed. 1985).

16. See Cochran, *Section 1983 Attorney Fee Awards in the Fifth Circuit,* 15 Tex. Tech.L.Rev. 1, 19–20 (1984).

17. The questions raised include: (i) the method by which fees should be calculated, see, *e.g.,* Blum v. Stenson, 465 U.S. 886 (1984); Hensley v. Eckerhart, 461 U.S. 424 (1983); (ii) whether an award of fees is unreasonable if it exceeds the amount of damages obtained, see City of Riverside v. Rivera, 477 U.S. 561 (1986) (approving such an award, 5–4, with no majority opinion); (iii) whether and how to apportion the fee when a lawyer's work on a § 1983 action is commingled with work on related causes of action as to which fees are not available, see, *e.g.,* Hensley v. Eckerhart, *supra,* at 434–37; (iv) whether fees can be recovered for time spent in related state administrative proceedings prior to a § 1983 action, see Webb v. Board of Educ., 471 U.S. 234 (1985) (disallowing such an award where no part of the work advanced the § 1983 litigation in court); (v) what constitutes "prevailing" for purposes of a fee award, *see* Hewitt v. Helms, 107 S.Ct. 2672 (1987); and (vi) whether plaintiff's acceptance of a settlement offer that conditions the provision of substantial benefits to the plaintiff on the waiver by plaintiff's counsel of statutory attorney's fees can be enforced to bar a claim for fees, see Evans v. Jeff D., 475 U.S. 717 (1986) (6–3) (enforcing such an agreement).

(8) *Bibliography.* There is a large literature on § 1983. Among the most helpful sources are Eisenberg, Paragraph (7), *supra;* Nahmod, Civil Rights and Liberties Litigation (2d ed. 1986); Schwartz & Kirklin, Section 1983 Litigation: Claims, Defenses, and Fees (1986); Eisenberg, note 5, *supra;* Whitman, Paragraph (1), *supra;* Zagrans, Paragraph (1), *supra;* Developments Note, 90 Harv.L.Rev. 1133 (1977).

(9) *Further Discussion of § 1983.* For discussion of other questions that arise in § 1983 actions, see, in addition to the material in the remainder of this Chapter, Chap. X, *infra,* and Chap. XII, pp. 1615–52, *infra.*

FURTHER NOTE ON 42 U.S.C. § 1983: INDIVIDUAL OFFICERS, LOCAL GOVERNMENTS, AND STATES AS DEFENDANTS

(1) *Individual Officers as Defendants: Personal Capacity Suits.* The great preponderance of § 1983 actions name individual officers as defendants. When damages are sought, the officer is ordinarily sued in his "personal" or "individual" capacity, which means that any judgment will be paid out of his own funds, rather than by the government that employs him. Similarly, in a personal capacity action, attorney's fees can be awarded only against the officer himself, not against the government. Kentucky v. Graham, 473 U.S. 159 (1985). And in such an action, the Eleventh Amendment is simply inapplicable, since the relief does not directly affect the state.

Ever since Tenney v. Brandhove, 341 U.S. 367 (1951), however, it has been clear that an official sued under § 1983 in his personal capacity may avail himself of immunity doctrines shielding him in many cases from damages liability. The Court has given extensive attention to the immunity doctrines applicable in § 1983 damage actions. These doctrines are discussed in detail in Section 3, *infra,* and for present purposes a summary of their broadest outlines will suffice. Most executive officials have a qualified immunity in § 1983 actions, which shields them from liability if their conduct, though unlawful, did not violate "clearly established statutory or constitutional rights of which a reasonable person would have knowledge." Harlow v. Fitzgerald, 457 U.S. 800, 812 (1982). But legislators, judges, and prosecutors have an absolute immunity from liability for conduct undertaken within their respective capacities.

(2) *Individual Officers as Defendants: Official Capacity Suits.* Some damage actions under § 1983 are filed against an officer in his "official" capacity. The designation of the individual as a defendant is a bit of a misnomer, as in an official capacity suit the plaintiff "must look to the government entity itself" as the source of any award, and that entity is the "real party in interest." Kentucky v. Graham, 473 U.S. 159, 166 (1985). Even though the government is not nominally the defendant, it can be ordered to pay damages and attorney's fees, provided that it had adequate notice and opportunity to defend. Brandon v. Holt, 469 U.S. 464 (1985). But because it will in fact be paid from the government treasury, a damage award in an official capacity suit is appropriate only in accordance with the rules about liability, immunity, and damages described in Paragraphs (4)–(6), (8), *infra,* governing actions against the government as such; the same appears to be true of awards of attorney's fees that are to be paid with

government funds. See Kentucky v. Graham, *supra*, at 167–68; note 6, *infra*.

When *equitable relief* is sought, the defendant official is ordinarily named in his official capacity. See, *e.g.*, Hutto v. Finney, 437 U.S. 678, 693 (1978); ACLU of Mississippi v. Finch, 638 F.2d 1336, 1338–42 (5th Cir.1981). Even in a suit thus captioned, the Eleventh Amendment interposes no bar, at least if the relief is deemed prospective in character. See pp. 1182–95, *supra*. (Don't be confused by the fact that even in an official capacity suit, the authority-stripping rationale of Ex parte Young (p. 1173, *supra*) applies, so that for purposes of the Eleventh Amendment the defendant is treated as stripped of his official character and subject, like any private tortfeasor, to an injunction against continuing harm).[1]

(3) *The Distinction Between Personal and Official Capacity Suits.* In Kentucky v. Graham, Paragraph (2), *supra*, the Supreme Court observed that the distinction between personal and official capacity suits "continues to confuse lawyers and confound lower courts." 473 U.S. at 165. In the case of equitable relief, it should make no difference whether the suit is labelled as one against the officer personally or against him in his official capacity.[2]

Insofar as plaintiff seeks damages, on the other hand, it is of some importance to know whether recovery is sought from the officer, the government entity, or both. The same is true when plaintiff seeks attorney's fees; since "fee liability runs with merits liability," Kentucky v. Graham, *supra*, at 168, the government is not liable for attorney's fees in a damage action unless the plaintiff has prevailed against it, and presumably an individual is not liable for fees in a suit against him in his official capacity. See Bender v. Williamsport Area School Dist., 475 U.S. 534, 543

---

1. Especially given the theory of Young, it is not clear that a suit seeking prospective relief against an officer "in his personal capacity" is defective. Surely any defect is sufficiently technical as to be remediable by amendment.

The label "personal" or "official" may have some practical importance in actions seeking equitable relief in which the named official ceases to hold office. Rule 25(d) of the Federal Rules of Civil Procedure and Rule 43(c)(1) of the Federal Rules of Appellate Procedure provide, in suits filed against an officer in his official capacity, for automatic substitution of his successor in office. (The 1961 Advisory Committee Note accompanying Rule 25(d) contemplated that suits for injunctive relief would be "official capacity" suits.) However, the plaintiff, in order to establish a right to equitable relief, must show continuation by the successor of the challenged policy or practice. See, *e.g.*, Spomer v. Littleton, 414 U.S. 514 (1974); Mayor v. Educational Equality League, 415 U.S. 605, 622–23 (1974).

2. Dictum in one footnote in Kentucky v. Graham states that "[t]here is no longer a need to bring official-capacity actions against local government officials, for un-

der Monell [v. Department of Social Services, 436 U.S. 658 (1978), Paragraph (4), *infra*, which established that local governments may be liable for violations of federal law pursuant to the local government's policy or custom,] local government units can be sued directly for damages and injunctive or declaratory relief" (p. 167 n. 14). Suppose, however, that a single police officer persistently harasses a particular citizen. Shouldn't the citizen be permitted to obtain an injunction if he can establish standing and his entitlement to equitable relief, even if the city could not itself be enjoined because the officer was not acting in accordance with city policy or custom? Indeed, doesn't the whole history of officers' suits support provision of injunctive relief against an official tortfeasor as if he were a private party? See pp. 1092–95, 1114–16, *supra*. Surely the Court's expansion in Monell of local government liability should not be understood to curtail the scope of available relief in suits against officers. In the example posed, then, isn't there still a need to bring official capacity actions against local government officials? Or would the Court hold that the suit should be filed against the officer personally?

n. 6 (1986) (by implication); but see Pulliam v. Allen, 466 U.S. 522 (1984), p. 1305, *infra* (state judge against whom declaratory and injunctive relief is awarded under § 1983 is also personally liable for attorney's fees).

Wouldn't it make sense, instead of using the somewhat elusive labels of official and personal capacity, simply to require the plaintiff to set forth in the complaint, or soon thereafter, the particular person or entity from which monetary relief or fees is sought? Naming the government rather than the official as the nominal defendant affects the plaintiff's ability to recover only when the plaintiff is seeking prospective relief against conduct of a state government; here, to avoid dismissal under the Eleventh Amendment, the plaintiff must name the official. But when monetary relief is sought from the government treasury, the plaintiff will have to establish that the government is liable under § 1983, and that the Eleventh Amendment poses no barrier to obtaining such relief in federal court—whether the nominal defendant is the government or an officer sued in his official capacity. So long as all defendants have fair notice, why should the caption of the complaint have significance?

(4) *Local Governments as Defendants: The Monell Decision.* Between 1961 and 1978 the Court reaffirmed and extended the subsidiary holding of Monroe v. Pape that municipalities are not "persons" within the meaning of § 1983. Thus, Moor v. Alameda County, 411 U.S. 693 (1973), refused to hold a county liable for damages under § 1983 even though the county had no immunity under state law, while City of Kenosha v. Bruno, 412 U.S. 507 (1973), held that municipalities could not be sued as such for equitable relief under § 1983.[3]

In Monell v. Department of Social Services, 436 U.S. 658 (1978), the Supreme Court shifted course, holding that Monroe v. Pape had misread the legislative history of § 1983, and that Congress did intend to include local governments among the "persons" it rendered liable. In this case, a class of female employees sued municipal agencies for back pay and injunctive relief, challenging defendants' policy of requiring pregnant employees to take unpaid leaves of absence. Reversing the lower courts, the Supreme Court, with Justice Brennan writing, ruled that cities and counties may be sued directly under § 1983 for damages or for declaratory and injunctive relief "where * * * the action that is alleged to be unconstitutional implements or executes a policy statement, ordinance, regulation or decision officially adopted and promulgated by that body's officers. Moreover * * * local governments * * * may be sued for constitutional deprivations visited pursuant to governmental 'custom' even though such a custom has not received formal approval through the body's official decisionmaking channels" (pp. 690–91).

The opinion's lengthy reexamination of the legislative history of the Civil Rights Act of 1871 led the Court to conclude that Monroe v. Pape had misinterpreted the import of the 42d Congress's rejection of the so-called Sherman Amendment. That amendment would have made municipalities liable not simply for violations of federal rights by municipal officials, but also for certain wrongful acts of *private citizens* within the municipality.

---

3. See also Aldinger v. Howard, 427 U.S. 1 (1976), holding that an action against a county under *state* law could not be joined to a § 1983 action against county officials on a theory of pendent jurisdiction. The Court reasoned that upholding pendent jurisdiction would violate Congress's intent not to make governmental bodies answerable in federal court under § 1983 and 28 U.S.C. § 1343(3).

In the view of the Monell Court, the rejection of that amendment could not justify an inference that Congress sought to exclude municipal liability for conduct of *officials*. The Court found support for municipal liability in the legislative debates, and in the general understanding in 1871 that the term "person" included municipal corporations.

The Court clearly stated, albeit in dictum, that "a municipality cannot be held liable *solely* because it employs a tortfeasor—or, in other words, a municipality cannot be held liable under § 1983 on a *respondeat superior* theory" (p. 691). The language of the statute—in particular, "[a]ny person who * * * shall subject, or causes to be subjected," any person to the deprivation of federal rights—"cannot be easily read to impose liability vicariously on governing bodies solely on the basis of the existence of an employer-employee relationship" (pp. 691–92). The Court viewed the primary rationales for *respondeat superior* liability—loss-spreading and reduction of harm—as too close to the justifications for the Sherman Amendment to be the predicate for municipal liability. Thus, "it is [only] when execution of a government's policy or custom, whether made by its lawmakers or by those whose edicts or acts may fairly be said to represent official policy, inflicts the injury that the government as an entity is responsible under § 1983" (p. 694).[4]

Justice Stevens concurred in part, refusing to join the Court's dictum rejecting *respondeat superior* liability. He later expressed his views on this question in a lone dissent in Oklahoma City v. Tuttle, 471 U.S. 808 (1985). Section 1983 was enacted, he argued, against a recognized background of *respondeat superior* liability in tort suits in general and specifically in tort suits against municipal corporations. The debate over the Sherman Amendment showed that Congress contemplated making municipalities more broadly (rather than more narrowly) liable than were private parties in 1871. Because the Fourteenth Amendment regulates only state action, an individual official can be liable under § 1983 only by virtue of his relationship to his government employer; that same relationship, Justice Stevens argued, justifies the application of normal principles of *respondeat superior*. He suggested that the policy considerations supporting the application of *respondeat superior* in common law tort suits against municipal corporations—compensation of victims, deterrence of misconduct, and fairness to individual officers "performing difficult and dangerous work"—also apply in constitutional tort actions (p. 844). The fear that broadened liability would bankrupt municipalities, though legitimate, was in Justice Stevens' view a matter primarily for Congress to consider, and in any event related to the question of damages rather than to the question of which classes of defendants could be held liable.[5]

(5) *The Scope of Municipal Damage Liability After Monell.* Even prior to Monell, local government entities could be effectively bound in injunc-

4. Both the Court's opinion and Justice Powell's concurrence contain elaborate explanations why, notwithstanding *stare decisis*, it was thought appropriate to overrule Monroe v. Pape on this issue.

Justice Rehnquist, joined by Chief Justice Burger, dissented.

5. For discussion of municipal liability roughly contemporaneous with Monell, see Blum, *From Monroe to Monell: Defining the Scope of Municipal Liability in Federal Courts*, 51 Temple L.J. 409 (1978); Levin, *The Section 1983 Municipal Immunity Doctrine*, 65 Geo.L.J. 1483 (1977); Schnapper, *Civil Rights Litigation After Monell*, 79 Colum.L.Rev. 213 (1979); Comment, 46 U.Chi.L.Rev. 935 (1979); Note, 79 Colum.L. Rev. 304 (1979).

tive or declaratory proceedings through the technique of suing their officials.[6] The important consequence of Monell is, therefore, to render city,
county, and school board treasuries liable in damage actions for violations
of constitutional and statutory rights by their officials—but only when the
violation is pursuant to government policy or custom. Note that Monell
thus adopts the same line that Justice Frankfurter argued should govern
the whole of § 1983 liability—a view the Court rejected in Monroe v. Pape.
Is that line more appropriately invoked in measuring local government
liability than in measuring the liability of individual officers? If not, does
it argue for adoption of Frankfurter's position more generally, or for
adoption of broad *respondeat superior* liability for local governments, as
Justice Stevens advocated?

Note that the imposition of governmental damage liability *always*
creates vicarious liability, in the sense that in the end it is the taxpayers
who foot the bill.[7] Does this fact call for hesitation in holding local
governments liable? One aspect of this question was at issue in Owen v.
City of Independence, 445 U.S. 622, 638 (1980). There, the Court held, 5–4,
that a municipality sued under Monell for violations committed by its
officials does not have a qualified immunity from damages liability under
§ 1983, even if it can show that the officials would themselves be entitled
to such an immunity in a § 1983 action against them personally.[8] Justice
Brennan's opinion for the Court argued that officers' immunity was already
deeply embedded in the common law when § 1983 was passed, so that the
42d Congress should be deemed to have enacted § 1983 in contemplation of
such a defense; by contrast, there existed at the time no common-law
tradition of immunity in actions against municipalities. Moreover, allowing the municipality to avail itself of the immunity of its officials would
interfere with both the compensatory and the deterrent purposes of § 1983.
The Court concluded by asserting that its holding, together with its previous decisions, "properly allocates [the costs of federal violations] among the
three principals in the scenario of the § 1983 cause of action: the victim of
the constitutional deprivation; the officer whose conduct caused the injury;
and the public, as represented by the municipal entity. The innocent
individual who is harmed by an abuse of governmental authority is assured
that he will be compensated for his injury. The offending official, so long
as he conducts himself in good faith, may go about his business secure in
the knowledge that a qualified immunity will protect him from personal
liability for damages that are more appropriately chargeable to the popu-
lace as a whole. And the public will be forced to bear only the costs of

6. In Hutto v. Finney, p. 1192, *supra*, a
suit for injunctive relief nominally against
individual officers in their official capacities, the Court upheld an award of attorney's fees to be paid by the state government. Should a state or local
government's liability for fees in a suit for
equitable relief depend upon a showing
that the action that was enjoined was itself
part of governmental policy or custom—
the showing that is necessary to establish
the liability of the government as such
under § 1983? In most cases, won't a
showing that is adequate for the award of
injunctive relief also establish governmental custom or policy? But *cf.* note 2, *supra*.

7. Compare the issue whether high city
officials may be sued for invasions of constitutional rights by their subordinates on
the theory that they encouraged (or failed
to prevent) such invasions. This theory
does not present a question of vicarious
liability or "respondeat superior". For an
example of such a suit, see Rizzo v. Goode,
423 U.S. 362 (1976).

8. *Cf.* the analogous holdings under the
Federal Tort Claims Act, p. 1147, note 11,
supra, that the United States is liable in
tort even when the misbehaving officer
would have an immunity defense.

injury inflicted by the 'execution of a government's policy or custom, whether made by its lawmakers or by those whose edicts or acts may fairly be said to represent official policy' [citing Monell]" (p. 657).[9]

Justice Powell's dissent, which was joined by Chief Justice Burger and Justices Stewart and Rehnquist, objected to the imposition of municipal liability in damages in a case in which government officials had violated "a constitutional right that was unknown when the events in this case occurred." He repeatedly characterized the effect of the case as the imposition of "strict liability" on municipalities: "This strict liability approach inexplicably departs from this Court's prior decisions under § 1983 and runs counter to the concerns of the 42d Congress when it enacted the statute.[10] The Court's ruling also ignores the vast weight of common-law precedent as well as the current state law of municipal immunity" (p. 658).[11] Justice Powell also disputed the Court's assertion that municipal liability will not unduly inhibit officials in their decision-making.

Is Justice Brennan's reasoning in Owen consistent with his rejection of *respondeat superior* liability in Monell?[12] Do you agree with the Court that there is nothing unfair about imposing liability on taxpayers for official conduct where there was no reason to believe that the conduct violated constitutional norms? *Cf.* City of Newport v. Fact Concerts, Inc., 453 U.S. 247, 258–71 (1981), where the Court held that municipalities may not be held liable under § 1983 for punitive damages. The opinion stressed that the common law did not subject municipalities to punitive damage awards, but also expressed the view that such an award would be a windfall to the plaintiff, while unfairly punishing "blameless or unknowing taxpayers" (p. 267).

(6) *The Meaning of "Policy" or "Custom".* The Supreme Court has discussed the meaning of Monell's "custom or policy" standard in three subsequent cases.

Oklahoma City v. Tuttle, 471 U.S. 808 (1985), was a § 1983 action alleging unconstitutional use of excessive force by a police officer. The jury's $1.5 million verdict against the city was overturned by the Supreme Court. Seven Justices found fault with the jury charge, which stated that

---

9. Owen did not present for decision the question whether local governments may be liable for acts by officials who are shielded by an absolute (rather than merely a qualified) immunity. The major thrust of the opinion, however, is that all individual immunity defenses are irrelevant to suits against governmental entities, and the cases distinguished include holdings that an official is absolutely immune.

10. [Ed.] Is it helpful to characterize the liability created by Owen as "strict" liability? Consider this question in connection with the evolving standards for municipal liability suggested by various Justices in the cases in Paragraph (6), *infra,* and the scienter requirements that must be met to show the underlying constitutional violations, see pp. 1269–70, *infra.*

11. On this point, Justice Brennan had argued that the common-law tort immuni-

ty of a municipality in connection with its "governmental" functions was irrelevant, on the ground that § 1983, by making municipalities liable at all, automatically abrogated doctrines that derive from or are allied to sovereign immunity. Justice Brennan dealt with the common-law immunity of municipalities in connection with their "discretionary" functions by declaring that a "municipality has no 'discretion' to violate the Federal Constitution; its dictates are absolute and imperative" (p. 649).

12. In Owen, Justice Brennan tried to reconcile the holdings: "when it is the local government itself that is responsible for the constitutional deprivation • • • it is perfectly reasonable to distribute the loss to the public as a cost of the administration of government" (p. 655 n. 39).

"a single, unusually excessive use of force may be sufficiently out of the ordinary to warrant an inference that it was attributable to inadequate training or supervision amounting to 'deliberate indifference' or 'gross negligence' on the part of the officials in charge" (p. 813). Justice Rehnquist, writing for a four-Justice plurality, expressed doubt that inadequate training could constitute a "policy" in the absence of proof that decisionmakers "deliberately chose a training program which would prove inadequate" (p. 823). He also doubted that a policy that (unlike the one in Monell) was not *itself* unconstitutional could be the basis for liability;[13] at a minimum, plaintiff would need to show an "affirmative link" between such a policy and the violation (p. 823). Justice Brennan (joined by Justices Marshall and Blackmun), concurred in part and concurred in the judgment. He agreed that the "single incident" instruction was erroneous, but disagreed with the majority's doubts that inadequate training could be an adequate basis for municipal liability. In his view, § 1983 requires proof only that an action undertaken in accordance with municipal policy or custom "subjected" or "caused [plaintiff] to be subjected" to a deprivation of a constitutional right (p. 828).[14]

In the second case, Pembaur v. City of Cincinnati, 475 U.S. 469 (1986), a physician, alleging that the county prosecutor had instructed police to make an unconstitutional entry into his clinic, sued the county under § 1983. The Supreme Court ruled that a single decision of a high official like the county prosecutor, who had authority under state law to decide whether the officers should enter and whose decision " 'may fairly be said to represent official policy,' " was an adequate basis for imposing governmental liability under § 1983 (p. 480, quoting Monell).[15] Justice Powell, joined by Chief Justice Burger and Justice Rehnquist, dissented. He accused the Court of imposing what Monell rejected—*respondeat superior* liability—at least with regard to employees having final authority to make policy (p. 499). Because the prosecutor's *ad hoc* decision did not establish a "rule of general applicability," and was made "without time for thoughtful consideration or consultation," it did not, in Justice Powell's view, establish a policy within the meaning of Monell (pp. 499–501).

In a third decision, City of St. Louis v. Praprotnik, 108 S.Ct. 915 (1988), the Court confronted the question of which officials' decisions can render a

13. In City of St. Louis v. Praprotnik, 108 S.Ct. 915 (1988), pp. 1255–56, *infra*, the plurality of four suggested in dictum that municipal liability must rest on the existence of an unconstitutional municipal policy. Justice Brennan, concurring in the judgment, took issue with that suggestion; he urged, as he had in Tuttle, that liability can be predicated on a policy that, although not unconstitutional in itself, gives rise to constitutional deprivations.

Cf. Polk County v. Dodson, 454 U.S. 312, 325–26 (1981). There, the plaintiff alleged that a public defender failed to provide effective assistance of counsel on appeal. The Court ruled that the county could not be held liable, because any policy its public defenders had of not pursuing frivolous appeals was not unconstitutional, and plaintiff failed to allege that the violation

was caused by a constitutionally forbidden policy. See also Snyder, *The Final Authority Analysis: A Unified Approach to Municipal Liability Under Section 1983*, 1986 Wis.L.Rev. 633, 675 n. 252.

14. Justice Stevens dissented, arguing that recovery was justified on a *respondeat superior* theory. See Paragraph (4), *supra.* Justice Powell did not participate.

15. Justice White's concurring opinion in Pembaur stressed that the entry was not illegal under federal or state law at the time it was made; he doubted that a high official's decision to effect an arrest in violation of prevailing federal or state law would constitute official policy. Compare Owen v. City of Independence, Paragraph (5), *supra.*

municipality liable under § 1983. There a municipal employee brought suit contending that the Director of Urban Design (UD) (to whom plaintiff reported) in the St. Louis Community Development Agency (CDA), and CDA's Director, had violated the First Amendment by discharging plaintiff in retaliation for earlier appeals to the city's Civil Service Commission. The Supreme Court ruled, 7–1, that the city could not be held liable for these acts. Justice O'Connor's plurality opinion (joined by Chief Justice Rehnquist and Justices White and Scalia) affirmed that state law determines who is a policymaking official; found that under state and local regulations, only the mayor and aldermen of St. Louis, and the Civil Service Commission, had policymaking authority over personnel decisions; and then found that no policymaker had adopted an unconstitutional municipal policy authorizing retaliatory discharges. The mere fact that policymakers had delegated to the Directors of UD and of CDA discretion to act—even if these subordinates' decisions were not in turn given de novo review by the policymakers—did not give the subordinate officials policymaking authority so as to make the municipality liable for their conduct.

Justice Brennan (joined by Justices Marshall and Blackmun) concurred in the judgment, agreeing that the record showed that the two subordinate officials lacked final authority to establish city policy. He questioned, however, the plurality's exclusive reliance on state statutory law in determining who the policymakers were. Instead, he argued that a factfinder must determine where policymaking authority actually resides, and not merely in whom the law formally purports to vest it. Justice Brennan disagreed in particular with the plurality's view that an official whose decisions are formally subject to review by others cannot be deemed a policymaker when, because that review is never exercised, the official effectively makes final policy.[16]

These decisions have left open many questions about the meaning of Monell, and the case law in the lower courts is extensive, particularly in police misconduct cases. Consider, for example, whether a victim of a policeman's use of excessive force establishes a governmental policy or custom of using excessive force by showing that policymaking officials (i) failed to implement a training program for police officers, (ii) provided a program that is inadequate, or (iii) did not discipline officers who committed similar acts in the past? In Kibbe v. City of Springfield, 777 F.2d 801 (1st Cir.1985), the court of appeals brushed aside the doubts of the plurality in Tuttle, and held that gross negligence in police training could constitute a municipal "policy" or "custom." The Supreme Court granted certiorari, but later dismissed the writ as improvidently granted. 107 S.Ct. 1114 (1987). Justice O'Connor, joined by Chief Justice Rehnquist, Justice White, and Justice Powell, dissented from that decision, and on the merits found the causal link between the inadequate training and the injury too attenuated to permit liability to be imposed absent proof of "reckless disregard for or deliberate indifference to the rights of persons within the city's domain" (p. 1121).

The dissenters in Kibbe seemed to assume that the scienter of the *city* was at issue. If § 1983 does not generally require proof of scienter beyond that needed to establish the predicate constitutional violation, see p. 1269,

---

16. Justice Stevens dissented, arguing that the city should be held liable for decisions made by "high officials" such as an agency head. Justice Kennedy did not participate.

infra, why should such proof be required in the case of municipal liability? Consider, also, whether the concept of governmental scienter is coherent. See Whitman, *Government Responsibility for Constitutional Torts,* 85 Mich. L.Rev. 225 (1986). Is the government's scienter the same as the scienter of one or more policymaking officials? How might a plaintiff establish that particular officials had the requisite scienter? By showing that the officials were aware of past incidents of similar misconduct? How many? How similar must they be? What kind of evidence can the officials offer to rebut the claim that such a policy or custom exists?

An equally difficult problem is raised in considering how a court determines that a policymaker's practice or custom, not itself unconstitutional, caused a low level official's constitutional violation. Are the dissenters in Kibbe correct in suggesting that greater culpability of high officials helps to establish the necessary causation?

Most fundamentally, note that the Justices seem to be trying to hold local governments liable only when the conduct in question was "really" that of the local government rather than that of the employee. See, *e.g.,* Pembaur, *supra,* at 479–80 (Brennan, J., joined by five other Justices); Tuttle, *supra,* 471 U.S. at 821 (Rehnquist, J, joined by three other Justices.). Doesn't the whole history of the sovereign immunity of the United States, and of the Eleventh Amendment, cast doubt on the intelligibility of such a distinction? [17]

With the liability of local governments under § 1983, contrast the liability of the federal government under the Federal Tort Claims Act. The United States is generally liable on a simple *respondeat superior* theory for the common law torts of its employees, 28 U.S.C. § 1346(b); there is an exception, however, for acts undertaken with "due care, in the execution of a statute or regulation, whether or not * * * valid," *id.* § 2680(a). Is there some reason to believe that opposing views of governmental liability are appropriate at the local and federal levels?

(7) *Implied Remedies Against Local Governments.* Prior to Monell, a number of lower courts, relying on the authority of the Bivens case, had implied a damage remedy directly under the Constitution against municipalities or other local governments for violations of constitutional rights by individual officials.[18] See Note, 89 Harv.L.Rev. 922 (1976). Were such decisions justifiable against the background of Monroe v. Pape's holding that Congress, in enacting § 1983, had not imposed any liability upon local governments? Is governmental liability in any event so sensitive a political matter as to call into question the wisdom of its imposition by federal judges rather than by Congress? Is it relevant to the latter question that the Constitution itself, in the Eleventh Amendment, has been interpreted to deny federal courts the authority to impose damage liability on one form of governmental entity, the state? Or does the fact that local governments are treated no differently from individual defendants under the Eleventh

---

17. For discussion of recent decisional law under Monell, see, *e.g.,* Mead, *42 U.S.C. § 1983 Municipal Liability: The Monell Sketch Becomes A Distorted Picture,* 65 N.C.L.Rev. 517 (1987); Oliver, *Municipal Liability for Police Misconduct under 42 U.S.C. § 1983 after City of Oklahoma City v. Tuttle,* 64 Wash.U.L.Rev. 151 (1986); Snyder, note 13, *supra.*

18. The Supreme Court granted certiorari in a case raising this issue, but disposed of the case on other grounds. See Mt. Healthy City Sch. Dist. Bd. of Educ. v. Doyle, 429 U.S. 274 (1977).

Amendment undercut any suggestion that the Amendment itself argues against judicial authority to imply a remedy against local governments? [19]

After Monell, a plaintiff would need to seek an implied damage remedy directly under the Fourteenth Amendment against a city or county only in a "pure" *respondeat superior* case. The lower courts facing this issue since Monell have generally thought implication of a remedy in such a case to be inappropriate in view of the congressional judgment in § 1983 not to provide an express remedy. See Zagrans, *"Under Color of" What Law: A Reconstructed Model of Section 1983 Liability,* 71 Va.L.Rev. 499, 591 n. 472 (1985). Professor Davis has criticized these decisions: he argues that, just as Carlson v. Green, p. 931, *supra,* held that an express statutory remedy (the Federal Tort Claims Act) did not preempt an implied remedy under the Constitution, the express remedy in § 1983 should not be deemed to preempt an implied remedy under the Constitution, at least where the implied remedy serves some important purposes more satisfactorily than the express remedy. See 5 Davis, Administrative Law Treatise § 27:26, at 152–54 (1984). Does this view give adequate weight to Congress's decision to limit the scope of governmental liability under § 1983?

(8) *States and State Agencies as Defendants.* Quern v. Jordan, 440 U.S. 332 (1979), p. 1218, *supra,* held that Congress did not clearly manifest an intention in § 1983 to override the states' Eleventh Amendment immunity. Accordingly, the Amendment bars federal court actions under § 1983 that seek retrospective relief to be paid from the state treasury as well as actions that are nominally against the state or a state agency. Note that Quern did not necessarily hold that § 1983 creates no rights against a state, but only that a federal court lacks power to enforce, against an unconsenting state, whatever rights were created by § 1983.

In Della Grotta v. Rhode Island, 781 F.2d 343 (1st Cir.1986), the court of appeals held that if a state has consented to federal court suit, it may then be held liable *in federal court* under § 1983 for violations pursuant to state "policy or custom," as defined by Monell and successive cases. Other decisions have held that because the Eleventh Amendment does not apply in state court actions, states or their agencies may be liable under § 1983 *in state court,* again at least for violations pursuant to policy or custom. The precedents are not unanimous on either point. See Zagrans, Paragraph (7), *supra,* at 561 n. 325.

If § 1983 were interpreted to provide a cause of action against a state for a constitutional tort committed pursuant to state policy or custom, would a state court be obliged in a § 1983 suit against the state as such to provide injunctive relief? A damage remedy? See pp. 581–89, *supra.*

---

19. See also Amar, *Of Sovereignty and Federalism,* 96 Yale L.J. 1425, 1484–92 (1987) (arguing that the Constitution demands full and adequate remedies for constitutional violations, and that imposition of governmental liability in damages, apparently through a judicially-implied remedy, will often be necessary to provide effective redress).

PARRATT v. TAYLOR

451 U.S. 527, 101 S.Ct. 1908, 68 L.Ed.2d 420 (1981).
Certiorari to the United States Court of the Appeals for the Eighth Circuit.

JUSTICE REHNQUIST delivered the opinion of the Court.

The respondent is an inmate at the Nebraska Penal and Correctional Complex who ordered by mail certain hobby materials valued at $23.50. The hobby materials were lost and respondent brought suit under 42 U.S.C. § 1983 to recover their value. At first blush one might well inquire why respondent brought an action in federal court to recover damages of such a small amount for negligent loss of property, but because 28 U.S.C. § 1343, the predicate for the jurisdiction of the United States District Court, contains no minimum dollar limitation, he was authorized by Congress to bring his action under that section if he met its requirements and if he stated a claim for relief under 42 U.S.C. § 1983. Respondent claimed that his property was negligently lost by prison officials in violation of his rights under the Fourteenth Amendment to the United States Constitution. More specifically, he claimed that he had been deprived of property without due process of law.

The United States District Court for the District of Nebraska entered summary judgment for respondent, and the United States Court of Appeals for the Eighth Circuit affirmed in a *per curiam* order. We granted certiorari.

I

The facts underlying this dispute are not seriously contested. Respondent paid for the hobby materials he ordered with two drafts drawn on his inmate account by prison officials. The packages arrived at the complex and were signed for by two employees who worked in the prison hobby center. One of the employees was a civilian and the other was an inmate. Respondent was in segregation at the time and was not permitted to have the hobby materials. Normal prison procedures for the handling of mail packages is that upon arrival they are either delivered to the prisoner who signs a receipt for the package or the prisoner is notified to pick up the package and to sign a receipt. No inmate other than the one to whom the package is addressed is supposed to sign for a package. After being released from segregation, respondent contacted several prison officials regarding the whereabouts of his packages. The officials were never able to locate the packages or to determine what caused their disappearance.

In 1976, respondent commenced this action against the petitioners, the Warden and Hobby Manager of the prison, in the District Court seeking to recover the value of the hobby materials which he claimed had been lost as a result of the petitioners' negligence. Respondent alleged that petitioners' conduct deprived him of property without due process of law in violation of the Fourteenth Amendment of the United States Constitution. Respondent chose to proceed in the United States District Court under 28 U.S.C. § 1343 and 42 U.S.C. § 1983, even though the State of Nebraska had a tort claims procedure which provided a remedy to persons who suffered tortious losses at the hands of the State.

* * *

II

* * *

Nothing in the language of § 1983 or its legislative history limits the statute solely to intentional deprivations of constitutional rights. In Baker v. McCollan, [443 U.S. 137 (1979)], we suggested that simply because a wrong was negligently as opposed to intentionally committed did not foreclose the possibility that such action could be brought under § 1983. We explained:

"[T]he question whether an allegation of simple negligence is sufficient to state a cause of action under § 1983 is more elusive than it appears at first blush. It may well not be susceptible of a uniform answer across the entire spectrum of conceivable constitutional violations which might be the subject of a § 1983 action." 443 U.S., at 139–140.

Section 1983, unlike its criminal counterpart, 18 U.S.C. § 242, has never been found by this Court to contain a state-of-mind requirement.[2] The Court recognized as much in Monroe v. Pape, 365 U.S. 167 (1961), when we explained after extensively reviewing the legislative history of § 1983, that

"[i]t is abundantly clear that one reason the legislation was passed was to afford a federal right in federal courts because, by reason of prejudice, passion, neglect, intolerance or otherwise, state laws might not be enforced and the claims of citizens to the enjoyment of rights, privileges and immunities guaranteed by the Fourteenth Amendment might be denied by the state agencies." *Id.*, at 180. * * *

Both Baker v. McCollan and Monroe v. Pape suggest that § 1983 affords a "civil remedy" for deprivations of federally protected rights caused by persons acting under color of state law without any express requirement of a particular state of mind. Accordingly, in any § 1983 action the initial inquiry must focus on whether the two essential elements to a § 1983 action are present: (1) whether the conduct complained of was committed by a person acting under color of state law; and (2) whether this conduct deprived a person of rights, privileges, or immunities secured by the Constitution or laws of the United States.

III

Since this Court's decision in Monroe v. Pape, *supra*, it can no longer be questioned that the alleged conduct by the petitioners in this case satisfies the "under color of state law" requirement. Petitioners were, after all, state employees in positions of considerable authority. They do not seriously contend otherwise. Our inquiry, therefore, must turn to the second requirement—whether respondent has been deprived of any right, privilege, or immunity secured by the Constitution or laws of the United States.

---

2. Title 18 U.S.C. § 242 provides in pertinent part:

"Whoever, under color of any law, statute, ordinance, regulation, or custom, *willfully* subjects any inhabitant of any State, Territory, or District to the deprivation of any rights, privileges, or immunities secured or protected by the Constitution or laws of the United States * * * shall be fined not more than $1,000 or imprisoned not more than one year, or both; and if death results shall be subject to imprisonment for any term of years or for life." (Emphasis supplied.)

The only deprivation respondent alleges in his complaint is that "his rights under the Fourteenth Amendment of the Constitution of the United States were violated. That he was deprived of his property and Due Process of Law." As such, respondent's claims differ from the claims which were before us in Monroe v. Pape, *supra,* which involved violations of the Fourth Amendment, and the claims presented in Estelle v. Gamble, 429 U.S. 97 (1976), which involved alleged violations of the Eighth Amendment. Both of these Amendments have been held applicable to the States by virtue of the adoption of the Fourteenth Amendment. See Mapp v. Ohio, 367 U.S. 643 (1961); Robinson v. California, 370 U.S. 660 (1962). Respondent here refers to no other right, privilege, or immunity secured by the Constitution or federal laws other than the Due Process Clause of the Fourteenth Amendment *simpliciter.* * * *

Unquestionably, respondent's claim satisfies three prerequisites of a valid due process claim: the petitioners acted under color of state law; the hobby kit falls within the definition of property; and the alleged loss, even though negligently caused, amounted to a deprivation. Standing alone, however, these three elements do not establish a violation of the Fourteenth Amendment. Nothing in that Amendment protects against all deprivations of life, liberty, or property by the State. The Fourteenth Amendment protects only against deprivations "without due process of law." Baker v. McCollan, 443 U.S., at 145. Our inquiry therefore must focus on whether the respondent has suffered a deprivation of property without due process of law. In particular, we must decide whether the tort remedies which the State of Nebraska provides as a means of redress for property deprivations satisfy the requirements of procedural due process.

This Court has never directly addressed the question of what process is due a person when an employee of a State negligently takes his property. In some cases this Court has held that due process requires a predeprivation hearing before the State interferes with any liberty or property interest enjoyed by its citizens. In most of these cases, however, the deprivation of property was pursuant to some established state procedure and "process" could be offered before any actual deprivation took place. For example, in Mullane v. Central Hanover Trust Co., 339 U.S. 306 (1950), the Court struck down on due process grounds a New York statute that allowed a trust company, when it sought a judicial settlement of its trust accounts, to give notice by publication to all beneficiaries even if the whereabouts of the beneficiaries were known. The Court held that personal notice in such situations was required and stated that "when notice is a person's due, process which is a mere gesture is not due process." *Id.,* at 315. * * * See also Boddie v. Connnecticut, 401 U.S. 371 (1971); Goldberg v. Kelly, 397 U.S. 254 (1970); and Sniadach v. Family Finance Corp., 395 U.S. 337 (1969). In all these cases, deprivations of property were authorized by an established state procedure and due process was held to require predeprivation notice and hearing in order to serve as a check on the possibility that a wrongful deprivation would occur.

We have, however, recognized that postdeprivation remedies made available by the State can satisfy the Due Process Clause. In such cases, the normal predeprivation notice and opportunity to be heard is pretermitted if the State provides a postdeprivation remedy. In North American Cold Storage Co. v. Chicago, 211 U.S. 306 (1908), we upheld the right of a State to seize and destroy unwholesome food without a preseizure hearing.

The possibility of erroneous destruction of property was outweighed by the fact that the public health emergency justified immediate action and the owner of the property could recover his damages in an action at law after the incident. * * * In Bowles v. Willingham, 321 U.S. 503 (1944), we upheld in the face of a due process challenge the authority of the Administrator of the Office of Price Administration to issue rent control orders without providing a hearing to landlords before the order or regulation fixing rents became effective. * * * These cases recognize that either the necessity of quick action by the State or the impracticality of providing any meaningful predeprivation process, when coupled with the availability of some meaningful means by which to assess the propriety of the State's action at some time after the initial taking, can satisfy the requirements of procedural due process. * * *

Our past cases mandate that some kind of hearing is required at some time before a State finally deprives a person of his property interests. The fundamental requirement of due process is the opportunity to be heard and it is an "opportunity which must be granted at a meaningful time and in a meaningful manner." Armstrong v. Manzo, 380 U.S. 545, 552 (1965). However, as many of the above cases recognize, we have rejected the proposition that "at a meaningful time and in a meaningful manner" *always* requires the State to provide a hearing prior to the initial deprivation of property. This rejection is based in part on the impracticability in some cases of providing any preseizure hearing under a state-authorized procedure, and the assumption that at some time a full and meaningful hearing will be available.

The justifications which we have found sufficient to uphold takings of property without any predeprivation process are applicable to a situation such as the present one involving a tortious loss of a prisoner's property as a result of a random and unauthorized act by a state employee. In such a case, the loss is not a result of some established state procedure and the State cannot predict precisely when the loss will occur. It is difficult to conceive of how the State could provide a meaningful hearing before the deprivation takes place. The loss of property, although attributable to the State as action under "color of law," is in almost all cases beyond the control of the State. Indeed, in most cases it is not only impracticable, but impossible, to provide a meaningful hearing before the deprivation. That does not mean, of course, that the State can take property without providing a meaningful postdeprivation hearing. The prior cases which have excused the prior-hearing requirement have rested in part on the availability of some meaningful opportunity subsequent to the initial taking for a determination of rights and liabilities.

A case remarkably similar to the present one is Bonner v. Coughlin, 517 F.2d 1311 (CA7 1975), modified en banc, 545 F.2d 565 (1976), cert. denied, 435 U.S. 932 (1978). There, a prisoner alleged that prison officials "made it possible by leaving the door of Plaintiff's cell open, for others without authority to remove Plaintiff's trial transcript from the cell." 517 F.2d, at 1318. The question presented was whether negligence may support a recovery under § 1983. Then Judge Stevens, writing for a panel of the Court of Appeals for the Seventh Circuit, recognized that the question that had to be decided was "whether it can be said that the deprivation was 'without due process of law.'" *Ibid.* He concluded:

"It seems to us that there is an important difference between a challenge to an established state procedure as lacking in due process and a property damage claim arising out of the misconduct of state officers. In the former situation the facts satisfy the most literal reading of the Fourteenth Amendment's prohibition against 'State' deprivations of property; in the latter situation, however, even though there is action 'under color of' state law sufficient to bring the amendment into play, the state action is not necessarily complete. For in a case such as this the law of Illinois provides, in substance, that the plaintiff is entitled to be made whole for any loss of property occasioned by the unauthorized conduct of the prison guards. We may reasonably conclude, therefore, that the existence of an adequate state remedy to redress property damage inflicted by state officers avoids the conclusion that there has been any constitutional deprivation of property without due process of law within the meaning of the Fourteenth Amendment." *Id.,* at 1319.

We believe that the analysis recited above in Bonner is the proper manner in which to approach a case such as this. This analysis is also quite consistent with the approach taken by this Court in Ingraham v. Wright, 430 U.S. 651 (1977), where the Court was confronted with the claim that corporal punishment in public schools violated due process. Arguably, the facts presented to the Court in Ingraham were more egregious than those presented here inasmuch as the Court was faced with both an intentional act (as opposed to negligent conduct) and a deprivation of liberty. However, we reasoned:

"'At some point the benefit of an additional safeguard to the individual affected * * * and to society in terms of increased assurance that the action is just, may be outweighed by the cost.' Mathews v. Eldridge, 424 U.S., at 348. We think that point has been reached in this case. In view of the low incidence of abuse, the openness of our schools, *and the common-law safeguards that already exist,* the risk of error that may result in violation of a schoolchild's substantive rights can only be regarded as minimal. Imposing additional administrative safeguards as a constitutional requirement might reduce that risk marginally, but would also entail a significant intrusion into an area of primary educational responsibility." *Id.,* at 682. (Emphasis supplied.)

IV

Application of the principles recited above to this case leads us to conclude the respondent has not alleged a violation of the Due Process Clause of the Fourteenth Amendment. Although he has been deprived of property under color of state law, the deprivation did not occur as a result of some established state procedure. Indeed, the deprivation occurred as a result of the unauthorized failure of agents of the State to follow established state procedure. There is no contention that the procedures themselves are inadequate nor is there any contention that it was practicable for the State to provide a predeprivation hearing. Moreover, the State of Nebraska has provided respondent with the means by which he can receive redress for the deprivation. The State provides a remedy to persons who believe they have suffered a tortious loss at the hands of the State. See Neb.Rev.Stat. § 81–8,209 *et seq.* (1976). Through this tort claims procedure the State hears and pays claims of prisoners housed in its penal institutions. This procedure was in existence at the time of the loss here in question but respondent did not use it. It is argued that the State does not adequately protect the respondent's interests because it provides only for an action against the State as opposed to its individual employees, it contains no provisions for punitive damages, and there is no right to a trial by jury. Although the state remedies may not provide the respondent with all the relief which may have been available if he could have proceeded under § 1983, that does not mean that the state remedies are not adequate to satisfy the requirements of due process. The remedies provided could have fully compensated the respondent for the property loss he suffered, and we hold that they are sufficient to satisfy the requirements of due process.

Our decision today is fully consistent with our prior cases. To accept respondent's argument that the conduct of the state officials in this case constituted a violation of the Fourteenth Amendment would almost necessarily result in turning every alleged injury which may have been inflicted by a state official acting under "color of law" into a violation of the Fourteenth Amendment cognizable under § 1983. It is hard to perceive any logical stopping place to such a line of reasoning. Presumably, under this rationale any party who is involved in nothing more than an automobile accident with a state official could allege a constitutional violation under § 1983. Such reasoning "would make of the Fourteenth Amendment a font of tort law to be superimposed upon whatever systems may already be administered by the States." Paul v. Davis, 424 U.S. 693, 701 (1976). We do not think that the drafters of the Fourteenth Amendment intended the Amendment to play such a role in our society.

Accordingly, the judgment of the Court of Appeals is reversed.

JUSTICE STEWART, concurring.

It seems to me extremely doubtful that the property loss here, even though presumably caused by the negligence of state agents, is the kind of deprivation of property to which the Fourteenth Amendment is addressed. If it is, then so too would be damages to a person's automobile resulting from a collision with a vehicle negligently operated by a state official. To hold that this kind of loss is a deprivation of property within the meaning of the Fourteenth Amendment seems not only to trivialize, but grossly to distort the meaning and intent of the Constitution.

But even if Nebraska has deprived the respondent of his property in the constitutional sense, it has not deprived him of it without due process of law. By making available to the respondent a reparations remedy, Nebraska has done all that the Fourteenth Amendment requires in this context.

On this understanding, I join the opinion of the Court.

JUSTICE WHITE, concurring.

I join the opinion of the Court but with the reservations stated by my Brother Blackmun in his concurring opinion.

JUSTICE BLACKMUN, concurring.

While I join the Court's opinion in this case, I write separately to emphasize my understanding of its narrow reach. This suit concerns the deprivation only of property and was brought only against supervisory personnel, whose simple "negligence" was assumed but, on this record, not actually proved. I do not read the Court's opinion as applicable to a case concerning deprivation of life or of liberty. *Cf.* Moore v. East Cleveland, 431 U.S. 494 (1977). I also do not understand the Court to intimate that the sole content of the Due Process Clause is procedural regularity. I continue to believe that there are certain governmental actions that, even if undertaken with a full panoply of procedural protection, are, in and of themselves, antithetical to fundamental notions of due process. See, *e.g.,* Boddie v. Connecticut, 401 U.S. 371 (1971); Roe v. Wade, 410 U.S. 113 (1973).

Most importantly, I do not understand the Court to suggest that the provision of "postdeprivation remedies" * * * within a state system would cure the unconstitutional nature of a state official's intentional act that deprives a person of property. While the "random and unauthorized" nature of negligent acts by state employees makes it difficult for the State to "provide a meaningful hearing before the deprivation takes place," * * * it is rare that the same can be said of intentional acts by state employees. When it is possible for a State to institute procedures to contain and direct the intentional actions of its officials, it should be required, as a matter of due process, to do so. See Sniadach v. Family Finance Corp., 395 U.S. 337 (1969); Fuentes v. Shevin, 407 U.S. 67 (1972); Goldberg v. Kelly, 397 U.S. 254 (1970). In the majority of such cases, the failure to provide adequate process prior to inflicting the harm would violate the Due Process Clause. The mere availability of a subsequent tort remedy before tribunals of the same authority that, through its employees, deliberately inflicted the harm complained of, might well not provide the due process of which the Fourteenth Amendment speaks.

JUSTICE POWELL, concurring in the result.

* * * Unlike the Court, I do not believe that * * * negligent acts by state officials constitute a deprivation of property within the meaning of the Fourteenth Amendment, regardless of whatever subsequent procedure a State may or may not provide. I therefore concur only in the result.

The Court's approach begins with three "unquestionable" facts concerning respondent's due process claim: "the petitioners acted under color of state law; the hobby kit falls within the definition of property; and the alleged loss, even though negligently caused, amounted to a deprivation." It then goes on to reject respondent's claim on the theory that procedural due process is satisfied in such a case where a State provides a "postdeprivation" procedure for seeking redress—here a tort claims procedure. I would not decide this case on that ground for two reasons. First, the Court passes over a threshold question—whether a negligent act by a state official that results in loss of or damage to property constitutes a deprivation of property for due process purposes.[1] Second, in doing so, the Court suggests a narrow, wholly procedural view of the limitation imposed on the States by the Due Process Clause.

The central question in this case is whether *unintentional* but negligent acts by state officials, causing respondent's loss of property, are actionable under the Due Process Clause. In my view, this question

---

1. Assuming that there was a "deprivation" of the hobby kit under color of state law in this case, I would agree with the Court's conclusion that state tort remedies provide adequate procedural protection. *Cf.* Ingraham v. Wright, 430 U.S. 651, 674–682 (1977) (common-law remedies are adequate to afford procedural due process in cases of corporal punishment of students).

requires the Court to determine whether intent is an essential element of a due process claim, just as we have done in cases applying the Equal Protection Clause and the Eighth Amendment's prohibition of "cruel and unusual punishment." The intent question cannot be given "a uniform answer across the entire spectrum of conceivable constitutional violations which might be the subject of a § 1983 action," Baker v. McCollan, 443 U.S. 137, 139–140 (1979). Rather, we must give close attention to the nature of the particular constitutional violation asserted, in determining whether intent is a necessary element of such a violation.

In the due process area, the question is whether intent is required before there can be a "deprivation" of life, liberty, or property. In this case, for example, the negligence of the prison officials caused respondent to lose his property. Nevertheless, I would not hold that such a negligent act, causing unintended loss of or injury to property, works a deprivation in the *constitutional sense*. Thus, no procedure for compensation is constitutionally required.

A "deprivation" connotes an intentional act denying something to someone, or, at the very least, a deliberate decision not to act to prevent a loss. The most reasonable interpretation of the Fourteenth Amendment would limit due process claims to such active deprivations. This is the view adopted by an overwhelming number of lower courts, which have rejected due process claims premised on negligent acts without inquiring into the existence or sufficiency of the subsequent procedures provided by the States. In addition, such a rule would avoid trivializing the right of action provided in § 1983. That provision was enacted to deter real *abuses* by state officials in the exercise of governmental powers. It would make no sense to open the federal courts to lawsuits where there has been no affirmative abuse of power, merely a negligent deed by one who happens to be acting under color of state law.

The Court appears unconcerned about this prospect, probably because of an implicit belief in the availability of state tort remedies in most cases. In its view, such remedies will satisfy procedural due process, and relegate cases of official negligence to nonfederal forums. But the fact is that this rule would "make of the Fourteenth Amendment a font of tort law," Paul v. Davis, 424 U.S. 693, 701 (1976), whenever a State has failed to provide a remedy for negligent invasions of liberty or property interests. Moreover, despite the breadth of state tort remedies, such claims will be more numerous than might at first be supposed. In Kent v. Prasse, 385 F.2d 406 (CA3 1967) (*per curiam*), for example, a state prisoner was forced to work on a faulty machine, sustained an injury, and brought suit against prison officials. The United States Court of Appeals for the Third Circuit noted that the State, unfortunately, did not provide compensation for this injury, but stated:

> "Nor are we able to perceive that a tort committed by a state official acting under color of law is, in and of itself, sufficient to show an invasion of a person's right under [§ 1983]. While not dispositive, we note that there is no allegation that defendants violated any state criminal law or acted out of bad motive. Nor [is it] alleged that any state law was not enforced by the defendants." *Id.*, at 407.

Rather than reject this reasoning, I would adopt the view that negligent official acts do not provide any basis for inquiries by federal courts into the existence, or procedural adequacy, of applicable state tort remedies.

Such an approach has another advantage; it avoids a somewhat disturbing implication in the Court's opinion concerning the scope of due process guarantees. The Court analyzes this case solely in terms of the procedural rights created by the Due Process Clause. Finding state procedures adequate, it suggests that no further analysis is required of more substantive limitations on state action located in this Clause. *Cf.* Paul v. Davis, *supra*, at 712–714 (assessing the claim presented in terms of the "substantive aspects of the Fourteenth Amendment"); Ingraham v. Wright, 430 U.S. 651, 679, n. 47 (1977) (leaving open the question whether "corporal punishment of a public school child may give rise to an independent federal cause of action to vindicate substantive rights under the Due Process Clause").

The Due Process Clause imposes substantive limitations on state action, and under proper circumstances these limitations may extend to intentional and malicious deprivations of liberty and property, even where compensation is available under state law. The Court, however, fails altogether to discuss the possibility that the kind of state action alleged here constitutes a violation of the substantive guarantees of the Due Process Clause. As I do not consider a negligent act the kind of deprivation that implicates the procedural guarantees of the Due Process Clause, I certainly would not view negligent acts as violative of these substantive guarantees. But the Court concludes that there has been such a deprivation. And yet it avoids entirely the question whether the Due Process Clause may place substantive limitations on this form of governmental conduct.

In sum, it seems evident that the reasoning and decision of the Court today, even if viewed as compatible with our precedents, create new uncertainties as well as invitations to litigate under a statute that already has burst its historical bounds.

JUSTICE MARSHALL, concurring in part and dissenting in part.

I join the opinion of the Court insofar as it holds that negligent conduct by persons acting under color of state law may be actionable under 42 U.S.C. § 1983. * * * I also agree with the majority that in cases involving claims of *negligent* deprivation of property without due process of law, the availability of an adequate postdeprivation cause of action for damages under state law may preclude a finding of a violation of the Fourteenth Amendment. I part company with the majority, however, over its conclusion that there was an adequate state-law remedy available to respondent in this case. My disagreement with the majority is not because of any shortcomings in the Nebraska tort claims procedure. Rather, my problem is with the majority's application of its legal analysis to the facts of this case.

It is significant, in my view, that respondent is a state prisoner whose access to information about his legal rights is necessarily limited by his confinement. Furthermore, there is no claim that either petitioners or any other officials informed respondent that he could seek redress for the alleged deprivation of his property by filing an action under the Nebraska tort claims procedure. This apparent failure takes on additional significance in light of the fact that respondent pursued his complaint about the missing hobby kit through the prison's grievance procedure. In cases such as this, I believe prison officials have an affirmative obligation to inform a prisoner who claims that he is aggrieved by official action about the remedies available under state law. If they fail to do so, then they should not be permitted to rely on the existence of such remedies as adequate alternatives to a § 1983 action for wrongful deprivation of property. Since these prison officials do not represent that respondent was informed about his rights under state law, I cannot join in the judgment of the Court in this case.

Thus, although I agree with much of the majority's reasoning, I would affirm the judgment of the Court of Appeals.

NOTE ON THE RELATIONSHIP BETWEEN COMMON LAW TORTS AND CONSTITUTIONAL TORTS IN ACTIONS AGAINST STATE AND LOCAL OFFICIALS

(1) *Common Law and Constitutional Torts.* Nearly every common law tort deprives the injured party of liberty or property. Should every common law tort committed by an official acting under color of law give rise to a constitutional tort action under § 1983 for a deprivation of liberty or property without due process? Note how broadly such a regime would displace state law with federal law and, by making resort to § 1983 available, displace state courts with federal courts.

If such a regime is to be avoided, should the Court (a) follow the approach of the majority in Parratt; (b) limit the kinds of harms that are considered deprivations of liberty or property, see Paragraph (2), *infra;* (c) adopt Justice Powell's suggestion that negligently inflicted harms do not deprive the victim of due process, see Paragraph (3), *infra;* or (d) reconsider some aspects of Monroe v. Pape, see Paragraph (9), *infra?* This Note examines these questions.

(2) *The Limits of Liberty and Property.* In Paul v. Davis, 424 U.S. 693 (1976), police officials circulated to local merchants a list of "active shoplifters" that included Davis' name. Davis filed a § 1983 action, contending that this conduct, taken without a prior hearing, denied him liberty and property without due process. The Supreme Court held that Davis' interest in reputation was not an interest in liberty or property protected by the Constitution. The decision has been widely criticized. See, *e.g.,* Monaghan, *Of "Liberty" and "Property",* 62 Cornell L.Rev. 405, 423–29 (1977); Shapiro, *Mr. Justice Rehnquist: A Preliminary View,* 90 Harv.L.Rev. 293, 322–38 (1976). See also Glennon, *Constitutional Liberty and Property: Federal Common Law and Section 1983,* 51 S.Cal.L.Rev. 355 (1978).

In Baker v. McCollan, 443 U.S. 137 (1979), the plaintiff had been mistakenly held in custody for eight days by the police, who confused him with his brother. The mistake was understandable, but could have been remedied had the police more promptly checked their records. The Supreme Court ruled that though the plaintiff might have a state law action for false imprisonment, he had not suffered a deprivation of liberty under the Fourteenth Amendment.

After Parratt v. Taylor, should cases like these be handled differently—not by denying that a deprivation has occurred, but rather by arguing that, so long as postdeprivation remedies exist, there is no denial of due process? See Smolla, *The Displacement of Federal Due Process Claims by*

State Tort Remedies: Parratt v. Taylor and Logan v. Zimmerman Brush Co., 1982 U.Ill.L.Rev. 831, 842–43. See Chap. V, Sec. 2(A), pp. 575–80, *supra.*

(3) *Scienter in Constitutional Tort Actions.* In a § 1983 action, three distinct issues of scienter may arise: (i) Does § 1983 itself require any distinctive scienter? (ii) Is scienter required to establish a violation (for which relief under § 1983 is sought) of the constitutional provision in question? (iii) Does an official sued have a qualified immunity from damages if his conduct did not violate clearly established legal norms? (On the last of these, see Sec. 3, *infra*). See generally Gildin, *The Standard of Culpability in Section 1983 and Bivens Actions: The Prima Facie Case, Qualified Immunity and the Constitution,* 11 Hof.L.Rev. 557, 558–59 (1983).

The first two of these questions had divided the lower courts prior to Parratt,[1] and a number of years after Parratt, in Daniels v. Williams, 474 U.S. 327 (1986), the Supreme Court shifted course. The case was a § 1983 action brought by an inmate of a city jail, who alleged that he had injured his back when he slipped on a pillow negligently left on a prison stairway by a deputy. The complaint alleged that the deputy's negligence had deprived plaintiff of his liberty without due process. The Supreme Court, per Rehnquist, J., adhered to Parratt's conclusion that § 1983 "contains no state-of-mind requirement independent of that necessary to state a violation of the underlying constitutional right" (p. 330).[2] But the Court overruled Parratt "to the extent that it states that mere lack of due care by a state official may 'deprive' an individual of life, liberty or property under the Fourteenth Amendment" (pp. 330–31).

The Court explained that the Due Process Clause, by requiring the government to follow appropriate procedures, promotes fair treatment of individuals, and by barring certain actions regardless of the procedures followed, "serves to prevent governmental power from being used for purposes of oppression * * *. * * * We think that the actions of prison custodians in leaving a pillow on the prison stairs, or mislaying an inmate's property, are quite remote from the concerns just discussed. * * * To hold that injury caused by such conduct is a deprivation within the meaning of the Fourteenth Amendment would trivialize the centuries-old principle of due process of law" (pp. 331–32). Though perhaps other constitutional provisions could be violated by the mere lack of due care, such conduct "does not implicate the Due Process Clause of the Fourteenth Amendment" (p. 334).[3]

---

1. See generally Friedman, *Parratt v. Taylor: Opening and Closing the Door on Section 1983,* 9 Hastings Const.L.Q. 545 (1982); Kirkpatrick, *Defining a Constitutional Tort under Section 1983: The State-of-Mind Requirement,* 46 U.Cinn.L.Rev. 45 (1977).

2. Recall, however, that some courts have interpreted § 1983's requirement of custom or policy in suits against local governments to call for proof of scienter on the part of high government officials. See pp. 1256–57, *supra.* See also Gregory v. Pittsfield, 470 U.S. 1018, 1022 (1985) (O'Connor, J., dissenting from the denial of certiorari).

3. The prisoner, in support of his argument that negligent conduct can deny due process, posited a case in which the state negligently failed to provide an inmate with a hearing before revoking his good time credit, as required by Wolff v. McDonnell, 418 U.S. 539, 558 (1974). The Court responded that "the relevant action of the prison officials in that situation is their deliberate decision to deprive the inmate of good-time credit, not their hypothetically negligent failure to accord him the procedural protections of the Due Process Clause" (pp. 333–34). Compare Logan v. Zimmerman Brush Co., Paragraph (4)(c), *infra.*

The Court relied on Daniels in disposing of the companion case of Davidson v. Cannon, 474 U.S. 344 (1986), which held that the failure of prison officials to protect one prisoner from an attack by another, even if negligent, did not constitute a deprivation of liberty.

In both Daniels and Davidson, Justice Stevens concurred in the judgment on the ground that each state had provided an adequate remedy, so that under Parratt there was no denial of due process. He disagreed, however, with the Court's conclusion that negligently inflicted harm could not constitute a deprivation of liberty or property (474 U.S. at 341): " 'Deprivation,' it seems to me, identifies, not the actor's state of mind, but the victim's infringement or loss. The harm to a prisoner is the same whether a pillow is left on a stair negligently, recklessly, or intentionally; so too, the harm resulting to a prisoner from an attack is the same whether his request for protection is ignored negligently, recklessly, or deliberately."

Justice Blackmun (joined by Justice Marshall) concurred in the judgment in Daniels, but dissented in Davidson, finding the two cases quite different. The incarceration of Daniels "left intact his own faculties for avoiding a slip and a fall. But the State prevented Davidson from defending himself, and therefore assumed some responsibility to protect him from the dangers to which he was exposed" (p. 350). Thus, though in Daniels (as in most cases), defendants' negligence did not constitute an abuse of power, the negligent conduct in Davidson was "the 'arbitrary action' against which the Due Process Clause protects" (p. 354).

Justice Blackmun argued in the alternative that Davidson's case should be remanded for review of his contention that the evidence established that the defendants had been reckless. In Daniels, the Court had reserved the question whether reckless or grossly negligent behavior would suffice to establish liability (p. 334 n. 3). Justice Blackmun noted that Estelle v. Gamble, 429 U.S. 97, 104 (1976), had held that a showing that an official's denial of medical care to a prisoner resulted from "deliberate indifference" could constitute a violation of the Eighth Amendment's Cruel and Unusual Punishment Clause, and he argued that nothing more should be required to establish that Davidson had suffered a deprivation of liberty (p. 357).[4]

(4) *The Reach of Parratt in Procedural Due Process Cases.*

(a) *Intentional Conduct.* Parratt was applied in Hudson v. Palmer, 468 U.S. 517 (1984), to a case of intentional deprivation of property. There, a prisoner alleged that during a search of his cell, a guard had intentionally destroyed certain personal property without justification. The Supreme Court unanimously held that the rationale of Parratt applied to intentional conduct, thereby resolving an issue that had split the circuits. The plaintiff missed the point, the Court said, in arguing that the *official* who acted intentionally could have provided predeprivation process. The key, rather, was that "[t]he *state* can no more anticipate and control in advance the random and unauthorized intentional conduct of its employees than it can anticipate similar negligent conduct" (p. 533; emphasis added). The

4. Justice Brennan dissented from the disposition in Davidson; he agreed with the Court that proof of mere negligence was insufficient, but agreed with Justice Blackmun that proof of recklessness should suffice and that a remand on that issue was appropriate. 474 U.S. at 349.

Court found that Parratt's reliance on Ingraham v. Wright, 430 U.S. 651 (1977), had foreshadowed the applicability of its reasoning to intentional conduct. See generally Note, 71 Calif.L.Rev. 253, 255–58 (1983); Note, 85 Colum.L.Rev. 837, 863–65 (1985).

(b) *Deprivation of Liberty.* Does Parratt's reliance on Ingraham also suggest that Parratt's reasoning extends to a deprivation of *liberty?* Isn't the theory of Parratt—that the state cannot practicably provide predeprivation process for a random and unauthorized incident of official misconduct—equally applicable whether, for example, a prison guard deliberately and unjustifiably destroys a prisoner's property or breaks his arm? Or is a postdeprivation remedy less likely to be adequate in cases involving injury to liberty interests? See generally Moore, *Parratt, Liberty, and the Devolution of Due Process: A Time for Reflection,* 13 W.St.U.L.Rev. 201 (1985); *cf.* Ingraham v. Wright, 430 U.S. at 701 (Stevens, J., dissenting).

In his separate opinion in Davidson, Justice Blackmun argued (p. 358) that the postdeprivation remedy was inadequate "[e]ven assuming" that Parratt applies to deprivation of liberty. See also Blackmun, *Section 1983 and Federal Protection of Individual Rights—Will the Statute Remain Alive or Fade Away?,* 60 N.Y.U.L.Rev. 1, 24–25 (1985): "The holdings of Parratt and Hudson have been confined to unauthorized deprivations of property, and I would hope that they would continue to be so confined." By contrast, Justice Stevens, in his separate opinion in Daniels and Davidson, found that there was a deprivation of liberty in each case but, following Parratt's reasoning, no denial of due process in view of the postdeprivation remedy.[5]

(c) *Conduct Pursuant to Established State Procedures.* The Court's opinion in Hudson v. Palmer stated that "postdeprivation remedies do not satisfy due process where a deprivation of property is caused by conduct pursuant to established state procedure, rather than random and unauthorized action" (468 U.S. at 532). The Hudson Court cited Logan v. Zimmerman Brush Co., 455 U.S. 422 (1982), as supporting that proposition. In Logan, an individual claiming employment discrimination filed a charge with the state equal opportunity commission, as required by state law. By statute, the commission had 120 days to schedule a factfinding conference, but, apparently due to inadvertence, it failed to do so within that time. Ruling on a motion of the employer, the Illinois Supreme Court held that because the 120-day limit was jurisdictional, the commission must dismiss the charge. The Supreme Court unanimously reversed, holding that Logan's cause of action was a property interest of which he had been deprived without due process. The employer argued that, because Logan could sue the commission in state court for damages, under Parratt there was no deprivation without due process, but the Court was unconvinced (p. 436): "Here * * * it is the state system itself that destroys a complainant's property interest, by operation of law, whenever the Commission fails to

---

5. The lower courts have generally agreed that Parratt extends to deprivations of liberty. See, *e.g.,* Thibodeaux v. Bordelon, 740 F.2d 329, 336–37 (5th Cir. 1984); Wilson v. Beebe, 770 F.2d 578 (6th Cir.1985) (en banc). See generally Moore, *supra,* at 215–53.

Does Parratt extend, also, to deprivations of life? Compare, *e.g.,* State Bank of St. Charles v. Camic, 712 F.2d 1140, 1147 (7th Cir.1983) (Parratt applies) (alternative holding), with Roberts v. Troy, 773 F.2d 720, 727–29 (6th Cir.1985) (Celebrezze, J., concurring) (wrongful death action not adequate because it does not come at a "meaningful time").

convene a timely conference * * *. * * * Unlike the complainant in Parratt, Logan is challenging not the Commission's error, but the 'established state procedure' that destroys his entitlement without according him proper procedural safeguards."

Recall the difficulties that the courts have had in determining, for purposes of local government liability under § 1983, when conduct is undertaken pursuant to government policy or custom. See pp. 1254–57, *supra.* Don't Hudson and Logan together require the drawing of a similar line—to distinguish conduct that is random and unauthorized from conduct undertaken pursuant to established state procedure? Is official conduct that violates state or local law nonetheless not random and unauthorized within the meaning of Hudson and Parratt if the actor is a "policymaking" official? What if the conduct violates state law but is a regular practice of the governmental agency? See generally Levinson, *Due Process Challenges to Governmental Actions: The Meaning of Parratt and Hudson,* 18 Urb. Law. 189, 194–99 (1986).

(5) *The Relationship of Parratt to Home Telephone and Telegraph and Monroe v. Pape.* Recall that Home Telephone and Telegraph, p. 1221, *supra,* held that a single incident of official conduct can violate the Due Process Clause even if the conduct was unauthorized under state law. Recall, also, that Monroe v. Pape held that § 1983 provides a statutory remedy for official conduct in violation of the Fourth Amendment (as incorporated by the Fourteenth), even if the conduct violated state law and found no sanction in local policy or custom. Can Parratt and Hudson be squared with Home Telephone and Monroe?

Is it possible to limit Parratt and Hudson to procedural due process cases? In his separate opinion in Davidson v. Cannon, Paragraph (3), *supra,* Justice Stevens set forth three categories of Due Process violations: first, violations of specific provisions of the Bill of Rights, like the Fourth Amendment, which are incorporated by the Fourteenth Amendment; second, violations of "substantive due process," which invalidates certain government actions regardless of the fairness of the procedures followed; and third, procedural due process violations. In his view, the approach of Parratt and Hudson applies only to the last of these categories. 474 U.S. at 337–38; see also Hudson v. Palmer, 468 U.S. at 541 n. 4 (opinion of Stevens, J., joined by Brennan, Marshall, and Blackmun, JJ.) (joining the Court's opinion on the understanding that it does not apply to "actions governmental officials may not take no matter what procedural protections accompany them"). The lower courts have followed Justice Stevens' view, uniformly permitting § 1983 actions alleging violations of the Bill of Rights or of substantive due process without regard to the availability of state remedies.[6] And in § 1983 actions alleging violations of Bill of Rights provisions, the Supreme Court has affirmed an award of damages, Smith v. Wade, 461 U.S. 30 (1983), or remanded for trial, see Tennessee v. Garner,

---

6. See, *e.g.,* Gilmere v. City of Atlanta, 774 F.2d 1495, 1499–1500 (11th Cir.1985) (en banc), and cases cited; Nahmod, *Due Process, State Remedies, and Section 1983,* 34 U.Kan.L.Rev. 217, 233–52 (1985).

Is it an objection to this view that Parratt reversed the judgment for plaintiff

without considering whether the loss of the hobby kit was a violation of substantive due process? See Monaghan, *State Law Wrongs, State Law Remedies, and the Fourteenth Amendment,* 86 Colum.L.Rev. 979, 985 (1986).

471 U.S. 1 (1985), without considering whether a meaningful state postdeprivation remedy might be available.

Why isn't the availability of a state tort remedy in a case like Monroe—alleging a violation of Fourth Amendment protections—an adequate substitute for a federal damage remedy, thus constituting the "process that is due" under the Fourteenth Amendment? [7] Is it an answer that in a procedural due process case, unlike Monroe, the issue is not one of choice between remedies to compensate for an "independent" constitutional wrong, but rather of the existence or nonexistence of the constitutional wrong itself? [8]

What would you think of an approach asserting that, on the ultimate question whether the state has deprived a person of liberty or property without the process that is due, state law remedies are *always* an aspect of the very question whether the state has committed the constitutional wrong? Would such an approach require a reconsideration of Home Telephone & Telegraph? Could it apply in suits seeking equitable as well as damages relief? See generally Bator, *Some Thoughts On Applied Federalism,* 6 Harv.J.L.Pub.Pol. 51 (1982).[9] Would it be desirable to curtail so radically the federal courts' role in adjudicating and redressings claims of federal constitutional right? Would it be ironic that under this view, the more clearly illegal an act is—when it violates not only federal but also state law—the less available federal relief would be? What would be the implications of this view for congressional power to criminalize conduct by state officials that also violates state law? See Paragraph (9), *infra.*

7. If a state official unjustifiably beats an individual, should the victim be able to sue under § 1983 if he is a prisoner (because the claim lies under the Eighth Amendment, as incorporated by the Fourteenth Amendment), but not if he is an ordinary citizen at liberty (in which case the claim would lie under the Fourteenth Amendment's Due Process Clause *simpliciter*)? See Mann v. City of Tucson, 782 F.2d 790, 796–98 (9th Cir.1986), in which Judge Sneed, in a concurring opinion, posed this question and argued that Parratt should extend to all suits alleging constitutional deprivations, so long as the violation was not pursuant to an unconstitutional law, policy, or practice. See also Judge Easterbrook's opinion concurring in the judgment in Gumz v. Morrissette, 772 F.2d 1395, 1409 (7th Cir.1985).

8. Consider the special problem of takings cases. In Williamson County Regional Planning Com'n v. Hamilton Bank, 473 U.S. 172 (1985), the Supreme Court held that a landowner's § 1983 suit claiming that defendants had taken his property without just compensation was not ripe because plaintiff "did not seek compensation through the procedures the State has provided [for compensation]" (p. 194). The Court analogized the case to Parratt, and said that "the State's action is not 'complete' in the sense of causing a constitu-

tional injury 'unless or until the State fails to provide an adequate postdeprivation remedy for the property loss' " (p. 195, quoting Hudson v. Palmer).

Why should a challenge under § 1983 to *authorized* conduct be immediately cognizable in federal court if it alleges a denial of due process, see Paragraph 4(c), *supra,* but not if it alleges a taking without just compensation? Is it pertinent that the Constitution implicitly authorizes takings, and bars only takings without just compensation? See 473 U.S. at 195 n. 14.

On the Hamilton Bank case, see Symposium, 29 Wash.U.J.Urb. & Contemp.L. 3 (1986).

9. Consider this further question: on such an approach, what would be the Supreme Court's scope of direct review of a state court judgment that, for instance, rejected on the merits—after full and fair procedures—a claim that evidence in a criminal case must be suppressed because obtained in violation of the Fourth Amendment? Compare the discussion, in connection with cases such as Frank v. Mangum, Brown v. Allen, and Stone v. Powell, pp. 1477–1524, *infra,* of what detentions are to be deemed to be in "violation" of the Constitution for purposes of exercising federal habeas corpus jurisdiction.

In considering these questions, is it pertinent that procedural due process, because it protects a far broader range of individual interests than the Bill of Rights or substantive due process, implicates concerns about excessive federal intervention to a far greater extent?

(6) *Procedural versus Substantive Due Process.* Was the Court mistaken in Parratt (and ever since) to view this line of cases as raising *procedural* due process claims? Procedural due process protections, after all, are designed primarily to reduce the risk of official error and to provide an opportunity for an individual to participate in decisions importantly affecting his welfare. A postdeprivation remedy cannot serve either of these purposes in a case like Parratt, Hudson, Daniels, or Davidson.

On this view, would the prisoner in Hudson v. Palmer be able to state a valid substantive due process claim—for the unconstitutional destruction of his property—on which he could seek immediate access to federal court, whether or not meaningful postdeprivation remedies exist? *Cf.* Whitley v. Albers, 475 U.S. 312, 326–27 (1986) (treating the complaint of a prisoner shot by prison officials who were attempting to quell a riot as raising a substantive but not a procedural due process claim, though denying relief on the merits). A substantive due process claim of this sort would presumably be meritorious only if the official's conduct crossed some threshold of seriousness. (How might such a threshold be defined?) If it did not, then federal law would provide no protection at all, and the victim would obtain only the relief (if any) that the state chose to provide. *Cf.* Martinez v. California, note 11, *infra.*

See generally, Wells & Eaton, *Substantive Due Process and the Scope of Constitutional Torts*, 18 Ga.L.Rev. 201 (1984).

(7) *The Adequacy of State Postdeprivation Remedies.* Parratt and Hudson bar federal relief for random and unauthorized conduct (at least in procedural due process cases) only so long as the state provides a "meaningful" postdeprivation remedy. It is clear from Parratt that a constitutionally "meaningful" remedy need not track § 1983's procedures and remedies even in very important respects. Parratt did state, however, that the state remedies available in that case "could have fully compensated the [plaintiff] for the property loss he suffered." In Hudson v. Palmer, Paragraph (4) (a), *supra*, the Court articulated its reasoning somewhat differently: "that Palmer might not be able to recover under these [state] remedies the full amount which he might receive in a § 1983 action is not ∗ ∗ ∗ determinative of the adequacy of the state remedies" (468 U.S. at 535).

In Davidson v. Cannon, Paragraph (3), *supra,* Justice Blackmun (joined by Justice Marshall) and Justice Stevens, having found that a deprivation of liberty had occurred, proceeded to consider whether the state provided an adequate postdeprivation remedy. The question revolved around a state statute that immunized all public officials and entities from liability in an action by one prisoner claiming injury by another prisoner. For Justice Stevens, this statute did not render the state's postdeprivation procedure constitutionally invalid so as to permit a § 1983 action. Just as "defenses such as contributory negligence or statutes of limitations may defeat recovery in particular cases without raising any question about the constitutionality of a State's procedures for disposing of tort litigation," so the provision of an immunity defense "does not justify the conclusion that [the state's] remedial system is constitutionally inadequate" (474 U.S. at 342).

Aren't contributory negligence and limitations defenses distinguishable? The former in effect denies that a wrong was committed, while the latter does not bar relief altogether but simply conditions its provision on compliance with reasonable procedural rules.

Justice Blackmun disagreed, arguing that the state remedy was obviously inadequate (p. 359): "Conduct that is wrongful under § 1983 surely cannot be immunized by state law." Doesn't Justice Blackmun put the cart before the horse by assuming the conduct was wrongful under § 1983, without first determining whether the state deprived the plaintiff of liberty with due process? Unless that determination has been made, there is no Fourteenth Amendment violation, and § 1983 accordingly is not implicated.

How, then, should a court determine whether, when a deprivation of liberty or property has occurred, the existence of immunities in any state court action denies the process that is due? If the state's sovereign and official immunity rules permit damage liability whenever, in a § 1983 action, damage liability could be imposed, is the state remedy plainly adequate? If, instead, the immunities in state court are broader than those applicable in § 1983 actions, does the state now plainly deny due process? [10] Recall that under Parratt, the question of adequacy is measured not by comparison to § 1983 actions, but to a constitutionally-based standard of adequacy.[11]

Immunity laws are only one of a seemingly endless number of provisions applicable in postdeprivation proceedings which plaintiffs have contended make that process inadequate within the meaning of Parratt.[12] Is a

---

10. The question whether broad immunities render state processes inadequate has divided the lower courts. For opinions stating that broad immunities render state processes inadequate, see, *e.g.,* Davidson v. O'Lone, 752 F.2d 817, 834 (3d Cir.1984) (en banc) (Seitz, J., dissenting), *aff'd sub nom.* Davidson v. Cannon, Paragraph (3), *supra;* Ausley v. Mitchell, 748 F.2d 224, 227–28 (4th Cir.1984) (en banc) (Winter, J., concurring in part); for contrary views, see, *e.g.,* Rittenhouse v. DeKalb County, 764 F.2d 1451 (11th Cir.1985); Daniels v. Williams, 720 F.2d 792, 798 (4th Cir.1983), *adhered to on other grounds,* 748 F.2d 229 (4th Cir. 1984) (en banc), *aff'd,* 474 U.S. 327 (1986).

Cf. Gregory v. Pittsfield, 470 U.S. 1018, 1022–23 (1985) (O'Connor, J., dissenting from the denial of certiorari) (doubting the adequacy of state remedies permitting a claimant who was improperly denied welfare benefits to obtain benefits one year later, without providing for damages for intervening harm).

11. Consider the bearing of Martinez v. California, 444 U.S. 277 (1980). There, a state court action against state parole officials, brought by the representatives of an individual murdered by a released convict, was dismissed under a state statute conferring absolute immunity on public officials and public entities. The Supreme Court affirmed. It found plaintiffs' § 1983 claim

without merit because the officials had not proximately caused the harm. Plaintiffs' state law wrongful death claim could, the Court admitted, be viewed as a property interest, but the state's interest in fashioning immunity rules was held to be paramount to any federal interest involved, except perhaps the interest in protecting individuals from wholly arbitrary action (a problem not raised by the immunity provision).

Is Martinez' highly deferential standard of review applicable only to "pure" state law claims like the wrongful death action?

12. Consider, for example, such holdings as these: (i) a state remedy for recovery of excess taxes assessed is inadequate because it permits no compensation for mental anguish, Rutherford v. United States, 702 F.2d 580, 584 (5th Cir.1983); (ii) state *administrative* remedies are not necessarily inadequate, Dusanek v. Hannon, 677 F.2d 538 (7th Cir.1982); but *cf.* Holman v. Hilton, 712 F.2d 854, 860–63 (3d Cir.1983) (administrative determination based exclusively on written presentations inadequate); (iii) state judicial review of an agency's decision arguably depriving a tow-truck operator of a property right provides an adequate remedy, even though the operator's § 1983 suit sought damages, Alfaro Motors, Inc. v. Ward, 814 F.2d 883 (2d Cir. 1987); (iv) state provision of damages but

state tort remedy inadequate if it applies a remedial or procedural rule that
would not be "incorporated" in a § 1983 suit (presumably because it was
deemed either "deficient" in promoting, or inconsistent with, federal policies, see pp. 953–59, 1247–48, *supra*)?

For general discussion of these problems, see Smolla, Paragraph (2),
supra, at 871–81; Note, 65 B.U.L.Rev. 607 (1985); Comment, 37 Baylor
L.Rev. 425 (1985).

(8) *Res Judicata.* Suppose that after an individual's property is intentionally destroyed by a state official acting without authorization, the
individual obtains in state court a remedy he believes to be inadequate. If
he now brings a § 1983 action in federal court claiming a denial of due
process, can that suit be defeated by a plea of claim preclusion? (On claim
preclusion, see generally Chap. XII, pp. 1626–27, *infra*.)

The federal plaintiff might try to avoid the plea by arguing that the
§ 1983 claim did not arise until after the state remedy proved to be
inadequate. Would it matter if the state remedy was plainly inadequate,
but the plaintiff nonetheless initially sought a state law remedy in state
court, and only later filed a § 1983 claim in federal court? See Flores v.
Edinburg Consolidated Ind. School Dist., 741 F.2d 773, 777–79 (5th Cir.1984)
(finding claim preclusion applicable in such a case). What if the claimant
had first filed a federal court § 1983 action in the face of uncertainty
whether the state remedy was adequate? See, *e.g.*, Loftin v. Thomas, 681
F.2d 364, 365 (5th Cir.1982) (dismissing § 1983 suit, with the caveat that
plaintiff may again seek relief under § 1983 if state court relief proves
inadequate); *cf.* England v. Louisiana State Bd. of Medical Examiners, p.
1376, *infra*.

Note the perils to the plaintiff of making the wrong guess: if he first
files in federal court when the state court in fact would provide adequate
relief, any state action that he later files may be time-barred; if he first
files in state court when the state court clearly does not provide meaningful
postdeprivation process, claim preclusion may defeat any subsequent federal action, see Flores, *supra*. See generally Kupfer, *Restructuring the
Monroe Doctrine: Current Litigation Under Section 1983*, 9 Hastings Const.
L.Q. 463, 474–75 (1982); Note, Paragraph (7), *supra*, at 637.

(9) *Parratt and Legislative Policy.* An alternative to the various approaches of Parratt, Daniels and Davidson, and Paul v. Davis—each of
which in some way limits the scope of *constitutional* protection—would be
to modify Monroe v. Pape's interpretation of § 1983, so as to exclude some
constitutional claims from the purview of § 1983, or to make the existence
of state remedies pertinent to the availability of federal relief.[13] Would
this approach to limiting federal intervention be preferable, either because
it can be squared more easily with Home Telephone and Telegraph, or

not specific relief for wrongful seizure of
personal property of sentimental value is
inadequate, Bumgarner v. Bloodworth, 738
F.2d 966 (8th Cir.1984) (per curiam).

13. In a dissent from a denial of certiorari, Justice Rehnquist expressed the view
that "the time may now be ripe for a
reconsideration of the Court's conclusion in

Monroe that the 'federal remedy is supplementary to the state remedy, and the latter need not be first sought and refused
before the federal one is invoked.'" He
was joined by Chief Justice Burger and
Justice Blackmun. City of Columbus v.
Leonard, 443 U.S. 905, 910–11 (1979).

because it permits legislative modification? See Monaghan, note 6, *supra,* at 996.[14]

(10) *The Pertinence of Parratt and Hudson to Constitutional Tort Actions Against Federal Officials.* How should a federal court deal with a Bivens-type action seeking damages, under the Fifth Amendment, for a procedural due process violation arising from the random and unauthorized conduct of federal officials? In Weiss v. Lehman, 676 F.2d 1320 (9th Cir. 1982), the Supreme Court had vacated and remanded, "for further consideration in light of Parratt v. Taylor," a prior judgment of the court of appeals that had upheld a damage award in such a case. On remand, the court of appeals ruled that because the plaintiff had an adequate remedy under the Federal Tort Claims Act, no due process violation had occurred. Recall that the FTCA (i) makes actionable wrongs defined by state law rather than the federal Constitution, (ii) affords no jury trial, (iii) establishes governmental but not individual liability, and (iv) forbids punitive damages. These were the very "defects" that the Court held in Carlson v. Green, p. 931, *supra,* made the FTCA less effective than a Bivens suit, and therefore made it inappropriate not to imply a Bivens remedy in an action directly under the Eighth Amendment. On the other hand, the state remedy that Parratt found adequate to redress a deprivation of property under the Fourteenth Amendment's Due Process Clause had all four of these "defects."

Aren't Parratt's concerns about excessive federal interference with state officials and state courts less forceful in suits against federal officials? Is that enough reason, however, to give different interpretations to the Due Process Clauses of the Fifth and Fourteenth Amendments? See Smolla, Paragraph (2), *supra,* at 881–83.

SECTION 3: OFFICIAL IMMUNITY

BUTZ v. ECONOMOU

438 U.S. 478, 98 S.Ct. 2894, 57 L.Ed.2d 895 (1978).
Certiorari to the United States Court of Appeals for the Second Circuit.

MR. JUSTICE WHITE delivered the opinion of the Court.

This case concerns the personal immunity of federal officials in the Executive Branch from claims for damages arising from their violations of citizens' constitutional rights. Respondent filed suit against a number of officials in the Department of Agriculture claiming that they had instituted an investigation and an administrative proceeding against him in retaliation for his criticism of that agency. The District Court dismissed the action on the ground that the individual defendants, as federal officials, were entitled to absolute immunity for all discretionary acts within the scope of their authority. The Court of Appeals reversed, holding that the

---

14. Suppose Congress wished today to permit a claimant like the prisoner in Hudson v. Palmer to seek federal court relief even if state remedies were adequate. Would it have power under § 5 of the Fourteenth Amendment to so legislate? See Monaghan, note 6, *supra,* at 997–98, expressing doubts.

defendants were entitled only to the qualified immunity available to their counterparts in state government. Because of the importance of immunity doctrine to both the vindication of constitutional guarantees and the effective functioning of government, we granted certiorari.

I

Respondent controls Arthur N. Economou and Co., Inc., which was at one time registered with the Department of Agriculture as a commodity futures commission merchant. Most of respondent's factual allegations in this lawsuit focus on an earlier administrative proceeding in which the Department of Agriculture sought to revoke or suspend the company's registration. On February 19, 1970, following an audit, the Department of Agriculture issued an administrative complaint alleging that respondent, while a registered merchant, had willfully failed to maintain the minimum financial requirements prescribed by the Department. After another audit, an amended complaint was issued on June 22, 1970. A hearing was held before the Chief Hearing Examiner of the Department, who filed a recommendation sustaining the administrative complaint. The Judicial Officer of the Department, to whom the Secretary had delegated his decisional authority in enforcement proceedings, affirmed the Chief Hearing Examiner's decision. On respondent's petition for review, the Court of Appeals for the Second Circuit vacated the order of the Judicial Officer. It reasoned that "the essential finding of willfulness * * * was made in a proceeding instituted without the customary warning letter, which the Judicial Officer conceded might well have resulted in prompt correction of the claimed insufficiencies."

While the administrative complaint was pending before the Judicial Officer, respondent filed this lawsuit in Federal District Court. Respondent sought initially to enjoin the progress of the administrative proceeding, but he was unsuccessful in that regard. On March 31, 1975, respondent filed a second amended complaint seeking damages. Named as defendants were the individuals who had served as Secretary and Assistant Secretary of Agriculture during the relevant events; the Judicial Officer and Chief Hearing Examiner; several officials in the Commodity Exchange Authority; the Agriculture Department attorney who had prosecuted the enforcement proceeding; and several of the auditors who had investigated respondent or were witnesses against respondent.

The complaint stated that prior to the issuance of the administrative complaints respondent had been "sharply critical of the staff and operations of Defendants and carried on a vociferous campaign for the reform of Defendant Commodity Exchange Authority to obtain more effective regulation of commodity trading." The complaint also stated that some time prior to the issuance of the February 19 complaint, respondent and his company had ceased to engage in activities regulated by the defendants. The complaint charged that each of the administrative complaints had been issued without the notice or warning required by law; that the defendants had furnished the complaints "to interested persons and others without furnishing respondent's answers as well"; and that following the issuance of the amended complaint, the defendants had issued a "deceptive" press release that "falsely indicated to the public that [respondent's] financial resources had deteriorated, when Defendants knew that their statement was untrue and so acknowledge[d] previously that said assertion was untrue."

The complaint then presented 10 "causes of action," some of which purported to state claims for damages under the United States Constitution. For example, the first "cause of action" alleged that respondent had been denied due process of law because the defendants had instituted unauthorized proceedings against him without proper notice and with the knowledge that respondent was no longer subject to their regulatory jurisdiction. The third "cause of action" stated that by means of such actions "the Defendants discouraged and chilled the campaign of criticism [plaintiff] directed against them, and thereby deprived the [plaintiff] of [his] rights to free expression guaranteed by the First Amendment of the United States Constitution." [5]

The defendants moved to dismiss the complaint on the ground that "as to the individual defendants it is barred by the doctrine of official immunity * * *." The defendants relied on an affidavit submitted earlier in the litigation by the attorney who had prosecuted the original administrative complaint against respondent. He stated that the Secretary of Agriculture had had no involvement with the case and that each of the other named defendants had acted "within the course of his official duties."

The District Court, apparently relying on the plurality opinion in Barr v. Matteo, 360 U.S. 564 (1959), held that the individual defendants would be entitled to immunity if they could show that "their alleged unconstitutional acts were within the outer perimeter of their authority and discretionary." After examining the nature of the acts alleged in the complaint, the District Court concluded: "Since the individual defendants have shown that their alleged unconstitutional acts were both within the scope of their authority and discretionary, we dismiss the second amended complaint as to them."

The Court of Appeals for the Second Circuit reversed the District Court's judgment of dismissal with respect to the individual defendants. Economou v. U.S. Department of Agriculture, 535 F.2d 688 (1976). The Court of Appeals reasoned that Barr v. Matteo, *supra,* did not "represen[t] the last word in this evolving area," 535 F.2d, at 691, because principles governing the immunity of officials of the Executive Branch had been elucidated in later decisions dealing with constitutional claims against state officials. *E.g.,* Pierson v. Ray, 386 U.S. 547 (1967); Scheuer v. Rhodes, 416 U.S. 232 (1974); Wood v. Strickland, 420 U.S. 308 (1975). These opinions were understood to establish that officials of the Executive Branch exercising discretionary functions did not need the protection of an absolute immunity from suit, but only a qualified immunity based on good faith and reasonable grounds. * * *

5. In the second "cause of action," respondent stated that the defendants had issued administrative orders "illegal and punitive in nature" against him when he was no longer subject to their authority. The fourth "cause of action" alleged, *inter alia,* that respondent's rights to due process of law and to privacy as guaranteed by the Federal Constitution had been infringed by the furnishing of the administrative complaints to interested persons without respondent's answers. The fifth "cause of action" similarly alleged as a violation of due process that defendants had issued a press release containing facts the defendants knew or should have known were false. Respondent's remaining "causes of action" allege common-law torts: abuse of legal process, malicious prosecution, invasion of privacy, negligence, and trespass.

* * * The court concluded that all of the defendants were "adequately protected by permitting them to avail themselves of the defense of qualified 'good faith, reasonable grounds' immunity of the type approved by the Supreme Court in Scheuer and Wood." After noting that summary judgment would be available to the defendants if there were no genuine factual issues for trial, the Court of Appeals remanded the case for further proceedings.

II

The single submission by the United States on behalf of petitioners is that all of the federal officials sued in this case are absolutely immune from any liability for damages even if in the course of enforcing the relevant statutes they infringed respondent's constitutional rights and even if the violation was knowing and deliberate. Although the position is earnestly and ably presented by the United States, we are quite sure that it is unsound and consequently reject it.

The Government places principal reliance on Barr v. Matteo, 360 U.S. 564 (1959). In that case, the acting director of an agency had been sued for malicious defamation by two employees whose suspension for misconduct he had announced in a press release. The defendant claimed an absolute or qualified privilege, but the trial court rejected both and the jury returned a verdict for plaintiff.

[The Court of Appeals ruled that the press release was protected by a qualified privilege, which could be defeated by a finding that the defendant had acted maliciously, or had spoken without reasonable grounds for believing that his statement was true; it remanded for a new trial on those issues. The Supreme Court reversed, ruling that the defendant could not be held liable for damages. There was no majority opinion. Speaking for a plurality of four *, Justice Harlan] inquired whether the conduct complained of was among those "matters committed by law to [the official's] control" and concluded, after an analysis of the specific circumstances, that the press release was within the "outer perimeter of [his] line of duty" and was "an appropriate exercise of the discretion which an officer of that rank must possess if the public service is to function effectively." Id., at 575. The plurality then held that under Spalding v. Vilas, 161 U.S. 483 (1896), the act was privileged and that the officer could not be held liable for the tort of defamation despite the allegations of malice.[12] Barr clearly held that a false and damaging publication, the issuance of which was otherwise

---

* [Ed.] Justice Black, concurring in the result, supplied the fifth vote for reversal; he stressed that no law forbade issuance of the press release, and that the criticism of "the way the Agency or its employees perform their duties" should not be subject to the restraint of libel actions (p. 577).

Justice Stewart approved Justice Harlan's opinion as a "lucid and persuasive analysis of the principles that should guide decision in this troublesome area of law." He dissented on the view that the press release was not "action in the line of duty" but designed only to defend the "individual reputation" of the petitioner (p. 592).

Dissenting opinions were filed by Chief Justice Warren, joined by Justice Douglas, and by Justice Brennan. Both opinions supported a qualified privilege but objected to affording absolute immunity.

12. The Court wrote a similar opinion and entered a similar judgment in a companion case, Howard v. Lyons, 360 U.S. 593 (1959). There a complaint for defamation under state law alleged the publication of a deliberate and knowing falsehood by a federal officer. Judgment was entered for the officer before trial on the ground that the release was within the limits of his authority. The judgment was reversed in part by the Court of Appeals on the ground that in

within the official's authority, was not itself actionable and would not become so by being issued maliciously. The Court did not choose to discuss whether the director's privilege would be defeated by showing that he was without reasonable grounds for believing his release was true or that he knew that it was false, although the issue was in the case as it came from the Court of Appeals.

Barr does not control this case. It did not address the liability of the acting director had his conduct not been within the outer limits of his duties, but from the care with which the Court inquired into the scope of his authority, it may be inferred that had the release been unauthorized, and surely if the issuance of press releases had been expressly forbidden by statute, the claim of absolute immunity would not have been upheld. The inference is supported by the fact that Mr. Justice Stewart, although agreeing with the principles announced by Mr. Justice Harlan, dissented and would have rejected the immunity claim because the press release, in his view, was not action in the line of duty. 360 U.S., at 592. It is apparent also that a quite different question would have been presented had the officer ignored an express statutory or constitutional limitation on his authority.

Barr did not, therefore, purport to depart from the general rule, which long prevailed, that a federal official may not with impunity ignore the limitations which the controlling law has placed on his powers. The immunity of federal executive officials began as a means of protecting them in the execution of their federal statutory duties from criminal or civil actions based on state law. See Osborn v. Bank of the United States, 9 Wheat. 738, 865–866 (1824). A federal official who acted outside of his federal statutory authority would be held strictly liable for his trespassory acts. For example, Little v. Barreme, 2 Cranch 170 (1804), held the commander of an American warship liable in damages for the seizure of a Danish cargo ship on the high seas. Congress had directed the President to intercept any vessels reasonably suspected of being en route *to* a French port, but the President had authorized the seizure of suspected vessels whether going *to* or *from* French ports, and the Danish vessel seized was en route *from* a forbidden destination. The Court, speaking through Mr. Chief Justice Marshall, held that the President's instructions could not "change the nature of the transaction, or legalize an act which, without those instructions, would have been a plain trespass." *Id.*, at 179. Although there was probable cause to believe that the ship was engaged in traffic with the French, the seizure at issue was not among that class of seizures that the Executive had been authorized by statute to effect.

* * *

As these cases demonstrate, a federal official was protected for action tortious under state law only if his acts were authorized by controlling federal law. "To make out his defence he must show that his authority was sufficient in law to protect him." Cunningham v. Macon & Brunswick R. Co., 109 U.S. 446, 452 (1883); Belknap v. Schild, 161 U.S. 10, 19 (1896). Since an unconstitutional act, even if authorized by statute, was viewed as not authorized in contemplation of law, there could be no immunity

some respects the defendant was entitled
to only a qualified privilege. This Court
reversed, ruling that Barr controlled.

defense.[15] See United States v. Lee, 106 U.S. 196, 218–223 (1882); Virginia Coupon Cases, 114 U.S. 269, 285–292 (1885).[16]

In * * * Barreme * * *, the officer [   ] did not merely mistakenly conclude that the circumstances warranted a particular seizure, but failed to observe the limitations on [his] authority by making seizures not within the category or type of seizures [he was] authorized to make. Kendall v. Stokes, 3 How. 87 (1845), addressed a different situation. The case involved a suit against the Postmaster General for erroneously suspending payments to a creditor of the Post Office. Examining and, if necessary, suspending payments to creditors were among the Postmaster's normal duties, and it appeared that he had simply made a mistake in the exercise of the discretion conferred upon him. He was held not liable in damages since "a public officer, acting to the best of his judgment and from a sense of duty, in a matter of account with an individual [is not] liable in an action for an error of judgment." Id., at 97–98. * * *

In Spalding v. Vilas, 161 U.S. 483 (1896), on which the Government relies, the principal issue was whether the malicious motive of an officer would render him liable in damages for injury inflicted by his official act that otherwise was within the scope of his authority. The Postmaster General was sued for circulating among the postmasters a notice that assertedly injured the reputation of the plaintiff and interfered with his contractual relationships. The Court first inquired as to the Postmaster General's Authority to issue the notice. In doing so, it "recognize[d] a distinction between action taken by the head of a Department in reference to matters which are manifestly or palpably beyond his authority, and action having more or less connection with the general matters committed by law to his control or supervision." Id., at 498. Concluding that the circular issued by the Postmaster General "was not unauthorized by law, nor beyond the scope of his official duties," the Court then addressed the major question in the case—whether the act could be "maintained because of the allegation that what the officer did was done maliciously?" Id., at 493. Its holding was that the head of a department could not be "held liable to a civil suit for damages on account of official communications made by him pursuant to an act of Congress, and in respect of matters within his authority," however improper his motives might have been. Id., at 498. * * *

Spalding made clear that a malicious intent will not subject a public officer to liability for performing his authorized duties as to which he would otherwise not be subject to damages liability. But Spalding did not involve conduct manifestly or otherwise beyond the authority of the official, nor did it involve a mistake of either law or fact in construing or applying the statute. It did not purport to immunize officials who ignore limitations on

---

15. Indeed, there appears to have been some doubt as to whether even an Act of Congress would immunize federal officials from suits seeking damages for constitutional violations. See Milligan v. Hovey, 17 F.Cas. 380 (No. 9,605) (CC Ind.1871); Griffin v. Wilcox, 21 Ind. 370, 372–373 (1863). See generally Engdahl, *Immunity and Accountability for Positive Governmental Wrongs*, 44 U.Colo.L.Rev. 1, 50–51 (1972).

16. While the Virginia Coupon Cases, like United States v. Lee, involved a suit for the return of specific property, the principles espoused therein are equally applicable to a suit for damages and were later so applied. Atchison, Topeka & Santa Fe R. Co. v. O'Connor, 223 U.S. 280, 287 (1912).

their authority imposed by law. * * * It is also evident that Spalding presented no claim that the officer was liable in damages because he had acted in violation of a limitation placed upon his conduct by the United States Constitution. * * *

Insofar as cases in this Court dealing with the immunity or privilege of federal officers are concerned, this is where the matter stood until Barr v. Matteo. * * * The plurality opinion and judgment in Barr also appear— although without any discussion of the matter—to have extended absolute immunity to an officer who was authorized to issue press releases, who was assumed to know that the press release he issued was false and who therefore was deliberately misusing his authority. Accepting this extension of immunity with respect to state tort claims, however, we are confident that Barr did not purport to protect an official who has not only committed a wrong under local law, but also violated those fundamental principles of fairness embodied in the Constitution.[22] Whatever level of protection from state interference is appropriate for federal officials executing their duties under federal law, it cannot be doubted that these officials, even when acting pursuant to congressional authorization, are subject to the restraints imposed by the Federal Constitution.

The liability of officials who have exceeded constitutional limits was not confronted in either Barr or Spalding. Neither of those cases supports the Government's position. Beyond that, however, neither case purported to abolish the liability of federal officers for actions manifestly beyond their line of duty; and if they are accountable when they stray beyond the plain limits of their statutory authority, it would be incongruous to hold that they may nevertheless willfully or knowingly violate constitutional rights without fear of liability.

Although it is true that the Court has not dealt with this issue with respect to federal officers, we have several times addressed the immunity of state officers when sued under 42 U.S.C. § 1983 for alleged violations of constitutional rights. These decisions are instructive for present purposes.

III

Pierson v. Ray, 386 U.S. 547 (1967), decided that § 1983 was not intended to abrogate the immunity of state judges which existed under the common law and which the Court had held applicable to federal judges in Bradley v. Fisher, 13 Wall. 335 (1872). Pierson also * * * held that police officers were entitled to a defense of "good faith and probable cause," even though an arrest might subsequently be proved to be unconstitutional. We observed, however, that "[t]he common law has never granted police officers an absolute and unqualified immunity, and the officers in this case do not claim that they are entitled to one." 386 U.S., at 555.

In Scheuer v. Rhodes, supra, the issue was whether "higher officers of the executive branch" of state governments were immune from liability under § 1983 for violations of constitutionally protected rights. 416 U.S., at 246. There, the Governor of a State, the senior and subordinate officers of the state National Guard, and a state university president had been sued on the allegation that they had suppressed a civil disturbance in an

---

22. We view this case, in its present posture, as concerned only with constitutional issues. * * *

unconstitutional manner. We explained that the doctrine of official immunity from § 1983 liability, although not constitutionally grounded and
essentially a matter of statutory construction, was based on two mutually
dependent rationales:

> "(1) the injustice, particularly in the absence of bad faith, of subjecting
> to liability an officer who is required, by the legal obligations of his
> position, to exercise discretion; (2) the danger that the threat of such
> liability would deter his willingness to execute his office with the
> decisiveness and the judgment required by the public good." *Id.*, at
> 240.

The opinion also recognized that executive branch officers must often act
swiftly and on the basis of factual information supplied by others, constraints which become even more acute in the "atmosphere of confusion,
ambiguity, and swiftly moving events" created by a civil disturbance. *Id.*,
at 246–247. Although quoting at length from Barr v. Matteo, we did not
believe that there was a need for absolute immunity from § 1983 liability
for these high-ranking state officials. Rather the considerations discussed
above indicated:

> "[I]n varying scope, a qualified immunity is available to officers of the
> executive branch of government, the variation being dependent upon
> the scope of discretion and responsibilities of the office and all the
> circumstances as they reasonably appeared at the time of the action on
> which liability is sought to be based. It is the existence of reasonable
> grounds for the belief formed at the time and in light of all the
> circumstances, coupled with good-faith belief, that affords a basis for
> qualified immunity of executive officers for acts performed in the
> course of official conduct." 416 U.S., at 247–248.

Subsequent decisions have applied the Scheuer standard in other
contexts. In Wood v. Strickland, 420 U.S. 308 (1975), school administrators
were held entitled to claim a similar qualified immunity. A school board
member would lose his immunity from a § 1983 suit only if "he knew or
reasonably should have known that the action he took within his sphere of
official responsibility would violate the constitutional rights of the student
affected, or if he took the action with the malicious intention to cause a
deprivation of constitutional rights or other injury to the student." 420
U.S., at 322. In O'Connor v. Donaldson, 422 U.S. 563 (1975), we applied the
same standard to the superintendent of a state hospital. In Procunier v.
Navarette, 434 U.S. 555 (1978), we held that prison administrators would be
adequately protected by the qualified immunity outlined in Scheuer and
Wood. We emphasized, however, that, at least in the absence of some
showing of malice, an official would not be held liable in damages under
§ 1983 unless the constitutional right he was alleged to have violated was
"clearly established" at the time of the violation.

        * * *

        * * * [I]n the absence of congressional direction to the contrary,
there is no basis for according to federal officials a higher degree of
immunity from liability when sued for a constitutional infringement as
authorized by Bivens than is accorded state officials when sued for the
identical violation under § 1983. The constitutional injuries made actionable by § 1983 are of no greater magnitude than those for which federal
officials may be responsible. The pressures and uncertainties facing deci-

sionmakers in state government are little if at all different from those affecting federal officials. We see no sense in holding a state governor liable but immunizing the head of a federal department; in holding the administrator of a federal hospital immune where the superintendent of a state hospital would be liable; in protecting the warden of a federal prison where the warden of a state prison would be vulnerable; or in distinguishing between state and federal police participating in the same investigation. * * *

The Government argues that the cases involving state officials are distinguishable because they reflect the need to preserve the effectiveness of the right of action authorized by § 1983. But * * * the cause of action recognized in Bivens v. Six Unknown Fed. Narcotics Agents, 403 U.S. 388 (1971), would similarly be "drained of meaning" if federal officials were entitled to absolute immunity for their constitutional transgressions.

Moreover, the Government's analysis would place undue emphasis on the congressional origins of the cause of action in determining the level of immunity. * * *

* * * *

Accordingly, without congressional directions to the contrary, we deem it untenable to draw a distinction for purposes of immunity law between suits brought against state officials under § 1983 and suits brought directly under the Constitution against federal officials. * * * To create a system in which the Bill of Rights monitors more closely the conduct of state officials than it does that of federal officials is to stand the constitutional design on its head.

IV

* * * [T]he decision in Bivens established that a citizen suffering a compensable injury to a constitutionally protected interest could invoke the general federal-question jurisdiction of the district courts to obtain an award of monetary damages against the responsible federal official. As Mr. Justice Harlan, concurring in the judgment, pointed out, the action for damages recognized in Bivens could be a vital means of providing redress for persons whose constitutional rights have been violated. The barrier of sovereign immunity is frequently impenetrable. Injunctive or declaratory relief is useless to a person who has already been injured. "For people in Bivens' shoes, it is damages or nothing." 403 U.S., at 410.

* * * *

The extension of absolute immunity from damages liability to all federal executive officials would seriously erode the protection provided by basic constitutional guarantees. The broad authority possessed by these officials enables them to direct their subordinates to undertake a wide range of projects—including some which may infringe such important personal interests as liberty, property, and free speech. It makes little sense to hold that a Government agent is liable for warrantless and forcible entry into a citizen's house in pursuit of evidence, but that an official of higher rank who actually orders such a burglary is immune simply because of his greater authority. Indeed, the greater power of such officials affords a greater potential for a regime of lawless conduct. * * *

* * *

This is not to say that considerations of public policy fail to support a limited immunity for federal executive officials. We consider here, as we did in Scheuer, the need to protect officials who are required to exercise their discretion and the related public interest in encouraging the vigorous exercise of official authority. Yet Scheuer and other cases have recognized that it is not unfair to hold liable the official who knows or should know he is acting outside the law, and that insisting on an awareness of clearly established constitutional limits will not unduly interfere with the exercise of official judgment. We therefore hold that, in a suit for damages arising from unconstitutional action, federal executive officials exercising discretion are entitled only to the qualified immunity specified in Scheuer, subject to those exceptional situations where it is demonstrated that absolute immunity is essential for the conduct of the public business.

* * *

V

Although a qualified immunity from damages liability should be the general rule for executive officials charged with constitutional violations, our decisions recognize that there are some officials whose special functions require a full exemption from liability. *E.g.,* Bradley v. Fisher, 13 Wall. 335 (1872); Imbler v. Pachtman, 424 U.S. 409 (1976). In each case, we have undertaken "a considered inquiry into the immunity historically accorded the relevant official at common law and the interests behind it." *Id.,* at 421.

In Bradley v. Fisher, the Court analyzed the need for absolute immunity to protect judges from lawsuits claiming that their decisions had been tainted by improper motives. The Court began by noting that the principle of immunity for acts done by judges "in the exercise of their judicial functions" had been "the settled doctrine of the English courts for many centuries, and has never been denied, that we are aware of, in the courts of this country." 13 Wall., at 347. The Court explained that the value of this rule was proved by experience. Judges were often called to decide "[c]ontroversies involving not merely great pecuniary interests, but the liberty and character of the parties, and consequently exciting the deepest feelings." *Id.,* at 348. Such adjudications invariably produced at least one losing party, who would "accep[t] anything but the soundness of the decision in explanation of the action of the judge." *Ibid.* * * * If a civil action could be maintained against a judge by virtue of an allegation of malice, judges would lose "that independence without which no judiciary can either be respectable or useful." *Id.,* at 347. Thus, judges were held to be immune from civil suit "for malice or corruption in their action whilst exercising their judicial functions within the general scope of their jurisdiction." *Id.,* at 354.[36]

The principle of Bradley was extended to federal prosecutors through the summary affirmance in Yaselli v. Goff, 275 U.S. 503 (1927), *aff'g* 12 F.2d 396 (CA2 1926). * * *

We recently reaffirmed the holding of Yaselli v. Goff in Imbler v. Pachtman, *supra,* a suit against a state prosecutor under § 1983. * * *

---

36. In Pierson v. Ray, 386 U.S. 547 (1967), we recognized that state judges sued on constitutional claims pursuant to § 1983 could claim a similar absolute immunity. * * *

Despite these precedents, the Court of Appeals concluded that all of the defendants in this case—including the Chief Hearing Examiner, Judicial Officer, and prosecuting attorney—were entitled to only a qualified immunity. The Court of Appeals reasoned that officials within the Executive Branch generally have more circumscribed discretion and pointed out that, unlike a judge, officials of the Executive Branch would face no conflict of interest if their legal representation was provided by the Executive Branch. The Court of Appeals recognized that "some of the Agriculture Department officials may be analogized to criminal prosecutors, in that they initiated the proceedings against [respondent], and presented evidence therein," but found that attorneys in administrative proceedings did not face the same "serious constraints of time and even information" which this Court has found to be present frequently in criminal cases. *See* Imbler v. Pachtman, 424 U.S., at 425.

We think that the Court of Appeals placed undue emphasis on the fact that the officials sued here are—from an administrative perspective— employees of the Executive Branch. Judges have absolute immunity not because of their particular location within the Government but because of the special nature of their responsibilities. This point is underlined by the fact that prosecutors—themselves members of the Executive Branch—are also absolutely immune. "It is the functional comparability of their judgments to those of the judge that has resulted in both grand jurors and prosecutors being referred to as 'quasi-judicial' officers, and their immunities being termed 'quasi-judicial' as well." *Id.,* at 423 n. 20.

The cluster of immunities protecting the various participants in judge-supervised trials stems from the characteristics of the judicial process rather than its location. As the Bradley Court suggested, 13 Wall., at 348– 349, controversies sufficiently intense to erupt in litigation are not easily capped by a judicial decree. The loser in one forum will frequently seek another, charging the participants in the first with unconstitutional animus. See Pierson v. Ray, 386 U.S., at 554. Absolute immunity is thus necessary to assure that judges, advocates, and witnesses can perform their respective functions without harassment or intimidation.

At the same time, the safeguards built into the judicial process tend to reduce the need for private damages actions as a means of controlling unconstitutional conduct. The insulation of the judge from political influence, the importance of precedent in resolving controversies, the adversary nature of the process, and the correctability of error on appeal are just a few of the many checks on malicious action by judges. Advocates are restrained not only by their professional obligations, but by the knowledge that their assertions will be contested by their adversaries in open court. Jurors are carefully screened to remove all possibility of bias. Witnesses are, of course, subject to the rigors of cross-examination and the penalty of perjury. Because these features of the judicial process tend to enhance the reliability of information and the impartiality of the decisionmaking process, there is a less pressing need for individual suits to correct constitutional error.

We think that adjudication within a federal administrative agency shares enough of the characteristics of the judicial process that those who participate in such adjudication should also be immune from suits for damages. * * *

There can be little doubt that the role of the modern federal hearing examiner or administrative law judge within this framework is "functionally comparable" to that of a judge. His powers are often, if not generally, comparable to those of a trial judge: He may issue subpoenas, rule on proffers of evidence, regulate the course of the hearing, and make or recommend decisions. More importantly, the process of agency adjudication is currently structured so as to assure that the hearing examiner exercises his independent judgment on the evidence before him, free from pressures by the parties or other officials within the agency. * * *

In light of these safeguards, we think that the risk of an unconstitutional act by one presiding at an agency hearing is clearly outweighed by the importance of preserving the independent judgment of these men and women. We therefore hold that persons subject to these restraints and performing adjudicatory functions within a federal agency are entitled to absolute immunity from damages liability for their judicial acts. Those who complain of error in such proceedings must seek agency or judicial review.

We also believe that agency officials performing certain functions analogous to those of a prosecutor should be able to claim absolute immunity with respect to such acts. The decision to initiate administrative proceedings against an individual or corporation is very much like the prosecutor's decision to initiate or move forward with a criminal prosecution. * * *

The discretion which executive officials exercise with respect to the initiation of administrative proceedings might be distorted if their immunity from damages arising from that decision was less than complete. *Cf.* Imbler v. Pachtman, 424 U.S., at 426 n. 24. * * *

* * *

We turn finally to the role of an agency attorney in conducting a trial and presenting evidence on the record to the trier of fact. We can see no substantial difference between the function of the agency attorney in presenting evidence in an agency hearing and the function of the prosecutor who brings evidence before a court. * * * We therefore hold that an agency attorney who arranges for the presentation of evidence on the record in the course of an adjudication is absolutely immune from suits based on the introduction of such evidence.

VI

There remains the task of applying the foregoing principles to the claims against the particular petitioner-defendants involved in this case. Rather than attempt this here in the first instance, we vacate the judgment of the Court of Appeals and remand the case to that court with instructions to remand the case to the District Court for further proceedings consistent with this opinion.

So ordered.

MR. JUSTICE REHNQUIST, with whom THE CHIEF JUSTICE, MR. JUSTICE STEWART, and MR. JUSTICE STEVENS join, concurring in part and dissenting in part.

I concur in that part of the Court's judgment which affords absolute immunity to those persons performing adjudicatory functions within a federal agency, * * * those who are responsible for the decision to initiate or continue a proceeding subject to agency adjudication, * * * and those agency personnel who present evidence on the record in the course of an adjudication * * *. I cannot agree, however, with the Court's conclusion that in a suit for damages arising from allegedly unconstitutional action federal executive officials, regardless of their rank or the scope of their responsibilities, are entitled to only qualified immunity even when acting within the outer limits of their authority. The Court's protestations to the contrary notwithstanding, this decision seriously misconstrues our prior decisions, finds little support as a matter of logic or precedent, and perhaps most importantly, will, I fear, seriously "dampen the ardor of all but the most resolute, or the most irresponsible, in the unflinching discharge of their duties," Gregoire v. Biddle, 177 F.2d 579, 581 (CA2 1949) (Learned Hand, J.).

Most noticeable is the Court's unnaturally constrained reading of the landmark case of Spalding v. Vilas, 161 U.S. 483 (1896). The Court in that case did indeed hold that the actions taken by the Postmaster General were within the authority conferred upon him by Congress, and went on to hold that even though he had acted maliciously in carrying out the duties conferred upon him by Congress he was protected by official immunity. But the Court left no doubt that it would have reached the same result had it been alleged the official acts were unconstitutional.

"We are of the opinion that the same general considerations of public policy and convenience which demand for judges of courts of superior jurisdiction immunity from civil suits for damages arising from acts done by them in the course of the performance of their judicial functions, apply to a large extent to official communications made by heads of Executive Departments when engaged in the discharge of duties imposed upon them by law. The interests of the people require that due protection be accorded to them in respect of their official acts." *Id.*, at 498. * * *

Indeed, the language from Spalding quoted above unquestionably applies with equal force in the case at bar. No one seriously contends that the Secretary of Agriculture or the Assistant Secretary, who are being sued for $32 million in damages, had wandered completely off the official reservation in authorizing prosecution of respondent for violation of regulations promulgated by the Secretary for the regulation of "futures commission merchants," 7 U.S.C. § 6 (1976 ed.). This is precisely what the Secretary and his assistants were empowered and required to do. That they would on occasion be mistaken in their judgment that a particular merchant had in fact violated the regulations is a necessary concomitant of any known system of administrative adjudication; that they acted "maliciously" gives no support to respondent's claim against them unless we are to overrule Spalding.

The Court's attempt to distinguish Spalding may be predicated on a simpler but equally erroneous concept of immunity. At one point the Court observes that even under Spalding "an executive officer would be vulnerable if he took action 'manifestly or palpably' beyond his authority or ignored a clear limitation on his enforcement powers." * * * From that proposition, which is undeniably accurate, the Court appears to conclude that anytime a plaintiff can paint his grievance in constitutional colors, the official is subject to damages unless he can prove he acted in good faith. * * *

Putting to one side the illogic and impracticability of distinguishing between constitutional and common-law claims for purposes of immunity, which will be discussed shortly, this sort of immunity analysis badly misses the mark. It amounts to saying that an official has immunity until someone alleges he has acted unconstitutionally. But that is no immunity at all: The "immunity" disappears at the very moment when it is needed. The critical inquiry in determining whether an official is entitled to claim immunity is not whether someone has in fact been injured by his action; that is part of the plaintiff's case in chief. The immunity defense turns on whether the action was one taken "when engaged in the discharge of duties imposed upon [the official] by law," Spalding, 161 U.S., at 498, or in other words, whether the official was acting within the outer bounds of his authority. Only if the immunity inquiry is approached in this manner does it have any meaning. That such a rule may occasionally result in individual injustices has never been doubted, but at least until today, immunity has been accorded nevertheless. * * *

Barr v. Matteo, 360 U.S. 564 (1959), unfortunately fares little better at the Court's hand than Spalding. * * * Barr is distinguished * * * on the ground that it did not involve a violation of "those fundamental principles of fairness embodied in the Constitution." * * * But if we allow a mere allegation of unconstitutionality, obviously unproved at the time made, to require a Cabinet-level official, charged with the enforcement of the responsibilities to which the complaint pertains, to lay aside his duties and defend such an action on the merits, the defense of official immunity will have been abolished in fact if not in form. The ease with which a constitutional claim may be pleaded in a case such as this, where a violation of statutory or judicial limits on agency action may be readily converted by any legal neophyte into a claim of denial of procedural due process under the Fifth Amendment, will assure that. The fact that the claim fails when put to trial will not prevent the consumption of time, effort, and money on the part of the defendant official in defending his actions on the merits. The result can only be damage to the "interests of the people," Spalding, *supra*, at 498, which "require[s] that due protection be accorded to [Cabinet officials] in respect of their official acts."

It likewise cannot seriously be argued that an official will be less deterred by the threat of liability for unconstitutional conduct than for activities which might constitute a common-law tort. The fear that inhibits is that of a long, involved lawsuit and a significant money judgment, not the fear of liability for a certain type of claim. Thus, even viewing the question functionally—indeed, *especially* viewing the question functionally—the basis for a distinction between constitutional and common-law torts in this context is open to serious question. Even the logical justification for raising such a novel distinction is far from clear. That the Framers thought some rights sufficiently susceptible of legislative derogation that they should be enshrined in the Constitution does not necessarily indicate that the Framers likewise intended to establish an immutable hierarchy of rights in terms of their importance to individuals. The most heinous common-law tort surely cannot be less important to, or have less of an impact on, the aggrieved individual than a mere technical violation of a constitutional proscription.

* * *

The Court also suggests in sweeping terms that the cause of action recognized in Bivens would be " 'drained of meaning' if federal officials were entitled to absolute immunity for their constitutional transgressions." * * * But Bivens is a slender reed on which to rely when abrogating official immunity for Cabinet-level officials. In the first place, those officials most susceptible to claims under Bivens have historically been given only a qualified immunity. As the Court observed in Pierson v. Ray, 386 U.S. 547, 555 (1967), "[t]he common law has never granted police officers an absolute and unqualified immunity * * *." In any event, it certainly does not follow that a grant of absolute immunity to the Secretary and Assistant Secretary of Agriculture requires a like grant to federal law enforcement officials. * * *

* * *

My biggest concern, however, is not with the illogic or impracticality of today's decision, but rather with the potential for disruption of Government that it invites. The steady increase in litigation, much of it directed against governmental officials and virtually all of which could be framed in constitutional terms, cannot escape the notice of even the most casual observer. * * *

The Court, of course, recognizes this problem and suggests two solutions. First, judges, ever alert to the artful pleader, supposedly will weed out insubstantial claims. * * * That, I fear, shows more optimism than prescience. Indeed, this very case, unquestionably frivolous in the extreme, belies any hope in that direction. And summary judgment on affidavits and the like is even more inappropriate when the central, and perhaps only, inquiry is the official's state of mind. * * *

The second solution offered by the Court is even less satisfactory. The Court holds that in those special circumstances "where it is demonstrated that absolute immunity is essential for the conduct of the public business," absolute immunity will be extended. * * * But this is a form of "absolute immunity" which in truth exists in name only. If, for example, the Secretary of Agriculture may never know until inquiry, by a trial court whether there is a possibility that vexatious constitutional litigation will interfere with his decision-making process, the Secretary will obviously think not only twice but thrice about whether to prosecute a litigious commodities merchant who has played fast and loose with the regulations for his own profit. Careful consideration of the rights of every individual subject to his jurisdiction is one thing; a timorous reluctance to prosecute any of such individuals who have a reputation for using litigation as a defense weapon is quite another. * * *

* * *

* * * That part of the Court's present opinion from which I dissent will, I fear, result in one of two evils, either one of which is markedly worse than the effect of according absolute immunity to the Secretary and the Assistant Secretary in this case. The first of these evils would be a significant impairment of the ability of responsible public officials to carry out the duties imposed upon them by law. If that evil is to be avoided after today, it can be avoided only by a necessarily unprincipled and erratic judicial "screening" of claims such as those made in this case, an adherence to the form of the law while departing from its substance. Either one of these evils is far worse than the occasional failure to award damages caused by official wrongdoing, frankly and openly justified by the rule of Spalding v. Vilas, Barr v. Matteo, and Gregoire v. Biddle.

NOTE ON OFFICERS' ACCOUNTABILITY IN DAMAGES FOR OFFICIAL MISCONDUCT

(1) *The Basis for Official Immunity.* Questions of official immunity ordinarily arise in suits (like Butz) seeking damages to be paid by individual officers personally, rather than by the government. (For discussion of individual officers' immunity from relief other than damages, see *Note on the Immunity of Government Officers From Relief Other Than Damages,* which follows this Note.)

A classic statement of the rationale for official immunity is found in Gregoire v. Biddle, 177 F.2d 579 (2d Cir.1949) (L. Hand, J.), upholding the absolute immunity not only of the Attorney General, but also of mid-level Justice Department officials, in a suit claiming that the defendants had, with malice and without justification, falsely imprisoned the plaintiff. The court wrote (p. 581):

"It does indeed go without saying that an official, who is in fact guilty of using his powers to vent his spleen upon others, or for any other personal motive not connected with the public good, should not escape liability for the injuries he may so cause; and, if it were possible in practice to confine such complaints to the guilty, it would be monstrous to deny recovery. The justification for doing so is that it is impossible to know whether the claim is well founded until the case has been tried, and that to submit all officials, the innocent as well as the guilty, to the burden of a trial and to the inevitable danger of its outcome, would dampen the ardor of all but the most resolute, or the most irresponsible, in the unflinching discharge of their duties. Again and again the public interest calls for action which may turn out to be founded on a mistake, in the face of which an official may later find himself hard put to it to satisfy a jury of his good faith. There must indeed be means of punishing public officers who have been truant to their duties; but that is quite another matter from exposing such as have been honestly mistaken to suit by anyone who has suffered from their errors. As is so often the case, the answer must be found in a balance between the evils inevitable in either alternative. In this instance it has been thought in the end better to leave unredressed the wrongs done by dishonest officers than to subject those who try to do their duty to the constant dread of retaliation. Judged as res nova, we should not hesitate to follow the path laid down in the books."

This view represents a major shift from nineteenth century practice, under which officials sued in tort generally were treated like private tortfeasors and not shielded by any distinctive immunity—although pockets of immunity did evolve, as for judges and high federal officials. See generally Engdahl, *Immunity and Accountability for Positive Governmental Wrongs,* 44 U.Colo.L.Rev. 1, 41–56 (1972).[1] Is broadened immunity necessi-

---

1. Engdahl argues that the expansion of sovereign immunity in the late nineteenth century "was considered to be consistent with the tradition of effective re- dress for positive governmental wrongs" only because of the reaffirmation of the personal liability of officials (p. 47).

tated by the increase in litigation against public officials as well as the expansion of constitutional restrictions on their conduct? [2]

(2) *The Relationship of State and Federal Immunity Rules.* Whether state or federal law governs the immunity issue in a damage action depends on whether the conduct is alleged to violate state or federal law, and whether the defendant is a state or a federal official.

(a) *State Law Actions.* Butz indicates that in state law tort actions against federal officials performing discretionary functions, federal law governs, and establishes a shield of absolute immunity from damage liability for actions within the "outer perimeter of [officials'] line of duty," Barr v. Matteo, 360 U.S. at 575 (plurality opinion).[3]

The immunity of *state* officials in actions based on state law is itself governed by state law, for absent wholly arbitrary action by the state, there is no distinctive federal interest. See Martinez v. California, 444 U.S. 277 (1980). This rule applies even in actions that fall within the federal courts' jurisdiction. See, *e.g.*, Oyler v. National Guard Ass'n, 743 F.2d 545 (7th Cir. 1984).

(b) *Federal Law Actions.* The remainder of this Note focuses primarily upon the immunity rules in actions based on federal law, especially constitutional tort actions. Federal law governs the immunity in such actions, even when brought against state officials. Consider this set of questions:

First, has the Court been correct in assuming that the immunities of state officials in § 1983 actions and of federal officials in Bivens actions should be co-extensive? [4] Is it possible that Congress, in enacting § 1983, should be understood to have provided an extraordinary remedy not restricted by the immunities available in other contexts? See Matasar, *Personal Immunities Under Section 1983: The Limits of the Court's Historical Analysis,* 40 Ark.L.Rev. 741 (1987). Had that understanding been accepted, could the state have protected its interest in not having officials' conduct influenced by the fear of litigation and liability by agreeing to provide counsel for and to indemnify officials sued under § 1983? See Eisenberg, *Section 1983: Doctrinal Foundations and an Empirical Study,* 67 Cornell L.Rev. 482, 491–504 (1982). Or is the Court right in assuming that if the 42d Congress had intended § 1983 to abrogate immunities recognized at common law, that intent would have been more clearly signalled in the statute?

Second, on what sources should the Court rely in determining the scope of official immunity? In Tower v. Glover, 467 U.S. 914, 920 (1984), a

---

2. Note that in July of 1986, the Department of Justice reported that there were nearly 3000 claims pending against federal employees personally, that since 1971 (when Bivens was decided) over 12,000 such claims had been filed, and that the Department was aware of only 32 adverse judgments against individual employees. 51 Fed.Reg. 27022 (1986). Recall, also, the statistics on the growth of § 1983 litigation, pp. 1242–43, *supra.*

3. In Westfall v. Erwin, 108 S.Ct. 580 (1988), the district court had dismissed a federal employee's suit against co-employ-

ees for workplace injuries, finding that the defendants' conduct was within the outer perimeter of their duties. The Supreme Court held that the dismissal was in error; immunity attaches only if the challenged actions were also discretionary in nature, an issue the Court left for determination on remand.

4. A limited exception to this parity is the absolute immunity of the President, see Paragraph (6), *infra;* state governors have only a qualified immunity, Scheuer v. Rhodes, 416 U.S. 232 (1974).

§ 1983 action, the Court described the appropriate inquiry this way: "If an official was accorded immunity from tort actions at common law when the Civil Rights Act was enacted in 1871, the Court next considers whether § 1983's history or purposes nonetheless counsel against recognizing the same immunity in § 1983 actions." Both of these inquiries may be quite open-ended. The common law history may be inapposite to the distinctive functions and organization of modern governments, or may simply be unclear. See generally Matasar, *supra.* Analysis of policy considerations may be quite indeterminate in view of the complexity of the competing goals, the paucity of pertinent empirical data, and the need to consider damage suits as just one of many remedies for official misconduct.

This leads to a third question: what are the respective roles of the courts, the Congress, and the Constitution in shaping immunities? In Bivens actions, the immunities are fashioned from federal common law. The Court has sometimes described the immunities in § 1983 actions also as federal common law, see, *e.g.,* United States v. Gillock, 445 U.S. 360, 372 n. 10 (1980), but has asserted on other occasions that the statutory basis of immunities in § 1983 suits imposes distinctive constraints on judicial lawmaking—as, for example, in the Court's insistence, in Tower v. Glover, *supra,* at 922–23, that when no analogous immunity was recognized at common law when the Civil Rights Act of 1871 was enacted, "[w]e do not have a license to establish immunities from § 1983 actions in the interests of what we judge to be sound public policy." But see Harlow v. Fitzgerald, 457 U.S. 800 (1982), Paragraph (8), *infra,* a Bivens action in which the Court, for public policy reasons, formulated a new standard for qualified immunity broader than that recognized at common law; the opinion expressly said that the new standard was meant to govern § 1983 actions as well.

Could Congress narrow or abolish immunities in § 1983 actions? In Bivens actions? On the other hand, could Congress constitutionally provide all officials with absolute immunity in all constitutional tort actions? See p. 934, *supra.* Does the answer to the latter question depend on whether Congress has made available other remedies—for example, a remedy directly against the government, as under the FTCA? (Note that the Department of Justice has issued a policy statement providing that the Department may indemnify its employees for any damage judgment against them resulting from conduct taken within the scope of their employment. 51 Fed.Reg. 27022, *codified at* 28 C.F.R. § 50.15 (1986).)

Fourth, is the Court correct, in § 1983 actions, to ignore the immunity law of the affected state? Suppose that a state prosecutor has only a qualified immunity from state tort actions. Is there any reason why the federal law applied in a § 1983 action should not incorporate state rules that would broaden, rather than narrow, the opportunities for recovery? Compare pp. 953–59, 1247–48, *supra. Cf.* note 17, *infra.*

(3) *Absolute vs. Qualified Immunity.* Absolute and qualified immunities differ both substantively and procedurally. Substantively, an absolute immunity cannot be defeated by proof that an official knew his conduct was unlawful, sought to injure the plaintiff, or otherwise acted without justification or with improper motivation. Procedurally, precisely because an official with absolute immunity has no obligation to justify his action, the suit can ordinarily be dismissed on a simple Rule 12(b)(6) motion; conse-

quently, unlike qualified immunity, absolute immunity eliminates nearly all of the possible burden, expense, and anxiety of litigation.

(4) *Absolute Immunities Associated With the Judicial Process.*

(a) *Judicial Immunity.* The justifications offered by the Court for absolute judicial immunity have been summarized as follows: "(1) the need for a judge to 'be free to act upon his own conviction, without apprehension of personal consequences to himself'; (2) the controversiality and importance of the competing interests adjudicated by judges and the likelihood that the loser, feeling aggrieved, would wish to retaliate; (3) the record-keeping to which self-protective judges would be driven in the absence of immunity; (4) the availability of alternative remedies, such as appeal and impeachment, for judicial wrongdoing; and (5) the ease with which bad faith can be alleged and made the basis for 'vexatious litigation.'" Schuck, Suing Government: Citizen Remedies for Official Wrongs 90 (1983).

The only way to circumvent judicial immunity is to show that a judge was acting "in the clear absence of all jurisdiction," or that he was not performing a "judicial act".[5] These tests, dating back at least to Bradley v. Fisher, 13 Wall. 335, 351 (U.S.1871), were applied in Stump v. Sparkman, 435 U.S. 349 (1978), in which an Indiana judge had approved *ex parte* a petition filed by parents of a fifteen year-old girl to have her sterilized without her knowledge. When she later sued the judge for damages under § 1983, the Supreme Court ruled that he was absolutely immune: since he presided over a court of general jurisdiction, he had not acted wholly outside his jurisdiction, and he did not lose his immunity simply because no state statute specifically authorized his conduct.

The Court also rejected the argument that because the petition was never docketed or filed with the clerk, no hearing was held, and no guardian *ad litem* was appointed, the judge's approval of the petition was not a "judicial act." In the Court's view, whether a judge's action is a "judicial act" depends on whether (i) it is a function normally performed by a judge, and (ii) the parties' expectations revealed that they were dealing with the judge in his judicial capacity. The Court found both criteria to be met, noting as to the former that Indiana judges are often called upon to approve petitions about minors' affairs (p. 362).

Justice Stewart, joined by Justices Marshall and Powell, wrote an angry dissent, arguing that *ex parte* approval of a parent's petition was not an act normally performed by Indiana judges. He continued by insisting (p. 367) that "false illusions as to a judge's power can hardly convert a judge's response to those illusions into a judicial act," and that "[a] judge is not free, like a loose cannon, to inflict indiscriminate damage whenever he announces that he is acting in his judicial capacity." Justice Powell's separate dissent emphasized (p. 370) that "[t]he complete absence of normal judicial process" made inoperative the assumption underlying judicial immunity that "there exist alternative forums and methods for vindicating [private] rights."[6]

---

5. Compare Dennis v. Sparks, 449 U.S. 24 (1980), holding that though a judge who allegedly conspired to accept a bribe was immune from suit, his private co-conspirators were not.

6. Compare Cleavinger v. Saxner, 474 U.S. 193 (1985), holding (6–3) that federal prison officials who are members of a prison's Institution Discipline Committee, on which they hear cases in which inmates

See generally Block, *Stump v. Sparkman and the History of Judicial Immunity,* 1980 Duke L.J. 879; Rosenberg, *Stump v. Sparkman: The Doctrine of Judicial Impunity,* 64 Va.L.Rev. 833 (1978).

After Stump, when will a judge or quasi-judicial officer be found to have acted outside his judicial capacity? Many of the cases so finding deal with offbeat situations.[7] But Forrester v. White, 108 S.Ct. 538 (1988), raised a more important issue. There, a state judge was sued by a probation officer who alleged that the judge had dismissed her on account of her sex, in violation of the Fourteenth Amendment. The Supreme Court unanimously ruled that the judge was acting in an administrative rather than a judicial capacity, and hence was not entitled to absolute immunity; the question of his entitlement to qualified immunity was not resolved.

(b) *Prosecutorial Immunity.* The purposes and scope of prosecutorial immunity are similar to those of judicial immunity. Imbler v. Pachtman, 424 U.S. 409 (1976), was a § 1983 damage action alleging that a state prosecutor had knowingly introduced perjured testimony at plaintiff's trial, resulting in an erroneous conviction. The Court found that prosecutorial immunity was well-established at common law, and necessary to protect the prosecutor; if only a qualified immunity attached, a criminal defendant could "transform his resentment ＊ ＊ ＊ into the ascription of improper and malicious actions to the State's advocate," and suits "could be expected with some frequency" (p. 425). These suits would require a retrial of the criminal case, could discourage the prosecutor from presenting relevant evidence to the trier of fact in the first instance, and might skew postconviction procedures because of a judge's subconscious knowledge that a decision favorable to the accused could lead to a prosecutor's civil liability. Accordingly, the Court held that a prosecutor is absolutely immune from damage suits arising from activities "intimately associated with the judicial phase of the criminal process." There was "no occasion," the Court added, "to consider whether like or similar reasons require immunity for those aspects of the prosecutor's responsibility that cast him in the role of an administrator or investigative officer rather than that of advocate" (pp. 430–31).[8]

In Mitchell v. Forsyth, 472 U.S. 511 (1985), the Court held with little discussion that former Attorney General Mitchell, in authorizing a warrantless wiretap for reasons of national security, was not acting in a prosecutorial capacity and hence was not shielded by absolute immunity.[9]

---

are charged with rules infractions, are not entitled to absolute immunity: though they perform an adjudicatory function, these officials are not professional hearing officers insulated from executive pressure, nor are they constrained by the kinds of procedural safeguards stressed in Butz.

7. See, *e.g.,* Zarcone v. Perry, 572 F.2d 52 (2d Cir.1978) (judge who ordered court officials to bring "before me in cuffs" the vendor of coffee that the judge thought tasted "putrid," and who then interrogated the vendor and threatened his "livelihood," acted outside his judicial capacity).

8. Concurring in the judgment, Justice White, joined by Justices Brennan and Marshall, "disagree[d] with any implica-

tion that absolute immunity ＊ ＊ ＊ extends to suits based on claims of unconstitutional suppression of evidence," as such a rule would undercut a key purpose of conferring immunity—namely, to encourage presentation of all pertinent evidence to the trier of fact (p. 433).

9. Public defenders do not ordinarily act under color of law, see Polk County v. Dodson, 454 U.S. 312 (1981), so that they are likely to be liable under § 1983 only if they conspire with state officials. Tower v. Glover, 467 U.S. 914 (1984), held that in such a § 1983 action a defender has no immunity, noting the absence of any common law immunity for a defense lawyer's intentional misconduct. *Cf.* Ferri v. Ack-

(5) *The Absolute Immunity of Legislators.* The only explicit source in the Constitution for official immunity of any kind is Article I, section 6, which states that Senators and Representatives "shall in all Cases, except Treason, Felony, and Breach of Peace, be privileged from Arrest during their Attendance at the Session of their respective Houses, and in going to and returning from the same; and for any Speech or Debate in either House, they shall not be questioned in any other Place." Unlike judges and prosecutors, federal legislators are immune not merely from damage actions, but also from any form of judicial process that requires inquiry into so-called legislative acts. See *Note on the Immunity of Government Officers From Relief Other Than Damages,* which follows this Note.

The Supreme Court first considered the Speech or Debate Clause in Kilbourn v. Thompson, 13 Otto 168, 200–05 (U.S.1880). Relying on the English tradition of parliamentary privilege, the Court held that federal legislators who had voted for a resolution ordering the plaintiff to be imprisoned for contempt of Congress were immune from damages liability in a suit for false imprisonment.[10] Subsequent cases have interpreted the Speech or Debate Clause to shield all "legislative acts"—matters that are "an integral part of the deliberative and communicative processes by which Members participate in committee and House proceedings with respect to the consideration and passage or rejection of proposed legislation or with respect to other matters which the Constitution places within the jurisdiction of either House." Gravel v. United States, 408 U.S. 606, 625 (1972).[11]

The Gravel case also held, contrary to prior authority,[12] that the immunity extends not only to members of Congress but also to their aides. The Court reasoned that in today's world a member cannot perform his tasks without the help of aides, and an aide must therefore be treated as a member's "alter ego" and immunized "insofar as [his conduct] would be a protected legislative act if performed by the Member himself" (pp. 616–18). See generally Comment, 91 Yale L.J. 961 (1982).

By its terms, the Speech or Debate Clause extends only to federal legislators. But in Tenney v. Brandhove, 341 U.S. 367 (1951), the Court held a state legislator absolutely immune from damages in a § 1983 action

erman, 444 U.S. 193 (1979) (attorney appointed to represent a defendant in a federal criminal trial has no federal law immunity from a state law malpractice action).

Jurors and witnesses in judicial proceedings also enjoy an absolute immunity. See Briscoe v. LaHue, 460 U.S. 325 (1983); Schwartz & Kirklin, Section 1983 Litigation: Claims, Defenses, and Fees § 7.9 (1986).

10. The Court ruled, however, that the Sergeant-at-Arms, who had carried out the arrest directed by the Members, was not immune.

11. Compare Doe v. McMillan, 412 U.S. 306 (1973) (House Members responsible for preparing a committee report were absolutely immune in a suit for invasion of privacy filed by schoolchildren identified in the report, though the Superintendent of Documents and the Public Printer, who

publicly disseminated the report, were not immune), with Hutchinson v. Proxmire, 443 U.S. 111 (1979) (Senator was not immune from a defamation action arising out of his publicizing his "Golden Fleece" award (for wasteful federal spending) in a press release, newsletter, and television program).

The question whether legislative immunity extends to suits seeking relief for employment discrimination has divided the lower courts. See Schwartz & Kirklin, note 9, *supra,* § 7.10; compare Forrester v. White, Paragraph (4)(a), *supra.*

12. Compare, *e.g.,* Powell v. McCormack, 395 U.S. 486 (1969) (action challenging Congressman's exclusion from the House dismissed as to Members of Congress but not as to congressional employees); note 10, *supra* (discussing Kilbourn v. Thompson).

that alleged that the defendant had called a hearing not for a legitimate legislative purpose, but instead to deprive plaintiff of his constitutional rights.

Like judicial immunity, legislative immunity attaches to functions, not offices. Thus, it extends to nonlegislative officials exercising legislative powers, such as judges who promulgate disciplinary rules for the bar. See Supreme Court of Virginia v. Consumers Union of the United States, Inc., 446 U.S. 719 (1980), p. 1303, infra.[13]

(6) *Absolute Immunity of the President and Presidential Aides.* In Nixon v. Fitzgerald, 457 U.S. 731 (1982), Fitzgerald, a well-known "whistleblower," sought damages from President Nixon, who allegedly was responsible for the elimination of Fitzgerald's federal job in violation of the First Amendment and federal statutes. Justice Powell's opinion for the Court ruled that the President enjoyed an absolute immunity from damage liability for all acts within the "outer perimeter" of his official responsibilities (p. 756). This immunity, he argued, was a "functionally mandated incident of the President's unique office, rooted in the constitutional tradition of the separation of powers" (p. 749).[14] The Court stressed that the President's prominence made him an easy target for damages actions, and that if he had only a qualified immunity, the resulting diversion of his energies in defending himself would jeopardize the effective functioning of government. Justice White wrote a vigorous dissent, in which Justices Brennan, Marshall, and Blackmun joined, accusing the Court of mistakenly conferring immunity on an office rather than a function, and finding nothing in the nature of executive personnel decisions to warrant absolute rather than qualified immunity.

The companion case of Harlow v. Fitzgerald, 457 U.S. 800 (1982), involved the liability of aides to President Nixon who allegedly had conspired with him to eliminate Fitzgerald's job. The aides argued that, like congressional aides, they should be accorded a derivative absolute immunity, but the Court found that Butz had impliedly rejected this argument. An executive official has absolute (rather than qualified) immunity, the Court reasoned, only when the public interest in shielding particular functions so requires. The Court found that no such need had been shown, while suggesting that absolute immunity might be appropriate for presidential aides with discretionary authority in national security matters or foreign affairs.

Harlow's suggestion was taken up in Mitchell v. Forsyth, 472 U.S. 511 (1985), a Bivens action against former Attorney General Mitchell for having authorized a warrantless wiretap for the purpose of protecting national security. Four of the seven Justices participating rejected Mitchell's claim of absolute immunity, finding no historical analog for it, and arguing that the secrecy of national security matters reduced both the

---

13. On legislative immunity, see generally Reinstein & Silverglate, *Legislative Privilege and the Separation of Powers,* 86 Harv.L.Rev. 1113 (1973); Bradley, *The Speech or Debate Clause: Bastion of Congressional Independence or Haven for Corruption,* 57 N.C.L.Rev. 197 (1979); Bolton, Vanderstar & Baldwin, *The Legislator's Shield: Speech or Debate Clause Protection* *Against State Interrogation,* 62 Marq.L. Rev. 351 (1979); Note, 88 Yale L.J. 1280 (1979).

14. The Court left open the question whether the President could be subjected to damages liability by explicit and affirmative congressional action (p. 748 n. 27).

likelihood of unfounded and burdensome lawsuits and the effectiveness of other possible mechanisms of restraining misconduct.

(7) *The Contrast Between Qualified and Absolute Immunity.* Consider Justice Rehnquist's criticism, in Butz, of the Court's refusal to extend absolute immunity generally to executive officials sued for constitutional torts (438 U.S. at 528 n. *):

"If one were to hazard an informed guess as to why such a distinction in treatment between judges and prosecutors, on the one hand, and other public officials on the other, obtains, mine would be that those who decide the common law know through personal experience the sort of pressures that might exist for such decisionmakers in the absence of absolute immunity, but may not know or may have forgotten that similar pressures exist in the case of nonjudicial public officials to whom difficult decisions are committed. But the cynical among us might not unreasonably feel that this is simply another unfortunate example of judges treating those who are not part of the judicial machinery as 'lesser breeds without the law.' "

If Justice Rehnquist is correct, does this argue for conferring absolute immunity on executive officials, see Schuck, Paragraph (4)(a), *supra,* at 90–91,[15] or only a qualified immunity on judges and prosecutors? See, *e.g.,* Maher, *Federally–Defined Judicial Immunity: Some Quixotic Reflections on an Unwarranted Imposition,* 88 Dick.L.Rev. 326 (1984). Or should executive officials have less complete protection, because, as compared to judges, their incentives for misconduct are greater, because they are subject to fewer alternative checks on possible misbehavior, and because they face smaller risks of harassment? See Cass, *Damages Suits Against Public Officers,* 129 U.Pa.L.Rev. 1110, 1146–47 (1981).

(8) *The Reshaping of Qualified Immunity: Harlow v. Fitzgerald.* In its important decision in Harlow v. Fitzgerald, 457 U.S. 800 (1982), the Supreme Court modified substantially the qualified immunity standard applied in Butz and earlier cases. (The facts in Harlow are described in Paragraph (6), *supra.*) Justice Powell, writing for the Court, argued that experience with that standard showed that "[t]he subjective element of the good faith defense frequently has proved incompatible with our admonition in Butz that insubstantial claims should not proceed to trial. * * * [A]n official's subjective good faith has been considered to be a question of fact that some courts have regarded as inherently requiring resolution by a jury" (pp. 815–16).

Moreover, he argued that "substantial costs attend the litigation of the subjective good faith of government officials. Not only are there the general costs of subjecting officials to the risks of trial—distraction of officials from their governmental duties, inhibition of discretionary action, and deterrence of able people from public service. There are special costs to 'subjective' inquiries of this kind * * * [, which] may entail broad-ranging discovery and the deposing of numerous persons, including an official's professional colleagues. Inquiries of this kind can be particularly disruptive of effective government.

" * * * [W]e conclude today that bare allegations of malice should not suffice to subject government officials either to the costs of trial or to

---

15. Schuck couples this argument with a proposal vastly to expand government liability for official misconduct.

the burdens of broad-reaching discovery. We therefore hold that government officials performing discretionary functions generally are shielded from liability for civil damages insofar as their conduct does not violate clearly established statutory or constitutional rights of which a reasonable person would have known" (pp. 816–18).

The Court stated that when an immunity defense is raised by motion for summary judgment, the judge should first determine whether the illegality of the official's conduct was clearly established at the time he acted. "Until this threshold immunity question is resolved, discovery should not be allowed. If the law was clearly established, the immunity defense ordinarily should fail * * *. Nevertheless, if the official pleading the defense claims extraordinary circumstances and can prove that he neither knew nor should have known of the relevant legal standard, the defense should be sustained. But again, the defense would turn primarily on objective factors" (pp. 818–19).[16]

Justice Brennan, joined by Justices Marshall and Blackmun, joined the Court's opinion, but added these concurring views (pp. 820–21): "I agree with the substantive standard announced by the Court today, imposing liability when a public-official defendant 'knew or should have known' of the constitutionally violative effect of his actions. * * * This standard would not allow the official who *actually knows* that he was violating the law to escape liability for his actions, even if he could not 'reasonably have been expected' to know what he actually did know."

Didn't Harlow hold (contrary to Justice Brennan's interpretation) that an official is immune so long as conduct did not violate "clearly established" legal standards? Put differently, isn't the "subjective" inquiry to which Justice Brennan refers meant to be only a second-tier one, which merely provides that if an official has violated clearly established law, he may nonetheless be immune if he can show that, due to extraordinary circumstances, he neither knew nor should have known of the relevant legal standard? Subsequent decisions by the Court applying the Harlow standard—for example, Davis v. Scherer, 468 U.S. 183, 191 (1984),[17] and Mitchell v. Forsyth, 472 U.S. 511, 517 (1985)—seem to so indicate.

Harlow's emphasis on facilitating dismissal of insubstantial suits agianst officials was visible in Mitchell v. Forsyth, *supra,* which held that a trial court's denial of a defendant's motion for summary judgment on the

---

16. Justice Powell also noted that though § 1983 was not involved in the case, it would be "untenable" to distinguish state from federal officials for purposes of immunity (p. 818 n. 30).

17. The Davis case was a § 1983 suit brought by a state employee who challenged his discharge as a violation of due process. He argued that the defendants lost their qualified immunity, because their conduct, even if not violative of clearly established law under the Fourteenth Amendment, violated clearly established state law. The Court acknowledged that the argument had some force, but declined to "disrupt the balance" established by Harlow, and held that the plaintiff can overcome qualified immunity only by

showing that the very law whose violation forms the basis of his federal action was clearly established (p. 195). The Court contended that a federal judge might have difficulty resolving issues of state law on summary judgment, and that state officials may be subject to a plethora of vague and contradictory state law rules.

Justices Brennan, Marshall, Blackmun, and Stevens, in dissent, argued that the discharge did violate clearly established federal constitutional law. See Paragraph (9)(a), *infra.* In passing, however, they expressed the view that a violation of state law is relevant in determining whether an immunity defense has been overcome (p. 204 n. 2).

ground of qualified immunity is immediately appealable as a "collateral order" under 28 U.S.C. § 1291. See Chapter XV, pp. 1800–13, *infra*.

(9) *Further Questions on the Meaning of Harlow.*

(a) *The Meaning of Clearly Established Law.* In Procunier v. Navarette, 434 U.S. 555 (1978), the Court (without dissent on this point) found no violation of clearly established law when, at the time prison officials interfered with a prisoner's outgoing mail, there was no decision of the Supreme Court, or of the pertinent federal circuit or district court, establishing the First Amendment right on which the suit was based, and other federal courts had divided on the First Amendment question. Davis v. Scherer, 468 U.S. 183 (1984), proved more difficult. There, the Court held, 5–4, that under the precedents as of 1977 (when the challenged conduct occurred), it was not clearly established that a permanent state employee who was terminated after various oral and written communications with his superiors had a right to a more formal hearing either before or promptly after his termination.

In many situations, the Supreme Court will not have addressed the legality of the conduct at issue. Can a single state court or lower federal court decision clearly establish the illegality of a practice if no other court has spoken? Even if all the circuits agree that a practice is illegal, isn't it possible that the Supreme Court would disagree?

Suppose instead that the lower courts have divided. Is an official immune if the legality of his conduct had previously been upheld by one court somewhere? What if that court is in Maine, the official works for the state of California, and both the California Supreme Court and the 9th Circuit had declared the practice unlawful before the conduct occurred?

In the absence of a generally accepted and clearcut theory of the role of precedent in adjudication—an especially complex problem in a federal system—how stable would you expect application of the "clearly established law" standard to be?

Many of the cases applying the Harlow standard involved a question about a general proposition of law. See, *e.g.*, Mitchell v. Forsyth, 472 U.S. 511 (1985) (Attorney General reasonably could have believed in 1970 that he had authority to conduct warrantless electronic surveillance for national security purposes). Anderson v. Creighton, 107 S.Ct. 3034 (1987), by contrast, was a case in which the governing principles of law were clear, but their application to the facts was in dispute. There, the court of appeals ruled that if a warrantless search of a home was unlawful, the officer could not obtain summary judgment on immunity grounds, because clearly established law prohibited entry of a dwelling absent probable cause and exigent circumstances. The Supreme Court reversed, holding that the court of appeals misapplied Harlow by identifying the legal rule that was violated at too high a level of generality: "The contours of the right must be sufficiently clear that a reasonable official would understand that what he is doing violates that right" (p. 3039).[18]

---

18. The Court also rejected the plaintiff's argument that since the Fourth Amendment prohibits "unreasonable searches and seizures," it is logically impossible to find an officer immune under Harlow, for to do so would imply that an officer "reasonably" acted unreasonably.

Justice Stevens (joined by Justices Brennan and Marshall) dissented.

(b) *The Pertinence of Subjective Motivation.* Halperin v. Kissinger, 807 F.2d 180 (D.C.Cir.1986), was a Bivens action against Henry Kissinger and other former officials for having wiretapped the plaintiffs' home telephone. The court of appeals (per Scalia, J., sitting by designation after his elevation from the court of appeals to the Supreme Court) first concluded that the wiretap would not have violated clearly established law at the time it was made if (but only if) its actual purpose was to protect national security—a matter of dispute between the parties. The court thus faced the question whether Harlow and subsequent cases meant to eliminate inquiry into "legitimizing or illegitimizing intent * * *—for example, invalidating intent to discriminate on the basis of race"—as distinguished from an official's "knowledge of the state of the law." Though "[r]espectable argument can be made that it did so," the court noted that "[t]he lower courts have been unwilling to rest such a massive expansion of official immunity upon the language of Harlow and later cases, without more specific indication that that was intended" (p. 186). The court held, however, that in the limited area of national security—in which Harlow's concerns about protecting the separation of powers, not dampening the ardor of public officials, and avoiding the intrusiveness of wide-ranging discovery are "especially prominent"—it was appropriate to adopt a "special rule" barring inquiry into the actual presence of legitimizing motivation (p. 187). Accordingly, "if the facts establish that the purported national security motivation would have been reasonable, the immunity defense will prevail" (p. 188). See generally Note, 95 Yale L.J. 126 (1985).

(c) *Advice of Counsel.* When would a "reasonable" official seek more specific advice from a government lawyer? If the lawyer advises an official that his contemplated action would be lawful though under the precedents it clearly would not be, is the officer immune? Is this last situation covered by Harlow's statement that even when an official's conduct violates clearly established law, he is still immune if he "claims extraordinary circumstances and can prove that he neither knew nor should have known of the relevant legal standard"?

See also Malley v. Briggs, 475 U.S. 335 (1986), in which a police officer presented arrest warrants to a state judge, who approved and signed them. The officer was later sued under § 1983 for having caused the arrest of individuals without probable cause. The Supreme Court refused to hold that the officer was absolutely immune because he had relied "on the judgment of a judicial officer in finding that probable cause exists and hence issuing the warrant" (p. 345). Though in an ideal system no judge would approve a defective application, it was not unreasonable to minimize the risk of error by holding an officer liable if "the warrant application is so lacking in indicia of probable cause as to render official belief in its existence unreasonable" (pp. 344–45). The Court remanded for application of the Harlow standard.[19]

On the application of Harlow, see generally Schwartz & Kirklin, note 9, *supra*, §§ 7.12–.15; Nahmod, *Constitutional Wrongs Without Remedies: Executive Official Immunity,* 62 Wash.U.L.Q. 221 (1984); Comment, 132 U.Pa.L.Rev. 901 (1984); Note, 38 Vand.L.Rev. 1543 (1985).

19. Dissenting in part, Justice Powell (joined by Justice Rehnquist) would have ruled that the defendant was immune under Harlow; he argued that the judge's determination was entitled to substantial evidentiary weight, and that on the facts a reasonable officer could have believed probable cause existed.

(10) *Official Immunity and Systems of Liability for Official Miscon-duct.* The question of the appropriate scope of official immunity implicates more general questions about how systems of liability for official misconduct should be structured. Those questions revolve around the relationship of governmental liability to individual officer liability, as well as the impact of governmental reimbursement of officials for damage awards and attorney's fees. Also implicated is the relationship among damage liability, other forms of judicial remedies (*i.e.,* equitable relief), and nonjudicial mechanisms for controlling government misconduct and for compensating injured individuals. These questions are complicated by the existence of both state law and federal law remedies for many forms of official misconduct.

There is a growing literature on these questions, much of it critical of reliance upon individual rather than governmental liability. See generally Schuck, Paragraph (4)(a), *supra;* Bermann, *Integrating Governmental and Officer Tort Liability,* 77 Colum.L.Rev. 1175 (1977); Cass, Paragraph (7), *supra;* Madden & Allard, *Advice on Official Liability and Immunity,* in 2 Administrative Conference of the United States: Reports and Recommendations 201–442 (1982); Whitman, *Government Responsibility for Constitutional Torts,* 85 Mich.L.Rev. 225 (1986); Wise, *Liability of Federal Officials: An Analysis of Alternatives,* 45 Pub.Ad.Rev. 746 (1985).

NOTE ON THE IMMUNITY OF GOVERNMENT OFFICERS FROM RELIEF OTHER THAN DAMAGES

(1) To what extent are principles of immunity developed in damage actions pertinent in suits for equitable relief?

In Eastland v. United States Servicemen's Fund, 421 U.S. 491 (1975), a Senate Committee subpoenaed the bank records of an organization that was critical of the Vietnam War. The organization sued to enjoin enforcement of the subpoenas as a violation of the First Amendment. The Supreme Court, without extended consideration, held that the suit was barred by the Speech or Debate Clause: "Just as a criminal prosecution infringes upon the independence which the Clause is designed to preserve, a private civil action, whether for an injunction or damages, creates a distraction and forces Members to divert their time, energy, and attention from their legislative tasks to defend the litigation" (p. 503).

Immunity from injunctive relief was extended to state officials acting in a legislative capacity in Supreme Court of Virginia v. Consumers Union of the United States, Inc., 446 U.S. 719 (1980). There a consumer group sued, *inter alia,* the Supreme Court of Virginia and its Chief Justice under § 1983, seeking to enjoin (as inconsistent with the First Amendment) state bar rules restricting plaintiff's ability to gather information about lawyers' fees. A three-judge federal court ultimately awarded the injunctive relief sought, as well as attorney's fees under 42 U.S.C. § 1988, against the Supreme Court of Virginia and the Chief Justice in his official capacity. On appeal, the Supreme Court unanimously ruled that officials acting in a legislative capacity could not be enjoined.[1]

1. Justice Powell did not participate.

The Court first reasoned that "in promulgating the disciplinary rules the Virginia Supreme Court acted in a legislative capacity" (p. 731). Given the decision in Eastland, and the Court's general practice of "equat[ing] the legislative immunity to which state legislators are entitled under § 1983 to that accorded Congressmen under the Constitution" (p. 733), there was little doubt that a state legislator would be immune from suit seeking an injunction.[2] Even conceding that not all officials exercising delegated rulemaking power are necessarily immune from suit, the Court rejected the contention that "in *no* circumstances do those who exercise delegated legislative power enjoy legislative immunity" (p. 734). The Supreme Court of Virginia was "exercising the State's entire legislative power" and its members were the state's legislators with respect to regulation of the Bar; they could not be enjoined in that capacity (p. 734).

The injunction was upheld, however, under a different theory. The Supreme Court noted that the Virginia court performed non-legislative functions in connection with attorney discipline—it both adjudicated (on appeal) violations of bar disciplinary rules and had independent enforcement authority. "We need not decide whether judicial immunity would bar prospective relief, for we believe that the Virginia Court and its chief justice properly were held liable in their enforcement capacities," much as prosecutors—who enjoy absolute immunity from damages liability—may be enjoined from enforcing laws that violate the Constitution (p. 736).

(2) Was the Court in Eastland justified in extending Speech or Debate Clause immunity to actions seeking prospective relief? To what extent do such lawsuits threaten to inhibit the fearless discharge by legislators of their duties, or to create injustice for individual legislators, given that Congress employs a legal staff to defend these actions? Does the answer to this question depend upon whether legislators may be held personally liable for attorney's fees? See Pulliam v. Allen, Paragraph (3), *infra*. In any event, don't suits for injunctive relief against prosecutors or other enforcement officials pose the same threats?

As Consumers Union itself shows, the extension of legislative immunity is relatively unimportant in suits seeking relief from unconstitutional legislation, precisely because enforcement officials are amenable to suit. But in legislative investigations, there may be no potential defendants other than legislators and their aides. Does Eastland mean that the only way to obtain judicial review of the constitutionality of committee process is to risk contempt?[3] Contrast the Court's argument in Consumers Union that prosecutors must be amenable to prospective relief, for otherwise "putative plaintiffs would have to await the institution of state-court proceedings against them in order to assert their federal constitutional claims" (p. 737). If an individual is held in contempt of Congress and

2. The Court did not mention Bond v. Floyd, 385 U.S. 116 (1966). There, Julian Bond, who had been elected to the Georgia House of Representatives, sought declaratory and injunctive relief after the House had excluded him because of his statements opposing the Vietnam War. A three-judge federal court found no constitutional violation, but the Supreme Court unanimously reversed, ruling that the exclusion violated Bond's First Amendment rights.

3. Indeed, in Eastland itself, because the subpoenas were directed at the bank, the plaintiff lacked even that option. Perhaps it could have sued the bank to bar compliance. *Cf.* United States v. American Tel. & Tel. Co., 551 F.2d 384 (D.C.Cir. 1976) (Justice Department moves to enjoin AT & T from complying with House subcommittee subpoena alleged to threaten national security), *on appeal after remand*, 567 F.2d 121 (1977).

detained, would legislators be immune from an action seeking a writ of habeas corpus?[4] If so, is there no remedy whatever? If not, can habeas relief after contempt and injunctive relief before contempt really be distinguished with respect to their impact on legislative independence?

(3) The question left open in Consumers Union—whether judicial immunity bars suits for prospective relief—was answered in Pulliam v. Allen, 466 U.S. 522 (1984). Pulliam, a state magistrate, had a practice in criminal cases involving nonjailable offenses of setting bail and incarcerating persons who could not post it. Two arrestees subjected to this policy brought suit under § 1983, seeking injunctive and declaratory relief. The district court ruled that the practice was unconstitutional, and enjoined Pulliam from continuing it. The court also awarded the plaintiffs $7691 in costs, of which $7038 was attorney's fees awarded under 42 U.S.C. § 1988.

Dividing 5–4, the Supreme Court upheld the injunction and the fee award. Justice Blackmun's opinion for the Court began by noting that the propriety of the award depended on whether judicial immunity barred the injunction. The Court conceded that at common law there were no injunctions against judges. But a lengthy review of English history showed, in the Court's view, that judicial immunity from injunctive orders developed merely to protect the common law courts from overreaching by the courts of equity. That immunity coexisted with the exercise of significant control by the King's Bench "over inferior and rival courts through the use of prerogative writs," particularly prohibition and mandamus (p. 532). Though in theory these writs were used only to control the proper exercise of lower courts' jurisdiction, in practice "the King's Bench used and continues to use the writs to prevent a judge from committing all manner of errors, including departing from the rules of natural justice, proceeding with a suit in which he has an interest, misconstruing substantive law, and rejecting legal evidence" (p. 533). That practice, though "not precisely paralleled in our system by the relationship between state and federal courts[,] * * * indicates that, at least in the view of the common law, there was no inconsistency between a principle of immunity that protected judicial authority from 'a wide, wasting, and harassing persecution,' * * * and the availability of collateral injunctive relief in exceptional cases" (pp. 535–36).

Justice Blackmun also contended that immunity from injunctive relief was far less necessary than immunity from damage awards. The need to show the lack of an adequate remedy at law and a serious risk of irreparable harm "severely curtail[s] the risk that judges will be harassed and their independence compromised by the threat of having to defend themselves against suits by disgruntled litigants," as does the need to satisfy Article III's requirements (pp. 537–38 & n. 18).

Turning to the award of costs and fees, Justice Blackmun conceded that "[t]here is, perhaps, some logic to [the defendant's] reasoning" that "the chilling effect of a damages award is no less chilling when the award is denominated attorney's fees" (p. 543). However, he found that Congress

---

4. In Marshall v. Gordon, 243 U.S. 521 (1917), the Court ordered issuance of the writ against the Sergeant–At–Arms of the House of Representatives. However, the case arose at a time when aides may have had less protection than they have today, see p. 1297 & note 10, supra, and might be also distinguished as involving conduct (legislative imposition of punishment for contempt) wholly outside the scope of legislative privilege.

had made unmistakable its intent that attorney's fees should be available "in any action to enforce a provision of § 1983[,] * * * even when damages would be barred or limited by 'immunity doctrines and special defenses available only to public officials'" (p. 543).

Justice Powell, joined by Chief Justice Burger and Justices Rehnquist and O'Connor, dissented. He found far more significance in the common law immunity of judges from injunctive relief, and less in the history of the writs of prohibition and mandamus, which "were intended only to control the proper exercise of jurisdiction" and therefore "posed no threat to judicial independence and implicated none of the policies of judicial immunity" (p. 550). In his view, the expansion of the writs through the "myth that misapplication of substantive common law affects the court's jurisdiction" was occasioned by the rivalry between the King's Bench and the ecclesiastical courts, a history without American parallel and therefore without relevance to the interpretation of § 1983 (pp. 550–51).

The dissent also argued (p. 554) that "the burdens of harassing litigation, rather than the threat of pecuniary loss," constitute the key threat to judicial independence, and suits for prospective relief pose that threat as much as damage actions. The threat is magnified if an injunction is issued, and a judge may risk contempt if a subsequent decision is deemed to run afoul of the order. Finally, the dissenters emphasized the impact of § 1988 in stimulating litigation, opining that "[s]ince its enactment in 1976, suits against state officials under § 1983 have increased geometrically," and that "[t]he Court * * * ignores reality when it suggests that the availability of injunctive relief under § 1983, combined with the prospect of attorney's fees under § 1988, poses no serious threat of harassing litigation with its potentially adverse consequences for judicial independence" (pp. 556–57).

(4) Consider whether the majority might be correct that immunity does not bar injunctive relief, but mistaken in permitting the award of attorney's fees. On the latter point, the Court relied in part on the understanding of § 1988 in Hutto v. Finney, p. 1192, *supra*. But while the judgment in Hutto enjoined state officials, the fee award was to be paid by the state itself.

Could § 1988 be interpreted to impose fee liability upon only those officials who could be held liable for damages? Would it pose a problem for this view if government liability for fees requires the same showing needed to establish government liability for damages—that the violation was pursuant to government policy or custom? See pp. 1251–57, *supra*. Isn't it likely that such a showing can be made, however, if the requisites for injunctive relief have been satisfied? And, at least where that showing is made, cannot judicial independence and Congress's policy in § 1988 both be honored by permitting fee awards only against the government?[5]

How helpful is the history of the King's Bench's issuance of prerogative writs in resolving these questions?

(5) Consumers Union indicates that executive officials in general have no immunity from suit for prospective relief—a conclusion supported by the

---

5. In the rare case in which an injunction issues against a official but government liability cannot be established, see p. 1250, note 2, *supra*, wouldn't it still be possible to read an exception into § 1988 so as to deny fees? Why should § 1988's authorization of attorney's fees be read as more absolute than § 1983's authorization of damage relief?

entire history of suits against officers as a means of ensuring governmental accountability. The President's amenability to an injunction or writ of mandamus, however, has never been authoritatively established. See *Note on Remedial Aspects of the Steel Case*, pp. 1134–39, *supra.*

(6) Government officials possess no general immunity from criminal process, though of course in particular instances their governmental status may permit a defense of privilege that could not be asserted by a private person. Thus, in Imbler v. Pachtman, 424 U.S. 409, 429 (1976), p. 1296, *supra,* the Court stressed that it had "never suggested that the policy considerations which compel civil immunity for certain governmental officials [in that case, for prosecutors] also place them beyond the reach of the criminal law. Even judges, who have long been cloaked with absolute immunity from damages, could be punished criminally for willful deprivations of constitutional rights on the strength of 18 U.S.C. § 242, the criminal analog of § 1983. O'Shea v. Littleton, 414 U.S. 488, 503 (1974) * * *. The prosecutor would fare no better for his willful acts."

The Speech or Debate Clause, however, does limit the reach of criminal process against federal legislators. Thus, in a federal bribery prosecution of a Congressman, the prosecution may not introduce evidence about the defendant's "legislative acts." United States v. Helstoski, 442 U.S. 477, 488–89 (1979). See also United States v. Johnson, 383 U.S. 169 (1966). Other kinds of evidence, however—that a Congressman accepted a bribe to perform a legislative act, Helstoski, *supra,* or that he attempted to influence the Justice Department, Johnson, *supra,*—may be introduced in a bribery trial, as such activities are not "related to the due functioning of the legislative process," *id.* at 172. See also Gravel v. United States, 408 U.S. 606 (1972) (senatorial aide is immune from grand jury questioning about a Senator's reading the Pentagon Papers in a subcommittee hearing, but not about the Senator's arrangements for their private publication).

United States v. Gillock, 445 U.S. 360 (1980), held that state legislators, unlike their federal counterparts, possess no immunity from the introduction, in a federal criminal prosecution, of evidence concerning their legislative acts. The defendant argued that here, as in constitutional tort actions, his immunity should be co-extensive with that enjoyed by federal legislators under the Speech or Debate Clause. But the Court responded that decisions affording state prosecutors and judges absolute immunity in § 1983 actions have been premised on the availability of federal criminal liability as a restraining influence on behavior, and argued that principles of comity to the state legislative process must yield to the needs of federal criminal prosecutions.

Chapter X

JUDICIAL FEDERALISM: LIMITATIONS ON DISTRICT COURT JURISDICTION OR ITS EXERCISE

INTRODUCTORY NOTE

Exercise of the jurisdiction in suits against state officials that was sanctioned in Ex parte Young and the Home Telephone case brought about a major shift in the distribution of power between state and nation. The significance of this change in the working "small-letter" constitution of the country largely escaped the attention of political scientists; but it was not overlooked by Congress, by the spokesmen for the interests adversely affected, or by the federal courts.

The congressional response was embodied in three important provisions of the Judicial Code: (1) the requirement that a district court of three judges be convened to hear actions seeking injunctive relief against state statutes or administrative orders alleged to be unconstitutional; (2) the Johnson Act of 1934, limiting federal district court jurisdiction to enjoin state public utility rate orders; and (3) the Tax Injunction Act of 1937, limiting federal district court jurisdiction to enjoin the collection of state taxes.[1] These measures are taken up in Section 1 below, which begins with consideration of a much older statute, the Anti–Injunction Act, first passed in 1793.

The federal courts themselves have played a major role in creating limits both on the jurisdiction sanctioned in Young and Home Telephone and on more traditional exercises of jurisdiction in federal question and diversity cases. Section 2 of this Chapter considers a range of judicially-fashioned doctrines calling for the federal courts to abstain from adjudicating cases that fall within the literal terms of congressional grants of jurisdiction.

---

1. A fourth provision, enacted in 1913, directed a three-judge federal district court to suspend its proceedings whenever a state court stayed proceedings under the challenged statute or order, pending state court determination of an action to enforce the same. The provision was largely ineffectual, see Pogue, *State Determination of State Law and the Judicial Code*, 41 Harv. L.Rev. 623 (1928); Hutcheson, *A Case for Three Judges*, 47 Harv.L.Rev. 795, 822–25 (1934), and was repealed in 1976.

SECTION 1. STATUTORY LIMITATIONS ON FEDERAL COURT JURISDICTION

SUBSECTION A: THE ANTI-INJUNCTION ACT

ATLANTIC COAST LINE R.R. v. BROTHERHOOD OF LOCOMOTIVE ENGINEERS

398 U.S. 281, 90 S.Ct. 1739, 26 L.Ed.2d 234 (1970).
Certiorari to the United States Court of Appeals for the Fifth Circuit.

MR. JUSTICE BLACK delivered the opinion of the Court.

Congress in 1793, shortly after the American Colonies became one united Nation, provided that in federal courts "a writ of injunction [shall not] be granted to stay proceedings in any court of a state." Act of March 2, 1793, § 5, 1 Stat. 335. Although certain exceptions to this general prohibition have been added, that statute, directing that state courts shall remain free from interference by federal courts, has remained in effect until this time. Today that amended statute provides:

> "A court of the United States may not grant an injunction to stay proceedings in a State court except as expressly authorized by Act of Congress, or where necessary in aid of its jurisdiction, or to protect or effectuate its judgments." 28 U.S.C. § 2283.

Despite the existence of this longstanding prohibition, in this case a federal court did enjoin the petitioner, Atlantic Coast Line Railroad Co. (ACL), from invoking an injunction issued by a Florida state court which prohibited certain picketing by respondent Brotherhood of Locomotive Engineers (BLE). The case arose in the following way.

In 1967 BLE began picketing the Moncrief Yard, a switching yard located near Jacksonville, Florida, and wholly owned and operated by ACL.[2] As soon as this picketing began ACL went into federal court seeking an injunction. When the federal judge denied the request, ACL immediately went into state court and there succeeded in obtaining an injunction. No further legal action was taken in this dispute until two years later in 1969, after this Court's decision in Brotherhood of Railroad Trainmen v. Jacksonville Terminal Co., 394 U.S. 369. In that case the Court considered the validity of a state injunction against picketing by the BLE and other unions at the Jacksonville Terminal, located immediately next to Moncrief Yard. The Court reviewed the factual situation surrounding the Jacksonville Terminal picketing and concluded that the unions had a federally protected right to picket under the Railway Labor Act, 45 U.S.C. § 151 et seq., and that that right could not be interfered with by state court injunctions. Immediately after a petition for rehearing was denied in that

---

2. There is no present labor dispute between the ACL and the BLE or any other ACL employees. ACL became involved in this case as a result of a labor dispute between the Florida East Coast Railway Co. (FEC) and its employees. FEC cars are hauled into and out of Moncrief Yard and switched around to make up trains in that yard. The BLE picketed the yard, encouraging ACL employees not to handle any FEC cars. * * *

case, 394 U.S. 1024 (1969), the respondent BLE filed a motion in state court to dissolve the Moncrief Yard injunction, arguing that under the Jacksonville Terminal decision the injunction was improper. The state judge refused to dissolve the injunction, holding that this Court's Jacksonville Terminal decision was not controlling. The union did not elect to appeal that decision directly, but instead went back into the federal court and requested an injunction against the enforcement of the state court injunction. The District Judge granted the injunction * * *. The Court of Appeals summarily affirmed on the parties' stipulation, and we granted a petition for certiorari to consider the validity of the federal court's injunction against the state court. * * *

* * *

I

Before analyzing the specific legal arguments advanced in this case, we think it would be helpful to discuss the background and policy which led Congress to pass the anti-injunction statute in 1793. While all the reasons that led Congress to adopt this restriction on federal courts are not wholly clear, it is certainly likely that one reason stemmed from the essentially federal nature of our national government. When this Nation was established by the Constitution each State surrendered only a part of its sovereign power to the national government. But those powers that were not surrendered were retained by the States and unless a State was restrained by "the supreme Law of the Land" as expressed in the Constitution, laws or treaties of the United States, it was free to exercise those retained powers as it saw fit. One of the reserved powers was the maintenance of state judicial systems for the decision of legal controversies.

* * *

While the lower federal courts were given certain powers in the [Judiciary Act of 1789], they were not given any power to review directly cases from state courts, and they have not been given such powers since that time. Only the Supreme Court was authorized to review on direct appeal the decisions of state courts. Thus from the beginning we have had in this country two essentially separate legal systems. Each system proceeds independently from the other with ultimate review in this Court of the federal questions raised in either system. Understandably this dual court system was bound to lead to conflicts and frictions. Litigants who foresaw the possibility of more favorable treatment in one or the other system would predictably hasten to invoke the powers of whichever court it was believed would present the best chance of success. Obviously this dual system could not function if state and federal courts were free to fight each other for control of a particular case. Thus, in order to make the dual system work and "to prevent needless friction between state and federal courts," Oklahoma Packing Co. v. Oklahoma Gas & Electric Co., 309 U.S. 4, 9 (1940), it was necessary to work out lines of demarcation between the two systems. Some of these limits were spelled out in the 1789 Act. Others have been added by later statutes as well as judicial decisions. The 1793 anti-injunction Act was at least in part a response to these pressures.

On its face the present Act is an absolute prohibition against enjoining state court proceedings, unless the injunction falls within one of three specifically defined exceptions. The respondent here has intimated that the Act only establishes a "principle of comity," not a binding rule on the power of the federal courts. The argument implies that in certain circumstances a federal court may enjoin state court proceedings even if that action cannot be justified by any of the three exceptions. We cannot accept any such contention. In 1954 when this Court interpreted this statute, it stated: "This is not a statute conveying a broad general policy for appropriate *ad hoc* application. Legislative policy is here expressed in a clear-cut prohibition qualified only by specifically defined exceptions." Amalgamated Clothing Workers v. Richman Brothers, 348 U.S. 511, 515–516 (1955). Since that time Congress has not seen fit to amend the statute and we therefore adhere to that position and hold that any injunction against state court proceedings otherwise proper under general equitable principles must be based on one of the specific statutory exceptions to § 2283 if it is to be upheld. Moreover since the statutory prohibition against such injunctions in part rests on the fundamental constitutional independence of the States and their courts, the exceptions should not be enlarged by loose statutory construction. Proceedings in state courts should normally be allowed to continue unimpaired by intervention of the lower federal courts, with relief from error, if any, through the state appellate courts and ultimately this Court.

II

In this case the Florida Circuit Court enjoined the union's intended picketing, and the United States District Court enjoined the railroad "from giving effect to or availing themselves of the benefits of" that state court order. Both sides agree that although this federal injunction is in terms directed only at the railroad it is an injunction "to stay proceedings in a state court." It is settled that the prohibition of § 2283 cannot be evaded by addressing the order to the parties or prohibiting utilization of the results of a completed state proceeding. * * * Thus if the injunction against the Florida court proceedings is to be upheld, it must be "expressly authorized by Act of Congress," "necessary in aid of [the District Court's] jurisdiction," or "to protect or effectuate [that court's] judgments."

Neither party argues that there is any express Congressional authorization for injunctions in this situation and we agree with that conclusion. The respondent union does contend that the injunction was proper either as a means to protect or effectuate the District Court's 1967 order, or in aid of that court's jurisdiction. We do not think that either alleged basis can be supported.

A

The argument based on protecting the 1967 order is not clearly expressed, but in essence it appears to run as follows: In 1967 the railroad sought a temporary restraining order which the union opposed. In the course of deciding that request, the United States District Court determined that the union had a federally protected right to picket Moncrief Yard and that this right could not be interfered with by state courts. When the Florida Circuit Court enjoined the picketing, the United States District Court could, in order to protect and effectuate its prior determination, enjoin enforcement of the state court injunction. Although the record on this point is not unambiguously clear, we conclude that no such interpretation of the 1967 order can be supported.

When the railroad initiated the federal suit it filed a complaint with three counts, each based entirely on alleged violations of federal law. The first two counts alleged violations of the Railway Labor Act, 45 U.S.C. § 151 et seq., and the third alleged a violation of that Act and the Interstate Commerce Act as well. Each of the counts concluded with a prayer for an injunction against the picketing. * * * [T]he union * * * appeared at a hearing on a motion for a temporary restraining order and argued against the issuance of such an order. The union argued that it was a party to a labor dispute with the FEC,* that it had exhausted the administrative remedies required by the Railway Labor Act, and that it was thus free to engage in "self-help," or concerted economic activity. Then the union argued that such activity could not be enjoined by the federal court. In an attempt to clarify the basis of this argument the District Judge asked: "You are basing your case solely on the Norris–LaGuardia Act?" The union's lawyer replied: "Right. I think at this point of the argument, since Norris–LaGuardia is clearly in point here." At no point during the entire argument did either side refer to state law, the effects of that law on the picketing, or the possible preclusion of state remedies as a result of overriding federal law. The next day the District Court entered an order denying the requested restraining order. In relevant part that order included these conclusions of law:

"3. The parties of the BLE–FEC 'major dispute,' having exhausted the procedures of the Railway Labor Act, 45 U.S.C. § 151, *et seq.,* are now free to engage in self-help. * * *

"4. The conduct of the FEC pickets and that of the responding ACL employees are a part of the FEC–BLE major dispute. * * *

* * *

"7. The Norris–LaGuardia Act, 29 U.S.C. § 101, and the Clayton Act, 29 U.S.C. § 52, are applicable to the conduct of the defendants here involved."

In this Court the union asserts that the determination that it was "free to engage in self-help" was a determination that it had a federally protected right to picket and that state law could not be invoked to negate that right. The railroad, on the other hand, argues that the order merely determined that the *federal* court could not enjoin the picketing, in large part because of the general prohibition in the Norris–LaGuardia Act, 47 Stat. 70, 29 U.S.C. § 101 *et seq.,* against issuance by federal courts of injunctions in labor disputes. Based solely on the state of the record when the order was entered, we are inclined to believe that the District Court did not determine whether federal law precluded an injunction based on state law. * * *

Any lingering doubts we might have as to the proper interpretation of the 1967 order are settled by references to the positions adopted by the parties later in the litigation. * * *

* * *

This record, we think, conclusively shows that neither the parties themselves nor the District Court construed the 1967 order as the union now contends it should be construed. Rather we are convinced that the union in effect tried to get the Federal District Court to decide that the state court judge was wrong in distinguishing the Jacksonville Terminal

* [Ed.] See footnote 2.

decision. Such an attempt to seek appellate review of a state decision in the Federal District Court cannot be justified as necessary "to protect or effectuate" the 1967 order. The record simply will not support the union's contention on this point.

B

This brings us to the second prong of the union's argument in which it is suggested that even if the 1967 order did not determine the union's right to picket free from state interference, once the decision in Jacksonville Terminal was announced, the District Court was then free to enjoin the state court on the theory that such action was "necessary to aid [the District Court's] jurisdiction." Again the argument is somewhat unclear, but it appears to go in this way: The District Court had acquired jurisdiction over the labor controversy in 1967 when the railroad filed its complaint, and it determined at that time that it did have jurisdiction. The dispute involved the legality of picketing by the union and the Jacksonville Terminal decision clearly indicated that such activity was not only legal, but was protected from state court interference. The state court had interfered with that right, and thus a federal injunction was "necessary in aid of its jurisdiction." For several reasons we cannot accept the contention.

First, a federal court does not have inherent power to ignore the limitations of § 2283 and to enjoin state court proceedings merely because those proceedings interfere with a protected federal right or invade an area preempted by federal law, even when the interference is unmistakably clear. * * * This conclusion is required because Congress itself set forth the only exceptions to the statute, and those exceptions do not include this situation. Second, if the District Court does have jurisdiction, it is not enough that the requested injunction is related to that jurisdiction, but it must be "*necessary in aid of*" that jurisdiction. While this language is admittedly broad, we conclude that it implies something similar to the concept of injunctions to "protect or effectuate" judgments. Both exceptions to the general prohibition of § 2283 imply that some federal injunctive relief may be necessary to prevent a state court from so interfering with a federal court's consideration or disposition of a case as to seriously impair the federal court's flexibility and authority to decide that case. Third, no such situation is presented here. * * * [T]he state and federal courts had concurrent jurisdiction in this case, and neither court was free to prevent either party from simultaneously pursuing claims in both courts. Kline v. Burke Constr. Co., 260 U.S. 226 (1922); *cf.* Donovan v. City of Dallas, 377 U.S. 408 (1964). Therefore the state court's assumption of jurisdiction over the state law claims and the federal preclusion issue did not hinder the federal court's jurisdiction so as to make an injunction *necessary* to aid that jurisdiction. An injunction was no more necessary because the state court may have taken action which the federal court was certain was improper under the Jacksonville Terminal decision. Again, lower federal courts possess no power whatever to sit in direct review of state court decisions. If the union was adversely affected by the state court's decision, it was free to seek vindication of its federal right in the Florida appellate courts and ultimately, if necessary, in this Court. Similarly if, because of the Florida Circuit Court's action, the union faced the threat of immediate irreparable injury sufficient to justify an injunction under usual equitable principles, it was undoubtedly free to seek such relief from the Florida appellate courts, and might possibly in certain emergency circumstances seek such relief from this Court as well. * * * Unlike the Federal District Court, this Court does have potential appellate jurisdiction over federal questions raised in state court proceedings, and that broader jurisdiction allows this Court correspondingly broader authority to issue injunctions "necessary in aid of its jurisdiction."

III

This case is by no means an easy one. The arguments in support of the union's contentions are not insubstantial. But whatever doubts we may have are strongly affected by the general prohibition of § 2283. Any doubts as to the propriety of a federal injunction against state court proceedings should be resolved in favor of permitting the state courts to proceed in an orderly fashion to finally determine the controversy. The explicit wording of § 2283 itself implies as much, and the fundamental principle of a dual system of courts leads inevitably to that conclusion.

The injunction issued by the District Court must be vacated. Since that court has not yet proceeded to a final judgment in the case, the cause is remanded to it for further proceedings in conformity with this opinion.

MR. JUSTICE MARSHALL took no part in the consideration or decision of this case.

MR. JUSTICE HARLAN, concurring.

* * *

MR. JUSTICE BRENNAN, with whom MR. JUSTICE WHITE joins, dissenting.

My disagreement with the Court in this case is a relatively narrow one. I do not disagree with much that is said concerning the history and policies underlying 28 U.S.C. § 2283. * * * Nevertheless, in my view the District Court had discretion to enjoin the state proceedings in the present case because it acted pursuant to an explicit exception to the prohibition of § 2283, that is, "to protect or effectuate [the District Court's] judgments."
* * *

In my view, what the District Court decided in 1967 was that BLE had a federally protected right to picket at the Moncrief Yard and, by necessary implication, that this right could not be subverted by resort to state proceedings. I find it difficult indeed to ascribe to the District Judge the views which the Court now says he held, namely, that ACL, merely by marching across the street to the state court, could render wholly nugatory the District Judge's declaration that BLE had a federally protected right to strike at the Moncrief Yard. * * *

* * *

Accordingly, I would affirm the judgment of the Court of Appeals sustaining the District Court's grant of injunctive relief against petitioner's giving effect to, or availing itself of, the benefit of the state injunction.

MITCHUM v. FOSTER

407 U.S. 225, 92 S.Ct. 2151, 32 L.Ed.2d 705 (1972).
Appeal from the United States District Court for the
Northern District of Florida.

Mr. Justice Stewart delivered the opinion of the Court.

The federal anti-injunction statute provides that a federal court "may not grant an injunction to stay proceedings in a State court except as expressly authorized by Act of Congress, or where necessary in aid of its jurisdiction, or to protect or effectuate its judgments." An Act of Congress, 42 U.S.C. § 1983, expressly authorizes a "suit in equity" to redress "the deprivation," under color of state law, "of any rights, privileges, or immunities secured by the Constitution. * * *" The question before us is whether this "Act of Congress" comes within the "expressly authorized" exception of the anti-injunction statute so as to permit a federal court in a § 1983 suit to grant an injunction to stay a proceeding pending in a state court. * * *

I

The prosecuting attorney of Bay County, Florida, brought a proceeding in a Florida court to close down the appellant's bookstore as a public nuisance under the claimed authority of Florida law. The state court entered a preliminary order prohibiting continued operation of the bookstore. After further inconclusive proceedings in the state courts, the appellant filed a complaint in the United States District Court for the Northern District of Florida, alleging that the actions of the state judicial and law enforcement officials were depriving him of rights protected by the First and Fourteenth Amendments. Relying upon 42 U.S.C. § 1983, he asked for injunctive and declaratory relief against the state court proceedings, on the ground that Florida laws were being unconstitutionally applied by the state court so as to cause him great and irreparable harm. * * *

II

In denying injunctive relief, the District Court relied on this Court's decision in Atlantic Coast Line R. Co. v. Brotherhood of Locomotive Engineers, 398 U.S. 281. The Atlantic Coast Line case did not deal with the "expressly authorized" exception of the anti-injunction statute, but the Court's opinion in that case * * * rejected the view that the anti-injunction statute merely states a flexible doctrine of comity, and made clear that the statute imposes an absolute ban upon the issuance of a federal injunction against a pending state court proceeding, in the absence of one of the recognized exceptions * * *.

It follows, in the present context, that if 42 U.S.C. § 1983 is not within the "expressly authorized" exception of the anti-injunction statute, then a federal equity court is wholly without power to grant any relief in a § 1983 suit seeking to stay a state court proceeding.

Last Term, in Younger v. Harris, 401 U.S. 37, and its companion cases, the Court dealt at length with the subject of federal judicial intervention in pending state criminal prosecutions. In Younger a three-judge federal district court in a § 1983 action had enjoined a criminal prosecution pending in a California court. In asking us to reverse that judgment, the appellant argued that the injunction was in violation of the federal anti-injunction statute. But the Court carefully eschewed any reliance on the statute in reversing the judgment, basing its decision instead upon what the Court called "Our Federalism"—upon "the national policy forbidding federal courts to stay or enjoin pending state court proceedings except under special circumstances."

* * * At the same time, however, the Court clearly left room for federal injunctive intervention in a pending state court prosecution in certain exceptional circumstances—where irreparable injury is "both great and immediate," where the state law is " 'flagrantly and patently violative of express constitutional prohibitions,' " or where there is a showing of "bad faith, harassment, or * * * other unusual circumstances that would call for equitable relief." * * *

While the Court in Younger and its companion cases expressly disavowed deciding the question now before us—whether § 1983 comes within the "expressly authorized" exception of the anti-injunction statute—it is evident that our decisions in those cases cannot be disregarded in deciding this question. In the first place, if § 1983 is not within the statutory exception, then the anti-injunction statute would have absolutely barred the injunction issued in Younger, as the appellant in that case argued, and there would have been no occasion whatever for the Court to decide that case upon the "policy" ground of "Our Federalism." Secondly, if § 1983 is not within the "expressly authorized" exception of the anti-injunction statute, then we must overrule Younger and its companion cases insofar as they recognized the permissibility of injunctive relief against pending criminal prosecutions in certain limited and exceptional circumstances. * * *

The Atlantic Coast Line and Younger cases thus serve to delineate both the importance and the finality of the question now before us. And it is in the shadow of those cases that the question must be decided.

III

The anti-injunction statute goes back almost to the beginnings of our history as a Nation. In 1793, Congress enacted a law providing that no "writ of injunction be granted [by any federal court] to stay proceedings in any court of a state. * * *" Act of March 2, 1793; 1 Stat. 335. The precise origins of the legislation are shrouded in obscurity,[10] but the

10. "The history of this provision in the Judiciary Act of 1793 is not fully known. We know that on December 31, 1790, Attorney General Edmund Randolph reported to the House of Representatives on desirable changes in the Judiciary Act of 1789. * * * The most serious question raised by Randolph concerned the arduousness of the circuit duties imposed on the Supreme Court justices. But the Report also suggested a number of amendments dealing with procedural matters. A section of the proposed bill submitted by him provided that 'no injunction in equity shall be granted by a district court to a judgment at law of a State court.' Randolph explained * * *[:] 'It is enough to split the same suit into one at law, and another in equity, without adding a further separation, by throwing the common law side of the question into the State courts, and the equity side into the federal courts.' * * * No action was taken until after Chief Justice Jay and his associates wrote the President that their circuit-riding duties were too burdensome. In response to this complaint, which was transmitted to Congress, the Act of March 2, 1793, was passed, containing in § 5, *inter alia*, the prohibition against staying state court proceedings.
* * *

consistent understanding has been that its basic purpose is to prevent "needless friction between state and federal courts." Oklahoma Packing Co. v. Gas Co., 309 U.S. 4, 9. The law remained unchanged until 1874, when it was amended to permit a federal court to stay state court proceedings that interfered with the administration of a federal bankruptcy proceeding. The present wording of the legislation was adopted with the enactment of Title 28 of the United States Code in 1948.

Despite the seemingly uncompromising language of the anti-injunction statute prior to 1948, the Court soon recognized that exceptions must be made to its blanket prohibition if the import and purpose of other Acts of Congress were to be given their intended scope. So it was that, in addition to the bankruptcy law exception that Congress explicitly recognized in 1874, the Court through the years found that federal courts were empowered to enjoin state court proceedings, despite the anti-injunction statute, in carrying out the will of Congress under at least six other federal laws. These covered a broad spectrum of congressional action: (1) legislation providing for removal of litigation from state to federal courts,[12] (2) legislation limiting the liability of shipowners,[13] (3) legislation providing for federal interpleader actions,[14] (4) legislation conferring federal jurisdiction over farm mortgages,[15] (5) legislation governing federal habeas corpus proceedings,[16] and (6) legislation providing for control of prices.[17]

"There is no record of any debates over the statute. See 3 Annals of Congress (1791–93). It has been suggested that the provision reflected the then strong feeling against the unwarranted intrusion of federal courts upon state sovereignty. Chisholm v. Georgia, 2 Dall. 419, was decided on February 18, 1793, less than two weeks before the provision was enacted into law. The significance of this proximity is doubtful. Compare Warren, Federal and State Court Interference, 43 Harv.L. Rev. 345, 347–348, with Gunter v. Atlantic Coast Line R. Co., 200 U.S. 273, 291–292. Much more probable is the suggestion that the provision reflected the prevailing prejudices against equity jurisdiction. * * *" Toucey v. New York Life Ins. Co., 314 U.S. 118, 130–132.

12. See French v. Hay, 22 Wall. 250; Kline v. Burke Construction Co., 260 U.S. 226. The federal removal provisions, both civil and criminal, 28 U.S.C. §§ 1441–1450, provide that once a copy of the removal petition is filed with the clerk of the state court, the "State court shall proceed no further unless and until the case is remanded." 28 U.S.C. § 1446(e).

13. See Providence & N.Y.S.S. Co. v. Hill Mfg. Co., 109 U.S. 578. The Act of 1851, 9 Stat. 635, as amended, provides that once a shipowner has deposited with the court an amount equal to the value of his interest in the ship, "all claims and proceedings against the owner with respect to the matter in question shall cease." 46 U.S.C. § 185.

14. See Treinies v. Sunshine Mining Co., 308 U.S. 66. The Interpleader Act of 1926, 44 Stat. 416, as currently written provides that in "any civil action of interpleader * * * a district court may * * * enter its order restraining [all claimants] * * * from instituting or prosecuting any proceeding in any State or United States court affecting the property, instrument or obligation involved in the interpleader action." 28 U.S.C. § 2361.

15. See Kalb v. Feuerstein, 308 U.S. 433. The Frazier–Lemke Farm–Mortgage Act, as amended in 1935, 49 Stat. 944, provides that in situations to which it is applicable a federal court shall "stay all judicial or official proceedings in any court." 11 U.S.C. § 203(s)(2) (1940 ed.).

16. See Ex parte Royall, 117 U.S. 241, 248–249. The Federal Habeas Corpus Act provides that a federal court before which a habeas corpus proceeding is pending may "stay any proceeding against the person detained in any State Court * * * for any matter involved in the habeas corpus proceeding." 28 U.S.C. § 2251.

17. Section 205(a) of the Emergency Price Control Act of 1942, 56 Stat. 33, provided that the Price Administrator could request a federal district court to enjoin acts that violated or threatened to violate the Act. In Porter v. Dicken, 328 U.S. 252, we held that this authority was broad enough to justify an injunction to restrain state court proceedings. The Emergency Price Control Act was thus considered a congressionally authorized excep-

In addition to the exceptions to the anti-injunction statute found to be embodied in these various Acts of Congress, the Court recognized other "implied" exceptions to the blanket prohibition of the anti-injunction statute. One was an "*in rem*" exception, allowing a federal court to enjoin a state court proceeding in order to protect its jurisdiction of a res over which it had first acquired jurisdiction. Another was a "relitigation" exception, permitting a federal court to enjoin relitigation in a state court of issues already decided in federal litigation. Still a third exception, more recently developed, permits a federal injunction of state court proceedings when the plaintiff in the federal court is the United States itself, or a federal agency asserting "superior federal interests."

In Toucey v. New York Life Ins. Co., 314 U.S. 118, the Court in 1941 issued an opinion casting considerable doubt upon the approach to the anti-injunction statute reflected in its previous decisions. The Court's opinion expressly disavowed the "relitigation" exception to the statute, and emphasized generally the importance of recognizing the statute's basic directive "of 'hands off' by the federal courts in the use of the injunction to stay litigation in a state court." The congressional response to Toucey was the enactment in 1948 of the anti-injunction statute in its present form in 28 U.S.C. § 2283, which, as the Reviser's Note makes evident, served not only to overrule the specific holding of Toucey, but to restore "the basic law as generally understood and interpreted prior to the Toucey decision."

We proceed, then, upon the understanding that in determining whether § 1983 comes within the "expressly authorized" exception of the anti-injunction statute, the criteria to be applied are those reflected in the Court's decisions prior to Toucey. A review of those decisions makes reasonably clear what the relevant criteria are. In the first place, it is evident that, in order to qualify under the "expressly authorized" exception of the anti-injunction statute, a federal law need not contain an express reference to that statute. * * * Indeed, none of the previously recognized statutory exceptions contains any such reference.[24] Secondly, a federal law need not expressly authorize an injunction of a state court proceeding in order to qualify as an exception. Three of the six previously recognized statutory exceptions contain no such authorization.[25] Thirdly, it is clear that, in order to qualify as an "expressly authorized" exception to the anti-injunction statute, an Act of Congress must have created a specific and uniquely federal right or remedy, enforceable in a federal court of equity, that could be frustrated if the federal court were not empowered to enjoin a state court proceeding. This is not to say that in order to come within the exception an Act of Congress must, on its face and in every one of its provisions, be totally incompatible with the prohibition of the anti-injunction statute. The test, rather, is whether an Act of Congress, clearly creating a federal right or remedy enforceable in a federal court of equity, could be given its intended scope only by the stay of a state court proceeding. * * *

With these criteria in view, we turn to consideration of 42 U.S.C. § 1983.

tion to the anti-injunction statute. Section 205(a) expired in 1947.

24. See nn. 12, 13, 14, 15, 16, and 17, *supra*.

25. See nn. 12, 13, and 17, *supra*.
* * *

IV

Section 1983 was originally § 1 of the Civil Rights Act of 1871. * * * The predecessor of § 1983 was thus an important part of the basic alteration in our federal system wrought in the Reconstruction era through federal legislation and constitutional amendment. As a result of the new structure of law that emerged in the post-Civil War era—and especially of the Fourteenth Amendment, which was its centerpiece—the role of the Federal Government as a guarantor of basic federal rights against state power was clearly established. * * *

It is clear from the legislative debates surrounding passage of § 1983's predecessor that the Act was intended to enforce the provisions of the Fourteenth Amendment "against State action, * * * whether that action be executive, legislative, or *judicial.* " Ex parte Virginia, 100 U.S. 339, 346 (emphasis supplied). Proponents of the legislation noted that state courts were being used to harass and injure individuals, either because the state courts were powerless to stop deprivations or were in league with those who were bent upon abrogation of federally protected rights.

As Representative Lowe stated, the "records of the [state] tribunals are searched in vain for evidence of effective redress [of federally secured rights]. * * * What less than this [the Civil Rights Act of 1871] will afford an adequate remedy? The Federal Government cannot serve a writ of mandamus upon State Executives or upon State courts to compel them to protect the rights, privileges and immunities of citizens. * * * The case has arisen * * * when the Federal Government must resort to its own agencies to carry its own authority into execution. Hence this bill throws open the doors of the United States courts to those whose rights under the Constitution are denied or impaired." Cong. Globe, 42d Cong., 1st Sess., 374–376 (1871). This view was echoed by [other legislators]. * * *

* * *

This legislative history makes evident that Congress clearly conceived that it was altering the relationship between the States and the Nation with respect to the protection of federally created rights; it was concerned that state instrumentalities could not protect those rights; it realized that state officers might, in fact, be antipathetic to the vindication of those rights; and it believed that these failings extended to the state courts.

V

Section 1983 was thus a product of a vast transformation from the concepts of federalism that had prevailed in the late 18th century when the anti-injunction statute was enacted. The very purpose of § 1983 was to interpose the federal courts between the States and the people, as guardians of the people's federal rights—to protect the people from unconstitutional action under color of state law, "whether that action be executive, legislative, or judicial." Ex parte Virginia, 100 U.S., at 346. In carrying out that purpose, Congress plainly authorized the federal courts to issue injunctions in § 1983 actions, by expressly authorizing a "suit in equity" as one of the means of redress. And this Court long ago recognized that federal injunctive relief against a state court proceeding can in some circumstances be essential to prevent great, immediate, and irreparable loss of a person's constitutional rights. Ex parte Young, 209 U.S. 123 * * *. For these reasons we conclude that, under the criteria established in our previous decisions construing the anti-injunction statute, § 1983 is an Act of Congress that falls within the "expressly authorized" exception of that law.

In so concluding, we do not question or qualify in any way the principles of equity, comity, and federalism that must restrain a federal court when asked to enjoin a state court proceeding. These principles, in the context of state criminal prosecutions, were canvassed at length last Term in Younger v. Harris, 401 U.S. 37, and its companion cases. * * * Today we decide only that the District Court in this case was in error in holding that, because of the anti-injunction statute, it was absolutely without power in this § 1983 action to enjoin a proceeding pending in a state court under any circumstances whatsoever.

The judgment is reversed and the case is remanded to the District Court for further proceedings consistent with this opinion.

[Justices Powell and Rehnquist did not participate. Chief Justice Burger, joined by Justices White and Blackmun, filed a concurring opinion stressing that the Court had not yet decided whether the principles of equity, comity, and federalism set forth in Younger v. Harris, Sec. 2(C), *infra*, restricted federal injunctive relief against pending state *civil* proceedings. He urged the district court on remand to consider that question before proceeding to the merits.]

NOTE ON 28 U.S.C. § 2283

(1) *History and Purpose.* The view of the Anti–Injunction Act's purpose set forth in Atlantic Coast Line and Mitchum has not gone unchallenged. Professor Mayton concludes that the original Act of 1793 was designed merely to prohibit a *single Justice* of the Supreme Court from enjoining such proceedings while riding circuit. Mayton, *Ersatz Federalism under the Anti–Injunction Statute,* 78 Colum.L.Rev. 330 (1978). Professor Mayton marshalls considerable support for this view, including the language of the statute itself,[1] though he does have some difficulty explaining the statute's syntax and its use at one point of the phrase "court or judge." *Id.* at 335. He concedes that the 1948 revision had a broader

---

1. He relies in part on the fact that the bar on injunctions was included in the middle of section 5 of the 1793 Act, which governed the powers of a single Justice. He also observes that for over fifty years, the federal courts did not rely on the statute in considering requests for injunctions against state court proceedings, disposing of such cases instead on "equitable principles, * * * standards of comity * * *, and on general principles of federalism" (p. 338). The original meaning, Mayton argues, was lost when, in Peck v. Jenness, 7 How. 612 (U.S.1849), the Supreme Court asserted without discussion that the 1793 Act barred federal injunctions against state court proceedings. That view was followed when the anti-injunction language was separated from the rest of section 5 in an 1874 statutory revision, which was not supposed to effect substantive changes (p. 346). See also Reaves & Golden, *The Federal Anti–Injunction Statute in the Aftermath of Atlantic Coast Line Railroad,* 5 Ga.L.Rev. 294, 297–99 (1971).

The thesis of Comment, *Federal Court Stays of State Court Proceedings: A Reexamination of Original Congressional Intent,* 38 U.Chi.L.Rev. 612 (1971), is "that Congress in 1793 did not intend to prevent stays effected by writs other than injunction, and that Congress specifically approved the use of the [common-law] writ of certiorari to stay state proceedings" (p. 613).

purpose, but argues that its true intent was only to authorize the exercise of a sound discretion to protect the federal courts and the exercise of their subject-matter jurisdiction.

(2) *Duplicative Proceedings in State Courts.* No general rule of federal law requires a federal court to abate or stay a proceeding otherwise within its jurisdiction merely on a plea of prior action pending in a state court. Stanton v. Embrey, 93 U.S. 548 (1877).

And federal courts have long been held to be barred by the predecessor of 28 U.S.C. § 2283 from enjoining parties from prosecuting pending in personam proceedings in a state court merely on the ground of duplication or overlapping of proceedings *previously* begun and still pending in the federal court.

The leading case on the application of the statute to the problem of duplicative state proceedings is Kline v. Burke Constr. Co., 260 U.S. 226 (1922). After stating the rule, discussed below, that permits a state or federal court, by injunction or otherwise, to protect its prior jurisdiction over a specific res, Justice Sutherland said (p. 230) that as to in personam actions, "[e]ach court is free to proceed in its own way and in its own time, without reference to the proceedings in the other court. Whenever a judgment is rendered in one of the courts and pleaded in the other, the effect of that judgment is to be determined by the application of the principles of *res adjudicata* by the court in which the action is still pending * * *. The rule, therefore, has become generally established that where the action first brought is *in personam* and seeks only a personal judgment, another action for the same cause in another jurisdiction is not precluded."

(3) *The Evolution of Exceptions to the Act.* A number of qualifications and limitations on the anti-injunction statute had been recognized prior to the important decision in Toucey v. New York Life Ins. Co., 314 U.S. 118 (1941), discussed in Paragraph (4), below.

(a) *Congressional Authorization.* Some of these qualifications were based on express provision or judicial construction of other Acts of Congress; they are summarized in Mitchum.

(b) *The Res Exception.* In addition, as Mitchum also notes, a line of cases beginning with Hagan v. Lucas, 10 Pet. 400 (U.S.1836), announced an implied exception to the Anti–Injunction Act by declaring that the court (state or federal) that first assumes jurisdiction over property is entitled to maintain and exercise jurisdiction, to the exclusion of any other court, even to the point of enjoining another court's proceedings. *Cf.* Freeman v. Howe, 24 How. 450 (U.S.1860), p. 1685, *infra.* See also Paragraph (8), *infra;* and see the immediately following *Note on the Power of State Courts to Enjoin Federal Court Actions.* Notwithstanding the frequent reiteration of this principle, no Supreme Court case has been found actually upholding an injunction against state proceedings issued to protect the federal court's control over property in a pending litigation.

There is a good deal of mystery, and even mysticism, surrounding the concept of judicial jurisdiction over property. The traditional distinction between in rem and in personam jurisdiction has been criticized as standing in the way of useful analysis, see, *e.g.,* Mullane v. Central Hanover Bank & Trust Co., 339 U.S. 306 (1950); von Mehren & Trautman, *Jurisdiction to Adjudicate: A Suggested Analysis,* 79 Harv.L.Rev. 1121 (1966), and more recently significant erosion has occurred, see, *e.g.,* Shaffer v. Heitner,

433 U.S. 186 (1977). Thus, it is not surprising that the problem of the scope of the res exception has been a troublesome one.[2]

(c) *Fraudulent State Court Judgments.* Several Supreme Court decisions sustained the power of federal courts to enjoin litigants from enforcing judgments fraudulently obtained in state courts. *E.g.,* Marshall v. Holmes, 141 U.S. 589 (1891); Simon v. Southern Ry., 236 U.S. 115 (1915). It was unclear, however, whether this power rested on the premise that the anti-injunction statute was inapplicable because the state proceeding had been completed, see Simon v. Southern Ry., *supra,* or that an exception to the anti-injunction statute existed with respect to the enforcement of state judgments fraudulently obtained, see Hill v. Martin, 296 U.S. 393, 403 (1935). See also Paragraph 10(b), *infra.*[3]

(4) *The Toucey Decision.* In Toucey v. New York Life Ins. Co., 314 U.S. 118 (1941), the Court broke with this tradition of implying exceptions to the Act. Toucey rejected the view—supported by such decisions as Supreme Tribe of Ben–Hur v. Cauble, 255 U.S. 356 (1921)—that the federal courts had authority to enjoin state relitigation of issues settled in a prior federal action. Justice Frankfurter's opinion for the majority found in existing precedent at most a "tenuous basis for the exception which we are now asked explicitly to sanction. Whatever justification there may be for turning past error into law when reasonable expectations would thereby be defeated, no such justification can be urged on behalf of a procedural doctrine in the distribution of power between federal and state courts. It denies reality to suggest that litigants have shaped their conduct in reliance upon some loose talk in past decisions * * *. We must be scrupulous in our regard for the limits within which Congress has confined the authority of the courts of its own creation" (pp. 131, 135, 140–41).

(5) *The 1948 Revision.* The Reviser's notes to § 2283, enacted in 1948, constitute the only legislative history of the provision. The substance of those notes is as follows:

"An exception as to acts of Congress relating to bankruptcy was omitted and the general exception substituted to cover all exceptions.

"The phrase 'in aid of its jurisdiction' was added to conform to section 1651 of this title and to make clear the recognized power of the Federal courts to stay proceedings in State cases removed to the district courts.

2. Princess Lida of Thurn and Taxis v. Thompson, 305 U.S. 456 (1939), held that the filing of trust accounts gave a state court quasi in rem jurisdiction and empowered it to enjoin a later federal action against the trustees for an accounting and other relief. Compare, on the other hand, Mandeville v. Canterbury, 318 U.S. 47 (1943), where the plaintiff sued in a federal court to determine rights in a trust, and the defendant trustees then sued in a state court to quiet title to the trust property. The Supreme Court held that the federal action was in personam and that the state action accordingly could not be enjoined. Compare the holdings in the converse situation, where the first action is in rem or quasi in rem and the second in personam. See Markham v. Allen, 326 U.S. 490 (1946), p. 1454, *infra,* and cases cited in that opinion and the following Note, especially United States v. Klein, 303 U.S. 276 (1938).

3. There were also several lower court decisions prior to 1941 that appeared to suggest an "ancillary exception" to the anti-injunction statute. See Comment, *Federal Injunctions Against Proceedings in State Courts,* 35 Calif.L.Rev. 545, 549–50 (1947). A typical case is Alliance Ins. Co. v. Jamerson, 12 F.Supp. 957 (E.D.Ill.1935), *aff'd,* 87 F.2d 253 (7th Cir.1937). There ten insurance companies brought a diversity suit to cancel defendant's insurance policies and to enjoin actions on each of the policies pending in state courts. They got the injunction. Accord: American Optometric Ass'n v. Ritholtz, 101 F.2d 883 (7th Cir. 1939). Can these cases be squared with Kline v. Burke Constr. Co., *supra?*

"The exceptions specifically include the words 'to protect or effectuate its judgments,' for lack of which the Supreme Court held that the Federal courts are without power to enjoin relitigation of cases and controversies fully adjudicated by such courts. (See Toucey v. New York Life Ins. Co., * * *. A vigorous dissenting opinion * * * notes that at the time of the 1911 revision of the Judicial Code, the power of the courts of the United States to protect their judgments was unquestioned and that the revisers of that code noted no change and Congress intended no change).

"Therefore the revised section restores the basic law as generally understood and interpreted prior to the Toucey decision.

"Changes were made in phraseology."

One comment on § 2283 when it was still only a proposal (35 Calif.L. Rev. 545, 563) concluded: " * * * [A]ny amendment should properly solve more questions than it raises. The proposed revision does not appear to have this virtue." Consider the clairvoyance of this comment in light of the post–1948 case law.

(6) *Judicially Implied Exceptions to § 2283.* Both Atlantic Coast Line and Mitchum clearly state that § 2283's ban is absolute unless the case falls within one of the three express exceptions. Is this interpretation convincing when it is recalled that the 1948 revision (i) was enacted against a background of judicially implied exceptions to the Act, and (ii) was designed to expand the scope of federal court power to issue injunctions? Is it likely that Congress could have foreseen all of the appropriate exceptions to a broad organic provision like § 2283?

Consider the application of the Anti–Injunction Act to cases in which the United States or a federal agency seeks to enjoin state proceedings. Both before and after the 1948 revision, there was uncertainty about its application to these cases. The question was partially settled in 1957, in Leiter Minerals v. United States, 352 U.S. 220 (1957), when the Court held the statute inapplicable to injunctions sought by the United States. Justice Frankfurter, who less than two years earlier had spoken of § 2283 as a "clear-cut prohibition qualified only by specifically defined exceptions" (Amalgamated Clothing Workers v. Richman Bros., 348 U.S. 511, 516 (1955)) now said (352 U.S. at 225–26):

" * * * The statute is designed to prevent conflict between federal and state courts. This policy is much more compelling when it is the litigation of private parties which threatens to draw the two judicial systems into conflict than when it is the United States which seeks to prevent a threatened irreparable injury to a national interest. The frustration of superior federal interests that would ensue from precluding the Federal Government from obtaining a stay of state court proceedings except under the severe restrictions of 28 U.S.C. § 2283 would be so great that we cannot reasonably impute such a purpose to Congress from the general language of § 2283 alone. It is always difficult to feel confident about construing an ambiguous statute * * * but the interpretation excluding the United States from the coverage of the statute seems to us preferable in the context of healthy federal-state relations." [4]

4. The state court action in Leiter Minerals was brought by Leiter against lessees of the United States. Leiter sought to have itself declared owner of the mineral rights under the land and also sought an accounting for minerals taken by the lessees. After the state action began, the United States brought a federal court ac-

In NLRB v. Nash–Finch Co., 404 U.S. 138 (1971), the Court extended the Leiter rationale to an application for an injunction by the National Labor Relations Board.

Although the expansive view expressed in Leiter appeared as a harbinger of further judicial creativity, the later discussions in Atlantic Coast Line and Mitchum seem to have closed the door on efforts by several lower courts to read into § 2283 a general exception in cases of particularly compelling circumstances.[5]

(7) *"As Expressly Authorized by Act of Congress"*.

(a) *The Reach of § 1983*. The breadth of Mitchum's holding is apparent when viewed in conjunction with the holding nine years later in Maine v. Thiboutot, 448 U.S. 1 (1980), p. 1254, *supra*, that § 1983 provides a remedy for a violation, by a person acting under color of state law, not only of federal rights conferred by the Constitution, or by legislation relating to equal rights, but also of rights created by federal statutes generally.

The scope of Mitchum thus depends importantly on when state court litigation between private parties is deemed to be "under color of law" for purposes of § 1983. In Lugar v. Edmondson Oil Co., Inc., 457 U.S. 922 (1982), a creditor brought suit on a debt, and, pursuant to a state statute, obtained ex parte a prejudgment attachment of the defendant's property. The Court held that though "a private party's mere invocation of state legal procedures" was not action under color of law, the attachment was and hence could be challenged under § 1983. Chief Justice Burger and Justices Powell, Rehnquist, and O'Connor dissented from the latter conclusion.[6] And the issuance of a state court injunction, temporary or permanent, surely constitutes action "under color of law." See, e.g., Henry v. First Nat. Bank, 595 F.2d 291, 299–300 (5th Cir.1979); Machesky v. Bizzell, 414 F.2d 283, 286 (5th Cir.1969); cf. Shelley v. Kraemer, 334 U.S. 1 (1948).[7]

How applicable is the legislative history of the reconstruction era, on which Mitchum placed great weight, to a § 1983 suit like Lugar, or to one alleging that state officials violated rules governing a federal benefit program?

Note that Mitchum creates a regime—in federal law actions seeking injunctions against state court proceedings involving conduct under color of law—very much like that advocated more generally by Professor Mayton,

tion against Leiter and others to quiet title to the mineral rights, and sought to enjoin the state proceedings. Could the federal injunction have been sustained on the res exception? On the argument that the injunction was "necessary in aid of" federal jurisdiction?

5. See, *e.g.*, Machesky v. Bizzell, 414 F.2d 283 (5th Cir.1969); Baines v. City of Danville, 337 F.2d 579 (4th Cir.1964).

6. See also Pennzoil Co. v. Texaco, Inc., 107 S.Ct. 1519 (1987), p. 1437, *infra*, in which Justices Brennan, Marshall, Blackmun, and Stevens, concurring in the judgment, expressly stated that a judgment creditor's invocation of state postjudgment collection procedures constitutes action under color of state law; the five Justices

joining the Court's opinion did not reach the issue.

7. Reconsider the facts of Atlantic Coast Line. Assuming issuance of the injunction constituted conduct under color of law, could the union have based its claim for relief on § 1983, arguing that the Railway Labor Act conferred a federal right to be free from preempted state court proceedings? Several circuit court decisions suggest not, holding that a claim of preemption, though a basis for Supreme Court review of a state court decision, does not assert a "right secured" to an individual by a law of the United States, and hence is not cognizable under § 1983. See p. 1243, note 8, *supra*.

see Paragraph (1), *supra:* federal relief is not absolutely barred, but is limited by principles of comity, equity and federalism.

(b) *Other "Express" Exceptions.* A careful look at footnotes 12–17 of Mitchum shows that in five of the six statutes that had previously been found expressly to authorize injunctive relief against state proceedings, Congress clearly indicated that state proceedings should cease. (The exception is the Emergency Price Control Act of 1942). Whether or not an indication of that kind necessarily authorizes such federal intervention— the Supremacy Clause, after all, obliges a state court to stay its own proceedings if federal law so dictates—isn't Mitchum still a further step, given the lack of any such indication in § 1983?

The possibility that after Mitchum, the "expressly authorized" exception to § 2283 would receive a broad construction in other areas may have been dimmed by the result in Vendo Co. v. Lektro–Vend Corp., 433 U.S. 623 (1977). Vendo sued Lektro–Vend (and others) in a state court for breach of an agreement not to compete. Lektro–Vend countered by bringing a federal court action against Vendo alleging that the agreement violated the federal antitrust laws. When the highest state court affirmed a judgment against Lektro–Vend for over $7 million, the federal district court enjoined enforcement of the judgment, holding that § 16 of the Clayton Act, 15 U.S.C. § 26 (authorizing private suits for injunctive relief against antitrust violations) was an "expressly authorized" exception to § 2283.

The Seventh Circuit affirmed; but the Supreme Court, though unable to muster a majority for any rationale, reversed. Justice Rehnquist, for himself and Justices Stewart and Powell, argued that, unlike § 1983, § 16 of the Clayton Act was not an act that could be given "its intended scope" only by a stay of state court proceedings. There was no indication that Congress, in enacting § 16, "was concerned with the possibility that state-court proceedings would be used to violate the Sherman or Clayton Acts" (p. 634); acceptance of respondents' argument on this score would "eviscerate" § 2283 "since the ultimate logic of this position can mean no less than that virtually *all* federal statutes authorizing injunctive relief are exceptions to § 2283" (p. 636). Implicitly rejected was any argument that significance should be attached to the congressional grant of exclusive jurisdiction to the federal courts in antitrust cases. *Cf.* note 10, *infra.*

Justice Blackmun, joined by the Chief Justice, concurred, but on the very different theory that (1) § 16 was an "expressly authorized" exception only in the "narrowly limited circumstances" where state court proceedings "are themselves part of a 'pattern of baseless, repetitive claims' that are being used as an anticompetitive device" (p. 644), and (2) no such pattern was or could have been found on the present record. Justice Stevens, speaking for four dissenters, argued that there were circumstances, like those in the case at bar, when the prosecution of even a single state-court proceeding could constitute a violation of the federal antitrust laws. To deny an injunction under those circumstances would be to deny § 16 its intended scope; thus under the test of Mitchum v. Foster, the case qualified as an "expressly authorized" exception to § 2283.

Note that the significant difference between the four dissenting and the two concurring Justices is over the circumstances when the prosecution of state court litigation will violate the federal antitrust laws. Can it then be contended that after Vendo, any federal statute providing for injunctive relief against unlawful action is an "expressly authorized" exception to § 2283 whenever it can be shown that the prosecution of a state court suit either constitutes or is a significant part of such unlawful action? See generally Redish, *The Anti-Injunction Statute Reconsidered*, 44 U.Chi.L. Rev. 717 (1977), arguing, *inter alia*, that the three opinions in Vendo demonstrate the unworkability of the Mitchum test.[8]

(8) *"In Aid of Its Jurisdiction"*. The Reviser's notes state that the § 2283's phrase "necessary in aid of its jurisdiction" confirms the recognized power of the federal courts to stay proceedings in state cases that have been removed.[9] On that explanation, why shouldn't the federal courts be able to protect their jurisdiction by also enjoining (a) concurrent state proceedings commenced after federal jurisdiction was acquired, thus overruling Kline v. Burke Constr. Co., Paragraph (2), *supra*, and (b) all state court cases that fall within the federal courts' exclusive jurisdiction?[10] Atlantic Coast Line makes clear that Kline is good law, but doesn't attempt to distinguish the removal situation.[11]

In Capital Service, Inc. v. NLRB, 347 U.S. 501 (1954), an employer, after having obtained a state court injunction against a union's secondary boycott, filed with the NLRB an unfair labor practice charge. After issuing a complaint, the NLRB obtained a federal court injunction against the boycott and against enforcement of the state court injunction, on the ground that federal law preempts state court jurisdiction over unfair labor practices. The Supreme Court affirmed the order as "necessary in aid of

8. Is Fed.R.Civ.Proc. 23 ever an authorized exception permitting injunctions against state court proceedings deemed to interfere with federal court class actions? In one mass tort case, there was an unsettled issue whether a defendant could be held liable under applicable state law for punitive damages in more than one suit arising out of a single occurrence. A federal district court certified two class actions under rule 23(b)(1)(B), which authorizes class suit (without a right to opt-out) when separate actions would effectively dispose of the interests of nonparties or substantially impair their ability to protect their interests. The district court enjoined all class members, including those with pending actions in state court, from settling their punitive damage claims until the federal court had resolved the issue. The court of appeals reversed that order as a violation of the Anti-Injunction Act. In re Federal Skywalk Cases, 680 F.2d 1175 (8th Cir.1982).

Could the injunction have been upheld by analogy to the federal interpleader statute, see footnote 14 in Mitchum, which has been held to be an expressly authorized exception?

For exploration of the interaction of Rule 23 and § 2283, see Larimore, *Exploring the Interface Between Rule 23 Class Actions and the Anti-Injunction Act*, 18 Ga.L.Rev. 259 (1984); Sherman, *Class Actions and Duplicative Litigation*, 62 Ind. L.J. 507, 528–36 (1987).

9. Mitchum, however, viewed the power to enjoin in removed cases as "expressly authorized by act of Congress" rather than "in aid of jurisdiction".

10. A grant of exclusive jurisdiction to the federal courts, combined with statutory authority to enjoin violations, may in some circumstances be construed as an authorized exception to § 2283. See Bowles v. Willingham, 321 U.S. 503, 510–11 (1944); *cf.* Studebaker Corp. v. Gittlin, 360 F.2d 692 (2d Cir.1966). But as Atlantic Coast Lines suggests, a grant of exclusive jurisdiction to the federal courts or a federal agency, standing alone, has not been thought a sufficient basis to enjoin state proceedings in cases within that jurisdiction. See, *e.g.*, T. Smith & Son, Inc. v. Williams, 275 F.2d 397 (5th Cir.1960); H.J. Heinz Co. v. Owens, 189 F.2d 505 (9th Cir.1951). For an argument favoring the contrary position, see Comment, note 1, *supra*.

11. In the Vendo case, Paragraph (7), *supra*, the Court declined to uphold the district court injunction as "necessary in aid of" that court's jurisdiction. Justice Rehnquist's plurality opinion for three members of the court reaffirmed Kline, emphasizing that the federal and state actions were in personam, not in rem. Chief Justice Burger and Justice Blackmun, concurring, tacitly accepted this analysis, and it was not discussed in the dissent.

jurisdiction": to make effective its statutory power to seek injunctions, the NLRB "must have authority to take all steps necessary to preserve its case" (p. 505).[12]

Capital Service was distinguished in Amalgamated Clothing Workers v. Richman Brothers, 348 U.S. 511 (1955), in which a union sought to enjoin, as preempted under the NLRA, a state-court suit against the union's picketing. The Supreme Court affirmed the district court's refusal to issue an injunction: no statute authorized the union (as distinguished from the NLRB) to file the federal court suit; the federal injunction was thus not ancillary to an independently-based, ongoing proceeding (pp. 516–17).[13]

Most courts have viewed the "necessary in aid of jurisdiction" language as confirming the "res" exception previously recognized in the federal courts[14]—despite the failure of the Reviser's notes to refer to that exception.

(9) *The Relitigation Exception.* Is the relitigation exception, revived in 1948, a sound one?

If an injunction is sought "to protect or effectuate" a federal judgment, is it sufficient to show that the matter sought to be litigated in the state proceeding has already been litigated between the parties in federal court? The author of Note, *Anti-Suit Injunctions Between State and Federal Courts*, 32 U.Chi.L.Rev. 471, 486 (1965), states that under the cases such a showing is sufficient, but criticizes this development. What further burden of establishing a need for equitable relief should the plaintiff bear? Should he have to establish that the state action is vexatious? That it is brought in a highly inconvenient forum? That there is need for speedier relief than can be afforded by a plea of res judicata in the state court?

Consider how this question is affected by Parsons Steel, Inc. v. First Alabama Bank, 474 U.S. 518 (1986). There, the plaintiffs sued the bank in separate actions in federal and state court. The federal action came to judgment first, with the bank prevailing. The bank's assertion in state court of res judicata defenses, based on the federal judgment, was rejected, leading to a $4 million jury verdict against the bank.

The bank then returned to federal district court, and obtained an injunction against the state court proceeding on the ground that state court claims could have been raised as pendent claims in the prior federal action, and accordingly should have been held by the state court to have been precluded. The Supreme Court unanimously overturned the injunction.

---

12. Today the injunction could be upheld under the subsequent decisions in Leiter Minerals and NLRB v. Nash–Finch Co., Paragraph (6), *supra*.

13. Compare Ex parte Peru, 318 U.S. 578 (1943), p. 347, *supra*, permitting the issuance of mandamus by the Supreme Court under 28 U.S.C. § 1651 to a lower federal court in aid of jurisdiction not yet acquired but likely to be acquired in the future. In Richman Brothers, 348 U.S. at 519–20 n. 5, the Court suggested that an order may more freely be deemed "necessary" in cases involving one sovereign than in cases involving two. (Note also that § 1651 speaks of writs necessary "or appropriate" in aid of jurisdiction.)

14. For a collection of cases, see 17 Wright, Miller & Cooper, Federal Practice & Procedure § 4225 (1978 & Supp.1986). For arguments criticizing the in personam/in rem distinction and suggesting that Kline should be overruled, or at least confined to its facts—a diversity case involving essentially state law issues, in which plaintiff was seeking an injunction "solely to protect his choice of a federal forum"— see Mayton, Paragraph (1), *supra*, at 359; *cf.* Redish, Paragraph (7), *supra*, at 745–60, proposing that Kline be rejected altogether and that a far broader interpretation of the exception be adopted.

The Court noted that the full faith and credit statute, 28 U.S.C. § 1738, generally requires a federal court to give a state court judgment the same effect that it would have under state law, see Chap. XII, pp. 1615–30, *infra;* that the Anti–Injunction Act was not an exception to § 1738; and that the relitigation exception was limited "to those situations in which the state court has not yet ruled on the merits of the res judicata issue. Once the state court has finally rejected a claim of res judicata, * * * federal courts must turn to state law to determine the preclusive effect of the state court's decision" (p. 772).

After Parsons Steel, what should a litigant who has obtained a favorable federal judgment do if there is any doubt that the state court will properly recognize the judgment's res judicata effect? Shouldn't he immediately seek, under the "relitigation exception," a federal injunction against state court adjudication of issues or claims that are precluded by the federal judgment? Will the likely response produce more or less federal-state friction?

Does the reference to the protection or effectuation of judgments cover non-appealable, interlocutory orders? See Sperry Rand Corp. v. Rothlein, 288 F.2d 245 (2d Cir.1961) (order enjoining state court use of evidence obtained in the course of federal discovery is needed to "effectuate" earlier federal court order in the same proceeding relating to priority of discovery) (alternative holding). But *cf.* Commerce Oil Ref. Corp. v. Miner, 303 F.2d 125, 128 (1st Cir.1962) (although "protectible rights may be conferred by something short of a final judgment," defendant may not be enjoined from relitigating in state proceeding a question resolved against him by federal district court in denying his motion to dismiss pending federal action). Does the unavailability of a res judicata defense in the state court in such a case support the availability of a federal injunction? Is a non-appealable, interlocutory order a "judgment"? See Wright, Miller, & Cooper, note 14, *supra,* § 4226 (urging application of the exception only to orders—final or interlocutory—that are appealable as of right), and cases collected therein.

(10) *The Meaning of "Proceedings".*

(a) *Commencement of Proceedings.* When do the "proceedings" referred to in § 2283 begin? Ex parte Young, 209 U.S. 123 (1908), p. 1173, *supra,* held that the Anti–Injunction Act did not apply to an injunction against criminal proceedings not yet instituted.[15] Consider how critical that holding has been to the vindication of federal rights.[16]

---

15. See also Dombrowski v. Pfister, 380 U.S. 479, 484 n. 2 (1965), p. 1397, *infra;* Brooks v. Briley, 274 F.Supp. 538, 553 (M.D.Tenn.1967), *aff'd,* 391 U.S. 361 (1968) ("the Court is of the opinion that the arrest and the issuance of a warrant by a magistrate, a state judicial officer, formally charging the plaintiffs with criminal violations, constitute 'proceedings' within the meaning of Sec. 2283"); McSurely v. Ratliff, 282 F.Supp. 848 (E.D.Ky.1967), *appeal dismissed,* 390 U.S. 412 (1968) (no state proceeding was pending, even after arrest, since no indictment had been issued and indictment was prerequisite to prosecution) (alternative holding).

16. A related question: At what stage in the federal proceeding does one determine whether state court proceedings are pending? Dombrowski v. Pfister, 380 U.S. 479, 484 n. 2 (1965), appears to hold (in the alternative) that when grand jury indictments are returned after the filing of a federal complaint seeking interlocutory and permanent injunctive relief but before such relief is issued, "no state 'proceedings' are pending within the intendment of § 2283." See Fiss, *Dombrowski,* 86 Yale L.J. 1103, 1108–09 (1977) (criticizing this holding). In Barancik v. Investors Funding Corp. of New York, 489 F.2d 933 (7th Cir.1973) (Stevens, J.), the court nonethe-

In Lynch v. Household Finance Corp., 405 U.S. 538 (1972), the Court held that a Connecticut prejudgment garnishment was not a "proceeding" in state court within the scope of § 2283, and hence could be enjoined by a federal court, even though the garnishment might be necessary to the effectiveness of any subsequent in personam judgment obtained by the creditor. The opinion emphasized that the garnishment could be instituted by the creditor's attorney, without judicial order, prior to the commencement of a creditor's suit (pp. 553–55). Justice White, joined by Chief Justice Burger and Justice Blackmun, dissented, stressing (p. 558) that the debtor's federal action to enjoin the garnishment was brought "more than seven months after the writ had been executed, the summons and complaint [in the debt action] served, process returned, and the case docketed in Connecticut." The garnishment "may be characterized as separate from the underlying action, but it is nonetheless a proceeding and derives its legitimacy from the suit it accompanies" (p. 560).[17]

(b) *Termination of Proceedings.* As to the termination of state proceedings, the problem is tied in with the authority of a federal court to enjoin enforcement of a fraudulently obtained state judgment, see Paragraph 3(c), *supra*. The line of cases recognizing such authority was questioned by the majority in Toucey v. New York Life Ins. Co., 314 U.S. 118 (1941) (as was Ex parte Young), and the lower courts are divided on whether such authority still exists. See Wright, Miller, & Cooper, note 14, *supra*, § 4223, at 326. After Atlantic Coast Line, and particularly the Court's statement that § 2283 "cannot be evaded by * * * prohibiting utilization of the results of a completed state proceeding", can an injunction in this situation be sustained? On the theory that there is no pending state proceeding? That the injunction is "in aid of" the federal court's jurisdiction to entertain an independent action to set aside the state court judgment?

(c) *State Court Proceedings Against Different Parties.* In County of Imperial v. Munoz, 449 U.S. 54 (1980), the county obtained a state court injunction against a landowner barring him from selling water from a well on his property for use outside the county. Three persons who had agreements to buy water for use in Mexico then sued the county in federal court, alleging that the state court injunction violated the Commerce Clause. The district court issued preliminary injunctive relief, which the court of appeals affirmed. The Supreme Court reversed, rejecting as contrary to the square holding of Atlantic Coast Line the court of appeals' view that the state court proceedings had terminated.

The federal plaintiffs also relied on Hale v. Bimco Trading, Inc., 306 U.S. 375 (1939). There, after one party obtained a state court order requiring a state agency to enforce a state statute, a different person obtained a federal court injunction barring, as a violation of the Commerce

---

less indicated that the mere fact that the federal complaint was filed before the state proceeding was commenced did not preclude operation of the Anti–Injunction Act, but went on to hold § 2283 inapplicable on the ground that the state proceeding in question was not filed until after the motion for federal injunctive relief had been made. *Contra,* Roth v. Bank of the Commonwealth, 583 F.2d 527 (6th Cir.1978), *cert. dismissed,* 442 U.S. 925 (1979).

Cf. Hicks v. Miranda, 422 U.S. 332 (1975), p. 1416 *infra,* holding that the equitable restraint doctrine of Younger v. Harris applies "in full force" when a state prosecution is filed after the federal action but "before any proceedings of substance on the merits" in federal court.

17. Lynch explicitly did not reach the question, decided later the same Term in Mitchum v. Foster, whether § 1983 was an exception to § 2283.

Clause, the agency's enforcement of the statute. The Hale opinion upheld
that injunction, rejecting the view that the Anti–Injunction Act in effect
bars federal suit by strangers to a state court proceeding who seek to enjoin
a statute that was the subject of that proceeding (pp. 377–78). In Munoz, a
majority of five Justices ruled that unless the federal plaintiffs were
"strangers," the injunction they sought was barred by § 2283; the case was
remanded for an appropriate determination (p. 60). Justice Powell joined
the majority but expressed his willingness to overrule Hale. Justice
Blackmun, concurring in result, was disturbed by the Court's implication
that that Act, rather than being an absolute ban, does not apply when the
state litigation involves different parties.[18]

Wouldn't acceptance of Justice Blackmun's view effectively transform
a state court proceeding like that in Munoz into a defendant class action,
without any due process safeguards? See Vestal, *Protecting A Federal
Court Judgment*, 42 Tenn.L.Rev. 635, 661–63 (1975).[19]

(11) *Declaratory Judgments.* When § 2283 bars an injunction, may a
federal plaintiff nonetheless obtain a declaratory judgment? This question
was once of particular importance in suits challenging state or local official
action as unlawful under federal law. But because these suits fall under
§ 1983, under Mitchum even injunctions are no longer barred.[20] An
example of a case in which the question of the availability of a declaratory
judgment may still arise under § 2283 is Thiokol Chemical Corp. v. Burlington Industries, Inc., 448 F.2d 1328 (3d Cir.1971), where the court said it
would be proper to award a declaratory judgment as to the validity of a
patent even though a parallel state proceeding involving the same patent
could not be enjoined. "Normally, the policy that precludes federal injunctions against state actions is also applied to prohibit declaratory judgments
* * *. But if the state suit is likely to turn on a question of federal law
with which a federal court is likely to be more familiar and experienced
than the state court, and if the state court * * * manifests willingness to
hold its hand pending federal decision on that question, we think it is
neither necessary nor desirable to construe section 2283 as precluding the
federal court from issuing a declaratory judgment on the common federal
question" (p. 1332).

Assuming that a federal declaratory judgment has res judicata effect,[21]
could the federal plaintiff then turn the declaratory judgment into an
injunction—either in every case, or at least whenever the state court
refused to honor it? In Munoz, Paragraph (10)(c), *supra*, the Court rejected
the plaintiffs' argument that (i) § 2283 did not bar declaratory relief, (ii)
such relief without an injunction would be a nullity, and (iii) therefore an
injunction was necessary "in aid of" the federal court's jurisdiction. While
expressing no opinion about the first premise, the Court said that the
argument "proves too much, since by its reasoning the exception, and not

---

18. Justices Brennan and Stevens dissented, finding no reason to believe that
two of the three plaintiffs were strangers.
Justice Marshall also dissented, but would
have dismissed the writ of certiorari as
improvidently granted.

19. Similar questions arise in the application to nonparties of the equitable restraint doctrine of Younger v. Harris. See
pp. 1428–29, *infra*.

20. A year before Mitchum, Justice
Brennan, concurring in part and dissenting
in part in Perez v. Ledesma, 401 U.S. 82,
128–29 n. 18 (1971), expressed the view
that § 2283 does not extend to federal declarations; Justices White and Marshall
joined that opinion.

21. For discussion of this question, see
p. 1426, *infra*.

the rule, would always apply." 449 U.S. at 60 n. 4. If the plaintiff in Thiokol, having secured a declaratory judgment, invoked the relitigation exception in order to obtain a federal injunction, should the argument fare better? See generally Note, 83 Harv.L.Rev. 1870 (1970).

The question whether restrictions on federal injunctions should also govern federal declaratory judgments is examined in detail in connection with Younger v. Harris and its doctrine of equitable restraint, discussed in Sec. 2(C), pp. 1426–28, infra.[22] Are the same considerations pertinent under § 2283?

(12) *Possible Revision of § 2283.* Should Congress repeal § 2283 and leave such matters to be worked out in accordance with principles of equity, comity, and federalism? That is the regime that Mitchum creates for § 1983 litigation;[23] is it less appropriate in suits between private parties involving rights created by federal law, or in disputes about state law in which the federal courts have diversity jurisdiction?

Under a more flexible approach, how would a court deal, for example, with Atlantic Coast Line? Bear in mind that, in labor disputes, the timing of economic pressure by either side may be critical, and a state court's preliminary injunction may effectively moot the controversy. *Cf.* Local No. 438, Constr. and General Laborers' Union v. Curry, 371 U.S. 542 (1963), p. 697, *supra.* Would it be preferable to retain § 2283, but to amend the jurisdictional statutes to permit removal to federal court based on a federal defense, at least if the defense is one of federal preemption?

NOTE ON THE POWER OF STATE COURTS TO ENJOIN FEDERAL COURT ACTIONS

(1) No federal statute in terms forbids state courts from enjoining the prosecution of an overlapping or duplicative action filed in federal court, but 2 Story, Equity Jurisprudence 186 (1st ed. 1836) states that "the State Courts cannot injoin proceedings in the Courts of the United States." One commentator contends, however, that "in 1836 * * * there was in existence no reported case actually holding that state courts might not enjoin federal proceedings." Arnold, *State Court Power to Enjoin Federal Court Proceedings,* 51 Va.L.Rev. 59, 65 (1965). On the early precedents, see also Comment, 32 U.Chi.L.Rev. 471 (1965).

(2) Donovan v. City of Dallas, 377 U.S. 408 (1964), provided about as strong a case as can be imagined for a state court injunction against federal in personam proceedings. There, 46 citizens brought a state court class action to enjoin expansion of an airport and issuance of municipal bonds for that purpose. After losing in state court and exhausting their appeals, 27 of the named plaintiffs, together with nearly 100 other plaintiffs, brought a federal court action seeking similar relief. Under Texas law, no bonds

---

22. Analogous questions have arisen under several other congressional statutes limiting federal court interference with state court proceedings. See Sec. 1(B), *infra.*

23. It may also be the regime created under each of the other recognized excep-

tions to § 2283. See, *e.g.,* Wright, Miller, & Cooper, note 14, *supra,* § 4226 n. 34; Vestal, Paragraph (10)(c), *supra,* at 667–71; but *cf.* Redish, Paragraph (7), *supra,* at 723–24 & n. 31.

could be issued so long as there was pending litigation challenging their validity.

The city not only moved to dismiss the federal court action, but also obtained a state court writ of prohibition, based upon a finding that plaintiffs had filed "vexatious and harassing litigation." The writ barred all of the federal plaintiffs from prosecuting their federal action, and enjoined them, "individually and as a class," from filing any further actions contesting the validity of the bonds. On review, the Supreme Court reversed, 6–3, stating (pp. 412–13):

"* * * It may be that a full hearing in an appropriate court would justify a finding that the state-court judgment in favor of Dallas in the first suit barred the issues raised in the second suit, a question as to which we express no opinion. But plaintiffs in the second suit chose to file that case in the federal court. They had a right to do this, a right which is theirs by reason of congressional enactments passed pursuant to congressional policy. And whether or not a plea of *res judicata* in the second suit would be good is a question for the federal court to decide. While Congress has seen fit to authorize courts of the United States to restrain state-court proceedings in some special circumstances, it has in no way relaxed the old and well-established judicially declared rule that state courts are completely without power to restrain federal-court proceedings in *in personam* actions like the one here. And it does not matter that the prohibition here was addressed to the parties rather than to the federal court itself. * * *

"Petitioners being properly in the federal court had a right granted by Congress to have the court decide the issues they presented * * * [, a right that] cannot be taken away by the State."

Justice Harlan's dissenting opinion expressed doubt that any of the precedents did or should negate the power of a state court to enjoin vexatious, duplicative federal litigation whose effect was to thwart an unfavorable state court judgment.

For criticism of the rationale but not the result in Donovan, *see* Arnold, Paragraph (1), *supra.*[1] See also Comment, Paragraph (1), *supra;* Note, 75 Yale L.J. 150 (1965).

(3) That Donovan's reasoning also bars a state court injunction prohibiting the institution of future litigation was made clear in General Atomic Co. v. Felter, 434 U.S. 12, 18 (1977) (per curiam), which stressed the existence of a federal statutory right to federal court access. Given that § 2283 does not bar injunctions against future litigation, was application of the judge-made doctrine of Donovan to future litigation inevitable? Was it desirable?

(4) Why should state power to restrain federal court proceedings be more limited than federal power to restrain state court proceedings? Justice Rehnquist, the lone dissenter in the General Atomic case, suggested that a state court should have injunctive authority against vexatious

---

1. Arnold argues that though state court injunctions may create undesirable friction, such friction may be necessary in some cases to do justice. Nonetheless, he believes the state court order was not necessary in Donovan. While recognizing that simply allowing the city to plead res judicata in federal court might prove inadequate, since the pendency of any suit barred issuance of the bonds, he suggests that the federal court could have stayed the action before it and enjoined the filing of any further lawsuits. If this is true in Donovan, won't it always be true?

federal court proceedings of the same scope as a federal court's authority under the Anti–Injunction Act. Compare the ALI Study's proposal to authorize a state court injunction when "necessary to protect against vexatious and harassing relitigation of matters determined by an existing judgment of the state court in a civil action" (proposed § 1373).

How persuasive is the Donovan Court's reliance upon protecting the right of access to federal court, when, as Section 2 of this Chapter shows, the Court in other cases has created a wide variety of doctrines of abstention and restraint limiting federal jurisdiction in deference to state courts and ongoing state proceedings? See generally Secs. 2(B)–2(E), *infra*.

(5) Donovan and General Atomic are both expressly limited to in personam actions; Donovan clearly affirms (377 U.S. at 412) that a state court may enjoin the continued prosecution of a federal proceeding when it has custody of property in quasi in rem or in rem proceedings, and the injunction is needed to protect that custody. See p. 1322, note 2, *supra*.[2] But is a state court injunction in such a case consistent with Donovan's theory that state courts may not curtail federal jurisdiction? Or should the state court's in rem jurisdiction be deemed to be exclusive, so that there was no federal jurisdiction that could be curtailed? See Hornstein & Nagle, *State Court Power to Enjoin Federal Judicial Proceedings: Donovan v. City of Dallas Revisited*, 60 Wash.U.L.Q. 1 (1982), arguing that the in rem cases support state court power to enjoin litigants from filing federal actions that in fact fall outside the federal courts' jurisdiction. Compare the rule of Tarble's Case, p. 484, *supra*, and other materials in Chap. IV, Sec. 2.

SUBSECTION B: OTHER STATUTORY RESTRICTIONS ON FEDERAL COURT JURISDICTION

NOTE ON THREE–JUDGE DISTRICT COURTS, THE JOHNSON ACT OF 1934, AND THE TAX INJUNCTION ACT OF 1937

Introduction

This Note considers three congressional responses to the recognition, in Ex parte Young and Home Telephone, of the federal courts' jurisdiction to enjoin state officials: (1) the three-judge court requirement; (2) the Johnson Act of 1934; and (3) the Tax Injunction Act of 1937.

1. The Rise and Decline of Three–Judge District Courts

(1) *The Reaction to Ex parte Young.* In the storm that followed the decision in Ex parte Young, controversy centered on the power of a single

---

2. Accord, Colorado River Water Conservation Dist. v. United States, 424 U.S. 800, 817 (1976), p. 1438, *infra*. See Moody v. State ex rel. Payne, 295 Ala. 299, 329 So. 2d 73 (1976), whose issuance of an injunction was later approved in Sumrall v. Moody, 620 F.2d 548 (5th Cir.1980), *opinion supplemented*, 632 F.2d 1351 (1980). But

cf. Meridian Investing & Develop. Corp. v. Suncoast Highland Corp., 628 F.2d 370, 372 & nn. 3–4 (5th Cir.1980) (state court entertaining in rem proceeding may enjoin only a federal court in rem action, not an in personam action); Mills v. Roanoke Indus. Loan and Thrift, 70 F.R.D. 448 (W.D.Va. 1975).

federal judge to stop state legislation in its tracks. Senator Overman of North Carolina protested that "there are 150 cases of this kind now where one federal judge has tied the hands of the state officers, the governor, and the attorney general. * * * Whenever [that happens], * * * public sentiment is stirred, * * * and you find the people of the State rising up in rebellion." [1]

Responding to the particular abuses of *ex parte* restraining orders and interlocutory injunctions, Congress in 1910 required that applications for interlocutory injunctions against enforcement of state statutes on constitutional grounds be heard by a district court of three judges (at least one of whom had to be a judge of the court of appeals), with appeal as of right directly to the Supreme Court. 36 Stat. 557.[2] The statute was extended in 1913 to cover interlocutory injunctions against state administrative orders, and was broadened in 1925 and 1948 to cover permanent as well as interlocutory injunctions.

From 1948–76, the provision was codified as 28 U.S.C. § 2281. A parallel provision, enacted in 1937 and codified from 1948–76 as 28 U.S.C. § 2282, required a three-judge court in suits seeking to enjoin federal statutes as unconstitutional.

(2) *Experience With Three–Judge Courts.* The burdens of arranging for and conducting three-judge court hearings proved to be substantial, as did the burden on the Supreme Court's docket resulting from the appeal as of right; in some years over 20% of the cases argued before the Supreme Court were mandatory appeals from three-judge courts.[3] Over time, numerous proposals for limitation or outright repeal of the requirement appeared.[4]

In 1976, Congress abolished nearly all three-judge courts. It repealed 28 U.S.C. §§ 2281–82, while enacting a new provision (now codified as 28 U.S.C. § 2284) that calls for three-judge courts only in suits "challenging the constitutionality of the apportionment of congressional districts or the apportionment of any statewide legislative body," or "when otherwise required by Act of Congress." 90 Stat. 1119 (1976).[5] The latter phrase refers primarily to provisions of the Civil Rights Act of 1964, 42 U.S.C. §§ 1971(g), 2000a–5(b), 2000e–6(b), and the Voting Rights Act of 1965, as amended, *id.* §§ 1973b(a), 1973c, 1973h(c), 1973aa–2, 1973bb–(a)(2), though other statutes occasionally employ the device. See generally Williams,

---

1. 45 Cong.Rec. 7256 (1910). See generally Frankfurter, *Distribution of Judicial Power Between United States and State Courts,* 13 Cornell L.Q. 499, 519 (1928); Lilienthal, *The Federal Courts and State Regulation of Public Utilities,* 43 Harv.L. Rev. 379 (1930); Lockwood, Maw, and Rosenberry, *The Use of the Federal Injunction in Constitutional Litigation,* 43 Harv. L.Rev. 426 (1930); Hutcheson, *A Case for Three Judges,* 47 Harv.L.Rev. 795 (1934).

2. This device had previously been used in certain antitrust cases, see 32 Stat. 823 (1903), and in suits challenging ICC orders, see 34 Stat. 584, 592 (1906).

3. S.Rep. No. 201, 94th Cong., 2d Sess. 4 (1976).

4. For a summary, see Jacoby, *Recent Proposals and Legislative Efforts to Limit Three–Judge Court Jurisdiction,* 26 Case W.Res.L.Rev. 32 (1975).

5. In 1974, the requirement of three-judge courts in certain antitrust actions, see note 2, *supra,* had been abolished, 88 Stat. 1706, and the following year, the requirement in suits to enjoin ICC orders was also repealed, 88 Stat. 1918. Still earlier, a provision for three-judge courts in condemnation suits involving the TVA, see 16 U.S.C. § 831x (1964), had been repealed. 82 Stat. 885 (1968).

The New Three–Judge Courts of Reapportionment and Continuing Problems of Three Judge–Court Procedure, 65 Geo.L.J. 971 (1977).

Under the original three-judge court provisions, the doctrines governing when three judges were required, and how to obtain appellate review of an order by or relating to a three-judge court, were enormously complex and confusing. Some of these problems remain of interest today in the limited areas in which the requirement survives, and hence are briefly discussed below.

(3) *Actions Subject to the Requirement.* In determining what actions required convening of a three-judge court, the Supreme Court treated § 2281 "not as a measure of broad social policy to be construed with great liberality, but as an enactment technical in the strict sense of the term and to be applied as such." Phillips v. United States, 312 U.S. 246, 251 (1941).

(a) *Suits Against State Officers Challenging State Statutes.* Section 2281 was limited to suits against *state* officers seeking to restrain *state* statutes. It thus did not require a three-judge court for suits challenging local ordinances, or for suits against local officials unless they were functioning pursuant to a policy of statewide concern. See generally, *e.g.,* Moody v. Flowers, 387 U.S. 97, 101–02 (1967).

(b) *The Meaning of "Constitutional" Challenge.* The Supreme Court repeatedly stated that § 2281 was limited to federal constitutional challenges. See, *e.g.,* Ex parte Williams, 277 U.S. 267, 271 (1928); In re Buder, 271 U.S. 461, 465 (1926). In Buder, *supra,* and Ex parte Bransford, 310 U.S. 354 (1940), the Court held that a suit alleging that a state statute conflicts with a federal statute, and hence is invalid under the Supremacy Clause, does not raise a "constitutional" claim for this purpose. After a brief lapse in Kesler v. Department of Public Safety, 369 U.S. 153 (1962), that position was reaffirmed in Swift & Co. v. Wickham, 382 U.S. 111 (1965).

(c) *Pendent Nonconstitutional Claims.* Florida Lime and Avocado Growers, Inc. v. Jacobsen, 362 U.S. 73 (1960), held that a properly convened three-judge court had jurisdiction under former § 2281 over related nonconstitutional challenges to a state statute. Despite contrary intimations in the Florida Lime case, the Court later held that a single judge could grant injunctive relief on a pendent nonconstitutional challenge. Hagans v. Lavine, 415 U.S. 528, 543–45 (1974).

(d) *Declaratory Judgment Actions.* In Kennedy v. Mendoza–Martinez, 372 U.S. 144 (1963), the Court held that an action for a declaration that a federal statute was unconstitutional was properly heard by a single judge rather than three judges (under former § 2282), because in the face of a mere declaration the government could continue to apply the law pending appellate review. Is this ruling best explained as an effort to give a "technical" and narrow reading to a measure viewed as imposing great burdens on the Supreme Court and lower federal courts?[6] The present

---

6. For criticism of Mendoza–Martinez, *see* Currie, *The Three–Judge District Court in Constitutional Litigation,* 32 U.Chi.L. Rev. 1, 13–19 (1964).

Contrast this decision with the equation of declaratory and injunctive relief under the Johnson Act and the Tax Injunction Act, both discussed in this Note, *infra.* See, further, the detailed discussion of the distinction between declaratory and injunctive relief in connection with the equitable restraint doctrine of Younger v. Harris, Sec. 2(C), pp. 1426–28, *infra.*

statute refers generally to suits challenging statutes without distinguishing injunctive from declaratory relief.

(e) *Mandatory or Permissive.* The three-judge court provisions were long held to be jurisdictional, requiring the convening of a three-judge court in a proper case whether or not the parties so requested. The present statute says that a three-judge court "shall be convened" in a case meeting the specifications, 28 U.S.C. § 2284(a), but in § 2284(b)(1) states that the special court shall be convened "[u]pon the filing of a request for three judges." The legislative history does not explain this apparent discrepancy; for an explanation of its origins and an argument that a three-judge court should not be required if neither party so moves, see 17 Wright, Miller & Cooper, Federal Practice & Procedure § 4235 (1978).

(4) *The Powers of a Single Judge.* The Supreme Court rejected the view that the original three-judge court statute left undisturbed a single judge's power to *deny* injunctive relief, Ex parte Metropolitan Water Co., 220 U.S. 539 (1911), even if the denial was based not on the constitutional merits but rather on the failure to show the need for equitable relief. See Idlewild Bon Voyage Liquor Corp. v. Epstein, 370 U.S. 713 (1962).

In Ex parte Poresky, 290 U.S. 30 (1933), however, the Court held that a single judge may pass on the existence of jurisdiction, and hence may dismiss a bill on the "jurisdictional" ground, see p. 1022, *supra,* that it presents no substantial federal question. Subsequent cases have said such dismissals will be "rare indeed." See, *e.g.,* Hagans v. Lavine, Paragraph (3) (c), *supra,* at 537–43. See also Gonzalez v. Automatic Employees Credit Union, 419 U.S. 90, 100 (1974) (single judge may dismiss for lack of standing). The lower courts have followed these holdings in decisions under the 1976 law. See, *e.g.,* Simkins v. Gressette, 631 F.2d 287 (4th Cir. 1980); Ryan v. State Bd. of Elections, 661 F.2d 1130 (7th Cir.1981).

The Supreme Court also reached the surprising conclusion that a single judge had power under former § 2281 to award injunctive relief in situations at the other end of the spectrum, where "prior decisions make frivolous any claim that a state statute on its face is not unconstitutional." Bailey v. Patterson, 369 U.S. 31, 33 (1962) (per curiam).

The present law, in § 2284(b)(3), bars a single district judge from "enter[ing] judgment on the merits." Is the holding in Bailey valid under the current law?

(5) *Review in Three-Judge Cases.* The sole route of appeal of a decision on the merits of a properly convened three-judge court is in the Supreme Court under 28 U.S.C. § 1253, a provision not modified in 1976. Short of that easy case, the decisions on appellate review under former §§ 2281–82 presented a shifting and complex picture.

In a reversal of prior decisions, the Court held that dispositions by three-judge courts on issues "short of the merits" are appealable to the court of appeals, not directly to the Supreme Court. See, *e.g.,* Gonzalez v. Automatic Employees Credit Union, 419 U.S. 90 (1974) (lack of standing); MTM, Inc. v. Baxley, 420 U.S. 799 (1975) (dismissal under the equitable restraint doctrine of Younger v. Harris, Sec. 2(C), *infra*). However, a three-judge court's injunction based on pendent nonconstitutional grounds is appealable directly to the Supreme Court, even where only the pendent statutory claim is presented for review. Philbrook v. Glodgett, 421 U.S. 707, 712 n. 8 (1975).[7]

Where a three-judge court was erroneously convened, an appeal could be taken only to the court of appeals, and the Supreme Court lacked jurisdiction to review—though it could remand the case to permit the district court to reenter a decree from which an appeal to the court of appeals could be taken. Phillips v. United States, 312 U.S. 246 (1941).

The precedents on the proper route of appeal where a single judge erroneously decided an issue that should have been assigned to a three-judge court took an uneven course. See generally Currie, *Appellate Review of the Decision Whether or Not to Empanel a Three–Judge Federal Court,* 37 U.Chi.L.Rev. 159 (1969). In the end, the Court suggested that appeal should be taken to the court of appeals, Menglekoch v. Industrial Welfare Com'n, 393 U.S. 83 (1968), which was empowered not to review the decision of the issue in the court below, but only to give guidance on whether a three-judge court should have been convened, see Schackman v. Arnebergh, 387 U.S. 427 (1967).

2. The Johnson Act of 1934

(1) *Origins.* The Johnson Act of 1934, 48 Stat. 775, now 28 U.S.C. § 1342, was the culmination of a quarter of a century of effort by advocates of state utility regulation. The Act deprives the district courts of jurisdiction to enjoin the operation of, or compliance with, any order of a state administrative agency or local rate-making body fixing rates for a public utility, whenever four conditions are met:

"(1) Jurisdiction is based solely on diversity of citizenship or repugnance of the order to the Federal Constitution; and,

(2) The order does not interfere with interstate commerce; and,

(3) The order has been made after reasonable notice and hearing; and,

(4) A plain, speedy and efficient remedy may be had in the courts of such State."

Notice how this statute overrides traditional doctrines of federal equity. Federal injunctive relief is now barred not only, as before, when there is an adequate remedy at law available on the law side of the federal court (which seldom happens in rate cases), but also when there is a sufficient remedy in the state courts either in equity, in an ordinary action at law, or by way of statutory appeal from the order. This approach was followed by Congress three years later in the Tax Injunction Act of 1937, as this Note discusses below, and is also reflected in the judicially-created equitable restraint doctrine, see Younger v. Harris, Subsection 2(C), *infra.*

Should the Act be read as "jurisdictional," in the sense that its observance is required even if neither party raises it, or raises it only on appeal?

(2) *The Statutory Criteria.* The Johnson Act comes into play only if all four statutory criteria are satisfied.

---

7. See also Supreme Court of Virginia v. Consumers Union, 446 U.S. 719, 737 n. 16 (1980) (though Supreme Court could not directly review attorney's fees question alone, it may consider that question along with the issues on the merits on appeal).

(a) *The Basis of Federal Jurisdiction.* Though the first criterion in the statute appears to have little significance, consider Aluminum Co. of America v. Utilities Com'n of North Carolina, 713 F.2d 1024, 1027–28 (4th Cir.1983) and IBEW v. Public Serv. Com'n, 614 F.2d 206, 211 (9th Cir.1980), holding that the Act does not apply to a suit challenging a state utility rate order as preempted by a federal statute. Why should federal courts be allowed to hear preemption claims but not, for example, claims that a rate order is unconstitutional because confiscatory? It is because, as the court suggested (p. 211) in the IBEW case, the former "involves more confining legal analysis and can hardly be thought to raise the worrisome possibilities that economic or political predilections will find their way into a judgment"?

(b) *Interference With Interstate Commerce.* Is the second criterion anything other than the question on the merits whether the rate order is constitutional under the Commerce Clause? Why should Commerce Clause challenges, unlike other constitutional challenges, always be cognizable in federal court?[1]

(c) *Reasonable Notice and Hearing.* The third criterion—the adequacy of notice and hearing—is governed by federal law, see City of Meridian v. Mississippi Valley Gas Co., 214 F.2d 525 (5th Cir.1954), and is ordinarily quite straightforward. Two courts of appeals have held, however, that no injunction can issue, even absent notice and hearing, if there was no issue of fact and the only disputed question involved the utility's power to issue the rate order in question. See General Inv. & Serv. Corp. v. Wichita Water Co., 236 F.2d 464 (10th Cir.1956); City of Monroe v. United Gas Corp., 253 F.2d 377 (5th Cir.1958).

(d) *Plain, Speedy, and Efficient Remedy.* The fourth criterion is the most important one, and litigation has centered on the availability of an interlocutory stay in state court. In both Mountain States Power Co. v. Public Serv. Com'n of Montana, 299 U.S. 167 (1936), and Driscoll v. Edison Light & Power Co., 307 U.S. 104 (1939), the Supreme Court assumed that there was no plain, speedy, and efficient remedy absent an opportunity at least to appeal to the discretion of the state court for a stay *pendente lite.* In discussing whether a stay could be obtained, the Court in Mountain States argued (299 U.S. at 170) that the existence of a remedy displacing federal jurisdiction "cannot be predicated upon the problematical outcome of future consideration"—thereby following the suggestion in the early case of Corporation Com'n of Oklahoma v. Cary, 296 U.S. 452 (1935), that substantial doubts would be resolved against the ouster of jurisdiction.

Suppose a state court empowered to issue a stay refuses to do so. May a federal district court review the state court's exercise of discretion and assume jurisdiction if it thinks the stay was wrongly denied? See generally Note, 50 Harv.L.Rev. 813 (1937); Comment, 44 Yale L.J. 119 (1934). If so, should the federal court simply grant interim relief pending further state

---

1. For cases in which the second criterion prevented the ouster of jurisdiction, see Public Util. Com'n v. United Fuel Gas Co., 317 U.S. 456 (1943); Charter Limousine, Inc. v. Dade County Bd. of County Com'rs, 678 F.2d 586 (5th Cir.1982); Tri–State Generation & Transmission Ass'n v. Public Serv. Com'n, 412 F.2d 115 (10th Cir.1969). But *cf.* Kansas–Nebraksa Natural Gas Co. v. City of St. Edward, 234 F.2d 436 (8th Cir. 1956) (allegation of burden on interstate commerce does not permit federal jurisdiction).

court review, or proceed to hear the entire case? *Cf.* ALI Study, proposed § 1371(d).

(3) *Declaratory Judgments.* The lower courts have interpreted the Act as barring a federal court from issuing not only injunctive but also declaratory relief when the four conditions are satisfied. See, *e.g.,* Hanna Mining Co. v. Minnesota Power and Light Co., 739 F.2d 1368, 1370 (8th Cir. 1984); Bridgeport Hydraulic Co. v. Council on Water, 453 F.Supp. 942, 954 (D.Conn.1977) (alternate holding), *aff'd,* 439 U.S. 999 (1978); Tennyson v. Gas Serv. Co., 506 F.2d 1135, 1139 (10th Cir.1974) (relying on precedents under the Tax Injunction Act, which is discussed in the next section of this Note).

(4) *Exceptions.* The Act has been held not to apply to suits brought by the United States. See, *e.g.,* United States v. Public Util. Com'n of Cal., 141 F.Supp. 168 (N.D.Cal.1956), *aff'd,* 355 U.S. 534 (1958); United States v. Public Serv. Com'n of Maryland, 422 F.Supp. 676, 678 (D.Md.1976); *cf.* Department of Employment v. United States, 385 U.S. 355 (1966), p. 1345, *infra* (similar holding under Tax Injunction Act). There is no special exception for suits under 42 U.S.C. § 1983, however, see, *e.g.,* Stanislaus Food Prods. Co. v. Public Util. Com'n, 560 F.Supp. 114 (N.D.Cal.1982); Klotz v. Consolidated Edison Co., 386 F.Supp. 577, 584–85 (S.D.N.Y.1974), as the Act's purpose was precisely to limit federal court jurisdiction in federal constitutional challenges.

3. The Tax Injunction Act of 1937

(1) *Origins.* By the Tax Injunction Act of 1937, 50 Stat. 738, now 28 U.S.C. § 1341, Congress restricted federal district court jurisdiction over a second major subject matter. The Act forbids an injunction against "the assessment, levy or collection of any tax under State law" so long as "a plain, speedy and efficient remedy may be had in the courts of such state." For purposes of the Act, local taxes have uniformly been held to be collected "under State law." See 17 Wright, Miller & Cooper, Federal Practice & Procedure § 4237 (1978).

Like the Johnson Act, this statute was a response to what was viewed as an unwarranted expansion of federal jurisdiction in the wake of Ex parte Young. The Act was also designed to eliminate disparities in treatment between taxpayers who could obtain injunctive relief in federal court—usually out-of state corporations asserting diversity jurisdiction— and other taxpayers left to the state courts, which generally required taxpayers to pay first and litigate later. Congress was also concerned that taxpayers, with the aid of a federal injunction, could withhold large sums, thereby disrupting governmental finances. S.Rep. No. 1035, 75th Cong., 1st Sess. 1–2 (1937); Rosewell v. LaSalle National Bank, 450 U.S. 503, 522– 23 & nn. 28–29, 527 (1981).

The Act, like the Johnson Act, displaces federal equity power when the complainant has a sufficient remedy either at law or equity in the state courts or by way of statutory appeal. Also like the Johnson Act, the Tax Injunction Act as originally enacted was a restriction on the district courts' *jurisdiction;* though the 1948 statutory revision removed any reference to jurisdiction, the Act's restriction of federal court power has been inter- preted to be "jurisdictional" and hence nonwaivable. See, *e.g.,* Sipe v. Amerada Hess Corp., 689 F.2d 396 (3d Cir.1982); City of Burbank v.

Nevada, 658 F.2d 708, 709 (9th Cir.1981); *cf.* California v. Grace Brethren Church, 457 U.S. 393, 408 (1982) (the Act "divests" district courts of jurisdiction); *id.* at 409 n. 22.

(2) *"Plain, Speedy and Efficient Remedy".*

(a) *The Relationship to Equity Practice.* Is "a plain, speedy, and efficient remedy" synonymous with an "adequate" remedy in equity doctrine prior to 1937? In early cases the Supreme Court often seemed to use the terms interchangeably, and on occasion even suggested that the Act merely incorporated the prior equity standard.[1] But the argument that, though the statute has its roots in equity practice, Congress meant to establish a more stringent standard for federal intervention was found persuasive in Rosewell v. LaSalle National Bank, 450 U.S. 503, 524–27 (1981).[2] But *cf.* Fair Assessment in Real Estate Ass'n v. McNary, 454 U.S. 100, 117 n. 8 (1981), Paragraph (4), *infra* (discerning no significant difference between remedies that are "plain, speedy and efficient" under § 1341, and those that are "plain, adequate, and complete" as that phrase has been used in articulating the doctrine of equitable restraint, discussed in Sec. 2(C), *infra*).

(b) *The Adequacy of State Remedies.* A taxpayer who has no offensive remedy in state court, but only a defensive one in an action to collect the tax, nonetheless has an adequate remedy. Kohn v. Central Distributing Co., Inc., 306 U.S. 531 (1939) (alternative holding). Also adequate, as the Act's purposes make clear, is a refund remedy conditioned upon payment under protest. See, *e.g.,* California v. Grace Brethren Church, 457 U.S. 393, 412 & n. 28 (1982).[3] That a taxpayer has forfeited a state remedy that was formerly available does not make the remedy inadequate. See, *e.g.,* Sacks Bros. Loan Co., Inc. v. Cunningham, 578 F.2d 172 (7th Cir.1978); Randall v. Franchise Tax Board, 453 F.2d 381 (9th Cir.1971).

The litigation burdens imposed by state remedies are pertinent to its "efficiency." A state remedy was found wanting where it "would require the filing of over three hundred separate claims in fourteen different counties to protect the single federal claim asserted by [the taxpayer]." Georgia R.R. & Banking Co. v. Redwine, 342 U.S. 299, 303 (1952). In Tully v. Griffin, Inc., 429 U.S. 68, 73 (1976), however, the Court said that a remedy is not inefficient merely because a taxpayer must travel across a state line to obtain it.

The Court first considered whether a remedy was "speedy" in Rosewell v. LaSalle National Bank, 450 U.S. 503 (1981). There, after reviewing statistics showing the serious delays in state and federal urban trial courts, the Court held that a customary delay of two years from payment under protest until receipt of a refund by a taxpayer after state court litigation, though regrettable, was not so unusual as to make the remedy not "speedy."

1. See, *e.g.,* Great Lakes Dredge & Dock Co. v. Huffman, 319 U.S. 293 (1943), discussed in Paragraph (3), *infra;* Spector Motor Service, Inc. v. McLaughlin, 323 U.S. 101, 105–06 (1944); Township of Hillsborough v. Cromwell, 326 U.S. 620 (1946), Paragraph (2)(b), *infra.*

2. Accord, Comment, 93 Harv.L.Rev. 1016, 1021–22 (1980); Note, 59 Harv.L.Rev.

780, 784 (1946); Note, 70 Yale L.J. 636, 643 (1961).

3. What if a taxpayer lacks the funds to pay before litigating? See Wood v. Sargeant, 694 F.2d 1159 (9th Cir.1982) (federal relief nonetheless barred), and cases cited.

Certainty that the remedy exists is also important. In Township of Hillsborough v. Cromwell, 326 U.S. 620, 625–26 (1946), the Court held that where it was at best "speculative" whether New Jersey followed the federal constitutional rule that a state may not "impos[e] on him against whom the discrimination has been directed the burden of seeking an upward revision of the taxes of other members of the class," federal jurisdiction would lie (p. 623). In Tully, *supra*, at 76, the Court, though reiterating that "uncertainty concerning a State's remedy may make it less than 'plain' under 28 U.S.C. § 1341," was convinced after a detailed inquiry into state law that an adequate remedy existed.

More generally, and more recently, the Court has stated that the "exception" to § 1341 permitting federal injunctions when state remedies are not plain, speedy, and efficient should be narrowly construed. California v. Grace Brethren Church, 457 U.S. 393, 413 (1982).

(c) *The LaSalle National Bank Decision.* In Rosewell v. LaSalle National Bank, *supra*, the Court considered whether Illinois provided a "plain, speedy, and efficient" remedy by authorizing refund actions, but without any interest. The taxpayer, alleging that her property was assessed at more than 300% of the amount specified by statute, and that the customary delay in refund actions was two years, brought suit in federal court under 42 U.S.C. § 1983, alleging a violation of the Fourteenth Amendment, and seeking to enjoin collection of the tax. The Supreme Court, per Brennan, J., held that the suit should have been dismissed, advancing (450 U.S. at 512) a purely "procedural interpretation" of "plain, speedy and efficient." The legislative history of the Act emphasized the need for a taxpayer to have a "full hearing and judicial determination" (pp. 513–14). Illinois clearly provided that much, and so long as the taxpayer could raise in state court all substantive constitutional objections to the tax (including her claim of a federal right to interest), the federal court was stripped of jurisdiction to enjoin.[4]

Justice Stevens, joined by Justices Stewart, Marshall, and Powell, filed a vigorous dissent. He emphasized the roots of the Act in equity practice, under which the substance of available state remedies was considered. He conceded that the Act was designed to impose new limits on federal equity jurisdiction, but argued that it did so by reversing the prior rule that an adequate state equitable remedy would not defeat federal equity jurisdiction (p. 534 & n. 7). The Court had considered the substance of state remedies in the past, he argued,[5] and "there would be little purpose in denying a federal remedy to a litigant and sending him to state court to pursue a state remedy—albeit a quick and certain one—that provided no relief" (p. 537). On the specific question of interest, he suggested that its provision had been deemed necessary to make state remedies adequate under both early equity cases and post-Act cases (p. 541). Without deciding whether the failure to pay interest always renders a state remedy inadequate, he argued that on the facts of this case, where the assessment was so excessive, the state remedy did not bar federal intervention.

4. The Court left open the question whether the state's failure to reassess the property in question after plaintiff's successful challenges (under state procedures) to prior years' assessments rendered the remedy deficient as to more recent tax years.

5. In the Township of Hillsborough case, Paragraph (2)(b), *supra*, the Court had indicated (p. 624) that even if the state's rule had been clear, the remedy would have been inadequate.

Assume for the moment that the Constitution requires the provision of interest on the facts of the LaSalle National Bank case. Wasn't the Court right to 'hold that the state remedies were not inadequate when the taxpayer was free to raise that constitutional claim in state court? Suppose, however, that the Illinois Supreme Court, in hearing her claim, proceeded to hold that the Constitution never requires payment of interest on claims for the refund of unconstitutional taxes. Should a different taxpayer, who subsequently raises a federal constitutional claim (for a refund and interest) that is virtually identical to that in LaSalle National Bank, also be barred from federal court—even though the Illinois Supreme Court's recent decision virtually guarantees that the state courts will not award interest? If so, the second taxpayer could ultimately seek Supreme Court review of an unfavorable state court decision, but only after a futile and wasteful exercise before state tribunals. Compare the rules governing exhaustion of remedies in federal habeas corpus, p. 1552–60, *infra,* which do not require a prisoner to resort to state remedies where it would be futile to do so. And *cf.* Fuchs, *Prerequisites to Judicial Review of Administrative Agency Action,* 51 Ind.L.J. 817, 909 (1976), citing numerous cases to support the proposition that administrative remedies need not be exhausted "if the agency, although legally empowered to consider the challenger's contention, has become rigidly precommitted against it."

Note, on the other hand, that permitting the second taxpayer to file in federal court (i) would undercut the policy of the Act whenever a taxpayer asserts that the state court precedents on an issue of federal law are erroneous, and (ii) would require the federal court, as part of its jurisdictional inquiry, to determine whether the precedents in the state courts make it futile to seek relief there. Does the existence of unfavorable or even clearly erroneous precedent constitute a denial of a "full and fair opportunity" to litigate under, for example, the doctrine of res judicata?

(3) *Declaratory Judgments.* The Tax Injunction Act was passed just three years after the federal declaratory judgment act, now 28 U.S.C. § 2201. In Great Lakes Dredge & Dock Co. v. Huffman, 319 U.S. 293 (1943), the Court avoided the question whether § 1341 itself bars a federal declaratory judgment concerning state taxes, ruling instead that declaratory relief ought not to be given in a situation in which, under traditional equity practice, the federal court would have stayed its hand. Even before the Act was passed, "the federal courts, in the exercise of the sound discretion which has traditionally guided courts of equity in granting or withholding the extraordinary relief which they may afford, [would] not ordinarily restrain state officers from collecting state taxes where state law afford[ed] an adequate remedy to the taxpayer" (p. 297). A declaration "may in every practical sense operate to suspend collection of the state taxes until the litigation is ended" (p. 299), and thus a federal court should exercise its equitable discretion to deny such relief when state remedies are adequate.[6]

Nearly 40 years later, in California v. Grace Brethren Church, 457 U.S. 393 (1982), the Court squarely ruled that § 1341 bars the issuance of declaratory judgments. The case was brought by religious institutions, seeking (i) to enjoin the Secretary of Labor from conditioning his approval

---

6. Note that in Standard Dredging Co. v. Murphy, 319 U.S. 306 (1943), a case decided on the same day as Great Lakes, the very same tax was upheld on the merits.

of a state unemployment insurance program on its coverage of the plaintiffs' employees,[7] and (ii) to enjoin the state from collecting both tax information and the tax itself. The Court relied upon the language from Great Lakes, just quoted, equating the practical effect of a declaration and an injunction, and on the Act's prohibition of actions that not only "enjoin" but also "suspend or restrain" collection of state taxes, as support for its holding (p. 408). To be sure, the Act focuses on injunctions, but only because they were "the principal weapon used by business to delay or avoid state taxes"; Congress was concerned not with the form of relief, but rather with federal court interference with state tax administration (p. 409 n. 22).[8]

The question whether a declaratory judgment differs from an injunction in ways that are pertinent to the appropriateness of federal court intervention is examined in detail at pp. 1426–28, *infra,* in connection with the equitable restraint doctrine of Younger v. Harris. Do the considerations discussed there also apply under the Tax Injunction Act?

(4) *Damage Actions.* A still more expansive limitation on federal court relief from state taxation was set forth in Fair Assessment in Real Estate Ass'n, Inc. v. McNary, 454 U.S. 100 (1981), decided one year before Grace Brethren Church. The plaintiffs brought suit under § 1983, alleging that the defendants (local officials in Missouri) had violated the Fourteenth Amendment by their unequal taxation of real property, and by targeting for reassessment taxpayers who had successfully appealed their assessments the previous year. Plaintiffs sought actual and punitive damages for past overassessments and for expenses incurred in combatting them. The Court, with Justice Rehnquist writing, deemed it unnecessary to decide whether § 1341 barred plaintiffs' action, as "the principle of comity bars federal courts from granting damages relief" (p. 107), much as comity had been held to bar declaratory relief in Great Lakes.[9] That principle barred any federal intervention whose practical effect was to suspend collection of state taxes, regardless of the form of federal relief sought (p. 111).

The Court rejected the taxpayers' argument that their § 1983 suit did not disrupt the collection of taxes since the suit sought damages from individual officers rather than from the county, and those officers would be shielded by a qualified immunity. Rather, the Court stated that in a damages action, the district court must "in effect * * * first enter a declaratory judgment like that barred in Great Lakes," a prospect as disruptive as an equitable remedy itself (p. 113). Moreover, the Court feared the disruptive effect of the litigation itself: plaintiffs' suit, hauling virtually every county tax official into federal court, with the risk of

---

7. Employers are entitled to a credit of up to 90% on their federal unemployment tax liability for payments to a federally-approved state unemployment compensation plan.

8. Justice Stevens, joined by Justice Blackmun, dissented. He stressed that the Act was directed in part against having federal courts adjudicate questions of state law under their diversity jurisdiction, a concern inapplicable to a First Amendment challenge. And he viewed it as odd that the statute was being stretched beyond its literal wording to prohibit a declaratory judgment in federal court in a

case about whether a *federal*-state cooperative program violated the *federal* Constitution—especially since one of the defendants was the federal Secretary of Labor, who could remove any state court action to federal court.

9. A footnote stated that "[w]e need not decide in this case whether * * * comity * * * would also bar a claim under § 1983 which requires no scrutiny whatever of state tax assessment practices, such as a facial attack on tax laws colorably claimed to be discriminatory as to race" (p. 107 n. 4).

punitive damages and attorney's fee liability, could have a chilling effect upon the officials' conduct of their duties (pp. 115–16).

Justice Brennan, joined by Justices Marshall, Stevens, and O'Connor, concurred in the judgment. In his view, the principle of comity was associated with the discretion of a court of equity in exercising its extraordinarily intrusive powers, a view that he believed Great Lakes had followed. "There is little room for the 'principle of comity' in actions at law where, apart from matters of administration, judicial discretion is at a minimum" (pp. 121–22). In enacting § 1983, Congress clearly intended federal adjudication of damage actions for constitutional violations by state officials; the precedents prior to passage of the Tax Injunction Act supported federal court power to award damages in actions seeking a refund of state taxes; and the legislative history of the Act expressly suggested that refund actions would be permitted.

Justice Brennan noted, however, that in First Nat. Bank of Greeley v. Board of County Com'rs, 264 U.S. 450, 456 (1924), the Court held that a federal refund action based on an alleged violation of the Fourteenth Amendment was barred by the taxpayers' failure to exhaust state administrative remedies.[10] He acknowledged that more recent cases suggested that in general no exhaustion should be required in § 1983 actions. (On this point, see generally Section 2(A) of this Chapter, *infra*.) But he argued that whether or not the Tax Injunction Act itself created an exception to the no exhaustion rule under § 1983, the Act's purpose was clearly consistent with requiring exhaustion in state tax cases (p. 137). Thus, "[w]here administrative remedies are a precondition to suit for monetary relief in state court, absent some substantial consideration compelling a contrary result in a particular case, those remedies should be deemed a precondition to suit in federal court as well" (*ibid.*).

Can McNary be squared with the view of § 1983 articulated in Monroe v. Pape and Mitchum v. Foster? Are the concerns raised by the majority implicated in the context of a suit in which the taxpayer has already paid? To the extent they are, are they not also implicated in every § 1983 action? See Bravemen, *Fair Assessment And Federal Jurisdiction in Civil Rights Cases*, 45 U.Pitt.L.Rev. 351 (1984); Note, 46 U.Chi.L.Rev. 736 (1979).

(5) *Section 1983 Actions in State Courts.* By its terms, the Tax Injunction Act governs only the federal district courts. Suppose a taxpayer brings a § 1983 action in state court. Is the state court obliged to hear the claim—and to provide all relief ordinarily available in § 1983 actions (including attorney's fees), regardless of limitations under state law on remedies in tax cases? If so, won't there always be a plain, speedy and efficient remedy in state court when the taxpayer's suit is based on a federal constitutional or statutory provision? (In McNary itself, the Court found that state remedies were adequate, referring both to Missouri's own remedies and to the fact that Missouri's courts "ha[d] expressly held that

---

10. Justice Brennan rejected the effort to distinguish the decision in First National Bank of Greeley on the ground that it was a refund suit brought against the county itself, rather than against officers as in McNary. He noted that if the plaintiffs in McNary were required to exhaust administrative remedies, they might obtain some relief against the county, which in turn, would reduce the potential damage liability of the individual defendants. Moreover, in McNary the county might itself be liable under § 1983 if, as appeared to have been alleged, the challenged taxation was pursuant to an official policy or custom (p. 135 & n. 24).

plaintiffs such as petitioners may assert a § 1983 claim in state court" (p. 116).) [11]   Aren't many of McNary's concerns about chilling state officials equally applicable to state court litigation? Indeed, wouldn't even the view of the Tax Injunction Act's policy expressed in Justice Brennan's concurrence in McNary—"to provide assurance that federal courts exercise at least the same restraint in dealing with questions of state tax administration as the courts of the State that levied the tax"—permit state courts to refuse relief under § 1983, so long as the state provides an adequate remedy for the underlying statutory or constitutional violation?

In Spencer v. South Carolina Tax Com'n, 281 S.C. 492, 316 S.E.2d 386 (1984), *aff'd by an equally divided court,* 471 U.S. 82 (1985), state taxpayers sued for and obtained a refund of less than $600, but their effort to frame the suit as one under § 1983, so as to obtain attorney's fees (which were not permitted under state law), was rebuffed by the state supreme court. That court did not refer to § 1341, McNary, or the special nature of tax cases, stating more generally that "[s]tate remedies for asserting rights may not be circumvented by invoking § 1983" (281 S.C. at 497, 316 S.E.2d at 389). In Arkansas Writers' Project, Inc. v. Ragland, 107 S.Ct. 1722, 1730 (1987), the state court had rejected a First Amendment challenge to a state tax, but the Supreme Court reversed on the merits. The Court remanded for the state court to decide in the first instance whether it would exercise jurisdiction over the challenge if framed as a § 1983 cause of action in which attorney's fees were sought. After referring to § 1341, the Court remarked that "whether state courts must assume jurisdiction over [§ 1983 suits challenging state taxation] is not entirely clear," and noted that the affirmance by an equally divided Court in Spencer had no precedential weight (p. 1730 n. 7). See generally Note, 95 Yale L.J. 414 (1985).

Doesn't the possibility that the Court's doctrine of comity could wholly foreclose plenary damage relief under § 1983 and attorney's fees under § 1988 highlight the problematic nature of McNary?

(6) *Suits Filed by a State or by the United States.* In Department of Employment v. United States, 385 U.S. 355 (1966), the Supreme Court held that the Act does not bar suits by the United States, or by a federal instrumentality, to enjoin state taxation of the instrumentality's employees, who claimed they had a federal immunity from the taxation.[12]   In Maryland v. Louisiana, 451 U.S. 725, 745 n. 21 (1981), the Court held that § 1341, which literally applies only to the district courts, does not affect suits between two states in the original jurisdiction of the Supreme Court.

---

11. The Supreme Court of Missouri subsequently ruled that the state courts have no jurisdiction over § 1983 actions in tax cases so long as the state itself provides a plain, speedy, and efficient remedy. Stuflebaum v. Panethiere, 691 S.W.2d 271 (Mo.1985).

12. See also Moe v. Confederated Salish and Kootenai Tribes, 425 U.S. 463 (1976), holding that § 1341 does not bar a suit by an Indian tribe that could have been brought by the United States on behalf of the tribe.

SECTION 2. JUDICIALLY-DEVELOPED LIMITATIONS ON FEDERAL COURT JURISDICTION: DOCTRINES OF EQUITY, COMITY, AND FEDERALISM

INTRODUCTORY NOTE

The central issue of this Section is whether, and in what circumstances, it is appropriate for federal courts to abstain from entertaining actions that appear to fall within the literal terms of congressional grants of jurisdiction. (That question has previously been raised by the decisions in McNary and in Great Lakes Dredge & Dock, pp. 1342–43, *supra*, notably in Justice Brennan's separate opinion in the former case). These materials consider the courts' response to continuing and conflicting pressures: the desire to avoid premature constitutional determinations, to defer to state tribunals on questions of state law, to avoid duplicative proceedings, and to interfere as little as possible with state processes, on the one hand; and the desire to uphold a litigant's choice of a federal forum and to vindicate federal rights without undue delay, on the other. The primary though not exclusive focus of the materials that follow is on federal actions against state officials.

The Section divides the judicially developed doctrines limiting district court jurisdiction into five groupings: (1) the requirement of exhaustion of state administrative and other nonjudicial remedies; (2) the doctrine derived from the Pullman case, often referred to as "Pullman abstention," and related abstention doctrines; (3) the doctrine, derived from equity practice, restricting the availability of federal equitable relief from pending state enforcement actions—particularly the rule against enjoining criminal prosecutions; (4) the doctrine calling for a federal court to stay its hand in exceptional circumstances because of the pendency of a parallel proceeding in state court; and (5) the rules restricting the exercise of federal jurisdiction in probate and domestic relations matters.

In connection with all of these limitations, consider Shapiro, *Jurisdiction and Discretion*, 60 N.Y.U.L.Rev. 543, 543–45, 574–75 (1985) (some paragraphing omitted):

"Judges and lawyers have often said that the federal courts are obligated to exercise the jurisdiction conferred on them by the Constitution and by Congress. * * * Only three Terms ago, Justice Brennan warned that the federal courts have a 'virtually unflagging obligation * * * to exercise the jurisdiction given them.'[3] * * *

"[S]uggestions of an overriding obligation, subject only and at most to a few narrowly drawn exceptions, are far too grudging in their recognition of judicial discretion in matters of jurisdiction. * * * [T]he existence of this discretion is much more pervasive than is generally realized, and * * * it has ancient and honorable roots at common law as well as in equity. * * *

"**3.** Moses H. Cone Memorial Hosp. v. Mercury Constr. Co., 460 U.S. 1, 15 (1983) [p. 1449, *infra*]. * * *"

"My point is not that the Constitution expressly 'provides' that a grant of jurisdiction carries with it certain discretion not to proceed, or that Congress necessarily 'intends' to confer such discretion when it authorizes the exercise of jurisdiction. Rather, I submit that, as experience and tradition teach, the question whether a court must exercise jurisdiction and resolve a controversy on its merits is difficult, if not impossible, to answer in gross. And the courts are functionally better adapted to engage in the necessary fine tuning than is the legislature. * * *

"A grant of jurisdiction obligates the court to receive and consider the plaintiff's complaint and, on appropriate occasions, to determine whether the ends of justice will be served best by declining to proceed. At the same time, nothing in our history or traditions permits a court to interpret a normal grant of jurisdiction as conferring unbridled authority to hear cases simply at its pleasure. * * * [W]hen jurisdiction is conferred, I believe that there is at least a 'principle of preference' that a court should entertain and resolve on its merits an action within the scope of the jurisdictional grant. For this preference to yield in a particular case, the court must provide an explanation based on the language of the grant, the historical context in which the grant was made, or the common law tradition behind it." In Shapiro's view, experience suggests that the criteria for channeling discretion in matters of jurisdiction may be grouped under four headings—"equitable discretion, federalism and comity, separation of powers, and judicial administration"—that "in general, are to be weighed against the presumption favoring the assertion and exercise of jurisdiction" (p. 579).

Consider, also, Bator, *The State Courts and Federal Constitutional Litigation*, 22 Wm. & Mary L.Rev. 605, 622 n. 49 (1981):

"Statutes such as § 1983 and the Habeas Corpus Act use language which, if woodenly and anachronistically read, can be interpreted to provide an 'absolute' right of access to the federal courts. But these statutes were themselves passed against the background of a large body of standing law on matters of substance, remedy, and jurisdiction. As is true of all legislation, it is a major problem of *interpretation* how to fit the new enactment into this preexisting texture. No statute recreates the entire legal universe. The fact that a given remedial doctrine is not explicitly mentioned therefore does not automatically mean that the new statute was intended wholly to supersede it."

See also Wells, *Why Professor Redish is Wrong About Abstention*, 19 Ga.L.Rev. 1097 (1985). For a contrasting view, see Redish, *Abstention, Separation of Powers, and the Limits of the Judicial Function*, 94 Yale L.J. 71 (1984).

SUBSECTION A: EXHAUSTION OF STATE NONJUDICIAL REMEDIES

NOTE ON EXHAUSTION OF STATE NONJUDICIAL REMEDIES

(1) In the same year in which Ex parte Young was decided, the Court was confronted with an appeal from a decree of a federal circuit court

enjoining the enforcement of a rate order of the Virginia State Corporation Commission. Prentis v. Atlantic Coast Line Co., 211 U.S. 210 (1908). The main contention of the appellants was that the commission, under the Virginia statutes, had the characteristics and powers of a court and that the injunction was prohibited by the Anti–Injunction Act, now 28 U.S.C. § 2283. But the Court, speaking through Justice Holmes, held that, whatever the status of the commission in other types of proceedings, "the establishment of a rate is the making of a rule for the future, and therefore is an act legislative not judicial in kind" (p. 226), so that the prohibition was inapplicable to the order in question.

However, the Court also noted that the Virginia statute provided an appeal as of right to the Supreme Court of Appeals of Virginia, upon the record made in the commission, and that "that court, if it reverses what has been done, is to substitute such order as in its opinion the commission should have made" (p. 224). *Cf.* Federal Radio Comm'n v. General Elec. Co., 281 U.S. 464 (1930), p. 291, note 8, *supra.* In ruling that the railroads should have taken such an appeal before resorting to the federal court, Justice Holmes said (pp. 229–30):

" * * * Considerations of comity and convenience have led this court ordinarily to decline to interfere by habeas corpus where the petitioner had open to him a writ of error to a higher court of a State, in cases where there was no merely logical reason for refusing the writ. The question is whether somewhat similar considerations ought not to have some weight here.

"We admit at once that they have not the same weight in this case. The question to be decided, we repeat, is legislative, whether a certain rule shall be made. * * * We should hesitate to say, as a general rule, that a right to resort to the courts could be made always to depend upon keeping a previous watch upon the bodies that make laws, and using every effort and all the machinery available to prevent unconstitutional laws from being passed. * * *

"But this case hardly can be disposed of on purely general principles. The question that we are considering may be termed a question of equitable fitness or propriety, and must be answered on the particular facts. * * * The railroads went into evidence before the commission. They very well might have taken the matter before the Supreme Court of Appeals. No new evidence and no great additional expense would have been involved.

"The State of Virginia has endeavored to impose the highest safeguards possible upon the exercise of the great power given to the State Corporation Commission, not only by the character of the members of that commission, but by making its decisions dependent upon the assent of the same historic body that is entrusted with the preservation of the most valued constitutional rights, if the railroads see fit to appeal. It seems to us only a just recognition of the solicitude with which their rights have been guarded, that they should make sure that the State in its final legislative action would not respect what they think their rights to be, before resorting to the courts of the United States.

"If the rate should be affirmed by the Supreme Court of Appeals and the railroads still should regard it as confiscatory, it will be understood from what we have said that they will be at liberty then to renew their application to the Circuit Court, without fear of being met by a plea of res judicata. It will not be necessary to wait for a prosecution by the commission." [1]

(2) The limits of the Prentis doctrine were plainly marked, and its rationale made unmistakable, in Bacon v. Rutland R.R., 232 U.S. 134 (1914). There, in a suit to enjoin the Public Service Commission of Vermont from enforcing an order concerning a passenger station, the Prentis case was invoked by the defendants in support of an objection that the railroad had failed to utilize its statutory right of appeal to the Supreme Court of Vermont. But the Court, speaking again through Justice Holmes, pointed out expressly that at the judicial stage the railroads had a right to resort to the courts of the United States at once; and, finding that no legislative powers had been conferred upon the Supreme Court of Vermont, it sustained the jurisdiction.

(3) Does it follow from the Prentis case that the losing party in a case in which the highest state court acts legislatively cannot go directly to the Supreme Court of the United States? Would the Supreme Court in such a case be exercising appellate jurisdiction?

In the Prentis case itself (211 U.S. at 226), Justice Holmes said that a writ of error would not lie to review the decision of the Virginia Corporation Commission but was silent about the Virginia Court of Appeals. For the unsupported view that the utility in such a case has an option to go to the Supreme Court or to a district court, see Lilienthal, *The Federal Courts and State Regulation of Public Utilities*, 43 Harv.L.Rev. 379, 400 (1930). But *cf.* Note, 50 Harv.L.Rev. 813, 816 n. 12 (1937); Corporation Comm'n of Oklahoma v. Cary, 296 U.S. 452 (1935).[2]

(4) Whether a state court's role is characterized as "legislative" or "judicial" clearly determines whether a litigant must first take an appeal in the state courts before mounting a federal challenge. But whenever a litigant does appeal in the state courts (whether or not he was obliged to do so), this characterization also determines the proper forum in which to seek federal review of the state court's decision. If that decision is "legislative," the federal district courts have jurisdiction, while the Supreme Court may not, see Paragraph (3), *supra*; if the state court's decision is "judicial," the

---

1. Accord, Porter v. Investors Syndicate, 286 U.S. 461 (1932), 287 U.S. 346 (1932), holding that a legislative remedy in a state district court against an administrative order under a state blue sky law must be exhausted before resort to a federal court.

But *cf.* Pacific Tel. & Tel. Co. v. Kuykendall, 265 U.S. 196, 204–05 (1924), where the utility alleged that existing rates were confiscatory and that no stay was available. "Under such circumstances comity yields to constitutional right, and the fact that the procedure on appeal in the legislative fixing of rates has not been concluded will not prevent a federal court of equity from suspending the daily confiscation, if it finds the case to justify it." See also Oklahoma Natural Gas Co. v. Russell, 261 U.S. 290 (1923).

2. The Cary case raised the question of the effect of the Johnson Act when a state's highest court acts legislatively on a statutory appeal from a rate order. The utility in that case, after having taken an unsuccessful appeal to the state supreme court (which, it was agreed on all sides, had power to act legislatively), obtained a federal court injunction against the commission's order. On appeal to the Supreme Court, the commission argued that the utility could have obtained Supreme Court review of the state court's decision, and its failure to do so barred the action for an injunction. *Cf.* pp. 1630–38 *infra*, discussing the "Rooker–Feldman" doctrine. But the Court ignored that contention, instead treating the case as if the only issue it raised was whether there was jurisdiction in equity in any state court to review judicially the decision of the state's highest court. Finding the remedy uncertain, the Court held that the Johnson Act did not bar the federal injunction.

Supreme Court has jurisdiction and the district courts do not, see pp. 1630–38, *infra*, discussing the "Rooker–Feldman" doctrine.

Is that characterization governed by state or federal law? In Oklahoma Packing Co. v. Oklahoma Gas & Elec. Co., 309 U.S. 4 (1940), the Supreme Court, after first upholding a plea of res judicata, withdrew its former opinion and overruled the plea in light of an intervening state court opinion characterizing the review as legislative.

(5) Analogous to the Prentis doctrine, and of more general importance today, is the doctrine that a federal court will not entertain an action against a state officer if the plaintiff has not yet exhausted remedies before a state administrative agency. Such a requirement of exhaustion has frequently been imposed as a precondition to federal challenge. *E.g.*, Pacific Live Stock Co. v. Lewis, 241 U.S. 440 (1916); First Nat. Bank of Greeley v. Board of County Com'rs, 264 U.S. 450 (1924); Illinois Commerce Com'n v. Thomson, 318 U.S. 675, 686 (1943). There are important limits upon exhaustion in this (and other) contexts: it has not generally been required when undue delay would result, when the state remedy is inadequate, or when exhaustion would be futile. See generally 17 Wright, Miller & Cooper, Federal Practice & Procedure § 4233 (1978).[3]

(6) In Patsy v. Board of Regents of the State of Florida, 457 U.S. 496 (1982), the Supreme Court ruled that exhaustion of state administrative remedies is not required in actions under 42 U.S.C. § 1983. The plaintiff had filed suit in district court, alleging that her employer, a state university, had discriminated against her on the basis of race and sex. The district court dismissed on the ground that she had not exhausted the university's administrative remedies. (The Supreme Court did not elaborate on those remedies, but the court of appeals' opinion indicates that the plaintiff could have complained to her supervisor, and then to others in the university's "chain of command," and also could have filed a complaint with the state Human Relations Commission.) The en banc court of appeals reversed, ruling that a § 1983 plaintiff was required to exhaust administrative remedies only when (1) an orderly system of review is provided by statute or agency rule; (2) the agency can grant relief more or less commensurate with the claim; (3) relief is available without undue delay; (4) the procedures are fair, not burdensome, and are not used to harass those with legitimate claims; and (5) interim relief is available in appropriate cases. It remanded for the district court to determine whether exhaustion was appropriate under those standards.

The Supreme Court, per Justice Marshall, reversed. The Court noted that it had ruled in McNeese v. Board of Education, 373 U.S. 668 (1963), that exhaustion should not be required in § 1983 actions, and had adhered to that view in seven subsequent cases. The view was also supported by the legislative history of § 1 of the Civil Rights of 1871, the precursor to § 1983, whose " 'very purpose * * * was to interpose the federal courts between the States and the people, as guardians of the people's federal rights * * *' " (p. 503, quoting Mitchum v. Foster, Sec. 1(A), *supra*). Though Congress in 1871 did not consider the question of exhaustion, the Court believed that the "tenor of the debates" did not support an exhaus-

---

3. What if a litigant failed to avail himself of state administrative remedies that are no longer available because of limitations periods? Consider, by way of analo-gy, (i) Huffman v. Pursue, Ltd., p. 1429, *infra*, and (ii) Wainwright v. Sykes, p. 1524 *infra*.

tion requirement (p. 502). That conclusion was based upon three recurring themes in the legislative history: Congress's assignment "to the federal courts [of] a paramount role in protecting constitutional rights" (p. 503); Congress's belief "that the state authorities had been unable or unwilling to protect the constitutional rights of individuals or to punish those who violated those rights" (p. 505); and "the fact that many legislators interpreted the bill to provide dual or concurrent forums in the state and federal system, enabling the plaintiff to choose the forum in which to seek relief" (p. 506).

Justice Marshall also found support for the Court's holding in a 1980 amendment to the Civil Rights of Institutionalized Persons Act, 42 U.S.C. § 1997 *et seq.* That amendment requires adult prisoners, before seeking relief under § 1983, to exhaust administrative remedies that satisfy statutorily specified conditions. See Paragraph (8)(b), *infra.* In the Court's view, "[t]his detailed scheme is inconsistent with discretion to impose, on an ad hoc basis, a judicially developed exhaustion rule in other cases" (p. 511).

Justice Powell, joined by Chief Justice Burger, dissented. The court of appeals' exhaustion requirement was, he said, based on "sound considerations. It does not defeat federal-court jurisdiction, it merely defers it. It permits the States to correct violations through their own procedures, and it encourages the establishment of such procedures. It is consistent with the principles of comity that apply whenever federal courts are asked to review state action or supersede state proceedings" (pp. 532–33). A rule requiring exhaustion also conserves federal court resources, Justice Powell argued, a matter particularly important given the rapid growth of § 1983 litigation.

In Justice Powell's view, many of the Court's past decisions suggesting that exhaustion was not required in a § 1983 action "can be explained as applications of traditional exceptions to the exhaustion requirement. Other decisions speak to the question in an offhand and conclusory fashion without full briefing and argument" (p. 533). Nor did § 1997e support the Court's decision: that provision focused on the particular question of prisoners' suits, and simply did not bear on the general question of exhaustion in § 1983 actions.[4]

(7) Contrast with the Patsy decision the Court's careful articulation of the judge-made rule that, subject to some limited exceptions, administrative remedies must be exhausted in suits challenging federal administrative action. That requirement is said to avoid premature interruption of agency procedures, permit proper factual development, take advantage of the agency's distinctive expertise and processes, give the agency the chance to correct its own errors, and to promote efficiency in both the judicial and administrative processes. See generally Fuchs, *Prerequisites to Judicial Review of Administrative Agency Action,* 51 Ind.L.J. 817, 859–911 (1976). Did the Court in Patsy confuse the question of exhaustion of state remedies in general (which Monroe v. Pape held is not required) with the question of exhaustion of distinctively administrative remedies?

---

4. Justice O'Connor wrote a concurring opinion, in which Justice Rehnquist joined, endorsing an exhaustion requirement as sound policy, but noting that, "for the reasons set forth in the Court's opinion," that view had already been rejected by prior decisions. Justice White concurred in part, expressing his disagreement with the Court's view that Congress's enactment of § 1997e supported the Court's decision.

Why should a claim of federal right under § 1983 be immediately cognizable in court, when that same right could not be asserted in court, in a challenge to federal administrative action, before administrative remedies were exhausted? Because Congress has more confidence in federal administrative processes it has created than in state administrative remedies over which it lacks formal and informal mechanisms of control? Can the problem of possibly deficient state (or local) administrative remedies be dealt with by applying the kinds of criteria set forth by the court of appeals in Patsy? See Comment, 41 U.Chi.L.Rev. 537 (1974). If Patsy and the university differ about the adequacy of the administrative remedies, must a court take evidence on the remedies' effectiveness? Mightn't that be a very burdensome inquiry—an especially troublesome prospect since exhaustion is a threshold doctrine?

Note, however, that some state administrative regimes were created in response to federal court decisions holding that the failure to provide such administrative procedures denied due process. Is it ironic that Patsy authorizes litigants to bypass these regimes altogether?

How pertinent is the legislative history of the Civil Rights Act of 1871 in resolving these questions?

Note Justice Powell's assertion that exhaustion does not heavily burden the federal plaintiff; "[i]t does not defeat federal-court jurisdiction, it merely defers it." Compare University of Tennessee v. Elliott, 106 S.Ct. 3220 (1986), p. 1629, *infra,* holding that when a state administrative agency acting in a judicial capacity makes factual findings after the parties have had a fair opportunity to litigate, a federal court in a § 1983 action must give those findings the same preclusive effect that they would have in the state's courts. On the facts of Patsy, a rule requiring exhaustion might not have resulted in preclusion, but that would not be true under many other administrative regimes.

(8) Patsy's general rule that exhaustion of administrative remedies is not required in § 1983 actions is subject to important limitations:

(a) The ruling in Fair Assessment in Real Estate Ass'n v. McNary, 454 U.S. 100 (1981), p. 1343, *supra,* interprets principles of comity to require federal courts to decline jurisdiction in suits seeking a remedy from state taxation whenever the state provides a plain, adequate, and complete remedy. Though the four concurring Justices would not have required the federal court to decline jurisdiction where state *judicial* remedies were available, they agreed that when the state courts would require exhaustion of *administrative* remedies before entertaining a challenge to state taxes in which monetary relief was sought, a federal court entertaining a § 1983 action should ordinarily do likewise.

(b) In § 1983 actions filed by prisoners, 42 U.S.C. § 1997e authorizes a court to continue a case for a period not to exceed ninety days if it believes exhaustion of administrative remedies would be "appropriate and in the interests of justice," *id.* § 1997e(a)(1), and if the Attorney General or the court has determined that there exist prison grievance procedures that are in substantial compliance with federal standards established by regulation by the Attorney General, *id.* § 1997(e)(2). The standards require an advisory role for prison employees and inmates, time limits for processing grievances, protection against reprisals, and a decisionmaker who is independent of the warden. (Detailed regulations have been issued and are codified at 28 C.F.R. §§ 40.1–40.22). As of March of 1987, the procedures of only three states and the District of Columbia had been certified (even partially or conditionally) by the Attorney General. Lewis v. Meyer, 815 F.2d 43, 44 (7th Cir.1987). Judge Lay reports that states have been reluctant to create grievance procedures and to seek certification for several reasons: some have not been plagued with prisoner suits, or believe that the procedures will not forestall them; others note that certification "buys" only a 90 day delay; still others resist inmate participation. Lay, *Exhaustion of Grievance Procedures for State Prisoners Under Section 1997e of the Civil Rights Act,* 71 Iowa L.Rev. 935, 949–51 (1986).

Suppose that, when a case is continued to permit exhaustion, the prisoner fails to file a grievance within the time or in the manner specified by the administrative scheme. May he then be barred from filing a § 1983 action? See Lewis v. Meyer, *supra,* at 45, and Rocky v. Vittorie, 813 F.2d 734, 736 (5th Cir.1987), arguing that the sanction of dismissal is necessary to ensure that the prisoner actually resorts to the scheme. In the latter case, the court ruled, however, that dismissal would be inappropriate where the prisoner had tried in good faith to comply with the administrative requirements.

(c) Parratt v. Taylor, p. 1259, *supra,* held that a state's provision of adequate postdeprivation *judicial* remedies can negate an allegation that due process was denied. The lower courts have held that postdeprivation *administrative* remedies may have the same effect. See p. 1275, note 12, *supra.* In such cases, then, an adequate state administrative remedy is not simply a prerequisite to suit, as would be true if Patsy had required exhaustion; instead, because of that remedy there is no federal violation for which relief under § 1983 could be sought in any forum.

(d) In Williamson County Regional Planning Com'n v. Hamilton Bank of Johnson City, 473 U.S. 172 (1985), a landowner filed a § 1983 action, contending that a local zoning agency's disapproval of its development plan, on the ground that the plan violated local zoning regulations, constituted a taking of property without just compensation. The Supreme Court held that the challenged administrative action was not a final, reviewable decision because the plaintiff had not sought a variance from the agency, and hence the suit was premature. Though finality and exhaustion doctrines overlapped, the Court explained that they are distinct doctrines: "the finality requirement is concerned with whether the initial decisionmaker has arrived at a definitive position on the issue that inflicts an actual, concrete injury; the exhaustion requirement generally refers to administrative * * * procedures by which an injured party may seek review of an adverse decision and obtain a remedy if the decision is found to be unlawful or otherwise inappropriate. Patsy concerned the latter, not the former" (p. 193).[5]

(9) Does Patsy's rule of non-exhaustion apply to § 1983 suits filed in the state courts? The state courts are divided, with the majority refusing to require exhaustion. See Schwartz & Kirklin, Section 1983 Litigation: Claims, Defenses, and Fees § 8.3 (1986). Justice White has twice dissented from the denial of certiorari seeking review of state court decisions requir-

---

5. In an alternate holding, the Court ruled that the claim was not ripe because plaintiff had not availed itself of state procedures for obtaining compensation (p. 194).

ing exhaustion, see Caylor v. City of Red Bluff, 474 U.S. 1037 (1985); Kramer v. Horton, 107 S.Ct. 324 (1986); his dissent in Caylor, which Justice Brennan joined, called the state court's ruling "questionable." See generally Note, 69 Iowa L.Rev. 1037 (1984).

SUBSECTION B: ABSTENTION: PULLMAN AND RELATED DOCTRINES

RAILROAD COMMISSION OF TEXAS v. PULLMAN CO.

312 U.S. 496, 61 S.Ct. 643, 85 L.Ed. 971 (1941).
Appeal from the United States District Court for the Western District of Texas.

MR. JUSTICE FRANKFURTER delivered the opinion of the Court.

In those sections of Texas where the local passenger traffic is slight, trains carry but one sleeping car. These trains, unlike trains having two or more sleepers, are without a Pullman conductor; the sleeper is in charge of a porter who is subject to the train conductor's control. As is well known, porters on Pullmans are colored and conductors are white. Addressing itself to this situation, the Texas Railroad Commission after due hearing ordered that "no sleeping car shall be operated on any line of railroad in the State of Texas * * * unless such cars are continuously in the charge of an employee * * * having the rank and position of Pullman conductor". Thereupon, the Pullman Company and the railroads affected brought this action in a federal district court to enjoin the Commission's order. Pullman porters were permitted to intervene as complainants, and Pullman conductors entered the litigation in support of the order. Three judges having been convened, the court enjoined enforcement of the order. From this decree, the case came here directly.

The Pullman Company and the railroads assailed the order as unauthorized by Texas law as well as violative of the Equal Protection, the Due Process and the Commerce Clauses of the Constitution. The intervening porters adopted these objections but mainly objected to the order as a discrimination against Negroes in violation of the Fourteenth Amendment.

The complaint of the Pullman porters undoubtedly tendered a substantial constitutional issue. It is more than substantial. It touches a sensitive area of social policy upon which the federal courts ought not to enter unless no alternative to its adjudication is open. Such constitutional adjudication plainly can be avoided if a definitive ruling on the state issue would terminate the controversy. It is therefore our duty to turn to a consideration of questions under Texas law.

The Commission found justification for its order in a Texas statute which we quote in the margin.[1] It is common ground that if the order is

1. Vernon's Anno. Texas Civil Statutes, Article 6445:

"Power and authority are hereby conferred upon the Railroad Commission of Texas over all railroads, and suburban, belt and terminal railroads, and over all public wharves, docks, piers, elevators, warehouses, sheds, tracks and other property used in connection therewith in this State, and over all persons, associations and corporations, private or municipal, owning or operating such railroad, wharf, dock, pier, elevator, warehouse, shed, track or other property to fix, and it is hereby

within the Commission's authority its subject matter must be included in the Commission's power to prevent "unjust discrimination * * * and to prevent any and all other abuses" in the conduct of railroads. Whether arrangements pertaining to the staffs of Pullman cars are covered by the Texas concept of "discrimination" is far from clear. What practices of the railroads may be deemed to be "abuses" subject to the Commission's correction is equally doubtful. Reading the Texas statutes and the Texas decisions as outsiders without special competence in Texas law, we would have little confidence in our independent judgment regarding the application of that law to the present situation. The lower court did deny that the Texas statutes sustained the Commission's assertion of power. And this represents the view of an able and experienced circuit judge of the circuit which includes Texas and of two capable district judges trained in Texas law. Had we or they no choice in the matter but to decide what is the law of the state, we should hesitate long before rejecting their forecast of Texas law. But no matter how seasoned the judgment of the district court may be, it cannot escape being a forecast rather than a determination. The last word on the meaning of Article 6445 of the Texas Civil Statutes, and therefore the last word on the statutory authority of the Railroad Commission in this case, belongs neither to us nor to the district court but to the supreme court of Texas. In this situation a federal court of equity is asked to decide an issue by making a tentative answer which may be displaced tomorrow by a state adjudication. Glenn v. Field Packing Co., 290 U.S. 177; Lee v. Bickell, 292 U.S. 415. The reign of law is hardly promoted if an unnecessary ruling of a federal court is thus supplanted by a controlling decision of a state court. The resources of equity are equal to an adjustment that will avoid the waste of a tentative decision as well as the friction of a premature constitutional adjudication.

An appeal to the chancellor, as we had occasion to recall only the other day, is an appeal to the "exercise of the sound discretion, which guides the determination of courts of equity". Beal v. Missouri Pacific R.R., 312 U.S. 45, decided January 20, 1941. The history of equity jurisdiction is the history of regard for public consequences in employing the extraordinary remedy of the injunction. There have been as many and as variegated applications of this simple principle as the situations that have brought it into play. See, for modern instances, Beasley v. Texas & Pacific Ry., 191 U.S. 492; Harrisonville v. Dickey Clay Co., 289 U.S. 334; United States v. Dern, 289 U.S. 352. Few public interests have a higher claim upon the discretion of a federal chancellor than the avoidance of needless friction with state policies, whether the policy relates to the enforcement of the criminal law, Fenner v. Boykin, 271 U.S. 240; Spielman Motor Co. v. Dodge, 295 U.S. 89; or the administration of a specialized scheme for liquidating embarrassed business enterprises, Pennsylvania v. Williams, 294 U.S. 176; or the final authority of a state court to interpret doubtful regulatory laws of the state, Gilchrist v. Interborough Co., 279 U.S. 159; cf.

---

made the duty of the said Commission to adopt all necessary rates, charges and regulations, to govern and regulate such railroads, persons, associations and corporations, and to correct abuses and prevent unjust discrimination in the rates, charges and tolls of such railroads, persons, associations and corporations, and to fix division of rates, charges and regulations between railroads and other utilities and common carriers where a division is proper and correct, and to prevent any and all other abuses in the conduct of their business and to do and perform such other duties and details in connection therewith as may be provided by law."

Hawks v. Hamill, 288 U.S. 52, 61. These cases reflect a doctrine of abstention appropriate to our federal system whereby the federal courts, "exercising a wise discretion", restrain their authority because of "scrupulous regard for the rightful independence of the state governments" and for the smooth working of the federal judiciary. See Cavanaugh v. Looney, 248 U.S. 453, 457; Di Giovanni v. Camden Ins. Ass'n, 296 U.S. 64, 73. This use of equitable powers is a contribution of the courts in furthering the harmonious relation between state and federal authority without the need of rigorous congressional restriction of those powers. * * *

Regard for these important considerations of policy in the administration of federal equity jurisdiction is decisive here. If there was no warrant in state law for the Commission's assumption of authority there is an end of the litigation; the constitutional issue does not arise. The law of Texas appears to furnish easy and ample means for determining the Commission's authority. Article 6453 of the Texas Civil Statutes gives a review of such an order in the state courts. Or, if there are difficulties in the way of this procedure of which we have not been apprised, the issue of state law may be settled by appropriate action on the part of the State to enforce obedience to the order. Beal v. Missouri Pacific R.R., *supra;* Article 6476, Texas Civil Statutes. In the absence of any showing that these obvious methods for securing a definitive ruling in the state courts cannot be pursued with full protection of the constitutional claim, the district court should exercise its wise discretion by staying its hands. Compare Thompson v. Magnolia Co., 309 U.S. 478.

We therefore remand the cause to the district court, with directions to retain the bill pending a determination of proceedings, to be brought with reasonable promptness, in the state court in conformity with this opinion. Compare Atlas Ins. Co. v. W.I. Southern, Inc., 306 U.S. 563, 573, and cases cited.

Reversed and remanded.

MR. JUSTICE ROBERTS took no part in the consideration or decision of this case.

NOTE ON ABSTENTION IN CASES INVOLVING A FEDERAL QUESTION

(1) *The Background of Pullman.* Even before Pullman, the Supreme Court had endorsed federal court abstention on difficult, unsettled questions of state law.[1] One pre-Pullman decision providing an important part of the background is Siler v. Louisville & N. R.R., 213 U.S. 175 (1909), p. 1044, *supra.* There, it will be recalled, the Court held that if a controverted

----

1. See, *e.g.,* Gilchrist v. Interborough Rapid Transit Co., 279 U.S. 159 (1929) (federal court action to prevent state commission from interfering with fare increase; action was filed only a few hours before commission sued in state court to compel compliance with existing fare); Railroad Com'n v. Rowan & Nichols Oil Co., 310 U.S. 573 (1940), rehear. denied, 311 U.S. 614 (1940) (rejecting on the merits a federal due process challenge to a regulatory order, and refusing to decide whether under state law there was a "reasonable basis" for the commission's order, so as to avoid supplanting the commission's expert judgment). See also Thompson v. Magnolia Petroleum Co., 309 U.S. 478 (1940) (although federal bankruptcy court had jurisdiction to determine the title to property in trustee's possession, trustee should be directed to bring state court proceeding to settle the issue).

question of state law underlay the question of federal law, it was the federal district court's duty to decide the state question first (even though the court had only pendent jurisdiction with respect to that question) in order to avoid, if possible, a federal constitutional question.

(2) *The Evolution of Pullman Abstention.* After Pullman, the Supreme Court frequently required abstention on unsettled state law issues when resolution of those issues was preliminary to consideration of a federal constitutional question. See, *e.g.*, Spector Motor Serv., Inc. v. McLaughlin, 323 U.S. 101 (1944); Albertson v. Millard, 345 U.S. 242 (1953); City of Meridian v. Southern Bell Tel. & Tel. Co., 358 U.S. 639 (1959). During the 1960s, however, the Court expressed concern about the delays abstention entails. One commentator, writing in 1967, noted that in all seven cases raising a Pullman question after Justice Frankfurter's retirement in 1962, the Court had managed to find reasons not to require abstention, and called the doctrine a "judicial orphan." Note, 80 Harv.L. Rev. 604, 608 & n. 3 (1967).[2] The doctrine staged something of a comeback in the Burger Court, see, *e.g.*, Babbitt v. United Farm Workers Nat. Union, 442 U.S. 289 (1979); Harris County Com'rs Court v. Moore, 420 U.S. 77 (1975); Lake Carriers' Ass'n v. MacMullan, 406 U.S. 498 (1972), although since 1979 the Court has found it applicable in only one instance. See Virginia v. American Booksellers Ass'n, Inc., 108 S.Ct. 636 (1988).

(3) *The Impact of Pennhurst.* In Pennhurst State School & Hosp. v. Halderman, 465 U.S. 89 (1984), p. 1195, *supra*, the Court held that the Eleventh Amendment denies federal courts jurisdiction to award injunctive relief against state officials based upon state law. Pennhurst does not bar federal court suits challenging state action under both state and federal law if the relief is not of the kind barred by the Eleventh Amendment—as is true of relief against a local government or its officials, and of damages to be paid out of the public official's pocket. But if the Pullman case were filed today in federal court, under Pennhurst the court would lack power altogether to entertain a claim to enjoin the order as unauthorized by Texas law; that state claim could be adjudicated only if the Pullman Company filed a second action in state court.

In such a case, should the federal court stay its hand pending resolution of the state law issue? In Askew v. Hargrave, 401 U.S. 476 (1971), Florida citizens filed a federal class action challenging a state school financing program under the Equal Protection Clause. A pending state action by a school board challenged the same law under the Florida constitution. The Court remanded for consideration whether to abstain, noting (p. 478) that the "claims under the Florida Constitution * * *, if sustained, will obviate the necessity of determining the [Equal Protection] question." Note that in Askew, unlike Pullman itself, abstention could be justified only to avoid a federal constitutional question, but not to prevent misconstruction of state law or the possibly unjustified interference with a state program. Werhan, *Pullman Abstention After Pennhurst: A Comment on Judicial Federalism,* 27 Wm. & Mary L.Rev. 449, 490–99 (1986).[3]

2. The cases were McNeese v. Board of Educ., 373 U.S. 668 (1963); Griffin v. County School Bd., 377 U.S. 218 (1964); Hostetter v. Idlewild Bon Voyage Liquor Corp., 377 U.S. 324 (1964); Davis v. Mann, 377 U.S. 678 (1964); Baggett v. Bullitt, 377 U.S. 360 (1964); Dombrowski v. Pfister, 380 U.S.

479 (1965); and Harman v. Forssenius, 380 U.S. 528 (1965).

3. Werhan also notes that a different abstention doctrine, dealing specifically with the problem of a parallel pending proceeding in state court, might apply.

What if, in a case like Pullman, neither the federal plaintiff nor anyone else files a parallel state court action? See Muskegon Theatres, Inc. v. City of Muskegon, 507 F.2d 199, 204 (6th Cir.1974) (refusing to permit the "simple expedient" of not raising the state law claim at all to "frustrate the policies underlying the doctrine of abstention"); Allendale Leasing, Inc. v. Stone, 614 F.Supp. 1440 (D.R.I.1985) (first dismissing, under Pennhurst, pendent state law challenges to the validity of certain state regulations, and then refusing to adjudicate the federal constitutional challenges to the regulations until the state courts could hear the state law challenges).

(4) *The Relevance of the Jurisdictional Basis: Diversity, Federal Question, and Civil Rights Cases.* In Pullman, jurisdiction was asserted under the general federal question statute, 28 U.S.C. § 1331. Is Pullman abstention any more or less appropriate in a suit within the diversity jurisdiction? In a suit under 42 U.S.C. § 1983?

With respect to diversity, a major purpose of the jurisdictional grant— to provide a neutral forum for the determination of state law issues, both hard and easy—is at least attenuated by abstention, whether or not the state law issue is preliminary to a federal question. *Cf. Note on the Abstention Doctrine In Cases Not Involving a Federal Question,* which follows this Note. The Court has, however, approved abstention in diversity cases involving federal questions, without discussing the significance of diversity jurisdiction. See, *e.g.,* Fornaris v. Ridge Tool Co., 400 U.S. 41 (1970); United Gas Pipe Line Co. v. Ideal Cement Co., 369 U.S. 134 (1962); Clay v. Sun Ins. Office, Ltd., 363 U.S. 207 (1960).

With respect to civil rights actions, recall the holdings of (i) Monroe v. Pape, refusing to limit the scope of § 1983 to suits challenging conduct authorized by state law or custom, and (ii) Patsy v. Board of Regents, refusing to require exhaustion of state administrative remedies in § 1983 actions. There is some tension between these decisions and Pullman. But an "exception" for § 1983 cases would swallow the rule, as that section extends to all constitutional violations by those acting under color of state law. Should particular classes of civil rights cases—for example, those raising equal protection or voting rights claims—be exempt from Pullman abstention? [4]

Harrison v. NAACP, 360 U.S. 167 (1959), involved a First Amendment challenge to five Virginia statutes dealing with litigation and lobbying activities, particularly as related to racial matters. A three-judge district court found that the statutes were enacted in an attempt to nullify Brown v. Board of Education, and enjoined three of them, but abstained as to the other two until a state court interpretation could be obtained. On the state's appeal, the Supreme Court ruled that the district court should not have issued the injunction, as the Court was "unable to agree that the terms of these three statutes leave no reasonable room for a construction by the Virginia courts which might avoid in whole or in part the necessity for federal constitutional adjudication, or at least materially change the nature of the problem" (p. 177). There was no discussion (beyond simple

See Canaday v. Koch, 608 F.Supp. 1460 (S.D.N.Y.), *aff'd,* 768 F.2d 501 (2d Cir. 1985). See generally Sec. 2(D), *infra.*

4. For two such proposals, see Wechsler, *Federal Jurisdiction and the Revision* of the Judicial Code, 13 Law & Contemp. Prob. 216, 230 (1948), and ALI Study, proposed § 1371(g), each of which would appear to preclude abstention on the facts of Pullman itself.

descriptive reference) of the jurisdictional basis for the litigation. Justice Douglas, joined by Chief Justice Warren and Justice Brennan, dissented, quoting from the legislative history of the Civil Rights Act of 1871, and asserting the special importance of a federal forum in civil rights cases. For other decisions abstaining in cases brought under § 1983, see, *e.g.*, Bellotti v. Baird, 428 U.S. 132 (1976); Carey v. Sugar, 425 U.S. 73 (1976); Boehning v. Indiana State Employees Ass'n, Inc., 423 U.S. 6 (1975) (per curiam).

In Babbitt v. United Farm Workers Nat. Union, 442 U.S. 289 (1979), and Virginia v. American Booksellers Ass'n, Inc., 108 S.Ct. 636 (1988), the Court declined to consider First Amendment challenges to state statutes before the state courts had the chance to construe them. Compare City of Houston v. Hill, 107 S.Ct. 2502 (1987), where the plaintiff challenged a municipal ordinance making it a misdemeanor "to assault, strike, or in any manner oppose, molest, abuse or interrupt any policeman in the execution of his duty * * *." When the city appealed from the court of appeals' decision that the ordinance was substantially overbroad, the Supreme Court ruled that there was no need to abstain, stating that " 'abstention * * * is inappropriate for cases [where] * * * statutes are justifiably attacked on their face as abridging free expression' " (p. 2513, quoting Dombrowski v. Pfister, 380 U.S. 479, 489–90 (1965)), and that " 'the delay of state-court proceedings might itself effect the impermissible chilling of the very constitutional right [plaintiff] seeks to protect,' " (p. 2513, quoting Zwickler v. Koota, 389 U.S. 241, 252 (1967)). The Court also ruled that abstention was inappropriate in any event because the ordinance was unambiguous. Justice Powell, joined by Chief Justice Rehnquist and Justices Scalia and O'Connor, concurred in the judgment on this issue, but did not agree that abstention is generally inappropriate in facial challenges under the First Amendment.

See also Mayor v. Educational Equality League, 415 U.S. 605, 628 (1974) ("abstention is not favored in an equal protection civil rights case brought * * * under 42 U.S.C. § 1983").[5]

(5) *The Meaning of Unsettled State Law.* When is an issue of state law sufficiently "unsettled" or "unclear" to warrant abstention under the Pullman doctrine? The answer does not emerge easily from analysis of the decisions, since the Court frequently announces only its conclusion on the point with little elaboration of its reasons.

Harrison v. NAACP, Paragraph (4), *supra,* took a fairly broad view of this criterion, the Court stating that it was "unable to agree that the terms of these three statutes leave no reasonable room" for a limiting construction (p. 177). Similar language can be found in Fornaris v. Ridge Tool Co., 400 U.S. 41, 44 (1970), and Reetz v. Bozanich, 397 U.S. 82, 86–87 (1970). Yet in other cases the Court has articulated a narrower standard. See, *e.g.*, Hawaii Housing Auth. v. Midkiff, 467 U.S. 229 (1984), in which the Court stated without dissent that although "[i]n the abstract" the possibility of a limiting construction always exists, "the relevant inquiry is not whether there is a bare, though unlikely possibility that state courts *might* render adjudication of the federal question unnecessary. Rather, '[w]e have fre-

---

5. For a collection of lower court cases exhibiting reluctance to abstain in First Amendment, voting rights, equal protection, or § 1983 suits, see Davies, *Pullman and Burford Abstention: Clarifying the Roles of State and Federal Courts in Constitutional Cases,* 20 U.C. Davis L.Rev. 1, 17 n. 83 (1986).

quently emphasized that abstention is not to be ordered unless the statute is of an uncertain nature, and is obviously susceptible of a limiting construction' " (p. 237, quoting Zwickler v. Koota, 389 U.S. 241, 251 & n. 14 (1967)).

The newness of a state statute and the total absence of judicial precedent are clearly significant considerations. See, *e.g.,* the Pullman case itself; Lake Carriers' Ass'n v. MacMullen, Paragraph (2), *supra;* Harrison, *supra.* On the other hand, the mere presence of judicially unconstrued state law does not automatically require abstention. See, *e.g.,* Brockett v. Spokane Arcades, Inc., 472 U.S. 491 (1985); Wisconsin v. Constantineau, 400 U.S. 433, 439 (1971); Toomer v. Witsell, 334 U.S. 385 (1948).

Most important, the uncertainty in state law must be such that construction by the state court might obviate the need for (or at least help to limit) decision of the federal constitutional question. Thus, in Baggett v. Bullitt, 377 U.S. 360 (1964), a Washington statute requiring a particular oath of all teachers was attacked as unconstitutionally vague on its face. A three-judge district court had refused to adjudicate the injunction action, in the absence of state court construction of the oath. The Supreme Court reversed. In rejecting the argument for abstention, Justice White said (pp. 375–78):

" * * * The abstention doctrine is not an automatic rule applied whenever a federal court is faced with a doubtful issue of state law; it rather involves a discretionary exercise of a court's equity powers. Ascertainment of whether there exists the 'special circumstances,' Propper v. Clark, 337 U.S. 472, prerequisite to its application must be made on a case-to-case basis. Those special circumstances are not present here. We doubt, in the first place, that a contruction of the oath provisions, in light of the vagueness challenge, would avoid or fundamentally alter the constitutional issue raised in this litigation. In the bulk of abstention cases in this Court, including those few cases where vagueness was at issue, the unsettled issue of state law principally concerned the applicability of the challenged statute to a certain person or a defined course of conduct, whose resolution in a particular manner would eliminate the constitutional issue and terminate the litigation. Here the * * * challenged oath is not open to one or a few interpretations, but to an indefinite number. There is no uncertainty that the oath applies to the appellants and the issue they raise is not whether the oath permits them to engage in certain definable activities. Rather their complaint is that they, about 64 in number, cannot understand the required promise, cannot define the range of activities in which they might engage in the future, and do not want to foreswear doing all that is literally or arguably within the purview of the vague terms. In these circumstances it is difficult to see how an abstract construction of the challenged terms, such as precept, example, allegiance, institutions, and the like, in a declaratory judgment action could eliminate the vagueness from these terms. It is fictional to believe that anything less than extensive adjudications, under the impact of a variety of factual situations, would bring the oath within the bounds of permissible constitutional certainty. Abstention does not require this.

"Other considerations also militate against abstention here. Construction of this oath in the state court, abstractly and without reference to concrete, particularized situations so necessary to bring into focus the impact of the terms on constitutionally protected rights of speech and association, Ashwander v. Tennessee Valley Authority, 297 U.S. 288, 341 (Brandeis, J., concurring), would not only hold little hope of eliminating the issue of vagueness but also would very likely pose other constitutional issues for decision, a result not serving the abstention-justifying end of avoiding constitutional adjudication."

Justices Clark and Harlan dissented.

(6) *Unsettled State Constitutional Questions.* Do different considerations apply when the uncertain state law is the state's constitution rather than a state statute or common-law rule—when, for example, a state statute is attacked under both the state and federal constitutions? Two decisions a year apart seemed to point in opposite directions. In Reetz v. Bozanich, 397 U.S. 82 (1970), plaintiff sought a declaration that Alaska fishing laws and regulations, which limited eligibility to receive certain commercial fishing licenses, violated (i) the Fourteenth Amendment of the federal Constitution, and (ii) two provisions of the Alaska constitution—one reserving fishing rights to the people, and the other proscribing exclusive fishing rights. A three-judge court upheld both contentions, but the Supreme Court vacated and remanded with directions to abstain, emphasizing that the Alaska constitutional provisions "have never been interpreted by an Alaska court" and that management of fish resources was "a matter of great state concern" (p. 86). See also Askew v. Hargrave, Paragraph (3), *supra.*

But in Wisconsin v. Constantineau, 400 U.S. 433 (1971), the Court upheld the decision of a three-judge district court invalidating a Wisconsin statute providing for the public posting, without notice or hearing to the person affected, of the name of any person whose excessive drinking produced specified social problems. (The statute prohibited the provision of intoxicating beverages to any such person.) Chief Justice Burger and Justices Black and Blackmun urged in dissent that abstention was appropriate because the statute (whose meaning had never been tested in state court) might be construed to provide basic rights of procedural due process. The Chief Justice added (p. 440): "For all we know, the state courts would find this statute invalid under the State Constitution, but no one on either side of the case thought to discuss this or exhibit any interest in the subject."[6] The majority refused to abstain; it did not allude to the state constitution, and concluded that the statute contained no ambiguity.

The Court sought to reconcile these decisions in Harris County Com'rs Court v. Moore, 420 U.S. 77 (1975), which ordered abstention to obtain a state court construction of the state constitution. The Court said (pp. 84–85 n. 8) that in Constantineau "we declined to order abstention where the federal due process claim was not complicated by an unresolved state-law question, even though the plaintiffs might have sought relief under a

---

6. A footnote to the Chief Justice's opinion at this point stated: "Although Wisconsin has no due process clause as such, Art. I, § 1, of the Wisconsin Constitution has been held by the Wisconsin Supreme Court to be substantially equivalent to the limitation on state action contained in the Due Process and Equal Protection Clauses of the Fourteenth Amendment" (p. 440 n. 1).

If Chief Justice Burger was correct in his analysis of the Wisconsin constitutional law, would a state decision invalidating the state law under the state constitution necessarily have been reviewable by the Supreme Court? See Chap. V, Sec. 2(A), *supra.* Is the answer to that question relevant to the decision whether to abstain?

similar provision of the state constitution. But where the challenged statute is part of an integrated scheme of related constitutional provisions, statutes, and regulations, and where the scheme as a whole calls for clarifying interpretation by the state courts, we have regularly required the district courts to abstain [citing Reetz]."

The theme of Harris was repeated in Examining Board of Engineers v. Flores de Otero, 426 U.S. 572, 597–98 (1976). There, in refusing to abstain because a challenged Puerto Rico statute might violate Puerto Rico's constitutional guarantees of equal protection and nondiscrimination, the Court said those provisions were not "so interrelated" with the statute that the law of Puerto Rico was ambiguous. Moreover, to require abstention because of the "broad and sweeping" provisions of the Puerto Rico constitution "would convert abstention from an exception into a general rule" (p. 598). See also Hawaii Housing Auth. v. Midkiff, 467 U.S. 229, 237 n. 4 (1984). Since most state constitutions contain guarantees analogous to those in the Bill of Rights, isn't the Court's last point the nub of the matter?[7]

(7) *Avoidance of Nonconstitutional Questions.* In Propper v. Clark, 337 U.S. 472, 490 (1949), the Court stated that abstention was an inappropriate means of avoiding decision of a federal nonconstitutional issue. Justice Frankfurter dissented, arguing that in any event "regard for the respective orbits of State and federal tribunals is the best of reasons, as a matter of judicial administration, for requiring a definitive adjudication by * * * [state] courts * * *" (p. 497). Most lower courts have resisted efforts to circumvent Propper by characterizing federal statutory challenges to state action as constitutional challenges under the Supremacy Clause. See, *e.g.,* United Services Automobile Ass'n v. Muir, 792 F.2d 356 (3d Cir.1986); 17 Wright, Miller, & Cooper, Federal Practice and Procedure § 4242 (1978 and 1986 Supp.); *cf.* Swift & Co. v. Wickham, p. 1335, *supra.*

(8) *Discretion to Abstain, Equitable and Otherwise.*

(a) *Law vs. Equity.* The Pullman decision is expressly rooted in the distinctive discretion of equity jurisdiction. See also, *e.g.,* Baggett v. Bullitt, Paragraph (5), *supra;* NAACP v. Bennett, 360 U.S. 471 (1959) (per curiam). Yet in subsequent cases, Pullman abstention has been applied in actions at law. In Clay v. Sun Ins. Office, Ltd., 363 U.S. 207 (1960), a diversity action for contract damages between private parties, the court of appeals had ruled that application of the forum's choice of law rules would deny due process. The Supreme Court reversed, holding that the lower courts should have certified the question of state law to the Florida Supreme Court before reaching the federal due process question. (On certification, see *Note on Certification of Questions of State Law,* pp. 1381–83, *infra.*) There was no allusion to the movement from equity to law in Clay, or in the subsequent decisions in Fornaris v. Ridge Tool Co., 400 U.S. 41 (1970), and United Gas Pipe Line Co. v. Ideal Cement Co., 369 U.S. 134 (1962).

---

7. Professor Currie responds to this point by saying: "But that should be no cause for misgivings. If the doctrine itself is sound, it should be applied to all cases within its purpose. Perhaps the Court's unprincipled limitation of abstention indicates a healthy disaffection with the doctrine itself. If so, it would be more consistent to abolish abstention altogether." Currie, *The Supreme Court and Federal Jurisdiction: 1975 Term,* 1976 Sup.Ct.Rev. 183, 212.

(b) *Whose Discretion: The Parties' or the Courts'?* As the Pullman case itself shows, the Court may decide on its own motion to abstain. See, *e.g.,* Ohio Bureau of Employment Services v. Hodory, 431 U.S. 471, 480 n. 11 (1977) (though appeal from three-judge district court's award of injunctive relief did not contest the failure to abstain, "Pullman abstention, where deference to the state process may result in elimination or material alteration of the constitutional issue, surely does not require that this Court defer to the wishes of the parties concerning adjudication"); Bellotti v. Baird, 428 U.S. 132, 143 n. 10 (1976); Wisconsin v. Constantineau, Paragraph (6), *supra.* But *cf.* Vance v. Universal Amusement Co., Inc., 445 U.S. 308, 315 n. 11 (1980): "At oral argument, appellants' counsel invited us also to review issues relating to [construction of the state statute] and the question whether the District Court should have abstained. Since the former contention would require us to review a construction ＊ ＊ ＊ which all members of the en banc Court of Appeals ultimately accepted, and since the latter contention was not raised in the Court of Appeals, we decline the invitation." See generally pp. 1707–09, *infra.*

(c) *Discretion and Prudence.* Recall Pullman's emphasis upon the existence of "a sensitive area of social policy upon which the federal courts ought not to enter unless no alternative to its adjudication is open." Is it equally plausible to argue that the equal protection issue in Pullman called insistently for resolution? Are discretionary judgments about the relative sensitivity of particular constitutional challenges at particular times an appropriate basis for jurisdictional decisions? Compare Professor Bickel's endorsement of "the passive virtues," pp. 87–88, *supra.*

The Court's recent decisions have not devoted much attention to the sensitivity of the state program, see, *e.g.,* Hawaii Housing Auth. v. Midkiff, Paragraph (5), *supra,* and it is not obvious that the issue in Clay v. Sun Ins. Office, Paragraph (8)(a), *supra,* for example, was particularly sensitive or affected an important state program. In struggling to honor Pullman's concern about "sensitive" areas, the lower courts have often tried to judge whether the matter in controversy is important to state or local governmental bodies. See generally Davies, note 5, *supra,* at 18–20.[8] But *cf.* Garcia v. San Antonio Metro. Transit Auth., 469 U.S. 528, 546–47 (1985) ("Any rule of state immunity that looks to the 'traditional,' 'integral,' or 'necessary' nature of governmental functions inevitably invites an unelected federal judiciary to make decisions about which state policies it favors and which it dislikes[,] ＊ ＊ ＊ leads to inconsistent results[, and] disserves principles of democratic self-governance ＊ ＊ ＊").

(9) *The Problem of Delay.* One of the principal costs of abstention is the prolonged delay it often brings in its wake. In Spector Motor Serv., Inc. v. O'Connor, for example, over six years elapsed between the Supreme Court's decision requiring abstention, 323 U.S. 101 (1944), and the Court's ultimate decision on the merits, 340 U.S. 602 (1951); in United States v.

---

8. In Note, *Land Use Regulation, the Federal Courts, and the Abstention Doctrine,* 89 Yale L.J. 1134, 1142 (1980), the author argues that the federal courts, which have historically been disinclined to enter local land use disputes, have stretched Pullman abstention (as well as so-called Burford abstention, see Paragraph (10), *infra,* and the equitable restraint doctrine of Younger v. Harris, Sec. 2(C), *infra*), so that abstention in land use cases "may in fact have become the rule." The writer advocates a general policy of abstention in land use cases; for a similar proposal, see Ryckman, *Land Use Litigation, Federal Jurisdiction, and the Abstention Doctrines,* 69 Calif.L.Rev. 377 (1981).

Leiter Minerals, Inc., 381 U.S. 413 (1965), the case was dismissed as moot eight years after abstention was ordered. The burdens of delay seemed great enough to Justice Douglas to warrant a complete reexamination of the Pullman doctrine, see England v. Louisiana State Bd. of Medical Exam'rs, 375 U.S. 411, 423 (1964) (concurring opinion).[9] And though other members of the Court have not gone that far, protracted delay and its consequences have not infrequently been cited among the reasons for refusing abstention in particular cases. See, *e.g.*, Harman v. Forssenius, 380 U.S. 528 (1965); Hostetter v. Idlewild Bon Voyage Liquor Corp., 377 U.S. 324 (1964); Griffin v. School Bd. of Prince Edward County, 377 U.S. 218, 228–29 (1964).

Compare Michigan v. Long, 463 U.S. 1032 (1983), Chap. V, Sec. 2(A), *supra*, which involved the Supreme Court's jurisdiction to review a state court decision that might, but does not clearly, rest on an adequate and independent state constitutional ground. The Court in Long rejected the option of vacating and remanding the case for clarification because of the resulting "delay and decrease in efficiency of judicial administration" and because of the "significant burdens" this approach would place on state courts (pp. 1040–41). Pullman abstention ordinarily involves greater delay and more significant burdens than would a simple remand by the Supreme Court. Can the approaches in these two areas be reconciled?

(10) *Burford Abstention.* The cases so far discussed involved challenges to state action on both federal and state grounds where resolution of an unsettled state law issue could eliminate the need to decide (or could at least narrow) the federal issue. Is abstention ever justified where this element is missing? Can considerations of comity—the desire to avoid friction with a state in the administration of its policies—justify abstention where, for instance, issues of state law appear to be inseparably intertwined with the federal issues? What if there is no issue of state law in the case at all? *Cf.* the Tax Injunction Act, 28 U.S.C. § 1341, and the Johnson Act, 28 U.S.C. § 1342, both discussed in Sec. 1(B), *supra*.

Two key cases considering these questions are Burford v. Sun Oil Co., 319 U.S. 315 (1943), and Alabama Pub. Serv. Comm'n v. Southern Ry., 341 U.S. 341 (1951), which are often regarded as establishing a distinct form of abstention, often called "Burford" or "administrative" abstention. Burford was an action to enjoin the execution of an order of the Railroad Commission of Texas granting a neighboring leaseholder a permit to drill new wells. The order was attacked on federal constitutional and state grounds, and jurisdiction rested both on the presence of the federal question and on diversity of citizenship. The Court held, 5–4, that the federal district court "as a matter of sound equitable discretion" should have declined to exercise jurisdiction and dismissed the case.

Justice Black's opinion noted the complexity of the problems of oil and gas regulation and condemned the results of previous federal court injunctions, particularly those which had proved to be based on "misunderstanding of local law". He said (pp. 325–26, 332–34):

9. Many commentators have urged abolition of Pullman abstention. See, *e.g.*, Kurland, *Toward a Co-operative Judicial Federalism: The Federal Court Abstention Doctrine*, 24 F.R.D. 481 (1959); Wright, *The Abstention Doctrine Reconsidered*, 37 Tex. L.Rev. 815 (1959); Field, *The Abstention Doctrine Today*, 125 U.Pa.L.Rev. 590, 605 (1977); Currie, *The Federal Courts and the American Law Institute, Part II*, 36 U.Chi. L.Rev. 268, 317 (1969).

"In describing the relation of the Texas court to the Commission, no useful purpose will be served by attempting to label the court's position as legislative, Prentis v. Atlantic Coast Line Co., [p. 1348, *supra*] * * *, or judicial, Bacon v. Rutland Railroad Co., [p. 1349, *supra*] * * *—suffice it to say that the Texas courts are working partners with the Railroad Commission in the business of creating a regulatory system for the oil industry. * * *

"To prevent the confusion of multiple review of the same general issues, the legislature provided for concentration of all direct review of the Commission's orders in the state district courts of Travis County. * * * * * *

"These questions of regulation of the industry by the state administrative agency, whether involving gas or oil prorationing programs or [well spacing] cases, so clearly involve basic problems of Texas policy that equitable discretion should be exercised to give the Texas courts the first opportunity to consider them. * * *

"The State provides a unified method for the formation of policy and determination of cases by the Commission and by the state courts. The judicial review of the Commission's decisions in the state courts is expeditious and adequate. Conflicts in the interpretation of state law, dangerous to the success of state policies, are almost certain to result from the intervention of the lower federal courts. On the other hand, if the state procedure is followed from the Commission to the State Supreme Court, ultimate review of the federal questions is fully preserved here. * * * Under such circumstances, a sound respect for the independence of state action requires the federal equity court to stay its hand." [10]

Justice Frankfurter, speaking for three other Justices, dissented vigorously. He found no such uncertainty in the state law as in the Pullman case. Rather, he said, the case depended upon "narrowly defined standards of law established by Texas for review of the orders of its Railroad Commission," which federal judges "are certainly not incompetent to apply" (p. 342). And, apparently regarding the federal issues as minor, he distinguished Pullman as "merely illustrative of one phase of the basic constitutional doctrine that substantial constitutional issues should be adjudicated only when no alternatives are open" (p. 338). In this view he considered the decision at odds with the basic presuppositions of the grant of diversity jurisdiction.

In Alabama Pub. Serv. Comm'n, the Southern Railway brought a federal action to enjoin the enforcement of the Commission's refusal to permit discontinuance of two intrastate trains. Jurisdiction was based on diversity of citizenship and on a federal question, the railroad alleging that the refusal constituted confiscation of property in violation of the Fourteenth Amendment. A three-judge court granted the requested injunction and on appeal the Supreme Court reversed, ordering dismissal of the complaint. Chief Justice Vinson, writing for the Court, apparently conceded that there were no issues of unsettled state law in the case and no challenge to the constitutionality of the state statute on its face. But, he said (pp. 346–50):

10. Justices Douglas and Murphy concurred specially on the ground that "this decision is but an application of the principle expressed in" Pennsylvania v. Williams, p. 1369, *infra.*

"* * * This Court has held that regulation of intrastate railroad service is 'primarily the concern of the state.' North Carolina v. United States, 325 U.S. 507, 511 (1945) * * *. Statutory appeal from an order of the Commission is an integral part of the regulatory process under the Alabama Code. Appeals, concentrated in one circuit court, are 'supervisory in character.' * * * As adequate state court review of an administrative order based upon predominantly local factors is available to appellee, intervention of a federal court is not necessary for the protection of federal rights. * * * 'Few public interests have a higher claim upon the discretion of a federal chancellor than the avoidance of needless friction with state policies' [citing Pullman] * * *."

Justice Frankfurter, joined by Justice Jackson, concurred in the result on the basis that the complaint failed to state a substantial claim, but dissented from the abstention rationale (pp. 360–62):

"Here the plaintiff has exhausted its nonjudicial remedies. * * * Concededly there is no State statute to construe. There is no consideration which should make a court of equity, as a matter of discretion, decline to entertain a bill for an injunction. Nor does the situation in this suit involve a specialized field of State law in which out-of-State federal judges are not at home. * * *

"* * * [I]t was never a doctrine of equity that a federal court should exercise its judicial discretion to dismiss a suit merely because a State court could entertain it.

"This is so because discretion based solely on the availability of a remedy in the State courts would for all practical purposes repeal the Act of 1875. * * *

"I regret my inability to make clear to the majority of this Court that its opinion is in flagrant contradiction with the unbroken course of decisions in this Court for seventy-five years."

Does it make sense to speak of a constitutional or other federal issue as being too "local" for the cognizance of a federal court having jurisdiction? Did Southern Railway so broaden the Burford rationale that "abstention is likely to be applied in any attempt to enjoin a state regulatory body in federal court"? Note, 73 Yale L.J. 850, 851 (1964).

The Supreme Court has not invoked Burford abstention since the Southern Railway decision. In McNeese v. Board of Education, 373 U.S. 668 (1963), the Court refused, over Justice Harlan's lone dissent, to abstain in a school desegregation case where the state claimed to have administrative procedures for handling the dispute; Burford was distinguishable, because here the federal right was not "entangled in a skein of state law" and the legality under state law of the conduct was not at issue (p. 674). The Court also stressed the importance of federal court jurisdiction in civil rights cases. And in Colorado River Water Conservation Dist. v. United States, 424 U.S. 800 (1976), Sec. 2(D), *infra,* a suit by the United States to adjudicate complex claims to water rights, the Court again found Burford abstention inappropriate, emphasizing that the state law was settled, and that although a federal decision might conflict with that of a state tribunal, it would not "impermissibly" impair state water policy.[11] How well do these considerations distinguish Burford and Southern Railway?

See also Zablocki v. Redhail, 434 U.S. 374, 379 n. 5 (1978), affirming that "there is, of course, no doctrine requiring abstention merely because resolution of a federal question may result in the overturning of a state policy"; *cf.* Kaiser Steel Corp. v. W.S. Ranch Co., 391 U.S. 593 (1968), p. 1373, *infra.*

The lower courts have, not surprisingly, found the Supreme Court's pronouncements less than pellucid, and the decisions are contradictory. See Davies, note 5, *supra,* at 16–21; Comment, 46 U.Chi.L.Rev. 971 (1979).[12]

(d) *The Relationship to § 1983.* The plaintiffs in both Burford and Southern Railway could have but did not frame their federal challenges as § 1983 actions. Abstention doctrines are in some tension with Monroe v. Pape insofar as they, in effect, call for exhaustion of state judicial remedies. Insofar as Burford abstention is based on the notion that a specialized state court has some attributes of an administrative agency, isn't it hard to square with the decision in Patsy, Sec. 2(A), *supra?* Indeed, in Burford abstention (unlike Pullman abstention), the federal court defers to the state court on federal as well as state issues, and unless the Supreme Court reviews the case, res judicata would preclude federal litigation of the federal issues. The majority in Patsy was unwilling, by contrast, to postpone federal jurisdiction over a § 1983 suit even on the apparent assumption that any state administrative proceeding would not preclude plenary federal litigation.[13]

(e) *Possible Legislative Responses.* Justice Frankfurter noted in his dissent in Burford that the Johnson Act limits federal court jurisdiction over one class of public utility orders, those dealing with rates. See Sec. 1(B), *supra.* Does that limitation call into question the decisions in Burford and Southern Railway? Is that limitation justified as a matter of legislative policy? The ALI Study, § 1371(b), would have extended the Johnson Act so as to limit federal court jurisdiction in suits challenging state orders relating to "conservation, production, or use of minerals, water, or other like natural resource of the state."

(11) *Bibliography.* For general discussion of the issues raised in this note, see, in addition to the sources already cited, Field, *Abstention in Constitutional Cases: The Scope of the Pullman Abstention Doctrine,* 122 U.Pa.L.Rev. 1071 (1974); Bezanson, *Abstention: The Supreme Court and Allocation of Judicial Power,* 27 Vand.L.Rev. 1107 (1974); Schoenfeld,

---

11. In a footnote, the Court noted (p. 815 n. 21) that Burford and Southern Railway both involved federal constitutional questions, and stated that "the presence of a federal basis for jurisdiction may raise the level of justification needed for abstention."

The Court did order the federal court to stay its proceedings in deference to a parallel state proceeding under Colorado's elaborate procedures for handling disputes about water rights, but viewed that as a rationale distinct from Burford abstention.

12. On the application of Burford abstention to land use cases, see Ryckman, note 8, *supra;* Note, note 8, *supra.*

13. The lower courts have continued to invoke Burford abstention in cases decided since Patsy. For citations, see, *e.g.,* 17 Wright, Miller, & Cooper, Federal Practice & Procedure, § 4244, at 172 n. 15 (1986 Supp.); Davies, note 5, *supra,* at 18 nn. 88–89, 21 n. 96.

American Federalism and the Abstention Doctrine in the Supreme Court, 73
Dick.L.Rev. 605 (1969).

NOTE ON ABSTENTION IN CASES NOT INVOLVING A FEDERAL QUESTION

(1) Ever since Pullman the question whether abstention could be
proper in cases where no question of federal law is involved at all has posed
impressive difficulty for the courts. Notice that in such a case one
significant policy stressed in Pullman—avoiding premature and perhaps
unnecessary decision of federal constitutional questions—is by hypothesis
irrelevant; the function of abstention would be simply to have a state
rather than a federal court decide a case governed entirely by state law.
Note too that in virtually all such cases federal jurisdiction would have to
be based on diversity of citizenship. Finally, notice that if all the issues in
the case are issues of state law, the usual consequence of abstention would
be not merely to postpone but to relinquish the exercise of federal jurisdiction. (But see Louisiana Power & Light Co. v. City of Thibodaux, Paragraph (4), *infra.*)

In view of these circumstances, is a federal court ever justified in
declining to decide such a case? If so, when? Is it enough if the state law
issue in the case is difficult and unsettled? Is the importance of the issue
relevant? Is it material whether or not the litigation involves the validity
of official action? Or the validity of a state regulatory scheme?

Consider these issues in reading the materials which follow. See also
Sec. 2(D), *infra.*

(2) In a few cases prior to Pullman the Supreme Court had indicated
that under certain circumstances a federal court should refrain from
deciding a case governed entirely by state law. Thus in Hawks v. Hamill,
288 U.S. 52 (1933), the complainants, claiming a perpetual franchise for a
toll bridge, brought suit to enjoin interference with their operation of the
bridge against state officers, who took the view that the franchise was void
under the state constitution. The complainants asserted no federal rights,
jurisdiction resting only on diversity of citizenship. The Court thought
decisions of the state supreme court to be controlling against the complainants, but said (p. 60):

"＊ ＊ ＊ There is another path of approach that brings us to the
same goal, an approach along the line of equitable remedies. ＊ ＊ ＊ The
members of the State Highway Commission believe it to be their official
duty to take possession of the bridge, and propose to act accordingly. The
Attorney General of the state is about to institute proceedings at law and
in equity to vindicate the public rights or what he believes to be such
rights. The County Attorneys of McClain and Cleveland Counties propose
to sue for fines and penalties. All these activities ＊ ＊ ＊ have been
enjoined by the decree under review. Only a case of manifest oppression
will justify a federal court in laying such a check upon administrative
officers acting *colore officii* in a conscientious endeavor to fulfill their duty
to the state. A prudent self-restraint is called for at such times if state and
national functions are to be maintained in stable equilibrium. Reluctance
there has been to use the process of federal courts in restraint of state

officials though the rights asserted by the complainants are strictly federal in origin. * * * There must be reluctance even greater when the rights are strictly local, jurisdiction having no other basis than the accidents of residence." See also Pennsylvania v. Williams, 294 U.S. 176 (1935) (federal diversity court should defer to impending state statutory proceeding for liquidating insolvent building and loan association); *cf.* Thompson v. Magnolia Petroleum Co., 309 U.S. 478 (1940).

(3) Meredith v. Winter Haven, 320 U.S. 228 (1943), was a municipal bondholders' action to enjoin the retirement of bonds on allegedly unlawful terms. Jurisdiction rested solely on diversity of citizenship; the key issue in the case was whether the City was authorized under Florida law to issue the bonds without a referendum. The court of appeals directed that the cause be dismissed without prejudice to the plaintiffs' right to proceed in the state courts. The Supreme Court reversed. After a careful review of the cases Chief Justice Stone found no basis for refusing to exercise diversity jurisdiction merely because a case "involve[s] state law or because the law is uncertain or difficult to determine. * * * Decision here does not require the federal court to determine or shape state policy governing administrative agencies. It entails no interference with such agencies or with the state courts. No litigation is pending in the state courts in which the questions here presented could be decided. We are pointed to no public policy or interest which would be served by withholding from petitioners the benefit of the jurisdiction which Congress has created with the purpose that it should be availed of and exercised subject only to such limitations as traditionally justify courts in declining to exercise the jurisdiction which they possess. * * *

"Erie R. Co. v. Tompkins, *supra,* did not free the federal courts from the duty of deciding questions of state law in diversity cases. Instead it placed on them a greater responsibility for determining and applying state laws in all cases within their jurisdiction in which federal law does not govern. Accepting this responsibility, as was its duty, this Court has not hesitated to decide questions of state law when necessary for the disposition of a case brought to it for decision * * *. Even though our decisions could not finally settle the questions of state law involved, they did adjudicate the rights of the parties with the aid of such light as was afforded by the materials for decision at hand, and in accordance with the applicable principles for determining state law" (pp. 236–38).

(4) Louisiana Power & Light Co. v. City of Thibodaux, 360 U.S. 25 (1959), was a proceeding by the City to take by eminent domain property owned by the Company. The Company removed the proceeding to federal court on the basis of diversity of citizenship. The issue in the case—aside from the question of amount of compensation—was whether as a matter of Louisiana law municipalities had the authority to condemn public utility properties. The district court stayed the action pending the institution of a state declaratory judgment action and decision of this issue by the state Supreme Court. The court of appeals reversed, but was in turn reversed by the Supreme Court. Justice Frankfurter stressed that eminent domain proceedings are "special and peculiar," and "intimately involved with sovereign prerogative," particularly where the issue "concerns the apportionment of governmental powers between City and State" (p. 28). He continued (pp. 29–30):

"The special nature of eminent domain justifies a district judge, when his familiarity with the problems of local law so counsels him, to ascertain the meaning of a disputed state statute from the only tribunal empowered to speak definitively—the courts of the State under whose statute eminent domain is sought to be exercised—rather than himself make a dubious and tentative forecast. This course does not constitute abnegation of judicial duty. On the contrary, it is a wise and productive discharge of it. There is only postponement of decision for its best fruition. Eventually the District Court will award compensation if the taking is sustained. If for some reason a declaratory judgment is not promptly sought from the state courts and obtained within a reasonable time, the District Court, having retained complete control of the litigation, will doubtless assert it to decide also the question of the meaning of the state statute. The justification for this power, to be exercised within the indicated limits, lies in regard for the respective competence of the state and federal court systems and for the maintenance of harmonious federal-state relations in a matter close to the political interests of a State. * * *

" * * * In providing on his own motion for a stay in this case, an experienced district judge was responding in a sensible way to a quandary about the power of the City of Thibodaux into which he was placed by an opinion of the Attorney General of Louisiana in which it was concluded that in a strikingly similar case a Louisiana city did not have the power here claimed by the City. A Louisiana statute apparently seems to grant such a power. But that statute has never been interpreted, in respect to a situation like that before the judge, by the Louisiana courts and it would not be the first time that the authoritative tribunal has found in a statute less than meets the outsider's eye. Informed local courts may find meaning not discernible to the outsider. The consequence of allowing this to come to pass would be that this case would be the only case in which the Louisiana statute is construed as we would construe it, whereas the rights of all other litigants would be thereafter governed by a decision of the Supreme Court of Louisiana quite different from ours." [1]

Herewith are extracts from Justice Brennan's long and vigorous dissent (pp. 31–33, 37–38, 39, 42, 44), which was joined by Chief Justice Warren and Justice Douglas:

"Until today, the standards for testing this order of the District Court sending the parties to this diversity action to a state court for decision of a state law question might have been said to have been reasonably consistent with the imperative duty of a District Court, imposed by Congress under 28

---

1. In a footnote (p. 27 n. 2) Justice Frankfurter said: "The issue in Meredith v. City of Winter Haven, 320 U.S. 228, is, of course, decisively different from the issue now before the Court. Here the issue is whether an experienced district judge, especially conversant with Louisiana law, who, when troubled with the construction which Louisiana courts may give to a Louisiana statute, himself initiates the taking of appropriate measures for securing construction of this doubtful and unsettled statute (and not at all in response to any alleged attempt by petitioner to delay a decision by that judge), should be jurisdic-

tionally disabled from seeking the controlling light of the Louisiana Supreme Court. The issue in Winter Haven was not that. It was whether jurisdiction must be surrendered to the state court. * * *

"In Winter Haven the Court of Appeals directed the action to be dismissed. In this case the Court of Appeals denied a conscientious exercise by the federal district judge of his discretionary power merely to stay disposition of a retained case until he could get controlling light from the state court."

U.S.C. §§ 1332 and 1441, to render prompt justice in cases between citizens of different States. To order these suitors out of the federal court and into a state court in the circumstances of this case passes beyond disrespect for the diversity jurisdiction to plain disregard of this imperative duty. The doctrine of abstention, in proper perspective, is an extraordinary and narrow exception to this duty, and abdication of the obligation to decide cases can be justified under this doctrine only in the exceptional circumstances where the order to the parties to repair to the state court would clearly serve one of two important countervailing interests: either the avoidance of a premature and perhaps unnecessary decision of a serious federal constitutional question, or the avoidance of the hazard of unsettling some delicate balance in the area of federal-state relationships.[2]

  * * *

"But neither of the two recognized situations justifying abstention is present in the case before us. * * *

" * * * [T]he decision in Meredith v. Winter Haven, 320 U.S. 228, long recognized as a landmark in this field, is squarely contrary to today's holding. * * * Although there was present the obvious irritant to state-federal relations of a federal court injunction against City officials, which is not present in this case, this Court in Winter Haven held that it was incumbent on the Federal District Court to perform its duty and adjudicate the case. I am unable to see a distinction, so far as concerns noninterference with the exercise of state sovereignty, between decision as to the City of Winter Haven's authority under Florida's statutes and constitution to issue deferred-interest bonds without a referendum, and decision as to the City of Thibodaux's authority under Louisiana's statutes and constitution to expropriate the Power and Light Company's property. Since the Court suggests no adequate basis of distinction between the two cases, it should frankly announce that Meredith v. Winter Haven is overruled, for no other conclusion is reasonable. * * *

" * * * It is true that there are no Louisiana decisions interpreting Act 111, and that there is a confusing opinion of the State's Attorney General on the question. But mere difficulty of construing the state statute is not justification for running away from the task. 'Questions may occur which we would gladly avoid; but we cannot avoid them. All we can do is, to exercise our best judgment, and conscientiously to perform our duty.' Cohens v. Virginia, 6 Wheat. 264, 404. * * *

"Not only has the Court departed from any precedential basis for its action, but the decision encourages inefficiency in administration of the federal courts and leads to unnecessary delay, waste and added expense for the parties. * * *

" * * * One must regret that this Court's departure from the long-settled criteria governing abstention should so richly fertilize the Power and Light Company's strategy of delay which now has succeeded, I dare say, past the fondest expectation of counsel who conceived it. It is especially unfortunate in that departure from these criteria fashions an opening

---

2. [Ed.] Most of the cases cited by Justice Brennan at this point as examples of abstention on the latter ground, e.g., Burford v. Sun Oil Co., 319 U.S. 315 (1943), and Alabama Pub. Serv. Comm'n v. Southern Ry., 341 U.S. 341 (1951), were not pure state-law cases, but rather involved federal constitutional claims. See pp. 1356–68, supra. Hawks v. Hamill, p. 1368, supra, was, however, also cited by Justice Brennan as an example.

wedge for District Courts to refer hard cases of state law to state courts in even the routine diversity negligence and contract actions."

(5) Note that Justice Brennan appears to concede that, in principle, the avoidance of friction with significant state policies is an independent justification for abstention. Is his conclusion, that federal adjudication of the state law issue in Thibodaux created no significant risk of such friction, correct? To support that conclusion, Justice Brennan stressed that this case did not involve a request for a federal injunction but, rather, was an action "at law" removed to federal court, and that it would not involve the use of *federal* law to strike down state action but rather would test such action by state law. Are these arguments persuasive? *Cf.* Pennhurst State Hosp. v. Halderman, p. 1195, *supra,* especially Justice Stevens' dissent.

(6) A reading of the Court's opinion in Thibodaux would surely justify the conclusion that the fact that eminent domain is involved tips the scales heavily in favor of abstention. That this conclusion may not be warranted, however, was indicated in County of Allegheny v. Frank Mashuda Co., 360 U.S. 185 (1959), decided on the same day as Thibodaux. This case also involved issues of power under state law to take property by eminent domain, the question being whether land taken by the County and then leased to a private party was validly condemned under Pennsylvania law. Alleging that the taking was for a "private" and not a "public" use, plaintiffs brought an action in federal court, on the basis of diversity, seeking a judgment of ouster and damages against Allegheny County and the private party. A proceeding to assess the amount of compensation for the taking was pending at the time in the state courts. The federal district court dismissed the suit on the ground that it "should not interfere with the administration of the affairs of a political subdivision acting under color of State Law in a condemnation proceeding." Affirming the court of appeals, the Supreme Court held that it was error for the district court to dismiss the case.

Justice Brennan's opinion for the 5–4 majority is an almost verbatim gloss of parts of his dissent in Thibodaux. It rejects any notion that federal adjudication of cases involving the eminent domain power of the states involves any special risks of friction with state authority. And it states (p. 196):

"Aside from the complete absence of any possibility that a District Court adjudication in this case would necessitate decision of a federal constitutional issue or conflict with state policy, the state law that the District Court was asked to apply is clear and certain. All that was necessary for the District Court to dispose of this case was to determine whether, as a matter of fact, the respondents' property was taken for the private use of * * * [the non-County respondents]. The propriety of a federal adjudication in this case follows *a fortiori* from the established principle that Federal District Courts should apply settled state law without abstaining from the exercise of jurisdiction even though this course would require decision of difficult federal constitutional questions."

Justice Clark's dissent was joined by Justices Black, Frankfurter and Harlan, all of whom were in the Thibodaux majority. It stressed that abstention was particularly appropriate in view of the fact that a state proceeding to determine the amount of damages was already pending.

(7) Note that the Court's opinion in Thibodaux repeatedly suggests that the trial judge's discretion should count heavily in determining whether abstention on grounds of comity is justified. But Mashuda, although it too phrased the issue in terms of whether the district court had "discretion" to order abstention, reversed the trial judge's decision. (Is it relevant in this connection that in the latter case the district judge had dismissed rather than stayed the action?) Would it be sound to leave broad discretion to trial courts to decide whether the case is one where federal adjudication would entail a serious risk of friction with significant state policies? See generally Wright, *The Abstention Doctrine Reconsidered,* 37 Tex.L.Rev. 815, 824–27 (1959).

(8) Of the nine Justices, seven evidently felt that Thibodaux and Mashuda were indistinguishable and dissented in either one or the other of the cases. Justices Stewart and Whittaker alone were in the majority in both cases. Only Justice Stewart attempted an explanation. In a concurrence in Thibodaux (p. 31), he said: "In a conscientious effort to do justice the District Court deferred immediate adjudication of this controversy pending authoritative clarification of a controlling state statute of highly doubtful meaning. Under the circumstances presented, I think the course pursued was clearly within the District Court's allowable discretion. For that reason I concur in the judgment.

"The case is totally unlike County of Allegheny v. Mashuda Co., decided today, except for the coincidence that both cases involve eminent domain proceedings. In Mashuda the Court holds that it was error for the District Court to dismiss the complaint. The Court further holds in that case that, since the controlling state law is clear and only factual issues need be resolved, there is no occasion in the interest of justice to refrain from prompt adjudication."

(9) The taking in Mashuda involved the enlargement and improvement of the Pittsburgh Airport; the property in controversy was leased by the County to a contractor on that project for the purpose of storing necessary materials and supplies. The issue was whether this was a private or a public use under Pennsylvania law.

Are Justices Brennan and Stewart correct in characterizing this as an issue of fact and therefore distinguishable from the issue in Thibodaux?

Even if the answer to this question is "no", is there a basis for distinction? Do the two cases raise issues of equal breadth and import? In which case would a "wrong" decision of the question by a federal court create graver consequences for the effectuation of state policy? Was there an equal need in the two cases for affording the kind of protection to out-of-staters for which the diversity jurisdiction was designed?

For discussion of these cases, see, *e.g.,* Gowen & Izlar, *Federal Court Abstention in Diversity of Citizenship Cases,* 43 Tex.L.Rev. 194 (1964); Note, 30 Mo.L.Rev. 460 (1965).

(10) Kaiser Steel Corp. v. W.S. Ranch Co., 391 U.S. 593 (1968), was a diversity action involving a dispute over rights to water on private land. The question was whether a New Mexico statute had authorized the defendant to take water, and, if so, whether the statute was valid under the state constitution, which permits takings only for "public use". The district court and the court of appeals decided these issues on the merits, but the Supreme Court held that the suit should be stayed pending their

adjudication in a state declaratory judgment action. (Such an action had in fact been commenced by the defendant after the court of appeals decision.) The Court's per curiam said: "The Court of Appeals erred in refusing to stay its hand. The state law issue which is crucial in this case is one of vital concern in the arid State of New Mexico, where water is one of the most valuable natural resources. The issue, moreover, is a truly novel one. The question will eventually have to be resolved by the New Mexico courts, and since a declaratory judgment action is actually pending there, in all likelihood that resolution will be forthcoming soon. Sound judicial administration requires that the parties in this case be given the benefit of the same rule of law which will apply to all other businesses and landowners concerned with the use of this vital state resource" (p. 594).[3]

The Court did not cite Thibodaux or Mashuda. Justice Brennan's brief concurrence, joined by Justices Douglas and Marshall, stressed that the importance of the issue of water use for New Mexico was a "special circumstance" justifying abstention, and included "*cf.*" cites to Burford and Southern Railway—which the majority did not cite.[4]

(11) Given the difficulties of understanding and reconciling the Supreme Court decisions, it should not occasion surprise to discover that the courts of appeals' decisions on when abstention is proper in state-law cases are not harmonious. The most extreme position was that adopted by the Fifth Circuit in its *en banc* decision in United Serv. Life Ins. Co. v. Delaney, 328 F.2d 483 (5th Cir.1964). This was a diversity case involving actions to recover the proceeds of life insurance policies covering "passengers" on air carriers; the question was whether pilots were passengers within the meaning of the policy; no official state action or state regulatory program was involved in any way. The court nevertheless ordered abstention on the ground that the Texas decisions left the answer to the question in obscurity. The decision has been extensively criticized in the commentaries, questioned in subsequent Fifth Circuit cases, see Boston Old Colony Ins. Co. v. Balbin, 591 F.2d 1040, 1045 (5th Cir.1979); Barrett v. Atlantic Richfield Co., 444 F.2d 38, 45 & n. 4 (5th Cir.1971), and rejected in a number of other circuits. See generally 17 Wright, Miller & Cooper, Federal Practice & Procedure § 4264, at 497–99 (1978).

(12) What is the relationship, if any, of abstention in cases such as Burford and Southern Railway (discussed in Paragraph (10) of the preceding note) and in pure state-law cases such as Thibodaux? The two groups of cases share at least one common characteristic: the Pullman purpose of avoiding the necessity for federal constitutional adjudication is not relevant. Are the remaining criteria bearing on abstention similar in the two types of situations?

---

3. The Supreme Court of New Mexico subsequently reached a result in the declaratory judgment action diametrically opposite to that reached by the court of appeals. 81 N.M. 414, 467 P.2d 986 (1970).

4. Note also the discussion in Colorado River Water Cons. Dist. v. United States, 424 U.S. 800 (1976), Sec. 2(D), *infra*, where, citing Kaiser Steel and Thibodaux, the Court said (p. 814): "Abstention is also appropriate where there have been presented difficult questions of state law bearing on policy problems of substantial public import whose importance transcends the result in the case then at bar."

NOTE ON PROCEDURAL ASPECTS OF ABSTENTION

(1) *Commencing A State Proceeding.* If a federal court decides to abstain on an issue of state law, what assurance does the plaintiff have that he can get a determination of the issue in a state court? A state proceeding raising the issue may already be pending, as in Askew v. Hargrave, p. 1357, *supra,* but if (again as in Askew) the state proceeding involves different parties, the plaintiff may be unhappy with the adequacy of presentation of the issue and may be denied intervention. The plaintiff may have to start the same lawsuit all over again in a state court, and run all the risks of procedural obstacles to adjudication that a litigant normally runs. Or he may be able to take advantage of declaratory judgment legislation, adopted in virtually every state, and seek a declaration limited to the precise issue on which abstention was ordered. But the existence of declaratory judgment legislation is no assurance that the state courts will entertain an action in the abstention context. In United Serv. Life Ins. Co. v. Delaney, Paragraph (11) of the preceding Note, after the Fifth Circuit abstained (reserving jurisdiction to enter final judgment), the Texas Supreme Court held that declaratory relief was unavailable because the decision of the issue of state law would be only an "advisory opinion." 396 S.W.2d 855 (Tex.1965). Do you agree that in a state court that is constitutionally limited to cases and controversies as federal courts are, such a request for declaratory relief is nonjusticiable?

(2) *Dismissal vs. Stay of Federal Proceedings.* When a federal court decides to abstain, should jurisdiction be retained or should the action be dismissed? In a case like Southern Railway, p. 1365, *supra,* there is a strong argument for dismissal because the federal issues in the case are left to the state court to decide. But in most Pullman abstention cases, a federal court retains jurisdiction to permit it to resolve the federal question if that is ultimately necessary.[1] Retaining jurisdiction also enables the federal court to guard against the possibility of unreasonable delay or an unforeseen bar to relief in the state courts, and, where appropriate, to provide interim relief pending the outcome of the state court litigation.[2]

(3) *Resolution of the Federal Questions.* Whether or not the federal court retains jurisdiction, the parties may present their federal as well as

---

1. Harris County Com'rs Court v. Moore, 420 U.S. 77 (1975), ordered abstention in a case arising in Texas, and in view of Texas' refusal in the Delaney case, Paragraph (1), *supra,* to issue what it viewed as an "advisory opinion," ruled that the district court should dismiss instead of retaining jurisdiction. "The dismissal," the Court specified, "should be without prejudice so that any remaining federal claim may be raised in a federal forum after the Texas courts have been given the opportunity to address the state law questions in this case" (pp. 88–89). This approach has since been followed by the federal courts in Texas cases; do you think it should persuade the Texas courts to distinguish their position in Delaney? Does your answer depend on whether you think Delaney was sound?

2. On the latter point, consider Babbitt v. United Farm Workers Nat. Union, 442 U.S. 289, 312 n. 18 (1979). There the Court found abstention appropriate in a First Amendment challenge to state law. In responding to plaintiff's request for an injunction against enforcement of the statute at issue pending the state court proceeding, the Court said simply that "this is a matter that is best addressed by the District Court in the first instance." Compare Catrone v. Massachusetts State Racing Com'n, 535 F.2d 669, 672 (1st Cir.1976) and Cox Cable Comm'n, Inc. v. Simpson, 569 F.Supp. 507 (D.Neb.1983), endorsing such relief. See generally Wells, *Preliminary Injunctions and Abstention: Some Problems in Federalism,* 63 Cornell L.Rev. 65 (1977).

their state contentions to the state court for decision, and the loser may seek Supreme Court review. This was the course followed after Harrison v. NAACP, p. 1358, *supra*, and in NAACP v. Button, 371 U.S. 415 (1963), the Supreme Court ultimately passed on the constitutionality of the state statutes on certiorari to the Virginia Supreme Court of Appeals, saying (p. 427): "Where ✳ ✳ ✳ the party remitted to the state courts elects to seek a complete and final adjudication of his rights in the state courts, the District Court's reservation of jurisdiction is purely formal, and does not impair our jurisdiction to review directly an otherwise final judgment."

But may a party elect not to submit the federal questions for state court decision? At least where those questions involve a constitutional challenge to the state statute being construed, the state court must be made aware of the nature of that challenge. In Government & Civic Employees Organizing Committee, CIO v. Windsor, 353 U.S. 364 (1957), the district court first abstained, and then, following a state court's construction of a state statute ruled that the statute was constitutional. The Supreme Court vacated that ruling, because (p. 366): "The bare adjudication by the Alabama Supreme Court ✳ ✳ ✳ does not suffice, since that court was not asked to interpret the statute in light of the constitutional objections presented to the District Court. If appellants' freedom-of-expression and equal protection arguments had been presented to the state court, it might have construed the statute in a different manner. Accordingly, the judgment of the District Court is vacated, and this cause is remanded to it with directions to retain jurisdiction until efforts to obtain an appropriate adjudication in the state courts have been exhausted."

(4) *The England Case.* Suppose the state supreme court, presented with the federal questions, chooses to decide them, and the litigant prefers not to seek Supreme Court review (or review is denied). May he return to the federal court, or is the state decision res judicata? The question was finally answered in England v. Louisiana State Bd. of Medical Examiners, 375 U.S. 411 (1964), holding that a party is bound by the state court determination *only* if he did in fact elect, in the words of Button, *supra*, "to seek a complete and final adjudication of his rights in a state court". In England, the Court reasoned (pp. 415–16):

"There are fundamental objections to any conclusion that a litigant who has properly invoked the jurisdiction of a Federal District Court to consider federal constitutional claims can be compelled, without his consent and through no fault of his own, to accept instead a state court's determination of those claims.[3] ✳ ✳ ✳ [Abstention's] recognition of the role of state courts as the final expositors of state law implies no disregard for the primacy of the federal judiciary in deciding questions of federal law. ✳ ✳ ✳

"It is true that, after a post-abstention determination and rejection of his federal claims by the state courts, a litigant could seek direct review in this Court. But such review, even when available by appeal rather than only by a discretionary writ of certiorari, is an inadequate substitute for the initial District Court determination ✳ ✳ ✳. This is true as to issues of law; it is especially true as to issues of fact. Limiting the litigant to review

3. In a footnote, the Court added (p. 415 n. 5): "At least this is true in a case, like the instant one, not involving the possibili- ty of unwarranted disruption of a state administrative process [citing Burford and Southern Railway]."

here would deny him the benefit of a federal trial court's role in constructing a record and making fact findings. How the facts are found will often dictate the decision of federal claims. * * * "

As to the hazards involved in the presentation required by Windsor, the Court said (pp. 421–22):

" * * * [A] party may readily forestall any conclusion that he has elected not to return to the District Court. He may accomplish this by making on the state record the 'reservation to the disposition of the entire case by the state courts' that we referred to in Button. That is, he may inform the state courts that he is exposing his federal claims there only for the purpose of complying with Windsor, and that he intends, should the state courts hold against him on the question of state law, to return to the District Court for disposition of his federal contentions. Such an explicit reservation is not indispensable; the litigant is in no event to be denied his right to return to the District Court unless it clearly appears that he voluntarily did more than Windsor required and fully litigated his federal claims in the state courts. When the reservation has been made, however, his right to return will in all events be preserved." [4]

After England, may a party obtain Supreme Court review of a state court decision of the federal question despite his own effort to reserve the question for the district court? If review is denied, may he then return to the district court?

After England, may a party submit some federal questions for binding state court decision and reserve others? Might not a party be willing to have a question of the validity of a statute on its face decided by a state court (with a right of appeal to the Supreme Court if the statute is upheld), reserving for federal court decision any questions involving determinations of fact or application of law to fact? *Cf.* Mishkin, *The Federal "Question" in the District Courts,* 53 Colum.L.Rev. 157, 172–75 (1953). If a state court determination of fact is relevant to both the state and federal questions, is the state court determination binding in the federal court after England?

In England itself, the Court (p. 422 n. 13) said: "The reservation [of the right to litigate the federal question in a federal court] may be made by any party to the litigation. Usually the plaintiff will have made the original choice to litigate in the federal court, but the defendant also, by virtue of the removal jurisdiction, 28 U.S.C. § 1441(b), has a right to litigate the federal question there. * * * The latter may protect his right by either declining to oppose the plaintiff's federal claim in the state court or opposing it with the appropriate reservation." Did the Court mean that a defendant may *always* make such a reservation, or may do so only when the original action was removable?

For further discussion of these issues, see Liebenthal, *A Dialogue on England: The England Case, its Effect on the Abstention Doctrine, and Some Suggested Solutions,* 18 West.Res.L.Rev. 157 (1966).

(5) *The Consequences of Not Abstaining.* What is the impact in subsequent state court litigation if a federal court does not abstain from deciding

---

4. In the specific case before it, the Court found that the litigants had submitted the federal question to the state court, but only in the belief that the Windsor case required them to do so; on this basis, the Court was unwilling to apply its new rule to them, and held that the district court should pass on the merits of their federal contention.

a question of state law? Is the state court free to construe its statute in a way that would save its validity even after it has been held invalid by the federal court? By the Supreme Court? In Planned Parenthood v. Danforth, 428 U.S. 52 (1976), the majority reviewed a lower federal court decision, construed the state statutory provision under challenge, held the provision unseverable, and declared it wholly invalid. The dissenters urged that, instead of taking such action, the federal courts should have abstained on the questions of construction and severability. They added: "The majority's construction of state law is, of course, not binding on the Missouri courts. If they should disagree with the majority's reading of state law on one or both of the points treated by the majority, the State could validly enforce the relevant parts of the statute—*at least against all those people not parties to this case*" (p. 101 n. 4) (emphasis added). If principles of res judicata are applicable, as the italicized phrase suggests, why isn't the state prosecutor (a defendant in the case) bound in a subsequent effort by him to enforce the statute against non-parties under the rationale of Blonder–Tongue Labs, Inc. v. University of Illinois Foundation, 402 U.S. 313 (1971)? Should the availability of collateral estoppel to a non-party, as authorized by Blonder–Tongue, be limited to questions of fact? To unitary systems? See Restatement (Second) of Judgments § 29 (1982). Are the dissenters in Danforth perhaps wrong in suggesting that even as to the parties themselves, the construction of state law by the federal courts is binding in a subsequent state-court proceeding? See generally Shapiro, *State Courts and Federal Declaratory Judgments,* 74 Nw. U.L.Rev. 759 (1979).

(6) *Appealability of Decisions Whether to Abstain.* For discussion of the appealability of orders granting or denying abstention, see Chapter XV, Sec. 1, *infra.*

(7) *The Option of Certification.* As an alternative to requiring the parties to commence a declaratory judgment action at the bottom of the state judicial ladder and to go as far up that ladder as they can, state law in nearly two-thirds of the states allows a federal court to certify an unsettled question of state law directly to the highest court. Consider, in light of the case and Note that follow, whether the availability of that procedure affects the appropriateness of abstention.

LEHMAN BROTHERS v. SCHEIN
416 U.S. 386, 94 S.Ct. 1741, 40 L.Ed.2d 215 (1974).
Certiorari to the United States Court of Appeals for the Second Circuit.

MR. JUSTICE DOUGLAS delivered the opinion of the Court.

* * *

These are suits brought in the District Court for the Southern District of New York. Lum's, one of the respondents in the Lehman Bros. petition, is a Florida corporation with headquarters in Miami. Each of the three petitions, which we consolidated for oral argument, involves shareholders' derivative suits naming Lum's and others as defendants; and the basis of federal jurisdiction is diversity of citizenship, 28 U.S.C. § 1332(a)(1), about which there is no dispute.

The complaints allege that Chasen, president of Lum's, called Simon, a representative of Lehman Bros., and told him about disappointing projections of Lum's earnings, estimates that were confidential, not public. Simon is said to have told an employee of IDS [Investors Diversified Services] about them. On the next day, it is alleged that the IDS defendants sold 83,000 shares of Lum's on the New York Stock Exchange for about $17.50 per share. Later that day the exchanges halted trading in Lum's stock and on the next trading day it opened at $14 per share, the public being told that the projected earnings would be "substantially lower" than anticipated. The theory of the complaints was that Chasen was a fiduciary but used the inside information along with others for profit and that Chasen and his group are liable to Lum's for their unlawful profits.

Lehman and Simon defended on the ground that the IDS sale was not made through them and that neither one benefited from the sales. Nonetheless plaintiffs claimed that Chasen and the other defendants were liable under Diamond v. Oreamuno, 24 N.Y.2d 494, 248 N.E.2d 910 (1969). Diamond proceeds on the theory that "inside" information of an officer or director of a corporation is an asset of the corporation which had been acquired by the insiders as fiduciaries of the company and misappropriated in violation of trust.

The District Court looked to the choice-of-law rules of the State of New York, Klaxon Co. v. Stentor Electric Mfg. Co., 313 U.S. 487 (1941), and held that the law of the State of incorporation governs the existence and extent of corporate fiduciary obligations, as well as the liability for violation of them. * * *

The District Court in examining Florida law concluded that, although the highest court in Florida has not considered the question, several district courts of appeal indicate that a complaint which fails to allege both wrongful acts and damage to the corporation must be dismissed. The District Court went on to consider whether if Florida followed the Diamond rationale, defendants would be liable. It concluded that the present complaints go beyond Diamond, as Chasen, the only fiduciary of Lum's involved in the suits, never sold any of his holdings on the basis of inside information. The other defendants were not fiduciaries of Lum's. The District Court accordingly dismissed the complaints, 335 F.Supp. 329 (1971).

The Court of Appeals by a divided vote reversed the District Court. 478 F.2d 817 (CA2 1973). While the Court of Appeals held that Florida law was controlling, it found none that was decisive. So it then turned to the law of other jurisdictions, particularly that of New York, to see if Florida "would probably" interpret Diamond to make it applicable here. The Court of Appeals concluded that the defendants had engaged with Chasen "to misuse corporate property," and that the theory of Diamond reaches that situation, "viewing the case as the Florida court would probably view it." Ibid. There were emanations from other Florida decisions that made the majority on the Court of Appeals feel that Florida would follow that reading of Diamond. Such a construction of Diamond, the Court of Appeals said, would have "the prophylactic effect of providing a disincentive to insider trading." Id., at 823. And so it would. Yet under the regime of Erie R. Co. v. Tompkins, 304 U.S. 64 (1938), a State can make just the opposite her law, providing there is no overriding federal rule which preempts state law by reason of federal curbs on trading in the stream of commerce.

The dissenter on the Court of Appeals urged that that court certify the state-law question to the Florida Supreme Court as is provided in Fla.Stat. Ann. § 25.031 and its Appellate Rule 4.61. That path is open to this Court and to any court of appeals of the United States. We have, indeed, used it before [5] as have courts of appeals.

Moreover when state law does not make the certification procedure available, a federal court not infrequently will stay its hand, remitting the parties to the state court to resolve the controlling state law on which the federal rule may turn. Kaiser Steel Corp. v. W.S. Ranch Co., 391 U.S. 593 (1968). Numerous applications of that practice are reviewed in Meredith v. Winter Haven, 320 U.S. 228 (1943), which teaches that the mere difficulty in ascertaining local law is no excuse for remitting the parties to a state tribunal for the start of another lawsuit. We do not suggest that where there is doubt as to local law and where the certification procedure is available, resort to it is obligatory. It does, of course, in the long run save time, energy, and resources and helps build a cooperative judicial federalism. Its use in a given case rests in the sound discretion of the federal court.

Here resort to it would seem particularly appropriate in view of the novelty of the question and the great unsettlement of Florida law, Florida being a distant State. When federal judges in New York attempt to predict uncertain Florida law, they act, as we have referred to ourselves on this Court in matters of state law, as "outsiders" lacking the common exposure to local law which comes from sitting in the jurisdiction.

"Reading the Texas statutes and the Texas decisions as outsiders without special competence in Texas law, we would have little confidence in our independent judgment regarding the application of that law to the present situation. The lower court did deny that the Texas statutes sustained the Commission's assertion of power. And this represents the view of an able and experienced circuit judge of the circuit which includes Texas and of two capable district judges trained in Texas law." Railroad Comm'n v. Pullman Co., 312 U.S. 496, 499 (1941).

The judgment of the Court of Appeals is vacated and the cases are remanded so that that court may reconsider whether the controlling issue of Florida law should be certified to the Florida Supreme Court pursuant to Rule 4.61 of the Florida Appellate Rules.

MR. JUSTICE REHNQUIST, concurring.

* * *

State certification procedures are a very desirable means by which a federal court may ascertain an undecided point of state law, especially where, as is the case in Florida, the question can be certified directly to the court of last resort within the State. But in a purely diversity case such as this one, the use of such a procedure is more a question of the considerable discretion of the federal court in going about the decisionmaking process

5. Aldrich v. Aldrich, 375 U.S. 249 (1963); Dresner v. City of Tallahassee, 375 U.S. 136 (1963).

than it is a question of a choice trenching upon the fundamentals of our federal-state jurisprudence.

While certification may engender less delay and create fewer additional expenses for litigants than would abstention, it entails more delay and expense than would an ordinary decision of the state question on the merits by the federal court. * * *

If a district court or court of appeals believes that it can resolve an issue of state law with available research materials already at hand, and makes the effort to do so, its determination should not be disturbed simply because the certification procedure existed but was not used. The question of whether certification on the facts of this case, particularly in view of the lateness of its suggestion by petitioners, would have advanced the goal of correctly disposing of this litigation on the state law issue is one which I would leave, and I understand that the Court would leave, to the sound judgment of the court making the initial choice. But since the Court has today for the first time expressed its view as to the use of certification procedures by the federal courts, I agree that it is appropriate to vacate the judgment of the Court of Appeals and remand the cases in order that the Court of Appeals may reconsider certification in light of the Court's opinion.

[On remand, the court of appeals certified the questions of state law to the Florida Supreme Court, which declared that there was no liability under Florida law. The court of appeals then reversed its initial determination and ordered dismissal of the action. 519 F.2d 453 (2d Cir.1975).]

NOTE ON CERTIFICATION OF QUESTIONS OF STATE LAW

(1) The Supreme Court first ordered a lower federal court to avail itself of state certification procedures in Clay v. Sun Ins. Office, Ltd., 363 U.S. 207 (1960), described at p. 1362, *supra*. Chief Justice Warren and Justices Black and Douglas dissented; the dissent of Justice Douglas (who wrote the Lehman Brothers opinion) objected to the delay involved.

The Clay case arose in Florida, which from 1945–65 was the only state with a statute authorizing its courts to answer certified questions. It is reported that as of 1986, 36 jurisdictions (including Puerto Rico) had enacted laws or rules providing for certification, with many states basing their provisions on the Uniform Certification of Questions of Law Act, 12 U.L.A. 52 (1967), adopted by the Commissioners on Uniform State Laws. See 17 Wright, Miller & Cooper, Federal Practice & Procedure § 4248 (1978 & 1986 Supp.).

(2) All states with certification procedures will respond to a question certified from the Supreme Court or a federal court of appeals; most but not all will also accept certified questions from a federal district court. See Seron, Certifying Questions of State Law: Experience of Federal Judges 2 (Federal Judicial Center 1983).[1] A federal court certifying a question of state law retains jurisdiction while awaiting a response.

---

1. Most states require that the certified question be potentially determinative of the case. Thus, in Abrams v. West Virginia Racing Com'n, 164 W.Va. 315, 263 S.E.2d 103 (1980), the Court refused to decide a certified question because it believed that federal law would control regardless of the answer. Some states, however, impose the stricter requirement that the answer will certainly determine the case.

Is the state court's response as much entitled to full faith and credit under 28 U.S.C. § 1738 as an ordinary state court judgment?

(3) Certification tends to involve less time, money, and procedural complexity than other methods of shuttling back and forth between federal and state courts. A recent study of 48 cases in which certification was used found a median time of six months from certification to obtaining the state's answer, though the range extended from less than one month to two and a half years. Seron, Paragraph (2), *supra*, at 16. Some federal courts have nonetheless been reluctant to certify questions in view of the anticipated delay. See, *e.g.*, State ex rel. Shevin v. Exxon Corp., 526 F.2d 266, 275–76 (5th Cir.1976); Roth, *Certified Questions from the Federal Courts: Review and Re-proposal*, 34 U.Miami L.Rev. 1 (1979).

The majority of commentators have been enthusiastic about certification, especially as a substitute for a state declaratory judgment action. But there is always the danger that the certified question will be badly drafted, too abstract,[2] or misunderstood by the state court, or that the federal court will be unsure of the significance of the answer.

(4) Should the Supreme Court's enthusiasm in Lehman Brothers for certification carry over from diversity cases to federal question cases? When Pullman abstention is warranted in any event, should federal courts use certification if it is available? See Field, *The Abstention Doctrine Today*, 125 U.Pa.L.Rev. 590, 605–09 (1977). Does Congress have the power to require states to entertain certified questions—and if so, should that power be exercised? Compare Kurland, *Mr. Justice Frankfurter, The Supreme Court and the Erie Doctrine in Diversity Cases*, 67 Yale L.J. 187, 214 (1957), with ALI Study at 295.

Should the availability of certification make a federal court more willing to abstain in Pullman-type cases? In Bellotti v. Baird, 428 U.S. 132, 151 (1976), the Court said: "The importance of speed in resolution of the instant litigation is manifest. * * * Although we do not mean to intimate that abstention would be improper in this case were certification not possible, the availability of certification greatly simplifies the analysis." See also Elkins v. Moreno, 435 U.S. 647, 662 n. 15 (1978); Planned Parenthood Ass'n of Kansas City, Mo., Inc. v. Ashcroft, 462 U.S. 476, 493 n. 21 (1983) (noting as one reason for refusing to abstain that Missouri had no certification procedure, and that "[s]uch a procedure 'greatly simplifie[d]' our analysis in Bellotti * * *.") But *cf.* Houston v. Hill, 107 S.Ct. 2502, 2514–15 (1987) (the availability of certification, though important in deciding whether to abstain, "is not in itself sufficient to render abstention appropriate"). Is there a risk that the availability of certification procedures will invite improvident abstention in Pullman-type cases?[3]

See Note, 59 Notre Dame L.Rev. 1339, 1349 (1984). How often will an answer *either way* determine the outcome? Doesn't this stricter requirement make certification virtually unavailable in Pullman-type cases?

2. In In re Richards, 223 A.2d 827 (Me. 1966), the Maine Supreme Judicial Court refused to answer a certified question on the ground that, because appropriate findings had not been made by the federal court, the question was not ripe for determination. Most states require, however,

that the certified question be accompanied by a statement of facts, which is often drafted by the parties. See Note, note 1, *supra*, at 1354–55.

3. The study mentioned above found some reluctance on the part of federal judges to certify questions in constitutional or civil rights cases; nearly two-thirds of all certified questions arose in diversity actions like Lehman Brothers. Seron, Paragraph (2), *supra*, at 7–10.

(5) Judge Butzner reported in 1985 that the Fourth Circuit had certified fewer than a half-dozen of the approximately 23,000 cases filed since 1972. Butzner & Kelly, *Certification: Assuring the Primacy of State Law in the Fourth Circuit,* 42 Wash. & Lee L.Rev. 449, 455 (1985). And several years earlier, Chief Judge Brown stated that the Fifth Circuit has "reserved certification only for use in cases where important, probably recurrent state issues are involved." Brown, *Certification—Federalism in Action,* 7 Cumb.L.Rev. 455, 457 (1977). But some decisions suggest a degree of enthusiasm for the device more likely to lead to its routine use than to its reservation for unusually important issues. See Walters v. Inexco Oil Co., 670 F.2d 476 (5th Cir.1982), a diversity case in which Judge Brown, in certifying a "narrow" question of Mississippi law to the state supreme court, without any finding that the issue was recurrent or of special significance, "seize[d] the opportunity to praise, extol, laud and proclaim the virtues of this wonderful device" (pp. 477–78).

(6) Can Lehman Brothers be squared with the ruling in Meredith v. Winter Haven, p. 1369, *supra,* that a federal court should not refuse to exercise diversity jurisdiction merely because the case involves a difficult question of state law? The Court went out of its way to reaffirm Meredith in dictum in McNeese v. Board of Educ., 373 U.S. 668, 673 n. 5 (1963); see also Colorado River Water Cons. Dist. v. United States, 424 U.S. 800 (1976), Sec. 2(D), *infra.*

Does Lehman Brothers suggest that certification is always appropriate in a case involving unsettled law of a state outside the federal court's jurisdiction? Should federal courts be less willing to certify unsettled issues of the law of local states? What standards can a lower court judge distill from the opinion in Lehman Brothers to guide the exercise of "sound discretion" in deciding whether to abstain?

(7) For further discussion of certification procedures, *see,* in addition to the sources cited above, Lillich & Mundy, *Federal Court Certification of Doubtful State Law Questions,* 18 U.C.L.A.L.Rev. 888 (1971); McKusick, *Certification: A Procedure for Cooperation between State and Federal Courts,* 16 Me.L.Rev. 33 (1964); Mattis, *Certification of Questions of State Law: An Impractical Tool in the Hands of the Federal Courts,* 23 U.Miami L.Rev. 717 (1969); Note, 111 U.Pa.L.Rev. 344 (1963).

SUBSECTION C: EQUITABLE RESTRAINT

YOUNGER v. HARRIS

401 U.S. 37, 91 S.Ct. 746, 27 L.Ed.2d 669 (1971).
Appeal from the United States District Court for the Central
District of California.

MR. JUSTICE BLACK delivered the opinion of the Court.

Appellee, John Harris, Jr., was indicted in a California state court, charged with violation of the California Penal Code §§ 11400 and 11401, known as the California Criminal Syndicalism Act ∗ ∗ ∗. He then filed a complaint in the Federal District Court, asking that court to enjoin the appellant, Younger, the District Attorney of Los Angeles County, from prosecuting him, and alleging that the prosecution and even the presence of the Act inhibited him in the exercise of his rights of free speech and press, rights guaranteed him by the First and Fourteenth Amendments. Appellees Jim Dan and Diane Hirsch intervened as plaintiffs in the suit, claiming that the prosecution of Harris would inhibit them as members of the Progressive Labor Party from peacefully advocating the program of their party, which was to replace capitalism with socialism and to abolish the profit system of production in this country. Appellee Farrell Broslawsky, an instructor in history at Los Angeles Valley College, also intervened claiming that the prosecution of Harris made him uncertain as to whether he could teach about the doctrines of Karl Marx or read from the Communist Manifesto as part of his classwork. All claimed that unless the United States court restrained the state prosecution of Harris each would suffer immediate and irreparable injury. A three-judge Federal District Court, convened pursuant to 28 U.S.C. § 2284, held that it had jurisdiction and power to restrain the District Attorney from prosecuting, held that the State's Criminal Syndicalism Act was void for vagueness and overbreadth in violation of the First and Fourteenth Amendments, and accordingly restrained the District Attorney from "further prosecution of the currently pending action against plaintiff Harris for alleged violation of the Act."

The case is before us on appeal by the State's District Attorney Younger, pursuant to 28 U.S.C. § 1253. In his notice of appeal and his jurisdictional statement appellant presented two questions: (1) whether the decision of this Court in Whitney v. California, 274 U.S. 357, holding California's law constitutional in 1927 was binding on the District Court and (2) whether the State's law is constitutional on its face. In this Court the brief for the State of California, filed at our request, also argues that only Harris, who was indicted, has standing to challenge the State's law, and that issuance of the injunction was a violation of a longstanding judicial policy and of 28 U.S.C. § 2283 * * *. Without regard to the questions raised about Whitney v. California, *supra*, since overruled by Brandenburg v. Ohio, 395 U.S. 444 (1969), or the constitutionality of the state law, we have concluded that the judgment of the District Court, enjoining appellant Younger from prosecuting under these California statutes, must be reversed as a violation of the national policy forbidding federal courts to stay or enjoin pending state court proceedings except under special circumstances.[2] We express no view about the circumstances under which federal courts may act when there is no prosecution pending in state courts at the time the federal proceeding is begun.

I

Appellee Harris has been indicted, and was actually being prosecuted by California for a violation of its Criminal Syndicalism Act at the time this suit was filed. He thus has an acute, live controversy with the State and its prosecutor. But none of the other parties plaintiff in the District

---

2. Appellees did not explicitly ask for a declaratory judgment in their complaint. They did, however, ask the District Court to grant "such other and further relief as to the Court may seem just and proper," and the District Court in fact granted a declaratory judgment. For the reasons stated in our opinion today in Samuels v. Mackell, 401 U.S. 66, we hold that declaratory relief is also improper when a prosecution involving the challenged statute is pending in state court at the time the federal suit is initiated.

Court, Dan, Hirsch, or Broslawsky, has such a controversy. None has been indicted, arrested, or even threatened by the prosecutor. * * *

Whatever right Harris, who is being prosecuted under the state syndicalism law may have, Dan, Hirsch, and Broslawsky cannot share it with him. If these three had alleged that they would be prosecuted for the conduct they planned to engage in, and if the District Court had found this allegation to be true—either on the admission of the State's district attorney or on any other evidence—then a genuine controversy might be said to exist. But here appellees, Dan, Hirsch, and Broslawsky do not claim that they have ever been threatened with prosecution, that a prosecution is likely, or even that a prosecution is remotely possible. They claim the right to bring this suit solely because, in the language of their complaint, they "feel inhibited." We do not think this allegation even if true, is sufficient to bring the equitable jurisdiction of the federal courts into play to enjoin a pending state prosecution. A federal lawsuit to stop a prosecution in a state court is a serious matter. And persons having no fears of state prosecution except those that are imaginary or speculative, are not to be accepted as appropriate plaintiffs in such cases. See Golden v. Zwickler, 394 U.S. 103 (1969). Since Harris is actually being prosecuted under the challenged laws, however, we proceed with him as a proper party.

II

Since the beginning of this country's history Congress has, subject to few exceptions, manifested a desire to permit state courts to try state cases free from interference by federal courts. In 1793 an Act unconditionally provided: "[N]or shall a writ of injunction be granted to stay proceedings in any court of a state * * *." A comparison of the 1793 Act with 28 U.S.C. § 2283, its present-day successor, graphically illustrates how few and minor have been the exceptions granted from the flat, prohibitory language of the old Act. During all this lapse of years from 1793 to 1970 the statutory exceptions to the 1793 congressional enactment have been only three: (1) "except as expressly authorized by Act of Congress"; (2) "where necessary in aid of its jurisdiction"; and (3) "to protect or effectuate its judgments." In addition, a judicial exception to the longstanding policy evidenced by the statute has been made where a person about to be prosecuted in a state court can show that he will, if the proceeding in the state court is not enjoined, suffer irreparable damages. See Ex parte Young, 209 U.S. 123 (1908).

The precise reasons for this longstanding public policy against federal court interference with state court proceedings have never been specifically identified but the primary sources of the policy are plain. One is the basic doctrine of equity jurisprudence that courts of equity should not act, and particularly should not act to restrain a criminal prosecution, when the moving party has an adequate remedy at law and will not suffer irreparable injury if denied equitable relief. The doctrine may originally have grown out of circumstances peculiar to the English judicial system and not applicable in this country, but its fundamental purpose of restraining equity jurisdiction within narrow limits is equally important under our Constitution, in order to prevent erosion of the role of the jury and avoid a duplication of legal proceedings and legal sanctions where a single suit would be adequate to protect the rights asserted. This underlying reason for restraining courts of equity from interfering with criminal prosecutions is reinforced by an even more vital consideration, the notion of "comity," that is, a proper respect for state functions, a recognition of the fact that the entire country is made up of a Union of separate state governments, and a continuance of the belief that the National Government will fare best if the States and their institutions are left free to perform their separate functions in their separate ways. This, perhaps for lack of a better and clearer way to describe it, is referred to by many as "Our Federalism," and one familiar with the profound debates that ushered our Federal Constitution into existence is bound to respect those who remain loyal to the ideals and dreams of "Our Federalism." The concept does not mean blind deference to "States' Rights" any more than it means centralization of control over every important issue in our National Government and its courts. The Framers rejected both these courses. What the concept does represent is a system in which there is sensitivity to the legitimate interests of both State and National Governments, and in which the National Government, anxious though it may be to vindicate and protect federal rights and federal interests, always endeavors to do so in ways that will not unduly interfere with the legitimate activities of the States. It should never be forgotten that this slogan, "Our Federalism," born in the early struggling days of our Union of States, occupies a highly important place in our Nation's history and its future.

This brief discussion should be enough to suggest some of the reasons why it has been perfectly natural for our cases to repeat time and time again that the normal thing to do when federal courts are asked to enjoin pending proceedings in state courts is not to issue such injunctions. In Fenner v. Boykin, 271 U.S. 240 (1926), suit had been brought in the Federal District Court seeking to enjoin state prosecutions under a recently enacted state law that allegedly interfered with the free flow of interstate commerce. The Court, in a unanimous opinion made clear that such a suit, even with respect to state criminal proceedings not yet formally instituted, could be proper only under very special circumstances:

> "Ex parte Young, 209 U.S. 123, and following cases have established the doctrine that, when absolutely necessary for protection of constitutional rights, courts of the United States have power to enjoin state officers from instituting criminal actions. But this may not be done, except under extraordinary circumstances, where the danger of irreparable loss is both great and immediate. Ordinarily, there should be no interference with such officers; primarily, they are charged with the duty of prosecuting offenders against the laws of the state, and must decide when and how this is to be done. The accused should first set up and rely upon his defense in the state courts, even though this involves a challenge of the validity of some statute, unless it plainly appears that this course would not afford adequate protection." *Id.*, at 243–244.

These principles, made clear in the Fenner case, have been repeatedly followed and reaffirmed in other cases involving threatened prosecutions. See, *e.g.*, Spielman Motor Sales Co. v. Dodge, 295 U.S. 89 (1935); Beal v. Missouri Pac. R. Co., 312 U.S. 45 (1941); Watson v. Buck, 313 U.S. 387 (1941); Williams v. Miller, 317 U.S. 599 (1942); Douglas v. City of Jeannette, 319 U.S. 157 (1943).

In all of these cases the Court stressed the importance of showing irreparable injury, the traditional prerequisite to obtaining an injunction. In addition, however, the Court also made clear that in view of the fundamental policy against federal interference with state criminal prosecutions, even irreparable injury is insufficient unless it is "both great and immediate." Fenner, *supra*. Certain types of injury, in particular, the cost, anxiety, and inconvenience of having to defend against a single criminal prosecution, could not by themselves be considered "irreparable" in the special legal sense of that term. Instead, the threat to the plaintiff's federally protected rights must be one that cannot be eliminated by his defense against a single criminal prosecution. * * *

This is where the law stood when the Court decided Dombrowski v. Pfister, 380 U.S. 479 (1965), and held that an injunction against the enforcement of certain state criminal statutes could properly issue under the circumstances presented in that case.[4] In Dombrowski, unlike many of the earlier cases denying injunctions, the complaint made substantial allegations that: "the threats to enforce the statutes against appellants are not made with any expectation of securing valid convictions, but rather are part of a plan to employ arrests, seizures, and threats of prosecution under color of the statutes to harass appellants and discourage them and their supporters from asserting and attempting to vindicate the constitutional rights of Negro citizens of Louisiana."

The appellants in Dombrowski had offered to prove that their offices had been raided and all their files and records seized pursuant to search and arrest warrants that were later summarily vacated by a state judge for lack of probable cause. They also offered to prove that despite the state court order quashing the warrants and suppressing the evidence seized, the prosecutor was continuing to threaten to initiate new prosecutions of appellants under the same statutes, was holding public hearings at which photostatic copies of the illegally seized documents were being used, and was threatening to use other copies of the illegally seized documents to obtain grand jury indictments against the appellants on charges of violating the same statutes. These circumstances, as viewed by the Court sufficiently establish the kind of irreparable injury, above and beyond that associated with the defense of a single prosecution brought in good faith,

---

4. Neither the cases dealing with standing to raise claims of vagueness or overbreadth, *e.g.*, Thornhill v. Alabama, 310 U.S. 88 (1940), nor the loyalty oath cases, *e.g.*, Baggett v. Bullitt, 377 U.S. 360 (1964), changed the basic principles governing the propriety of injunctions against state criminal prosecutions. In the standing cases we allowed attacks on overly broad or vague statutes in the absence of any showing that the defendant's conduct could not be regulated by some properly drawn statute. But in each of these cases the statute was not merely vague or overly broad "on its face"; the statute was held to be vague or overly broad as construed and *applied* to a particular defendant in a particular case. If the statute had been too vague as written but sufficiently narrow as applied, prosecutions and convictions under it would ordinarily have been permissible.

See Dombrowski, *supra*, 380 U.S., at 491 n. 7.

In Baggett and similar cases we enjoined state officials from discharging employees who failed to take certain loyalty oaths. We held that the States were without power to exact the promises involved, with their vague and uncertain content concerning advocacy and political association, as a condition of employment. Apart from the fact that any plaintiff discharged for exercising his constitutional right to refuse to take the oath would have had no adequate remedy at law, the relief sought was of course the kind that raises no special problem—an injunction against allegedly unconstitutional state action (discharging the employees) that is not part of a criminal prosecution.

that had always been considered sufficient to justify federal intervention. See, *e.g.*, Beal, *supra*, 312 U.S., at 50. Indeed, after quoting the Court's statement in Douglas [v. City of Jeanette, *supra*] concerning the very restricted circumstances under which an injunction could be justified, the Court in Dombrowski went on to say:

"But the allegations in this complaint depict a situation in which defense of the State's criminal prosecution will not assure adequate vindication of constitutional rights. They suggest that a substantial loss of or impairment of freedoms of expression will occur if appellants must await the state court's disposition and ultimate review in this Court of any adverse determination. These allegations, if true, clearly show irreparable injury." 380 U.S., at 485–486.

And the Court made clear that even under these circumstances the District Court issuing the injunction would have continuing power to lift it at any time and remit the plaintiffs to the state courts if circumstances warranted. 380 U.S., at 491, 492. * * *

It is against the background of these principles that we must judge the propriety of an injunction under the circumstances of the present case. Here a proceeding was already pending in the state court, affording Harris an opportunity to raise his constitutional claims. There is no suggestion that this single prosecution against Harris is brought in bad faith or is only one of a series of repeated prosecutions to which he will be subjected. In other words, the injury that Harris faces is solely "that incidental to every criminal proceeding brought lawfully and in good faith," Douglas, *supra*, and therefore under the settled doctrine we have already described he is not entitled to equitable relief "even if such statutes are unconstitutional," Buck, *supra*.

The District Court, however, thought that the Dombrowski decision substantially broadened the availability of injunctions against state criminal prosecutions and that under that decision the federal courts may give equitable relief, without regard to any showing of bad faith or harassment, whenever a state statute is found "on its face" to be vague or overly broad, in violation of the First Amendment. We recognize that there are some statements in the Dombrowski opinion that would seem to support this argument. But, as we have already seen, such statements were unnecessary to the decision of that case, because the Court found that the plaintiffs had alleged a basis for equitable relief under the long-established standards. In addition, we do not regard the reasons adduced to support this position as sufficient to justify such a substantial departure from the established doctrines regarding the availability of injunctive relief. It is undoubtedly true, as the Court stated in Dombrowski, that "[a] criminal prosecution under a statute regulating expression usually involves imponderables and contingencies that themselves may inhibit the full exercise of First Amendment freedoms." 380 U.S., at 486. But this sort of "chilling effect," as the Court called it, should not by itself justify federal intervention. In the first place, the chilling effect cannot be satisfactorily eliminated by federal injunctive relief. In Dombrowski itself the Court stated that the injunction to be issued there could be lifted if the State obtained an "acceptable limiting construction" from the state courts. The Court then made clear that once this was done, prosecutions could then be brought for conduct occurring before the narrowing construction was made, and proper convictions could stand so long as the defendants were not deprived of fair warning. 380 U.S., at 491 n. 7. The kind of relief granted in Dombrowski thus does not effectively eliminate uncertainty as to the coverage of the state statute and leaves most citizens with virtually the same doubts as before regarding the danger that their conduct might eventually be subjected to criminal sanctions. The chilling effect can, of course, be eliminated by an injunction that would prohibit any prosecution whatever for conduct occurring prior to a satisfactory rewriting of the statute. But the States would then be stripped of all power to prosecute even the socially dangerous and constitutionally unprotected conduct that had been covered by the statute, until a new statute could be passed by the state legislature and approved by the federal courts in potentially lengthy trial and appellate proceedings. Thus, in Dombrowski itself the Court carefully reaffirmed the principle that even in the direct prosecution in the State's own courts, a valid narrowing construction can be applied to conduct occurring prior to the date when the narrowing construction was made, in the absence of fair warning problems.

Moreover, the existence of a "chilling effect," even in the area of First Amendment rights, has never been considered a sufficient basis, in and of itself, for prohibiting state action. Where a statute does not directly abridge free speech, but—while regulating a subject within the State's power—tends to have the incidental effect of inhibiting First Amendment rights, it is well settled that the statute can be upheld if the effect on speech is minor in relation to the need for control of the conduct and the lack of alternative means for doing so. Just as the incidental "chilling effect" of such statutes does not automatically render them unconstitutional, so the chilling effect that admittedly can result from the very existence of certain laws on the statute books does not in itself justify prohibiting the State from carrying out the important and necessary task of enforcing these laws against socially harmful conduct that the State believes in good faith to be punishable under its laws and the Constitution.

Beyond all this is another, more basic consideration. Procedures for testing the constitutionality of a statute "on its face" in the manner apparently contemplated by Dombrowski, and for then enjoining all action to enforce the statute until the State can obtain court approval for a modified version, are fundamentally at odds with the function of the federal courts in our constitutional plan. The power and duty of the judiciary to declare laws unconstitutional is in the final analysis derived from its responsibility for resolving concrete disputes brought before the courts for decision; a statute apparently governing a dispute cannot be applied by judges, consistently with their obligations under the Supremacy Clause, when such an application of the statute would conflict with the Constitution. Marbury v. Madison, 5 U.S. (1 Cranch) 137 (1803). But this vital responsibility, broad as it is, does not amount to an unlimited power to survey the statute books and pass judgment on laws before the courts are called upon to enforce them. Ever since the Constitutional Convention rejected a proposal for having members of the Supreme Court render advice concerning pending legislation it has been clear that, even when suits of this kind involve a "case or controversy" sufficient to satisfy the requirements of Article III of the Constitution, the task of analyzing a proposed statute, pinpointing its deficiencies, and requiring correction of these deficiencies before the statute is put into effect, is rarely if ever an appropriate task for the judiciary. The combination of the relative remoteness of the controversy, the impact on the legislative process of the relief sought, and above all the speculative and amorphous nature of the required line-by-line analysis of detailed statutes ordinarily results in a kind of case that is wholly unsatisfactory for deciding constitutional questions, whichever way they might be decided. In light of this fundamental conception of the Framers as to the proper place of the federal courts in the governmental processes of passing and enforcing laws, it can seldom be appropriate for these courts to exercise any such power of prior approval or veto over the legislative process.

For these reasons, fundamental not only to our federal system but also to the basic functions of the Judicial Branch of the National Government under our Constitution, we hold that the Dombrowski decision should not be regarded as having upset the settled doctrines that have always confined very narrowly the availability of injunctive relief against state criminal prosecutions. We do not think that opinion stands for the proposition that a federal court can properly enjoin enforcement of a statute solely on the basis of a showing that the statute "on its face" abridges First Amendment rights. There may, of course, be extraordinary circumstances in which the necessary irreparable injury can be shown even in the absence of the usual prerequisites of bad faith and harassment. For example, as long ago as the Buck case, *supra,* we indicated:

"It is of course conceivable that a statute might be flagrantly and patently violative of express constitutional prohibitions in every clause, sentence and paragraph, and in whatever manner and against whomever an effort might be made to apply it." 313 U.S., at 402.

Other unusual situations calling for federal intervention might also arise, but there is no point in our attempting now to specify what they might be. It is sufficient for purposes of the present case to hold, as we do, that the possible unconstitutionality of a statute "on its face" does not in itself justify an injunction against good-faith attempts to enforce it, and that appellee Harris has failed to make any showing of bad faith, harassment, or any other unusual circumstance that would call for equitable relief. Because our holding rests on the absence of the factors necessary under equitable principles to justify federal intervention, we have no occasion to consider whether 28 U.S.C. § 2283, which prohibits an injunction against state court proceedings "except as expressly authorized by Act of Congress" would in and of itself be controlling under the circumstances of this case.

The judgment of the District Court is reversed, and the case is remanded for further proceedings not inconsistent with this opinion.

MR. JUSTICE BRENNAN with whom MR. JUSTICE WHITE and MR. JUSTICE MARSHALL join, concurring in the result.

I agree that the judgment of the District Court should be reversed. Appellee Harris had been indicted for violations of the California Criminal Syndicalism Act before he sued in federal court. He has not alleged that the prosecution was brought in bad faith to harass him. His constitutional contentions may be adequately adjudicated in the state criminal proceeding, and federal intervention at his instance was therefore improper.

* * *

MR. JUSTICE STEWART, with whom MR. JUSTICE HARLAN joins, concurring.

The questions the Court decides today are important ones. Perhaps as important, however, is a recognition of the areas into which today's holdings do not necessarily extend. In all of these cases, the Court deals only with the proper policy to be followed by a federal court when asked to intervene by injunction or declaratory judgment in a criminal prosecution which is contemporaneously pending in a state court.

In basing its decisions on policy grounds, the Court does not reach any questions concerning the independent force of the federal anti-injunction statute, 28 U.S.C. § 2283. Thus we do not decide whether the word "injunction" in § 2283 should be interpreted to include a declaratory judgment, or whether an injunction to stay proceedings in a state court is "expressly authorized" by § 1 of the Civil Rights Act of 1871, now 42 U.S.C. § 1983. And since all these cases involve state criminal prosecutions, we do not deal with the considerations that should govern a federal court when it is asked to intervene in state civil proceedings, where, for various reasons, the balance might be struck differently.[2] Finally, the Court today does not resolve the problems involved when a federal court is asked to give injunctive or declaratory relief from *future* state criminal prosecutions.

The Court confines itself to deciding the policy considerations that in our federal system must prevail when federal courts are asked to interfere with pending state prosecutions. Within this area, we hold that a federal court must not, save in exceptional and extremely limited circumstances, intervene by way of either injunction or declaration in an existing state criminal prosecution.[3] Such circumstances exist only when there is a threat of irreparable injury "both great and immediate." A threat of this nature might be shown if the state criminal statute in question were patently and flagrantly unconstitutional on its face ∗ ∗ ∗ or if there has been bad faith and harassment—official lawlessness—in a statute's enforcement ∗ ∗ ∗. ∗ ∗ ∗

MR. JUSTICE DOUGLAS, dissenting.

∗ ∗ ∗

Dombrowski represents an exception to the general rule that federal courts should not interfere with state criminal prosecutions. The exception does not arise merely because prosecutions are threatened to which the First Amendment will be the proffered defense. Dombrowski governs statutes which are a blunderbuss by themselves or when used *en masse* — those that have an "overbroad" sweep. ∗ ∗ ∗

∗ ∗ ∗

Harris' "crime" was distributing leaflets advocating change in industrial ownership through political action. The statute under which he was

2. Courts of equity have traditionally shown greater reluctance to intervene in criminal prosecutions than in civil cases. See Younger v. Harris, 401 U.S., at 43–44; Douglas v. City of Jeannette, 319 U.S. 157, 163–164. The offense to state interests is likely to be less in a civil proceeding. A State's decision to classify conduct as criminal provides some indication of the importance it has ascribed to prompt and unencumbered enforcement of its law. By contrast, the State might not even be a party in a proceeding under a civil statute.

These considerations would not, to be sure, support any distinction between civil and criminal proceedings should the ban of 28 U.S.C. § 2283, which makes no such distinction, be held unaffected by 42 U.S.C. § 1983.

3. The negative pregnant in this sentence—that a federal court may, as a matter of policy, intervene when such "exceptional and extremely limited circumstances" are found—is subject to any further limitations that may be placed on such intervention by 28 U.S.C. § 2283.

indicted was the one involved in Whitney v. California, 274 U.S. 357, a decision we overruled in Brandenburg v. Ohio, 395 U.S. 444, 449.

If the "advocacy" which Harris used was an attempt at persuasion through the use of bullets, bombs, and arson, we would have a different case. But Harris is charged only with distributing leaflets advocating political action toward his objective. He tried unsuccessfully to have the state court dismiss the indictment on constitutional grounds. He resorted to the state appellate court for writs of prohibition to prevent the trial, but to no avail. He went to the federal court as a matter of last resort in an effort to keep this unconstitutional trial from being saddled on him.

* * *

NOTE ON THE HISTORY OF THE EQUITABLE RESTRAINT DOCTRINE

(1) *The Problem of Equitable Restraint: English Origins.* A venerable maxim is that equity will not enjoin a criminal proceeding. It is unclear whether this rule arose from the English Court of Chancery's exclusive concern with matters involving property rights, or its renunciation of criminal jurisdiction when the common law courts began to enforce criminal sanctions. See Shapiro, *Jurisdiction and Discretion,* 60 N.Y.U.L.Rev. 543, 550 n. 37 (1985); Whitten, *Federal Declaratory and Injunctive Interference with State Court Proceedings: The Supreme Court and the Limits of Judicial Discretion,* 53 N.C.L.Rev. 591, 597–600 (1975). But from the beginning that principle was subject to exceptions: for example, a court of equity would enjoin a party from litigating the same matter in a later-commenced criminal action, *id.* at 598, and some American cases permitted an injunction against a criminal prosecution that would infringe property rights, see Davis & Farnum Mfg. Co. v. Los Angeles, 189 U.S. 207, 277 (1903); Fitts v. McGhee, 172 U.S. 516, 531–32 (1899).

Also of importance are the maxims that equity will not provide relief unless (i) there is no adequate remedy at law and (ii) the plaintiff is threatened with irreparable injury. Although often treated together, these were, at least in origin, distinct requirements: the former addressed the jurisdictional boundaries of the courts of law and equity, while the latter went to the propriety of awarding relief that the court was empowered to grant. See Shapiro, *supra,* at 548. The legal remedy of defending a criminal proceeding was ordinarily considered adequate, so that absent unusual circumstances—for example, the threat of multiple prosecutions under an invalid law—equity would not intervene to spare a defendant the burdens of a criminal prosecution. Whitten, *supra,* at 600–04.

(2) *Reception in the United States.* Section 16 of the First Judiciary Act stated that "suits in equity shall not be sustained in * * * the courts of United States, in any case where plain, adequate, and complete remedy may be had at law," 1 Stat. 82, a limitation repealed in 1948, see p. 808, *supra.* That provision defeated the plaintiff's case for equitable relief, however, only if the remedy was available on the law side of a *federal* court; it was not intended to affect the plaintiff's right to a federal—as against a state—forum. See Atlas Life Ins. Co. v. W.I. Southern, Inc., 306 U.S. 563, 569 (1939).

What should be the relevance of a *state* court remedy, by way of defense to a criminal prosecution, in an action seeking federal equitable relief against state prosecution? How does the availability of such a remedy bear on the question whether the criminal defendant faces the threat of irreparable injury? See Soifer & Macgill, *The Younger Doctrine: Reconstructing Reconstruction,* 55 Tex.L.Rev. 1141, 1158 (1977). Does the answer depend on whether federal relief is sought against prosecution for past conduct, as in Younger, rather than against conduct to be carried out in the future?

(3) *Ex Parte Young.* Ex parte Young, p. 1173, *supra,* though best known for its Eleventh Amendment holding, is also a key precedent for federal equitable intervention in state prosecutions.[1] The lower court, it will be recalled, had enjoined the Attorney General of Minnesota from enforcing certain railroad rate regulations alleged to deny due process. In upholding the injunction, the Supreme Court stated that, to the "general rule" that "equity has no jurisdiction to enjoin [state] criminal proceedings, * * * there are exceptions. When such * * * [a] proceeding is brought to enforce an alleged unconstitutional statute, which is the subject matter of inquiry in a suit already pending in a Federal court, the latter court having first obtained jurisdiction over the subject matter, has the right, in both civil and criminal cases, to hold and maintain such jurisdiction, to the exclusion of all other courts, until its duty is fully performed. But the Federal court cannot, of course, interfere in a case where the proceedings were already pending in a state court" (pp. 161–62).

The Court in Young also rejected the Attorney General's argument that the railroads had an adequate remedy at law—namely, to disobey the statute and then challenge its constitutionality in a subsequent prosecution. In part this conclusion was based on the difficulty for the railroad of finding an employee willing to risk imprisonment in order to set up a test case. But the opinion also contains a broader argument. On the one hand, compliance with the law prior to an ultimate determination of its unconstitutionality would result in a taking of the company's property without possibility of recovery. On the other hand, "to await proceedings against the company in a state court grounded upon a disobedience of the act [and then if necessary seek Supreme Court review] would place the company in great risk of large loss and its agents in peril of fines and imprisonment if it should be finally determined that the act was valid. This risk the company ought not to be required to take" (p. 165).

(4) *Douglas v. City of Jeannette.* Alongside Ex parte Young and similar cases are other federal decisions expressing deep reluctance to interfere with criminal proceedings. An influential statement of this view is found in Douglas v. City of Jeannette, 319 U.S. 157 (1943). The suit was a class action by Jehovah's Witnesses—whose religious practice was to distribute books door-to-door—seeking to restrain, as a violation of the First Amendment, their threatened prosecution under a city ordinance forbidding solicitation of orders for merchandise without a license. The com-

---

1. For discussion of the precedents prior to Young, see Isseks, *Jurisdiction of the Lower Federal Courts to Enjoin Unauthorized Action of State Officials,* 40 Harv.L. Rev. 969 (1927); Taylor & Willis, *The Power of Federal Courts to Enjoin Proceedings in State Courts,* 42 Yale L.J. 1169, 1190–92 (1942); Warren, *Federal and State Court Interference,* 43 Harv.L.Rev. 345, 372–74 (1930); B. Wechsler, *Federal Courts, State Criminal Law and the First Amendment,* 49 N.Y.U.L.Rev. 740, 753–62 (1974); Whitten, Paragraph (1), *supra,* at 629–30.

plaint alleged that the plaintiffs had already been arrested and prosecuted for violating the ordinance, and that continued enforcement of the ordinance was threatened.

The Court, per Stone, C.J., held that the suit should be dismissed for want of equity (pp. 162–64):

"The power reserved to the states under the Constitution to provide for the determination of controversies in their courts may be restricted by federal district courts only in obedience to Congressional legislation in conformity to the judiciary Article of the Constitution. Congress, by its legislation, has adopted the policy, with certain well defined statutory exceptions, of leaving generally to the state courts the trial of criminal cases arising under state laws, subject to review by this Court of any federal questions involved. Hence, courts of equity in the exercise of their discretionary powers should conform to this policy by refusing to interfere with or embarrass threatened proceedings in state courts save in those exceptional cases which call for the interposition of a court of equity to prevent irreparable injury which is clear and imminent; and equitable remedies infringing this independence of the states—though they might otherwise be given—should be withheld if sought on slight or inconsequential grounds.   *   *   *

"It is a familiar rule that courts of equity do not ordinarily restrain criminal prosecutions. No person is immune from prosecution in good faith for his alleged criminal acts. Its imminence, even though alleged to be in violation of constitutional guaranties, is not a ground for equity relief since the lawfulness or constitutionality of the statute or ordinance on which the prosecution is based may be determined as readily in the criminal case as in a suit for an injunction. Davis & Farnum Mfg. Co. v. Los Angeles, 189 U.S. 207; Fenner v. Boykin, 271 U.S. 240. Where the threatened prosecution is by state officers for alleged violations of a state law, the state courts are the final arbiters of its meaning and application, subject only to review by this Court on federal grounds appropriately asserted. Hence the arrest by the federal courts of the processes of the criminal law within the states, and the determination of questions of criminal liability under state law by a federal court of equity, are to be supported only on a showing of danger of irreparable injury 'both great and immediate.'   *   *   * "

Is it appropriate to use "doctrines of equity—doctrines forged in the battles of English Chancery—to further views of federalism, a political principle central to American Government"? See Fiss, *Dombrowski*, 86 Yale L.J. 1103, 1107 (1977), for a negative view. Compare the line of equity cases declining, both prior and subsequent to enactment of the Tax Injunction Act, to restrain collection of state taxes in the face of an adequate *state* remedy at law. See pp. 1339–42, *supra.*

(5) *The Meaning of Douglas.* Douglas has sometimes been taken as representing a general policy restricting federal injunctions against the enforcement of state criminal laws. See, *e.g.,* Dombrowski v. Pfister, Paragraph (6), *infra.*[2] But the earlier case law had already made clear that

---

2. On the same day Douglas was decided, the Court, in reviewing the criminal convictions of some Jehovah's Witnesses who had already violated the ordinance, held it unconstitutional. Murdock v. Pennsylvania, 319 U.S. 105 (1943). In view of that authoritative ruling, the plaintiffs in Douglas did not face the same dilemma, as to their continuing conduct, faced by the plaintiffs in Ex parte Young—either obey-

the impact of this equity rule must be assessed in light of the highly varied situations in which it might be deemed to have relevance:

(a) *Past Conduct.* Is a court of equity ever warranted in enjoining a threatened prosecution for an act already done, simply to protect the complainant from the stigma or burden of a criminal prosecution, when there is no showing of threatened interference with a continuing course of conduct? Injunctions were denied in situations seemingly of this type in Fenner v. Boykin, 271 U.S. 240 (1926), and Spielman Motor Sales Co. v. Dodge, 295 U.S. 89 (1935); in neither case did there appear to be a pending prosecution.

(b) *Future Conduct.* Suppose the plaintiff seeks a federal injunction to avoid the risk of prosecution for a future act or series of acts? In this case, the federal plaintiff cannot litigate the constitutional issue as a defendant in a state court without first violating the statute. And Ex parte Young makes it clear that a past violation is not a precondition for a federal court constitutional challenge.[3]

(c) *Continuing Conduct.* The Douglas case involves a kind of hybrid of the prior two situations: there has already been a past violation of the statute that is or could be the subject of pending prosecution; but the actors wish to engage in similar conduct in the future. In denying relief, the Court relied upon Fenner and Spielman, *supra* (though those cases are readily distinguishable in that they involved past conduct only), as well as two other cases.

In one, Beal v. Missouri Pac. R.R. Corp., 312 U.S. 45 (1941), a railroad brought a diversity action alleging that it was in compliance with a state full train crew law, but that state officials had misconstrued the statute and threatened prosecution. Each running of the train was a separate violation, and the railroad had surely violated the statute already, but no prosecution had been commenced. The Court ordered dismissal (pp. 50–52):

"Here the court below found danger of irreparable injury in the threatened multiplicity of prosecutions and risk that the aggregate fines which might be imposed would be very large. But whether more than one criminal prosecution is threatened was by the pleadings made an issue of fact which the district court did not resolve. If it had found after a hearing, as the answer alleges, that only a single suit is contemplated, we

ing an ordinance they believed to be unconstitutional, or risking criminal prosecution if they disobeyed and it were then held to be valid. The Douglas opinion recognizes this point, see 319 U.S. at 165, though its language is far broader.

3. That case and others involving a continuing course of conduct did not make close inquiry into the actual danger of multiple prosecutions. *E.g.,* Hygrade Provision Co. v. Sherman, 266 U.S. 497, 500 (1925). Is the case for intervention less strong when there is no risk of multiple prosecutions? Consider Terrace v. Thompson, 263 U.S. 197 (1923), in which a landowner and an alien sued to enjoin enforcement of an alien land law. The case involved in part this situation of risk of criminal liability (although the alien would

have been liable only for failure to disclose his ownership if he bought the land) and in part the risk of escheat. The Court said (263 U.S. at 216):

" * * * The owners have an interest in the freedom of the alien, and he has an interest in their freedom, to make the lease. The state act purports to operate directly upon the consummation of the proposed transaction between them, and the threat and purpose of the Attorney General to enforce the punishments and forfeiture prescribed prevent each from dealing with the other. * * * They are not obliged to take the risk of prosecution, fines and imprisonment and loss of property in order to secure an adjudication of their rights."

could not say that any such irreparable injury is threatened as would justify staying the prosecution and withdrawing the determination of the legal question from the state courts, whose appointed function is to decide it. * * *

"If its decision should be favorable to respondent no reason is shown for anticipating further prosecutions. If it were adverse, penalties in large amount, it is true, might be incurred, but they may well be the consequence of violations of state law. No question is here presented of the constitutional validity of the statute because the penalties which it inflicts are so great as to prevent recourse to the courts for the adjudication of respondent's rights under it. See Ex parte Young, 209 U.S. 123, 144."

Note, in considering how broadly this language should be read, that (i) the case raised no challenge to the statute under the federal Constitution, jurisdiction being based only on diversity of citizenship, and (ii) the opinion argued that the state courts could more appropriately determine the meaning of the state statute.

The other case, Watson v. Buck, 313 U.S. 387 (1941), involved a broad facial challenge to state antitrust legislation that had apparently already been violated. The Court refused to hear most of the challenge on the ground that it was not ripe, relying in part on the fact that enforcement was not imminently threatened, and in part (citing Pullman) on the desirability of first permitting the state courts to provide a narrowing construction of the challenged legislation.[4]

In a careful study of the origins of the equitable restraint doctrine, Professor Laycock concludes that while the language used in Douglas, Fenner, Spielman, Beal, and Watson suggests that federal injunctions should ordinarily not be issued to restrain threatened state prosecutions, neither they nor any other case squarely holds relief unavailable in a case seeking relief as to future rather than past conduct. Laycock, *Federal Interference with State Prosecutions: The Cases* Dombrowski *Forgot*, 46 U.Chi.L.Rev. 636, 644–45, 656 (1979). But *cf.* the summary affirmance in Williams, note 4, *supra*. Laycock further notes that both before and after the Douglas case, the Supreme Court approved federal injunctions against threatened prosecution for future conduct, even when the federal plaintiff wishing to engage in a continuous course of conduct was already the subject of a pending state prosecution for past conduct. See Laycock, *supra*, at 666 & n. 201. For example, in Cline v. Frink Dairy Co., 274 U.S. 445, 452–53, 466 (1927), a three-judge court had permanently enjoined state officials from bringing criminal prosecutions under an unconstitutional state statute. The Supreme Court reversed the grant of relief as to a prosecution already pending when the federal suit was filed, but affirmed the grant as to the institution of future prosecutions.

(d) *Federal Interference Short of Enjoining the Prosecution Altogether.* Under what, if any, circumstances may a federal court interfere with the use of specific evidence or testimony in a state criminal proceeding? In Stefanelli v. Minard, 342 U.S. 117 (1951), a district court was asked to

---

4. A final decision in this line—cited in Younger, but not in Douglas—is Williams v. Miller, 317 U.S. 599 (1942). In that case, a landowner who wished to build, and two prospective employees, challenged a statute requiring the work to be performed by a licensed contractor. The lower court dismissed, and the Supreme Court summarily affirmed (p. 599): "[T]he bill does not allege facts which would warrant the granting of equitable relief by a federal court to restrain enforcement of the state statute."

enjoin the use, in a state criminal proceeding, of evidence seized by state police officers in violation of the Federal Constitution. The Supreme Court held that the injunction should not issue, saying that the equity rule of Douglas v. City of Jeannette applies *a fortiori* where the request is "to intervene piecemeal to try collateral issues" in a criminal proceeding.

At the time of Stefanelli, state courts were not required to exclude such illegally seized evidence, see Wolf v. Colorado, 338 U.S. 25 (1949). Quite aside from the Douglas doctrine, therefore, was it not clear that the plaintiff's claim lacked substantive merit?

For the subsequent, often complex, development of the Stefanelli principle, see Rea v. United States, 350 U.S. 214 (1956) (federal officers enjoined from testifying in state criminal proceeding as to evidence obtained by them in violation of Fed.R.Crim.P. 41); Wilson v. Schnettler, 365 U.S. 381 (1961) (upholding refusal to enjoin federal officers from testifying where allegation that the evidence was illegally obtained was insufficient); Pugach v. Dollinger, 365 U.S. 458 (1961) (refusing to enjoin state officer from testifying as to illegal wiretap); Cleary v. Bolger, 371 U.S. 392 (1963) (reversing grant of injunction prohibiting state officer from testifying as to evidence illegally gathered by federal officers).

(6) *The Dombrowski Case.* Dombrowski v. Pfister, 380 U.S. 479 (1965), discussed at length in Younger, was an action brought by a civil rights group and affiliated individuals to enjoin state officials from prosecuting or threatening to prosecute the plaintiffs for alleged violations of two Louisiana statutes criminalizing subversive activities. The complaint alleged that the statutes were overbroad and therefore violated the First Amendment, and that the threats to enforce the statutes were "not made with any expectation of securing valid convictions," but rather as part of a plan to harass the plaintiffs and discourage their constitutionally protected activity (p. 482). After the three-judge federal district court dismissed the suit on grounds of equitable restraint, the individual plaintiffs were in fact indicted.

The Supreme Court reversed the denial of relief. Justice Brennan's majority opinion accepted as the general rule the position of the Douglas case that "the mere possibility of erroneous initial application of constitutional standards will usually not amount to the irreparable injury necessary to justify a disruption of orderly state proceedings" (pp. 484–85). But in the Court's view, the plaintiffs' allegations that the statutes were overbroad, if true, would establish the threat of "irreparable injury" warranting relief. The majority argued that when statutes are overbroad, "[t]he assumption that defense of a criminal prosecution will generally assure ample vindication of constitutional rights is unfounded * * *. * * * The chilling effect upon the exercise of First Amendment rights may derive from the fact of the prosecution, unaffected by the prospects of its success or failure" (pp. 486–87). The Court noted that the repeated invocation (and threatened invocation) of state criminal prosecutions, and concomitant searches and seizures, had frightened off potential members of the organization and "paralyzed operations," making the need for "immediate resolution" of the First Amendment claims especially pressing (p. 489).

The Court also concluded that the district court "erred in holding that it should abstain pending authoritative interpretation of the statutes in state court * * *. We hold the abstention doctrine is inappropriate for cases such as the present one where, unlike Douglas v. City of Jeannette, statutes are justifiably attacked on their face as abridging free expression, or as applied for the purpose of discouraging protected activities" (pp. 489–90). A state court's limiting construction would not eliminate the threat of bad faith harassment; moreover, citing Baggett v. Bullitt, 377 U.S. 360, 378 (1964), the Court stressed that "no readily apparent limiting construction suggests itself," and that plaintiffs were entitled to be free from the burdens of defending the multiple prosecutions necessary to hammer out the statute's meaning (p. 491).

The Court held that plaintiffs were entitled to an injunction against enforcement of the overbroad sections of one of the statutes. It then remanded, ordering the district court to frame a specific decree, to adjudicate the merits of attacks on the other challenged provisions, and to hear plaintiffs' allegations that the defendants "threaten to enforce both statutes solely to discourage [plaintiffs] from continuing their civil rights activities" (p. 497).[5]

Although the facts of Dombrowski may well have sufficed to establish bad faith, the Court's decision (and disposition) in fact appeared to create a special rule permitting federal intervention in First Amendment overbreadth cases. See Fiss, Paragraph (4), *supra*, at 1112. Does that rule survive Younger?

For discussion of the lower courts' reaction to Dombrowski prior to the Younger decision, see especially Maraist, *Federal Injunctive Relief Against State Court Proceedings: The Significance of Dombrowski*, 48 Tex.L.Rev. 535 (1970).

NOTE ON YOUNGER v. HARRIS AND THE DOCTRINE OF EQUITABLE RESTRAINT

(1) *Companion Cases.* On the day Younger was decided, the Supreme Court handed down important decisions in two companion cases.

(a) In Samuels v. Mackell, 401 U.S. 66 (1971), the Court held that the Younger doctrine applies not only to injunctive but also to declaratory relief against a pending state criminal prosecution. The Court relied heavily on Great Lakes Dredge & Dock Co. v. Huffman, 319 U.S. 293 (1943), p. 1342, *supra*, which, though not literally extending the Tax Injunction Act to restrict declaratory judgments, had as an exercise of equitable discretion refused federal declaratory relief against the imposition of state taxes.[1] Justice Black, writing for the Court, said (p. 72):

5. Justices Black and Stewart did not participate. Justice Harlan, joined by Justice Clark, dissented, objecting that "[t]his decision abolishes the doctrine of federal judicial abstention in all suits attacking state criminal statutes for vagueness on First–Fourteenth Amendment grounds," and that "[i]n practical effect the Court's decision means that a State may no longer carry on prosecutions under statutes challengeable for vagueness on 'First Amendment' grounds without the prior approval of the federal courts" (p. 498).

1. The Court subsequently held that the Tax Injunction Act itself bars federal declaratory relief. See California v. Grace Brethren Church, 457 U.S. 393 (1982), p. 1342, *supra.*

Samuels did not refer to Kennedy v. Mendoza–Martinez, 372 U.S. 144 (1963), p. 1335, *supra*, in which the Court refused to equate declaratory and injunctive relief for purposes of the three-judge court requirement.

"[O]rdinarily a declaratory judgment will result in precisely the same interference with and disruption of state proceedings that the long-standing policy limiting injunctions was designed to avoid. This is true for at least two reasons. In the first place, the Declaratory Judgment Act provides that after a declaratory judgment is issued the district court may enforce it by granting '[f]urther necessary or proper relief,' 28 U.S.C. § 2202, and therefore a declaratory judgment issued while state proceedings are pending might serve as the basis for a subsequent injunction against those proceedings to 'protect or effectuate' the declaratory judgment, 28 U.S.C. § 2283, and thus result in a clearly improper interference with the state proceedings. Secondly, even if the declaratory judgment is not used as a basis for actually issuing an injunction, the declaratory relief alone has virtually the same practical impact as a formal injunction would. As we said in [Public Service Comm'n of Utah v. Wycoff Co., 344 U.S. 237, 247 (1952)]:

> 'Is the declaration contemplated here to be res judicata, so that the [state court] cannot hear evidence and decide any matter for itself? If so, the federal court has virtually lifted the case out of the State [court] before it could be heard. If not, the federal judgment serves no useful purpose as a final determination of rights.' "

Justice Black conceded, however, that there might be "unusual circumstances" in which, despite a plaintiff's "strong claim for relief," an injunction would be withheld because it would have been "particularly intrusive or offensive," but in which "a declaratory judgment might be appropriate" (p. 73). He "express[ed] no views on the propriety of declaratory relief when no state proceeding is pending at the time the federal suit is begun" (pp. 73–74).[2]

(b) In Perez v. Ledesma, 401 U.S. 82 (1971), the federal plaintiffs were being prosecuted in state court under state and local obscenity laws. A three-judge district court had upheld the constitutionality of the *state* obscenity law, but, finding that the arrest of plaintiffs and the seizure from them of allegedly obscene materials were unlawful, issued an injunction ordering that the materials be returned to plaintiffs and not used in evidence by state prosecutors. While recognizing that a three-judge court lacked jurisdiction over the question of the validity of a local ordinance without statewide applicability, the court expressed its view that the local ordinance was unconstitutional. Thereafter, the single district judge who initially referred the case to a court of three judges issued a declaratory judgment that the *local* ordinance was unconstitutional.

On direct review, the Supreme Court applied Younger to vacate the decision upholding the *state* statute's constitutionality on the merits, holding that the three-judge court should have dismissed the action. The Court reversed the injunction against use of the seized materials, noting that that order would "effectively stifle the then-pending state criminal prosecution" (p. 84), and that "[t]he propriety of arrests and the admissibility of evidence in state criminal prosecutions are ordinarily matters to be resolved by state tribunals, see Stefanelli v. Minard, 342 U.S. 117 (1951) [p. 1396, *supra*],

---

2. Justice Douglas wrote a separate concurring opinion stressing that the prosecutions were not "palpably unconstitutional". Justice Brennan, joined by Justices White and Marshall, concurred in the judgment on the ground that the state indictment preceded the federal suit, and there were no allegations amounting to bad faith harassment.

subject, of course, to review by certiorari or appeal in this Court or, in a proper case, on federal habeas corpus" (pp. 84–85).[3] Finally, the Court ruled that it lacked jurisdiction to review directly the single judge's decision that the *local* ordinance was unconstitutional; appeal from that decision should have been taken to the court of appeals.

Justice Brennan, joined by Justices White and Marshall, dissented on this last point, concluding that the Court did have jurisdiction to review the declaratory judgment as to the local ordinance. He then argued that because criminal charges under the local ordinance had been dismissed before the three-judge court was convened, the declaratory judgment did not interfere with pending prosecutions. In a preview of the position he took for the Court in Steffel v. Thompson, p. 1406, *infra,* he argued that in such a situation, a declaratory judgment—which he called a "milder alternative" to an injunction—should be available.[4]

(2) *The Relationship of Younger to Mitchum v. Foster.* The question reserved in Younger—whether 28 U.S.C. § 2283 would bar an injunction in that case—was decided a year later in Mitchum v. Foster, 407 U.S. 225 (1972), p. 1315, *supra.* Mitchum held that injunctive relief under 42 U.S.C. § 1983 to restrain state court proceedings was "expressly authorized by Act of Congress" within the meaning of § 2283 and therefore not prohibited by that statute.

Was it appropriate for the Court in Younger to decide the case on the basis of a judge-made doctrine of equitable restraint without determining the reach of § 2283? Should the Court have suggested in dicta that in certain narrow situations an injunction against pending state prosecutions would be proper without considering § 2283? Was it in turn appropriate for the Court in Mitchum to justify its construction of § 2283 by relying on Younger's dicta?

Most federal actions seeking injunctions against state prosecution are, like the Younger case itself, in fact filed under 42 U.S.C. § 1983. Note the tension between Younger and the emphasis on the importance of federal court jurisdiction in § 1983 actions expressed in cases like Mitchum and Patsy v. Board of Regents of the State of Florida, p. 1350, *supra.*

(3) *The Relationship of Younger to Pullman Abstention.* Note the differences between the Pullman "abstention" doctrine and the equitable restraint doctrine of Younger. In a conventional Pullman-type case, the issue is whether the federal plaintiff should himself be forced to commence a state proceeding that might not otherwise occur at all. In the normal

---

3. Justice Douglas alone dissented from this part of the ruling.

For a refusal to issue similar relief, *see* O'Shea v. Littleton, 414 U.S. 488, 499–504 (1974).

4. In two other companion cases, Dyson v. Stein, 401 U.S. 200 (1971) and Byrne v. Karalexis, 401 U.S. 216 (1971), the Court vacated district court injunctions and remanded for reconsideration in light of Younger and Samuels.

A somewhat different issue was presented in a final companion case, Boyle v. Landry, 401 U.S. 77 (1971). This was an action by a group of black residents of Chicago, who alleged that a number of state statutes and city ordinances—for example, laws prohibiting mob action, resisting arrest, aggravated assault and intimidation—were being used to harass them. The only part of the case before the Court was the district court's decree enjoining the defendants from enforcing one section of the statute prohibiting certain kinds of "intimidation." The Supreme Court reversed. Stressing that none of the plaintiffs had ever been arrested, charged, prosecuted, or even threatened with prosecution under the statute, it held that the complaint did not allege the requisite irreparable injury to justify injunctive relief.

Younger-type case, on the other hand, the whole point is that a state proceeding either has been or is about to be commenced by the state authorities, and the holding is that the whole case should be litigated in that proceeding.

Note, moreover, the different impact of the two doctrines on the federal plaintiff's ability to obtain a federal court resolution of the federal questions on which he relies. The Pullman doctrine ordinarily entails postponement, not relinquishment, of federal jurisdiction to pass on claims of federal right; the point of abstention is characteristically to permit the state courts to resolve issues of state law, and thereafter, to permit the litigants to return to federal court with their federal questions, as the England case, p. 1376, *supra*, strongly reaffirms.[5] On the other hand, although at times equitable restraint is justified in part by the desirability of giving the state courts a chance to provide narrowing constructions, see, *e.g.*, Pennzoil Co. v. Texaco, Inc., 107 S.Ct. 1519, 1526 (1987); Moore v. Sims, 442 U.S. 415, 429–30 (1979), the principal thrust of Younger is that a state criminal defendant's *federal* constitutional claims should usually be raised and definitively adjudicated in the state criminal case, subject only to Supreme Court review. And as the Court later held in Allen v. McCurry, 449 U.S. 90 (1980), p. 1615, *infra*, that state court adjudication will have full res judicata effect in a subsequent federal court proceeding, even one under 42 U.S.C. § 1983. Thus, Younger bars federal litigation under § 1983 while state proceedings are pending, and res judicata ordinarily bars federal relitigation under § 1983 once those proceedings have come to judgment. (Notwithstanding Younger, a state criminal defendant may ultimately reach federal court by filing a federal habeas corpus petition, but important limits apply to this remedy: (i) it comes only after state remedies have been exhausted; (ii) it is available only to defendants who are still "in custody" after exhaustion of state remedies; (iii) it ordinarily does not permit plenary federal litigation of the facts; and (iv) it ordinarily does not extend to Fourth Amendment claims.)

(4) *Exceptions to the Younger Doctrine.* Younger suggested that there might be exceptional cases warranting federal equitable relief against pending state criminal prosecutions. Subsequent decisions have stressed the narrowness of the possible openings. See generally Comment, 67 Calif. L.Rev. 1318 (1979). (As is discussed in detail in the *Note on the Application of Equitable Restraint in the Face of Pending Civil State Court or Administrative Proceedings*, pp. 1433–38, *infra*, the Younger doctrine has been extended to bar federal interference in some kinds of state court *civil* proceedings, and many of the cases discussed in this Paragraph involve intervention in civil matters.)

---

5. Not all of the abstention cases conform to this "pure" model. In particular, *see* Alabama Pub. Serv. Comm'n v. Southern Ry., p. 1365, *supra*, holding abstention appropriate to secure a state court decision of federal (not state law) questions; here, abstention entailed relinquishment and not mere postponement of federal trial-court adjudication.

Moreover, at times abstention is invoked when there is already a pending state court proceeding. See, *e.g.*, Askew v. Har-grave, p. 1357, *supra*; Kaiser Steel Corp. v. W.S. Ranch Co., p. 1373, *supra*.

The terminology should not confuse the important underlying issues: (i) Is it state or federal questions that would be decided if the federal court stays its hand? (ii) Is federal jurisdiction being relinquished or postponed? (iii) Is the federal court deferring to a pending state proceeding, or will one have to be initiated? (iv) Are there timing or ripeness problems as well as federal-state comity problems?

(a) *Bad Faith Prosecution or Harassment.* The Dombrowski case argued that allegations of bad faith and harassment made *Pullman abstention* inappropriate, but Younger interpreted Dombrowski as authorizing an exception to the *equitable restraint doctrine* when such allegations are made. (By the way, are bad faith and harassment different concepts or only different labels?) The Supreme Court has never authorized intervention under this exception. In Cameron v. Johnson, 390 U.S. 611 (1968), the Court, in refusing to permit intervention, rejected the notion that bad faith could be inferred from the innocence of the accused; the question was whether enforcement was undertaken "with no expectation of convictions but only to discourage exercise of protected rights" (p. 621).

The Court's fullest discussion is found in Hicks v. Miranda, 422 U.S. 332, 350–51 (1975), p. 1416, *infra.* There, the three-judge district court had found official harassment and bad faith in the use of obscenity statutes to bar exhibition of the movie "Deep Throat," but the Court reversed, ruling that the findings were "vague and conclusory" (p. 350). The lower court's reference to the "pattern of seizure" of the movie did not make out bad faith and harassment since each step in the pattern was authorized by judicial order; even a showing "that the state courts were in error on some one or more issues of state or federal law" would not necessarily establish bad faith or harassment (p. 351).[6]

For a collection of a small number of lower court cases upholding federal interference under this exception, see 17 Wright, Miller & Cooper, Federal Practice and Procedure § 4255 (1978 & 1986 Supp.).

If Younger itself is right, why should there be such an exception? Is a state court unable to determine whether a prosecutor is acting in bad faith? Even if the harm in such a case results from the fact of prosecution itself, regardless of its outcome, do the burdens of defending a criminal prosecution—which do not themselves constitute irreparable injury—become more irreparable merely because the prosecutor has no expectation of conviction? Or is the real problem one of harassment—of repeated, unfounded prosecutions that are dismissed before the defendant can obtain a favorable ruling?

(b) *Patent and Flagrant Unconstitutionality.* Younger also suggested that federal courts might be justified in restraining prosecutions under statutes that are "flagrantly and patently violative of express constitutional prohibitions in every clause, sentence, and paragraph, and in whatever manner and against whomever an effort might be made to apply it." The language is from Watson v. Buck, 313 U.S. 387, 402 (1941), p. 1396, *supra,* which refused to enjoin an entire statute when parts could be severed or the legislation could be given a narrowing construction. Not much is left of this "exception" after Trainor v. Hernandez, 431 U.S. 434, 446–47 (1977).[7] There, the defendants in a state court action filed a federal suit

---

6. The Court also refused to find bad faith in Juidice v. Vail, 430 U.S. 327, 338 (1977), p. 1434, *infra.* There, a debtor, who had been held in civil contempt in the course of a state court action by his creditor to satisfy a prior default judgment, filed a federal action challenging the constitutionality of the contempt procedures. Though the complaint alleged bad faith on the part of the creditors, it failed to include what the Supreme Court deemed neces-

sary: allegations of bad faith on the part of the state judges who issued the contempt order.

7. Indeed, what was left of this exception after Younger itself? A year after the three-judge court's decision in Younger, and two years before its own Younger decision, the Court, in Brandenburg v. Ohio, 395 U.S. 444 (1969), had invalidated a stat-

challenging the constitutionality of a state court attachment against their property; the attachment had been obtained without any prior hearing, as authorized by state law. The lower court, in enjoining the attachment, stated that the state's attachment procedure was "on its face patently violative of the due process clause." 405 F.Supp. at 762. Dividing 5–4, the Supreme Court reversed. Without clearly stating whether there was an exception to Younger for statutes found to be flagrantly unconstitutional, the majority simply said that if the lower court's statement constituted such a finding, it "would have not been warranted in light of our cases. *Compare* North Georgia Finishing, Inc. v. Di-Chem, Inc., 419 U.S. 601 (1975), with Mitchell v. W.T. Grant Co., 416 U.S. 600 (1974)."

Justices Brennan, Stewart, Marshall, and Stevens dissented. Justice Brennan's dissent argued that "a requirement that the * * * formulation [defining this exception] must be literally satisfied renders the exception meaningless" (p. 457). Analyzing the statute in some detail, Justice Brennan found it clearly unconstitutional under North Georgia Finishing and clearly distinguishable from the statute upheld in W.T. Grant. Justice Stevens' dissent objected that the majority's view made the exception inapplicable whenever the statute had a separability clause, and argued that there was no reason "why all sections of any statute must be considered invalid in order to justify an injunction against a portion that is itself flagrantly unconstitutional" (p. 463).

Why, however, should there be such an exception at all? Isn't it a particular insult to the state courts to suggest that they will be unable to detect patent unconstitutionality in state statutes? Indeed, isn't it arguable that a defendant faces no risk of irreparable injury in the state court prosecution if a Supreme Court decision is clearly (and favorably) on point? *Cf.* the discussion of Douglas v. City of Jeannette and Murdock v. Pennsylvania, pp. 1393–94 & note 2, *supra;* Roe v. Wade, 410 U.S. 113, 166 (1973).

(c) *Other Extraordinary Circumstances.* What else might constitute "extraordinary circumstances" meriting an exception to Younger's policy of non-interference? In Gibson v. Berryhill, 411 U.S. 564 (1973), the Court refused to apply Younger to require deference to administrative proceedings before a state agency that the lower court had found to be "incompetent by reason of bias to adjudicate the issues pending before it. If the District Court's conclusion was correct in this regard, it was also correct that it need not defer to the Board. Nor, in these circumstances, would a different result be required simply because judicial review, de novo or otherwise, would be forthcoming at the conclusion of the administrative proceedings" (p. 577).[8]

Justice Stevens has gone one step further, advancing the view that Younger should *never* apply if the federal constitutional challenge relates to the validity of the very state procedures to which Younger would, if applied, remit the federal plaintiff. See, *e.g.,* Juidice v. Vail, 430 U.S. 327, 340–41 (1977) (Stevens, J., concurring in the judgment); Trainor v. Her-

---

ute almost identical to the one under which Harris was being prosecuted.

8. In Kugler v. Helfant, 421 U.S. 117, 125 n. 4 (1975), the Court described Gibson as an example of an "extraordinary circumstance," other than bad faith/harass-

ment or patent unconstitutionality, but concluded that because the plaintiff's claim that he could not obtain a fair hearing in the state courts was without merit, the case was distinguishable.

nandez, *supra*, at 460, 469 (Stevens, J., dissenting). The contention has considerable surface plausibility, but will it withstand analysis? Is a state court—particularly a state supreme court—automatically disqualified from passing on the fairness and validity of all procedural rules? [9] The majority of the Court has never accepted this view.

Compare Gerstein v. Pugh, 420 U.S. 103 (1975), holding unconstitutional Florida's procedures whereby a person arrested without a warrant and charged by information could be held in jail pending trial without a judicial determination of probable cause. The suit was a federal class action by pretrial detainees in Florida. The Court brushed aside in a footnote the contention that Younger was applicable (p. 108 n. 9): "The injunction was not directed at the state prosecutions as such, but only at the legality of pretrial detention without a judicial hearing, an issue that could not be raised in defense of the criminal prosecution. The order to hold preliminary hearings could not prejudice the conduct of the trial on the merits."

Gerstein presents the classic case where remitting a plaintiff to the state forum will irrevocably prejudice the vindication of the claimed federal right. Compare the decisions holding that exhaustion of state remedies is not required as a prerequisite to federal habeas jurisdiction where irreparable damage to the underlying federal claim is threatened by the very imposition of the requirement, p. 1552–53, *infra*.

Should the applicability of Younger, like the applicability of the Tax Injunction Act's bar on federal interference, depend upon the existence of a "plain, speedy, and effective" remedy in state court? See Rosenfeld, *The Place of State Courts in the Era of Younger v. Harris*, 59 B.U.L.Rev. 597, 655–58 (1979); Comment, *supra*. Is there, or should there be, a parallel here to doctrines that permit federal intervention if—but only if—there was not a full and fair opportunity to litigate the constitutional question in state court? See Bator, *The State Courts and Federal Constitutional Litigation*, 22 Wm. & Mary L.Rev. 605, 626 (1981); Collins, *The Right to Avoid Trial: Justifying Federal Court Intervention into Ongoing State Court Proceedings*, 66 N.C.L.Rev. 49 (1987).

(5) *Younger and Pending Court–Martial Proceedings.* In Schlesinger v. Councilman, 420 U.S. 738 (1975), a district court enjoined pending court-martial proceedings on the ground that the offense was not service-connected and the military courts therefore could not constitutionally exercise jurisdiction.[10] The Supreme Court reversed, finding that the policies of Younger (which it said were echoed in the exhaustion requirement in federal habeas corpus actions and, to some extent, in the requirement that federal administrative remedies be exhausted) barred relief: "While the peculiar demands of federalism are not implicated, the deficien-

9. In Trainor, Justice Stevens' dissent also argued that the state statute under attack effectively foreclosed a challenge to the validity of the attachment procedures in the state's courts. On remand, the three-judge district court reached the same conclusion and held that therefore Younger was inapplicable. The district court's judgment was then unanimously and summarily affirmed by the Supreme Court. Quern v. Hernandez, 440 U.S. 951 (1979). Does that decision give inadequate recognition to the Supremacy Clause? *Compare*

the decision in Rosewell v. LaSalle National Bank, 450 U.S. 503 (1981), p. 1341, *supra*, on whether a state's remedy for allegedly unconstitutional taxation is plain, speedy, and efficient so as to bar federal equitable relief under the Tax Injunction Act.

10. See O'Callahan v. Parker, 395 U.S. 258 (1969), *overruled*, Solorio v. United States, 107 S.Ct. 2924 (1987), Chap. IV, Sec. 1A, p. 394, note 3, *supra*.

cy is supplied by factors equally compelling"—the special need for deference to the military court system (pp. 757–58). The Court distinguished prior cases permitting anticipatory federal court relief against courts-martial acting in excess of their constitutional jurisdiction [11] as involving civilians; their federal court actions contested "the right of the military to try them at all," and "the expertise of military courts [did not extend] to the consideration of constitutional claims of the type presented" in those cases (p. 759). Justices Douglas, Brennan, and Marshall dissented, believing that these considerations applied equally to the lawsuit at bar.

What does this case suggest about whether Younger bars a federal suit seeking relief from a pending state court proceeding on the ground that the state court lacks jurisdiction? *Cf.* Ohio Civil Rights Com'n v. Dayton Christian Schools, Inc., 477 U.S. 619 (1986), p. 1435, *infra.*

(6) *Equitable Restraint—Mandatory or Permissive?.* In Ohio Bureau of Employment Services v. Hodory, 431 U.S. 471 (1977), the state, in appealing a three-judge court's injunction against a state statute, argued for reversal on the merits but not for dismissal under Younger. The Supreme Court reached the merits and reversed, over the suggestion of an amicus that Younger called for dismissal. On this point, the Court said (p. 480): "If the State voluntarily chooses to submit to a federal forum, principles of comity do not demand that the federal court force the case back into the State's own system." Accord, Brown v. Hotel & Rest. Employees & Bartenders Local 54, 468 U.S. 491, 500 n. 9 (1984).[12] By contrast, in Hodory the Court stated that it was not required to defer to the parties' wishes regarding Pullman abstention, which may result in avoidance of a constitutional question (p. 480 n. 11), though on the facts it found Pullman abstention inappropriate. Is the distinction valid, especially in view of the suggestion in some decisions, see Paragraph (3), *supra,* that equitable restraint under Younger may also help to avoid decision of constitutional questions?

(7) *Appealability.* Decisions dismissing a federal action on Younger grounds are plainly appealable. On the appealability of the refusal to dismiss an action, see Chap. XV, p. 1809, note 7, pp. 1818–19, *infra.*

(8) *Bibliography.* The commentary on Younger is extensive. For a compilation of sources, see 17 Wright, Miller & Cooper, Paragraph (4), *supra,* § 4252 n. 1 (1978 & 1986 Supp.).

---

11. See Toth v. Quarles, 350 U.S. 11 (1955); Reid v. Covert, 354 U.S. 1 (1957); McElroy v. U.S. ex rel. Guagliardo, 361 U.S. 281 (1960). See also Noyd v. Bond, 395 U.S. 683, 696 n. 8 (1969).

12. In Ohio Civil Rights Comm'n v. Dayton Christian Schools, 106 S.Ct. 2718 (1986), the federal plaintiff contended that the defendant had waived any claim for equitable restraint under Younger, because though the claim was raised in the federal district court and in oral argument before the Supreme Court, the defendant conceded in the district court that that court had jurisdiction. The Supreme Court ruled that this waiver argument "misconceive[d] the nature of Younger abstention," which is founded not on lack of jurisdiction but on "strong policies" of noninterference (p. 2722). Hodory and Brown showed, the Court said, that a state may voluntarily submit to federal jurisdiction even though it could have invoked Younger, but in those two cases the state expressly urged federal court adjudication of the merits; "there was no similar consent or waiver here, and we therefore address the [Younger issue]" (pp. 2722–23).

STEFFEL v. THOMPSON

415 U.S. 452, 94 S.Ct. 1209, 39 L.Ed.2d 505 (1974).
Certiorari to the United States Court of Appeals for the Fifth Circuit.

MR. JUSTICE BRENNAN delivered the opinion of the Court.

When a state criminal proceeding under a disputed state criminal statute is pending against a federal plaintiff at the time his federal complaint is filed, Younger v. Harris, 401 U.S. 37 (1971), and Samuels v. Mackell, 401 U.S. 66 (1971), held, respectively, that, unless bad-faith enforcement or other special circumstances are demonstrated, principles of equity, comity, and federalism preclude issuance of a federal injunction restraining enforcement of the criminal statute and, in all but unusual circumstances, a declaratory judgment upon the constitutionality of the statute. This case presents the important question reserved in Samuels v. Mackell, *id.*, at 73–74, whether declaratory relief is precluded when a state prosecution has been threatened, but is not pending, and a showing of bad-faith enforcement or other special circumstances has not been made.

Petitioner, and others, filed a complaint in the District Court for the Northern District of Georgia, invoking the Civil Rights Act of 1871, 42 U.S.C. § 1983, and its jurisdictional implementation, 28 U.S.C. § 1343. The complaint requested a declaratory judgment pursuant to 28 U.S.C. §§ 2201–2202, that Ga.Code Ann. § 26–1503 (1972) was being applied in violation of petitioner's First and Fourteenth Amendment rights, and an injunction restraining respondents—the Solicitor of the Civil and Criminal Court of DeKalb County, the chief of the DeKalb County Police, the owner of the North DeKalb Shopping Center, and the manager of that shopping center—from enforcing the statute so as to interfere with petitioner's constitutionally protected activities.

The parties stipulated to the relevant facts: On October 8, 1970, while petitioner and other individuals were distributing handbills protesting American involvement in Vietnam on an exterior sidewalk of the North DeKalb Shopping Center, shopping center employees asked them to stop handbilling and leave. They declined to do so, and police officers were summoned. The officers told them that they would be arrested if they did not stop handbilling. The group then left to avoid arrest. Two days later petitioner and a companion returned to the shopping center and again began handbilling. The manager of the center called the police, and petitioner and his companion were once again told that failure to stop their handbilling would result in their arrests. Petitioner left to avoid arrest. His companion stayed, however, continued handbilling, and was arrested and subsequently arraigned on a charge of criminal trespass in violation of § 26–1503. Petitioner alleged in his complaint that, although he desired to return to the shopping center to distribute handbills, he had not done so because of his concern that he, too, would be arrested for violation of § 26–1503; the parties stipulated that, if petitioner returned and refused upon request to stop handbilling, a warrant would be sworn out and he might be arrested and charged with a violation of the Georgia statute.

After hearing, the District Court denied all relief and dismissed the action, finding that "no meaningful contention can be made that the state has [acted] or will in the future act in bad faith," and therefore "the rudiments of an active controversy between the parties * * * [are] lacking." Petitioner appealed only from the denial of declaratory relief. The Court of Appeals for the Fifth Circuit, one judge concurring in the result, affirmed the District Court's judgment refusing declaratory relief.

* * *

We granted certiorari, 410 U.S. 953 (1973), and now reverse.

I

At the threshold we must consider whether petitioner presents an "actual controversy," a requirement imposed by Art. III of the Constitution and the express terms of the Federal Declaratory Judgment Act, 28 U.S.C. § 2201.

Unlike three of the appellees in Younger v. Harris, 401 U.S., at 41, petitioner has alleged threats of prosecution that cannot be characterized as "imaginary or speculative," id., at 42. He has been twice warned to stop handbilling that he claims is constitutionally protected and has been told by the police that if he again handbills at the shopping center and disobeys a warning to stop he will likely be prosecuted. The prosecution of petitioner's handbilling companion is ample demonstration that petitioner's concern with arrest has not been "chimerical," Poe v. Ullman, 367 U.S. 497, 508 (1961). In these circumstances, it is not necessary that petitioner first expose himself to actual arrest or prosecution to be entitled to challenge a statute that he claims deters the exercise of his constitutional rights. See, e.g., Epperson v. Arkansas, 393 U.S. 97 (1968). Moreover, petitioner's challenge is to those specific provisions of state law which have provided the basis for threats of criminal prosecution against him. Cf. Boyle v. Landry, 401 U.S. 77, 81 (1971); Watson v. Buck, 313 U.S. 387, 399–400 (1941).

* * *

II

We now turn to the question of whether the District Court and the Court of Appeals correctly found petitioner's request for declaratory relief inappropriate.

Sensitive to principles of equity, comity, and federalism, we recognized in Younger v. Harris, supra, that federal courts should ordinarily refrain from enjoining ongoing state criminal prosecutions. We were cognizant that a pending state proceeding, in all but unusual cases, would provide the federal plaintiff with the necessary vehicle for vindicating his constitutional rights, and, in that circumstance, the restraining of an ongoing prosecution would entail an unseemly failure to give effect to the principle that state courts have the solemn responsibility, equally with the federal courts "to guard, enforce, and protect every right granted or secured by the constitution of the United States. * * *" Robb v. Connolly, 111 U.S. 624, 637 (1884). In Samuels v. Mackell, supra, the Court also found that the same principles ordinarily would be flouted by issuance of a federal declaratory judgment when a state proceeding was pending, since the intrusive effect of declaratory relief "will result in precisely the same interference with and disruption of state proceedings that the long-standing policy limiting injunctions was designed to avoid." 401 U.S., at 72.[11] We

11. The Court noted that under 28 U.S.C. § 2202 a declaratory judgment might serve as the basis for issuance of a later injunction to give effect to the declar-

therefore held in Samuels that, "in cases where the state criminal prosecution was begun prior to the federal suit, the same equitable principles relevant to the propriety of an injunction must be taken into consideration by federal district courts in determining whether to issue a declaratory judgment. * * *" *Id.,* at 73.

Neither Younger nor Samuels, however, decided the question whether federal intervention might be permissible in the absence of a pending state prosecution. * * *

These reservations anticipated the Court's recognition that the relevant principles of equity, comity, and federalism "have little force in the absence of a pending state proceeding." Lake Carriers' Assn. v. MacMullan, 406 U.S. 498, 509 (1972). When no state criminal proceeding is pending at the time the federal complaint is filed, federal intervention does not result in duplicative legal proceedings or disruption of the state criminal justice system; nor can federal intervention, in that circumstance, be interpreted as reflecting negatively upon the state court's ability to enforce constitutional principles. In addition, while a pending state prosecution provides the federal plaintiff with a concrete opportunity to vindicate his constitutional rights, a refusal on the part of the federal courts to intervene when no state proceeding is pending may place the hapless plaintiff between the Scylla of intentionally flouting state law and the Charybdis of foregoing what he believes to be constitutionally protected activity in order to avoid becoming enmeshed in a criminal proceeding. *Cf.* Dombrowski v. Pfister, 380 U.S. 479, 490 (1965).

When no state proceeding is pending and thus considerations of equity, comity, and federalism have little vitality, the propriety of granting federal declaratory relief may properly be considered independently of a request for injunctive relief. Here, the Court of Appeals held that, because injunctive relief would not be appropriate since petitioner failed to demonstrate irreparable injury—a traditional prerequisite to injunctive relief, *e.g.,* Dombrowski v. Pfister, *supra*—it followed that declaratory relief was also inappropriate. Even if the Court of Appeals correctly viewed injunctive relief as inappropriate—a question we need not reach today since petitioner has abandoned his request for that remedy,[12] the court erred in treating the requests for injunctive and declaratory relief as a single issue. "[W]hen no state prosecution is pending and the only question is whether declaratory relief is appropriate[,] * * * the congressional scheme that makes the federal courts the primary guardians of constitutional rights, and the express congressional authorization of declaratory relief, afforded because

atory judgment, and that a declaratory judgment might have a res judicata effect on the pending state proceeding. 401 U.S., at 72.

12. We note that, in those cases where injunctive relief has been sought to restrain an imminent, but not yet pending, prosecution *for past conduct,* sufficient injury has not been found to warrant injunctive relief, see Beal v. Missouri Pacific R. Co., 312 U.S. 45 (1941); Spielman Motor Sales Co. v. Dodge, 295 U.S. 89 (1935); Fenner v. Boykin, 271 U.S. 240 (1926). There is some question, however, whether a showing of irreparable injury might be

made in a case where, although no prosecution is pending or impending, an individual demonstrates that he will be required to *forego* constitutionally protected activity in order to avoid arrest. Compare Dombrowski v. Pfister, 380 U.S. 479 (1965); Hygrade Provision Co., Inc. v. Sherman, 266 U.S. 497 (1925); and Terrace v. Thompson, 263 U.S. 197, 214, 216 (1923), with Douglas v. City of Jeannette, 319 U.S. 157 (1943); see generally Note, Implications of the Younger Cases for the Availability of Federal Equitable Relief When No State Prosecution is Pending, 72 Col.L.Rev. 874 (1972).

it is a less harsh and abrasive remedy than the injunction, become the factors of primary significance." Perez v. Ledesma, 401 U.S. 82, 104 (1971) (separate opinion of Brennan, J.).

The subject matter jurisdiction of the lower federal courts was greatly expanded in the wake of the Civil War. A pervasive sense of nationalism led to enactment of the Civil Rights Act of 1871, 17 Stat. 13, empowering the lower federal courts to determine the constitutionality of actions, taken by persons under color of state law, allegedly depriving other individuals of rights guaranteed by the Constitution and federal law, see 42 U.S.C. § 1983, 28 U.S.C. § 1343(3). Four years later, in the Judiciary Act of March 3, 1875, 18 Stat. 470, Congress conferred upon the lower federal courts, for but the second time in their nearly century-old history, general federal-question jurisdiction subject only to a jurisdictional-amount requirement, see 28 U.S.C. § 1331. With this latter enactment, the lower federal courts "ceased to be restricted tribunals of fair dealing between citizens of different states and became the *primary* and powerful reliances for vindicating every right given by the Constitution, the laws, and treaties of the United States." F. Frankfurter & J. Landis, The Business of the Supreme Court 65 (1928) (emphasis added). These two statutes, together with the Court's decision in Ex parte Young, 209 U.S. 123 (1908)—holding that state officials who threaten to enforce an unconstitutional state statute may be enjoined by a federal court of equity and that a federal court may, in appropriate circumstances, enjoin future state criminal prosecutions under the unconstitutional Act—have "established the modern framework for federal protection of constitutional rights from state interference." Perez v. Ledesma, *supra,* 401 U.S., at 107 (separate opinion of Brennan, J.).

A "storm of controversy" raged in the wake of Ex parte Young, focusing principally on the power of a single federal judge to grant *ex parte* interlocutory injunctions against the enforcement of state statutes, H. Hart & H. Wechsler, The Federal Courts and the Federal System 967 (2d ed. 1973). This uproar was only partially quelled by Congress' passage of legislation, 36 Stat. 557, requiring the convening of a three-judge district court before a preliminary injunction against enforcement of a state statute could issue, and providing for direct appeal to this Court from a decision granting or denying such relief. See 28 U.S.C. §§ 2281, 1253. From a State's viewpoint the granting of injunctive relief—even by these courts of special dignity—"rather clumsily" crippled state enforcement of its statutes pending further review. Furthermore, plaintiffs were dissatisfied with this method of testing the constitutionality of state statutes, since it placed upon them the burden of demonstrating the traditional prerequisites to equitable relief—most importantly, irreparable injury. See, e.g., Fenner v. Boykin, 271 U.S. 240, 243 (1926).

To dispel these difficulties, Congress in 1934 enacted the Declaratory Judgment Act, 28 U.S.C. §§ 2201–2202. That Congress plainly intended declaratory relief to act as an alternative to the strong medicine of the injunction and to be utilized to test the constitutionality of state criminal statutes in cases where injunctive relief would be unavailable is amply evidenced by the legislative history of the Act, traced in full detail in Perez v. Ledesma, *supra,* at 111–115 (separate opinion of Brennan, J.). The highlights of that history, particularly pertinent to our inquiry today, emphasize that:

"* * *

"The express purpose of the Federal Declaratory Judgment Act was to provide a milder alternative to the injunction remedy. * * * Of particular significance on the question before us, the Senate report makes it even clearer that the declaratory judgment was designed to be available to test state criminal statutes in circumstances where an injunction would not be appropriate. * * *

" * * * Moreover, the Senate report's clear implication that declaratory relief would have been appropriate in Pierce v. Society of Sisters, 268 U.S. 510 (1925), and Village of Euclid v. Ambler Realty Co., 272 U.S. 365 (1926), both cases involving federal adjudication of the constitutionality of a state statute carrying criminal penalties, and the report's quotation from Terrace v. Thompson, [p. 1395, note 3, *supra*,] which also involved anticipatory federal adjudication of the constitutionality of a state criminal statute, make it plain that Congress anticipated that the declaratory judgment procedure would be used by the federal courts to test the constitutionality of state criminal statutes." [18]

It was this history that formed the backdrop to our decision in Zwickler v. Koota, 389 U.S. 241 (1967), where a state criminal statute was attacked on grounds of unconstitutional overbreadth and no state prosecution was pending against the federal plaintiff. There, we found error in a three-judge district court's considering, as a single question, the propriety of granting injunctive and declaratory relief. Although we noted that injunctive relief might well be unavailable under principles of equity jurisprudence canvassed in Douglas v. City of Jeannette, 319 U.S. 157 (1943), we held that "a federal district court has the duty to decide the appropriateness and the merits of the declaratory request irrespective of its conclusion as to the propriety of the issuance of the injunction." 389 U.S., at 254. Only one year ago, we reaffirmed the Zwickler v. Koota holding in Roe v. Wade, 410 U.S. 113 (1973), and Doe v. Bolton, 410 U.S. 179 (1973). In those two cases, we declined to decide whether the District Courts had properly denied to the federal plaintiffs, against whom no prosecutions were pending, injunctive relief restraining enforcement of the Texas and Georgia criminal abortion statutes; instead, we affirmed the issuance of declaratory judgments of unconstitutionality, anticipating that these would be given effect by state authorities. * * *

The "different considerations" entering into a decision whether to grant declaratory relief have their origins in the preceding historical

---

18. As Professor Borchard, a principal proponent and author of the Federal Declaratory Judgment Act, said in a written statement introduced at the hearings on the Act:

"It often happens that courts are unwilling to grant injunctions to restrain the enforcement of penal statutes or ordinances, and relegate the plaintiff to his option, either to violate the statute and take his chances in testing constitutionality on a criminal prosecution, or else to [forgo], in the fear of prosecution, the exercise of his claimed rights. Into this dilemma no civilized legal system operating under a constitution should force any person.

The court, in effect, by refusing an injunction informs the prospective victim that the only way to determine whether the suspect is a mushroom or a toadstool, is to eat it. Assuming that the plaintiff has a vital interest in the enforcement of the challenged statute or ordinance, there is no reason why a declaratory judgment should not be issued, instead of compelling a violation of the statute as a condition precedent to challenging its constitutionality." Hearings on H.R. 5623 before a Subcommittee of the Senate Committee on the Judiciary, 70th Cong., 1st Sess., 75–76 (1928). See E. Borchard, Declaratory Judgments x–xi (2d ed. 1941).

summary. First, as Congress recognized in 1934, a declaratory judgment will have a less intrusive effect on the administration of state criminal laws. As was observed in Perez v. Ledesma, 401 U.S., at 124–126 (separate opinion of Brennan, J.):

> " * * * [W]here the highest court of a State has had an opportunity to give a statute regulating expression a narrowing or clarifying construction but has failed to do so, and later a federal court declares the statute unconstitutionally vague or overbroad, it may well be open to a state prosecutor, after the federal court decision, to bring a prosecution under the statute if he reasonably believes that the defendant's conduct is not constitutionally protected and that the state courts may give the statute a construction so as to yield a constitutionally valid conviction. * * * [E]ven though a declaratory judgment has 'the force and effect of a final judgment,' 28 U.S.C. § 2201, it is a much milder form of relief than an injunction. Though it may be persuasive, it is not ultimately coercive; noncompliance with it may be inappropriate, but is not contempt." [19]

Second, engrafting upon the Declaratory Judgment Act a requirement that all of the traditional equitable prerequisites to the issuance of an injunction be satisfied before the issuance of a declaratory judgment is considered would defy Congress' intent to make declaratory relief available in cases where an injunction would be inappropriate. * * *

Thus, the Court of Appeals was in error when it ruled that a failure to demonstrate irreparable injury * * * precluded the granting of declaratory relief.

The only occasions where this Court has disregarded these "different considerations" and found that a preclusion of injunctive relief inevitably led to a denial of declaratory relief have been cases in which principles of federalism militated altogether against federal intervention in a class of adjudications. See Great Lakes Dredge & Dock Co. v. Huffman, 319 U.S. 293 (1943) (federal policy against interfering with the enforcement of state tax laws); Samuels v. Mackell, 401 U.S. 66 (1971). In the instant case, principles of federalism not only do not preclude federal intervention, they compel it. Requiring the federal courts totally to step aside when no state criminal prosecution is pending against the federal plaintiff would turn federalism on its head. When federal claims are premised on 42 U.S.C. § 1983 and 28 U.S.C. § 1343(3)—as they are here—we have not required exhaustion of state judicial or administrative remedies, recognizing the paramount role Congress has assigned to the federal courts to protect constitutional rights. See, *e.g.*, McNeese v. Board of Education, 373 U.S. 668 (1963); Monroe v. Pape, 365 U.S. 167 (1961). But exhaustion of state remedies is precisely what would be required if both federal injunctive and declaratory relief were unavailable in a case where no state prosecution had been commenced.

---

19. The pending prosecution of petitioner's handbilling companion does not affect petitioner's action for declaratory relief. In Roe v. Wade, 410 U.S. 113 (1973), while the pending prosecution of Dr. Hallford under the Texas Abortion law was found to render his action for declaratory and injunctive relief impermissible, this did not prevent our granting plaintiff Roe, against whom no action was pending, a declaratory judgment that the statute was unconstitutional.

III

Respondents, however, relying principally upon our decision in Cameron v. Johnson, 390 U.S. 611 (1968), argue that, although it may be appropriate to issue a declaratory judgment when no state criminal proceeding is pending and the attack is upon the *facial validity* of a state criminal statute, such a step would be improper where, as here, the attack is merely upon the constitutionality of the statute as applied, since the State's interest in unencumbered enforcement of its laws outweighs the minimal federal interest in protecting the constitutional rights of only a single individual. We reject the argument. * * *

* * * Our holding in Cameron was * * * that the state courts in which prosecutions were already pending would have to be given the first opportunity to correct any misapplication of the state criminal laws; Cameron is plainly not authority for the proposition that, in the absence of a pending state proceeding, a federal plaintiff may not seek a declaratory judgment that the state statute is being applied in violation of his constitutional rights.

Indeed, the State's concern with potential interference in the administration of its criminal laws is of lesser dimension when an attack is made upon the constitutionality of a state statute as applied. A declaratory judgment of a lower federal court that a state statute is invalid *in toto* — and therefore incapable of any valid application — or is overbroad or vague — and therefore no person can properly be convicted under the statute until it is given a narrowing or clarifying construction, see, *e.g.*, United States v. Thirty-seven Photographs, 402 U.S. 363, 369 (1971); Gooding v. Wilson, 405 U.S. 518, 520 (1972)—will likely have a more significant potential for disruption of state enforcement policies than a declaration specifying a limited number of impermissible applications of the statute. While the federal interest may be greater when a state statute is attacked on its face, since there exists the potential for eliminating any broad-ranging deterrent effect on would-be actors, see Dombrowski v. Pfister, 380 U.S. 479 (1965), we do not find this consideration controlling. The solitary individual who suffers a deprivation of his constitutional rights is no less deserving of redress than one who suffers together with others.[21]

We therefore hold that, regardless of whether injunctive relief may be appropriate, federal declaratory relief is not precluded when no state prosecution is pending and a federal plaintiff demonstrates a genuine threat of enforcement of a disputed state criminal statute, whether an attack is made on the constitutionality of the statute on its face or as applied. The judgment of the Court of Appeals is reversed, and the case is remanded for further proceedings consistent with this opinion.

It is so ordered.

MR. JUSTICE STEWART, with whom THE CHIEF JUSTICE joins, concurring.

---

21. Abstention, a question "entirely separate from the question of granting declaratory or injunctive relief," Lake Carriers' Assn. v. MacMullan, 406 U.S. 498, 509 n. 13 (1972), might be more appropriate when a challenge is made to the state statute as applied, rather than upon its face, since the reach of an uncertain state statute might, in that circumstance, be more susceptible of a limiting or clarifying construction that would avoid the federal constitutional question. *Cf.* Zwickler v. Koota, 389 U.S., at 249–252, 254; Baggett v. Bullitt, 377 U.S. 360, 375–378 (1964).

While joining the opinion of the Court, I add a word by way of emphasis.

Our decision today must not be understood as authorizing the invocation of federal declaratory judgment jurisdiction by a person who thinks a state criminal law is unconstitutional, even if he genuinely feels "chilled" in his freedom of action by the law's existence, and even if he honestly entertains the subjective belief that he may now or in the future be prosecuted under it. * * *

The petitioner in this case has succeeded in objectively showing that the threat of imminent arrest, corroborated by the actual arrest of his companion, has created an actual concrete controversy between himself and the agents of the State. He has, therefore, demonstrated "a genuine threat of enforcement of a disputed state criminal statute * * *." Cases where such a "genuine threat" can be demonstrated will, I think be exceedingly rare.

Mr. Justice White, concurring.

I offer the following few words in light of Mr. Justice Rehnquist's concurrence in which he discusses the impact on a pending federal action of a later filed criminal prosecution against the federal plaintiff, whether a federal court may enjoin a state criminal prosecution under a statute the federal court has earlier declared unconstitutional at the suit of the defendant now being prosecuted, and the question whether that declaratory judgment is res judicata in such a later filed state criminal action.

It should be noted, first, that his views on these issues are neither expressly nor impliedly embraced by the Court's opinion filed today. Second, my own tentative views on these questions are somewhat contrary to my Brother's.

At this writing at least, I would anticipate that a final declaratory judgment entered by a federal court holding particular conduct of the federal plaintiff to be immune on federal constitutional grounds from prosecution under state law should be accorded res judicata effect in any later prosecution of that very conduct. There would also, I think, be additional circumstances in which the federal judgment should be considered as more than a mere precedent bearing on the issue before the state court.

Neither can I at this stage agree that the federal court, having rendered a declaratory judgment in favor of the plaintiff, could not enjoin a later state prosecution for conduct that the federal court has declared immune. The Declaratory Judgment Act itself provides that a "declaration shall have the force and effect of a final judgment or decree," 28 U.S.C. § 2201; eminent authority anticipated that declaratory judgments would be res judicata, E. Borchard, Declaratory Judgments 10–11 (2d ed. 1941); and there is every reason for not reducing declaratory judgments to mere advisory opinions. Toucey v. New York Life Insurance Co., 314 U.S. 118 (1941), once expressed the view that 28 U.S.C. § 2283 forbade injunctions against relitigation in state courts of federally decided issues, but the section was then amended to overrule that case, the consequence being that "[i]t is clear that the Toucey rule is gone, and that to protect or effectuate its judgment a federal court may enjoin relitigation in the state court." C. Wright, Federal Courts 180 (2d ed. 1970). I see no more reason here to hold that the federal plaintiff must always rely solely on his plea of res judicata in the state courts. The statute provides for "[f]urther necessary or proper relief * * * against any adverse party whose rights have been determined by such judgment," 28 U.S.C. § 2202, and it would not seem improper to enjoin local prosecutors who refuse to observe adverse federal judgments.

Finally, I would think that a federal suit challenging a state criminal statute on federal constitutional grounds could be sufficiently far along so that ordinary consideration of economy would warrant refusal to dismiss the federal case solely because a state prosecution has subsequently been filed and the federal question may be litigated there.

MR. JUSTICE REHNQUIST, with whom THE CHIEF JUSTICE joins, concurring.

I concur in the opinion of the Court. Although my reading of the legislative history of the Declaratory Judgment Act of 1934 suggests that its primary purpose was to enable persons to obtain a definition of their rights before an actual injury had occurred, rather than to palliate any controversy arising from Ex parte Young, 209 U.S. 123 (1908), Congress apparently was aware at the time it passed the Act that persons threatened with state criminal prosecutions might choose to forego the offending conduct and instead seek a federal declaration of their rights. Use of the declaratory judgment procedure in the circumstances presented by this case seems consistent with that congressional expectation. * * *

* * * The Court quite properly leaves for another day whether the granting of a declaratory judgment by a federal court will have any subsequent res judicata effect or will perhaps support the issuance of a later federal injunction. But since possible resolutions of those issues would substantially undercut the principles of federalism reaffirmed in Younger v. Harris, 401 U.S. 37 (1971), and preserved by the decision today, I feel it appropriate to add a few remarks.

First, the legislative history of the Declaratory Judgment Act and the Court's opinion in this case both recognize that the declaratory judgment procedure is an alternative to pursuit of the arguably illegal activity. There is nothing in the Act's history to suggest that Congress intended to provide persons wishing to violate state laws with a federal shield behind which they could carry on their contemplated conduct. Thus I do not believe that a federal plaintiff in a declaratory judgment action can avoid, by the mere filing of a complaint, the principles so firmly expressed in Samuels, *supra*. The plaintiff who continues to violate a state statute after the filing of his federal complaint does so both at the risk of state prosecution and at the risk of dismissal of his federal lawsuit. For any arrest prior to resolution of the federal action would constitute a pending prosecution and bar declaratory relief under the principles of Samuels.

Second, I do not believe that today's decision can properly be raised to support the issuance of a federal injunction based upon a favorable declaratory judgment. The Court's description of declaratory relief as " 'a milder alternative to the injunction remedy,' " having a "less intrusive effect on the administration of state criminal laws" than an injunction, indicates to me critical distinctions which make declaratory relief appropriate where injunctive relief would not be. It would all but totally obscure these important distinctions if a successful application for declaratory relief came to be regarded, not as the conclusion of a lawsuit, but as a giant step toward obtaining an injunction against a subsequent criminal prosecution.

* * *

A declaratory judgment is simply a statement of rights, not a binding order supplemented by continuing sanctions. State authorities may choose to be guided by the judgment of a lower federal court, but they are not compelled to follow the decision by threat of contempt or other penalties. If the federal plaintiff pursues the conduct for which he was previously threatened with arrest and is in fact arrested, he may not return the controversy to federal court, although he may, of course, raise the federal declaratory judgment in the state court for whatever value it may prove to have.[3] In any event, the defendant at that point is able to present his case for full consideration by a state court charged, as are the federal courts, to preserve the defendant's constitutional rights. Federal interference with this process would involve precisely the same concerns discussed in Younger and recited in the Court's opinion in this case.

Third, attempts to circumvent Younger by claiming that enforcement of a statute declared unconstitutional by a federal court is *per se* evidence of bad faith should not find support in the Court's decision in this case.

* * *

If the declaratory judgment remains, as I think the Declaratory Judgment Act intended, a simple declaration of rights without more, it will not be used merely as a dramatic tactical maneuver on the part of any state defendant seeking extended delays. Nor will it force state officials to try cases time after time first in the federal courts and then in the state courts. I do not believe Congress desired such unnecessary results, and I do not think that today's decision should be read to sanction them. Rather the Act, and the decision, stand for the sensible proposition that both a potential state defendant, threatened with prosecution but not charged, and the State itself, confronted by a possible violation of its criminal laws, may benefit from a procedure which provides for a declaration of rights without activation of the criminal process. If the federal court finds that the threatened prosecution would depend upon a statute it judges unconstitutional, the State may decide to forgo prosecution of similar conduct in the future, believing the judgment persuasive. Should the state prosecutors not find the decision persuasive enough to justify forbearance, the successful federal plaintiff will at least be able to bolster his allegations of unconstitutionality in the state trial with a decision of the federal district court in the immediate locality. The state courts may find the reasoning convincing even though the prosecutors did not. Finally, of course, the state legislature may decide, on the basis of the federal decision, that the statute would be better amended or repealed. All these possible avenues of relief would be reached voluntarily by the States and would be completely consistent with the concepts of federalism discussed above. Other more intrusive forms of relief should not be routinely available. * * *

---

3. The Court's opinion notes that the possible res judicata effect of a federal declaratory judgment in a subsequent state court prosecution is a question "not free from difficulty." * * * I express no opinion on that issue here. * * *

HICKS v. MIRANDA

422 U.S. 332, 95 S.Ct. 2281, 45 L.Ed.2d 223 (1975).
Appeal from the United States District Court for the Central
District of California.

MR. JUSTICE WHITE delivered the opinion of the Court.

This case poses issues under Younger v. Harris, 401 U.S. 37 (1971); Samuels v. Mackell, 401 U.S. 66 (1971), and related cases * * *.

I

On November 23 and 24, 1973, pursuant to four separate warrants issued seriatim, the police seized four copies of the film "Deep Throat," each of which had been shown at the Pussycat Theatre in Buena Park, Orange County, California. On November 26 an eight-count criminal misdemeanor charge was filed in the Orange County Municipal Court against two employees of the theater, each film seized being the subject matter of two counts in the complaint. Also on November 26, the Superior Court of Orange County ordered appellees to show cause why "Deep Throat" should not be declared obscene, an immediate hearing being available to appellees, who appeared that day, objected on state law grounds to the court's jurisdiction to conduct such a proceeding, purported to "reserve" all federal questions and refused further to participate. Thereupon, on November 27 the Superior Court held a hearing, viewed the film, took evidence and then declared the movie to be obscene and ordered seized all copies of it that might be found at the theater. This judgment and order were not appealed by appellees.

Instead, on November 29, they filed this suit in the District Court against appellants—four police officers of Buena Park and the District Attorney and Assistant District Attorney of Orange County. The complaint recited the seizures and the proceedings in the Superior Court, stated in the body of the complaint that the action was for an injunction against the enforcement of the California obscenity statute, prayed for judgment declaring the obscenity statute unconstitutional and for an injunction ordering the return of all copies of the film, but permitting one of the films to be duplicated before its return.

A temporary restraining order was requested and denied, the District Judge finding the proof of irreparable injury to be lacking and an insufficient likelihood of prevailing on the merits to warrant an injunction. He requested the convening of a three-judge court, however, to consider the constitutionality of the statute. Such a court was then designated on January 8, 1974.

Service of the complaint was completed on January 14, 1974, and answers and motions to dismiss, as well as a motion for summary judgment, were filed by appellants. Appellees moved for a preliminary injunction. None of the motions was granted and no hearings held, all of the issues being ordered submitted on briefs and affidavits. * * *

Meanwhile, on January 15, the criminal complaint pending in the Municipal Court had been amended by naming appellees as additional parties defendant and by adding four conspiracy counts, one relating to each of the seized films. * * *

On June 4, 1974, the three-judge court issued its judgment and opinion declaring the California obscenity statute to be unconstitutional * * * and ordering appellants to return to appellees all copies of "Deep Throat" which had been seized as well as to refrain from making any additional seizures. Appellants' claim that Younger v. Harris, *supra,* and Samuels v. Mackell, *supra,* required dismissal of the case was rejected, the court holding that no criminal charges were pending in the state court against appellees and that in any event the pattern of search warrants and seizures demonstrated bad faith and harassment on the part of the authorities, all of which relieved the court from the strictures of Younger v. Harris, *supra,* and its related cases.

* * *

III

The District Court committed error in reaching the merits of this case despite the State's insistence that it be dismissed under Younger v. Harris, *supra,* and Samuels v. Mackell, *supra.* When they filed their federal complaint, no state criminal proceedings were pending against appellees by name; but two employees of the theater had been charged and four copies of "Deep Throat" belonging to appellees had been seized, were being held and had been declared to be obscene and seizable by the Superior Court. Appellees had a substantial stake in the state proceedings, so much so that they sought federal relief, demanding that the state statute be declared void and their films be returned to them. Obviously, their interest and those of their employees were intertwined; and as we have pointed out, the federal action sought to interfere with the pending state prosecution. Absent a clear showing that appellees, whose lawyers also represented their employees, could not seek the return of their property in the state proceedings and see to it that their federal claims were presented there, the requirements of Younger v. Harris could not be avoided on the ground that no criminal prosecution was pending against appellees on the date the federal complaint was filed. The rule in Younger v. Harris is designed to "permit state courts to try state cases free from interference by federal courts," 401 U.S., at 43, particularly where the party to the federal case may fully litigate his claim before the state court. Plainly, "the same comity considerations apply," Allee v. Medrano, 416 U.S. 802, 831 (Burger, C.J., concurring), where the interference is sought by some, such as appellees, not parties to the state case.

What is more, on the day following the completion of service of the complaint, appellees were charged along with their employees in Municipal Court. Neither Steffel v. Thompson, 415 U.S. 452, nor any other case in this Court has held that for Younger v. Harris to apply, the state-criminal proceedings must be pending on the day the federal case is filed. Indeed, the issue has been left open; [17] and we now hold that where state criminal proceedings are begun against the federal plaintiffs after the federal complaint is filed but before any proceedings of substance on the merits have taken place in the federal court, the principles of Younger v. Harris should apply in full force. Here, appellees were charged on January 15,

---

17. At least some Justices have thought so. Perez v. Ledesma, 401 U.S. 82, at 117 n. 9 (opinion of Mr. Justice Brennan, joined by Justices White and Marshall). Also, Steffel v. Thompson, *supra,* did not decide whether an injunction, as well as a declaratory judgment, can be issued when no state prosecution is pending.

prior to answering the federal case and prior to any proceedings whatsoever before the three-judge court. Unless we are to trivialize the principles of Younger v. Harris, the federal complaint should have been dismissed on the State's motion absent satisfactory proof of those extraordinary circumstances calling into play one of the limited exceptions to the rule of Younger v. Harris and related cases.

[The Court then rejected the district court's finding of official harassment and bad faith. See p. 1402, *supra.*][20] * * *

* * * The District Court should have dismissed the complaint before it and we accordingly reverse its judgment.

MR. CHIEF JUSTICE BURGER, concurring.

* * *

MR. JUSTICE STEWART, with whom MR. JUSTICE DOUGLAS, MR. JUSTICE BRENNAN, and MR. JUSTICE MARSHALL join, dissenting.

* * *

In Steffel v. Thompson, 415 U.S. 452, the Court unanimously held that the principles of equity, comity, and federalism embodied in Younger v. Harris, 401 U.S. 37, and Samuels v. Mackell, 401 U.S. 66, do not preclude a federal district court from entertaining an action to declare unconstitutional a state criminal statute when a state criminal prosecution is threatened but not pending at the time the federal complaint is filed. Today the Court holds that the Steffel decision is inoperative if a state criminal charge is filed at any point after the commencement of the federal action "before any proceedings of substance on the merits have taken place in the federal court." Any other rule, says the Court, would "trivialize" the principles of Younger v. Harris. I think this ruling "trivializes" Steffel, decided just last Term, and is inconsistent with those same principles of equity, comity, and federalism.[1]

There is, to be sure, something unseemly about having the applicability of the Younger doctrine turn solely on the outcome of a race to the

20. It has been noted that appellees did not appeal the Superior Court's order of November 27, 1973, declaring "Deep Throat" obscene and ordering all copies of it seized. It may be that under Huffman v. Pursue, 420 U.S. 592, decided March 18, 1975, the failure of appellees to appeal the Superior Court order of November 27, 1973, would itself foreclose resort to federal court, absent extraordinary circumstances bringing the case within some exception to Younger v. Harris. Appellees now assert, seemingly contrary to their prior statement before Judge Ferguson, that the November 27 order was not appealable. In view of our disposition of the case, we need not pursue the matter further.

1. There is the additional difficulty that the precise meaning of the rule the Court today adopts is a good deal less than apparent. What are "proceedings of substance on the merits"? Presumably, the proceedings must be both "on the merits" and "of substance." Does this mean, then, that months of discovery activity would be in-sufficient, if no question on the merits is presented to the court during that time? What proceedings "on the merits" are sufficient is also unclear. An application for a temporary restraining order or a preliminary injunction requires the court to make an assessment about the likelihood of success on the merits. Indeed, in this case, appellees filed an application for a temporary restraining order along with six supporting affidavits on November 29, 1973. Appellants responded on December 3, 1973, with six affidavits of their own as well as additional documents. On December 28, 1973, Judge Lydick denied the request for a temporary restraining order, in part because appellees "have failed totally to make that showing of * * * likelihood of prevailing on the merits needed to justify the issuance of a temporary restraining order." These proceedings, the Court says implicitly, were not sufficient to satisfy the test it announces. Why that should be, even in terms of the Court's holding, is a mystery.

courthouse. The rule the Court adopts today, however, does not eliminate that race; it merely permits the State to leave the mark later, run a shorter course, and arrive first at the finish line. This rule seems to me to result from a failure to evaluate the state and federal interests as of the time the state prosecution was commenced.

As of the time when its jurisdiction is invoked in a Steffel situation, a federal court is called upon to vindicate federal constitutional rights when no other remedy is available to the federal plaintiff. The Court has recognized that at this point in the proceedings no substantial state interests counsel the federal court to stay its hand. * * *

The duty of the federal courts to adjudicate and vindicate federal constitutional rights is, of course, shared with state courts, but there can be no doubt that the federal courts are "the primary and powerful reliances for vindicating every right given by the Constitution, the laws, and treaties of the United States." Frankfurter & Landis, The Business of the Supreme Court: A Study of the Federal Judicial System 65. The statute under which this action was brought, 42 U.S.C. § 1983, established in our law "the role of the Federal Government as a guarantor of basic federal rights against state power." Mitchum v. Foster, 407 U.S. 225, 239. Indeed, "[t]he very purpose of § 1983 was to interpose the federal courts between the States and the people." *Id.*, at 242. And this central interest of a federal court as guarantor of constitutional rights is fully implicated from the moment its jurisdiction is invoked. How, then, does the subsequent filing of a state criminal charge change the situation from one in which the federal court's dismissal of the action under Younger principles "would turn federalism on its head" to one in which *failure* to dismiss would "trivialize" those same principles?

A State has a vital interest in the enforcement of its criminal law, and this Court has said time and again that it will sanction little federal interference with that important state function. *E.g.*, Kugler v. Helfant, 421 U.S. 117. But there is nothing in our decision in Steffel that requires a State to stay its hand during the pendency of the federal litigation. If, in the interest of efficiency, the State wishes to refrain from actively prosecuting the criminal charge pending the outcome of the federal declaratory judgment suit, it may, of course, do so. But no decision of this Court requires it to make that choice.

The Court today, however, goes much further than simply recognizing the right of the State to proceed with the orderly administration of its criminal law; it ousts the federal courts from their historic role as the "primary reliances" for vindicating constitutional freedoms. This is no less offensive to "Our Federalism" than the federal injunction restraining pending state criminal proceedings condemned in Younger v. Harris. The concept of federalism requires "sensitivity to the legitimate interests of *both* State and National Governments." *Id.*, 401 U.S., at 44 (emphasis added). Younger v. Harris and its companion cases reflect the principles that the federal judiciary must refrain from interfering with the legitimate functioning of state courts. But surely the converse is a principle no less valid.

The Court's new rule creates a reality which few state prosecutors can be expected to ignore. It is an open invitation to state officials to institute state proceedings in order to defeat federal jurisdiction. One need not impugn the motives of state officials to suppose that they would rather prosecute a criminal suit in state court than defend a civil case in a federal forum. Today's opinion virtually instructs state officials to answer federal complaints with state indictments. Today, the State must file a criminal charge to secure dismissal of the federal litigation; perhaps tomorrow an action "akin to a criminal proceeding" will serve the purpose, see Huffman v. Pursue, Ltd., 420 U.S. 592; and the day may not be far off when any state civil action will do.

The doctrine of Younger v. Harris reflects an accommodation of competing interests. The rule announced today distorts that balance beyond recognition.

FURTHER NOTE ON ENJOINING STATE PROCEEDINGS

(1) *Doran v. Salem Inn, Inc.* A week after the decision in Hicks v. Miranda the Court decided Doran v. Salem Inn, Inc., 422 U.S. 922 (1975). An ordinance passed by the Town of North Hempstead, on Long Island, prohibited topless dancing in bars; the case involved three local bars where topless dancing had until then been featured. All three bars initially complied with the ordinance. The three corporate bar owners (M & L, Salem, and Tim–Robb) then brought suit in federal court seeking a declaration that the ordinance was unconstitutional as well as a temporary restraining order and a preliminary injunction against its enforcement. The day after the complaint was filed, M & L (but not the other two plaintiffs) resumed topless dancing; a criminal prosecution against it was commenced immediately. The district court granted plaintiffs' prayer for a preliminary injunction, and the Court of Appeals for the Second Circuit affirmed.

The Supreme Court first concluded that the three plaintiffs should not "be thrown into the same hopper for Younger" purposes; while there "may be some circumstances in which legally distinct parties are so closely related that they should all be subjected to the Younger considerations which govern any one of them, this is not such a case" (p. 928).[1] The court then held that M & L was barred from securing an injunction by Younger, and a declaratory judgment by Samuels v. Mackell. "When the criminal summonses issued against M & L on the days immediately following the filing of the federal complaint, the federal litigation was in an embryonic stage" (p. 929). With regard to Salem and Tim–Robb, the Court said that their prayers for declaratory relief were squarely governed by Steffel, since they were not subject to state criminal prosecution at any time. Further, the Court held that under the circumstances the issuance of a preliminary injunction restraining defendants from enforcing the ordinance was not subject to the restrictions of Younger. The Court reasoned that, at the end of trial on the merits, the plaintiffs' interests can generally be protected by a declaratory judgment; but "prior to final judgment there is no established declaratory remedy comparable to a preliminary injunction; unless preliminary relief is available upon a proper showing, plaintiffs in some situations may suffer unnecessary and substantial irreparable harm" (p. 931).

1. The Court noted that, although the plaintiffs were represented by common counsel, they were unrelated in terms of ownership or management.

Turning to the merits, and stressing the narrow scope of appellate review, the Court held that it was not an abuse of discretion to grant the preliminary injunction, since a sufficient showing of both irreparable harm *pendente lite* and likelihood of ultimate success on the merits had been made.

(2) *Relief Against Prosecution for Future Conduct.* Consider the case of plaintiffs such as Salem and Tim–Robb, who have not yet violated a criminal statute, but fear irreparable injury if they are prevented from continuing the proscribed activity while it is finally determined whether the statute is constitutional. Anticipatory federal relief is important to relieve them from having to choose between forgoing conduct they believe to be constitutionally protected and risking criminal prosecution. In these circumstances, a declaratory judgment is plainly available under Steffel; Doran adds that enforcement can, in an appropriate case, be enjoined *pendente lite;* and Hicks would not come into play because, by hypothesis, there is no past violation for which charges could be filed.

The major problem in cases relating to future conduct is one of "ripeness." In Doran, Salem's and Tim–Robb's conduct prior to enactment of the ordinance, and the quick prosecution of M & L, made the case obviously ripe. Note, however, Justice Stewart's suggestion in Steffel that cases where a genuine threat of prosecution can be demonstrated will be "exceedingly rare," and his emphasis on Steffel's having engaged in similar conduct in the past and on the prosecution of his companion. Shouldn't someone who wishes to engage in activity he believes to be constitutionally protected have a way of obtaining a determination whether he can be punished for it short of engaging in the prohibited conduct in order to demonstrate his bona fides? Though the Court's ripeness decisions have not taken a straight path, they clearly have not followed Justice Stewart's suggestion; one commentator concludes that the Court "routinely entertain[s] suits to declare statutes unconstitutional, invoking the ripeness requirement only occasionally." Laycock, Modern American Remedies 1211 (1985). See also Ohio Civil Rights Com'n v. Dayton Christian Schools, Inc., 477 U.S. 619 (1986), p. 1435, *infra.* See generally Chap. II, Sec. 5, pp. 239–51, *supra.*

(3) *Relief Against Prosecution for Continuing Conduct.* More difficult than a case involving only future conduct is the case of a plaintiff engaged in a continuing course of conduct—someone who has already violated a criminal statute, but who seeks federal equitable relief from prosecution for similar actions not yet undertaken. Doran (as to M & L) and Hicks exemplify this situation: in each case the federal plaintiff had already engaged in conduct alleged to violate state law, but undoubtedly would continue that conduct if the threat of prosecution were removed.

(a) *The Importance of Anticipatory Relief.* In such a case, anticipatory federal intervention offers the federal plaintiff distinctive advantages over defending against state prosecution. First, in appropriate cases like Doran, interlocutory relief is available, thereby largely eliminating the need for the federal plaintiff to choose, *pendente lite,* between desisting from conduct he believes to be constitutionally protected and risking additional criminal penalties. And second, if the federal court awards equitable relief based upon the protected nature of the plaintiff's conduct, he has secure protection against a second prosecution for similar conduct undertaken in the future.[2] By contrast, a victory in the pending state criminal case will not necessarily preclude his prosecution for engaging thereafter in the same conduct: an acquittal, or even a trial judge's dismissal of the charges, may not have preclusive effect, especially where the state could not appeal. See generally Laycock, *Federal Interference With State Prosecutions: The Need for Prospective Relief,* 1977 Sup.Ct.Rev. 193.[3] Note that these considerations do not call into question Younger's refusal to permit federal intervention in a situation involving only past conduct; if there is not, in addition, a ripe controversy about the federal plaintiff's future activities, he does not have an important need for either relief *pendente lite* or for a judgment that, if favorable, would clearly preclude additional prosecutions.

(b) *The Relationship of Hicks and Doran.* In a situation involving continuing conduct, is there an underlying inconsistency between Hicks and Doran? Steffel permits federal intervention so long as no state prosecution is pending. Under Hicks, however, the state can preempt the federal action by commencing a prosecution before substantial proceedings occur in the federal case, and thereby bar federal relief even as to conduct not yet undertaken; that, indeed, is what happened to M & L in Doran.[4] But under Doran, the district court may issue a preliminary injunction against enforcement of the statute if the requisites for such relief have been satisfied. Doesn't Doran, therefore, shut the door opened by Hicks v. Miranda in any case where a district court, at the outset of the federal litigation, concludes that, *pendente lite,* injunctive relief is appropriate?

Of course, merely filing a motion for a preliminary injunction does not constitute "proceedings of substance on the merits," as Hicks itself demonstrates, and a prosecutor can often file charges before much has happened in connection with that motion. A plaintiff might seek still earlier federal intervention by way of a temporary restraining order, but even then he would have to give prior notice to the defendant, unless it were clear that irreparable injury would result before notice could be provided, see Fed.R. Civ.Proc. 65(b). Isn't Hicks likely to give an alert prosecutor a "reverse removal power"? See Fiss, *Dombrowski,* 86 Yale L.J. 1103, 1136 (1977).

(c) *The Possibility of Limited Federal Relief Pendente Lite.* In Doran, didn't M & L, during the pendency of the state prosecution against it, have just as much need as the other plaintiffs to avoid having either to suffer economic injury from not showing topless dancing or to run the risk of multiple prosecutions if the dancing continued? Given a proper showing of likely success on the merits and irreparable injury, why wasn't the district judge in Doran right, then, to grant M & L a preliminary injunction restraining the enforcement of the ordinance with respect to violations by

---

2. This assumes a federal declaratory judgment would be accorded res judicata effect in a subsequent state prosecution, see Paragraph (5)(a), *infra.*

3. Professor Laycock also notes that the criminal case may be disposed of without reaching the federal constitutional question.

In addition, Laycock suggests a third advantage to federal intervention—the availability of class relief.

4. See also Roe v. Wade, 410 U.S. 113 (1973), where a doctor who had already

been indicted for performing abortions sought an injunction against further prosecution for performing additional abortions. The Supreme Court held that under Younger, this request for prospective relief was barred in view of the pending prosecution. (Of course, the Court's ruling on the merits as to other plaintiffs in Roe largely eliminated any need for relief, much as was true in Douglas v. City of Jeannette and Murdock v. Pennsylvania, pp. 1393–94 & note 2, *supra*).

M & L occurring *after* the injunction was granted and before the constitutional issues were settled on the merits? (For suggestions along this line, see Laycock, *supra,* 1977 Sup.Ct.Rev. at 238; *The Supreme Court, 1974 Term,* 89 Harv.L.Rev. 151–69 (1975).) This would have allowed the state to prosecute the single *past violation* and thus to preempt a full federal trial on the merits under Hicks; on the other hand, the preliminary injunction would have permitted M & L to continue the disputed activity while the issue of constitutionality was being settled (either in the state prosecution or, if none were brought, in federal court). See Spartacus, Inc. v. Borough of McKees Rocks, 694 F.2d 947, 949 n. 3 (3d Cir.1982), note 14, *infra,* awarding such relief; *cf.* Cline v. Frink Dairy Co., 274 U.S. 445, 452–53, 466 (1927), p. 1396, *supra.*

Does the need for interim relief disappear if the state officials promise not to seek additional sanctions for further violations pending resolution of the issue in the pending prosecution? Is such a promise enforceable? See Laycock, Modern American Remedies 1178–79 (1985).

(d) *The Effect of Preliminary Relief.* When preliminary relief is awarded—as it was in fact in Doran to Salem and Tri–Robb—does it immunize the plaintiff from criminal prosecution for acts taken after the injunction issued, even if the statute is ultimately held to be constitutional in further proceedings in state or federal court? The claim that it does was urged in Edgar v. MITE Corp., 457 U.S. 624 (1982), as part of an argument that a federal action seeking to restrain enforcement of a state statute was moot because (i) the only past violation occurred during the pendency of a preliminary injunction forbidding the statute's enforcement, and (ii) the plaintiff did not plan any future violations of the challenged statute. The Court brushed aside the mootness argument (p. 630): "While, as Justice Stevens' concurrence indicates, [the claim of immunity] is not a frivolous question by any means; it is an issue to be decided when and if the [state official charged with enforcing the statute] initiates an action."

Of the five Justices in the majority, only Justice Stevens reached the question. In his concurring opinion he contended that whether or not such immunity would be wise, federal judges were not empowered to confer it. He suggested that even a final judgment declaring a state law unconstitutional would not confer immunity from prosecution for post-judgment conduct if the judgment were later reversed on appeal.

Justice Marshall's dissent on the mootness point—which Justice Brennan joined and with which Justice Powell expressed his general agreement—argued that federal courts have the power to confer such immunity; that "whether a particular injunction provides temporary or permanent protection becomes a question of interpretation"; and that "in the ordinary case * * * it should be presumed that an injunction secures permanent protection from penalties for violations that occurred during the period it was in effect" (p. 657). He insisted that people will be "reluctant to challenge [the validity of state statutes] unless they can obtain permanent immunity from penalties," and that "short-term protection is often only marginally better than no protection at all" (pp. 657 n. 1, 658).[5] See also Paragraph (5)(c), *infra.*

5. Justice Rehnquist found the case moot on other grounds without reaching the immunity issue.

None of the opinions cited Oklahoma Operating Co. v. Love, 252 U.S. 331 (1920) (Brandeis, J.), where in unanimously af-

(e) *The Relationship Between Ongoing State and Federal Proceedings.*
Suppose that M & L had been permitted to obtain a preliminary injunction
pendente lite, notwithstanding the filing of a state prosecution against it.
Note that the ultimate question of constitutionality would be resolved by
the state court; at that point, the preliminary injunction would presumably
be dissolved as unnecessary.

Should the federal court's role be so limited? While the state prosecution is pending (but before it has come to judgment), should the federal
court be denied the power to enter a *final* judgment declaring the ordinance invalid, and *permanently* enjoining the institution of prosecutions
against M & L for any conduct that occurs in the future? Courts sometimes proceed to enter final judgment after hearing a motion for preliminary relief when the legal issues are so well-developed that further proceedings are unnecessary. And note that a final injunction could presumably
be entered, in an appropriate case, as to Salem and Tri–Robb, who had not
yet violated the statute. Would M & L obtain any advantage from a final
federal judgment in its favor, as compared to a federal preliminary injunction followed by a victory in the pending state prosecution? *See* Paragraph
(3)(a), *supra.* Could the award of permanent federal relief be reconciled
with Younger itself? Does the answer to the latter question depend on
whether a final judgment favorable to M & L would preclude relitigation of
the constitutional question in the pending state prosecution against M &
L?[6] Recall that in Cline v. Frink Dairy Co., 274 U.S. 445, 452–53, 466
(1927), p. 1396, *supra,* the Supreme Court, per Brandeis, J., affirmed the
issuance of final injunctive relief against the institution of *future* prosecutions even though a state prosecution was pending when the federal action
was filed.

(4) *The Significance of the Pending/Not Pending Distinction.*

(a) *Cases Involving Past Conduct.* Most of Justice Brennan's arguments in Steffel supporting federal relief in cases where a state proceeding
has not yet commenced really apply only to those cases where a federal
plaintiff seeks a declaratory judgment immunizing future (rather than
past) conduct from prosecution. See *The Supreme Court, 1973 Term,* 88
Harv.L.Rev. 203–13 (1974). Declaratory relief designed to immunize past,
noncontinuing conduct from state prosecution cannot spare a litigant the
choice between violating the statute and forgoing possibly lawful activity;
that choice has already been made. And if the state prevails in the federal

---

firming the award of a preliminary injunction against allegedly confiscatory rate regulation, the Court said (p. 338): "If upon
final hearing the maximum rates fixed
should be found not to be confiscatory, a
permanent injunction should, nevertheless,
issue to restrain enforcement of penalties
accrued *pendente lite*, provided that it also
be found that the plaintiff had reasonable
ground to contest them as being confiscatory." See generally Laycock, Modern
American Remedies 1227, 1230 (1985).

6. It is unlikely, but not impossible,
that a similar question might arise as to
the res judicata effect of a federal judgment merely awarding preliminary relief.
The Restatement (Second) of Judgments,

§ 13, Illustration 1 (1982), suggests that a
decision on a motion for preliminary injunction can (but does not necessarily)
have preclusive effect, and that suggestion
has been endorsed in some cases. See, *e.g.,*
Commodity Futures Trading Com'n v.
Board of Trade, 701 F.2d 653, 656–58 (7th
Cir.1983); Miller Brewing Co. v. Jos.
Schlitz Brewing Co., 605 F.2d 990, 995–96
(7th Cir.1979); *cf.* Lummus Co. v. Commonwealth Oil Refining Co., 297 F.2d 80, 89 (2d
Cir.1961). But see United Books, Inc. v.
Conte, 739 F.2d 30, 33 (1st Cir.1984) (asserting in passing and without qualification
that a preliminary injunction against future prosecution would not have preclusive
effect in a pending state prosecution).

action, a subsequent prosecution is likely to be highly duplicative, since the federal litigation will have at best very limited res judicata effect against the state criminal defendant.[7]

Doesn't *Younger* suggest that federal equitable intervention is unjustified if its only advantage over a state defense is the immediate provision of a *federal* forum? Is the point equally valid whether or not the state has chosen to file charges for the past violation?[8] The pertinent precedents on this issue prior to *Younger* and *Steffel* include Fenner v. Boykin, 271 U.S. 240 (1926), and Spielman Motor Sales Co. v. Dodge, 295 U.S. 89 (1935), discussed at p. 1395, *supra*, both of which denied relief even though there was no pending prosecution when the federal action was instituted. Is *Steffel* unsound insofar as it suggests that federal declaratory relief might be appropriate in a case of past conduct only? If it is unsound, note that the disagreement between majority and dissent in *Hicks* becomes moot, since the pendency of state proceedings would not affect the appropriateness of federal relief against prosecution for past conduct alone.

Or are there cases in which a litigant threatened with prosecution for a single past act should be able to seek federal intervention to remove the threat—to force the state to fish or cut bait? Would the "bad faith/harassment" exception permit federal intervention in these cases? Is there likely to be a ripeness problem in this situation?

(b) *Continuing Conduct.* On the facts of *Hicks*, one can safely assume that the theatre owners were engaged in a pattern of continuing conduct: they had already shown the film, and surely wished to continue doing so. If no state prosecution were ever filed, there would appear to be no barrier to the issuance of a federal declaratory judgment that the film was constitutionally protected expression, and perhaps an injunction forbidding prosecution for future showings. *Hicks* asserts that such federal relief becomes inappropriate, however, if a state prosecution is filed shortly after the federal suit but before "proceedings of substance on the merits." Do you agree?

Hicks is contrary to the settled rule that equity jurisdiction is not destroyed because an adequate legal remedy has become available after the equitable action was filed. See, *e.g.*, American Life Ins. Co. v. Stewart, 300 U.S. 203, 215 (1937) (Cardozo, J.); Dawson v. Kentucky Distilleries & Warehouse Co., 255 U.S. 288, 296 (1921) (Brandeis, J.). See also the quotation from Ex parte Young, 209 U.S. 123, 162 (1908), p. 1393, *supra*; Cline v. Frink Dairy Co., 274 U.S. 445, 453 (1927), p. 1396, *supra*.[9]

---

7. Although preclusion might apply to a pure issue of law—such as the facial validity of a statute—differences in the burden of proof in civil and criminal cases would ordinarily require relitigation of the application of law to fact. See generally Restatement (Second) of Judgments §§ 27, 28 (1982).

Does this suggest that there may be a stronger argument for federal intervention in cases involving past conduct if the federal plaintiff is challenging the state statute on its face rather than merely as applied?

8. On the applicability of *Younger* when grand jury proceedings are underway, see p. 1436, *infra*.

9. Neither the majority nor dissent in *Hicks* paid attention to the alternate holding in Dombrowski v. Pfister, 380 U.S. 479, 484 n. 2 (1965), that when grand jury indictments are returned after the filing of a federal complaint seeking interlocutory and permanent injunctive relief but before such relief is issued, "no state 'proceedings' were pending within the intendment of [the Anti–Injunction Act, 28 U.S.C.] § 2283." See p. 1328, note 15, *supra*.

(c) *The Meaning of "Proceedings of Substance on the Merits".* What suffices to constitute "proceedings of substance on the merits" in the federal action? The not insignificant proceedings on the motion for a temporary restraining order in Hicks obviously did not suffice, a result that Justice Stewart deemed a "mystery."

Ordinarily, if a plaintiff obtains a temporary restraining order or preliminary injunction, the State will be barred from instituting suit. But suppose any injunctive order is later vacated, or is limited in scope, or indeed is defied; are the federal proceedings leading to the issuance of that order substantial enough to permit the federal court to retain jurisdiction notwithstanding a subsequently filed state proceeding? In Hawaii Housing Auth. v. Midkiff, 467 U.S. 229 (1984), the Supreme Court found that Younger did not bar consideration of a federal action seeking injunctive relief against a state land reform scheme, stating (p. 238): "Whether issuance of the February temporary restraining order was a substantial federal court action or not, issuance of the June preliminary injunction certainly was"; the court had by then "proceeded well beyond the 'embryonic stage,'" and no state judicial proceedings had yet been filed.

(5) *Declaratory v. Injunctive Relief.* Can the distinction between declaratory and injunctive relief bear the weight that Justice Brennan placed on it in Steffel? That question raises a number of distinct considerations.

(a) *The Res Judicata Effect of a Federal Declaratory Judgment on an Issue of Federal Law.* Suppose that, on remand in Steffel, the district court entered a declaratory judgment that the plaintiff's leafletting was constitutionally protected, and thereafter the state indicted him for criminal trespass. In the state prosecution, could he invoke issue preclusion on the federal constitutional question, based upon the federal judgment? Doubts were expressed in Steffel, especially in Justice Rehnquist's concurrence. See also Green v. Mansour, p. 1194, *supra.* But "[t]he very purpose of the declaratory judgment proceeding would appear to be thwarted were this determination to be regarded, in a subsequent proceeding between the same parties, as no more than the view of a coordinate court." Shapiro, *State Courts and Federal Declaratory Judgments,* 74 Nw.U.L.Rev. 759, 764 (1979); accord, Restatement (Second) of Judgments § 33.[10]

Assuming Steffel could invoke the preclusive effect of a favorable federal judgment, does it follow that a fellow protester who was not a party to the federal proceeding should be able to do so? See Shapiro, *supra,* at 770–76, arguing that to permit nonmutual preclusion could prevent the full ventilation of issues of law regarding matters of public importance. See also pp. 1605–15, *infra.* (If, however, the federal suit can be and is filed as a class action, there may be no one outside the class against whom the state can bring an action.)

Suppose instead that the federal district court declared that the statute was *constitutional* as applied to Steffel's conduct. Should Steffel be precluded in the criminal case from relitigating the constitutional question?

(b) *The Choice Between Declaratory and Injunctive Relief.* Assuming that a declaratory judgment ordinarily will have preclusive effect, isn't its

---

10. There should be no problem, should there, with binding the state in the criminal case on the basis of a federal action that, because of Eleventh Amendment constraints, named an official rather than the state as a defendant? See Shapiro, *supra,* at 764; *cf.* Duncan v. United States, p. 1125, *supra.*

intended effect the same as that of an injunction? Of course, if a state prosecutor subsequently brings an action that "violates" a declaration, the prosecutor would not be in contempt, as he would be had an injunction issued. But wouldn't the plaintiff surely seek and be entitled to a supplementary injunction under 28 U.S.C. §§ 2201–2202; indeed, wouldn't the prosecutor have acted in "bad faith" by bringing a prosecution in which, by virtue of the preclusive effect of the declaration, he knew he could not prevail? *Cf.* the "relitigation exception" to 28 U.S.C. § 2283, p. 1327, *supra*.

Is there any virtue in leaving the threat of a federal contempt sanction an extra step away? *Cf.* General Atomic Co. v. Felter and Deen v. Hickman, Chap. V, Sec. 1, p. 519, *supra*. *Per contra*, in some settings repeated prosecutions can be used by officials as a weapon in an ongoing political struggle; might a refusal to issue an immediate injunction result in irreparable injury to the plaintiffs?

Does a declaration leave the state with more freedom than it would have under an injunction to prosecute other persons under the statute and thereby to salvage its constitutional applications? If such flexibility is desired, couldn't an injunction be drawn to permit it?

Does all of this suggest that the difference between injunctive and declaratory relief should not have the kind of significance that Justice Brennan gives it in Steffel? [11]

If there is reason to prefer a declaratory judgment to an injunction, at least in the first instance, when should a federal plaintiff be entitled to injunctive relief as well? In Wooley v. Maynard, 430 U.S. 705 (1977), the Court upheld a permanent injunction barring New Hampshire officials from enforcing against the plaintiffs a state law making it a misdemeanor to "obscure" the phrase "Live Free or Die" on state license plates. Maynard had previously been convicted three times for violating the statute. The Court held that "[t]he threat of repeated prosecutions in the future against both [Maynard] and his wife, and the effect of such a continuing threat on their ability to perform the ordinary tasks of daily life which require an automobile, is sufficient to justify injunctive relief" (p. 712). Justice White, joined by Justices Blackmun and Rehnquist, dissented on the Younger issue, arguing that there was no reason to believe that the state officials—who had simply been performing their jobs in obtaining the three prior convictions—would not comply with a declaration, and hence there was no special need for injunctive relief.

In more recent cases involving threatened prosecution for future conduct, the Court has approved the issuance of final injunctions (rather than declaratory judgments) without comment or dissent. See, *e.g.,* Bellotti v. Baird, 443 U.S. 622, 651 (1979); Ray v. Atlantic Richfield Co., 435 U.S. 151, 156–57 (1978); Zablocki v. Redhail, 434 U.S. 374, 377 (1978).

(c) *Federal Judgments Involving Issues of State Law.* Suppose that in the Steffel case, the federal district court on remand determined that (i) Steffel's conduct was not constitutionally protected, but (ii) the criminal trespass statute was nonetheless invalid because it reached other constitutionally protected conduct, and as a matter of state law no narrowing construction was possible. Might not a federal *injunction* against prosecutions under the statute risk depriving the state of the opportunity, through

---

11. Compare California v. Grace Brethren Church, p. 1342, *supra* (Tax Injunction Act bars a federal action for declaratory judgment as to state taxes).

further litigation, to obtain the state courts' authoritative resolution of the state law issue?

Of course, the state could in any event bring a state court declaratory action against Steffel to determine whether a narrowing construction could be given. In such an action, should the federal judgment on the state law issue have preclusive effect? For a negative answer, see Shapiro, *supra*, at 769. If the state court were to supply a valid narrowing construction that would make application of the statute to Steffel's conduct constitutional, could Steffel then be prosecuted for conduct he undertook prior to the narrowing construction, but after the initial federal declaration that the state statute was invalid? A dictum in Dombrowski v. Pfister, 380 U.S. 479, 491 n. 7 (1965) rather clearly suggested yes, but Shapiro, *supra*, at 769–70, finds it unpersuasive because of the evident notice problem. See also Shuttlesworth v. Birmingham, 394 U.S. 147 (1969), p. 185, *supra*, where the state supreme court, in upholding a conviction under a city ordinance prohibiting demonstrations without a permit, construed the ordinance so as to restrict the city's freedom to deny a permit. The Supreme Court assumed the narrowing construction would pass constitutional muster, but nonetheless reversed, noting that city officials clearly indicated that no demonstration would be permitted under any circumstances, and that the defendant would have needed "extraordinary clairvoyance" to anticipate the construction ultimately given to the ordinance. *Cf.* the related question, discussed but not resolved in Edgar v. MITE, Paragraph (3)(d), *supra*, whether an actor is immune from liability for conduct following issuance of a preliminary injunction in his favor if the final resolution on the merits goes against him.

(6) *The Pertinence of Pending Actions Against Nonparties.* Notice the contrary indications in Hicks and Doran with respect to the question whether Younger ever bars X from obtaining federal relief because of the pendency of state proceedings against Y? [12] Did the Court in Hicks really mean to hold so casually (albeit in the alternative) that for Younger purposes a criminal prosecution against Y can oust X's right to litigate a constitutional claim in federal court because X and Y's interests are "intertwined", X and Y share the same lawyer, and X has not made a "clear showing" that he cannot protect his rights in state court? Compare the Court's refusal in Doran to withhold federal relief in favor of two bar owners because of the pending prosecution of the third: "while [the three owners] are represented by common counsel, * * * they are apparently unrelated in terms of ownership, control, and management" (pp. 928–29). Hicks, decided one week earlier, was not cited.

Aren't the interests of employees and owners potentially quite divergent in Hicks? Suppose, for example, the prosecutor were to offer a favorable plea to the employees if they agree to implicate the owners. See Wood v. Georgia, 450 U.S. 261 (1981) (vacating the convictions of two employees of a theatre for distributing obscene materials, and remanding the case, because of a possible conflict of interest; the employees' lawyer was paid by their employer, who may have been more interested in

---

12. In Steffel the Court dismissed the argument that the pendency of a prosecution against Steffel's handbilling companion barred Steffel's federal action. 415 U.S. at 471 n. 19. See also Roe v. Wade, 410 U.S. 113, 126–27 (1973) (pending prosecution against a physician who was a plaintiff-intervenor does not bar challenge to same statute by a different plaintiff).

creating a test case than in representing the employees' distinctive interests). Shouldn't X be barred from seeking federal relief only if he would be deemed to be a privy (and hence to have had his day in court) in the pending state court proceeding against Y? [13]

(7) *Exhaustion of State Remedies and Res Judicata.* Once the doctrine of equitable restraint closes the door to the federal courthouse because a state proceeding is pending, does there ever come a time—for example, after the state trial court has rendered judgment—when access to a federal court is no longer barred? The answer to this question may depend on whether further state-court remedies are available at the time the federal suit is filed.

(a) *State Remedies Still Available.* In Huffman v. Pursue, Ltd., 420 U.S. 592 (1975), the state had brought a civil action under its obscenity laws to "abate" the showing of obscene movies by Pursue. After the state trial court had issued a final order of abatement, Pursue filed a § 1983 action in federal court challenging the validity of the state obscenity statute. The Supreme Court first ruled that Younger applied when this form of *civil* proceeding was pending in state court—a question discussed at pp. 1433–38, *infra.* The Court then ruled that a party in Pursue's position "must exhaust his state appellate remedies before seeking relief in the District Court, unless he can bring himself within one of the exceptions specified in Younger" (p. 608), and noted that at the time the federal action was commenced Pursue still had the right to appeal the state trial court's order. Refusing to "assum[e] that state judges will not be faithful to their constitutional responsibilities" (p. 611), the Court held that the exhaustion requirement is not excused merely because the prospects for success in the state courts are poor.

Is there any reason for saying that a state proceeding still open to review by the state appellate courts is not "pending" for Younger purposes? Is it possible nonetheless to find that an appeal is futile, given the state's precedents, without accusing the state courts of constitutional infidelity? Compare the exhaustion requirement in federal habeas corpus, p. 1552, *infra.* Even if Younger were held not to apply when state remedies are futile, however, res judicata would presumably foreclose any federal action based upon a federal issue that was fully and fairly litigated in state court.

(b) *State Remedies No Longer Available.* Suppose that at the time he files a federal action, the federal plaintiff has forfeited state court appellate remedies of which he could have availed himself at an earlier point. This may have been the case in Huffman: the Court was not sure whether at the time the federal district court issued its injunction Pursue could still have appealed the state court's order, but said that it "may not avoid the standards of Younger by simply failing to comply with the procedures of perfecting its appeal within the Ohio judicial system" (p. 611 n. 22). It may also have been the case in Hicks. See footnote 20 of the Hicks opinion.

A similar question was presented in Ellis v. Dyson, 421 U.S. 426 (1975), decided two months after Huffman. On the basis of their pleas of *nolo contendre,* several individuals were convicted in a Texas municipal court of

13. Compare County of Imperial v. Munoz, 449 U.S. 54 (1980), p. 1329, *supra,* holding that the plaintiffs' federal action seeking to set aside on federal grounds a state court injunction against a different person was barred under the Anti-Injunction Act, 28 U.S.C. § 2283, unless the federal plaintiffs were "strangers" to the state court litigation.

loitering, and fined $10 each. Under Texas law, they were entitled to trial de novo in a county court and thereafter to appellate review. But, fearing higher fines on reconviction, they allowed the municipal court convictions to become final. They then brought suit in federal district court, seeking (a) a declaratory judgment that the loitering ordinance was unconstitutional and could not be applied to them in the future, and (b) an order "expunging" the records of the municipal court convictions. The court of appeals affirmed the district court's holding that the federal plaintiffs were not entitled to relief absent a showing of bad faith. The Supreme Court, in a confusing and opaque opinion, reversed and remanded for reconsideration in light of the intervening decision in Steffel, with particular instructions to determine whether there existed a real and continuing case or controversy. Justice Powell, dissenting, argued that the collateral attack on the convictions raised an issue not of equitable restraint, but of res judicata. He then concluded that plaintiffs' challenge was in any event barred by the doctrine that a defendant who enters a constitutionally valid guilty plea cannot litigate in a federal habeas corpus proceeding alleged violations of constitutional rights, see Tollett v. Henderson, 411 U.S. 258 (1973), p. 1523, *infra;* as a result, there was no need to decide whether § 1983 could be used as a basis for collateral attack on state court judgments.

Justice Powell is right, isn't he, that if a federal § 1983 suit challenges the validity of a state statute under which a conviction has already become final, the real issue is res judicata rather than Younger and exhaustion? Is there any reason why the federal plaintiff's forfeiture of state remedies should preclude the § 1983 suit when res judicata doctrine would not?

On this point, consider Wooley v. Maynard, 430 U.S. 705 (1977), Paragraph (5)(b), *supra.* There, Maynard, who had not appealed any of his three state convictions for obscuring his license plate, later joined with his wife in bringing a § 1983 action to enjoin enforcement of the state law under which he had been convicted. In finding no bar to the action, the Court distinguished Huffman: there, the plaintiff was trying to "annul the results of a state trial"; by contrast, Maynard sought relief that was "wholly prospective, to preclude further prosecution," and did not seek expungement of his prior convictions or relief from their consequences (p. 711). Federal intervention was appropriate to avoid the dilemma of either risking punishment under state law or forgoing conduct that might be constitutionally protected.[14]

The Court proceeded to award the Maynards federal injunctive relief without discussing whether the prior state judgment precluded the federal suit. The three-judge district court in Wooley had addressed this question, ruling that the Maynards were not precluded from challenging the statute's constitutionality because that issue was not actually litigated in the criminal prosecutions. 406 F.Supp. at 1385 n. 6. And though the district

---

14. Is this reasoning consistent with Doran's denial of all relief (including relief from prosecution for conduct *pendente lite*) to a litigant (M & L) against whom a state prosecution was pending? Doran surely suggests that even if, in Huffman, the plaintiff had not sought expungement of his conviction, federal relief would be barred until appellate remedies had been exhausted. Does Wooley require reconsideration of this aspect of Doran? See Spartacus, Inc. v. Borough of McKees Rocks, 694 F.2d 947, 949 n. 3 (3d Cir.1982), citing Wooley and Doran in holding that Younger does not bar a federal action seeking preliminary injunctive relief only against future enforcement of a local ordinance, even though the federal plaintiff had pending in state court an appeal from a conviction for violating the ordinance in the past.

court did not say this, claim preclusion could not be invoked, since Maynard could not have counterclaimed in a misdemeanor prosecution for an injunction against enforcement of a state statute. But see Currie, *Res Judicata: The Neglected Defense*, 45 U.Chi.L.Rev. 317, 336–47, 349–50 (1978), questioning the lower court's reasoning, though not necessarily its result.

(8) *Younger and Federal Damage Actions.* In Juidice v. Vail, 430 U.S. 327, 339 n. 16 (1977), the Supreme Court noted but reserved the question "as to the applicability of Younger–Huffman principles to a § 1983 suit seeking only [damage] relief." This question can arise in different contexts.

(a) Consider first Martin v. Merola, 532 F.2d 191 (2d Cir.1976). The defendants in a pending state criminal case, alleging a denial of their fair trial rights, brought a damage action against a state prosecutor. The court of appeals held that the complaint had to be dismissed as premature. The court went on to opine that, in any event, it would "offend the principle of comity for a federal district court to inquire into plaintiffs' ability to secure a fair trial in a pending state prosecution. See Younger v. Harris * * *" (pp. 194–95).

Isn't the court's principal holding—that a damage remedy should not be available until the damage is done—correct? Is the citation to Younger apposite?

(b) A more general problem is posed by § 1983 damage actions that necessarily require testing the validity of a state criminal conviction. The ordinary route for a federal challenge to a state conviction itself is a federal habeas corpus action, which is subject to certain limitations, most importantly that the petitioner first exhaust state remedies. May he circumvent the exhaustion requirement by filing a § 1983 action for damages? In Tower v. Glover, 467 U.S. 914 (1984), a state convict filed such an action, but he had already exhausted or forfeited all state remedies. The Court said "[w]e therefore have no occasion to decide if a Federal District Court should abstain from deciding a § 1983 suit for damages stemming from an unlawful conviction pending the collateral exhaustion of state-court attacks on the conviction itself" (p. 923). Justices Brennan, Marshall, Blackmun, and Stevens concurred in all but this part of the Court's opinion, complaining that the issue reserved by the Court was never raised or briefed and "has absolutely no bearing on the disposition of this case" (p. 924). Some courts of appeals have required exhaustion in this situation. See, *e.g.,* Parkhurst v. State of Wyoming, 641 F.2d 775 (10th Cir.1981) (per curiam); Miner v. Brackney, 719 F.2d 954 (8th Cir.1983) (per curiam).

On the relationship between § 1983 and federal habeas corpus, see generally Preiser v. Rodriguez, p. 1638, *infra.*

(c) In Giulini v. Blessing, 654 F.2d 189 (2d Cir.1981), the Second Circuit indicated that its broad dictum in Martin v. Merola, *supra,* about the applicability of Younger to damage actions should not be taken seriously. Guilini found that a § 1983 damage action challenging a local zoning ordinance was not barred by Younger, even though there was pending in state court an action against the federal plaintiff for a previous violation. The court of appeals strongly suggested, however, that on remand the district court should exercise its discretion to stay the action in view of the parallel state proceeding. See generally Sec. 2(D), *infra.*

See also Deakins v. Monaghan, 108 S.Ct. 523 (1988). There, the court of appeals had reversed the district court's dismissal, under Younger, of a damages claim, ruling that the case should instead have been stayed. Before the Supreme Court, the plaintiffs represented that on remand they would seek to stay the damage claims pending resolution of state prosecutions then pending. In this posture, the Supreme Court affirmed the court of appeals' disposition, without deciding whether Younger applied to damage claims. Justice White (joined by Justice O'Connor) would have reached that question. He argued that Younger's policy of avoiding the preemption of state proceedings was fully implicated by federal damage claims, whose decision would presumably be res judicata in any state prosecution.[15]

(9) *Equitable Restraint and State Executive Functions.* Rizzo v. Goode, 423 U.S. 362 (1976), was a lawsuit under § 1983 charging the mayor and other high officials of the City of Philadelphia with responsibility for a wide variety of discriminatory and arbitrary police practices. The Supreme Court held that there was no justification for equitable relief against the named defendants, since there was no showing that they had themselves invaded or authorized any invasions of the plaintiffs' constitutional rights. The opinion then went on, quite unnecessarily, to suggest that "principles of federalism" would independently bar relief. After citing Doran and Huffman, the Court said (p. 380): "Thus the principles of federalism which play such an important part in governing the relationship between federal courts and state governments, though initially expounded and perhaps entitled to their greatest weight in cases where it was sought to enjoin a criminal prosecution in progress, have not been limited either to that situation or indeed to a criminal proceeding itself. We think these principles likewise have applicability where injunctive relief is sought, not against the judicial branch of the state government, but against those in charge of an executive branch of an agency of state or local governments such as petitioners here." Accord, City of Los Angeles v. Lyons, 461 U.S. 95, 112–13 (1983).

Do you think this is an appropriate use of the Younger doctrine?[16] Do you understand the *content* of a rule that would take the Younger doctrine of non-interference with state judicial proceedings and convert it by analogy into a principle of non-interference with state executive officials?

This aspect of Rizzo has been extensively criticized. See, *e.g.*, Weinberg, *The New Judicial Federalism,* 29 Stan.L.Rev. 1191, 1219–27 (1977); Eisenberg & Yeazell, *The Ordinary and the Extraordinary in Institutional*

---

15. Does Fair Assessment in Real Estate Ass'n, Inc. v. McNary, 454 U.S. 100 (1981), p. 1343, *supra,* argue for holding Younger applicable to federal damage actions? In McNary, the Court ruled that "the principle of comity bars federal courts from granting damages relief" in a § 1983 action against state tax officials. Though the Tax Anti–Injunction Act did not itself apply, the Court found that the "principle of comity"—which was given its "fullest articulation" in Younger—was applicable and barred relief, even in the absence of a pending state proceeding (pp. 111–13); a key argument was that before damages could be awarded, the district court would "[i]n effect [have to] enter a declaratory judgment" (p. 113). Should McNary be limited to the special problem of federal interference with state tax administration?

16. Just two years earlier in Allee v. Medrano, 416 U.S. 802 (1974), in approving a district court decree barring certain law enforcement practices, the Court said (p. 814) that it "creates no interference with prosecutions pending in the state courts, so that the special considerations relevant to cases like Younger v. Harris, 401 U.S. 37, do not apply here." Chief Justice Burger's dissent, joined by Justices Rehnquist and White, relied heavily on Younger; Justice Powell did not participate. Only Justice Stewart joined the majority in both cases.

Litigation, 93 Harv.L.Rev. 465, 503–06 (1980); Fiss, Paragraph (3)(b), *supra,* at 1159.

NOTE ON THE APPLICATION OF EQUITABLE RESTRAINT IN THE CONTEXT OF PENDING CIVIL STATE COURT OR ADMINISTRATIVE PROCEEDINGS

(1) In Huffman v. Pursue, Ltd., 420 U.S. 592 (1975) (also discussed at p. 1429, *supra*), the state brought a civil action under its obscenity laws to "abate" the showing of obscene movies by Pursue. The Supreme Court held that Younger applies to bar federal relief when "[t]he State is a party to the ＊ ＊ ＊ proceeding, and the proceeding is both in aid of and closely related to criminal statutes" (p. 604).

In the Court's view, the federalism strain of Younger—its policies of avoiding interference with state officials, duplicative proceedings, and negative reflection upon the state courts—all counseled restraint. The Court conceded, however, that Younger's equitable component—the traditional reluctance to enjoin criminal proceedings—was not "strictly" on point. "But whatever may be the weight attached to this factor in civil litigation involving private parties, we deal here with a state proceeding which in important respects is more akin to a criminal prosecution than are most civil cases" (p. 604).

The Court rejected the argument that restraint was inappropriate because the defendant in a state civil proceeding, unlike a state criminal defendant, cannot ultimately present his federal constitutional claims to a federal court on habeas corpus. Pointing out that a state civil defendant can always seek Supreme Court review (in Pursue's case, by appeal), the Court said (p. 606) that in any event, the "unarticulated major premise," that every litigant with a federal claim "is entitled to have it decided on the merits by a federal, rather than a state, court," at best establishes a right to *relitigate* a federal issue adversely decided by the state courts.[1] Even if valid—a question not reached—this premise would not preclude the application of Younger, which requires only that the states be allowed initially to decide the federal claims. The question whether Pursue could relitigate its first amendment claim in a federal court (in a § 1983 action following completion of the state proceedings) was left open. (The Court has since held that res judicata applies and can foreclose such an action. See pp. 1615–30, *infra.*)

Justice Brennan's dissent, joined by Justices Douglas and Marshall, complained that the Court was taking a "first step toward extending to state *civil* proceedings generally the holding of Younger v. Harris" (p. 613). He argued that such a course would undermine Mitchum v. Foster, which, on virtually identical facts, held a federal court § 1983 action not barred by the Anti–Injunction Act, 28 U.S.C. § 2283.[2] Further, he argued, there are

---

1. Should the majority have questioned the minor premise that a criminal defendant can always obtain federal review via habeas corpus? What if the defendant is only fined, or has completed a brief sentence before his state remedies are exhausted? See p. 1569, *infra.*

2. Can one argue that § 2283 in fact supports the Court's holding? After all, (i) Younger relied heavily upon that Act as a source of the federal policy of noninterference, and (ii) the Act does not distinguish criminal from civil proceedings.

functional differences between state civil and criminal proceedings: while many safeguards are provided against the initiation of unfair or unjust criminal proceedings, state civil proceedings may be initiated "merely upon the filing of a complaint, whether or not well founded" (p. 615). (The ease of filing a civil complaint may also facilitate a state official's availing himself of the "reverse removal power" established by Hicks v. Miranda.)

To what extent does Younger's "bad faith" exception adequately address Justice Brennan's concern about the ease of filing state civil proceedings? See p. 1402, *supra*.

One other difference between pending civil and criminal cases deserves mention. Unlike a criminal defendant, a civil defendant in state court will often be able to counterclaim for relief against enforcement of the challenged enactment—including declaratory relief, class relief, and relief *pendente lite*. But if a civil defendant fails to counterclaim, compulsory counterclaim and claim preclusion rules may bar later federal court consideration of the federal constitutional claim, even if the constitutional issue was not raised or decided in state court. Compare Wooley v. Maynard, p. 1430, *supra*.

(2) Juidice v. Vail, 430 U.S. 327 (1977), buried the notion that Huffman was limited to civil proceedings "in aid of" criminal statutes. There, following a default judgment against him in a debt collection case, Vail was found in civil contempt of a New York court's order to attend a deposition to provide information relevant to satisfying the judgment. Vail then filed a federal class action to enjoin New York's judges from using the state's statutory contempt procedures, which, he alleged, denied due process. The Court held that Younger and Huffman barred the injunction. The state's interest in its contempt processes, "through which it vindicates the regular operation of its judicial system," is important enough to warrant the application of Younger, "so long as that system itself affords the opportunity to pursue federal claims within it," even though no criminal or "quasi-criminal" law was being enforced (p. 335).[3]

(3) After several decisions in which it applied the Juidice rationale,[4] the Court, in Middlesex Ethics Comm. v. Garden State Bar Ass'n, 457 U.S.

3. Justice Stevens concurred in the result on the ground that the New York procedure was valid, but did not agree that it was appropriate to invoke Younger. Justice Brennan (joined by Justice Marshall) and Justice Stewart each dissented; the latter thought that Pullman abstention was called for.

4. Trainor v. Hernandez, 431 U.S. 434 (1977), involved a state court civil action brought by the State of Illinois to recover welfare payments that the defendants had allegedly obtained by fraud. After the state, at the outset of the action, attached some funds of the defendants, they brought a federal challenge to the constitutional validity of Illinois' attachment procedures. The Supreme Court held, 5–4, that Younger applied: "[T]he suit and the accompanying writ of attachment were brought to vindicate important state policies" (p. 444). The Court did acknowledge, however, that

federal interference would be warranted if it would not be possible to challenge the validity of the attachment procedures in the Illinois litigation, and remanded the case for a determination of that question. In dissent, Justice Brennan (joined by Justice Marshall) continued to criticize the application of Younger to pending civil proceedings. In addition, he and Justice Stevens (who also wrote an opinion) argued that the case fell within exceptions to Younger for challenges to (i) "patently and flagrantly unconstitutional" statutes and (ii) the constitutionality of state procedures themselves. (For discussion of these points, see pp. 1401–04, *supra*.) Justice Stewart stated that he agreed "substantially" with both dissents.

In Moore v. Sims, 442 U.S. 415 (1979), Younger was held to foreclose interference with a pending state proceeding in which the state was seeking custody of children

423 (1982), extended Younger once again. The case involved New Jersey's system for the discipline of attorneys, for which the state supreme court had ultimate responsibility. By rule, the court had established local district ethics committees to investigate complaints and hold hearings on any charges issued, subject to review by a statewide board and in some cases by the state supreme court. A lawyer who had referred to a pending murder trial as "a travesty," a "legalized lynching," and a "kangaroo court" was charged with violating a bar rule prohibiting conduct "prejudicial to the administration of justice." Rather than defend himself before the local ethics committee, the lawyer filed a federal action challenging the rule under the First Amendment, but the Supreme Court held the suit barred by Younger.

The Court first noted that under state law, a local committee was "an arm of the [New Jersey Supreme Court]" and its disciplinary proceedings were "judicial in nature" (pp. 433–34). Because those proceedings implicate the state's extremely important interests in assuring the professional conduct of attorneys, federal interference was inappropriate, so long as the lawyer had an adequate opportunity to raise his First Amendment claim. The Court rejected his argument that the local ethics committee lacked authority to consider that claim. In addition, citing Hicks v. Miranda, the Court held that it could take account of the fact that the New Jersey Supreme Court had recently undertaken review of the disciplinary case, leaving no doubt that the First Amendment issue could be raised in the pending state proceeding.

Justice Marshall, joined by Justices Brennan, Blackmun, and Stevens, concurred in the judgment, finding Younger applicable only because of the state supreme court's recent intervention. In a separate concurrence, Justice Brennan said that "[t]he traditional * * * responsibility of state courts for [bar discipline] and the quasi-criminal nature of bar disciplinary procedures call for exceptional deference by the federal courts" (p. 438).

(4) Younger's applicability to pending state *administrative* proceedings was raised in Ohio Civil Rights Com'n v. Dayton Christian Schools, Inc., 106 S.Ct. 2718 (1986). There, the Ohio Civil Rights Commission had filed a formal administrative complaint against a religious school for terminating the employment of a pregnant teacher. The school then filed a federal court § 1983 action to enjoin the administrative proceedings as a violation of the Religion Clauses of the First Amendment. Relying in part upon Middlesex County, the Court ruled that Younger bars interference with a pending state administrative proceeding involving sufficiently important state interests, of which combatting discrimination was one (p. 2723). The Court rejected on the merits the school's argument that the investigation itself was prohibited by the First Amendment (p. 2724). And it then found that the school had an adequate opportunity to raise its First Amendment objections: even if they could not be raised in the administrative hearing, it sufficed that they could be heard in state court judicial review of any administrative decision (p. 2724).[5]

who had allegedly been abused by their parents. The Court divided 5–4 on the question whether the state proceedings afforded the federal plaintiffs a meaningful opportunity to raise their federal constitutional claims.

5. The case was consistent, the Court explained, with the rule that § 1983 plaintiffs need not exhaust state administrative remedies, *see* Patsy v. Florida Board of Regents, 457 U.S. 496 (1982), p. 1350, *supra*: "Unlike Patsy, the administrative

The Court had to distinguish Hawaii Housing Auth. v. Midkiff, 467 U.S. 229 (1984). That case was a federal challenge to a Hawaii land redistribution program. Before the federal preliminary injunction issued, a state agency had started the process for acquiring land owned by the federal plaintiffs, ordering them to submit to compulsory arbitration as provided by state law. The Supreme Court found Younger inapplicable: under Hawaii law the administrative proceedings were not "judicial," and "Younger is not a bar to federal court action when state judicial proceedings have not themselves commenced" (pp. 238–39). In the Ohio case, the Court, citing Midkiff, said "if state law expressly indicates that the administrative proceedings are not even 'judicial in nature,' abstention may not be appropriate" (106 S.Ct. at 2723 n. 2).

Finding the school's challenge not ripe, Justice Stevens, joined by Justices Brennan, Marshall, and Blackmun, concurred in the judgment, but criticized the Court's reliance on Younger: "That disposition would presumably deny the School a federal forum to adjudicate the constitutionality of a provisional administrative remedy, such as reinstatement pending resolution of the complainant's charges, even though * * * the Commission refuses to address the merits of the constitutional claims" (p. 2726 n. 5).

In the Midkiff case, had Hawaii deemed the arbitration proceeding "judicial," should the Younger issue have come out the other way? Wasn't Justice Stevens correct in the Ohio case that the critical question is not the state's label, but whether the pending proceedings are before a tribunal competent to adjudicate the federal constitutional issue? Isn't federal interference justified in an otherwise ripe case if the administrative agency lacks that competence? *Cf.* Gibson v. Berryhill, p. 1403, *supra*.

A suggestion along this line was offered in Monaghan v. Deakins, 798 F.2d 632 (3d Cir.1986). The suit arose from an allegedly unconstitutional search and seizure of documents by state officials. After finding that Younger did not bar a damages claim, the court ruled that an injunction ordering return of the documents was not barred by the pendency of a state grand jury investigation of the federal plaintiffs. The court read Middlesex and Midkiff as mandating noninterference only when there is a pending proceeding before a tribunal with "authority to *adjudicate* the merits of a federal plaintiff's federal claims" (p. 637). Was this decision, however persuasive, consistent with the Ohio Civil Rights Commission decision, which had been handed down a month earlier?

The issue presented changed considerably when some of the federal plaintiffs were thereafter indicted. Before the Supreme Court, all the plaintiffs represented that they wished to withdraw their federal equitable claim, which the Court accordingly ruled should be dismissed with prejudice as moot. Deakins v. Monaghan, 108 S.Ct. 523 (1988). (On the Court's treatment of the damage claims, see p. 1432, *supra*.)

(5) Can Younger sometimes bar an injunction against a pending civil action between *private* parties? Note that in order to escape the bar of § 2283 under Mitchum v. Foster, the federal suit must be filed under

proceedings here are coercive rather than remedial, began before any substantial advancement in the federal action took place, and involve an important state interest" (p. 2723 n. 2).

§ 1983; this requires that the private defendant in that suit have acted under color of state law, see pp. 1240–41, *supra.*

The issue arose in Juidice, Paragraph (2), *supra,* though the state judge who issued the contempt citation might in some sense have been viewed as a party to the contempt proceeding that was being challenged in federal court. A purer example is Pennzoil Co. v. Texaco, Inc., 107 S.Ct. 1519 (1987). Pennzoil had obtained an $11 billion jury verdict against Texaco in a Texas court. Texas law gave Pennzoil two important rights after judgment: (i) to obtain a writ of execution permitting it to levy execution on Texaco's assets unless Texaco posted a sufficient bond (Texas law appeared to call for a bond equal to the judgment and interest, though it was not certain that such an extraordinary amount would be required); and (ii) to secure liens on Texaco's real property in Texas, without regard to the posting of a bond.

Before judgment on the verdict was entered in state court, Texaco brought suit in federal court in New York (where it was headquartered) to enjoin Pennzoil from taking action to enforce the Texas judgment soon to be entered. Such an injunction, Texaco argued, rather than interfering with state proceedings, was necessary to permit an appeal to go forward. The district court issued a preliminary injunction along the lines requested, finding that application of the lien and bond provisions would probably force Texaco into bankruptcy and hence denied due process. The court of appeals substantially affirmed, though it rejected some of the district court's reasoning and stressed the "extraordinary circumstances" arising from a judgment of "unprecedented" amount (784 F.2d at 1157).

The Supreme Court reversed. Without considering whether the lower courts were correct in holding that the suit was properly brought under § 1983 (and hence not barred by § 2283),[6] Justice Powell's opinion for five Justices stated that Younger applied when, as here, "the State's interests in the proceeding are so important that exercise of the federal judicial power would disregard the comity between the States and the National Government" (p. 1526). As in Juidice, the pending proceeding implicated the state's interest in enforcing the orders and judgments of its courts. Justice Powell added that the Texas courts might interpret state law to provide some relief from the lien and bond provisions; federal noninterference was thus also supported by the policy of constitutional avoidance. In a footnote, he asserted that the Court was not holding that Younger applies whenever a civil case is pending in state court (p. 1527 n. 12).

Four Justices concurred in the judgment but rejected the Court's Younger analysis.[7] Justice Brennan's opinion (with which Justices Marshall, Blackmun and Stevens agreed on this point) repeated his view that Younger should be generally inapplicable to civil proceedings, and argued that since Texas law directs state officials merely to "do Pennzoil's bidding" in enforcing the judgment, it was only Pennzoil, not Texas, that had an interest in the pending proceedings (pp. 1530–31). (For further discussion of the Pennzoil case, see Chap. XII, pp. 1634–38, *infra.*)

6. The four concurring Justices addressed this issue, agreeing with the lower courts. *See* Justices Brennan's and Stevens' separate opinions.

7. Justices Brennan, Marshall, and Stevens concluded that Texaco's due process argument lacked merit. Justice Marshall further argued that the district court lacked jurisdiction under the "Rooker–Feldman" doctrine, pp. 1630–38, *infra.* Justice Blackmun favored Pullman abstention.

For commentary on the application of Younger to civil cases, see, *e.g.*, Bartels, *Avoiding a Comity of Errors: A Model for Adjudicating Federal Civil Rights Suits That "Interfere" With State Civil Proceedings,* 29 Stan.L. Rev. 27 (1976); Aldisert, *On Being Civil to* Younger, 11 Conn.L.Rev. 181 (1979); Edwards, *The Changing Notion of "Our Federalism",* 33 Wayne L.Rev. 1015 (1987).

———

After the extension of Younger to many kinds of civil proceedings, and the decision in Hicks v. Miranda permitting a later-filed state proceeding to oust federal jurisdiction, how much is left of the rule, stated in Kline v. Burke Constr. Co., 260 U.S. 226, 230 (1922), Sec. 1(A), p. 1321, *supra,* that when in personam actions are pending in state and federal courts, "[e]ach court is free to proceed in its own way * * * without reference to the proceeding in the other court"? Consider this question in light of the materials that follow.

———

SUBSECTION D: PARALLEL PROCEEDINGS

———

COLORADO RIVER WATER CONSERVATION DISTRICT v. UNITED STATES

424 U.S. 800, 96 S.Ct. 1236, 47 L.Ed.2d 483 (1976).
Certiorari to the United States Court of Appeals for the Tenth Circuit.

MR. JUSTICE BRENNAN delivered the opinion of the Court.

The McCarran Amendment, 66 Stat. 560, 43 U.S.C. § 666, provides that "consent is hereby given to join the United States as a defendant in any suit (1) for the adjudication of rights to the use of water of a river system or other source, or (2) for the administration of such rights, where it appears that the United States is the owner of or is in the process of acquiring water rights by appropriation under State law, by purchase, by exchange, or otherwise, and the United States is a necessary party to such suit." The questions presented by this case concern the effect of the McCarran Amendment upon the jurisdiction of the federal district courts under 28 U.S.C. § 1345 over suits for determination of water rights brought by the United States as trustee for certain Indian tribes and as owner of various non-Indian Government claims.

I

It is probable that no problem of the Southwest section of the Nation is more critical than that of scarcity of water. As southwestern populations have grown, conflicting claims to this scarce resource have increased. To meet these claims, several Southwestern States have established elaborate procedures for allocation of water and adjudication of conflicting claims to that resource. In 1969, Colorado enacted its Water Rights Determination and Administration Act in an effort to revamp its legal procedures for determining claims to water within the State.

Under the Colorado Act, the State is divided into seven Water Divisions, each Division encompassing one or more entire drainage basins for the larger rivers in Colorado. Adjudication of water claims within each Division occurs on a continuous basis. Each month, Water Referees in each Division rule on applications for water rights filed within the preceding five months or refer those applications to the Water Judge of their Division. Every six months, the Water Judge passes on referred applications and contested decisions by Referees. A State Engineer and engineers for each Division are responsible for the administration and distribution of the waters of the State according to the determinations in each Division.

Colorado applies the doctrine of prior appropriation in establishing rights to the use of water. Under that doctrine, one acquires a right to water by diverting it from its natural source and applying it to some beneficial use. Continued beneficial use of the water is required in order to maintain the right. In periods of shortage, priority among confirmed rights is determined according to the date of initial diversion.

The reserved rights of the United States extend to Indian reservations, Winters v. United States, 207 U.S. 564 (1908), and other federal lands, such as national parks and forests, Arizona v. California, 373 U.S. 546 (1963). The reserved rights claimed by the United States in this case affect waters within Colorado Water Division No. 7. On November 14, 1972, the Government instituted this suit in the United States District Court for the District of Colorado, invoking the court's jurisdiction under 28 U.S.C. § 1345. The District Court is located in Denver, some 300 miles from Division 7. The suit, against some 1,000 water users, sought declaration of the Government's rights to waters in certain rivers and their tributaries located in Division 7. In the suit, the Government asserted reserved rights on its own behalf and on behalf of certain Indian tribes, as well as rights based on state law. It sought appointment of a water master to administer any waters decreed to the United States. Prior to institution of this suit, the Government had pursued adjudication of non-Indian reserved rights and other water claims based on state law in Water Divisions 4, 5, and 6, and the Government continues to participate fully in those Divisions.

Shortly after the federal suit was commenced, one of the defendants in that suit filed an application in the state court for Division 7, seeking an order directing service of process on the United States in order to make it a party to proceedings in Division 7 for the purpose of adjudicating all of the Government's claims, both state and federal. On January 3, 1973, the United States was served pursuant to authority of the McCarran Amendment. Several defendants and intervenors in the federal proceeding then filed a motion in the District Court to dismiss on the ground that under the Amendment, the court was without jurisdiction to determine federal water rights. Without deciding the jurisdictional question, the District Court, on June 21, 1973, granted the motion in an unreported oral opinion stating that the doctrine of abstention required deference to the proceedings in Division 7. On appeal, the Court of Appeals for the Tenth Circuit reversed, United States v. Akin, 504 F.2d 115 (1974), holding that the suit of the United States was within district-court jurisdiction under 28 U.S.C. § 1345, and that abstention was inappropriate. * * * We reverse.

II

We first consider the question of district-court jurisdiction under 28 U.S.C. § 1345. That section provides that the district courts shall have original jurisdiction over all civil actions brought by the Federal Government "[e]xcept as otherwise provided by Act of Congress." It is thus necessary to examine whether the McCarran Amendment is such an Act of Congress excepting jurisdiction under § 1345.

The McCarran Amendment does not by its terms, at least, indicate any repeal of jurisdiction under § 1345. ＊ ＊ ＊

＊ ＊ ＊

＊ ＊ ＊ The immediate effect of the Amendment is to give consent to jurisdiction in the state courts concurrent with jurisdiction in the federal courts over controversies involving federal rights to the use of water. There is no irreconcilability in the existence of concurrent state and federal jurisdiction. Such concurrency has, for example, long existed under federal diversity jurisdiction. Accordingly, we hold that the McCarran Amendment in no way diminished federal-district-court jurisdiction under § 1345 and that the District Court had jurisdiction to hear this case.[15]

III

We turn next to the question whether this suit nevertheless was properly dismissed in view of the concurrent state proceedings in Division 7.

A

First, we consider whether the McCarran Amendment provided consent to determine federal reserved rights held on behalf of Indians in state court. This is a question not previously squarely addressed by this Court, and given the claims for Indian water rights in this case, dismissal clearly would have been inappropriate if the state court had no jurisdiction to decide those claims. We conclude that the state court had jurisdiction over Indian water rights under the Amendment.

＊ ＊ ＊

B

Next, we consider whether the District Court's dismissal was appropriate under the doctrine of abstention. We hold that the dismissal cannot be supported under that doctrine in any of its forms.

Abstention from the exercise of federal jurisdiction is the exception, not the rule. "The doctrine of abstention, under which a District Court may decline to exercise or postpone the exercise of its jurisdiction, is an extraordinary and narrow exception to the duty of a District Court to adjudicate a controversy properly before it. Abdication of the obligation to decide cases can be justified under this doctrine only in the exceptional circumstances where the order to the parties to repair to the State court would clearly serve an important countervailing interest." County of Allegheny v. Frank Mashuda Co., 360 U.S. 185, 188–189 (1959). "[I]t was never a doctrine of equity that a federal court should exercise its judicial discretion to dismiss a suit merely because a State court could entertain it." Alabama Pub. Serv. Comm'n v. Southern R. Co., 341 U.S. 341, 361 (1951)

---

15. The District Court also would have had jurisdiction of this suit under the general federal-question jurisdiction of 28 U.S.C. § 1331. For the same reasons, the McCarran Amendment did not affect jurisdiction under § 1331 either.

(Frankfurter, J., concurring in result). Our decisions have confined the circumstances appropriate for abstention to three general categories.

(a) Abstention is appropriate "in cases presenting a federal constitutional issue which might be mooted or presented in a different posture by a state court determination of pertinent state law." County of Allegheny v. Frank Mashuda Co., *supra*, at 189. See, *e.g.*, Railroad Comm'n of Texas v. Pullman Co., 312 U.S. 496 (1941). This case, however, presents no federal constitutional issue for decision.

(b) Abstention is also appropriate where there have been presented difficult questions of state law bearing on policy problems of substantial public import whose importance transcends the result in the case then at bar. Louisiana Power & Light Co. v. City of Thibodaux, 360 U.S. 25 (1959), for example, involved such a question. In particular, the concern there was with the scope of the eminent domain power of municipalities under state law. See also Kaiser Steel Corp. v. W.S. Ranch Co., 391 U.S. 593 (1968). In some cases, however, the state question itself need not be determinative of state policy. It is enough that exercise of federal review of the question in a case and in similar cases would be disruptive of state efforts to establish a coherent policy with respect to a matter of substantial public concern. In Burford v. Sun Oil Co., 319 U.S. 315 (1943), for example, the Court held that a suit seeking review of the reasonableness under Texas state law of a state commission's permit to drill oil wells should have been dismissed by the District Court. The reasonableness of the permit in that case was not of transcendent importance, but review of reasonableness by the federal courts in that and future cases, where the State had established its own elaborate review system for dealing with the geological complexities of oil and gas fields, would have had an impermissibly disruptive effect on state policy for the management of those fields. See also Alabama Pub. Serv. Comm'n v. Southern R. Co., *supra*.[21]

The present case clearly does not fall within this second category of abstention. While state claims are involved in the case, the state law to be applied appears to be settled. No questions bearing on state policy are presented for decision. Nor will decision of the state claims impair efforts to implement state policy as in Burford. To be sure, the federal claims that are involved in the case go to the establishment of water rights which may conflict with similar rights based on state law. But the mere potential for conflict in the results of adjudications, does not, without more, warrant staying exercise of federal jurisdiction. See Meredith v. Winter Haven,

---

21. We note that Burford v. Sun Oil Co., and Alabama Pub. Serv. Comm'n v. Southern R. Co., differ from Louisiana Power & Light Co. v. City of Thibodaux, and County of Allegheny v. Frank Mashuda Co., in that the former two cases, unlike the latter two, raised colorable constitutional claims and were therefore brought under federal-question, as well as diversity, jurisdiction. While abstention in Burford and Alabama Pub. Serv. had the effect of avoiding a federal constitutional issue, the opinions indicate that this was not an additional ground for abstention in those cases. See Alabama Pub. Serv. Comm'n v. Southern R. Co., 341 U.S., at 344; Burford v. Sun Oil Co., 319 U.S., at 334; H. Hart & H. Wechsler, The Federal Courts and the Federal System 1005 (2d ed. 1973) ("The two groups of cases share at least one common characteristic: the Pullman purpose of avoiding the necessity for federal constitutional adjudication is not relevant"). We have held, of course, that the opportunity to avoid decision of a constitutional question does not alone justify abstention by a federal court. See Harman v. Forssenius, 380 U.S. 528 (1965); Baggett v. Bullitt, 377 U.S. 360 (1964). Indeed, the presence of a federal basis for jurisdiction may raise the level of justification needed for abstention. See Burford v. Sun Oil Co., *supra*, at 318 n. 5; Hawks v. Hamill, 288 U.S. [52, 61 (1933)].

320 U.S. 228 (1943); Kline v. Burke Constr. Co., 260 U.S. 226 (1922); McClellan v. Carland, 217 U.S. 268 (1910). The potential conflict here, involving state claims and federal claims, would not be such as to impair impermissibly the State's effort to effect its policy respecting the allocation of state waters. Nor would exercise of federal jurisdiction here interrupt any such efforts by restraining the exercise of authority vested in state officers.

(c) Finally, abstention is appropriate where, absent bad faith, harassment, or a patently invalid state statute, federal jurisdiction has been invoked for the purpose of restraining state criminal proceedings, Younger v. Harris, 401 U.S. 37 (1971); Douglas v. City of Jeannette, 319 U.S. 157 (1943); state nuisance proceedings antecedent to a criminal prosecution, which are directed at obtaining the closure of places exhibiting obscene films, Huffman v. Pursue, Ltd., 420 U.S. 592 (1975); or collection of state taxes, Great Lakes Dredge & Dock Co. v. Huffman, 319 U.S. 293 (1943). Like the previous two categories, this category also does not include this case. * * * [23] * * *

C

Although this case falls within none of the abstention categories, there are principles unrelated to considerations of proper constitutional adjudication and regard for federal-state relations which govern in situations involving the contemporaneous exercise of concurrent jurisdictions, either by federal courts or by state and federal courts. These principles rest on considerations of "[w]ise judicial administration, giving regard to conservation of judicial resources and comprehensive disposition of litigation." Kerotest Mfg. Co. v. C–O–Two Fire Equipment Co., 342 U.S. 180, 183 (1952). Generally, as between state and federal courts, the rule is that "the pendency of an action in the state court is no bar to proceedings concerning the same matter in the Federal court having jurisdiction. * * * " McClellan v. Carland, *supra*, at 282. As between federal district courts, however, though no precise rule has evolved, the general principle is to avoid duplicative litigation. See Kerotest Mfg. Co. v. C–O–Two Fire Equipment Co., *supra*. This difference in general approach between state-federal concurrent jurisdiction and wholly federal concurrent jurisdiction stems from the virtually unflagging obligation of the federal courts to exercise the jurisdiction given them. England v. Medical Examiners, 375 U.S. 411, 415 (1964); Cohens v. Virginia, 6 Wheat. 264, 404 (1821) (dictum). Given this obligation, and the absence of weightier considerations of constitutional adjudication and state-federal relations, the circumstances permitting the dismissal of a federal suit due to the presence of a concurrent state proceeding for reasons of wise judicial administration are considerably more limited than the circumstances appropriate for abstention. The former circumstances, though exceptional, do nevertheless exist.

It has been held, for example, that the court first assuming jurisdiction over property may exercise that jurisdiction to the exclusion of other courts. Donovan v. City of Dallas, [377 U.S. 408, 412 (1964)]; Princess Lida

---

23. Our reasons for finding abstention inappropriate in this case make it unnecessary to consider when, if at all, abstention would be appropriate where the Federal Government seeks to invoke federal jurisdiction. *Cf.* Leiter Minerals, Inc. v. United States, 352 U.S. 220 (1957).

v. Thompson, 305 U.S. 456, 466 (1939). But *cf.* Markham v. Allen, 326 U.S. 490 (1946). This has been true even where the Government was a claimant in existing state proceedings and then sought to invoke district-court jurisdiction under the jurisdictional provision antecedent to 28 U.S.C. § 1345. In assessing the appropriateness of dismissal in the event of an exercise of concurrent jurisdiction, a federal court may also consider such factors as the inconvenience of the federal forum, *cf.* Gulf Oil Corp. v. Gilbert, 330 U.S. 501 (1947); the desirability of avoiding piecemeal litigation, *cf.* Brillhart v. Excess Ins. Co., 316 U.S. 491, 495 (1942); and the order in which jurisdiction was obtained by the concurrent forums, Pacific Live Stock Co. v. Oregon Water Bd., 241 U.S. 440, 447 (1916). No one factor is necessarily determinative; a carefully considered judgment taking into account both the obligation to exercise jurisdiction and the combination of factors counselling against that exercise is required. Only the clearest of justifications will warrant dismissal.

Turning to the present case, a number of factors clearly counsel against concurrent federal proceedings. The most important of these is the McCarran Amendment itself. The clear federal policy evinced by that legislation is the avoidance of piecemeal adjudication of water rights in a river system. This policy is akin to that underlying the rule requiring that jurisdiction be yielded to the court first acquiring control of property, for the concern in such instances is with avoiding the generation of additional litigation through permitting inconsistent dispositions of property. This concern is heightened with respect to water rights, the relationships among which are highly interdependent. Indeed, we have recognized that actions seeking the allocation of water essentially involve the disposition of property and are best conducted in unified proceedings. The consent to jurisdiction given by the McCarran Amendment bespeaks a policy that recognizes the availability of comprehensive state systems for adjudication of water rights as the means for achieving these goals.

As has already been observed, the Colorado Water Rights Determination and Administration Act established such a system for the adjudication and management of rights to the use of the State's waters. As the Government concedes and as this Court recognized in [prior cases], the Act established a single continuous proceeding for water rights adjudication which antedated the suit in District Court. * * *

Beyond the congressional policy expressed by the McCarran Amendment and consistent with furtherance of that policy, we also find significant (a) the apparent absence of any proceedings in the District Court, other than the filing of the complaint, prior to the motion to dismiss, (b) the extensive involvement of state water rights occasioned by this suit naming 1,000 defendants, (c) the 300-mile distance between the District Court in Denver and the court in Division 7, and (d) the existing participation by the Government in Division 4, 5, and 6 proceedings. We emphasize, however, that we do not overlook the heavy obligation to exercise jurisdiction. We need not decide, for example, whether, despite the McCarran Amendment, dismissal would be warranted if more extensive proceedings had occurred in the District Court prior to dismissal, if the involvement of state water rights were less extensive than it is here, or if the state proceeding were in some respect inadequate to resolve the federal claims. But the opposing factors here, particularly the policy underlying the McCarran Amendment, justify the District Court's dismissal in this particular case.[26]

The judgment of the Court of Appeals is reversed and the judgment of the District Court dismissing the complaint is affirmed for the reasons here stated.

MR. JUSTICE STEWART, with whom MR. JUSTICE BLACKMUN and MR. JUSTICE STEVENS concur, dissenting.

The Court says that the United States District Court for the District of Colorado clearly had jurisdiction over this lawsuit. I agree. The Court further says that the McCarran Amendment "in no way diminished" the District Court's jurisdiction. I agree. The Court also says that federal courts have a "virtually unflagging obligation * * * to exercise the jurisdiction given them." I agree. And finally, the Court says that nothing in the abstention doctrine "in any of its forms" justified the District Court's dismissal of the Government's complaint. I agree. These views would seem to lead ineluctably to the conclusion that the District Court was wrong in dismissing the complaint. Yet the Court holds that the order of dismissal was "appropriate." With that conclusion I must respectfully disagree.

In holding that the United States shall not be allowed to proceed with its lawsuit, the Court relies principally on cases reflecting the rule that where "control of the property which is the subject of the suit [is necessary] in order to proceed with the cause and to grant the relief sought, the jurisdiction of one court must of necessity yield to that of the other." Penn General Casualty Co. v. Pennsylvania ex rel. Schnader, 294 U.S. 189, 195. See also Donovan v. City of Dallas, 377 U.S. 408; Princess Lida v. Thompson, 305 U.S. 456. But, as those cases make clear, this rule applies only when exclusive control over the subject matter is necessary to effectuate a court's judgment. Here the federal court did not need to obtain *in rem* or *quasi in rem* jurisdiction in order to decide the issues before it. The court was asked simply to determine as a matter of federal law whether federal reservations of water rights had occurred, and, if so, the date and scope of the reservations. The District Court could make such a determination without having control of the river.

The rule invoked by the Court thus does not support the conclusion that it reaches. In the Princess Lida case, for example, the reason for the surrender of federal jurisdiction over the administration of a trust was the fact that a state court had already assumed jurisdiction over the trust estate. But the Court in that case recognized that this rationale "ha[d] no application to a case in a federal court * * * wherein the plaintiff seeks merely an adjudication of his right or his interest as a basis of a claim against a fund in the possession of a state court. * * *" The Court stressed that "[n]o question is presented in the federal court as to the right of any person to participate in the res or as to the quantum of his interest in it." Similarly, in the Bank of New York case, *supra*, the Court stressed that the "object of the suits is to take the property from the depositaries and from the control of the state court, and to vest the property in the United States. * * *" "The suits are not merely to establish a debt or a

---

26. Whether similar considerations would permit dismissal of a water suit brought by a private party in federal dis- trict court is a question we need not now decide.

right to share in property, and thus to obtain an adjudication which might be had without disturbing the control of the state court." * * *

The precedents cited by the Court thus not only fail to support the Court's decision in this case, but expressly point in the opposite direction. The present suit, in short, is not analogous to the administration of a trust, but rather to a claim of a "right to participate," since the United States in this litigation does not ask the court to control the administration of the river, but only to determine its specific rights in the flow of water in the river. This is an almost exact analogue to a suit seeking a determination of rights in the flow of income from a trust.

The Court's principal reason for deciding to close the doors of the federal courthouse to the United States in this case seems to stem from the view that its decision will avoid piecemeal adjudication of water rights.[6] To the extent that this view is based on the special considerations governing *in rem* proceedings, it is without precedential basis, as the decisions discussed above demonstrate. To the extent that the Court's view is based on the realistic practicalities of this case, it is simply wrong, because the relegation of the Government to the state courts will not avoid piecemeal litigation.

The Colorado courts are currently engaged in two types of proceedings under the State's water-rights law. First, they are processing new claims to water based on recent appropriations. Second, they are integrating these new awards of water rights with all past decisions awarding such rights into one all-inclusive tabulation for each water source. The claims of the United States that are involved in this case have not been adjudicated in the past. Yet they do not involve recent appropriations of water. In fact, these claims are wholly dissimilar to normal state water claims, because they are not based on actual beneficial use of water but rather on an intention formed at the time the federal land use was established to reserve a certain amount of water to support the federal reservations. The state court will, therefore, have to conduct separate proceedings to determine these claims. And only after the state court adjudicates the claims will they be incorporated into the water source tabulations. If this suit were allowed to proceed in federal court the same procedures would be followed, and the federal court decree would be incorporated into the state

---

6. The Court lists four other policy reasons for the "appropriateness" of the District Court's dismissal of this lawsuit. All of those reasons are insubstantial. First, the fact that no significant proceedings had yet taken place in the federal court at the time of the dismissal means no more than that the federal court was prompt in granting the defendants' motion to dismiss. At that time, of course, no proceedings involving the Government's claims had taken place in the state court either. Second, the geographic distance of the federal court from the rivers in question is hardly a significant factor in this age of rapid and easy transportation. Since the basic issues here involve the determination of the amount of water the Government intended to reserve rather than the amount it actually appropriated on a given date, there is little likelihood that live testimony by

water district residents would be necessary. In any event, the Federal District Court in Colorado is authorized to sit at Durango, the headquarters of Water Division 7. 28 U.S.C. § 85. Third, the Government's willingness to participate in some of the state proceedings certainly does not mean that it had no right to bring this action, unless the Court has today unearthed a new kind of waiver. Finally, the fact that there were many defendants in the federal suit is hardly relevant. It only indicates that the federal court had all the necessary parties before it in order to issue a decree finally settling the Government's claims. Indeed, the presence of all interested parties in the federal court made the lawsuit the kind of unified proceeding envisioned by Pacific Live Stock Co. v. Oregon Water Bd., 241 U.S. 440, 447–449.

tabulation, as other federal court decrees have been incorporated in the past. Thus, the same process will occur regardless of which forum considers these claims. Whether the virtually identical separate proceedings take place in a federal court or a state court, the adjudication of the claims will be neither more nor less "piecemeal." Essentially the same process will be followed in each instance.

As the Court says, it is the virtual "unflagging obligation" of a federal court to exercise the jurisdiction that has been conferred upon it. Obedience to that obligation is particularly "appropriate" in this case, for at least two reasons.

First, the issues involved are issues of federal law. A federal court is more likely than a state court to be familiar with federal water law and to have had experience in interpreting the relevant federal statutes, regulations, and Indian treaties. * * *

Second, some of the federal claims in this lawsuit relate to water reserved for Indian reservations. It is not necessary to determine that there is no state-court jurisdiction of these claims to support the proposition that a federal court is a more appropriate forum than a state court for determination of questions of life-and-death importance to Indians. * * *

The Court says that "[o]nly the clearest of justifications will warrant dismissal" of a lawsuit within the jurisdiction of a federal court. In my opinion there was no justification at all for the District Court's order of dismissal in this case.

I would affirm the judgment of the Court of Appeals.

MR. JUSTICE STEVENS, dissenting.

[While agreeing with Justice Stewart, Justice Stevens added three points: (1) "the holding that United States may not litigate a federal claim in a federal court having jurisdiction thereof [is] particularly anomalous"; (2) the Court's holding would restrict private water users' access to federal courts—a "surprising byproduct of the McCarran Amendment"—since private persons could hardly have greater access than the United States to a federal court; [1] and (3) in any event the Court should defer to the judgment of the Court of Appeals, rather than evaluate itself the balance of factors for and against the exercise of jurisdiction.]

NOTE ON FEDERAL COURT DEFERENCE TO PARALLEL STATE COURT PROCEEDINGS

(1) Colorado River refers to the dictum in Cohens v. Virginia, 6 Wheat. 264, 404 (U.S.1821), where Chief Justice Marshall said:

"It is most true, that this court will not take jurisdiction if it should not: but it is equally true, that it must take jurisdiction, if it should. The judiciary cannot, as the legislature may, avoid a measure, because it

---

1. [Ed.] Justice Stevens' prophecy was fulfilled in Arizona v. San Carlos Apache Tribe of Arizona, 463 U.S. 545 (1983), upholding a district court's dismissal, in deference to pending state court proceedings, of federal water rights claims brought by Indian Tribes. The Court stressed that both water rights adjudication and the McCarran Amendment were "unique" (p. 571). Justices Stevens, Marshall, and Blackmun dissented.

approaches the confines of the constitution.   *   *   *   With whatever doubts, with whatever difficulties, a case may be attended, we must decide it, if it be brought before us. We have no more right to decline the exercise of jurisdiction which is given, than to usurp that which is not given. The one or the other would be treason to the constitution."

In McClellan v. Carland, 217 U.S. 268 (1910), the complainants brought a bill in a federal circuit court to have themselves adjudicated the sole heirs at law of a decedent. The circuit court stayed action to permit the state of South Dakota to bring a proceeding in the state courts to determine an escheat—which would have been binding on all parties, including the complainants. The Supreme Court held the stay improper. The circuit court, it said (p. 281), "practically abandoned its jurisdiction over a case of which it had cognizance, and turned the matter over for adjudication to the state court. This, it has steadily been held, a Federal court may not do." [1]

Recall the criticism of dicta like these in the excerpts from Shapiro, *Jurisdiction and Discretion*, 60 N.Y.U.L.Rev. 543 (1985), quoted at pp. 1346–47, *supra*. See also the other authorities cited thereafter, and see Note, 59 Yale L.J. 978, 980–81 (1950).

(2) Several instances should be noted in which the Supreme Court, prior to the Colorado River case, had approved federal deference to pending state proceedings.

In Langnes v. Green, 282 U.S. 531 (1931), the Court held that a federal district court should have stayed a shipowner's petition to limit his liability (pursuant to a federal statute) to the value of his interest in the vessel, where he showed only one personal injury claim pending against him in a state court and it was doubtful whether other claims existed. The Court emphasized the importance of preserving, if possible, the right of the state claimant to a common-law remedy. (Can this decision be viewed as resting on ripeness grounds?)

Brillhart v. Excess Ins. Co., 316 U.S. 491 (1942), has broader implications. There the petitioner, after recovering a default judgment against the tortfeasor, instituted garnishment proceedings in a state court against the insurer. The respondent, a reinsurer, then brought a federal action, *inter alia*, for a declaratory judgment to determine its rights under the reinsurance agreement. Thereafter, the insurer having become insolvent, the reinsurer was joined as a party defendant in the state garnishment proceedings, where it challenged the court's jurisdiction.

That is how matters stood when the district court dismissed the federal complaint, without considering whether the claims could be raised in the state garnishment proceeding. The court of appeals reversed and directed a trial on the merits. The Supreme Court in turn reversed, holding that the district court should be told to consider "whether the claims of all parties in interest can be satisfactorily adjudicated in" the state proceeding.

Justice Frankfurter, for the Court, said (pp. 494–95):

"Although the District Court had jurisdiction of the suit under the Federal Declaratory Judgments Act, it was under no compulsion to exercise that jurisdiction. The petitioner's motion to dismiss the bill was addressed

---

1. McClellan v. Carland rejected the suggestion that the federal court should stay its hand in favor of state proceedings that had not even been instituted. For an instance in which such a suggestion was approved, see Thompson v. Magnolia Petroleum Co., 309 U.S. 478 (1940).

to the discretion of the Court. * * * Ordinarily it would be uneconomical as well as vexatious for a federal court to proceed in a declaratory judgment suit where another suit is pending in a state court presenting the same issues, not governed by federal law, between the same parties. Gratuitous interference with the orderly and comprehensive disposition of a state court litigation should be avoided."

See also Provident Tradesman Bank v. Patterson, 390 U.S. 102, 126 (1968), reaffirming Brillhart in dictum.

Does Brillhart rest on the discretionary nature of the declaratory judgment jurisdiction?

In Scott v. Germano, 381 U.S. 407 (1965), the Court directed the district court to stay its hand in an action challenging a state legislative apportionment. The stay was warranted, the Court held, by a similar proceeding then pending in which the state supreme court had held the apportionment statute invalid. The state proceeding was filed after the federal one, and the Court did not say whether the same parties were involved.

In Kaiser Steel Corp. v. W.S. Ranch Co., 391 U.S. 593 (1968), p. 1373, *supra*, the Court unanimously agreed that the federal courts should abstain in a private diversity action for trespass that raised questions about the construction and validity of a state statute governing the use of water rights. After the federal court of appeals had decided the case on the merits, Kaiser (defendant in the federal suit) commenced a declaratory judgment action raising the same issues in the state court. The matter was thought by the Supreme Court to involve a truly novel issue of vital concern in an arid state, and three concurring Supreme Court justices emphasized the special circumstances that led them to join in the decision to defer to the pending state proceeding.[2]

(3) Is there any general principle to be derived from the Colorado River case? Or did it rest not only on the unique character of disputes over water rights but also on the specific purpose underlying the McCarran amendment? Those questions were no closer to resolution after Will v. Calvert Fire Ins. Co., 437 U.S. 655 (1977), in which no rationale commanded a majority of the Court.

In the Calvert case, American Mutual Reinsurance Co. sued Calvert in a state court for a declaration that a reinsurance pool agreement was still in effect. Calvert raised several defenses and counterclaims based on both the federal securities law (including the Securities Exchange Act of 1934) and various state laws. On the same day that its answer was filed, Calvert sued American in federal district court on many of the same grounds as those asserted in its state pleadings, but also added a claim for damages under the 1934 Act (SEC Rule 10b–5)—a claim over which the federal courts have exclusive jurisdiction. In response to American's motion to dismiss or abate the federal action, Judge Will deferred proceedings until completion of the state action, except for the Rule 10b–5 claim for damages. On that issue, he heard argument but did not rule on the question whether

---

2. Numerous lower courts had dealt with the problem of duplicative proceedings before Colorado River, often choosing to defer. See Comment, 44 U.Chi.L.Rev. 641, 653–66 (1977), which views Colorado River as narrowing discretion to decline jurisdiction.

For discussions of the Colorado River case itself, see authorities cited in Mullenix, *A Branch Too Far: Pruning the Abstention Doctrine*, 75 Geo.L.J. 99, 107 n. 33 (1986).

Calvert's interest in the reinsurance pool was a "security" within the meaning of the 1934 Act.

Calvert petitioned for mandamus, seeking an order requiring Judge Will to adjudicate Calvert's claim under the 1934 Act for equitable relief as well as for damages. The Seventh Circuit granted the petition, deciding that the case did not fit any of the grounds for abstention specified in Colorado River (handed down after the district judge's action) and ordered him to "proceed immediately" with Calvert's claims under the 1934 Act.

The Supreme Court reversed, 5–4. In an opinion for four members of the Court, Justice Rehnquist found the case inappropriate for mandamus. See p. 1825, *infra.* Relying heavily on Brillhart, Paragraph (2), *supra,* as well as on cases involving conflicts between federal courts, *e.g.,* Kerotest Mfg. Co. v. C–O–Two Fire Equipment Co., 342 U.S. 180 (1952), p. 1789, *infra,* he concluded that Colorado River was consistent with the view that "the decision [whether or not to defer] is largely committed to the 'carefully considered judgment,' Colorado River, at 818, of the district court" (p. 663). And the exercise of that judgment was essentially unreviewable on mandamus.

Justice Brennan (the author of the Court's opinion in Colorado River), dissenting for himself and three other Justices, would have affirmed the court of appeals. Brillhart, he argued, was different because it was both a diversity suit and an action for declaratory relief, where the court is vested with discretion not to proceed. Colorado River cut against reversal because it rested heavily on the clear federal policy "evinced by the McCarran Amendment" (p. 673) and because it emphasized " 'the virtually unflagging obligation of the federal courts to exercise the jurisdiction given them' " (p. 669, quoting Colorado River, 424 U.S. at 817).[3]

Justice Blackmun cast the swing vote, stating that in his view Brillhart—a diversity case—was not applicable, that Colorado River set a stricter standard for abstention in federal issue cases, and that the whole matter should therefore be remanded to the district judge for reconsideration in light of Colorado River, which was decided since his ruling.[4]

(4) Any doubt about the vitality, after Calvert, of Colorado River's "exceptional circumstances" test was removed in Moses H. Cone Memorial Hosp. v. Mercury Constr. Corp., 460 U.S. 1 (1983). The case revolved around a construction contract between the hospital and a contractor,

3. Justice Brennan's dissent also discussed whether the state court judgment could have preclusive effect in an action within the federal courts' exclusive jurisdiction. See generally Chap. XII, pp. 1627–29, *infra.* If so, he argued that a stay would thwart the policy of the 1934 Act; if not, he argued that a stay was unjustified, because the state court proceedings could not affect the federal action.

See also Note, *Judicial Abstention and Exclusive Federal Jurisdiction: A Reconciliation,* 67 Cornell L.Rev. 219 (1981).

4. The case was remanded for reconsideration to Judge Will, who adhered to his original decision, arguing that Colorado River was based on considerations of "wise judicial administration," was not intended to limit district court discretion, and concerned a dismissal of a federal action, not just a stay. He also pointed out that Calvert could have removed the state court action on the basis of diversity, but chose instead to bring a "wasteful duplicative and reactive" federal suit, adding only a "dubious 10b–5 claim" to the matters at issue in state court. 459 F.Supp. 859, 863–64 (N.D.Ill.1978). The Seventh Circuit affirmed, stressing the finding that Calvert's federal suit was "vexatious." 600 F.2d 1228, 1235–36 (7th Cir.1979). Perhaps as a result of fatigue, Calvert did not seek certiorari.

For discussion of Calvert, see the authorities in Mullenix, note 2, *supra,* at 109–10 n. 51.

which provided that disputed claims, after initial referral to the architect, were subject to arbitration. After construction was complete, the contractor filed with the architect a claim against the hospital. Following various discussions between the parties, the hospital sued the contractor and architect in state court, seeking declarations (i) that the hospital was not liable to the contractor, (ii) that if the hospital were liable, it would be entitled to indemnity from the architect, and (iii) that the contractor had no present right to arbitration. A stay of arbitration was also sought. Soon thereafter, the contractor filed a federal diversity action to compel arbitration under the Federal Arbitration Act, 9 U.S.C. § 4. The district court stayed the suit in view of the pending state court action, but on appeal under 28 U.S.C. § 1291, the court of appeals reversed, instructing the district court to issue an order compelling arbitration.

The Supreme Court, with Justice Brennan writing, affirmed. After ruling that the district court's order was in fact appealable,[5] the Court rejected the argument that Calvert had undermined the "exceptional circumstances" test of Colorado River (p. 16). Justice Brennan noted that Justice Rehnquist's opinion in Calvert commanded only four votes, and contended that the "key to Calvert was the standard for issuance of a writ of mandamus under 28 U.S.C. § 1651" (p. 18). Though the question of deference is "necessarily left to the discretion of the district court in the first instance," that discretion is not unreviewable. Rather, it must be exercised under the proper standard, namely, "Colorado River's exceptional circumstances test, as elucidated by the factors discussed in that case" (p. 19).

Applying that test, the Court found the district court's stay unjustified. Of the four factors supporting the dismissal in Colorado River, the first two—the state court's assumption of jurisdiction over a res, and that court's greater convenience—were simply not applicable.[6] Nor did the suit implicate the third factor—avoidance of piecemeal litigation (which Justice Brennan described (p. 19) as the "paramount" consideration in Colorado River); piecemeal litigation might indeed result, for only the contractor's claim against the hospital, not the hospital's indemnity claim, was arbitrable; but a stay of the federal action could not avoid that problem. And fourth, the order of suit did not support the stay: though the state action had been filed first, the hospital's claim of priority was "too mechanical"; "[t]his factor, as with the other Colorado River factors, is to be applied in a pragmatic, flexible manner," and here "the federal suit was running well ahead of the state suit * * *" (pp. 21–22).

Two other factors, Justice Brennan continued, were pertinent. The first was that the federal action in Moses Cone was governed by federal law (here, pertaining to the arbitrability of the dispute), which "must always be a major consideration weighing against surrender" (p. 26).[7] And second,

---

5. The Court held both that the order was "final" and that it qualified as a "collateral order" appealable whether or not final. See generally Chap. XV, Sec. 1, *infra*.

6. Note that in Moses Cone, as in Colorado River and Calvert, the federal district court was located in the same state in which the related proceedings were pending. When the federal action is located in a different state, convenience may be a more important factor. See, *e.g.*, Centronics Data Computer Corp. v. Merkle Korff Indus., 503 F.Supp. 168 (D.N.H.1980), deferring to a suit in Illinois state court.

7. Justice Brennan noted the "anomaly" that the Federal Arbitration Act creates a federal right to arbitration that cannot be enforced under the federal question jurisdiction (p. 25 n. 32). "But we empha-

because of uncertainty whether the Federal Arbitration Act obliges state as well as federal courts to issue orders compelling arbitration,[8] the state court proceeding was "probabl[y] inadequa[te]" to protect the contractor's rights (p. 26).

Finally, the Court rejected the hospital's argument that a *stay* of a federal action could be justified more easily than a *dismissal* (as in Colorado River), finding that in either event, the district court must conclude "that the parallel state-court litigation will be an adequate vehicle for the complete and prompt resolution of the issues between the parties. * * * Thus, the decision to invoke Colorado River necessarily contemplates that the federal court will have nothing further to do in resolving any substantive part of the case, whether it stays or dismisses" (p. 28).[9]

Justice Rehnquist, joined by Chief Justice Burger and Justice O'Connor, dissented on the question of appealability, expressing no view on the appropriateness of a stay.[10]

(5) Moses Cone identifies six factors governing the appropriateness of abstention in the face of pending proceedings. How clear are they? What should a court do when they pull in different directions?

Is it consistent with the Supreme Court's decisions, and otherwise appropriate, for a district court also to consider in such cases (a) whether the federal action seeks declaratory relief; [11] (b) whether the federal suit is meritless, or interposed for delay or harassment; [12] (c) whether the federal plaintiff could have filed the pending state proceeding in, or removed it to, federal court; [13] (d) whether the federal plaintiff is also the plaintiff in state

size that our task in cases such as this is not to find some substantial reason for the *exercise* of federal jurisdiction, [but rather] * * * to ascertain whether there exist 'exceptional' circumstances, 'the clearest of justifications,' that can suffice under Colorado River to justify the *surrender* of that jurisdiction" (pp. 25–26).

According to Justice Brennan (p. 23 & n. 29), that the governing law in Colorado River was federal had been of "ambiguous relevance," given (i) the McCarran Act's policy approving state court litigation of federal water rights, and (ii) the fact that the bulk of the litigation concerned state law rights of the nonfederal parties. But five Justices (Justice Blackmun and the four dissenters) stressed this factor in Calvert, where it was more important because federal jurisdiction was exclusive.

8. Subsequently, in Southland Corp. v. Keating, 465 U.S. 1 (1984), the Court ruled that the Act preempts a state law purporting to limit state court power to enforce arbitration agreements, and in Perry v. Thomas, 107 S.Ct. 2520 (1987), similarly ruled that the Act preempts a state statute purporting to require judicial resolution of wage claims that the contracting parties agreed to resolve by arbitration.

9. Consider, however, the view that a stay is preferable because if the state case for any reason does not conclude the mat-

ter, the federal action will remain before the same judge and will not be time-barred. Lumen Constr., Inc. v. Brant Constr. Co., Inc., 780 F.2d 691, 697–98 (7th Cir. 1985); *cf.* the similar argument in Pullman abstention cases, p. 1375, *supra.*

10. For discussion of Moses Cone, see the authorities cited by Mullenix, note 2, *supra*, at 112 n. 65.

11. See Brillhart, Paragraph (2), *supra*, and the discussion thereof in the opinions in Calvert. Compare, *e.g.*, Mission Ins. Co. v. Puritan Fashions Corp., 706 F.2d 599, 601–02 & nn. 1, 3 (5th Cir.1983) (declaratory jurisdiction may be declined in view of pending proceedings even absent "exceptional circumstances"), with, *e.g.*, Mobil Oil Corp. v. City of Long Beach, 772 F.2d 534, 542 (9th Cir.1985) (declaratory actions governed by Colorado River criteria), *questioned in* Transamerica Occidental Life Ins. Co. v. Digregorio, 811 F.2d 1249, 1253–55 (9th Cir.1987).

12. See the remand in Calvert, note 4, *supra*. In Moses Cone, the Court said there was "considerable merit" in giving weight to vexatiousness, but did not rely on that consideration (p. 18 n. 20).

13. See, *e.g.*, Microsoftware Computer Systems, Inc. v. Ontel Corp., 686 F.2d 531, 537 (7th Cir.1982).

court, having filed parallel claims in two fora, or is the state court defendant, having filed a federal claim incorporating issues that could be raised as defenses or counterclaims in state court; [14] (e) whether the subject matter implicates important state interests; [15] (f) whether either the federal or state court offers particular procedural advantages; (g) whether the state court has stayed its own proceedings; [16] (h) whether the federal action is filed under § 1983; [17] or (i) whether the federal action will be burdensome? [18] (On the last point, note that in Moses Cone the federal court was required only to compel arbitration, and that federal law *might* have compelled the state court to do likewise, see note 8, *supra.*)

(6) The practice of deferring to pending state proceedings has not gone uncriticized. A recent article suggests that Congress's failure to repeal the diversity jurisdiction has led the Court to "sanction the fabrication of an artificial abstention doctrine as a means of docket clearing," thereby extending abstention beyond its justified purpose of promoting comity and federalism into the realm of "an unprincipled judicial self-help remedy"; the ill-defined "exceptional circumstances test," moreover, is said to permit *ad hoc* and unpredictable decisionmaking. Mullenix, note 2, *supra*, at 101, 103–04, 156. Consider these criticisms separately:

(a) Is abstention less justified in the service of judicial administration than in the service of comity and federalism? Are the decisions (see Chap. XIV, Sec. 5, *infra*) staying (for reasons of judicial administration) one federal action to permit a second, overlapping federal action to proceed wholly inapplicable to a case like Colorado River, because they still permit some federal court to adjudicate?

Even if a federal court should consider the avoidance of duplication in deciding whether to exercise jurisdiction, how much weight can be assigned to this concern without undercutting the presumption that federal jurisdiction is to be exercised even in the face of a pending state court proceeding? See Sonenshein, *Abstention: The Crooked Course of Colorado River*, 59 Tul. L.Rev. 651, 693–94 (1985). Should Colorado River be viewed more narrowly—as focusing on the avoidance not of duplication but of piecemeal litigation?

14. See generally Vestal, *Repetitive Litigation*, 45 Iowa L.Rev. 525 (1960).

15. Recall the discussion in Colorado River; *cf.* Louisiana Power & Light Co. v. City of Thibodaux, p. 1369, *supra.*

16. *Cf.* United States v. Adair, 723 F.2d 1394, 1404–05 (9th Cir.1983), finding no abuse of discretion in a refusal to stay a federal water rights claim brought by an Indian Tribe—notwithstanding San Carlos Apache Tribe, p. 1446 note 1, *supra* —in part because the state court proceedings had been effectively stayed.

17. The obligation to exercise federal jurisdiction has been deemed especially weighty in such cases, see, *e.g.,* Signad, Inc. v. City of Sugar Land, 753 F.2d 1338, 1340 (5th Cir.1985), though in Lumen Constr., Inc. v. Brant Constr. Co., 780 F.2d 691, 696–98 (7th Cir.1985) (Will, J.), the court nonetheless deferred.

18. Concern about the workload of the federal courts has influenced other interpretations of the scope of federal jurisdiction—for example, the meaning of "arising under" in § 1331, or the breadth of Supreme Court review under § 1257. *Cf.* Justice Douglas' concurring opinion in England v. Louisiana State Bd. of Medical Examiners, 375 U.S. 411, 430 n. 2 (1964), p. 1376, *supra* (urging reevaluation of all abstention doctrines, and criticizing lower court decisions that, prior to Colorado River, had deferred to state proceedings as "baldly deny[ing] a suitor the remedy granted by Congress because it is not convenient to the district judge to decide the case"). See also Thermtron Prods., Inc. v. Hermansdorfer, 423 U.S. 336, 344 (1976), p. 1825, *infra* (holding improper the remand of a properly removed case because the district court considered itself too busy).

(b) Given the flexibility and multiplicity of Moses Cone's criteria—not to mention additional possible criteria, see Paragraph (5), *supra*—can overburdened district courts be trusted to exercise proper restraint in invoking a doctrine that helps to clear their dockets, especially of diversity cases? Can clearer standards be developed?

(7) Do you think, in view of these problems, that a doctrine permitting deference to pending proceedings is wholly improper, even as limited to "exceptional circumstances"? Might not district courts in effect "stay" proceedings anyway, in the guise of arranging priorities on their dockets? *Cf.* Calvert, Paragraph (3), *supra*, 437 U.S. at 665 (plurality opinion). Would the absence of *any* limit on duplicative proceedings invite each litigant to race to secure a judgment in his preferred forum, in order to permit preclusion of litigation in the other forum? (Under the current doctrine, isn't there some reason to fear a race to generate substantial proceedings? *Cf.* Hicks v. Miranda, p. 1416, *supra*.)

Consider the quite different suggestion that the judicial code should be amended to require a state or federal court to stay any action whose subject matter is already at issue in another court, so long as the other court can resolve the rights of all of the parties. Kurland, *Toward a Co-operative Judicial Federalism: The Federal Court Abstention Doctrine*, 24 F.R.D. 481, 491–92 (1959); accord, Currie, *The Federal Courts and the American Law Institute (II)*, 36 U.Chi.L.Rev. 268, 335 (1969). Should the dice be loaded so heavily in favor of the first filed action? Would this approach generate a race to the courthouse, rather than a race to judgment? Is the former a less wasteful race?

(8) Moses Cone establishes that an order staying or dismissing a federal action is appealable. See generally Chap. XV, Sec. 1, *infra*. The courts of appeals divided, however, on whether a refusal to stay or dismiss the action is appealable. The issue was resolved in Gulfstream Aerospace Corp. v. Mayacamas Corp., 108 S.Ct. 1133 (1988), p. 1809, note 7, p. 1819, *infra*, which held that such a refusal is not an appealable order. See also Note, 59 Ind.L.Rev. 65 (1983).

(9) What is the scope of appellate review of a decision to enter a stay? In Mobil Oil Corp. v. City of Long Beach, 772 F.2d 534, 540 (9th Cir.1985), the court said that though review was for abuse of discretion, the district court's discretion was not as broad here as when, for example, it rules on pretrial motions or evidentiary questions.

Compare the scope of review in related settings. The standard governing review of decisions whether to abstain under Pullman, although articulated somewhat differently, is not dissimilar. The appellate court undertakes de novo review of the "essentially legal" questions whether state law is unsettled and whether a narrowing construction is possible, see D'Iorio v. County of Delaware, 592 F.2d 681, 686 (3d Cir.1978); a district court has some discretion to forgo abstention even where it might be proper, Shamrock Development Co. v. City of Concord, 656 F.2d 1380, 1385 (9th Cir.1981), but little or no discretion to abstain when the stated requirements are not met, United Services Auto Ass'n v. Muir, 792 F.2d 356, 361 (3d Cir.1986). (If review in the former situation comes only after the case has been litigated to final judgment, won't reversal be especially costly?) By contrast, the decision whether to certify an issue to a state court rests in the "sound discretion" of the federal court, see Lehman

Brothers, Sec. 2(B), *supra;* note that the case was remanded to permit the court of appeals, rather than the district court, to exercise its discretion. In Younger cases, however, the Supreme Court appears to have recognized virtually no discretion in the lower courts. See also Loyd v. Loyd, 731 F.2d 393, 397 (7th Cir.1984), discussed in Sec. 2(E), p. 1459, note 3, *infra,* recognizing some district court discretion in deciding whether to decline to exercise jurisdiction over probate and domestic relations matters.

SUBSECTION E: MATTERS OF PROBATE AND DOMESTIC RELATIONS

MARKHAM, ALIEN PROPERTY CUSTODIAN v. ALLEN
326 U.S. 490, 66 S.Ct. 296, 90 L.Ed. 256 (1946).
Certiorari to the Circuit Court of Appeals for the Ninth Circuit.

MR. CHIEF JUSTICE STONE delivered the opinion of the Court.

The question is whether a district court of the United States has jurisdiction of a suit brought by the Alien Property Custodian against an executor and resident heirs to determine the Custodian's asserted right to share in decedent's estate which is in course of probate administration in a state court.

On January 23, 1943, petitioner, the Alien Property Custodian, ∗ ∗ ∗ issued vesting order No. 762, by which he purported to vest in himself as Custodian all right, title and interest of German legatees in the estate of Alvina Wagner, who died testate, a resident of California, whose will was admitted to probate and whose estate is being administered in the Superior Court of California. Previously, on December 30, 1942, six of the other heirs-at-law of decedent, residing in the United States, filed a petition in the Superior Court of California for determination of heirship, asserting that under the provisions of California Statutes, 1941, chap. 895, p. 2473, § 1,[1] the German legatees were ineligible as beneficiaries, and that the American heirs were therefore entitled to inherit decedent's estate. This proceeding is still pending.

On April 6, 1943, the Custodian brought the present suit in the district court for the northern district of California against the executor and the six California claimants, seeking a judgment determining that the resident claimants have no interest in the estate, and that the Custodian, by virtue of his vesting order, is entitled to the entire net estate of the decedent after payment of expenses of administration, debts, and taxes, and is the owner of specified real estate of decedent passing under the will. ∗ ∗ ∗ [T]he district court gave judgment for petitioner, Crowley v. Allen, 52 F.Supp. 850. The court held that it had jurisdiction to enforce the vesting order of petitioner; that its jurisdiction is derived from the Constitution and laws of the United States and is not subject to restriction or ouster by state legislation; and that California Statutes, 1941, chap. 895, § 1, is invalid.
∗ ∗ ∗

---

1. This statute purports to limit inheritance by non-resident aliens to nationals of countries which grant reciprocal rights of inheritance to American citizens.

Without passing upon the merits, the Court of Appeals for the Ninth Circuit reversed and ordered the cause dismissed, upon the ground that the district court was without jurisdiction of the subject matter of the action. 147 F.2d 136. The court thought that since "the matter is within probate jurisdiction and that court is in possession of the property, its right to proceed to determine heirship cannot be interfered with by the federal court."

It is not denied that the present suit is a suit "of a civil nature * * * in equity," brought by an officer of the United States, authorized to sue, of which district courts are given jurisdiction by § 24(1), 28 U.S.C. § 41(1), of the Judicial Code [now 28 U.S.C. § 1345]. But respondents argue, as the Circuit Court of Appeals held, that as the district courts of the United States are without jurisdiction over probate matters, see In re Broderick's Will, 21 Wall. 503, 517; Byers v. McAuley, 149 U.S. 608, 615, which the court of appeals thought are not "cases or controversies within the meaning of Art. III of the Constitution," and since the present suit to determine heirship of property being administered in a state probate court is an exercise of probate jurisdiction, the district court is without jurisdiction.

It is true that a federal court has no jurisdiction to probate a will or administer an estate, the reason being that the equity jurisdiction conferred by the Judiciary Act of 1789, 1 Stat. 73, and § 24(1) of the Judicial Code, which is that of the English Court of Chancery in 1789, did not extend to probate matters. But it has been established by a long series of decisions of this Court that federal courts of equity have jurisdiction to entertain suits "in favor of creditors, legatees and heirs" and other claimants against a decedent's estate "to establish their claims" so long as the federal court does not interfere with the probate proceedings or assume general jurisdiction of the probate or control of the property in the custody of the state court. Waterman v. Canal–Louisiana Bank & Trust Co., 215 U.S. 33, 43, and cases cited.

Similarly while a federal court may not exercise its jurisdiction to disturb or affect the possession of property in the custody of a state court, Penn General Casualty Co. v. Pennsylvania, 294 U.S. 189, 195–196 and cases cited; United States v. Bank of New York & Trust Co., supra, 296 U.S. 477–478 and cases cited, it may exercise its jurisdiction to adjudicate rights in such property where the final judgment does not undertake to interfere with the state court's possession save to the extent that the state court is bound by the judgment to recognize the right adjudicated by the federal court. Commonwealth Trust Co. v. Bradford, supra, 297 U.S. 619; United States v. Klein, supra, 303 U.S. 281, and cases cited.

Although in this case petitioner sought a judgment in the district court ordering defendant executor to pay over the entire net estate to the petitioner upon an allowance of the executor's final account, the judgment declared only that petitioner "is entitled to receive the net estate of the late Alvina Wagner in distribution, after the payment of expenses of administration, debts, and taxes." The effect of the judgment was to leave undisturbed the orderly administration of decedent's estate in the state probate court and to decree petitioner's right in the property to be distributed after its administration. This, as our authorities demonstrate, is not an exercise of probate jurisdiction or an interference with property in the possession or custody of a state court.

There remains the question whether the district court having jurisdiction should, in the exercise of its discretion, have declined to entertain the suit which involves issues of state law and have remitted the petitioner to his remedy in the state probate proceeding. See Thompson v. Magnolia Petroleum Co., 309 U.S. 478, 483 * * *. The mere fact that the district court, in the exercise of the jurisdiction which Congress has conferred upon it, is required to interpret state law is not in itself a sufficient reason for withholding relief to petitioner. Meredith v. Winter Haven, 320 U.S. 228. This is the more so in this case because § 17 of the Trading with the Enemy Act, 50 U.S.C.App. § 17, specially confers on the district court, independently of the statutes governing generally jurisdiction of federal courts, jurisdiction to enter "all such orders and decrees * * * as may be necessary and proper in the premises to enforce the provisions" of the Act. Although the district court has jurisdiction of the present case under § 24(1) of the Judicial Code, irrespective of § 17, the latter section plainly indicates that Congress has adopted the policy of permitting the custodian to proceed in the district courts to enforce his rights under the Act, whether they depend on state or federal law. The cause was therefore within the jurisdiction of the district court, which could appropriately proceed with the case, and the Court of Appeals erroneously ordered its dismissal.

The judgment is reversed and the cause remanded to the Circuit Court of Appeals for further proceedings in conformity to this opinion.

MR. JUSTICE JACKSON took no part in the consideration or decision of this case.

MR. JUSTICE RUTLEDGE is of the opinion that the cause should be remanded to the district court and jurisdiction should be retained by it pending the state court's decision as to the persons entitled to receive the net estate.

NOTE ON FEDERAL JURISDICTION IN MATTERS OF PROBATE AND ADMINISTRATION

(1) The probate of wills and the grant of letters of administration were the distinctive functions of the ecclesiastical courts in England. No federal court seems ever to have undertaken to do either of these things.

Even before 1789, however, the English chancery courts took jurisdiction over the administration of estates of personalty. See Ballow, A Treatise of Equity 193 (1756); Note, *Federal Jurisdiction in Matters Relating to Probate and Administration*, 43 Harv.L.Rev. 462, 465 (1930). But the Supreme Court has regularly rebuked the few efforts of lower federal courts to take over, generally, the administration of a decedent's estate. *E.g.*, Hook v. Payne, 14 Wall. 252 (U.S.1872); Byers v. McAuley, 149 U.S. 608 (1893). *Cf.* Waterman v. Canal–Louisiana Bank & Trust Co., 215 U.S. 33 (1909), denying jurisdiction, in an otherwise proper case, of a prayer for an accounting of an estate.

Sometimes this has been on the ground that the state court's possession of a *res* ought not to be interfered with (see pp. 1321–22 & note 2, *supra*), sometimes on the ground that complete diversity was lacking among all the interested parties (see Chap. XIII, Sec. 2, *infra*), and sometimes on the ground, suggested in the Markham opinion, that administration was part of the exclusive probate jurisdiction of the state courts.

(2) Numerous cases support the holding of the Markham case that federal courts may entertain actions *inter partes* against administrators or executors, or other claimants, for such purposes as the establishment of (a) a right to a distributive share, under a will or in intestacy, Payne v. Hook, 7 Wall. 425 (U.S.1869), p. 808, *supra;* Byers v. McAuley, *supra;* Waterman v. Canal–Louisiana Bank & Trust Co., *supra;* McClellan v. Carland, 217 U.S. 268 (1910), p. 1447, *supra;* or (b) a lien on a distributive share, Ingersoll v. Coram, 211 U.S. 335 (1908); or (c) a debt due from the decedent, Hess v. Reynolds, 113 U.S. 73 (1885).[1]

In these cases the Court has repeatedly insisted that the judgment or decree must not interfere with the orderly handling by the state court of an estate under administration. Federal jurisdiction, in the cases prior to Markham v. Allen, was predicated on diversity of citizenship.

In both Payne v. Hook and Hess v. Reynolds, the Court disregarded a state statute that attempted to confine litigation of the type in question to the state probate courts. Compare Ledbetter v. Taylor, 359 F.2d 760 (10th Cir.1966).

(3) Actions to annul wills or set aside an order of probate have been treated as raising special problems.

Sutton v. English, 246 U.S. 199 (1918), was a bill in equity brought by the heirs-at-law of one Mary Jane Hubbard seeking a series of determinations: first, that a joint will of the decedent and her husband, who had predeceased her, was inefficacious to dispose of the community property; second, that a state court judgment, obtained by some of the defendants, establishing their title to the community property as against Hubbard, be set aside; third, that Hubbard's will be annulled so far as it gave the property in question to another of the defendants; and fourth, that the community property, thus having been shown to have been the separate estate of Hubbard and not to have been devised by her, be decreed to have passed to the plaintiffs and be partitioned among them.

In an opinion for the Court, Justice Pitney said (pp. 205–06):

"By a series of decisions in this court it has been established that since it does not pertain to the general jurisdiction of a court of equity to set aside a will or the probate thereof, or to administer upon the estates of decedents *in rem*, matters of this character are not within the ordinary equity jurisdiction of the federal courts; that as the authority to make wills is derived from the States, and the requirement of probate is but a regulation to make a will effective, matters of strict probate are not within the jurisdiction of courts of the United States; that where a State, by statute or custom, gives to parties interested the right to bring an action or

---

1. The law is less clear on the existence of jurisdiction over an action against an executor or administrator personally for fraud or mismanagement. Compare, *e.g.,* Hamilton v. Nielson, 678 F.2d 709 (7th Cir. 1982) (allowing an action for breach of fiduciary duty), *noted,* 48 Mo.L.Rev. 564 (1983); Bassler v. Arrowood, 500 F.2d 138 (8th Cir.1974) (allowing a fraud action), with, *e.g.,* Bedo v. McGuire, 767 F.2d 305 (6th Cir.1985) and Starr v. Rupp, 421 F.2d 999 (6th Cir.1970) (both dismissing an action for breach of fiduciary duty). The courts in these cases consider whether the state probate court's jurisdiction over such actions is exclusive within the state's court system, and whether a final accounting has been rendered in a state probate proceeding or the matter is still pending.

suit *inter partes,* either at law or in equity, to annul a will or to set aside the probate, the courts of the United States, where diversity of citizenship and a sufficient amount in controversy appear, can enforce the same remedy, but that this relates only to independent suits, and not to procedure merely incidental or ancillary to the probate; and further, that questions relating to the interests of heirs, devisees, or legatees, or trusts affecting such interests, which may be determined without interfering with probate or assuming general administration, are within the jurisdiction of the federal courts where diversity of citizenship exists and the requisite amount is in controversy.

"It is the contention of appellants that the United States District Court had original jurisdiction of this cause (there being diversity of citizenship and a sufficient amount in controversy) because jurisdiction over a suit in equity of the same character would have existed in the county or district courts of the State.

"In order to test this, we must consider the nature and extent of the jurisdiction of the courts referred to, as established by the constitution of Texas and statutes passed in pursuance thereof * * *."

Examining the jurisdiction of a Texas district court, the Court concluded (pp. 207–08):

" * * * it may be assumed that an independent suit in equity [like the federal suit under consideration] could be entertained by that court, and therefore—under the decisions of this court to which reference has been made—might be brought in the United States District Court * * *. But * * * even could complainants succeed in showing that Hubbard at the time of her death was entitled to the community property, her will giving all the residue of her property to Cora D. Spencer still stands in the way of their succeeding to it as heirs-at-law, and hence their prayer to have that will annulled with respect to the residuary clause is essential to their right to any relief in the suit.

"But it is established by repeated decisions of the Supreme Court of Texas that under the present constitution the district courts have no jurisdiction to annul by an original proceeding the action of a county court in probating a will, their jurisdiction in the premises being confined to a review by appeal or certiorari, which are in effect but a continuation of the probate proceedings. It is further held that under a statutory provision (Art. 5699) * * * such a suit must be instituted in the court in which the will was admitted to probate, that is to say, in the county court; and that it calls for an exercise of original probate jurisdiction. * * *

"The present suit being, in an essential feature, a suit to annul the will of Mary Jane Hubbard, and a proceeding of this character being by the laws of Texas merely supplemental to the proceedings for probate of the will and cognizable only by the probate court, it follows from what we have said that the controversy is not within the jurisdiction of the courts of the United States."

For a similarly careful analysis of state law reaching a similar conclusion in a similar case, see Farrell v. O'Brien, 199 U.S. 89 (1905).[2] And see generally 13B Wright, Miller & Cooper, Federal Practice and Procedure

---

2. For representative lower court decisions, see Lamberg v. Callahan, 455 F.2d 1213 (2d Cir.1972); Kausch v. First Wichita Nat. Bank, 470 F.2d 1068 (5th Cir.1972); Davis v. Hunter, 323 F.Supp. 976 (D.Conn. 1970).

§ 3610, at 499–500 (1984); Vestal & Foster, *Implied Limitations on the Diversity Jurisdiction of Federal Courts,* 41 Minn.L.Rev. 1, 13–23 (1956); Note, 45 Ind.L.J. 387 (1970).

(4) If the Alien Property Custodian had been advancing the claim in Sutton v. English, Paragraph (3), *supra,* should the result differ?

(5) Is the jurisdiction of the English Court of Chancery in 1789 an appropriate criterion of contemporary federal jurisdiction in probate matters? This criterion was strongly criticized in Dragan v. Miller, 679 F.2d 712 (7th Cir.1982) (Posner, J.), yet the court concluded that "however shoddy the historical underpinnings of the probate exception, it is too well established a feature of our federal system to be lightly discarded, and by an inferior court at that" (p. 713). Uncertain whether Markham controlled the case of an action to set aside a will on the ground of undue influence, the court followed the "practical" approach of examining "the purposes that the probate exception * * * might be thought to serve," (p. 714) and proceeded to explore considerations—such as legal certainty, judicial economy, and relative judicial expertise—that might favor state court exclusivity.

If the lower courts lack the authority to abandon the probate exception, do they have the authority to redefine its boundaries in light of these kinds of "practical" considerations? Is Dragan's approach likely to increase litigation about where to litigate?

(6) In Rice v. Rice Foundation, 610 F.2d 471 (7th Cir.1979), the court of appeals remanded a case to the district court to consider whether the proceeding was within the probate exception, rather than disposing of the issue on appeal: "Even where a particular probate-like case is found to be outside the scope of the probate exception, the district court may, in its discretion, decline to exercise its jurisdiction. * * * Discretionary abstention in probate-related matters is suggested not only by the strong state interest in such matters generally but also by special circumstances in particular cases" (pp. 477–78).[3] Can workable criteria be developed for the exercise of such discretion?

A similar notion has emerged in cases involving domestic relations matters. (See Paragraph (5) of the following Note.) When jurisdiction does exist and, as is ordinarily the case, is founded on diversity, is discretionary abstention more appropriate than in other diversity cases involving state law? See Subsections 2(B) and 2(D) of this Chapter, *supra.* Consider Giardina v. Fontana, 733 F.2d 1047 (2d Cir.1984), finding that the district court erred in declining to exercise diversity jurisdiction over a plaintiff's claim that her assignment of her interest in an estate was obtained by undue influence and fraud. The court ruled that the case did not fall within any of the exceptions recognized by Colorado River and Moses Cone, pp. 1438–51, *supra,* and emphasized the district courts' " 'virtually unflagging obligation * * * to exercise the jurisdiction given them' " (p. 1052, quoting Colorado River, 424 U.S. at 817).

---

3. See also Loyd v. Loyd, 731 F.2d 393, 397 (7th Cir.1984). There the district court, applying Dragan's practical approach, entertained jurisdiction. In affirming that decision, the court of appeals treated it as "an exercise of discretion" and found no abuse: "[i]n candor, if the district court had found originally that the probate exception was applicable, we doubt we would have faulted him" (p. 397).

NOTE ON FEDERAL JURISDICTION IN MATTERS OF
DOMESTIC RELATIONS

(1) In Barber v. Barber, 21 How. 582 (U.S.1859), the Court upheld the jurisdiction of a federal district court in Wisconsin to enforce an award of alimony made by a New York state court against a wandering husband, in favor of a home-staying wife, as part of a decree of divorce *a mensa et thoro*.[1] The Court said (p. 584):

"Our first remark is—and we wish it to be remembered—that this is not a suit asking the court for the allowance of alimony. The court in Wisconsin was asked to interfere to prevent that decree from being defeated by fraud.

"We disclaim altogether any jurisdiction in the courts of the United States upon the subject of divorce, or for the allowance of alimony, either as an original proceeding in chancery or as an incident to divorce *a vinculo*, or to one from bed and board."

The remark was remembered, and the dictum established lasting law. In another dictum in In re Burrus, 136 U.S. 586, 593–94 (1890), the Court, broadening the disclaimer, flatly stated that "The whole subject of the domestic relations of husband and wife, parent and child, belongs to the laws of the States and not to the laws of the United States." The Burrus case actually involved only the question of the power of a United States district court, under the habeas corpus statutes, to make an award of an infant's custody in the absence of diversity of citizenship jurisdiction. The question of power, given diversity jurisdiction, was expressly reserved (136 U.S. at 597).[2] But the quoted dictum nevertheless has generally been taken as referring more generally to judicial competence. See the further dicta in Simms v. Simms, 175 U.S. 162, 167 (1899), and Williams v. North Carolina, 325 U.S. 226, 233 (1945).

Popovici v. Popovici, 30 F.2d 185 (N.D.Ohio 1927), was a suit for divorce in a federal district court by an Ohio wife against a Rumanian vice-consul and subject. Deferring to the Supreme Court's earlier dicta, the court reluctantly denied its jurisdiction. Later the wife got her divorce in the Ohio state courts, in the face of the explicit grant to the federal courts of exclusive jurisdiction in actions against consuls. The Supreme Court, in its first square holding in this field, upheld the decree, on the ground that there was an implied exception in the grant of federal jurisdiction which was an exception also to the provision for exclusivity. Ohio ex rel. Popovici v. Agler, 280 U.S. 379, 383 (1930). See Chap. III, Sec. 2, p. 346, *supra*.

(2) The domestic relations exception is firmly established in the lower courts, but its boundaries are unsettled. The "core" of the exception includes cases asking a court "to grant a divorce or annulment, determine support payments, or award custody of a child." Csibi v. Fustos, 670 F.2d 134, 137 (9th Cir.1982). And most courts will not hear cases where "the primary issue concerns the status of parent and child or husband and

---

1. Usually translated "from bed to board"—a form of judicial separation (rather than a dissolution of the marriage) first provided by the ecclesiastical courts.

2. In re Burrus did not contemplate that a federal habeas corpus petitioner might raise a federal constitutional question in a custody dispute. See Paragraph (6), *infra*.

wife." Buechold v. Ortiz, 401 F.2d 371 (9th Cir.1968). See generally Rush, *Domestic Relations Law: Federal Jurisdiction and State Sovereignty in Perspective*, 60 Notre Dame L.Rev. 1, 8 n. 33 (1984); Note, 83 Colum.L.Rev. 1824, 1828 & nn. 29–31 (1983).

The decisions are less uniform in suits arising in a domestic relations context, but involving claims traditionally adjudicated in federal courts. For the most part, federal courts will hear cases "whose essence is in, for example, tort or contract, and which do not require the federal court to exceed its competence." Bennett v. Bennett, 682 F.2d 1039, 1042 (D.C.Cir. 1982). For example, Wasserman v. Wasserman, 671 F.2d 832 (4th Cir.1982) and Lloyd v. Loeffler, 694 F.2d 489 (7th Cir.1982) upheld jurisdiction over tort damage actions for interference with child custody, which was not itself in dispute;[3] but *cf.* Sutter v. Pitts, Paragraph (5), *infra*. And Crouch v. Crouch, 566 F.2d 486 (5th Cir.1978) upheld jurisdiction in an action for breach of a separation agreement also involving no dispute about custody.[4] But similar suits have been dismissed for lack of jurisdiction on the ground that they (i) involve ongoing familial disputes, see, *e.g.*, Jagiella v. Jagiella, 647 F.2d 561, 565 (5th Cir.1981) (tort claim for intentional infliction of mental anguish arising out of the "dissolved but still stormy relationship"); (ii) would require too close an inquiry into a marital or parent-child relationship, see, *e.g.*, Solomon v. Solomon, 516 F.2d 1018 (3d Cir.1975) (divorced wife's contract claim for nonsupport that revolves around dispute over visitation rights), or (iii) implicate agreements that are modifiable under state law, see, *e.g.*, Morris v. Morris, 273 F.2d 678, 682 (7th Cir.1960) (action to enforce separation decree's payment provisions, which might be modified in light of changing circumstances).[5]

(3) What is the ground for the exclusion of federal jurisdiction in domestic relations matters? In Fontain v. Ravenel, 17 How. 369 (U.S.1854), Chief Justice Taney, dissenting from the Court's decision refusing on the merits to enforce a charitable bequest, contended that the federal circuit court lacked jurisdiction (p. 393):

"The 2d section of the 3d article of the constitution declares that the judicial power of the United States shall extend to all cases in law and equity specified in the section. These words obviously confer judicial power, and nothing more; and cannot, upon any fair construction, be held to embrace the prerogative powers, which the king, as *parens patriae*, in England, exercised through the courts. And the chancery jurisdiction of the courts of the United States, as granted by the constitution, extends only

---

3. The court in Lloyd expressed concern, however, with a provision of the judgment awarding plaintiff an additional $2,000/month in punitive damages until the child was returned. The coercive effect of that award, the court feared, might make it tantamount to an injunction directing the child's return, and such an injunction was held to fall within the domestic relations exception in the Bennett case, *supra*.

4. The courts have also entertained actions focusing on the validity of a divorce decree. See Keating v. Keating, 542 F.2d 910 (4th Cir.1976) (jurisdiction to determine validity of conflicting decrees and to

provide enforcement); Southard v. Southard, 305 F.2d 730 (2d Cir.1962) (upholding jurisdiction to determine whether Connecticut divorce decree was invalid for failure to give full faith and credit to a prior Nevada decree); Harrison v. Harrison, 214 F.2d 571 (4th Cir.1954) (upholding jurisdiction to declare Mexican divorce invalid, and to order payment of alimony under an Ohio decree); Spindel v. Spindel, Paragraph (4), *infra*.

5. For an argument favoring federal enforcement of state decrees so long as it does not prejudice the right to seek modification in state court, see Comment, 50 U.Chi.L. Rev. 1357 (1983).

to cases over which the court of chancery had jurisdiction, in its judicial character as a court of equity. The wide discretionary power which the chancellor of England exercises over infants, lunatics, or idiots, or charities, has not been conferred.

"These prerogative powers, which belong to the sovereign as *parens patriae*, remain with the States. They may legalize charitable bequests within their own respective dominions, to the extent to which the law upon that subject has been carried in England; and they may require any tribunal of the State, which they think proper to select for that purpose, to establish such charities, and to carry them into execution. But state laws will not authorize the courts of the United States to exercise any power that is not in its nature judicial; nor can they confer on them the prerogative powers over minors, idiots, and lunatics, or charities, which the English chancellor possesses. Nobody will for a moment suppose that a court of equity of the United States could, in virtue of a state law, take upon itself the guardianship over all the minors, idiots, or lunatics in the State. Yet these powers in the English chancellor stand upon the same ground, and are derived from the same authority, as its power in cases of charitable bequests."

In De La Rama v. De La Rama, 201 U.S. 303, 307 (1906), the Court, in reviewing and reversing a territorial court's refusal to grant a divorce, with award of alimony, spoke of the regular federal courts as lacking jurisdiction in such proceedings "both by reason of fact that the husband and wife cannot usually be citizens of different States, so long as the marriage relation continues (a rule which has been somewhat relaxed in recent cases), and for the further reason that a suit for divorce in itself involves no pecuniary value".

(4) The whole development of federal doctrine in matters of domestic relations was subjected to searching analysis and criticism in Spindel v. Spindel, 283 F.Supp. 797 (E.D.N.Y.1968), in which the court sustained its jurisdiction to entertain a diversity action by a wife challenging the validity of a Mexican divorce and seeking damages from her husband for fraud in inducing the marriage and procuring the divorce. In the course of his opinion, Judge Weinstein challenged the assumption as to citizenship in De La Rama, *supra*, as well as the view—exemplified by Chief Justice Taney's dissent in Fontain v. Ravenel, *supra*—that matrimonial matters were handled exclusively in the ecclesiastical courts and not in chancery acting in its judicial capacity. He also argued that Article III requires only a "controversy" (not a "case in law or equity") between citizens of different states for federal jurisdiction to exist and that Congress could therefore confer on the federal courts authority to grant divorces in such cases;[6] pointed out the distinction between holding and dicta in all of the Supreme Court decisions except Ohio ex rel. Popovici v. Agler, Paragraph (1), *supra*; noted the precedents supporting jurisdiction in matrimonial cases where divorce is not sought; and concluded that in the case before him there was no valid basis for not exercising federal jurisdiction.

6. Judge Weinstein relied heavily on the Simms and De La Rama cases, *supra*, as demonstrating the power of federal courts to handle divorce cases under Article III. How else, he asks, could the Supreme Court have reviewed the decisions of the territorial courts in these cases?

The commentators have recognized the force of Judge Weinstein's analysis.[7] Several courts have also, though they have been quick to add that the exception is "too well established to be questioned any longer by a lower court," Lloyd v. Loeffler, Paragraph (2), *supra,* 694 F.2d at 492, or that many factors other than history support its continued observance, including " 'the strong state interest in domestic relations matters, the competence of state courts in settling family disputes,[8] the possibility of incompatible federal and state court decrees in cases of continuing judicial supervision by the state, and the problem of congested dockets in the federal courts.' " Ruffalo by Ruffalo v. Civiletti, 702 F.2d 710, 717 (8th Cir. 1983), *quoting* Crouch v. Crouch, 566 F.2d 486, 487 (5th Cir.1978).[9]

(5) Although the domestic relations exception has traditionally been viewed as a limitation of jurisdictional power, see, *e.g.,* Phillips, Nizer, Benjamin, Krim and Ballon v. Rosenstiel, 490 F.2d 509, 512–515 (2d Cir. 1973), some courts—perhaps in response to the points raised by Judge Weinstein—have recently begun to view it as an exercise in discretionary abstention. See, *e.g.,* Huynh Thi Anh v. Levi, 586 F.2d 625, 632 (6th Cir. 1978). Other courts follow a combined view, regarding the exception as a limitation of power in "core" cases and a matter of discretion in "peripheral" cases. See, *e.g.,* Sutter v. Pitts, 639 F.2d 842 (1st Cir.1981) (abstaining in a suit under state civil rights law for damages and equitable relief against divorced husband for disobeying state custody decree); Peterson v. Babbitt, 708 F.2d 465, 466 (9th Cir.1983) (abstaining in a prisoner's constitutional challenge to denial of child visitation rights). Does the choice between a jurisdictional and discretionary view affect the breadth of federal adjudication? Whether an objection to federal adjudication is waivable? The scope of appellate review of trial court decisions? See generally Ward, note 7, *supra,* at 323–24.

Is this notion of a penumbra around the court's jurisdiction, in which it may choose to abstain, an appropriate one? See McIntyre v. McIntyre, 771 F.2d 1316 (9th Cir.1985) (dismissal of tort action for violation of visitation agreement was abuse of discretion; abstention is proper only in the categories of cases identified in Colorado River); *cf.* the discussion, in Paragraph (6) of the preceding Note, of the same question in the probate setting.

(6) The domestic relations exception arose as a limitation only on federal diversity jurisdiction. Some courts have also refused, on an abstention theory, to exercise federal question jurisdiction in domestic relations

---

7. Some have suggested outright abolition. See Wand, *A Call for the Repudiation of the Domestic Relations Exception to Federal Jurisdiction,* 30 Vill.L.Rev. 307 (1985); Note, 24 B.C.L.Rev. 661 (1983); Comment, 71 Marq.L.Rev. 141 (1987). Others have urged limiting the scope of the exception, see Rush, Paragraph (2), *supra,* or serving its purposes by use of more general abstention doctrines, see, *e.g.,* Atwood, *Domestic Relations Cases in Federal Court: Toward a Principled Exercise of Jurisdiction,* 35 Hastings L.J. 571 (1984); Note, 1983 Duke L.J. 1095.

8. [Ed.] *Cf.* Currie, *Suitcase Divorce in the Conflict of Laws: Simons, Rosenstiel,*

and Borax, 34 U.Chi.L.Rev. 26, 49–53 (1966), arguing that a state whose divorce law is to be applied may properly confine divorce litigation to its own (often specialized) courts to avoid the serious risk of error in adjudication in other fora.

9. See Phillips, Nizer, Benjamin, Krim & Ballon v. Rosenstiel, 490 F.2d 509, 514 (2d Cir.1973) (Friendly, J.) ("It is beyond the realm of reasonable belief that, in these days of congested dockets, Congress would wish the federal courts to seek to regain territory, even if the cession of 1859 was unjustified.")

matters. See Bergstrom v. Bergstrom, 623 F.2d 517 (8th Cir.1980) (abstaining in custody fight involving child's claim of a constitutional right to remain in the United States), and Peterson v. Babbitt, Paragraph (5), *supra*. But see Hooks v. Hooks, 771 F.2d 935 (6th Cir.1985) (upholding jurisdiction over § 1983 claim that plaintiff was deprived of custody without due process). See generally Comment, 31 U.C.L.A.L.Rev. 843 (1984).

In Lehman v. Lycoming County Children's Services Agency, 458 U.S. 502 (1982), a mother's parental rights over her children had been involuntarily terminated in a state proceeding; custody was awarded to a county agency, which placed the children in a private foster home. After the award was upheld on appeal and the Supreme Court denied certiorari, the mother filed a federal habeas corpus petition under 28 U.S.C. § 2254, challenging the county's custody on the ground that the statute under which it had been awarded denied due process. In ruling that § 2254 did not confer federal jurisdiction over such a case, the Supreme Court distinguished the situation of the children from that of a petitioner whose custody arises from a criminal conviction.[10] Though it did not advert to the domestic relations exception per se, the Court did stress the special solicitude that federal courts have traditionally shown in "family and family-property arrangements" (p. 512), and the importance to the state of certainty and finality in child custody disputes.[11]

(7) The Parental Kidnaping Prevention Act of 1980, 94 Stat. 3568–73 (1980), codified in pertinent part as 28 U.S.C. § 1738A, requires (except in certain limited circumstances) that a state recognize and enforce child custody decrees rendered by other states in accordance with the Act's provisions. Resolving a circuit conflict, the Supreme Court ruled in Thompson v. Thompson, 108 S.Ct. 513 (1988) that the Act does not create an implied federal right of action permitting federal court suit to enjoin state court proceedings in violation of the Act. The Court noted that Congress, when enacting this statute, had rejected a proposal to extend the diversity jurisdiction to actions seeking enforcement of state custody orders. Federal court determination of which of two conflicting decrees should be given effect, the Court added, would offend the "longstanding tradition of reserving domestic-relations matters to the States" (p. 520 n. 4).

---

10. The Court reserved the question of federal habeas jurisdiction when the child is confined in a state institution (p. 511 n. 12).

11. Justice Blackmun, joined by Justices Brennan and Marshall, dissented, finding that the history of habeas corpus and the language of § 2254 supported federal court power to issue the writ, though noting that in the exercise of that power the district court might as a matter of discretion have denied relief on the ground that the petitioner was no longer a proper "next friend" who could seek the writ on the children's behalf. He did not discuss whether his argument was consistent with the domestic relations exception.

Chapter XI

FEDERAL HABEAS CORPUS

SECTION 1. INTRODUCTION

NOTE ON THE JURISDICTIONAL STATUTES

(1) Section 14 of the First Judiciary Act provided (1 Stat. 81–82):

"That all the before-mentioned courts of the United States, shall have power to issue writs of *scire facias, habeas corpus,* and all other writs not specially provided for by statute, which may be necessary for the exercise of their respective jurisdictions, and agreeable to the principles and usages of law. And that either of the justices of the supreme court, as well as judges of the district courts, shall have power to grant writs of *habeas corpus* for the purpose of an inquiry into the cause of commitment.—*Provided,* That writs of *habeas corpus* shall in no case extend to prisoners in gaol, unless where they are in custody, under or by colour of the authority of the United States, or are committed for trial before some court of the same, or are necessary to be brought into court to testify."

The view that this provision authorized the courts to issue the writ only as an auxiliary to jurisdiction otherwise conferred upon them was rejected in Ex parte Bollman, 4 Cranch 75 (U.S.1807), p. 354 *supra*.[1] The power expressly conferred on the justices and judges to inquire by the writ into the cause of commitment was held to be vested by implication in the courts. And where commitment was by order of a lower federal court, issuance of the writ by the Supreme Court was held to be an exercise of appellate jurisdiction, even though no appeal to the Court from a judgment of conviction was provided by the statutes. See pp. 354–55, *supra*.

The Bollman case also made it clear, however, that the jurisdiction of the federal courts to issue the writ must be conferred by statute, and is not an "inherent" power. And Ex parte Dorr, 3 How. 103 (U.S.1845) affirmed that, as a consequence, the statute's proviso deprived these courts of the power to issue the writ to one held under state law.

(2) Subsequent enactments progressively reduced the class of prisoners excluded from the writ by the proviso, articulating, at the same time, specific grounds on which the writ might issue.

(a) The Force Act of 1833, countering South Carolina's resistance to the "Tariff of Abominations", provided in section 7 (4 Stat. 634–35) that "either of the justices of the Supreme Court, or a judge of any district court of the United States, in addition to the authority already conferred by law, shall have power to grant writs of habeas corpus in all cases of a prisoner or prisoners, in jail or confinement, where he or they shall be committed or

---

1. For an interesting article maintaining that Marshall misread the statute, see Paschal, *The Constitution and Habeas Corpus,* 1970 Duke L.J. 605.

confined on, or by any authority or law, for any act done, or omitted to be done, in pursuance of a law of the United States, or any order, process, or decree, of any judge or court thereof, anything in any act of Congress to the contrary notwithstanding."

(b) The Act of Aug. 29, 1842, 5 Stat. 539–40, was enacted following British diplomatic protest that the trial of a Canadian soldier by New York for murder constituted an infringement of the law of nations—the homicide being claimed to be an act of state. See People v. McCleod, 25 Wend. 483 (1841); 2 Warren, The Supreme Court in United States History 98 (rev. ed. 1947). It authorized justices and district judges to "grant writs of habeas corpus" in certain cases involving prisoners who are "subjects or citizens of a foreign State, and domiciled therein" and are held under federal or state law. Decisions of justices and judges were made appealable to the circuit court and then to the Supreme Court.

(c) The most significant expansion of the reach of the writ—to encompass generally persons held under state law—came with the Act of February 5, 1867, 14 Stat. 385, which provided broadly that "the several courts of the United States, and the several justices and judges of such courts, within their respective jurisdictions, in addition to the authority already conferred by law, shall have power to grant writs of habeas corpus in all cases where any person may be restrained of his or her liberty in violation of the constitution, or of any treaty or law of the United States * * *." The Act also prescribed the procedure on the writ (in terms later applied to all cases of its use), authorized appeals to the circuit court from decisions of justices, judges or inferior courts and from the circuit court to the Supreme Court [2] and declared void all state proceedings against the prisoner, pending a determination on the writ.[3]

(3) The foregoing provisions were codified in Title 13 of the Revised Statutes of 1874, §§ 751–766, and survived without important change until 1948. See 28 U.S.C. § 451 et seq. (1940).

The 1948 revision collected the provisions with respect to habeas corpus in Chapter 153 of the Judicial Code, 28 U.S.C. §§ 2241–55. The revision did not make significant changes in the provisions governing the prisoners to whom the writ extends and the grounds on which detention may be challenged. See § 2241. But it effected some important alterations of procedure.[4] In addition, it gave statutory formulation for the first

---

2. This was the provision repealed by the Act of March 27, 1868, 15 Stat. 44, involved in Ex parte McCardle, p. 364, *supra.*

3. Decisions under each of the foregoing statutory formulations are collected in 18 Fed. 68 (1884).

4. Prior to the 1948 revision, the statute provided that on an application for habeas, the court, justice or judge shall "forthwith award a writ of habeas corpus, unless it appears from the petition itself that the party is not entitled thereto." Rev.Stat. § 755, 28 U.S.C. § 455 (1940). It also provided that the "person making the return shall at the same time bring the body of the party before the judge who granted the writ." Rev.Stat. § 758, 28

U.S.C. § 458 (1940). Walker v. Johnston, 312 U.S. 275 (1941), however, sustained the practice of issuing a rule to show cause rather than the writ itself. Justice Roberts said (p. 284):

"* * * By this procedure the facts on which the opposing parties rely may be exhibited, and the court may find that no issue of fact is involved. In this way useless grant of the writ with consequent production of the prisoner and of witnesses may be avoided where from undisputed facts or from incontrovertible facts, such as those recited in a court record, it appears, as matter of law, no cause for granting the writ exists. On the other hand, on the facts admitted, it may appear that, as matter of law, the prisoner is entitled to the

time to the rule requiring exhaustion of state remedies prior to seeking the writ in federal court. See § 2254(b) and (c). And, finally, in § 2255, it created a new statutory motion for federal prisoners making collateral attack on their convictions; habeas corpus for such a prisoner was declared to be available only if the new statutory motion "is inadequate or ineffective to test the legality of his detention".

(4) In 1966 Congress, seeking further specification of the rules governing the effect of previous adjudications on habeas corpus litigation, added subsections (b) and (c) to 28 U.S.C. § 2244. It also enacted 28 U.S.C. § 2254(d), specifying the circumstances when a habeas corpus court should take evidence in a case involving a state prisoner. See further p. 1561, *infra*.

NOTE ON THE FUNCTIONS OF THE WRIT

(1) This Chapter deals with the writ of *habeas corpus ad subjiciendum*, the so-called Great Writ. But this was only one form of the writ at common law. The other forms enumerated by Blackstone were: (1) *ad respondendum* (to remove a prisoner confined by process of an inferior court to answer to an action in a higher court); (2) *ad satisfaciendum* (to remove a prisoner to a higher court to be charged with process of execution); (3) *ad prosequendum, testificandum, deliberandum* (to remove a prisoner to enable him to prosecute or testify or to be tried in the proper jurisdiction); (4) *ad faciendum et recipiendum* (to remove a cause at the prisoner's behest from an inferior court to Westminster). 3 Commentaries 129–132.[1]

(2) In McNally v. Hill, 293 U.S. 131 (1934), the Court described *habeas corpus ad subjiciendum* as follows (pp. 136–37): "The statute [Judicial Code] does not define the term habeas corpus. To ascertain its meaning and the appropriate use of the writ in the federal courts, recourse must be had to the common law, from which the term was drawn, and to the decisions of

writ and to a discharge. This practice has long been followed by this court and by the lower courts. It is a convenient one, deprives the petitioner of no substantial right, if the petition and traverse are treated, as we think they should be, as together constituting the application for the writ, and the return to the rule as setting up the facts thought to warrant its denial, and if issues of fact emerging from the pleadings are tried as required by the statute."

This aspect of the Walker decision was ratified by § 2243 of the 1948 revision. The requirement that testimony be given as in other civil cases *ore tenus* or by deposition was qualified, however, by making admissible in evidence "the certificate of the judge who presided at the trial resulting in the judgment, setting forth the facts occurring at the trial" (§ 2245), and by authorizing the taking of evidence "by deposition, or, in the discretion of the judge, by affidavit" subject to the right "to propound written interrogatories to the affiants, or to file answering affidavits" (§ 2246). See

Parker, *Limiting the Abuse of Habeas Corpus,* 8 F.R.D. 171, 174–75 (1949).

1. See also Ex parte Bollman, 4 Cranch 75, 97–98 (U.S.1807); Price v. Johnston, 334 U.S. 266, 281 (1948). None of these forms included use of the writ to compel the production of a prisoner to argue his own appeal, but in the Price case a court of appeals was declared to have the power to issue a writ "in the nature of *habeas corpus*" for this purpose under § 262 of the Judicial Code (now 28 U.S.C. § 1651). Use of the writ when "necessary" to bring the prisoner "into court to testify or for trial" is specifically authorized by 28 U.S.C. § 2241(c)(5).

Carbo v. United States, 364 U.S. 611 (1961), upheld, under 28 U.S.C. § 2241, the power of a federal district court in California to issue a writ of *habeas corpus ad prosequendum* directing a New York City prison official to deliver a prisoner held in New York for trial on an indictment pending in the California court.

this Court interpreting and applying the common law principles which define its use when authorized by the statute. * * *

"Originating as a writ by which the superior courts of the common law and the chancellor sought to extend their jurisdiction at the expense of inferior or rival courts, it ultimately took form and survived as the writ of *habeas corpus ad subjiciendum,* by which the legality of the detention of one in the custody of another could be tested judicially. See Holdsworth, History of the English Law, vol. 9, 108–125. Its use was defined and regulated by the Habeas Corpus Act of 1679, 31 Car. II, c. 2. This legislation and the decisions of the English courts interpreting it have been accepted by this Court as authoritative guides in defining the principles which control the use of the writ in the federal courts. * * *

"The purpose of the proceeding defined by the statute was to inquire into the legality of the detention, and the only judicial relief authorized was the discharge of the prisoner or his admission to bail, and that only if his detention were found to be unlawful. In this, the statute conformed to the traditional form of the writ, which put in issue only the disposition of the custody of the prisoner according to law. There is no warrant in either the statute or the writ for its use to invoke judicial determination of questions which could not affect the lawfulness of the custody and detention, and no suggestion of such a use has been found in the commentaries on the English common law."

(3) The Great Writ always serves the function of precipitating a judicial inquiry into a claim of illegality in the petitioner's detention for the purpose of commanding his release, or other appropriate disposition, if he is found to be illegally detained. The underlying premise is, of course, that only law can justify detention, the specific contribution of the English struggle with royal prerogative in which the writ played an historic part.[2] The custodian, whether an official or a private citizen [3] must point to law to defend the restraint. But law is not a simple concept for this purpose, consisting as it does of rules distributing authority to make decisions as well as rules that govern the decisions to be made. There is a sense, therefore, in which a prisoner can be deemed to be legally detained if he is held pursuant to the judgment or decision of a competent tribunal or authority, even though the decision to detain rested on an error as to law or fact.

That there must be some room for limiting conceptions of this kind seems clear enough: the writ cannot be made the instrument for re-determining the merits of all cases in the legal system that have ended in detention. See generally Bator, *Finality in Criminal Law and Federal*

2. For the British development, see Duker, *The English Origins of the Writ of Habeas Corpus: A Peculiar Path to Fame,* 53 N.Y.U.L.Rev. 983 (1978), and the survey and the literature cited in *Developments in the Law—Federal Habeas Corpus,* 83 Harv. L.Rev. 1038, 1042–45 (1970). See also Walker, Constitutional and Legal Developments of Habeas Corpus as the Writ of Liberty (1960).

3. Restraints by private citizens are not normally reached by the federal writ (except within the District of Columbia).

Whether the writ might issue (in a case involving a private detention) under the "all writs" section in aid of diversity jurisdiction was reserved in Ex parte Burrus, 136 U.S. 586, 597 (1890) and Matters v. Ryan, 249 U.S. 375 (1919). A case involving such restraint would present difficult problems with respect to the jurisdictional amount requirement, and if it involved a question of child custody, would encounter the limitations of federal jurisdiction in cases of domestic relations. See p. 1460, *supra.*

Habeas Corpus for State Prisoners, 76 Harv.L.Rev. 441 (1963).[4] But how severe the limitations ought to be and in what terms they should be formulated are questions that have posed impressive difficulty to the courts. Concepts such as "jurisdiction," "power," or "authority," distinctions between actions that are "void" and merely "voidable," while traditional and relevant in marking boundaries of this order, serve less often to explain than to express conclusions as to whether relief on the writ shall lie. Other factors may have a more generative influence upon results, such as the nature and importance of the legal right asserted to establish illegality, the need for speed in the determination and the availability of other remedies, the extent to which the inquiry upon the writ will further or will thwart the ordinary processes of law administration, the impact of the inquiry on tender areas of power distribution like the relation between federal and state or civilian and military courts.

These complexities must be kept well in mind in reading the traditional encomiums about the writ. There is over-statement coupled with the truth in assertions such as Dicey's that the writ provides "adequate security that every one who without legal justification is placed in confinement shall be able to get free." Law of the Constitution 213 (10th ed. 1959).

(4) This chapter focuses primarily on the use of the writ as an extraordinary post-conviction remedy for prisoners who urge a federal defect in their convictions. This is the area where there has been the most development and difficulty in the course of recent years. Other uses of the writ should not, however, be ignored. Of these, some of the most important have been noted earlier in Chapter IV (pp. 411–23, *supra*). The writ provides a ready mechanism for a constitutional attack upon official claims of power to detain (other than to answer charges in a civil court).[5] It serves

---

4. " * * * [O]n this underlying premise [—that a detention may not be considered lawful unless the proceedings leading to it were, in some ultimate sense, free of error—] the conclusion is inescapable that no detention can ever be finally determined to be lawful; for if legality turns on 'actual' freedom from errors of either fact or law, whenever error is alleged the court passing on legality will necessarily have to satisfy itself by determining the merits whether in fact error occurred. After all, there is no ultimate guarantee that *any* tribunal arrived at the correct result * * *. * * *

"Surely, then, it is naive and confusing to think of detention as lawful only if the previous tribunal's proceedings were 'correct' in this ultimate sense. If any detention whatever is to be validated, the concept of 'lawfulness' must be defined in terms more complicated than 'actual' freedom from error; or, if you will, the concept of 'freedom from error' must eventually include a notion that some complex of institutional processes is empowered definitively to *establish* whether or not there was error, even though in the very nature of things no such processes can give us ultimate assurances. * * * The task of

assuring legality is to define and create a set of arrangements and procedures which provide a reasoned and acceptable probability that justice will be done, that the facts found will be 'true' and the law applied 'correct'." Bator, *supra,* at 446–48.

5. See, *e.g.,* Ex parte Milligan, 4 Wall. 2 (U.S.1866) (power of military to try civilian); Duncan v. Kahanamoku, 327 U.S. 304 (1946) (same); Jurney v. MacCracken, 294 U.S. 125 (1935) (power of Senate to order arrest for contempt of a Committee); Ex parte Quirin, 317 U.S. 1 (1942) (military commission); In re Yamashita, 327 U.S. 1 (1946) (same); Ex parte Endo, 323 U.S. 283 (1944) (power to hold loyal citizen of Japanese descent in Relocation Center); Ludecke v. Watkins, 335 U.S. 160 (1948) (power to repatriate enemy without due process hearing); Kwong Hai Chew v. Colding, 344 U.S. 590 (1953) (power to exclude resident alien without hearing).

See also Lehman v. Lycoming County Children's Services Agency, 458 U.S. 502 (1982), p. 1464, *supra,* holding that § 2254 does not confer jurisdiction over a petition brought by a mother to challenge as unconstitutional a state adjudication terminating her parental rights and awarding custody

to provide such judicial review of decisions of other agencies resulting in detention as the constitution guarantees.[6] It also performs traditional, though marginal, preliminary functions in connection with charges of crime: testing the sufficiency of cause for a commitment on complaint [7] or for removal,[8] the denial of bail,[9] the legality of interstate rendition,[10] or of extradition to a foreign country.[11] And, finally, the writ has been much used to test the legality of the conditions of confinement.[12]

(5) For a comprehensive survey of the field of habeas corpus, see 17 Wright, Miller & Cooper, Federal Practice and Procedure: Jurisdiction §§ 4261–68 (1978 & 1987 Supp.) (hereafter cited as 17 Federal Practice). For an earlier survey, see *Developments in the Law—Federal Habeas Corpus*, 83 Harv.L.Rev. 1038 (1970) (hereafter cited as *Developments*).[13] Other general accounts of habeas corpus are Bator, *supra* (hereafter cited as Bator, *Finality*); Hart, *The Supreme Court, 1958 Term, Foreword: The Time Chart of the Justices*, 73 Harv.L.Rev. 84, 101–25 (1959) (hereafter cited as Hart, *Foreword*); Wechsler, *Habeas Corpus and the Supreme Court: Reconsidering the Reach of the Great Writ*, 59 U.Colo.L.Rev. 167 (1988); Yackle, *Explaining Habeas Corpus*, 60 N.Y.U.L.Rev. 991 (1985); and Symposium, *State Prisoner Use of Federal Habeas Corpus Procedures*, 44 Ohio St.L.J. 269 (1983). For empirical studies, see Shapiro, *Federal Habeas Corpus: A Study in Massachusetts*, 87 Harv.L.Rev. 321 (1973); Robinson,

of her children to a county agency, which placed the children in a private foster home. The Court reserved the question of federal habeas jurisdiction when the child is confined in a state institution.

6. For a survey of the use of federal habeas corpus to review administrative restraints in three areas (military administrative decisions, conscription, and deportation and exclusion of aliens), see *Developments*, note 2, *supra*, at 1238–63. Habeas corpus review of court martial determinations is described in Section 3, p. 1590, *infra*.

7. See, *e.g.*, Ex parte Bollman, 4 Cranch 75 (U.S.1807).

8. See, *e.g.*, Tinsley v. Treat, 205 U.S. 20 (1907); Henry v. Henkel, 235 U.S. 219 (1914); Rodman v. Pothier, 264 U.S. 399 (1924); United States ex rel. Kassin v. Mulligan, 295 U.S. 396 (1935). The narrow review sanctioned by these decisions has been further limited by Rule 40 of the Rules of Criminal Procedure under which an indictment is sufficient for removal upon proof of the identity of the defendant. Moreover, the Act of June 29, 1938, 52 Stat. 1232, eliminated an appeal from final orders on the writ when used to test detention for removal. See 28 U.S.C. § 2253.

9. Though one of the main purposes of the Habeas Corpus Act of 1679 was to provide for vindication of the right to bail of persons charged with bailable offenses, the writ is rarely needed for this purpose in federal courts. Bail is normally allowed at the preliminary hearing and an application to the court or to a judge or justice

may be made if it is not. See 18 U.S.C. §§ 3041, 3141; Rule 46, Rules of Criminal Procedure. In Stack v. Boyle, 342 U.S. 1 (1951), the proper remedy for a reduction of excessive bail was held to be a motion in the district court and an appeal from its denial.

As to the power of a single Justice to admit to bail pending review of a denial of habeas corpus, see the opinion of Jackson, J., in Stack v. Boyle, *supra;* and compare the opinion of Jackson, J., in In the Matter of Pirinsky, 70 S.Ct. 232 (1949) with that of Douglas, J., in Petition of Johnson, 72 S.Ct. 1028 (1952).

10. See, *e.g.*, Roberts v. Reilly, 116 U.S. 80 (1885); Drew v. Thaw, 235 U.S. 432 (1914); Biddinger v. Commissioner of Police, 245 U.S. 128 (1917). But *cf.* Sweeney v. Woodall, 344 U.S. 86 (1952) (escaped prisoner). For a case discussing the limits the Extradition Act, 18 U.S.C. § 3182, imposes upon state habeas corpus challenges to extradition warrants, see California v. Superior Court, 107 S.Ct. 2433 (1987). See generally Note, 83 Colum.L.Rev. 975 (1983); Note, 74 Yale L.J. 78 (1964).

11. See, *e.g.*, Fernandez v. Phillips, 268 U.S. 311 (1925); Factor v. Laubenheimer, 290 U.S. 276 (1933); *cf.* 18 U.S.C. § 3184 (procedure prior to issuance of warrant).

12. See, *e.g.*, Wilwording v. Swenson, 404 U.S. 249 (1971); Johnson v. Avery, 393 U.S. 483 (1969).

13. See also the surveys at Notes, 61 Harv.L.Rev. 657 (1948), and 35 Colum.L. Rev. 404 (1935).

An Empirical Study of Federal Habeas Corpus Review of State Court Judgments (U.S. Dep't of Justice) (1979); and Allen, Schachtman & Wilson, *Federal Habeas Corpus and its Reform: An Empirical Analysis,* 13 Rutgers L.J. 675 (1982).

——————

NOTE ON COURTS, JUSTICES, AND JUDGES AUTHORIZED
TO GRANT THE WRIT

(1) The present statute vests authority to grant the writ in the Supreme Court and the district courts, any justice of the Supreme Court and any circuit judge "within their respective jurisdictions" (28 U.S.C. § 2241). This represents a change from prior law in the unexplained exclusion of the district judges, see 28 U.S.C. § 452 (1940), though not in the exclusion of the courts of appeals, which have never had authority to grant the writ,[1] except under the "all writs" provision, 28 U.S.C. § 1651, in aid of appellate jurisdiction in a pending case.[2]

(2) For an admirable account of the development of the law and the current practice of the Supreme Court with respect to applications for habeas corpus directed to it in the first instance, see Oaks, *The "Original" Writ of Habeas Corpus in the Supreme Court,* 1962 Sup.Ct.Rev. 153. The Court's early practice was to exercise jurisdiction if the petition made the necessary showing of defect of "jurisdiction" in the lower court authorizing the detention. See, *e.g.,* Ex parte Siebold, 100 U.S. 371 (1879).[3] In Ex parte Yarbrough, 110 U.S. 651, 653 (1884) the Court declared it "well settled that when a prisoner is held under the sentence of any court of the United States in regard to a matter wholly beyond or without the jurisdiction of that court, it is not only within the authority of the Supreme Court, but it is its duty to inquire into the cause of commitment when the matter is properly brought to its attention, and if found to be as charged, a matter of which such a court had no jurisdiction, to discharge a prisoner from confinement."

The Court's practice and its concept of judicial duty went through drastic change. As stated in Ex parte Abernathy, 320 U.S. 219 (1943): "the jurisdiction conferred on this Court ∗ ∗ ∗ to issue writs of habeas corpus in aid of its appellate jurisdiction ∗ ∗ ∗ is discretionary ∗ ∗ ∗ and this Court does not, save in exceptional circumstances, exercise it in cases where an adequate remedy may be had in a lower federal court ∗ ∗ ∗ or, if the relief sought is from the judgment of a state court, where the petitioner has not exhausted his remedies in the state courts ∗ ∗ ∗." *Cf.* Ex parte Peru, 318 U.S. 578 (1943), p. 347, *supra.*

Three major factors seem to have produced the change: (1) the Act of March 3, 1885, 23 Stat. 437, restoring an appeal to the Supreme Court from circuit court judgments in habeas cases, as provided by the Act of 1867 and

1. See Whitney v. Dick, 202 U.S. 132 (1906).

2. See Adams v. United States, 317 U.S. 269 (1942); Price v. Johnston, 334 U.S. 266 (1948).

From 1911 until corrected by the Judiciary Act of 1925, 43 Stat. 940, circuit judges lacked authority to grant the writ unless

specially assigned to hold a district court. See Craig v. Hecht, 263 U.S. 255, 271 (1923).

3. *Cf.* Ex parte Virginia, 100 U.S. 339 (1879), where the petition was entertained before trial on a challenge to the statute underlying the indictment.

withdrawn in 1868 (see p. 364, *supra*); (2) the decisions in Ex parte Royall, 117 U.S. 241, 254 (1886), affirming broad discretion in the Supreme Court and in the circuit courts to deny the writ to a state prisoner seeking to challenge in advance of trial the validity of the state statute under which he was indicted; (3) the establishment in 1889 and 1891 of an appeal from convictions [4] in federal criminal cases. For milestones on the course of this development, see, *e.g.,* Ex parte Mirzan, 119 U.S. 584 (1887); Ex parte Lancaster, 137 U.S. 393 (1890); In re Chapman, 156 U.S. 211 (1895); In re Lincoln, 202 U.S. 178 (1906); Ex parte Tracy, 249 U.S. 551 (1919).

In this century, the Court appears to have granted relief in cases involving direct recourse to its habeas jurisdiction in only three instances. In Ex parte Hudgings, 249 U.S. 378 (1919), the writ was sustained where a district court had summarily adjudged the petitioner in contempt on the ground that his testimony as a witness was perjured. Holding that perjury is not, as such, contempt, the Court said (p. 384): "In view of the nature of the case, of the relation which the question which it involves bears generally to the power and duty of courts in the performance of their functions, of the dangerous effect on the liberty of the citizen when called upon as a witness in a court which might result if the erroneous doctrine upon which the order under review was based were not promptly corrected, we are of opinion that the case is an exception to the general rules of procedure to which we have at the outset referred, and therefore that our duty exacts that we finally dispose of the questions in the proceeding for habeas corpus which is before us."

See also Matter of Heff, 197 U.S. 488 (1905) (petitioner's attack on constitutionality of statute under which he was convicted had already been rejected by court of appeals in another case; statute held unconstitutional and prisoner discharged); Ex parte Grossman, 267 U.S. 87 (1925) (commitment for criminal contempt despite Presidential pardon; Attorney General, urging Presidential power, supported petitioner; prisoner discharged).

(3) The principle that now guides the Supreme Court on original applications for the writ is presumably followed by its members in the exercise of their authority as justices. For an express statement to this effect, see the opinion of Justice Douglas in United States ex rel. Norris v. Swope, 72 S.Ct. 1020 (1952); *cf.* Rosoto v. Warden, 83 S.Ct. 1788 (1963) (Harlan, J.). Such applications have, however, been occasionally denied on the merits. See, *e.g.,* the opinions of Justice Reed in Ex parte Taylor Seals, September 4 and November 23, 1943 (unreported) in which he said: "As I look upon the petition submitted to me as entirely lacking in merit, I am entering an order denying the petition without referring it to the Court."

The power of a justice to grant a writ returnable before the full court was affirmed in Ex parte Clarke, 100 U.S. 399, 403 (1879).

(4) The Supreme Court, Supreme Court justices, and circuit judges, are now expressly authorized to "decline to entertain an application for the writ" and to transfer it to the district court "having jurisdiction to entertain it." 28 U.S.C. § 2241(b). What was their authority for so declining prior to 1948? The statute provided that the "court, or justice, or judge to whom such application is made shall forthwith award a writ of habeas

---

4. See Frankfurter & Landis, The Business of the Supreme Court 109 (1928); pp. 1794–95, *infra.*

corpus, unless it appears from the petition itself that the party is not entitled thereto." Rev.Stat. § 755; 28 U.S.C. § 455 (1940); *cf.* 28 U.S.C. § 2243.

For instances of the Court's exercise of the transfer power granted by the 1948 revision, see, *e.g.,* Chaapel v. Chochran, 369 U.S. 869 (1962); Hayes v. Maryland, 370 U.S. 931 (1962); Byrnes v. Walker, 371 U.S. 937 (1962); *cf.* Wharton v. Crouse, 393 U.S. 815 (1968) (motion for leave to file denied; three justices would have transferred). See Oaks, Paragraph (2), *supra,* at 194.

(5) It is only "within their respective jurisdictions" that courts, justices and judges have been authorized to grant the writ.

Ahrens v. Clark, 335 U.S. 188 (1948), held that this limitation precluded the District Court for the District of Columbia from issuing the writ for persons detained at Ellis Island, New York, though they were held by order of the Attorney General who had the power to produce them in the District and expressed a willingness to waive objection that the application was not filed in the Southern District of New York. The Court, as noted previously, p. 422, *supra,* held the presence of the person detained within the territorial jurisdiction of the district court essential to its jurisdiction.

The provisions construed in Ahrens were legislatively modified: as to federal prisoners, by the 1948 revision, see 28 U.S.C. § 2255 (federal prisoners must attack their convictions in the sentencing court, not the district of incarceration); as to state prisoners, by the Act of September 19, 1966, 80 Stat. 811, see 28 U.S.C. § 2241(d) (prisoners attacking convictions by states comprising two or more districts may seek habeas in district where incarcerated *or* where convicting court sat). See Nelson v. George, 399 U.S. 224, 228 n. 5 (1970).

The rule of Ahrens v. Clark was overruled in Braden v. 30th Judicial Circuit Court, 410 U.S. 484 (1973). Braden was an application for habeas corpus by a petitioner serving a sentence in an Alabama prison. The prisoner had been indicted three years previously on an unrelated charge in Kentucky, and a detainer had been filed to assure that he would be turned over to Kentucky on the expiration of his Alabama sentence. The petitioner (relying on Smith v. Hooey, 393 U.S. 374 (1969)) alleged denial of his constitutional right to a speedy trial in Kentucky and sought an order compelling his immediate trial there. The petition was filed in the District Court for the Western District of Kentucky.

The Supreme Court (after holding that exhaustion requirements were satisfied, that petitioner was "in custody," and that the petition was not premature) held that Kentucky was the proper forum for the action. It concluded that the language of § 2241(a), authorizing courts to grant the writ only "within their respective jurisdictions," "requires nothing more than that the court issuing the writ have jurisdiction over the custodian" (pp. 494–95).

The Court stated that "developments since Ahrens have had a profound impact on the continuing vitality of that decision" (p. 497). It pointed to §§ 2255 and 2241(d) as exemplifying Congress' recognition of the desirability of having habeas cases resolved in a court with close contact with the underlying controversy. It pointed out that § 2243 reduces the number of occasions when the prisoner must personally attend the hearing. It referred to the decisions allowing habeas in the District of Columbia for prisoners held abroad. Finally, it stated, a "critical development" since Ahrens had been "the emergence of new classes of prisoners who are able to petition for habeas corpus because of the adoption of a more expansive definition of the 'custody' requirement" (p. 498) [see pp. 1569–72, *infra*]; it is this development that permitted a "petitioner held in one State to attack a detainer lodged against him by another" (p. 498). Petitioner's "dispute" was with Kentucky, not Alabama and "[w]e cannot assume that Congress intended" to require "Kentucky to defend its action in a distant State" (p. 499).

The Court concluded that Ahrens should be confined to its facts rather than taken to create a rigid jurisdictional rule.[5]

In a footnote, the Court carefully stated that "nothing in this opinion should be taken to preclude the exercise of concurrent habeas corpus jurisdiction * * * in the district of confinement" (p. 499 n. 15). Section 1404(a) was stated to be available to transfer a habeas case brought in an inconvenient venue.[6]

(6) What if there is no *custodian* within the territorial reach of the district court? In Schlanger v. Seamans, 401 U.S. 487 (1971), the Court held that the Arizona district court could not entertain a petition from an Air Force enlisted man on temporary duty in Arizona, since nobody who could be deemed his "custodian" (*i.e.*, his commanding officer or the Secretary of the Air Force) was in the state. But the teeth of this decision were drawn in the next Term in Strait v. Laird, 406 U.S. 341 (1972), holding that an inactive Army reservist could petition for habeas (to review a failure to grant discharge as a conscientious objector) in California, where *he* was domiciled, even though all of his superior officers were in Indiana. The majority argued that, since the petitioner's Indiana superiors processed his discharge application through Army personnel in California, they were "present" in California and would have been amenable to process there under the test of International Shoe Co. v. Washington, 326 U.S. 310 (1945). (Four dissenters said the decision "emasculates" Schlanger.)

Compare the decision in Ex parte Endo, 323 U.S. 283 (1944). Here the application for the writ was made and denied by the District Court for the Northern District of California and an appeal perfected from the denial while petitioner was held in a Relocation Center in that district. It was held that her subsequent removal to Utah did not cause the District Court to "lose jurisdiction where a person in whose custody she is remains within the District" (p. 306). The person viewed as a custodian within the district was an assistant director of the War Relocation Authority, the agency in the Department of Interior in charge of the Relocation Centers. The decision was explained in Ahrens v. Clark, *supra,* as "in conformity with the policy underlying [then] Rule 45(1) of the Court" which provided that pending "review of a decision refusing a writ of habeas corpus, the custody of the prisoner shall not be disturbed." See Supreme Court Rule 41.1 (1980).[7]

5. The Court pointed out that under traditional venue rules Ahrens was correct on its facts: the prisoners and those holding them were all located in New York, and no showing was made that the District of Columbia was a more convenient forum.

6. Justice Rehnquist, joined by Chief Justice Burger and Justice Powell, dissented, arguing that the task of bringing § 2241(a) into line with new developments was for Congress, not the Court.

7. What happens if no custodian remains within the district? In United States ex rel. Innes v. Crystal, 319 U.S. 755 (1943), the petitioner was held pursuant to a judgment of a court martial. After denial of the writ by the district court and affirmance by the circuit court of appeals

(7) Distinguish from the above problem—involving mootness where the prisoner or the custodian leaves the territory of the district during the action—the question whether a prisoner's release from confinement upon expiration of his sentence moots a habeas corpus case commenced before such release; as to this, see p. 1570, *infra.*

NOTE ON HABEAS CORPUS PROCEDURE

(1) *Rules for § 2254 Cases.* On February 1, 1977, "Rules Governing Section 2254 Cases in the United States District Courts" went into effect.[1]

The new rules apply of their own force only to habeas cases brought under § 2254 to challenge a present or future detention pursuant to a state court *judgment;* in habeas attacks on prejudgment state detentions under § 2241, and in federal prisoner habeas corpus cases, "these rules may be applied at the discretion of the United States district court" (Rule 1(b)). (Why do you suppose the scope of the rules was so limited?)

A noteworthy innovation in the new rules is a laches provision. According to Rule 9(a), a "petition may be dismissed if it appears that the state of which the respondent is an officer has been prejudiced in its ability to respond to the petition by delay in its filing unless the petitioner shows that it is based on grounds of which he could not have had knowledge by the exercise of reasonable diligence before the circumstances prejudicial to the state occurred. [If the petition is filed more than five years after the judgment of conviction, there shall be a presumption, rebuttable by the petitioner, that there is prejudice to the state. When a petition challenges the validity of an action, such as revocation of probation or parole, which occurs after judgment of conviction, the five-year period as to that action shall start to run at the time the order in the challenged action took place.]" (The two bracketed sentences were in the rule as transmitted, but were eliminated by Congress in Public Law 94–426.)[2]

but before the filing of a petition for certiorari, he was transferred to a federal penitentiary in a different district and circuit. The commanding officer, not the warden of the penitentiary, was the respondent. The Supreme Court denied the petition on the ground the cause was moot.

So, too, in United States ex rel. Lynn v. Downer, 322 U.S. 756 (1944), the petitioner, who claimed that he had been illegally inducted into the Army, was sent out of the district after judgment of the district court remanding him to custody and had been transferred to the South Pacific before the argument of his appeal in the circuit court of appeals. The respondent named was the commanding officer in New York at the time of the induction, who was no longer in the Army. Certiorari was denied on the ground "that the case is moot, it appearing that petitioner no longer is in respondent's custody," citing the Innes case as authority. Leave to file a petition for the writ was also denied by the Court, without assigning reasons. Lynn v. Ulio, 323 U.S. 678 (1944).

1. The Rules were drafted in response to a suggestion in the Court's opinion in Harris v. Nelson, 394 U.S. 286, 300 n. 7 (1969). In that case, the Court held that the federal discovery rules did not apply to habeas corpus, but said that the habeas corpus statutes gave the district courts broad discretion to fashion procedures to allow full development of the facts, and that under the All Writs Act, 28 U.S.C. § 1651, district courts could resort to discovery devices analogous to those created by the civil rules. Rule 6 of the § 1254 rules now entitles a party to use federal discovery processes "if, and to the extent that, the judge in the exercise of his discretion and for good cause shown grants leave to do so, but not otherwise."

2. See 90 Stat. 1334 (1976) (approving the rules with certain amendments). See generally Clinton, *Rule 9 of the Federal Habeas Corpus Rules: A Case Study on the Need for Reform of the Rules Enabling Acts,* 63 Iowa L.Rev. 15 (1977).

Do you think Rule 9(a) as proposed would have been valid under the Rules Enabling Act, 28 U.S.C. § 2072? Or does it "abridge" or "modify" a "substantive right"? Would the Court have authority to promulgate a similar rule for ordinary federal question cases where Congress has enacted no statute of limitations? For all diversity cases? For diversity cases where no state statute exists? [3]

In Vasquez v. Hillery, 474 U.S. 254 (1986), the Court ruled that difficulties in retrying the defendant caused by a delay in filing the petition are not "prejudice" within the meaning of Rule 9(a); the Court noted that a proposed amendment to Rule 9(a), specifying that dismissal might be had in the event of delay prejudicing the state's ability to retry the defendant, had not been adopted. For other applications of Rule 9(a), see 17 Federal Practice § 4268.

Rule 9(b) creates a modified res judicata rule: "A second or successive petition may be dismissed if the judge finds that it fails to allege new or different grounds for relief and the prior determination was on the merits or, if new and different grounds are alleged, the judge finds that the failure of the petitioner to assert those grounds in a prior petition constituted an abuse of the writ." Cf. Federal Rules of Criminal Procedure, Rule 12(b)(2), and Davis v. United States, 411 U.S. 233 (1973), discussed at pp. 1584–85, infra.

Before the adoption of the § 2254 rules, Rule 81(a)(2) of the Federal Rules of Civil Procedure had provided that those rules were applicable to habeas corpus proceedings, subject to statutes of the United States (e.g., the procedural rules set out in the habeas corpus statutes themselves), but only to the extent "that the practice in such proceedings * * * has heretofore conformed to the practice in civil actions". The draftsmen provided no guidance to the meaning of this second, opaque, reservation. The § 2254 rules continue the tradition that the Federal Rules of Civil Procedure (to the extent not inconsistent with the new rules) may be applied, "when appropriate," to petitions filed under the new rules (Rule 11).[4]

(2) *Rules for § 2255 Cases.* Also in February 1977, parallel "Rules Governing Section 2255 Proceedings in the United States District Courts" went into effect. (Habeas cases brought by federal prisoners may be governed, at the discretion of the court, by the § 2254 rules. See § 2254 Rule 1(b).) These rules contain parallel laches (Rule 9(a)) and res judicata (Rule 9(b)) provisions.

(3) *Role of Magistrates.* 28 U.S.C. § 636(b)(1) expressly permits a district judge to "designate a magistrate to conduct hearings, including evidentiary hearings, * * * of applications for posttrial relief made by individuals convicted of criminal offenses." Any party may object to any of the magistrate's proposed findings and recommendations, and the district

---

3. Cf. Goldberg, *The Influence of Procedural Rules on Federal Jurisdiction,* 28 Stan.L.Rev. 395 (1976), for the argument that the Court has a wide latitude under the Rules Enabling Act to promulgate quasi-jurisdictional rules; compare Ely, *The Irrepressible Myth of Erie,* 87 Harv.L.Rev. 693 (1974), and Clinton, note 2, *supra.*

4. See further Blackledge v. Allison, 431 U.S. 63 (1977) (suggesting summary judgment under Fed.R.Civ.P. 56 may be appropriate in a habeas case); Browder v. Director, Dept. of Corrections, 434 U.S. 257 (1978) (applying Fed.R.Civ.P. 52(b) and 59 to habeas cases for purposes of testing the timeliness of postjudgment motions, and ruling also that habeas is a civil proceeding and thus subject to the 30–day time-to-appeal rule of Fed.R.App.P. 4(a)).

judge must make a "de novo determination" with respect to any such contested matter. In United States v. Raddatz, 447 U.S. 667 (1980) (see p. 436, *supra*), the obligation to make a "de novo determination" was held not to require the district judge to rehear the evidence even with respect to critical issues of demeanor credibility. (Raddatz involved a motion to suppress evidence, and there are phrases in the Court's opinion which would permit it to distinguish such a motion from an application for habeas corpus.)

Under the Federal Magistrate Act of 1979, 28 U.S.C. § 636(c)(1), a magistrate may, "[u]pon the consent of the parties," be designated by the district court to conduct "any or all proceedings in a jury or nonjury civil matter" (presumably including habeas corpus), and to order the entry of judgment in the case. See pp. 54–55, *supra,* for further discussion of this Act.

(4) *Class Actions.* Although Rule 23, providing for class actions, is not formally applicable to habeas corpus, a number of courts have exercised habeas jurisdiction on a class-wide basis, finding authority to do so in the All Writs Act, 28 U.S.C. § 1651. See, *e.g.,* United States ex rel. Sero v. Preiser, 506 F.2d 1115 (2d Cir.1974) (economies and improvements in quality of representation provided by common processing of claims create a "compelling justification for allowing a multi-party proceeding similar to the class action authorized by the Rules" (p. 1125)); United States ex rel. Morgan v. Sielaff, 546 F.2d 218 (7th Cir.1976); Martin v. Strasburg, 689 F.2d 365 (2d Cir.1982). For early comment on this development see Note, 81 Harv.L.Rev. 1482 (1968). Many questions potentially raised by "class action" habeas corpus remain to be answered: What is the scope of the district court's power to fashion decrees reaching beyond the custodian of the named representatives of the class? To grant relief to class members not confined within the district? Is multi-district consolidation available? What are the res judicata effects of a judgment adverse to the class? [5]

SECTION 2.   COLLATERAL ATTACK ON STATE JUDGMENTS OF CONVICTION

BROWN v. ALLEN

344 U.S. 443, 73 S.Ct. 397, 97 L.Ed. 469 (1953).
Certiorari to the United States Court of Appeals for the Fourth Circuit.

[Brown v. Allen was decided together with two other cases: Daniels v. Allen and Speller v. Allen. Those parts of the opinions relating to Speller are omitted; those relating to Daniels are discussed at p. 1539, *infra.*

[Brown was convicted of rape in North Carolina and sentenced to death. In his appeal to the state supreme court, Brown claimed his conviction violated the federal Constitution because of the admission of a coerced confession and racial discrimination in the selection of grand and

---

5. For a general survey of current habeas corpus procedure, see 17 Federal Practice § 4268.

petit juries. These issues had been fully litigated, with the aid of counsel, in the trial court through procedures not themselves alleged to have been in any way unfair. The state supreme court affirmed the conviction, rejecting the defendant's federal contentions on the merits in a reasoned opinion. Certiorari was denied. The prisoner then sought federal habeas corpus.

[The Supreme Court's handling of Brown and its companion cases was somewhat strange. There are two opinions for the Court, those of Justice Reed and Justice Frankfurter, even though on one issue Justice Reed spoke for only a minority and even though Justice Frankfurter (in a second, separate, opinion) dissented from the Court's disposition of all the cases. Much of the lengthy opinions (omitted here) is given over to a discussion of the question whether a district court considering a habeas corpus petition should give "weight" to the Supreme Court's denial of certiorari in the case; Justice Frankfurter, speaking for the Court, answered "no". The constitutional issues were carefully canvassed on the merits, and on behalf of a majority (Justices Black, Douglas, and Frankfurter dissenting) Justice Reed held that the defendants' federal rights were not violated. And the opinions also engage in an extended discussion of the question whether, on habeas corpus, the district court must hold a hearing with respect to questions of *fact* already canvassed in the state courts. (As to this issue, see further *Note on Relitigating the Facts on Habeas Corpus,* p. 1561, *infra.*)

[The brief extracts from Brown reprinted here comprise—surprisingly—the only parts of the opinions that discuss the question whether an issue fully and fairly adjudicated by a state court is cognizable at all on habeas corpus.]

MR. JUSTICE REED delivered the opinion of the Court.

* * *

II. Effect of Former Proceedings.

* * *

So far as weight to be given the proceedings in the courts of the state is concerned, a United States district court, with its familiarity with state practice is in a favorable position to recognize adequate state grounds in denials of relief by state courts without opinion. *A fortiori,* where the state action was based on an adequate state ground, no further examination is required, unless no state remedy for the deprivation of federal constitutional rights ever existed. Mooney v. Holohan, 294 U.S. 103; Ex parte Hawk, 321 U.S. 114. Furthermore, where there is material conflict of fact in the transcripts of evidence as to deprivation of constitutional rights, the District Court may properly depend upon the state's resolution of the issue. Malinski v. New York, 324 U.S. 401, 404. In other circumstances the state adjudication carries the weight that federal practice gives to the conclusion of a court of last resort of another jurisdiction on federal constitutional issues. It is not *res judicata.*

* * *

III. Right to a Plenary Hearing.

* * *

Jurisdiction over applications for federal habeas corpus is controlled by statute.[11] The Code directs a court entertaining an application to award the writ. But an application is not "entertained" by a mere filing. Liberal as the courts are and should be as to practice in setting out claimed violations of constitutional rights, the applicant must meet the statutory test of alleging facts that entitle him to relief.

The word "entertain" presents difficulties. Its meaning may vary according to its surroundings. In § 2243 and § 2244 we think it means a federal district court's conclusion, after examination of the application with such accompanying papers as the court deems necessary, that a hearing on the merits legal or factual is proper. * * * Even after deciding to entertain the application, the District Court may determine later from the return or otherwise that the hearing is unnecessary.

It is clear by statutory enactment that a federal district court is not required to entertain an application for habeas corpus if it appears that "the legality of such detention has been determined by a judge or court of the United States on a prior application for a writ of habeas corpus." The Reviser's Notes to this section in House Report No. 308, 80th Cong., 1st Sess., say that no material change in existing practice is intended. Nothing else indicates that the purpose of Congress was to restrict by the adoption of the Code of 1948 the discretion of the District Court, if it had such discretion before, to entertain petitions from state prisoners which raised the same issues raised in the state courts.

Furthermore, in enacting 28 U.S.C. § 2254, dealing with persons in custody under state judgments, Congress made no reference to the power of a federal district court over federal habeas corpus for claimed wrongs previously passed upon by state courts. A federal judge on a habeas corpus application is required to "summarily hear and determine the facts, and dispose of the matter as law and justice require," 28 U.S.C. § 2243. This has long been the law. R.S. § 761, old 28 U.S.C. § 461. * * *

Applications to district courts on grounds determined adversely to the applicant by state courts should follow the same principle—a refusal of the writ without more, if the court is satisfied, by the record, that the state process has given fair consideration to the issues and the offered evidence, and has resulted in a satisfactory [sic] conclusion. Where the record of the application affords an adequate opportunity to weigh the sufficiency of the allegations and the evidence, and no unusual circumstances calling for a hearing are presented, a repetition of the trial is not required. However, a trial may be had in the discretion of the federal court or judge hearing the new application. A way is left open to redress violations of the Constitution. Moore v. Dempsey, 261 U.S. 86. Although they have the power, it is not necessary for federal courts to hold hearings on the merits, facts or law a second time when satisfied that federal constitutional rights have been protected. It is necessary to exercise jurisdiction to the extent of determining by examination of the record whether or not a hearing would serve the ends of justice. Cf. 28 U.S.C. § 2244. As the state and federal courts have the same responsibilities to protect persons from violation of their constitu-

---

11. 28 U.S.C. § 2241(a).

tional rights, we conclude that a federal district court may decline, without a rehearing of the facts, to award a writ of habeas corpus to a state prisoner where the legality of such detention has been determined, on the facts presented, by the highest state court with jurisdiction, whether through affirmance of the judgment on appeal or denial of post-conviction remedies.

As will presently appear, this case involves no extraordinary situation. Since the complete record was before the District Court, there was no need for rehearing or taking of further evidence. Treating the state's response to the application as a motion to dismiss, the court properly granted that motion. Discharge from conviction through habeas corpus is not an act of judicial clemency but a protection against illegal custody.

The need for argument is a matter of judicial discretion. All issues were adequately presented. There was no abuse.

IV. Disposition of Constitutional Issues.

[Justice Reed then addressed at length the merits of Brown's arguments that his rape conviction was constitutionally invalid, first because of discrimination against blacks in the selection of grand and petit jurors, and second, because his confession, admitted into evidence, had been given involuntarily. (Was the fact that he did so consistent with the foregoing parts of his opinion?) Justice Reed concluded that the record before the Court showed no unconstitutional exclusions of blacks from the grand or petit juries in this case, and that petitioner's confession had not been involuntary simply because given during an eighteen day detention that preceded petitioner's preliminary hearing. Accordingly, the judgment was affirmed.]

* * *

MR. JUSTICE FRANKFURTER.

* * *

II.

The issue of the significance of the denial of certiorari raises a sharp division in the Court. This is not so as to the bearing of the proceedings in the State courts upon the disposition of the application for a writ of habeas corpus in the Federal District Courts. This opinion is designed to make explicit and detailed matters that are also the concern of Mr. Justice Reed's opinion. The uncommon circumstances in which a district court should entertain an application ought to be defined with greater particularity, as should be the criteria for determining when a hearing is proper. The views of the Court on these questions may thus be drawn from the two opinions jointly.

I deem it appropriate to begin by making explicit some basic considerations underlying the federal habeas corpus jurisdiction. Experience may be summoned to support the belief that most claims in these attempts to obtain review of State convictions are without merit. Presumably they are adequately dealt with in the State courts. Again, no one can feel more strongly than I do that a casual, unrestricted opening of the doors of the federal courts to these claims not only would cast an undue burden upon those courts, but would also disregard our duty to support and not weaken the sturdy enforcement of their criminal laws by the States. That wholesale opening of State prison doors by federal courts is, however, not at all the real issue before us is best indicated by a survey recently prepared in the Administrative Office of the United States Courts for the Conference of Chief Justices: of all federal question applications for habeas corpus, some not even relating to State convictions, only 67 out of 3,702 applications were granted in the last seven years. And "only a small number" of these 67 applications resulted in release from prison: "a more detailed study over the last four years ∗ ∗ ∗ shows that out of 29 petitions granted, there were only 5 petitioners who were released from state penitentiaries." [11] The meritorious claims are few, but our procedures must ensure that those few claims are not stifled by undiscriminating generalities. The complexities of our federalism and the workings of a scheme of government involving the interplay of two governments, one of which is subject to limitations enforceable by the other, are not to be escaped by simple, rigid rules which, by avoiding some abuses, generate others.

For surely it is an abuse to deal too casually and too lightly with rights guaranteed by the Federal Constitution, even though they involve limitations upon State power and may be invoked by those morally unworthy. Under the guise of fashioning a procedural rule, we are not justified in wiping out the practical efficacy of a jurisdiction conferred by Congress on the District Courts. Rules which in effect treat all these cases indiscriminately as frivolous do not fall far short of abolishing this head of jurisdiction.

Congress could have left the enforcement of federal constitutional rights governing the administration of criminal justice in the States exclusively to the State courts. These tribunals are under the same duty as the federal courts to respect rights under the United States Constitution. See The Federalist, No. 82; Claflin v. Houseman, 93 U.S. 130; Testa v. Katt, 330 U.S. 386; Note, 60 Harv.L.Rev. 966. Indeed, the jurisdiction given to the federal courts to issue writs of habeas corpus by the First Judiciary Act, § 14, 1 Stat. 81–82, extended only to prisoners in custody under authority of the United States. It was not until the Act of 1867 that the power to issue the writ was extended to an applicant under sentence of a State court. It is not for us to determine whether this power should have been vested in the federal courts. As Mr. Justice Bradley, with his usual acuteness, commented not long after the passage of that Act, "although it may appear unseemly that a prisoner, after conviction in a state court, should be set at liberty by a single judge on *habeas corpus,* there seems to be no escape from the law." Ex parte Bridges, 2 Woods (5th Cir.) 428, 432. His feeling has been recently echoed in a proposal of the Judicial Conference of Senior Circuit Judges that these cases be heard by three-judge courts. See Rep. Jud.Conf.1943, p. 23. But the wisdom of such a modification in the law is for Congress to consider, particularly in view of the effect of the expanding concept of due process upon enforcement by the States of their criminal laws. It is for this Court to give fair effect to the habeas corpus jurisdiction as enacted by Congress. By giving the federal courts that jurisdiction, Congress has imbedded into federal legislation the historic function of habeas corpus adapted to reaching an enlarged area of claims. See, *e.g.,* Mooney v. Holohan, 294 U.S. 103; Johnson v. Zerbst, 304 U.S. 458.

11. Habeas Corpus Cases in the Federal   istrative Office of the United States Courts
Courts Brought by State Prisoners, Admin-   4 (Dec. 16, 1952).

In exercising the power thus bestowed, the District Judge must take due account of the proceedings that are challenged by the application for a writ. All that has gone before is not to be ignored as irrelevant. But the prior State determination of a claim under the United States Constitution cannot foreclose consideration of such a claim, else the State court would have the final say which the Congress, by the Act of 1867, provided it should not have. *Cf.* Ex parte Royall, 117 U.S. 241, 248–250. A State determination may help to define the claim urged in the application for the writ and may bear on the seriousness of the claim. That most claims are frivolous has an important bearing upon the procedure to be followed by a district judge. The prior State determination may guide his discretion in deciding upon the appropriate course to be followed in disposing of the application before him. The State record may serve to indicate the necessity of further pleadings or of a quick hearing to clear up an ambiguity, or the State record may show the claim to be frivolous or not within the competence of a federal court because solely dependent on State law.

It may be a matter of phrasing whether we say that the District Judge summarily denies an application for a writ by accepting the ruling of the State court or by making an independent judgment, though he does so on the basis of what the State record reveals. But since phrasing mirrors thought, it is important that the phrasing not obscure the true issue before a federal court. Our problem arises because Congress has told the District Judge to act on those occasions, however rare, when there are meritorious causes in which habeas corpus is the ultimate and only relief and designed to be such. Vague, undefined directions permitting the District Court to give "consideration" to a prior State determination fall short of appropriate guidance for bringing to the surface the meritorious case. They may serve indiscriminately to preclude a hearing where one should have been granted, and yet this basis for denial may be so woven into the texture of the result that an improper deference to a State court treatment of a constitutional issue cannot even be corrected on review. If we are to give effect to the statute and at the same time avoid improper intrusion into the State criminal process by federal judges—and there is no basis for thinking there is such intrusion unless "men think dramatically, not quantitatively," Holmes, Collected Legal Papers, p. 293—we must direct them to probe the federal question while drawing on available records of prior proceedings to guide them in doing so.

Of course, experience cautions that the very nature and function of the writ of habeas corpus precludes the formulation of fool-proof standards which the 225 District Judges can automatically apply. Here as elsewhere in matters of judicial administration we must attribute to them the good sense and sturdiness appropriate for men who wield the power of a federal judge. Certainly we will not get these qualities if we fashion rules assuming the contrary. But it is important, in order to preclude individualized enforcement of the Constitution in different parts of the Nation, to lay down as specifically as the nature of the problem permits the standards or directions that should govern the District Judges in the disposition of applications for habeas corpus by prisoners under sentence of State courts.

First. Just as in all other litigation, a prima facie case must be made out by the petitioner. The application should be dismissed when it fails to state a federal question, or fails to set forth facts which, if accepted at face value, would entitle the applicant to relief. * * *

Second. Failure to exhaust an available State remedy is an obvious ground for denying the application. An attempt must have been made in the State court to present the claim now asserted in the District Court, in compliance with § 2254 of the Judicial Code. * * *

Third. If the record of the State proceedings is not filed, the judge is required to decide, with due regard to efficiency in judicial administration, whether it is more desirable to call for the record or to hold a hearing. * * *

Fourth. When the record of the State court proceedings is before the court, it may appear that the issue turns on basic facts and that the facts (in the sense of a recital of external events and the credibility of their narrators) have been tried and adjudicated against the applicant. Unless a vital flaw be found in the process of ascertaining such facts in the State court, the District Judge may accept their determination in the State proceeding and deny the application. On the other hand, State adjudication of questions of law cannot, under the habeas corpus statute, be accepted as binding. It is precisely these questions that the federal judge is commanded to decide. * * *

Fifth. Where the ascertainment of the historical facts does not dispose of the claim but calls for interpretation of the legal significance of such facts, see Baumgartner v. United States, 322 U.S. 665, 670–671, the District Judge must exercise his own judgment on this blend of facts and their legal values. Thus, so-called mixed questions or the application of constitutional principles to the facts as found leave the duty of adjudication with the federal judge.

For instance, the question whether established primary facts underlying a confession prove that the confession was coerced or voluntary cannot rest on the State decision. See, *e.g.,* Haley v. Ohio, 332 U.S. 596, 601 (concurring opinion) and Stroble v. California, 343 U.S. 181, 190. * * * Although there is no need for the federal judge, if he could, to shut his eyes to the State consideration of such issues, no binding weight is to be attached to the State determination. The congressional requirement is greater. The State court cannot have the last say when it, though on fair consideration and what procedurally may be deemed fairness, may have misconceived a federal constitutional right.

Sixth. A federal district judge may under § 2244 take into consideration a prior denial of relief by a federal court, and in that sense § 2244 is of course applicable to State prisoners. * * *

These standards, addressed as they are to the practical situation facing the District Judge, recognize the discretion of judges to give weight to whatever may be relevant in the State proceedings, and yet preserve the full implication of the requirement of Congress that the District Judge decide constitutional questions presented by a State prisoner even after his claims have been carefully considered by the State courts. Congress has the power to distribute among the courts of the States and of the United States jurisdiction to determine federal claims. It has seen fit to give this Court power to review errors of federal law in State determinations, and in addition to give to the lower federal courts power to inquire into federal claims, by way of habeas corpus. Such power is in the spirit of our inherited law. It accords with, and is thoroughly regardful of, "the liberty of the subject," from which flows the right in England to go from judge to judge, any one of whose decisions to discharge the prisoner is final. Our rule is not so extreme as in England; § 2244 does place some limits on repeating applications to the Federal Courts. But it would be in disregard of what Congress has expressly required to deny State prisoners access to the federal courts.

The reliable figures of the Administrative Office of the United States Courts, showing that during the last four years five State prisoners, all told, were discharged by federal district courts, prove beyond peradventure that it is a baseless fear, a bogeyman, to worry lest State convictions be upset by allowing district courts to entertain applications for habeas corpus on behalf of prisoners under State sentence. Insofar as this jurisdiction enables federal district courts to entertain claims that State Supreme Courts have denied rights guaranteed by the United States Constitution, it is not a case of a lower court sitting in judgment on a higher court. It is merely one aspect of respecting the Supremacy Clause of the Constitution whereby federal law is higher than State law. It is for the Congress to designate the member in the hierarchy of the federal judiciary to express the higher law. The fact that Congress has authorized district courts to be the organ of the higher law rather than a Court of Appeals, or exclusively this Court, does not mean that it allows a lower court to overrule a higher court. It merely expresses the choice of Congress how the superior authority of federal law should be asserted. ＊ ＊ ＊

The uniqueness of habeas corpus in the procedural armory of our law cannot be too often emphasized. It differs from all other remedies in that it is available to bring into question the legality of a person's restraint and to require justification for such detention. Of course this does not mean that prison doors may readily be opened. It does mean that explanation may be exacted why they should remain closed. ＊ ＊ ＊

The significance of the writ for the moral health of our kind of society has been amply attested by all the great commentators, historians and jurists, on our institutions. It has appropriately been characterized by Hallam as "the principal bulwark of English liberty." But the writ has potentialities for evil as well as for good. Abuse of the writ may undermine the orderly administration of justice and therefore weaken the forces of authority that are essential for civilization.

The circumstances and conditions for bringing into action a legal remedy having such potentialities obviously cannot be defined with a particularity appropriate to legal remedies of much more limited scope. To attempt rigid rules would either give spuriously concrete form to wide-ranging purposes or betray the purposes by strangulating rigidities. Equally unmindful, however, of the purposes of the writ—its history and its functions—would it be to advise the Federal District Courts as to their duty in regard to habeas corpus in terms so ambiguous as in effect to leave their individual judgment unguided. This would leave them free to misuse the writ by being either too lax or too rigid in its employment. The fact that we cannot formulate rules that are absolute or of a definiteness almost mechanically applicable does not discharge us from the duty of trying to be as accurate and specific as the nature of the subject permits.

It is inadmissible to deny the use of the writ merely because a State court has passed on a federal constitutional issue. The discretion of the lower courts must be canalized within banks of standards governing all federal judges alike, so as to mean essentially the same thing to all and to leave only the margin of freedom of movement inevitably entailed by the nature of habeas corpus and the indefinable variety of circumstances which bring it into play.   *   *   *

MR. JUSTICE JACKSON, concurring in the result.

Controversy as to the undiscriminating use of the writ of habeas corpus by federal judges to set aside state court convictions is traceable to three principal causes: (1) this Court's use of the generality of the Fourteenth Amendment to subject state courts to increasing federal control, especially in the criminal law field; (2) *ad hoc* determination of due process of law issues by personal notions of justice instead of by known rules of law; and (3) the breakdown of procedural safeguards against abuse of the writ. *   *   *

The fact that the substantive law of due process is and probably must remain so vague and unsettled as to invite farfetched or borderline petitions makes it important to adhere to procedures which enable courts readily to distinguish a probable constitutional grievance from a convict's mere gamble on persuading some indulgent judge to let him out of jail. Instead, this Court has sanctioned progressive trivialization of the writ until floods of stale, frivolous and repetitious petitions inundate the docket of the lower courts and swell our own. Judged by our own disposition of habeas corpus matters, they have, as a class, become peculiarly undeserving. It must prejudice the occasional meritorious application to be buried in a flood of worthless ones. He who must search a haystack for a needle is likely to end up with the attitude that the needle is not worth the search. Nor is it any answer to say that few of these petitions in any court really result in the discharge of the petitioner. That is the condemnation of the procedure which has encouraged frivolous cases. In this multiplicity of worthless cases, states are compelled to default or to defend the integrity of their judges and their official records, sometimes concerning trials or pleas that were closed many years ago. State Attorneys General recently have come habitually to ignore these proceedings, responding only when specially requested and sometimes not then. Some state courts have wearied of our repeated demands upon them and have declined to further elucidate grounds for their decisions. The assembled Chief Justices of the highest courts of the states have taken the unusual step of condemning the present practice by resolution.[13]

It cannot be denied that the trend of our decisions is to abandon rules of pleading or procedure which would protect the writ against abuse. Once upon a time the writ could not be substituted for appeal or other reviewing process but challenged only the legal competence or jurisdiction of the committing court. We have so departed from this principle that the profession now believes that the issues we *actually consider* on a federal prisoner's habeas corpus are substantially the same as would be considered on appeal.

Conflict with state courts is the inevitable result of giving the convict a virtual new trial before a federal court sitting without a jury. Whenever decisions of one court are reviewed by another, a percentage of them are

13. Conference of Chief Justices—1952, 25 State Government, No. 11, p. 249 (Nov. 1952).

reversed. That reflects a difference in outlook normally found between personnel comprising different courts. However, reversal by a higher court is not proof that justice is thereby better done. There is no doubt that if there were a super-Supreme Court, a substantial proportion of our reversals of state courts would also be reversed. We are not final because we are infallible, but we are infallible only because we are final. * * *

It is sometimes said that *res judicata* has no application whatever in habeas corpus cases and surely it does not apply with all of its conventional severity. Habeas corpus differs from the ordinary judgment in that, although an adjudication has become final, the application is renewable, at least if new evidence and material is discovered or if, perhaps as the result of a new decision, a new law becomes applicable to the case. This is quite proper so long as its issues relate to jurisdiction. But call it *res judicata* or what one will, courts ought not to be obliged to allow a convict to litigate again and again exactly the same question on the same evidence. Nor is there any good reason why an identical contention rejected by a higher court should be reviewed on the same facts in a lower one. * * *

My conclusion is that whether or not this Court has denied certiorari from a state court's judgment in a habeas corpus proceeding, no lower federal court should entertain a petition except on the following conditions: (1) that the petition raises a jurisdictional question involving federal law on which the state law allowed no access to its courts, either by habeas corpus or appeal from the conviction, and that he therefore has no state remedy; or (2) that the petition shows that although the law allows a remedy, he was actually improperly obstructed from making a record upon which the question could be presented, so that his remedy by way of ultimate application to this Court for certiorari has been frustrated. There may be circumstances so extraordinary that I do not now think of them which would justify a departure from this rule, but the run-of-the-mill case certainly does not.

Whether one will agree with this general proposition will depend, I suppose, on the latitude he thinks federal courts should exercise in retrying *de novo* state court criminal issues. If the federal courts are to test a state court's decision by hearing new evidence in a new proceeding, the pretense of exhaustion of state remedies is a sham, for the state courts could not have given a remedy on evidence which they had no chance to hear. I cannot see why federal courts should hear evidence that was not presented to the state court unless the prisoner has been prevented from making a record of his grievance, with the result that there is no record of it to bring here on certiorari. Such circumstances would seem to call for an original remedy in the district courts which would be in a position to take evidence and make the record on which we ultimately must pass if there develops a conflict of law between a federal and state court.

If this Court were willing to adopt this doctrine of federal self-restraint, it could settle some procedures, rules of pleading and practices which would weed out the abuses and frivolous causes and identify the worthy ones. I know the difficulty of formulating practice rules and their pitfalls. Nor do I underestimate the argument that the writ often is petitioned for by prisoners without counsel and that they should not be held to the artificialities in pleading that we expect in lawyers. But I know of no way that we can have equal justice under law except we have some law. * * *

MR. JUSTICE BLACK, with whom MR. JUSTICE DOUGLAS concurs, dissenting.

* * *

I agree with the Court that the District Court had habeas corpus jurisdiction in all the cases including power to release either or all of the prisoners if held as a result of violation of constitutional rights. This I understand to be a reaffirmance of the principle embodied in Moore v. Dempsey, 261 U.S. 86. I also agree that in the exercise of this jurisdiction the District Court had power to hear and consider all relevant facts bearing on the constitutional contentions asserted in these cases. I disagree with the Court's conclusion that petitioners failed to establish those contentions.

* * *

———

NOTE ON THE ISSUES COGNIZABLE ON HABEAS CORPUS: HEREIN OF THE RULE OF BROWN v. ALLEN AND ITS BACKGROUND

(1) Brown v. Allen squarely established the proposition that federal constitutional questions litigated fully and fairly in state criminal cases are subject to collateral review on habeas corpus.[1] The arguments in favor of the rule of Brown v. Allen are strongly made in, *e.g.*, Peller, *In Defense of Federal Habeas Corpus Relitigation*, 16 Harv.C.R.–C.L.Rev. 579 (1982); Reitz, *Federal Habeas Corpus: Postconviction Remedy for State Prisoners*, 108 U.Pa.L.Rev. 461 (1960); Amsterdam, *Search, Seizure and Section 2255: A Comment*, 112 U.Pa.L.Rev. 378, 379–80 (1964); Wright & Sofaer, *Federal Habeas Corpus for State Prisoners: The Allocation of Fact–Finding Responsibility*, 75 Yale L.J. 895, 897–906 (1966); and *Developments* 1056–62. For more reserved appraisals, see Bator, *Finality* 499–523; and Friendly, *Is Innocence Irrelevant? Collateral Attack on Criminal Judgments*, 38 U.Chi. L.Rev. 142 (1970).

"[Brown v. Allen] seems to say that due process of law in the case of state prisoners is not primarily concerned with the adequacy of the state's corrective process or of the prisoner's personal opportunity to avail himself of this process * * * but relates essentially to the avoidance in the end of any underlying constitutional error * * *. The decision manifestly broke new ground. But perhaps it can be both explained and justified as resting on the principle that a state prisoner ought to have an opportunity for a hearing on a federal constitutional claim in a federal constitutional court, and that, if the Supreme Court in its discretion denies this opportunity on petition for certiorari, it ought to be available on habeas corpus in a federal district court." Hart, *Foreword* 106–07.

Do you agree? What is the stated principle based on? For an argument that habeas is best explained as providing a federal forum in which to enforce federal rights and remedies that may be unpopular with the states, see Yackle, p. 1470, *supra*.

The rule of Brown v. Allen is usually thought to rest primarily on the assumption that constitutional rights cannot be adequately protected by direct Supreme Court review of state court judgments resulting in deten-

———

1. Insofar as Justice Reed's ambiguous language casts doubt on this proposition, the point is definitively established by his exhaustive review of the merits of Brown's constitutional claims, and by Justice Frankfurter's opinion in the case.

tion. Is the assumption justified? What justifies it? The inability of the Court, in view of its docket, to review all such cases in which a constitutional question is raised? The inability of the Court to go behind the factual records made in the state courts? The unsatisfactory and incoherent condition of many of these records?

(2) The historical legitimacy of Brown was the central focus of disagreement between Justices Brennan and Harlan in their opinions in Fay v. Noia, 372 U.S. 391 (1963). Noia was convicted in New York state court of murder, after a confession later agreed by the state to have been coerced was admitted into evidence. Both his codefendants, also convicted on the basis of coerced confessions, pursued state appeals and in subsequent proceedings had their convictions reversed. Noia, however, failed to raise his coerced-confession claim on appeal before the time allowed for a direct appeal to be taken had lapsed. The issue actually presented for decision was whether the consequence of Noia's failure to raise his federal contentions in accordance with state procedural rules was that he forfeited his right to raise them on federal habeas corpus. Justice Brennan, writing for the majority, held that it was not, and as to this holding Noia has essentially been limited to its facts in Wainwright v. Sykes, p. 1524, *infra*. But much of the Noia Court's opinion was devoted to establishing a different proposition: that it had always been the law that a federal constitutional claim may be raised for decision on the merits on habeas corpus, no matter how fully and fairly that same claim had been litigated in the state courts. Much of Justice Harlan's dissenting opinion, on the other hand, is devoted to showing that prior to Brown v. Allen, habeas would not lie for a federal claim already fully and fairly considered by the state courts.

Here is Justice Brennan's version of the historical development of the writ (pp. 401–424):

" * * * It is no accident that habeas corpus has time and again played a central role in national crises, wherein the claims of order and of liberty clash most acutely, not only in England in the seventeenth century, but also in America from our very beginnings, and today. Although in form the Great Writ is simply a mode of procedure, its history is inextricably intertwined with the growth of fundamental rights of personal liberty. For its function has been to provide a prompt and efficacious remedy for whatever society deems to be intolerable restraints. Its root principle is that in a civilized society, government must always be accountable to the judiciary for a man's imprisonment: if the imprisonment cannot be shown to conform with the fundamental requirements of law, the individual is entitled to his immediate release. Thus there is nothing novel in the fact that today habeas corpus in the federal courts provides a mode for the redress of denials of due process of law. Vindication of due process is precisely its historic office. * * *

"Of course standards of due process have evolved over the centuries. But the nature and purpose of habeas corpus have remained remarkably constant. History refutes the notion that until recently the writ was available only in a very narrow class of lawless imprisonments. For example, it is not true that at common law habeas corpus was exclusively designed as a remedy for executive detentions; it was early used by the great common-law courts to effect the release of persons detained by order of inferior courts. The principle that judicial as well as executive restraints may be intolerable received dramatic expression in Bushell's Case, Vaughan, 135, 124 Eng.Rep. 1006, 6 Howell's State Trials 999 (1670). Bushell was one of the jurors in the trial, held before the Court of Oyer and Terminer at the Old Bailey, of William Penn and William Mead on charges of tumultuous assembly and other crimes. When the jury brought in a verdict of not guilty, the court ordered the jurors committed for contempt. Bushell sought habeas corpus, and the Court of Common Pleas, in a memorable opinion by Chief Justice Vaughan, ordered him discharged from custody. The case is by no means isolated, and when habeas corpus practice was codified in the Habeas Corpus Act of 1679, 31 Car. II, c. 2, no distinction was made between executive and judicial detentions.

"Nor is it true that at common law habeas corpus was available only to inquire into the jurisdiction, in a narrow sense, of the committing court. Bushell's Case is again in point. Chief Justice Vaughan did not base his decision on the theory that the Court of Oyer and Terminer had no jurisdiction to commit persons for contempt, but on the plain denial of due process, violative of Magna Charta, of a court's imprisoning the jury because it disagreed with the verdict * * *.

* * *

"Thus, at the time that the Suspension Clause was written into our Federal Constitution and the first Judiciary Act was passed conferring habeas corpus jurisdiction upon the federal judiciary, there was respectable common-law authority for the proposition that habeas was available to remedy any kind of governmental restraint contrary to fundamental law. In this connection it is significant that neither the Constitution nor the Judiciary Act anywhere defines the writ, although the Act does intimate, 1 Stat. 82, that its issuance is to be 'agreeable to the principles and usages of law'—the common law, presumably. * * *

"The early decision of this Court in Ex parte Watkins, 3 Pet. 193, which held that the judgment of a federal court of competent jurisdiction could not be impeached on habeas, seems to have viewed the power more narrowly; see also Ex parte Kearney, 7 Wheat. 38. But Watkins may have been compelled by factors, affecting peculiarly the jurisdiction of this Court, which are not generally applicable to federal habeas corpus powers. * * *

"* * * But even as to this Court's power, the life of the principles advanced in Watkins was relatively brief. In Ex parte Lange, 18 Wall. 163, again a case of direct application to this Court for the writ, the Court ordered the release of one duly convicted in a Federal Circuit Court. The trial judge, after initially imposing upon the defendant a sentence in excess of the legal maximum, had attempted to correct the error by resentencing him. The Court held this double-sentencing procedure unconstitutional, on the ground of double jeopardy, and while conceding that the Circuit Court had a general competence in criminal cases, reasoned that it had no jurisdiction to render a patently lawless judgment.

"This marked a return to the common-law principle that restraints contrary to fundamental law, by whatever authority imposed, could be redressed by writ of habeas corpus. See also Ex parte Wells, 18 How. 307; Ex parte Parks, 93 U.S. 18, 21. The principle was clearly stated a few years after the Lange decision by Mr. Justice Bradley, writing for the Court in Ex parte Siebold, 100 U.S. 371, 376–377:

"' * * * The validity of the judgments is assailed on the ground that the acts of Congress under which the indictments were found are unconstitutional. If this position is well taken, it affects the foundation of the whole proceedings. An unconstitutional law is void, and is as no law. An offence created by it is not a crime. A conviction under it is not merely erroneous, but is illegal and void, and cannot be a legal cause of imprisonment. It is true, if no writ of error lies, the judgment may be final, in the sense that there may be no means of reversing it. But personal liberty is of so great moment in the eye of the law that the judgment of an inferior court affecting it is not deemed so conclusive but that * * * the question of the court's authority to try and imprison the party may be reviewed on habeas corpus * * *.'

"The course of decisions of this Court from Lange and Siebold to the present makes plain that restraints contrary to our fundamental law, the Constitution, may be challenged on federal habeas corpus even though imposed pursuant to the conviction of a federal court of competent jurisdiction.

"The same principles have consistently been applied in cases of state prisoners seeking habeas corpus in the federal courts, although the development of the law in this area was at first delayed for several reasons. The first Judiciary Act did not extend federal habeas to prisoners in state custody, Ex parte Dorr, 3 How. 103; and shortly after Congress removed this limitation in 1867, it withdrew from this Court jurisdiction of appeals from habeas decisions by the lower federal courts and did not restore it for almost 20 years. Moreover, it was not until this century that the Fourteenth Amendment was deemed to apply some of the safeguards of criminal procedure contained in the Bill of Rights to the States. Yet during the period of the withdrawal of the Supreme Court's jurisdiction of habeas appeals, the lower federal courts did not hesitate to discharge state prisoners whose convictions rested on unconstitutional statutes or had otherwise been obtained in derogation of constitutional rights. After its jurisdiction had been restored, this Court adhered to the pattern set by the lower federal courts and to the principles enunciated in Ex parte Siebold and the other federal-prisoner cases. More recently, further applications of the Fourteenth Amendment in state criminal proceedings have led the Court to find correspondingly more numerous occasions upon which federal habeas would lie.

"Mr. Justice Holmes expressed the rationale behind such decisions in language that sums up virtually the whole history of the Great Writ:

"' * * * [H]abeas corpus cuts through all forms and goes to the very tissue of the structure. It comes in from the outside, not in subordination to the proceedings, and although every form may have been preserved opens the inquiry whether they have been more than an empty shell.

'The argument for the appellee in substance is that the trial was in a court of competent jurisdiction * * *. But * * * [w]hatever disagreement there may be as to the scope of the phrase "due process of law," there can be no doubt that it embraces the fundamental conception of a fair trial * * *. We are not speaking of mere disorder, or mere irregularities in procedure, but of a case where the processes of justice are actually subverted. In such a case, the Federal court has jurisdiction to issue the writ. The fact that the state court still has its general jurisdiction and is otherwise a competent court does not make it impossible to find that a jury has been subjected to intimidation in a particular case. The loss of jurisdiction is not general, but particular, and proceeds from the control of a hostile influence.' [22] * * *

"But, it is argued, a different result is compelled by the exigencies of federalism, which played no role in Bushell's case.

"We can appraise this argument only in light of the historical accommodation that has been worked out between the state and federal courts respecting the administration of federal habeas corpus. Our starting point is the Judiciary Act of February 5, 1867, c. 28, § 1, 14 Stat. 385–386, which first extended federal habeas corpus to state prisoners generally, and which survives, except for some changes in wording, in the present statutory codification. * * * Although the Act of 1867, like its English and American predecessors, nowhere defines habeas corpus, its expansive language and imperative tone, viewed against the background of post-Civil War efforts in Congress to deal severely with the States of the former Confederacy, would seem to make inescapable the conclusion that Congress was enlarging the habeas remedy as previously understood, not only in extending its coverage to state prisoners, but also in making its procedures more efficacious. In 1867, Congress was anticipating resistance to its Reconstruction measures and planning the implementation of the post-war constitutional Amendments. Debated and enacted at the very peak of the Radical Republicans' power, see 2 Warren, The Supreme Court in United States History (1928), 455–497, the measure that became the Act of 1867 seems plainly to have been designed to furnish a method additional to and independent of direct Supreme Court review of state court decisions for the vindication of the new constitutional guarantees. Congress seems to have had no thought, thus, that a state prisoner should abide state court determination of his constitutional defense—the necessary predicate of direct review by this Court—before resorting to federal habeas corpus. Rather, a remedy almost in the nature of *removal* from the state to the federal courts of state prisoners' constitutional contentions seems to have been envisaged. * * *

"The elaborate provisions in the Act for taking testimony and trying the facts anew in habeas hearings lend support to this conclusion, as does the legislative history of House bill No. 605, which became, with slight changes, the Act of February 5, 1867. * * *

"In thus extending the habeas corpus power of the federal courts evidently to what was conceived to be its constitutional limit, the Act of February 5, 1867, clearly enough portended difficult problems concerning the relationship of the state and federal courts in the area of criminal administration. Such problems were not slow to mature. Only eight years after passage of the Act, Mr. Justice Bradley, sitting as Circuit Justice, held that a convicted state prisoner who had not sought any state appellate or collateral remedies could nevertheless win immediate release on federal habeas if he proved the unconstitutionality of his conviction; although the

"22. Frank v. Mangum, 237 U.S. 309, 346–347 (dissenting opinion). The principles advanced by Mr. Justice Holmes in his dissenting opinion in Frank were later adopted by the Court in Moore v. Dempsey, 261 U.S. 86, and have remained the law.

judgment was not final within the state court system, the federal court had
the power to inquire into the legality of the prisoner's detention. * * *
This holding flowed inexorably from the clear congressional policy of
affording a federal forum for the determination of the federal claims of
state criminal defendants, and it was explicitly approved by the full Court
in Ex parte Royall, 117 U.S. 241, 253, a case in which habeas had been
sought in advance of trial. The Court held that even in such a case the
federal courts had the *power* to discharge a state prisoner restrained in
violation of the Federal Constitution, see 117 U.S., at 245, 250–251, but that
ordinarily the federal court should stay its hand on habeas pending
completion of the state court proceedings. * * *

"These decisions fashioned a doctrine of abstention, whereby full play
would be allowed the States in the administration of their criminal justice
without prejudice to federal rights enwoven in the state proceedings. Thus
the Court has frequently held that application for a writ of habeas corpus
should have been denied 'without prejudice to a renewal of the same after
the accused had availed himself of such remedies as the laws of the state
afforded * * *.' Minnesota v. Brundage, 180 U.S. 499, 500–501. See also
Ex parte Royall, *supra*, 117 U.S., at 254. With refinements, this doctrine
requiring the exhaustion of state remedies is now codified in 28 U.S.C.
§ 2254. * * *

"The reasoning of Ex parte Royall and its progeny suggested that after
the state courts had decided the federal question on the merits against the
habeas petitioner, he could return to the federal court on habeas and there
relitigate the question, else a rule of timing would become a rule circum-
scribing the power of the federal courts on habeas, in defiance of unmistakable congressional intent. And so this Court has consistently held, save
only in Frank v. Mangum, 237 U.S. 309. In that case, the State Supreme
Court had rejected on the merits petitioner's contention of mob domination
at his trial, and this Court held that habeas would not lie because the State
had afforded petitioner corrective process. However, the decision seems
grounded not in any want of power, for the Court described the federal
courts' habeas powers in the broadest terms, 237 U.S., at 330–331, but
rather in a narrow conception of due process in state criminal justice. The
Court felt that so long as Frank had had an opportunity to challenge his
conviction in some impartial tribunal, such as the State Supreme Court, he
had been afforded the process he was constitutionally due.

"The majority's position in Frank, however, was substantially repudiated in Moore v. Dempsey, 261 U.S. 86, a case almost identical in all
pertinent respects to Frank. Mr. Justice Holmes, writing for the Court in
Moore (he had written the dissenting opinion in Frank), said: 'if in fact a
trial is dominated by a mob so that there is an actual interference with the
course of justice, there is a departure from due process of law; * * * [if]
the State Courts fail to correct the wrong, * * * perfection in the
machinery for correction * * * can [not] prevent this Court from securing
to the petitioners their constitutional rights.' 261 U.S., at 90–91. It was
settled in Moore, restoring what evidently had been the assumption until
Frank, * * * that the state courts' view of the merits was not entitled to
conclusive weight. We have not deviated from that position.[30] Thus, we

"30. * * * The argument has recent-   vanced by the Court in Frank v. Mangum
ly been advanced that the Moore decision   (that habeas would lie only if the state
did not in fact discredit the position ad-   courts had failed to afford petitioner cor-

have left the weight to be given a particular state court adjudication of a federal claim later pressed on habeas substantially in the discretion of the Federal District Court: 'the state adjudication carries the weight that federal practice gives to the conclusion of a court * * * of another jurisdiction on federal constitutional issues. It is not res judicata.' Brown v. Allen, *supra*, 344 U.S., at 458 (opinion of Mr. Justice Reed). '* * * [N]o binding weight is to be attached to the State determination. The congressional requirement is greater. The State court cannot have the last say when it, though on fair consideration and what procedurally may be deemed fairness, may have misconceived a federal constitutional right.' 344 U.S., at 508 (opinion of Mr. Justice Frankfurter). Even if the state court adjudication turns wholly on primary, historical facts, the Federal District Court has a broad *power* on habeas to hold an evidentiary hearing and determine the facts.

"The breadth of the federal courts' power of independent adjudication on habeas corpus stems from the very nature of the writ * * *. Hence, the familiar principle that res judicata is inapplicable in habeas proceedings * * * is really but an instance of the larger principle that void judgments may be collaterally impeached. * * * This is not to say that a state criminal judgment resting on a constitutional error is void for all purposes. But conventional notions of finality in criminal litigation cannot be permitted to defeat the manifest federal policy that federal constitutional rights of personal liberty shall not be denied without the fullest opportunity for plenary federal judicial review."

(3) Compare Justice Harlan's account of the history in his dissent (pp. 450–61):

"1. *Pre–1915 period.*—The formative stage of the development of habeas corpus jurisdiction may be said to have ended in 1915, the year in which Frank v. Mangum, 237 U.S. 309, was decided. During this period the federal courts, on applications for habeas corpus complaining of detention pursuant to a judgment of conviction and sentence, purported to examine *only* the jurisdiction of the sentencing tribunal. In the leading case of Ex parte Watkins, 3 Pet. 193, the Court stated:

" 'An imprisonment under a judgment cannot be unlawful, unless that judgment be an absolute nullity; and it is not a nullity if the court has general jurisdiction of the subject, although it should be erroneous.' 3 Pet., at 203.

"Many subsequent decisions, dealing with both state and federal prisoners, and involving both original applications to this Court for habeas corpus and review of lower court decisions, reaffirmed the limitation of the

rective process), and that this position was first upset in Brown v. Allen. Bator, Finality in Criminal Law and Federal Habeas Corpus for State Prisoners, 76 Harv.L.Rev. 441, 488–500 (1963). The argument would seem untenable in light of certain factors: (1) The opinion of the Court in Moore, written by Mr. Justice Holmes, is a virtual paraphrase of his dissenting opinion in Frank. (2) The thesis of the Frank majority finds no support in other decisions of the Court; though the availability of corrective process is sometimes mentioned as a factor bearing upon grant or denial of federal habeas, such language typically appears in the context of the exhaustion problem; indeed, "available State corrective process" is part of the language of 28 U.S.C. § 2254. See, *e.g.*, White v. Ragen, 324 U.S. 760, 764. (3) None of the opinions in Brown v. Allen even remotely suggests that the Court was changing the existing law in allowing coerced confessions and racial discrimination in jury selection to be challenged on habeas notwithstanding state court review of the merits of these constitutional claims.

writ to consideration of the sentencing court's jurisdiction over the person of the defendant and the subject matter of the suit. *E.g.,* Ex parte Parks, 93 U.S. 18; Andrews v. Swartz, 156 U.S. 272; In re Belt, 159 U.S. 95; In re Moran, 203 U.S. 96.

"The concept of jurisdiction, however, was subjected to considerable strain during this period, and the strain was not lessened by the fact that until the latter part of the last century, federal criminal convictions were not generally reviewable by the Supreme Court. The expansion of the definition of jurisdiction occurred primarily in two classes of cases: (1) those in which the conviction was for violation of an allegedly unconstitutional statute, and (2) those in which the Court viewed the detention as based on some claimed illegality in the sentence imposed, as distinguished from the judgment of conviction. An example of the former is Ex parte Siebold, 100 U.S. 371, in which the Court considered on its merits the claim that the acts under which the indictments were found were unconstitutional, reasoning that '[a]n unconstitutional law is void, and is as no law,' and therefore 'if the laws are unconstitutional and void, the Circuit Court acquired no jurisdiction of the causes.' 100 U.S., at 376–377. An example of the latter is Ex parte Lange, 18 Wall. 163, in which this Court held that if a valid sentence had been carried out, and if the governing statute permitted only one sentence, the sentencing judge lacked jurisdiction to impose further punishment:

" '[W]hen the prisoner * * * by reason of a valid judgment, had fully suffered one of the alternative punishments to which alone the law subjected him, the power of the court to punish further was gone.' 18 Wall., at 176.

"It was also during this period that Congress, in 1867, first made habeas corpus available by statute to prisoners held under state authority. Act of February 5, 1867, c. 28, § 1, 14 Stat. 385. In this 1867 Act the Court now seems to find justification for today's decision, relying on the statement of one of its proponents that the bill was 'coextensive with all the powers that can be conferred' on the courts and judges of the United States. Cong.Globe, 39th Cong., 1st Sess. 4151. But neither the statute itself, its legislative history, nor its subsequent interpretation lends any support to the view that habeas corpus jurisdiction since 1867 has been exercisable whether or not the state detention complained of rested on decision of a federal question.

"*First,* there is nothing in the language of the Act—which spoke of the availability of the writ to prisoners 'restrained of * * * liberty in violation of the constitution * * *'—to suggest that there was any change in the *nature* of the writ as applied to one held pursuant to a judgment of conviction. The language was that typically employed in habeas corpus cases, and, as we have seen, it was not believed that a person so held was restrained in violation of law if the sentencing court had personal and subject matter jurisdiction. Rather, the change accomplished by the language of the Act related to the *classes* of prisoners (in particular, state as well as federal) for whom the writ would be available.

"*Second,* what little legislative history there is does not suggest any change in the nature of the writ. The extremely brief debates indicated only a lack of understanding as to what the Act would accomplish, coupled with an effort by the proponents to make it clear that the purpose was to extend the availability of the writ to persons not then covered; there was no indication of any intent to alter its substantive scope. Thus, less than 20 years after enactment, a congressional committee could say of the 1867 Act that it was not 'contemplated by its framers or * * * properly * * * construed to authorize the overthrow of the final judgments of the State courts of general jurisdiction, by the inferior Federal judges * * *.'

"*Third,* cases decided under the Act during this period made it clear that the Court did not regard the Act as changing the character of the writ. In considering the lawfulness of the detention of state prisoners, the Court continued to confine itself to questions it regarded as 'jurisdictional.' See, *e.g.,* In re Rahrer, 140 U.S. 545; Harkrader v. Wadley, 172 U.S. 148; Pettibone v. Nichols, 203 U.S. 192. And the Court repeatedly held that habeas corpus was not available to a state prisoner to consider errors, even constitutional errors, that did not go to the jurisdiction of the sentencing court. *E.g.,* In re Wood, 140 U.S. 278; Andrews v. Swartz, 156 U.S. 272; Bergemann v. Backer, 157 U.S. 655.

"At the same time, in dealing with applications by state prisoners the Court developed the doctrine of exhaustion of state remedies, a doctrine now embodied in 28 U.S.C. § 2254. In Ex parte Royall, 117 U.S. 241, the prisoner had brought federal habeas corpus seeking release from his detention pending a state prosecution, and alleging that the statute under which he was to be tried was void under the Contract Clause. The *power* of the federal court to act in this case, if the allegations could be established, was clear since under accepted principles the State would have lacked 'jurisdiction' to detain the prisoner. But the Court observed that the question of constitutionality would be open to the prisoner at his state trial and, absent any showing of urgency, considerations of comity counseled the exercise of discretion to withhold the writ at this early stage. * * *

"There can be no doubt of the limited scope of habeas corpus during this formative period, and of the consistent efforts to confine the writ to questions of jurisdiction. * * *

"2. *1915–1953 period.*—The next stage of development may be described as beginning in 1915 with Frank v. Mangum, 237 U.S. 309, and ending in 1953 with Brown v. Allen, 344 U.S. 443. In Frank, the prisoner had claimed before the state courts that the proceedings in which he had been convicted for murder had been dominated by a mob, and the State Supreme Court, after consideration not only of the record but of extensive affidavits, had concluded that mob domination had not been established. Frank then sought federal habeas, and this Court affirmed the denial of relief. But in doing so the Court recognized that Frank's allegation of mob domination raised a constitutional question which he was entitled to have considered by a competent tribunal uncoerced by popular pressures. Such 'corrective process' had been afforded by the State Supreme Court, however, and since Frank had received 'notice and a hearing, or an opportunity to be heard' on his constitutional claims (237 U.S., at 326), his detention was not in violation of federal law and habeas corpus would not lie.

"It is clear that a new dimension was added to habeas corpus in this case, for in addition to questions previously thought of as 'jurisdictional,' the federal courts were now to consider whether the applicant had been given an adequate opportunity to raise his constitutional claims before the state courts. And if no such opportunity had been afforded in the state courts, the federal claim would be heard on its merits. * * *

"In no case prior to Brown v. Allen, I submit, was there any substantial modification of the concepts articulated in the Frank decision. In Moore v. Dempsey, 261 U.S. 86, this Court did require a hearing on federal habeas of a claim similar to that in Frank, of mob domination of the trial, even though the state appellate court had purported to pass on the claim, but only by refusing to 'assume that the trial was an empty ceremony.' The decision of this Court is sufficiently ambiguous that it seems to have meant all things to all men. But I suggest that the decision cannot be taken to have overruled Frank; it did not purport to do so, and indeed it was joined by two Justices who had joined in the Frank opinion. Rather, what the Court appears to have held was that the state appellate court's perfunctory treatment of the question of mob domination, amounting to nothing more than reliance on the presumptive validity of the trial, was not in fact acceptable corrective process and federal habeas would therefore lie to consider the merits of the claim. Until today, the Court has consistently so interpreted the opinion, as in Ex parte Hawk, 321 U.S. 114, 118, where Moore was cited as an example of a case in which 'the remedy afforded by state law proves in practice unavailable or seriously inadequate.' See also Jennings v. Illinois, 342 U.S. 104, 111. * * *

"Subsequent decisions involving state prisoners continued to indicate that the controlling question on federal habeas—apart from matters going to lack of state jurisdiction in light of federal law—was whether or not the State had afforded adequate opportunity to raise the federal claim. If not, the federal claim could be considered on its merits. See, *e.g.,* Mooney v. Holohan, 294 U.S. 103 * * *.

"A development paralleling that in Frank v. Mangum took place during this period with regard to federal prisoners. The writ remained unavailable to consider questions that were or could have been raised in the original proceedings, or on direct appeal, see Sunal v. Large, 332 U.S. 174, but it was employed to permit consideration of constitutional questions that could not otherwise have been adequately presented to the courts. *E.g.,* Johnson v. Zerbst, 304 U.S. 458; Walker v. Johnston, 312 U.S. 275; Waley v. Johnston, 316 U.S. 101. * * *

"To recapitulate, then, prior to Brown v. Allen, habeas corpus would not lie for a prisoner who was in custody pursuant to a state judgment of conviction by a court of competent jurisdiction if he had been given an adequate opportunity to obtain full and fair consideration of his federal claim in the state courts. * * *

"3. *Post–1953, Brown v. Allen, period.* * * *

"It is manifest that [Brown v. Allen] substantially expanded the scope of inquiry on an application for federal habeas corpus. Frank v. Mangum and Moore v. Dempsey had denied that the federal courts in habeas corpus sat to determine whether errors of law, even constitutional law, had been made in the original trial and appellate proceedings. Under the decision in Brown, if a petitioner could show that the validity of a state decision to detain rested on a determination of a constitutional claim, and if he alleged that determination to be erroneous, the federal court had the right and the duty to satisfy itself of the correctness of the state decision. * * *"

(4) The opinions of Justices Brennan and Harlan in Noia, taken together, paint a fair picture in conveying the impression that in the 30-year period between Moore v. Dempsey (1923) and Brown v. Allen (1953) it was simply not clear what the "theory" of habeas corpus for state prisoners was. Was it an instrument for review on the merits of all federal constitutional questions in state criminal litigation? For review of some but not all such questions? Or was it an instrument for vindicating constitutional rights only where the state did not provide adequate "corrective process" (that is, an opportunity for the full and fair litigation of those constitutional rights) in the state courts?

But the further claim, repeatedly made by Justice Brennan—that from the time of its common law origins through its 19th century American development, it was the central and acknowledged function of the writ to permit collateral attack on criminal convictions whenever the allegation was that the convicting court committed an error on an issue of "fundamental" or "constitutional" law—cannot be sustained.

On the reach of the writ under British law in the 17th and 18th centuries, see the critical analysis of Justice Brennan's version of history in Oaks, *Legal History in the High Court—Habeas Corpus*, 64 Mich.L.Rev. 451 (1966),[2] concluding (p. 468): "The seventeenth and eighteenth century law of habeas corpus posed three insurmountable obstacles to any attempt to use the writ of habeas corpus for the 'vindication of due process,' if that phrase denotes the sort of 'fundamental law' or 'intolerable restraint' considerations invoked to free the petitioner in Fay v. Noia. First, * * * a general return that the petitioner had been committed for treason or felony was a sufficient return to a writ of habeas corpus. Second, petitioners were forbidden to challenge the truth of particulars set out in the respondent's return to the writ. Third, once a person had been convicted by a superior court of general jurisdiction, a court disposing of a habeas corpus petition could not go behind the conviction for any purpose other than to verify the formal jurisdiction of the committing court. In view of these three limitations, it may be said that practically every kind of 'intolerable restraint' or violation of 'fundamental law' that the twentieth century lawyer might imagine—except an imprisonment without *stated* legal justification, such as the imprisonment involved in Bushell—could be shielded from inquiry by a general return, a valid judgment, or the rule against controverting facts set out in the return, and a court would be virtually powerless to supply a remedy by habeas corpus. Concededly, there should be a remedy for every violation of law involving a person's liberty, and perhaps in our day the remedy should be through the writ of

---

2. Professor Oaks points out (p. 461) that the general rule, confirmed by the Habeas Corpus Act of 1679, was that habeas corpus was not grantable at all where a person "is in execution on a criminal charge, after judgment, on an indictment according to the course of the common law" (quoting Lord Campbell). He then demonstrates (pp. 461–67) that Justice Brennan's use of Bushell's case in Noia was misleading (e.g., "it is questionable whether the portion of the Bushell report quoted by the Supreme Court is even a part of Chief Justice Vaughan's opinion" (p. 463); the case was a contempt case, where special rules obtained; as indicated by the title appearing before the quoted extract and by portions of the text "edited out in the version quoted by the Supreme Court", the language quoted by the Court goes solely to the question whether the writ can issue out of the Common Pleas "when there was no issue of privilege"; the writ issued in Bushell because the return failed to state any sufficient basis for the commitment).

habeas corpus. But it is misleading to claim support for this proposition in the holding or language of Bushell's Case." [3]

On the 19th century American development, see the survey (by student authors who warmly espoused the *policy* of broad federal relitigation) in *Developments* 1045–50, which fully supports the account given by Justice Harlan.[4]

On Justice Brennan's interpretation of the specific history of the Act of 1867, see the examination of the materials in Mayers, *The Habeas Corpus Act of 1867: The Supreme Court as Legal Historian*, 33 U.Chi.L.Rev. 31 (1965), concluding that the Court's claim—that it was the dominant purpose of the 1867 Act to give the federal courts a broad power to review constitutional issues already decided in state criminal cases—"is without historical foundation" (p. 58).[5]

(5) Frank v. Mangum, 237 U.S. 309 (1915), discussed in the Noia opinions, was the first of the great 20th century habeas corpus cases. Recall Justice Harlan's formulation of the proposition of the case: if it is found that the state tribunals have failed to provide "corrective process" (in the sense of giving the petitioner a fair opportunity to raise and litigate his constitutional claim) in the state courts, then the federal habeas corpus court may proceed to adjudicate the merits of that claim; but if it is found that a state court of competent jurisdiction has fully and fairly adjudicated

3. See also Duker, p. 1468, note 2, *supra*, concluding (p. 1054) that "[f]rom the fourteenth to the seventeenth century, habeas corpus was a convenient weapon wielded by the courts of England in their maneuvers to increase and to safeguard their jurisdictions. A subject imprisoned by one court could be released by means of the writ issued by a rival court on the holding that the committing court lacked jurisdiction in the case."

4. The authors concluded: (i) that for a century the Supreme Court adhered to the "common law principles" which limited use of the writ to cases attacking the jurisdiction of the sentencing court; (ii) that the post-Civil War expansion of the concept of "lack of jurisdiction" was, as Justice Harlan asserted, limited to cases such as Ex parte Lange, 18 Wall. 163 (U.S.1873), challenging a particular sentence (rather than the conviction), and to cases such as Ex parte Siebold, 100 U.S. 371 (1879), challenging the constitutionality of the statute creating the crime; (iii) that these two exceptional categories are perhaps best explained by the fact that they involved cases otherwise wholly unappealable ("this thesis is supported by the Court's implicit rejection of Siebold after direct review was established" (p. 1047)); (iv) that the Court squarely held many constitutional issues not cognizable on habeas corpus; and (v) that the passage of the Act of 1867, making habeas corpus available to state prisoners, did not lead to expansion of the substantive scope of the writ: "To the contrary, the Court declined to extend the writ to

questions other than the competency of the trial court, excepting only claims of convictions under unconstitutional statutes. * * * The broad language of the 1867 Act was not taken as an invitation to review all federal questions once decided by the state court. The traditional test remained: the petitioner would be released only if the committing court was without jurisdiction" (pp. 1049–50).

5. In contrast to Mayers, Amsterdam, *Criminal Prosecutions Affecting Federally Guaranteed Civil Rights: Federal Removal and Habeas Corpus Jurisdiction to Abort State Court Trial*, 113 U.Pa.L.Rev. 793 (1965), argues that the history justifies a generally broad view of the purposes of the Act of 1867. And Professor Amsterdam does in footnote assert that it was the "overriding purpose" of the Act of 1867 "to give all state prisoners both a federal trial forum and access to the Supreme Court for litigation of their federal claims, whatever those claims might be" (p. 839 n. 191). But neither that article, nor the other article cited in support (Amsterdam, *Search, Seizure and Section 2255: A Comment*, 112 U.Pa.L.Rev. 378, 379–80, 384–85 n. 33 (1964)) refers to any historical materials which would support the proposition that it was the purpose of the 1867 Act to broaden the *substantive* scope of the writ by permitting relitigation of all constitutional questions already litigated in the state courts. For another argument for a broad interpretation of the 1867 Act, see Peller, p. 1487, *supra*, at 618–20.

the merits of the defendant's constitutional claim, then that decision is immune from collateral attack, and alleged error on the merits of the federal question should be reviewed by the Supreme Court on direct review.[6]

Note that even on the view that the actual authority of Frank was fleeting, the case is significant, because the foregoing proposition suggests at least *an* intelligible and coherent "model" or theory for the use of federal habeas corpus for state prisoners, which can be evaluated in comparison to the model or theory embodied in the rule of Brown v. Allen.

Suppose the theory of federal habeas corpus espoused in Frank v. Mangum had remained good law; would this have left federal constitutional interests insufficiently protected? Note that even on the Frank theory, a federal habeas corpus court has wide power to supervise the fairness of the methods by which the states must adjudicate claims of federal right. The question is thus the comparatively narrow one whether it is necessary to go beyond this, whether a federal district court should have power to redetermine the facts and the law in cases where the state appears to have provided a full and conscientious—albeit perhaps erroneous—adjudication of the federal claim.

---

6. Justice Pitney said for the Court (pp. 335–36):

"We of course agree that if a trial is in fact dominated by a mob, so that the jury is intimidated and the trial judge yields, and so that there is an actual interference with the course of justice, there is, in that court, a departure from due process of law in the proper sense of that term. And if the State, supplying no corrective process, carries into execution a judgment of death or imprisonment based on a verdict thus produced by mob domination, the State deprives the accused of his life or liberty without due process of law.

"But the State may supply such corrective process as to it seems proper. Georgia has adopted the familiar procedure of a motion for a new trial followed by an appeal to its Supreme Court, not confined to the mere record of conviction but going at large, and upon evidence adduced outside of that record, into the question whether the processes of justice have been interfered with in the trial court. * * *

"Such an appeal was accorded to the prisoner in the present case * * * and the Supreme Court, upon a full review, decided appellant's allegations of fact, so far as matters now material are concerned, to be unfounded. Owing to considerations already adverted to (arising not out of comity merely, but out of the very right of the matter to be decided, in view of the relations existing between the States and the Federal Government), we hold that such a determination as was thus made by the court of last resort of Georgia respecting the alleged interference with the trial

through disorder and manifestations of hostile sentiment cannot in this collateral inquiry be treated as a nullity, but must be taken as setting forth the truth of the matter, certainly until some reasonable ground is shown for an inference that the court which rendered it either was wanting in jurisdiction, or at least erred in the exercise of its jurisdiction, and that the mere assertion by the prisoner that the facts of the matter are other than the state court upon full investigation determined them to be will not be deemed sufficient to raise an issue respecting the correctness of that determination; especially not, where the very evidence upon which the determination was rested is withheld by him who attacks the finding."

Justices Holmes and Hughes dissented (pp. 347–48): "Mob law does not become due process of law by securing the assent of a terrorized jury. We are not speaking of mere disorder, or mere irregularities in procedure, but of a case where the processes of justice are actually subverted. In such a case, the Federal court has jurisdiction to issue the writ. The fact that the state court still has its general jurisdiction and is otherwise a competent court does not make it impossible to find that a jury has been subjected to intimidation in a particular case. The loss of jurisdiction is not general, but particular, and proceeds from the control of a hostile influence.

"When such a case is presented, it cannot be said, in our view, that the state court decision makes the matter res judicata. * * *"

In considering this question it is of course crucial to take into account the role of the Supreme Court in reviewing state court judgments and the effectiveness of such review to assure the uniformity and supremacy of federal constitutional law. In particular reconsider the materials in Chapter V, Sec. 2(c), p. 639, *supra,* relating to the scope of the Supreme Court's review of questions of fact in cases involving federal rights coming from the state courts. Consider also the possible relevance of the fact that, shortly after the decision in Frank, the jurisdictional statutes for the first time gave the Supreme Court discretion (on certiorari) to refuse to review on the merits many cases where a state criminal defendant's federal contentions had been rejected by the state courts.[7]

(6) Moore v. Dempsey, 261 U.S. 86 (1923), the next significant case, is fully discussed in the Noia opinions. Note that those opinions consider only two alternative interpretations of the case: on the one hand, that Moore was consistent with Frank; on the other hand, that it held that all constitutional claims were cognizable on habeas, without regard to the state's previous consideration of the issues.

Is there a possible middle ground? Can Moore be seen as holding that certain *types* of constitutional claims—such as an allegation of mob domination—would always be cognizable on habeas, without regard to whether and through what process the state had already inquired into them? But that other types of claims, which do not go to the basic integrity of the state's criminal process (albeit they may be "constitutional" claims) would not be cognizable on federal habeas corpus if fairly considered by the state tribunals?[8]

Can an intelligible and principled line be drawn between defects which are so fundamental and grave that they should be considered on federal collateral attack without regard to previous state corrective process, and other constitutional claims? Consider whether the cases discussed in the next paragraph can be seen as an attempt to draw such a line, and, if so, whether they succeeded in doing so.

(7) In the period between Moore and Brown v. Allen, the Court's most significant decisions with respect to the scope of federal habeas corpus were

---

7. Act of September 6, 1916, ch. 448, § 237, 39 Stat. 726; see p. 502, *supra.*

8. The Moore opinion was written by Justice Holmes (who had dissented in Frank). Acknowledging that, under Frank, "the corrective process supplied by the State may be so adequate that interference by habeas corpus ought not to be allowed", Justice Holmes said that "if the case is that the whole proceeding is a mask—that counsel, jury and judge were swept to the fatal end by an irresistible wave of public passion, and that the State Courts failed to correct the wrong, neither perfection in the machinery of correction nor the possibility that the trial court and counsel saw no other way of avoiding an immediate outbreak of the mob can prevent this Court from securing to the peti-

tioners their constitutional rights." And, after reciting the course the case took in the state courts, Justice Holmes added: "We shall not say more concerning the corrective process afforded to the petitioners than that it does not seem to us sufficient to allow a Judge of the United States to escape the duty of examining the facts for himself when if true as alleged they make the trial absolutely void" (pp. 91, 92). The ambiguities of these passages are explored in Bator, *Finality* 488–90 & n. 131.

For further insight into Justice Holmes' views on the writ, see his 1927 opinion as Circuit Justice, denying the petition in the case of Sacco and Vanzetti; this is reprinted in Michael & Wechsler, Criminal Law and its Administration 1230–31 (1940).

Mooney v. Holohan, Johnson v. Zerbst, and Waley v. Johnston.[9]   None casts a very clear light on the functions of the writ.[10]

(a) Mooney v. Holohan, 294 U.S. 103 (1935) was a motion for leave to file a petition for habeas corpus in the Supreme Court. The petitioner alleged that he was convicted of murder in California on the basis of perjured testimony "which was knowingly used by the prosecuting authorities in order to obtain that conviction"; that "these authorities deliberately suppressed evidence which would have impeached and refuted the testimony thus given against him"; and that "he could not by reasonable diligence have discovered prior to the denial of his motion for a mistrial, and his appeal to the Supreme Court of the State, the evidence which was subsequently developed and which proved the testimony against him to have been perjured." It was contended (p. 110) that "the State deprives him of his liberty without due process of law by its failure, in the circumstances set forth, to provide any corrective judicial process by which a conviction so obtained may be set aside."

The Supreme Court said (pp. 112–13) that the requirement of due process "cannot be deemed to be satisfied by mere notice and hearing if a State has contrived a conviction through the pretense of a trial which in truth is but used as a means of depriving a defendant of liberty through a deliberate deception of court and jury by the presentation of testimony known to be perjured. Such a contrivance by a state to procure the conviction and imprisonment of a defendant is as inconsistent with the rudimentary demands of justice as is the obtaining of a like result by intimidation. And the action of prosecuting officers on behalf of the State, like that of administrative officers in the execution of its laws, may constitute a state action within the purview of the Fourteenth Amendment. * * *"

Leave to file was denied, however, on the ground that petitioner had not applied to the state court for a writ of habeas corpus and that "corrective judicial process" is "not shown to be unavailable." [11]

(b) Johnson v. Zerbst, 304 U.S. 458 (1938), involved a federal prisoner convicted of counterfeiting; at his trial he did not have the assistance of counsel. The Court held that the "Sixth Amendment withholds from federal courts, in all criminal proceedings, the power and authority to deprive an accused of his life or liberty unless he has or waives the

9. Other significant pre-Brown cases bearing on the scope of review on habeas corpus are Ex parte Hawk, 321 U.S. 114 (1944), see p. 1553, *infra*; House v. Mayo, 324 U.S. 42 (1945); White v. Ragen, 324 U.S. 760 (1945); Wade v. Mayo, 334 U.S. 672 (1948); and Jennings v. Illinois, 342 U.S. 104 (1951); all are discussed in Bator, *Finality* 495–99. See also Bowen v. Johnston, 306 U.S. 19 (1939) (federal prisoner); Sunal v. Large, 332 U.S. 174 (1947) (federal prisoner); Dowd v. Cook, 340 U.S. 206 (1951).

10. Hart, *Foreword* 104–06, reads these cases (as well as Moore) as having significantly loosened the scope of inquiry on habeas corpus. Bator, *Finality* 488–95, argues that they can all be read consistently with Frank.

11. For the prior history of the Mooney case see People v. Mooney, 175 Cal. 666, 166 Pac. 999 (1917) (Attorney General's stipulation for reversal on grounds extrinsic to the record rejected); 176 Cal. 105, 167 Pac. 696 (1917) (same); 177 Cal. 642, 171 Pac. 690 (1918) (conviction sustained); 178 Cal. 525, 174 Pac. 325 (1918), cert. denied, Mooney v. California, 248 U.S. 579 (1918) (review of denial of relief on coram nobis denied). For its subsequent history, see In re Mooney, 10 Cal.2d 1, 73 P.2d 554 (1937) (habeas corpus discharged), cert. denied, Mooney v. Smith, 305 U.S. 598 (1938); Ex parte Mooney, 305 U.S. 573 (1938) (leave to file petition for habeas corpus denied). Shortly thereafter Mooney was pardoned by Governor Olson.

assistance of counsel" (p. 463). It then went on to hold that the question whether counsel was effectively waived—not previously canvassed by any tribunal—could be tested on federal habeas corpus. The Court said (pp. 467–68):

"Since the Sixth Amendment constitutionally entitles one charged with crime to the assistance of counsel, compliance with this constitutional mandate is an essential jurisdictional prerequisite to a federal court's authority to deprive an accused of his life or liberty. ＊ ＊ ＊ A court's jurisdiction at the beginning of trial may be lost 'in the course of the proceedings' due to failure to complete the court—as the Sixth Amendment requires—by providing counsel for an accused who is unable to obtain counsel, who has not intelligently waived this constitutional guaranty, and whose life or liberty is at stake. If this requirement of the Sixth Amendment is not complied with, the court no longer has jurisdiction to proceed. The judgment of conviction pronounced by a court without jurisdiction is void, and one imprisoned thereunder may obtain release by habeas corpus." [12]

(c) In Waley v. Johnston, 316 U.S. 101 (1942), the habeas corpus petitioner (a federal prisoner) alleged that his plea of guilty was coerced. The Court finally abandoned the kissing of the jurisdictional book [13] in holding the writ available (pp. 104–05):

"＊ ＊ ＊ If the allegations are found to be true, petitioner's constitutional rights were infringed. For a conviction on a plea of guilty coerced by a federal law enforcement officer is no more consistent with due process than a conviction supported by a coerced confession. ＊ ＊ ＊ And if his plea was so coerced as to deprive it of validity to support the conviction, the coercion likewise deprived it of validity as a waiver of his right to assail the conviction. Johnson v. Zerbst, ＊ ＊ ＊.

"The issue here was appropriately raised by the habeas corpus petition. The facts relied on are dehors the record and their effect on the judgment was not open to consideration and review on appeal. In such circumstances the use of the writ in the federal courts to test the constitutional validity of a conviction for crime is not restricted to those cases where the judgment of conviction is void for want of jurisdiction of the trial court to render it. It extends also to those exceptional cases where the conviction has been in disregard of the constitutional rights of the accused, and where the writ is the only effective means of preserving his rights." [14]

(8) "The Court did not, after Frank, give any rounded consideration to the reaches and purposes of the habeas jurisdiction. Most of the cases of the period are explicitly concerned not with the problem of relitigation of federal questions already canvassed in state courts, but with the complications created by the exhaustion doctrine and with the vexing question whether a prisoner must seek direct Supreme Court review of a state judgment as a condition of the right to seek habeas corpus. Several times the Court stressed that technically res judicata does not apply in habeas proceedings; and ＊ ＊ ＊ its dicta state that state-court adjudications of the merits of federal questions reviewed or left undisturbed by the Supreme

12. A claim by a *state* prisoner that at trial he had been denied his constitutional right to counsel was held cognizable on federal habeas corpus in House v. Mayo, 324 U.S. 42 (1945).

13. The phrase is borrowed from Friendly, p. 1487, *supra*, at 151.

14. See also Walker v. Johnston, 312 U.S. 275 (1941).

Court will not 'ordinarily' be redetermined on habeas. And there are some opinions which could be taken to intimate that the writ automatically reaches the merits of all federal constitutional questions. Furthermore, there can be no doubt that, by 1952, the integrity and continuing authority of the doctrine of Frank v. Mangum had been endangered, as it were, * * * by the ambiguities introduced by the Moore case, [and] by the abandonment, in Waley, of the language of 'jurisdictional' error; psychologically, at least, this may have served as an invitation to further widenings of the writ. * * *

"On the other hand, what is equally clear is that at no time did the Court hold that the habeas jurisdiction is appropriately exercised in cases where a federal question has been fully considered by the state, where there has been adequate corrective process. And the essential purpose of the writ as affording a forum where the state fails to provide such process was, as we have seen, stressed again and again." Bator, *Finality* 496–99.[15]

(9) In evaluating the rule of Brown v. Allen, note that the question is one that touches not only the proper relations between state and federal courts in the effectuation of constitutional rights. It touches also the more general problem of creating effective, humane, and sensible procedures for enforcing the criminal law. What role should interests of finality play in those procedures? See generally the authorities cited in Paragraph (1), *supra,* for discussions of this issue. Note, too, the words of the Court in the Sanders case, p. 1566, *infra:* "Conventional notions of finality of litigation have no place where life or liberty is at stake and infringement of constitutional rights is alleged". Friendly, p. 1487, *supra,* responds (pp. 149–50): "Why do they have *no* place? One will readily agree that 'where life or liberty is at stake,' different rules should govern the determination of guilt than when only property is at issue * * *. * * * But this shows only that 'conventional notions of finality' should not have *as much* place in criminal as in civil litigation, not that they should have *none.*"

(10) The rule of Brown v. Allen appears to be limited to questions of *constitutional* law; but in the case of state prisoners the limitation would not appear to be significant. In this connection, consider also Friendly, Paragraph (1), *supra,* who chronicled some of the many claims of error that, by 1970, could be grounded in the Constitution, and then wrote (pp. 156–57):

"I am not now concerned with the merits of these decisions which, whether right or wrong, have become part of our way of life. What I do challenge is the assumption that simply because a claim can be characterized as 'constitutional,' it should necessarily constitute a basis for collateral attack when there has been fair opportunity to litigate it at trial and on appeal. Whatever may have been true when the Bill of Rights was read to protect a state criminal defendant only if the state had acted in a manner 'repugnant to the conscience of mankind,' the rule prevailing when Brown v. Allen was decided, the 'constitutional' label no longer assists in appraising how far society should go in permitting relitigation of criminal convictions. It carries a connotation of outrage—the mob-dominated jury, the confession extorted by the rack, the defendant deprived of counsel—which

15. For criticism of Bator's view of the cases between 1915 and 1953, see Peller, p. 1487, *supra,* at 643–61.

is wholly misplaced when, for example, the claim is a pardonable but allegedly mistaken belief that probable cause existed for an arrest or that a statement by a person not available for cross-examination came within an exception to the hearsay rule. A judge's overly broad construction of a penal statute can be much more harmful to a defendant than unwarranted refusal to compel a prosecution witness on some peripheral element of the case to reveal his address. If a second round on the former is not permitted, and no one suggests it should be, I see no justification for one on the latter in the absence of a colorable showing of innocence."

(11) Note that within the whole vast area covered by the Supreme Court's discretionary certiorari jurisdiction, the "principle" inherent in Brown and Noia—that litigants should have a right to have questions of federal constitutional law arising in a state court decided by some federal court—applies generally only to criminal cases, and then only to those eventuating in custody. State court civil judgments, and state criminal convictions followed by a fine, have not been thought to be subject to collateral attack in a federal court simply because a federal constitutional question was decided and the Supreme Court failed to review on certiorari.

Is the distinction between criminal cases ending in custody and all other cases justified? In terms of constitutional rights, is access to a federal forum in a case such as NAACP v. Alabama, 377 U.S. 288 (1964), p. 520, *supra*, less important than in a case such as Henry v. Mississippi, 379 U.S. 443 (1965), 610, *supra*?

Res judicata questions with respect to previous state court adjudications are discussed in Chapter XII, pp. 1615–30, *infra*.

(12) The development of new constitutional principles governing the states' criminal procedures has, when combined with the wide scope of federal habeas corpus, created a special complexity. Suppose a state court correctly decides an issue of constitutional law in a criminal case; but after that case becomes "final" the Supreme Court changes the governing constitutional principle. Is the prisoner to be deemed to be unlawfully detained for purposes of federal habeas corpus? [16]

This question has never been answered (or even addressed) as such by the Court. Rather, it has merged into a novel and intricate body of law governing the question whether new constitutional doctrines should be "retroactively" or "prospectively" applied.[17] The most striking feature of this body of law is the Court's assertion of a general power to decide

---

16. This problem became acute when Mapp v. Ohio, 367 U.S. 643 (1961), overruled Wolf v. Colorado, 338 U.S. 25 (1949), and raised the question with respect to all state prisoners against whom illegally seized evidence had been admitted under the rule of the Wolf case. See Traynor, *Mapp v. Ohio at Large in the Fifty States*, 1962 Duke L.J. 319; Bender, *The Retroactive Effect of an Overruling Constitutional Decision: Mapp v. Ohio*, 110 U.Pa.L.Rev. 650 (1962). The Court eventually held that the Mapp exclusionary rule did not apply in cases where a conviction had become final before Mapp had been decided. Linkletter v. Walker, 381 U.S. 618 (1965). See further p. 88, *supra*.

17. Some constitutional doctrines have been declared fully retroactive (*e.g.*, the right to counsel under Gideon v. Wainwright, 372 U.S. 335 (1963)); some are applied only to cases still open on direct review (*e.g.*, the self-incrimination rule of Griffin v. California, 380 U.S. 609 (1965)); some are applied in the very case producing the new rule but otherwise only to cases not yet tried at the time of its announcement (*e.g.*, the Escobedo and Miranda rules, under Johnson v. New Jersey, 384 U.S. 719 (1966)); and some are applied in the immediate case and in cases where the police activity in question occurred after the new rule was announced (*e.g.*, the rules governing searches incident to arrest, un-

whether, and to what extent, new doctrines of constitutional law should apply retrospectively; and no firm distinction—at least no distinction *in principle*—has thus far been drawn for this purpose between cases involving collateral attack and cases still open to direct attack (or even untried) when the new doctrine was announced.

In Williams v. United States and Mackey v. United States, 401 U.S. 646, 667 (1971), the Court rejected a powerful plea by Justice Harlan that a fundamental distinction be drawn between cases still open to direct review and cases where the conviction is "final" in the sense that only collateral relief is available. New constitutional doctrines must be fully retroactive within the former category, Justice Harlan argued, if the Court is to comply with the premises which govern judicial review under Marbury v. Madison. But if the case is in the courts on habeas corpus, the "finality" interest in "a visible end to the litigable aspect of the criminal process" was, Justice Harlan believed, overriding. It required that, subject to a few special exceptions,[18] constitutional errors be defined for habeas purposes "according to the law in effect when a conviction became final."

In Griffith v. Kentucky, 107 S.Ct. 708, 713 (1987), the Court explicitly adopted Justice Harlan's views of retroactivity in the context of decisions pending on direct review: "[F]ailure to apply a newly declared constitutional rule to criminal cases pending on direct review violates basic norms of constitutional adjudication." Moreover, the recognition in Griffith that "the retroactivity analysis for convictions that have become final must be different from the analysis for convictions that are not final at the time the new decision is issued" (p. 713), together with heavy reliance in that case on Justice Harlan's analysis in Mackey, suggest that the Court may be moving towards the position that new constitutional rules operate only prospectively as to convictions that are already final.[19]

Yates v. Aiken, cert. granted 107 S.Ct. 1601 (1987), argued during the 1987 Term, may provide the Court with an opportunity to adopt this view. In Yates, petitioner collaterally attacked his final state court conviction in state habeas corpus proceedings. While petitioner's appeal of the denial of habeas was pending in the state courts, the Supreme Court decided Francis v. Franklin, 471 U.S. 307 (1985), holding jury instructions similar to those used in Yates' trial to be unconstitutional. The state supreme court later declined to apply Franklin in Yates' case, on the ground that decisions announcing new constitutional rules applied retroactively only to cases still on direct appeal. The Supreme Court granted certiorari on the retroactivity issue.

---

der Williams v. United States, 401 U.S. 646 (1971)).

18. These exceptions were for newly announced rules of *substantive* due process, placing "individual conduct beyond the power of the criminal law-making authority to proscribe;" and for rules specifying "bedrock procedural elements" that are "implicit in the concept of ordered liberty," such as "the right to counsel at trial" (pp. 792–93).

19. The retroactivity problem has spawned a large literature. See, *e.g.*, Mishkin, *The Supreme Court, 1964 Term, Foreword: The High Court, The Great Writ, and the Due Process of Time and Law*, 79 Harv.L.Rev. 56 (1965); Haddad, *The Finality Distinction in Supreme Court Retroactivity Analysis: An Inadequate Surrogate for Modification of the Scope of Federal Habeas Corpus*, 79 Nw.U.L.Rev. 1062 (1984); see also p. 88, *supra*.

STONE v. POWELL

428 U.S. 465, 96 S.Ct. 3037, 49 L.Ed.2d 1067 (1976).
Certiorari to the United States Court of Appeals for the Ninth Circuit.

MR. JUSTICE POWELL delivered the opinion of the Court.

Respondents in these cases were convicted of criminal offenses in state courts, and their convictions were affirmed on appeal. The prosecution in each case relied upon evidence obtained by searches and seizures alleged by respondents to have been unlawful. Each respondent subsequently sought relief in a federal district court by filing a petition for a writ of federal habeas corpus under 28 U.S.C. § 2254. The question presented is whether a federal court should consider, in ruling on a petition for habeas corpus relief filed by a state prisoner, a claim that evidence obtained by an unconstitutional search or seizure was introduced at his trial, when he has previously been afforded an opportunity for full and fair litigation of his claim in the state courts. The issue is of considerable importance to the administration of criminal justice.

I

We summarize first the relevant facts and procedural history of these cases.

A

Respondent Lloyd Powell was convicted of murder in June 1968 after trial in a California state court. At about midnight on February 17, 1968, he and three companions entered the Bonanza Liquor Store in San Bernardino, Cal., where Powell became involved in an altercation with Gerald Parsons, the store manager, over the theft of a bottle of wine. In the scuffling that followed Powell shot and killed Parsons' wife. Ten hours later an officer of the Henderson, Nev., Police Department arrested Powell for violation of the Henderson vagrancy ordinance, and in the search incident to the arrest discovered a .38 caliber revolver with six expended cartridges in the cylinder.

Powell was extradited to California and convicted of second-degree murder in the Superior Court of San Bernardino County. Parsons and Powell's accomplices at the liquor store testified against him. A criminologist testified that the revolver found on Powell was the gun that killed Parsons' wife. The trial court rejected Powell's contention that testimony by the Henderson police officer as to the search and the discovery of the revolver should have been excluded because the vagrancy ordinance was unconstitutional. In October 1969, the conviction was affirmed by a California District Court of Appeal. * * * The Supreme Court of California denied Powell's petition for habeas corpus relief.

In August 1971 Powell filed an amended petition for a writ of federal habeas corpus under 28 U.S.C. § 2254 in the United States District Court for the Northern District of California, contending that the testimony concerning the .38 caliber revolver should have been excluded as the fruit of an illegal search. He argued that his arrest had been unlawful because the Henderson vagrancy ordinance was unconstitutionally vague, and that the arresting officer lacked probable cause to believe that he was violating it. The District Court concluded that the arresting officer had probable cause and held that even if the vagrancy ordinance was unconstitutional, the deterrent purpose of the exclusionary rule does not require that it be applied to bar admission of the fruits of a search incident to an otherwise valid arrest. In the alternative, that court agreed with the California District Court of Appeal that the admission of the evidence concerning Powell's arrest, if error, was harmless beyond a reasonable doubt.

In December 1974, the Court of Appeals for the Ninth Circuit reversed. 507 F.2d 93. The Court concluded that the vagrancy ordinance was unconstitutionally vague, that Powell's arrest was therefore illegal, and that although exclusion of the evidence would serve no deterrent purpose with regard to police officers who were enforcing statutes in good faith, exclusion would serve the public interest by deterring legislators from enacting unconstitutional statutes. *Id.,* at 98. After an independent review of the evidence the court concluded that the admission of the evidence was not harmless error since it supported the testimony of Parsons and Powell's accomplices. *Id.,* at 99.

B

* * *

[The Court's description of the co-defendant Rice's case is omitted.]

Petitioners Stone and Wolff, the wardens of the respective state prisons where Powell and Rice are incarcerated, petitioned for review of these decisions, raising questions concerning the scope of federal habeas corpus and the role of the exclusionary rule upon collateral review of cases involving Fourth Amendment claims. We granted their petitions for certiorari. 422 U.S. 1055 (1975). We now reverse.

II

* * *

[After a discussion of the history of the writ, and especially its expansion in Brown v. Allen, Justice Powell continued:]

During the period in which the substantive scope of the writ was expanded, the Court did not consider whether exceptions to full review might exist with respect to particular categories of constitutional claims. Prior to the Court's decision in Kaufman v. United States, 394 U.S. 217 (1969), however, a substantial majority of the federal courts of appeals had concluded that collateral review of search-and-seizure claims was inappropriate on motions filed by federal prisoners under 28 U.S.C. § 2255, the modern post-conviction procedure available to federal prisoners in lieu of habeas corpus. The primary rationale advanced in support of those decisions was that Fourth Amendment violations are different in kind from denials of Fifth or Sixth Amendment rights in that claims of illegal search and seizure do not "impugn the integrity of the fact-finding process or challenge evidence as inherently unreliable; rather, the exclusion of illegally seized evidence is simply a prophylactic device intended generally to deter Fourth Amendment violations by law enforcement officers." *Id.,* at 224. See Thornton v. United States, 125 U.S.App.D.C. 114, 368 F.2d 822 (1966).

Kaufman rejected this rationale and held that search-and-seizure claims are cognizable in § 2255 proceedings. The Court noted that "the federal habeas remedy extends to state prisoners alleging that unconstitutionally obtained evidence was admitted against them at trial," 394 U.S., at 225, citing, *e.g.,* Mancusi v. DeForte, 392 U.S. 364 (1968); Carafas v. LaVallee, 391 U.S. 234 (1968), and concluded, as a matter of statutory construction, that there was no basis for restricting "access by federal prisoners with illegal search-and-seizure claims to federal collateral remedies, while placing no similar restriction on access by state prisoners," 394 U.S., at 226. Although in recent years the view has been expressed that the Court should re-examine the substantive scope of federal habeas jurisdiction and limit collateral review of search-and-seizure claims "solely to the question of whether the petitioner was provided with a fair opportunity to raise and have adjudicated the question in state courts," Schneckloth v. Bustamonte, 412 U.S. 218, 250 (1973) (Powell, J., concurring), the Court, without discussion or consideration of the issue, has continued to accept jurisdiction in cases raising such claims. See Lefkowitz v. Newsome, 420 U.S. 283 (1975); Cady v. Dombrowski, 413 U.S. 433 (1973); Cardwell v. Lewis, 417 U.S. 583 (1974) (plurality opinion).

The discussion in Kaufman of the scope of federal habeas corpus rests on the view that the effectuation of the Fourth Amendment, as applied to the States through the Fourteenth Amendment, requires the granting of habeas corpus relief when a prisoner has been convicted in state court on the basis of evidence obtained in an illegal search or seizure since those Amendments were held in Mapp v. Ohio, 367 U.S. 643 (1961), to require exclusion of such evidence at trial and reversal of conviction upon direct review.[15] Until this case we have not had occasion fully to consider the validity of this view. See, *e.g.,* Schneckloth v. Bustamonte, *supra,* at 249 n. 38; Cardwell v. Lewis, *supra,* at 596 and n. 12. Upon examination, we conclude, in light of the nature and purpose of the Fourth Amendment exclusionary rule, that this view is unjustified.[16] We hold, therefore, that where the State has provided an opportunity for full and fair litigation of a Fourth Amendment claim, the Constitution does not require that a state prisoner be granted federal habeas corpus relief on the ground that evidence obtained in an unconstitutional search or seizure was introduced at his trial.

III

* * *

The exclusionary rule was a judicially created means of effectuating the rights secured by the Fourth Amendment. * * *

Decisions prior to Mapp [v. Ohio, 367 U.S. 643 (1961)] advanced two principal reasons for application of the rule in federal trials. The Court in

---

15. As Mr. Justice Black commented in dissent, Kaufman v. United States, 394 U.S. 217, 231, 239 (1969), the Kaufman majority made no effort to justify its result in light of the long-recognized deterrent purpose of the exclusionary rule. Instead, the Court relied on a series of prior cases as implicitly establishing the proposition that search-and-seizure claims are cognizable in federal habeas corpus proceedings.

* * *

16. The issue in Kaufman was the scope of § 2255. Our decision today rejects

the dictum in Kaufman concerning the applicability of the exclusionary rule in federal habeas corpus review of state court decisions pursuant to § 2254. To the extent the application of the exclusionary rule in Kaufman did not rely upon the supervisory role of this Court over the lower federal courts, *cf.* Elkins v. United States, 364 U.S. 206 (1960), the rationale for its application in that context is also rejected.

Elkins, for example, in the context of its special supervisory role over the lower federal courts, referred to the "imperative of judicial integrity," suggesting that exclusion of illegally seized evidence prevents contamination of the judicial process. 364 U.S., at 222. But even in that context a more pragmatic ground was emphasized:

"The rule is calculated to prevent, not to repair. Its purpose is to deter—to compel respect for the constitutional guaranty in the only effectively available way—by removing the incentive to disregard it." *Id.*, at 217.

The Mapp majority justified the application of the rule to the States on several grounds, but relied principally upon the belief that exclusion would deter future unlawful police conduct. 367 U.S., at 658.

Although our decisions often have alluded to the "imperative of judicial integrity," *e.g.*, United States v. Peltier, 422 U.S. 531, 536–539 (1975), they demonstrate the limited role of this justification in the determination whether to apply the rule in a particular context. Logically extended this justification would require that courts exclude unconstitutionally seized evidence despite lack of objection by the defendant, or even over his assent. *Cf.* Henry v. Mississippi, 379 U.S. 443 (1965). It also would require abandonment of the standing limitations on who may object to the introduction of unconstitutionally seized evidence, Alderman v. United States, 394 U.S. 165 (1969), and retreat from the proposition that judicial proceedings need not abate when the defendant's person is unconstitutionally seized, Gerstein v. Pugh, 420 U.S. 103, 119 (1975); Frisbie v. Collins, 342 U.S. 519 (1952). Similarly, the interest in promoting judicial integrity does not prevent the use of illegally seized evidence in grand jury proceedings. United States v. Calandra, 414 U.S. 338 (1974). Nor does it require that the trial court exclude such evidence from use for impeachment of a defendant, even though its introduction is certain to result in convictions in some cases. Walder v. United States, 347 U.S. 62 (1954). The teaching of these cases is clear. While courts, of course, must ever be concerned with preserving the integrity of the judicial process, this concern has limited force as a justification for the exclusion of highly probative evidence. The force of this justification becomes minimal where federal habeas corpus relief is sought by a prisoner who previously has been afforded the opportunity for full and fair consideration of his search-and-seizure claim at trial and on direct review.

The primary justification for the exclusionary rule then is the deterrence of police conduct that violates Fourth Amendment rights. Post-Mapp decisions have established that the rule is not a personal constitutional right. It is not calculated to redress the injury to the privacy of the victim of the search or seizure, for any "[r]eparation comes too late." Linkletter v. Walker, 381 U.S. 618, 637 (1965). Instead, "the rule is a judicially created remedy designed to safeguard Fourth Amendment rights generally through its deterrent effect. * * *" United States v. Calandra, 414 U.S. at 348. * * *

* * * The decision in Kaufman, as noted above, is premised on the view that implementation of the Fourth Amendment also requires the consideration of search-and-seizure claims upon collateral review of state convictions. But despite the broad deterrent purpose of the exclusionary rule, it has never been interpreted to proscribe the introduction of illegally

seized evidence in all proceedings or against all persons. As in the case of any remedial device, "the application of the rule has been restricted to those areas where its remedial objectives are thought most efficaciously served." United States v. Calandra, 414 U.S. at 348.[24] * * *

IV

We turn now to the specific question presented by these cases. Respondents allege violations of Fourth Amendment rights guaranteed them through the Fourteenth Amendment. The question is whether state prisoners—who have been afforded the opportunity for full and fair consideration of their reliance upon the exclusionary rule with respect to seized evidence by the state courts at trial and on direct review—may invoke their claim again on federal habeas corpus review. The answer is to be found by weighing the utility of the exclusionary rule against the costs of extending it to collateral review of Fourth Amendment claims.

The costs of applying the exclusionary rule even at trial and on direct review are well known: the focus of the trial, and the attention of the participants therein, is diverted from the ultimate question of guilt or innocence that should be the central concern in a criminal proceeding. Moreover, the physical evidence sought to be excluded is typically reliable and often the most probative information bearing on the guilt or innocence of the defendant. * * * Application of the rule thus deflects the truthfinding process and often frees the guilty. The disparity in particular cases between the error committed by the police officer and the windfall afforded a guilty defendant by application of the rule is contrary to the idea of proportionality that is essential to the concept of justice. Thus, although the rule is thought to deter unlawful police activity in part through the nurturing of respect for Fourth Amendment values, if applied indiscriminately it may well have the opposite effect of generating disrespect for the law and administration of justice. These long-recognized costs of the rule persist when a criminal conviction is sought to be overturned on collateral review on the ground that a search-and-seizure claim was erroneously rejected by two or more tiers of state courts.[31]

24. As Professor Amsterdam has observed:

"The rule is unsupportable as reparation or compensatory dispensation to the injured criminal; its sole rational justification is the experience of its indispensibility in 'exert[ing] general legal pressures to secure obedience to the Fourth Amendment on the part of * * * law-enforcing officers.' As it serves this function, the rule is a needed, but grudingly [sic] taken, medicament; no more should be swallowed than is needed to combat the disease. Granted that so many criminals must go free as will deter the constables from blundering, pursuance of this policy of liberation beyond the confines of necessity inflicts gratuitous harm on the public interest. * * * " Amsterdam, Search, Seizure, and Section 2255: A Comment, 112 U.Pa.L.Rev. 378, 388–389 (1964) (footnotes omitted).

31. Resort to habeas corpus, especially for purposes other than to assure that no innocent person suffers an unconstitutional loss of liberty, results in serious intrusions on values important to our system of government. They include "(i) the most effective utilization of limited judicial resources, (ii) the necessity of finality in criminal trials, (iii) the minimization of friction between our federal and state systems of justice, and (iv) the maintenance of the constitutional balance upon which the doctrine of federalism is founded." Schneckloth v. Bustamonte, 412 U.S., at 259 (Powell, J., concurring). See also Kaufman v. United States, 394 U.S., at 231 (Black, J., dissenting); Friendly, [p. 1487, *supra*].

We nevertheless afford broad habeas corpus relief, recognizing the need in a free society for an additional safeguard against compelling an innocent man to suffer an

Evidence obtained by police officers in violation of the Fourth Amendment is excluded at trial in the hope that the frequency of future violations will decrease. Despite the absence of supportive empirical evidence, we have assumed that the immediate effect of exclusion will be to discourage law enforcement officials from violating the Fourth Amendment by removing the incentive to disregard it. More importantly, over the long term, this demonstration that our society attaches serious consequences to violation of constitutional rights is thought to encourage those who formulate law enforcement policies, and the officers who implement them, to incorporate Fourth Amendment ideals into their value system.

We adhere to the view that these considerations support the implementation of the exclusionary rule at trial and its enforcement on direct appeal of state court convictions. But the additional contribution, if any, of the consideration of search-and-seizure claims of state prisoners on collateral review is small in relation to the costs. To be sure, each case in which such claim is considered may add marginally to an awareness of the values protected by the Fourth Amendment. There is no reason to believe, however, that the overall educative effect of the exclusionary rule would be appreciably diminished if search-and-seizure claims could not be raised in federal habeas corpus review of state convictions. Nor is there reason to assume that any specific disincentive already created by the risk of exclusion of evidence at trial or the reversal of convictions on direct review would be enhanced if there were the further risk that a conviction obtained in state court and affirmed on direct review might be overturned in collateral proceedings often occurring years after the incarceration of the defendant. The view that the deterrence of Fourth Amendment violations would be furthered rests on the dubious assumption that law enforcement authorities would fear that federal habeas review might reveal flaws in a search or seizure that went undetected at trial and on appeal.[35] Even if one rationally could assume that some additional incremental deterrent effect would be present in isolated cases, the resulting advance of the legitimate goal of furthering Fourth Amendment rights would be out-

unconstitutional loss of liberty. * * * But in the case of a typical Fourth Amendment claim, asserted on collateral attack, a convicted defendant is usually asking society to redetermine an issue that has no bearing on the basic justice of his incarceration.

35. The policy arguments that respondents marshal in support of the view that federal habeas corpus review is necessary to effectuate the Fourth Amendment stem from a basic mistrust of the state courts as fair and competent forums for the adjudication of federal constitutional rights. The argument is that state courts cannot be trusted to effectuate Fourth Amendment values through fair application of the rule, and the oversight jurisdiction of this Court on certiorari is an inadequate safeguard. The principal rationale for this view emphasizes the broad differences in the respective institutional setting within which federal judges and state judges operate. Despite differences in institutional environment and the unsympathetic attitude

to federal constitutional claims of some state judges in years past, we are unwilling to assume that there now exists a general lack of appropriate sensitivity to constitutional rights in the trial and appellate courts of the several States. State courts, like federal courts, have a constitutional obligation to safeguard personal liberties and to uphold federal law. Martin v. Hunter's Lessee, 14 U.S. (1 Wheat.) 304, 341–344 (1816). Moreover, the argument that federal judges are more expert in applying federal constitutional law is especially unpersuasive in the context of search-and-seizure claims, since they are dealt with on a daily basis by trial level judges in both systems. In sum, there is "no intrinsic reason why the fact that a man is a federal judge should make him more competent, or conscientious, or learned with respect to the [consideration of Fourth Amendment claims] than his neighbor in the state courthouse." Bator, [*Finality*], at 50.

weighted by the acknowledged costs to other values vital to a rational system of criminal justice.

In sum, we conclude that where the State has provided an opportunity for full and fair litigation of a Fourth Amendment claim, a state prisoner may not be granted federal habeas corpus relief on the ground that evidence obtained in an unconstitutional search or seizure was introduced at his trial.[37] In this context the contribution of the exclusionary rule, if any, to the effectuation of the Fourth Amendment is minimal and the substantial societal costs of application of the rule persist with special force.

Accordingly, the judgments of the Courts of Appeals are

Reversed.

MR. CHIEF JUSTICE BURGER, concurring.

I concur in the Court's opinion. By way of dictum, and somewhat hesitantly, the Court notes that the holding in this case leaves undisturbed the exclusionary rule as applied to criminal trials. For reasons stated in my dissent in Bivens v. Six Unknown Named Federal Agents, 403 U.S. 388, 414 (1971), it seems clear to me that the exclusionary rule has been operative long enough to demonstrate its flaws. The time has come to modify its reach, even if it is retained for a small and limited category of cases. * * *

MR. JUSTICE BRENNAN, with whom MR. JUSTICE MARSHALL concurs, dissenting.*

The Court today holds "that where the State has provided an opportunity for full and fair litigation of a Fourth Amendment claim, a state prisoner may not be granted federal habeas corpus relief on the ground that evidence obtained in an unconstitutional search or seizure was introduced at his trial." To be sure, my Brethren are hostile to the continued vitality of the exclusionary rule as part and parcel of the Fourth Amendment's prohibition of unreasonable searches and seizures * * *. But these cases, despite the veil of Fourth Amendment terminology employed by the Court, plainly do not involve any question of the right of a defendant to have evidence excluded from use against him in his criminal trial when that evidence was seized in contravention of rights ostensibly secured by the Fourth and Fourteenth Amendments. Rather, they involve the question of the availability of a *federal forum* for vindicating those federally

---

37. The dissent characterizes the Court's opinion as laying the groundwork for a "drastic withdrawal of federal habeas jurisdiction, if not for all grounds * * *, then at least [for many] * * *." * * *

With all respect, the hyperbole of the dissenting opinion is misdirected. Our decision today is *not* concerned with the scope of the habeas corpus statute as authority for litigating constitutional claims generally. We do reaffirm that the exclusionary rule is a judicially created remedy rather than a personal constitutional right, and we emphasize the minimal utility of the rule when sought to be applied to Fourth Amendment claims in a habeas corpus proceeding. * * * In sum, we hold only that a federal court need not apply the exclusionary rule on habeas review of a Fourth Amendment claim absent a showing that the state prisoner was denied an opportunity for a full and fair litigation of that claim at trial and on direct review. Our decision does not mean that the federal court lacks jurisdiction over such a claim, but only that the application of the rule is limited to cases in which there has been both such a showing and a Fourth Amendment violation.

* [Ed.] Only brief extracts from the lengthy dissenting opinion of Justice Brennan are printed here.

guaranteed rights.   Today's holding portends substantial evisceration of federal habeas corpus jurisdiction, and I dissent.

The Court's opinion does not specify the particular basis on which it denies federal habeas jurisdiction over claims of Fourth Amendment violations brought by state prisoners.   The Court insists that its holding is based on the Constitution, but in light of the explicit language of 28 U.S.C. § 2254 (significantly not even mentioned by the Court), I can only presume that the Court intends to be understood to hold either that respondents are not, as a matter of statutory construction, "in custody in violation of the Constitution or laws of the United States," or that "considerations of comity and concerns for the orderly administration of criminal justice," are sufficient to allow this Court to rewrite jurisdictional statutes enacted by Congress.   Neither ground of decision is tenable; the former is simply illogical, and the latter is an arrogation of power committed solely to the Congress.

*

I

Much of the Court's analysis implies that respondents are not entitled to habeas relief because they are not being unconstitutionally detained. Although purportedly adhering to the principle that the Fourth and Fourteenth Amendments "require exclusion" of evidence seized in violation of their commands, the Court informs us that there has merely been a "view" in our cases that "the effectuation of the Fourth Amendment ∗ ∗ ∗ requires the granting of habeas corpus relief when a prisoner has been convicted in state court on the basis of evidence obtained in an illegal search or seizure ∗ ∗ ∗." Applying a "balancing test," the Court then concludes that this "view" is unjustified and that the policies of the Fourth Amendment would not be implemented if claims to the benefits of the exclusionary rule were cognizable in collateral attacks on state court convictions.

Understandably the Court must purport to cast its holding in constitutional terms, because that avoids a direct confrontation with the incontrovertible facts that the habeas statutes have heretofore always been construed to grant jurisdiction to entertain Fourth Amendment claims of both state and federal prisoners, that Fourth Amendment principles have been applied in decisions on the merits in numerous cases on collateral review of final convictions, and that Congress has legislatively accepted our interpretation of congressional intent as to the necessary scope and function of habeas relief.   Indeed, the Court reaches its result without explicitly overruling any of our plethora of precedents inconsistent with that result or even discussing principles of *stare decisis*.   Rather, the Court asserts, in essence, that the Justices joining those prior decisions or reaching the merits of Fourth Amendment claims simply overlooked the obvious constitutional dimension to the problem in adhering to the "view" that granting collateral relief when state courts erroneously decide Fourth Amendment issues would effectuate the principles underlying that Amendment.   But shorn of the rhetoric of "interest balancing" used to obscure what is at stake in this case, it is evident that today's attempt to rest the decision on the Constitution must fail so long as Mapp v. Ohio, 367 U.S. 643 (1961), remains undisturbed.

Under Mapp, as a matter of federal constitutional law, a state court *must* exclude evidence from the trial of an individual whose Fourth and Fourteenth Amendment rights were violated by a search or seizure that directly or indirectly resulted in the acquisition of that evidence. * * * When a state court admits such evidence, it has committed a *constitutional* error, and unless that error is harmless under federal standards, see *e.g.,* Chapman v. California, 386 U.S. 18 (1967), it follows ineluctably that the defendant has been placed "in custody in violation of the Constitution" within the comprehension of 28 U.S.C. § 2254. In short, it escapes me as to what logic can support the assertion that the defendant's unconstitutional confinement obtains during the process of direct review, no matter how long that process takes, but that the unconstitutionality then suddenly dissipates at the moment the claim is asserted in a collateral attack on the conviction. * * *

The Court, assuming without deciding that respondents were convicted on the basis of unconstitutionally obtained evidence erroneously admitted against them by the state trial courts, acknowledges that respondents had the right to obtain a reversal of their convictions on appeal in the state courts or on certiorari to this Court. Indeed, since our rules relating to the time limits for applying for certiorari in criminal cases are nonjurisdictional, certiorari could be granted respondents even today and their convictions could be reversed despite today's decisions. And the basis for reversing those convictions would of course have to be that the States, in rejecting respondents' Fourth Amendment claims, had deprived them of a right in derogation of the Federal Constitution. It is simply inconceivable that that constitutional deprivation suddenly vanishes after the appellate process has been exhausted. And as between this Court on certiorari, and federal district courts on habeas, it is for *Congress* to decide what the most efficacious method is for enforcing *federal* constitutional rights and asserting the primacy of federal law. The Court, however, simply ignores the settled principle that for purposes of adjudicating constitutional claims Congress, which has the power to do so under Art. III of the Constitution, has effectively cast the district courts sitting in habeas in the role of surrogate Supreme Courts.[10]

10. The failure to confront this fact forthrightly is obviously a core defect in the Court's analysis. For to the extent Congress has accorded the Federal District Courts a role in our constitutional scheme functionally equivalent to that of the Supreme Court with respect to review of state court resolutions of federal constitutional claims, it is evident that the Court's direct/collateral review distinction for constitutional purposes simply collapses. Indeed, logically extended, the Court's analysis, which basically turns on the fact that law enforcement officials cannot anticipate a second court finding constitutional errors after one court has fully and fairly adjudicated the claim and found it to be meritless, would preclude any Supreme Court review on direct appeal or even state appellate review if the trial court fairly addressed the Fourth Amendment claim on the merits. * * *

Another line of analysis exposes the fallacy of treating today's holding as a constitutional decision. Constitutionally, no barrier precludes a state defendant from immediately seeking a federal court's injunction against any state use of unconstitutionally seized evidence against him at trial. However, equitable principles have operated to foreclose cutting short the normal *initial* adjudication of such constitutional defenses in the course of a criminal prosecution, Dombrowski v. Pfister, 380 U.S. 479, 485 n. 3 (1965), subject to ultimate federal review either on direct review or collaterally through habeas. See also, *e.g.,* Younger v. Harris, 401 U.S. 37 (1971). Moreover, considerations of comity, now statutorily codified as the exhaustion requirement of § 2254, and not lack of power, dictate that federal habeas review be delayed pending the initial state court determination. * * * Although the federal

The Court adheres to the holding of Mapp that the Constitution "require[d] exclusion" of the evidence admitted at respondents' trials. However, the Court holds that the Constitution "does not require" that respondents be accorded habeas relief if they were accorded "an opportunity for full and fair litigation of [their] Fourth Amendment claim[s]" in state courts. Yet once the Constitution was interpreted by Mapp to require exclusion of certain evidence at trial, the Constitution became irrelevant to the manner in which that constitutional right was to be enforced in the federal courts; *that* inquiry is only a matter of respecting Congress' allocation of federal judicial power between this Court's appellate jurisdiction and a federal district court's habeas jurisdiction. Indeed, by conceding that today's "decision does not mean that the federal [district] court lacks jurisdiction over [respondents'] claim[s]," the Court admits that respondents have sufficiently alleged that they are "in custody in violation of the Constitution" within the meaning of § 2254 and that there is no "constitutional" rationale for today's holding. Rather, the constitutional "interest balancing" approach to this case is untenable, and I can only view the constitutional garb in which the Court dresses its result as a disguise for rejection of the longstanding principle that there are no "second class" constitutional rights for purposes of federal habeas jurisdiction; it is nothing less than an attempt to provide a veneer of respectability for an obvious usurpation of Congress' Art. III power to delineate the jurisdiction of the federal courts.

II

Therefore, the real ground of today's decision—a ground that is particularly troubling in light of its portent for habeas jurisdiction generally—is the Court's novel reinterpretation of the habeas statutes; this would read the statutes as requiring the District Courts routinely to deny habeas relief to prisoners "in custody in violation of the Constitution or laws of the United States" as a matter of judicial "discretion"—a "discretion" judicially manufactured today contrary to the express statutory language—because such claims are "different in kind" from other constitutional violations in that they "do not 'impugn the integrity of the fact-finding process,'" and because application of such constitutional strictures "often frees the guilty." Much in the Court's opinion suggests that a construction of the habeas statutes to deny relief for non-"guilt-related" constitutional violations, based on this Court's vague notions of comity and federalism, is the actual premise for today's decision, and although the Court attempts to bury its underlying premises in footnotes, those premises mark this case as a harbinger of future eviscerations of the habeas statutes that plainly does violence to congressional power to frame the statutory contours of habeas jurisdiction. * * * I am therefore justified in apprehending that the groundwork is being laid today for a drastic withdrawal of federal habeas

courts could have been the forum for the initial "opportunity for a full and fair hearing" of Fourth Amendment claims of state prisoners that the Court finds constitutionally sufficient, nonconstitutional concerns dictated temporary abstention; but having so abstained, federal courts are now ousted by this Court from ever determining the claims, since the courts to which they initially deferred are all that this Court deems necessary for protecting rights essential to preservation of the Fourth Amendment. Such hostility to federal jurisdiction to redress violations of rights secured by the Federal Constitution, despite congressional conferral of that jurisdiction, is profoundly disturbing.

jurisdiction, if not for all grounds of alleged unconstitutional detention, then at least for claims—for example, of double jeopardy, entrapment, self-incrimination, Miranda violations, and use of invalid identification procedures—that this Court later decides are not "guilt-related."

To the extent the Court is actually premising its holding on an interpretation of 28 U.S.C. § 2241 or § 2254, it is overruling the heretofore settled principle that federal habeas relief is available to redress *any* denial of asserted constitutional rights, whether or not denial of the right affected the truth or fairness of the fact-finding process. * * * This Court has on numerous occasions accepted jurisdiction over collateral attacks by state prisoners premised on Fourth Amendment violations, often over dissents that as a statutory matter such claims should not be cognizable. * * *

* * * In effect, habeas jurisdiction is a deterrent to unconstitutional actions by trial and appellate judges, and a safeguard to ensure that rights secured under the Constitution and federal laws are not merely honored in the breach. * * *

At least since Brown v. Allen detention emanating from judicial proceedings in which constitutional rights were denied has been deemed "contrary to fundamental law," and all constitutional claims have thus been cognizable on federal habeas corpus. There is no foundation in the language or history of the habeas statutes for discriminating between types of constitutional transgressions, and efforts to relegate certain categories of claims to the status of "second-class rights" by excluding them from that jurisdiction have been repulsed. Today's opinion, however, marks the triumph of those who have sought to establish a hierarchy of constitutional rights, and to deny for all practical purposes a federal forum for review of those rights that this Court deems less worthy or important. Without even paying the slightest deference to principles of *stare decisis* or acknowledging Congress' failure for two decades to alter the habeas statutes in light of our interpretation of congressional intent to render all federal constitutional contentions cognizable on habeas, the Court today rewrites Congress' jurisdictional statutes as heretofore construed and bars access to federal courts by state prisoners with constitutional claims distasteful to a majority of my Brethren. But even ignoring principles of *stare decisis* dictating that Congress is the appropriate vehicle for embarking on such a fundamental shift in the jurisdiction of the federal courts, I can find no adequate justification elucidated by the Court for concluding that habeas relief for all federal constitutional claims is no longer compelled under the reasoning of Brown, Fay, and Kaufman. * * *

* * * State judges popularly elected may have difficulty resisting popular pressures not experienced by federal judges given lifetime tenure designed to immunize them from such influences, and the federal habeas statutes reflect the Congressional judgment that such detached federal review is a salutary safeguard against *any* detention of an individual "in violation of the Constitution or laws of the United States."

Federal courts have the duty to carry out the congressionally assigned responsibility to shoulder the ultimate burden of adjudging whether detentions violate federal law, and today's decision substantially abnegates that duty. The Court does not, because it cannot, dispute that institutional constraints totally preclude any possibility that this Court can adequately oversee whether state courts have properly applied federal law, and does not controvert the fact that federal habeas jurisdiction is partially designed to ameliorate that inadequacy. Thus, although I fully agree that state courts "have a constitutional obligation to safeguard personal liberties and to uphold federal law," and that there is no "general lack of appropriate sensitivity to constitutional rights in the trial and appellate courts of the several States," I cannot agree that it follows that, as the Court today holds, federal court determination of almost all Fourth Amendment claims of state prisoners should be barred and that state court resolution of those issues should be insulated from the federal review Congress intended.

* * *

MR. JUSTICE WHITE, dissenting.

For many of the reasons stated by Mr. Justice Brennan, I cannot agree that the writ of habeas corpus should be any less available to those convicted of state crimes where they allege Fourth Amendment violations than where other constitutional issues are presented to the federal court. Under the amendments to the habeas corpus statute, which were adopted after Fay v. Noia, 372 U.S. 391 (1963), and represented an effort by Congress to lend a modicum of finality to state criminal judgments, I cannot distinguish between Fourth Amendment and other constitutional issues.

Suppose, for example, that two confederates in crime, Smith and Jones, are tried separately for a state crime and convicted on the very same evidence, including evidence seized incident to their arrest allegedly made without probable cause. Their constitutional claims are fully aired, rejected and preserved on appeal. Their convictions are affirmed by the State's highest court. Smith, the first to be tried, does not petition for certiorari, or does so but his petition is denied. Jones, whose conviction was considerably later, is more successful. His petition for certiorari is granted and his conviction reversed because this Court, without making any new rule of law, simply concludes that on the undisputed facts the arrests were made without probable cause and the challenged evidence was therefore seized in violation of the Fourth Amendment. The State must either retry Jones or release him, necessarily because he is deemed in custody in violation of the Constitution. It turns out that without the evidence illegally seized, the State has no case; and Jones goes free. Smith then files his petition for habeas corpus. He makes no claim that he did not have a full and fair hearing in the state courts, but asserts that his Fourth Amendment claim had been erroneously decided and that he is being held in violation of the Federal Constitution. He cites this Court's decision in Jones' case to satisfy any burden placed on him by § 2254 to demonstrate that the state court was in error. Unless the Court's reservation, in its present opinion, of those situations where the defendant has not had a full and fair hearing in the state courts is intended to encompass all those circumstances under which a state criminal judgment may be reexamined under § 2254—in which event the opinion is essentially meaningless and the judgment erroneous—Smith's petition would be dismissed, and he would spend his life in prison while his colleague is a free man. I cannot believe that Congress intended this result. * * *

I feel constrained to say, however, that I would join four or more other Justices in substantially limiting the reach of the exclusionary rule as presently administered under the Fourth Amendment in federal and state criminal trials. * * *

FURTHER NOTE ON THE ISSUES COGNIZABLE ON HABEAS CORPUS

(1) The Court's opinion in Stone v. Powell was prefigured in Justice Powell's concurring opinion in Schneckloth v. Bustamonte, 412 U.S. 218, 250 (1973). This was also a habeas case attacking a state conviction on the ground that illegal evidence was admitted at trial. A majority of the Court held that the search was lawful. Justice Powell, joined by Chief Justice Burger and Justice Rehnquist,[1] stated that he would hold that federal collateral review of Fourth Amendment claims should be permitted only where the petitioner did not have a fair opportunity to litigate those claims in the state courts.

Many of the arguments with respect to the exclusionary rule subsequently appearing in Stone v. Powell were made in Schneckloth. But in the latter case Justice Powell also made a more general attack on the version of federal habeas corpus created in Brown v. Allen and Fay v. Noia. Starting with the question of "the nature of the writ at the time of its incorporation in our Constitution and at the time of the Habeas Corpus Act of 1867" (p. 252), Justice Powell stated: "[R]ecent scholarship has cast grave doubt on Fay's version of the writ's historic function.

"It has been established that both the Framers of the Constitution and the authors of the 1867 Act expected that the scope of habeas corpus would be determined with reference to the writ's historic, common-law development.[3] * * *

"It thus becomes important to understand exactly what was the common-law scope of the writ both when embraced by our Constitution and incorporated into the Habeas Corpus Act of 1867. Two respected scholars have recently explored these questions. Their efforts have been both meticulous and revealing. Their conclusions differ significantly from those of the Court in Fay v. Noia, that habeas corpus traditionally has been available 'to remedy any kind of governmental restraint contrary to fundamental law.' 372 U.S., at 405.

"* * * The historical evidence demonstrates that the purposes of the writ, at the time of the adoption of the Constitution, were tempered by a due regard for the finality of the judgment of the committing court. This regard was maintained substantially intact when Congress, in the Habeas Corpus Act of 1867, first extended federal habeas review to the delicate interrelations of our dual court systems. * * *

"Recent decisions, however, have tended to depreciate the importance of the finality of prior judgments in criminal cases. * * * This trend may be a justifiable evolution of the use of habeas corpus where the one in state custody raises a constitutional claim bearing on his innocence. But

---

1. Justice Blackmun stated that he agreed with "nearly all" of Justice Powell's opinion, but did not formally join it.

"3. Bator, *Finality in Criminal Law and Federal Habeas Corpus for State Pris-* oners, 76 Harv.L.Rev. 441, 466 (1963); Oaks, *Legal History in the High Court— Habeas Corpus,* 64 Mich.L.Rev. 451, 451–56 (1966).

the justification for disregarding the historic scope and function of the writ is measurably less apparent in the typical Fourth Amendment claim asserted on collateral attack. In this latter case, a convicted defendant is most often asking society to redetermine a matter with no bearing at all on the basic justice of his incarceration.

"Habeas corpus indeed *should* provide the added assurance for a free society that no innocent man suffers an unconstitutional loss of liberty.
* * *

"I am aware that history reveals no exact tie of the writ of habeas corpus to a constitutional claim relating to innocence or guilt. Traditionally, the writ was unavailable even for many constitutional pleas grounded on the claimant's innocence, while many contemporary proponents of expanded employment of the writ would permit its issuance for one whose deserved confinement was never in doubt. We are now faced, however, with the task of accommodating the historic respect for the finality of the judgment of a committing court with recent Court expansions of the role of the writ. This accommodation can best be achieved, with due regard to all of the values implicated, by recourse to the central reason for habeas corpus: the affording of means, through an extraordinary writ, of redressing an *unjust* incarceration.

"Federal habeas review of search and seizure claims is rarely relevant to this reason. * * *

"When raised on federal habeas, a claim generally has been considered by two or more tiers of state courts. It is the solemn duty of these courts, no less than federal ones, to safeguard personal liberties and consider federal claims in accord with federal law. The task which federal courts are asked to perform on habeas is thus most often one that has or should have been done before. The presumption that 'if a job can be well done once, it should not be done twice' is sound and one calculated to utilize best 'the intellectual, moral, and political resources involved in the legal system.' [13] * * *

"The present scope of federal habeas corpus also has worked to defeat the interest of society in a rational point of termination for criminal litigation. * * *

"No effective judicial system can afford to concede the continuing theoretical possibility that there is error in every trial and that every incarceration is unfounded. At some point the law must convey to those in custody that a wrong has been committed, that consequent punishment has been imposed, that one should no longer look back with the view to resurrecting every imaginable basis for further litigation but rather should look forward to rehabilitation and to becoming a constructive citizen.
* * *

"Finally, the present scope of habeas corpus tends to undermine the values inherent in our federal system of government. To the extent that every state criminal judgment is to be subject indefinitely to broad and repetitive federal oversight, we render the actions of state courts a serious disrespect in derogation of the constitutional balance between the two systems. The present expansive scope of federal habeas review has prompted no small friction between state and federal judiciaries. * * *

"13. Bator, *supra*, n. 3, at 451. * * *

"Perhaps no single development of the criminal law has had consequences so profound as the escalating use over the past two decades, of federal habeas corpus to reopen and readjudicate state criminal judgments. * * * If these consequences flowed from the safeguarding of constitutional claims of innocence they should, of course, be accepted as a tolerable price to pay for cherished standards of justice at the same time that efforts are pursued to find more rational procedures. * * * It is this paradox of a system, which so often seems to subordinate substance to form, that increasingly provokes criticism and lack of confidence. Indeed, it is difficult to explain why a system of criminal justice deserves respect which allows repetitive reviews of convictions long since held to have been final at the end of the normal process of trial and appeal where the basis for reexamination is not even that the convicted defendant was innocent. There has been a halo about the 'Great Writ' that no one would wish to dim. Yet one must wonder whether the stretching of its use far beyond any justifiable purpose will not in the end weaken rather than strengthen the writ's vitality" (pp. 253–65, 274–75).

(2) Justice Brennan expressed the fear in dissent in Stone v. Powell that the decision laid the groundwork for "a drastic withdrawal of federal habeas jurisdiction * * * for claims * * * that this Court later decides are not 'guilt-related'." No such development has in fact occurred.

Rose v. Mitchell, 443 U.S. 545 (1979), involved an allegation by prisoners convicted of murder in Tennessee that there was racial discrimination in selecting the grand jury which indicted them. The Supreme Court decided (5–2 on this issue) not to extend the rationale of Stone v. Powell to such a claim.[2] Justice Blackmun wrote that in Stone the Court confined its ruling to "cases involving the judicially created exclusionary rule, which had minimal utility when applied in a habeas corpus proceeding. * * * [A] claim of discrimination in the selection of the grand jury differs * * * fundamentally * * *" (p. 560). The Court stressed, first, that the latter claim involves an allegation that the trial court itself—rather than the police—violated the Constitution, and that therefore there is doubt whether the claim can receive a full and fair hearing in the state courts. Second, the grand jury claim involves a violation of the direct commands of the Equal Protection Clause and statutes passed under it, rather than the judicially created exclusionary rule. Third, habeas corpus will serve as an effective remedy for violations of the rule prohibiting discrimination in the selection of the grand jury. Finally, the Court stated that grand jury discrimination issues involve a "concern with judicial integrity" and touch on constitutional interests which are "substantially more compelling" than those at issue in Stone v. Powell (pp. 563–64). Justice Powell, in dissent on this issue, complained that the Court's ruling was an "extreme example" of the "loss of historical perspective" which has converted habeas corpus into a repetitive duplication of the appellate process (p. 581); he reiterated the arguments he advanced in Schneckloth v. Bustamonte and concluded: "Because the need to protect the innocent [from unjust convictions] is not

2. Two Justices did not express their opinion on the Stone v. Powell question. The Court also ruled that the claim of grand jury discrimination was not "harmless error" although raised by a defendant convicted beyond a reasonable doubt by a petit jury conceded to be properly constituted. In doing so it rejected an argument to the contrary by Justice Stewart, which in turn revived an argument made by Justice Jackson in dissent in Cassell v. Texas, 339 U.S. 282 (1950). On the merits the Court rejected the claim of unconstitutional discrimination.

implicated in cases such as this, the writ of habeas corpus is not an appropriate remedy" (p. 587).[3]

(3) Another major case involving the rule of Stone v. Powell was Jackson v. Virginia, 443 U.S. 307 (1979), p. 682, *supra*. Recall that in Jackson the Court first ruled that the federal constitutional right not to be convicted of crime unless the jury finds the defendant guilty beyond a reasonable doubt means that the question whether the evidence in the case supports the finding of guilt beyond reasonable doubt is itself a federal constitutional question reviewable in the federal courts. The Court then went on to hold that the question is not to be subjected to the limited review authorized by Stone v. Powell but, rather, is to be fully available on habeas corpus without regard to whether it has been given a full and fair hearing in the state courts.

Note that in Jackson the Court ruled that Stone v. Powell was inapposite because the question at issue did bear on the guilt or innocence of the prisoner; and that in Rose it ruled that Stone v. Powell was inapposite despite the fact that the question at issue did not bear on guilt or innocence. Do the two cases leave any room for the application of Stone v. Powell beyond the confines of the Fourth Amendment?

(4) Kimmelman v. Morrison, 477 U.S. 365 (1986), held that Stone v. Powell would not be extended to foreclose habeas review of a Sixth Amendment claim of ineffective assistance of counsel, even though the inadequacy alleged was counsel's failure to file a timely motion to suppress evidence on the ground that it had been seized in violation of the Fourth Amendment. Rejecting the state's argument that the claim being made was "in fact, if not in form, a Fourth Amendment one" controlled by Stone, Justice Brennan stated that to make out a Sixth Amendment claim under Strickland v. Washington, 466 U.S. 668 (1984), a defendant had to prove both inadequate representation and prejudice: "In order to prevail, the defendant must show * * * that counsel's representation fell below an objective standard of reasonableness * * *. Where defense counsel's failure to litigate a Fourth Amendment claim competently is the principal allegation of ineffectiveness, the defendant must also prove that this Fourth Amendment claim is meritorious and that there is a reasonable probability that the verdict would have been different absent the excludable evidence in order to demonstrate actual prejudice. Thus, while respondent's defaulted Fourth Amendment claim is one element of proof of his Sixth Amendment claim, the two claims have separate identities * * * " (p. 375). Justice Brennan also noted that the Fourth and Sixth Amendment claims reflected different constitutional values—privacy and fair and reliable trials, respectively (pp. 374–75).

Justice Brennan rejected too the state's argument that Stone's rationale and purposes applied to Sixth Amendment claims based on counsel's failure competently to argue Fourth Amendment claims. He noted, first,

3. In Vasquez v. Hillery, 474 U.S. 254 (1986), p. 1476, *supra,* involving a 1962 conviction, the majority, following Rose, affirmed the grant of a habeas petition because there had been racial discrimination in selecting the grand jury that indicted the prisoner. In dissent, Justice Powell stressed that the state might no longer be able to retry the prisoner. The majority noted, however, that Congress and a Judicial Conference rules committee had refused to adopt proposals that would permit or require dismissal of a petition simply on the ground of passage of time prejudicial to the state's ability to retry.

that the Court in Stone had distinguished personal constitutional rights—such as that to effective assistance of counsel—from the judicially created remedy excluding illegally obtained evidence. And, second, he argued that while the Stone Court had stressed the minimal deterrent utility of applying the exclusionary rule in habeas cases, "collateral review will frequently be the only means through which an accused can effectuate the right to counsel * * *. * * * Indeed, an accused will often not realize that he has a meritorious ineffectiveness claim until he begins collateral review proceedings, particularly if he retained trial counsel on direct appeal. Were we to extend Stone and hold that criminal defendants may not raise ineffective assistance claims that are based primarily on incompetent handling of Fourth Amendment issues on federal habeas, we would deny most defendants whose trial attorneys performed incompetently in this regard the opportunity to vindicate their right to effective trial counsel. We would deny all defendants whose appellate counsel performed inadequately with respect to Fourth Amendment issues the opportunity to protect their right to effective appellate counsel. * * * Thus, we cannot say, as the Court was able to say in Stone, that restriction of federal habeas review would not severely interfere with the protection of the constitutional right asserted by the habeas petitioner" [4] (pp. 378–79).

Justice Powell, with whom Chief Justice Burger and Justice Rehnquist joined, concurred on the ground that Stone was inapplicable. He doubted, however, "whether the admission of illegally seized but reliable evidence can ever constitute 'prejudice' under Strickland" (p. 391). Since the parties had not raised the issue, Justice Powell declined to decide it.

(6) Justice Powell's suggestions that "innocence" should be a factor relevant to the scope of habeas review resurfaced in Kuhlmann v. Wilson, 477 U.S. 436 (1986), in the context of a habeas application by a state prisoner who had raised the identical issue in a previous habeas petition. That case is further discussed in the *Note on Relitigating the Facts on Habeas Corpus: Herein Also of Second and Subsequent Applications,* p. 1561, *infra.*[5]

(7) Articles critical of Stone v. Powell include Seidman, *Factual Guilt and the Burger Court: An Examination of Continuity and Change in Criminal Procedure,* 80 Colum.L.Rev. 436 (1980), and Soloff, *Litigation and Relitigation: The Uncertain Status of Federal Habeas Corpus for State Prisoners,* 6 Hofstra L.Rev. 297 (1978). More supportive of Stone is Halpern, *Federal Habeas Corpus and the Mapp Exclusionary Rule After Stone v. Powell,* 82 Colum.L.Rev. 1 (1982). See also Cover and Aleinikoff, *Dialectical Federalism: Habeas Corpus and the Court,* 86 Yale L.J. 1035, 1086–1100 (1977). On Hillery, Kimmelman and Kuhlmann, see Robbins, *Whither (or Wither) Habeas Corpus?: Observations on the Supreme Court's 1985 Term,* 111 F.R.D. 265 (1986).

---

4. Justice Brennan added that "the restriction on federal habeas relief established by Stone v. Powell, was predicated on the existence at trial and on direct review of 'an opportunity for full and fair litigation' of the constitutional claim advanced by the habeas petitioner. 428 U.S 465, 494 (1976). In general, no comparable, meaningful opportunity exists for the full and fair litigation of a habeas petitioner's ineffective assistance claims at trial and on direct review."

5. The Court's recent procedural default cases also show a concern with the question of the petitioner's guilt or innocence. See Murray v. Carrier, p. 1547, *infra.*

For a collection of lower court cases considering the question whether a Fourth Amendment claim was given a full and fair hearing in the state courts within the meaning of Stone v. Powell, see 17 Federal Practice § 4263 nn. 23–31. A recurrent question has been the relationship between the test of Stone v. Powell and the test laid down in Townsend v. Sain, p. 1561, *infra*, for determining when a habeas court must rehear the facts. See Halpern, *supra*, at 14–16, citing the lower court cases discussing this issue, and Michael, *The "New" Federalism and the Burger Court's Deference to the States in Federal Habeas Proceedings*, 64 Iowa L.Rev. 233 (1979).

(8) Even prior to Stone v. Powell, the Court had decided to resist one possible line of expansion in the rule of Brown v. Allen. In Tollett v. Henderson, 411 U.S. 258 (1973), the Court made it clear that alleged violations of constitutional rights (in Tollett, the allegation was racial discrimination in the selection of the grand jury) could not be litigated on habeas corpus if the detention was authorized by a guilty plea which was itself constitutionally valid.[6] The Court stated that "a guilty plea represents a break in the chain of events" (p. 267). The fact that, at the time of the plea, the facts relating to the alleged racial discrimination were unknown (so that no intelligent "waiver" occurred) is irrelevant. "The focus of federal habeas inquiry is the nature of the [attorney's] advice and the voluntariness of the plea, not the existence as such of an antecedent constitutional infirmity"; "while claims of prior constitutional deprivation may play a part in evaluating the advice rendered by counsel, they are not themselves independent grounds for federal collateral relief" (pp. 266, 267).

Compare Lefkowitz v. Newsome, 420 U.S. 283 (1975). Here a New York defendant pleaded guilty, but thereafter was permitted by the New York courts to appeal a prior adverse ruling on a motion to suppress evidence on the ground of its illegal seizure, under a New York statute which explicitly allows appellate review of such rulings notwithstanding the fact that the "judgment of conviction is predicated upon a plea of guilty." The New York courts having ruled that the search and seizure in question were valid, the defendant sought habeas. The Supreme Court held 5–4 that the writ was available to test the legality of the search and seizure notwithstanding the guilty plea.[7] The Court stated that where state law authorizes the raising of the constitutional issue, and the state courts in fact consider it, all the prerequisites for habeas jurisdiction have been satisfied without regard to the guilty plea, and Tollett is "inapposite". Justice White's dissent emphasized that if the guilty plea is constitutionally valid, there can be no "custody in violation of the Constitution" within the meaning of the habeas corpus statutes. The Tollett rule, argued Justice

---

6. What constitutes a valid guilty plea is a question that had been canvassed in three cases in 1970; the Court held that guilty pleas based on the advice of reasonably competent counsel are generally valid. See Brady v. United States, 397 U.S. 742 (1970); McMann v. Richardson, 397 U.S. 759 (1970); Parker v. North Carolina, 397 U.S. 790 (1970). *Cf.* Blackledge v. Perry, 417 U.S. 21 (1974) (guilty plea in a case where the state wholly lacks power under the due process clause to prosecute is open to attack); Menna v. New York, 423 U.S. 61, 63 n. 2 (1975) ("a plea of guilty to a charge does not waive a claim that—judged

on its face—the charge is one which the State may not constitutionally prosecute [here a double jeopardy claim]"). These cases are discussed in Westen, *Away From Waiver: A Rationale for the Forfeiture of Constitutional Rights in Criminal Procedure*, 75 Mich.L.Rev. 1214 (1977); Saltzburg, *Pleas of Guilty and the Loss of Constitutional Rights: The Current Price of Pleading Guilty*, 76 Mich.L.Rev. 1265 (1978).

7. Of course under Stone v. Powell there would now in any event be no collateral attack in Newsome.

White, under which preceding constitutional violations "merge" into the guilty plea, is not a rule of procedure about how federal questions are "preserved"; it is a substantive constitutional rule limiting the federal constitutional grounds on which a defendant may attack a judgment based on a guilty plea.

Isn't the crucial question in Newsome whether the Tollett rule is a "waiver" rule or a substantive rule? Given the fact that in Tollett the facts about racial discrimination were unknown when the guilty plea was entered, what should the answer be?

WAINWRIGHT v. SYKES

433 U.S. 72, 97 S.Ct. 2497, 53 L.Ed.2d 594 (1977).
Certiorari to the United States Court of Appeals for the Fifth Circuit.

MR. JUSTICE REHNQUIST delivered the opinion of the Court.

We granted certiorari to consider the availability of federal habeas corpus to review a state convict's claim that testimony was admitted at his trial in violation of his rights under Miranda v. Arizona, 384 U.S. 436 (1966), a claim which the Florida courts have previously refused to consider on the merits because of noncompliance with a state contemporaneous-objection rule. Petitioner Wainwright, on behalf of the State of Florida, here challenges a decision of the Court of Appeals for the Fifth Circuit ordering a hearing in state court on the merits of respondent's contention.

Respondent Sykes was convicted of third-degree murder after a jury trial in the Circuit Court of DeSoto County. He testified at trial that on the evening of January 8, 1972, he told his wife to summon the police because he had just shot Willie Gilbert. Other evidence indicated that when the police arrived at respondent's trailer home, they found Gilbert dead of a shotgun wound, lying a few feet from the front porch. Shortly after their arrival, respondent came from across the road and volunteered that he had shot Gilbert, and a few minutes later respondent's wife approached the police and told them the same thing. Sykes was immediately arrested and taken to the police station.

Once there, it is conceded that he was read his Miranda rights, and that he declined to seek the aid of counsel and indicated a desire to talk. He then made a statement, which was admitted into evidence at trial through the testimony of the two officers who heard it, to the effect that he had shot Gilbert from the front porch of his trailer home. There were several references during the trial to respondent's consumption of alcohol during the preceding day and to his apparent state of intoxication, facts which were acknowledged by the officers who arrived at the scene. At no time during the trial, however, was the admissibility of any of respondent's statements challenged by his counsel on the ground that respondent had not understood the Miranda warnings. Nor did the trial judge question their admissibility on his own motion or hold a factfinding hearing bearing on that issue.

Respondent appealed his conviction, but apparently did not challenge the admissibility of the inculpatory statements. He later filed in the trial court a motion to vacate the conviction and, in the State District Court of Appeals and Supreme Court, petitions for habeas corpus. These filings, apparently for the first time, challenged the statements made to police on grounds of involuntariness. In all of these efforts respondent was unsuccessful.

Having failed in the Florida courts, respondent initiated the present action under 28 U.S.C. § 2254, asserting the inadmissibility of his statements by reason of his lack of understanding of the Miranda warnings. * * *

The simple legal question before the Court calls for a construction of the language of 28 U.S.C. § 2254(a), which provides that the federal courts shall entertain an application for a writ of habeas corpus "in behalf of a person in custody pursuant to the judgment of a state court only on the ground that he is in custody in violation of the Constitution or laws or treaties of the United States." But, to put it mildly, we do not write on a clean slate in construing this statutory provision.[6] Its earliest counterpart, applicable only to prisoners detained by federal authority, is found in the Judiciary Act of 1789. Construing that statute for the Court in Ex parte Watkins, 3 Pet. 193, 202 (1830), Mr. Chief Justice Marshall said:

> "An imprisonment under a judgment cannot be unlawful, unless that judgment be an absolute nullity; and it is not a nullity if the Court has general jurisdiction of the subject, although it should be erroneous."

See Ex parte Kearney, 7 Wheat. 38 (1822).

In 1867 Congress expanded the statutory language so as to make the writ available to one held in state as well as federal custody. For more than a century since the 1867 amendment, this Court has grappled with the relationship between the classical common-law writ of habeas corpus and the remedy provided in 28 U.S.C. § 2254. Sharp division within the Court has been manifested on more than one aspect of the perplexing problems which have been litigated in this connection. Where the habeas petitioner challenges a final judgment of conviction rendered by a state court, this Court has been called upon to decide no fewer than four different questions, all to a degree interrelated with one another: (1) What types of federal claims may a federal habeas court properly consider? (2) Where a federal claim is cognizable by a federal habeas court, to what extent must that court defer to a resolution of the claim in prior state proceedings? (3) To what extent must the petitioner who seeks federal habeas exhaust state remedies before resorting to the federal court? (4) In what instances will an adequate and independent state ground bar consideration of otherwise cognizable federal issues on federal habeas review?

Each of these four issues has spawned its share of litigation. * * *

There is no need to consider here in greater detail these first three areas of controversy attendant to federal habeas review of state convictions. Only the fourth area—the adequacy of state grounds to bar federal habeas

---

6. For divergent discussions of the historic role of federal habeas corpus, compare: Hart, *The Supreme Court, 1958 Term, Foreword: The Time Chart of the Justices,* 73 Harv.L.Rev. 84 (1959); Reitz, *Federal Habeas Corpus: Impact of an Abortive State Proceeding,* 74 Harv.L.Rev. 1315 (1961); Brennan, *Federal Habeas Corpus and State Prisoners: An Exercise in Federalism,* 7 Utah L.Rev. 423 (1961); Bator, *Finality in Criminal Law and Federal Habeas Corpus for State Prisoners,* 76 Harv.L.Rev. 441, 468 (1963); Oaks, *Legal History in the High Court—Habeas Corpus,* 64 Mich.L.Rev. 451 (1966); Friendly, *Is Innocence Irrelevant? Collateral Attack on Criminal Judgments,* 38 U.Chi.L.Rev. 142, 170, 171 (1970); and *Note, Developments in the Law—Federal Habeas Corpus,* 83 Harv.L.Rev. 1038 (1970).

review—is presented in this case. The foregoing discussion of the other three is pertinent here only as it illustrates this Court's historic willingness to overturn or modify its earlier views of the scope of the writ, even where the statutory language authorizing judicial action has remained unchanged.

As to the role of adequate and independent state grounds, it is a well-established principle of federalism that a state decision resting on an adequate foundation of state substantive law is immune from review in the federal courts. Fox Film Corp. v. Muller, 296 U.S. 207 (1935); Murdock v. Memphis, 20 Wall. 590 (1875). The application of this principle in the context of a federal habeas proceeding has therefore excluded from consideration any questions of state *substantive* law, and thus effectively barred federal habeas review where questions of that sort are either the only ones raised by a petitioner or are in themselves dispositive of his case. The area of controversy which has developed has concerned the reviewability of federal claims which the state court has declined to pass on because not presented in the manner prescribed by its *procedural* rules. The adequacy of such an independent state procedural ground to prevent federal habeas review of the underlying federal issue has been treated very differently than where the state-law ground is substantive. The pertinent decisions marking the Court's somewhat tortuous efforts to deal with this problem are: Ex parte Spencer, 228 U.S. 652 (1913); Brown v. Allen, 344 U.S. 443 (1953); Fay v. Noia, *supra;* Davis v. United States, 411 U.S. 233 (1973); and Francis v. Henderson, 425 U.S. 536 (1976).

In Brown, *supra,* petitioner Daniels' lawyer had failed to mail the appeal papers to the State Supreme Court on the last day provided by law for filing, and hand delivered them one day after that date. Citing the state rule requiring timely filing, the Supreme Court of North Carolina refused to hear the appeal. This Court, relying in part on its earlier decision in Ex parte Spencer, *supra,* held that federal habeas was not available to review a constitutional claim which could not have been reviewed on direct appeal here because it rested on an independent and adequate state procedural ground. 344 U.S., at 486–487.

In Fay v. Noia, *supra,* respondent Noia sought federal habeas to review a claim that his state-court conviction had resulted from the introduction of a coerced confession in violation of the Fifth Amendment to the United States Constitution. While the convictions of his two codefendants were reversed on that ground in collateral proceedings following their appeals, Noia did not appeal and the New York courts ruled that his subsequent *coram nobis* action was barred on account of that failure. This Court held that petitioner was nonetheless entitled to raise the claim in federal habeas, and thereby overruled its decision 10 years earlier in Brown v. Allen, *supra:*

> "[T]he doctrine under which state procedural defaults are held to constitute an adequate and independent state law ground barring direct Supreme Court review is not to be extended to limit the power granted the federal courts under the federal habeas statute." 372 U.S., at 399.

As a matter of comity but not of federal power, the Court acknowledged "a limited discretion in the federal judge to deny relief * * * to an applicant who had deliberately by-passed the orderly procedure of the state courts and in so doing has forfeited his state court remedies." *Id.*, at 438. In so stating, the Court made clear that the waiver must be knowing and actual—" 'an intentional relinquishment or abandonment of a known right or privilege.' " *Id.*, at 439, quoting Johnson v. Zerbst, 304 U.S., at 464. Noting petitioner's "grisly choice" between acceptance of his life sentence and pursuit of an appeal which might culminate in a sentence of death, the Court concluded that there had been no deliberate bypass of the right to have the federal issues reviewed through a state appeal.[8]

A decade later we decided Davis v. United States, *supra,* in which a federal prisoner's application under 28 U.S.C. § 2255 sought for the first time to challenge the makeup of the grand jury which indicted him. The Government contended that he was barred by the requirement of Fed.Rule Crim.Proc. 12(b)(2) providing that such challenges must be raised "by motion before trial." The Rule further provides that failure to so object constitutes a waiver of the objection, but that "the court for cause shown may grant relief from the waiver." We noted that the Rule "promulgated by this Court and, pursuant to 18 U.S.C. § 3771, 'adopted' by Congress, governs by its terms the manner in which the claims of defects in the institution of criminal proceedings may be waived," 411 U.S., at 241, and held that this standard contained in the Rule, rather than the Fay v. Noia concept of waiver, should pertain in federal habeas as on direct review. Referring to previous constructions of Rule 12(b)(2), we concluded that review of the claim should be barred on habeas, as on direct appeal, absent a showing of cause for the noncompliance and some showing of actual prejudice resulting from the alleged constitutional violation.

Last Term, in Francis v. Henderson, *supra,* the rule of Davis was applied to the parallel case of a state procedural requirement that challenges to grand jury composition be raised before trial. The Court noted that there was power in the federal courts to entertain an application in such a case, but rested its holding on "considerations of comity and concerns for the orderly administration of criminal justice * * *." 425 U.S., at 538–539. While there was no counterpart provision of the state rule which allowed an exception upon some showing of cause, the Court concluded that the standard derived from the Federal Rule should nonetheless be applied in that context since " '[t]here is no reason to * * * give greater preclusive effect to procedural defaults by federal defendants than to similar defaults by state defendants.' " *Id.*, at 542, quoting Kaufman v.

---

8. Not long after Fay, the Court in Henry v. Mississippi, 379 U.S. 443 (1965), considered the question of the adequacy of a state procedural ground to bar direct Supreme Court review, and concluded that failure to comply with a state contemporaneous-objection rule applying to the admission of evidence did not necessarily foreclose consideration of the underlying Fourth Amendment claim. The state procedural ground would be "adequate," and thus dispositive of the case on direct appeal to the United States Supreme Court, only where "the State's insistence on compliance with its procedural rule serves a legitimate state interest." *Id.*, at 447. Because, the Court reasoned, the purposes of the contemporaneous-objection rule were largely served by the motion for a directed verdict at the close of the State's case, enforcement of the contemporaneous-objection rule was less than essential and therefore lacking in the necessary "legitimacy" to make it an adequate state ground.

Rather than searching the merits of the constitutional claim, though, the Court remanded for determination whether a separate adequate state ground might exist—that is, whether petitioner had knowingly and deliberately waived his right to object at trial for tactical or other reasons. This was the same type of waiver which the Court in Fay had said must be demonstrated in order to bar review on state procedural grounds in a federal habeas proceeding.

United States, 394 U.S. 217, 228 (1969). As applied to the federal petitions of state convicts, the Davis cause-and-prejudice standard was thus incorporated directly into the body of law governing the availability of federal habeas corpus review.

To the extent that the dicta of Fay v. Noia may be thought to have laid down an all-inclusive rule rendering state contemporaneous-objection rules ineffective to bar review of underlying federal claims in federal habeas proceedings—absent a "knowing waiver" or a "deliberate bypass" of the right to so object—its effect was limited by Francis, which applied a different rule and barred a habeas challenge to the makeup of a grand jury. Petitioner Wainwright in this case urges that we further confine its effect by applying the principle enunciated in Francis to a claimed error in the admission of a defendant's confession. * * *

We * * * conclude that Florida procedure did, consistently with the United States Constitution, require that respondent's confession be challenged at trial or not at all, and thus his failure to timely object to its admission amounted to an independent and adequate state procedural ground which would have prevented direct review here. See Henry v. Mississippi, 379 U.S. 443 (1965). We thus come to the crux of this case. Shall the rule of Francis v. Henderson, *supra*, barring federal habeas review absent a showing of "cause" and "prejudice" attendant to a state procedural waiver, be applied to a waived objection to the admission of a confession at trial?[11] We answer that question in the affirmative.

As earlier noted in the opinion, since Brown v. Allen, 344 U.S. 443 (1953), it has been the rule that the federal habeas petitioner who claims he is detained pursuant to a final judgment of a state court in violation of the United States Constitution is entitled to have the federal habeas court make its own independent determination of his federal claim, without being bound by the determination on the merits of that claim reached in the state proceedings. This rule of Brown v. Allen is in no way changed by our holding today. Rather, we deal only with contentions of federal law which were *not* resolved on the merits in the state proceeding due to respondent's failure to raise them there as required by state procedure. We leave open for resolution in future decisions the precise definition of the "cause"-and-"prejudice" standard, and note here only that it is narrower than the standard set forth in dicta in Fay v. Noia, 372 U.S. 391 (1963), which would make federal habeas review generally available to state convicts absent a knowing and deliberate waiver of the federal constitutional contention. It is the sweeping language of Fay v. Noia, going far beyond the facts of the case eliciting it, which we today reject.[12]

11. Petitioner does not argue, and we do not pause to consider, whether a bare allegation of a Miranda violation, without accompanying assertions going to the actual voluntariness or reliability of the confession, is a proper subject for consideration on federal habeas review where there has been a full and fair opportunity to raise the argument in the state proceeding. See Stone v. Powell, 428 U.S. 465 (1976). We do not address the merits of that question because of our resolution of the case on alternative grounds.

12. We have no occasion today to consider the Fay rule as applied to the facts there confronting the Court. Whether the Francis rule should preclude federal habeas review of claims not made in accordance with state procedure where the criminal defendant has surrendered, other than for reasons of tactical advantage, the right to have all of his claims of trial error considered by a state appellate court, we leave for another day.

The Court in Fay stated its knowing-and-deliberate-waiver rule in language which

The reasons for our rejection of it are several. The contemporaneous-objection rule itself is by no means peculiar to Florida, and deserves greater respect than Fay gives it, both for the fact that it is employed by a coordinate jurisdiction within the federal system and for the many interests which it serves in its own right. A contemporaneous objection enables the record to be made with respect to the constitutional claim when the recollections of witnesses are freshest, not years later in a federal habeas proceeding. It enables the judge who observed the demeanor of those witnesses to make the factual determinations necessary for properly deciding the federal constitutional question. While the 1966 amendment to § 2254 requires deference to be given to such determinations made by state courts, the determinations themselves are less apt to be made in the first instance if there is no contemporaneous objection to the admission of the evidence on federal constitutional grounds.

A contemporaneous-objection rule may lead to the exclusion of the evidence objected to, thereby making a major contribution to finality in criminal litigation. Without the evidence claimed to be vulnerable on federal constitutional grounds, the jury may acquit the defendant, and that will be the end of the case; or it may nonetheless convict the defendant, and he will have one less federal constitutional claim to assert in his federal habeas petition.[13] If the state trial judge admits the evidence in question after a full hearing, the federal habeas court pursuant to the 1966 amendment to § 2254 will gain significant guidance from the state ruling in this regard. Subtler considerations as well militate in favor of honoring a state contemporaneous-objection rule. An objection on the spot may force the prosecution to take a hard look at its hole card, and even if the prosecutor thinks that the state trial judge will admit the evidence he must contemplate the possibility of reversal by the state appellate courts or the ultimate issuance of a federal writ of habeas corpus based on the impropriety of the state court's rejection of the federal constitutional claim.

We think that the rule of Fay v. Noia, broadly stated, may encourage "sandbagging" on the part of defense lawyers, who may take their chances on a verdict of not guilty in a state trial court with the intent to raise their constitutional claims in a federal habeas court if their initial gamble does not pay off. The refusal of federal habeas courts to honor contemporaneous-objection rules may also make state courts themselves less stringent in their enforcement. Under the rule of Fay v. Noia, state appellate courts know that a federal constitutional issue raised for the first time in the proceeding before them may well be decided in any event by a federal habeas tribunal. Thus, their choice is between addressing the issue notwithstanding the petitioner's failure to timely object, or else face the prospect that the federal habeas court will decide the question without the benefit of their views.

applied not only to the waiver of the right to appeal, but to failures to raise individual substantive objections in the state trial. Then, with a single sentence in a footnote, the Court swept aside all decisions of this Court "to the extent that [they] may be read to suggest a standard of discretion in federal habeas corpus proceedings different from what we lay down today * * *." 372 U.S., at 439 n. 44. We do not choose to paint with a similarly broad brush here.

13. Responding to concerns such as these, Mr. Justice Powell's concurring opinion last Term in Estelle v. Williams, 425 U.S. 501, 513 (1976), proposed an "inexcusable procedural default" test to bar the availability of federal habeas review where the substantive right claimed could have been safeguarded if the objection had been raised in a timely manner at trial.

The failure of the federal habeas courts generally to require compliance with a contemporaneous-objection rule tends to detract from the perception of the trial of a criminal case in state court as a decisive and portentous event. A defendant has been accused of a serious crime, and this is the time and place set for him to be tried by a jury of his peers and found either guilty or not guilty by that jury. To the greatest extent possible all issues which bear on this charge should be determined in this proceeding: the accused is in the courtroom, the jury is in the box, the judge is on the bench, and the witnesses, having been subpoenaed and duly sworn, await their turn to testify. Society's resources have been concentrated at that time and place in order to decide, within the limits of human fallibility, the question of guilt or innocence of one of its citizens. Any procedural rule which encourages the result that those proceedings be as free of error as possible is thoroughly desirable, and the contemporaneous-objection rule surely falls within this classification.

We believe the adoption of the Francis rule in this situation will have the salutary effect of making the state trial on the merits the "main event," so to speak, rather than a "tryout on the road" for what will later be the determinative federal habeas hearing. There is nothing in the Constitution or in the language of § 2254 which requires that the state trial on the issue of guilt or innocence be devoted largely to the testimony of fact witnesses directed to the elements of the state crime, while only later will there occur in a federal habeas hearing a full airing of the federal constitutional claims which were not raised in the state proceedings. If a criminal defendant thinks that an action of the state trial court is about to deprive him of a federal constitutional right there is every reason for his following state procedure in making known his objection.

The "cause"-and-"prejudice" exception of the Francis rule will afford an adequate guarantee, we think, that the rule will not prevent a federal habeas court from adjudicating for the first time the federal constitutional claim of a defendant who in the absence of such an adjudication will be the victim of a miscarriage of justice. Whatever precise content may be given those terms by later cases, we feel confident in holding without further elaboration that they do not exist here. Respondent has advanced no explanation whatever for his failure to object at trial,[14] and, as the proceeding unfolded, the trial judge is certainly not to be faulted for failing to question the admission of the confession himself. The other evidence of guilt presented at trial, moreover, was substantial to a degree that would negate any possibility of actual prejudice resulting to the respondent from the admission of his inculpatory statement.

We accordingly conclude that the judgment of the Court of Appeals for the Fifth Circuit must be reversed, and the cause remanded to the United States District Court for the Middle District of Florida with instructions to dismiss respondent's petition for a writ of habeas corpus.

14. In Henry v. Mississippi, 379 U.S., at 451, the Court noted that decisions of counsel relating to trial strategy, even when made without the consultation of the defendant, would bar direct federal review of claims thereby forgone, except where "the circumstances are exceptional."

Last Term in Estelle v. Williams, *supra*, the Court reiterated the burden on a defendant to be bound by the trial judgments of his lawyer. "Under our adversary system, once a defendant has the assistance of counsel the vast array of trial decisions, strategic and tactical, which must be made before and during trial rests with the accused and his attorney." 425 U.S., at 512.

It is so ordered.

MR. CHIEF JUSTICE BURGER, concurring.

I concur fully in the judgment and in the Court's opinion. I write separately to emphasize one point which, to me, seems of critical importance to this case. In my view, the "deliberate bypass" standard enunciated in Fay v. Noia, 372 U.S. 391 (1963), was never designed for, and is inapplicable to, errors—even of constitutional dimension—alleged to have been committed during trial.

In Fay v. Noia, the Court applied the "deliberate bypass" standard to a case where the critical procedural decision—whether to take a criminal appeal—was entrusted to a convicted defendant. Although Noia, the habeas petitioner, was represented by counsel, he himself had to make the decision whether to appeal or not; the role of the attorney was limited to giving advice and counsel. In giving content to the new deliberate-bypass standard, Fay looked to the Court's decision in Johnson v. Zerbst, 304 U.S. 458 (1938), a case where the defendant had been called upon to make the decision whether to request representation by counsel in his federal criminal trial. Because in both Fay and Zerbst, important rights hung in the balance of the *defendant's own decision,* the Court required that a waiver impairing such rights be a knowing and intelligent decision by the defendant himself. As Fay put it:

> "If a habeas applicant, after consultation with competent counsel or otherwise, understandingly and knowingly forewent the privilege of seeking to vindicate his federal claims in the state courts * * * then it is open to the federal court on habeas to deny him all relief * * *."
> 372 U.S., at 439.

The touchstone of Fay and Zerbst, then, is the exercise of volition by the defendant himself with respect to his own federal constitutional rights. In contrast, the claim in the case before us relates to events during the trial itself. Typically, habeas petitioners claim that unlawfully secured evidence was admitted, but see Stone v. Powell, 428 U.S. 465 (1976), or that improper testimony was adduced, or that an improper jury charge was given, but see Henderson v. Kibbe, 431 U.S. 145, 157 (1977) (Burger, C.J., concurring in judgment), or that a particular line of examination or argument by the prosecutor was improper or prejudicial. But unlike Fay and Zerbst, preservation of this type of claim under state procedural rules does not generally involve an assertion by the defendant himself; rather, the decision to assert or not to assert constitutional rights or constitutionally based objections at trial is necessarily entrusted to the defendant's attorney, who must make on-the-spot decisions at virtually all stages of a criminal trial. As a practical matter, a criminal defendant is rarely, if ever, in a position to decide, for example, whether certain testimony is hearsay and, if so, whether it implicates interests protected by the Confrontation Clause; indeed, it is because " '[e]ven the intelligent and educated layman has small and sometimes no skill in the science of law' " that we held it constitutionally required that every defendant who faces the possibility of incarceration be afforded counsel. Argersinger v. Hamlin, 407 U.S. 25 (1972); Gideon v. Wainwright, 372 U.S. 335, 345 (1963).

Once counsel is appointed, the day-to-day conduct of the defense rests with the attorney. He, not the client, has the immediate—and ultimate— responsibility of deciding if and when to object, which witnesses, if any, to call, and what defenses to develop. Not only do these decisions rest with the attorney, but such decisions must, as a practical matter, be made without consulting the client.[1] The trial process simply does not permit the type of frequent and protracted interruptions which would be necessary if it were required that clients give knowing and intelligent approval to each of the myriad tactical decisions as a trial proceeds.[2]

Since trial decisions are of necessity entrusted to the accused's attorney, the Fay–Zerbst standard of "knowing and intelligent waiver" is simply inapplicable. The dissent in this case, written by the author of Fay v. Noia, implicitly recognizes as much. According to the dissent, Fay imposes the knowing-and-intelligent-waiver standard "where possible" during the course of the trial. In an extraordinary modification of Fay, Mr. Justice Brennan would now require "that the lawyer actually exercis[e] his expertise and judgment in his client's service, and with his client's knowing and intelligent participation *where possible*"; he does not intimate what guidelines would be used to decide when or under what circumstances this would actually be "possible." (Emphasis supplied.) What had always been thought the standard governing the *accused's* waiver of his own constitutional rights the dissent would change, in the trial setting, into a standard of conduct imposed upon the defendant's *attorney*. This vague "standard" would be unmanageable to the point of impossibility.

The effort to read this expanded concept into Fay is to no avail; that case simply did not address a situation where the defendant had to look to his lawyer for vindication of constitutionally based interests. I would leave the core holding of Fay where it began, and reject this illogical uprooting of an otherwise defensible doctrine.

MR. JUSTICE STEVENS, concurring.

Although the Court's decision today may be read as a significant departure from the "deliberate bypass" standard announced in Fay v. Noia, 372 U.S. 391, I am persuaded that the holding is consistent with the way other federal courts have actually been applying Fay.[1] The notion that a client must always consent to a tactical decision not to assert a constitu-

---

1. Only such basic decisions as whether to plead guilty, waive a jury, or testify in one's own behalf are ultimately for the accused to make. See ABA Project on Standards for Criminal Justice, The Prosecution Function and Defense Function § 5.2, pp. 237–238 (App.Draft 1971).

2. One is left to wonder what use there would have been to an objection to a confession corroborated by witnesses who heard Sykes freely admit the killing at the scene within minutes after the shooting.

1. The suggestion in Fay, 372 U.S., at 439, that the decision must be made personally by the defendant has not fared well, see United States ex rel. Cruz v. LaVallee, 448 F.2d 671, 679 (CA2 1971); United States ex rel. Green v. Rundle, 452 F.2d 232, 236 (CA3 1971), although a decision by counsel may not be binding if made over the objection of the defendant. Paine v. McCarthy, 527 F.2d 173, 175–176 (CA9 1975). Courts have generally found a "de-

liberate bypass" where counsel could reasonably have decided not to object. United States ex rel. Terry v. Henderson, 462 F.2d 1125, 1129 (CA2 1972); Whitney v. United States, 513 F.2d 326, 329 (CA8 1974); United States ex rel. Broaddus v. Rundle, 49 F.2d 791, 795 (CA3 1970), but they have not found a bypass when they consider the right "deeply embedded" in the Constitution, Frazier v. Roberts, 441 F.2d 1224, 1230 (CA8 1971), or when the procedural default was not substantial. Minor v. Black, 527 F.2d 1, 5 n. 3 (CA6 1975); Black v. Beto, 382 F.2d 758, 760 (CA5 1967). Sometimes, even a deliberate choice by trial counsel has been held not to be a "deliberate bypass" when the result would be unjust. Moreno v. Beto, 415 F.2d 154 (CA5 1969). In short, the actual disposition of these cases seems to rest on the court's perception of the totality of the circumstances, rather than on mechanical application of the "deliberate bypass" test.

tional objection to a proffer of evidence has always seemed unrealistic to me.[2] Conversely, if the constitutional issue is sufficiently grave, even an express waiver by the defendant himself may sometimes be excused.[3] Matters such as the competence of counsel, the procedural context in which the asserted waiver occurred, the character of the constitutional right at stake, and the overall fairness of the entire proceeding, may be more significant than the language of the test the Court purports to apply. I therefore believe the Court has wisely refrained from attempting to give precise content to its "cause"-and-"prejudice" exception to the rule of Francis v. Henderson, 425 U.S. 536.[4]

In this case I agree with the Court's holding that collateral attack on the state-court judgment should not be allowed. The record persuades me that competent trial counsel could well have made a deliberate decision not to object to the admission of the respondent's in-custody statement. That statement was consistent, in many respects, with the respondent's trial testimony. It even had some positive value, since it portrayed the respondent as having acted in response to provocation, which might have influenced the jury to return a verdict on a lesser charge. To extent that it was damaging, the primary harm would have resulted from its effect in impeaching the trial testimony, but it would have been admissible for impeachment in any event, Harris v. New York, 401 U.S. 222. Counsel may well have preferred to have the statement admitted without objection when it was first offered rather than making an objection which, at best, could have been only temporarily successful.

Moreover, since the police fully complied with Miranda, the deterrent purpose of the Miranda rule is inapplicable to this case. Finally, there is clearly no basis for claiming that the trial violated any standard of fundamental fairness. Accordingly, no matter how the rule is phrased, this case is plainly not one in which a collateral attack should be allowed. I therefore join the opinion of the Court.

MR. JUSTICE WHITE, concurring in the judgment. * * *

MR. JUSTICE BRENNAN, with whom MR. JUSTICE MARSHALL joins, dissenting.

2. "If counsel is to have the responsibility for conducting a contested criminal trial, quite obviously he must have the authority to make important tactical decisions promptly as a trial progresses. The very reasons why counsel's participation is of such critical importance in assuring a fair trial for the defendant, see Powell v. Alabama, 287 U.S. 45, 68–69, make it inappropriate to require that his tactical decisions always be personally approved, or even thoroughly understood, by his client. Unquestionably, assuming the lawyer's competence, the client must accept the consequences of his trial strategy. A rule which would require the client's participation in every decision to object, or not to object, to proffered evidence would make a shambles of orderly procedure." United States ex rel. Allum v. Twomey, 484 F.2d 740, 744–745 (CA7 1973).

3. The test announced in Fay was not actually applied in that case. The Court held that habeas relief was available notwithstanding the client's participation in the waiver decision, and notwithstanding the fact that the decision was made on a tactical basis. The client apparently feared that the State might be able to convict him even without the use of his confession, and that he might be sentenced to death if reconvicted. See Fay, supra, at 397 n. 3, 440.

4. As Fay v. Noia, supra, at 438, makes clear, we are concerned here with a matter of equitable discretion rather than a question of statutory authority; and equity has always been characterized by its flexibility and regard for the necessities of each case, cf. Swann v. Charlotte–Mecklenburg Board of Education, 402 U.S. 1, 15.

Over the course of the last decade, the deliberate-bypass standard announced in Fay v. Noia, 372 U.S. 391, 438–439 (1963), has played a central role in efforts by the federal judiciary to accommodate the constitutional rights of the individual with the States' interests in the integrity of their judicial procedural regimes. The Court today decides that this standard should no longer apply with respect to procedural defaults occurring during the trial of a criminal defendant. In its place, the Court adopts the two-part "cause"-and-"prejudice" test originally developed in Davis v. United States, 411 U.S. 233 (1973), and Francis v. Henderson, 425 U.S. 536 (1976). As was true with these earlier cases,[1] however, today's decision makes no effort to provide concrete guidance as to the content of those terms. More particularly, left unanswered is the thorny question that must be recognized to be central to a realistic rationalization of this area of law: How should the federal habeas court treat a procedural default in a state court that is attributable purely and simply to the error or negligence of a defendant's trial counsel? Because this key issue remains unresolved, I shall attempt in this opinion a re-examination of the policies [2] that should inform—and in Fay did inform—the selection of the standard governing the availability of federal habeas corpus jurisdiction in the face of an intervening procedural default in the state court.

1. The Court began its retreat from the deliberate-bypass standard of Fay in Davis v. United States, where a congressional intent to restrict the bypass formulation with respect to collateral review under 28 U.S.C. § 2255 was found to inhere in Fed. Rule Crim.Proc., 12(b)(2). By relying upon Congress' purported intent, Davis managed to evade any consideration of the justifications and any shortcomings of the bypass test. Subsequently, in Francis v. Henderson, a controlling congressional expression of intent no longer was available, and the Court therefore employed the shibboleth of "considerations of comity and federalism" to justify application of Davis to a § 2254 proceeding. 425 U.S., at 541. Again, any coherent analysis of the bypass standard or the waivability of constitutional rights was avoided—as it was that same day in Estelle v. Williams, 425 U.S. 501 (1976), which proceeded to find a surrender of a constitutional right in an opinion that was simply oblivious to some 40 years of existing case law. Thus, while today's opinion follows from Davis, Francis, and Estelle, the entire edifice is a mere house of cards whose foundation has escaped any systematic inspection.

2. I use the term "policies" advisedly, for it is important to recognize the area of my disagreement with the Court. This Court has never taken issue with the foundation principle established by Fay v. Noia—that in considering a petition for the writ of habeas corpus, federal courts possess the *power* to look beyond a state procedural forfeiture in order to entertain the contention that a defendant's constitutional rights have been abridged. 372 U.S., at 398–399. Indeed, only last Term, the Court reiterated: "There can be no question of a federal district court's power to entertain an application for a writ of habeas corpus in a case such as this." Francis v. Henderson, 425 U.S., at 538. Today's decision reconfirms this federal power by authorizing federal intervention under the "cause"-and-"prejudice" test. Were such power unavailable, federal courts would be bound by Fla.Rule Crim. Proc. 3.190, which contains no explicit provision for relief from procedural defaults. Our disagreement, therefore, centers upon the standard that should govern a federal district court in the exercise of this power to adjudicate the constitutional claims of a state prisoner—which, in turn, depends upon an evaluation of the competing policies and values served by collateral review weighted against those furthered through strict deference to a State's procedural rules.

It is worth noting that because we deal with the standards governing the exercise of the conceded power of federal habeas courts to excuse a state procedural default, Congress, as the primary expositor of federal-court jurisdiction, remains free to undo the potential restrictiveness of today's decision by expressly defining the standard of intervention under 28 U.S.C. § 2254. *Cf.* Davis v. United States, 411 U.S., at 241–242.

I

I begin with the threshold question: What is the meaning and import of a procedural default? If it could be assumed that a procedural default more often than not is the product of a defendant's conscious refusal to abide by the duly constituted, legitimate processes of the state courts, then I might agree that a regime of collateral review weighted in favor of a State's procedural rules would be warranted. Fay, however, recognized that such rarely is the case; and therein lies Fay's basic unwillingness to embrace a view of habeas jurisdiction that results in "an airtight system of [procedural] forfeitures." 372 U.S., at 432.

This, of course, is not to deny that there are times when the failure to heed a state procedural requirement stems from an intentional decision to avoid the presentation of constitutional claims to the state forum. Fay was not insensitive to this possibility. Indeed, the very purpose of its bypass test is to detect and enforce such intentional procedural forfeitures of outstanding constitutionally based claims. * * * For this reason, the Court's assertion that it "think[s]" that the Fay rule encourages intentional "sandbagging" on the part of the defense lawyers is without basis; certainly the Court points to no cases or commentary arising during the past 15 years of actual use of the Fay test to support this criticism. Rather, a consistent reading of case law demonstrates that the bypass formula has provided a workable vehicle for protecting the integrity of state rules in those instances when such protection would be both meaningful and just.

But having created the bypass exception to the availability of collateral review, Fay recognized that intentional, tactical forfeitures are not the norm upon which to build a rational system of federal habeas jurisdiction. In the ordinary case, litigants simply have no incentive to slight the state tribunal, since constitutional adjudication on the state and federal levels are not mutually exclusive. * * * Under the regime of collateral review recognized since the days of Brown v. Allen, and enforced by the Fay bypass test, no rational lawyer would risk the "sandbagging" feared by the Court. If a constitutional challenge is not properly raised on the state level, the explanation generally will be found elsewhere than in an intentional tactical decision.

In brief then, any realistic system of federal habeas corpus jurisdiction must be premised on the reality that the ordinary procedural default is born of the inadvertence, negligence, inexperience, or incompetence of trial counsel. See, *e.g.,* Hill, *The Inadequate State Ground,* 65 Colum.L.Rev. 943, 997 (1965). The case under consideration today is typical. * * *

II

What are the interests that Sykes can assert in preserving the availability of federal collateral relief in the face of his inadvertent state procedural default? Two are paramount.

As is true with any federal habeas applicant, Sykes seeks access to the federal court for the determination of the validity of his federal constitutional claim. Since at least Brown v. Allen, it has been recognized that the "fair effect [of] the habeas corpus jurisdiction as enacted by Congress" entitles a state prisoner to such federal review. 344 U.S., at 500 (opinion of Frankfurter, J.). While some of my Brethren may feel uncomfortable with this congressional choice of policy, see, *e.g.,* Stone v. Powell, 428 U.S. 465 (1976), the Legislative Branch nonetheless remains entirely free to determine that the constitutional rights of an individual subject to state custody, like those of the civil rights plaintiff suing under 42 U.S.C. § 1983, are best preserved by "interpos[ing] the federal courts between the States and the people, as guardians of the people's federal rights * * *." Mitchum v. Foster, 407 U.S. 225, 242 (1972).

With respect to federal habeas corpus jurisdiction, Congress explicitly chose to effectuate the federal court's primary responsibility for preserving federal rights and privileges by authorizing the litigation of constitutional claims and defenses in a district court after the State vindicates its own interest through trial of the substantive criminal offense in the state courts. This, of course, was not the only course that Congress might have followed: As an alternative, it might well have decided entirely to circumvent all state procedure through the expansion of existing federal removal statutes such as 28 U.S.C. §§ 1442(a)(1) and 1443, thereby authorizing the pretrial transfer of all state criminal cases to the federal courts whenever federal defenses or claims are in issue. But liberal post-trial federal review is the redress that Congress ultimately chose to allow and the consequences of a state procedural default should be evaluated in conformance with this policy choice. Certainly, we can all agree that once a state court has assumed jurisdiction of a criminal case, the integrity of its own process is a matter of legitimate concern. The Fay bypass test, by seeking to discover intentional abuses of the rules of the state forum, is, I believe, compatible with this state institutional interest. But whether Fay was correct in penalizing a litigant solely for his intentional forfeitures properly must be read in light of Congress' desired norm of widened post-trial access to the federal courts. If the standard adopted today is later construed to require that the simple mistakes of attorneys are to be treated as binding forfeitures, it would serve to subordinate the fundamental rights contained in our constitutional charter to inadvertent defaults of rules promulgated by state agencies, and would essentially leave it to the States, through the enactment of procedure and the certification of the competence of local attorneys, to determine whether a habeas applicant will be permitted the access to the federal forum that is guaranteed him by Congress.[9]

Thus, I remain concerned that undue deference to local procedure can only serve to undermine the ready access to a federal court to which a state defendant otherwise is entitled. But federal review is not the full measure of Sykes' interest, for there is another of even greater immediacy: assuring that his constitutional claims can be addressed to *some* court. For the obvious consequence of barring Sykes from the federal courthouse is to insulate Florida's alleged constitutional violation from any and all judicial review because of a lawyer's mistake. From the standpoint of the habeas petitioner, it is a harsh rule indeed that denies him "any review at all where the state has granted none," Brown v. Allen, 344 U.S., at 552 (Black, J., dissenting)—particularly when he would have enjoyed both state and federal consideration had his attorney not erred. * * *

9. Of course, even under the Court's new standard, traditional principles continue to apply, and the federal judiciary is not bound by state rules of procedure that are unreasonable on their face, or that are either unreasonably or inconsistently applied. See, *e.g.,* Henry v. Mississippi, 379 U.S. 443 (1965); NAACP v. Alabama, 377 U.S. 288 (1964); Staub v. City of Baxley, 355 U.S. 313 (1958); Williams v. Georgia, 349 U.S. 375 (1955).

A * * * recent development in the law of habeas corpus suggests that adherence to the deliberate-bypass test may be more easily justified today than it was when Fay was decided. It also suggests that the "prejudice" prong of the Court's new test may prove to be a redundancy. Last Term the Court ruled that alleged violations of the Fourth Amendment in most circumstances no longer will be cognizable in habeas corpus. Stone v. Powell, 428 U.S. 465 (1976). While, for me, the principle that generated this conclusion was not readily apparent, I expressed my concern that the Stone decision contains the seeds for the exclusion from collateral review of a variety of constitutional rights that my Brethren somehow deem to be unimportant—perhaps those that they are able to conclude are not "guilt-related." See *id.*, at 517–518 (dissenting opinion). If this trail is to be followed, it would be quite unthinkable that an unintentional procedural default should be allowed to stand in the way of vindication of constitutional rights bearing upon the guilt or innocence of a defendant. Indeed, if as has been argued, a key to decision in this area turns upon a comparison of the importance of the constitutional right at stake with the state procedural rule, Sandalow, *Henry v. Mississippi and the Adequate State Ground: Proposals for a Revised Doctrine,* 1965 Sup.Ct.Rev. 187, 236–237, then the Court's threshold effort to identify those rights of sufficient importance to be litigated collaterally should largely predetermine the outcome of this balance. * * *

III

A regime of federal habeas corpus jurisdiction that permits the reopening of state procedural defaults does not invalidate any state procedural rule as such; Florida's courts remain entirely free to enforce their own rules as they choose, and to deny any and all state rights and remedies to a defendant who fails to comply with applicable state procedure. The relevant inquiry is whether more is required—specifically, whether the fulfillment of important interests of the State necessitates that federal courts be called upon to impose additional sanctions for inadvertent noncompliance with state procedural requirements such as the contemporaneous-objection rule involved here. * * *

Punishing a lawyer's unintentional errors by closing the federal courthouse door to his client is both a senseless and misdirected method of deterring the slighting of state rules. It is senseless because unplanned and unintentional action of any kind generally is not subject to deterrence; and, to the extent that it is hoped that a threatened sanction addressed to the defense will induce greater care and caution on the part of trial lawyers, thereby forestalling negligent conduct or error, the potential loss of all valuable state remedies would be sufficient to this end. And it is a misdirected sanction because even if the penalization of incompetence or carelessness will encourage more thorough legal training and trial preparation, the habeas applicant, as opposed to his lawyer, hardly is the proper recipient of such a penalty. Especially with fundamental constitutional rights at stake, no fictional relationship of principal-agent or the like can justify holding the criminal defendant accountable for the naked errors of his attorney. This is especially true when so many indigent defendants are without any realistic choice in selecting who ultimately represents them at trial. Indeed, if responsibility for error must be apportioned between the parties, it is the State, through its attorney's admissions and certification policies, that is more fairly held to blame for the fact that practicing lawyers too often are ill-prepared or ill-equipped to act carefully and knowledgeably when faced with decisions governed by state procedural requirements. * * *

IV

Perhaps the primary virtue of Fay is that the bypass test at least yields a coherent yardstick for federal district courts in rationalizing their power of collateral review. In contrast, although some four years have passed since its introduction in Davis v. United States, 411 U.S. 233 (1973), the only thing clear about the Court's "cause"-and-"prejudice" standard is that it exhibits the notable tendency of keeping prisoners in jail without addressing their constitutional complaints. Hence, as of today, all we know of the "cause" standard is its requirement that habeas applicants bear an undefined burden of explanation for the failure to obey the state rule. Left unresolved is whether a habeas petitioner like Sykes can adequately discharge this burden by offering the commonplace and truthful explanation for his default: attorney ignorance or error beyond the client's control. The "prejudice" inquiry, meanwhile, appears to bear a strong resemblance to harmless-error doctrine. * * * I disagree with the Court's appraisal of the harmlessness of the admission of respondent's confession, but if this is what is meant by prejudice, respondent's constitutional contentions could be as quickly and easily disposed of in this regard by permitting federal courts to reach the merits of his complaint. In the absence of a persuasive alternative formulation to the bypass test, I would simply affirm the judgment of the Court of Appeals and allow Sykes his day in court on the ground that the failure of timely objection in this instance was not a tactical or deliberate decision but stemmed from a lawyer's error that should not be permitted to bind his client.

One final consideration deserves mention. Although the standards recently have been relaxed in various jurisdictions, it is accurate to assert that most courts, this one included, traditionally have resisted any realistic inquiry into the competency of trial counsel. There is nothing unreasonable, however, in adhering to the proposition that it is the responsibility of a trial lawyer who takes on the defense of another to be aware of his client's basic legal rights and of the legitimate rules of the forum in which he practices his profession. If he should unreasonably permit such rules to bar the assertion of the colorable constitutional claims of his client, then his conduct may well fall below the level of competence that can fairly be expected of him. For almost 40 years it has been established that inadequacy of counsel undercuts the very competence and jurisdiction of the trial court and is always open to collateral review. Johnson v. Zerbst, 304 U.S. 458 (1938). Obviously, as a practical matter, a trial counsel cannot procedurally waive his own inadequacy. If the scope of habeas jurisdiction previously governed by Fay v. Noia is to be redefined so as to enforce the errors and neglect of lawyers with unnecessary and unjust rigor, the time may come when conscientious and fair-minded federal and state courts, in adhering to the teaching of Johnson v. Zerbst, will have to reconsider whether they can continue to indulge the comfortable fiction that all lawyers are skilled or even competent craftsmen in representing the fundamental rights of their clients.

NOTE ON FEDERAL HABEAS CORPUS AND STATE PROCEDURAL DEFAULT

(1) The question of the effect of a state procedural default on the right to seek federal habeas corpus was dramatically raised in Daniels v. Allen, a companion case to Brown v. Allen, p. 1477, *supra,* and decided by the same opinions, see 344 U.S. at 482–87 (Reed, J., for the Court), 552–54 (Black, J., dissenting), 556–60 (Frankfurter, J., dissenting). In Daniels the two petitioners were convicted of murder in North Carolina and sentenced to death. At their trial they raised federal questions similar to those determined on the merits in Brown v. Allen. They also sought to appeal from the judgments of conviction but their appeals were rejected by the Supreme Court of North Carolina without consideration of the merits on the ground that the case on appeal was served a day later than the sixty days allowed for the purpose by the trial court. Under North Carolina practice, late filing precluded an appeal as of right. The state supreme court also refused certiorari to review the constitutional contentions and rejected two applications for a writ of error coram nobis on the ground that the petition did not make a *prima facie* showing of substance. Certiorari was denied by the United States Supreme Court.

The federal claims were then renewed on petitions for habeas corpus in the district court which dismissed after a hearing, sustaining the state determinations on the merits. The court of appeals and the Supreme Court affirmed. Holding the failure to serve the case on appeal in the time allowed "decisive" (p. 483), Justice Reed said (pp. 485–87):

"This situation confronts us. * * * The state furnished an adequate and easily-complied-with method of appeal. This included a means to serve the statement of the case on appeal in the absence of the prosecutor from his office. Yet petitioners' appeal was not taken and the State of North Carolina, although the full trial record and statement on appeal were before it, refused to consider the appeal on its merits. * * *

"Of course, federal habeas corpus is allowed where time has expired without appeal when the prisoner is detained without opportunity to appeal because of lack of counsel, incapacity, or some interference by officials. Also, this Court will review state habeas corpus proceedings even though no appeal was taken, if the state treated habeas corpus as permissible. Federal habeas corpus is available following our refusal to review such state habeas corpus proceedings. Failure to appeal is much like a failure to raise a known and existing question of unconstitutional proceeding or action prior to conviction or commitment. Such failure, of course, bars subsequent objection to conviction on those grounds.

"North Carolina has applied its law in refusing this out-of-time review. This Court applies its jurisdictional statute in the same manner. Preston v. Texas, 343 U.S. 917, 933. We cannot say that North Carolina's action in refusing review after failure to perfect the case on appeal violates the Federal Constitution. A period of limitation accords with our conception of proper procedure.

"* * * A failure to use a state's available remedy, in the absence of some interference or incapacity * * * bars federal habeas corpus. The statute requires that the applicant exhaust available state remedies. To show that the time has passed for appeal is not enough to empower the Federal District Court to issue the writ. The judgment must be affirmed."[1]

Justice Black said (pp. 552–54):

"Here also evidence establishes an unlawful exclusion of Negroes from juries because of race. The State Supreme Court refused to review this evidence on state procedural grounds. Absence of state court review on this ground is now held to cut off review in federal habeas corpus proceedings. But in the two preceding cases where the State Supreme Court did review the evidence, this Court has also reviewed it. I find it difficult to agree with the soundness of a philosophy which prompts this Court to grant a second review where the state has granted one but to deny any review at all where the state has granted none. * * *

"The Court thinks that to review this question and grant petitioners the protections guaranteed by the Constitution would 'subvert the entire system of state criminal justice and destroy state energy in the detection and punishment of crime.' I cannot agree. State systems are not so feeble. And the object of habeas corpus is to search records to prevent illegal imprisonments. To hold it unavailable under the circumstances here is to degrade it. I think Moore v. Dempsey, 261 U.S. 86, forbids this. * * * I read Moore v. Dempsey, as standing for the principle that it is never too late for courts in habeas corpus proceedings to look straight through procedural screens in order to prevent forfeiture of life or liberty in flagrant defiance of the Constitution. Perhaps there is no more exalted judicial function. I am willing to agree that it should not be exercised in cases like these except under special circumstances or in extraordinary situations. But I cannot join in any opinion that attempts to confine the Great Writ within rigid formalistic boundaries."

Justice Frankfurter said (pp. 557–58):

"We were given to understand on the argument that if petitioners' lawyer had mailed his 'statement of case on appeal' on the 60th day and the prosecutor's office had received it on the 61st day the law of North Carolina would clearly have been complied with, but because he delivered it by hand on the 61st day all opportunities for appeal, both in the North Carolina courts and in the federal courts, are cut off although the North Carolina courts had discretion to hear this appeal. For me it is important to emphasize the fact that North Carolina does not have a fixed period for taking an appeal. The decisive question is whether a refusal to exercise a discretion which the Legislature of North Carolina has vested in its judges is an act so arbitrary and so cruel in its operation, considering that life is at stake, that in the circumstances of this case it constitutes a denial of due process in its rudimentary procedural aspect." [2]

1. Earlier in the Brown opinion, Justice Reed had said (p. 458): "So far as weight to be given the proceedings in the courts of the state is concerned, a United States district court, with its familiarity with state practice is in a favorable position to recognize adequate state grounds in denials of relief by state courts without opinion. *A fortiori*, where the state action was based on an adequate state ground, no further examination is required, unless no state remedy for the deprivation of federal constitutional rights ever existed."

2. In his other opinion in the same case, Justice Frankfurter wrote (p. 503):

"Of course, nothing we have said suggests that the federal habeas corpus jurisdiction can displace a state's procedural rule requiring that certain errors be raised on appeal. Normally rights under the Federal Constitution may be waived at the

(2) In Fay v. Noia, p. 1488, *supra,* the Court rejected the Daniels rule. Noia had failed to take a timely appeal from a conviction based primarily on a confession that he alleged was coerced. The Court held that his failure to appeal did not bar habeas. It first ruled that the exhaustion requirement was inapplicable, because state remedies were no longer available when habeas corpus was sought.[3] (By restricting the exhaustion requirement to remedies still available when the writ was sought, the Court in Fay finally eliminated a confusing overlap between two issues—(a) whether procedural default bars habeas; (b) whether the petition is premature because state remedies are still available. That confusion was created by Justice Reed's opinion in Daniels and Justice Brennan's own opinion in Irvin v. Dowd, 359 U.S. 394, 406 (1959). See further *Note on Exhaustion of State Court Remedies,* p. 1552, *infra.*)

The Court then turned to the effect, on habeas jurisdiction, of Noia's failure to take an appeal. Though that default could bar direct review by the Supreme Court, Justice Brennan held that the Court's habeas jurisdiction was not affected (pp. 428–34; 438–39):

"It is a familiar principle that this Court will decline to review state court judgments which rest on independent and adequate state grounds, notwithstanding the co-presence of federal grounds. See, *e.g.,* N.A.A.C.P. v. Alabama ex rel. Patterson, 357 U.S. 449; Fox Film Corp. v. Muller, 296 U.S. 207. * * * Murdock [v. City of Memphis] was a case involving state substantive grounds, but the principle is also applicable in cases involving procedural grounds. See, *e.g.,* Herb v. Pitcairn, 324 U.S. 117; Davis v. Wechsler, 263 U.S. 22; Ward v. Board of County Comm'rs, 253 U.S. 17. Thus, a default such as Noia's, if deemed adequate and independent (a question on which we intimate no view), would cut off review by this Court of the state *coram nobis* proceeding in which the New York Court of Appeals refused him relief. It is contended that it follows from this that the remedy of federal habeas corpus is likewise cut off.

"The fatal weakness of this contention is its failure to recognize that the adequate state-ground rule is a function of the limitations of *appellate* review. Most of the opinion in the Murdock case is devoted to demonstrating the Court's lack of jurisdiction on direct review to decide questions of state law in cases also raising federal questions. It followed from this holding that if the state question was dispositive of the case, the Court could not decide the federal question. The federal question was moot; nothing turned on its resolution. And so we have held that the adequate

---

trial, Adams v. United States ex rel. McCann, 317 U.S. 269, and may likewise be waived by failure to assert such errors on appeal. Compare Frank v. Mangum, 237 U.S. 309, 343. When a State insists that a defendant be held to his choice of trial strategy and not be allowed to try a different tack on State habeas corpus, he may be deemed to have waived his claim and thus have no right to assert on federal habeas corpus. Such considerations of orderly appellate procedure give rise to the conventional statement that habeas corpus should not do service for an appeal. See Adams v.

United States ex rel. McCann, *supra,* at 274. Compare Sunal v. Large, 332 U.S. 174, with Johnson v. Zerbst, 304 U.S. 458, 465–469. However, this does not touch one of those extraordinary cases in which a substantial claim goes to the very foundation of a proceeding, as in Moore v. Dempsey, 261 U.S. 86. *Cf.* Ex parte Lange, 18 Wall. 163; Ex parte Royall, 117 U.S. 241."

3. The Noia Court adopted Professor Hart's view as to the scope of the exhaustion doctrine. See Hart, *Foreword* 112–14.

state-ground rule is a consequence of the Court's obligation to refrain from rendering advisory opinions or passing upon moot questions.[40]

"But while our appellate function is concerned only with the judgments or decrees of state courts, the habeas corpus jurisdiction of the lower federal courts is not so confined. The jurisdictional prerequisite is not the judgment of a state court but detention *simpliciter*. The entire course of decisions in this Court elaborating the rule of exhaustion of state remedies is wholly incompatible with the proposition that a state court *judgment* is required to confer federal habeas jurisdiction. And the broad power of the federal courts under 28 U.S.C. § 2243 summarily to hear the application and to 'determine the facts, and dispose of the matter as law and justice require,' is hardly characteristic of an appellate jurisdiction. Habeas lies to enforce the right of personal liberty; when that right is denied and a person confined, the federal court has the power to release him. Indeed, it has no other power; it cannot revise the state court judgment; it can act only on the body of the petitioner. In re Medley, Petitioner, 134 U.S. 160, 173.

"To be sure, this may not be the entire answer to the contention that the adequate state-ground principle should apply to the federal courts on habeas corpus as well as to the Supreme Court on direct review of state judgments. The Murdock decision may be supported not only by the factor of mootness, but in addition by certain characteristics of the federal system. The first question the Court had to decide in Murdock was whether it had the power to review state questions in cases also raising federal questions. It held that it did not, thus affirming the independence of the States in matters within the proper sphere of their lawmaking power from federal judicial interference. For the federal courts to refuse to give effect in habeas proceedings to state procedural defaults might conceivably have some effect upon the States' regulation of their criminal procedures. But the problem is crucially different from that posed in Murdock of the federal courts' deciding questions of substantive state law. In Noia's case the only relevant substantive law is federal—the Fourteenth Amendment. State law appears only in the procedural framework for adjudicating the substantive federal question. The paramount interest is federal. *Cf.* Dice v. Akron, C. & Y.R. Co., 342 U.S. 359. That is not to say that the States have not a substantial interest in exacting compliance with their procedural rules from criminal defendants asserting federal defenses. Of course orderly criminal procedure is a desideratum, and of course there must be sanctions for the flouting of such procedure. But that state interest 'competes * * * against an ideal * * * [the] ideal of fair procedure.' Schaefer, *Federalism and State Criminal Procedure,* 70 Harv.L.Rev. 1, 5 (1956). And the only concrete impact the assumption of federal habeas jurisdiction in the face of a procedural default has on the state interest we have described, is that it prevents the State from closing off the convicted defendant's last opportunity to vindicate his constitutional rights, thereby

"40. * * * We need not decide whether the adequate state-ground rule is constitutionally compelled or merely a matter of the construction of the statutes defining this Court's appellate review. Murdock itself was predicated on statutory construction, and the present statute governing our review of state court decisions, 28 U.S.C. § 1257, limited as it is to "*judgments or decrees* rendered by the highest court of a State in which a decision could be had" (italics supplied), provides ample statutory warrant for our continued adherence to the principles laid down in Murdock.

punishing him for his default and deterring others who might commit similar defaults in the future.

"Surely this state interest in an airtight system of forfeitures is of a different order from that, vindicated in Murdock, in the autonomy of state law within the proper sphere of its substantive regulation. * * *

"A practical appraisal of the state interest here involved plainly does not justify the federal courts' enforcing on habeas corpus a doctrine of forfeitures under the guise of applying the adequate state-ground rule. We fully grant that the exigencies of federalism warrant a limitation whereby the federal judge has the discretion to deny relief to one who has deliberately sought to subvert or evade the orderly adjudication of his federal defenses in the state courts. Surely no stricter rule is a realistic necessity. A man under conviction for crime has an obvious inducement to do his very best to keep his state remedies open, and not stake his all on the outcome of a federal habeas proceeding which, in many respects, may be less advantageous to him than a state court proceeding. See Rogers v. Richmond, 365 U.S. 534, 547–548. And if because of inadvertence or neglect he runs afoul of a state procedural requirement, and thereby forfeits his state remedies, appellate and collateral, as well as direct review thereof in this Court, those consequences should be sufficient to vindicate the State's valid interest in orderly procedure. Whatever residuum of state interest there may be under such circumstances is manifestly insufficient in the face of the federal policy, drawn from the ancient principles of the writ of habeas corpus, embodied both in the Federal Constitution and in the habeas corpus provisions of the Judicial Code, and consistently upheld by this Court, of affording an effective remedy for restraints contrary to the Constitution. For these several reasons we reject as unsound in principle, as well as not supported by authority, the suggestion that the federal courts are without power to grant habeas relief to an applicant whose federal claims would not be heard on direct review in this Court because of a procedural default furnishing an adequate and independent ground of state decision. * * *

"Although we hold that the jurisdiction of the federal courts on habeas corpus is not affected by procedural defaults incurred by the applicant during the state court proceedings, we recognize a limited discretion in the federal judge to deny relief to an applicant under certain circumstances. Discretion is implicit in the statutory command that the judge, after granting the writ and holding a hearing of appropriate scope, 'dispose of the matter as law and justice require,' 28 U.S.C. § 2243; and discretion was the flexible concept employed by the federal courts in developing the exhaustion rule. Furthermore, habeas corpus has traditionally been regarded as governed by equitable principles. United States ex rel. Smith v. Baldi, 344 U.S. 561, 573 (dissenting opinion). Among them is the principle that a suitor's conduct in relation to the matter at hand may disentitle him to the relief he seeks. Narrowly circumscribed, in conformity to the historical role of the writ of habeas corpus as an effective and imperative remedy for detentions contrary to fundamental law, the principle is unexceptionable. We therefore hold that the federal habeas judge may in his discretion deny relief to an applicant who has deliberately bypassed the orderly procedure of the state courts and in so doing has forfeited his state court remedies.

"But we wish to make very clear that this grant of discretion is not to be interpreted as a permission to introduce legal fictions into federal habeas corpus. The classic definition of waiver enunciated in Johnson v. Zerbst, 304 U.S. 458, 464—'an intentional relinquishment or abandonment of a known right or privilege'—furnishes the controlling standard. If a habeas applicant, after consultation with competent counsel or otherwise, understandingly and knowingly forewent the privilege of seeking to vindicate his federal claims in the state courts, whether for strategic, tactical, or any other reasons that can fairly be described as the deliberate by-passing of state procedures, then it is open to the federal court on habeas to deny him all relief if the state courts refused to entertain his federal claims on the merits—though of course only after the federal court has satisfied itself, by holding a hearing or by some other means, of the facts bearing upon the applicant's default. *Cf.* Price v. Johnston, 334 U.S. 266, 291. At all events we wish it clearly understood that the standard here put forth depends on the considered choice of the petitioner. * * * A choice made by counsel not participated in by the petitioner does not automatically bar relief. Nor does a state court's finding of waiver bar independent determination of the question by the federal courts on habeas, for waiver affecting federal rights is a federal question. *E.g.,* Rice v. Olson, 324 U.S. 786."

Justice Harlan, in dissent, said (pp. 468–70):

"The adequate state ground doctrine * * * finds its source in basic constitutional principles, and the question before us is whether this is as true in a collateral attack in habeas corpus as on direct review. Assume, then, that after dismissal of the writ of certiorari in * * * [a case where a state defendant failed to make a timely challenge to the composition of the grand jury], the prisoner seeks habeas corpus in a Federal District Court, again complaining of the composition of the grand jury that indicted him. Is that federal court constitutionally more free than the Supreme Court on direct review to 'ignore' the adequate state ground, proceed to the federal question, and order the prisoner's release?

"The answer must be that it is not. Of course, as the majority states, a judgment is not a 'jurisdictional prerequisite' to a habeas corpus application, but that is wholly irrelevant. The point is that if the applicant is detained *pursuant* to a judgment, termination of the detention necessarily nullifies the judgment. The fact that a District Court on habeas has fewer choices than the Supreme Court, since it can *only* act on the body of the prisoner, does not alter the significance of the exercise of its power. In habeas as on direct review, ordering the prisoner's release invalidates the judgment of conviction and renders ineffective the state rule relied upon to sustain that judgment. Try as the majority does to turn habeas corpus into a roving commission of inquiry into every possible invasion of the applicant's civil rights that may ever have occurred, it cannot divorce the writ from a judgment of conviction if that judgment is the basis of the detention.

"Thus in the present case if this Court had granted certiorari to review the State's denial of *coram nobis,* had considered the coerced confession claim, and had ordered Noia's release, the necessary effects of that disposition would have been (1) to set aside the conviction and (2) to invalidate application of the New York rule requiring the claim to be raised on direct appeal in order to be preserved. It is, I think, beyond dispute that the Court does exactly the same thing by affirming the decision below in this case. In doing so, the Court exceeds its constitutional power if in fact the state ground relied upon to sustain the judgment of conviction is an adequate one. The effect of the approach adopted by the Court is, indeed, to do away with the adequate state ground rule entirely in every state case, involving a federal question, in which detention follows from a judgment."

(3) The governing habeas corpus statute, 28 U.S.C. § 2241, authorizes the federal courts to issue the writ to a prisoner in custody "in violation of the Constitution or laws or treaties of the United States". Was not the central problem of the Noia case this: How can a prisoner be deemed to be in custody in violation of the Constitution when his detention is authorized by a judgment which is by hypothesis unreversible by the Supreme Court because it rests on a dispositive state law ground which is constitutional and adequate?

Does Justice Brennan answer this question? Is it a persuasive answer to say that while the Court's "appellate function is concerned only with the judgments or decrees of state courts, the habeas corpus jurisdiction of the lower federal courts is not so confined", and that "[t]he jurisdictional prerequisite is not the judgment of a state court but detention *simpliciter*"? What does it mean, to pass on the lawfulness of a detention *simpliciter*? How can one determine the lawfulness of a detention without considering the lawfulness of the judgment which authorized it? [4]

Notice that Justice Brennan also argues that issuing the habeas writ is less of an interference with state procedures than a direct reversal because on habeas the state court judgment stands unreversed and the federal court acts only "on the body of the petitioner". Is this persuasive? In terms of the purpose being served by the state's judgment, does it matter whether a prisoner is released as a consequence of reversal or through the issuance of the writ? And what is the effectiveness of a state procedural rule requiring a constitutional claim to be raised in a certain manner, if noncompliance with the rule does not preclude consideration of the claim on habeas? [5]

Should we conclude that it is impossible to justify the rule of Fay v. Noia by the argument that there is a logical distinction in kind between direct review and review on habeas corpus? Does not the essential instability of the distinction account for the fact that two years after Noia the availability of habeas in the face of an adequate state ground was used by Justice Brennan as an argument for widening access to direct review? See Henry v. Mississippi, p. 610, *supra*. And is this instability not evidenced by the subsequent history of the Noia rule?

---

4. Notice Justice Brennan's next sentence: "The entire course of decisions in this Court elaborating the rule of exhaustion of state remedies is wholly incompatible with the proposition that a state court *judgment* is required to confer federal habeas jurisdiction." This is a *non-sequitur*, isn't it? Of course a federal court may inquire into the lawfulness of a state arrest or detention prior to a state trial and judgment. But once the detention is justified by a judgment, how can one pass on the validity of the detention without passing on the validity of the justification?

5. But see Sofaer, Note, *Federal Habeas Corpus for State Prisoners: The Isolation Principle*, 39 N.Y.U.L.Rev. 78, 94 (1964), for the argument that the habeas court, "by acting only upon the body of the petitioner", avoids "a declaration of the rule's institutional invalidity". The same line of argument had been advanced prior to Noia in Reitz, *Federal Habeas Corpus: Impact of an Abortive State Proceeding*, 74 Harv.L. Rev. 1314, 1347–48 (1961). Much of the reasoning in Noia in fact derives from this article. See also the preview of the Noia opinion, delivered as a lecture, in Brennan, *Federal Habeas Corpus and State Prisoners: An Exercise in Federalism*, 7 Utah L.Rev. 423 (1961).

On the other hand, couldn't Fay v. Noia have been justified on the deeper basis that it is suggested by the rule of Brown v. Allen? Doesn't Brown v. Allen imply that state-court determinations are irrelevant? Given the Brown principle that any decision of the federal question by the state court will be nondispositive in any event, why should we insist that the state court defendant jump through hoops in order to obtain that nondispositive decision?

(4) As indicated in the Wainwright opinion, the erosion of Fay v. Noia began with a federal prisoner case, Davis v. United States (discussed further at p. 1584, *infra*). Francis v. Henderson then transposed the Davis standard to the case of a state prisoner; the opinion completely ignored Fay v. Noia and cast no light whatever on the question of what cases were to be governed by it and what cases would continue to be governed by Noia. The use of Davis as governing precedent (and the ignoring of Noia) in Francis was made possible by the coincidence that the Louisiana rule governing the timeliness of motions attacking the composition of the grand jury was in substance the replica of Federal Rule of Criminal Procedure 12(b)—the very rule which had been held to supersede the Noia standard in Davis. The Court in Francis was thus moved primarily by the notion that it would offend "comity and federalism" to apply to habeas a federal rule governing the timeliness of a motion and then to fail to enforce in the same terms the identical state rule. This left it unclear whether Francis had any relevance to cases where a state did not have a rule identical to a federal rule of criminal procedure. (It was also unclear whether it was essential for the application of Francis that the state's forfeiture rule be in the form of a statute or a formal court-issued rule of procedure—that is, whether a state judge-made rule of waiver could replace the Noia standard.)[6]

(5) Wainwright left "cause and prejudice" to be defined in later cases. (For a discussion of possible lines of interpretation, see Marcus, *Federal Habeas Corpus After State Court Default: A Definition of Cause and Prejudice,* 53 Ford.L.Rev. 663 (1985).) To date, the meaning of "cause" has received more attention. Engle v. Isaac, 456 U.S. 107 (1982), involved habeas petitions by prisoners who had claimed self-defense at trial and had not at that time objected to jury charges stating that the defendant bore the burden of persuasion on the self-defense issue. The Court stated that the petitioners had a colorable constitutional claim (under Mullaney v. Wilbur, 421 U.S. 684 (1975), and Patterson v. New York, 432 U.S. 197 (1977)) that the state must disprove self-defense.[7] The Court then considered whether there had been "cause" for the petitioners' failure to conform to Ohio's contemporaneous objection rule. Justice O'Connor's opinion rejected the notion that the supposed futility of raising the objection—Ohio had long required defendants to prove self-defense—constituted cause,

---

6. On the same day as the decision in Francis the Court also gave Fay v. Noia the silent treatment in Estelle v. Williams, 425 U.S. 501 (1976). Petitioner was convicted of assault with intent to murder in a Texas court, and his conviction was affirmed. On habeas he alleged that he had been compelled to stand trial in prison clothes, in violation of the due process clause. Although petitioner had asked a jailer for civilian clothes, no objection was made to the prison attire at any time in the state courts. The Supreme Court, without a single reference to Noia, held that habeas was unavailable (pp. 512–13).

7. Patterson had been held to apply retroactively in Hankerson v. North Carolina, 432 U.S. 233 (1977).

saying that "[e]ven a state court that has previously rejected a constitutional argument may decide, upon reflection, that the contention is valid" (p. 130). As to the argument that petitioners could not have known of the constitutional claim at the time of trial, before Mullaney and Patterson were decided, the Court said that In re Winship, 397 U.S. 358 (1970),[8] had laid the basis for such a claim well before the trial, and had been relied on by some lawyers making similar claims; therefore it could not be said that the petitioners had "lacked the tools to construct" a constitutional argument. Though not "every astute counsel" would have recognized in Winship the basis for a constitutional objection, "the Constitution * * * does not insure that defense counsel will recognize and raise every conceivable constitutional claim" (pp. 133–34).

(6) The Court left open in Isaac the question "whether the novelty of a constitutional claim ever establishes cause for a failure to object" (p. 131). That question was answered affirmatively in Reed v. Ross, 468 U.S. 1 (1984) (5–4), which involved the same burden of proof issue as Isaac. Ross had failed to challenge the correctness of the burden of proof instructions on appeal, thus violating a North Carolina requirement for preserving postconviction claims for relief. At the time of appeal, however, Winship had not yet been decided. Stating that "the cause requirement may be satisfied under certain circumstances when a procedural failure is not attributable to an intentional decision by counsel made in pursuit of his client's interests" (p. 14), Justice Brennan held that there was cause for the procedural default in Ross' case because at the time of appeal counsel could not reasonably have been expected to know his client had a constitutional argument. In dissent, Justice Rehnquist first questioned whether the novelty of an argument should ever be equated with cause, and then went on to argue that in any event Ross' claim was not novel, because the Winship approach had been adopted in two decisions—one state, one federal—reached some months prior to the time for Ross' appeal.

(7) In Murray v. Carrier, 477 U.S. 478 (1986), the Court refused to develop the suggestion in Ross that cause might generally be found for procedural failures not attributable to intentional decisions by counsel. In Carrier, counsel had inadvertently failed to include in the appeal from his client's rape and abduction convictions a claim that the trial court had erred by not permitting counsel to examine the victim's statements to the police. Under Virginia law, this procedural default barred state collateral review. The Court, in an opinion by Justice O'Connor that relied heavily on Engle v. Isaac, held that the default also barred federal habeas review. The Court emphasized the "considerable costs" associated with habeas review, costs which "do not disappear when the default stems from counsel's ignorance or inadvertence rather than from a deliberate decision, for whatever reason, to withhold a claim." Indeed, Justice O'Connor said, these costs would increase if procedural defaults were treated differently according to the reason for them, because "federal habeas courts would routinely be required to hold evidentiary hearings to determine what prompted counsel's failure to raise the claim in question" (p. 487). The Court then went on to hold "that the question of cause for a procedural default does not turn on whether counsel erred or on the kind of error

8. In Winship the Court had held that "the Due Process Clause protects the accused against conviction except upon proof beyond a reasonable doubt of every fact necessary to constitute the crime with which he is charged" (p. 364).

counsel may have made. So long as a defendant is represented by counsel whose performance is not constitutionally ineffective under the standard established in Strickland v. Washington [466 U.S. 668 (1984)], we discern no inequity in requiring him to bear the risk of attorney error that results in the procedural default. Instead, we think that the existence of cause for a procedural default must ordinarily turn on whether the prisoner can show that some objective factor external to the defense impeded counsel's efforts to comply with the State's procedural rule. Without attempting an exhaustive catalog * * *, we note that a showing that the factual or legal basis for a claim was not reasonably available to counsel, see Reed v. Ross * * *, or that 'some interference by officials,' Brown v. Allen, 344 U.S. [at] 486, * * * made compliance impracticable, would constitute cause under this standard.

"Similarly, if the procedural default is the result of ineffective assistance of counsel, the Sixth Amendment itself requires that responsibility for the default be imputed to the State * * *. Ineffective assistance of counsel, then, is cause for a procedural default. However, we think that the exhaustion doctrine * * * generally requires that a claim of ineffective assistance be presented to the state courts as an independent claim before it may be used to establish cause for a procedural default. [Otherwise] the federal habeas court would find itself in the anomalous position of adjudicating an unexhausted constitutional claim for which state court review might still be available * * *" (pp. 488–89).

Justice O'Connor did state, however, that "in an extraordinary case, where a constitutional violation has probably resulted in the conviction of one who is actually innocent, a federal habeas court may grant the writ even in the absence of a showing of cause for the procedural default" (p. 496).

The habeas petitioner also argued in Carrier that "cause" means something different in the case of procedural default on appeal than at trial, and that counsel's ignorance or inadvertence was cause for default occurring on appeal. The Court refused to draw any such distinction, stating that "[a] State's procedural rules serve vital purposes at trial, on appeal, and on state collateral attack. * * * [T]he standard for cause should not vary depending on the timing of a procedural default or on the strength of an uncertain and difficult assessment of the relative magnitude of the benefits attributable to the state procedural rules that attach at each successive stage of the judicial process. * * * It is apparent that the frustration of the State's interests that occurs when an appellate procedural rule is broken is not significantly diminished when counsel's breach results from ignorance or inadvertence rather than a deliberate decision * * *" (pp. 490–91).

Concurring in the result in Carrier (a remand), Justice Stevens (joined by Justice Blackmun) stated that the majority's "'cause and prejudice' formula * * * is not dispositive when the fundamental fairness of a prisoner's conviction is at issue. That formula is of recent vintage, particularly in comparison to the writ for which it is invoked. It is, at most, part of a broader inquiry into the demands of justice" (p. 501). According to Justice Stevens, this inquiry "requires a consideration, not only of the nature and strength of the constitutional claim, but also of the nature and strength of the state procedural rule that has not been observed" (p. 506).

And "with an appellate default, the state interest in procedural rigor is weaker than at trial, and the transcendence of the Great Writ is correspondingly clearer" (p. 507). Justice Stevens found Reed v. Ross of assistance in applying his balancing test: "[i]f the state's interest in the finality of its judgment is not sufficient to defeat a meritorious federal claim that was not raised on appeal because the prisoner's lawyer did not have the ability to anticipate a later development in the law, there is no reason why the same state interest should defeat a meritorious federal claim simply because the prisoner's lawyer did not exercise due care in prosecuting an appeal" (pp. 514–15).

Justices Brennan and Marshall, in dissent, repeated the assertion that Wainwright was wrong in abandoning Fay v. Noia's "deliberate bypass" standard. They went on to argue that, even under Wainwright, and balancing the state's and the litigant's interests, counsel's inadvertent default constituted cause. The state's interest "in maintaining the integrity of its rules and proceedings" is weaker in the case of inadvertent default than in the case of a tactical decision to bypass a state procedure. As Justice Brennan explained, "[w]here counsel is unaware of a claim or of the duty to raise it at a particular time, the procedural default rule cannot operate as a specific deterrent to noncompliance with the State's procedural rules. Consequently, the State's interest in ensuring that the federal court help prevent circumvention of the State's procedural rules by imposing the same forfeiture sanction is much less compelling [and] simply is not sufficient to overcome the heavy presumption against a federal court's refusing to exercise jurisdiction clearly granted by Congress" (p. 524).[9]

Cf. Taylor v. Illinois, 108 S.Ct. 646, 664–66 (1988), where Justice Brennan said in dissent that counsel's failure to disclose (in response to a discovery request) the names of defense witnesses should not have the consequence of prohibiting the testimony of the witnesses whose names had been omitted. Sanctioning the defendant for attorney misconduct, he said, was both unfair and less effective in deterring violations than a direct sanction against the attorney. The majority disagreed, but did note that there are some rights—to trial, to jury trial, to be present during trial—that can be waived only by the defendant personally. *Id.* at 657 n. 24.

(8) Applying Carrier in a case decided the same day, Smith v. Murray, 477 U.S. 527 (1986), the Court held that the petitioner had not shown cause where his counsel had deliberately not pressed a constitutional claim because he thought it unlikely to succeed. The issue in Smith was sharpened because the state courts had later accepted the claim counsel had predicted would fail, and because the alleged constitutional error—the

---

9. Justice Brennan also criticized the majority's identification of the costs of habeas review after procedural default, especially the "reduction in the finality of litigation." He said that "'finality' concerns have no bearing on the question whether a federal court should refuse to exercise its habeas jurisdiction because of a procedural default. From the standpoint of the State's finality interests, there is no difference whatever between making habeas review available after the state court has denied a claim on the merits, and making such review available after the state court has denied the claim on procedural default grounds. In both situations, the State has determined that the litigation is at an end * * *. No one questions the availability of habeas relief where the state court has denied the claim on the merits. Accordingly, treating likes alike, such relief should also be available where the claim is denied because of procedural default unless the State's interest in enforcing its procedural default rules requires a different result" (p. 520, n. 2) (emphasis omitted).

admission of testimony about petitioner's past conduct—occurred at a sentencing hearing at which the petitioner had been sentenced to death. The minority argued that in capital cases failure to reach the constitutional question was so prejudicial that any colorable constitutional claim should be entertained on habeas. But Justice O'Connor, for a bare majority, "reject[ed] the suggestion that the principles of Wainwright v. Sykes apply differently depending on the nature of the penalty a State imposes for the violation of its criminal laws." And finding no indication that petitioner had been improperly sentenced as a result of the alleged error, she did not "believe that refusal to consider the defaulted claim on federal habeas carries with it the risk of a manifest miscarriage of justice" (p. 538).

Four Justices dissented, with Justices Brennan and Stevens each writing an opinion based on the analysis in their respective separate opinions in Carrier. Both dissents urged that greater forgiveness of defaults is required in a capital case.[10]

(9) The major case in which the Supreme Court has discussed the meaning of "prejudice" is United States v. Frady, 456 U.S. 152 (1982), which involved a § 2255 motion by a federal prisoner. It is discussed in Section 3, p. 1584, *infra,* dealing with collateral relief for federal prisoners.

(10) Does the Fay v. Noia deliberate bypass standard retain any vitality after the recent cases on cause and prejudice? Note that in Murray v. Carrier, while the majority held that "counsel's failure to raise a *particular* claim or claims on appeal is to be scrutinized under the cause and prejudice standard," it expressed "no opinion as to whether counsel's decision not to take an appeal at all might require treatment under" Noia's deliberate bypass standard (p. 492).

(11) What is the relationship of the "cause and prejudice" test to the test of "adequacy" of state procedural grounds on direct review? The Court's cases have not explicitly reconstructed the bridge between standards of forfeiture for direct review cases and collateral attack cases that had been so radically severed in Noia. (For arguments why it should do so, see Meltzer, *State Court Forfeitures of Federal Rights,* 99 Harv.L.Rev. 1130 (1986).) Does the cause and prejudice test in effect do so? Recall in this connection that Wainwright involved the same kind of "contemporaneous objection" rule at issue in Henry v. Mississippi. Is Wainwright more or less stringent in enforcing a rule of forfeiture than Henry?

Suppose a state criminal defendant fails to comply with a state procedural rule under circumstances where the default would not bar direct review, because the rule (on its face or in its application in this case) would be deemed "inadequate." Would it be tolerable to hold that there was insufficient "cause" or "prejudice" and that the same default therefore barred habeas corpus? *Per contra,* if noncompliance with a state procedural rule would bar direct review because the state judgment rested on an

---

10. As this book went to press, the Supreme Court heard argument in another capital case involving the meaning of "cause." In Amadeo v. Kemp, 816 F.2d 1502 (11th Cir. 1987), cert. granted, 108 S.Ct. 257 (1987), the district court had held the petitioner had cause for not raising at trial his claim of discrimination in drawing up the master jury list, because county officials had concealed a memorandum evidencing the discrimination. The Eleventh Circuit reversed on the ground that counsel would readily have discovered the memorandum had they not decided for tactical reasons to forego review of the jury lists.

"adequate" ground, should we at the same time conclude that there was good "cause" for the noncompliance for purposes of habeas review?

(12) It is evident that a majority of the Court is extremely concerned about the heavy burdens imposed on the effective administration of criminal justice, and on the ideals of federalism, by a system that allows easy access to repetitious proceedings through collateral federal review. It is equally evident that the Court is relying, almost exclusively, on a harsh system of forfeitures in order to give expression to these concerns. Is this an intelligent choice of techniques? Is the elaboration of an exquisitely detailed set of standards for what constitutes "cause" and "prejudice" a sensible way to limit the reach of federal habeas corpus? Shouldn't the Court return to fundamentals rather than further embroider the aridities of "cause"? If the Court thinks that repetitious review imposes intolerable burdens on the federal system and on the criminal justice system, why doesn't it worry more about federal review of cases where the defendant *did* get a full and fair state-court hearing on the merits of his federal claim, rather than cases where he didn't? Why doesn't it focus on the question of the reach of Brown v. Allen, rather than the question whether we have been too lax in administering our system of forfeitures?

(13) What should be the relationship between the standards for forgiving procedural defaults (on federal issues) applied by the federal courts, on direct or collateral review of state court convictions, and those applied by the state courts in the first instance? In Noia, the Court stated that a federal court's refusal to give effect to a state court forfeiture did not bar the state from enforcing the underlying procedural requirement in the future. The regime thus created, the Court contended, had two advantages: (i) it minimized federal interference with the state courts; and (ii) under the deliberate bypass standard, it ensured virtually every criminal defendant an ultimate federal adjudication of his federal constitutional claims—even claims not properly raised in state court. See also the articles by Reitz and Sofaer, note 5, *supra*.

These contentions are challenged in Meltzer, Paragraph (11), *supra*. On the first point, he notes that there is often considerable pressure on states to hear claims that will ultimately be heard by a federal habeas court; his review of state decisions shows that during Noia's ascendency, many (though not all) states did relax their rules for just this reason. On the second point, he notes that the habeas corpus jurisdiction does not effectively guarantee a federal forum for review of forfeited federal claims: many convicted defendants will not be in custody by the time state remedies are exhausted; others will simply fail to seek relief; and any relief will come only after months or years of confinement.

Meltzer argues that the rules that permit a defendant to have a federal court hear the merits of his federal constitutional claim, notwithstanding noncompliance with state procedural requirements, should be characterized as rules of federal common law. As such, they should be binding on the states, like other forms of federal common law, with the states bound to forgive any defaults that would not block direct or collateral review in federal court. "[I]f the state's interest in imposing a forfeiture * * * is not sufficiently weighty to bar the Supreme Court or a federal habeas court from reviewing the federal issue, that interest is also not weighty enough to bar review of the federal issue in state court in the first instance" (pp.

1189–90). Meltzer then proceeds to argue for more forgiveness of defaults than is provided under the cause and prejudice test.

Compare Brilmayer, *State Forfeiture Rules and Federal Review of State Criminal Convictions,* 49 U.Chi.L.Rev. 741 (1982) (state law governs the validity of forfeitures in state courts and on direct review in the Supreme Court; but the grant of habeas jurisdiction authorizes federal habeas courts to develop rules relieving prisoners of state court forfeitures); for a critical response, see Meltzer, *supra,* at 1146 n. 90, 1196–1202 & n. 369.

(14) None of the recent developments in the law of forfeitures has affected the traditional rule, that if the state courts overlook procedural default and reach the merits of the federal claim, the federal courts on habeas have jurisdiction in turn to consider the claim. This settled doctrine was reaffirmed in Warden v. Hayden, 387 U.S. 294, 297 n. 3 (1967).

(15) For discussions of the application of the Noia "waiver" test, see White, *Federal Habeas Corpus: The Impact of the Failure to Assert a Constitutional Claim at Trial,* 58 Va.L.Rev. 67 (1972); Wright & Sofaer, *Federal Habeas Corpus for State Prisoners: The Allocation of Fact–Finding Responsibility,* 75 Yale L.J. 895, 960–79 (1966). For comment on the general situation created by Wainwright, see Cover & Aleinikoff, p. 1522, *supra;* Hill, *The Forfeiture of Constitutional Rights in Criminal Cases,* 78 Colum.L.Rev. 1050 (1978); Spritzer, *Criminal Waiver, Procedural Default, and the Burger Court,* 126 U.Pa.L.Rev. 473 (1978); Guttenberg, *Federal Habeas Corpus, Constitutional Rights, and Procedural Forfeitures: The Delicate Balance,* 12 Hofstra L.Rev. 617 (1984); Note, 85 Mich.L.Rev. 1393 (1985).

NOTE ON EXHAUSTION OF STATE COURT REMEDIES AND ON THE STATES' OBLIGATION TO PROVIDE THEM

(1) The requirement that state prisoners exhaust state court remedies before resorting to federal habeas corpus [1] derives from Ex parte Royall, 117 U.S. 241 (1886). The petitioner had been indicted for violation of a Virginia statute and was detained awaiting trial. Alleging that this statute was unconstitutional, he sought habeas corpus in the federal district court, which dismissed the writ.[2] On appeal the Supreme Court affirmed: though the district court has power in advance of trial to inquire into the allegation, it need not and should not do so pending consideration of the question in the normal course of trial by the state court. The Court said (p. 251): "We cannot suppose that Congress intended to compel * * * [the federal] courts * * * to draw to themselves, in the first instance, the control of all criminal prosecutions commenced in State courts * * *. The injunction to hear the case summarily, and thereupon 'to dispose of the party as law and justice require' does not deprive the court of discretion as

1. See generally Yackle, *The Exhaustion Doctrine in Federal Habeas Corpus: An Argument for a Return to First Principles,* 44 Ohio St.L.J. 393 (1983); Amsterdam, *Criminal Prosecutions Affecting Federally Guaranteed Civil Rights: Federal Removal and Habeas Corpus Jurisdiction to Abort State Court Trial,* 113 U.Pa.L.Rev. 793, 884–96 (1965); 17 Federal Practice

§ 4264. See also Comment, 50 U.Chi.L. Rev. 354 (1983).

2. Note that the issue presented for decision in Royall, the constitutionality of the Virginia statute, was deemed cognizable on habeas corpus as "jurisdictional" under the doctrine of Ex parte Siebold, pp. 1490, 1494, *supra.*

to the time and mode in which it will exert the powers conferred upon it. That discretion should be exercised in the light of the relations existing, under our system of government, between the judicial tribunals of the Union and of the States, and in recognition of the fact that the public good requires that those relations be not disturbed by unnecessary conflict between courts equally bound to guard and protect rights secured by the Constitution."

The Court subsequently made it clear that the references in Royall to the trial court's "discretion" were not to be taken seriously; it routinely reversed grants of the writ prior to exhaustion of state remedies where no special circumstances were present.[3]

Cases following Royall held that habeas corpus should be denied while a prisoner seeks to vindicate his federal rights in the state appellate courts[4] and through state postconviction procedures.[5] And still another line of cases established that even after all state remedies were exhausted, habeas corpus should be denied and the prisoner put to his writ of error in the United States Supreme Court.[6]

See also Mooney v. Holohan, p. 1501, *supra.*

In a well known per curiam opinion in Ex parte Hawk, 321 U.S. 114 (1944), the Court stated the doctrine as follows (pp. 116–18):

"Ordinarily an application for habeas corpus by one detained under a state court judgment of conviction for crime will be entertained by a federal court only after all state remedies available, including all appellate remedies in the state courts and in this Court by appeal or writ of certiorari, have been exhausted. * * * And where those remedies have been exhausted this Court will not ordinarily entertain an application for the writ before it has been sought and denied in a district court or denied by a circuit or district judge. * * *

"Where the state courts have considered and adjudicated the merits of his contentions, and this Court has either reviewed or declined to review the state court's decision, a federal court will not ordinarily re-examine upon writ of habeas corpus the questions thus adjudicated. Salinger v. Loisel, 265 U.S. 224, 230–32. But where resort to state court remedies has failed to afford a full and fair adjudication of the federal contentions raised, either because the state affords no remedy, see Mooney v. Holohan, *supra,* or because in the particular case the remedy afforded by state law proves in practice unavailable or seriously inadequate, *cf.* Moore v. Dempsey, 261 U.S. 86; Ex parte Davis, 318 U.S. 412, a federal court should entertain his petition for habeas corpus, else he would be remediless. In such a case he should proceed in the federal district court before resorting to this Court by petition for habeas corpus."[7]

3. See, *e.g.,* New York v. Eno, 155 U.S. 89 (1894); Baker v. Grice, 169 U.S. 284 (1898); Fitts v. McGhee, 172 U.S. 516 (1899); Minnesota v. Brundage, 180 U.S. 499 (1901); Urquhart v. Brown, 205 U.S. 179 (1907).

4. Ex parte Fonda, 117 U.S. 516 (1886); In re Duncan, 139 U.S. 449 (1891); Minnesota v. Brundage, 180 U.S. 499 (1901); Reid v. Jones, 187 U.S. 153 (1902).

5. Pepke v. Cronan, 155 U.S. 100 (1894).

6. In re Frederich, 149 U.S. 70 (1893); Bergemann v. Backer, 157 U.S. 655 (1895); Tinsley v. Anderson, 171 U.S. 101 (1898); Markuson v. Boucher, 175 U.S. 184 (1899); Urquhart v. Brown, 205 U.S. 179 (1907).

7. For other cases dealing with the requirement in the period preceding Brown v. Allen, see, *e.g.,* Ex parte Botwinski, 314 U.S. 586 (1942); Ex parte Davis, 317 U.S. 592 (1942); Ex parte Abernathy, 320 U.S. 219 (1943); Marino v. Ragen, 332 U.S. 561 (1947); Young v. Ragen, 337 U.S. 235

(2) In 1948 Congress codified some aspects of the exhaustion rule in 28 U.S.C. § 2254(b) and (c). For an account of the legislative history, see the opinion of Justice Reed in Brown v. Allen, 344 U.S. at 447–50; the Court relied on this history in holding that, in spite of the language of 2254(c), if the federal question has been fully and properly presented in the state appellate proceedings, "[i]t is not necessary * * * for the prisoner to ask the state for collateral relief, based on the same evidence and issues already decided by direct review * * *." Nor need a prisoner resubmit his federal contention to the state courts even though there has been some change in state law that suggests a second attempt would be successful. Francisco v. Gathright, 419 U.S. 59 (1974); Roberts v. LaVallee, 389 U.S. 40 (1967).[8] If the claim is properly presented to the state court, state remedies are exhausted even if the claim is ignored in the state court's opinion. Smith v. Digmon, 434 U.S. 332 (1978).

On the other hand, Picard v. Connor, 404 U.S. 270 (1971), reaffirmed the principle that the exhaustion requirement is satisfied only where the prisoner has presented the *same* claim he is now urging on habeas: "[t]he rule would serve no purpose if it could be satisfied by raising one claim in the state courts and another in the federal courts" (p. 276). See also Anderson v. Harless, 459 U.S. 4, 7 n. 3 (1982) (exhaustion requirement not satisfied by presenting federal claim to state court by citing a state court decision, predicated on state law, in which another defendant had advanced the federal claim). *Cf.* Vasquez v. Hillery, p. 1476, *supra* (holding that the relevant claim had been presented to state court, though district court hearing the habeas petition had exercised its power to require the parties to provide supplemental evidence consisting of affidavits and computer analysis; new evidence "did not fundamentally alter the legal claim already considered by the state courts").

As the statute makes clear, resort to state remedies is not required where a state remedy is not available at all—either generally or for the particular prisoner; or when the remedy is unduly burdensome or ineffective; or where resort to the state courts would clearly be futile. See, *e.g.,* Wilwording v. Swenson, 404 U.S. 249 (1971); and see generally the authorities cited in 17 Federal Practice § 4264.

(3) Most circuits had ruled that a petitioner could obtain a federal decision on an exhausted claim, even though it was asserted in a petition that also included unexhausted claims. The Supreme Court rejected this position, however, in Rose v. Lundy, 455 U.S. 509 (1982), adopting a "total exhaustion" requirement for such mixed petitions for reasons of comity. Writing for the majority, Justice O'Connor said that "[a] rigorously enforced total exhaustion rule will encourage state prisoners to seek full relief first from the state courts, thus giving those courts the first opportunity to review all claims of constitutional error. As the number of prisoners who exhaust all of their federal claims increases, state courts

_____

(1949); Dowd v. United States ex rel. Cook, 340 U.S. 206 (1951); Jennings v. Illinois, 342 U.S. 104 (1951).

8. *Cf.* Pitchess v. Davis, 421 U.S. 482 (1975) (application to state court for extraordinary writ of prohibition on a question which can be raised in the ordinary course of state proceedings does not consti-

tute adequate exhaustion); Mabry v. Klimas, 448 U.S. 444 (1980) (prisoner could not raise for first time on habeas his claim that he was entitled to be resentenced because of amendment to state recidivist statute; state courts had to be given an opportunity to interpret the statute).

may become increasingly familiar with and hospitable toward federal constitutional issues. * * * Equally as important, federal claims will more often be accompanied by a complete factual record to aid the federal courts in their review" (pp. 518–19).

According to six of the Justices, under the total exhaustion rule a district court is required to dismiss mixed habeas petitions (p. 522). This leaves the petitioner the choice of returning to state court to exhaust all his claims, or amending his petition to proceed only with his exhausted claims, in which case (according to four Justices) he risks dismissal on grounds of abuse of the writ of any subsequent petition that raises his previously unexhausted claims (pp. 520–21). Justice Blackmun, concurring, believed that the appropriate order in the case of a mixed petition was to dismiss only the unexhausted claims, not the entire petition. He warned that, otherwise, the total exhaustion rule would "operate[ ] as a trap for the uneducated and indigent pro se prisoner-applicant" (p. 522), who "will consolidate all conceivable grounds for relief in an attempt to accelerate review and minimize costs. But, under the Court's approach, if he unwittingly includes in a § 2254 motion a claim not yet presented to the state courts, he risks dismissal of the entire petition and substantial delay before a ruling on the merits of his exhausted claims" (p. 530).

(4) Despite the omission from § 2254(b) and (c) of any reference to a requirement that habeas be preceded by an application to the Supreme Court for direct review of the state court determination, Darr v. Burford, 339 U.S. 200 (1950), reaffirmed the existence of such a requirement, relying in part on the reviser's note that the "new section is declaratory of existing law as affirmed by the Supreme Court. See Ex parte Hawk, 1944, 321 U.S. 114." The Hawk per curiam, see Paragraph (1), *supra,* had referred to the requirement, but the problem had given the Court considerable difficulty. See, *e.g.,* White v. Ragen, 324 U.S. 760 (1945); Wade v. Mayo, 334 U.S. 672 (1948). Darr v. Burford was overruled in Fay v. Noia, 372 U.S. at 435–38, on the ground that the statute specifically required only that a petitioner exhaust "remedies available in the courts of the *State.*" See also Ulster County Court v. Allen, 442 U.S. 140, 149 n. 7 (1979) (rejecting, for the same reason, an argument that habeas corpus review was unavailable prior to an appeal to the Supreme Court under 28 U.S.C. § 1257(2)).

(5) Two empirical studies have shown that failure to exhaust state remedies is a major obstacle to adjudication of habeas petitions on the merits. In a study of Massachusetts habeas cases, Professor Shapiro found that 135 out of 257 petitions filed in a three-year period were dismissed wholly or in part on exhaustion grounds. Concluding that the system was not functioning well, he recommended several changes in law and practice, including a proposal that states limit the time available for their post-conviction processes, and a proposal that plainly unmeritorious petitions not be dismissed for lack of exhaustion. Shapiro, *Federal Habeas Corpus: A Study in Massachusetts,* 87 Harv.L.Rev. 321 (1973). A later study found that of 1899 petitions filed in six district courts and one court of appeals between 1975 and 1977, 37 per cent were denied for failure to exhaust state remedies. Allen, Schachtman & Wilson, *Federal Habeas Corpus and its Reform: An Empirical Analysis,* 13 Rutgers L.J. 675 (1982).

One of Shapiro's proposals has recently been adopted in part. In Granberry v. Greer, 107 S.Ct. 1671 (1987), a unanimous Court held that when a petitioner filed an unexhausted claim, but the state failed to raise its exhaustion defense in the district court, the court hearing the petitioner's appeal was not required to treat the state's omission as a definitive waiver precluding the state from raising the issue on appeal. Nor must the court dismiss the petition for failure to exhaust. Pointing out that it is well established that the exhaustion doctrine is not jurisdictional, see Strickland v. Washington, 466 U.S. 668, 684 (1984), the Court stated in Granberry that "[a]lthough there is a strong presumption in favor of requiring the prisoner to pursue his available state remedies, his failure to do so is not an absolute bar to appellate consideration of his claims. * * * [I]t seems unwise to adopt a rule that would permit, and might even encourage, the State to seek a favorable ruling on the merits in the district court while holding the exhaustion defense in reserve for use on appeal if necessary. If the habeas petition is meritorious, such a rule would prolong the prisoner's confinement for no other reason than the State's postponement of the exhaustion defense to the appellate level. Moreover, if the court of appeals is convinced that the petition has no merit, a belated application of the exhaustion rule might simply require useless litigation in the state courts." Where the state has failed to raise its exhaustion defense in the district court, the court of appeals "should determine whether the interests of comity and federalism will be better served by addressing the merits forthwith or by requiring a series of additional state and district court proceedings before reviewing the merits of the petitioner's claim. * * * [I]f it is perfectly clear that the applicant does not raise even a colorable federal claim, the interests of the petitioner, the warden, the state attorney general, the state courts, and the federal courts will all be well served even if the State fails to raise the exhaustion defense, the district court denies the habeas petition, and the court of appeals affirms the judgment of the district court forthwith." Similarly, the nonexhaustion defense may be held waived "if a full trial has been held in the district court and it is evident that a miscarriage of justice has occurred" (pp. 1674–76).

Granberry involved the exhaustion defense raised for the first time in the court of appeals. Does it have any application in the district courts? Suppose the state fails to raise the issue in the district court, but the court raises it of its own motion. If it is clear that the petitioner has no colorable federal claim, must the district court dismiss and return the petitioner to the state courts, or may it exercise discretion to decide whether the administration of justice would be better served by reaching the merits (in which case the petition will usually be denied on the merits in order to prevent "useless litigation in the state courts")? See Plunkett v. Johnson, 828 F.2d 954 (2d Cir.1987) (divided court applied Granberry's reasoning to require district courts to exercise their discretion in this situation to determine what effect to give the state's waiver).

On waiver of the exhaustion defense, see generally Comment, 50 U.Chi.L.Rev. 354 (1983); Note, 52 Geo.Wash.L.Rev. 419 (1984); Note, 97 Harv.L.Rev. 511 (1983).

(6) The requirement of exhaustion has led to some celebrated procedural tangles, particularly in the period of the 40's. The Hawk case is a cautionary tale:

The petitioner was sentenced to life imprisonment for murder in 1936, the sentence to begin upon completion of a prior federal sentence. He filed a petition for habeas corpus in the state court, apparently attacking the validity of the sentence. The petition was denied without a hearing on the ground that it did not state a case for release. Hawk v. O'Grady, 137 Neb. 639 (1940), cert. denied, 311 U.S. 645 (1940). He then filed a petition in the federal district court which was denied without a hearing, the circuit court of appeals affirming on the ground that he had not exhausted his state remedies on the new points raised in the petition. Hawk v. Olson, 130 F.2d 910 (8th Cir.1942), cert. denied, 317 U.S. 697 (1943). A second state petition was then denied without a hearing or opinion, and in Ex parte Hawk, 318 U.S. 746 (1943), the Court denied a motion for leave to file without prejudice to application in the district court. Such application was then made and denied, and, leave to appeal being denied, Hawk moved again for leave to file in the Supreme Court. Leave was again denied in Ex parte Hawk, 321 U.S. 114 (1944), on the ground that he had still not exhausted state remedies because on the points made in this petition he had applied for state habeas only in the state Supreme Court, not a district court, and also had not invoked coram nobis. He then filed a petition for habeas in a state district court which denied relief without a hearing and was sustained on appeal. Hawk v. Olson, 145 Neb. 306 (1944). The Supreme Court granted certiorari and reversed, hold that the petition stated a case for relief, entitling the petitioner to a hearing. Hawk v. Olson, 326 U.S. 271 (1945). A motion to enforce the mandate was, however, denied by the state court on the ground that habeas was not a proper remedy unless a judgment was absolutely void. Hawk v. Olson, 146 Neb. 875 (1946). An application was then made for federal habeas and denied upon the ground that petitioner must first apply for coram nobis in the state courts. Hawk v. Olson, 66 F.Supp. 195 (D.Neb.1946), aff'd sub nom. Hawk v. Jones, 160 F.2d 807 (8th Cir.1947), cert. denied, 332 U.S. 779 (1947). When, thereafter, he applied for coram nobis the state courts denied relief, partly on the ground that his rights were not infringed, partly in the view that the points made were lost by the original failure to appeal. Hawk v. State, 151 Neb. 717 (1949), cert. denied, 339 U.S. 923 (1950). In Hawk v. Hann, 103 F.Supp. 138 (D.Neb.1952), the district court concluded: "Indubitably no further remedies are available to petitioner in the courts of the state of Nebraska" (103 F.Supp. at 140). After a hearing on the writ the court concluded that denial of due process at the trial was established and it ordered Hawk's discharge.[9]

(7) In the Royall case Justice Harlan stated that the discretion to withhold jurisdiction on habeas is "to be subordinated to any special circumstances requiring immediate action" (p. 253), and suggested that federal interference prior to exhaustion of state remedies might be justified in "cases of urgency, involving the authority and operations of the General Government, or the obligations of this country to, or its relations with, foreign nations" (p. 251).

9. For the story of the "Illinois merry-go-round," involving repeated attempts by a baffled Supreme Court to deal with the complexities of the Illinois remedial law, see White v. Ragen, 324 U.S. 760 (1945); Woods v. Nierstheimer, 328 U.S. 211 (1946); Marino v. Ragen, 332 U.S. 561 (1947); Loftus v. Illinois, 334 U.S. 804 (1948); Young v. Ragen, 337 U.S. 235 (1949); and Jennings v. Illinois, 342 U.S. 104 (1951).

Under this standard, determination of the federal claim on habeas was deemed appropriate before trial in Wildenhus Case, 120 U.S. 1 (1887) (state indictment of foreign seaman for crime on vessel in port urged to contravene treaty); In re Neagle, 135 U.S. 1 (1890) (state indictment of federal deputy marshal for murder; claim that homicide was in justifiable performance of his duty to defend Justice Field); In re Loney, 134 U.S. 372 (1890) (state indictment for perjury in making deposition before notary for transmittal to House of Representatives in connection with election contest; claimed to infringe exclusive federal jurisdiction). But *cf.* Drury v. Lewis, 200 U.S. 1 (1906) (state indictment of military officer for murder; claim that homicide was committed in course of duty; evidence conflicting; circuit court "properly exercised" discretion not to intervene).

The federal claim was entertained and determined after trial and judgment in Ohio v. Thomas, 173 U.S. 276 (1899) (prosecution of governor of soldiers' home for serving oleomargarine without notice required by state statute; application of statute held interference with performance of federal function); Boske v. Comingore, 177 U.S. 459 (1900) (Collector of Internal Revenue committed for contempt of state court for refusing to produce copies of reports filed with Treasury pursuant to regulation of Secretary forbidding disclosure); Hunter v. Wood, 209 U.S. 205 (1908) (railroad ticket agent convicted of violating rate statute after federal interlocutory injunction restraining its enforcement). See generally Amsterdam, note 1, *supra,* at 892–99.

In such cases it seems clear that intervention before trial on habeas is still permissible, though the broad provision for removal of state prosecutions of federal officials [28 U.S.C. §§ 1442(a)(1), (3), (4), see p. 1057, *supra*] may provide ground in some cases for declining to grant the writ. Indeed, 28 U.S.C. § 2254 was amended in the course of its enactment to limit its exhaustion requirement to cases of custody pursuant to a "judgment of a state court," excluding language that would have applied it also to custody pursuant to "authority of a State officer." See H.R. 7124, 79th Cong., 2d Sess. 138 (1948). But is intervention after judgment now precluded by § 2254? Are these cases where state corrective process is "ineffective to protect the rights of the prisoner"? Should § 2254 have been made inapplicable to cases where habeas is sought under 28 U.S.C. § 2241(c)(2) and (c)(4)?

For a powerful argument that federal habeas corpus should be available prior to state trial whenever the prospective state defendant makes a "colorable showing that the conduct for which he is prosecuted was conduct protected by the federal constitutional guarantees of civil rights," see Amsterdam, *supra* note 1. *Cf.* In re Shuttlesworth, 369 U.S. 35 (1962), discussed by Amsterdam at 895–96, where the Court appears to have held that habeas corpus should be available in advance of state appeal where the shortness of the sentence might moot the case (which raised substantial equal protection issues).

(8) In Braden v. 30th Judicial Circuit Court, 410 U.S. 484 (1973), p. 1473, *supra,* a major issue was whether petitioner was barred by the exhaustion requirement. The Court held that habeas was now available: "It is true, of course, that he has not yet been tried on the Kentucky indictment, and he can assert a speedy trial defense when, and if, he is finally brought to trial. It is also true, as our Brother Rehnquist points out

in dissent, that federal habeas corpus does not lie, absent 'special circumstances,' to adjudicate the merits of an affirmative defense to a state criminal charge prior to a judgment of conviction by a state court. Ex parte Royall, 117 U.S. 241, 253 (1886). Petitioner does not, however, seek at this time to litigate a federal defense to a criminal charge, but only to demand enforcement of the Commonwealth's affirmative constitutional obligation to bring him promptly to trial. * * * He has made repeated demands for trial to the courts of Kentucky * * *. Under these circumstances it is clear that he has exhausted all available state court remedies for consideration of that constitutional claim. * * * He has already presented his federal constitutional claim of a *present* denial of a speedy trial to the courts of Kentucky. The state courts rejected the claim, apparently on the ground that since he had once escaped from custody the Commonwealth should not be obligated to incur the risk of another escape by returning him for trial. * * * Moreover, petitioner made no effort to abort a state proceeding or to disrupt the orderly functioning of state judicial processes. He comes to federal court, not in an effort to forestall a state prosecution, but to enforce the Commonwealth's obligation to provide him with a state court forum" (pp. 489–91).

Does Braden make pre-trial habeas automatically available to test the right to a speedy trial? The courts of appeals have not so held. See, *e.g.*, Atkins v. Michigan, 644 F.2d 543 (6th Cir.1981); Brown v. Estelle, 530 F.2d 1280 (5th Cir.1976); Moore v. DeYoung, 515 F.2d 437 (3d Cir.1975) (each distinguishing Braden). See also Note, 1977 Duke L.J. 707.

What about a pre-trial claim of double jeopardy? In Justices of Boston Municipal Court v. Lydon, 466 U.S. 294 (1984), a defendant had elected a bench trial in Municipal Court, from which there was no appeal, but after which he had an absolute right to a trial de novo before a jury. After conviction in the bench trial, the defendant first requested a trial de novo, and then sought dismissal of the charge, arguing that a new jury trial would violate the Double Jeopardy Clause absent some prior determination that the evidence at the first trial was sufficient to sustain a conviction. Having exhausted state remedies on the double jeopardy claim, the defendant sought habeas review. Ruling against petitioner on the merits, the Court held that the petitioner had met the exhaustion requirement, citing "the unique nature of the double jeopardy right." Justice White reasoned that this "right cannot be fully vindicated on appeal following final judgment, since in part the Double Jeopardy Clause protects 'against being twice put to *trial* for the same offense'" (pp. 302–03).

(9) The exhaustion rule places a requirement on the habeas corpus petitioner. For a discussion of the converse question—whether the constitution imposes a "duty" on the states to provide post-conviction remedies for the litigation of federal constitutional rights, see Chap. V, Sec. 2(a), p. 589, *supra*.

In view of the rule of Brown v. Allen, would it make sense at the present time to impose such a duty? Why should the states be required to create special remedies for the litigation of federal claims if those claims are in any event going to be relitigated in a federal district court? Whatever the duty, should it not in any event be allowed to remain inchoate until such time as the federal courts are unavailable to hear such claims? Indeed, is this not the explanation for the fact that, although there are cases which talk about the existence of such a duty, the operative remedy for the failure of a state to provide post-conviction process has always been assumed to be federal habeas corpus? See p. 589, *supra.*

Note that the same kinds of questions can be raised in connection with the issue of desirable directions for state law reform. The habeas corpus literature is full of repeated suggestions that the states expand the availability of their collateral remedies in order to assure that all federal claims be fully heard in the state courts.[10] Is the suggestion sensible? See generally the interesting discussion in Note, *State Court Withdrawal From Habeas Corpus,* 114 U.Pa.L.Rev. 1081 (1966); see also Friendly, p. 1487, *supra,* at 167–69.[11]

(10) In connection with the issues just discussed, consider the relevance of the scattering of cases holding that where a federal habeas corpus court finds that a state court has resolved a federal claim under an erroneous standard or through impermissible procedures, the proper remedy is, not for the federal court to decide the federal question on the merits, but to grant the writ subject to a new and proper adjudication of the federal question by the *state* court. See, *e.g.,* Rogers v. Richmond, 365 U.S. 534 (1961) (state trial judge's use of improper legal standard in testing voluntariness of confession may have "tainted" his findings of fact on that issue; however, federal court is not to decide this issue itself; writ granted and prisoner ordered released subject to state's right to retry him); Jackson v. Denno, 378 U.S. 368 (1964) (state may not leave the issue of the voluntariness of a confession to the jury trying guilt; petitioner must be released subject to state's right to retry him or to hold a hearing (before a judge) limited to issue of voluntariness, with release to be ordered if judge finds the confession coerced); Pate v. Robinson, 383 U.S. 375 (1966) (hearing in state court on issue of petitioner's competency to stand trial inadequate; writ will issue subject to state's right to retry him).

By what criteria should it be determined whether the habeas court should proceed to decide the underlying federal question, or should resort to the alternative of having the question decided anew in the state court? If the latter alternative is chosen, and after the state retrial or rehearing is completed, is the underlying federal claim cognizable anew on federal habeas corpus? Presumably the answer is yes. On this new collateral inquiry, does the federal judge still have plenary power to retry all the facts? Presumably yes.

Does all of this make sense?

---

10. See, *e.g.,* Brennan, *Some Aspects of Federalism,* 39 N.Y.U.L.Rev. 945 (1964). For a survey of state post-conviction procedures, see Yackle, Postconviction Remedies, Chap. 1 (1981 & 1987 Supp.).

11. Compare the suggestion that Congress create uniform procedural rules for the presentation of federal constitutional claims in state criminal proceedings, and that it also create a uniform federal post-conviction proceeding for such claims *to be brought and determined in the state courts.* All these state determinations would then be reviewed by a new, single nationwide federal appellate tribunal, rather than on habeas in the district courts. Mayers, *Federal Review of State Convictions: The Need for Procedural Reappraisal,* 34 Geo.Wash. L.Rev. 615 (1966).

NOTE ON RELITIGATING THE FACTS ON HABEAS CORPUS; HEREIN ALSO OF SECOND AND SUBSEQUENT APPLICATIONS

(1) Both Justices Reed and Frankfurter, in their opinions for the Court in Brown v. Allen, stated that a habeas court might sometimes be obligated to conduct a hearing. If there were "unusual circumstances" (Reed) or a "vital flaw" (Frankfurter) in the state proceedings, a hearing was mandatory; otherwise the habeas court had discretion whether to hold a hearing (pp. 463–64; 507).

In Townsend v. Sain, 372 U.S. 293 (1963), the Court transformed these generalities into a detailed code specifying when a hearing must be held. Here the habeas petitioner alleged that his confession had been coerced because it had been caused by his injection with a supposed "truth serum." The district court had refused to hold a hearing on the voluntariness of the confession, though the state trial judge had made no findings on the admissibility of the confession, and the voluntariness issue had been left to the jury. Chief Justice Warren wrote for the majority (pp. 311–12):

"[T]he Act of February 5, 1867, * * * in extending the federal writ to state prisoners described the power of the federal courts to take testimony and determine the facts *de novo* in the largest terms * * *. The hearing provisions of the 1867 Act remain substantially unchanged in the present codification. 28 U.S.C. § 2243. In construing the mandate of Congress, so plainly designed to afford a trial-type proceeding in federal court for state prisoners aggrieved by unconstitutional detentions, this Court has consistently upheld the power of the federal courts on habeas corpus to take evidence relevant to claims of such detention. * * *

"The rule could not be otherwise. The whole history of the writ—its unique development—refutes a construction of the federal courts' habeas corpus powers that would assimilate their task to that of courts of appellate review. The function on habeas is different. It is to test by way of an original civil proceeding, independent of the normal channels of review of criminal judgments, the very gravest allegations. * * * It is the typical, not the rare, case in which constitutional claims turn upon the resolution of contested factual issues. Thus a narrow view of the hearing power would totally subvert Congress' specific aim in passing the Act of February 5, 1867, of affording state prisoners a forum in the federal trial courts for the determination of claims of detention in violation of the Constitution. The language of Congress, the history of the writ, the decisions of this Court, all make clear that the power of inquiry on federal habeas corpus is plenary. Therefore, where an applicant for a writ of habeas corpus alleges facts which, if proved, would entitle him to relief, the federal court to which the application is made has the power to receive evidence and try the facts anew."

The Chief Justice went on (pp. 312–13) to set out "the considerations which in certain cases may make exercise of that power mandatory":

"Where the facts are in dispute, the federal court in habeas corpus must hold an evidentiary hearing if the habeas applicant did not receive a full and fair evidentiary hearing in a state court, either at the time of the trial or in a collateral proceeding. In other words a federal evidentiary hearing is required unless the state-court trier of fact has after a full hearing reliably found the relevant facts.[9]

"It would be unwise to overly particularize this test. The federal district judges are more intimately familiar with state criminal justice, and with the trial of fact, than are we, and to their sound discretion must be left in very large part the administration of federal habeas corpus. But experience proves that a too general standard—the 'exceptional circumstances' and 'vital flaw' tests of the opinions in Brown v. Allen—does not serve adequately to explain the controlling criteria for the guidance of the federal habeas corpus courts. Some particularization may therefore be useful. We hold that a federal court must grant an evidentiary hearing to a habeas applicant under the following circumstances: If (1) the merits of the factual dispute were not resolved in the state hearing; (2) the state factual determination is not fairly supported by the record as a whole; (3) the fact-finding procedure employed by the state court was not adequate to afford a full and fair hearing; (4) there is a substantial allegation of newly discovered evidence; (5) the material facts were not adequately developed at the state-court hearing; or (6) for any reason it appears that the state trier of fact did not afford the habeas applicant a full and fair fact hearing."

The Court held that the district court erred in not affording the petitioner a hearing on the voluntariness of his confession. "The state trial judge rendered neither an opinion, conclusions of law, nor findings of fact. He made no charge to the jury setting forth the constitutional standards governing the admissibility of confessions. In short, there are no indicia which would indicate whether the trial judge applied the proper standard of federal law in ruling upon the admissibility of the confession" (p. 320).

Justice Stewart, for the four dissenters, agreed with the basic principle that the habeas court must hold a hearing where the petitioner did not receive a full and fair evidentiary hearing in the state court, but strongly doubted the wisdom of "cataloguing in advance a set of standards which are inflexibly to compel district judges to grant evidentiary hearings in habeas corpus proceedings" (p. 326). The dissenters disagreed with the majority's holding that a hearing was required in the particular case before the Court. According to Justice Stewart, the trial court's instructions to the jury "were couched in terms of voluntariness, and they clearly establish that the trial judge was aware of the correct constitutional standards to be applied. Nothing in the record indicates that an incorrect standard was applied at the suppression hearing. * * * Where, as here, a record is totally devoid of any indication that a state trial judge employed an erroneous constitutional standard, the presumption should surely be that the judge knew the law and correctly applied it. Certainly it is improper to presume that the trial judge did *not* know the law which the Constitution commands him to

"9. In announcing this test we do not mean to imply that the state courts are required to hold hearings and make findings which satisfy this standard, because such hearings are governed to a large extent by state law.

"The existence of the exhaustion of state remedies requirement (announced in Ex parte Royall, 117 U.S. 241, and now codified in 28 U.S.C. § 2254) lends support to the view that a federal hearing is not always required. It presupposes that the State's adjudication of the constitutional issue can be of aid to the federal court sitting in habeas corpus.

follow. Yet that is precisely the presumption which the Court makes in this case" (pp. 330–31).

(2) In fiscal 1960 a total of 868 state-prisoner habeas corpus cases were terminated in the federal district courts; of these 2.6% (23) were disposed of after an evidentiary hearing or trial.[1] In fiscal 1965, the first full year after Townsend, out of a total of 4243 such cases, 11% (468) involved an evidentiary hearing. Thus the increase in tried state-prisoner cases was almost 2000%, compared to an increase of just under 500% in habeas cases altogether, and a 233% increase in all private[2] federal question cases reaching trial. In 1965, out of a total of 2026 private federal question trials, more than one in five was a state-prisoner habeas case.

Since 1965, the percentage of state-prisoner habeas cases reaching trial has steadily declined. Out of 8423 state-prisoner habeas cases in fiscal 1970, 4.8% (403) reached trial, so that both the percentage and number of trials declined since 1965, in the face of an accelerating caseload. In fiscal 1979, only 2.3% of such cases reached trial. In fiscal 1985, a little under 1% of all habeas cases terminated (115) proceeded to a hearing, and most of these (91) lasted one day or less. The burdens imposed by Townsend have also been mitigated by the Federal Magistrate Act of 1976, see p. 1476, *supra*, which permits magistrates to hold hearings in habeas cases. But see Allen, Schachtman & Wilson, p. 1555, *supra*, at 720–24 (finding generally infrequent use of magistrates as fact-finders).

(3) The Townsend criteria and their application in the lower courts are exhaustively analyzed in 17 Federal Practice § 4265.

Is the district courts' power to order a new hearing plenary? Or is it subject to control if discretion is abused? Can you think of a case where a hearing should be had even though none of the Townsend criteria is met and it is found that the state gave a full and fair hearing within the meaning of Townsend? What is the purpose of giving the district court "discretion" to do so?

Is it appropriate to make the right to a plenary hearing on habeas corpus a matter of discretion at all? And consider the position of a district judge who has to exercise this discretion: given what is at stake, is it sound, psychologically, to ask the judge to decide without specifying firm legal standards?

(4) Consider 28 U.S.C. § 2254(d), added to the statute in 1966.[3] What is the relation of § 2254(d) to the Townsend rules? A number of early

1. The figures in this paragraph are derived from the Annual Reports of the Director of the Administrative Office of the United States Courts.

2. "Private" as used in the Director's Annual Reports refers to all federal question cases in which the United States or its officers or agencies are not plaintiffs or defendants. These figures thus exclude § 2255 cases involving federal prisoners.

3. The statute lists eight possible deficiencies in state court fact-findings (rather than the Townsend six); but their relevance is to the question whether the state findings are to be "presumed" correct. Further, if none of the eight deficiencies is

shown, the effect is not to negate the power of the judge to call a hearing, but to shift to the petitioner the burden to show at a hearing that the state findings were erroneous. The statute also leaves it unclear whether, if one of the eight deficiencies is established, the burden of proof on all facts shifts to the state.

Of the eight statutory criteria, three (lack of jurisdiction in state court; failure to appoint counsel when this was constitutionally required; denial of due process in the state court proceedings) are not found in Townsend (but would not appear to change the law). The remaining five appear to subsume the Townsend six.

lower court cases held that the section merely codified the Townsend criteria and required no change in approach. See, *e.g.,* Maxwell v. Turner, 411 F.2d 805 (10th Cir.1969); United States ex rel. Hughes v. McMann, 405 F.2d 773, 776 (2d Cir.1968). Though the Court did once say that the statute "codifies most of the criteria set out in Townsend," Brewer v. Williams, 430 U.S. 387, 395 (1977), it more usually and more accurately calls Townsend "the precursor of § 2254(d)," *e.g.,* Cuyler v. Sullivan, 446 U.S. 335, 341 (1980). Note, for instance, that unlike Townsend, the statute does not purport to define when a federal evidentiary hearing is mandatory; it appears merely to state a set of rather confused burden of proof rules to guide the district courts which are to hold such hearings.

The operation of the § 2254(d) burden of proof rules was addressed in LaVallee v. Delle Rose, 410 U.S. 690 (1973). The habeas petitioner argued in that case that a state court's finding that his confessions had been voluntary was not entitled to the presumption of correctness accorded by § 2254(d) because the court had failed to articulate any finding as to the credibility of the petitioner's testimony that the confessions had been coerced, and so had failed to resolve the merits of the factual dispute as required under § 2254(d)(1). The district court accepted this argument, held a hearing, found the confessions involuntary, and granted the writ. The Supreme Court, however, held that it was obvious from the state court's finding of voluntariness that it had not credited the petitioner's testimony. Thus the state court's determination was to be presumed correct and "[t]he burden was * * * on [petitioner] to establish in the District Court by convincing evidence that the state court's determination was erroneous" (p. 695). In dissent, Justice Marshall noted that "[t]he Court * * * does not hold that the District Court erred in holding a *de novo* evidentiary hearing * * *. That is a question distinct from the presumption of validity and the special burden of proof established by 28 U.S.C. § 2254(d). Section 2254(d) says nothing concerning when a district judge may hold an evidentiary hearing * * *. So far as I understand, the question whether such a hearing is appropriate * * * continues to be controlled exclusively by our decision in Townsend * * *" (p. 701 n. 2).

The LaVallee statement as to the effect of § 2254(d) was reiterated in Sumner v. Mata [I], 449 U.S. 539 (1981). The California Court of Appeal had rejected the defendant's argument that the pretrial identification admitted as evidence against him at his murder trial had been based on impermissibly suggestive procedures. The Ninth Circuit, however, granted habeas on the ground that these identification procedures were suggestive and hence unconstitutional. The Supreme Court reversed because the Ninth Circuit had not included in its opinion "a statement tying the generalities of § 2254(d) to the particular facts of the case" (p. 551). In order to enforce the "mandate of Congress" that a habeas petitioner must show state court factual determinations to be erroneous by "convincing evidence" rather than the usual "preponderance of the evidence," the Court held "that a habeas court should include in its opinion granting the writ the reasoning which led it to conclude that any of the first seven [§ 2254(d)] factors were present, or the reasoning which led it to conclude that the state finding was 'not fairly supported by the record'" (p. 551).[4]

---

4. Sumner I also determined that § 2254(d) applies to factual findings by state appellate as well as trial courts. Fur- thermore, the majority held it proper to consider the applicability of § 2254(d) though the issue had not been raised be-

(5) Recent cases have devoted substantial attention to the application of § 2254(d). The primary significance of this new jurisprudence has been the emergence of a strict rule that § 2254(d) requires deference to state court determinations of "historical" fact, though not to "mixed" rulings of law and fact. The Court has, however, had trouble defining this line; and the cases leave the sense that the line-drawing is, to some extent, driven by the Court's eagerness to restrict the scope of federal habeas review.

In Cuyler v. Sullivan, 446 U.S. 335 (1980), noting that § 2254(d) does not apply to review of a state court's determinations of mixed questions of law and fact, the Court concluded that findings about the roles various attorneys played in representing codefendants were findings as to "basic, primary, or historical facts" (quoting Townsend). However, it also stated that "the holding that lawyers who played those roles did not engage in multiple representation is a mixed determination of law and fact that requires the application of legal principles to the historical facts of this case. * * * That holding is open to review on collateral attack in a federal court" (p. 342).

In Sumner v. Mata [II], 455 U.S. 591 (1982), the Court held that the question whether a state's pretrial photographic identification procedure was impermissibly suggestive was a mixed question of law and fact. In Strickland v. Washington, 466 U.S. 668, 698 (1984), "both the performance and prejudice components of the ineffectiveness [of counsel] inquiry" were said to be mixed questions, not "subject to the deference requirements of § 2254(d)." And, finally, in Miller v. Fenton, 474 U.S. 104 (1985), the Court held that "the ultimate question of the admissibility of a confession merits treatment as a legal inquiry requiring plenary federal review" (p. 115).

In other cases, however, the Court found state court determinations to be ones of historical fact. See, e.g., Marshall v. Lonberger, 459 U.S. 422 (1983) (distinguishing between the question whether a guilty plea is voluntary for constitutional purposes, which is for the habeas court, and questions of historical fact about whether the defendant understood what he was pleading to, as to which state court determinations had to be presumed correct under § 2254(d)); Maggio v. Fulford, 462 U.S. 111 (1983) (court of appeals had granted habeas because it questioned the state court's ruling (based upon the trial court's observation of the defendant and its disbelief of a psychiatrist's testimony) that defendant was competent to stand trial; Supreme Court reversed, 6–3, holding that state court finding was supported by the record and did not fall within § 2254(d)(8)).[5]

low, because the question was one of subject matter jurisdiction: the habeas statute was the "successor to 'the first congressional grant of jurisdiction to the federal courts' * * * and the 1966 amendments embodied in § 2254(d) were intended by Congress as limitations on the exercise of that jurisdiction" (p. 547 n. 2).

Should a burden of proof statute be classified as "jurisdictional"?

5. See also Wainwright v. Goode, 464 U.S. 78 (1983) (state supreme court's finding—that sentencing judge in death penalty case had not relied on defendant's future dangerousness—was one of historical fact adequately supported by the record);

Rushen v. Spain, 464 U.S. 114 (1983) (state court's finding that ex parte communication between trial judge and juror had no effect on juror impartiality was one of fact); Patton v. Yount, 467 U.S. 1025 (1984) (whether jurors had opinions that disqualify them was a question of fact); Wainwright v. Witt, 469 U.S. 412 (1985) (whether a person was properly excludable for cause from a jury in a capital case, because of his opposition to the death penalty, was a question of fact). This series of decisions prompted Justice Brennan to complain in dissent in Witt about "the Court's increasingly expansive definition of 'questions of fact' calling for application of the presump-

In her opinion in Miller v. Fenton, *supra,* Justice O'Connor admitted that "the Court has not charted an entirely clear course" on what are questions of fact and what are mixed questions of law and fact for purposes of § 2254(d).

"In the § 2254(d) context, as elsewhere, the appropriate methodology for distinguishing questions of fact from questions of law has been, to say the least, elusive.   *   *   *   A few principles, however, are by now well established. For example, that an issue involves an inquiry into state of mind is not at all inconsistent with treating it as a question of fact [citing Maggio, *supra*]. Equally clearly, an issue does not lose its factual character merely because its resolution is dispositive of the ultimate constitutional issue.   *   *   *   But beyond these elemental propositions, negative in form, the Court has yet to arrive at 'a rule or principle that will unerringly distinguish a factual finding from a legal conclusion.' Pullman Standard v. Swint, 456 U.S. 276 (1982).

"Perhaps much of the difficulty in this area stems from the practical truth that the decision to label an issue a 'question of law,' a 'question of fact,' or a 'mixed question of law and fact' is sometimes as much a matter of allocation as it is of analysis. See Monaghan, *Constitutional Fact Review,* 85 Colum.L.Rev. 229, 237 (1985). At least in those instances in which Congress has not spoken and in which the issue falls somewhere between a pristine legal standard and a simple historical fact, the fact/law distinction at times has turned on a determination that, as a matter of the sound administration of justice, one judicial actor is better positioned than another to decide the issue in question" (pp. 113–14).

How well does Justice O'Connor's explanation account for the cases discussed in this section?

(6) The cases heretofore studied in this Chapter define the deference due to previous state proceedings. What about the deference owing to a previous federal habeas corpus proceeding? This was the issue addressed in Sanders v. United States, 373 U.S. 1 (1963).

Sanders was a postconviction motion by a federal prisoner under 28 U.S.C. § 2255; but the Court held that the standards governing second and subsequent applications under § 2255 are precisely the same as the standards (codified in 1948 in 28 U.S.C. § 2244)[6] governing state-prisoner habeas applicants who have made previous application for federal habeas corpus.[7] The Court then announced the following "basic rules to guide the lower federal courts" (pp. 15–17):

tion of correctness of 28 U.S.C. § 2254(d) to thwart vindication of fundamental rights in the federal courts" (p. 463).

6. In the 1948 codification, § 2244 had but one subsection; this was essentially the present § 2244(a), but drafted to be applicable to state as well as federal prisoners. When subsections (b) and (c) were added to § 2244 in 1966, (a) was amended to eliminate its application to state prisoners. Thus, presently, state prisoners are governed exclusively by § 2244(b) and (c); and federal prisoners either by § 2255 or (if they are entitled to habeas rather than having to proceed under § 2255) by § 2244(a).

As to § 2244(c), see Neil v. Biggers, 409 U.S. 188 (1972) (4–4 affirmance by Supreme Court held not to render an issue "actually adjudicated" within meaning of § 2244(c)).

7. The Court based its finding of equivalence on the conclusion that § 2255 was not intended to narrow a federal prisoner's habeas corpus rights; it rejected as insignificant the verbal discrepancy between § 2244 and the relevant sentence in § 2255 ("The sentencing court shall not be required to entertain a second or successive motion for similar relief").

"Controlling weight may be given to denial of a prior application for federal habeas corpus or § 2255 relief only if (1) the same ground presented in the subsequent application was determined adversely to the applicant on the prior application, (2) the prior determination was on the merits, and (3) the ends of justice would not be served by reaching the merits of the subsequent application.

"(1) By 'ground,' we mean simply a sufficient legal basis for granting the relief sought by the applicant. For example, the contention that an involuntary confession was admitted in evidence against him is a distinct ground for federal collateral relief. But a claim of involuntary confession predicated on alleged psychological coercion does not raise a different 'ground' than does one predicated on alleged physical coercion. In other words, identical grounds may often be proved by different factual allegations. So also, identical grounds may often be supported by different legal arguments, * * * or be couched in different language * * *. Should doubts arise in particular cases as to whether two grounds are different or the same, they should be resolved in favor of the applicant.

"(2) The prior denial must have rested on an adjudication of the merits of the ground presented in the subsequent application. * * * This means that if factual issues were raised in the prior application, and it was not denied on the basis that the files and records conclusively resolved these issues, an evidentiary hearing was held. * * *

"(3) Even if the same ground was rejected on the merits on a prior application, it is open to the applicant to show that the ends of justice would be served by permitting the redetermination of the ground. If factual issues are involved, the applicant is entitled to a new hearing upon showing that the evidentiary hearing on the prior application was not full and fair; we canvassed the criteria of a full and fair evidentiary hearing recently in Townsend v. Sain, *supra*, and that discussion need not be repeated here. If purely legal questions are involved, the applicant may be entitled to a new hearing upon showing an intervening change in the law or some other justification for having failed to raise a crucial point or argument in the prior application. Two further points should be noted. *First*, the foregoing enumeration is not intended to be exhaustive; the test is 'the ends of justice' and it cannot be too finely particularized. *Second*, the burden is on the applicant to show that, although the ground of the new application was determined against him on the merits on a prior application, the ends of justice would be served by a redetermination of the ground." [8]

Justice Harlan, joined by Justice Clark, dissented, protesting, *inter alia*, against "these 'guideline' decisions" which "suffer the danger of pitfalls that usually go with judging in a vacuum" (p. 32).

(7) When subsections (b) and (c) were added to § 2244 in 1966, the "ends of justice" rubric that the Sanders Court had drawn from the prior version of § 2244 was omitted. Kuhlmann v. Wilson, 477 U.S. 436 (1986), concerned a second habeas petition; both petitions raised the same Sixth Amendment claim, that petitioner had been denied the right to counsel

---

8. Full consideration of second or subsequent applications, continued the Court, based on new grounds or grounds not previously adjudicated on the merits, could be denied only if the petitioner is guilty of "abuse of the writ"; abuse of the writ may be found if the failure to litigate the present claim on the previous application constituted a deliberate bypass or waiver within the meaning of Noia.

when his cellmate, a police informant, reported certain of his statements to the police. These statements were later admitted into evidence. The government argued in Kuhlmann that as a result of the omission from the 1966 amendments, "federal courts no longer must consider the 'ends of justice' before dismissing a successive petition" (p. 451). The eight members of the Court who addressed the issue rejected this argument. They disagreed, however, as to whether the "ends of justice" could ever require reconsideration of a claim already raised on habeas absent a colorable showing that the petitioner was innocent. Justice Powell, speaking for a plurality of four, said (p. 454):

"In the light of the historic purpose of habeas corpus and the interests implicated by successive petitions for federal habeas relief from a state conviction, we conclude that the 'ends of justice' require federal courts to entertain such petitions only where the prisoner supplements his constitutional claim with a colorable showing of factual innocence. This standard was proposed by Judge Friendly more than a decade ago as a prerequisite for federal habeas review generally. Friendly, *Is Innocence Irrelevant? Collateral Attack on Criminal Judgments*, 38 U. Chi. L. Rev. 142 (1970). As Judge Friendly persuasively argued then, a requirement that the prisoner come forward with a colorable showing of innocence identifies those habeas petitioners who are justified in again seeking relief from their incarceration. We adopt this standard now to effectuate the clear intent of Congress that successive federal habeas review should be granted only in rare cases, but that it should be available when the ends of justice so require. The prisoner may make the requisite showing by establishing that under the probative evidence he has a colorable claim of factual innocence. The prisoner must make his evidentiary showing even though—as argued in this case—the evidence of guilt may have been unlawfully admitted."

Justice Brennan, disagreeing, stated that "we simply have never held that federal habeas review * * * is limited either to constitutional protections that advance the accuracy of the fact finding process at trial or is available solely to prisoners who make out a colorable showing of factual innocence" (p. 466). Justice Stevens, on the other hand, said that in determining whether the ends of justice required reconsideration of a claim, "one of the facts that may properly be considered is whether the petitioner has advanced a 'colorable claim of innocence,'" but that "this is not an essential element of every just disposition of a successive petition" (p. 476).

(8) Rule 9(b) of the § 2254 Rules provides that "[a] second or successive petition may be dismissed if the judge finds that it fails to allege new or different grounds for relief and the prior determination was on the merits or, if new and different grounds are alleged, the judge finds that the failure of the petitioner to assert those grounds in a prior petition constituted an abuse of the writ." In Rose v. Lundy, p. 1554, *supra*, Justice O'Connor said for four Justices that under this Rule a prisoner whose mixed petition of exhausted and unexhausted claims was dismissed, and who thereafter elected to proceed only with his exhausted claims, risked dismissal for abuse of the writ of any subsequent habeas petition raising the previously unexhausted claims. Four other Justices, however, stated that they would require a more rigorous showing of abuse in such circumstances; Justice Stevens did not address the issue.

NOTE ON PROBLEMS OF CUSTODY AND REMEDY

(1) The habeas corpus statute adopts the common law in making it a jurisdictional criterion for relief that the prisoner be in "custody" when seeking the writ, see 28 U.S.C. § 2241(c); see also *Note on the Functions of the Writ*, p. 1467, *supra*. Until the 1960s the custody requirement was strictly interpreted. See, *e.g.*, Wales v. Whitney, 114 U.S. 564 (1885) (Naval officer's challenge to order confining him to city limits; no jurisdiction); Stallings v. Splain, 253 U.S. 339 (1920) (habeas will not lie if petitioner has been released on bail); Weber v. Squier, 315 U.S. 810 (1942) (parole). Nor was the writ available after the petitioner was released, Ex parte Baez, 177 U.S. 378 (1900), even if he was in custody when the application was filed, Parker v. Ellis, 362 U.S. 574 (1960).

(2) In Jones v. Cunningham, 371 U.S. 236 (1963) this aspect of the law was revolutionized by the holding that a state prisoner free on parole was in "custody" within the meaning of § 2241 and could challenge the validity of his conviction.[1] The Court said that "[w]hile petitioner's parole releases him from immediate physical imprisonment, it imposes conditions which significantly confine and restrain his freedom; this is enough to keep him in the 'custody' of the members of the Virginia Parole Board within the meaning of the habeas corpus statute * * *" (p. 243). The Court referred to several different types of constraints which justified this conclusion, but did not specify whether all or any were essential to it: restrictions on lawful physical movements (*e.g.*, not permitted to leave city or to change residence without permission); other requirements which constrained freedom (*e.g.*, not permitted to drive an automobile without permission; required to report monthly to his parole officer); the threat of reimprisonment for even the slightest violation of the conditions of parole; and the fact that reimprisonment could occur without further judicial proceedings and other procedural safeguards.

The trend towards a wider definition of "custody" continued with Hensley v. Municipal Court, 411 U.S. 345 (1973), involving a habeas petitioner who had been convicted and sentenced to jail by a state court. Petitioner had then exhausted all state remedies, by appeal and collateral attack, available to him to set aside his conviction. When he filed his petition he was, however, still free on his own recognizance, awaiting execution of the sentence. The Court held that a person free on bail or recognizance is in "custody" and may petition for the writ. Petitioner is "subject to restraints 'not shared by the public generally'"; he cannot "come and go as he pleases," his freedom resting in the hands of state judicial officials "who may demand his presence at any time"; "disobedience is itself a criminal offense" (p. 351). In any event, said the Court, petitioner remains at large only by grace of a stay granted by the federal courts; custody is imminent and certain, not speculative. No important state interest is jeopardized by acting now rather than postponing adjudication until actual imprisonment. See also Justices of Boston Municipal Court v. Lydon, p. 1559, *supra*, at 300–02 (petitioner in custody, though his conviction was vacated when he applied for trial de novo and he was released on his own recognizance, because the Massachusetts statute pro-

---

1. For a criticism of the use of history and precedent in the Jones case, see Oaks, p. 1497, *supra*. For an inquiry into the reasons for the expansion of the custody concept, see Yackle, *Explaining Habeas Corpus*, p. 1470, *supra*, at 998–1010.

viding for trial de novo required that he appear for trial and not leave the jurisdiction without permission).

Note that a person on bail or recognizance will often have difficulty in satisfying the exhaustion requirement even though he is deemed to be in custody.

(3) Where all or most of the constraints incident to parole and stressed by the Court in Jones also accompany other forms of restraint, the lower courts have not hesitated since Jones to entertain applications for habeas corpus; the obvious examples are probation [2] and release on a conditionally suspended sentence.[3]

Some broad language in Jones ("besides physical imprisonment, there are other restraints on a man's liberty, restraints not shared by the public generally, which have been thought sufficient in the English-speaking world to support the issuance of habeas corpus" (p. 240)) have the potential of pushing the law even further. Is any special disability or constraint, not shared by the public generally, sufficient to constitute custody for purposes of supporting habeas jurisdiction? Can the imposition of a fine be tested by habeas? Can a fully served sentence be challenged on habeas if there are civil disabilities which still adhere? No cases appear to support these extensions;[4] but are the lines of resistance to them likely to be stable? Is there a principled line once the notion of physical custody is abandoned?[5]

(4) In Jones the petitioner was still in prison when he first applied for the writ; release on parole came later; and the case could have been put on the ground that the release on parole of a prisoner does not moot a habeas proceeding properly begun. But the Court's opinion cannot be read as resting on such a principle and holds squarely that parole is itself a form of "custody".

On the other hand a different approach was taken in Carafas v. LaVallee, 391 U.S. 234 (1968). Here the applicant was also in prison when the habeas petition was filed; during the course of the litigation, however, his sentence expired and he was unconditionally released. Overruling its prior decision in Parker v. Ellis, 362 U.S. 574 (1960), the Court held that release did not moot the proceeding. The fact that civil disabilities and burdens accompanied the prisoner after his release was seen as justification for the conclusion that the case was not moot. On the other hand the Court did not hold that those civil disabilities constituted a "custody" which would independently support an application for the writ. Cf. North Carolina v. Rice, 404 U.S. 244 (1971).

Carafas was subsequently limited by Lane v. Williams, 455 U.S. 624 (1982). Following a plea bargain Williams had pleaded guilty and was imprisoned. On release he was subject to a special parole term that was mandatory under state law but of which he had not been informed at the

2. Bruno v. Greenlee, 569 F.2d 775 (3d Cir.1978); Hahn v. Burke, 430 F.2d 100 (7th Cir.1970); United States v. Re, 372 F.2d 641 (2d Cir.1967) (federal prisoner).

3. United States ex rel. Wojtycha v. Hopkins, 517 F.2d 420 (3d Cir.1975); Radford v. Webb, 446 F.Supp. 608 (W.D.N.C.1978).

4. E.g., Ward v. Knoblock, 738 F.2d 134 (6th Cir.1984) (sentence fully served);

Spring v. Caldwell, 692 F.2d 994 (5th Cir. 1982) (fine).

5. The Developments authors, at 1078–79, suggest that, absent physical custody, the essential element should be the possibility of reincarceration by administrative action without judicial hearing. Compare Comment, 14 U.Mich.J.L.Ref. 465 (1981) (arguing custody requirement should be abandoned altogether).

time his plea had been accepted. He violated parole and was reimprisoned. He then filed for habeas corpus on the ground that he had been deprived of due process when the state court failed to inform him of the parole term; he did not ask the federal court to set aside his conviction and allow him to plead anew, only that he be freed from imprisonment and from "all future liability" under his original sentence (p. 627). After the petition had been granted by the district court and while appeal was pending, the parole term expired and Williams was released. Justice Stevens held the petition moot because the sentence—which was all the petition attacked—had expired:

"The doctrine of Carafas * * * is not applicable in this case. No civil disabilities such as those present in Carafas result from a finding that an individual has violated parole. At most, certain nonstatutory consequences may occur; employment prospects, or the sentence imposed in a future criminal proceeding, could be affected. * * * The discretionary decisions that are made by an employer or a sentencing judge, however, are not governed by the mere presence or absence of a recorded violation of parole; these decisions may take into consideration, and are more directly influenced by, the underlying conduct that formed the basis for the parole violation. Any disabilities that flow from whatever respondents did to evoke revocation of parole are not removed—or even affected—by a District Court order that simply recites that their parole terms are 'void' " (pp. 632–33).

(5) The correlative of the doctrine that a habeas applicant must be in "custody" was the notion that the only appropriate habeas corpus remedy is release from confinement.[6] In the celebrated case of McNally v. Hill, 293 U.S. 131 (1934), this notion was the basis for the holding that a prisoner serving the first of two consecutive sentences may not attack the second sentence while still serving the first. The Court said that a "sentence which the prisoner has not begun to serve cannot be the cause of restraint which the statute makes the subject of inquiry" (p. 138).

The McNally prematurity doctrine clearly barred habeas attacks on sentences which the petitioner had not yet begun to serve. Lower courts, relying on some sweeping language in the case (stressing that the writ can be sought only if a ruling for the petitioner would result in his "immediate release" (pp. 137–38)), read it as also barring challenges to one of two concurrent sentences,[7] to the first of several consecutive sentences,[8] and to an excessively long sentence before completion of the valid portion.[9] In 1968 the Supreme Court started the process of eroding McNally by disapproving of these holdings and restricting its doctrine to cases where the petitioner had not yet begun to serve the sentence under attack. See Walker v. Wainright, 390 U.S. 335 (1968), holding that the validity of a

---

6. But see the cases holding that the writ is available to test the validity of conditions of confinement in prison, e.g., Wilwording v. Swenson, 404 U.S. 249 (1971); Johnson v. Avery, 393 U.S. 483 (1969). See also *Developments* 1079–87. For further light on this problem, see Preiser v. Rodriguez, p. 1638, *infra.*

7. See, e.g., Wilson v. Gray, 345 F.2d 282, 286 (9th Cir.1965); Lowther v. Maxwell, 347 F.2d 941 (6th Cir.1965).

8. See, e.g., Wells v. California, 352 F.2d 439 (9th Cir.1965), *Cf.* Tucker v. Peyton, 357 F.2d 115 (4th Cir.1966), allowing one serving a second sentence to attack the validity of a first sentence already served, where the effect of the first sentence was to extend the duration of the second and where immediate release would be in order.

9. See, e.g., Carpenter v. Crouse, 358 F.2d 701 (10th Cir.1966).

sentence presently being served may be attacked even though another sentence awaits the prisoner.

(6) Later in the same Term, the Court overruled McNally in Peyton v. Rowe, 391 U.S. 54 (1968), holding that a prisoner may use habeas to challenge the validity of the second of two consecutive sentences while still serving the first. The principal reason given was a practical one: if the first sentence is a long one, the validity of the second will be tested long after the event, when witnesses have disappeared and memories dimmed. Moreover, said the Court, the prematurity rule prejudices the ultimately successful petitioner by forcing him to enter upon his confinement before he litigates its validity.[10]

In Rowe the Court characterized the "custody" as being "under the aggregate of the consecutive sentences imposed" (p. 64), and thus as satisfying the statutory requirement that the writ extend to a prisoner only if "He is in custody in violation of the Constitution * * *". Does this mean that a prisoner may not test a future sentence which cannot meaningfully be "aggregated" with his current one, for instance, a sentence in a different jurisdiction? In Nelson v. George, 399 U.S. 224 (1970) the Court stated that a North Carolina sentence could be challenged in a California district court by a prisoner presently still serving a California sentence, at least where North Carolina had issued a detainer to the California warden which allegedly affected the petitioner's conditions of confinement in California and his chances of parole from that imprisonment.[11] *Cf.* Braden v. 30th Judicial Circuit Court, p. 1473, *supra* (prisoner serving an Alabama sentence while under detainer from Kentucky may file for the writ in federal court in Kentucky to litigate the question whether Kentucky is under a constitutional obligation to grant him immediate trial).

(7) In United States v. Morgan, 346 U.S. 502 (1954), a state prisoner, whose state sentence was lengthened by the fact that he was deemed a second offender, wished to attack the federal sentence resulting from his first offense, which he had already served. The Supreme Court held that the district courts have power to grant relief "in the nature of a writ of error coram nobis" under the All Writs Act, 28 U.S.C. § 1651. Rule 60(b) of the Civil Rules, abolishing coram nobis, was deemed inapplicable on the ground that the application was a step in a criminal case. Relief under § 2255 was deemed both unavailable and non-exclusive.[12]

---

10. Under Rowe prisoners have generally been permitted to mount habeas attacks where the result would be to shorten the total period of confinement, though not to obtain immediate release. See, *e.g.*, Jensen v. Satran, 688 F.2d 76 (8th Cir.1982).

Can habeas be used to challenge one of two equally long concurrent sentences? One court, simply citing Rowe, has said yes. Velasquez v. Rhay, 408 F.2d 9 (9th Cir.1969). Such an adjudication may conceivably affect the conditions of confinement or eligibility for parole. But if such an effect is not alleged, should the case be adjudicated?

11. The actual holding of Nelson v. George was that habeas must await the

exhaustion of petitioner's remedies in the California courts. The theory was that the effect of the North Carolina detainer with respect to the conditions of petitioner's California confinement should first be passed on by California.

12. On the authority of Morgan, the Ninth Circuit recently held that coram nobis should be granted to vacate petitioner's federal convictions for violating wartime military orders that excluded Japanese Americans from certain areas and imposed a curfew on them; the court cited the War Department's concealment of a report explaining the basis for the orders and evidencing racial prejudice. Hirabayashi v. United States, 828 F.2d 591 (9th

NOTE ON HABEAS CORPUS REFORM

(1) Is the present structure of habeas corpus jurisdiction for state prisoners sound? If not, what change is needed? Should it come by legislation or should it be left to judicial formulation? What constitutional limits are there on the possibilities of legislative change?

(2) That the habeas jurisdiction imposes a serious burden on the federal courts cannot be gainsaid.[1] State prisoners filed 871 habeas petitions in fiscal 1960, 9063 in 1970.[2] This figure declined somewhat during the next decade, to 7843 in 1975 and 7031 in 1980. But filings rebounded after 1980, reaching 11939 in 1985 and 10724 in 1986. In addition, 1186 § 2255 motions were filed in 1982 and 1556 in 1986.

A study reviewing data from fiscal years 1975–76 found that 10% of the filings categorized as habeas corpus petitions by the Administrative Office in fact were not § 2254 petitions, but other actions (*e.g.,* § 2255 petitions or § 1983 suits). Allen, Schachtman & Wilson, p. 1555, *supra,* at 680 n. 8. Of the habeas petitions filed, roughly 70% attacked convictions or sentences; the rest related to pretrial matters, conditions of confinement, or revocation of probation or parole. See *id.* at 755 n. 367; Meltzer, p. 1550, *supra,* at 1192 n. 323.

In assessing the need for changes in the habeas jurisdiction, consider the pioneering study of the actual operations of habeas corpus (and related reform proposals) made by Shapiro, p. 1555, supra. See also the important information collected in Robinson, An Empirical Study of Federal Habeas Corpus Review of State Court Judgments (U.S. Dep't of Justice, Office for Improvements in the Administration of Justice 1979), discussed in Allen, Schachtman & Wilson, p. 1555, *supra.* Robinson studied all habeas petitions filed in a two-year period in six district courts and in one court of appeals (the Seventh Circuit). Among his findings: A majority of petitioners had been convicted of serious violent offenses, and 80% had pled not guilty. The most common interval between conviction and filing was 1½ years. Over 30% of the petitioners had filed at least one previous petition. At least two grounds for relief were offered in 80% (and at least three in 50%) of the petitions. About 80% of the petitions were filed *in forma pauperis* and *pro se.* 55% of the petitions were never considered on the merits because of procedural defects; of these, 60% failed on exhaustion grounds. Magistrates screened 45% of the petitions. Hearings were relatively rare: magistrates held hearings in 3.2% of the cases referred to them, and district judges held hearings in 6.2% of the cases. Nevertheless, the burden imposed on the judiciary and on the state was substantial (particularly in the more than 25% of the cases which were appealed). Only 3.2% of the petitions were successful, but this figure hides some interesting disparities. The success rate at the court of appeals level was the highest

---

Cir.1987). Petitioner's convictions had been upheld more than forty years earlier, in Hirabayashi v. United States, 320 U.S. 81 (1943). See also Korematsu v. United States, 584 F.Supp. 1406 (N.D.Cal.1984), again relying on Morgan, granting coram nobis to vacate a conviction (for violating the exclusion order) that had been upheld at 323 U.S. 214 (1944).

1. See Friendly, p. 1487, *supra,* at 143–49; but see Robbins, p. 1522, *supra,* at 266–67, and Note, 52 Va.L.Rev. 486 (1966).

2. The figures in this Paragraph come from the Annual Reports of the Director of the Administrative Office of the United States Courts. They are for petitions *filed,* whereas those given on p. 1563 are for cases *terminated.*

(12.3%), as might be predicted. The six districts ranged widely: four had a success rate of between 1 and 2%; one of 3.4%; and one (N.D.Ill.) of 8.7%. Three judges (5.9% of the 51 judges surveyed) accounted for 30% of petitions granted. Petitioners who are represented by counsel are much more likely to be successful than those who appear *pro se:* only .8% of the *pro se* cases at the district level resulted in the grant of the writ, whereas 12.6% of the counseled cases were successful. (The most significant disparity appears in the fact that 45.8% of the *pro se* cases were dismissed on procedural grounds, in contrast to 19.2% of the counseled cases.)

See also Mikva & Godbold, *"You Don't Have to be a Bleeding Heart",* 14 Human Rights 22 (1987), and Godbold, *Pro Bono Representation of Death Sentenced Inmates,* 42 Rec. of Ass'n of Bar of New York City 862 (1987) (arguing that in death penalty cases habeas is granted in a significant number of cases because of constitutional deficiencies).

For comparative perspectives, see Robbins, Comparative Postconviction Remedies (1980).

(3) What is surely true in any event is that every petition should receive serious and conscientious attention. Is this possible, in view of what the above figures reveal that of the habeas petitions actually filed, few are meritorious and most are completely frivolous? [3] The fact that few cases eventuate in release is usually adduced as a reason for concluding that the existence of the jurisdiction exacts few costs.[4] But see Friendly, p. 1487, *supra,* at 148–49, suggesting that a "remedy that produces no result in the overwhelming majority of cases" may be a "gigantic waste of effort",[5] and continuing: "[T]he most serious evil with today's proliferation of collateral attack is its drain upon the resources of the community— judges, prosecutors, and attorneys * * *. Today of all times we should be conscious of the falsity of the bland assumption that these are in endless supply. Everyone concerned with the criminal process * * * agrees that our greatest single problem is the long delay in bringing accused persons to trial. The time of judges, prosecutors, and lawyers now devoted to collateral attacks, most of them frivolous, would be much better spent in trying cases."

Nevertheless, it is also the case that serious injustices and serious invasions of constitutional interests have been remedied only because the habeas writ was available.[6] If the issue were whether the writ should be retained or abolished, then we would be reduced to deciding whether such

---

3. For the kind of psychological atmosphere which the flood of frivolous petitions creates, see the account by Judge Pope, *Suggestions for Lessening the Burden of Frivolous Applications,* 33 F.R.D. 409, 410 (1964): "As these applications have come before us day after day, and week after week, many of them no more than duplicates or repetitions of former applications filed by the same individuals, and as we have had to dig through hundreds of petitions, many of them nearly unintelligible, in an effort to find out what the petitioner is trying to say, I have felt like the operator of a dredge who is required to sift through vast quantities of gravel in order to find a few stray colors of gold. General-

ly speaking, the results have been so meager that one feels like the dredge owner who finally decides to abandon the whole operation."

4. See Frankfurter, J., in Brown v. Allen, *supra,* 344 U.S. at 510; Brennan, *Federal Habeas Corpus and State Prisoners: An Exercise in Federalism,* 7 Utah L.Rev. 423, 440–41 (1961); *Developments* 1041.

5. Judge Friendly adds that even among the few cases where the applicant prevails the result is often "unjust" in the sense that the prisoner is guilty of the underlying crime.

6. See Reitz, p. 1487, *supra;* Wright & Sofaer, p. 1487, *supra,* at 898–99.

cases justify the costs incurred. But that is not the issue, is it? Shouldn't the inquiry rather be whether the jurisdiction can be reshaped to avoid some of the costs without sacrificing the major benefits?

(4) In 1955 the Judicial Conference of the United States recommended enactment of the following addition to § 2254:[7]

"A Justice of the Supreme Court, a Circuit Judge or a District Court or Judge shall entertain an application for a writ of habeas corpus in behalf of a person in custody pursuant to a judgment of a State court, only on a ground which presents a substantial Federal constitutional question (1) which was not theretofore raised and determined (2) which there was no fair and adequate opportunity theretofore to raise and have determined and (3) which cannot thereafter be raised and determined in a proceeding in the State court, by an order or judgment subject to review by the Supreme Court of the United States on writ of certiorari.

"An order denying an application for a writ of habeas corpus by a person in custody pursuant to a judgment of a State court shall be reviewable only on a writ of certiorari by the Supreme Court of the United States. The petition for the writ of certiorari shall be filed within 30 days after the entry of such order."

This bill was twice passed by the House, but never the Senate.[8] Is it a good bill?[9]

Beginning in 1959 the Judicial Conference repeatedly urged that habeas corpus cases in the federal courts should be heard by three-judge courts. As the number of petitions skyrocketed in the 60's, however, this proposal was withdrawn in 1965.[10]

(5) See Friendly, *supra,* for the thesis that "with a few important exceptions, convictions should be subject to collateral attack only when the prisoner supplements his constitutional plea with a colorable claim of innocence" (p. 142). The suggested exceptions involve four categories: (i) where the original tribunal lacked jurisdiction or where the criminal process so broke down that the defendant did not receive the kind of trial the Constitution guarantees (*e.g.,* mob domination); (ii) where the constitutional claim is based on facts outside the record and only collateral attack can vindicate the claim; (iii) where the state has failed to provide a proper procedure for making a defense at trial and on appeal; and (iv) where there has been a change in the governing constitutional law, which is a "special case." Compare the suggestion of the (then) Assistant Attorney General Rehnquist of the Office of Legal Counsel that habeas be limited to cases where the "claimed constitutional right is one which has as its primary purpose the protection of the reliability of either the fact finding process at the trial or the appellate process on appeal from the judgment of conviction

7. See *Hearings on H.R. 5649 Before Subcommittee No. 3 of the House Committee on the Judiciary,* 84th Cong., 1st Sess., sec. 6, at 89–90 (1955).

8. See 102 Cong.Rec. 940 (84th Cong. 1956); 104 *id.* 4675 (85th Cong.1958).

9. The bill received the support of the Judicial Conference of the United States, the Conference of State Chief Justices, the Association of Attorneys General, the ABA, and the Department of Justice. See Hearings, *supra* note 7, at 7. It was criticized in Schaefer, *Federalism and State Criminal Procedure,* 70 Harv.L.Rev. 1 (1956); Pollak, *Proposals to Curtail Federal Habeas Corpus for State Prisoners: Collateral Attack on the Great Writ,* 66 Yale L.J. 50 (1956).

10. See H.R.Rep. No. 1892, 89th Cong., 2d Sess (1966).

* * *." Hearings on S. 895 Before the Subcommittee on Constitutional Rights, Sen. Comm. on the Judiciary, 92d Cong., 1st Sess. 264–72 (1971).

(6) The Reagan Administration has proposed legislative reforms in habeas corpus, though without success. See Habeas Corpus Reform Act of 1982, S. 2216, 97th Cong., 2d Sess., 128 Cong.Rec. S2172 (daily ed. Apr. 1, 1982); H.R. 6050, 97th Cong., 2d Sess., Cong.Rec. H1405 (daily ed. Mar. 16, 1982). Section 5 of S. 2216 would have added a subsection to § 2254 stating that habeas corpus "shall not be granted with respect to any claim that has been fully and fairly adjudicated in state court proceedings."

As to fact relitigation on habeas, current § 2254(d) would be replaced by a new subsection providing that in habeas litigation "a full and fair determination of a factual issue made in the case by a state court shall be presumed to be correct. The applicant shall bear the burden of rebutting this presumption by clear and convincing evidence." This provision omits the eight standards currently set out in the statute (derived in part from Townsend v. Sain) that indicate when habeas courts may reconsider factual findings of the state courts. It also omits the current requirement that state court findings will bind habeas courts only if the state court held a hearing and the finding is evidenced in writing.

Section 2 of S. 2216 would have added a new subsection to § 2254 governing habeas corpus after state procedural default.[11] See Sallet & Goodman, *Closing the Door to Federal Habeas Corpus: A Comment on Legislative Proposals to Restrict Access in State Procedural Default Cases*, 20 Am.Crim.L.Rev. 465 (1983). For a critical discussion, see Yackle, *The Reagan Administration's Habeas Corpus Proposals*, 68 Iowa L.Rev. 609 (1983).

(7) One reform directed not at the scope of the writ but at the institutional structure for dealing with habeas petitions has been the use of magistrates in processing habeas applications. See p. 1476, *supra.* For a proposal similarly aimed at institutional structure, see Friendly, *supra,* at 166–67, raising the possibility of routing appeals from state criminal cases to an intermediate court of appeals. Compare Meador, *Straightening Out Federal Review of State Criminal Cases*, 44 Ohio St.L.J. 273 (1983). Along a different line is the suggestion for a federal statute of limitations for federal habeas corpus, designed to deal with the problem that the longer the prisoner withholds his application, the harder it is to retry him if the writ issues.[12] Recent proposals include a three-year statute of limitations,

---

11. "When a person in custody pursuant to the judgment of a State court fails to raise a claim in state proceedings at the time or in the manner required by State rules of procedure, the claim shall not be entertained in an application for a writ of habeas corpus unless actual prejudice resulted to the applicant from the alleged denial of the federal right asserted and—

(1) the failure to raise the claim properly or to have it heard in State proceedings was the result of State action in violation of the Constitution or laws of the United States;

(2) the federal right asserted was not recognized prior to the procedural default; or

(3) the factual predicate of the claim could not have been discovered through the exercise of reasonable diligence prior to the procedural default."

12. See Bator, *Finality* 517. But see Wright & Sofaer, p. 1487, *supra,* at 900 n. 18: "The suggestion that a time limit be placed on the writ's availability * * * runs afoul of Mr. Justice Harlan's eloquent reminder 'that the overriding responsibility of this Court is to the Constitution of the United States, no matter how late it may be that a violation of the Constitution is found to exist.' Chessman v. Teets, 354 U.S. 156, 165 (1957)." Do you suppose Justice Harlan meant that all constitutional claims must be allowed to be raised with-

see *Attorney General's Task Force on Violent Crime, Final Report,* Rec. 42 (1981); or a one year statute in § 2254 cases and a two-year statute in § 2255 cases, Habeas Corpus Reform Act of 1982, *supra.* These are criticized in Yackle, *supra,* at 612 n. 22.

(8) To what extent does the Constitution constrain legislative exploration of avenues of reform of the kinds outlined above? Would any of the proposed changes run afoul of the Suspension Clause? The Due Process Clause?

Note the language of the Suspension Clause: "The Privilege of the Writ of Habeas Corpus shall not be suspended, unless when in cases of Rebellion or Invasion the public Safety may require it" (Art. I, § 9, cl. 2). The proceedings of the Convention do not cast much direct light on just what the Framers assumed the "privilege" of the writ to be; but it was of course the clear contemporaneous understanding that the fundamental function of the writ was to test executive detentions and that convictions by a criminal court of competent jurisdiction could not be reexamined on habeas corpus at all.[13] In Swain v. Pressley, 430 U.S. 372 (1977), the Court held that the statutory motion created by the District of Columbia Code for collateral attack on District convictions was "commensurate" with habeas corpus and therefore involved no suspension of the writ. Chief Justice Burger, joined by Justices Blackmun and Rehnquist, concurred, arguing that the Suspension Clause protects only the writ as known at the time of the Framers and therefore imposes no requirement on Congress to provide any collateral review of convictions entered by a court of competent jurisdiction.

Recall the constitutional understanding (already accepted by the Convention when the Suspension Clause was adopted) leaving it up to Congress whether or not there should be lower federal courts, and what their jurisdiction should be if Congress should choose to create them. In light of this understanding, how can it be plausibly argued that there is a constitutional right to seek habeas corpus specifically in a lower *federal* court?[14] See Chap. I, pp. 10–11, *supra;* and see generally Chap. IV, Sec. 1(a), *supra.*

In any event, how can the Suspension Clause be read to create such a right in the case of detentions under *state* law? What the Framers feared was imprisonment by federal authority. State prisoners did not have access to the writ in the federal courts at all until 1867. Was the writ under suspension as to them all that time? Or is the right to federal habeas corpus for state prisoners to be deemed a creation of the Fourteenth Amendment?

Is it plausible to suppose that the Suspension Clause had anything whatever to do with collateral attacks on judgments of conviction by courts of competent jurisdiction? See Friendly, p. 1487, *supra,* at 170–72.

out limit of time, whether or not there is excuse for the delay, and no matter how stale?

13. For a survey of the historical materials on the Suspension Clause, see *Developments* 1263–66; and see Paschal, *The Constitution and Habeas Corpus,* 1970 Duke L.J. 605. With respect to the contemporaneous understanding about habeas corpus, *see* Oaks, p. 1497, *supra.*

14. Compare Collings, *Habeas Corpus for Convicts—Constitutional Right or Legislative Grace,* 40 Calif.L.Rev. 335 (1952), with *Developments* 1266–74. And see Paschal, *supra* note 13, for the thesis that it was the purpose of the Suspension Clause to direct all superior courts of record, state and federal, to make the privileges of the writ "routinely" available.

Should the practice of collateral relitigation of all constitutional issues be frozen into the Constitution? Should either the Suspension or the Due Process Clause be read to do more than to guarantee one fair hearing of all constitutional claims by a competent and fairly constituted tribunal using constitutional processes of decision? Particularly where that decision is subject to review in the Supreme Court?

SECTION 3. COLLATERAL ATTACK ON FEDERAL JUDGMENTS OF CONVICTION

UNITED STATES v. HAYMAN

342 U.S. 205, 72 S.Ct. 263, 96 L.Ed. 232 (1952).
Certiorari to the United States Court of Appeals for the Ninth Circuit.

MR. CHIEF JUSTICE VINSON delivered the opinion of the Court.

In its 1948 revision of the Judicial Code, Congress provided that prisoners in custody under sentence of a federal court may move the sentencing court to vacate, set aside or correct any sentence subject to collateral attack. 28 U.S.C. (Supp. IV) § 2255.

Respondent, confined at the McNeil Island penitentiary in the Western District of Washington, invoked this new procedure by filing a motion to vacate his sentence and grant a new trial in the District Court for the Southern District of California. That court had imposed a sentence of twenty years' imprisonment in 1947 for forging Government checks and related violations of federal law.

In his motion, respondent alleged that he did not enjoy the effective assistance of counsel guaranteed defendants in federal courts by the Sixth Amendment. Specifically, he alleged that one Juanita Jackson, a principal witness against respondent at his trial and a defendant in a related case, was represented by the same lawyer as respondent. * * *

For three days, the District Court received testimony in connection with the issues of fact raised by the motion. This proceeding was conducted without notice to respondent and without ordering the presence of respondent. On the basis of this *ex parte* investigation, the District Court found as a fact that respondent's counsel had also represented Juanita Jackson but that he "did so only with the knowledge and consent, and at the instance and request of [respondent]." Pursuant to this finding, the District Court entered an order denying respondent's motion to vacate his sentence and to grant a new trial.

On appeal to the Court of Appeals for the Ninth Circuit, the majority, acting *sua sponte*, raised questions as to the adequacy and constitutionality of Section 2255. The court addressed itself to the provision that an application for a writ of habeas corpus "shall not be entertained" where the sentencing court has denied relief "unless it also appears that the remedy by motion is inadequate or ineffective to test the legality of his detention." Considering that the proceedings in the District Court were proper under the terms of Section 2255, the court below held, one judge dissenting, that the Section 2255 procedure could not be adequate or effective in this case and, in the alternative, that the Section, in precluding resort to habeas corpus, amounted to an unconstitutional "suspension" of the writ of habeas corpus as to respondent.

On rehearing below, and again in this Court, the Government conceded that respondent's motion raised factual issues which required respondent's presence at a hearing. The Court of Appeals, however, refused either to affirm the denial of respondent's motion or to accept the Government's concession and remand the case for a hearing with respondent present. Instead, it treated Section 2255 as a nullity and ordered respondent's motion dismissed so that respondent might proceed by habeas corpus in the district of his confinement. 187 F.2d 456.

We granted certiorari in this case, 1951, 341 U.S. 930, to review the decision that Section 2255 must be considered a nullity, a holding that stands in conflict with cases decided in other circuits. We do not reconsider the concurrent findings of both courts below that respondent's motion states grounds to support a collateral attack on his sentence and raises substantial issues of fact calling for an inquiry into their verity.

First. The need for Section 2255 is best revealed by a review of the practical problems that had arisen in the administration of the federal courts' habeas corpus jurisdiction. * * *

Under the 1867 Act, United States District Courts have jurisdiction to determine whether a prisoner has been deprived of liberty in violation of constitutional rights, although the proceedings resulting in incarceration may be unassailable on the face of the record. Under that Act, a variety of allegations have been held to permit challenge of convictions on facts *dehors* the record.

One aftermath of these developments in the law has been a great increase in the number of applications for habeas corpus filed in the federal courts by state and federal prisoners. The annual volume of applications had nearly tripled in the years preceding enactment of Section 2255.[13] In addition to the problems raised by a large volume of applications for habeas corpus that are repetitious [14] and patently frivolous, serious administrative problems developed in the consideration of applications which appear meritorious on their face. Often, such applications are found to be wholly lacking in merit when compared with the records of the sentencing court. But, since a habeas corpus action must be brought in the district of confinement, those records are not readily available to the habeas corpus court.

13. During 1936 and 1937, an annual average of 310 applications for habeas corpus were filed in the District Courts and an annual average of 22 prisoners were released. By 1943, 1944 and 1945, however, the annual average of filings reached 845, although an average of only 26 prisoners were released per year. Figures from tables submitted to the Chairmen of the House and Senate Judiciary Committees. * * *

These figures do not include the District Court for the District of Columbia where a similar increase in the volume of applica-

tions for habeas corpus had been reported. See Dorsey v. Gill, 1945, 80 U.S.App.D.C. 9, 14, 148 F.2d 857, 862.

14. In several districts, up to 40% of all applications for habeas corpus filed during the years 1943, 1944 and 1945 were so-called repeater petitions. Speck, Statistics on Federal Habeas Corpus, 10 Ohio St.L.J. 337, 352 (1949). See also Price v. Johnston, 1948, 334 U.S. 266; Dorsey v. Gill, note 13, *supra;* Goodman, Use and Abuse of the Writ of Habeas Corpus, 1947, 7 F.R.D. 313.

Walker v. Johnston, 1941, 312 U.S. 275, illustrates a further practical problem * * * [in that a] hearing had to be held in the habeas corpus court in California although the federal officers involved were stationed in Texas and the facts occurred in Texas.

These practical problems have been greatly aggravated by the fact that the few District Courts in whose territorial jurisdiction major federal penal institutions are located were required to handle an inordinate number of habeas corpus actions far from the scene of the facts, the homes of the witnesses and the records of the sentencing court solely because of the fortuitous concentration of federal prisoners within the district.[18]

Second. The Judicial Conference of the United States, addressing itself to the problems raised by the increased habeas corpus business in 1942, * * * recommended adoption of two proposed bills, a "procedural bill" containing provisions designed to prevent abuse of the habeas corpus writ and a "jurisdictional bill," Section 2 of which established a procedure whereby a federal prisoner might collaterally attack his conviction in the sentencing court. The Judicial Conference repeatedly reaffirmed its approval of this forerunner of Section 2255.

In 1944, the two bills approved by the Judicial Conference were submitted to the Congress on behalf of the Conference. In the letter of transmittal and accompanying memorandum, Section 2 of the "jurisdictional bill" was described as requiring prisoners convicted in federal courts to apply by motion in the sentencing court "instead of making application for habeas corpus in the district in which they are confined." At the request of the Chairman of the House and Senate Judiciary Committees, a "Statement" describing the necessity and purposes of the bills was submitted to Congress * * *. The Statement * * * described Section 2 of the "jurisdictional bill" as follows:

"This section applies only to Federal sentences. It creates a statutory remedy consisting of a motion before the court where the movant has been convicted. The remedy is in the nature of, but much broader than, *coram nobis.* The motion remedy broadly covers all situations where the sentence is 'open to collateral attack.' As a remedy, it is intended to be as broad as habeas corpus."

While the bills proposed by the Judicial Conference were pending, the Committee on Revision of the Laws of the House of Representatives had drafted a bill revising the entire Judicial Code. Portions of this bill dealing with habeas corpus were drafted to conform with the bills approved by the Judicial Conference, including Section 2255, modeled after Section 2 of the "jurisdictional bill" approved by the Judicial Conference. According to the Reviser's Note on Section 2255:

18. Of all habeas corpus applications filed by federal prisoners, 63% were filed in but five of the eighty-four District Courts. And, although habeas corpus trials average only 3% of all trials in all districts, the proportion of habeas corpus trials in those five districts has run from 20% to as high as 65% of all trials conducted in the district.

The basic data, compiled by Speck, note 14, *supra,* covers the six years immediately preceding enactment of Section 2255 in 1948. Again, the figures do not include the District Court for the District of Columbia. The five districts are: Northern California (Alcatraz); Northern Georgia (Atlanta); Kansas (Leavenworth); Western Washington (McNeil Is.); and Western Missouri (Springfield Medical Center).

"This section restates, clarifies and simplifies the procedure in the nature of the ancient writ of error coram nobis. It provides an expeditious remedy for correcting erroneous sentences without resort to habeas corpus. It has the approval of the Judicial Conference of the United States. * * * " * * *

This review of the history of Section 2255 shows that it was passed at the instance of the Judicial Conference to meet practical difficulties that had arisen in administering the habeas corpus jurisdiction of the federal courts. Nowhere in the history of Section 2255 do we find any purpose to impinge upon prisoners' rights of collateral attack upon their convictions. On the contrary, the sole purpose was to minimize the difficulties encountered in habeas corpus hearings by affording the same rights in another and more convenient forum.[29]

Third. The crucial issue of fact presented by respondent's motion under Section 2255 was whether his attorney appeared as counsel for Juanita Jackson "with the knowledge and consent" of respondent. The Court of Appeals found, and the Government now agrees, that respondent's presence at a hearing on this issue is required if the Section 2255 procedure is to be adequate and effective in this case. In holding that Section 2255 should be treated as a nullity in this case, the court below found that the Section contemplated and permitted the *ex parte* investigation conducted by the District Court without notice to respondent and without respondent's presence.

We do not find in Section 2255 the disturbing inadequacies found by the court below. The issues raised by respondent's motion were not determined by the "files and records" in the trial court. In such circumstances, Section 2255 requires that the trial court act on the motion as follows: " * * * cause notice thereof to be served upon the United States attorney, *grant a prompt hearing thereon,* determine the issues and make findings of fact and conclusions of law with respect thereto." (Emphasis supplied.) In requiring a "hearing," the Section "has obvious reference to the tradition of judicial proceedings".[30] Respondent, denied an opportunity to be heard, "has lost something indispensable, however convincing the *ex parte* showing." [31] We conclude that the District Court did not proceed in conformity with Section 2255 when it made findings on controverted issues of fact relating to respondent's own knowledge without notice to respondent and without his being present.

The court below also held that the sentencing court could not hold the required hearing because it was without power to order the presence of a prisoner confined in another district. * * *

The very purpose of Section 2255 is to hold any required hearing in the sentencing court because of the inconvenience of transporting court officials and other necessary witnesses to the district of confinement. The District Court is not impotent to accomplish this purpose, at least so long as it may invoke the statutory authority of federal courts to issue "all writs necessary or appropriate in aid of their respective jurisdictions and agreea-

29. Parker, Limiting the Abuse of Habeas Corpus, 1948, 8 F.R.D. 171, 175. Judge Parker served as Chairman of the Judicial Conference Committee on Habeas Corpus Procedure.

30. See Morgan v. United States, 1936, 298 U.S. 468, 480.

31. Snyder v. Commonwealth of Massachusetts, 1934, 291 U.S. 97, 116.

ble to the usages and principles of law." [33]   An order to secure respondent's presence in the sentencing court to testify or otherwise prosecute his motion is "necessary or appropriate" to the exercise of its jurisdiction under Section 2255 and finds ample precedent in the common law. * * *

The existence of power to produce the prisoner does not, of course, mean that he should be automatically produced in every Section 2255 proceeding. This is in accord with procedure in habeas corpus actions.[38] Unlike the criminal trial where the guilt of the defendant is in issue and his presence is required by the Sixth Amendment, a proceeding under Section 2255 is an independent and collateral inquiry into the validity of the conviction. Whether the prisoner should be produced depends upon the issues raised by the particular case. Where, as here, there are substantial issues of fact as to events in which the prisoner participated, the trial court should require his production for a hearing.

Fourth. Nothing has been shown to warrant our holding at this stage of the proceeding that the Section 2255 procedure will be "inadequate or ineffective" if respondent is present for a hearing in the District Court on remand of this case. In a case where the Section 2255 procedure is shown to be "inadequate or ineffective", the Section provides that the habeas corpus remedy shall remain open to afford the necessary hearing.[40] Under such circumstances, we do not reach constitutional questions. This Court will not pass upon the constitutionality of an act of Congress where the question is properly presented unless such adjudication is unavoidable, much less anticipate constitutional questions.

We conclude that the District Court erred in determining the factual issues raised by respondent's motion under Section 2255 without notice to respondent and without his presence. We hold that the required hearing can be afforded respondent under the procedure established in Section 2255. The Court of Appeals correctly reversed the order of the District Court but should have remanded the case for a hearing under Section 2255 instead of ordering that respondent's motion be dismissed. Accordingly, we vacate the judgment of the Court of Appeals and remand the case to the District Court for further proceedings in conformity with this opinion.

Vacated and remanded.

MR. JUSTICE BLACK and MR. JUSTICE DOUGLAS concur in the result.

MR. JUSTICE MINTON took no part in the consideration or decision of this case.

NOTE ON COLLATERAL ATTACK BY FEDERAL PRISONERS

(1) Kaufman v. United States, 394 U.S. 217 (1969), decided six years after Fay v. Noia, determined that the expansive version of collateral relief

---

33. 28 U.S.C. (Supp.IV) § 1651(a).

38. Walker v. Johnston, *supra*, at page 284. According to the Reviser's Note, 28 U.S.C. (Supp.IV) § 2243, governing the requirements for presence of a prisoner in habeas corpus actions, was drafted to conform with the practice described in the Walker case.

40. If Section 2255 had not expressly required that the extraordinary remedy of habeas corpus be withheld pending resort to established procedures providing the same relief, the same result would have followed under our decisions. Stack v. Boyle, 1951, 342 U.S. 1, 6–7; Johnson v. Hoy, 1913, 227 U.S. 245; Ex parte Royall, 1886, 117 U.S. 241.

adopted in Brown v. Allen and ratified in Fay v. Noia should extend to federal prisoners who seek relief under § 2255, as well as to state prisoners. The particular issue in Kaufman was whether a federal prisoner could use § 2255 to raise the question whether illegally seized evidence had been admitted into evidence against him at his trial. The Court said that the Fourth Amendment question, like all other constitutional questions, was cognizable under the rule of Brown v. Allen; that Fay v. Noia's "deliberate bypass" standard should govern the question whether the constitutional issue had been waived; and that Townsend v. Sain should govern the question of the § 2255 court's obligation and discretion to try the facts anew.[1]

The Court rejected the government's argument that Brown v. Allen was inapposite because Kaufman had already had one fair chance to litigate his Fourth Amendment claim in a *federal* court. "The opportunity to assert federal rights in a federal forum is clearly not the sole justification for federal post-conviction relief; otherwise there would be no need to make such relief available to federal prisoners at all. The provision of federal collateral remedies rests more fundamentally upon a recognition that adequate protection of constitutional rights relating to the criminal trial process requires the continuing availability of a mechanism for relief. This is no less true for federal prisoners than it is for state prisoners.
* * *

"The approach * * * pressed upon us here exalts the value of finality in criminal judgments at the expense of the interest of each prisoner in the vindication of his constitutional rights. Such regard for the benefits of finality runs contrary to the most basic precepts of our system for post-conviction relief. * * * Plainly the interest in finality is the same with regard to both federal and state prisoners. With regard to both, Congress has determined that the full protection of their constitutional rights requires the availability of a mechanism for collateral attack. The right then is not merely to a federal forum but to full and fair consideration of constitutional claims. Federal prisoners are no less entitled to such consideration than are state prisoners. There is no reason to treat federal trial errors as less destructive of constitutional guarantees than state trial errors, nor to give greater preclusive effect to procedural defaults by federal defendants than to similar defaults by state defendants. To hold otherwise would reflect an anomalous and erroneous view of federal-state relations" (pp. 226–28).

In footnote 8, the Court added that the effect of previous consideration of the constitutional question by the sentencing court should be assimilated to the standards announced in Sanders v. United States, 373 U.S. 1 (1963) (p. 1566, *supra*), governing *successive* motions under § 2255.

1. The Court held that only the third Townsend criterion, requiring that the habeas court scrutinize the trial court's fact-finding procedure, did not apply in a § 2255 case: "[F]ederal fact-finding procedures are by hypothesis adequate to assure the integrity of the underlying constitutional rights. Thus, when a request for relief under § 2255 asserts a claim of unconstitutional search and seizure which was tested by a motion to suppress at or before trial under Fed.Rule Crim.Proc. 41(e), the § 2255 court need not stop to review the adequacy of the procedure established by that Rule. * * * We perceive no differences between the situations of state and federal prisoners which should make allegations of the other circumstances listed in Townsend v. Sain less subject to scrutiny by a § 2255 court" (p. 227).

Justices Black, Harlan, and Stewart dissented.[2]

(2) In Stone v. Powell, p. 1506, *supra*, Kaufman was rejected with respect to its particular holding that Fourth Amendment claims may automatically be relitigated on collateral attack.[3]

But Kaufman's *general* rule—that Brown v. Allen applies to federal prisoners and allows collateral attack with respect to all constitutional issues (other than Fourth Amendment ones)—remains the law. See, *e.g.*, United States v. Dukes, 727 F.2d 34 (2d Cir.1984); Thor v. United States, 574 F.2d 215 (5th Cir.1978).

(3) Davis v. United States, 411 U.S. 233 (1973), which is described by Justice Rehnquist in his opinion in Wainwright v. Sykes, p. 1527, *supra*, sharply reduced the role of the Noia waiver rule in cases involving procedural default in federal courts. Recall the holding in Davis: if a federal defendant failed to comply with Rule 12(b) of the Rules of Criminal Procedure, which specified that "objections based on defects in the institution of prosecution or in the indictment * * * may be raised only by motion before trial," the case is governed by the express provision in the Rule that this "constitutes a waiver," and the objection may not be raised later in a § 2255 motion. The Court distinguished Kaufman on the ground that there the Court was "not dealing with the sort of express waiver provision contained in Rule 12(b)(2)" (p. 239), and that the Rule, "adopted by Congress, governs by its terms the manner in which the claims of defects in the institution of criminal proceedings may be waived" (p. 241). Justices Marshall, Brennan and Douglas dissented.

Although Davis itself was based on the specific waiver rule set out in Rule 12(b)(2), it has become clear since Davis that waiver in the § 2255 setting is governed generally by the Wainwright cause and prejudice standard. The lower courts had assumed this to be the case, see 3 Federal Practice § 596.1 & n. 13, and the Supreme Court confirmed it in United States v. Frady, 456 U.S. 152 (1982). Indeed, Frady is the leading case on the meaning of the "prejudice" requirement. In Frady, a federal prisoner had filed a § 2255 motion to vacate his life sentence for murder, on the ground that, nineteen years previously, the jury had been wrongly instructed as to proof of malice. The prisoner had not made this challenge at trial, on appeal, or in any of his numerous prior collateral attacks. Applying the Wainwright standard, the Court refused to permit § 2255 review, holding that Frady, who admitted the killing for which he had been convicted, had suffered no prejudice as a result of the procedural default. Prejudice does not follow simply from the fact that a jury instruction is erroneous, the Court held. Rather, the degree of prejudice caused by an error must be

---

2. Kaufman was subjected to withering criticism by Friendly, *Is Innocence Relevant? Collateral Attack on Criminal Judgments*, 38 U.Chi.L.Rev. 142, 161–62 (1970). Judge Friendly relied in part on the analysis of Professor Amsterdam suggesting that collateral attack is unjustified for Fourth Amendment issues. See Amsterdam, *Search, Seizure, and Section 2255: A Comment*, 112 U.Pa.L.Rev. 378 (1960).

3. The Court stated in a footnote in Stone v. Powell that "[t]o the extent the application of the exclusionary rule in Kaufman did not rely upon the supervisory role of this Court over the lower federal courts * * * the rationale for its application in [the § 2255] context is * * * rejected" (p. 481 n. 16). The Court has not, however, drawn any distinction between § 2254 and § 2255 cases based upon this "supervisory role," and it is clear that the Stone v. Powell standard applies on an undifferentiated basis to § 2255 cases. See 3 Wright, Federal Practice and Procedure: Criminal 2d § 594 & n. 35 (1982 & 1987 Supp.) (hereafter cited as 3 Federal Practice).

evaluated in the context of the whole trial, and is only sufficient to satisfy the Wainwright test when the error has so infected the trial that the conviction violates due process (p. 169). The petitioner must show that errors at trial "worked to his *actual* and substantial disadvantage, infecting his entire trial with error of constitutional dimensions" (p. 170). Since Frady had never presented colorable evidence to contradict strong evidence in the record that he had acted with malice, he had failed to show prejudice.[4]

Prior to Frady, lower courts had occasionally suggested that § 2255 collateral attack is available for *constitutional* claims that were not raised on appeal, provided there was no "deliberate bypass" on the issue. See, *e.g.,* United States v. Capua, 656 F.2d 1033, 1037 (5th Cir.1981). There seems little doubt, however, that the "deliberate bypass" standard has now been entirely replaced for federal prisoners by the Wainwright "cause and prejudice" test. See, *e.g.,* Norris v. United States, 687 F.2d 899 (7th Cir. 1982). On the issue of the continued vitality of the Noia standard in this area, see 3 Federal Practice § 596.1 n. 20.

(4) Despite the formal equivalence between state prisoner and federal prisoner cases posited by Kaufman and Frady, note how much more restricted in real life § 2255 is. In a simple case in which there is no change in governing law and no new evidence or other reason to relitigate the facts, a state prisoner can nevertheless obtain a new determination from a federal habeas court on a constitutional claim already rejected by the state courts. A federal prisoner, by contrast, cannot ordinarily attack his conviction under § 2255 in such a case. If the federal court of appeals already rejected the federal prisoner's claim on the merits, that precedent will, as a practical matter, be deemed binding, and the § 2255 motion will be dismissed out of hand (even if formally the court has jurisdiction and res judicata is inapplicable). See 3 Federal Practice § 593, at 439 n. 26. If the federal prisoner's claim was not previously resolved on the merits by the court of appeals, the cause and prejudice test will nearly always bar relief. Thus, unlike § 2254, § 2255 is effectively limited to cases in which (i) there was some defect in the factfinding at trial (*e.g.,* new evidence has been discovered), (ii) the governing law has changed, see Paragraph (6), *infra,* or (iii) the prisoner can show cause for and prejudice from a procedural default.

(5) Note that § 2255 refers to sentences "imposed in violation of the Constitution *or laws* of the United States". Is an error which is neither constitutional, nor "jurisdictional" in the conventional sense (as to which see Bowen v. Johnston, 306 U.S. 19 (1939)), automatically the basis for collateral relief under the statute?

Sunal v. Large, 332 U.S. 174 (1947),[5] and Hill v. United States, 368 U.S. 424 (1962), both cited in this connection in Kaufman, indicate that the answer is probably "no".

4. In dissent, Justice Brennan said that Fed.R.Crim.Proc. 52(b) (the plain error rule), not the Wainwright standard, should apply to § 2255 motions. Rule 52(b) should apply in the § 2255 context even if it does not govern § 2254 review, because the latter is a civil collateral review for state prisoners, whereas § 2255 provides a criminal review procedure for federal pris-

oners. This result, Justice Brennan said, "merely allows federal courts the discretion common to most [state] courts to waive procedural defaults where justice requires" (p. 184).

5. Sunal was a habeas corpus case, decided a year before § 2255 was enacted. Note, however, that the habeas statute,

Sunal v. Large shows, however, that it is by no means clear that "constitutional" issues are inevitably more important or always bear more significantly on the justice of a conviction than nonconstitutional issues. The petitioners were convicted of violating the Selective Training and Service Act of 1940 by refusing to submit to induction. At their trials they sought to show that they were illegally denied exempt classification as ministers of religion. The trial courts excluded the evidence, holding the classification incontestable in a criminal prosecution. There was no appeal from the convictions. Almost a year thereafter the Supreme Court's decision in Estep v. United States, 327 U.S. 114 (1946), p. 405, *supra,* showed that the trial courts erred in excluding an attack on the selective service classification.

The Supreme Court held habeas corpus was not available to test whether there was a basis in fact for the classifications. Justice Douglas said (332 U.S. at 177–83):

"The normal and customary method of correcting errors of the trial is by appeal. Appeals could have been taken in these cases, but they were not.   *   *   *

" *   *   * So far as convictions obtained in the federal courts are concerned, the general rule is that the writ of habeas corpus will not be allowed to do service for an appeal.   *   *   * There have been, however, some exceptions.   *   *   *

" *   *   * At the time these defendants were convicted the Estep and Smith cases were pending before the appellate courts. The petition in the Smith case was, indeed, filed here about two weeks before Kulick's conviction and about a month after Sunal's conviction. The same road was open to Sunal and Kulick as the one Smith and Estep took. Why the legal strategy counseled taking appeals in the Smith and Estep cases and not in these we do not know. Perhaps it was based on the facts of these two cases. For the question of law had not been decided by the Court; and counsel was pressing for a decision here. The case, therefore, is not one where the law was changed after the time for appeal had expired. It is rather a situation where at the time of the convictions the definitive ruling on the question of law had not crystallized. Of course, if Sunal and Kulick had pursued the appellate course and failed, their cases would be quite different. But since they chose not to pursue the remedy which they had, we do not think they should now be allowed to justify their failure by saying they deemed any appeal futile.   *   *   *

"An endeavor is made to magnify the error in these trials to constitutional proportions by asserting that the refusal of the proffered evidence robbed the trial of vitality by depriving defendants of their only real defense. But as much might be said of many rulings during a criminal trial. Defendants received throughout an opportunity to be heard and enjoyed all procedural guaranties granted by the Constitution."

Justices Frankfurter, Murphy, and Rutledge dissented.

Suppose that an appeal had been taken in Sunal. Suppose that the court of appeals had affirmed on the basis of the pre-Estep law, and certiorari had thereupon been denied. Do you read the opinion as indicat-

§ 2241(c)(3), also refers to custody in violation of the "laws" (as well as of the Constitution) of the United States.

ing that collateral relief would then have been available after Estep? Or is the talk about appeal meant to indicate that the issue raised can only be litigated on direct review?

In Hill v. United States the claim was that the sentencing judge violated Rule 32(a) of the Criminal Rules by failing to give the defendant an opportunity to speak prior to sentencing. The Court held that the claim could not be raised under § 2255 (368 U.S. at 428–29): "The failure of a trial court to ask a defendant represented by an attorney whether he has anything to say before sentence is imposed is not of itself an error of the character or magnitude cognizable under a writ of habeas corpus. It is an error which is neither jurisdictional nor constitutional. It is not a fundamental defect * * *. Whether § 2255 relief would be available if a violation of Rule 32(a) occurred in the context of other aggravating circumstances is a question we therefore do not consider."

The question whether nonconstitutional errors can be considered on collateral attack under § 2255 was further explored in Davis v. United States, 417 U.S. 333 (1974) (referred to as Davis II herein, in order to avoid confusion with the unrelated Davis case, discussed in Paragraph (3)). Petitioner was convicted for refusing to obey an order of induction. He sought § 2255 relief on the ground that the regulation authorizing his induction for "delinquency" (failing to report for a physical examination) was invalid because not authorized by the statute.[6] The Court, with only Justice Rehnquist in dissent on this point, held that the nonconstitutional issue was cognizable on a § 2255 motion, since § 2255 refers to sentences imposed in violation of the "laws" as well as the Constitution of the United States. The Court reasoned that, as held in Hayman, § 2255 was intended to be as broad as habeas corpus, which under § 2254 encompasses cases where a state custody is "in violation of the Constitution *or laws*" of the United States. Since nonconstitutional grounds are available under § 2254, they must be under § 2255.

Is this reasoning persuasive? The case where a *state* prisoner can allege that his detention violates federal *non*constitutional law will be a very rare one indeed; can you think of such a case? Opening up § 2255 to nonconstitutional claims thus cannot be fairly described as merely honoring Congress' intent to create *equivalence* between federal and state prisoners, can it?

The Court distinguished Sunal, stating that that case was premised essentially on the fact that no appeal had been taken rather than on the unavailability of § 2255 to test the issue sought to be raised.

Finally, the Court warned that not "every asserted error of law can be raised on a § 2255 motion," and reasserted the authority of the test suggested in Hill v. United States: was the "claimed error of law 'a fundamental defect which inherently results in a complete miscarriage of justice,' " and is the case one presenting " 'exceptional circumstances where the need for the remedy * * * is apparent' " (p. 346). The Court concluded that Davis' claim—that he was in effect punished for conduct the statute did not make criminal—met these standards.

6.   Davis' legal position was in fact later upheld in Gutknecht v. United States, 396 U.S. 295 (1970).

The restrictive language of Hill and Davis II was applied later in United States v. Timmreck, 441 U.S. 780 (1979) (§ 2255 is not available when all that can be shown is a purely "formal" violation of Rule 11 (governing the taking of guilty pleas)); see also United States v. Addonizio, 442 U.S. 178, 186 (1979) ("the claimed error here—that the judge [in imposing sentence] was incorrect about the future course of parole proceedings—does not meet any of the established standards of collateral attack"). See generally the cases cited at 3 Federal Practice § 593 n. 15.

(6) Davis II was also notable because it radically—albeit casually—expanded the opportunities for § 2255 relitigation of issues already adjudicated by a federal tribunal. As noted above, the Court said in a footnote in Kaufman that where a constitutional issue has previously been considered by the convicting court (or by another § 2255 court), the availability of relitigation is governed by the test in Sanders v. United States, p. 1566, *supra* (as to which, in the § 2255 context, see 3 Federal Practice § 602). Davis' claim had been raised at his criminal trial and rejected by the panel of the court of appeals that affirmed his conviction. Thereafter, a different panel of the same court of appeals upheld, in an unrelated case, the same legal claim Davis had made. The question was whether, under Sanders, Davis could relitigate his legal claim in a § 2255 proceeding. The Court without discussion held that the intervening inconsistent opinion by another panel of the same court of appeals constitutes "an intervening change in the law" within the meaning of the Sanders test, and that Davis could therefore raise the question again.

Does this make sense? Should collateral relitigation of a claim already fully litigated and rejected by a federal court of appeals be permitted in the absence of an intervening change in law which would now be *authoritative* (*e.g.*, an inconsistent ruling by the Supreme Court or by the court of appeals *en banc*)? Note that on Davis' § 2255 motion, the district court will be free to follow *either* the first Davis holding or the inconsistent holding. Whichever way it rules, the question of what panel of the court of appeals will then hear the § 2255 motion on appeal is a matter of pure chance. The case may come before the same panel (or a majority of the same panel) which decided the Davis case on *direct* appeal. What are the judges of this panel supposed to do? Does it make sense to ask them to reconsider the matter? In any event, they are free to stick to their guns, aren't they? And even if the case comes before a panel whose judges agree with the intervening decision, is it appropriate for three members of a court of appeals to hold illegal—in the absence of intervening law from the Supreme Court—the very sentence whose legality has just been affirmed by three of their colleagues? Shouldn't the court of appeals at least hear the next case *en banc*?

Note that in many circuits the practice now is that decisions by a panel are regarded as authoritative within the circuit unless overruled by the court *en banc*, so that *intra*-circuit conflicts such as the one in Davis cannot arise. But does Davis II mean that a federal prisoner may collaterally relitigate a claim fully litigated and rejected on the merits by a court of appeals if thereafter *another* court of appeals takes a different view of the law? What is the first court of appeals supposed to do when the § 2255 case now comes before it?

Notice that the holding of Davis II is responsive to a grave and troubling general problem in the administration of justice: what to do when differences among coordinate tribunals lead to release of an accused in one case and to incarceration in another, undistinguishable, one. (Surely the existence of this factor enormously exacerbated the difficulties of Noia's case.) The question nevertheless remains whether the doctrine created in Davis II is an intelligent way of dealing with this problem: is it wise to destabilize the law by allowing collateral attack on a judgment where the only new event is an inconsistent holding by a coordinate tribunal? And if we do decide to permit collateral attack in such a case, shouldn't we then at least make certain that there is an assured method of securing an *authoritative* resolution of the conflict?

(7) In the Hill case a bare majority of the Court held that a Rule 32(a) violation could not be raised as an attack on an "illegal sentence" under Criminal Rule 35, which allows such a sentence to be corrected without limit of time. Rule 35 was construed as limited to claims alleging that the actual punishment imposed was illegal, and not available to test errors in the proceedings at trial and prior to sentencing. Compare Heflin v. United States, 358 U.S. 415 (1959), Paragraph (9), *infra.*

Is it sensible to allow attacks on the illegality of the sentence to be made at any time, but to limit attacks on the legality of the conviction to direct review—unless, of course, the issue is constitutional, jurisdictional, or nonconstitutional but "fundamental," in which cases there is again no time limit?

Compare Rule 33, allowing a motion for a new trial on the basis of newly discovered evidence to be made only within two years of final judgment. But, recall again, if the newly discovered evidence goes to a question cognizable under § 2255, this is one of the Townsend factors calling for collateral rehearing.[7]

(8) The courts apply to federal prisoners an exhaustion of remedies doctrine analogous to that imposed on state prisoners. See Riggins v. United States, 199 U.S. 547, 551 (1905) (habeas corpus sought by federal prisoner awaiting trial on indictment; writ ordered dismissed; no special circumstances justified departure "from the regular course of judicial procedure"); see also Bowen v. Johnston, 306 U.S. 19, 26–27 (1939). And a § 2255 application will be dismissed in the absence of extraordinary circumstances if direct appeal is still available.[8]

(9) In spite of the language of § 2255 that the motion for relief "may be made at any time," Heflin v. United States, 358 U.S. 415 (1959), held that present "custody" was a jurisdictional prerequisite for § 2255 motions, so that no attack could be made under that section on a sentence that the prisoner had not yet begun to serve.[9] The "equivalence" between § 2255 and habeas corpus established in the Hayman and Sanders cases means, however, that Peyton v. Rowe necessarily overruled the Heflin case,[10] and

7. For detailed analysis of Rules 32, 33, and 35, see 5 Rhodes, Orfield's Criminal Procedure Under the Federal Rules (2d ed. 1987).

8. See, *e.g.*, United States v. Gordon, 634 F.2d 638 (1st Cir.1980); United States ex rel. Calabro v. United States Marshall, 466 F.2d 1350 (2d Cir.1972).

9. The Court also held, however, that Fed.R.Crim.Proc. 35 could be used to test Heflin's claim that it was illegal to impose three consecutive sentences because the petitioner had committed only one offense.

10. See Simmons v. United States, 437 F.2d 156, 158 (5th Cir.1971).

that the Jones v. Cunningham definition of "custody" applies to § 2255. See pp. 1569–72, *supra*; and see generally 3 Federal Practice § 596 and cases cited.

BURNS v. WILSON

346 U.S. 137, 73 S.Ct. 1045, 97 L.Ed. 1508 (1953).
Certiorari to the United States Court of Appeals for the
District of Columbia Circuit.

MR. CHIEF JUSTICE VINSON announced the judgment of the Court in an opinion in which MR. JUSTICE REED, MR. JUSTICE BURTON and MR. JUSTICE CLARK join.

Tried separately by Air Force courts-martial on the Island of Guam, petitioners were found guilty of murder and rape and sentenced to death. The sentences were confirmed by the President, and petitioners exhausted all remedies available to them under the Articles of War for review of their convictions by the military tribunals. They then filed petitions for writs of habeas corpus in the United States District Court for the District of Columbia.

In these applications petitioners alleged that they had been denied due process of law in the proceedings which led to their conviction by the courts-martial. They charged that they had been subjected to illegal detention; that coerced confessions had been extorted from them; that they had been denied counsel of their choice and denied effective representation; that the military authorities on Guam had suppressed evidence favorable to them, procured perjured testimony against them and otherwise interfered with the preparation of their defenses. Finally, petitioners charged that their trials were conducted in an atmosphere of terror and vengeance, conducive to mob violence instead of fair play.

The District Court dismissed the applications without hearing evidence, and without further review, after satisfying itself that the courts-martial which tried petitioners had jurisdiction over their persons at the time of the trial and jurisdiction over the crimes with which they were charged as well as jurisdiction to impose the sentences which petitioners received. 104 F.Supp. 310, 312. The Court of Appeals affirmed the District Court's judgment, after expanding the scope of review by giving petitioners' allegations full consideration on their merits, reviewing in detail the mass of evidence to be found in the transcripts of the trial and other proceedings before the military court. 91 U.S.App.D.C. 208, 202 F.2d 335.

We granted certiorari, 344 U.S. 903. Petitioners' allegations are serious, and, as reflected by the divergent bases for decision in the two courts below, the case poses important problems concerning the proper administration of the power of a civil court to review the judgment of a court-martial in a habeas corpus proceeding.

In this case, we are dealing with habeas corpus applicants who assert—rightly or wrongly—that they have been imprisoned and sentenced to death as a result of proceedings which denied them basic rights guaranteed by the Constitution. The federal civil courts have jurisdiction over such applications. By statute, Congress has charged them with the exercise of that power. Accordingly, our initial concern is not whether the District Court has any power at all to consider petitioners' applications; rather our concern is with the manner in which the Court should proceed to exercise its power.

The statute which vests federal courts with jurisdiction over applications for habeas corpus from persons confined by the military courts is the same statute which vests them with jurisdiction over the applications of persons confined by the civil courts. But in military habeas corpus the inquiry, the scope of matters open for review, has always been more narrow than in civil cases. Hiatt v. Brown, 339 U.S. 103 (1950). Thus the law which governs a civil court in the exercise of its jurisdiction over military habeas corpus applications cannot simply be assimilated to the law which governs the exercise of that power in other instances. It is *sui generis;* it must be so, because of the peculiar relationship between the civil and military law.

Military law, like state law, is a jurisprudence which exists separate and apart from the law which governs in our federal judicial establishment. This Court has played no role in its development; we have exerted no supervisory power over the courts which enforce it; the rights of men in the armed forces must perforce be conditioned to meet certain overriding demands of discipline and duty, and the civil courts are not the agencies which must determine the precise balance to be struck in this adjustment. The Framers expressly entrusted that task to Congress.

Indeed, Congress has taken great care both to define the rights of those subject to military law, and provide a complete system of review within the military system to secure those rights. Only recently the Articles of War were completely revised, and thereafter, in conformity with its purpose to integrate the armed services, Congress established a Uniform Code of Military Justice applicable to all members of the military establishment. These enactments were prompted by a desire to meet objections and criticisms lodged against court-martial procedures in the aftermath of World War II. Nor was this a patchwork effort to plug loopholes in the old system of military justice. The revised Articles and the new Code are the result of painstaking study; they reflect an effort to reform and modernize the system—from top to bottom.

Rigorous provisions guarantee a trial as free as possible from command influence, the right to prompt arraignment, the right to counsel of the accused's own choosing, and the right to secure witnesses and prepare an adequate defense. The revised Articles, and their successor—the new Code—also establish a hierarchy within the military establishment to review the convictions of courts-martial, to ferret out irregularities in the trial, and to enforce the procedural safeguards which Congress determined to guarantee to those in the Nation's armed services.[7] And finally Congress has provided a special post-conviction remedy within the military establishment, apart from ordinary appellate review, whereby one convict-

---

7. 10 U.S.C. (Supp.II) § 1521. The Uniform Code of Military Justice established the Court of Military Appeals, which is composed of civilians. It automatically reviews all capital cases and has discretionary jurisdiction over other cases. It is the highest court in the military system. 50 U.S.C. (Supp. V) § 654. See Walker and Niebank, *The Court of Military Appeals—Its History, Organization and Operation,* 6 Vand.L.Rev. 228 (1953).

ed by a court-martial may attack collaterally the judgment under which he stands convicted.[8]

The military courts, like the state courts, have the same responsibilities as do the federal courts to protect a person from a violation of his constitutional rights. In military habeas corpus cases, even more than in state habeas corpus cases, it would be in disregard of the statutory scheme if the federal civil courts failed to take account of the prior proceedings—of the fair determinations of the military tribunals after all military remedies have been exhausted. Congress has provided that these determinations are "final" and "binding" upon all courts.[9] We have held before that this does not displace the civil courts' jurisdiction over an application for habeas corpus from the military prisoner. Gusik v. Schilder, 340 U.S. 128 (1950). But these provisions do mean that when a military decision has dealt fully and fairly with an allegation raised in that application, it is not open to a federal civil court to grant the writ simply to re-evaluate the evidence. Whelchel v. McDonald, 340 U.S. 122 (1950).

We turn, then, to this case.

Petitioners' applications, as has been noted, set forth serious charges—allegations which, in their cumulative effect, were sufficient to depict fundamental unfairness in the process whereby their guilt was determined and their death sentences rendered. Had the military courts manifestly refused to consider those claims, the District Court was empowered to review them *de novo*. For the constitutional guarantee of due process is meaningful enough, and sufficiently adaptable, to protect soldiers—as well as civilians—from the crude injustices of a trial so conducted that it becomes bent on fixing guilt by dispensing with rudimentary fairness rather than finding truth through adherence to those basic guarantees which have long been recognized and honored by the military courts as well as the civil courts. * * *

Answering the habeas corpus applications, respondents denied that there had been any violation of petitioners' rights and attached to their answer copies of the record of each trial, the review of the Staff Judge Advocate, the decision of the Board of Review in the office of the Judge Advocate General, the decision (after briefs and oral argument) of the Judicial Council in the Judge Advocate General's office, the recommendation of the Judge Advocate General, the action of the President confirming the sentences, and also the decision of the Judge Advocate General denying petitions for new trials under Article 53 of the Articles of War.

These records make it plain that the military courts have heard petitioners out on every significant allegation which they now urge. Accordingly, it is not the duty of the civil courts simply to repeat that process—to re-examine and reweigh each item of evidence of the occurrence of events which tend to prove or disprove one of the allegations in the applications for habeas corpus. It is the limited function of the civil courts

---

8. 62 Stat. 639, 10 U.S.C. (Supp.III) § 1525. See Gusik v. Schilder, 340 U.S. 128 (1950). This provision was also made a part of the Uniform Code of Military Justice. 64 Stat. 132, 50 U.S.C. (Supp. V) § 660; 64 Stat. 147, 50 U.S.C. (Supp. V) § 740.

9. The revisions of the Articles of War, 10 U.S.C. (Supp. II) § 1521(h), and the Uniform Code of Military Justice, 50 U.S.C. (Supp. V) § 663, both provided that the decisions of the appellate military tribunals should be "final" and should be "binding" upon the courts.

to determine whether the military have given fair consideration to each of these claims. Whelchel v. McDonald, *supra*. We think they have.

The military reviewing courts scrutinized the trial records before rejecting petitioners' contentions. In lengthy opinions, they concluded that petitioners had been accorded a complete opportunity to establish the authenticity of their allegations, and had failed. Thus, the trial records were analyzed to show that the circumstances fully justified the decision to remove Dennis' original choice of defense counsel; that each petitioner had declared, at the beginning of his trial, that he was ready to proceed; that each was ably represented; that the trials proceeded in an orderly fashion—with that calm degree of dispassion essential to a fair hearing on the question of guilt; that there was exhaustive inquiry into the background of the confessions—with the taking of testimony from the persons most concerned with the making of these statements, including petitioner Dennis who elected to take the stand. And finally it was demonstrated that the issues arising from the charges relating to the use of perjured testimony and planted evidence were either explored or were available for exploration at the trial.

Petitioners have failed to show that this military review was legally inadequate to resolve the claims which they have urged upon the civil courts. They simply demand an opportunity to make a new record, to prove *de novo* in the District Court precisely the case which they failed to prove in the military courts. We think, under the circumstances, that due regard for the limitations on a civil court's power to grant such relief precludes such action. We think that although the Court of Appeals may have erred in reweighing each item of relevant evidence in the trial record, it certainly did not err in holding that there was no need for a further hearing in the District Court. Accordingly its judgment must be

Affirmed.

MR. JUSTICE JACKSON concurs in the result.

MR. JUSTICE MINTON, concurring in the affirmance of the judgment.

I do not agree that the federal civil courts sit to protect the constitutional rights of military defendants, except to the limited extent indicated below. Their rights are committed by the Constitution and by Congress acting in pursuance thereof to the protection of the military courts, with review in some instances by the President. Nor do we sit to review errors of law committed by military courts. * * *

If error is made by the military courts, to which Congress has committed the protection of the rights of military personnel, that error must be corrected in the military hierarchy of courts provided by Congress. We have but one function, namely, to see that the military court has jurisdiction, not whether it has committed error in the exercise of that jurisdiction.

The rule was clearly stated in the early case of In re Grimley, 137 U.S. 147, 150, in these words:

"It cannot be doubted that the civil courts may in any case inquire into the jurisdiction of a court-martial, and if it appears that the party condemned was not amenable to its jurisdiction, may discharge him from the sentence. And, on the other hand, it is equally clear that by habeas corpus the civil courts exercise no supervisory or correcting power over the proceedings of a court-martial; and that no mere errors in their proceedings are open to consideration. The single inquiry, the test, is jurisdiction. * * *"

This case was cited and an excerpt from the above quoted with approval in Hiatt v. Brown, 339 U.S. 103, 111. After approving In re Grimley, we rejected the broader claim of the respondent for review to determine whether certain action of the military court had denied him due process of law and said:

"In this case the court-martial had jurisdiction of the person accused and the offense charged, and acted within its lawful powers. The correction of any errors it may have committed is for the military authorities which are alone authorized to review its decision. * * *"

With this understanding, I concur in affirming the judgment.

Mr. Justice Frankfurter. * * *

[Justice Frankfurter urged that the case be set down for reargument. In October, 1953, when a petition for rehearing was denied, he dissented in an opinion which argued that the scope of review should be reconsidered in light of Johnson v. Zerbst, p. 1501, *supra.* 346 U.S. 844.]

Mr. Justice Douglas, with whom Mr. Justice Black concurs, dissenting.

The charges which are made concerning the confessions exacted from these accused are quite lurid. But the basic, undisputed facts, though not dramatic, leave the clear impression that one of the petitioners was held incommunicado and repeatedly examined over a 5–day period until he confessed. * * *

I think petitioners are entitled to a judicial hearing on the circumstances surrounding their confessions. * * *

The * * * Court gives binding effect to the ruling of the military tribunal on the constitutional question, provided it has given fair consideration to it.

If the military agency has fairly and conscientiously applied the standards of due process formulated by this Court, I would agree that a rehash of the same facts by a federal court would not advance the cause of justice. But where the military reviewing agency has not done that, a court should entertain the petition for habeas corpus. In the first place, the military tribunals in question are federal agencies subject to no other judicial supervision except what is afforded by the federal courts. In the second place, the rules of due process which they apply are constitutional rules which we, not they, formulate.

The *undisputed* facts in this case make a prima facie case that our rule on coerced confessions expressed in Watts v. Indiana, 338 U.S. 49, was violated here. No court has considered the question whether repetitious questioning over a period of 5 days while the accused was held incommunicado without benefit of counsel violated the Fifth Amendment. The highest reviewing officer, the Judge Advocate General of the Air Force, said only this:

"After reading and re-reading the record of trial, there is no reasonable doubt in my mind that all the confessions were wholly voluntary, as the court decided, and were properly admitted. Where the evidence as to whether there was coercion is conflicting, or where different inferences may fairly be drawn from the admitted facts, the question whether a confession was voluntary is for the triers of the facts (Lyons v. Oklahoma, 322 U.S. 596; Lisenba v. California, 314 U.S. 219). Thus the court's decision on the voluntary nature of the testimony, arrived at from first-hand hearing and observation, is presumptively correct and will not be disturbed unless manifestly erroneous (MGM Corporation v. Fear, 104 F.2d 892; ACM 3597, Maddle, 4 Court–Martial Reports [AF] 573)."

There has been at no time any considered appraisal of the facts surrounding these confessions in light of our opinions. Before these men go to their death, such an appraisal should be made.

NOTE ON COLLATERAL ATTACK ON COURT MARTIAL CONVICTIONS

(1) As Justice Minton pointed out, only three years before Burns the Court reaffirmed the principle that "the single inquiry, the test, is jurisdiction" in Hiatt v. Brown, 339 U.S. 103 (1950), thereby reversing the trend (actuated by the widening scope of habeas review of civilian convictions) towards softening that requirement in the lower courts. See *Developments,* p. 1470, *supra,* at 1208–15 for a full account of the pre-Burns law; see also, generally, Bishop, *Civilian Judges and Military Justice: Collateral Review of Court–Martial Convictions,* 61 Colum.L.Rev. 40 (1961); Katz & Nelson, *The Need for Clarification in Military Habeas Corpus,* 27 Ohio St.L.J. 193 (1966); Notes, 73 Mich.L.Rev. 886 (1975), 69 Colum.L.Rev. 1259 (1969), and 76 Yale L.J. 380 (1966).

Since Burns, the Court has decided on the merits a number of cases dealing with the jurisdiction of courts martial, see, *e.g.,* Kinsella v. United States ex rel. Singleton, 361 U.S. 234 (1960) (military courts do not have power to try serviceman's wife); and on one occasion it has refused to pass on the question whether a sentence imposed by a court martial was too harsh, see Fowler v. Wilkinson, 353 U.S. 583, 585 (1957) ("We have determined that the board of review had jurisdiction to modify the sentence. Our inquiry cannot extend beyond that question"). The Court did reach the merits of petitioner's constitutional claims in Parker v. Levy, 417 U.S. 733 (1974) (denying claim that the Military Code provisions prohibiting "conduct unbecoming to an officer and a gentleman," among others, was unconstitutionally vague and overbroad), and in Middendorf v. Henry, 425 U.S. 25 (1976) (rejecting claim that summary court martial procedure denied defendant's right to counsel).

The lower courts have generally assumed that the middle position stated by the Chief Justice in Burns represents the law, though they have taken varying approaches to the issue when a constitutional question has been given such "fair consideration" by the courts in the military hierarchy that habeas inquiry is barred. See the discussions of these decisions in the authorities cited above.

(2) What is the justification for giving the decisions of military tribunals greater deference than is given state and federal courts? See Justice Rehnquist's opinion in Parker v. Levy, *supra,* 417 U.S. at 743–52, discussing "very significant differences between military law and civilian law and between the military community and the civilian community."

Recall that the early court martial cases defining a narrow scope of inquiry were decided when the scope of inquiry in cases involving civilian convictions was equally narrow. Prior to Hiatt v. Brown, *supra,* most lower courts assumed that the widening range of habeas review in civilian cases was equally relevant to military cases (albeit acknowledging, of course, that the content of constitutional rules may be very different in court martial proceedings).

Do the opinions in Burns and Parker furnish a persuasive explanation why military determinations of constitutional questions should receive such special consideration?

(3) One convicted by court martial must exhaust available military remedies before seeking federal habeas corpus. See Gusik v. Schilder, 340 U.S. 128 (1950); Noyd v. Bond, 395 U.S. 683 (1969). Compare Parisi v. Davidson, 405 U.S. 34 (1972), involving a soldier whose application for discharge as a conscientious objector was denied by the Army; administrative remedies for review of that decision were duly exhausted. Alleging that the refusal was without warrant, the petitioner sought federal habeas corpus. Thereafter court martial charges were instituted against him for refusal to obey an order to board a plane for Viet Nam. The Supreme Court held that it was error to stay the habeas proceeding pending final decision by the court martial. Justice Stewart said (pp. 41–42): "Under accepted principles of comity, the court should stay its hand only if the relief the petitioner seeks—discharge as a conscientious objector—would also be available to him with reasonable promptness and certainty through the machinery of the military judicial system in its processing of the court-martial charge." Although an unlawful failure to grant a discharge could be a defense in the court-martial proceeding, continued Justice Stewart, it is doubtful whether that proceeding could effectuate the petitioner's discharge even if the defense is upheld. He concluded: "[T]he pendency of court-martial proceedings must not delay a federal district court's prompt determination of the conscientious objector claim of a serviceman who has exhausted all administrative remedies * * *. * * * But our decision today should not be understood as impinging upon the basic principles of comity that must prevail between civilian courts and the military judicial system. * * * Accordingly, a federal district court, even though upholding the merits of the conscientious objector claim of a serviceman against whom court-martial charges are pending, should give careful consideration to the appropriate demands of comity in effectuating its habeas corpus decree" (pp. 45–46).

On the exhaustion question generally, see Sherman, *Judicial Review of Military Determinations and the Exhaustion of Remedies Requirement,* 55 Va.L.Rev. 483 (1969). On the scope of habeas corpus inquiry into military determinations other than convictions by court martial, see also Sherman, and see *Developments* 1238–63.

(4) An important case on the jurisdiction of the federal courts to pass on the validity of court-martial proceedings is Schlesinger v. Councilman, 420 U.S. 738 (1975).[1] Court-martial charges were preferred against Councilman, an army captain, accusing him of selling marijuana. Alleging that the offense was not "service connected" (within the law defining court-

1. The case is commented on in Note, *Courts for the Servicemember Not in Custo-Post–Conviction Review in the Federal dy,* 73 Mich.L.Rev. 886 (1975).

martial jurisdiction at that time), Councilman, after an unsuccessful attempt to get the charges dismissed, brought suit in federal district court seeking an injunction against the pending court martial; jurisdiction was based on 28 U.S.C. § 1331. The Supreme Court rejected the government's contention that habeas corpus was the exclusive remedy for testing the question whether there is some fundamental or jurisdictional defect in a court-martial proceeding. It observed that trespass and backpay actions were traditional methods to test the question whether a judgment by court martial was or was not void. Nor did the finality provision of Article 76 of the Uniform Code of Military Justice, providing that the "proceedings, findings, and sentences of courts-martial * * * are final and conclusive," indicate a congressional purpose to restrict collateral attack on courts martial to habeas corpus: "nothing in Article 76 distinguishes between habeas corpus and other remedies also consistent with well-established rules governing collateral attack" (p. 751).

The Court then went on to hold, however, that, even though the district court had subject-matter jurisdiction, relief should be denied as a matter of equitable discretion. Citing the Younger rule, the requirement of exhaustion in habeas cases, and the rule requiring exhaustion of federal administrative remedies, the Court stated that similar considerations apply to the propriety of equitable intervention into pending court-martial proceedings (p. 758): "[J]udgments of the military court system remain subject in proper cases to collateral impeachment. But implicit in the congressional scheme embodied in the Code is the view that the military court system generally is adequate to and responsibly will perform its assigned task. We think this congressional judgment must be respected and that it must be assumed that the military court system will vindicate servicemen's constitutional rights. We have recognized this, as well as the practical considerations common to all exhaustion requirements, in holding that federal courts normally will not entertain habeas petitions by military prisoners unless all available military remedies have been exhausted. * * * The same principles are relevant to striking the balance governing the exercise of equity power. We hold that when a serviceman charged with crimes by military authorities can show no harm other than that attendant to resolution of his case in the military court system, the federal district courts must refrain from intervention, by way of injunction or otherwise." [2]

2. [Ed.] The Court distinguished the cases in which civilians had been permitted to test court-martial jurisdiction over them without exhaustion, such as Toth v. Quarles, 350 U.S. 11 (1955), and Reid v. Covert, 354 U.S. 1 (1957). It held that there is "no injustice" in requiring a person admittedly in the military to submit initially to military justice; and that the expertise of military courts is relevant to the resolution of the very question at issue: whether Councilman's offense was service-connected.

Chapter XII

ADVANCED PROBLEMS IN JUDICIAL FEDERALISM: HEREIN OF RES JUDICATA AND OTHER ASPECTS OF CONCURRENT OR SUCCESSIVE JURISDICTION

NOTE ON THE RES JUDICATA EFFECT OF FEDERAL JUDGMENTS

(1) When a federal court renders a judgment on a federal question it has generally been assumed—usually without discussion—that federal law governs the preclusive effects of that judgment in a subsequent action in a federal court. See 18 Wright, Miller & Cooper, Federal Practice and Procedure § 4466 (1981 & 1987 Supp.) (hereafter cited "18 Federal Practice"); Degnan, *Federalized Res Judicata,* 85 Yale L.J. 741, 755–73 (1976) (hereafter cited "Degnan"); see also Restatement (Second) of Judgments § 87 (1982) (hereafter cited "Restatement 2d") ("Federal law determines the effects under the rules of res judicata of a judgment of a federal court").

Res judicata law is almost entirely judge-made.[1] The federal courts have consequently made substantial contributions to the common law of preclusion as they have gone about developing this body of federal res judicata law. Although it is not the purpose of this Note to provide a comprehensive survey of this body of federal law, a scattering of particularly celebrated cases will serve to illustrate it.

(a) United States v. Moser, 266 U.S. 236 (1924), Commissioner v. Sunnen, 333 U.S. 591 (1948), and Montana v. United States, 440 U.S. 147 (1979), are considered the leading cases on the problem of when rulings on question of law have preclusive effect.[2] Moser involved the question whether a retired naval captain's service at the Naval Academy had amounted to "service during the civil war" within the meaning of a federal statute; if it did he was entitled to a higher pension. The Court of Claims answered the question in the affirmative, and in two later actions to recover pension installments it held the issue of Moser's entitlement to be res judicata, despite an intervening decision involving another person in which the same court had declined to follow the interpretation of the applicable statute adopted in the first Moser case. In Moser's fourth action to recover an installment of the pension, the Supreme Court held that his

---

1. The term "res judicata" is used herein, as in the Restatement 2d, to refer both to claim preclusion and issue preclusion (collateral estoppel).

2. It is usually said that the doctrine of res judicata does not apply to "pure" questions of law, at least where the two actions involve substantially unrelated claims.

Montana v. United States, 440 U.S. 147, 162–63 (1979); Restatement 2d § 28(2)(a). The courts' pronouncements on "pure" issues of law exercise power in subsequent cases through the ordinary rules of stare decisis, not through res judicata. The cases in the text thus concern issues of law application.

right to his pension was res judicata, stating that "a fact, question or right distinctly adjudged in the original action cannot be disputed in a subsequent action, even though the determination was reached upon an erroneous view or by an erroneous application of the law. That would be to affirm the principle in respect of the thing adjudged but, at the same time, deny it all efficacy by sustaining a challenge to the grounds upon which the judgment was based. * * * A determination in respect of the status of an individual upon which his right to recover depends is as conclusive as a decision upon any other matter" (p. 242).

In Commissioner v. Sunnen, a taxpayer had won a decision in the Board of Tax Appeals that he was not liable for taxes for the years 1929 through 1931 on royalties paid under a contract he had assigned to his wife in 1928. The contract was renewed in 1938 and the Commissioner again sought a decision that Sunnen was liable for taxes, this time for 1937 (for royalties paid under the 1928 contract) and 1938 through 1941 (under the new contract). As to liability for 1937, the Court held that issue preclusion did not apply, despite "complete identity of facts, issues and parties as between the earlier Board proceeding and the instant one," because a series of intervening Supreme Court decisions had "vitally altered" the legal situation and made it clear that the Board had reached an erroneous result.[3] Regarding liability under the 1938 contract, the Court denied the Board decision preclusive effect on the distinct ground that different facts were involved. The Court held that "if the relevant facts in the two cases are separable, even though they be similar or identical, collateral estoppel does not govern the legal issues which recur in the second case. Thus the second proceeding may involve an instrument or transaction identical with, but in form separable from, the one dealt with in the first proceeding. In that situation, a court is free in the second proceeding to make an independent examination of the legal matters at issue" (p 601).

Montana v. United States involved attacks by the United States on the validity of Montana's gross receipts tax on contractors for public construction projects; the government claimed the tax discriminated against the United States. The Montana Supreme Court upheld the tax in a state-court litigation brought by contractors but controlled and financed by the United States. No appeal was taken. The United States in the meantime had brought its own action to invalidate the tax in a federal district court. The Supreme Court held that the United States was bound by the state-court judgment, since it was in privity with the plaintiffs there and since there had not been the "major changes in the law governing intergovernmental tax immunity" required under Sunnen to create an exception to res judicata.[4]

(b) The Supreme Court has also made significant contributions to the erosion of the doctrine of mutuality of estoppel, under which "neither party could use a prior judgment as an estoppel against the other unless both parties were bound by the judgment." Parklane Hosiery Co., Inc. v. Shore, 439 U.S. 322, 326–27 (1979). The mutuality rule prevented a new plaintiff

---

3. On the sorts of changes in legal climate that have been held sufficient to bar issue preclusion, see 18 Federal Practice § 4425, at 261–64.

4. Montana involved a state court, not a federal court judgment, but the Supreme Court apparently assumed that federal law governs the preclusion question. *Cf. Note on § 1738 and the Res Judicata Effect of State Judgments*, p. 1624, *infra*.

or defendant from making offensive or defensive use of a prior judgment against a former party.

In Blonder-Tongue Laboratories, Inc. v. University of Illinois Foundation, 402 U.S. 313 (1971), a patentee brought an infringement suit. In a prior infringement action by the same patentee against a different defendant, the patent had been held invalid. Emphasizing the burden on courts and defendants of permitting relitigation of the issue of validity, the Supreme Court held that the prior holding of invalidity was preclusive provided the plaintiff had had a "full and fair opportunity to litigate" the question at the first trial.

In Parklane Hosiery, *supra*, the Court made a major pronouncement on the issue of "offensive" nonmutual preclusion. The SEC had obtained an injunction against false and misleading proxy statements in violation of the securities laws. A private stockholders' action for damages was then brought against the same defendant on account of the same statements. The Court held that the defendant was precluded by the first judgment from relitigating the issues adjudicated in the first case. The Court noted that offensive nonmutual preclusion—unlike defensive use of findings against a former party—may be problematic;[5] but it said that these problems can be solved by giving the district courts "broad discretion to determine" whether to allow a nonparty to the former litigation to make offensive use of findings made in that litigation. The Court said that such use should be denied when the plaintiff "could easily have joined in the earlier action" or where preclusion "would be unfair to the defendants."[6]

For other important cases on the federal common law of res judicata, see, *e.g.*, Federated Department Stores, Inc. v. Moitie, 452 U.S. 394 (1981) (leading case on the question whether there is a general "fairness" exception to res judicata); Lawlor v. National Screen Service Corp., 349 U.S. 322 (1955) (scope of claim preclusion).

(2) Special res judicata problems arise when a federal judgment is collaterally attacked in a subsequent action on the ground that the first court lacked subject matter jurisdiction. The rules limiting the federal courts to cases within their subject matter jurisdiction have always been given special force. Thus, under the rule in the Mansfield case, discussed further in Chap. XIV, Sec. 1, *infra*, a challenge to a federal court's subject matter jurisdiction may be made at any time during the course of proceedings, and the court may raise the question sua sponte. Does this policy go so far, however, as to permit a federal court's judgment to be collaterally attacked on this ground? Or does the policy against relitigation cut in?

5. The Court noted two problems: (a) offensive preclusion may encourage potential plaintiffs not to join the first action, because they have everything to win (by a favorable judgment) and nothing to lose (by an unfavorable one); (b) offensive preclusion may be unfair if the defendant had little incentive to litigate in the first action (because, for instance, the amount involved was small), or if the judgment relied on was itself inconsistent with earlier judgments involving the same defendant, or if in the first action the defendant was incon-

venienced by difficulties in obtaining proof or calling witnesses.

6. The Court rejected the defendants' claim that it violated their Seventh Amendment rights to give preclusive effect in a damages action (in which they had a right to jury trial) to a decision against defendants in an equitable action (in which they did not), reasoning in part that the effect of preclusion is that "there is no further factfinding function for the jury to perform" (p. 336).

In McCormick v. Sullivant, 10 Wheat. 192 (U.S.1825), the Court was called upon to decide whether a prior "general decree of dismissal" by a federal district court acted as a bar to a second action on the same claim. The record in the first suit did not show that the parties were of diverse citizenship; on this basis, plaintiffs claimed that the previous action was *coram non judice* and the prior decree void. The Supreme Court responded:

"But this reason proceeds upon an incorrect view of the character and jurisdiction of the inferior courts of the United States. They are all of limited jurisdiction; but they are not, on that account, inferior courts, in the technical sense of those words, whose judgments, taken alone, are to be disregarded. If the jurisdiction be not alleged in the proceedings, their judgments and decrees are erroneous, and may, upon a writ of error or appeal, be reversed for that cause. But they are not absolute nullities." The decree in the prior suit "whilst it remains unreversed, is a valid bar of the present suit" (p. 199).

In McCormick the record in the first case merely failed to disclose the citizenship of the parties. But in Des Moines Navig. & R. Co. v. Iowa Homestead Co., 123 U.S. 552 (1887), the record showed affirmatively that there was no diversity of citizenship or any other basis of jurisdiction. The Court held that this made no difference. Both cases were relied on in Dowell v. Applegate, 152 U.S. 327, 340 (1894), where the objection was that the court in the first case was wrong as a matter of law in assuming jurisdiction on the ground that the action was one arising under the laws of the United States.

In Chicot County Drainage District v. Baxter State Bank, 308 U.S. 371 (1940), a federal district court had approved a plan of municipal reorganization under a jurisdictional statute which the Supreme Court in other litigation afterwards held unconstitutional. Relying in part on McCormick, the Court decided that the judgment was res judicata against participating bondholders in a second action in the same district court, despite the fact that the issue of constitutionality had not been litigated in the first case. *Cf.* Stoll v. Gottlieb, 305 U.S. 165 (1938), holding that an order of a district court in bankruptcy proceedings releasing a guarantor of the debtor's bonds, although assumed to have been entered without jurisdiction, was res judicata in a later action in a state court against the guarantor brought by a bondholder who had received notice of the district court's hearing and had later failed in a petition to the court to set aside its order for want of jurisdiction. See also Jackson v. Irving Trust Co., 311 U.S. 494 (1941). *Cf.* Durfee v. Duke, 375 U.S. 106 (1963), holding that a Nebraska state court decision determining after litigation that the land in issue was in Nebraska was binding in a subsequent action in federal court in Missouri, even though the Nebraska court had jurisdiction only if the land was in that state.[7]

7. The Restatement 2d (§ 10 comment *d*, and Reporter's Note, p. 107; *cf. id.* § 11, comment *b*) suggests that Durfee involved territorial rather than subject-matter jurisdiction. Nevertheless, Durfee was relied on in Underwriters Nat'l Assurance Co. v. North Carolina Life & Acc. Health Ins. Guar. Ass'n, 455 U.S. 691 (1982), holding that North Carolina violated the Full Faith and Credit Clause by failing to give res judicata effect to an Indiana adjudication which had concluded that the Indiana court had subject matter jurisdiction over an action involving rights to a $100,000 deposit an Indiana insurance company had made in North Carolina to qualify to do insurance business in that state. The issue of the Indiana court's jurisdiction had been

However, in United States v. United States Fidelity & Guaranty Co., 309 U.S. 506 (1940), the Court held that the United States and the Indian Nations under its tutelage were immune from suit; that the immunity could not be waived by failure to assert it; and that a judgment against them was open to collateral attack in a later proceeding. Justice Reed said (pp. 514–15):

"In the Chicot County case no inflexible rule as to collateral objection in general to judgments was declared. We explicitly limited our examination to the effect of a subsequent invalidation of the applicable jurisdictional statute upon an existing judgment in bankruptcy. To this extent the case definitely extended the area of adjudications that may not be the subject of collateral attack. No examination was made of the susceptibility to such objection of numerous groups of judgments concerning status, extra-territorial action of courts, or strictly jurisdictional and quasi-jurisdictional facts. No solution was attempted of the legal results of a collision between the desirable principle that rights may be adequately vindicated through a single trial of an issue and the sovereign right of immunity from suit. We are of the opinion, however, that without legislative action the doctrine of immunity should prevail."

See also Kalb v. Feuerstein, 308 U.S. 433 (1940), in which a judgment of foreclosure and a foreclosure sale by a state court while a petition was pending under Section 75 of the Bankruptcy Act (the Frazier–Lemke Act) were held void in a later action by the mortgagors to recover possession.

Can the last two cases be reconciled with the others? See, generally, Boskey & Braucher, *Jurisdiction and Collateral Attack*, 40 Colum.L.Rev. 1006 (1940); Note, 87 Yale L.J. 164 (1977). And see the formulation in Restatement (First) of Judgments (1942) § 10:

"[1] Where a court has jurisdiction over the parties and determines that it has jurisdiction over the subject matter, the parties cannot collaterally attack the judgment on the ground that the court did not have jurisdiction over the subject matter, unless the policy underlying the doctrine of res judicata is outweighed by the policy against permitting the court to act beyond its jurisdiction.

"[2] Among the factors appropriate to be considered in determining that collateral attack should be permitted are that—

(a) the lack of jurisdiction over the subject matter was clear;

(b) the determination as to jurisdiction depended upon a question of law rather than of fact;

(c) the court was one of limited and not of general jurisdiction;

(d) the question of jurisdiction was not actually litigated;

(e) the policy against the court's acting beyond its jurisdiction is strong."

litigated in Indiana in a proceeding in which the North Carolina objector had intervened. The Court said that North Carolina had "failed to recognize the limited scope of review one court may conduct to determine whether a foreign court had jurisdiction" (p. 706). Since the Indiana court had "fully and fairly" considered the question of jurisdiction, its conclusion was preclusive.

Compare Restatement 2d § 12:

"When a court has rendered a judgment in a contested action, the judgment precludes the parties from litigating the question of the court's subject matter jurisdiction in subsequent litigation except if:

"(1) The subject matter of the action was so plainly beyond the court's jurisdiction that its entertaining the action was a manifest abuse of authority; or

"(2) Allowing the judgment to stand would substantially infringe the authority of another tribunal or agency of government; or

"(3) The judgment was rendered by a court lacking capability to make an adequately informed determination of a question concerning its own jurisdiction and as a matter of procedural fairness the party seeking to avoid the judgment should have the opportunity belatedly to attack the court's subject matter jurisdiction."

Do you think the new provision is an improvement?

Cf. the cases on the question whether the jurisdiction of a federal court may be challenged by way of defense to contempt proceedings for violation of an interlocutory injunction; see, *e.g.*, United States v. United Mine Workers, 330 U.S. 258 (1947); Walker v. City of Birmingham, 388 U.S. 307 (1967), p. 620, *supra*.

(3) There is no explicit constitutional or legislative text providing that the preclusive effect of federal judgments in state courts should be measured by federal law. But such a rule "is indispensible to federalism"; "[w]ere there no such rule, it would be necessary to invent one—so invent it the Supreme Court did." Degnan, at 749. Beginning with Dupasseur v. Rochereau, 21 Wall. 130, 134 (U.S.1874), the Court has consistently held that a claim under a federal court judgment is "a title or right * * * claimed under an authority exercised under the United States," and that it therefore has jurisdiction on review of state court decisions to determine whether proper effect has been given to such a judgment. See Metcalf v. Watertown, 153 U.S. 671 (1894); Stoll v. Gottlieb, *supra*, 305 U.S. at 167. There is, nevertheless, a good deal of confusion as to what makes the preclusive effects of federal judgments in state cases a federal matter. Compare, *e.g.*, Embry v. Palmer, 17 Otto 3, 9 (U.S.1883) (application of the full faith and credit statute, now § 28 U.S.C. 1738, to federal judgments was authorized, despite statutory language that seems to apply only to state court judgments, by provisions of the Constitution other than the Full Faith and Credit Clause, "such as those which declare the extent of the judicial power of the United States, which authorize all legislation necessary and proper for executing the powers vested by the Constitution in the government of the United States, or in any department or officer thereof, and which declare the supremacy of the authority of the national government within the limits of the Constitution"), with Dupasseur v. Rochereau, *supra*, 21 Wall. at 134 (res judicata effect of circuit court judgment is a question arising under the laws "establishing the Circuit Court and vesting it with jurisdiction; * * * and it is clearly within the chart of appellate power given to this court, over cases arising in and decided by the State courts").

(4) That the preclusive effect of a federal judgment is a federal *question* does not mean that federal res judicata *rules* will in fact always govern

preclusion in a state action in a particular case. It is clear that where the federal court decided a federal question, federal res judicata rules govern. See Deposit Bank v. Frankfort, 191 U.S. 499 (1903); Stoll v. Gottlieb, *supra.* But where the first judgment was in a diversity action, or decided questions of state law pursuant to the court's pendent jurisdiction, federal courts reviewing the subsequent state court action have often borrowed state preclusion rules. In the Dupasseur case, for example, concerning the preclusive effect of a judgment in a diversity action, Justice Bradley said that "[t]he only effect that can be justly claimed for the judgment in the Circuit Court of the United States, is such as would belong to judgments of the State courts [in the state in which the circuit court was sitting] rendered under similar circumstances" (p. 135). This statement has been frequently repeated. See, *e.g.,* Crescent City Live Stock Co. v. Butchers' Union Slaughter House Co., 120 U.S. 141, 146–47 (1887); Metcalf v. Watertown, *supra,* 153 U.S. at 676; Pittsburgh, C. C. & St.L.Ry. v. Long Island Loan & Trust Co., 172 U.S. 493, 507–10 (1899). See generally 18 Federal Practice § 4472; Restatement 2d § 87 comment *b.*

Similarly, where the question is the preclusive effect of a federal judgment on a state law issue in a second federal diversity action, state preclusion rules are frequently applied without significant discussion. See, *e.g.,* Iowa Electric Light & Power Co. v. Mobile Aerial Towers, Inc., 723 F.2d 50 (8th Cir.1983). On the other hand, where the court finds some affirmative federal policy with respect to preclusion, that policy governs even if the case is a diversity case. Thus, Federal Rule of Civil Procedure 41(b) provides that dismissal of an action "operates as an adjudication upon the merits." In Kern v. Hettinger, 303 F.2d 333 (2d Cir.1962), the preclusive effect of a diversity judgment rendered by a district court in California was held to be measured by Rule 41(b) rather than by California law (under which the dismissal would have been without prejudice). Judge Medina stated, in a well-known passage, that "[o]ne of the strongest policies a court can have is that of determining the scope of its own judgments. * * * It would be destructive of the basic principles of the Federal Rules of Civil Procedure to say that the effect of a judgment of a federal court was governed by the law of the state where the court sits simply because the source of federal jurisdiction is diversity. The rights and obligations of the parties are fixed by state law. * * * But we think it would be strange doctrine to allow a state to nullify the judgments of federal courts. * * * The Erie doctrine is not applicable here * * *" (p. 340).

Some courts have declined to apply state preclusion rules even where there is no strong conflicting federal policy. See, *e.g.,* Aerojet–General Corp. v. Askew, 511 F.2d 710 (5th Cir.1975).[8] Compare the rule suggested in Degnan, at 773: "A valid judgment rendered in any judicial system within the United States must be recognized by all other judicial systems within the United States, and the claims and issues precluded by that judgment, and the parties bound thereby, are determined by the law of the system which rendered the judgment."

8. "We see no persuasive reason to look to state law for some elements of res judicata, such as the scope of the cause of action or similarity of the parties, in light of the prominent influence of federal law on other elements of the doctrine. To do so would sacrifice the uniformity of the law which federal courts must apply" (511 F.2d at 717).

Should federal law adopt state law as the measure of the effect of a judgment in a case involving only state-created rights? In what circumstances? Even if state law is incorporated, would it follow that the state has legislative jurisdiction to enact provisions with regard to the effect of the judgments of federal courts sitting in the state?

In connection with all of these questions, consider Burbank, *Interjurisdictional Preclusion, Full Faith and Credit and Federal Common Law: A General Approach,* 71 Cornell L.Rev. 733, 747–97 (and especially 791–97) (1986). Professor Burbank, disagreeing with Professor Degnan, argues that neither the Full Faith and Credit Clause nor the Federal Rules of Civil Procedure provide preclusion rules for federal judgments; that the only putative rules of federal law on this question are rules of federal common law, and that the usual methodology regarding the use of federal common law should apply; and that when a federal diversity court adjudicates issues of state law, the Court's Erie precedents are also relevant and should be "integrated" with the Court's federal common law precedents.

(5) Do the normal rules with respect to the preclusive effects of federal judgments differ if the federal court entered a declaratory judgment? See the comprehensive discussion in Shapiro, *State Courts and Federal Declaratory Judgments,* 74 Nw.U.L.Rev. 759 (1979). Suppose that a federal district court has declared a state statute unconstitutional on the ground that it made criminal some constitutionally protected activity. Is the state collaterally estopped from prosecuting the plaintiff in the federal suit under that statute? From prosecuting someone else under it? What if the federal court's decision was that the statute was overbroad?

As to these problems, see also the discussion in Chap. X, Sec. 2(C), pp. 1426–28, *supra.*

UNITED STATES v. MENDOZA
464 U.S. 154, 104 S.Ct. 568, 78 L.Ed.2d 379 (1984).
Certiorari to the United States Court of Appeals for the Ninth Circuit.

JUSTICE REHNQUIST delivered the opinion of the Court.

In 1978 respondent Sergio Mendoza, a Filipino national, filed a petition for naturalization under a statute which by its terms had expired 32 years earlier. Respondent's claim for naturalization was based on the assertion that the Government's administration of the Nationality Act denied him due process of law. Neither the District Court nor the Court of Appeals for the Ninth Circuit ever reached the merits of his claim, because they held that the Government was collaterally estopped from litigating that constitutional issue in view of an earlier decision against the Government in a case brought by other Filipino nationals in the United States District Court for the Northern District of California. We hold that the United States may not be collaterally estopped on an issue such as this, adjudicated against it in an earlier lawsuit brought by a different party. We therefore reverse the judgment of the Court of Appeals.

The facts bearing on respondent's claim to naturalization are not in dispute. In 1942 Congress amended the Nationality Act, § 701 of which provided that noncitizens who served honorably in the Armed Forces of the United States during World War II were exempt from some of the usual requirements for nationality. In particular, such veterans were exempt from the requirement of residency within the United States and literacy in the English language. Congress later provided by amendment that all naturalization petitions seeking to come under § 701 must be filed by December 31, 1946. Act of Dec. 28, 1945, § 202(c), 59 Stat. 658. Section 702 of the Act provided for the overseas naturalization of aliens in active service who were eligible for naturalization under § 701 but who were not within the jurisdiction of any court authorized to naturalize aliens. In order to implement that provision, the Immigration and Naturalization Service from 1943 to 1946 sent representatives abroad to naturalize eligible alien servicemen.

Respondent Mendoza served as a doctor in the Philippine Commonwealth Army from 1941 until his discharge in 1946. Because Japanese occupation of the Philippines had made naturalization of alien servicemen there impossible before the liberation of the Islands, the INS did not designate a representative to naturalize eligible servicemen there until 1945. Because of concerns expressed by the Philippine Government to the United States, however, to the effect that large numbers of Filipinos would be naturalized and would immigrate to the United States just as the Philippines gained their independence, the Attorney General subsequently revoked the naturalization authority of the INS representative. Thus all naturalizations in the Philippines were halted for a 9–month period from late October 1945 until a new INS representative was appointed in August 1946.

Respondent's claim for naturalization is based on the contention that that conduct of the Government deprived him of due process of law in violation of the Fifth Amendment to the United States Constitution, because he was present in the Philippines during part, but not all, of the 9–month period during which there was no authorized INS representative there. The naturalization examiner recommended denial of Mendoza's petition, but the District Court granted the petition without reaching the merits of Mendoza's constitutional claim. The District Court concluded that the Government could not relitigate the due process issue because that issue had already been decided against the Government in In re Naturalization of 68 Filipino War Veterans, 406 F.Supp. 931 (ND Cal.1975) (hereinafter 68 Filipinos), a decision which the Government had not appealed.[2]

2. In 68 Filipinos, the District Court considered the naturalization petitions of 68 Filipino World War II veterans filed pursuant to §§ 701–702 of the Nationality Act. Fifty-three of those veterans, whom the District Court designated as Category II veterans, like Mendoza, had made no effort to become naturalized before the expiration of the statutory provisions. Like Mendoza, they claimed that the failure of the United States to station an INS representative in the Philippines for the entire period of time in which rights under § 702 were available to them discriminated against Filipinos as a class. Rejecting the Government's arguments that INS v. Hibi, 414 U.S. 5 (1973) (per curiam), was controlling, that the issue was nonjusticiable, and that petitioners were not protected by the Federal Constitution during the period at issue, the court applied strict scrutiny to petitioners' claim and held that the Government had not offered sufficient justification for its conduct. 406 F.Supp., at 940–951.

Although the Government initially docketed an appeal from that decision, the Court of Appeals granted the Government's motion to withdraw the appeal on November 30, 1977. The Government made that motion after a new administration and a new INS Commissioner had taken office. Eventually the Government reevaluated its position and decided to take appeals from all orders granting naturalization to so-called Category II petitioners, with the exception of orders granting naturalization to petitioners who filed petitions prior to the withdrawal of the appeal in 68

Noting that the doctrine of nonmutual offensive collateral estoppel has been conditionally approved by this Court in Parklane Hosiery Co. v. Shore, 439 U.S. 322 (1979), the Court of Appeals concluded that the District Court had not abused its discretion in applying that doctrine against the United States in this case. 672 F.2d 1320, 1322 (1982). The Court of Appeals rejected the Government's argument that Parklane Hosiery should be limited to private litigants. Although it acknowledged that the Government is often involved in litigating issues of national significance where conservation of judicial resources is less important than "getting a second opinion," it concluded that litigation concerning the rights of Filipino war veterans was not such a case. For the reasons which follow, we agree with the Government that Parklane Hosiery's approval of nonmutual offensive collateral estoppel is not to be extended to the United States.

Under the judicially developed doctrine of collateral estoppel, once a court has decided an issue of fact or law necessary to its judgment, that decision is conclusive in a subsequent suit based on a different cause of action involving a party to the prior litigation. Montana v. United States, 440 U.S. 147, 153 (1979). Collateral estoppel, like the related doctrine of res judicata,[3] serves to "relieve parties of the cost and vexation of multiple lawsuits, conserve judicial resources, and, by preventing inconsistent decisions, encourage reliance on adjudication." Allen v. McCurry, 449 U.S. 90, 94 (1980). In furtherance of those policies, this Court in recent years has broadened the scope of the doctrine of collateral estoppel beyond its common-law limits. It has done so by abandoning the requirement of mutuality of parties, Blonder–Tongue Laboratories, Inc. v. University of Illinois Foundation, 402 U.S. 313 (1971), and by conditionally approving the "offensive" use of collateral estoppel by a nonparty to a prior lawsuit. Parklane Hosiery, *supra.*[4]

In Standefer v. United States, 447 U.S. 10, 24 (1980), however, we emphasized the fact that Blonder–Tongue and Parklane Hosiery involved disputes over private rights between private litigants. We noted that "[i]n such cases, no significant harm flows from enforcing a rule that affords a litigant only one full and fair opportunity to litigate an issue, and [that] there is no sound reason for burdening the courts with repetitive litigation." Here, as in Montana v. United States [p. 1598, *supra*], the party against whom the estoppel is sought is the United States; but here, unlike in Montana, the party who seeks to preclude the Government from relitigating the issue was not a party to the earlier litigation.

We have long recognized that "the Government is not in a position identical to that of a private litigant," INS v. Hibi, 414 U.S. 5, 8 (1973) (*per*

Filipinos. Brief for United States 11–12, and n. 13; Olegario v. United States, 629 F.2d 204, 214 (CA2 1980). Mendoza's petition for naturalization was filed after the Government withdrew its appeal in 68 Filipinos.

3. Under res judicata, a final judgment on the merits bars further claims by parties or their privies on the same cause of action. Montana v. United States, 440 U.S., at 153; Parklane Hosiery Co. v. Shore, 439 U.S. 322, 326, n. 5 (1979). The Restatement of Judgments speaks of res judicata as "claim preclusion" and of col-

lateral estoppel as "issue preclusion." Restatement (Second) of Judgments § 27 (1982).

4. Offensive use of collateral estoppel occurs when a plaintiff seeks to foreclose a defendant from relitigating an issue the defendant has previously litigated unsuccessfully in another action against the same or a different party. Defensive use of collateral estoppel occurs when a defendant seeks to prevent a plaintiff from relitigating an issue the plaintiff has previously litigated unsuccessfully in another action against the same or a different party.

curiam), both because of the geographic breadth of Government litigation and also, most importantly, because of the nature of the issues the Government litigates. It is not open to serious dispute that the Government is a party to a far greater number of cases on a nationwide basis than even the most litigious private entity; in 1982, the United States was a party to more than 75,000 of the 206,193 filings in the United States District Courts. Administrative Office of the United States Courts, Annual Report of the Director 98 (1982). In the same year the United States was a party to just under 30% of the civil cases appealed from the District Courts to the Court of Appeals. *Id.*, at 79, 82. Government litigation frequently involves legal questions of substantial public importance; indeed, because the proscriptions of the United States Constitution are so generally directed at governmental action, many constitutional questions can arise only in the context of litigation to which the Government is a party. Because of those facts the Government is more likely than any private party to be involved in lawsuits against different parties which nonetheless involve the same legal issues.

A rule allowing nonmutual collateral estoppel against the Government in such cases would substantially thwart the development of important questions of law by freezing the first final decision rendered on a particular legal issue. Allowing only one final adjudication would deprive this Court of the benefit it receives from permitting several courts of appeals to explore a difficult question before this Court grants certiorari. See E.I. du Pont de Nemours & Co. v. Train, 430 U.S. 112, 135, n. 26 (1977); see also Califano v. Yamasaki, 442 U.S. 682, 702 (1979). Indeed, if nonmutual estoppel were routinely applied against the Government, this Court would have to revise its practice of waiting for a conflict to develop before granting the Government's petitions for certiorari. See this Court's Rule 17.1.

The Solicitor General's policy for determining when to appeal an adverse decision would also require substantial revision.[6] The Court of Appeals faulted the Government in this case for failing to appeal a decision that it now contends is erroneous. But the Government's litigation conduct in a case is apt to differ from that of a private litigant. Unlike a private litigant who generally does not forgo an appeal if he believes that he can prevail, the Solicitor General considers a variety of factors, such as the limited resources of the Government and the crowded dockets of the courts, before authorizing an appeal. Brief for United States 30–31. The application of nonmutual estoppel against the Government would force the Solicitor General to abandon those prudential concerns and to appeal every adverse decision in order to avoid foreclosing further review.

In addition to those institutional concerns traditionally considered by the Solicitor General, the panoply of important public issues raised in governmental litigation may quite properly lead successive administrations of the Executive Branch to take differing positions with respect to the resolution of a particular issue. While the Executive Branch must of course defer to the Judicial Branch for final resolution of questions of constitutional law, the former nonetheless controls the progress of Government litigation through the federal courts. It would be idle to pretend that

---

6. The Attorney General has delegated discretionary authority to the Solicitor General to determine when to appeal from a judgment adverse to the interests of the United States. 28 CFR § 0.20(b) (1983).

the conduct of Government litigation in all its myriad features, from the decision to file a complaint in the United States district court to the decision to petition for certiorari to review a judgment of the court of appeals, is a wholly mechanical procedure which involves no policy choices whatever.

For example, in recommending to the Solicitor General in 1977 that the Government's appeal in 68 Filipinos be withdrawn, newly appointed INS Commissioner Castillo commented that such a course "would be in keeping with the policy of the [new] Administration," described as "a course of compassion and amnesty." Brief for United States 11. But for the very reason that such policy choices are made by one administration, and often reevaluated by another administration, courts should be careful when they seek to apply expanding rules of collateral estoppel to Government litigation. The Government of course may not now undo the consequences of its decision not to appeal the District Court judgment in the 68 Filipinos case; it is bound by that judgment under the principles of res judicata. But we now hold that it is not further bound in a case involving a litigant who was not a party to the earlier litigation.

The Court of Appeals did not endorse a routine application of nonmutual collateral estoppel against the Government, because it recognized that the Government does litigate issues of far-reaching national significance which in some cases, it concluded, might warrant relitigation. But in this case it found no "record evidence" indicating that there was a "crucial need" in the administration of the immigration laws for a redetermination of the due process question decided in 68 Filipinos and presented again in this case. The Court of Appeals did not make clear what sort of "record evidence" would have satisfied it that there *was* a "crucial need" for redetermination of the question in this case, but we pretermit further discussion of that approach; we believe that the standard announced by the Court of Appeals for determining when relitigation of a legal issue is to be permitted is so wholly subjective that it affords no guidance to the courts or to the Government. Such a standard leaves the Government at sea because it cannot possibly anticipate, in determining whether or not to appeal an adverse decision, whether a court will bar relitigation of the issue in a later case. By the time a court makes its subjective determination that an issue cannot be relitigated, the Government's appeal of the prior ruling of course would be untimely.

We hold, therefore, that nonmutual offensive collateral estoppel simply does not apply against the Government in such a way as to preclude relitigation of issues such as those involved in this case.[7] The conduct of Government litigation in the courts of the United States is sufficiently different from the conduct of private civil litigation in those courts so that what might otherwise be economy interests underlying a broad application of collateral estoppel are outweighed by the constraints which peculiarly affect the Government. We think that our conclusion will better allow thorough development of legal doctrine by allowing litigation in multiple forums. Indeed, a contrary result might disserve the economy interests in

---

7. The Government does not base its argument on the exception to the doctrine of collateral estoppel for "unmixed questions of law" arising in "successive actions involving unrelated subject matter." Montana v. United States, 440 U.S., at 162; see United States v. Stauffer Chemical Co., [464 U.S. at] 165; United States v. Moser, 266 U.S. 236, 242 (1924). Our holding in no way depends on that exception.

whose name estoppel is advanced by requiring the Government to abandon virtually any exercise of discretion in seeking to review judgments unfavorable to it. The doctrine of res judicata, of course, prevents the Government from relitigating the same cause of action against the parties to a prior decision, but beyond that point principles of nonmutual collateral estoppel give way to the policies just stated.

Our holding in this case is consistent with each of our prior holdings to which the parties have called our attention, and which we reaffirm. Today in a companion case we hold that the Government may be estopped under certain circumstances from relitigating a question when the parties to the two lawsuits are the same. United States v. Stauffer Chemical Co., post, p. 165; see also Montana v. United States, 440 U.S. 147 (1979); United States v. Moser, 266 U.S. 236 (1924). None of those cases, however, involve the effort of a party to estop the Government in the absence of mutuality.

The concerns underlying our disapproval of collateral estoppel against the Government are for the most part inapplicable where mutuality is present, as in Stauffer Chemical, Montana, and Moser. The application of an estoppel when the Government is litigating the same issue with the same party avoids the problem of freezing the development of the law because the Government is still free to litigate that issue in the future with some other party. And, where the parties are the same, estopping the Government spares a party that has already prevailed once from having to relitigate—a function it would not serve in the present circumstances. We accordingly hold that the Court of Appeals was wrong in applying nonmutual collateral estoppel against the Government in this case. Its judgment is therefore reversed.

NOTE ON RES JUDICATA IN FEDERAL GOVERNMENT LITIGATION AND ON THE PROBLEM OF ACQUIESCENCE

(1) Suppose the 68 Filipinos case could have been, and was, certified as a class action. Should the result in Mendoza be different?

(2) As indicated at the end of the Mendoza opinion, the Supreme Court considered the applicability of *mutual* collateral estoppel against the government in United States v. Stauffer Chemical Co., 464 U.S. 165 (1984), decided on the same day. Stauffer had refused to allow private contractors hired by EPA to inspect one of its chemical plants in Wyoming. In the suit that followed, the Tenth Circuit held that private contractors were not "authorized representatives" of the Administrator of EPA with authority (under the Clean Air Act, 42 U.S.C. § 7414(a)(2)) to inspect the plant. Stauffer Chemical Co. v. EPA, 647 F.2d 1075 (10th Cir.1981) (Stauffer I). Two weeks after the attempted inspection in Wyoming, the EPA tried to inspect a Stauffer plant in Tennessee, again using private contractors. When Stauffer refused to allow the contractors to enter the plant, the EPA obtained an administrative warrant authorizing the inspection. Stauffer failed to honor the warrant and the EPA then began civil contempt proceedings. The Sixth Circuit held that the government was collaterally estopped from relitigating against Stauffer the question of statutory interpretation settled in Stauffer I. The Supreme Court affirmed. Writing for the Court, Justice Rehnquist said (p. 173):

"The Government ∗ ∗ ∗ argues here, as it did in United States v. Mendoza, that the application of collateral estoppel in Government litigation involving recurring issues of public importance will freeze the development of the law. But we concluded in United States v. Mendoza that that argument is persuasive only to prevent the application of collateral estoppel against the Government in the absence of mutuality. When estoppel is applied in a case where the Government is litigating the same issue arising under virtually identical facts against the same party, as here, the Government's argument loses its force. The Sixth Circuit's decision prevents EPA from relitigating the § 114(a)(2) issue with Stauffer, but it still leaves EPA free to litigate the same issue in the future with other litigants.[6] "

Unlike the Tenth Circuit, the Ninth Circuit (in an unrelated case) had interpreted § 114(a)(2) to authorize inspection by private contractors. Bunker Hill Company Lead & Zinc Smelter v. EPA, 658 F.2d 1280 (9th Cir. 1981). The EPA argued in Stauffer II that "if it is foreclosed from relitigating the statutory issue with Stauffer, then Stauffer plants within the Ninth Circuit will benefit from a rule precluding inspections by private contractors while plants of Stauffer's competitors will be subject to the Ninth Circuit's contrary rule," and "an inequitable administration of the law" would result (p. 174). Compare Restatement 2d § 28(2)(b) comment c (problems of inequality are particularly significant if "one of the parties is a government agency responsible for continuing administration of a body of law that affects members of the public generally, as in the case of tax law"). The Court, however, refused to address the question whether collateral estoppel would operate against the EPA in an action against Stauffer in the Ninth Circuit.[1]

Justice White, concurring, agreed that further litigation on the statutory interpretation issue was foreclosed between the EPA and Stauffer in the Tenth Circuit, but thought that "[o]utside the Tenth Circuit, the policies of judicial economy and consistency are much less compelling. At least where ∗ ∗ ∗ one party is a governmental agency administering a public law, judicial economy is not advanced; the Government can always force a

"**6.** Thus the application of an estoppel in cases such as this one will require no alteration of this Court's practice of waiting for conflicts to develop before granting the Government's petitions for certiorari, nor in the Solicitor General's policy of circumspection in determining when to pursue appeals or file certiorari petitions.

∗ ∗ ∗

"The Government argues, however, that in deciding whether to appeal an adverse decision, the Solicitor General has no way of knowing whether future litigation will arise with the same or a different party. The Government thus argues that the mere possibility of being bound in the future will influence the Solicitor General to appeal or seek certiorari from adverse decisions when such action would otherwise be unwarranted. The Government lists as an example Stauffer I, from which the Government did not seek certiorari because there was no circuit conflict at the time of the Tenth Circuit's decision. Yet, taking the issue here as an example, the Govern-

ment itself asserts that "thousands of businesses are affected each year by the question of contractor participation in Section 114 inspections." Brief for United States 28. It is thus unrealistic to assume that the Government would be driven to pursue an unwarranted appeal here because of fear of being unable to relitigate the § 114 issue in the future with a different one of those thousands of affected parties."

1. The Government also argued in Stauffer II that the issue of statutory interpretation was "an unmixed question of law," and that under Commissioner v. Sunnen, *supra,* there is no issue preclusion unless the two cases arise from the very same transaction. The Court rejected this argument, holding that under Montana v. United States, *supra,* legal issues will be res judicata in a subsequent action where there is mutuality and there has been no change in the law, unless the claims in the two actions are substantially unrelated. *Cf.* Restatement 2d § 29 comment *i.*

ruling on the merits by suing someone else. * * * And if the circuit has ruled on the merits in another case, reliance on *stare decisis* is no more burdensome than reliance on collateral estoppel. The policy against inconsistent decisions is much less relevant outside the original circuit. Conflicts in the circuits are generally accepted and in some ways even welcomed" (p. 177).

Justice White was prepared to give Stauffer the benefit of collateral estoppel in the Sixth Circuit, which had not previously ruled on the statutory issue, on the ground that this "would spare Stauffer the burden of fighting a battle that it has won once" (p. 177). But he stated that he would not give Stauffer the benefit of estoppel in a circuit that had adopted a contrary rule on the merits, as had the Ninth Circuit: "Judicial economy is not served for the simple reason that no litigation is prevented; the prior litigant is subject to one black-letter rule rather than another. For the same reason, there is no concern about protecting the prior litigant from repetitious, vexatious, or harassing litigation" (p. 178). Moreover, preclusion in such circumstances would create inconsistency "more dramatic and more troublesome than a normal circuit split; by definition, it compounds that problem. It would be dubious enough were the EPA unable to employ private contractors to inspect Stauffer's plants within the Ninth Circuit even though it can use such contractors in inspecting other plants. But the disarray is more extensive. By the same application of mutual collateral estoppel, the EPA could presumably use private contractors to inspect Bunker Hill's plants in circuits like the Tenth, despite the fact that other companies are not subject to such inspections. Furthermore * * * the EPA can relitigate this matter as to other companies. As a result, in, say, the First Circuit, the EPA must follow one rule as to Bunker Hill, the opposite as to Stauffer, and, depending on any ruling by that Circuit, one or the other or a third as to other companies" (p. 178–79).

Would Justice White's solution cause complexities of its own? Suppose the Sixth Circuit were later to decide in the EPA's favor in a suit brought against a different defendant. Would Stauffer be able to rely on collateral estoppel in the Sixth Circuit thereafter?

(3) Under Mendoza and Stauffer, there can be no collateral estoppel against the government without mutuality. Questions can therefore arise whether the government party in the second suit is the same government party that was involved in the first suit. Sunshine Anthracite Coal Co. v. Adkins, 310 U.S. 381, 402–03 (1940), a case involving an IRS claim of issue preclusion resulting from a prior judgment in favor of the National Bituminous Coal Commission, held that "a judgment in a suit between a party and a representative of the United States is *res judicata* in relitigation of the same issue between that party and another officer of the government." *Cf.* Montana v. United States, 440 U.S. 147 (1979), p. 1598, *supra.* Compare the materials discussing the question of when the United States is bound by judgments rendered in actions against its individual officials, in Chap. IX, pp. 1125–26, *supra.*[2] Compare also the rule that double jeopardy does not bar a federal government prosecution for conduct that a state government

---

2. Parallel issues of privity can arise in litigation involving state officials. If in a federal court action brought against a state officer (on account of the Eleventh Amendment) rather than the state itself, it is held that a state statute is unconstitutional, is the state barred from prosecuting the federal plaintiff for violating the statute? Shapiro, *State Courts and Federal Declaratory Judgments,* 74 Nw.U.L.Rev. 759, 764 & n. 31 (1979), argues that the answer is yes.

has already prosecuted, and vice versa. See United States v. Wheeler, 435 U.S. 313 (1978); Bartkus v. Illinois, 359 U.S. 121 (1959).

(4) Difficult questions about the fair administration of justice can arise when the government is faced with lower court rulings it believes to be wrong. Mendoza established that res judicata does not bar the government from relitigating the issue against a new party. And the policy arguments that the Supreme Court relied on in Mendoza make it plain that it is not improper for the government to relitigate issues in order to persuade other courts that the first decision was erroneous.

But should there there be limits on the government's privilege to relitigate? Suppose that the government loses on an issue in Circuit A. May it—and should it—take the position that, even in Circuit A, it will not "acquiesce" in the decision—that it will require citizens to litigate the question in district courts even though those courts are bound to reject the government's position? Why should private parties be burdened by the obligation to litigate cases that the government knows it is bound to lose? Isn't this simply bullying, by putting pressure on citizens who cannot afford to litigate to forgo their rights? Can it be justified if the government's purpose is to generate an intra-circuit conflict, or perhaps an *en banc* reconsideration by Circuit A? If in the meantime well considered opinions elsewhere have rejected the views of Circuit A? If the question at issue is one that demands uniform nationwide administration as a matter of effective and fair policy?

Or suppose that the government's position on an issue is rejected in three or four—or seven or eight—circuits. Is the government free to—and should it—relitigate the issue in the remaining circuits?

Should these problems be solved by legal rules enforced by courts and binding on the government? Or is the matter one that should be worked out by the development of fair and sensible rules within the executive branch?

All of these issues have generated intense controversy. A number of federal agencies have regularly refused to acquiesce in circuit court decisions. See Carter, *The Commissioner's Nonacquiescence: A Case for a National Court of Tax Appeals*, 59 Temp.L.Q. 879 (1986) (IRS); Weis, *Agency Non-Acquiescence—Respectful Lawlessness or Legitimate Disagreement?*, 48 U.Pitt.L.Rev. 845 (1987) (NLRB); Comment, *Administrative Agency Intracircuit Nonacquiescence*, 85 Colum.L.Rev. 582 (1985) (SSA). Between 1981 and 1984, for example, the Social Security Administration—acting at the instance of Congress in re-evaluating all cases where disability payments were being made—terminated an unusually high number of disability payments. By 1984, all but one circuit had struck down the SSA's termination criteria. The SSA nevertheless refused to acquiesce in these decisions, prompting at least one judge to threaten the Secretary with contempt proceedings, see Hillhouse v. Harris, 715 F.2d 428, 430 (8th Cir. 1983) (McMillian, J., concurring), and at one point causing the Ninth Circuit to uphold a preliminary injunction ordering the Secretary to reinstate beneficiaries terminated pursuant to the nonacquiescence policy. Lopez v. Heckler, 725 F.2d 1489 (9th Cir.1984), vacated and remanded, 469 U.S. 1082 (1984). See generally Comment, *supra,* at 584–87.

Judge Weis has complained that "[t]he non-acquiescence policy of an agency results in intolerable and inexcusable expense to litigants, as well as in the unnecessary and wasteful expenditure of scarce judicial resources. But perhaps most objectionable is the disrespect for the administration of justice generated by the spectacle of a federal agency which refuses to acknowledge that a court's ruling applies to it as well as to other litigants." Weis, *supra*, at 851–52.[3]

In view of the policy considerations outlined in Mendoza, isn't the criticism too general? Too harsh? But are there not cases where it could be apt?

For further discussion of this problem see Maranville, *Nonacquiescence: Outlaw Agencies, Imperial Courts, and the Perils of Pluralism*, 39 Vand.L. Rev. 471 (1986); and see Notes, 99 Harv.L.Rev. 847 (1986); 53 Geo.Wash. U.L.Rev. 147 (1984–85); 60 So.Cal.L.Rev. 1143 (1987); 42 Wash. & Lee.L. Rev. 1233 (1985). In 1984, in connection with the Social Security Disability Benefits Reform Act of 1984 the House included in its bill a provision requiring the administration under certain circumstances to acquiesce in the law of the circuit, but the provision was removed by the conference committee.[4]

(5) Chilicky v. Schweiker, 796 F.2d 1131 (9th Cir.1986), was a Bivens action for damages against federal government officials alleging that defendants, in terminating social security disability benefits, had violated plaintiffs' Fifth Amendment rights. The complaint alleged, *inter alia*, that defendants had "illegally nonacquiesced" in the law of the Ninth Circuit in terminating plaintiffs' benefits, and that this was unconstitutional action. The court of appeals held that defendants were entitled to qualified immunity with respect to these allegations. The court said (p. 1138): "Our examination of relevant statutory and decisional law at the time of the termination of benefits compels us to concur with the district court's evaluation: the law was not sufficiently clear in 1981 so as to expose to civil liability under Bivens those public officials who in effect terminated disability benefits. At that time, there were no reported cases that held nonacquiescence by the Executive Branch in judicial decisions to be clearly unlawful. The officials charged with the responsibility of implementing and administering the CDR process were confronted with a congressionally mandated program designed to terminate benefits, a Presidential directive to implement that program some 10 months earlier than its effective date, and an administrative policy guideline instructing Social Security Administration officials to ignore certain case authority. In view of these factors,

---

3. See also Goodman's Furniture Co. v. United States Postal Service, 561 F.2d 462, 465–66 (3d Cir.1977) (Weis, J., concurring) (criticizing relitigation of an issue of statutory interpretation in a *different* circuit as "unseemly," "unsettling to the course of justice," "disrespectful toward the courts," "expensive and time consuming"). Do you agree? Should the decision of the first circuit to consider a matter be authoritative? Doesn't Mendoza answer this question?

4. The conference report stated: "The conference agreement deletes ∗ ∗ ∗ [the House] language. The conferees do not intend that [this] ∗ ∗ ∗ be interpreted as approval of 'non-acquiescence' by a federal agency to an interpretation of a U.S. Circuit Court of Appeals as a general practice. On the contrary, the conferees note that questions have been raised about the constitutional basis of non-acquiescence and many of the conferees have strong concerns about some of the ways in which this policy has been applied, even if constitutional. Thus, the conferees urge that a policy of non-acquiescence be followed only in situations where the Administration has initiated or has the reasonable expectation and intention of initiating the steps necessary to receive a review of the issue in the Supreme Court." See H.R.Rep. No. 1039, 98th Cong., 2d Sess. 36–38 (1984). On the effect of this legislative history see Hyatt v. Heckler, 757 F.2d 1455 (4th Cir.1985); and see further 807 F.2d 376 (4th Cir.1986).

we find that appellees acted within the bounds of Harlow's reasonable person standard. The constant tension between the Executive and Judicial Branches over the appropriate standard for terminating disability benefits together with the Secretary's nonacquiescence policy, rendered assessment of the legality of the CDR process by even a legal scholar extremely difficult."

On October 5, 1987, the Supreme Court granted certiorari. 108 S.Ct. 64. How should the Court decide the case?

(6) Problems of "acquiescence" can also arise, of course, in the context of litigation involving state and local governments. Should state government refrain from further prosecution after a ruling by a federal district court—for instance in a habeas case—that a state criminal statute is unconstitutional?

————

ALLEN v. McCURRY

449 U.S. 90, 101 S.Ct. 411, 66 L.Ed.2d 308 (1980).
Certiorari to the United States Court of Appeals for the Eighth Circuit.

JUSTICE STEWART delivered the opinion of the Court.

At a hearing before his criminal trial in a Missouri court, the respondent, Willie McCurry, invoked the Fourth and Fourteenth Amendments to suppress evidence that had been seized by the police. The trial court denied the suppression motion in part, and McCurry was subsequently convicted after a jury trial. The conviction was later affirmed on appeal. State v. McCurry, 587 S.W.2d 337 (Mo.App.1979). Because he did not assert that the state courts had denied him a "full and fair opportunity" to litigate his search and seizure claim, McCurry was barred by this Court's decision in Stone v. Powell, 428 U.S. 465, from seeking a writ of habeas corpus in a federal district court. Nevertheless, he sought federal-court redress for the alleged constitutional violation by bringing a damages suit under 42 U.S.C. § 1983 against the officers who had entered his home and seized the evidence in question. We granted certiorari to consider whether the unavailability of federal habeas corpus prevented the police officers from raising the state courts' partial rejection of McCurry's constitutional claim as a collateral estoppel defense to the § 1983 suit against them for damages. 444 U.S. 1070.

I

In April 1977, several undercover police officers, following an informant's tip that McCurry was dealing in heroin, went to his house in St. Louis, Mo., to attempt a purchase. Two officers, petitioners Allen and Jacobsmeyer, knocked on the front door, while the other officers hid nearby. When McCurry opened the door, the two officers asked to buy some heroin "caps." McCurry went back into the house and returned soon thereafter, firing a pistol at and seriously wounding Allen and Jacobsmeyer. After a gun battle with the other officers and their reinforcements, McCurry retreated into the house; he emerged again when the police demanded that he surrender. Several officers then entered the house without a warrant, purportedly to search for other persons inside. One of the officers seized drugs and other contraband that lay in plain view, as well as additional contraband he found in dresser drawers and in auto tires on the porch.

McCurry was charged with possession of heroin and assault with intent to kill. At the pretrial suppression hearing, the trial judge excluded the evidence seized from the dresser drawers and tires, but denied suppression of the evidence found in plain view. McCurry was convicted of both the heroin and assault offenses.

McCurry subsequently filed the present § 1983 action for $1 million in damages against petitioners Allen and Jacobsmeyer, other unnamed individual police officers, and the city of St. Louis and its police department. The complaint alleged a conspiracy to violate McCurry's Fourth Amendment rights, an unconstitutional search and seizure of his house, and an assault on him by unknown police officers after he had been arrested and handcuffed. The petitioners moved for summary judgment. The District Court apparently understood the gist of the complaint to be the allegedly unconstitutional search and seizure and granted summary judgment, holding that collateral estoppel prevented McCurry from relitigating the search-and-seizure question already decided against him in the state courts. 466 F.Supp. 514 (ED Mo.1978).

The Court of Appeals reversed the judgment and remanded the case for trial. 606 F.2d 795 (CA8 1979). The appellate court said it was not holding that collateral estoppel was generally inapplicable in a § 1983 suit raising issues determined against the federal plaintiff in a state criminal trial. But noting that Stone v. Powell, *supra*, barred McCurry from federal habeas corpus relief, and invoking "the special role of the federal courts in protecting civil rights," the court concluded that the § 1983 suit was McCurry's only route to a federal forum for his constitutional claim and directed the trial court to allow him to proceed to trial unencumbered by collateral estoppel.[4]

II

The federal courts have traditionally adhered to the related doctrines of res judicata and collateral estoppel. Under res judicata, a final judgment on the merits of an action precludes the parties or their privies from relitigating issues that were or could have been raised in that action. Cromwell v. County of Sac, 94 U.S. 351, 352. Under collateral estoppel, once a court has decided an issue of fact or law necessary to its judgment, that decision may preclude relitigation of the issue in a suit on a different cause of action involving a party to the first case. Montana v. United States, 440 U.S. 147, 153.[5] As this Court and other courts have often recognized, res judicata and collateral estoppel relieve parties of the cost and vexation of multiple lawsuits, conserve judicial resources, and, by preventing inconsistent decisions, encourage reliance on adjudication.

In recent years, this Court has reaffirmed the benefits of collateral estoppel in particular, finding the policies underlying it to apply in contexts

---

4. Nevertheless, relying on the doctrine of Younger v. Harris, 401 U.S. 37, the Court of Appeals directed the District Court to abstain from conducting the trial until McCurry had exhausted his opportunities for review of his claim in the state appellate courts.

5. * * * Contrary to a suggestion in the dissenting opinion, n. 12, this case does not involve the question whether a § 1983 claimant can litigate in federal court an issue he might have raised but did not raise in previous litigation.

not formerly recognized at common law. Thus, the Court has eliminated the requirement of mutuality in applying collateral estoppel to bar relitigation of issues decided earlier in federal-court suits, Blonder–Tongue Laboratories, Inc. v. University of Illinois Foundation, 402 U.S. 313, and has allowed a litigant who was not a party to a federal case to use collateral estoppel "offensively" in a new federal suit against the party who lost on the decided issue in the first case, Parklane Hosiery Co. v. Shore, 439 U.S. 322. But one general limitation the Court has repeatedly recognized is that the concept of collateral estoppel cannot apply when the party against whom the earlier decision is asserted did not have a "full and fair opportunity" to litigate that issue in the earlier case. Montana v. United States, *supra*, at 153; Blonder–Tongue Laboratories, Inc. v. University of Illinois Foundation, *supra*, at 328–329.[7]

The federal courts generally have also consistently accorded preclusive effect to issues decided by state courts. *E.g.*, Montana v. United States, *supra*; Angel v. Bullington, 330 U.S. 183. Thus, res judicata and collateral estoppel not only reduce unnecessary litigation and foster reliance on adjudication, but also promote the comity between state and federal courts that has been recognized as a bulwark of the federal system. See Younger v. Harris, 401 U.S. 37, 43–45.

Indeed, though the federal courts may look to the common law or to the policies supporting res judicata and collateral estoppel in assessing the preclusive effect of decisions of other federal courts, Congress has specifically required all federal courts to give preclusive effect to state-court judgments whenever the courts of the State from which the judgments emerged would do so:

> "[J]udicial proceedings [of any court of any State] shall have the same full faith and credit in every court within the United States and its Territories and Possessions as they have by law or usage in the courts of such State. * * *"   28 U.S.C. § 1738.[8]

Huron Holding Corp. v. Lincoln Mine Operating Co., 312 U.S. 183, 193; Davis v. Davis, 305 U.S. 32, 40. It is against this background that we examine the relationship of § 1983 and collateral estoppel, and the decision of the Court of Appeals in this case.

---

7. Other factors, of course, may require an exception to the normal rules of collateral estoppel in particular cases. *E.g.*, Montana v. United States, 440 U.S., at 162 (unmixed questions of law in successive actions between the same parties on unrelated claims).

Contrary to the suggestion of the dissent, our decision today does not "fashion" any new, more stringent doctrine of collateral estoppel, nor does it hold that the collateral-estoppel effect of a state-court decision turns on the single factor of whether the State gave the federal claimant a full and fair opportunity to litigate a federal question. Our decision does not "fashion" any doctrine of collateral estoppel at all. Rather, it construes § 1983 to determine wheth-

er the conventional doctrine of collateral estoppel applies to the case at hand. It must be emphasized that the question whether any exceptions or qualifications within the bounds of that doctrine might ultimately defeat a collateral-estoppel defense in this case is not before us.

8. This statute has existed in essentially unchanged form since its enactment just after the ratification of the Constitution, Act of May 26, 1790, ch. 11, 1 Stat. 122, and its re-enactment soon thereafter, Act of Mar. 27, 1804, ch. 56, 2 Stat. 298–299. Congress has also provided means for authenticating the records of the state proceedings to which the federal courts are to give full faith and credit. 28 U.S.C. § 1738.

III

This Court has never directly decided whether the rules of res judicata and collateral estoppel are generally applicable to § 1983 actions. But in Preiser v. Rodriguez, 411 U.S. 475, 497, the Court noted with implicit approval the view of other federal courts that res judicata principles fully apply to civil rights suits brought under that statute. See also Huffman v. Pursue, Ltd., 420 U.S. 592, 606, n. 18; Wolff v. McDonnell, 418 U.S. 539, 554, n. 12. And the virtually unanimous view of the Courts of Appeals since Preiser has been that § 1983 presents no categorical bar to the application of res judicata and collateral estoppel concepts.[10] These federal appellate court decisions have spoken with little explanation or citation in assuming the compatibility of § 1983 and rules of preclusion, but the statute and its legislative history clearly support the courts' decisions.

Because the requirement of mutuality of estoppel was still alive in the federal courts until well into this century * * *, the drafters of the 1871 Civil Rights Act, of which § 1983 is a part, may have had less reason to concern themselves with rules of preclusion than a modern Congress would. Nevertheless, in 1871 res judicata and collateral estoppel could certainly have applied in federal suits following state-court litigation between the same parties or their privies, and nothing in the language of § 1983 remotely expresses any congressional intent to contravene the common-law rules of preclusion or to repeal the express statutory requirements of the predecessor of 28 U.S.C. § 1738. Section 1983 creates a new federal cause of action.[11] It says nothing about the preclusive effect of state-court judgments.[12]

10. *E.g.,* Robbins v. District Court, 592 F.2d 1015 (CA8 1979); Jennings v. Caddo Parish School Bd., 531 F.2d 1331 (CA5 1976); Lovely v. Laliberte, 498 F.2d 1261 (CA1 1974); Brown v. Georgia Power Co., 491 F.2d 117 (CA5 1974); Tang v. Appellate Division, 487 F.2d 138 (CA2 1973).

A very few courts have suggested that the normal rules of claim preclusion should not apply in § 1983 suits in one peculiar circumstance: Where a § 1983 plaintiff seeks to litigate in federal court a federal issue which he could have raised but did not raise in an earlier state-court suit against the same adverse party. Graves v. Olgiati, 550 F.2d 1327 (CA2 1977); Lombard v. Board of Ed. of New York City, 502 F.2d 631 (CA2 1974); Mack v. Florida Bd. of Dentistry, 430 F.2d 862 (CA5 1970). These cases present a narrow question not now before us, and we intimate no view as to whether they were correctly decided.

11. * * *

It has been argued that, since there remains little federal common law after Erie R. Co. v. Tompkins, 304 U.S. 64, to hold that the creation of a federal cause of action by itself does away with the rules of

preclusion would take away almost all meaning from § 1738. Currie, Res Judicata: The Neglected Defense, 45 U.Chi.L. Rev. 317, 328 (1978).

12. By contrast, the roughly contemporaneous statute extending the federal writ of habeas corpus to state prisoners expressly rendered "null and void" any state-court proceeding inconsistent with the decision of a federal habeas court, Act of Feb. 5, 1867, ch. 28, § 1, 14 Stat. 385, 386 (current version at 28 U.S.C. § 2254), and the modern habeas statute also expressly adverts to the effect of state-court criminal judgments by requiring the applicant for the writ to exhaust his state-court remedies, 28 U.S.C. § 2254(b), and by presuming a state-court resolution of a factual issue to be correct except in eight specific circumstances, § 2254(d). In any event, the traditional exception to res judicata for habeas corpus review, see Preiser v. Rodriguez, 411 U.S. 475, 497, provides no analogy to § 1983 cases, since that exception finds its source in the unique purpose of habeas corpus—to release the applicant for the writ from unlawful confinement. Sanders v. United States, 373 U.S. 1, 8.

Moreover, the legislative history of § 1983 does not in any clear way suggest that Congress intended to repeal or restrict the traditional doctrines of preclusion. The main goal of the Act was to override the corrupting influence of the Ku Klux Klan and its sympathizers on the governments and law enforcement agencies of the Southern States, see Monroe v. Pape, 365 U.S. 167, 174, and of course the debates show that one strong motive behind its enactment was grave congressional concern that the state courts had been deficient in protecting federal rights, Mitchum v. Foster, 407 U.S. 225, 241–242; Monroe v. Pape, *supra,* at 180. But in the context of the legislative history as a whole, this congressional concern lends only the most equivocal support to any argument that, in cases where the state courts have recognized the constitutional claims asserted and provided fair procedures for determining them, Congress intended to override § 1738 or the common-law rules of collateral estoppel and res judicata. Since repeals by implication are disfavored, * * * much clearer support than this would be required to hold that § 1738 and the traditional rules of preclusion are not applicable to § 1983 suits.

As the Court has understood the history of the legislation, Congress realized that in enacting § 1983 it was altering the balance of judicial power between the state and federal courts. See Mitchum v. Foster, *supra,* at 241. But in doing so, Congress was adding to the jurisdiction of the federal courts, not subtracting from that of the state courts.[14] * * *

To the extent that it did intend to change the balance of power over federal questions between the state and federal courts, the 42d Congress was acting in a way thoroughly consistent with the doctrines of preclusion. In reviewing the legislative history of § 1983 in Monroe v. Pape, the Court inferred that Congress had intended a federal remedy in three circumstances: where state substantive law was facially unconstitutional, where state procedural law was inadequate to allow full litigation of a constitutional claim, and where state procedural law, though adequate in theory, was inadequate in practice. In short, the federal courts could step in where the state courts were unable or unwilling to protect federal rights. This understanding of § 1983 might well support an exception to res judicata and collateral estoppel where state law did not provide fair procedures for the litigation of constitutional claims, or where a state court failed to even acknowledge the existence of the constitutional principle on which a litigant based his claim. Such an exception, however, would be essentially the same as the important general limit on rules of preclusion that already exists: Collateral estoppel does not apply where the party against whom an earlier court decision is asserted did not have a full and fair opportunity to litigate the claim or issue decided by the first court. But the Court's view of § 1983 in Monroe lends no strength to any argument that Congress intended to allow relitigation of federal issues decided after a full and fair hearing in a state court simply because the state court's decision may have been erroneous.[17]

14. To the extent that Congress in the post-Civil War period did intend to deny full faith and credit to state-court decisions on constitutional issues, it expressly chose the very different means of postjudgment removal for state-court defendants whose civil rights were threatened by biased state courts and who therefore "are denied or cannot enforce [their civil rights] in the courts or judicial tribunals of the State." Act of Apr. 9, 1866, ch. 31, § 3, 14 Stat. 27.

17. The dissent suggests that the Court's decision in England v. Medical Examiners, 375 U.S. 411, demonstrates the impropriety of affording preclusive effect

The Court of Appeals in this case acknowledged that every Court of Appeals that has squarely decided the question has held that collateral estoppel applies when § 1983 plaintiffs attempt to relitigate in federal court issues decided against them in state criminal proceedings. But the court noted that the only two federal appellate decisions invoking collateral estoppel to bar relitigation of Fourth Amendment claims decided adversely to the § 1983 plaintiffs in state courts came before this Court's decision in Stone v. Powell, 428 U.S. 465. It also noted that some of the decisions holding collateral estoppel applicable to § 1983 actions were based at least in part on the estopped party's access to another federal forum through habeas corpus. The Court of Appeals thus concluded that since Stone v. Powell had removed McCurry's right to a hearing of his Fourth Amendment claim in federal habeas corpus, collateral estoppel should not deprive him of a federal judicial hearing of that claim in a § 1983 suit.

Stone v. Powell does not provide a logical doctrinal source for the court's ruling. This Court in Stone assessed the costs and benefits of the judge-made exclusionary rule within the boundaries of the federal courts' statutory power to issue writs of habeas corpus, and decided that the incremental deterrent effect that the issuance of the writ in Fourth Amendment cases might have on police conduct did not justify the cost the writ imposed upon the fair administration of criminal justice. The Stone decision concerns only the prudent exercise of federal-court jurisdiction under 28 U.S.C. § 2254. It has no bearing on § 1983 suits or on the question of the preclusive effect of state-court judgments.

The actual basis of the Court of Appeals' holding appears to be a generally framed principle that every person asserting a federal right is entitled to one unencumbered opportunity to litigate that right in a federal district court, regardless of the legal posture in which the federal claim arises. But the authority for this principle is difficult to discern. It cannot lie in the Constitution, which makes no such guarantee, but leaves the scope of the jurisdiction of the federal district courts to the wisdom of Congress. And no such authority is to be found in § 1983 itself. For reasons already discussed at length, nothing in the language or legislative history of § 1983 proves any congressional intent to deny binding effect to a state-court judgment or decision when the state court, acting within its proper jurisdiction, has given the parties a full and fair opportunity to litigate federal claims, and thereby has shown itself willing and able to protect federal rights. And nothing in the legislative history of § 1983 reveals any purpose to afford less deference to judgments in state criminal proceedings than to those in state civil proceedings. There is, in short, no

to the state-court decision in this case. The England decision is inapposite to the question before us. In the England case, a party first submitted to a federal court his claim that a state statute violated his constitutional rights. The federal court abstained and remitted the plaintiff to the state courts • • •. This Court held that in such a circumstance, a plaintiff who properly reserved the federal issue by informing the state courts of his intention to return to federal court, if necessary, was not precluded from litigating the federal question in federal court. The holding in England depended entirely on this Court's view of the purpose of abstention in such a case: Where a plaintiff properly invokes federal court jurisdiction in the first instance on a federal claim, the federal court has a duty to accept that jurisdiction. Abstention may serve only to postpone, rather than to abdicate, jurisdiction, since its purpose is to determine whether resolution of the federal question is even necessary, or to obviate the risk of a federal court's erroneous construction of state law. These concerns have no bearing whatsoever on the present case.

reason to believe that Congress intended to provide a person claiming a federal right an unrestricted opportunity to relitigate an issue already decided in state court simply because the issue arose in a state proceeding in which he would rather not have been engaged at all.

Through § 1983, the 42d Congress intended to afford an opportunity for legal and equitable relief in a federal court for certain types of injuries. It is difficult to believe that the drafters of that Act considered it a substitute for a federal writ of habeas corpus, the purpose of which is not to redress civil injury, but to release the applicant from unlawful physical confinement, Preiser v. Rodriguez, 411 U.S., at 484; Fay v. Noia, 372 U.S. 391, 399, n. 5,[24] particularly in light of the extremely narrow scope of federal habeas relief for state prisoners in 1871.

The only other conceivable basis for finding a universal right to litigate a federal claim in a federal district court is hardly a legal basis at all, but rather a general distrust of the capacity of the state courts to render correct decisions on constitutional issues. It is ironic that Stone v. Powell provided the occasion for the expression of such an attitude in the present litigation, in view of this Court's emphatic reaffirmation in that case of the constitutional obligation of the state courts to uphold federal law, and its expression of confidence in their ability to do so.

The Court of Appeals erred in holding that McCurry's inability to obtain federal habeas corpus relief upon his Fourth Amendment claim renders the doctrine of collateral estoppel inapplicable to his § 1983 suit.[25] Accordingly, the judgment is reversed, and the case is remanded to the Court of Appeals for proceedings consistent with this opinion.

It is so ordered.

JUSTICE BLACKMUN, with whom JUSTICE BRENNAN and JUSTICE MARSHALL join, dissenting.

The legal principles with which the Court is concerned in this civil case obviously far transcend the ugly facts of respondent's criminal convictions in the courts of Missouri for heroin possession and assault.

The Court today holds that notions of collateral estoppel apply with full force to this suit brought under 42 U.S.C. § 1983. In my view, the Court, in so ruling, ignores the clear import of the legislative history of that statute and disregards the important federal policies that underlie its enforcement. It also shows itself insensitive both to the significant differences between the § 1983 remedy and the exclusionary rule, and to the pressures upon a criminal defendant that make a free choice of forum illusory. I do not doubt that principles of preclusion are to be given such effect as is appropriate in a § 1983 action. In many cases, the denial of res judicata or collateral estoppel effect would serve no purpose and would harm relations between federal and state tribunals. Nonetheless, the Court's analysis in this particular case is unacceptable to me. It works injustice on this § 1983 plaintiff, and it makes more difficult the consistent

24. Under the modern statute, federal habeas corpus is bounded by a requirement of exhaustion of state remedies and by special procedural rules, 28 U.S.C. § 2254, which have no counterparts in § 1983, and which therefore demonstrate the continuing illogic of treating federal habeas and § 1983 suits as fungible remedies for constitutional violations.

25. We do not decide *how* the body of collateral-estoppel doctrine or 28 U.S.C. § 1738 should apply in this case.

protection of constitutional rights, a consideration that was at the core of the enacters' intent. Accordingly, I dissent.

In deciding whether a common-law doctrine is to apply to § 1983 when the statute itself is silent, prior cases uniformly have accorded the intent of the legislators great weight. * * * In the present case, however, the Court minimizes the significance of the legislative history and discounts its own prior explicit interpretations of the statute. Its discussion is limited to articulating what it terms the single fundamental principle of res judicata and collateral estoppel.

Respondent's position merits a quite different analysis. Although the legislators of the 42d Congress did not expressly state whether the then existing common-law doctrine of preclusion would survive enactment of § 1983, they plainly anticipated more than the creation of a federal statutory remedy to be administered indifferently by either a state or a federal court. The legislative intent, as expressed by supporters and understood by opponents, was to restructure relations between the state and federal courts. Congress deliberately opened the federal courts to individual citizens in response to the States' failure to provide justice in their own courts. Contrary to the view presently expressed by the Court, the 42d Congress was not concerned solely with procedural regularity. Even where there was procedural regularity, which the Court today so stresses, Congress believed that substantive justice was unobtainable. The availability of the federal forum was not meant to turn on whether, in an individual case, the state procedures were adequate. Assessing the state of affairs as a whole, Congress specifically made a determination that federal oversight of constitutional determinations through the federal courts was necessary to ensure the effective enforcement of constitutional rights.

That the new federal jurisdiction was conceived of as concurrent with state jurisdiction does not alter the significance of Congress' opening the federal courts to these claims. * * *

[Justice Blackmun's analysis of the legislative history is omitted.]

I appreciate that the legislative history is capable of alternative interpretations. I would have thought, however, that our prior decisions made very clear which reading is required. [Justice Blackmun here discusses Monroe v. Pape, p. 1229, *supra;* Mitchum v. Foster, p. 1315, *supra;* and England v. Medical Examiners, p. 1376, *supra.*] * * *

The Court now fashions a new doctrine of preclusion, applicable only to actions brought under § 1983, that is more strict and more confining than the federal rules of preclusion applied in other cases. In Montana v. United States, 440 U.S. 147 (1979), the Court pronounced three major factors to be considered in determining whether collateral estoppel serves as a barrier in the federal court:

"[W]hether the issues presented * * * are in substance the same * * *; whether controlling facts or legal principles have changed significantly since the state-court judgment; and finally, whether other special circumstances warrant an exception to the normal rules of preclusion."

But now the Court states that the collateral-estoppel effect of prior state adjudication should turn on only one factor, namely, what it considers the "one general limitation" inherent in the doctrine of preclusion: "that the concept of collateral estoppel cannot apply when the party against whom the earlier decision is asserted did not have a 'full and fair opportunity' to litigate that issue in the earlier case." If that one factor is present, the Court asserts, the litigant properly should be barred from relitigating the issue in federal court.[12] One cannot deny that this factor is an important one. I do not believe, however, that the doctrine of preclusion requires the inquiry to be so narrow, and my understanding of the policies underlying § 1983 would lead me to consider all relevant factors in each case before concluding that preclusion was warranted.

In this case, the police officers seek to prevent a criminal defendant from relitigating the constitutionality of their conduct in searching his house, after the state trial court had found that conduct in part violative of the defendant's Fourth Amendment rights and in part justified by the circumstances. I doubt that the police officers, now defendants in this § 1983 action, can be considered to have been in privity with the State in its role as prosecutor. Therefore, only "issue preclusion" is at stake.

The following factors persuade me to conclude that this respondent should not be precluded from asserting his claim in federal court. First, at the time § 1983 was passed, a non-party's ability, as a practical matter, to invoke collateral estoppel was nonexistent. One could not preclude an opponent from relitigating an issue in a new cause of action, though that issue had been determined conclusively in a prior proceeding, unless there was "mutuality." Additionally, the definitions of "cause of action" and "issue" were narrow. As a result, and obviously, no preclusive effect could arise out of a criminal proceeding that would affect subsequent *civil* litigation. Thus, the 42d Congress could not have anticipated or approved that a criminal defendant, tried and convicted in state court, would be precluded from raising against police officers a constitutional claim arising out of his arrest.

Also, the process of deciding in a state criminal trial whether to exclude or admit evidence is not at all the equivalent of a § 1983 proceeding. The remedy sought in the latter is utterly different. In bringing the civil suit the criminal defendant does not seek to challenge his conviction collaterally. At most, he wins damages. In contrast, the exclusion of evidence may prevent a criminal conviction. A trial court, faced with the decision whether to exclude relevant evidence, confronts institutional pressures that may cause it to give a different shape to the Fourth Amendment right from what would result in civil litigation of a damages claim. Also, the issue whether to exclude evidence is subsidary to the purpose of a criminal trial, which is to determine the guilt or innocence of the defendant, and a trial court, at least subconsciously, must weigh the potential damage to the truth-seeking process caused by excluding relevant evidence.

* * *

A state criminal defendant cannot be held to have chosen "voluntarily" to litigate his Fourth Amendment claim in the state court. The risk of conviction puts pressure upon him to raise all possible defenses. He also faces uncertainty about the wisdom of forgoing litigation on *any* issue, for there is the possibility that he will be held to have waived his right to

---

12. This articulation of the preclusion doctrine of course would bar a § 1983 litigant from relitigating any issue he *might* have raised, as well as any issue he actually litigated in his criminal trial.

appeal on that issue. The "deliberate bypass" of state procedures, which the imposition of collateral estoppel under these circumstances encourages, surely is not a preferred goal. To hold that a criminal defendant who raises a Fourth Amendment claim at his criminal trial "freely and without reservation submits his federal claims for decision by the state courts," see England v. Medical Examiners, 375 U.S., at 419, is to deny reality. The criminal defendant is an involuntary litigant in the state tribunal, and against him all the forces of the State are arrayed. To force him to a choice between forgoing either a potential defense or a federal forum for hearing his constitutional civil claim is fundamentally unfair.

I would affirm the judgment of the Court of Appeals.

NOTE ON 28 U.S.C. § 1738 AND THE RES JUDICATA EFFECT OF STATE JUDGMENTS

(1) At the time that Allen v. McCurry was decided, there was wide disagreement among commentators about the preclusive effect of state court judgments on subsequent § 1983 actions. See, e.g., Currie, *Res Judicata: The Neglected Defense*, 45 U.Chi.L.Rev. 317 (1978); Averitt, *Federal Section 1983 Actions After State Court Judgment*, 44 U.Colo.L.Rev. 191 (1972); *Developments in the Law—Section 1983 and Federalism*, 90 Harv.L.Rev. 1133, 1330–54 (1977); Note, 78 Colum.L.Rev. 610 (1978). The decisions, too, were in disarray, although the courts did not go as far as suggesting that § 1983 allows the same scope for relitigating state-court rulings on questions of federal law as is permitted when the federal courts exercise habeas corpus jurisdiction. Oddly, much of the judicial consideration of the question took no account of § 1738 at all.

(2) Allen v. McCurry affirmed that § 1983 does not simply negate the application of res judicata and that "normal" res judicata principles apply. But note how many ambiguities stud the opinion. (i) The Court noted the relevance of § 1738 as "background," but did not unequivocally state that the central principle of § 1738—that the federal court must measure the preclusive effect of the state court adjudication by the res judicata law of the rendering state—holds in § 1983 litigation. In fact the Court insisted that it was not deciding exactly "how" res judicata applies in § 1983 actions. (ii) The Court reserved the question whether preclusion could apply to claims that could have been but were not raised in the state courts. It did not indicate whether this issue turned on federal or state law. (iii) Nor did the Court specify the source or content of the rule that res judicata does not apply when there was no "full and fair opportunity" to litigate. (Is the latter a constitutional principle that generally limits res judicata? Is it simply a short-hand for res judicata exceptions found inside the law of res judicata in most states? Or is it a federal rule derived from § 1983?)

Many of these ambiguities have, however, been removed from the law by the Court's later opinions, which we now survey. See generally Shreve, *Preclusion and Federal Choice of Law*, 64 Tex.L.Rev. 1209 (1986). The Court's approach to § 1738 is criticized in Burbank, p. 1605, *supra*, at 805–29.

(3) In Kremer v. Chemical Construction Corp., 456 U.S. 461 (1982), the Court moved unequivocally to the position that § 1738 provides an authoritative command to the federal courts to give the same preclusive effect to state court resolutions of federal questions as would be given in the courts of the rendering state, absent a clear countervailing command to be found in another federal statute. Kremer involved not § 1983, but Title VII of the Civil Rights Act of 1964, which provides that employment discrimination charges must initially be filed with the state agency that administers state antidiscrimination laws. Thereafter, a complainant may file a claim with the federal EEOC, which is required to "accord substantial weight" to the state agency decision. Title VII also gives a complainant the right, after state and federal agency determinations of his claim, to a trial de novo in federal court. In Kremer the complainant had unsuccessfully appealed an unfavorable state agency determination to the New York courts before filing with the EEOC and, after failing there, bringing suit in a federal district court. By a bare majority the Supreme Court held that neither the grant in Title VII of a right to a trial de novo, nor the provision that state findings be accorded "substantial weight" by the EEOC, worked an implied partial repeal of § 1738; the state courts' rejection of the claim was therefore preclusive to the same extent that it would be in a second action in the New York state courts. The Court said:

"No provision of Title VII requires claimants to pursue in state court an unfavorable state administrative action, nor does the Act specify the weight a federal court should afford a final judgment by a state court if such a remedy is sought. While we have interpreted the 'civil action' authorized to follow consideration by federal and state *agencies* to be a 'trial *de novo*,' * * * neither the statute nor our decisions indicate that the final judgment of a state *court* is subject to redetermination at such a trial. Similarly, the congressional directive that the EEOC should give 'substantial weight' to findings made in state proceedings * * * indicates only the minimum level of deference the EEOC must afford all state determinations; it does not bar affording the greater preclusive effect which may be required by § 1738 if judicial action is involved. To suggest otherwise, to say that either the opportunity to bring a 'civil action' or the 'substantial weight' requirement implicitly repeals § 1738, is to prove far too much. For if that is so, even a full trial on the merits in state court would not bar a trial de novo in federal court and would not be entitled to more than 'substantial weight' before the EEOC" (pp. 469–70).

The Court went on to review the legislative history of Title VII, concluding that "[w]hile striving to craft an optimal niche for the States in the overall enforcement scheme, the legislators did not envision full litigation of a single claim in both state and federal forums" (pp. 473–74).

The state court in Kremer had determined only that the state agency's decision had not been "arbitrary or capricious." In dissent, Justice Blackmun argued that because "the Appellate Division made no finding one way or the other concerning the *merits* " of the discrimination claim, "although it claims to grant a state *court* decision preclusive effect, in fact the Court bars petitioner's suit based on the state *agency's* decision of no probable cause. The Court thereby disregards the express provisions of Title VII, for * * * Congress has decided that an adverse state agency decision will not prevent a complainant's subsequent Title VII suit" (pp. 492–93).

The Court in Kremer also considered the "full and fair opportunity to litigate" exception to preclusion. Noting that neither the source nor content of the exception had been specified in previous cases, the Court stated that "for present purposes, where we are bound by the statutory directive of § 1738, state proceedings need do no more than satisfy the minimum procedural requirements of the Fourteenth Amendment's Due Process Clause in order to qualify for the full faith and credit guaranteed by federal law" (p. 481). Since a state "may not grant preclusive effect in its own courts to a constitutionally infirm judgment," this requirement is consistent with § 1738; "other state and federal courts would still be providing a state court judgment with the 'same' preclusive effect as the courts of the State from which the judgment emerged. In such a case, there could be no constitutionally recognizable preclusion at all" (pp. 482–83).

(4) Many of the remaining ambiguities of Allen v. McCurry were settled in the important decision in Migra v. Warren City School District, 465 U.S. 75 (1984), in an opinion—this time for a surprisingly unanimous Court—written by Justice Blackmun.[1]

Migra involved an elementary school supervisor who had been fired from her job. She brought a successful suit in the Ohio courts for damages and reinstatement, alleging only breach of contract and tortious interference with an employment contract. Thereafter she brought a second action under § 1983 in federal court, this time alleging that her dismissal violated the First, Fifth, and Fourteenth Amendments, and seeking *inter alia* punitive damages. The Supreme Court held that § 1738 governs and requires claim preclusion to the same extent as would be applied by the Ohio courts. It rejected plaintiff's argument that the Court should "interpret the interplay between § 1738 and § 1983 in such a way as to accord state-court judgments preclusive effect in § 1983 suits only as to issues actually litigated in state courts" (pp. 83–85):

"It is difficult to see how the policy concerns underlying § 1983 would justify a distinction between the issue preclusive and claim preclusive effects of state-court judgments. The argument that state-court judgments should have less preclusive effect in § 1983 suits than in other federal suits is based on Congress' expressed concern over the adequacy of state courts as protectors of federal rights. * * * Allen recognized that the enactment of § 1983 was motivated partially out of such concern, but Allen nevertheless held that § 1983 did not open the way to relitigation of an issue that had been determined in a state criminal proceeding. Any distrust of state courts that would justify a limitation on the preclusive

1. Between Kremer and Migra the Court decided Haring v. Prosise, 462 U.S. 306 (1983), holding that a state court guilty plea to a charge of manufacturing illegal drugs did not preclude a § 1983 action against state police who had obtained the evidence leading to the charge. The Court said that § 1738 does not require preclusion, because the relevant state law did not require it. The Court also went on, however, to engage in some confusing dicta suggesting that preclusion may be negated as a matter of federal policy or by special circumstances. See the full discussion in 18 Federal Practice §§ 4471, 4474, at 255–59, 303–06 (1987 Supp.).

Would a state rule giving sweeping preclusive effect to all issues subsumed in a guilty plea violate Due Process? To the extent it did not, may § 1738 be ignored? (Note that exactly the same problem could arise with respect to interstate full faith and credit.)

See generally Shapiro, *Should a Guilty Plea Have Preclusive Effect?*, 70 Iowa L.Rev. 27 (1984).

effect of state judgments in § 1983 suits would presumably apply equally to issues that actually were decided in a state court as well as to those that could have been. If § 1983 created an exception to the general preclusive effect accorded to state-court judgments, such an exception would seem to require similar treatment of both issue preclusion and claim preclusion. Having rejected in Allen the view that state-court judgments have no issue preclusive effect in § 1983 suits, we must reject the view that § 1983 prevents the judgment in petitioner's state-court proceeding from creating a claim preclusion bar in this case.

"Petitioner suggests that to give state-court judgments full issue preclusive effect but not claim preclusive effect would enable litigants to bring their state claims in state court and their federal claims in federal court, thereby taking advantage of the relative expertise of both forums. Although such a division may seem attractive from a plaintiff's perspective, it is not the system established by § 1738. That statute embodies the view that it is more important to give full faith and credit to state-court judgments than to ensure separate forums for federal and state claims. This reflects a variety of concerns, including notions of comity, the need to prevent vexatious litigation, and a desire to conserve judicial resources.

"In the present litigation, petitioner does not claim that the state court would not have adjudicated her federal claims had she presented them in her original suit in state court. Alternatively, petitioner could have obtained a federal forum for her federal claim by litigating it first in a federal court.[7] Section 1983, however, does not override state preclusion law and guarantee petitioner a right to proceed to judgment in state court on her state claims and then turn to federal court for adjudication of her federal claims. We hold, therefore, that petitioner's state-court judgment in this litigation has the same claim preclusive effect in federal court that the judgment would have in the Ohio state courts."

The Court remanded the case to the district court with the order to "interpret Ohio preclusion law and apply it" (p. 87).

Justice White's concurrence, joined by Chief Justice Burger and Justice Powell, stated that it would be desirable to allow federal courts to use federal res judicata law to give state court judgments preclusive effect even if res judicata would not bar relitigation in the state courts. However, in view of the "long standing" construction of § 1738 as allowing a federal court to give a state judgment "no greater efficacy" than would the judgment-rendering state, Justice White agreed with the Court's disposition (p. 88).

(5) Marrese v. American Academy of Orthopaedic Surgeons, 470 U.S. 373 (1985), touches on the thorny question of the preclusive effect of a state court judgment on a later federal action within the exclusive jurisdiction of the federal courts.[2] This case involved an action brought in state court

---

"7. The author of this opinion was in dissent in Allen. The rationale of that dissent, however, was based largely on the fact that the § 1983 plaintiff in that case first litigated his constitutional claim in state court in the posture of his being a *defendant* in a criminal proceeding. See 449 U.S., at 115–116. In this case, petitioner was in an offensive posture in her state-court proceeding, and could have proceeded

first in federal court had she wanted to litigate her federal claim in a federal forum. * * *"

2. In Kremer v. Chemical Constr. Co., *supra*, the Court found it unnecessary to determine whether federal courts have exclusive jurisdiction over actions under Title VII.

asserting that the Academy's denial of membership to plaintiff violated the Illinois constitution and common law. After a defeat in the state courts, plaintiff brought a new action in federal court, alleging a violation of the federal antitrust laws—a claim over which the federal courts have exclusive jurisdiction and which could not, therefore, have been joined in the state action. The Seventh Circuit, in an interesting array of opinions, ruled that the federal action was barred by res judicata, applying federal law. 726 F.2d 1150 (7th Cir.1984). In the Supreme Court Justice O'Connor said that the lower courts had erred in not taking account of Illinois preclusion law under § 1738, which "requires a federal court to look first to state preclusion law in determining the preclusive effect of a state court judgment" (p. 381). Acknowledging that Illinois law would have no "occasion to address the specific question whether a state judgment has issue or claim preclusive effect in a later action that can be brought only in federal court," the Court pointed out that Illinois res judicata law might nevertheless address the more general question whether claim preclusion forecloses related claims that were not within the jurisdiction of the rendering court. Ordinarily, the Court said, claim preclusion does not apply in such situations. If Illinois adheres to that rule, the federal courts under § 1738 must also do so and may not give preclusive effect to the Illinois judgment. "States * * * determine the preclusive scope of their own courts' judgments. * * * These concerns certainly are not made less compelling because state courts lack jurisdiction over federal antitrust claims. We therefore reject a judicially created exception to § 1738 that effectively holds as a matter of federal law that a plaintiff can bring state law claims initially in state court only at the cost of forgoing subsequent federal antitrust claims" (pp. 385–86).

The Court then went on, surprisingly, to state that it would not determine whether preclusion *would* be required if the preclusion law of Illinois did apply to closely related claims even when one was not within the jurisdiction of the rendering court. The Court stated that in determining whether an exception is to be made to § 1738 for a particular class of federal claims, such as an antitrust claim, the question is "whether the concerns underlying a particular grant of exclusive jurisdiction justify a finding of an implied partial repeal of § 1738" (p. 386). The case was remanded for an inquiry into the relevant Illinois law.[3]

(6) The Marrese case apparently settles the point that, under § 1738, the federal courts may not give greater res judicata effect to a state judgment than the state itself would give. But it leaves unexplored the difficult question whether and when state preclusion rules can be defeated by the policies that led Congress to make federal jurisdiction over a certain class of claims exclusive. The extraordinary array of approaches to this question are explored in depth in 18 Federal Practice § 4470. A celebrated treatment of the issue is Judge Learned Hand's opinion in Lyons v. Westinghouse Elec. Corp., 222 F.2d 184 (2d Cir.1955),[4] holding that a state

3. Chief Justice Burger, concurring, argued in favor of a broad federal rule of preclusion.

4. In Westinghouse Judge Hand stated the issue as being "whether, when Congress gave exclusive jurisdiction to the district court over wrongs committed under the Antitrust Acts, it only meant that the 'person who shall be injured' must sue in the district court to recover damages; or whether it also meant that the district court must have unfettered power to decide the claim, regardless of the findings of any other courts, even when these were essential to the decision of actions over which their jurisdiction was unquestioned. A priori either reading seems permissible" (p. 188).

court determination of an antitrust defense in a contract action did not bind the federal court in a later federal antitrust action. On the other hand the Third Circuit held that where a patentee, suing to recover royalties under a license agreement, lost in state court on the ground that the patent did not cover the defendant's goods, the patentee was barred thereafter from maintaining a federal patent infringement suit with respect to the identical goods. Vanderveer v. Erie Malleable Iron Co., 238 F.2d 510 (3d Cir.1956). The question is also of significance in areas such as securities litigation and bankruptcy.

The Restatement 2d § 26 provides that rules against splitting causes of action do not apply where the plaintiff was barred from submitting a "certain theory of the case" because of limitations on the subject matter jurisdiction of the rendering court; and a specific illustration (p. 237) states that if A sues B on a state antitrust action and loses on the merits, A is not thereafter barred from bringing a federal antitrust action in federal court. Compare § 28, Subsection (2) and Comment *d* (flexible rule with respect to issue preclusion).

Should there be a single answer to this problem? Should not the answer depend, both on the nature and strength of the policies that led Congress to the decision to make federal jurisdiction exclusive, and on the particular sort of preclusion in question (*e.g.,* issue preclusion with respect to an issue of fact or law? mutual or nonmutual preclusion?)? [5]

(7) The Court pushed the notion that the preclusive effect of state proceedings on the federal courts is to be measured by state law yet another step in University of Tennessee v. Elliott, 478 U.S. 788 (1986).[6] A state administrative law judge determined that Elliott's discharge from his university job had not been motivated by racial prejudice, and this finding was upheld on administrative appeal. Rather than seeking review of these agency determinations in the Tennessee courts, Elliott filed Title VII and § 1983 claims in a federal district court. The Supreme Court ruled that § 1738 was inapplicable, because it governs only the preclusive effect of "judicial" proceedings.[7] Nevertheless, the Court noted that it had "frequently fashioned federal common-law rules of preclusion in the absence of a governing statute," and that "because § 1738 antedates the development of administrative agencies it clearly does not represent a congressional determination that the decisions of state administrative agencies should not be given preclusive effect" (pp. 794–95). The Court held that a rule giving unreviewed state administrative proceedings preclusive effect would be inconsistent with Title VII's provision for a trial de

---

5. Consider, for instance, a holding by a state court, in adjudicating a defense in a contract action, that the plaintiff's patent is invalid. Even if that holding is binding in a subsequent federal infringement action by the plaintiff against the same defendant, should it be binding, under the Blonder Tongue case, in an infringement action against a new defendant?

6. See also Parsons Steel, Inc. v. First Alabama Bank, 474 U.S. 518 (1986) (whether state-court rejection of res judicata claim with respect to earlier federal judgment is itself res judicata in a later federal action to enjoin the enforcement of the state court judgment depends, under § 1738, on the state's res judicata law; 28 U.S.C. § 2283 does not create an implied exception to § 1738). See further pp. 1327–28, *supra.*

7. The Court had held that the award of a state arbitration tribunal that has not been reviewed or enforced by any state court is not a "judicial proceeding" and does not have preclusive effect in the federal courts under § 1738. McDonald v. City of West Branch, 466 U.S. 284 (1984). After Elliott, what would be the effect—apart from § 1738—of such an award by a state that does give it preclusive effect?

novo following agency action. As to § 1983 actions, however, the Court held that factfinding by a state agency acting in a judicial capacity was to be given the preclusive effect to which it would be entitled in the state's courts. Citing Allen v. McCurry for the proposition that Congress had not intended § 1983 "to repeal or restrict the traditional doctrines of preclusion," and United States v. Utah Construction & Mining Co., 384 U.S. 394 (1966), for the proposition that federal agency factfinding has preclusive effect, the Court held that the traditional purposes of preclusion are "equally implicated whether factfinding is done by a federal or state agency" (p. 798).[8]

Recall that in Patsy v. Florida Board of Regents, p. 1350, *supra,* the Court held that a § 1983 plaintiff does not have to exhaust state administrative remedies. In light of that holding, was it wise for the Court to discourage voluntary resort to state administrative procedures by creating a risk that administrative findings may bar the § 1983 action entirely? On the other hand, recall also the holding in Ohio Civil Rights Comm'n v. Dayton Christian Schools, p. 1435, *supra,* that Younger bars interference with a pending state administrative enforcement proceeding. The consequences of that holding are enormously intensified, are they not, by the Elliott case?

Do Patsy, Dayton Christian Schools, and Elliott, together, create a sensible system of deference to state administrative processes?

Suppose that state law does not give unreviewed administrative findings res judicata effect, but provides for a narrow scope of review of such findings by the state courts. Should a federal court in a § 1983 action, brought before any judicial review is sought in the state courts, think of such state law as analogous to state preclusion rules and thus applicable under Elliott?

ROOKER v. FIDELITY TRUST COMPANY

263 U.S. 413, 44 S.Ct. 149, 68 L.Ed. 362 (1923).
Appeal From the District Court of the United States for the District of Indiana.

MR. JUSTICE VAN DEVANTER delivered the opinion of the Court.

This is a bill in equity to have a judgment of a circuit court in Indiana, which was affirmed by the Supreme Court of the State, declared null and void, and to obtain other relief dependent on that outcome. An effort to have the judgment reviewed by this Court on writ of error had failed because the record did not disclose the presence of any question constituting a basis for such a review. Rooker v. Fidelity Trust Co., 261 U.S. 114. The parties to the bill are the same as in the litigation in the state court, but with an addition of two defendants whose presence does not need special notice. All are citizens of the same State. The grounds advanced for resorting to the District Court are that the judgment was rendered and

---

8. Dissenting as to the § 1983 issue, Justice Stevens said preclusion would not serve finality or federalism objectives, because the complainant could still take his companion Title VII claim to federal court, and because "litigants apprised of this decision will presumably forgo state administrative determinations for the same reason they currently forgo state judicial review of those determinations—to protect their entitlement to a federal forum" (p. ___).

affirmed in contravention of the contract clause of the Constitution of the United States and the due process of law and equal protection clauses of the Fourteenth Amendment, in that it gave effect to a state statute alleged to be in conflict with those clauses and did not give effect to a prior decision in the same cause by the Supreme Court of the State which is alleged to have become the "law of the case." The District Court was of opinion that the suit was not within its jurisdiction as defined by Congress, and on that ground dismissed the bill. The plaintiffs have appealed directly to this court under § 238 of the Judicial Code.

The appellees move that the appeal be dismissed, or in the alternative that the decree be affirmed.

The appeal is within the first clause of § 238; so the motion to dismiss must be overruled. But the suit is so plainly not within the District Court's jurisdiction as defined by Congress that the motion to affirm must be sustained.

It affirmatively appears from the bill that the judgment was rendered in a cause wherein the circuit court had jurisdiction of both the subject matter and the parties; that a full hearing was had therein; that the judgment was responsive to the issues, and that it was affirmed by the Supreme Court of the State on an appeal by the plaintiffs. 191 Ind. 141. If the constitutional questions stated in the bill actually arose in the cause, it was the province and duty of the state courts to decide them; and their decision, whether right or wrong, was an exercise of jurisdiction. If the decision was wrong, that did not make the judgment void, but merely left it open to reversal or modification in an appropriate and timely appellate proceeding. Unless and until so reversed or modified, it would be an effective and conclusive adjudication. * * * Under the legislation of Congress, no court of the United States other than this Court could entertain a proceeding to reverse or modify the judgment for errors of that character. Judicial Code, § 237, as amended September 6, 1916, c. 448, § 2, 39 Stat. 726. To do so would be an exercise of appellate jurisdiction. The jurisdiction possessed by the District Courts is strictly original. Judicial Code, § 24. Besides, the period within which a proceeding might be begun for the correction of errors such as are charged in the bill had expired before it was filed, Act September 6, 1916, c. 448, § 6, 39 Stat. 726, and * * * after that period elapses an aggrieved litigant cannot be permitted to do indirectly what he no longer can do directly.

Some parts of the bill speak of the judgment as given without jurisdiction and absolutely void; but this is merely mistaken characterization. A reading of the entire bill shows indubitably that there was full jurisdiction in the state courts and that the bill at best is merely an attempt to get rid of the judgment for alleged errors of law committed in the exercise of that jurisdiction.

In what has been said we have proceeded on the assumption that the constitutional questions alleged to have arisen in the state courts respecting the validity of a state statute, Acts 1915, c. 62, and the effect to be given to a prior decision in the same cause by the Supreme Court of the State, 185 Ind. 172, were questions of substance, but we do not hold that they were such,—the assumption being indulged merely for the purpose of testing the nature of the bill and the power of the District Court to entertain it. * * *

Decree affirmed.

NOTE ON THE ROOKER DOCTRINE AND ON PENNZOIL v. TEXACO: HEREIN OF THE INTERPLAY BETWEEN RES JUDICATA, EXCLUSIVE JURISDICTION, AND COMITY

(1) The Rooker case, apparently holding that the grant of statutory jurisdiction to the Supreme Court to review state court judgments furnished an independent basis for prohibiting collateral attack on those judgments, was largely forgotten until revived in Chang, *Rediscovering the Rooker Doctrine: Section 1983, Res Judicata and the Federal Courts*, 31 Hastings L.J. 1337 (1980).

Rooker's analysis was thereafter used as the basis for the Court's decision in District of Columbia Court of Appeals v. Feldman, 460 U.S. 462 (1983). In that case two applicants for membership in the District of Columbia bar asked the District of Columbia Court of Appeals—the court authorized by statute to supervise D.C. bar admission matters—to waive the normal rule that requires applicants to have graduated from an ABA-accredited law school. In both cases, after various proceedings, that court by per curiam order denied the applications for waivers, notwithstanding the applicants' arguments that denial would deprive them of constitutional rights. Applicants thereafter filed complaints in the United States District Court for the District of Columbia, challenging the denial of the waiver applications and the constitutional validity of the relevant bar admission rules. The district court dismissed for lack of subject matter jurisdiction, but was reversed by the court of appeals.

The Supreme Court held that the district court did not have jurisdiction over the actions to challenge the validity of the waivers. Noting the provision of the D.C.Code making final judgments of the D.C. Court of Appeals reviewable by the Supreme Court under § 1257, and the amendment of § 1257 specifying that the term "highest court of a State" included that court, the Supreme Court held that the district court "is without authority to review final determinations of the District of Columbia Court of Appeals in judicial proceedings [citing Rooker]" (p. 476). It then considered whether the rulings of the D.C. Court of Appeals, denying the petitions for waiver, constituted "judicial" proceedings, and concluded that the Supreme Court's precedents "clearly establish that the proceedings * * * surrounding Feldman's and Hickey's petitions for waiver were judicial in nature. The proceedings were not legislative, ministerial, or administrative. * * * Instead, the proceedings * * * involved a 'judicial inquiry' in which the court was called upon to investigate, declare, and enforce 'liabilities as they [stood] on present or past facts and under laws supposed already to exist.' Prentis v. Atlantic Coast Line Co., 211 U.S. at 226 [see p. 1348, *supra*]" (p. 479). Consequently, said the Court, the district court lacked subject matter jurisdiction over these complaints; applicants "should have sought review of the District of Columbia Court of Appeals' judgments in this Court." [1]

The Court held, on the other hand, that the applicants' "general challenge" to the constitutionality of the rule requiring graduation from a law school for bar admission was within the district court's jurisdiction. The Court stated that there is a distinction between "seeking review in a federal district court of a state court's final judgment in a bar admission matter and challenging the validity of a state bar admission rule" (pp. 483–84).

The Court "expressly" did not reach the question "whether the doctrine of res judicata forecloses litigation of the latter claims" (p. 487).

Justice Stevens, dissenting, said (pp. 489–90):

"[E]ven if the refusal to grant a waiver were an adjudication, the federal statute that confers jurisdiction upon the United States District Court to entertain a constitutional challenge to the rules themselves also authorizes that court to entertain a collateral attack upon the unconstitutional application of those rules. The Court's opinion fails to distinguish between two concepts: appellate review and collateral attack. If a challenge to a state court's decision is brought in United States district court and alleges violations of the United States Constitution, then by definition it does not seek appellate review. It is plainly within the federal-question jurisdiction of the federal court. There may be other reasons for denying relief to the plaintiff—such as failure to state a cause of action, claim or issue preclusion, or failure to prove a violation of constitutional rights. But it does violence to jurisdictional concepts for this Court to hold, as it does, that the federal district court has no *jurisdiction* to conduct independent review of a specific claim that a licensing body's action did not comply with federal constitutional standards. The fact that the licensing function in the legal profession is controlled by the judiciary is not a sufficient reason to immunize allegedly unconstitutional conduct from review in the federal courts."

(2) What do Rooker and Feldman add to the doctrine of res judicata and to § 1738?

(a) Suppose, first, that a collateral challenge to a state court judgment would be barred in the courts of the state by the law of res judicata. Wouldn't a collateral challenge in a federal court be barred by § 1738? Does § 1257 now furnish an independent statutory basis for that result? What turns on labeling the result a lack of jurisdiction in the district court to review the state court judgment, rather than an application of res judicata? (Does the reformulation suggest that the case might be dismissed even if the defendant does not object to the action?)

Note that the Court in Feldman held that the district court had "jurisdiction" to consider the plaintiffs' attack on the validity of the bar

---

1. In an elaborate footnote (p. 482 n. 16) the Court noted that Supreme Court review of the denial of applicants' requests for admission might be barred if they failed to raise their constitutional claims in the "state" court. It then went on expressly to disapprove the holding of the Fifth Circuit in Dasher v. Supreme Court of Texas, 658 F.2d 1045 (1981), that in such a case a district court may review a bar admission denial precisely because the Supreme Court could not. "[T]he fact that we may not have jurisdiction to review a final state court judgment because of a petitioner's failure to raise his constitutional claims in state court does not mean that a United States district court should have jurisdiction over the claims."

admission rules, but left open the question whether this latter attack was barred by preclusion. Do the resulting distinctions make sense? Is the Court saying that the preclusive effect of a state court's ruling on the validity *as applied* of a state bar admission rule is governed by § 1257's grant of exclusive appellate jurisdiction to the Supreme Court, whereas the preclusive effect of its judgment on the question whether that same rule is valid on its face is tested by the law of res judicata? If so, why should this be so?

(b) Now assume that an original action of the sort at issue in Feldman, challenging on constitutional grounds the state supreme court's denial of waiver, *could* be maintained in the state courts. Does the Rooker–Feldman doctrine hold that a federal action is impermissible nevertheless? What would this do to the Court's insistence, in its § 1738 cases, that the preclusive effect in a federal court of a state court judgment must be measured by state law? To the rule that a state court judgment should not have greater "efficacy" in a federal court than it does in the courts of the rendering state? See *Note on § 1738 and the Res Judicata Effect of State Judgments,* p. 1624, *supra.*

When a federal district court is asked to reopen issues already adjudicated by another federal district court, we usually rely on the law of res judicata to determine whether this is permissible. Would it help the analysis to ask, independently, whether the second inquiry is precluded by 28 U.S.C. § 1291—the statute governing the federal courts of appeals' "exclusive" jurisdiction to review final district court judgments?

The possibility of appellate review is, of course, an important reason for the existence of res judicata rules barring relitigation on collateral attack. But should statutes providing for appellate review be read as generating an independent set of rules to the same end?

(3) Rooker and Feldman both involved state court proceedings that were complete when district court challenges were initiated; there was no occasion to inquire whether state remedies should be exhausted before the federal action is entertained, or whether comity principles barred the action. But note that the "exclusive jurisdiction" notion underlying Rooker–Feldman could, theoretically, also be relevant in cases where state proceedings are still underway, and where the applicable doctrines in play have been thought to be those of comity, abstention, and exhaustion, rather than res judicata. (See, in this connection, the discussion of Huffman v. Pursue and related cases in Chap. X, Sec. 2(C), p. 1433, *supra.*)

The relationship among all of these doctrines was dramatically presented by the celebrated case of Pennzoil Co. v. Texaco, Inc., 107 S.Ct. 1519 (1987).

(a) *The facts.* Pennzoil obtained a $10.53 billion judgment against Texaco for tortious interference with Pennzoil's contract to purchase Getty Oil Co. Under Texas law, such a judgment was the basis for recording a lien on Texaco's assets, unless Texaco filed a supersedeas bond "at least [equal in] amount to the judgment" pending an appeal.

Texaco, without raising the issue of the constitutional validity of these bond and lien provisions in the Texas courts, brought a § 1983 action in the federal district court in New York, alleging that these provisions violated the federal Constitution by impermissibly burdening Texaco's right to appeal the Texas judgment in the state courts.[2]   The district court, ruling that Texaco's claims had a "clear probability of success" on the merits, entered an injunction barring any action by Pennzoil to enforce its state-court judgment pending state appellate review.   The court of appeals affirmed.   The Supreme Court reversed unanimously, with five Justices ruling that, under Younger, the federal court was barred from interfering with the course of the state court litigation.   (This aspect of the case is discussed in connection with the Younger rule at p. 1437, *supra*.)   The four remaining Justices concurred on other grounds.

Consider the various elements of state-federal court relations potentially in play in the Pennzoil case.

(b) *The Anti–Injunction Act.*   Texaco's action would clearly have been barred by § 2283, the Anti–Injunction Act, unless it was properly brought as a § 1983 action and thus covered by the ruling in Mitchum v. Foster, p. 1315, *supra*, holding that in § 1983 actions injunctions against state proceedings are "expressly authorized" within the meaning of § 2283.   The court of appeals had held that Texaco's suit was a proper § 1983 action because Pennzoil was a "state actor" in enforcing the Texas bond and lien provisions.[3]   The Supreme Court's majority did not pass on this issue, although four Justices indicated agreement with the court of appeals.

In its jurisdictional statement (J.S.), Pennzoil argued (p. 12):

"By vastly expanding the application of § 1983 to private conduct, the holding below retroactively pumps new meaning into the exemption authorized by Mitchum v. Foster and thereby drastically erodes the force of the Anti–Injunction Act.   That Act by its very terms comes into play only where state judicial proceedings have been invoked.   But if the invocation of state judicial proceedings makes a private litigant a state actor whose conduct is actionable under § 1983 whenever a constitutional complaint against him can be invented, § 2283 will be cannibalized.   Even if the Second Circuit's ruling is limited to state-court judgment winners, the result will be to render § 2283 inoperative with respect to federal court interference with state post-trial and appellate processes.   Surely this is not what this Court contemplated when it decided Mitchum v. Foster, which was a real § 1983 action against a real government officer whose official activities constituted the sort of action at the core of Congress' concern when it 'expressly authorized' injunctive relief under § 1983."

Texaco replied (Motion to Affirm p. 19):

"A ruling that a particular private party is a state actor has *no* impact on the breadth of the Section 1983 exception to the Anti–Injunction Act.   If a state proceeding deprives the state court defendant of federally protected rights, thereby creating a *meritorious* Section 1983 claim, the state court defendant can always institute a Section 1983 injunction action against the state officials involved in the proceeding (who are clearly state actors under Section 1983), rather than against the private state court plaintiff.   Such an action would not be barred by the Anti–Injunction Act, even if the private state court plaintiff were *not* itself deemed a state actor."

2.   Texaco also attacked the merits of the Texas judgment on various federal grounds.   These latter claims were held by the court of appeals to be improper under Rooker and Feldman, and were not before the Supreme Court.

3.   The Second Circuit—and Texaco—relied on Lugar v. Edmondson Oil Co., 457 U.S. 922 (1982), pp. 1241, 1324, *supra*, holding that a private actor who, *prior* to judgment, seeks to invoke state attachment statutes, is a "state actor" under § 1983.

Who has the better of the argument?

Could Texaco have obtained relief against the use of the Texas bond and lien provisions by suing state officials? If so, why didn't it?

(c) *Younger v. Harris.* The court of appeals had ruled that Younger does not apply to "private" proceedings in the state courts, and that to apply Younger here would undermine Mitchum.[4] In response, Pennzoil argued (J.S. at 14, 15–16):

"The court of appeals created a zone within which *all* rules of comity are rendered entirely inoperative. It thereby made nonsense of the law. If Pennzoil is to be deemed 'the state' for § 1983 purposes, this must be *because* its activities implicate the *public* powers of the state. But if the public powers of the state are in fact implicated, Younger concerns come into play for that very reason: the point of the Younger doctrine is to assure that the use of state courts for the effectuation of the state's public policies not be subject to federal interference, except in narrowly defined extraordinary circumstances. To conclude, as the court below did, that a § 1983 action is so private that it escapes Younger is a contradiction in terms: *by definition* the § 1983 action is an action against *public* authorities to curb the exercise of *public* power—power 'under color * * * of state law'—and sensitivity to comity interests therefore becomes absolutely imperative. * * *

"The court of appeals opined that to allow Younger to operate here 'would broaden Younger to cover almost every § 1983 case and thus undermine the Supreme Court's holding in Mitchum that federal courts are empowered by § 1983 to enjoin ongoing state proceedings.' But Mitchum itself made it absolutely clear that its ruling is not in any way 'undermined' by the applicability of Younger; in fact, the Court *justified* its conclusion in Mitchum by noting that Younger comity principles will be operative even though § 2283 is not. Mitchum thus clearly stands for the proposition that, in *real* § 1983 actions seeking to enjoin *real* state officials and agencies from litigating in state courts, Younger is fully applicable.

"The court below now holds that, when a self-styled § 1983 action is brought against private persons, federal injunctions may be granted entirely without comity constraints. This has the perverse result of making § 1983 a far more radical instrument for federal intervention against private litigants—who are at the margins of the policies of § 1983—than against the state officials who are the central focus of those policies."

Texaco replied (Motion to Affirm at 22):

"[A]ccording to Pennzoil, whenever state action exists for Section 1983 purposes, there is a 'vital' state interest for Younger purposes.

"Pennzoil in fact has things reversed. In the present context, a private party is considered a state actor for Section 1983 purposes only when the state has ceded to him the power to invoke and control, in an unsupervised manner, the conduct of state officials. That is *inconsistent* with a finding of a 'vital' state interest. Under Pennzoil's theory, the less control the

---

4. Also at issue, in connection with the application of Younger, was the question whether the Texas courts would consider Texaco's constitutional claim.

state exercises and the more control it abdicates to private parties, the more 'vital' its interest.

"If Pennzoil's argument were correct—and it is not—it would automatically extend Younger to ' "every pending proceeding between a State and a federal plaintiff" ', a result 'not remotely suggest[ed]' by this Court's prior decisions—indeed, it would, contrary to Pennzoil's disclaimer, automatically extend Younger to all ' "purely" private' civil state court lawsuits. Pennzoil's theory would also (a) mechanically bar relief, under Younger, in every Section 1983 action, thereby significantly eroding Mitchum v. Foster, 407 U.S. 225 (1972); and (b) render inexplicable this Court's careful focus in each Younger decision on the particular subject matter of the state court litigation—as opposed to the mere pendency of the proceeding."

Who has the better of this argument? [5]

(d) *Rooker–Feldman.*   Pennzoil argued that, in any event, the Rooker–Feldman doctrine barred the federal action: it is wrong "to suppose that the Rooker–Feldman doctrine may be limited to instances in which a federal court is literally asked to review the result of a state court adjudication.   The whole point of that doctrine is that Congress has never conferred upon the lower federal courts the authority to *displace* state courts (and ultimately this Court) in the appellate process.   It matters not whether such displacement takes the form of direct review by a lower federal court of a state court judgment, or the form of collateral attack on the validity * * * of state laws rendering the judgment immediately enforceable" (J.S. at 21).

Six Justices indicated in Pennzoil that they rejected this application of the Rooker doctrine.

Where a litigant seeks to enjoin a pending state proceeding, what independent significance should the Rooker doctrine have?   If an injunction is permissible under Younger, should the Rooker doctrine cut in to prevent it?   *Per contra,* if interference is prohibited by Younger (as supplemented by Huffman v. Pursue), what need is there for Rooker? [6]

---

5. In holding that Younger applied to this Texas proceeding, the Supreme Court did not address the issue of the relationship between § 1983 and § 2283.   See p. 1437, *supra.*

6. In the lower courts, the parties argued at length about the implications of Henry v. First Nat'l Bank, 595 F.2d 291 (5th Cir.1979).   There, white merchants in Mississippi sued the NAACP in state court alleging that a boycott of the plaintiffs' businesses, organized by the NAACP to protest racial discrimination, violated state antitrust laws.   When the merchants obtained a pre-trial writ attaching the NAACP's bank accounts, the NAACP went to federal court and obtained an order forbidding enforcement of the attachment.   A state court trial on the merits ensued and resulted in a judgment for the plaintiffs, an injunction against continuation of the protest, and a damage award in excess of $1 million.

Under state law, the NAACP could avert enforcement of the judgment pending appeal only by posting a bond equal to 125% of the judgment.   The NAACP first sought without success to obtain an emergency stay of the judgment, without having to post the bond, from the state trial and appeals courts.   It then brought a § 1983 action in federal court against the merchants, seeking to restrain (as a violation of the First Amendment) enforcement of the injunction and execution on the damage award, pending the NAACP's appeals from the state court judgment.   The district court granted the relief requested, and the Fifth Circuit affirmed.

Does the ruling in Henry survive the Pennzoil decision?

Cf. Robinson v. Ariyoshi, 753 F.2d 1468 (9th Cir.1985), vacated and remanded, 106 S.Ct. 3269 (1986) (federal court attack on Hawaii adjudication respecting entitlements to state water rights).

(4) Would there be anything problematic about reformulating Rooker so that, instead of operating as an independent doctrine, it would simply serve to remind courts that where a collateral attack is mounted on a pending or completed state proceeding, one of the consequences of allowing the attack is to interfere with Congress's contemplated plan for review of state court judgments by the Supreme Court under § 1257?

PREISER v. RODRIGUEZ

411 U.S. 475, 93 S.Ct. 1827, 36 L.Ed.2d 439 (1973).
Certiorari to the United States Court of Appeals for the Second Circuit.

MR. JUSTICE STEWART delivered the opinion of the Court.

The respondents in this case were state prisoners who were deprived of good-conduct-time credits by the New York State Department of Correctional Services as a result of disciplinary proceedings. They then brought actions in a federal district court, pursuant to the Civil Rights Act of 1871, 42 U.S.C. § 1983. Alleging that the Department had acted unconstitutionally in depriving them of the credits, they sought injunctive relief to compel restoration of the credits, which in each case would result in their immediate release from confinement in prison. The question before us is whether state prisoners seeking such redress may obtain equitable relief under the Civil Rights Act, even though the federal habeas corpus statute, 28 U.S.C. § 2254, clearly provides a specific federal remedy.

The question is of considerable practical importance. For if a remedy under the Civil Rights Act is available, a plaintiff need not first seek redress in a state forum. Monroe v. Pape, 365 U.S. 167, 183 (1961) * * *. If, on the other hand, habeas corpus is the exclusive federal remedy in these circumstances, then a plaintiff cannot seek the intervention of a federal court until he has first sought and been denied relief in the state courts, if a state remedy is available and adequate. 28 U.S.C. § 2254(b).

The present consolidated case originated in three separate actions, brought individually by the three respondents. The respondent Rodriguez, having been convicted in a New York state court of perjury and attempted larceny, was sentenced to imprisonment for an indeterminate term of from one and one-half to four years. Under New York Correction Law § 803 and Penal Law §§ 70.30(4)(a), 70.40(1)(b), a prisoner serving an indeterminate sentence may elect to participate in a conditional-release program by which he may earn up to 10 days per month good-behavior-time credit toward reduction of the maximum term of his sentence. Rodriguez elected to participate in this program. Optimally, such a prisoner may be released on parole after having served approximately two-thirds of his maximum sentence (20 days out of every 30); but accrued good-behavior credits so earned may at any time be withdrawn, in whole or in part, for bad behavior or for violation of the institutional rules. N.Y. Correction Law § 803(1).

Rodriguez was charged in two separate disciplinary action reports with possession of contraband material in his cell. The deputy warden determined that as punishment, 120 days of Rodriguez' earned good-conduct-time credits should be canceled, and that Rodriguez should be placed in segregation, where he remained for more than 40 days. * * *

Rodriguez then filed in the District Court a complaint pursuant to § 1983, combined with a petition for a writ of habeas corpus. He asserted that he was not really being punished for possession of the contraband material, but for refusal to disclose how he had obtained it, and that he had received no notice or hearing on the charges for which he had ostensibly been punished. Thus, he contended that he had been deprived of his good-conduct-time credits without due process of law.

After a hearing, the District Court held that Rodriguez' suit had properly been brought under the Civil Rights Act, that the habeas corpus claim was "merely a proper adjunct to insure full relief if [Rodriguez] prevails in the dominant civil rights claim," 307 F.Supp. 627, 628–629 (1969), and that therefore Rodriguez was not required to exhaust his state remedies, as he would have had to do if he had simply filed a petition for habeas corpus. On the merits, the District Court agreed with Rodriguez * * *.

The Court of Appeals reversed this decision by a divided vote. The appellate court not only disagreed with the District Court on the merits, but also held that Rodriguez' action was really a petition for habeas corpus and, as such, should not have been entertained by the District Court because Rodriguez had not exhausted his state remedies in accordance with § 2254(b). * * *

[The Court's description of the other two cases is omitted.]

After rehearing *en banc* of the three now-consolidated cases, the Court of Appeals, with three dissents, affirmed the judgments of the District Court in all of the cases "upon consideration of the merits and upon the authority of Wilwording v. Swenson" [404 U.S. 249]. 456 F.2d 79, 80 (1972). Although eight judges wrote separate opinions, it is clear that the majority of the Court relied primarily on our opinion in the Wilwording case, holding that complaints of state prisoners relating to the conditions of their confinement were cognizable either in federal habeas corpus or under the Civil Rights Act, and that as civil rights actions they were not subject to any requirement of exhaustion of state remedies.

We granted certiorari in order to consider the bearing of the Wilwording decision upon the situation before us—where state prisoners have challenged the actual duration of their confinement on the ground that they have been unconstitutionally deprived of good-conduct-time credits, and where restoration of those credits would result in their immediate release from prison or in shortening the length of their confinement. * * *

The problem involves the interrelationship of two important federal laws. * * *

It is clear, not only from the language of §§ 2241(c)(3) and 2254(a), but also from the common-law history of the writ, that the essence of habeas corpus is an attack by a person in custody upon the legality of that custody, and that the traditional function of the writ is to secure release from illegal custody. * * * [7]

7. It was not until quite recently that habeas corpus was made available to challenge less obvious restraints. In 1963, the Court held that a prisoner released on parole from immediate physical confinement was nonetheless sufficiently restrained in his freedom as to be in custody for purposes of federal habeas corpus. Jones v. Cunningham, 371 U.S. 236. In Carafas v. LaVallee, 391 U.S. 234 (1968), the Court for

* * *

In the case before us, the respondents' suits in the District Court fell squarely within this traditional scope of habeas corpus. They alleged that the deprivation of their good-conduct-time credits was causing or would cause them to be in illegal physical confinement, *i.e.,* that once their conditional-release date had passed, any further detention of them in prison was unlawful; and they sought restoration of those good-time credits, which, by the time the District Court ruled on their petitions, meant their immediate release from physical custody.

Even if the restoration of the respondents' credits would not have resulted in their immediate release, but only in shortening the length of their actual confinement in prison, habeas corpus would have been their appropriate remedy. For recent cases have established that habeas corpus relief is not limited to immediate release from illegal custody, but that the writ is available as well to attack future confinement and obtain future releases. In Peyton v. Rowe, 391 U.S. 54 (1968), the Court held that a prisoner may attack on habeas the second of two consecutive sentences while still serving the first. * * *

Although conceding that they could have proceeded by way of habeas corpus, the respondents argue that the Court of Appeals was correct in holding that they were nonetheless entitled to bring their suits under § 1983 so as to avoid the necessity of first seeking relief in a state forum. Pointing to the broad language of § 1983, they argue that since their complaints plainly came within the literal terms of that statute, there is no justifiable reason to exclude them from the broad remedial protection provided by that law. * * *

The broad language of § 1983, however, is not conclusive of the issue before us. The statute is a general one, and, despite the literal applicability of its terms, the question remains whether the specific federal habeas corpus statute, explicitly and historically designed to provide the means for a state prisoner to attack the validity of his confinement, must be understood to be the exclusive remedy available in a situation like this where it so clearly applies. The respondents' counsel acknowledged at oral argument that a state prisoner challenging his underlying conviction and sentence on federal constitutional grounds in a federal court is limited to habeas corpus. It was conceded that he cannot bring a § 1983 action, even though the literal terms of § 1983 might seem to cover such a challenge, because Congress has passed a more specific act to cover that situation, and, in doing so, has provided that a state prisoner challenging his conviction must first seek relief in a state forum, if a state remedy is available. It is clear to us that the result must be the same in the case of a state prisoner's challenge to the fact or duration of his confinement, based, as here, upon the alleged unconstitutionality of state administrative action. Such a challenge is just as close to the core of habeas corpus as an attack on the prisoner's conviction, for it goes directly to the constitutionality of

the first time decided that once habeas corpus jurisdiction has attached, it is not defeated by the subsequent release of the prisoner. And just this Term, in Hensley v. Municipal Court, we held that a person, who, after conviction, is released on bail or on his own recognizance, is "in custody" within the meaning of the federal habeas corpus statute. But those cases marked no more than a logical extension of the traditional meaning and purpose of habeas corpus—to effect release from illegal custody.

his physical confinement itself and seeks either immediate release from that confinement or the shortening of its duration.

In amending the habeas corpus laws in 1948, Congress clearly required exhaustion of adequate state remedies as a condition precedent to the invocation of federal judicial relief under those laws. It would wholly frustrate explicit congressional intent to hold that the respondents in the present case could evade this requirement by the simple expedient of putting a different label on their pleadings. In short, Congress has determined that habeas corpus is the appropriate remedy for state prisoners attacking the validity of the fact or length of their confinement, and that specific determination must override the general terms of § 1983.

The policy reasons underlying the habeas corpus statute support this conclusion. The respondents concede that the reason why only habeas corpus can be used to challenge a state prisoner's underlying conviction is the strong policy requiring exhaustion of state remedies in that situation— to avoid the unnecessary friction between the federal and state court systems that would result if a lower federal court upset a state court conviction without first giving the state court system an opportunity to correct its own constitutional errors. But they argue that * * * the whole purpose of the exhaustion requirement, now codified in § 2254(b), is to give state *courts* the first chance at remedying *their own* mistakes, and thereby to avoid "the unseemly spectacle of federal district courts trying the regularity of proceedings had in *courts* of coordinate jurisdiction." Parker, Limiting the Abuse of Habeas Corpus, 8 F.R.D. 171, 172–173 (1948) (emphasis added). This policy, the respondents contend, does not apply when the challenge is not to the action of a state court, but, as here, to the action of a state administrative body. * * *

We cannot agree. The respondents, we think, view the reasons for the exhaustion requirement of § 2254(b) far too narrowly. The rule of exhaustion in federal habeas corpus actions is rooted in considerations of federal-state comity. * * * That comity considerations are not limited to challenges to the validity of state court convictions is evidenced by cases such as Morrissey v. Brewer, [408 U.S. 471 (1972)], where the petitioners' habeas challenge was to a state administrative decision to revoke their parole, and Braden v. 30th Judicial Circuit Court of Kentucky, [410 U.S. 484 (1973)], where the petitioner's habeas attack was on the failure of state prosecutorial authorities to afford him a speedy trial.

It is difficult to imagine an activity in which a State has a stronger interest, or one that is more intricately bound up with state laws, regulations, and procedures, than the administration of its prisons. The relationship of state prisoners and the state officers who supervise their confinement is far more intimate than that of a State and a private citizen. * * * Since these internal problems of state prisons involve issues so peculiarly within state authority and expertise, the States have an important interest in not being bypassed in the correction of those problems. Moreover, because most potential litigation involving state prisoners arises on a day-to-day basis, it is most efficiently and properly handled by the state administrative bodies and state courts, which are, for the most part, familiar with the grievances of state prisoners and in a better physical and practical position to deal with those grievances. In New York, for example, state judges sit on a regular basis at all but one of the State's correctional facilities, and thus inmates may present their grievances to a court at the place of their confinement, where the relevant records are available and where potential witnesses are located. The strong considerations of comity that require giving a state court system that has convicted a defendant the first opportunity to correct its own errors thus also require giving the States the first opportunity to correct the errors made in the internal administration of their prisons.

Requiring exhaustion in situations like that before us means, of course, that a prisoner's state remedy must be adequate and available, as indeed § 2254(b) provides. The respondents in this case concede that New York provided them with an adequate remedy for the restoration of their good-time credits, through § 79–c of the New York Civil Rights Law, which explicitly provides for injunctive relief to a state prisoner "for improper treatment where such treatment constitutes a violation of his constitutional rights." (Supp.1972–1973.)

But while conceding the availability in the New York courts of an opportunity for equitable relief, the respondents contend that confining state prisoners to federal habeas corpus, after first exhausting state remedies, could deprive those prisoners of any damages remedy to which they might be entitled for their mistreatment, since damages are not available in federal habeas corpus proceedings, and New York provides no damages remedy at all for state prisoners. * * * They argue that even if such a prisoner were to bring a subsequent federal civil rights action for damages, that action could be barred by principles of *res judicata* where the state courts had previously made an adverse determination of his underlying claim, even though a federal habeas court had later granted him relief on habeas corpus.

The answer to this contention is that the respondents here sought no damages, but only equitable relief—restoration of their good-time credits—and our holding today is limited to that situation. If a state prisoner is seeking damages, he is attacking something other than the fact or length of his confinement, and he is seeking something other than immediate or more speedy release—the traditional purpose of habeas corpus. In the case of a damages claim, habeas corpus is *not* an appropriate or available federal remedy. Accordingly, as petitioners themselves concede, a damages action by a state prisoner could be brought under the Civil Rights Act in federal court without any requirement of prior exhaustion of state remedies. * * *

   * * *

Principles of *res judicata* are, of course, not wholly applicable to habeas corpus proceedings. 28 U.S.C. § 2254(d). See Salinger v. Loisel, 265 U.S. 224, 230 (1924). Hence, a state prisoner in the respondents' situation who has been denied relief in the state courts is not precluded from seeking habeas relief on the same claims in federal court. On the other hand, *res judicata* has been held to be fully applicable to a civil rights action brought under § 1983. * * * Accordingly, there would be an inevitable incentive for a state prisoner to proceed at once in federal court by way of a civil rights action, lest he lose his right to do so. This would have the unfortunate dual effect of denying the state prison administration and the state courts the opportunity to correct the errors committed in the State's own prisons, and of isolating those bodies from an understanding of and hospitality to the federal claims of state prisoners in situations such as those before us. Federal habeas corpus, on the other hand, serves the important function of allowing the State to deal with these peculiarly local problems on its own, while preserving for the state prisoner an expeditious federal forum for the vindication of his federally protected rights, if the State has denied redress.

The respondents place a great deal of reliance on our recent decisions upholding the right of state prisoners to bring federal civil rights actions to challenge the conditions of their confinement. Cooper v. Pate, 378 U.S. 546 (1964); Houghton v. Shafer, 392 U.S. 639 (1968); Wilwording v. Swenson, 404 U.S. 249 (1971); Haines v. Kerner, 404 U.S. 519 (1972). But none of the state prisoners in those cases was challenging the fact or duration of his physical confinement itself, and none was seeking immediate release or a speedier release from that confinement—the heart of habeas corpus. In Cooper, the prisoner alleged that, solely because of his religious beliefs, he had been denied permission to purchase certain religious publications and had been denied other privileges enjoyed by his fellow prisoners. In Houghton, the prisoner's contention was that prison authorities had violated the Constitution by confiscating legal materials which he had acquired for pursuing his appeal, but which, in violation of prison rules, had been found in the possession of another prisoner. In Wilwording, the prisoners' complaints related solely to their living conditions and disciplinary measures while confined in maximum security. And in Haines, the prisoner claimed that prison officials had acted unconstitutionally by placing him in solitary confinement as a disciplinary measure, and he sought damages for claimed physical injuries sustained while so segregated. It is clear, then, that in all those cases, the prisoners' claims related solely to the States' alleged unconstitutional treatment of them while in confinement. None sought, as did the respondents here, to challenge the very fact or duration of the confinement itself. Those cases, therefore, merely establish that a § 1983 action is a proper remedy for a state prisoner who is making a constitutional challenge to the conditions of his prison life, but not to the fact or length of his custody. Upon that understanding, we reaffirm those holdings.[14]

This is not to say that habeas corpus may not also be available to challenge such prison conditions. See Johnson v. Avery, 393 U.S. 483 (1969); Wilwording v. Swenson, *supra*, at 251. When a prisoner is put under additional and unconstitutional restraints during his lawful custody, it is arguable that habeas corpus will lie to remove the restraints making the custody illegal. See Note, Developments in the Law—Habeas Corpus, 83 Harv.L.Rev. 1038, 1084 (1970).

But we need not in this case explore the appropriate limits of habeas corpus as an alternative remedy to a proper action under § 1983. That question is not before us. What is involved here is the extent to which § 1983 is a permissible alternative to the traditional remedy of habeas corpus. Upon that question, we hold today that when a state prisoner is challenging the very fact or duration of his physical imprisonment, and the

---

14. If a prisoner seeks to attack both the conditions of his confinement and the fact or length of that confinement, his latter claim, under our decision today, is cognizable only in federal habeas corpus, with its attendant requirement of exhaustion of state remedies. But, consistent with our prior decisions, that holding in no way precludes him from simultaneously litigating in federal court, under § 1983, his claim relating to the conditions of his confinement.

relief he seeks is a determination that he is entitled to immediate release or a speedier release from that imprisonment, his sole federal remedy is a writ of habeas corpus. Accordingly, we reverse the judgment before us.

It is so ordered.

MR. JUSTICE BRENNAN, with whom MR. JUSTICE DOUGLAS and MR. JUSTICE MARSHALL join, dissenting.

The question presented by this case is one that I, like the Court of Appeals, had thought already resolved by our decision last Term in Wilwording v. Swenson, 404 U.S. 249 (1971). We held there that the Ku Klux Klan Act of 1871, 42 U.S.C. § 1983, confers jurisdiction on the United States District Courts to entertain a state prisoner's application for injunctive relief against allegedly unconstitutional conditions of confinement. * * * At the same time, we held that "[t]he remedy provided by these Acts 'is supplementary to the state remedy, and the latter need not be first sought and refused before the federal one is invoked.' Monroe v. Pape, 365 U.S. 167, 183 (1961). State prisoners are not held to any stricter standard of exhaustion than other civil rights plaintiffs." Wilwording v. Swenson, supra, at 251.

Regrettably, the Court today eviscerates that proposition by drawing a distinction that is both analytically unsound and, I fear, unworkable in practice. The net effect of the distinction is to preclude respondents from maintaining these actions under § 1983, leaving a petition for writ of habeas corpus the only available federal remedy. As a result, respondents must exhaust state remedies before their claims can be heard in a federal district court. I remain committed to the principles set forth in Wilwording v. Swenson, and I therefore respectfully dissent.

* * *

The Court's conclusion that Wilwording is not controlling is assertedly justified by invocation of a concept, newly invented by the Court today, variously termed the "core of habeas corpus," the "heart of habeas corpus," and the "essence of habeas corpus." In the Court's view, an action lying at the "core of habeas corpus" is one that "goes directly to the constitutionality of [the prisoner's] physical confinement itself and seeks either immediate release from that confinement or the shortening of its duration." With regard to such actions, habeas corpus is now considered the prisoner's exclusive remedy. In short, the Court does not graft the habeas corpus exhaustion requirement onto prisoner actions under the Ku Klux Klan Act, but it reaches what is functionally the same result by holding that the District Court's jurisdiction under the Act is in some instances displaced by the habeas corpus remedy. Henceforth, in such cases a prisoner brings an action in the nature of habeas corpus—or he brings no federal court action at all.

At bottom, the Court's holding today rests on an understandable apprehension that the no-exhaustion rule of § 1983 might, in the absence of some limitation, devour the exhaustion rule of the habeas corpus statute. The problem arises because the two statutes necessarily overlap. Indeed, every application by a state prisoner for federal habeas corpus relief against his jailers could, as a matter of logic and semantics, be viewed as an action under the Ku Klux Klan Act to obtain injunctive relief against "the deprivation," by one acting under color of state law, "of any rights, privileges, or immunities secured by the Constitution and laws" of the

United States. 42 U.S.C. § 1983. To prevent state prisoners from nullifying the habeas corpus exhaustion requirement by invariably styling their petitions as pleas for relief under § 1983, the Court today devises an ungainly and irrational scheme that permits some prisoners to sue under § 1983, while others may proceed only by way of petition for habeas corpus. And the entire scheme operates in defiance of the purposes underlying both the exhaustion requirement of habeas corpus and the absence of a comparable requirement under § 1983.

I

At the outset, it is important to consider the nature of the line that the Court has drawn. The Court holds today that "when a state prisoner is challenging the very fact or duration of his physical imprisonment, and the relief he seeks is a determination that he is entitled to immediate release or a speedier release from that imprisonment, his sole federal remedy is a writ of habeas corpus." But, even under the Court's approach, there are undoubtedly some instances where a prisoner has the option of proceeding either by petition for habeas corpus or by suit under § 1983.

In Johnson v. Avery, 393 U.S. 483 (1969), we held that the writ of habeas corpus could be used to challenge allegedly unconstitutional conditions of confinement. * * * And in Wilwording v. Swenson, *supra*, where the petitioners challenged "only their living conditions and disciplinary measures while confined in maximum security at Missouri State Penitentiary," we held explicitly that their claims were cognizable in habeas corpus. * * *

Yet even though a prisoner may challenge the conditions of his confinement by petition for writ of habeas corpus, he is not precluded by today's opinion from raising the same or similar claim, without exhaustion of state remedies, by suit under the Ku Klux Klan Act, provided he attacks only the conditions of his confinement and not its fact or duration. To that extent, at least, the Court leaves unimpaired our holdings in Wilwording v. Swenson, and the other cases in which we have upheld the right of prisoners to sue their jailers under § 1983 without exhaustion of state remedies. * * * Accordingly, one can only conclude that some instances remain where habeas corpus provides a supplementary but not an exclusive remedy—or, to put it another way, where an action may properly be brought in habeas corpus, even though it is somehow sufficiently distant from the "core of habeas corpus" to avoid displacing concurrent jurisdiction under the Ku Klux Klan Act. * * *

II

Putting momentarily to one side the grave analytic shortcomings of the Court's approach, it seems clear that the scheme's unmanageability is sufficient reason to condemn it. For the unfortunate but inevitable legacy of today's opinion is a perplexing set of uncertainties and anomalies. And the nub of the problem is the definition of the Court's new-found and essentially ethereal concept, the "core of habeas corpus."

* * *

[S]erious difficulties will arise whenever a prisoner seeks to attack in a single proceeding both the conditions of his confinement and the deprivation of good-time credits. And the addition of a plea for monetary damages exacerbates the problem.

If a prisoner's sole claim is that he was placed in solitary confinement pursuant to an unconstitutional disciplinary procedure, he can obtain federal injunctive relief and monetary damages in an action under § 1983. The unanswered question is whether he loses the right to proceed under § 1983 if, as punishment for his alleged misconduct, his jailers have not only subjected him to unlawful segregation and thereby inflicted an injury that is compensable in damages, but have compounded the wrong by improperly depriving him of good-time credits. Three different approaches are possible.

First, we might conclude that jurisdiction under § 1983 is lost whenever good-time credits are involved, even where the action is based primarily on the need for monetary relief or an injunction against continued segregation. If that is the logic of the Court's opinion, then the scheme creates an undeniable, and in all likelihood irresistible, incentive for state prison officials to defeat the jurisdiction of the federal courts by adding the deprivation of good-time credits to whatever other punishment is imposed. And if all of the federal claims must be held in abeyance pending exhaustion of state remedies, a prisoner's subsequent effort to assert a damages claim under § 1983 might arguably be barred by principles of res judicata. * * *

As an alternative, we might reject outright the premises of the first approach and conclude that a plea for money damages or for an injunction against continued segregation is sufficient to bring all related claims, including the question of good-time credits, under the umbrella of § 1983. That approach would, of course, simplify matters considerably. And it would make unnecessary the fractionation of the prisoner's claims into a number of different issues to be resolved in duplicative proceedings in state and federal courts. * * *

In any event, the Court today rejects, perhaps for the reasons suggested above, both of the foregoing positions. Instead, it holds that insofar as a prisoner's claim relates to good-time credits, he is required to exhaust state remedies; but he is not precluded from simultaneously litigating in federal court, under § 1983, his claim for monetary damages or an injunction against continued segregation. Under that approach, state correctional authorities have no added incentive to withdraw good-time credits, since that action cannot, standing alone, keep the prisoner out of federal court. And, at the same time, it does not encourage a prisoner to assert an unnecessary claim for damages or injunctive relief as a means of bringing his good-time claim under the purview of § 1983. Nevertheless, this approach entails substantial difficulties—perhaps the greatest difficulties of the three. In the first place, its extreme inefficiency is readily apparent. For in many instances a prisoner's claims will be under simultaneous consideration in two distinct forums, even though the identical legal and factual questions are involved in both proceedings. * * * Moreover, if the federal court is the first to reach decision, and if that court concludes that the procedures are, in fact, unlawful, then the entire state proceeding must be immediately aborted, even though the state court may have devoted substantial time and effort to its consideration of the case. By the same token, if traditional principles of res judicata are applicable to suits under § 1983, the prior conclusion of the state court suit would effectively set at naught the entire federal court proceeding. This is plainly a curious prescription for improving relations between state and federal courts.

Since some of the ramifications of this new approach are still unclear, the unfortunate outcome of today's decision—an outcome that might not be immediately surmised from the seeming simplicity of the basic concept, the "core of habeas corpus"—is almost certain to be the further complication of prison-conditions litigation. In itself that is disquieting enough. But it is especially distressing that the remaining questions will have to be resolved on the basis of pleadings, whether in habeas corpus or suit under § 1983, submitted by state prisoners, who will often have to cope with these questions without even minimal assistance of counsel.

III

The Court's conclusion that respondents must proceed by petition for habeas corpus is unfortunate, not only because of the uncertainties and practical difficulties to which the conclusion necessarily gives rise, but also because it derives from a faulty analytic foundation. The text of § 1983 carries no explanation for today's decision; prisoners are still, I assume, "persons" within the meaning of the statute. Moreover, prior to our recent decisions expanding the definition of "custody," and abandoning the "prematurity" doctrine, it is doubtful that habeas corpus would even have provided them a remedy. Since their claims could not, in all likelihood, have been heard on habeas corpus at the time the present habeas corpus statute was enacted in 1867, or at the time the exhaustion doctrine was first announced in Ex parte Royall, 117 U.S. 241 (1886), or at the time the requirement was codified in 1948, it is surely hard to view these acts as a determination to preclude suit under § 1983 and leave habeas corpus the prisoner's only remedy. Nevertheless, to prevent state prisoners from invoking the jurisdictional grant of § 1983 as a means of circumventing the exhaustion requirement of the habeas corpus statute, the Court finds it necessary to hold today that in this one instance jurisdiction under § 1983 is displaced by the habeas corpus remedy.

The concern that § 1983 not be used to nullify the habeas corpus exhaustion doctrine is, of course, legitimate. But our effort to preserve the integrity of the doctrine must rest on an understanding of the purposes that underlie it. * * *

By enactment of the Ku Klux Klan Act in 1871, and again by the grant in 1875 of original federal-question jurisdiction to the federal courts, Congress recognized important interests in permitting a plaintiff to choose a federal forum in cases arising under federal law. * * *

* * * *

It is against this background that we have refused to require exhaustion of state remedies by civil rights plaintiffs. * * *

* * * *

[T]he absence of an exhaustion requirement in § 1983 is not an accident of history or the result of careless oversight by Congress or this Court. On the contrary, the no-exhaustion rule is an integral feature of the statutory scheme. Exhaustion of state remedies is not required precisely because such a requirement would jeopardize the purposes of the Act. For that reason, the imposition of such a requirement, even if done indirectly by means of a determination that jurisdiction under § 1983 is displaced by an alternative remedial device, must be justified by a clear statement of congressional intent, or, at the very least, by the presence of the most persuasive considerations of policy. In my view, no such justification can be found.

Crucial to the Court's analysis of the case before us is its understanding of the purposes that underlie the habeas corpus exhaustion requirement. But just as the Court pays too little attention to the reasons for a no-exhaustion rule in actions under § 1983, it also misconceives the purposes of the exhaustion requirement in habeas corpus. * * *

Although codified in the habeas corpus statute in 1948, 28 U.S.C. § 2254(b), the exhaustion requirement is a "judicially crafted instrument which reflects a careful balance between important interests of federalism and the need to preserve the writ of habeas corpus as a 'swift and imperative remedy in all cases of illegal restraint or confinement.' Secretary of State for Home Affairs v. O'Brien, [1923] A.C. 603, 609 (H.L.)." Braden v. 30th Judicial Circuit, 410 U.S. 484, 490 (1973). The indisputable concern of all our decisions concerning the doctrine has been the relationship "between the *judicial tribunals* of the Union and of the States. * * * [T]he public good requires that those relations be not disturbed by unnecessary conflict between *courts* equally bound to guard and protect rights secured by the Constitution." Ex parte Royall, 117 U.S., at 251 (emphasis added). Ex parte Royall is, of course, the germinal case, and its concern with the relations between state and federal *courts* is mirrored in our subsequent decisions. * * * We have grounded the doctrine squarely on the view that "it would be unseemly in our dual system of government for a federal district court to upset a *state court conviction* without an opportunity to the state courts to correct a constitutional violation." Fay v. Noia, 372 U.S. 391, 419–420 (1963) (emphasis added).

That is not to say, however, that the purposes of the doctrine are implicated only where an attack is directed at a state court *conviction* or *sentence.* Ex parte Royall itself did not involve a challenge to a state conviction, but rather an effort to secure a prisoner's release on habeas corpus "in advance of his trial in the [state] court in which he [was] indicted." *Id.,* at 253. But there, too, the focus was on relations between the state and federal *judiciaries.* * * *

With these considerations in mind, it becomes clear that the Court's decision does not serve the fundamental purposes behind the exhaustion doctrine. For although respondents were confined pursuant to the judgment of a state judicial tribunal, their claims do not relate to their convictions or sentences, but only to the administrative action of prison officials who subjected them to allegedly unconstitutional treatment, including the deprivation of good-time credits. This is not a case, in other words, where federal intervention would interrupt a state proceeding or jeopardize the orderly administration of state judicial business. Nor is it a case where an action in federal court might imperil the relationship between state and federal courts. * * *

To be sure, respondents do call into question the constitutional validity of action by state officials, and friction between those officials and the federal court is by no means an inconceivable result. But standing alone, that possibility is simply not enough to warrant application of an exhaustion requirement.   *   *   *

[T]he situation that exists in the case before us—an attack on state administrative rather than judicial action—is the stereotypical situation in which relief under § 1983 is authorized.   See, *e.g.,* McNeese v. Board of Education, 373 U.S. 668 (1963) (attack on school districting scheme); Damico v. California, 389 U.S. 416 (1967) (attack on welfare requirements); Monroe v. Pape, 365 U.S., at 183 (attack on police conduct).   In each of these cases the exercise of federal jurisdiction was potentially offensive to the State and its officials.   In each of these cases the attack was directed at an important state function in an area in which the State has wide powers of regulation.   Yet in each of these cases we explicitly held that exhaustion of state remedies was not required.   *   *   *

[I]f the Court is correct in assuming that the exhaustion requirement must be applied whenever federal jurisdiction might be a source of substantial friction with the State, then I simply do not understand why the Court stops where it does in rolling back the district courts' jurisdiction under § 1983.   Application of the exhaustion doctrine now turns on whether or not the action is directed at the fact or duration of the prisoner's confinement.   It seems highly doubtful to me that a constitutional attack on prison conditions is any less disruptive of federal-state relations than an attack on prison conditions joined with a plea for restoration of good-time credits.   Chief Judge Friendly expressed the view, as did the judges in dissent below, that "petitions of state prisoners complaining of the time or conditions of their confinement have the same potentialities for exacerbating federal-state relations as petitions attacking the validity of their confinement—perhaps even more."   456 F.2d, at 80.   Yet the Court holds today that exhaustion is required where a prisoner attacks the deprivation of good-time credits, but not where he challenges only the conditions of his confinement.   It seems obvious to me that both of those propositions cannot be correct.   *   *   *

*   *   *

Since I share the Court's view that exhaustion of state judicial remedies is not required in any suit properly brought in federal court under § 1983, and since I am convinced that respondents have properly invoked the jurisdictional grant of § 1983, I would affirm the judgment of the Court of Appeals.

NOTE ON THE RELATIONSHIP OF HABEAS CORPUS AND SECTION 1983

(1) The limits of Preiser v. Rodriguez were tested in Wolff v. McDonnell, 418 U.S. 539 (1974).   This was a state prisoners' § 1983 action, alleging that certain prison disciplinary proceedings had violated the Due Process Clause, and raising constitutional complaints with respect to the prison legal aid program and the prison mail censorship system.   The complaint sought damages as well as the restoration of good-time credits. The Court held that the § 1983 action could go forward: "The complaint in this case sought restoration of good-time credits, and the Court of Appeals correctly held this relief foreclosed under Preiser.   But the complaint also sought damages; and Preiser expressly contemplated that claims properly

brought under § 1983 could go forward while actual restoration of good-time credits is sought in state proceedings. Respondents' damage claim was therefore properly before the District Court and required determination of the validity of the procedures employed for imposing sanctions, including loss of good time, for flagrant or serious misconduct. Such a declaratory judgment as a predicate to a damage award would not be barred by Preiser; and because under that case only an injunction restoring good time improperly taken is foreclosed, neither would it preclude a litigant with standing from obtaining by way of ancillary relief an otherwise proper injunction enjoining the prospective enforcement of invalid prison regulations. We therefore conclude that it was proper for the Court of Appeals and the District Court to determine the validity of the procedures for revoking good-time credits and to fashion appropriate remedies for any constitutional violations ascertained, short of ordering the actual restoration of good time already cancelled" (pp. 554–55).

(2) Does Wolff make it easy to evade Preiser? Suppose a prisoner seeks to attack his conviction and secure his release, and wants to do so in a § 1983 action, which Preiser says may not be done. May he get an adjudication of the validity of his conviction in a § 1983 *damage* action without exhausting state court remedies? If he does, is this res judicata in a subsequent state-court habeas proceeding?

The courts of appeals have struggled mightily with this and related problems created by the borderline between Preiser and Wolff.[1] Many of them have resisted the implications of Wolff and have held that when a declaratory or damage action would serve as a predicate in a later action for release, exhaustion should be required. An example of this approach is Hamlin v. Warren, 664 F.2d 29 (4th Cir.1981). Hamlin was convicted in North Carolina for armed robbery. While his appeal was pending in the state supreme court, he filed a § 1983 action in federal court, alleging that state police officials had conspired to procure his conviction by perjured testimony. He sought a declaratory judgment that his conviction violated the Constitution, and compensatory and punitive damages. The district court dismissed, holding that the exhaustion requirement of § 2254(b) applied. The Fourth Circuit affirmed.

With respect to the declaratory judgment count, Judge Haynsworth said that, although Hamlin did not ask for release in his federal action, his purpose was to establish a "predicate" for release, since a federal declaration that the conviction was invalid would be binding in a subsequent state-court habeas corpus proceeding (and in any event upon a later federal habeas proceeding).

With respect to the damage count, the opinion stated that Preiser and Wolff did not require that count to be adjudicated immediately, since those cases involved attacks on state administrative rather than state judicial action. Not to apply the exhaustion requirement in this case "would be to substantially undermine it"; "anyone who could state a viable civil rights claim could subvert it [the exhaustion requirement] by postponing a claim for release until his substantive rights had been adjudicated in a federal forum" (p. 32).

1. See, for an early account of the case law, Note, 77 Colum.L.Rev. 742 (1977).

The court also said (p. 32): "Holding the exhaustion ∗ ∗ ∗ requirement applicable opens the possibility that a later civil rights claim in a federal court will be foreclosed, upon principles of collateral estoppel, by an adverse state court judgment. Principles of collateral estoppel, however, have only limited applicability [on habeas corpus] ∗ ∗ ∗. If, after exhaustion of state remedies [plaintiff returns to the federal court and obtains federal habeas relief] ∗ ∗ ∗ there is no reason to believe that the federal judgment would not also relieve him of the collateral estoppel effect of the state judgment with respect to an ancillary civil rights claim."

Do you agree with Judge Haynsworth's dictum that if a federal claim, rejected by the state courts, is subsequently vindicated in a federal habeas corpus proceeding, a § 1983 action is free thereafter from the preclusive effects of the state judgment? What is the relevance of § 1738 at that point?

Suppose exhaustion had not been required. Would Younger and Huffman in any event have barred the federal declaratory claim? What about Rooker? Would these cases bar a federal damage action? See pp. 1431–32, *supra.*[2]

The Supreme Court has indicated it may wish to reconsider the implications of Wolff. In Tower v. Glover, 467 U.S. 914, 923 (1984), it observed that it had "no occasion to decide if a Federal District Court should abstain from deciding a § 1983 suit for damages stemming from an unlawful conviction pending the collateral exhaustion of state-court attacks on the conviction itself."

Is there a sensible reason (other than historical accident) why exhaustion should be required in the habeas context and not required in the § 1983 context? If not, might this explain why the courts are having such a difficult time drawing the line?

(3) Suppose that a sentence of imprisonment has been fully served, or the sentence consists solely of a fine, so that habeas corpus relief is clearly unavailable because there is no "custody", see p. 1569, *supra.* Is an injunctive or declaratory action to "expunge" such a conviction or a damage action to recover such a fine available under § 1983? The courts are in disagreement. Compare Hanson v. Circuit Court, 591 F.2d 404 (7th Cir.1979), and Battieste v. City of Baton Rouge, 732 F.2d 439 (5th Cir.1984), with Strader v. Troy, 571 F.2d 1263 (4th Cir.1978), and Maurer v. Los Angeles County Sheriff's Dept., 691 F.2d 434 (9th Cir.1982).[3]

---

2. For other authorities, see, *e.g.*, the discussion in Offet v. Solem, 823 F.2d 1256, 1258 (8th Cir.1987) ("because a prisoner who wins a § 1983 action in federal court for damages or declaratory relief for the unconstitutional deprivation of good time credits thereby establishes an irrefutable claim for early or immediate release under habeas, we hold that in such a case the federal court should stay the § 1983 claim until the plaintiff has satisfied the exhaustion requirement with respect to the underlying constitutional issue"). Compare Georgevich v. Strauss, 772 F.2d 1078, 1087 (3d Cir.1985) (§ 1983 challenge to parole procedures allowed even though success

"might increase the chance for early release"). In a series of cases ending with Serio v. Louisiana State Bd. of Pardons, 821 F.2d 1112 (1987), the Fifth Circuit has tried to create general guidelines to help solve the question whether exhaustion is required.

3. See Note, 64 B.U.L. Rev. 683 (1984). *Cf.* Neely v. United States, 546 F.2d 1059 (3d Cir.1976) (class action by federal prisoners to annul convictions and to recover fines and penalties after Supreme Court in another case declared the relevant criminal statute unconstitutional; "civil" class action held maintainable).

Shouldn't Allen v. McCurry and the cases in its line be deemed to settle this issue?

Is Rooker relevant?

CONCLUDING NOTE ON THE JURISDICTION OF FEDERAL AND STATE COURTS IN CASES INVOLVING FEDERAL LAW CHALLENGES TO STATE OFFICIAL ACTION

(1) Consider the various rules that govern the jurisdiction of federal and state courts (and the relationship among them) when an individual claims that state or local government action—past, present or future—is violative of a federal right or immunity. Here is an attempt at a summary (and simplified) Restatement of those rules:

I. Where No State Court Enforcement Proceeding Is Underway

A. The plaintiff, subject to justiciability requirements, may bring an action against an appropriate official for injunction and/or damages, alleging past, present, or future violation of a federal constitutional right (Ex parte Young; Monroe v. Pape).

B. It is irrelevant whether an adequate remedy exists in the state courts (Home Telephone; Monroe), *unless*

    (i) the action falls under the Johnson Act of 1934 or the Tax Injunction Act of 1937, in which case the existence of an adequate remedy in state court ousts federal jurisdiction; *or*

    (ii) the existence of fair state procedures, constituting the "process" that is "due", negates the claimed constitutional liability (Parratt).

C. It is irrelevant whether the official's action was authorized by state law or state policy (Monroe), *unless* the action is against a local governmental body (Monell).

D. In an injunction action, the plaintiff may not (absent a relevant consent (Smith v. Reeves)) append a state law claim to a federal claim against officials of the state (Pennhurst), but must either split his action or pursue both claims in state court.

E. Nevertheless, if antecedent or parallel state law issues are present in the case, the federal court may abstain and send the plaintiff over to state court for resolution of those issues (Pullman). But the plaintiff may, by reservation, guarantee a return to the federal court for disposition of the unmooted federal claims notwithstanding normal res judicata rules (England).

F. Plaintiff may, if he chooses, take his claim first to state court, but will then be subject to normal res judicata rules (see "III", *infra*).

II. Where A State Court Proceeding Is Underway (Or Imminent) When The Federal Action Is Commenced

A. If the federal action is not a § 1983 action, it may be barred by the Anti–Injunction Act (§ 2283).

B. If the plaintiff is in custody, and the effect of the relief sought would be to end or shorten custody, the action will be deemed a habeas corpus action, and exhaustion requirements will apply (Preiser).

C. If the action is a § 1983 action, § 2283 is not a bar (Mitchum). But the Younger doctrine will normally prevent a federal court from aborting, by injunction or declaratory judgment, a pending (or, sometimes, an impending) state court enforcement proceeding (Younger; Hicks) throughout its course (Huffman). It is uncertain whether a concurrent damage action based on the same constitutional claims is allowable.

D. In addition, the federal court may decline to adjudicate where "exceptional circumstances" call for deference to pending state proceedings (Colorado River).

E. Nor may the state court proceeding be removed to federal court, *unless*

(i) the defendant is a federal official; *or*

(ii) the stringent rules for civil rights removal under § 1443 are met.

III. Where State Court Proceedings Are Complete

A. If the result of the state court proceeding is custody, habeas relitigation of the federal question is permissible (Brown), *unless*

(i) the federal issue is a Fourth Amendment issue, and there was a full and fair opportunity to litigate it in the state courts (Stone); *or*

(ii) state remedies are still available; *or*

(iii) the federal question was not raised or decided, and the resulting forfeiture is not excused by cause and prejudice (Sykes).

B. Further, if there is custody, and the relief requested would be to end or shorten the custody, the action will be deemed a habeas action, and exhaustion will be required (Preiser).

C. If the result of the state proceeding is not custody, the issue and claim preclusion rules of the rendering state apply in a subsequent federal action, whether the litigant was plaintiff or defendant in the state proceeding (Allen; Migra; Kremer), *unless*

(i) state preclusion law is overcome by strong federal statutory policies, such as a grant of exclusive federal jurisdiction (Marrese); *or*

(ii) the state's preclusion law violates due process because it did not give a full and fair opportunity to litigate (Allen; Kremer).

D. Resort to federal court after completed state proceedings (except by direct review) may also be independently barred by the Rooker doctrine.

IV. Effect Of State Administrative Proceedings

A. If the federal plaintiff is seeking relief that entails the ending or shortening of confinement, exhaustion of remedies, including administrative remedies, is required (Preiser).

B. If the plaintiff does not seek the end or shortening of confinement, and reaches federal court before state administrative proceedings have begun (and otherwise has a proper § 1983 action), exhaustion of state administrative procedures is not required (Patsy), *unless* another superseding federal statute is deemed to require exhaustion.

C. If administrative enforcement proceedings have begun when the plaintiff reaches federal court, an injunctive action is prohibited by Younger (Dayton Christian Schools).

D. If a state administrative proceeding has been completed, and there is no proceeding for judicial review underway in the state courts, a § 1983 action may be brought, but is subject to any relevant state law giving preclusive effect to state administrative findings (Elliott).

E. If the state administrative proceeding has gone to the state courts, the rules of "II" and "III" apply.

* * *

(2) Note the enormous weight the law places on the question whether a state *court* has undertaken to inquire into the dispute between the citizen and the state. If it has not, the citizen can normally proceed immediately to federal court and ask for adjudication of the relevant federal issues without regard to state administrative or judicial remedies; even if abstention intervenes, an eventual federal adjudication is guaranteed. On the other hand, once a state court proceeding is underway, we enter a different universe: no removal, no injunctive action, and full res judicata. Even in cases where habeas is available, it must await exhaustion and is subject to harsh forfeiture rules.

Does the radical difference in attitudes make sense? Why is access to a federal court so freely available for plaintiffs, but made so difficult for state-court defendants? Why isn't the claim for a federal trial forum when federal rights are at stake taken at face value after a state court has commenced proceedings? *Per contra,* if rules of comity demand that there be a showing that state process is inadequate before a federal court is allowed to adjudicate a dispute between the citizen and state or local government, why does this demand become irrelevant when the plaintiff reaches the federal courthouse first?

(3) Our existing extraordinary array of rules developed, of course, within different pigeon-holes, with little cross-reference among the doctrinal frameworks. (That is why some of the borderline problems discussed in this Chapter are so difficult.)

Has the time come for a systematic review? What would such a review lead to? Should it reenact the existing radical disassociation between the universe of Ex parte Young and Monroe v. Pape and Mitchum, on the one hand, and the universe of Younger and Rachel and the § 1738 cases, on the other? Should it adopt as a universal model the schemes of the Tax Injunction Act and the Johnson Act, restricting federal courts to cases where no adequate remedy is available in the state courts? (If it did, should a habeas exception continue to exist? For all constitutional questions? For a few exceptionally grave ones?)

Or should it adopt the philosophy of Monroe v. Pape across the board and freely allow defendants access to federal courts by removal or injunction or collateral attack?

(4) Note also the extraordinary array of formulations that govern the question whether the usual rules of comity are overcome because the state

courts do not provide an adequate forum for the litigation of the federal right:

(a) The Johnson Act and the Tax Injunction Act allow attacks on the constitutional validity of state rate orders and state taxes where a "plain, speedy, and efficient remedy" cannot be had in the state courts (§§ 1341, 1342).

(b) The Younger doctrine will not prevent a federal action to abort pending state enforcement proceedings if those proceedings are in "bad faith" or there are other "extraordinary circumstances" (Younger).

(c) The Anti-Injunction Act, when it applies, has its own statutory exceptions; none is couched in terms of a "fair opportunity" to litigate a question in the state courts (§ 2283).

(d) A private state court defendant may remove an enforcement proceeding to federal court if he is "denied or cannot enforce" in state courts a right under the statutes protecting equal civil rights (§ 1443).

(e) A state prisoner may raise Fourth Amendment claims on habeas corpus if the state did not provide an opportunity for a "full and fair litigation" of that claim (Stone).

(f) Habeas exhaustion is excused if there is "an absence of available state corrective process" or if the circumstances render "such process ineffective" (§ 2254(b)).

(g) A failure to raise a federal question in a state criminal case will not lead to forfeiture of a habeas remedy if there was "cause" for the failure and if the prisoner was "prejudiced" as a result.

(h) Res judicata will not bar federal consideration of a federal question if there was no "full and fair opportunity" to litigate in the state courts (Allen). If the state proceeding afforded due process, this will be deemed to provide a "full and fair opportunity" (Kremer).

Would it not be sensible in any event to think of these formulations as responding to a common set of concerns? See Bator, *The State Courts and Federal Constitutional Litigation*, 22 Wm. & Mary L.Rev. 605, 626 (1981); Collins, *The Right to Avoid Trial: Justifying Federal Court Intervention Into Ongoing State Proceedings*, 66 N.C.L.Rev. 49 (1987). Shouldn't we attempt to develop a unifying framework—a field theory—that could encompass them all? Consider, for instance, the realms of habeas, Younger, and res judicata. In all these contexts, the courts are grappling with the question of when failure to resort to the state courts should be excused and the doors of the federal courthouse opened because of some failing in the state court system for adjudicating federal rights. Is it intelligent to think of these as entirely distinct problems?

What should a common formulation look like? When are state processes or remedies "inadequate"? Should we insist that the very question of inadequacy be put first to the state courts, and then subjected to normal Supreme Court review?

(5) In cases where federal court trial jurisdiction is justified, what is the best technique for affording it? Removal before or after judgment? Independent injunctive or declaratory actions in the federal courts to test the federal right? Post-judgment audit of the state court adjudication by collateral attack? Or some mix of all of the above?

Chapter XIII

THE DIVERSITY JURISDICTION OF THE FEDERAL DISTRICT COURTS

SECTION 1. INTRODUCTION

STATUTORY DEVELOPMENT

Act of 1789

" * * * [T]he circuit courts shall have original cognizance, concurrent with the courts of the several States, of all suits of a civil nature at common law or in equity, where the matter in dispute exceeds, exclusive of costs, the sum or value of five hundred dollars, and * * * an alien is a party, or the suit is between a citizen of the State where the suit is brought, and a citizen of another State." Act of Sept. 24, 1789, Sec. 11, 1 Stat. 73, 78.

Act of 1875

" * * * in which there shall be a controversy between citizens of different States or * * * a controversy between citizens of a State and foreign states, citizens, or subjects * * *." Act of Mar. 3, 1875, Sec. 1, 18 Stat. 470.

Act of 1887

" * * * where the matter in dispute exceeds, exclusive of interest and costs, the sum or value of two thousand dollars * * *." Act of Mar. 3, 1887, Sec. 1, 24 Stat. 552.

Judicial Code of 1911

" * * * where the matter in controversy exceeds, exclusive of interest or costs, the sum or value of three thousand dollars * * *." Act of Mar. 3, 1911, Sec. 24, 36 Stat. 1087, 1091.

Act of 1940

" * * * (b) Is between citizens of different States, or citizens of the District of Columbia, the Territory of Hawaii, or Alaska, and any State or Territory." Act of Apr. 20, 1940, 54 Stat. 143.

Revised Judicial Code of 1948

" (a) The district courts shall have original jurisdiction of all civil actions where the matter in controversy exceeds the sum or value of $3000 exclusive of interest and costs, and is between:

1656

" (1) Citizens of different States:

" (2) Citizens of a State, and foreign states or citizens or subjects thereof;

" (3) Citizens of different States and in which foreign states or citizens or subjects thereof are additional parties.

" (b) The word 'States', as used in this section, includes the Territories and the District of Columbia."   Act of June 25, 1948, Sec. 1, 62 Stat. 930.

Act of 1956

" * * * (b) The word 'States', as used in this section, includes the Territories, the District of Columbia, and the Commonwealth of Puerto Rico."   Act of July 26, 1956, c. 740, 70 Stat. 658.

Act of 1958

" (a) * * * where the matter in controversy exceeds the sum or value of $10,000, exclusive of interest and costs * * *.

" (b) Except when express provision therefor is otherwise made in a statute of the United States, where the plaintiff who files the case originally in the federal courts is finally adjudged to be entitled to recover less than the sum or value of $10,000, computed without regard to any setoff or counterclaim to which the defendant may be adjudged to be entitled, and exclusive of interest and costs, the district court may deny costs to the plaintiff and, in addition, may impose costs on the plaintiff.

" (c) For the purposes of this section and section 1441 of this title, a corporation shall be deemed a citizen of any State by which it has been incorporated and of the State where it has its principal place of business.

" (d) The word 'States', as used in this section, includes the Territories, the District of Columbia, and the Commonwealth of Puerto Rico."   Act of July 25, 1958, Sec. 2, 72 Stat. 415.

Act of 1964

" * * * (c) * * *: *Provided further,* That in any direct action against the insurer of a policy or contract of liability insurance, whether incorporated or unincorporated, to which action the insured is not joined as a party-defendant, such insurer shall be deemed a citizen of the State of which the insured is a citizen, as well as of any State by which the insurer has been incorporated and of the State where it has its principal place of business."   Act of Aug. 14, 1964, Sec. 1, 78 Stat. 445.

Act of 1976

" (a) * * *

" (2) citizens of a State and citizens or subjects of a foreign state;

" (3) citizens of different States and in which citizens or subjects of a foreign state are additional parties; and

" (4) a foreign state, defined in section 1603(a) of this title, as plaintiff and citizens of a State or of different States." Act of Oct. 21, 1976, Sec. 3, 90 Stat. 2891.[1]

NOTE ON THE HISTORICAL BACKGROUND OF THE DIVERSITY JURISDICTION

(1) The conventional explanation of the diversity jurisdiction has referred it solely to the last of the six "descriptions of cases" which Hamilton listed as proper for a federal jurisdiction at the beginning of The Federalist, No. 80, q.v., p. 23, *supra*. The most quoted statement is Marshall's in Bank of the United States v. Deveaux, 5 Cranch 61, 87 (U.S.1809):

" * * * However true the fact may be, that the tribunals of the states will administer justice as impartially as those of the nation, to parties of every description, it is not less true, that the constitution itself either entertains apprehensions on this subject, or views with such indulgence the possible fears and apprehensions of suitors, that it has established national tribunals for the decision of controversies between aliens and a citizen, or between citizens of different states."

In Martin v. Hunter's Lessee, 1 Wheat. 304, 347 (U.S.1816), Justice Story said of diversity cases:

" * * * The constitution has presumed (whether rightly or wrongly we do not inquire) that state attachments, state prejudices, state jealousies, and state interests, might sometimes obstruct, or control, or be supposed to obstruct or control, the regular administration of justice * * *. No other reason than that which has been stated can be assigned, why some, at least, of those cases should not have been left to the cognizance of the state courts."

(2) The evidence concerning the origins of the diversity jurisdiction is examined in Friendly, *The Historic Basis of the Diversity Jurisdiction*, 41 Harv.L.Rev. 483 (1928). The principal discussion took place in the debates on ratification, in which the proposed jurisdiction was bitterly denounced. What Friendly finds "astounding", however, "is not the vigor of the attack but the apathy of the defense" (p. 487). Hamilton's argument from the privileges and immunities clause he dismisses as "specious" (p. 492 n. 44). And he questions the "sincerity" of the argument from apprehension of local prejudice because of the failure of Madison and others who made it to adduce specific examples of prejudice. Reviewing the scanty reports of contemporary decisions, he finds that the evidence "entirely fails to show the existence of prejudice on the part of the state judges".

---

1. The 1976 amendment to § 1332 was enacted in connection with the Foreign Sovereign Immunities Act of that year, 28 U.S.C. §§ 1602–11. The references to foreign states as parties were stricken from subsections (a)(2) and (a)(3), and a new subsection (a)(4) was added conferring jurisdiction over suits brought by foreign states as defined by the new act. Suits against foreign states, as defined by that act, were dealt with in new § 1330 of Title 28, which conferred on the district courts "original jurisdiction without regard to amount in controversy of any nonjury civil action against a foreign state as defined in section 1603(a) of this title as to any claim for relief in personam with respect to which the foreign state is not entitled to immunity either under sections 1605–1607 of this title or under any applicable international agreement." The corresponding provision for removal of actions brought in state courts was new § 1441(d) of Title 28.

What Friendly does find is that "the real fear was not of state courts so much as of state legislatures. * * * In summary, we may say that the desire to protect creditors against legislation favorable to debtors was a principal reason for the grant of diversity jurisdiction, and that as a reason it was by no means without validity" (pp. 495–97). To this he adds lack of confidence in elected judges and fear of the practice of legislative review prevailing in some states. "Not unnaturally the commercial interests of the country were reluctant to expose themselves to the hazards of litigation before such courts as these. They might be good enough for the inhabitants of their respective states, but merchants from abroad felt themselves entitled to something better. There was a vague feeling that the new courts would be strong courts, creditors' courts, business men's courts" (p. 498).

Friendly's conclusions are challenged in Yntema & Jaffin, *Preliminary Analysis of Concurrent Jurisdiction,* 79 U.Pa.L.Rev. 869, 873–76 (1931), on the ground that the available evidence "precludes extensive inference", and that "the theory of no local prejudice is presumptively improbable."

Frank, *Historical Bases of the Federal Judicial System,* 13 Law & Contemp.Prob. 3, 22–28 (1948), reviews the question and concludes:

"To summarize, the diversity jurisdiction in the federal Constitution may fairly be said to be the product of three factors, the relative weights of which cannot now be assessed:

"1. The desire to avoid regional prejudice against commercial litigants, based in small part on experience and in large part on common-sense anticipation.

"2. The desire to permit commercial, manufacturing, and speculative interests to litigate their controversies, and particularly their controversies with other classes, before judges who would be firmly tied to their own interests.

"3. The desire to achieve more efficient administration of justice for the classes thus benefited".

(3) For the full story of the use made of the diversity authority in the first Judiciary Act, and the related effort in the same Congress to eliminate the diversity clause by constitutional amendment, see Warren, *New Light on the History of the Federal Judiciary Act of 1789,* 37 Harv.L.Rev. 49 (1923). For more recent discussions of the origins of the diversity jurisdiction, with particular emphasis on the nationalizing functions which it served, see Marbury, *Why Should We Limit Federal Diversity Jurisdiction?,* 46 A.B.A.J. 379 (1960); Moore & Weckstein, *Diversity Jurisdiction: Past, Present, and Future,* 43 Texas L.Rev. 1 (1964).

SECTION 2. ELEMENTS OF DIVERSITY JURISDICTION

NOTE ON THE KINDS OF DIVERSE CITIZENSHIP THAT CONFER JURISDICTION

A. The Meaning of State Citizenship

From the beginning the Court has steadily insisted that state citizenship, for the purposes of the diversity jurisdiction, is dependent upon two elements: first, United States citizenship; and second, domicile in the state, in the traditional sense of the conflict of laws.[1] See, *e.g.*, Brown v. Keene, 8 Pet. 112 (U.S.1834).

The second of these requirements has been reflected in innumerable holdings that a mere allegation of residence in a state is insufficient to found diversity jurisdiction, since such an allegation may or may not connote citizenship. *E.g.*, Wolfe v. Hartford Life & Annuity Ins. Co., 148 U.S. 389 (1893). For reasons that reflection will make clear, this doctrine survived the Fourteenth Amendment, despite the use in the amendment of the term "resides". See the discussion in Robertson v. Cease, 97 U.S. 646, 648–50 (1879).

This doctrine, of course, is initially one of pleading, and a pleading error may often be remedied by amendment. But beneath the point of pleading remains a point of substance. It is possible to be a citizen of the United States without being a citizen of any state or federal territory. See Paragraph B(7) of this Note. And a natural person cannot be a citizen of more than one state.

B. The Kinds of Diverse Citizenship

1. *Actions between a citizen of the forum state and a citizen of another state.*

Notice that from 1789 to 1875 the diversity jurisdiction (apart from aliens) extended only to cases of this first type. (Here, and throughout this Note, the existence of the requisite amount in controversy is assumed.)

Notice that it made no difference, and never has, what law was applicable, or (with respect to original jurisdiction) whether the out-of-state citizen was plaintiff or defendant.

But if the plaintiff elected to sue in the state court, only an out-of-state defendant could, or now can, remove to the federal court. Is there a sound reason for this difference?

2. *Actions between citizens of two different non-forum states.*

Jurisdiction in this class of cases was first conferred in 1875 and still exists. If the case is brought in a state court, the defendant can remove.

---

1. Professor Currie has argued that the test of "domicile" in the conflict of laws sense is not an appropriate standard for determining diversity. He admits the difficulty of formulating an alternative, but expresses the hope that "the courts in problem cases would pay less heed to intention and more to physical facts than is suggested by the traditional concept of domicile". Currie, *The Federal Courts and the American Law Institute*, 36 U.Chi.L. Rev. 1, 10–12 (1968).

What justification is there for this jurisdiction? Did the Klaxon case, p. 791, *supra*, remove whatever justification there was? Or is there warrant for it in the fact that, on many occasions, one noncitizen may have much closer ties to the forum state than his noncitizen adversary?

3. *Actions between an alien (or a foreign state) and a citizen of the forum state.*

This jurisdiction has existed since 1789. Note that the present statute appears to exclude from the jurisdiction an alien who is "stateless", and it has been so held. *E.g.*, Shoemaker v. Malaxa, 241 F.2d 129 (2d Cir.1957). Is this result compelled by Article III?[2]

4. *Actions between an alien (or a foreign state) and a citizen of a non-forum state.*

Unlike the comparable jurisdiction in class 2, this jurisdiction has existed since 1789.

Are there special dangers of prejudice here which do not exist in class 2? If the rule of the Klaxon case is accepted for conflicts between the laws of different states, does it follow that it should be applied also to conflicts between the law of a state and that of a foreign state? *Cf.* Banco Nacional de Cuba v. Sabbatino, 376 U.S. 398 (1964), p. 901, *supra*.

5. *Actions between a citizen of the District of Columbia and (a) a citizen of the forum state; or (b) a citizen of a non-forum state; or (c) an alien; or (d) a citizen of Puerto Rico; or (e) a citizen of a territory.*

Actions between a citizen of a territory and (a) a citizen of the forum state; or (b) a citizen of a non-forum state; or (c) an alien; or (d) a citizen of Puerto Rico; or (e) a citizen of another territory.

Actions between a citizen of Puerto Rico and (a) a citizen of the forum state; or (b) a citizen of a non-forum state; or (c) an alien.

Does the decision in the Tidewater case, p. 473, *supra*, settle the constitutionality of the jurisdiction in all the sub-classes in this class? See, *e.g.*, Americana of Puerto Rico, Inc. v. Kaplus, 368 F.2d 431 (3d Cir.1966) (upholding jurisdiction in an action by a Puerto Rican corporation against New Jersey defendants brought in a New Jersey federal court). In which of the sub-classes is there substantial justification for the jurisdiction?

Observe that all these cases are also within the removal jurisdiction, except when a citizen of the forum state is defendant.

6. *Actions (a) between aliens or (b) between a foreign state and an alien who is a subject of that or of a different state, or (c) between different foreign states.*

There is not and never has been jurisdiction in any of these cases. Should there be?[3]

2. On the applicability of § 1332 to dual nationals, compare Aguirre v. Nagel, 270 F.Supp. 535 (E.D.Mich.1967) (upholding jurisdiction in action by a citizen of both the United States and Mexico against a citizen of the United States; both parties were domiciled in Michigan), with Sadat v. Mertes, 615 F.2d 1176 (7th Cir.1980) (denying jurisdiction in action by a citizen of both the United States and Egypt against citizens of the United States; plaintiff was domiciled abroad and defendants were domiciled in Connecticut and Wisconsin).

3. In Hodgson v. Bowerbank, 5 Cranch 303 (U.S.1809), the Court construed an ambiguous provision of the First Judiciary Act as not authorizing the exercise of jurisdiction solely on the basis of the alienage of one of the parties. See p. 478, *supra*.

7. *Actions in which one of the parties is a citizen of the United States but not of any state or territory or of the District of Columbia or Puerto Rico.*

This class of American citizens includes Americans domiciled abroad. See, *e.g.,* Smith v. Carter, 545 F.2d 909 (5th Cir.1977); Van Der Schelling v. U.S. News & World Report, Inc., 213 F.Supp. 756 (E.D.Pa.), *aff'd per curiam,* 324 F.2d 956 (3d Cir.1963). In both cases, motions to dismiss were sustained on the ground that such persons are not within the grant of diversity jurisdiction. Is this result compelled by Article III?

8. *Actions in which one of the parties is a citizen of a state but not of the United States.*

If the position of the Court stated at the outset of this Note is sound, as it seems to be, this situation is double-talk and really involves one of the situations in class 3–6. Article III, in other words, refers only to citizens of a state who are also citizens of the United States. (Compare the discussion of class 9, below.)

9. *Actions in which one of the parties is a citizen of a territory but not of the United States.*

The first question in dealing with this class—a question on which there is a notable lack of authority—is to determine the meaning of "Territory" under § 1332(d). Does it include all territories and possessions of the United States regardless of their formal designation? American Samoa and Swains Island, for example, are defined as "outlying possessions" in 8 U.S.C. § 1101(a)(29).[4]

Persons born in the outlying possessions are "nationals, but not citizens, of the United States". 8 U.S.C. § 1408. They are clearly not aliens. Are they within the diversity jurisdiction if domiciled in an outlying possession? In a state?

NOTE ON THE TIME WHEN JURISDICTION ATTACHES AND ITS OUSTER BY SUBSEQUENT EVENTS

It is commonly said that the original jurisdiction of a federal trial court depends upon the facts existing when the action was begun. For a statement of a similar but double requirement in removed actions, see Mansfield, Coldwater & Lake Michigan Ry. v. Swan, p. 1701, *infra.* As a corollary, it is said that jurisdiction, once having attached, whether in an original or a removed action, will not be ousted by later events. Mollan v. Torrance, 9 Wheat. 537 (U.S.1824).

The problem of ouster of jurisdiction may arise as a result simply of the happening of extra-litigation events. These events may or may not have been within the control of a party, who in turn may or may not have acted with a view to defeating federal jurisdiction. The Court early said that jurisdiction, once attached, would not be defeated by a party's later change of domicile. Mollan v. Torrance, *supra.* And it said the same thing

4. In United States v. Standard Oil Co., 404 U.S. 558 (1972), the Supreme Court, reversing per curiam a lower court decision, held that American Samoa is a "Territory of the United States" within the meaning of § 3 of the Sherman Antitrust Act. The term, the Court said in quoting from an earlier opinion, was " 'used in its most comprehensive sense' " (p. 559).

of the death of a party and the substitution of a non-diverse representative. Dunn v. Clarke, 8 Pet. 1, 2 (U.S.1834).

Changes in the record that are not simply unavoidable responses to external events may be thought to raise different problems. However, in Hardenbergh v. Ray, 151 U.S. 112, 118 (1894), the Court relied on the Mollan and Dunn cases in holding that the substitution, on his own motion, of a non-diverse landlord as the defendant in an action of ejectment brought originally against the tenant left the jurisdiction unimpaired. The Court relied also on Phelps v. Oaks, 117 U.S. 236, 240 (1886), which had reached the same result in a case of intervention by the landlord. See generally 13B Wright, Miller & Cooper, Federal Practice and Procedure § 3608 (1984).

More difficult problems are involved when one of the parties tries by amendment or responsive pleading to present a case or question that would not, in the first instance, have been within the court's jurisdiction. The Court has squarely held that the plaintiff may not, after removal by the defendant, defeat the jurisdiction by reducing the *ad damnum* below the jurisdictional amount. Saint Paul Mercury Indemnity Co. v. Red Cab Co., 303 U.S. 283 (1938). On the other hand, when a separable controversy with a diverse party served as the basis of removal, an amendment eliminating that controversy was held to require the remand of the remnant of the case to the state court. Texas Transp. Co. v. Seeligson, 122 U.S. 519 (1887).

Other aspects of the question of ouster of jurisdiction are developed later in this chapter. Consider, after reflecting on these aspects, whether the cases can be reconciled on the basis of the principle that jurisdiction will be ousted by a later amendment only when the jurisdiction was ancillary and the amendment eliminated entirely the primary claim upon which it depended. Compare the statement in United Mine Workers v. Gibbs, p. 1042, *supra*, that "if the federal claims are dismissed before trial, even though not insubstantial in a jurisdictional sense, the state claims should be dismissed as well." And see generally Schlesinger & Strasburger, *Divestment of Federal Jurisdiction: A Trapdoor Section in the Judicial Code*, 39 Colum.L.Rev. 595 (1939).

STRAWBRIDGE v. CURTISS

3 Cranch 267, 2 L.Ed. 435 (U.S.1806).
Appeal from the Circuit Court for the District of Massachusetts.

MARSHALL, CH.J., delivered the opinion of the court.

The court has considered this case, and is of opinion that the jurisdiction cannot be supported.

The words of the act of congress are, "where an alien is a party; or the suit is between a citizen of a state where the suit is brought, and a citizen of another state."

The court understands these expressions to mean, that each distinct interest should be represented by persons, all of whom are entitled to sue, or may be sued, in the federal courts. That is, that where the interest is joint, each of the persons concerned in that interest must be competent to sue, or liable to be sued, in those courts.

But the court does not mean to give an opinion in the case where several parties represent several distinct interests, and some of those parties are, and others are not, competent to sue, or liable to be sued, in the courts of the United States.

Decree affirmed.

NOTE ON MULTIPLE ORIGINAL PARTIES: HEREIN OF ALIGNMENT AND INTERPLEADER

(1) Under all the varying formulations of the general grant of diversity jurisdiction in successive judiciary acts, the Strawbridge decision has been consistently interpreted as requiring that there be diversity of citizenship as between each plaintiff and each defendant.[1] Should the decision have been limited to cases in which the interests of the several plaintiffs and defendants were "joint"? Does the co-citizenship of two adverse parties always assure impartiality in the disposition of every aspect of the litigation?

(2) In applying the doctrine of Strawbridge v. Curtiss, the court is not controlled by the plaintiff's alignment of the parties. It "will look beyond the pleadings and arrange the parties according to their sides in the dispute", whether the result is to establish or to defeat jurisdiction. See Dawson v. Columbia Ave. Savings Fund, Safe Dep., Title & Trust Co., 197 U.S. 178, 180 (1905) (realigning to defeat jurisdiction); Indianapolis v. Chase Nat. Bank, 314 U.S. 63 (1941) (same).

The problem of realignment is particularly important in stockholders' derivative suits, since the defendants are often directors or officers of the corporation and thus co-citizens of the corporation.[2] Early decisions like Dodge v. Woolsey, 18 How. 331 (U.S.1856), and Hawes v. Oakland, 104 U.S. 450 (1882), established criteria for determining when a shareholder could maintain a derivative action—criteria now reflected in significant part in Fed.Rule 23.1. In Doctor v. Harrington, 196 U.S. 579 (1905), the Court, while reversing a decision realigning a corporate defendant as a plaintiff in a derivative action, apparently recognized the possibility that realignment might be appropriate. Even though a corporation stands to benefit from the suit, the Court said (p. 587) that the corporation should not be realigned as a plaintiff if it is "under a control antagonistic to him [the shareholder plaintiff], and made to act in a way detrimental to his rights".

The circumstances in which realignment was required in these cases remained cloudy at least until Smith v. Sperling, 354 U.S. 91 (1957), and its companion case, Swanson v. Traer, 354 U.S. 114 (1957). The plaintiff in Smith had brought a derivative action in a federal court on behalf of Warner Brothers (a Delaware corporation), against United States Pictures, Inc. (another Delaware corporation), certain directors of Warner, and

---

1. Does the Strawbridge rule apply when there is an independent basis of federal jurisdiction over the controversy between the nondiverse parties? See Comment, 82 Colum.L.Rev. 784, 797 (1982) (arguing persuasively, on the basis of the Romero case, p. 1071, *supra*, that the Strawbridge rule does not apply).

2. When a derivative suit is brought, the only shareholder whose citizenship is taken into account in determining diversity is the one in whose name the action is filed. 7C Wright, Miller & Kane, Federal Practice and Procedure § 1822 (1986).

others, challenging the fairness of various agreements between Warner and United. The district court, after a 15–day hearing, ordered Warner realigned as a plaintiff and dismissed the action for lack of diversity, finding that the stockholders, officers, and directors of Warner were not "antagonistic to the financial interests" of the company and that none of the officers and directors "wrongfully participated" in the acts complained of.

After affirmance by the court of appeals, the Supreme Court reversed, 5–4, with both sides relying on existing precedent. Justice Douglas, for the majority, said (pp. 96–97):

"It seems to us that the proper course [for deciding the alignment question] is not to try out the issues presented by the charges of wrongdoing but to determine the issue of antagonism on the face of the pleadings and by the nature of the controversy. The bill and answer normally determine whether the management is antagonistic to the stockholder * * *. Whenever the management refuses to take action to undo a business transaction or whenever, as in this case, it so solidly approves it that any demand to rescind would be futile, antagonism is evident. The cause of action, to be sure, is that of the corporation. But the corporation has become through its managers hostile and antagonistic to the enforcement of the claim.

"Collusion to satisfy the jurisdictional requirements of the District Courts may, of course, always be shown; and it will always defeat jurisdiction. Absent collusion, there is diversity jurisdiction when the real collision of issues * * * is between citizens of different States."

For Justice Frankfurter, in dissent, the Court "purporting to interpret [a] half-century of precedents, sweeps them away" and "[i]n so doing, it greatly expands the diversity jurisdiction," perhaps beyond constitutional bounds (p. 105). In his view, a corporation on whose behalf a derivative action is brought may properly be regarded as a defendant only when it is "in fact the tool of the very people against whom a judgment is sought".

Does the Smith case hold that an allegation of antagonism and satisfaction of the other pleading requirements of Rule 23.1 is sufficient to insure that the corporation will be aligned as a defendant? Some commentators think so, e.g., Wright, Federal Courts § 73 (4th ed. 1983), and it is hard to see what else the majority is asking the plaintiff to do. Is there an acceptable alternative that does not involve a lengthy hearing that is bound to duplicate in part the hearing on the merits? Do the constitutional doubts expressed by the dissent have any substance if complete diversity is not constitutionally required? See Paragraph (4), infra.

The majority in Smith states that collusion "may always be shown". How? Suppose that a corporation has 1000 stockholders, most of whom are co-citizens of the corporation and its directors. If a derivative action is brought against the directors by a shareholder who is not a co-citizen, is collusion shown by the fact that he is morally and financially supported by shareholders who are? Apparently not. Sias v. Johnson, 86 F.2d 766 (6th Cir.1936). But cf. Hood v. James, 256 F.2d 895 (5th Cir.1958). Compare Amar v. Garnier Enterprises, Inc., 41 F.R.D. 211 (C.D.Cal.1966), where an outsider from another state was brought into a family dispute over a close corporation so that the suit might be brought in a federal court, and collusion was found. See generally 7C Wright, Miller & Kane, Federal Practice and Procedure § 1830 (1986).

Smith v. Sperling has had its impact in cases other than derivative suits. In Reed v. Robilio, 376 F.2d 392 (6th Cir.1967), the plaintiff sued on behalf of the executors of her parents' estate to set aside certain contracts, and the court relied heavily on Smith in holding that the executors, who had refused to sue and had shown considerable hostility to the plaintiff's claim, should not have been realigned as plaintiffs.

The possibility of realignment, however, is still a very real one, at least in other contexts. See, *e.g.*, Standard Oil Co. of California v. Perkins, 347 F.2d 379 (9th Cir.1965), holding that parties who had refused to join as plaintiffs and who had been added as defendants because they were indispensable (see Fed.Rule 19(a)) should be realigned as plaintiffs, thus preserving diversity jurisdiction.

(3) Did the Strawbridge decision have any bearing on the power of Congress to provide for jurisdiction when complete diversity was lacking? The question remained open until 1967, and generated considerable discussion. McGovney, *A Supreme Court Fiction: Corporations in the Diverse Citizenship Jurisdiction of the Federal Courts,* 56 Harv.L.Rev. 853, 1090, 1103–11 (1943), argued that complete diversity was probably required by Article III, that the likelihood of prejudice was obviated if either result in the case would cut against a citizen of the forum state, and that an action in which there was only partial diversity, while not a suit between citizens of the same state, was also not a suit between "citizens of different states". A number of commentators disagreed, including the reporters for the ALI Study, who argued both from the standpoint of precedent[3] and policy. ALI Study, Supporting Memorandum A, 426–36.

The matter came to a head in 1967 in a federal interpleader case. There are today two kinds of federal interpleader: statutory interpleader, under the successively broadened federal interpleader acts now codified in 28 U.S.C. §§ 1335, 1397, and 2361; and what may be called equity interpleader, developed under the old equity practice now liberalized and codified in Fed.Rule 22.[4] In the absence of a ground for federal question jurisdiction under § 1331, jurisdiction in equity interpleader must be based on the general grant of diversity jurisdiction, and its exercise is subject to the rules of process and venue ordinarily applicable in diversity cases. Such interpleader has been treated as involving a controversy between the stakeholder on one side and all the claimants on the other, whether or not the stakeholder disputed the existence or extent of his liability. See Wright, Federal Courts § 74, at 497 (4th ed. 1984).

In statutory interpleader, the jurisdictional amount is only $500. Under § 1397, venue may be laid in any judicial district where one or more claimants reside, and under § 2361, process may be served in any district where a claimant resides or may be found. The requirement of citizenship under § 1335 is expressed in the words: "Two or more adverse claimants,

3. *E.g.*, Barney v. Latham, 103 U.S. 205 (1881) (removal under the "separable controversy" provision); Supreme Tribe of Ben–Hur v. Cauble, 255 U.S. 356 (1921) (class action).

4. See generally the series of articles by Professor Chafee: *Modernizing Interpleader,* 30 Yale L.J. 814 (1921); *Interpleader in the United States Courts,* 41 Yale L.J. 1134, 42 *id.* 41 (1932); *The Federal Interpleader Act of 1936,* 45 Yale L.J. 963 (1936); *Federal Interpleader Since the Act of 1936,* 49 Yale L.J. 377 (1940); *Broadening the Second Stage of Interpleader,* 56 Harv.L.Rev. 541 (1943); *Broadening the Second Stage of Federal Interpleader,* 56 Harv.L.Rev. 929 (1943).

of diverse citizenship as defined in section 1332 of this title". Under the prior act, 49 Stat. 1096 (1936), the parenthetical phrase after "claimants" was "citizens of different States". Under both acts, lower courts had generally held that diversity between any two adverse claimants was sufficient. The constitutional question posed by these holdings was dealt with by the Supreme Court in State Farm Fire & Cas. Co. v. Tashire, 386 U.S. 523 (1967), an interpleader case in which the provisions of 28 U.S.C. § 2361 had been used to achieve service of process although there was not complete diversity among all the adverse claimants. Raising the issue of diversity jurisdiction on its own motion, the Court held with almost no discussion that "minimal diversity"—diversity between any two adverse parties—was enough. Citing its own precedents as implicitly recognizing this rule "in a variety of contexts," the Court stated that "[f]ull-dress arguments for the constitutionality of 'minimal diversity' in situations like interpleader * * * need not be rehearsed here". The ALI Study and other secondary sources were also cited (p. 531 and n. 7).

Does the Tashire case stand for the proposition that minimal diversity is always enough to satisfy Article III? Can the proposition be defended on the ground that Article III should be read as authorizing Congress in the broadest terms to decide when, if ever, it is appropriate to take jurisdiction over controversies in which there are persons of diverse citizenship on different sides?

NOTE ON THE EFFECTS OF MISJOINDER AND NONJOINDER OF PARTIES

(1) If a person who has not been joined as a party is indispensable within the meaning of Fed.Rule 19, and if his joinder would destroy diversity, the action cannot go forward. See Provident Tradesmens Bank & Trust Co. v. Patterson, 390 U.S. 102, 108 (1968). But what if a person who has been joined, and whose presence destroys diversity, is not indispensable? May he be dropped as a party without dismissal of the case? Fed. Rule 21 states that he may, "at any stage of the action and on such terms as are just".

(2) Suppose that an action against two defendants, one of whom is a co-citizen of the plaintiff, goes to trial and to judgment for the plaintiff, and the jurisdictional defect is noticed for the first time on appeal. Rule 21 applies only to the district courts, but 28 U.S.C. § 1653 appears to permit an amendment of the pleadings on appeal in such a case. If the co-citizen defendant is dropped as a party, may the judgment stand against the other defendant? What of the rule that subsequent events cannot ordinarily create or defeat jurisdiction? See Note on the Time When Jurisdiction Attaches and its Ouster by Subsequent Events, p. 1662, supra. Should it matter whether or not the remaining defendant may have been prejudiced by the presence of the non-diverse defendant? If so, how and where should the determination of possible prejudice be made? Compare, e.g., Dollar S.S. Lines v. Merz, 68 F.2d 594 (9th Cir.1934) (new trial required because trial court lacked jurisdiction to conduct the initial trial), with, e.g., Fifty Associates v. Prudential Ins. Co., 446 F.2d 1187 (9th Cir.1970) (case remand-ed for exercise of discretion by district court).

KELLY v. UNITED STATES STEEL CORP.

284 F.2d 850 (1960).

United States Court of Appeals for the Third Circuit.

Before GOODRICH, KALODNER and STALEY, CIRCUIT JUDGES.

GOODRICH, CIRCUIT JUDGE.

These are appeals from a series of decisions in the United States District Court for the Western District of Pennsylvania in which judgment has been entered for the defendant. The appeals all raise the same question. That question is whether the United States Steel Corporation has its principal place of business in Pennsylvania. If it has, the decision of the court below is correct since all these appellants are Pennsylvania citizens and there is, consequently, no diversity of citizenship on which to base the jurisdiction of a federal court.

The question arises under the 1958 statute, § 1332(c) of Title 28. * * * The new provision is, as appears in its legislative history, an effort to reduce the number of cases coming to federal courts on the ground of diversity of citizenship only.

* * * The simplest case [under this statute] is probably that of a corporation which gets a charter in one state but carries on all its business operations in another state. Obviously, in such a case the connection with the state of charter is nominal and the principal place of business is where the corporate activity is carried on. But from there the question becomes more difficult. A corporation may carry on much of its activity in the state of charter but have another state or perhaps more than one state where a great deal of its business activities take place. In such circumstances one is tempted to try to find some one criterion by which the question can be decided.

The place of the meeting of shareholders will not do. Corporations under modern statutes may have shareholders' meetings in a state other than the state of charter and that place of meeting may be the only corporate act which takes place in that state. The place of meeting of the Board of Directors offers a tempting criterion. * * * That spot, of course, may change from time to time as the seasons and the board personnel change.

One may also look to the place where physical activity is carried on. We can suppose a mining corporation where the actual digging of iron ore is on the Mesabi Range in Minnesota, the corporation has a New Jersey charter but all the directive activity of the corporation is conducted at its office in Superior, Wisconsin. Should the state of digging be called the principal place of business when all the contracts, sales and plans for expansion or contraction, the bank accounts and all the rest that make up this corporation's business activity take place in Wisconsin? In the absence of a simple single test we are forced to analyze our question further and endeavor to pick out as best we can the factor or combination of factors that seem to point to one place as the "principal" place of business. The concept may get artificial in some cases as indeed it is in the case before us. This great corporation has fourteen divisions of the parent corporation and eleven principal subordinate companies. Its various manufacturing activities are spread over practically all the United States and extend to foreign countries. It has literally dozens of important places of business one of which we must pick out as the principal one because the statute says so.

The appellants urge upon us that the test should be where the "nerve center" of the corporation's business is and they urge that the nerve center is New York. We do not find the figure of speech helpful. Dorland's Medical Dictionary tells us that a nerve center is "any group of cells of gray nerve substance having a common function." We think there will be, in the case of United States Steel Corporation, a good many collections of nerve cells serving the common function of making the corporate enterprise go.

We turn, therefore, from a pleasant and alluring figure of speech to a consideration of the facts of the Steel Corporation's life. The appellants in a very well constructed brief list for us the activities of the United States Steel Corporation which to their minds make New York its principal place of business. We make little out of the fact that the federal income tax return is filed in New York. As will be seen from enumeration of other things which take place in that state, New York would be the natural filing place for its tax return. We move then to things more important on the New York side of the question. The Board of Directors regularly meets in New York. It has, however, met in Pittsburgh and as already pointed out the Board can choose its own place of meeting. The Chairman of the Board is in New York, spending one day a week in Pittsburgh. The President divides his time evenly between New York and Pittsburgh. The Executive Committee of the Board meets regularly in New York. So does the Finance Committee. The Secretary of the corporation lives and has his office in New York and the Treasurer, Comptroller and General Counsel have their offices there. The company owns the building at 71 Broadway. From New York is mailed the annual report. Dividends are declared in New York. The Public Relations Department of the corporate enterprise is centered in New York. The Steel Corporation's major banking activities are there. The cash on hand and its government securities are managed and controlled in New York and the corporation's pension funds are invested in New York. To us this adds up to the conclusion that as at present conducted the final decisions through the Board of Directors, the President and top executive officers are made in New York state. If the test of "principal place of business" is where such final decisions are made on corporate policy, including its financing, then the appellants are right in pointing to New York as the principal place of business.

After balancing these important and significant facts with those pointing to Pennsylvania, we reach the conclusion that Pennsylvania and not New York is the principal place of business. It is in Pennsylvania that the Operation Policy Committee sits and conducts its affairs. The Board of Directors has delegated to this committee the duty of conducting the business of the corporation relating to manufacturing, mining, transportation and general operation. It is composed of the Chairman of the Board, the President, the Chairman of the Finance Committee, the General Counsel and the seven Executive Vice Presidents. It makes policy decisions, of course subject to the Board of Directors. It appoints division presidents and corporate officers through the rank of Administrative Vice President. The seven Executive Vice Presidents, one at the head of each of the seven great branches of the corporation, have headquarters and staffs in Pittsburgh. All but one of the seventeen Administrative Vice Presidents and twenty-two out of the twenty-five Vice Presidents are located in Pittsburgh with their staffs. So, too, is the General Solicitor and his staff. In Pennsylvania almost thirty-four per cent of the employees classified as exempt under the Fair Labor Standards Act (29 U.S.C.A. § 201 *et seq.*) are located. This is fourteen times as many as there are in New York.

All this points to us the conclusion that business by way of activities is centered in Pennsylvania and we think it is the activities rather than the occasional meeting of policy-making Directors which indicate the principal place of business.

To this center of corporate activity we may add some other facts having to do with physical location of employer's plants and the like. We think these elements are of lesser importance, but added to the items already enumerated pointing to the center of corporate activity, we think they have some significance. For instance, Pennsylvania has 32.13 per cent of employee personnel, twenty-five times as many as New York and more than twice as many as any other state. More than one-third of the $2,547,594,414 worth of tangible property is in Pennsylvania. In New York there is less than one per cent. Pennsylvania leads in steel productive capacity. This is about thirty-five per cent of the total capacity of the corporation. New York has none. Other items could be added to this list but we have picked those which we think most significant. It is true that Pennsylvania does not have the majority of the productive capacity of this corporation nor the majority of the employees of this corporation. It does have, however, more than any other state. These facts, added to what we have found to be the headquarters of day-to-day corporate activity and management, add up to the irresistible conclusion that the principal place of business of this giant corporation is in Pennsylvania. * * *

The judgments of the district court will be affirmed.

NOTE ON CORPORATE CITIZENSHIP

(1) Does the conferring of citizenship on corporations for diversity purposes raise any constitutional issues? Prior to the addition of § 1332(c) to the Code in 1958, what was the basis on which corporations were treated as citizens for diversity purposes?

In the Supreme Court's first major pronouncement on the subject, Chief Justice Marshall said, "That invisible, intangible, and artificial being, that mere legal entity, a corporation aggregate, is certainly not a citizen; * * *." Bank of the United States v. Deveaux, 5 Cranch 61, 86 (U.S.1809).

From this premise the Court might have moved to any one of three possible conclusions: first, that despite its admitted capacity to sue and be sued, a corporation was barred altogether from the diversity jurisdiction; second, that actions by and against corporations should be regarded as conducted, in behalf of the stockholders, by the president and directors, and that the citizenship of these managers controlled for diversity purposes; and third, that such actions should be treated as, in substance, actions by or against all the stockholders, and that it was the stockholders' citizenship which was controlling. In the Deveaux case, the Court reached the third of these conclusions. Taken together with the rule of Strawbridge v. Curtiss, this approach effectively closed the doors of federal courts to most corporate litigants, in diversity cases, so long as it prevailed.

Thirty-five years later, the Court yielded to the pressure of the bar for a different result. Louisville, C. & C.R.R. v. Letson, 2 How. 497 (U.S.1844). The Court said (p. 555):

"* * * A corporation created by a state to perform its functions under the authority of that state and only suable there, though it may have members out of the state, seems to us to be a person, though an artificial one, inhabiting and belonging to that state, and therefore entitled, for the purpose of suing and being sued, to be deemed a citizen of that state".

While the Letson opinion said that a corporation was "entitled to be deemed" a citizen, and elsewhere that it was "substantially" a citizen, it carefully avoided saying that it *was* a citizen. Under the vigorous hammering of a minority of the Justices, the Court ten years later rephrased its position so as to bring it into closer accord with the Deveaux decision. Marshall v. Baltimore & O.R.R., 16 How. 314, 329 (U.S.1854). As Chief Justice Taney later explained it, the Court decided "that where a corporation is created by the laws of a State, the legal presumption is, that its members are citizens of the State * * * and that a suit by or against a corporation, in its corporate name, must be presumed to be a suit by or against citizens of the State which created the corporate body; and that no averment or evidence to the contrary is admissible * * *." Ohio & M.R.R. v. Wheeler, 1 Black 286, 296 (U.S.1861). See also Steamship Co. v. Tugman, 106 U.S. 118 (1882), applying a similar presumption to corporations created by foreign states.

The story here summarized is told in detail, but from sharply conflicting points of view, in McGovney, *A Supreme Court Fiction*, 56 Harv.L.Rev. 853, 1090, 1225 (1943), and Green, *Corporations as Persons, Citizens, and Possessors of Liberty*, 94 U.Pa.L.Rev. 202 (1946). See also Henderson, The Position of Foreign Corporations in American Constitutional Law (1918), particularly Chap. IV; Moore & Weckstein, *Corporations and Diversity of Citizenship Jurisdiction: A Supreme Court Fiction Revisited*, 77 Harv.L. Rev. 1426 (1964).

Professor McGovney saw this judicial development as part of a larger effort by the federal courts to free business interests from state control. Speaking of the presumption of the Marshall case, he concluded (56 Harv.L. Rev. at 1258):

"In this era of candor and intellectual integrity in judicial decision it is inconceivable that the present Court would now create the fiction. Nothing but *stare decisis* stands in the way of its recall, and *stare decisis* was ignored by the justices who adopted it. Is it not time for the Supreme Court to say of it, as Mr. Justice Holmes said of the doctrine of Swift v. Tyson, that it is 'an unconstitutional assumption of powers by the Courts of the United States which no lapse of time or respectable array of opinion should make us hesitate to correct'?" (Although he might have been somewhat mollified by the dual citizenship provisions of § 1332(c), McGovney would undoubtedly have been distressed at Congress's decision in 1958 to become an accessory after the fact to the Marshall presumption.)

The following excerpts indicate Professor Green's position (94 U.Pa.L. Rev. at 217, 218, 227–28):

"A state which calls a corporation into being endows its members with corporate existence and capacities. It holds them responsible as a corporation for the abuse of their corporate privileges. It exercises a control in some respects greater than it has over its human residents. The fulfillment of the legitimate purposes of incorporation requires that if the corporation is looked upon as a body of members it be also recognized that the members in their organized capacity are the adopted citizens of the state that has made them into a body. To that state the incorporated group stands in a relation which for the purposes of the jurisdictional clauses of the Constitution seems identical with that of an individual citizen to his state. * * *

"* * * The so-called presumption of citizenship is not a fictitious presumption as to what the facts are, but a characterization of the actual facts. It is not a presumption about persons, who happen to be members of a corporation, to the effect that they are individually citizens of the state of incorporation; it is a doctrine about corporations, to the effect that their members, as members, are citizens of the corporation's state. * * *

"It was the Deveaux case and not the later cases that was founded on fiction, for a suit by or against a corporation is not a suit by or against its members."

(2) Prior to the 1958 amendment, the courts struggled continuously with the problem of the corporation incorporated in more than one state. The question arose in a variety of contexts, and the story of the Supreme Court's own inconsistency and confusion on the subject is fully and entertainingly told in Currie, Federal Courts 338–40 (3d ed. 1982). After a per curiam opinion in Jacobson v. New York, N.H. & H.R.R., 347 U.S. 909 (1954), the chances were excellent that a corporation would be considered a citizen of the forum state and *only* of the forum state if it was incorporated there, at least if it had not been compelled to incorporate in that state as a condition of doing business. Thus the fact of dual incorporation might sometimes be used to create and sometimes to defeat diversity jurisdiction. Did such a rule make sense?

Was all this confusion swept away by the 1958 amendment, making a corporation a citizen of "any" state in which it was incorporated? Friedenthal, *New Limitations on Federal Jurisdiction,* 11 Stan.L.Rev. 213, 236–41 (1959), expressed some doubts and noted the absence of any useful legislative history. The matter, unfortunately, is yet to be laid to rest, and some courts still hold that there is diversity if a citizen of A brings an action in B against a corporation incorporated in both A and B, at least if the corporation's principal place of business is not in A. See Wright, Federal Courts § 27, at 151 and authorities cited nn. 21, 23 (4th ed. 1983); Majewski v. New York Cent. R.R., 227 F.Supp. 950 (W.D.Mich.1964) (holding that jurisdictional barriers prevent such a case from being transferred to A under 28 U.S.C. § 1404(a)!).

What more could Congress do to resolve the problem? The ALI recommended that "any" be changed to "every" (proposed § 1301(b)(1)), but Professor Currie thought even this might not work. Currie, *The Federal Courts and the American Law Institute,* 36 U.Chi.L.Rev. 1, 39–43 (1968). Do you agree?

No matter how the statute is drafted, isn't there a problem if an A corporation is required to incorporate in B as a condition of doing business there and then is considered a citizen of *B* for diversity purposes? Can or should such a condition imposed by a state lead to the closing of the doors of the federal court for disputes between the corporation and the citizens of *B*? See Rudisill v. Southern Ry., 424 F.Supp. 1102, 1104 (W.D.N.C.1976), *aff'd,* 548 F.2d 488 (4th Cir.1977) (upholding jurisdiction); *cf.* Terral v. Burke Constr. Co., 257 U.S. 529 (1922), p. 831, *supra.*

(3) The most frequently litigated issue under § 1332(c) is the location of a corporation's principal place of business. Is there one and only one such place for each corporation? The language seems to suggest so, and the legislative history so indicates. See S.Rep. No. 1830, 85th Cong., 2d Sess. 5 (1958); H.R.Rep. No. 1706, 85th Cong., 2d Sess. 4 (1958).

According to Professor Wright, the early cases "seemed to take two different views on how to determine the principal place of business of a corporation with significant activities in several states." On one view, the principal place was the one in which the "home office" was located, since this was "the nerve center" of the corporation. The other view looked to "the place where the corporation carried on the bulk of its activity." Later cases, however, tended to reconcile these decisions and to apply "a single rule," which "looks to the place where the bulk of the corporate activity takes place, if there is any one state in which this is true, while resorting to the location of the home office only if the corporation's activities are dispersed among several states and no one state clearly predominates." Wright, Federal Courts § 27, at 152–53 (4th ed. 1983).

How do the result and rationale of the Kelly case fit into this analysis? Should a court in deciding this issue ever consider the effect on its jurisdiction in the case as a factor in the decision?

If sued after Kelly in a New York federal court by a New York citizen, should U.S. Steel be allowed to argue that its principal place of business is New York? What if its New York adversary had sued in a state court and was seeking to block removal to a federal court on this ground?

(4) Does § 1332(c) have any impact on a corporation incorporated abroad with its principal place of business in the United States? What if, for example, a Panamanian corporation with its headquarters in Florida sues (or is sued by) a Florida citizen? One leading decision sustained diversity jurisdiction in such a case. Eisenberg v. Commercial Union Assurance Co., 189 F.Supp. 500 (S.D.N.Y.1960) (alternative holding), but several later decisions have held to the contrary. *E.g.,* Jerguson v. Blue Dot Investment, Inc., 659 F.2d 31 (5th Cir.1981). See also Note, 84 Colum. L.Rev. 177 (1984) (arguing that an alien corporation with its principal place of business in a state of the United States should not have dual citizenship but should be regarded only as a citizen of that state). If the Jerguson case is followed, could the Panamanian corporation in the hypothetical sue a Mexican national in a federal court?

(5) What is the status for diversity purposes of a corporation incorporated under the laws of the United States but not of any state? 28 U.S.C. § 1348 provides that national banking associations shall "be deemed citizens of the States in which they are respectively located". This provision codified a result that had previously been reached without the aid of statute, and has also been reached with respect to federal corporations other than national banks. Should a similar result be reached with respect to other nationally chartered corporations, at least if "localized" within one

state? Compare, *e.g.*, Feuchtwanger Corp. v. Lake Hiawatha Fed. Credit Union, 272 F.2d 453 (3d Cir.1959) (yes), with, *e.g.*, Hancock Fin. Corp. v. Federal Savs. & Loan Ins. Corp., 492 F.2d 1325 (9th Cir.1975) (no) (alternative holding). See generally 13B Wright, Miller & Cooper, Federal Practice and Procedure § 3627 (1984). Is the Feuchtwanger result consistent with the provisions of 28 U.S.C. § 1349? With the rationale of the Bouligny case, which follows this Note? Observe that the only effect of a decision like Feuchtwanger is to expand the reach of the diversity jurisdiction.

(6) A state itself is not a "citizen of a state." Postal Tel. Cable Co. v. Alabama, 155 U.S. 482, 487 (1894). But a political subdivision is, "unless it is merely an alter ego" of the state itself. See 13B Wright, Miller & Cooper, Federal Practice and Procedure § 3602 (1984). Note that the presumption of Marshall v. Baltimore & O.R.R., *supra*, has a real foundation of probability in such cases.

(7) For discussion of the proviso to § 1332(c), *see* p. 1694, *infra*.

UNITED STEELWORKERS v. R.H. BOULIGNY, INC.

382 U.S. 145, 86 S.Ct. 272, 15 L.Ed.2d 317 (1965).
Certiorari to the United States Court of Appeals for the Fourth Circuit.

MR. JUSTICE FORTAS delivered the opinion of the Court.

Respondent, a North Carolina corporation, brought this action in a North Carolina state court. It sought $200,000 in damages for defamation alleged to have occurred during the course of the United Steelworkers' campaign to unionize respondent's employees. The Steelworkers, an unincorporated labor union whose principal place of business purportedly is Pennsylvania, removed the case to a Federal District Court. The union asserted not only federal-question jurisdiction, but that for purposes of the diversity jurisdiction it was a citizen of Pennsylvania, although some of its members were North Carolinians.

The corporation sought to have the case remanded to the state courts, contending that its complaint raised no federal questions and relying upon the generally prevailing principle that an unincorporated association's citizenship is that of each of its members. But the District Court retained jurisdiction. The District Judge noted "a trend to treat unincorporated associations in the same manner as corporations and to treat them as citizens of the state wherein the principal office is located." Divining "no common sense reason for treating an unincorporated national labor union differently from a corporation," he declined to follow what he styled "the poorer reasoned but more firmly established rule" of Chapman v. Barney, 129 U.S. 677.

On interlocutory appeal the Court of Appeals for the Fourth Circuit reversed and directed that the case be remanded to the state courts. 336 F.2d 160. Certiorari was granted so that we might decide whether an unincorporated labor union is to be treated as a citizen for purposes of federal diversity jurisdiction, without regard to the citizenship of its members. Because we believe this properly a matter for legislative consideration which cannot adequately or appropriately be dealt with by this Court, we affirm the decision of the Court of Appeals.

Article III, § 2, of the Constitution provides:

"The judicial Power shall extend * * * to Controversies * * * between Citizens of different States * * *."

Congress lost no time in implementing the grant. In 1789 it provided for federal jurisdiction in suits "between a citizen of the State where the suit is brought, and a citizen of another State." * * * [The Court here summarizes the judicial development of the concept of corporate citizenship to 1875, see pp. 1670–71, *supra.*]

Congress re-entered the lists in 1875, significantly expanding diversity jurisdiction by deleting the requirement imposed in 1789 that one of the parties must be a citizen of the forum State. The resulting increase in the quantity of diversity litigation, however, cooled enthusiasts of the jurisdiction, and in 1887 and 1888 Congress enacted sharp curbs. It quadrupled the jurisdictional amount, confined the right of removal to nonresident defendants, reinstituted protections against jurisdiction by collusive assignment, and narrowed venue.

It was in this climate that the Court in 1889 decided Chapman v. Barney, *supra.* On its own motion the Court observed that plaintiff was a joint stock company and not a corporation or natural person. It held that although plaintiff was endowed by New York with capacity to sue, it could not be considered a "citizen" for diversity purposes. 129 U.S., at 682.

In recent years courts and commentators have reflected dissatisfaction with the rule of Chapman v. Barney. The distinction between the "personality" and "citizenship" of corporations and that of labor unions and other unincorporated associations, it is increasingly argued, has become artificial and unreal. The mere fact that a corporation is endowed with a birth certificate is, they say, of no consequence. In truth and in fact, they point out, many voluntary associations and labor unions are indistinguishable from corporations in terms of the reality of function and structure, and to say that the latter are juridical persons and "citizens" and the former are not is to base a distinction upon an inadequate and irrelevant difference. They assert, with considerable merit, that it is not good judicial administration, nor is it fair, to remit a labor union or other unincorporated association to vagaries of jurisdiction determined by the citizenship of its members and to disregard the fact that unions and associations may exist and have an identity and a local habitation of their own.

The force of these arguments in relation to the diversity jurisdiction is particularized by petitioner's showing in this case. Petitioner argues that one of the purposes underlying the jurisdiction—protection of the nonresident litigant from local prejudice—is especially applicable to the modern labor union. According to the argument, when the nonresident defendant is a major union, local juries may be tempted to favor local interests at its expense. Juries may also be influenced by the fear that unionization would adversely affect the economy of the community and its customs and practices in the field of race relations. In support of these contentions, petitioner has exhibited material showing that during organizational campaigns like that involved in this case, localities have been saturated with propaganda concerning such economic and racial fears. Extending diversity jurisdiction to unions, says petitioner, would make available the advantages of federal procedure, Article III judges less exposed to local pressures than their state court counterparts, juries selected from wider geographical areas, review in appellate courts reflecting a multistate perspective, and more effective review by this Court.

We are of the view that these arguments, however appealing, are addressed to an inappropriate forum, and that pleas for extension of the diversity jurisdiction to hitherto uncovered broad categories of litigants ought to be made to the Congress and not to the courts.

Petitioner urges that in People of Puerto Rico v. Russell & Co., 288 U.S. 476, we have heretofore breached the doctrinal wall of Chapman v. Barney and, that step having been taken, there is now no necessity for enlisting the assistance of Congress. But Russell does not furnish the precedent which petitioner seeks. The problem which it presented was that of fitting an exotic creation of the civil law, the *sociedad en comandita*, into a federal scheme which knew it not. The Organic Act of Puerto Rico conferred jurisdiction upon the federal court if all the parties on either side of a controversy were citizens of a foreign state or "citizens of a State, Territory, or District of the United States not domiciled in Porto Rico." All of the *sociedad's* members were nonresidents of Puerto Rico, and jurisdiction lay in the federal court if they were the "parties" to the action. But this Court held that the *sociedad* itself, not its members, was the party, doing so on a basis that is of no help to petitioner. It did so because, as Justice Stone stated for the Court, in "[t]he tradition of the civil law, as expressed in the Code of Puerto Rico," "the *sociedad* is consistently regarded as a juridical person." 288 U.S., at 480–481. Accordingly, the Court held that the *sociedad*, Russell & Co., was a citizen domiciled in Puerto Rico, within the meaning of the Organic Act, and ordered the case remanded to the insular courts. It should be noted that the effect of Russell was to contract jurisdiction of the federal court in Puerto Rico.

If we were to accept petitioner's urgent invitation to amend diversity jurisdiction so as to accommodate its case, we would be faced with difficulties which we could not adequately resolve. Even if the record here were adequate, we might well hesitate to assume that petitioner's situation is sufficiently representative or typical to form the predicate of a general principle. We should, for example, be obliged to fashion a test for ascertaining of which State the labor union is a citizen. Extending the jurisdiction to corporations raised no such problem, for the State of incorporation was a natural candidate, its arguable irrelevance in terms of the policies underlying the jurisdiction being outweighed by its certainty of application. But even that easy and apparent solution did not dispose of the problem; in 1958 Congress thought it necessary to enact legislation providing that corporations are citizens both of the State of incorporation and of the State in which their principal place of business is located. Further, in contemplating a rule which would accommodate petitioner's claim, we are acutely aware of the complications arising from the circumstance that petitioner, like other labor unions, has local as well as national organizations and that these perhaps, should be reckoned with in connection with "citizenship" and its jurisdictional incidents.

Whether unincorporated labor unions ought to be assimilated to the status of corporations for diversity purposes, how such citizenship is to be determined, and what if any related rules ought to apply, are decisions which we believe suited to the legislative and not the judicial branch, regardless of our views as to the intrinsic merits of petitioner's argument—

merits stoutly attested by widespread support for the recognition of labor unions as juridical personalities.

We affirm the decision below.

_____

NOTE ON UNINCORPORATED ORGANIZATIONS

(1) Did the Court in Bouligny make too much, or too little, of the addition of § 1332(c) in 1958 or of its amendment in 1964 (discussed at p. 1672, *supra*)? The legislative history shows no consideration of the Bouligny problem, or of the rule of Chapman v. Barney, at either time. Would it "amend diversity jurisdiction" for the Court to overrule its own prior decision in Chapman? Did the Court exaggerate the difficulties that overruling would bring in its wake? How would the overruling have affected an unincorporated association organized under the laws of state *A* and having its principal place of business in state *B* ? Is the problem likely to arise? Aside from any practical difficulties, is there a rational basis for distinguishing between a corporation and a labor union?[1]

(2) When a partnership sues or is sued, the citizenship of each of its members must be considered in determining diversity jurisdiction. See 13B Wright, Miller & Cooper, Federal Practice and Procedure § 3630 (1954). But in Navarro Sav. Ass'n v. Lee, 446 U.S. 458 (1980), the Court decided that individual trustees of a Massachusetts business trust could invoke diversity jurisdiction on the basis of their own citizenship without regard to the citizenship of the trust's beneficial shareholders. The Court began with the proposition that diversity jurisdiction should rest on the citizenship of the "real parties to the controversy" (p. 461) and took note of a line of decisions establishing that a trustee is such a party "when he possesses certain customary powers to hold, manage, and dispose of assets for the benefit of others" (p. 464). The business trust in Navarro, though different from a conventional trust in some respects, was one in which there were "active trustees whose control over the assets held in their names is real and substantial" (p. 465). The Court stressed the value of simplicity in determining jurisdictional issues, and observed that there was a rough correspondence between the test of citizenship it had applied and that for determining capacity to sue under Fed.R.Civ.P. 17(a).

Did the Court in Navarro pay sufficient heed to the rationale of Bouligny? Or can it be said that Bouligny simply reaffirmed the unavailability of entity status to organizations other than corporations, leaving open the question of determining those individuals in an organization whose citizenship should be looked to when diversity jurisdiction is invoked?

1. Did the Court in Bouligny adequately distinguish its own prior decision in Puerto Rico v. Russell & Co., 288 U.S. 476 (1933)? The Second Circuit in Mason v. American Express Co., 334 F.2d 392 (2d Cir.1964), a decision rendered before Bouligny, concluded that Russell had implicitly overruled Chapman and that a joint stock company organized and existing under the laws of New York was a citizen of New York for diversity purposes. Like the sociedad in Russell, the court argued, the joint stock company was virtually the same as a corporation in its essential legal characteristics. Even the lack of a limitation on the liability of the joint stock company was more of a theoretical than a practical difference, said the court, and in any event limited liability was not a universal attribute of all corporations.

Could the holding in Mason, as distinct from its rationale, survive Bouligny?

(3) Navarro resolved one conflict among the lower courts; another still remains with respect to limited partnerships in which there are both "general" and "limited" partners. Compare, *e.g.,* New York State Teachers Retirement System v. Kalkus, 764 F.2d 1015 (4th Cir.1985) (citizenship of limited as well as general partners must be looked to in determining diversity), with, *e.g.,* Mesa Operating Limited Partnership v. Louisiana Interstate Gas Corp., 797 F.2d 238 (5th Cir.1986) (only citizenship of general partners is relevant). Such partnerships are governed in every state by the Uniform Limited Partnership Act, under which limited partners have very narrow rights with respect to management, do not have an interest in the property of the partnership but only a right to a distributive share of the profits, are not personally liable to third persons for the debts or torts of the partnership, and cannot sue or be sued on behalf of the partnership. See Comment, 45 U.Chi.L.Rev. 384, 403–04 (1978).

Does the Supreme Court's decision in Navarro suggest or require a particular result in the limited partnership case? Is either result more consistent with the purposes of diversity jurisdiction as you understand them? What is the significance of Great Southern Fire Proof Hotel Co. v. Jones, 177 U.S. 449 (1900)? That case involved a "limited partnership association" in which *all* partners were limited partners under state law; the Court held that diversity jurisdiction depended on the citizenship of each of the partners composing the association.

(4) Supreme Tribe of Ben–Hur v. Cauble, 255 U.S. 356 (1921), established that in a class action the citizenship of the named representatives is controlling. The class action device has been successfully invoked to circumvent the limitations of the Chapman rule. See, *e.g.,* Calagaz v. Calhoon, 309 F.2d 248 (5th Cir.1962); 13B Wright, Miller & Cooper, Federal Practice and Procedure § 3630, at 702–08 (1984). Note also that Fed.Rule 23.2, added in 1966, relates specifically to actions "by or against the members of an unincorporated association as a class."

Is the Calagaz result sound? Note that it does not render the Chapman–Bouligny problem academic since even if the other prerequisites for a class action are met, the court may conclude that the only members of the unincorporated association who would adequately represent the class of all members are those whose citizenship would destroy diversity. And there is a danger that the named representative may be held to have been "improperly or collusively made or joined to invoke the jurisdiction" of the federal court. 28 U.S.C. § 1359. See also Underwood v. Maloney, 256 F.2d 334 (3d Cir.1958), holding that the class action device may not be used to circumvent diversity requirements if under the forum state's law the unincorporated association in question may sue or be sued *only* as an entity. (The court relied on Fed.Rule 17(b) in reaching this result. Was the reliance warranted?)

(5) Several proposals would deal with the Bouligny problem through a statutory provision giving a partnership or other unincorporated association state citizenship for diversity purposes, and in particular by providing that the association shall be deemed a citizen of the state where it has its principal place of business. See, *e.g.,* ALI Study § 1301(b)(2); Note, 60 N.C.L.Rev. 194 (1981).

Would the adoption of such a proposal be likely to reduce or to expand the number of cases falling within diversity jurisdiction? Should its applicability in a particular case depend on the capacity of the association to sue or be sued under state law? *Cf.* Fed.Rule 17(b).

SECTION 3.   ANCILLARY JURISDICTION

OWEN EQUIPMENT AND ERECTION COMPANY v. KROGER

437 U.S. 365, 98 S.Ct. 2396, 57 L.Ed.2d 274 (1978).
Certiorari to the United States Court of Appeals for the Eighth Circuit.

MR. JUSTICE STEWART delivered the opinion of the Court.

In an action in which federal jurisdiction is based on diversity of citizenship, may the plaintiff assert a claim against a third-party defendant when there is no independent basis for federal jurisdiction over that claim? The Court of Appeals for the Eighth Circuit held in this case that such a claim is within the ancillary jurisdiction of the federal courts. We granted certiorari because this decision conflicts with several recent decisions of other Courts of Appeals.

I

On January 18, 1972, James Kroger was electrocuted when the boom of a steel crane next to which he was walking came too close to a high-tension electric power line. The respondent (his widow, who is the administratrix of his estate) filed a wrongful-death action in the United States District Court for the District of Nebraska against the Omaha Public Power District (OPPD). Her complaint alleged that OPPD's negligent construction, maintenance, and operation of the power line had caused Kroger's death. Federal jurisdiction was based on diversity of citizenship, since the respondent was a citizen of Iowa and OPPD was a Nebraska corporation.

OPPD then filed a third-party complaint pursuant to Fed.Rule Civ. Proc. 14(a) against the petitioner, Owen Equipment and Erection Co. (Owen), alleging that the crane was owned and operated by Owen, and that Owen's negligence had been the proximate cause of Kroger's death.[3] OPPD later moved for summary judgment on the respondent's complaint against it. While this motion was pending, the respondent was granted leave to file an amended complaint naming Owen as an additional defendant. Thereafter, the District Court granted OPPD's motion for summary judgment in an unreported opinion. The case thus went to trial between the respondent and the petitioner alone.

The respondent's amended complaint alleged that Owen was "a Nebraska corporation with its principal place of business in Nebraska." Owen's answer admitted that it was "a corporation organized and existing under the laws of the State of Nebraska," and denied every other allegation

---

3. Under Rule 14(a), a third-party defendant may not be impleaded merely because he may be liable to the *plaintiff.* While the third-party complaint in this case alleged merely that Owen's negligence caused Kroger's death, and the basis of Owen's alleged liability *to OPPD* is nowhere spelled out, OPPD evidently relied upon the state common-law right of contribution among joint tortfeasors. * * *

of the complaint. On the third day of trial, however, it was disclosed that the petitioner's principal place of business was in Iowa, not Nebraska,[5] and that the petitioner and the respondent were thus both citizens of Iowa. The petitioner then moved to dismiss the complaint for lack of jurisdiction. The District Court reserved decision on the motion, and the jury thereafter returned a verdict in favor of the respondent. In an unreported opinion issued after the trial, the District Court denied the petitioner's motion to dismiss the complaint.

The judgment was affirmed on appeal. 558 F.2d 417. * * *

II

It is undisputed that there was no independent basis of federal jurisdiction over the respondent's state-law tort action against the petitioner, since both are citizens of Iowa. And although Fed.Rule Civ.Proc. 14(a) permits a plaintiff to assert a claim against a third-party defendant, it does not purport to say whether or not such a claim requires an independent basis of federal jurisdiction. Indeed, it could not determine that question, since it is axiomatic that the Federal Rules of Civil Procedure do not create or withdraw federal jurisdiction.

In affirming the District Court's judgment, the Court of Appeals relied upon the doctrine of ancillary jurisdiction, whose contours it believed were defined by this Court's holding in Mine Workers v. Gibbs, 383 U.S. 715 [p. 1040, *supra*]. The Gibbs case differed from this one in that it involved pendent jurisdiction, which concerns the resolution of a plaintiff's federal- and state-law claims against a single defendant in one action. By contrast, in this case there was no claim based upon substantive federal law, but rather state-law tort claims against two different defendants. Nonetheless, the Court of Appeals was correct in perceiving that Gibbs and this case are two species of the same generic problem: Under what circumstances may a federal court hear and decide a state-law claim arising between citizens of the same State?[8] But we believe that the Court of Appeals failed to understand the scope of the doctrine of the Gibbs case.

* * *

Gibbs delineated the constitutional limits of federal judicial power. But even if it be assumed that the District Court in the present case had constitutional power to decide the respondent's lawsuit against the petitioner, it does not follow that the decision of the Court of Appeals was correct. Constitutional power is merely the first hurdle that must be overcome in determining that a federal court has jurisdiction over a particular controversy. For the jurisdiction of the federal courts is limited not only by the provisions of Art. III of the Constitution, but also by Acts of Congress.

That statutory law as well as the Constitution may limit a federal court's jurisdiction over nonfederal claims is well illustrated by two recent

---

5. The problem apparently was one of geography. Although the Missouri River generally marks the boundary between Iowa and Nebraska, Carter Lake, Iowa, where the accident occurred and where Owen had its main office, lies west of the river, adjacent to Omaha, Neb. Apparently the river once avulsed at one of its bends, cutting Carter Lake off from the rest of Iowa.

8. No more than in Aldinger v. Howard, 427 U.S. 1, is it necessary to determine here "whether there are any 'principled' differences between pendent and ancillary jurisdiction; or, if there are, what effect Gibbs had on such differences." *Id.*

decisions of this Court, Aldinger v. Howard, 427 U.S. 1 [p. 1050, *supra*], and Zahn v. International Paper Co., 414 U.S. 291 [p. 1764, *infra*]. * * *

[These cases] make clear that a finding that federal and nonfederal claims arise from a "common nucleus of operative fact," the test of Gibbs, does not end the inquiry into whether a federal court has power to hear the nonfederal claims along with the federal ones. Beyond this constitutional minimum, there must be an examination of the posture in which the nonfederal claim is asserted and of the specific statute that confers jurisdiction over the federal claim, in order to determine whether "Congress in [that statute] has * * * expressly or by implication negated" the exercise of jurisdiction over the particular nonfederal claim. Aldinger v. Howard, *supra*, 427 U.S., at 18.

III

The relevant statute in this case, 28 U.S.C. § 1332(a)(1), * * * and its predecessors have consistently been held to require complete diversity of citizenship. That is, diversity jurisdiction does not exist unless each defendant is a citizen of a different State from *each* plaintiff. Over the years Congress has repeatedly re-enacted or amended the statute conferring diversity jurisdiction, leaving intact this rule of complete diversity. Whatever may have been the original purposes of diversity-of-citizenship jurisdiction, this subsequent history clearly demonstrates a congressional mandate that diversity jurisdiction is not to be available when any plaintiff is a citizen of the same State as any defendant.

Thus it is clear that the respondent could not originally have brought suit in federal court naming Owen and OPPD as codefendants, since citizens of Iowa would have been on both sides of the litigation. Yet the identical lawsuit resulted when she amended her complaint. Complete diversity was destroyed just as surely as if she had sued Owen initially. In either situation, in the plain language of the statute, the "matter in controversy" could not be "between * * * citizens of different States."

It is a fundamental precept that federal courts are courts of limited jurisdiction. The limits upon federal jurisdiction, whether imposed by the Constitution or by Congress, must be neither disregarded nor evaded. Yet under the reasoning of the Court of Appeals in this case, a plaintiff could defeat the statutory requirement of complete diversity by the simple expedient of suing only those defendants who were of diverse citizenship and waiting for them to implead nondiverse defendants.[17] If, as the Court of Appeals thought, a "common nucleus of operative fact" were the only requirement for ancillary jurisdiction in a diversity case, there would be no principled reason why the respondent in this case could not have joined her cause of action against Owen in her original complaint as ancillary to her claim against OPPD. Congress' requirement of complete diversity would thus have been evaded completely.

It is true, as the Court of Appeals noted, that the exercise of ancillary jurisdiction over nonfederal claims has often been upheld in situations

---

17. This is not an unlikely hypothesis, since a defendant in a tort suit such as this one would surely try to limit his liability by impleading any joint tortfeasors for indemnity or contribution. * * *

involving impleader, cross-claims or counterclaims.[18] But in determining whether jurisdiction over a nonfederal claim exists, the context in which the nonfederal claim is asserted is crucial. And the claim here arises in a setting quite different from the kinds of nonfederal claims that have been viewed in other cases as falling within the ancillary jurisdiction of the federal courts.

First, the nonfederal claim in this case was simply not ancillary to the federal one in the same sense that, for example, the impleader by a defendant of a third-party defendant always is. A third-party complaint depends at least in part upon the resolution of the primary lawsuit. Its relation to the original complaint is thus not mere factual similarity but logical dependence. The respondent's claim against the petitioner, however, was entirely separate from her original claim against OPPD, since the petitioner's liability to her depended not at all upon whether or not OPPD was also liable. Far from being an ancillary and dependent claim, it was a new and independent one.

Second, the nonfederal claim here was asserted by the plaintiff, who voluntarily chose to bring suit upon a state-law claim in a federal court. By contrast, ancillary jurisdiction typically involves claims by a defending party haled into court against his will, or by another person whose rights might be irretrievably lost unless he could assert them in an ongoing action in a federal court. A plaintiff cannot complain if ancillary jurisdiction does not encompass all of his possible claims in a case such as this one, since it is he who has chosen the federal rather than the state forum and must thus accept its limitations. "[T]he efficiency plaintiff seeks so avidly is available without question in the state courts." Kenrose Mfg. Co. v. Fred Whitaker Co., 512 F.2d 890, 894 (CA4).

It is not unreasonable to assume that, in generally requiring complete diversity, Congress did not intend to confine the jurisdiction of federal courts so inflexibly that they are unable to protect legal rights or effectively to resolve an entire, logically entwined lawsuit. Those practical needs are the basis of the doctrine of ancillary jurisdiction. But neither the convenience of litigants nor considerations of judicial economy can suffice to justify extension of the doctrine of ancillary jurisdiction to a plaintiff's cause of action against a citizen of the same State in a diversity case. Congress has established the basic rule that diversity jurisdiction exists under 28 U.S.C. § 1332 only when there is complete diversity of citizenship. "The policy of the statute calls for its strict construction." Healy v. Ratta, 292 U.S. 263, 270. To allow the requirement of complete diversity to be circumvented as it was in this case would simply flout the congressional command.[21]

---

18. The ancillary jurisdiction of the federal courts derives originally from cases such as Freeman v. Howe, 24 How. 450, which held that when federal jurisdiction "effectively controls the property or fund under dispute, other claimants thereto should be allowed to intervene in order to protect their interests, without regard to jurisdiction." Aldinger v. Howard, 427 U.S., at 11. More recently, it has been said to include cases that involve multiparty practice, such as compulsory counterclaims, *e.g.*, Moore v. New York Cotton

Exchange, 270 U.S. 593; impleader, *e.g.*, H.L. Peterson Co. v. Applewhite, 383 F.2d 430, 433 (CA5); Dery v. Wyer, 265 F.2d 804 (CA2); cross-claims, *e.g.*, LASA Per L'Industria Del Marmo Soc. Per Azioni v. Alexander, 414 F.2d 143 (CA6); or intervention as of right, *e.g.*, Phelps v. Oaks, 117 U.S. 236, 241; Smith Petroleum Service, Inc. v. Monsanto Chemical Co., 420 F.2d 1103, 1113–1115 (CA5).

21. Our holding is that the District Court lacked power to entertain the re-

Accordingly, the judgment of the Court of Appeals is reversed.

MR. JUSTICE WHITE, with whom MR. JUSTICE BRENNAN joins, dissenting.

* * *

In Mine Workers v. Gibbs, we held that once a claim has been stated that is of sufficient substance to confer subject-matter jurisdiction on the federal district court, the court has judicial power to consider a nonfederal claim if it and the federal claim are derived from "a common nucleus of operative fact." Although the specific facts of that case concerned a state claim that was said to be pendent to a federal-question claim, the Court's language and reasoning were broad enough to cover the instant factual situation. * * * Accordingly, as far as Art. III of the Constitution is concerned, the District Court had power to entertain Mrs. Kroger's claim against Owen.

The majority correctly points out, however, that the analysis cannot stop here. As Aldinger v. Howard teaches, the jurisdictional power of the federal courts may be limited by Congress, as well as by the Constitution.

* * *

In the present case, the only indication of congressional intent that the Court can find is that contained in the diversity jurisdictional statute, 28 U.S.C. § 1332(a) * * *. Because this statute has been interpreted as requiring complete diversity of citizenship between each plaintiff and each defendant, the Court holds that the District Court did not have ancillary jurisdiction over Mrs. Kroger's claim against Owen. In so holding, the Court unnecessarily expands the scope of the complete-diversity requirement while substantially limiting the doctrine of ancillary jurisdiction.

The complete-diversity requirement, of course, could be viewed as meaning that in a diversity case, a federal district court may adjudicate only those claims that are between parties of different States. Thus, in order for a defendant to implead a third-party defendant, there would have to be diversity of citizenship; the same would also be true for cross-claims between defendants and for a third-party defendant's claim against a plaintiff. Even the majority, however, refuses to read the complete-diversity requirement so broadly; it recognizes with seeming approval the exercise of ancillary jurisdiction over nonfederal claims in situations involving impleader, cross-claims, and counterclaims. Given the Court's willingness to recognize ancillary jurisdiction in these contexts, despite the requirements of § 1332(a), I see no justification for the Court's refusal to approve the District Court's exercise of ancillary jurisdiction in the present case.

It is significant that a plaintiff who asserts a claim against a third-party defendant is not seeking to add a new party to the lawsuit. In the present case, for example, Owen had already been brought into the suit by OPPD, and, that having been done, Mrs. Kroger merely sought to assert against Owen a claim arising out of the same transaction that was already before the court. Thus the situation presented here is unlike that in Aldinger * * *.

Because in the instant case Mrs. Kroger merely sought to assert a claim against someone already a party to the suit, considerations of judicial

spondent's lawsuit against the petitioner. Thus, the asserted inequity in the respondent's alleged concealment of its citizenship is irrelevant. Federal judicial power does not depend upon "prior action or consent of the parties." American Fire & Cas. Co. v. Finn, 341 U.S., at 17–18.

economy, convenience, and fairness to the litigants—the factors relied upon in Gibbs—support the recognition of ancillary jurisdiction here. Already before the court was the whole question of the cause of Mr. Kroger's death. Mrs. Kroger initially contended that OPPD was responsible; OPPD in turn contended that Owen's negligence had been the proximate cause of Mr. Kroger's death. In spite of the fact that the question of Owen's negligence was already before the District Court, the majority requires Mrs. Kroger to bring a separate action in state court in order to assert that very claim. Even if the Iowa statute of limitations will still permit such a suit, considerations of judicial economy are certainly not served by requiring such duplicative litigation.[4]

The majority, however, brushes aside such considerations of convenience, judicial economy, and fairness because it concludes that recognizing ancillary jurisdiction over a plaintiff's claim against a third-party defendant would permit the plaintiff to circumvent the complete-diversity requirement and thereby "flout the congressional command." Since the plaintiff in such a case does not bring the third-party defendant into the suit, however, there is no occasion for deliberate circumvention of the diversity requirement, absent collusion with the defendant. In the case of such collusion, of which there is absolutely no indication here, the court can dismiss the action under the authority of 28 U.S.C. § 1359. In the absence of such collusion, there is no reason to adopt an absolute rule prohibiting the plaintiff from asserting those claims that he may properly assert against the third-party defendant pursuant to Fed.Rule Civ.Proc. 14(a). The plaintiff in such a situation brings suit against the defendant only with absolutely no assurance that the defendant will decide or be able to implead a particular third-party defendant. Since the plaintiff has no control over the defendant's decision to implead a third party, the fact that he could not have originally sued that party in federal court should be irrelevant. Moreover, the fact that a plaintiff in some cases may be able to foresee the subsequent chain of events leading to the impleader does not seem to me to be a sufficient reason to declare that a district court does not have the *power* to exercise ancillary jurisdiction over the plaintiff's claims against the third-party defendant.[7]

*   *   *

4. It is true that prior to trial OPPD was dismissed as a party to the suit and that, as we indicated in Gibbs, the dismissal prior to trial of the federal claim will generally require the dismissal of the nonfederal claim as well. Given the unusual facts of the present case, however—in particular, the fact that the actual location of Owen's principal place of business was not revealed until the third day of trial—fairness to the parties would lead me to conclude that the District Court did not abuse its discretion in retaining jurisdiction over Mrs. Kroger's claim against Owen. Under the Court's disposition, of course, it would not matter whether or not the federal claim is tried, for in either situation the court would have no jurisdiction over the plaintiff's nonfederal claim against the third-party defendant.

7. Under the Gibbs analysis, recognition of the district court's power to hear a plaintiff's nonfederal claim against a third-party defendant in a diversity suit would not mean that the court would be required to entertain such claims in all cases. The district court would have the discretion to dismiss the nonfederal claim if it concluded that the interests of judicial economy, convenience, and fairness would not be served by the retention of the claim in the federal lawsuit. *   *   *

NOTE ON ANCILLARY JURISDICTION IN DIVERSITY CASES

(1) What are the origins of and justifications for ancillary jurisdiction in diversity cases? What is its proper relationship to the doctrine of pendent jurisdiction developed in such federal question cases as United Mine Workers v. Gibbs, 383 U.S. 715 (1966), p. 1040, *supra?*[1] In considering these questions, what significance should be accorded the general grant of diversity jurisdiction and its construction in Strawbridge v. Curtiss? These issues were all raised in the Kroger case, and are addressed in this Note.

(2) One of the earliest cases on this subject is Freeman v. Howe, 24 How. 450 (U.S.1860), cited in Kroger at footnote 18. In that case the Court held that a state court was without jurisdiction of an action of replevin brought by claimants to property that had previously been attached in a federal diversity action. Answering the objection that the claimants would then be "utterly remediless in the Federal courts, inasmuch as both parties were citizens of Massachusetts" the Court said (p. 460):

"The principle is, that a bill filed on the equity side of the [federal] court to restrain or regulate judgments or suits at law in the same court, and thereby prevent injustice, or an inequitable advantage under mesne or final process, is not an original suit, but ancillary and dependent, supplementary merely to the original suit, out of which it had arisen, and is maintained without reference to the citizenship or residence of the parties."

Rejecting the suggestion in Dunn v. Clarke, 8 Pet. 1 (U.S.1834), that the principle was "limited to a case between the parties to the original suit", the Court said that "any party may file the bill whose interests are affected by the suit at law".

Note that "[o]nce it is agreed that a state court cannot interfere with property in the control of the federal court, the notion of ancillary jurisdiction put forward in Freeman v. Howe cannot be avoided. Unless the federal court has ancillary jurisdiction to hear the claims of all persons to the property, regardless of their citizenship, some persons, with a valid claim to the property, would be deprived of any forum in which to press that claim." Wright, Federal Courts § 9, at 29 (4th ed. 1983).

From Freeman and related holdings, the Court moved almost imperceptibly to the recognition of an ancillary jurisdiction to effectuate or to reexamine judgments after they had become final. See, *e.g.,* Minnesota Co. v. St. Paul Co., 2 Wall. 609, 631–35 (U.S.1864) (upholding an ancillary bill brought by the defendant in a foreclosure suit against various persons, including purchasers at the foreclosure sale, for a construction of the decree and other relief); Dietzsch v. Huidekoper, 103 U.S. 494 (1880) (upholding district court jurisdiction, after judgment for the plaintiff in a

---

1. As indicated in footnote 8 in Kroger, the Supreme Court has never undertaken to draw a precise distinction between pendent and ancillary jurisdiction, and some commentators think that no sound distinction exists. The term "pendent" jurisdiction is generally used when a plaintiff seeks (as in Gibbs) to join with a federal claim a non-federal claim over which the court has no independent basis of jurisdiction. "Ancillary" jurisdiction is generally used with respect to claims asserted after the filing of the original complaint. See Corporacion Venezolana De Fomento v. Vintero Sales Corp., 477 F.Supp. 615, 622 n. 13 (S.D.N.Y.1979).

removed action of replevin, to enjoin the prosecution of an action against the plaintiff in a state court on the plaintiff's replevin bond).

A key case in this development is Supreme Tribe of Ben–Hur v. Cauble, 255 U.S. 356 (1921). A class action had been brought in a federal court against a fraternal benefit association organized under the laws of Indiana. The action was brought by certificate holders from states other than Indiana, and a judgment was rendered favorable to the association. Indiana certificate holders then commenced a state court action against the association, designed to litigate the same questions, and the association thereupon filed a bill in federal court against the Indiana plaintiffs seeking to enjoin them from prosecuting the state court action on the ground that they were bound by the federal decree. The Supreme Court reversed a dismissal for lack of jurisdiction and held that the requested injunction should issue. The Court stated that even though their joinder as plaintiffs at the outset of the initial federal action would have defeated jurisdiction, the Indiana certificate holders were bound by the judgment rendered in that action as members of the class represented.[2] "The intervention of the Indiana citizens in the suit [after it had begun]," the Court noted (p. 366), "would not have defeated the jurisdiction already acquired. Stewart v. Dunham [115 U.S. 61]." The Court then disposed of the remaining jurisdictional issue—that the adversaries in the second federal proceeding were not of diverse citizenship—in a single sentence (p. 367): "As to the other question herein involved, holding, as we do, that the [Indiana certificate holders] * * * were concluded by the decree of the District Court, an ancillary bill may be prosecuted from the same court to protect the rights secured to all in the class by the decree rendered."

Was the determination that the Indiana certificate holders could have intervened in the initial action essential to the result? Consistent with Strawbridge? See *Note on the Time When Jurisdiction Attaches and Its Ouster by Subsequent Events,* p. 1662, *supra.* Was the need to uphold ancillary jurisdiction as great in Ben–Hur as in Freeman v. Howe? Could the Supreme Court have reviewed an Indiana state court decision adverse to the contentions of the association?

(3) Several Supreme Court decisions prior to Kroger dealt directly with the question of the effect of intervention on diversity jurisdiction. *E.g.,* Phelps v. Oaks, 117 U.S. 236 (1886) (cited with apparent approval in Kroger at footnote 18); Wichita R.R. & Light Co. v. Public Util. Com'n, 260 U.S. 48 (1922). In Wichita the Court said (p. 54):

"* * * Jurisdiction once acquired on [the ground of diversity of citizenship] * * * is not divested by a subsequent change in the citizenship of the parties. * * * Much less is such jurisdiction defeated by the intervention, by leave of the court, of a party whose presence is not essential to a decision of the controversy between the original parties."

If it appears that an intervenor is an indispensable party within the meaning of Rule 19 and could not have been joined originally without destroying diversity of citizenship, it seems clear that the case must be dismissed or remanded to the state court. An intervention needed to cure

---

2. The Court defended this conclusion by stating (p. 367): "If the federal courts are to have the jurisdiction in class suits to which they are obviously entitled, the de- cree when rendered must bind all of the class properly represented. The parties and the subject-matter are within the court's jurisdiction."

an otherwise fatal defect of parties can scarcely be regarded as ancillary. See, *e.g.,* Duggins v. Kentucky Natural Gas Corp., 165 F.2d 1011 (6th Cir. 1948); Chance v. County Board, 332 F.2d 971 (7th Cir.1964).

Would it be sound to conclude that, at least in the absence of any such prior bar to the main action, an intervention as of right under Rule 24(a)— even as that concept has been broadened by the amendment of the rule in 1966—should always be treated as ancillary? Can the suggested conclusion be justified, in view of the provision of Rule 82 that the rules shall not be construed to extend or limit the jurisdiction of the district courts?

Most commentators suggest, and the lower courts generally hold, that permissive intervention under Rule 24(b) must be supported by independent grounds of jurisdiction. Is this sound? In principle, should not the controlling question be whether the applicant is seeking a judgment that will improve his position or trying only to prevent a judgment that will worsen it? Are any of the situations governed by Rule 24(b) of the latter type?

See generally 7C Wright, Miller & Kane, Federal Practice and Procedure § 1917 (1986); Shapiro, *Some Thoughts on Intervention Before Courts, Agencies, and Arbitrators,* 81 Harv.L.Rev. 721, 760–64 (1968).

(4) The Ben–Hur decision itself indicated that ancillary jurisdiction would support intervention in a class action by a member of the class without regard to that member's citizenship. Under former Rule 23, however, there was sharp disagreement with respect to intervention in a "spurious" class action (former Rule 23(a)(3)), which was described by some as no more than a device for permissive joinder. See *Developments in the Law: Multiparty Litigation in the Federal Courts,* 71 Harv.L.Rev. 874, 941– 42, and authorities cited n. 493 (1958). Under the revised rule, which contemplates that in a class action all members of the class not properly excluded will be bound by the judgment, the "spurious" class action no longer exists, and ancillary jurisdiction may support intervention by class members in all cases. See 7C Wright, Miller & Kane, *supra,* at 470–72. Again, however, Rule 82 may cause difficulty. *Cf.* Snyder v. Harris, 394 U.S. 332 (1969), p. 1759, *infra* (relying in part on Rule 82 in disallowing aggregation of claims for purposes of satisfying the jurisdictional amount requirements in a class action).

(5) Would (and should) the Kroger case have come out the same way if OPPD had not obtained summary judgment—if the case had gone to trial with all three parties still in it?

It is possible that the significance of the Kroger decision may lie at least as much in the kinds of ancillary jurisdiction apparently recognized in the Court's discussion as in the Court's specific holding in the case before it.[3] Note that the Court does not foreclose the possibility that in a case like Kroger, the third-party defendant might be allowed to assert a claim against the original plaintiff arising out of the subject matter of the original action.[4] If such a claim is allowed, shouldn't the door be open for

---

3. Cited with apparent approval in footnote 18 were cases involving intervention (see Paragraphs (3), (4), *supra*), compulsory counterclaims, and cross-claims. Also, the Court appeared to agree with the decisions holding that a third-party defendant may be impleaded even in the absence of

diversity between it and the original defendant.

4. See Wright, Federal Courts § 76, at 517, and authorities cited n. 53 (4th ed. 1983).

the assertion of a "compulsory" counterclaim by the plaintiff against the third-party defendant?[5] Would the resulting pattern be a sensible one? Does it cast doubt on the central distinction between parties drawn in Kroger itself?

Comment on the Kroger case has varied widely. Compare, *e.g.*, *The Supreme Court, 1977 Term*, 92 Harv.L.Rev. 57, 241–53 (1978) (supporting the result), with, *e.g.*, Garvey, *The Limits of Ancillary Jurisdiction*, 57 Tex. L.Rev. 697, 709–11 (1979).

(6) Prior to the Kroger decision, several lower courts, drawing on notions of pendent jurisdiction in federal question cases, had allowed plaintiffs in diversity suits to assert "pendent claims" for less than the jurisdictional amount or against non-diverse parties. See, *e.g.*, Borror v. Sharon Steel Co., 327 F.2d 165 (3d Cir.1964) (claim against non-diverse party); Hatridge v. Aetna Cas. & Sur. Co., 415 F.2d 809 (8th Cir.1969) (claim for less than jurisdictional amount). Whatever the policy arguments in favor of these results, they would appear to be precluded by the combined weight of the Kroger and Zahn decisions.[6] See Wright, Federal Courts § 36 (4th ed. 1983); Hixon v. Sherwin–Williams Co., 671 F.2d 1005 (7th Cir.1982).

(7) Have the lines between permissible and impermissible ancillary claims been sensibly drawn? Is the argument for entertaining such a claim weaker with respect to a plaintiff in a diversity case than with respect to a plaintiff in a federal question case because of the state law basis of the claim? Because of the problematic nature of the diversity jurisdiction itself? (See pp. 1695–1700, *infra*.)

If diversity jurisdiction is to be retained, how strong an argument can be made for overruling Strawbridge v. Curtiss and for substituting discretion in the district court with respect to all ancillary claims that can be joined under the present rules of civil procedure? If you favor such a step, do you think it should be taken by the Court or by Congress?

SECTION 4. DEVICES FOR CREATING OR AVOIDING DIVERSITY JURISDICTION

KRAMER v. CARIBBEAN MILLS, INC.

394 U.S. 823, 89 S.Ct. 1487, 23 L.Ed.2d 9 (1969).
Certiorari to the United States Court of Appeals for the Fifth Circuit.

Mr. Justice Harlan delivered the opinion of the Court.

5. The word "compulsory" is here used in the sense of a counterclaim arising out of the same transaction or occurrence. It is clear that if there is no jurisdiction over the counterclaim, its assertion in a subsequent action is not precluded by Fed.R.Civ. P. 13.

6. In Zahn v. International Paper Co., 414 U.S. 291 (1975), the Court held that in a diversity class action under Fed.R.Civ.P. 23(b)(3), the claim of each member of the plaintiff class must independently satisfy the jurisdictional amount requirement. The Zahn case, which was relied on in Kroger, is also discussed at pp. 1764–65, *infra*.

The sole question presented by this case is whether the Federal District Court in which it was brought had jurisdiction over the cause, or whether that court was deprived of jurisdiction by 28 U.S.C. § 1359. * * *

The facts were these. Respondent Caribbean Mills, Inc. (Caribbean) is a Haitian corporation. In May 1959 it entered into a contract with an individual named Kelly and the Panama and Venezuela Finance Company (Panama), a Panamanian Corporation. The agreement provided that Caribbean would purchase from Panama 125 shares of corporate stock, in return for payment of $85,000 down and an additional $165,000 in 12 annual installments.

No installment payments ever were made, despite requests for payment by Panama. In 1964, Panama assigned its entire interest in the 1959 contract to petitioner Kramer, an attorney in Wichita Falls, Texas. The stated consideration was $1. By a separate agreement dated the same day, Kramer promised to pay back to Panama 95% of any net recovery on the assigned cause of action, "soley as a Bonus."

Kramer soon thereafter brought suit against Caribbean for $165,000 in the United States District Court for the Northern District of Texas, alleging diversity of citizenship between himself and Caribbean. The District Court denied Caribbean's motion to dismiss for want of jurisdiction. The case proceeded to trial, and a jury returned a $165,000 verdict in favor of Kramer.

On appeal, the Court of Appeals for the Fifth Circuit reversed, holding that the assignment was "improperly or collusively made" within the meaning of 28 U.S.C. § 1359, and that in consequence the District Court lacked jurisdiction. We granted certiorari, 393 U.S. 819 (1968). For reasons which follow, we affirm the judgment of the Court of Appeals.

I.

The issue before us is whether Kramer was "improperly or collusively made" a party "to invoke the jurisdiction" of the District Court, within the meaning of 28 U.S.C. § 1359. We look first to the legislative background.

Section 1359 has existed in its present form only since the 1948 revision of the Judicial Code. Prior to that time, the use of devices to create diversity was regulated by two federal statutes. The first, known as the "assignee clause," provided that, with certain exceptions not here relevant:

"No district court shall have cognizance of any suit * * * to recover upon any promissory note or other chose in action in favor of any assignee * * * unless such suit might have been prosecuted in such court * * * if no assignment had been made." [3]

The second pre–1948 statute, 28 U.S.C. § 80 (1940 ed.),[4] stated that a district court should dismiss an action whenever: "it shall appear to the satisfaction of the * * * court * * * that such suit does not really and substantially involve a dispute or controversy properly within the jurisdiction of [the] court, or that the parties to said suit have been improperly or

3. 28 U.S.C. § 41(1) (1940 ed.). The clause first appeared as § 11 of the Judiciary Act of 1789, 1 Stat. 79.

4. This statute was first enacted in 1875. See 18 Stat. 470.

collusively made or joined * * * for the purpose of creating [federal jurisdiction]."

As part of the 1948 revision, § 80 was amended to produce the present § 1359. The assignee clause was simultaneously repealed. The Reviser's Note describes the amended assignee clause as a " 'jumble of legislative jargon,' " and states that "[t]he revised section changes this clause by confining its application to cases wherein the assignment is improperly or collusively made * * *. Furthermore, * * * the original purpose of [the assignee] clause is better served by substantially following section 80." That purpose was said to be "to prevent the manufacture of Federal jurisdiction by the device of assignment." *Ibid.*

II.

Only a small number of cases decided under § 1359 have involved diversity jurisdiction based on assignments, and this Court has not considered the matter since the 1948 revision. Because the approach of the former assignee clause was to forbid the grounding of jurisdiction upon *any* assignment, regardless of its circumstances or purpose, decisions under that clause are of little assistance. However, decisions of this Court under the other predecessor statute, 28 U.S.C. § 80 (1940 ed.), seem squarely in point. These decisions, together with the evident purpose of § 1359, lead us to conclude that the Court of Appeals was correct in finding that the assignment in question was "improperly or collusively made."

The most compelling precedent is Farmington Village Corp. v. Pillsbury, 114 U.S. 138 (1885). There Maine holders of bonds issued by a Maine village desired to test the bonds' validity in the federal courts. In an effort to accomplish this, they cut the coupons from their bonds and transferred them to a citizen of Massachusetts, who gave in return a non-negotiable two-year note for $500 and a promise to pay back 50% of the net amount recovered above $500. The jurisdictional question was certified to this Court, which held that there was no federal jurisdiction because the plaintiff had been "improperly or collusively" made a party within the meaning of the predecessor statute to 28 U.S.C. § 80 (1940 ed.). The Court pointed out that the plaintiff could easily have been released from his non-negotiable note, and found that apart from the hoped-for creation of federal jurisdiction the only real consequence of the transfer was to enable the Massachusetts plaintiff to "retain one-half of what he collects for the use of his name and his trouble in collecting." 114 U.S., at 146. The Court concluded that "the transfer of the coupons was 'a mere contrivance, a pretense, the result of a collusive arrangement to create' " federal jurisdiction. *Ibid.*

We find the case before us indistinguishable from Farmington and other decisions of like tenor. When the assignment to Kramer is considered together with his total lack of previous connection with the matter and his simultaneous reassignment of a 95% interest back to Panama, there can be little doubt that the assignment was for purposes of collection, with Kramer to retain 5% of the net proceeds "for the use of his name and his trouble in collecting." [9] If the suit had been unsuccessful, Kramer

---

9. Hence, we have no occasion to re-examine the cases in which this Court has held that where the transfer of a claim is absolute, with the transferor retaining no interest in the subject matter, then the transfer is not "improperly or collusively

would have been out only $1, plus costs. Moreover, Kramer candidly admits that the "assignment was in substantial part motivated by a desire by [Panama's] counsel to make diversity jurisdiction available ∗ ∗ ∗."

The conclusion that this assignment was "improperly or collusively made" within the meaning of § 1359 is supported not only by precedent but also by consideration of the statute's purpose. If federal jurisdiction could be created by assignments of this kind, which are easy to arrange and involve few disadvantages for the assignor, then a vast quantity of ordinary contract and tort litigation could be channeled into the federal courts at the will of one of the parties. Such "manufacture of Federal jurisdiction" was the very thing which Congress intended to prevent when it enacted § 1359 and its predecessors.

III.

Kramer nevertheless argues that the assignment to him was not "improperly or collusively made" within the meaning of § 1359, for two main reasons. First, he suggests that the undisputed legality of the assignment under Texas law necessarily rendered it valid for purposes of federal jurisdiction. We cannot accept this contention. The existence of federal jurisdiction is a matter of federal, not state law. Under the predecessor section, 28 U.S.C. § 80 (1940 ed.), this Court several times held that an assignment could be "improperly or collusively made" even though binding under state law, and nothing in the language or legislative history of § 1359 suggests that a different result should be reached under that statute. Moreover, to accept this argument would render § 1359 largely incapable of accomplishing its purpose; this very case demonstrates the ease with which a party may "manufacture" federal jurisdiction by an assignment which meets the requirements of state law.

Second, Kramer urges that this case is significantly distinguishable from earlier decisions because it involves diversity jurisdiction under 28 U.S.C. § 1332(a)(2), arising from the alienage of one of the parties, rather than the more common diversity jurisdiction based upon the parties' residence in different States. We can perceive no substance in this argument: by its terms, § 1359 applies equally to both types of diversity jurisdiction, and there is no indication that Congress intended them to be treated differently.

made," regardless of the transferor's motive. See, *e.g.*, Cross v. Allen, 141 U.S. 528 (1891); South Dakota v. North Carolina, 192 U.S. 286 (1904); Black & White Taxicab & Transfer Co. v. Brown & Yellow Taxicab & Transfer Co., 276 U.S. 518 (1928); *cf.* Williamson v. Osenton, 232 U.S. 619 (1914).

Nor is it necessary to consider whether, in cases in which suit is required to be brought by an administrator or guardian, a motive to create diversity jurisdiction renders the appointment of an out-of-state representative "improper" or "collusive." *See, e.g.,* McSparran v. Weist, 402 F.2d 867 (3 Cir.1968); *cf.* Mecom v. Fitzsimmons Drilling Co., 284 U.S. 183 (1931). Cases involving representatives vary in several respects from those in which jurisdiction is based on assignments: (1) in the former situation, some representative must be appointed before suit can be brought, while in the latter the assignor normally is himself capable of suing in state court; (2) under state law, different kinds of guardians and administrators may possess discrete sorts of powers; and (3) all such representatives owe their appointment to the decree of a state court, rather than solely to an action of the parties. It is not necessary to decide whether these distinctions amount to a difference for purposes of § 1359.

IV.

In short, we find that this assignment falls not only within the scope of § 1359 but within its very core. It follows that the District Court lacked jurisdiction to hear this action, and that petitioner must seek his remedy in the state courts. The judgment of the Court of Appeals is affirmed.

Affirmed.

NOTE ON DEVICES FOR CREATING OR AVOIDING FEDERAL JURISDICTION

(1) The Court in footnote 9 of the Kramer opinion refers to the appointment of an administrator or guardian for the purpose of creating diversity jurisdiction. The problem presented by this practice had become particularly acute in the Eastern District of Pennsylvania, where it was common for lawyers in Philadelphia to arrange for the appointment—as guardians, administrators, or executors—of secretaries or other office staff who commuted to work from New Jersey, thus laying the basis for a diversity action against a Pennsylvania defendant.[1] This device was aided by the established practice of regarding the fiduciary's citizenship (and not that of his beneficiary) as controlling in an action between the fiduciary and a third person. *E.g.*, Chappedelaine v. Dechenaux, 4 Cranch 306 (U.S.1808) (executor); Dodge v. Tulleys, 144 U.S. 451 (1892) (trustee). The status of guardians was a bit fuzzier, but the Supreme Court in Mexican Cent. Ry. v. Eckman, 187 U.S. 429 (1903), had held the citizenship of a general guardian for a minor to be controlling, and had disregarded the citizenship of the minor. (The case spoke in terms of jurisdiction, although it appeared to involve a question of venue.) The Eckman decision did not provide the same beacon for all the lower courts, compare Martineau v. City of St. Paul, 172 F.2d 777 (8th Cir.1949) (citizenship of ward controlling), with Fallat v. Gouran, 220 F.2d 325 (3d Cir.1955) (citizenship of guardian controlling), and the whole matter was clouded by the uncertain impact of Erie and of the provisions of Fed.Rule 17. But the Third Circuit in Fallat had given an expansive reading to Eckman, and in Corabi v. Auto Racing, Inc., 264 F.2d 784 (3d Cir.1959), the court held that in the absence of collusion between plaintiff and defendant, 28 U.S.C. § 1359 did not bar an action even if the sole purpose of the appointment of an out-of-state administrator was to create diversity jurisdiction.

In McSparran v. Weist, 402 F.2d 867 (3d Cir.1968), decided a few months before Kramer, the Third Circuit reversed field and squarely overruled Corabi and related decisions. The case was one in which the plaintiff conceded that the fiduciary was "a straw party, chosen solely to create diversity jurisdiction" (p. 869). Although McSparran involved a guardian for a minor, and Corabi an administrator of a decedent's estate, the court did not rely on the distinction in holding § 1359 applicable (pp. 873–75):

---

1. As part of the ALI project, a study was made of actions filed in the Eastern District of Pennsylvania from November 10, 1958, to July 7, 1959. Of more than 1000 cases, 530 were based on diversity of citizenship. Of these, 107 were brought by out-of-state representatives of Pennsylvania decedents against Pennsylvania defendants. ALI Study 469–71.

" * * * [A] nominal party designated simply for the purpose of creating diversity of citizenship, who has no real or substantial interest in the dispute or controversy, is improperly or collusively named.

"The impropriety or collusion is not any conduct between the plaintiff and the defendant, for as Chief Judge Biggs pointed out in Corabi, the defendant may even oppose the guardian's prosecution of the action. The collusion exists between the nonresident guardian and the applicant for his appointment in the state proceeding as a result of which one who would not otherwise have been named as guardian has achieved the status from which he claims the right to sue because of his artificial selection solely for the purpose of creating jurisdiction. He is not chosen because of his capacity to manage the property of his ward, and indeed need have no experience in the management of property. He is outside the jurisdiction of the court which is to supervise his nominal activity. In truth none of the considerations which normally lead to the selection of a guardian affects the local appointing court's determination because it knows that in the 'manufactured' diversity case the guardian is not expected to manage any property for his supposed ward and usually will not continue in office or exercise any real function after any funds are recovered in the litigation. He is no more than a representative of the minor's counsel whom counsel provides in order to establish a diversity of citizenship which will permit him to bring the action in the federal court. As a straw party he does not stand in the position of a true fiduciary whose involvement in litigation is incidental to his general duty to protect the interests of those for whom he is responsible."

In a companion case, Esposito v. Emery, 402 F.2d 878, 881–82 (3d Cir. 1968), Judge Biggs registered strong objection to the overruling of Corabi:

"The reasoning and the rulings of the majority seem to turn on the statement: 'Here plaintiff [Esposito] has added nothing to a record which shows on its face a *naked arrangement* for the selection of an out-of-state guardian in order to prosecute a diversity suit.' (Emphasis added). The condition of a 'naked arrangement' as a bar to the application of Section 1359 will prove, I think, most troublesome. * * *

" * * * [I]n ascertaining what is a 'naked arrangement', would not the United States district court in almost every case, at its peril and at the peril of the litigants, have to determine what the purpose, 'naked', 'primary', or otherwise, [was] which caused or prompted someone on behalf of some kind of a fiduciary to bring suit in the United States court? * * * While purporting to abolish the 'manufacture' of diversity jurisdiction, the majority rule would elevate such manufacturing to an art difficult to define and even more difficult to combat."

(2) What do you think of the distinctions between Kramer and McSparran suggested by the Kramer Court in footnote 9? According to one commentator, subsequent lower court cases "have held with one voice that the distinctions * * * do not amount to a difference," and have followed the trail blazed by McSparran in actions brought by representatives. Wright, Federal Courts § 31, at 168 (4th ed. 1983). Most of these decisions hold that § 1359 bars jurisdiction on the basis of the representative's citizenship if the purpose of his appointment was to create diversity. *E.g.*, Bianca v. Parke–Davis Pharmaceutical Division, 723 F.2d 392 (5th Cir. 1984). But one court held this purpose not to be a bar when the represen-

tative had a personal stake in the outcome. Hackney v. Newman Memorial Hospital, Inc., 621 F.2d 1069 (10th Cir.1980). And (conversely) another held, in the case of an administrator, that the lack of any personal stake operates as a bar even if the appointment was *not* for the purpose of creating jurisdiction. See Vaughan v. Southern Ry. Co., 542 F.2d 641 (4th Cir.1976).

In view of this disparity, as well as the difficulty of determining motive or purpose, should Congress address this issue? If so, should it adopt a bright-line test that looks to the citizenship of the person represented, or of the real parties to the controversy? See ALI Study, proposed § 1301(b)(4); Mullenix, *Creative Manipulation of Federal Jurisdiction: Is There Diversity After Death?*, 70 Cornell L.Rev. 1011 (1985).

(3) The Kramer Court deliberately left open the status under § 1359 of a variety of events, thus casting doubt on a number of its own precedents. As stated in the Court's footnote 9, an absolute transfer not subject to the former assignee clause has been held not improper or collusive, regardless of the transferor's motive. *E.g.*, Cross v. Allen, 141 U.S. 528 (1891). And if the plaintiff effectively changed his domicile prior to the bringing of suit, it did not matter that his sole motive was to create jurisdiction. Williamson v. Osenton, 232 U.S. 619 (1914). Finally, although reincorporation would fail to create diversity jurisdiction if the old corporation continued in existence with power to control the new, *e.g.*, Lehigh Mining & Mfg. Co. v. Kelly, 160 U.S. 327 (1895), the device would succeed if the new corporation was a genuine one not subject to control by any predecessor, Black and White Taxicab & Transfer Co. v. Brown and Yellow Taxicab & Transfer Co., 276 U.S. 518 (1928).

Should any or all of these holdings be overruled? See Greater Development Co. v. Amelung, 471 F.2d 338 (1st Cir.1973) (criticizing and distinguishing the Black and White case).

(4) In the 1964 amendment to 28 U.S.C. § 1332(c), Congress dealt with one device for obtaining federal diversity jurisdiction. Statutes of a few states (notably, Louisiana) permitted an injured person to bring suit directly against a liability insurer without joining the insured, and this made it possible, for example, for a case in which one Louisiana citizen had injured another to be litigated in a federal court if the alleged tortfeasor had an out-of-state insurer. Lumbermen's Mut. Cas. Co. v. Elbert, 348 U.S. 48 (1954). Such cases were pouring into the Louisiana federal courts until Congress provided that the insurer defendant in a direct action must be deemed a citizen of the insured's state as well as of its own.

Was Congress correct in concluding that such cases are less fitting for original diversity jurisdiction than other cases in which an in-state citizen sues an out-of-state citizen? See the criticism of the statute in Weckstein, *The 1964 Diversity Amendment: Congressional Indirect Action Against State 'Direct Action' Laws*, 1965 Wis.L.Rev. 268.

(5) No statutory provision aids a district court in disregarding devices to avoid federal jurisdiction, and such devices have often been successful. In Provident Savings Life Assurance Society v. Ford, 114 U.S. 635 (1885), the Court held that if an assignment to the plaintiff was "merely colorable" and made to prevent removal, the matter was at most one of defense to the action in the state court; the case could not be removed. See also Oakley v. Goodnow, 118 U.S. 43 (1886) (assignment to defeat jurisdiction precludes

removal); Mecom v. Fitzsimmons Drilling Co., 284 U.S. 183 (1931) (appointment of co-citizen administrator to defeat jurisdiction precludes removal).

But the tide may be turning. In Gentle v. Lamb–Weston, Inc., 302 F.Supp. 161 (D.Me.1969), the plaintiffs, citizens of Maine, each transferred 1% of his claim to an Oregon citizen (a law school classmate of their Maine attorney), and the Oregon citizen then joined as a plaintiff in an action against an Oregon defendant in a Maine state court. The admitted purpose of the transfer was to prevent removal, yet Judge Gignoux denied a motion to remand the case to the state court. He managed to distinguish each of the Supreme Court cases cited above (as involving either total assignments or state-court approved appointments), and relied on the Kramer rationale as well as on cases in which "fraudulent joinder" of an in-state defendant failed to preclude removal. As to the partial transfer in the case before him, "the essential diversity of citizenship of the parties at bar has not been vitiated by plaintiffs' sham transaction" (p. 166). The case was noted at 83 Harv.L.Rev. 465 (1969), and has been followed in several other districts. See, *e.g.*, Carter v. Seaboard Coast Line R.R., 318 F.Supp. 368 (D.S.C.1970); *cf.* Miller v. Perry, 456 F.2d 63 (4th Cir.1972) (criticizing and distinguishing Mecom and holding that plaintiff's appointment of a North Carolina administrator did not preclude removal to a federal court by North Carolina defendants). See generally Wright, Federal Courts § 31, at 170–75 (4th ed. 1983).

SECTION 5. THE FUTURE OF DIVERSITY JURISDICTION

NOTE ON THE PRESENT–DAY UTILITY OF THE JURISDICTION

(1) Does Erie R.R. v. Tompkins weaken or strengthen the case for limiting or abolishing the diversity jurisdiction?[1] For a review of the problem, written after Erie and before the 1948 revision of the Judicial Code, see Wechsler, *Federal Jurisdiction and the Revision of the Judicial Code*, 13 Law & Contemp.Prob., 216, 234–40 (1948):

"Those who defend the jurisdiction point, of course, to the original fear of prejudice against the litigant from out of state and argue that the danger is not gone today. I share the view that this provides an insufficient answer, that when this sentiment exists and works unfairness, the protec-

---

1. The controversy over the diversity jurisdiction did not begin with the Erie decision. For conflicting views in the decade prior to Erie, see Frankfurter, *Distribution of Judicial Power between United States and State Courts*, 13 Corn.L.Q. 499, 520–30 (1928); Yntema & Jaffin, *Preliminary Analysis of Concurrent Jurisdiction*, 79 U.Pa.L.Rev. 869 (1931); Frankfurter, *A Note on Diversity Jurisdiction—In Reply to Professor Yntema*, 79 U.Pa.L.Rev. 1097 (1931); *Limiting Jurisdiction of Federal Courts—Pending Bills—Comments by Members of Chicago University Law Faculty*, 31 Mich.L.Rev. 59 (1932); Charles E. Clark, *Diversity of Citizenship Jurisdiction of the Federal Courts*, 19 A.B.A.J. 499 (1933); Ball, *Revision of Federal Diversity Jurisdiction*, 28 Ill.L.Rev. 356 (1933).

For a summary of earlier views, see Frankfurter & Landis, The Business of the Supreme Court 86–102, 136–41 (1928).

tion must be found, as in the case of other prejudices threatening administration of state justice, in state appellate processes—including, when due process is denied, review by the Supreme Court. It is, indeed, a rather startling thought that this least troublesome of all the prejudices should be the basis of a special federal forum which none of the hostilities that flow from faction, interest, race, or creed is deemed sufficient to provide. But even if the prejudice hypothesis is thought to warrant federal intervention, it is quite plain that the diversity jurisdiction is not defined in terms that are responsive to the theory.

" * * * What is needed is a total reconsideration of the jurisdiction, guided by the principle that federal judicial energy should be preserved for vindication of those interests which, because the Congress has considered them of national importance, have become the subject of the federal substantive law. * * *

"There is, I think, a solid case for preservation of the jurisdiction in any instance where a concrete showing of state prejudice can be established. There may be cases, too, where there is need for process that outruns state borders, as in the interpleader under present law. I do not argue that diversity should not be utilized to grant a federal forum on such principles. To do so is to premise federal intervention on a current finding of a state inadequacy. The problem is to limit intervention to the situations where it is in fact responsive to such need.

"A program of this kind does not, it must be recognized, present solid political attraction. No major economic interest now feels outraged by diversity jurisdiction, as in the days when it was portion of the target in labor's fight against the federal injunction. And Erie v. Tompkins operates to keep down deep resentment founded on the overt nullification of state law. Support must come, therefore, from the disinterested sources, the judiciary and the bar—including the law members of the Congress— content to view the issue in its right dimension as a problem of the uses of the federal courts. Such support may be forthcoming at a time when there is widespread interest in the organization of the federal government and the surrender of unnecessary functions now in federal hands."

(2) Think about the possible uses of the diversity jurisdiction:

(a) *As a vehicle for building up and administering a uniform body of judge-made law in areas in which Congress either has not legislated or could not.*

This was the great experiment of Swift v. Tyson on which, presumably, the books are now closed.

(b) *As a means of encouraging out-of-state individuals and enterprises to engage in local investment and other activities, by providing an assurance of impartial decision of disputes growing out of those activities.*

Notice the varying kinds of injustice against which safeguard may be desired: *e.g.,* invocation of unjust or discriminatory rules of law; unjust application of law to the facts; delays and inefficiencies in judicial administration.

Consider the other instruments of federal protection against these evils: *e.g.,* the Privileges and Immunities Clause of Article IV, § 2; the Privileges and Immunities Clause of the Fourteenth Amendment; the

Commerce Clause; the Due Process Clause of the Fourteenth Amendment; the Equal Protection Clause.

In view of these safeguards on the one hand, and in view of the lessening of provincialism and the improvement of state judicial systems on the other hand, is there substantial present need on this score for maintaining the diversity jurisdiction?[2]

(c) *As a means of providing for the just resolution of conflicts of laws in controversies between citizens of different states.*

Was Klaxon Co. v. Stentor Elec. Mfg. Co., 313 U.S. 487 (1941), p. 791, *supra*, a mistake? Should legislative or judicial action be taken under the Full Faith and Credit Clause to achieve the suggested objective?

(d) *As a means of facilitating the settlement of controversies that because of the multiplicity of parties and their diversity of citizenship, cannot be effectually settled in the courts of any one state.*

Consider the distinctive function served by the Federal Interpleader Act and various provisions of the federal rules with respect to multi-party litigation.

Are there amendments of the Judicial Code that would enable this function to be better performed?

(e) *As a means of assuring out-of-state litigants and their attorneys that a familiar procedural system will be available for the adjudication of their disputes.*

The adoption of the Federal Rules of Civil Procedure in 1938 made it possible to think about this objective as a justification for the jurisdiction. Has its value been undercut by the extent to which those very rules have influenced the development of procedural systems in virtually every state?

(f) *As a means of facilitating interchange between state and federal systems on matters of substance and procedure.*

For discussion of the possible values of diversity jurisdiction in supporting the "migration of ideas" between state and federal courts, see Shapiro, *Federal Diversity Jurisdiction: A Survey and a Proposal*, 91 Harv.L.Rev. 317, 324–27 (1977). See also Posner, note 2, *supra*, at 144, concluding that "[e]ven in the years since the Erie decision eliminated or, more realistically, confined their creative lawmaking role in diversity cases, the federal courts have made a disproportionate contribution to the shaping of the common law * * *."

2. A provision of the former removal statute, tracing back to the Act of March 2, 1867, 14 Stat. 559, authorized a defendant to remove a case "when it shall be made to appear to said district court that from prejudice or local influence he will not be able to obtain justice" in any available state court. This provision was repealed in 1948, the revisers saying in their notes that provisions "born of the bitter sectional feelings engendered by the Civil War and the Reconstruction period, have no place in the jurisprudence of a nation since united by three wars against foreign powers." If the revisers were correct in their conclusion that specifically demonstrated local prejudice was an inappropriate ground of federal jurisdiction, what of presumed local prejudice?

For the view that some diversity jurisdiction may be warranted not so much by the danger of prejudice against all out-of-staters as by regional or sectional prejudices, see the ALI Study, discussed in Paragraph (3), *infra*. For an argument that the diversity jurisdiction may be justified in at least those situations in which a state's residents (including the judges they have chosen) may have an *economic* incentive to discriminate against nonresidents, see Posner, The Federal Courts: Crisis and Reform 175–77 (1985).

Are there other uses of the diversity jurisdiction to which consideration should be given? Should it matter if the federal courts of first instance are in fact, or are perceived to be, of higher quality than their state counterparts? For an argument that it should not, see Friendly, Federal Jurisdiction: A General View 145–47 (1973).

(3) Concern with the questions of policy raised by the scope of the diversity jurisdiction was brought to a head, once again, in 1968 by the recommendations of the ALI Study. The Study considered the diversity jurisdiction in the context of current conditions and concluded that the goal of encouraging free movement and business activity throughout the country had been "spectacularly achieved", and that abrogation of the diversity jurisdiction today would not give rise to significant apprehension about crossing state borders. It recognized, however, that the pledge of federal justice to travelers from other states was "woven into the fabric of our society" and "should not lightly be withdrawn". Further, it saw the jurisdiction as guarding against the still-existing dangers of prejudice towards those from far-removed sections of the country and against other possible shortcomings of state justice for which the out-of-stater could not be held responsible and which were beyond his power to remedy. Finally, the Study noted that whatever the actual defects of state justice, the out-of-stater (and especially the alien) who loses his case is far less likely to blame his defeat on the bias or incompetence of the tribunal if his case is tried in a federal court. See ALI Study 105–08.

After rejecting other arguments in favor of diversity, the Study proposed a series of changes designed to bring the jurisdiction into harmony with this rationale. In some respects, the Study recommended expansion of the jurisdiction.[3] At the same time, it concluded that invocation of diversity jurisdiction by persons who had close ties with the forum state was inconsistent with the underlying rationale of diversity jurisdiction and should not be allowed. Thus one who was a "citizen" of the forum state under present definitions would be barred from invoking the jurisdiction. Invocation would also be barred by out-of-state corporations and other businesses having "local establishments" (as defined) in the state, if the suit arose out of the activities of that establishment, and by persons who regularly commuted to work in the state (proposed § 1302). In such instances, the Study argued, there was no basis for overcoming the normal presumption that the proper allocation of functions in a federal system requires state law cases to be tried in the state courts.

The response of the profession to the recommendations of the ALI Study was mixed.[4] By far the most detailed analysis of those recommendations was Currie, *The Federal Courts and the American Law Institute*, 36 U.Chi.L.Rev. 1, 268 (1968, 1969). Largely disenchanted with the diversity aspects of the proposals, and horrified at the complexity of the new multiparty provisions (see note 3, *supra*), Currie concluded that "the impossibili-

---

3. Most notable was a proposed new head of federal jurisdiction designed to cover multi-party, multi-state cases that were thought to fall beyond the reach of the state courts. (See proposed §§ 2371–76.) For a simpler, and broader, proposal, see Rowe & Sibley, *Beyond Diversity: Federal Multistate, Multiparty Jurisdiction*, 135 U.Pa.L.Rev. 7 (1987).

4. Compare, *e.g.*, Frank, *For Maintaining Diversity Jurisdiction*, 73 Yale L.J. 7 (1963), and Moore & Weckstein, *Diversity Jurisdiction: Past, Present, and Future*, 43 Texas L.Rev. 1 (1964), with, *e.g.*, Wright, *Restructuring Federal Jurisdiction: The American Law Institute Proposals*, 26 W. & L.L.Rev. 185 (1969).

ty of drafting sensible and workable limits for diversity cases is reason enough to abandon the jurisdiction." *Id.* at 6.

(4) In 1978, a bill abolishing the diversity jurisdiction, except in alienage and interpleader cases, was approved by the House of Representatives, H.R. 9622, 95th Cong., 2d Sess. (1978), but died in a subcommittee of the Senate Judiciary Committee.[5] Similar bills have been introduced in later Congresses, but none has been approved in either House.

Renewed interest in legislative change has been accompanied by extensive commentary. Among those favoring abolition of diversity jurisdiction under § 1332(a)(1) were Judge Friendly in Federal Jurisdiction: A General View 3–4, 139–52 (1973), and Chief Justice Burger in *Annual Report on the State of the Judiciary,* 62 A.B.A.J. 443, 444 (1976). See also Rowe, *Abolishing Diversity Jurisdiction: Positive Side Effects and Potential for Further Reforms,* 92 Harv.L.Rev. 963, 966 (1979), concluding that abolition is supported not only by arguments traditionally made—"the lack of positive reasons for it, the need for a reduction in federal caseloads and jury trials, and the appropriateness of merging more fully the power to interpret state law with the responsibility of applying it"—but also by the "additional effects of abolition—elimination or reduction of some of the most vexing problems in federal practice, demystified interpretations, and facilitation of reforms." [6]

With the foregoing, compare, *e.g.,* Frank, *The Case for Diversity Jurisdiction,* 16 Harv.J.Legis. 403 (1979); Posner, The Federal Courts: Crisis and Reform 139–47 (1985) (advocating adoption of a higher jurisdictional amount, together with the ALI's proposed limitations on invocation of diversity jurisdiction); Shapiro, Paragraph (2)(f), *supra,* at 319 (suggesting a " 'local option plan,' under which each federal district would have limited freedom to retain, curtail, or virtually eliminate diversity jurisdiction within its borders").

The number of diversity cases filed in the district courts has continued to increase, but the ratio of such cases to all civil actions filed in those courts has been declining—from approximately ⅓ in 1960 to ¼ today. See the discussion of the business of the district courts at pp. 50–55, *supra.*

(5) Only in recent decades has there been any empirical investigation of the reasons why litigants and their lawyers choose the federal courts in diversity cases. Two of the earliest studies, in the 1960s, seemed to point toward quite different conclusions. Summers, *Analysis of Factors that Influence Choice of Forum in Diversity Cases,* 47 Iowa L.Rev. 933 (1962), found that of a total of 164 reasons given by Wisconsin attorneys for the choice of a federal court in 82 cases, local bias against a nonresident client was indicated only 7 times, and was never the sole factor. Geographical convenience, on the other hand, was listed 30 times; better discovery 26 times; and higher awards 23 times. In the other study, Note, *The Choice*

---

5. See *Hearings on S. 2094. S. 2389 and H.R. 9622 Before the Subcommittee on Improvements in Judicial Machinery of the Senate Comm. on the Judiciary,* 95th Cong., 2d Sess. (1978), especially the statement and testimony of Professor Wright at 44–63; *Hearings on S. 679 Before the Senate Comm. on the Judiciary,* 96th Cong., 1st Sess. (1979), especially the statement of Professor Wechsler at 144–53.

6. Many of the authorities favoring the general abolition of diversity jurisdiction support its retention in alienage and interpleader cases; Professor Rowe goes one step further and urges that any requirement of complete diversity in alienage cases should be eliminated, 92 Harv.L.Rev. at 966–68.

Between State and Federal Court in Diversity Cases in Virginia, 51 Va.L. Rev. 178 (1965), local prejudice against an out-of-state client was listed as a reason for choosing a federal court by 60.3% of the surveyed attorneys; local prejudice against an out-of-state adversary was indicated as a reason for preferring a state court by 52.1% of the same group. (The studies differed in methodology in several respects, one of which was that the Virginia study asked attorneys about the factors that *would* lead them to prefer a federal or state court, rather than—as with the Wisconsin study— the factors that *did* influence them in actual cases.)

In a later survey, taken in Cook County, Illinois, it was reported, *inter alia,* that 40% of the surveyed attorneys who had filed diversity cases (originally or on removal) in federal court cited "local bias against an out-of-state resident" as a relevant factor in making the choice of courts. Goldman & Marks, *Diversity Jurisdiction and Local Bias: A Preliminary Empirical Inquiry,* 9 J.Leg.Stud. 93, 97–99 (1980). Although the authors suggest that "many of the reports of local bias ∗ ∗ ∗ are likely to be confused with other types of bias," they conclude that pending further investigation, "the evidence from this study would seem to indicate that the door to the federal courthouse be kept open for out-of-state litigants" (p. 104).

Finally, in Bumiller, *Choice of Forum in Diversity Cases: Analysis of a Survey and Implications for Reform,* 15 Law & Soc'y Rev. 749 (1980–81), the author found "local bias" to be a significant factor in the choice of a federal court only in rural districts. This and other variables indicating the greater utility of diversity jurisdiction within particular geographical areas led her to support the local option plan proposed in Shapiro, Paragraph (2) (f), *supra.*

For the results of a survey of federal judges on the question whether diversity jurisdiction should be retained, in whole or in part, or abolished, see Shapiro, Paragraph 2(f), *supra,* at 332–39. For the results of a survey of lawyers, see *Lawpoll,* 66 A.B.A.J. 148, 149 (1980).

Chapter XIV

ADDITIONAL PROBLEMS OF DISTRICT COURT JURISDICTION

SECTION 1. CHALLENGES TO JURISDICTION

MANSFIELD, COLDWATER & LAKE MICHIGAN RY.
v. SWAN

111 U.S. 379, 4 S.Ct. 510, 28 L.Ed. 462 (1884).
In Error to the Circuit Court of the United States for the
Northern District of Ohio.

MR. JUSTICE MATTHEWS delivered the opinion of the Court.

This was an action at law originally brought in the court of common pleas of Fulton county, Ohio, by John Swan, S.C. Rose, F.M. Hutchinson, and Robert McMann, as partners under the name of Swan, Rose & Co., against the plaintiffs in error. The object of the suit was the recovery of damages for alleged breaches of a contract for the construction of the railroad of the defendants below. It was commenced June 10, 1874. Afterwards, on October 28, 1879, the cause being at issue, the defendants below filed a petition for its removal to the circuit court of the United States. They aver therein that one of the petitioners is a corporation created by the laws of Ohio alone, and the other, a corporation consolidated under the laws of Michigan and Ohio, the constituent corporations having been organized under the laws of those states respectively, and that they are, consequently, citizens, one of Ohio, and one of both Michigan and Ohio. It is also alleged, in the petition for removal, "that the plaintiffs, John Swan and Frank M. Hutchinson, at the time of the commencement of this suit, were, and still are, citizens of the state of Pennsylvania; that the said Robert H. McMann was then (according to your petitioners' recollection) a citizen of the state of Ohio, but that he is not now a citizen of that state, but where he now resides or whereof he is now a citizen (except that he is a citizen of one of the states or territories comprising the United States) your petitioners are unable to state; * * *" The petition, being accompanied with a satisfactory bond, was allowed, and an order made for the removal of the cause. The plaintiffs below afterwards, on December 13, 1879, moved to remand the cause on the ground, among others, that the circuit court had no jurisdiction, because the "real and substantial controversy in the cause is between real and substantial parties who are citizens of the same state and not of different states." But the motion was denied. Subsequently a trial took place upon the merits, which resulted in a verdict and judgment in favor of the plaintiffs, the defendants in error, for $238,116.18 against the defendants jointly, and the further sum of $116,468.32 against one of them. Many exceptions to the rulings of the court during the trial were taken, and are embodied in a bill of exceptions, on which errors have been assigned, and the writ of error is prosecuted by the defendants below to reverse this judgment.

An examination of the record, however, discloses that the circuit court had no jurisdiction to try the action, and as, for this reason, we are constrained to reverse the judgment, we have not deemed it within our province to consider any other questions involved in it. It appears from the petition for removal, and not otherwise by the record elsewhere, that, at the time the action was first brought in the state court, one of the plaintiffs, and a necessary party, McMann, was a citizen of Ohio, the same state of which the defendants were citizens. It does not affirmatively appear that at the time of the removal he was a citizen of any other state. The averment is that he was not then a citizen of Ohio, and that his actual citizenship was unknown, except that he was a citizen of one of the states or territories. It is consistent with this statement that he was not a citizen of any state. He may have been a citizen of a territory; and, if so, the requisite citizenship would not exist. New Orleans v. Winter, 1 Wheat. 91. According to the decision in Gibson v. Bruce, 108 U.S. 561, the difference of citizenship on which the right of removal depends must have existed at the time when the suit was begun, as well as at the time of the removal; and, according to the uniform decisions of this court, the jurisdiction of the circuit court fails, unless the necessary citizenship affirmatively appears in the pleadings or elsewhere in the record. Grace v. American Cent. Ins. Co., 109 U.S. 278–283; Robertson v. Cease, 97 U.S. 646. It was error, therefore, in the circuit court to assume jurisdiction in the case, and not to remand it, on the motion of the plaintiffs below.

It is true that the plaintiffs below, against whose objection the error was committed, do not complain of being prejudiced by it, and it seems to be an anomaly and a hardship that the party at whose instance it was committed should be permitted to derive an advantage from it; but the rule, springing from the nature and limits of the judicial power of the United States, is inflexible and without exception which requires this court, of its own motion, to deny its own jurisdiction, and, in the exercise of its appellate power, that of all other courts of the United States, in all cases where such jurisdiction does not affirmatively appear in the record on which, in the exercise of that power, it is called to act. On every writ of error or appeal the first and fundamental question is that of jurisdiction, first, of this court, and then of the court from which the record comes. This question the court is bound to ask and answer for itself, even when not otherwise suggested, and without respect to the relation of the parties to it. This rule was adopted in Capron v. Van Noorden, 2 Cranch, 126, decided in 1804, where a judgment was reversed on the application of the party against whom it had been rendered in the circuit court, for want of the allegation of his own citizenship, which he ought to have made to establish the jurisdiction which he had invoked. * * *

In the Dred Scott Case, 19 How. 393–400, it was decided that a judgment of the circuit court, upon the sufficiency of a plea in abatement, denying its jurisdiction, was open for review upon a writ of error sued out by the party in whose favor the plea had been overruled. And in this view Mr. Justice Curtis, in his dissenting opinion, concurred; and we adopt from that opinion the following statement of the law on the point: " * * * The true question is not what either of the parties may be allowed to do, but whether this court will affirm or reverse a judgment of the circuit court on the merits, when it appears on the record, by a plea to the jurisdiction, that it is a case to which the judicial power of the United States does not extend. The course of the court is, when no motion is made by either party, on its own motion, to reverse such a judgment for want of jurisdiction, not only in cases where it is shown, negatively, by a plea to the jurisdiction, that jurisdiction does not exist, but even when it does not appear, affirmatively, that it does exist. Pequignot v. Pennsylvania R. Co., 16 How. 104. It acts upon the principle that the judicial power of the United States must not be exerted in a case to which it does not extend, even if both parties desire to have it exerted. Cutler v. Rae, 7 How. 729. I consider, therefore, that when there was a plea to the jurisdiction of the circuit court in a case brought here by a writ of error, the first duty of this court is, *sua sponte*, if not moved to it by either party, to examine the sufficiency of that plea, and thus to take care that neither the circuit court nor this court shall use the judicial power of the United States in a case to which the constitution and laws of the United States have not extended that power" [19 How. 566].

This is precisely applicable to the present case, for the motion of the plaintiffs below to remand the cause was equivalent to a special plea to the jurisdiction of the court; but the doctrine applies equally in every case where the jurisdiction does not appear from the record. * * *

The judgment of the circuit court is accordingly reversed, with costs against the plaintiffs in error, and the cause is remanded to the circuit court, with directions to render a judgment against them for costs in that court, and to remand the cause to the court of common pleas of Fulton county, Ohio; and it is so ordered.

––––––––––

NOTE ON CHALLENGING THE EXISTENCE OF FEDERAL JURISDICTION IN REGULAR COURSE OF TRIAL AND APPELLATE REVIEW

(1) Requirements for alleging jurisdiction and the proper manner for raising the defense of lack of jurisdiction are specified in Rules 8(a) and 12(b)(1) of the Federal Rules of Civil Procedure. Rule 12(h)(3) requires dismissal whenever it appears that jurisdiction over the subject matter is lacking.

(2) The principle declared in the Mansfield case and codified in the Federal Rules is reflected not only in the requirements of proper pleadings and requests for review but in the accepted form of briefing and oral argument. The first duty of counsel is to make clear to the court the basis of its jurisdiction as a federal court. The first duty of the court is to make sure that jurisdiction exists. If the record fails to disclose a basis for federal jurisdiction, the court not only will but must refuse to proceed further with the determination of the merits of the controversy unless the failure can be cured. This is true whether the case is at the trial stage or the appellate stage, and whether the defect is called to the court's attention "by suggestion of the parties or otherwise." The rest of this book might be

filled with citations and thumbnail abstracts of cases illustrating the application of this principle.[1]

This is established practice. Is it fetishism?[2] Or is it grounded on solid considerations of policy and of legislative and judicial statesmanship? Why should not a party who has invoked federal jurisdiction, or failed seasonably to object to it, be held to have waived any defect, or be estopped from asserting it?

(3) A federal court always has jurisdiction to decide whether it has jurisdiction and, if it decides that it does not, to take appropriate action. And a federal appellate court has jurisdiction to decide whether the court or courts below had jurisdiction and, if not, to take appropriate action. Commonly the appropriate disposition will be to reverse the judgment under review with directions to the court of first instance to dismiss the action, or if it was a removed action to remand it to the state court for want of jurisdiction. But what if jurisdiction exists in fact but merely has not been properly alleged?

At the time of the Mansfield case, and prior to the Act of March 3, 1915, c. 90, 38 Stat. 956, the appellate court in this situation had no choice but reversal. In an original action the trial court might thereafter permit an appropriate amendment of the pleadings, if it were satisfied of the existence of jurisdiction in fact. Robertson v. Cease, 97 U.S. 646, 650–51 (1878). But not in a removed action. Cameron v. Hodges, 127 U.S. 322, 326 (1888). Why the difference?

The 1915 act provided that in a case in which "diverse citizenship in fact existed at the time the suit was brought or removed, though defectively alleged, either party may amend at any stage of the proceedings and in the appellate court upon such terms as the court may impose, so as to show on the record" the existence of jurisdiction. Why the discrimination in favor of diversity litigation?

The present statute, 28 U.S.C. § 1653, provides generally that "defective allegations of jurisdiction may be amended, upon terms, in the trial or appellate courts".

(4) A lack of jurisdiction at the time the complaint is filed may be cured by a subsequent statutory change. In Andrus v. Charlestone Stone Products Co., Inc., 436 U.S. 604, 607–08 n. 6 (1978), and in Duke Power Co. v. Carolina Environmental Study Group, Inc., 438 U.S. 59, 70 n. 14 (1978), the Supreme Court raised the issue of federal jurisdiction *sua sponte*. It

1. For a noteworthy but evidently unsuccessful effort by one lower court to depart from the principle, see Paragraph (6), *infra*.

The Supreme Court itself has shown no tendency to retreat explicitly from the principle. See, *e.g.,* Firestone Tire and Rubber Co. v. Risjord, 449 U.S. 368, 379–80 and n. 15 (1981), holding that a "jurisdictional ruling [that an appeal could not be heard for lack of a final judgment] may never be made prospective only." But the Court has not infrequently overlooked some jurisdictional issues. Thus before the 1976 repeal of the jurisdictional amount requirement under § 1331, the Court often dealt with a case without reference to that requirement, even though a substantial question appeared to exist. See, *e.g.,* Flast v. Cohen, 392 U.S. 83 (1968); Kleindienst v. Mandel, 408 U.S. 753 (1972); United States v. Richardson, 418 U.S. 166 (1974). And the Court has occasionally refused to resolve an unusually difficult issue of jurisdiction in a case where decision in another, related case effectively disposed of the action on the merits. See Philbrook v. Glodgett, 421 U.S. 707 (1975); Secretary of the Navy v. Avrech, 418 U.S. 676 (1974).

2. See Ryan, *The Dajongi Experience: A Comparative Study in Federal Jurisdiction,* 18 Stan.L.Rev. 451 (1966).

then held that failure to assert any "amount in controversy" in actions against federal officers instituted in 1973 was immaterial on the basis of the 1976 amendment to § 1331 eliminating the jurisdictional amount requirement in such actions—an amendment adopted several years after each suit had been commenced. The absence from each complaint of any explicit reference to § 1331 was deemed insignificant because the facts alleged were sufficient to establish jurisdiction under the section.

(5) At the time of the Mansfield decision, Section 5 of the Act of March 3, 1875, c. 137, 18 Stat. 470, 472, provided:

"That if, in any suit commenced in a circuit court or removed from a State court to a circuit court of the United States, it shall appear to the satisfaction of said circuit court, at any time after such suit has been brought or removed thereto, that such suit does not really and substantially involve a dispute or controversy properly within the jurisdiction of said circuit court, or that the parties to said suit have been improperly or collusively made or joined, either as plaintiffs or defendants, for the purpose of creating a case cognizable or removable under this act, the said circuit court shall proceed no further therein, but shall dismiss the suit or remand it to the court from which it was removed as justice may require, and shall make such order as to costs as shall be just * * *."

This provision appeared as Section 37 of the Judicial Code of 1911 and as Section 80 of the original Title 28 of the United States Code. It was relied upon in innumerable cases decided between 1875 and 1948 in which the court at either the trial or the appellate stage, on its own motion or on the belated suggestion of a party, took notice of a defect of jurisdiction and dismissed or directed dismissal of the action. It was also the primary ground for holding that the burden of proof of all the elements requisite for federal jurisdiction rested on the party invoking the jurisdiction. See McNutt v. General Motors Acc. Corp., 298 U.S. 178 (1936). Does this mean that these results would have been different in the absence of the provision?

The question is not academic. In the 1948 revision, the provision was combined with the famous assignee clause (see pp. 362, 1689, *supra*) and the two reduced to the following sentence [§ 1359. Parties collusively joined or made]:

"A district court shall not have jurisdiction of a civil action in which any party, by assignment or otherwise, has been improperly or collusively made or joined to invoke the jurisdiction of such court."

The revisers explained their treatment of Section 80 as follows:

"Provisions of section 80 * * * for dismissal of an action not really and substantially involving a dispute or controversy within the jurisdiction of a district court, were omitted as unnecessary. Any court will dismiss a case not within its jurisdiction when its attention is drawn to the fact, or even on its own motion."

Were the revisers well-advised in what they did?

(6) The revisers' prophecy—self-fulfilling or otherwise—has generally prevailed. The federal courts have continued to accept jurisdictional attacks at any time, *e.g.,* even when the party that had invoked federal jurisdiction challenged it after losing the case on the merits, American Fire

& Cas. Co. v. Finn, 341 U.S. 6 (1951),[3] or when the objection was withheld until after the statute of limitations had run on a possible state court action, Knee v. Chemical Leaman Tank Lines, 293 F.Supp. 1094 (E.D.Pa. 1968).

One effort to carve out an exception occurred in Di Frischia v. New York Central R.R., 279 F.2d 141 (3d Cir.1960). In this case, defendant objected to the jurisdiction of the court, asserting a lack of diversity. It then filed a stipulation withdrawing the objection, and the case proceeded through pretrial stages. Twenty-three months later, after the statute of limitations had run, defendant renewed its original objection. The trial court dismissed the action after hearing, but the Third Circuit reversed, tartly commenting that "[a] defendant may not play fast and loose with the judicial machinery and deceive the courts" (p. 144). See also Klee v. Pittsburgh & W. Va. Ry. Co., 22 F.R.D. 252 (W.D.Pa.1958), and Stephens, *Estoppel to Deny Federal Jurisdiction—Klee and Di Frischia Break Ground,* 68 Dick.L.Rev. 39 (1963). Is this response to a "fast and loose" play consistent with the Mansfield rule? For an interesting argument that it is, as well as for a narrow reading of Mansfield generally,[4] see Dobbs, *Beyond Bootstrap: Foreclosing the Issue of Subject–Matter Jurisdiction Before Final Judgment,* 51 Minn.L.Rev. 491 (1967). *Cf.* Dobbs, *The Decline of Jurisdiction by Consent,* 40 N.C.L.Rev. 49 (1961).

But the Di Frishcia assault on the principle has not proved generative. See, *e.g.,* Sadat v. Mertes, 615 F.2d 1176, 1189 (7th Cir.1980); Eisler v. Stritzler, 535 F.2d 148, 151–52 (1st Cir.1976); Lackawanna Refuse Removal, Inc. v. Proctor & Gamble Paper Products Co., 86 F.R.D. 330 (M.D.Pa.1979).[5] And it was at least implicitly disapproved by the Supreme Court in Owen Equipment & Erection Co. v. Kroger, 437 U.S. 365 (1978), p. 1679, *supra.* Defendant Owen's answer had admitted diversity jurisdiction, but on the third day of trial it appeared that the requisite diversity did not exist, and Owen then moved to dismiss for want of jurisdiction. The Third Circuit, relying in part on the view that Owen's conduct created an estoppel, affirmed denial of the motion. The Supreme Court reversed, concluding (p. 377 n. 21): "Our holding is that the District Court lacked power to entertain the respondent's lawsuit against the petitioner. Thus, the asserted inequity in the respondent's alleged concealment of its citizenship is irrelevant."

(7) The American Law Institute proposed to overturn the Mansfield rule and to preclude raising of jurisdictional issues by the parties or the courts after the beginning of trial except in specified circumstances—

3. The Court of Appeals did subsequently enter a new judgment on the original verdict in this case after plaintiff had dismissed as to the party whose presence had barred jurisdiction. Finn v. American Fire & Cas. Co., 207 F.2d 113 (5th Cir.1953).

4. Recall that in Mansfield, the jurisdictional defect was apparent on the face of the record. (Also, as the Supreme Court noted, the question of jurisdiction had been raised below by the plaintiffs. Plaintiffs, of course, did not press the issue on the defendant's appeal.)

5. But see Ferguson v. Neighborhood Housing Services, Inc., 780 F.2d 549, 551 (8th Cir.1986). In this case, the defendant sought on the eve of trial to amend its answer to withdraw its admission that it was an employer subject to the Fair Labor Standards Act. A divided court of appeals upheld the district court's refusal to permit the amendment, holding that although parties could not confer jurisdiction by consent, a party could be held bound to an admission of a "jurisdictional fact."

Is the suggested distinction valid? Is the fact at issue in the Ferguson case "jurisdictional" in the same sense as the question of citizenship in a diversity case?

principally involving either previously unknown and unavailable facts or collusion between the parties. ALI Study § 1386. The Commentary gave as the "principal purpose of the revisions * * * to provide every incentive to both sides to seek resolution of the issue of subject-matter jurisdiction prior to the commencement of trial. At the same time, an effort has been made not to preclude the raising of issues even after the beginning of trial if those issues could not reasonably be expected to have been raised and resolved earlier."

Would the proposed jurisdictional foreclosure be constitutional? In a case that was shown, while still pending, to fall outside the competence of the federal courts under Article III?

(8) The materials in this section do not deal with the problem of challenging a district court's assumption of jurisdiction, or its refusal to assume jurisdiction, either by interlocutory appeal or by prohibition or mandamus from a higher court. As to this, *see* in addition to Ex parte Peru, p. 347, *supra*, the materials in Chap. XV, Sec. 1, *infra*.

(9) On challenges to subject-matter jurisdiction after final judgment, see Chap. XII, pp. 1600–03, *supra*.

NOTE ON RAISING OTHER QUESTIONS OF "JURISDICTION" IN THE REGULAR COURSE OF THE PROCEEDING

The prior Note dealt only with questions of the jurisdiction of the court as a federal court. Usually, these are questions whether the case is founded on federal law or whether the requisite diversity of citizenship exists. If the jurisdictional amount requirement is applicable, they include questions of whether the requisite amount is involved.

Other types of questions, however, may be raised which are in some sense questions of jurisdiction—of the power of the federal tribunal to decide this kind of case.[1] Are these questions which the court should raise on its own motion, treating the objection as beyond the power of the parties to waive? The trial court only? Or the appellate court also? To which, if any, of them is Rule 12(h) applicable? Which, if any, of them is within the principle relied on by the revisers that "any court will dismiss a case not within its jurisdiction when its attention is called to the fact"?

Consider the following other types of objections:

(1) *Lack of personal jurisdiction.* Look again at Rules 12(b) and 12(h). See also Insurance Corp. of Ireland Ltd. v. Compagnie des Bauxites de Guinee, 456 U.S. 694 (1982); Petrowski v. Hawkeye–Security Ins. Co., 350 U.S. 495 (1956).

(2) *Improper venue.* In Neirbo Co. v. Bethlehem Shipbuilding Corp., 308 U.S. 165, 167–68 (1939), Justice Frankfurter said:

"The jurisdiction of the federal courts—their power to adjudicate—is a grant of authority to them by Congress and thus beyond the scope of litigants to confer. But the locality of a law suit—the place where judicial

---

1. A related question is the extent to which state law may permit waiver of a challenge to state court authority based on federal grounds. See, *e.g.*, International Longshoremen's Ass'n v. Davis, 476 U.S. 380, 389 (1986) (defense that federal labor law preempts state law claim involves a "nonwaivable foreclosure of the state court's very jurisdiction to adjudicate").

authority may be exercised—though defined by legislation relates to the convenience of litigants and as such is subject to their disposition. * * * Section 51 [the then venue statute] 'merely accords to the defendant a personal privilege respecting the venue, or place of suit, which he may assert, or may waive, at his election.' * * *

"Being a privilege, it may be lost. It may be lost by failure to assert it seasonably, by formal submission in a cause, or by submission through conduct."[2]

(3) *Lack of equity jurisdiction.* Many cases say in substance what Justice Stone said in Di Giovanni v. Camden Fire Ins. Ass'n, 296 U.S. 64, 69 (1935):

" * * * Whether a suitor is entitled to equitable relief in the federal courts, other jurisdictional requirements being satisfied, is strictly not a question of jurisdiction in the sense of the power of a federal court to act. It is a question only of the merits; whether the case is one for the peculiar type of relief which only a federal court of equity is competent to give."

(4) *Abstention.* See Chap. X, p. 1405, *supra.*

(5) *Sovereign Immunity.* See Chap. IX, p. 1213, *supra.*

(6) *Failure to Satisfy Statutory Conditions on Availability of Habeas Corpus.* In Sumner v. Mata, 449 U.S. 539, 547–48 n. 2 (1981), the Court said: "Whether or not the petitioner specifically directed the Court of Appeals' attention to [28 U.S.C.] § 2254(d)[3] makes no difference as to the outcome of this case. * * * [The provisions of the habeas corpus statute are jurisdictional and as stated in Louisville & N. Ry. v. Mottley, 211 U.S. 149, 152 (1908)] 'it is the duty of this Court to see to it that the jurisdiction of the [District Court], which is defined and limited by the statute, is not exceeded.' "

But in Granberry v. Greer, 107 S.Ct. 1671 (1987), the Court held that the statutory requirement of exhaustion of state remedies did not go to the jurisdiction of a federal court to entertain a habeas petition. At the same time, it held that when the state failed to raise an exhaustion claim, the federal court was not obligated to entertain the petition but rather had discretion to determine whether exhaustion should be required.

(7) *Justiciability.* Claims that a case is moot, or unripe, or that a plaintiff lacks standing, are considered nonwaivable. See generally the materials in Chap. II, *supra.*

2. In Leroy v. Great Western United Corp., 443 U.S. 173, 180 (1979), the Court chose to pretermit a difficult question of personal jurisdiction and to order dismissal on the ground of improper venue. It said: "The question of personal jurisdiction, which goes to the court's power to exercise control over the parties, is typically decided in advance of venue, which is primarily a matter of choosing a convenient forum. * * * On the other hand, neither personal jurisdiction nor venue is fundamentally preliminary in the sense that subject-matter jurisdiction is, for both are personal privileges of the defendant, rather than absolute strictures on the court, and both may be waived by the parties. * * * Accordingly, when there is a sound prudential justification for doing so, * * * a court may reverse the normal order of considering personal jurisdiction and venue."

See, further, Section 2 of this chapter.

3. This provision specifies what an applicant for habeas corpus must show in order to overcome the presumed correctness of a state court determination of a factual issue.

Are there any threads running through these diverse areas and holdings that make possible the formulation of general criteria with respect to waiver?

SECTION 2. PROCESS AND VENUE IN ORIGINAL ACTIONS

ROBERTSON v. RAILROAD LABOR BOARD

268 U.S. 619, 45 S.Ct. 621, 69 L.Ed. 1119 (1925).
Appeal from the District Court of the United States for the
Northern District of Illinois.

MR. JUSTICE BRANDEIS delivered the opinion of the Court.

[Robertson appealed from a decree of the district court overruling his motion to quash service of original process upon him in a suit brought by the Board to compel him to appear before it as a witness and to testify. The ground of the motion was that the district court for the northern district of Illinois lacked personal jurisdiction over him, since process had been served upon him in the northern district of Ohio where he resided.

[Robertson had previously failed to respond to a subpoena from the Board, served upon him in Ohio, commanding him to appear and testify on a day named at the Board's offices in Chicago. The present action was brought pursuant to § 310(b) of the Transportation Act of February 28, 1920, 41 Stat. 456, 472, which provided:

["In case of failure to comply with any subpoena [to testify] * * *, the Board may invoke the aid of any United States district court. Such court may thereupon order the witness to comply with the requirements of such subpoena * * *."]

* * * The case is here on appeal under section 238 of the Judicial Code (Comp.St. § 1215), the questions of jurisdiction having been duly certified. Whether the court acquired jurisdiction over Robertson is the only question requiring decision.

Robertson contends that by the term "any United States District Court" Congress meant any such court "of competent jurisdiction"; and that, under the applicable law, no District Court is of competent jurisdiction to compel a defendant to obey its decree except that of the district of which he is an inhabitant or of one in which he is found. The Board contends that Congress intended by the phrase to confer not only liberty to invoke the aid of the court for any district, but power to compel the person named as defendant to litigate in the district selected by the Board, although he is not a citizen or inhabitant of it and is not found therein. The question presented is one of statutory construction. Congress clearly has the power to authorize a suit under a federal law to be brought in any inferior federal court. Congress has power, likewise, to provide that the process of every District Court shall run into every part of the United States. Toland v. Sprague, 12 Pet. 300; United States v. Union Pacific R.R.

Co., 98 U.S. 569, 604. But it has not done so either by any general law or in terms by § 310 of Transportation Act 1920. The precise question is whether it has impliedly done so by that provision.

In a civil suit in personam, jurisdiction over the defendant, as distinguished from venue, implies, among other things, either voluntary appearance by him or service of process upon him at a place where the officer serving it has authority to execute a writ of summons. Under the general provisions of law, a United States District Court cannot issue process beyond the limits of the district. Harkness v. Hyde, 98 U.S. 476; Ex parte Graham, 3 Wash. 456. And a defendant in a civil suit can be subjected to its jurisdiction in personam only by service within the district. Toland v. Sprague, 12 Pet. 300, 330. Such was the general rule established by Judiciary Act Sept. 24, 1789, c. 20, § 11, 1 Stat. 73, 79, in accordance with the practice at the common law. Piquet v. Swan, 5 Mason, 35, 39 *et seq.*, Fed.Cas.No. 11,134. And such has been the general rule ever since. Munter v. Weil Corset Co., 261 U.S. 276, 279. No distinction has been drawn between the case where the plaintiff is the Government and where he is a private citizen.

Section 51 of the Judicial Code (Comp.St. § 1033) is a general provision regulating venue. The part pertinent here is that, with certain inapplicable exceptions, "no civil suit shall be brought in any District Court against any person by any original process or proceeding in any other district than that whereof he is an inhabitant." [2] It is obvious that jurisdiction, in the sense of personal service within a district where suit has been brought, does not dispense with the necessity of proper venue. It is equally obvious that proper venue does not eliminate the requisite of personal jurisdiction over the defendant. The general provision as to venue contained in Judicial Code, § 51, has been departed from in various specific provisions which allow the plaintiff, in actions not local in their nature, some liberty in the selection of venue. Unrestricted choice was conferred upon the Labor Board by the section of Transportation Act 1920, here involved (§ 310). So far as venue is concerned, there is no ambiguity in the words "any United States District Court."

Congress has also made a few clearly expressed and carefully guarded exceptions to the general rule of jurisdiction in personam stated above. In one instance, the Credit Mobilier Act March 3, 1873, c. 226, § 4, 17 Stat. 485, 509, it was provided that writs of subpoena to bring in parties defendant should run into any district. This broad power was to be exercised at the instance of the Attorney General in a single case in which, in order to give complete relief, it was necessary to join in one suit defendants living in different States. United States v. Union Pacific Railroad, 98 U.S. 569. Under similar circumstances, but only for the period of three years, authority was granted generally by Act Sept. 19, 1922, c. 345, 42 Stat. 849, to institute a civil suit by or on behalf of the United States, either in the district of the residence of one of the necessary defendants or in that in which the cause of action arose; and to serve the process upon a defendant in any district. The Sherman Act (Act July 2, 1890, c. 647, § 5, 26 Stat. 209, 210), provides that when "it shall appear to the court" in which a proceeding to restrain violations of the act is pending

---

2. . . . The rule applies even where it may result in barring the jurisdiction of every federal court because all the defen-

dants are indispensable parties. Shields v. Barrow, 17 How. 130, 140, 142 . . . .

"that the ends of justice require that other parties should be brought before the court," it may cause them to be summoned although they reside in some other district. The Clayton Act (Act Oct. 15, 1914, c. 323, § 15, 38 Stat. 730, 737), contains a like provision. But no act has come to our attention in which such power has been conferred in a proceeding in a Circuit or District Court where a private citizen is the sole defendant and where the plaintiff is at liberty to commence the suit in the district of which the defendant is an inhabitant or in which he can be found.

As the Railroad Labor Board is charged generally with the adjustment of disputes between carriers and their employees, it may prove desirable to hold hearings at any place within the United States; and power to do so was expressly conferred. The Board may demand answers or the production of documentary evidence from one who attends such a hearing. The contumacy of a witness appearing before the Board in any designated place of hearing was thus one contingency for which it was necessary to make provision. Congress also granted to the Labor Board in explicit language the broad power of compelling a person to come from any place in the United States to any designated place of hearing to furnish evidence. The refusal of such person, who might be in any district in the United States, to comply with such a subpoena was obviously a second contingency to be provided for. Unrestricted liberty of venue in invoking the aid of a District Court, referred to before, was clearly essential to the complete exercise of the Board's powers and the effective performance of its functions. Moreover, this unrestricted choice cannot subject to undue hardship any defendant actually found within the district in which the suit is brought. But no reason is suggested why Congress should have wished to compel every person summoned either to obey the Board's administrative order without question, or to litigate his right to refuse to do so in such district, however remote from his home or temporary residence, as the Board might select. The Interstate Commerce Commission which, throughout 38 years, has dealt in many different ways with most of the railroads of the United States, has never exercised, nor asserted, or sought to secure for itself, such broad powers.

We are of opinion that by the phrase "any District Court of the United States" Congress meant any such court "of competent jurisdiction." The phrase "any court" is frequently used in the federal statutes and has been interpreted under similar circumstances as meaning "any court of competent jurisdiction." By the general rule the jurisdiction of a District Court in personam has been limited to the district of which the defendant is an inhabitant or in which he can be found. It would be an extraordinary thing if, while guarding so carefully all departure from the general rule, Congress had conferred the exceptional power here invoked upon a board whose functions are purely advisory, and which enters the District Court, not to enforce a substantive right, but in an auxiliary proceeding to secure evidence from one who may be a stranger to the matter with which the Board is dealing. We think it has made no such extension by section 310 of Transportation Act 1920. It is not lightly to be assumed that Congress intended to depart from a long-established policy.

Reversed.

NOTE ON THE DEVELOPMENT OF THE RULES GOVERNING PROCESS AND VENUE IN THE DISTRICT COURTS

(1) Are there any constitutional limitations on the reach of process issuing from the district courts? Language in a number of Supreme Court opinions, including Robertson, indicates that there are not, at least within national boundaries. Could Congress then authorize any action within federal jurisdiction to be brought in any federal court, with nationwide process issuing from that court, regardless of the connections between the district, state, or territory in which the court sits and the claim asserted? Recall that territorial limitations on process rooted in notions of sovereignty, see Pennoyer v. Neff, 95 U.S. 714 (1877), have been supplemented, and to some extent superseded, by limitations based on principles of fairness and convenience, see International Shoe Co. v. Washington, 326 U.S. 310 (1945).[1] Are not such principles to be found in the Due Process Clause of the Fifth Amendment as well as the Due Process Clause of the Fourteenth? Do they extend beyond questions of the adequacy of notice to the appropriateness of the particular forum? If so, can such questions in any event be resolved by transfer of the case to an appropriate forum (pp. 1732–46, *infra*) rather than dismissal?[2]

Isn't it clear that whatever the constitutional limitations on the reach of federal process, there is little if any significance to a state or district line, at least in a civil case, since district boundaries are matters of congressional choice? (But note that with the sole exception of the short-lived Midnight Judges Act of 1801, p. 961, *supra*, Congress has never chosen to create districts crossing state lines.) Justice Black argued that in diversity cases state lines may well be constitutionally controlling: "Whatever power Congress might have in these other areas to extend a District Court's power to serve process across state lines, such power does not, I think, provide sound argument to justify reliance upon diversity jurisdiction to destroy a man's constitutional right to have his civil lawsuit tried in his own State."

---

1. In Omni Capital International v. Rudolf Wolff & Co., Ltd., 108 S.Ct. 404, 412 (1987) (p. 1726, *infra*), the Court relied upon the Robertson case for the rule that "At common law a court lacked authority to issue process outside its district." It then noted that the principles of territoriality underlying that rule had been undercut by International Shoe, but "express[ed] no view as to the continuing validity of Robertson's rationales" (p. 412 n. 10).

2. See the dissenting opinion in Stafford v. Briggs, 444 U.S. 527, 554 (1980), a case discussed more fully at Paragraph (8), *infra*. The dissent rejected the argument that nationwide service in a federal court suit against a federal official might violate the Fifth Amendment, since "due process requires only certain minimum contacts between the defendant and the sovereign that has created the court." In the Omni case, note 1, *supra*, the Court expressly declined to "consider the constitutional issues raised by this theory" (108 S.Ct. at 408–09 n. 5)

For lower Court decisions on these issues, compare, *e.g.*, Securities Investor Protection Corp. v. Vigman, 764 F.2d 1309 (9th Cir.1985) (following the approach of the Stafford dissent), with *e.g.*, Oxford First Corp. v. PNC Liquidating Corp., 372 F.Supp. 191 (E.D.Pa.1974) (applying a "fairness" test derived from the Fifth Amendment).

Commentators have expressed a variety of views on these questions. See, *e.g.*, Abrams, *Power, Convenience, and the Elimination of Personal Jurisdiction in the Federal Courts*, 58 Ind.L.J. 1 (1982); Fullerton, *Constitutional Limits on Nationwide Personal Jurisdiction in the Federal Courts*, 79 Nw.U.L.Rev. 1 (1984); Seidelson, *The Jurisdictional Reach of a Federal Court Hearing a Federal Cause of Action: A Path Through the Maze*, 23 Duquesne L.Rev. 323 (1984); Note, 61 B.U.L.Rev. 403 (1981); Note, 59 Temple L.Q. 1267 (1986).

National Equip. Rental, Ltd. v. Szukhent, 375 U.S. 311, 318, 331 (1964) (dissenting opinion). What effect would such a conclusion have on the provision for nationwide service in interpleader cases, 28 U.S.C. § 2361? How does the constitutional right asserted by Justice Black square with his own support of state long-arm process in such cases as International Shoe, and McGee v. International Life Ins. Co., 355 U.S. 220 (1957)?

Constitutional questions aside, what considerations should guide Congress in framing policy? What is the appropriate function of a restriction on service of process as distinguished from a venue requirement? Is there any reason why the two concepts should be kept separate? See Currie, *The Federal Courts and the American Law Institute (II)*, 36 U.Chi.L.Rev. 268, 299–307 (1969); Barrett, *Venue and Service of Process in the Federal Courts—Suggestions for Reform*, 7 Vand.L.Rev. 608 (1954).

(2) Fed.R.Civ.P. 4(f) relaxed the rule for service of process in actions in the district courts by providing that process "may be served anywhere within the territorial limits of the state in which the district court is held."

In Mississippi Publishing Corp. v. Murphree, 326 U.S. 438 (1946), this rule was attacked as in violation of the provision of the Enabling Act that the rules "shall neither abridge, enlarge, nor modify the substantive rights of any litigant", and as inconsistent with the provision of Rule 82 that the rules "shall not be construed to extend or limit the jurisdiction of the district courts of the United States or the venue of actions therein". The Court explained that Rule 82 must be treated as "referring to venue and jurisdiction of the subject matter * * *, rather than the means of bringing the defendant before the court already having venue and jurisdiction of the subject matter". Concerning the charge of violation of the Enabling Act, it said (pp. 445–46):

"* * * Undoubtedly most alterations of the rules of practice and procedure may and often do affect the rights of litigants. Congress' prohibition of any alteration of substantive rights of litigants was obviously not addressed to such incidental effects as necessarily attend the adoption of the prescribed new rules of procedure upon the rights of litigants who, agreeably to rules of practice and procedure, have been brought before a court authorized to determine their rights. Sibbach v. Wilson & Co., 312 U.S. 1, 11–14 [p. 765, *supra*]. The fact that the application of Rule 4(f) will operate to subject petitioner's rights to adjudication by the district court for northern Mississippi will undoubtedly affect those rights. But it does not operate to abridge, enlarge or modify the rules of decision by which that court will adjudicate its rights. It relates merely to 'the manner and the means by which a right to recover * * * is enforced.' Guaranty Trust Co. v. York, 326 U.S. 99, 109. In this sense the rule is a rule of procedure and not of substantive right, and is not subject to the prohibition of the Enabling Act." [3]

Substantial amendments of Rule 4 became effective in 1963 and in 1983. The 1963 amendments are fully discussed in Kaplan, *Amendments of the Federal Rules of Civil Procedure, 1961–1963(I)*, 77 Harv.L.Rev. 601, 619–

---

3. *Cf.* 28 U.S.C. § 1693, which still precludes a person from being "arrested" in one district for trial of a civil action in another district. One commentator would reconcile this section with Rule 4 by applying the section only to the relatively rare civil actions begun by arrest of the defendant pursuant to a writ of *capias ad respondendum,* and not those begun by other forms of process. Note, 31 U.Chi.L.Rev. 752, 759–60 (1964).

39 (1964), and the 1983 amendments in Siegel, *Practice Commentary on Amendments of Federal Rule 4 (Eff. Feb. 26, 1983) With Special Statute of Limitations Precautions*, 96 F.R.D. 88 (1983). The 1983 amendments included a provision authorizing service in most cases by mail or by "any person who is not a party and is not less than 18 years of age," and a provision requiring service within 120 days unless good cause is shown for a longer period. The 1963 amendments included addition of a special subsection (i), relating to service in a foreign country; explicit permission in subsection (e) for federal courts to make use of state provisions for extraterritorial service and for attachment and garnishment actions against nonresidents; and creation in subsection (f) of a "100–mile bulge" around the federal courthouse for service of persons brought in as parties under Rule 14, or as additional parties under Rule 19. This last provision enables a court in the Eastern District of Pennsylvania, for example, to reach into four other states to bring in additional parties to a pending action. Would Justice Black have regarded it as unconstitutional to use this provision in a diversity case?[4]

For further discussion of the significance of Rule 4 in determining questions of personal jurisdiction, see pp. 1725–28, *infra*.

(3) Several special provisions for service beyond the borders of a state have been mentioned in this Note; others cited in the Robertson case are still in existence. Still others are collected in 2 Moore, Federal Practice ¶ 4.42[1] (2d ed. 1986). But the norm, even in federal question cases, remains that imposed by the provisions of Rule 4.

(4) May a defendant summoned under a special provision for nationwide service of process be required to answer additional claims filed by other parties, if they would otherwise be proper under the rules? Only if they are "pendent" within the meaning of United Mine Workers v. Gibbs, 383 U.S. 715 (1966), p. 1040, *supra?* The courts are divided on these questions. For discussion and a survey of the cases, see Mills, *Pendent Jurisdiction and Extraterritorial Service Under the Federal Securities Laws*, 70 Colum.L.Rev. 423 (1970); Ferguson, *Pendent Personal Jurisdiction in the Federal Courts*, 11 Vill.L.Rev. 56 (1965); 4 Wright & Miller, Federal Practice and Procedure § 1075, at 481–82 (1987).

Should the Klaxon rule (Klaxon Co. v. Stentor Elec. Mfg. Co., p. 791, *supra*) apply whenever the pendent claim in such a case is governed by state law? If your answer is yes, would you consider a modification of the rule looking to the state where the party is *served* rather than the state in which the district court sits?

(5) Venue and personal jurisdiction were scarcely distinguishable concepts in federal practice prior to the Judiciary Act of March 3, 1887, 24 Stat. 552, as corrected by the Act of August 13, 1888, 25 Stat. 433. The earlier venue provision was as follows: "And no civil suit shall be brought before either of said courts [circuit or district] against any person by any original process or proceeding in any other district than that whereof he is an inhabitant, or in which he shall be found ＊ ＊ ＊." Act of March 3, 1875, 18 Stat. 470, based on § 11 of the Judiciary Act of September 24,

---

4. For criticism of the Murphree rationale, and an argument that Rule 4, as currently written and interpreted, raises serious questions under the Enabling Act, see Whitten, *Separation of Powers Restrictions on Rulemaking: A Case Study of Federal Rule 4*, 40 Me.L.Rev. 41 (1988).

1789, 1 Stat. 73, 78. By virtue of the latter clause the acquisition of personal jurisdiction automatically satisfied the requirement of venue.

Until 1963, the general venue statute (28 U.S.C. § 1391), as it applied to natural persons, did not substantially depart from the provision introduced in 1887. An ordinary two-party action had to be brought in the district where the defendant resided, unless jurisdiction was founded "solely" on diversity of citizenship, in which case the plaintiff also had the option of bringing it in the district of his own residence.[5] In multi-party cases, venue based on the residence of a defendant had to be in the district of "all defendants",[6] and venue based on a plaintiff's residence in the district of residence of "all plaintiffs". This phrasing of § 1391, which precluded venue altogether in some multi-party cases, codified the prior interpretation of the statute when it referred to each party only in the singular. Camp v. Gress, 250 U.S. 308 (1919).

In 1963, the restrictions were eased by a provision allowing venue in certain motor vehicle tort cases to be laid in the district where "the act or omission complained of occurred". 77 Stat. 473. In 1966, this provision was repealed, and venue was made proper generally in the district "in which the claim arose". The relationship between this provision and the expanding reach of personal jurisdiction is manifest; but in cases where personal jurisdiction cannot be obtained in the district where the claim arose, or where that district is for some other reason unacceptable to the plaintiff, the old problems raised by § 1391 still survive.

(6) The concept of state citizenship, for purposes of diversity jurisdiction, is considered to be substantially the same as the concept of domicile in the conflict of laws; thus a natural person can be a citizen, for diversity purposes, of only one state. Should the term "residence" in the venue statute be similarly restricted? One treatise, relying in part on Ex parte Shaw, 145 U.S. 444 (1892), argues that it should, and most courts agree. See 15 Wright, Miller & Cooper, Federal Practice and Procedure § 3805, at 33–36 (1986). But see, *e.g.*, Townsend v. Bucyrus–Eric Co., 144 F.2d 106 (10th Cir.1944) (place of abode where defendant intended to remain for an indefinite period was sufficient to found venue, though defendant was domiciled in another state); Kahane v. Carlson, 527 F.2d 492, 494 (2d Cir. 1975) (though domicile is usually the best measure of residence, special considerations of fairness and convenience warrant the conclusion that a party who may be domiciled abroad is a resident of the Eastern District of New York). *Cf.* 28 U.S.C. § 1391(c) (venue in actions involving corporations), discussed at pp. 1729–30, *infra.*

---

5. Why has federal law thus discriminated against plaintiffs who want to bring federal questions into federal courts? Neither the legislative history nor the decisions yield any answer to the enigma. The bill passed by the House in 1887 proposed simply to restrict venue in diversity cases: an action could be brought where the defendant could be found, except that if jurisdiction was founded solely on diverse citizenship venue was restricted to the district of residence either of the plaintiff or the defendant. 18 Cong.Rec. Pt. 1, p. 613. (The exception was apparently an effort to restore the limitations on diversity juris-diction embodied in § 11 of the First Judiciary Act, 1 Stat. 73, 78 (1789).) The Senate version, accepted by the House, retained the provision for venue in diversity cases, but sharply narrowed the venue for other cases to that of the defendant's residence. 18 Cong.Rec. Pt. 3, pp. 2542–46, 2651.

6. 28 U.S.C. § 1392(a) provides a choice of districts when defendants reside in different districts in the same state. See also 28 U.S.C. § 1393(b), relating to defendants residing in different divisions of the same district.

(7) Section 1391(d), providing that an alien may be sued in any district, appeared for the first time in the Judicial Code of 1948.[7] As early as 1893, however, the Court held the general venue statute inapplicable in a suit against an alien defendant; thus such a defendant could be sued in any district in which valid service could be made. In re Hohorst, 150 U.S. 653 (1893). In Brunette Machine Works, Ltd. v. Kockum Industries, Inc., 406 U.S. 706 (1972), the Court stated (p. 714): "§ 1391(d) is properly regarded, not as a venue restriction at all, but rather as a declaration of the long-established rule that suits against aliens are wholly outside the operation of all the federal venue laws, general and special." Thus a patent infringement suit against an alien corporation could be brought in the district where valid service of process was made and without regard to the special venue provision for patent cases, 28 U.S.C. § 1400(b).

May an alien plaintiff domiciled in the United States who is suing a U.S. citizen in a federal court lay venue under § 1391(a) in the state of his domicile? Evidently not. See 15 Wright, Miller & Cooper, Federal Practice and Procedure § 3810, and cases cited n. 7 (1986).

(8) The basic statutory provision governing venue and service of process for suits against federal officials and agencies is § 1391(e).[8] This provision, originally enacted in 1962 as part of the Mandamus and Venue Act (see p. 1094, *supra*), gives the plaintiff a number of choices, including the district of his own residence. Expressly preserved are the specific venue provisions of various statutes authorizing actions against federal officers or agencies to review particular administrative acts.

Prior to the enactment of § 1391(e), a litigant suing a subordinate government official in his individual capacity frequently found the action dismissed on the ground that the superior officer was an indispensable party. Despite the Supreme Court's attempts to ease this difficulty in Williams v. Fanning, 332 U.S. 490 (1947), and Shaughnessy v. Pedreiro, 349 U.S. 48 (1955), many cases continued to hold that superior officers were indispensable parties. Thus litigants often found it difficult or impossible to bring suit outside the District of Columbia. The Committee Report recommending the enactment of § 1391(e) concluded that this state of affairs was "contrary to the sound and equitable administration of justice," and that requiring the government to defend certain suits outside Washington would aid private citizens without imposing an undue burden on the government itself. See H.R.Rep. No. 536, 87th Cong., 1st Sess. 3-4 (1961).

---

7. As part of the Foreign Sovereign Immunities Act of 1976, see p. 1658, note 1, *supra*, Congress enacted a new statutory provision, 28 U.S.C. § 1391(f), governing venue in civil actions against a foreign state.

8. In federal criminal prosecutions, the Sixth Amendment gives the accused a right to trial by a jury "of the State and District wherein the crime shall have been committed," and Fed.R.Cr.P. 18 states that, except as otherwise provided by law, the prosecution shall be had in "a district in which the offense was committed." (Rule 18 thus appears to recognize the fact that many federal crimes have no single locus of commission but rather are continuous in time and space.) In addition, 18 U.S.C.

§ 3238 deals with the trial of offenses "begun or committed on the high seas, or elsewhere out of the jurisdiction of any particular State or district," and 49 U.S.C. § 1473 contains similar provisions for aircraft cases.

In the absence of a special venue statute (*e.g.*, 28 U.S.C. § 1395, covering actions for fines, penalties, seizures, and forfeitures), civil actions brought by the United States are subject to the general venue provisions of § 1391(b). Civil actions brought against the United States in its own name are, for the most part, governed by 28 U.S.C. § 1402. See 15 Wright, Miller & Cooper, Federal Practice and Procedure § 3814 (1986).

A district court must still determine whether a superior officer not named as a defendant must be joined as a party. A finding of "indispensability" can usually be surmounted, however, by refiling or amending to add the essential party. Moreover, plaintiffs can relieve judges of a difficult decision on dispensability by always joining a superior officer. Then the court need only make the relatively easy decision whether joinder is permissible under Rule 20.

In Stafford v. Briggs, 444 U.S. 527 (1980), the Supreme Court came to the surprising conclusion that § 1391(e) does not apply to actions for money damages brought against federal officials in their individual capacities, even though the activity complained of was "under color of legal authority" within the meaning of the statute.[9] The Court read the legislative history of the Act to indicate that "Congress intended nothing more than to provide nationwide venue for the convenience of individual plaintiffs in actions which are nominally against an individual officer but are in reality against the Government" (p. 542). Justice Stewart, joined by Justice Brennan, dissented, emphasizing the "plain meaning" of the statutory language and the fact that the Department of Justice "has long assumed a special responsibility for representing federal officers sued for money damages for actions taken under color of legal authority" (p. 552).

Although § 1391(e) is not entirely clear on the point, courts and commentators have interpreted the section to authorize nationwide service by certified mail to the officer or agency whenever the provision's venue requirements are satisfied. See 2 Moore, Federal Practice ¶ 4.29, at 244–45 (2d ed. 1986). This interpretation appears to have been endorsed in Stafford v. Briggs, *supra*, when the Court said that § 1391(e) rendered defendants amenable to suit "in any one of the 95 federal district courts covering the 50 states and other areas within federal jurisdiction" (444 U.S. at 544).

(9) The phrase "in which the claim arose" in the 1966 amendment to § 1391 was first considered by the Supreme Court in Leroy v. Great Western United Corp., 443 U.S. 173 (1979). Great Western, a Delaware corporation with headquarters in the Northern District of Texas, made a bid to take over a Washington corporation with executive offices and substantial assets in Idaho. Idaho officials objected that Great Western had failed to satisfy the filing requirements of Idaho's Corporate Takeover Act and entered an order delaying the effective date of Great Western's tender offer.

Great Western then brought suit in the federal court for the Northern District of Texas against several defendants, including the Idaho officials responsible for enforcing Idaho's Takeover Act. It sought a declaration of the invalidity of the Idaho Act as applied, on the ground of federal preemption, and the district court upheld the claim on the merits after rejecting challenges to subject matter jurisdiction, personal jurisdiction, and venue. (Subject matter jurisdiction was upheld under 28 U.S.C. §§ 1331, 1332, and 1337, as well as the Securities Exchange Act of 1934, 15 U.S.C. § 78aa, and venue was upheld under the same provision of the 1934 Act.) On appeal, the Fifth Circuit affirmed, but added its view that venue was also proper under § 1391(b) because the suit had been brought in the

9. In an earlier decision, Schlanger v. Seamans, 401 U.S. 487 (1971), the Court had held § 1391(e) inapplicable to habeas corpus proceedings.

district in which the claim arose. (Why wasn't venue also proper in that district because it was the residence of the plaintiff? See note 5, *supra*.)

The Supreme Court reversed, without reaching the merits or the issue of personal jurisdiction, on the ground that venue did not lie against the Idaho defendants in the Northern District of Texas. The venue provision of the 1934 Securities Exchange Act was held inapplicable (over three dissents) on the ground that it applied only in actions seeking to enforce a duty imposed by that Act, and no such duty was imposed on the defendant state officials. The Court then held that the claim did not arise in Texas within the meaning of § 1391(b). Venue provisions, the Court reasoned, were generally designed to protect defendants and, whatever gaps the "claim arose" language was designed to fill, it was not intended to give plaintiffs an "unfettered choice among a host of different districts" (p. 185). The Court declined to decide whether a claim could ever arise in more than one district within the meaning of the law: "In our view * * * the broadest interpretation of the language of § 1391(b) that is even arguably acceptable is that in the unusual case in which it is not clear that the claim arose in only one specific district, a plaintiff may choose between those two (or conceivably even more) districts that with approximately equal plausibility—in terms of the availability of witnesses, the accessibility of relevant evidence, and the convenience of the defendant (but *not* of the plaintiff)— may be assigned as the locus of the claim" (id.). The present case was held not to fit that category, despite any impact that the actions of the defendants may have had in Texas and elsewhere; the claim arose in the District of Idaho and only in that district.

Is the Court correct that only in an "unusual" case can a claim arise in more than one district? Is this because the statute refers to "the district," or are there deeper policy reasons? (Compare the language in the proposed ALI venue provisions, §§ 1303(a)(1), 1314(a)(1): where "a substantial part of the events or omissions giving rise to the claim occurred, or where a substantial part of the property that is the subject of the action is situated.") In any event, when such an "unusual" case is encountered, why is the convenience of the plaintiff an irrelevant factor? [10]

(10) The established doctrine that venue is merely a personal privilege that may be waived is codified in Fed.R.Civ.P. 12(b), (g), and (h) and in 28 U.S.C. § 1406(b).

Waiver may take place in other ways than by failure to "interpose timely and sufficient objection" in the particular action. See, *e.g.,* General Elec. Co. v. Marvel Rare Metals Co., 287 U.S. 430 (1932), holding that a plaintiff in a federal court waives any objection on the score of venue to any counterclaim the federal rules permit to be asserted against him. See also Neirbo Co. v. Bethlehem Shipbuilding Corp., 308 U.S. 165 (1939), and related problems discussed in the *Note on Bringing Corporations and Unincorporated Organizations Into Court,* p. 1725, *infra*.

Prior to 1948, a federal district court had no choice but to dismiss an action as to any defendant who duly asserted a proper objection to the venue. If there was only one defendant, or if the objecting defendant was an indispensable party, the entire action had to be dismissed.

10. For discussion and criticism of Leroy, see Comment, 31 S.C.L.Rev. 579 (1980).

Section 1406(a) of Title 28 introduced a striking innovation, transforming the whole theory of federal venue. In its original form this section made it mandatory for a district judge who found the venue improper, to "transfer such case to any district or division in which it could have been brought". The 1949 amendments, however, modified the direction to provide that the judge "shall dismiss, or if it be in the interest of justice, transfer such case * * *." See *Note on Forum Non Conveniens and Change of Venue*, p. 1738, *infra*.

(11) Recall the materials on pendent and ancillary jurisdiction, pp. 1040–52, 1679–88, *supra*. Should any claim maintainable on an ancillary jurisdiction theory—for example, a cross-claim, counterclaim against an additional party, or third-party claim—be freed from the venue requirements on an "ancillary venue" theory? Generally, the courts have answered in the affirmative. See Note, 73 Harv.L.Rev. 1164 (1960); Wright, Federal Courts § 9, at 32 (4th ed. 1983). Should it matter whether the party objecting to the venue on one claim is already a party to the proceeding with respect to another claim?

(12) There are a large number of special venue provisions in the United States Code. Some, like 28 U.S.C. §§ 1397 (interpleader), 1400 (patents and copyrights), 1401 (stockholders derivative actions), and 1402 (United States as defendant), are in the Judicial Code, but an extraordinary number are not. (The ALI Study, pp. 498–501, listed over 300 special venue provisions not in Title 28.) Such provisions are often combined with special provisions for service of process, as in the case of interpleader. But the reasons for many of these special venue provisions are hard to come by, and although a number may have been justified by the rigidity of the general venue law before 1966, their usefulness may now be questioned.[11]

(13) 28 U.S.C. § 1392(b) provides that any civil action "of a local nature" involving property located in different districts in the same state may be brought in any of such districts. But the phrase "of a local nature" is nowhere defined, nor does the Code specify what happens when such an action involves property in only one district.

Under the common-law doctrine of local actions, certain proceedings involving real property may be tried only in the jurisdiction where the land is located.[12] As developed in the federal courts and in many states, the doctrine extends beyond actions in rem to such in personam actions as trespass to land and nuisance. See, *e.g.*, Livingston v. Jefferson, 15 Fed. Cas. 660 (No. 8411) (C.C.D.Va.1811). Among the unanswered questions raised by the doctrine in the federal courts are: Is the doctrine one of

---

11. There is a judge-made exception to the general venue provisions in the area of admiralty and maritime claims, where venue lies in an in personam action wherever the defendant can be served or his goods or credits can be attached. See 7A Moore, Federal Practice ¶ .66[3] (2d ed. 1986); Atkins v. Disintegrating Co., 18 Wall. 272 (U.S.1873); In re Louisville Underwriters, 134 U.S. 488 (1890). This exception is reflected in Fed.Rule 82, providing that admiralty and maritime claims shall not be regarded as civil actions for purposes of 28 U.S.C. §§ 1391–1393. The ALI proposals preserved the exception intact, see pro-

posed § 1318, a decision leading Professor Currie to conclude that the Institute was "bamboozled by the antiquarian crustaceans of the admiralty bar". Currie, *The Federal Courts and the American Law Institute (II)*, 36 U.Chi.L.Rev. 268, 303 (1969).

12. One decision indicated that if an action is local, the district where the property is located becomes simply another available venue. Coffey v. Managed Properties, Inc., 85 F.2d 88 (2d Cir.1936). But other cases support the proposition in text.

subject matter jurisdiction (and thus not waivable), as Ellenwood v. Marietta Chair Co., 158 U.S. 105 (1895), would indicate, or is it one of venue, as suggested by the reference in § 1392 and by cases allowing transfer under 28 U.S.C. § 1406(a), *e.g.,* Wheatley v. Phillips, 228 F.Supp. 439, 442 (W.D. N.C.1964)? Must an action that is local also satisfy the general statutory venue requirements, as indicated by Ladew v. Tennessee Copper Co., 218 U.S. 357 (1910), or is it enough that it be brought where the land is located, as indicated by Casey v. Adams, 102 U.S. 66 (1880)? What is the effect in a federal diversity case of a rule in the forum state that differs from the rule developed in the federal courts? See Still v. Rossville Crushed Stone Co., 370 F.2d 324 (6th Cir.1966) (state rule is determinative); Central Transport, Inc. v. Theurer, Inc., 430 F.Supp. 1076 (E.D.Mich.1977) (venue is determined by federal law, but state substantive law must be analyzed to determine whether the action is local or transitory).[13] The question is important because some states have drastically curtailed or eliminated the operation of the doctrine, while others may define a local action more expansively than would a federal court.

When a case falls within 28 U.S.C. § 1655, several of these questions are resolved. That section, which was derived from a provision limited to equity cases, 17 Stat. 196, 198 (1872), authorizes extraterritorial service in actions "to enforce any lien upon or claim to, or to remove any incumbrance or lien or cloud upon the title to, real or personal property within the district"; if the defendant does not appear or plead, the court is empowered to render an adjudication affecting only the property that is the subject of the action. The section has been held to authorize venue in the district where the land is located. See Shuford v. Anderson, 352 F.2d 755 (10th Cir.1965). But it does not apply to all local actions, see Ladew v. Tennessee Copper Co., *supra* (action to enjoin a nuisance), and has been limited to "a lien or title existing anterior to the suit, and not one caused by the institution of the suit itself." Dormitzer v. Illinois & St. Louis Bridge Co., 6 Fed. 217, 218 (C.C.D.Mass.1881); see Nowell v. Nowell, 417 F.2d 902, 905 (1st Cir.1969).

Considerable relief from some of these problems was afforded by the 1966 amendment to § 1391, since the claim in a local action case will almost invariably have arisen where the land is located. This provision, coupled with the increasing number of state long-arm statutes applying to one who commits a tort in the state, makes it unlikely that, as in Livingston v. Jefferson, *supra,* the plaintiff will be remediless for lack of a forum.

Does the doctrine of local actions have any proper place in the federal courts? See Note, *Local Actions in the Federal Courts,* 70 Harv.L.Rev. 708 (1957).

(14) Although they have long been held removable if state statutory requirements are satisfied, proceedings commenced by attachment or garnishment could not originate in the federal courts prior to the 1963 amendment of Fed.Rule 4(e). But the significance of this amendment was in turn reduced by later Supreme Court decisions invalidating state court

---

13. One commentator criticizes the tendency of lower federal courts to regard state law as controlling, and attributes it to an "erroneous dictum" in Huntington v. Attrill, 146 U.S. 657, 669–70 (1892), "mis- reading Marshall [in Livingston v. Jefferson]." 15 Wright, Miller & Cooper, Federal Practice and Procedure § 3822, at 208 (1986).

assertions of "quasi in rem" jurisdiction. Shaffer v. Heitner, 433 U.S. 186 (1977); Rush v. Savchuck, 444 U.S. 320 (1980). In these cases, the Court held that the relevant standards for determining the validity of such jurisdiction under the Due Process Clause of the Fourteenth Amendment were those set forth in International Shoe Co. v. Washington, 326 U.S. 310 (1945).

The applicability of these decisions to federal court actions is not entirely clear, but they would presumably be controlling in diversity cases where the reach of federal court jurisdiction is determined by state law. For consideration of their applicability in a maritime attachment proceeding under the Supplemental Rules for Admiralty and Maritime Claims, see Culp, *Charting a New Course: Proposed Amendments to the Supplemental Rules for Admiralty Arrest and Attachment*, 103 F.R.D. 319, 334–38 (1985), and cases cited therein.

PENROD DRILLING COMPANY v. JOHNSON

United States Court of Appeals for the Fifth Circuit.
414 F.2d 1217 (1969).

Before JOHN R. BROWN, CHIEF JUDGE, and BELL and THORNBERRY, CIRCUIT JUDGES.

JOHN R. BROWN, CHIEF JUDGE:

This case, simple in setting but not so easy of determination, is before us as an interlocutory appeal, 28 U.S.C.A. § 1292(b). The appeal presents the single issue of whether a partnership may be sued under the special venue provisions of the Jones Act in a district in which the partnership is doing business but in which neither the partnership's principal office is located nor any partner resides. It splices the main brace to state it in more realistic terms. The question is whether the cherished ward of the admiralty—a seaman, whether salt water, pure and unadulterated or of a Sieracki–Ryan–Yaka variety—who sustains an injury on navigable waters within or offshore of Louisiana, must, in making a Jones Act claim against the multimillion dollar shipowner-employer whose extensive operations are widely scattered over the nation, the high seas and perhaps the terrestrial globe, pursue this employer in Dallas, Texas, where the dream of oceangoing vessels up the Trinity is an enticing but unrealized community hope and where the admiralty Judge must dispense his justice not from any juridical quarterdeck but from a non-nautical bench high and dry above maritime waters.

The District Court held that venue in the Eastern District (in addition to the Northern District—Dallas) was proper. We affirm.

The Seamen [4] sued Shipowner in the Eastern District of Texas for damages under the Jones Act, 46 U.S.C.A. § 688. Shipowner, a partnership whose partners reside in Dallas, Texas, and whose principal office is in Dallas, filed a motion seeking to have the action either dismissed or transferred to the Northern District of Texas. The motion was denied by the District Judge. This Court granted a § 1292(b) interlocutory appeal from that ruling, which appeared to be on a controlling question of law.

---

4. One was injured on an amphibious rig on internal navigable waters in Louisi-   ana, the other on an offshore rig some 50 miles out in the Gulf of Mexico.

The special venue provision of the Jones Act reads:

"Jurisdiction in such actions shall be under the court of the district in which the defendant employer resides or in which his principal office is located."

It has long been settled that even though this provision reads in jurisdictional terms, it refers to venue only. Pure Oil Co. v. Suarez, 1966, 384 U.S. 202; Panama R.R. Co. v. Johnson, 1924, 264 U.S. 375. As this statute was originally enacted and interpreted, "residence" for a partnership would most certainly have been limited to the residences of the individual partners. McCullough v. Jannson, 9 Cir.1923, 292 F. 377. But Seamen contend that the expanded concept of corporate residence for venue purposes, as set forth in 28 U.S.C.A. § 1391(c), is applicable to this large business organization sued as a shipowner under the Jones Act.

At the outset, certain things warrant emphasis. First, there is no question of subject-matter jurisdiction which rests on the Jones Act, a federal statute. Second, on jurisdiction over the person there is no doubt that Shipowner had sufficient contacts with the Eastern District to be amenable to *in personam* process under F.R.Civ.P. 4(d)(3). Last, for a federal statutory claim, F.R.Civ.P. 17(b)(1), accords partnerships express capacity to be sued. Of greatest importance is the fact that *jurisdiction* is in no sense in question, so this case does not involve the problem confronting the Supreme Court in United Steelworkers of America v. Bouligny, 1965, 382 U.S. 145. There the Court held that for purposes of diversity jurisdiction an unincorporated association was not a citizen and that its citizenship was that of its individual members.

The problem comes down to the purely procedural question whether a multistate unincorporated business organization "resides" or has a "residence" for Jones Act venue purposes in a district in which it is doing business, but which is not the location of its principal office or the place where its owner-partners live. We answer this question in the affirmative. Since in that answer we draw directly on the Supreme Court's holding that corporate venue standards apply to give meaning to "residence" or similar concepts concerning unincorporated associations, we are led to the subsidiary question whether for *venue* purposes—we repeat, *venue*—there can be any recognizable difference between the unincorporated partnership and the unincorporated association. That we answer in the negative. In this binary world, that plus and minus adds up to affirmance.

A good place to start is Pure Oil Co. v. Suarez, *supra,* because it deals with this very part of the Jones Act. In that case the Supreme Court held that in a suit against a corporation under the Jones Act, venue was proper in a state that was neither the state of incorporation nor the place of the principal office, but in which the corporation was doing business. This inverted form of statutory interpretation, reading the general provision of § 1391(c) into the specific provision of the Jones Act was thought justifiable in light of the liberalizing policy of § 1391(c) and the generality of the language used. Thus the word "residence" as used in the Jones Act was thought to do nothing more than refer to general doctrines of venue rules, which might change from time to time. The change might come from legislative or judicial action or a combination of both.

But the quest cannot end there. For a partnership is not a corporation, even though persuasive arguments may be made that the entity theory of partnerships has now so engulfed the aggregate theory as to make nice distinctions between the two forms of business associations almost meaningless. But while the Suarez Court did not decide our specific question, it did accomplish a number of things. It established the principle that venue provisions of the Jones Act should receive treatment consistent with the liberal application of that legislation. Next, it recognized that the legislative addition of § 1391(c) was made "to bring venue law in tune with modern concepts of corporate operations." 384 U.S. at 204. To this end the change was held to be applicable not only to the general diversity and federal-question venue provisions, § 1391(a) and (b), but also "to all venue statutes using residence as a criterion, at least in the absence of contrary restrictive indications in any such statute." *Id.* at 205. On that score, the Court concluded that "there is nothing to the legislative history of [the venue] provision of the Jones Act to indicate that its framers meant to use 'residence' as anything more than a referent to more general doctrines of venue rules, which might alter in the future. *Id.* (footnotes omitted).

Perhaps with this liberal approach nothing more would have been needed to reach our result here. But we are spared the travail of speculating whether a small step by that Court would have meant a big leap for us unaided by any decision subsequent to Suarez for the recent case of Denver & R.G.W.R.R. v. Brotherhood of R.R. Trainmen, 1967, 387 U.S. 556, affords an adequate gravitational basis. In that case the defendant was an unincorporated association—a labor union. The Court reaffirmed that for venue purposes the defendant should be suable as an entity and recognized that the critical factor was the residence of the entity, rather than the residence of the individual members of the association. Faced with the question of where that entity "resided", the Court then proceeded to hold for the first time that an unincorporated association should be analogized to a corporation. With that it applied to the assimilated "corporation" § 1391(c), which in 1948 brought in for corporate venue any district in which the corporation was "doing business." [10] Until this decision the lower courts had been hopelessly divided on the question of where proper venue lay for an unincorporated association.

The decision in the Denver case leads inevitably to the conclusion that if two seamen were suing an unincorporated association such as a labor union for injuries sustained in the operations of an excursion vessel owned and operated by the union as a shipowner, then venue under § 688 could properly be laid wherever that unincorporated-business-association-shipowner was doing business, for that would be one of its "residences" for venue purposes. But, is it much of a step from Denver's holding to a holding in the present case that this huge unincorporated business enterprise should likewise be treated as "residing" wherever "it is doing business"? That query leads to two further questions. First, is the holding in Denver to be broadly construed or is it to be limited to labor unions? Second, for *venue* purposes, are there any significant differences between a partnership and an unincorporated association?

As to the first—the scope of the holding in Denver—we perceive no great difficulty. Venue is primarily a question of convenience for litigants and witnesses, Denver & R.G.W.R.R. Co. v. Brotherhood of R.R. Trainmen,

---

10. The Court was careful to point out that United Steelworkers of America v. H. & W.—Fed.Cts. & Sys. 3d Ed. UCB—39   Bouligny dealt with diversity jurisdiction, not capacity or venue, 387 U.S. at 559–560.

1967, 387 U.S. at 560, and venue provisions should be treated in practical terms. Rutland Ry. Corp. v. Brotherhood of Locomotive Eng., 2 Cir., 1962, 307 F.2d 21, 29, *cert. denied*, 1963, 372 U.S. 954. These guidelines become especially applicable when dealing with the Jones Act. To hold that labor unions will be the only unincorporated associations to be likened to corporations would be to exclude myriad other unincorporated associations, many of them very large, such as agricultural societies, co-ops, banking associations, charitable associations, news associations, and religious societies, from the sound result of the Denver decision. This would force the law back to the restrictive rule allowing unincorporated associations other than labor unions to be sued only at the location of their principal place of business. Not only would that be illogical, but it would subject litigants bringing suit against such associations to unfair, discriminatory burdens. Furthermore, it would run counter to the general trend to allow suits to be brought at the place liabilities are being created.

On the second question, exploring the legal theory behind an unincorporated association to determine the difference between that form of enterprise and a partnership can certainly be an exercise in futility. Platitudes and generalities abound. Most are question begging. Few sharp legal boundaries appear.

* * * [O]ne of the immediate distinctions urged by Shipowner is that an unincorporated association may be formed for some political or benevolent enterprise, while a partnership is nearly always formed to earn a profit. We think this is bad economics and, at least, incomplete law. Worse, for venue purposes the distinction is meaningless. An unincorporated association formed for the most worthy of non-profit purposes could still create liabilities where it was doing business. Extending this argument, Shipowner urges that since many unincorporated associations—especially unions—have grown so large and pervasive in their influence, the Supreme Court opted to hold them suable where they were doing business. But partnerships, too, can grow to immense proportions, as Shipowner's activities attest. It operates under an assumed name, employs over seven hundred people, owns twenty-five drilling rigs, and operates in at least three states and on the high seas. Of all things, the most irrelevant is the domicile or residence of those individuals who happen to own the enterprise. It acts like a business. It acts like a big business. It is a big business. The plea that partnership venue must be geared to the small neighborhood self-made business can hardly be voiced by this industrial Goliath. The problem does not arise until business activities expand geographically beyond personal residence (or principal place of business).

The little case law and other authority on the problem almost all point toward treating unincorporated associations and partnerships the same for venue purposes. * * * [17] [In addition] two provisions of the rules are persuasive in indicating an assimilation. F.R.Civ.P. 17(b)(1) gives "a partnership or other unincorporated association" capacity to sue and be sued in federal question cases. Rule 4(d)(3) outlines the requirements for service of

---

17. In considering the venue cases, Shipowner has failed to make a distinction that must be kept in mind. The cases arising on diversity jurisdiction have apparently proceeded on the reasoning that since F.R.Civ.P. 17(b) requires the court to look to state law to determine capacity to sue and be sued, state law should also determine whether an unincorporated association or partnership is an entity and has a separate residence for venue purposes. These cases are not persuasive in a case like the present one, which arises under federal law.

process upon "a partnership or other unincorporated association." In these rules the partnership is not only recognized as an entity but is assimilated into the generic term "unincorporated association." The notes of the Advisory Committee and the commentary make clear that Rule 17(b) did not change the law concerning the capacity to sue or be sued but merely codified existing case law. Rule 17(b) is based primarily on Coronado. (United Mine Workers v. Coronado Coal Co., 1922, 259 U.S. 344.) In Denver the Court said: "The Coronado case dealt with capacity to be sued, not with venue, but it did legitimate suing the unincorporated association as an entity. Although that entity has no citizenship independent of its members for purposes of diversity jurisdiction, * * * we think that the question of the proper venue for such a defendant, like the question of capacity, should be determined by looking to the residence of the association itself rather than that of its individual members." The Court then went on to hold: "We think it most nearly approximates the intent of Congress to recognize the reality of the multi-state, unincorporated association such as a labor union and to permit suit against that entity, like the analogous corporate entity, wherever it is 'doing business.'"

This tiny step of assimilating partnerships with unincorporated associations for venue purposes is in keeping with the strong trend—judicial and legislative—toward making modern business entities amenable to suit in places where their business activities give rise to liabilities and obligations.

Thus, while the Venue Act of 1887 severely limited venue from what it had been since 1789, the trend since that time has been expansive. * * * [Since 1966] all suits may be brought where the cause of action arose. All changes, legislative and judicial, have been designed to effectuate one purpose—to make the venue provisions serve litigants and witnesses, not to allow nice but meaningless distinctions to place stumbling blocks in their way.

Affirmed.

NOTE ON BRINGING CORPORATIONS AND UNINCORPORATED ORGANIZATIONS INTO COURT

(1) Fed. Rules 4(c)(2)(C) and 4(d)(3) tell *how* service of process is to be made on a corporation or on a partnership or other unincorporated association subject to suit under a common name, but do not appear to tell *when* these organizations are amenable to process.[1] Rule 4(e) refers to federal and state law for authority to serve a party outside the state. Rule 4(f) sets the boundaries of the state as the limits of service unless otherwise authorized by statute or rule.

What, then, is the relevance of state law in determining whether a corporation, partnership, or unincorporated association is amenable to process issuing from a particular district court?

1. There is some support in case and commentary for the view that these provisions of Rule 4 deal not only with the method of service but also with amenability to process. See, *e.g.*, Seidelson, p. 1712, note 2, *supra.* For a forceful refutation of this view, see Fullerton, p. 1712, note 2, *supra*, at 80–85.

(a) Consider first an action founded on a federal question in which no federal statute or rule authorizes service outside the boundaries of the forum state. The defendant is a corporation, partnership, or unincorporated association organized under the laws of another state and with its principal place of business in that state. Even though service is made within the forum state on a person described in Rule 4(d)(3), this clearly should not be the end of the inquiry. If, for example, the person in question was traveling through the state at the time of service, and the organization had no other contacts with the state, Rule 4(d)(3) surely should not be held to authorize the assertion of personal jurisdiction. (See also p. 1712, *supra,* with respect to the constitutional issues in such a case.)

What if service must be made under Rule 4(e) in the manner authorized by state law? Is the court free to ignore the limitations in that law on amenability to service? What of the limitations imposed on the reach of state process by the Fourteenth Amendment? Are they controlling, or should the reach of federal process in such a case be measured by looking to the existence of minimum contacts with the United States as a whole (subject to any additional requirements of fairness imposed by the Due Process Clause of the Fifth Amendment)?

After years of uncertainty in the lower courts on these questions, a number of them were resolved by the decision in Omni Capital International v. Rudolf Wolff & Co., Ltd., 108 S.Ct. 404 (1987). This case was a federal question suit, brought in a federal court in Louisiana under the Commodity Exchange Act (CEA); the suit involved an alien corporate defendant and an alien individual defendant, neither of whom could be served in the state of Louisiana. The Court first held that the CEA itself did not authorize service upon a person who could not be served within the state; it then concluded that these defendants were not subject to service under Rule 4(e) because the requirements of Louisiana law for amenability to long-arm service of process had not been met. (Since the Louisiana statute concededly did not permit service on these defendants, the Court did not reach the question whether, as a matter of due process, the defendants could be subjected to service.)

The Court in the Omni case specifically declined the invitation of the dissenters in the court below to fashion a common law rule filling the "interstices in the law inadvertently left by legislative enactment" (p. 412, quoting 795 F.2d 415, 431–32). Citing the "assumption that federal courts cannot add to the scope of service Congress has authorized," the Court said that "the strength of this longstanding assumption, and the network of statutory enactments and judicial decisions tied to it," argued strongly against its abandonment (p. 412).[2]

(b) There seems to be general agreement that, subject to any limitations imposed by the Fifth Amendment, Congress or the rulemakers may depart from state law in matters of process in diversity cases. But should a departure be inferred from Rule 4(d)(3)? Is there any reason in federal policy why Rule 4(d)(3) should be construed to subject a foreign organization to federal diversity jurisdiction in a particular state when it is beyond the reach of that state's process?

2. Recognizing that a rule subjecting the alien defendants to service in such a case might "well serve the ends of the CEA and other statutes," the Court said that responsibility to create such a rule "better rests with those who propose the Federal Rules of Civil Procedure and with Congress" (p. 413).

In considering this question, recall the decision in Szantay v. Beech Aircraft Corp., 349 F.2d 60 (4th Cir.1965), p. 840, *supra*. What if the state's limitation on suit by one out-of-stater against another had been built into its statutory provisions for service of process? Should the result be different? Note that in Szantay, one of the reasons for not dismissing the out-of-state defendant was the desirability of resolving a multi-party controversy in a single lawsuit. Not all such cases are covered by the nationwide service provision of the interpleader statute, 28 U.S.C. § 2361, or by the 100–mile bulge of Rule 4(f).

On the other hand, would not significant state interests be affected if state law were to be disregarded in a diversity case? Shouldn't that law, if constitutional, at least establish the floor for service on defendant? Isn't it often arguable (though perhaps not in Szantay) that it should also establish a ceiling because the state may desire not to discourage foreign businesses from coming in by subjecting them to the threat of inconvenient litigation? In view of the Klaxon rule, wouldn't a broader reach of federal process interfere with the interests of states other than the forum by depriving them of the chance to have their choice-of-law rules applied? Is it possible under Klaxon to separate questions of the reach of process from questions of the reach of substantive law? (Compare the discussion of the 100–mile bulge, subparagraph (c), below.)

Does this line of questions suggest that in diversity cases, state law on amenability should ordinarily control unless in the specific case there is some clear basis in federal policy for departing from it? That in the absence of a statute or rule, such a basis should not lightly be found?

There are many federal decisions in this area, collected and discussed in 4 Wright & Miller, Federal Practice and Procedure § 1075 (1987). The most significant, and influential, is still Arrowsmith v. United Press Int'l, 320 F.2d 219 (2d Cir.1963), in which the court, sitting en banc, held state law to be controlling in the absence of a specific federal provision to the contrary. Judge Clark filed a vigorous dissent.[3]

(c) What standard should be applied in measuring amenability within the 100–mile bulge of Rule 4(f)? See Annot., 8 A.L.R.Fed. 784, 798–806 (1971). Arrowsmith reserved this question, but the same court in Coleman v. American Export Isbrandtsen Lines, Inc., 405 F.2d 250, 252 (2d Cir.1968), suggested that the controlling law was that of the state in which service was made. See also Pierce v. Globemaster Baltimore, Inc., 49 F.R.D. 63 (D.Md.1969). Should this be so? Doesn't Rule 4(f) reflect a federal policy in favor of resolving the whole controversy in a multi-party dispute, and if so, shouldn't amenability be pressed to the full extent permitted by the Constitution? See Note, *Bulge Service Amenability: A Federal Standard,* 41 U.Pitt.L.Rev. 801 (1980). But if this approach is taken in a diversity case, to what extent should the forum state's choice of law rules be held to govern? *Cf.* Griffin v. McCoach, 313 U.S. 498 (1941), p. 799, *supra*.

(d) Some commentators have suggested that doubt was cast on Arrowsmith by the Supreme Court's decision in National Equip. Rental, Ltd. v. Szukhent, 375 U.S. 311 (1964). See, *e.g.*, Currie, Federal Courts 414 (3d ed. 1982). In Szukhent, the question was whether a New York federal court

---

3. It is interesting to note the agreement of the majority and dissenting judges that in a removed case, the action would have to be dismissed if the defendant were beyond the reach of state court process.

had jurisdiction over a Michigan farmer whose "agent" (*i.e.*, the person so designated in the equipment rental agreement sued upon) had been served with process in New York. The Court held, or strongly implied, that a federal standard governed the definition of an "agent" for purposes of service on an individual under Rule 4(d)(1). Professor Wright, however, finds no undermining of Arrowsmith because "in Szukhent the Court was dealing with manner of service, rather than amenability to process". Wright, Federal Courts § 64, at 421 (4th ed. 1983). In any event, since the majority in Szukhent perceived no difference between federal and state policies on the question before it, it seems inappropriate to read the decision as establishing a federal standard of amenability.

(e) Whenever state law is controlling for purposes of amenability, is it necessary or appropriate to consider whether it would be constitutional for the state courts to apply that law in the case at hand? Assuming that the constitutional standards applicable to the state courts are not the same as those applicable to the federal courts, is it possible to attach federal consequences to an unconstitutional state law? And if it is—perhaps on a theory of "incorporation" of state rules into federal law—what purpose would be served by doing so?

(2) Solution of problems both of venue and of personal jurisdiction in actions against corporations was long vexed by the dogma that a corporation "must dwell in the place of its creation, and cannot migrate to another sovereignty". Bank of Augusta v. Earle, 13 Pet. 519, 588 (U.S.1839).

As the Bank of Augusta case itself showed, a corporation could migrate as a plaintiff, in the absence of valid state action to exclude it. But not until 1877 did the Court work out a basis for overcoming difficulties of venue and process when a foreign corporation was a defendant. It did this through a theory of consent. At a time when venue depended, alternatively, on the defendant's being an "inhabitant" of or "found" within the district of suit, Ex parte Schollenberger, 96 U.S. 369 (1877), held that the defendant had consented to be so "found" by designating an agent for service of process in actions in courts of the state in which the federal district court was located.

However, after venue in 1887 had been made to depend solely on residence, the Court, harking back to early notions, held that a corporation could be a "resident" only of the state in which it was incorporated and of the district in that state in which its principal offices were located. Shaw v. Quincy Mining Co., 145 U.S. 444 (1892). Most lower federal courts interpreted these decisions as involving an abandonment of the theory of venue by prior consent or waiver.

Nearly fifty years later, in Neirbo Co. v. Bethlehem Shipbuilding Corp., 308 U.S. 165 (1939), the Supreme Court reaffirmed the Schollenberger principle. There New Jersey plaintiffs brought a diversity action in a federal district court in New York against a New York corporation and a Delaware corporation. It was held that the Delaware company had waived its venue privilege by a prior general designation of an agent "as the person upon whom a summons may be served within the State of New York".

The Neirbo decision greatly eased the problems of suing foreign corporations in federal courts. But it made federal venue in such actions dependent *pro tanto* upon state law. The state must have power to exact a valid consent. And application of the doctrine, for example, to causes of action arising outside the state, depended presumably upon the state court's construction of the consent.

Uncertainties as to the scope of the decision abounded. Should the consent be construed as extending also to federal causes of action? If the action were within the exclusive jurisdiction of the federal court? Or only if the state courts had a concurrent jurisdiction? Must the consent on which the waiver was based be express, as by the designation of an agent for service of process? What if the corporation was required to designate such an agent but failed to do so? (A footnote to the Neirbo opinion, 308 U.S. at 173–74, n. 15, said that "the decisive difference" between that case and In re Keasbey & Mattison Co., 160 U.S. 221 (1895), was that "in the latter case the designation under state law which is the basis of consent had in fact not been made".) Could a waiver be found in an implied consent attached by state law simply to the doing of certain acts within the state? See generally Comment, *The Aftermath of the Neirbo Case,* 42 Ill.L. Rev. 780 (1948).

Section 1391(c) of Title 28, enacted in 1948, seems to have been primarily designed to eliminate the possibility that a corporation failing to comply with state law requirements would be better off than one that had complied. Does the provision make the Neirbo doctrine entirely obsolete? In Olberding v. Illinois Cent. R.R., 346 U.S. 338 (1953), a divided Court upheld a challenge to the venue by an out-of-state individual defendant who had been involved in an accident in the state but who had no other connections with it and had not designated an agent for service. Section 1391(c) was not applicable, and the fact that the state's long-arm statute reached this defendant was held to be of no help, since "implied consent" was a pure fiction not equivalent to actual consent within the meaning of Neirbo.

Note that the problem in the Olberding case would now be obviated by the provision for venue in the district "in which the claim arose".

(3) What is the purpose and effect of the last clause in § 1391(c)?

Does it operate to control the meaning of "residence" and "reside" in other special venue provisions? Generally, yes, as shown by the decision in Pure Oil Co. v. Suarez, 384 U.S. 202 (1966), followed in Penrod. One exception, however, is the special venue provision applicable to patent cases, 28 U.S.C. § 1400(b);[4] the Supreme Court held in Fourco Glass Co. v. Transmirra Products Corp., 353 U.S. 222 (1957), that a corporation "resides" only in the state of its incorporation within the meaning of that provision. *Cf.* Brunette Machine Works, Ltd. v. Kockum Industries, Inc., p. 1716, *supra.*

Does the last clause of § 1391(c) also enlarge a corporation's opportunities of access to federal courts as a plaintiff? This natural reading of the clause apparently never occurred to the revisers, see Note, 28 Ind.L.J. 256 (1953), and would certainly promote widespread forum shopping by corporate plaintiffs doing business in many states. At the same time it would enlarge the possibilities of transfer under § 1404, see Note, *Federal Venue and the Corporate Plaintiff,* 37 Ind.L.J. 363 (1962). The Supreme Court

---

4. That section provides that an action for patent infringement may be brought in the district where the defendant "resides" or where he "has committed acts of infringement and has a regular and established place of business."

expressly left the question open, noting that it "is a difficult one, with far-reaching effects." Abbott Laboratories v. Gardner, 387 U.S. 136, 156–57 n. 20 (1967). But every court of appeals to consider the question has relied on the history of § 1391(c), and on the policy underlying it, to hold it inapplicable to corporate plaintiffs. See 15 Wright, Miller & Cooper, Federal Practice and Procedure § 3811 (1986).

(4) By what standard should courts decide whether a corporation is "doing business" within the meaning of § 1391(c)? There is a consensus that a federal standard is appropriate, but little agreement on its content. Some courts have held that if the defendant meets the "minimum contacts" test for amenability to service, it is doing business for venue purposes. *E.g.,* Du–Al Corp. v. Rudolph Beaver, Inc., 540 F.2d 1230 (4th Cir.1976). Others believe the standard for venue is more stringent, requiring some degree of continuity and substantiality. *E.g.,* Damon Coats, Inc. v. Munsingwear, Inc., 431 F.Supp. 1303 (E.D.Pa.1977). Doesn't the latter approach make more sense in view of (a) the expansion of state long-arm jurisdiction to cases involving a single contact with the state; (b) the origins of § 1391(c) in the Neirbo doctrine of waiver by those licensed to carry on business activities; and (c) the provision that venue will also lie where "the claim arose"? [5]

(5) As the Penrod decision and Rule 4(d)(3) indicate, the question of litigating capacity becomes important when considering the amenability to suit of a partnership or unincorporated association. Note the provisions of Rule 17(b) on this point, particularly the distinction drawn between cases involving federal claims and all other cases. Is the distinction sound? Does it imply that for purposes of federal law, an unincorporated association may have rights and liabilities distinct from those of its members? [6] If so, is it consistent with the Enabling Act? *Cf.* § 301(b) of the Labor–Management Relations Act of 1947, 29 U.S.C. § 185(b), providing that for certain purposes a labor organization may sue or be sued "as an entity" in the federal courts and that "[a]ny money judgment against a labor organization in a district court of the United States shall be enforceable only against the organization as an entity and against its assets, and shall not be enforceable against any individual member or his assets".

(6) Can the Penrod decision—and the Supreme Court decision on which it relied, Denver & R.G.W.R.R. v. Brotherhood of Railroad Trainmen, 387 U.S. 556 (1967)—be squared with United Steelworkers v. Bouligny, Inc., 382 U.S. 145 (1965), p. 1674, *supra?* In the Denver decision, the Supreme Court noted that Congress in enacting § 1391(c) was addressing itself to a question involving corporations "while maintaining its silence with regard

5. See Note, 65 Tex.L.Rev. 153, 173 (1986) (arguing that venue based on "doing business" should be proper only "when the defendant corporation has such continuous and substantial contacts with the forum as would allow general jurisdiction" (*i.e.,* the maintenance of any claim against the defendant) in that forum).

6. As noted in Penrod, the provision of Rule 17(b) relating to federal claims is drawn from United Mine Workers v. Coronado Coal Co., 259 U.S. 344 (1922). In Coronado, the Court reversed on the merits a Sherman Act judgment against several

unions and others but held that the unions' motion to dismiss, on the ground they could not be sued in their own names, was properly denied. Chief Justice Taft, after reviewing the large body of state and federal legislation recognizing the existence and lawfulness of labor unions, concluded (p. 391): "In this state of federal legislation, we think that such organizations are suable in the federal courts for their acts, and that funds accumulated to be expended in conducting strikes are subject to execution in suits for torts committed by such unions in strikes."

to the unincorporated association" (p. 561). And unlike the rules relating to diversity jurisdiction, "[t]here was no settled construction of the [venue] law" as it applied to such associations in 1948 "and there is none yet". *Id.* Finally, the Court suggested that there could be more judicial innovation in matters of venue than in matters affecting the scope of jurisdiction.

Note how a plaintiff can be squeezed between the two rules. He may be forced to bring a class action against representative members of an association, in order to satisfy the diversity requirements, but may find himself far more limited in his choice of venue than if he could sue the association directly.

(7) The ALI Study, in proposed § 1314, provided that in federal question cases, venue would lie only in (1) a district where a substantial part of the events occurred or the property that is the subject of the action is situated, (2) the district where all defendants reside, or (3) a district where any defendant may be found if no other venue is available. Corporate residence was limited to the state of incorporation and of the principal place of business; the residence of unincorporated associations was limited to the principal place of business. Nationwide service of process was then provided.[7] Proposed § 1303, on venue in diversity cases, was essentially the same, except that no provision for service of process was included.[8]

Professor Currie applauded the adoption of a "single test" for place of trial in federal question cases as "an original and brilliant advance" and jeered at the retention of a "double test" of venue and personal jurisdiction in diversity cases (as well as the failure to revise the rules in admiralty) as "plodding and myopic". Currie, *The Federal Courts and the American Law Institute (II)*, 36 U.Chi.L.Rev. 268, 299–307 (1969). Like Professor Barrett, *Venue and Service of Process in the Federal Courts—Suggestions for Reform*, 7 Vand.L.Rev. 608 (1954), Currie urged that federal standards should govern the place of trial in all cases. But unlike the ALI in its federal question proposals, Currie would make these standards part of a statute on the reach of process—a federal long-arm statute governing the issuance of process by the district courts—and would scrap the venue concept altogether. (Do you see what the difference between the two approaches would be, in view of the fact that objections to process as well as to venue are waivable?) Both Barrett and Currie would abrogate the Klaxon rule as an incident of such a revision of the power of the district courts.

---

7. The ALI recommended that after adoption of this proposal, there be a systematic reexamination of the hundreds of special venue provisions in the United States Code, with the expectation that most of them could be repealed.

8. Special venue and process provisions were included in the separate chapter dealing with multi-party multi-state diversity cases. See proposed §§ 2372, 2374(a).

VAN DUSEN v. BARRACK

376 U.S. 612, 84 S.Ct. 805, 11 L.Ed.2d 945 (1964).

Certiorari to the United States Court of Appeals for the Third Circuit.

MR. JUSTICE GOLDBERG delivered the opinion of the Court. * *

* * * On October 4, 1960, shortly after departing from a Boston airport, a commercial airliner, scheduled to fly from Boston to Philadelphia, plunged into Boston Harbor. As a result of the crash, over 150 actions for personal injury and wrongful death have been instituted against the airline, various manufacturers, the United States, and, in some cases, the Massachusetts Port Authority. In most of these actions the plaintiffs have alleged that the crash resulted from the defendants' negligence in permitting the aircraft's engines to ingest some birds. More than 100 actions were brought in the United States District Court for the District of Massachusetts, and more than 45 actions in the United States District Court for the Eastern District of Pennsylvania.

The present case concerns 40 of the wrongful death actions brought in the Eastern District of Pennsylvania by personal representatives of victims of the crash. The defendants, petitioners in this Court, moved under [28 U.S.C.] § 1404(a) to transfer these actions to the District of Massachusetts, where it was alleged that most of the witnesses resided and where over 100 other actions are pending. The District Court granted the motion, holding that the transfer was justified regardless of whether the transferred actions would be governed by the laws and choice-of-law rules of Pennsylvania or of Massachusetts. 204 F.Supp. 426. The District Court also specifically held that transfer was not precluded by the fact that the plaintiffs had not qualified under Massachusetts law to sue as representatives of the decedents. The plaintiffs, respondents in this Court, sought a writ of mandamus from the Court of Appeals and successfully contended that the District Court erred and should vacate its order of transfer. 309 F.2d 953. The Court of Appeals held that a § 1404(a) transfer could be granted only if at the time the suits were brought, the plaintiffs had qualified to sue in Massachusetts, the State of the transferee District Court. The Court of Appeals relied in part upon its interpretation of Rule 17(b) of the Federal Rules of Civil Procedure.

We granted certiorari to review important questions concerning the construction and operation of § 1404(a). For reasons to be stated below, we hold that the judgment of the Court of Appeals must be reversed, that both the Court of Appeals and the District Court erred in their fundamental assumptions regarding the state law to be applied to an action transferred under § 1404(a), and that accordingly the case must be remanded to the District Court.[3]

3. Although it is clear that this Court has jurisdiction to review the judgment of the Court of Appeals, the Government, a defendant in this case, urges that the judgment below be reversed because mandamus was an improper remedy. * * * Since in our opinion the courts below erred in interpreting the legal limitations upon and criteria for a § 1404(a) transfer, we find it unnecessary to consider the mandamus contentions advanced by the Government. Cf. Platt v. Minnesota Mining & Mfg. Co., 376 U.S., at 240.

I. WHERE THE ACTION "MIGHT HAVE BEEN BROUGHT."

Section 1404(a) reflects an increased desire to have federal civil suits tried in the federal system at the place called for in the particular case by considerations of convenience and justice. Thus, as the Court recognized in Continental Grain Co. v. Barge F.B.L.–585, 364 U.S. 19, 26, 27, the purpose of the section is to prevent the waste "of time, energy and money" and "to protect litigants, witnesses and the public against unnecessary inconvenience and expense * * *." To this end it empowers a district court to transfer "any civil action" to another district court if the transfer is warranted by the convenience of parties and witnesses and promotes the interest of justice. This transfer power is, however, expressly limited by the final clause of § 1404(a) restricting transfer to those federal districts in which the action "might have been brought." Although in the present case the plaintiffs were qualified to bring suit as personal representatives under Pennsylvania law (the law of the State of the transferor federal court), the Court of Appeals ruled that the defendants' transfer motion must be denied because at the time the suits were brought in Pennsylvania (the transferor forum) the complainants had not obtained the appointments requisite to initiate such actions in Massachusetts (the transferee forum). At the outset, therefore, we must consider whether the incapacity of the plaintiffs at the time they commenced their actions in the transferor forum to sue under the state law of the transferee forum renders the latter forum impermissible under the "might-have-been-brought" limitation.

There is no question concerning the propriety either of venue or of jurisdiction in the District of Massachusetts, the proposed transferee forum. The Court of Appeals conceded that it was "quite likely" that the plaintiffs could have obtained ancillary appointment in Massachusetts but held this legally irrelevant. In concluding that the transfer could not be granted, the Court of Appeals relied upon Hoffman v. Blaski, 363 U.S. 335, as establishing that "unless the plaintiff *had an unqualified right to bring suit* in the transferee forum at the time he filed his original complaint, transfer to that district is not authorized by § 1404(a)." (Emphasis in original.) * * *

A. In Hoffman v. Blaski this Court first considered the nature of the limitation imposed by the words "where it might have been brought." The plaintiff opposed the defendant's motion to transfer on the ground that the proposed transferee forum lacked both "venue over the action and ability to command jurisdiction over the * * *" defendant. 363 U.S., at 337. The question, as stated by the Court, was "whether a District Court, in which a civil action has been properly brought, is empowered by § 1404(a) to transfer the action, on the motion of the defendant, to a district in which the plaintiff did not have a *right* to bring it." *Id.,* 363 U.S. at 336. (Emphasis in original.) The defendant emphasized that "venue, like jurisdiction over the person, may be waived." *Id.,* 363 U.S. at 343. This Court held that, despite the defendant's waivers or consent, a forum which had been improper for both venue and service of process was not a forum where the action "might have been brought."

In the present case the Court of Appeals concluded that transfer could not be granted because here, as in Hoffman v. Blaski, the plaintiffs did not have an "independent" or "unqualified" right to bring the actions in the transferee forum. The propriety of this analogy to Hoffman turns, however, on the validity of the assumption that the "where-it-might-have-been-brought" clause refers not only to federal venue statutes but also to the laws applied in the State of the transferee forum. It must be noted that the instant case, unlike Hoffman, involves a motion to transfer to a district in which both venue and jurisdiction are proper. This difference plainly demonstrates that the Court of Appeals extended the Hoffman decision and increased the restrictions on transfers to convenient federal forums. The issue here is not that presented in Hoffman but instead is whether the limiting words of § 1404(a) prevent a change of venue within the federal system because, under the law of the State of the transferee forum, the plaintiff was not qualified to sue or might otherwise be frustrated or prejudiced in pursuing his action.

* * *

In summary, then, we hold that the words "where it might have been brought" must be construed with reference to the federal laws delimiting the districts in which such an action "may be brought" and not with reference to laws of the transferee State concerning the capacity of fiduciaries to bring suit.

B. The Court of Appeals, in reversing the District Court, relied in part upon Rule 17(b) of the Federal Rules of Civil Procedure. * * * The reliance placed on Rule 17(b) necessarily assumes that its language—which is not free from ambiguity—requires the application of the law of the State of the transferee district court rather than that of the transferor district court. * * *

* * * [I]n our opinion the underlying and fundamental question is whether, in a case such as the present, a change of venue within the federal system is to be accompanied by a change in the applicable state law. * * * In view of the facts of this case and their bearing on this basic question, we must consider first, insofar as is relevant, the relationship between a change of venue under § 1404(a) and the applicable state law.

II. "THE INTEREST OF JUSTICE": EFFECT OF A CHANGE OF VENUE UPON APPLICABLE STATE LAW.

A. The plaintiffs contend that the change of venue ordered by the District Court was necessarily precluded by the likelihood that it would be accompanied by a highly prejudicial change in the applicable state law. The prejudice alleged is not limited to that which might flow from the Massachusetts laws governing capacity to sue. Indeed, the plaintiffs emphasize the likelihood that the defendants' "ultimate reason for seeking transfer is to move to a forum where recoveries for wrongful death are restricted to sharply limited punitive damages rather than compensation for the loss suffered." It is argued that Pennsylvania choice-of-law rules would result in the application of laws substantially different from those that would be applied by courts sitting in Massachusetts. * * *

The possibilities suggested by the plaintiffs' argument illustrate the difficulties that would arise if a change of venue, granted at the motion of a defendant, were to result in a change of law. Although in the present case the contentions concern rules relating to capacity to sue and damages, in other cases the transferee forum might have a shorter statute of limitations or might refuse to adjudicate a claim which would have been actionable in the transferor State. In such cases a defendant's motion to transfer could be tantamount to a motion to dismiss. In light, therefore, of this background and the facts of the present case, we need not and do not consider the merits of the contentions concerning the meaning and proper application of Pennsylvania's laws and choice of law rules. For present purposes it is enough that the potential prejudice to the plaintiffs is so substantial as to require review of the assumption that a change of state law would be a permissible result of transfer under § 1404(a).

The decisions of the lower federal courts, taken as a whole, reveal that courts construing § 1404(a) have been strongly inclined to protect plaintiffs against the risk that transfer might be accompanied by a prejudicial change in applicable state laws. * * *

Of course these cases allow plaintiffs to retain whatever advantages may flow from the state laws of the forum they have initially selected. There is nothing, however, in the language or policy of § 1404(a) to justify its use by defendants to defeat the advantages accruing to plaintiffs who have chosen a forum which, although it was inconvenient, was a proper venue. In this regard the transfer provisions of § 1404(a) may be compared with those of § 1406(a). Although both sections were broadly designed to allow transfer instead of dismissal, § 1406(a) provides for transfer from forums in which venue is wrongly or improperly laid, whereas, in contrast, § 1404(a) operates on the premises that the plaintiff has properly exercised his venue privilege. This distinction underlines the fact that Congress, in passing § 1404(a), was primarily concerned with the problems arising where, despite the propriety of the plaintiff's venue selection, the chosen forum was an inconvenient one.

In considering the Judicial Code, Congress was particularly aware of the need for provisions to mitigate abuses stemming from broad federal venue provisions. The venue provision of the Federal Employers' Liability Act was the subject of special concern. However, while the Judicial Code was pending, Congress considered and rejected the Jennings bill which, as the Court stated in Ex parte Collett, 337 U.S. 55, 64, "was far more drastic than § 1404(a)," and which "would in large part have repealed [the venue section] of the Liability Act" by severely delimiting the permissible forums. This legislative background supports the view that § 1404(a) was not designed to narrow the plaintiff's venue privilege or to defeat the state-law advantages that might accrue from the exercise of this venue privilege but rather the provision was simply to counteract the inconveniences that flowed from the venue statutes by permitting transfer to a convenient federal court. The legislative history of § 1404(a) certainly does not justify the rather startling conclusion that one might "get a change of law as a bonus for a change of venue." Indeed, an interpretation accepting such a rule would go far to frustrate the remedial purposes of § 1404(a). If a change of law were in the offing, the parties might well regard the section primarily as a forum-shopping instrument. And, more importantly, courts would at least be reluctant to grant transfers, despite considerations of convenience, if to do so might conceivably prejudice the claim of a plaintiff who had initially selected a permissible forum. We believe, therefore, that both the history and purposes of § 1404(a) indicate that it should be regarded as a federal judicial housekeeping measure, dealing with the placement of litigation in the federal courts and generally intended, on the basis of convenience and fairness, simply to authorize a change of court-rooms.[36]

Although we deal here with a congressional statute apportioning the business of the federal courts, our interpretation of that statute fully accords with and is supported by the policy underlying Erie R. Co. v. Tompkins, 304 U.S. 64. * * * [W]e should ensure that the "accident" of federal diversity jurisdiction does not enable a party to utilize a transfer to achieve a result in federal court which could not have been achieved in the courts of the State where the action was filed. This purpose would be defeated in cases such as the present if nonresident defendants, properly subjected to suit in the transferor State (Pennsylvania), could invoke § 1404(a) to gain the benefits of the laws of another jurisdiction (Massachusetts). What Erie and the cases following it have sought was an identity or uniformity between federal and state courts; and the fact that in most instances this could be achieved by directing federal courts to apply the laws of the States "in which they sit" should not obscure that, in applying the same reasoning to § 1404(a), the critical identity to be maintained is between the federal district court which decides the case and the courts of the State in which the action was filed.

We conclude, therefore, that in cases such as the present, where the defendants seek transfer, the transferee district court must be obligated to apply the state law that would have been applied if there had been no change of venue. A change of venue under § 1404(a) generally should be, with respect to state law, but a change of courtrooms.[40]

We, therefore, reject the plaintiffs' contention that the transfer was necessarily precluded by the likelihood that a prejudicial change of law would result. In so ruling, however, we do not and need not consider whether in all cases § 1404(a) would require the application of the law of the transferor, as opposed to the transferee, State.[41] We do not attempt to determine whether, for example, the same considerations would govern if a plaintiff sought transfer under § 1404(a) or if it was contended that the transferor State would simply have dismissed the action on the ground of *forum non conveniens*.

---

36. For recent proposals, see A.L.I., Study of the Division of Jurisdiction between State and Federal Courts (Tent. Draft No. 1, 1963), §§ 1306, 1307, 1308. The commentary on the proposed § 1306 notes that, where the defendant seeks transfer, the section would provide "that the transferee court shall apply the rules which the transferor court would have been bound to apply. * * * The effect is to give the plaintiff the benefit which traditionally he has had in the selection of a forum with favorable choice-of-law rules. * * * It may be thought undesirable to let the plaintiff reap a choice-of-law benefit from the deliberate selection of an inconvenient forum. In a sense this is so, but the alternatives seem even more undesirable. If the rules of the State where the transferee district is located were to control, the judge exercising his discretion upon a motion for transfer might well make a ruling decisive of the merits of the case. Whether he should simply decide the appropriate place for trial, letting the choice-of-law bonus fall as it may, or include in his consideration of 'the interest of justice' the 'just' choice-of-law rule, the result is unfortunate. * * *" *Id.*, at 65–66.

40. Of course the transferee District Court may apply its own rules governing the conduct and dispatch of cases in its court. We are only concerned here with those state laws of the transferor State which would significantly affect the outcome of the case.

41. We do not suggest that the application of transferor state law is free from constitutional limitations. See, *e.g.*, Watson v. Employers Liability Assurance Corp., Ltd., 348 U.S. 66; Hughes v. Fetter, 341 U.S. 609. * * *

B. It is in light of the foregoing analysis that we must consider the interpretation of Rule 17(b) of the Federal Rules of Civil Procedure and the relationship between that Rule and the laws applicable following a § 1404(a) transfer.

Since in this case the transferee district court must under § 1404(a) apply the laws of the State of the transferor district court, it follows in our view that Rule 17(b) must be interpreted similarly so that the capacity to sue will also be governed by the laws of the transferor State. Where a § 1404(a) transfer is thus held not to effect a change of law but essentially only to authorize a change of courtrooms, the reference in Rule 17(b) to the law of the State "in which the district court is held" should be applied in a corresponding manner so that it will refer to the district court which sits in the State that will generally be the source of applicable laws. We conclude, therefore, that the Court of Appeals misconceived the meaning and application of Rule 17(b) and erred in holding that it required the denial of the § 1404(a) transfer.

III. APPLICABLE LAW: EFFECT ON THE CONVENIENCE OF PARTIES AND WITNESSES.

The holding that a § 1404(a) transfer would not alter the state law to be applied does not dispose of the question of whether the proposed transfer can be justified when measured against the relevant criteria of convenience and fairness. * * *

It is apparent that the desirability of transfer might be significantly affected if Pennsylvania courts decided that, in actions such as the present, they would recognize the cause of action based on the Massachusetts Death Act but would not apply that statute's culpability principle and damage limitation. In regard to this possibility it is relevant to note that the District Court in transferring these actions generally assumed that transfer to Massachusetts would facilitate the consolidation of these cases with those now pending in the Massachusetts District Court and that, as a result, transfer would be accompanied by the full benefits of consolidation and uniformity of result. Since, however, Pennsylvania laws would govern the trial of the transferred cases, insofar as those laws may be significantly different from the laws governing the cases already pending in Massachusetts, the feasibility of consolidation and the benefits therefrom may be substantially altered. Moreover, if the transferred actions would not be subject to the Massachusetts culpability and damage limitation provisions, then the plaintiffs might find a relatively greater need for compensatory damage witnesses to testify with regard to the economic losses suffered by individuals. It is possible that such a difference in damage rules could make the plaintiffs relatively more dependent upon witnesses more conveniently located for a trial in Pennsylvania. In addition, it has long been recognized that: "There is an appropriateness * * * in having the trial of a diversity case in a forum that is at home with the state law that must govern the case, rather than having a court in some other forum untangle problems in conflict of laws, and in law foreign to itself." Gulf Oil Corp. v. Gilbert, 330 U.S. 501, 509. Thus, to the extent that Pennsylvania laws are difficult or unclear and might not defer to Massachusetts laws, it may be advantageous to retain the actions in Pennsylvania where the judges possess a more ready familiarity with the local laws.

If, on the other hand, Pennsylvania courts would apply the Massachusetts Death Act in its entirety, these same factors might well weigh quite differently. Consolidation of the transferred cases with those now pending in Massachusetts might be freed from any potential difficulties and rendered more desirable. The plaintiffs' need for witnesses residing in Pennsylvania might be significantly reduced. And, of course, the trial would be held in the State in which the causes of action arose and in which the federal judges are more familiar with the governing laws.

In pointing to these considerations, we are fully aware that the District Court concluded that the relevant Pennsylvania law was unsettled, that its determination involved difficult questions, and that in the near future Pennsylvania courts might provide guidance. We think that this uncertainty, however, should itself have been considered as a factor bearing on the desirability of transfer. Section 1404(a) provides for transfer to a more convenient forum, not to a forum likely to prove equally convenient or inconvenient. We do not suggest that elements of uncertainty in transferor state law would alone justify a denial of transfer; but we do think that the uncertainty is one factor, among others, to be considered in assessing the desirability of transfer. * * *

Accordingly, the judgment of the Court of Appeals for the Third Circuit is reversed and the cause remanded to the District Court for further proceedings in conformity with this opinion.

Reversed and remanded.

MR. JUSTICE BLACK concurs in the reversal substantially for the reasons set forth in the opinion of the Court, but he believes that, under the circumstances shown in the opinion, this Court should now hold it was error to order these actions transferred to the District of Massachusetts.

NOTE ON FORUM NON CONVENIENS AND CHANGE OF VENUE

(1) Section 1404 of Title 28 originated in the revision of the Judicial Code in 1948.[1] Prior to that time, the Court had held the principle of forum non conveniens applicable in an action at law in the federal courts: "[A] court [by dismissing the action] may resist imposition upon its jurisdiction even when jurisdiction is authorized by the letter of a general venue statute." Gulf Oil Corp. v. Gilbert, 330 U.S. 501, 507 (1947).[2] After noting that the doctrine "presupposes at least two forums in which the defendant

---

1. Other transfer provisions include 28 U.S.C. § 1406 (see Paragraph (6), *infra*); 28 U.S.C. § 1407 (see Paragraph (9), *infra*); 28 U.S.C. § 1631 (transfer "to cure want of jurisdiction"); 28 U.S.C. § 2112(a) (proceedings instituted in two or more courts of appeals with respect to the same administrative order); 46 U.S.C. § 742 (admiralty suits against the United States); Fed.R.Civ. P., Supplementary Rule F(9) (limitation proceedings); Fed.R.Cr.P. 21 (criminal proceedings).

2. Gulf Oil was a diversity action for damages resulting from alleged negligence.

Earlier decisions had permitted dismissal on similar grounds in admiralty and equity proceedings. See, *e.g.*, Canada Malting Co. v. Paterson S.S., Ltd., 285 U.S. 413 (1932); Rogers v. Guaranty Trust Co., 288 U.S. 123 (1933). But in Baltimore & O.R.R. v. Kepner, 314 U.S. 44 (1941), the Court indicated that no such power to dismiss existed in an FELA case because the broad venue provision of the FELA conferred an unqualified privilege on the plaintiff-employee.

is amenable to process," the Court in Gulf Oil described the factors that were to be considered (pp. 508–09):

"If the combination and weight of factors requisite to given results are difficult to forecast or state, those to be considered are not difficult to name. An interest to be considered, and the one likely to be most pressed, is the private interest of the litigant. Important considerations are the relative ease of access to sources of proof; availability of compulsory process for attendance of unwilling, and the cost of obtaining attendance of willing, witnesses; possibility of view of premises, if view would be appropriate to the action; and all other practical problems that make trial of a case easy, expeditious and inexpensive. There may also be questions as to the enforcibility of a judgment if one is obtained. The court will weigh relative advantages and obstacles to fair trial. It is often said that the plaintiff may not, by choice of an inconvenient forum, 'vex,' 'harass,' or 'oppress' the defendant by inflicting upon him expense or trouble not necessary to his own right to pursue his remedy. But unless the balance is strongly in favor of the defendant, the plaintiff's choice of forum should rarely be disturbed.

"Factors of public interest also have place in applying the doctrine. Administrative difficulties follow for courts when litigation is piled up in congested centers instead of being handled at its origin. Jury duty is a burden that ought not to be imposed upon the people of a community which has no relation to the litigation. In cases which touch the affairs of many persons, there is reason for holding the trial in their view and reach rather than in remote parts of the country where they can learn of it by report only. There is a local interest in having localized controversies decided at home. There is an appropriateness, too, in having the trial of a diversity case in a forum that is at home with the state law that must govern the case, rather than having a court in some other forum untangle problems in conflict of laws, and in law foreign to itself."

(2) The Reviser's Notes to § 1404(a) explained the provision as follows:

"Subsection (a) was drafted in accordance with the doctrine of *forum non conveniens,* permitting transfer to a more convenient forum, even though the venue is proper. As an example of the need of such a provision, see Baltimore & Ohio R. Co. v. Kepner, 314 U.S. 44 (1941), which was prosecuted under the Federal Employer's Liability Act in New York, although the accident occurred and the employee resided in Ohio. The new subsection requires the court to determine that the transfer is necessary for convenience of the parties and witnesses, and further, that it is in the interest of justice to do so." [3]

The provision does not deprive the court of discretion to dismiss on grounds of forum non conveniens when it concludes that the case ought to be litigated in a forum to which it cannot be transferred. Thus in Piper Aircraft Co. v. Reyno, 454 U.S. 235 (1981), the Supreme Court upheld as within the district court's discretion a decision to dismiss a wrongful death action brought on behalf of the Scottish victims of an air crash that had occurred in Scotland. The Court sustained the dismissal although the

---

3. Partly on the basis of this citation of the Kepner case, the Court concluded in Ex parte Collett, 337 U.S. 55 (1949), that § 1404(a) was applicable in an FELA case. See also Continental Grain Co. v. Barge FBL–585, 364 U.S. 19 (1960) (upholding transfer under § 1404(a) of admiralty action in which in rem and in personam proceedings were joined.)

defendants were American companies and although Scottish law was less favorable to the plaintiffs than American law on issues of capacity to sue, liability, and damages. Among the factors supporting the dismissal were the Scottish citizenship and residence of the victims and their survivors, the location of evidence in Scotland, the ability to implead third parties there, the interest of United States courts in avoiding complex problems of choice of law, and the danger that refusal to dismiss would "increase and further congest already crowded courts" in this country (p. 252). The Court did state, however, that dismissal might not be in the interest of justice "if the remedy provided by the alternative forum is so clearly inadequate or unsatisfactory that it is no remedy at all ∗ ∗ ∗" (p. 254).[4]

(3) The doctrine of forum non conveniens is recognized in many but not all of the states. (Most state court dismissals involve suits between nonresidents on foreign causes of action. Some involve questions of the "internal affairs" of a foreign corporation.) Should a federal court transfer a diversity case (or if transfer is unavailable, dismiss) if the case is one that the forum state would dismiss on forum non conveniens grounds?[5] *Cf.* Szantay v. Beech Aircraft Corp., 349 F.2d 60 (4th Cir.1965), p. 840, *supra*. In Parsons v. Chesapeake & O. Ry. Co., 375 U.S. 71, 74 (1963), the Supreme Court held in an FELA case that a prior state court dismissal on the basis of forum non conveniens can "never serve to divest a federal district judge of the discretionary power vested in him" under § 1404(a). Noting that there were differences between the state's criteria for dismissal and the federal court's criteria for transfer, the Supreme Court sustained the trial court's refusal to transfer the action. The precise question in Parsons was the applicability of res judicata to a motion for transfer in a federal question case, but the Parsons rationale was relied on, along with a number of other factors, in a well-reasoned opinion in a diversity case refusing to follow state law on a motion to dismiss. Lapides v. Doner, 248 F.Supp. 883 (E.D.Mich.1965). See also Michell v. General Motors Corp., 439 F.Supp. 24 (N.D.Ohio 1977).

4. The Court in Piper emphasized the fact that the action had been brought on behalf of persons who were not U.S. citizens or residents. How much weight should be accorded this factor in deciding whether to defer to the plaintiff's choice of forum? See Alcoa S.S. Co., Inc. v. M/V Nordic Regent, 654 F.2d 147 (2d Cir.1978) (upholding forum non conveniens dismissal although the plaintiff was a U.S. corporation and the law of Trinidad—the place found to be the more appropriate forum— imposed a much lower limit on recovery than did the law of the United States); Yellen, *Forum Non Conveniens: Standards for the Dismissal of Actions From United States Federal Courts to Foreign Tribunals,* 5 Fordham Int'l L.J. 533 (1982).

The Piper decision was relied on by the Second Circuit in affirming a dismissal on forum non conveniens grounds in In re Union Carbide Corp. Gas Plant Disaster at Bhopal, India, in December 1984, 809 F.2d 195 (2d Cir.1987).

For broad-ranging criticisms of current forum non conveniens doctrine, see Stein, *Forum Non Conveniens and the Redundancy of Court Access Doctrine,* 133 U.Pa.L. Rev. 781 (1985); Stewart, *Forum Non Conveniens: A Doctrine in Search of a Role,* 74 Calif.L.Rev. 1259 (1986); Robertson, *Forum Non Conveniens in America and England: "A Rather Fantastic Fiction,"* 103 L.Q.Rev. 398 (1987).

5. In the Gulf Oil case, the Court observed that "[t]he law of New York as to the discretion of a court to apply the doctrine of forum non conveniens, and as to the standards that guide discretion is, so far as here involved, the same as the federal rule. ∗ ∗ ∗ It would not be profitable, therefore, to pursue inquiry as to the source from which our rule must flow." 330 U.S. at 509. See also Piper Aircraft Co. v. Reyno, Paragraph (2), *supra,* at 248 n. 13.

(4) The Court's decision in Hoffman v. Blaski, construing "where it might have been brought" in § 1404(a), is discussed and distinguished in Van Dusen. Although neither decision makes it completely clear whether a case can be transferred to a district in which venue is proper but personal jurisdiction over the defendant cannot be obtained, it is generally believed that such transfer is unavailable. See Wright, Federal Courts § 44, at 263 n. 44 (4th ed. 1983).

A vigorous dissent in Hoffman was filed by Justice Frankfurter, who argued that the language of § 1404(a) did not compel the result reached and that the policies of the section would best be served by holding that the defendant's motion for transfer obviates any objections to process or venue in the transferee forum. But what of the argument that the venue provisions are designed for the convenience of both parties and that while the plaintiff cannot be heard to object when he selects the forum, he should be able to object if the defendant is trying to choose the place of trial? Justice Frankfurter answered (363 U.S. at 361–62):

"* * * This would be a powerful argument if, under § 1404(a), a transfer were to be made whenever requested by the defendant. Such is not the case, and this bears emphasis. A transfer can be made under § 1404(a) to a place where the action might have been brought only when 'convenience' and 'justice' so dictate, not whenever the defendant so moves. A legitimate objection by the plaintiff to proceeding in the transferee forum will presumably be reflected in a decision that the interest of justice does not require the transfer, and so it becomes irrelevant that the proposed place of transfer is deemed one where the action 'might have been brought.' If the plaintiff's objection to proceedings in the transferee court is not consonant with the interests of justice, a good reason is wanting why the transfer should not be made."

Are you satisfied with the answer? If Justice Frankfurter's position is sound, shouldn't it be applicable to a plaintiff's motion for transfer as well? Would Justice Frankfurter agree? Was he perhaps thinking of § 1404(a) as only a defendant's remedy?[6] If the answer to either of the last two questions is yes, what meaning did Justice Frankfurter attribute to "where it might have been brought"?

Given the result in Hoffman v. Blaski, should § 1404(a) be changed to delete the phrase "where it might have been brought"? What of the similar language in § 1406(a)?[7]

(5) What considerations should guide a judge in deciding whether to order a transfer? In Norwood v. Kirkpatrick, 349 U.S. 29 (1955), the Court held that the relevant factors remained those described in Gulf Oil Corp. v. Gilbert, *supra*, but that a "lesser showing of inconvenience" (p. 32) was needed to support transfer than was required for dismissal. Dismissal, the

---

6. Although the question has not been squarely ruled upon by the Supreme Court, it is now generally held that transfer may be granted on plaintiff's motion under § 1404(a). See 15 Wright, Miller & Cooper, Federal Practice and Procedure § 3844, at 330 (1986). Forum non conveniens is a defendant's remedy, and the Reviser's notes say nothing about making transfer under § 1404(a) available to plaintiffs. Why might a plaintiff want transfer if he cannot use it to avoid venue and process requirements?

7. Does the language of § 1404(a) allow transfer of an action commenced by the attachment of property? See Continental Grain Co. v. Barge FBL–585, note 3, *supra*; Comment, 31 U.Chi.L.Rev. 373 (1964); Wright, Federal Courts § 44, at 260–61 (4th ed. 1983). Is the question affected by the holding in Shaffer v. Heitner, 433 U.S. 186 (1977), summarized at p. 1721, *supra*?

Court noted, was a far harsher remedy than transfer. Does the Reviser's note support this result? Is it sound in view of the fact that dismissal under forum non conveniens presupposes another available forum? Should a heavier burden be imposed on a plaintiff seeking transfer than is imposed on a defendant?

For an excellent discussion, see Kitch, *Section 1404(a) of the Judicial Code: In the Interest of Justice or Injustice?*, 40 Ind.L.J. 99, 131–37 (1965). See also Annot., 1 A.L.R.Fed. 15 (1969).

(6) 28 U.S.C. § 1406(a) provides for transfer in lieu of dismissal, in the discretion of the court, in a case "laying venue in the wrong division or district". Section 1406(a) is plainly designed to aid plaintiffs who have chosen the wrong court. Somewhat surprisingly, this section has been held applicable to a case in which venue is improper *and* the defendant has not been subjected to the jurisdiction of the court. Goldlawr, Inc. v. Heiman, 369 U.S. 463 (1962). What is the advantage of transfer over dismissal in such a case?

Is transfer available if the plaintiff has selected the right venue but has not obtained personal jurisdiction over the defendant? See, *e.g.*, Dubin v. United States, 380 F.2d 813 (5th Cir.1967) (transfer allowed under § 1406(a)); Ellis v. Great Southwestern Corp., 646 F.2d 1099, 1106 (5th Cir. 1981) (transfer allowed under § 1404(a)).[8]

(7) An order granting or denying transfer is not an appealable final judgment, and is not ordinarily thought to be within the scope of the interlocutory appeal provisions of 28 U.S.C. § 1292(b). See Wright, Federal Courts § 44, at 266 (4th ed. 1983).[9] Thus immediate review of such an order is generally limited to an application for mandamus or prohibition, see p. 1827, *infra,* and each circuit seems to have its own standard governing the availability of the writ. While the Supreme Court has avoided any direct pronouncements, such decisions as Hoffman and Van Dusen indicate that it regards issuance of the writ to be proper when the district court has ordered a transfer to a district that is not one where the action "might have been brought". What if it is argued that the district court has relied on an inappropriate factor or refused to take a relevant factor into account? *Cf.* Platt v. Minnesota Mining & Mfg. Co., 376 U.S. 240 (1964). That it has evaluated relevant factors incorrectly? See General Tire & Rubber Co. v. Watkins, 373 F.2d 361 (4th Cir.1967); Chicago, R.I. & P.R.R. v. Igoe, 220 F.2d 299 (7th Cir.1955).

Although the decisions of the various circuits differ in both language and result, it seems almost impossible to obtain reversal in most courts of appeals on an application for mandamus if the argument is simply that the trial court abused its discretion in ordering or denying a transfer. For a forceful statement that such abuse should not be a basis for issuance of the writ, see Judge Friendly's concurring opinion in A. Olinick & Sons v. Dempster Bros., 365 F.2d 439, 445–48 (2d Cir.1966).

---

8. See Piper Aircraft Co. v. Reyno, Paragraph (2), *supra*, at 240–41 (district court transferred action against two defendants in which venue was proper but personal jurisdiction was lacking with respect to one of the defendants; transferee court then dismissed on forum non conveniens grounds.)

Would 28 U.S.C. § 1631 be of any assistance in such a case? See note 1, *supra*.

9. But see Continental Grain Co. v. Barge FBL–585, note 3, *supra*, in which an appeal to the court of appeals was allowed under § 1292(b). The question of appealability was not discussed by the Supreme Court.

Is there any reason why the party aggrieved by a grant or denial of transfer may be unable to obtain an effective remedy on appeal after final judgment? Would any error relating to transfer be likely to be considered harmless at that stage? See Ford Motor Co. v. Ryan, 182 F.2d 329, 330 (2d Cir.1950).[10] If so, how can the issuance of mandamus at an earlier stage be said to be "in aid of" the court's appellate jurisdiction under 28 U.S.C. § 1651? On the basis that the phrase contemplates use of the writ when its denial would immunize a lower court decision from appellate review?

(8) One conceptual problem in these cases is to decide where a case "is" when a district court has ordered it transferred to a district in another circuit. Once a case has been transferred, can the court of appeals in the transferor circuit cause the case to be brought back by instructing the district judge to vacate the order of transfer? See In re Nine Mile Limited, 673 F.2d 242 (8th Cir.1982) (after district court in 8th circuit transferred file to district court in 4th circuit, 8th circuit had no jurisdiction to review on writ of mandamus; transferor court should request transferee court to return the record.)[11]

Conceptual questions aside, should review of a transfer order occur in the transferor or in the transferee circuit? To avoid a judicial ping-pong game, shouldn't a decision by the transferor circuit refusing to require vacation of the transfer order be considered the "law of the case" in the transferee circuit? In Hoffman v. Blaski, the transferee circuit had ordered the case transferred back after the transferor circuit had denied mandamus, and the Supreme Court affirmed over Justice Frankfurter's dissenting argument that "res judicata" should be applied.

(9) Following the experience in handling pretrial discovery in the almost 2,000 separate antitrust suits filed in 36 districts against electrical equipment manufacturers in the early 1960s,[12] Congress enacted 28 U.S.C. § 1407 in 1968. The statute, based on the recommendations of a committee of the Judicial Conference, provides for transfers of actions involving one or more questions of fact "to any district for coordinated or consolidated pretrial proceedings." Transfers are made by a "judicial panel on multidistrict litigation," consisting of seven circuit and district judges named by the Chief Justice, no two of whom may be from the same circuit.

The Administrative Office of the United States Courts, in its 1986 Annual Report (at p. 128), stated that since the creation of the judicial panel in 1968, 15,026 civil actions had been centralized for pretrial proceedings, and 9,458 of these had been transferred from other districts. Of this total, 1,367 were still pending and subject to § 1407, and another 2,597 had been remanded to the transferor district for trial. The remainder had been terminated (by settlement or otherwise) in the transferee district.

10. It is generally held that if a case is transferred from a district court in one circuit to a district court in another, the initial decision may not be reviewed by a court of appeals in the transferee circuit. See, *e.g.*, Roofing & Sheet Metal Services, Inc. v. La Quinta Motor Inns, Inc., 689 F.2d 982 (11th Cir.1982). But this limitation may be finessed by a motion in the transferee district court to send the case back. Denial of that motion would presumably be subject to review by the court of appeals in the transferee circuit.

11. For an interesting variation on this conceptual problem, see Koehring v. Hyde Constr. Co., 382 U.S. 362 (1966).

12. See Neal & Goldberg, *The Electrical Equipment Antitrust Cases: Novel Judicial Administration*, 50 A.B.A.J. 621 (1964).

May a transferee court acting under § 1407 order some or all of the cases transferred to itself for trial under § 1404(a) or § 1406? Both the Rules of the Judicial Panel and the decisions indicate that it may.[13]

(10) Can the result in Van Dusen be squared with the fact that, prior to the enactment of § 1404, a dismissal would have required the commencement of a new action with the applicable law being determined in and by the second forum? Does the answer lie in part in the greater availability of transfer under Norwood v. Kirkpatrick, Paragraph (5), *supra?* For an argument that, in spite of Klaxon, there should be independent federal choice of law rules in transfer cases, see the unduly long Note, 75 Yale L.J. 90 (1965). For the view that the approach represented by Van Dusen is probably the best of several unsatisfactory alternatives, see B. Currie, *Change of Venue and the Conflict of Laws: A Retraction,* 27 U.Chi.L.Rev. 341 (1960). Wasn't Justice Goldberg right when he said that any other approach would lead litigants to use § 1404 to shop for the most favorable substantive rules and would make courts reluctant, for that very reason, to grant the transfer remedy?

What does the Van Dusen Court mean by the statement that the transferee may apply its own rules governing the "conduct and dispatch of cases"?

What law should govern the liability of a party who is added to the case after transfer?

Are the questions of applicable law on transfer different if state law applies interstitially in a federal question case?

(11) Note the questions reserved by the Court in Van Dusen: What law should govern if transfer is granted under § 1406(a), or at the behest of the plaintiff under § 1404(a)? Should it matter in either case whether the law of the transferor state is more favorable to the plaintiff than the law of the transferee state? See Martin v. Stokes, 623 F.2d 469 (6th Cir.1980) (law of transferor state should apply in cases transferred under § 1404(a), and law of transferee state in cases transferred under § 1406(a)); Note, 63 Cornell L.Rev. 149 (1977) (relied on in Martin v. Stokes); 15 Wright, Miller & Cooper, Federal Practice and Procedure § 3846, at 365–67 (1986).

The question of which state's law to apply has arisen in several cases in which transfer is granted to a plaintiff who has been unable to obtain jurisdiction over the defendant in the transferor district. (See Paragraph (6), *supra.*) Is the action barred if it was originally filed after the transferee state's statute of limitations had run? Yes, according to several courts, *e.g.,* Carson v. U–Haul Co., 434 F.2d 916 (6th Cir.1970), even if the action was timely filed under the transferor state's law. What if the transferee state's statute ran after the action was filed in the transferor district? The action is not barred, according to Mayo Clinic v. Kaiser, 383 F.2d 653 (8th

---

13. See Jud.Pan.Mult.Lit.Rule 11(b); Pfizer v. Lord, 447 F.2d 122 (2d Cir.1971); In re Yarn Processing Patent Validity Litigation, 472 F.Supp. 174 (S.D.Fla.1979) (also raising issues of the use of collateral estoppel in actions not eligible for transfer under § 1404(a) or § 1406).

For further discussion of § 1407 and its administration, see Herndon & Higginbotham, *Complex Multidistrict Litigation—An Overview,* 31 Baylor L.Rev. 33 (1979); Weigel, *The Judicial Panel on Multidistrict Litigation, Transferor Courts and Transferee Courts,* 78 F.R.D. 575 (1978); Note, 87 Harv.L.Rev. 1001 (1974); 15 Wright, Miller & Cooper, Federal Practice and Procedure §§ 3861–3867 (1986).

Cir.1967). Whose law governs the tolling effect of an action filed in the wrong court? [14]

(12) Isn't the weakest case for application of the transferor state's law one also reserved by the Court in Van Dusen—that in which a state court in the transferor district would have dismissed for forum non conveniens? Aside from the difficulty of determining whether the state court would have dismissed—a difficulty that may well be dispositive of the problem— wouldn't it be consistent with Klaxon, and eminently sensible, to have a federal choice of law rule in such a case? Even if the case is not transferred? [15] Currie, Paragraph (10), *supra*, at 350–51, argues that application of the transferor state's substantive law in such a case may raise constitutional issues under the Due Process and Full-Faith-and-Credit Clauses.[16]

Are any difficult questions of applicable law likely to arise under § 1407? [17] What, for example, of a claim of privilege in the course of a deposition to be used in cases from many different districts?

(13) Professor Kitch has argued that the best legislative course would be to improve the venue statutes and to repeal the transfer provisions for cases in which initial venue is proper. Kitch, *Section 1404(a) of the Judicial Code: In the Interest of Justice or Injustice?*, 40 Ind.L.J. 99 (1965). Once the defects in the general venue provisions were remedied, the marginal benefits from finding a better forum in the occasional case would, in his view, be far outweighed by the enormous costs to litigants and courts of protracted disputes about the place of trial. Such costs, he believes, are amply demonstrated by the experience under present law.

But Kitch tells us nothing about the relationship between the number of cases transferred without substantial delay under present law and the cases in which appeals or other time consuming tactics are employed. Nor

---

14. *Cf.* Atkins v. Schmutz Mfg. Co., 435 F.2d 527 (4th Cir.1970). The plaintiff in this diversity case had filed his action originally in a federal court in Kentucky, but the Kentucky statute of limitations was held to be a bar. Following dismissal by the Kentucky district court, plaintiff filed in a federal court in Virginia, and the court of appeals (sitting in banc) held the action timely. The Virginia statute of limitations had run while the first action was pending and before the second was commenced, but a majority of the court, sitting en banc, held that the Virginia statute was tolled as a matter of federal law by the filing of the first action, whether or not the Virginia state courts would reach a similar result. Can this decision be squared with Guaranty Trust Co. v. York? Judge Haynsworth, in an opinion for the majority that is well worth reading, thought it could, but two members of the court disagreed. The decision is praised in Note, 71 Colum.L. Rev. 865 (1971), and criticized in 1971 Duke L.J. 785.

15. But see In re Air Crash Disaster at Boston, Mass., 399 F.Supp. 1106, 1119–22 (D.Mass.1975), discussed in Caffrey, *The Role of the Transferee Judge in Multidis-*

trict Litigation, 69 F.R.D. 289, 294–98 (1976). In this case, Judge Caffrey held that the law of the transferor state would apply, even though the courts of that state would have dismissed for forum non conveniens. He argued that the transferor district court was not obliged to dismiss or to transfer because of state law (compare the discussion in Paragraph (3), *supra*), and had it retained the case, would have applied the transferor state's law.

16. In a federal question case, which circuit's rule should govern if the controlling precedents differ in the transferor and transferee circuits? See Marcus, *Conflicts Among Circuits and Transfers Within the Federal Judicial System*, 93 Yale L.J. 677 (1984) (arguing that the transferee's rule should govern).

17. See Atwood, *The Choice-of-Law Dilemma in Mass Tort Litigation: Kicking Around Erie, Klaxon, and Van Dusen*, 19 Conn.L.Rev. 9, 51 (1986) (arguing forcefully that "in mass tort actions transferred and consolidated under section 1407," federal courts should apply "uniform choice-of-law rules").

does he tell us how commonly motions for transfer are used, or what the experience of judges and lawyers has been since § 1404 was enacted in 1948.[18] Don't we have to have such empirical data before any well-informed judgments about the utility of transfer can be made?

SECTION 3.   JURISDICTIONAL AMOUNT

INTRODUCTORY NOTE

(1) The Judiciary Act of 1789, 1 Stat. 73, 78, fixed the requisite jurisdictional amount, in those cases in which some amount was requisite, at $500.[1] Ninety-eight years later, 24 Stat. 552 (1887), this was raised to $2,000. In 1911, 36 Stat. 1087, 1091, it was set at $3,000 and in 1958, 72 Stat. 415, at $10,000, where it remains today in diversity cases brought under 28 U.S.C. § 1332.[2] In interpleader, the figure is lower—$500. 28 U.S.C. § 1335. (Why the difference?)

(2) From 1875, when general federal question jurisdiction was first enacted, to 1976, there was a jurisdictional amount requirement in such cases identical to that in diversity cases. But many statutes, *e.g.*, 28 U.S.C. § 1333 (admiralty), 28 U.S.C. § 1337 (cases arising under any act of Congress regulating commerce), 28 U.S.C. § 1343 (certain civil rights cases) authorized suits to be brought without regard to that requirement. And in cases involving constitutional claims that could be brought in federal court, if at all, only under § 1331 (the general federal question statute), some decisions ignored the requirement,[3] or stretched it to accommodate the case,[4] or even raised a question about its constitutionality,[5] while others insisted rigorously that it be satisfied.[6] The difficulty was significantly

---

18. A letter from the Administrative Office of the United States Courts reports that in fiscal 1980, 1981, and 1982 the total number of § 1404(a) transfers granted were:

1980	2,120
1981	2,435
1982	2,445

This figure was slightly more than 1% of the total number of civil cases commenced in the district courts during this period. There is no indication, however, of how many transfer motions were denied or how many of those granted were contested in the district courts or in proceedings for appellate review.

1. For a fuller review of the jurisdictional amount requirement from 1789 to the present, see Baker, *The History and Tradition of the Amount in Controversy Requirement: A Proposal to "Up the Ante" in Diversity Jurisdiction*, 102 F.R.D. 299 (1985). For the history of specified amounts in controversy as prerequisites for taking an appeal, see p. 34, *supra*, p. 1794, *infra*.

2. Note that the amount in controversy must exceed $10,000 to confer federal jurisdiction under § 1332. Compare 28 U.S.C. § 1346 (district court jurisdiction over certain civil actions against the United States is concurrent with that of the Claims Court only as to claims "not exceeding $10,000 in amount").

3. See, *e.g.*, Flast v. Cohen, 392 U.S. 83 (1968); Kleindienst v. Mandel, 408 U.S. 753 (1972).

4. See, *e.g.*, Spock v. David, 469 F.2d 1047 (3d Cir.1972).

5. See, *e.g.*, Cortright v. Resor, 325 F.Supp. 797 (E.D.N.Y.1971), *reversed on other grounds*, 447 F.2d 245 (2d Cir.1971); Murray v. Vaughn, 300 F.Supp. 688 (D.R.I.1969). See also Note, 71 Colum.L. Rev. 1474 (1971).

6. See, *e.g.*, Goldsmith v. Sutherland, 426 F.2d 1395 (6th Cir.1970); McGaw v. Farrow, 472 F.2d 952 (4th Cir.1973); Senate Select Comm. on Presidential Campaign Activities v. Nixon, 366 F.Supp. 51 (D.D.C.1973).

alleviated, however, in 1976, when Congress excepted actions against federal officers and agencies from the jurisdictional amount requirement of § 1331,[7] and was virtually eliminated in 1980 when the requirement was deleted from the section altogether.[8] Only a few federal statutes remain in which access to a federal court is conditioned on a specified amount in controversy.[9]

(3) If it was appropriate to abolish the jurisdictional amount requirement in federal question cases, should it be retained in diversity cases?[10] Professor Currie at one time proposed eliminating the requirement across the board. Currie, *The Federal Courts and the American Law Institute (II)*, 36 U.Chi.L.Rev. 268, 292–98 (1969). Are there significant differences between the two heads of jurisdiction which, at least in theory, support the distinction? Isn't there a greater justification for imposing on a federal court the burden of litigating a "small" case when that case arises under federal law than when it arises under state law? Note too that state courts may be better equipped, through the use of special tribunals and procedures, to adjudicate such cases. And consider the burden on a defendant who is forced to litigate a small case in a distant, unfamiliar federal court rather than in a nearby state court; isn't that burden easier to explain if the rights and liabilities at stake are themselves federal? Do the practical difficulties in administration of the amount requirement, the ease of circumventing it in many cases, and the possible unfairness of judging a case's importance in terms of a dollar figure, outweigh these considerations? You should keep these questions in mind in reading the materials that follow.[11]

BURNS v. ANDERSON

502 F.2d 970 (1974).

United States Court of Appeals for the Fifth Circuit.

Before BROWN, CHIEF JUDGE, and THORNBERRY and AINSWORTH, CIRCUIT JUDGES.

JOHN R. BROWN, CHIEF JUDGE:

The question on this appeal is whether a district court may dismiss a personal injury diversity suit where it appears "to a legal certainty" that the claim was "really for less than the jurisdictional amount."[1]

7. Act of Oct. 21, 1976, 90 Stat. 2721.

8. Act of Dec. 1, 1980, 94 Stat. 2369.

9. *E.g.*, 15 U.S.C. § 2072 (actions under Consumer Product Safety Act); 15 U.S.C. § 2310(d) (actions under Consumer Product Warranties Act); 28 U.S.C. §§ 1337, 1445(b) (suits under 49 U.S.C. § 20 for freight damage or loss); 42 U.S.C. § 1395 ff(b) (judicial review of benefits under the Medicare Act). With respect to the last of these provisions, see Bartlett v. Bowen, 816 F.2d 695, 697 (D.C.Cir.1987) (holding that Congress "did not intend to bar judicial review [in cases falling below the jurisdictional amount] of constitutional challenges to the underlying Act").

10. The ALI Study proposed deleting the requirement in original federal question cases, but not in diversity cases (proposed §§ 1301, 1311).

11. A number of proposals for a further increase in the jurisdictional amount have been made, partly to take account of inflation and partly to reduce the pressure on federal dockets. See, *e.g.*, Posner, The Federal Courts: Crisis and Reform 146 (1985) ($50,000).

1. St. Paul Mercury Indemnity Co. v. Red Cab Co., 1938, 303 U.S. 283, 289.

The suit grew out of an auto accident in which plaintiff Burns' automobile was struck amidships by that of defendant Anderson. Burns' principal injury was a broken thumb. He brought the action in the Eastern District of Louisiana, claiming $1,026.00 in lost wages and medical expenses and another $60,000.00 for pain and suffering. After a pre-trial conference and considerable discovery, the District Court dismissed for want of jurisdiction. Plaintiff appeals.

The test for jurisdictional amount was established by the Supreme Court in St. Paul Mercury Indemnity Co. v. Red Cab Co.[2] There, the Court held that the determinant is plaintiff's good faith claim and that to justify dismissal it must appear to a legal certainty that the claim is really for less than the jurisdictional amount. There is no question but that this is a test of liberality,[3] and it has been treated as such by this Court. This does not mean, however, that Federal Courts must function as small claims courts. The test is an objective one and, once it is clear that as a matter of law the claim is for less than $10,000.00, the Trial Judge is required to dismiss.

In the instant case, the District Judge dismissed only after examination of an extensive record. This record included the testimony of three doctors who treated Burns, as well as his own deposition. The accident occurred on May 26. The evidence is without contradiction that by the middle of August only very minimal disability remained. By December, even this minor condition had disappeared. Burns' actions speak even more strongly than the medical testimony. In his deposition he testified that he took a job as a carpenter's assistant on June 21 or 22—less than a month after the accident. He did heavy manual labor for the remainder of the summer with absolutely no indication of any difficulty with his thumb. It is equally clear that any pain he suffered was not of very great magnitude or lasting duration. Burns admitted that by the end of July there was no pain whatsoever. As a matter of fact, the evidence reveals that the only medication he ever received was a single prescription on the day of the accident for Empirin, a mild aspirin compound. Nor did his special damages take him a significant way down the road to the $10,000.00 minimum. His total medical bills were less than $250.00. Although he claims $800.00 in lost wages, it is difficult to see how this could have amounted to even $300.00 at Burns' rate of pay that summer.[5]

The point of this fact recitation is that it really does appear to a legal certainty that the amount in controversy is less than $10,000. This is no Plimsoll case,[6] where dismissal was based on "bare bones pleadings" alone. The present situation differs from that case also in that this dismissal was for lack of subject matter jurisdiction not for failure to state a claim. Here the Trial Court examined an extensive record and determined as a matter of law that the requisite amount in controversy was not present. Indeed, had the case gone to trial and had the jury returned an award of $10,000, a Gorsalitz-girded Judge would have been compelled as a matter of law to order a remittitur. He would have inescapably found that the verdict was "so inordinately large as obviously to exceed the maximum of the reasona-

2. *Id.*

3. See Bell v. Preferred Life Assurance Society, 1943, 320 U.S. 238; Horton v. Liberty Mutual Ins. Co., 1961, 367 U.S. 348.

5. Burns was making the minimum wage, $1.65 an hour. Four forty-hour work weeks at this wage grosses $264.00.

6. Cook & Nichol, Inc. v. Plimsoll Club, 5 Cir., 1971, 451 F.2d 505.

ble range within which the jury may properly operate.[7]" Of course, we decline to make any more precise determination of plaintiff's loss since to do so might prejudice his right to a trial in another court.

Neither are we affected by plaintiff's plaintive plea that he is being deprived of a jury trial. The question in this case is not whether Burns is entitled to a trial by jury but rather where that trial is to be. We hold only that the case cannot be tried in the Federal Court because competence over it has not been granted to that Court by Congress.

Affirmed.

NOTE ON THE EFFECT OF PLAINTIFF'S AD DAMNUM IN UNLIQUIDATED DAMAGES CASES

(1) In St. Paul Mercury Indem. Co., v. Red Cab Co., 303 U.S. 283 (1938), cited in the Burns opinion, the Court held in a removed case that jurisdiction, once having attached by virtue of the plaintiff's good faith claim in excess of $3,000, was not defeated by the plaintiff's later amendment reducing the ad damnum below $3,000. Would it ever be possible to find bad faith in a claim for unliquidated damages where the defendant rather than the plaintiff had invoked federal jurisdiction?

For unliquidated damage cases in which the Supreme Court has upheld the invocation of federal jurisdiction by the plaintiff against a challenge to the amount in controversy, see, e.g., Bell v. Preferred Life Assurance Society, 320 U.S. 238, 243 (1943) (although actual damages could not exceed $1,000, "we are unable to say that under petitioner's complaint evidence could not be introduced at a trial justifying a jury verdict for actual and punitive damages exceeding $3,000"); Barry v. Edmunds, 116 U.S. 550 (1886).

(2) Following these decisions the lower federal courts had generally held that the plaintiff's claim in an action for unliquidated damages was virtually conclusive on the issue of amount in controversy. E.g., Deutsch v. Hewes St. Realty Corp., 359 F.2d 96 (2d Cir.1966); Wade v. Rogala, 270 F.2d 280 (3d Cir.1959). But a number of later decisions, of which Burns is representative, have shown a willingness to take a much closer look. See, e.g., Nelson v. Keefer, 451 F.2d 289 (3d Cir.1971); Sanders v. Hiser, 479 F.2d 71 (8th Cir.1973); Hupp v. Port Brownsville Shipyard, Inc., 515 F.Supp. 546 (S.D.Tex.1981).

Granted a genuine concern over crowded federal dockets, is the game really worth the candle? Might motions to dismiss on this ground, coupled with extensive discovery designed to show lack of a colorable claim, lead to a net increase in the expenditure of judicial time?

Was plaintiff's jury trial argument in Burns properly disposed of? See Note, 48 Iowa L.Rev. 471 (1963); 14A Wright, Miller & Cooper, Federal Practice and Procedure § 3702, at 27–28 (1985) (arguing that there is no jury trial right on jurisdictional fact issues even if they are related to the merits of the case).[1]

---

7. Gorsalitz v. Olin Mathieson Chemical Corp., 5 Cir., 1970, 429 F.2d 1033, 1046.

1. After this decision, is a state court jury still free to award plaintiff more than $10,000? See McAuliffe v. Colonial Imports, Inc., 116 N.H. 398, 399, 359 A.2d 630, 631 (1976) (dismissal for lack of jurisdictional amount does not bar subsequent

(3) Suppose it is established at trial that plaintiff is entitled to recover, but not more than $10,000, or that he is not entitled to recover at all. Should the action be dismissed for lack of jurisdiction? See Rosado v. Wyman, 397 U.S. 397, 405 n. 6 (1970); Mt. Healthy City School Dist. Bd. of Educ. v. Doyle, 429 U.S. 274 (1977). In Mt. Healthy, the plaintiff had sought $50,000 damages and reinstatement but was awarded only $5,158 damages and reinstatement. The Court said (p. 277): "Even if the District Court had chosen to award only compensatory damages [of $5,158] and not reinstatement, it was far from a 'legal certainty' at the time of suit that Doyle would not have been entitled to more than $10,000." But cf. City of Boulder v. Snyder, 396 F.2d 853 (10th Cir.1968) (ordering dismissal for lack of jurisdiction after plaintiff recovered less than $10,000 at trial); Sanders v. Hiser, Paragraph (2), supra (same); Ross v. Inter–Ocean Ins. Co., 693 F.2d 659 (7th Cir.1982) (reversing summary judgment for defendant in removed case and ordering dismissal for lack of jurisdiction). But such dismissals are (and for reasons of judicial economy surely should be) extremely rare.

Section 1332(b), enacted in 1958, provides that a plaintiff who recovers less than the jurisdictional amount may be saddled with the opponent's court costs. The provision avoids the difficulties inherent in pretrial and post-trial dismissals for lack of jurisdiction, but does not seem to have had much impact.[2] See Wright, Federal Courts § 33, at 185–86 (4th ed. 1983). Note the difficulty of imposing such a sanction on the plaintiff himself, when in all probability it was plaintiff's lawyer who chose the forum. Does this suggest that the provisions of Fed.R.Civ.P. 11 (subjecting lawyers to sanctions for filing pleadings that are not "well grounded in fact") afford a more appropriate basis for relief? See generally Note, 27 B.C.L.Rev. 385 (1986).

HEALY v. RATTA

292 U.S. 263, 54 S.Ct. 700, 78 L.Ed. 1248 (1934).
Appeal from the Circuit Court of Appeals for the First Circuit.

MR. JUSTICE STONE delivered the opinion of the Court.

This case comes here on appeal from a decree of the Court of Appeals for the First Circuit, affirming a decree of the District Court for New Hampshire, which enjoined appellant, the chief of police for the city of Manchester, from enforcing the Hawkers' and Peddlers' Act, chapter 102, New Hampshire Laws of 1931, as an infringement of the Fourteenth Amendment. An appeal taken directly to this Court from the District Court, three judges sitting, was dismissed for want of jurisdiction here

state court action; "[h]owever, the federal judgment of dismissal is a conclusive adjudication of issues material to determination of jurisdiction and actually decided"—in this case that "as a matter of legal certainty the claim did not exceed $10,000").

2. "The costs sanction has apparently been invoked very infrequently, and the fear of it does not seem to have played any significant part in the choice of forum. See Lutz v. McNair, 233 F.Supp. 871, 873–874 (E.D.Va.1964). The records of the Ad-ministrative Office of judgments after trial in diversity cases terminated in the fiscal year 1961 (some few of which were probably filed before the 1958 increase in jurisdictional amount became effective) show that 614 out of 1,268 reported judgments, 48 percent of the total, were for less than $10,000, and that the amount of the median judgment in these cases was $3,793. The amount of the median claim in these same cases [except for the few where no specific claim was reported] was $32,000." ALI Study 120.

since, in the lower court, appellee had waived his prayer for temporary relief. 289 U.S. 701; see Smith v. Wilson, 273 U.S. 388, 391.

The act, effective April 14, 1931, requires payment of an annual license tax or fee for every hawker or peddler, defined to be "any person, either principal or agent, who goes from town to town or from place to place in the same town selling or bartering, or carrying for sale or barter or exposing therefor, any goods, wares or merchandise." Section 1. The tax is $50 for a state-wide license. Local licenses are obtainable at a rate graduated according to population. That for Manchester is stated to be $85 for each license. Violation of the act is punishable by a fine of not more than $200. Appellee's chief ground of attack upon the statute, sustained by both the courts below, is that it denies the equal protection of the laws by excepting from its operation certain classes of hawkers and peddlers, in which appellee and his agents are not included.

The bill of complaint alleges that, until the effective date of the act, appellee, a resident of Massachusetts, was engaged in Manchester and elsewhere in New Hampshire in the distribution of vacuum cleaners through their sale and delivery to purchasers by traveling salesmen; that the business was conducted in such a manner as to subject the salesmen to the tax, which they were unwilling or unable to pay; and that their arrest and prosecution, which appellant threatens if they continue to sell without paying the tax, would destroy appellee's business. The value of his business and his loss on account of the enforcement of the act are each alleged to be more than $3,000. Appellant's answer and motion to dismiss the cause, as not within the jurisdiction of the District Court, admit the facts stated in the complaint, so far as now material, except that they deny the allegation that the matter in controversy exceeds $3,000, the jurisdictional amount.

On this issue a trial was had, in the course of which evidence was given to show the extent of appellee's business in Manchester and elsewhere in New Hampshire and in adjoining states, and the profits derived from it in New Hampshire both before and after the enactment of the taxing statute. No interlocutory injunction was sought, and after the effective date of the statute appellee changed the method of doing his business in New Hampshire in a way to avoid the necessity of a license, sales being made by sample, with later delivery by shipping the merchandise directly to the purchaser from outside the state. The business was carried on in this manner in 1931 at a loss. It appeared that the total number of salesmen employed in conducting appellee's business in Manchester during 1931, when the statute was enacted, was six, and that in earlier years a larger number had been employed. During those years from twenty-two to twenty-seven salesmen were employed elsewhere in the state.

It is appellee's contention that the matter in controversy is either the tax which he would be required to pay annually in order to continue his business in New Hampshire, or his right to conduct the business there without payment of the tax, and that the value of each exceeds $3,000. He argues upon the evidence that the expenditure for payment of the tax which he would be obliged to bear in order to continue his business in Manchester is at least $350 per annum, and that the capitalized value of this expenditure would exceed $3,000.

The District Court concluded that, as the tax which would be imposed for the conduct of appellee's business in Manchester would amount to at least $300 per annum, its capitalized value, which would exceed $3,000, satisfies the jurisdictional requirement. The Court of Appeals thought that the matter in controversy was appellee's right to do business throughout the state, which it valued at more than $3,000.

It is conceded that the authority of appellant, as chief of police, to make arrests for violation of the statute is restricted to the City of Manchester. * * * Appellee neither asks, nor could he properly be awarded a decree in the present suit restraining enforcement of the law by police officers elsewhere, and the collateral effect of the decree, by virtue of stare decisis, upon other and distinct controversies, may not be considered in ascertaining whether the jurisdictional amount is involved, even though their decision turns on the same question of law. Lion Bonding & Surety Co. v. Karatz, 262 U.S. 77, 85 * * *.

If the threatened action of appellant is not restrained, the consequence will be either the payment of the tax by appellee, or the suppression of his business in Manchester because of his failure to pay it. Hence we disregard evidence of injury to appellee's business outside the city and of the cost of licenses for doing it, and confine ourselves to the inquiry whether his right to do the business in Manchester or the tax which must be paid for doing the business there is the matter in controversy, and whether the record shows that its value does not exceed $3,000.

That the issue between the parties is the right of the state to collect the tax cannot be gainsaid. There is no question of the authority of a state to suppress the conduct of a business for the nonpayment of an exaction lawfully imposed upon it, or of the appellant's authority to suppress the business here, by threat of criminal prosecution of the salesmen, if this tax is valid. The dispute as to the lawfulness of the tax is the controversy which alone gives vitality to the litigation. Once that is resolved, no other issue survives for decision.

It has been said that it is the value of the "object of the suit" which determines the jurisdictional amount in the federal courts, Mississippi & Missouri R.R. Co. v. Ward, 2 Black, 485; Packard v. Banton, 264 U.S. 140, 142. But this does not mean objects which are merely collateral or incidental to the determination of the issue raised by the pleadings. * * * Whether and in what manner the penalty for nonpayment may be enforced in the event the tax is valid are but collateral and incidental to the determination whether payment may be exacted. Only when the suit is brought to restrain imposition of a penalty already accrued by reason of failure to comply with the statute or order assailed can the penalty be included as any part of the matter in controversy. See McNeil v. Southern Ry. Co., 202 U.S. 343 * * *.

The case of a tax or fee exacted for the privilege of doing a particular business presents no different considerations. * * * The disputed tax is the matter in controversy, and its value, not that of the penalty or loss which payment of the tax would avoid, determines the jurisdiction. See Washington & Georgetown R.R. v. District of Columbia, 146 U.S. 227; compare Elliott v. Empire Natural Gas Co., C.C.A., 4 F.2d 493.

* * *

The contested license fees must be paid annually as a condition precedent to doing the business. But it does not follow that capitalization of the tax is the method of determining the value of the matter in controversy. The bill of complaint does not allege, nor can it be assumed, that the appellant will act to compel compliance with the statute by appellee in future years for which no tax is yet payable, or that the appellee will seek to continue his business in Manchester indefinitely in the future, or that the taxing act will be continued on the statute books, unmodified either as to the amount of the tax or the features to which the appellee objects. These, or like considerations, have led to the conclusion that, in suits to enjoin the collection of a tax payable annually or the imposition of penalties in case it is not paid, the sum due or demanded is the matter in controversy, and the amount of the tax, not its capitalized value, is the measure of the jurisdictional amount. Washington & Georgetown R.R. Co. v. District of Columbia, *supra* * * *.

A different question is presented where the matter in controversy is the validity of a permanent exemption by contract from an annual property tax, Berryman v. Whitman College, 222 U.S. 334, 348; *see* Riverside & A. Ry. Co. v. City of Riverside, C.C., 118 F. 736; or the validity of an order of a state commission directing a railroad to construct and maintain an unremunerative spur track. Western & Atlantic R.R. v. Railroad Commission, 261 U.S. 264, 267. There the value of the matter drawn into controversy, the contract providing permanent immunity from taxation, or the order to maintain a permanent structure for an unlimited time, is more than a limited number of the annual payments demanded. Compare Glenwood Light & Water Co. v. Mutual Light, Heat & Power Co., 239 U.S. 121. In such a case the burden which rests on a defendant who challenges the plaintiff's allegation of the jurisdictional amount, see Hunt v. New York Cotton Exchange, 205 U.S. 322, 333, may well not be sustained by the mere showing that the annual payment is less than the jurisdictional amount.

Here the record shows affirmatively that the total amount of the tax demanded, or which may be demanded, within any time reasonably required to conclude the litigation, is less than the jurisdictional amount; that any action by appellant to compel compliance by appellee or his salesmen with the taxing act in future years is at most conjectural; and that the effect of any decree rendered in the present suit upon the tax for other years, or with respect to appellee's business outside the city of Manchester is collateral to the present controversy. The decree will be reversed, with instructions to the district court to dismiss the cause for want of jurisdiction.

Reversed.

NOTE ON THE ADMISSIBLE ELEMENTS IN VALUATION

(1) Aside from the problem of determining what is a "joint interest", see p. 1764, *infra*, do you have any comments on the following as a restatement of existing law?

"The amount in controversy in an action in a federal district court is the value to the plaintiff (or to any group of plaintiffs having a joint interest) of the relief he (or they) would get from the defendant (or from any group of defendants having a joint interest) as a direct consequence of the judgment sought, provided that the claim for relief is stated in good faith and without manifest error in law."

(2) The Healy case applied doctrine standard in tax litigation: the amount in controversy is to be measured by the amount of the tax rather than of the penalty. See, *e.g.*, Henneford v. Northern Pac. Ry., 303 U.S. 17 (1938). Can these cases be explained in part on the basis of a policy of avoiding undue friction with the administration of state tax laws, a policy now reflected in 28 U.S.C. § 1341? With these decisions, compare Hunt v. New York Cotton Exch., 205 U.S. 322 (1907) (in suit to enjoin unauthorized use of stock quotations, amount in controversy is value to exchange of right to control their distribution, not the cost of a subscription by the defendant).

Consider also the much-cited decision and statement in Mississippi & M.R.R. v. Ward, 2 Black 485 (U.S.1862). That was a suit, on the theory of abatement of nuisance, to enjoin the continued maintenance of a bridge over the Mississippi. The Court upheld the jurisdiction, and seemed to say that the damage to the plaintiff's navigation business was not controlling. It said (p. 492):

"But the want of a sufficient amount of damage having been sustained to give the Federal Courts jurisdiction, will not defeat the remedy, as the removal of the obstruction is the matter of controversy, and the value of the object must govern."

(3) Granting that the stare decisis value of a judgment ought not to be taken into account, as the Healy case holds, why not the res judicata value? Is the Court's refusal to take into account the amount of taxes for future years based simply on the uncertainty of the taxes or on a general principle that only the value of the relief currently sought can be counted—the value so to speak, by way only of direct and not of collateral estoppel?

In Clark v. Paul Gray, Inc., 306 U.S. 583, 589 (1939), a suit to enjoin the enforcement of a California statute imposing license fees aggregating $15 for each automobile caravaned into the state for sale, the Court said:

"Examination of the record shows that only in the case of a single appellee, Paul Gray, Inc., is there any allegation or proof tending to show the amount in controversy. As to it the bill of complaint alleged that 'it causes to be caravaned into the said state * * * approximately one hundred fifty (150) automobiles each year.' This allegation is supported by evidence that this appellee is regularly engaged in the business and tending to show that its volume exceeded that amount when the act went into effect July 2, 1937. Since the amount in controversy in a suit to restrain illegal imposition of fees or taxes is the amount of the fees or taxes which would normally be collected during the period of the litigation, Healy v. Ratta, 292 U.S. 263, we cannot say, upon this state of the record, that jurisdiction was not established as to appellee Paul Gray, Inc." [1]

---

1. The Court held that the suit should be dismissed as to all the appellees except Gray. It defended this conclusion by stating (p. 590): "Otherwise an appellate court could be called on to sustain a decree in favor of a plaintiff who had not shown that his claim involved the jurisdictional amount, even though the suit were dismissed on the merits as to the other plaintiffs who had established the jurisdictional amount for themselves. Although it appears that such a result could not follow here, we think it better practice to dismiss the suit for want of the jurisdictional

Elgin v. Marshall, 106 U.S. 578 (1882), was an action to recover the amount due on certain coupons detached from bonds, the defense being that both bonds and coupons were void. The Court held that the amount in controversy was the value of the coupons in suit only, although it recognized that a decision would be res judicata as to other coupons and as to the bonds themselves. And in cases involving the right to recover on a policy of disability insurance, the courts have generally refused to consider future installments in computing the amount in controversy; unless the controversy relates to the validity of the policy, only the installments allegedly due at the commencement of suit are included. *E.g.,* Mutual Life Ins. Co. v. Wright, 276 U.S. 602 (1928), *affirming* 19 F.2d 117 (5th Cir.1927); Lenox v. S.A. Healy Co., 463 F.Supp. 51 (D.Md.1978); *cf.* New York Life Ins. Co. v. Viglas, 297 U.S. 672 (1936). Nor does it appear to avail the plaintiff to seek a declaratory judgment that he is in fact permanently disabled and entitled to future installments. Beaman v. Pacific Mut. Life Ins. Co., 369 F.2d 653 (4th Cir.1966); Rudder v. Ohio State Life Ins. Co., 208 F.Supp. 577 (E.D.Ky. 1962). See generally Annot., 11 A.L.R.Fed. 120 (1972).[2]

(4) When is capitalization of the amount currently due or to be expended proper? Is the distinction satisfactory which the Healy case draws between the facts there involved and Berryman v. Whitman College?

In Aetna Cas. & Sur. Co. v. Flowers, 330 U.S. 464 (1947), a widow brought an action for death benefits under a state workers' compensation statute, and the action was removed to a federal court. The statute sued on provided for maximum payments of $18 per week, for a maximum of 400 weeks (but not to exceed $5,000), with payments to be terminated on the death or remarriage of the widow, plus the death or attainment of the age of eighteen by the children. The Court held that a remand for lack of the jurisdictional amount was improper, distinguishing the disability cases cited in the preceding Paragraph on the ground that the state law creating liability for the award in Flowers "contemplates a single action for the determination of claimant's right to benefits and a single judgment for the award granted" (pp. 467–68). Are you satisfied with the distinction? Is it like the difference between a contingent remainder and a vested remainder subject to divestment? *Cf.* Western & A.R.R. v. Railroad Comm'n, 261 U.S. 264, 267 (1923) (in a suit to enjoin an order to build a side track, the "permanent annual burden" of interest on the cost of construction, of depreciation, and of maintenance and operation of the side track, capitalized at a reasonable rate, should be taken into account in computing the amount in controversy).

Though not cited, the Flowers case was followed (and perhaps extended) in Weinberger v. Wiesenfeld, 420 U.S. 636, 642 n. 10 (1975). In upholding jurisdiction in an action for survivors' benefits under the Social Security Act, the Court said: "[W]here an injunction commanding future payments is sought, there is no need to await accrual of $10,000 in back benefits to bring suit." The disability cases, though not cited, were implicitly distinguished: "[U]nlike disability benefits, * * * these survivors' benefits do not depend upon ability to earn, but only upon actual earnings. Thus, they give a potential recipient a choice between staying home

amount as to all appellees except Paul Gray, Inc."

2. But *cf.* Goldberg, *The Influence of Procedural Rules on Federal Jurisdiction,*

28 Stan.L.Rev. 395, 424–27 (1976), discussing some of the older decisions.

* * * and working. This opportunity for choice * * * certainly has a present value of $10,000 * * *."

The relevance of future harm to the determination of the amount in controversy was further underscored in Hunt v. Washington State Apple Advertising Com'n, 432 U.S. 333 (1977). In this case, an agency of the state of Washington brought a federal court action seeking a declaration of the unconstitutionality, and an injunction against enforcement, of a North Carolina law effectively prohibiting the use by Washington apple growers and dealers of their own state's system for grading apples destined for North Carolina. The requested relief was granted below and the Supreme Court unanimously affirmed. After holding that the state agency had standing to sue as representative of its constituent growers and dealers, see p. 159, *supra,* the Court held the jurisdictional amount requirement satisfied on the basis of an analysis of "the losses [to growers and dealers] that will follow from the statute's enforcement" (p. 347). Such losses, in various instances, included lost sales in North Carolina, the costs of altering containers, and the loss of competitive advantage associated with the widely known Washington grades. Given the substantial volume of sales of Washington apples in North Carolina, and "the continuing nature of the statute's interference, * * * [we cannot say] 'to a legal certainty,' on this record, that such losses and expenses will not, *over time, if they have not done so already,* amount to the requisite $10,000 *for at least some of the individual growers and dealers.* That is sufficient to sustain the District Court's jurisdiction [under § 1331]" (p. 348) (emphasis added).

The analysis seems eminently sound, and the first italicized phrase seems consistent with Weinberger v. Weisenfeld. Is the second phrase consistent with the Zahn case, p. 1764, *infra?* Does it at least suggest a way around the Zahn result if the right plaintiff can be found and the "class action" label avoided?

Note that Weinberger and Hunt were both federal question cases—arising before the 1980 amendment to § 1331 eliminated the amount requirement. Do you think that fact made the Court more receptive to the arguments favoring jurisdiction than it would have been in a diversity case?

(5) In an action for other than monetary relief, is the "good faith" test applicable to the amount alleged by the plaintiff to be in controversy? Healy v. Ratta and many of the cases discussed in this Note indicate that it is not—that the plaintiff must satisfy the court as to the objective facts. See Justice Roberts' opinion in Hague v. CIO, 307 U.S. 496, 507–08 (1939). See also City of Milwaukee v. Saxbe, 546 F.2d 693, 702 (7th Cir.1976). (But see, *e.g.,* Opelika Nursing Home, Inc. v. Richardson, 448 F.2d 658 (5th Cir. 1971).) What if the plaintiff attempts to satisfy his burden by showing that although the value of the requested relief to him is not over $10,000, the cost of that relief to defendant is?[3] What if the defendant argues in the converse case that the crucial figure is the cost of the relief to him?

---

3. Professor Currie suggests that the question may be meaningless because "If the * * * [right sought to be protected] is worth only $1000 to the plaintiff, cannot the defendant buy it from him for $1000.01?" Currie, Federal Courts 362 (3d ed. 1982). Professor Wright replies that the answer "will not always be 'Yes,' either because of stubbornness or because a right may have intangible value to a party, not included among the elements used in measuring the value of the right for purposes of amount in controversy." Wright, Federal Courts § 34, at 192 n. 12 (4th ed. 1983).

Glenwood Light & Water Co. v. Mutual Light, Heat & Power Co., 239 U.S. 121 (1915), was a suit to enjoin the defendant from maintaining its poles and wires in such a way as to interfere with the complainant's poles and wires. The Court, finding that the damage to the plaintiff from the interference exceeded $3,000, held it to be irrelevant that the defendant could remove the offending equipment for $500. See also Hunt v. New York Cotton Exch., Paragraph (2), *supra.* But compare Mississippi & M.R.R. v. Ward, Paragraph (2), *supra.*

In Ronzio v. Denver & Rio Grande Co., 116 F.2d 604 (10th Cir.1940), a suit to quiet title to water rights, it appeared that while the value of the water to the plaintiff for farming purposes was less than $3,000, its value to the defendant railroad materially exceeded that amount. The court upheld the jurisdiction.[4]

Should the restatement proposed at the outset of this Note be redrafted so as to recognize either value to the plaintiff or cost to the defendant, *whichever is the greater?* For an answer in the negative, see Dobie, *Jurisdictional Amount in the United States District Court,* 38 Harv.L.Rev. 733 (1925). But if the major purpose of the jurisdictional amount limitation is to keep relatively small cases out of the federal courts, why shouldn't the value to either party suffice? Indeed, to the extent the limitation is designed to protect defendants against harassment by suit in distant courts, shouldn't the value to the defendant be critical? (Note that in some cases the presence of a readily ascertainable value to the defendant may eliminate the necessity of a highly speculative judgment as to the value to the plaintiff.) See generally Note, 73 Harv.L.Rev. 1369 (1960); Note, 11 Loyola of L.A.L.Rev. 637 (1978); Wright, Federal Courts § 34, at 192–93 (4th ed. 1983); *Cf. Note on Joinder and Aggregation of Claims,* p. 1763, *infra.*

(6) How is the amount in controversy determined in a declaratory judgment action? "Usually the right or nonliability sought to be established in a declaratory suit might be adjudicated in a present or potential coercive action by one of the parties. The potential monetary value of the right, or amount of the liability, in such a coercive action, is normally considered to be the amount in controversy in the declaratory suit. * * * If a breach of a contractual condition is in issue, the amount of the probable liability is the amount in controversy." *Developments in the Law—Declaratory Judgments,* 62 Harv.L.Rev. 787, 801 (1949).

(7) Suppose the plaintiff's claim does not exceed the jurisdictional amount: what then is the relevance of a counterclaim by the defendant? Does it matter whether the question arises in an original action, or in a removed action where the counterclaim was asserted before removal? Whether the counterclaim is permissive or compulsory? Whether the counterclaim itself exceeds the jurisdictional amount or must be added to the claim before the minimum is reached? For a survey of the range of judicial responses to these questions, see 1 Moore, Federal Practice ¶ 0.98

---

4. See also McCarty v. Amoco Pipeline Co., 595 F.2d 389 (7th Cir.1979), noted, 29 De Paul L.Rev. 933 (1980); Oklahoma Retail Grocers Ass'n v. Wal–Mart Stores, Inc., 605 F.2d 1155 (10th Cir.1979).

Ronzio and other authorities supporting an "either party" viewpoint were cited with approval in Illinois v. City of Milwaukee, 406 U.S. 91, 98 (1972), p. 898, *supra.* The citation followed the cryptic comment that the "considerable interests involved in the purity of interstate waters would seem to put beyond question the jurisdictional amount provided in § 1331(a)."

(2d ed. 1986); 14A Wright, Miller & Cooper, Federal Practice and Procedure § 3706 (1985). Does Louisville & Nashville R.R. v. Mottley, 211 U.S. 149 (1908), p. ___, *supra,* have any bearing?

In Horton v. Liberty Mut. Ins. Co., 367 U.S. 348 (1961), Horton had filed a claim for $14,035 with the Texas Industrial Accident Board and had received an award for $1,050. On the basis of diversity of citizenship, the insurance company brought an action in a Texas federal court to set aside the award, alleging that Horton had claimed and would claim $14,035. (Under Texas law, the filing of a suit by either party had the effect of nullifying the award and placing the burden of proof on the claimant of establishing the amount to which he was entitled.) Subsequently, Horton filed a suit in a Texas state court for $14,035,[5] moved to dismiss the federal action for lack of the jurisdictional amount, and filed a "conditional" compulsory counterclaim in the federal suit for $14,035. The Supreme Court held, 5–4, that the requisite jurisdictional amount existed. Relying on all the record facts described above, the Court said (pp. 353–54):

"* * * No denial of these allegations in the complaint has been made, no attempted disclaimer or surrender of any part of the original claim has been made by petitioner [Horton], and there has been no other showing * * * of any lack of good faith on the part of the respondent * * *. No matter which party brings it into court, the controversy remains the same; it involves the same amount of money and is to be adjudicated under the same rules. Unquestionably, therefore, the amount in controversy is in excess of $10,000."

Does the Horton case mean that a plaintiff may always survive a challenge to the amount in controversy by making a good faith allegation that the defendant will counterclaim for more than $10,000? What if the defendant simply refuses to file the counterclaim until disposition of his motion to dismiss, as Horton could certainly have done?[6] Can the Horton case be explained as simply an example of the principle referred to in Paragraph (6) governing actions for a declaratory judgment? Is the company's action any different from a request for a determination of non-liability? In the view of the dissenters, a rationale based on an analogy to a declaratory judgment proceeding was unacceptable because "[t]he complaint filed in the District Court was not styled a declaratory judgment action, and it did not seek such relief. More importantly, respondent has succeeded in avoiding the element of discretion permitted by the [declaratory judgment] statute. * * * Moreover, it is even questionable whether respondent has satisfied the jurisdictional amount requirement for such actions" (pp. 359–60).

(8) On the statutory exclusion of interest and costs, *see* Note, 94 U.Pa. L.Rev. 401 (1946); Note, 45 Iowa L.Rev. 832 (1960). The interest exclusion has caused difficulty. There are plainly times when interest must be

---

5. Under a 1958 provision, 28 U.S.C. § 1445(c), a state court action arising under the workers' compensation laws of that state is not removable. The Horton case, and cases like it, thus involve a race to the courthouse by the two parties—a race often won by the insurance company. In Horton the dissenters noted that the federal action was filed within hours of the state board's rendition of the award.

6. *Cf.* Hardware Mut. Cas. Co. v. McIntyre, 304 F.2d 566 (5th Cir.1962) (on facts similar to Horton, court dismisses for lack of jurisdiction when claimant files counterclaim limited to $9,000; claimant had already initiated a state court action on the same claim for $12,827). The case is noted in 41 Texas L.Rev. 587 (1963).

included in determining the amount in controversy—in an action on a bond coupon for example—but shouldn't any interest accruing *after* the cause of action arose be excluded? It would seem so if the purpose of the interest exclusion is to prevent the plaintiff from profiting from his own delay in bringing suit, yet artful pleading sometimes enables the plaintiff to defeat this purpose. See, cases cited in Wright, Federal Courts § 35, at 195 n. 18 (4th ed. 1983).

SNYDER v. HARRIS

394 U.S. 332, 89 S.Ct. 1053, 22 L.Ed.2d 319 (1969).
Certiorari to the United States Court of Appeals for the Eighth Circuit.

MR. JUSTICE BLACK delivered the opinion of the Court. * * *

Each of these cases involves a single plaintiff suing on behalf of himself and "all others similarly situated." In No. 109, Mrs. Margaret E. Snyder, a shareholder of Missouri Fidelity Union Trust Life Insurance Company, brought suit against members of the company's board of directors alleging that they had sold their shares of the company's stock for an amount far in excess of its fair market value, that this excess represented payment to these particular directors to obtain complete control of the company, and that under Missouri law the excess should properly be distributed among all the shareholders of the company and not merely to a few of them. The suit was brought in the United States District Court for the Eastern District of Missouri, 268 F.Supp. 701, diversity of citizenship being alleged as the basis for federal jurisdiction. Since petitioner's allegations showed that she sought for herself only $8,740 in damages, respondent moved to dismiss on the grounds that the matter in controversy did not exceed $10,000. Petitioner contended, however, that her claim should be aggregated with those of the other members of her class, approximately 4,000 shareholders of the company stock. If all 4,000 potential claims were aggregated, the amount in controversy would be approximately $1,200,000. The District Court held that the claims could not thus be aggregated to meet the statutory test of jurisdiction and the Court of Appeals for the Eighth Circuit * * * affirmed, 390 F.2d 204 (1968).

In No. 117, Otto R. Coburn, a resident of Kansas, brought suit in the United States District Court for the District of Kansas against the Gas Service Company, a corporation marketing natural gas in Kansas. Jurisdiction was predicated upon diversity of citizenship. The complaint alleged that the Gas Service Company had billed and illegally collected a city franchise tax from Coburn and others living outside city limits. Coburn alleged damages to himself of only $7.81. Styling his complaint as a class action, however, Coburn sought relief on behalf of approximately 18,000 other Gas Service Company customers living outside of cities. The amount by which other members of the class had been overcharged was, and is, unknown, but the complaint alleged that the aggregation of all these claims would in any event exceed $10,000. The District Court overruled the Gas Company's motion to dismiss for failure to satisfy the jurisdictional amount and, on interlocutory appeal, the Court of Appeals for the Tenth Circuit affirmed * * *. We granted certiorari to resolve the conflict * * *.

The traditional judicial interpretation under all of [the statutes dealing with jurisdictional amount] * * * has been from the beginning that the separate and distinct claims of two or more plaintiffs cannot be aggregated in order to satisfy the jurisdictional amount requirement. Aggregation has been permitted only (1) in cases in which a single plaintiff seeks to aggregate two or more of his own claims against a single defendant and (2) in cases in which two or more plaintiffs unite to enforce a single title or right in which they have a common and undivided interest. It is contended, however, that the adoption of a 1966 amendment to Rule 23 effectuated a change in this jurisdictional doctrine. Under old Rule 23, class actions were divided into three categories which came to be known as "true", "hybrid," and "spurious." True class actions were those in which the rights of the different class members were common and undivided; in such cases aggregation was permitted. Spurious class actions, on the other hand, were in essence merely a form of permissive joinder in which parties with separate and distinct claims were allowed to litigate those claims in a single suit simply because the different claims involved common questions of law or fact. In such cases aggregation was not permitted: each plaintiff had to show that his individual claim exceeded the jurisdictional amount. The 1966 amendment to Rule 23 replaced the old categories with a functional approach to class actions. The new Rule establishes guidelines for the appropriateness of class actions, makes provision for giving notice to absent members, allows members of the class to remove themselves from the litigation and provides that the judgment will include all members of the class who have not requested exclusion. In No. 117, Gas Service Company, the Court of Appeals for the Tenth Circuit held that these changes in Rule 23 changed the jurisdictional amount doctrine as well. * * * We disagree and conclude, as did the Courts of Appeal for the Fifth and Eighth Circuits, that the adoption of amended Rule 23 did not and could not have brought about this change in the scope of the congressionally enacted grant of jurisdiction to the district courts.

The doctrine that separate and distinct claims could not be aggregated was never, and is not now, based upon the categories of old Rule 23 or of any rule of procedure. That doctrine is based rather upon this Court's interpretation of the statutory phrase "matter in controversy." The interpretation of this phrase as precluding aggregation substantially predates the 1938 Federal Rules of Civil Procedure. In 1911 this Court said in Troy Bank v. G.A. Whitehead & Co.:

"When two or more plaintiffs, having separate and distinct demands, unite for convenience and economy in a single suit, it is essential that the demand of each be of the requisite jurisdictional amount * * *." 222 U.S. 39.

By 1916 this Court was able to say in Pinel v. Pinel, 240 U.S. 594, that it was "settled doctrine" that separate and distinct claims could not be aggregated to meet the required jurisdictional amount. In Clark v. Paul Gray, Inc., 306 U.S. 583 (1939), this doctrine, which had first been declared in cases involving joinder of parties, was applied to class actions under the then recently passed Federal Rules. In that case numerous individuals, partnerships, and corporations joined in bringing a suit challenging the validity of a California statute which exacted fees of $15 on each automobile driven into the State. Raising the jurisdictional amount question *sua sponte,* this Court held that the claims of the various fee payers could not be aggregated "where there are numerous plaintiffs having no joint or common interest or title in the subject matter of the suit." 306 U.S., at

588. Nothing in the amended Rule 23 changes this doctrine. The class action plaintiffs in the two cases before us argue that since the new Rule will include in the judgment all members of the class who do not ask to be out by a certain date, the "matter in controversy" now encompasses all the claims of the entire class. But it is equally true that where two or more plaintiffs join their claims under the joinder provisions of Rule 20, each and every joined plaintiff is bound by the judgment. And it was in joinder cases of this very kind that the doctrine that distinct claims could not be aggregated was originally enunciated. Troy Bank v. G.A. Whitehead & Co., 222 U.S. 39 (1911); Pinel v. Pinel, 240 U.S. 594 (1916). The fact that judgments under class actions formerly classified as spurious may now have the same effect as claims brought under the joinder provisions is certainly no reason to treat them *differently* from joined actions for purposes of aggregation.

Any change in the Rules that did purport to effect a change in the definition of "matter in controversy" would clearly conflict with the command of Rule 82 that "[t]hese rules shall not be construed to extend or limit the jurisdiction of the United States district courts ＊ ＊ ＊." In Sibbach v. Wilson & Co., this Court held that the rule-making authority was limited by "the inability of a court, by rule, to extend or restrict the jurisdiction conferred by a statute." 312 U.S. 1, 10 (1941). We have consistently interpreted the jurisdictional statute passed by Congress as not conferring jurisdiction where the required amount in controversy can be reached only by aggregating separate and distinct claims. The interpretation of that statute cannot be changed by a change in the Rules.

For the reasons set out above, we think that it is unmistakably clear that the 1966 changes in Rule 23 did not and could not have changed the interpretation of the statutory phrase "matter in controversy." ＊ ＊ ＊

To overrule the aggregation doctrine at this late date would run counter to the congressional purpose in steadily increasing through the years the jurisdictional amount requirement. That purpose was to check, to some degree, the rising caseload of the federal courts, especially with regard to the federal courts' diversity of citizenship jurisdiction. ＊ ＊ ＊

Finally, it has been argued that unless the established aggregation principles are overturned, the functional advantages alleged to inhere in the new class action Rule will be undercut by resort to the old forms. But the disadvantageous results are overemphasized, we think, since lower courts have developed largely workable standards for determining when claims are joint and common, and therefore entitled to be aggregated, and when they are separate and distinct and therefore not aggregable. Moreover, while the class action device serves a useful function across the entire range of legal questions, the jurisdictional amount requirement applies almost exclusively to controversies based upon diversity of citizenship. ＊ ＊ ＊ If there is a present need to expand the jurisdiction of those courts we cannot overlook the fact that the Constitution specifically vests that power in the Congress, not in the courts.

The judgment in No. 109 is Affirmed.

The judgment in No. 117 is Reversed.

MR. JUSTICE FORTAS, with whom MR. JUSTICE DOUGLAS joins, dissenting.

The Court today refuses to conform the judge-made formula for computing the amount in controversy in class actions with the 1966 amendment to Rule 23 of the Federal Rules of Civil Procedure. The effect of this refusal is substantially to undermine a generally welcomed and long-needed reform in federal procedure.

* * *

The artificial, awkward, and unworkable distinctions between "joint," "common," and "several" claims and between "true," "hybrid," and "spurious" class actions which the amendment of Rule 23 sought to terminate is now re-established in federal procedural law. Litigants, lawyers, and federal courts must now continue to be ensnared in their complexities in all cases where one or more of the coplaintiffs have a claim of less than the jurisdictional amount, usually $10,000.

It was precisely this morass that the 1966 amendment to Rule 23 sought to avoid. * * *

* * *

II.

Whatever the pre–1966 status of the aggregation doctrines in class action cases, the amendment of the Rules in that year permits and even requires a re-examination of the application of the doctrines to such cases. The fundamental change in the law of class actions effected by the new Rule 23 requires that prior subsidiary judicial doctrine developed for application to the old Rule be harmonized with the new procedural law. By Act of Congress, the Rules of Procedure, when promulgated according to the statutorily defined process, have the effect of law and supersede all prior laws in conflict with them. 28 U.S.C. § 2072 (1964 ed., Supp. III). Thus, even if the old aggregation doctrines were embodied in statute—as they are not—they could not stand if they conflicted with the new Rule.

Under the pre–1966 version of Rule 23 the very availability of the class action device depended on the "joint" or "common" "character of the right sought to be enforced." If the right were merely "several," only a "spurious" class action could be maintained and only those members of the class who actually appeared as parties were bound by the judgment. It was in this context of a law of class actions already heavily dependent on categorization of interests as "joint" or "several" that the traditional aggregation doctrines were originally applied to class actions under the Federal Rules. In such a context those aggregation doctrines which the majority now perpetuates in the quite different context of the new Rule, whatever their other defects, were at least not anomalous and eccentric.

* * * Under the new Rule the focus shifts from the abstract character of the right asserted to explicit analysis of the suitability of the particular claim to resolution in a class action. The decision that a class action is appropriate is not to be taken lightly; the district court must consider the full range of relevant factors specified in the Rule. However, whether a claim is, in traditional terms, "joint" or "several" no longer has any necessary relevance to whether a class action is proper. Thus, the amended Rule 23, which in the area of its operation has the effect of a statute, states a new method for determining when the common interests of many individuals can be asserted and resolved in a single litigation.

The jurisdictional amount statutes require placing a value on the "matter in controversy" in a civil action. Once it is decided under the new Rule that an action may be maintained as a class action, it is the claim of the whole class and not the individual economic stakes of the separate members of the class which is the "matter in controversy." That this is so is perhaps most clearly indicated by the fact that the judgment in a class action properly maintained as such includes all members of the class. Rule 23(c)(3). This effect of the new Rule in broadening the scope of the "controversy" in a class action to include the combined interests of all the members of the class is illustrated by the facts of No. 117. That class action, if allowed to proceed, would, under the Rule, determine not merely whether the gas company wrongfully collected $7.81 in taxes from Mr. Coburn. It would also result in a judgment which, subject to the limits of due process, would determine—authoritatively and not merely as a matter of precedent—the status of the taxes collected from the 18,000 other people allegedly in the class Coburn seeks to represent. That being the case, it is hard to understand why the fact that the alleged claims are, in terms of the old Rule categories, "several" rather than "joint," means that the "matter in controversy" for jurisdictional amount purposes must be regarded as the $7.81 Mr. Coburn claims instead of the thousands of dollars of alleged overcharges of the whole class, the status of all of which would be determined by the judgment.

＊ ＊ ＊ [T]he majority result will continue to make determinative of the maintainability of a class action just that obsolete conceptualism the amended Rule sought to make irrelevant. In this sense, continued adherence to the old aggregation doctrines conflicts with the new Rule and is improper under 28 U.S.C. § 2072 (1964 ed., Supp. III).

III.

Permitting aggregation in class action cases does not involve any violation of the principle, expressed in Rule 82 and inherent in the whole procedure for the promulgation and amendment of the Federal Rules, that the courts cannot by rule expand their own jurisdictions. While the Rules cannot change subject-matter jurisdiction, changes in the forms and practices of the federal courts through changes in the Rules frequently and necessarily will affect the occasions on which subject-matter jurisdiction is exercised because they will in some cases make a difference in what cases the federal courts will hear and who will be authoritatively bound by the judgment. ＊ ＊ ＊

For these reasons, I would measure the value of the "matter in controversy" in a class action found otherwise proper under the amended Rule 23 by the monetary value of the claim of the whole class.

NOTE ON JOINDER AND AGGREGATION OF CLAIMS

(1) The Court in Snyder implies that a single plaintiff may aggregate two or more of his own claims against a single defendant even if there is no relationship among the claims. Why should this be so? Is it consistent with the purpose of the jurisdictional amount requirement?

For a case in which the rules on aggregation were surmounted by a transfer of claims to a small group of plaintiffs, see Bullard v. City of Cisco, 290 U.S. 179 (1933). Compare Woodside v. Beckham, 216 U.S. 117 (1910) (when transferee was not in fact the owner of the claims sued upon, jurisdiction depended on the ability of the transferors to sue). See *Note on Devices for Creating or Avoiding Federal Jurisdiction,* p. 1692, *supra.*

(2) Recall the majority's argument in Snyder that a contrary result would necessitate the overruling of cases dealing with permissive joinder (like Pinel v. Pinel, 240 U.S. 594 (1916)) because in those cases, as in class actions, each person whose claim is involved would be bound by the judgment. Is this argument adequately answered by the dissent?

(3) Why doesn't an answer to the majority in Snyder lie in the suggestion at p. 1757, *supra,* that the controlling amount is either the value to the plaintiff or the cost to the defendant, whichever is higher? If the suggestion is sound, why isn't the total potential liability of each defendant in a case like Snyder sufficient to meet the requirement? See Colvin v. Jacksonville, 158 U.S. 456 (1895) (in a taxpayer's bill to enjoin a bond issue, taxpayer's interest and not amount of bond issue held controlling). See also, *e.g.,* Lonnquist v. J.C. Penney Co., 421 F.2d 597, 599 (10th Cir.1970), a class action in which the court refused to permit aggregation and attempted to distinguish Ronzio v. Denver & Rio Grande Co., 116 F.2d 604 (10th Cir.1940), p. 1757, *supra,* by stating: "Although the court [in Ronzio] said that the test was the pecuniary value to either party, the decision is not pertinent because a single right was asserted by a single plaintiff and the question was the value of that right. No problem of aggregation was presented." But see Committee for GI Rights v. Callaway, 518 F.2d 466, 473 (D.C.Cir.1975) (alternative holding).

Unless a theory analogous to that adopted in Ronzio is used, how could federal jurisdiction have existed in a case like Flast v. Cohen, 392 U.S. 83 (1968), p. 138, *supra?* See Note, 79 Yale L.J. 1577 (1970). The problem was not alluded to in Flast itself, or in later decisions dealing on the merits with the constitutionality of government aid to schools with religious affiliations. Lemon v. Kurtzman, 403 U.S. 602 (1971); Tilton v. Richardson, 403 U.S. 672 (1971).[1]

(4) In commenting on the Snyder majority's reference to "largely workable standards for determining when claims are joint and common", Professor Wright says: "It would have been helpful if the Court had indicated what these standards are or where they are to be found." Wright, Federal Courts § 36, at 198 (4th ed. 1983). A review of the decisions dealing with aggregation of multiple claims offers convincing evidence of Wright's skepticism. See 14A Wright, Miller & Cooper, Federal Practice and Procedure § 3704 (1985).

(5) After Snyder, the question arose whether federal jurisdiction existed in a class action in which (a) the interests were not joint and common, and (b) some but not all members of the class had the requisite amount in controversy. In Zahn v. International Paper Co., 414 U.S. 291 (1973), the Supreme Court upheld the decision of the district court that in a Rule 23(b)(3) class action "each plaintiff * * * must satisfy the jurisdictional

---

1. The jurisdictional amount question in such cases was, of course, mooted by the 1980 amendment to § 1331.

amount, and any plaintiff who does not must be dismissed from the case * * *" (p. 301). The Court began by noting that, though the named plaintiffs did satisfy the jurisdictional amount requirement, some unnamed class members did not. Describing a Rule 23(b)(3) "spurious class action" as, "in effect, but a congeries of separate suits," the Court evoked the requirement of Clark v. Paul Gray, Inc., cited and discussed in Snyder v. Harris, that named plaintiffs in such a suit who did not meet the jurisdictional requirements had to be dismissed (pp. 296–300). Reasoning that unnamed members of a class should not "enjoy advantages not shared by named plaintiffs," the Court applied "the rule governing named plaintiffs joining in an action to the unnamed members of a class" (pp. 300–01 n. 9). The Court concluded by refusing to reconsider Snyder and "the Court's longstanding construction of the 'matter in controversy' requirement of § 1332" (p. 301).

Justices Brennan, Douglas, and Marshall, dissenting, drew a distinction between "civil actions" and "individual claimants and individual claims," asserting that the "matter in controversy" requirement applied only to the former (p. 303). Arguing that the claims of the unnamed class members should be entertained as within the district court's ancillary jurisdiction, the dissent described the governing policies as "accommodations that take into account the impact of the adjudication on parties and third persons, the susceptibility of the dispute or disputes in the case to resolution in a single adjudication, and the structure of the litigation as governed by the Federal Rules of Civil Procedure" (p. 305). "Class actions were born of necessity," the dissent continued; "the alternatives were joinder of the entire class, or redundant litigation of the common issues" (p. 307). Concluding that Clark v. Paul Gray, Inc., should be limited so as to allow unnamed class members' claims to be adjudicated within a single suit, the dissent urged that both precedent (*e.g.*, Strawbridge v. Curtiss, 3 Cranch 267 (U.S. 1806); Supreme Tribe of Ben Hur v. Cauble, 255 U.S. 356 (1921)), and the impact of a decision on nonappearing class members justified such a use of ancillary jurisdiction (pp. 309–10).

Can the result in Zahn be squared with the prevailing doctrines of ancillary jurisdiction in other areas? (See pp. 1679–88, *supra*.) With the settled rule that in a class action the citizenship of the named representative is controlling for diversity purposes? With the Court's approach to the question of mootness in class actions? (See Chap. II, Sec. 4, *supra*.)

What is the effect of Zahn on the availability of ancillary jurisdiction in a case in which A and B join in suing C on closely related claims but only A has the requisite amount in controversy?[2]

(6) One type of class action in which aggregation is not a problem is a stockholder's derivative action. The Court has held that the measure of the amount in controversy in such cases is not the possible benefit to the plaintiff shareholder but the damage asserted to have been sustained by the corporation. Koster v. (American) Lumbermens Mut. Cas. Co., 330 U.S. 518 (1947). Was the Koster holding inconsistent with the Court's observation in the same case that the corporation was properly aligned as a defendant for diversity purposes because it was in "antagonistic hands"?

2. The authorities are divided on this and related questions of the applicability of Zahn outside the class action context. See Wright, Federal Courts § 36, at 199–201 (4th ed. 1983); 14A Wright, Miller & Cooper, Federal Practice and Procedure § 3704, at 88–95 (1985).

(7) Since Snyder, Congress has dealt with the problem of aggregation in a class action in the Consumer Product Warranties Act (the Magnuson–Moss Act), 15 U.S.C. §§ 2301–12. After establishing certain federal standards for consumer warranties, the statute vests jurisdiction in state and federal courts in consumer actions for breach of any obligation under the Act or "under a written warranty, implied warranty, or service contract." It then explicitly bars a federal action:

"(A) if the amount in controversy of any individual claim is less than the sum or value of $25;

"(B) if the amount in controversy is less than the sum or value of $50,000 (exclusive of interest and costs) computed on the basis of all claims to be determined in this suit; or

"(C) if the action is brought as a class action, and the number of named plaintiffs is less than one hundred." 15 U.S.C. § 2310(d)(1)(3).

Given the broad remedial provisions of this statute, it poses many difficult questions of definition and of applicable law. See, *e.g.,* Skelton v. General Motors Corp., 660 F.2d 311 (7th Cir.1981). See also Schroeder, *Private Action Under the Magnuson–Moss Warranty Act,* 66 Calif.L.Rev. 1 (1978). Some of these questions may also implicate issues of the constitutional reach of federal court jurisdiction. *Cf.* Textile Workers Union v. Lincoln Mills and the following Note, pp. 975, 983, *supra.*

(8) In the Snyder case, and to a lesser extent in Zahn, the Court relied on Rule 82 as a barrier to the sustaining of jurisdiction. Professor Goldberg, in *The Influence of Procedural Rules on Federal Jurisdiction,* 28 Stan.L.Rev. 395 (1976), has challenged this reliance. Pointing to a number of areas in which the courts, resting in part on the federal rules, have sustained federal jurisdiction on a theory of pendent or ancillary jurisdiction without even alluding to the prohibition of Rule 82, she argues that Rule 82 is not required by either the Enabling Act or the Constitution but rather is a rule of judicial self-restraint. It should therefore be construed in harmony with Rule 1, she urges, with respect to procedural changes that serve "some procedural purpose in one or more situations in which jurisdiction is not a barrier to the rule's implementation" (p. 442).

Do you agree with Professor Goldberg that Rule 82 is not required by the Enabling Act or the Constitution? In the absence of Rule 82, could the rulemakers, consistently with the Enabling Act and the Constitution, abolish the diversity jurisdiction? Eliminate the jurisdictional amount limitation under § 1332? [3]

---

3. With respect to the limitations imposed by the Enabling Act, see Burbank, *The Rules Enabling Act of 1934,* 130 U.Pa. L.Rev. 1015 (1982).

SECTION 4. REMOVAL JURISDICTION AND PROCEDURE *

INTRODUCTORY NOTE

(1) Since 1789 the judiciary acts have continuously provided two ways of removing a case from a state to a federal court: first, by review in the Supreme Court after the state courts have had their final say; and second, by transfer to a lower federal court for trial in the first instance. For the cases upholding the power of Congress thus to displace the state courts, see pp. 481–84, *supra*.

What purposes should the removal jurisdiction serve? Primarily to equalize, in cases of concurrent jurisdiction, the opportunity of both parties to gain access to a federal court? Is there justification in some cases for denying the defendant this choice even though the plaintiff had it? May there be a justification in others for allowing removal (by the defendant or by either party) even though the plaintiff's only initial choice was to sue in the state court? As, for example, if a federal defense is raised? See pp. 1052–57, *supra*.

(2) From 1789 to 1887 the requirements of jurisdiction on removal were stated in terms independent of the requirements for original jurisdiction.

In the Judiciary Act of 1789, 1 Stat. 73, 79–80, the removal privilege was given only in cases in which more than five hundred dollars was in dispute, and then only to three classes of parties: (a) to a defendant who was an alien; (b) to a defendant who was a citizen of another state, sued by a citizen of the state of the forum; and (c) to either party, where title to land was in dispute under conflicting grants of different states and the non-removing party claimed under a grant of the forum state.

Between 1789 and 1872 Congress enacted a series of relatively specific removal statutes, most of them prompted by occasions of sharp conflict with state authority and designed to give added protection to federal officers or federal law. See pp. 1057–58, *supra*. In addition the Separable Controversy Act of July 27, 1866, 14 Stat. 306, introduced a new principle of general importance, allowing removal by one or less than all of the defendants on the basis of the nature of the controversy with the removing defendants rather than of the case as a whole. The problems involved in the current version of this legislation are dealt with below in this section.

The Act of March 3, 1875, 18 Stat. 470, enormously broadened the removal as well as the original jurisdiction. Removal was made a privilege equally of a plaintiff and a defendant. The general removal provision did retain the jurisdictional amount requirement of five hundred dollars. But otherwise the classes of removable cases covered substantially the entire gamut authorized by Article III.

---

* Issues relating to removal are also dealt with in several other chapters. See Chap. IV, pp. 481–84, *supra* (power of Congress to provide for removal); Chap. VIII, Sec. 5, *supra* (removal on the basis of a federal question); Chap. XV, pp. 1825–26, *infra* (appealability of remand orders).

The present pattern of the removal jurisdiction was fixed by the Judiciary Act of 1887. Act of March 3, 1887, 24 Stat. 552, corrected by Act of August 13, 1888, 25 Stat. 433.

For the first time the requirements of removal jurisdiction, under the general removal provision, were expressly tied together with those for original jurisdiction. Then as now there were other provisions for removal in special classes of cases. But the general provision applied only if the case was one "of which the circuit courts of the United States are given original jurisdiction by the preceding section". The present general removal provision, 28 U.S.C. § 1441(a), states the basic condition for removal in substantially the same way; the action must be one "of which the district courts of the United States have original jurisdiction". Special removal provisions with independent requirements are contained in § 1442 (federal officers sued or prosecuted); § 1443 (civil rights cases); and § 1444 (foreclosure action against the United States).

The present statute follows the 1887 act also in restricting the privilege of removal to defendants. All the defendants (or if removal is based on a separate or independent claim against some of the defendants, all defendants interested in the separate claim) must join in the petition for removal. The defendant's residence is immaterial if jurisdiction is "founded on a claim or right arising under the Constitution, treaties or laws of the United States". But any other action "shall be removable only if none of the parties in interest properly joined and served as defendants is a citizen of the State in which such action is brought".

(3) Sometimes Congress has deliberately denied to defendants the choice of forum given to plaintiffs. Notice that this is true in diversity cases in which the defendant is a resident of the state in which the action is brought. Removal is expressly forbidden also in a number of statutes creating new federal rights of action. See, e.g., 28 U.S.C. § 1445(a) (FELA). In these instances, plaintiff alone has the choice of forum.

(4) Should a plaintiff against whom a counterclaim has been filed setting forth an independent cause of action be permitted to remove as a defendant to the counterclaim?

In Shamrock Oil & Gas Corp. v. Sheets, 313 U.S. 100 (1941), the Supreme Court, resolving conflicting decisions in the lower courts, held that the plaintiff could not remove in such a case. This was a diversity case in which both the original claim and the counterclaim exceeded $3,000. But the Court went out of its way to say that it would have made no difference if the plaintiff had never had a choice of suing in the federal court. It said (p. 108):

"[T]he question here is not of waiver but of the acquisition of a right which can only be conferred by Act of Congress. We can find no basis for saying that Congress, by omitting from the present statute all reference to 'plaintiffs,' intended to save a right of removal to some plaintiffs and not to others. * * *

"Not only does the language of the Act of 1887 evidence the Congressional purpose to restrict the jurisdiction of the federal courts on removal, but the policy of the successive acts of Congress regulating the jurisdiction of federal courts is one calling for the strict construction of such legislation."

Shamrock did not discuss the question whether the defendant could rely on a counterclaim as a basis for removal. Should it matter whether such a counterclaim is permissive or compulsory? What is the relevance of Louisville & N.R.R. v. Mottley, 211 U.S. 149 (1908), p. 989, *supra?* For a discussion of the issues and citation of the divided cases, see Wright, Federal Courts § 37, at 203 (4th ed. 1983).[1]

(5) Section 1441 and succeeding sections contain their own venue provisions. Removal is "to the district court of the United States for the district and division embracing the place where such action is pending." For the tangled history of venue on removal under earlier statutes, see Lee v. Chesapeake & O. Ry., 260 U.S. 653 (1923).

(6) The right of removal is a privilege that may be lost if it is not asserted in time and in due conformity with the provisions of the statute. Moreover, even before the time for removal has expired the defendant may take steps in the state court that will be construed as a waiver of the right to remove. See p. 1777, *infra.* As to waiver by voluntary agreement in advance of any litigation, see p. 831, *supra.*

(7) For discussion of § 1447(d), prohibiting review of remand orders, and of its interpretation by the Supreme Court, see Chap. XV, Sec. 1, pp. 1825–26, *infra.*

GRANNY GOOSE FOODS, INC. v. BROTHERHOOD OF TEAMSTERS

415 U.S. 423, 94 S.Ct. 1113, 39 L.Ed.2d 435 (1974).
Certiorari to the United States Court of Appeals for the Ninth Circuit.

MR. JUSTICE MARSHALL delivered the opinion of the Court.

This case concerns the interpretation of 28 U.S.C. § 1450, which provides in pertinent part: "Whenever any action is removed from a State court to a district court of the United States * * * [a]ll injunctions, orders, and other proceedings had in such action prior to its removal shall remain in full force and effect until dissolved or modified by the district court." The District Court held respondent Union in criminal contempt for violating a temporary restraining order issued by the California Superior Court on May 18, 1970, prior to the removal of the case from the Superior Court to the District Court. The Court of Appeals reversed, one judge dissenting, on the ground that the temporary restraining order had expired long before November 30, 1970, the date of the alleged contempt. 472 F.2d 764. The court reasoned that under both § 527 of the California Code of Civil Procedure and of Fed.Rule Civ.Proc. 65(b), the temporary restraining order must have expired no later than June 7, 1970, 20 days after its issuance. The court rejected petitioners' contention that the life of the order was indefinitely prolonged by § 1450 "until dissolved or modified by the district court" * * *.

1. Though the Supreme Court has never decided whether counterclaims (or third-party or cross claims) are removable by any party under § 1441(c) (considered in more detail at pp. 1778–86, *infra*), most commentators and lower courts have concluded that they are not. See 14A Wright, Miller & Cooper § 3724, at 388–94 (1985).

I

On May 15, 1970, petitioners Granny Goose Foods, Inc., and Sunshine Biscuits, Inc., filed a complaint in the Superior Court of California for the county of Alameda alleging that respondent, a local Teamsters Union, and its officers and agents, were engaging in strike activity in breach of national and local collective-bargaining agreements recently negotiated by multiunion-multiemployer bargaining teams. Although the exact nature of the underlying labor dispute is unclear, its basic contours are as follows: The Union was unwilling to comply with certain changes introduced in the new contracts; it believed it was not legally bound by the new agreements because it had not been a part of the multiunion bargaining units that negotiated the contracts; and it wanted to negotiate separate contracts with petitioner employers.

The same day the complaint was filed, the Superior Court issued a temporary restraining order enjoining all existing strike activity and ordering the defendants to show cause on May 26, 1970, why a preliminary injunction should not issue during the pendency of the suit. An amended complaint adding petitioner Standard Brands, Inc., was filed on May 18, and a modified temporary restraining order was issued that same day adding a prohibition against strike activities directed toward that employer.

On May 19, 1970, after having been served with the May 15 restraining order but before the scheduled hearing on the order to show cause, the Union and the individual defendants removed the proceeding to the District Court on the ground that the action arose under § 301 of the Labor Management Relations Act, 1974. On May 20, 1970 an amended removal petition was filed to take into account the modified temporary restraining order of May 18.

Simultaneously with the filing of the removal petition, the defendants filed a motion in the District Court to dissolve the temporary restraining order. * * * *

The employers then filed a motion to remand the case to the Superior Court, alleging that the defendants had waived their right to removal by submitting to the jurisdiction of the state court. The Union's motion to dissolve and the employers' motion to remand came on for a hearing on May 27, 1970. The motion to remand was denied from the bench. * * * Three days later, on June 4, 1970, the District Court entered a brief order denying the motion to dissolve the state court temporary restraining order * * *.

Evidently picketing and strike activity stopped and the labor dispute remained dormant after June 4. The flame was rekindled, however, when on November 9, 1970, the Union sent the employers telegrams requesting bargaining to arrive at a collective-bargaining agreement and expressing the Union's continued belief that it was not bound by the national and local agreements negotiated by the multiunion-multiemployer groups. The employers answered that there was no need to bargain because, in their view, the Union was bound by the national and local agreements. The conflict remained unresolved, and on November 30, 1970, the Union commenced its strike activity once again.

The next day the employers moved the District Court to hold the Union, its agents, and officers in contempt of the modified temporary restraining order issued by the Superior Court on May 18. A hearing was held on the motion the following day. The Union's argument that the temporary restraining order had long since expired was rejected by the District Court on two grounds. First, the court concluded that its earlier action denying the motion to dissolve the temporary restraining order gave the order continuing force and effect. Second, the court found that § 1450 itself served to continue the restraining order in effect until affirmatively dissolved or modified by the court. Concluding after the hearing that the Union had willfully violated the restraining order, the District Court held it in criminal contempt and imposed a fine of $200,000.

II

Leaving aside for the moment the question whether the order denying the motion to dissolve the temporary restraining order was effectively the grant of a preliminary injunction, it is clear that whether California law or Rule 65(b) is controlling, the temporary restraining order issued by the Superior Court expired long before the date of the alleged contempt. Section 527 of the California Code of Civil Procedure, under which the order was issued, provides that temporary restraining orders must be returnable no later than 15 days from the date of the order, 20 days if good cause is shown, and unless the party obtaining the order then proceeds to submit its case for a preliminary injunction, the temporary restraining order must be dissolved. Similarly, under Rule 65(b), temporary restraining orders must expire by their own terms within 10 days after entry, 20 days if good cause is shown.

Petitioners argue, however, that notwithstanding the time limitations of state law, § 1450 keeps all state court injunctions, including *ex parte* temporary restraining orders, in full force and effect after removal until affirmatively dissolved or modified by the district court. To the extent this reading of § 1450 is inconsistent with the time limitations of Rule 65(b), petitioners contend the statute must control.

In our view, however, § 1450 can and should be interpreted in a manner which fully serves its underlying purposes, yet at the same time places it in harmony with the important congressional policies reflected in the time limitations in Rule 65(b).

* * *

* * * [W]hile Congress clearly intended to preserve the effectiveness of state court orders after removal, there is no basis for believing that § 1450 was designed to give injunctions or other orders *greater* effect after removal to federal court than they would have had if the case had remained in state court. * * *

More importantly, once a case has been removed to federal court, it is settled that federal rather than state law governs the future course of proceedings, notwithstanding state court orders issued prior to removal. Section 1450 implies as much by recognizing the district court's authority to dissolve or modify injunctions, orders, and all other proceedings had in state court prior to removal. This Court resolved this issue long ago in Ex parte Fisk, 113 U.S. 713 (1885). There it was argued that an order to take the deposition of a witness issued by the state court prior to removal was binding in federal court and could not be reconsidered by the federal court, notwithstanding its inconsistency with certain federal statutes governing procedure in federal courts. The Court rejected this contention, and said that the predecessor of § 1450

"declares orders of the State court, in a case afterwards removed, to be in force until dissolved or modified by the Circuit Court. This fully recognizes the power of the latter court over such orders. And it was not intended to enact that an order made in the State court, which affected or might affect the mode of trial yet to be had, could change or modify the express directions of an act of Congress on that subject.

"The petitioner having removed his case into the Circuit Court has a right to have its further progress governed by the law of the latter court, and not by that of the court from which it was removed; and if one of the advantages of this removal was an escape from this examination, he has a right to that benefit if his case was rightfully removed." *Id.*, at 725–726.

By the same token, respondent Union had a right to the protections of the time limitation in Rule 65(b) once the case was removed to the District Court. The Federal Rules of Civil Procedure, like other provisions of federal law, govern the mode of proceedings in federal court after removal. See Fed.Rule Civ.Proc. 81(c). * * * The stringent restrictions * * * on the availability of *ex parte* temporary restraining orders reflect the fact that our entire jurisprudence runs counter to the notion of court action taken before reasonable notice and an opportunity to be heard has been granted both sides of a dispute. *Ex parte* temporary restraining orders are no doubt necessary in certain circumstances, but under federal law they should be restricted to serving their underlying purpose of preserving the status quo and preventing irreparable harm just so long as is necessary to hold a hearing, and no longer.

We can find no indication that Congress intended § 1450 as an exception to its broader, longstanding policy of restricting the duration of *ex parte* restraining orders. The underlying purpose of § 1450—ensuring that no lapse in a state court temporary restraining order will occur simply by removing the case to federal court—and the policies reflected in Rule 65(b) can easily be accommodated by applying the following rule: An *ex parte* temporary restraining order issued by a state court prior to removal remains in force after removal no longer than it would have remained in effect under state law, but in no event does the order remain in force longer than the time limitations imposed by Rule 65(b), measured from the date of removal.

* * * Accordingly, no order was in effect on November 30, 1970, and the Union violated no order when it resumed its strike at that time.

III

We now turn to petitioners' argument that, apart from the operation of § 1450, the District Court's denial of the Union's motion to dissolve the temporary restraining order effectively converted the order into a preliminary injunction of unlimited duration. The Court of Appeals rejected this argument out of hand, stating that "[t]he Union's unsuccessful effort to dissolve the order before it died a natural death did not convert the temporary restraining order into a preliminary injunction or estop it from relying on the death certificate." 472 F.2d, at 767. We reach essentially the same conclusion.

* * *

Judgment affirmed.

MR. JUSTICE REHNQUIST, with whom THE CHIEF JUSTICE, MR. JUSTICE STEWART, and MR. JUSTICE POWELL join, concurring in the judgment.

I agree with the Court that the judgment of the Court of Appeals for the Ninth Circuit in this case should be affirmed, since there was no injunctive order in effect at the time that respondent's allegedly contemptuous conduct occurred. But I do not join that portion of the Court's opinion which lays down a "rule" for all cases involving 28 U.S.C. § 1450, the statute which all parties agree is controlling in the case before us. In my view, the announcement of this "rule" is neither necessary to the decision of this case nor consistent with the provisions of the statute itself.

The Court persuasively demonstrates in its opinion that the temporary restraining order issued by the California Superior Court had expired by its own terms long before the alleged contempt occurred. And I see nothing in the language or legislative history of 28 U.S.C. § 1450 * * * which would indefinitely extend the Superior Court's restraining order beyond the time of its normal expiration under state law. Since the temporary restraining order, had the case remained in state court, concededly would have expired in early June, respondent's actions in November and December could not have constituted a contempt of that order.

The Court also persuasively demonstrates that none of the proceedings occurring after removal of the case to the United States District Court had the effect of converting the subsisting state court temporary restraining order into a preliminary injunction of indefinite duration. Those proceedings addressed markedly different issues and certainly did not give the state court order a new, independent federal existence.

Having said this much, the Court has disposed of the case before it. The opinion then goes on, however, to devise a "rule" that

> "[a]n *ex parte* temporary restraining order issued by a state court prior to removal remains in force after removal no longer than it would have remained in effect under state law, but in no event does the order remain in force longer than the time limitations imposed by Rule 65(b), measured from the date of removal."

But the determination that mere removal of a case to a federal district court does not extend the duration of a previously issued state court order past its original termination date makes quite unnecessary to this case any further discussion about time limitations contained in Fed.Rules Civ.Proc. 65(b). More importantly, the second clause of the "rule" devised by the Court seems quite contrary to the specific language of 28 U.S.C. § 1450.

The Court apparently bases this latter clause of the "rule" upon the observation that "respondent Union had a right to the protections of the time limitation in Rule 65(b) once the case was removed to the District Court." While this premise probably has a good deal to recommend it as a matter of practicality or of common sense, the language of the statute gives no hint that rules of practice governing issuance of federal injunctions in the first instance were automatically to be incorporated in applying its terms. The statute says that the state court's temporary restraining order "shall remain in full force and effect until dissolved or modified by the district court." This Court's "rule," however, says that it shall *not* remain in full force and effect, even though not dissolved or modified by the District Court, if it would have a life beyond the time limitations imposed by Rule 65(b).

I think it likely that the interest in limiting the duration of temporary restraining orders which is exemplified in Rule 65(b) can be fully protected in cases removed to the district court by an application to modify or dissolve a state court restraining order which is incompatible with those terms. Such a procedure would be quite consistent with § 1450, which specifically contemplates dissolution or modification by the district court upon an appropriate showing, in a way that the "rule" devised by the Court in this case is not. It is unlikely that many orders issued under rules of state procedure, primarily designed, after all, to provide suitable procedures for state courts rather than to frustrate federal procedural rules in removed actions, would by their terms remain in effect for a period of time far longer than that contemplated by the comparable Federal Rule of Civil Procedure. But in the rare case where such a condition obtains, it is surely not asking too much of a litigant in a removed case to comply with § 1450 and affirmatively move for appropriate modification of the state order.

Therefore, although I cannot subscribe to the rule which the Court fashions to govern cases of this type, I concur in its conclusion that respondent's activity in November and December 1970 did not violate any injunctive order which was in force at that time.

NOTE ON SOME SPECIAL PROBLEMS OF THE RELATION BETWEEN STATE AND FEDERAL LAW IN REMOVED CASES

(1) In its interpretation of § 1450, the majority in Granny Goose relied heavily on the decision in Ex parte Fisk, 113 U.S. 713 (1885), which held that a state court order to take a deposition was subject to reconsideration after removal. Doesn't that case actually lend support to the argument of the concurrence—that a state court order may be modified or dissolved in accordance with federal law but remains in effect until and unless such action is taken?

Federal Rule of Civil Procedure 81(c), also referred to by the majority, provides that the rules apply to removed actions and "govern procedure after removal." But the pre-1948 provision of the Judicial Code that the district court, after removal, shall "proceed therein as if the suit had been originally commenced in said district court" was not carried forward in the new § 1447. Doesn't this omission lend further support to the position of the concurrence?

(2) Until 1986, subject matter jurisdiction in cases removed under § 1441 turned not only on the existence of original federal court jurisdiction in the removed case but also on the existence of state subject matter jurisdiction. Thus if a removed case was one within exclusive federal

jurisdiction, the federal court was required to dismiss. See, *e.g.*, Lambert Run Coal Co. v. Baltimore & Ohio R.R., 258 U.S. 377 (1922).[1]

Academic reaction to this rule was generally critical, see, *e.g.*, Moore, Commentary on the U.S. Judicial Code 219 n. 6 (1949) ("[p]ractical judicial administration can look with little favor upon this technical and subtle doctrine"), and it was finally overturned by the 99th Congress, which added a new subsection (e) to § 1441 (100 Stat. 637 (1986)):

"The court to which such civil action is removed is not precluded from hearing and determining any claim in such civil action because the State court from which such civil action is removed did not have jurisdiction over that claim."

(3) An objection that the state court had not obtained personal jurisdiction over the defendant is not waived by removal to a federal court, Cain v. Commercial Publishing Co., 232 U.S. 124 (1914); and the state court's decision upholding jurisdiction may be reexamined by the district court, at least if the decision was interlocutory under state law, General Inv. Co. v. Lake Shore & M.S. Ry., 260 U.S. 261, 267 (1922), or is open to constitutional challenge, Goldey v. Morning News, 156 U.S. 518 (1895).

If the objection is sustained, and valid service cannot be made, the action should presumably be dismissed and not remanded. But 28 U.S.C. §§ 1447(a) and 1448 preserve the plaintiff's right to make or perfect service after removal. See 14A Wright, Miller & Cooper § 3722, at 290 (1985).

(4) An interesting question of the relation between state and federal law in a removed criminal case arose in Arizona v. Manypenny, 451 U.S. 232 (1981). A state criminal prosecution of a federal official was removed to a federal district court under 28 U.S.C. § 1442(a)(1). After the jury rendered a guilty verdict, the trial judge upheld the defendant's immunity defense and entered a judgment of acquittal. When the state sought to appeal under the general appeal provisions of § 1291, the defendant invoked the rule of federal law that bars an appeal by the prosecution in a criminal case in the absence of express authorization by Congress. The Court held, over two dissents, that since the prosecution was authorized to appeal under state law, the appeal should be allowed. "[T]he Court's prior decisions restricting the availability of § 1291 in a criminal context flow from a tradition of requiring that a prosecutorial appeal be affirmatively authorized by the same sovereign that sponsors the prosecution. * * * [Thus] Arizona can rely on § 1291 combined with appellate authorization from the Arizona Legislature" (p. 249).

---

1. This notion that removal jurisdiction was "derivative" was not carried to its logical extreme, however. In Freeman v. Bee Machine Co., 319 U.S. 448 (1943), the Court held that the rule did not bar amendments to the complaint, otherwise proper, merely because the amended complaint would not have come within the jurisdiction of the state court had the action not been removed. And in one extraordinary case, Federated Dept. Stores, Inc. v. Moitie, 452 U.S. 394, 397 n. 2 (1981), the Court overlooked the rule entirely and said, in passing, that the case had been properly removed to a federal court.

NOTE ON THE PROCEDURE FOR DETERMINING
REMOVABILITY AND ON THE TIME FOR REMOVAL

(1) Before 1948, removal procedure varied according to the ground of removal. The 1948 revision eliminated these discrepancies, save for a few provisions peculiar to criminal prosecutions. The uniform procedure differs in important respects from the procedure under the former statute. The key to the difference is that the petition for removal and the bond required by federal law (28 U.S.C. § 1446(d)) are now filed in the first instance in the federal court instead of the state court and these steps, coupled with notice to adverse parties and to the state court, "shall effect the removal and the State court shall proceed no further unless and until the case is remanded". 28 U.S.C. § 1446(e). Questions of the sufficiency of the petition and of removability are passed on by the federal court.

(2) Under the former procedure the state court had first to decide whether, on the face of the record including the petition, a case for removal had been made out. If the state court denied the petition, the defendant could (a) remain in the state courts and, if he lost on the merits, urge the denial as ground for reversal, Railroad Co. v. Koontz, 104 U.S. 5 (1881); (b) file a transcript of the record in the federal court, disregard the state proceedings and thus run the risk of a binding state judgment if the case was ultimately held nonremovable, Metropolitan Cas. Ins. Co. v. Stevens, 312 U.S. 563 (1941); or (c) litigate in both courts at once in order to safeguard all his flanks. A federal court did have authority under the old procedure to protect the defendant from the danger of (b) or the burden of (c) by enjoining the plaintiff from further proceedings in the state court. See, *e.g.*, Madisonville Traction Co. v. Saint Bernard Mining Co., 196 U.S. 239 (1905).

(3) Does the 1948 revision eliminate the possibilities of inconvenience and conflict? Under the revision, state courts have held that once the required procedural steps are taken in a civil case,[1] all subsequent state action is void, even if the case is nonremovable, unless and until the case is remanded. *E.g.*, Hopson v. North Am. Ins. Co., 71 Idaho 461, 233 P.2d 799 (1951); Artists' Representatives Ass'n v. Haley, 26 A.D.2d 918, 274 N.Y.S.2d 442 (1966). But see Wilson v. Sandstrom, 317 So.2d 732 (Fla.1975), criticized in 30 U.Miami L.Rev. 739 (1976). But what if the removal petition reveals on its face that it has been filed out of time? What if the state court action is taken between the filing of the petition and the receipt of notice by the parties and the state court? See 14A Wright, Miller & Cooper, Federal Practice and Procedure § 3737, at 550 (1985) (suggesting that "the sounder rule" is that removal is not effective until all required steps have been taken).

(4) Do the authorities discussed in Paragraph (3) mean that if a petition for removal is filed in the middle of a state court jury trial, the trial must stop no matter how frivolous the claim for removal? Apparently so, at least if the petition does not reveal on its face that it has been filed out of time. See ALI Study 358–60 and authorities there cited. But see Burlington N.R.R. v. Bell, 107 S.Ct. 3197 (1987) (White, J., dissenting from denial of certiorari). Isn't this rule a powerful weapon in the hands of an

---

1. In 1977, Congress amended § 1446(c) and (e) to distinguish between civil and criminal cases with respect to the authori- ty of a state court over a removed action. For the history of these amendments, see S.Rep. No. 95–354, at 12–13 (1977).

unscrupulous defendant? (Note that the bond required for removal does serve as a deterrent.) The ALI proposed that in a case removed "while a trial is in progress, the trial may be completed in the State court, and judgment thereafter entered if the case is remanded" (proposed § 1383(a)).

(5) Before 1948, a petition for removal under the general removal statute had to be filed "at the time, or any time before the defendant is required by the laws of the State * * * to answer or plead to the declaration or complaint of the plaintiff". 24 Stat. 554 (1887), as amended, 25 Stat. 435 (1888). The provision yielded a mass of litigation over what happened when a case became removable only after this time had expired.

The 1948 revisers decided to replace the prior law's indefinite period for removal of a civil case with a definite period of twenty days (changed in 1965 to thirty days) from the date of filing the initial pleading. This change, they said, would "give adequate time and operate uniformly throughout the federal jurisdiction." [2] But the revisers overlooked the problem of post-filing events (such as voluntary dismissal of a party) that might make a non-removable case removable, and the provision had to be amended in 1949. Under the amended provision, the period begins to run, if the case was not at first removable, upon "receipt by the defendant, through service or otherwise, of a copy of an amended pleading, motion, order or other paper from which it may first be ascertained that the case is one which is or has become removable."

(6) Some difficult questions have arisen as to when, if ever, the existence of the requisite amount in controversy is sufficiently established to start the clock running on the right to removal. In states that do not require a specific sum to be demanded in the pleading, or in which such a demand is forbidden, may the defendant remove if he can show that a recovery of more than $10,000 is possible, or likely? If so, when does the time start to run? In states following the pattern of Fed.Rule 54(c) (allowing a grant of the relief to which the winner is entitled, even if not demanded in the pleadings), what is the effect of a specific demand for less than the jurisdictional amount if the complaint shows damages of more? Of a statement by counsel at the trial of such a case that more than $10,000 is sought? Of a jury verdict for $20,000 if no prior demand for judgment in excess of $10,000 has been made? See Justices v. Murray, 9 Wall. 274 (U.S. 1870), p. 484, supra. See generally 14A Wright, Miller & Cooper, Federal Practice and Procedure § 3725 (1985).

(7) The defendant may waive his right of removal, before the statutory period has expired, by action in the state court which is deemed inconsistent with it. See Rosenthal v. Coates, 148 U.S. 142 (1893), in which the Supreme Court referred to "the spirit of the removal acts, which do not contemplate that a plaintiff may experiment on his case in the state court, and, upon an adverse decision, then transfer it to the Federal court". See also 14A Wright, Miller & Cooper, Federal Practice and Procedure § 3721, at 223–24 (1985).

Given the 30–day time limit on removal, does the waiver doctrine have any rational basis?

---

2. In the 1977 amendments to § 1446 (note 1, *supra*), Congress also changed the time limits for removal of a criminal case. Prior to that amendment, removal was allowed "at any time before trial."

AMERICAN FIRE & CASUALTY CO. v. FINN

341 U.S. 6, 71 S.Ct. 534, 95 L.Ed. 702 (1951).

Certiorari to the United States Court of Appeals for the Fifth Circuit.

MR. JUSTICE REED delivered the opinion of the Court. * * *

Petitioner, the American Fire and Casualty Company, a Florida corporation, and its codefendant, the Indiana Lumbermens Mutual Insurance Company, an Indiana corporation, removed, in accordance with 28 U.S.C. § 1446, a suit brought by respondent Finn in a Texas state court against the two corporations and an individual, Reiss, local agent of both corporations and a resident of Texas. The suit was for a fire loss on Texas property suffered by respondent, a resident of Texas. Respondent tried to have the case remanded before trial but was unsuccessful. After special issues were found by the jury, judgment was entered against petitioner for the amount of insurance claimed and costs, and in favor of the other two defendants. The District Court denied the motion to vacate the judgment and the Court of Appeals affirmed. 181 F.2d 845. The latter court concluded there were causes of action against the foreign insurance companies "separate and independent" from that stated against the resident individual. Since the causes against the companies would have been removable if sued on alone, the entire suit was removable. 28 U.S.C. § 1441(c). That ruling required consideration of the changes concerning removal made by § 1441(c), which superseded 28 U.S.C. (1946 ed.) § 71. The Court of Appeals said:

"The difference, if any, between separable controversies under the old statute and separate and independent claims under the new one is in degree, not in kind. It is difficult to distinguish between the two concepts, but it is not necessary to attempt it in a case like this, which would be removable under either statute."

Consideration of the ruling on the motion to vacate the judgment requires a determination of whether the suit contained separate and independent causes of action under § 1441(c), and, if the conclusion is that it did not, a ruling on the effect of a judgment after a removal without right, initiated by the party against whom the judgment was ultimately rendered. As prompt, economical and sound administration of justice depends to a large degree upon definite and finally accepted principles governing important areas of litigation, such as the respective jurisdictions of federal and state courts, we granted certiorari. * * *

I.

The removal took place after September 1, 1948, the effective date of the revision of the laws relating to judicial procedure. The former provision governing removal, 28 U.S.C. (1946 ed.) § 71, read:

"And when in any suit mentioned in this section there shall be a controversy which is wholly between citizens of different States, and which can be fully determined as between them, then either one or more of the defendants actually interested in such controversy may remove said suit into the district court of the United States for the proper district."

* * *

One purpose of Congress in adopting the "separate and independent claim or cause of action" test for removability by § 1441(c) of the 1948 revision in lieu of the provision for removal of 28 U.S.C. (1946 ed.) § 71, was by simplification to avoid the difficulties experienced in determining the meaning of that provision. Another and important purpose was to limit removal from state courts. Section 71 allowed removal when a controversy was wholly between citizens of different states and fully determinable between them. Such a controversy was said to be "separable." * * * Often plaintiffs in state actions joined other state residents as defendants with out-of-state defendants so that removable controversies wholly between citizens of different states would not be pleaded. The effort frequently failed, see Pullman Co. v. Jenkins, 305 U.S. at page 538, and removal was allowed. Our consideration of the meaning and effect of 28 U.S.C. § 1441(c), should be carried out in the light of the congressional intention.

The Congress, in the revision, carried out its purpose to abridge the right of removal. Under the former provision, 28 U.S.C. (1946 ed.) § 71, separable controversies authorized removal of the suit. * * * In § 71 the removable "controversy" was interpreted as any possible separate suit that a litigant might properly bring in a federal court so long as it was wholly between citizens of different states. So, before the revision, when a suit in a state court had such a separable federally cognizable controversy, the entire suit might be removed to the federal court.[4]

A separable controversy is no longer an adequate ground for removal unless it also constitutes a separate and independent claim or cause of action. * * * Of course, "separate cause of action" restricts removal more than "separable controversy." In a suit covering multiple parties or issues based on a single claim, there may be only one cause of action and yet be separable controversies. The addition of the word "independent" gives emphasis to congressional intention to require more complete disassociation between the federally cognizable proceedings and those cognizable only in state courts before allowing removal.

The effectiveness of the restrictive policy of Congress against removal depends upon the meaning ascribed to "separate and independent * * * cause of action". § 1441. * * *

* * * Considering the previous history of "separable controversy," the broad meaning of "cause of action," and the congressional purpose in the revision resulting in 28 U.S.C. § 1441(c), we conclude that where there is a single wrong to plaintiff, for which relief is sought, arising from an interlocked series of transactions, there is no separate and independent claim or cause of action under § 1441(c).

In making this determination we look to the plaintiff's pleading, which controls. Pullman Co. v. Jenkins, 305 U.S. 534, 538. The single wrong for which relief is sought is the failure to pay compensation for the loss on the property. Liability lay among three parties, but it was uncertain which one was responsible. Therefore, all were joined as defendants in one

---

4. Barney v. Latham, 103 U.S. 205, is a good illustration. This Court held that there were separable controversies in a state court suit against a local corporation and nonresident individuals for an accounting on land sales. One group of sales was by the nonresidents before conveyance to the corporation; the other by the corporation after conveyance.

See also Pullman Co. v. Jenkins, 305 U.S. 534. * * *

petition. First, facts were stated that made the petitioner, American Fire and Casualty Company, liable. It was alleged that the company, through its agent Reiss, insured the property destroyed for the amount claimed, that Reiss gave plaintiff credit for the premium, controlled her insurance, agreed to keep the property insured at all times. She further alleged that the Company issued the policy but Reiss retained the document in his possession and refused to deliver it after the fire. Then followed a prayer for judgment against the Company.

The next portion of the complaint stated, in the alternative, an obligation by the Indiana Lumbermens Insurance Company to pay the same loss. The policy with Lumbermens was attached as an exhibit, and allegations concerning Reiss similar to those in the first portion were made. A second prayer was added for recovery against Lumbermens.

The last portion of the complaint, alternative to both the preceding, alleged that Reiss, American Fire and Casualty Company and Indiana Lumbermens Insurance Company were jointly and severally liable for the loss. Reiss was said to be plaintiff's insurance broker, responsible for keeping her house insured. Plaintiff alleged Reiss insured her property with Lumbermens and never notified her of any cancellation or expiration. Reiss was alleged to have agreed later to insure her property with American, to have promised after the fire to deliver the policy, to have failed to make the promised delivery. She claimed that Reiss was responsible for "anything that results in the defeat of her recovery on either one of said policies" and that he was "the direct cause of the condition, of said insurance, and the proximate cause of all of plaintiff's troubles and confusion." The pleader then asserted:

"That such acts and conduct on the part of said Joe Reiss as agent for the said two insurance companies, renders said Joe Reiss, agent, the Joe Reiss Insurance Agency and the American Fire and Casualty Insurance Company of Orlando, Florida, and the Indiana Lumbermens Mutual Insurance Company of Indianapolis, Indiana, jointly and severally liable for the full amount of the damages that plaintiff has suffered by reason of said fire in the amount of Five Thousand Dollars."

The petition concluded with a prayer for joint and several judgment against all three defendants, based on the third set of allegations.

The past history of removal of "separable" controversies, the effort of Congress to create a surer test, and the intention of Congress to restrict the right of removal leads us to the conclusion that separate and independent causes of action are not stated. The facts in each portion of the complaint involve Reiss, the damage comes from a single incident. The allegations in which Reiss is a defendant involve substantially the same facts and transactions as do the allegations in the first portion of the complaint against the foreign insurance companies. It cannot be said that there are separate and independent claims for relief as § 1441(c) requires. Therefore, we conclude there was no right to removal.

II.

There are cases which uphold judgments in the district courts even though there was no right to removal. In those cases the federal trial court would have had original jurisdiction of the controversy had it been brought in the federal court in the posture it had at the time of the actual trial of the cause or of the entry of the judgment. That is, if the litigation had been initiated in the federal court on the issues and between the parties that comprised the case at the time of trial or judgment, the federal court would have had cognizance of the case. This circumstance was relied upon as the foundation of the holdings.[15] The defendant who had removed the action was held to be estopped from protesting that there was no right to removal. Since the federal court could have had jurisdiction originally, the estoppel did not endow it with a jurisdiction it could not possess.

In this case, however, the District Court would not have had original jurisdiction of the suit, as first stated in the complaint, because of the presence on each side of a citizen of Texas. 28 U.S.C. § 1332. The posture of this case even at the time of judgment also barred federal jurisdiction. A Texas citizen was and remained a party defendant. The trial court judgment, after decreeing recovery against American Fire and Casualty Company on the jury's verdict, added, over American's objection,

"It Is Further Ordered, Adjudged and Decreed that the Plaintiff take nothing as against Defendants, Indiana Lumbermens Mutual Insurance Company and Joe Reiss, individually and doing business as the Joe Reiss Insurance Agency, and that such Defendants go hence without day with their costs."

By this decree the merits of the litigation against Reiss were finally adjudicated. The request of respondent to dismiss Reiss after the judgment was not acted upon by the trial court.

The jurisdiction of the federal courts is carefully guarded against expansion by judicial interpretation or by prior action or consent of the parties. To permit a federal trial court to enter a judgment in a case removed without right from a state court where the federal court could not have original jurisdiction of the suit even in the posture it had at the time of judgment, would by the act of the parties work a wrongful extension of federal jurisdiction and give district courts power the Congress has denied them.

The judgment of the Court of Appeals must be reversed and the cause remanded to the District Court with directions to vacate the judgment entered and, if no further steps are taken by any party to affect its jurisdiction,[18] to remand the case to the District Court of Harris County, Texas, with costs against petitioner.

It is so ordered.

Judgment of Court of Appeals reversed, and cause remanded with directions.

MR. JUSTICE DOUGLAS, with whom MR. JUSTICE BLACK and MR. JUSTICE MINTON concur, dissenting.

15. E.g., in Baggs v. Martin, 179 U.S. 206, the federal court had jurisdiction over the property in the hands of the receiver and it was not a proceeding wherein "mere consent, or even voluntary action by the parties, * * * [conferred] jurisdiction upon a court which would not have possessed it without such consent or action." 179 U.S. at page 209.

18. Issues not raised in the records or briefs are not passed upon, such as the propriety of the District Court's allowing, after vacation of judgment, a motion to dismiss Reiss, the resident defendant; or the associated problem: whether, if such a dismissal is allowed, a new judgment can be entered on the old verdict without a new trial. These questions and like matters are for the consideration and decision of the District Court.

I think petitioner, having asked for and obtained the removal of the case to the Federal District Court, and having lost its case in that court, is now estopped from having it remanded to the state court. * * *

The argument [against estoppel] is that the suit against Reiss, the individual defendant, could not be removed since both he and the plaintiff were residents of Texas, and that the suits against the two nonresident corporations could not be removed because the claim asserted against them was not "separate and independent."

But the judgment sought to be reviewed here was rendered by the District Court only against petitioner who could have been sued there originally and who invoked the jurisdiction of the District Court. As the court observed in the closely analogous case of Bailey v. Texas Co., *supra,* 47 F.2d at page 155, "the resulting situation is equivalent to initiating an action in the District Court in which the defendant appears."[3] I think it is abusive of the interests of justice when the challenge now made is raised to the dignity of a jurisdictional question. Any requirement of § 1441(c) that was not met in this case rose to no level higher than an irregularity, so far as petitioner is concerned. Both Reiss and the other nonresident defendant have been dismissed from the case. The only judgment before the Court is one which satisfies the requirements of original jurisdiction. Petitioner— the one who invoked federal jurisdiction and as a result suffered the consequences of this judgment—should not now be heard to complain. Baggs v. Martin [179 U.S. 206], should govern this case.

NOTE ON SEPARATE AND INDEPENDENT CLAIMS OR CAUSES OF ACTION

(1) The original Separable Controversy Act of July 27, 1866, 14 Stat. 306, authorized removal to the federal court only of the separable controversy. But the 1875 act, as construed in Barney v. Latham, provided that the whole suit should be removed. The court, in other words, had first to inquire whether the suit included a controversy "which is wholly between citizens of different States, and which can be fully determined as between them", and then, if it found a controversy which was thus separable from the main suit, it was directed *not* to separate it. In this way the federal courts were called upon to determine many claims between co-citizens founded solely upon state law.

What was the constitutional justification, if any, for this jurisdiction? That it was ancillary to the exercise of jurisdiction over a controversy independently within Article III, and hence within the power of Congress to authorize under the necessary and proper clause? See Texas Employers Ins. Ass'n v. Felt, 150 F.2d 227, 233–35 (5th Cir.1945). Or that Strawbridge v. Curtiss did not state a constitutional principle, and that the whole suit was within Article III? See generally Note, 94 U.Pa.L.Rev. 239 (1946).

(2) Notice that the 1948 revision made three major changes in the former provisions relating to "separable controversies":

3. In that case the parties who could not have been brought to the District Court by removal were after removal dismissed out of the case and judgment was rendered against a defendant who could have been sued in the District Court.

First, the introduction of the new standard of "a separate and independent claim or cause of action", discussed in the Finn case;

Second, the provision for remand, in the district court's discretion, of matters not within the court's original jurisdiction; and

Third, the elimination of the former restriction to controversies "wholly between citizens of different States", and the extension of the authority to remove to cases in which federal jurisdiction over the separate claim is based on the presence of a federal question, alienage, or any other ground.

The Reviser's notes explained the changes as follows:

"Subsection (c) has been substituted for the provision in section 71 of Title 28, U.S.C., 1940 ed., 'and when in any suit * * * [quoting]'.

"This quoted language has occasioned much confusion. The courts have attempted to distinguish between separate and separable controversies, a distinction which is sound in theory but illusory in substance. (See 41 Harv.L.Rev. 1048; 35 Ill.L.Rev. 576.)

"Subsection (c) permits the removal of a separate cause of action but not of a separable controversy unless it constitutes a separate and independent claim or cause of action within the original jurisdiction of United States District Courts. In this respect it will somewhat decrease the volume of Federal litigation.

"Rules 18, 20, and 23 of the Federal Rules of Civil Procedure permit the most liberal joinder of parties, claims, and remedies in civil actions. Therefore there will be no procedural difficulty occasioned by the removal of the entire action. Conversely, if the court so desires, it may remand to the State court all nonremovable matters."

Was this an accurate explanation or an adequate disclosure of what was actually being done?

(3) In three main classes of cases prior to 1948 the courts had recognized what were called "separate and independent causes of action" within a state court proceeding, as distinguished from mere "separable controversies".

Two consequences followed from the distinction. The *separate* cause of action was removable under the general removal statute—not the separable controversy provision. Thus, diverse citizenship was not necessary, if the cause of action was independently within a grant of federal question jurisdiction. By parity of reasoning, the rest of the state court proceeding stayed in the state court. Thus, the courts were saying, in effect, that the connection between the federal part of the original proceeding and the state part was so remote, in such cases, that the removability of the federal part should be determined independently, and ancillary jurisdiction over the state part was unwarranted.

The first of these classes of cases involved multiple claims of a single plaintiff against multiple defendants, where separate relief was sought against each defendant and the only basis of joinder was a common question of law or fact. *E.g.,* Pacific Railroad Removal Cases (Union Pac. Ry. v. City of Kansas), 115 U.S. 1, 18–23 (1885) (condemnation and benefit assessment proceeding against several land owners, of whom one, a corporation, was allowed to remove separately because of its federal charter).

A second and similar class of cases involved multiple claims of multiple plaintiffs against a single defendant, where separate judgments were likewise demanded and a common question of law and fact provided the only basis of joinder. *E.g.,* Young v. Southern Pac. Co., 15 F.2d 280 (2d Cir.1926) (claims only of those plaintiffs who were of diverse citizenship removed).

A third and distinct class of cases involved multiple claims of a single plaintiff against a single defendant, where the claims had no relation other than the fact that they involved the same parties. *E.g.,* Tillman v. Russo-Asiatic Bank, 51 F.2d 1023 (2d Cir.1931) (separable controversy provision inapplicable because defendant an alien; removal of first cause of action approved; second cause of action held nonremovable because of assignee clause and remanded).

These were the cases drawing the distinction which the revisers called "sound in theory but illusory in substance" and then utilized nevertheless as a new criterion of removability.

Consider whether the following is an unfair paraphrase of § 1441(c): "When a matter that would be independently within federal jurisdiction is associated in a state court proceeding with matters that would not be independently within federal jurisdiction, the whole proceeding can be removed to the federal court if the state and federal matters are sufficiently *disconnected.*"

Does this make sense?

(4) Under the interpretation announced in the Finn case, can § 1441(c) have any constitutional sphere of operation in cases in which federal jurisdiction is based on the presence of a federal question? See Lewin, *The Federal Courts' Hospitable Back Door—Removal of "Separate and Independent" Non-Federal Causes of Action,* 66 Harv.L.Rev. 423 (1953); Cohen, *Problems in the Removal of a "Separate and Independent Claim or Cause of Action,"* 46 Minn.L.Rev. 1 (1961). Even if Hurn v. Oursler, 289 U.S. 238 (1933), didn't carry pendent jurisdiction to the limit of the constitutional concept of a "case," doesn't United Mine Workers v. Gibbs, 383 U.S. 715, (1966), p. 1040, *supra,* do just that? (Note that removal of a state pendent claim in a federal question case can be had under § 1441(a) and (b).)

Under the holding in State Farm Fire & Cas. Co. v. Tashire, 386 U.S. 523 (1967), p. 1667, *supra,* the rule of Strawbridge v. Curtiss does not reflect a constitutional limitation. Does it follow that federal jurisdiction can be extended to all claims involved in each of the three classes of cases described in Paragraph (3) above? Is diversity between any two adverse parties enough to give constitutional jurisdiction over any combination of claims that a state may choose to call a "case"?

(5) Constitutional limitations aside, what are the kinds of cases that can be removed under § 1441(c) as now interpreted? Does the Court in Finn put forward a useful definition of "claim or cause of action" or does it, as one commentator suggested, nod in several directions at once? See Cohen, *supra,* at 16–17.

Suppose that the petitioner in Finn had insured only part of the risk and that the claim against Reiss touched only the question of the remainder of the risk with the other company. Would the claim against the petitioner then have been "separate and independent"?

For the view that "separate and independent claims are presented * * * if recovery upon one of the claims would not preclude enforcement of the other, as it would have in the Finn case," see Note, *The Supreme Court, 1950 Term*, 65 Harv.L.Rev. 107, 166–68 (1951). Can this test be maintained in view of the Court's statement in Finn that Barney v. Latham would not now be removable? There the plaintiffs sought an accounting for sales of land in which they claimed their ancestor had had an interest as a joint adventurer. But the recovery sought from the nonresident defendants was only for sales prior to transfer of the land to the resident defendant, and the two groups of claims were neither alternative nor overlapping.

Would it be accurate, at least, to say that separate and independent claims are *not* presented if recovery upon one *would* preclude enforcement of the other? If so, the 1948 revision settled substantial doubts, under the prior law, as to the removability not only of alternative claims but of certain kinds of claims for entire liability on account of acts of concurrent negligence. See the majority and concurring opinions in Pullman Co. v. Jenkins, 305 U.S. 534 (1939).

For the view that after Finn, it is hard to imagine a diversity case that would satisfy state rules for joinder of claims and would at the same time be removable under § 1441(c), see Wright, Federal Courts § 39, at 222–23 (4th ed. 1983). Indeed, there are relatively few such cases in the reports, and most if not all are quite debatable. See, *e.g.*, Hudson v. Smith, 618 F.2d 642, 644–45 (10th Cir.1980) (removing party challenges jurisdiction after losing on merits; court says that "we are disinclined to disturb [the district court's] resolution of the matter"); Crosby v. Paul Hardeman, Inc., 414 F.2d 1 (8th Cir.1969) (claims against original contractor and surety held separate and independent from claims against successor contractor and others; entire case is removable); Climax Chem. Co. v. C.F. Braun & Co., 370 F.2d 616, 619 (10th Cir.1966) (claims against multiple defendants, for breach of their contracts in connection with a construction project, held removable under § 1441(c): "If the Court [in Finn] was sounding the death knell of section 1441(c), we believe it would have said so").[1]

(6) Suppose that in an action by a single plaintiff against a single defendant, the complaint contains a claim under the FELA, which is specified to be nonremovable by 28 U.S.C. § 1445(a), and a separate and independent claim under state common law. If there is diversity of citizenship, should the defendant be able to remove the whole case under § 1441(c)? Compare Hoges v. Aliquippa & So. R.R., 427 F.Supp. 889 (W.D. Pa.1977) (yes), with Gamble v. Central of Ga. Ry. Co., 486 F.2d 781 (5th Cir. 1973) (no). Can it be argued that given the head-on collision between two statutory policies expressed in the same chapter of the Judicial Code, the only adequate solution is to allow removal of the state claim and remand of the FELA claim to the state court? Does the remand provision of § 1441(c) preclude such a result? Is remand of a federal claim and retention of a state claim in such a case too ironic to contemplate? See 14A Wright, Miller & Cooper, Federal Practice and Procedure § 3724, at 408–09 (1985).

(7) What is the relevance of state substantive law, in actions to enforce state-created rights, in determining whether a claim is "separate and

1. On the question of the applicability of § 1441(c) to counterclaims, cross-claims, and third-party claims, see p. 1769, note 1, *supra*.

independent"? What did the Court mean in the Finn case by saying that "we look to the plaintiff's pleading, which controls", in deciding whether "a separate and independent claim or cause of action" is presented?

Would it be accurate to say that the plaintiff, being the master of his pleading, determines what liability he wishes to assert, that state law determines whether the asserted liability is well-founded, and that federal law determines whether a well-founded assertion of liability of that kind is "a separate and independent claim"?

Suppose that several defendants, by separate acts, have contributed to the pollution of a stream and thus to the injury of the plaintiff's land. Suppose that it is doubtful whether, under the state law, each is liable for the whole damage or only for the part which he himself has done. Suppose that the plaintiff, in good faith, seeks judgment for the full amount against each. Should a nonresident defendant be able to remove? Would the case be different if the claim of entire liability were tenuous and unsound?

(8) Suppose that in the Finn case there had been no basis for the plaintiff's claim against Reiss.

The doctrine has long been recognized that the "fraudulent" joinder of a resident defendant is no bar to removal. If a petition for removal contained allegations sufficient, if proved, to show "fraud", the state court was bound to grant the petition, leaving the proof to be made in the federal court. But the mere purpose to defeat removal did not constitute fraud, even though the resident defendant was known to be judgment-proof. Illinois Cent. R.R. v. Sheegog, 215 U.S. 308 (1909). The plaintiff must be shown to have known that his claim was groundless in fact or in law, or else to have closed his eyes to evidence that would have shown it to be so. Wecker v. National Enameling & Stamping Co., 204 U.S. 176 (1907); Parks v. New York Times Co., 308 F.2d 474 (5th Cir.1962).

NOTE ON THE DOCTRINE OF ESTOPPEL AND ON THE EFFECT UPON REMOVAL JURISDICTION OF POST–REMOVAL EVENTS

(1) What did Justice Douglas mean in the Finn case by saying that the judgment sought to be reviewed was rendered "only against petitioner", and that "both Reiss and the other nonresident defendant have been dismissed from the case"? The dismissal was on the merits and still stood. Should the fact that the petitioner alone appealed have the effect of severing the case as to it?

(2) In Baggs v. Martin, cited in both Finn opinions, an action for damages brought in the state court against a railroad receiver had been removed by the receiver to the federal circuit court which had appointed him. After judgment had gone against the receiver on the merits, he raised the question of jurisdiction for the first time in the circuit court of appeals. Answering certified questions, the Supreme Court assumed that the case was not within the removal statute, but held "that, in the present case, the receiver, having voluntarily brought the cause into the Circuit Court by whose appointment he held his office, cannot, after that court has passed upon the matter in controversy, be heard to object to the power of

that court to render judgment therein". Explaining this holding, the Court went on (179 U.S. at 209):

"We do not mean to be understood to say that mere consent, or even voluntary action by the parties, can confer jurisdiction upon a court which would not have possessed it without such consent or action. But here the Circuit Court had, independently of the citizenship of the parties in the damage suit, jurisdiction over the railroad and its property in the hands of its receiver. It may be that its jurisdiction was not, by reason of the act of March 3, 1887, exclusive of that of other courts in controversies like the present one. But when the receiver, waiving any right he might have had to have the cause tried in a state court, brought it before the court whose officer he was, he cannot successfully dispute its jurisdiction." [1]

The reasoning in Baggs v. Martin was more fully developed in Mackay v. Uinta Dev. Co., 229 U.S. 173 (1913). A Wyoming corporation had sued Mackay, a citizen of Utah, in a Wyoming state court upon a non-federal claim for less than the jurisdictional amount. Mackay then counter-claimed upon a federal claim for more than the jurisdictional amount, and thereafter removed the entire case to the federal circuit court, where the company had judgment on the merits. The circuit court of appeals raised the jurisdictional question on its own motion and certified it to the Supreme Court.

The Supreme Court assumed without deciding that the removal was improper, but upheld the jurisdiction. It said (pp. 176–77):

"* * * The case was removed in fact, and, while the parties could not give jurisdiction by consent, there was the requisite amount and the diversity of citizenship necessary to give the United States Circuit Court jurisdiction of the cause. The case, therefore, resolves itself into an inquiry as to whether, if irregularly removed, it could be lawfully tried and determined.

"Removal proceedings are in the nature of process to bring the parties before the United States court. * * * When that result is accomplished by * * * voluntary attendance, the court will not, of its own motion, inquire as to the regularity of the issue or service of process,—or, indeed, whether there was any process at all, since it could be waived, in whole or in part, either expressly or by failing seasonably to object. Powers v. C. & O. Ry., 169 U.S. 92, 98.

"What took place in the state court may, therefore, be disregarded by the court because it was waived by the parties, and regardless of the manner in which the case was brought or how the attendance of the parties in the United States court was secured, there was presented to the Circuit Court a controversy between citizens of different States in which the amount claimed by one non-resident was more than $2,000, exclusive of interest and costs. As the court had jurisdiction of the subject-matter the parties could have been realigned by making Mackay plaintiff and the Development Company defendant, if that had been found proper. But if there was any irregularity in docketing the case or in the order of the

---

1. The assumption in Baggs v. Martin that the state court had jurisdiction of the case and that the statute did not authorize its removal crystallized into a holding later in the same term in Gableman v. Peoria, D. & E. Ry., 179 U.S. 335 (1900), in which the Court, while reaffirming the earlier decision, decided that it was the duty of the circuit court in a similar situation to grant a timely motion to remand.

pleadings such an irregularity was waivable and neither it nor the method of getting the parties before the court operated to deprive it of the power to determine the cause."

(3) Look again at the flat direction of 28 U.S.C. § 1447(c). Does this shake the Baggs–Mackay principle? No court has so held, and the most recent Supreme Court decision applying the principle, Grubbs v. General Elec. Credit Corp., 405 U.S. 699 (1972), makes no mention of the provision.

(4) Should the Baggs–Mackay estoppel be extended to bar the removing defendant from objecting to any curative amendment offered by the plaintiff for the purpose of establishing jurisdiction retroactively? On remand of the Finn case, the district court allowed dismissal as to all defendants except American Fire & Casualty Co., and then ordered a second trial. On appeal by Finn from a judgment for defendant following the second trial, the court of appeals held that after dismissal of the other four defendants, judgment for the plaintiff should have been entered on the original record. Finn v. American Fire & Cas. Co., 207 F.2d 113 (5th Cir.1953). See *Note on the Effects of Misjoinder and Nonjoinder of Parties*, p. 1667, *supra.*

(5) If jurisdiction exists at the time of removal, should the plaintiff have power by a later amendment to oust it?

A plaintiff unquestionably can defeat removal jurisdiction by dismissing his complaint in the federal court. Thereafter he can try to state a non-removable case in a fresh action in the state court. Mecom v. Fitzsimmons Drilling Co., 284 U.S. 183 (1931) (dismissal, followed by substitution of new administrator with same citizenship as defendant). (Observe the limitation Fed.Rule 41(a)(1) places on the repetition of this device.)

What of steps short of outright dismissal, such as amendment of the complaint (a) to reduce the ad damnum below the jurisdictional amount, or (b) to eliminate the federal claim on which removal jurisdiction was based, leaving only a state claim for adjudication? Although (a) has long been held not to oust jurisdiction, or to permit remand, St. Paul Mercury Indemnity Co. v. Red Cab Co., 303 U.S. 283 (1938), the Supreme Court in 1988 resolved a conflict among the lower courts by holding that (b) did leave the court with discretion to remand, as well as to dismiss. Carnegie-Mellon University v. Cohill, 108 S.Ct. 614 (1988). The decision does seem consistent with the discretionary scope of pendent jurisdiction articulated in UMW v. Gibbs, p. 1040, *supra*, and the Court distinguished St. Paul Mercury on that ground, adding that "forum manipulation concerns" (p. 622 n. 12) could be dealt with by the court in the exercise of that discretion. Broad language in Thermtron Products, Inc. v. Hermansdorfer, p. 1825, *infra*—to the effect that a court may never remand a case to a state court on a ground not specified in the removal statute—was also distinguished on the basis of the discretionary nature of pendent jurisdiction. See generally Swing, *Federal Common Law Power to Remand a Removed Case*, 136 U.Pa. L.Rev. 583 (1987).

SECTION 5. CONFLICTS OF JURISDICTION AMONG FEDERAL COURTS

KEROTEST MANUFACTURING CO. v. C–O–TWO FIRE EQUIPMENT CO.

342 U.S. 180, 72 S.Ct. 219, 96 L.Ed. 200 (1952).
Certiorari to the United States Court of Appeals for the Third Circuit.

MR. JUSTICE FRANKFURTER delivered the opinion of the Court.

The C–O–Two Fire Equipment Company, the respondent here, owns two patents, one issued on November 23, 1948, and the other reissued on August 23, 1949, for squeeze-grip valves and discharge heads for portable fire extinguishers. C–O–Two, incorporated in Delaware, has offices in Newark, New Jersey. On January 17, 1950, it commenced in the District Court for the Northern District of Illinois an action against the Acme Equipment Company for "making and causing to be made and selling and using" devices which were charged with infringing C–O–Two's patents.

On March 9, 1950, the petitioner Kerotest began in the District Court of Delaware this proceeding against C–O–Two for a declaration that the two patents sued on in the Illinois action are invalid and that the devices which Kerotest manufactures and supplies to Acme, the Illinois defendant, do not infringe the C–O–Two patents. Kerotest, a Pennsylvania corporation, has its offices in Pittsburgh, but was subject to service of process in Illinois. C–O–Two on March 22, 1950, filed an amendment to its complaint joining Kerotest as a defendant in the Illinois action.

In Delaware, C–O–Two moved for a stay of the declaratory judgment action and Kerotest sought to enjoin C–O–Two from prosecuting the Illinois suit "whether as against Kerotest alone, or generally, as [the Delaware District Court might] deem just and proper." The District Court stayed the Delaware proceeding and refused to enjoin that in Illinois, subject to reexamination of the questions after 90 days. On appeal by Kerotest, the Court of Appeals for the Third Circuit affirmed, holding that the District Court had not abused its discretion in staying the Delaware action for 90 days to permit it to get "more information concerning the controverted status of Kerotest in the Illinois suit".

During the 90-day period the Illinois District Court allowed the joinder of Kerotest as a defendant, denying a motion by Acme to stay the Illinois proceeding pending disposition of the Delaware suit, and Kerotest made a general appearance. After 90 days both parties renewed their motions in Delaware, with Kerotest this time asking that C–O–Two be enjoined from prosecuting the Illinois suit only as to Kerotest. The District Court, a different judge sitting, enjoined C–O–Two from proceeding in the Illinois suit against Kerotest, and denied the stay of the Delaware action, largely acting on the assumption that rulings by its own and other Courts of Appeals required such a result except in "exceptional cases," since the Delaware action between C–O–Two and Kerotest was commenced before Kerotest was made a defendant in the Illinois suit. On appeal, the Court of Appeals for the Third Circuit reversed, saying in part: " * * * the whole of the war and all the parties to it are in the Chicago theatre and there only can it be fought to a finish as the litigations are now cast. On the other hand if the battle is waged in the Delaware arena there is a strong probability that the Chicago suit nonetheless would have to be proceeded with for Acme is not and cannot be made a party to the Delaware litigation. The Chicago suit when adjudicated will bind all the parties in both cases. Why, under the circumstances, should there be two litigations where one will suffice? We can find no adequate reason. We assume, of course, that there will be prompt action in the Chicago theatre."

A petition for rehearing was granted and the Court of Appeals, the seven circuit judges sitting *en banc,* in an expanded opinion to which two judges dissented, adhered to the views of the court of three judges. Inasmuch as a question of importance to the conduct of multiple litigation in the federal judicial system was involved, we granted certiorari.

The Federal Declaratory Judgments Act, facilitating as it does the initiation of litigation by different parties to many-sided transactions, has created complicated problems for coordinate courts. Wise judicial administration, giving regard to conservation of judicial resources and comprehensive disposition of litigation, does not counsel rigid mechanical solution of such problems. The factors relevant to wise administration here are equitable in nature. Necessarily, an ample degree of discretion, appropriate for disciplined and experienced judges, must be left to the lower courts. The conclusion which we are asked to upset derives from an extended and careful study of the circumstances of this litigation. Such an estimate has led the Court of Appeals twice to conclude that all interests will be best served by prosecution of the single suit in Illinois. Even if we had more doubts than we do about the analysis made by the Court of Appeals, we would not feel justified in displacing its judgment with ours.[3]

It was strongly pressed upon us that the result below may encourage owners of weak patents to avoid a real test of their patents' validity by successive suits against customers in forums inconvenient for the manufacturer, or selected because of greater hospitality to patents. Such apprehension implies a lack of discipline and of disinterestedness on the part of the lower courts, hardly a worthy or wise basis for fashioning rules of procedure. It reflects an attitude against which we were warned by Mr. Justice Holmes, speaking for the whole Court, likewise in regard to a question of procedure: "Universal distrust creates universal incompetence." Graham v. United States, 231 U.S. 474, 480. If in a rare instance a district judge abuses the discretionary authority the want of which precludes an effective, independent judiciary, there is always the opportunity for corrective review by a Court of Appeals and ultimately by this Court.

The manufacturer who is charged with infringing a patent cannot stretch the Federal Declaratory Judgments Act to give him a paramount right to choose the forum for trying out questions of infringement and validity. He is given an equal start in the race to the courthouse, not a headstart. If he is forehanded, subsequent suits against him by the patentee can within the trial court's discretion be enjoined pending determination of the declaratory judgment suit, and a judgment in his favor bars suits against his customers. If he is anticipated, the court's discretion is

3. Other cases in Courts of Appeals which present at all comparable situations do not show any rigid rule such as that under which the District Court felt constrained. * * *

broad enough to protect him from harassment of his customers. If the patentee's suit against a customer is brought in a district where the manufacturer cannot be joined as a defendant, the manufacturer may be permitted simultaneously to prosecute a declaratory action against the patentee elsewhere. And if the manufacturer is joined as an unwilling defendant in a *forum non conveniens,* he has available upon an appropriate showing the relief provided by § 1404(a) of the Judiciary Code.

The judgment below must be affirmed.

Affirmed.

THE CHIEF JUSTICE and MR. JUSTICE BLACK dissent.

NOTE ON THE TREATMENT OF DUPLICATIVE ACTIONS IN THE FEDERAL COURTS

(1) Should it be a postulate of federal judicial administration that there ought to be no more than one trial of a controversy between the same parties at the same time in the federal courts, and that accordingly, when duplicating actions of this kind are instituted, the only problem is to decide which action should be allowed to proceed?

Are the three-fold devices of stay (or abatement), injunction against the other proceeding, and transfer to the other district under 28 U.S.C. § 1404(a), pp. 1732–46, *supra,* adequate to accomplish such an objective? When one proceeding includes additional parties not joined in the other? When decisions in each district are subject to revision by different courts of appeals?

(2) The common law plea of a prior action pending called for the abatement of the second action, when both courts were in the same jurisdiction and the parties and cause of action were identical. See Clark, Code Pleading 505, 603 (2d ed. 1947).

A more flexible instrument than abatement is the discretionary power of a court to stay its proceedings, which may be exercised where abatement would not be permissible or appropriate. The considerable latitude of the federal courts in granting stays is illustrated by the landmark decision in Landis v. North American Co., 299 U.S. 248 (1936), recognizing a limited power to stay an action pending the outcome of other proceedings having only a stare decisis bearing on the case at bar. Justice Cardozo said (p. 254):

"* * * [T]he power to stay proceedings is incidental to the power inherent in every court to control the disposition of the causes on its docket with economy of time and effort for itself, for counsel, and for litigants".[1]

(3) It has long been held that, where a controversy between the same parties is simultaneously before two state courts of coordinate jurisdiction, whether in the same or different states, the first court to obtain jurisdiction may in its discretion enjoin the parties (not the court) from carrying on the second proceeding. See 2 Story, Equity Jurisprudence 560 (14th ed. 1918).

---

1. For recent cases in which lower courts have failed to find a "clear case of hardship or inequity [to the defendant] in being required to go forward" (Landis, 229 U.S. at 255), and have thus refused a stay, see, *e.g.,* Look Magazine Enterprises S.A. v. Look, Inc., 596 F.Supp. 774 (D.Del.1984); Bedel v. Thompson, 103 F.R.D. 78, 81–83 (S.D.Ohio 1984).

Assertion of the power of a federal court to enjoin proceedings in another federal court was a later development. In Steelman v. All Continent Corp., 301 U.S. 278 (1937), the Court upheld the power of a bankruptcy court to enjoin an allegedly fraudulent action against the trustee in bankruptcy in another district court. The power came, Justice Cardozo said, from the all-writs section, now 28 U.S.C. § 1651, and the provision of the Bankruptcy Act investing the bankruptcy court with equity jurisdiction.

The earliest court of appeals case upholding intra-federal injunctions seems to be In re Georgia Power Co., 89 F.2d 218 (5th Cir.1937) (plaintiff in first action enjoined from joining others in suing defendant in a second action). For later cases, see, *e.g.,* Columbia Plaza Corp. v. Security Nat. Bank, 525 F.2d 620 (D.C.Cir.1975); William Gluckin & Co. v. International Playtex Corp., 407 F.2d 177 (2d Cir.1969).

(4) What is the precise holding in Kerotest? Whose discretion is to be left largely undisturbed? That of the courts in the first district or in the second? That of the district court or of the court of appeals? *Cf.* Semmes Motors, Inc. v. Ford Motor Co., 429 F.2d 1197, 1203 (2d Cir.1970) (there are "insufficient grounds for * * * [the district court's departure] from the general rule that in the absence of sound reasons the second action should give way to the first").

In Note, *The Supreme Court, 1951 Term,* 66 Harv.L.Rev. 89, 169–70 (1952), it is suggested that the danger of conflicting decisions in different districts and circuits might have been avoided in Kerotest "by the adoption of a strict rule to determine the proper court to decide which action should be given priority". What should be the content of such a rule?

(5) In evaluating Kerotest, what weight should be given to the fact that a declaratory judgment action was involved? See p. 234, *supra. Cf.* Brillhart v. Excess Ins. Co. of America, 316 U.S. 491 (1942), discussed at p. 1447, *supra.*

(6) A difficult problem of conflicting federal court orders under the Freedom of Information Act, 5 U.S.C. § 552, was resolved as a matter of statutory construction in GTE Sylvania, Inc. v. Consumers Union, 445 U.S. 375 (1980). When the Consumer Product Safety Commission (CPSC) was contemplating releasing to Consumers Union (CU) certain documents CU had requested under the Freedom of Information Act, GTE and others brought suit against the CPSU in the District of Delaware and elsewhere to enjoin release, claiming that such disclosure was prohibited by the Consumer Product Safety Act, 15 U.S.C. § 2055, and other laws. The Delaware federal court issued a preliminary injunction and, ultimately, a permanent injunction against release that was affirmed by the Third Circuit. CU did not seek to intervene in that action but instead (after the filing of the Delaware action and the issuance of certain temporary restraining orders but before the Delaware court's issuance of the preliminary injunction) filed suit against the CPSC in the District of Columbia to compel release under the Freedom of Information Act. The district court dismissed the action for want of a case or controversy.

The D.C. Circuit reversed, holding that there was a sufficient controversy and that the suit was not foreclosed by the Delaware action; it adhered to this position even after the Supreme Court had remanded (434 U.S. 1030 (1978)) for reconsideration in light of the intervening issuance of a permanent injunction by the Delaware district court. The Supreme Court granted certiorari to review the decisions of both circuits.

Reversing the decision of the D.C. Circuit before deciding the Third Circuit case on the merits, the Supreme Court unanimously held that (a) there was an Article III case or controversy, see p. 198, *supra*, and (b) the CPSC could not be ordered to release the documents because those documents had not been "improperly" withheld within the meaning of the Freedom of Information Act, 5 U.S.C. § 552(a)(4)(B). The Delaware district court plainly had jurisdiction to issue its decrees; they had more than a "frivolous pretense to validity" (p. 386, quoting Walker v. Birmingham, 388 U.S. 307, 315 (1967)); and the CPSC's lawful obedience of a federal court injunction thus could not be considered as improper.

Does this decision have any implications for the doctrines of res judicata (since CU was not a party to the Delaware action) or of comity between federal courts? Or is its significance confined to the precise question of statutory construction decided by the Supreme Court? (See p. 387 n. 11, where the Court says that it "need not address" the issue of comity.)

(7) For extensive treatment of conflicts of jurisdiction between federal and state courts, see Chap. X Sec. 2(D), *supra*.

Chapter XV

APPELLATE REVIEW OF FEDERAL DECISIONS AND THE CERTIORARI POLICY

STATUTORY DEVELOPMENT

(1) The court structure established by the First Judiciary Act and the system of appellate review thus created are described in broad outline in Chapter I. They were maintained more than a century, with changes only of detail, before the Evarts Act [1] laid the foundation of the present plan. Long before 1891, however, it was acknowledged that the circuit courts were ill-equipped for the performance of appellate duties and that reviewing both the circuit and the district courts placed an intolerable burden on the Supreme Court. [2] Only the slow development of criminal appeals [3] and jurisdictional amount requirements in some, but not all, cases [4] stood between most unsuccessful litigants and a determination of their cases by the highest court.

(2) The Evarts Act interposed the circuit courts of appeals between the Supreme Court and the circuit and district courts, stripping the circuit courts of their appellate jurisdiction.

Section 5 provided a direct Supreme Court review of the circuit or the district court in the following cases:

"In any case in which the jurisdiction of the court is in issue; in such cases the question of jurisdiction alone shall be certified to the Supreme Court from the court below for decision.

"From the final sentences and decrees in prize causes.

"In cases of conviction of a capital or otherwise infamous crime.

"In any case that involves the construction or application of the Constitution of the United States.

"In any case in which the constitutionality of any law of the United States, or the validity or construction of any treaty made under its authority, is drawn in question.

"In any case in which the constitution or law of a State is claimed to be in contravention of the Constitution of the United States."

1. Act of March 3, 1891, 26 Stat. 826.

2. See Frankfurter & Landis, The Business of the Supreme Court 56–102 (1928).

3. Until 1889 criminal cases were reviewable by the Supreme Court only in the event of a division of opinion in the circuit court on a question of law (Act of April 29, 1802, § 6, 2 Stat. 156, 159–61 [certification]; Act of June 1, 1872, § 1, 17 Stat. 196) or within the limited range of issues that could be raised by habeas corpus. The Act of February 6, 1889, § 6, 25 Stat. 655, 656 granted a writ of error in capital cases only, extended by the Evarts Act to "infamous crimes."

4. The jurisdictional amount, fixed in 1789 at $2000, was raised to $5000 in 1875. Many types of cases were reviewable, however, without regard to amount.

Section 6 conferred jurisdiction on the circuit courts of appeals to review a "final decision" in all other cases, "unless otherwise provided by law." It declared that the circuit court of appeals decision "shall be final in all cases in which the jurisdiction is dependent entirely upon the opposite parties to the suit or controversy, being aliens and citizens of the United States or citizens of different States; also in all cases arising under the patent laws, under the revenue laws, and under the criminal laws and in admiralty cases," subject to the power of the court of appeals to certify to the Supreme Court "any questions or propositions of law concerning which it desires the instruction of that court for its proper decision" and the power of the Supreme Court "to require, by certiorari or otherwise, any such case to be certified * * * for its review and determination * * * as if it had been carried by appeal or writ of error to the Supreme Court."

Except in cases where the decision of the circuit court of appeals was thus declared to be final, courts of appeals decisions were reviewable by the Supreme Court as of right "where the matter in controversy shall exceed one thousand dollars besides costs."

Section 7 of the Act, initiating a departure from the general finality requirement, authorized an appeal to a circuit court of appeals from "an interlocutory order or decree granting or continuing" an injunction in a case in which a final decree would be appealable to the circuit court of appeals.

(3) The distribution of appellate jurisdiction effected by the Evarts Act was not drastically altered until the enactment of the Judges' Bill in 1925.[5] There were, however, some important changes in the intervening years:

(a) The provision for direct appeal of convictions of "infamous crimes" was broadly construed in In re Claasen, 140 U.S. 200 (1891), to include all offenses punishable by a penitentiary sentence. It was modified in 1897 to route appeals in all but capital cases through the circuit courts of appeals, with only discretionary review by the Supreme Court.[6] Capital cases were so treated too by the Judicial Code of 1911.[7]

(b) The legislation establishing the Court of Appeals of the District of Columbia in 1893 provided a much broader right to Supreme Court review of its decisions than obtained for decisions of the circuit courts of appeals.[8]

(c) Despite the provisions of the Evarts Act for direct Supreme Court review of cases involving the constitutionality of federal laws, the Supreme Court held that a judgment quashing an indictment on the ground that it was based on an invalid statute could not be reviewed at the instance of the government.[9] The Criminal Appeals Act of 1907 [10] filled this gap, its enactment stimulated by the unreviewable decision blocking prosecution of the Beef Trust.[11]

5. Act of February 13, 1925, 43 Stat. 936.

6. Act of Jan. 20, 1897, 29 Stat. 492.

7. Act of March 3, 1911, §§ 128, 240, 36 Stat. 1087, 1133, 1157. See Stephan v. United States, 319 U.S. 423 (1943).

8. Act of Feb. 9, 1893, § 8, 27 Stat. 434, 436. The right was narrowed by Section 250 of the Judicial Code of 1911 to cases involving "the construction of any law of the United States."

9. United States v. Sanges, 144 U.S. 310 (1892).

10. Act of March 2, 1907, 34 Stat. 1246.

11. United States v. Armour & Co., 142 F. 808 (N.D.Ill.1906). See Frankfurter & Landis, *supra* note 2, at 113–19.

(d) The Expediting Act of 1903 and later legislation providing for a special three judge court in certain cases also provided for direct review of its determinations by the Supreme Court.[12]

(e) Under the Evarts Act decisions of the circuit courts of appeals were reviewable as of right in the Supreme Court in many types of cases; and the number grew as Congress enacted new substantive legislation.[13] The principle of discretionary review was or came to be applied, however, to cases under the Trademark Act of 1905,[14] other trademark cases, all bankruptcy cases [15] and, most important, cases under the Federal Employers' Liability Act.[16]

(f) The provision made for appellate review of interlocutory orders granting or continuing an injunction was extended to orders denying such relief [17] as well as to orders appointing a receiver.[18]

(4) The Judges' Bill of 1925 dealt a blow to obligatory Supreme Court review of circuit court of appeals decisions, including those of the Court of Appeals of the District of Columbia. Under its terms such review was preserved in but one case: "where is drawn in question the validity of a statute of any state, on the grounds of its being repugnant to the Constitution, treaties or laws of the United States, and the decision is against its validity"; and even then obligatory review was "restricted to an examination and decision of the Federal questions presented" and could be sought only by the party relying on the state law.[19] In all other situations the jurisdiction of the Supreme Court could be invoked to pass on court of appeals decisions only by certificate [20] or, before as well as after final judgment of the court of appeals, by certiorari.[21] It could, however, be invoked without regard to jurisdictional amount.

Court of claims decisions too became reviewable only on certificate or certiorari; [22] and the limited review on certiorari only of the Court of Customs Appeals was not changed.[23] For the complex arrangement that obtained in the review of territorial tribunals,[24] the Act retained discretionary Supreme Court review in some cases of the Supreme Court of the Philippines [25] but routed all other territorial cases subject to review through a circuit court of appeals.[26]

---

12. See pp. 1333–37, *supra.*

13. See the enumeration by Chief Justice Taft quoted in Frankfurter & Landis, *supra* note 2, at 261–62.

14. Act of Feb. 20, 1905, § 18, 33 Stat. 724, 729.

15. Act of Jan. 28, 1915, §§ 2, 4, 38 Stat. 803, 804.

16. Act of Sept. 6, 1916, § 3, 39 Stat. 726, 727.

17. Act of Feb. 18, 1895, 28 Stat. 666; see also Act of April 14, 1906, 34 Stat. 116.

18. Act of June 6, 1900, 31 Stat. 660; Judicial Code, § 129, 36 Stat. 1087, 1134. The tangled story of this legislation is told in Frankfurter & Landis, *supra* note 2, at 124–27.

19. Judicial Code § 240(b), 28 U.S.C. § 347(b) (1940).

20. Judicial Code § 239, 28 U.S.C. § 346 (1940).

21. Judicial Code § 240(a), 28 U.S.C. § 347(a) (1940).

22. Act of Feb. 13, 1925, § 3, 43 Stat. 939, 28 U.S.C. § 288 (1940).

23. See also Act of Aug. 22, 1914, c. 267, 38 Stat. 703; Act of June 17, 1930, § 647, 46 Stat. 762.

24. See Frankfurter & Landis, *supra* note 2, at 266–70.

25. Act of Feb. 13, 1925, § 7, 43 Stat. 940, 28 U.S.C. § 349 (1940).

26. Judicial Code § 128, 28 U.S.C. § 225 (1940). (In 1961, Congress repealed a provision for court of appeals review of decisions of the Supreme Court of the Commonwealth of Puerto Rico and substituted a provision for direct review by the Supreme Court. 28 U.S.C. § 1258.)

The Act also contracted greatly the area of direct Supreme Court review of the district courts. The categories of cases in which the Evarts Act preserved direct review were all eliminated, shifting appellate jurisdiction to the circuit courts of appeals. Direct review was maintained, however, in a group of important cases where it had been authorized by later legislation: suits in equity brought by the United States to restrain violations of the Anti–Trust or Interstate Commerce Acts; suits to enjoin enforcement of certain orders of the Interstate Commerce Commission or of the Secretary of Agriculture under the Packers and Stockyards Act; suits to enjoin enforcement of state statutes or administrative orders governed by Section 266 of the Judicial Code; and government appeals under the Criminal Appeals Act.[27] All but the criminal cases involved were required to be heard in the first instance by a three-judge court (some only on certificate of the Attorney General), a tribunal of comparable dignity to a circuit court of appeals. Where direct review was thus preserved, it was maintained as a matter of right.

(5) The provisions for direct review by the Supreme Court were extended in a number of instances after 1925,[28] but a movement towards reduction, and perhaps virtual elimination, of a right of appeal to the Supreme Court from the lower federal courts began again in 1950. In that year, Congress substituted court of appeals review for the Urgent Deficiencies Act procedure as the mode of challenging orders issued under the Federal Communications Act, Packers and Stockyards Act, Perishable Agricultural Commodities Act, and the Shipping Acts.[29] In 1974, partly as a result of dissatisfaction expressed by Supreme Court Justices themselves, see United States v. Singer Mfg. Co., 374 U.S. 174, 175 n. 1 (1963), Congress eliminated the provision of the Expediting Act requiring direct appeals to the Supreme Court on all antitrust and Interstate Commerce Act cases in which the United States was a party.[30] And the following year, Congress repealed the

27. Judicial Code § 238, 28 U.S.C. § 345 (1940). See also California v. United States, 320 U.S. 577, 579 (1944).

28. These instances included: (a) extending the Expediting Act to civil suits to enforce Title II of the Communications Act (see Act of June 19, 1934, § 401(d), 48 Stat. 1093); (b) requiring a three-judge court in suits to restrain other administrative orders (see, e.g., Act of June 10, 1930, § 11, 46 Stat. 535); (c) requiring a three-judge court in suits to enjoin the enforcement of an Act of Congress on constitutional grounds, with direct Supreme Court review of a judgment granting or denying injunctive relief (see Act of August 24, 1937, § 3, 50 Stat. 752); (d) providing for an appeal to the Supreme Court from any judgment invalidating a federal statute when the United States or a federal officer or agency is a party (see id., § 2; 28 U.S.C. § 1252): and (e) providing for a three-judge court, and a direct appeal to the Supreme Court, in certain cases arising under the Voting Rights Acts of 1965 and 1970 (see 42 U.S.C. §§ 1973b, 1973c (1965 Act); 42 U.S.C. §§ 1973aa-2, 1973bb-2 (1970 Act)) and the Civil Rights Act of 1964 (see 42 U.S.C. §§ 1971(g), 2000a-5(b), 2000e-6(b)).

29. 64 Stat. 1129 (1950) (the relevant provisions are now contained in 28 U.S.C. § 2342).

30. Sections 4–6, 88 Stat. 1708–09 (1974), 15 U.S.C. §§ 28, 29, 49 U.S.C. §§ 44, 45. Section 1 now provides that if a certificate of general importance is filed by the Attorney General in an action covered by the Act, the action must be expedited but is no longer to be heard by a three-judge court. Section 2 now provides that appeals are to be taken to the court of appeals unless upon application of a party after final judgment the district judge enters an order "stating that immediate consideration of the appeal by the Supreme Court is of general public importance in the administration of justice"; in that event the Supreme Court may either dispose of the appeal and any cross appeal or, in its discretion, deny direct appeal and remand the case to the court of appeals. The end result of the statute is only marginally different from certiorari practice—under which certiorari may be granted before as well as after judgment in the courts of appeals. 28 U.S.C. § 1254(1).

requirement that suits for injunctive relief from Interstate Commerce Commission orders be heard by three-judge courts, subject to direct Supreme Court review.[31]

Perhaps most important, Congress in 1976 repealed the three-judge court provisions of 28 U.S.C. §§ 2281 (relating to actions to enjoin the enforcement of state statutes) and 2282 (relating to certain actions to enjoin the operation of federal statutes), substituting a far more limited requirement of a three-judge court in certain apportionment cases.[32] The effect of these repeals was to render inapplicable to such cases the provision for direct Supreme Court review in 28 U.S.C. § 1253.

(6) A further significant change in the Supreme Court's appellate jurisdiction was the elimination of direct appeals from the district courts in certain criminal cases—a change incorporated in the Omnibus Crime Control Act of 1970.[33] The Criminal Appeals Act of 1907, Paragraph (3)(c), *supra*, was not affected by the Judges' Bill of 1925, and had been carried forward, as amended, in 18 U.S.C. § 3731. The provision had caused continual difficulties for the Supreme Court—because of the statute's own ambiguities, the Court's reluctance to review directly the decisions of the district courts, and the problems of double jeopardy often posed by Government appeals in criminal cases. See, *e.g.*, United States v. Sisson, 399 U.S. 267 (1970). See also Kurland, *The Mersky Case and the Criminal Appeals Act: A Suggestion for Amendment of the Statute*, 28 U.Chi.L.Rev. 419 (1961).

The Amendment in the Act of 1970 provided that any appeal by the United States from a dismissal of one or more counts of an indictment or information shall lie to a court of appeals "except that no appeal shall lie where the double jeopardy clause of the Constitution prohibits further prosecution." [34]

While the 1970 Act has freed the Supreme Court of the burden of direct criminal appeals, it has imposed on it the difficult task of marking the boundaries of the government's right to appeal to the court of appeals by defining the constitutional limits established by the Double Jeopardy Clause.[35]

(7) As part of the Military Justice Act of 1983, Pub.L. No. 98–209, Congress added to the certiorari jurisdiction of the Supreme Court certain categories of decisions of the United States Court of Military Appeals, 28 U.S.C. § 1259. This provision—the first authorizing direct review by an

---

31. Section 9, 88 Stat. 1918 (1975).

32. 90 Stat. 1119 (1976). The story of these provisions and of their repeal is more fully told at pp. 1333–37, *supra*.

33. 18 U.S.C. § 3731, as amended by Act of Jan. 2, 1971, § 14(a), 84 Stat. 1890.

34. The amendment also continued, with some modification, the prior provision for appeals by the United States from certain orders suppressing or excluding evidence, or requiring the return of seized property, but provided that such appeals shall lie only to a court of appeals. For other provisions authorizing appeals by the government in criminal cases, see 18 U.S.C. §§ 2518(10)(b), 3576.

35. See, *e.g.*, United States v. Martin Linen Supply Co., 430 U.S. 564 (1977); Finch v. United States, 433 U.S. 676 (1977); United States v. Scott, 437 U.S. 82 (1978); Sanabria v. United States, 437 U.S. 54 (1978). For a perceptive discussion of these cases, see Cooper, *Government Appeals in Criminal Cases, The 1978 Decisions*, 81 F.R.D. 539 (1979).

As part of the Comprehensive Crime Control Act of 1984, Pub.L. 98–473, 98 Stat. 1986, 2153, Congress amended 18 U.S.C. § 3731 to authorize government appeals from certain orders granting release of a prisoner, as well as from orders "granting a new trial after verdict or judgment."

Article III court of the judgments of a military tribunal—is discussed in Boskey & Gressman, *The Supreme Court's New Certiorari Jurisdiction Over Military Appeals,* 102 F.R.D. 329 (1985).

(8) The time limits for seeking review on appeal or certiorari in the Supreme Court may be found in 28 U.S.C. § 2101 and Sup.Ct.Rules 11, 12, 20. For valuable discussions of these provisions and of the entire subject of Supreme Court procedure, see Stern, Gressman & Shapiro, Supreme Court Practice (6th ed. 1986); Boskey & Gressman, *The Supreme Court's New Rules for the Eighties,* 85 F.R.D. 487 (1980).

(9) One important change in the statutory jurisdiction of the courts of appeals was the enactment in 1958 of the Interlocutory Appeals Act, 28 U.S.C. § 1292(b), on the recommendation of the Judicial Conference. This act provides for an appeal of any interlocutory order of a district court when the trial judge finds that certain conditions exist and the court of appeals, in its discretion, decides to allow the appeal. See pp. 1819–20, *infra,* for further discussion.

(10) There are, in addition, many special provisions relating to appeals in particular kinds of cases or from particular tribunals. (A number of these provisions appear outside the Judicial Code). Examples include provisions for appeals of federal administrative orders, of final orders in habeas corpus proceedings, 28 U.S.C. § 2253, of decisions by magistrates in cases tried by consent, 28 U.S.C. § 636(c), of decisions in bankruptcy cases, 28 U.S.C. § 158, and of cases within the jurisdiction of the Court of Appeals for the Federal Circuit, 28 U.S.C. § 1295. These provisions often raise their own difficult questions of interpretation. See, *e.g.,* United States v. Hohri, 107 S.Ct. 2246 (1987) (jurisdiction of the Federal Circuit). See also the discussion of appeals of magistrates' decisions in 15 Wright, Miller & Cooper, Federal Practice and Procedure § 3901 (Supp.1986), at 1–15, and of appeals in bankruptcy cases in 16 *id.* § 3926 (Supp.1986), at 67–76.

(11) The time limits for appeals from the district courts to the courts of appeals (and from the Claims Court) may be found in 28 U.S.C. §§ 1292(b), 2107, and 2522, and in Federal Rules of Appellate Procedure 4–6. Until 1968, the procedures governing such appeals were set out in Rules 73–76 of the Civil Rules, Rules 37–39 of the Criminal Rules, and the separately adopted and varying provisions of the rules of each of the eleven courts of appeals. In that year the Federal Rules of Appellate Procedure, a uniform set of rules applicable to all cases in the courts of appeals, went into effect following their submission to Congress by the Supreme Court. *See* 389 U.S. 1063 (1968). For detailed discussion of these rules and their innovations, see 16 Wright, Miller, Cooper & Gressman, Federal Practice and Procedure §§ 3945–3994 (1977 & Supp.1985).

(12) For discussion of further proposed changes in the jurisdiction of the courts of appeals and of the Supreme Court to review decisions of lower federal tribunals, see Chap. I, pp. 43–45, *supra.* For discussion of the explosive growth in the caseloads of the courts of appeals, and of responses to that growth, see Chap. I, pp. 55–57, *supra.*

SECTION 1. JURISDICTION OF THE COURTS OF APPEALS

FIRESTONE TIRE & RUBBER CO. v. RISJORD

449 U.S. 368, 101 S.Ct. 669, 66 L.Ed.2d 571 (1981).
Certiorari to the United States Court of Appeals for the Eighth Circuit.

JUSTICE MARSHALL delivered the opinion of the Court.

This case presents the question whether a party may take an appeal, pursuant to 28 U.S.C. § 1291, from a district court order denying a motion to disqualify counsel for the opposing party in a civil case. The United States Court of Appeals for the Eighth Circuit held that such orders are not appealable, but made its decision prospective only and therefore reached the merits of the challenged order. We hold that orders denying motions to disqualify counsel are not appealable final decisions under § 1291, and we therefore vacate the judgment of the Court of Appeals and remand with instructions that the appeal be dismissed for lack of jurisdiction.

I

Respondent is lead counsel for the plaintiffs in four product liability suits seeking damages from petitioner and other manufacturers of multipiece truck tire rims for injuries caused by alleged defects in their products. The complaints charge petitioner and the other defendants with various negligent, willful or intentional failures to correct or to warn of the supposed defects in the rims. Plaintiffs seek both compensatory and exemplary damages.

Petitioner was at all relevant times insured by Home Insurance Company (Home) under a contract providing that Home would be responsible only for some types of liability beyond a minimum "deductible" amount. Home was also an occasional client of respondent's law firm. Based on these facts, petitioner in May 1979 filed a motion to disqualify respondent from further representation of the plaintiffs. Petitioner argued that respondent had a clear conflict of interest because his representation of Home would give him an incentive to structure plaintiff's claims for relief in such a way as to enable the insurer to avoid any liability. This in turn, petitioner argued, could increase its own potential liability. Home had in fact advised petitioner in the course of the litigation that its policy would cover neither an award of compensatory damages for willful or intentional acts nor any award of exemplary or punitive damages. The District Court entered a pretrial order requiring that respondent terminate his representation of the plaintiffs unless both the plaintiffs and Home consented to his continuing representation.

In accordance with the District Court's order, respondent filed an affidavit in which he stated that he had informed both the plaintiffs and Home of the potential conflict and that neither had any objection to his continuing representation of them both. He filed supporting affidavits executed by the plaintiffs and by a representative of Home. Because he had satisfied the requirements of the pretrial order, respondent was able to continue his representation of the plaintiffs. Petitioner objected to the

District Court's decision to permit respondent to continue his representation if he met the stated conditions, and therefore filed a notice of appeal pursuant to 28 U.S.C. § 1291.[7]

Although it did not hear oral argument on the appeal, the Eighth Circuit decided the case en banc and affirmed the trial court's order permitting petitioner to continue representing the plaintiffs.[8] Before considering the merits of the appeal, the court reconsidered and overruled its prior decisions holding that orders denying disqualification motions were immediately appealable under § 1291. The Court of Appeals reasoned that such orders did not fall within the collateral order doctrine of Cohen v. Beneficial Industrial Loan Corp., 337 U.S. 541 (1949), which allows some appeals prior to final judgment. Because it was overruling prior cases, the court stated that it would reach the merits of the challenged order "[i]n fairness to the appellant in the instant case," but held that in the future, appellate review of such orders would have to await final judgment on the merits of the main proceeding. 612 F.2d, at 378–379. We granted certiorari, to resolve a conflict among the circuits on the appealability question.

II

Under § 1291, the Courts of Appeals are vested with "jurisdiction of appeals from all final decisions of the district courts * * * except when a direct review may be had in the Supreme Court." We have consistently interpreted this language as indicating that a party may not take an appeal under this section until there has been "a decision by the District Court that 'ends the litigation on the merits and leaves nothing for the court to do but execute the judgment.'" Coopers & Lybrand v. Livesay, 437 U.S. 463, 467 (1978), quoting Catlin v. United States, 324 U.S. 229 (1945). This rule, that a party must ordinarily raise all claims of error in a single appeal following final judgment on the merits, serves a number of important purposes. It emphasizes the deference that appellate courts owe to the trial judge as the individual initially called upon to decide the many questions of law and fact that occur in the course of a trial. Permitting piecemeal appeals would undermine the independence of the District Judge, as well as the special role that individual plays in our judicial system. In addition, the rule is in accordance with the sensible policy of "avoid[ing] the obstruction to just claims that would come from permitting the harassment and cost of a succession of separate appeals from the various rulings to which a litigation may give rise, from its initiation to entry of judgment." Cobbledick v. United States, 309 U.S. 323, 325 (1940). * * * The rule also serves the important purpose of promoting efficient

---

7. The District Court certified its pretrial order on disqualification for interlocutory appeal pursuant to 28 U.S.C. § 1292(b). * * *.

Neither party elected to proceed under § 1292(b). Respondent chose to comply with the order rather than appeal. Petitioner chose to appeal the denial of its motion under § 1291 rather than under § 1292(b). After filing its notice of appeal, petitioner moved that respondent be held in contempt for allegedly failing to comply with the pretrial order, but this motion was subsequently withdrawn.

8. The Court of Appeals also stated that orders *granting* motions to disqualify counsel would be appealable under § 1291. That question is not presented by the instant petition, and we express no opinion on it. Neither do we express any view on whether an order denying a disqualification motion in a criminal case would be appealable under § 1291.

judicial administration. Eisen v. Carlisle & Jacquelin, 417 U.S. 156, 170 (1974).

Our decisions have recognized, however, a narrow exception to the requirement that all appeals under § 1291 await final judgment on the merits. In Cohen v. Beneficial Industrial Loan Corp., *supra,* we held that a "small class" of orders that did not end the main litigation were nevertheless final and appealable pursuant to § 1291. Cohen was a shareholder's derivative action in which the Federal District Court refused to apply a state statute requiring a plaintiff in such a suit to post security for costs. The defendant appealed the ruling without awaiting final judgment on the merits, and the Court of Appeals ordered the trial court to require that costs be posted. We held that the Court of Appeals properly assumed jurisdiction of the appeal pursuant to § 1291 because the District Court's order constituted a final determination of a claim "separable from, and collateral to," the merits of the main proceeding, because it was "too important to be denied review," and because it was "too independent of the cause itself to require that appellate consideration be deferred until the whole case is adjudicated." *Id.,* at 546. Cohen did not establish new law; rather, it continued a tradition of giving § 1291 a "practical rather than a technical construction." *Ibid.* See, *e.g.,* United States v. River Rouge Improvement Co., 269 U.S. 411, 413–414 (1926); Bronson v. LaCrosse & Milwaukee Railroad Co., 67 U.S. 524–531 (1863); Forgay v. Conrad, 47 U.S. 201, 203 (1848); Whiting v. Bank of the United States, 38 U.S. 6, 15 (1839). We have recently defined this limited class of final "collateral orders" in these terms: "[T]he order must conclusively determine the disputed question, resolve an important issue completely separate from the merits of the action, and be effectively unreviewable on appeal from a final judgment." Coopers & Lybrand v. Livesay, *supra,* 437 U.S. at 468 * * *.

Because the litigation from which the instant petition arises had not reached final judgment at the time the notice of appeal was filed, the order denying petitioner's motion to disqualify respondent is appealable under § 1291 only if it falls within the Cohen doctrine. The Court of Appeals held that it does not, and 5 of the other 10 circuits have also reached the conclusion that denials of disqualification motions are not immediately appealable "collateral orders." We agree with these courts that under Cohen such an order is not subject to appeal prior to resolution of the merits.

An order denying a disqualification motion meets the first part of the "collateral order" test. It "conclusively determine[s] the disputed question," because the only issue is whether challenged counsel will be permitted to continue his representation. In addition, we will assume, although we do not decide, that the disqualification question "resolve[s] an important issue completely separate from the merits of the action," the second part of the test. Nevertheless, petitioner is unable to demonstrate that an order denying disqualification is "effectively unreviewable on appeal from a final judgment" within the meaning of our cases.

In attempting to show why the challenged order will be effectively unreviewable on final appeal, petitioner alleges that denying immediate review will cause it irreparable harm. It is true that the finality requirement should "be construed so as not to cause crucial collateral claims to be lost and potentially irreparable injuries to be suffered," Mathews v. Eldridge, 424 U.S. 319, 331, n. 11 (1976). In support of its assertion that it will be irreparably harmed, petitioner hints at "the possibility that the course of the proceedings may be indelibly stamped or shaped with the fruits of a breach of confidence or by acts or omissions prompted by a divided loyalty," and at "the effect of such a tainted proceeding in frustrating public policy." But petitioner fails to supply a single concrete example of the indelible stamp or taint of which it warns. The only ground that petitioner urged in the District Court was that respondent might shape the products-liability plaintiffs' claims for relief in such a way as to increase the burden on petitioner. Our cases, however, require much more before a ruling may be considered "effectively unreviewable" absent immediate appeal.

To be appealable as a final collateral order, the challenged order must constitute "a complete, formal and, in the trial court, a final rejection," Abney v. United States, *supra*, 431 U.S. at 659, of a claimed right "where denial of immediate review would render impossible any review whatsoever," United States v. Ryan, 402 U.S. 530, 533 (1971). Thus we have permitted appeals prior to criminal trials when a defendant has claimed that he is about to be subjected to forbidden double jeopardy, Abney v. United States, *supra*, or a violation of his constitutional right to bail, Stack v. Boyle, 342 U.S. 1 (1957), because those situations, like the posting of security for costs involved in Cohen, "each involved an asserted right the legal and practical value of which would be destroyed if it were not vindicated before trial." United States v. MacDonald, 435 U.S. 850, 860 (1978). By way of contrast, we have generally denied review of pretrial discovery orders, see, *e.g.*, United States v. Ryan, *supra;* Cobbledick v. United States, *supra*. Our rationale has been that in the rare case when appeal after final judgment will not cure an erroneous discovery order, a party may defy the order, permit a contempt citation to be entered against him, and challenge the order on direct appeal of the contempt ruling. See Cobbledick v. United States, *supra*, at 327. We have also rejected immediate appealability under § 1291 of claims that "may fairly be assessed" only after trial, United States v. MacDonald, *supra*, at 860, and those involving "considerations that are 'enmeshed in the factual and legal issues comprising the plaintiff's cause of action,'" Coopers & Lybrand v. Livesay, *supra*, 437 U.S. at 469, quoting Mercantile Nat'l Bank v. Langdeau, 371 U.S. 555, 558 (1963).

An order refusing to disqualify counsel plainly falls within the large class of orders that are indeed reviewable on appeal after final judgment, and not within the much smaller class of those that are not. The propriety of the District Court's denial of a disqualification motion will often be difficult to assess until its impact on the underlying litigation may be evaluated, which is normally only after final judgment. The decision whether to disqualify an attorney ordinarily turns on the peculiar factual situation of the case then at hand, and the order embodying such a decision will rarely, if ever, represent a final rejection of a claim of fundamental right that cannot effectively be reviewed following judgment on the merits. In the case before us, petitioner has made no showing that its opportunity for meaningful review will perish unless immediate appeal is permitted. On the contrary, should the Court of Appeals conclude after the trial has ended that permitting continuing representation was prejudicial error, it would retain its usual authority to vacate the judgment appealed from and order a new trial. That remedy seems plainly adequate should petitioner's concerns of possible injury ultimately prove well-founded. As the Second Circuit has recently observed, the potential harm that might be caused by requiring that a party await final judgment before it may appeal even when the denial of its disqualification motion was erroneous does not "diffe[r] in any significant way from the harm resulting from other interlocutory orders that may be erroneous, such as orders requiring discovery over a work-product objection or orders denying motions for recusal of the trial judge." Armstrong v. McAlpin, 625 F.2d 433, 438 (1980), petition for certiorari pending, No. 80–433. But interlocutory orders are not appealable "on the mere ground that they may be erroneous." Will v. United States, 389 U.S. 90, 98, n. 6 (1967). Permitting wholesale appeals on that ground not only would constitute an unjustified waste of scarce judicial resources, but would transform the limited exception carved out in Cohen into a license for broad disregard of the finality rule imposed by Congress in § 1291. This we decline to do.[13]

III

We hold that a district court's order denying a motion to disqualify counsel is not appealable under § 1291 prior to final judgment in the underlying litigation. Insofar as the Eighth Circuit reached this conclusion, its decision is correct. But because its decision was contrary to precedent in the circuit, the court went further and reached the merits of the order appealed from. This approach, however, overlooks the fact that the finality requirement embodied in § 1291 is jurisdictional in nature. If the appellate court finds that the order from which a party seeks to appeal does not fall within the statute, its inquiry is over. A court lacks discretion to consider the merits of a case over which it is without jurisdiction, and thus, by definition, a jurisdictional ruling may never be made prospective only. We therefore hold that because the Court of Appeals was without jurisdiction to hear the appeal, it was without authority to decide the merits. Consequently, the judgment of the Eighth Circuit is vacated and the case remanded with instructions to dismiss the appeal for want of jurisdiction. * * *

So ordered.

JUSTICE REHNQUIST, with whom THE CHIEF JUSTICE joins, concurring.

13. Although there may be situations in which a party will be irreparably damaged if forced to wait until final resolution of the underlying litigation before securing review of an order denying its motion to disqualify opposing counsel, it is not necessary, in order to resolve those situations, to create a general rule permitting the appeal of all such orders. In the proper circumstances, the moving party may seek sanctions short of disqualification, such as a protective order limiting counsel's ability to disclose or to act on purportedly confidential information. If additional facts in support of the motion develop in the course of the litigation, the moving party might ask the trial court to reconsider its decision. Ultimately, if dissatisfied with the result in the District Court and absolutely determined that it will be harmed irreparably, a party may seek to have the question certified for interlocutory appellate review pursuant to 28 U.S.C. § 1292(b), and, in the exceptional circumstances for which it was designed, a writ of mandamus from the court of appeals might be available. * * * We need not be concerned with the availability of such extraordinary procedures in the case before us, because petitioner has made no colorable claim that the harm it might suffer if forced to await the final outcome of the litigation before appealing the denial of its disqualification motion is any greater than the harm suffered by any litigant forced to wait until the termination of the trial before challenging interlocutory orders it considers erroneous.

I agree with the result in this case and the analysis of the Court so far as it concerns the question whether an order denying disqualification of counsel is "effectively unreviewable on appeal from the final judgment." The Court's answer to this question is dispositive on the appealability issue. Since it is completely unnecessary to do so, however, I would not state, as the Court does:

> "An order denying a disqualification motion meets the first part of the 'collateral order' test. It 'conclusively determines the disputed question,' because the only issue is whether challenged counsel will be permitted to continue his representation."

In Cohen v. Beneficial Industrial Loan Corp., 337 U.S. 541 (1949), Mr. Justice Jackson stressed that the order before the Court was "a final disposition of a claimed right" and specifically distinguished a case in which the matter was "subject to reconsideration from time to time." *Id.*, at 546–547. Just recently in Coopers & Lybrand v. Livesay, 437 U.S. 463 (1978), we held that an order denying class certification was not appealable under the collateral order doctrine, in part because such an order is "subject to revision in the District Court." *Id.*, at 469. The possibility that a district judge would reconsider his determination was highly significant in United States v. MacDonald, 435 U.S. 850, 858–859 (1978), where the Court held that the denial of a pretrial motion to dismiss an indictment on speedy trial grounds was not appealable under the collateral order doctrine. The Court noted that speedy trial claims necessitated a careful assessment of the particular facts of the case, and that "The denial of a pretrial motion to dismiss an indictment on speedy trial grounds does not indicate that a like motion made after trial—when prejudice can be better gauged—would also be denied."

It is not at all clear to me, nor has it been to courts considering the question, that an order denying a motion for disqualification of counsel conclusively determines the disputed question. The District Court remains free to reconsider its decision at any time. * * * Petitioner's claim is that respondent will advance only those theories of liability which absolve the insurer, or will advance those theories more strenuously than others. Although it is impossible to discern if this is true before trial, the issue may become clearer as trial progresses and respondent actually does present his theories. As in MacDonald, it cannot be assumed that a motion made at a later point in the proceedings—"when prejudice can be better gauged"—will be denied.

Because of what seem to me to be totally unnecessary and very probably incorrect statements as to this minor point in the opinion, I concur in the result only.

NOTE ON "FINAL DECISIONS"

(1) The policies favoring limitation of appeals to final judgments are articulated in the Firestone opinion. See also Note, 75 Harv.L.Rev. 351 (1961). There is little indication, however, that those policies underlay the development of the common law rule from which the present statutory provisions are derived. The original motives appear to have been largely

formalistic. See Crick, *The Final Judgment as a Basis for Appeal,* 41 Yale L.J. 539, 540–44 (1932).

Countering the policies supporting the final judgment rule are a number of factors that may favor earlier appeals in particular cases: the avoidance of hardship that would be difficult or impossible to remedy if appeal were postponed, the need to oversee the work of the lower courts on matters that seldom if ever arise on appeal from a final judgment, and the interest in conserving the time and energy of courts and litigants by the correction of error at an early stage. The story of judicial and legislative attempts to work out a sensible system of appeals is in large part the story of the continuing effort to reconcile these conflicting interests.[1]

(2) As the Court notes in Firestone, the final judgment rule has never been construed to mean that the litigation must be concluded in every respect before the time for appeal begins to run. In the case of actions for declaratory or injunctive relief in which relief is granted, the possibilities of modification or of supplemental relief might prevent that point from ever being reached, and even a judgment in a routine action for damages is subject to being reopened. See Fed.R.Civ.P. 60(b). And the Court has not insisted that all incidental questions, like those of costs, for example, must be resolved before the point of finality is reached. See St. Louis, I.M. & S.R.R. v. Southern Express Co., 108 U.S. 24, 28–29 (1883). Even the denial of a temporary restraining order may be final if the likely effect of the denial is to moot the case and thus to deny the ultimate relief sought. See United States v. Wood, 295 F.2d 772 (5th Cir.1961).

But a "practical" approach of this kind, appropriate as it may be, brings difficult issues to the fore. If incidental questions of costs need not be resolved, for example, what of a question of an award of attorney's fees? The courts of appeals were at one time sharply divided on this question, with at least one being forced to resolve an intracircuit conflict by an en banc decision. See Croker v. Boeing Co., 662 F.2d 975 (3d Cir.1981) (judgment not final until court determines amount of attorney's fees to be awarded). The question has been resolved, however, in favor of the finality of the judgment before the fee is determined—at least when the fee is claimed under authority of a separate statute like 42 U.S.C. § 1988. White v. New Hampshire Dep't of Employment Security, 455 U.S. 445 (1982).[2]

(3) The rule of Cohen v. Beneficial Industrial Loan Corp., explained and applied in Firestone at pp. 1802–04, *supra,* has its roots in similar

1. For a comprehensive effort to rationalize and restate the law governing appeals in the federal courts, see *Federal Civil Appellate Jurisdiction: An Interlocutory Restatement,* 47 Law & Contemp.Probs., Spring 1984, at 13. Building on this effort, Professor Carrington has proposed a revision of the governing statutes that would authorize appeals both from "final" decisions and from certain "interlocutory orders"; included under the latter heading would be those appeals "essential to protect substantial rights which cannot be effectively enforced on review after final decision." Carrington, *Toward a Federal Civil Interlocutory Appeals Act,* 47 Law & Contemp. Probs., Summer 1984, at 165, 167.

2. *Cf.* Boeing Co. v. Van Gemert, 444 U.S. 472 (1980) (holding final an award of attorney's fees before determination of the amount of those fees or other questions relating to them).

The lower courts remain divided, however, on the question whether the White case establishes a bright line rule governing *all* disputes over attorneys' fees. See Beckwith Machine Co. v. Travelers Indemnity Co., 815 F.2d 286 (3d Cir.1987), and authorities cited therein at 288–90. See also Budinich v. Becton Dickinson & Co., 807 F.2d 155 (10th Cir.1986), *cert. granted,* 108 S.Ct. 226 (1987) (raising question of effect of state law in a diversity case).

practical considerations: although the litigation may not be at an end, a particular matter of importance has been finally determined, and effective review at a later stage may be difficult or impossible. Areas in which the Court has had to grapple with this rule in recent years include pretrial appeals by defendants in criminal cases, appeals from denials of immunity claims in actions against government officials, appeals from the denial of certification in class action suits, and appeals from decisions to abstain in favor of state proceedings.

(a) *Criminal cases.* In Abney v. United States, 431 U.S. 651 (1977), discussed in Firestone, the Court permitted appeal before trial of a denial of a motion to dismiss an indictment on grounds of double jeopardy. The Court emphasized that the rights conferred on a criminal defendant by the Double Jeopardy Clause are significantly undermined by the very occurrence of a second trial, regardless of the outcome.[3]

Was the Court in Firestone correct when it characterized Abney as involving a right whose "legal and practical value" would be "destroyed" if not vindicated before trial? Surely the Court did not mean that the defendant's right is solely a right not to be tried, so that a conviction in these circumstances would not be set aside. Does this verbal overkill in the description of Abney make the Firestone case seem more distinguishable than it really was?[4]

(b) *Claims of immunity.* Relying on the Abney rationale, the Court in Nixon v. Fitzgerald, 457 U.S. 731 (1982), unanimously held immediately appealable a district court denial of a claim of absolute presidential immunity from civil prosecution for damages. But the unanimity dissolved in Mitchell v. Forsyth, 472 U.S. 511 (1985), where the question was the appealability of denial of a claim of qualified immunity in a damage action against a former Attorney General. For the majority, the denial was immediately appealable, to the extent it turned on an issue of law, because "qualified immunity is in fact an entitlement not to stand trial under certain circumstances" (p. 525). For Justice Brennan (joined by Justice Marshall) in dissent, the immunity claim was not sufficiently separable from the merits and was not appropriately characterized as a right not to stand trial—any more than a claim based on the statute of limitations, a right to jury trial, or a venue limitation (p. 547 n. 4).

Can a satisfactory line be drawn between those rights that would be seriously impaired by the holding of further proceedings and those rights that can be adequately vindicated when the proceedings have been concluded? Do you agree that a defendant's claim—that, as a present or former government official, he cannot be held accountable in damages for his unlawful actions—fits into the former category?[5]

3. The Court stated that a case falling within the Cohen rationale was a "final decision" under § 1291 even though not a "final judgment" (p. 658). But it also noted that its holding of appealability did not extend to other claims contained in the motion to dismiss.

4. Since Abney, the Court has on several occasions refused to allow an appeal from a pretrial order in a criminal case, concluding in each instance that the right involved could be adequately protected by an appeal after conviction. United States v. MacDonald, 435 U.S. 850 (1978) (claim of right to speedy trial); United States v. Hollywood Motor Car Co., Inc., 458 U.S. 263 (1982) (claim of prosecutorial vindictiveness). But cf. Helstoski v. Meanor, 442 U.S. 500 (1979) (applying the Abney rationale to a claim of immunity from criminal prosecution on the basis of the Speech or Debate Clause).

5. The Mitchell case has created uncertainty in the lower courts about the mater-

(c) *Class action certification.* The Supreme Court first spoke on this problem in Eisen v. Carlisle & Jacquelin, 417 U.S. 156 (1974), holding final a trial court order (allowing the suit to proceed as a class action) which required the defendants to pay 90% of the costs of notifying class members. The Court analogized the order imposing costs to the order held final in Cohen and went on to uphold appellate authority to review all aspects of the class action notice problems in the case.

Four years later, the Court settled over a decade of controversy in the lower courts by unanimously holding that, despite the implications of Eisen, a district court order denying class certification (and, a fortiori, an order granting certification) is not final and appealable under § 1291. Coopers & Lybrand v. Livesay, 437 U.S. 463 (1978). The Cohen rule did not apply because the order denying certification was subject to later revision in the district court, because the issues were closely related to the factual and legal issues on the merits, and because such an order was "subject to effective review after final judgment at the behest of the named plaintiff or intervening class members" (p. 469).[6] The "death knell" doctrine that had been developed in some circuits—allowing an appeal when a denial of class certification to the plaintiff made it extremely unlikely that the plaintiff could or would pursue the action on his own behalf—was given the coup de grace by the Court. Its reasons were that (a) if based solely on the amount in controversy, the death-knell approach involved an invasion of the legislative province, (b) if based on a multi-factor analysis, the approach would impose too heavy a burden on the courts, and (c) the approach would in any event authorize indiscriminate interlocutory review inconsistent with the procedures and criteria provided in the Interlocutory Appeals Act, § 1292(b).

Did the Court in Coopers & Lybrand end up effectively precluding any appeal as of right of a trial court's denial of class action certification whenever the plaintiff cannot afford to pursue the action on an individual basis? *Cf.* pp. 1815, 1817, *infra.* What if a plaintiff whose motion is denied submits to a judgment of involuntary dismissal of his individual action under Rule 41(b)—perhaps for failure to prosecute—and then raises the certification issue on appeal? See Huey v. Teledyne, Inc., 608 F.2d 1234 (9th Cir.1979) (denial of class certification not reviewable on appeal of

ials that may properly be considered on appeal from denial of a claim of immunity. Compare, *e.g.*, Bonitz v. Fair, 804 F.2d 164, 167 (1st Cir.1986) (even after two years of discovery, the court should consider "only the plaintiff's allegations rather than the undisputed facts as revealed by depositions, affidavits, and other discovery materials"), with, *e.g.*, Green v. Carlson, 826 F.2d 647 (7th Cir.1987) (the court should review the entire record and consider the qualified immunity issue in light of all the undisputed facts).

For a question of appealability closely related to Mitchell, see Van Cauwenberghe v. Biard, 108 S.Ct. 326 (1987) (granting certiorari from a decision holding unappealable a district court order denying an extradited person's claim of absolute immunity from civil process).

6. Two years after Coopers & Lybrand, a sharply divided Supreme Court confronted some aspects of the appealability of a denial of class certification in the face of a claim of mootness. See United States Parole Com'n v. Geraghty, 445 U.S. 388 (1980), p. 212, *supra,* and the following Note. In the course of his dissent from the decision allowing an appeal in Geraghty, Justice Powell referred to the statement quoted in text from Coopers & Lybrand— that an order denying certification is reviewable after final judgment "at the behest of the named plaintiff"—as a "gratuitous sentence" that "apparently is elevated by the Court's opinion in this case to the status of new doctrine." 445 U.S. at 416–17.

dismissal for failure to prosecute); Comment, 48 U.Chi.L.Rev. 912, 927–35 (1981) (forcefully criticizing the Huey decision).

(d) *Abstention in favor of state proceedings.* In Moses H. Cone Memorial Hospital v. Mercury Construction Corp., 460 U.S. 1 (1983), the district court stayed a diversity action to compel arbitration pending resolution of a state court action between the same parties involving similar issues. The Supreme Court held that order final and appealable. It reasoned that (a) the only substantial issue in the case (that of arbitrability) would not be further litigated in federal court, since the state court's determination of that issue would be res judicata and (b) "[i]n any event," the case met the criteria for the "exception to the finality rule" under Cohen and its progeny (p. 11). (The Court went on to hold that the decision to abstain was an abuse of discretion. See p. 1449, *supra.*)

Justice Rehnquist (joined by the Chief Justice and Justice O'Connor) dissented on the question of appealability. He argued that the stay order was "tentative" and "subject to change at any time" and that the decision constituted "an unwarranted limitation upon the power of district courts to control their own cases" (pp. 30–31). And he urged that the decision lacked both the conclusiveness and the importance to warrant an appeal under the Cohen rationale.

Does this decision mean that any stay of proceedings is an appealable decision? How can the result be squared with the rejection of the "death knell" doctrine in Coopers & Lybrand, Paragraph (3)(c), *supra*? The Court attempted to answer both questions in its opinion (pp. 10–11, n. 11), stating that (a) "most stays do not put the plaintiff 'effectively out of court,' " and (b) unlike the death-knell cases, the order appealed from in Cone had the *legal* effect of preventing further litigation in federal court.[7]

(4) Accepting the Firestone opinion's analysis of the application of the Cohen rule to an order denying disqualification, would you distinguish the case in which a motion to disqualify is granted? If the party deprived of the counsel of choice by such an order later lost on the merits, would an appellate court simply presume that the change of counsel had been prejudicial, or would some showing of prejudice be required? If, as many observers have noted, motions to disqualify are being increasingly used by litigants as a dilatory tactic, would allowing an appeal of a grant of disqualification be as supportive of that tactic as allowing an appeal of a denial?

Without answering the question whether a showing of prejudice is required, the Court after Firestone held orders granting disqualification to be nonappealable in both criminal and civil contexts. See Flanagan v. United States, 465 U.S. 259 (1984) (criminal); Richardson–Merrell, Inc. v. Koller, 472 U.S. 424 (1985) (civil). The reasoning was explained in Richardson–Merrell:

"[I]f establishing a violation of one's right to counsel of choice in civil cases requires no showing of prejudice, then, 'a pretrial order violating the right does not meet the third condition for coverage by the collateral order exception: it is not "effectively unreviewable on appeal from a final judgment." ' * * * [If a showing of prejudice is required,] then a disqual-

---

7. In Gulfstream Aerospace Corp. v. Mayacamas Corp., 108 S.Ct. 1133 (1988), the Supreme Court held that an order de- *nying* a request for abstention is not immediately appealable under § 1291 or § 1292(a)(1).

ification order, though 'final,' is not independent of the issues to be tried" (pp. 438–39).

(5) Forgay v. Conrad, 6 How. 201 (U.S.1848), was a case in which a federal circuit court had ordered the defendants to turn over certain property to an assignee in bankruptcy. Although the case was to continue in the circuit court for an accounting, the Supreme Court held this order final and appealable, since immediate execution, sale of the property, and distribution of the proceeds to creditors was contemplated.

In recent years, the Forgay case has apparently not been viewed by the Supreme Court as establishing an independent rationale for determining the finality of a district court order. Rather, as in Firestone, it seems to have been assimilated to the Cohen "collateral order" rule.[8] But the order in Forgay was in no sense "collateral" to the merits of the controversy over distribution of the bankrupt's estate among his creditors. It was the element of hardship from the impending execution and sale of the property that, standing alone, supported the determination of finality. Indeed, the opinion suggested that an order simply directing transfer of the property to the control of the court would not be final. See generally 15 Wright, Miller & Cooper, Federal Practice & Procedure § 3910 (1976).

(6) In the 1960s and '70s, the Court had a brief flirtation with a considerably more relaxed approach to finality than that evidenced by its recent decisions under § 1291. The high water mark of this period was Gillespie v. United States Steel Corp., 379 U.S. 148 (1964), a case not even cited in Firestone. In Gillespie, the plaintiff, administrator of her son's estate, sued for damages under the Jones Act and (under Ohio's wrongful death law) for unseaworthiness. She sought recovery both for herself and for her son's surviving brother and sisters. The district court struck all references in the complaint to Ohio law, to unseaworthiness, and to recovery for the benefit of the brother and sisters. On appeal from this order, the court of appeals decided the controversy on the merits, as did the Supreme Court after holding, 7–2, that the order was appealable under § 1291. The basis of the decision on appealability appeared to be that the cost of holding the order unappealable would exceed the benefits:

"It is true that the review of this case by the Court of Appeals could be called 'piecemeal'; but it does not appear that the inconvenience and cost of trying this case will be greater because the Court of Appeals decided the issues raised instead of compelling the parties to go to trial with them unanswered. We cannot say that the Court of Appeals chose wrongly under the circumstances. And it seems clear now that the case is before us that the eventual costs, as all the parties recognize, will certainly be less if we now pass on the questions presented here rather than send the case back with those issues undecided. Moreover, delay of perhaps a number of years in having the brother's and sisters' rights determined might work a great injustice on them, since the claims for recovery for their benefit have been effectively cut off so long as the District Judge's ruling stands. * * * It is true that if the District Judge had certified the case to the Court of Appeals under 28 U.S.C. § 1292(b) * * *, the appeal unquestionably would have been proper; in light of the circumstances we believe that

---

8. The case has occasionally been relied on, however, as a basis for allowing review of state court judgments under 28 U.S.C. § 1257. See, e.g., Radio Station WOW, Inc. v. Johnson, 326 U.S. 120, 125–26 (1945); North Dakota State Bd. of Pharmacy v. Snyder's Drug Stores, Inc., 414 U.S. 156, 162 (1973). Cf. Paragraph (8), infra.

the Court of Appeals properly implemented the same policy Congress sought to promote in § 1292(b) by treating this obviously marginal case as final and appealable under 28 U.S.C. § 1291 * * * " (pp. 153–54).

Gillespie did have some impact in the lower courts, moving them toward a greater willingness to entertain appeals on the basis of a balance of costs and benefits. See, *e.g.,* Norman v. McKee, 431 F.2d 769 (9th Cir. 1970). But its generative force in cases arising under § 1291 was not great, especially at the Supreme Court level.[9] See Redish, *The Pragmatic Approach to Appealability in the Federal Courts,* 75 Colum.L.Rev. 89, 120–24 (1975). And in 1978, in Coopers & Lybrand, Paragraph (3), *supra,* the Court confined it to the limbo of its particular facts.[10]

Assuming that the statutory language of § 1291 permits the kind of balancing employed in Gillespie, do you think the Court weighed all relevant elements in the scale? What of the impact on the costs of administration and of litigation that such an open-ended, case-by-case approach might entail? In Gillespie itself, was there any harm that could be shown aside from the delay that would result from having to wait for a final decision and the possible extra expense of a second trial?

(7) Should orders to testify or to produce documents in a pending judicial proceeding ever be regarded as final? In general, they are not. See, *e.g.,* Cobbledick v. United States, 309 U.S. 323 (1940); United States v. Ryan, 402 U.S. 530 (1971). And indeed, although a criminal or civil contempt order against a nonparty is considered final, a civil contempt order against a party is not, see Doyle v. London Guar. & Accident Co., 204 U.S. 599 (1907)—a rule that is sometimes honored in the breach, as in Sibbach v. Wilson & Co., 312 U.S. 1 (1941). The distinction has been forcefully criticized on the ground that both civil and criminal contempt adjudications cause the kind of hardships that decisions like Forgay v. Conrad, Paragraph (5), *supra,* have sought to prevent. Andre, *The Final Judgment Rule and Party Appeals of Civil Contempt Orders: Time for a Change,* 55 N.Y.U.L.Rev. 1041 (1980).

In two instances, appeals even prior to a contempt adjudication have been allowed. The first was a case in which the owner of documents in possession of the court petitioned to bar their use before a grand jury, and his petition was denied; the Court noted that to deny an appeal at that stage would be to deny any appeal, since the petitioner was unable to resist production by placing himself in contempt. Perlman v. United States, 247 U.S. 7 (1918).[11] In the second, President Nixon was allowed to appeal from the denial of his motion to quash a subpoena to produce the "Watergate" tapes before a grand jury. United States v. Nixon, 418 U.S. 683 (1974). The extraordinary rationale of this case—that it would be "unseemly" to require a President to place himself in contempt just to "trigger" appellate review (pp. 691–92)—evidently does not extend to members of the Presi-

9. Gillespie was relied on, however, in Cox Broadcasting Corp. v. Cohn, 420 U.S. 469, 478 n. 7 (1975), p. 694, *supra.*

10. In a parting footnote in Coopers & Lybrand, the Court emphasized the importance of the substantive issue in Gillespie and the late stage at which the finality issue had been presented to the Supreme Court. "If Gillespie were extended beyond the unique facts of that case," it concluded, "§ 1291 would be stripped of all significance" (p. 477 n. 30).

11. For discussion of the range of lower court opinions interpreting and applying the Perlman exception, and an argument for a "narrow reading" of that exception, see Note, 49 U.Chi.L.Rev. 798, 799 (1982).

dent's cabinet. See In re Attorney General, 596 F.2d 58 (2d Cir.1979), and Justice White's dissent from the denial of certiorari in Socialist Workers Party v. Attorney General, 444 U.S. 903 (1979).

(8) Should the criteria for determining what is a "final decision" under § 1291 be any different from those used in applying 28 U.S.C. § 1257, which provides for Supreme Court review of "final judgments or decrees" of "the highest court of a State"? See Chap. V, Sec. 3, *supra*. The Supreme Court has often cited cases under one statute when applying the other. See, *e.g.*, Cox Broadcasting Corp. v. Cohn, 420 U.S. 469, 478 (1975); National Socialist Party v. Village of Skokie, 432 U.S. 43, 44 (1977). But consider the following possible bases for drawing some distinctions:

(a) The language of the two statutes;

(b) Problems of federalism and comity involved in federal review of state court judgments (see Justice Rehnquist's dissent in the Cox Broadcasting case, 420 U.S. at 502–05);

(c) The availability in the lower federal courts, but not on Supreme Court review of state courts, of alternative avenues to appellate review (*e.g.*, 28 U.S.C. §§ 1292(a)(1), 1292(b));

(d) The possibility that the federal issues in a case in the state courts might be finally disposed of by the highest state court long before the case is concluded, and that the federal interest might be defeated absent immediate review; [12]

(e) The relative difficulties for a court in administering a flexible standard governing its own appellate jurisdiction (§ 1257), and in supervising the administration of a standard governing the appellate jurisdiction of thirteen lower courts (§ 1291); and

(f) The fact that, at least on petitions for certiorari governed by 28 U.S.C. § 1254(1), there is no final judgment required for Supreme Court review of the decisions of the federal courts of appeals.

(9) When a close question of finality is presented in the course of litigation, must the party aggrieved file an appeal in order to preserve his rights? Congress has provided thirty days for the filing of an appeal, 28 U.S.C. § 2107, and the failure to appeal from a "final" order during that time has been held fatal, even though the action did not go to judgment until more than a year later. Dickinson v. Petroleum Conversion Corp., 338 U.S. 507 (1950).[13] But in Corey v. United States, 375 U.S. 169 (1963), the Court, over Justice Harlan's dissent, held that the petitioner, a defendant in a criminal case, had an option to appeal either (1) when he was committed under 18 U.S.C. § 4208(b), pending receipt of a report from the Bureau of Prisons, or (2) when he was resentenced following receipt of the report over three months later.[14] And in several cases since Abney, Paragraph 3(a), *supra*, lower courts have held that although denial of a pretrial motion to dismiss on double jeopardy grounds is immediately

---

12. See, *e.g.*, Mercantile National Bank v. Langdeau, 371 U.S. 555 (1963), p. 697, *supra*. (Would an extraordinary writ like mandamus or prohibition be available in a case like Langdeau if an appeal did not lie? See 28 U.S.C. § 1651.)

13. See also White v. New Hampshire Dept. of Employment Security, 455 U.S.

445 (1982); Boeing Co. v. Van Gemert, 444 U.S. 472, 489 (1980) (Rehnquist, J., dissenting); Swanson v. American Consumer Indus., Inc., 517 F.2d 555 (7th Cir.1975).

14. *Cf.* Rosenblatt v. American Cyanamid Co., 86 S.Ct. 1, 3 n. 6 (1965) (Goldberg, J., on application for a stay).

appealable, appeal at that stage is not "mandatory"; the claim may be raised on appeal after conviction. *E.g.,* United States v. Gamble, 607 F.2d 820 (9th Cir.1979). Perhaps with tongue in cheek, the court in Gamble said that its holding would "avoid piecemeal appeals" (p. 823).

Are there, then, two kinds of final orders—those that may be treated as final at the option of the litigants and those that must be appealed now if at all? How are they to be distinguished? Does a case fall into the latter category if the party contemplating an appeal cannot be affected by anything remaining for determination in the trial court? Only in such circumstances? [15] *Cf.* Chap. V, Sec 3, p. 709, *supra* (discussing an analogous question with respect to Supreme Court review of state court decisions).

(10) The notion that the statutory limits on appellate review are "jurisdictional" is of ancient lineage, and its announcement and application in Firestone was not too surprising. But this application may be seen as driving one more nail into the coffin of the Gillespie case, Paragraph (6), *supra.* Some observers viewed Gillespie as moderating a strict jurisdictional view—as saying that even when an appeal had been improperly taken, dismissal might not be required if the case had been decided on the merits below and argued on the merits in the Supreme Court. See, *e.g.,* 15 Wright, Miller & Cooper, Federal Practice and Procedure § 3905 (1976). Firestone is surely a rejection of any such approach. If a matter is "jurisdictional," does it follow ineluctably (as the Firestone Court held) that a judicial overruling of prior precedent must be retrospective? [16] See generally Chap. XIV, Sec. 1, *supra.*

NOTE ON RULE 54(b): APPEALS IN MULTI–PARTY AND MULTI–CLAIM CASES

(1) Before the adoption of the federal rules in 1938, the Supreme Court had held that an appeal from the disposition of one claim in a single or multi-party case could not be taken if other claims remained undecided. *E.g.,* Collins v. Miller, 252 U.S. 364 (1920). The rulemakers originally addressed the problem by providing, in Rule 54(b), that an order disposing of a single claim in a multi-claim case "shall terminate the action with respect to the claim so disposed of." Later, in 1946, the rule was amended to permit the resolution of doubts, and the limitation of appeals, at the district court level; the amended rule stated that "The [district] court may direct the entry of a final judgment upon one or more but less than all of the claims only upon an express determination that there is no just reason for delay"; in the absence of such a determination and direction, "any order * * * shall not terminate the action as to any of the claims."

In Sears, Roebuck & Co. v. Mackey, 351 U.S. 427 (1956), the Court rejected an attack on the validity of this rule, holding that it was not "an

---

15. A question that may be raised in an interlocutory appeal is not lost if no such appeal is taken; if it has not become moot, it may also be raised on appeal from a final judgment. See, *e.g.,* United States v. Clark, 445 U.S. 23, 25 n. 2 (1980) (interpreting 28 U.S.C. § 1252).

16. In his proposed statute, Professor Carrington would provide that "[a] defect of appellate jurisdiction * * * may be waived and appellate jurisdiction conferred by consent of the parties. Rules of court may be promulgated * * * which limit the time for making motions to dismiss appeals for unripeness or untimeliness." Carrington, note 1, *supra,* at 170.

unauthorized extension of § 1291. * * * The District Court *cannot* in the exercise of its discretion, treat as 'final' that which is not 'final' within the meaning of § 1291. But the District Court *may,* by the exercise of its discretion in the interest of sound judicial administration, release for appeal final decisions upon one or more, but less than all, claims in multiple claim actions. * * * [A]ny abuse of that discretion remains reviewable by the Court of Appeals" (pp. 436–37) (emphasis in original). Cases like Collins v. Miller were shunted aside as resting on a construction of the judicial unit "developed from the common law which had dealt with litigation generally less complicated than much of that of today" (p. 432).

(2) In a separate opinion concurring in Sears and dissenting in a companion case (Cold Metal Process Co. v. United Eng. & Foundry Co., 351 U.S. 445 (1956)), Justice Frankfurter stated (p. 439): "The Court could have said that Rule 54(b), promulgated under congressional authority and having the force of statute, has qualified 28 U.S.C. § 1291." Do you agree? Does the provision in the Enabling Act, 28 U.S.C. § 2072, that "[a]ll laws in conflict with such rules shall be of no further force and effect" mean that the Court could by rule provide for an appeal as of right from all interlocutory orders of the district courts, or from any category of interlocutory orders not now appealable? *Cf.* Rule 82; Shapiro, *Federal Diversity Jurisdiction: A Survey and a Proposal,* 91 Harv.L.Rev. 317, 343–48 (1977).

(3) A 1961 amendment to Rule 54(b) explicitly made the rule applicable to a judgment in a multi-party case determining the rights of "fewer than all the parties". But the question of the dimensions of a "claim for relief" remains important. In Sears itself, the district court order, which it certified under Rule 54(b), had dismissed only Counts I and II of a multi-count complaint, and the Supreme Court, in upholding the appealability of the order, noted that "the claim dismissed by striking out Count I is based on the Sherman Act, while Counts III and IV do not rely on, or even refer to, that Act. They are largely predicated on common-law rights. The basis of liability in Count I is independent of that on which the claims in Counts III and IV depend. But the claim in Count I does rest in part on some of the facts that are involved in Counts III and IV. The claim stated in Count II is clearly independent of those in Counts III and IV" (p. 437 n. 9).[1]

In Seatrain Shipbldg. Co. v. Shell Oil Co., 444 U.S. 572, 579–84 (1980), the Court held that plaintiff's complaint asserted two claims: (1) that the Secretary of Commerce had no authority to grant a release from certain restrictions on the operation of a vessel, and (2) that in any event the granting of a release in the particular case was an abuse of discretion. Thus an appeal would lie under Rule 54(b) from a "final disposition" of the first claim, on proper certification by the district court, even though the second claim had not been finally disposed of. Was the Supreme Court here and in Sears using a narrower definition of a claim than the "transactional" approach adopted in the Restatement (Second) of Judgments § 24 (1982)? Is this appropriate? Would dividing a case into claims on the basis

---

1. *Cf.* Liberty Mut. Ins. Co. v. Wetzel, 424 U.S. 737, 743 n. 4 (1976) (order granting partial summary judgment on liability, but leaving unresolved requests for injunctive relief, damages, and fees, was not appealable under Rule 54(b) or on any other ground; "a complaint asserting only one legal right, even if seeking multiple remedies * * * states a single claim for relief").

of, say, legal theories, or sources of governing law, encourage too many piecemeal appeals? [2]

(4) Although the opinion in Sears indicated that the district court's exercise of discretion under Rule 54(b) was subject to review, the Court later made it clear that this exercise should not be lightly set aside for abuse. In Curtiss–Wright Corp. v. General Elec. Co., 446 U.S. 1 (1980), Curtiss–Wright had sued General Electric on several claims, including a claim for a balance of $19 million due on contracts performed, and General Electric had filed a substantial counterclaim. The district court entered summary judgment for Curtiss–Wright on the $19 million claim and ruled it entitled to prejudgment interest on that claim at the New York statutory rate. After full consideration of the relevant factors, the district court then determined that there was "no just reason for delay" and granted Curtiss–Wright's motion to certify the court's orders as final judgments under Rule 54(b). A divided court of appeals ruled that the district court's certification was an abuse of discretion because in the appellate court's view, the presence of a non-frivolous counterclaim that could result in a set-off weighed heavily against the decision to certify. The Supreme Court reversed the judgment of the court of appeals, noting that the presence of the counterclaim had been considered by the district court, along with other factors, and that its assessment of the equities was reasonable. "The question in cases such as this is likely to be close, but the task of weighing and balancing the contending factors is peculiarly one for the trial judge, who can explore all the facets of a case. As we have noted, that assessment merits substantial deference on review" (p. 12).

(5) May Rule 54(b) be used to appeal the denial of a motion to certify an action as a class action, on the theory that the denial is a final disposition of the claim on behalf of the class (as distinct from the claim of the named plaintiff)? Compare Windham v. American Brands, Inc., 539 F.2d 1016, 1020 (4th Cir.1976) (allowing Rule 54(b) review), *rev'd on other grounds on rehearing en banc*, 565 F.2d 59 (4th Cir.1977), with West v. Capital Fed. Sav. & Loan Ass'n, 558 F.2d 977 (10th Cir.1977). Can the Windham approach survive the decisions in Coopers & Lybrand, p. 1808, *supra*, and Gardner v. Westinghouse Broadcasting Co., p. 1817, *infra?*

(6) To what degree is there an overlap between Rule 54(b) and other statutory and judicially developed rules allowing appeals? In theory at least, Rule 54(b) and 28 U.S.C. § 1292(b), pp. 1819–20, *infra*, are mutually exclusive—though the line between a "final" order subject to Rule 54(b) certification and an "interlocutory" order eligible for § 1292(b) certification may often be indistinct. What of a collateral order within the rationale of the Cohen case? Clearly, not all collateral orders raise a question of the applicability of Rule 54(b). But might there be a collateral order that, say,

---

2. For a lower court decision proposing the Restatement's transactional approach as a "rule of thumb" in determining the meaning of "claim" under Rule 54(b), see Tolson v. United States, 732 F.2d 998 (D.C. Cir.1984). Although the Sears decision was cited, as possibly inconsistent with this approach, Seatrain was not discussed. See also Note, 75 Harv.L.Rev. 351, 360–61 (1961) (suggesting that despite Supreme Court decisions, lower courts have continued to rely on a transactional or "pragmatic" approach).

involved the final disposition of a single claim in a multi-claim case?[3] If so, would the absence of the requisite district court certification under Rule 54(b) bar an appeal? The commentators don't think so, but the discussion sometimes bogs down in the metaphysics of defining a "claim for relief." See 10 Wright, Miller & Kane, Federal Practice and Procedure § 2658.4 (1983); 6 Moore, Federal Practice ¶ 54.31 (2d ed. 1986). And though the question has not been squarely addressed by the Supreme Court, it has generally been given fairly short shrift in the lower courts. See, *e.g.*, In re General Motors Corp. Engine Interchange Litigation, 594 F.2d 1106, 1118 n. 12 (7th Cir.1979) (a "collateral order" final within the Cohen doctrine is appealable without certification under Rule 54(b)).

NOTE ON INTERLOCUTORY APPEALS

(1) Section 1292 of Title 28 authorizes interlocutory appeals in a number of situations, the most important of which is that specified in subsection (a)(1): orders "granting, continuing, modifying, refusing or dissolving injunctions, or refusing to modify or dissolve injunctions, except where direct review may be had in the Supreme Court."

Some insight into the meaning and purpose of this provision is given by the decision in Carson v. American Brands, Inc., 450 U.S. 79 (1981). In Carson, the district court had refused to enter a proposed consent decree in a case brought under Title VII of the Civil Rights Act of 1964—a decree that would have imposed significant obligations on the defendant with respect to the hiring, promotion, and transfer of employees. The Supreme Court, reversing the court of appeals, held that this action was appealable under § 1292(a)(1). It was not sufficient, however, that the district court's action had the practical effect of denying injunctive relief: "Unless a litigant can show that an interlocutory order of the District Court might have 'serious, perhaps irreparable consequence,' and that the order can be 'effectually challenged' only by immediate appeal, the general congressional policy against piecemeal appeal will preclude interlocutory appeal" (p. 84). In the present case, those stringent criteria were met because the district court's order might deny the parties "their right to compromise their dispute on mutually agreeable terms" (p. 88), and because the plaintiffs might be irrevocably harmed by the delay resulting from a trial.

(2) Was the order in Carson also appealable under § 1291? (The Court noted the question in its opinion but did not resolve it.)

(3) What basis did the Court in Carson have for saying that for an interlocutory order to be immediately appealable under § 1292(a)(1), a litigant must show *more* than that the order has the practical effect of refusing an injunction? Granted that one purpose of the statute is to facilitate prompt review in cases most likely to involve immediate hardship to the litigants, does the statute make a showing of hardship the test of appealability?

Does the Carson decision mean that, to resolve the issue of appealability under § 1291(a)(1), each case must be judged on its particular facts to

---

3. In Cohen itself, for example, could the demand of security for costs be considered a separate "claim for relief"? The majority spoke of the state security-for-costs statute as creating "a new liability where none existed before" (337 U.S. at 555).

determine the seriousness of the consequences? If so, does this requirement apply only to orders effectively denying or refusing injunctive relief
and not to orders *granting* such relief? [1] (Consider, for example, a case in
which a court, in a preliminary injunction, orders the parties to maintain
the status quo, and in which neither party can show any serious or
irreparable harm as a result of the order.)

In Switzerland Cheese Ass'n, Inc. v. E. Horne's Market, Inc., 385 U.S.
23 (1966), relied on in Carson, the denial of plaintiffs' motion for summary
judgment was held not immediately appealable even though its practical
effect was to deny them the permanent injunction they had sought in the
motion. But the denial did not preclude the plaintiffs from immediately
seeking preliminary relief and only postponed the question of permanent
relief until trial. Did it require a close analysis of the actual consequences
to conclude that the order was not appealable under § 1292(a)(1)?

(4) In Gardner v. Westinghouse Broadcasting Co., 437 U.S. 478 (1978),
also relied on in Carson, the Court held that an order denying class
certification was not appealable under § 1292(a)(1) even though the order
might significantly affect the scope of any ultimate injunctive relief. No
motion for preliminary relief had been filed, the Court noted, and the
district court had not "entirely disposed of" the prayer for permanent
relief. Moreover, the denial of class action status was itself conditional and
"did not pass on the legal sufficiency of any claims for injunctive relief";
thus, as in Switzerland Cheese, the order had "no direct or irreparable
impact on the merits of the controversy" (pp. 480–82).

In Gardner, the plaintiff was also seeking injunctive relief on her own
behalf. What if it were clear in such a case that the individual plaintiff
would not be entitled to an injunction—that such relief could only be
granted on behalf of the class? Should the conditional nature of the denial
of class action status in itself be sufficient to preclude review under
§ 1292(a)(1)?

Suppose that in a class action case, a district court issues an order (a)
denying class action status and (b) denying preliminary relief. May both
aspects of the order be reviewed in an appeal under § 1292(a)(1)? See
Kershner v. Mazurkiewicz, 670 F.2d 440 (3d Cir.1982) (deciding, en banc,
that the class certification issue is not reviewable in such a case "unless the
preliminary injunction issue cannot properly be decided without reference
to the class certification question" (p. 449).

(5) Among the most troublesome cases under § 1292(a)(1) are those
concerned with the order of trial or with a stay of proceedings in one
tribunal pending adjudication in another.

---

1. Section 1292(a)(1) had its origin in
the Evarts Act of 1891, see p. 1795, *supra*,
and originally provided for interlocutory
appeals only from orders granting or continuing injunctions. For analysis of subsequent revisions, and the suggestion that in
extending the statute to denials of relief,
Congress "was thinking primarily of the
case where erroneous denial of a *temporary*
injunction may cause injury quite as irreparable as an erroneous grant of one," *see*
Stewart-Warner Corp. v. Westinghouse

Elec. Corp., 325 F.2d 822, 830 (2d Cir.1963)
(Friendly, J., dissenting).

Though the final judgment rule existed
at common law, it never developed in
courts of equity. *See* Crick, *The Final
Judgment Rule as a Basis for Appeal,* 41
Yale L.J. 539, 545–48 (1932). There is no
clear indication of why the First Judiciary
Act limited appeals to final judgments and
decrees at law *and* in equity.

In Enelow v. New York Life Ins. Co., 293 U.S. 379 (1935), the plaintiff brought an action on a life insurance policy. Relying on then § 274b of the Judicial Code, 28 U.S.C. § 398 (1928), permitting equitable defenses in actions at law, the defendant alleged that the policy had been obtained by fraud, tendered judgment for the premiums, prayed for cancellation of the policy and petitioned that the "equitable" issue be heard by the court without a jury prior to determination of the "legal" issues. The district court granted the petition and on appeal from the decree the court of appeals affirmed. The Supreme Court, reversing on the merits, held the decree appealable. Chief Justice Hughes said (p. 383): "[W]hen an order or decree is made under § 274b, requiring, or refusing to require, that an equitable defense shall first be tried, the court, exercising what is essentially an equitable jurisdiction, in effect grants or refuses an injunction restraining proceedings at law precisely as if the court had acted upon a bill of complaint in a separate suit for the same purpose."

The same problem arose after the promulgation of the Federal Rules in Ettelson v. Metropolitan Life Ins. Co., 317 U.S. 188, 192 (1942), and was decided the same way, in the view that the "plaintiffs are * * * in no different position than if a state equity court had restrained them from proceeding in the law action". The single civil action of the Federal Rules was held to make no difference. "The relief afforded by § 129 [now § 1292(a)(1)] is not restricted by the terminology used. The statute looks to the substantial effect of the order made."

Morgantown v. Royal Ins. Co., 337 U.S. 254 (1949), presented the issue in reverse. The insurer brought an action to reform and correct a policy for mutual mistake and the insured counterclaimed upon the policy as written. Demand for jury trial by the insured was overruled and the case set for trial without a jury. The court of appeals dismissed the appeal and the Supreme Court affirmed.

Finally, in Baltimore Contractors, Inc. v. Bodinger, 348 U.S. 176 (1955), the Court held that no appeal could be taken from a district court order denying a stay pending arbitration in an action for an accounting of the profits in a joint venture. After holding that "The Morgantown case controls here," the Court conceded (at pp. 184–85):

"The reliance on the analogy of equity power to enjoin proceedings in other courts has elements of fiction in this day of one form of action. The incongruity of taking jurisdiction from a stay in a law type and denying jurisdiction in an equity type proceeding springs from the persistence of outmoded procedural differentiations. * * * The distinction has been applied for years, however, and we conclude that it is better judicial practice to follow the precedents which limit appealability of interlocutory orders, leaving Congress to make such amendments as it may find proper."

Assuming Enelow to have been correctly decided, what of the other cases in the series?

(6) Application of the Enelow line of cases to requests for abstention, or for a stay relating to arbitration, became a source of disagreement and confusion in the lower courts. In the context of arbitration, the question could arise in connection with orders granting or denying a stay of an arbitration proceeding or with orders granting or denying a stay of the court's own proceedings pending arbitration. And the judicial proceeding

itself could be characterized as one in equity or law, depending on the nature of the complaint.

Criticism of the Enelow line, from the standpoint both of its historical accuracy and its current value, was widespread. After a full review of this criticism, the Supreme Court, in Gulfstream Areospace Corp. v. Mayacamas Corp., 108 S.Ct. 1133 (1988), p. 1809, note 7, *supra*, unanimously voted to "overturn the cases establishing the Enelow-Ettelson rule and hold that orders granting or denying stays of 'legal' proceedings on 'equitable' grounds are not automatically appealable under § 1292(a)(1)" (p. 1142). "The case against perpetuation of this sterile and antiquated doctrine seems to us conclusive. * * * This holding will not prevent interlocutory review of district court orders when such review is truly needed * * * [as in the case of] orders that have the practical effect of granting or denying injunctions and have 'serious, perhaps irreparable, consequence.' [citing discussion in Carson, Paragraph (1), *supra*]" (pp. 1442–43).

(7) An order granting, denying, or dissolving a temporary restraining order is not ordinarily appealable under § 1292(a)(1). See 16 Wright, Miller, Cooper & Gressman § 3922 (1977). But in Sampson v. Murray, 415 U.S. 61, 86–87 n. 58 (1974), the Court quoted with approval, and applied, the reasoning of the Second Circuit that "continuation of the temporary restraining order beyond the period of statutory authorization [*i.e.*, the time permissible under Federal Rule 65(b)] having, as it does, the same practical effect as the issuance of a preliminary injunction, is appealable within the meaning and intent of 28 U.S.C. § 1292(a)(1)" (quoting from Pan American World Airways, Inc. v. Flight Engineers' Intern. Ass'n, 306 F.2d 840, 843 (2d Cir.1962)). Also, the grant or denial of a temporary restraining order may under special circumstances be so clear a disposition of the merits (because of the threat of mootness) as to be an appealable final order under § 1291. See, *e.g.*, Virginia v. Tenneco, Inc., 538 F.2d 1026 (4th Cir.1976).

(8) The enactment in 1958 of § 1292(b) added one more string to the bow of a losing party in a civil action who wants prompt review of an interlocutory order. But the statute requires approval of an appeal by both the district and appellate courts, and at neither level has there been an inclination to allow free and easy use of its provisions. Thus a study of the administration of the statute in 1975 reported that only 53% of applications to the courts of appeals for leave to appeal under § 1292(b) were accepted and that the ratio of such appeals to the total number of appeals was 1.2%. Note, 88 Harv.L.Rev. 607, 607 n. 5, 627 n. 87 (1975).[2]

(a) Among the possible reasons for permitting appeals before final judgment are the avoidance of hardship, the need to supervise the administration of the law in the lower courts on matters not often presented on appeal from final judgments, and the desire to increase efficiency and reduce costs. Does § 1292(b) contemplate the allowance of interlocutory appeals on any or all of these grounds? The Harvard Law Review note, *supra*, argues that in light of the language and history of the statute, only the last of these grounds may be viewed as a basis for use of this procedure.

---

2. Note that applications may be made only after the district court has granted leave to appeal. Moreover, as the Harvard Note reports (pp. 616–17), the courts of appeals have consistently refused to issue mandamus to review a trial court denial of certification.

(b) What is a "controlling question of law" within the meaning of the statute? Must the question be one that will be dispositive of the action? Or is it enough that reversal would have a substantial effect on the course of litigation? May a question involving the exercise of discretion ever be reviewed under this section?[3]

(c) Does the condition that an immediate appeal "may materially advance the ultimate termination of the litigation" limit the applicability of § 1292(b) to protracted cases? Must the time and expense of the appeal be countered by a greater potential saving of time and expense at the trial level? Given this requirement, as well as that of a "controlling question of law," may an order to transfer a case under § 28 U.S.C. § 1404, or refusing to transfer, ever be reviewable under this section?[4]

(d) In addition to the Harvard Law Review Note, *supra,* see generally 16 Wright, Miller, Cooper & Gressman, Federal Practice and Procedure §§ 3929–3931 (1977); Note, 54 Geo.L.J. 940 (1966).

WILL v. UNITED STATES

389 U.S. 90, 88 S.Ct. 269, 19 L.Ed.2d 305 (1967).
Certiorari to the United States Court of Appeals for the Seventh Circuit.

MR. CHIEF JUSTICE WARREN delivered the opinion of the Court.

The question in this case is the propriety of a writ of mandamus issued by the Court of Appeals for the Seventh Circuit to compel the petitioner, a United States District Judge, to vacate a portion of a pretrial order in a criminal case.

Simmie Horwitz, the defendant in a criminal tax evasion case pending before petitioner in the Northern District of Illinois, filed a motion for a bill of particulars, which contained thirty requests for information. The Government resisted a number of the requests, and over the course of several hearings most of these objections were either withdrawn by the Government or satisfied by an appropriate narrowing of the scope of the bill of particulars by petitioner. Ultimately the dispute centered solely on defendant's request number 25. This request sought certain information concerning any oral statements of the defendant relied upon by the Government to support the charge in the indictment. It asked the names and addresses of the persons to whom such statements were made, the times and places at which they were made, whether the witnesses to the statements were government agents and whether any transcripts or memoranda of the statements had been prepared by the witnesses and given to the Government. After considerable discussion with counsel for both sides, petitioner ordered the Government to furnish the information. The United

---

3. In Coopers & Lybrand v. Livesay, 437 U.S. 463 (1978), p. 1808, *supra,* the Supreme Court cited with apparent approval several lower court decisions reviewing "discretionary class determinations" under § 1292(b) (pp. 475–76 n. 27). But *cf.* Link v. Mercedez-Benz of North America, Inc., 550 F.2d 860 (3d Cir.1977) (en banc).

4. In Continental Grain Co. v. Barge FBL–585, 364 U.S. 19 (1960), p. 1739, note

3, *supra,* the court of appeals had allowed a § 1292(b) appeal of a transfer order; the question of appealability was not discussed by the Supreme Court. *Cf., e.g.,* Garner v. Wolfinbarger, 433 F.2d 117 (5th Cir.1970) (§ 1292(b) is appropriate for review of questions of "law" but not of "discretion" in transfer cases); 9 Moore, Federal Practice ¶ 110.13[6] (2d ed. 1986).

States Attorney declined to comply with the order on the grounds that request number 25 constituted a demand for a list of prosecution witnesses and that petitioner had no power under Rule 7(f) of the Federal Rules of Criminal Procedure to require the Government to produce such a list.

Petitioner indicated his intention to dismiss the indictments against Horwitz because of the Government's refusal to comply with his order for a bill of particulars. Before the order of dismissal was entered, however, the Government sought and obtained *ex parte* from the Seventh Circuit a stay of all proceedings in the case. The Court of Appeals also granted the Government leave to file a petition for a writ of mandamus and issued a rule to show cause why such a writ should not issue to compel petitioner to strike request number 25 from his bill of particulars order. This case was submitted on the briefs, and the Court of Appeals at first denied the writ. The Government petitioned for reconsideration, however, and the Court of Appeals, without taking new briefs or hearing oral argument, reversed itself and without opinion issued a writ of mandamus directing petitioner "to vacate his order directing the Government to answer question 25 in defendant's motion for bill of particulars." We granted certiorari because of the wide implications of the decision below for the orderly administration of criminal justice in the federal courts. We vacate the writ and remand the case to the Court of Appeals for further proceedings.

Both parties have devoted substantial argument in this Court to the propriety of petitioner's order. In our view of the case, however, it is unnecessary to reach this question.[4] The peremptory writ of mandamus has traditionally been used in the federal courts only "to confine an inferior court to a lawful exercise of its prescribed jurisdiction or to compel it to exercise its authority when it is its duty to do so." Roche v. Evaporated Milk Assn., 319 U.S. 21, 26 (1943). While the courts have never confined themselves to an arbitrary and technical definition of "jurisdiction," it is clear that only exceptional circumstances amounting to a judicial "usurpation of power" will justify the invocation of this extraordinary remedy. De Beers Consol. Mines, Ltd. v. United States, 325 U.S. 212, 217 (1945). Thus the writ has been invoked where unwarranted judicial action threatened "to embarrass the executive arm of the government in conducting foreign relations," Ex parte Republic of Peru, 318 U.S. 578, 588 (1943), where it was the only means of forestalling intrusion by the federal judiciary on a delicate area of federal-state relations, State of Maryland v. Soper, 270 U.S. 9 (1926), where it was necessary to confine a lower court to the terms of an appellate tribunal's mandate, United States v. United States Dist. Court, 334 U.S. 258 (1948), and where a district judge displayed a persistent disregard of the Rules of Civil Procedure promulgated by this Court, La Buy v. Howes Leather Co., 352 U.S. 249 (1957) * * *. And the party seeking mandamus has "the burden of showing that its right to issuance of the writ is 'clear and indisputable.'" Bankers Life & Cas. Co. v. Holland, 346 U.S. 379, 384 (1953). * * *

4. It is likewise unnecessary for us to reach the question whether the writ in the circumstances of this case may be said to issue in aid of an exercise of the Court of Appeals' appellate jurisdiction. See 28 U.S.C. § 1651; Roche v. Evaporated Milk Assn., 319 U.S. 21, 25 (1943). * * * In our view, even assuming that the possible future appeal in this case would support the Court of Appeals' mandamus jurisdiction, it was an abuse of discretion for the court to act as it did in the circumstances of this case.

We also approach this case with an awareness of additional considerations which flow from the fact that the underlying proceeding is a criminal prosecution. All our jurisprudence is strongly colored by the notion that appellate review should be postponed, except in certain narrowly defined circumstances, until after final judgment has been rendered by the trial court. * * * This general policy against piecemeal appeals takes on added weight in criminal cases, where the defendant is entitled to a speedy resolution of the charges against him. * * * Nor is the case against permitting the writ to be used as a substitute for interlocutory appeal "made less compelling * * * by the fact that the Government has no later right to appeal." DiBella v. United States, 369 U.S. 121, 130 (1962).[5] This is not to say that mandamus may never be used to review procedural orders in criminal cases. It has been invoked successfully where the action of the trial court totally deprived the Government of its right to initiate a prosecution, Ex parte United States, 287 U.S. 241 (1932), and where the court overreached its judicial power to deny the Government the rightful fruits of a valid conviction, Ex parte United States, 242 U.S. 27 (1916). But this Court has never approved the use of the writ to review an interlocutory procedural order in a criminal case which did not have the effect of a dismissal. We need not decide under what circumstances, if any, such a use of mandamus would be appropriate. It is enough to note that we approach the decision in this case with an awareness of the constitutional precepts that a man is entitled to a speedy trial and that he may not be placed twice in jeopardy for the same offense.

In light of these considerations and criteria, neither the record before us nor the cryptic order of the Court of Appeals justifies the invocation of the extraordinary writ in this case.

We do not understand the Government to argue that petitioner was in any sense without "jurisdiction" to order it to file a bill of particulars.[6] Suffice it to note that Rule 7(f) of the Federal Rules of Criminal Procedure specifically empowers the trial court to "direct the filing of a bill of particulars," and that federal trial courts have always had very broad discretion in ruling upon requests for such bills * * *.

The Government seeks instead to justify the employment of the writ in this instance on the ground that petitioner's conduct displays a "pattern of manifest noncompliance with the rules governing federal criminal trials." It argues that the federal rules place settled limitations upon pretrial discovery in criminal cases, and that a trial court may not, in the absence

---

5. Thus it is irrelevant, and we do not decide, whether the Government could appeal in the event petitioner dismissed the Horwitz indictments because of its refusal to comply with his bill of particulars order.

* * *

[Ed.] Would a dismissal of the indictments be appealable today? See p. 1798, supra.

6. Nor do we understand the Government to argue that a judge has no "power" to enter an erroneous order. Acceptance of this semantic fallacy would undermine the settled limitations upon the power of an appellate court to review interlocutory orders. Neither "jurisdiction" nor "pow-

er" can be said to "run the gauntlet of reversible errors." Bankers Life & Cas. Co. v. Holland, 346 U.S. 379, 382 (1953). Courts faced with petitions for the peremptory writs must be careful lest they suffer themselves to be misled by labels such as "abuse of discretion" and "want of power" into interlocutory review of nonappealable orders on the mere ground that they may be erroneous. "Certainly Congress knew that some interlocutory orders might be erroneous when it chose to make them nonreviewable." De Beers Consol. Mines, Ltd. v. United States, 325 U.S. 212, 223, 225 (1945) (dissenting opinion of Justice Douglas).

of compelling justification, order the Government to produce a list of its witnesses in advance of trial. It argues further that in only one category of cases, *i.e.*, prosecutions for treason and other capital offenses, is the Government required to turn over to the defense such a list of its witnesses. A general policy of requiring such disclosure without a particularized showing of need would, it is contended, offend the informant's privilege. Petitioner, according to the Government, adopted "a uniform rule in his courtroom requiring the government in a criminal case to furnish the defense, on motion for a bill of particulars, a list of potential witnesses." The Government concludes that since petitioner obviously had no power to adopt such a rule, mandamus will lie under this Court's decision in La Buy v. Howes Leather Co., 352 U.S. 249 (1957), to correct this studied disregard of the limitations placed upon the district courts by the federal rules.[10]

The action of the Court of Appeals cannot, on the record before us, bear the weight of this justification. There is absolutely no foundation in this record for the Government's assertions concerning petitioner's practice. The legal proposition that mandamus will lie in appropriate cases to correct willful disobedience of the rules laid down by this Court is not controverted. But the position of the Government rests on two central factual premises: (1) that petitioner in effect ordered it to produce a list of witnesses in advance of trial; and (2) that petitioner took this action pursuant to a deliberately adopted policy in disregard of the rules of criminal procedure. Neither of these premises finds support in the record.

* * *

Even more important in our view, however, than these deficiencies in the record is the failure of the Court of Appeals to attempt to supply any reasoned justification of its action. * * * There is no evidence in this record concerning petitioner's practice in other cases, aside from his own remark that the Government was generally dissatisfied with it, and his statements do not reveal any intent to evade or disregard the rules. We do not know what he ordered the Government to reveal under what circumstances in other cases. This state of the record renders the silence of the Court of Appeals all the more critical. We recognized in La Buy that the familiarity of a court of appeals with the practice of the individual district courts within its circuit was relevant to an assessment of the need for mandamus as a corrective measure. See 352 U.S., at 258. But without an opinion from the Court of Appeals we do not know what role, if any, this factor played in the decision below. In fact, we are in the dark with respect to the position of the Court of Appeals on all the issues crucial to an informed exercise of our power of review. * * * We cannot properly identify the questions for decision in the case before us without illumination of this unclear record by the measured and exposed reflection of the Court of Appeals. * * *

Mandamus is not a punitive remedy. The entire thrust of the Government's justification for mandamus in this case, moreover, is that the writ

---

10. We note in passing that La Buy and the other decisions of this Court approving the use of mandamus as a means of policing compliance with the procedural rules were civil cases. * * * We have pointed out that the fact this case involves a criminal prosecution has contextual relevance. In view of our reading of the record, how-ever, we need not venture an abstract pronouncement on the question whether this fact imposes a more stringent standard for the invocation of mandamus by the Government where the allegation is that a district judge has deviated from the federal rules.

serves a vital corrective and didactic function. While these aims lay at the core of this Court's decisions in La Buy and Schlagenhauf v. Holder, 379 U.S. 104 (1964), we fail to see how they can be served here without findings of fact by the issuing court and some statement of the court's legal reasoning. A mandamus from the blue without rationale is tantamount to an abdication of the very expository and supervisory functions of an appellate court upon which the Government rests its attempt to justify the action below.

* * * What might be the proper decision upon a more complete record, supplemented by the findings and conclusions of the Court of Appeals, we cannot and do not say. Hence the writ is vacated and the cause is remanded to the Court of Appeals for the Seventh Circuit for further proceedings not inconsistent with this opinion. It is so ordered.

Writ vacated and cause remanded.

MR. JUSTICE BLACK, concurring.

I concur in the Court's judgment to vacate and agree substantially with its opinion, but would like to add a few words, which I do not understand to be in conflict with what the Court says, concerning the writ of mandamus. I agree that mandamus is an extraordinary remedy which should not be issued except in extraordinary circumstances. And I also realize that sometimes the granting of mandamus may bring about the review of a case as would an appeal. Yet this does not deprive a court of its power to issue the writ. Where there are extraordinary circumstances, mandamus may be used to review an interlocutory order which is by no means "final" and thus appealable under federal statutes. Finality, then, while relevant to the right of appeal, is not determinative of the question when to issue mandamus. Rather than hinging on this abstruse and infinitely uncertain term, the issuance of the writ of mandamus is proper where a court finds exceptional circumstances to support such an order. In the present case it is conceivable that there are valid reasons why the Government should not be forced to turn over the requested names and that compliance with the order would inflict irreparable damage on its conduct of the case. The trouble here, as I see it, is that neither of the courts below gave proper consideration to the possible existence of exceptional facts which might justify the Government's refusal to disclose the names. Having no doubt as to the appropriateness of mandamus, if the circumstances exist to justify it, I would vacate the judgment below and remand the case to the Court of Appeals for further deliberation on whether there are special circumstances calling for the issuance of mandamus.

NOTE ON THE EXTRAORDINARY WRITS IN THE COURTS OF APPEALS

(1) The Court in Will relied on its 1943 decision in Roche v. Evaporated Milk Ass'n, 319 U.S. 21 (1943), in which it reversed a lower court's use of mandamus to review a decision of a pretrial motion in a criminal case. Since Roche, there has been a good deal of oscillation in the Supreme Court's approach to the availability of mandamus under the All Writs Act, now embodied in 28 U.S.C. § 1651. In recent years, however, the trend has

been in the direction of greater restraint,[1] although the standard is still far from clear, and the Court may take a close look at the merits in the course of holding mandamus unavailable.[2]

A particularly interesting case is Will v. Calvert Fire Ins. Co., 437 U.S. 655 (1978), p. 1448, *supra*, in which the Court reversed an appellate court's grant of mandamus to compel the district court to adjudicate a claim pending between the same parties in a state court. A plurality opinion for four Justices said that mandamus did not lie because the district court had neither exceeded the bounds of its jurisdiction nor refused to exercise its authority when it had a duty to do so. The district court's decision to defer to the state court was essentially a discretionary one, and the opinion strongly suggested that even an abuse of discretion was not subject to review on mandamus: "Although in at least one instance we approved the issuance of the writ upon a *mere* showing of abuse of discretion, LaBuy v. Howes Leather Co., 352 U.S. 249, 257 (1957), we warned soon thereafter against the dangers of such a practice" (p. 665 n. 7) (emphasis added).

Justice Blackmun, in a brief opinion concurring only in the judgment, said that the court below should have remanded for reconsideration in the light of Colorado River, p. 1438, *supra*, decided after the district court's action. With respect to the appropriateness of mandamus, he said only that its issuance had been "premature" (p. 668). (How could the court of appeals have required the district court to do anything without granting the petition in some form?) Four dissenters argued that the issuance of mandamus was appropriate "[w]hether evaluated under the 'clear abuse of discretion' standard set forth [in LaBuy] or under the prong of [Will v. United States] that permits the use of mandamus 'to compel [an inferior court] to exercise its authority when it is its duty to do so' " (p. 676).

The nature of Justice Blackmun's swing vote in this case has not only complicated the problem of determining the applicable standard for the availability of mandamus; it also caused difficulties for the lower courts in Calvert itself in deciding what the significance of the Supreme Court's remand was. See p. 1449, note 4, *supra*.

(2) During this period of retrenchment, however, the Supreme Court did hold, in Thermtron Products, Inc. v. Hermansdorfer, 423 U.S. 336 (1976), that mandamus was available to review a district court remand order, despite the prohibitory language of 28 U.S.C. § 1447(d), because the order was not issued under § 1447(c), *i.e.,* the district court had not relied on the ground that the case had been removed "improvidently and without jurisdiction". Only cases remanded under § 1447(c), the Court held, were unreviewable under § 1447(d), and this was not such a case since the district court had in effect conceded that the case had been properly removed.

1. See, *e.g.,* Kerr v. United States Dist. Court, 426 U.S. 394 (1976) (mandamus unavailable to review district court order compelling the government to disclose documents); Helstoski v. Meanor, 442 U.S. 500, 506 (1979) (mandamus unavailable to obtain pretrial review of denial of claim of immunity from criminal prosecution; though no timely appeal had been taken, denial was appealable under § 1291); Allied Chemical Corp. v. Daiflon, Inc., 449 U.S. 33, 35 (1980) (per curiam reversal of grant of mandamus to review new trial order; "[o]nly exceptional circumstances, amounting to a judicial usurpation of power, will justify invocation of this extraordinary remedy").

2. See, *e.g.,* Kerr v. United States, note 1, *supra.* For an example at the court of appeals level, see Kaufman v. Edelstein, 539 F.2d 811, 816–22 (2d Cir.1976).

Justice Rehnquist, speaking for himself and two other Justices, dissented. He disagreed with the majority's view of the legislative history of the relevant statutory provisions, urged that the plain language of § 1447(d) precluded the result, and asked what would now happen if a remanding court used "the rubric of § 1447(c), but the papers plainly demonstrate such a conclusion to be absurd? * * * If the Court's grant of certiorari and order of reversal in this case are to have any meaning, it would seem that such avenues of attack should clearly be open. * * * Yet it is equally clear that such devices would soon render meaningless Congress' express, and heretofore fully effective, directive prohibiting such tactics because of their potential for abuse by those seeking only to delay" (p. 357).

If you were a legislator determined to avoid the delays inherent in review of remand orders, and thus to prohibit *all* such review, how would you write the statutory provision? Could you have drafted clearer language than that contained in § 1447(d)? Did the majority in Thermtron imply that some errors of law are so egregious that prohibitions on review will simply be ignored? Is there any justification for such action?

Whether Thermtron was correct or not, its scope has been severely confined by the brief per curiam decision in Gravitt v. Southwestern Bell Tel. Co., 430 U.S. 723 (1977). In reversing an appellate court's grant of mandamus to review a district court's remand order, the Supreme Court made it clear that, whether right or wrong, a remand order was not reviewable so long as it purported to rest on a ground within the scope of § 1447(c).[3]

(3) Whatever the precise standard for the availability of mandamus— whether phrased in terms of "jurisdiction," "excess of power," or "clear abuse of discretion"—the cases in the courts of appeals continue to indicate that an order to show cause will issue, and mandamus or its equivalent will be granted, when the court is satisfied that sound judicial administration so requires and when no other adequate remedy exists.[4] There are variations in approach among and even within circuits, of course, and there is an ungrudging recognition of the congressional policy favoring review only after final decision. But that policy has, after all, been considerably diluted by judicial decision, by rule, and by statutory exception. Indeed, it is not too difficult to imagine a party in a civil case who wants to bring an issue up for review seeking a certification from the trial judge under Rule 54(b) or § 1292(b) in the alternative, and failing in that, arguing to the

---

3. But *cf.* Sheet Metal Workers' Intern. Ass'n v. Carter, 450 U.S. 949 (1981) (Rehnquist, J., dissenting from denial of certiorari).

4. See, *e.g.*, Evans v. Buchanan, 582 F.2d 750 (3d Cir.1978) (mandamus lies to require further proceedings to evaluate a taxation scheme adopted by the petitioning state in response to an earlier district court order); In re Attorney General, 596 F.2d 58 (2d Cir.1979) (mandamus lies to review order holding Attorney General in civil contempt); Halkin v. Helms, 598 F.2d 1 (D.C.Cir.1978) (mandamus lies to review order prohibiting plaintiffs from public discussion of material obtained through discovery); Central Microfilm Service Corp. v. Basic/Four Corp., 688 F.2d 1206 (8th Cir.

1982) (mandamus lies to review second new trial order that was erroneous as a matter of law); In re American Cable Publications, Inc., 768 F.2d 1194 (10th Cir.1985) (mandamus lies to review order disqualifying plaintiff's law partner from representing him).

In Firestone Tire & Rubber Co. v. Risjord, 449 U.S. 368, 379 n. 13 (1981), p. 1800, *supra,* the Court, while holding not final an order refusing to disqualify counsel, said that "in the exceptional circumstances for which it was designed, a writ of mandamus from the court of appeals might be available." Would mandamus ever be available to review an order denying class action certification—an order that is similarly not final for purposes of appeal under § 1291?

court of appeals that (a) the decision below is final under § 1291; (b) if not, it is appealable under § 1292(a)(1); and (c) if not, mandamus should issue. (See p. 1806 n. 1, *supra,* for reference to proposed legislation designed to simplify the task of lawyers and judges in such a case.)

(4) What is the meaning of the limitation in the All Writs Act to writs necessary or appropriate "in aid of [the courts'] respective jurisdictions"? (See footnote 4 of the Court's opinion in the Will case.) The phrase has not been construed to mean that the case must then be pending in the court issuing the writ. Is it enough that the case is one that may at some future time come within the court's appellate jurisdiction? If the issue would not come before the appellate court in the ordinary course of review of a final judgment, either because it would then be moot or because any error would likely be held harmless at that stage, how can the granting of mandamus aid the court in the exercise of appellate jurisdiction? If the issue would come up in ordinary course after final judgment, how can the use of mandamus simply to advance appellate consideration be defended? Is the strongest case for the exercise of mandamus one in which the trial judge has acted or failed to act in a way that would prevent the controversy from being adjudicated and thus would defeat appellate review, *e.g.,* a refusal to render a ruling or to allow the case to proceed? [5]

For discussion of similar issues as they affect the power of the Supreme Court, see Ex parte Peru, 318 U.S. 578 (1943), and the following Note, p. 347, *supra.*

(5) Two trial court actions as to which mandamus is most frequently sought are denials of jury trial claims and grants or denials of requested transfers of venue. With respect to transfer, Supreme Court decisions indicate that the writ is available to review certain errors of law by the district court,[6] but there is less guidance on the availability of the writ to review the exercise of discretion.[7] With respect to a claim of the right to a jury trial, the Court has said: "Whatever differences of opinion there may be in other types of cases, we think the right to grant mandamus to require jury trial where it has been improperly denied is settled." Beacon Theatres, Inc. v. Westover, 359 U.S. 500, 511 (1959). Has it been settled correctly?

(6) When mandamus is used not as a remedy against a judge for wrongful conduct but simply as a means of reviewing the merits of his

---

5. See generally FTC v. Dean Foods Co., 384 U.S. 597, 603–04 (1966). See also United States v. Christian, 660 F.2d 892 (3d Cir. 1981), in which the court entertained a petition for mandamus to require a district court to summon a grand jury to investigate possible violations of the antitrust laws. After reviewing a number of decisions, the court concluded that "where a district court, by action not committed to its discretion, prevents a nascent controversy from being adjudicated and thereby defeats appellate review, the subject matter of the court's action is within the 'jurisdiction' of the appellate court for purposes of the All Writs Act" (p. 896).

6. See Hoffman v. Blaski, 363 U.S. 335, 340 n. 9 (1960); Van Dusen v. Barrack, 376

U.S. 612, 615 n. 3 (1964). The discussion in these opinions is less than fully enlightening, but they appear to support use of the writ at least when transfer has been ordered to a district that is not one where the action "might have been been brought."

7. The variation among the lower courts is fully set forth in 15 Wright, Miller & Cooper, Federal Practice and Procedure, § 3855 (1986). For a particularly helpful discussion, see A. Olinick & Sons v. Dempster Bros., 365 F.2d 439, 445–48 (2d Cir.1966) (concurring opinion). See also pp. 1742–43, *supra.*

decision on an issue of law, it seems inappropriate for the judge to appear in the reviewing court as a litigant. And the problem is aggravated if after working with a party to have his ruling upheld on review, the judge returns to his role as adjudicator when the case goes forward in the district court. For an imaginative and controversial effort to deal with this problem, see Rapp v. Van Dusen, 350 F.2d 806, 812–13 (3d Cir.1965). Rule 21 of the Federal Rules of Appellate Procedure, promulgated after the Rapp decision, provides that in an application for prohibition or mandamus, all parties other than the petitioner shall be considered respondents, along with the named judge or judges. It further provides that the judge may, if he wishes, choose not to appear in the proceeding, and such a choice shall not be taken as an admission of the allegations of the petition.[8]

(7) Mandamus and its fraternal twin, prohibition, are not the only writs falling within the scope of the All Writs Act. See, *e.g.,* Kanatser v. Chrysler Corp., 199 F.2d 610 (10th Cir.1952) (granting a common law writ of certiorari to review the district court's award of a new trial, more than six months after the entry of judgment, on a ground not asserted in a timely new trial motion); FTC v. Dean Foods Co., 384 U.S. 597 (1966) (holding, 5–4, that a court of appeals may exercise its authority under the All Writs Act to enjoin a corporate merger pending adjudication of the lawfulness of the proposed merger before the Federal Trade Commission).

(8) The quantity of applications to the courts of appeals for extraordinary writs has not been great, although like all business in the federal courts, it has been growing. In fiscal 1970, of 11,662 cases filed in the courts of appeals, only 241 were original proceedings. Annual Report of the Director of the Administrative Office of the U.S. Courts 1970, Table B–1. Sixteen years later, the figure had grown to 703 of 34,292 cases docketed in the courts of appeals. Annual Report 1986, Table B–1. (Over 95% of these original proceedings are applications for mandamus, and most of the remainder are applications for prohibition. See letter from J.A. McCafferty, Administrative Office, to David Shapiro (August 26, 1982).)

(9) For valuable discussion of the availability of mandamus and other writs in the courts of appeals, see generally 16 Wright, Miller, Cooper & Gressman, Federal Practice and Procedure §§ 3932–3936 (1977); 9 Moore, Federal Practice ¶ 110.28 (2d ed. 1985); Note, *Mandamus as a Means of Federal Interlocutory Review,* 38 Ohio St.L.J. 301 (1977); Kitch, *Section 1404(a) of the Judicial Code: In the Interest of Justice or Injustice?,* 40 Ind. L.J. 99, 110–31 (1964).

---

8. The local rules of several courts of appeals now provide that a petition for mandamus or prohibition shall not bear the name of the district judge and that, unless otherwise ordered, the judge shall be represented pro forma by counsel opposing the requested relief. *E.g.,* § 21 of the Rules of the Second Circuit.

SECTION 2.   REVIEW OF FEDERAL DECISIONS BY THE SUPREME COURT

SUBSECTION A: OBLIGATORY REVIEW

CALIFORNIA v. GRACE BRETHREN CHURCH

457 U.S. 393, 102 S.Ct. 2498, 73 L.Ed.2d 93 (1982).
Appeal from the United States District Court for the
Central District of California.

[The Federal Unemployment Tax Act (FUTA) established a cooperative federal-state scheme to provide benefits to unemployed workers. The Act required employers to pay an excise tax on wages paid to employees in "covered" employment, but entitled them to a credit on the federal tax for contributions paid into federally approved state unemployment compensation programs. The Act, in 26 U.S.C. § 3309(b), exempted from mandatory state coverage employees of, *inter alia,* "an organization which is operated primarily for religious purposes and which is operated, supervised, controlled, or principally supported by a church or convention or association of churches." A number of California churches and religious schools, including religious schools unaffiliated with any church, brought suit in Federal District Court to enjoin the Secretary of Labor from conditioning his approval of the California unemployment insurance program on its coverage of plaintiffs' employees, and to enjoin the State from collecting both tax information and the state unemployment compensation tax. The District Court conducted various proceedings and issued several opinions and orders extending over almost a year and a half. Concluding that the benefit entitlement decisions for employees of the religious schools unaffiliated with churches (described in the opinion as Category III schools) risked excessive entanglement with religion in violation of the Establishment Clause of the First Amendment, the court permanently enjoined the state defendants from collecting unemployment taxes from such schools. It did not issue an injunction against the federal defendants as to those schools, however, because it had no information as to what response the Secretary of Labor would make to the court's conclusion that the state defendants could not constitutionally impose state unemployment taxes on the employees of such schools. The court said that if the Secretary instituted decertification proceedings against California for failing to collect the taxes on behalf of such employees, the parties could apply to the court for further relief.]*

JUSTICE O'CONNOR delivered the opinion of the Court.

* * * *

An initial matter requiring our attention is whether this Court has jurisdiction to hear these appeals. * * *

* [Ed.] This summary is taken from the
Syllabus prepared by the Reporter of decisions.

The only possible doubt regarding our appellate jurisdiction under this provision is the requirement that the District Court hold "an Act of Congress unconstitutional."

In McLucas v. DeChamplain, 421 U.S. 21 (1975), we stated that § 1252 was an unambiguous exception to the policy of minimizing the mandatory docket of this Court. Indeed, the "language of the statute sufficiently demonstrates its purpose: to afford immediate review in this Court in civil actions to which the United States or its officers are parties and thus will be bound by a holding of unconstitutionality." *Id.*, at 31. Moreover, this Court has appellate jurisdiction under § 1252 "when the ruling of unconstitutionality is made in the application of the statute to a particular circumstance, * * * rather than upon the challenged statute as a whole." Fleming v. Rhodes, 331 U.S. 100, 102–103 (1947) (discussing the predecessor to § 1252, Act of Aug. 24, 1937, 50 Stat. 751). Finally, § 1252 provides jurisdiction even though the lower court did not expressly declare a federal statute unconstitutional, so long as a determination that a statutory provision was unconstitutional "was a necessary predicate to the relief" that the lower court granted. United States v. Clark, 445 U.S. 23, 26 n. 2 (1980).[16]

In the present case, the District Court did not expressly hold § 3309(b) of FUTA unconstitutional as applied to the Category III appellees, but the effect of its several opinions and orders was to make "the United States or its officers * * * bound by a holding of unconstitutionality." McLucas v. DeChamplain, *supra*, at 31. For example, while discussing the Establishment Clause claim of the Category III schools, the District Court held:

> "Since such entanglement [involving the resolution of questions of faith and doctrine by secular tribunals] is inevitable during the benefit eligibility determination process if religious schools are brought within the scope of the unemployment compensation tax *scheme,* constitutional considerations bar the *application of the scheme* to them." (Emphasis added).

Examination of other portions of the court's opinion makes clear that the court's use of the word "scheme" refers to the combined federal and state provisions. * * * Moreover, the District Court's analysis leading to its order holding the California provision unconstitutional is based solely on its understanding of the operation and effect of FUTA, which of course prompted the passage of the corresponding state statute in the first place.[18] * * * Finally, in its Second Supplemental Opinion, the court made clear

---

16. In Clark, the Court of Claims simply ordered relief based on its earlier decision in another case. In that earlier decision, the court had declared the challenged statutory provision unconstitutional. See Gentry v. United States, 212 Ct.Cl. 1, 546 F.2d 343 (1976), rehearing denied, 212 Ct. Cl. 27, 551 F.2d 852 (1977).

18. The court's analysis of Category I and II schools also demonstrates that it believed FUTA, as applied to Category III schools, to be unconstitutional. In its discussion of Category I and II schools, the court held that if it were to follow the Secretary's interpretation of § 3309, *i.e.,* if *no* exemption existed, then FUTA would be

unconstitutional as applied to those schools in part because of the excessive governmental entanglement in the benefit eligibility hearing. Since the court also found an entanglement problem with respect to benefit eligibility hearings for Category III schools, and since there is no statutory exemption for those schools, it follows that the District Court must have believed that FUTA was unconstitutional as applied to the Category III plaintiffs.

[Ed.] Categories I and II embraced schools affiliated with churches. No appeal was taken from the district court's holding with respect to them.

that if the Secretary "institutes decertification proceedings against the State of California" for failing to collect unemployment compensation taxes on behalf of Category III employees, "the parties may apply to this Court for further relief," which can only mean injunctive relief against the Secretary. Under these circumstances, it is clear that the Secretary is "bound by a holding of unconstitutionality," and that this Court has jurisdiction under § 1252 to hear this appeal.

* * * [The Court went on to hold, 7–2, that 28 U.S.C. § 1341, the Tax Injunction Act, deprived the district court of jurisdiction to grant injunctive or declaratory relief. See p. 1342, *supra*.]

NOTE ON APPEALS TO THE SUPREME COURT FROM THE LOWER FEDERAL COURTS

(1) As a result of the significant reduction in the federal cases reviewable as of right in the Supreme Court, see pp. 1797–98, *supra,* the principal provisions for such appeals that remain on the books are 28 U.S.C. §§ 1252 (decisions invalidating acts of Congress), 1253 (decisions of three-judge courts, which are now required only in limited cases, see p. 1334, *supra*), and 1254(2) (decisions holding state statutes invalid).[1] There have been continuing efforts to repeal these provisions as well. See p. 45, *supra;* Gressman, *Requiem for the Supreme Court's Obligatory Jurisdiction,* 65 A.B.A.J. 1325 (1979); Letter signed by all Supreme Court Justices, *id.* at 1328. *Cf.* Tushnet, *The Mandatory Jurisdiction of the Supreme Court— Some Recent Developments,* 46 U.Cin.L.Rev. 347 (1977).

(2) Section 1252 applies only if "the United States, or any of its agencies, or any officer or employee thereof, as such officer or employee, is a party." Participation may occur through intervention, and 28 U.S.C. § 2403 requires that the Attorney General be notified, and permitted to intervene, in any case to which the United States is not a party and in which "the constitutionality of any Act of Congress affecting the public interest is drawn in question."

Does § 1252 authorize an appeal in a criminal case, or does "civil" modify "suit or proceeding" as well as "action"? Compare 17 Wright, Miller & Cooper, Federal Practice and Procedure § 4037, at 57–58 (1978) (allowance of appeal in criminal as well as civil cases is consistent with the history of the section), with 12 Moore's Federal Practice ¶ 411.17(3) (2d ed. 1982) (section is "sufficiently broad to include any non-criminal action, * * * [but] does not, of course, embrace a criminal proceeding").

As noted in Grace Brethren Church, an appeal may be taken under § 1252 when the statute is declared unconstitutional on its face or as applied.[2] But an appeal does not lie if the lower court's holding was directed only to the unconstitutionality of the "*method* by which [a statute]

---

1. See also 15 U.S.C. §§ 28, 29, discussed at p. 1797, *supra;* 2 U.S.C. § 437h (provision of The Federal Election Campaign Act for appeal to the Supreme Court as part of special expedited procedures in certain circumstances). The latter provision was narrowly construed in Bread Political Action Comm. v. FEC, 455 U.S. 577 (1982).

2. In his dissent in Fleming v. Rhodes, 331 U.S. 100, 109 (1947), Justice Frankfurter argued that § 1252 should not be construed in pari materia with the provisions of § 1257 governing appeals from state courts. (See Dahnke–Walker Milling Co. v. Bondurant, 257 U.S. 282 (1921), p. 711, *supra.*) "There is an important difference," he said, "between review of State

was enforced." United States v. Christian Echoes Nat. Ministry, Inc., 404 U.S. 561, 564 (1972) (district court held that plaintiff-appellee qualified for tax-exempt status and that methods used by IRS in deciding to revoke that status violated the First, and Fifth Amendments). To say the least, the line is a difficult one to draw, and may require microscopic analysis of the language of the complaint and of the lower court's opinion.

In an appeal under § 1252, the Court's jurisdiction extends to the whole case, not just to the question of unconstitutionality. See, *e.g.,* United States v. Rock Royal Co-op., Inc., 307 U.S. 533 (1939). Moreover, the Court held in McLucas v. DeChamplain, 421 U.S. 21, 32 (1975), that an appeal would lie under § 1252 even if the district court lacked jurisdiction to issue the order appealed from. See also Williams v. Zbaraz, 448 U.S. 358, 367–68 (1980).[3] Compare Weinberger v. Salfi, 422 U.S. 749, 763 n. 8 (1975) (appeal lies under § 1252 from a declaration of unconstitutionality even though it would not lie under § 1253 if the three-judge court that issued the declaration had been improperly convened).

(3) A difficult question posed by several recent cases is whether an appeal lies to the Supreme Court under § 1252 (and thus not to a court of appeals under § 1291) if the holding of invalidity is itself not challenged on the appeal. In Heckler v. Edwards, 465 U.S. 870 (1984), the government, in appealing to a court of appeals from a district court judgment, accepted the district court's holding of unconstitutionality and challenged only the remedy. The court of appeals held that it lacked jurisdiction of the appeal since the case fell within the scope of § 1252, but the Supreme Court unanimously disagreed. Recognizing that the literal language of § 1252 supported the view of the court of appeals, the Supreme Court concluded that the language was "at loggerheads" with the "natural sense" of the provision that the holding of unconstitutionality was what Congress wished the Supreme Court to review (p. 879). When that holding is not at issue on an appeal, the Court noted, the case is less likely to implicate separation of powers issues or to require speedy resolution of a restraint on the federal government's administration of the law.[4]

court decisions and decisions of the district courts. The latter are subject to review as a matter of course by the circuit courts of appeals. They are not dependent on [federal] review by grace through *certiorari,* as would be comparable State decisions except for the Dahnke–Walker doctrine."

3. In McLucas, a single judge district court had preliminarily enjoined the appellants from proceeding with a court martial of the appellee, on grounds of (1) the unconstitutionality of the article of the Uniform Code of Military Justice under which he was charged, and (2) excessive restrictions that had been placed on appellee's access to certain documents. The Supreme Court held that even if the three-judge court provisions then in force precluded such action by a single judge, the case was properly before the Court on appeal under § 1252.

In Williams, a federal district court had ruled both a state abortion statute and the federal "Hyde Amendment" unconstitutional. On appeal under § 1252, the Court held that since none of the parties had challenged the validity of the Hyde Amendment, and since the ruling on the state statute was a sufficient basis for award of all the relief sought, there was no case or controversy on the Hyde Amendment issue. Nevertheless, the Court held that it had jurisdiction over the whole case under § 1252 and went on to consider the other issues presented.

4. The Court in Heckler distinguished its own earlier opinion in INS v. Chadha, 462 U.S. 919 (1983), which had allowed an appeal under § 1252, on the ground that although the Executive Branch in that case had agreed with the holding of unconstitutionality in the court below, Congress had intervened as a party and had contested that holding on appeal.

(4) Section 1254(2) provides an appeal for a party "relying on a State statute held by a court of appeals to be invalid as repugnant to the Constitution, treaties or laws of the United States." The appeal is limited to the "Federal questions presented." (Healy v. Ratta, 292 U.S. 263 (1934), indicates, though the point was not discussed in the opinion, that this limitation does not confine review to the issue of the statute's validity; the Supreme Court reversed the judgment below because the district court lacked jurisdiction.)

Suppose the Supreme Court wanted to construe a statute in a way that would avoid the question of validity. Is the Court precluded by § 1254 from deciding on that ground? Should it be? *Cf.* United States v. CIO, 335 U.S. 106 (1948). Is there any purpose that may be ascribed to the limitation other than to exclude appeals from circuit court decisions that rest alternatively on state and federal grounds? *Cf.* Roth v. Delano, 338 U.S. 226 (1949); Williams v. Mayor, 289 U.S. 36 (1933).

Under the cases, "State statute" appears to extend to state laws of local as well as general application, Dusch v. Davis, 387 U.S. 112 (1967); to municipal ordinances, Doran v. Salem Inn, Inc., 422 U.S. 922, 927 n. 2 (1975); and to orders of state administrative bodies exercising "legislative power", see United States v. Howard, 352 U.S. 212, 215 (1957).[5]

Note that appeal under § 1254(2) "preclude[s] review by writ of certiorari" at the instance of the appellant. But a 1962 amendment to 28 U.S.C. § 2103—which permits the Court to treat improvident appeals from state courts as petitions for certiorari—extended the statute to improvident appeals from a court of appeals. The two provisions have been reconciled by a holding that the preclusion of § 1254(2) applies only when an appeal has been *properly* taken. El Paso v. Simmons, 379 U.S. 497, 501-03 (1965).

(5) A question that has arisen under both § 1252 and § 1254(2) is the extent to which those provisions apply to interlocutory decisions. In Thornburgh v. American College of Obstetricians and Gynecologists, 476 U.S. 747, 754-55 (1986), the Court held that it had no appellate jurisdiction under § 1254(2) when the court below had not rendered a final decision but had remanded the case to the district court for further consideration. (Treating the jurisdictional statement as a petition for certiorari, the Court granted the writ and went on to decide the merits. See Paragraph (4), *supra.*)

Unlike § 1254(2), § 1252 explicitly authorizes an appeal from an "interlocutory or final" judgment, decree, or order. And in the McLucas case, Paragraph (2), *supra,* the Court unanimously allowed an appeal from an order granting a preliminary injunction on the basis of the unconstitutionality of the statute under attack. The Court was sharply divided, however, in Walters v. National Ass'n of Radiation Survivors, 473 U.S. 305 (1985). In this case, the government sought to appeal under § 1252 from a

---

5. But the phrase does not extend to the provisions of a collective bargaining agreement between a local board of education and a teachers' union. Perry Education Ass'n v. Perry Local Educators' Ass'n, 460 U.S. 37 (1983).

See also Silkwood v. Kerr-McGee Corp., 464 U.S. 238 (1984). In this case the Court held that a lower federal court decision invalidating an exercise of authority under state law was not appealable under § 1254 because the lower court had acted "without reference to the state statute" (p. 247). Cases interpreting § 1257, pp. 721-23, *supra,* were relied on because of the "history of • • • close relationship" between the two provisions (p. 247 n. 9).

preliminary injunction against the enforcement of a statutory limitation on the fees payable to an attorney in proceedings before the Veterans' Administration. Although the district court had stated only that plaintiffs were highly likely to prevail on the merits, the majority decided that the case was "controlled by McLucas. It is true that in McLucas the District Court actually stated its holding that the statute was unconstitutional, whereas here the court's statements are less direct. But that is merely a semantic difference in the case; * * * any conclusions reached at the preliminary injunction stage are subject to revision * * *" (p. 317). The majority then went on to reverse on the merits, holding that the evidence in the record fell "far short of the kind which would warrant upsetting Congress' judgment" (p. 334). Justice O'Connor (joined by Justice Blackmun) concurred in the opinion and judgment, emphasizing her understanding that in reversing the preliminary injunction, the Court was ruling on the challenge to the validity of the fee limitation on its face but not on the claim that the rule was invalid as applied. "[D]irect appeal of a preliminary injunction under § 1252," she argued, "is appropriate in the rare case such as this where a district court has issued a nationwide injunction that in practical effect invalidates a federal law" (p. 336).

Justice Brennan (joined by Justice Marshall) argued in a lengthy dissent that appellate jurisdiction in the case was not authorized by § 1252 since the district court had based its preliminary injunction only on its assessment of the balance of hardship in light of the likelihood of success. Pointing to the differences in the rationale of the majority and concurring opinions, he stated his disagreement with both (p. 358): "Unlike Justice O'Connor, I do not believe that § 1252 requires this Court directly to police the injunctive process in constitutional challenges in the first instance. Unlike the opinion for the Court, I do not believe that § 1252 may be invoked in such cases to short-circuit the process of orderly and principled constitutional adjudication." [6]

In view of the McLucas decision and the language of § 1252, isn't there virtue in a bright line test allowing direct appeal to the Supreme Court of any preliminary injunction based on a determination that plaintiffs are likely to prevail on a claim of unconstitutionality? Note that since Justice Brennan was not prepared to overrule McLucas, his approach would appear to require a cautious appellant to docket appeals in such cases both in the court of appeals and in the Supreme Court.[7]

NOTE ON SUMMARY AFFIRMANCE AND ON DISMISSAL OF APPEALS FROM LOWER FEDERAL COURTS

(1) Under Sup.Ct.Rule 16, an appellee who seeks a summary disposition of an appeal on the ground of the insubstantiality of the questions presented should file a motion to dismiss if the appeal is from a state court and a motion to affirm if the appeal is from a federal court. Under Rule 16.1(d) the Court states that it "will receive a motion to dismiss or affirm

---

6. Justice Stevens, joined by Justices Brennan and Marshall, dissented on the merits.

7. The question of the standard of review of a preliminary injunction is, of course, a different one, and on this point the concurring opinion serves as a helpful gloss on the majority.

on any other ground the appellee wishes to present as a reason why the Court should not set the case for argument". Stern, Gressman & Shapiro, Supreme Court Practice § 7.12, at 419 (6th ed. 1986) read the substantially identical predecessor of this provision as indicating "that an important purpose of a motion to dismiss or affirm is the same as that of a brief in opposition to a petition for certiorari—*i.e.*, to present *all* reasons why oral argument is not justified and why the decision below should not be altered or reviewed, without limitation to jurisdictional defects or lack of substantiality of the questions".

(2) In Socialist Labor Party v. Gilligan, 406 U.S. 583 (1972), the Party, its officers and members, brought a federal court action against the Governor of Ohio and others seeking to invalidate certain election laws of the state of Ohio. A three-judge panel, convened under 28 U.S.C. § 2281, ruled in favor of the plaintiffs except with respect to a provision requiring the filing of an oath in order to obtain a position on the ballot. Both sides appealed to the Supreme Court under 28 U.S.C. § 1253, but while the appeal was pending, changes in governing state law rendered moot all the issues except the validity of the oath requirement. As to that issue, the Court held that the appeal should be dismissed because of the inadequacy of the record and the abstractness of the questions presented. Relying heavily on Rescue Army v. Municipal Court, 331 U.S. 549 (1947), p. 735, *supra*, the Court stated (p. 588): "Problems of prematurity and abstractness may well present 'insuperable obstacles' to the exercise of the Court's jurisdiction, even though that jurisdiction is technically present."

Justice Douglas was the sole dissenter. He urged (pp. 592–93, n. 3) that it was "an undue extension of Rescue Army to apply it to an appeal from a federal court which properly heard and considered a federal constitutional question."

The Rescue Army doctrine raises troublesome questions. See pp. 740–48, *supra*. But is it more, or less, defensible to apply that doctrine to an appeal from a lower federal court than to an appeal from a state court? Should the Court in the Socialist Labor Party case, instead of dismissing the appeal, have remanded to the district court with directions to dismiss the complaint? Does its failure to do so mean that the district court's decision on the merits will stand?

(3) On the differences and similarities between a summary disposition of an appeal and a denial of certiorari, see pp. 1859–63, *infra;* Chap. V, Sec. 4(B), (C) *supra,* and especially the discussion of Hicks v. Miranda and related cases at pp. 730–34. Note that the major reduction in the jurisdiction of three-judge courts makes the problem of summary disposition less significant on appeal of federal decisions than on appeal of state decisions under § 1257(2).[1]

---

1. But in recent years there have been a substantial number of summary affirmances of appeals under § 1254(2). See Hellman, *Error Correction, Lawmaking, and the Supreme Court's Exercise of Discretionary Review,* 44 U.Pitt.L.Rev. 795, 813 (1983); Letter from Arthur Hellman to David Shapiro (March 22, 1985) (reporting 24 such affirmances in the 1980–83 Terms).

NATIONAL LABOR RELATIONS BOARD v.
WHITE SWAN CO.

313 U.S. 23, 61 S.Ct. 751, 85 L.Ed. 1165 (1941).
Certificate from the Circuit Court of Appeals for the Fourth Circuit.

MR. JUSTICE DOUGLAS delivered the opinion of the Court.

A certificate from the Circuit Court of Appeals for the Fourth Circuit submitted pursuant to § 239 of the Judicial Code [now 28 U.S.C. § 1254(3)] is as follows:

This is a petition for enforcement of an order of the National Labor Relations Board, which directed the White Swan Company, a corporation of Wheeling, West Virginia, engaged in the operation of a laundry and dry cleaning business, to cease and desist from certain unfair labor practices and to offer employment with back pay to certain employees held to have been discharged because of union affiliation and activities. The findings of the Board with respect to the unfair labor practices and discriminatory discharge of employees are sustained by substantial evidence; but a question has arisen, as to which the members of the Court are divided and in doubt, with respect to the jurisdiction of the Board in the premises.

The respondent, White Swan Company, operates a combined laundry and dry cleaning establishment in the city of Wheeling, West Virginia. While certain of its supplies are obtained from without the state, the volume of the interstate business thus involved is not sufficient, in our opinion, to bring the business within the jurisdiction of the Board. The record shows that these supplies consist of soap, bluing, bleach, solvent, coal, water, paper, tape and padding, and that respondent's purchases thereof during 1938 amounted to $38,333.15, of which $10,810.90 came from without the state. Respondent, however, operates delivery trucks in Ohio as well as in West Virginia, three of the delivery routes from its plant being in Ohio and eleven in West Virginia. The business involved is necessarily of a purely local character, as the record shows that a radius of fifteen miles is the practical limit for a laundry or dry-cleaning business in this territory. The fact that business is done in Ohio outside the state in which respondent's laundry is located, results from the fact that this purely local business is located in a city on a state line. Respondent transports garments in its trucks from those of its customers who reside in Ohio to its plant in West Virginia to be serviced, and then after servicing returns the garments in its trucks to the customers. Approximately 12.93 per cent of its gross income for 1938 was derived from this source. In addition thereto, approximately 5 per cent of its gross income during 1938 was derived from the servicing of garments which persons not in its employment collected in Ohio, brought to its plant for servicing and delivered in Ohio after they had been serviced. Respondent's total gross income in 1938 was $128,752.96. The total income from the business obtained from persons in Ohio during this period was $28,088.43.

We recognize that the collection and delivery of garments across state lines, as above described, constitutes interstate commerce. We are advertent, however, to the admonition of the court that in applying the act we are to bear in mind "the distinction between what is national and what is local in the activities of commerce." National Labor Relations Board v. Jones & Laughlin Steel Corp. (301 U.S. 1, 30). And although the letter of the National Labor Relations Act may cover such collections and deliveries in interstate commerce as are here involved, the question arises whether a proper interpretation of the Act, in view of the intent of Congress, would include them. We are divided and in doubt as to whether such collection and delivery, which results from the fact that business of a local character, such as a laundry, is located on a state line, is sufficient to bring such business within the jurisdiction of the Board under the National Labor Relations Act. To so hold would be to bring under the jurisdiction of the Board a great variety of businesses of purely local character simply because they maintain a delivery service in cities located on state lines. As there are many such cities in the United States, the question seems to us one of sufficient importance to justify us in certifying it to the Supreme Court so that it may be definitely settled.

Being divided and in doubt, therefore, this Court respectfully certifies to the Supreme Court of the United States, for its instruction and advice, the following questions of law, the determination of which is indispensable to a proper decision of the case.

1. Should the National Labor Relations Act be interpreted as having application to a business of purely local character, such as a laundry, merely because such business is located in a city on a state line and derives a substantial portion of its income from business which involves collections or deliveries of articles in a state other than that in which the business is located?

2. Where a local business, such as a laundry, is located in a city on a state line, and is not engaged in interstate commerce, except in so far as it may collect articles to be serviced and may make deliveries to customers living across the state line, is such business, by reason of such collections and deliveries, deemed engaged in "commerce" within the meaning of Subsection 6 of Section 2 of the Act of July 5, 1935, ch. 372, 29 U.S.C.A. § 152(6), so that an unfair labor practice on its part would be an unfair labor practice "affecting commerce" within the meaning of Subsection 7 of said section, 29 U.S.C.A. § 152(7), and Subsection (a) of Section 10, 29 U.S.C.A. § 160(a)? [1]

The certificate must be dismissed.

* * *

The questions do not focus "the controversy in its setting." Lowden v. Northwestern National Bank & Trust Co., 298 U.S. 160, 163. From the certificate we do not know on what grounds the Board based its jurisdiction—that the business was "in commerce" or that it was embraced within the other categories described in § 2(7) of the Act. The terms "business of purely local character" and "local business" are meaningful for purposes of § 10(a) of the Act only in light of specific findings of the Board. To answer the questions we would have to make a supposition as to the sense in which the Board made its finding under § 10(a) that the unfair labor practices were "affecting commerce". The necessity of making that supposition reveals the hypothetical and abstract quality of the questions. And the fact that on the whole record the answer might be clear whichever the theory of the Board's findings does not make the questions any the less defective. The reviewing court is passing on the validity of a specific order

1. The court denied a motion made by the Solicitor General to amend the certificate by embodying the purchase of supplies in interstate commerce as well as the collections and deliveries.

of the Board. Since the questions certified do not reflect the precise conclusions of the Board and the precise findings on which those conclusions were based, they necessarily have an "objectionable generality". See United States v. Mayer, 235 U.S. 55, 66 * * *. And if, in this case, they did reflect those conclusions and findings, they would be defective as calling for a "decision of the whole case". News Syndicate Co. v. New York Central Railroad Co., 275 U.S. 179, 188.

Dismissed.

WISNIEWSKI v. UNITED STATES
353 U.S. 901, 77 S.Ct. 633, 1 L.Ed.2d 658 (1957).
On Certificate from the United States Court of Appeals for the Eighth Circuit.

PER CURIAM.

Defendant was convicted of violation of 26 C.F.R. § 175.121, a Regulation promulgated by the Secretary of the Treasury under the authority of § 2871 of the Internal Revenue Code of 1939, 26 U.S.C. § 2871, and providing that:

"No liquor bottle shall be reused for the packaging of distilled spirits for sale, except as provided in § 175.63 [exceptions not here relevant], nor shall the original contents, or any portion of such original contents, remaining in a liquor bottle be increased by the addition of any substance."

The Court of Appeals for the Eighth Circuit has certified to this Court the following question: "Does the phrase 'any substance' as employed in 26 C.F.R., Section 175.121, 1952 Cumulative Pocket Supplement, include tax paid distilled spirits?"

It appears that the question certified by the Court of Appeals was decided by another panel of that court less than a year and a half before the present certification, on reviewing the dismissal of the indictment in this very case. United States v. Goldberg, 8 Cir., 225 F.2d 180. Because of the volume of business, all but two Circuits have more than three Circuit Judges. This undoubtedly raises problems when one panel has doubts about a previous decision by another panel of the same court. Whatever procedure a Court of Appeals follows to resolve these problems—and desirable judicial administration commends consistency at least in the more or less contemporaneous decisions of different panels of a Court of Appeals—doubt about the respect to be accorded to a previous decision of a different panel should not be the occasion for invoking so exceptional a jurisdiction of this Court as that on certification. It is primarily the task of a Court of Appeals to reconcile its internal difficulties. See In re Burwell, 350 U.S. 521; Western Pacific R. Corp. v. Western Pacific R. Co., 345 U.S. 247. It is also the task of a Court of Appeals to decide all properly presented cases coming before it, except in the rare instances, as for example the pendency of another case before this Court raising the same issue, when certification may be advisable in the proper administration and expedition of judicial business.

The certificate must be dismissed.

NOTE ON CERTIFICATION

(1) Sup.Ct.Rule 24.1 provides: "When a federal court of appeals or the Court of Claims shall certify to this Court a question or proposition of law * * * the certificate shall contain a statement of the nature of the cause and the facts on which such question or proposition of law arises. Questions of fact cannot be certified. Only questions or propositions of law may be certified, and they must be distinct and definite."

Rule 24.2 provides that "When a question is certified by a federal court of appeals, and if it appears that there is special reason therefor, this Court, on application or on its own motion, may consider and decide the entire matter in controversy".

In a case like White Swan, in which the certifying court was the first judicial tribunal to review the action of an administrative agency, would any constitutional problem be presented if the Supreme Court chose to decide the "entire matter in controversy" (28 U.S.C. § 1254(3)) at the certification stage? See Stern, Gressman & Shapiro, Supreme Court Practice 43–44 (6th ed. 1986); *cf.* Wheeler Lumber Bridge & Supply Co. v. United States, 281 U.S. 572, 576 (1930) (stating, in dictum, that determination of the entire case on certification from the Court of Claims "would be an [unconstitutional] exercise of original jurisdiction by this Court"). But *cf.* United States v. Jones, 119 U.S. 477 (1886) (holding, without discussing any question of original vs. appellate jurisdiction, that an appeal lay from the Court of Claims to the Supreme Court at a time when the Court of Claims was not an Article III court). Would a similar problem be presented by the disposition of a single issue in White Swan? See Old Colony Trust Co. v. Commissioner, 279 U.S. 716, 728–29 (1929).

(2) In News Syndicate Co. v. New York Cent. R.R., 275 U.S. 179, 188 (1927), the Court answered three certified questions, but with respect to the fourth—"Did the District Court err in sustaining the demurrer to the said petition?"—it declined to answer on the ground that "The inquiry calls for decision of the whole case. It is not specific or confined to any distinct question or proposition of law and therefore need not be answered." Yet it is not a difficulty that the answer to a "distinct and definite" question of law may be dispositive. United States v. Mayer, 235 U.S. 55, 66 (1914); Wheeler Lumber, Bridge & Supply Co. v. United States, *supra* at 1585.

Is the limitation endorsed in News Syndicate required by the statute? Does it rest on solid policy? Why should such an inquiry be unacceptable, if the facts on which the answer turns are adequately set forth in the certificate? Compare the questions in Chicago, B. & Q. Ry. v. Williams, 205 U.S. 444 (1907), and their restatement in 214 U.S. 493–95 (1909); see also the dissent of Justice Holmes, 214 U.S. at 495.

(3) Assuming the propriety of the Supreme Court's reluctance in Wisniewski to resolve an intra-circuit conflict on an insubstantial question, what is the source of its authority for refusing a certificate that poses such a question? Moore & Vestal, *Present and Potential Role of Certification in Federal Appellate Procedure*, 35 Va.L.Rev. 1, 42 (1949), state that: "One present difficulty arises from the fact that certification invokes the Supreme Court's obligatory jurisdiction," and then urge that response to certified questions should be made discretionary.

(4) From 1927–36, 85 certificates were filed in the Supreme Court, including 13 from the Court of Claims, and from 1937–46, there were only 20, all from the courts of appeals. Moore & Vestal, *supra*, at 26. Since United States v. Rice, 327 U.S. 742 (1946), only three certificates have been accepted by the Court: in United States v. Barnett, 376 U.S. 681 (1964) (court of appeals, which was sitting in banc and was equally divided, certified the question whether Governor Barnett of Mississippi was entitled to a jury in an original contempt proceeding in that court); in Moody v. Albemarle Paper Co., 417 U.S. 622 (1974) (court of appeals certified the question whether a senior judge of the court, who had been a member of the original panel hearing a case, could vote to determine whether the case should be reheard in banc); and in Iran National Airlines Corp. v. Marschalk Co., Inc., 453 U.S. 919 (1981) (court of appeals certified three questions relating to the scope, validity, and effect of the Executive Orders carrying out the agreement with Iran under which American hostages were released).[1]

(5) Since the certification procedure is "virtually, but not quite, a dead letter," [2] and since the Court plainly is not happy about giving a measure of control over its docket to the courts of appeals, why shouldn't § 1254(3) be repealed? Can you think of a case in which the question raised in a certificate could not also be presented to the Court, at some point, in a petition for certiorari or for an extraordinary writ? See Bernard, *Certified Questions in the Supreme Court*, 83 Dick.L.Rev. 31 (1978), arguing that the law should be retained because it serves a useful purpose in those infrequent cases when the courts of appeals require authoritative guidance before proceeding. But see 17 Wright, Miller & Cooper, Federal Practice and Procedure § 4038 at 73–74 (1978): "The apparent unseemliness of * * * frank abdication of statutory jurisdiction doubtless accounts for the veiled nature of the statement in the Wisniewski decision. The Court may very well be right that discretionary control of its own docket requires abolition of certification. That result has been virtually accomplished in fact. The sooner it is accomplished by explicit statutory amendment, the better."

---

1. In Marschalk, the Court on the same day had decided a similar controversy, in a full opinion, in a case in which certiorari had been granted before judgment in the court of appeals. Dames & Moore v. Regan, 453 U.S. 654 (1981). The Court answered the three questions in Marschalk—the third only in part—and appended a citation to Dames & Moore to each answer. In dissent, Justice Powell, joined by Justices Marshall and Stevens, said that he would dismiss the certificate with a citation to Dames & Moore. "Having rendered an opinion on the subject of those questions, we should not answer them in monosyllables nor attempt a syllabus of a portion of the Court's opinion" (pp. 919–20).

With the Barnett, Moody and Marschalk cases, compare, *e.g.*, Atkins v. United States, 426 U.S. 944 (1976) (dismissing certificate, 6–3, without opinion), in which federal judges had brought suit in the Court of Claims alleging entitlement to a cost-of-living salary increase and the judges of the Court of Claims had certified the question whether they were disqualified for financial interest.

2. Stern, Gressman & Shapiro, Supreme Court Practice 461 (6th ed. 1986).

SUBSECTION B: DISCRETIONARY REVIEW

EX PARTE REPUBLIC OF PERU

The report of this decision appears at p. 347, *supra.**

DAVIS v. JACOBS

454 U.S. 911, 102 S.Ct. 417, 70 L.Ed.2d 226 (1981).
Petition for Certiorari to the United States Court of Appeals
for the Second Circuit.

The petitions for writs of certiorari [in Davis and in 16 other, similar cases] are denied.

Opinion of JUSTICE STEVENS respecting the denial of the petitions for writs of certiorari.

The question raised by the dissenting opinion is whether the order to be entered in these seventeen cases should be a dismissal or a denial. Although this question might be characterized as a procedural technicality—because its resolution is a matter of complete indifference to the litigants—the argument made in the dissent merits a response because it creates the impression that the Court's answer to this arcane inquiry demonstrates that the Court is discharging its responsibilities in a lawless manner. The impression is quite incorrect.

The petitioners in these cases are state prisoners. None of them has a meritorious claim. Their habeas corpus petitions were all dismissed by federal district judges and they all unsuccessfully sought review in the United States Court of Appeals. Because none of the petitioners obtained a certificate of probable cause, none of these cases was properly "in" the Court of Appeals and therefore 28 U.S.C. § 1254 does not give this Court jurisdiction over the petitions for certiorari. It is perfectly clear, however, that if there were merit to the petitions, the Court would have ample authority to review them in either of two ways.

First, as the Court expressly decided in 1945 in a case that is procedurally identical to these, this Court has jurisdiction under 28 U.S.C. § 1651. In House v. Mayo, 324 U.S. 42 (1945), the Court conceded that it lacked certiorari jurisdiction under the predecessor to § 1254, but squarely held that the All Writs Act, now 28 U.S.C. § 1651, authorized the Court to "grant a writ of certiorari to review the action of the court of appeals in declining to allow an appeal to it" and to review the "questions on the

---

* *Cf.* Jackson, J., in Ex parte Fahey, 332 U.S. 258, 259–60 (1947):

"Mandamus, prohibition and injunction against judges are drastic and extraordinary remedies. We do not doubt power in a proper case to issue such writs. But they have the unfortunate consequence of making the judge a litigant, obliged to obtain personal counsel or to leave his defense to one of the litigants before him. These remedies should be resorted to only when appeal is a clearly inadequate remedy. We are unwilling to utilize them as substitutes for appeals. As extraordinary remedies, they are reserved for really extraordinary causes."

See also the Notes following Ex parte Peru; *Note on Courts, Justices and Judges Authorized to Grant the Writ* (Habeas Corpus), p. 1471, *supra;* Oaks, *The "Original" Writ of Habeas Corpus in the Supreme Court,* 1962 Sup.Ct.Rev. 153.

merits sought to be raised by the appeal." 324 U.S., at 44–45.[1] The Court has consistently followed House v. Mayo for over 35 years.

Second, as the dissent notes, "a Circuit Justice, or this Court itself, may issue a certificate of probable cause. * * *" Because we have that authority, it is part of our responsibility in processing these petitions to determine whether they have arguable merit notwithstanding the failure of a district or circuit judge to authorize an appeal to the Court of Appeals.

A complete explanation of the Court's conclusion that these cases have insufficient merit to warrant the exercise of its jurisdiction should therefore include three elements: (1) the petitioner has incorrectly invoked our jurisdiction under 28 U.S.C. § 1254 because no certificate of probable cause was issued; (2) the Court has decided not to exercise its jurisdiction under 28 U.S.C. § 1651; and (3) neither the Circuit Justice nor the Court has decided to issue a certificate of probable cause. Instead of entering detailed orders of this kind in all of these cases, the Court wisely has adopted the practice of entering simple denials. Ironically, the dissenters argue that this settled practice creates "more paper work."

As a practical matter, given the volume of frivolous, illegible, and sometimes unintelligible petitions that are filed in this Court, our work is facilitated by the practice of simply denying certiorari once a determination is made that there is no merit to the petitioner's claim. * * *

JUSTICE REHNQUIST, with whom THE CHIEF JUSTICE and JUSTICE POWELL join, dissenting.

In Jeffries v. Barksdale, 453 U.S. 914 (1981), The Chief Justice, Justice Powell, and I dissented from a simple denial of the writ of certiorari, contending that the writ should instead be *dismissed* because we had no jurisdiction to consider it. Further reflection and research has only strengthened my belief that where a specific statutory enactment dealing with our jurisdiction to consider decisions of the Courts of Appeals limits that jurisdiction to "[c]ases in the courts of appeals", 28 U.S.C. § 1254, we are bound by that statutory provision just as we would be bound by any other statutory provision, unless we were to hold it violative of some provision of the Constitution.

In each of these cases, the petitioner was convicted in a state court. He then sought habeas corpus relief in a United States District Court, and the District Court dismissed the action or denied the writ and refused to issue a certificate of probable cause to appeal. * * *

---

1. The dissenting opinion makes the entirely unwarranted assumption that United States Alkali Export Assn. v. United States, 325 U.S. 196 (1945), and its companion case, De Beers Consolidated Mines, Ltd. v. United States, 325 U.S. 212 (1945), decided only a few weeks after House, implicitly overruled that case. In those cases, the petitioners had sought by writs of certiorari interlocutory review of orders issued by federal district courts, and the statutes that expressly conferred upon this Court appellate jurisdiction did not provide for interlocutory review. Despite its language that "[t]he writs may not be used as a substitute for an authorized appeal," 325 U.S., at 203, the Court reasoned that in both cases there were countervailing interests that so outweighed the interest in avoidance of piecemeal review that review by certiorari was appropriate. The holdings in Alkali and De Beers actually reinforce the holding in House because the interest in granting habeas relief in a deserving case clearly outweighs the interest in terminating frivolous appeals, especially when certiorari petitions are filed with this Court despite the refusals of the lower courts to grant certificates of probable cause. See Oaks, The "Original" Writ of Habeas Corpus in the Supreme Court, 1962 Sup.Ct.Rev. 153, 187 & n. 158 (distinguishing De Beers from House on the ground that the former involved property rights).

The effect of [28 U.S.C. § 2253], which could not have been drafted in plainer terms, is clear: a certificate of probable cause is an indispensable prerequisite to an appeal from the District Court to the appropriate Court of Appeals. This has long been recognized by the courts, and by distinguished commentators, see, *e.g.*, Blackmun, Allowance of In Forma Pauperis Appeals in § 2255 and Habeas Corpus Cases, 43 F.R.D. 343, 351 (1967). Our cases are not entirely in harmony as to their reasoning on this issue, though all concede that there is no jurisdiction to grant a writ of certiorari where both the District Court and the Court of Appeals have denied a habeas corpus petitioner a certificate of probable cause to appeal. See Bilik v. Strassheim, 212 U.S. 551, (1908); Ex parte Patrick, 212 U.S. 555, (1908); House v. Mayo, 324 U.S. 42, 44 (1945). In House, however, this Court held that although it could not entertain a petition for certiorari, it had jurisdiction under the All Writs Act to determine the merits of the habeas petition, as well as whether the Court of Appeals had abused its discretion in denying the petitioner a certificate of probable cause to appeal. *Id.*, at 44–45. In reaching this conclusion, it relied on a series of cases interpreting the scope of the common law writ of certiorari under the All Writs Act. See, *e.g.*, * * * In re 620 Church St. Corp., 299 U.S. 24 (1936).

This reasoning, however, would seem to conflict with the principles established in United States Alkali Export Assn. v. United States, 325 U.S. 196, 203 (1945), and its companion case DeBeers Consolidated Mines, Ltd. v. United States, 325 U.S. 212 (1945). These two cases hold that where Congress has withheld appellate review, the All Writs Act cannot be used as a substitute for an authorized appeal. Review by common law certiorari or any other extraordinary writ is not permissible in the face of a legislative purpose to foreclose review in a particular set of circumstances. Alkali Export, *supra*, 325 U.S., at 203.

Congress, in enacting 28 U.S.C. § 2253, has determined that an indispensable prerequisite to an appeal in a habeas corpus proceeding is a certificate of probable cause. * * * Where the statutory scheme permits appellate review only upon the issuance of such a certificate, review by extraordinary writ in the absence of a certificate collides with Congress' express purpose to foreclose review.*

We should not fear that a more exacting application of § 2253 will result in meritorious petitions for habeas corpus slipping by unobservant or callous Courts of Appeals, thereby evading any review by this Court.

---

* Although the concurring opinion correctly notes that this Court utilized the common law writ in Alkali Export, *supra*, to review an interlocutory order by the District Court, this hardly "reinforce[s] the holding in House v. Mayo." The questions in Alkali Export involved the propriety of an exercise of the District Court's equitable jurisdiction, where there was an apparent conflict between its jurisdiction and that of the agency specifically charged by Congress with the duty of enforcing the antitrust laws under the circumstances present in that case. Thus, the common law writ was utilized by this Court in Alkali Export only to determine whether the District Court's assumption of jurisdiction *conflicted* with Congress' intent to foreclose such jurisdiction pending a determination of a particularly sensitive issue by the Federal Trade Commission. Alkali Export, *supra*, 325 U.S., at 203–204. In contrast, use of the common law writ to review uncertificated petitions does not operate to ensure that a lower court is exercising its jurisdiction in accord with congressional intent. It has precisely the opposite effect of providing uncertificated petitioners with certiorari review in the teeth of a congressional mandate that such review should not be available.

Pursuant to § 2253, a Circuit Justice, or this Court itself, may issue a certificate of probable cause. * * *

But the practice from which I dissented in Jeffries, in addition to creating more paper work with no observable change in the results of a case, has at least two singularly undesirable side-effects. Presumably a case where a Court of Appeals has refused to grant leave to appeal, and thus has neither examined the accuracy of petitioner's factual assertions nor articulated the reasons for its conclusion that petitioner's legal contentions lack merit, is not an ideal candidate for certiorari here entirely apart from the importance of the issues presented by such a petition. * * *

But an even more important consequence of the disregard of congressional provisions as to our jurisdiction is a tendency to weaken the authority of this Court when it can demonstrate in a principled manner that it has either the constitutional or statutory authority to decide a particular issue. The necessary concomitant of our tri-partite system of government that the other two branches of government obey judgments rendered within our jurisdiction is sapped whenever we decline for any reason other than the exercise of our own constitutional duties to similarly follow the mandates of Congress and the Executive within their spheres of authority.

NOTE ON COMMON LAW AND STATUTORY CERTIORARI

(1) Both opinions in Davis start from the proposition that the case was not "in" the court of appeals for purposes of determining the availability of statutory certiorari under 28 U.S.C. § 1254(1). This proposition is squarely supported by House v. Mayo, 324 U.S. 42 (1945).

Is the proposition sound? What if an appeal to a court of appeals is dismissed by that court for lack of a final decision, i.e., for lack of jurisdiction? The Supreme Court has statutory jurisdiction to review that dismissal, doesn't it? See, e.g., Gardner v. Westinghouse Broadcasting Co., 437 U.S. 478 (1978). Indeed, in Nixon v. Fitzgerald, 457 U.S. 731 (1982), the Court first determined that the court of appeals erred in dismissing for lack of a final decision and then went on to decide the appeal on the merits. How different is the Davis situation?

Note that in Holiday v. Johnston, 313 U.S. 342, 348 (1941), the Supreme Court used the common law writ of certiorari to review and reverse a court of appeals decision refusing to allow an appeal in forma pauperis. But after a change in the statutory provisions governing these appeals, see 28 U.S.C. § 1915, the Court, without discussion, reviewed similar denials of leave apparently on statutory writ under § 1254(1). See, e.g., Coppedge v. United States, 369 U.S. 438 (1962).[1] Similarly, although there has been no analogous statutory change in § 2253, the Court appears to have granted statutory certiorari in a few cases in which a court of appeals has denied a habeas petitioner's application for a certificate of probable cause. E.g., Smith v. Digmon, 434 U.S. 332 (1978); cases cited in

---

1. In Coppedge and similar cases, review was granted simply on petition for certiorari, without insisting on prior resort to a motion for leave to file. (The latter procedure was then required by the Supreme Court Rules on any application for common law certiorari or other extraordinary writ. New Sup.Ct. Rule 27 no longer requires such a preliminary motion.)

Justice Stevens opinion in Davis, at n. 2. See Oaks, *The "Original" Writ of Habeas Corpus in the Supreme Court*, 1962 Sup.Ct.Rev. 153, 186 nn. 151, 152.

(2) If statutory certiorari is not available in a case like Davis, is Justice Rehnquist correct that common law certiorari should not be available either? To the extent that Justice Rehnquist is relying on § 2253, how does he answer Justice Stevens' point that this provision goes only to the jurisdiction of the court of appeals? To the extent he is relying on § 1254(1), is he arguing that common law certiorari under the All Writs Act, 28 U.S.C. § 1651, should be available only to correct actions by lower courts in excess of their jurisdiction?[2] Professor Oaks, Paragraph (1), *supra*, at 182–89, concluded from his research that at common law, the writ was available to correct nonjurisdictional errors.

(3) The statutory writ runs to the courts of appeals in any case "before or after rendition of judgment or decree." A final judgment in the court of appeals is not required. But grant of certiorari before *any* court of appeals judgment is quite rare, being generally reserved for cases of "imperative public importance" in which there is a need for prompt settlement of the issues.[3] And in a few such instances, certiorari has been granted on petition by the United States even though it was the prevailing party in the district court.[4]

The policy of the Court in the exercise of its discretion to review by certiorari is examined in Section 3, *infra*.

SUBSECTION C: LIMITATIONS ON REVIEW

SCHACHT v. UNITED STATES
398 U.S. 58, 90 S.Ct. 1555, 26 L.Ed.2d 44 (1970).
Certiorari to the United States Court of Appeals for the Fifth Circuit.

MR. JUSTICE BLACK delivered the opinion of the Court.

The petitioner, Daniel Jay Schacht, was indicted in a United States District Court for violating 18 U.S.C. § 702, which makes it a crime for any person "without authority [to wear] the uniform or a distinctive part thereof * * * of any of the armed forces of the United States, * * *" He was tried and convicted by a jury, and on February 29, 1968, he was sentenced to pay a fine of $250 and to serve a six-month prison term, the maximum sentence allowable under 18 U.S.C. § 702. There is no doubt that Schacht did wear distinctive parts of the uniform of the United States Army and that he was not a member of the Armed Forces. He has defended his conduct since the beginning, however, on the ground that he

---

2. See n. * of Justice Rehnquist's opinion, discussing United States Alkali Export Ass'n v. United States, 325 U.S. 196 (1945).

3. See Sup.Ct. Rule 18; *see also e.g.*, United States v. United Mine Workers, 330 U.S. 258 (1947); Youngstown Sheet & Tube Co. v. Sawyer, 343 U.S. 579 (1952); United States v. Nixon, 418 U.S. 683 (1974); Dames & Moore v. Regan, 453 U.S. 654 (1981).

4. *E.g.*, United States v. United Mine Workers, note 3, *supra*.

was authorized to wear the uniform by an Act of Congress, 10 U.S.C. § 772(f), which provides as follows:

"When wearing by persons not on active duty authorized.

* * *

"(f) While portraying a member of the Army, Navy, Air Force, or Marine Corps, an actor in a theatrical or motion picture production may wear the uniform of that armed force *if the portrayal does not tend to discredit that armed force.*" (Emphasis added.)

Schacht argued in the trial court and in this Court that he wore the army uniform as an "actor" in a "theatrical production" performed several times between 6:30 and 8:30 A.M. on December 4, 1967, in front of the Armed Forces Induction Center at Houston, Texas. The street skit in which Schacht wore the army uniform as a costume was designed, in his view, to expose the evil of the American presence in Vietnam and was part of a larger, peaceful anti-war demonstration at the induction center that morning. * * *

[In Part I of the opinion, the Court held that Schacht had participated in a "theatrical production" within the meaning of § 772. It further held that, in order to preserve the constitutionality of that provision, the final clause must be sticken.]

II

The Government's brief and argument seriously contend that this Court is without jurisdiction to consider and decide the merits of this case on the ground that the petition for certiorari was not timely filed under Rule 22(2) of the Rules of this Court. This Rule provides that a petition for certiorari to review a court of appeals' judgment in a criminal case "shall be deemed in time when * * * filed with the Clerk within thirty days after the entry of such judgment." * We cannot accept the view that this time requirement is jurisdictional and cannot be waived by the Court. Rule 22(2) contains no language that calls for so harsh an interpretation, and it must be remembered that this Rule was not enacted by Congress but was promulgated by this Court under authority of Congress to prescribe rules concerning the time limitations for taking appeals and applying for certiorari in criminal cases. See 18 U.S.C. § 3772; Rule 37, Fed.Rule Crim. Proc. The procedural rules adopted by the Court for the orderly transaction of its business are not jurisdictional and can be relaxed by the Court in the exercise of its discretion when the ends of justice so require. This discretion has been expressly declared in several opinions of the Court. See Taglianetti v. United States, 394 U.S. 316 n. 1; Heflin v. United States, 358 U.S. 415, 418 n. 7. See also Stern and Gressman, Supreme Court Practice (4th ed., 1969), at 242–244, and the cases cited therein. It is true that the Taglianetti and Heflin cases dealt with this time question only in footnotes. But this is no reason to disregard their holdings and in fact indicates the Court deemed a footnote adequate treatment to give the issue.

When the petition for certiorari was filed in this case it was accompanied by a motion, supported by affidavits, asking that we grant certiorari

---

* [Ed.] The present provision may be found in Rule 20.1, which states that a certiorari petition "to review the judgment in a criminal case of a state court of last resort or of a federal court of appeals shall be deemed in time when it is filed with the Clerk within 60 days after the entry of such judgment."

despite the fact that the petition was filed 101 days after the appropriate period for filing the petition had expired. Affidavits filed with the motion, not denied or challenged by the Government, present facts showing that petitioner had acted in good faith and that the delay in filing the petition for certiorari was brought about by circumstances largely beyond his control. Without detailing these circumstances, it is sufficient to note here that after consideration of the motion and affidavits this Court on December 15, 1969, granted the motion, three Justices dissenting. The decision of this Court waiving the time defect and permitting the untimely filing of the petition was thus made several months ago, and no new facts warranting a reconsideration of that decision have been presented to us.

For the reasons stated in Parts I and II of this opinion, the judgment of the Court of Appeals is reversed.

Reversed.

MR. JUSTICE HARLAN, concurring.

I join Part I of the Court's opinion. With respect to Part II, I agree with the Court's rejection of the Government's "jurisdictional" contention premised on the untimely filing of the petition for certiorari. In my view, however, that contention deserves fuller consideration than has been accorded it in the Court's opinion.

I

The Court's opinion does not fully come to grips with the Solicitor General's position. The Court rejects the argument that untimeliness under Rule 22(2) should be given jurisdictional effect by stating, in part, that the Rule "contains no language that calls for so harsh an interpretation." In this regard, however, the time limitation found in Rule 22(2) is no different from those established by statute;[1] neither makes explicit reference to waivers of the limitation. In the absence of language providing for waiver, we have without exception treated the statutory limitations as jurisdictional. The Solicitor General asks why we should not do the same under our Rule. This issue, i.e., why we treat time requirements under our Rule differently from the requirements imposed by statute, is hardly acknowledged in the Court's opinion. Moreover, although it is true that Taglianetti v. United States, 394 U.S. 316 n. 1, and Heflin v. United States, 358 U.S. 415, 418 n. 7, held that the Court could waive untimeliness under our Rule, neither opinion explained why this is so. The Solicitor General does not belittle those two cases merely because each dealt with the problem in a footnote, but rather urges that they are inconclusive because neither gave reasons for the conclusion.

II

My own analysis of the issue presented here begins with an examination of the statutory authority for Rule 22(2). This is found in what is now 18 U.S.C. § 3772, a provision authorizing this Court to prescribe post-verdict rules of practice and procedure in criminal cases. Section 3772 specifically delegates to this Court the power to promulgate rules prescrib-

---

1. Compare Rule 22(2) with, e.g., 28 U.S.C. § 2101(b), (c). Both the Rule and this statute provide for limited extensions of time. There was, however, no extension in the case before us.

ing "the times for and manner of taking appeals [to the Courts of Appeals] and applying for writs of certiorari * * *." While the legislative history of this provision evinces a congressional concern over undue delays in the disposition of criminal cases, the broad terms of the statutory language, as well as what was written in the Committee reports, convince me that Congress' purpose was to give this Court the freedom to decide what time limits should apply.

Under the unqualified delegation found in § 3772, I have no doubts concerning this Court's authority to promulgate a rule that required certiorari petitions to be filed within 30 days of the judgment below but that expressly provided that this requirement could be waived for good cause shown, in order to avoid unfairness in extraordinary cases. I also think the Court might promulgate a rule that expressly provided that untimeliness could not be waived even for "excusable neglect,"—in other words a "jurisdictional rule."

Rule 22(2), as promulgated, contains no express provision allowing for waiver. It is clear from prior decisions that the Court has interpreted the rule to allow for such a waiver, however. So interpreted, I find Rule 22(2) no less authorized under 18 U.S.C. § 3772 than would be a rule that by its terms provided expressly for the possibility of a waiver.

Nor do I find it at all anomalous that this Court on occasion waives the time limitations imposed by its own Rules and yet treats time requirements imposed by statute as jurisdictional. As a matter of statutory interpretation, the Court has not presumed the right to extend time limits specified in statutes where there is no indication of a congressional purpose to authorize the Court to do so. Because we cannot "waive" congressional enactments, the statutory time limits are treated as jurisdictional. On the other hand, for the time requirement of Rule 22(2), established under a broad statutory delegation, it is appropriate to apply the "general principle" that "[i]t is always within the discretion of a court or an administrative agency to relax or modify its procedural rules adopted for the orderly transaction of business before it when in a given case the ends of justice require it," American Farm Lines v. Black Ball, 397 U.S. 532, 539 (1970), quoting from N.L.R.B. v. Monsanto Chemical Co., 205 F.2d 763, 764 (C.A. 8th Cir.1953).

III

Although I therefore conclude that this Court possesses the discretion to waive the time requirements of Rule 22(2), it must be recognized that such requirements are essential to an orderly appellate process. Consequently, I believe our discretion must be exercised sparingly, and only when an adequate reason exists to excuse noncompliance with our Rules. In the present case, I agree with the Court that petitioner has adequately explained why he failed to meet our time requirements. On this basis I concur in Part II of the Court's opinion.

NOTE ON TIME LIMITATIONS FOR CERTIORARI
AND APPEAL

As indicated in the Schacht opinions, the statutory time limitations for certiorari and appeal are regarded as jurisdictional.[1] The time is calculated from the day of entry of the judgment below, without counting that day, but the period is tolled by the filing of a timely petition for rehearing in the court below and begins to run anew from the date of the order denying the petition. *See* Department of Banking v. Pink, 317 U.S. 264, 266 (1942). The filing of an untimely petition tolls the period for seeking review only if the court below "allows the filing and, after considering the merits, denies [or otherwise acts upon] the petition." Bowman v. Loperena, 311 U.S. 262, 266 (1940). But in FTC v. Minneapolis–Honeywell Regulator Co., 344 U.S. 206 (1952), the Court held that when no petition for rehearing is filed, a modification in a judgment that does not affect the portion on which review is sought does not extend the time for seeking review. Subsequent decisions, however, have held petitions for certiorari to be timely despite at least an arguable resemblance to the facts of Minneapolis–Honeywell. See United States v. Adams, 383 U.S. 39 (1966) (petition held timely although it was filed more than 90 days after the initial judgment and raised issues apparently unaffected by a second judgment entered in response to a timely motion to amend); FTC v. Colgate–Palmolive Co., 380 U.S. 374, 378–84 (1965) (period for filing petition commenced on the date of the second judgment below because, after the first judgment, the Commission issued a revised order in a good-faith attempt to comply with the appellate court's first mandate). See generally Stern, Gressman & Shapiro, Supreme Court Practice §§ 6.3, 6.4 (6th ed. 1986). The governing statute and rule permit extensions of time for petitioning for certiorari to be granted for good cause shown. 28 U.S.C. § 2101(c); Sup.Ct.Rule 20.1. And although no extensions may be granted for filing notices of appeal to the Supreme Court, extensions of the time for docketing an appeal (payment of docket fee and filing of jurisdictional statement) are authorized. Sup.Ct.Rule 12.2; see State Bd. of Election Comm'rs v. Evers, 405 U.S. 1001, 1005 (1972) (dissenting opinion), where Justice Douglas said: "[T]his Court has failed to develop even the shadow of a consistent practice concerning the effect to be given an appellant's failure to docket within the prescribed time. * * * I cannot acquiesce in an arbitrary practice which permits the Court to sweep unpleasant cases under the rug. Unless we are willing to prescribe criteria for guiding our granting of waivers * * * we should either enforce Rule 13(1) [the predecessor of present Rule 12.2] for all or for none."

---

1. See 28 U.S.C. § 2101.

REDRUP v. NEW YORK

386 U.S. 767, 87 S.Ct. 1414, 18 L.Ed.2d 515 (1967).

Certiorari to the Appellate Term of the Supreme Court of New York, First Judicial Department.*

PER CURIAM.

These three cases arise from a recurring conflict—the conflict between asserted state power to suppress the distribution of books and magazines through criminal or civil proceedings, and the guarantees of the First and Fourteenth Amendments of the United States Constitution.

I.

In No. 3, Redrup v. New York, the petitioner was a clerk at a New York City newsstand. A plainsclothes patrolman approached the newsstand, saw two paperback books on a rack—Lust Pool, and Shame Agent—and asked for them by name. The petitioner handed him the books and collected the price of $1.65. As a result of this transaction, the petitioner was charged in the New York City Criminal Court with violating a state criminal law. He was convicted, and the conviction was affirmed on appeal.

In No. 16, Austin v. Kentucky, the petitioner owned and operated a retail bookstore and newsstand in Paducah, Kentucky. A woman resident of Paducah purchased two magazines from a salesgirl in the petitioner's store, after asking for them by name—High Heels, and Spree. As a result of this transaction the petitioner stands convicted in the Kentucky courts for violating a criminal law of that State.

In No. 50, Gent v. Arkansas, the prosecuting attorney of the Eleventh Judicial District of Arkansas brought a civil proceeding under a state statute to have certain issues of various magazines declared obscene, to enjoin their distribution and to obtain a judgment ordering their surrender and destruction. The magazines proceeded against were: Gent, Swank, Bachelor, Modern Man, Cavalcade, Gentleman, Ace, and Sir. The County Chancery Court entered the requested judgment after a trial with an advisory jury, and the Supreme Court of Arkansas affirmed, with minor modifications.

In none of the cases was there a claim that the statute in question reflected a specific and limited state concern for juveniles. * * * In none was there any suggestion of an assault upon individual privacy by publication in a manner so obtrusive as to make it impossible for an unwilling individual to avoid exposure to it. * * * And in none was there evidence of the sort of "pandering" which the Court found significant in Ginzburg v. United States, 383 U.S. 463.

II.

The Court originally limited review in these cases to certain particularized questions, upon the hypothesis that the material involved in each case

---

* Together with No. 16, Austin v. Kentucky, on certiorari to the Circuit Court of McCracken County, Kentucky, argued on October 10–11, 1966, and No. 50, Gent et al. v. Arkansas, on appeal from the Supreme Court of Arkansas, argued October 11, 1966.

was of a character described as "obscene in the constitutional sense" in A Book Named "John Cleland's Memoirs of a Woman of Pleasure" v. Attorney General of Com. of Massachusetts, 383 U.S. 413, 418. But we have concluded that the hypothesis upon which the Court originally proceeded was invalid, and accordingly that the cases can and should be decided upon a common and controlling fundamental constitutional basis, without prejudice to the questions upon which review was originally granted. We have concluded, in short, that the distribution of the publications in each of these cases is protected by the First and Fourteenth Amendments from governmental suppression, whether criminal or civil, *in personam* or *in rem.*[6]

Two members of the Court have consistently adhered to the view that a State is utterly without power to suppress, control or punish the distribution of any writings or pictures upon the ground of their "obscenity." A third has held to the opinion that a State's power in this area is narrowly limited to a distinct and clearly identifiable class of material. Others have subscribed to a not dissimilar standard, holding that a State may not constitutionally inhibit the distribution of literary material as obscene unless "(a) the dominant theme of the material taken as a whole appeals to a prurient interest in sex; (b) the material is patently offensive because it affronts contemporary community standards relating to the description or representation of sexual matters; and (c) the material is utterly without redeeming social value," emphasizing that the "three elements must coalesce," and that no such material can "be proscribed unless it is found to be *utterly* without redeeming social value." A Book Named "John Cleland's Memoirs of a Woman of Pleasure" v. Attorney General of Com. of Massachusetts, 383 U.S. 413, 418–419. Another Justice has not viewed the "social value" element as an independent factor in the judgment of obscenity. *Id.,* at 460–462 (dissenting opinion).

Whichever of these constitutional views is brought to bear upon the cases before us, it is clear that the judgments cannot stand. Accordingly, the judgment in each case is reversed. It is so ordered.

Judgments reversed.

MR. JUSTICE HARLAN, whom MR. JUSTICE CLARK joins, dissenting.

Two of these cases, Redrup v. New York and Austin v. Kentucky, were taken to consider the standards governing the application of the *scienter* requirement announced in Smith v. People of State of California, 361 U.S. 147, for obscenity prosecutions. There it was held that a defendant criminally charged with purveying obscene material must be shown to have had some kind of knowledge of the character of such material; the quality of that knowledge, however, was not defined. The third case, Gent v. Arkansas, was taken to consider the validity of a comprehensive Arkansas anti-obscenity statute, in light of the doctrines of "vagueness" and "prior restraint." The writs of certiorari in Redrup and Austin, and the notation of probable jurisdiction in Gent, were respectively limited to these issues, thus laying aside, for the purposes of these cases, the permissibility of the state determinations as to the obscenity of the challenged publications.

---

6. In each of the cases before us, the contention that the publications involved were basically protected by the First and Fourteenth Amendments was timely but unsuccessfully asserted in the state proceedings. In each of these cases, this contention was properly and explicitly presented for review here.

Accordingly the obscenity *vel non* of these publications was not discussed in the briefs or oral arguments of any of the parties.

The three cases were argued together at the beginning of this Term. Today, the Court rules that the materials could not constitutionally be adjudged obscene by the States, thus rendering adjudication of the other issues unnecessary. In short, the Court disposes of the cases on the issue that was deliberately excluded from review, and refuses to pass on the questions that brought the cases here.

In my opinion these dispositions do not reflect well on the processes of the Court, and I think the issues for which the cases were taken should be decided. Failing that, I prefer to cast my vote to dismiss the writs in Redrup and Austin as improvidently granted and, in the circumstances, to dismiss the appeal in Gent for lack of a substantial federal question. I deem it more appropriate to defer an expression of my own views on the questions brought here until an occasion when the Court is prepared to come to grips with such issues.

NOTE ON LIMITED REVIEW

(1) Redrup and the companion cases all arose from state courts, but such limited grants also occur in cases coming from the federal appellate courts.[1] See, *e.g.,* Louisiana Power & Light Co. v. City of Thibodaux, 360 U.S. 25, 26 n. 1 (1959); Gregg v. United States, 393 U.S. 932 (1968); Whiteley v. Warden, 401 U.S. 560, 562 n. 3 (1971). And, as in Redrup, the Court has on occasion gone beyond the scope of its grant in deciding the case. *E.g.,* Olmstead v. United States, 277 U.S. 438, 466, 468 (1928); Piper Aircraft Co. v. Reyno, 454 U.S. 235, 246–47 n. 12 (1981).[2]

(2) Suppose that in Redrup and Austin the Court had confined itself to the questions on which certiorari had been granted and had affirmed the convictions. Would you be troubled by the fact that the Court's decision would have sustained, on the merits, convictions for engaging in constitutionally protected activity? That the Court's failure to reverse was in no way attributable to any procedural default by the petitioners? (Similar questions could be asked about an affirmance of the civil judgment in Gent.) Can or should the Court, operating within the limits imposed by Article III, decide a case without passing on a question that is within its jurisdiction, that is properly presented, and that is not mooted by the Court's disposition of any other question in the case? Is it enough of an answer that the Court must be able to exercise control over its own docket?[3]

---

1. A study published in 1975 reported that over a period of eleven terms, the Court limited the grant of review in an average of 4.3% per term of the cases in which certiorari was granted. See Bice, *The Limited Grant of Certiorari and the Justification of Judicial Review,* 1975 Wis. L.Rev. 343, 356–57 n. 61.

2. And the Court has, over strong dissent, asked the parties to brief and argue a question not presented in the certiorari petition. See Colorado v. Connelly, 474 U.S. 1050 (1986).

3. In an exhaustive analysis of the issues involved, Bice, note 1, *supra,* concludes that the practice of limited grants is both desirable and legitimate. He argues that at least at the highest appellate level, Congress by statute (as in 28 U.S.C. § 1254(2)) and the Court in its discretion may limit the issues for decision, even though a similar limitation at the trial court level might raise serious constitutional problems. He does suggest, however, that in certain areas, notably that of jurisdiction, Supreme Court consideration

(3) Whatever your answers to the questions in Paragraph (2), aren't you troubled by Justice Harlan's vote to dismiss the appeal in Gent for lack of a substantial federal question? Did Justice Harlan mean that the appealable issues, which the majority did not reach, were insubstantial? (The issues are stated in the notation of probable jurisdiction, 384 U.S. 937 (1966).) If not, what did he mean?

————

NOTE ON CROSS–APPEALS, CROSS–PETITIONS, AND REVIEW OF ERRORS NOT ASSIGNED IN THE PETITION

(1) Without a cross-appeal or cross-petition, the appellee or respondent is precluded from attacking the judgment or decree "with a view either to enlarging his own rights thereunder or of lessening the rights of his adversary, whether what he seeks is to correct an error or to supplement the decree with respect to a matter not dealt with below."[1] He is not barred, however, from urging in support of the judgment "any matter appearing in the record, although his argument may involve an attack upon the reasoning of the lower court or an insistence upon matter overlooked or ignored by it."[2]

Nor is it necessary to support the judgment that the point be one urged below, if it is grounded in the record. Bondholders Committee v. Commissioner, 315 U.S. 189, 192 n. 2 (1942). The Supreme Court may prefer, however, to reverse and permit the initial consideration of such new contentions on remand. See, e.g., United States v. Ballard, 322 U.S. 78, 88 (1944).[3]

The same principles apply in the courts of appeals upon review of district court decisions. Morley Constr. Co. v. Maryland Cas. Co., 300 U.S. 185 (1937). See also Note, 64 Harv.L.Rev. 652 (1951).

(2) Some question has arisen in recent years about the application of these principles in a case in which (a) the rationale urged by respondent could support a result more favorable to him than the judgment below but (b) the respondent is willing to accept that judgment. In Strunk v. United States, 412 U.S. 434 (1973), the petitioner had prevailed in the court of

of an issue should not be excluded by a limited grant of certiorari. He also urges that when, as in Redrup, the Court goes outside such a limited grant, the parties should be given an opportunity to brief and argue the additional issues.

1. United States v. American Ry. Exp. Co., 265 U.S. 425, 435 (1924). Even under these circumstances, an issue may be raised if it goes to subject matter jurisdiction. See Lake Country Estates, Inc. v. Tahoe Regional Planning Agency, 440 U.S. 391, 398 (1979).

2. United States v. American Ry. Exp. Co., 265 U.S. 425, 435 (1924). See also, e.g., Thigpen v. Roberts, 468 U.S. 27 (1984); Langnes v. Green, 282 U.S. 531 (1931); Hutchinson v. Proxmire, 443 U.S. 111, 121 n. 10 (1979).

One apparent exception is a claim of improper venue, which has been held to be waived if not raised by cross-appeal. Peoria & Pekin Union Ry. v. United States, 263 U.S. 528, 536 (1924). Another possible exception involves claims of untimeliness. See Stern, Gressman & Shapiro, Supreme Court Practice 383–84 (6th ed. 1986).

3. But cf. United States v. Erika, Inc., 456 U.S. 201, 211 n. 14 (1982) (refusing to consider a constitutional question raised by respondent at oral argument, when respondent had not presented the question below, or included it among the questions presented in the briefs in opposition or on the merits, or argued it to any substantial extent in the body of the brief on the merits).

Of course, the point must not have been lost through failure to make a timely objection in the lower courts. See, e.g., Fed.R. Civ.P. 12(h)(1) (waiver of certain defenses).

appeals on his claim of violation of his right to a speedy trial, and certiorari was granted on his claim that he was entitled to dismissal of the charge, not merely to a reduction of his sentence. The government, as respondent, sought to argue that petitioner's speedy trial right had not been violated, although it indicated its willingness to accept the reduced sentence ordered by the court of appeals. The Supreme Court refused to consider the argument, holding that "in the absence of a cross-petition for certiorari * * * the only question properly before us for review is the propriety of the remedy fashioned by the Court of Appeals" (p. 437).[4]

Perhaps in response to scholarly criticism,[5] the Court appears to have retreated from the implication that it lacks power to consider a question raised by a respondent in these circumstances, noting instead its discretion to do so. See, *e.g.,* United States v. ITT Continental Baking Co., 420 U.S. 223, 226–27 n. 2 (1975);[6] United States v. New York Tel. Co., 434 U.S. 159, 166 n. 8 (1977). In New York Telephone, the Court did in fact consider the questions raised, although the grounds urged by respondent might have justified greater relief than that accorded below. The Court said that "[t]he only relief sought by the [respondent] Company is that granted by the Court of Appeals."

The result in New York Telephone, as well as the Court's emphasis on its discretion to accept or decline consideration, is applauded in Stern, Gressman & Shapiro, Supreme Court Practice § 6.35 (6th ed. 1986).

(3) Compare the limitations on review of errors not assigned or presented in the petition for certiorari. Sup.Ct. Rule 21.1(a); see Pollard v. United States, 352 U.S. 354, 358–59 (1957); Stern, Gressman & Shapiro, Supreme Court Practice § 6.27 (6th ed. 1986); *cf.* Neely v. Martin K. Eby Constr. Co., 386 U.S. 317, 320–21 (1967) (in granting certiorari, the Court requested the parties to argue certain questions not presented in the petition); Blonder–Tongue Labs., Inc. v. University of Illinois Foundation, 402 U.S. 313, 320 n. 6 (1971) ("Rule 23(1)(c) [the predecessor of Rule 21.1(a)] * * * does not limit our power to decide important questions not raised by the parties"); Vance v. Terrazas, 444 U.S. 252, 258–59 n. 5 (1980) (same). In Vance, the issue did not appear in the jurisdictional statement and had not been presented in the court of appeals. Blonder–Tongue was cited in support of the holding; Vachon v. New Hampshire, p. 601, *supra,* a more debatable decision—involving as it did review of a state court judgment— was also cited as "*Cf.*"

---

4. The opinion went on to say: "Whether in some circumstances, and as to some questions, the Court might deal with an issue involving constitutional claims, absent its being raised by cross-petition, we need not resolve" (p. 437).

5. Especially Stern, *When to Cross-Appeal or Cross-Petition—Certainty or Confusion?,* 87 Harv.L.Rev. 763 (1974).

6. The Court, citing Strunk and other cases, said: "Ordinarily * * * as a matter of practice and control of our docket, if

not of our power, we do not entertain a challenge to a decision on the merits where the only petition for certiorari presents solely a question as to the remedy granted for a liability found to exist, even if the respondent is willing to accept whatever judgment has already been entered against him. * * * We follow that rule of practice in this case, particularly because the issue of whether there were any violations * * * would not merit this Court's grant of a petition for certiorari."

SECTION 3. THE CERTIORARI POLICY

INTRODUCTORY NOTE: THE CONSIDERATION AND DISPOSITION OF PETITIONS

(1) At the present time, well over 4000 cases are docketed in the Supreme Court each Term.[1] Less than 10% of these cases are within the Court's obligatory appellate jurisdiction,[2] and only a handful (usually fewer than 5) within the original jurisdiction. Virtually all of the remainder are petitions for statutory certiorari under 28 U.S.C. § 1254(1) or § 1257(3).

The Court has traditionally denied the large majority of these petitions. Until the early 1980s, the number of petitions filed and granted had been growing, but in recent Terms both numbers have leveled off. These developments are highlighted if paid cases are separated from in forma pauperis cases:

Terms [3]

	1960	1970	1981	1983	1984	1985	1986
Paid Cases [4]							
Cases docketed during term [5]	718	1540	2413	2168	2036	2171	2071
Review granted	87 (12.1%)	101 (7.8%)	299 (12.4%)	247 (11.3%)	241 (11.8%)	244 (11.2%)	242 (11.7%)
In Forma Pauperis [6]							
Cases docketed during term [5]	950	1771	2004	2050	2007	2239	2165
Review granted	16 (1.7%)	83 [7] (4.8%)	13 (0.6%)	14 (0.7%)	23 (1.1%)	29 (1.3%)	26 (1.2%)

(2) For all of the Justices, the burden of considering certiorari petitions is lightened by the work of their law clerks, who prepare memoranda summarizing the petitions and recommending dispositions.[8] Moreover, the majority of petitions are not discussed by the Justices in conference. The concept of a "special" or "dead" list was introduced by Chief Justice Hughes; he and his clerks compiled and circulated, in advance, a list of

---

1. See, *e.g.,* the figures for the 1984, 1985, and 1986 Terms, summarized in 56 U.S.L.W. 3102 (1987).

2. See Provine, Case Selection in the United States Supreme Court 10 (1980).

3. The figures in this table are taken from the statistics published each November as part of the Supreme Court Note by the Harvard Law Review and from those published each summer in the Supreme Court edition of United States Law Week.

4. These figures include all paid cases except those on the original docket, whether filed as appeals or as petitions for certiorari.

5. This category includes cases in which review was granted that were carried over to a subsequent Term, but not cases summarily decided without opinion. The percentage is computed by using as the divisor all cases docketed during the Term. (The divisor thus does not include cases remaining on the dockets from prior Terms.)

6. These figures include all cases filed in forma pauperis, whether filed as appeals or as petitions for certiorari.

7. This figure was disproportionately high because of a large number of capital cases that were vacated and remanded. See 403 U.S. 946–48 (1971).

8. A number of Justices reportedly use "pool memos" prepared by a clerk of one of the Justices and distributed to the others in the group. See Stevens, *The Life Span of a Judge–Made Rule,* 58 N.Y.U.L.Rev. 1, 13–14 (1983); Stern, Gressman & Shapiro, Supreme Court Practice 258 n. 13 (6th ed. 1986).

cases that would not be discussed. Any Justice could remove a case from the list at or before conference, and those remaining on the list at the end of the conference would automatically be denied review. The increase in filings has changed the practice, first with the Miscellaneous Docket and then with the Appellate Docket, so that the list now consists of those cases scheduled *for* discussion, and any Justice may add a case to the list or delay its disposition.[9]

(3) Despite these time-saving devices, the burden involved in the exercise of discretion is clearly great, though the extent of that burden and the desirability of change have been the subject of vigorous debate.[10] For further discussion of this and related problems of Supreme Court caseload, and of proposals for change, see p. 1875, *infra*; Chap. I, pp. 43–45, *supra*.

SINGLETON v. COMMISSIONER OF INTERNAL REVENUE

439 U.S. 940, 99 S.Ct. 335, 58 L.Ed.2d 335 (1978).
Petition for Certiorari to the United States Court of Appeals
for the Fifth Circuit.

The petition for a writ of certiorari is denied.

MR. JUSTICE BLACKMUN, with whom MR. JUSTICE MARSHALL and MR. JUSTICE POWELL join, dissenting.

The issue in this federal income tax case is whether a cash distribution that petitioner husband (hereafter petitioner) received in 1965 with respect to his shares in Capital Southwest Corporation (CSW) was taxable to him as a dividend, as the United States Court of Appeals for the Fifth Circuit held, or whether that distribution was a return of capital and therefore not taxable, as the Tax Court held. I regard the issue as of sufficient importance in the administration of the income tax laws to justify review here, and I dissent from the Court's failure to grant certiorari.

* * *

I hope that the Court's decision to pass this case by is not due to a natural reluctance to take on another complicated tax case that is devoid of glamour and emotion and that would be remindful of the recent struggles, upon argument and reargument, in United States v. Foster Lumber Co., 429 U.S. 32 (1976), and Laing v. United States, 423 U.S. 161 (1976).*

Opinion of MR. JUSTICE STEVENS respecting the denial of the petition for writ of certiorari.

What is the significance of this Court's denial of certiorari? That question is asked again and again; it is a question that is likely to arise whenever a dissenting opinion argues that certiorari should have been granted. Almost 30 years ago Mr. Justice Frankfurter provided us with an answer to that question that should be read again and again.

---

9. For a fuller description, see Provine, note 2, *supra*, at 28–29.

10. See, *e.g.*, Symposium, *The Supreme Court Workload*, 11 Hastings Const. L.Q. 353–504 (1984); authorities cited pp. 43–46, *supra*. For earlier discussion, see, *e.g.*, Gressman, *Much Ado About Certiorari*, 52 Geo.L.J. 742 (1964); Hart, *Foreword—The Time Chart of the Justices*, 73 Harv.L.Rev.

84 (1959); Harlan, *Manning the Dikes*, 13 Record Ass'n B. City N.Y. 541 (1958).

* The point Mr. Justice Stevens would make by his separate opinion was answered effectively 25 years ago by Mr. Justice Jackson, concurring in the result, in Brown v. Allen, 344 U.S. 443, 542–544 (1953).

"This Court now declines to review the decision of the Maryland Court of Appeals. The sole significance of such denial of a petition for writ of certiorari need not be elucidated to those versed in the Court's procedures. It simply means that fewer than four members of the Court deemed it desirable to review a decision of the lower court as a matter 'of sound judicial discretion.' Rule 38, paragraph 5. A variety of considerations underlie denials of the writ, and as to the same petition different reasons may lead different Justices to the same result. This is especially true of petitions for review on writ of certiorari to a State court. Narrowly technical reasons may lead to denials. Review may be sought too late; the judgment of the lower court may not be final; it may not be the judgment of a State court of last resort; the decision may be supportable as a matter of State law, not subject to review by this Court, even though the State court also passed on issues of federal law. A decision may satisfy all these technical requirements and yet may commend itself for review to fewer than four members of the Court. Pertinent considerations of judicial policy here come into play. A case may raise an important question but the record may be cloudy. It may be desirable to have different aspects of an issue further illumined by the lower courts. Wise adjudication has its own time for ripening.

"Since there are these conflicting and, to the uninformed, even confusing reasons for denying petitions for certiorari, it has been suggested from time to time that the Court indicate its reasons for denial. Practical considerations preclude. In order that the Court may be enabled to discharge its indispensable duties, Congress has placed the control of the Court's business, in effect, within the Court's discretion. During the last three terms the Court disposed of 260, 217, 224 cases, respectively, on their merits. For the same three terms the Court denied, respectively, 1,260, 1,105, 1,189 petitions calling for discretionary review. If the Court is to do its work it would not be feasible to give reasons, however brief, for refusing to take these cases. The time that would be required is prohibitive, apart from the fact as already indicated that different reasons not infrequently move different members of the Court in concluding that a particular case at a particular time makes review undesirable. It becomes relevant here to note that failure to record a dissent from a denial of a petition for writ of certiorari in nowise implies that only the member of the Court who notes his dissent thought the petition should be granted.

"Inasmuch, therefore, as all that a denial of a petition for a writ of certiorari means is that fewer than four members of the Court thought it should be granted, this Court has rigorously insisted that such a denial carries with it no implication whatever regarding the Court's views on the merits of a case which it has declined to review. The Court has said this again and again; again and again the admonition has to be repeated." Opinion respecting the denial of the petition for writ of certiorari in Maryland v. Baltimore Radio Show, 338 U.S. 912, 917–919.

When those words were written, Mr. Justice Frankfurter and his colleagues were too busy to spend their scarce time writing dissents from denials of certiorari. Such opinions were almost nonexistent.[1] It was then obvious that if there was no need to explain the Court's action in denying the writ, there was even less reason for individual expressions of opinion about why certiorari should have been granted in particular cases.

Times have changed. Although the workload of the Court has dramatically increased since Mr. Justice Frankfurter's day,[2] most present Members of the Court frequently file written dissents from certiorari denials. It is appropriate to ask whether the new practice serves any important goals or contributes to the strength of the institution.

One characteristic of all opinions dissenting from the denial of certiorari is manifest. They are totally unnecessary. They are examples of the purest form of dicta, since they have even less legal significance than the orders of the entire Court which, as Mr. Justice Frankfurter reiterated again and again, have no precedential significance at all.

Another attribute of these opinions is that they are potentially misleading. Since the Court provides no explanation of the reasons for denying certiorari, the dissenter's arguments in favor of a grant are not answered and therefore typically appear to be more persuasive than most other opinions. Moreover, since they often omit any reference to valid reasons for denying certiorari, they tend to imply that the Court has been unfaithful to its responsibilities or has implicitly reached a decision on the merits when, in fact, there is no basis for such an inference.

In this case, for example, the dissenting opinion suggests that the Court may have refused to grant certiorari because the case is "devoid of glamour and emotion." I am puzzled by this suggestion because I have never witnessed any indication that any of my colleagues has ever considered "glamour and emotion" as a relevant consideration in the exercise of his discretion or in his analysis of the law. With respect to the Court's action in this case, the absence of any conflict among the Circuits is plainly a sufficient reason for denying certiorari. Moreover, in allocating the Court's scarce resources, I consider it entirely appropriate to disfavor complicated cases which turn largely on unique facts. A series of decisions by the courts of appeals may well provide more meaningful guidance to the bar than an isolated or premature opinion of this Court. As Mr. Justice Frankfurter reminded us, "wise adjudication has its own time for ripening."

Admittedly these dissenting opinions may have some beneficial effects. Occasionally a written statement of reasons for granting certiorari is more persuasive than the Justice's oral contribution to the Conference. For that reason the written document sometimes persuades other Justices to change their votes and a case is granted that would otherwise have been denied. That effect, however, merely justifies the writing and circulating of these memoranda within the Court; it does not explain why a dissent which has not accomplished its primary mission should be published.

It can be argued that publishing these dissents enhances the public's understanding of the work of the Court. But because they are so seldom answered, these opinions may also give rise to misunderstanding or incor-

1. There were none in 1945 or 1946, and I have been able to find only one in the 1947 Term. See dissent in Chase National Bank v. Cheston, and companion cases, 332 U.S. 793, 800.

2. By way of comparison to the figures cited by Mr. Justice Frankfurter, the Court during the three most recent Terms reviewed and decided 362, 483, and 323 cases respectively. And during each of these Terms, the Court denied certiorari in well over 3,000 cases.

rect impressions about how the Court actually works. Moreover, the selected bits of information which they reveal tend to compromise the otherwise secret deliberations in our Conferences. There are those who believe that these Conferences should be conducted entirely in public or, at the very least, that the votes on all Conference matters should be publicly recorded. The traditional view, which I happen to share, is that confidentiality makes a valuable contribution to the full and frank exchange of views during the decisional process; such confidentiality is especially valuable in the exercise of the kind of discretion that must be employed in processing the thousands of certiorari petitions that are reviewed each year. In my judgment, the importance of preserving the tradition of confidentiality outweighs the minimal educational value of these opinions.

In all events, these are the reasons why I have thus far resisted the temptation to publish opinions dissenting from denials of certiorari.

NOTE ON DENIALS OF CERTIORARI

(1) Do you agree with Justice Frankfurter's statement in the Baltimore Radio Show Case, quoted by Justice Stevens in Singleton, that the Court should not state its reasons for denying certiorari? If it is assumed that a denial of certiorari, without more, has no significance with respect to the merits of a case, might there not be times when the Court would want the denial to carry some specific meaning? See, *e.g.,* Bryant v. Ohio, 362 U.S. 906 (1960) (certiorari denied "in the light of the representation made by respondent in its brief in opposition that 'Petitioner may at this time perfect an appeal to the Supreme Court of Ohio *in forma pauperis,* which appeal will be heard by that Court.'") See also Stern, Gressman & Shapiro, Supreme Court Practice § 5.5 and cases cited (6th ed. 1986).[1] Justice Frankfurter himself, in Rosenberg v. United States, 344 U.S. 889, 890 (1952), thought it appropriate to point out—in a statement attached to the Court's denial of rehearing on a certiorari petition—that "A sentence imposed by a United States district court, even though it be a death sentence, is not within the power of this Court to revise."

Is it ever proper for the Court, in denying certiorari, to purport to construe the opinion below? In United States ex rel. Rogers v. Richmond, 252 F.2d 807 (2d Cir.1958)—a habeas corpus proceeding attacking a state conviction—the court of appeals appeared to say that in the absence of some "vital flaw" or "unusual circumstance" in the state proceedings, the federal judge would not be warranted in holding a de novo hearing on the

---

1. In the 1950s and '60s the Court not infrequently stated that the denial of certiorari to a state prisoner was "without prejudice to an application for writ of habeas corpus in an appropriate United States District Court." *E.g.,* Grace v. California, 360 U.S. 940 (1959). These notations might have been nothing more than gratuitous legal advice to often unrepresented prisoners. But they did carry the unfortunate connotation that a denial in which the words were omitted was *with prejudice* to such an application. *See* Reitz, *Federal Habeas Corpus: Postconviction Remedy for State Prisoners,* 108 U.Pa. L.Rev. 461, 503–13 (1960).

As a result of changes in the requirement of exhaustion of state remedies, this practice appears to have ended. See 16 Wright, Miller, Cooper & Gressman, Federal Practice and Procedure 512 (1977). But *cf.* Jurek v. Estelle, 430 U.S. 951 (1977) (certiorari denied "[w]ithout intimating any views on the merits" of petitioner's pending habeas corpus application); Shippy v. Estelle, 440 U.S. 968 (1979) (certiorari denied because petitioner would not be executed "[a]s long as [he] is actively pursuing his right to a writ of habeas corpus").

admissibility of certain confessions. The Supreme Court denied certiorari, 357 U.S. 220 (1958), saying: "We read the opinion of the Court of Appeals as holding that while the District Judge may, unless he finds a vital flaw in the State Court proceedings, accept the determination in such proceedings, he need not deem such determination binding, and may take testimony." One commentator pointedly inquired about the meaning and legal effect of the Supreme Court's "reading", observing: "If the Court had granted certiorari and remanded with a similar statement on its own authority, at least one reader would have understood its action as a modification of the decision of the court of appeals." Brown, *Foreword: Process of Law,* 72 Harv.L.Rev. 77, 93 (1958).[2]

(2) As Justice Stevens indicated, the practice of noting dissents from certiorari denials, and of writing opinions in support of such dissents, has become increasingly common. Justice Douglas alone dissented from the denial of certiorari 477 times in the 1973 Term,[3] and even after his departure from the Court, the level of recorded dissents has been high. As part of an exhaustive study of Supreme Court certiorari practice,[4] Professor Linzer gives the following figures for the 1978 Term:

Analysis of Individual Notations to Denials of Certiorari, October Term, 1978

Justice	Total Individual Dissents and Notations	Dissents Indicating Position on Merits	Dissents Indicating Reasons for Granting Cert., but Not Discussing Merits	Dissents Without Opinions	Notations Other Than Dissents
Brennan	131	86	0	43	2
Marshall	121	88	1	32	0
Stewart	47	29	0	17	1
White	41	2	2	37	0
Blackmun	34	3	4	26	1
Powell	23	7	1	15	0
Rehnquist	8	6	0	2	0
Burger	5	1	0	3	1
Stevens	3	0	0	0	3
Grand Totals	413	222	8	175	8

(In accordance with the views expressed in Singleton, Justice Stevens has generally declined to note his dissents to denials of certiorari, but in three

2. For a later chapter in these proceedings, see Rogers v. Richmond, 365 U.S. 534 (1961) (reversing the court of appeals and instructing it to hold the case in order to give the state an opportunity to retry the petitioner under proper standards for determining the admissibility of his confession).

3. Linzer, *The Meaning of Certiorari Denials,* 79 Colum.L.Rev. 1227, 1257 n. 217

(1979). Had certiorari been granted in all the cases, the Court's plenary docket at that time would have more than doubled.

4. Linzer, note 3, *supra,* at 1258. Copyright 1979 by the Directors of the Columbia Law Review Association, Inc. This table and other excerpts reproduced with permission.

instances in the 1978 Term and on a number of other occasions, as in Singleton, he has defended the Court's denial against a dissent. See, *e.g.,* Castorr v. Brundage, 459 U.S. 928 (1982); Coleman v. Balkcom, 451 U.S. 949 (1981).[5]

Are published dissents from denials of certiorari always as inappropriate as Justice Stevens thinks they are?[6] Justice Frankfurter's separate statement in Baltimore Radio Show, while not labeled a dissent, left little doubt that he had voted to grant the petition. And Justice Harlan, while saving his notations of dissent for "rare instances," was occasionally willing to go public in cases he thought to be particularly important. *E.g.,* Lance v. Plummer, 384 U.S. 929, 932–33 (1966).

Are such dissents of value in informing the bar and the public of possible directions the law may take, and of areas of interest to particular Justices? If the decision to accept or reject a petition is a judicial act, is the expression of dissent any more "unnecessary" than a dissent from any other judicial act? Is the problem with such dissents that in the absence of a defender like Justice Stevens, the majority's unexplained denial is too easy a target? Note, however, that the threat of dissent may serve to keep the Court from rejecting cases that ought to be accepted under the standards set forth by the Court in its own rules.

Linzer concludes, 79 Colum.L.Rev. at 1267, that dissents on the merits from denials of certiorari "can be put in three broad categories: those finding something offensive about the application of law in the particular case; 'irredentist' dissents, in which a minority reiterates its opposition to a clear precedent; and those urging the majority to consider an apparently uncontroversial point."

A few Justices have also used the dissent to express their views on the Supreme Court's workload and on the desirability of proposed legislation. See, *e.g.,* Brown Transp. Co. v. Atcon, Inc., 439 U.S. 1014 (1978), in which Chief Justice Burger, Justice White, and Justice Brennan each wrote separate opinions dealing with the need for and possible shape of changes in the structure of the federal judicial system.

Are such questions of judicial administration appropriate subjects of debate in the pages of the U.S. Reports on the occasion of a denial of certiorari?

(3) Justice Jackson, concurring in Brown v. Allen, 344 U.S. 443 (1953), p. 1477, *supra,* had this to say about denials of certiorari (pp. 542–43):

"The Court is not quite of one mind on the subject. Some say denial means nothing, others say it means nothing much. Realistically, the first position is untenable and the second is unintelligible. How can we say that the prisoner must present his case to us and at the same time say that what we do with it means nothing to anybody? We might conceivably take

---

5. In Coleman v. Balkcom, Justice Rehnquist, dissenting from the denial of certiorari in a capital case, argued that in order to reduce the inordinate delays in capital cases, the Supreme Court should grant certiorari in each such case coming up from a state court—thus precluding subsequent federal habeas corpus review of the same grounds, 28 U.S.C. § 2244(c). Justice Stevens challenged Justice Rehnquist's willingness to fill up some 50% of

the Court's calendar with those cases, as well as his assumption that a policy of automatic review would have an appreciable impact on existing delays.

But *cf.* Stephens v. Kemp, 469 U.S. 1098 (1984) (Stevens, J., dissenting from a denial of certiorari in a capital case).

6. For an elaborate statement of an opposing view, see Trope, *Dissent to Silence,* 18 Beverly Hills B.A.J. 75 (1984).

either position but not, rationally, both, for the two will not only burden our own docket and harass the state authorities but it makes a prisoner's legitimate quest for federal justice an endurance contest.

"True, neither those outside of the Court, nor on many occasions those inside of it, know just what reasons led six Justices to withhold consent to a certiorari. But all know that a majority, larger than can be mustered for a good many decisions, has found reason for not reviewing the case here. Because no one knows all that a denial means, does it mean that it means nothing? Perhaps the profession could accept denial as meaningless before the custom was introduced of noting dissents from them. Lawyers and lower judges will not readily believe that Justices of this Court are taking the trouble to signal a meaningless division of opinion about a meaningless act. It is just one of the facts of life that today every lower court does attach importance to denials and to presence or absence of dissents from denials, as judicial opinions and lawyers' arguments show.

"The fatal sentence that in real life writes *finis* to many causes cannot in legal theory be a complete blank. I can see order in the confusion as to its meaning only by distinguishing its significance under the doctrine of *stare decisis,* from its effect under the doctrine of *res judicata.* I agree that, as *stare decisis,* denial of certiorari should be given no significance whatever. It creates no precedent and approves no statement of principle entitled to weight in any other case. But, for the case in which certiorari is denied, its minimum meaning is that this Court allows the judgment below to stand with whatever consequences it may have upon the litigants involved under the doctrine of *res judicata* as applied either by state or federal courts. A civil or criminal judgment usually becomes *res judicata* in the sense that it is binding and conclusive even if new facts are discovered and even if a new theory of law were thought up, except for some provision for granting a new trial, which usually is discretionary with the trial court and limited in time."

Justice Jackson's opinion focused on the question of the significance of a denial of certiorari in a subsequent habeas corpus action brought by the same petitioner. (See generally Chap. XI, Sec. 2, *supra.*) Didn't Justice Blackmun miscite that opinion when he invoked it as a justification for his dissent in Singleton?

(4) In United States v. Kras, 409 U.S. 434 (1973), Justice Blackmun, speaking for the Court, placed heavy emphasis on the denial of certiorari in an identical case some time earlier, a denial made in the face of a claim that the decision below was wrong in light of a still earlier Supreme Court precedent. The denial, he said, was surely "not without some significance as to * * * the Court's attitude * * *" (p. 443). Justice Marshall, in dissent, was sharply critical of the Court's willingness to draw any inference whatever from the denial of certiorari.[7] Other categories of cases in which Linzer, Paragraph (2), *supra,* notes a tendency on the part of lower courts to rely on denials of certiorari as indicating the Supreme Court's view on the merits are (1) cases in which certiorari was denied despite the

---

7. Note that Justice Marshall was one of those who joined Justice Blackmun's dissent in Singleton.

In Hughes Tool Co. v. TWA, Inc., 409 U.S. 363, 366 n. 1 (1973), decided the same day as Kras, the Court referred with ap-

proval to "the well-settled view that denial of certiorari imparts no implication or inference concerning the Court's view of the merits" [citing Justice Frankfurter's dissent in Baltimore Radio Show].

"great importance and controversial nature" of the holding below, (2) "cases in which the Supreme Court had remanded a case to a lower court and then had denied certiorari" after the lower court had acted on remand, and (3) "cases involving limited grants of certiorari" (p. 1278).

Do you think it is proper to place weight on the denial in any or all of these situations? Linzer concludes that a "certiorari denial is often not based on the merits and never should bind anyone * * *. Yet it seems time to stop pretending that denial of certiorari means nothing. Many times it gives us a glimpse, imperfect to be sure, into the Justices' preliminary attitudes on a given issue." And dissents and other separate opinions "can provide starting points for reexamination of an issue" (pp. 1304–05). But whatever their value as signposts, he urges that "[w]ise litigants should continue to refrain from citing certiorari denials to bolster their arguments on the merits" and "neither the Supreme Court nor the courts below need be embarrassed about ignoring them" (id).

(5) Studies indicate that the Supreme Court reverses the judgment below in 60 to 70 percent of the cases in which certiorari is granted. See Stern, Gressman & Shapiro, Supreme Court Practice 223 n. 70 (6th ed. 1986). See also Hellman, *Error Correction, Lawmaking, and the Supreme Court's Exercise of Discretionary Review*, 44 U.Pitt.L.Rev. 795, 875 (1983) ("[C]onsideration of the correctness of the lower court's decision also plays a role in the selection of cases for the plenary docket. This proposition is hardly novel, but the data provide some striking illustrations of its continuing validity.").

Does the Court's tendency to reverse in the cases in which it grants certiorari cast any light on its views in the cases in which certiorari is denied? Even if it tells us something about those cases as a group, does it provide any useful information about the Court's attitude in a *particular* case?

(6) For discussion of the issues of certiorari policy raised by Justice Blackmun's dissent in Singleton, see *Concluding Note on the Certiorari Policy*, p. 1872, *infra*.

ROGERS v. MISSOURI PACIFIC RAILROAD CO.

352 U.S. 500, 77 S.Ct. 443, 1 L.Ed.2d 493 (1957).
Certiorari to the Supreme Court of Missouri.

WEBB v. ILLINOIS CENTRAL RAILROAD CO.

352 U.S. 512, 77 S.Ct. 451, 1 L.Ed.2d 503 (1957).
Certiorari to the United States Court of Appeals for the Seventh Circuit.

HERDMAN v. PENNSYLVANIA RAILROAD CO.

352 U.S. 518, 77 S.Ct. 455, 1 L.Ed.2d 508 (1957).
Certiorari to the United States Court of Appeals for the Sixth Circuit.

FERGUSON v. MOORE–McCORMACK LINES, INC.

352 U.S. 521, 77 S.Ct. 457, 1 L.Ed.2d 511 (1957).
Certiorari to the United States Court of Appeals for the Second Circuit.

[All four of these cases were decided on the same day. Three of them—Rogers, Webb, and Herdman—arose under the FELA, and the fourth—Ferguson—arose under the Jones Act. In each of the four cases, the court below had held that the evidence was not sufficient to take the case to the jury. In all but Herdman, the Supreme Court disagreed and reversed the judgment. Justice Brennan, writing for the Court in Rogers, defended the decision to grant certiorari in such cases:

["Cognizant of the duty to effectuate the intention of the Congress to secure the right to a jury determination, this Court is vigilant to exercise its power of review in any case where it appears that the litigants have been improperly deprived of that determination. * * * The kind of misconception evidenced in the opinion below, which fails to take into account the special features of this statutory negligence action that make it significantly different from the ordinary common-law negligence action, has required this Court to review a number of cases. In a relatively large percentage of the cases reviewed, the Court has found that lower courts have not given proper scope to this integral part of the congressional scheme. * * * Special and important reasons for the grant of certiorari in these cases are certainly present when lower federal and state courts persistently deprive litigants of their right to a jury determination."

[The opinions that follow are that of Justice Frankfurter, dissenting in all four cases, and that of Justice Harlan, concurring in Herdman and dissenting in the other three cases.]

MR. JUSTICE FRANKFURTER, dissenting.

"The Federal Employers' Liability Act gives to railroad employees a somewhat liberalized right of recovery for injuries on the job. A great number of cases under the Act have been brought to the Supreme Court, many of them cases in which the court of appeals had set aside, on the evidence, verdicts for the employees. Despite the human appeal of these cases, Brandeis never allowed himself to regard them as the proper business of the appellate jurisdiction of the Supreme Court." Paul A. Freund, The Liberalism of Justice Brandeis, address at a meeting of the American Historical Association in St. Louis, December 28, 1956.

In so discharging his judicial responsibility, Mr. Justice Brandeis did not disclose an idiosyncracy in a great judge. His attitude expressed respect for the standards formulated by the Court in carrying out the mandate of Congress regarding this Court's appellate jurisdiction in cases arising under the Federal Employers' Liability Act, 45 U.S.C.A. § 51 *et seq.* For he began his work on the Court just after Congress had passed the Act of September 6, 1916, 39 Stat. 726, relieving the Court of its obligatory jurisdiction over Federal Employers' Liability Act decisions by the highest state courts and the Circuit Courts of Appeals. Mr. Justice Brandeis' general outlook on the formulation by the Supreme Court of the public law appropriate for an evolving society has more and more prevailed; his concept of the role of the Supreme Court in our judicial system, and his consequent regard for the bearing on the judicial product of what business comes to the Court and how the Court deals with it, have often been neglected in the name of "doing justice" in individual cases. To him these were not technicalities, in the derogatory sense, for the conduct of judicial business. He deemed wise decisions on substantive law within the indispensable area of the Court's jurisdiction dependent on a limited volume of business and on a truly deliberative process.

One field of conspicuous disregard of these vital considerations is that large mass of cases under the Federal Employers' Liability Act in which the sole issue is the sufficiency of the evidence for submission to the jury.[2] For many years, I reluctantly voted on the merits of these negligence cases that had been granted review. In the last ten years, and more particularly within the past few years, as the Court has been granting more and more of these petitions, I have found it increasingly difficult to acquiesce in a practice that I regard as wholly incompatible with the certiorari policy embodied in the 1916 Act, the Judiciary Act of 1925, 43 Stat. 936, and the Rules formulated by the Court to govern certiorari jurisdiction for its own regulation and for the guidance of the bar. I have therefore felt compelled to vote to dismiss petitions for certiorari in such cases as improvidently granted without passing on the merits. In these cases I indicated briefly the reasons why I believed that this Court should not be reviewing decisions in which the sole issue is the sufficiency of the evidence for submission to the jury. In view of the increasing number of these cases that have been brought here for review—this dissent is to four decisions of the Court—and in view of the encouragement thereby given to continuing resort to this Court, I deem it necessary to enlarge upon the considerations that have guided me in the conviction that writs in this class of cases are "improvidently granted."

At the outset, however, I should deal briefly with a preliminary problem. It is sometimes said that the "integrity of the certiorari process" as expressed in the "rule of four" (that is, this Court's practice of granting certiorari on the vote of four Justices) requires all the Justices to vote on the merits of a case when four Justices have voted to grant certiorari and no new factor emerges after argument and deliberation. There are two reasons why there can be no such requirement. Last Term, for example,

---

2. Throughout this opinion I have dealt with the issue of granting certiorari in this type of case almost entirely in terms of the Federal Employers' Liability Act because the greatest abuse of the certiorari policy has occurred in that field. The problem is not confined to that Act, however, since the same or similar issues arise under other Acts, such as the Jones Act, 41 Stat. 1007, 46 U.S.C. § 688 * * *. Indeed, one of the decisions to which this dissent is written, No. 59, arises under the Jones Act.

the Court disposed of 1,361 petitions for certiorari. With such a volume of certiorari business, not to mention the remainder of the Court's business, the initial decision to grant a petition for certiorari must necessarily be based on a limited appreciation of the issues in a case, resting as it so largely does on the partisan claims in briefs of counsel. * * * The Court does not, indeed it cannot and should not try to, give to the initial question of granting or denying a petition the kind of attention that is demanded by a decision on the merits. The assumption that we know no more after hearing and deliberating on a case than after reading the petition for certiorari and the response is inadmissible in theory and not true in fact. Even an FELA case sometimes appears in quite a different light after argument than it appeared on the original papers. Surely this must be acknowledged regarding one of today's cases, No. 46, and see McCarthy v. Bruner, certiorari granted, 322 U.S. 718, certiorari dismissed, 323 U.S. 673. The course of argument and the briefs on the merits may disclose that a case appearing on the surface to warrant a writ of certiorari does not warrant it, see Layne & Bowler Corp. v. Western Well Works, Inc., 261 U.S. 387, or may reveal more clearly that the only thing in controversy is an appraisal of facts on which this Court is being asked to make a second guess, to substitute its assessment of the testimony for that of the court below.

But there is a more basic reason why the "integrity of the certiorari process" does not require me to vote on the merits of these cases. The right of a Justice to dissent from an action of the Court is historic. Of course self-restraint should guide the expression of dissent. But dissent is essential to an effective judiciary in a democratic society, and especially for a tribunal exercising the powers of this Court. Not four, not eight, Justices can require another to decide a case that he regards as not properly before the Court. The failure of a Justice to persuade his colleagues does not require him to yield to their views, if he has a deep conviction that the issue is sufficiently important. Moreover, the Court operates ultimately by majority. Even though a minority may bring a case here for oral argument, that does not mean that the majority has given up its right to vote on the ultimate disposition of the case as conscience directs. This is not a novel doctrine. As a matter of practice, members of the Court have at various times exercised this right of refusing to pass on the merits of cases that in their view should not have been granted review.

This does not make the "rule of four" a hollow rule. I would not change the practice. No Justice is likely to vote to dismiss a writ of certiorari as improvidently granted after argument has been heard, even though he has not been convinced that the case is within the rules of the Court governing the granting of certiorari. In the usual instance, a doubting Justice respects the judgment of his brethren that the case does concern issues important enough for the Court's consideration and adjudication. But a different situation is presented when a class of cases is systematically taken for review. Then a Justice who believes that such cases raise insignificant and unimportant questions—insignificant and unimportant from the point of view of the Court's duties—and that an increasing amount of the Court's time is unduly drained by adjudication of these cases cannot forego his duty to voice his dissent to the Court's action.

The "rule of four" is not a command of Congress. It is a working rule devised by the Court as a practical mode of determining that a case is deserving of review, the theory being that if four Justices find that a legal question of general importance is raised, that is ample proof that the question has such importance. This is a fair enough rule of thumb on the assumption that four Justices find such importance on an individualized screening of the cases sought to be reviewed. The reason for deference to a minority view no longer holds when a class of litigation is given a special and privileged position.

The history of the Federal Employers' Liability Act reveals the continuing nature of the problem of review by this Court of the vast litigation under that Act in both the federal and state courts. * * *

        * * *

This unvarnished account of Federal Employers' Liability Act litigation in this Court relating to sufficiency of the evidence for submission of cases to the jury is surely not an exhilarating story. For the Supreme Court of the United States to spend two hours of solemn argument, plus countless other hours reading the briefs and record and writing opinions, to determine whether there was evidence to support an allegation that it could reasonably be foreseen that an ice-cream server on a ship would use a butcher's knife to scoop out ice cream that was too hard to be scooped with a regular scoop, is surely to misconceive the discretion that was entrusted to the wisdom of the Court for the control of its calendar. The Court may or may not be "doing justice" in the four insignificant cases it decides today; it certainly is doing injustice to the significant and important cases on the calendar and to its own role as the supreme judicial body of the country. * * *

I would dismiss all four writs of certiorari as improvidently granted.
        * * *

MR. JUSTICE HARLAN, concurring in No. 46 and dissenting in Nos. 28, 42 and 59.

I.

I am in full agreement with what my Brother Frankfurter has written in criticism of the Court's recurring willingness to grant certiorari in cases of this type. For the reasons he has given, I think the Court should not have heard any of these four cases. Nevertheless, the cases having been taken, I have conceived it to be my duty to consider them on their merits, because I cannot reconcile voting to dismiss the writs as "improvidently granted" with the Court's "rule of four." In my opinion due adherence to that rule requires that once certiorari has been granted a case should be disposed of on the premise that it is properly here, in the absence of considerations appearing which were not manifest or fully apprehended at the time certiorari was granted. In these instances I am unable to say that such considerations exist, even though I do think that the arguments on the merits underscored the views of those of us who originally felt that the cases should not be taken because they involved only issues of fact, and presented nothing of sufficient general importance to warrant this substantial expenditure of the Court's time.

I do not think that, in the absence of the considerations mentioned, voting to dismiss a writ after it has been granted can be justified on the basis of an inherent right of dissent. In the case of a petition for certiorari that right, it seems to me—again without the presence of intervening factors—is exhausted once the petition has been granted and the cause set for argument.[1] Otherwise the "rule of four" surely becomes a meaningless thing in more than one respect. *First,* notwithstanding the "rule of four," five objecting Justices could undo the grant by voting, after the case has been heard, to dismiss the writ as improvidently granted—a course which would hardly be fair to litigants who have expended time, effort, and money on the assumption that their cases would be heard and decided on the merits. While in the nature of things litigants must assume the risk of "improvidently granted" dismissals because of factors not fully apprehended when the petition for certiorari was under consideration, short of that it seems to me that the Court would stultify its own rule if it were permissible for a writ of certiorari to be annulled by the later vote of five objecting Justices. Indeed, if that were proper, it would be preferable to have the vote of annulment come into play the moment after the petition for certiorari has been granted, since then at least the litigants would be spared useless effort in briefing and preparing for the argument of their cases. *Second,* permitting the grant of a writ to be thus undone would undermine the whole philosophy of the "rule of four," which is that any case warranting consideration in the opinion of such a substantial minority of the Court will be taken and disposed of. It appears to me that such a practice would accomplish just the contrary of what representatives of this Court stated to Congress as to the "rule of four" at the time the Court's certiorari jurisdiction was enlarged by the Judiciary Act of 1925. In effect the "rule of four" would, by indirection, become a "rule of five." *Third,* such a practice would, in my opinion, be inconsistent with the long-standing and desirable custom of not announcing the Conference vote on petitions for certiorari. For in the absence of the intervening circumstances which may cause a Justice to vote to dismiss a writ as improvidently granted, such a disposition of the case on his part is almost bound to be taken as reflecting his original Conference vote on the petition. And if such a practice is permissible, then by the same token I do not see how those who voted in favor of the petition can reasonably be expected to refrain from announcing their Conference votes at the time the petition is acted on.

My Brother Frankfurter states that the course he advocates will not result in making of the "rule of four" an empty thing, suggesting that in individual cases "a doubting Justice" will normally respect "the judgment of his brethren that the case does concern issues important enough for the Court's consideration and adjudication," and that it is only "when a class of cases is systematically taken for review" that such a Justice "cannot forego his duty to voice his dissent to the Court's action." However, it seems to me that it is precisely in that type of situation where the exercise of the right of dissent may well result in nullification of the "rule of four" by the action of five Justices. For differences of view as to the desirability of the Court's taking particular "classes" of cases—the situation we have here—

---

1. In some instances where the Court has granted certiorari and simultaneously summarily disposed of the case on the merits, individual Justices (including the writer) have merely noted their dissent to the grant without reaching the merits. See, *e.g.,* Anderson v. Atlantic Coast Line R. Co., 350 U.S. 807; Cahill v. New York, N.H. & H.R. Co., 350 U.S. 898. Even here, I am bound to say, it would probably be better practice for a Justice, who has unsuccessfully opposed certiorari, to face the merits, and to dissent from the summary disposition rather than from the grant of certiorari if he is not prepared to reach the merits without full-dress argument.

are prone to lead to more or less definite lines of cleavage among the Justices, which past experience has shown may well involve an alignment of four Justices who favor granting certiorari in such cases and five who do not. If in such situations it becomes the duty of one Justice among the disagreeing five not to "forego" his right to dissent, then I do not see why it is not equally the duty of the remaining four, resulting in the "rule of four" being set at naught. I thus see no basis in the circumstance that a case is an "individual" one rather than one of a "class" for distinctions in what may be done by an individual Justice who disapproves of the Court's action in granting certiorari.

Although I feel strongly that cases of this kind do not belong in this Court, I can see no other course, consistent with the "rule of four," but to continue our Conference debates, with the hope that persuasion or the mounting calendars of the Court will eventually bring our differing brethren to another point of view.

II.

Since I can find no intervening circumstances which would justify my voting now to dismiss the writs in these cases as improvidently granted, I turn to the merits of the four cases before us. * * *

NOTE ON THE RULE OF FOUR

(1) When, if ever, is it appropriate to dismiss a writ as improvidently granted over four dissents?

(2) "There is ample indication that Congress had the rule of four in mind when it approved the Judges Bill [in 1925]." Leiman, *The Rule of Four,* 57 Colum.L.Rev. 975, 985 (1957). The rule was frequently mentioned by the Justices in their testimony and cited both in Committee reports and on the floor in defense of the fairness of the certiorari process. *Id.* at 985–86 (citing H.R.Rep. No. 1075, 68th Cong., 2d Sess. 3 (1925)). But how was the rule understood? In Leiman's view, it meant only that the vote of four would commit all nine to a more extended look at the case; it would not commit anyone to a vote on the merits if a majority were convinced, after briefing and oral argument, that the writ should be dismissed as improvidently granted. In the absence of such a majority, however, an individual Justice should not vote to dismiss except for a jurisdictional defect.[1]

A view similar to Leiman's was adopted by Justice Stevens (and perhaps by the majority) in New York v. Uplinger, 467 U.S. 246 (1984). In that case, the majority dismissed a writ of certiorari as improvidently granted because of the ambiguity of the state court opinion below and the possibility that it rested on state law. Four dissenters said that the merits of the decision below were "properly before us and should be addressed" (p. 252). The majority did not discuss the significance of the rule of four, but Justice Stevens, concurring, did (pp. 250–51):

"It might be suggested that [under the rule of four] the case must be decided unless there has been an intervening development that justifies a

---

1. Leiman notes one case, Parker v. Illinois, 334 U.S. 816 (1948), in which Justice Jackson's vote to dismiss the writ left the Court equally divided on the merits. Thus his vote was effectively a vote to affirm.

dismissal. ∗ ∗ ∗ I am now persuaded, however, that there is *always* an important intervening development that may be decisive. The Members of the Court have always considered a case more carefully after full briefing and argument on the merits than they could at the time of the certiorari conference, when almost 100 petitions must be considered each week. ∗ ∗ ∗ [T]he Rule of Four is a valuable, though not immutable, device for deciding when a case must be argued, but its force is largely spent once the case has been heard."

For further discussion of this question, see Triangle Improvement Council v. Ritchie, 402 U.S. 497, 502 (Harlan, J., concurring), 508 (Douglas, J., dissenting) (1971); [2] Donnelly v. DeChristoforo, 416 U.S. 637, 648 (1974); [3] Burrell v. McCray, 426 U.S. 471 (1976); [4] Blumstein, *The Supreme Court's Jurisdiction—Reform Proposals, Discretionary Review, and Writ Dismissals,* 26 Vand.L.Rev. 895 (1973).

(3) The question of the obligation imposed on the majority by a grant of certiorari has also been raised in the context of a request for a stay of execution in a capital case. In Darden v. Wainwright, 473 U.S. 927 (1985), the Court (within a few hours) first denied an application for a stay by a vote of 5–4, then granted a petition for certiorari, and then granted the application for a stay, again by a vote of 5–4. Explaining his ultimate vote to grant the stay, Justice Powell indicated that only four Justices had voted to grant certiorari and that he had not been one of them. Of the four Justices who dissented from grant of the stay, Chief Justice Burger said he thought that the case was wholly without merit and that the grant of certiorari was an abuse of discretion.

In another capital case during the same Term, the Court (after oral argument in Darden, *supra*) voted to hold the petition for certiorari pending disposition of Darden, but then, by a vote of 5–4, vacated its earlier stay of execution. Straight v. Wainwright, 476 U.S. 1132 (1986). (In his concurring opinion, Justice Powell indicated that there had been four votes to hold the case, though Justice Brennan disclosed in a later opinion that

---

2. Justice Harlan, concurring in a 5–4 dismissal, concluded that the writ was properly dismissed because the case had "changed posture" after certiorari had been granted (p. 502). Justice Douglas, dissenting, argued that such action should not be taken by those who had originally opposed granting the writ.

In Iowa Beef Packers, Inc. v. Thompson, 405 U.S. 228, 232 (1972), Justice Douglas went further and said in his dissent that certiorari should be dismissed as improvidently granted "only in exceptional situations and where all nine members of the Court agree."

3. Five Justices expressed the view that certiorari should not have been granted, but all nine voted on the merits (dividing 6–3). Justice Stewart, joined by Justice White, said he felt obligated to address the merits because as many as four colleagues "remain so minded after oral argument" (p. 648).

4. The Court, after oral argument, dismissed a writ of certiorari as improvidently granted over the dissent of three Justices who would have affirmed the judgment below. Justice Stevens, concurring, noted that he would have voted to deny certiorari had he been on the Court when the writ was granted, that the concurrence in the dismissal by one Justice who had voted to grant the petition meant the rule of four was not violated, and that there was ground for the dismissal because further study indicated the law to be sufficiently clear that there was no need for an opinion of the Court. (Was Justice Stevens expressing an opinion on the merits?) Justice Brennan, in dissent, argued that there was nothing to indicate that the conditions originally thought to warrant issuance of the writ were not in fact present and that under those circumstances, a Justice who originally voted to deny certiorari should not vote to dismiss.

"[t]hree votes suffice to hold a case." Watson v. Butler, 108 S.Ct. 6, 7 (1987) (Brennan, J., dissenting from denial of a stay of execution).)

What is the nature of the Court's obligation to attempt to preserve its jurisdiction once certiorari has been granted? Is that obligation greater in a capital case? Greater than in a case in which a minority of four (or three) has voted only to hold a petition for the disposition of another case? These and a number of other issues relating to the rule of four and to the "hold" rule are perceptively discussed in Revesz & Karlan, *Non–Majority Rules and the Supreme Court*, 136 U.Pa.L.Rev. 1067 (1988).

(4) In support of the rule of four, Justice Douglas argued that only minority control makes the Court's power over its own docket tolerable. See Douglas, *Managing the Docket of the Supreme Court of the United States*, 25 Record Ass'n B. City N.Y. 279, 298 (1970). But Justice Stevens, concerned about that very same power of a minority to force a hearing on an unwilling majority, has recently urged consideration of a change to a rule of five. See Stevens, *The Life Span of a Judge–Made Rule*, 58 N.Y. U.L.Rev. 1 (1983). He contends that the rule was adopted in 1924 in order to allay fears that the Court would not accept enough cases if its discretion to deny review was increased, and suggests that the reason for the rule has therefore ceased to exist.

(5) In Board of Education, Island Trees Union Free School Dist. No. 26 v. Pico, 457 U.S. 853 (1982), the majority, relying on the First Amendment, agreed with the court of appeals that summary judgment should not have been granted to the defendant school board. Justice White, concurring, said that he saw no need for a discussion of the First Amendment issue, since it was enough at this stage to conclude that there was a material issue of fact precluding summary judgment. Justice Rehnquist, dissenting for himself and two other Justices, said in a footnote that Justice White's refusal to reach the First Amendment issue was "inconsistent with the 'rule of four'" (p. 904 n. 1). Citing the Harlan opinion in Rogers *et al.*, he said that Justice White's concurrence, "although not couched in such language, is in effect a single vote to dismiss the writ of certiorari as improvidently granted" (*id.*).

Justice Rehnquist is plainly wrong, isn't he?[5] If the rule of four does require a justice to reach the merits of a particular case—at least when there is no objection to jurisdiction—does it also require him to submit to someone else's view of the *issues* that must be decided in order to dispose of the case?

(6) In a few instances, a petition for certiorari has been denied over four dissents. In Gay v. United States, 411 U.S. 974 (1973), the four dissenters did not object to the denial; rather they would have summarily reversed. Should this be regarded as a waiver of the dissenters' power to have the petition granted?[6]

In a series of obscenity cases in 1974 and 1975, the Supreme Court denied certiorari over four dissents, but in each case three of the dissenters stated: "Although four of us would grant certiorari and reverse the judgment, the Justices who join this opinion do not insist that the case be

---

5. For a later expression by Justice Rehnquist of a similar view, see his dissenting opinion in Thigpen v. Roberts, 468 U.S. 27, 33 (1984).

6. See also Drake v. Zant, 449 U.S. 999 (1980) (denying certiorari over four dissents).

decided on the merits." *E.g.,* Trinkler v. Alabama, 418 U.S. 917, 918 n. *
(1974). In many of these cases, unlike Gay, it was clear that the dissenters
were expressing a view that had already been rejected by the majority in
prior decisions. But in some of the cases, the dissenters urged that denial
of certiorari was improper on the basis of the Court's own prior decisions.
E.g., J–R Distributors, Inc. v. Washington, 418 U.S. 949 (1974).

When Justice Stevens replaced Justice Douglas in the 1975 Term, the
number of votes dissenting from the denial of certiorari in these obscenity
cases went down from four to three. Without rejecting the views of the
dissenters on the merits, Justice Stevens concurred in the denial of certiorari in one such case, saying:

"＊ ＊ ＊ [T]here is no reason to believe that the majority of the Court
＊ ＊ ＊ is any less adamant than the minority. Accordingly, regardless of
how I might vote on the merits after full argument, it would be pointless to
grant certiorari in case after case of this character only to have [our prior
decisions] reaffirmed time after time.

"Since my dissenting Brethren have recognized the force of this reasoning in the past, I believe they also could properly vote to deny certiorari in
this case without acting inconsistently with their principled views on the
merits. In all events, until a valid reason for voting to grant one of these
petitions is put forward, I shall continue to vote to deny. In the interest of
conserving scarce law library space, I shall not repeat this explanation
every time I cast such a vote." Liles v. Oregon, 425 U.S. 963–64 (1976).

(7) Are four votes required to grant a petition for certiorari when only
eight Justices are sitting on a case? When only seven Justices are sitting?
Although Justice Douglas said in 1970 that the vote of three Justices would
suffice when seven were sitting,[7] the Court on several occasions has denied
certiorari in these circumstances over three dissents.[8] No objection to this
practice was noted by the dissenters.

CONCLUDING NOTE ON THE CERTIORARI POLICY

(1) Professor Hart, agreeing with Justice Frankfurter in Rogers, described the Court's determination to engage in case-by-case policing in
FELA and related cases as "a grievous frittering away of the judicial
resources of the nation". Hart, *Foreword: The Time Chart of the Justices,*
73 Harv.L.Rev. 84, 98 (1959). Thurman Arnold replied that the enforcement of proper standards for jury verdicts in FELA cases is "vital to the
security of lowly litigants" and "directly or indirectly affects the lives of
millions". Arnold, *Professor Hart's Theology,* 73 Harv.L.Rev. 1298, 1302,
1304 (1960).

Did review of these decisions consume a substantial segment of the
Court's time? Justice Douglas thought not. In a concurring opinion in a
1959 FELA case, he noted that in the more than ten years from January
31, 1949, to October 19, 1959, there had been 110 petitions for certiorari in
FELA cases. Of these, 77 were denied, and of the 33 granted 16 were

---

7. Douglas, Paragraph (3), *supra,* at
298.

8. See, *e.g.,* Donaldson v. California, 404
U.S. 968 (1971); Stanley v. United States,

404 U.S. 996 (1971); Delaware State Bd. of
Educ. v. Evans, 434 U.S. 880 (1977).

reversed without oral argument. Of the 17 argued, 5 were disposed of with brief per curiam opinions, leaving an average of slightly more than one full opinion per year in FELA cases for the period in question. Harris v. Pennsylvania R.R., 361 U.S. 15, 16–25 (1959). Compare Note, 69 Harv.L. Rev. 1441 (1956).

Justice Douglas's figures do not tell the whole story. A policy that encourages the filing of certiorari petitions on a given question increases the total workload even if many or most of the petitions are denied. And a case that requires review of the record to determine the sufficiency of the evidence may well take more time to dispose of than a case presenting a purely legal issue.

(2) The controversy over FELA cases is no longer a live one. But disagreements persist within the Court over the willingness to grant certiorari in certain categories of cases. Justice Stevens, for example, has been especially critical of the increase in petitions granted at the behest of the prosecution in state criminal cases. "The result," he complains, "is a docket swollen with requests by the state to reverse judgments that their courts have rendered in favor of their citizens." Michigan v. Long, 463 U.S. 1032, 1070 (1983) (dissenting opinion). See also Paragraph (7), *infra.*

(3) Note the provisions of Sup.Ct.Rule 17: "Considerations governing review on certiorari." How satisfactory are the criteria there articulated? How consistent are they with the view that the Court sits to adjudicate only those cases, within its jurisdiction, of most far-reaching, general importance?

Rule 17, which became effective in 1980, embodied a number of organizational and stylistic changes from its predecessor, and two substantive changes: (1) the new rule omits the reference in the former rule to a federal court of appeals decision of "an important state or territorial question * * * in conflict with applicable state or territorial law"; and (2) the new rule adds a reference to a decision of a federal question by a state court of last resort "in a way in conflict with the decision of another state court of last resort or of a federal court of appeals." The omission "doubtless reflects the Court's lack of interest in reviewing diversity cases where the only certiorari ground is an alleged conflict with state law." Stern, Gressman & Shapiro, Supreme Court Practice 195 (6th ed. 1986). And the addition brought within the text of the rule a situation that "has long been recognized in practice" as a basis for certiorari. Boskey & Gressman, *The Supreme Court's New Rules for the Eighties,* 85 F.R.D. 487, 505 (1980).

Each of the subparagraphs of Rule 17.1 includes a reference to a conflict (for example, a conflict between decisions of the federal courts of appeals, or between state and federal decisions on a federal question, as well as a conflict with applicable decisions of the Supreme Court) as a basis for certiorari. Should the petitioner in such a case have to show in addition that present resolution of the conflict is required by such factors as the national importance of the issue or the nature of the interests affected?

While the existence of a conflict is clearly a significant factor in the consideration of a certiorari petition (see Stern, Gressman & Shapiro, *supra,* §§ 4.3–4.10), it was reported as early as 1953 that the Court would not automatically grant certiorari when there was a conflict among the federal courts of appeals. Stern, *Denial of Certiorari Despite a Conflict,* 66 Harv.L.Rev. 465, 472 (1953). And in a study published in 1975, which canvassed certiorari petitions over two Terms, it was concluded that the Court was denying certiorari in approximately 60–65 cases each Term despite the existence of a "direct conflict" in all of those cases.[1] (A recent reexamination of 40 of the cases in the 1975 study, however, applied different standards of evaluation and concluded that the number of "square conflicts" was considerably lower, and that the number of "intolerable conflicts" was lower still.[2])

Commentators on the work of the Court are not of one mind about the Supreme Court's responsibility for the resolution of conflicts. In the view of some, the Court should allow issues to "percolate" in the lower courts unless there is some pressing reason to resolve a conflict at an early stage; this process, they contend, will assure a wiser and more informed resolution in the long run. See, *e.g.,* Estreicher & Sexton, Redefining the Supreme Court's Role 47–52, 73–74 (1986); Posner, The Federal Courts: Crisis and Reform 163 (1985). In the view of others, this argument transforms the sensible caution against a rush to judgment into an inflated excuse for failing to take steps sorely needed to restore the health of our system of national law. See, *e.g.,* Baker & McFarland, *The Need for a New National Court,* 100 Harv.L.Rev. 1400, 1408–09 (1987); Bator, *What is Wrong with the Supreme Court?,* 50 U.Pitt.L.Rev. ___ (1988); Bator, *The Judicial Universe of Judge Posner* (Book Review), 52 U.Chi.L.Rev. 1146, 1154–55 (1985).

(4) In a book growing out of the NYU Supreme Court Project, note 2, *supra,* Professors Estreicher and Sexton propose a number of "modest reforms" of Supreme Court practice, one of which is to revise Rule 17 to establish a "principled set of case selection criteria [that] would send clearer signals to the Bar." Estreicher & Sexton, Redefining the Supreme Court's Role 116, 118 (1986). Although they do not submit a suggested draft, they do refer to their own criteria, which embrace both a "priority" and "discretionary" docket. Among the cases in the first category are those involving "intolerable intercourt conflicts" (defined as conflicts involving three or more circuits, as well as those conflicts creating a substantial opportunity for forum shopping or making it difficult for multi-state actors to conduct their affairs), conflict with Supreme Court precedent, resolution of "profound vertical federalism disputes," resolution of interbranch disputes, and resolution of interstate disputes (pp. 52–62). Included in the second category are such cases as those involving "a significant interference with federal executive responsibility" and "vehicles for advances in the development of federal law" (pp. 62–69).

1. Feeney, *Conflicts Involving Federal Law: A Review of Cases Presented to the Supreme Court,* 67 F.R.D. 301, 320 (1975). Professor Feeney's study was prepared under the aegis of of the Hruska Commission (see Chap. I, p. 44, *supra*), and was relied on by that Commission in its decision to recommend the creation of a National Court of Appeals. See 67 F.R.D. 195, 298 (1975).

Justice White has frequently dissented from denials of certiorari in cases of

claimed conflict. See Stern, Gressman & Shapiro, Supreme Court Practice 198 n. 29 (4th ed. 1986) (reporting 22 such dissents in the 1984 Term alone).

2. See Note, 59 N.Y.U.L.Rev. 1007 (1984). This reexamination was part of the New York University Supreme Court Project published in three issues of the New York University Law Review.

Do you think that such an effort to sharpen the applicable criteria would affect the rate of irresponsible certiorari petitions? Of improvident grants? Would it help on the first of these questions to fine attorneys who file frivolous petitions? See Sup.Ct. Rule 56(4).

(5) The complaint typified by Justice Blackmun's dissent in the Singleton case (p. 1856, *supra*)—that there are significant areas of federal law where the Court is failing to give sufficient guidance—is one that, in the view of many observers, transcends issues of certiorari policy.[3] These critics argue that the Supreme Court simply lacks the capacity to insure the stability, clarity, and uniformity of the huge body of national law being interpreted and applied in many thousands of state and federal court cases each year. Thus they have urged that consideration be given to fundamental changes in the structure of the federal judiciary—changes that would enable the Supreme Court to share some of its responsibility for the elaboration and clarification of national law.

For a discussion of the evolution and content of these proposed changes, and of the debate over their desirability, see Chap. I, pp. 43–45, *supra.*

(6) Perhaps the most important of the avoidance devices discussed by Professor Bickel in The Least Dangerous Branch—The Supreme Court at the Bar of Politics (1962), see p. 87, *supra,* is the Court's discretionary certiorari jurisdiction. Taking as an illustration the case of Times Film Corp. v. Chicago, 365 U.S. 43 (1961), Bickel suggested (pp. 141–43) that instead of rejecting the petitioner's challenge to Chicago's film censorship ordinance on its merits, the Court should have denied review. Since the issue as posed by the parties was the constitutionality of censorship per se (the film was not even in the record), since the Constitution did not in Bickel's view furnish a basis for invalidation, and since Bickel feared the impetus that would be given to the undesirable practice of censorship by a decision favoring the city, he would have opted for the "comparatively inoffensive expedient" of denying certiorari.

Professor Gunther was sharply critical of this line of argument. Gunther, *The Subtle Vices of the "Passive Virtues"—A Comment on Principle and Expediency in Judicial Review,* 64 Colum.L.Rev. 1 (1964). He suggested (p. 14) that it was "manipulative dissimilation" and "intervention in the political process" (using phrases of Bickel's) "when the Court concludes that the Constitution imposes no absolute ban on prior restraints but decides not to say so * * * because of the likely effect in current social and political circumstances, of the judgment of 'legitimation.'" Further, Gunther argued, "Bickel's approach to certiorari * * * undercuts his goal of a principled, candid evolution of constitutional interpretation" (p. 14). While Gunther agreed that valid reasons existed for denying certiorari in Times Film—especially the fact that the parties had framed a test case in a

---

3. Professor Bator has argued that the problem is especially severe in the private sector and in areas of business and tax law. In the latter areas, it appears that only the government can persuade the Court to take a case; in the four Terms of Court from 1980 to 1983, for example, all 15 tax cases heard on the merits in the Supreme Court were cases in which the government had either filed the certiorari petition or agreed that it should be granted because of a conflict. Bator, *What Is Wrong with the Supreme Court* ?, Paragraph (3), *supra.*

manner that "narrowed" the Court's "line of vision" (p. 13)—he rejected the asserted evils of "legitimation" as one of them.[4]

A similar controversy surfaced in 1978, in a dissent by Justice Rehnquist from a denial of certiorari. Ratchford v. Gay Lib, 434 U.S. 1080 (1978). Writing for himself and Justice Blackmun, he argued that the case—involving the validity of a state university's denial of recognition to a student organization—was one in which the Court's criteria in what is now Rule 17 had plainly been satisfied. The existence of discretion to decline to hear a case, he concluded, "does not imply that it should be used as a sort of judicial storm cellar to which we may flee to escape from controversial or sensitive cases" (p. 1081).

(7) During the Warren Court era, the Court frequently engaged in the practice of summarily reversing the judgment below on the certiorari papers and with no more than a citation or two of explanation. The practice was forcefully criticized by several observers, see, *e.g.,* Brown, *Foreword: Process of Law,* 72 Harv.L.Rev. 77 (1958), and its frequency was substantially reduced by the Burger Court. See Hellman, *Error Correction, Lawmaking, and the Supreme Court's Exercise of Discretionary Review,* 44 U.Pitt.L.Rev. 795, 824–25 (1983). But the Court continued in a number of instances to reverse the decision below on the certiorari papers and without plenary consideration, usually accompanying the disposition with a brief per curiam opinion explaining the Court's reasoning. See *id.* at 825–36. The practice continues to come under heavy attack. See, *e.g.,* Rosenberg, *Notes from the Underground: A Substantive Analysis of Summary Adjudication by the Burger Court (Part II),* 19 Houston L.Rev. 831, 869–94 (1982).[5]

The Court in recent years has had its internal critics of summary reversal. The most forceful has been Justice Stevens, often joined by Justices Brennan and Marshall.[6] In some instances, they have urged that the case is too unimportant to be considered at all;[7] in others that it is too important to be treated summarily.[8] On one occasion they called the majority's action "unprecedented and drastic" because the Court appeared to grant a petition for certiorari and then to reject the petitioner's arguments in a footnote solely to enable it to grant the government's cross-petition and to reverse summarily on the basis of arguments in that cross-petition. Snepp v. United States, 444 U.S. 507, 517 (1980). On another, they complained that in these summary dispositions, which were frequently

---

4. Gunther is even more critical of Bickel's further suggestion that once certiorari had been granted, the appropriate disposition was a "jurisdictional dismissal for lack of ripeness". Bickel, *supra,* at 143. In Gunther's view, this prescription "is not merely bad but lawless judgment" (64 Colum.L.Rev. at 13) since the "jurisdictional" principle relied on has no basis in any statute or in the Constitution. *Cf.* the discussion of Naim v. Naim, 350 U.S. 891 (1955), in Chap. V, Sec. 5, p. 744, *supra.*

5. Professor Rosenberg's attack in this article and in Part I (19 Houston L.Rev. 607 (1982)) extends also to a number of other forms of summary adjudication, including summary affirmance.

6. *E.g.,* County of Los Angeles v. Kling, 474 U.S. 936 (1985); Florida v. Meyers, 466

U.S. 380, 383 (1984); Illinois v. Batchelder, 463 U.S. 1112, 1119 (1983); Idaho Dept. of Employment v. Smith, 434 U.S. 100, 103 (1977); Pennsylvania v. Mimms, 434 U.S. 106, 115 (1977). In the Kling case, Justice Stevens was especially critical of the Court's one sentence per curiam reversal of a case in which the court of appeals had issued an unpublished opinion. "[L]ike a court of Appeals that issues an opinion that may not be published or cited, this Court ＊ ＊ ＊ engages in decision-making without the discipline and accountability that the preparation of opinions requires" (p. 303).

7. *E.g.,* Board of Educ. v. McCluskey, 458 U.S. 966, 971 (1982).

8. *E.g.,* Hutto v. Davis, 454 U.S. 370, 381 (1982).

granted in favor of a government petition, the Court was "primarily concerned with vindicating the will of the majority and less interested in its role as protector of the individual's constitutional rights." Florida v. Meyer, 466 U.S. 380, 386 (1984).[9]

Is there ever a case appropriate for summary reversal? What if the lower court has committed a manifest and grievous error in a case plainly not worth the time required for full briefing and argument? Should the Court in any event act summarily only when it is unanimous? Would even such action smack of unfairness to the losing party unless an opportunity were afforded for the filing of briefs on the merits? [10]

(8) In the last several decades, there has been a considerable body of literature, much of it emanating from political and social scientists, reporting and analyzing the Court's practices in the exercise of its discretionary jurisdiction. One of the earliest studies, by Professor Harper and others, reviewed the Court's dockets over four Terms and concluded that the Court was taking cases it shouldn't, not taking cases it should, and fostering unnecessary petitions by failing to articulate what it was doing.[11]

Later studies have included:

• An analysis of FELA cases by Professor Schubert, suggesting that a bloc of Justices used the certiorari power in those cases to force the majority to reach certain policy results on the merits; [12]

• A study by Professor Tanenhaus and associates concluding that the existence of certain factors operated as "cues" to stimulate closer consideration and favorable response by the Court—notably the presence of the United States as petitioner; a disagreement between the trial and appellate courts; and the presence of certain civil liberties issues; [13] and

• Several studies by Professor Ulmer suggesting a close relationship between the Justices' votes to grant certiorari and their views on the merits.[14]

---

9. In a memorandum filed in Colorado v. Connelly, 474 U.S. 1050 (1986), Justice Brennan (joined by Justice Stevens) complained that of 30 criminal cases in which the Court had summarily reversed without briefing or oral argument in three and one half years, 26 were decided in favor of the prosecutor or warden.

10. See Montana v. Hall, 107 S.Ct. 1825, 1830 (1987), in which Justice Marshall, dissenting from a summary reversal, said that "when the Court contemplates a summary disposition, it should, at the very least, invite the parties to file supplemental briefs on the merits *at their option*. • • • [This device] would go a long way toward achieving the fairness and accuracy that the Nation rightfully expects from its court of last resort."

11. The four articles were entitled *What the Supreme Court Did Not Do During the [1949, 1950, 1951, 1952] Term* and appeared in the University of Pennsylvania Law Review: Harper & Rosenthal, 99 U.Pa.L.Rev. 293 (1950); Harper &

Etherington, 100 U.Pa.L.Rev. 354 (1951); Harper & Pratt, 101 U.Pa.L.Rev. 439 (1953); Harper & Leibowitz, 102 U.Pa.L. Rev. 427 (1954).

12. Schubert, *The Certiorari Game,* in Quantitative Analysis of Judicial Behavior 210 (Schubert ed. 1959); Schubert, *Policy Without Law: An Extension of the Certiorari Game,* 14 Stan.L.Rev. 284 (1962).

13. Tanenhaus, Schick, Muraskin & Rosen, *The Supreme Court's Certiorari Jurisdiction: Cue Theory,* in Judicial Decision-Making 111 (Schubert ed. 1963).

14. Ulmer, *The Decision to Grant Certiorari as an Indicator to Decision "On the Merits,"* 4 Polity 429 (1972); Ulmer, *Supreme Court Justices as Strict and Not-so-Strict Constructionists: Some Implications,* 8 Law & Soc.Rev. 13 (1973); cf. Ulmer, *Revising the Jurisdiction of the Supreme Court: Mere Administrative Reform or Substantive Policy Change?,* 58 Minn.L. Rev. 121 (1973).

Perhaps the most thoughtful and penetrating of these analyses is Provine, Case Selection in the United States Supreme Court (1980). This book is based in significant part on an intensive study of the records and papers of Justice Burton—papers that cover the 1945–1957 Terms and that include the recorded vote of every Justice on certiorari petitions during this period. Her basic conclusion—a most important one in light of other criticisms of the Court's work—is that the Justices' perceptions of their role and of the role of the Court serve as a significant intervening variable between their votes on certiorari and their policy preferences. Thus she concludes, for example, that as a result of these perceptions, the use of the certiorari power for dispute avoidance is rare (Chap. II); that "cue theory" serves as an inadequate explanation of certiorari decisions (Chap. III); that a Justice's political and policy orientation is not the sole or determining variable in the exercise of discretion, nor is there strong evidence that a Justice will characteristically vote to deny certiorari if he fears that his view will not prevail on the merits (Chap. IV); and that the record in FELA cases does not substantiate the bloc voting hypothesis (Chap. V). She urges that the Court's discretionary power be retained but that, in the interest of public awareness and scholarly study, the votes on certiorari petitions should be disclosed.[15]

One of the most interesting tables in this book reveals the high degree of unanimity on certiorari petitions. From the 1947 Term through the 1957 Term, a less than unanimous vote was recorded on only 18% of the petitions: 11% in which certiorari was denied and 7% in which it was granted (Table 1.4, p. 32).

15. If this policy is adopted, should dis-   be deferred until the case has been disclosure of the votes on a grant of certiorari   posed of?

INDEX

†